# 2022 OHIO ELDER LAW HANDBOOK

Containing:

Chapter 173: Department of Aging

Chapter 2103: Dower

Chapter 2105: Descent and Distribution

Chapter 2106: Rights of Surviving Spouses

Chapter 2112: Adult Guardianship and Protective Proceedings Jurisdiction Act

Chapter 2133: Modified Uniform Rights of the Terminally Ill Act and the DNR Identification and Do-Not-Resuscitate Order Law

Chapter 3721: Nursing Homes; Residential Care Facilities

Selected Chapters from Title 51: Public Welfare

And Miscellaneous Related Statutes as amended by the Ohio General Assembly and filed with the Secretary of State through File 100 of the 134th General Assembly

Selected Medicaid and related regulations from the Ohio Administrative Code as amended through March 26, 2022

LexisNexis®

QUESTIONS ABOUT THIS PUBLICATION?

For CUSTOMER SERVICE ASSISTANCE concerning replacement pages, shipments, billing, reprint permission, or other matters,

please contact Customer Support at our self-service portal available 24/7 at *support.lexisnexis.com/print*
or call us at 800-833-9844

For EDITORIAL **content questions** concerning this publication,

please email: *llp.clp@lexisnexis.com*

For **information on other LEXISNEXIS MATTHEW BENDER publications,**

please call us at 800-223-1940
or visit our online bookstore at *www.lexisnexis.com/bookstore*

---

ISBN: 978-1-66334-388-8



LexisNexis

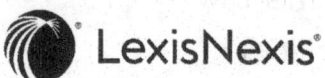

Matthew Bender & Company, Inc.
Editorial Offices
9443 Springboro Pike
Miamisburg, OH 45342
800-833-9844
www.lexisnexis.com

(Pub. 33054)

# TABLE OF CONTENTS

## TITLE 21: COURTS—PROBATE—JUVENILE

Chapter



## TITLE 29: CRIMES—PROCEDURE

Chapter



## TITLE 31: DOMESTIC RELATIONS—CHILDREN

Chapter



## TITLE 33: EDUCATION—LIBRARIES

Chapter



## TITLE 37: HEALTH—SAFETY—MORALS

Chapter



## TITLE 39: INSURANCE

Chapter



## TITLE 41: LABOR AND INDUSTRY

Chapter

## TITLE 45: MOTOR VEHICLES—AERONAUTICS—WATERCRAFT



## TITLE 47: OCCUPATIONS—PROFESSIONS



## TITLE 51: PUBLIC WELFARE



## TITLE 53: REAL PROPERTY



## TITLE 57: TAXATION



## OHIO ADMINISTRATIVE CODE

## DIVISION 4501:1 BUREAU OF MOTOR VEHICLES



## DIVISION 5101:4 DIVISION OF FOOD STAMPS



## DIVISION 5160 MEDICAID SERVICES

## DIVISION 5160:1 MEDICAID GENERAL PRINCIPLES

Chapter

# SECTIONS AFFECTED BY 2021 LEGISLATION

**NOTE:** In addition to the sections listed below, users of this edition should be aware that additional section and case note annotations have also been appropriately incorporated throughout this publication. The sections with new and/or revised annotations do not appear in this listing.

| Section | Action | Effective Date | File | Bill No. | Sec. No. |
|---|---|---|---|---|---|
| 1.14 | Amended | 30-Sep-21 | 30 | HB 110 | 101.01 |
| 173.012 | Added | 30-Sep-21 | 30 | HB 110 | 101.01 |
| 173.27 | Amended | 22-Dec-21 | 62 | SB 217 | 1 |
| 173.38 | Amended | 30-Sep-21 | 30 | HB 110 | 101.01 |
| 173.38 | Amended | 22-Dec-21 | 62 | SB 217 | 1 |
| 173.381 | Amended | 30-Sep-21 | 30 | HB 110 | 101.01 |
| 173.381 | Amended | 22-Dec-21 | 62 | SB 217 | 1 |
| 173.39 | Amended | 30-Sep-21 | 30 | HB 110 | 101.01 |
| 173.391 | Amended | 30-Sep-21 | 30 | HB 110 | 101.01 |
| 173.392 | Amended | 30-Sep-21 | 30 | HB 110 | 101.01 |
| 173.393 | Amended | 30-Sep-21 | 30 | HB 110 | 101.01 |
| 323.153 | Amended | 30-Sep-21 | 30 | HB 110 | 101.01 |
| 1337.11 | Amended | 30-Sep-21 | 30 | HB 110 | 101.01 |
| 2106.13 | Amended | 17-Aug-21 | 17 | HB 7 | 1 |
| 2108.05 | Amended | 17-Aug-21 | 17 | HB 7 | 1 |
| 2108.05 | Amended | 1-Oct-22 | 50 | HB 21 | 1 |
| 2108.06 | Amended | 17-Aug-21 | 17 | HB 7 | 1 |
| 2108.07 | Amended | 17-Aug-21 | 17 | HB 7 | 1 |
| 2108.23 | Amended | 17-Aug-21 | 17 | HB 7 | 1 |
| 2108.23 | Amended | 1-Oct-22 | 50 | HB 21 | 1 |
| 2108.24 | Amended | 17-Aug-21 | 17 | HB 7 | 1 |
| 2108.34 | Amended | 17-Aug-21 | 17 | HB 7 | 1 |
| 2108.34 | Amended | 1-Oct-22 | 50 | HB 21 | 1 |
| 2131.12 | Amended | 30-Jun-21 | 5 | HB 74 | 101.01 |
| 2133.01 | Amended | 30-Sep-21 | 30 | HB 110 | 101.01 |
| 2133.07 | Amended | 17-Aug-21 | 17 | HB 7 | 1 |
| 2133.16 | Repealed | 17-Aug-21 | 17 | HB 7 | 3 |
| 3721.60 | Added | 23-Mar-22 | 66 | SB 58 | 1 |
| 3721.61 | Added | 23-Mar-22 | 66 | SB 58 | 1 |
| 3721.62 | Added | 23-Mar-22 | 66 | SB 58 | 1 |
| 3721.63 | Added | 23-Mar-22 | 66 | SB 58 | 1 |
| 3721.64 | Added | 23-Mar-22 | 66 | SB 58 | 1 |
| 3721.65 | Added | 23-Mar-22 | 66 | SB 58 | 1 |
| 3721.66 | Added | 23-Mar-22 | 66 | SB 58 | 1 |
| 3721.67 | Added | 23-Mar-22 | 66 | SB 58 | 1 |
| 3721.68 | Added | 23-Mar-22 | 66 | SB 58 | 1 |
| 3721.69 | Added | 23-Mar-22 | 65 | HB 122 | 1 |
| 3721.99 | Amended | 23-Mar-22 | 66 | SB 58 | 1 |
| 4503.066 | Amended | 30-Sep-21 | 30 | HB 110 | 101.01 |
| 5101.63 | Amended | 30-Sep-21 | 30 | HB 110 | 101.01 |
| 5101.741 | Amended | 30-Sep-21 | 30 | HB 110 | 101.01 |
| 5162.06 | Amended | 13-Jun-22 | 83 | HB 136 | 1 |
| 5162.82 | Added | 30-Sep-21 | 30 | HB 110 | 101.01 |
| 5163.06 | Amended | 30-Sep-21 | 30 | HB 110 | 101.01 |
| 5163.061 | Amended | 30-Sep-21 | 30 | HB 110 | 101.01 |
| 5163.52 | Added | 1-Jan-22 | 30 | HB 110 | 101.01 |
| 5164.291 | Added | 23-Mar-22 | 65 | HB 122 | 1 |
| 5164.34 | Amended | 30-Sep-21 | 30 | HB 110 | 101.01 |
| 5164.342 | Amended | 30-Sep-21 | 30 | HB 110 | 101.01 |
| 5164.95 | Amended | 23-Mar-22 | 65 | HB 122 | 1 |
| 5165.01 | Amended | 30-Sep-21 | 30 | HB 110 | 101.01 |
| 5165.15 | Amended | 30-Jun-21 | 30 | HB 110 | 101.01 |
| 5165.151 | Amended | 30-Jun-21 | 30 | HB 110 | 101.01 |
| 5165.16 | Amended | 30-Sep-21 | 30 | HB 110 | 101.01 |
| 5165.17 | Amended | 30-Sep-21 | 30 | HB 110 | 101.01 |
| 5165.191 | Amended | 30-Sep-21 | 30 | HB 110 | 101.01 |
| 5165.25 | Repealed | 30-Sep-21 | 30 | HB 110 | 105.01 |
| 5165.26 | Amended | 30-Jun-21 | 30 | HB 110 | 101.01 |

| Section | Action | Effective Date | File | Bill No. | Sec. No. |
|---|---|---|---|---|---|
| 5165.261 | Added | 30-Sep-21 | 30 | HB 110 | 101.01 |
| 5165.36 | Amended | 30-Jun-21 | 30 | HB 110 | 101.01 |
| 5165.771 | Amended | 30-Sep-21 | 30 | HB 110 | 101.01 |

# SECTIONS AFFECTED BY 2022 LEGISLATION

**NOTE:** In addition to the sections listed below, users of this edition should be aware that additional section and case note annotations have also been appropriately incorporated throughout this publication. The sections with new and/or revised annotations do not appear in this listing.

| Section | Action | Effective Date | File | Bill No. | Sec. No. |
|---|---|---|---|---|---|
| 3721.20 | Added | 21-Jul-22 | 94 | HB 120 | 1 |

# OHIO ELDER LAW HANDBOOK

## OHIO REVISED CODE GENERAL PROVISIONS



## CHAPTER 1
## DEFINITIONS; RULES OF CONSTRUCTION

Construction



## CONSTRUCTION

### § 1.14 First day excluded and last day included in computing time; exceptions; legal holiday defined.

The time within which an act is required by law to be done shall be computed by excluding the first and including the last day; except that, when the last day falls on Sunday or a legal holiday, the act may be done on the next succeeding day that is not Sunday or a legal holiday.

When a public office in which an act, required by law, is to be performed is closed to the public for the entire day that constitutes the last day for doing the act or before its usual closing time on that day, the act may be performed on the next succeeding day that is not a Sunday or a legal holiday as defined in this section.

"Legal holiday" as used in this section means the following days:

(A) The first day of January, known as New Year's day;

(B) The third Monday in January, known as Martin Luther King day;

(C) The third Monday in February, known as Washington-Lincoln day;

(D) The day designated in the "Act of June 28, 1968," 82 Stat. 250, 5 U.S.C. 6103, as amended, for the commemoration of Memorial day;

(E) The nineteenth day of June, known as Juneteenth day;

(F) The fourth day of July, known as Independence day;

(G) The first Monday in September, known as Labor day;

(H) The second Monday in October, known as Columbus day;

(I) The eleventh day of November, known as Veterans' day;

(J) The fourth Thursday in November, known as Thanksgiving day;

(K) The twenty-fifth day of December, known as Christmas day;

(L) Any day appointed and recommended by the governor of this state or the president of the United States as a holiday.

If any day designated in this section as a legal holiday falls on Sunday, the next succeeding day is a legal holiday.

**HISTORY:**

RS § 4951; S&C 1130; 51 v 57, § 597; GC § 10216; Bureau of Code Revision, 10-1-53; 129 v 1073 (Eff 10-11-61); 133 v H 5 (Eff 1-1-71); 135 v H 460 (Eff 7-1-74); 136 v S 18 (Eff 8-1-75); 138 v S 93 (Eff 4-14-81); 139 v S 68 (Eff 5-17-81); 140 v H 364 (Eff 3-14-85); 148 v H 738. Eff 4-10-2001; 2021 hb110, § 101.01, effective September 30, 2021.

**Editor's Notes**

The provisions of § 3 of HB 364 of 1985 read as follows:

SECTION 3. In the case of collective bargaining agreements between private employers and bona fide labor organizations that are in effect on the effective date of sections 1.14 and 124.19 of the Revised Code as amended by this act, the day designated in the "Act of September 18, 1975," 89 Stat. 479, 5 U.S.C. 6103, as now or hereafter amended, for the commemoration of Memorial Day shall be observed as Decoration or Memorial Day unless the agreement specifically identifies another day as the one on which Decoration or Memorial Day will be observed.

**Amendment Notes**

The 2021 amendment by HB 110 added (E); and made related changes.

#### NOTES TO DECISIONS

Analysis

Act required by law
Appeal
Applicability
Civil Rules
Closing of public office
Computation of limitations periods
Construction
Contracts
Criminal cases
Election cases
History
Holiday
Judicial act not prohibited
Last day on Sunday, holiday
Speedy trial
Time limitations

**Act required by law**

A written demand for jury trial, required to prevent a waiver of the right to jury trial, is "an act, required by law" within the meaning of R.C. 1.14: Athens v. White, 28 Ohio St. 2d 35, 57 Ohio Op. 2d 155, 274 N.E.2d 760, 1971 Ohio LEXIS 416 (Ohio 1971).

**Appeal**

R.C. 1.14 governs the computation of the time within which the appeal of an administrator's decision must be filed with the unemployment compensation board pursuant to R.C. 4141.28: Perry v. Giles, 60 Ohio Misc. 40, 14 Ohio Op. 3d 117, 395 N.E.2d 1369, 1979 Ohio Misc. LEXIS 70 (Ohio C.P. 1979).

**Applicability**

Summary judgment was properly granted to a doctor in a re-filed medical negligence action, as the claim was filed more than one year after the original action was voluntarily dismissed pursuant to Civ.R. 41(A)(1) for purposes of R.C. 2305.19(A), and the limitations period of R.C. 2305.113(A) had expired; as the filing dates were not on a weekend or a legal holiday, Civ.R. 6(A) or R.C. 1.14 did not apply. Crump v. Batie, 2013-Ohio-2345, 2013 Ohio App. LEXIS 2273 (Ohio Ct. App., Clark County 2013).

Under R.C. 1.14, an insurer should exclude the day of mailing in computing the ten-day period required in a notice of cancellation for nonpayment of the premium: Love v. Motorists Mut. Ins. Co., 86 Ohio App. 3d 394, 620 N.E.2d 987, 1993 Ohio App. LEXIS 802 (Ohio Ct. App., Athens County 1993).

Based upon R.C. 1.14, the five-year period in former R.C. 1309.40(B)(1) is to be computed by excluding the day of filing and including the fifth anniversary date of the filing; thus, the continuation statement was timely filed with the secretary of state of Ohio in order to continue the effectiveness of that financing statement: Gordon Square Pharmacy, Inc. v. Harris Wholesale Co., 138 B.R. 533, 1992 Bankr. LEXIS 530 (Bankr. N.D. Ohio 1992).

R.C. 1.14 and Civ.R. 6(A) are applicable to the computation of the limitations period of R.C. 2125.02(D) for wrongful death actions. Therefore, where the two-year limitations period of R.C. 2125.02(D) expires on a Saturday, Sunday, or legal holiday, those days are excluded from the computation of the limitations period, and a complaint filed on the next day which is not a Saturday, Sunday or legal holiday is timely: Ritz v. Brown, 61 Ohio App. 3d 65, 572 N.E.2d 159, 1989 Ohio App. LEXIS 706 (Ohio Ct. App., Putnam County 1989).

No action may be filed for forcible entry and detainer under R.C. Chapter 1923. until expiration of the three-day notice period in R.C. 1923.04(A). The three-day period is calculated by excluding the day of service and then counting the next three days. The following day, the fourth day, is the earliest date an action can be filed under R.C. Chapter 1923.: Wintrow v. Smith, 32 Ohio Misc. 2d 12, 513 N.E.2d 363, 1987 Ohio Misc. LEXIS 146 (Ohio Mun. Ct. 1987).

In computing a period of one year from the happening of a particular event, the year begins the day following the day the event occurs and ends at the close of the first anniversary date the event occurred: Schon v. National Tea Co., 19 Ohio App. 2d 222, 48 Ohio Op. 2d 358, 250 N.E.2d 890, 1969 Ohio App. LEXIS 578 (Ohio Ct. App., Mahoning County 1969).

Where a statute requires an application to be filed in a public office within a certain number of calendar days, the time within which such filing can be made should be computed by excluding the first and including the last day and, when the last day falls on Saturday, then the filing may be done on the following Monday: Van Meter v. Segal-Schadel Co., 5 Ohio St. 2d 185, 34 Ohio Op. 2d 345, 214 N.E.2d 664, 1966 Ohio LEXIS 406 (Ohio 1966).

In computing periods of time, such as a thirty-day grace period, this section is applicable and the first day of the period must be excluded: Frontier-Embers Supper Club, Inc. v. Board of Liquor Control, 112 Ohio App. 325, 15 Ohio Op. 2d 393, 172 N.E.2d 717, 85 Ohio Law Abs. 97, 1960 Ohio App. LEXIS 673 (Ohio Ct. App., Franklin County 1960).

The language used in the wrongful death statute (R.C. 2125.02) providing for the term within which such action must be commenced after the death of the deceased person, must be construed so that the first day of the period named is excluded and the last-named day included. The provisions of this section are applicable to GC § 10509-167 (R.C. 2125.02): Young v. New York C. R. Co., 64 Ohio App. 362, 18 Ohio Op. 149, 28 N.E.2d 687, 1939 Ohio App. LEXIS 357 (Ohio Ct. App., Lorain County 1939).

In computing the time within which a suit in partition can be brought by a devisee under a will providing that the property remain as a whole and be managed by a trustee, and that it be "not sold or partitioned or divided for a period of twenty-five years after" testator's decease, the day of the testator's death must be excluded: Reibold v. McKerrow, 48 Ohio App. 115, 1 Ohio Op. 81, 192 N.E. 535, 16 Ohio Law Abs. 294, 1934 Ohio App. LEXIS 412 (Ohio Ct. App., Montgomery County 1934).

**Civil Rules**

Rules of Civil Procedure apply only to court proceedings and Ohio Civ.R. 6(A) does not apply to a teacher's request for an administrative hearing before the education board. Moffett v. Salem City Sch. Dist. Bd. of Educ., 2003-Ohio-7007, 2003 Ohio App. LEXIS 6396 (Ohio Ct. App., Columbiana County 2003).

R.C. 1.14, when construed together with CivR 6(A) with which it is in pari materia, provides that the period for commencing an action is extended to the next work day when the last day of the statutory period falls on a Saturday: Rahm v. Hemsoth, 53 Ohio App. 2d 147, 7 Ohio Op. 3d 136, 372 N.E.2d 358, 1976 Ohio App. LEXIS 5919 (Ohio Ct. App., Lucas County 1976).

**Closing of public office**

For purposes of R.C. 1.14, the village clerk's office was closed to the public. Thus the referendum petition was timely filed: Truman v. Village of Clay Center, 2005-Ohio-1385, 160 Ohio App. 3d 78, 825 N.E.2d 1182, 2005 Ohio App. LEXIS 1348 (Ohio Ct. App., Ottawa County 2005).

The words "such day" in this section do not require the conclusion that, where a public office in which an application is to be filed is closed on Saturday afternoon, it is not closed before its usual closing time on such day merely because R.C. 5.30 makes Saturday afternoon a legal holiday: Van Meter v. Segal-Schadel Co., 5 Ohio St. 2d 185, 34 Ohio Op. 2d 345, 214 N.E.2d 664, 1966 Ohio LEXIS 406 (Ohio 1966).

Where the office of clerk of courts is for any reason closed on a day that is not a legal holiday, and such day is one on which business is usually transacted, this section, by its terms tolls the statute of limitations, and a petition may then be filed on the next succeeding business day: Hackett v. Kibbee, 4 Ohio App. 2d 246, 33 Ohio Op. 2d 287, 211 N.E.2d 892, 1965 Ohio App. LEXIS 506 (Ohio Ct. App., Lorain County 1965).

**Computation of limitations periods**

Appellee accomplished service of her motion to vacate, modify, or correct an arbitration award within the three-month time limit in R.C. 2711.13 because under R.C. 1.14 and Civ.R. 6(A), the three-month period began the day after the arbitration award was delivered; in accordance with R.C. 1.45, appellee sent notice of her motion by certified mail on the same numerical day three months later; and under Civ.R. 5(B)(2)(c), service was complete at the time of mailing and was therefore timely. Cox v. Dayton Pub. Schs. Bd. of Educ., 2016-Ohio-5505, 147 Ohio St. 3d 298, 64 N.E.3d 977, 2016 Ohio LEXIS 2107 (Ohio 2016).

**Construction**

Based on the computation of time rules pursuant to R.C. 1.14 and Ohio Crim.R. 45(A), the time in which the State had to bring defendant to trial began running on the day after he was arrested and released on bail for purposes of a speedy trial under R.C. 2945.71(C)(2); the period between defendant's initial arrest and the date he waived his preliminary hearing and the case was bound over to the grand jury, as well as the time through the period taken in the grand jury process, was all chargeable to the State. State v. Alexander, 2009-Ohio-1401, 2009 Ohio App. LEXIS 1170 (Ohio Ct. App., Scioto County 2009).

**Contracts**

R.C. 1.14, which allows for relief when the last day for taking the action falls upon a Saturday, Sunday or legal holiday, is limited to acts required by law and does not apply to limitations periods established by the parties' contract: Kumar v. Metropolitan Property & Liability Ins. Co., 1992 Ohio App. LEXIS 5977 (Ohio Ct. App., Montgomery County Nov. 23, 1992).

In the interpretation of contracts, in the absence of an applicable statutory provision, time is computed by excluding the first day and including the last: McCarty v. Grange Mut. Casualty Co., 27 Ohio App. 2d 181, 56 Ohio Op. 2d 346, 273 N.E.2d 345, 1971 Ohio App. LEXIS 497 (Ohio Ct. App., Franklin County 1971).

The day of arrest is not counted in computing the time for trial under R.C. 2945.71: State v. Lautenslager, 112 Ohio App. 3d 108, 677 N.E.2d 1263, 1996 Ohio App. LEXIS 2835 (Ohio Ct. App., Marion County 1996).

**Criminal cases**

Pursuant to Crim.R. 45(A), the arrest date is not chargeable to the State of Ohio in computing speedy trial time. State v. Juarez-Hernandez, 2012-Ohio-4835, 2012 Ohio App. LEXIS 4232 (Ohio Ct. App., Franklin County 2012).

Trial court abused its discretion in a DUI and aggravated vehicular assault prosecution by denying a pretrial motion to suppress evidence as untimely under Ohio Crim.R. 12(D) where trial was set less than 35 days from arraignment and the motion to suppress could not have been filed seven days before trial because the seventh day was a Monday holiday; thus, the motion was timely under R.C. 1.14. State v. Jones, 2010-Ohio-2777, 2010 Ohio App. LEXIS 2280 (Ohio Ct. App., Cuyahoga County 2010).

Motion to dismiss was properly denied because there was no violation of U.S. Const. amend. VI or Ohio Const. art. I, § 10 where defendant was brought to trial within the 270 day time limit in R.C. 2945.71 where the counting started the day after defendant's arrest; even though the triple count provision applied to some of the time that defendant was in jail, the speedy trial clock was tolled due to a continuance motion, a speedy trial motion, and a motion seeking the identity of a confidential informant. The appellate court did not address defendant's argument that another time period that she spent in jail should have been considered because the speedy trial clock was tolled during that time; moreover, the State was not precluded from arguing that defendant's discovery motion tolled the speedy trial clock, even though that issue was not raised before the trial court. State v. Toler, 2009-Ohio-6669, 2009 Ohio App. LEXIS 5589 (Ohio Ct. App., Ross County 2009).

Date of arrest is not included when calculating the time in which an accused must be brought to trial. State v. Foden, 2009-Ohio-6532, 2009 Ohio App. LEXIS 5452 (Ohio Ct. App., Columbiana County 2009).

The day of arrest is not to be included when computing the time within which a defendant must be brought to trial under R.C. 2945.71: State v. Steiner, 71 Ohio App. 3d 249, 593 N.E.2d 368, 1991 Ohio App. LEXIS 994 (Ohio Ct. App., Summit County 1991).

Where the trial of a defendant charged with violation of a local ordinance was first inadvertently scheduled on Martin Luther King day, a state holiday under R.C. 1.14, and was then later rescheduled for the 99th day after his arrest, such continuance to the next available trial date was not facially unreasonable, and the defendant failed to introduce any evidence to the contrary. The defendant was thus not entitled to an acquittal under the "speedy trial" statute, R.C. 2945.73(B): Aurora v. Patrick, 61 Ohio St. 2d 107, 15 Ohio Op. 3d 150, 399 N.E.2d 1220, 1980 Ohio LEXIS 621 (Ohio 1980).

**Election cases**

Candidate was not entitled to a writ of mandamus directing a board of elections to place the candidate's name on a ballot because (1) there was conflicting evidence as to whether the candidate was a resident of the community in which the candidate sought to run for city council, under R.C. 3503.02, and a court would not substitute its judgment for that of a board of elections in such an event, and (2) a protest to the candidate's candidacy was timely filed, under R.C. 3513.263 and 1.14, because the sixty-fourth day prior to the general election fell on a holiday, so the protest could be filed the next day. State ex rel. Duncan v. Portage County Bd. of Elections, 2007-Ohio-5346, 115 Ohio St. 3d 405, 875 N.E.2d 578, 2007 Ohio LEXIS 2513 (Ohio 2007).

Where a county board of elections properly computed the time for certification of an initiative petition by a city auditor to the board for purposes of placing an issue on an election ballot, pursuant to R.C. 731.28, a registered voter's request for a writ of prohibition to prevent placement of the issue on the ballot was dismissed sua sponte by the court; the time computation was based on the liberal construction afforded by R.C. 1.14, as well as by the interpretation of R.C. 731.28 pursuant to an Ohio Supreme Court judicial precedent. Ramser v. Cuyahoga County Bd. of Elections,

2005-Ohio-5731, 2005 Ohio App. LEXIS 5163 (Ohio Ct. App., Cuyahoga County 2005).

R.C. 1.14 may be applied in election cases: State ex rel. Comm. to Repeal Ordinance No. 146-02 v. City of Lakewood, 2003-Ohio-5771, 100 Ohio St. 3d 252, 798 N.E.2d 362, 2003 Ohio LEXIS 2785 (Ohio 2003).

An action challenging the ballot language of a proposed constitutional amendment filed later than 64 days before the election was barred by Ohio Const. art XVI, § 1; the fact that the 64th day before the election fell on Labor Day did not modify this result because the Ohio Constitution does not contain a provision similar to R.C. 1.14, which applies to statutory time requirements: State ex rel. Ohio Roundtable v. Taft, 76 Ohio St. 3d 643, 670 N.E.2d 231, 1996 Ohio LEXIS 1211 (Ohio 1996).

**History**

For history of this section, see Kilgore v. Krabach, 117 Ohio App. 439, 24 Ohio Op. 2d 245, 192 N.E.2d 664, 1963 Ohio App. LEXIS 834 (Ohio Ct. App., Franklin County 1963).

**Holiday**

May 28, 1984, a national holiday, was a "legal holiday" within the meaning of R.C. 1.14(K): Shreve v. General Motors Corp., Elyria Div., 35 Ohio App. 3d 170, 520 N.E.2d 266, 1987 Ohio App. LEXIS 10494 (Ohio Ct. App., Lorain County 1987).

**Judicial act not prohibited**

Trial court did not err by entering the foreclosure judgment on Veterans' Day, a legal holiday under R.C. 1.14 as there was no statute containing a mandatory provision forbidding judges of courts to hear and determine matters on a legal holiday; thus, a judicial proceeding on such day was not void. Moreover, Montgomery County, Ohio, Ct. C.P. R. 1.37 allowed courts to electronically file documents 24 hours a day, 7 days a week. Bank of N.Y. Mellon v. Ackerman, 2012-Ohio-956, 2012 Ohio App. LEXIS 836 (Ohio Ct. App., Montgomery County 2012), dismissed, 2017-Ohio-4038, 149 Ohio St. 3d 1416, 75 N.E.3d 235, 2017 Ohio LEXIS 1014 (Ohio 2017).

**Last day on Sunday, holiday**

Developer's administrative appeal was timely as: (1) assuming the Clerk's September 25, 2015 letter constituted the final order, the 30th day, October 25, 2015, fell on a Sunday and the notice of appeal was served on the City on October 26, 2015; (2) R.C. 1.14 extended the deadline for filing an appeal, even though it was not included in R.C. 2505.07; and (3) as the 30th day following the mailing of the city council's decision was a Sunday, the developer could file its notice of appeal the next day that was not a Saturday, Sunday, or legal holiday. If the final order were issued at a later date, the October 26, 2015, notice of appeal was also timely and effective. NVR, Inc. v. City of Centerville, 2016-Ohio-6960, 71 N.E.3d 745, 2016 Ohio App. LEXIS 3822 (Ohio Ct. App., Champaign County 2016).

Employee presented enough evidence to withstand the employer's motion to dismiss for lack of subject matter jurisdiction; the evidence included a dated, certified mail return receipt, which showed that the employer received the written notice of a retaliatory discharge claim within the time limitations of R.C. 4123.90. Although the notice was received on the 91st day after the employee's discharge, the 90th day was a Sunday. Coon v. Tech. Constr. Specialties, Inc., 2010-Ohio-417, 2010 Ohio App. LEXIS 346 (Ohio Ct. App., Summit County 2010).

Where the last day for filing a motion to alter or amend a final judgment pursuant to Fed. R. Civ. P. 59(e) fell on the third Monday in January, which is an Ohio legal holiday under R.C. 1.14 known as Martin Luther King day, that day was to be excluded in computing the time for filing the motion, and the motion was therefore timely filed on the following day: Ohio Inns, Inc. v. Nye, 542 F.2d 673, 1976 U.S. App. LEXIS 6788 (6th Cir. Ohio 1976), cert. denied, 430 U.S. 946, 97 S. Ct. 1583, 51 L. Ed. 2d 794, 1977 U.S. LEXIS 1308 (U.S. 1977).

Where, in an action in forcible entry and detainer grounded on the default of defendant in failing to pay an installment of rent on the first day of the month as required by written lease, there is sufficient basis for a determination that defendant made reasonable effort to tender a check for such installment, by special delivery letter on the Monday following Sunday, the due date, such attempt constitutes a sufficient compliance with the term for payment, under provisions of this section, requiring the exclusion of Sunday in the computation of time when the last day falls on Sunday: Rea v. Helsley, 86 Ohio App. 114, 40 Ohio Op. 518, 90 N.E.2d 168, 1949 Ohio App. LEXIS 744 (Ohio Ct. App., Franklin County 1949).

**Speedy trial**

Where defendant was charged with two misdemeanors, the trial court properly denied his motion to dismiss because the State did not violate his right to a speedy trial; the speedy-trial period did not begin to run until the day after the charges were refiled and he was served with summons of the refiled charges. The remaining untolled time from this date until he filed his motion to dismiss, which was the date that the trial was scheduled, was well within the permissible 90-day period. State v. McIntyre, 2016-Ohio-5363, 2016 Ohio App. LEXIS 3232 (Ohio Ct. App., Ross County 2016).

**Time limitations**

Evidence indicated that the customer simply failed to file her complaint within applicable statute of limitations; because the customer failed to file complaint before the statute of limitations had expired, there was no action for the savings statute to save, and the store's motion for judgment on the pleadings was granted. Smith v. Wal-Mart Stores East, LP, 2019-Ohio-5037, 150 N.E.3d 499, 2019 Ohio App. LEXIS 5108 (Ohio Ct. App., Allen County 2019).

When a litigant sued a company under the Telephone Consumer Protection Act, 47 U.S.C.S. § 277, four years and one day after he received an unsolicited fax from the company, his complaint was untimely because, under R.C. 1.14, when calculating a period within which a required act was to be performed, a year began the day after the fax was received and ended at the close of the first anniversary of the day the fax was received, so the complaint was filed one day too late. Mokrytzky v. Super Sys., 2007-Ohio-404, 2007 Ohio App. LEXIS 340 (Ohio Ct. App., Cuyahoga County 2007).

Ohio courts consistently interpreted a "year," as set forth in R.C. 1.14, to begin the day following the date on which the event occurred and end at the close of the first anniversary of the day the event occurred, and, except in those instances where the last day of a period of limitation fell on a Sunday or on a holiday, the "last day" was universally included in the computation of time under a statute of limitations. Mokrytzky v. Super Sys., 2007-Ohio-404, 2007 Ohio App. LEXIS 340 (Ohio Ct. App., Cuyahoga County 2007).

## ATTORNEY GENERAL OPINIONS

The national day of prayer and thanksgiving, proclaimed by the President for a 24 hour period beginning 7:00 p.m., Saturday, January 27, 1973, was not a "holiday" for purposes of R.C. 143.12 and 1.14(J): 1973 Ohio Op. Att'y Gen. No. 069 (1973).

County employees, for the year 1970, are entitled to those holidays which are defined as legal holidays in R.C. 1.14, as such section is presently in effect; as of January 1, 1971, county employees will be entitled to the holidays specified in R.C. 1.14 as amended by Am. Sub. H.B. No. 5: 1970 Ohio Op. Att'y Gen. No. 012 (1970).

## RESEARCH REFERENCES AND PRACTICE AIDS

**Cross-References to Related Sections**

Computation of time in limitation of actions, RC § 2305.03.
Fractions of day, priority of legal rights, RC § 1.15.
Holidays and time, RC § 5.20 et seq.
Paid holidays—
County employees, RC § 325.19.
Nonteaching school employees, RC § 3319.087.
Township employees, RC § 511.10.

**Ohio Rules**

Time computation, CivR 6(A); CrimR 45(A); JuvR 18(A); AppR 14(A).

# TITLE 1
# STATE GOVERNMENT



## CHAPTER 109
## ATTORNEY GENERAL

Patient Abuse or Neglect



## PATIENT ABUSE OR NEGLECT

**§ 109.86 Investigation of abuse or neglect of care facility patient; prosecution.**

(A) The attorney general shall investigate any activity the attorney general has reasonable cause to believe is in violation of section 2903.34 of the Revised Code. Upon written request of the governor, the general assembly, the auditor of state, or the director of health, job and family services, aging, mental health and addiction services, or developmental disabilities, the attorney general shall investigate any activity these persons believe is in violation of section 2903.34 of the Revised Code. If after an investigation the attorney general has probable cause to prosecute for the commission of a crime, the attorney general shall refer the evidence to the prosecuting attorney, director of law, or other similar chief legal officer having jurisdiction over the matter. If the prosecuting attorney decides to present the evidence to a grand jury, the prosecuting attorney shall notify the attorney general in writing of the decision within thirty days after referral of the matter and shall present the evidence prior to the discharge of the next regular grand jury. If the director of law or other chief legal officer decides to prosecute the case, the director or officer shall notify the attorney general in writing of the decision within thirty days and shall initiate prosecution within sixty days after the matter was referred to the director or officer.

(B) If the prosecuting attorney, director of law, or other chief legal officer fails to notify the attorney general or to present evidence or initiate prosecution in accordance with division (A) of this section, the attorney general may present the evidence to a regular grand jury drawn and impaneled pursuant to sections 2939.01 to 2939.24 of the Revised Code, or to a special grand jury drawn and impaneled pursuant to section 2939.17 of the Revised Code, or the attorney general may initiate and prosecute any action in any court or tribunal of competent jurisdiction in this state. The attorney general, and any assistant or special counsel designated by the attorney general, have all the powers of a prosecuting attorney, director of law, or other chief legal officer when proceeding under this section. Nothing in this section shall limit or prevent a prosecuting attorney, director of law, or other chief legal officer from investigating and prosecuting criminal activity committed against a resident or patient of a care facility.

**HISTORY:**

141 v H 566 (Eff 9-17-86); 148 v H 471. Eff 7-1-2000; 153 v S 79, § 1, eff. 10-6-09; 2013 HB 59, § 101.01, eff. Sept. 29, 2013.

**Amendment Notes**

The 2013 amendment inserted "and addiction services" in the second sentence of (A).

153 v S 79, effective October 6, 2009, deleted "mental retardation and" preceding "developmental disabilities" throughout.

**RESEARCH REFERENCES AND PRACTICE AIDS**

**Cross-References to Related Sections**

Investigation by attorney general of alleged violation of resident's rights at care facility, RC § 3721.18.

Patient abuse; neglect, RC § 2903.34.

## CHAPTER 121
## STATE DEPARTMENTS

Miscellaneous



## MISCELLANEOUS

**§ 121.36 Contracts for provision of services to home care dependent adults.**

(A) As used in this section, "home care dependent adult" means an individual who resides in a private home or other noninstitutional and unlicensed living arrangement, without the presence of a parent or guardian, but has health and safety needs that require the provision of regularly scheduled home care services to remain in the home or other living arrangement because one of the following is the case:

(1) The individual is at least twenty-one years of age but less than sixty years of age and has a physical disability or mental impairment.

(2) The individual is sixty years of age or older, regardless of whether the individual has a physical disability or mental impairment.

(B) Except as provided in division (D) of this section, the departments of developmental disabilities, aging, job and family services, and health shall each implement this section with respect to all contracts entered into by the department for the provision of home care services to home care dependent adults that are paid for in whole or in part with federal, state, or local funds. Except as provided in division (D) of this section, each department shall also require all public and private entities that receive money from or through the department to comply with this section when entering into contracts for the provision of home care services to home care dependent adults that are paid for in whole or in part with federal, state, or local funds. Such entities may include county boards of developmental disabilities, area agencies on aging, county departments of job and family services, and boards of health of city and general health districts.

(C) Beginning one year after September 26, 2003, each contract subject to this section shall include terms requiring that the provider of home care services to home care dependent adults have a system in place that effectively monitors the delivery of the services by its employees. To be considered an effective monitoring system for purposes of the contract, the system established by a provider must include at least the following components:

(1) When providing home care services to home care dependent adults who have a mental impairment or life-threatening health condition, a mechanism to verify whether the provider's employees are present at the location where the services are to be provided and at the time the services are to be provided;

(2) When providing home care services to all other home care dependent adults, a system to verify at the end of each working day whether the provider's employees have provided the services at the proper location and time;

(3) A protocol to be followed in scheduling a substitute employee when the monitoring system identifies that an employee has failed to provide home care services at the proper location and time, including standards for determining the length of time that may elapse without jeopardizing the health and safety of the home care dependent adult;

(4) Procedures for maintaining records of the information obtained through the monitoring system;

(5) Procedures for compiling annual reports of the information obtained through the monitoring system, including statistics on the rate at which home care services were provided at the proper location and time;

(6) Procedures for conducting random checks of the accuracy of the monitoring system. For purposes of conducting these checks, a random check is considered to be a check of not more than five per cent of the home care visits the provider's employees make to different home care dependent adults within a particular work shift.

(D) In implementing this section, the departments shall exempt providers of home care services who are self-employed providers with no other employees or are otherwise considered by the departments not to be agency providers. The departments shall conduct a study on how the exempted providers may be made subject to the requirement of effectively monitoring whether home care services are being provided and have been provided at the proper location and time. Not later than two years after September 26, 2003, the departments shall prepare a report of their findings and recommendations. The report shall be submitted to the president of the senate and the speaker of the house of representatives.

(E) The departments of developmental disabilities, aging, job and family services, and health shall each adopt rules as necessary to implement this section. The rules shall be adopted in accordance with Chapter 119. of the Revised Code.

**HISTORY:**

150 v H 95, § 1, eff. 9-26-03; 153 v S 79, § 1, eff. 10-6-09.

**Amendment Notes**

153 v S 79, effective October 6, 2009, deleted "mental retardation and" preceding "developmental disabilities" throughout; and, in the introductory language of (C) and in (D), substituted "September 26, 2003" for "the effective date of this section".

# CHAPTER 173
# DEPARTMENT OF AGING

## § 173.01 Powers and duties of department of aging.

The department of aging shall:

(A) Be the designated state agency to administer programs of the federal government relating to the aged, requiring action within the state, that are not the specific responsibility of another state agency under federal or state statutes. The department shall be the sole state agency to administer funds granted by the federal government under the "Older Americans Act of 1965," 79 Stat. 219, 42 U.S.C. 3001, as amended. The department shall not supplant or take over for the counties or municipal corporations or from other state agencies or facilities any of the specific responsibilities borne by them on November 23, 1973. The department shall cooperate with such federal and state agencies, counties, and municipal corporations and private agencies or facilities within the state in furtherance of the purposes as set forth in this chapter.

(B) Administer state funds appropriated for its use for administration and for grants and may use appropriated state funds as state match for federal grants. All federal funds received shall be reported to the director of budget and management.

(C) Review all proposed plans, programs, and rules primarily affecting persons sixty years of age or older, and shall be sent a copy of all proposed and final rules, as well as proposals for plans and programs that primarily affect persons sixty years of age or older and notices of all hearings on such rules, plans, and programs. Any state agency proposing a plan, program, or rule that primarily affects persons sixty years of age or older shall submit a copy of such proposal to the department for its written comments. No such proposed plan, program, or rule shall take effect until the department's comments have been requested. The department shall review the proposal and submit a written comment on such proposal to the agency making the proposal, within thirty days from the date the department receives the proposal. If the department does not agree that the proposed plan, program, or rule shall take effect as proposed, the department shall set forth in writing its reasons and its suggestions for changes in the proposed plan, program, or rule. If the agency making the proposal does not choose to comply with the suggestions of the department, the agency making the proposal shall send the department, no later than thirty days before the proposal becomes final, written notice of its intention not to comply with such suggestions and its reason for such noncompliance.

This section does not apply to plans or revisions adopted under section 5101.46 of the Revised Code.

(D) Plan, initiate, coordinate, and evaluate statewide programs, services, and activities for elderly people;

(E) Disseminate information concerning the problems of elderly people and establish and maintain a central clearinghouse of information on public programs at all levels of government that would be of interest or benefit to the elderly;

(F) Report annually to the governor and the general assembly on the department's programs;

(G) Have authority to contract with public or private groups to perform services for the department;

(H) Adopt rules in accordance with Chapter 119. of the Revised Code to govern the operation of services and facilities for the elderly that are provided, operated, contracted for, or supported by the department, and determine that those services and facilities are operated in conformity with the rules;

(I) Determine the needs of the elderly and represent their interests at all levels of government;

(J) Establish and operate a state long-term care ombudsman program pursuant to sections 307 and 712 of the "Older Americans Act of 1965," 42 U.S.C. 3027 and 3058.

**HISTORY:**

RC § 173.03, 135 v H 384 (Eff 11-23-73); 136 v S 351 (Eff 8-27-76); 137 v H 1 (Eff 8-26-77); RC § 173.01, 140 v H 660 (Eff 7-26-84); 141 v H 201. Eff 7-1-85; 2017 hb49, § 101.01, effective September 29, 2017.

**Amendment Notes**

The 2017 amendment by HB 49 deleted former (H), which read: "Conduct investigations under section 3721.17 of the Revised Code"; deleted (I), which formerly read: "Hire investigators to conduct investigations of alleged violations of sections 3721.10 to 3721.17 of the Revised Code pursuant to section 3721.17 of the Revised Code; deleted (J), which formerly read: "Adopt rules under Chapter 119. of the Revised Code to govern investigations conducted under section 3721.17 of the Revised Code"; redesignated former (K) through (M) as (H) through (J); substituted "rules in accordance with" for "rules pursuant to" in (K); and in (J), substituted "state long-term care" for "long-term care," and "pursuant to sections 307 and 712 of the 'Older Americans Act of 1965', 42 U.S.C. 3027 and 3058" for "pursuant to section 307(a)(12)(A) of the 'Older Americans Act of 1965,' as amended by the 'Comprehensive Older Americans Act Amendments of 1978,' 92 Stat. 1524, 42 U.S.C.A. 3027, and amendments thereto."

**RESEARCH REFERENCES AND PRACTICE AIDS**

**Cross-References to Related Sections**

Office of state long-term care ombudsman program, RC § 173.15.
Duties of state ombudsperson, RC § 173.17.
Persons excepted from long-term care ombudsman training program, RC § 173.21.
Rights of residents in rest homes, other homes, RC § 3721.10 et seq.
Investigation by attorney general of alleged violations, RC § 3721.18.

**Ohio Administrative Code**

Department of aging. OAC ch. 173-1 et seq.
Division of long-term care. OAC ch. 173:3-1.

**Comparative Legislation**

Commission on aging:
CA—Cal Wel & Inst Code § 9200 et seq
IL—20 Ill. Comp. Stat. § 105/4
KY—KRS § 205.201
MI—MCLS § 400.583
PA—71 P.S. § 581-3

## § 173.011 Planning and service areas for administration of Older Americans Act.

(A) When administering funds granted under the "Older Americans Act of 1965," 79 Stat. 219, 42 U.S.C. 3001, as amended, the department of aging may divide the state into separate multi-county regions that shall be known as planning and service areas. If the department divides the state into those areas, then, consistent with the rules adopted under division (C)(1) of this section, it shall designate one public entity or one private nonprofit entity as each area's agency on aging. That agency shall administer programs on behalf of the department under the Older Americans Act of 1965 within its planning and service area.

(B) Consistent with the rules adopted under division (C)(2) of this section and following an adjudication hearing conducted in accordance with Chapter 119. of the Revised Code, the department may issue an adjudication order that withdraws or provisionally maintains the designation of an entity as an agency on aging.

(C) The department shall adopt rules under Chapter 119. of the Revised Code that do both of the following:

(1) Establish criteria to be used for designating an agency on aging;

(2) Provide procedures and grounds for withdrawing or provisionally maintaining the designation of an entity as an agency on aging of a planning and service area.

**HISTORY:**

148 v H 283. Eff 9-29-99.

**RESEARCH REFERENCES AND PRACTICE AIDS**

**Ohio Administrative Code**

Designation of new area agencies on aging. OAC 173-2-02; de-designation. OAC 173-2-04.
Designation of planning and service areas. OAC 173-1-03.

## § 173.012 Training programs for area agencies on aging, long-term care facilities, and providers of long-term care services; fees.

The department of aging may develop and offer training programs to area agencies on aging, long-term care facilities, providers of long-term care services, and other interested parties. The department may charge fees for the training programs. Amounts collected from charging the fees shall be deposited into the state treasury to the credit of the senior community outreach fund, which is hereby created. Money credited to the fund may be used by the department to administer this section and to develop and offer additional training programs.

**HISTORY:**

2021 hb110, § 101.01, effective September 30, 2021.

## § 173.02 Additional duties of department; adoption of rules.

The department of aging shall adopt, and may rescind, rules as necessary to carry out the provisions of Chapter 173. of the Revised Code and may:

(A) Provide technical assistance and consultation to public and private nonprofit agencies with respect to programs, services, and activities for elderly people;

(B) Cooperate with federal agencies, other state agencies or departments, and organizations to conduct studies and surveys on the special problems of the aged in such matters as mental and physical health, housing, transportation, family relationships, employment, income, vocational rehabilitation, recreation, and education; make such reports as are appropriate to the governor and other federal and state agencies; and develop recommendations for administrative or legislative action to alleviate such problems;

(C) Develop and strengthen the services available for the aging in the state by coordinating the existing services provided by federal, state, and local departments and agencies, and private agencies and facilities;

(D) Extend and expand services for the aged through coordinating the interests and efforts of local communities in studying the problems of the aged citizens of this state;

(E) Encourage, promote, and aid in the establishment of programs and services on the local level for the betterment of the living conditions of the aged by making it possible for the aged to more fully enjoy and participate in family and community life;

(F) Sponsor voluntary community rehabilitation and recreational facilities for the purpose of improving the general welfare of the elderly;

(G) Stimulate the training of workers in the field of aging;

(H) Provide consultants to agencies, associations, or individuals providing services supported by the department;

(I) Provide support which shall include, but not be limited to, financial support for the Martin Janis multipurpose senior center in Columbus;

(J) Recommend methods of improving the effectiveness of state services for elderly citizens;

(K) Adopt rules pursuant to Chapter 119. of the Revised Code to request fees, if not prohibited by any federal or state law, from persons using services or facilities for the elderly that are provided, operated, contracted for, or supported by the department, provided that requesting the fees will not disqualify the department from receiving federal or state funds;

(L) Publish a description of the organization and functions of the department so that all interested agencies and individuals may receive information about, and be better able to solicit assistance from, the department.

**HISTORY:**

140 v H 660 (Eff 7-26-84); 147 v H 215. Eff 6-30-97.

**RESEARCH REFERENCES AND PRACTICE AIDS**

**Ohio Administrative Code**

Division of long-term care —
PASSPORT program. OAC ch. 173:3-1.

**§ 173.021 Renumbered.**

Amended and renumbered RC § 173.04 in 140 v H 660. Eff 7-26-84.

**§ 173.022 Renumbered.**

Amended and renumbered RC § 173.05 in 140 v H 660. Eff 7-26-84.

**§ 173.03 Advisory council for aging.**

(A) There is hereby created the Ohio advisory council for the aging, which shall consist of twelve members to be appointed by the governor with the advice and consent of the senate. Two ex officio members of the council shall be members of the house of representatives appointed by the speaker of the house of representatives and shall be members of two different political parties. Two ex officio members of the council shall be members of the senate appointed by the president of the senate and shall be members of two different political parties. The medicaid director and directors of mental health and addiction services, developmental disabilities, health, and job and family services, or their designees, shall serve as ex officio members of the council. The council shall carry out its role as defined under the "Older Americans Act of 1965," 79 Stat. 219, 42 U.S.C. 3001, as amended.

At the first meeting of the council, and annually thereafter, the members shall select one of their members to serve as chairperson and one of their members to serve as vice-chairperson.

(B) Members of the council shall be appointed for a term of three years, except that for the first appointment members of the Ohio commission on aging who were serving on the commission immediately prior to July 26, 1984, shall become members of the council for the remainder of their unexpired terms. Thereafter, appointment to the council shall be for a three-year term by the governor. Each member shall hold office from the date of appointment until the end of the term for which the member was appointed. Any member appointed to fill a vacancy occurring prior to the expiration of the term for which the member's predecessor was appointed shall hold office for the remainder of the term. No member shall continue in office subsequent to the expiration date of the member's term unless reappointed under the provisions of this section, and no member shall serve more than three consecutive terms on the council.

(C) Membership of the council shall represent all areas of Ohio and shall be as follows:

(1) A majority of members of the council shall have attained the age of fifty and have a knowledge of and continuing interest in the affairs and welfare of the older citizens of Ohio. The fields of business, labor, health, law, and human services shall be represented in the membership.

(2) No more than seven members shall be of the same political party.

(D) Any member of the council may be removed from office by the governor for neglect of duty, misconduct, or malfeasance in office after being informed in writing of the charges and afforded an opportunity for a hearing. Two consecutive unexcused absences from regularly scheduled meetings constitute neglect of duty.

(E) The director of aging may reimburse a member for actual and necessary traveling and other expenses incurred in the discharge of official duties. But reimbursement shall be made in the manner and at rates that do not exceed those prescribed by the director of budget and management for any officer, member, or employee of, or consultant to, any state agency.

(F) Council members are not limited as to the number of terms they may serve.

(G)(1) The department of aging may award grants to or enter into contracts with a member of the advisory council or an entity that the member represents if any of the following apply:

(a) The department determines that the member or the entity the member represents is capable of providing the goods or services specified under the terms of the grant or contract.

(b) The member has not taken part in any discussion or vote of the council related to whether the council should recommend that the department of aging award the grant to or enter into the contract with the member of the advisory council or the entity that the member represents.

(2) A member of the advisory council is not in violation of Chapter 102. or section 2921.42 of the Revised Code with regard to receiving a grant or entering into a contract under this section if the conditions of division (G)(1)(a) and (b) of this section have been met.

**HISTORY:**

140 v H 660 (Eff 7-26-84); 141 v H 428 (Eff 12-23-86); 144 v S 331 (Eff 11-13-92); 148 v H 471. Eff 7-1-2000; 153 v S 79, § 1, eff. 10-6-09; 2011 SB 171, § 1, eff. June 30, 2011; 2013 HB 59, § 101.01, eff. Sept. 29, 2013.

**Editor's Notes**

The provisions of § 4 of H.B. 516 (150 v —) read in part as follows:

SECTION 4. The following agencies shall be retained pursuant to division (D) of section 101.83 of the Revised Code and shall expire on December 31, 2010:

| AGENCY NAME | REVISED CODE OR UNCODIFIED SECTION |
|---|---|
| ○○○ | ○○○ |
| Ohio Advisory Council for the Aging | 173.03 |
| ○○○ | ○○○ |

**Amendment Notes**

The 2013 amendment substituted "medicaid director and directors of mental health and addiction services" for "directors of mental health" in the fourth sentence of the first paragraph of (A); and substituted "age of fifty" for "age of sixty" in the first sentence of (C)(1).

The 2011 amendment, in the last sentence of (B), substituted "No member shall" for "Any member may" and "unless reappointed under the provisions of this section, and no member shall serve more than three consecutive terms on the council" for "until a successor takes office and shall be compensated for the period served between the expiration of the member's term and the beginning of the successor's term"; and rewrote (E) and (G).

153 v S 79, effective October 6, 2009, deleted "mental retardation and" preceding "developmental disabilities" throughout.

**RESEARCH REFERENCES AND PRACTICE AIDS**

**Ohio Constitution**

Appointments subject to advice and consent of Senate, Ohio Const. art III, § 21.

**§ 173.04 Programs relating to Alzheimer's disease; task force.**

(A) As used in this section:

(1) Respite care means short-term, temporary care or supervision provided to a person who has dementia in the absence of the person who normally provides that care or supervision.

(2) "Dementia" includes Alzheimer's disease or other dementia.

(B) Through the internet web site maintained by the department of aging, the director of aging shall disseminate dementia training materials for licensed physicians, registered nurses, licensed practical nurses, administrators of health care programs, social workers, and other health care and social service personnel who participate or assist in the care or treatment of persons who have dementia. The training materials disseminated through the web site may be developed by the director or obtained from other sources.

(C) To the extent funds are available, the director shall administer respite care programs and other supportive services for persons who have dementia and their families or care givers. Respite care programs shall be approved by the director and shall be provided for the following purposes:

(1) Giving persons who normally provide care or supervision for a person who has dementia relief from the stresses and responsibilities that result from providing such care;

(2) Preventing or reducing inappropriate institutional care and enabling persons who have dementia to remain at home as long as possible.

(D) The director may provide services under this section to persons with dementia and their families regardless of the age of the persons with dementia.

(E) The director may adopt rules in accordance with Chapter 119. of the Revised Code governing respite care programs and other supportive services, the distribution of funds, and the purpose for which funds may be utilized under this section.

**HISTORY:**

RC § 3701.18, 141 v S 256 (Eff 6-7-86); RC § 173.04, 145 v H 152. Eff 7-1-93; 152 v H 119, § 101.01, eff. 9-29-07; 2011 SB 171, § 1, eff. June 30, 2011; 2019 hb166, § 101.01, effective October 17, 2019.

**Editor's Notes**

The provisions of § 4 of H.B. 516 (150 v —) read in part as follows:

SECTION 4. The following agencies shall be retained pursuant to division (D) of section 101.83 of the Revised Code and shall expire on December 31, 2010:

| AGENCY | REVISED CODE OR UNCODIFIED SECTION |
| --- | --- |
| ○○○ | ○○○ |
| Alzheimer's Disease Task Force | 173.04(F) |
| ○○○ | ○○○ |

**Amendment Notes**

The 2019 amendment by HB 166 added the (A)(1) designation; substituted "dementia" for "Alzheimer's disease" wherever it appears in (A)(1) and (B) through (D); added (A)(2); and made a stylistic and a related change.

The 2011 amendment substituted "may adopt" for "shall adopt" in (E); and deleted (F), pertaining to the creation of an Alzheimer's disease and related disorders task force by the director.

152 v H 119, effective September 29, 2007, in (B), substituted "Through the internet web site maintained by the department of aging, the director of aging shall disseminate Alzheimer's disease" for "The director of aging shall develop and disseminate new training materials of disseminate existing", and added the last sentence; and rewrote (F).

**RESEARCH REFERENCES AND PRACTICE AIDS**

**Comparative Legislation**

Alzheimer's disease and related dementias services research:
42 USCS § 11201 et seq
CA—Cal Health & Saf Code § 125280
IL—410 Ill. Comp. Stat. § 410/1 et seq
MI—MCLS § 333.5511 et seq

## § 173.05 Acting director.

Deputy director of the aging shall be the acting director when the director is absent or disabled or the position is vacant. The director shall specify who shall be the acting director if no deputy director has been appointed.

**HISTORY:**

RC § 173.02.1, 136 v S 351 (Eff 8-27-76); RC § 173.02.2, 137 v H 1084 (Eff 1-5-79); RC § 173.05, 140 v H 660. Eff 7-26-84.

## § 173.06 Golden buckeye card program.

(A) The director of aging shall establish a golden buckeye card program and provide a golden buckeye card to any resident of this state who applies to the director for a card and is sixty years of age or older or is a person with a disability and is eighteen years of age or older. The director shall devise programs to provide benefits of any kind to card holders, and encourage support and participation in them by all persons, including governmental organizations. Card holders shall be entitled to any benefits granted to them by private persons or organizations, the laws of this state, or ordinances or resolutions of political subdivisions. This section does not require any person or organization to provide benefits to any card holder. The department of aging shall bear all costs of the program.

(B) Before issuing a golden buckeye card to any person, the director shall establish the identity of any person who applies for a card and shall ascertain that such person is sixty years of age or older or is a person with a disability and is eighteen years of age or older. The director shall adopt rules under Chapter 119. of the Revised Code to prevent the issuance of cards to persons not qualified to have them. Cards shall contain the signature of the card holder and any other information the director considers necessary to carry out the purposes of the golden buckeye card program under this section. Any card that the director issues shall be held in perpetuity by the original card holder and shall not be transferable to any other person. A person who loses the person's card may obtain another card from the director upon providing the same information to the director as was required for the issuance of the original card.

(C) No person shall use a golden buckeye card except to obtain a benefit for the holder of the card to which the holder is entitled under the conditions of the offer.

(D) As used in this section, "person with a disability" means a person who has some impairment of body or mind and has been certified as permanently and totally disabled by an agency of this state or the United States having the function of so classifying persons.

**HISTORY:**

RC § 173.13, 138 v S 243 (Eff 3-27-80); RC § 173.06, 140 v H 660 (Eff 7-26-84); 141 v H 186 (Eff 10-9-85); 149 v S 261. Eff 9-4-2002; 150 v H 95, § 1, eff. 9-26-03; 151 v H 468, § 4, eff. 7-1-07.

**Amendment Notes**

Section 4, 151 v H 468, effective July 1, 2007, in (A), deleted "except that the department is not required to bear any costs related to the prescription drug programs established pursuant to section 173.061 of the Revised Code" from the end.

**RESEARCH REFERENCES AND PRACTICE AIDS**

**Ohio Administrative Code**

Golden buckeye card program. OAC ch. 173-6.

## § 173.061 Disclosure of card program records.

Records identifying the recipients of golden buckeye cards issued under section 173.06 of the Revised Code are not public records subject to inspection or copying under section 149.43 of the Revised Code and may be disclosed only at the discretion of the director of aging. The director may disclose only information in records identifying the recipients of golden buckeye cards that does not contain the recipient's medical history.

**HISTORY:**

149 v S 261. Eff 9-4-2002; 150 v H 95, § 1, eff. 9-26-03; 151 v H 468, § 4, eff. 7-1-07.

**Publisher's Note:**

This section was amended and renumbered from RC § 173.062 by 151 v H 468, effective July 1, 2007.

**Amendment Notes**

Section 4, 151 v H 468, effective July 1, 2007, deleted "or prescription drug cards issued under section 173.061 of the Revised Code" preceding "are not public records", "or prescription drug cards" following "buckeye cards", and "or prescription drug utilization history" from the end.

**RESEARCH REFERENCES AND PRACTICE AIDS**

**Ohio Administrative Code**

Golden buckeye card program. OAC ch. 173-6.

## § 173.062 Renumbered.

Amended and renumbered RC § 173.061 by 151 v H 468. Eff 7-1-07

## § 173.07 Repealed.

Repealed, 151 v H 468, § 5 [149 v S 261. Eff 9-4-2002; 150 v H 95, § 1, eff. 9-26-03]. Eff 7-1-07.

**Editor's Notes**

This section concerned reports on prescription drug programs.

### § 173.071 Repealed.

Repealed, 151 v H 468, § 5 [149 v S 261. Eff 9-4-2002; 150 v H 95, § 1, eff. 9-26-03]. Eff 7-1-07.

**Editor's Notes**

This section concerned source and contents of reports.

### § 173.072 Repealed.

Repealed, 151 v H 468, § 5 [149 v S 261. Eff 9-4-2002]. Eff 7-1-07.

**Editor's Notes**

This section concerned distribution of reports.

### § 173.08 Resident services coordinator program.

(A) The resident services coordinator program is established in the department of aging to fund resident services coordinators. The coordinators shall provide information to low-income and special-needs tenants, including the elderly, who live in financially assisted rental housing complexes, and assist those tenants in identifying and obtaining community and program services and other benefits for which they are eligible.

(B) The resident services coordinator program fund is hereby created in the state treasury to support the resident services coordinator program established pursuant to this section. The fund consists of all moneys the department of development sets aside pursuant to division (A)(3) of section 174.02 of the Revised Code and moneys the general assembly appropriates to the fund.

**HISTORY:**

150 v H 95, § 1, eff. 6-26-03; 150 v H 431, § 1, eff. 7-1-05; 153 v H 1, § 101.01, eff. 10-16-09.

**Amendment Notes**

153 v H 1, effective October 16, 2009, substituted "division (A)(3)" for "division (A)(4)" in the second sentence of (B).

### § 173.09 Repealed.

Repealed, 139 v H 694, § 2 [136 v S 351]. Eff 11-15-81.

**Editor's Notes**

This section concerned interdepartmental committee on aging.

### § 173.10 Repealed.

Repealed, 146 v H 117, § 2 [145 v H 152]. Eff 9-29-95.

**Editor's Notes**

This section concerned assisted living facilities for older adults and community-based long-term care services.

### § 173.11 Multipurpose senior centers.

The department of aging shall, as appropriate and feasible and to the extent federal, state, and local funding is available, develop a system of community multipurpose senior centers for the purposes of:

(A) Providing centralized, coordinated medical, social, supportive, and rehabilitative services to older adults;

(B) Encouraging older adults to maintain physical, social, and emotional well-being and to live dignified and reasonably independent lives in their own homes;

(C) Diminishing the rate of inappropriate entry and placement of older adults in nursing homes, sheltered housing for older adults, and related facilities.

The department shall, in accordance with Chapter 119. of the Revised Code, adopt rules under which counties, townships, municipal corporations, or local nonprofit organizations may make application to the department to operate a multipurpose senior center or to participate in a multipurpose senior center program. Procedures shall be established for the maximum feasible participation by older adults and representatives of organizations of older adults in the planning of these programs. The area agency on aging, established under the "Older Americans Act of 1965," 79 Stat. 219, 42 U.S.C. 3001, as amended, shall be given the opportunity to review and comment on all applications for the establishment of a center or the expansion of the scope of services provided by a senior center operated as part of the social services system under the agency's area plan.

The department shall plan, coordinate, and monitor, and, to the extent feasible, provide funds for services for older adults under this section and section 173.12 of the Revised Code. In order to carry out the purposes of such sections, the department or the designated local entity may accept gifts and grants and enter into contracts for the purchase of services.

The multipurpose senior centers shall be centrally located and easily accessible to any public transportation available in such location. The centers may provide transportation for older adults who wish to utilize services available in the facility, but are unable to reach it because of the lack of financial resources or physical impairment. Centers shall be designed to provide ease of access and use considering the infirmities of frail and handicapped older adults. Special safety features shall be provided as unobtrusively as possible. In establishing the location of multipurpose senior centers, the department shall, to the extent feasible, give precedence to the use of existing buildings and facilities, which may be renovated, over the construction of new buildings and facilities.

**HISTORY:**

137 v H 1084 (Eff 1-5-79); 138 v H 827 (Eff 8-7-80); 140 v H 660. Eff 7-26-84.

**ATTORNEY GENERAL OPINIONS**

Under R.C. 173.11 and 505.70(B), a township has authority to purchase a building to be used as a multipurpose senior center: 1987 Ohio Op. Att'y Gen. No. 106.

**RESEARCH REFERENCES AND PRACTICE AIDS**

**Cross-References to Related Sections**

Contracting for services provided at senior center, RC § 173.12.

Trustees may give financial assistance to and cooperate with other agencies, RC § 505.70.

### § 173.12 Services to be available at centers; liability insurance for volunteers.

The services provided by a multipurpose senior center shall be available to all residents of the area served by the center who are sixty years of age or older, except where legal requirements for the use of funds available for a component program specify other age limits. Persons who receive services from the center may be encouraged to make voluntary contributions to the center, but no otherwise eligible person shall be refused services because of inability to make a contribution.

Services provided by the center may include, but are not limited to, the following:

(A) Services available within the facility:

(1) Preventive medical services, diagnostic and treatment services, emergency health services, and counseling on health matters, which are provided on a regular basis by a licensed physician, pharmacist, or registered nurse or other qualified health professional;

(2) A program to locate full-or part-time employment opportunities;

(3) Information and counseling by professional or other persons specially trained or qualified to enable older adults to make decisions on personal matters, including income, health, housing, transportation, and social relationships;

(4) A listing of services available in the community for older adults to assist in identifying the type of assistance needed, to place them in contact with appropriate services, and to determine whether services have been received and identified needs met;

(5) Legal advice and assistance by an attorney or a legal assistant acting under the supervision of an attorney;

(6) Recreation, social activities, and educational activities.

(B) Services provided outside the facility:

(1) Routine health services necessary to help functionally impaired older adults to maintain an appropriate standard of personal health, provided to them in their homes by licensed physicians, registered nurses, or other qualified health service personnel;

(2) Household services, such as light housekeeping, laundering, meal preparation, personal and grocery shopping, check cashing and bill paying, friendly visiting, minor household repairs, and yard chores, that are necessary to help functionally impaired older adults meet the normal demands of daily living;

(3) The delivery, on a regular schedule, of hot or cold nourishing meals to functionally impaired older adults and the determination of the nutritional needs of such persons;

(4) Door-to-door vehicular transportation for functionally impaired or other older adults.

Other services, including social and recreational services, adult education courses, reassurance by telephone, escort services, and housing assistance may be added to the center's program as appropriate, to the extent that resources are available.

Services may be furnished by public agencies or private persons or organizations, but all services shall be coordinated by a single management unit, operating within the center, that is established, staffed, and equipped for this purpose.

The department of aging, or the local entity approved by the department under section 173.11 of the Revised Code for the operation of a center, may contract for any or all of the services provided by the center with any other state agency, county, township, municipal corporation, school district, community or technical college district, health district, person, or organization.

The department shall provide for the necessary insurance coverage to protect all volunteers from the normal risks of personal liability while they are acting within the scope of their volunteer assignments for the provision of services under this section.

As used in this section, "functionally impaired older adult" means an individual sixty years of age or older who requires help from others in order to cope with the normal demands of daily living.

**HISTORY:**

137 v H 1084 (Eff 1-5-79); 138 v H 827 (Eff 8-7-80); 140 v H 660. Eff 7-26-84; 2018 sb265, § 1, effective April 5, 2019.

**Amendment Notes**

The 2018 amendment by SB 265 substituted "pharmacist, or registered nurse" for "or by a registered nurse" in (A)(1).

### ATTORNEY GENERAL OPINIONS

The adoption by the Department of Aging of OAC 173:1-3-05(D), part of which requires that a facility "have adequate insurance, or be self-insured for its staff, including volunteers" prior to designation by the Department as a community multipurpose senior center, satisfies the Department's obligation under R.C. 173.12 to provide for personal liability insurance for volunteers serving at community multipurpose senior centers: 1992 Ohio Op. Att'y Gen. No. 042 (1992).

### RESEARCH REFERENCES AND PRACTICE AIDS

**Cross-References to Related Sections**

Center may conduct bingo games, RC § 173.121.

Multipurpose senior centers; provision of funds, RC § 173.11.

Trustees may give financial assistance to and cooperate with other agencies, RC § 505.70.

## § 173.121 Center may conduct bingo games.

(A) As used in this section, "bingo," "bingo game operator," and "participant" have the same meanings as in section 2915.01 of the Revised Code.

(B) Notwithstanding sections 2915.07 to 2915.13 of the Revised Code, a multipurpose senior center may conduct bingo games described in division (O)(1) of section 2915.01 of the Revised Code, but only if it complies with all of the following requirements:

(1) All bingo games are conducted only on the premises of the facility.

(2) All participants are twenty-one years of age or older.

(3) All bingo game operators are sixty years of age or older and receive no compensation for serving as operators.

(4) No participant is charged an admission fee, and no participant is charged more than twenty-five cents to purchase a bingo card or sheet.

(5) All proceeds from games are used only for any of the following:

(a) To pay winners monetary or nonmonetary prizes;

(b) To provide refreshments;

(c) To defray any costs directly related to conducting the games;

(d) To defray costs of services the facility provides in accordance with section 173.12 of the Revised Code.

**HISTORY:**

143 v H 573 (Eff 4-10-91); 149 v H 512. Eff 7-1-03; 150 v H 87, § 24, eff. 3-31-03; 2012 HB 386, § 1, eff. June 11, 2012.

**Editor's Notes**

The provisions of § 24 of H.B. 87 (150 v —) read as follows:

SECTION 24. Sections 1 to 9 of Am.Sub. H.B. 512 of the 124th General Assembly take effect July 1, 2003.

This section is not subject to the referendum. Therefore, under Ohio Constitution, Article II, Section 1d and section 1.471 of the Revised Code, this section goes into immediate effect when this act becomes law.

**Amendment Notes**

The 2012 amendment substituted "division (O)(1)" for "division (S)(1)" in the introductory language of (B); and substituted "twenty-one years" for "sixty years" in (B)(2).

## § 173.13 Rights of continuing care facility residents.

(A) As used in this section:

(1) "Continuing care" means the provision under a written agreement of board, lodging, medical services, nursing, and other health-related services to a person sixty years of age or older, unrelated by consanguinity or affinity to the provider, for the life of the person or for a period in excess of one year in return for the payment of an entrance fee or of periodic charges.

(2) "Entrance fee" means an initial or deferred payment of a sum of money or other property made or promised to be made by or on behalf of a person entering into a written agreement with a facility for the provision of continuing care services in consideration for acceptance of the person as a resident in the facility.

(B) The residents of a facility that provides continuing care may determine annually whether they wish to elect a resident of the facility to serve on the board of directors, board of trustees, or other board that operates the facility. Election of a resident to serve on the board shall be by a simple majority vote of all residents attending a meeting called to determine if residents of the facility wish to have representation on the board. The individual organizing the meeting shall give residents at least seven days' notice of the meeting. A board to which a resident is elected under this section shall accept the resident as a nonvoting member and give him notice of and permit him to attend all meetings of the board.

(C) Every facility that provides continuing care shall, upon request, provide its residents and prospective residents with copies of any of its audited annual financial reports.

(D) Residents of facilities that provide continuing care shall have the right of self-organization.

(E) Each board of directors, board of trustees, or other board that operates a facility that provides continuing care, or a committee of the board, shall hold meetings at least quarterly with the residents of the facility, or with a committee of the residents, for the purpose of discussing facility income, expenditures, and financial matters and proposed changes in facility policies, programs, and services. The board shall give residents or the committee of residents at least seven days' notice of each such meeting.

(F) A resident of a facility that provides continuing care may bring a civil action to enforce any of the rights granted under this section.

**HISTORY:**
142 v H 253. Eff 10-20-87.

## LONG-TERM CARE OMBUDSPERSON PROGRAM

### § 173.14 Definitions.

As used in sections 173.14 to 173.28 of the Revised Code:

(A)(1) Except as otherwise provided in division (A)(2) of this section, "long-term care facility" includes any residential facility that provides personal care services for more than twenty-four hours for one or more unrelated adults, including all of the following:

(a) A "nursing home," "residential care facility," or "home for the aging," as those terms are defined in section 3721.01 of the Revised Code;

(b) A facility authorized to provide extended care services under Title XVIII of the "Social Security Act," 49 Stat. 620 (1935), 42 U.S.C. 301, as amended, including a long-term acute care hospital that provides medical and rehabilitative care to patients who require an average length of stay greater than twenty-five days and is classified by the centers for medicare and medicaid services as a long-term care hospital pursuant to 42 C.F.R. 412.23(e);

(c) A county home or district home operated pursuant to Chapter 5155. of the Revised Code;

(d) A residential facility licensed under section 5119.34 of the Revised Code that provides accommodations, supervision, and personal care services for three to sixteen unrelated adults or accommodations and personal care services for only one or two adults who are receiving payments under the residential state supplement program established under section 5119.41 of the Revised Code;

(e) A facility approved by the veterans administration under section 104(a) of the "Veterans Health Care Amendments of 1983," 97 Stat. 993, 38 U.S.C. 630, as amended, and used exclusively for the placement and care of veterans.

(2) "Long-term care facility" does not include a residential facility licensed under section 5123.19 of the Revised Code.

(B) "Resident" means a resident of a long-term care facility and, where appropriate, includes a prospective, previous, or deceased resident of a long-term care facility.

(C) "Community-based long-term care services" means health and social services provided to persons in their own homes or in community care settings, and includes any of the following:

(1) Case management;

(2) Home health care;

(3) Homemaker services;

(4) Chore services;

(5) Respite care;

(6) Adult day care;

(7) Home-delivered meals;

(8) Personal care;

(9) Physical, occupational, and speech therapy;

(10) Transportation;

(11) Any other health and social services provided to persons that allow them to retain their independence in their own homes or in community care settings.

(D) "Recipient" means a recipient of community-based long-term care services and, where appropriate, includes a prospective, previous, or deceased recipient of community-based long-term care services.

(E) "Sponsor" means an adult relative, friend, or guardian who has an interest in or responsibility for the welfare of a resident or a recipient.

(F) "Personal care services" has the same meaning as in section 3721.01 of the Revised Code.

(G) "Regional long-term care ombudsman program" means an entity, either public or private and nonprofit, designated as a regional long-term care ombudsman program by the state long-term care ombudsman.

(H) "Representative of the office of the state long-term care ombudsman program" means the state long-term care ombudsman or a member of the ombudsman's staff, or a person certified as a representative of the office under section 173.21 of the Revised Code.

(I) "Area agency on aging" means an area agency on aging established under the "Older Americans Act of 1965," 79 Stat. 219, 42 U.S.C. 3001, as amended.

(J) "Long-term care provider" means a long-term care facility or a provider of community-based long-term care services.

(K) "Advocacy visit" means a visit by a representative of the office of the state long-term care ombudsman program to a long-term care provider, a resident, or a recipient when the purpose of the visit is one or more of the following:

(1) To establish a regular presence that creates awareness of the availability of the office of the long-term care ombudsman program;

(2) To increase awareness of the services the office provides;

(3) To address any other matter not related to the representative's investigation of a specific complaint.

An advocacy visit may unexpectedly involve addressing uncomplicated complaints or lead to an investigation of a complaint when needed.

**HISTORY:**
143 v H 359 (Eff 6-12-90); 145 v H 152 (Eff 7-1-93); 146 v H 117 (Eff 9-29-95); 146 v H 670. Eff 12-2-96; 150 v H 95, § 1, eff. 9-26-03; 151 v H 530, § 101.01, eff. 6-30-06; 2011 HB 153, § 101.01, eff. Sept. 29, 2011; 2012 HB 487, § 101.01, eff. Sept. 10, 2012; 2013 HB 59, § 101.01, eff. Sept. 29, 2013; 2017 hb49, § 101.01, effective September 29, 2017.

**Editor's Notes**

Pursuant to 2011 HB 153, § 812.30, the amendments to subdivisions (A)(1)(d) and (f) are effective July 1, 2011. All other amendments by this act take effect September 29, 2011.

**Amendment Notes**

The 2017 amendment by HB 49 substituted "173.28 of the Revised Code" for "173.27 of the Revised Code" in the introductory language; added "those terms" in (A)(1)(a); in (A)(1)(d), added "payments under the" and "established under section 5119.41 of the Revised Code"; substituted "42 U.S.C. 3001" for "42 U.S.C.A. 3001" in (I); and added (J) and (K).

The 2013 amendment, in (A)(1)(d), substituted "section 5119.34" for "section 5119.22" and "receiving" for "recipients under the"; substituted "ombudsman" for "ombudsperson" or variants wherever it appears in (G) and (H).

The 2012 amendment substituted "one or more" for "two or more" in the introductory language of (A)(1); rewrote (A)(1)(d), which formerly read: "An 'adult care facility' as defined in section 5119.70 of the Revised Code"; deleted (A)(1)(f), which read: "An adult foster home certified under section 5119.692 of the Revised Code"; in (A)(2), deleted "a 'residential facility' as defined in section 5119.22 of the Revised Code or" following "does not include" and substituted "licensed under" for "as defined in"; and made related and stylistic changes.

The 2011 amendment added the language beginning "including a long-term" to the end of (A)(1)(b); substituted "section 5119.70" for "section 3722.01" in (A)(1)(d); and substituted "section 5119.692" for "section 173.36" in (A)(1)(f).

151 v H 530, effective June 30, 2006, inserted (C)(10) and redesignated former (C)(10) as (C)(11); and corrected internal references.

**RESEARCH REFERENCES AND PRACTICE AIDS**

**Ohio Administrative Code**
Definitions. OAC 173-14-01.

### § 173.15 Office of state long-term care ombudsman program; appointment of state ombudsman; conflicts of interest.

The state long-term care ombudsman program established by the department of aging pursuant to division (J) of section 173.01 of the Revised Code shall be known as "the office of the state long-term care ombudsman program." It shall consist of the state long-term care ombudsman, the ombudsman's staff, and regional long-term care ombudsman programs. In establishing and operating the office, the department shall consider the views of area agencies on aging, individuals age sixty or older, and agencies and other entities that provide services to individuals age sixty and older.

The department of aging shall appoint the state ombudsman, who shall serve at the pleasure of the department. The department shall appoint as state ombudsman an individual who has no conflict of interest with the position and is capable of administering the office impartially, has an understanding of long-term care issues, and has experience related to the concerns of residents and recipients, such as experience in the fields of aging, health care, and long-term care; work with community programs and health care providers; and work with and involvement in volunteer programs. No individual or entity whose interests are in conflict with the responsibilities of the state ombudsman shall be involved in the ombudsman's appointment.

The department shall ensure that no employee or representative of the office and no individual involved in the designation of the head of any regional long-term care ombudsman program has any interest that is, or may be, in conflict with the interests and concerns of the office and shall ensure that mechanisms are in place to remedy any conflicts.

For purposes of this section, conflicts of interest may include, but are not limited to, employment by a long-term care provider within two years prior to being employed by or associated with the office of the state long-term care ombudsman program, affiliation with or financial interest in a long-term care provider, and affiliation with or financial interest in a membership organization of long-term care providers.

**HISTORY:**

143 v H 359. Eff 6-12-90; 2017 hb49, § 101.01, effective September 29, 2017.

**Amendment Notes**

The 2017 amendment by HB 49, in the first paragraph, in the first sentence, substituted "state long-term care ombudsman" for "long-term care ombudsman" and "division (J)" for "division (M), and substituted "state long-term care ombudsman, the ombudsman's staff" for "state long-term care ombudsman and his staff" in the second sentence; substituted "the ombudsman's appointment" for "his appointment" in the last sentence of the second paragraph; and substituted "long-term care provider" for "long-term care facility or a provider of community-based long-term care services" twice in the last paragraph.

### RESEARCH REFERENCES AND PRACTICE AIDS

**Cross-References to Related Sections**

Cooperation of agencies, RC § 173.25.
Definitions, RC § 173.14.
Duties of state ombudsperson, RC § 173.17.
Immunity of representatives; legal counsel, RC § 173.23.

**Ohio Administrative Code**

Conflicts of interest. OAC 173-14-15.

## § 173.16 Designation of regional programs.

(A) The department of aging shall designate regions to be served by regional long-term care ombudsman programs.

(B) Except as otherwise provided in division (C) of this section, the state long-term care ombudsman shall designate regional programs in accordance with criteria established by the department of aging in rules which the department shall adopt under Chapter 119. of the Revised Code. The criteria shall include specifications regarding the sites of the regional programs' offices and requirements concerning staffing, levels of training required for staff members, program review, and tax exempt status for federal income tax purposes.

(C) An entity serving as a regional program on the effective date of this section shall be designated as a regional program unless the state ombudsman determines that the entity does not meet the requirements established under division (B) of this section. Except that the state ombudsman may designate as a regional program an entity that does not meet the requirements if it is serving as a regional program on the effective date of this section and the state ombudsman determines that it is the best qualified program to serve the region.

(D) In an adjudication conducted in accordance with Chapter 119. of the Revised Code, the state ombudsman may issue an adjudication order withdrawing or provisionally maintaining the designation of an entity as a regional program if it ceases to meet the criteria established pursuant to division (B) of this section or a conflict of interest develops between the regional program or a person associated with it and the office. If the designation of a regional program is provisionally maintained, the state ombudsman shall notify the program of the reasons for its provisional status, the changes or corrections necessary for the removal of its provisional status, the length of time it has to make the changes or corrections, and that the state ombudsman will withdraw the designation if the program does not comply with the requirements specified in the notice. If the designation of a regional program is withdrawn, the state ombudsman shall provide for the continuation of ombudsman services for that region.

**HISTORY:**

143 v H 359. Eff 6-12-90.

### RESEARCH REFERENCES AND PRACTICE AIDS

**Cross-References to Related Sections**

Definitions, RC § 173.14.
Duties of regional programs, RC § 173.18.
Immunity of representatives; legal counsel, RC § 173.23.

**Ohio Administrative Code**

Designated long-term care ombudsman regions. OAC 173-14-20.
Development of ombudsman plans by all programs. OAC ch. 173-14-23.
Initial designation of existing regional programs. OAC 173-14-21, OAC 173-14-22.
Program review for continued designation. OAC 173-14-24.
Provisional designation; de-designation; voluntary withdrawal. OAC 173-14-25.
Staffing requirements and qualifications. OAC 173-14-14.

## § 173.17 Duties of state ombudsperson.

(A) The state long-term care ombudsman shall do all of the following:

(1) Appoint a staff and direct and administer the work of the staff;

(2) Oversee the performance and operation of the office of the state long-term care ombudsman program, including the operation of regional long-term care ombudsman programs;

(3) Establish and maintain a statewide uniform reporting system to collect and analyze information relating to complaints and conditions in long-term care facilities and complaints regarding the provision of community-based long-term care services for the purpose of identifying and resolving significant problems;

(4) Provide for public forums to discuss concerns and problems relating to action, inaction, or decisions that may adversely affect the health, safety, welfare, or rights of residents, recipients and their representatives with respect to services by long-term care providers, public agencies and entities, and social service agencies. This may include any of the following: conducting public hearings; sponsoring workshops and conferences; holding meetings for the purpose of obtaining information about residents and recipients, discussing and publicizing their needs, and advocating solutions to their problems; and promoting the development of citizen organizations.

(5) Encourage, cooperate with, and assist in the development and operation of services to provide current, objective, and verified information about long-term care;

(6) Develop and implement, with the assistance of regional programs, a continuing program to publicize, through the media and civic organizations, the office, its purposes, and its methods of operation;

(7) Maintain written descriptions of the duties and qualifications of representatives of the office;

(8) Evaluate and make known concerns and issues regarding long-term care by doing all of the following:

(a) Preparing an annual report containing information and findings regarding the types of problems experienced by residents and recipients and the complaints made by or on behalf of residents and recipients. The report shall include recommendations for policy, regulatory, and legislative changes to solve problems, resolve complaints, and improve the quality of care and life for residents and recipients. The report shall be submitted to the governor, the speaker of the house of representatives, the president of the senate, the director of health, the medicaid director, the director of job and family services, the director of mental health and addiction services, and the assistant secretary for aging of the United States department of health and human services.

(b) Monitoring and analyzing the development and implementation of federal, state, and local laws, rules, and policies regarding long-term care services in this state and recommending to officials changes the office considers appropriate in those laws, rules, and policies;

(c) Providing information and making recommendations to public agencies, members of the general assembly, and others regarding problems and concerns of residents and recipients.

(9) Conduct training for employees and volunteers on the ombudsman's staff and for representatives of the office employed by regional programs;

(10) Monitor the training of representatives of the office who provide volunteer services to regional programs, and provide technical assistance to the regional programs in conducting the training;

(11) Issue certificates attesting to the successful completion of training and specifying the level of responsibility for which a representative of the office who has completed training is qualified;

(12) Register as a residents' rights advocate with the department of health under division (B) of section 3701.07 of the Revised Code;

(13) Conduct advocacy visits and authorize other representatives of the office of the state long-term care ombudsman program to conduct advocacy visits;

(14) Perform other duties specified by the department of aging.

(B) The state ombudsman may delegate to any member of the ombudsman's staff any of the ombudsman's authority or duties set forth in sections 173.14 to 173.28 of the Revised Code other than any authority or duty required by federal law to be exercised or performed by the ombudsman. The state ombudsman is responsible for any authority or duties the ombudsman delegates.

**HISTORY:**

143 v H 359 (Eff 6-12-90); 146 v H 670 (Eff 12-2-96); 148 v H 471. Eff 7-1-2000; 2013 HB 59, § 101.01, eff. Sept. 29, 2013; 2017 hb49, § 101.01, effective September 29, 2017.

**Amendment Notes**

The 2017 amendment by HB 49 deleted former (A)(2), which read: "Supervise the nursing home investigative unit established under division (I) of section 173.01 of the Revised Code"; redesignated former (A)(3) through (A)(13) as (A)(2) through (A)(12); substituted "rights of residents, recipients and their representatives with respect to services by long-term care providers" for "rights of residents and recipients of services by providers of long-term care and their representatives" in (A)(4); rewrote (A)(8)(a); substituted "in those laws" for "in these laws" in (A)(8)(b); added (A)(13); and rewrote (B).

The 2013 amendment substituted "ombudsman" for "ombudsperson" or variants wherever it appears in the section.

**RESEARCH REFERENCES AND PRACTICE AIDS**

**Cross-References to Related Sections**

Access to long-term care facilities; private communication with residents and sponsors, RC § 173.19.

Definitions, RC § 173.14.

Immunity of representatives; legal counsel, RC § 173.23.

**Ohio Administrative Code**

Representatives of the office—

Duties. OAC 173-14-03.

Separation of representatives from the office. OAC 173-14-12.

Types. OAC 173-14-02.

## § 173.18 Duties of regional programs.

Each regional long-term care ombudsman program designated under section 173.16 of the Revised Code shall do all of the following:

(A) Provide ombudsman services for the region in which it is located;

(B) Employ representatives of the office of the state long-term care ombudsman program or receive services from volunteers certified under section 173.21 of the Revised Code as representatives of the office, or both;

(C) Submit reports to the state long-term care ombudsman as he may require;

(D) Register as a residents' rights advocate with the department of health under division (B) of section 3701.07 of the Revised Code.

**HISTORY:**

143 v H 359. Eff 6-12-90.

**RESEARCH REFERENCES AND PRACTICE AIDS**

**Cross-References to Related Sections**

Access to long-term care facilities; private communication with residents and sponsors, RC § 173.19.

Definitions, RC § 173.14.

Duties of state ombudsperson, RC § 173.17.

Immunity of representatives; legal counsel, RC § 173.23.

## § 173.19 Investigation and resolution of complaints.

(A) The office of the state long-term care ombudsman program, through the state long-term care ombudsman and the regional long-term care ombudsman programs, shall receive, investigate, and attempt to resolve complaints made by residents, recipients, sponsors, long-term care providers, or any person acting on behalf of a resident or recipient, relating to either of the following:

(1) The health, safety, welfare, or civil rights of a resident or recipient or any violation of a resident's rights described in sections 3721.10 to 3721.17 of the Revised Code;

(2) Any action or inaction or decision by any of the following that may adversely affect the health, safety, welfare, or rights of a resident or recipient: a long-term care provider or a representative of a long-term care provider; a medicaid managed care organization, as defined in section 5167.01 of the Revised Code; a government entity; or a private social service agency.

(B) The department of aging shall adopt rules in accordance with Chapter 119. of the Revised Code regarding the handling of complaints received under this section, including procedures for conducting investigations of complaints. The rules shall include procedures to ensure that no representative of the office investigates any complaint involving a long-term care provider with which the representative was once employed or associated.

The state ombudsman and regional programs shall establish procedures for handling complaints consistent with the department's rules. Complaints shall be dealt with in accordance with the procedures established under this division.

(C) The office of the state long-term care ombudsman program may decline to investigate any complaint if it determines any of the following:

(1) That the complaint is frivolous, vexatious, or not made in good faith;

(2) That the complaint was made so long after the occurrence of the incident on which it is based that it is no longer reasonable to conduct an investigation;

(3) That an adequate investigation cannot be conducted because of insufficient funds, insufficient staff, lack of staff expertise, or any other reasonable factor that would result in an inadequate investigation despite a good faith effort;

(4) That an investigation by the office would create a real or apparent conflict of interest.

(D) If a regional long-term care ombudsman program declines to investigate a complaint, it shall refer the complaint to the state long-term care ombudsman.

(E) Each complaint to be investigated by a regional program shall be assigned to a representative of the office of the state long-term care ombudsman program. If the representative determines that the complaint is valid, the representative shall assist the parties in attempting to resolve it. If the representative is unable to resolve it, the representative shall refer the complaint to the state ombudsman.

In order to carry out the duties of sections 173.14 to 173.28 of the Revised Code, a representative has the right to private communication with residents and their sponsors and access to long-term care facilities, including the right to tour resident areas unescorted and the right to tour facilities unescorted as reasonably necessary to the investigation of a complaint. Access to facilities shall be during reasonable hours or, during investigation of a complaint, at other times appropriate to the complaint.

When community-based long-term care services are provided at a location other than the recipient's home, a representative has the right to private communication with the recipient and the recipient's sponsors and access to the community-based long-term care site, including the right to tour the site unescorted. Access to the site shall be during reasonable hours or, during the investigation of a complaint, at other times appropriate to the complaint.

(F) The state ombudsman shall determine whether complaints referred to the ombudsman under division (D) or (E) of this section warrant investigation. The ombudsman's determination in this matter is final.

(G) No long-term care provider or other entity, no person employed by a long-term care provider or other entity, and no other individual shall do either of the following:

(1) Knowingly deny a representative of the office of the state long-term care ombudsman program the right to private communication or access described in division (E) of this section;

(2) Engage in willful interference.

As used in division (G)(2) of this section, "willful interference" means any action or inaction that is intended to prevent, interfere with, or impede a representative of the office of the state long-term care ombudsman program from exercising any of the rights or performing any of the duties of an ombudsman set forth in sections 173.14 to 173.28 of the Revised Code.

**HISTORY:**

143 v H 359 (Eff 6-12-90); 146 v H 670 (Eff 12-2-96); 148 v H 403. Eff 7-1-2000; 2013 HB 59, § 101.01, eff. Sept. 29, 2013; 2017 hb49, § 101.01, effective September 29, 2017.

**Amendment Notes**

The 2017 amendment by HB 49 substituted "residents, recipients, sponsors, long-term care providers" for "residents, recipients, sponsors, providers of long-term care" in the introductory language of (A); in (A)(2), substituted "decision by any of the following" for "decision by a provider of long-term care or representative of a provider, a governmental entity, or a private social service agency" and added "a long-term care provider or a representative of a long-term care provider; a medicaid managed care organization, as defined in section 5167.01 of the Revised Code; a government entity; or a private social service agency"; substituted "long-term care provider" for "provider of long-term care" in the second sentence of (B); substituted "sections 173.14 to 173.28 of the Revised Code" for "sections 173.14 to 173.26 of the Revised Code" in first sentence of the second paragraph of (E); and added (G).

The 2013 amendment substituted "ombudsman" for "ombudsperson" or variants wherever it appears in the section.

**RESEARCH REFERENCES AND PRACTICE AIDS**

**Cross-References to Related Sections**

Definitions, RC § 173.14.

Immunity of representatives; legal counsel, RC § 173.23.

**Ohio Administrative Code**

Complaint handling protocol. OAC 173-14-16 to 173-14-19.

## § 173.20 Access to records of resident, recipient or provider; subpoenas; injunction; referral of complaints.

(A) If consent is given and unless otherwise prohibited by law, a representative of the office of the state long-term care ombudsman program shall have access to any records, including medical records, of a resident or a recipient that are reasonably necessary for investigation of a complaint. Consent may be given in any of the following ways:

(1) In writing by the resident or recipient;

(2) Orally by the resident or recipient, witnessed in writing at the time it is given by one other person;

(3) In writing by the guardian of the resident or recipient;

(4) In writing by the attorney in fact of the resident or recipient, if the resident or recipient has authorized the attorney in fact to give such consent;

(5) In writing by the executor or administrator of the estate of a deceased resident or recipient.

(B) If consent to access to records is not refused by a resident or recipient or the resident's or recipient's legal representative but cannot be obtained and any of the following circumstances exist, a representative of the office of the state long-term care ombudsman program, on approval of the state long-term care ombudsman, may inspect the records of a resident or a recipient, including medical records, that are reasonably necessary for investigation of a complaint:

(1) The resident or recipient is unable to express written or oral consent and there is no guardian or attorney in fact;

(2) There is a guardian or attorney in fact, but the guardian or attorney in fact cannot be contacted within three working days;

(3) There is a guardianship or durable power of attorney, but its existence is unknown by the long-term care provider and the representative of the office at the time of the investigation;

(4) There is no executor or administrator of the estate of a deceased resident or recipient.

(C) If a representative of the office of the state long-term care ombudsman program has been refused access to records by a guardian or attorney in fact, but has reasonable cause to believe that the guardian or attorney in fact is not acting in the best interests of the resident or recipient, the representative may, on approval of the state long-term care ombudsman, inspect the records of the resident or recipient, including medical records, that are reasonably necessary for investigation of a complaint.

(D) A representative of the office of the state long-term care ombudsman program shall have access to any records of a long-term care provider reasonably necessary to an investigation conducted under this section, including but not limited to: incident reports, dietary records, policies and procedures of a facility required to be maintained under section 5165.06 of the Revised Code, admission agreements, staffing schedules, any document depicting the actual staffing pattern of the provider, any financial records that are matters of public record, resident council and grievance committee minutes, and any waiting list maintained by a facility in accordance with section 5165.08 of the Revised Code, or any similar records or lists maintained by a provider of community-based long-term care services. Pursuant to division (E) of this section, a representative shall be permitted to make or obtain copies of any of these records after giving the long-term care provider twenty-four hours" notice. A long-term care provider may impose a charge for providing copies of records under this division that does not exceed the actual and necessary expense of making the copies.

(E) Each long-term care provider shall designate one or more of its employees to be responsible for releasing records for copying to representatives of the office of the state long-term care ombudsman program who request permission to make or obtain copies of records specified in division (D) of this section. In the event that a designated employee is not available when a representative of the office makes the request, the long-term care provider shall designate another employee to release the records for copying.

(F) A long-term care provider or any employee of such a provider is immune from civil or criminal liability or action taken pursuant to a professional disciplinary procedure for the release or disclosure of records to a representative of the office pursuant to this section.

(G) A state or local government agency or entity with records relevant to a complaint or investigation being conducted by a representative of the office shall provide the representative access to the records.

(H) The state ombudsman, with the approval of the director of aging, may issue a subpoena to compel any person the ombudsman reasonably believes may be able to provide information to appear before the ombudsman or the ombudsman's designee and give sworn testimony and to produce documents, books, records, papers, or other evidence the state ombudsman believes is relevant to the investigation. On the refusal of a witness to be sworn or to answer any question put to the witness, or if a person disobeys a subpoena, the ombudsman shall apply to the Franklin county court of common pleas for a contempt order, as in the case of disobedience of the requirements of a subpoena issued from the court, or a refusal to testify in the court.

(I) The state ombudsman may petition the court of common pleas in the county in which a long-term care facility is located to issue an injunction against any long-term care facility in violation of sections 3721.10 to 3721.17 of the Revised Code.

(J) To the extent permitted by federal law, a representative of the office may report to an appropriate authority any suspected violation of state law discovered during the course of an advocacy visit or investigation.

(K) The department of aging shall adopt rules in accordance with Chapter 119. of the Revised Code for referral by the state ombudsman and regional long-term care ombudsman programs of complaints to other public agencies or entities. A public agency or entity to which a complaint is referred shall keep the state ombudsman or regional program handling the complaint advised and notified in writing in a timely manner of the disposition of the complaint to the extent permitted by law.

**HISTORY:**

143 v H 359. Eff 6-12-90; 2013 HB 59, § 101.01, eff. Sept. 29, 2013; 2017 hb49, § 101.01, effective September 29, 2017.

**Amendment Notes**

The 2017 amendment by HB 49 deleted "and, if the records involved are being maintained by a long-term care provider, also by an employee of the long-term care provider designated under division (E)(1) of this section" at the end of (A)(2); in (D), substituted "Pursuant to division (E)" for "Pursuant to division (E)(2)" in the second sentence of the first paragraph and deleted the former second paragraph; redesignated and rewrote former (E)(1) and (E)(2) as (E); and rewrote (J).

The 2013 amendment, in the first sentence of the first paragraph of (D), substituted "section 5165.06" for "section 5111.21" and "section 5165.08" for "section 5111.31"; and made stylistic changes.

## NOTES TO DECISIONS

**Subpoenas**

The state ombudsman has authority to issue a subpoena as part of his or her investigatory authority and, if the subpoena is disobeyed, he or she may apply for a contempt order from the Franklin County Court of Common Pleas. No section of the Ohio Revised Code provides a forum for a deponent to file a motion to quash a subpoena served pursuant to R.C. 173.20(H): In re Investigation of Laplow, 96 Ohio App. 3d 386, 645 N.E.2d 103, 1994 Ohio App. LEXIS 3528 (Ohio Ct. App., Franklin County 1994).

## RESEARCH REFERENCES AND PRACTICE AIDS

**Cross-References to Related Sections**

Access to long-term care facilities; private communication with residents and sponsors, RC § 173.19.

Definitions, RC § 173.14.

Immunity of representatives; legal counsel, RC § 173.23.

Rules governing recipient information, RC § 5101.30.

**Ohio Rules**

Injunction, CivR 65.

Subpoena, CivR 45.

**Ohio Administrative Code**

Case records and reporting of complaint handling activities. OAC 173-14-19.

Referrals of complaints to—

Other agencies. OAC 173-14-18.

State long-term care ombudsman. OAC 173-14-17.

### § 173.21 Training and certification of representatives of state office; identification cards; continuing education; training of volunteers.

(A) The office of the state long-term care ombudsman program, through the state long-term care ombudsman and the regional long-term care ombudsman programs, shall require each representative of the office to complete a training and certification program in accordance with this section and to meet the continuing education requirements established under this section.

(B) The department of aging shall adopt rules in accordance with Chapter 119. of the Revised Code specifying the content of training programs for representatives of the office of the state long-term care ombudsman program. Training for representatives other than those who are volunteers providing services through regional long-term care ombudsman programs shall include instruction regarding federal, state, and local laws, rules, and policies on long-term care facilities and community-based long-term care services; investigative techniques; and other topics considered relevant by the department and shall consist of the following:

(1) A minimum of forty clock hours of basic instruction, which shall be completed before the trainee is permitted to handle complaints without the supervision of a representative of the office certified under this section;

(2) An additional sixty clock hours of instruction, which shall be completed within the first fifteen months of employment;

(3) An internship of twenty clock hours, which shall be completed within the first twenty-four months of employment, including instruction in, and observation of, basic nursing care and long-term care provider operations and procedures. The internship shall be performed at a site that has been approved as an internship site by the state long-term care ombudsman.

(4) One of the following, which shall be completed within the first twenty-four months of employment:

(a) Observation of a survey conducted by the director of health to certify a nursing facility to participate in the medicaid program;

(b) Observation of an inspection conducted by the director of mental health and addiction services to license a residential facility under section 5119.34 of the Revised Code that provides accommodations, supervision, and personal care services for three to sixteen unrelated adults.

(5) Any other training considered appropriate by the department.

(C) Any person who for a period of at least six months prior to June 11, 1990, served as an ombudsman through the long-term care ombudsman program established by the department of aging under section 173.01 of the Revised Code shall not be required to complete a training program. Such a person and persons who complete a training program shall take an examination administered by the department of aging. On attainment of a passing score, the person shall be certified by the department as a representative of the office. The department shall issue the person an identification card, which the representative shall show at the request of any person with whom the representative deals while performing the representative's duties and which shall be surrendered at the time the representative separates from the office.

(D) The state ombudsman and each regional program shall conduct training programs for volunteers on their respective staffs in accordance with the rules of the department of aging adopted under division (B) of this section. Training programs may be conducted that train volunteers to complete some, but not all, of the duties of a representative of the office. Each regional office shall bear the cost of training its representatives who are volunteers. On completion of a training program, the representative shall take an examination administered by the department of aging. On attainment of a passing score, a volunteer shall be certified by the department as a representative authorized to perform services specified in the certification. The department shall issue an identification card, which the representative shall show at the request of any person with whom the representative deals while performing the representative's duties and which shall be surrendered at the time the representative separates from the office. Except as a supervised part of a training program, no volunteer shall perform any duty unless the volunteer is certified as a representative having received appropriate training for that duty.

(E) The state ombudsman shall provide technical assistance to regional programs conducting training programs for volunteers and shall monitor the training programs.

(F) Prior to scheduling an observation of a certification survey or licensing inspection for purposes of division (B)(4) of this section, the state ombudsman shall obtain permission to have the survey or inspection observed from both the long-term care facility at which the survey or inspection is to take place and, as the case may be, the director of health or director of mental health and addiction services.

(G) The department of aging shall establish continuing education requirements for representatives of the office.

**HISTORY:**

143 v H 359 (Eff 6-12-90); 146 v S 162. Eff 10-29-95; 2011 HB 153, § 101.01, eff. July 1, 2011; 2012 HB 487, § 101.01, eff. Sept. 10, 2012; 2013 HB 59, § 101.01, eff. Sept. 29, 2013; 2017 hb49, § 101.01, effective September 29, 2017.

**Amendment Notes**

The 2017 amendment by HB 49 substituted "in accordance with Chapter 119. of the Revised Code" for "under Chapter 119. of the Revised Code" in the first sentence of the introductory paragraph of (B); deleted "division (M) of" following "department of aging under" in the first sentence of (C); substituted "the volunteer is certified" for "he is certified' in the last sentence of (D); and, in (F), deleted "the director of health and" preceding "the long-term care facility" and added "and, as the case may be, the director of health or director of mental health and addiction services."

The 2013 amendment substituted "ombudsman" for "ombudsperson" wherever it appears in (A), (B), and (D) through (F); substituted "nursing facility to participate in the medicaid program" for "facility to receive funds under sections 5111.20 to 5111.32 of the Revised Code" in (B)(4)(a); in (B)(4)(b), inserted "and addiction services" and substituted "section 5119.34" for "section 5119.22"; and, in (C), in the first sentence, substituted "Any person" for "Persons", "served as an ombudsman" for "served as ombudsmen", and "ombudsman program" for "ombudsperson program" and substituted "Such a person" for "These persons" in the second sentence.

The 2012 amendment, in (B)(4)(b), substituted "a residential" for "an adult care", substituted "section 5119.22" for "section 5119.73", and added "that provides accommodations, supervision, and personal care services for three to sixteen unrelated adults" to the end.

The 2011 amendment substituted "ombudsperson" for "ombudsman" throughout the section; in (B)(4)(b), inserted "mental" and substituted "section 5119.73" for "section 3722.04"; and made stylistic changes.

### RESEARCH REFERENCES AND PRACTICE AIDS

**Cross-References to Related Sections**

Duties of regional programs, RC § 173.18.

Immunity of representatives; legal counsel, RC § 173.23.

Representative of the office of the state long-term care ombudsperson program defined, RC § 173.14.

**Ohio Administrative Code**

Professional development for representatives of the office. OAC 173-14-04 to 173-14-07.

Certification; registration. OAC 173-14-10, OAC 173-14-11.

Continuing education requirements. OAC 173-14-13.

Notice rights and hearing requirements in decertification or removal. OAC 173-14-26.

Observation of survey or inspection. OAC 173-14-09.

## § 173.22 Confidentiality of information.

(A) The collection, compilation, analysis, and dissemination of information by the office of the state long-term care ombudsman program shall be performed in a manner that protects complainants, individuals providing information about a complaint, public entities, and confidential records of residents or recipients. The identity of a resident or recipient, a complainant who is not a resident or recipient, or an individual providing information about a complaint shall not be disclosed without the written consent of the resident or recipient, complainant, or individual, or a legal representative of any of the foregoing, or except as required by court order.

The investigative files of the office and any records contained in those files, including any proprietary records of a long-term care provider or records relating to advocacy visits, are not public records subject to inspection or copying under section 149.43 of the Revised Code and are exempt from the provisions of Chapter 1347. of the Revised Code. Information contained in investigative and other files maintained by the state long-term care ombudsman and regional long-term care ombudsman programs shall be disclosed only at the discretion of the state ombudsman or if disclosure is required by court order.

(B) No report prepared by the state ombudsman or a regional program shall include any information that violates the confidentiality requirements of this section. Proprietary records of a specific long-term care provider are subject to the confidentiality requirements of this section.

**HISTORY:**

143 v H 359. Eff 6-12-90; 2017 hb49, § 101.01, effective September 29, 2017.

**Amendment Notes**

The 2017 amendment by HB 49, in (A), substituted "or a legal representative of any of the foregoing" for "or his legal representative" in the second sentence of the first paragraph, and rewrote the second paragraph, which formerly read: "The investigative files, including any proprietary records of a long-term care provider contained in the files, of the office are not public records subject to inspection or copying under section 149.43 of the Revised Code. Information contained in investigative and other files maintained by the state long-term care ombudsman and regional long-term care ombudsman programs shall be disclosed only at the discretion of the state ombudsman or the regional program maintaining the records or if disclosure is required by court order."

### RESEARCH REFERENCES AND PRACTICE AIDS

**Cross-References to Related Sections**

Definitions, RC § 173.14.

Immunity of representatives; legal counsel, RC § 173.23.

## § 173.23 Immunity; legal counsel for representatives; false complaints.

(A) Representatives of the office of the state long-term care ombudsman program are immune from civil or criminal liability for any action taken in the good faith performance of their official duties under sections 173.14 to 173.26 of the Revised Code.

(B) A person acting in good faith is immune from civil or criminal liability incident to any of the following: providing information to the office, participating in registration of a complaint with the office, participating in investigation of a complaint by the office, or participating in an administrative or judicial proceeding resulting from a complaint.

(C) No person shall knowingly register a false complaint with the office, or knowingly swear or affirm the truth of a false complaint previously registered, when the statement is made with purpose to incriminate another.

(D) The attorney general shall provide legal counsel to the office of the state long-term care ombudsman program and to the regional long-term care ombudsman programs. The attorney general shall represent any representative of the office and any representative of a regional program against whom any legal action is brought in connection with the representative's official duties under sections 173.14 to 173.26 of the Revised Code.

**HISTORY:**

143 v H 359 (Eff 6-12-90); 146 v H 670. Eff 12-2-96; 2012 HB 487, § 101.01, eff. Sept. 10, 2012; 2013 HB 59, § 101.01, eff. Sept. 29, 2013.

**Amendment Notes**

The 2013 amendment substituted "ombudsman" for "ombudsperson" wherever it appears in (A) and the first sentence of (D).

The 2012 amendment deleted the second sentence of (A), which read: "The department of aging shall ensure that adequate legal counsel is available to the office of the state long-term care ombudsperson program for advice and consultation and that legal representation is provided to any representative of the office against whom any legal action is brought in connection with the representative's official duties under sections 173.14 to 173.26 of the Revised Code"; and added (D).

### NOTES TO DECISIONS

**Immunity**

When a relative asserted that the State Long Term Care Ombudsman's (SLTCO) office failed to investigate his complaint about the care received by a resident of a long term care facility, the Ohio Court of Claims had no jurisdiction to hear his complaint against the Ohio Department of Aging, which controlled the SLTCO, because (1) the Department's disinclination to investigate his complaint was covered by the immunity provision of R.C. 173.23(A), and (2) the relative's claims were beyond the state's statutorily established limited waiver of sovereign immunity because, under R.C. 2743.02, the state was liable in the court of claims only in accordance with the same rules of law applicable to suits between private parties, and there was no common law cause of action between private parties for the relative's claim that the Department refused to respond to his complaints. Fuerst v. Ohio Dep't of Aging, 2007-Ohio-1926, 2007 Ohio Misc. LEXIS 87 (Ohio Ct. Cl. 2007).

### RESEARCH REFERENCES AND PRACTICE AIDS

**Cross-References to Related Sections**

Penalties, RC § 173.99.
Definitions, RC § 173.14.

## § 173.24 Protection of employees of provider, residents, and recipients from retaliation.

(A) As used in this section:

(1) "Employee" and "employer" have the same meanings as in section 4113.51 of the Revised Code.

(2) "Retaliatory action" includes physical, mental, or verbal abuse; change of room assignment; withholding of services; failure to provide care in a timely manner; discharge; and termination of employment.

(B) An employee providing information to or participating in good faith in registering a complaint with the office of the state long-term care ombudsman program or participating in the investigation of a complaint or in administrative or judicial proceedings resulting from a complaint registered with the office shall have the full protection against disciplinary or retaliatory action provided by division (G) of section 3721.17 and by sections 4113.51 to 4113.53 of the Revised Code.

(C) No long-term care provider or other entity, no person employed by a long-term care provider or other entity, and no other individual shall knowingly subject any resident, recipient, employee, representative of the office of the state long-term care ombudsman program, or another individual to any form of retaliation, reprisal, discipline, or discrimination for doing any of the following:

(1) Providing information to the office;

(2) Participating in registering a complaint with the office;

(3) Cooperating with or participating in the investigation of a complaint by the office or in administrative or judicial proceedings resulting from a complaint registered with the office.

**HISTORY:**

143 v H 359. Eff 6-12-90; 2017 hb49, § 101.01, effective September 29, 2017.

**Amendment Notes**

The 2017 amendment by HB 49 redesignated and revised former (A) as the introductory language of (A) and (A)(1); added (A)(2); redesignated and revised former (C) as the introductory language of (C), (C)(1), (C)(2) and (C)(3).

### RESEARCH REFERENCES AND PRACTICE AIDS

**Cross-References to Related Sections**

Penalties, RC § 173.99.
Access to long-term care facilities; private communication with residents and sponsors, RC § 173.19.
Definitions, RC § 173.14.
Immunity of representatives; legal counsel, RC § 173.23.

## § 173.25 Cooperation of agencies.

The office of the state long-term care ombudsman program shall, in carrying out the provisions and purposes of sections 173.14 to 173.26 of the Revised Code, advise, consult, and cooperate with any agency, program, or other entity related to the purposes of the office. Any agency, program, or other entity related to the purposes of the office shall advise, consult, and cooperate with the office.

The office shall attempt to establish effective coordination with government-sponsored programs that provide legal services to the elderly and with protective and advocacy programs for individuals with developmental disabilities or mental illness.

**HISTORY:**

143 v H 359 (Eff 6-12-90); 146 v H 670. Eff 12-2-96; 2013 HB 59, § 101.01, eff. Sept. 29, 2013; 2016 hb158, § 1, effective October 12, 2016.

**Amendment Notes**

The 2016 amendment by HB 158 deleted "mental retardation" following "developmental disabilities" in the second paragraph.

The 2013 amendment substituted "ombudsman" for "ombudsperson" in the first sentence of the first paragraph.

### RESEARCH REFERENCES AND PRACTICE AIDS

**Cross-References to Related Sections**

Definitions, RC § 173.14.
Immunity of representatives; legal counsel, RC § 173.23.

## § 173.26 Payment for each bed maintained for resident; program fund; contributions.

(A) Each of the following facilities shall annually pay to the department of aging six dollars for each bed the facility was licensed or otherwise authorized to maintain during any part of the previous year:

(1) Nursing homes and residential care facilities, as defined in section 3721.01 of the Revised Code;

(2) Facilities authorized to provide extended care services under Title XVIII of the "Social Security Act," 49 Stat. 620 (1935), 42 U.S.C. 301, as amended, including a long-term acute care hospital that provides medical and rehabilitative care to patients who require an average length of stay greater than twenty-five days and is classified by the centers for medicare and medicaid services as a long-term care hospital pursuant to 42 C.F.R. 412.23(e);

(3) County homes and district homes operated pursuant to Chapter 5155. of the Revised Code;

(4) Residential facilities licensed under section 5119.34 of the Revised Code that provide accommodations, supervision, and personal care services for three to sixteen unrelated adults;

(5) Facilities approved by the Veterans Administration under Section 104(a) of the "Veterans Health Care Amendments of 1983," 97 Stat. 993, 38 U.S.C. 630, as amended, and used exclusively for the placement and care of veterans.

The department shall, by rule adopted in accordance with Chapter 119. of the Revised Code, establish deadlines for payments required by this section. A facility that fails, within ninety days after the established deadline, to pay a payment required by this section shall be assessed at two times the original invoiced payment.

(B) All money collected under this section shall be deposited in the state treasury to the credit of the office of the state long-term care ombudsman program fund, which is hereby created. Money credited to the fund shall be used solely to pay the costs of operating the regional long-term care ombudsman programs.

(C) The state long-term care ombudsman and the regional programs may solicit and receive contributions to support the operation of the office or a regional program, except that no contribution shall be solicited or accepted that would interfere with the independence or objectivity of the office or program.

**HISTORY:**

143 v H 359 (Eff 6-12-90); 145 v H 152 (Eff 7-1-93); 146 v H 117. Eff 9-29-95; 150 v H 95, § 1, eff. 9-26-03; 151 v H 66, § 101.01, eff. 9-29-05; 2011 HB 153, § 101.01, eff. Sept. 29, 2011; 2012 HB 487, § 101.01, eff. Sept. 10, 2012; 2013 HB 59, § 101.01, eff. Sept. 29, 2013.

**Editor's Notes**

Pursuant to 2011 HB 153, § 812.30, the amendment to subdivision (A)(4) is effective July 1, 2011. All other amendments by this act take effect September 29, 2011.

**Amendment Notes**

The 2013 amendment substituted "the facility was licensed or otherwise authorized to maintain" for "maintained by the facility for use by a resident" in the introductory language of (A); deleted "and homes for the aging" following "residential care facilities" in (A)(1); substituted "section 5119.34" for "section 5119.22" in (A)(4); substituted "ombudsman" for "ombudsperson" wherever it appears in (B) and (C); and made a related change.

The 2012 amendment rewrote (A)(4), which formerly read: "Adult care facilities as defined in section 5119.70 of the Revised Code."

The 2011 amendment added the language beginning "including a long-term" to the end of (A)(2); and substituted "section 5119.70" for "section 3722.01" in (A)(4).

151 v H 66, effective September 29, 2005, added the last sentence to the last paragraph of (A)(5).

### RESEARCH REFERENCES AND PRACTICE AIDS

**Cross-References to Related Sections**

Definitions, RC § 173.14.

Immunity of representatives; legal counsel, RC § 173.23.

### § 173.27 Criminal records check concerning applicant for employment; offenses precluding employment; conditional employment; civil actions.

(A) As used in this section:

(1) "Applicant" means a person who is under final consideration for employment by a responsible party in a full-time, part-time, or temporary position that involves providing ombudsman services to residents and recipients. "Applicant" includes a person who is under final consideration for employment as the state long-term care ombudsman or the head of a regional long-term care ombudsman program. "Applicant" does not include a person seeking to provide ombudsman services to residents and recipients as a volunteer without receiving or expecting to receive any form of remuneration other than reimbursement for actual expenses.

(2) "Criminal records check" has the same meaning as in section 109.572 of the Revised Code.

(3) "Disqualifying offense" means any of the offenses listed or described in divisions (A)(3) (a) to (e) of section 109.572 of the Revised Code.

(4) "Employee" means a person employed by a responsible party in a full-time, part-time, or temporary position that involves providing ombudsman services to residents and recipients. "Employee" includes the person employed as the state long-term care ombudsman and a person employed as the head of a regional long-term care ombudsman program. "Employee" does not include a person who provides ombudsman services to residents and recipients as a volunteer without receiving or expecting to receive any form of remuneration other than reimbursement for actual expenses.

(5) "Responsible party" means the following:

(a) In the case of an applicant who is under final consideration for employment as the state long-term care ombudsman or the person employed as the state long-term care ombudsman, the director of aging;

(b) In the case of any other applicant who is under final consideration for employment with the state long-term care ombudsman program or any other employee of the state long-term care ombudsman program, the state long-term care ombudsman;

(c) In the case of an applicant who is under final consideration for employment with a regional long-term care ombudsman program (including as the head of the regional program) or an employee of a regional long-term care ombudsman program (including the head of a regional program), the regional long-term care ombudsman program.

(B) A responsible party may not employ an applicant or continue to employ an employee in a position that involves providing ombudsman services to residents and recipients if any of the following apply:

(1) A review of the databases listed in division (D) of this section reveals any of the following:

(a) That the applicant or employee is included in one or more of the databases listed in divisions (D)(1) to (5) of this section;

(b) That there is in the state nurse aide registry established under section 3721.32 of the Revised Code a statement detailing findings by the director of health that the applicant or employee abused, neglected, or exploited a long-term care facility or residential care facility resident or misappropriated property of such a resident;

(c) That the applicant or employee is included in one or more of the databases, if any, specified in rules adopted under this section and the rules prohibit the responsible party from employing an applicant or continuing to employ an employee included in such a database in a position that involves providing ombudsman services to residents and recipients.

(2) After the applicant or employee is provided, pursuant to division (E)(2)(a) of this section, a copy of the form prescribed pursuant to division (C)(1) of section 109.572 of the Revised Code and the standard impression sheet prescribed pursuant to division (C)(2) of that section, the applicant or employee fails to complete the form or provide the applicant's or employee's fingerprint impressions on the standard impression sheet.

(3) Unless the applicant or employee meets standards specified in rules adopted under this section, the applicant or employee is found by a criminal records check required by this section to have been convicted of, pleaded guilty to, or been found eligible for intervention in lieu of conviction for a disqualifying offense.

(C) A responsible party or a responsible party's designee shall inform each applicant of both of the following at the time of the applicant's initial application for employment in a position that involves providing ombudsman services to residents and recipients:

(1) That a review of the databases listed in division (D) of this section will be conducted to determine whether the responsible party is prohibited by division (B)(1) of this section from employing the applicant in the position;

(2) That, unless the database review reveals that the applicant may not be employed in the position, a criminal records check of the applicant will be conducted and the applicant is required to provide a set of the applicant's fingerprint impressions as part of the criminal records check.

(D) As a condition of any applicant's being employed by a responsible party in a position that involves providing ombudsman services to residents and recipients, the responsible party or designee shall conduct a database review of the applicant in accordance with rules adopted under this section. If rules adopted under this section so require, the responsible party or designee shall conduct a database review of an employee in accordance with the rules as a condition of the responsible party continuing to employ the employee in a position that involves providing ombudsman services to residents and recipients. A database review shall determine whether the applicant or employee is included in any of the following:

(1) The excluded parties list system that is maintained by the United States general services administration pursuant to subpart 9.4 of the federal acquisition regulation and available at the federal web site known as the system for award management;

(2) The list of excluded individuals and entities maintained by the office of inspector general in the United States department of health and human services pursuant to section 1128 of the "Social Security Act," 94 Stat. 2619 (1980), 42 U.S.C. 1320a-7, as amended, and section 1156 of the "Social Security Act," 96 Stat. 388 (1982), 42 U.S.C. 1320c-5, as amended;

(3) The registry of developmental disabilities employees established under section 5123.52 of the Revised Code;

(4) The internet-based sex offender and child-victim offender database established under division (A)(11) of section 2950.13 of the Revised Code;

(5) The internet-based database of inmates established under section 5120.66 of the Revised Code;

(6) The state nurse aide registry established under section 3721.32 of the Revised Code;

(7) Any other database, if any, specified in rules adopted under this section.

(E)(1) As a condition of any applicant's being employed by a responsible party in a position that involves providing ombudsman services to residents and recipients, the responsible party or designee shall request that the superintendent of the bureau of criminal identification and investigation conduct a criminal records check of the applicant. If rules adopted under this section so require, the responsible party or designee shall request that the superintendent conduct a criminal records check of an employee at times specified in the rules as a condition of the responsible party continuing to employ the employee in a position that involves providing ombudsman services to residents and recipients. However, the responsible party or designee is not required to request the criminal records check of the applicant or employee if the responsible party is prohibited by division (B)(1) of this section from employing the applicant or continuing to employ the employee in a position that involves providing ombudsman services to residents and recipients. If an applicant or employee for whom a criminal records check request is required by this section does not present proof of having been a resident of this state for the five-year period immediately prior to the date the criminal records check is requested or provide evidence that within that five-year period the superintendent has requested information about the applicant or employee from the federal bureau of investigation in a criminal records check, the responsible party or designee shall request that the superintendent obtain information from the federal bureau of investigation as part of the criminal records check. Even if an applicant or employee for whom a criminal records check request is required by this section presents proof of having been a resident of this state for the five-year period, the responsible party or designee may request that the superintendent include information from the federal bureau of investigation in the criminal records check.

(2) A responsible party or designee shall do all of the following:

(a) Provide to each applicant and employee for whom a criminal records check request is required by this section a copy of the form prescribed pursuant to division (C)(1) of section 109.572 of the Revised Code and a standard impression sheet prescribed pursuant to division (C)(2) of that section;

(b) Obtain the completed form and standard impression sheet from the applicant or employee;

(c) Forward the completed form and standard impression sheet to the superintendent.

(3) A responsible party shall pay to the bureau of criminal identification and investigation the fee prescribed pursuant to division (C)(3) of section 109.572 of the Revised Code for each criminal records check the responsible party or the responsible party's designee requests under this section. The responsible party may charge an applicant a fee not exceeding the amount the responsible party pays to the bureau under this section if the responsible party or designee notifies the applicant at the time of initial application for employment of the amount of the fee.

(F)(1) A responsible party may employ conditionally an applicant for whom a criminal records check is required by this section prior to obtaining the results of the criminal records check if both of the following apply:

(a) The responsible party is not prohibited by division (B)(1) of this section from employing the applicant in a position that involves providing ombudsman services to residents and recipients;

(b) The responsible party or designee requests the criminal records check in accordance with division (E) of this section before conditionally employing the applicant.

(2) A responsible party shall terminate the employment of an applicant employed conditionally under division (F)(1) of this section if the results of the criminal records check, other than the results of any request for information from the federal bureau of investigation, are not obtained within the period ending sixty days after the date the request for the criminal records check is made. Regardless of when the results of the criminal records check are obtained, if the results indicate that the applicant has been convicted of, pleaded guilty to, or been found eligible for intervention in lieu of conviction for a disqualifying offense, the responsible party shall terminate the applicant's employment unless the applicant meets standards specified in rules adopted under this section that permit the responsible party to employ the applicant and the responsible party chooses to employ the applicant. Termination of employment under this division shall be considered just cause for discharge for purposes of division (D)(2) of section 4141.29 of the Revised Code if the applicant makes any attempt to deceive the responsible party or designee about the applicant's criminal record.

(G) The report of any criminal records check conducted pursuant to a request made under this section is not a public record for the purposes of section 149.43 of the Revised Code and shall not be made available to any person other than the following:

(1) The applicant or employee who is the subject of the criminal records check or the applicant's or employee's representative;

(2) The responsible party or designee;

(3) In the case of a criminal records check conducted for an applicant who is under final consideration for employment with a regional long-term care ombudsman program (including as the head of the regional program) or an employee of a regional long-term care ombudsman program (including the head of a regional program), the state long-term care ombudsman or a representative of the office of the state long-term care ombudsman program who is responsible for monitoring the regional program's compliance with this section;

(4) A court or hearing officerinvolved in a case dealing with any of the following:

(a) A denial of employment of the applicant or employee;

(b) Employment or unemployment benefits of the applicant or employee;

(c) A civil or criminal action regarding the medicaid program or a program the department of aging administers.

(5) Pursuant to a lawful subpoena or valid court order, any necessary individual not identified in division (G)(4) of this section who is involved in a case dealing with any issue, matter, or action described in division (G)(4)(a), (b), or (c) of this section.

(H) In a tort or other civil action for damages that is brought as the result of an injury, death, or loss to person or property caused by an applicant or employee who a responsible party employs in a position that involves providing ombudsman services to residents and recipients, all of the following shall apply:

(1) If the responsible party employed the applicant or employee in good faith and reasonable reliance on the report of a criminal records check requested under this section, the responsible party shall not be found negligent solely because of its reliance on the report, even if the information in the report is determined later to have been incomplete or inaccurate.

(2) If the responsible party employed the applicant in good faith on a conditional basis pursuant to division (F) of this section, the responsible party shall not be found negligent solely because it employed the applicant prior to receiving the report of a criminal records check requested under this section.

(3) If the responsible party in good faith employed the applicant or employee because the applicant or employee meets standards specified in rules adopted under this section, the responsible party shall not be found negligent solely because the applicant or employee has been convicted of, pleaded guilty to, or been found eligible for intervention in lieu of conviction for a disqualifying offense.

(I) The state long-term care ombudsman may not act as the director of aging's designee for the purpose of this section. The head of a regional long-term care ombudsman program may not act as the regional program's designee for the purpose of this section if the head is the employee for whom a database review or criminal records check is being conducted.

(J) The director of aging shall adopt rules in accordance with Chapter 119. of the Revised Code to implement this section.

(1) The rules may do the following:

(a) Require employees to undergo database reviews and criminal records checks under this section;

(b) If the rules require employees to undergo database reviews and criminal records checks under this section, exempt one or more classes of employees from the requirements;

(c) For the purpose of division (D)(7) of this section, specify other databases that are to be checked as part of a database review conducted under this section.

(2) The rules shall specify all of the following:

(a) The procedures for conducting database reviews under this section;

(b) If the rules require employees to undergo database reviews and criminal records checks under this section, the times at which the database reviews and criminal records checks are to be conducted;

(c) If the rules specify other databases to be checked as part of the database reviews, the circumstances under which a responsible party is prohibited from employing an applicant or continuing to employ an employee who is found by a database review to be included in one or more of those databases;

(d) Standards that an applicant or employee must meet for a responsible party to be permitted to employ the applicant or continue to employ the employee in a position that involves providing ombudsman services to residents and recipients if the applicant or employee is found by a criminal records check required by this section to have been convicted of, pleaded guilty to, or been found eligible for intervention in lieu of conviction for a disqualifying offense.

**HISTORY:**

151 v H 530, § 101.01, eff. 6-30-06; 151 v S 321, § 101.01, eff. 6-6-06; 2012 HB 487, § 101.01, eff. Jan. 1, 2013; 2013 HB 59, § 101.01, eff. Sept. 29, 2013; 2016 hb158, § 1, effective October 12, 2016; 2017 hb49, § 101.01, effective September 29, 2017; 2019 hb166, § 101.01, effective October 17, 2019; 2021 sb217, § 1, effective December 22, 2021.

**Editor's Notes**

Acts 2021, SB 217, § 3 provides: "This act is hereby declared to be an emergency measure necessary for the immediate preservation of the public peace, health, and safety. The reason for such necessity is that the changes that it makes to Ohio law are urgently needed to restrict access in specified circumstances to criminal records check information related to long-term care ombudsman programs, direct-care positions, community-based long-term care services, and municipal corporation tax administrators. Therefore, this act shall go into immediate effect."

**Amendment Notes**

The 2021 amendment by SB 217 substituted "A court or hearing officer" for "A court, hearing officer, or other necessary individual" in the introductory language of (G)(4); and added (G)(5).

The 2019 amendment by HB 166 substituted "before conditionally employing the applicant" for "not later than five business days after the applicant begins conditional employment" in (F)(1)(b).

The 2017 amendment by HB 49 substituted "applicant or employee abused, neglected, or exploited" for "applicant or employee neglected or abused" in (B)(1)(b).

The 2016 amendment by HB 158 substituted "developmental disabilities" for "MR/DD" in (D)(3).

The 2013 amendment rewrote the section.

The 2012 amendment rewrote the section.

151 v S 321, effective June 6, 2006, in (A)(1), inserted "but is not limited to"; and, in (E)(2), substituted "aging" for "health".

### § 173.28 Civil penalties against long-term care providers.

(A) As used in this section, "incident" means the occurrence of a violation with respect to a resident or recipient. A violation is a separate incident for each day it occurs and for each resident who is subject to it.

(B)(1) In lieu of the fine that may be imposed under division (A) of section 173.99 of the Revised Code for a criminal offense, the director of aging may, under Chapter 119. of the Revised Code, fine a long-term care provider or other entity, a person employed by a long-term care provider or other entity, or an individual for a violation of division (C) of section 173.24 of the Revised Code. The fine shall not exceed one thousand dollars per incident.

(2) In lieu of the fine that may be imposed under division (C) of section 173.99 of the Revised Code for a criminal offense, the director may, under Chapter 119. of the Revised Code, fine a long-term care provider or other entity, a person employed by a long-term care provider or other entity, or an individual for a violation of division (G)(1) or (2) of section 173.19 of the Revised Code. The fine shall not exceed five hundred dollars for each day the violation continued.

(C) On request of the director, the attorney general shall bring and prosecute to judgment a civil action to collect any fine imposed under division (B)(1) or (2) of this section that remains unpaid thirty days after the violator's final appeal is exhausted.

(D) All fines collected under this section shall be deposited into the state treasury to the credit of the state long-term care ombudsman program fund created under section 173.26 of the Revised Code.

**HISTORY:**

153 v H 1, § 101.01, eff. 10-16-09; 2013 HB 59, § 101.01, eff. Sept. 29, 2013; 2017 hb49, § 101.01, effective September 29, 2017.

**Amendment Notes**

The 2017 amendment by HB 49 redesignated former (A)(1) as (A); in the first sentence of (A), substituted "section" for "division" and deleted "as those terms are defined in section 173.14 of the Revised Code" at the end; redesignated former second paragraph of (A)(1) as (B)(1); in (B)(1), in the first sentence, added "for a criminal offense" and "an individual"; in (B)(2), in the first sentence, added "for a criminal offense" and substituted "an individual for a violation of division (G)(1) or (2) of section 173.19 of the Revised Code" for "for violating of division (E) of section 173.19 of the Revised Code by denying a representative of the office of the state long-term care ombudsman program the access required by that division; redesignated former (B) and (C) as (C) and (D); substituted "division (B)(1) or (2)" for "division (A)(1) or (2)" in (C); and made related changes.

The 2013 amendment substituted "ombudsman" for "ombudsperson" in the first sentence of (A)(2) and in (C).

## RESIDENTIAL STATE SUPPLEMENT PROGRAM

### § 173.35 Residential state supplement program [Renumbered].

**Editor's Notes**

This section was renumbered as RC § 5119.69 by 2011 HB 153, § 101.01, eff. July 1, 2011.

### § 173.351 Home first component [Renumbered].

**Editor's Notes**

This section was renumbered as RC § 5119.691 by 2011 HB 153, § 101.01, eff. July 1, 2011.

## CERTIFICATION OF ADULT FOSTER HOMES

### § 173.36 Standards for certification of adult foster homes [Renumbered].

**Editor's Notes**

This section was renumbered as RC § 5119.692 by 2011 HB 153, § 101.01, eff. July 1, 2011.

## CERTIFICATION OF PROVIDERS OF COMMUNITY-BASED LONG-TERM CARE SERVICES

### § 173.38 Criminal records check for certain applicants for employment.

(A) As used in this section:

(1) "Applicant" means a person who is under final consideration for employment with a responsible party in a full-time, part-time, or temporary direct-care position or is referred to a responsible party by an employment service for such a position. "Applicant" does not include a person being considered for a direct-care position as a volunteer.

(2) "Area agency on aging" has the same meaning as in section 173.14 of the Revised Code.

(3) "Chief administrator of a responsible party" includes a consumer when the consumer is a responsible party.

(4) "Community-based long-term care services" means community-based long-term care services, as defined in section 173.14 of the Revised Code, that are provided under a program the department of aging administers.

(5) "Consumer" means an individual who receives community-based long-term care services.

(6) "Criminal records check" has the same meaning as in section 109.572 of the Revised Code.

(7)(a) "Direct-care position" means an employment position in which an employee has either or both of the following:

(i) In-person contact with one or more consumers;

(ii) Access to one or more consumers' personal property or records.

(b) "Direct-care position" does not include a person whose sole duties are transporting individuals under Chapter 306. of the Revised Code.

(8) "Disqualifying offense" means any of the offenses listed or described in divisions (A)(3) (a) to (e) of section 109.572 of the Revised Code.

(9) "Employee" means a person employed by a responsible party in a full-time, part-time, or temporary direct-care position and a person who works in such a position due to being referred to a responsible party by an employment service. "Employee" does not include a person who works in a direct-care position as a volunteer.

(10) "PASSPORT administrative agency" has the same meaning as in section 173.42 of the Revised Code.

(11) "Provider" has the same meaning as in section 173.39 of the Revised Code.

(12) "Responsible party" means the following:

(a) An area agency on aging in the case of either of the following:

(i) A person who is an applicant because the person is under final consideration for employment with the agency in a full-time, part-time, or temporary direct-care position or is referred to the agency by an employment service for such a position;

(ii) A person who is an employee because the person is employed by the agency in a full-time, part-time, or temporary direct-care position or works in such a position due to being referred to the agency by an employment service.

(b) A PASSPORT administrative agency in the case of either of the following:

(i) A person who is an applicant because the person is under final consideration for employment with the agency in a full-time, part-time, or temporary direct-care position or is referred to the agency by an employment service for such a position;

(ii) A person who is an employee because the person is employed by the agency in a full-time, part-time, or temporary direct-care position or works in such a position due to being referred to the agency by an employment service.

(c) A provider in the case of either of the following:

(i) A person who is an applicant because the person is under final consideration for employment with the provider in a full-time, part-time, or temporary direct-care position or is referred to the provider by an employment service for such a position;

(ii) A person who is an employee because the person is employed by the provider in a full-time, part-time, or temporary direct-care position or works in such a position due to being referred to the provider by an employment service.

(d) A subcontractor in the case of either of the following:

(i) A person who is an applicant because the person is under final consideration for employment with the subcontractor in a full-time, part-time, or temporary direct-care position or is referred to the subcontractor by an employment service for such a position;

(ii) A person who is an employee because the person is employed by the subcontractor in a full-time, part-time, or temporary direct-care position or works in such a position due to being referred to the subcontractor by an employment service.

(e) A consumer in the case of either of the following:

(i) A person who is an applicant because the person is under final consideration for employment with the consumer in a full-time, part-time, or temporary direct-care position for which the consumer, as the employer of record, is to direct the person in the provision of community-based long-term care services the person is to provide the consumer or is referred to the consumer by an employment service for such a position;

(ii) A person who is an employee because the person is employed by the consumer in a full-time, part-time, or temporary direct-care position for which the consumer, as the employer of record, directs the person in the provision of community-based long-term care services the person provides to the consumer or who works in such a position due to being referred to the consumer by an employment service.

(13) "Subcontractor" has the meaning specified in rules adopted under this section.

(14) "Volunteer" means a person who serves in a direct-care position without receiving or expecting to receive any form of remuneration other than reimbursement for actual expenses.

(15) "Waiver agency" has the same meaning as in section 5164.342 of the Revised Code.

(B) This section does not apply to any individual who is subject to a database review or criminal records check under section 173.381 or 3701.881 of the Revised Code or to any individual who is subject to a criminal records check under section 3721.121 of the Revised Code.

(C) No responsible party shall employ an applicant or continue to employ an employee in a direct-care position if any of the following apply:

(1) A review of the databases listed in division (E) of this section reveals any of the following:

(a) That the applicant or employee is included in one or more of the databases listed in divisions (E)(1) to (5) of this section;

(b) That there is in the state nurse aide registry established under section 3721.32 of the Revised Code a statement detailing findings by the director of health that the applicant or employee abused, neglected, or exploited a long-term care facility or residential care facility resident or misappropriated property of such a resident;

(c) That the applicant or employee is included in one or more of the databases, if any, specified in rules adopted under this section and the rules prohibit the responsible party from employing an applicant or continuing to employ an employee included in such a database in a direct-care position.

(2) After the applicant or employee is provided, pursuant to division (F)(2)(a) of this section, a copy of the form prescribed pursuant to division (C)(1) of section 109.572 of the Revised Code and the standard impression sheet prescribed pursuant to division (C)(2) of that section, the applicant or employee fails to complete the form or provide the applicant's or employee's fingerprint impressions on the standard impression sheet.

(3) Unless the applicant or employee meets standards specified in rules adopted under this section, the applicant or employee is found by a criminal records check required by this section to have been convicted of, pleaded guilty to, or been found eligible for intervention in lieu of conviction for a disqualifying offense.

(D) Except as provided by division (G) of this section, the chief administrator of a responsible party shall inform each applicant of both of the following at the time of the applicant's initial application for employment or referral to the responsible party by an employment service for a direct-care position:

(1) That a review of the databases listed in division (E) of this section will be conducted to determine whether the responsible party is prohibited by division (C)(1) of this section from employing the applicant in the direct-care position;

(2) That, unless the database review reveals that the applicant may not be employed in the direct-care position, a criminal records check of the applicant will be conducted and the applicant is required to provide a set of the applicant's fingerprint impressions as part of the criminal records check.

(E) As a condition of employing any applicant in a direct-care position, the chief administrator of a responsible party shall conduct a database review of the applicant in accordance with rules adopted under this section. If rules adopted under this section so require, the chief administrator of a responsible party shall conduct a database review of an employee in accordance with the rules as a condition of continuing to employ the employee in a direct-care position. However, a chief administrator is not required to conduct a database review of an applicant or employee if division (G) of this section applies. A database review shall determine whether the applicant or employee is included in any of the following:

(1) The excluded parties list system that is maintained by the United States general services administration pursuant to subpart 9.4 of the federal acquisition regulation and available

at the federal web site known as the system for award management;

(2) The list of excluded individuals and entities maintained by the office of inspector general in the United States department of health and human services pursuant to the "Social Security Act," sections 1128 and 1156, 42 U.S.C. 1320a-7 and 1320c-5;

(3) The registry of developmental disabilities employees established under section 5123.52 of the Revised Code;

(4) The internet-based sex offender and child-victim offender database established under division (A)(11) of section 2950.13 of the Revised Code;

(5) The internet-based database of inmates established under section 5120.66 of the Revised Code;

(6) The state nurse aide registry established under section 3721.32 of the Revised Code;

(7) Any other database, if any, specified in rules adopted under this section.

(F)(1) As a condition of employing any applicant in a direct-care position, the chief administrator of a responsible party shall request that the superintendent of the bureau of criminal identification and investigation conduct a criminal records check of the applicant. If rules adopted under this section so require, the chief administrator of a responsible party shall request that the superintendent conduct a criminal records check of an employee at times specified in the rules as a condition of continuing to employ the employee in a direct-care position. However, the chief administrator is not required to request the criminal records check of the applicant or employee if division (G) of this section applies or the responsible party is prohibited by division (C)(1) of this section from employing the applicant or continuing to employ the employee in a direct-care position. If an applicant or employee for whom a criminal records check request is required by this section does not present proof of having been a resident of this state for the five-year period immediately prior to the date the criminal records check is requested or provide evidence that within that five-year period the superintendent has requested information about the applicant or employee from the federal bureau of investigation in a criminal records check, the chief administrator shall request that the superintendent obtain information from the federal bureau of investigation as part of the criminal records check. Even if an applicant or employee for whom a criminal records check request is required by this section presents proof of having been a resident of this state for the five-year period, the chief administrator may request that the superintendent include information from the federal bureau of investigation in the criminal records check.

(2) The chief administrator shall do all of the following:

(a) Provide to each applicant and employee for whom a criminal records check request is required by this section a copy of the form prescribed pursuant to division (C)(1) of section 109.572 of the Revised Code and a standard impression sheet prescribed pursuant to division (C)(2) of that section;

(b) Obtain the completed form and standard impression sheet from the applicant or employee;

(c) Forward the completed form and standard impression sheet to the superintendent.

(3) A responsible party shall pay to the bureau of criminal identification and investigation the fee prescribed pursuant to division (C)(3) of section 109.572 of the Revised Code for each criminal records check the responsible party requests under this section. A responsible party may charge an applicant a fee not exceeding the amount the responsible party pays to the bureau under this section if both of the following apply:

(a) The responsible party notifies the applicant at the time of initial application for employment of the amount of the fee and that, unless the fee is paid, the applicant will not be considered for employment.

(b) The medicaid program does not pay the responsible party for the fee it pays to the bureau under this section.

(G) Divisions (D) to (F) of this section do not apply with regard to an applicant or employee if the applicant or employee is referred to a responsible party by an employment service that supplies full-time, part-time, or temporary staff for direct-care positions and both of the following apply:

(1) The chief administrator of the responsible party receives from the employment service confirmation that a review of the databases listed in division (E) of this section was conducted of the applicant or employee.

(2) The chief administrator of the responsible party receives from the employment service, applicant, or employee a report of the results of a criminal records check of the applicant or employee that has been conducted by the superintendent within the one-year period immediately preceding the following:

(a) In the case of an applicant, the date of the applicant's referral by the employment service to the responsible party;

(b) In the case of an employee, the date by which the responsible party would otherwise have to request a criminal records check of the employee under division (F) of this section.

(H)(1) A responsible party may employ conditionally an applicant for whom a criminal records check request is required by this section prior to obtaining the results of the criminal records check if the responsible party is not prohibited by division (C)(1) of this section from employing the applicant in a direct-care position and either of the following applies:

(a) The chief administrator of the responsible party requests the criminal records check in accordance with division (F) of this section before conditionally employing the applicant.

(b) The applicant is referred to the responsible party by an employment service, the employment service or the applicant provides the chief administrator of the responsible party a letter that is on the letterhead of the employment service, the letter is dated and signed by a supervisor or another designated official of the employment service, and the letter states all of the following:

(i) That the employment service has requested the superintendent to conduct a criminal records check regarding the applicant;

(ii) That the requested criminal records check is to include a determination of whether the applicant has been convicted of, pleaded guilty to, or been found eligible for intervention in lieu of conviction for a disqualifying offense;

(iii) That the employment service has not received the results of the criminal records check as of the date set forth on the letter;

(iv) That the employment service promptly will send a copy of the results of the criminal records check to the chief administrator of the responsible party when the employment service receives the results.

(2) If a responsible party employs an applicant conditionally pursuant to division (H)(1)(b) of this section, the employment service, on its receipt of the results of the criminal records check, promptly shall send a copy of the results to the chief administrator of the responsible party.

(3) A responsible party that employs an applicant conditionally pursuant to division (H)(1)(a) or (b) of this section shall terminate the applicant's employment if the results of the criminal records check, other than the results of any request for information from the federal bureau of investigation, are not obtained within the period ending sixty days after the date the request for the criminal records check is made. Regardless of when the results of the criminal records check are obtained, if the results indicate that the applicant has been convicted of, pleaded guilty to, or been found eligible for intervention in lieu of conviction for a disqualifying offense, the responsible party shall terminate the applicant's employment unless the applicant meets standards specified in rules adopted under this section that permit the responsible party to employ the applicant and the responsible party chooses to employ the applicant. Termination of employment under this division shall be considered just cause for discharge for purposes of division (D)(2) of section 4141.29 of the Revised Code if the applicant makes any attempt to deceive the responsible party about the applicant's criminal record.

(I) The report of any criminal records check conducted pursuant to a request made under this section is not a public record for the purposes of section 149.43 of the Revised Code and shall not be made available to any person other than the following:

(1) The applicant or employee who is the subject of the criminal records check or the applicant's or employee's representative;

(2) The chief administrator of the responsible party requesting the criminal records check or the administrator's representative;

(3) The administrator of any other facility, agency, or program that provides community-based long-term care services that is owned or operated by the same entity that owns or operates the responsible party that requested the criminal records check;

(4) The employment service that requested the criminal records check;

(5) The director of aging or a person authorized by the director to monitor a responsible party's compliance with this section;

(6) The medicaid director and the staff of the department of medicaid who are involved in the administration of the medicaid program if any of the following apply:

(a) In the case of a criminal records check requested by a provider or subcontractor, the provider or subcontractor also is a waiver agency;

(b) In the case of a criminal records check requested by an employment service, the employment service makes the request for an applicant or employee the employment service refers to a provider or subcontractor that also is a waiver agency;

(c) The criminal records check is requested by a consumer who is acting as a responsible party.

(7) A court or hearing officer involved in a case dealing with any of the following:

(a) A denial of employment of the applicant or employee;

(b) Employment or unemployment benefits of the applicant or employee;

(c) A civil or criminal action regarding the medicaid program or a program the department of aging administers.

(8) Pursuant to a lawful subpoena or valid court order, any necessary individual not identified in division (I)(7) of this section who is involved in a case dealing with any issue, matter, or action described in division (I)(7)(a), (b), or (c) of this section.

(J) In a tort or other civil action for damages that is brought as the result of an injury, death, or loss to person or property caused by an applicant or employee who a responsible party employs in a direct-care position, all of the following shall apply:

(1) If the responsible party employed the applicant or employee in good faith and reasonable reliance on the report of a criminal records check requested under this section, the responsible party shall not be found negligent solely because of its reliance on the report, even if the information in the report is determined later to have been incomplete or inaccurate.

(2) If the responsible party employed the applicant in good faith on a conditional basis pursuant to division (H) of this section, the responsible party shall not be found negligent solely because it employed the applicant prior to receiving the report of a criminal records check requested under this section.

(3) If the responsible party in good faith employed the applicant or employee because the applicant or employee meets standards specified in rules adopted under this section, the responsible party shall not be found negligent solely because the applicant or employee has been convicted of, pleaded guilty to, or been found eligible for intervention in lieu of conviction for a disqualifying offense.

(K) The director of aging shall adopt rules in accordance with Chapter 119. of the Revised Code to implement this section.

(1) The rules may do the following:

(a) Require employees to undergo database reviews and criminal records checks under this section;

(b) If the rules require employees to undergo database reviews and criminal records checks under this section, exempt one or more classes of employees from the requirements;

(c) For the purpose of division (E)(7) of this section, specify other databases that are to be checked as part of a database review conducted under this section.

(2) The rules shall specify all of the following:

(a) The meaning of the term "subcontractor";

(b) The procedures for conducting database reviews under this section;

(c) If the rules require employees to undergo database reviews and criminal records checks under this section, the times at which the database reviews and criminal records checks are to be conducted;

(d) If the rules specify other databases to be checked as part of the database reviews, the circumstances under which a responsible party is prohibited from employing an applicant or continuing to employ an employee who is found by a database review to be included in one or more of those databases;

(e) Standards that an applicant or employee must meet for a responsible party to be permitted to employ the applicant or continue to employ the employee in a direct-care position if the applicant or employee is found by a criminal records check required by this section to have been convicted of, pleaded guilty to, or been found eligible for intervention in lieu of conviction for a disqualifying offense.

**HISTORY:**

146 v S 160 (Eff 1-27-97); 147 v S 96 (Eff 6-11-97); 147 v H 18. Eff. 1-30-98; 151 v H 530, § 101.01, eff. 6-30-06; 2012 HB 487, § 101.01, eff. Jan. 1, 2013; 2013 HB 59, § 101.01, eff. Sept. 29, 2013; 2014 HB 483, § 101.01, eff. Sept. 15, 2014; 2016 hb158, § 1, effective October 12, 2016; 2017 hb49, § 101.01, effective September 29, 2017; 2019 hb166, § 101.01, effective October 17, 2019; 2021 hb110, § 101.01, effective September 30, 2021; 2021 sb217, § 1, effective December 22, 2021.

**Publisher's Note:**

Former § 173.394 was amended and renumbered from RC § 173.41 by 151 v H 530, effective June 30, 2006.

**Editor's Notes**

Acts 2021, SB 217, § 3 provides: "This act is hereby declared to be an emergency measure necessary for the immediate preservation of the public peace, health, and safety. The reason for such necessity is that the changes that it makes to Ohio law are urgently needed to restrict access in specified circumstances to criminal records check information related to long-term care ombudsman programs, direct-care positions, community-based long-term care services, and municipal corporation tax administrators. Therefore, this act shall go into immediate effect."

This section was formerly codified as RC § 173.394.

**Amendment Notes**

The 2021 amendment by SB 217 substituted "A court or hearing officer" for "A court, hearing officer, or other necessary individual" in the introductory language of (I)(7); and added (I)(8).

The 2021 amendment by HB 110 substituted "3740.11" for "3701.881" in (B).

The 2019 amendment by HB 166 deleted the former second sentence of (B), which read: "If a provider or subcontractor also is a waiver agency, the provider or subcontractor may provide for applicants and employees to undergo database reviews and criminal records checks in accordance with section 5164.342 of the Revised Code rather than this section"; and substituted "before conditionally employing the applicant" for "not later than five business days after the applicant begins conditional employment" in (H)(1)(a).

The 2017 amendment by HB 49 substituted "applicant or employee abused, neglected, or exploited" for "applicant or employee neglected or abused" in (C)(1)(b).

The 2016 amendment by HB 158 substituted "developmental disabilities" for "MR/DD" in (E)(3).

The 2014 amendment by HB 483 inserted (A)(3); redesignated former (A)(3) through (A)(14) as (A)(4) through (A)(15); added (A)(12)(e) and (I)(6)(e); substituted "section 173.381 or 3701.881" for "section 3701.881" in the first sentence of (B); and made related stylistic changes.

The 2013 amendment rewrote the section.

The 2012 amendment rewrote the section.

151 v H 530, effective June 30, 2006, substituted "community-based long-term care" for "PASSPORT" throughout; substituted "individual" for "older adult" throughout; in (A)(2), substituted "has the same meaning" for "and 'older adult' have the same meanings"; deleted (A)(3), defining "PASSPORT agency"; in (D)(2)(b), substituted "medicaid" for "medical assistance"; and inserted (E)(4) and redesignated former (E)(4) as (5).

**§ 173.381 Issuance or award of a community-based long-term care services certificate or community-based long-term care services contract or grant; conditions; application review.**

(A) As used in this section:

(1) "Community-based long-term care services" means community-based long-term care services, as defined in section 173.14 of the Revised Code, that are provided under a program the department of aging administers.

(2) "Community-based long-term care services certificate" means a certificate issued under section 173.391 of the Revised Code.

(3) "Community-based long-term care services contract or grant" means a contract or grant awarded under section 173.392 of the Revised Code.

(4) "Criminal records check" has the same meaning as in section 109.572 of the Revised Code.

(5) "Disqualifying offense" means any of the offenses listed or described in divisions (A)(3) (a) to (e) of section 109.572 of the Revised Code.

(6) "Provider" has the same meaning as in section 173.39 of the Revised Code.

(7) "Self-employed provider" means a provider who works for the provider's self and has no employees.

(B) This section does not apply to any individual who is subject to a database review or criminal records check under section 3701.881 of the Revised Code.

(C)(1) The department of aging or its designee shall take the following actions when the circumstances specified in division (C)(2) of this section apply:

(a) Refuse to issue a community-based long-term care services certificate to a self-employed provider;

(b) Revoke a self-employed provider's community-based long-term care services certificate;

(c) Refuse to award a community-based long-term care services contract or grant to a self-employed provider;

(d) Terminate a self-employed provider's community-based long-term care services contract or grant awarded on or after September 15, 2014.

(2) The following are the circumstances that require the department of aging or its designee to take action under division (C)(1) of this section:

(a) A review of the databases listed in division (E) of this section reveals any of the following:

(i) That the self-employed provider is included in one or more of the databases listed in divisions (E)(1) to (5) of this section;

(ii) That there is in the state nurse aide registry established under section 3721.32 of the Revised Code a statement detailing findings by the director of health that the self-employed provider abused, neglected, or exploited a long-term care facility or residential care facility resident or misappropriated property of such a resident;

(iii) That the self-employed provider is included in one or more of the databases, if any, specified in rules adopted under this section and the rules require the department or its designee to take action under division (C)(1) of this section if a self-employed provider is included in such a database.

(b) After the self-employed provider is provided, pursuant to division (F)(2)(a) of this section, a copy of the form prescribed pursuant to division (C)(1) of section 109.572 of the Revised Code and the standard impression sheet prescribed pursuant to division (C)(2) of that section, the self-employed provider fails to complete the form or provide the self-employed provider's fingerprint impressions on the standard impression sheet.

(c) Unless the self-employed provider meets standards specified in rules adopted under this section, the self-employed provider is found by a criminal records check required by this section to have been convicted of, pleaded guilty to, or been found eligible for intervention in lieu of conviction for a disqualifying offense.

(D) The department of aging or its designee shall inform each self-employed provider of both of the following at the time of the self-employed provider's initial application for a community-based long-term care services certificate or initial bid for a community-based long-term care services contract or grant:

(1) That a review of the databases listed in division (E) of this section will be conducted to determine whether the department or its designee is required by division (C) of this section to refuse to issue or award a community-based long-term care services certificate or community-based long-term care services contract or grant to the self-employed provider;

(2) That, unless the database review reveals that the department or its designee is required to refuse to issue or award a community-based long-term care services certificate or community-based long-term care services contract or grant to the self-employed provider, a criminal records check of the self-employed provider will be conducted and the self-employed provider is required to provide a set of the self-employed provider's fingerprint impressions as part of the criminal records check.

(E) As a condition of issuing or awarding a community-based long-term care services certificate or community-based long-term care services contract or grant to a self-employed provider, the department of aging or its designee shall conduct a database review of the self-employed provider in accordance with rules adopted under this section. If rules adopted under this section so require, the department or its designee shall conduct a database review of a self-employed provider in accordance with the rules as a condition of not revoking or terminating the self-employed provider's community-based long-term care services certificate or community-based long-term care services contract or grant. A database review shall determine whether the self-employed provider is included in any of the following:

(1) The excluded parties list system that is maintained by the United States general services administration pursuant to subpart 9.4 of the federal acquisition regulation and available at the federal web site known as the system for award management;

(2) The list of excluded individuals and entities maintained by the office of inspector general in the United States department of health and human services pursuant to the "Social Security Act," 42 U.S.C. 1320a-7 and 1320c-5;

(3) The registry of developmental disabilities employees established under section 5123.52 of the Revised Code;

(4) The internet-based sex offender and child-victim offender database established under division (A)(11) of section 2950.13 of the Revised Code;

(5) The internet-based database of inmates established under section 5120.66 of the Revised Code;

(6) The state nurse aide registry established under section 3721.32 of the Revised Code;

(7) Any other database, if any, specified in rules adopted under this section.

(F)(1) As a condition of issuing or awarding a community-based long-term care services certificate or community-based long-term care services contract or grant to a self-employed provider, the department of aging or its designee shall request that the superintendent of the bureau of criminal identification and investigation conduct a criminal records check of the self-employed provider. If rules adopted under this section so require, the department or its designee shall request that the superintendent conduct a criminal records check of a self-employed provider at times specified in the rules as a condition of not revoking or terminating the self-employed provider's community-based long-term care services certificate or community-based long-term care services contract or grant. However, the department or its designee is not required to request the criminal records check of the self-employed provider if the department or its designee, because of circumstances specified in division (C)(2)(a) of this section, is required to refuse to issue or award a community-based long-term care services certificate or community-based long-term care services contract or grant to the self-employed provider or to revoke or terminate the self-employed provider's certificate or contract or grant.

If a self-employed provider for whom a criminal records check request is required by this section does not present proof of having been a resident of this state for the five-year period immediately prior to the date the criminal records check is requested or provide evidence that within that five-year period the superintendent has requested information about the self-employed provider from the federal bureau of investigation in a criminal records check, the department or its designee shall request that the superintendent obtain information from the federal bureau of investigation as part of the criminal records check. Even if a self-employed provider for whom a criminal records check request is required by this section presents proof of having been a resident of this state for the five-year period, the department or its designee may request that the superintendent include information from the federal bureau of investigation in the criminal records check.

(2) The department or its designee shall do all of the following:

(a) Provide to each self-employed provider for whom a criminal records check request is required by this section a copy of the form prescribed pursuant to division (C)(1) of section 109.572 of the Revised Code and a standard impression sheet prescribed pursuant to division (C)(2) of that section;

(b) Obtain the completed form and standard impression sheet from the self-employed provider;

(c) Forward the completed form and standard impression sheet to the superintendent.

(3) The department or its designee shall pay to the bureau of criminal identification and investigation the fee prescribed pursuant to division (C)(3) of section 109.572 of the Revised Code for each criminal records check of a self-employed provider the department or its designee requests under this section. The department or its designee may charge the self-employed provider a fee that does not exceed the amount the department or its designee pays to the bureau.

(G) The report of any criminal records check of a self-employed provider conducted pursuant to a request made under this section is not a public record for the purposes of section 149.43 of the Revised Code and shall not be made available to any person other than the following:

(1) The self-employed provider or the self-employed provider's representative;

(2) The department of aging, the department's designee, or a representative of the department or its designee;

(3) The medicaid director and the staff of the department of medicaid who are involved in the administration of the medicaid program if the self-employed provider is to provide, or provides, community-based long-term care services under a component of the medicaid program that the department of aging administers;

(4) A court or hearing officer involved in a case dealing with any of the following:

(a) A refusal to issue or award a community-based long-term services certificate or community-based long-term care services contract or grant to the self-employed provider;

(b) A revocation or termination of the self-employed provider's community-based long-term care services certificate or community-based long-term care services contract or grant;

(c) A civil or criminal action regarding a program the department of aging administers.

(5) Pursuant to a lawful subpoena or valid court order, any necessary individual not identified in division (G)(4) of this section who is involved in a case dealing with any issue, matter, or action described in division (G)(4)(a), (b), or (c) of this section.

(H) In a tort or other civil action for damages that is brought as the result of an injury, death, or loss to person or property caused by a self-employed provider, both of the following shall apply:

(1) If the department of aging or its designee, in good faith and reasonable reliance on the report of a criminal records check requested under this section, issued or awarded a community-based long-term care services certificate or community-based long-term care services contract or grant to the self-employed provider or did not revoke or terminate the self-employed provider's certificate or contract or grant, the department and its designee shall not be found negligent solely because of its reliance on the report, even if the information in the report is determined later to have been incomplete or inaccurate.

(2) If the department or its designee in good faith issued or awarded a community-based long-term care services certificate or community-based long-term care services contract or grant to the self-employed provider or did not revoke or terminate the self-employed provider's certificate or contract or grant because the self-employed provider meets standards specified in rules adopted under this section, the department and its designee shall not be found negligent solely because the self-employed provider has been convicted of, pleaded guilty to, or been found eligible for intervention in lieu of conviction for a disqualifying offense.

(I) The director of aging shall adopt rules in accordance with Chapter 119. of the Revised Code to implement this section.

(1) The rules may do the following:

(a) Require self-employed providers who have been issued or awarded community-based long-term care services certificates or community-based long-term care services contracts or grants to undergo database reviews and criminal records checks under this section;

(b) If the rules require self-employed providers who have been issued or awarded community-based long-term care services certificates or community-based long-term care services contracts or grants to undergo database reviews and criminal records checks under this section, exempt one or more classes of such self-employed providers from the requirements;

(c) For the purpose of division (E)(7) of this section, specify other databases that are to be checked as part of a database review conducted under this section.

(2) The rules shall specify all of the following:

(a) The procedures for conducting database reviews under this section;

(b) If the rules require self-employed providers who have been issued or awarded community-based long-term care services certificates or community-based long-term care services contracts or grants to undergo database reviews and criminal records checks under this section, the times at which the database reviews and criminal records checks are to be conducted;

(c) If the rules specify other databases to be checked as part of the database reviews, the circumstances under which the department of aging or its designee is required to refuse to issue or award a community-based long-term care services certificate or community-based long-term care services contract or grant to a self-employed provider or to revoke or terminate a self-employed provider's certificate or contract or grant when the self-employed provider is found by a database review to be included in one or more of those databases;

(d) Standards that a self-employed provider must meet for the department or its designee to be permitted to issue or award a community-based long-term care services certificate or community-based long-term care services contract or grant to the self-employed provider or not to revoke or terminate the self-employed provider's certificate or contract or grant if the self-employed provider is found by a criminal records check required by this section to have been convicted of, pleaded guilty to, or been found eligible for intervention in lieu of conviction for a disqualifying offense.

**HISTORY:**

2014 HB 483, § 101.01, eff. Sept. 15, 2014; 2016 hb158, § 1, effective October 12, 2016; 2017 hb49, § 101.01, effective September 29, 2017; 2021 hb110, § 101.01, effective September 30, 2021; 2021 sb217, § 1, effective December 22, 2021.

**Editor's Notes**

Acts 2021, SB 217, § 3 provides: "This act is hereby declared to be an emergency measure necessary for the immediate preservation of the public peace, health, and safety. The reason for such necessity is that the changes that it makes to Ohio law are urgently needed to restrict access in specified circumstances to criminal records check information related to long-term care ombudsman programs, direct-care positions, community-based long-term care services, and municipal corporation tax administrators. Therefore, this act shall go into immediate effect."

**Amendment Notes**

The 2021 amendment by SB 217 substituted "A court or hearing officer" for "A court, hearing officer, or other necessary individual" in the introductory language of (G)(4); and added (G)(5).

The 2021 amendment by HB 110 substituted "section 3740.11" for "section 3701.881" in (B).

The 2017 amendment by HB 49 substituted "self-employed provider abused, neglected, or exploited" for "self-employed provider neglected or abused" in (C)(2)(a)(ii).

The 2016 amendment by HB 158 substituted "September 15, 2014" for "the effective date of this section" in (C)(1)(d); and substituted "developmental disabilities" for "MR/DD" in (E)(3).

## § 173.39 Requirements for payment for providing community-based long-term care services.

(A) As used in sections 173.39 to 173.393 of the Revised Code:

(1) "Provider" means a person or government entity that provides any services, including community-based long-term care services, under a program the department of aging administers. "Provider" includes a person or government entity that provides home and community-based services to older adults through the PASSPORT program or assisted living program.

(2) "Community-based long-term care services" has the same meaning as in section 173.14 of the Revised Code.

(3) "PASSPORT program" and "assisted living program" have the same meanings as in section 173.51 of the Revised Code.

(B) The department of aging shall not pay a provider for providing any service, including community-based long-term care services, under the PASSPORT program or assisted living program unless the provider is certified under section 173.391 of the Revised Code and the service is in fact provided.

The department may require a provider under any other program the department administers to be certified under section 173.391 of the Revised Code. If the department requires this certification, the department shall not pay the provider for providing any service under that program unless the provider is certified under section 173.391 of the Revised Code and the service is in fact provided. If the department does not require this certification, the department shall not pay the provider for providing any service under that program unless the provider complies with section 173.392 of the Revised Code.

**HISTORY:**

151 v H 66, § 101.01, eff. 9-29-05; 151 v H 530, § 101.01, eff. 6-30-06; 2013 HB 59, § 101.01, eff. Sept. 29, 2013; 2021 hb110, § 101.01, effective September 30, 2021.

**Amendment Notes**

The 2021 amendment by HB 110, in (A)(1), added "any services, including" in the first sentence and substituted "program or assisted living program" for "program as defined in section 173.51 of the Revised Code" in the second sentence; added (A)(3); rewrote (B); and made a related change.

The 2013 amendment substituted "sections 173.39 to 173.393" for "sections 173.39 to 173.394" in the introductory language of (A); substituted "Provider" for "Community-based long-term care agency" in the first and second sentences of (A)(1); in (A)(1), deleted "regardless of whether the person or government entity is certified under section 173.391 or authorized to receive payment for the services from the department under section 173.392 of the Revised Code" from the end of the first sentence and substituted "as defined in section 173.51" for "created under section 173.40" in the second sentence; and substituted "provider" for "person or government entity" twice in (B).

151 v H 530, effective June 30, 2006, redesignated the former provisions as (A) and (B); and rewrote (A).

## § 173.391 Certification requirements; disciplinary actions.

(A) Subject to section 173.381 of the Revised Code, the department of aging or its designee shall do all of the following in accordance with Chapter 119. of the Revised Code:

(1) Certify a provider to provide services, including community-based long-term care services, under a program the department administers if the provider satisfies the requirements for certification established by rules adopted under division (B) of this section and pays the fee, if any, established by rules adopted under division (G) of this section;

(2) When required to do so by rules adopted under division (B) of this section, take one or more of the following disciplinary actions against a provider certified under division (A)(1) of this section:

(a) Issue a written warning;

(b) Require the submission of a plan of correction or evidence of compliance with requirements identified by the department;

(c) Suspend referrals;

(d) Remove clients;

(e) Impose a fiscal sanction such as a civil monetary penalty or an order that unearned funds be repaid;

(f) Suspend the certification;

(g) Revoke the certification;

(h) Impose another sanction.

(3) Except as provided in division (E) of this section, hold hearings when there is a dispute between the department or its designee and a provider concerning actions the department or its designee takes regarding a decision not to certify the provider under division (A)(1) of this section or a disciplinary action under divisions (A)(2)(e) to (h) of this section.

(B) The director of aging shall adopt rules in accordance with Chapter 119. of the Revised Code establishing certification requirements and standards for determining which type of disciplinary action to take under division (A)(2) of this section in individual situations. The rules shall establish procedures for all of the following:

(1) Ensuring that providers comply with sections 173.38 and 173.381 of the Revised Code;

(2) Evaluating the services provided by the providers to ensure that the services are provided in a quality manner advantageous to the individual receiving the services;

(3) In a manner consistent with section 173.381 of the Revised Code, determining when to take disciplinary action under division (A)(2) of this section and which disciplinary action to take;

(4) Determining what constitutes another sanction for purposes of division (A)(2)(h) of this section.

(C) The procedures established in rules adopted under division (B)(2) of this section shall require that all of the following be considered as part of an evaluation described in division (B)(2) of this section:

(1) The provider's experience and financial responsibility;

(2) The provider's ability to comply with standards for the services, including community-based long-term care services, that the provider provides under a program the department administers;

(3) The provider's ability to meet the needs of the individuals served;

(4) Any other factor the director considers relevant.

(D) The rules adopted under division (B)(3) of this section shall specify that the reasons disciplinary action may be taken under division (A)(2) of this section include good cause, including misfeasance, malfeasance, nonfeasance, confirmed abuse or neglect, financial irresponsibility, or other conduct the director determines is injurious, or poses a threat, to the health or safety of individuals being served.

(E) Subject to division (F) of this section, the department is not required to hold hearings under division (A)(3) of this section if any of the following conditions apply:

(1) Rules adopted by the director of aging pursuant to this chapter require the provider to be a party to a provider agreement; hold a license, certificate, or permit; or maintain a certification, any of which is required or issued by a state or federal government entity other than the department of aging, and either of the following is the case:

(a) The provider agreement has not been entered into or the license, certificate, permit, or certification has not been obtained or maintained.

(b) The provider agreement, license, certificate, permit, or certification has been denied, revoked, not renewed, or suspended or has been otherwise restricted.

(2) The provider's certification under this section has been denied, suspended, or revoked for any of the following reasons:

(a) A government entity of this state, other than the department of aging, has terminated or refused to renew any of the following held by, or has denied any of the following sought by, a provider: a provider agreement, license, certificate, permit, or certification. Division (E)(2)(a) of this section applies regardless of whether the provider has entered into a provider agreement in, or holds a license, certificate, permit, or certification issued by, another state.

(b) The provider or a principal owner or manager of the provider who provides direct care has entered a guilty plea for, or has been convicted of, an offense materially related to the medicaid program.

(c) A principal owner or manager of the provider who provides direct care has entered a guilty plea for, been convicted of, or been found eligible for intervention in lieu of conviction for an offense listed or described in divisions (A)(3)(a) to (e) of section 109.572 of the Revised Code, but only if the provider, principal owner, or manager does not meet standards specified by the director in rules adopted under section 173.38 of the Revised Code.

(d) The department or its designee is required by section 173.381 of the Revised Code to deny or revoke the provider's certification.

(e) The United States department of health and human services has taken adverse action against the provider and that action impacts the provider's participation in the medicaid program.

(f) The provider has failed to enter into or renew a provider agreement with the PASSPORT administrative agency, as that term is defined in section 173.42 of the Revised Code, that administers programs on behalf of the department of aging in the region of the state in which the provider is certified to provide services.

(g) The provider has not billed or otherwise submitted a claim to the department for payment under the medicaid program in at least two years.

(h) The provider denied or failed to provide the department or its designee access to the provider's facilities during the provider's normal business hours for purposes of conducting an audit or structural compliance review.

(i) The provider has ceased doing business.

(j) The provider has voluntarily relinquished its certification for any reason.

(3) The provider's provider agreement with the department of medicaid has been suspended under section 5164.36 of the Revised Code.

(4) The provider's provider agreement with the department of medicaid is denied or revoked because the provider or its owner, officer, authorized agent, associate, manager, or employee has been convicted of an offense that caused the provider agreement to be suspended under section 5164.36 of the Revised Code.

(F) If the department does not hold hearings when any condition described in division (E) of this section applies, the department shall send a notice to the provider describing a decision not to certify the provider under division (A)(1) of this section or the disciplinary action the department is taking under divisions (A)(2)(e) to (h) of this section. The notice shall be sent to the provider's address that is on record with the department and may be sent by regular mail.

(G) The director of aging may adopt rules in accordance with Chapter 119. of the Revised Code establishing a fee to be charged by the department of aging or its designee for certification issued under this section.

(H) Any amounts collected by the department or its designee under this section shall be deposited in the state treasury to the credit of the provider certification fund, which is hereby created. Money credited to the fund shall be used to pay for services, including community-based long-term care services, to pay for administrative costs associated with provider certification under this section, and to pay for administrative costs related to the publication of the Ohio long-term care consumer guide.

**HISTORY:**

151 v H 66, § 101.01, eff. 9-29-05; 151 v H 530, § 101.01, eff. 6-30-06; 2011 HB 153, § 101.01, eff. Sept. 29, 2011; 2012 HB 487, § 101.01, eff. Jan. 1, 2013; 2013 HB 59, § 101.01, eff. Sept. 29, 2013; 2014 HB 483, § 101.01, eff. Sept. 15, 2014; 2019 hb166, § 101.01, effective October 17, 2019; 2021 hb110, § 101.01, effective September 30, 2021.

**Amendment Notes**

The 2021 amendment by HB 110 added "services, including" in (A)(1), (C)(2) and in the second sentence of (H); added "to pay for" twice in the second sentence of (H); and made related changes.

The 2019 amendment by HB 166 deleted "division (C) of" following "under in (E)(3); substituted "section 5164.36" for "division (C) of section 5164.37" in (E)(3) and (E)(4); in (F), in the first sentence, substituted "shall" for "may" and "is taking under divisions (A)(2)(e)" for "proposes to take under division (A)(2)(e)"; added the (H) designation; and substituted "Any amounts" for "All fees" at the beginning of the first sentence of (H).

The 2014 amendment by HB 483 added "Subject to section 173.381 of the Revised Code" to the beginning of the introductory language of (A); substituted "sections 173.38 and 173.381" for "section 173.38" in (B)(1); added "In a manner consistent with section 173.381 of the Revised Code" to the beginning of (B)(3); deleted "The provider or" from the beginning of (E)(2)(c); inserted (E)(2)(d); and redesignated former (E)(2)(d) through (E)(2)(i) as (E)(2)(e) through (E)(2)(j).

The 2013 amendment substituted "provider" for "person or government entity" wherever it appears in (A); substituted "providers" for "community-based long-term care agencies" in (B)(1), (C)(1), and in the second sentence of the second paragraph of (G); "section 173.38" for "section 173.394" in (B)(1); substituted "provider" for "agency" in (B)(2), (C)(2), (C)(3), and (F); and rewrote (E).

The 2012 amendment, in (E)(2)(c), inserted "or been found eligible for intervention in lieu of conviction for", substituted "or described in divisions (A)(3)(a) to (e) of section 109.572" for "in division (C)(1)(a) of section 173.394", substituted "director" for "department", and deleted "division (F) of" following "adopted under"; and made related and stylistic changes.

The 2011 amendment added "and pays the fee, if any, established by rules adopted under division (G) of this section" in (A)(1); substituted "certified" for "issued a certificate" in the introductory language of (A)(2); added "or evidence of compliance with requirements identified by the department" in (A)(2)(b); inserted (A)(2)(f); redesignated former (A)(2)(f) and (A)(2)(g) as (A)(2)(g) and (A)(2)(h); rewrote (A)(3); inserted "by the agencies" in (B)(2); added (B)(4) and (E) through (G); rewrote (C); inserted "or poses a threat" in (D); and made stylistic changes.

151 v H 530, effective June 30, 2006, rewrote (B)(1).

## § 173.392 Payment of non-certified providers; contracts.

(A) In the case of a provider that the department of aging under section 173.39 of the Revised Code has not required to be certified under section 173.391 of the Revised Code, the department may pay the provider for providing services, including community-based long-term care services, under a program the department administers but only if all of the following are the case:

(1) The provider has a contract with the department of aging or the department's designee to provide the services in accordance with the contract or has received a grant from the department or its designee to provide the services in accordance with a grant agreement;

(2) The contract or grant agreement includes detailed conditions of participation for the provider and service standards that the provider is required to satisfy;

(3) The provider complies with the contract or grant agreement;

(4) The contract or grant is not for medicaid-funded services, other than services provided under the PACE program administered by the department of aging under section 173.50 of the Revised Code.

(B)(1) The director of aging shall adopt rules in accordance with Chapter 119. of the Revised Code governing both of the following:

(a) Contracts and grant agreements between the department of aging or its designee and providers;

(b) The department's payment for services, including community-based long-term care services, under this section.

(2) The rules adopted under this section shall be consistent with section 173.381 of the Revised Code.

**HISTORY:**

151 v H 66, § 101.01, eff. 9-29-05; 153 v H 1, § 101.01, eff. 10-16-09; 2013 HB 59, § 101.01, eff. Sept. 29, 2013; 2014 HB 483, § 101.01, eff. Sept. 15, 2014; 2021 hb110, § 101.01, effective September 30, 2021.

**Amendment Notes**

The 2021 amendment by HB 110, in the introductory language of (A), added "In the case of a provider that the department of aging under section 173.39 of the Revised Code has not required to be certified under section 173.391 of the Revised Code," and substituted "may pay the provider for providing services, including" for "of aging may pay a provider for providing" and "administers but only" for "administers, even though the provider is not certified under section 173.391 of the Revised Code"; added "services, including" in (B)(1)(b); and made a related change.

The 2014 amendment by HB 483 redesignated former (B)(1) and (B)(2) as (B)(1)(a) and (B)(1)(b); and added (B)(2).

The 2013 amendment substituted "provider" for "person or government entity" in the introductory language of (A) and in (A)(1) and (A)(3); in (A)(2), substituted "the provider" for "providers of services under a program the department administers" and "provider is" for "person or government entity is"; and substituted "providers" for "persons and government entities regarding community-based long-term care services provided under a program the department administers" in (B)(1).

153 v H 1, effective October 16, 2009, in (A)(1), added "in accordance with . . . a grant agreement", in (A)(2) and (A)(3), inserted "or grant agreement", and in (A)(4), inserted "or grant"; in (B)(1), inserted "and grant agreements" and "or its designee" and in (B)(2), substituted "under this section" for "provided under such a contract"; and made a stylistic change.

### § 173.393 Access to records of evaluation.

(A) Except as provided in division (B) of this section, the records of an evaluation conducted in accordance with rules adopted under division (B)(2) of section 173.391 of the Revised Code are public records for purposes of section 149.43 of the Revised Code and shall be made available on request of any person, including individuals receiving or seeking any services, including community-based long-term care services, under a program the department of aging administers.

(B) A part of a record of an evaluation that is otherwise available as a public record under division (A) of this section is not available as a public record if its release would violate a federal or state statute, regulation, or rule, including regulations adopted by the United States department of health and human services to implement the health information privacy provisions of the "Health Insurance Portability and Accountability Act of 1996," 110 Stat. 1955, 42 U.S.C. 1320d, et seq., as amended.

**HISTORY:**

151 v H 66, § 101.01, eff. 9-29-05; 2021 hb110, § 101.01, effective September 30, 2021.

**Amendment Notes**

The 2021 amendment by HB 110 added "any services, including" in (A); and made a related change.

### § 173.394 Criminal records check for certain applicants for employment [Renumbered].

**Editor's Notes**

This section was renumbered as RC § 173.38 by 2013 HB 59, § 101.01, effective September 29, 2013.

## PASSPORT PROGRAM

### § 173.40 PASSPORT program as alternative to nursing facility placement [Renumbered].

**Editor's Notes**

This section was renumbered as RC § 173 52 by 2013 HB 59, § 101.01, effective September 29, 2013.

### § 173.401 Home first component of PASSPORT program [Renumbered].

**Editor's Notes**

This section was renumbered as RC § 173.521 by 2013 HB 59, § 101.01, effective September 29, 2013.

### § 173.402 Kosher home-delivered meals under PASSPORT program [Renumbered].

**Editor's Notes**

This section was renumbered as RC § 173.524 by 2013 HB 59 § 101.01, effective September 29, 2013.

### § 173.403 Choices program [Renumbered].

**Editor's Notes**

This section was renumbered as RC § 173.53 by 2013 HB 59 § 101.01, effective September 29, 2013.

### § 173.404 Unified waiting list [Renumbered].

**Editor's Notes**

This section was renumbered as RC § 173.55 by 2013 HB 59 § 101.01, effective September 29, 2013.

### § 173.41 Statewide aging and disabilities resource network.

(A) The department of aging shall promote the development of a statewide aging and disabilities resource network through which older adults, adults with disabilities, and their caregivers are provided with both of the following:

(1) Information on any long-term care service options available to the individuals;

(2) Streamlined access to long-term care services, both publicly funded services and services available through private payment.

(B) Area agencies on aging shall establish the network throughout the state. In doing so, the agencies shall collaborate with centers for independent living and other locally funded organizations to establish a cost-effective and consumer-friendly network that builds on existing, local infrastructures of services that support consumers in their communities.

**HISTORY:**

2011 HB 153, § 101.01, eff. Sept. 29, 2011.

**RESEARCH REFERENCES AND PRACTICE AIDS**

**Cross-References to Related Sections**

Superintendent of the bureau of criminal identification and investigation; duties, RC §§ 109.57, 109.572.

**Ohio Administrative Code**

Department of aging, division of long-term care —
Background investigations by PASSPORT agencies. OAC 173-9-01.

## LONG-TERM CARE CONSULTATION PROGRAM

### § 173.42 Long-term care consultation program.

(A) As used in sections 173.42 to 173.434 of the Revised Code:

(1) "Area agency on aging" means a public or private nonprofit entity designated under section 173.011 of the Revised Code to administer programs on behalf of the department of aging.

(2) "Department of aging-administered medicaid waiver component" means each of the following:

(a) The medicaid-funded component of the PASSPORT program created under section 173.52 of the Revised Code;

(b) The medicaid-funded component of the assisted living program created under section 173.54 of the Revised Code;

(c) Any other medicaid waiver component, as defined in section 5166.01 of the Revised Code, that the department of aging administers pursuant to an interagency agreement with the department of medicaid under section 5162.35 of the Revised Code.

(3) "Home and community-based services covered by medicaid components the department of aging administers" means all of the following:

(a) Medicaid waiver services available to a participant in a department of aging-administered medicaid waiver component;

(b) The following medicaid state plan services available to a participant in a department of aging-administered medicaid waiver component as specified in rules adopted under section 5164.02 of the Revised Code:

(i) Home health services;
(ii) Private duty nursing services;
(iii) Durable medical equipment;
(iv) Services of a clinical nurse specialist;
(v) Services of a certified nurse practitioner.

(c) Services available to a participant of the PACE program.

(4) "Long-term care consultation" or "consultation" means the consultation service made available by the department of aging or a program administrator through the long-term care consultation program established pursuant to this section.

(5) "Nursing facility" has the same meaning as in section 5165.01 of the Revised Code.

(6) "PACE program" means the component of the medicaid program the department of aging administers pursuant to section 173.50 of the Revised Code.

(7) "PASSPORT administrative agency" means an entity under contract with the department of aging to provide administrative services regarding the PASSPORT program.

(8) "Program administrator" means an area agency on aging or other entity under contract with the department of aging to administer the long-term care consultation program in a geographic region specified in the contract.

(9) "Representative" means a person acting on behalf of an individual who is the subject of a long-term care consultation. A representative may be a family member, attorney, hospital social worker, or any other person chosen to act on behalf of the individual.

(B) The department of aging shall develop a long-term care consultation program whereby individuals or their representatives are provided with long-term care consultations and receive through these professional consultations information about options available to meet long-term care needs and information about factors to consider in making long-term care decisions. The long-term care consultations may be provided at any appropriate time, including either prior to or after the individual who is the subject of a consultation has been admitted to a nursing facility or granted assistance in receiving home and community-based services covered by medicaid components the department of aging administers.

(C) The long-term care consultation program shall be administered by the department of aging, except that the department may have the program administered on a regional basis by one or more program administrators. The department and each program administrator shall administer the program in such a manner that all of the following are included:

(1) Coordination and collaboration with respect to all available funding sources for long-term care services;

(2) Assessments of individuals regarding their long-term care service needs;

(3) Assessments of individuals regarding their on-going eligibility for long-term care services;

(4) Procedures for assisting individuals in obtaining access to, and coordination of, health and supportive services, including department of aging-administered medicaid waiver components;

(5) Priorities for using available resources efficiently and effectively.

(D) The program's long-term care consultations shall be provided by individuals certified by the department under section 173.422 of the Revised Code.

(E) The information provided through a long-term care consultation shall be appropriate to the individual's needs and situation and shall address all of the following:

(1) The availability of any long-term care options open to the individual;

(2) Sources and methods of both public and private payment for long-term care services;

(3) Factors to consider when choosing among the available programs, services, and benefits;

(4) Opportunities and methods for maximizing independence and self-reliance, including support services provided by the individual's family, friends, and community.

(F) An individual's long-term care consultation may include an assessment of the individual's functional capabilities. The consultation may incorporate portions of the determinations required under sections 5119.40, 5123.021, and 5165.03 of the Revised Code and may be provided concurrently with the assessment required under section 173.546 or 5165.04 of the Revised Code.

(G) Except as provided in division (I) of this section, a long-term care consultation shall be provided to each individual for whom the department or a program administrator determines such a consultation is appropriate.

(H) A long-term care consultation shall be completed within the applicable time frames specified in rules adopted under this section.

(I) An individual is not required to be provided a long-term care consultation if any of the following is the case:

(1) The department or a program administrator has attempted to provide the consultation, but the individual or the individual's representative refuses to cooperate;

(2) The individual is to receive care in a nursing facility under a contract for continuing care, as defined in section 173.13 of the Revised Code;

(3) The individual has a contractual right to admission to a nursing facility operated as part of a system of continuing care in conjunction with one or more facilities that provide a less intensive level of services, including a residential care facility licensed under Chapter 3721. of the Revised Code, a residential facility licensed under section 5119.34 of the Revised Code that provides accommodations, supervision, and personal care services for three to sixteen unrelated adults, or an independent living arrangement;

(4) The individual is to receive continual care in a home for the aged exempt from taxation under section 5701.13 of the Revised Code;

(5) The individual is seeking admission to a facility that is not a nursing facility with a provider agreement under section 5165.07, 5165.511, or 5165.512 of the Revised Code;

(6) Pursuant to rules that may be adopted under this section, the department or a program administrator has exempted the individual from receiving the long-term care consultation.

(J) As part of the long-term care consultation program, the department or a program administrator may assist an individual or individual's representative in accessing all sources of care and services that are appropriate for the individual and for which the individual is eligible, including all available home and community-based services covered by medicaid components the department of aging administers. The assistance may include providing for the conduct of assessments or other evaluations and the development of individualized plans of care or services under section 173.424 of the Revised Code.

(K) No nursing facility for which an operator has a provider agreement under section 5165.07, 5165.511, or 5165.512 of the Revised Code shall admit as a resident any individual described in division (G) of this section, unless the nursing facility has received evidence that a long-term care consultation has been completed for the individual or division (I) of this section is applicable to the individual.

(L) The director of aging shall adopt rules for the implementation and administration of this section. The rules shall be adopted in accordance with Chapter 119. of the Revised Code. The rules may specify any or all of the following:

(1) Procedures for providing long-term care consultations;

(2) Information to be provided through long-term care consultations regarding long-term care services that are available;

(3) Criteria and procedures to be used to identify and recommend appropriate service options for an individual receiving a long-term care consultation;

(4) Criteria for exempting individuals from receiving a long-term care consultation;

(5) Circumstances under which it may be appropriate to provide an individual's long-term care consultation after the individual's admission to a nursing facility rather than before admission;

(6) Criteria for identifying individuals for whom a long-term care consultation is appropriate, including nursing facility residents who would benefit from the consultation;

(7) A description of the types of information from a nursing facility that is needed under the long-term care consultation program to assist a resident with relocation from the facility;

(8) Standards to prevent conflicts of interest relative to the referrals made by a person who performs a long-term care consultation, including standards that prohibit the person from being employed by a provider of long-term care services;

(9) Procedures for providing notice and an opportunity for a hearing under division (N) of this section;

(10) Time frames for providing or completing a long-term care consultation;

(11) Any other standards or procedures the director considers necessary for the program.

(M) To assist the department and each program administrator with identifying individuals for whom a long-term care consultation is appropriate, the department and program administrator may ask to be given access to nursing facility resident assessment data collected through the use of the resident assessment instrument specified in rules authorized by section 5165.191 of the Revised Code for purposes of the medicaid program. Except when prohibited by state or federal law, the department of health, department of medicaid, or nursing facility holding the data shall grant access to the data on receipt of the request from the department of aging or program administrator.

(N)(1) The director of aging, after providing notice and an opportunity for a hearing, may fine a nursing facility an amount determined by rules the director shall adopt in accordance with Chapter 119. of the Revised Code for any of the following reasons:

(a) The nursing facility violates division (K) of this section;

(b) The nursing facility denies a person attempting to provide a long-term care consultation access to the facility or a resident of the facility;

(c) The nursing facility denies the department of aging or a program administrator access to the facility or a resident of the facility, as the department or administrator considers necessary to administer the program.

(2) In accordance with section 5162.66 of the Revised Code, all fines collected under division (N)(1) of this section shall be deposited into the state treasury to the credit of the residents protection fund.

**HISTORY:**

145 v H 152 (Eff 7-1-93); 145 v H 715 (Eff 7-22-94); 146 v H 117 (Eff 9-29-95); 148 v H 471. Eff 7-1-2000; 150 v H 95, § 1, eff. 6-26-03; 151 v H 66, § 101.01, eff. 9-29-05; 153 v H 1, § 101.01, eff. 10-16-09; 2011 HB 153, § 101.01, eff. Sept. 29, 2011; 2012 HB 487, § 101.01, eff. Sept. 10, 2012; 2013 HB 59, § 101.01, eff. Sept. 29, 2013; 2017 hb49, § 101.01, effective September 29, 2017.

**Publisher's Note:**

This section was amended and renumbered from RC § 5101.75 by 151 v H 66, effective September 29, 2005.

**Editor's Notes**

Pursuant to 2011 HB 153, § 812.30, the amendment to subdivision (I)(3) is effective July 1, 2011. All other amendments by this act take effect September 29, 2011.

The provisions of § 203.21.03 of 151 v H 66 read as follows:

SECTION 203.21.03. PRE-ADMISSION REVIEW FOR NURSING FACILITY ADMISSION.

Pursuant to an interagency agreement, the Department of Job and Family Services shall designate the Department of Aging to perform assessments under sections 173.42 and 5111.204 of the Revised Code. Of the foregoing appropriation item 490-403, PASSPORT, the Department of Aging may use not more than $2,586,648 in fiscal year 2006 and $2,651,315 in fiscal year 2007 to perform the assessments for persons not eligible for Medicaid under the department's interagency agreement with the Department of Job and Family Services and to assist individuals in planning for their long-term health care needs.

**Amendment Notes**

The 2017 amendment by HB 49 rewrote the section.

The 2013 amendment substituted "section 173.52" for "section 173.40" in (A)(2)(a); substituted "section 173.53" for "section 173.403" in (A)(2)(b); substituted "section 173.54" for "section 5111.89"; in (A)(2)(d), substituted "section 5166.01" for "section 5111.85" and "section 5162.35" for "section 5111.91"; substituted "of medicaid" for "of job and family services" in (A)(2)(d) and the second sentence of (M); substituted "section 5164.02" for "section 5111.02" in the introductory language of (A)(3)(b); deleted (A)(5), which read: "'Medicaid' means the medical assistance program established under Chapter 5111. of the Revised Code" and redesignated the remaining subsections accordingly; substituted "section 5165.01" for "section 5111.20" in present (A)(5); rewrote the second sentence of (F); substituted "section 5165.04" for "section 5111.204" in (H)(1)(a); substituted "section 5119.34" for "section 5119.22" in (I)(3); substituted "section 5165.07, 5165.511, or 5165.512" for "section 5111.22, 5111.671, or 5111.672" in (I)(5) and (K); substituted "authorized by section 5165.191" for "adopted under section 5111.02" in the first sentence of (M); and substituted "section 5162.66" for "section 5111.62" in (N)(2).

The 2012 amendment, in (I)(3), substituted "a residential facility licensed under section 5119.22" for "an adult care facility licensed under sections 5119.70 to 5119.88" and inserted "that provides accommodations, supervision, and personal care services for three to sixteen unrelated adults".

The 2011 amendment inserted "medicaid-funded component of the" in (A)(2)(a) and (A)(2)(c); and substituted "sections 5119.70 to 5119.88" for "Chapter 3722" in (I)(3).

153 v H 1, effective October 16, 2009, rewrote the section.

151 v H 66, effective September 29, 2005, rewrote the section.

## § 173.421 Periodic or follow-up consultations.

As part of the long-term care consultation program established under section 173.42 of the Revised Code, the department of aging may establish procedures for the conduct of periodic or follow-up long-term care consultations for residents of nursing facilities, including annual or more frequent reassessments of the residents' functional capabilities. If the procedures are established, the department or program administrator shall assign individuals to nursing facilities to serve as care managers within the facilities. The individuals assigned shall be individuals who are certified under section 173.422 of the Revised Code to provide long-term care consultations.

**HISTORY:**

153 v H 1, § 101.01, eff. 10-16-09.

## § 173.422 Certification of providers of long-term care consultations.

The department of aging shall certify individuals who meet certification requirements established by rule to provide long-term care consultations for purposes of sections 173.42 and 173.421 of the Revised Code. The director of aging shall adopt rules in accordance with Chapter 119. of the Revised Code governing the certification process and requirements. The rules shall specify the education, experience, or training in long-term care a person must have to qualify for certification.

**HISTORY:**

145 v H 152 (Eff 7-1-93); 146 v S 223 (Eff 3-18-97); 148 v H 471. Eff 7-1-2000; 151 v H 66, § 101.01, eff. 9-29-05; 153 v H 1, § 101.01, eff. 10-16-09.

**Publisher's Note:**

This section was amended and renumbered from RC § 5101.752 by 151 v H 66, effective September 29, 2005.

This section was amended and renumbered from RC § 173.43 by 153 v H 1, effective October 16, 2009.

**Amendment Notes**

153 v H 1, effective October 16, 2009, substituted "sections 173.42 and 173.421" for "section 173.42" in the first sentence.

151 v H 66, effective September 29, 2005, rewrote the section.

## § 173.423 Monitoring of home and community-based services.

If an individual who is the subject of a long-term care consultation is eligible for and elects to receive home and community-based services covered by medicaid components the department of aging administers, the department of aging or program administrator shall monitor the individual by doing either or both of the following at least once each year:

(A) Determining whether the services being provided to the individual are appropriate;

(B) Determining whether changes in the types of services being provided to the individual should be made.

**HISTORY:**

153 v H 1, § 101.01, eff. 10-16-09.

### § 173.424 Implementation of procedures necessary to comply with federal law.

If, under federal law, an individual's eligibility for the home and community-based services covered by medicaid components the department of aging administers is dependent on the conduct of an assessment or other evaluation of the individual's needs and capabilities and the development of an individualized plan of care or services, the department shall develop and implement all procedures necessary to comply with the federal law. The procedures may include the use of long-term care consultations.

**HISTORY:**

153 v H 1, § 101.01, eff. 10-16-09; 2017 hb49, § 101.01, effective September 29, 2017.

**Amendment Notes**

The 2017 amendment by HB 49 substituted "procedures may include" for "procedures shall include" in the second sentence.

### § 173.425 Annual report [Repealed].

Repealed by Acts 2013, HB 59, § 105.01, effective September 29, 2013.

**HISTORY:**

153 v H 1, § 101.01, eff. 10-16-09.

## UNIFIED LONG-TERM CARE BUDGET

### § 173.43 Interagency agreement regarding unified long-term care budget.

(A) The department of aging shall enter into an interagency agreement with the department of medicaid under section 5162.35 of the Revised Code under which the department of aging is required to establish for each biennium a unified long-term care budget for home and community-based services covered by medicaid components the department of aging administers. The interagency agreement shall require the department of aging to do all of the following:

(1) Administer the unified long-term care budget in accordance with sections 173.43 to 173.434 of the Revised Code and the general assembly's appropriations for home and community-based services covered by medicaid components the department of aging administers for the applicable biennium;

(2) Contract with each PASSPORT administrative agency for assistance in the administration of the unified long-term care budget;

(3) Provide individuals who are eligible for home and community-based services covered by medicaid components the department of aging administers a choice of services that meet the individuals' needs and improve their quality of life;

(4) Provide a continuum of services that meet the life-long needs of individuals who are eligible for home and community-based services covered by medicaid components the department of aging administers.

(B) The director of budget and management shall create new appropriation items as necessary for establishment of the unified long-term care budget.

**HISTORY:**

153 v H 1, § 101.01, eff. 10-16-09; 2013 HB 59, § 101.01, eff. Sept. 29, 2013.

**Amendment Notes**

The 2013 amendment, in the first sentence of the introductory language of (A), deleted "Subject to section 173.433 of the Revised Code" from the beginning and substituted "department of medicaid under section 5162.35" for "department of job and family services under section 5111.91".

### § 173.431 Services to be available under budget.

The department of aging shall ensure that the unified long-term care budget established under section 173.43 of the Revised Code is administered in a manner that provides medicaid coverage of and expands access to all of the following as necessary to meet the needs of individuals receiving home and community-based services covered by medicaid components the department of aging administers:

(A) To the extent permitted by the medicaid waivers authorizing department of aging-administered medicaid waiver components, all of the following medicaid waiver services provided under department of aging-administered medicaid waiver components:

(1) Personal care services;
(2) Home-delivered meals;
(3) Adult day-care;
(4) Homemaker services;
(5) Emergency response services;
(6) Medical equipment and supplies;
(7) Chore services;
(8) Social work counseling;
(9) Nutritional counseling;
(10) Independent living assistance;
(11) Medical transportation;
(12) Nonmedical transportation;
(13) Home care attendant services;
(14) Assisted living services;
(15) Community transition services;
(16) Enhanced community living services;
(17) All other medicaid waiver services provided under department of aging-administered medicaid waiver components.

(B) All of the following state medicaid plan services as specified in rules adopted under section 5164.02 of the Revised Code:

(1) Home health services;
(2) Private duty nursing services;
(3) Durable medical equipment;
(4) Services of a clinical nurse specialist;
(5) Services of a certified nurse practitioner.

(C) The services that the PACE program provides.

**HISTORY:**

153 v H 1, § 101.01, eff. 10-16-09; 2013 HB 59, § 101.01, eff. Sept. 29, 2013.

**Amendment Notes**

The 2013 amendment deleted "Subject to section 173.433 of the Revised Code" from the beginning of the introductory language; and substituted "section 5164.02" for "section 5111.02" in the introductory language of (B).

### § 173.432 Care management and authorization services.

The department of aging or its designee shall provide care management and authorization services with regard to the state plan services specified in division (B) of section 173.431 of the Revised Code that are provided to participants of department of aging-administered medicaid waiver components. The department or its designee shall ensure that no person providing the care management and authorization services performs an activity that may not be performed without a valid certificate or license issued by an agency of this state unless the person holds the valid certificate or license.

**HISTORY:**

153 v H 1, § 101.01, eff. 10-16-09; 2013 HB 59, § 101.01, eff. Sept. 29, 2013.

**Amendment Notes**

The 2013 amendment deleted "Subject to section 173.433 of the Revised Code" from the beginning of the first sentence.

### § 173.433 Federal approval [Repealed].

Repealed by 2013 HB 59, § 105.01, effective September 29, 2013.

**HISTORY:**

153 v H 1, § 101.01, eff. 10-16-09.

### § 173.434 Rules.

To the extent authorized by rules authorized by section 5162.021 of the Revised Code, the director of aging shall adopt rules that are needed to implement sections 173.43 to 173.432 of the Revised Code. The rules shall be adopted in accordance with Chapter 119. of the Revised Code.

**HISTORY:**

153 v H 1, § 101.01, eff. 10-16-09; 2013 HB 59, § 101.01, eff. Sept. 29, 2013.

**Amendment Notes**

The 2013 amendment, in the first sentence, substituted "To the extent authorized by rules authorized by section 5162.021" for "The director of job and family services shall adopt rules under section 5111.85", deleted "to authorize" preceding "the director of" and deleted "director of aging's" preceding "rules shall be" in the second sentence; and made a stylistic change.

# SURVEY OF NURSING HOMES AND RESIDENTIAL CARE FACILITIES

### § 173.44 Annual survey of nursing homes and residential care facilities.

(A) As used in this section, "nursing home" and "residential care facility" have the same meanings as in section 3721.01 of the Revised Code.

(B) The department of aging may conduct an annual survey of nursing homes and residential care facilities. The survey shall include questions about capacity, occupancy, and private pay charges. The department may contract with an outside entity to conduct the survey and analyze the results. The results of the survey and any analysis completed by the department or its designee shall be made available to the general assembly, other state agencies, nursing home and residential care facility providers, and the general public.

(C) No nursing home or residential care facility shall recklessly fail to complete the survey.

**HISTORY:**

151 v H 66, § 101.01, eff. 9-29-05.

# LONG-TERM CARE CONSUMER GUIDE; CUSTOMER SATISFACTION SURVEYS

### § 173.45 Definitions.

As used in this section and in sections 173.46 to 173.49 of the Revised Code:

(A) "Residential facility" means a residential facility licensed under section 5119.34 of the Revised Code that provides accommodations, supervision, and personal care services for three to sixteen unrelated adults.

(B) "Community-based long-term care services" has the same meaning as in section 173.14 of the Revised Code.

(C) "Long-term care facility" means a nursing home or residential care facility.

(D) "Nursing home" and "residential care facility" have the same meanings as in section 3721.01 of the Revised Code.

(E) "Nursing facility" has the same meaning as in section 5165.01 of the Revised Code.

**HISTORY:**

151 v H 66, § 101.01, eff. 9-29-05; 2011 HB 153, § 101.01, eff. Sept. 29, 2011; 2012 HB 487, § 101.01, eff. Sept. 10, 2012; 2013 HB 59, § 101.01, eff. Sept. 29, 2013.

**Amendment Notes**

The 2013 amendment substituted "section 5119.34" for "section 5119.22" in (A); and substituted "section 5165.01" for "section 5111.20" in (E).

The 2012 amendment rewrote (A), which formerly read: "'Adult care facility' has the same meaning as in section 5119.70 of the Revised Code."

The 2011 amendment added (A) and (B) and redesignated the remaining subsections accordingly.

### § 173.46 Long-term care consumer guide.

(A) The department of aging shall develop and publish a guide to long-term care facilities for use by individuals considering long-term care facility admission and their families, friends, and advisors. The guide, which shall be titled the Ohio long-term care consumer guide, may be published in printed form or in electronic form for distribution over the internet. The guide may be developed as a continuation or modification of the guide published by the department prior to September 29, 2005, under rules adopted under section 173.02 of the Revised Code.

(B) The Ohio long-term care consumer guide shall include information on each long-term care facility in this state. For each facility, the guide shall include the following information, as applicable to the facility:

(1) Information regarding the facility's compliance with state statutes and rules and federal statutes and regulations;

(2) Information generated by the centers for medicare and medicaid services of the United States department of health and human services from the quality measures developed as part of its nursing home quality initiative;

(3) Results of the customer satisfaction surveys conducted under section 173.47 of the Revised Code;

(4) Any other information the department specifies in rules adopted under section 173.49 of the Revised Code.

(C) The Ohio long-term care consumer guide may include information on residential facilities and providers of community-based long-term care services. The department may adopt rules under section 173.49 of the Revised Code to specify the information to be included in the guide pursuant to this division.

**HISTORY:**

151 v H 66, § 101.01, eff. 9-29-05; 2011 HB 153, § 101.01, eff. Sept. 29, 2011; 2012 HB 487, § 101.01, eff. Sept. 10, 2012.

**Amendment Notes**

The 2012 amendment substituted "residential facilities" for "adult care facilities" in the first sentence of (C).

The 2011 amendment substituted "September 29, 2005" for "the effective date of this section" in the last sentence of (A); and added (C).

### § 173.47 Customer satisfaction surveys.

(A) For purposes of publishing the Ohio long-term care consumer guide, the department of aging shall conduct or provide for the conduct of an annual customer satisfaction survey of each long-term care facility. The results of the surveys may include information obtained from long-term care facility residents, their families, or both.

(B) Each long-term care facility shall cooperate in the conduct of its annual customer satisfaction survey.

**HISTORY:**

151 v H 66, § 101.01, eff. 9-29-05; 2011 HB 153, § 101.01, eff. Sept. 29, 2011; 2011 SB 264, § 1, eff. July 1, 2012; 2013 HB 59, § 101.01, eff. Sept. 29, 2013; 2014 HB 483, § 101.01, eff. Sept. 15, 2014; 2015 hb64, § 101.01, effective July 1, 2016.

**Amendment Notes**

The 2015 amendment by HB 64 deleted the last two sentences of (A), which read: "A survey that is to include information obtained from nursing facility residents shall include the questions specified in divisions (C)(7)(a) and (b) of section 5165.25 of the Revised Code. A survey that is to include information obtained from the families of nursing facility residents shall include the questions specified in divisions (C)(8)(a) and (b) of section 5165.25 of the Revised Code."

The 2014 amendment by HB 483, in (A), substituted "divisions (C)(7)(a) and (b)" for "divisions (C)(7)(a) and (b) and (18) and (D)(7)(a) and (b)" in the third sentence and substituted "divisions (C)(8)(a) and (b)" for "divisions (C)(8)(a) and (b) and (19) and (D)(8)(a) and (b)" in the last sentence.

The 2013 amendment substituted "divisions (C)(7)(a) and (b) and (18) and (D)(7)(a) and (b)" for "divisions (C)(7)(a) and (b) and (18)" in the third sentence of (A); substituted "section 5165.25" for "section 5111.244" in the last two sentences of (A); and substituted "divisions (C)(8)(a) and (b) and (19) and (D)(8)(a) and (b) of section 5165.25" for "divisions (C)(8)(a) and (b) and (19) of section 5111.244" in the last sentence of (A).

The 2011 amendment by SB 264 added the last two sentences to (A).

The 2011 amendment by HB 153 deleted (B), pertaining to the fees charged for the conduction of annual customer satisfaction surveys; and redesignated former (C) as (B).

**§ 173.48 Long-term care consumer guide fund.**

(A)(1) The department of aging may charge annual fees to long-term care facilities for the publication of the Ohio long-term care consumer guide, as well as late penalties if applicable. The department may contract with any person or government entity to collect the fees on its behalf. All fees collected under this section shall be deposited in accordance with division (B) of this section.

(2) Except as provided in division (A)(3) of this section, the annual fees charged under this section shall not exceed the following amounts:

(a) For each long-term care facility that is a nursing home, six hundred fifty dollars;

(b) For each long-term care facility that is a residential care facility:

(i) Until June 30, 2016, three hundred dollars;

(ii) Beginning July 1, 2016, three hundred fifty dollars.

(3) The department, by rule adopted in accordance with Chapter 119. of the Revised Code, may establish deadlines for the payment of the annual fees charged under this section. If the annual fee is not received by the department within ninety days of any deadline established by the department, the rules may require a long-term care facility to pay a late penalty equal to and in addition to the amount of the annual fee charged under this section.

(4) Unless prohibited by federal law, fees paid by a long-term care facility that is a nursing facility, including late penalties, shall be reimbursed through the medicaid program.

(B) There is hereby created in the state treasury the long-term care consumer guide fund. Money collected from the fees charged for the publication of the Ohio long-term care consumer guide under division (A) of this section and any late penalties shall be credited to the fund. The department shall use money in the fund for costs associated with publishing the Ohio long-term care consumer guide, including, but not limited to, costs incurred in conducting or providing for the conduct of customer satisfaction surveys.

**HISTORY:**

151 v H 66, § 101.01, eff. 9-29-05; 2011 HB 153, § 101.01, eff. Sept. 29, 2011; 2013 HB 59, § 101.01, eff. Sept. 29, 2013; 2015 hb64, § 101.01, effective September 29, 2015; 2017 hb49, § 101.01, effective September 29, 2017.

**Amendment Notes**

The 2017 amendment by HB 49 added "as well as late penalties if applicable" in the first sentence of (A)(1); added "Except as provided in division (A)(3) of this section" in the introductory language of (A)(2); redesignated and revised former (A)(3) as (A)(3) and (A)(4); and added "and any late penalties" in the second sentence of (B).

The 2015 amendment by HB 64 deleted "Three hundred dollars" from the beginning of (A)(2)(b); added (A)(2)(b)(i) and (A)(2)(b)(ii); and made a related change.

The 2013 amendment deleted "operated under Chapter 5111. of the Revised Code" from the end of (A)(3).

The 2011 amendment added (A); redesignated the former provisions as (B); in the second sentence of present (B), substituted "publication of the Ohio long-term care consumer guide" for "conduct of customer satisfaction surveys", inserted "division (A) of this", and deleted "173.47 of the Revised Code" preceding "shall be credited"; and deleted "of aging" following "The department" in the last sentence of present (B).

**§ 173.49 Rules.**

The department of aging shall adopt rules as the department considers necessary to implement and administer sections 173.45 to 173.48 of the Revised Code. The rules shall be adopted under Chapter 119. of the Revised Code.

**HISTORY:**

151 v H 66, § 101.01, eff. 9-29-05.

# OTHER DEPARTMENT OF AGING PROGRAMS

**§ 173.50 PACE program.**

(A) Pursuant to a contract entered into with the department of medicaid as an interagency agreement under section 5162.35 of the Revised Code, the department of aging shall carry out the day-to-day administration of the component of the medicaid program known as the program of all-inclusive care for the elderly or PACE. The department of aging shall carry out its PACE administrative duties in accordance with the provisions of the interagency agreement and all applicable federal laws, including the "Social Security Act," section 1934, 42 U.S.C. 1396u-4.

(B) To the extent authorized by rules authorized by section 5162.021 of the Revised Code, the director of aging may adopt rules in accordance with Chapter 119. of the Revised Code regarding the PACE program, including rules establishing priorities for enrolling in the program pursuant to section 173.501 of the Revised Code. The rules shall address only those issues that are not addressed in rules adopted by the medicaid director for the PACE program.

**HISTORY:**

151 v H 66, § 101.01, eff. 9-29-05; 153 v H 1, § 101.01, eff. 10-16-09; 2013 HB 59, § 101.01, eff. Sept. 29, 2013.

**Amendment Notes**

The 2013 amendment, in (A), in the first sentence, substituted "department of medicaid" for "department of job and family services", substituted "section 5162.35" for "section 5111.91", and deleted "established under Chapter 5111. of the Revised Code" and substituted "section 1934, 42 U.S.C. 1396u" for "79 Stat. 286 (1965) U.S.C. 1396u-4, as amended"; and rewrote (B), which formerly read: "The department of aging may adopt rules in accordance with Chapter 119. of the Revised Code regarding the PACE program, including rules establishing priorities for enrolling in the program pursuant to section 173.501 of the Revised Code. The department's rules are subject to both of the following: (1) The rules shall be authorized by rules adopted by the department of job and family services. (2) The rules shall address only those issues that are not addressed in rules adopted by the department of job and family services for the PACE program."

153 v H 1, effective October 16, 2009, in the introductory language of (B), added "including rules establishing priorities for enrolling in the program pursuant to section 173.501 of the Revised Code" in the first sentence and added "The department's rules are" in the second sentence.

**§ 173.501 Home first component of PACE program.**

(A) As used in this section:

"Nursing facility" has the same meaning as in section 5165.01 of the Revised Code.

"PACE provider" has the same meaning as in the "Social Security Act," section 1934(a)(3), 42 U.S.C. 1396u-4(a)(3).

(B) The department of aging shall establish a home first component of the PACE program under which eligible individuals may be enrolled in the PACE program in accordance with this section. An individual is eligible for the PACE program's home first component if both of the following apply:

(1) The individual has been determined to be eligible for the PACE program.

(2) At least one of the following applies:

(a) The individual has been admitted to a nursing facility.

(b) A physician has determined and documented in writing that the individual has a medical condition that, unless the individual is enrolled in home and community-based services such as the PACE program, will require the individual to be admitted to a nursing facility within thirty days of the physician's determination.

(c) The individual has been hospitalized and a physician has determined and documented in writing that, unless the individual is enrolled in home and community-based services such as the PACE program, the individual is to be transported directly from the hospital to a nursing facility and admitted.

(d) Both of the following apply:

(i) The individual is the subject of a report made under section 5101.63 of the Revised Code regarding abuse, neglect, or exploitation or such a report referred to a county department of job and family services under section 5126.31 of the Revised Code or has made a request to a county department for protective services as defined in section 5101.60 of the Revised Code.

(ii) A county department of job and family services and an area agency on aging have jointly documented in writing that, unless the individual is enrolled in home and community-based services such as the PACE program, the individual should be admitted to a nursing facility.

(C) Each month, the department of aging shall identify individuals who are eligible for the home first component of the PACE program. When the department identifies such an individual, the department shall notify the PACE provider serving the area in which the individual resides. The PACE provider shall determine whether the PACE program is appropriate for the individual and whether the individual would rather participate in the PACE program than continue or begin to reside in a nursing facility. If the PACE provider determines that the PACE program is appropriate for the individual and the individual would rather participate in the PACE program than continue or begin to reside in a nursing facility, the PACE provider shall so notify the department of aging. On receipt of the notice from the PACE provider, the department of aging shall approve the individual's enrollment in the PACE program in accordance with priorities established in rules adopted under section 173.50 of the Revised Code.

**HISTORY:**

153 v H 1, § 101.01, eff. 10-16-09; 153 v H 398, § 1, eff. 8-31-10; 2011 HB 153, § 101.01, eff. Sept. 29, 2011; 2013 HB 59, § 101.01, eff. Sept. 29, 2013; 2017 hb49, § 130.31, effective September 29, 2018.

**Amendment Notes**

The 2017 amendment by HB 49 substituted "section 5101.63" for "section 5101.61" in (B)(2)(d)(i).

The 2013 amendment substituted "section 5165.01" for "section 5111.20" in the second paragraph of (A); and inserted "the 'Social Security Act,' section 1934(a)(3)" in the last paragraph of (A).

The 2011 amendment substituted "both" for "all" in the second sentence of the introductory language of (B); inserted "has been determined to be" in (B)(1); deleted (B)(2), which read: "The individual is on the unified waiting list established under section 173.404 of the Revised Code"; redesignated former (B)(3) as (B)(2); deleted (D), which read: "Each quarter, the department of aging shall certify to the director of budget and management the estimated increase in costs of the PACE program resulting from enrollment of individuals in the PACE program pursuant to this section"; and made a stylistic change.

153 v H 398, effective August 31, 2010, rewrote the section.

## § 173.51 Definitions.

As used in sections 173.51 to 173.56 of the Revised Code:

"Area agency on aging" has the same meaning as in section 173.14 of the Revised Code.

"Assisted living program" means the program that consists of a medicaid-funded component created under section 173.54 of the Revised Code and a state-funded component created under section 173.543 of the Revised Code and provides assisted living services to individuals who meet the program's applicable eligibility requirements.

"Assisted living services" means the following home and community-based services: personal care, homemaker, chore, attendant care, companion, medication oversight, and therapeutic social and recreational programming.

"Assisted living waiver" means the federal medicaid waiver granted by the United States secretary of health and human services that authorizes the medicaid-funded component of the assisted living program.

"County or district home" means a county or district home operated under Chapter 5155. of the Revised Code.

"Long-term care consultation program" means the program the department of aging is required to develop under section 173.42 of the Revised Code.

"Long-term care consultation program administrator" or "administrator" means the department of aging or, if the department contracts with an area agency on aging or other entity to administer the long-term care consultation program for a particular area, that agency or entity.

"Medicaid waiver component" has the same meaning as in section 5166.01 of the Revised Code.

"Nursing facility" has the same meaning as in section 5165.01 of the Revised Code.

"PASSPORT program" means the preadmission screening system providing options and resources today program (PASSPORT) that consists of a medicaid-funded component created under section 173.52 of the Revised Code and a state-funded component created under section 173.522 of the Revised Code and provides home and community-based services as an alternative to nursing facility placement for individuals who are aged and disabled and meet the program's applicable eligibility requirements.

"PASSPORT waiver" means the federal medicaid waiver granted by the United States secretary of health and human services that authorizes the medicaid-funded component of the PASSPORT program.

"Representative" means a person acting on behalf of an applicant for the medicaid-funded component or state-funded component of the assisted living program. A representative may be a family member, attorney, hospital social worker, or any other person chosen to act on behalf of an applicant.

"Residential care facility" has the same meaning as in section 3721.01 of the Revised Code.

"Unified long-term services and support medicaid waiver component" means the medicaid waiver component authorized by section 5166.14 of the Revised Code.

**HISTORY:**

2013 HB 59, § 101.01, eff. Sept. 29, 2013; 2017 hb49, § 101.01, effective September 29, 2017.

**Editor's Notes**

Former § 173.51 [148 v H 403. Eff 7-1-2000], was repealed by 150 v H 95, effective June 26, 2003.

**Amendment Notes**

The 2017 amendment by HB 49 deleted the definition of "Choices program," which formerly read: "'Choices program' means the program created under section 173.53 of the Revised Code" following the definition of 'Assisted living waiver'."

## § 173.52 PASSPORT program as alternative to nursing facility placement.

(A) The department of medicaid shall create the medicaid-funded component of the PASSPORT program. In creating the medicaid-funded component, the department of medicaid shall collaborate with the department of aging.

(B) Unless the medicaid-funded component of the PASSPORT program is terminated under division (C) of this section, all of the following apply:

(1) The department of aging shall administer the medicaid-funded component through a contract entered into with the department of medicaid under section 5162.35 of the Revised Code.

(2) The medicaid-funded component shall be operated as a separate medicaid waiver component.

(3) For an individual to be eligible for the medicaid-funded component, the individual must be a medicaid recipient and meet the additional eligibility requirements applicable to the individual established in rules adopted under division (B)(4) of this section.

(4) To the extent authorized by rules authorization by section 5162.021 of the Revised Code, the director of aging shall adopt rules in accordance with Chapter 119. of the Revised Code to implement the medicaid-funded component.

(C) If the unified long-term services and support medicaid waiver component is created, the departments of aging and medicaid shall work together to determine whether the medicaid-funded component of the PASSPORT program should continue to operate as a separate medicaid waiver component or be terminated. If the departments determine that the medicaid-funded component of the PASSPORT program should be terminated, the medicaid-funded component shall cease to exist on a date the departments shall specify.

**HISTORY:**

145 v H 152 (Eff 7-1-93); 148 v H 471 (Eff 7-1-2000); 149 v H 94 (Eff 9-5-2001); 149 v S 261. Eff 6-5-2002; 151 v H 66, § 101.01, eff. 9-29-05; 153 v H 1, § 101.01, eff. 10-16-09; 2011 HB 153, § 101.01, eff. Sept. 29, 2011; 2012 HB 487, § 101.01, eff. Sept. 10, 2012; 2013 HB 59, § 101.01, eff. Sept. 29, 2013.

**Editor's Notes**

This section was formerly codified as RC § 173.40.

**Amendment Notes**

The 2013 amendment rewrote the section.

## § 173.521 Home first component of PASSPORT program.

(A) Unless the medicaid-funded component of the PASSPORT program is terminated pursuant to division (C) of section 173.52 of the Revised Code, the department shall establish a home first component of the PASSPORT program under which eligible individuals may be enrolled in the medicaid-funded component of the PASSPORT program in accordance with this section. An individual is eligible for the PASSPORT program's home first component if both of the following apply:

(1) The individual has been determined to be eligible for the medicaid-funded component of the PASSPORT program.

(2) At least one of the following applies:

(a) The individual has been admitted to a nursing facility.

(b) A physician has determined and documented in writing that the individual has a medical condition that, unless the individual is enrolled in home and community-based services such as the PASSPORT program, will require the individual to be admitted to a nursing facility within thirty days of the physician's determination.

(c) The individual has been hospitalized and a physician has determined and documented in writing that, unless the individual is enrolled in home and community-based services such as the PASSPORT program, the individual is to be transported directly from the hospital to a nursing facility and admitted.

(d) Both of the following apply:

(i) The individual is the subject of a report made under section 5101.63 of the Revised Code regarding abuse, neglect, or exploitation or such a report referred to a county department of job and family services under section 5126.31 of the Revised Code or has made a request to a county department for protective services as defined in section 5101.60 of the Revised Code.

(ii) A county department of job and family services and an area agency on aging have jointly documented in writing that, unless the individual is enrolled in home and community-based services such as the PASSPORT program, the individual should be admitted to a nursing facility.

(B) Each month, each area agency on aging shall identify individuals residing in the area that the agency serves who are eligible for the home first component of the PASSPORT program. When an area agency on aging identifies such an individual, the agency shall notify the long-term care consultation program administrator serving the area in which the individual resides. The administrator shall determine whether the PASSPORT program is appropriate for the individual and whether the individual would rather participate in the PASSPORT program than continue or begin to reside in a nursing facility. If the administrator determines that the PASSPORT program is appropriate for the individual and the individual would rather participate in the PASSPORT program than continue or begin to reside in a nursing facility, the administrator shall so notify the department of aging. On receipt of the notice from the administrator, the department shall approve the individual's enrollment in the medicaid-funded component of the PASSPORT program regardless of the unified waiting list established under section 173.55 of the Revised Code, unless the enrollment would cause the component to exceed any limit on the number of individuals who may be enrolled in the component as set by the United States secretary of health and human services in the PASSPORT waiver.

**HISTORY:**

152 v H 119, § 101.01, eff. 7-1-07; 153 v H 1, § 101.01, eff. 10-16-09; 153 v H 398, § 1, eff. 8-31-10; 2011 HB 153, § 101.01, eff. Sept. 29, 2011; 2013 HB 59, § 101.01, eff. Sept. 29, 2013; 2017 hb49, § 130.31, effective September 29, 2018.

**Editor's Notes**

This section was formerly codified as RC § 173.401.

**Amendment Notes**

The 2017 amendment by HB 49 substituted "section 5101.63" for "section 5101.61" in (A)(2)(d)(i).

The 2013 amendment deleted (A); redesignated former (B) and (C) as (A) and (C); in the first sentence of the introductory language of (B), substituted "Unless the medicaid-funded component of the PASSPORT program is terminated pursuant" for "Subject" and "division (C) of section 173.52" for "division (C)(2) of section 173.40"; and substituted "section 173.55" for "section 173.404" in the last sentence of present (B).

## § 173.522 Administration of state and federal PASSPORT components.

(A) The department of aging shall create and administer the state-funded component of the PASSPORT program. The state-funded component shall not be administered as part of the medicaid program.

(B) For an individual to be eligible for the state-funded component of the PASSPORT program, the individual must meet one of the following requirements and meet the additional eligibility requirements applicable to the individual established in rules adopted under division (D) of this section:

(1) The individual must have been enrolled in the state-funded component on September 1, 1991, (as the state-funded component was authorized by uncodified law in effect at that time) and have had one or more applications for enrollment in the medicaid-funded component of the PASSPORT program (or, if the medicaid-funded component is terminated under division (C) of section 173.52 of the Revised Code, the unified long-term services and support medicaid waiver component) denied.

(2) The individual must have an application for the medicaid-funded component of the PASSPORT program (or, if the medicaid-funded component is terminated under division (C) of section 173.52 of the Revised Code, the unified long-term services and support medicaid waiver component) pending and the department or the department's designee must have determined that the individual meets the nonfinancial eligibility requirements of the medicaid-funded component (or, if the medicaid-funded component is terminated under division (C) of section 173.52 of the Revised Code, the unified long-term services and support medicaid waiver component) and not have reason to doubt that the individual meets the financial eligibility requirements of the medicaid-funded component (or, if the medicaid-funded component is terminated under division (C) of section 173.52 of the Revised Code, the unified long-term services and support medicaid waiver component).

(C) An individual who is eligible for the state-funded component of the PASSPORT program because the individual meets the requirement of division (B)(2) of this section may participate in the component on that basis for a period of time specified in rules adopted under division (D) of this section.

(D)(1) The director of aging shall adopt rules in accordance with section 111.15 of the Revised Code to implement the state-funded component of the PASSPORT program.

The rules shall include all of the following:

(a) Additional eligibility requirements for an individual to be eligible for the state-funded component of the PASSPORT program;

(b) The duration that an individual eligible for the state-funded component of the PASSPORT program under division (B)(2) of this section may participate in that component;

(c) Any other rules the director considers appropriate to implement the state-funded component of the PASSPORT program.

(2) The additional eligibility requirements established in the rules may vary for the different groups of individuals specified in divisions (B)(1) and (2) of this section.

**HISTORY:**

2013 HB 59, § 101.01, eff. Sept. 29, 2013; 2015 hb64, § 101.01, effective September 29, 2015.

**Amendment Notes**

The 2015 amendment by HB 64 deleted (B)(2), which read: "The individual must have had the individual's enrollment in the medicaid-funded component of the PASSPORT program (or, if the medicaid-funded component is terminated under division (C) of section 173.52 of the Revised Code, the unified long-term services and support medicaid waiver component) terminated and the individual must still need the home and community-based services provided under the PASSPORT program to protect the individual's health and safety"; redesignated former (B)(3) as

(B)(2); substituted "a period of time specified in rules adopted under division (D) of this section" for "not more than ninety days" in (C); added the (D)(1) and (D)(2) designations; added the second paragraph of (D)(1); and made related and stylistic changes.

### § 173.523 Appeals for actions under the state component of PASSPORT.

(A) An individual who is an applicant for or participant or former participant in the state-funded component of the PASSPORT program may appeal an adverse action taken or proposed to be taken by the department of aging or an entity designated by the department concerning participation in or services provided under the component if the action will result in any of the following:

(1) Denial of enrollment or continued enrollment in the component;

(2) Denial of or reduction in the amount of services requested by or offered to the individual under the component;

(3) Assessment of any patient liability payment pursuant to rules adopted by the department under this section.

The appeal shall be made in accordance with section 173.56 of the Revised Code and rules adopted pursuant to that section.

(B) An individual who is an applicant for or participant or former participant in the state-funded component of the PASSPORT program may not bring an appeal under this or any other section of the Revised Code if any of the following is the case:

(1) The individual has voluntarily withdrawn the application for enrollment in the component;

(2) The individual has voluntarily terminated enrollment in the component;

(3) The individual agrees with the action being taken or proposed;

(4) The individual fails to submit a written request for a hearing to the director of aging within the time specified in the rules adopted pursuant to section 173.56 of the Revised Code;

(5) The individual has received services under the component for the maximum time permitted by section 173.522 of the Revised Code.

**HISTORY:**

2013 HB 59, § 101.01, eff. Sept. 29, 2013; 2015 hb64, § 101.01, effective September 29, 2015.

**Amendment Notes**

The 2015 amendment by HB 64 substituted "section 173.522 of the Revised Code" for "this section" in (B)(5).

### § 173.524 Kosher home-delivered meals under PASSPORT program.

An individual enrolled in the PASSPORT program may request that home-delivered meals provided to the individual under the PASSPORT program be kosher. If such a request is made, the department of aging or the department's designee shall ensure that each home-delivered meal provided to the individual under the PASSPORT program is kosher. In complying with this requirement, the department or department's designee shall require each entity that provides home-delivered meals to the individual to provide the individual with meals that meet, as much as possible, the requirements established in rules adopted under sections 173.52 and 173.522 of the Revised Code governing the home-delivered meal service while complying with kosher practices for meal preparation and dietary restrictions.

An entity that provides a kosher home-delivered meal to a PASSPORT program enrollee pursuant to this section shall be reimbursed for the meal at a rate equal to the rate for home-delivered meals furnished to PASSPORT program enrollees requiring a therapeutic diet.

**HISTORY:**

153 v H 1, § 101.01, eff. 10-16-09; 2013 HB 59, § 101.01, eff. Sept. 29, 2013.

**Editor's Notes**

This section was formerly codified as RC § 173.402.

**Amendment Notes**

The 2013 amendment substituted "sections 173.52 and 173.522" for "section 173.40" in the last sentence of the first paragraph.

### § 173.53 Choices program. [Repealed]

**HISTORY:**

153 v H 1, § 101.01, eff. 10-16-09; 2011 HB 153, § 101.01, eff. Sept. 29, 2011; 2013 HB 59, § 101.01, eff. Sept. 29, 2013; repealed by 2017 hb49, § 105.01, effective September 29, 2017.

### § 173.54 Definitions; assisted living program; department of aging to administer program; rules.

(A) The department of medicaid shall create the medicaid-funded component of the assisted living program. In creating the medicaid-funded component, the department of medicaid shall collaborate with the department of aging.

(B) Unless the medicaid-funded component of the assisted living program is terminated under division (C) of this section, all of the following apply:

(1) The department of aging shall administer the medicaid-funded component through a contract entered into with the department of medicaid under section 5162.35 of the Revised Code.

(2) The contract shall include an estimate of the medicaid-funded component's costs.

(3) The medicaid-funded component shall be operated as a separate medicaid waiver component.

(4) The medicaid-funded component may not serve more individuals than is set by the United States secretary of health and human services in the assisted living waiver.

(5) To the extent authorized by rules authorized by section 5162.021 of the Revised Code, the director of aging may adopt rules under Chapter 119. of the Revised Code regarding the medicaid-funded component .

(C) If the unified long-term services and support medicaid waiver component is created, the departments of aging and medicaid shall collaborate to determine whether the medicaid-funded component of the assisted living program should continue to operate as a separate medicaid waiver component or be terminated. If the departments determine that the medicaid-funded component of the assisted living program should be terminated, the medicaid-funded component shall cease to exist on a date the departments shall specify.

**HISTORY:**

151 v H 66, § 101.01, eff. 10-1-05; 152 v H 119, § 101.01, eff. 7-1-07; 152 v H 420, § 101.01, eff. 12-30-08; 153 v H 1, § 101.01, eff. 10-16-09; 2011 HB 153, § 101.01, eff. Sept. 29, 2011; 2012 HB 487, § 101.01, eff. Sept. 10, 2012; 2013 HB 59, § 101.01, eff. Sept. 29, 2013.

**Editor's Notes**

This section was formerly codified as RC § 5111.89.

**Amendment Notes**

The 2013 amendment rewrote the section.

### § 173.541 Eligibility for program.

To be eligible for the medicaid-funded component of the assisted living program, an individual must meet all of the following requirements:

(A) Need an intermediate level of care as determined by an assessment conducted under section 173.546 of the Revised Code;

(B) While receiving assisted living services under the medicaid-funded component, reside in a residential care facility that is authorized by a valid medicaid provider agreement to participate in the component, including both of the following:

(1) A residential care facility that is owned or operated by a metropolitan housing authority that has a contract with the United States department of housing and urban development to receive an operating subsidy or rental assistance for the residents of the facility;

(2) A county or district home licensed as a residential care facility.

(C) Meet all other eligibility requirements for the medicaid-funded component established in rules adopted under section 173.54 of the Revised Code.

**HISTORY:**

151 v H 66, § 101.01, eff. 10-1-05; 152 v H 119, § 101.01, eff. 7-1-07; 152 v H 420, § 101.01, eff. 12-30-08; 153 v H 1, § 101.01, eff. 10-16-09; 2011 HB 153, § 101.01, eff. Sept. 29, 2011; 2013 HB 59, § 101.01, eff. Sept. 29, 2013.

**Editor's Notes**

This section was formerly codified as RC § 5111.891.

**Amendment Notes**

The 2013 amendment substituted "by an assessment conducted under section 173.546 of the Revised Code" for "under rule 5101:3-3-06 of the Administrative Code" in (A); and substituted "under section 173.54" for "pursuant to division (C) of section 5111.89" in (C).

### § 173.542 Home first component of assisted living program.

(A) Unless the medicaid-funded component of the assisted living program is terminated pursuant to division (C) of section 173.54 of the Revised Code, the department of aging shall establish a home first component of the assisted living program under which eligible individuals may be enrolled in the medicaid-funded component of the assisted living program in accordance with this section. An individual is eligible for the assisted living program's home first component if both of the following apply:

(1) The individual has been determined to be eligible for the medicaid-funded component of the assisted living program.

(2) At least one of the following applies:

(a) The individual has been admitted to a nursing facility.

(b) A physician has determined and documented in writing that the individual has a medical condition that, unless the individual is enrolled in home and community-based services such as the assisted living program, will require the individual to be admitted to a nursing facility within thirty days of the physician's determination.

(c) The individual has been hospitalized and a physician has determined and documented in writing that, unless the individual is enrolled in home and community-based services such as the assisted living program, the individual is to be transported directly from the hospital to a nursing facility and admitted.

(d) Both of the following apply:

(i) The individual is the subject of a report made under section 5101.63 of the Revised Code regarding abuse, neglect, or exploitation or such a report referred to a county department of job and family services under section 5126.31 of the Revised Code or has made a request to a county department for protective services as defined in section 5101.60 of the Revised Code.

(ii) A county department of job and family services and an area agency on aging have jointly documented in writing that, unless the individual is enrolled in home and community-based services such as the assisted living program, the individual should be admitted to a nursing facility.

(B) Each month, each area agency on aging shall identify individuals residing in the area that the area agency on aging serves who are eligible for the home first component of the assisted living program. When an area agency on aging identifies such an individual and determines that there is a vacancy in a residential care facility participating in the medicaid-funded component of the assisted living program that is acceptable to the individual, the agency shall notify the long-term care consultation program administrator serving the area in which the individual resides. The administrator shall determine whether the assisted living program is appropriate for the individual and whether the individual would rather participate in the assisted living program than continue or begin to reside in a nursing facility. If the administrator determines that the assisted living program is appropriate for the individual and the individual would rather participate in the assisted living program than continue or begin to reside in a nursing facility, the administrator shall so notify the department of aging. On receipt of the notice from the administrator, the department shall approve the individual's enrollment in the medicaid-funded component of the assisted living program regardless of the unified waiting list established under section 173.55 of the Revised Code, unless the enrollment would cause the component to exceed any limit on the number of individuals who may participate in the component as set by the United States secretary of health and human services in the assisted living waiver.

**HISTORY:**

152 v H 119, § 101.01, eff. 7-1-07; 152 v H 420, § 101.01, eff. 12-30-08; 153 v H 1, § 101.01, eff. 10-16-09; 153 v H 398, § 1, eff. 8-31-10; 2011 HB 153, § 101.01, eff. Sept. 29, 2011; 2012 HB 487, § 101.01, eff. Sept. 10, 2012; 2013 HB 59, § 101.01, eff. Sept. 29, 2013; 2017 hb49, § 130.31, effective September 29, 2018.

**Editor's Notes**

This section was formerly codified as RC § 5111.894.

**Amendment Notes**

The 2017 amendment by HB 49 substituted "section 5101.63" for "section 5101.61" in (A)(2)(d)(i).

The 2013 amendment, in the first sentence of the introductory language of (A), substituted "Unless the medicaid-funded component of the assisted living program is terminated pursuant" for "Subject" and "division (C) of section 173.54" for "division (C)(2) of section 5111.89"; and substituted "section 173.55" for "section 173.404" in the last sentence of (B).

### § 173.543 Administration of state funded assisted living program.

The department of aging shall create and administer the state-funded component of the assisted living program. The state-funded component shall not be administered as part of the medicaid program.

An individual who is eligible for the state-funded component may participate in the component for a period of time specified in rules adopted under this section.

The director of aging shall adopt rules in accordance with section 111.15 of the Revised Code to implement the state-funded component. The rules shall specify the period that an individual eligible for the state-funded component may participate in the component.

**HISTORY:**

2013 HB 59, § 101.01, eff. Sept. 29, 2013; 2015 hb64, § 101.01, effective September 29, 2015.

**Amendment Notes**

The 2015 amendment by HB 64 substituted "a period of time specified in rules adopted under this section" for "not more than ninety days" in the second paragraph; added the second sentence to the last paragraph.

### § 173.544 State funded assisted living program; eligibilty.

To be eligible for the state-funded component of the assisted living program, an individual must meet all of the following requirements:

(A) The individual must need an intermediate level of care as determined by an assessment conducted under section 173.546 of the Revised Code.

(B) The individual must have an application for the medicaid-funded component of the assisted living program (or, if the medicaid-funded component is terminated under division (C) of section 173.54 of the Revised Code, the unified long-term services and support medicaid waiver component) pending and the department or the department's designee must have determined that the individual meets the nonfinancial eligibility requirements of the medicaid-funded component (or, if the medicaid-funded component is terminated under division (C) of section 173.54 of the Revised Code, the unified long-term services and support medicaid waiver component) and not have reason to doubt that the individual meets the financial eligibility requirements of the medicaid-funded component (or, if the medicaid-funded component is terminated under division (C) of section 173.54 of the Revised Code, the unified long-term services and support medicaid waiver component).

(C) While receiving assisted living services under the state-funded component, the individual must reside in a residential care facility that is authorized by a valid provider agreement to participate in the component, including both of the following:

(1) A residential care facility that is owned or operated by a metropolitan housing authority that has a contract with the United States department of housing and urban development to receive an operating subsidy or rental assistance for the residents of the facility;

(2) A county or district home licensed as a residential care facility.

(D) The individual must meet all other eligibility requirements for the state-funded component established in rules adopted under section 173.543 of the Revised Code.

**HISTORY:**

2011 HB 153, § 101.01, eff. Sept. 29, 2011; 2013 HB 59, § 101.01, eff. Sept. 29, 2013; 2015 hb64, § 101.01, effective September 29, 2015.

**Editor's Notes**

This section was formerly codified as RC § 5111.892.

**Amendment Notes**

The 2015 amendment by HB 64 substituted "section 173.543" for "section 173.54" in (D).

The 2013 amendment substituted "by an assessment conducted under section 173.546 of the Revised Code" for "under rule 5101:3-3-06 of the Administrative Code" in (A); substituted "division (C) of section 173.54" for "division (C)(2) of section 5111.89" wherever it appears in (B); substituted "section 173.54" for "division (D) of section 5111.89" in (D).

### § 173.545 Appeals of state funded assisted living program actions.

(A) An individual who is an applicant for or participant or former participant in the state-funded component of the assisted living program may appeal an adverse action taken or proposed to be taken by the department of aging or an entity designated by the department concerning participation in or services provided under the component if the action will result in any of the following:

(1) Denial of enrollment or continued enrollment in the component;

(2) Denial of or reduction in the amount of services requested by or offered to the individual under the component;

(3) Assessment of any patient liability payment pursuant to rules adopted by the department under this section.

The appeal shall be made in accordance with section 173.56 of the Revised Code and rules adopted pursuant to that section.

(B) An individual who is an applicant for or participant or former participant in the state-funded component of the assisted living program may not bring an appeal under this or any other section of the Revised Code if any of the following is the case:

(1) The individual has voluntarily withdrawn the application for enrollment in the component;

(2) The individual has voluntarily terminated enrollment in the component;

(3) The individual agrees with the action being taken or proposed;

(4) The individual fails to submit a written request for a hearing to the director of aging within the time specified in the rules adopted pursuant to section 173.56 of the Revised Code;

(5) The individual has received services under the component for the maximum time permitted by section 173.543 of the Revised Code.

**HISTORY:**

2013 HB 59, § 101.01, eff. Sept. 29, 2013; 2015 hb64, § 101.01, effective September 29, 2015.

**Amendment Notes**

The 2015 amendment by HB 64 substituted "section 173.543 of the Revised Code" for "this section" in (B)(5).

### § 173.546 Determination of a need for intermediate level care.

(A) Each applicant for the assisted living program shall undergo an assessment to determine whether the applicant needs an intermediate level of care. The department of medicaid or an agency under contract pursuant to division (C) of this section shall conduct the assessment. The assessment may be performed concurrently with a long-term care consultation provided under section 173.42 of the Revised Code.

(B) An applicant or applicant's representative has the right to appeal an assessment's findings. Section 5160.31 of the Revised Code applies to appeals regarding the medicaid-funded component of the assisted living program. The department or an agency under contract to conduct the assessment shall provide written notice of this right to the applicant or applicant's representative and the residential care facility in which the applicant intends to reside if enrolled in the assisted living program. The notice shall include an explanation of the appeal procedures. The department or agency under contract to conduct the assessment shall represent the state in any appeal of an assessment's findings.

(C) The department may contract with one or more agencies to perform assessments under this section. A contract shall specify the agency's responsibilities regarding the assessments.

**HISTORY:**

2013 HB 59, § 101.01, eff. Sept. 29, 2013.

### § 173.547 Facility staffing requirements.

A residential care facility providing services covered by the assisted living program to an individual enrolled in the program shall have staff on-site twenty-four hours each day who are able to do all of the following:

(A) Meet the scheduled and unpredicted needs of the individuals enrolled in the assisted living program in a manner that promotes the individuals' dignity and independence;

(B) Provide supervision services for those individuals;

(C) Help keep the individuals safe and secure.

**HISTORY:**

151 v H 66, § 101.01, eff. 10-1-05; 2011 HB 153, § 101.01, eff. Sept. 29, 2011; 2013 HB 59, § 101.01, eff. Sept. 29, 2013.

**Editor's Notes**

This section was formerly codified as RC § 5111.893.

### § 173.548 Program enrollee's right to choose single occupancy or multiple occupancy room.

An individual enrolled in the medicaid-funded component of the assisted living program may choose a single occupancy room or multiple occupancy room in the residential care facility in which the individual resides. The choice of a multiple occupancy room is subject to approval pursuant to a process the director of aging shall establish in rules adopted under section 173.54 of the Revised Code.

**HISTORY:**

2015 hb64, § 101.01, effective September 29, 2015.

### § 173.55 Unified waiting list.

(A) As used in this section:

(1) "Department of aging-administered medicaid waiver component" means both of the following:

(a) The medicaid-funded component of the PASSPORT program;

(b) The medicaid-funded component of the assisted living program.

(2) "PACE program" means the component of the medicaid program the department of aging administers pursuant to section 173.50 of the Revised Code.

(B) If the department of aging determines that there are insufficient funds to enroll all individuals who have applied and been determined eligible for department of aging-administered medicaid waiver components and the PACE program, the department shall establish a unified waiting list for the components and program. Only individuals eligible for a department of aging-administered medicaid waiver component or the PACE program may be placed on the unified waiting list. An individual who may be enrolled in a department of aging-administered medicaid waiver component or the PACE program through a home first component established under section 173.501, 173.521, or 173.542 of the Revised Code may be so enrolled without being placed on the unified waiting list.

**HISTORY:**

153 v H 398, § 1, eff. 8-31-10; 2011 HB 153, § 101.01, eff. Sept. 29, 2011; 2013 HB 59, § 101.01, eff. Sept. 29, 2013; 2017 hb49, § 101.01, effective September 29, 2017.

**Editor's Notes**

This section was formerly codified as RC § 173.404.

**Amendment Notes**

The 2017 amendment by HB 49 substituted "both of the following" for "each of the following" in the introductory language of (A)(1); deleted former (A)(1)(b), which read "The choices program"; and redesignated former (A)(1)(c) as (A)(1)(b).

The 2013 amendment deleted "created under section 173.40 of the Revised Code" from the end of (A)(1)(a); deleted "created under section 173.403 of the Revised Code" from the end of (A)(1)(b); deleted "created under section 5111.89 of the Revised Code" from the end of (A)(1)(c); and substituted "section 173.501, 173.521 or 173.542" for "section 173.401, 173.501, or 5111.894" in the last sentence of (B).

### § 173.56 Notice and opportunity of hearing for appeal.

(A) The department of aging shall adopt rules in accordance with section 111.15 of the Revised Code governing appeals brought under section 173.523 or 173.545 of the Revised Code. The rules shall require notice and the opportunity for a hearing. The rules may allow an appeal hearing to be conducted by telephone and permit the department to record hearings conducted by telephone. Chapter 119. of the Revised Code applies to a hearing under section 173.523 or 173.545 of the Revised Code only to the extent provided in rules the department adopts under this section.

(B) An appeal shall be commenced by submission of a written request for a hearing to the director of aging within the time specified in the rules adopted under this section. The hearing may be recorded, but neither the recording nor a transcript of the recording is part of the official record of the proceeding. The director shall notify the individual bringing the appeal of the director's decision and of the procedure for appealing the decision.

(C) The director's decision may be appealed to a court of common pleas pursuant to section 119.12 of the Revised Code. The appeal shall be governed by that section except as follows:

(1) The appeal shall be in the court of common pleas of the county in which the individual who brings the appeal resides or, if the individual does not reside in this state, to the Franklin county court of common pleas.

(2) The notice of appeal must be mailed to the department and filed with the court not later than thirty days after the department mails notice of the director's decision. For good cause shown, the court may extend the time for mailing and filing the notice of appeal, but the time cannot exceed six months from the date the department mails the notice of the director's decision.

(3) If an individual applies to the court for designation as an indigent and the court grants the application, the individual shall not be required to furnish the costs of the appeal.

(4) The department is required to file a transcript of the testimony of the state hearing with the court only if the court orders that the transcript be filed. The court shall make such an order only if it finds that the department and the individual bringing the appeal are unable to stipulate to the facts of the case and that the transcript is essential to a determination of the appeal. The department shall file the transcript not later than thirty days after such an order is issued.

**HISTORY:**

2013 HB 59, § 101.01, eff. Sept. 29, 2013.

**Editor's Notes**

Former § 173.56 [148 v H 403. Eff 7-1-2000], was repealed by 150 v H 95, effective June 26, 2003.

### § 173.57 Repealed.

Repealed 150 v H 95, § 2 [148 v H 403. Eff 7-1-2000]. Eff 6-26-03.

**Editor's Notes**

This section concerned rules.

### § 173.58 Repealed.

Repealed 150 v H 95, § 2 [148 v H 403 (Eff 7-1-2000); 148 v H 548. Eff 3-22-2001]. Eff 6-26-03.

**Editor's Notes**

This section concerned the advisory council.

### § 173.59 Repealed.

Repealed 150 v H 95, § 2 [148 v H 403 (Eff 7-1-2000)]. Eff 6-26-03.

**Editor's Notes**

This section concerned advertising restriction.

### § 173.60 Improvement of person centered care in nursing homes.

(A) As used in this section:

(1) "Nursing home" has the same meaning as in section 3721.01 of the Revised Code.

(2) "Person-centered care" means a relationship-based approach to care that honors and respects the opinions of individuals receiving care and those working closely with them.

(B) The department of aging shall implement a nursing home quality initiative to improve the provision of person-centered care in nursing homes. The office of the state long-term care ombudsman program shall assist the department with the initiative. The initiative shall include quality improvement projects that provide nursing homes with resources and on-site education promoting person-centered care strategies and positive resident outcomes, as well as other assistance designed to improve the quality of nursing home services. The department may offer any of the projects.

(C) The department shall make available a list of quality improvement projects that may be used by nursing homes in meeting the requirements of section 3721.072 of the Revised Code. In addition to any of the projects offered by the department pursuant to division (B) of this section, the list may include projects offered by any of the following:

(1) Other state agencies;

(2) A quality improvement organization under contract with the United States secretary of health and human services to carry out in this state the functions described in the "Social Security Act," section 1154, 42 U.S.C. 1320c-3;

(3) The Ohio person-centered care coalition;

(4) Any other academic, research, or health care entity identified by the department.

(D) The director of aging may adopt rules in accordance with Chapter 119. of the Revised Code as necessary to implement this section.

**HISTORY:**

2013 HB 59, § 101.01, eff. Sept. 29, 2013.

### § 173.70 Contract for provision of outpatient prescription drug discounts.

(A) The director of aging may enter into a contract with any person under which the person operates a program for the provision of outpatient prescription drug discounts to any or all of the following:

(1) Individuals who are sixty years of age or older;

(2) Individuals whose family incomes do not exceed three hundred per cent of the federal poverty guidelines, as revised annually by the United States department of health and human services in accordance with section 673(2) of the "Omnibus Budget Reconciliation Act of 1981," 95 Stat. 511, 42 U.S.C. 9902, as amended;

(3) Individuals who are persons with disabilities, as defined in section 173.06 of the Revised Code.

(B) The director may disclose to the person under contract information that identifies the individuals who participated in and individuals who applied for participation in the Ohio's best Rx program that was operated under former sections 173.71 to 173.91 of the Revised Code.

**HISTORY:**
153 v H 1, § 101.01, eff. 7-17-09.

## OHIO'S BEST RX PROGRAM

### § 173.71 Repealed.

Repealed, 153 v H 1, § 105.01 [150 v H 311, § 1, eff. 12-18-03; 151 v H 468, § 1, eff. 4-6-07; 151 v H 468, § 4, eff. 7-1-07; 152 v H 119, § 101.01, eff. 9-29-07; 153 v H 1, § 101.01, eff. 7-17-09]. Eff 7-17-09.

**Editor's Notes**
This section concerned definitions.

### § 173.72 Repealed.

Repealed, 153 v H 1, § 105.01 [150 v H 311, § 1, eff. 12-18-03; 151 v H 468, § 1, eff. 4-6-07; 151 v H 468, § 4, eff. 7-1-07]. Eff 7-17-09.

**Editor's Notes**
The section established Ohio's best Rx program.

### § 173.721 Repealed.

Repealed, 153 v H 1, § 105.01 [151 v H 468, § 1, eff. 4-6-07; 151 v H 468, § 4, eff. 7-1-07]. Eff 7-17-09.

**Editor's Notes**
This section concerned administration by department of aging.

### § 173.722 Repealed.

Repealed, 153 v H 1, § 105.01 [150 v H 311, § 1, eff. 12-18-03; 151 v H 468, § 4, eff. 7-1-07]. Eff 7-17-09.

**Editor's Notes**
This section concerned outreach efforts.

### § 173.723 Repealed.

Repealed, 153 v H 1, § 105.01 [150 v H 311, § 1, eff. 12-18-03; 151 v H 468, § 4, eff. 7-1-07]. Eff 7-17-09.

**Editor's Notes**
This section concerned ombudspersons.

### § 173.724 Repealed.

Repealed, 153 v H 1, § 105.01 [150 v H 311, § 1, eff. 12-18-03; 151 v H 468, § 1, eff. 4-6-07; 151 v H 468, § 4, eff. 7-1-07]. Eff 7-17-09.

**Editor's Notes**
This section concerned coordination with the golden buckeye card program or state employee health benefit plan.

### § 173.73 Repealed.

Repealed, 153 v H 1, § 105.01 [151 v H 468, § 1, eff. 4-6-07; 151 v H 468, § 4, eff. 7-1-07]. Eff 7-17-09.

**Editor's Notes**
This section concerned the consulting pharmacy benefit manager.

### § 173.731 Repealed.

Repealed, 153 v H 1, § 105.01 [151 v H 468, § 1, eff. 4-6-07; 151 v H 468, § 4, eff. 7-1-07]. Eff 7-17-09.

**Editor's Notes**
This section concerned selection of the consulting pharmacy benefit manager.

### § 173.732 Repealed.

Repealed, 153 v H 1, § 105.01 [151 v H 468, § 1, eff. 4-6-07; 151 v H 468, § 4, eff. 7-1-07]. Eff 7-17-09.

**Editor's Notes**
This section concerned audits to determine whether manager has provided valid information.

### § 173.74 Repealed.

Repealed, 153 v H 1, § 105.01 [151 v H 468, § 1, eff. 4-6-07; 151 v H 468, § 4, eff. 7-1-07]. Eff 7-17-09.

**Editor's Notes**
This section concerned the establishment of base price for each drug.

### § 173.741 Repealed.

Repealed, 153 v H 1, § 105.01 [151 v H 468, § 1, eff. 4-6-07; 151 v H 468, § 4, eff. 7-1-07]. Eff 7-17-09.

**Editor's Notes**
This section concerned designation of formulas for determining base price and modifications.

### § 173.742 Repealed.

Repealed, 153 v H 1, § 105.01 [151 v H 468, § 1, eff. 4-6-07; 151 v H 468, § 4, eff. 7-1-07]. Eff 7-17-09.

**Editor's Notes**
This section concerned verification of drug pricing information and reviews concerning brand name and generic drugs.

### § 173.75 Repealed.

Repealed, 153 v H 1, § 105.01 [151 v H 468, § 1, eff. 4-6-07; 151 v H 468, § 4, eff. 7-1-07]. Eff 7-17-09.

**Editor's Notes**
This section concerned establishment of amount participant to be charged for drug.

### § 173.751 Repealed.

Repealed, 153 v H 1, § 105.01 [150 v H 311, § 1, eff. 12-18-03; 151 v H 468, § 1, eff. 4-6-07; 151 v H 468, § 4, eff. 7-1-07]. Eff 7-17-09.

**Editor's Notes**
This section concerned price and fee information reported to distributor and mail order system.

### § 173.752 Repealed.

Repealed, 153 v H 1, § 105.01 [151 v H 468, § 1, eff. 4-6-07; 151 v H 468, § 4, eff. 7-1-07]. Eff 7-17-09.

**Editor's Notes**
This section concerned determination of amount saved by participant.

### § 173.753 Repealed.

Repealed, 153 v H 1, § 105.01 [150 v H 311, § 1, eff. 12-18-03; 151 v H 66, § 101.01, eff. 9-29-05; 151 v H 468, § 1, eff. 4-6-07; 151 v H 468, § 4, eff. 7-1-07]. Eff 7-17-09.

**Editor's Notes**
This section concerned determination of average percentage savings.

### § 173.76 Repealed.

Repealed, 153 v H 1, § 105.01 [150 v H 311, § 1, eff. 12-18-03; 151 v H 468, § 1, eff. 4-6-07; 151 v H 468, § 4, eff. 7-1-07]. Eff 7-17-09.

**Editor's Notes**
This section concerned eligibility for program.

### § 173.77 Repealed.

Repealed, 153 v H 1, § 105.01 [151 v H 468, § 1, eff. 4-6-07; 151 v H 468, § 4, eff. 7-1-07]. Eff 7-17-09.

**Editor's Notes**
This section concerned application for participation.

### § 173.771 Repealed.

Repealed, 153 v H 1, § 105.01 [150 v H 311, § 1, eff. 12-18-03; 151 v H 468, § 1, eff. 4-6-07; 151 v H 468, § 4, eff. 7-1-07]. Eff 7-17-09.

**Editor's Notes**
This section concerned Medicaid information provided to applicant.

### § 173.772 Repealed.

Repealed, 153 v H 1, § 105.01 [150 v H 311, § 1, eff. 12-18-03; 151 v H 468, § 1, eff. 4-6-07; 151 v H 468, § 4, eff. 7-1-07]. Eff 7-17-09.

**Editor's Notes**
This section concerned eligibility determinations.

### § 173.773 Repealed.

Repealed, 153 v H 1, § 105.01 [150 v H 311, § 1, eff. 12-18-03; 151 v H 468, § 1, eff. 4-6-07; 151 v H 468, § 4, eff. 7-1-07]. Eff 7-17-09.

**Editor's Notes**
This section concerned issuance of enrollment cards and confirmation of enrollment.

### § 173.78 Repealed.

Repealed, 153 v H 1, § 105.01 [151 v H 468, § 1, eff. 4-6-07; 151 v H 468, § 4, eff. 7-1-07]. Eff 7-17-09.

**Editor's Notes**
This section concerned the drug mail order system.

### § 173.79 Repealed.

Repealed, 153 v H 1, § 105.01 [150 v H 311, § 1, eff. 12-18-03; 151 v H 468, § 1, eff. 4-6-07; 151 v H 468, § 4, eff. 7-1-07]. Eff 7-17-09.

**Editor's Notes**
This section concerned agreements with terminal distributors of dangerous drugs.

### § 173.791 Repealed.

Repealed, 153 v H 1, § 105.01 [150 v H 311, § 1, eff. 12-18-03; 151 v H 468, § 1, eff. 4-6-07; 151 v H 468, § 4, eff. 7-1-07]. Eff 7-17-09.

**Editor's Notes**
This section prohibited nonparticipating terminal distributors from being barred from other programs.

### § 173.80 Repealed.

Repealed, 153 v H 1, § 105.01 [150 v H 311, § 1, eff. 12-18-03; 151 v H 468, § 1, eff. 4-6-07; 151 v H 468, § 4, eff. 7-1-07]. Eff 7-17-09.

**Editor's Notes**
This section concerned submission of claims.

### § 173.801 Repealed.

Repealed, 153 v H 1, § 105.01 [150 v H 311, § 1, eff. 12-18-03; 151 v H 468, § 1, eff. 4-6-07; 151 v H 468, § 4, eff. 7-1-07]. Eff 7-17-09.

**Editor's Notes**
This section concerned payment for complete and timely claim.

### § 173.802 Repealed.

Repealed, 153 v H 1, § 105.01 [150 v H 311, § 1, eff. 12-18-03; 151 v H 468, § 1, eff. 4-6-07; 151 v H 468, § 4, eff. 7-1-07]. Eff 7-17-09.

**Editor's Notes**
This section concerned charges for submitting or processing claim prohibited.

### § 173.803 Repealed.

Repealed, 153 v H 1, § 105.01 [150 v H 311, § 1, eff. 12-18-03; 151 v H 468, § 1, eff. 4-6-07; 151 v H 468, § 4, eff. 7-1-07]. Eff 7-17-09.

**Editor's Notes**
This section concerned claims that may not be paid.

## MANUFACTURER AGREEMENTS

### § 173.81 Repealed.

Repealed, 153 v H 1, § 105.01 [151 v H 468, § 1, eff. 4-6-07; 151 v H 468, § 4, eff. 7-1-07]. Eff 7-17-09.

**Editor's Notes**
This section concerned manufacturer agreements to make payments for drugs purchased.

### § 173.811 Repealed.

Repealed, 153 v H 1, § 105.01 [151 v H 468, § 1, eff. 4-6-07; 151 v H 468, § 4, eff. 7-1-07]. Eff 7-17-09.

**Editor's Notes**
This section concerned terms of manufacturer agreement.

### § 173.812 Repealed.

Repealed, 153 v H 1, § 105.01 [151 v H 468, § 1, eff. 4-6-07; 151 v H 468, § 4, eff. 7-1-07]. Eff 7-17-09.

**Editor's Notes**
This section concerned manufacturer payment amount.

### § 173.813 Repealed.

Repealed, 153 v H 1, § 105.01 [151 v H 468, § 1, eff. 4-6-07; 151 v H 468, § 4, eff. 7-1-07]. Eff 7-17-09.

**Editor's Notes**
This section concerned information used in negotiations with manufacturer.

### § 173.814 Repealed.

Repealed, 153 v H 1, § 105.01 [151 v H 468, § 1, eff. 4-6-07; 151 v H 468, § 4, eff. 7-1-07]. Eff 7-17-09.

**Editor's Notes**
This section concerned manufacturer payment sample.

### § 173.815 Repealed.

Repealed, 153 v H 1, § 105.01 [151 v H 468, § 1, eff. 4-6-07; 151 v H 468, § 4, eff. 7-1-07]. Eff 7-17-09.

**Editor's Notes**
This section concerned Medicaid best price.

### § 173.82 Repealed.

Repealed, 153 v H 1, § 105.01 [151 v H 468, § 1, eff. 4-6-07; 151 v H 468, § 4, eff. 7-1-07]. Eff 7-17-09.

**Editor's Notes**
This section concerned manufacturer audit claims.

## MISCELLANEOUS

### § 173.83 Repealed.

Repealed, 153 v H 1, § 105.01 [150 v H 311, § 1, eff. 12-18-03; 150 v S 189, § 1, eff. 6-29-04; 151 v H 468, § 1, eff. 4-6-07; 151 v H 468, § 4, eff. 7-1-07]. Eff 7-17-09.

**Editor's Notes**
This section concerned rules.

### § 173.831 Repealed.

Repealed, 153 v H 1, § 105.01 [150 v H 311, § 1, eff. 12-18-03; 151 v H 66, § 101.01, eff. 6-30-05; 151 v H 468, § 1, eff. 4-6-07; 151 v H 468, § 4, eff. 7-1-07]. Eff 7-17-09.

**Editor's Notes**
This section concerned reviews of amount of professional fee charged to participants and limitations.

### § 173.832 Repealed.

Repealed, 153 v H 1, § 105.01 [150 v H 311, § 1, eff. 12-18-03; 151 v H 468, § 1, eff. 4-6-07; 151 v H 468, § 4, eff. 7-1-07]. Eff 7-17-09.

**Editor's Notes**
This section concerned administrative fees.

### § 173.833 Repealed.

Repealed, 153 v H 1, § 105.01 [150 v H 311, § 1, eff. 12-18-03; 151 v H 468, § 1, eff. 4-6-07; 151 v H 468, § 4, eff. 7-1-07]. Eff 7-17-09.

**Editor's Notes**
This section concerned determination of percentage of manufacturer payment retained to pay administrative costs.

### § 173.84 Repealed.

Repealed, 153 v H 1, § 105.01 [150 v H 311, § 1, eff. 12-18-03; 151 v H 468, § 4, eff. 7-1-07]. Eff 7-17-09.

**Editor's Notes**
This section concerned conformance to or coordination with federally funded program.

### § 173.85 Repealed.

Repealed, 153 v H 1, § 105.01 [150 v H 311, § 1, eff. 12-18-03; 151 v H 468, § 1, eff. 4-6-07; 151 v H 468, § 4, eff. 7-1-07; 152 v H 119, § 101.01, eff. 9-29-07]. Eff 7-17-09.

**Editor's Notes**
This section concerned Ohio's best Rx program fund created.

### § 173.86 Repealed.

Repealed, 153 v H 1, § 105.01 [150 v H 311, § 1, eff. 12-18-03; 151 v H 468, § 1, eff. 4-6-07; 151 v H 468, § 4, eff. 7-1-07; 152 v H 119, § 101.01, eff. 9-29-07]. Eff 7-17-09.

**Editor's Notes**
This section concerned administration fund.

### § 173.861 Repealed.

Repealed, 153 v H 1, § 105.01 [151 v H 468, § 1, eff. 4-6-07; 151 v H 468, § 4, eff. 7-1-07]. Eff 7-17-09.

**Editor's Notes**
This section concerned subsidies provided to participants.

### § 173.87 Repealed.

Repealed, 153 v H 1, § 105.01 [150 v H 311, § 1, eff. 12-18-03; 151 v H 468, § 4, eff. 7-1-07]. Eff 7-17-09.

**Editor's Notes**
This section created the Ohio's best Rx program council.

### § 173.871 Repealed.

Repealed, 153 v H 1, § 105.01 [150 v H 311, § 1, eff. 12-18-03; 151 v H 468, § 4, eff. 7-1-07]. Eff 7-17-09.

**Editor's Notes**
This section concerned members.

### § 173.872 Repealed.

Repealed, 153 v H 1, § 105.01 [150 v H 311, § 1, eff. 12-18-03; 151 v H 468, § 4, eff. 7-1-07]. Eff 7-17-09.

**Editor's Notes**
This section concerned appointments to council.

### § 173.873 Repealed.

Repealed, 153 v H 1, § 105.01 [150 v H 311, § 1, eff. 12-18-03; 151 v H 468, § 4, eff. 7-1-07]. Eff 7-17-09.

**Editor's Notes**
This section concerned co-chairs and representatives of legislative officers.

### § 173.874 Repealed.

Repealed, 153 v H 1, § 105.01 [150 v H 311, § 1, eff. 12-18-03; 151 v H 468, § 4, eff. 7-1-07]. Eff 7-17-09.

**Editor's Notes**
This section prohibited compensation and reimbursement.

### § 173.875 Repealed.

Repealed, 153 v H 1, § 105.01 [150 v H 311, § 1, eff. 12-18-03; 151 v H 468, § 4, eff. 7-1-07]. Eff 7-17-09.

**Editor's Notes**
This section concerned access to council records.

### § 173.876 Repealed.

Repealed, 153 v H 1, § 105.01 [150 v H 311, § 1, eff. 12-18-03; 151 v H 468, § 4, eff. 7-1-07]. Eff 7-17-09.

**Editor's Notes**
This section concerned exemption from sunset review provisions.

### § 173.88 Repealed.

Repealed, 153 v H 1, § 105.01 [150 v H 311, § 1, eff. 12-18-03; 151 v H 468, § 1, eff. 4-6-07; 151 v H 468, § 4, eff. 7-1-07]. Eff 7-17-09.

**Editor's Notes**
This section concerned manufacturer agreement list and list of terminal distributors and mail order system.

# CONFIDENTIALITY OF PROGRAM AND CONSUMER INFORMATION

### § 173.89 Repealed.

Repealed, 153 v H 1, § 105.01 [150 v H 311, § 1, eff. 12-18-03; 151 v H 468, § 1, eff. 4-6-07; 151 v H 468, § 4, eff. 7-1-07]. Eff 7-17-09.

**Editor's Notes**

This section concerned state and federal confidentiality requirements.

### § 173.891 Repealed.

Repealed, 153 v H 1, § 105.01 [150 v H 311, § 1, eff. 12-18-03; 151 v H 468, § 1, eff. 4-6-07; 151 v H 468, § 4, eff. 7-1-07]. Eff 7-17-09.

**Editor's Notes**

This section concerned protection of trade secrets.

### § 173.892 Repealed.

Repealed, 153 v H 1, § 105.01 [150 v H 311, § 1, eff. 12-18-03; 151 v H 468, § 1, eff. 4-6-07; 151 v H 468, § 4, eff. 7-1-07]. Eff 7-17-09.

**Editor's Notes**

This section concerned permissible disclosures.

### § 173.90 Repealed.

Repealed, 153 v H 1, § 105.01 [150 v H 311, § 1, eff. 12-18-03; 151 v H 468, § 1, eff. 4-6-07; 151 v H 468, § 4, eff. 7-1-07]. Eff 7-17-09.

**Editor's Notes**

This section concerned confidentiality of applicant or participant information.

### § 173.91 Repealed.

Repealed, 153 v H 1, § 105.01 [150 v H 311, § 1, eff. 12-18-03; 151 v H 468, § 1, eff. 4-6-07; 151 v H 468, § 4, eff. 7-1-07]. Eff 7-17-09.

**Editor's Notes**

This section concerned use and preservation of records.

### § 173.95 Best practices and standards for preventing elder fraud and financial exploitation; education; access to available services and resources.

(A) The director of aging, the director of commerce, the director of job and family services, and the attorney general or the attorney general's designee, in consultation with county departments of job and family services, adult protective services agencies, the Ohio bankers league, the community bankers association of Ohio, the securities industry and financial markets association, and the Ohio credit union league, shall work together to do all of the following:

(1) Develop best practices and standards for preventing elder fraud and financial exploitation;

(2) Provide education on elder fraud and financial exploitation;

(3) Ensure that victims of elder fraud and exploitation have access to available services and resources.

(B) The director of aging, the director of commerce, and the director of job and family services shall create a report of the best practices and standards developed under division (A)(1) of this section and shall provide a copy of that report to the governor, the president and minority leader of the senate, and the speaker and minority leader of the house of representatives not later than December 1, 2019.

**HISTORY:**

2018 sb158, § 1, effective March 20, 2019.

# PENALTIES

### § 173.99 Penalties.

(A) Whoever violates division (C) of section 173.24 of the Revised Code is subject to a fine not to exceed one thousand dollars for each violation.

(B) Whoever violates division (C) of section 173.23 of the Revised Code is guilty of registering a false complaint, a misdemeanor of the first degree.

(C) Whoever violates division (G)(1) or (2) of section 173.19 of the Revised Code is subject to a fine not to exceed five hundred dollars for each violation.

(D) Whoever violates division (C) of section 173.44 of the Revised Code is subject to a fine of one hundred dollars.

**HISTORY:**

143 v H 359. Eff 6-12-90; 151 v H 66, § 101.01, eff. 9-29-05; 151 v H 468, § 4, eff. 7-1-07; 153 v H 1, § 101.01, eff. 7-17-09; 2013 HB 59, § 101.01, eff. Sept. 29, 2013; 2017 hb49, § 101.01, effective September 29, 2017.

**Amendment Notes**

The 2017 amendment by HB 49 substituted "Whoever violates" for "A long-term care provider, person employed by a long-term care provider, other entity, or employee of such other entity that violates" in (A); and in (C), substituted "Whoever violates" for "A long-term care provider, other entity, or person employed by a long-term care provider or other entity that violates" and "division (G)(1) or (2)" for "division (E)," and deleted "by denying a representative of the office of the state long-term care ombudsman program the access required by that division" following "Revised Code."

The 2013 amendment substituted "ombudsman" for "ombudsperson" in (C).

153 v H 1, effective July 17, 2009, deleted former (E), which read: "Whoever violates division (B) of section 173.90 of the Revised Code is guilty of a misdemeanor of the first degree".

Section 4, 151 v H 468, effective July 1, 2007, added (E).

151 v H 66, effective September 29, 2005, added (C) and (D).

#### RESEARCH REFERENCES AND PRACTICE AIDS

**Cross-References to Related Sections**

Penalties for misdemeanor, RC § 2929.21.

# TITLE 3

# COUNTIES



# CHAPTER 317

# RECORDER



### § 317.41 Free distribution of living will and durable power of attorney for health care forms.

A county recorder, upon request, may distribute to any person free of charge a copy of the printed form of the declaration described in section 2133.07 of the Revised Code and a copy of the printed form of the durable power of attorney for health care described in section 1337.17 of the Revised Code.

**HISTORY:**

146 v H 644. Eff 11-6-96.

# CHAPTER 323

# COLLECTION OF TAXES



# VALUATION OF HOMESTEAD PROPERTY

### § 323.151 Definitions.

As used in sections 323.151 to 323.159 of the Revised Code:

(A)(1) "Homestead" means either of the following:

(a) A dwelling, including a unit in a multiple-unit dwelling and a manufactured home or mobile home taxed as real property pursuant to division (B) of section 4503.06 of the Revised Code, owned and occupied as a home by an individual whose domicile is in this state and who has not acquired ownership from a person, other than the individual's spouse, related by consanguinity or affinity for the purpose of qualifying for the real property tax reduction provided in section 323.152 of the Revised Code.

(b) A unit in a housing cooperative that is occupied as a home, but not owned, by an individual whose domicile is in this state.

(2) The homestead shall include so much of the land surrounding it, not exceeding one acre, as is reasonably necessary for the use of the dwelling or unit as a home. An owner includes a holder of one of the several estates in fee, a vendee in possession under a purchase agreement or a land contract, a mortgagor, a life tenant, one or more tenants with a right of survivorship, tenants in common, and a settlor of a revocable or irrevocable inter vivos trust holding the title to a homestead occupied by the settlor as of right under the trust. The tax commissioner shall adopt rules for the uniform classification and valuation of real property or portions of real property as homesteads.

(B) "Sixty-five years of age or older" means a person who has attained age sixty-four prior to the first day of January of the year of application for reduction in real estate taxes.

(C) "Total income" means Ohio adjusted gross income of the owner and the owner's spouse for the year preceding the year in which application for a reduction in taxes is made, as determined under division (A) of section 5747.01 of the Revised Code.

(D) "Permanently and totally disabled" means that a person other than a disabled veteran has, on the first day of January of the year of application for reduction in real estate taxes, some impairment in body or mind that makes the person unable to work at any substantially remunerative employment that the person is reasonably able to perform and that will, with reasonable probability, continue for an indefinite period of at least twelve months without any present indication of recovery therefrom or has been certified as permanently and totally disabled by a state or federal agency having the function of so classifying persons.

(E) "Housing cooperative" means a housing complex of at least two units that is owned and operated by a nonprofit corporation that issues a share of the corporation's stock to an individual, entitling the individual to live in a unit of the complex, and collects a monthly maintenance fee from the individual to maintain, operate, and pay the taxes of the complex.

(F) "Disabled veteran" means a person who is a veteran of the armed forces of the United States, including reserve components thereof, or of the national guard, who has been discharged or released from active duty in the armed forces under honorable conditions, and who has received a total disability rating or a total disability rating for compensation based on individual unemployability for a service-connected disability or combination of service-connected disabilities as prescribed in Title 38, Part 4 of the Code of Federal Regulations, as amended.

(G) "Public service officer" means a peace officer, firefighter, first responder, EMT-basic, EMT-I, or paramedic, or an individual holding any equivalent position in another state.

(H) "Killed in the line of duty" means either of the following:

(1) Death in the line of duty;

(2) Death from injury sustained in the line of duty, including heart attack or other fatal injury or illness caused while in the line of duty.

(I) "Peace officer" has the same meaning as in section 2935.01 of the Revised Code.

(J) "Firefighter" means a firefighter, whether paid or volunteer, of a lawfully constituted fire department.

(K) "First responder," "EMT-basic," "EMT-I," and "paramedic" have the same meanings as in section 4765.01 of the Revised Code.

**HISTORY:**

134 v H 475 (Eff 12-20-71); 134 v S 535 (Eff 6-30-72); 136 v H 23 (Eff 5-1-75); 136 v S 24 (Eff 11-7-75); 136 v S 489 (Eff 9-1-76); 136 v H 920 (Eff 10-11-76); 137 v H 1 (Eff 8-26-77); 140 v H 260 (Eff 9-27-83); 140 v S 201 (Eff 4-4-85); 141 v S 121 (Eff 10-17-85); 141 v H 182 (Eff 3-13-87); 144 v H 66 (Eff 7-11-91); 144 v H 641 (Eff 10-6-92); 146 v H 117 (Eff 6-30-95); 147 v S 142 (Eff 3-30-99); 148 v S 6 (Eff 8-12-99); 148 v H 595. Eff 4-5-2001; 150 v H 369, § 1, eff. 11-26-04; 152 v H 119, § 101.01, eff. 6-30-07; 152 v H 130, § 1, eff. 4-7-09; 2013 HB 59, § 101.01, eff. Sept. 29, 2013; 2014 HB 85, § 1, eff. Sept. 11, 2014; 2015 sb10, § 1, effective March 23, 2016; 2019 hb166, § 101.01, effective October 17, 2019; 2020 hb17, § 1, effective January 15, 2021.

**Editor's Notes**

Acts 2015, SB 10, § 3 provides: "The amendment by this act of section 323.151 of the Revised Code applies to tax year 2015 and thereafter."

The provisions of § 803.06 of 152 v H 119 read as follows:

SECTION 803.06. The amendments by this act to sections 323.151, 323.152, 323.153, and 323.154 of the Revised Code are first effective for tax year 2007, and the amendments to sections 4503.064, 4503.065, 4503.066, and 4503.067 of the Revised Code are first effective for tax year 2008, and the following provisions shall apply:

(A) Notwithstanding the filing deadlines set forth in sections 323.153 and 4503.066 of the Revised Code, original applications requesting reductions pursuant to division (A) of section 323.152 or section 4503.065 of the Revised Code may be filed not later than October 1, 2007. Notwithstanding the deadlines set forth in division (A) of section 323.153 of the Revised Code for homesteads in a housing cooperative, not later than August 1, 2007, the nonprofit corporation that owns and operates the housing cooperative shall obtain original applications from the county auditor and provide one to each occupant in the cooperative. Not later than September 1, 2007, any occupant who may be eligible for the reduction in taxes under division (A) of section 323.152 of the Revised Code shall submit the completed application to the corporation. Not later than October 1, 2007, the corporation shall file all completed applications and the information required by division (B) of section 323.159 of the Revised Code with the county auditor of the county in which the occupants' homesteads are located.

(B) Notwithstanding the deadlines set forth in sections 323.154 and 4503.067 of the Revised Code, if an application requesting the reduction under division (A) of section 323.152 of the Revised Code for tax year 2007 or under section 4503.065 of the Revised Code for tax year 2008 is not approved or the county auditor otherwise determines that the homestead does not qualify for a reduction in taxes, the auditor's deadline to notify the applicant of the reasons for such denial shall be extended to November 1, 2007.

The provisions of § 3 of HB 672 (148 v —) read as follows:

SECTION 3. Sections 323.151, 323.152, 323.154, and 323.155 of the Revised Code, as amended by Am. Sub. S.B. 142 of the 122nd General Assembly, and sections 323.153 and 323.156 of the Revised Code, as amended by this act, apply to 2000 and thereafter.

The provisions of § 3(A) of SB 6 (148 v —) read as follows:

SECTION 3. (A)(1) Except as otherwise provided in division (A)(2) of this section, the amendments made by this act to division (C) of section 323.151 and division (A) of section 323.152 of the Revised Code first apply to tax year 1999. A person whose homestead first becomes eligible for the reduction in taxable value or is entitled to an increased reduction for tax year 1999 because of the amendments made to either of those divisions may apply for the reduction or increase therein for that year not later than 90 days after the effective date of this section, notwithstanding filing requirements to the contrary under division (A)(3) of section 323.153 of the Revised Code.

(2) Notwithstanding division (A)(3) of section 323.152 of the Revised Code, as amended by this act, the adjustment to the dollar amount by which taxable value is reduced under that division shall be made first in calendar year 2001 and thereafter. The reduction resulting from that adjustment first applies to tax years 2002 and thereafter.

**Amendment Notes**

The 2020 amendment by HB 17 added (G) through (K).

The 2019 amendment by HB 166 in (C), substituted "modified adjusted gross income, as that term is defined in section 5747.01 of the Revised Code" for "Ohio adjusted gross income" and deleted "as determined under division (A) of section 5747.01 of the Revised Code" following "is made" at the end."

The 2015 amendment by SB 10, in (F), substituted "been discharged or released from active duty in the armed forces under honorable conditions, and who has received a" for "received a permanent", inserted "for compensation based on individual unemployability", and substituted "as prescribed in Title 38" for "for which the schedule for rating disabilities in Schedule 38".

The 2014 amendment by HB 85 substituted "that a person other than a disabled veteran" for "a person who" in (D); and added (F).

The 2013 amendment inserted (C); and redesignated former (C) and (D) as (D) and (E).

152 v H 130, effective April 7, 2009, redesignated the former provisions of (A) as (A)(1) and (2); in present (A)(2), inserted "or irrevocable"; and, in (D), deleted "hundred fifty" following "two".

152 v H 119, effective June 30, 2007, deleted (C) and (D), defining "total income", "old age and survivors benefits received pursuant to the 'Social Security Act' ", and "tier I railroad retirement benefits received pursuant to the 'Railroad Retirement Act' ", and redesignated the remaining subsections accordingly.

**Applicability**

Acts 2020, HB 17, § 3 provides: "The amendment by this act of sections 323.151, 323.152, and 323.153 of the Revised Code applies to tax year 2020 and every tax year thereafter. The amendment by this act of sections 4503.064, 4503.065, and 4503.066 of the Revised Code applies to tax year 2021 and every tax year thereafter."

Acts 2019, HB 166, § 757.150 provides: "(A) The amendment by this act of section 323.151 of the Revised Code applies to section 323.152 of the Revised Code for tax year 2020 and every tax year thereafter and to section 4503.065 of the Revised Code for tax year 2021 and every tax year thereafter.

"(B) Except as provided in division (C) of this section, the amendment or repeal by this act of sections 5747.01, 5747.02, 5747.022, 5747.025, 5747.05, 5747.054, 5747.055, 5747.06, 5747.29, 5747.65, and 5748.01 of the Revised Code applies to taxable years beginning on or after January 1, 2019.

"(C) The amendment by this act of divisions (A)(31), (B), and (HH) of section 5747.01 of the Revised Code applies to taxable years beginning on or after January 1, 2020."

## NOTES TO DECISIONS

Analysis

Contruction with other law
Owner

**Contruction with other law**

Taxpayer's explicit claim under former R.C. 5747.24(B)(1) to be domiciled outside Ohio did not bind the tax commissioner because the statement was false, as the evidence, including a contradictory application for a homestead exemption on an Ohio home, established that the taxpayers were Ohio domiciliaries under the common law for the tax year at issue; therefore, the taxpayer was not entitled to the irrebuttable presumption against Ohio domicile. Cunningham v. Testa, 2015-Ohio-2744, 144 Ohio St. 3d 40, 40 N.E.3d 1096, 2015 Ohio LEXIS 1715 (Ohio 2015).

**Owner**

Although the auditor urged that recognizing a trustee's status as owner would lead to absurd results that the General Assembly did not intend and the auditor pointed out that in many cases a bank or an unrelated third party might be the trustee, and rhetorically asked whether those trustees would be entitled to the Homestead Exemption in derogation of the rights of the beneficiaries, the plain terms of R.C. 323.151 limited the exemption to a dwelling "owned and occupied as a home by an individual," along with other personal restrictions. As a result, a bank-trustee would not qualify because a bank was not an individual and would not be able to occupy a dwelling as its home; nor did the court anticipate that fiduciary duty and trust terms would usually permit an individual trustee to occupy a dwelling as a home apart from a familial relationship with the settlor or beneficiary, and the statute restricted the availability of the exemption where related persons transferred the property for the purpose of creating an entitlement to the exemption. Gilman v. Hamilton County Bd. of Revision, 127 Ohio St. 3d 154, 2010 Ohio 4992, 937 N.E.2d 109, 2010 Ohio LEXIS 2657 (2010), remanded by 2011 Ohio Tax LEXIS 44 (Ohio B.T.A. Jan. 11, 2011).

"Owner" for purposes of R.C. 323.151(A)(2) encompassed the trustee of a trust to which real property was subject. Gilman v. Hamilton County Bd. of Revision, 127 Ohio St. 3d 154, 2010 Ohio 4992, 937 N.E.2d 109, 2010 Ohio LEXIS 2657 (2010), remanded by 2011 Ohio Tax LEXIS 44 (Ohio B.T.A. Jan. 11, 2011).

Although the county auditor contended that when property was held in trust, the property qualified for the homestead exemption under R.C. 323.151(A)(2) only if the settlor of the trust was the resident and occupant of the property, the court held that "owner" for purposes of R.C. 323.151(A)(2) encompassed the trustee of a trust to which real property was subject, and it followed that when the other requirements of the statute were satisfied, a dwelling that was held in trust may qualify as a "homestead" when the trustee was an individual who occupied the property as a home. "Owner" encompassed holders of legal title without regard to any division of legal and equitable estates, and accordingly, the trustee qualified as an owner under R.C. 323.151(A)(2) by virtue of her authority over the property as trustee; therefore, the BTA acted reasonably and lawfully when it reversed the determination of the county Board of Revision and granted the homestead exemption for tax year 2007. Gilman v. Hamilton County Bd. of Revision, 127 Ohio St. 3d 154, 2010 Ohio 4992, 937 N.E.2d 109, 2010 Ohio LEXIS 2657 (2010), remanded by 2011 Ohio Tax LEXIS 44 (Ohio B.T.A. Jan. 11, 2011).

## ATTORNEY GENERAL OPINIONS

When a taxpayer, who qualified as of January 1st for a homestead exemption, filed an application for the tax reduction, but sells the property later in the year, the real property taxes on that particular piece of property are reduced for that calendar year, and such reduction shall be recorded on the general tax list and duplicate pursuant to R.C. 323.15.4 and 323.15.5. Where a qualifying taxpayer filed an application for the homestead exemption and then dies, the real property taxes on the homestead are reduced for that calendar year, even though the surviving spouse is not 65 years of age: 1973 Ohio Op. Att'y Gen. No. 027 (1973).

The land which a taxpayer owns, and on which he lives in a mobile home, is a part of the taxpayer's homestead, and the real property taxes on such land may be reduced pursuant to R.C. 323.15.1 et seq: 1973 Ohio Op. Att'y Gen. No. 003 (1973).

Under R.C. 319.30.1 the county auditor is required to apply the ten per cent tax rollback, and then to submit a tax duplicate and a certificate of reduction under the homestead exemption to the county treasurer, who then applies the homestead exemption pursuant to R.C. 323.15.1 et seq: 1972 Ohio Op. Att'y Gen. No. 115 (1972).

Neither the five per cent tax rollback provided in § 6 of Am Sub H No. 475, effective Dec. 20, 1971, nor a reduction in taxes pursuant to R.C. 323.15.1 et seq (homestead exemption), is forfeited because of delinquency in tax payments: 1973 Ohio Op. Att'y Gen. No. 022 (1973).

Under R.C. 323.151(A), a person who owns a life estate in a homestead is an owner of a homestead for purposes of R.C. 323.152. The county auditor is not required to notify anyone other than a life estate owner in a homestead who applies for a reduction in real property taxes under R.C. 323.152(A) when the auditor denies the life estate owner's application for the reduction or determines that the life estate owner does not qualify for the reduction. 2007 Ohio Op. Att'y Gen. No. 021 (2007).

## RESEARCH REFERENCES AND PRACTICE AIDS

**Cross-References to Related Sections**

Application for reduction in real property taxes, RC § 323.15.3.

Costs of administering exemption paid from general revenue fund, RC § 323.15.6.

Employees; rules, RC § 323.15.7.

Schedule of reduction in taxable value, RC § 323.15.2.

Tax commissioner shall furnish forms, RC § 5715.30.

**Comparative Legislation**

Definitions; valuation of homestead property:

IL—35 Ill. Comp. Stat. § 200/15-170

KY—KRS § 132.810

MI—MCLS § 211.7

NY—NY CLS RPTL § 467

**Practice Manuals and Treatises**

Anderson's Ohio Elder Law Practice Manual § 3.9 Funding Choices

## § 323.152 Computation of reduction in taxable value.

In addition to the reduction in taxes required under section 319.302 of the Revised Code, taxes shall be reduced as provided in divisions (A) and (B) of this section.

(A)(1)(a) Division (A)(1) of this section applies to any of the following persons:

(i) A person who is permanently and totally disabled;

(ii) A person who is sixty-five years of age or older;

(iii) A person who is the surviving spouse of a deceased person who was permanently and totally disabled or sixty-five years of age or older and who applied and qualified for a reduction in taxes under this division in the year of death, provided the surviving spouse is at least fifty-nine but not sixty-five or more years of age on the date the deceased spouse dies.

(b) Real property taxes on a homestead owned and occupied, or a homestead in a housing cooperative occupied, by a person to whom division (A)(1) of this section applies shall be reduced for each year for which an application for the reduction has been approved. The reduction shall equal one of the following amounts, as applicable to the person:

(i) If the person received a reduction under division (A)(1) of this section for tax year 2006, the greater of the reduction for that tax year or the amount computed under division (A)(1)(c) of this section;

(ii) If the person received, for any homestead, a reduction under division (A)(1) of this section for tax year 2013 or under division (A) of section 4503.065 of the Revised Code for tax year 2014 or the person is the surviving spouse of such a person and the surviving spouse is at least fifty-nine years of age on the date the deceased spouse dies, the amount computed under division (A)(1)(c) of this section. For purposes of divisions (A)(1)(b)(ii) and (iii) of this section, a person receives a reduction under division (A)(1) of this section or under division (A) of section 4503.065 of the Revised Code for tax year 2013 or 2014, respectively, if the person files a late application for that respective tax year that is approved by the county auditor under section 323.153 or 4503.066 of the Revised Code.

(iii) If the person is not described in division (A)(1)(b)(i) or (ii) of this section and the person's total income does not exceed thirty thousand dollars, as adjusted under division (A)(1)(d) of this section, the amount computed under division (A)(1)(c) of this section.

(c) The amount of the reduction under division (A)(1)(c) of this section equals the product of the following:

(i) Twenty-five thousand dollars of the true value of the property in money;

(ii) The assessment percentage established by the tax commissioner under division (B) of section 5715.01 of the Revised Code, not to exceed thirty-five per cent;

(iii) The effective tax rate used to calculate the taxes charged against the property for the current year, where "effective tax rate" is defined as in section 323.08 of the Revised Code;

(iv) The quantity equal to one minus the sum of the percentage reductions in taxes received by the property for the current tax year under section 319.302 of the Revised Code and division (B) of section 323.152 of the Revised Code.

(d) Each calendar year, the tax commissioner shall adjust the total income threshold described in division (A)(1)(b)(iii) of this section by completing the following calculations in September of each year:

(i) Determine the percentage increase in the gross domestic product deflator determined by the bureau of economic analysis of the United States department of commerce from the first day of January of the preceding calendar year to the last day of December of the preceding calendar year;

(ii) Multiply that percentage increase by the total income threshold for the current tax year;

(iii) Add the resulting product to the total income threshold for the current tax year;

(iv) Round the resulting sum to the nearest multiple of one hundred dollars.

The commissioner shall certify the amount resulting from the adjustment to each county auditor not later than the first day of December each year. The certified amount applies to the following tax year for persons described in division (A)(1)(b)(iii) of this section. The commissioner shall not make the adjustment in any calendar year in which the amount resulting from the adjustment would be less than the total income threshold for the current tax year.

(2) Real property taxes on a homestead owned and occupied, or a homestead in a housing cooperative occupied, by a disabled veteran shall be reduced for each year for which an application for the reduction has been approved. The reduction shall equal the product obtained by multiplying fifty thousand dollars of the true value of the property in money by the amounts described in divisions (A)(1)(c)(ii) to (iv) of this section. The reduction is in lieu of any reduction under section 323.158 of the Revised Code or division (A)(1) or (3) of this section. The reduction applies to only one homestead owned and occupied by a disabled veteran.

If a homestead qualifies for a reduction in taxes under division (A)(2) of this section for the year in which the disabled veteran dies, and the disabled veteran is survived by a spouse who occupied the homestead when the disabled veteran died and who acquires ownership of the homestead or, in the case of a homestead that is a unit in a housing cooperative, continues to occupy the homestead, the reduction shall continue through the year in which the surviving spouse dies or remarries.

(3) Real property taxes on a homestead owned and occupied, or a homestead in a housing cooperative occupied, by the surviving spouse of a public service officer killed in the line of duty shall be reduced for each year for which an application for the reduction has been approved. The reduction shall equal the product obtained by multiplying fifty thousand dollars of the true value of the property in money by the amounts described in divisions (A)(1)(c)(ii) to (iv) of

this section. The reduction is in lieu of any reduction under section 323.158 of the Revised Code or division (A)(1) or (2) of this section. The reduction applies to only one homestead owned and occupied by such a surviving spouse. A homestead qualifies for a reduction in taxes under division (A)(3) of this section for the tax year in which the public service officer dies through the tax year in which the surviving spouse dies or remarries.

(B) To provide a partial exemption, real property taxes on any homestead, and manufactured home taxes on any manufactured or mobile home on which a manufactured home tax is assessed pursuant to division (D)(2) of section 4503.06 of the Revised Code, shall be reduced for each year for which an application for the reduction has been approved. The amount of the reduction shall equal two and one-half per cent of the amount of taxes to be levied by qualifying levies on the homestead or the manufactured or mobile home after applying section 319.301 of the Revised Code. For the purposes of this division, "qualifying levy" has the same meaning as in section 319.302 of the Revised Code.

(C) The reductions granted by this section do not apply to special assessments or respread of assessments levied against the homestead, and if there is a transfer of ownership subsequent to the filing of an application for a reduction in taxes, such reductions are not forfeited for such year by virtue of such transfer.

(D) The reductions in taxable value referred to in this section shall be applied solely as a factor for the purpose of computing the reduction of taxes under this section and shall not affect the total value of property in any subdivision or taxing district as listed and assessed for taxation on the tax lists and duplicates, or any direct or indirect limitations on indebtedness of a subdivision or taxing district. If after application of sections 5705.31 and 5705.32 of the Revised Code, including the allocation of all levies within the ten-mill limitation to debt charges to the extent therein provided, there would be insufficient funds for payment of debt charges not provided for by levies in excess of the ten-mill limitation, the reduction of taxes provided for in sections 323.151 to 323.159 of the Revised Code shall be proportionately adjusted to the extent necessary to provide such funds from levies within the ten-mill limitation.

(E) No reduction shall be made on the taxes due on the homestead of any person convicted of violating division (D) or (E) of section 323.153 of the Revised Code for a period of three years following the conviction.

**HISTORY:**

134 v H 475 (Eff 12-20-71); 134 v S 535 (Eff 6-30-72); 135 v H 86 (Eff 6-29-73); 135 v S 247 (Eff 7-17-73); 135 v H 1064 (Eff 7-26-74); 136 v H 23 (Eff 5-1-75); 136 v S 24 (Eff 11-7-75); 138 v S 6 (Eff 6-7-79); 138 v H 204 (Eff 1-1-80); 138 v H 1238 (Eff 12-19-80); 141 v H 182 (Eff 3-13-87); 144 v H 66 (Eff 7-11-91); 146 v H 117 (Eff 6-30-95); 147 v S 142 (Eff 3-30-99); 148 v S 6 (Eff 8-12-99); 148 v H 595 (Eff 4-5-2001); 149 v S 200. Eff 9-6-2002; 150 v H 127, § 1, eff. 3-11-04; 151 v H 66, § 101.01, eff. 6-30-05; 152 v H 119, § 101.01, eff. 6-30-07; 152 v H 130, § 1, eff. 4-7-09; 2013 HB 59, § 101.01, eff. Sept. 29, 2013; 2013 HB 72, § 1, eff. Jan. 30, 2014; 2013 HB 311, § 1, eff. Jan. 30, 2014; 2014 HB 85, § 1, eff. Sept. 11, 2014; 2020 hb17, § 1, effective January 15, 2021.

**Editor's Notes**

Acts 2013, HB 311, § 6 provides: "Sections 323.152 and 4503.065 of the Revised Code are amended by this act and also by H.B. 72 of the 130th General Assembly (effective January 30, 2014). The amendments of H.B. 72 are included in this act to confirm the intention to retain them, but are not intended to be effective until January 30, 2014."

See provisions of § 803.06 of 152 v H 119 following RC § 323.151.

The provisions of § 557.15 of 151 v H 66 read as follows:

SECTION 557.15. The amendment by this act of sections 319.302 and 323.152 of the Revised Code first applies in tax year 2005.

The provisions of § 10, H.B. 127 (150 v —), read as follows:

Section 10. (A) The amendment by this act of section 323.152 of the Revised Code applies to tax year 2004 and thereafter.

See provisions, § 3 of HB 672 (148 v —) following RC § 323.151.

See provisions, § 3(A) of SB 6 (148 v —), following RC § 323.151.

**Amendment Notes**

The 2020 amendment by HB 17 added "or (3)" in the second to the last sentence of the first paragraph of (A)(2); and added (A)(3).

The 2014 amendment by HB 85 redesignated former (A)(1) through (A)(4) as (A)(1)(a) through (A)(1)(d); inserted "division (A) of" in the first and second sentences of (A)(1)(b)(ii); added present (A)(2); and made related and stylistic changes.

The 2013 amendment by HB 311 inserted "for any homestead" in the first sentence of (A)(2)(b).

The 2013 amendment by HB 72, in the first sentence of (A)(2)(b), substituted "section 4503.065" for "section 4503.066" and inserted "or the person is the surviving spouse of such a person and the surviving spouse is at least fifty-nine years of age on the date the deceased spouse dies"; and substituted "is not described in division (A)(2)(a) or (b) of this section" for "did not receive a reduction under division (A) of this section or under section 4503.066 of the Revised Code for tax year 2013" in (A)(2)(c).

The 2013 amendment by HB 59 added "persons" to the end of the introductory language of (A)(1); substituted "one of the following amounts, as applicable to the person" for "the greater of the reduction granted for the tax year preceding the first tax year to which this section applies pursuant to Section 803.06 of Am. Sub. H.B. 119 of the 127th general assembly, if the taxpayer received a reduction for that preceding tax year, or" in the second sentence of the introductory language of (A)(2); added (A)(2)(a) through (A)(2)(c) and (A)(4); added the (A)(3) designation; added "The amount of the reduction under division (A)(3) of this section equals" to the beginning of the introductory language of (A)(3); and in (B), inserted "by qualifying levies" in the second sentence and added the last sentence.

152 v H 130, effective April 7, 2009, substituted "an application for the reduction has been approved" for "the owner obtains a certificate of reduction from the county auditor under section 323.154 of the Revised Code or for which the occupant obtains a certificate of reduction in accordance with section 323.159 of the Revised Code" in the introductory language of (A)(2), and substituted the same for "the owner obtains a certificate of reduction from the county auditor under section 323.154 of the Revised Code" in (B); and corrected internal references.

152 v H 119, effective June 30, 2007, rewrote (A)(2); and deleted (A)(3), pertaining to calculations to a schedule of total income versus taxable value required by the tax commissioner.

151 v H 66, effective June 30, 2005, in (B), added "To provide a partial exemption" to the beginning, and substituted "two and one-half per cent of the amount of taxes to be levied" for "one-fourth of the amount by which the taxes charged and payable" and "after applying section 319.301" for "are reduced for such year under section 319.302".

**Applicability**

Acts 2020, HB 17, § 3 provides: "The amendment by this act of sections 323.151, 323.152, and 323.153 of the Revised Code applies to tax year 2020 and every tax year thereafter. The amendment by this act of sections 4503.064, 4503.065, and 4503.066 of the Revised Code applies to tax year 2021 and every tax year thereafter."

Acts 2019, HB 166, § 757.150 provides: "(A) The amendment by this act of section 323.151 of the Revised Code applies to section 323.152 of the Revised Code for tax year 2020 and every tax year thereafter and to section 4503.065 of the Revised Code for tax year 2021 and every tax year thereafter."

## NOTES TO DECISIONS

Analysis

Constitutionality
January First

**Constitutionality**

Denial of appellants' application for homestead exemption was proper, because plain language of R.C. 323.11 did not establish a new tax lien date for newly platted parcels, but rather merely permitted apportionment of taxes between portions of a parcel that existed as of January 1, based upon the value as of January 1; the parcel did not exist as a stand-alone parcel on January 1, 2007, and in May 2007, appellants applied for homestead exemption for the parcel for tax year 2007. Dugan v. Franklin County Bd. of Revision, 2014-Ohio-4491, 2014 Ohio App. LEXIS 4388 (Ohio Ct. App., Franklin County 2014).

The provision in R.C. 323.15.2(B) for the "rollback" or partial exemption from taxes charged and payable on homesteads is not such a classification that would be violative of the equal protection section of Ohio Const. art I, § 2: State ex rel. Swetland v. Kinney, 62 Ohio St. 2d 23, 16 Ohio Op. 3d 14, 402 N.E.2d 542, 1980 Ohio LEXIS 682 (Ohio 1980).

Revised Code § 323.15.2(B), which partially exempts a "homestead" as defined within R.C. 323.15.1(A) from real estate taxation, is a valid exercise of the General Assembly's power to tax real property, and to exempt certain classifications of real property as provided by Ohio Const. art XII, § 2: State ex rel. Swetland v. Kinney, 62 Ohio St. 2d 23, 16 Ohio Op. 3d 14, 402 N.E.2d 542, 1980 Ohio LEXIS 682 (Ohio 1980).

**January First**

County board of revision erred in denying an owner's "late" application for the homestead exemption for the tax year 2013 on the basis that he did not own the residence as of January 1, 2013 because the owner, who took title to the residence on August 30, 2013, was not required to occupy the residence as of January 1, 2013, for the tax year 2013 homestead exemption. Devan v. Cuyahoga County Bd. of Revision, 2015-Ohio-4279, 45 N.E.3d 661, 2015 Ohio App. LEXIS 4169 (Ohio Ct. App., Cuyahoga County 2015).

Denial of appellants' application for homestead exemption was proper, because plain language of R.C. 323.11 did not establish a new tax lien date for newly platted parcels, but rather merely permitted apportionment of taxes between portions of a parcel that existed as of January 1, based upon the value as of January 1; the parcel did not exist as a stand-alone parcel on January 1, 2007, and in May 2007, appellants applied for homestead exemption for the parcel for tax year 2007. Dugan v. Franklin County Bd. of Revision, 2014-Ohio-4491, 2014 Ohio App. LEXIS 4388 (Ohio Ct. App., Franklin County 2014).

### ATTORNEY GENERAL OPINIONS

Under R.C. 319.30.1 the county auditor is required to apply the ten per cent tax rollback, and then to submit a tax duplicate and a certificate of reduction under the homestead exemption to the county treasurer, who then applies the homestead exemption pursuant to R.C. 323.15.1 et seq: 1972 Ohio Op. Att'y Gen. No. 115 (1972).

Where a qualifying taxpayer filed an application for the homestead exemption and then dies, the real property taxes on the homestead are reduced for that calendar year, even though the surviving spouse is not 65 years of age: 1973 Ohio Op. Att'y Gen. No. 027 (1973).

Under R.C. 323.151(A), a person who owns a life estate in a homestead is an owner of a homestead for purposes of R.C. 323.152. The county auditor is not required to notify anyone other than a life estate owner in a homestead who applies for a reduction in real property taxes under R.C. 323.152(A) when the auditor denies the life estate owner's application for the reduction or determines that the life estate owner does not qualify for the reduction. 2007 Ohio Op. Att'y Gen. No. 021 (2007).

Neither the five per cent tax rollback provided in § 6 of Am Sub H No. 475, effective Dec. 20, 1971, nor a reduction in taxes pursuant to R.C. 323.15.1 et seq (homestead exemption), is forfeited because of delinquency in tax payments. The ten per cent penalty, imposed by R.C. 5719.17 on delinquent taxes, is computed after application of the five per cent tax rollback (or ten per cent rollback under R.C. 319.30.1, as the case may be) and the homestead exemption (OAG No. 73-008, approved and followed): 1973 Ohio Op. Att'y Gen. No. 022 (1973).

### RESEARCH REFERENCES AND PRACTICE AIDS

**Cross-References to Related Sections**

Application for reduction, RC § 323.15.3.
Certain property tax reduced by ten percent, RC § 319.30.2.
Certificate of reduction issued by county auditor, RC § 323.154.
Costs of administering exemption paid from general revenue fund, RC § 323.15.6.
Homestead defined, RC § 323.15.1.
Homestead exemption defined in re manufactured home, RC § 4503.06.4.
Lower rate for owners receiving homestead exemption, RC § 322.07.
Partial tax exemption on homesteads in counties with major league teams, RC § 323.15.8.
Property tax deduction subsequent to receipt of certificate, RC § 323.155.
Statement by grantee of real property re homestead exemption required, RC § 319.20.2.
Tax commissioner shall furnish forms, RC § 5715.30.
Tax on manufactured or mobile home, RC § 4503.06.
Tax valuation defined, RC § 133.01.

## § 323.153 Application for reduction.

(A) To obtain a reduction in real property taxes under division (A) or (B) of section 323.152 of the Revised Code or in manufactured home taxes under division (B) of section 323.152 of the Revised Code, the owner shall file an application with the county auditor of the county in which the owner's homestead is located.

To obtain a reduction in real property taxes under division (A) of section 323.152 of the Revised Code, the occupant of a homestead in a housing cooperative shall file an application with the nonprofit corporation that owns and operates the housing cooperative, in accordance with this paragraph. Not later than the first day of March each year, the corporation shall obtain applications from the county auditor's office and provide one to each new occupant. Not later than the first day of May, any occupant who may be eligible for a reduction in taxes under division (A) of section 323.152 of the Revised Code shall submit the completed application to the corporation. Not later than the fifteenth day of May, the corporation shall file all completed applications, and the information required by division (B) of section 323.159 of the Revised Code, with the county auditor of the county in which the occupants' homesteads are located. Continuing applications shall be furnished to an occupant in the manner provided in division (C)(4) of this section.

(1) An application for reduction based upon a physical disability shall be accompanied by a certificate signed by a physician, and an application for reduction based upon a mental disability shall be accompanied by a certificate signed by a physician or psychologist licensed to practice in this state, attesting to the fact that the applicant is permanently and totally disabled. The certificate shall be in a form that the tax commissioner requires and shall include the definition of permanently and totally disabled as set forth in section 323.151 of the Revised Code. An application for reduction based upon a disability certified as permanent and total by a state or federal agency having the function of so classifying persons shall be accompanied by a certificate from that agency.

An application by a disabled veteran for the reduction under division (A)(2) of section 323.152 of the Revised Code shall be accompanied by a letter or other written confirmation from the United States department of veterans affairs, or its predecessor or successor agency, showing that the veteran qualifies as a disabled veteran.

An application by the surviving spouse of a public service officer killed in the line of duty for the reduction under division (A)(3) of section 323.152 of the Revised Code shall be accompanied by a letter or other written confirmation from an employee or officer of the board of trustees of a retirement or pension fund in this state or another state or from the chief or other chief executive of the department, agency, or other employer for which the public service officer served when killed in the line of duty affirming that the public service officer was killed in the line of duty.

An application for a reduction under division (A) of section 323.152 of the Revised Code constitutes a continuing application for a reduction in taxes for each year in which the dwelling is the applicant's homestead.

(2) An application for a reduction in taxes under division (B) of section 323.152 of the Revised Code shall be filed only if the homestead or manufactured or mobile home was transferred in the preceding year or did not qualify for and receive the reduction in taxes under that division for the preceding tax year. The application for homesteads transferred in the preceding year shall be incorporated into any form used by the county auditor to administer the tax law in respect to the conveyance of real property pursuant to section 319.20 of the Revised Code or of used manufactured homes or used mobile homes as defined in section 5739.0210 of the Revised Code. The owner of a manufactured or mobile home who has elected under division (D)(4) of section 4503.06 of the Revised Code to be taxed under division (D)(2) of that section for the ensuing year may file the application at the time of making that election. The application shall contain a statement that failure by the applicant to affirm on the application that the dwelling on the property conveyed is the applicant's homestead prohibits the owner from receiving the reduction in taxes until a proper application is filed within the period prescribed by division (A)(3) of this section. Such an application constitutes a continuing application for a reduction in taxes for each year in which the dwelling is the applicant's homestead.

(3) Failure to receive a new application filed under division (A)(1) or (2) or notification under division (C) of this section after an application for reduction has been approved is prima-facie evidence that the original applicant is entitled to the reduction in taxes calculated on the basis of the information contained in the original application. The original application and any subsequent application, including any late application, shall be in the form of a signed statement and shall be filed on or before the thirty-first day of December of the year for which the reduction is sought. The original application and any subsequent application for a reduction in manufactured home taxes shall be filed in the year preceding the year for which the reduction is sought. The statement shall be on a form, devised

and supplied by the tax commissioner, which shall require no more information than is necessary to establish the applicant's eligibility for the reduction in taxes and the amount of the reduction, and, except for homesteads that are units in a housing cooperative, shall include an affirmation by the applicant that ownership of the homestead was not acquired from a person, other than the applicant's spouse, related to the owner by consanguinity or affinity for the purpose of qualifying for the real property or manufactured home tax reduction provided for in division (A) or (B) of section 323.152 of the Revised Code. The form shall contain a statement that conviction of willfully falsifying information to obtain a reduction in taxes or failing to comply with division (C) of this section results in the revocation of the right to the reduction for a period of three years. In the case of an application for a reduction in taxes for persons described in division (A)(1)(b)(iii) of section 323.152 of the Revised Code, the form shall contain a statement that signing the application constitutes a delegation of authority by the applicant to the tax commissioner or the county auditor, individually or in consultation with each other, to examine any tax or financial records relating to the income of the applicant as stated on the application for the purpose of determining eligibility for the exemption or a possible violation of division (D) or (E) of this section.

(B) A late application for a tax reduction for the year preceding the year in which an original application is filed, or for a reduction in manufactured home taxes for the year in which an original application is filed, may be filed with the original application. If the county auditor determines the information contained in the late application is correct, the auditor shall determine the amount of the reduction in taxes to which the applicant would have been entitled for the preceding tax year had the applicant's application been timely filed and approved in that year.

The amount of such reduction shall be treated by the auditor as an overpayment of taxes by the applicant and shall be refunded in the manner prescribed in section 5715.22 of the Revised Code for making refunds of overpayments. The county auditor shall certify the total amount of the reductions in taxes made in the current year under this division to the tax commissioner, who shall treat the full amount thereof as a reduction in taxes for the preceding tax year and shall make reimbursement to the county therefor in the manner prescribed by section 323.156 of the Revised Code, from money appropriated for that purpose.

(C)(1) If, in any year after an application has been filed under division (A)(1) or (2) of this section, the owner does not qualify for a reduction in taxes on the homestead or on the manufactured or mobile home set forth on such application, the owner shall notify the county auditor that the owner is not qualified for a reduction in taxes.

(2) If, in any year after an application has been filed under division (A)(1) of this section, the occupant of a homestead in a housing cooperative does not qualify for a reduction in taxes on the homestead, the occupant shall notify the county auditor that the occupant is not qualified for a reduction in taxes or file a new application under division (A)(1) of this section.

(3) If the county auditor or county treasurer discovers that an owner of property or occupant of a homestead in a housing cooperative not entitled to the reduction in taxes under division (A) or (B) of section 323.152 of the Revised Code failed to notify the county auditor as required by division (C)(1) or (2) of this section, a charge shall be imposed against the property in the amount by which taxes were reduced under that division for each tax year the county auditor ascertains that the property was not entitled to the reduction and was owned by the current owner or, in the case of a homestead in a housing cooperative, occupied by the current occupant. Interest shall accrue in the manner prescribed by division (B) of section 323.121 or division (G)(2) of section 4503.06 of the Revised Code on the amount by which taxes were reduced for each such tax year as if the reduction became delinquent taxes at the close of the last day the second installment of taxes for that tax year could be paid without penalty. The county auditor shall notify the owner or occupant, by ordinary mail, of the charge, of the owner's or occupant's right to appeal the charge, and of the manner in which the owner or occupant may appeal. The owner or occupant may appeal the imposition of the charge and interest by filing an appeal with the county board of revision not later than the last day prescribed for payment of real and public utility property taxes under section 323.12 of the Revised Code following receipt of the notice and occurring at least ninety days after receipt of the notice. The appeal shall be treated in the same manner as a complaint relating to the valuation or assessment of real property under Chapter 5715. of the Revised Code. The charge and any interest shall be collected as other delinquent taxes.

(4) Each year during January, the county auditor shall furnish by ordinary mail a continuing application to each person receiving a reduction under division (A) of section 323.152 of the Revised Code. The continuing application shall be used to report changes in total income, ownership, occupancy, disability, and other information earlier furnished the auditor relative to the reduction in taxes on the property. The continuing application shall be returned to the auditor not later than the thirty-first day of December; provided, that if such changes do not affect the status of the homestead exemption or the amount of the reduction to which the owner is entitled under division (A) of section 323.152 of the Revised Code or to which the occupant is entitled under section 323.159 of the Revised Code, the application does not need to be returned.

(5) Each year during February, the county auditor, except as otherwise provided in this paragraph, shall furnish by ordinary mail an original application to the owner, as of the first day of January of that year, of a homestead or a manufactured or mobile home that transferred during the preceding calendar year and that qualified for and received a reduction in taxes under division (B) of section 323.152 of the Revised Code for the preceding tax year. In order to receive the reduction under that division, the owner shall file the application with the county auditor not later than the thirty-first day of December. If the application is not timely filed, the auditor shall not grant a reduction in taxes for the homestead for the current year, and shall notify the owner that the reduction in taxes has not been granted, in the same manner prescribed under section 323.154 of the Revised Code for notification of denial of an application. Failure of an owner to receive an application does not excuse the failure of the owner to file an original application. The county auditor is not required to furnish an application under this paragraph for any homestead for which application has previously been made on a form incorporated into any form used by the county auditor to administer the tax law in respect to the conveyance of real property or of used manufactured homes or used mobile homes, and an owner who previously has applied on such a form is not required to return an application furnished under this paragraph.

(D) No person shall knowingly make a false statement for the purpose of obtaining a reduction in the person's real property or manufactured home taxes under section 323.152 of the Revised Code.

(E) No person shall knowingly fail to notify the county auditor of changes required by division (C) of this section that have the effect of maintaining or securing a reduction in taxes under section 323.152 of the Revised Code.

(F) No person shall knowingly make a false statement or certification attesting to any person's physical or mental condition for purposes of qualifying such person for tax relief pursuant to sections 323.151 to 323.159 of the Revised Code.

**HISTORY:**

134 v H 475 (Eff 12-20-71); 134 v S 535 (Eff 6-30-72); 135 v S 247 (Eff 7-17-73); 135 v H 1064 (Eff 7-26-74); 136 v H 23 (Eff 5-1-75); 136 v S 24 (Eff 11-7-75); 136 v H 920 (Eff 10-11-76); 138 v H 204 (Eff 1-1-80); 140 v H 260 (Eff 9-27-83); 141 v H 201 (Eff 7-1-85); 144 v H 641 (Eff 10-6-92); 145 v H 207 (Eff 6-30-93); 147 v H 177 (Eff 9-16-98); 147 v S 201 (Eff 12-21-98); 147 v S 142 (Eff 3-30-99); 148 v H 595 (Eff 4-5-2001); 148 v H 672. Eff 4-9-2001; 152 v H 119, § 101.01, eff. 6-30-07; 152 v H 130, § 1, eff. 4-7-09; 2013 HB 59, § 101.01, eff. Sept. 29, 2013; 2014 HB 85, § 1, eff. Sept. 11, 2014; 2016 hb166, § 1, effective September 8, 2016; 2020 hb17, § 1, effective January 15, 2021; 2021 hb110, § 101.01, effective September 30, 2021.

**Editor's Notes**

See provisions of § 803.06 of 152 v H 119 following RC § 323.151.

The provisions of § 824.03 of 152 v H 119 read in part as follows:

SECTION 824.03. The General Assembly, applying the principle stated in division (B) of section 1.52 of the Revised Code that amendments are to be harmonized if reasonably capable of simultaneous operation, finds that the following sections, presented in this act as composites of the sections as amended by the acts indicated, are the resulting versions of the sections in effect prior to the effective date of the sections as presented in this act:

* * *

Section 323.153 of the Revised Code as amended by both Am. H.B. 595 and Am. Sub. H.B. 672 of the 123rd General Assembly.

* * *

The finding in this section takes effect at the same time as the section referenced in the finding takes effect.

The provisions of § 5 of HB 672 (148 v —) read, in part, as follows:

SECTION 5. Section 323.153 of the Revised Code is presented in this act as a composite of the section as amended by Am. Sub. H.B. 177, Am. Sub. S.B. 201, and Am. Sub. S.B. 142, all of the 122nd General Assembly, with the new language of none of the acts shown in capital letters. * * * This is in recognition of the principle stated in division (B) of section 1.52 of the Revised Code that such amendments are to be harmonized where not substantively irreconcilable and constitutes a legislative finding that such is the resulting version in effect prior to the effective date of this act.

The provisions of § 3 of HB 595 (148 v —) read as follows:

SECTION 3. Section 323.153 of the Revised Code is presented in this act as a composite of the section as amended by Am. Sub. H.B. 177, Am. Sub. S.B. 201, and Am. Sub. S.B. 142, all of the 122nd General Assembly, with the new language of none of the acts shown in capital letters. This is in recognition of the principle stated in division (B) of section 1.52 of the Revised Code that such amendments are to be harmonized where not substantively irreconcilable and constitutes a legislative finding that such is the resulting version in effect prior to the effective date of this act.

See provisions, § 3 of HB 672 (148 v —) following RC § 323.151.

See provisions, § 3(A) of SB 6 (148 v —) following RC § 323.151.

**Amendment Notes**

The 2021 amendment by HB 110, in (C)(3), in the first sentence, substituted "an owner of property or occupant of a homestead in a housing cooperative" for "the owner of property," and added "(A) or," "or (2)" and "or, in the case of a homestead in a housing cooperative, occupied by the current occupant," in the third sentence, substituted "the owner or occupant" for "the owner" twice and added "or occupant's," and added "or occupant" in the fourth sentence.

The 2020 amendment by HB 17 redesignated the former last sentence of the first paragraph of (A)(1) as the second paragraph of (A)(1); and added the third paragraph of (A)(1).

The 2016 amendment by HB 166, in the second sentence of (A)(3), substituted "on or before the thirty-first day of December of" for "after the first Monday in January and not later than the first Monday in June" and deleted "The original application and any subsequent application for a reduction in real property taxes shall be filed in" preceding "the year for"; deleted "On the first day of July of each year" from the beginning of the second sentence of (B); and substituted "thirty-first day of December" for "first Monday in June" in the last sentence of (C)(4) and in the second sentence of (C)(5).

The 2014 amendment by HB 85 added the last sentence to the first paragraph of (A)(1); and substituted "division (A)(1)(b)(iii)" for "division (A)(2)(c)" in the last sentence of (A)(3).

The 2013 amendment added the last sentence to (A)(3); substituted "division (A)(1)" for "division (A)" twice in (C)(2); and inserted "total income" in the second sentence of (C)(4).

152 v H 130, effective April 7, 2009, in (A)(3), substituted "an application for the reduction has been approved" for "a certificate of reduction has been issued under section 323.154 of the Revised Code, or failure to receive a new application filed under division (A)(1) or notification under division (C) of this section after a certificate of reduction has been issued under section 323.159 of the Revised Code" and "except for homesteads that are units in a housing cooperative" for "for a certificate of reduction issued under section 323.154 of the Revised Code"; and, in (C)(4), substituted "receiving a reduction" for "issued a certificate of reduction under section 323.154 or 323.59 of the Revised Code with respect to a reduction in taxes", and deleted "of the homestead, including changes in or revocation of a revocable inter vivos trust, changes in" following "occupancy" and made related changes.

152 v H 119, effective June 30, 2007, in the present second paragraph of (A)(1), substituted "An application for a reduction under division (A) of section 323.152 of the Revised Code" for "Such an application", and deleted "and the amount of the reduction in taxable value to which the applicant is entitled does not exceed either the amount or percentage of the reduction to which the applicant was entitled for the year in which the application was first filed" from the end; deleted the last sentence of (A)(3), pertaining to guidelines for an application for a reduction in taxes; in (C)(1), deleted "or qualifies for a reduction in taxes that is to be based upon a reduction in taxable value less than either the percentage or amount of the reduction in taxable value to which the owner was entitled in the year the application was filed" preceding "the owner shall" and "or file a new application under division (A)(1) or (2) of this section" from the end; in (C)(4), deleted "changes in total income that would have the effect of increasing or decreasing the reduction in taxable value to which the person is entitled" following "used to report"; in (E), deleted "in taxable value of homestead property or a reduction" preceding "in taxes" and "in excess of the reduction allowed" following "in taxes"; and corrected internal references.

**Applicability**

Acts 2020, HB 17, § 3 provides: "The amendment by this act of sections 323.151, 323.152, and 323.153 of the Revised Code applies to tax year 2020 and every tax year thereafter. The amendment by this act of sections 4503.064, 4503.065, and 4503.066 of the Revised Code applies to tax year 2021 and every tax year thereafter."

### NOTES TO DECISIONS

**January First**

County board of revision erred in denying an owner's "late" application for the homestead exemption for the tax year 2013 on the basis that he did not own the residence as of January 1, 2013 because the owner, who took title to the residence on August 30, 2013, was not required to occupy the residence as of January 1, 2013, for the tax year 2013 homestead exemption. Devan v. Cuyahoga County Bd. of Revision, 2015-Ohio-4279, 45 N.E.3d 661, 2015 Ohio App. LEXIS 4169 (Ohio Ct. App., Cuyahoga County 2015).

Denial of appellants' application for homestead exemption was proper, because plain language of R.C. 323.11 did not establish a new tax lien date for newly platted parcels, but rather merely permitted apportionment of taxes between portions of a parcel that existed as of January 1, based upon the value as of January 1; the parcel did not exist as a stand-alone parcel on January 1, 2007, and in May 2007, appellants applied for homestead exemption for the parcel for tax year 2007. Dugan v. Franklin County Bd. of Revision, 2014-Ohio-4491, 2014 Ohio App. LEXIS 4388 (Ohio Ct. App., Franklin County 2014).

### RESEARCH REFERENCES AND PRACTICE AIDS

**Cross-References to Related Sections**

Penalty, RC § 323.99.

Certificate of reduction issued by county auditor, RC § 323.154.

Notice to homeowner of right to 2 ½% reduction, RC § 5713.01.1.

Prohibition on reduction of taxes, when, RC § 323.15.2.

Tax commissioner shall furnish forms, RC § 5715.30.

## § 323.154 Approval or denial of application by county auditor; appeal.

The county auditor shall approve or deny an application for reduction under section 323.152 of the Revised Code and shall so notify the applicant within thirty days after the application is approved or denied. Notification shall be provided on a form prescribed by the tax commissioner. If the application is approved, upon issuance of the notification the county auditor shall record the amount of reduction in taxes in the appropriate column on the general tax list and duplicate of real and public utility property and on the manufactured home tax list. If the application is denied, the notification shall inform the applicant of the reasons for the denial.

If an applicant believes that the application for reduction has been improperly denied or that the reduction is for less than that to which the applicant is entitled, the applicant may file an appeal with the county board of revision not later than sixty days after the notification was issued under this section. The appeal shall be treated in the same manner as a complaint relating to the valuation or assessment of real property under Chapter 5715. of the Revised Code.

**HISTORY:**

134 v H 475 (Eff 12-20-71); 135 v S 247 (Eff 7-17-73); 135 v H 1064 (Eff 7-26-74); 136 v S 24 (Eff 11-7-75); 136 v H 920 (Eff 10-11-76); 138 v H 204 (Eff 1-1-80); 138 v H 1238 (Eff 12-19-80); 140 v H 260 (Eff 9-27-83); 145 v H 207 (Eff 6-30-93); 147 v S 142 (Eff 3-30-99); 148 v H 595. Eff 4-5-2001; 152 v H 119, § 101.01, eff. 6-30-07; 152 v H 130, § 1, eff. 4-7-09; 2020 hb197, § 1, effective March 27, 2020.

**Editor's Notes**

See provisions of § 803.06 of 152 v H 119 following RC § 323.151.

See provisions, § 3 of HB 672 (148 v —) following RC § 323.151.

**Amendment Notes**

The 2020 amendment by HB 197 substituted "within thirty days after the application is approved or denied" for "not later than the first Monday in October" in the first sentence of the first paragraph; and substituted "sixty days after the notification was issued under this section" for "the date of closing of the collection for the first half of real and public utility property taxes or manufactured home taxes" in the first sentence of the second paragraph.

152 v H 130, effective April 7, 2009, rewrote the section.

152 v H 119, effective June 30, 2007, in the first paragraph, deleted "amount of the reduction in taxable value and the" preceding "total reduction".

### NOTES TO DECISIONS

**January First**

County board of revision erred in denying an owner's "late" application for the homestead exemption for the tax year 2013 on the basis that he did not own the residence as of January 1, 2013 because the owner, who took title to the residence on August 30, 2013, was not required to occupy the residence as of January 1, 2013, for the tax year 2013 homestead exemption. Devan v. Cuyahoga County Bd. of Revision, 2015-Ohio-4279, 45 N.E.3d 661, 2015 Ohio App. LEXIS 4169 (Ohio Ct. App., Cuyahoga County 2015).

Denial of appellants' application for homestead exemption was proper, because plain language of R.C. 323.11 did not establish a new tax lien date for newly platted parcels, but rather merely permitted apportionment of taxes between portions of a parcel that existed as of January 1, based upon the value as of January 1; the parcel did not exist as a stand-alone parcel on January 1, 2007, and in May 2007, appellants applied for homestead exemption for the parcel for tax year 2007. Dugan v. Franklin County Bd. of Revision, 2014-Ohio-4491, 2014 Ohio App. LEXIS 4388 (Ohio Ct. App., Franklin County 2014).

### ATTORNEY GENERAL OPINIONS

When a taxpayer, who qualifies as of January 1st for a homestead exemption, filed an application for the tax reduction, but sells the property later in the year, the real property taxes on that particular piece of property are reduced for that calendar year, and such reduction shall be recorded on the general tax list and duplicate pursuant to R.C. 323.15.4 and 323.15.5. Where a qualifying taxpayer filed an application for the homestead exemption and then dies, the real property taxes on the homestead are reduced for that calendar year, even though the surviving spouse is not 65 years of age: 1973 Ohio Op. Att'y Gen. No. 027 (1973).

### RESEARCH REFERENCES AND PRACTICE AIDS

**Cross-References to Related Sections**

Application for reduction in taxes, RC § 323.15.3.

Costs of administering exemption paid from general revenue fund, RC § 323.15.6.

Employees; rules, RC § 323.15.7.

Lower rate for owners receiving homestead exemption, RC § 322.07.

Schedule of reduction in taxable value, RC § 323.15.2.

Tax commissioner shall furnish forms, RC § 5715.30.

## § 323.155 Tax bill; reduction disregarded in determining eligibility under Title LI.

The tax bill prescribed under section 323.131 of the Revised Code shall indicate the net amount of taxes due following the reductions in taxes under sections 319.301, 319.302, 323.152, and 323.16 of the Revised Code.

Any reduction in taxes under section 323.152 of the Revised Code shall be disregarded as income or resources in determining eligibility for any program or calculating any payment under Title LI of the Revised Code.

**HISTORY:**

134 v H 475 (Eff 12-20-71); 135 v S 247 (Eff 7-17-73); 138 v H 1238 (Eff 12-19-80); 147 v S 142 (Eff 3-30-99); 148 v H 595. Eff 4-5-2001; 152 v H 130, § 1, eff. 4-7-09; 2019 hb166, § 101.01, effective October 17, 2019; 2020 hb197, § 1, effective March 27, 2020.

**Editor's Notes**

See provisions, § 3 of HB 672 (148 v —) following RC § 323.151.

**Amendment Notes**

The 2020 amendment by HB 197 substituted "and 323.16" for "323.16" in the first paragraph.

The 2019 amendment by HB 166 added "323.16" in the first paragraph; and made a related change.

152 v H 130, effective April 7, 2009, rewrote the section.

**Applicability**

Acts 2019, HB 166, § 757.340 provides: "As used in this section, 'qualified property' means any property that satisfies the qualifications for tax exemption under the terms of section 5709.08 of the Revised Code and that is owned by a municipal corporation that, within the preceding twenty-five years, (A) was part of an area subject to a federal disaster declaration on the basis of severe storms or flooding and (B) following that declaration, obtained the title to one or more parcels pursuant to the terms of a hazard mitigation grant from the Federal Emergency Management Agency.

"Notwithstanding section 5713.081 of the Revised Code, when qualified property has not received tax exemption due to a failure to comply with Chapter 5713. or section 5715.27 of the Revised Code, the municipal corporation that owns the property, at any time on or before twelve months after the effective date of this act, may file with the Tax Commissioner an application requesting that the property be placed on the tax-exempt list and that all unpaid taxes, penalties, and interest on the property be abated.

"The application shall be made on the form prescribed by the Commissioner under section 5715.27 of the Revised Code and shall list the name of the county in which the property is located; the property's parcel number or legal description; its assessed value; the amount in dollars of the unpaid taxes, penalties, and interest; and any other information required by the Commissioner. The county auditor shall supply the required information upon request of the applicant.

"After receiving and considering the application, the Commissioner shall determine if the applicant meets the qualifications set forth in this section. If so, the Commissioner shall issue an order directing that the property be placed on the tax-exempt list of the county and that all unpaid taxes, penalties, and interest be abated. If the Commissioner finds that the property is not now being used for an exempt purpose or is otherwise ineligible for abatement of taxes, penalties, and interest under this section, the Commissioner shall issue an order denying the application.

"If the Commissioner finds that the property is not entitled to tax exemption and to the abatement of unpaid taxes, penalties, and interest, the Commissioner shall order the county treasurer of the county in which the property is located to collect all taxes, penalties, and interest due on the property for those years in accordance with law.

"The Commissioner may apply this section to any qualified property that is the subject of an application for exemption pending before the Commissioner on the effective date of this section without requiring the property owner to file an additional application."

## § 323.156 Costs of administering exemption paid from general revenue fund.

(A) Within thirty days after a settlement of taxes under divisions (A) and (C) of section 321.24 of the Revised Code, the county treasurer shall certify to the tax commissioner one-half of the total amount of taxes on real property that were reduced pursuant to section 323.152 of the Revised Code for the preceding tax year. The commissioner, within thirty days of the receipt of such certifications, shall provide for payment to the county treasurer, from the general revenue fund, of the amount certified, which shall be credited upon receipt to the county's undivided income tax fund, and an amount equal to two per cent of the amount by which taxes were reduced, which shall be credited upon receipt to the county general fund as a payment, in addition to the fees and charges authorized by sections 319.54 and 321.26 of the Revised Code, to the county auditor and treasurer for the costs of administering the exemption provided under sections 323.151 to 323.159 of the Revised Code.

(B) On or before the second Monday in September of each year, the county treasurer shall certify to the tax commissioner the total amount by which the manufactured home taxes levied in that year were reduced pursuant to division (B) of section 323.152 of the Revised Code, as evidenced by the certificates of reduction and the tax duplicate certified to the county treasurer by the county auditor. The commissioner, within ninety days after the receipt of such certifications, shall provide for payment to the county treasurer, from the general revenue fund, of the amount certified, which shall be credited upon receipt to the county's undivided income tax fund, and an amount equal to two per cent of the amount by which taxes were reduced, which shall be credited upon receipt to the county general fund as a payment, in addition to the fees and charges authorized by sections 319.54 and 321.26 of the Revised Code, to the county auditor and treasurer for the costs of administering the exemption provided under sections 323.151 to 323.159 of the Revised Code.

(C) Immediately upon receipt of funds into the county undivided income tax fund under this section, the auditor shall distribute the full amount thereof among the taxing districts in the county as though the total had been paid as taxes by each person for whom taxes were reduced under sections 323.151 to 323.159 of the Revised Code.

**HISTORY:**

134 v H 475 (Eff 12-20-71); 135 v S 247 (Eff 7-17-73); 141 v H 201 (Eff 7-1-85); 147 v S 142 (Eff 3-30-99); 148 v H 595 (Eff 4-5-2001); 148 v H 672. Eff 4-9-2001; 152 v H 130, § 1, eff. 4-7-09; 153 v H 1, § 101.01, eff. 7-17-09.

**Editor's Notes**

The provisions of § 6 of 152 v H 130 read as follows:

SECTION 6. Section 323.156 of the Revised Code is presented in this act as a composite of the section as amended by both Am. H.B. 595 and Am. Sub. H.B. 672 of the 123rd General Assembly. The General Assembly, applying the principle stated in division (B) of section 1.52 of the Revised Code that amendments are to be harmonized if reasonably capable of simultaneous operation, finds that the composite is the resulting version of the section in effect prior to the effective date of the section as presented in this act.

**Amendment Notes**

153 v H 1, effective July 17, 2009, in the first sentence of (A), substituted "divisions (A) and (C)" for "divisions (A), (C), and (H)" and deleted "and one-half of the total amount of taxes on manufactured and mobile homes that were reduced pursuant to division (B) of section 323.152 of the Revised Code for the current tax year" from the end; inserted (B); and added the (C) designation.

152 v H 130, effective April 7, 2009, in the first paragraph, deleted "as evidenced by the certificates of reduction and the tax duplicate certified to the county treasurer by the county auditor" from the end of the first sentence.

**RESEARCH REFERENCES AND PRACTICE AIDS**

**Cross-References to Related Sections**

Application for reduction in taxes, RC § 323.15.3.

Current revenue notes in anticipation of ad valorem property taxes issued by municipality during fiscal emergency period, RC § 118.23.

Distribution of income tax moneys in general revenue fund; payments to be credited to county's undivided income tax fund, RC § 5747.03.

Subtraction from payments to school district; payments to community school, RC § 3314.08.

### § 323.157 Employees; rules.

Each county treasurer and county auditor shall employ the assistants, clerks, and other employees necessary to carry out the duties imposed by sections 323.151 to 323.159 of the Revised Code. The tax commissioner shall promulgate rules necessary to facilitate the reduction of taxes on homesteads, reimbursement by the state, the determination of "total income," and the administration of sections 323.151 to 323.159 of the Revised Code.

**HISTORY:**

134 v H 475 (Eff 12-20-71); 136 v H 920 (Eff 10-11-76); 140 v H 260 (Eff 9-27-83); 148 v H 595. Eff 4-5-2001.

# CHAPTER 340

# ALCOHOL, DRUG ADDICTION, AND MENTAL HEALTH SERVICES



### § 340.05 Report or complaint of abuse or neglect of adult care facility resident.

If a community addiction services provider or community mental health services provider receives a complaint alleging abuse or neglect of an individual with mental illness or severe mental disability, or an individual receiving addiction services, who resides in a residential facility licensed under section 5119.34 of the Revised Code, the provider shall report the complaint to the board of alcohol, drug addiction, and mental health services serving the alcohol, drug addiction, and mental health service district in which the residential facility is located. A board of alcohol, drug addiction, and mental health services that receives such a report from a community addiction services provider or community mental health services provider of such a complaint shall report the complaint to the director of mental health and addiction services for the purpose of the director conducting an investigation under section 5119.34 of the Revised Code. The board may enter the facility with or without the director and, if the health and safety of a resident is in immediate danger, take any necessary action to protect the resident. The board's action shall not violate any resident's rights specified in rules adopted by the department of mental health and addiction services under section 5119.34 of the Revised Code. The board shall immediately report to the director regarding the board's actions under this section.

**HISTORY:**

148 v H 283. Eff 9-29-99; 2011 HB 153, § 101.01, eff. July 1, 2011; 2012 HB 487, § 101.01, eff. Sept. 10, 2012; 2013 HB 59, § 101.01, eff. Sept. 29, 2013; 2015 hb64, § 101.01, effective September 29, 2015; 2016 sb319, § 1, effective July 1, 2017.

**Editor's Notes**

Not analogous to former RC § 340.05, amended and renumbered RC § 340.03.2 in 138 v S 160, eff 10-31-80.

**Amendment Notes**

The 2016 amendment by SB 319 substituted "addiction services provider or community" for "addiction or" in the first and second sentences; in the first sentence, added "If" at the beginning, substituted "provider receives" for "provider that receives", and added "the provider"; and deleted "complaint or a" following "receives such a" in the second sentence.

The 2015 amendment by HB 64, substituted "licensed under" for "as defined in division (A)(9)(b) of" in the first sentence.

The 2013 amendment substituted "addiction or mental health services provider" for "mental health agency" in the first and second sentences; inserted "or an individual receiving addiction services" in the first sentence; substituted "section 5119.34" for "section 5119.22" in the first, second, and fourth sentences; and substituted "mental health and addiction services" for "mental health" in the second and fourth sentences.

The 2012 amendment, in the first sentence, deleted "under section 5119.87 of the Revised Code" following "receives a complaint", substituted "a residential facility as defined in division (A)(9)(b) of section 5119.22 of the Revised Code" for "an adult care facility", and substituted "residential" for "adult care" preceding "facility is located"; substituted "section 5119.22" for "section 5119.87" in the second sentence; deleted "adult care" following "may enter the" in the third sentence; and, in the fourth sentence, substituted "specified in rules" for "under section 5119.81 of the Revised Code and rules" and "section 5119.22" for "sections 5119.70 to 5119.88".

The 2011 amendment, in the first and second sentences, inserted "community" and substituted "section 5119.87" for "section 3722.17"; inserted "mental" in the second sentence; and, in the fourth sentence, substituted "section 5119.81" for "section 3722.12", "department of mental health" for "public health council", and " sections 5119.70 to 5119.88 of the Revised Code" for "that chapter".

**RESEARCH REFERENCES AND PRACTICE AIDS**

**Cross-References to Related Sections**

Persons authorized to enter facility, RC § 5119.84.

General Provisions — Titles 1-7

# TITLE 5

# TOWNSHIPS



# CHAPTER 505

# TRUSTEES



### § 505.102 Realty transactions with nonprofit senior citizens' organization.

Notwithstanding section 505.10 of the Revised Code, the board of township trustees may sell, lease, or transfer any real property belonging to the township and not needed for public use to a nonprofit senior citizens' organization to be used for public purposes involving the provision of housing, health, social services, or recreational activities for the benefit of older persons, upon such terms and conditions as may be agreed upon by the board of township trustees and the organization. The nonprofit senior citizens' organization shall report annually to the board of township trustees on the nature of the activities for which the property is being used and shall provide such other information regarding the property that the board may require. Any deed conveying real property under this section may state that if the real property is used at any time for purposes other than those enumerated in this section, all right, title, and interest in the property shall revert to the township.

**HISTORY:**
140 v S 148. Eff 6-13-84.

#### ATTORNEY GENERAL OPINIONS

A board of county commissioners and board of education may enter into an agreement whereby the county agrees to lease to the school district a building and underlying land that are no longer needed for the county's use, with an option for the school district to purchase the property for a nominal amount at the end of the lease. The board of county commissioners is not required to competitively bid the conveyance. Payments may not extend for more than five years, however, and the board of education must secure voter approval of a special tax levy under R.C. 5705.21 or otherwise provide for levying and collecting a tax to meet future payments. (1986 Op. Att'y Gen. No. 86-031; 1957 Op. Att'y Gen. No. 398, p. 118; 1945 Op. Att'y Gen. No. 143, p. 110; and, 1939 Op. Att'y Gen. No. 1267, vol. III, p. 1867, overruled due to statutory change.) OAG No. 2004-012 (2004).

If the board of township trustees decides to allow the public to use a former school building that the township owns, the board may, without competitive bidding, lease the building under such terms as are agreed upon, pursuant to R.C. 505.102, 505.11(A), or 511.03. OAG No. 2004-002 (2004).

## TOWNSHIP POLICE DISTRICTS

### § 505.706 Senior citizen services and facilities.

The board of township trustees of a township may expend money for providing and maintaining services and facilities for senior citizens.

**HISTORY:**
145 v H 184. Eff 9-20-93.

# TITLE 7
# MUNICIPAL CORPORATIONS



## CHAPTER 717
## SPECIFIC POWERS



### § 717.01 Powers of municipal corporations.

Each municipal corporation may do any of the following:

(A) Acquire by purchase or condemnation real estate with or without buildings on it, and easements or interests in real estate;

(B) Extend, enlarge, reconstruct, repair, equip, furnish, or improve a building or improvement that it is authorized to acquire or construct;

(C) Erect a crematory or provide other means for disposing of garbage or refuse, and erect public comfort stations;

(D) Purchase turnpike roads and make them free;

(E) Construct wharves and landings on navigable waters;

(F) Construct infirmaries, workhouses, prisons, police stations, houses of refuge and correction, market houses, public halls, public offices, municipal garages, repair shops, storage houses, and warehouses;

(G) Construct or acquire waterworks for supplying water to the municipal corporation and its inhabitants and extend the waterworks system outside of the municipal corporation limits;

(H) Construct or purchase gas works or works for the generation and transmission of electricity, for the supplying of gas or electricity to the municipal corporation and its inhabitants;

(I) Provide grounds for cemeteries or crematories, enclose and embellish them, and construct vaults or crematories;

(J) Construct sewers, sewage disposal works, flushing tunnels, drains, and ditches;

(K) Construct free public libraries and reading rooms, and free recreation centers;

(L) Establish free public baths and municipal lodging houses;

(M) Construct monuments or memorial buildings to commemorate the services of soldiers, sailors, and marines of the state and nation;

(N) Provide land for and improve parks, boulevards, and public playgrounds;

(O) Construct hospitals and pesthouses;

(P) Open, construct, widen, extend, improve, resurface, or change the line of any street or public highway;

(Q) Construct and improve levees, dams, waterways, waterfronts, and embankments and improve any watercourse passing through the municipal corporation;

(R) Construct or improve viaducts, bridges, and culverts;

(S)(1) Construct any building necessary for the police or fire department;

(2) Purchase fire engines or fire boats;

(3) Construct water towers or fire cisterns;

(4) Place underground the wires or signal apparatus of any police or fire department.

(T) Construct any municipal ice plant for the purpose of manufacturing ice for the citizens of a municipal corporation;

(U) Construct subways under any street or boulevard or elsewhere;

(V) Acquire by purchase, gift, devise, bequest, lease, condemnation proceedings, or otherwise, real or personal property, and thereon and thereof to establish, construct, enlarge, improve, equip, maintain, and operate airports, landing fields, or other air navigation facilities, either within or outside the limits of a municipal corporation, and acquire by purchase, gift, devise, lease, or condemnation proceedings rights-of-way for connections with highways, waterways, and electric, steam, and interurban railroads, and improve and equip such facilities with structures necessary or appropriate for such purposes. No municipal corporation may take or disturb property or facilities belonging to any public utility or to a common carrier engaged in interstate commerce, which property or facilities are required for the proper and convenient operation of the utility or carrier, unless provision is made for the restoration, relocation, or duplication of the property or facilities elsewhere at the sole cost of the municipal corporation.

(W) Provide by agreement with any regional airport authority, created under section 308.03 of the Revised Code, for the making of necessary surveys, appraisals, and examinations preliminary to the acquisition or construction of any airport or airport facility and pay the portion of the expense of the surveys, appraisals, and examinations as set forth in the agreement;

(X) Provide by agreement with any regional airport authority, created under section 308.03 of the Revised Code, for the acquisition, construction, maintenance, or operation of any airport or airport facility owned or to be owned and operated by the regional airport authority or owned or to be owned and operated by the municipal corporation and pay the portion of the expense of it as set forth in the agreement;

(Y) Acquire by gift, purchase, lease, or condemnation, land, forest, and water rights necessary for conservation of forest reserves, water parks, or reservoirs, either within or without the limits of the municipal corporation, and improve and equip the forest and water parks with structures, equipment, and reforestation necessary or appropriate for any purpose for the utilization of any of the forest and water benefits that may properly accrue therefrom to the municipal corporation;

(Z) Acquire real property by purchase, gift, or devise and construct and maintain on it public swimming pools, either within or outside the limits of the municipal corporation;

(AA) Construct or rehabilitate, equip, maintain, operate, and lease facilities for housing of elderly persons and for persons of low and moderate income, and appurtenant facilities. No municipal corporation shall deny housing accommodations to or withhold housing accommodations from elderly persons or persons of low and moderate income because of race, color, religion, sex, familial status as defined in section 4112.01 of the Revised Code, military status as defined in that section, disability as defined in that section, ancestry, or national origin. Any elderly person or person of low or moderate income who is denied housing accommodations or has them withheld by a municipal corporation because of race, color, religion, sex, familial status as defined in section 4112.01 of the Revised Code, military status as defined in that section, disability as defined in that section, ancestry, or national origin may file a charge with the Ohio civil rights commission as provided in Chapter 4112. of the Revised Code.

(BB) Acquire, rehabilitate, and develop rail property or rail service, and enter into agreements with the Ohio rail development commission, boards of county commissioners, boards of township trustees, legislative authorities of other municipal corporations, with other governmental agencies or organizations, and with private agencies or organizations in order to achieve those purposes;

(CC) Appropriate and contribute money to a soil and water conservation district for use under Chapter 940. of the Revised Code;

(DD) Authorize the board of county commissioners, pursuant to a contract authorizing the action, to contract on the municipal corporation's behalf for the administration and enforcement within its jurisdiction of the state building code by another county or another municipal corporation located within or outside the county. The contract for administration and enforcement shall provide for obtaining certification pursuant to division (E) of section 3781.10 of the Revised Code for the exercise of administration and enforcement authority within the municipal corporation seeking those services and shall specify which political subdivision is responsible for securing that certification.

(EE) Expend money for providing and maintaining services and facilities for senior citizens.

"Airport," "landing field," and "air navigation facility," as defined in section 4561.01 of the Revised Code, apply to division (V) of this section.

As used in divisions (W) and (X) of this section, "airport" and "airport facility" have the same meanings as in section 308.01 of the Revised Code.

As used in division (BB) of this section, "rail property" and "rail service" have the same meanings as in section 4981.01 of the Revised Code.

**HISTORY:**

RS § 2835; 76 v 158; 90 v 229; 95 v 318; 97 v 291; 98 v 63; GC § 3939; 100 v 53; 102 v 153; 102 v 262; 106 v 536; 107 v 553; 110 v 373; 111 v 45; 112 v 364(379), § 2; 114 v 122, § 3; 115 v 187; 121 v 253(264), § 14; 122 v 519; Bureau of Code Revision, 10-1-53; 129 v 1282 (Eff 10-2-61); 136 v H 439 (Eff 1-17-77); 141 v S 289 (Eff 6-24-86); 141 v H 595 (Eff 3-11-87); 143 v H 715 (Eff 7-18-90); 144 v H 321 (Eff 6-30-92); 145 v H 184 (Eff 9-20-93); 145 v H 250 (Eff 10-20-94); 148 v H 264. Eff 3-17-2000; 152 v H 372, § 1, eff. 3-24-08; 2015 hb64, § 101.01, effective January 1, 2016.

**Editor's Notes**

The provisions of 151 v S 167 read as follows:

SECTION 1. As used in Sections 2 to 7 of this act:

(A) "Blighted area" has the same meaning as in section 303.26 of the Revised Code, but also includes an area in a municipal corporation.

(B) "Public body" means any entity of the state government, and any county, municipal corporation, township, commission, district, authority, or other political subdivision of the state, that has the power to take private property by eminent domain.

SECTION 2. (A) Notwithstanding any provision of the Revised Code to the contrary, until December 31, 2006, no public body shall use eminent domain to take, without the consent of the owner, private property that is not within a blighted area, as determined by the public body, when the primary purpose for the taking is economic development that will ultimately result in ownership of that property being vested in another private person.

(B)(1) Until December 31, 2006, if any public body uses eminent domain to take, without the consent of the owner, private property that is not within a blighted area, as determined by the public body, when the primary purpose for the taking is economic development that will ultimately result in ownership of that property being vested in another private person, each of the following shall apply:

(a) The Ohio Public Works Commission shall not award or distribute to the public body any funding under a capital improvement program created under Chapter 164. of the Revised Code.

(b) The Department of Development shall not award or distribute to the public body any funding under a shovel ready sites program created under section 122.083 of the Revised Code.

(c) The public body shall not receive any funding designated for capital purposes in any act of the General Assembly.

(2) Until December 31, 2006, any public body seeking to obtain funds described in division (B)(1) of this section, shall certify in writing to the grantor of the funds that the public body has not used its eminent domain authority on or after the effective date of this act to take private property in violation of the moratorium established by this act.

(C) Divisions (A) and (B) of this section do not apply to the use of eminent domain for the taking of private property to be used as follows:

(1) In the construction, maintenance, or repair of streets, roads, or walkways, paths, or other ways open to the public's use, including rights of way immediately adjacent to those public ways, including, but not limited to, such use pursuant to authority granted under Title LV of the Revised Code;

(2) For a public utility purpose;

(3) By a common carrier;

(4) For parks or recreation areas open to the public;

(5) In the construction, maintenance, or repair of buildings and grounds used for governmental purposes.

SECTION 3. (A) There is hereby created the Legislative Task Force to Study Eminent Domain and Its Use and Application in the State. The Task Force shall consist of the following twenty-five members:

(1) Three members of the House of Representatives, appointed by the Speaker of the House of Representatives in consultation with the Minority Leader of the House of Representatives. The Speaker of the House of Representatives shall designate one of the members the Speaker appoints to serve as co-chairperson of the Task Force.

(2) Three members of the Senate, appointed by the President of the Senate in consultation with the Minority Leader of the Senate. The President of the Senate shall designate one of the members the President appoints to serve as co-chairperson of the Task Force.

(3) One member representing the home building industry in the state, appointed jointly by the Speaker of the House of Representatives and the President of the Senate;

(4) One member who shall be a statewide advocate on the issues raised in *Kelo v. City of New London* (2005), 125 S. Ct. 2655, insofar as they affect eminent domain, appointed jointly by the Speaker of the House of Representatives and the President of the Senate;

(5) One member representing the agricultural industry in the state, appointed jointly by the Speaker of the House of Representatives and the President of the Senate;

(6) One member representing the commercial real estate industry in the state, appointed jointly by the Speaker of the House of Representatives and the President of the Senate;

(7) One member representing licensed realtors in the state, appointed jointly by the Speaker of the House of Representatives and the President of the Senate;

(8) One member representing the Ohio Prosecuting Attorneys Association or the Ohio Association of Probate Judges, appointed jointly by the Speaker of the House of Representatives and the President of the Senate;

(9) One member who shall be an attorney who is knowledgeable on the issues confronting the Task Force and who represents persons who own property and reside within Ohio, appointed jointly by the Speaker of the House of Representatives and the President of the Senate;

(10) One member knowledgeable on the issues confronting the Task Force who represents persons who own property and reside within Ohio, appointed jointly by the Speaker of the House of Representatives and the President of the Senate;

(11) One member representing the planning industry in the state, one member representing an Ohio labor organization, one member representing a statewide historic preservation organization that works within commercial districts, one member representing municipal corporations, one member representing counties, and one member representing townships, each appointed by the Governor;

(12) The Director of Development or the Director's designee;

(13) The Director of Transportation or the Director's designee;

(14) Two members who shall be attorneys with expertise in eminent domain issues, each appointed by the Attorney General;

(15) One member representing small businesses, appointed jointly by the Speaker of the House of Representatives and the President of the Senate.

(B) Appointments to the Task Force shall be made not later than thirty days after the effective date of this section. Any vacancy in the membership of the Task Force shall be filled in the same manner as the original appointment. Members of the Task Force shall serve without compensation.

(C)(1) The Task Force shall study each of the following:

(a) The use of eminent domain and its impact on the state;

(b) How the decision of the United States Supreme Court in *Kelo v. City of New London* (2005), 125 S. Ct. 2655, affects state law governing the use of eminent domain in the state;

(c) The overall impact of state laws governing the use of eminent domain on economic development, residents, and local governments in Ohio.

(2) The Task Force shall prepare and submit to the General Assembly by not later than April 1, 2006, a report that shall include the findings of its study and recommendations concerning the use of eminent domain and its impact on the state, and by not later than August 1, 2006, a report that shall include findings and recommendations regarding the updating of state law governing eminent domain. On submission of the report due not later than August 1, 2006, the Task Force shall cease to exist.

(D) The Legislative Service Commission shall provide any technical, professional, and clerical employees that are necessary for the Task Force to perform its duties.

(E) All meetings of the Task Force are declared to be public meetings open to the public at all times. A member of the Task Force shall be present in person at a meeting that is open to the public in order to be considered present or to vote at the meeting and for the purposes of determining whether a quorum is present. The Task Force shall promptly prepare and maintain the minutes of its meetings, which shall be public records under section 149.43 of the Revised Code. The Task Force shall give reasonable notice of its meetings so that any person may determine the time and place of all scheduled meetings. The Task Force shall not hold a meeting unless it gives at least twenty-four hours advance notification to the news media organizations that have requested such notification.

SECTION 4. The General Assembly hereby makes the following statements of findings and intent:

(A) On June 23, 2005, the United States Supreme Court rendered its decision in *Kelo v. City of New London* (2005), 125 S. Ct. 2655, which allows the taking of private property that is not within a blighted area by eminent domain for the purpose of economic development even when the ultimate result of the taking is ownership of the property being vested in another private person. As a result of this decision, the General Assembly believes the interpretation and use of the state's eminent domain law could be expanded to allow the taking of private property that is not within a blighted area, ultimately resulting in ownership of that property being vested in another private person in violation of Sections 1 and 19 of Article I, Ohio Constitution, which protect the rights of Ohio citizens to maintain property as inviolate, subservient only to the public welfare. Thus, the General Assembly finds it is necessary to enact a moratorium on any takings of this nature by any public body until further legislative remedies may be considered.

(B) The General Assembly finds that it is a matter of statewide concern to enact the moratorium. The moratorium is necessary to protect the general welfare and the rights of citizens under Sections 1 and 19 of Article I, Ohio Constitution, and to ensure that these rights are not violated due to the *Kelo* decision. In enacting this provision, the General Assembly wishes to ensure uniformity throughout the state.

SECTION 5. Section 2 of this act applies only to taking actions initiated on or after the effective date of this act. As used in this section, "initiated" means the adoption of a resolution or ordinance of necessity by the public body or filing of a court action, but excludes taking actions for which a resolution or ordinance of necessity or other official action of a public body has been taken and public funds have been expended in connection with that taking action prior to the effective date of this act.

SECTION 6. If any item of law that constitutes the whole or part of an uncodified section of law contained in this act, or if any application of any item of law that constitutes the whole or part of an uncodified section of law contained in this act, is held invalid, the invalidity does not affect other items of law or applications of items of law that can be given effect without the invalid item of law or application. To this end, the items of law of which the uncodified sections contained in this act are composed, and their applications, are independent and severable.

SECTION 7. Nothing in this act shall be construed to imply that any public body with eminent domain authority has prior to the enactment of this act abused that authority or engaged in any wrongdoing in the exercise of its eminent domain authority conferred by statute or the Ohio Constitution.

SECTION 8. This act is hereby declared to be an emergency measure necessary for the immediate preservation of the public peace, health, and safety. The reason for the necessity is that the United States Supreme Court decision in *Kelo v. City of New London* (2005), 125 S. Ct. 2655, could allow the taking of private property that is not within a blighted area, ultimately resulting in ownership of that property being vested in another private person in violation of Sections 1 and 19 of Article I, Ohio Constitution, and, as a result, warrants a moratorium on any takings of this type until further legislative remedies may be considered. Therefore, this act shall go into immediate effect.

**Amendment Notes**

The 2015 amendment by HB 64 substituted "Chapter 940." for "Chapter 1515." in (CC).

152 v H 372, effective March 24, 2008, in (AA), twice inserted "military status as defined in that section".

## NOTES TO DECISIONS

Analysis



**Abortion**

**—Constitutionality**

A penal ordinance that lacks explanatory regulations is void for vagueness. In the absence of a reasonable connection between a right to exercise legislative power and the actual exercise thereof such effort is void. Where an effort by the council of a municipal corporation violates a holding of the Supreme Court of the United States mandating noninterference with persons seeking first trimester abortions, such effort is void ab initio: Planned Parenthood Assn. v. City of Cincinnati, 632 F. Supp. 994 (S.D. 1986).

**Airports**

By authority of Ohio Const. art XVIII, § 3 and GC § 3677 (R.C. 719.01) and this section, a municipality has power to acquire, own and operate an air landing field: State ex rel. Hile v. Cleveland, 26 Ohio App. 265, 160 N.E. 241, 5 Ohio Law Abs. 307, 1927 Ohio App. LEXIS 540 (Ohio Ct. App., Cuyahoga County), dismissed, State ex rel. Hile v. City of Cleveland, 5 Ohio Law Abs. 823, 25 Ohio L. Rep. 618 (Ohio Ct. App. 1927).

**—Constitutionality**

A general grant of power given by constitutional authority to a municipal corporation to condemn land within or without its corporate limits for the establishment of public utilities such as airports, landing fields, or other air navigation facilities does not extend to the appropriation of a public street in another municipal corporation which is maintained by such municipal corporation in the performance of a governmental function: Blue Ash v. Cincinnati, 173 Ohio St. 345, 19 Ohio Op. 2d 274, 182 N.E.2d 557, 1962 Ohio LEXIS 702 (Ohio 1962).

**—Interstate commerce**

The operation of a municipal airport is an integral governmental function within the meaning of National League of Cities v. Usery, 426 US 833. Such function is within the state sovereignty limitation upon congressional power under the interstate commerce clause. Thus municipal employees assigned to the airport are not covered by the minimum wage and maximum hour provisions of the fair labor standards act: Amersbach v. Cleveland, 598 F.2d 1033, 1979 U.S. App. LEXIS 14781 (6th Cir. Ohio 1979), disapproved, Garcia v. San Antonio Metro. Transit Auth., 469 U.S. 528, 105 S. Ct. 1005, 83 L. Ed. 2d 1016, 1985 U.S. LEXIS 48 (U.S. 1985).

**—Public utilities**

Under the power conferred by Ohio Const. art XVIII, § 4, GC § 3677 (R.C. 710.01) and GC § 3939 (R.C. 717.01), a municipal corporation may purchase or lease and operate a landing field and place improvements thereon so as to make a fully equipped aircraft and transportation terminal; and, as such, it is a public utility: Toledo v. Jenkins, 143 Ohio St. 141, 28 Ohio Op. 72, 54 N.E.2d 656, 1944 Ohio LEXIS 389 (Ohio 1944).

An airport established by municipality under power to purchase or condemn land therefor, is a public utility subject to laws applicable to municipally owned utilities (this section; Ohio Const. art 18, § 8): State ex rel. Chandler v. Jackson, 121 Ohio St. 186, 167 N.E. 396, 7 Ohio Law Abs. 367, 1929 Ohio LEXIS 304 (Ohio 1929).

**Applicability**

General Code §§ 3298-15d and 3298-15e (R.C. 5573.13, 5573.14) apply to townships, and do not repeal by implication this section, which applies to municipal corporations: State ex rel. Steller v. Zangerle, 100 Ohio St. 414, 126 N.E. 413, 17 Ohio L. Rep. 345, 1919 Ohio LEXIS 143 (Ohio 1919).

**Construction**

Whether this section as amended in 102 v 153 or as amended in 102 v 262 was in force thereafter was immaterial as to cases which were controlled by a language which was identical in each act: Heffner v. Krinn, 98 Ohio St. 1, 120 N.E. 221, 1918 Ohio LEXIS 215 (Ohio 1918).

**Indebtedness**

**—Limitations**

Grant of power from the legislature is not a prerequisite to a municipality's borrowing money, and under the provisions of Ohio Const. art XVIII, § 13, the indebtedness which may be incurred for such purpose is subject only to the limitation prescribed by the legislature as to the extent of general tax levies and the aggregate amount of indebtedness that may be incurred for all local purposes: State ex rel. Toledo v. Weiler, 101 Ohio St. 123, 128 N.E. 88, 1920 Ohio LEXIS 164 (Ohio 1920).

**Libraries**

**—Issuance of bonds**

A municipality may issue bonds to provide funds to construct and equip a free public library building in the municipality, where the building will be leased to the county public library for operation by that county library as a free public library: State ex rel. Buescher v. Linton, 6 Ohio St. 2d 218, 35 Ohio Op. 2d 341, 217 N.E.2d 201, 1966 Ohio LEXIS 374 (Ohio 1966).

**Power to construct**

A municipality may contract with a nonprofit corporation to provide shelter for homeless persons: Franklinton Coalition v. Open Shelter, Inc., 13 Ohio App. 3d 399, 469 N.E.2d 861, 1983 Ohio App. LEXIS 11426 (Ohio Ct. App., Franklin County 1983).

The General Assembly has not affirmatively granted the specific power to a municipal corporation to provide or construct a bomb shelter, community blast and fallout shelter, or any facility whatever to protect against thermo-nuclear conflict: Schnoerr v. Miller, 4 Ohio App. 2d 99, 33 Ohio Op. 2d 150, 212 N.E.2d 671, 1963 Ohio App. LEXIS 610 (Ohio Ct. App.,

Hamilton County 1963), aff'd, 2 Ohio St. 2d 121, 31 Ohio Op. 2d 192, 206 N.E.2d 902, 1965 Ohio LEXIS 501 (Ohio 1965).

While a municipality does not have the power to establish a free public library, it does have the power under this section to construct free public library buildings and under the provisions of GC § 3711 (R.C. 721.22) to lease such buildings to a county library district: State ex rel. Daley v. Parma, 123 N.E.2d 295, 68 Ohio Law Abs. 577, 1952 Ohio App. LEXIS 846 (Ohio Ct. App., Cuyahoga County 1952).

A general power to construct sewers empowers a municipal corporation to acquire and to contract for acquisition of sewer rights outside its corporation limits, even though the statute conferring the power to construct sewers is silent on the subject of acquiring or contracting for land or rights therein outside its corporate limits: Cleveland v. Cuyahoga Heights, 81 Ohio App. 191, 36 Ohio Op. 522, 75 N.E.2d 99, 49 Ohio Law Abs. 78, 1947 Ohio App. LEXIS 635 (Ohio Ct. App., Cuyahoga County 1947).

**Water rates**

**—Tax charges**

Water rates or charges or "rents" collected by a municipality cannot be classed as taxes so long as their use is limited to the waterworks purposes enumerated in this section; but if employed as a mere device to lessen the burden of taxation for general governmental purposes, such funds should be considered in the category of taxes: Himebaugh v. Canton, 145 Ohio St. 237, 30 Ohio Op. 471, 61 N.E.2d 483, 1945 Ohio LEXIS 416 (Ohio 1945).

**Water rent**

**—Standing**

Water-rent payers possess the legal capacity to bring an action against a municipality for an accounting and restoration of a trust fund held by the city as a trustee solely for waterworks purposes as defined in this section: Himebaugh v. Canton, 145 Ohio St. 237, 30 Ohio Op. 471, 61 N.E.2d 483, 1945 Ohio LEXIS 416 (Ohio 1945).

## ATTORNEY GENERAL OPINIONS

Pursuant to R.C. 307.20, 308.03(G), 308.06(K), and 717.01(X), a board of county commissioners may contract with a regional airport authority for the county to provide county employees to serve as staff for the airport: 1990 Ohio Op. Att'y Gen. No. 067 (1990).

Inherent in the power provided for in § 717.01(V) is the authority to charge reasonable fees for facilities and services related to the operation of an airport. Therefore, the board of county commissioners has the authority to charge tie-down fees on county airport property: 1970 Ohio Op. Att'y Gen. No. 099 (1970).

It is not within the power of the council of a noncharter city to create by ordinance a municipal airport board to control the operations of the municipal airport and administer the affairs of the municipality with reference thereto: 1929 Ohio Op. Att'y Gen. No. 1276 (1929).

A county and city may not legally enter into a joint ownership agreement with respect to that portion of a county home farm, not needed for public use, for purpose of equipping an airport: 1928 OAG No. 2843 (1928).

Municipalities may submit bond issues for disposal plant, and bond issues for airport on the same ballot: 1929 Ohio Op. Att'y Gen. No. 1361 (1929).

A municipal corporation may not lease lands outside its corporate limits for the purpose of providing a landing field for aircraft: 1928 OAG No. 3097 (1928).

A municipality may not issue bonds for the general purpose of flood control: 1922 OAG No. 4099 (1922).

A city and a county may, through a cooperative agreement, share the cost of repairing a bridge located on a county road within a municipality: 1988 Ohio Op. Att'y Gen. No. 039 (1988).

A city has implied power to insure its public property, and like power to enter into a contract for indemnity insurance in so far as its proprietary functions are concerned: 1937 OAG No. 615 (1937).

A city and a county may obtain financing through the Ohio Building Authority, pursuant to R.C. 307.021, for the purpose of jointly acquiring, constructing, or renovating a city-county jail facility under R.C. 153.61, R.C. 307.01, R.C. 341.01-.33, R.C. 715.16, and R.C. 717.01(F). The board of county commissioners may then enter into an agreement, pursuant to R.C. 307.15, with the boards of county commissioners of other counties whereby the board undertakes to perform for those counties the functions those counties are otherwise empowered and under a duty to perform with respect to the construction and operation of county jail facilities: 1986 Ohio Op. Att'y Gen. No. 084 (1986).

A city may not lease part of a proposed city building to a county for county purposes prior to the actual construction of said municipal building and a determination that such part contemplated to be leased is not needed for municipal purposes: 1938 OAG No. 1909 (1938).

A municipality, which claims no such charter power, lacks authority to adopt an ordinance which would legally permit it to pay from public funds membership dues or fees in an association or conference of municipalities: 1941 OAG No. 4506 (1941).

## RESEARCH REFERENCES AND PRACTICE AIDS

**Cross-References to Related Sections**

No limitation on municipal authority —

Regional transit authorities, RC § 306.32.

Resolution relative to tax levy in excess of ten-mill limitation, RC § 5705.19.

**Ohio Constitution**

Powers of municipalities, Ohio Const. art XVIII, § 3.

**Ohio Administrative Code**

Department of commerce—

Board of building appeals. OAC ch. 4101:13-1.

Specific local boards. OAC ch. 4101:2-78.

Board of building standards. OAC ch. 4101:1-1 et seq.

Local building departments, certification of. OAC ch. 4101:2-70 et seq, OAC ch. 4101:2-94 et seq.

**Comparative Legislation**

Powers of municipal corporation:

CA—Cal Gov Code § 34409 et seq

FL—Fla. Const. Art. VIII, § 2

IL—65 Ill. Comp. Stat. § 5/1-1-6

IN—Burns Ind. Code Ann. § 36-1-3-5

KY—KRS § 83.420

MI—MCLS § 117.3

NY—NY CLS Gen City § 20

PA—53 P.S. § 306

**Practice Manuals and Treatises**

Anderson's Ohio Civil Practice with Forms § 21.02 Appropriation by a Municipality

# TITLE 11

# FINANCIAL INSTITUTIONS



## CHAPTER 1109

## BANKS — POWERS

Deposit Accounts



## DEPOSIT ACCOUNTS

### § 1109.07 Deposits in name of two or more persons; deposits payable on death.

(A) When a deposit is made in the name of two or more persons, payable to either or the survivor, the bank may pay all of the deposit, any part of the deposit, or any interest earned on the deposit, to either of the named persons, or the guardian of the estate of either of the named persons, whether or not the other person is living. The receipt or acquittance of the person paid is a sufficient release and discharge of the bank for any payments made from the account to that person.

(B) A bank may enter into a written contract with a natural person for the proceeds of the person's deposits to be payable on the death of that person to another person or to any entity or organization in accordance with the terms, restrictions, and limitations set forth in sections 2131.10 and 2131.11 of the Revised Code.

**HISTORY:**

RC § 1107.08, 132 v S 97 (Eff 1-1-68); 140 v H 348 (Eff 9-20-84); RC § 1109.07, 146 v H 538 (Eff 1-1-97); 148 v H 313. Eff 8-29-2000.

#### NOTES TO DECISIONS

Analysis



**Appeal**

Although Thompson reallocated to the joint survivor the burden of proof of intent and the joint survivor would have no opportunity to meet that burden without a remand for a new trial, it is permissible and proper to deny a remand when the record clearly demonstrates a new trial would be futile because the joint survivor could not reasonably meet his burden of proof: (decided under former analogous section) Gillota v. Gillota, 4 Ohio St. 3d 222, 448 N.E.2d 802, 1983 Ohio LEXIS 701 (Ohio 1983).

**Bank liability**

Bank was not liable for withdrawals made by a bank customer's children from a joint savings account in the name of the customer and the children. Tsepas v. JPMorgan Chase Bank, N.A., 2017-Ohio-1272, 2017 Ohio App. LEXIS 1271 (Ohio Ct. App., Stark County 2017).

**Banking defined**

The purpose of this statute is to permit banks to enter into joint and survivorship accounts, and if they pay the survivor the money they are discharged from any obligation regardless of the ultimate decision concerning whether the asset belongs in the probate estate or to the survivor. This section is not part of the probate code and does not determine whether there is in fact a true joint and survivorship account: (decided under former analogous section) Eger v. Eger, 39 Ohio App. 2d 14, 68 Ohio Op. 2d 150, 314 N.E.2d 394, 1974 Ohio App. LEXIS 2670 (Ohio Ct. App., Cuyahoga County 1974).

**Beneficiaries**

The 1984 amendment to R.C. 2131.10 permits artificial persons to be named as beneficiaries of POD accounts: (decided under former analogous section) Estate of Kinsey v. Janes, 82 Ohio App. 3d 822, 613 N.E.2d 686, 1992 Ohio App. LEXIS 5220 (Ohio Ct. App., Franklin County 1992).

When R.C. 1107.08(B), 2131.10 and 2131.11 are read in pari materia, it is clear that the General Assembly intended that only natural persons may be designated as the beneficiaries of "P.O.D." (payable on death) accounts; hence, a corporation may not be a beneficiary of a "P.O.D." account: (decided under former analogous section) Powell v. City Nat'l Bank & Trust Co., 2 Ohio App. 3d 1, 440 N.E.2d 560, 1981 Ohio App. LEXIS 9888 (Ohio Ct. App., Franklin County 1981).

**Breach of contract**

Trial court erred in rendering summary judgment in favor of the bank on the contract and conversion claims because, under the unambiguous terms of the contract between the decedent and the bank, his accounts were not payable on death (POD) accounts and should have been paid instead to the decedent's estate for distribution under his will. To establish the existence of POD beneficiaries, both R.C. 1109.07(B) and R.C. 2131.10 required a written contract signed by the account owner and the bank could not produce a written signature card, and its internal records were insufficient to substitute for the statutory requirements. Hillier v. Fifth Third Bank, 2020-Ohio-3679, 154 N.E.3d 1266, 2020 Ohio App. LEXIS 2623 (Ohio Ct. App., Miami County 2020).

A beneficiary to a payable-on-death account has a vested interest in the proceeds of the account and, as a third-party beneficiary to the agreement between a defendant-bank and the decedent-depositor, has a right to enforce this interest. Thus, where the bank pays the account proceeds to an estate creditor, a genuine issue of material fact exists as to whether the bank breached its contract with the depositor to pay the proceeds to the beneficiary upon the depositor's death: (decided under former analogous section) Taylor v. First Nat'l Bank, 31 Ohio App. 3d 49, 508 N.E.2d 1006, 1986 Ohio App. LEXIS 10110 (Ohio Ct. App., Hamilton County 1986).

**Burden of proof**

A valid P.O.D. account may be established despite the lack of the decedent's signature on the signature card. A party seeking to void a P.O.D. account due to lack of mental capacity has the burden of proof by clear and convincing evidence: (decided under former analogous section) Giurbino v. Giurbino, 89 Ohio App. 3d 646, 626 N.E.2d 1017, 1993 Ohio App. LEXIS 3654 (Ohio Ct. App., Cuyahoga County 1993).

**Constructive trust**

Presumption of equal ownership of a joint and survivorship account is rebuttable by evidence of individual net contributions. Before a constructive trust can be imposed, there must be adequate tracing from the time of the wrongful deprivation of the relevant assets to the specific property over which the constructive trust should be placed. When property was subsequently transferred to third parties, a constructive trust could be imposed: Estate of Cowling v. Estate of Cowling, 2006-Ohio-2418, 109 Ohio St. 3d 276, 847 N.E.2d 405, 2006 Ohio LEXIS 1567 (Ohio 2006).

**Conversion of funds**

Where a codepositor in a joint account has a vested right of survivorship, but does not have true ownership in the account during the lifetime of the other codepositor, his conversion of the funds into an account solely in his own name during the other codepositor's lifetime destroys his right of survivorship and makes him liable to the true owner for the amount converted: (decided under former analogous section) In re Webb, 18 Ohio App. 2d 287, 47 Ohio Op. 2d 452, 249 N.E.2d 83, 1969 Ohio App. LEXIS 630 (Ohio Ct. App., Cuyahoga County 1969).

**Deposit contracts**

Where a bank provides by rule, which rule becomes contractually binding on depositors, for the right to setoff funds in a joint and survivorship account against debts owed the bank by a party to the account, the bank may lawfully setoff such funds without violating the public policy of this state, although the funds in the account are supplied exclusively by a non-debtor depositor: (decided under former analogous section) Chickerneo v. Society Nat'l Bank, 58 Ohio St. 2d 315, 12 Ohio Op. 3d 298, 390 N.E.2d 1183, 1979 Ohio LEXIS 436 (Ohio 1979).



**Fraud**

Wife's complaint against her deceased husband's children, asserting a claim of civil conspiracy, was properly dismissed on summary judgment because the husband's use of marital property, during the marriage of the husband and the wife, to purchase certificates of deposit and bonds, placing them in joint and survivorship with the children, resulted in complete gifts intervivos to children and caused the property to pass to the children by contract under R.C. 1109.07. Any alleged financial misconduct of the decedent during the marriage did not rise to the level of fraud for purposes of supporting a claim of civil conspiracy. Click v. Unknown Ex'r (Estate of Click), 2007-Ohio-3029, 2007 Ohio App. LEXIS 2783 (Ohio Ct. App., Lawrence County 2007).

A court may properly make a finding of fraud where the funds of an elderly parent who does not understand the nature of joint accounts are deposited in a joint account with his child and then depleted by the child during the parent's lifetime: (decided under former analogous section) Ross v. Barker, 101 Ohio App. 3d 611, 656 N.E.2d 363, 1995 Ohio App. LEXIS 1007 (Ohio Ct. App., Montgomery County 1995).

**Garnishment**

In responding to a garnishment order, banks have no duty to determine the proportions of ownership in a joint account or to determine what funds came from exempt personal earnings: Ingram v. Hocking Valley Bank, 125 Ohio App. 3d 210, 708 N.E.2d 232, 1997 Ohio App. LEXIS 6000 (Ohio Ct. App., Athens County 1997).

**Inducement to marriage**

Where a decedent established a joint and survivorship account as an inducement to a party to marry him, the party was not entitled to the proceeds where she declined to do so: In re Schwechlik, 89 Ohio Misc. 2d 10, 692 N.E.2d 1103, 1997 Ohio Misc. LEXIS 304 (Ohio C.P. 1997).

**Intent**

Where there is clear and convincing evidence that the decedent did not intend to create a present interest in the named survivor, the account is properly deemed to be an asset of the decedent's estate: (decided under former analogous section) Offret v. DiDomenico, 88 Ohio App. 3d 63, 623 N.E.2d 128, 1993 Ohio App. LEXIS 2678 (Ohio Ct. App., Summit County 1993).

A depository institution has no obligation to determine whether the parties to a joint account actually intended that each of them have the sole right to all the funds in the account. There is no distinction between a withdrawal and a pledge of the funds: (decided under former analogous section) Wilhelm v. Peoples Federal Sav. & Loan Ass'n, 72 Ohio App. 3d 258, 594 N.E.2d 635, 1991 Ohio App. LEXIS 286 (Ohio Ct. App., Stark County 1991).

No right of survivorship is created where it is clear that the decedent-depositor did not intend to create a present interest in the joint tenant: (decided under former analogous section) Pontius v. Nadolske, 65 Ohio App. 3d 522, 584 N.E.2d 1228, 1989 Ohio App. LEXIS 4526 (Ohio Ct. App., Summit County 1989).

To support a finding of a gift inter vivos there must exist clear and convincing evidence of a present intention on the part of the donor to transfer title and right of possession as well as evidence of a completed delivery of the subject matter of the gift with the donor relinquishing ownership, dominion and control over it. Where a confidential or fiduciary relationship exists between a donor and a donee, the transfer is looked upon with some suspicion that undue influence may have been brought to bear on the donor by the donee: (decided under former analogous section) Studniewski v. Krzyzanowski, 65 Ohio App. 3d 628, 584 N.E.2d 1297, 1989 Ohio App. LEXIS 4703 (Ohio Ct. App., Lucas County 1989).

In order to create a true joint and survivorship account, the creator must intend to transfer a present interest as well as a survivorship interest in the account to the other. The presumption of a right to survivorship may be rebutted by evidence that during the creator's life he kept the passbook, and that even when in need the survivor borrowed from the creator rather than withdrew from the account: (decided under former analogous section) In re Estate of Tyler, 42 Ohio App. 3d 123, 536 N.E.2d 1188, 1987 Ohio App. LEXIS 10845 (Ohio Ct. App., Ross County 1987).

The intent of the party or parties opening a joint and survivorship account, rather than the contractual nature of the account, is the crucial criterion for determining whether a joint and survivorship account has actually been created: (decided under former analogous section) Corrigan v. Coughlin, 11 Ohio App. 3d 176, 463 N.E.2d 1258, 1983 Ohio App. LEXIS 11269 (Ohio Ct. App., Cuyahoga County 1983).

Where the decedent merely signed blank signature cards which were returned to several banks for the purpose of establishing joint and survivorship accounts, such act does not sufficiently show an intention to create a present existing interest in the survivors: (decided under former analogous section) In re Estate of Kapatch, 73 Ohio Op. 2d 422 (Ohio C.P. 1975).

**Joint account**

Decedent did not take any action to make her attorney in fact a joint owner of the savings account. The bank's error in transferring the account to the attorney in fact, resulting in her receiving a request to pay taxes on the account, did not create a joint account with rights of survivorship: In re Estate of Kirkland, 2008-Ohio-421, 175 Ohio App. 3d 73, 885 N.E.2d 271, 2008 Ohio App. LEXIS 378 (Ohio Ct. App., Clark County 2008).

Joint and survivorship accounts created when the decedent signed signature cards passed to the survivor, the decedent's attorney in fact, upon the decedent's death. Joint and survivorship account created by the attorney in fact with the decedent's funds became an estate asset where the attorney in fact did not rebut the presumption of undue influence: Rusnak v. Fleming, 2007-Ohio-6752, 879 N.E.2d 865, 2007 Ohio Misc. LEXIS 525 (Ohio C.P. 2007).

Trial court did not err in finding a decedent's bank account was not a joint account with rights of survivorship; however, the trial court erred in including the entire account in the estate of the deceased. In re Estate of Lowe, 2003-Ohio-6865, 2003 Ohio App. LEXIS 6209 (Ohio Ct. App., Licking County 2003).

A bank may not pay money from a joint account on the garnishment order of a creditor of a single depositor if that depositor could not himself withdraw funds without the signature of the other joint depositor: (decided under former analogous section) Ross v. Thrift Sav. & Loan Co., 60 Ohio App. 3d 94, 573 N.E.2d 788, 1989 Ohio App. LEXIS 3864 (Ohio Ct. App., Hamilton County 1989).

**Joint account during divorce**

A bank account established by spouses to freeze their funds pending a divorce, which requires two signatures for withdrawal, is not a joint and survivorship account with equal ownership presumed: (decided under former analogous section) Ross v. Thrift Sav. & Loan Co., 60 Ohio App. 3d 94, 573 N.E.2d 788, 1989 Ohio App. LEXIS 3864 (Ohio Ct. App., Hamilton County 1989).

**Joint and survivorship account defined**

A joint and survivorship bank account is an inter vivos contract creating a present, equal, joint vested interest in the parties named therein and either party may withdraw the funds at any time and upon the death of one of the parties, the survivor becomes the absolute owner of the bank account by the operative provisions of the contract: (decided under former analogous section) Eger v. Eger, 39 Ohio App. 2d 14, 68 Ohio Op. 2d 150, 314 N.E.2d 394, 1974 Ohio App. LEXIS 2670 (Ohio Ct. App., Cuyahoga County 1974); Benson v. Harmon, 39 Ohio App. 2d 92, 68 Ohio Op. 2d 248, 315 N.E.2d 821, 1974 Ohio App. LEXIS 2675 (Ohio Ct. App., Cuyahoga County 1974).

**Notice**

Once a depositor's knowledge of and voluntary acceptance of the terms and conditions of a joint and survivorship account are placed into question, former R.C. 1107.06 does not relieve the bank of responsibility to show that it provided the depositor with a reasonable means of understanding the consequences of the deposit contract: (decided under former analogous section) Rives v. Krupzsield, 60 Ohio App. 3d 97, 573 N.E.2d 1199, 1989 Ohio App. LEXIS 3535 (Ohio Ct. App., Lucas County 1989).

**Ownership**

During the lifetime of the owners of a joint and survivorship account, the funds belong to the parties in proportion to their net contributions to the account: Slaughter v. Ohio Operating Eng'rs Fed. Credit Union, 2005-Ohio-3004, 161 Ohio App. 3d 666, 831 N.E.2d 1034, 2005 Ohio App. LEXIS 2798 (Ohio Ct. App., Cuyahoga County 2005).

During the lifetime of all the parties to a joint and survivorship account, the funds belong to the parties in proportion to their contributions unless there is clear and convincing evidence of a different intent: (decided under former analogous section) Estate of Averiett v. Averiett, 1993 Ohio App. LEXIS 4048 (Ohio Ct. App., Summit County Aug. 18, 1993).

A joint and survivorship account belongs, during the lifetime of all parties, to the parties in proportion to the net contributions by each to the sums on deposit, unless there is clear and convincing evidence of a different intent: (decided under former analogous section) Gillota v. Gillota, 4 Ohio

St. 3d 222, 448 N.E.2d 802, 1983 Ohio LEXIS 701 (Ohio 1983); In re Estate of Thompson, 66 Ohio St. 2d 433, 20 Ohio Op. 3d 371, 423 N.E.2d 90, 1981 Ohio LEXIS 528 (Ohio 1981), overruled, Wright v. Bloom, 1994-Ohio-153, 69 Ohio St. 3d 596, 635 N.E.2d 31, 1994 Ohio LEXIS 1497 (Ohio 1994).

**Presumption of ownership**

Transfers from a joint and survivorship bank account by the noncontributor to a joint investment account do not affect the presumption that the funds were intended to pass to the noncontributor upon the death of the person contributing the funds. However, a constructive trust arises where the noncontributor transfers fund to his or her individual account: (decided under former analogous section) In re Estate of Mayer, 105 Ohio App. 3d 483, 664 N.E.2d 583, 1995 Ohio App. LEXIS 3196 (Ohio Ct. App., Lucas County 1995).

A party attempting to uphold a joint and survivorship account is entitled to a rebuttable presumption and to the benefit of other relevant evidence that the party is at least to share equally in the ownership of the funds; however, the other party is entitled to rebut this presumption by showing the realities of ownership: (decided under former analogous section) Craig v. Curtiss, 64 Ohio App. 2d 72, 18 Ohio Op. 3d 49, 411 N.E.2d 197, 1979 Ohio App. LEXIS 8418 (Ohio Ct. App., Lucas County 1979).

The party seeking to uphold the joint and survivorship contract is benefited by a presumption that both parties to the contract are rebuttably presumed to share equally in the funds on deposit: (decided under former analogous section) Vetter v. Hampton, 54 Ohio St. 2d 227, 8 Ohio Op. 3d 198, 375 N.E.2d 804, 1978 Ohio LEXIS 549 (Ohio 1978).

The existence of a joint survivorship bank account raises a rebuttable presumption that co-owners of the account share equally in the ownership of the funds on deposit: (decided under former analogous section) Vetter v. Hampton, 54 Ohio St. 2d 227, 8 Ohio Op. 3d 198, 375 N.E.2d 804, 1978 Ohio LEXIS 549 (Ohio 1978).

When a joint and survivorship account is the subject of a court challenge, and the evidence shows it was not intended to create a present, equal joint vested interest in the party claiming ownership, a true joint and survivorship account was not created. Under these circumstances a survivor cannot take the proceeds of the account upon the death of the other party because the survivorship provision of a joint and survivorship account does not stand alone: (decided under former analogous section) Eger v. Eger, 39 Ohio App. 2d 14, 68 Ohio Op. 2d 150, 314 N.E.2d 394, 1974 Ohio App. LEXIS 2670 (Ohio Ct. App., Cuyahoga County 1974); Benson v. Harmon, 39 Ohio App. 2d 92, 68 Ohio Op. 2d 248, 315 N.E.2d 821, 1974 Ohio App. LEXIS 2675 (Ohio Ct. App., Cuyahoga County 1974).

The fact that a bank account is carried in the names of two persons jointly with the right of survivorship is not always conclusive as to the ownership of the account. It only raises a rebuttable presumption that the co-owners of the account share equally in the funds on deposit. Where a controversy arises after the death of one of the parties as to the ownership of such accounts, evidence is admissible to show the true situation, and where the realities of ownership are not in accord with the form of the contract the asset does not go to the survivor but into the estate of the decedent: (decided under former analogous section) Eger v. Eger, 39 Ohio App. 2d 14, 68 Ohio Op. 2d 150, 314 N.E.2d 394, 1974 Ohio App. LEXIS 2670 (Ohio Ct. App., Cuyahoga County 1974); Benson v. Harmon, 39 Ohio App. 2d 92, 68 Ohio Op. 2d 248, 315 N.E.2d 821, 1974 Ohio App. LEXIS 2675 (Ohio Ct. App., Cuyahoga County 1974).

**Question of fact**

The issue of whether an account was created merely for the decedent's own convenience is a factual question to be resolved by the trial court: (decided under former analogous section) Cork v. Bray, 52 Ohio St. 3d 35, 555 N.E.2d 936, 1990 Ohio LEXIS 245 (Ohio 1990).

**"Realities of ownership"**

The possession of a joint certificate of deposit by the nondepositor is merely evidence of one of the "realities of ownership" and is not conclusive as to whether the bank erred in paying the proceeds of the certificate to the depositor upon completion of an affidavit declaring the certificate to be lost: (decided under former analogous section) Kristofik v. Bank One, Akron, N.A., 34 Ohio App. 3d 104, 517 N.E.2d 272, 1986 Ohio App. LEXIS 10317 (Ohio Ct. App., Summit County 1986).

The party contending that no valid joint and survivorship contract was created may show the "realities of ownership"; to do this, the challenger must show either that there was no present interest created or that no right of survivorship was intended: (decided under former analogous section) In re Estate of Stevenson, 64 Ohio App. 2d 187, 18 Ohio Op. 3d 144, 412 N.E.2d 409, 1979 Ohio App. LEXIS 8431 (Ohio Ct. App., Lucas County 1979).

A party contending that no valid joint and survivorship contract was created by asserting "realities of ownership" must show either that no present interest was created or that no right of survivorship was intended: (decided under former analogous section) Vetter v. Hampton, 54 Ohio St. 2d 227, 8 Ohio Op. 3d 198, 375 N.E.2d 804, 1978 Ohio LEXIS 549 (Ohio 1978).

The fact that a bank account is carried in the names of two persons jointly, with right of survivorship, is not always conclusive as to the ownership of the account, and, when a controversy arises as to the ownership of such an account, the party contending that no valid joint and survivorship contract was created may present evidence to show the "realities of ownership": (decided under former analogous section) Vetter v. Hampton, 54 Ohio St. 2d 227, 8 Ohio Op. 3d 198, 375 N.E.2d 804, 1978 Ohio LEXIS 549 (Ohio 1978).

The existence of a joint and survivorship account raises only a rebuttable presumption that both or all codepositors share equally in the true ownership of the funds deposited, and such presumption is overcome by evidence showing that the "realities of ownership" are different from the appearance of equality of interest: (decided under former analogous section) In re Webb, 18 Ohio App. 2d 287, 47 Ohio Op. 2d 452, 249 N.E.2d 83, 1969 Ohio App. LEXIS 630 (Ohio Ct. App., Cuyahoga County 1969).

**Rights**

In litigation to determine the rights of parties to the funds in a joint and survivorship account instituted during the joint lives of the parties, a joint control provision of the account does not irrevocably terminate any rights of the parties to an inter vivos distribution: (decided under former analogous section) Craig v. Curtiss, 64 Ohio App. 2d 72, 18 Ohio Op. 3d 49, 411 N.E.2d 197, 1979 Ohio App. LEXIS 8418 (Ohio Ct. App., Lucas County 1979).

**Rights defined**

The rights of parties to a joint and survivorship bank account are governed by the contract and not by the principles of the law of gifts: (decided under former analogous section) Vetter v. Hampton, 54 Ohio St. 2d 227, 8 Ohio Op. 3d 198, 375 N.E.2d 804, 1978 Ohio LEXIS 549 (Ohio 1978).

**Setoff by bank**

Where a parent provided all the funds for a joint CD with his sons, a bank which acquired the assets of the bank where the CD was opened could not appropriate those funds to satisfy a debt owed by one of the sons: Smaltz v. National City Bank, 136 Ohio App. 3d 203, 736 N.E.2d 95, 2000 Ohio App. LEXIS 504 (Ohio Ct. App., Mahoning County 2000).

A bank may not setoff a debt against a joint account which has not been pledged as collateral without inquiring into the "realities of ownership" of the account: Citizens Fed. Bank, F.S.B. v. Zierolf, 119 Ohio App. 3d 46, 694 N.E.2d 496, 1997 Ohio App. LEXIS 1300 (Ohio Ct. App., Montgomery County 1997).

**Simultaneous death of joint owners**

When the owners of a joint account with right of survivorship die simultaneously, rights to the fund are to be determined without respect to the matter of survivorship, and the proceeds of the account belong to the estates of the parties in proportion to their net contributions, absent clear and convincing evidence of a different intent: (decided under former analogous section) In re Estate of Jenkins, 29 Ohio App. 3d 235, 504 N.E.2d 1178, 1985 Ohio App. LEXIS 10409 (Ohio Ct. App., Madison County 1985).

**Survivorship rights**

When a decedent's sister-in-law sought the imposition of a constructive trust on funds the decedent's grandson withdrew from the decedent's account containing a payable on death certificate of deposit, of which the grandson and sister-in-law were beneficiaries, the grandson and the decedent's daughter were not entitled to a directed verdict against the sister-in-law, under Civ.R. 50(A)(4), because the grandson's right to withdraw those funds pursuant to R.C. 1109.07 was not superior to the sister-in-law's right of ownership in those funds, since the sister-in-law was a beneficiary of that account. Weyand v. Barnes, 2009-Ohio-3239, 2009 Ohio App. LEXIS 2767 (Ohio Ct. App., Franklin County 2009).

The survivorship rights under a joint and survivorship account of the co-party or co-parties to the sums remaining on deposit at the death of the depositor may not be defeated by extrinsic evidence that the decedent did not intend to create in such surviving party or parties a present interest in the account during the decedent's lifetime. The opening of a joint and survivorship account in the absence of fraud, duress, undue influence or lack of capacity on the part of the decedent is conclusive evidence of his or her intention to transfer to the surviving party or parties a survivorship interest in the balance remaining in the account at his or her death. The opening of a joint or alternative account without a provision for survivorship shall be conclusive evidence, in the absence of fraud or mistake, of the depositor's intention not to transfer a survivorship interest to the joint or alternative party or parties in the balance of funds contributed by such depositor remaining in the account at his or her death. Such funds shall belong in such case exclusively to the depositor's estate, subject only to claims arising under other rules of law: (decided under former analogous section) Wright v. Bloom, 1994-Ohio-153, 69 Ohio St. 3d 596, 635 N.E.2d 31, 1994 Ohio LEXIS 1497 (Ohio 1994).

When only one joint tenant with the right of survivorship to a certificate of deposit signs a security agreement and pledges the certificate as collateral to secure his or her loan, and such joint tenant dies before the loan is satisfied, the joint tenant survivor(s) is entitled to the entire amount of the certificate, as the bank's interest is immediately extinguished upon the death of the debtor joint tenant: (decided under former analogous section) In re Certificates of Deposit Issued by Hocking Valley Bank, 58 Ohio St. 3d 172, 569 N.E.2d 484, 1991 Ohio LEXIS 698 (Ohio 1991).

Sums remaining on deposit at the death of a party to a joint and survivorship account belong to the surviving party against the estate of the decedent unless there is clear and convincing evidence of a different intent: (decided under former analogous section) Witt v. Ward, 60 Ohio App. 3d 21, 573 N.E.2d 201, 1989 Ohio App. LEXIS 439 (Ohio Ct. App., Preble County 1989).

When one joint tenant with the right of survivorship to a certificate of deposit uses the certificate of deposit as collateral to secure his consumer loan, and such joint tenant dies before the loan is paid off, the surviving joint tenant is entitled to the full amount of the certificate of deposit since the bank's right of setoff is subordinate to the survivor's right of survivorship; the bank's security interest is extinguished upon the death of the debtor joint tenant: (decided under former analogous section) Franke v. Third Nat'l Bank & Trust Co., 31 Ohio App. 3d 189, 509 N.E.2d 955, 1986 Ohio App. LEXIS 10145 (Ohio Ct. App., Montgomery County 1986).

Sums remaining on deposit at the death of a party to a joint and survivorship account belong to the surviving party or parties as against the estate of the decedent unless there is clear and convincing evidence of a different intention at the time the account is created. If there are two or more surviving parties, their respective ownership during their lifetime shall be in proportion to their previous ownership interests augmented by an equal share for each survivor of any interest the decedent may have owned in the account immediately before his death; and the right of survivorship continues between the surviving parties: (decided under former analogous section) In re Estate of Thompson, 66 Ohio St. 2d 433, 20 Ohio Op. 3d 371, 423 N.E.2d 90, 1981 Ohio LEXIS 528 (Ohio 1981), overruled, Wright v. Bloom, 1994-Ohio-153, 69 Ohio St. 3d 596, 635 N.E.2d 31, 1994 Ohio LEXIS 1497 (Ohio 1994).



**Treatment of incompetency**

The mental incompetency of a codepositor in a joint and survivorship account effectively terminates the account. When a joint and survivorship account is terminated by the mental incompetency of a codepositor, each codepositor, including the incompetent, is entitled to the portion of the funds representing his contribution thereto. A depositor who has knowledge of a codepositor's mental incompetency prior to such adjudication has no right as against such codepositor to withdraw for his own use more than the portion attributable to his own contribution: (decided under former analogous section) In re Webb, 18 Ohio App. 2d 287, 47 Ohio Op. 2d 452, 249 N.E.2d 83, 1969 Ohio App. LEXIS 630 (Ohio Ct. App., Cuyahoga County 1969).

**Unauthorized withdrawals**

Any allegedly unauthorized withdrawal from a joint and survivorship account must be challenged prior to the death of the depositor. Only challenges based on fraud, duress, undue influence, or lack of capacity are permitted after the death of the depositor: In re Estate of Platt, 2002-Ohio-3382, 148 Ohio App. 3d 132, 772 N.E.2d 198, 2002 Ohio App. LEXIS 3390 (Ohio Ct. App., Trumbull County 2002).

## RESEARCH REFERENCES AND PRACTICE AIDS

**Practice Manuals and Treatises**

Anderson's Ohio Civil Practice with Forms § 28.02 Liability Arising from Bank Deposits

# TITLE 13
# COMMERCIAL TRANSACTIONS — OTHER COMMERCIAL TRANSACTIONS



# CHAPTER 1337
# POWER OF ATTORNEY



## § 1337.01 Power of attorney.

A power of attorney for the conveyance, mortgage, or lease of any interest in real property shall be signed, acknowledged, and certified as provided in section 5301.01 of the Revised Code.

**HISTORY:**

RS § 4108; S&C 464; 29 v 346, § 3; 80 v 79; 84 v 132, 133; GC § 8512; Bureau of Code Revision, 10-1-53; 149 v H 279. Eff 2-1-2002.

### NOTES TO DECISIONS

Analysis

Generally
Leases
Mental competence
Mortgages
Power of attorney
Power of sale
Witnesses

**Generally**

Substantial compliance with R.C. 5301.01 is sufficient to generate a valid power of attorney and/or mortgage: Huntington Nat'l Bank v. Kazmaier, 2008-Ohio-603, 175 Ohio App. 3d 130, 885 N.E.2d 314, 2008 Ohio App. LEXIS 516 (Ohio Ct. App., Wood County 2008).

**Leases**

An option to cancel a lease given the lessor by agreements between tenant and agency managing building constituting corpus of trust estate, modifying rent provisions and other terms of lease, conveyed no "interest in realty" and was merely an "executory agreement," and hence trustee's authorization to agency to enter into agreements need not be executed in conformity with statute of conveyance: Schofield v. John R. Thompson Co., 109 F.2d 432, 17 Ohio Op. 75, 1940 U.S. App. LEXIS 3922 (6th Cir. Ohio 1940).

Agent's authority to execute lease of principal's property must be executed as required by statute, though lease is temporary: Hodesh v. Hallerman, 45 Ohio App. 278, 186 N.E. 921, 14 Ohio Law Abs. 395, 39 Ohio L. Rep. 45, 1933 Ohio App. LEXIS 554 (Ohio Ct. App., Hamilton County 1933).

The validity of a lease, as between the parties thereto, is not affected by the fact that such power of attorney was not recorded, but the want of acknowledgment thereof renders a lease executed by the agent invalid for want of authority to execute it: Lithograph Bldg. Co. v. Watt, 96 Ohio St. 74, 117 N.E. 25, 1917 Ohio LEXIS 220 (Ohio 1917).

Under the provisions of R.C. 1337.01, a power of attorney to authorize the execution of a lease of any estate or interest in real property for a period of five years is required to be acknowledged by the principal, and under the provisions of GC § 8536 (R.C. 1337.04), it is required to be recorded: Lithograph Bldg. Co. v. Watt, 96 Ohio St. 74, 117 N.E. 25, 1917 Ohio LEXIS 220 (Ohio 1917).

**Mental competence**

The creation of a power of attorney requires that the principal be mentally competent at the time the power is executed: Testa v. Roberts, 44 Ohio App. 3d 161, 542 N.E.2d 654, 1988 Ohio App. LEXIS 723 (Ohio Ct. App., Lucas County 1988).

**Mortgages**

Validity of a real estate mortgage that was signed by a debtor for her incapacitated husband per a valid and recorded power of attorney (POA) was sustained despite claims in a Chapter 7 trustee's adversary complaint under 11 U.S.C.S. § 544(a)(3) to avoid the lien created by the mortgage per 11 U.S.C.S. § 101(54)(A) and to recover the interest on behalf of the estate pursuant to 11 U.S.C.S. § 551 because both the POA and the mortgage complied with R.C. 1337.01, with R.C. 1337.02, and with R.C. 1337.04, and with R.C. 5301.01(A) and because the only signature that mattered — which was that of the debtor — was properly acknowledged and certified. Drown v. Nat'l City Bank (In re Ingersoll), 403 B.R. 505, 2009 Bankr. LEXIS 975 (Bankr. S.D. Ohio), aff'd, 420 B.R. 414, 2009 Bankr. LEXIS 3824 (B.A.P. 6th Cir. 2009).

**Power of attorney**

Summary judgment to a bank in its foreclosure action was proper where a mortgagor's power of attorney over the mortgagor's parents' real property was in substantial compliance with the requirements of R.C. 5301.01(A), and accordingly, there was authority for the mortgagor to obtain a credit line secured by a mortgage on the property pursuant to R.C. 1337.01. Huntington Nat'l Bank v. Kazmaier, 2008-Ohio-603, 175 Ohio App. 3d 130, 885 N.E.2d 314, 2008 Ohio App. LEXIS 516 (Ohio Ct. App., Wood County 2008).

**Power of sale**

A power of attorney granting to the attorney the right to "sell and dispose of" certain premises does not authorize him to exchange them for other real estate: Raymond v. Raymond, 31 Ohio Cir. Dec. 57, 34 Ohio Cir. Dec. 57, 22 Ohio C.C. (n.s.) 569, 1915 Ohio Misc. LEXIS 90 (Ohio Ct. App., Cuyahoga County 1915).

**Witnesses**

Decedent's power of attorney that designated her nephew as the attorney-in-fact was properly executed under R.C. 1337.01 and 5301.01(B)(1), as no witnesses were required. Estate of Niemi v. Niemi, 2009-Ohio-2090, 2009 Ohio App. LEXIS 1749 (Ohio Ct. App., Trumbull County 2009).

### RESEARCH REFERENCES AND PRACTICE AIDS

**Cross-References to Related Sections**

Instruments executed out of state, RC § 5301.06.

Personal property, record of power of attorney authorizing, RC § 1337.08.

Power of attorney to convey registered land, RC § 5309.74.

**Comparative Legislation**

Power of attorney:

CA—Cal Prob Code § 4401

FL— Fla. Stat. §§ 695.01, 709.01

IL—755 Ill. Comp. Stat. § 45/1-1 et seq

IN—Burns Ind. Code Ann. § 30-5-1-1 et seq

MI—MCLS §§ 565.631, 565.632

NY—NY CLS Gen Oblig § 5-1501 et seq

**Practice Manuals and Treatises**

Anderson's Ohio Elder Law Practice Manual § 2.14 Conflicts, Execution and Recording

**Practice Guides**

Anderson's Ohio Probate Practice and Procedure § 52.02 Formalities and effect of power of attorney

**Practice Checklists**

Related and Subsequent Procedures, Ohio Transaction Guide: Family Law & Forms § 7.07

**Practice Forms**

Durable general power of attorney, Couse's Ohio Form Book Form 41.22

Durable limited power of attorney, Couse's Ohio Form Book Form 41.23

Contract between agent and owner for management of property, Couse's Ohio Form Book Form 42.8

## § 1337.02 Form and effect of power of attorney.

A deed, mortgage, or lease of any interest in real property, made by virtue of a power of attorney, must contain the name of the grantor, mortgagor, or lessor, and shall convey, mortgage, or lease the interest of such grantor, mortgagor, or lessor as fully as if such deed, mortgage, or lease were executed by such grantor, mortgagor, or lessor, in person. At any time previous to the conveyance, mortgage, or lease, the grantor, mortgagor, or lessor may revoke such power of attorney.

**HISTORY:**

RS § 4109; S&C 464; 29 v 346, § 4; 84 v 132, 133; GC § 8513; Bureau of Code Revision. Eff 10-1-53.

### NOTES TO DECISIONS

Analysis



**Power to mortgage realty**

Validity of a real estate mortgage that was signed by a debtor for her incapacitated husband per a valid and recorded power of attorney (POA) was sustained despite claims in a Chapter 7 trustee's adversary complaint under 11 U.S.C.S. § 544(a)(3) to avoid the lien created by the mortgage per 11 U.S.C.S. § 101(54)(A) and to recover the interest on behalf of the estate pursuant to 11 U.S.C.S. § 551 because both the POA and the mortgage complied with R.C. 1337.01, with R.C. 1337.02, and with R.C. 1337.04, and with R.C. 5301.01(A) and because the only signature that mattered — which was that of the debtor — was properly acknowledged and certified. Drown v. Nat'l City Bank (In re Ingersoll), 403 B.R. 505, 2009 Bankr. LEXIS 975 (Bankr. S.D. Ohio), aff'd, 420 B.R. 414, 2009 Bankr. LEXIS 3824 (B.A.P. 6th Cir. 2009).

**Power to sell realty**

If a will confers upon the executor the power to sell realty, and such power is personal, the administrator with a will annexed does not possess such power. If on the other hand, the will shows that such power is annexed to the office and is a part of the trust, it passes to the administrator with the will annexed: Westwater v. Guitner, 30 Ohio Dec. 370, 18 Ohio N.P. (n.s.) 209, 1915 Ohio Misc. LEXIS 60 (Ohio C.P. 1915).

### RESEARCH REFERENCES AND PRACTICE AIDS

**Cross-References to Related Sections**

Instruments executed out of state, RC § 5301.06.

**Comparative Legislation**

Real property transactions:

CA—Cal Prob Code § 4451

FL— Fla. Stat. §§ 696.01, 696.03

IL—755 Ill. Comp. Stat. § 45/1-1 et seq

IN—Burns Ind. Code Ann. § 30-5-5-2

MI—MCLS §§ 565.631, 565.632

NY—NY CLS Gen Oblig § 5-1502A

**Practice Guides**

Anderson's Ohio Probate Practice and Procedure § 52.02 Formalities and effect of power of attorney

**Practice Forms**

Deed executed by attorney in fact, Couse's Ohio Form Book Form 35.7

## § 1337.03 Validity of certain acts of attorney in fact.

No deed executed by a person acting for another, under a power of attorney, acknowledged, and recorded, is invalid or defective because he, instead of his principal, is named in such deed as such attorney as grantor; nor because his name, as such attorney, is subscribed to such deed, instead of the name of his principal; nor because the certificate of acknowledgment, instead of setting forth that the deed was acknowledged by the principal, by his attorney, sets forth that it was acknowledged by the person who executed it, as such attorney. All such deeds shall be as valid and effectual, in all respects, within the authority conferred by such powers of attorney, as if they had been executed by the principals of such attorneys, in person.

**HISTORY:**

RS § 4110; S&C 474; 49 v 103; GC § 8514; Bureau of Code Revision. Eff 10-1-53.

RESEARCH REFERENCES AND PRACTICE AIDS

**Cross-References to Related Sections**
Instruments executed out of state, RC § 5301.06.

**Practice Guides**
Anderson's Ohio Probate Practice and Procedure § 52.02 Formalities and effect of power of attorney

**Practice Forms**
Deed executed by attorney in fact, Couse's Ohio Form Book Form 35.7

## § 1337.04 Recording of powers of attorney.

A power of attorney for the conveyance, mortgage, or lease of an interest in real property must be recorded in the office of the county recorder of the county in which such property is situated, previous to the recording of a deed, mortgage, or lease by virtue of such power of attorney.

**HISTORY:**
RS § 4131; S&C 465; 54 v 218, § 2; 84 v 133, 134; GC § 8536; 120 v 226; Bureau of Code Revision. Eff 10-1-53.

NOTES TO DECISIONS

Analysis

Annexation petition
Leases
Mortgages

**Annexation petition**
A person who possesses a power of attorney and who signs a petition for annexation does not fall within the recording requirements of R.C. 1337.04: In re Petition for Annexation, 52 Ohio App. 3d 8, 556 N.E.2d 200, 1988 Ohio App. LEXIS 4014 (Ohio Ct. App., Franklin County 1988).

**Leases**
Under GC § 8512 (R.C. 1337.01), a power of attorney to authorize the execution of a lease of any estate or interest in real property for a period of five years is required to be acknowledged by the principal and under the provisions of R.C. 1337.04, it is required to be recorded: Lithograph Bldg. Co. v. Watt, 96 Ohio St. 74, 117 N.E. 25, 1917 Ohio LEXIS 220 (Ohio 1917).

**Mortgages**
Because there was no evidence that the property owner's obligations under the mortgage were in any way affected by the assignment, she did not have standing to challenge the mortgage assignment at issue. Although there was no evidence to show that a power of attorney was recorded as required, contrary to her argument that she was the third-party that the statute was intended to protect, the recording statute was not enacted for the benefit of mortgagors, but for the protection of third persons who might acquire legal interests in the property. Bank of N.Y. Mellon v. Workman, 2020-Ohio-3330, 2020 Ohio App. LEXIS 2263 (Ohio Ct. App., Lake County 2020).

With respect to a mortgagee's claim for an equitable lien on property, it should have been on notice that inquiry was necessary where a power of attorney from a decedent who owned the property to his daughter had not been filed prior to the recording of a quitclaim deed to the property, as required by R.C. 1337.04. Campbell v. Krupp, 2011-Ohio-2694, 195 Ohio App. 3d 573, 961 N.E.2d 205, 2011 Ohio App. LEXIS 2299 (Ohio Ct. App., Lucas County 2011).

In the foreclosure action, the trial court properly found, as a matter of law, that the bank had a valid mortgage on the property because the father had transferred the property to his son, the mortgagor, in 2005. There was sufficient evidence that the father executed a valid power of attorney appointing his daughter as his attorney-in-fact, despite the fact that the power of attorney had not been recorded, and she then, at the father's direction, transferred the property to his son. Wells Fargo Bank, N.A. v. Todt, 2011-Ohio-1376, 2011 Ohio App. LEXIS 1187 (Ohio Ct. App., Cuyahoga County 2011).

Validity of a real estate mortgage that was signed by a debtor for her incapacitated husband per a valid and recorded power of attorney (POA) was sustained despite claims in a Chapter 7 trustee's adversary complaint under 11 U.S.C.S. § 544(a)(3) to avoid the lien created by the mortgage per 11 U.S.C.S. § 101(54)(A) and to recover the interest on behalf of the estate pursuant to 11 U.S.C.S. § 551 because both the POA and the mortgage complied with R.C. 1337.01, with R.C. 1337.02, and with R.C. 1337.04, and with R.C. 5301.01(A) and because the only signature that mattered — which was that of the debtor — was properly acknowledged and certified. Drown v. Nat'l City Bank (In re Ingersoll), 403 B.R. 505, 2009 Bankr. LEXIS 975 (Bankr. S.D. Ohio), aff'd, 420 B.R. 414, 2009 Bankr. LEXIS 3824 (B.A.P. 6th Cir. 2009).

R.C. 1337.04 was not enacted for the benefit of mortgagors, but for the protection of third persons who might acquire legal interests in the property. As between parties, the validity of the mortgage is not affected by the statute: Henry v. BancOhio Nat'l Bank, 74 Ohio App. 3d 209, 598 N.E.2d 766, 1991 Ohio App. LEXIS 2426 (Ohio Ct. App., Franklin County 1991).

RESEARCH REFERENCES AND PRACTICE AIDS

**Comparative Legislation**
Power of attorney recorded — notice of revocation:
CA—Cal Civ Code § 1216
FL—Fla. Stat. § 696.03
IN—Burns Ind. Code Ann. §§ 30-5-3-3, 30-5-10-1
MI—MCLS §§ 565.631, 565.632, 700.5504
NY—NY CLS Real P § 326

**Practice Manuals and Treatises**
Anderson's Ohio Elder Law Practice Manual § 2.14 Conflicts, Execution and Recording

**Practice Guides**
Anderson's Ohio Probate Practice and Procedure § 52.03 Recording; real and personal property

**Practice Forms**
Contract between agent and owner for management of property, Couse's Ohio Form Book Form 42.8



## § 1337.05 Revocation of power of attorney must be recorded.

No instrument containing a power of attorney for the conveyance, mortgage, or lease of an interest in real property, which has been recorded, will be revoked by any act of the person by whom it was executed, unless the instrument containing such revocation is also recorded in the same office in which the instrument containing the power of attorney was recorded.

**HISTORY:**
RS § 4132; 84 v 132, 134; GC § 8537; Bureau of Code Revision. Eff 10-1-53.

RESEARCH REFERENCES AND PRACTICE AIDS

**Practice Manuals and Treatises**
Anderson's Ohio Elder Law Practice Manual § 2.15 Revocation and Other Termination

**Practice Guides**
Anderson's Ohio Probate Practice and Procedure § 52.03 Recording; real and personal property

## § 1337.06 Execution and evidence of power of attorney.

A power of attorney for the transfer of personal property or the transaction of business relating to the transfer of personal property, in order to be admitted to record as provided in section 1337.07 of the Revised Code, shall be signed and acknowledged in the same manner as deeds and mortgages under section 5301.01 of the Revised Code. When so executed, acknowledged, and recorded, a copy of the record, certified by the county recorder, with the recorder's official seal affixed to it, shall be received in all courts and places within this state as prima-facie evidence of the existence of that instrument and as conclusive evidence of the existence of that record.

**HISTORY:**
RS § 4132-2; 90 v 356, § 2; GC § 8540; Bureau of Code Revision, 10-1-53; 126 v 392 (Eff 3-17-55); 149 v H 279. Eff 2-1-2002.

NOTES TO DECISIONS

Analysis

Premium finance agreement
Signature

**Premium finance agreement**

A power of attorney in a premium finance agreement authorizing the creditor to discontinue its obligation to incur further indebtedness when the debtor is delinquent in his obligation to the creditor need not rigidly adhere to the formalities set forth in R.C. 1337.06: Black v. Globe American Casualty Co., 19 Ohio App. 3d 58, 482 N.E.2d 1278, 1984 Ohio App. LEXIS 10541 (Ohio Ct. App., Montgomery County 1984).

**Signature**

Because no valid alternative dispute resolution agreement existed between the operators of a skilled nursing and residential health care facility and a decedent, the trial court correctly denied the operators' motion to stay an executor's proceedings against them; the operators relied on a copy of a "durable power of attorney," but it did not contain the decedent's signature or indicate that the executor's authority to act on the decedent's behalf extended to her health care. Templeman v. Kindred Healthcare, Inc., 2013-Ohio-3738, 2013 Ohio App. LEXIS 3885 (Ohio Ct. App., Cuyahoga County 2013).



### RESEARCH REFERENCES AND PRACTICE AIDS

**Cross-References to Related Sections**

Dealer or salesperson may witness power of attorney for transfer of title, RC § 4505.071.

**Comparative Legislation**

Personal property transactions:
- CA—Cal Prob Code § 4450
- FL—Fla. Stat. § 709.01
- IN—Burns Ind. Code Ann. § 30-5-5-3
- MI—MCLS § 700.8101 et seq
- NY—NY CLS Gen Oblig § 5-1502B et seq

**Practice Guides**

Anderson's Ohio Probate Practice and Procedure § 52.03 Recording; real and personal property

## § 1337.07 Admission of power of attorney to record.

Any person interested may have a power of attorney authorizing the transfer of personal property or the transaction of any business relating thereto admitted to record in the office of the county recorder of the county in which such property is situated, or in which any of such business is to be transacted.

**HISTORY:**

RS § 4132-2; 90 v 356, § 2; GC § 8539; Bureau of Code Revision. Eff 10-1-53.

### RESEARCH REFERENCES AND PRACTICE AIDS

**Cross-References to Related Sections**

Execution and evidence of power of attorney, RC § 1337.06.

**Practice Guides**

Anderson's Ohio Probate Practice and Procedure § 52.03 Recording; real and personal property

## § 1337.08 Record of power of attorney authorizing transfer of personal property.

The county recorder shall record in the official records all powers of attorney authorizing the transfer of personal property or the transaction of any business relating thereto. Upon presentation of such a power of attorney, the county recorder shall endorse thereon the date of its presentation, and after it is recorded endorse thereon the time at which the instrument was recorded, and the number or letter and page of the official records in which it is recorded. The county recorder also shall keep an index of each power of attorney so recorded as provided in section 317.18 of the Revised Code.

**HISTORY:**

RS § 4132-1; 90 v 355; GC § 8538; Bureau of Code Revision, 10-1-53; 139 v S 114. Eff 10-27-81; 2013 HB 72, § 1, eff. Jan. 30, 2014.

**Amendment Notes**

The 2013 amendment substituted "record in the official records all" for "keep a record, in which shall be recorded" in the first sentence; in the second sentence, inserted "county" and substituted "official records" for "book"; in the last sentence, deleted "alphabetical" preceding "index" and added "as provided in section 317.18 of the Revised Code" to the end; and made stylistic changes.

### ATTORNEY GENERAL OPINIONS

R.C. 1337.08 has not been repealed by implication or rendered inoperative by the 1947 amendment of GC § 2757 (R.C. 317.08), and such powers of attorney, when filed with the county recorder for recording, should be recorded in the separate record book which R.C. 1337.08 requires the recorder to keep for that purpose: 1947 OAG No. 2272 (1947).

## § 1337.09 Durable power of attorney; nomination of guardian for minor or incompetent adult child [Repealed].

Repealed by 2011 SB 117, § 1337.09, effective March 22, 2012.

**HISTORY:**

136 v S 165 (Eff 7-12-76); 140 v S 115 (Eff 10-14-83); 142 v S 228 (Eff 3-22-89); 146 v H 288. Eff 1-14-97; 152 v S 157, § 1, eff. 5-14-08.

## § 1337.091 Effect of execution of power [Repealed].

Repealed by 2011 SB 117, § 1337.091, effective March 22, 2012.

**HISTORY:**

136 v S 165 (Eff 7-12-76); 138 v S 317 (Eff 3-23-81); 149 v H 279. Eff 2-1-2002; 150 v S 64, § 1, eff. 10-21-03.

## § 1337.092 When attorney in fact is not personally liable on contract or for debt of principal.

(A) If an attorney in fact enters into a contract in the representative capacity of the attorney in fact, if the contract is within the authority of the attorney in fact, and if the attorney in fact discloses in the contract that it is being entered into in the representative capacity of the attorney in fact, the attorney in fact is not personally liable on the contract, unless the contract otherwise specifies. If the words or initialism "attorney in fact," "as attorney in fact," "AIF," "power of attorney," "POA," or any other word or words or initialism indicating representative capacity as an attorney in fact are included in a contract following the name or signature of an attorney in fact, the inclusion is sufficient disclosure for purposes of this division that the contract is being entered into in the attorney in fact's representative capacity as attorney in fact.

(B) An attorney in fact is not personally liable for a debt of the attorney in fact's principal, unless one or more of the following applies:

(1) The attorney in fact agrees to be personally responsible for the debt.

(2) The debt was incurred for the support of the principal, and the attorney in fact is liable for that debt because of another legal relationship that gives rise to or results in a duty of support relative to the principal.

(3) The negligence of the attorney in fact gave rise to or resulted in the debt.

(4) An act of the attorney in fact that was beyond the attorney in fact's authority gave rise to or resulted in the debt.

(5) An agreement to assist in the recovery of funds under section 169.13 of the Revised Code was the subject of the power of attorney that gave rise to or resulted in the debt.

(C) This section applies but is not limited to, and the terms "power of attorney" and "attorney in fact" include but are not limited to, an agency agreement and an agent under an agency agreement.

**HISTORY:**

146 v H 391. Eff 10-1-96; 2011 SB 117, § 1, eff. Mar. 22, 2012.

**Editor's Notes**

Acts 2011, SB 117, § 4 provides: "The General Assembly hereby declares its intent by this act to clarify the procedure for resolution of issues created by the past or future repeal or reenactment of the federal estate tax, federal generation-skipping transfer tax, and Ohio estate tax."

**Amendment Notes**

The 2011 amendment added (C).

## NOTES TO DECISIONS

Analysis

Applicability
Attorney in fact
Breach of contract
Breach of fiduciary duty and negligence claim.
Breach of fiduciary duty and negligence claims
Exemption
Personal liability
Recognizance bond

**Applicability**

Trial court did not err by dismissing the nursing facility's complaint because the facility waived any argument concerning the applicability of the statute for purposes of appeal by failing to allege the applicability of the statute in its second amended complaint or in its case-in-chief. Vancrest Mgmt. Corp. v. Mullenhour, 2019-Ohio-2958, 140 N.E.3d 1051, 2019 Ohio App. LEXIS 3044 (Ohio Ct. App., Allen County 2019).

Nursing home's choice not to employ the statute and the exceptions to an attorney-in-fact's liability therein as a basis for recovery precluded its application. Extendicare Health Servs. v. Dunkerton, 2017-Ohio-427, 84 N.E.3d 92, 2017 Ohio App. LEXIS 428 (Ohio Ct. App., Portage County 2017).

**Attorney in fact**

Since an ambiguity existed as to the capacity in which a bail bondsman signed the recognizance of accused and whether he intended to be personally responsible for the debt or signed as the attorney in fact under R.C. 1337.092, the trial court needed to make further findings of fact as to whether the parties intended that the bondsman be personally bound by the obligation. State v. Slider, 2009-Ohio-4179, 184 Ohio App. 3d 68, 919 N.E.2d 775, 2009 Ohio App. LEXIS 3544 (Ohio Ct. App., Washington County 2009).

**Breach of contract**

Borrower's breach of contract claim against a mortgage servicer failed because the mortgage servicer, which signed a trial period plan (TTP) only in its representative capacity as attorney in fact for a lender, was not a party to the TPP pursuant to R.C. 1337.092(A). Gilchrist v. Saxon Mortg. Servs., 2013-Ohio-949, 2013 Ohio App. LEXIS 846 (Ohio Ct. App., Franklin County 2013).

**Breach of fiduciary duty and negligence claim.**

Trial court's judgment in favor of defendant, patient's attorney in fact, on the statutory claim was not against the manifest weight of the evidence because nursing facility had a conversation with defendants about redirecting patient's funds, and she did, defendant testified she acted pursuant to patient's direction and the funds were used for patient's benefit; although receipts were not maintained, defendant testified the funds were withdrawn and/or transferred for and on behalf of patient. Montefiore Home v. Fields, 2021-Ohio-3734, 2021 Ohio App. LEXIS 3648 (Ohio Ct. App., Cuyahoga County 2021).

**Breach of fiduciary duty and negligence claims**

Because a bank did not act as an attorney-in-fact and was not required to do so pursuant to the provisions of a construction loan agreement which provided for the disbursement of loan funds from the bank to a general contractor, the bank was not liable for any negligent behavior under R.C. 1337.092(B)(3) when a subcontractor was not paid by the general contractor. Huntington Nat'l Bank v. Val Homes, Inc., 2012-Ohio-526, 2012 Ohio App. LEXIS 461 (Ohio Ct. App., Geauga County 2012).

A creditor of the principal did not prove claims of breach of fiduciary duty and negligence against the attorney in fact: Aristocrat Lakewood Nursing Home v. Mayne, 133 Ohio App. 3d 651, 729 N.E.2d 768, 1999 Ohio App. LEXIS 2076 (Ohio Ct. App., Cuyahoga County 1999).

**Exemption**

grant of summary judgment in favor of the son as to the unpaid account of his father was proper because, despite the son's failure to sign the contract on the "Resident" line and specifically designate himself as power of attorney for the father, the son was acting as his father's attorney-in-fact rather than in his individual capacity when he executed the contract with the facility as the father's "Representative." Given that fact, the facility waived any argument that the son was subject to individual liability under one of statutory exceptions as the facility did not raise the applicability prior. Vill. at the Greene v. Smith, 2020-Ohio-4088, 2020 Ohio App. LEXIS 2974 (Ohio Ct. App., Montgomery County 2020).

In an action for breach of contract filed by a nursing home, a son lost the exemption to sign as an attorney in fact for his father under R.C. 1337.092(B)(4) because he refused to allow the transfer of his father to another residential facility; therefore, the son was personally responsible for the balance due on his father's account. Briarwood v. Bratanov, 2007-Ohio-2476, 2007 Ohio App. LEXIS 2304 (Ohio Ct. App., Summit County 2007).

**Personal liability**

Representative of a resident of a skilled-nursing facility was not entitled to summary judgment on the facility's claim of power-of-attorney negligence and/or unauthorized acts because the representative represented to the facility that the representative would act on the resident's behalf. Further, the evidence established that the representative depleted or transferred the resident's assets and did not direct any of the assets to the facility to address the resident's accruing debt. Montefiore Home v. Fields, 2019-Ohio-1989, 2019 Ohio App. LEXIS 2061 (Ohio Ct. App., Cuyahoga County 2019).

Dismissal sua sponte by a trial court under Ohio R. Civ. P. 12(B)(6) to a patient's attorney-in-fact in a health care company's action, seeking payment under a promissory note signed by the attorney-in-fact for the patient's care, was error, as the parties did not receive notice of the trial court's intention to dismiss under Rule 12(B)(6), and the action was not frivolous or clearly lacking in merit; the company's assertion that the attorney-in-fact had misappropriated the patient's funds for purposes of payment under the promissory note, such that the attorney-in-fact was personally liable under R.C. 1337.092(B)(1)-(5), was not addressed. Concord Health Care, Inc. v. Schroeder, 2008-Ohio-3392, 177 Ohio App. 3d 228, 894 N.E.2d 351, 2008 Ohio App. LEXIS 2874 (Ohio Ct. App., Trumbull County 2008).

**Recognizance bond**

By "revoking" the bond, the trial court did not release the surety from liability. Because R.C. 2937.36 clearly sets forth the timeframe for conducting forfeiture proceedings, reference to the Civil Rules is not necessary or required. Personal judgment against the attorney in fact on a recognizance bond was remanded where there was an ambiguity in the recognizance form. Trial court did not err by failing to grant remission where the surety did not request remission or offer evidence entitling him to it. Trial court did not err by refusing to grant additional time to secure the attendance of the accused: State v. Slider, 2009-Ohio-4179, 184 Ohio App. 3d 68, 919 N.E.2d 775, 2009 Ohio App. LEXIS 3544 (Ohio Ct. App., Washington County 2009).



## RESEARCH REFERENCES AND PRACTICE AIDS

**Cross-References to Related Sections**

Agency agreement included, RC § 1337.093.

**Practice Manuals and Treatises**

Anderson's Ohio Elder Law Practice Manual § 2.11 Protecting the Agent

**Practice Guides**

Anderson's Ohio Probate Practice and Procedure § 52.02 Formalities and effect of power of attorney

Anderson's Ohio Probate Practice and Procedure § 52.09 Agency relationships

## § 1337.093 Agency agreement included [Repealed].

Repealed by 2011 SB 117, § 1337.093, effective March 22, 2012.

**HISTORY:**

RC § 1337.09.2, 138 v S 317 (Eff 3-23-81); RC § 1337.09.3, 146 v H 391. Eff 10-1-96.

## § 1337.10 Fees of recorder.

The county recorder shall charge the same fee for the recording of a power of attorney authorizing the transfer of personal property or the transaction of business relating to the transfer of personal property, the indexing of that instrument, and for making a certified copy of the record of the instrument, that the recorder is allowed by section 317.32 of the Revised Code to charge for similar services in regard to other instruments.

In a county in which the county recorder has determined to use the microfilm process as provided by section 9.01 of the Revised Code, the recorder may require that all cancellations, releases, or other actions affecting recorded powers of attorney be by separate instrument, signed and acknowledged as provided by section 5301.01 of the Revised Code. The original instrument bearing the proper endorsement may be used as that separate instrument. Any cancellations, releases, or other actions described in this section shall be recorded in the books in which the powers of attorney were recorded. The fee for recordation shall be as set forth in this section.

**HISTORY:**

RS § 4132-3; 90 v 356; GC § 8541; Bureau of Code Revision, 10-1-53; 135 v S 341 (Eff 12-17-73); 145 v H 152 (Eff 7-1-93); 149 v H 279. Eff 2-1-2002.

# DURABLE POWER FOR HEALTH CARE

Titles 11 — 37

### § 1337.11 Definitions.

As used in sections 1337.11 to 1337.17 of the Revised Code:

(A) "Adult" means a person who is eighteen years of age or older.

(B) "Attending physician" means the physician to whom a principal or the family of a principal has assigned primary responsibility for the treatment or care of the principal or, if the responsibility has not been assigned, the physician who has accepted that responsibility.

(C) "Comfort care" means any of the following:

(1) Nutrition when administered to diminish the pain or discomfort of a principal, but not to postpone death;

(2) Hydration when administered to diminish the pain or discomfort of a principal, but not to postpone death;

(3) Any other medical or nursing procedure, treatment, intervention, or other measure that is taken to diminish the pain or discomfort of a principal, but not to postpone death.

(D) "Consulting physician" means a physician who, in conjunction with the attending physician of a principal, makes one or more determinations that are required to be made by the attending physician, or to be made by the attending physician and one other physician, by an applicable provision of sections 1337.11 to 1337.17 of the Revised Code, to a reasonable degree of medical certainty and in accordance with reasonable medical standards.

(E) "Declaration for mental health treatment" has the same meaning as in section 2135.01 of the Revised Code.

(F) "Guardian" means a person appointed by a probate court pursuant to Chapter 2111. of the Revised Code to have the care and management of the person of an incompetent.

(G) "Health care" means any care, treatment, service, or procedure to maintain, diagnose, or treat an individual's physical or mental condition or physical or mental health.

(H) "Health care decision" means informed consent, refusal to give informed consent, or withdrawal of informed consent to health care.

(I) "Health care facility" means any of the following:

(1) A hospital;

(2) A hospice care program, pediatric respite care program, or other institution that specializes in comfort care of patients in a terminal condition or in a permanently unconscious state;

(3) A nursing home;

(4) A home health agency;

(5) An intermediate care facility for individuals with intellectual disabilities;

(6) A regulated community mental health organization.

(J) "Health care personnel" means physicians, nurses, physician assistants, emergency medical technicians-basic, emergency medical technicians-intermediate, emergency medical technicians-paramedic, medical technicians, dietitians, other authorized persons acting under the direction of an attending physician, and administrators of health care facilities.

(K) "Home health agency" has the same meaning as in section 3740.01 of the Revised Code.

(L) "Hospice care program" and "pediatric respite care program" have the same meanings as in section 3712.01 of the Revised Code.

(M) "Hospital" has the same meanings as in sections 3701.01, 3727.01, and 5122.01 of the Revised Code.

(N) "Hydration" means fluids that are artificially or technologically administered.

(O) "Incompetent" has the same meaning as in section 2111.01 of the Revised Code.

(P) "Intermediate care facility for individuals with intellectual disabilities" has the same meaning as in section 5124.01 of the Revised Code.

(Q) "Life-sustaining treatment" means any medical procedure, treatment, intervention, or other measure that, when administered to a principal, will serve principally to prolong the process of dying.

(R) "Medical claim" has the same meaning as in section 2305.113 of the Revised Code.

(S) "Mental health treatment" has the same meaning as in section 2135.01 of the Revised Code.

(T) "Nursing home" has the same meaning as in section 3721.01 of the Revised Code.

(U) "Nutrition" means sustenance that is artificially or technologically administered.

(V) "Permanently unconscious state" means a state of permanent unconsciousness in a principal that, to a reasonable degree of medical certainty as determined in accordance with reasonable medical standards by the principal's attending physician and one other physician who has examined the principal, is characterized by both of the following:

(1) Irreversible unawareness of one's being and environment.

(2) Total loss of cerebral cortical functioning, resulting in the principal having no capacity to experience pain or suffering.

(W) "Person" has the same meaning as in section 1.59 of the Revised Code and additionally includes political subdivisions and governmental agencies, boards, commissions, departments, institutions, offices, and other instrumentalities.

(X) "Physician" means a person who is authorized under Chapter 4731. of the Revised Code to practice medicine and surgery or osteopathic medicine and surgery.

(Y) "Political subdivision" and "state" have the same meanings as in section 2744.01 of the Revised Code.

(Z) "Professional disciplinary action" means action taken by the board or other entity that regulates the professional conduct of health care personnel, including the state medical board and the board of nursing.

(AA) "Regulated community mental health organization" means a residential facility as defined and licensed under section 5119.34 of the Revised Code or a community mental health services provider as defined in section 5122.01 of the Revised Code.

(BB) "Terminal condition" means an irreversible, incurable, and untreatable condition caused by disease, illness, or injury from which, to a reasonable degree of medical certainty as determined in accordance with reasonable medical standards by a principal's attending physician and one other physician who has examined the principal, both of the following apply:

(1) There can be no recovery.

(2) Death is likely to occur within a relatively short time if life-sustaining treatment is not administered.

(CC) "Tort action" means a civil action for damages for injury, death, or loss to person or property, other than a civil action for damages for a breach of contract or another agreement between persons.

**HISTORY:**

143 v S 13 (Eff 9-27-89); 144 v S 1 (Eff 10-10-91); 146 v S 150 (Eff 11-24-95); 146 v S 143. Eff 3-5-96; 150 v H 95, § 1, eff. 9-26-03; 150 v H 72, § 1, eff. 10-29-03; 152 v H 529, § 1, eff. 4-7-09; 2012 HB 303, § 1, eff. Mar. 20, 2013; 2013 HB 59, § 101.01, eff. Sept. 29, 2013; 2021 hb110, § 101.01, effective September 30, 2021.

**Editor's Notes**

The provisions of § 3 of 152 v H 529 read as follows:

SECTION 3. Section 1337.11 of the Revised Code was amended by both Am. H.B. 72 and Am. Sub. H.B. 95 of the 125th General Assembly. Comparison of these amendments in pursuance of section 1.52 of the Revised Code discloses that while certain of the amendments of these acts are reconcilable, certain other of the amendments are substantively irreconcilable. Am. H.B. 72 was passed on June 10, 2003; Am. Sub. H.B. 95 was passed on June 19, 2003. Section 1337.11 of the Revised Code is therefore presented in this act as it results from Am. Sub. H.B. 95 and such of the amendments of Am. H.B. 72 as are not in conflict with the amendments of Am. Sub. H.B. 95. The General Assembly, applying the principle stated in division (B) of section 1.52 of the Revised Code that amendments are to be harmonized if reasonably capable of simultaneous operation, finds that the composite is the resulting version of the section in effect prior to the effective date of the section as presented in this act.

**Amendment Notes**

The 2021 amendment by HB 110 substituted "section 3740.01" for "section 3701.881" in (K).

The 2013 amendment substituted "individuals with intellectual disabilities" for "the mentally retarded" in (I)(5) and (P); substituted " section 5124.01" for " section 5111.20" in (P); and in (AA), substituted " section 5119.34" for " section 5119.22" and "services provider" for "agency".

The 2012 amendment inserted "pediatric respite care program" in (I)(2); substituted "and 'pediatric respite care program' have" for "has" in (L); and made a stylistic change.

152 v H 529, effective April 7, 2009, corrected internal references.

## NOTES TO DECISIONS

Analysis

Authority of probate court
Authorized representative
Insurance coverage
Wrongful administration of life-prolonging medical treatment

**Authority of probate court**

Under appropriate circumstances, a probate court may authorize withdrawal of nutrition and hydration from a permanently vegetative patient: In re Guardianship of Crum, 61 Ohio Misc. 2d 596, 580 N.E.2d 876, 1991 Ohio Misc. LEXIS 19 (Ohio P. Ct. 1991).

**Authorized representative**

Decision to designate an authorized representative for Medicaid purposes was a decision on informed consent to care, treatment, service, or procedure to maintain, diagnose, or treat a principal's physical or mental health or condition; while decisions about health care were covered by a health care power of attorney (POA), decisions about how to pay for health care would be covered by a financial power of attorney, and the son did not have the authority under the decedent's health care POA to designate the nursing home as her authorized Medicaid representative. Campbell v. Ohio Dep't of Job & Family Servs., 2020-Ohio-298, 2020 Ohio App. LEXIS 267 (Ohio Ct. App., Montgomery County 2020).

**Insurance coverage**

Husband did not violate the divorce decree by adding his children to his new wife's health insurance policy without obtaining consulting the former wife, because the requirement in the divorce decree that the husband consult the former wife before making major decisions on health care issues contemplated decisions concerning actual medical treatment, and not issues relating to health insurance coverage for that treatment. Masters v. Masters, 2010-Ohio-5961, 191 Ohio App. 3d 308, 945 N.E.2d 1118, 2010 Ohio App. LEXIS 5043 (Ohio Ct. App., Hamilton County 2010).

**Wrongful administration of life-prolonging medical treatment**

Ohio does not recognize a claim for wrongful administration of life-prolonging medical treatment. Any damages must be based on negligence or battery: Anderson v. St. Francis-St. George Hosp., 77 Ohio St. 3d 82, 671 N.E.2d 225, 1996 Ohio LEXIS 1693 (Ohio 1996).

## RESEARCH REFERENCES AND PRACTICE AIDS

**Cross-References to Related Sections**

Application for driver's license or identification card; re valid durable power of attorney for health care, RC §§ 4506.07, 4507.06, 4507.51.

Health care benefits not to be affected; transfer to willing physician or facility; emergency situations, RC § 1337.16.

Immunity of physicians and other persons, RC § 1337.15.

Patient or representative may request copy of medical record, RC § 3701.74.

**Comparative Legislation**

Durable power of attorney for health care:

CA— Cal Civ Code §§ 56, 4603, 4606, 4609, 4612, 4615, 4618.
FL—Fla. Stat. § 765.202
IN—Burns Ind. Code Ann. § 30-5-5-16 et seq
MI—MCLS § 700.5501
NY—NY CLS Pub Health § 2980 et seq

**Practice Manuals and Treatises**

Anderson's Ohio Elder Law Practice Manual § 8.3 Nutrition and Hydration

Anderson's Ohio Elder Law Practice Manual § 8.4 Persistent Vegetative State and Terminal Condition

Anderson's Ohio Elder Law Practice Manual § 9.2 Ohio Statute

**Practice Guides**

Anderson's Ohio Probate Practice and Procedure § 52.06 Durable power of attorney for health care

## § 1337.12 Durable power of attorney for health care; witnesses; acknowledgment.

(A)(1) An adult who is of sound mind voluntarily may create a valid durable power of attorney for health care by executing a durable power of attorney, in accordance with section 1337.24 of the Revised Code, that authorizes an attorney in fact as described in division (A)(2) of this section to make health care decisions for the principal at any time that the attending physician of the principal determines that the principal has lost the capacity to make informed health care decisions for the principal. The durable power of attorney for health care may authorize the attorney in fact, commencing immediately upon the execution of the instrument or at any subsequent time and regardless of whether the principal has lost the capacity to make informed health care decisions, to obtain information concerning the principal's health, including protected health information as defined in 45 C.F.R. 160.103. Except as otherwise provided in divisions (B) to (F) of section 1337.13 of the Revised Code, the authorization may include the right to give informed consent, to refuse to give informed consent, or to withdraw informed consent to any health care that is being or could be provided to the principal. Additionally, to be valid, a durable power of attorney for health care shall satisfy both of the following:

(a) It shall be signed at the end of the instrument by the principal and shall state the date of its execution.

(b) It shall be witnessed in accordance with division (B) of this section or be acknowledged by the principal in accordance with division (C) of this section.

(2) Except as otherwise provided in this division, a durable power of attorney for health care may designate any competent adult as the attorney in fact. The attending physician of the principal and an administrator of any nursing home in which the principal is receiving care shall not be designated as an attorney in fact in, or act as an attorney in fact pursuant to, a durable power of attorney for health care. An employee or agent of the attending physician of the principal and an employee or agent of any health care facility in which the principal is being treated shall not be designated as an attorney in fact in, or act as an attorney in fact pursuant to, a durable power of attorney for health care, except that these limitations do not preclude a principal from designating either type of employee or agent as the principal's attorney in fact if the individual is a competent adult and related to the principal by blood, marriage, or adoption, or if the individual is a competent adult and the principal and the individual are members of the same religious order.

(3) A durable power of attorney for health care shall not expire, unless the principal specifies an expiration date in the instrument. However, when a durable power of attorney contains an expiration date, if the principal lacks the capacity to make informed health care decisions for the principal on the expiration date, the instrument shall continue in effect until the principal regains the capacity to make informed health care decisions for the principal.

(B) If witnessed for purposes of division (A)(1)(b) of this section, a durable power of attorney for health care shall be witnessed by at least two individuals who are adults and who are not ineligible to be witnesses under this division. Any person who is related to the principal by blood, marriage, or adoption, any person who is designated as the attorney in fact or alternate attorney in fact in the instrument, the attending physician of the principal, and the administrator of any nursing home in which the principal is receiving care are ineligible to be witnesses.

The witnessing of a durable power of attorney for health care shall involve the principal signing, or acknowledging the principal's signature, at the end of the instrument in the presence of each witness. Then, each witness shall subscribe the witness's signature after the signature of the principal and, by doing so, attest to the witness's belief that the principal appears to be of sound mind and not under or subject to duress, fraud, or undue influence. The signatures of the principal and the witnesses under this division are not required to appear on the same page of the instrument.

(C) If acknowledged for purposes of division (A)(1)(b) of this section, a durable power of attorney for health care shall be acknowledged before a notary public, who shall make the certification described in section 147.53 of the Revised Code and also shall attest that the principal appears to be of sound mind and not under or subject to duress, fraud, or undue influence.

(D)(1) If a principal has both a valid durable power of attorney for health care and a valid declaration, division (B) of section 2133.03 of the Revised Code applies. If a principal has both a valid durable power of attorney for health care and a DNR identification that is based upon a valid declaration and if the declaration supersedes the durable power of attorney for health care under division (B) of section 2133.03 of the Revised Code, the DNR identification supersedes the durable power of attorney for health care to the extent of any conflict between the two. A valid durable power of attorney for health care supersedes any DNR identification that is based upon a do-not-resuscitate order that a physician issued for the principal which is inconsistent with the durable power of attorney for health care or a valid decision by the attorney in fact under a durable power of attorney.



(2) As used in division (D) of this section:

(a) "Declaration" has the same meaning as in section 2133.01 of the Revised Code.

(b) "Do-not-resuscitate order" and "DNR identification" have the same meanings as in section 2133.21 of the Revised Code.

(E)(1) In a durable power of attorney for health care, a principal may nominate a guardian of the principal's person, estate, or both for consideration by a court if proceedings for the appointment of a guardian for the principal's person, estate, or both are commenced at a later time. The principal may authorize the person nominated as the guardian or the attorney in fact to nominate a successor guardian for consideration by the court. The principal's nomination of a guardian of the principal's person, estate, or both is revoked by the principal's subsequent nomination of a guardian of the principal's person, estate, or both, and, except for good cause shown or disqualification, the court shall make its appointment in accordance with the principal's most recent nomination.

(2) The principal may direct that bond be waived for a person nominated as guardian or successor guardian under division (E)(1) of this section.

(3) A durable power of attorney for health care that contains the nomination of a person to be the guardian of the person, estate, or both of the principal may be filed with the probate court for safekeeping, and the probate court shall designate the nomination as the nomination of a standby guardian.

(4) If a guardian is appointed for the principal, a durable power of attorney for health care is not terminated, and the authority of the attorney in fact continues unless the court, pursuant to its authority under section 2111.50 of the Revised Code, limits, suspends, or terminates the power of attorney after notice to the attorney in fact and upon a finding that the limitation, suspension, or termination is in the best interest of the principal.

**HISTORY:**

143 v S 13 (Eff 9-27-89); 144 v S 1 (Eff 10-10-91); 147 v H 354 (Eff 7-9-98); 148 v H 494. Eff 3-15-2001; 2011 SB 117, § 1, eff. Mar. 22, 2012; 2013 HB 126, § 1, eff. Mar. 20, 2014.

**Editor's Notes**

Acts 2011, SB 117, § 4 provides: "The General Assembly hereby declares its intent by this act to clarify the procedure for resolution of issues created by the past or future repeal or reenactment of the federal estate tax, federal generation-skipping transfer tax, and Ohio estate tax."

The provisions of § 3(A) of HB 494 (148 v —) read as follows

SECTION 3. (A) The amendments made by this act to sections 1337.12, 1337.13, and 1337.17 of the Revised Code do not invalidate an otherwise valid durable power of attorney for health care that was executed prior to the effective date of this act in conformity with those sections as they existed on the date of the execution of the durable power of attorney for health care.

* * *

**Amendment Notes**

The 2013 amendment inserted the second sentence of the introductory language of (A)(1); inserted "or alternate attorney in fact" in the second sentence of the first paragraph of (B); and added (E).

The 2011 amendment substituted "section 1337.24" for "division (B) of section 1337.09" in the first sentence of the introductory language of (A)(1).

## NOTES TO DECISIONS

Analysis

Generally
Arbitration agreement
Removal
Validity
Wrongful prolongation of life

**Generally**

Because no valid alternative dispute resolution agreement existed between the operators of a skilled nursing and residential health care facility and a decedent, the trial court correctly denied the operators' motion to stay an executor's proceedings against them; the operators relied on a copy of a "durable power of attorney," but it did not contain the decedent's signature or indicate that the executor's authority to act on the decedent's behalf extended to her health care. Templeman v. Kindred Healthcare, Inc., 2013-Ohio-3738, 2013 Ohio App. LEXIS 3885 (Ohio Ct. App., Cuyahoga County 2013).

In the absence of advance directives, the administration or withdrawal of life-sustaining treatment should be based on medical expertise, consistent with the patient's wishes, as they are expressed by family members: In re Guardianship of McInnis, 61 Ohio Misc. 2d 790, 584 N.E.2d 1389, 1991 Ohio Misc. LEXIS 41 (Ohio P. Ct. 1991).

**Arbitration agreement**

Nursing facility's motion to stay proceedings and compel arbitration was properly denied because the patient's daughter was not authorized under the health care power of attorney to waive his right to access to courts and agree to binding arbitration and she lacked the apparent authority to enter into the arbitration agreement on his behalf. The decision to waive the right to arbitrate was a legal determination, not a health care decision. Primmer v. Healthcare Indus. Corp., 2015-Ohio-4104, 43 N.E.3d 788, 2015 Ohio App. LEXIS 3932 (Ohio Ct. App., Athens County 2015).

**Removal**

Trial court properly granted summary judgment to a church official in an action by a decedent's nephews and nieces, alleging that he engaged in negligence after he undertook a duty to remove the church pastor from the decedent's legal documents, including her healthcare power of attorney, as only the decedent had the authority to remove the pastor from the power of attorney and to designate the beneficiaries of her will pursuant to R.C. 1337.12(A)(1) and 2107.02. Kitchen v. Teeters, 2012-Ohio-4343, 2012 Ohio App. LEXIS 3802 (Ohio Ct. App., Clermont County 2012).

Trial court properly granted summary judgment to a church pastor in an action by a decedent's nephews and nieces, alleging that he engaged in negligence after he undertook a duty to remove himself from the decedent's legal documents, including her healthcare power of attorney, as only the decedent had the authority to remove the pastor from the power of attorney under R.C. 1337.12(A)(1). Kitchen v. Teeters, 2012-Ohio-4343, 2012 Ohio App. LEXIS 3802 (Ohio Ct. App., Clermont County 2012).

**Validity**

In a guardianship proceeding, the magistrate's decision was not against the manifest weight of the evidence, as powers of attorney in favor of the ward's son were not valid either due to the ward's disability or the lack of statutorily required language. In re Austin, 2016-Ohio-667, 2016 Ohio App. LEXIS 587 (Ohio Ct. App., Franklin County 2016).

**Wrongful prolongation of life**

Damages were not recoverable on a claim of wrongful prolongation of life. Unwanted medical care did not constitute a battery: Allore v. Flower Hosp., 121 Ohio App. 3d 229, 699 N.E.2d 560, 1997 Ohio App. LEXIS 2753 (Ohio Ct. App., Lucas County 1997).

## RESEARCH REFERENCES AND PRACTICE AIDS

**Cross-References to Related Sections**

Authority of attorney in fact, RC § 1337.13.
Definitions, RC § 1337.11.

Do not resuscitate orders, RC § 2133.25.
Health care benefits not to be affected; transfer to willing physician or facility; emergency situations, RC § 1337.16.
Immunity of physicians and other persons, RC § 1337.15.
Fees of the county recorder, RC § 317.32.
Records to be kept by county recorder, RC § 317.08.
Revocation of durable power of attorney, RC § 1337.14.

**Ohio Administrative Code**
Department of health—
Do not resuscitate (DNR) protocol. OAC ch. 3701-62.
Department of job and family services, division of medical assistance —

**Comparative Legislation**
Requirements for valid durable power of attorney for health care:
CA— Cal Prob Code §§ 4121, 4122, 4700, 4701, 4773
FL—Fla. Stat. § 765.203
IL—755 Ill. Comp. Stat. § 45/4-3
IN—Burns Ind. Code Ann. §§ 16-36-1-1 et seq, 30-5-5-16 et seq
MI—MCLS § 700.5501 et seq
NY—NY CLS Pub Health § 2981

**Practice Manuals and Treatises**
Anderson's Ohio Elder Law Practice Manual § 9.1 Authority in General
Anderson's Ohio Elder Law Practice Manual § 9.2 Ohio Statute
Anderson's Ohio Elder Law Practice Manual § 9.7 Common Statutory Provisions
Anderson's Ohio Elder Law Practice Manual § 9.8 Drafting Considerations

**Practice Guides**
Anderson's Ohio Probate Practice and Procedure § 52.06 Durable power of attorney for health care
Anderson's Ohio Probate Practice and Procedure § 59.01 Living will

## § 1337.13 Authority of attorney in fact.

(A)(1) An attorney in fact under a durable power of attorney for health care shall make health care decisions for the principal only if the instrument substantially complies with section 1337.12 of the Revised Code and specifically authorizes the attorney in fact to make health care decisions for the principal, and only if the attending physician of the principal determines that the principal has lost the capacity to make informed health care decisions for the principal. If authorized in the instrument, the attorney in fact, commencing immediately upon the execution of the instrument or at any subsequent time specified in the instrument and regardless of whether the principal has lost the capacity to make informed health care decisions, may obtain information concerning the principal's health, including protected health information as defined in 45 C.F.R. 160.103. Except as otherwise provided in divisions (B) to (F) of this section and subject to any specific limitations in the instrument, the attorney in fact may make health care decisions for the principal to the same extent as the principal could make those decisions for the principal if the principal had the capacity to do so. Except as otherwise provided in divisions (B) to (F) of this section, in exercising that authority, the attorney in fact shall act consistently with the desires of the principal or, if the desires of the principal are unknown, shall act in the best interest of the principal.

(2) This section does not affect, and shall not be construed as affecting, any right that the person designated as attorney in fact in a durable power of attorney for health care may have, apart from the instrument, to make or participate in the making of health care decisions on behalf of the principal.

(3) Unless the right is limited in a durable power of attorney for health care, when acting pursuant to the instrument, the attorney in fact has the same right as the principal to receive information about proposed health care, to review health care records, and to consent to the disclosure of health care records.

(B)(1) An attorney in fact under a durable power of attorney for health care does not have authority, on behalf of the principal, to refuse or withdraw informed consent to life-sustaining treatment, unless the principal is in a terminal condition or in a permanently unconscious state and unless the applicable requirements of divisions (B)(2) and (3) of this section are satisfied.

(2) In order for an attorney in fact to refuse or withdraw informed consent to life-sustaining treatment for a principal who is in a permanently unconscious state, the consulting physician associated with the determination that the principal is in the permanently unconscious state shall be a physician who, by virtue of advanced education or training, of a practice limited to particular diseases, illnesses, injuries, therapies, or branches of medicine and surgery or osteopathic medicine and surgery, of certification as a specialist in a particular branch of medicine or surgery or osteopathic medicine and surgery, or of experience acquired in the practice of medicine and surgery or osteopathic medicine and surgery, is qualified to determine whether the principal is in a permanently unconscious state.

(3) In order for an attorney in fact to refuse or withdraw informed consent to life-sustaining treatment for a principal who is in a terminal condition or in a permanently unconscious state, the attending physician of the principal shall determine, in good faith, both of the following:

(a) To a reasonable degree of medical certainty, and in accordance with reasonable medical standards, that there is no reasonable possibility that the principal will regain the capacity to make informed health care decisions for the principal;

(b) That the attorney in fact is competent to make such a decision under division (H) of this section.

(C) Except as otherwise provided in this division, an attorney in fact under a durable power of attorney for health care does not have authority, on behalf of the principal, to refuse or withdraw informed consent to health care necessary to provide comfort care. This division does not preclude, and shall not be construed as precluding, an attorney in fact under a durable power of attorney for health care from refusing or withdrawing informed consent to the provision of nutrition or hydration to the principal if, under the circumstances described in division (E) of this section, the attorney in fact would not be prohibited from refusing or withdrawing informed consent to the provision of nutrition or hydration to the principal.

(D) An attorney in fact under a durable power of attorney for health care does not have authority to refuse or withdraw informed consent to health care for a principal who is pregnant if the refusal or withdrawal of the health care would terminate the pregnancy, unless the pregnancy or the health care would pose a substantial risk to the life of the principal, or unless the principal's attending physician and at least one other physician who has examined the principal determine, to a reasonable degree of medical certainty and in accordance with reasonable medical standards, that the fetus would not be born alive.

(E) An attorney in fact under a durable power of attorney for health care does not have authority to refuse or withdraw informed consent to the provision of nutrition or hydration to the principal, unless the principal is in a terminal condition or in a permanently unconscious state and unless the following apply:

(1) The principal's attending physician and at least one other physician who has examined the principal determine, to a reasonable degree of medical certainty and in accordance with reasonable medical standards, that nutrition or hydration will not or no longer will serve to provide comfort to, or alleviate pain of, the principal.

(2) If the principal is in a permanently unconscious state, the principal has authorized the attorney in fact to refuse or withdraw informed consent to the provision of nutrition or hydration to the principal when the principal is in a permanently unconscious state by doing both of the following in the durable power of attorney for health care:

(a) Including a statement in capital letters or other conspicuous type, including, but not limited to, a different font, bigger type, or boldface type, that the attorney in fact may refuse or withdraw informed consent to the provision of nutrition or hydration to the principal if the principal is in a permanently unconscious state and if the determination described in division (E)(1) of this section is made, or checking or otherwise marking a box or line that is adjacent to a similar statement on a printed form of a durable power of attorney for health care;

(b) Placing the principal's initials or signature underneath or adjacent to the statement, check, or other mark described in division (E)(2)(a) of this section.

(3) If the principal is in a permanently unconscious state, the principal's attending physician determines, in good faith, that the principal authorized the attorney in fact to refuse or withdraw informed consent to the provision of nutrition or hydration to the principal when the principal is in a permanently unconscious state by complying with the requirements of divisions (E)(2)(a) and (b) of this section.

(4) The principal's attending physician determines, in good faith, that the attorney in fact is competent to make such a decision under division (H) of this section.

(F) An attorney in fact under a durable power of attorney for health care does not have authority to withdraw informed consent to any health care to which the principal previously consented, unless at least one of the following applies:

(1) A change in the physical condition of the principal has significantly decreased the benefit of that health care to the principal.

(2) The health care is not, or is no longer, significantly effective in achieving the purposes for which the principal consented to its use.

(G) An attorney in fact under a durable power of attorney for health care does not have authority to make decisions pertaining to the use or continuation of life-sustaining treatment or the provision of nutrition or hydration to the principal unless the attorney in fact is competent to make those decisions under division (H) of this section.

(H) An attorney in fact is competent to make decisions under division (B), (E), or (G) of this section unless the attorney in fact is subject to a temporary protection order, civil protection order, or any other protection order issued by a court in this state or another state in which the principal is the alleged victim.

Titles 11 — 37

**HISTORY:**

143 v S 13 (Eff 9-27-89); 144 v S 1 (Eff 10-10-91); 148 v H 494. Eff 3-15-2001; 2013 HB 126, § 1, eff. Mar. 20, 2014; 2016 hb451, § 1, effective April 6, 2017.

**Editor's Notes**

See provisions, § 3(A) of HB 494 (148 v —) following RC § 1337.12.

**Amendment Notes**

The 2016 amendment by HB 451 redesignated and rewrote the former introductory language of (B)(3) as (B)(3)(a) and (b); inserted (E)(4); and added (G) and (H).

The 2013 amendment inserted the second sentence of (A)(1).

### NOTES TO DECISIONS

Analysis

Authority
Withdrawal of hydration or nutrition

**Authority**

No evidence existed showing that the decedent had lost the capacity to make informed health-care decisions for herself, let alone evidence that her attending physician ever made this determination. Campbell v. Ohio Dep't of Job & Family Servs., 2020-Ohio-298, 2020 Ohio App. LEXIS 267 (Ohio Ct. App., Montgomery County 2020).

Nursing facility's motion to stay proceedings and compel arbitration was properly denied because the patient's daughter was not authorized under the health care power of attorney to waive his right to access to courts and agree to binding arbitration and she lacked the apparent authority to enter into the arbitration agreement on his behalf. The decision to waive the right to arbitrate was a legal determination, not a health care decision. Primmer v. Healthcare Indus. Corp., 2015-Ohio-4104, 43 N.E.3d 788, 2015 Ohio App. LEXIS 3932 (Ohio Ct. App., Athens County 2015).

Trial court erred in granting the nursing home's motion stay proceedings pending the outcome of arbitration and compel or enforce arbitration because, at the time the representative signed the arbitration agreement, the health care power of attorney was not in effect since there was no evidence that the decedent had lost the capacity to make her own health care decisions. McFarren v. Emeritus at Canton, 2013-Ohio-3900, 997 N.E.2d 1254, 2013 Ohio App. LEXIS 4058 (Ohio Ct. App., Stark County 2013).

Because no valid alternative dispute resolution agreement existed between the operators of a skilled nursing and residential health care facility and a decedent, the trial court correctly denied the operators' motion to stay an executor's proceedings against them; the operators relied on a copy of a "durable power of attorney," but it did not contain the decedent's signature or indicate that the executor's authority to act on the decedent's behalf extended to her health care. Templeman v. Kindred Healthcare, Inc., 2013-Ohio-3738, 2013 Ohio App. LEXIS 3885 (Ohio Ct. App., Cuyahoga County 2013).

Nursing home owner's motion to stay the case pending arbitration was properly denied because the daughter lacked authority to sign the arbitration agreement on behalf of her mother. The daughter signed the agreement as her mother's representative under a health care power of attorney that had specific provisions regarding when that power existed and, according to the record, that power of attorney had not yet come into being because no one had declared the mother mentally unfit to make her own health care decisions. Tedeschi v. Atrium Ctrs., L.L.C., 2012-Ohio-2929, 2012 Ohio App. LEXIS 2560 (Ohio Ct. App., Cuyahoga County 2012).

**Withdrawal of hydration or nutrition**

The public policy of this state as announced by the General Assembly in its enactment of R.C. 1337.11 through 1337.17, forbids the withdrawal of hydration or nutrition from a comatose patient in a persistent vegetative state with no realistic prospect of recovery, where the withdrawal of nutrition or hydration is likely to result in the death of the patient. Such withdrawal is prohibited notwithstanding previous oral statements of the patient himself that he would not desire the use of artificial life support to prolong his existence: Couture v. Couture, 48 Ohio App. 3d 208, 549 N.E.2d 571, 1989 Ohio App. LEXIS 3300 (Ohio Ct. App., Montgomery County 1989).

### RESEARCH REFERENCES AND PRACTICE AIDS

**Cross-References to Related Sections**

Creation of valid durable power of attorney for health care, RC § 1337.12.

Definitions, RC § 1337.11.

Health care benefits not to be affected; transfer to willing physician or facility; emergency situations, RC § 1337.16.

Immunity of physicians and other persons, RC § 1337.15.

Revocation of durable power of attorney, RC § 1337.14.

**Practice Manuals and Treatises**

Anderson's Ohio Elder Law Practice Manual § 8.3 Nutrition and Hydration

Anderson's Ohio Elder Law Practice Manual § 8.5 Non-exclusivity of Advance Directive Statutes

Anderson's Ohio Elder Law Practice Manual § 9.2 Ohio Statute

**Practice Guides**

Anderson's Ohio Probate Practice and Procedure § 52.06 Durable power of attorney for health care

## § 1337.14 Revocation of power.

(A) A principal who creates a valid durable power of attorney for health care may revoke that instrument or the designation of the attorney in fact under it.

The principal may so revoke at any time and in any manner. The revocation shall be effective when the principal expresses an intention to so revoke, except that, if the principal made the principal's attending physician aware of the durable power of attorney for health care, the revocation shall be effective upon its communication to the attending physician by the principal, a witness to the revocation, or other health care personnel to whom the revocation is communicated by such a witness. Absent actual knowledge to the contrary, the attending physician of the principal and other health care personnel who are informed of the revocation of a durable power of attorney for health care by an alleged witness may rely on the information and act in accordance with the revocation.

(B) Upon the communication as described in division (A) of this section to the attending physician of a principal of the fact that the principal's durable power of attorney for health care has been revoked, the attending physician or other health care personnel acting under the direction of the attending physician shall make the fact a part of the principal's medical record.

(C) Unless the instrument provides otherwise, a valid durable power of attorney for health care revokes a prior, valid durable power of attorney for health care.

(D) Regardless of when the declaration is drafted, the execution of a declaration for mental health treatment does not revoke a valid durable power of attorney for health care. A declaration for mental health treatment executed in accordance with Chapter 2135. of the Revised Code supersedes a valid durable power of attorney for health care with regard to mental health treatment and the designation of a proxy to make decisions regarding mental health treatment.

**HISTORY:**

143 v S 13 (Eff 9-27-89); 144 v S 1. Eff 10-10-91; 150 v H 72, § 1, eff. 10-29-03.

**RESEARCH REFERENCES AND PRACTICE AIDS**

**Cross-References to Related Sections**

Definitions, RC § 1337.11.

Health care benefits not to be affected; transfer to willing physician or facility; emergency situations, RC § 1337.16.

Immunity of physicians and other persons, RC § 1337.15.

**Comparative Legislation**

Revocation of power:

CA—Cal Prob Code § 4727

FL—Fla. Stat. § 765.104

IL—755 Ill. Comp. Stat. § 45/4-6

IN—Burns Ind. Code Ann. §§ 16-36-1-6, 30-5-10-1

MI—MCLS § 700.5504

NY—NY CLS Pub Health § 2981

**Practice Manuals and Treatises**

Anderson's Ohio Elder Law Practice Manual § 9.7 Common Statutory Provisions

## § 1337.15 Immunity of physicians and other persons.

(A) Subject to division (H) of this section, an attending physician of a principal is not subject to criminal prosecution or professional disciplinary action and is not liable in damages in a tort or other civil action for actions taken in good faith and in reliance on a health care decision when all of the following are satisfied:

(1) The decision is made by an attorney in fact under a durable power of attorney for health care after the attorney in fact receives information sufficient to satisfy the requirements of informed consent or refusal or withdrawal of informed consent, and the attending physician, in good faith, believes that the attorney in fact is authorized to make the decision.

(2) The attending physician, in good faith, believes that the decision is consistent with the desires of the principal, or the attorney in fact informs the attending physician that the desires of the principal are unknown and the attending physician, in good faith, believes that the desires of the principal are unknown and that the decision is in the best interest of the principal.

(3) The attending physician determines, in good faith, to a reasonable degree of medical certainty, and in accordance with reasonable medical standards, that the principal has lost the capacity to make informed health care decisions for the principal.

(4) If the decision is to withhold or withdraw life-sustaining treatment, the attending physician attempts, in good faith, to determine the desires of the principal to the extent that the principal is able to convey them and places a report of the attempt in the health care records of the principal.

(5) If the decision is to withhold or withdraw life-sustaining treatment, the attending physician determines, in good faith, to a reasonable degree of medical certainty, and in accordance with reasonable medical standards, that both of the following apply:

(a) The principal is in a terminal condition or in a permanently unconscious state.

(b) There is no reasonable possibility that the principal will regain the capacity to make informed health care decisions for the principal.

(6) If the decision pertains to a principal who is pregnant and if the withholding or withdrawal of health care would terminate the pregnancy, the attending physician makes, in good faith, to a reasonable degree of medical certainty, and in accordance with reasonable medical standards, a determination whether or not the pregnancy or health care involved would pose a substantial risk to the life of the principal or a determination whether or not the fetus would be born alive.

(7) If the decision pertains to the provision of nutrition or hydration to a principal who is in a terminal condition or in a permanently unconscious state, the attending physician determines, in good faith, to a reasonable degree of medical certainty, and in accordance with reasonable medical standards, that nutrition or hydration will not or no longer will serve to provide comfort to, or alleviate pain of, the principal.

(8) If the decision pertains to the provision of nutrition or hydration to a principal who is in a permanently unconscious state, the attending physician determines, in good faith, that the principal authorized the attorney in fact to refuse or withdraw informed consent to the provision of nutrition or hydration to the principal when the principal is in a permanently unconscious state by complying with the requirements of divisions (E)(2)(a) and (b) of section 1337.13 of the Revised Code.

(B)(1) Notwithstanding the health care decision of the attorney in fact, subject to division (H) of this section, an attending physician of a principal is not subject to criminal prosecution or professional disciplinary action and is not liable in damages in a tort or other civil action for providing or for failing to withdraw life-sustaining treatment.

(2) Subject to division (H) of this section, an attending physician who is carrying out in good faith and in a manner consistent with divisions (C) and (E) of section 1337.13 of the Revised Code the responsibility to provide comfort care to a principal in a terminal condition or in a permanently unconscious state is not subject to criminal prosecution or professional disciplinary action and is not liable in damages in a tort or other civil action for prescribing, dispensing, administering, or causing to be administered any particular medical procedure, treatment, intervention, or other measure to the principal, including, but not limited to, prescribing, personally furnishing, administering, or causing to be administered by judicious titration or in another manner any form of medication, for the purpose of diminishing the principal's pain or discomfort and not for the purpose of postponing or causing the principal's death, even though the medical procedure, treatment, intervention, or other measure may appear to hasten or increase the risk of the principal's death.

(C) Subject to division (H) of this section, a consulting physician is not subject to criminal prosecution or professional disciplinary action and is not liable in damages in a tort or other civil action as follows:

(1) If the health care decision involved is one other than the health care decision described in division (C)(2), (3), or (4) of this section, the consulting physician made a determination, in good faith, to a reasonable degree of medical certainty, and in accordance with reasonable medical standards, in conjunction with the attending physician of a principal.

(2) If the decision is to withhold or withdraw life-sustaining treatment, the consulting physician determines, in good faith, to a reasonable degree of medical certainty, and in accordance with reasonable medical standards, after examining the principal, that the principal is in a terminal condition or in a permanently unconscious state.

(3) If the health care decision involved pertains to a principal who is pregnant and if the withholding or withdrawal of health care would terminate the pregnancy, the consulting physician makes, in good faith, to a reasonable degree of medical certainty, and in accordance with reasonable medical standards, a determination whether or not the pregnancy or health care involved would pose a substantial risk to the life of the principal or a determination whether or not the fetus would be born alive.

(4) If the decision pertains to the provision of nutrition or hydration to a principal who is in a terminal condition or in a permanently unconscious state, the consulting physician determines, in good faith, to a reasonable degree of medical certainty, and in accordance with reasonable medical standards, that nutrition or hydration will not or no longer will serve to provide comfort to, or alleviate pain of, the principal.

(D) Subject to division (H) of this section, a person is not subject to criminal prosecution or professional disciplinary action and is not liable in damages in a tort or other civil action for actions taken, in good faith, while relying on a durable power of

Titles 11 — 37

attorney for health care if the person does not have actual knowledge of either of the following facts:

(1) The durable power of attorney has been revoked pursuant to section 1337.14 of the Revised Code.

(2) The durable power of attorney does not substantially comply with sections 1337.11 to 1337.17 of the Revised Code.

(E)(1) Subject to division (H) of this section, a consulting physician, an employee or agent of any health care facility or the attending physician of a principal, and health care personnel acting under the direction of the attending physician of a principal are not subject to criminal prosecution or professional disciplinary action and are not liable in damages in a tort or other civil action for any action described in division (A), (B), (C), or (D) of this section that was undertaken, in good faith, pursuant to the direction of the attending physician of the principal.

(2) Subject to division (H) of this section, health care personnel who are acting under the direction of the principal's attending physician and who carry out the responsibility to provide comfort care to a principal in a terminal condition or in a permanently unconscious state in good faith and in a manner consistent with divisions (C) and (E) of section 1337.13 of the Revised Code are not subject to criminal prosecution or professional disciplinary action and are not liable in damages in a tort or other civil action for dispensing, administering, or causing to be administered any particular medical procedure, treatment, intervention, or other measure to the principal, including, but not limited to, personally furnishing, administering, or causing to be administered by judicious titration or in another manner any form of medication, for the purpose of diminishing the principal's pain or discomfort and not for the purpose of postponing or causing the principal's death, even though the medical procedure, treatment, intervention, or other measure may appear to hasten or increase the risk of the principal's death.

(F) Subject to division (H) of this section, a health care facility is not subject to criminal prosecution or professional disciplinary action and is not liable in damages in a tort or other civil action for any action that properly was undertaken pursuant to division (A), (B), (C), (D), or (E) of this section.

(G) Subject to division (H) of this section, an attorney in fact is not subject to criminal prosecution or professional disciplinary action and is not liable in damages in a tort or other civil action for health care decisions made in good faith while acting pursuant to the attorney in fact's authority under a durable power of attorney for health care.

(H)(1) Sections 1337.11 to 1337.17 of the Revised Code and a durable power of attorney for health care do not affect or limit any potential tort or other civil liability of an attending or consulting physician, an employee or agent of a health care facility or an attending physician, health care personnel acting under the direction of an attending physician, a health care facility, an attorney in fact, or any other person, including, but not limited to, liability associated with a medical claim, that satisfies both of the following:

(a) The liability arises out of a negligent action or omission in connection with the medical diagnosis, care, or treatment of a principal under a durable power of attorney for health care or arises out of any deviation from reasonable medical standards.

(b) The liability is based on the fact that the negligent action or omission, or the deviation, as described in division (H)(1)(a) of this section caused or contributed to the principal under the durable power of attorney for health care having a terminal condition or being in a permanently unconscious state, or otherwise caused or contributed to any injury to or the wrongful death of the principal.

(2) Sections 1337.11 to 1337.17 of the Revised Code and a durable power of attorney for health care do not grant an immunity from criminal or civil liability or from professional disciplinary action to health care personnel for actions that are outside the scope of their authority.

**HISTORY:**

143 v S 13 (Eff 9-27-89); 144 v S 1 (Eff 10-10-91); 145 v H 343 (Eff 7-22-94); 147 v S 66. Eff 7-22-98.

**RESEARCH REFERENCES AND PRACTICE AIDS**

**Cross-References to Related Sections**

Definitions, RC § 1337.11.

Health care benefits not to be affected; transfer to willing physician or facility; emergency situations, RC § 1337.16.

**Comparative Legislation**

Physician immunity:

CA—Cal Prob Code § 4750
FL—Fla. Stat. § 765.109
IL—755 Ill. Comp. Stat. § 45/4-8
IN—Burns Ind. Code Ann. §§ 16-36-1-4, 30-5-9-10
MI—MCLS § 700.5501 et seq
NY—NY CLS Pub Health § 2986

**Practice Manuals and Treatises**

Anderson's Ohio Elder Law Practice Manual § 9.7 Common Statutory Provisions

Anderson's Ohio Elder Law Practice Manual § 9.8 Drafting Considerations

### § 1337.16 Health care benefits not to be affected; refusal to follow instructions; transfer to willing physician or facility; emergencies; notification of certain persons; complaint by objecting person; power executed in another state.

(A) No physician, health care facility, other health care provider, person authorized to engage in the business of insurance in this state under Title XXXIX [39] of the Revised Code, health insuring corporation, other health care plan, or legal entity that is self-insured and provides benefits to its employees or members shall require an individual to create or refrain from creating a durable power of attorney for health care, or shall require an individual to revoke or refrain from revoking a durable power of attorney for health care, as a condition of being admitted to a health care facility, being provided health care, being insured, or being the recipient of benefits.

(B)(1) Subject to division (B)(2) of this section, an attending physician of a principal or a health care facility in which a principal is confined may refuse to comply or allow compliance with the instructions of an attorney in fact under a durable power of attorney for health care on the basis of a matter of conscience or on another basis. An employee or agent of an attending physician of a principal or of a health care facility in which a principal is confined may refuse to comply with the instructions of an attorney in fact under a durable power of attorney for health care on the basis of a matter of conscience.

(2)(a) An attending physician of a principal who, or health care facility in which a principal is confined that, is not willing or not able to comply or allow compliance with the instructions of an attorney in fact under a durable power of attorney for health care to use or continue, or to withhold or withdraw, health care that were given under division (A) of section 1337.13 of the Revised Code, or with any probate court reevaluation order issued pursuant to division (D)(6) of this section, shall not prevent or attempt to prevent, or unreasonably delay or attempt to unreasonably delay, the transfer of the principal to the care of a physician who, or a health care facility that, is willing and able to so comply or allow compliance.

(b) If the instruction of an attorney in fact under a durable power of attorney for health care that is given under division (A) of section 1337.13 of the Revised Code is to use or continue life-sustaining treatment in connection with a principal who is in a terminal condition or in a permanently unconscious state, the attending physician of the principal who, or the health care facility in which the principal is confined that, is not willing or not able to comply or allow compliance with that instruction shall use or continue the life-sustaining treatment or cause it to be used or continued until a transfer as described in division (B)(2)(a) of this section is made.

(C) Sections 1337.11 to 1337.17 of the Revised Code and a durable power of attorney for health care created under section 1337.12 of the Revised Code do not affect or limit the authority of a physician or a health care facility to provide or not to provide health care to a person in accordance with reasonable medical standards applicable in an emergency situation.

(D)(1) If the attending physician of a principal and one other physician who examines the principal determine that the principal is in a terminal condition or in a permanently unconscious state, if the attending physician additionally determines that the principal has lost the capacity to make informed health care decisions for the principal and that there is no reasonable possibility that the principal will regain the capacity to make informed health care decisions for the principal, and if the attorney in fact under the principal's durable power of attorney for health care makes a health care decision pertaining to the use or continuation, or the withholding or withdrawal, of life-sustaining treatment, the attending physician shall do all of the following:

(a) Record the determinations and health care decision in the principal's medical record;

(b) Make a good faith effort, and use reasonable diligence, to notify the appropriate individual or individuals, in accordance with the following descending order of priority, of the determinations and health care decision:

(i) If any, the guardian of the principal. This division does not permit or require the appointment of a guardian for the principal.

(ii) The principal's spouse;

(iii) The principal's adult children who are available within a reasonable period of time for consultation with the principal's attending physician;

(iv) The principal's parents;

(v) An adult sibling of the principal or, if there is more than one adult sibling, a majority of the principal's adult siblings who are available within a reasonable period of time for such consultation.

(c) Record in the principal's medical record the names of the individual or individuals notified pursuant to division (D)(1)(b) of this section and the manner of notification;

(d) Afford time for the individual or individuals notified pursuant to division (D)(1)(b) of this section to object in the manner described in division (D)(3)(a) of this section.

(2)(a) If, despite making a good faith effort, and despite using reasonable diligence, to notify the appropriate individual or individuals described in division (D)(1)(b) of this section, the attending physician cannot notify the individual or individuals of the determinations and health care decision because the individual or individuals are deceased, cannot be located, or cannot be notified for some other reason, the requirements of divisions (D)(1)(b), (c), and (d) of this section and, except as provided in division (D)(3)(b) of this section, the provisions of divisions (D)(3) to (6) of this section shall not apply in connection with the principal. However, the attending physician shall record in the principal's medical record information pertaining to the reason for the failure to provide the requisite notices and information pertaining to the nature of the good faith effort and reasonable diligence used.

(b) The requirements of divisions (D)(1)(b), (c), and (d) of this section and, except as provided in division (D)(3)(b) of this section, the provisions of divisions (D)(3) to (6) of this section shall not apply in connection with the principal if only one individual would have to be notified pursuant to division (D)(1)(b) of this section and that individual is the attorney in fact under the durable power of attorney for health care. However, the attending physician of the principal shall record in the principal's medical record information indicating that no notice was given pursuant to division (D)(1)(b) of this section because of the provisions of division (D)(2)(b) of this section.

(3)(a) Within forty-eight hours after receipt of a notice pursuant to division (D)(1) of this section, any individual so notified shall advise the attending physician of the principal whether the individual objects on a basis specified in division (D)(4)(c) of this section. If an objection as described in that division is communicated to the attending physician, then, within two business days after the communication, the individual shall file a complaint as described in division (D)(4) of this section in the probate court of the county in which the principal is located. If the individual fails to so file a complaint, the individual's objections as described in division (D)(4)(c) of this section shall be considered to be void.

(b) Within forty-eight hours after the priority individual or any member of a priority class of individuals receives a notice pursuant to division (D)(1) of this section or within forty-eight hours after information pertaining to an unnotified priority individual or unnotified priority class of individuals is recorded in a principal's medical record pursuant to division (D)(2)(a) or (b) of this section, the individual or a majority of the individuals in the next class of individuals that pertains to the principal in the descending order of priority set forth in divisions (D)(1)(b)(i) to (v) of this section shall advise the attending physician of the principal whether the individual or majority object on a basis specified in division (D)(4)(c) of this section. If an objection as described in that division is communicated to the attending physician, then, within two business days after the communication, the objecting individual or majority shall file a complaint as described in division (D)(4) of this section in the probate court of the county in which the principal is located. If the objecting individual or majority fails to file a complaint, the objections as described in division (D)(4)(c) of this section shall be considered to be void.

(4) A complaint of an individual that is filed in accordance with division (D)(3)(a) of this section or of an individual or majority of individuals that is filed in accordance with division (D)(3)(b) of this section shall satisfy all of the following:

(a) Name any health care facility in which the principal is confined;

(b) Name the principal, the principal's attending physician, and the consulting physician associated with the determination that the principal is in a terminal condition or in a permanently unconscious state;

(c) Indicate whether the plaintiff or plaintiffs object on one or more of the following bases:

(i) To the attending physician's determination that the principal has lost the capacity to make informed health care decisions for the principal;

(ii) To the attending physician's determination that there is no reasonable possibility that the principal will regain the capacity to make informed health care decisions for the principal;

(iii) That, in exercising the attorney in fact's authority, the attorney in fact is not acting consistently with the desires of the principal or, if the desires of the principal are unknown, in the best interest of the principal;

(iv) That the durable power of attorney for health care has expired or otherwise is no longer effective;

(v) To the attending physician's and consulting physician's determinations that the principal is in a terminal condition or in a permanently unconscious state;

(vi) That the attorney in fact's health care decision pertaining to the use or continuation, or the withholding or withdrawal, of life-sustaining treatment is not authorized by the durable power of attorney for health care or is prohibited under section 1337.13 of the Revised Code;

(vii) That the durable power of attorney for health care was executed when the principal was not of sound mind or was under or subject to duress, fraud, or undue influence;

(viii) That the durable power of attorney for health care otherwise does not substantially comply with section 1337.12 of the Revised Code.

(d) Request the probate court to issue one or more of the following types of orders:

(i) An order to the attending physician to reevaluate, in light of the court proceedings, the determination that the principal has lost the capacity to make informed health care decisions for the principal, the determination that the principal is in a terminal condition or in a permanently unconscious state, or the determination that there is no reasonable possibility that the principal will regain the capacity to make informed health care decisions for the principal;

(ii) An order to the attorney in fact to act consistently with the desires of the principal or, if the desires of the principal are unknown, in the best interest of the principal in exercising the attorney in fact's authority, or to make only health care decisions pertaining to life-sustaining treatment that are authorized by the durable power of attorney for health care and that are not prohibited under section 1337.13 of the Revised Code;

(iii) An order invalidating the durable power of attorney for health care because it has expired or otherwise is no longer effective, it was executed when the principal was not of sound mind or was under or subject to duress, fraud, or undue influence, or it otherwise does not substantially comply with section 1337.12 of the Revised Code.

(e) Be accompanied by an affidavit of the plaintiff or plaintiffs that includes averments relative to whether the plaintiff is an individual or the plaintiffs are individuals as described in division (D)(1)(b)(i), (ii), (iii), (iv), or (v) of this section and to the factual basis for the plaintiff's or the plaintiffs' objections;

(f) Name any individuals who were notified by the attending physician in accordance with division (D)(1)(b) of this section and who are not joining in the complaint as plaintiffs;

(g) Name, in the caption of the complaint, as defendants the attending physician of the principal, the attorney in fact under the durable power of attorney for health care, the consulting physician associated with the determination that the principal is in a terminal condition or in a permanently unconscious state, any health care facility in which the principal is confined, and any individuals who were notified by the attending physician in accordance with division (D)(1)(b) of this section and who are not joining in the complaint as plaintiffs.

(5) Notwithstanding any contrary provision of the Revised Code or of the Rules of Civil Procedure, the state and persons other than an objecting individual as described in division (D)(3)(a) of this section, other than an objecting individual or majority of individuals as described in division (D)(3)(b) of this section, and other than persons described in division (D)(4)(g) of this section are prohibited from commencing a civil action under division (D) of this section and from joining or being joined as parties to an action commenced under division (D) of this section, including joining by way of intervention.

(6)(a) A probate court in which a complaint as described in division (D)(4) of this section is filed within the period specified in division (D)(3)(a) or (b) of this section shall conduct a hearing on the complaint after a copy of it and a notice of the hearing have been served upon the defendants. The clerk of the probate court in which the complaint is filed shall cause the complaint and the notice of the hearing to be so served in accordance with the Rules of Civil Procedure, which service shall be made, if possible, within three days after the filing of the complaint. The hearing shall be conducted at the earliest possible time, but no later than the third business day after such service has been completed. Immediately following the hearing, the court shall enter on its journal its determination whether a requested order will be issued.

(b) If the health care decision of the attorney in fact authorized the use or continuation of life-sustaining treatment and if the plaintiff or plaintiffs requested a reevaluation order to the attending physician of the principal or an order to the attorney in fact as described in division (D)(4)(d)(i) or (ii) of this section, the court shall issue the requested order only if it finds that the plaintiff or plaintiffs have established a factual basis for the objection or objections involved by clear and convincing evidence and, if applicable, to a reasonable degree of medical certainty and in accordance with reasonable medical standards.

(c) If the health care decision of the attorney in fact authorized the withholding or withdrawal of life-sustaining treatment and if the plaintiff or plaintiffs requested a reevaluation order to the attending physician of the principal or an order to the attorney in fact as described in division (D)(4)(d)(i) or (ii) of this section, the court shall issue the requested order only if it finds that the plaintiff or plaintiffs have established a factual basis for the objection or objections involved by a preponderance of the evidence and, if applicable, to a reasonable degree of medical certainty and in accordance with reasonable medical standards.

(d) If the plaintiff or plaintiffs requested an invalidation order as described in division (D)(4)(d)(iii) of this section, the court shall issue the order only if it finds that the plaintiff or plaintiffs have established a factual basis for the objection or objections involved by clear and convincing evidence.

(e) If the court issues a reevaluation order to the principal's attending physician pursuant to division (D)(6)(b) or (c) of this section, the attending physician shall make the requisite reevaluation. If, after doing so, the attending physician again determines that the principal has lost the capacity to make informed health care decisions for the principal, that the principal is in a terminal condition or in a permanently unconscious state, or that there is no reasonable possibility that the principal will regain the capacity to make informed health care decisions for the principal, the attending physician shall notify the court in writing of the determination and comply with division (B)(2) of this section.

(E)(1) In connection with the provision of comfort care in a manner consistent with divisions (C) and (E) of section 1337.13 of the Revised Code to a principal who is in a terminal condition or in a permanently unconscious state, nothing in sections 1337.11 to 1337.17 of the Revised Code precludes the attending physician of the principal who carries out the responsibility to provide comfort care to the principal in good faith and while acting within the scope of the attending physician's authority from prescribing, dispensing, administering, or causing to be administered any particular medical procedure, treatment, intervention, or other measure to the principal, including, but not limited to, prescribing, personally furnishing, administering, or causing to be administered by judicious titration or in another manner any form of medication, for the purpose of diminishing the principal's pain or discomfort and not for the purpose of postponing or causing the principal's death, even though the medical procedure, treatment, intervention, or other measure may appear to hasten or increase the risk of the principal's death. In connection with the provision of comfort care in a manner consistent with divisions (C) and (E) of section 1337.13 of the Revised Code to a principal who is in a terminal condition or in a permanently unconscious state, nothing in sections 1337.11 to 1337.17 of the Revised Code precludes health care personnel acting under the direction of the principal's attending physician who carry out the responsibility to provide comfort care to the principal in good faith and while acting within the scope of their authority from dispensing, administering, or causing to be administered any particular medical procedure, treatment, intervention, or other measure to the principal, including, but not limited to, personally furnishing, administering, or causing to be administered by judicious titration or in another manner any form of medication, for the purpose of diminishing the principal's pain or discomfort and not for the purpose of postponing or causing the principal's death, even though the medical procedure, treatment, intervention, or other measure may appear to hasten or increase the risk of the principal's death.

(2) If, at any time, a priority individual or any member of a priority class of individuals under division (D)(1)(b) of this section or if, at any time, the individual or a majority of the individuals in the next class of individuals that pertains to the principal in the descending order of priority set forth in that division, believes in good faith that both of the following circumstances apply, the priority individual, the member of the priority class of individuals, or the individual or majority of individuals in the next class of individuals that pertains to the principal may commence an action in the probate court of the county in which a principal who is in a terminal condition or permanently unconscious state is located for the issuance of an order mandating the use or continuation of comfort care in connection with the principal in a manner that is consistent with sections 1337.11 to 1337.17 of the Revised Code:

(a) Comfort care is not being used or continued in connection with the principal.

(b) The withholding or withdrawal of the comfort care is contrary to sections 1337.11 to 1337.17 of the Revised Code.

(F) Except as provided in divisions (D) and (E) of this section in connection with principals who are in a terminal condition or in a permanently unconscious state, sections 1337.11 to 1337.17 of the Revised Code do not authorize the commencement of any civil action in a probate court or court of common pleas for the purpose of obtaining an order relative to a health care decision made by an attorney in fact under a durable power of attorney for health care.

(G) A durable power of attorney for health care, or other document, that is similar to a durable power of attorney for health care authorized by sections 1337.11 to 1337.17 of the Revised Code, that is or has been executed under the law of another state prior to, on, or after October 10, 1991, and that substantially complies with that law or with sections 1337.11 to 1337.17 of the Revised Code shall be considered to be valid for purposes of those sections.

**HISTORY:**

143 v S 13 (Eff 9-27-89); 144 v S 1 (Eff 10-10-91); 145 v H 343 (Eff 7-22-94); 147 v S 67 (Eff 6-4-97); 147 v S 66. Eff 7-22-98.

### NOTES TO DECISIONS

**Unwanted medical care**

Ohio does not recognize a claim for wrongful administration of life-prolonging medical treatment. Any damages must be based on negligence or battery: Anderson v. St. Francis-St. George Hosp., 77 Ohio St. 3d 82, 671 N.E.2d 225, 1996 Ohio LEXIS 1693 (Ohio 1996).

### ATTORNEY GENERAL OPINIONS

Existing statutes and case law do not expressly authorize a member of a rescue squad, acting in an emergency situation and without direction of a physician, to honor the request of a relative of a resident of a rest home to provide no extraordinary care to the resident: 1993 Ohio Op. Att'y Gen. No. 062 (1993).

The statutes governing living wills and durable powers of attorney for health care do not provide for the application of those documents when a rescue squad is acting in an emergency situation and without the direction of an individual's attending physician: 1993 Ohio Op. Att'y Gen. No. 062 (1993).

### RESEARCH REFERENCES AND PRACTICE AIDS

**Cross-References to Related Sections**

Definitions, RC § 1337.11.
Immunity of physicians and other persons, RC § 1337.15.
Jurisdiction of probate court, RC § 2101.24.

**Comparative Legislation**

Validity of power executed in another state:
CA—Cal Prob Code § 4653
FL—Fla. Stat. § 765.112
IN—Burns Ind. Code Ann. § 30-5-3-2
NY—NY CLS Pub Health § 2990

**Practice Manuals and Treatises**

Anderson's Ohio Elder Law Practice Manual § 9.2 Ohio Statute
Anderson's Ohio Elder Law Practice Manual § 9.7 Common Statutory Provisions

## § 1337.17 Use of printed form; notice to principal.

A printed form of durable power of attorney for health care may be sold or otherwise distributed in this state for use by adults who are not advised by an attorney. By use of such a printed form, a principal may authorize an attorney in fact to make health care decisions on the principal's behalf, but the printed form shall not be used as an instrument for granting authority for any other decisions. Any printed form that is sold or otherwise distributed in this state for the purpose described in this section shall include the following notice:

Notice to Adult Executing This Document

This is an important legal document. Before executing this document, you should know these facts:

This document gives the person you designate (the attorney in fact) the power to make most* health care decisions for you if you lose the capacity to make informed health care decisions for yourself. This power is effective only when your attending physician determines that you have lost the capacity to make informed health care decisions for yourself and, notwithstanding this document, as long as you have the capacity to make informed health care decisions for yourself, you retain the right to make all medical and other health care decisions for yourself.

You may include specific limitations in this document on the authority of the attorney in fact to make health care decisions for you.

Subject to any specific limitations you include in this document, if your attending physician determines that you have lost the capacity to make an informed decision on a health care matter, the attorney in fact generally* will be authorized by this document to make health care decisions for you to the same extent as you could make those decisions yourself, if you had the capacity to do so. The authority of the attorney in fact to make health care decisions for you generally* will include the authority to give informed consent, to refuse to give informed consent, or to withdraw informed consent to any care, treatment, service, or procedure to maintain, diagnose, or treat a physical or mental condition.

However, even if the attorney in fact has general authority to make health care decisions for you under this document, the attorney in fact never* will be authorized to do any of the following:

(1) Refuse or withdraw informed consent to life-sustaining treatment (unless your attending physician and one other physician who examines you determine, to a reasonable degree of medical certainty and in accordance with reasonable medical standards, that either of the following applies:

(a) You are suffering from an irreversible, incurable, and untreatable condition caused by disease, illness, or injury from which (i) there can be no recovery and (ii) your death is likely to occur within a relatively short time if life-sustaining treatment is not administered, and your attending physician additionally determines, to a reasonable degree of medical certainty and in accordance with reasonable medical standards, that there is no reasonable possibility that you will regain the capacity to make informed health care decisions for yourself.

(b) You are in a state of permanent unconsciousness that is characterized by you being irreversibly unaware of yourself and your environment and by a total loss of cerebral cortical functioning, resulting in you having no capacity to experience pain or suffering, and your attending physician additionally determines, to a reasonable degree of medical certainty and in accordance with reasonable medical standards, that there is no reasonable possibility that you will regain the capacity to make informed health care decisions for yourself);

(2) Refuse or withdraw informed consent to health care necessary to provide you with comfort care (except that, if the attorney in fact is not prohibited from doing so under (4) below, the attorney in fact could refuse or withdraw informed consent to the provision of nutrition or hydration to you as described under (4) below). (You should understand that comfort care is defined in Ohio law to mean artificially or technologically administered sustenance (nutrition) or fluids (hydration) when administered to diminish your pain or discomfort, not to postpone your death, and any other medical or nursing procedure, treatment, intervention, or other measure that would be taken to diminish your pain or discomfort, not to postpone your death. Consequently, if your attending physician were to determine that a previously described medical or nursing procedure, treatment, intervention, or other measure will not or no longer will serve to provide comfort to you or alleviate your pain, then, subject to (4) below, your attorney in fact would be authorized to refuse or withdraw informed consent to the procedure, treatment, intervention, or other measure.);

(3) Refuse or withdraw informed consent to health care for you if you are pregnant and if the refusal or withdrawal would terminate the pregnancy (unless the pregnancy or health care would pose a substantial risk to your life, or unless your attending physician and at least one other physician who examines you determine, to a reasonable degree of medical certainty and in accordance with reasonable medical standards, that the fetus would not be born alive);

(4) Refuse or withdraw informed consent to the provision of artificially or technologically administered sustenance (nutrition) or fluids (hydration) to you, unless:

(a) You are in a terminal condition or in a permanently unconscious state.

(b) Your attending physician and at least one other physician who has examined you determine, to a reasonable degree of medical certainty and in accordance with reasonable medical standards, that nutrition or hydration will not or no longer will serve to provide comfort to you or alleviate your pain.

(c) If, but only if, you are in a permanently unconscious state, you authorize the attorney in fact to refuse or withdraw informed consent to the provision of nutrition or hydration to you by doing both of the following in this document:

(i) Including a statement in capital letters or other conspicuous type, including, but not limited to, a different font, bigger type, or boldface type, that the attorney in fact may refuse or withdraw informed consent to the provision of nutrition or hydration to you if you are in a permanently unconscious state and if the determination that nutrition or hydration will not or no longer will serve to provide comfort to you or alleviate your pain is made, or checking or otherwise marking a box or line (if any) that is adjacent to a similar statement on this document;

(ii) Placing your initials or signature underneath or adjacent to the statement, check, or other mark previously described.

(d) Your attending physician determines, in good faith, that you authorized the attorney in fact to refuse or withdraw informed consent to the provision of nutrition or hydration to you if you are in a permanently unconscious state by complying with the requirements of (4)(c)(i) and (ii) above.

(5) Withdraw informed consent to any health care to which you previously consented, unless a change in your physical condition has significantly decreased the benefit of that health care to you, or unless the health care is not, or is no longer, significantly effective in achieving the purposes for which you consented to its use;

(6) Provide, refuse, or withdraw informed consent to life-sustaining treatment, or the provision of artificially or technologically administered sustenance (nutrition) or fluids (hydration) to you, if the attorney in fact is subject to a temporary protection order, civil protection order, or any other protection order in this state or another state in which you are the alleged victim.

Additionally, when exercising authority to make health care decisions for you, the attorney in fact will have to act consistently with your desires or, if your desires are unknown, to act in your best interest. You may express your desires to the attorney in fact by including them in this document or by making them known to the attorney in fact in another manner.

When acting pursuant to this document, the attorney in fact generally* will have the same rights that you have to receive information about proposed health care, to review health care records, and to consent to the disclosure of health care records. You can limit that right in this document if you so choose.

Generally, you may designate any competent adult as the attorney in fact under this document. However, you cannot* designate your attending physician or the administrator of any nursing home in which you are receiving care as the attorney in fact under this document. Additionally, you cannot* designate an employee or agent of your attending physician, or an employee or agent of a health care facility at which you are being treated, as the attorney in fact under this document, unless either type of employee or agent is a competent adult and related to you by blood, marriage, or adoption, or unless either type of employee or agent is a competent adult and you and the employee or agent are members of the same religious order.

This document has no expiration date under Ohio law, but you may choose to specify a date upon which your durable power of attorney for health care generally will expire. However, if you specify an expiration date and then lack the capacity to make informed health care decisions for yourself on that date, the document and the power it grants to your attorney in fact will continue in effect until you regain the capacity to make informed health care decisions for yourself.

You have the right to revoke the designation of the attorney in fact and the right to revoke this entire document at any time and in any manner. Any such revocation generally will be effective when you express your intention to make the revocation. However, if you made your attending physician aware of this document, any such revocation will be effective only when you communicate it to your attending physician, or when a witness to the revocation or other health care personnel to whom the revocation is communicated by such a witness communicate it to your attending physician.

If you execute this document and create a valid durable power of attorney for health care with it, it will revoke any prior, valid durable power of attorney for health care that you created, unless you indicate otherwise in this document.

This document is not valid as a durable power of attorney for health care unless it is acknowledged before a notary public or is signed by at least two adult witnesses who are present when you sign or acknowledge your signature. No person who is related to you by blood, marriage, or adoption may be a witness. The attorney in fact, your attending physician, and the administrator of any nursing home in which you are receiving care also are ineligible to be witnesses.

If there is anything in this document that you do not understand, you should ask your lawyer to explain it to you.

In the preceding notice, the single words, and the two sentences in the second set of parentheses in paragraph (2), followed by an asterisk and all of paragraph (4) shall appear in the printed form in capital letters or other conspicuous type, including, but not limited to, a different font, bigger type, or boldface type.

**HISTORY:**

143 v S 13 (Eff 9-27-89); 144 v S 1 (Eff 10-10-91); 148 v H 494. Eff 3-15-2001; 2016 hb451, § 1, effective April 6, 2017.

**Amendment Notes**

The 2016 amendment by HB 451 inserted (6).

**Editor's Notes**

See provisions, § 3(A) of HB 494 (148 v —) following RC § 1337.12.

## RESEARCH REFERENCES AND PRACTICE AIDS

**Cross-References to Related Sections**

Definitions, RC § 1337.11.

Free distribution of living will and durable power of attorney for health care forms, RC § 317.41.

Health care benefits not to be affected; transfer to willing physician or facility; emergency situations, RC § 1337.16.

Immunity of physicians and other persons, RC § 1337.15.

Revocation of durable power of attorney, RC § 1337.14.

**Comparative Legislation**

Notice to principal executing printed form:

CA— Cal Prob Code §§ 4704, 4771, 4772
FL— Fla. Stat. §§ 765.203, 765.204
IL—755 Ill. Comp. Stat. § 45/4-10
IN—Burns Ind. Code Ann. § 16-36-1-6
MI—MCLS §§ 700.5504, 700.8101
NY—NY CLS Pub Health § 2981

**Practice Manuals and Treatises**

Anderson's Ohio Elder Law Practice Manual § 9.2 Ohio Statute

Anderson's Ohio Elder Law Practice Manual § 9.8 Drafting Considerations

**Practice Guides**

Anderson's Ohio Probate Practice and Procedure § 52.06 Durable power of attorney for health care

**Practice Forms**

Health Care Power of Attorney, Anderson's Ohio Elder Law Practice Manual Form 9.2

Durable power of attorney for health care with reference to living will declaration—witnessed, Couse's Ohio Form Book Form 41.27

# STATUTORY FORM FOR CREATION OF POWER OF ATTORNEY

### § 1337.18 Form for creation of power of attorney [Repealed].

Repealed by 2011 SB 117, § 1337.18, effective March 22, 2012.

**HISTORY:**
151 v H 246, § 1, eff. 3-29-06.

### § 1337.19 General powers of attorney in fact under power of attorney [Repealed].

Repealed by 2011 SB 117, § 1337.19, effective March 22, 2012.

**HISTORY:**
151 v H 246, § 1, eff. 3-29-06.

### § 1337.20 Construction of powers of attorney in fact [Repealed].

Repealed by 2011 SB 117, § 1337.20, effective March 22, 2012.

**HISTORY:**
151 v H 246, § 1, eff. 3-29-06.

### § 1337.21 Uniform power of attorney act.

Sections 1337.21 to 1337.64 of the Revised Code may be cited as the uniform power of attorney act.

**HISTORY:**
2011 SB 117, § 1, eff. Mar. 22, 2012.

**Editor's Notes**
Acts 2011, SB 117, § 4 provides: "The General Assembly hereby declares its intent by this act to clarify the procedure for resolution of issues created by the past or future repeal or reenactment of the federal estate tax, federal generation-skipping transfer tax, and Ohio estate tax."

### § 1337.22 Definitions.

As used in sections 1337.21 to 1337.64 of the Revised Code:

(A) "Agent" means a person granted authority to act for a principal under a power of attorney, whether denominated an agent, attorney in fact, or otherwise. "Agent" includes an original agent, coagent, successor agent, and a person to which an agent's authority is delegated.

(B) "Durable," with respect to a power of attorney, means not terminated by the principal's incapacity.

(C) "Electronic" means relating to technology having electrical, digital, magnetic, wireless, optical, electromagnetic, or similar capabilities.

(D) "Good faith" means honesty in fact.

(E) "Incapacity" means inability of an individual to manage property or business affairs for either of the following reasons:

(1) The individual has an impairment in the ability to receive and evaluate information or make or communicate decisions even with the use of technological assistance.

(2) The individual is any of the following:

(a) Missing;

(b) Detained, including incarcerated in a penal system;

(c) Outside the United States and unable to return.

(F) "Person" means an individual, corporation, business trust, estate, trust, partnership, limited liability company, association, joint venture, public corporation, government or governmental subdivision, agency, or instrumentality, or any other legal or commercial entity.

(G) "Power of attorney" means a writing or other record that grants authority to an agent to act in the place of the principal, whether or not the term power of attorney is used.

(H) "Presently exercisable general power of appointment," with respect to property or a property interest subject to a power of appointment, means power exercisable at the time in question to vest absolute ownership in the principal individually, the principal's estate, the principal's creditors, or the creditors of the principal's estate. The term includes a power of appointment not exercisable until the occurrence of a specified event, the satisfaction of an ascertainable standard, or the passage of a specified period only after the occurrence of the specified event, the satisfaction of the ascertainable standard, or the passage of the specified period. The term does not include a power exercisable in a fiduciary capacity or only by will.

(I) "Principal" means an individual who grants authority to an agent in a power of attorney.

(J) "Property" means anything that may be the subject of ownership, whether real or personal, or legal or equitable, or any interest or right therein.

(K) "Record" means information that is inscribed on a tangible medium or that is stored in an electronic or other medium and is retrievable in perceivable form.

(L) "Sign" means, with present intent to authenticate or adopt a record, to execute or adopt a tangible symbol or to attach to or logically associate with the record an electronic sound, symbol, or process.

(M) "State" means a state of the United States, the District of Columbia, Puerto Rico, the United States Virgin Islands, or any territory or insular possession subject to the jurisdiction of the United States.

(N) "Stocks and bonds" means stocks, bonds, mutual funds, and all other types of securities and financial instruments, whether held directly, indirectly, or in any other manner, but does not include commodity futures contracts or call or put options on stocks or stock indexes.

**HISTORY:**
2011 SB 117, § 1, eff. Mar. 22, 2012.

**Editor's Notes**
Acts 2011, SB 117, § 4 provides: "The General Assembly hereby declares its intent by this act to clarify the procedure for resolution of issues created by the past or future repeal or reenactment of the federal estate tax, federal generation-skipping transfer tax, and Ohio estate tax."

### § 1337.23 Exceptions.

Sections 1337.21 to 1337.64 of the Revised Code apply to all powers of attorney except the following:

(A) A power to the extent it is coupled with an interest in the subject of the power, including a power given to or for the benefit of a creditor in connection with a credit transaction;

(B) A power to make health-care decisions;

(C) A proxy or other delegation to exercise voting rights or management rights with respect to an entity;

(D) A power created on a form prescribed by a government or governmental subdivision, agency, or instrumentality for a governmental purpose.

**HISTORY:**
2011 SB 117, § 1, eff. Mar. 22, 2012.

**Editor's Notes**
Acts 2011, SB 117, § 4 provides: "The General Assembly hereby declares its intent by this act to clarify the procedure for resolution of issues created by the past or future repeal or reenactment of the federal estate tax, federal generation-skipping transfer tax, and Ohio estate tax."

### § 1337.24 Durable power of attorney.

A power of attorney created under sections 1337.21 to 1337.64 of the Revised Code is durable unless it expressly provides that it is terminated by the incapacity of the principal.

**HISTORY:**
2011 SB 117, § 1, eff. Mar. 22, 2012.

**Editor's Notes**
Acts 2011, SB 117, § 4 provides: "The General Assembly hereby declares its intent by this act to clarify the procedure for resolution of issues created by the past or future repeal or reenactment of the federal estate tax, federal generation-skipping transfer tax, and Ohio estate tax."

### § 1337.25 Signature.

A power of attorney must be signed by the principal or in the principal's conscious presence by another individual directed by the principal to sign the principal's name on the power of attorney. A signature on a power of attorney is presumed to be genuine if the principal acknowledges the signature before a notary public or other individual authorized by law to take acknowledgments.

**HISTORY:**
2011 SB 117, § 1, eff. Mar. 22, 2012.

**Editor's Notes**
Acts 2011, SB 117, § 4 provides: "The General Assembly hereby declares its intent by this act to clarify the procedure for resolution of issues created by the past or future repeal or reenactment of the federal estate tax, federal generation-skipping transfer tax, and Ohio estate tax."

#### NOTES TO DECISIONS

**Requirements**
There was no genuine issue of material fact regarding a breach of contract claim against a medical facility by the purported attorney in fact, who was also the notary and the principal's son, because the notary had a conflict of interest and was invalid, and, thus, the execution of the power of attorney did not comply with statutory requirements, rendering the power of attorney invalid and insufficient as the basis for any contract. Estate of Armatas v. Cleveland Clinic Found., 2020-Ohio-3338, 2020 Ohio App. LEXIS 2271 (Ohio Ct. App., Stark County 2020).

Appellee's signature and notation of "P.O.A." had no legal effect and could not bind appellee's mother to the arbitration agreement in documentation signed by appellee in admitting her mother to appellant's nursing home facility because it was undisputed that the mother had never granted appellee power of attorney in the manner required under this statute. Scott v. Kindred Transitional Care & Rehab., 2016-Ohio-495, 2016 Ohio App. LEXIS 418 (Ohio Ct. App., Cuyahoga County 2016).

Because no valid alternative dispute resolution agreement existed between the operators of a skilled nursing and residential health care facility and a decedent, the trial court correctly denied the operators' motion to stay an executor's proceedings against them; the operators relied on a copy of a "durable power of attorney," but it did not contain the decedent's signature or indicate that the executor's authority to act on the decedent's behalf extended to her health care. Templeman v. Kindred Healthcare, Inc., 2013-Ohio-3738, 2013 Ohio App. LEXIS 3885 (Ohio Ct. App., Cuyahoga County 2013).

### § 1337.26 Execution.

(A) A power of attorney executed in this state on or after the effective date of this section is valid if its execution complies with section 1337.25 of the Revised Code.

(B) A power of attorney executed in this state before the effective date of this section is valid if its execution complied with the law of this state as it existed at the time of execution.

(C) A power of attorney executed other than in this state is valid in this state if, when the power of attorney was executed, the execution complied with the law of the jurisdiction that determines the meaning and effect of the power of attorney pursuant to section 1337.27 of the Revised Code or with the requirements for a military power of attorney pursuant to 10 U.S.C. 1044b.

(D) Except as otherwise provided by statute other than sections 1337.21 to 1337.64 of the Revised Code, a photocopy or electronically transmitted copy of an original power of attorney has the same effect as the original.

**HISTORY:**
2011 SB 117, § 1, eff. Mar. 22, 2012.

**Editor's Notes**
Acts 2011, SB 117, § 4 provides: "The General Assembly hereby declares its intent by this act to clarify the procedure for resolution of issues created by the past or future repeal or reenactment of the federal estate tax, federal generation-skipping transfer tax, and Ohio estate tax."

### § 1337.27 Meaning and effect determined by jurisdiction indicated in the power of attorney.

The meaning and effect of a power of attorney is determined by the law of the jurisdiction indicated in the power of attorney and, in the absence of an indication of jurisdiction, by the law of the jurisdiction in which the power of attorney was executed.

**HISTORY:**
2011 SB 117, § 1, eff. Mar. 22, 2012.

**Editor's Notes**
Acts 2011, SB 117, § 4 provides: "The General Assembly hereby declares its intent by this act to clarify the procedure for resolution of issues created by the past or future repeal or reenactment of the federal estate tax, federal generation-skipping transfer tax, and Ohio estate tax."

### § 1337.28 Nomination of guardian; bond waiver.

(A) In a power of attorney, a principal may nominate a guardian of the principal's person, estate, or both and may nominate a guardian of the person, the estate, or both of one or more of the principal's minor children or incompetent adult children, whether born at the time of the execution of the power of attorney or afterward. The nomination is for consideration by a court if proceedings for the appointment of a guardian for the principal's person, estate, or both or if proceedings for the appointment of a guardian of the person, the estate, or both of one or more of the principal's minor children or incompetent adult children are commenced at a later time. The principal may authorize the person nominated as guardian or the agent to nominate a successor guardian for consideration by a court. The principal's nomination of a guardian of the principal's person, estate, or both or the principal's nomination of a guardian of the person, the estate, or both of one or more of the principal's minor children or incompetent adult children is revoked by the principal's subsequent nomination of a guardian of the principal's person, estate, or both or the principal's subsequent nomination of a guardian of the person, the estate, or both of one or more of the principal's minor children or incompetent adult children, and, except for good cause shown or disqualification, the court shall make its appointment in accordance with the principal's most recent nomination. Nomination of a person as a guardian or successor guardian of the person, the estate, or both of one or more of the principal's minor children or incompetent adult children under this division, and any subsequent appointment of the guardian or successor guardian as guardian under section 2111.02 of the Revised Code, does not vacate the jurisdiction of any other court that previously may have exercised jurisdiction over the person of the minor or incompetent adult child.

(B) The principal may direct that bond be waived for a person nominated as guardian or as a successor guardian.

(C) If, after a principal executes a power of attorney, a court appoints a guardian of the principal's estate or other fiduciary charged with the management of some or all of the principal's property, the agent is accountable to the fiduciary as well as to the principal. The power of attorney is not terminated and the agent's authority continues unless limited, suspended, or terminated by the court after notice to the agent and upon a finding that the limitation, suspension, or termination would be in the best interest of the principal.

(D) A power of attorney that contains the nomination of a person to be the guardian of the person, the estate, or both of one or more of the principal's minor children or incompetent adult children under this division may be filed with the probate court for safekeeping, and the probate court shall designate the nomination as the nomination of a standby guardian.

(E) As used in this section, "incompetent" has the same meaning as in section 2111.01 of the Revised Code.

**HISTORY:**
2011 SB 117, § 1, eff. Mar. 22, 2012; 2012 HB 247, § 1, eff. Mar. 22, 2013; 2013 HB 126, § 1, eff. Mar. 20, 2014.

**Editor's Notes**
Acts 2011, SB 117, § 4 provides: "The General Assembly hereby declares its intent by this act to clarify the procedure for resolution of issues created by the past or future repeal or reenactment of the federal estate tax, federal generation-skipping transfer tax, and Ohio estate tax."

**Amendment Notes**
The 2013 amendment added "The principal's nomination of a guardian of the principal's person, estate, or both or the principal's nomination of a

guardian of the person, the estate, or both of one or more of the principal's minor children or incompetent adult children is revoked by the principal's subsequent nomination of a guardian of the principal's person, estate, or both or the principal's subsequent nomination of a guardian of the person, the estate, or both of one or more of the principal's minor children or incompetent adult children, and" to the beginning of the fourth sentence of (A).

The 2012 amendment added "or incompetent adult children" wherever it appears in (A) and (D); and added (E).

## § 1337.29 Effective Date.

(A) A power of attorney is effective when executed unless the principal provides in the power of attorney that it becomes effective at a future date or upon the occurrence of a future event or contingency.

(B) If a power of attorney becomes effective upon the occurrence of a future event or contingency, the principal, in the power of attorney, may authorize one or more persons to determine in a writing or other record that the event or contingency has occurred.

(C) If a power of attorney becomes effective upon the principal's incapacity and the principal has not authorized a person to determine whether the principal is incapacitated, or the person authorized is unable or unwilling to make the determination, the power of attorney becomes effective upon one of the following determinations made in a writing or other record:

(1) A determination by a physician who has examined the principal or a licensed psychologist who has evaluated the principal that the principal is incapacitated within the meaning of division (E)(1) of section 1337.22 of the Revised Code;

(2) A determination by an attorney at law, a judge, or an appropriate governmental official that the principal is incapacitated within the meaning of division (E)(2) of section 1337.22 of the Revised Code.

(D) A person authorized by the principal in the power of attorney to determine that the principal is incapacitated may act as the principal's personal representative pursuant to 42 U.S.C. 1320d to 1320d-8, and applicable regulations, to obtain access to the principal's health-care information and communicate with the principal's health-care provider.

**HISTORY:**
2011 SB 117, § 1, eff. Mar. 22, 2012.

**Editor's Notes**
Acts 2011, SB 117, § 4 provides: "The General Assembly hereby declares its intent by this act to clarify the procedure for resolution of issues created by the past or future repeal or reenactment of the federal estate tax, federal generation-skipping transfer tax, and Ohio estate tax."

### NOTES TO DECISIONS

**Motion denied**
Nursing home owner's motion to stay the case pending arbitration was properly denied because the daughter lacked authority to sign the arbitration agreement on behalf of her mother. The daughter signed the agreement as her mother's representative under a health care power of attorney that had specific provisions regarding when that power existed and, according to the record, that power of attorney had not yet come into being because no one had declared the mother mentally unfit to make her own health care decisions. Tedeschi v. Atrium Ctrs., L.L.C., 2012-Ohio-2929, 2012 Ohio App. LEXIS 2560 (Ohio Ct. App., Cuyahoga County 2012).

## § 1337.30 Termination.

(A) A power of attorney terminates when any of the following occurs:

(1) The principal dies;

(2) The principal becomes incapacitated, if the power of attorney is not durable;

(3) The principal revokes the power of attorney;

(4) The power of attorney provides that it terminates;

(5) The purpose of the power of attorney is accomplished;

(6) The principal revokes the agent's authority or the agent dies, becomes incapacitated, or resigns, and the power of attorney does not provide for another agent to act under the power of attorney.

(B) An agent's authority terminates when any of the following occurs:

(1) The principal revokes the authority;

(2) The agent dies, becomes incapacitated, or resigns;

(3) An action is filed for the divorce, dissolution, or annulment of the agent's marriage to the principal or their legal separation, unless the power of attorney otherwise provides;

(4) The power of attorney terminates.

(C) Unless the power of attorney otherwise provides, an agent's authority is exercisable until the authority terminates under division (B) of this section, notwithstanding a lapse of time since the execution of the power of attorney.

(D) Termination of an agent's authority or of a power of attorney is not effective as to the agent or another person that, without actual knowledge of the termination, acts in good faith under the power of attorney. An act so performed, unless otherwise invalid or unenforceable, binds the principal and the principal's successors in interest.

(E) Incapacity of the principal of a power of attorney that is not durable does not revoke or terminate the power of attorney as to an agent or other person that, without actual knowledge of the incapacity, acts in good faith under the power of attorney. An act so performed, unless otherwise invalid or unenforceable, binds the principal and the principal's successors in interest.

(F) The execution of a power of attorney does not revoke a power of attorney previously executed by the principal unless the subsequent power of attorney provides that the previous power of attorney is revoked or that all other powers of attorney are revoked.

**HISTORY:**
2011 SB 117, § 1, eff. Mar. 22, 2012.

**Editor's Notes**
Acts 2011, SB 117, § 4 provides: "The General Assembly hereby declares its intent by this act to clarify the procedure for resolution of issues created by the past or future repeal or reenactment of the federal estate tax, federal generation-skipping transfer tax, and Ohio estate tax."

### NOTES TO DECISIONS

**Lapse of designation**
Even if appellant, a nursing home, previously had been designated the resident's authorized representative, that designation lapsed upon the resident's death; a proper party to represent the resident's estate in an administrative appeal would have been an estate administrator, and there was no authority to support the proposition that would allow the trial court's appointment of a special administrator in this case to relate back to the time of the filing of the notice of appeal. Saber Health Care v. Ohio Dep't of Job & Family Servs., 2020-Ohio-4044, 2020 Ohio App. LEXIS 2936 (Ohio Ct. App., Adams County 2020).

## § 1337.31 Coagents.

(A) A principal may designate two or more persons to act as coagents. Unless the power of attorney otherwise provides, each coagent may exercise its authority independently.

(B) A principal may designate one or more successor agents to act if an agent resigns, dies, becomes incapacitated, is not qualified to serve, or declines to serve. A principal may grant authority to designate one or more successor agents to an agent or other person designated by name, office, or function. Unless the power of attorney otherwise provides, a successor agent has the same authority as that granted to the original agent and may not act until all predecessor agents have resigned, died, become incapacitated, are no longer qualified to serve, or have declined to serve.

(C) Except as otherwise provided in the power of attorney and division (D) of this section, an agent that does not participate in or conceal a breach of fiduciary duty committed by another agent, including a predecessor agent, is not liable for the actions of the other agent.

(D) An agent that has actual knowledge of a breach or imminent breach of fiduciary duty by another agent shall notify the principal and, if the principal is incapacitated, take any action reasonably appropriate in the circumstances to safeguard the principal's best interest. An agent that fails to notify the principal or take action as required by this division is liable for the reasonably foreseeable damages that could have been avoided if the agent had notified the principal or taken action as required by this division.

**HISTORY:**
2011 SB 117, § 1, eff. Mar. 22, 2012.

**Editor's Notes**
Acts 2011, SB 117, § 4 provides: "The General Assembly hereby declares its intent by this act to clarify the procedure for resolution of issues created by the past or future repeal or reenactment of the federal estate tax, federal generation-skipping transfer tax, and Ohio estate tax."



### § 1337.32 Reimbursement of agent's expenses.

Unless the power of attorney otherwise provides, an agent is entitled to reimbursement of expenses reasonably incurred on behalf of the principal and to compensation that is reasonable under the circumstances.

**HISTORY:**
2011 SB 117, § 1, eff. Mar. 22, 2012.

**Editor's Notes**
Acts 2011, SB 117, § 4 provides: "The General Assembly hereby declares its intent by this act to clarify the procedure for resolution of issues created by the past or future repeal or reenactment of the federal estate tax, federal generation-skipping transfer tax, and Ohio estate tax."

### § 1337.33 Acceptance of appointment.

Except as otherwise provided in the power of attorney, a person accepts appointment as an agent under a power of attorney by exercising authority or performing duties as an agent or by any other assertion or conduct indicating acceptance.

**HISTORY:**
2011 SB 117, § 1, eff. Mar. 22, 2012.

**Editor's Notes**
Acts 2011, SB 117, § 4 provides: "The General Assembly hereby declares its intent by this act to clarify the procedure for resolution of issues created by the past or future repeal or reenactment of the federal estate tax, federal generation-skipping transfer tax, and Ohio estate tax."

### § 1337.34 Duties of agent; breach of duty.

(A) Notwithstanding provisions in the power of attorney, an agent that has accepted appointment shall do all of the following:

(1) Act in accordance with the principal's reasonable expectations to the extent actually known by the agent and, otherwise, in the principal's best interest;

(2) Act in good faith;

(3) Act only within the scope of authority granted in the power of attorney;

(4) Attempt to preserve the principal's estate plan to the extent actually known by the agent if preserving the plan is consistent with the principal's best interest based on all relevant factors, including all of the following:

(a) The value and nature of the principal's property;

(b) The principal's foreseeable obligations and need for maintenance;

(c) Minimization of taxes, including income, estate, inheritance, generation-skipping transfer, and gift taxes;

(d) Eligibility for a benefit, a program, or assistance under a statute or regulation.

(B) Except as otherwise provided in the power of attorney, an agent that has accepted appointment shall do all of the following:

(1) Act loyally for the principal's benefit;

(2) Act so as not to create a conflict of interest that impairs the agent's ability to act impartially in the principal's best interest;

(3) Act with the care, competence, and diligence ordinarily exercised by agents in similar circumstances;

(4) Keep a record of all receipts, disbursements, and transactions made on behalf of the principal;

(5) Cooperate with a person that has authority to make health-care decisions for the principal to carry out the principal's reasonable expectations to the extent actually known by the agent and, otherwise, act in the principal's best interest.

(C) An agent that acts in good faith is not liable to any beneficiary of the principal's estate plan for failure to preserve the plan.

(D) An agent that acts with care, competence, and diligence for the best interest of the principal is not liable solely because the agent also benefits from the act or has an individual or conflicting interest in relation to the property or affairs of the principal.

(E) If an agent is selected by the principal because of special skills or expertise possessed by the agent or in reliance on the agent's representation that the agent has special skills or expertise, the special skills or expertise must be considered in determining whether the agent has acted with care, competence, and diligence under the circumstances.

(F) Absent a breach of duty to the principal, an agent is not liable if the value of the principal's property declines.

(G) An agent that exercises authority to delegate to another person the authority granted by the principal or that engages another person on behalf of the principal is not liable for an act, error of judgment, or default of that person if the agent exercises care, competence, and diligence in selecting and monitoring the person.

(H) Except as otherwise provided in the power of attorney, an agent is not required to disclose receipts, disbursements, or transactions conducted on behalf of the principal unless ordered by a court or requested by the principal, a guardian, a conservator, another fiduciary acting for the principal, a governmental agency having authority to protect the welfare of the principal, or, upon the death of the principal, by the personal representative or successor in interest of the principal's estate. If so requested, within thirty days the agent shall comply with the request or provide a writing or other record substantiating why additional time is needed and shall comply with the request within an additional thirty days.

**HISTORY:**
2011 SB 117, § 1, eff. Mar. 22, 2012.

**Editor's Notes**
Acts 2011, SB 117, § 4 provides: "The General Assembly hereby declares its intent by this act to clarify the procedure for resolution of issues created by the past or future repeal or reenactment of the federal estate tax, federal generation-skipping transfer tax, and Ohio estate tax."

#### NOTES TO DECISIONS

**Applicability**
To the extent that a sister had standing to pursue an accounting via this section, the court was required to consider, within its discretion, whether she was entitled to such. If the court found merit in her request, it would issue an order and her brother, in his capacity as economic power of attorney for their mother, would be required to submit an accounting. Colburn v. Cooper, 2018-Ohio-5190, 2018 Ohio App. LEXIS 5501 (Ohio Ct. App., Lake County 2018).

### § 1337.35 Relieving agent of liability for breach of duty.

A provision in a power of attorney relieving an agent of liability for breach of duty is binding on the principal and the principal's successors in interest except to the extent that either of the following applies:

(A) The provision relieves the agent of liability for breach of duty committed dishonestly, with an improper motive, or with reckless indifference to the purposes of the power of attorney or the best interest of the principal.

(B) The provision was inserted as a result of an abuse of a confidential or fiduciary relationship with the principal.

**HISTORY:**
2011 SB 117, § 1, eff. Mar. 22, 2012.

**Editor's Notes**
Acts 2011, SB 117, § 4 provides: "The General Assembly hereby declares its intent by this act to clarify the procedure for resolution of issues created by the past or future repeal or reenactment of the federal estate tax, federal generation-skipping transfer tax, and Ohio estate tax."

NOTES TO DECISIONS

**Applicability**

Trial court did not abuse its discretion in ordering the agent to pay $302,257.27 to his mother's estate because the agent was completely indifferent to his responsibilities as set forth in the power-of-attorney (POA), the agent admitted that the subject POA did not contain an exoneration clause, and the POA did not imply an exoneration clause; there was ample evidence to support a finding that the agent's conduct fell outside the scope of any exoneration clause. In re Estate of Baughman, 2020-Ohio-6928, 2020 Ohio App. LEXIS 4765 (Ohio Ct. App., Licking County 2020).

## § 1337.36 Review of agent's conduct.

(A) Any of the following persons may petition a court to construe a power of attorney or review the agent's conduct and grant appropriate relief:

(1) The principal or the agent;

(2) A guardian, conservator, or other fiduciary acting for the principal, including an executor or administrator of the estate of a deceased principal;

(3) A person authorized to make health-care decisions for the principal;

(4) The principal's spouse, parent, or descendant;

(5) An individual who would qualify as a presumptive heir of the principal;

(6) A person named as a beneficiary to receive any property, benefit, or contractual right on the principal's death or as a beneficiary of a trust created by or for the principal that has a financial interest in the principal's estate;

(7) A governmental agency having regulatory authority to protect the welfare of the principal;

(8) The principal's caregiver or another person that demonstrates sufficient interest in the principal's welfare;

(9) A person asked to accept the power of attorney.

(B) Upon motion by the principal, the court shall dismiss a petition filed under this section, unless the court finds that the principal lacks capacity to revoke the agent's authority or the power of attorney.

**HISTORY:**

2011 SB 117, § 1, eff. Mar. 22, 2012.

**Editor's Notes**

Acts 2011, SB 117, § 4 provides: "The General Assembly hereby declares its intent by this act to clarify the procedure for resolution of issues created by the past or future repeal or reenactment of the federal estate tax, federal generation-skipping transfer tax, and Ohio estate tax."

NOTES TO DECISIONS

Analysis



**Final order**

Judgment entry appealed from was a final appealable order because the order was entered in a proceeding under this statute, making it an appeal from a provisional remedy under R.C. 2505.02. In re Baughman, 2017-Ohio-2966, 2017 Ohio App. LEXIS 1989 (Ohio Ct. App., Licking County 2017).

**Standing**

In a sister's action against her brother, in his capacity as economic power of attorney for their mother, the sister's status as either a presumptive heir or designated beneficiary under her mother's will provided her with statutory standing to move the court for an accounting prior to the mother's death. Colburn v. Cooper, 2018-Ohio-5190, 2018 Ohio App. LEXIS 5501 (Ohio Ct. App., Lake County 2018).

To the extent that a sister had standing to pursue an accounting via this section, the court was required to consider, within its discretion, whether she was entitled to such. If the court found merit in her request, it would issue an order and her brother, in his capacity as economic power of attorney for their mother, would be required to submit an accounting. Colburn v. Cooper, 2018-Ohio-5190, 2018 Ohio App. LEXIS 5501 (Ohio Ct. App., Lake County 2018).

Only those persons named as a beneficiary on the principal's death may petition the court to review an agent's conduct; former beneficiaries were outside the purview of the statute, and there was no scenario under which the former beneficiary could become a beneficiary within the meaning of the statute. Wisner v. Wisner, 2016-Ohio-5095, 2016 Ohio App. LEXIS 2980 (Ohio Ct. App., Hancock County 2016).

## § 1337.37 Agent liable to principle for breach of duty.

An agent that violates sections 1337.21 to 1337.64 of the Revised Code is liable to the principal or the principal's successors in interest for the amount required to restore the value of the principal's property to what it would have been had the violation not occurred and the amount required to reimburse the principal or the principal's successors in interest for the attorney's fees and costs paid on the agent's behalf.

**HISTORY:**

2011 SB 117, § 1, eff. Mar. 22, 2012.

**Editor's Notes**

Acts 2011, SB 117, § 4 provides: "The General Assembly hereby declares its intent by this act to clarify the procedure for resolution of issues created by the past or future repeal or reenactment of the federal estate tax, federal generation-skipping transfer tax, and Ohio estate tax."



## § 1337.38 Agent resignation.

Unless the power of attorney provides a different method for an agent's resignation, an agent may resign by giving notice to the principal and, if the principal is incapacitated, to whichever of the following applies:

(A) The guardian, if one has been appointed for the principal, and any coagent or successor agent;

(B) If there is no person described in division (A) of this section, to any of the following:

(1) The principal's caregiver;

(2) Another person reasonably believed by the agent to have sufficient interest in the principal's welfare;

(3) A governmental agency having authority to protect the welfare of the principal.

**HISTORY:**

2011 SB 117, § 1, eff. Mar. 22, 2012.

**Editor's Notes**

Acts 2011, SB 117, § 4 provides: "The General Assembly hereby declares its intent by this act to clarify the procedure for resolution of issues created by the past or future repeal or reenactment of the federal estate tax, federal generation-skipping transfer tax, and Ohio estate tax."

## § 1337.39 Principles of law and equity.

Unless displaced by a provision of sections 1337.21 to 1337.64 of the Revised Code, the principles of law and equity supplement those sections.

**HISTORY:**

2011 SB 117, § 1, eff. Mar. 22, 2012.

**Editor's Notes**

Acts 2011, SB 117, § 4 provides: "The General Assembly hereby declares its intent by this act to clarify the procedure for resolution of issues created by the past or future repeal or reenactment of the federal estate tax, federal generation-skipping transfer tax, and Ohio estate tax."

## § 1337.40 Power of attorney provisions control in conflict with other provisions of the Revised Code.

In the event of a conflict between any provision of sections 1337.21 to 1337.64 of the Revised Code and any other provision of law applicable to financial institutions or other entities, the other provision of law controls.

**HISTORY:**

2011 SB 117, § 1, eff. Mar. 22, 2012.

**Editor's Notes**

Acts 2011, SB 117, § 4 provides: "The General Assembly hereby declares its intent by this act to clarify the procedure for resolution of issues created by the past or future repeal or reenactment of the federal estate tax, federal generation-skipping transfer tax, and Ohio estate tax."

## § 1337.41 Remedies do not abrogate any rights under other provisions of law.

The remedies provided under sections 1337.21 to 1337.64 of the Revised Code are not exclusive and do not abrogate any right or remedy under any other provision of law of this state.

**HISTORY:**

2011 SB 117, § 1, eff. Mar. 22, 2012.

**Editor's Notes**

Acts 2011, SB 117, § 4 provides: "The General Assembly hereby declares its intent by this act to clarify the procedure for resolution of issues created by the past or future repeal or reenactment of the federal estate tax, federal generation-skipping transfer tax, and Ohio estate tax."

Titles 11 — 37

## § 1337.42 Grant of specific duties on behalf of the principle or with the principle's property.

(A) An agent under a power of attorney may do any of the following on behalf of the principal or with the principal's property only if the power of attorney expressly grants the agent the authority and if exercise of the authority is not otherwise prohibited by another agreement or instrument to which the authority or property is subject, and, with respect to a revocable trust of which the principal was the settlor, if the trust agreement expressly authorizes the agent to exercise the principal's powers with respect to the revocation, amendment, or distribution:

(1) Create, amend, revoke, or terminate an inter vivos trust to the extent permitted by section 5801.05 of the Revised Code or any other provision of Title LVIII of the Revised Code;

(2) Make a gift;

(3) Create or change rights of survivorship;

(4) Create or change a beneficiary designation;

(5) Delegate authority granted under the power of attorney;

(6) Waive the principal's right to be a beneficiary of a joint and survivor annuity, including a survivor benefit under a retirement plan;

(7) Exercise fiduciary powers that the principal has authority to delegate.

(B) Notwithstanding a grant of authority to do an act described in division (A) of this section, unless the power of attorney otherwise provides, an agent that is not an ancestor, spouse, or descendant of the principal may not exercise authority under a power of attorney to create in the agent, or in an individual to whom the agent owes a legal obligation of support, an interest in the principal's property, whether by gift, right of survivorship, beneficiary designation, disclaimer, or otherwise.

(C) Subject to divisions (A), (B), (D), and (E) of this section, if a power of attorney grants to an agent authority to do all acts that a principal could do, the agent has the general authority described in sections 1337.45 to 1337.57 of the Revised Code.

(D) Unless the power of attorney otherwise provides, a grant of authority to make a gift is subject to section 1337.58 of the Revised Code.

(E) Subject to divisions (A), (B), and (D) of this section, if the subjects over which authority is granted in a power of attorney are similar or overlap, the broadest authority controls.

(F) Authority granted in a power of attorney is exercisable with respect to property that the principal has when the power of attorney is executed or acquires later, whether or not the property is located in this state and whether or not the authority is exercised or the power of attorney is executed in this state.

(G) An act performed by an agent pursuant to a power of attorney has the same effect and inures to the benefit of and binds the principal and the principal's successors in interest as if the principal had performed the act.

**HISTORY:**

2011 SB 117, § 1, eff. Mar. 22, 2012.

**Editor's Notes**

Acts 2011, SB 117, § 4 provides: "The General Assembly hereby declares its intent by this act to clarify the procedure for resolution of issues created by the past or future repeal or reenactment of the federal estate tax, federal generation-skipping transfer tax, and Ohio estate tax."

### NOTES TO DECISIONS

**Authorized acts**

Power of attorney from the decedent to the son failed to expressly authorize him to change the daughter's rights of survivorship and to change her beneficiary designation to the various bank accounts. The son testified at trial the decedent was fully competent when he read and signed the general power of attorney and by accepting that evidence in the record, the decedent intended to expressly fail to authorize in the power of attorney any changes pursuant to R.C. 1337.42(A)(3)-(4). In re Estate of Zoltanski v. Zoltanski, 2020-Ohio-3908, 2020 Ohio App. LEXIS 2808 (Ohio Ct. App., Wood County 2020).

In a suit to challenge the distribution of trust assets, the trial court erred by returning a verdict for plaintiff and compensatory damages for conversion because the durable power of attorney specifically authorized defendant to create an irrevocable inter vivos trust and no evidence demonstrated wrongful conduct in execution of the trust. Hutchings v. Hutchings, 2019-Ohio-5362, 150 N.E.3d 548, 2019 Ohio App. LEXIS 5427 (Ohio Ct. App., Sandusky County 2019).

## § 1337.43 General authority.

(A) An agent has authority described in sections 1337.42 to 1337.58 of the Revised Code if the power of attorney refers to general authority with respect to the descriptive term for the subjects stated in sections 1337.45 to 1337.58 of the Revised Code or cites the section of the Revised Code in which the authority is described.

(B) A reference in a power of attorney to general authority with respect to the descriptive term for a subject in sections 1337.45 to 1337.58 of the Revised Code or a citation to any of those sections incorporates the entire section as if it were set out in full in the power of attorney.

(C) A principal may modify authority incorporated by reference.

**HISTORY:**

2011 SB 117, § 1, eff. Mar. 22, 2012.

**Editor's Notes**

Acts 2011, SB 117, § 4 provides: "The General Assembly hereby declares its intent by this act to clarify the procedure for resolution of issues created by the past or future repeal or reenactment of the federal estate tax, federal generation-skipping transfer tax, and Ohio estate tax."

## § 1337.44 Authority of Agent.

Except as otherwise provided in the power of attorney, by executing a power of attorney that incorporates by reference a subject described in sections 1337.45 to 1337.58 of the Revised Code or that grants to an agent authority to do all acts that a principal could do pursuant to division (C) of section 1337.42 of the Revised Code, a principal authorizes the agent, with respect to that subject, to do all of the following:

(A) Demand, receive, and obtain by litigation or otherwise, money or another thing of value to which the principal is, may become, or claims to be entitled, and conserve, invest, disburse, or use anything so received or obtained for the purposes intended;

(B) Contract in any manner with any person, on terms agreeable to the agent, to accomplish a purpose of a transaction and perform, rescind, cancel, terminate, reform, restate, release, or modify the contract or another contract made by or on behalf of the principal;

(C) Execute, acknowledge, seal, deliver, file, or record any instrument or communication the agent considers desirable to accomplish a purpose of a transaction, including creating at any time a schedule listing some or all of the principal's property and attaching it to the power of attorney;

(D) Initiate, participate in, submit to alternative dispute resolution, settle, oppose, or propose or accept a compromise with respect to a claim existing in favor of or against the principal or intervene in litigation relating to the claim;

(E) Seek on the principal's behalf the assistance of a court or other governmental agency to carry out an act authorized in the power of attorney;

(F) Engage, compensate, and discharge an attorney, accountant, discretionary investment manager, expert witness, or other advisor;

(G) Prepare, execute, and file a record, report, or other document to safeguard or promote the principal's interest under a statute or regulation;

(H) Communicate with any representative or employee of a government or governmental subdivision, agency, or instrumentality, on behalf of the principal;

(I) Access communications intended for, and communicate on behalf of the principal, whether by mail, electronic transmission, telephone, or other means;

(J) Do any lawful act with respect to the subject and all property related to the subject.

**HISTORY:**
2011 SB 117, § 1, eff. Mar. 22, 2012.

**Editor's Notes**
Acts 2011, SB 117, § 4 provides: "The General Assembly hereby declares its intent by this act to clarify the procedure for resolution of issues created by the past or future repeal or reenactment of the federal estate tax, federal generation-skipping transfer tax, and Ohio estate tax."

## § 1337.45 General authority real property.

Unless the power of attorney otherwise provides, language in a power of attorney granting general authority with respect to real property authorizes the agent to do all of the following:

(A) Demand, buy, lease, receive, accept as a gift or as security for an extension of credit, or otherwise acquire or reject an interest in real property or a right incident to real property;

(B) Sell; exchange; convey with or without covenants, representations, or warranties; quitclaim; release; surrender; retain title for security; encumber; partition; consent to partitioning; subject to an easement or covenant; subdivide; apply for zoning or other governmental permits; plat or consent to platting; develop; grant an option concerning; lease; sublease; contribute to an entity in exchange for an interest in that entity; or otherwise grant or dispose of an interest in real property or a right incident to real property;

(C) Pledge or mortgage an interest in real property or right incident to real property as security to borrow money or pay, renew, or extend the time of payment of a debt of the principal or a debt guaranteed by the principal;

(D) Release, assign, satisfy, or enforce by litigation or otherwise a mortgage, deed of trust, conditional sale contract, encumbrance, lien, or other claim to real property that exists or is asserted;

(E) Manage or conserve an interest in real property or a right incident to real property owned or claimed to be owned by the principal, including all of the following:

(1) Insure against liability or casualty or other loss;

(2) Obtain or regain possession of or protect the interest or right by litigation or otherwise;

(3) Pay, assess, compromise, or contest taxes or assessments or apply for and receive refunds in connection with taxes;

(4) Purchase supplies, hire assistance or labor, and make repairs or alterations to the real property.

(F) Use, develop, alter, replace, remove, erect, or install structures or other improvements upon real property in or incident to which the principal has, or claims to have, an interest or right;

(G) Participate in a reorganization with respect to real property or an entity that owns an interest in or right incident to real property and receive, and hold, and act with respect to stocks and bonds or other property received in a plan of reorganization, including all of the following:

(1) Sell or otherwise dispose of them;

(2) Exercise or sell an option, right of conversion, or similar right with respect to them;

(3) Exercise any voting rights in person or by proxy.

(H) Change the form of title of an interest in or right incident to real property;

(I) Dedicate to public use, with or without consideration, easements or other real property in which the principal has, or claims to have, an interest.

**HISTORY:**
2011 SB 117, § 1, eff. Mar. 22, 2012.

**Editor's Notes**
Acts 2011, SB 117, § 4 provides: "The General Assembly hereby declares its intent by this act to clarify the procedure for resolution of issues created by the past or future repeal or reenactment of the federal estate tax, federal generation-skipping transfer tax, and Ohio estate tax."

## § 1337.46 General authority tangible personal property.

Unless the power of attorney otherwise provides, language in a power of attorney granting general authority with respect to tangible personal property authorizes the agent to do all of the following:

(A) Demand, buy, receive, accept as a gift or as security for an extension of credit, or otherwise acquire or reject ownership or possession of tangible personal property or an interest in tangible personal property;

(B) Sell; exchange; convey with or without covenants, representations, or warranties; quitclaim; release; surrender; create a security interest in; grant options concerning; lease; sublease; or otherwise dispose of tangible personal property or an interest in tangible personal property;

(C) Grant a security interest in tangible personal property or an interest in tangible personal property as security to borrow money or pay, renew, or extend the time of payment of a debt of the principal or a debt guaranteed by the principal;

(D) Release, assign, satisfy, or enforce by litigation or otherwise a security interest, lien, or other claim on behalf of the principal with respect to tangible personal property or an interest in tangible personal property;

(E) Manage or conserve tangible personal property or an interest in tangible personal property on behalf of the principal, including all of the following:

(1) Insure against liability or casualty or other loss;

(2) Obtain or regain possession of or protect the property or interest by litigation or otherwise;

(3) Pay, assess, compromise, or contest taxes or assessments or apply for and receive refunds in connection with taxes or assessments;

(4) Move the property from place to place;

(5) Store the property for hire or on a gratuitous bailment;

(6) Use and make repairs, alterations, or improvements to the property.

(F) Change the form of title of an interest in tangible personal property.

**HISTORY:**
2011 SB 117, § 1, eff. Mar. 22, 2012.

**Editor's Notes**
Acts 2011, SB 117, § 4 provides: "The General Assembly hereby declares its intent by this act to clarify the procedure for resolution of issues created by the past or future repeal or reenactment of the federal estate tax, federal generation-skipping transfer tax, and Ohio estate tax."

## § 1337.47 General authority stocks and bonds.

Unless the power of attorney otherwise provides, language in a power of attorney granting general authority with respect to stocks and bonds authorizes the agent to do all of the following:

(A) Buy, sell, and exchange stocks and bonds;

(B) Establish, continue, modify, or terminate an account with respect to stocks and bonds;

(C) Pledge stocks and bonds as security to borrow, pay, renew, or extend the time of payment of a debt of the principal;

(D) Receive certificates and other evidences of ownership with respect to stocks and bonds;

(E) Exercise voting rights with respect to stocks and bonds in person or by proxy, enter into voting trusts, and consent to limitations on the right to vote.

**HISTORY:**
2011 SB 117, § 1, eff. Mar. 22, 2012.

**Editor's Notes**
Acts 2011, SB 117, § 4 provides: "The General Assembly hereby declares its intent by this act to clarify the procedure for resolution of issues created

by the past or future repeal or reenactment of the federal estate tax, federal generation-skipping transfer tax, and Ohio estate tax."

### § 1337.48 General authority commodities and options.

Unless the power of attorney otherwise provides, language in a power of attorney granting general authority with respect to commodities and options authorizes the agent to do both of the following:

(A) Buy, sell, exchange, assign, settle, and exercise commodity futures contracts and call or put options on stocks or stock indexes traded on a regulated option exchange;

(B) Establish, continue, modify, and terminate option accounts.



**HISTORY:**

2011 SB 117, § 1, eff. Mar. 22, 2012.

**Editor's Notes**

Acts 2011, SB 117, § 4 provides: "The General Assembly hereby declares its intent by this act to clarify the procedure for resolution of issues created by the past or future repeal or reenactment of the federal estate tax, federal generation-skipping transfer tax, and Ohio estate tax."

### § 1337.49 General authority banks and other financial institutions.

Unless the power of attorney otherwise provides, language in a power of attorney granting general authority with respect to banks and other financial institutions authorizes the agent to do all of the following:

(A) Continue, modify, and terminate an account or other banking arrangement made by or on behalf of the principal;

(B) Establish, modify, and terminate an account or other banking arrangement with a bank, trust company, savings and loan association, credit union, thrift company, brokerage firm, or other financial institution selected by the agent;

(C) Contract for services available from a financial institution, including renting a safe deposit box or space in a vault;

(D) Withdraw, by check, order, electronic funds transfer, or otherwise, money or property of the principal deposited with or left in the custody of a financial institution;

(E) Receive statements of account, vouchers, notices, and similar documents from a financial institution and act with respect to them;

(F) Enter a safe deposit box or vault and withdraw or add to the contents;

(G) Borrow money and pledge as security personal property of the principal necessary to borrow money or pay, renew, or extend the time of payment of a debt of the principal or a debt guaranteed by the principal;

(H) Make, assign, draw, endorse, discount, guarantee, and negotiate promissory notes, checks, drafts, and other negotiable or nonnegotiable paper of the principal or payable to the principal or the principal's order, transfer money, receive the cash or other proceeds of those transactions, and accept a draft drawn by a person upon the principal and pay it when due;

(I) Receive for the principal and act upon a sight draft, warehouse receipt, or other document of title whether tangible or electronic, or other negotiable or nonnegotiable instrument;

(J) Apply for, receive, and use letters of credit, credit and debit cards, electronic transaction authorizations, and traveler's checks from a financial institution and give an indemnity or other agreement in connection with letters of credit;

(K) Consent to an extension of the time of payment with respect to commercial paper or a financial transaction with a financial institution.

**HISTORY:**

2011 SB 117, § 1, eff. Mar. 22, 2012.

**Editor's Notes**

Acts 2011, SB 117, § 4 provides: "The General Assembly hereby declares its intent by this act to clarify the procedure for resolution of issues created by the past or future repeal or reenactment of the federal estate tax, federal generation-skipping transfer tax, and Ohio estate tax."

### § 1337.50 General authority operation of an entity or business.

Subject to the terms of a document or an agreement governing an entity or an entity ownership interest, and unless the power of attorney otherwise provides, language in a power of attorney granting general authority with respect to the operation of an entity or business authorizes the agent to do all of the following:

(A) Operate, buy, sell, enlarge, reduce, or terminate an ownership interest;

(B) Perform a duty or discharge a liability and exercise in person or by proxy a right, power, privilege, or option that the principal has, may have, or claims to have;

(C) Enforce the terms of an ownership agreement;

(D) Initiate, participate in, submit to alternative dispute resolution, settle, oppose, or propose or accept a compromise with respect to litigation to which the principal is a party because of an ownership interest;

(E) Exercise in person or by proxy, or enforce by litigation or otherwise, a right, power, privilege, or option the principal has or claims to have as the holder of stocks and bonds;

(F) Initiate, participate in, submit to alternative dispute resolution, settle, oppose, or propose or accept a compromise with respect to litigation to which the principal is a party concerning stocks and bonds;

(G) With respect to an entity or business owned solely by the principal, do all of the following:

(1) Continue, modify, renegotiate, extend, and terminate a contract made by or on behalf of the principal with respect to the entity or business before execution of the power of attorney;

(2) Determine all of the following:

(a) The location of its operation;

(b) The nature and extent of its business;

(c) The methods of manufacturing, selling, merchandising, financing, accounting, and advertising employed in its operation;

(d) The amount and types of insurance carried;

(e) The mode of engaging, compensating, and dealing with its employees and accountants, attorneys, or other advisors.

(3) Change the name or form of organization under which the entity or business is operated and enter into an ownership agreement with other persons to take over all or part of the operation of the entity or business;

(4) Demand and receive money due or claimed by the principal or on the principal's behalf in the operation of the entity or business and control and disburse the money in the operation of the entity or business.

(H) Put additional capital into an entity or business in which the principal has an interest;

(I) Join in a plan of reorganization, consolidation, conversion, domestication, or merger of the entity or business;

(J) Sell or liquidate all or part of an entity or business;

(K) Establish the value of an entity or business under a buy-out agreement to which the principal is a party;

(L) Prepare, sign, file, and deliver reports, compilations of information, returns, or other papers with respect to an entity or business and make related payments;

(M) Pay, compromise, or contest taxes, assessments, fines, or penalties and perform any other act to protect the principal from illegal or unnecessary taxation, assessments, fines, or penalties, with respect to an entity or business, including attempts to recover, in any manner permitted by law, money paid before or after the execution of the power of attorney.

**HISTORY:**

2011 SB 117, § 1, eff. Mar. 22, 2012.

**Editor's Notes**

Acts 2011, SB 117, § 4 provides: "The General Assembly hereby declares its intent by this act to clarify the procedure for resolution of issues created by the past or future repeal or reenactment of the federal estate tax, federal generation-skipping transfer tax, and Ohio estate tax."

### § 1337.51 General authority insurance and annuities.

Unless the power of attorney otherwise provides, language in a power of attorney granting general authority with respect to insurance and annuities authorizes the agent to do all of the following:

(A) Continue, pay the premium or make a contribution on, modify, exchange, rescind, release, or terminate a contract procured by or on behalf of the principal that insures or provides an annuity to either the principal or another person, whether or not the principal is a beneficiary under the contract;

(B) Procure new, different, and additional contracts of insurance and annuities for the principal and the principal's spouse, children, and other dependents and select the amount, type of insurance or annuity, and mode of payment;

(C) Pay the premium or make a contribution on, modify, exchange, rescind, release, or terminate a contract of insurance or annuity procured by the agent;

(D) Apply for and receive a loan secured by a contract of insurance or annuity;

(E) Surrender and receive the cash surrender value on a contract of insurance or annuity;

(F) Exercise an election;

(G) Exercise investment powers available under a contract of insurance or annuity;

(H) Change the manner of paying premiums on a contract of insurance or annuity;

(I) Change or convert the type of insurance or annuity with respect to which the principal has or claims to have authority described in this section;

(J) Apply for and procure a benefit or assistance under a statute or regulation to guarantee or pay premiums of a contract of insurance on the life of the principal;

(K) Collect, sell, assign, hypothecate, borrow against, or pledge the interest of the principal in a contract of insurance or annuity;

(L) Select the form and timing of the payment of proceeds from a contract of insurance or annuity;

(M) Pay from proceeds or otherwise, compromise or contest, and apply for refunds in connection with a tax or assessment levied by a taxing authority with respect to a contract of insurance or annuity or its proceeds or liability accruing by reason of the tax or assessment.

**HISTORY:**

2011 SB 117, § 1, eff. Mar. 22, 2012.

**Editor's Notes**

Acts 2011, SB 117, § 4 provides: "The General Assembly hereby declares its intent by this act to clarify the procedure for resolution of issues created by the past or future repeal or reenactment of the federal estate tax, federal generation-skipping transfer tax, and Ohio estate tax."

### § 1337.52 General authority estates, trusts and other beneficial interests.

(A) As used in this section, "estate, trust, or other beneficial interest" means a trust, probate estate, guardianship, conservatorship, escrow, or custodianship or a fund from which the principal is, may become, or claims to be entitled to a share or payment.

(B) Unless the power of attorney otherwise provides, language in a power of attorney granting general authority with respect to estates, trusts, and other beneficial interests authorizes the agent to do all of the following:

(1) Accept, receive, receipt for, sell, assign, pledge, or exchange a share in or payment from an estate, trust, or other beneficial interest;

(2) Demand or obtain money or another thing of value to which the principal is, may become, or claims to be entitled by reason of an estate, trust, or other beneficial interest, by litigation or otherwise;

(3) Exercise for the benefit of the principal a presently exercisable general power of appointment held by the principal;

(4) Initiate, participate in, submit to alternative dispute resolution, settle, oppose, or propose or accept a compromise with respect to litigation to ascertain the meaning, validity, or effect of a deed, will, declaration of trust, or other instrument or transaction affecting the interest of the principal;

(5) Initiate, participate in, submit to alternative dispute resolution, settle, oppose, or propose or accept a compromise with respect to litigation to remove, substitute, or surcharge a fiduciary;

(6) Conserve, invest, disburse, or use anything received for an authorized purpose;

(7) Transfer an interest of the principal in real property, stocks and bonds, accounts with financial institutions or securities intermediaries, insurance, annuities, and other property to the trustee of a revocable trust created by the principal as settlor;

(8) Reject, renounce, disclaim, release, or consent to a reduction in or modification of a share in or payment from an estate, trust, or other beneficial interest.

**HISTORY:**

2011 SB 117, § 1, eff. Mar. 22, 2012.

**Editor's Notes**

Acts 2011, SB 117, § 4 provides: "The General Assembly hereby declares its intent by this act to clarify the procedure for resolution of issues created by the past or future repeal or reenactment of the federal estate tax, federal generation-skipping transfer tax, and Ohio estate tax."



### § 1337.53 General authority claims and litigation.

Unless the power of attorney otherwise provides, language in a power of attorney granting general authority with respect to claims and litigation authorizes the agent to do all of the following:

(A) Assert and maintain before a court or administrative agency a claim, claim for relief, cause of action, counterclaim, offset, recoupment, or defense, including an action to recover property or other thing of value, recover damages sustained by the principal, eliminate or modify tax liability, or seek an injunction, specific performance, or other relief;

(B) Bring an action to determine adverse claims or intervene or otherwise participate in litigation;

(C) Seek an attachment, garnishment, order of arrest, or other preliminary, provisional, or intermediate relief and use an available procedure to effect or satisfy a judgment, order, or decree;

(D) Make or accept a tender, offer of judgment, or admission of facts, submit a controversy on an agreed statement of facts, consent to examination, and bind the principal in litigation;

(E) Submit to alternative dispute resolution, settle, and propose or accept a compromise;

(F) Waive the issuance and service of process upon the principal, accept service of process, appear for the principal, designate persons upon which process directed to the principal may be served, execute and file or deliver stipulations on the principal's behalf, verify pleadings, seek appellate review, procure and give surety and indemnity bonds, contract and pay for the preparation and printing of records and briefs, receive, execute, and file or deliver a consent, waiver, release, confession of judgment, satisfaction of judgment, notice, agreement, or other instrument in connection with the prosecution, settlement, or defense of a claim or litigation;

(G) Act for the principal with respect to bankruptcy or insolvency, whether voluntary or involuntary, concerning the principal or some other person, or with respect to a reorganization, receivership, or application for the appointment of a receiver or trustee that affects an interest of the principal in property or other thing of value;

(H) Pay a judgment, award, or order against the principal or a settlement made in connection with a claim or litigation;

(I) Receive money or other thing of value paid in settlement of or as proceeds of a claim or litigation.

**HISTORY:**

2011 SB 117, § 1, eff. Mar. 22, 2012.

**Editor's Notes**

Acts 2011, SB 117, § 4 provides: "The General Assembly hereby declares its intent by this act to clarify the procedure for resolution of issues created by the past or future repeal or reenactment of the federal estate tax, federal generation-skipping transfer tax, and Ohio estate tax."

### § 1337.54 General authority personal and family maintenance.

(A) Unless the power of attorney otherwise provides, language in a power of attorney granting general authority with respect to personal and family maintenance authorizes the agent to do all of the following:

(1) Perform the acts necessary to maintain the customary standard of living of the principal, the principal's spouse, and the following individuals, whether living when the power of attorney is executed or later born:

(a) Other individuals legally entitled to be supported by the principal;

(b) The individuals whom the principal has customarily supported or indicated the intent to support.

(2) Make periodic payments of child support and other family maintenance required by a court or governmental agency or an agreement to which the principal is a party;

(3) Provide living quarters for the individuals described in division (A)(1) of this section by doing either of the following:

(a) Purchasing, leasing, or otherwise contracting;

(b) Paying the operating costs, including interest, amortization payments, repairs, improvements, and taxes, for premises owned by the principal or occupied by those individuals.

(4) Provide normal domestic help, usual vacations and travel expenses, and funds for shelter, clothing, food, appropriate education, including postsecondary and vocational education, and other current living costs for the individuals described in division (A)(1) of this section;

(5) Pay expenses for necessary health care and custodial care on behalf of the individuals described in division (A)(1) of this section;

(6) Act as the principal's personal representative pursuant to 42 U.S.C. 1320d to 1320d-9 and applicable regulations in making decisions related to the past, present, or future payment for the provision of health care consented to by the principal or anyone authorized under the law of this state to consent to health care on behalf of the principal;

(7) Continue any provision made by the principal for automobiles or other means of transportation, including registering, licensing, insuring, and replacing them, for the individuals described in division (A)(1) of this section;

(8) Maintain credit and debit accounts for the convenience of the individuals described in division (A)(1) of this section and open new accounts;

(9) Continue payments incidental to the membership or affiliation of the principal in a religious institution, club, society, order, or other organization or to continue contributions to those organizations.

(B) Authority with respect to personal and family maintenance is neither dependent upon, nor limited by, authority that an agent may or may not have with respect to gifts under sections 1337.21 to 1337.64 of the Revised Code.

**HISTORY:**

2011 SB 117, § 1, eff. Mar. 22, 2012.

**Editor's Notes**

Acts 2011, SB 117, § 4 provides: "The General Assembly hereby declares its intent by this act to clarify the procedure for resolution of issues created by the past or future repeal or reenactment of the federal estate tax, federal generation-skipping transfer tax, and Ohio estate tax."

### § 1337.55 General authority social security, medicare, and medicaid.

(A) As used in this section, "benefits from governmental programs or civil or military service" means any benefit, program, or assistance provided under a statute or regulation, including social security, medicare, and medicaid.

(B) Unless the power of attorney otherwise provides, language in a power of attorney granting general authority with respect to benefits from governmental programs or civil or military service authorizes the agent to do all of the following:

(1) Execute vouchers in the name of the principal for allowances and reimbursements payable by the United States or a foreign government or by a state or subdivision of a state to the principal, including allowances and reimbursements for transportation of the individuals described in division (A)(1) of section 1337.54 of the Revised Code, and for shipment of their household effects;

(2) Take possession and order the removal and shipment of property of the principal from a post, warehouse, depot, dock, or other place of storage or safekeeping, either governmental or private, and execute and deliver a release, voucher, receipt, bill of lading, shipping ticket, certificate, or other instrument for that purpose;

(3) Enroll in, apply for, select, reject, change, amend, or discontinue, on the principal's behalf, a benefit or program;

(4) Prepare, file, and maintain a claim of the principal for a benefit or assistance, financial or otherwise, to which the principal may be entitled under a statute or regulation;

(5) Initiate, participate in, submit to alternative dispute resolution, settle, oppose, or propose or accept a compromise with respect to litigation concerning any benefit or assistance the principal may be entitled to receive under a statute or regulation;

(6) Receive the financial proceeds of a claim described in division (B)(4) of this section and conserve, invest, disburse, or use for a lawful purpose anything so received.

**HISTORY:**

2011 SB 117, § 1, eff. Mar. 22, 2012.

**Editor's Notes**

Acts 2011, SB 117, § 4 provides: "The General Assembly hereby declares its intent by this act to clarify the procedure for resolution of issues created by the past or future repeal or reenactment of the federal estate tax, federal generation-skipping transfer tax, and Ohio estate tax."

### § 1337.56 Retirement plan.

(A) As used in this section, "retirement plan" means a plan or account created by an employer, the principal, or another individual to provide retirement benefits or deferred compensation of which the principal is a participant, beneficiary, or owner, including any of the following plans or accounts:

(1) An individual retirement account under section 408 of the Internal Revenue Code of 1986, 26 U.S.C. 408;

(2) A Roth individual retirement account under section 408A of the Internal Revenue Code of 1986, 26 U.S.C. 408A;

(3) A deemed individual retirement account under section 408(q) of the Internal Revenue Code of 1986, 26 U.S.C. 408(q);

(4) An annuity or mutual fund custodial account under section 403(b) of the Internal Revenue Code of 1986, 26 U.S.C. 403(b);

(5) A pension, profit-sharing, stock bonus, or other retirement plan qualified under section 401(a) of the Internal Revenue Code of 1986, 26 U.S.C. 401(a);

(6) A plan under section 457(b) of the Internal Revenue Code of 1986, 26 U.S.C. 457(b);

(7) A nonqualified deferred compensation plan under section 409A of the Internal Revenue Code of 1986, 26 U.S.C. 409A.

(B) Unless the power of attorney otherwise provides, language in a power of attorney granting general authority with respect to retirement plans authorizes the agent to do all of the following:

(1) Select the form and timing of payments under a retirement plan and withdraw benefits from a plan;

(2) Make a rollover, including a direct trustee-to-trustee rollover, of benefits from one retirement plan to another;

(3) Establish a retirement plan in the principal's name;

(4) Make contributions to a retirement plan;

(5) Exercise investment powers available under a retirement plan;

(6) Borrow from, sell assets to, or purchase assets from a retirement plan.

**HISTORY:**

2011 SB 117, § 1, eff. Mar. 22, 2012.

**Editor's Notes**

Acts 2011, SB 117, § 4 provides: "The General Assembly hereby declares its intent by this act to clarify the procedure for resolution of issues created by the past or future repeal or reenactment of the federal estate tax, federal generation-skipping transfer tax, and Ohio estate tax."

### § 1337.57 General authority taxes.

Unless the power of attorney otherwise provides, language in a power of attorney granting general authority with respect to taxes authorizes the agent to do all of the following:

(A) Prepare, sign, and file federal, state, local, and foreign income, gift, payroll, property, Federal Insurance Contributions Act, and other tax returns, claims for refunds, requests for extension of time, petitions regarding tax matters, and any other tax-related documents, including receipts, offers, waivers, consents, including consents and agreements under section 2032A of the Internal Revenue Code of 1986, 26 U.S.C. 2032A, closing agreements, and any power of attorney required by the internal revenue service or other taxing authority with respect to a tax year upon which the statute of limitations has not run and the following twenty-five tax years;

(B) Pay taxes due, collect refunds, post bonds, receive confidential information, and contest deficiencies determined by the internal revenue service or other taxing authority;

(C) Exercise any election available to the principal under federal, state, local, or foreign tax law;

(D) Act for the principal in all tax matters for all periods before the internal revenue service, or other taxing authority.

**HISTORY:**
2011 SB 117, § 1, eff. Mar. 22, 2012.

**Editor's Notes**
Acts 2011, SB 117, § 4 provides: "The General Assembly hereby declares its intent by this act to clarify the procedure for resolution of issues created by the past or future repeal or reenactment of the federal estate tax, federal generation-skipping transfer tax, and Ohio estate tax."

### § 1337.571 Power of attorney with respect to digital assest makes agent an authorized user.

Unless the power of attorney otherwise provides, language in a power of attorney granting general authority with respect to digital assets causes the agent to be an authorized user for the purpose of applicable computer fraud and unauthorized computer access laws and authorizes the agent to do all of the following:

(A) Have access to any catalogue of electronic communications sent or received by the principal;

(B) Have access to any other digital asset in which the principal has a right or interest;

(C) Have the right to access any of the principal's tangible personal property capable of receiving, storing, processing, or sending a digital asset;

(D) Take any action concerning the asset to the extent of the account holder's authority;

(E) Have access to the content of electronic communications sent or received by the principal.

**HISTORY:**
2016 hb432, § 1, effective April 6, 2017.

### § 1337.58 General authority gifts.

(A) As used in this section, a gift "for the benefit of" a person includes a gift to a trust, an account under the Uniform Transfers to Minors Act, and a tuition savings account or prepaid tuition plan as defined under section 529 of the Internal Revenue Code of 1986, 26 U.S.C. 529.

(B) Unless the power of attorney otherwise provides, language in a power of attorney granting general authority with respect to gifts authorizes the agent to do only the following:

(1) Make outright to, or for the benefit of, a person, a gift of any of the principal's property, including by the exercise of a presently exercisable general power of appointment held by the principal, in an amount per donee not to exceed the annual dollar limits of the federal gift tax exclusion under section 2503(b) of the Internal Revenue Code of 1986, 26 U.S.C. 2503(b), without regard to whether the federal gift tax exclusion applies to the gift, or if the principal's spouse agrees to consent to a split gift pursuant to section 2513 of the Internal Revenue Code of 1986, 26 U.S.C. 2513, in an amount per donee not to exceed twice the annual federal gift tax exclusion limit;

(2) Consent, pursuant to section 2513 of the Internal Revenue Code of 1986, 26 U.S.C. 2513, to the splitting of a gift made by the principal's spouse in an amount per donee not to exceed the aggregate annual gift tax exclusions for both spouses.

(C) An agent may make a gift of the principal's property, outright or by amending, creating, or funding a trust, only as the agent determines is consistent with the principal's objectives if actually known by the agent and, if unknown, as the agent determines is consistent with the principal's best interest based on all relevant factors, including all of the following:

(1) The value and nature of the principal's property;

(2) The principal's foreseeable obligations and need for maintenance;

(3) Minimization of taxes, including income, estate, inheritance, generation-skipping transfer, and gift taxes;

(4) Eligibility for a benefit, a program, or assistance under a statute or regulation;

(5) The principal's personal history of making or joining in making gifts.

**HISTORY:**
2011 SB 117, § 1, eff. Mar. 22, 2012.

**Editor's Notes**
Acts 2011, SB 117, § 4 provides: "The General Assembly hereby declares its intent by this act to clarify the procedure for resolution of issues created by the past or future repeal or reenactment of the federal estate tax, federal generation-skipping transfer tax, and Ohio estate tax."

### § 1337.59 Use of former statutory power of attorney form.

In a power of attorney executed on or after March 29, 2006, and before the effective date of this section that either uses the statutory power of attorney form contained in former section 1337.18 of the Revised Code or that incorporates by reference any one or more of the powers contained in former section 1337.20 of the Revised Code, the powers granted shall be construed in accordance with former section 1337.20 of the Revised Code.

**HISTORY:**
2011 SB 117, § 1, eff. Mar. 22, 2012.

**Editor's Notes**
Acts 2011, SB 117, § 4 provides: "The General Assembly hereby declares its intent by this act to clarify the procedure for resolution of issues created by the past or future repeal or reenactment of the federal estate tax, federal generation-skipping transfer tax, and Ohio estate tax."

### § 1337.60 Statutory power of attorney form.

A document substantially in the following form may be used to create a statutory form power of attorney that has the meaning and effect prescribed by sections 1337.21 to 1337.64 of the Revised Code.

[INSERT NAME OF JURISDICTION]

STATUTORY FORM POWER OF ATTORNEY

IMPORTANT INFORMATION

This power of attorney authorizes another person (your agent) to make decisions concerning your property for you (the principal). Your agent will be able to make decisions and act with respect to your property (including your money) whether or not you are able to act for yourself. The meaning of authority over subjects listed on this form is explained in the Uniform Power of Attorney Act (sections 1337.21 to 1337.64 of the Revised Code).

This power of attorney does not authorize the agent to make health-care decisions for you.

You should select someone you trust to serve as your agent. Unless you specify otherwise, generally the agent's authority will continue until you die or revoke the power of attorney or the agent resigns or is unable to act for you.

Your agent is entitled to reasonable compensation unless you state otherwise in the Special Instructions.

This form provides for designation of one agent. If you wish to name more than one agent you may name a coagent in the Special Instructions. Coagents are not required to act together unless you include that requirement in the Special Instructions.

If your agent is unable or unwilling to act for you, your power of attorney will end unless you have named a successor agent. You may also name a second successor agent.

This power of attorney becomes effective immediately unless you state otherwise in the Special Instructions.

ACTIONS REQUIRING EXPRESS AUTHORITY

Unless expressly authorized and initialed by me in the Special Instructions, this power of attorney does not grant authority to my agent to do any of the following:

(1) Create a trust;

(2) Amend, revoke, or terminate an inter vivos trust, even if specific authority to do so is granted to the agent in the trust agreement;

(3) Make a gift;

(4) Create or change rights of survivorship;

(5) Create or change a beneficiary designation;

(6) Delegate authority granted under the power of attorney;

(7) Waive the principal's right to be a beneficiary of a joint and survivor annuity, including a survivor benefit under a retirement plan;

(8) Exercise fiduciary powers that the principal has authority to delegate.

CAUTION: Granting any of the above eight powers will give your agent the authority to take actions that could significantly reduce your property or change how your property is distributed at your death.

If you have questions about the power of attorney or the authority you are granting to your agent, you should seek legal advice before signing this form.

DESIGNATION OF AGENT

I, ................ (Name of Principal) name the following person as my agent:

................Name of Agent:

................Agent's Address:

....Agent's Telephone Number:

DESIGNATION OF SUCCESSOR AGENT(S) (OPTIONAL)

If my agent is unable or unwilling to act for me, I name as my successor agent:

................Name of Successor Agent:

................Successor Agent's Address:

....Successor Agent's Telephone Number:

If my successor agent is unable or unwilling to act for me, I name as my second successor agent:

................Name of Second Successor Agent:

................Second Successor Agent's Address:

....Second Successor Agent's Telephone Number:

GRANT OF GENERAL AUTHORITY

I grant my agent and any successor agent general authority to act for me with respect to the following subjects as defined in the Uniform Power of Attorney Act (sections 1337.21 to 1337.64 of the Revised Code):

(INITIAL each subject you want to include in the agent's general authority. If you wish to grant general authority over all of the subjects you may initial "All Preceding Subjects" instead of initialing each subject.)

(...) Real Property

(...) Tangible Personal Property

(...) Stocks and Bonds

(...) Commodities and Options

(...) Banks and Other Financial Institutions

(...) Operation of Entity or Business

(...) Insurance and Annuities

(...) Estates, Trusts, and Other Beneficial Interests

(...) Claims and Litigation

(...) Personal and Family Maintenance

(...) Benefits from Governmental Programs or Civil or Military Service

(...) Retirement Plans

(...) Taxes

(...) Digital Assets

All Preceding Subjects

(...) My agent shall have access to the content of electronic communications sent or received by me.

LIMITATION ON AGENT'S AUTHORITY

An agent that is not my ancestor, spouse, or descendant MAY NOT use my property to benefit the agent or a person to whom the agent owes an obligation of support unless I have included that authority in the Special Instructions.

SPECIAL INSTRUCTIONS (OPTIONAL)

You may give special instructions on the following lines:

..........................................................................................
..........................................................................................
..........................................................................................
..........................................................................................
..........................................................................................
..........................................................................................
..........................................................................................
..........................................................................................
..........................................................................................

EFFECTIVE DATE

This power of attorney is effective immediately unless I have stated otherwise in the Special Instructions.

NOMINATION OF GUARDIAN (OPTIONAL)

If it becomes necessary for a court to appoint a guardian of my estate or my person, I nominate the following person(s) for appointment:

................Name of Nominee for guardian of my estate:

................Nominee's Address:

....Nominee's Telephone Number:

................Name of Nominee for guardian of my person:

................Nominee's Address:

....Nominee's Telephone Number:

RELIANCE ON THIS POWER OF ATTORNEY

Any person, including my agent, may rely upon the validity of this power of attorney or a copy of it unless that person knows it has terminated or is invalid.

SIGNATURE AND ACKNOWLEDGMENT

................................ ................

Your Signature Date

IMPORTANT INFORMATION FOR AGENT

Agent's Duties

When you accept the authority granted under this power of attorney, a special legal relationship is created between you and the principal. This relationship imposes upon you legal duties that continue until you resign or the power of attorney is terminated or revoked. You must:

(1) Do what you know the principal reasonably expects you to do with the principal's property or, if you do not know the principal's expectations, act in the principal's best interest;

(2) Act in good faith;

(3) Do nothing beyond the authority granted in this power of attorney;

(4) Attempt to preserve the principal's estate plan if you know the plan and preserving the plan is consistent with the principal's best interest;

(5) Disclose your identity as an agent whenever you act for the principal by writing or printing the name of the principal and signing your own name as "agent" in the following manner:

(Principal's Name) by (Your Signature) as Agent

Unless the Special Instructions in this power of attorney state otherwise, you must also:

(1) Act loyally for the principal's benefit;

(2) Avoid conflicts that would impair your ability to act in the principal's best interest;

(3) Act with care, competence, and diligence;

(4) Keep a record of all receipts, disbursements, and transactions made on behalf of the principal;

(5) Cooperate with any person that has authority to make health-care decisions for the principal to do what you know the principal reasonably expects or, if you do not know the principal's expectations, to act in the principal's best interest.

Termination of Agent's Authority

You must stop acting on behalf of the principal if you learn of any event that terminates this power of attorney or your authority under this power of attorney. Events that terminate a power of attorney or your authority to act under a power of attorney include:

(1) The death of the principal;

(2) The principal's revocation of the power of attorney or your authority;

(3) The occurrence of a termination event stated in the power of attorney;

(4) The purpose of the power of attorney is fully accomplished;

(5) If you are married to the principal, a legal action is filed with a court to end your marriage, or for your legal separation, unless the Special Instructions in this power of attorney state that such an action will not terminate your authority.

Liability of Agent

The meaning of the authority granted to you is defined in the Uniform Power of Attorney Act (sections 1337.21 to 1337.64 of the Revised Code). If you violate the Uniform Power of Attorney Act or act outside the authority granted, you may be liable for any damages caused by your violation.

If there is anything about this document or your duties that you do not understand, you should seek legal advice.

**HISTORY:**

2011 SB 117, § 1, eff. Mar. 22, 2012; 2016 hb432, § 1, effective April 6, 2017.

**Amendment Notes**

The 2016 amendment by HB 432 in the form GRANT OF GENERAL AUTHORITY, inserted "Digital Assets" and "My agent shall have access to the content of electronic communications sent or received by me".

**Editor's Notes**

Acts 2011, SB 117, § 4 provides: "The General Assembly hereby declares its intent by this act to clarify the procedure for resolution of issues created by the past or future repeal or reenactment of the federal estate tax, federal generation-skipping transfer tax, and Ohio estate tax."

## § 1337.61 Optional form to certify facts.

The following optional form may be used by an agent to certify facts concerning a power of attorney.

AGENT'S CERTIFICATION AS TO THE VALIDITY OF POWER OF ATTORNEY AND AGENT'S AUTHORITY

State of Ohio

County of ............................

I, ............................ (Name of Agent), certify under penalty of perjury that ............................ (Name of Principal) granted me authority as an agent or successor agent in a power of attorney dated ............................

I further certify that to my knowledge:

(1) The Principal is alive and has not revoked the Power of Attorney or my authority to act under the Power of Attorney and the Power of Attorney and my authority to act under the Power of Attorney have not terminated;

(2) If the Power of Attorney was drafted to become effective upon the happening of an event or contingency, the event or contingency has occurred;

(3) If I was named as a successor agent, the prior agent is no longer able or willing to serve;

(4) ............................................................

(Insert other relevant statements).

SIGNATURE AND ACKNOWLEDGMENT

............................ ....................

Agent's Signature Date

Agent's Name Printed

Agent's Address

Agent's Telephone Number

State of Ohio

County of ............................

This document was acknowledged before me on .................... (Date) by ............................ (Name of Agent).

............................................................

Signature of Notary

My commission expires:

This document prepared by:

**HISTORY:**

2011 SB 117, § 1, eff. Mar. 22, 2012.

**Editor's Notes**

Acts 2011, SB 117, § 4 provides: "The General Assembly hereby declares its intent by this act to clarify the procedure for resolution of issues created by the past or future repeal or reenactment of the federal estate tax, federal generation-skipping transfer tax, and Ohio estate tax."

## § 1337.62 Consideration to promote uniformity of the law.

In applying and construing sections 1337.21 to 1337.64 of the Revised Code, consideration shall be given to the need to promote uniformity of the law with respect to its subject matter among the states that enact it.

**HISTORY:**

2011 SB 117, § 1, eff. Mar. 22, 2012.

**Editor's Notes**

Acts 2011, SB 117, § 4 provides: "The General Assembly hereby declares its intent by this act to clarify the procedure for resolution of issues created by the past or future repeal or reenactment of the federal estate tax, federal generation-skipping transfer tax, and Ohio estate tax."



## § 1337.63 Electronic signatures.

Sections 1337.21 to 1337.64 of the Revised Code modify, limit, and supersede the "Electronic Signatures in Global and National Commerce Act," 15 U.S.C. 7001 et seq., with the exception of section 101(c) of that act, 15 U.S.C. 7001(c). Sections 1337.21 to 1337.64 of the Revised Code do not authorize electronic delivery of any of the notices described in section 103(b) of that act, 15 U.S.C. 7003(b).

**HISTORY:**

2011 SB 117, § 1, eff. Mar. 22, 2012.

**Editor's Notes**

Acts 2011, SB 117, § 4 provides: "The General Assembly hereby declares its intent by this act to clarify the procedure for resolution of issues created by the past or future repeal or reenactment of the federal estate tax, federal generation-skipping transfer tax, and Ohio estate tax."

## § 1337.64 Application.

(A) Except as otherwise provided in sections 1337.21 to 1337.64 of the Revised Code, on the effective date of this section, those sections apply to all of the following:

(1) A power of attorney created before, on, or after the effective date of this section;

(2) A judicial proceeding concerning a power of attorney commenced on or after the effective date of this section;

(3) A judicial proceeding concerning a power of attorney commenced before the effective date of this section, unless the court finds that application of a provision of sections 1337.21 to 1337.64 of the Revised Code would substantially interfere with the effective conduct of the judicial proceeding or prejudice the rights of a party, in which case that provision does not apply and the superseded law applies.

(B) Sections 1337.21 to 1337.64 of the Revised Code do not affect an act done before the effective date of this section.

**HISTORY:**

2011 SB 117, § 1, eff. Mar. 22, 2012.

**Editor's Notes**

Acts 2011, SB 117, § 4 provides: "The General Assembly hereby declares its intent by this act to clarify the procedure for resolution of issues created by the past or future repeal or reenactment of the federal estate tax, federal generation-skipping transfer tax, and Ohio estate tax."

# TITLE 17

# CORPORATIONS — PARTNERSHIPS



## CHAPTER 1733

## CREDIT UNIONS



### § 1733.241 Joint accounts; payable on death accounts.

(A) When a share, share account, or deposit is made in the name of two or more persons, payable to either or the survivor, the credit union may pay all of the share, share account, deposit, any part of the share, share account, deposit, or any interest earned on the share, share account, or deposit, to either of the named persons, or the guardian of the estate of either of the named persons, whether or not the other person is living. The receipt or acquittance of the person paid is a sufficient release and discharge of the credit union for any payments made from the account to that person.

(B) A credit union may enter into a written contract with a natural person for the proceeds of the person's shares, share accounts, or deposits to be payable on the death of that person to another person or to any entity or organization in accordance with the terms, restrictions, and limitations set forth in sections 2131.10 and 2131.11 of the Revised Code.

**HISTORY:**

152 v S 247, § 1, eff. 9-11-08.

# TITLE 21

# COURTS — PROBATE — JUVENILE



# CHAPTER 2101

# PROBATE COURT — JURISDICTION; PROCEDURE



### § 2101.24 Jurisdiction of probate court.

(A)(1) Except as otherwise provided by law, the probate court has exclusive jurisdiction:

(a) To take the proof of wills and to admit to record authenticated copies of wills executed, proved, and allowed in the courts of any other state, territory, or country. If the probate judge is unavoidably absent, any judge of the court of common pleas may take proof of wills and approve bonds to be given, but the record of these acts shall be preserved in the usual records of the probate court.

(b) To grant and revoke letters testamentary and of administration;

(c) To direct and control the conduct and settle the accounts of executors and administrators and order the distribution of estates;

(d) To appoint the attorney general to serve as the administrator of an estate pursuant to section 2113.06 of the Revised Code;

(e) To appoint and remove guardians, conservators, and testamentary trustees, direct and control their conduct, and settle their accounts;

(f) To grant marriage licenses;

(g) To make inquests respecting persons who are so mentally impaired as a result of a mental or physical illness or disability, as a result of intellectual disability, or as a result of chronic substance abuse, that they are unable to manage their property and affairs effectively, subject to guardianship;

(h) To qualify assignees, appoint and qualify trustees and commissioners of insolvents, control their conduct, and settle their accounts;

(i) To authorize the sale of lands, equitable estates, or interests in lands or equitable estates, and the assignments of inchoate dower in such cases of sale, on petition by executors, administrators, and guardians;

(j) To authorize the completion of real property contracts on petition of executors and administrators;

(k) To construe wills;

(*l*) To render declaratory judgments, including, but not limited to, those rendered pursuant to Chapter 5817. of the Revised Code;

(m) To direct and control the conduct of fiduciaries and settle their accounts;

(n) To authorize the sale or lease of any estate created by will if the estate is held in trust, on petition by the trustee;

(o) To terminate a testamentary trust in any case in which a court of equity may do so;

(p) To hear and determine actions to contest the validity of wills;

(q) To make a determination of the presumption of death of missing persons and to adjudicate the property rights and obligations of all parties affected by the presumption;

(r) To act for and issue orders regarding wards pursuant to section 2111.50 of the Revised Code;

(s) To hear and determine actions against sureties on the bonds of fiduciaries appointed by the probate court;

(t) To hear and determine actions involving informed consent for medication of persons hospitalized pursuant to section 5122.141 or 5122.15 of the Revised Code;

(u) To hear and determine actions relating to durable powers of attorney for health care as described in division (D) of section 1337.16 of the Revised Code;

(v) To hear and determine actions commenced by objecting individuals, in accordance with section 2133.05 of the Revised Code;

(w) To hear and determine complaints that pertain to the use or continuation, or the withholding or withdrawal, of life-sustaining treatment in connection with certain patients allegedly in a terminal condition or in a permanently unconscious state pursuant to division (E) of section 2133.08 of the Revised Code, in accordance with that division;

(x) To hear and determine applications that pertain to the withholding or withdrawal of nutrition and hydration from certain patients allegedly in a permanently unconscious state pursuant to section 2133.09 of the Revised Code, in accordance with that section;

(y) To hear and determine applications of attending physicians in accordance with division (B) of section 2133.15 of the Revised Code;

(z) To hear and determine actions relative to the use or continuation of comfort care in connection with certain principals under durable powers of attorney for health care, declarants under declarations, or patients in accordance with division (E) of either section 1337.16 or 2133.12 of the Revised Code;

(aa) To hear and determine applications for an order relieving an estate from administration under section 2113.03 of the Revised Code;

(bb) To hear and determine applications for an order granting a summary release from administration under section 2113.031 of the Revised Code;

(cc) To hear and determine actions relating to the exercise of the right of disposition, in accordance with section 2108.90 of the Revised Code;

(dd) To hear and determine actions relating to the disinterment and reinterment of human remains under section 517.23 of the Revised Code;

(ee) To hear and determine petitions for an order for treatment of a person suffering from alcohol and other drug abuse filed under section 5119.93 of the Revised Code and to order treatment of that nature in accordance with, and take other actions afforded to the court under, sections 5119.90 to 5119.98 of the Revised Code.

(2) In addition to the exclusive jurisdiction conferred upon the probate court by division (A)(1) of this section, the probate court shall have exclusive jurisdiction over a particular subject matter if both of the following apply:

(a) Another section of the Revised Code expressly confers jurisdiction over that subject matter upon the probate court.

(b) No section of the Revised Code expressly confers jurisdiction over that subject matter upon any other court or agency.

(B)(1) The probate court has concurrent jurisdiction with, and the same powers at law and in equity as, the general division of the court of common pleas to issue writs and orders, and to hear and determine actions as follows:

(a) If jurisdiction relative to a particular subject matter is stated to be concurrent in a section of the Revised Code or has been construed by judicial decision to be concurrent, any action that involves that subject matter;

(b) Any action that involves an inter vivos trust; a trust created pursuant to section 5815.28 of the Revised Code; a charitable trust or foundation; subject to divisions (A)(1)(t) and (y) of this section, a power of attorney, including, but not limited to, a durable power of attorney; the medical treatment of a competent adult; or a writ of habeas corpus;

(c) Subject to section 2101.31 of the Revised Code, any action with respect to a probate estate, guardianship, trust, or post-death dispute that involves any of the following:

(i) A designation or removal of a beneficiary of a life insurance policy, annuity contract, retirement plan, brokerage account, security account, bank account, real property, or tangible personal property;

(ii) A designation or removal of a payable-on-death beneficiary or transfer-on-death beneficiary;

(iii) A change in the title to any asset involving a joint and survivorship interest;

(iv) An alleged gift;

(v) The passing of assets upon the death of an individual otherwise than by will, intestate succession, or trust.

(2) Any action that involves a concurrent jurisdiction subject matter and that is before the probate court may be transferred by the probate court, on its order, to the general division of the court of common pleas.

(3) Notwithstanding that the probate court has exclusive jurisdiction to render declaratory judgments under Chapter 5817. of the Revised Code, the probate court may transfer the proceeding to the general division of the court of common pleas pursuant to division (A) of section 5817.04 of the Revised Code.

(C) The probate court has plenary power at law and in equity to dispose fully of any matter that is properly before the court, unless the power is expressly otherwise limited or denied by a section of the Revised Code.

(D) The jurisdiction acquired by a probate court over a matter or proceeding is exclusive of that of any other probate court, except when otherwise provided by law.

**HISTORY:**

GC §§ 10501-53, 10501-55; 114 v 320; Bureau of Code Revision, 10-1-53; 125 v 903(960); 127 v 27 (Eff 9-9-57); 129 v 7 (Eff 10-5-61); 130 v 611 (Eff 10-14-63); 136 v S 145 (Eff 1-1-76); 136 v S 466 (Eff 5-26-76); 137 v H 1 (Eff 8-26-77); 137 v S 112 (Eff 11-1-77); 137 v H 505 (Eff 1-1-79); 140 v H 84 (Eff 3-19-85); 141 v S 135 (Eff 3-13-86); 143 v S 46 (Eff 1-1-90); 143 v H 764 (Eff 4-10-91); 144 v S 1 (Eff 10-10-91); 144 v S 124 (Eff 4-16-93); 146 v H 167 (Eff 11-15-95); 148 v H 313. Eff 8-29-2000; 151 v H 426, § 1, eff. 10-12-06; 151 v H 416, § 1, eff. 1-1-07; 2011 SB 124, § 1, eff. Jan. 13, 2012; 2011 SB 117, § 1, eff. Mar. 22, 2012; 2012 HB 479, § 1, eff. Mar. 27, 2013; 2013 HB 59, § 101.01, eff. Sept. 29, 2013; 2013 SB 23, § 1, eff. Mar. 20, 2015; 2016 hb158, § 1, effective October 12, 2016; 2018 hb595, § 1, effective March 22, 2019.

**Amendment Notes**

The 2018 amendment by HB 595, substituted "pursuant to Chapter 5817." for "pursuant to section 2107.084" in (A)(1)(*l*); and added (B)(3).

The 2016 amendment by HB 158 substituted "as a result of intellectual disability" for "or mental retardation" in (A)(1)(g).

**Comment, Legislative Service Commission**

Section 2101.24 of the Revised Code is amended by Sub. H.B. 416 and Sub. H.B. 426 of the 126th General Assembly. Comparison of these amendments in pursuance of section 1.52 of the Revised Code discloses that they are not irreconcilable so that they are required by that section to be harmonized to give effect to each amendment.

## NOTES TO DECISIONS

Analysis



**Constitutionality**

General Code § 10510-10 (R.C. 2127.08) and this section were held not unconstitutional as violative of Ohio Const. art IV, § 8: (decided under former analogous section) Hatch v. Buckeye State Bldg. & Loan Co., 32 Ohio N.P. 297 (1934).

Former GC §§ 10494, 10495 and 10497 (repealed, 114 v 320 [475]) are valid enactments, and not so inseparably united with the appeal provision of former GC § 10496 (repealed, 114 v 320 [475]), that they are unconstitutional and void: (decided under former analogous section) Geiger v. Geiger, 117 Ohio St. 451, 160 N.E. 28, 5 Ohio Law Abs. 829, 1927 Ohio LEXIS 210 (Ohio 1927).

**Abuse of discretion**

Probate court did not abuse its discretion in finding that an executrix's decision to transfer estate property to two acquaintances was improper and

Titles 11 — 37

that the transfer constituted a fraudulent conveyance where the transfer was made with the intent to defraud the only other beneficiary of the estate besides herself and a creditor of the estate; the property was transferred without a reasonable equivalent value in exchange; she transferred the property to pay an untimely claim against the estate by one transferee and a personal loan that the other transferee made to her; and she transferred the property without notice to the probate court even though it was the subject of much controversy and litigation. In re Estate of Brate, 2019-Ohio-446, 2019 Ohio App. LEXIS 466 (Ohio Ct. App., Warren County 2019).

Although removal of a fiduciary was a matter within the sound discretion of the probate court, it abused its discretion in allowing an executrix to continue in her role after finding clear grounds for her removal, including the fraudulent conveyance of estate property, commingling of estate assets with her personal assets, and failing to establish an estate checking account. In re Estate of Brate, 2019-Ohio-446, 2019 Ohio App. LEXIS 466 (Ohio Ct. App., Warren County 2019).

**Accounts**

In a case in which the executor of the decedent's estate withdrew $15,000 from a guardianship account before the guardian filed the final accounting associated with the guardianship, the probate court's jurisdiction over the final accounting did not extend to compelling the executor of the estate to return funds to the guardianship account because the guardianship terminated upon the death of the decedent; and the guardian could complete and submit a final accounting without the return of the funds. In re Guardianship of Siman, 2020-Ohio-4472, 158 N.E.3d 955, 2020 Ohio App. LEXIS 3329 (Ohio Ct. App., Cuyahoga County 2020).

**Attorney's fees**

Probate court properly exercised it plenary jurisdiction when it considered and ruled on a motion for a charging lien; the parties were not strangers to the underlying lawsuit, the probate court had knowledge of the value of the underlying trust dispute, and the record supported the conclusion that the attorney's representation helped secure the judgment obtained in the underlying trust dispute. Galloway v. Galloway, 2017-Ohio-87, 80 N.E.3d 1225, 2017 Ohio App. LEXIS 74 (Ohio Ct. App., Cuyahoga County 2017).

**Best interest of ward**

Probate court did not have exclusive jurisdiction over a daughter's claims because the complaint alleged her mother, a ward of the state, was the perpetrator of improper acts and did not call into question the guardian's conduct; although, the guardian had a duty to protect and control the ward, that was not sufficient to convey exclusive jurisdiction to the probate court over a ward's conduct, especially since the allegations stemmed from actions that occurred prior to the guardianship. Sosnoswsky v. Koscianski, 2018-Ohio-3045, 118 N.E.3d 403, 2018 Ohio App. LEXIS 3298 (Ohio Ct. App., Cuyahoga County 2018).

**Birth certificates**

Probate court lacked authority to change an applicant's race and nationality on the birth record he provide because the birth record did not contain any race or nationality classification, and, as such, the applicant was asking the probate court to amend his birth certificate to add classifications, rather than to correct "required facts." In re Easterling, 2019-Ohio-1516, 135 N.E.3d 496, 2019 Ohio App. LEXIS 1616 (Ohio Ct. App., Hamilton County 2019).

**Breach of fiduciary duty**

Where co-trustee essentially prevented the trusts from collecting on certain promissory notes, first by stopping payment as president of the family companies and later by refusing to enforce the notes as co-trustee, the probate court did not error or exceed the scope of prayed-for relief when it ordered him to pay the amount due and owing on the notes, plus accrued interest. Zarlenga v. Zarlenga, 2020-Ohio-6947, 2020 Ohio App. LEXIS 4779 (Ohio Ct. App., Mahoning County 2020).

**Concurrent jurisdiction**

Because none of the enumerated exceptions in subsection (B)(1) conferred probate court concurrent jurisdiction, the jurisdictional-priority rule did not apply; jurisdiction was proper in the general division of the common pleas court, and thus, the trial court erred when it dismissed the daughter's complaint for lack of subject matter jurisdiction. Sosnoswsky v. Koscianski, 2018-Ohio-3045, 118 N.E.3d 403, 2018 Ohio App. LEXIS 3298 (Ohio Ct. App., Cuyahoga County 2018).

Probate court did not err in declaring that another common pleas court had exerted jurisdiction in a tax foreclosure action involving the decedent's real estate, such that the probate court was not the appropriate forum to resolve a land contract issue between the former co-executor and his brother, who was also a co-executor that had been removed. In re Estate of Fields, 2016-Ohio-5358, 2016 Ohio App. LEXIS 3224 (Ohio Ct. App., Wood County 2016).

**Constitutionality of ordinance**

A probate court is without jurisdiction to entertain an original action wherein plaintiff seeks to obtain a declaratory judgment by that court that an ordinance of a municipality is unconstitutional as it relates to plaintiff's property, together with injunctive and equitable relief; a declaratory judgment rendered by such court, without jurisdiction, is void and of no effect: (decided under former analogous section) State ex rel. Mayfield Heights v. Bartunek, 12 Ohio App. 2d 141, 41 Ohio Op. 2d 222, 231 N.E.2d 326, 1967 Ohio App. LEXIS 392 (Ohio Ct. App., Cuyahoga County 1967).

**Generally**

Pursuant to R.C. 2101.24(A)(1)(c), a probate court had "exclusive" jurisdiction to direct and control the conduct and settle the accounts of executors and administrators. Holik v. Lafferty, 2006-Ohio-2652, 2006 Ohio App. LEXIS 2482 (Ohio Ct. App., Ashtabula County 2006).

Probate court's plenary jurisdiction at law and in equity under R.C. 2101.24(C) authorized any relief required to fully adjudicate the subject matter within the probate court's exclusive jurisdiction, and claims for breach of fiduciary duty, which inexorably implicated the control over the conduct of the fiduciaries, were within that subject-matter jurisdiction by virtue of R.C. 2101.24(A)(1)(c). Holik v. Lafferty, 2006-Ohio-2652, 2006 Ohio App. LEXIS 2482 (Ohio Ct. App., Ashtabula County 2006).

When a decedent's former wife, who was also the administrator of his estate, sued his brother, both in her capacity as the estate's administrator and individually, claiming that the decedent's transfers of properties to the brother were fraudulent, the trial court could not address her claims as the estate's administrator because, under R.C. 2101.24 and 2721.05, the probate court had exclusive jurisdiction over them, because, while she couched her claims as being brought under the Uniform Fraudulent Transfer Act, R.C. 1336.01 et seq., they, in essence, sought to have the trial court declare the transfers to the brother were invalid, thus having the properties revert to the decedent's estate. Lamar v. Washington, 2006-Ohio-1414, 2006 Ohio App. LEXIS 1298 (Ohio Ct. App., Allen County 2006).

Because the son's claims pertained to the guardian's conduct in his capacity as a guardian, the trial court did not err in dismissing the claim under Civ.R. 12(B)(1) as it lacked subject matter jurisdiction. The probate court had exclusive jurisdiction pursuant to R.C. 2101.24 and the son's prayer for money damages did not divest the probate court of its jurisdiction over the matter. Rowan v. McLaughlin, 2005-Ohio-3473, 2005 Ohio App. LEXIS 3226 (Ohio Ct. App., Cuyahoga County 2005).

Neither R.C. 2101.24 nor R.C. 2109.50 to 2109.56 confer subject matter jurisdiction on probate courts to issue prejudgment attachment orders relating to personal property. Wrongful death settlement proceeds are not estate assets: State ex rel. Goldberg v. Mahoning County Probate Court, 2001-Ohio-1297, 93 Ohio St. 3d 160, 753 N.E.2d 192, 2001 Ohio LEXIS 2186 (Ohio 2001).

General Code § 11215 (R.C. 2305.01) is an old and general statute, while this section is recent and special; therefore, under the canons of statutory construction, the latter must take precedence over the former: (decided under former analogous section) Unger v. Wolfe, 134 Ohio St. 69, 11 Ohio Op. 483, 15 N.E.2d 955, 1938 Ohio LEXIS 317 (Ohio 1938).

**Abuse of discretion**

Probate court abused its discretion when it overruled siblings' motion to continue a case and erred as a matter of law when it approved the guardian's final accounts because Hocking County, Ohio, Ct. C.P. Prob. Div. R. 32(B) required that the siblings, who were interested parties under R.C. 2109.33 and had the right to receive notice and file exceptions, were to be served with notice of the hearing under R.C. 2109.32(A) on the guardian's final accounts. However, the siblings did not receive either a copy of the accounts or notice of the hearing on the accounts. In re Guardianship of Snyder, 2010-Ohio-3899, 2010 Ohio App. LEXIS 3332 (Ohio Ct. App., Hocking County 2010).

**Accounts**

Probate court acted pursuant to its plenary power by accepting an account and complied with its duty to act as the superior guardian of the ward when it determined that, even though the guardians did not comply with all of the statutory requirements, the guardians had cared for the ward's best interest. In re Guardianship of Lindsey, 2015-Ohio-4235, 2015 Ohio App. LEXIS 4126 (Ohio Ct. App., Preble County 2015).

It is the duty of the probate court to require of the guardian of the estate of a minor a full account of the guardian's care or lack of care of the assets belonging to the ward. It is the duty of the probate court to fix the liability, if any, of a guardian for his failure on final settlement to account fully for the estate of the ward: (decided under former analogous section) Guardianship of Zimmerman, 141 Ohio St. 207, 25 Ohio Op. 326, 47 N.E.2d 782, 1943 Ohio LEXIS 409 (Ohio 1943).

The probate court has jurisdiction to hear exceptions to the account of the superintendent of banks in charge of liquidation of an Ohio bank as to a trust for which such bank, before its liquidation, was trustee through appointment by that court; to settle such account; to surcharge the bank as such trustee; and to direct the superintendent of banks to such trustee; and to direct the superintendent of banks to issue a certificate of claim against the assets of such bank to and in favor of a successor trustee; but such court does not have jurisdiction to render a money judgment against the bank or superintendent of banks, or to determine the character of the claim as to preferences, or to impress a lien upon property held by the bank as trustee, in favor of the successor trustee: (decided under former analogous section) In re Binder's Estate, 137 Ohio St. 26, 17 Ohio Op. 364, 27 N.E.2d 939, 1940 Ohio LEXIS 418 (Ohio 1940).

There is no authority in the probate court to set aside the final account of an administrator and reopen the estate, where no exception was filed by a party in interest within eight months of the settlement of said account, which is conclusive unless attacked for fraud or corrected by the court upon the filing of a subsequent and correct account. But when a mistake has been made in the former and final account as to the existence of debts against the estate and credits due the administrator, said former and final account may be opened up by the probate court upon the filing of a subsequent account showing the existence of such debts and credits: (decided under former analogous section) Hunter v. Yocum, 27 Ohio Dec. 31, 18 Ohio N.P. (n.s.) 14, 1914 Ohio Misc. LEXIS 74 (Ohio C.P. 1914).

After the expiration of the eight months allowed by GC § 10834 (see now R.C. 2109.35) for filing exceptions when the account is settled in the absence of a person interested and without actual notice to him, the judgment of a probate court settling the final account of an executor or an administrator becomes absolute and conclusive and cannot be attacked except for fraud of the prevailing party: (decided under former analogous section) Crawford v. Zeigler, 84 Ohio St. 224, 95 N.E. 743, 9 Ohio L. Rep. 94, 1911 Ohio LEXIS 98 (Ohio 1911).



**Administrator for nonresident**

The prohibition action against the probate court was erroneously dismissed where that court appointed an administrator for the intestate estate of a nonresident: State ex rel. Lee v. Trumbull County Probate Court, 1998-Ohio-51, 83 Ohio St. 3d 369, 700 N.E.2d 4, 1998 Ohio LEXIS 2739 (Ohio 1998).

**Administrators**

Probate court did not abuse its discretion under R.C. 2101.24(A)(1)(c) by compelling a decedent's estate administrator to sign authorization forms in order to enable an attorney to obtain the decedent's medical, school, and employment records for use in a wrongful death action on the children's behalf, as such documents were necessary for the preparation of the claim and it was in their best interests. The attorney represented the father of the children, who was the decedent's former husband and who was the childrens' next friend in the wrongful death action, and the court-appointed guardian of the children. Estate of Sarantino, 2006-Ohio-3641, 2006 Ohio App. LEXIS 3567 (Ohio Ct. App., Trumbull County 2006).

**Agreement between beneficiary and decedent**

Where a decedent obtained an auto loan for her niece because the niece had bad credit, and the niece agreed in writing to pay that loan, the probate court had authority to require that the niece save the estate harmless as to such debt by a charge against her distributive share. Estate of Shively v. Peterman, 2004-Ohio-3644, 2004 Ohio App. LEXIS 3279 (Ohio Ct. App., Delaware County 2004).

**Applicability**

Because the power of attorney which the decedent gave to the decedent's adult child did not authorize self-dealing, and the transactions whereby the child transferred real property appeared invalid due to the child's fiduciary relationship to the decedent, the administrator of the decedent's estate had remedies pursuant to R.C. 2101.24(A)(1 )(l) or 2721.03, among others, and should have filed as complaint under one of these sections. In re Estate of Rotilio, 2013-Ohio-2878, 2013 Ohio App. LEXIS 2922 (Ohio Ct. App., Belmont County 2013).

**Appointment of successor trustees**

Since no one designated by a trust was willing to serve as successor trustee, since the trust beneficiaries were not in agreement as to a successor, and since the first daughter's claims of mismanagement and theft were not substantiated, the probate court was authorized by R.C. 2101.24, 5807.04 to appoint the mother and second daughter as successor trustees. Franklin v. Franklin, 2010-Ohio-4251, 2010 Ohio App. LEXIS 3599 (Ohio Ct. App., Cuyahoga County 2010).

**Attorney malpractice**

Common pleas court which had exclusive jurisdiction over a legal client's malpractice action against an attorney, arising from the attorney's settlement of the client's wrongful death action involving the client's daughter, had subject matter jurisdiction over the matter until its conclusion; although a probate court had jurisdiction pursuant to R.C. 2101.24 to approve settlements of wrongful death matters, it had no jurisdiction over the malpractice claim. Batteiger v. Deutsch, 2008-Ohio-1582, 2008 Ohio App. LEXIS 1333 (Ohio Ct. App., Montgomery County 2008).

**Attorney-in-fact's power**

Even considering an executor's evidence of a decedent's estate planning, the executor exceeded his power under a power of attorney as he cashed savings bonds titled in the name of a decedent and her son under a power of attorney, deposited the proceeds into a joint account with a right of survivorship in the names of the decedent and the executor, moved the proceeds to his own account after the decedent's death, did not list the proceeds in the initial inventory of the estate, and later transferred the proceeds to the estate's accounts; the finding that the decedent intended for her son to receive the bond proceeds was reasonable as the executor became the sole owner of the funds due to his actions, the executor did not hold the funds in trust for the decedent's son, and the executor and the executor's son were the major beneficiaries under the will. In re Estate of Leach, 2006-Ohio-3755, 2006 Ohio App. LEXIS 3721 (Ohio Ct. App., Montgomery County 2006).

**Attorney's fees**

Ohio probate courts have equitable powers, under R.C. 2101.24(C), and, in rare cases, a probate court may authorize the payment of reasonable fees from an estate to an attorney employed by an heir or beneficiary where the attorney's services were rendered to the benefit of the whole estate. Compensation is based on the equitable doctrine that where one has created, augmented, or preserved a fund he may be compensated therefrom, and, where the beneficiary is reasonably justified in bringing suit, attorney fees are justified as long as they benefit the estate. In re Estate of Romero, 2007-Ohio-2157, 2007 Ohio App. LEXIS 2029 (Ohio Ct. App., Preble County 2007).

When a decedent's mother, who was appointed as the decedent's administratrix, and the decedent's former mother-in-law, who was appointed as the decedent's special administrator by another state's court, each were involved in a wrongful death suit prosecuted on account of the decedent's death, and each of them sought an award of attorney's fees, it was not an abuse of discretion, under R.C. 2101.24(C), to award attorney's fees to the former mother-in-law because the actions of the former mother-in-law's counsel benefitted the estate. In re Estate of Romero, 2007-Ohio-2157, 2007 Ohio App. LEXIS 2029 (Ohio Ct. App., Preble County 2007).

The probate court had exclusive jurisdiction over the subject of the division of attorney fees where several attorneys represented a minor in a personal injury action at different times during the action: Waterman v. Elk & Elk Co., L.P.A., 96 Ohio App. 3d 772, 645 N.E.2d 1326, 1994 Ohio App. LEXIS 4089 (Ohio Ct. App., Summit County 1994).

A probate court may allow payment of reasonable fees from the estate to an attorney employed by an heir or beneficiary where such attorney's services were necessarily and successfully rendered to the benefit of the whole estate. However, an attorney is not entitled to compensation for an unsuccessful effort: In re Estate of Fugate, 86 Ohio App. 3d 293, 620 N.E.2d 966, 1993 Ohio App. LEXIS 785 (Ohio Ct. App., Meigs County 1993).

A probate court, in order to maintain control over any personal injury settlement entered into on behalf of a ward under its protection, has subject matter jurisdiction over the entire amount of settlement funds, which includes attorney fees to be drawn therefrom. A probate court's approval of a fee-splitting agreement between counsel, without affording notice or opportunity to be heard to all parties in the agreement, violates the right to due process: In re Guardianship of Jadwisiak, 64 Ohio St. 3d 176, 593 N.E.2d 1379, 1992 Ohio LEXIS 1453 (Ohio 1992).

Where services are rendered by an attorney for a widow in effecting a settlement of all her rights and claims in and to the estate of her deceased husband the probate court has jurisdiction to hear and determine an application by the attorney for the allowance of compensation out of the estate; but, although it may have been fortuitous for the estate that a settlement of many problems may have been effected, such circumstances do not justify payment of attorney fees by the estate: (decided under former analogous section) In re Estate of Colosimo, 104 Ohio App. 342, 5 Ohio Op. 2d 24, 149 N.E.2d 31, 1957 Ohio App. LEXIS 924 (Ohio Ct. App., Montgomery County 1957).

Under the provisions of this section, the probate court has exclusive jurisdiction as to the allowance of fees to an attorney for his services in the unsuccessful prosecution of an application for the removal of the guardian of an incompetent: (decided under former analogous section) Unger v. Wolfe, 134 Ohio St. 69, 11 Ohio Op. 483, 15 N.E.2d 955, 1938 Ohio LEXIS 317 (Ohio 1938).

The probate court has jurisdiction of an application of an heir to the administratrix of an estate for an allowance for attorney fees incurred when he resisted a claim against the estate previously allowed as valid, which claim was substantially reduced through the applicant's efforts, such jurisdiction being granted by Ohio Const. art IV, § 8 and by this section: (decided under former analogous section) In re Estate of Helfrich, 3 Ohio Op. 162 (Ohio C.P. 1935).

Under Ohio Const. art IV, § 8 and GC § 10492 the claim for attorney's fees expended by an heir in contesting with partial success a claim against the estate by filing requisition for rejection in the probate court should be presented to the probate court for allowance and cannot be allowed by the common pleas court: (decided under former analogous section) Koelble v. Runyan, 25 Ohio App. 426, 158 N.E. 279, 6 Ohio Law Abs. 41, 1927 Ohio App. LEXIS 515 (Ohio Ct. App., Brown County 1927).

**Birth certificates**

Public policy in Ohio concerning changes to birth certificates is to allow a court to correct errors or mistakes only on the original birth record and not changes in the sexual designation when the original designation is correct. In re Application of Marriage License for Nash, 2003-Ohio-7221, 2003 Ohio App. LEXIS 6513 (Ohio Ct. App., Trumbull County 2003).

**Breach of fiduciary duty**

Probate court did not err in declining to dismiss the complaint for lack of jurisdiction under Civ.R. 12(B)(1). Because the sisters' claims against the attorney were for breach of fiduciary duty arising out of the administration of their father's estate, seeking to enhance the estate in the wake of the attorney's depletion of the estate by $50,000, and to have the estate distributed according to law, the matter was properly before the probate court. Ivancic v. Enos, 2012-Ohio-3639, 978 N.E.2d 927, 2012 Ohio App. LEXIS 3218 (Ohio Ct. App., Lake County 2012).

**Child custody**

Juvenile court properly dismissed the case for lack of jurisdiction and the probate court's order appointing the father of the child's half-siblings as the child's guardian was a valid judgment. The juvenile court could not determine the child's custody because she was a ward of the probate court when the grandmother filed her complaint for legal custody. In re I.B., 2015-Ohio-4181, 2015 Ohio App. LEXIS 4039 (Ohio Ct. App., Cuyahoga County 2015).

Although guardianship applications over adult children were within the exclusive jurisdiction of a probate court except as provided by law, pursuant to R.C. 2101.24(A)(1)(e), where a domestic relations court which handled parents' divorce and ancillary custody issues over their mentally impaired autistic son continued to exercise jurisdiction in that area, the probate court declined jurisdiction over the guardianship applications of the parents; the domestic relations court had the first opportunity to decide whether to exercise or decline jurisdiction due to the continuing nature of its jurisdiction under R.C. 3105.011 and 3109.05. In re Guardianship of Campbell, 2006-Ohio-1764, 2006 Ohio App. LEXIS 1614 (Ohio Ct. App., Mahoning County 2006).

Where the probate court had the power to determine custody, pursuant to R.C. 2111.06, it also had the power to determine visitation rights. In re Hoke, 2003-Ohio-4704, 2003 Ohio App. LEXIS 4210 (Ohio Ct. App., Franklin County 2003).

Under R.C. 2101.24(A)(1)(e), a probate court retained exclusive jurisdiction over modification of its custody decision and appointment of a guardian even after a minor became the subject of a neglect/dependency complaint within the exclusive jurisdiction of a juvenile court under R.C. 2151.23(A)(1). In re Guardianship of Pierce, 2003-Ohio-3997, 2003 Ohio App. LEXIS 3559 (Ohio Ct. App., Ross County 2003).

**Child support**

Husband failed to cite to any authority in support of his claim that a common pleas court lacked subject matter jurisdiction over the issue of child support for an adult-aged mentally retarded daughter, such that his claim failed under App.R. 16(A)(7); further, pursuant to R.C. 2101.24(D), 3109.05(A)(1), and 3105.011, the common pleas court had jurisdiction over the child support issue despite the fact that the parents had been appointed as guardians over the daughter. In re Edgell, 2010-Ohio-6435, 2010 Ohio App. LEXIS 5325 (Ohio Ct. App., Lake County 2010).

**Child support arrearage**

Juvenile court had no jurisdiction to determine estate matters, and its judgment finding that child support arrearages owed to the mother were not an asset of her estate was vacated. Miller v. McMichael, 2003-Ohio-6713, 2003 Ohio App. LEXIS 6081 (Ohio Ct. App., Paulding County 2003).

The domestic relations court had implicit authority under R.C. 3105.011 and 3105.21 to establish a guardianship to facilitate child support payments. That court also properly reduced arrearages to a lump sum. The probate court exercised its authority as superior guardian when it denied the request to distribute funds in a lump sum: In re Derakhshan, 110 Ohio App. 3d 190, 673 N.E.2d 954, 1996 Ohio App. LEXIS 1227 (Ohio Ct. App., Lake County 1996).

**Collateral attack on judgment**

The rule that the judgments of the probate court cannot be set aside, collaterally, except for fraud, applies to judgments approving accounts of executors: (decided under former analogous section) Truss v. Clouse, 23 Ohio Law Abs. 610, 1937 Ohio Misc. LEXIS 1237 (Ohio Ct. App., Miami County Jan. 21, 1937).

**Common law marriage**

As an incident to a hearing upon exceptions to an inventory pursuant to R.C. 2109.58, the probate court has jurisdiction to determine the issue of a common law marriage: (decided under former analogous section) In re Estate of Soeder, 7 Ohio App. 2d 271, 36 Ohio Op. 2d 404, 220 N.E.2d 547, 1966 Ohio App. LEXIS 443 (Ohio Ct. App., Cuyahoga County 1966).

**Concealment of assets**

Probate court did not patently and unambiguously lack jurisdiction over the action concerning concealment of assets on the basis that the assets were allegedly take prior to creation of the guardianship estate. Automatic stay provision of the Bankruptcy Code did not patently and unambiguously deprive the probate court of jurisdiction to proceed on the concealment of assets action: Goldberg v. Maloney, 2006-Ohio-5485, 111 Ohio St. 3d 211, 855 N.E.2d 856, 2006 Ohio LEXIS 3224 (Ohio 2006).

**Concurrent jurisdiction**

Trial court erred by acting under his probate authority, but only those actions taken that were inconsistent with the civil procedural rules in the general division were void, where the action was filed in the general division, but the probate division technically had the statutory authority to take subject matter jurisdiction over the action as: (1) the trial court had to maintain jurisdiction in the general division, where it was commenced; (2) the Ohio Constitution created a separate probate division within a court of common pleas; (3) R.C. 2101.24(B) established concurrent jurisdiction between general divisions and probate divisions; (4) the case could not be transferred to the probate division under Civ.R. 73(B); and (5) the trial judge never journalized the transfer. Demery v. Baluk, 2012-Ohio-4486, 2012 Ohio App. LEXIS 3921 (Ohio Ct. App., Erie County 2012).

**Constitutional claims**

To the extent that the property owners argued that the assessment by the county board of commissioners constituted an unconstitutional taking of property without due process of law, seeking a declaratory judgment and injunction, that claim was cognizable by the trial court, and thus the complaint should not have been dismissed for lack of jurisdiction. Bollenbacher v. Wayne County Bd. of Comm'rs, 2012-Ohio-4198, 2012 Ohio App. LEXIS 3693 (Ohio Ct. App., Wayne County 2012).

**Contract for division of estate**

A probate court does not have jurisdiction to render a declaratory judgment as to the validity or enforceability of a contract providing for a division of the testator's estate different from that provided in the will. Such contracts are not directly related to the administration of the testator's estate: Zuendel v. Zuendel, 63 Ohio St. 3d 733, 590 N.E.2d 1260, 1992 Ohio LEXIS 1000 (Ohio 1992).

**Correction of court records**

The mother may decide what surname will appear on a child's new birth certificate following the father's acknowledgment of paternity. A probate court has jurisdiction to correct an error in its records: In re Mantia-Allen, 108 Ohio App. 3d 302, 670 N.E.2d 570, 1996 Ohio App. LEXIS 52 (Ohio Ct. App., Montgomery County 1996).

**Declaratory judgments generally**

After plaintiff administrator's wife died intestate, the family home, which was titled only in her name, was damaged in a fire; the probate court did not err in dismissing plaintiffs complaint for declaratory judgment against defendant insurer because it lacked subject matter jurisdiction to address issues relating to defendant's obligations to plaintiff under his homeowner's insurance policy, as the matter involved a contract dispute between the parties that was unrelated to the administration of the estate. Wiggins v. Safeco Ins. Co. of Ind., 2019-Ohio-312, 2019 Ohio App. LEXIS 309 (Ohio Ct. App., Montgomery County 2019).

After plaintiff administrator's wife died intestate, the family home, which was titled only in her name, was damaged in a fire; the probate court did not err in dismissing plaintiffs complaint for declaratory judgment against defendant homeowners insurer because it lacked concurrent jurisdiction under over plaintiffs action since it did not involve a designation or removal of a beneficiary of a life insurance policy, annuity contract, retirement plan, brokerage account, security account, bank account, real property, or tangible personal property. Wiggins v. Safeco Ins. Co. of Ind., 2019-Ohio-312, 2019 Ohio App. LEXIS 309 (Ohio Ct. App., Montgomery County 2019).

Although the park district could seek relief from contract disputes, the probate court lacked jurisdiction to enter declaratory judgments over contract disputes. In re Creation of a Park Dist. Within Chester Twp., 2017-Ohio-4031, 91 N.E.3d 26, 2017 Ohio App. LEXIS 2074 (Ohio Ct. App., Geauga County 2017).

When a trustee sought a declaratory judgment construing an assessment agreement signed by the trust's settlor, a probate court had jurisdiction because (1) claims had been made against trust property, so the case was not so removed from trust governance to bar jurisdiction under R.C. 2101.24(B)(1)(b), and (2) such jurisdiction provided jurisdiction over the trustee's other claims. Revocable Living Trust of Mandel v. Lake Erie Utils. Co., 2012-Ohio-5718, 2012 Ohio App. LEXIS 4928 (Ohio Ct. App., Cuyahoga County 2012).

R.C. § § 2101.24 and 2721.05, taken together, give the probate court exclusive jurisdiction over declaratory judgment actions brought to determine any question arising out of the administration of an estate. A declaratory judgment action may be brought in the probate court to determine the validity of inter vivos transfers where the property transferred would revert to the estate if the transfers are invalidated. The judgment of the general division did not constitute res judicata because that court lacked subject matter jurisdiction: Grimes v. Grimes, 2007-Ohio-5653, 173 Ohio App. 3d 537, 879 N.E.2d 247, 2007 Ohio App. LEXIS 4975 (Ohio Ct. App., Washington County 2007).

It was not the purpose of the General Assembly, by the enactment of the uniform declaratory judgments act, to alter or broaden the jurisdiction of the probate court over parties and subject matter, but only to provide a new procedural device or vehicle of relief in the disposition of the matters properly coming before it: (decided under former analogous section) State ex rel. Mayfield Heights v. Bartunek, 12 Ohio App. 2d 141, 41 Ohio Op. 2d 222, 231 N.E.2d 326, 1967 Ohio App. LEXIS 392 (Ohio Ct. App., Cuyahoga County 1967).

**Distribution of estates**

Because the probate court had neither approved and settled the final account nor discharged the administrator, the estate remained open and the questions posed in the declaratory judgment action arose in the administration of the pending estate. The probate court did not abuse its discretion in rendering relief because it had statutory authority to grant or deny declaratory relief. Hodge v. Callinan, 2018-Ohio-227, 104 N.E.3d 56, 2018 Ohio App. LEXIS 247 (Ohio Ct. App., Warren County 2018).

Probate court did not act improperly in distributing funds from the estates of a mother and father under the exclusive jurisdiction established by R.C. 2101.24(A)(1)(c) in finding that a son was entitled to funds that had originated in a jointly-owned account with the mother; the mother's incompetence did not terminate the account's survivorship nature and funds transferred to other accounts retained their survivorship identity. In re Estate of Lilley, 2006-Ohio-5510, 2006 Ohio App. LEXIS 5491 (Ohio Ct. App., Warren County 2006).

When a will directed that intangible property was to pass to a trust and that tangible property would pass to an executrix, and it was determined that the decedent's corporation was intangible property, the probate court had jurisdiction, under R.C. 2101.24(A)(1)(c), to order the corporation to issue stock in itself naming the trustee of the trust to which it passed as the corporation's owner because the probate court had the authority to order the distribution of estates. Kasapis v. High Point Furniture Co., 2006-Ohio-255, 2006 Ohio App. LEXIS 211 (Ohio Ct. App., Summit County 2006).

Will's in terrorem clause did not have the effect of placing an executrix's conduct beyond the reach of the probate court, as a probate court continued to retain the power to supervise a fiduciary's actions, under R.C. 2101.24(A)(1)(m), which included the power to review how the executrix disposed of probate assets. Kasapis v. High Point Furniture Co., 2006-Ohio-255, 2006 Ohio App. LEXIS 211 (Ohio Ct. App., Summit County 2006).

Probate court is not prevented from construing a will while it is also determining the validity of a will. Children can be completely disinherited by implication if a testator completely disposes of all of his property by will: Estate of Snell v. Kilburn, 2005-Ohio-7076, 165 Ohio App. 3d 352, 846 N.E.2d 572, 2005 Ohio App. LEXIS 6382 (Ohio Ct. App., Monroe County 2005).

Where the only asset of a testator's estate was a mortgage because the testator had sold the underlying real estate and no longer had an interest in it, pursuant to R.C. 2101.24, a magistrate and the trial court erroneously considered the real estate transfers that occurred before and during the estate's administration. In re Estate of Mizer, 2005-Ohio-862, 2005 Ohio App. LEXIS 879 (Ohio Ct. App., Tuscarawas County 2005).

Probate court erred in determining it had jurisdiction to hear the matter where the estate had already rejected the creditor's claim that the creditor, who lived with the decedent for several years and helped with the rental properties, was entitled to assets of the estate; accordingly, its judgment was void ab initio. Kraus v. Hanna, 2004-Ohio-3928, 2004 Ohio App. LEXIS 3579 (Ohio Ct. App., Portage County 2004).

The probate court had jurisdiction over a declaratory judgment action concerning allegedly misappropriated property which should have been included in a decedent's estate: Sayer v. Epler, 121 Ohio App. 3d 329, 699 N.E.2d 1000, 1997 Ohio App. LEXIS 3341 (Ohio Ct. App., Licking County 1997).

Probate court had jurisdiction to render a declaratory judgment involving administration of the estate. The terms of the will bequeathed decedent's entire interest in a mortgage to his daughters pursuant to a separation agreement with the mother of his 2 youngest daughters; the interpretation of such a clause was a matter of law: Johnson v. Wheeler, 1996 Ohio App. LEXIS 953 (Ohio Ct. App., Franklin County Mar. 14, 1996).

A declaratory judgment action may be brought in the probate court to determine the validity of inter vivos transfers where the property transferred would revert to the estate if the transfers are invalidated: State ex rel. Lipinski v. Cuyahoga County Common Pleas Court, 1995-Ohio-96, 74 Ohio St. 3d 19, 655 N.E.2d 1303, 1995 Ohio LEXIS 2190 (Ohio 1995).

R.C. 2101.24(C) and 2721.05 permit a plaintiff personally interested in an estate to bring a declaratory judgment action in the probate court to determine the title to estate assets and to adjudicate questions directly affecting the administration of an estate: Wozniak v. Wozniak, 90 Ohio App. 3d 400, 629 N.E.2d 500, 1993 Ohio App. LEXIS 4608 (Ohio Ct. App., Summit County 1993).

The probate court lacked the jurisdiction to order that a criminal fine against the decedent's spouse be paid from the decedent's estate: In re Estate of Wolfe, 71 Ohio App. 3d 501, 594 N.E.2d 1055, 1991 Ohio App. LEXIS 1166 (Ohio Ct. App., Wood County 1991).

A probate court has jurisdiction to consider a declaratory judgment action challenging the validity of alleged inter vivos transfer by the decedent of property which should in fact be part of the estate: Bobko v. Sagen, 61 Ohio App. 3d 397, 572 N.E.2d 823, 1989 Ohio App. LEXIS 1881 (Ohio Ct. App., Cuyahoga County 1989).

In a hearing on exceptions to the inventory, the court lacks jurisdiction to impose a constructive trust on savings bonds which it finds are not in fact estate assets: In re Estate of Etzensperger, 9 Ohio St. 3d 19, 457 N.E.2d 1161, 1984 Ohio LEXIS 998 (Ohio 1984).

The probate court has exclusive jurisdiction to direct and control the conduct and settle the accounts of executors and administrators and order the distribution of estates: (decided under former analogous section) Border v. Ohio Sav. & Trust Co., 26 Ohio Misc. 273, 55 Ohio Op. 2d 410, 267 N.E.2d 120, 1970 Ohio Misc. LEXIS 327 (Ohio C.P. 1970).

A probate court has no jurisdiction to consider the validity or effect of a contract between the distributee of a decedent's estate and one who contracted to collect their share of the estate for a percentage thereof, where the purported contract has no bearing on the assets of the estate, the duties of the administrator or the court's supervision of his administration: (decided under former analogous section) In re Estate of Porter, 17 Ohio Misc. 136, 46 Ohio Op. 2d 180, 243 N.E.2d 794, 1969 Ohio Misc. LEXIS 308 (Ohio P. Ct. 1969).

The power of the probate court in relation to a decedent's estate is strictly limited to matters involving the enhancement or depletion of such estate and the distribution of its assets to the lawful heirs: (decided under former analogous section) In re Estate of Porter, 17 Ohio Misc. 136, 46 Ohio Op. 2d 180, 243 N.E.2d 794, 1969 Ohio Misc. LEXIS 308 (Ohio P. Ct. 1969).

The determination by the probate court in the summary proceeding provided for by R.C. 2115.16 that assets should be included in an estate makes the question of title res judicata as between all parties to the proceeding, but the judgment of the probate court may be attacked in a subsequent action by other interested persons who were not parties to the proceeding in probate court: (decided under former analogous section) Cole v. Ottawa Home & Sav. Ass'n, 18 Ohio St. 2d 1, 47 Ohio Op. 2d 1, 246 N.E.2d 542, 1969 Ohio LEXIS 355 (Ohio 1969).

Under the provisions of this section a probate court does not have jurisdiction in action on rejected claims, and cannot assert jurisdiction over such claims through a petition for declaratory judgment: (decided under former analogous section) Mainline Const. Co. v. Warren, 11 Ohio Misc. 233, 40 Ohio Op. 2d 509, 227 N.E.2d 432 (PC 1967).

By virtue of the provisions of Ohio Const. art IV, § 8 and R.C. Title 21, a probate court has jurisdiction to pass upon a claim against an estate filed individually by one of the co-administrators of such estate; but such court has no jurisdiction in such proceeding to examine into a claim of such estate against such co-administrator and her husband for moneys allegedly owing the estate on promissory notes: (decided under former analogous section) In re Estate of Stutz, 1 Ohio App. 2d 188, 30 Ohio Op. 2d 212, 204 N.E.2d 248, 1964 Ohio App. LEXIS 540 (Ohio Ct. App., Darke County 1964).

Where the assets of an estate have (in accordance with the terms of a will) been distributed to life tenants, the estate has been closed and the final account has been settled and determined, and the life tenants die, in the absence of a motion, filed in accordance with R.C. 2109.35 to vacate the order of the probate court, such court lacks jurisdiction to entertain an application by the remaindermen to commit securities formerly in the estate to a trustee: (decided under former analogous section) State ex rel. Beedle v. Kiracofe, 176 Ohio St. 149, 27 Ohio Op. 2d 25, 198 N.E.2d 61, 1964 Ohio LEXIS 890 (Ohio 1964).

By the constitution and statutory enactments, the probate court is invested with the power and jurisdiction to adjudicate a matter relating to the title to and status of personal property, where, during the administration of a decedent's estate in such court, decedent's widow files her petition asking for a declaration that certain personal property is an asset of the estate and must be administered as such, as against the claim that such property was effectually disposed of by the decedent during his lifetime through a written declaration of trust: (decided under former analogous section) In re Morrison's Estate, 159 Ohio St. 285, 50 Ohio Op. 291, 112 N.E.2d 13, 1953 Ohio LEXIS 575 (Ohio 1953).

The probate court is a court authorized to determine the validity of claims of all claimants to decedent's property. Since the petition (in common pleas court) states an ordinary action in replevin and fails to assert reasons why the probate court cannot grant the relief requested under the statutes vesting responsibility and authority in the administrator, an action does not lie in the court of common pleas: (decided under former analogous section) Service Transport Co. v. Matyas, 108 N.E.2d 741, 63 Ohio Law Abs. 236, 244, 1952 Ohio App. LEXIS 861 (Ohio Ct. App., Cuyahoga County 1952), rev'd, 159 Ohio St. 300, 50 Ohio Op. 298, 112 N.E.2d 20, 1953 Ohio LEXIS 668 (Ohio 1953).

Where probate court, in proceedings by village against township for a division of property, made an order of division of funds and assets, such order terminated the jurisdiction of the court, which jurisdiction did not continue over the divided property so as to enable the court to entertain a proceeding by the village attorney to impress such property with a lien: (decided under former analogous section) Eastlake v. Davis, 94 Ohio App. 71, 51 Ohio Op. 279, 114 N.E.2d 627, 1952 Ohio App. LEXIS 603 (Ohio Ct. App. 1952).

Titles 11 — 37

A judgment of the court of common pleas, in an action for declaratory judgment, ordering the distribution of assets of an estate in the hands of the executor thereof is invalid by virtue of this section, giving the exclusive right to order the distribution of estates to the probate court: (decided under former analogous section) Mally v. Kekich, 71 N.E.2d 305, 47 Ohio Law Abs. 120, 1946 Ohio App. LEXIS 750 (Ohio Ct. App., Cuyahoga County 1946).

Where the administratrix of an estate files an action in the probate court of a county against a savings and loan company, a resident of such county, and the receiver of a park association, a nonresident of such county, the petition in the action charging fraud in the decedent's oral transaction with the park association and seeking a declaration of rights to a certain stock certificate of the company alleged to have been given by the deceased to the association as consideration in such transaction, an order of dismissal of the petition is justifiable, the court having no jurisdiction of the subject matter of the action and there being an improper joinder of parties defendant: (decided under former analogous section) Sherrets v. Tuscarawas Sav. & Loan Co., 78 Ohio App. 307, 34 Ohio Op. 21, 70 N.E.2d 127, 1945 Ohio App. LEXIS 527 (Ohio Ct. App., Tuscarawas County 1945).

The probate court does not have jurisdiction, in a proceeding upon exceptions to the inventory filed in a decedent's estate, to determine the title to real or personal property that had been duly transferred, and possession thereof delivered, by the decedent before her death: (decided under former analogous section) In re Brunskill's Estate, 63 Ohio App. 529, 17 Ohio Op. 265, 27 N.E.2d 492, 1940 Ohio App. LEXIS 996 (Ohio Ct. App., Summit County 1940).

**Domicile**

Probate court found that a township, rather than a city, was the decedent's domicile at the time of the decedent's death because, although the decedent owned residences in both the city and later the township as well, the decedent abandoned the decedent's domicile in the city and acquired a new domicile in the township and continued to maintain that domicile until the decedent's death. City of Warren v. Rebhan, 2011-Ohio-2941, 163 Ohio Misc. 2d 29, 950 N.E.2d 250, 2011 Ohio Misc. LEXIS 239 (Ohio C.P.), aff'd, 2011-Ohio-6340, 2011 Ohio App. LEXIS 5205 (Ohio Ct. App., Trumbull County 2011).

**Estate assets**

Probate court had jurisdiction to distribute the death benefits of a deceased mother's annuities because the court properly found the annuities' beneficiary designations were invalid. Schiavoni v. Roy, 2012-Ohio-4435, 2012 Ohio App. LEXIS 3897 (Ohio Ct. App., Medina County 2012).

Because a settlement agreement did not preserve any right to bring additional claims for punitive damages and attorney fees after settlement of the probate case, and those claims were previously litigated and settled, they were barred by res judicata; with plenary power in both law and equity, the probate court had jurisdiction under R.C. 2101.24 to hear the claims for both punitive damages and attorney fees related to the conversion claims a father and children brought against a mother. Lanzalaco v. Lanzalaco, 2012-Ohio-4053, 976 N.E.2d 309, 2012 Ohio App. LEXIS 3558 (Ohio Ct. App., Cuyahoga County 2012).

Trial court did not abuse its discretion when it included certain proceeds of savings bonds a now-deceased ward had purchased for the ward's grandchildren in the ward's decedent's estate, despite the ward's apparent intention, because, when the ward's guardian was allowed to deposit the proceeds in savings accounts, and, thereafter, in the guardianship estate's checking account, those savings accounts, while joint accounts, were not survivorship accounts, so the proceeds could not pass directly to the grandchildren upon the ward's death. In re Estate of Pallay, 2007-Ohio-2754, 2007 Ohio App. LEXIS 2534 (Ohio Ct. App., Washington County 2007).

Trial court abused its discretion when it included certain stock purchased with the funds of a now-deceased ward's guardianship estate in the ward's decedent's estate because, when the ward's guardian was allowed to purchase the stock, it was on the condition that the stock be given a payable on death (POD) or similar designation, and, when the stock was not given this designation, it retained its intended identity as a POD account, so, upon the ward's death, it passed directly to the ward's grandchildren without passing through the ward's decedent's estate. In re Estate of Pallay, 2007-Ohio-2754, 2007 Ohio App. LEXIS 2534 (Ohio Ct. App., Washington County 2007).

**Exceptions to account**

Where a guardian was acting in good faith, a sale and commission benefited the estate pursuant to R.C. 2111.14(B), and an executor did not object to the commission, there was competent, credible evidence supporting the probate court's decision to overrule the exception to the accounting. In re Rolfe, 2003-Ohio-5879, 2003 Ohio App. LEXIS 5225 (Ohio Ct. App., Fayette County 2003).

**Exclusive jurisdiction**

Complaint by the Ohio Bureau of Workers' Compensation, seeking to recover its alleged subrogation interest against third parties with whom a widow of a deceased employee had settled wrongful death claims, was within the probate court's exclusive jurisdiction, such that dismissal by the trial court was proper. Mal-Sarkar v. Cleveland State Univ., 2015 Ohio 1025, 2015 Ohio App. LEXIS 965.

Domestic relations court did not abuse its discretion in determining it lacked jurisdiction over certain jewelry and cash and instead directed the husband to litigate his claims in the probate court because the husband's father died testate, and the jewelry and cash were assets of the husband's parents that were subject to probate and within the probate court's exclusive jurisdiction. Bauer v. Bauer, 2020-Ohio-425, 2020 Ohio App. LEXIS 388 (Ohio Ct. App., Warren County 2020).

Trial court erred by granting summary judgment because the son's claim was for the recovery of damages for fraud. Therefore, there was no basis for concluding that the probate court had exclusive jurisdiction. Gibson v. Shepard, 2020-Ohio-4569, 2020 Ohio App. LEXIS 3446 (Ohio Ct. App., Cuyahoga County 2020).

Trial court lacked jurisdiction to distribute or intercept the retirement funds at issue upon the decedent's death because the probate court had exclusive jurisdiction over claims made against the estate, and the Child Support Enforcement Agency and the decedent's ex-wife, who were claimants to the estate, should have filed their claims with the probate court. Dana v. Taylor, 2018-Ohio-2925, 2018 Ohio App. LEXIS 3143 (Ohio Ct. App., Stark County 2018).

Trial court erred in dismissing a daughter's complaint for lack of subject matter jurisdiction because the probate court did not have exclusive jurisdiction since the daughter alleged her mother, a ward, was the perpetrator of improper acts; although the guardian had a duty to protect and control the ward, that was insufficient to convey exclusive jurisdiction to the probate court over a ward's conduct, especially since the allegations stemmed from actions that occurred before the guardianship. Sosnowsky v. Koscianski, 2018-Ohio-3045, 118 N.E.3d 403, 2018 Ohio App. LEXIS 3298 (Ohio Ct. App., Cuyahoga County 2018).

Statute does not provide for jurisdiction over claims made against a ward. Sosnowsky v. Koscianski, 2018-Ohio-3045, 118 N.E.3d 403, 2018 Ohio App. LEXIS 3298 (Ohio Ct. App., Cuyahoga County 2018).

Domestic court correctly denied a former husband's motion for a constructive trust because it lacked jurisdiction to grant the relief requested since only the probate court could direct and control the actions of the testamentary trustee; the probate court had exclusive jurisdiction to direct and control the husband's actions involving life insurance proceeds out of custodial accounts that were subject to the control of the probate court. Kasper v. Kasper, 2014-Ohio-1256, 2014 Ohio App. LEXIS 1135 (Ohio Ct. App., Franklin County 2014).

Probate court had jurisdiction over a deceased mother's annuities, under R.C. 2101.24(B)(1)(b), because the court could decide if the mother's son (1) properly used a power of attorney to buy an annuity, and (2) unduly influenced a change-of-beneficiary form regarding another annuity, since the son completed most of the form and was with the mother when the mother signed the form. Schiavoni v. Roy, 2012-Ohio-4435, 2012 Ohio App. LEXIS 3897 (Ohio Ct. App., Medina County 2012).

To the extent that the property owners challenged the apportionment of the assessment by the county board of commissioners as not compliant with R.C. Chapter 6117, seeking a declaratory judgment and injunction, the trial court correctly dismissed the complaint because such a challenge was proper only before the probate court, pursuant to R.C. 2101.24(A)(2). Bollenbacher v. Wayne County Bd. of Comm'rs, 2012-Ohio-4198, 2012 Ohio App. LEXIS 3693 (Ohio Ct. App., Wayne County 2012).

Trial court lacked jurisdiction to consider the daughter's guardian-removal claim because, under R.C. 2101.24(A)(1)(e), the probate court had exclusive jurisdiction to appoint and remove guardians, conservators, and testamentary trustees, direct and control their conduct, and settle their accounts. Under Civ.R. 73(B), the guardian-removal claim had to be transferred to the probate court. Florkey v. Malott, 2011-Ohio-5199, 2011 Ohio App. LEXIS 4285 (Ohio Ct. App., Highland County 2011).

Pursuant to R.C. 2101.24(A)(1)(c), a probate court had "exclusive" jurisdiction to direct and control the conduct and settle the accounts of executors and administrators. Holik v. Lafferty, 2006-Ohio-2652, 2006 Ohio App. LEXIS 2482 (Ohio Ct. App., Ashtabula County 2006).

Probate court's plenary jurisdiction at law and in equity under R.C. 2101.24(C) authorized any relief required to fully adjudicate the subject matter within the probate court's exclusive jurisdiction, and claims for breach of fiduciary duty, which inexorably implicated the control over the conduct of the fiduciaries, were within that subject-matter jurisdiction by virtue of R.C. 2101.24(A)(1)(c). Holik v. Lafferty, 2006-Ohio-2652, 2006 Ohio App. LEXIS 2482 (Ohio Ct. App., Ashtabula County 2006).

Beneficiary of a decedent's estate could not sue the estate's administrator in the trial court's general division for claims that (1) the administrator charged the beneficiary rent to live in the beneficiary's deceased mother's house, (2) the administrator increased his hourly fee to administer the estate, (3) the administrator allegedly sold the deceased mother's house at below market value, and (4) the administrator allegedly charged an excessive fee to adminster the estate because all of these claims were within the exclusive jurisdiction of the probate court, under R.C. 2101.24(A)(1)(c), and, even if the trial court's general division somehow had jurisdiction, the probate court had resolved them, so the doctrine of res judicata barred their relitigation in the trial court's general division. Holik

v. Lafferty, 2006-Ohio-2652, 2006 Ohio App. LEXIS 2482 (Ohio Ct. App., Ashtabula County 2006).

When a decedent's former wife, who was also the administrator of his estate, sued his brother, both in her capacity as the estate's administrator and individually, claiming that the decedent's transfers of properties to the brother were fraudulent, the trial court could not address her claims as the estate's administrator because, under R.C. 2101.24 and 2721.05, the probate court had exclusive jurisdiction over them, because, while she couched her claims as being brought under the Uniform Fraudulent Transfer Act, R.C. 1336.01 et seq., they, in essence, sought to have the trial court declare the transfers to the brother were invalid, thus having the properties revert to the decedent's estate. Lamar v. Washington, 2006-Ohio-1414, 2006 Ohio App. LEXIS 1298 (Ohio Ct. App., Allen County 2006).

Because the son's claims pertained to the guardian's conduct in his capacity as a guardian, the trial court did not err in dismissing the claim under Civ.R. 12(B)(1) as it lacked subject matter jurisdiction. The probate court had exclusive jurisdiction pursuant to R.C. 2101.24 and the son's prayer for money damages did not divest the probate court of its jurisdiction over the matter. Rowan v. McLaughlin, 2005-Ohio-3473, 2005 Ohio App. LEXIS 3226 (Ohio Ct. App., Cuyahoga County 2005).



**Expectancy of inheritance**

Because the siblings' accusations of fraud, embezzlement, undue influence, and breach of fiduciary duty against their sister could be brought in probate court under R.C. 2107.46 and R.C. 2109.50, the sister was entitled to summary judgment in the siblings' action for intentional interference with expectancy of inheritance. Wickline v. Hoyer, 2012-Ohio-945, 2012 Ohio App. LEXIS 822 (Ohio Ct. App., Franklin County 2012).

Parties claiming that they were wrongfully deprived of their expectancy of an inheritance were not required to obtain a determination that the will was valid; there is no procedure by which parties may obtain such a determination in a probate court. Elderly decedent's poor health made her vulnerable to undue influence and fraud: Sull v. Kaim, 2007-Ohio-3269, 172 Ohio App. 3d 297, 874 N.E.2d 865, 2007 Ohio App. LEXIS 3035 (Ohio Ct. App., Cuyahoga County 2007).

A probate court lacks jurisdiction over a claim for intentional interference with expectancy of inheritance. Such a claim may not be pursued if adequate relief is available through probate procedures: Roll v. Edwards, 2004-Ohio-767, 156 Ohio App. 3d 227, 805 N.E.2d 162, 2004 Ohio App. LEXIS 719 (Ohio Ct. App., Ross County 2004).

**Federal courts**

Exclusive jurisdiction of probate matters, including breach of fiduciary duty, is vested in the probate court under Ohio law. Accordingly the district court lacked jurisdiction to hear an action brought by heirs of decedent against executrix on basis of alleged breach of fiduciary duty: Bedo v. McGuire, 767 F.2d 305, 1985 U.S. App. LEXIS 20525 (6th Cir. Ohio 1985).

Jurisdiction of an action involving an alleged breach of fiduciary duties is lodged in the probate court, and the federal court was without jurisdiction over the subject matter: (decided under former analogous section) Starr v. Rupp, 421 F.2d 999, 25 Ohio Misc. 224, 53 Ohio Op. 2d 169, 1970 U.S. App. LEXIS 10735 (6th Cir. Ohio 1970).

The action of an Ohio probate court in removing for neglect and incompetency an executor under a will during the pendency of an action to contest such will in the common pleas court of the same county, is not subject to review by a federal court: (decided under former analogous section) Pettiford v. George, 125 F.2d 144, 22 Ohio Op. 460, 1942 U.S. App. LEXIS 4332 (6th Cir. Ohio 1942).

**Foreign court**

Trial court properly dismissed for lack of jurisdiction because only the Florida probate court had jurisdiction over those items that were mistakenly omitted from the estate. Since the probate court had not yet distributed those assets due to a mistake of the personal representative, the Ohio county court could not grant to said personal representative the right to obtain estate assets that were omitted from the estate and never distributed. Doyle v. Morgan, 2009-Ohio-795, 2009 Ohio App. LEXIS 652 (Ohio Ct. App., Mahoning County 2009).

**Former guardian**

Probate court had authority and jurisdiction under R.C. 2101.24(A)(1)(s), (C), and 2111.50 to grant a preliminary injunction that prevented a former guardian of an adjudicated incompetent from residing at or visiting the incompetent's home, as the elements necessary for the grant of the injunction were met. The court had jurisdiction to impose the order, as it did not actually evict the guardian, but instead, it found him to be a disruptive influence on the incompetent and ordered him to leave the premises. In re Guardianship of Norwood, 2006-Ohio-4504, 2006 Ohio App. LEXIS 4404 (Ohio Ct. App., Cuyahoga County 2006).

**Fraud**

Suit by children of a deceased seeking money damages for fraud against the deceased's widow based on her application for a summary release from administration in the probate court pursuant to R.C. 2113.031 was within the exclusive jurisdiction of the probate court under R.C. 2101.24(A)(1)(c) and (cc). Estate of Dombroski v. Dombroski, 2014-Ohio-5827, 2014 Ohio App. LEXIS 5642 (Ohio Ct. App., Harrison County 2014).

A probate court lacks jurisdiction over actions seeking money damages for fraud: Dumas v. Estate of Dumas, 1994-Ohio-312, 68 Ohio St. 3d 405, 627 N.E.2d 978, 1994 Ohio LEXIS 498 (Ohio 1994).

Probate courts have no jurisdiction over claims for money damages resulting from fraud: Alexander v. Compton, 57 Ohio App. 2d 89, 11 Ohio Op. 3d 81, 385 N.E.2d 638, 1978 Ohio App. LEXIS 7548 (Ohio Ct. App., Clinton County 1978).

A probate court has inherent power to vacate, after term, a judgment procured by fraud: (decided under former analogous section) In re Adoption of Sladky, 109 Ohio App. 120, 10 Ohio Op. 2d 304, 161 N.E.2d 554, 81 Ohio Law Abs. 264, 1958 Ohio App. LEXIS 636 (Ohio Ct. App., Franklin County 1958).

**Guardians**

Trial court did not err by dismissing the guardianship proceeding for lack of jurisdiction because the alleged incompetent's Declaration of Domicile indicated his physical relocation to Florida and noted his intent to remain there indefinitely. Absent any evidence to the contrary, it was found that the alleged incompetent voluntarily changed his residence and legal settlement to Florida. In re Guardianship of Shelar, 2013-Ohio-4737, 2013 Ohio App. LEXIS 4951 (Ohio Ct. App., Lucas County 2013).

Trial court's dismissal of a ward's claims against various guardians, arising from a guardianship that was initiated in the probate court against the ward until the probate court determined that the ward was not incompetent and the guardianship was not needed, was proper, as the probate court had exclusive jurisdiction over all matters incident to the guardianship pursuant to R.C. 2101.24(A)(1)(e); the fact that the guardianship had terminated did not divest the probate court of jurisdiction. Keith v. Bringardner, 2008-Ohio-950, 2008 Ohio App. LEXIS 833 (Ohio Ct. App., Franklin County 2008).

Considering that the probate court is limited to resolving only those claims properly before it and acknowledging that party who was a minor when injured was, at the time of the hearing regarding disbursement of proceeds, an adult no longer requiring the assistance of a guardian, the court lacked jurisdictional authority to decide the disbursement of funds as to party's claim: In re Altomare, 2001-Ohio-3540, 2001 Ohio App. LEXIS 260 (Ohio Ct. App., Columbiana County 2001).

The determination whether guardians must obtain, and banks must require, a probate court order authorizing a withdrawal before guardianship funds must be removed from a financial institution concerned the conduct of guardians and the administration of guardianships. Therefore, the probate court possessed subject matter jurisdiction over the matter: Ohio Farmers Ins. Co. v. Bank One, 1998 Ohio App. LEXIS 3854 (Ohio Ct. App., Montgomery County Aug. 21, 1998).

A financial institution that conveys funds to a guardian under circumstances that create liability to the estate falls within the ambit of R.C. 2109.50, and a probate court has jurisdiction pursuant to R.C. 2101.24. Issuance of a debit card to a guardian, in connection with a restricted guardianship account, does not necessarily create liability on the part of the bank: Rinehart v. Bank One, N.A., 125 Ohio App. 3d 719, 709 N.E.2d 559, 1998 Ohio App. LEXIS 1393 (Ohio Ct. App., Franklin County), dismissed, 82 Ohio St. 3d 1480, 696 N.E.2d 1087, 1998 Ohio LEXIS 2084 (Ohio 1998).

A probate court has exclusive jurisdiction over an action by a legatee of his parent's estate for breach of fiduciary duties against the parent's co-guardians, co-executors and the surety on the guardians' bond: Goff v. Ameritrust Co., N.A., 1994 Ohio App. LEXIS 1916 (Ohio Ct. App., Cuyahoga County May 5, 1994).

A probate court has jurisdiction to award money damages against a guardian who fails to sell or rent the ward's vacant residence when such action was appropriate under the circumstances: In re Guardianship of McPheter, 95 Ohio App. 3d 440, 642 N.E.2d 690, 1994 Ohio App. LEXIS 3384 (Ohio Ct. App., Huron County 1994).

Where the probate court acts as guardian, the court has the full power to make or approve medical treatment decisions for a ward, including life and death issues of removing life supports or life-sustaining treatment: In re Guardianship of Myers, 62 Ohio Misc. 2d 763, 610 N.E.2d 663, 1993 Ohio Misc. LEXIS 5 (Ohio C.P. 1993).

A probate court does not have authority to order a guardian to accept a settlement offer on a minor's personal injury claim: In re Guardianship of Hicks, 63 Ohio Misc. 2d 280, 624 N.E.2d 1125, 1993 Ohio Misc. LEXIS 54 (Ohio C.P. 1993).

The fact that the probate court has jurisdiction for oversight of the ward's funds and of the accounts and other proceedings of her guardian for deposit and expenditure of the ward's funds is not evidence proving that the court is trustee of an express trust, nor is it probative of the existence of an express trust: Gorenflo v. Ohio Dep't of Human Servs., 81 Ohio App. 3d 500, 611 N.E.2d 425, 1992 Ohio App. LEXIS 3319 (Ohio Ct. App., Marion County 1992).

Pursuant to R.C. 2101.24 and 2111.13(A)(4), the probate court has subject matter jurisdiction over all matters concerning a guardian's expenditure of a ward's funds, including the proposed expenditure of the ward's funds to pay for the medical expenses of his wife: In re Rauscher, 40 Ohio

App. 3d 106, 531 N.E.2d 745, 1987 Ohio App. LEXIS 10725 (Ohio Ct. App., Cuyahoga County 1987).

In a divorce proceeding, where the wife has a guardian of the person appointed by the probate court, the court of common pleas, division of domestic relations, has no jurisdiction to require the husband to pay expenses incurred by the guardian, i.e., the probate court has exclusive jurisdiction in this area: Caudill v. Caudill, 29 Ohio App. 3d 51, 502 N.E.2d 703, 1986 Ohio App. LEXIS 9987 (Ohio Ct. App., Franklin County 1986).

Once the probate court appoints a guardian for a minor, the juvenile court is without jurisdiction to grant custody of the ward to another person, until the guardianship has been terminated: In re Miller, 33 Ohio App. 3d 224, 515 N.E.2d 635, 1986 Ohio App. LEXIS 10269 (Ohio Ct. App., Cuyahoga County 1986).

Under the statutory scheme set out in R.C. Chapter 2111 regarding guardianships, the probate court has jurisdiction in the appointment and control of guardians which extends to all matters touching the guardianship, including the custody of the minor and the visitation rights of third parties: In re Zahoransky, 22 Ohio App. 3d 75, 488 N.E.2d 944, 1985 Ohio App. LEXIS 10077 (Ohio Ct. App., Cuyahoga County 1985).

Civil Rule 17(B) clearly authorizes a court other than the probate court to appoint a guardian ad litem for the protection of an individual the court believes to be an incompetent. Probate courts do not possess exclusive jurisdiction in these matters: Dailey v. Dailey, 11 Ohio App. 3d 121, 463 N.E.2d 427, 1983 Ohio App. LEXIS 11258 (Ohio Ct. App., Montgomery County 1983).

The probate court has jurisdiction to entertain the application of a guardian to enter into a trust agreement with minor children and to exercise that jurisdiction to the full extent authorized or referable to the authority granted in this section, notwithstanding the irregularity in failing to appoint a guardian ad litem for the minors and to have an answer filed in their behalf: (decided under former analogous section) Pence v. Pence, 43 N.E.2d 924, 36 Ohio Law Abs. 369, 1942 Ohio App. LEXIS 862 (Ohio Ct. App., Shelby County 1942).

**—Appointment**

Probate court, with plenary authority as the superior guardian, may upon notice from a county board of developmental disabilities conduct proceedings to remove a guardian; there was sufficient cause for the probate court to call the guardian in for a hearing after it heard allegations that, three months later, one of the guardians arrived unexpectedly late at night and intoxicated at the home of the son's service providers and threatening to remove him from a stable placement. In re Guardianship of Spangler, 2010-Ohio-2471, 126 Ohio St. 3d 339, 933 N.E.2d 1067, 2010 Ohio LEXIS 1384 (Ohio 2010).

Where the probate court of one county has lawfully and properly assumed jurisdiction over the estate of a minor and appointed a guardian of such estate, the jurisdiction of such probate court is exclusive and the attempted appointment of another as guardian by the probate court of another county, even at the request of the ward, is null and void: (decided under former analogous section) Kollmeyer, 113 N.E.2d 122, 64 Ohio Law Abs. 577, 64 Ohio Law Abs. 578, 1952 Ohio App. LEXIS 1378 (Ohio Ct. App., Darke County 1952).

**—Death of ward**

Despite the death of the ward, the probate court's orders for the return of improperly transferred assets to the guardianship estate were necessary to the winding up of the estate's affairs and within the court's continuing jurisdiction: In re Guardianship of Hards, 2008-Ohio-630, 175 Ohio App. 3d 168, 885 N.E.2d 980, 2008 Ohio App. LEXIS 562 (Ohio Ct. App., Lake County 2008).

Jurisdiction of a guardianship court does not completely terminate upon the ward's death; those powers and duties necessarily involved in the proper accounting and settlement of the guardianship continue. Prohibition was not available to prevent the court from awarding fees to a special master commissioner: State ex rel. Estate of Hards v. Klammer, 2006-Ohio-3670, 110 Ohio St. 3d 104, 850 N.E.2d 1197, 2006 Ohio LEXIS 2179 (Ohio 2006).

**—Divorce of ward**

The appointment by the probate court of a guardian of an incompetent's person and estate will not interfere with the jurisdiction of the court of common pleas in a pending divorce action over the "assets of the marriage": (decided under former analogous section) In re Guardianship of Stephens, 2 Ohio Misc. 47, 30 Ohio Op. 2d 325, 202 N.E.2d 458, 1964 Ohio Misc. LEXIS 211 (Ohio P. Ct. 1964).

**—Mentally ill ward**

R.C. 2101.24 which grants the probate court authority to make inquests respecting insane persons subject to guardianship, also provides that such jurisdiction is exclusive unless otherwise provided by law: (decided under former analogous section) In re Appropriation for Highway Purposes, 19 Ohio Misc. 81, 47 Ohio Op. 2d 420, 246 N.E.2d 626 (CP 1969).

The court of common pleas does not have jurisdiction to appoint a general guardian for an incompetent person: (decided under former analogous section) In re Guardianship of Stephens, 2 Ohio Misc. 47, 30 Ohio Op. 2d 325, 202 N.E.2d 458, 1964 Ohio Misc. LEXIS 211 (Ohio P. Ct. 1964).

**—Minors**

When a guardianship is predicated exclusively on a ward's minor status, the guardian's power and the probate court's jurisdiction both terminate when the ward reaches the age of majority: In re Guardianship of Hollins, 2007-Ohio-4555, 114 Ohio St. 3d 434, 872 N.E.2d 1214, 2007 Ohio LEXIS 2192 (Ohio 2007).

**—Removal**

Appellant, a guardian removed from her duties is not precluded from raising the issue of the nonresidency status of a co-guardian for the first time on appeal: In re Guardianship of Coller, 74 Ohio App. 3d 386, 599 N.E.2d 292, 1991 Ohio App. LEXIS 2487 (Ohio Ct. App., Wood County 1991).

**—Termination**

Biological mother's motion to intervene and have her minor child returned to her was properly dismissed in her action, which was in effect a request to terminate the guardianship over the child, because the probate court had exclusive jurisdiction over the matter. In re O.S., 2015-Ohio-912, 2015 Ohio App. LEXIS 859 (Ohio Ct. App., Fulton County 2015).

Petition for writ of habeas corpus failed substantively because while petitioner framed her petition as one seeking release from a guardianship, what petitioner essentially sought was a termination of a guardianship, which was a matter that fell under the exclusive jurisdiction of the probate court. Elmer v. Moore, 2014-Ohio-3709, 2014 Ohio App. LEXIS 3631 (Ohio Ct. App., Erie County 2014).

The probate court has no jurisdiction to determine custody of a minor once it terminates the guardianship of that minor. Once the guardianship is terminated, the juvenile court then has exclusive jurisdiction to determine the custody of the child under R.C. 2151.23(A)(2): In re Guardianship of Harrison, 60 Ohio App. 3d 19, 572 N.E.2d 855, 1989 Ohio App. LEXIS 3079 (Ohio Ct. App., Hamilton County 1989).

**Humane society**

Under the provisions of Chap.V, Title IX, Div. VI, of the General Code (GC §§ 10062 to 10084 [R.C. 1717.01 to 1717.14]), providing for the organization and powers of humane societies, a probate judge, when called upon to approve the appointment of an agent for such society, has discretion to determine not only whether the person named is a proper person for the discharge of such duties, but also whether there is such necessity for the appointment as would justify the payment of the expense out of the public treasury: (decided under former analogous section) State ex rel. Coshocton Humane Soc. v. Ashman, 90 Ohio St. 200, 107 N.E. 337, 12 Ohio L. Rep. 14, 1914 Ohio LEXIS 209 (Ohio 1914).

**Inter vivos transfers**

When the executor of a decedent's estate sued the executor's brother in the general division of the trial court for a declaratory judgment regarding inter vivos transfers to the brother by the decedent, and then refiled those claims in the probate division, it was error for the probate court to decline to exercise jurisdiction over those claims because, since the decedent owned the transferred property immediately before the property was transferred, the property would revert to the decedent's estate if those transfers were declared invalid, so the executor's claims related to the administration of the decedent's estate and the probate court had exclusive jurisdiction over those claims, under R.C. 2101.24(A)(1)(c), 2101.24(A)(1)(l), and 2721.05. Grimes v. Grimes, 2007-Ohio-5653, 173 Ohio App. 3d 537, 879 N.E.2d 247, 2007 Ohio App. LEXIS 4975 (Ohio Ct. App., Washington County 2007).

**Interpleader**

The probate court had jurisdiction under R.C. 2101.24(C) and 2125.02(C) to determine the insurer's total liability as part of the interpleader action: Kniskern v. Township of Somerford, 112 Ohio App. 3d 189, 678 N.E.2d 273, 1996 Ohio App. LEXIS 2744 (Ohio Ct. App., Franklin County 1996), dismissed, 77 Ohio St. 3d 1485, 673 N.E.2d 145, 1996 Ohio LEXIS 2790 (Ohio 1996), cert. denied, 521 U.S. 1120, 117 S. Ct. 2513, 138 L. Ed. 2d 1015, 1997 U.S. LEXIS 4089 (U.S. 1997).

**Investigations by court**

The probate court abused its discretion by conducting its own investigation of the guardian's fees and performance and then holding a hearing on its own exceptions to the guardian's accounts, without giving the guardian a proper opportunity to respond: In re Lauder, 2002-Ohio-6102, 150 Ohio App. 3d 277, 780 N.E.2d 1025, 2002 Ohio App. LEXIS 5943 (Ohio Ct. App., Franklin County 2002).

**Involuntary administration of drugs**

An injunction against the involuntary administration of drugs by the department of mental health should have been dissolved where an amendment to R.C. 2101.24 granted exclusive jurisdiction over such matters to the probate court: Cleveland v. Ohio Dep't of Mental Health, 84 Ohio App.

3d 769, 618 N.E.2d 244, 1992 Ohio App. LEXIS 6790 (Ohio Ct. App., Franklin County 1992).

**Judicial immunity**

Mother's claim for interference with parental interests against the magistrate was properly dismissed for failure to state a claim because it was barred by the doctrine of judicial immunity. Since the alleged conduct took place prior to her termination of the conservatorship, the face of the complaint established that the magistrate had jurisdiction over the matter and the request of the conservator's status report was a function normally performed by a judge, and the parties dealt with the magistrate in a judicial capacity. Jacobson-Kirsch v. Kaforey, 2012-Ohio-3553, 2012 Ohio App. LEXIS 3138 (Ohio Ct. App., Summit County 2012).

A probate judge who ordered sterilization of plaintiff acted wholly without jurisdiction in the matter and hence was not protected by the doctrine of judicial immunity, where there was no set of conditions or circumstances under Ohio law which would permit the probate judge to order plaintiff to submit to sterilization, and where the proceeding which resulted in plaintiff's sterilization commenced on an affidavit filed by the county child welfare board alleging that plaintiff was a feeble minded person: (decided under former analogous section) Wade v. Bethesda Hospital, 337 F. Supp. 671, 61 Ohio Op. 2d 147, 1971 U.S. Dist. LEXIS 11739 (S.D. Ohio 1971).



**Jurisdiction**

Court of common pleas erred by dismissing the foreclosure action for want of jurisdiction because based on the record, there was no action taken by the estate to invoke the probate court's jurisdiction over that matter considering that the insolvency proceedings, the appraisal of the real property, and the parties' correspondence did not demonstrate that the probate court acquired jurisdiction over the sale of the real property at issue. Fifth Third Bank, N.A. v. Leveck, 2022-Ohio-546, 2022 Ohio App. LEXIS 470 (Ohio Ct. App., Miami County 2022).

Decedent's executor was entitled to summary judgment on her declaratory judgment claim because, since the bond issue was only pending before the trial court, the jurisdictional-priority rule did not apply, and the trial court had the authority to resolve the parties' dispute regarding the interpretation of the separation agreement. Szokan v. Szokan, 2020-Ohio-7001, 2020 Ohio App. LEXIS 4845 (Ohio Ct. App., Lake County 2020).

Ruling with respect to the trial court's show cause order did not mean that the trial court lacked jurisdiction over the matter. Because the record did not indicate that the brother obtained a stay of a judgment awarding costs, the trial court had jurisdiction to take steps to execute on the judgment and, while the trial court erred in its method of execution, that did not mean that it lacked jurisdiction over the matter. Dibert v. Carpenter, 2018-Ohio-1054, 98 N.E.3d 350, 2018 Ohio App. LEXIS 1133 (Ohio Ct. App., Champaign County 2018).

Probate court had jurisdiction over plaintiff's refiled complaint requesting a constructive trust and an action for accounting, breach of fiduciary duty, fraud, and conversion of an estate by a person under a guardianship, because the first complaint was dismissed under Civ.R. 41(a) without prejudice; with the operation of the savings statute, plaintiff could refile her claims in probate court. Sosnoswsky v. Koscianski, 2018-Ohio-1409, 110 N.E.3d 849, 2018 Ohio App. LEXIS 1552 (Ohio Ct. App., Cuyahoga County), vacated, sub. op., 2018-Ohio-3045, 118 N.E.3d 403, 2018 Ohio App. LEXIS 3298 (Ohio Ct. App., Cuyahoga County 2018).

Probate court's plenary jurisdiction at law and in equity authorized it to impose a constructive trust on a decedent's vacation cottage; the court's exclusive jurisdiction to direct and control the conduct of fiduciaries, such as the decedent's wife, and settle their accounts authorized it to resolve the children's exceptions to the estate inventory submitted by the wife as the decedent's administrator. Jamison v. Jamison, 2018-Ohio-1626, 2018 Ohio App. LEXIS 1767 (Ohio Ct. App., Cuyahoga County 2018).

Probate court had jurisdiction to order the payment of annuity proceeds to the estate of the first contingent beneficiary because the probate court exercised authority over the estate and the challengers themselves, not the financial company who issued the annuity, seeing as the estate's attorney was in possession of the annuity. In re Estate of Harries, 2018-Ohio-3725, 2018 Ohio App. LEXIS 4036 (Ohio Ct. App., Belmont County 2018).

Trial court did not err in making a determination on the testamentary intent of a handwritten document, as appellant's position that the court lacked jurisdiction to consider testamentary intent, based upon a claim that the only matter properly before the court was limited to the execution of the document and excluded the surrounding circumstances, was without merit; the complaint specifically set forth that it was contesting the "facts and circumstances surrounding the execution." Schroeder v. Meyers, 2018-Ohio-2982, 2018 Ohio App. LEXIS 3226 (Ohio Ct. App., Williams County 2018).

There was no error in the probate court's decision denying the daughter's motion to revoke the admission to probate of her mother's will because its jurisdiction to probate the will was not a race to see which court could first render a decision on a then pending matter. The filing of the Application for Authority to Administer Estate in that county together with its service and the holding of a hearing on the application, with all parties present, prior to the filing of an application in the other county vested the probate court with jurisdiction in the matter. In re Estate of Torbett, 2017-Ohio-417, 2017 Ohio App. LEXIS 418 (Ohio Ct. App., Fayette County 2017).

Appellant's complaint did not allege a cause of action that the probate court had authority to decide, since the complaint for declaratory relief did not request the registration of an unrecorded birth or the correction of a birth record and was subject to dismissal by the probate court for lack of subject matter jurisdiction. R.C. Chapter 2721 did not expand the probate court's jurisdiction beyond that conferred by statute. Zimmerman v. Montgomery Cnty. Pub. Health Dep't, 2016-Ohio-1423, 2016 Ohio App. LEXIS 1301 (Ohio Ct. App., Montgomery County 2016).

Probate court did not err or exceed its jurisdictional authority by entering an order fully disposing of the case after conducting a full hearing on the issues and allocating a proper distribution of past and prospective wrongful death proceeds. Accordingly, any argument raised as to the status of the parties was irrelevant, specifically with respect to the intervening death of the mother, whose status as their father's surviving spouse was fixed as of the time of his death. In re Estate of Molitor, 2016-Ohio-1429, 2016 Ohio App. LEXIS 1311 (Ohio Ct. App., Brown County 2016).

Township trustees' writ of prohibition seeking to prohibit a probate judge from issuing or enforcing rulings against them was denied because the township trustees have not shown that the probate court patently and unambiguously lacked jurisdiction to issue orders attempting to correct activities by the park-district commissioners and the township trustees that frustrated the purpose of the original probate court order creating the park district. State ex rel. Chester Twp. v. Grendell, 2016-Ohio-1520, 147 Ohio St. 3d 366, 66 N.E.3d 683, 2016 Ohio LEXIS 936 (Ohio 2016).

Trial court had jurisdiction over a sister's petition for a domestic violence civil protection order because although the genesis of the dispute between the sister and her brother could have been a probate case, that matter was wholly unrelated to whether a domestic violence civil protection order could be issued. Barrett v. Soltesz, 2015-Ohio-794, 2015 Ohio App. LEXIS 782 (Ohio Ct. App., Erie County 2015).

Jurisdiction was appropriate because the claim was that an inter vivos transaction was improper and that the property in question belonged to the estate. Furthermore, the trial court clearly concluded in its decision that the transfer of the checks was not a valid inter vivos gift to the son. Bayes v. Dornon, 2015-Ohio-3053, 37 N.E.3d 181, 2015 Ohio App. LEXIS 2952 (Ohio Ct. App., Clark County 2015).

Probate court had jurisdiction over the trusts, and it was fully within the court's power to consider amounts recovered by the charitable organization under the restitution order when evaluating whether distributions from the Interim Trust were equitable. In re Estate of Hersh, 2014-Ohio-612, 2014 Ohio App. LEXIS 591 (Ohio Ct. App., Hamilton County 2014).

Daughter's claims arose out of the alleged conduct by her mother as guardian, the attorney for the guardian, and the bank's handling of the funds, as well as the probate court's approval to terminate the guardianship and allow the mother to access the estate funds, and these claims touched the guardianship and were within the exclusive jurisdiction of the probate court under the statute. Rheinhold v. Reichek, 2014-Ohio-31, 2014 Ohio App. LEXIS 24 (Ohio Ct. App., Cuyahoga County 2014).

Fact that the guardianship had terminated did not foreclose the probate court's exclusive jurisdiction. Rheinhold v. Reichek, 2014-Ohio-31, 2014 Ohio App. LEXIS 24 (Ohio Ct. App., Cuyahoga County 2014).

Probate court had authority to grant a second successor trustee's motion to expend funds for the primary beneficiary's funeral and burial from an inter vivos trust because the court retained jurisdiction over the administration of the irrevocable trust and the record was replete with the court's combined exercise of judicial supervision of the irrevocable trust as ordered by its judgment entries and the parties' reliance on the probate court's continuing jurisdiction by their continual filings. In re Cletus P. McCauley & Mary A. McCauley Irrevocable Trust, 2014-Ohio-3692, 2014 Ohio App. LEXIS 3624 (Ohio Ct. App., Stark County 2014).

Accounting and trust construction claims alleged actions by the executor, as successor trustee, were issues that related to the administration of the estate and therefore the trial court properly found that those claims were within the jurisdiction of the probate court. Phillips v. Deskin, 2013-Ohio-3025, 2013 Ohio App. LEXIS 3067 (Ohio Ct. App., Richland County 2013).

Since the results of executor's conduct or omissions pre-testamentary were at issue, the claims under the declaratory judgment action were not related to issues regarding the administration of the estate and were not subject to the probate court's jurisdiction. Phillips v. Deskin, 2013-Ohio-3025, 2013 Ohio App. LEXIS 3067 (Ohio Ct. App., Richland County 2013).

Dismissal by the general division of a court of common pleas of a plaintiff's claims for a declaratory judgment, unjust enrichment, and tortious interference with expectancy of inheritance was appropriate because the probate court, pursuant to R.C. 2101.24(A)(1)(l) and 2721.05(C), was the court vested with jurisdiction to hear the plaintiff's claims relating to the administration of an estate. Patterson v. Church, 2013-Ohio-1906, 2013 Ohio App. LEXIS 1785 (Ohio Ct. App., Cuyahoga County 2013).

Probate court properly exercised jurisdiction and venue over a will contest matter, based upon the applicable statutory provisions of R.C. 2101.24(A) and 2107.71 because (1) there was no dispute that the court had jurisdiction to hear and determine actions to contest the validity of wills pursuant to R.C. 2101.24(A)(1)(p); and (2) the parties did not dispute that the will contest action was filed in the same county in which the will was admitted to probate pursuant to the venue provisions of R.C. 2107.71(A). Daubel v. Dineen, 2012-Ohio-5924, 2012 Ohio App. LEXIS 5107 (Ohio Ct. App., Lorain County 2012).

General division of a trial court was not the proper court to litigate the parties' claims, regarding the parties' parent giving money to certain of the parties, because once a guardian was appointed for the parties' parent the action then became within the probate court's exclusive jurisdiction, under R.C. 2101.24 and 2111.50(A)(1), as it touched upon the guardianship. Accordingly, the general division of the trial court should have transferred the case to the probate court under Civ.R. 73(B). Barber v. Williamson, 2012-Ohio-4925, 2012 Ohio App. LEXIS 4307 (Ohio Ct. App., Ross County 2012).

Although trustees argued that the probate court had exclusive or concurrent jurisdiction with the general division of the court of common pleas over trusts, the trustees did not provide any controlling authority that prevented a domestic relations court from undertaking proceedings involving a trust that may have had property related to matters before the domestic relations division; therefore, the trustees were not entitled to a writ of prohibition. State ex rel. Lavelle v. Karner, 2012-Ohio-4297, 2012 Ohio App. LEXIS 3774 (Ohio Ct. App., Cuyahoga County 2012).

Probate court had exclusive subject-matter jurisdiction over the guardianship action and the husband raised neither an objection for want of personal jurisdiction nor for improper venue within the circumstances described in Civ.R. 12(G). Such defenses were, therefore, waived. In re Guardianship of Lavers, 2012-Ohio-1668, 2012 Ohio App. LEXIS 1457 (Ohio Ct. App., Lucas County 2012).

Probate court did not have any statutory authority under R.C. 2101.24 and 2721.05áto render a declaratory judgment in a case because the issues in the case did not relate to the ongoing administration of an estate and were not a matter properly before the probate court. Weathington v. Hill, 2011-Ohio-5875, 2011 Ohio App. LEXIS 4809 (Ohio Ct. App., Marion County 2011).

Probate court had jurisdiction under R.C. 2101.24 to order a distribution by the trustee of a trust that was created by the decedent, before the decedent died, to the administrator of the decedent's estate and a beneficiary because of the financial hardship that the litigation had caused the estate, which was significantly less than what they were entitled to under the terms of the declaration of trust and will. Heslet v. Artz, 2011-Ohio-2961, 2011 Ohio App. LEXIS 2572 (Ohio Ct. App., Sandusky County 2011).

Nephew's argument that a probate court had jurisdiction over a claim was rejected because R.C. 2109.50 did not apply where a trust was not shown to be part of an estate; moreover, the nephew had already filed an action in a general division of a common pleas court, and the jurisdictional priority rule applied. In re Estate of Scanlon, 2011-Ohio-1097, 2011 Ohio App. LEXIS 942 (Ohio Ct. App., Cuyahoga County 2011).

Probate court has jurisdiction to hear and determine actions involving the misuse of a power of attorney, pursuant to R.C. 2101.24(B)(1)(b). Letson v. McCardle, 2010-Ohio-3676, 2010 Ohio App. LEXIS 3148 (Ohio Ct. App., Trumbull County 2010).

Common pleas court erred by dismissing the complaint because it did not appear that the uncle's claims for reformation of documents and imposition of a constructive trust, as an equitable owner, were cognizable in the probate court nor barred by subsequent action in the common pleas court; the real and personal property was not held by bona fide purchasers, but rather by the sons of the decedent (the nephews), as heirs. Thus, there being no requirement for the uncle to either except to the inventory or file a creditor's claim with the time allotted under the creditor's claim statute, and in light of the reasoning suggesting that an owner's interest in recovering his property outweighed the interests of finality of estate administration, there was nothing which should have prohibited the common pleas court from exercising jurisdiction over the claims. Bishop v. Bishop, 2010-Ohio-2958, 188 Ohio App. 3d 98, 934 N.E.2d 420, 2010 Ohio App. LEXIS 2459 (Ohio Ct. App., Jackson County 2010).

Probate court had jurisdiction to determine whether the proceeds of a life insurance policy and an accident insurance policy properly belonged to the decedent's estate. Pursuant to the probate court's plenary power and its jurisdiction over the inventories of the estates, the probate court had subject matter jurisdiction over the insurance proceeds, and the proceeds were included as an asset of the estate. In re Estate of Boone, 2010-Ohio-6269, 190 Ohio App. 3d 799, 944 N.E.2d 307, 2010 Ohio App. LEXIS 5246 (Ohio Ct. App., Mahoning County 2010).

After a general division court adopted a settlement agreement in a trust action, it lacked jurisdiction to prohibit an executor from proceeding in a federal lawsuit, notwithstanding an express reservation of jurisdiction in its order, because R.C. 2101.24(A)(1)(c) provided that this was within the exclusive jurisdiction of a probate court. Rieser v. Rieser, 2010-Ohio-6227, 191 Ohio App. 3d 616, 947 N.E.2d 222, 2010 Ohio App. LEXIS 5229 (Ohio Ct. App., Montgomery County 2010).

As an Ohio common pleas court lacked subject matter jurisdiction under R.C. 2101.24(C) and 2727.03 to determine a putative heir's claim for injunctive relief against his sister and her husband, wherein he alleged that assets from their deceased mother's estate were wrongfully transferred, dismissal of the action was proper; such a claim was exclusively within a probate court's jurisdiction. Bunting v. Estate of Bunting, 2009-Ohio-3136, 2009 Ohio App. LEXIS 2691 (Ohio Ct. App., Stark County 2009).

Probate court had jurisdiction under R.C. 2101.24(B)(1)(b) to determine whether a decedent's transfer of real estate to her deceased nephew and his wife should be voided due to an alleged misuse by the nephew of a power of attorney granted to him by the decedent. Estate of Niemi v. Niemi, 2009-Ohio-2090, 2009 Ohio App. LEXIS 1749 (Ohio Ct. App., Trumbull County 2009).

When a decedent's grandchildren filed claims alleging conspiracy to defraud the decedent, fraud upon the decedent, breach of fiduciary duties owed to the decedent, conversion of the decedent's assets, and incapacity of the decedent to enter a contract, as well as a claim for a fiduciary accounting, the general division of a court of common pleas properly found that the court had no jurisdiction to consider the claims because, (1) under R.C. 2101.24(A)(1)(l) and 2721.05(C), a probate court had exclusive jurisdiction over such claims, even though no estate was administered because the decedent's assets passed to recipients by beneficiary designation outside of the probate process, since, as to claims of conspiracy, fraud, conversion, and incapacity to contract, a challenge to such a transfer remained within the exclusive jurisdiction of the probate court because the setting aside of such a transfer would cause the assets to revert to the decedent's probate estate, and (2) the claims belonged to the decedent's estate and could not be asserted by a third party. Treadway v. Free Pentecostal Pater Ave. Church of God, Inc., 2008-Ohio-1663, 2008 Ohio App. LEXIS 1433 (Ohio Ct. App., Butler County 2008).



As a ward improperly instituted an action dealing with a guardianship in the general division of the common pleas court when it properly should have been within the probate court's exclusive jurisdiction pursuant to R.C. 2101.24, the trial court should have granted the ward's request to transfer the matter to the probate division pursuant to CivR 73(B), rather than dismissing it. Keith v. Bringardner, 2008-Ohio-950, 2008 Ohio App. LEXIS 833 (Ohio Ct. App., Franklin County 2008).

As a decedent was not an Ohio resident, a probate court lacked jurisdiction pursuant to R.C. 2101.24(A)(1)(b), (c), and 2113.01 to appoint an estate administrator; as such appointment was void, the probate court's judgment was subject to collateral attack in a wrongful death action brought by the administrator, who was deemed to lack standing to bring the action pursuant to R.C. 2125.02(A)(1). Black v. Aristech Chem. Co., 2008-Ohio-7038, 2008 Ohio App. LEXIS 5890 (Ohio Ct. App., Scioto County 2008).

When a decedent's grandchildren filed claims alleging conspiracy to defraud the decedent, fraud upon the decedent, breach of fiduciary duties owed to the decedent, conversion of the decedent's assets, and incapacity of the decedent to enter a contract, as well as a claim for a fiduciary accounting, the general division of a court of common pleas properly found that the court had no jurisdiction to consider the claims because, (1) under R.C. 2101.24(A)(1)(l) and 2721.05(C), a probate court had exclusive jurisdiction over such claims, even though no estate was administered because the decedent's assets passed to recipients by beneficiary designation outside of the probate process, since, as to claims of conspiracy, fraud, conversion, and incapacity to contract, a challenge to such a transfer remained within the exclusive jurisdiction of the probate court because the setting aside of such a transfer would cause the assets to revert to the decedent's probate estate, and (2) the claims belonged to the decedent's estate and could not be asserted by a third party. Treadway v. Free Pentecostal Pater Ave. Church of God, Inc., 2008-Ohio-1663, 2008 Ohio App. LEXIS 1433 (Ohio Ct. App., Butler County 2008).

Common pleas court which had exclusive jurisdiction over a legal client's malpractice action against an attorney, arising from the attorney's settlement of the client's wrongful death action involving the client's daughter, had subject matter jurisdiction over the matter until its conclusion; although a probate court had jurisdiction pursuant to R.C. 2101.24 to approve settlements of wrongful death matters, it had no jurisdiction over the malpractice claim. Batteiger v. Deutsch, 2008-Ohio-1582, 2008 Ohio App. LEXIS 1333 (Ohio Ct. App., Montgomery County 2008).

As a ward improperly instituted an action dealing with a guardianship in the general division of the common pleas court when it properly should have been within the probate court's exclusive jurisdiction pursuant to R.C. 2101.24, the trial court should have granted the ward's request to transfer the matter to the probate division pursuant to Civ.R. 73(B), rather than dismissing it. Keith v. Bringardner, 2008-Ohio-950, 2008 Ohio App. LEXIS 833 (Ohio Ct. App., Franklin County 2008).

Trial court's dismissal of a ward's claims against various guardians, arising from a guardianship that was initiated in the probate court against the ward until the probate court determined that the ward was not incompetent and the guardianship was not needed, was proper, as the probate court had exclusive jurisdiction over all matters incident to the guardianship pursuant to R.C. 2101.24(A)(1)(e); the fact that the guardianship had terminated did not divest the probate court of jurisdiction. Keith v. Bringardner, 2008-Ohio-950, 2008 Ohio App. LEXIS 833 (Ohio Ct. App., Franklin County 2008).

Because the controversy concerned the administration of the decedent's estate, including the duty of the decedent's sister as executrix to file an account of estate assets pursuant to R.C. 2109.30, the probate court did not err in ruling upon the issue because it had jurisdiction. In re Estate of Perry, 2008-Ohio-351, 2008 Ohio App. LEXIS 296 (Ohio Ct. App., Butler County 2008).

Pursuant to R.C. 2101.24, 2721.03, and 2721.05, the probate court had jurisdiction to determine the validity of the July 18, 1999 writing; the evidence demonstrated that the assets described in the writing should have been treated as if they were in the estate, in accordance with the agreement of the parties. The probate court did have jurisdiction to determine the declaratory judgment action pending before it and it was the proper forum for rendering a declaratory judgment on a contract or writing constituting a contract because the property transferred was related to the administration of the estate. Kozak v. Jackson, 2008-Ohio-50, 2008 Ohio App. LEXIS 45 (Ohio Ct. App., Cuyahoga County 2008).

Probate court properly exercised jurisdiction over a successor trustee's declaratory judgment action, seeking construction of a decedent's trust and construction of an antenuptial agreement between the decedent and his surviving wife which encompassed the decedent's intentions regarding his estate, as it had plenary power of such a matter pursuant to R.C. 2101.24(C). Nat'l City Bank v. de Laville, 2006-Ohio-5909, 170 Ohio App. 3d 317, 867 N.E.2d 416, 2006 Ohio App. LEXIS 5858 (Ohio Ct. App., Lucas County 2006).

Probate court had authority and jurisdiction under R.C. 2101.24(A)(1)(s), (C), and 2111.50 to grant a preliminary injunction that prevented a former guardian of an adjudicated incompetent from residing at or visiting the incompetent's home, as the elements necessary for the grant of the injunction were met; further, the court had jurisdiction to impose the order, as it did not actually evict the guardian, but instead, it found him to be a disruptive influence on the incompetent and ordered him to leave the premises. In re Guardianship of Norwood, 2006-Ohio-4504, 2006 Ohio App. LEXIS 4404 (Ohio Ct. App., Cuyahoga County 2006).

When a will directed that intangible property was to pass to a trust and that tangible property would pass to an executrix, and it was determined that the decedent's corporation was intangible property, the probate court had jurisdiction, under R.C. 2101.24(A)(1)(c), to order the corporation to issue stock in itself naming the trustee of the trust to which it passed as the corporation's owner because the probate court had the authority to order the distribution of estates. Kasapis v. High Point Furniture Co., 2006-Ohio-255, 2006 Ohio App. LEXIS 211 (Ohio Ct. App., Summit County 2006).

Pursuant to R.C. 2101.24(A)(1)(e), 2101.06, and 2101.07, a probate court judge had jurisdiction to appoint a special master commissioner to resolve attorney fee disputes in a guardianship matter, as well as the authority to remove a guardian for her mother and her mother's estate, and to appoint a successor guardian; although a guardianship ended upon the death of a ward, the successor guardian had the power to make a proper accounting and settlement of any acts taken with respect to the ward's assets, and fees awarded to the commissioner were proper. State ex rel. Estate of Hards v. Klammer, 2006-Ohio-3670, 110 Ohio St. 3d 104, 850 N.E.2d 1197, 2006 Ohio LEXIS 2179 (Ohio 2006).

Jurisdiction of a "guardianship" court does not completely terminate immediately after the ward's death, as that court has continuing jurisdiction to settle all pending matters in the action and render a judgment as to the final accounting of the estate. State ex rel. Estate of Hards v. Klammer, 2005-Ohio-2655, 2005 Ohio App. LEXIS 2501 (Ohio Ct. App., Lake County 2005), aff'd, 2006-Ohio-3670, 110 Ohio St. 3d 104, 850 N.E.2d 1197, 2006 Ohio LEXIS 2179 (Ohio 2006).

When a master commissioner was appointed in a guardianship case, the trial court in that case had jurisdiction to consider the master commissioner's petition for approval of his fee after the ward died because, while the ward's death terminated the guardianship, the trial court had continuing jurisdiction under R.C. 2101.24(A)(1)(d) to settle the guardianship final account, which included the assessment of court costs, including the master commissioner's fee, under R.C. 2101.07. State ex rel. Estate of Hards v. Klammer, 2005-Ohio-2655, 2005 Ohio App. LEXIS 2501 (Ohio Ct. App., Lake County 2005), aff'd, 2006-Ohio-3670, 110 Ohio St. 3d 104, 850 N.E.2d 1197, 2006 Ohio LEXIS 2179 (Ohio 2006).

Probate court lacked jurisdiction pursuant to R.C. 2101.24 over a claim of tortious interference with an expectation of inheritance; although it had the same element of undue influence that was often presented in a will contest, the tort claim also required proof of other elements not properly before a probate court. Hoopes v. Hoopes, 2007 Ohio App. LEXIS 1582 (Ohio Ct. App., Stark County Apr. 9, 2007).

Son was incorrect that the daughter's sole remedy in challenging the exclusion of the family Bible from the estate inventory was to file a concealment/embezzlement action, under R.C. 2109.50, or an action for declaratory judgment, under R.C. 2721.05, because a probate court can determine title to personal property on exceptions to an inventory and it was a matter of discretion whether the exceptor shall be ordered to pursue other remedies. The probate court has concurrent jurisdiction, under R.C. 2101.24(B)(1)(b), to determine title to disputed assets in addition to the jurisdiction granted under R.C. 2109.50 in concealment/embezzlement actions. In re Estate of Kelsey, 2006-Ohio-1171, 165 Ohio App. 3d 680, 847 N.E.2d 1277, 2006 Ohio App. LEXIS 1052 (Ohio Ct. App., Lake County 2006).

Probate court had jurisdiction regarding the recovering of funds by inter vivos transactions since the validity of the underlying transfers was challenged. Also, because the matter was tried in a dual manner considering the application of R.C. 2109.50 and R.C. 2101.24, the probate court had concurrent jurisdiction to entertain the action for concealed or embezzled assets under R.C. 2109.50, pertaining to power of attorney issues. Burwell v. Rains, 2005-Ohio-1893, 2005 Ohio App. LEXIS 1802 (Ohio Ct. App., Trumbull County 2005).

Writ of prohibition was issued at the request of an estate executrix against a probate court judge, who had appointed counsel to represent the estate for purposes of appealing a reversal of the judge's order that had reduced a law firm's fees and expenses, arising from the firm's settlement of wrongful death claims, as the judge exceeded his authority in assuming that it was in the estate's best interests to appeal that determination. While the probate court had authority under R.C. 2101.24(C) to dispose fully of any matter that was properly before it, seeking to appeal that order was not an issue that was properly before it, as the estate was concluded except for the final resolution of the wrongful death claims, which were not estate assets. State ex rel. Marsteller v. Maloney, 2005-Ohio-1836, 2005 Ohio App. LEXIS 1746 (Ohio Ct. App., Mahoning County 2005).

Because a probate court had jurisdiction over an incompetent, its jurisdiction continued by virtue of a guardian's complaint for land sale pending before it; consequently, the common pleas court did not err by dismissing a daughter's complaint and action for declaratory judgment for lack of jurisdiction. Brady v. McCaffrey, 2005-Ohio-1197, 2005 Ohio App. LEXIS 1180 (Ohio Ct. App., Cuyahoga County 2005).

Although a probate court had jurisdiction under R.C. 2101.24(A)(1), (b), (c), (l) and (m) to remove the daughter as executrix, the R.C. 2113.05 notice was lacking. In re Estate of Mizer, 2005-Ohio-862, 2005 Ohio App. LEXIS 879 (Ohio Ct. App., Tuscarawas County 2005).

Since a probate court had jurisdiction to hear a will contest, and the tort claim for intentional interference with expectancy of inheritance required proof of elements that were not relevant or necessary to the probate court's resolution of the will contest, the probate court did not have jurisdiction over that claim. Thus, the claim was properly dismissed. Roll v. Edwards, 2004-Ohio-767, 156 Ohio App. 3d 227, 805 N.E.2d 162, 2004 Ohio App. LEXIS 719 (Ohio Ct. App., Ross County 2004).

Probate court had jurisdiction over an action to recover funds given to a family by a challenged inter vivos transaction, and the court could render a declaratory judgment that all transfers to the family were invalid. Rudloff v. Efstathiadis, 2003-Ohio-6686, 2003 Ohio App. LEXIS 5943 (Ohio Ct. App., Trumbull County 2003).

Mandamus will not issue to compel the general division of a court of common pleas to decide claims against an executor, rather than transfer them to the probate division, where the claims are arguably within the exclusive jurisdiction of the probate court and the relators have an adequate remedy by way of appeal: State ex rel. Lewis v. Moser, 1995-Ohio-148, 72 Ohio St. 3d 25, 647 N.E.2d 155, 1995 Ohio LEXIS 814 (Ohio 1995).

The probate court had exclusive jurisdiction as to the action against the executor for conversion of estate assets and against the guardian of the decedent's child for breach of fiduciary duties: Johnson v. Allen, 101 Ohio App. 3d 181, 655 N.E.2d 240, 1995 Ohio App. LEXIS 348 (Ohio Ct. App., Cuyahoga County 1995).

R.C. 2107.11(B) provides a probate court with jurisdiction over intangible assets deemed located in that Ohio county. Jurisdiction is not lost due to the disputed nature of the assets: Carlin v. Mambuca, 96 Ohio App. 3d 500, 645 N.E.2d 737, 1994 Ohio App. LEXIS 2084 (Ohio Ct. App., Cuyahoga County 1994).

Where courts have concurrent jurisdiction, the first court to acquire jurisdiction over the parties and the subject matter precludes the second court from assuming jurisdiction. It is sufficient that the first court has acquired jurisdiction over some of the parties and the subject matter to preclude the second court from assuming jurisdiction. Once a court has obtained jurisdiction, it must exercise it and cannot dismiss the action because a subsequent action involving the same parties and same subject matter and seeking the same relief is filed in another court: DeMar v. Mosley, 63 Ohio Misc. 2d 102, 619 N.E.2d 1239, 1993 Ohio Misc. LEXIS 21 (Ohio C.P. 1993).

The court of claims does not have exclusive jurisdiction when an action is solely for a declaratory judgment or injunctive relief against the state and no monetary damages are sought. A probate court has jurisdiction to grant relief in equity on probate matters against the state: Oakar v. Ohio Dep't of Mental Retardation, 88 Ohio App. 3d 332, 623 N.E.2d 1296, 1993 Ohio App. LEXIS 2902 (Ohio Ct. App., Cuyahoga County 1993).

Proceedings in probate court are restricted to those actions permitted by statute and by the constitution, since the probate court is a court of limited jurisdiction. (Schucker v. Metcalf, 22 Ohio St. 3d 33, 488 N.E.2d 210, 1986 Ohio LEXIS 574 (Ohio 1986).

A court having general jurisdiction of the subject matter of an action has authority to determine its own jurisdiction on the issue raised, and a party challenging its jurisdiction has a remedy at law in appeal from an adverse holding of the court that it has such jurisdiction, and may not maintain a proceeding in prohibition to prevent the prosecution of such action: State ex rel. Smith v. Court of Common Pleas, Probate Div., 70 Ohio St. 2d 213, 24 Ohio Op. 3d 320, 436 N.E.2d 1005, 1982 Ohio LEXIS 666 (Ohio 1982).

While the powers of the probate division of the court of common pleas are plenary, they are so only with respect to matters "properly before the court." R.C. 2101.24(O): Oncu v. Bell, 49 Ohio App. 2d 109, 3 Ohio Op. 3d 175, 359 N.E.2d 712, 1976 Ohio App. LEXIS 5809 (Ohio Ct. App., Medina County 1976).

The probate division of the court of common pleas is without jurisdiction either to reform a deed executed prior to an owner's death or to order a series of conveyances to correct alleged defects in that deed: Oncu v. Bell, 49 Ohio App. 2d 109, 3 Ohio Op. 3d 175, 359 N.E.2d 712, 1976 Ohio App. LEXIS 5809 (Ohio Ct. App., Medina County 1976).

The probate court and the court of common pleas have concurrent jurisdiction of an action to foreclose a mortgage on the real estate of a deceased mortgagor of whose estate an administratrix has been appointed and qualified, when it is necessary to sell the real estate to pay decedent's debts, and the court which first acquires jurisdiction thereof retains it to the exclusion of the other: (decided under former analogous section) Government Nat'l Mortg. Ass'n v. Smith, 28 Ohio App. 2d 300, 57 Ohio Op. 2d 453, 277 N.E.2d 233, 1971 Ohio App. LEXIS 464 (Ohio Ct. App., Hamilton County 1971).

The probate court has plenary power at law and in equity fully to dispose of any matter properly before the court unless the power is expressly otherwise limited or denied by statute: (decided under former analogous section) Wolfrum v. Wolfrum, 2 Ohio St. 2d 237, 31 Ohio Op. 2d 501, 208 N.E.2d 537, 1965 Ohio LEXIS 538 (Ohio 1965).

The probate court was without jurisdiction to declare the validity of a purported contract, in a declaratory judgment action, where such contract had no bearing on the assets of the estate, duties of the executor, or the court's supervision of the administration of the estate: (decided under former analogous section) In re Estate of Martin, 115 Ohio App. 515, 21 Ohio Op. 2d 166, 185 N.E.2d 785, 1962 Ohio App. LEXIS 709 (Ohio Ct. App., Fayette County 1962).

In an action for a declaratory judgment brought by a person in possession of personal property claimed by the executor of decedent's estate and which the party in possession claims by virtue of a gift inter vivos, a probate court has jurisdiction to determine the title to such personal property: (decided under former analogous section) Renee v. Sanders, 102 Ohio App. 21, 2 Ohio Op. 2d 7, 131 N.E.2d 846, 73 Ohio Law Abs. 449, 1956 Ohio App. LEXIS 618 (Ohio Ct. App., Cuyahoga County 1956).

By reason of GC § 10501-53 (R.C. 2101.24), the probate court has exclusive jurisdiction, unless otherwise provided by law, as to all matters specifically set forth therein and as to all matters pertaining directly to the administration and settlement of estates: (decided under former analogous section) Jacobsen v. Jacobsen, 164 Ohio St. 413, 58 Ohio Op. 239, 131 N.E.2d 833, 1956 Ohio LEXIS 576 (Ohio 1956); Wolfrum v. Wolfrum, 2 Ohio St. 2d 237, 31 Ohio Op. 2d 501, 208 N.E.2d 537, 1965 Ohio LEXIS 538 (Ohio 1965).

The probate court in which a decedent's estate is being administered has jurisdiction to determine what rights, if any, the administratrix of the deceased's estate has in a purported oral lease of land occupied by the deceased at the time of his death: (decided under former analogous section) In re Estate of Logan, 131 N.E.2d 454, 71 Ohio Law Abs. 391, 1955 Ohio Misc. LEXIS 360 (Ohio P. Ct. 1955).

No relief for a probate court estate, upon a complaint to the probate court pursuant to GC § 10506-67 (R.C. 2109.50), can be given except with respect to property of such estate: (decided under former analogous section) In re Estate of Sexton, 163 Ohio St. 124, 56 Ohio Op. 2d 178, 56 Ohio Op. 178, 126 N.E.2d 129, 1955 Ohio LEXIS 531 (Ohio), cert. denied, 350 U.S. 838, 76 S. Ct. 75, 100 L. Ed. 747, 1955 U.S. LEXIS 489 (U.S. 1955).

General Code § 10501-53 (R.C. 2101.24), providing that "The probate court shall have plenary power at law and in equity to fully dispose of any matter properly before the court. . ." adds nothing to the jurisdiction conferred upon such court by Ohio Const. art IV, § 8: (decided under former analogous section) Foerster v. Foerster, 54 Ohio Op. 441, 122 N.E.2d 314, 71 Ohio Law Abs. 129, 1954 Ohio Misc. LEXIS 298 (Ohio P. Ct. 1954), disapproved, Sawyer v. Sawyer, 53 Ohio App. 2d 323, 7 Ohio Op. 3d 422, 374 N.E.2d 166, 1977 Ohio App. LEXIS 7002 (Ohio Ct. App., Hamilton County 1977).

Where probate court, on petition to sell real estate, found that deed from decedent to his grandson conveyed title to the real estate and that it was not an asset of the estate, such ruling terminated the court's jurisdiction precluding further determination of the issue of whether the state of Ohio had waived priority under trust mortgage executed by decedent upon receiving aid for aged: (decided under former analogous section) Piatt v. Piatt, 114 N.E.2d 441, 65 Ohio Law Abs. 284, 1952 Ohio App. LEXIS 889 (Ohio Ct. App., Darke County 1952).

The question of whether or not plaintiff is entitled to the return of his property, title to which he put in the name of the deceased under mistake of fact or because of the fraudulent conduct or representation of (his supposed wife) made by her during her lifetime states a cause of action coming within the equity power of the court of common pleas and the fact that defendant is an administrator does not oust it of such jurisdiction: (decided under former analogous section) Carter v. Birnbaum, 113 N.E.2d 102, 68 Ohio Law Abs. 97, 1953 Ohio App. LEXIS 886 (Ohio Ct. App., Cuyahoga County 1953).

General Code § 10509-185 (R.C. 2113.58), the purpose of which is to protect the interests of remaindermen under wills, contains two distinct remedies, either of which the court, in a proper case, may apply; the provisions of that section do not operate as a limitation on the plenary jurisdiction conferred on the probate court by Ohio Const. art IV, § 8, and this section: (decided under former analogous section) In re Miller's Estate, 95 Ohio App. 457, 54 Ohio Op. 98, 121 N.E.2d 26, 1953 Ohio App. LEXIS 737 (Ohio Ct. App., Franklin County 1953), aff'd, 160 Ohio St. 529, 52 Ohio Op. 437, 117 N.E.2d 598, 1954 Ohio LEXIS 624 (Ohio 1954).

Under authority of this section, the probate court has full power to hear and determine any matter properly before it, unless the power is expressly otherwise limited or denied by statute: (decided under former analogous section) In re Smith's Estate, 120 N.E.2d 632, 67 Ohio Law Abs. 409, 1952 Ohio Misc. LEXIS 310 (Ohio P. Ct. 1952).

This section modifies or limits the jurisdiction conferred on the common pleas court, with reference to the specific provisions incorporated therein, including jurisdiction to construe wills, in which respect GC § 11215 (R.C. 2305.01), is repealed by implication: (decided under former analogous section) Van Stone v. Van Stone, 95 Ohio App. 406, 53 Ohio Op. 438, 120 N.E.2d 154, 1952 Ohio App. LEXIS 593 (Ohio Ct. App., Lucas County 1952).

This section gives the probate court, in matters within its jurisdiction, the authority to exercise equity powers in disposing of matters where there is no legal remedy or where the legal remedy is inadequate: (decided under former analogous section) In re Dickey's Estate, 87 Ohio App. 255, 42 Ohio Op. 474, 94 N.E.2d 223, 57 Ohio Law Abs. 346, 1949 Ohio App. LEXIS 603 (Ohio Ct. App., Montgomery County 1949).

The exclusive jurisdiction of a probate court referred to in this section does not apply when otherwise provided by law: (decided under former analogous section) State ex rel. Overlander v. Brewer, 147 Ohio St. 386, 34 Ohio Op. 338, 72 N.E.2d 84, 1947 Ohio LEXIS 416 (Ohio 1947).

Jurisdiction of the probate court to redetermine its finding or modify its order or instruct its fiduciary is not limited by the power conferred by GC § 5339 (R.C. 5731.20), but includes broad powers conferred by GC § 10501-53 (R.C. 2101.24): (decided under former analogous section) In re Shafer's Estate, 74 Ohio App. 33, 29 Ohio Op. 233, 56 N.E.2d 926, 40 Ohio Law Abs. 496, 1943 Ohio App. LEXIS 616 (Ohio Ct. App., Butler County 1943).

By this section the probate court is given, inter alia, exclusive jurisdiction over the administration of decedents' estates: (decided under former analogous section) Saluppo v. Santangelo, 71 Ohio App. 185, 26 Ohio Op. 10, 48 N.E.2d 903, 39 Ohio Law Abs. 169, 1942 Ohio App. LEXIS 592 (Ohio Ct. App., Hamilton County 1942).

The specific grant of power to the probate court as contained in GC § 10501-17 (R.C. 2101.33) and this section does not confer upon such court general equity jurisdiction: (decided under former analogous section) Hooffstetter v. Adams, 67 Ohio App. 21, 21 Ohio Op. 70, 35 N.E.2d 896, 1941 Ohio App. LEXIS 799 (Ohio Ct. App., Summit County 1941).

While the authority of the court under a proceeding is very broad for the purpose of discovering concealed or embezzled assets, it is not broad enough to litigate all the issues in a case where there has been no concealment of assets. To that extent there is a limitation upon the "plenary power" granted to probate court in the [next to] the last paragraph of this section: (decided under former analogous section) Goodrich v. Anderson, 136 Ohio St. 509, 17 Ohio Op. 152, 26 N.E.2d 1016, 1940 Ohio LEXIS 534 (Ohio 1940).

Under this section the probate court has "plenary power at law and in equity fully to dispose of any matter properly before the court," unless otherwise provided by statute. There is no statutory provision which limits or denies to that court power to hear and determine fully and completely all questions raised by exceptions to an inventory of the assets of a decedent's estate: (decided under former analogous section) Bolles v. Toledo Trust Co., 136 Ohio St. 517, 17 Ohio Op. 156, 27 N.E.2d 145, 1940 Ohio LEXIS 536 (Ohio), cert. denied, 311 U.S. 673, 61 S. Ct. 37, 85 L. Ed. 433, 1940 U.S. LEXIS 430 (U.S. 1940).

In view of the "exclusive" jurisdiction and "plenary" power, both legal and equitable, given the probate court by this section, fraud on the part of a fiduciary must be challenged in that court: (decided under former analogous section) Neidecker v. Neidecker, 63 Ohio App. 416, 17 Ohio Op. 135, 26 N.E.2d 929, 1939 Ohio App. LEXIS 245 (Ohio Ct. App., Ottawa County 1939).

The common pleas court acquires jurisdiction of a mortgage foreclosure proceeding, although the mortgagor is dead, where a petition is duly filed and process issued and served, and such jurisdiction is not lost by the executor of the mortgagor filing in probate court, the following day, a petition to sell realty to pay debts of the estate: (decided under former analogous section) Home Owners' Loan Corp. v. Roth, 24 Ohio Law Abs. 693, 1937 Ohio Misc. LEXIS 1087 (Ohio Ct. App., Lorain County May 17, 1937).

This statute establishes the law to the effect that the jurisdiction of a probate court once acquired over an estate is exclusive of every other probate court: (decided under former analogous section) Ex parte Crist, 89 Ohio St. 33, 105 N.E. 71, 11 Ohio L. Rep. 295, 1913 Ohio LEXIS 553 (Ohio 1913); Children's Home of Marion County v. Fetter, 90 Ohio St. 110, 106 N.E. 761, 11 Ohio L. Rep. 518, 1914 Ohio LEXIS 215 (Ohio 1914); Addams

v. State, 104 Ohio St. 475, 135 N.E. 667, 1922 Ohio LEXIS 350 (Ohio 1922); State ex rel. Black v. White, 132 Ohio St. 58, 7 Ohio Op. 165, 5 N.E.2d 163, 1936 Ohio LEXIS 234 (Ohio 1936).

Where the evidence shows clearly that a deed executed by decedent was intended as security for a loan, the probate court has jurisdiction to determine the rights of parties, and have the conveyed property sold to pay debts of deceased: (decided under former analogous section) Helmbold v. Helmbold, 25 Ohio App. 32, 158 N.E. 499, 4 Ohio Law Abs. 532, 1926 Ohio App. LEXIS 474 (Ohio Ct. App., Lucas County), writ of error dismissed, 115 Ohio St. 727, 156 N.E. 216, 4 Ohio Law Abs. 726, 25 Ohio L. Rep. 45, 1926 Ohio LEXIS 252 (Ohio 1926).

**—Related to tort claim**

Trial court had jurisdiction over a claim of intentional interference with expectancy of inheritance by a decedent's daughter, even though the daughter did not pursue any remedies in the probate court, because the probate division had no jurisdiction over claims for money damages arising from allegations of fraud and the daughter sufficiently alleged the beneficiaries, who were the decedent's grandchildren, acted fraudulently and with undue influence to take the decedent's property. Widdig v. Watkins, 2013-Ohio-3858, 2013 Ohio App. LEXIS 4015 (Ohio Ct. App., Scioto County 2013).

Because the interference with an expectancy of an inheritance and fraud claims sounded in tort and fraud due to the executor's failure to carry out her father's wishes prior to his death, the claims were within the jurisdiction of the general division, not the probate division. Phillips v. Deskin, 2013-Ohio-3025, 2013 Ohio App. LEXIS 3067 (Ohio Ct. App., Richland County 2013).

Probate court lacked jurisdiction pursuant to R.C. 2101.24 over a claim of tortious interference with an expectation of inheritance; although it had the same element of undue influence that was often presented in a will contest, the tort claim also required proof of other elements not properly before a probate court. Hoopes v. Hoopes, 2007 Ohio App. LEXIS 1582 (Ohio Ct. App., Stark County Apr. 9, 2007).

**Jurisdiction as to title to realty**

Son was not entitled to a writ of prohibition to prevent a court from transferring property allegedly bequeathed to the son to anyone else because the son did not show the court patently and unambiguously lacked jurisdiction over will contests. State ex rel. Evans v. Scioto Cty. Common Pleas Court, 2018-Ohio-4696, 155 Ohio St. 3d 41, 118 N.E.3d 249, 2018 Ohio LEXIS 2764 (Ohio 2018).

The language of this section and R.C. 5303.03 does not subtract from or limit the full jurisdiction of the common pleas court in an action of ejectment to determine the legal title to land, be it by will, deed or otherwise, upon which to award possession of land: (decided under former analogous section) Avery v. Avery, 107 Ohio App. 199, 8 Ohio Op. 2d 91, 157 N.E.2d 917, 1958 Ohio App. LEXIS 727 (Ohio Ct. App., Wood County 1958).

**Marriage license**

Trial court, exercising its R.C. 2101.24(A)(1)(f) jurisdictional powers to grant or not grant marriage licenses, had given the Massachusetts' amended birth certificate (ABC) full faith and credit to the extent that Massachusetts would—the ABC created a rebuttable presumption that such person was a male and that presumption was then rebutted by other evidence (the original birth certificate and that person's prior marriage and divorce as a female) that indicated that the person was, under the Ohio common definition under R.C. 3101.01, for marriage license purposes, a female; denial of marriage license to female changed to male (under amended Massachusetts birth certificate) and female was proper as denial was found not to violate full faith and credit or equal protection since Ohio's gender definitions were traditional. In re Application of Marriage License for Nash, 2003-Ohio-7221, 2003 Ohio App. LEXIS 6513 (Ohio Ct. App., Trumbull County 2003).

With respect to R.C. 2101.24, 3101.01 and 3101.05, a probate court cannot be expected to turn a blind eye to evidence that comes before it that could possibly foreclose the issuance of a marriage license; rather, the probate court is permitted to proceed with the case accordingly, including requiring additional information or conducting an evidentiary hearing on the matter. In re Application of Marriage License for Nash, 2003-Ohio-7221, 2003 Ohio App. LEXIS 6513 (Ohio Ct. App., Trumbull County 2003).

**Missing persons**

The probate court, under this section, has authority to authorize a trustee for a missing person to bring an action for equitable partition of lands in which the missing person owned a fractional interest: (decided under former analogous section) In re Parrett, 86 Ohio App. 162, 41 Ohio Op. 20, 90 N.E.2d 425, 1949 Ohio App. LEXIS 676 (Ohio Ct. App., Franklin County 1949).

**Parentage**

Although a probate court had authority to render declaratory judgments pursuant to R.C. ch. 2721 and R.C. 2101.24 in limited situations, it lacked jurisdiction to make a parentage determination in order to declare biological parents as the true parents of a child who was carried during pregnancy pursuant to a surrogacy agreement; as the probate court lacked jurisdiction to make the parentage determination under R.C. 3111.381 and 3111.02(A), the biological parents' action seeking such a determination and the issuance of a birth certificate pursuant thereto was dismissed. Nemcek v. Paskey, 2006-Ohio-2059, 137 Ohio Misc. 2d 1, 849 N.E.2d 108, 2006 Ohio Misc. LEXIS 107 (Ohio C.P. 2006).

**Power of attorney**

Probate court had jurisdiction to hear and determine the action involving a power of attorney and to determine whether the son, as attorney-in-fact, properly placed his father's assets in a joint account. Fields v. Brackney, 2011-Ohio-1128, 2011 Ohio App. LEXIS 963 (Ohio Ct. App., Montgomery County 2011).

Trial court did not abuse its discretion by granting judgment against the bank for conversion because the evidence showed that the bank had actual knowledge of the fiduciary relationship between the decedent and the daughter's husband due to the issuance of the power of attorney by the husband to the bank; that the bank acted in bad faith, rather than mere negligence, when it allowed the husband to deposit the decedent's annuity check in his individual account; and that the bank was not protected by the Uniform Fiduciary Act, R.C. 5815.06. The bank also had actual knowledge that the husband was defrauding the decedent at the moment of the transaction at issue because the bank was aware of the fiduciary relationship as the bank was in possession of a copy of the power of attorney, which did not expressly give the power of the fiduciary to give gifts to himself. Letson v. McCardle, 2010-Ohio-3681, 2010 Ohio App. LEXIS 3143 (Ohio Ct. App., Trumbull County 2010).

Even considering an executor's evidence of a decedent's estate planning, the executor exceeded his power under a power of attorney as he cashed savings bonds titled in the name of a decedent and her son under a power of attorney, deposited the proceeds into a joint account with a right of survivorship in the names of the decedent and the executor, moved the proceeds to his own account after the decedent's death, did not list the proceeds in the initial inventory of the estate, and later transferred the proceeds to the estate's accounts; the finding that the decedent intended for her son to receive the bond proceeds was reasonable as the executor became the sole owner of the funds due to his actions, the executor did not hold the funds in trust for the decedent's son, and the executor and the executor's son were the major beneficiaries under the will. In re Estate of Leach, 2006-Ohio-3755, 2006 Ohio App. LEXIS 3721 (Ohio Ct. App., Montgomery County 2006).

When it was alleged that a sister, pursuant to a power of attorney appointing her as a mother's attorney in fact, converted the mother's certificates of deposit (CDs) to annuities and improperly, as to one annuity, added a provision that she was its per stirpes beneficiary, as such a provision was not found in the CDs used to buy the annuity, the probate court had jurisdiction, under R.C. 2101.24(C) and (B)(1)(b), to hear the matter and to order the sister's daughter, who had been appointed attorney in fact in the sister's place when the sister predeceased the mother, to pay a substantial sum back to the estate, plus a penalty. Levy v. Thompson, 2006-Ohio-5312, 2006 Ohio App. LEXIS 5292 (Ohio Ct. App., Montgomery County 2006).

Probate court properly held that it had subject matter jurisdiction under R.C. 2101.24(B)(1)(b) over a dispute involving the proceeds of savings bonds, titled in the names of a decedent and her son, which the executor cashed under a power of attorney, deposited into a joint account with a right of survivorship in the names of the executor and the decedent, transferred to the executor's own account, did not list in the initial inventory, and later deposited into the estate's accounts. Even though a probate court held that the assets were not assets of the estate, the probate court had ancillary jurisdiction as the funds were in the possession of the executor in estate accounts and all of the parties necessary to determine title participated in the hearing. In re Estate of Leach, 2006-Ohio-3755, 2006 Ohio App. LEXIS 3721 (Ohio Ct. App., Montgomery County 2006).

The probate court had authority, in protecting a ward, to revoke a durable power of attorney executed by the ward: In re Guardianship of Thomas, 2002-Ohio-1037, 148 Ohio App. 3d 11, 771 N.E.2d 882, 2002 Ohio App. LEXIS 1041 (Ohio Ct. App., Franklin County 2002).

Where, pursuant to a power of attorney, a party managed a decedent's assets for several years prior to her death, the probate court could require the party to reimburse the estate for missing and unaccounted for assets: Spitzer v. Jackson, 96 Ohio App. 3d 313, 644 N.E.2d 1122, 1994 Ohio App. LEXIS 3385 (Ohio Ct. App., Montgomery County 1994).

**Prenuptial, antenuptial agreements**

An action for divorce abates upon the death of a party. However, an action to enforce an antenuptial agreement may be brought subsequent to the death of a party. The probate division, not the domestic relations division, is the court in which the action must be brought: Diemer v. Diemer, 99 Ohio App. 3d 54, 649 N.E.2d 1285, 1994 Ohio App. LEXIS 5484 (Ohio Ct. App., Cuyahoga County 1994).

**Private mental health facility**

A probate court does not have authority to order the department of mental health to pay the cost of care of a mentally ill person placed in a private facility: Berger v. Clermont County Alcohol, Drug Addiction & Mental Health Servs. Bd., 86 Ohio App. 3d 349, 620 N.E.2d 1027, 1993 Ohio App. LEXIS 819 (Ohio Ct. App., Clermont County), dismissed, 67 Ohio St. 3d 1421, 616 N.E.2d 504, 1993 Ohio LEXIS 1646 (Ohio 1993).

The Juvenile court acts beyond the scope of its jurisdiction when it orders the Ohio Department of Mental Health to pay the cost of care of a child placed in a private, non-public psychiatric hospital: In re Hamil, 69 Ohio St. 2d 97, 23 Ohio Op. 3d 151, 431 N.E.2d 317, 1982 Ohio LEXIS 543 (Ohio 1982).

**Real property of decedent**

Trial court properly adopted a magistrate's decision, which granted the decedent's estate administrator's writ of restitution on a forcible entry and detainer complaint against the executrix, as a petition in the probate court for the executrix's removal from the property was not mandated where the will provided that the administrator was authorized to sell the property without a court order. Sed v. Mundy, 2016-Ohio-8431, 2016 Ohio App. LEXIS 5313 (Ohio Ct. App., Portage County 2016).

Probate court was the first court to assert jurisdiction over the decedent's realty, and the general division of the court of common pleas was required to dismiss the mortgage foreclosure action: United States Bank, N.A. v. Webb, 2006-Ohio-5462, 139 Ohio Misc. 2d 54, 860 N.E.2d 161, 2006 Ohio Misc. LEXIS 211 (Ohio C.P. 2006).

**Release of negligence claim**

The issue whether a release of a negligence claim executed in the probate court is void may be determined by a common pleas court in an action therein to recover for personal injury damages caused by such negligence: (decided under former analogous section) Carpenter v. Pontius, 119 Ohio App. 383, 28 Ohio Op. 2d 12, 200 N.E.2d 682, 1963 Ohio App. LEXIS 747 (Ohio Ct. App., Stark County 1963).

**Removal of trustee**

Where a trustee was appointed via an inter vivos trust agreement during the lifetime of the settlor, it was an "inter vivos trustee," and accordingly, the probate court had jurisdiction, pursuant to R.C. 2101.24(B)(1)(b), over a matter wherein a beneficiary of the trust alleged that the trustee had breached its fiduciary duties and the trustee's removal was sought so that a new appointment could be made. Martin v. Wayne County Nat'l Bank Trust & Inv. Div., 2004-Ohio-4194, 2004 Ohio App. LEXIS 3827 (Ohio Ct. App., Wayne County 2004).

**Renunciation of succession**

The probate court has exclusive jurisdiction of an action to rescind a renunciation of intestate succession properly filed with it: (decided under former analogous section) Wolfrum v. Wolfrum, 2 Ohio St. 2d 237, 31 Ohio Op. 2d 501, 208 N.E.2d 537, 1965 Ohio LEXIS 538 (Ohio 1965).

**Res judicata**

In a will contest action, the court rejected the will contestant's contention that the probate court erred by ruling on issues of will construction during a will contest action because nothing in R.C. 2101.24 prevents a probate court from construing a will while also determining the validity of a will, and both Civ.R. 18(A) and caselaw indicated that the failure to raise issues of will construction in an action determining the validity of a will acts as res judicata on a later action to construe the will. Thus, the probate court properly determined that res judicata applied to the will contestant's claims in his declaratory judgment action asking that the will be construed, which was brought after summary judgment was granted on the contestant's original will contest action, because the parties and the claims were the same in both actions. Estate of Snell v. Kilburn, 2005-Ohio-7076, 165 Ohio App. 3d 352, 846 N.E.2d 572, 2005 Ohio App. LEXIS 6382 (Ohio Ct. App., Monroe County 2005).

**Spendthrift trust, creation**

The probate court has the power to appoint a trustee for personal property bequeathed to a spendthrift life tenant (remainder to her children) in order to protect the property, even though the will expressly provides otherwise: (decided under former analogous section) In re Miller's Estate, 95 Ohio App. 457, 54 Ohio Op. 98, 121 N.E.2d 26, 1953 Ohio App. LEXIS 737 (Ohio Ct. App., Franklin County 1953), aff'd, 160 Ohio St. 529, 52 Ohio Op. 437, 117 N.E.2d 598, 1954 Ohio LEXIS 624 (Ohio 1954).

**Standing to appeal**

Appellant lacked standing to appeal judgments entered by a probate court regarding the termination and distribution of a testamentary trust because appellant had never been appointed as a trustee of the trust. In re Estate of Keisser, 2013-Ohio-2803, 2013 Ohio App. LEXIS 2848 (Ohio Ct. App., Lucas County 2013).

**State mental hospital costs**

In an action by the state to recover the cost of care in a mental hospital, the probate court properly declined jurisdiction and directed the parties to the general division: Ohio Dep't of Mental Health v. Baldauf, 107 Ohio App. 3d 467, 669 N.E.2d 39, 1995 Ohio App. LEXIS 5104 (Ohio Ct. App., Lake County 1995).

A county probate court possesses jurisdiction to issue an order of involuntary commitment for mental health treatment pursuant to R.C. 2101.24 and 5122.15. A probate court does not exceed its jurisdiction when it orders that the state assume the cost of mental health treatment which is integral to the commitment determination but for which no provision has been made in the mental health plan developed by the county and approved by the state: Ohio Dep't of Mental Health v. Clermont County Alcohol, Drug Addiction & Mental Health Servs. Bd. (In re Hays), 70 Ohio St. 3d 471, 639 N.E.2d 433, 1994 Ohio LEXIS 2229 (Ohio 1994).

**Subject matter jurisdiction**

Trial court properly exercised subject matter jurisdiction in an executor's action seeking monetary and injunctive relief for a joint savings account holder's alleged fraudulent transfer of real estate and bank account funds from a decedent because the basis for the executor's claims occurred during the decedent's lifetime and not after his death; thus, the claims did not directly concern the administration of the decedent's estate. Love v. Love, 2021-Ohio-558, 168 N.E.3d 554, 2021 Ohio App. LEXIS 579 (Ohio Ct. App., Jackson County 2021).

Probate court properly held that it had subject matter jurisdiction under R.C. 2101.24(B)(1)(b) over a dispute involving the proceeds of savings bonds, titled in the names of a decedent and her son, which the executor cashed under a power of attorney, deposited into a joint account with a right of survivorship in the names of the executor and the decedent, transferred to the executor's own account, did not list in the initial inventory, and later deposited into the estate's accounts; even though a probate court held that the assets were not assets of the estate, the probate court had ancillary jurisdiction as the funds were in the possession of the executor in estate accounts and all of the parties necessary to determine title participated in the hearing. In re Estate of Leach, 2006-Ohio-3755, 2006 Ohio App. LEXIS 3721 (Ohio Ct. App., Montgomery County 2006).

**Title to disputed property**

Son was incorrect that the daughter's sole remedy in challenging the exclusion of the family Bible from the estate inventory was to file a concealment/embezzlement action, under R.C. 2109.50, or an action for declaratory judgment, under R.C. 2721.05, because a probate court can determine title to personal property on exceptions to an inventory and it was a matter of discretion whether the exceptor shall be ordered to pursue other remedies. The probate court has concurrent jurisdiction, under R.C. 2101.24(B)(1)(b), to determine title to disputed assets in addition to the jurisdiction granted under R.C. 2109.50 in concealment/embezzlement actions. In re Estate of Kelsey, 2006-Ohio-1171, 165 Ohio App. 3d 680, 847 N.E.2d 1277, 2006 Ohio App. LEXIS 1052 (Ohio Ct. App., Lake County 2006).

**Trusts generally**

Probate court possessed the jurisdiction to carry out the only relief that the guardian requested—the establishment of a trust account with the pooled special needs trust on the ward's behalf for the purpose of Medicaid eligibility. The probate court was not required to declare that a pooled trust account that it opened on a ward's behalf complied with R.C. 5111.151(F)(3)(a) and OAC 5101:1-39-27.1(C)(3)(c). Kormanik v. Cooper, 2011-Ohio-5617, 195 Ohio App. 3d 790, 961 N.E.2d 1187, 2011 Ohio App. LEXIS 4596 (Ohio Ct. App., Franklin County 2011).

Pursuant to R.C. 2101.24(B)(1)(b) and 2721.05, the probate court had jurisdiction to order payment of the surviving spouse's statutory allowance from the assets of an inter vivos trust established by the decedent for his support. The trust specifically provided that, if the estate assets were insufficient, the trustee was to satisfy certain estate obligations, including the payment of statutory allowances: Zahn v. Nelson, 2007-Ohio-667, 170 Ohio App. 3d 111, 866 N.E.2d 58, 2007 Ohio App. LEXIS 601 (Ohio Ct. App., Highland County 2007).

Summary judgment was properly granted for the decedent's wife because R.C. 2101.24(B)(1)(b) granted the probate court concurrent jurisdiction with the general division of the court of common pleas to hear and determine any action involving an inter vivos trust, and R.C. 2721.05 permitted any interested person to seek a declaration of rights or legal relations regarding the administration of a trust. Zahn v. Nelson, 2007-Ohio-667, 170 Ohio App. 3d 111, 866 N.E.2d 58, 2007 Ohio App. LEXIS 601 (Ohio Ct. App., Highland County 2007).

Probate court has jurisdiction in an action for declaratory judgment to determine a surviving spouse's right to share in a decedent's estate—not just under the terms of a trust agreement, but also under the terms of a prenuptial agreement. Provisions concerning whether the marital trust A was to be reduced by estate taxes were ambiguous. As used in the trust, "net federal estate tax value" of the marital residence meant one-half of the full value of the residence, minus any encumbrances. Decedent intended the trustee to distribute payments of principal to the surviving spouse without considering any of her other income or resources, and that is the general rule of construction in Ohio: Nat'l City Bank v. de Laville, 2006-Ohio-5909, 170 Ohio App. 3d 317, 867 N.E.2d 416, 2006 Ohio App. LEXIS 5858 (Ohio Ct. App., Lucas County 2006).

Probate courts have jurisdiction over inter vivos trusts: State ex rel. Sladoje v. Belskis, 2002-Ohio-4505, 149 Ohio App. 3d 190, 776 N.E.2d 557, 2002 Ohio App. LEXIS 4638 (Ohio Ct. App., Franklin County 2002).

The probate court had jurisdiction to adjudicate the claims against the trustee by a beneficiary: Bank One Trust Co., N.A. v. Nye, 91 Ohio Misc. 2d 204, 698 N.E.2d 519, 1998 Ohio Misc. LEXIS 27 (Ohio P. Ct. 1998).

Where successive beneficiary questioned a trust transaction, court erred in appointing a "trust advisor" contrary to provisions and intent of trust where less intrusive measures were available, but did not err in appointing a trust investigator: In re Marchin Trust, 1996 Ohio App. LEXIS 1896 (Ohio Ct. App., Trumbull County May 10, 1996).

For a probate court to exercise its subject matter jurisdiction in a proceeding involving a trust and multistate beneficiaries, the court must have jurisdiction over the trust, the trust property or the trust parties. Personal jurisdiction over the beneficiaries is not necessary unless affirmative relief is demanded from them: Galbreath v. Del Valle, 91 Ohio App. 3d 829, 633 N.E.2d 1185, 1993 Ohio App. LEXIS 5671 (Ohio Ct. App., Franklin County 1993), dismissed, 69 Ohio St. 3d 1414, 630 N.E.2d 376, 1994 Ohio LEXIS 836 (Ohio 1994).

The general division of the court of common pleas had jurisdiction to construe the terms of a settlement requiring a trustee to vote for "independent business persons" as directors of a corporation: Sherman v. Fifth Third Bank, 93 Ohio App. 3d 57, 637 N.E.2d 929, 1992 Ohio App. LEXIS 836 (Ohio Ct. App., Montgomery County 1992).

The probate division has no control over the trustees of inter vivos trusts: Schucker v. Metcalf, 22 Ohio St. 3d 33, 488 N.E.2d 210, 1986 Ohio LEXIS 574 (Ohio 1986).

Though the jurisdiction of the probate court in Ohio is limited to testamentary trustees, it does not preclude the court from following the assets of a testamentary trust into an inter vivos trust, in furtherance of its jurisdiction of the testamentary trust, in order to fully dispose of the issues properly before it: (decided under former analogous section) Dollar Sav. & Trust Co. v. First Nat'l Bank, 32 Ohio Misc. 81, 61 Ohio Op. 2d 134, 285 N.E.2d 768, 1972 Ohio Misc. LEXIS 177 (Ohio C.P. 1972).

An action for money damages is not within the jurisdiction of the probate division of the common pleas court, although filed as a counterclaim to an action within the jurisdiction of that division by a trust adviser named in a will being administered under its authority: (decided under former analogous section) Kindt v. Cleveland Trust Co., 26 Ohio Misc. 1, 55 Ohio Op. 2d 53, 266 N.E.2d 84, 1971 Ohio Misc. LEXIS 266 (Ohio C.P. 1971), disapproved, Goff v. Ameritrust Co., N.A., 1994 Ohio App. LEXIS 1916 (Ohio Ct. App., Cuyahoga County May 5, 1994).

Generally, a change in circumstances and the needs of beneficiaries do not justify a court termination of a trust created in a will to meet the change in circumstances and conditions: (decided under former analogous section) Collins v. First Nat'l Bank, 20 Ohio App. 2d 1, 49 Ohio Op. 2d 1, 251 N.E.2d 610, 1969 Ohio App. LEXIS 486 (Ohio Ct. App., Hamilton County 1969).

Where there is no repugnancy in a will creating a trust and it is not against public policy, such trust cannot be judicially terminated before the objects of the trust have been fully accomplished: (decided under former analogous section) Collins v. First Nat'l Bank, 20 Ohio App. 2d 1, 49 Ohio Op. 2d 1, 251 N.E.2d 610, 1969 Ohio App. LEXIS 486 (Ohio Ct. App., Hamilton County 1969).

In ruling on petition, asking for the construction of the terms of a will, probate court has jurisdiction to pass on the question of the validity of an inter vivos trust which petitioner's decedent believed he had created: (decided under former analogous section) Knowles v. Knowles, 4 Ohio Misc. 153, 33 Ohio Op. 2d 218, 212 N.E.2d 88, 1965 Ohio Misc. LEXIS 313 (Ohio P. Ct. 1965).

A probate court does not have jurisdiction of an action in which plaintiff seeks an order that a trustee (not appointed by such court) of an inter vivos trust turn over to plaintiff, the surviving spouse of the deceased settlor, property delivered by the settlor, prior to her death, to, and held by, such trustee: (decided under former analogous section) Purcell v. Cleveland Trust Co., 6 Ohio App. 2d 235, 35 Ohio Op. 2d 426, 217 N.E.2d 876, 1965 Ohio App. LEXIS 462 (Ohio Ct. App., Cuyahoga County 1965).

Under this section, the probate court has jurisdiction to entertain an application by the beneficiary of a testamentary trust to direct and control the conduct of testamentary trustees in the payment, or the withholding of payment, of trust income which is payable to such beneficiary under the will of the decedent: (decided under former analogous section) In re Trust of Gallagher, 118 Ohio App. 477, 25 Ohio Op. 2d 394, 195 N.E.2d 601, 1963 Ohio App. LEXIS 817 (Ohio Ct. App., Mahoning County 1963).

A probate court has jurisdiction to render a declaratory judgment deciding whether or not the beneficiary of an inter vivos trust has capacity to take where that question is interwoven with the administration of the estate: (decided under former analogous section) National City Bank v. Baldwin, 21 Ohio Op. 2d 145, 90 Ohio Law Abs. 228, 1962 Ohio Misc. LEXIS 231 (Ohio P. Ct. 1962).

By virtue of GC § 10501-53 (R.C. 2101.24), and GC § 12102-4 (R.C. 2721.05), one who as trustee under a will and as an individual is interested in a provision of the will authorizing the removal of certain of testator's real estate from the trust and the substitution of a sum of money to take its place may bring and maintain an action for a declaratory judgment in the probate court to secure a determination and declaration as to his obligations as trustee and as an individual with respect to such matter and as to the rights of the trust beneficiaries, where there is a present bona fide dispute between or among those concerned as to the interpretation of the will and doubt exists as to the proper interpretation: (decided under former analogous section) Sessions v. Skelton, 163 Ohio St. 409, 56 Ohio Op. 370, 127 N.E.2d 378, 1955 Ohio LEXIS 565 (Ohio 1955).

Even though the probate court has the power to control the conduct of trustees under this section, ex parte orders without notice are not binding upon the life tenant: (decided under former analogous section) Holmes v. Hrobon, 93 Ohio App. 1, 50 Ohio Op. 178, 103 N.E.2d 845, 61 Ohio Law Abs. 113, 61 Ohio Law Abs. 241, 1951 Ohio App. LEXIS 576 (Ohio Ct. App., Franklin County 1951), aff'd in part and rev'd in part, 158 Ohio St. 508, 49 Ohio Op. 450, 110 N.E.2d 574, 1953 Ohio LEXIS 643 (Ohio 1953).

The grant of exclusive jurisdiction to the probate court by this section, is subject to the general limitation found therein, to wit, "such jurisdiction shall be exclusive in the probate court unless otherwise provided by law": (decided under former analogous section) Haag v. Meffley, 89 Ohio App. 471, 46 Ohio Op. 274, 103 N.E.2d 37, 1951 Ohio App. LEXIS 718 (Ohio Ct. App., Lucas County 1951).

Under Ohio Const. art IV, § 8, and GC §§ 5340 and 10501-53 (R.C. 5731.21 and 2101.24) the probate court is vested with plenary equity jurisdiction to hear and determine an application, filed after term, to modify an order determining inheritance taxes paid through a mistake of fact: (decided under former analogous section) In re Beckman's Estate, 91 Ohio App. 42, 48 Ohio Op. 236, 107 N.E.2d 538, 1951 Ohio App. LEXIS 606 (Ohio Ct. App., Mercer County 1951).

In controlling the administration of a testamentary trust, the probate court, under the jurisdiction vested in it by this section, has the power to determine the validity of a deed obtained from the beneficiary of the trust, where the validity of such conveyance is challenged on the ground of undue influence, mental incapacity or fraud: (decided under former analogous section) In re Stuckey's Will, 80 Ohio App. 421, 36 Ohio Op. 117, 73 N.E.2d 208, 1947 Ohio App. LEXIS 669 (Ohio Ct. App., Madison County 1947).

General Code § 11925 et seq (R.C. 5303.21 et seq) conferred jurisdiction on the court of common pleas to authorize sale of realty held in testamentary trust: (decided under former analogous section) State ex rel. Ehmann v. Schneider, 78 Ohio App. 27, 33 Ohio Op. 391, 67 N.E.2d 117, 45 Ohio Law Abs. 239, 1946 Ohio App. LEXIS 625 (Ohio Ct. App., Hamilton County 1946).

**Voting trust**

A probate court has concurrent jurisdiction with the general division of the court of common pleas over an irrevocable voting trust created pursuant to R.C. 1701.49: In re Lombardo, 1999-Ohio-132, 86 Ohio St. 3d 600, 716 N.E.2d 189, 1999 Ohio LEXIS 2952 (Ohio 1999).

**Will contest**

In a will contest action, the court rejected the will contestant's contention that the probate court erred by ruling on issues of will construction during a will contest action because nothing in R.C. 2101.24 prevents a probate court from construing a will while also determining the validity of a will, and both Civ.R. 18(A) and caselaw indicated that the failure to raise issues of will construction in an action determining the validity of a will acts as res judicata on a later action to construe the will. Thus, the probate court properly determined that res judicata applied to the will contestant's claims in his declaratory judgment action asking that the will be construed, which was brought after summary judgment was granted on the contestant's original will contest action, because the parties and the claims were the same in both actions. Estate of Snell v. Kilburn, 2005-Ohio-7076, 165 Ohio App. 3d 352, 846 N.E.2d 572, 2005 Ohio App. LEXIS 6382 (Ohio Ct. App., Monroe County 2005).

A party to a will contest action does not have the right to a jury trial; instead, a probate court has discretion to determine whether to sit as the trier of fact in a will contest action or to impanel a jury: State ex rel. Kear v. Court of Common Pleas, 67 Ohio St. 2d 189, 21 Ohio Op. 3d 118, 423 N.E.2d 427, 1981 Ohio LEXIS 566 (Ohio 1981).

**Wills**

Will's in terrorem clause did not have the effect of placing an executrix's conduct beyond the reach of the probate court, as a probate court continued to retain the power to supervise a fiduciary's actions, under R.C. 2101.24(A)(1)(m), which included the power to review how the executrix disposed of probate assets. Kasapis v. High Point Furniture Co., 2006-Ohio-255, 2006 Ohio App. LEXIS 211 (Ohio Ct. App., Summit County 2006).

**Workers' compensation settlement**

A settlement of a workers' compensation claim was not a tort claim. Thus the probate court did not have jurisdiction under R.C. 2323.584 to approve a transfer of payment rights: In re Stratcap Invs., Inc., 2003-Ohio-4589, 154 Ohio App. 3d 89, 796 N.E.2d 73, 2003 Ohio App. LEXIS 4081 (Ohio Ct. App., Clark County 2003).

**Wrongful death settlement**

Common pleas court, not the probate court, had jurisdiction over claims for legal malpractice and breach of contract even though they arose from the attorney's representation of the plaintiff in a wrongful death settlement: Buckman-Peirson v. Brannon, 2004-Ohio-6074, 159 Ohio App. 3d 12, 822 N.E.2d 830, 2004 Ohio App. LEXIS 5509 (Ohio Ct. App., Montgomery County 2004).

A probate court exercising jurisdiction granted by R.C. 2125.02(C) to approve a wrongful death settlement by the personal representative of the decedent has limited plenary jurisdiction under R.C. 2101.24 to construe a policy of liability insurance for the purpose of determining the amount of insurance coverage available to settle the wrongful death claim: Burris v. Grange Mut. Cos., 46 Ohio St. 3d 84, 545 N.E.2d 83, 1989 Ohio LEXIS 260 (Ohio 1989), overruled, Savoie v. Grange Mut. Ins. Co., 1993-Ohio-134, 67 Ohio St. 3d 500, 620 N.E.2d 809, 1993 Ohio LEXIS 2047 (Ohio 1993).

# CHAPTER 2103

# DOWER

Section



## § 2103.01 "Property" construed.

As used in sections 2103.01 to 2103.09 of the Revised Code, unless the context shows that another sense is intended, "property" includes real property and money, choses in action, evidences of debt, and other personal property.

**HISTORY:**

GC § 10502-9; 114 v 320(339); Bureau of Code Revision. Eff 10-1-53; 2011 SB 124, § 1, eff. Jan. 13, 2012.

**Editor's Notes**

Acts 2011, SB 124, § 3 provides: "The provisions of this act that relate to the estates of decedents apply to the estates of decedents who die on or after the effective date of this act."

**Amendment Notes**

The 2011 amendment added "As used"; deleted "inclusive" following "to 2103.09"; substituted "real property" for "lands, tenements, hereditaments"; deleted "chattels" following "money"; added "and other personal property" to the end; and made related and stylistic changes.

### RESEARCH REFERENCES AND PRACTICE AIDS

**Cross-References to Related Sections**

Application for registration of land titles on death of registered owner, RC § 5309.45.

Dower, RC § 2103.02.

Estate by curtesy abolished, RC § 2103.09.

Legal disability defined, RC § 2131.02.

Rights as to shares in corporation, RC § 2109.29.

Rights of surviving spouses, RC § 2106.01 et seq.

Rules and procedure of court of common pleas to govern, RC § 2101.32.

## § 2103.02 Dower.

A spouse who has not relinquished or been barred from it shall be endowed of an estate for life in one third of the real property of which the consort was seized as an estate of inheritance at any time during the marriage. Such dower interest shall terminate upon the death of the consort except:

(A) To the extent that any such real property was conveyed by the deceased consort during the marriage, the surviving spouse not having relinquished or been barred from dower therein;

(B) To the extent that any such real property during the marriage was encumbered by the deceased consort by mortgage, judgment, lien, except tax lien, or aliened by involuntary sale, the surviving spouse not having relinquished or been barred from dower therein. If such real property was encumbered or aliened prior to decease, the dower interest of the surviving spouse therein shall be computed on the basis of the amount of the encumbrance at the time of the death of such consort or at the time of such alienation, but not upon an amount exceeding the sale price of such property.

In lieu of such dower interest which terminates pursuant to this section, a surviving spouse shall be entitled to the distributive share provided by section 2105.06 of the Revised Code.

Dower interest shall terminate upon the granting of an absolute divorce in favor of or against such spouse by a court of competent jurisdiction within or without this state.

Wherever dower is referred to in Chapters 2101. to 2131., inclusive, of the Revised Code, it means the dower to which a spouse is entitled by this section.

**HISTORY:**

GC § 10502-1; 114 v 320(337); 116 v 385; Bureau of Code Revision, 10-1-53; 125 v 903(962). Eff 10-1-53.

### NOTES TO DECISIONS

Analysis

Generally
Bankruptcy
Conveyance prior to marriage
Dower interest
Evidence
Foreclosure
Forfeited property
Inchoate Nature
Interest denied
Marital residence
Partition
Release
Summary judgment

**Generally**

Ohio legislature in 1999 changed the actuarial tables to which courts had to look when calculating the present value of an inchoate dower interest—from the American Experience Table to the IRS Tables—but did not otherwise overrule the methodology for calculating the present value of an inchoate dower interest, which requires that the ages of both spouses be considered when calculating the present value of an inchoate dower interest. Drown v. JPMorgan Chase Bank, N.A. (In re Barnhart), 447 B.R. 551, 2011 Bankr. LEXIS 1002 (Bankr. S.D. Ohio 2011).

Release of a dower interest in a mortgage does not inure to the benefit of the owner-spouse's subsequent judgment creditors. The release only subordinates the dower interest to the mortgage interest. In a judicial sale, the present value of a dower interest is to be determined from an applicable IRS table: Stand Energy Corp. v. Epler, 2005-Ohio-4820, 163 Ohio App. 3d 354, 837 N.E.2d 1229, 2005 Ohio App. LEXIS 4348 (Ohio Ct. App., Franklin County 2005).

During the lifetime of both spouses, dower is a contingent inchoate right that becomes vested in the surviving spouse only upon the death of the other spouse: Short v. Conn, 1994 Ohio App. LEXIS 312 (Ohio Ct. App., Jackson County Jan. 25, 1994), dismissed, 69 Ohio St. 3d 1477, 634 N.E.2d 1023, 1994 Ohio LEXIS 1389 (Ohio 1994).

By incorporating in the first sentence of GC § 10502-1, and again in R.C. 2103.02, the same definition of dower which was included in the previous dower statute, GC § 8606, and earlier statutes, the legislature must have intended that inchoate dower should be limited in accordance with such definition: Central Trust Co. v. Gilardi, 21 Ohio Op. 2d 183, 186 N.E.2d 771 (Ohio C.P. 1962).

Inchoate right of dower is a contingent interest in the land of a consort, is of substantial value, and cannot be barred by any act of the consort: Grundstein v. Suburban Motor Freight, Inc., 92 Ohio App. 181, 49 Ohio Op. 312, 107 N.E.2d 368, 62 Ohio Law Abs. 252, 1952 Ohio App. LEXIS 703 (Ohio Ct. App., Franklin County 1952).

Dower is a creature of statute, is founded on reasons of public policy and is subject, while it remains inchoate, to such modifications and qualifications as legislative authority, for like reasons of public policy, may see proper to impose: Goodman v. Gerstle, 158 Ohio St. 353, 49 Ohio Op. 235, 109 N.E.2d 489, 1952 Ohio LEXIS 487 (Ohio 1952).

Although inchoate right of dower becomes choate only upon the death of a spouse, such right may be protected by a court in a judicial sale of real estate by sequestering from the proceeds of the sale, pending the determination of the contingency of such right, an amount equal in value to the calculated value of such dower interest: Liberty Folder Co. v. Anderson, 86 Ohio App. 433, 42 Ohio Op. 23, 90 N.E.2d 408, 55 Ohio Law Abs. 388, 1949 Ohio App. LEXIS 720 (Ohio Ct. App., Shelby County 1949).

The enactment of this section virtually abolished all vested dower except: (a) in such real estate conveyed during coverture without the spouse joining in the deed, (b) to the extent that such real property during coverture was encumbered by mortgage without the spouse joining in the mortgage or by judgment lien without the surviving spouse having relinquished, or being barred of, dower, and (c) to such real property alienated during coverture by judicial or other involuntary sale, the surviving spouse not having relinquished or having been barred of dower: Liberty Folder Co. v. Anderson, 86 Ohio App. 433, 42 Ohio Op. 23, 90 N.E.2d 408, 55 Ohio Law Abs. 388, 1949 Ohio App. LEXIS 720 (Ohio Ct. App., Shelby County 1949).

If the first donee dies survived by a widow and heirs of his body, and has not so aliened or encumbered his estate as to bring the case within the exceptions to the barring of dower as set out in this section, then by the provision of the statute the right to dower terminates upon his death: Miller v. Miller, 41 Ohio Op. 233, 83 N.E.2d 254, 52 Ohio Law Abs. 121, 1948 Ohio Misc. LEXIS 237 (Ohio C.P. 1948).

This section and GC § 10502-6 (R.C. 2103.06) provide the only statutory limitations against a husband disposing of his real property during his lifetime without the consent of his wife. A wife's right to her distributive share and that portion of the estate exempt from administration and a year's allowance, do not come into existence until the death of the husband and therefore any transfer of the property of the husband during his lifetime will be free of such claims: Neville v. Sawicki, 44 Ohio L. Ab. 408, 64 N.E.2d 685 (App 1945), affirmed 146 Ohio St. 539, 33 Ohio Op. 19, 67 N.E.2d 323.].

A vested dower right in real estate is a personal right which must be asserted during the life of the owner and no right thereto survives unless an action to have it assigned is commenced during that life: Dick v. Bauman, 73 Ohio App. 107, 28 Ohio Op. 176, 55 N.E.2d 137, 1943 Ohio App. LEXIS 669 (Ohio Ct. App., Sandusky County 1943).

Where the first donee in fee tail leaves no heir of his body, that issue having predeceased him leaving a widow and two children, such widow is not entitled to her share in lieu of dower under this section as the surviving spouse of the deceased son: Mays v. Mays, 42 N.E.2d 446, 37 Ohio Law Abs. 102, 1942 Ohio App. LEXIS 871 (Ohio Ct. App. 1942).

This section provides for inchoate but not vested dower, thereby abolishing the latter: Geiselman v. Wise, 137 Ohio St. 93, 17 Ohio Op. 430, 28 N.E.2d 199, 1940 Ohio LEXIS 426 (Ohio 1940).

An inchoate right of dower cannot be reached by a creditor's bill: Geiselman v. Wise, 137 Ohio St. 93, 17 Ohio Op. 430, 28 N.E.2d 199, 1940 Ohio LEXIS 426 (Ohio 1940).

A surviving spouse, having only a consummate dower right, is not entitled to possession, rents, profits, or right of entry on the premises of the deceased spouse until dower has been ascertained and set off to him: Huffman v. Huffman, 57 Ohio App. 33, 10 Ohio Op. 24, 11 N.E.2d 271, 25 Ohio Law Abs. 5, 1937 Ohio App. LEXIS 291 (Ohio Ct. App. 1937).

**Bankruptcy**

Husband and wife who declared Chapter 7 bankruptcy shortly after the wife's mother died intestate were allowed to claim a homestead exemption under Ohio Rev. Code Ann. § 2329.66 in a house the wife's mother owned at the time she died because they lived in the house, the wife acquired her mother's fee simple interest in the house upon her mother's death, pursuant to Ohio Rev. Code Ann. § 2105.06, even without the commencement of probate proceedings, and the husband had a dower interest in the property under Ohio Rev. Code Ann. § 2103.02. In re Pugh, 2015 Bankr. LEXIS 2911 (Bankr. N.D. Ohio Aug. 31, 2015).

Court used an Internal Revenue Service actuarial table to determine that debtor's dower interest in his residence was $ 24,511.09, and because literal application of the 11 U.S.C.S. § 522(f)(2)(A) formula in a situation where the debtor had only a fractional interest in the property would have produced an unreasonably high impairment, the court considered the portion of the debt the mortgage secured attributable to the debtor's share of the property, in place of the total debt secured by the mortgage, and determined that $ 7,309.56 of the creditor's lien was left unavoided under 11 U.S.C.S. § 522(f). In re Morrow, 2009 Bankr. LEXIS 1505 (Bankr. N.D. Ohio Feb. 12, 2009).

Debtor wife could not avoid creditors' lien on her residence under 11 U.S.C.S. § 522(f). When the creditors converted their certificate of judgment into a lien on the property under R.C. 2329.02, the husband had a fee simple interest in the property and the wife had a dower right in the property under Ohio Rev. Code Ann. § 2103.02; when the husband transferred the property to the wife, she took the property encumbered by the creditors' lien, and the creditors did nothing that "fixed" the lien on her interest. In re Jaber, 406 B.R. 756, 2009 Bankr. LEXIS 1289 (Bankr. N.D. Ohio 2009).

Once the spouse's bankruptcy case was terminated, his dower interest reverted to him as if no bankruptcy had ever been filed. His conveyance of dower rights through signing the mortgage thus became effective with the close of the bankruptcy case: Std. Fed. Bank v. Staff, 2006-Ohio-3601, 168 Ohio App. 3d 14, 857 N.E.2d 1245, 2006 Ohio App. LEXIS 3544 (Ohio Ct. App., Hamilton County 2006).

Bankruptcy debtors improperly included a dower interest in aggregating liens to support avoidance of a judicial lien under 11 U.S.C.S. § 522(f) as impairing the debtors' exemptions in their residence, since the dower interest was an interest in property rather than a lien under R.C. 2103.02, and it was irrelevant that the dower interest had priority over judicial liens in state foreclosure proceedings. In re Rudicil, 343 B.R. 181, 2006 Bankr. LEXIS 1023 (Bankr. S.D. Ohio 2006).

**Conveyance prior to marriage**

Vacation cottage was not marital property subject to a dower interest even though the cottage was titled in the decedent's name when he died, as the decedent's dissolution decree with his ex-wife clearly provided that the cottage was to be conveyed to a living trust to ensure that it would remain in the family for use by the decedent, his ex-wife, and their children and grandchildren regardless of any remarriage by the decedent; the decree ordered that the children would be the only remaindermen of the living trust upon the decedent's death, the living trust's terms did not allow for the trust to be terminated during the decedent's lifetime and no agreement to terminate was ever reached between the decedent, his ex-wife, and the children. Jamison v. Jamison, 2018-Ohio-1626, 2018 Ohio App. LEXIS 1767 (Ohio Ct. App., Cuyahoga County 2018).

A conveyance of realty to children of a former marriage, without consideration other than love and affection, by a man engaged to be married, without disclosure of the conveyance to his intended wife whom he later marries, does not defraud her of her right of dower, provided for in R.C. 2103.02: Perlberg v. Perlberg, 18 Ohio St. 2d 55, 47 Ohio Op. 2d 167, 247 N.E.2d 306, 1969 Ohio LEXIS 364 (Ohio 1969).

**Dower interest**

Borrower's right to dower never vested and, thus, the borrower did not lose the right to an interest in her spouse's property; any right to dower which could arguably have applied had terminated since divorce barred an ex-spouse from any dower right. Cianfaglione v. Lake Nat'l Bank, 2019-Ohio-1299, 134 N.E.3d 661, 2019 Ohio App. LEXIS 1396 (Ohio Ct. App., Lake County 2019).

Former wife had no interest in a foreclosure action and had no right to any of the proceeds resulting from the foreclosure because the dissolution of her marriage meant that she had lost her dower right in the mortgaged property. Wells Fargo Bank, N.A. v. Kessler, 2015-Ohio-5085, 2015 Ohio App. LEXIS 4918 (Ohio Ct. App., Franklin County 2015).

Husband had no dower rights when the buyers bought the property as his dower rights were extinguished when he and his wife were divorced in Hungary; the buyers were bona fide purchasers as they bought the property free of any prior dower interest since the husband and the wife had divorced, and there was no evidence that the buyers were aware of the alleged oral agreement requiring the wife to reconvey the property to the husband upon his demand. Soley v. Soley, 2014-Ohio-3965, 2014 Ohio App. LEXIS 3874 (Ohio Ct. App., Huron County 2014).

Although a property owner initially had a dower interest in the property because the owner was married to the owner's former spouse at the time the former spouse executed the mortgage, a final decree of dissolution was entered, which ultimately terminated any dower interest which the owner had in the property, pursuant to R.C. 2103.02 and 3105.65(B). United States Bank, N.A. v. Fitzgerrel, 2012-Ohio-4522, 2012 Ohio App. LEXIS 3983 (Ohio Ct. App., Clermont County 2012).

No sale of condominium property took place for purposes of a declaration and bylaws, or for purposes of the Ohio Condominium Act, R.C. ch. 5311, when a dentist conveyed the dentist's office unit in a professional office building by way of a quit-claim deed, with a transfer-on-death provision, to the dentist's wife because the dentist conveyed the dentist's fee simple interest to the dentist's wife after signing the condominium documents. The dentist, under R.C. 2103.02, retained a dower interest in the property, which was an estate for life in one-third of the property, and was not a legal interest, as the dentist's wife held full legal title to the property. DiPasquale v. Costas, 2010-Ohio-832, 186 Ohio App. 3d 121, 926 N.E.2d 682, 2010 Ohio App. LEXIS 676 (Ohio Ct. App., Montgomery County 2010).

Although the marital status of grantors in a deed was not set forth, the deed was not rendered invalid and further, even if a dower interest remained, such an interest was one for life and would have terminated with the death of the grantors' wives pursuant to R.C. 2103.02, such that it would not have interfered with a quiet title claim between adjacent property owners regarding the existence and validity of an easement; there was no evidence that any of the wives were still living in order to preclude summary judgment. Penn v. Esham, 2008-Ohio-3695, 177 Ohio App. 3d 201, 894 N.E.2d 131, 2008 Ohio App. LEXIS 3121 (Ohio Ct. App., Scioto County 2008).

Although a husband was involved in bankruptcy when he signed a mortgage with a mortgagee bank over real property, his claim that after the termination of the bankruptcy he still had his dower interest under R.C. 2103.02, for which he claimed he was owed payment prior to the mortgagee's collection from a foreclosure judgment of the amount due it under the mortgage, lacked merit; the interest was deemed abandoned under 11 U.S.C.S. § 554 and upon termination of the bankruptcy, it reverted to the husband and the mortgage that he signed conveying his interest became effective. Std. Fed. Bank v. Staff, 2006-Ohio-3601, 168 Ohio App. 3d 14, 857 N.E.2d 1245, 2006 Ohio App. LEXIS 3544 (Ohio Ct. App., Hamilton County 2006).

Bankruptcy debtors improperly included a dower interest in aggregating liens to support avoidance of a judicial lien under 11 U.S.C.S. § 522(f) as impairing the debtors' exemptions in their residence, since the dower interest was an interest in property rather than a lien under R.C. 2103.02, and it was irrelevant that the dower interest had priority over judicial liens in state foreclosure proceedings. In re Rudicil, 343 B.R. 181, 2006 Bankr. LEXIS 1023 (Bankr. S.D. Ohio 2006).

**Evidence**

Trial court's award of dower under R.C. 2103.02 based on the full amount of a mortgage interest on the property was supported by the evidence; the widow had not released her dower, the mortgage had not been released or satisfied, and there was no evidence that the amount of the mortgage had ever been reduced. Cunningham v. Shaffernocker, 2008-Ohio-7015, 2008 Ohio App. LEXIS 5871 (Ohio Ct. App., Stark County 2008).

**Foreclosure**

Lender's mortgage had priority over a wife's dower interest in foreclosure proceedings because the mortgage was granted to the wife's in-laws years before the wife received her dower interest, and, as such, the wife inherited her dower interest subject to the mortgage; the mortgage was issued in 2007 and the wife received her dower interest when her husband inherited title to the property in 2013. GE Credit Union v. Medow, 2016-Ohio-3266, 54 N.E.3d 1281, 2016 Ohio App. LEXIS 2128 (Ohio Ct. App., Hamilton County 2016).

Mortgage agreement was upheld because, although the husband did not sign the note and was not listed as a Borrower/Mortgagor on the first page of the mortgage, a paragraph of the mortgage made clear that a "Borrower" who signed the mortgage instrument, but did not execute the note, mortgaged the borrower's interest in the property without assuming liability for repayment of the debt. Furthermore, the husband initialed the pates of the mortgage and signed below the wife's name as a "Borrower," and there was no mention in the mortgage about the release of dower rights, nor was there any provision that suggested that the husband signed the mortgage for a purpose other than to mortgage the husband's interest in the property. SFJV 2005, LLC v. Ream, 2010-Ohio-1615, 187 Ohio App. 3d 715, 933 N.E.2d 819, 2010 Ohio App. LEXIS 1330 (Ohio Ct. App., Champaign County 2010).

Where the debtor wife of the mortgagor held an unreleased dower interest, under R.C. 2103.02, in the real property of the debtor husband, which predated the purchase money mortgage of the creditor, the dower interest had priority. Its value was to be determined under R.C. 2103.041. In re Rosario, 402 B.R. 223, 2009 Bankr. LEXIS 578 (Bankr. N.D. Ohio 2009).

In a foreclosure case, a mortgage was subject to the mortgagor's spouse's dower interest because the mortgagor was married to the spouse at the time of the execution of the mortgage, and the spouse did not join in the execution of the mortgage. Deutsche Bank Trust Co. Ams. v. Smith, 2008-Ohio-2778, 2008 Ohio App. LEXIS 2352 (Ohio Ct. App., Cuyahoga County 2008).

When a widower inherited property concerning which the widower's deceased spouse had granted a mortgage, the widower no longer had a dower interest in the property because that interest was extinguished when fee simple title was transferred to the widower because the dower interest merged into the fee simple title, so that interest did not have to be disposed of pursuant to R.C. 2103.041 when the mortgage was foreclosed on. First Bank Nat'l Ass'n v. Parker, 2007-Ohio-3066, 2007 Ohio App. LEXIS 2810 (Ohio Ct. App., Cuyahoga County 2007).

When a widower had not signed a mortgage granted by the widower's deceased spouse regarding property to which the spouse had fee simple title, the widower's dower interest in the property did not cause the mortgage not to be fully secured because the dower interest (1) could not be used to borrow money, (2) was personal, and (3) was not transferable. First Bank Nat'l Ass'n v. Parker, 2007-Ohio-3066, 2007 Ohio App. LEXIS 2810 (Ohio Ct. App., Cuyahoga County 2007).

The inchoate dower interest of a wife in real estate which was owned by her husband prior to a sheriff's sale in a foreclosure action must be computed on the surplus remaining after the satisfaction of the mortgage and payment of court costs and real estate taxes: Central Trust Co. v. Gilardi, 21 Ohio Op. 2d 183, 186 N.E.2d 771 (Ohio C.P. 1962).

**Forfeited property**

A spouse does not have dower rights in realty forfeited to the state due to a corrupt activity offense by the other spouse: State v. Thrower, 81 Ohio App. 3d 15, 610 N.E.2d 433, 1991 Ohio App. LEXIS 2495 (Ohio Ct. App., Summit County 1991).

**Inchoate Nature**

Wife's dower Interest, although technically vested in her as soon as her husband obtained title to the property at issue during their marriage, would remain inchoate for the balance of the husband's life. Drown v. JPMorgan Chase Bank, N.A. (In re Barnhart), 447 B.R. 551, 2011 Bankr. LEXIS 1002 (Bankr. S.D. Ohio 2011).

**Interest denied**

Probate court properly determined that a widow was not entitled to a dower interest pursuant to R.C. 2103.02 in property owned by her late husband where neither of the statutory circumstances existed; instead, she was properly provided with her distributive share under the statute of descent and distribution, R.C. 2105.06(D). In re Estate of French, 2011-Ohio-422, 2011 Ohio App. LEXIS 342 (Ohio Ct. App., Carroll County 2011).

**Marital residence**

Where the decedent conveyed his one-half interest in the marital residence without his spouse's consent, she was entitled to both that dower interest and a statutory distributive share of the rest of his estate: Armstrong v. Armstrong, 128 Ohio App. 3d 393, 715 N.E.2d 207, 1998 Ohio App. LEXIS 2705 (Ohio Ct. App., Wayne County), dismissed, State v. Jackson, 83 Ohio St. 3d 1446, 700 N.E.2d 330, 1998 Ohio LEXIS 2829 (Ohio 1998).

**Partition**

The spouse of a co-tenant is neither a necessary nor a proper party in an action in partition between co-tenants: Dunkle v. Dunkle, 2 Ohio Op. 2d 399, 137 N.E.2d 170, 73 Ohio Law Abs. 477, 1956 Ohio Misc. LEXIS 317 (Ohio C.P. 1956).

**Release**

Wife who signed three mortgages to secure promissory notes her husband signed relinquished dower interests she had under R.C. 2103.02 in three parcels of real property to the mortgagees when she joined her husband in signing the mortgages, even though she did not sign the notes. The bankruptcy court found that the Ohio Supreme Court, if faced with the issue, would have concluded that where a mortgage was properly signed, acknowledged, and certified as provided in R.C. 5301.01, no specific reference to "dower" in the mortgage was required to relinquish a dower interest in favor of the mortgagee, and language in the mortgages and riders the wife signed clearly and unambiguously provided that the wife was a "borrower" and was bound by the terms of mortgages and the riders. Nelson v. Countrywide Home Loans (In re Barger), 490 B.R. 744, 2012 Bankr. LEXIS 3044 (Bankr. S.D. Ohio 2012).

A dower interest was not released where it was not specifically released in the security agreement or the record: Ogan v. Ogan, 122 Ohio App. 3d 580, 702 N.E.2d 472, 1997 Ohio App. LEXIS 4021 (Ohio Ct. App., Fayette County 1997).

**Summary judgment**

Trial court properly denied the bank's motion for summary judgment because the bank failed to meet its initial Dresher burden of establishing the absence of a question of fact as to its claim for an equitable mortgage on the wife's dower interest; the owner's marriage to the wife predated the 2006 refinancing, to which the wife was not a party, and thus as to the couple, the bank was not a common creditor. Also, the bank failed to set forth any action of the wife warranting imposing an equitable lien on her interests and a question of material fact existed as to whether the bank's loss of priority was due to its own actions. BankUnited, F.S.B. v. Klug, 2013-Ohio-1599, 2013 Ohio App. LEXIS 1490 (Ohio Ct. App., Lorain County 2013).

Summary judgment to a decedent's estate administrator was error in her action against a property transferee, alleging that the decedent's real property was improperly transferred to the transferee, as genuine issues of material fact existed as to the validity of the real property transfer and whether it was subject to a dower right of the decedent's estranged wife under R.C. 2103.02 and 2103.05. Reigles v. Urban, 2010-Ohio-4427, 2010 Ohio App. LEXIS 3772 (Ohio Ct. App., Lake County 2010).

## RESEARCH REFERENCES AND PRACTICE AIDS

**Cross-References to Related Sections**

Action for dower not abated by death, RC § 2311.22.
Additional rights of surviving spouse, RC § 2106.24.
Assignment of dower, RC § 5305.01 et seq.
Conveyance in lieu of dower, RC § 2103.03.
Court may correct errors in deed, RC § 2719.06.
Court may order sale of mortgaged real property, RC § 1313.29 et seq.
Deeds; mortgages, RC § 5302.05 et seq.
Divorce, effect of, RC § 3105.10.
Separation agreement, RC § 3105.65.
Election to take under will, RC § 2106.05.
Estate by curtesy abolished, RC § 2103.09.
Execution of rights not to affect, RC § 2329.83.
Fees —
Commissioner, RC § 2335.01.
Sheriff, RC § 311.21.
Foreclosure; finding; sale, RC § 5721.19.
Interest in the property of the other, RC § 3103.04.
Partition proceedings, RC § 5307.17.
Set off, RC § 5307.18.

Probate court, jurisdiction over, RC § 2101.24.
Property construed, RC § 2103.01.
Registered land, attachment to, RC §§ 5309.70, 5309.85.
Sale by executor, etc., free of dower, RC §§ 2127.16, 2127.30.
Sale by guardian, compromise of, RC §§ 2111.21, 2111.28.
Taxes, forfeiture on failure to pay, RC §§ 323.41, 323.44.
Validity of instruments, RC § 5301.07.1.
Waste bars dower, RC § 2103.07.

**Comparative Legislation**
Dower:
CA—Cal Prob Code § 6412
FL—Fla. Stat. § 732.111
IL—755 Ill. Comp. Stat. § 5/2-9
IN—Burns Ind. Code Ann. § 29-1-2-11
KY—KRS § 392.020
MI—MCLS § 558.1
NY—NY CLS RPAPL § 1001
PA—20 P.S. § 2105



**Practice Manuals and Treatises**
Anderson's Ohio Residential Real Estate Manual § 9.08 Interest conveyed
Anderson's Ohio Probate Practice and Procedure Form 19.24 Answer of spouse of decedent consenting to sale free of dower
Anderson's Ohio Probate Practice and Procedure Form 19.78 Release of dower

**Practice Guides**
Anderson's Ohio Probate Practice and Procedure § 15.04 Remaining in the mansion house
Anderson's Ohio Probate Practice and Procedure § 58.03 Calculation of contingent dower interests

**Practice Forms**
Release of dower, Couse's Ohio Form Book Form 30.31

## § 2103.021 When affidavit required to preserve dower.

Whenever "trustee," "as trustee," or "agent" follows the name of the grantee in any deed of conveyance of land recorded in this state and no other instrument containing a description of such land has been recorded in the office of the recorder of the county in which such land is situated which puts upon inquiry any person dealing with such land that a spouse of such grantee would have a dower interest in such land, a conveyance of such land by such grantee to a bona fide purchaser conveys a title free from the claims of any spouse of such grantee in such land, for dower, inchoate, or otherwise, unless such spouse, prior to the recording of such conveyance by such grantee to said purchaser, has recorded in the office of the recorder of the county in which the land is situated an affidavit describing such land and setting forth the nature of such spouse's interest in such land.

**HISTORY:**
129 v 339. Eff 10-17-61.

### RESEARCH REFERENCES AND PRACTICE AIDS

**Practice Manuals and Treatises**
Anderson's Ohio Residential Real Estate Manual § 9.08 Interest conveyed
Anderson's Ohio Probate Practice and Procedure Form 19.79 Affidavit to preserve dower

## § 2103.03 Conveyance in lieu of dower.

If accepted by the grantee, the conveyance of an estate or interest in real property in lieu of dower, to take effect on the death of the grantor, will bar such grantee's right of dower in the real property of the grantor. If the conveyance was made when the grantee was a minor or during the marriage, the grantee may waive title to such real property and demand dower.

When a conveyance which is intended to be in lieu of dower fails through any defect to be a bar thereto, and the widow or widower availing of such defect demands dower, the estate or interest conveyed to such widow or widower shall cease.

**HISTORY:**
GC § 10502-2; 114 v 320(338); Bureau of Code Revision. Eff 10-1-53.

### RESEARCH REFERENCES AND PRACTICE AIDS

**Comparative Legislation**
Conveyance in lieu of dower:
IL—755 Ill. Comp. Stat. § 5/2-9
IN—Burns Ind. Code Ann. §§ 29-1-2-3.1, 29-1-2-11
KY—KRS § 392.120
NY—NY CLS RPAPL § 1002

**Practice Guides**
Anderson's Ohio Probate Practice and Procedure § 58.01 General

**Practice Forms**
Proposed Distribution in Application to Relieve Estate from Administration Where Assets Insufficient to Pay Creditors in Full C Butler County Form 465, 11 OH Forms of Pleading & Practice — Probate Form 2:1G

## § 2103.04 Eviction from premises conveyed in lieu of dower.

A widow or widower lawfully evicted from real property conveyed in lieu of dower, or any part thereof, shall be endowed with as much of the residue of the real property of the deceased consort as will equal that from which such widow or widower is evicted.

**HISTORY:**
GC § 10502-4; 114 v 320(338); Bureau of Code Revision. Eff 10-1-53.

## § 2103.041 Judicial sale of dower interest.

In any action involving the judicial sale of real property for the purpose of satisfying the claims of creditors of an owner of an interest in the property, the spouse of the owner may be made a party to the action, and the dower interest of the spouse, whether inchoate or otherwise, may be subjected to the sale without the consent of the spouse. The court shall determine the present value and priority of the dower interest in accordance with section 2131.01 of the Revised Code and shall award the spouse a sum of money equal to the present value of the dower interest, to be paid out of the proceeds of the sale according to the priority of the interest. To the extent that the owner and the owner's spouse are both liable for the indebtedness, the dower interest of the spouse is subordinate to the claims of their common creditors.

**HISTORY:**
137 v S 161 (Eff 11-16-77); 148 v H 59. Eff 10-29-99.

### NOTES TO DECISIONS

Analysis



**Generally**
Ohio legislature in 1999 changed the actuarial tables to which courts had to look when calculating the present value of an inchoate dower interest—from the American Experience Table to the IRS Tables—but did not otherwise overrule the methodology for calculating the present value of an inchoate dower interest, which requires that the ages of both spouses be considered when calculating the present value of an inchoate dower interest. Drown v. JPMorgan Chase Bank, N.A. (In re Barnhart), 447 B.R. 551, 2011 Bankr. LEXIS 1002 (Bankr. S.D. Ohio 2011).

In a foreclosure case, the mortgagor's spouse's dower interest in the subject property was not extinguished when the spouse did not file an answer or otherwise respond to the complaint because the language of R.C. 2103.041 did not require a spouse to assert a dower interest, be it inchoate or vested, and stated that the dower interest, be it inchoate or vested, could be subject to sale without the consent of the spouse, alleviating any need to join an unknown or known spouse, but it did not state that the dower interest, if extinguished with or without the consent of the spouse, could be subject to sale. Deutsche Bank Trust Co. Ams. v. Smith, 2008-Ohio-2778, 2008 Ohio App. LEXIS 2352 (Ohio Ct. App., Cuyahoga County 2008).

In a foreclosure case, the mortgagor's spouse's dower interest in the subject property was not extinguished when the spouse did not file an answer or otherwise respond to the complaint because the spouse's failure to release that interest when the mortgagor encumbered the property left the property subject to an outstanding, inchoate, interest, which vested upon the mortgagor's death and became a one-third life interest in the realty. Deutsche Bank Trust Co. Ams. v. Smith, 2008-Ohio-2778, 2008 Ohio App. LEXIS 2352 (Ohio Ct. App., Cuyahoga County 2008).

Release of a dower interest in a mortgage does not inure to the benefit of the owner-spouse's subsequent judgment creditors. The release only subordinates the dower interest to the mortgage interest. In a judicial sale, the present value of a dower interest is to be determined from an applicable IRS table: Stand Energy Corp. v. Epler, 2005-Ohio-4820, 163 Ohio App. 3d 354, 837 N.E.2d 1229, 2005 Ohio App. LEXIS 4348 (Ohio Ct. App., Franklin County 2005).

**Bankruptcy**

Court used an Internal Revenue Service actuarial table to determine that debtor's dower interest in his residence was $ 24,511.09, and because literal application of the 11 U.S.C.S. § 522(f)(2)(A) formula in a situation where the debtor had only a fractional interest in the property would have produced an unreasonably high impairment, the court considered the portion of the debt the mortgage secured attributable to the debtor's share of the property, in place of the total debt secured by the mortgage, and determined that $ 7,309.56 of the creditor's lien was left unavoided under 11 U.S.C.S. § 522(f). In re Morrow, 2009 Bankr. LEXIS 1505 (Bankr. N.D. Ohio Feb. 12, 2009).

Where the debtor wife of the mortgagor held an unreleased dower interest, under R.C. 2103.02, in the real property of the debtor husband, which predated the purchase money mortgage of the creditor, the dower interest had priority. Its value was to be determined under R.C. 2103.041. In re Rosario, 402 B.R. 223, 2009 Bankr. LEXIS 578 (Bankr. N.D. Ohio 2009).

Bankruptcy debtors improperly included a dower interest in aggregating liens to support avoidance of a judicial lien under 11 U.S.C.S. § 522(f) as impairing the debtors' exemptions in their residence, since the dower interest was an interest in property rather than a lien, and it was irrelevant that the dower interest had priority over judicial liens in state foreclosure proceedings under R.C. 2103.0241. In re Rudicil, 343 B.R. 181, 2006 Bankr. LEXIS 1023 (Bankr. S.D. Ohio 2006).

When a widower inherited property concerning which the widower's deceased spouse had granted a mortgage, the widower no longer had a dower interest in the property because that interest was extinguished when fee simple title was transferred to the widower because the dower interest merged into the fee simple title, so that interest did not have to be disposed of pursuant to R.C. 2103.041 when the mortgage was foreclosed on. First Bank Nat'l Ass'n v. Parker, 2007-Ohio-3066, 2007 Ohio App. LEXIS 2810 (Ohio Ct. App., Cuyahoga County 2007).

Where debtor wife had an inchoate dower interest in her co-debtor husband's real property, consistent with long-standing state law, the ages of both spouses, not just the age of the wife, had to be considered when calculating the present value of the inchoate dower interest. Drown v. JPMorgan Chase Bank, N.A. (In re Barnhart), 447 B.R. 551, 2011 Bankr. LEXIS 1002 (Bankr. S.D. Ohio 2011).

**Fair market value**

Although the extent of the deceased husband's ownership over the property was complicated by a mortgage, because he owned, or was "seised" of, the entire property during his marriage to the wife, the value of her dower interest had to be determined from the entire fair market value of the property, not the fair market value minus the mortgage interest, pursuant to R.C. 2103.041. Stand Energy Corp. v. Epler, 2005-Ohio-4820, 163 Ohio App. 3d 354, 837 N.E.2d 1229, 2005 Ohio App. LEXIS 4348 (Ohio Ct. App., Franklin County 2005).

**Foreclosure**

Lender was not required to join the borrower's wife in a collateral foreclosure proceeding to determine her dower interest in the subject real property because the wife's dower interest was acquired after the borrower entered into the purchase-money mortgage, the wife's rights were subordinate to the lender's mortgage lien, and the sale of the property generated no surplus after the payoff of the mortgage; thus, the trial court did not err in granting the lender's motion to quiet title. Jackson v. Moissis, 2017-Ohio-1000, 87 N.E.3d 591, 2017 Ohio App. LEXIS 954 (Ohio Ct. App., Geauga County 2017).

Lender's mortgage had priority over a wife's dower interest in foreclosure proceedings because the mortgage was granted to the wife's in-laws years before the wife received her dower interest, and, as such, the wife inherited her dower interest subject to the mortgage; the mortgage was issued in 2007 and the wife received her dower interest when her husband inherited title to the property in 2013. GE Credit Union v. Medow, 2016-Ohio-3266, 54 N.E.3d 1281, 2016 Ohio App. LEXIS 2128 (Ohio Ct. App., Hamilton County 2016).

In a foreclosure action, a wife's counterclaim regarding the establishment of a dower interest failed to state a claim under Civ.R. 12(B)(6) because the claim was devoid of any factual averments; the wife failed to set forth any allegations to suggest that she was entitled to judgment against an assignee under any particular theory of recovery. BAC Home Loans Servicing, LP v. Kolenich, 2011-Ohio-3345, 194 Ohio App. 3d 777, 958 N.E.2d 194, 2011 Ohio App. LEXIS 2836 (Ohio Ct. App., Butler County 2011).

When, in a foreclosure case filed by an owners' association against a homeowner, the association filed a new complaint naming the homeowner's spouse to dispose of the spouse's dower interest in the property, the affirmative defenses and counterclaims the spouse asserted were properly dismissed because the spouse did not have standing to assert those defenses and counterclaims, as the spouse did not hold title to the property. Bonnieville Towers Condo. Owners Ass'n v. Andrews, 2008-Ohio-1833, 2008 Ohio App. LEXIS 1559 (Ohio Ct. App., Cuyahoga County 2008).

When a widower inherited property concerning which the widower's deceased spouse had granted a mortgage, the widower no longer had a dower interest in the property because that interest was extinguished when fee simple title was transferred to the widower because the dower interest merged into the fee simple title, so that interest did not have to be disposed of pursuant to R.C. 2103.041 when the mortgage was foreclosed on. First Bank Nat'l Ass'n v. Parker, 2007-Ohio-3066, 2007 Ohio App. LEXIS 2810 (Ohio Ct. App., Cuyahoga County 2007).

Trial court properly denied the bank's motion for summary judgment because the bank failed to meet its initial Dresher burden of establishing the absence of a question of fact as to its claim for an equitable mortgage on the wife's dower interest; the owner's marriage to the wife predated the 2006 refinancing, to which the wife was not a party, and thus as to the couple, the bank was not a common creditor. Also, the bank failed to set forth any action of the wife warranting imposing an equitable lien on her interests and a question of material fact existed as to whether the bank's loss of priority was due to its own actions. BankUnited, F.S.B. v. Klug, 2013-Ohio-1599, 2013 Ohio App. LEXIS 1490 (Ohio Ct. App., Lorain County 2013).



### RESEARCH REFERENCES AND PRACTICE AIDS

**Cross-References to Related Sections**

Property construed, RC § 2103.01.

**Practice Guides**

Anderson's Ohio Probate Practice and Procedure § 58.02 Calculation of dower interests

## § 2103.05 Adultery a bar to dower.

A husband or wife who leaves the other and dwells in adultery will be barred from dower in the real property of the other, unless the offense is condoned by the injured consort.

**HISTORY:**

GC § 10502-5; 114 v 320(338); Bureau of Code Revision. Eff 10-1-53.

### NOTES TO DECISIONS

**Summary judgment**

Summary judgment to a decedent's estate administrator was error in her action against a property transferee, alleging that the decedent's real property was improperly transferred to the transferee, as genuine issues of material fact existed as to the validity of the real property transfer and whether it was subject to a dower right of the decedent's estranged wife under R.C. 2103.02 and 2103.05. Reigles v. Urban, 2010-Ohio-4427, 2010 Ohio App. LEXIS 3772 (Ohio Ct. App., Lake County 2010).

### RESEARCH REFERENCES AND PRACTICE AIDS

**Comparative Legislation**

Effect of living in adultery:

IL—755 Ill. Comp. Stat. § 5/2-9
IN—Burns Ind. Code Ann. § 29-1-2-14
KY—KRS § 392.090
PA—20 P.S. § 2106

## § 2103.06 Lands given up by fraud.

If a husband or wife gives up real property by collusion or fraud, or loses it by default, the widow or widower may recover dower therein.

**HISTORY:**

GC § 10502-6; 114 v 320(338); Bureau of Code Revision. Eff 10-1-53.

### NOTES TO DECISIONS

**Conveyance prior to marriage**

A conveyance of realty to children of a former marriage, without consideration other than love and affection, by a man engaged to be married, without disclosure of the conveyance to his intended wife whom he later marries, does not defraud her of her right of dower, provided for in R.C. 2103.02. (Ward v. Ward, 63 OS 125, overruled: Perlberg v. Perlberg, 18 Ohio St. 2d 55, 47 Ohio Op. 2d 167, 247 N.E.2d 306 (1969).

#### RESEARCH REFERENCES AND PRACTICE AIDS

**Ohio Constitution**

Nonforfeiture of estate, Ohio Const. art I, § 12.

### § 2103.07 Dower is forfeited by waste.

A tenant in dower in real property who commits or suffers waste thereto will forfeit that part of the property to which such waste is committed or suffered to the person having the immediate estate in reversion or remainder and will be liable in damages to such person for the waste committed or suffered thereto.

**HISTORY:**

GC § 10502-7; 114 v 320(338); Bureau of Code Revision. Eff 10-1-53.

#### RESEARCH REFERENCES AND PRACTICE AIDS

**Comparative Legislation**

Forfeiture for waste:

CA—Cal Civ Code § 826
KY—KRS § 381.350
MI—MCLS § 558.22
NY—NY CLS RPAPL § 801

**Practice Manuals and Treatises**

Anderson's Ohio Civil Practice with Forms § 143.01 Waste Generally

### § 2103.08 Assignment of dower.

Sections 5305.01 to 5305.22, inclusive, of the Revised Code apply to the assignment of the dower of a husband.

**HISTORY:**

GC § 10502-10; 114 v 320(339); Bureau of Code Revision. Eff 10-1-53.

### § 2103.09 Estate by curtesy abolished.

The estate by the curtesy is abolished; but sections 2103.01 to 2103.09, inclusive, of the Revised Code shall not affect vested rights nor any section of the Revised Code.

**HISTORY:**

GC § 10502-8; 114 v 320(339); Bureau of Code Revision. Eff 10-1-53.

#### RESEARCH REFERENCES AND PRACTICE AIDS

**Comparative Legislation**

Courtesy interest:

CA—Cal Prob Code § 6412
FL—Fla. Stat. § 732.111
IL—755 Ill. Comp. Stat. § 5/2-9
IN—Burns Ind. Code Ann. § 29-1-2-11
KY—KRS § 392.020
MI—MCLS § 558.1
NY—NY CLS Real P § 189
PA—20 P.S. § 2105

# CHAPTER 2105

# DESCENT AND DISTRIBUTION

Section



Section



### § 2105.01 No distinction between ancestral and nonancestral or real and personal property.

In intestate succession, there shall be no difference between ancestral and nonancestral property or between real and personal property.

**HISTORY:**

GC § 10503-1; 114 v 320(339); Bureau of Code Revision. Eff 10-1-53.

#### NOTES TO DECISIONS

**Generally**

Under the provisions of this section, in intestate succession there shall be no difference between ancestral and nonancestral property: In re Estate of Sherick, 167 Ohio St. 151, 4 Ohio Op. 2d 141, 146 N.E.2d 727, 1957 Ohio LEXIS 346 (Ohio 1957).

A distinction, in Ohio, between ancestral and nonancestral real and personal property was drawn by GC §§ 8573 and 8574 (see now R.C. 2105.06), in effect prior to 1932, but by virtue of this section, effective January 1, 1932, such a distinction no longer exists: Asher v. Asher, 87 Ohio App. 227, 42 Ohio Op. 454, 94 N.E.2d 582, 1948 Ohio App. LEXIS 594 (Ohio Ct. App., Tuscarawas County 1948).

#### RESEARCH REFERENCES AND PRACTICE AIDS

**Cross-References to Related Sections**

Afterborn or pretermitted heirs, RC § 2107.34.

Application for registration of land titles on death of registered owner, RC § 5309.45.

Commission issued to take election of spouse, RC § 2106.07.

Descent of real estate, RC § 2121.06.

Dower, RC § 2103.02.

Election made by one under legal disability, RC § 2106.08.

Escheat—

Application of provisions, RC § 2105.08.

Disposition of lands, RC § 2105.09.

Personal estate, RC § 2105.07.

Fiduciary defined, RC § 2109.01.

Guardians —

Foreign, RC § 2111.43.

Powers, RC § 2111.07.

Legal disability defined, RC § 2131.02.
Living and died construed, RC § 2105.02.
Permanent leasehold estates, RC § 2105.04.
Petition for judgment declaring validity of will, RC § 2107.081.
Declaration of validity; procedure for revoking or modifying will, RC § 2107.084.
Presentation of claims; acceleration of bar, RC § 2117.07.
Rights as to shares in corporation, RC § 2109.29.
Rules and procedure of court of common pleas to govern, RC § 2101.32.
Will construed, RC § 2107.01.
Notice of admission of will to probate, RC § 2107.19.

**Comparative Legislation**

No distinction between ancestral and nonancestral or real and personal property:
CA—Cal Prob Code § 6400
FL—Fla. Stat. § 732.101
IL—755 Ill. Comp. Stat. § 5/2-1
IN—Burns Ind. Code Ann. § 29-1-6-1
KY—KRS §§ 391.010, 391.030
MI—MCLS § 700.1106
PA—20 P.S. § 2101
Types of property:
FL—Fla. Stat. § 731.201
KY—KRS §§ 391.010, 391.030
PA—20 P.S. § 2104

**Practice Manuals and Treatises**

Anderson's Ohio Probate Practice and Procedure Form 18.02 Letter for incorporation by reference

**Practice Guides**

Anderson's Ohio Probate Practice and Procedure § 17.01 The language of succession

Anderson's Ohio Probate Practice and Procedure § 17.03 Statute of descent and distribution; Revised Code § 2105.06

## § 2105.02 Construction of "living" and "died."

When, in this chapter, a person is described as living, it means that the person was living at the time of the death of the intestate from whom the estate came and that the person lived for at least one hundred twenty hours following the death of the intestate, and when a person is described as having died, it means that the person died before such intestate or that the person failed to live for at least one hundred twenty hours following the death of the intestate.

**HISTORY:**

GC § 10503-3; 114 v 320(339); Bureau of Code Revision, 10-1-53; 149 v H 242. Eff 5-16-2002; 2016 hb432, § 1, effective April 6, 2017.

**Editor's Notes**

See provisions, § 5 of HB 345 (149 v —) following RC § 2105.39.

**Amendment Notes**

The 2016 amendment by HB 432 substituted "When, in this chapter" for "When, in Chapter 2105. of the Revised Code," inserted "and that the person lived for at least one hundred twenty hours following the death of the intestate" and "or that the person failed to live for at least one hundred twenty hours following the death of the intestate."

### RESEARCH REFERENCES AND PRACTICE AIDS

**Practice Guides**

Anderson's Ohio Probate Practice and Procedure § 58.02 Calculation of dower interests

## § 2105.03 Determination of next of kin.

In the determination of intestate succession, next of kin shall be determined by degrees of relationship computed by the rules of civil law.

**HISTORY:**

GC § 10503-2; 114 v 320(339); Bureau of Code Revision. Eff 10-1-53.

### NOTES TO DECISIONS

**Generally**

The provisions of this section, relating to intestate succession, and defining, for such purpose, the term "next of kin," have no application in the determination of the right to appointment as administrator of a decedent's estate: In re Fields' Estate, 65 N.E.2d 70, 44 Ohio Law Abs. 284, 1944 Ohio App. LEXIS 492 (Ohio Ct. App., Greene County 1944); In re Applegate's Estate, 45 Ohio Op. 24, 100 N.E.2d 322, 61 Ohio Law Abs. 277, 1951 Ohio Misc. LEXIS 424 (Ohio P. Ct. 1951).

"Next of kin" in this statute refers to those persons who take intestate property under the statutes of descent and distribution, meaning that the entire estate passes to the living next of kin and the legal representatives of deceased next of kin of the same class as the living next of kin: Weisflock v. Sigling, 116 Ohio St. 435, 156 N.E. 905, 4 Ohio Law Abs. 756, 5 Ohio Law Abs. 315, 25 Ohio L. Rep. 331, 1927 Ohio LEXIS 303 (Ohio 1927).

The phrase "nearest of kin" when employed in a last will and testament, in the absence of language in the will manifesting a different intention, is to be so construed as to embrace within its meaning such as would inherit under the statutes of descent and distribution, and in the order and proportion therein provided: Godfrey v. Epple, 100 Ohio St. 447, 126 N.E. 886, 1919 Ohio LEXIS 138 (Ohio 1919).

It has been held that aunts and uncles of the deceased and their representatives are the next of kin of the decedent instead of his grandparents: Ampey v. Hirsch, 20 Ohio N.P. 1 (1917).

### RESEARCH REFERENCES AND PRACTICE AIDS

**Comparative Legislation**

Next of kin determined:
CA—Cal Prob Code § 6402
FL—Fla. Stat. § 732.103
IL—755 Ill. Comp. Stat. § 5/2-1
IN—Burns Ind. Code Ann. § 29-1-6-6
KY—KRS § 391.010
MI—MCLS § 700.2103
NY—NY CLS EPTL §§ 2-1.1, 4-1.1
PA—20 P.S. § 2103

**Practice Guides**

Anderson's Ohio Probate Practice and Procedure § 17.01 The language of succession

Anderson's Ohio Probate Practice and Procedure § 17.03 Statute of descent and distribution; Revised Code § 2105.06

## § 2105.04 Permanent leases to descend same as estates in fee.

Permanent leasehold estates, renewable forever, are subject to Chapter 2105. of the Revised Code.

**HISTORY:**

GC § 10503-11; 114 v 320(341); Bureau of Code Revision, 10-1-53; 149 v H 242. Eff 5-16-2002.

**Editor's Notes**

See provisions, § 5 of HB 345 (149 v —) following RC § 2105.39.

### NOTES TO DECISIONS

**Generally**

A permanent leasehold estate, renewable forever, is not a fee simple although under the Ohio statutes it has many of the incidents thereof. The fee simple remains in the lessor, his heirs, devisees or assigns: Rawson v. Brown, 104 Ohio St. 537, 20 Ohio L. 44, 136 N.E. 209 (1922), affirming Brown v. Rawson, 15 Ohio App. 289, which, on appeal, rendered similar decree as 23 Ohio N.P. (n.s.) 105, 31 Ohio Dec. 447]; Rawson v. Brown, 104 Ohio St. 548, 136 N.E. 213 (1922), affirming Brown v. Rawson, 15 Ohio App. 289, which, on appeal, rendered similar decree as 23 Ohio N.P. (n.s.) 105, 31 Ohio Dec. 447.].

### RESEARCH REFERENCES AND PRACTICE AIDS

**Practice Guides**

Anderson's Ohio Probate Practice and Procedure § 27.02 Commencement of action

## § 2105.05 Repealed.

Repealed, 136 v S 466, § 2 [GC §§ 10503-19—10503-22; 114 v 320(343, 344); Bureau of Code Revision, 10-1-53]. Eff 5-26-76.

**Editor's Notes**

This section concerned advancements.

### § 2105.051 Advancements; time of valuation.

When a person dies, property that the person gave during the person's lifetime to an heir shall be treated as an advancement against the heir's share of the estate only if declared in a contemporaneous writing by the decedent or acknowledged in writing by the heir to be an advancement. For this purpose, property advanced is valued as of the time the heir came into possession or enjoyment of the property, or as of the time of death of the decedent, whichever occurs first. If the heir does not survive the decedent, the property shall not be taken into account in computing the intestate share to be received by the heir's issue, unless the declaration or acknowledgment provides otherwise.

**HISTORY:**

136 v S 145. Eff 1-1-76; 2011 SB 124, § 1, eff. Jan. 13, 2012.

**Editor's Notes**

Acts 2011, SB 124, § 3 provides: "The provisions of this act that relate to the estates of decedents apply to the estates of decedents who die on or after the effective date of this act."

**Amendment Notes**

The 2011 amendment made stylistic changes.

#### NOTES TO DECISIONS

Analysis

Division of marital assets
Intent of donor

**Division of marital assets**

Money provided to an ex-wife and an ex-husband by the ex-wife's parents for building the marital home was marital property under R.C. 3105.171 that should have been included in the division of marital assets; it was not an advancement of the ex-wife's inheritance under R.C. 2105.051 as there was no contemporaneous writing to that effect, and the marital home was deeded in the names of both the ex-wife and ex-husband. Dudley v. Dudley, 2008-Ohio-3760, 2008 Ohio App. LEXIS 3184 (Ohio Ct. App., Guernsey County 2008).

In an appeal from a divorce where the evidence showed that during the marriage the husband's mother gave real property to the parties, that both parties were named on the deed as grantees, and that the husband's mother testified that she never expected that the parties would get a divorce and that she made the gift to both of the parties as a family unit, the determination that the real property was marital was affirmed because the husband was unable to produce a contemporaneous writing showing that the gift was an advancement of his inheritance under R.C. 2105.051. Crish v. Crish, 2003-Ohio-4465, 2003 Ohio App. LEXIS 3962 (Ohio Ct. App., Mahoning County 2003).

**Intent of donor**

Whether an inter vivos gift is an advancement against the share received by an heir depends on the intent of the donor at the time the gift was made. R.C. 2105.051 limits proof of that intent to a declaration by contemporaneous writing of the decedent or written acknowledgement of the heir: King v. King, 82 Ohio App. 3d 747, 613 N.E.2d 251, 1992 Ohio App. LEXIS 4823 (Ohio Ct. App., Montgomery County 1992).

#### RESEARCH REFERENCES AND PRACTICE AIDS

**Cross-References to Related Sections**

Living and died construed, RC § 2105.02.

**Comparative Legislation**

Advancement:
CA—Cal Prob Code § 6409
FL—Fla. Stat. § 733.806
IL—755 Ill. Comp. Stat. § 5/2-5
IN—Burns Ind. Code Ann. § 29-1-2-10
KY—KRS § 391.140
MI—MCLS § 700.2608
NY—NY CLS EPTL § 2-1.5
PA—20 P.S. § 2109.1

**Practice Manuals and Treatises**

Anderson's Ohio Probate Practice and Procedure Form 21.12 Declaration that gift constitutes an advancement

Anderson's Ohio Probate Practice and Procedure Form 21.13 Acknowledgment that gift constitutes an advancement

**Practice Guides**

Anderson's Ohio Probate Practice and Procedure § 21.09 Gift made to beneficiary during testator's life

### § 2105.052 Debt not to be charged against intestate share.

Any debt owed to a decedent shall not be charged against the intestate share of any person except the debtor. If the debtor fails to survive decedent, the debt shall not be taken into account in computing the intestate share of the debtor's issue.

**HISTORY:**

136 v S 145. Eff 1-1-76.

#### RESEARCH REFERENCES AND PRACTICE AIDS

**Practice Guides**

Anderson's Ohio Probate Practice and Procedure § 21.04 Legacies, bequests, and devises

### § 2105.06 Statute of descent and distribution.

When a person dies intestate having title or right to any personal property, or to any real property or inheritance, in this state, the personal property shall be distributed, and the real property or inheritance shall descend and pass in parcenary, except as otherwise provided by law, in the following course:

(A) If there is no surviving spouse, to the children of the intestate or their lineal descendants, per stirpes;

(B) If there is a spouse and one or more children of the decedent or their lineal descendants surviving, and all of the decedent's children who survive or have lineal descendants surviving also are children of the surviving spouse, then the whole to the surviving spouse;

(C) If there is a spouse and one child of the decedent or the child's lineal descendants surviving and the surviving spouse is not the natural or adoptive parent of the decedent's child, the first twenty thousand dollars plus one-half of the balance of the intestate estate to the spouse and the remainder to the child or the child's lineal descendants, per stirpes;

(D) If there is a spouse and more than one child or their lineal descendants surviving, the first sixty thousand dollars if the spouse is the natural or adoptive parent of one, but not all, of the children, or the first twenty thousand dollars if the spouse is the natural or adoptive parent of none of the children, plus one-third of the balance of the intestate estate to the spouse and the remainder to the children equally, or to the lineal descendants of any deceased child, per stirpes;

(E) If there are no children or their lineal descendants, then the whole to the surviving spouse;

(F) Except as provided in section 2105.062 of the Revised Code, if there is no spouse and no children or their lineal descendants, to the parents of the intestate equally, or to the surviving parent;

(G) Except as provided in section 2105.062 of the Revised Code, if there is no spouse, no children or their lineal descendants, and no parent surviving, to the brothers and sisters, whether of the whole or of the half blood of the intestate, or their lineal descendants, per stirpes;

(H) Except as provided in section 2105.062 of the Revised Code, if there are no brothers or sisters or their lineal descendants, one-half to the paternal grandparents of the intestate equally, or to the survivor of them, and one-half to the maternal grandparents of the intestate equally, or to the survivor of them;

(I) Except as provided in section 2105.062 of the Revised Code, if there is no paternal grandparent or no maternal grandparent, one-half to the lineal descendants of the deceased grandparents, per stirpes; if there are no such lineal descendants, then to the surviving grandparents or their lineal descendants, per stirpes; if there are no surviving grandparents or their lineal descendants, then to the next of kin of the intestate, provided there shall be no representation among the next of kin;

(J) If there are no next of kin, to stepchildren or their lineal descendants, per stirpes;

**(K) If there are no stepchildren or their lineal descendants, escheat to the state.**

**HISTORY:**

GC § 10503-4; 114 v 320(339); 116 v 385; Bureau of Code Revision, 10-1-53; 128 v 155 (Eff 11-9-59); 136 v S 145 (Eff 1-1-76); 136 v S 466 (Eff 5-26-76); 141 v S 248 (Eff 12-17-86); 148 v S 152. Eff 3-22-2001; 2011 SB 124, § 1, eff. Jan. 13, 2012; 2014 sb207, § 1, effective March 23, 2015.

**Editor's Notes**

Acts 2011, SB 124, § 3 provides: "The provisions of this act that relate to the estates of decedents apply to the estates of decedents who die on or after the effective date of this act."

The provisions of § 3 of SB 152 (148 v —) read as follows:

SECTION 3. Sections 2105.06, 2105.061, 2106.11, and 2127.04 of the Revised Code, as amended by this act, shall apply to the estates of decedents who die on or after the effective date of this act.

**Amendment Notes**

The 2014 amendment by SB 207, added the exception to the beginning of (F) through (I).

The 2011 amendment substituted "real property" for "real estate" twice in the introductory language; and made a stylistic change.

## NOTES TO DECISIONS

Analysis



**Generally**

Lineal descendants of the parties to this action were coparceners (and thus cotenants) with respect to the property where there was no evidence of inter vivos conveyance by deed or of any testamentary conveyance or transfer of any interest in property subsequent to deed in 1910. Hoosier v. Heirs, 2014-Ohio-5810, 2014 Ohio App. LEXIS 5613 (Ohio Ct. App., Pike County 2014).

The right to inherit property is neither a natural nor an inherent right. Rather, it is a statutory right created by the legislature and, therefore, subject to the legislature's control: Winkelfoos v. Mann, 16 Ohio App. 3d 266, 475 N.E.2d 509, 1984 Ohio App. LEXIS 12376 (Ohio Ct. App., Huron County 1984).

The laws of descent are mere arbitrary rules for the transmission of property, enacted by the legislature, and cannot be modified by courts by reason of equitable consideration: Campbell v. Musart Soc. of Cleveland Museum of Art, 2 Ohio Op. 2d 517, 131 N.E.2d 279, 72 Ohio Law Abs. 46, 1956 Ohio Misc. LEXIS 368 (Ohio P. Ct. 1956).

The right to inherit property is not an inherent or natural right, but is entirely statutory and the legislature may create and change the right of inheritance as it sees fit: Frantz v. Florence, 131 N.E.2d 630, 72 Ohio Law Abs. 222, 1954 Ohio Misc. LEXIS 299 (Ohio C.P. 1954).

According to the general rules of interpreting statutes of descent and distribution, descendants of the nearest degree of consanguinity, however remote, take in their own right such shares as would come to them if all of the descendants of the same degree with the testator were living, and those of a more remote degree take per stirpes, or by representation, the shares of their deceased ancestors of the degree of consanguinity represented by living members: Oakley v. Davey, 49 Ohio App. 113, 1 Ohio Op. 144, 195 N.E. 406 (1934), reversing Davey v. Climo, 30 Ohio N.P. (n.s.) 457.].

**Administrator of estate**

Where a woman who is divorced dies survived by her four minor children, her former husband may be appointed administrator of her estate provided he is a "suitable person" as set forth in R.C. 2113.06: In re Estate of Robertson, 26 Ohio App. 3d 64, 498 N.E.2d 206, 1985 Ohio App. LEXIS 10225 (Ohio Ct. App., Cuyahoga County 1985).

**Adoption**

In the case of adoption by a stepfather or stepmother, the natural parent and the adoptive stepfather or stepmother are to be treated equally, and they have equal and joint rights and obligations to and from the child, including the right to share equally in the estate of the deceased adopted child: Mancino v. Smith, 30 Ohio Op. 2d 282, 201 N.E.2d 93, 95 Ohio Law Abs. 51, 1964 Ohio Misc. LEXIS 275 (Ohio P. Ct. 1964).

The provisions of the statutes creating the rights of inheritance between the parties to an adoption and the provisions of the law of descent and distribution of intestate estates are in pari materia and should, therefore, be construed together as one law: Campbell v. Musart Soc. of Cleveland Museum of Art, 2 Ohio Op. 2d 517, 131 N.E.2d 279, 72 Ohio Law Abs. 46, 1956 Ohio Misc. LEXIS 368 (Ohio P. Ct. 1956).

Where an adopted child's adoptive mother and adoptive grandparents predecease her leaving no lineal descendants surviving, the adoptive next of kin are the heirs of such child: Vodrey v. Quigley, 139 N.E.2d 108, 74 Ohio Law Abs. 29, 1956 Ohio Misc. LEXIS 344 (Ohio P. Ct.), aff'd, 143 N.E.2d 162, 75 Ohio Law Abs. 65, 1956 Ohio App. LEXIS 745 (Ohio Ct. App., Columbiana County 1956).

Even though an adoptive mother has perpetrated a fraud by adopting a child and using the child's estate for its support, thus neglecting the principal duty of a parent to support such child, such action alone is not enough to invalidate an otherwise legal adoption or to change the plan provided under the laws of descent and distribution: Vodrey v. Quigley, 139 N.E.2d 108, 74 Ohio Law Abs. 29, 1956 Ohio Misc. LEXIS 344 (Ohio P. Ct.), aff'd, 143 N.E.2d 162, 75 Ohio Law Abs. 65, 1956 Ohio App. LEXIS 745 (Ohio Ct. App., Columbiana County 1956).

This statute is in pari materia with the adoption statute, so where the words "brothers and sisters" are used, it is clear that such phrase is intended to include brothers and sisters by adoption: National Bank of Lima v. Hancock, 85 Ohio App. 1, 40 Ohio Op. 30, 88 N.E.2d 67, 1948 Ohio App. LEXIS 622 (Ohio Ct. App., Allen County 1948).

Under this section and GC § 10512-19 (R.C. 3107.10) an adopted child is entitled to inherit not only from an adopting parent, but also through such adopting parent from a deceased sister of the adopting parent: White v. Meyer, 66 Ohio App. 549, 21 Ohio Op. 38, 37 N.E.2d 546, 33 Ohio Law Abs. 151, 1940 Ohio App. LEXIS 808 (Ohio Ct. App., Cuyahoga County 1940).

**Appeal**

Probate court's decision to grant an estate executrix's motion to strike a surviving spouse's exercise of her elective share to take against the decedent's will pursuant to R.C. 2106.01(A) and 2105.06 was a final judgment which affected the spouse's substantial rights for purposes of R.C. 2505.02(B)(2), and the appellate court had jurisdiction to review the matter pursuant to Ohio Const. art. IV, § 3(B)(2). In re Estate of Riley, 2006-Ohio-956, 165 Ohio App. 3d 471, 847 N.E.2d 22, 2006 Ohio App. LEXIS 898 (Ohio Ct. App., Scioto County 2006).

**Applicability**

Probate court was directed to conduct a hearing on remand and order the distribution of wrongful death proceeds because the court erred by ordering and confirming the distribution of wrongful death proceeds pursuant to R.C. 2105.06, rather than by equitable considerations as was required by the wrongful death distribution statute, R.C. 2125.03(A)(1). In re Estate of Molitor, 2013-Ohio-525, 2013 Ohio App. LEXIS 461 (Ohio Ct. App., Brown County 2013).

**Bankruptcy**

Husband and wife who declared Chapter 7 bankruptcy shortly after the wife's mother died intestate were allowed to claim a homestead exemption under Ohio Rev. Code Ann. § 2329.66 in a house the wife's mother owned at the time she died because they lived in the house, the wife acquired her mother's fee simple interest in the house upon her mother's death, pursuant to Ohio Rev. Code Ann. § 2105.06, even without the commencement of probate proceedings, and the husband had a dower interest in the property under Ohio Rev. Code Ann. § 2103.02. In re Pugh, 2015 Bankr. LEXIS 2911 (Bankr. N.D. Ohio Aug. 31, 2015).

Debtors argued that, by virtue of their marriage, the husband should still be found to maintain a recognizable interest in his wife's vehicle for purposes of R.C. 2329.66. As for R.C. 2105.06, 3105.171, as cited to by debtors in support for their position, these provisions were best viewed in the circumstances as contingent restraints on alienation, as opposed to actual "interests" in property. In re Toland, 346 B.R. 444, 2006 Bankr. LEXIS 1509 (Bankr. N.D. Ohio 2006).

**Children of deceased siblings**

When an intestate dies leaving no spouse, no children or their lineal descendants, or no surviving parent and is preceded in death by two brothers, one of whom leaves one child and one of whom leaves two children surviving at the time of the death of the intestate, the children of such deceased brothers, being in an equal degree of consanguinity to the intestate, inherit per capita pursuant to R.C. 2105.12: Washburn v. Scurlock, 5 Ohio App. 3d 125, 449 N.E.2d 797, 1982 Ohio App. LEXIS 11031 (Ohio Ct. App., Jackson County 1982).



**Children out of wedlock**

Trial court properly held that appellant, an out-of-wedlock child of the decedent, was not entitled to inherit from him because based on the decedent's lack of action during his lifetime to indicate his desire to include appellant as an heir to his estate, any presumption of parentage created by appellant's birth certificate was rebutted for the purpose of inheritance under R.C. 2105.06. In re Estate of Burdette, 2016-Ohio-5866, 70 N.E.3d 1238, 2016 Ohio App. LEXIS 3710 (Ohio Ct. App., Montgomery County 2016).

Regarding the administration of the decedent's estate, there was prima facie evidence that paternity was established by agreement of the parties well before the statute of limitation under R.C. 3111.05 expired. There was testimony that the decedent and the mother of the three children held themselves out as married for several years, that the decedent claimed the children as his, and that after the death of their mother, the children were raised by the decedent as his children without any formal establishment of guardianship; all three of the birth certificates in question listed the decedent as the father. In re Estate of Collins, 2012-Ohio-5234, 2012 Ohio App. LEXIS 4585 (Ohio Ct. App., Allen County 2012).

Illegitimate children can inherit from their fathers under R.C. 2105.06 only if paternity is established prior to the death of the father. They may also inherit by bringing a parentage action after the death of the father. However, a probate court lacks jurisdiction to hear a parentage action under R.C. Chapter 3111: Byrd v. Trennor, 2004-Ohio-2736, 157 Ohio App. 3d 358, 811 N.E.2d 549, 2004 Ohio App. LEXIS 2432 (Ohio Ct. App., Clark County 2004).

An alleged child of a decedent cannot inherit from him under R.C. 2105.06 unless the child was "legitimized" in one of the recognized manners: In re Estate of Hicks, 90 Ohio App. 3d 483, 629 N.E.2d 1086, 1993 Ohio App. LEXIS 4803 (Ohio Ct. App., Erie County 1993).

Whatever procedures are used to establish paternity of a child born out of wedlock the child cannot inherit from the natural father unless the required acts were completed prior to the death of the father: Hunter-Martin v. Winchester Transp., Inc., 71 Ohio App. 3d 273, 593 N.E.2d 383, 1991 Ohio App. LEXIS 1110 (Ohio Ct. App., Shelby County 1991).

A child born out of wedlock who seeks to inherit from his father's estate may prove his paternity by genetic testing, and the probate court may permit disinterment to effect such a test: Alexander v. Alexander, 42 Ohio Misc. 2d 30, 537 N.E.2d 1310, 1988 Ohio Misc. LEXIS 13 (Ohio P. Ct. 1988), dismissed, 54 Ohio App. 3d 77, 560 N.E.2d 1337, 1989 Ohio App. LEXIS 5286 (Ohio Ct. App., Franklin County 1989).

A child born out of wedlock can inherit from his natural father through the means provided in R.C. Chapter 2105, or by an action to establish paternity under R.C. 3111.04: Garrison v. Smith, 55 Ohio App. 3d 14, 561 N.E.2d 1041, 1988 Ohio App. LEXIS 4360 (Ohio Ct. App., Lucas County 1988).

The word "child" as used in the Statute of Descent and Distribution, R.C. 2105.06, includes the child born out-of-wedlock as well as the legitimate child if the parent-child relationship has been established prior to death of the father pursuant to the parameters of R.C. Chapter 3111, as effective June 29, 1982: Beck v. Jolliff, 22 Ohio App. 3d 84, 489 N.E.2d 825, 1984 Ohio App. LEXIS 12693 (Ohio Ct. App., Knox County 1984).

The words "child" or "children" appearing in R.C. 2105.06, the statute of descent and distribution means all children, both legitimate and illegitimate: Green v. Woodard, 40 Ohio App. 2d 101, 69 Ohio Op. 2d 130, 318 N.E.2d 397, 1974 Ohio App. LEXIS 2624 (Ohio Ct. App., Cuyahoga County 1974).

The word "children," as it appears in the substitute beneficiary clause of a group life insurance policy, is to be construed to mean all offspring, regardless of whether they are born in or out of wedlock: Butcher v. Pollard, 32 Ohio App. 2d 1, 61 Ohio Op. 2d 1, 288 N.E.2d 204, 1972 Ohio App. LEXIS 348 (Ohio Ct. App., Cuyahoga County 1972).

**Class action members defined**

In a class action brought by family members of deceased relatives held in custody of a county morgue during a five-month period where the family members alleged that defendants either permitted or engaged in the practice of posing, disrupting, and photographing the remains of their relatives and that crime scene photographs and autopsy photographs of their relatives were illegally released to the public, the court found that "family member" in defining the class should be defined as encompassing only the surviving spouse of any decedent and, in the event, no surviving spouse then the next of kin in order of succession as defined by the Ohio statute of descent and distribution, R.C. 2105.06. Chesher v. Neyer, 2005 U.S. Dist. LEXIS 35536 (S.D. Ohio July 19, 2005).

**Conflict of laws**

Intestate succession to personal property is governed by the law of the deceased owner's domicile: Howard v. Reynolds, 30 Ohio St. 2d 214, 59 Ohio Op. 2d 228, 283 N.E.2d 629, 1972 Ohio LEXIS 448 (Ohio 1972).

**Construction**

Debtors argued that, by virtue of their marriage, the husband should still be found to maintain a recognizable interest in his wife's vehicle for purposes of R.C. 2329.66. As for R.C. 2105.06, 3105.171, as cited to by debtors in support for their position, these provisions were best viewed in the circumstances as contingent restraints on alienation, as opposed to actual "interests" in property. In re Toland, 346 B.R. 444, 2006 Bankr. LEXIS 1509 (Bankr. N.D. Ohio 2006).

**Construction with other laws**

Timing of the mother's intestate death was not relevant to whether a mechanic's lien later arose that was enforceable regarding the son's interest in the property as R.C. 1311.02 established that a mechanic's lien was on the improvement and all interests that the part owner may have or subsequently acquire in the land. United States Bank Nat'l Ass'n v. Unknown Heirs, 2019-Ohio-2021, 136 N.E.3d 879, 2019 Ohio App. LEXIS 2086 (Ohio Ct. App., Franklin County 2019).

Revised Code §§ 2105.06 and former 2107.39 (now 2106.01) concern the devolution of a decedent's property; they are to be read in pari materia and construed together: Winkelfoos v. Mann, 16 Ohio App. 3d 266, 475 N.E.2d 509, 1984 Ohio App. LEXIS 12376 (Ohio Ct. App., Huron County 1984).

The provisions of this section are controlling only "except as otherwise provided by law": Stocker v. Tranter, 31 Ohio N.P. 467 (1934).

**Descendant**

The word "descendant" should be construed to include all those to whom an estate descends, whether in a direct or collateral line from the intestate: Oakley v. Davey, 49 Ohio App. 113, 1 Ohio Op. 144, 195 N.E. 406 (1934), reversing Davey v. Climo, 30 Ohio N.P. (n.s.) 457.].

**Descendants of grandparents**

This section as amended provides for an equal division between the lineal descendants of each set of paternal and maternal grandparents, and no distinction is made between those of the half blood and those of the whole blood: Sheeler v. Burkhart, 45 Ohio Op. 415, 101 N.E.2d 401, 62 Ohio Law Abs. 356, 1951 Ohio Misc. LEXIS 396 (Ohio P. Ct. 1951).

Where the intestate's maternal grandmother had been married twice and had left lineal descendants from each marriage, and there were no kin more closely related to the decedent within the terms of par. 8 of this section [now par. (H)], the lineal descendants of both marriages are entitled to share in the estate of such decedent: In re Stephenson's Estate, 75 N.E.2d 834, 48 Ohio Law Abs. 624, 1946 Ohio Misc. LEXIS 200 (Ohio P. Ct. 1946).

Where the heirs of the decedent consist of one uncle on the maternal side, and three uncles, one aunt and nine children of a deceased uncle on the paternal side, one-half of the estate will go to the one uncle on the maternal side, he being the only lineal descendant of the maternal grandparents, and the other one-half will be divided in five equal parts, one part to go to each of the three uncles and the one aunt, and the fifth part to the children of the deceased uncle, they being the only lineal descendants of the paternal grandparents: Ryan v. Dixon, 12 Ohio Op. 185, 26 Ohio Law Abs. 450, 1938 Ohio Misc. LEXIS 1074 (Ohio P. Ct. 1938).

Where the mother of decedent's father had married three times and left lineal descendants from each marriage, all of such lineal descendants, by virtue of the provisions of par. 8 of this section [now par. (H)], were entitled to share in the estate of the decedent whether their ancestor was the first, second, or third husband of the decedent's grandmother: Shepard v. Wilson, 61 Ohio App. 191, 14 Ohio Op. 282, 22 N.E.2d 568, 28 Ohio Law Abs. 448, 1938 Ohio App. LEXIS 285 (Ohio Ct. App., Hamilton County 1938).

**Designation of heir**

An heir designated by virtue of R.C. 2105.15 is an heir under the statute of descent and distribution: Witten v. Landrum, 41 Ohio App. 2d 65, 70 Ohio Op. 2d 61, 322 N.E.2d 146, 1974 Ohio App. LEXIS 2608 (Ohio Ct. App., Van Wert County 1974).

**Election by surviving spouse**

Where a certified letter which notified a surviving spouse of her right to make an election regarding her deceased husband's will was properly served pursuant to Civ.R. 4.1(A) and 73(E)(3) when it was clearly delivered to the correct address and the spouse's son signed for the letter, the five-month statutory period to make such an election pursuant to R.C. 2105.06 and 2106.01(E) began to run. As the spouse made an election to take against her deceased husband's will beyond that five-month period, the probate court properly granted the executrix's motion to strike the election and the spouse was presumed to have elected to take pursuant to the will. In re Estate of Riley, 2006-Ohio-956, 165 Ohio App. 3d 471, 847 N.E.2d 22, 2006 Ohio App. LEXIS 898 (Ohio Ct. App., Scioto County 2006).

Since all necessary expenses were paid by Medicaid in order to care for the seventy-nine year old widow, it was in her best interests to take under the will, even though her deceased husband left her nothing: In re Estate of Cross, 1995 Ohio App. LEXIS 667 (Ohio Ct. App., Cuyahoga County Feb. 23, 1995), rev'd, 75 Ohio St. 3d 530, 664 N.E.2d 905, 1996 Ohio LEXIS 362 (Ohio 1996).

Where an authenticated copy of a will, executed and proved according to the laws of the state of the decedent's domicile, has been admitted to record pursuant to R.C. 2129.05, and where it is not established that the widow who was domiciled in that state had claimed anything under that will or otherwise elected to take thereunder and where the testator owned real estate in Ohio at his death, such widow has the right, with respect to that Ohio real estate, to elect not to take under the testator's will but to take under the Ohio statute of descent and distribution (R.C. 2105.06), even though no such election is permitted by the law of the state of the testator's domicile at death: Pfau v. Moseley, 9 Ohio St. 2d 13, 38 Ohio Op. 2d 8, 222 N.E.2d 639, 1966 Ohio LEXIS 286 (Ohio 1966).

Where a deceased husband, by his will, made a specific bequest of a certain number of shares of stock in a corporation for the creation of a trust for the benefit of one of his employees, and where the remaining portion of his estate is sufficient, after the payment of all debts and other obligations, to provide his relict, who elected not to take under the will, with the share of his net estate to which she is entitled under the provisions of R.C. 2105.06, the relict's share of the net estate is an undivided fractional interest in the real estate plus such additional amount of personal property not specifically bequeathed under the will, either in kind or in money, as shall make her total share of the net estate that amount to which she is entitled under the provisions of the statute: Winters Nat'l Bank & Trust Co. v. Riffe, 2 Ohio St. 2d 72, 31 Ohio Op. 2d 56, 206 N.E.2d 212, 1965 Ohio LEXIS 487 (Ohio 1965).

If a surviving spouse remains alive and competent and, within nine months after the appointment of the first fiduciary charged with the administration of the estate under the will of the deceased spouse, no citation is issued and served upon him to elect whether to take under the will or under R.C. 2105.06, and within such nine-month period he also fails voluntarily so to elect, he will be conclusively presumed to have elected to take under the will, regardless of whether or not the inventory, appraisement and schedule of debts are filed: In re Estate of Witteman, 3 Ohio St. 2d 66, 32 Ohio Op. 2d 49, 209 N.E.2d 427, 1965 Ohio LEXIS 593 (Ohio 1965).

Where the wills of a husband and wife were made in pursuance of a plan to minimize estate and inheritance taxes, and the wife's bequest of her entire estate directly to her children, rather than to her husband, was made to minimize the impact of federal estate taxes upon their joint estates, the Probate Court may properly make an election for the incompetent surviving husband to permit the wife's estate to pass directly to her legatees: In re Estate of Rieley, 28 Ohio Op. 2d 122, 194 N.E.2d 918, 92 Ohio Law Abs. 296, 1963 Ohio Misc. LEXIS 234 (Ohio P. Ct. 1963).

Where the surviving spouse elects to take against the will and under the statute of descent and distribution, there is an acceleration of the remainder interests which are dependent entirely upon the life tenancy of the widow: Ginder v. Ginder, 59 Ohio Op. 320, 134 N.E.2d 603, 82 Ohio Law Abs. 129, 1954 Ohio Misc. LEXIS 297 (Ohio P. Ct. 1954).

Where a widow elects under GC § 10504-55 (R.C. 2107.39), to take under the statute of descent and distribution and the applicable portions of that statute (GC § 10504-4), [R.C. 2105.06] provide that "personal property shall be distributed" and any "real estate or inheritance shall descend and pass in parcenary" in part to the surviving spouse, the amount of the federal estate tax on the decedent's estate should be deducted therefrom before computing the widow's share thereof. (GC §§ 10503-4, 10504-55, 10504-77, 10509-121, 10509-181, 10509-182 and 10510-2, [R.C. 2105.06, 2107.39, 2107.54, 2117.25, 2113.53, 2113.54 and 2127.02], and 26 U.S.C. § 812 (e), construed and applied. The syllabus in Tax Commission, ex rel. Price, Atty. Genl. v. Lamprecht, Admr., 107 OS 535, approved and followed. Paragraphs two, three and four of the syllabus and the decision in Miller et al., Exrx. v. Hammond, 156 OS 475, 46 OO 405, overruled. McDougall, Admr. v. Central National Bank of Cleveland, Trustee, 157 OS 45, 47 OO 60, distinguished: Campbell v. Lloyd, 162 Ohio St. 203, 55 Ohio Op. 102, 122 N.E.2d 695 (1954).

If an estate of such deceased husband consists wholly or in part of real estate, and his widow, as relict, elects not to take under his will but under the statute of descent and distribution, she takes her quantitative share in such real estate as an estate of inheritance, subject to sale, if necessary, to pay the debts of the estate of her deceased husband: Barlow v. Winters Nat. Bank & Trust Co., 145 Ohio St. 270, 30 Ohio Op. 484, 61 N.E.2d 603 (1945), reversing 27 Ohio Op. 187 (PC).].

In case the relict of a deceased husband takes title to any such real estate by reason of such election, she is entitled to the rentals from her share of such real estate from the date of the death of her husband: Barlow v. Winters Nat. Bank & Trust Co., 145 Ohio St. 270, 30 Ohio Op. 484, 61 N.E.2d 603 (1945), reversing 27 Ohio Op. 187 (PC).].

**Escheat to state**

Although the events (the death of the grandson and granddaughter prior to the death of the great-grandchildren) were not certain to occur, declaratory relief was nonetheless warranted, pursuant to R.C. 2721.05(C), because if neither great-grandson were beneficiaries of the trust, its assets had to be distributed in their entirety during the lives of the current beneficiaries in order to avoid an escheat to the state pursuant to R.C. 2105.06(J) of any balance remaining after their deaths, if there then were no other heirs at law of the trustor who could then benefit; that could produce a disorderly process the trustee has a duty to avoid. On the other hand, if either great-grandson could subsequently benefit, especially upon termination of the trust, such disorder may be avoided; therefore, declaratory relief was proper. Bank One Trust Co. N.A. v. Reynolds, 2007-Ohio-4197, 173 Ohio App. 3d 1, 877 N.E.2d 342, 2007 Ohio App. LEXIS 3794 (Ohio Ct. App., Montgomery County 2007).

For purposes of determining whether property should escheat to the state or go to persons claiming to be next of kin, affidavits and other extraneous evidence are acceptable to aid in a proper determination: Estate of Parks v. Hodge, 87 Ohio App. 3d 831, 623 N.E.2d 227, 1993 Ohio App. LEXIS 3528 (Ohio Ct. App., Cuyahoga County 1993).

The specific mandate of R.C. 2105.06 et seq., governing escheats of property to the state, must be strictly followed to create a valid finding and judgment by the Probate Court of the escheat of property to the state where a decedent leaves no heirs. To be valid, such judgment of escheat must be that there are no heirs, not that "to the knowledge of plaintiff there are no known next of kin": Borovskaya v. State, 54 Ohio App. 2d 79, 8 Ohio Op. 3d 132, 375 N.E.2d 57, 1977 Ohio App. LEXIS 7017 (Ohio Ct. App., Wood County 1977).

**Friend**

Decedent's friend would not be entitled to inherit by intestate succession if the decedent's Last Will were found to be invalid since he was not a blood relative. Cook v. Everhart, 2019-Ohio-3044, 2019 Ohio App. LEXIS 3134 (Ohio Ct. App., Cuyahoga County 2019).

**Net estate**

The "net estate" is that portion of the estate remaining after satisfaction of all the indebtedness of the decedent and the obligations of the estate. (Weeks v. Vandeveer, 13 Ohio St. 2d 15, 42 Ohio Op. 2d 25, 233 N.E.2d 502, 1968 Ohio LEXIS 457 (Ohio 1968).

**Next of kin**

Will admitted to probate bequeathed no property other than real property, and it did not contain a residuary clause. Thus, any settlement proceeds allocated to a survival claim passed to the decedent's father, because the decedent did not have a surviving spouse, surviving children, or surviving mother. In re Estate of Garza, 2013-Ohio-2750, 2013 Ohio App. LEXIS 2769 (Ohio Ct. App., Franklin County 2013).

Under R.C. 2105.06(I) (former subdivision 8 of GC § 10503-4), a subsection of the statute of descent and distribution, before it is required that an estate be divided into equal halves and descend to the heirs of both branches of the family, at least one grandparent must survive, or not surviving must leave lineal descendants and where both do not survive and both do not leave lineal descendants there is no division of the estate and the entire estate goes to the next of kin without representation: Vodrey v. Quigley, 139 N.E.2d 108, 74 Ohio Law Abs. 29, 1956 Ohio Misc. LEXIS 344 (Ohio P. Ct.), aff'd, 143 N.E.2d 162, 75 Ohio Law Abs. 65, 1956 Ohio App. LEXIS 745 (Ohio Ct. App., Columbiana County 1956).

In the enactment of subdivision 8 of GC § 10503-4 [R.C. 2105.06, paragraph (I)], the general assembly clearly intended to divide an estate between the two sides of a family only so long as there were surviving maternal or paternal grandparents or their lineal descendants; that, where there were no grandparents or their lineal descendants on one side, the one half should go to the surviving grandparents or their lineal descendants on the other side; and that the next of kin should inherit only where there were no surviving grandparents or their lineal descendants on either side: In re Estate of Kelly, 165 Ohio St. 259, 59 Ohio Op. 354, 135 N.E.2d 378, 1956 Ohio LEXIS 487 (Ohio 1956).

**Per stirpes**

The phrase "per stirpes" as used in par. 8 of this section [now par. (I)] modifies the word "descendants" and not the words "grandparent or grandparents": Oakley v. Davey, 49 Ohio App. 113, 1 Ohio Op. 144, 195 N.E. 406 (1934), reversing Davey v. Climo, 30 Ohio N.P. (n.s.) 457.].

**Presumption of paternity**

Ohio follows the common law rule that a child conceived during the existence of a lawful marital relation is presumed to be the legitimate issue of the marriage: Gray v. Richardson, 474 F.2d 1370, 1973 U.S. App. LEXIS 11383 (6th Cir. Ohio 1973).

**Realty purchased by one spouse**

Real estate which has been purchased and paid for solely by a wife, and title thereto taken jointly with her husband, but he having thereafter immediately conveyed his interest to her, passes, upon the wife's death intestate after her husband's decease, to her next of kin, under this section: Speidel v. Schaller, 73 Ohio App. 141, 28 Ohio Op. 252, 55 N.E.2d 346, 40 Ohio Law Abs. 190, 1943 Ohio App. LEXIS 708 (Ohio Ct. App., Clermont County 1943).

**Separation agreement**

A covenant in a separation agreement that the agreement is a full settlement of the rights of each party in the estate of the other is binding, even though one of the parties dies intestate while a petition for dissolution of the marriage is pending, if the agreement shows that it was intended to bind the parties independently of any dissolution proceeding: In re Estate of Hogrefe, 30 Ohio App. 3d 238, 507 N.E.2d 414, 1986 Ohio App. LEXIS 10078 (Ohio Ct. App., Henry County 1986).

**Siblings**

Claimant's brother and sisters were personal representatives within the meaning of Fed. R. App. P. 43(a)(1) and were therefore properly substituted parties because (1) the claimant's social security claim survived his death, and payment of any amount due should have been made to the legal representative of the estate of the deceased individual, if any, because his mother, in whose name the appeal was filed, died prior to any payment being completed, under 42 U.S.C.S. § 404(d)(7) and 20 C.F.R. § 404.503(b)(7); and (2) R.C. 2105.06(G) articulated the manner in which a decedent's estate passed when the decedent died intestate. Cunningham v. Astrue, 360 Fed. Appx. 606, 2010 FED App. 0007N, 2010 U.S. App. LEXIS 193 (6th Cir. Ohio 2010).

**Stepchildren**

Stepson is not an "interested person" despite maintaining a mother-son relationship, purchasing stepmother's house, or having had power of attorney over stepmother's assets: In re Guardianship of Dougherty, 63 Ohio App. 3d 289, 578 N.E.2d 832, 1989 Ohio App. LEXIS 1799 (Ohio Ct. App., Montgomery County), dismissed, 45 Ohio St. 3d 712, 545 N.E.2d 901, 1989 Ohio LEXIS 2394 (Ohio 1989).

An illegitimate child, whose mother subsequently marries a man, not the child's father, is a stepchild of such man for the purpose of determining the descent and distribution of property: Kest v. Lewis, 169 Ohio St. 317, 8 Ohio Op. 2d 317, 159 N.E.2d 449, 1959 Ohio LEXIS 604 (Ohio 1959).

**Surviving spouse generally**

In an estate dispute, the trial court did not err in finding that appellants' amended complaint did not allege sufficient facts to support a claim of a pour-over bequest to the living trust as appellants conceded that no trust was never drafted. The residuary estate descended to appellee as decedent's surviving spouse and next-of-kin, pursuant to the intestate rules of descent and distribution because the residue and remainder of the estate could not be poured-over to the living trust. Mackay v. Thomas, 2018-Ohio-4154, 121 N.E.3d 814, 2018 Ohio App. LEXIS 4469 (Ohio Ct. App., Tuscarawas County 2018).

Trial court did not err by granting summary judgment for the insurer because, undisputedly, a change of beneficiary designation card was not in existence and the terms of the insurance policy specifically provided for payment to others i.e., the surviving spouse, as a default beneficiary. Although the executor and the surviving children presented a "wish she could have, should have" argument, there was no showing that the insurer breached its duty of good faith or acted negligently in following the specific provisions of the insurance contract. Keny v. Anthem Life Ins. Co., 2015-Ohio-2939, 2015 Ohio App. LEXIS 2838 (Ohio Ct. App., Delaware County 2015).

Probate court properly determined that a widow was not entitled to a dower interest pursuant to R.C. 2103.02 in property owned by her late husband where neither of the statutory circumstances existed; instead, she was properly provided with her distributive share under the statute of descent and distribution, R.C. 2105.06(D). In re Estate of French, 2011-Ohio-422, 2011 Ohio App. LEXIS 342 (Ohio Ct. App., Carroll County 2011).

The revocable living trust executed by the husband and accompanied by the wife's waiver of rights was effective to waive her statutory rights as surviving spouse: Miller v. Miller, 139 Ohio App. 3d 512, 744 N.E.2d 778, 2000 Ohio App. LEXIS 3751 (Ohio Ct. App., Cuyahoga County 2000), dismissed, 91 Ohio St. 3d 1445, 742 N.E.2d 143, 2001 Ohio LEXIS 379 (Ohio 2001).

The first $30,000 [now $60,000] which a surviving spouse is to receive pursuant to R.C. 2105.06(C) is a distribution which is to be made from the net estate rather than a charge against and deduction from the gross estate: Winkelfoos v. Mann, 16 Ohio App. 3d 266, 475 N.E.2d 509, 1984 Ohio App. LEXIS 12376 (Ohio Ct. App., Huron County 1984).

The value of an automobile taken under former R.C. 2113.53.2 shall not be considered an asset for the estate in computing a surviving spouse's interest under R.C. 2105.06: In re Estate of Green, 63 Ohio Misc. 44, 17 Ohio Op. 3d 388, 410 N.E.2d 812, 1980 Ohio Misc. LEXIS 53 (Ohio P. Ct. 1980).

The value of the statutory allowance taken under former R.C. 2117.20 shall be deducted from the gross estate prior to computing a surviving spouse's interest under R.C. 2105.06: In re Estate of Green, 63 Ohio Misc. 44, 17 Ohio Op. 3d 388, 410 N.E.2d 812, 1980 Ohio Misc. LEXIS 53 (Ohio P. Ct. 1980).

There can be no doubt, by virtue of the provisions of this section and those of R.C. 2103.02, that the surviving spouse is an heir for the purposes of inheritance, being subject to and having all the rights of an heir, and this status is neither enlarged nor diminished by the special relationship of husband and wife: In re Estate of Morgan, 185 N.E.2d 822, 89 Ohio Law Abs. 225, 1962 Ohio Misc. LEXIS 249 (Ohio P. Ct. 1962).

The proper manner by which to compute the one-third interest of a widow under par. 3 of this section [now par. (C)] is to be arrived at by adding the appraised value of the specifically devised real estate to the amount of cash remaining after having converted the remainder of the estate into money and after having deducted therefrom the debts, funeral expenses, costs of administration, allowance to widow for year's support and the twenty per cent allowance under GC § 10509-54 (R.C. 2115.13): In re Thoroman's Estate, 76 Ohio App. 309, 32 Ohio Op. 16, 62 N.E.2d 530, 43 Ohio Law Abs. 259, 1945 Ohio App. LEXIS 646 (Ohio Ct. App., Montgomery County 1945).

**Trust residue**

When a decedent's will created a trust for the care of the decedent's father but did not contain a residuary clause, the trust residue, upon the father's death, was intestate property which, under the laws of descent and distribution, passed to the decedent's next of kin, which was the father, and, under R.C. 2105.06(F), the father was free to dispose of the residue as the father saw fit, so, when the father's will left the father's entire estate to the trust's trustee, the residue belonged solely to the trustee, because the law favored the immediate vesting of estates at the time of the decedent's death, absent the decedent's expression of a contrary intent, which was absent. Stevens v. Radey, 2008-Ohio-291, 117 Ohio St. 3d 65, 881 N.E.2d 855, 2008 Ohio LEXIS 242 (Ohio 2008).

**Vesting of estates**

Trial court properly denied summary judgment to a tenant in the landlord's action for, inter alia, unpaid rent because the landlord obtained title to the property pursuant to Ohio's statute of descent and distribution since the owner died intestate, the landlord's title vested immediately upon the owner's death, and, therefore, the landlord had authority to enter into the lease agreement. Hurton v. Boyer, 2020-Ohio-2790, 2020 Ohio App. LEXIS 1758 (Ohio Ct. App., Trumbull County 2020).

Unless a testator manifests a contrary intent in a will, the preference for the immediate vesting of estates requires interests to be assigned at the testator's death, not held in abeyance until a future uncertain date: Stevens v. Radey, 2008-Ohio-291, 117 Ohio St. 3d 65, 881 N.E.2d 855, 2008 Ohio LEXIS 242 (Ohio 2008).

**Vesting**

It is well settled that the law strongly favors the immediate vesting of estates, so the rights of beneficiaries become fixed and certain at the death of a testator unless a contrary intent is manifested, and, in the absence of some contrary intent expressed by the testator to postpone vesting, the preference for the vesting of all interests, including residuary interests, under R.C. 2131.04, in the testator's heirs at the earliest possible time is observed. Stevens v. Radey, 2008-Ohio-291, 117 Ohio St. 3d 65, 881 N.E.2d 855, 2008 Ohio LEXIS 242 (Ohio 2008).

Unless a testator manifests a contrary intent in a will, the preference for the immediate vesting of estates requires such interests to be assigned at the testator's death, not held in abeyance until a future uncertain date. Stevens v. Radey, 2008-Ohio-291, 117 Ohio St. 3d 65, 881 N.E.2d 855, 2008 Ohio LEXIS 242 (Ohio 2008).

**Will construction**

Where the terms of a will provide for a bequest or devise to a named person, per stirpes, without expressly designating the class of persons who are to take in the event that the named person does not survive the testatrix, and it is clear from the will taken as a whole, read in light of the circumstances surrounding the execution of the will, that a secondary gift was intended, then it will be assumed that a secondary gift is intended to go to the heirs at law of the named person as determined by the statutes of descent and distribution: Richland Trust Co. v. Becvar, 44 Ohio St. 2d 219, 73 Ohio Op. 2d 512, 339 N.E.2d 830, 1975 Ohio LEXIS 614 (Ohio 1975).

The legal meaning of the word, "heirs," denominating those designated by the statute of descent and distribution to inherit from the ancestor as of the time of application of such statute, will be followed unless it clearly and affirmatively appears that the testator intended a different meaning. (Holt v. Miller, 133 OS 418, 11 OO 85; Cultice v. Mills, 97 OS 112, followed: Casey v. Gallagher, 11 Ohio St. 2d 42, 40 Ohio Op. 2d 55, 227 N.E.2d 801 (1967).

Where will devised life estate to wife with provision that "all of my full blood and all of the half blood relatives shall share alike in the remainder, if any," and on death of testator only wife and cousins survived, the latter, upon the death of the wife, succeed to the title of devised real property per stirpes and not by equal distribution between the lineal descendants of the maternal and paternal branches: Parrett v. Paul, 115 Ohio App. 488, 21 Ohio Op. 2d 134, 185 N.E.2d 798, 1962 Ohio App. LEXIS 707 (Ohio Ct. App., Paulding County 1962).

Where a testator leaves all or a part of his estate "per stirpes among my heirs at law, according to the laws of descent and distribution now in force in the state of Ohio, which heirs at law shall be determined and distribution made as though my death had occurred at the time of the final termination of the trust hereby created," and where the law in effect at the testator's death is the same as the law in effect at the time the will was executed, the testator has expressed an intent that his "heirs at law" shall be determined as of the time of the termination of the trust but by the law in effect at the time the will was executed: Kraemer v. Hook, 168 Ohio St. 221, 6 Ohio Op. 2d 11, 152 N.E.2d 430, 1958 Ohio LEXIS 404 (Ohio 1958).

Where a testator gives the residue of his estate to his heirs in accordance with the laws and statutes of descent and distribution of Ohio in effect at the time of his decease, he clearly intends that said residue should be distributed to those individuals who would be entitled to the same in the event he should die intestate: Shook v. McConnell, 43 Ohio Op. 403, 97 N.E.2d 111, 59 Ohio Law Abs. 358, 1951 Ohio Misc. LEXIS 445 (Ohio P. Ct. 1951).

In determining heirs under a residuary clause in a will leaving the residue to the next of kin and heirs under the laws of descent, where there are no persons or classes of persons within the first seven paragraphs of this section, and the deceased left surviving him no paternal or maternal grandparents or their lineal descendants, the estate goes to the "next of kin," that is, the nearest of kindred to the deceased who are most nearly related by blood; where there is only one relative bearing a relationship of five degrees or less, such relative is his only next of kin: In re Morris' Estate, 29 Ohio Op. 173, 39 Ohio Law Abs. 187, 1943 Ohio Misc. LEXIS 254 (Ohio P. Ct. 1943).

Under former GC § 8573 (see now R.C. 2105.06) the son of a deceased nephew of the testator was held to take as "next of kin" under a will devising property "to the next of my kin, to them as they would take under statute of descent and distribution," where the testator died leaving no issue or surviving spouse: Jobe v. Shaffer, 25 Ohio Law Abs. 649, 1936 Ohio Misc. LEXIS 932 (Ohio Ct. App., Greene County Nov. 14, 1936).

**Wills**

**—Election**

Where a certified letter which notified a surviving spouse of her right to make an election regarding her deceased husband's will was properly served pursuant to Civ.R. 4.1(A) and 73(E)(3) when it was clearly delivered to the correct address and the spouse's son signed for the letter, the five-month statutory period to make such an election pursuant to R.C. 2105.06 and 2106.01(E) began to run; as the spouse made an election to take against her deceased husband's will beyond that five-month period, the probate court properly granted the executrix's motion to strike the election and the spouse was presumed to have elected to take pursuant to the will. In re Estate of Riley, 2006-Ohio-956, 165 Ohio App. 3d 471, 847 N.E.2d 22, 2006 Ohio App. LEXIS 898 (Ohio Ct. App., Scioto County 2006).

## ATTORNEY GENERAL OPINIONS

For purposes of R.C. 145.43 and 145.45, which provide for Public Employee Retirement System survivor benefits, and R.C. 3307.48 and 3307.49, which provide for State Teachers Retirement System survivor benefits, the term "child" does not include a stepchild. (1973 OAG No. 73-065 overruled): 1988 Ohio Op. Att'y Gen. No. 090 (1988).

## RESEARCH REFERENCES AND PRACTICE AIDS

**Cross-References to Related Sections**

Action to sell real estate, denial by court, RC § 2127.04.
Adopted child, legal rights, RC § 3107.15.
Authorizing agent for cremation, RC § 4717.22.
Capacity of illegitimate children to inherit, RC § 2105.17.
Dower, RC § 2103.02.
Election by surviving spouse, RC § 2106.01.
Citation to make election, RC § 2106.02.
Election made by one under legal disability, RC § 2106.08.
Election made in person, RC § 2106.06.
Election to receive mansion house, RC § 2106.10.
Estate tax not to be apportioned against property that passes as elective or intestate share under certain conditions, RC § 2113.86.
Gifts received by will not to be included in reports to ethics commission, RC §§ 102.02, 102.022.
Heirs of aliens may inherit, RC § 2105.16.
Living and died construed, RC § 2105.02.
Parentage actions, statutes of limitations, RC § 3111.05.
Parent who abandons minor child barred from intestate succession from child; status as next of kin or heir at law, RC § 2105.10.
Parties to will contest, RC § 2107.73.
Passing of real property subject to monetary charge of surviving spouse, RC § 2105.061.
Payment of specific monetary share to surviving spouse, RC § 2106.11.
Persons prohibited from benefiting by the death of another, RC § 2105.19.
Probate court as superior guardian of all wards, RC § 2111.50.
Proceedings in case of presumption of death, RC § 2121.02.
Release from administration, RC § 2113.03.
Sales of former executor or administrator valid, RC § 2113.23.
Uniform transfer-on-death security registration; heirs defined, RC § 1709.01.

**Ohio Constitution**

Nonforfeiture of estate, Ohio Const. art I, § 12.

**Comparative Legislation**

Distribution — intestate:
CA—Cal Prob Code § 6400 et seq
FL—Fla. Stat. § 732.101 et seq
IL—755 Ill. Comp. Stat. § 5/2-1
IN—Burns Ind. Code Ann. § 29-1-2-1
KY—KRS § 391.010
MI—MCLS §§ 700.2101-700.2103
NY—NY CLS EPTL § 4-1.1
PA—20 P.S. § 2101 et seq

**Practice Manuals and Treatises**

Anderson's The Simple Will in Ohio § 5.7 Right to Take Against Will
Anderson's The Simple Will in Ohio § 5.22 Exemption of Spouse's Share
Anderson's Ohio Civil Practice with Forms § 51.01 Substance of the Action
Anderson's Ohio Probate Practice and Procedure Form 6.01 Complaint to contest will and codicil
Anderson's Ohio Probate Practice and Procedure Form 15.11 Application for appointment of commissioner to take election
Anderson's Ohio Probate Practice and Procedure Form 15.15 Application for appointment of commissioner where spouse is under disability
Anderson's Ohio Probate Practice and Procedure Form 15.16 Journal entry appointing commissioner to ascertain values
Anderson's Ohio Probate Practice and Procedure Form 15.17 Commission to ascertain value of provision for surviving spouse under legal disability under will and value of rights at law
Anderson's Ohio Probate Practice and Procedure Form 15.18 Journal entry making election for surviving spouse under legal disability
Anderson's Ohio Probate Practice and Procedure Form 15.19 Election of surviving spouse to receive mansion house
Anderson's Ohio Probate Practice and Procedure Form 16.14 Probate issues in title examinations Ohio checklist
Anderson's Ohio Probate Practice and Procedure Form 21.08 Application for distribution of personal property to surviving spouse in satisfaction of specific monetary share
Anderson's Ohio Probate Practice and Procedure Form 53.01 Complaint as to presumption of death because of absence for five-year period [when person was domiciled in Ohio at time of disappearance]
Anderson's Ohio Probate Practice and Procedure Form 53.02 Complaint as to presumption of death because of absence for five-year period [when person at time of disappearance was domiciled outside Ohio]
Anderson's Ohio Probate Practice and Procedure Form 21.09 Order of distribution of personal property to surviving spouse in satisfaction of specific monetary share
Anderson's Ohio Probate Practice and Procedure Form 53.03 Complaint as to presumption of specific peril of death [when presumed decedent was exposed to a specific peril of death]
Anderson's Ohio Probate Practice and Procedure Standard Probate Form 1.0 Surviving Spouse, Children, Next of Kin, Legatees and Devisees
Anderson's Ohio Probate Practice and Procedure Outline No. § 45 Election by spouse under will-under legal disability

**Practice Guides**

Anderson's Ohio Probate Practice and Procedure § 8.01 General
Anderson's Ohio Probate Practice and Procedure § 15.05 Election to take the testamentary share or to take against the will
Anderson's Ohio Probate Practice and Procedure § 15.06 Election to receive the mansion house as part of intestate share and family allowance
Anderson's Ohio Probate Practice and Procedure § 16.01 The nature of the decedent's interest in real property
Anderson's Ohio Probate Practice and Procedure § 16.02 Descent
Anderson's Ohio Probate Practice and Procedure § 16.04 Certificate of transfer; unregistered land
Anderson's Ohio Probate Practice and Procedure § 17. Synopsis to Chapter 17 Descent and distribution; heirs
Anderson's Ohio Probate Practice and Procedure § 17.03 Statute of descent and distribution; Revised Code § 2105.06
Anderson's Ohio Probate Practice and Procedure § 17.07 Effect of the order of death on intestate succession

Anderson's Ohio Probate Practice and Procedure § 18.07 Identification of the beneficiaries; collateral heirs
Anderson's Ohio Probate Practice and Procedure § 18.08 Afterborn and pretermitted heirs
Anderson's Ohio Probate Practice and Procedure § 23.10 Apportionment of taxes among beneficiaries
Anderson's Ohio Probate Practice and Procedure § 26.03 Surviving spouse
Anderson's Ohio Probate Practice and Procedure § 26.05 Intestacy vs. wills
Anderson's Ohio Probate Practice and Procedure § 27.04 Beneficiaries
Anderson's Ohio Probate Practice and Procedure § 48.02 Revocable inter vivos trusts
Anderson's Ohio Probate Practice and Procedure § 55.03 Establishing parentage in juvenile court
Anderson's Ohio Probate Practice and Procedure § 58.02 Calculation of dower interests

**Practice Forms**
Complaint: Will Contest, Anderson's Ohio Civil Practice with Forms Form 144B.04
Surviving Spouse, Next of Kin, Legatees and Devisees, Couse's Ohio Form Book Form SPF 1.0
Application by Administrator or Executor for Distribution of Personal Property in Kind to Surviving Spouse 1, 12 OH Forms of Pleading & Practice — Probate Form 14:10



## § 2105.061 Passing of real property subject to monetary charge of surviving spouse.

Except any real property that a surviving spouse elects to receive under section 2106.10 of the Revised Code, the title to real property in an intestate estate shall descend and pass in parcenary to those persons entitled to it under division (B), (C), or (D) of section 2105.06 of the Revised Code, subject to the monetary charge of the surviving spouse. The administrator or executor shall file an application for a certificate of transfer as provided in section 2113.61 of the Revised Code, and the application shall include a statement of the amount of money that remains due and payable to the surviving spouse as found by the probate court. The certificate of transfer ordered by the probate court shall recite that the title to the real property described in the certificate is subject to the monetary charge in favor of the surviving spouse and shall recite the value in dollars of the charge on the title to the real property included in the certificate.

**HISTORY:**
143 v H 346 (Eff 5-31-90); 148 v S 152. Eff 3-22-2001.

**Editor's Notes**
See provisions, § 3 of SB 152 (148 v —), following RC § 2105.06.

### RESEARCH REFERENCES AND PRACTICE AIDS

**Practice Manuals and Treatises**
Anderson's Ohio Probate Practice and Procedure Outline No. § 87 Transfer of real property

**Practice Guides**
Anderson's Ohio Probate Practice and Procedure § 16.04 Certificate of transfer; unregistered land

## § 2105.062 Prohibition on inheritance.

As used in this section, "relative" includes a parent, grandparent, great-grandparent, stepparent, child, grandchild, aunt, uncle, cousin, sibling, and half sibling.

The parent, or a relative of the parent, of a child who was conceived as the result of the parent's violation of section 2907.02 or 2907.03 of the Revised Code shall not inherit the real property, personal property, or inheritance of the child or the child's lineal descendants as provided under section 2105.06 of the Revised Code.

**HISTORY:**
2014 sb207, § 1, effective March 23, 2015.

## § 2105.063 Renumbered.

Amended and renumbered RC §§ 2106.10, 2106.11 in 143 v H 346. Eff 5-31-90.

## § 2105.07 Escheat of personal estate.

When, under Chapter 2105. of the Revised Code, personal property escheats to the state, the prosecuting attorney of the county in which letters of administration are granted upon such estate shall collect and pay it over to the county treasurer. Such estate shall be applied exclusively to the support of the common schools of the county in which collected.

**HISTORY:**
GC § 10503-24; 114 v 320(344); Bureau of Code Revision, 10-1-53; 149 v H 242. Eff 5-16-2002.

**Editor's Notes**
See provisions, § 5 of HB 345 (149 v —) following RC § 2105.39.

### NOTES TO DECISIONS

Analysis

Generally
Unclaimed funds
Unknown heir

**Generally**
Escheat is an incident or attribute of sovereignty. In Ohio, by virtue of R.C. 2105.07, the right of the state to escheated funds has been relinquished to the county: Illes v. State, 10 Ohio App. 3d 111, 460 N.E.2d 707, 1983 Ohio App. LEXIS 11112 (Ohio Ct. App., Franklin County 1983).

A person died intestate leaving personal property only, and leaving no spouse relict, no heirs at law or next of kin. It was held that such personal estate is vested in the state under former GC § 8579 (see now R.C. 2105.07). (Children of the deceased wife by a former marriage claimed the property): Center v. Kramer, 112 Ohio St. 269, 147 N.E. 602, 3 Ohio Law Abs. 200, 1925 Ohio LEXIS 329 (Ohio 1925).

**Unclaimed funds**
The state in which intermediary banks, brokers, and depositories are incorporated has the right to escheat funds such as unclaimed dividends, interest, and other securities distributions belonging to beneficial owners who cannot be identified or located: Delaware v. New York, 507 U.S. 490, 113 S. Ct. 1550, 123 L. Ed. 2d 211, 1993 U.S. LEXIS 2553 (U.S. 1993).

**Unknown heir**
Where there is a living heir of a decedent, even though he may be unknown to the administrator at the time of administration of the estate, the state takes no title to the personal property of the estate by escheat: Borovskaya v. State, 54 Ohio App. 2d 79, 8 Ohio Op. 3d 132, 375 N.E.2d 57, 1977 Ohio App. LEXIS 7017 (Ohio Ct. App., Wood County 1977).

### ATTORNEY GENERAL OPINIONS

The term "common schools" has been used in Ohio law for many years and is ordinarily understood to mean "public schools," or schools that are administered by public agencies and maintained from public funds. Precisely which schools are included as common schools under a particular statute depends on the intent of the legislature in enacting that statute: 1995 Ohio Op. Att'y Gen. No. 031 (1995).

The provisions of R.C. 3315.32, repealed by 1985-1986 Ohio Laws, Part I, 1760, 2640 (Sub. H.B. 201, eff. July 1, 1985, with repeal eff. Aug. 1, 1985), might provide some guidance as to an interpretation of R.C. 2105.07 that could be considered reasonable: 1995 Ohio Op. Att'y Gen. No. 031 (1995).

In the absence of statutory direction, the county may distribute funds under R.C. 2105.07 to the support of the common schools of the county in any manner that it determines to be fair and equitable: 1995 Ohio Op. Att'y Gen. No. 031 (1995).

There is no provision of law authorizing the payment of interest by the county treasurer on funds paid to him as escheated but subsequently claimed by an heir: 1934 OAG No. 2257 (1934).

### RESEARCH REFERENCES AND PRACTICE AIDS

**Cross-References to Related Sections**
Proceedings in case of presumption of death, RC § 2121.02.

**Practice Manuals and Treatises**
Anderson's Ohio Probate Practice and Procedure Form 21.10 Disposition of escheated personal property
Anderson's Ohio Probate Practice and Procedure Form 21.11 Order of distribution of escheated personal property to county treasurer

### § 2105.08 Application of provisions relating to escheating estates.

Chapter 2105. of the Revised Code applies to any escheating estate of which possession has not been taken, or which has not been collected by the proper officers of the state or those acting under their authority. Right or claim of the state thereto is hereby relinquished to the person who would have been entitled thereto had such sections been in force when the intestate died.

**HISTORY:**

GC § 10503-25; 114 v 320(344); Bureau of Code Revision, 10-1-53; 149 v H 242. Eff 5-16-2002.

**Editor's Notes**

See provisions, § 5 of HB 345 (149 v —) following RC § 2105.39.

RESEARCH REFERENCES AND PRACTICE AIDS

**Practice Manuals and Treatises**

Anderson's Ohio Probate Practice and Procedure Form 21.10 Disposition of escheated personal property

Anderson's Ohio Probate Practice and Procedure Form 21.11 Order of distribution of escheated personal property to county treasurer

### § 2105.09 Disposition of escheated lands.

(A) The county auditor, unless the auditor acts pursuant to division (C) of this section, shall take possession of real property escheated to the state that is located in the auditor's county and outside the incorporated area of a city. The auditor shall take possession in the name of the state and sell the property at public auction, at the county seat of the county, to the highest bidder, after having given thirty days' notice of the intended sale in a newspaper of general circulation in the county or as provided in section 7.16 of the Revised Code.

On the application of the auditor, the court of common pleas shall appoint three disinterested freeholders of the county to appraise the real property. The freeholders shall be governed by the same rule as appraisers in sheriffs' or administrators' sales. The auditor shall sell the property at not less than two thirds of its appraised value and may sell it for cash, or for one-third cash and the balance in equal annual payments, the deferred payments to be amply secured. Upon payment of the whole consideration, the auditor shall execute a deed to the purchaser, in the name and on behalf of the state. The proceeds of the sale shall be paid by the auditor to the county treasurer.

If there is a regularly organized agricultural society within the county, the treasurer shall pay the greater of six hundred dollars or five per cent of the proceeds, in any case, to the society. The excess of the proceeds, or the whole thereof if there is no regularly organized agricultural society within the county, shall be distributed as follows:

(1) Twenty-five per cent shall be paid equally to the townships of the county;

(2) Seventy per cent shall be paid into the state treasury to the credit of the agro Ohio fund created under section 901.04 of the Revised Code;

(3) Five per cent shall be credited to the county general fund for such lawful purposes as the board of county commissioners provides.

(B) The legislative authority of a city within which are lands escheated to the state, unless it acts pursuant to division (C) of this section, shall take possession of the lands for the city, and the title to the lands shall vest in the city. The city shall use the premises primarily for health, welfare, or recreational purposes, or may lease them at such prices and for such purposes as it considers proper. With the approval of the tax commissioner, the city may sell the lands or any undivided interest in the lands, in the same manner as is provided in the sale of land not needed for any municipal purposes; provided, that the net proceeds from the rent or sale of the premises shall be devoted to health, welfare, or recreational purposes.

(C) As an alternative to the procedure prescribed in divisions (A) and (B) of this section, the county auditor, or if the real property is located within the incorporated area of a city, the legislative authority of that city by an affirmative vote of at least a majority of its members, may request the probate court to direct the administrator or executor of the estate that contains the escheated property to commence an action in the probate court for authority to sell the real property in the manner provided in Chapter 2127. of the Revised Code. The proceeds from the sale of real property that is located outside the incorporated area of a city shall be distributed by the court in the same manner as the proceeds are distributed under division (A) of this section. The proceeds from the sale of real property that is located within the incorporated area of a city shall be distributed by the court in the same manner as the proceeds are distributed under division (B) of this section.

**HISTORY:**

GC §§ 10503-26—10503-29; 114 v 320(344); 122 v 256; Bureau of Code Revision, 10-1-53; 136 v H 1098 (Eff 8-6-76); 136 v H 920 (Eff 10-11-76); 137 v H 42 (Eff 10-7-77); 140 v H 260 (Eff 9-27-83); 141 v H 201 (Eff 7-1-85); 141 v H 751. Eff 9-8-86; 2011 HB 153, § 101.01, eff. Sept. 29, 2011.

**Amendment Notes**

The 2011 amendment, in the second sentence of the first paragraph of (A), substituted "of general circulation in" for "published within" and added "or as provided in section 7.16 of the Revised Code" to the end; and made stylistic changes.

RESEARCH REFERENCES AND PRACTICE AIDS

**Cross-References to Related Sections**

Gifts or bequests credited to agro Ohio fund, RC § 901.04.

Proceedings in case of presumption of death, RC § 2121.02.

**Comparative Legislation**

Sale of estates which have escheated to state:

CA—Cal Code Civ Proc § 1370 et seq

FL—Fla. Stat. §§ 732.107, 733.816

IL—755 Ill. Comp. Stat. § 20/2

IN—Burns Ind. Code Ann. § 29-1-17-12

KY—KRS § 393.030

**Practice Manuals and Treatises**

Anderson's Ohio Probate Practice and Procedure Form 17.09 Application of county auditor for appointment of appraisers for escheated real estate

Anderson's Ohio Probate Practice and Procedure Form 17.10 Order appointing appraisers for escheated real estate

Anderson's Ohio Probate Practice and Procedure Form 17.11 Notice of public sale of escheated real estate

Anderson's Ohio Probate Practice and Procedure Form 17.12 Application requesting probate court to direct fiduciary to commence land sale proceeding

Anderson's Ohio Probate Practice and Procedure Form 17.13 Order directing fiduciary to commence land sale proceeding

### § 2105.10 Parent who abandons minor child barred from intestate succession from child; status as next of kin or heir at law.

(A) As used in this section:

(1) "Abandoned" means that a parent of a minor failed without justifiable cause to communicate with the minor, care for the minor, and provide for the minor's maintenance or support as required by law or judicial decree for a period of at least one year immediately prior to the date of the death of the minor.

(2) "Minor" means a person who is less than eighteen years of age.

(B) Subject to divisions (C), (D), and (E) of this section, a parent who has abandoned the parent's minor child who subsequently dies intestate as a minor shall not inherit the real or personal property of the deceased child pursuant to section 2105.06 of the Revised Code. If a parent is prohibited by this division from inheriting from the parent's deceased child, the real or personal property of the deceased child shall be distributed, or shall descend and pass in parcenary, pursuant to section 2105.06 of the Revised Code as if the parent had predeceased the deceased child.

(C) Subject to divisions (D) and (E) of this section, a parent who is alleged to have abandoned a child who died as an intestate minor shall be considered as a next of kin or an heir at law of the deceased child only for the following purposes:

(1) To receive any notice required to be given to the heirs at law of a decedent in connection with an application for release of an estate from administration under section 2113.03 of the Revised Code;

(2) To be named as a next of kin in an application for the appointment of a person as the administrator of the estate of the deceased child, if the parent is known to the person filing the application pursuant to section 2113.07 of the Revised Code, and to receive a citation issued by the probate court pursuant to that section.

(D)(1) The prohibition against inheritance set forth in division (B) of this section shall be enforceable only in accordance with a probate court adjudication rendered pursuant to this division.

(2) If the administrator of the estate of an intestate minor has actual knowledge, or reasonable cause to believe, that the minor was abandoned by a parent, the administrator shall file a petition pursuant to section 2123.02 of the Revised Code to obtain an adjudication that the parent abandoned the child and that, because of the prohibition against inheritance set forth in division (B) of this section, the parent shall not be considered to be an heir at law of, and shall not be entitled to inherit the real and personal property of, the deceased child pursuant to section 2105.06 of the Revised Code. That parent shall be named as a defendant in the petition and, whether or not that parent is a resident of this state, shall be served with a summons and a copy of the petition in accordance with the Rules of Civil Procedure. In the heirship determination proceeding, the administrator has the burden of proving, by a preponderance of the evidence, that the parent abandoned the child. If, after the hearing, the probate court finds that the administrator has sustained that burden of proof, the probate court shall include in its adjudication described in section 2123.05 of the Revised Code its findings that the parent abandoned the child and, because of the prohibition against inheritance set forth in division (B) of this section, the parent shall not be considered to be an heir at law of, and shall not be entitled to inherit the real and personal property of, the deceased child pursuant to section 2105.06 of the Revised Code. If the probate court so finds, then, upon the entry of its adjudication on its journal, the administrator may make a final distribution of the estate of the deceased child in accordance with division (B) of this section.

(3) An heirship determination proceeding resulting from the filing of a petition pursuant to this division shall be conducted in accordance with Chapter 2123. of the Revised Code, except to the extent that a provision of this section conflicts with a provision of that chapter, in which case the provision of this section shall control.

(E) If the administrator of the estate of an intestate minor has not commenced an heirship determination proceeding as described in division (D) of this section within four months from the date that the administrator receives the administrator's letters of administration, then that proceeding may not be commenced subsequently, no parent of the deceased child shall be prohibited from inheriting the real or personal property of the deceased child pursuant to division (B) of this section, and the probate of the estate of the deceased child in accordance with section 2105.06 and other relevant sections of the Revised Code shall be forever binding.

**HISTORY:**

144 v H 166. Eff 8-3-92; 2011 SB 124, § 1, eff. Jan. 13, 2012.

**Editor's Notes**

Acts 2011, SB 124, § 3 provides: "The provisions of this act that relate to the estates of decedents apply to the estates of decedents who die on or after the effective date of this act."

The provisions of § 3 of HB 166 (144 v —) read as follows:

SECTION 3. The provisions of section 2105.10 of the Revised Code, as enacted by this act, shall apply to all parents of minors who die intestate on or after the effective date of this act, whether or not the abandonment described in that section commenced prior to, on, or after the effective date of this act. The amendments to sections 2125.02 and 2125.03 of the Revised Code, as amended by this act, shall apply to all parents of minors who die on or after the effective date of this act, whether or not the abandonment, as described in section 2125.02 of the Revised Code, as amended by this act, commenced prior to, on, or after the effective date of this act.

**Amendment Notes**

The 2011 amendment made stylistic changes.

### NOTES TO DECISIONS

**Abandonment**

Even though a father had not communicated with his child or cared for the child within the year preceding the child's death, since the father had paid child support within the year prior to the child's death he had not "abandoned" the child, within the meaning of R.C. 2105.10(A)(1), and was entitled to share in the child's estate. Keybank Nat'l Ass'n v. Hanns, 2009-Ohio-1935, 2009 Ohio App. LEXIS 1658 (Ohio Ct. App., Montgomery County 2009).

Since R.C. 2125.02(G)(3), which defined "abandoned" for purposes of the wrongful death statute, was similar to R.C. 2105.10(A)(1), it was used as a guide in interpreting § 2105.10(A)(1). Section 2105.10(A)(1) should be read in the conjunctive, i.e., if a parent performed any of the three actions — communicating, caring, or providing for the child's maintenance and support — the parent had not "abandoned the child within the meaning of § 2105.10(A)(1). Keybank Nat'l Ass'n v. Hanns, 2009-Ohio-1935, 2009 Ohio App. LEXIS 1658 (Ohio Ct. App., Montgomery County 2009).

Ohio General Assembly's use of the conjunctive in R.C. 2105.10(A)(1) and 2125.02(G)(3) suggests that all three conditions must be met to constitute abandonment. Therefore, the estate bears the burden of establishing, by a preponderance of the evidence, that the alleged abandoning parent failed to perform all of the three parental duties under § 2105.10(A)(1). Keybank Nat'l Ass'n v. Hanns, 2009-Ohio-1935, 2009 Ohio App. LEXIS 1658 (Ohio Ct. App., Montgomery County 2009).

### RESEARCH REFERENCES AND PRACTICE AIDS

**Cross-References to Related Sections**

Application for appointment as executor or administrator, RC § 2113.07.
Descent and distribution, RC § 2105.06.
Finding and order of determination of heirship, RC § 2123.05.
Proceedings in case of presumption of death, RC § 2121.02.
Release from administration, RC § 2113.03.

## § 2105.11 Estate to descend equally to children of intestate.

When a person dies intestate leaving children and none of the children of the intestate have died leaving children or their lineal descendants, the estate shall descend to the children of the intestate living at the time of the intestate's death in equal proportions.

**HISTORY:**

GC § 10503-6; 114 v 320(340); Bureau of Code Revision. Eff 10-1-53; 2011 SB 124, § 1, eff. Jan. 13, 2012.

**Editor's Notes**

Acts 2011, SB 124, § 3 provides: "The provisions of this act that relate to the estates of decedents apply to the estates of decedents who die on or after the effective date of this act."

**Amendment Notes**

The 2011 amendment made stylistic changes.

### NOTES TO DECISIONS

**Construction with other laws**

Timing of the mother's intestate death was not relevant to whether a mechanic's lien later arose that was enforceable regarding the son's interest in the property as R.C. 1311.02 established that a mechanic's lien was on the improvement and all interests that the part owner may have or subsequently acquire in the land. United States Bank Nat'l Ass'n v. Unknown Heirs, 2019-Ohio-2021, 136 N.E.3d 879, 2019 Ohio App. LEXIS 2086 (Ohio Ct. App., Franklin County 2019).

### RESEARCH REFERENCES AND PRACTICE AIDS

**Cross-References to Related Sections**

Living and died construed, RC § 2105.02.
Proceedings in case of presumption of death, RC § 2121.02.

**Comparative Legislation**

Descent of property to children, no surviving spouse:
CA—Cal Prob Code § 6402
FL—Fla. Stat. § 732.103
IL—755 Ill. Comp. Stat. § 5/2-1

IN—Burns Ind. Code Ann. § 29-1-2-1
KY—KRS § 391.010
MI—MCLS §§ 700.2101-700.2103
NY—NY CLS EPTL § 4-1.1
PA—20 P.S. § 2103

## § 2105.12 Descent when all descendants of equal degree of consanguinity.

When all the descendants of an intestate, in a direct line of descent, are on an equal degree of consanguinity to the intestate, the estate shall pass to such persons in equal parts, however remote from the intestate such equal and common degree of consanguinity may be.

**HISTORY:**

GC § 10503-7; 114 v 320(341); Bureau of Code Revision. Eff 10-1-53.

### NOTES TO DECISIONS

Analysis

Generally
Common law
Construction with other laws
Wills

**Generally**

When an intestate dies leaving no spouse, no children or their lineal descendants, or no surviving parent and is preceded in death by two brothers, one of whom leaves one child and one of whom leaves two children surviving at the time of the death of the intestate, the children of such deceased brothers, being in an equal degree of consanguinity to the intestate, inherit per capita pursuant to R.C. 2105.12: Washburn v. Scurlock, 5 Ohio App. 3d 125, 449 N.E.2d 797, 1982 Ohio App. LEXIS 11031 (Ohio Ct. App., Jackson County 1982).

Where the heirs of the intestate consist of lineal descendants of both the paternal and maternal grandparents, even though such heirs are on an equal degree of consanguinity to the intestate, the estate will be divided in halves, in accordance with R.C. 2105.06: Reimer v. Finnegan, 32 Ohio Op. 391 (Ohio P. Ct. 1945); In re Stephenson's Estate, 75 N.E.2d 834, 48 Ohio Law Abs. 624, 1946 Ohio Misc. LEXIS 200 (Ohio P. Ct. 1946).

This section provides that when all the descendants of an intestate are of an equal degree of consanguinity they take equally: Snodgrass v. Bedell, 134 Ohio St. 311, 12 Ohio Op. 103, 16 N.E.2d 463, 1938 Ohio LEXIS 291 (Ohio 1938).

**Common law**

The rule with reference to distribution per capita and per stirpes which obtained in Ohio at common law and equity prior to this statute was not changed thereby: Ewers v. Follin, 9 Ohio St. 327, 1859 Ohio LEXIS 192 (Ohio 1859); Dutoit v. Doyle, 16 Ohio St. 400, 1865 Ohio LEXIS 81 (Ohio 1865); Parsons v. Parsons, 52 Ohio St. 470, 40 N.E. 165, 1895 Ohio LEXIS 148 (Ohio 1895).

**Construction with other laws**

Under the provisions of this section and GC §§ 10503-4, 10503-8 and 10503-9 (R.C. 2105.06 and 2105.13), which must be read in pari materia, nephews and nieces of a decedent who left no other nearer of kin surviving, take per capita, and the descendants of deceased nephews and nieces take per stirpes: Stocker v. Tranter, 31 Ohio N.P. 467 (1934); Schwaigert v. Vitzhum, 12 Ohio Op. 114, 26 Ohio Law Abs. 442, 1938 Ohio Misc. LEXIS 1116 (Ohio P. Ct. 1938).

**Wills**

A will giving property to life tenant, with remainder at her death to issue of her body then living, required distribution per stirpes among living children and children of deceased child (former GC § 8581 [see now R.C. 2105.12] et seq): Watson v. Watson, 34 Ohio App. 311, 171 N.E. 257, 1929 Ohio App. LEXIS 324 (Ohio Ct. App., Pickaway County 1929).

Under a provision in a will, "I give and devise to the children of A, and the children of B, and C, all said children being my grandchildren, the following real estate, to-wit: [Description of property], to have and to hold the same for the said grandchildren, their heirs and assigns forever," a distribution per capita, rather than a distribution per stirpes, will be presumed to have been intended by the testator, since the law favors equality rather than inequality; and if A has two children and B and C have twelve children, each of such grandchildren will take one-fourteenth of the estate: Broermann v. Kessling, 6 Ohio App. 7, 30 Ohio Cir. Dec. 103, 28 Ohio C.A. 321, 28 Ohio C.C. (n.s.) 321, 1914 Ohio App. LEXIS 184 (Ohio Ct. App., Hamilton County 1914).

Property which passed by devise to be distributed among all heirs of testator or some other person is to be distributed per stirpes in the absence of words showing a contrary intention: Eichenlaub v. Heschong, 18 Ohio Dec. 47, 5 Ohio N.P. (n.s.) 367, 1907 Ohio Misc. LEXIS 7 (Ohio C.P. 1907).

### RESEARCH REFERENCES AND PRACTICE AIDS

**Comparative Legislation**

Equal degree of consanguinity:
CA—Cal Prob Code § 6402
FL—Fla. Stat. § 732.104
IL—755 Ill. Comp. Stat. § 5/2-1
IN—Burns Ind. Code Ann. § 29-1-2-1
KY—KRS § 391.030
MI—MCLS § 700.2103
NY—NY CLS EPTL § 2-1.2
PA—20 P.S. § 2104

## § 2105.13 Descent when children and heirs of deceased children are living.

If some of the children of an intestate are living and others are dead, the estate shall descend to the children who are living and to the lineal descendants of the children who are dead, so that each child who is living will inherit the share to which the child who is living would have been entitled if all the children of the intestate were living, and the lineal descendants of the deceased child will inherit equal parts of that portion of the estate to which the deceased child would be entitled if the deceased child were living.

This section shall apply in all cases in which the descendants of the intestate, not more remote than lineal descendants of grandparents, entitled to share in the estate, are of unequal degree of consanguinity to the intestate, so that those who are of the nearest degree of consanguinity will take the share to which they would have been entitled, had all the descendants in the same degree of consanguinity with them who died leaving issue, been living.

**HISTORY:**

GC §§ 10503-8, 10503-9; 114 v 320(341); 116 v 385; Bureau of Code Revision. Eff 10-1-53; 2011 SB 124, § 1, eff. Jan. 13, 2012.

**Editor's Notes**

Acts 2011, SB 124, § 3 provides: "The provisions of this act that relate to the estates of decedents apply to the estates of decedents who die on or after the effective date of this act."

**Amendment Notes**

The 2011 amendment made stylistic changes.

### NOTES TO DECISIONS

Analysis

Generally
Construction with other laws
Debts of deceased child
Wills

**Generally**

Where those entitled to share in an estate are nieces, nephews, grandnieces and grandnephews of the intestate, the nieces and nephews take equally, per capita, according to the total number of nieces and nephews whether surviving or not, and the grandnieces and grandnephews take per stirpes or by representation the shares of their deceased parents: Kincaid v. Cronin, 61 Ohio App. 300, 15 Ohio Op. 198, 22 N.E.2d 576, 28 Ohio Law Abs. 475, 1939 Ohio App. LEXIS 447 (Ohio Ct. App., Hamilton County 1939).

Under GC § 10503-8 (R.C. 2105.13), if some of the descendants of an intestate are living and others are dead, leaving children, those living take the same per capita share to which they would be entitled if all were living, and the lineal descendants of those deceased take per stirpes: Snodgrass v. Bedell, 134 Ohio St. 311, 12 Ohio Op. 103, 16 N.E.2d 463, 1938 Ohio LEXIS 291 (Ohio 1938).

If realty which has descended from one spouse to another, passes on the death of the latter intestate, half to his heirs and half to hers, such relatives are not heirs of the surviving spouse, and therefore stand in unequal relationship to him, and they take per stirpes and not per capita: Newton v. Harris, 29 Ohio Dec. 251, 21 Ohio N.P. (n.s.) 329, 1918 Ohio Misc. LEXIS 39 (Ohio C.P. 1918).

**Construction with other laws**

The last part of the first paragraph of R.C. 2105.13 providing that "the lineal descendants of the deceased child will inherit equal parts of that portion of the estate to which such deceased child would be entitled if he were living," and the second paragraph applying the same rule to more remote next of kin, must be read in pari materia with R.C. 2105.06(F) (now (G)), relating to descent to brothers and sisters or their lineal descendants: Gruhler v. Hossapaus, 28 Ohio Op. 2d 477, 195 N.E.2d 387, 93 Ohio Law Abs. 71, 1963 Ohio Misc. LEXIS 213 (Ohio P. Ct. 1963).

**Debts of deceased child**

Nieces and nephews of an intestate decedent are subject to having a debt of their father, who predeceased the decedent, set off against their distributive share, when decedent has a brother and sister still living, in view of the provisions of this section, that "the lineal descendants of the deceased child will inherit equal parts of that portion of the estate to which such deceased child would be entitled if he were living": Gruhler v. Hossapaus, 28 Ohio Op. 2d 477, 195 N.E.2d 387, 93 Ohio Law Abs. 71, 1963 Ohio Misc. LEXIS 213 (Ohio P. Ct. 1963).



**Wills**

In a will which devised one-half of an estate to the lawful heirs of the testator and one-half to the lawful heirs of his wife, after the death of his only son without issue, and which contained specific provisions as to the disposition of the shares of his sister (if she should survive the testator) and of the sister and brother of his wife, the persons included in the designation "lawful heirs" to whom "my estate shall go," are to be ascertained as of the date of the death of the testator or his wife respectively per stirpes, the representatives of deceased brothers and sisters to take the share that would have gone to their ancestor if living, except where the will itself otherwise provides: Wilberding v. Miller, 90 Ohio St. 28, 106 N.E. 665 (1914), affirming on rehearing Miller v. Miller, 15 Ohio C.C. (n.s.) 481, 24 Ohio Cir. Dec. 43; which was modified in memorandum opinion, Wilberding v. Miller, 88 Ohio St. 609, and was on appeal from Miller v. Miller, 13 Ohio N.P. (n.s.) 1.].

A testator who provides, "all the remainder of my estate I desire shall descend and pass according to the laws of inheritance of the state of Ohio," intends that the residue of his estate shall be distributed the same as the personal property of an intestate would be distributed; and where such testator left surviving him two nephews and one niece and children of two other nieces, the residue of his estate will be divided in five parts of which the two nephews and the niece will each get one-fifth, and each set of children of the deceased nieces one-fifth to be equally divided among them: Elliott v. Shaw, 23 Ohio Dec. 662, 15 Ohio N.P. (n.s.) 81, 1913 Ohio Misc. LEXIS 26 (Ohio C.P. 1913).

### RESEARCH REFERENCES AND PRACTICE AIDS

**Cross-References to Related Sections**

Living and died construed, RC § 2105.02.
Proceedings in case of presumption of death, RC § 2121.02.

## § 2105.14 Posthumous child to inherit.

No descendant of an intestate shall inherit under this chapter unless surviving the intestate for at least one hundred twenty hours, or unless born within three hundred days after the death of the intestate and living for at least one hundred twenty hours after birth.

**HISTORY:**

GC § 10503-16; 114 v 320(342); Bureau of Code Revision. Eff 10-1-53; 2011 SB 124, § 1, eff. Jan. 13, 2012; 2016 sb232, § 1, effective March 14, 2017; 2016 hb432, § 1, effective April 6, 2017.

**Editor's Notes**

Acts 2011, SB 124, § 3 provides: "The provisions of this act that relate to the estates of decedents apply to the estates of decedents who die on or after the effective date of this act."

**Amendment Notes**

The 2016 amendment by SB 232 and HB 432 rewrote the section, which formerly read: "Descendants of an intestate begotten before the intestate's death, but born after the intestate's death, in all cases will inherit as if born in the lifetime of the intestate and surviving the intestate; but in no other case can a person inherit unless living at the time of the death of the intestate."

The 2011 amendment and made stylistic changes.

### NOTES TO DECISIONS

**Wills**

A bequest to a class of persons "living at the time of my death" includes in such class a child en ventre sa mere who is a viable unborn child capable of sustaining life outside the mother's womb even though not born until three days after the death of testatrix: Ebbs v. Smith, 59 Ohio Misc. 133, 11 Ohio Op. 3d 356, 394 N.E.2d 1034, 1979 Ohio Misc. LEXIS 66 (Ohio P. Ct. 1979).

### RESEARCH REFERENCES AND PRACTICE AIDS

**Cross-References to Related Sections**

Living and died construed, RC § 2105.02.
Proceedings in case of presumption of death, RC § 2121.02.

**Comparative Legislation**

Posthumous child:

- CA—Cal Prob Code § 6407
- FL—Fla. Stat. § 732.106
- IL—755 Ill. Comp. Stat. § 5/2-3
- IN—Burns Ind. Code Ann. § 29-1-2-6
- KY—KRS § 391.070
- MI—MCLS § 700.2106
- NY—NY CLS EPTL § 2-1.3
- PA—20 P.S. § 2104

## § 2105.15 Designation of heir at law.

A person of sound mind and memory may appear before the probate judge of the person's county and in the presence of the judge and two disinterested persons of that person's acquaintance, file a written declaration declaring that, as the person's free and voluntary act, the person did designate and appoint another, stating the name and place of residence of the other person specifically, to stand toward the person in the relation of an heir at law in the event of the person's death. The declaration shall be attested by the two disinterested persons and subscribed by the declarant. If satisfied that the declarant is of sound mind and memory and free from restraint, the judge shall enter that fact upon the judge's journal and make a complete record of the proceedings. From then on the person designated will stand in the same relation, for all purposes, to the declarant as the person designated could if a child born in lawful wedlock. The rules of inheritance will be the same between the person designated and the relations by blood of the declarant, as if so born. A certified copy of the record will be prima-facie evidence of the fact stated in the record, and conclusive evidence, unless impeached for actual fraud or undue influence. After a lapse of one year from the date of the designation, the declarant may have the designation vacated or changed by filing in that probate court an application to vacate or change the designation of heir; provided that there is compliance with the procedure, conditions, and prerequisites required in the making of the original declaration.

**HISTORY:**

GC § 10503-12; 114 v 320(341); 118 v 406; Bureau of Code Revision. Eff 10-1-53; 2011 SB 124, § 1, eff. Jan. 13, 2012.

**Editor's Notes**

Acts 2011, SB 124, § 3 provides: "The provisions of this act that relate to the estates of decedents apply to the estates of decedents who die on or after the effective date of this act."

**Amendment Notes**

The 2011 amendment substituted "the other person" for "such person" in the first sentence; deleted "thereupon" preceding "shall enter" in the third sentence; and made stylistic changes.

### NOTES TO DECISIONS

Analysis



**Generally**

An heir designated by virtue of R.C. 2105.15 is an heir under the statute of descent and distribution: Witten v. Landrum, 41 Ohio App. 2d 65, 70

Ohio Op. 2d 61, 322 N.E.2d 146, 1974 Ohio App. LEXIS 2608 (Ohio Ct. App., Van Wert County 1974).

A valid designation of an heir under this section amounts to the recognition by the designator of the designee as an adopted child: In re Estate of Gompf, 175 Ohio St. 400, 25 Ohio Op. 2d 388, 195 N.E.2d 806, 1964 Ohio LEXIS 1011 (Ohio 1964).

Under the statutes of descent and distribution, a person who has been designated and appointed by another as an heir at law, pursuant to this section, inherits from but not through his designator: Blackwell v. Bowman, 150 Ohio St. 34, 37 Ohio Op. 323, 80 N.E.2d 493 (1948), discussed in 9 Ohio St. L.J. 531; Uhl v. Armstrong, 140 N.E.2d 60, 78 Ohio Law Abs. 592, 1957 Ohio App. LEXIS 977 (Ohio Ct. App., Cuyahoga County 1957).

The designated heir of a brother of an intestate is not an heir of such intestate, and the intestate's niece, being the nearest of kin under the statutes of descent and distribution, inherits the estate: Southern Ohio Sav. Bank & Trust Co. v. Boyer, 66 Ohio App. 136, 19 Ohio Op. 398, 31 N.E.2d 161 (1940), discussed in 15 Ohio St. B. 214.

Neither this section, providing for designation of heirs, nor GC § 10512-9 (R.C. 3107.01), relative to adoption, contemplates giving an interest either to designated heir or adopted child, in the estate of any person other than that of the declarant, or of the adopting parent. Property may flow through the adopted child or the declared heir to others in the chain of title: Rogers v. Cromer, 37 N.E.2d 407, 24 Ohio Law Abs. 508, 1937 Ohio Misc. LEXIS 1144 (Ohio Ct. App., Miami County 1937).

A proceeding to designate an heir at law, as prescribed by this section, is ex parte, and the court's action in determining whether declarant is of sound mind and not under restraint is quasi-judicial; an expectant heir at law of such a declarant is without right to invoke the probate court's jurisdiction to set aside such designation on the ground it was not the free act of declarant, but the court, sua sponte, upon information furnished by such expectant heir, may modify or set aside its former action: Horine v. Horine, 16 Ohio Law Abs. 155, 1934 Ohio Misc. LEXIS 1403 (Ohio Ct. App., Darke County Jan. 11, 1934).

This section is constitutional, and it cannot be said that it deprives the prospective heirs of any right if they had no vested right in the property at the time of the designation: Davis v. Laws, 27 Ohio N.P. (n.s.) 193 (1928), affirmed, 34 Ohio App. 157, 170 N.E. 601.].

**Children out of wedlock**

Where a testamentary trust extended to the "lineal decedents" of the testator, a child born out of wedlock to the testator's grandson was a potential beneficiary, despite the lack of a prior determination of legal parentage, where DNA tests showed an overwhelming likelihood of paternity: Bank One Trust Co. N.A. v. Reynolds, 2007-Ohio-4197, 173 Ohio App. 3d 1, 877 N.E.2d 342, 2007 Ohio App. LEXIS 3794 (Ohio Ct. App., Montgomery County 2007).

Civ.R. 12 dismissal of a putative son's will contest (of a father's will) for lack of standing was proper; the son could not prove under R.C. 2105.15 that he was a son and an R.C. 2107.71 "person interested" by being acknowledged by the father during the father's lifetime to be a son; a prior alleged will naming the son was not executed with the proper R.C. 2107.03, 2107.26 formalities to be prima facie proof that he was acknowledged. Estate of Okos v. Farley, 2004-Ohio-2882, 2004 Ohio App. LEXIS 2542 (Ohio Ct. App., Lucas County 2004).

Whatever procedures are used to establish paternity of a child born out of wedlock the child cannot inherit from the natural father unless the required acts were completed prior to the death of the father: Hunter-Martin v. Winchester Transp., Inc., 71 Ohio App. 3d 273, 593 N.E.2d 383, 1991 Ohio App. LEXIS 1110 (Ohio Ct. App., Shelby County 1991).

An illegitimate child cannot inherit from or through his natural father unless the father takes some steps during his lifetime to permit such inheritance, such as acknowledgment pursuant to former R.C. 2105.18, designating the illegitimate as an heir pursuant to R.C. 2105.15, adopting the illegitimate, or providing for the illegitimate in his will: Moore v. Dague, 46 Ohio App. 2d 75, 75 Ohio Op. 2d 68, 345 N.E.2d 449, 1975 Ohio App. LEXIS 5826 (Ohio Ct. App., Franklin County 1975).

The designation of heir statute gives to the designated heir so far as the property of the declarant is concerned all the rights and privileges of children born in lawful wedlock (R.C. 2105.15): In re Estate of Powell, 168 N.E.2d 27, 82 Ohio Law Abs. 549, 1959 Ohio Misc. LEXIS 306 (Ohio P. Ct. 1959).

Designation of an heir under former GC § 8598 (see now R.C. 2105.15) gives to him rights of inheritance under the statute of descent and distribution, and the same right of property as if he were born in lawful wedlock: Cochrel v. Robinson, 113 Ohio St. 526, 149 N.E. 871, 3 Ohio Law Abs. 740, 23 Ohio L. Rep. 607, 1925 Ohio LEXIS 211 (Ohio 1925); In re Estate of Powell, 168 N.E.2d 27, 82 Ohio Law Abs. 549, 1959 Ohio Misc. LEXIS 306 (Ohio P. Ct. 1959).

An illegitimate son, designated as heir at law by his natural father, pursuant to the provision of this section, is not authorized under GC § 12079 (R.C. 2741.01) to bring an action to contest the will of the brother of the natural father, which brother died subsequent to the decease of the natural father: Blackwell v. Bowman, 150 Ohio St. 34, 37 Ohio Op. 323, 80 N.E.2d 493 (1948), discussed in 9 Ohio St. L.J. 531.

**Death of designated heir**

A designated heir dying prior to the death of his designator does not acquire the status of a child, and where the death of such designated heir occurs prior to the execution of a last will and testament of the designator, the children of the designated heir surviving the designator do not have as heirs at law or next of kin a right of inheritance in the estate of such designator and may not maintain an action to contest his will: Kirsheman v. Paulin, 155 Ohio St. 137, 44 Ohio Op. 134, 98 N.E.2d 26 (1951), discussed in 47 Ohio Op. 303.

**Estate tax**

To qualify under R.C. 5731.09(B) for a tax exemption when the property passes to or for the use of a "person recognized by the decedent as an adopted child and designated by such decedent as an heir ..... ," the successor must establish that during his minority his relationship to the decedent was similar to that of a parent and child and that he was designated as an heir by the decedent according to law, although such designation need not necessarily have occurred during the minority of such successor: In re Estate of George, 82 Ohio Law Abs. 452, 1959 Ohio Misc. LEXIS 300 (Ohio P. Ct. June 30, 1959).

Where testator began, during the minority of his stepdaughter and her daughter, to treat and refer to them as his daughter and grandchild respectively, and continued so to do during his lifetime, the relationship of adopted daughter and grandchild was established, and the stepdaughter became an adopted child within the meaning of R.C. 5731.09, providing an exemption from taxation for a "person" recognized by the decedent as an adopted child and designated by such decedent as an heir under a statute of this or any other state or county, or the lineal descendants thereof * * *." and where they were so designated as heirs by decedent both the stepdaughter and her daughter became entitled to the exemption so provided. (R.C. 2105.15): In re Estate of Powell, 168 N.E.2d 27, 82 Ohio Law Abs. 549, 1959 Ohio Misc. LEXIS 306 (Ohio P. Ct. 1959).

**Guardians**

"Heirs at law" designated in probate court under GC § 10503-12 (R.C. 2105.15) are not, during the lifetime of the person who designated them, "next of kin" entitled to written notice of the time and place of hearing of an application for appointment of a guardian for such person: In re Guardianship of Jones, 30 Ohio Law Abs. 499, 1939 Ohio Misc. LEXIS 904 (Ohio Ct. App., Franklin County Sept. 27, 1939).

**Trusts**

Where a trust provided that if a beneficiary did not survive a certain event, his interest was to pass to his "heirs at law," the beneficiary's designated heir did not qualify as an heir at law: PNC Bank, N.A. v. Stanton, 104 Ohio App. 3d 558, 662 N.E.2d 875, 1995 Ohio App. LEXIS 2403 (Ohio Ct. App., Hamilton County 1995).

**Wills**

This section does not render invalid and inoperative a provision in a will which provides "I hereby make my two granddaughters, A and B, each equal heirs with my own children": Moon v. Stewart, 87 Ohio St. 349, 101 N.E. 314 (1913), affirming Moon v. Harness, 15 Ohio C.C. (n.s.) 139, 23 Ohio Cir. Dec. 337.].

## RESEARCH REFERENCES AND PRACTICE AIDS

**Cross-References to Related Sections**

Adoption of child; effect on inheritance, RC § 3107.15.
Afterborn or pretermitted heirs, RC § 2107.34.
Proceedings in case of presumption of death, RC § 2121.02.
Relative defined, RC § 2107.52.

**Practice Manuals and Treatises**

Anderson's The Simple Will in Ohio § 5.9 Afterborn or Pretermitted Children

Anderson's Ohio Probate Practice and Procedure Form 17.04 Designation of heir-at-law

Anderson's Ohio Probate Practice and Procedure Outline No. § 34 Designation of heir-at-law

**Practice Guides**

Anderson's Ohio Probate Practice and Procedure § 17.05 Designation of an heir

Anderson's Ohio Probate Practice and Procedure § 18.06 Identification of the beneficiaries; issue

Anderson's Ohio Probate Practice and Procedure § 55.01 Illegitimate children's statutory rights of inheritance

Anderson's Ohio Probate Practice and Procedure § 55.02 Constitutionality of statutes

Anderson's Ohio Probate Practice and Procedure § 55.04 Summary

**Practice Forms**

Designation of Heir at Law 1, 12 OH Forms of Pleading & Practice — Probate Form 18:4

### § 2105.16 Heirs of aliens may inherit; aliens may hold lands.

No person who is capable of inheriting shall be deprived of the inheritance by reason of any of the person's ancestors having been aliens. Aliens may hold, possess, and enjoy real property within this state, either by descent, devise, gift, or purchase, as fully as any citizen of the United States or of this state may do.

**HISTORY:**

GC § 10503-13; 114 v 320(342); Bureau of Code Revision. Eff 10-1-53; 2011 SB 124, § 1, eff. Jan. 13, 2012.

**Editor's Notes**

Acts 2011, SB 124, § 3 provides: "The provisions of this act that relate to the estates of decedents apply to the estates of decedents who die on or after the effective date of this act."

**Amendment Notes**

The 2011 amendment substituted "real property" for "lands, tenements, and hereditaments" in the second sentence; and made a stylistic change.

#### NOTES TO DECISIONS

**Dower**

This section, permitting aliens to hold, possess and enjoy lands, is broad enough to include a claim of dower: Falkoff v. Sugerman, 26 Ohio N.P. 81 (1925).

#### ATTORNEY GENERAL OPINIONS

A foreign nation, in the absence of a treaty with the United States, may not hold title to real estate located in the state of Ohio without the express consent of the state: 1949 OAG No. 998 (1949).

#### RESEARCH REFERENCES AND PRACTICE AIDS

**Comparative Legislation**

Rights of aliens:
CA—Cal Const, Art I § 20; Cal Prob Code § 6411
FL—Fla. Stat. § 732.1101
IL—765 Ill. Comp. Stat. § 60/0.01
IN—Burns Ind. Code Ann. § 32-1-7-1
KY—KRS §§ 391.030, 391.060
MI—MCLS § 554.135
PA—20 P.S. § 2104

**Practice Guides**

Anderson's Ohio Probate Practice and Procedure § 17.08 Alien status

### § 2105.17 Children born out of wedlock.

Children born out of wedlock shall be capable of inheriting or transmitting inheritance from and to their mother, and from and to those from whom she may inherit, or to whom she may transmit inheritance, as if born in lawful wedlock.

**HISTORY:**

GC § 10503-14; 114 v 320(342); Bureau of Code Revision, 10-1-53; 136 v S 145. Eff 1-1-76.

#### NOTES TO DECISIONS

Analysis



**Constitutionality**

Section 12 of the Illinois Probate Act, which allows illegitimate children to inherit by intestate succession only from their mothers (though under Illinois law legitimate children may inherit by intestate succession from both their mothers and their fathers), held to violate the equal protection clause of USConst amend XIV: Trimble v. Gordon, 430 U.S. 762, 97 S. Ct. 1459, 52 L. Ed. 2d 31, 1977 U.S. LEXIS 77 (U.S. 1977).

Enactment of R.C. 2105.17 providing that illegitimate children can inherit from and through their mother as if born in lawful wedlock expanded and modified the word "child" or "children" appearing in R.C. 2105.06, the statute of descent and distribution, to include those children. After the enactment of R.C. 2105.17, the operation of the equal protection clause of the USConst amend XIV required that the words "child" or "children" include all children, both legitimate and illegitimate, whether inheriting from and through their mother or father: Green v. Woodard, 40 Ohio App. 2d 101, 69 Ohio Op. 2d 130, 318 N.E.2d 397, 1974 Ohio App. LEXIS 2624 (Ohio Ct. App., Cuyahoga County 1974).

**Generally**

An illegitimate child can inherit both from and through his mother, either directly or collaterally: Kest v. State, 77 Ohio L. Ab. 193, 4 Ohio Op. 2d 250, 146 N.E.2d 775 (PC 1957), affirmed 169 Ohio St. 317.].

This section removes the disabilities of illegitimates in inheriting from their mother and from any others from whom the mother could inherit and should be given a liberal construction: Porsberg v. Klein, 53 N.E.2d 63, 39 Ohio Law Abs. 470, 1942 Ohio App. LEXIS 782 (Ohio Ct. App., Cuyahoga County 1942).

An illegitimate child was adopted by one not its natural mother; and died intestate leaving its natural mother, its adopting parents and children of the adopting parents surviving. Under such circumstances the personal estate of such child passes to its natural mother to the exclusion of the adopting parents and their children: Upson v. Noble, 35 Ohio St. 655, 1880 Ohio LEXIS 199 (Ohio 1880).

Subsequently the foregoing statute was amended by the addition of the words "if the mother being dead the estate of such illegitimate child shall descend to the relatives on the part of the mother as if the intestate had been legitimate." Under this statute it was held that while an inheritance might pass from an illegitimate child to her mother's relatives, such inheritance could not pass from the relatives of the mother to the illegitimate child; and that such child could not take under a will giving property to the issue of her mother nor could she inherit from her mother's brother or niece; but she could take under that part of the estate which descended to her mother as intestate property: Gibson v. McNeely, 11 Ohio St. 131, 1860 Ohio LEXIS 132 (Ohio 1860), overruled, Long v. Long, 45 Ohio St. 2d 165, 74 Ohio Op. 2d 287, 343 N.E.2d 100, 1976 Ohio LEXIS 555 (Ohio 1976).

For a general statement with reference to inheritance by or from illegitimate children, see Lewis v. Eutsler, 4 Ohio St. 354, 1854 Ohio LEXIS 127 (Ohio 1854).

An earlier form of this statute permitted illegitimate children to be "capable of inheriting or transmitting inheritance on the part of their mother in like manner as if they had been born of lawful wedlock." This statute permitted an illegitimate child to inherit from or through its mother: Stevenson's Heirs v. Sullivant, 18 U.S. 207, 5 L. Ed. 70, 1820 U.S. LEXIS 252 (U.S. 1820).

**Life insurance**

The word "children," as it appears in the substitute beneficiary clause of a group life insurance policy, is to be construed to mean all offspring, regardless of whether they are born in or out of wedlock: Butcher v. Pollard, 32 Ohio App. 2d 1, 61 Ohio Op. 2d 1, 288 N.E.2d 204, 1972 Ohio App. LEXIS 348 (Ohio Ct. App., Cuyahoga County 1972).

**Wills**

Where the testator, with knowledge of the existence of an illegitimate child, makes specific bequests to his other children but makes no mention of the illegitimate child, it is to be presumed that the testator intended to disinherit the child: Birman v. Sproat, 47 Ohio App. 3d 65, 546 N.E.2d 1354, 1988 Ohio App. LEXIS 1232 (Ohio Ct. App., Miami County 1988).

A devise to the "issue of the body" is prima facie a devise to legitimate children or their descendants: Flora v. Anderson, 8 Ohio Fed. 660, 75 F. 217 (S.D. 1896).

#### RESEARCH REFERENCES AND PRACTICE AIDS

**Comparative Legislation**

Inheritances by and from mother by and from illegitimate child:
CA—Cal Prob Code § 21115
FL—Fla. Stat. § 732.108
IL—755 Ill. Comp. Stat. § 5/2-2
IN—Burns Ind. Code Ann. § 29-1-2-7
KY—KRS § 391.105
MI—MCLS § 700.2114
NY—NY CLS EPTL § 4-1.2
PA—20 P.S. § 2107

**Practice Guides**

Anderson's Ohio Probate Practice and Procedure § 17.03 Statute of descent and distribution; Revised Code § 2105.06

Anderson's Ohio Probate Practice and Procedure § 55.01 Illegitimate children's statutory rights of inheritance

Anderson's Ohio Probate Practice and Procedure § 55.02 Constitutionality of statutes

Anderson's Ohio Probate Practice and Procedure § 55.04 Summary

### § 2105.18 Renumbered.

Amended and renumbered RC § 5101.31.4 in 147 v H 352. Eff 1-1-98.

**Editor's Notes**

The effective date is set by section 4 of HB 352.

### § 2105.19 Persons prohibited from benefiting by the death of another.

(A) Except as provided in division (C) of this section, no person who is convicted of, pleads guilty to, or is found not guilty by reason of insanity of a violation of or complicity in the violation of section 2903.01, 2903.02, or 2903.03 of the Revised Code or a violation of division (A) of section 2903.04 of the Revised Code that is not a proximate result of a felony violation of section 2903.06 of the Revised Code, or of an existing or former law of any other state, the United States, or a foreign nation, substantially equivalent to a violation of or complicity in the violation of any of these sections, no person who is indicted for a violation of or complicity in the violation of any of those sections or laws and subsequently is adjudicated incompetent to stand trial on that charge, and no juvenile who is found to be a delinquent child by reason of committing an act that, if committed by an adult, would be a violation of or complicity in the violation of any of those sections or laws, shall in any way benefit by the death. All property of the decedent, and all money, insurance proceeds, or other property or benefits payable or distributable in respect of the decedent's death, shall pass or be paid or distributed as if the person who caused the death of the decedent had predeceased the decedent.

(B) A person prohibited by division (A) of this section from benefiting by the death of another is a constructive trustee for the benefit of those entitled to any property or benefit that the person has obtained, or over which the person has exerted control, because of the decedent's death. A person who purchases any such property or benefit from the constructive trustee, for value, in good faith, and without notice of the constructive trustee's disability under division (A) of this section, acquires good title, but the constructive trustee is accountable to the beneficiaries for the proceeds or value of the property or benefit.

(C) A person who is prohibited from benefiting from a death pursuant to division (A) of this section either because the person was adjudicated incompetent to stand trial or was found not guilty by reason of insanity, or the person's guardian appointed pursuant to Chapter 2111. of the Revised Code or other legal representative, may file a complaint to declare the person's right to benefit from the death in the probate court in which the decedent's estate is being administered or that released the estate from administration. The complaint shall be filed no later than sixty days after the person is adjudicated incompetent to stand trial or found not guilty by reason of insanity. The court shall notify each person who is a devisee or legatee under the decedent's will, or if there is no will, each person who is an heir of the decedent pursuant to section 2105.06 of the Revised Code that a complaint of that nature has been filed within ten days after the filing of the complaint. The person who files the complaint, and each person who is required to be notified of the filing of the complaint under this division, is entitled to a jury trial in the action. To assert the right, the person desiring a jury trial shall demand a jury in the manner prescribed in the Civil Rules.

A person who files a complaint pursuant to this division shall be restored to the person's right to benefit from the death unless the court determines, by a preponderance of the evidence, that the person would have been convicted of a violation of, or complicity in the violation of, section 2903.01, 2903.02, or 2903.03 of the Revised Code or a violation of division (A) of section 2903.04 of the Revised Code that is not a proximate result of a felony violation of section 2903.06 of the Revised Code, or of a law of another state, the United States, or a foreign nation that is substantially similar to any of those sections, if the person had been brought to trial in the case in which the person was adjudicated incompetent or if the person were not insane at the time of the commission of the offense.

**HISTORY:**

136 v H 490 (Eff 11-20-75); 136 v S 145 (Eff 1-1-76); 139 v S 176 (Eff 6-1-82); 141 v S 102. Eff 10-17-85; 2011 SB 124, § 1, eff. Jan. 13, 2012; 2018 hb595, § 1, effective March 22, 2019.

**Editor's Notes**

Acts 2011, SB 124, § 3 provides: "The provisions of this act that relate to the estates of decedents apply to the estates of decedents who die on or after the effective date of this act."

This section was enacted identically in S 145 and H 490.

**Amendment Notes**

The 2018 amendment by HB 595, added "or a violation of division (A) of section 2903.04 of the Revised Code that is not a proximate result of a felony violation of section 2903.06 of the Revised Code" in the first sentence of (A); and added "or a violation of division (A) of section 2903.04 of the Revised Code that is not a proximate result of a felony violation of section 2903.06 of the Revised Code" in the second paragraph of (C).

The 2011 amendment, in (C), inserted "of that nature" in the third sentence, substituted "complaint" for "motion" twice in the fourth sentence; and made stylistic changes.



#### NOTES TO DECISIONS

Analysis



**Constitutionality**

Revised Code § 2105.19 does not impair the obligation of contracts as set forth in both the Ohio and United States Constitutions: In re Estate of Fiore, 16 Ohio App. 3d 473, 476 N.E.2d 1093, 1984 Ohio App. LEXIS 12421 (Ohio Ct. App., Cuyahoga County 1984).

**Generally**

The involuntary manslaughter conviction precluded inheriting from the decedent. R.C. 2105.19 does not provide the exclusive means of disqualification: In re Estate of Cotton, 104 Ohio App. 3d 368, 662 N.E.2d 63, 1995 Ohio App. LEXIS 2365 (Ohio Ct. App., Franklin County 1995).

Where the employee was the only named beneficiary of the life insurance on his wife but was barred from collecting it after murdering her, the estate of the wife had no rights under the policy: Caliman v. American Gen. Fire & Casualty Co., 94 Ohio App. 3d 572, 641 N.E.2d 261, 1994 Ohio App. LEXIS 1974 (Ohio Ct. App., Hamilton County 1994).

The court violated R.C. 2105.19 where it ordered that a criminal fine levied on the decedent's spouse for murdering her be paid from the decedent's estate: In re Estate of Wolfe, 71 Ohio App. 3d 501, 594 N.E.2d 1055, 1991 Ohio App. LEXIS 1166 (Ohio Ct. App., Wood County 1991).

Revised Code § 2105.19, as it applies to disposition of insurance benefits, construed: Caliman v. American General Fire & Casualty Co., 1990 Ohio App. LEXIS 128 (Ohio Ct. App., Hamilton County Jan. 24, 1990).

The word "conviction," as used in R.C. 2105.19, signifies the giving of judgment against a defendant, and applies to a civil as well as a criminal action: Bosley v. Hawkins, 24 Ohio Misc. 2d 11, 494 N.E.2d 460, 1985 Ohio Misc. LEXIS 102 (Ohio C.P. 1985).

Property of a victim of a murder received by inheritance, bequest, devise or operation of law by the killer is subject to all the claims the decedent would have had had she survived the killer, regardless of when it is determined that he was the wrongful cause of the victim's death by reason of R.C. 2105.19: Home Sav. & Loan Asso. v. Potter, 21 Ohio Misc. 2d 1, 487 N.E.2d 927, 1984 Ohio Misc. LEXIS 213 (Ohio C.P. 1984).

Absent the application of R.C. 2105.19(A) which bars from recovery those persons convicted of or pleading guilty to certain designated homicide offenses, a person challenging the beneficiary's claim has the burden of proving the intentional and malicious killing: Huff v. Union Fidelity Life Ins. Co., 14 Ohio App. 3d 135, 470 N.E.2d 236, 1984 Ohio App. LEXIS 11259 (Ohio Ct. App., Cuyahoga County 1984).

Where a beneficiary under an insurance policy pleads guilty to manslaughter in the killing of the insured, the insurer must prove the killing was wilful and intentional in order to defeat the right of such beneficiary to the proceeds: (decided under former analogous section) Travelers Ins. Co. v.

Gray, 37 Ohio Misc. 27, 66 Ohio Op. 2d 64, 306 N.E.2d 189, 1973 Ohio Misc. LEXIS 189 (Ohio C.P. 1973).

Where plaintiff's evidence to support a petition by plaintiff as guardian of a minor ward to sell real property of such ward shows that the parents of the ward each owned an undivided one-half interest in real property, that the wife was convicted of murdering her husband but that no attempt was made under this section, to deprive her of a share in the estate of her husband who died intestate, and that, thereafter, the wife executed a quitclaim deed in which the grantee, her minor son, was designated as "Estate of . . . . , Ward"; such deed effectively divests the wife of all her right, title and interest in the real property and plaintiff has made a prima facie case. And it is not error for the court to overrule defendants' motion for a directed verdict at the close of plaintiff's evidence: (decided under former analogous section) Alston v. Alston, 4 Ohio App. 2d 270, 33 Ohio Op. 2d 311, 212 N.E.2d 65, 1964 Ohio App. LEXIS 478 (Ohio Ct. App., Franklin County 1964).

By reason of the provisions of this section, a husband, who has been finally adjudged guilty of murdering his wife, cannot take or receive anything which is provided for him as surviving spouse of such wife by the provisions of GC § 10509-54 (R.C. 2115.13 [repealed]): (decided under former analogous section) Bauman v. Hogue, 160 Ohio St. 296, 52 Ohio Op. 183, 116 N.E.2d 439, 1953 Ohio LEXIS 506 (Ohio 1953).

This section is not intended to abrogate or delimit common law rule, but to establish by fact of conviction for murder legal status of a person so convicted with respect to receiving any benefit from death of person unlawfully killed: (decided under former analogous section) Cook v. Western & Southern Life Ins. Co., 30 Ohio N.P. 247 (1932).



**Applicability**

Although the slayer's statute was inapplicable in a beneficiary's bad faith action against an insurer for its failure to pay her life insurance proceeds because she was not convicted of the death, the insurer relied on the correct principle of law in considering whether she was entitled to the life insurance proceeds. McNair v. State Farm Fire & Cas. Co., 2013-Ohio-5625, 2013 Ohio App. LEXIS 5906 (Ohio Ct. App., Lucas County 2013).

Although R.C. 2105.19 prevents persons from benefiting by the death of another the statute does not apply where a husband committed suicide after he shot his wife and was not convicted, or found not guilty by reason of insanity, of aggravated murder, murder or voluntary manslaughter, nor did he plead guilty to any of those offenses: In re Estate of Price, 62 Ohio Misc. 2d 26, 587 N.E.2d 995, 1990 Ohio Misc. LEXIS 65 (Ohio C.P. 1990).

Where one co-owner of joint bank account murdered the other and then committed suicide while in jail awaiting trial, the provisions of this section have no application since there was no criminal prosecution: (decided under former analogous section) Shuman v. Schick, 95 Ohio App. 413, 53 Ohio Op. 441, 120 N.E.2d 330, 1953 Ohio App. LEXIS 730 (Ohio Ct. App., Meigs County 1953).

This section, which disinherits persons finally adjudged guilty of murder in the first or second degree as to the property of the person killed, has no effect upon one never brought to trial or convicted: (decided under former analogous section) Demos v. Freemas, 26 Ohio Law Abs. 601, 1938 Ohio Misc. LEXIS 1227 (Ohio Ct. App., Franklin County Feb. 15, 1938).

This section, providing that no person finally adjudged guilty of murder should be entitled to inherit any of the estate of the person killed, is not applicable in suit by administrator of the murdered person to recover from her surviving husband who killed her, the proceeds of a life insurance policy in which the husband was named beneficiary, such money never being a part of the estate of decedent: (decided under former analogous section) Hennigh v. Neff, 27 Ohio Law Abs. 364, 1938 Ohio Misc. LEXIS 1104 (Ohio Ct. App., Franklin County May 13, 1938).

**Application to trust provisions**

As application of the Slayer Statute entailed treating a husband who had been involved in his wife's murder as predeceasing his wife, the trial court properly ruled that the husband's right to amend or revoke the trust he and his wife had created ceased on the date of the wife's death. Evans v. Evans, 2014-Ohio-4450, 20 N.E.3d 1139, 2014 Ohio App. LEXIS 4367 (Ohio Ct. App., Jackson County 2014).

Trial court properly applied the Slayer Statute to the trust interests of a husband settlor involved in the murder of his wife, treating the husband as if he had predeceased his wife; application of the statute in this manner did not deny the husband any vested rights as any rights he might have had could only vest if he survived his wife. Evans v. Evans, 2014-Ohio-4450, 20 N.E.3d 1139, 2014 Ohio App. LEXIS 4367 (Ohio Ct. App., Jackson County 2014).

As application of the Slayer Statute entailed treating a husband who had been involved in his wife's murder as predeceasing his wife, the trial court, in its equitable powers, had the authority to make an order directing the trustees to replace from the husband's separate property any distributions made on his behalf. Evans v. Evans, 2014-Ohio-4450, 20 N.E.3d 1139, 2014 Ohio App. LEXIS 4367 (Ohio Ct. App., Jackson County 2014).

**Civil proceedings establishing offender**

The identity of a person who intentionally and feloniously causes the death of another can be established in a civil proceeding in order to prevent the wrongdoer from receiving the proceeds of the deceased's life insurance policy: Shrader v. Equitable Life Assurance Soc., 20 Ohio St. 3d 41, 485 N.E.2d 1031, 1985 Ohio LEXIS 545 (Ohio 1985).

**Common law**

At common law, the beneficiary of a life insurance policy cannot recover the proceeds if he caused the insured's death by his intentional and felonious act: Huff v. Union Fidelity Life Ins. Co., 14 Ohio App. 3d 135, 470 N.E.2d 236, 1984 Ohio App. LEXIS 11259 (Ohio Ct. App., Cuyahoga County 1984).

**Constructive trust**

Application of the constructive trust doctrine and R.C. 2105.19 will treat the victim's contribution to her "as if" estate, at least until completely exhausted, as prior in time to any later contributions made by others, even innocent persons acting without knowledge: Home Sav. & Loan Asso. v. Potter, 21 Ohio Misc. 2d 1, 487 N.E.2d 927, 1984 Ohio Misc. LEXIS 213 (Ohio C.P. 1984).

**Federal preemption**

ERISA preempted R.C. § 2105.19 as to employer-provided life insurance: Ahmed v. Ahmed, 158 Ohio App. 3d 527, 2004 Ohio 5120, 817 N.E.2d 424, Ohio App. LEXIS 4677 (2004).

**Joint and survivorship accounts**

Revised Code § 2105.19 provides that all money or other property or benefits payable or distributable in respect to the death of the decedent shall pass or be paid as if the guilty person had predeceased the decedent. Thus, for purposes of R.C. 2105.19, where the decedent and the guilty party had a joint and survivorship bank account, the guilty party is considered to have predeceased the decedent and the decedent is to be treated as the survivor: In re Estate of Fiore, 16 Ohio App. 3d 473, 476 N.E.2d 1093, 1984 Ohio App. LEXIS 12421 (Ohio Ct. App., Cuyahoga County 1984).

**Justifiable killing**

A justifiable killing in defense of oneself or another will not disqualify a beneficiary from recovering benefits resulting from that death: Huff v. Union Fidelity Life Ins. Co., 14 Ohio App. 3d 135, 470 N.E.2d 236, 1984 Ohio App. LEXIS 11259 (Ohio Ct. App., Cuyahoga County 1984).

**Juveniles**

The judgment entry of the juvenile court finding that a minor is a delinquent child by reason of having committed acts which if committed by an adult would constitute aggravated murder is a judgment entry of conviction of this offense and, therefore, such minor is not entitled to benefit from the estate of the victim, pursuant to R.C. 2105.19: Bosley v. Hawkins, 24 Ohio Misc. 2d 11, 494 N.E.2d 460, 1985 Ohio Misc. LEXIS 102 (Ohio C.P. 1985).

A minor whose age precludes convictions that statutorily bar recovery for an adult can still forfeit beneficial rights under the common-law rule: Huff v. Union Fidelity Life Ins. Co., 14 Ohio App. 3d 135, 470 N.E.2d 236, 1984 Ohio App. LEXIS 11259 (Ohio Ct. App., Cuyahoga County 1984).

Revised Code § 2105.19 does not preclude a juvenile adjudicated delinquent by reason of having murdered his father from inheriting from his father's estate: In re Estate of Birt, 18 Ohio Misc. 2d 7, 481 N.E.2d 1387, 1983 Ohio Misc. LEXIS 443 (Ohio C.P. 1983).

**No contest plea**

A plea of "no contest" to a charge of murder under R.C. 2903.02, followed by a finding of guilty, does not bar the application of R.C. 2105.19: In re Estate of Fiore, 16 Ohio App. 3d 473, 476 N.E.2d 1093, 1984 Ohio App. LEXIS 12421 (Ohio Ct. App., Cuyahoga County 1984).

**Relationship to other laws**

Relator was entitled to X-rays, photographs, and written reports created during the autopsy of his daughter, because as her biological father, he had a clear legal right to the records under R.C. 313.10(C)(1), he possessed no other adequate remedy to obtain the records from the coroner, and the coroner had a clear legal duty to provide the records. Neither R.C. 149.43 or R.C. 2105.19 were statutes related to R.C. 313.10 and thus were not required to be read in para materia with it. State ex rel. Clay v. Cuyahoga Cnty. Med. Exam'rs Office, 2016-Ohio-407, 58 N.E.3d 552, 2016 Ohio App. LEXIS 1224 (Ohio Ct. App., Cuyahoga County 2016), aff'd on other grounds, 2017-Ohio-8714, 152 Ohio St. 3d 163, 94 N.E.3d 498, 2017 Ohio LEXIS 2380 (Ohio 2017).

**Statutory share of surviving spouse**

A husband who has been adjudged guilty of first degree manslaughter in the death of his wife is entitled to the statutory share of a surviving spouse in his wife's estate: (decided under former analogous section) Wadsworth v. Siek, 23 Ohio Misc. 112, 50 Ohio Op. 2d 507, 254 N.E.2d 738, 1970 Ohio Misc. LEXIS 261 (Ohio P. Ct. 1970).

RESEARCH REFERENCES AND PRACTICE AIDS

**Ohio Constitution**
Nonforfeiture of estate, Ohio Const. art I, § 12.

**Comparative Legislation**
Inheritance from estate by person causing death:
CA—Cal Prob Code § 250 et seq
FL—Fla. Stat. § 732.802
IL—755 Ill. Comp. Stat. § 5/2-6
IN—Burns Ind. Code Ann. § 29-1-2-12.1
KY—KRS § 381.280
MI—MCLS § 700.2803
PA—20 P.S. §§ 2106, 2507

**Practice Guides**
Anderson's Ohio Probate Practice and Procedure § 17.09 Escheat by attainder
Anderson's Ohio Probate Practice and Procedure § 27.10 Distribution of proceeds
Anderson's Ohio Probate Practice and Procedure § 39.02 Constructive trusts

**Practice Checklists**
Master Checklist: Jury Selection, 1-4-1 Ohio Litigation Checklists § 1.01
Checklist: Initial Selection of Jury, 1-4-1 Ohio Litigation Checklists § 1.02

## § 2105.20 Waste by tenant for life.

A tenant for life in real property who commits or suffers waste thereto shall forfeit that part of the property, to which such waste is committed or suffered, to the person having the immediate estate in reversion or remainder and such tenant will be liable in damages to such person for the waste committed or suffered thereto.

**HISTORY:**
GC § 10503-23; 114 v 320(344); Bureau of Code Revision. Eff 10-1-53.

NOTES TO DECISIONS

Analysis

Generally
Accrual of right of action
Appeal
Assignment by life tenant
Oil

**Generally**
Since an action seeking a forfeiture of a life estate for waste under authority of this section is a special statutory proceeding and forfeitures, generally, are not favored by the law, the evidence must be strictly construed: Folden v. Folden, 26 Ohio Op. 2d 240, 188 N.E.2d 193, 90 Ohio Law Abs. 218, 1962 Ohio App. LEXIS 772 (Ohio Ct. App., Meigs County 1962).

An action, predicated upon this section, may be maintained only by the person or persons having the immediate estate in reversion or remainder in the real property: Cook v. Hardin County Bank Co., 76 Ohio App. 203, 31 Ohio Op. 498, 63 N.E.2d 686, 1945 Ohio App. LEXIS 513 (Ohio Ct. App., Hancock County 1945).

An earlier form of this statute applied to wastes committed by a widow; and subsequently by amendment such statute was made to apply to all cases of tenancy for life: Brenneman v. Brenneman, 3 Ohio Dec. 392, 1 Ohio N.P. 332 (Ohio C.P. 1895).

This section does not apply to cases where a life tenant is interposed between the estate of the tenant who commits waste and the estate in reversion or remainder: Hatch v. Hatch, 1 Ohio Dec. 271 (1893).

**Accrual of right of action**
The right of action for waste accrues under this section at the time the waste is committed or suffered with respect to the right to damages for that particular item of waste: Reams v. Henney, 88 Ohio App. 409, 44 Ohio Op. 196, 97 N.E.2d 37, 58 Ohio Law Abs. 507, 1950 Ohio App. LEXIS 662 (Ohio Ct. App., Franklin County 1950).

**Appeal**
Action to forfeit life estate on ground of waste is legal in character, and not appealable: Oglesbee v. Miller, 125 Ohio St. 223, 181 N.E. 26, 1932 Ohio LEXIS 285 (Ohio 1932).

**Assignment by life tenant**
A life tenant of conventional life estate who assigns all his interest in and surrenders possession to his assignee is not liable for subsequent waste: Howell v. Howell, 122 Ohio St. 543, 172 N.E. 528, 8 Ohio Law Abs. 337, 1930 Ohio LEXIS 258 (Ohio 1930).

**Oil**
One acquiring a life estate in land before commencement of mining operations cannot operate for oil, or make oil lease thereon, without committing enjoinable waste: Fourth & Central Trust Co. v. Woolley, 31 Ohio App. 259, 165 N.E. 742, 28 Ohio L. Rep. 497, 1928 Ohio App. LEXIS 320 (Ohio Ct. App., Hamilton County 1928).

RESEARCH REFERENCES AND PRACTICE AIDS

**Practice Manuals and Treatises**
Anderson's Ohio Civil Practice with Forms § 143.01 Waste Generally

**Practice Guides**
Anderson's Ohio Probate Practice and Procedure § 39.02 Constructive trusts



## § 2105.21 Repealed.

Repealed, 149 v H 242, § 2 [GC § 10503-18; 114 v 320(343); Bureau of Code Revision, 10-1-53; 125 v 903(963); 125 v 411]. Eff 5-16-2002.

**Editor's Notes**
This section concerned presumption of order of death. See now RC §§ 2105.31 to 2105.39.
See provisions, § 5 of HB 345 (149 v —) following RC § 2105.39.

## § 2105.25 Filing of declaration that man is adult child's father.

(A) As used in this section and section 2105.26 of the Revised Code:

(1) "Adult child" means a person born in this state who is twenty-three years old or older.

(2) "Genetic test" has the same meaning as in section 3111.09 of the Revised Code.

(B) A man alleging himself to be the father of an adult child, the adult child's mother, and the adult child may appear together before the probate judge of the county in which the man resides and jointly file a declaration stating that the man is the adult child's father and requesting that the court issue an order declaring the man to be the adult child's father. The declaration must state that the adult child's birth certificate does not designate anyone as the adult child's father, the request for the order is made freely and voluntarily by all parties appearing before the court, and genetic test results show the man is the adult child's father. A copy of the birth certificate and the genetic test results must be attached to the declaration.

(C) The man alleging himself to be the adult child's father and the adult child may appear before the court without the adult child's mother and file the declaration if the mother is deceased or has been adjudicated incompetent. If the man alleging himself to be the adult child's father is not a resident of this state, appearance under this section may be made before a probate judge of any county of this state.

**HISTORY:**
149 v H 85. Eff 10-31-2001.

RESEARCH REFERENCES AND PRACTICE AIDS

**Cross-References to Related Sections**
Order declaring man to be adult child's father. RC § 2105.26.

## § 2105.26 Order declaring man to be adult child's father.

(A) If the probate court determines the following, it shall issue the order requested under section 2105.25 of the Revised Code declaring the man alleging himself to be the father of the adult child to be the adult child's father:

(1) The order was freely and voluntarily requested.

(2) No person is designated as the father on the birth certificate of the adult child.

(3) Genetic test results show that the man is the father of the adult child.

(4) It is in the best interests of the man and adult child that the order be issued.

(B) As part of the order, the court shall order the adult child's birth certificate to be changed to designate the man as the adult child's father.

(C) After issuance of an order under this section, the adult child shall be considered the child of the man declared to be the father as if born to him in lawful wedlock, except that the adult child and the adult child's mother shall not be awarded child support from the man for the time the adult child was a minor.

Titles 11 — 37

**HISTORY:**
149 v H 85. Eff 10-31-2001.

### RESEARCH REFERENCES AND PRACTICE AIDS

**Cross-References to Related Sections**
Designation of father on birth certificate, RC § 3705.09.

# UNIFORM SIMULTANEOUS DEATH ACT

## § 2105.31 Definitions.

As used in sections 2105.31 to 2105.40 of the Revised Code:

(A) "Co-owners with right of survivorship" includes joint tenants, tenants by the entireties, and other co-owners of property or accounts held under circumstances that entitle one or more individuals to the whole of the property or account on the death of the other individual or individuals.

(B) "Governing instrument" means a deed, will, trust, insurance or annuity policy, account with a transfer-on-death designation or the abbreviation TOD, account with a payable-on-death designation or the abbreviation POD, transfer-on-death designation affidavit, pension, profit-sharing, retirement, or similar benefit plan, instrument creating or exercising a power of appointment or a power of attorney, or a dispositive, appointive, or nominative instrument of any similar type.

(C) "Payor" means a trustee, insurer, business entity, employer, government, governmental agency, political subdivision or instrumentality, or any other person authorized or obligated by law or a governing instrument to make payments or transfers.

**HISTORY:**
149 v H 242. Eff 5-16-2002; 151 v H 81, § 1, eff. 4-14-06; 2016 hb432, § 1, effective April 6, 2017.

**Editor's Notes**
See provisions, § 5 of HB 345 (149 v —) following RC § 2105.39.

**Amendment Notes**
The 2016 amendment by HB 432 substituted "sections 2105.31 to 2105.40" for "sections 2105.31 to 2105.39" in the introductory language; in (A); substituted "co-owners of property or other accounts" for "co-owners of real or personal property; insurance or other policies; or bank, savings bank, credit union, or other accounts," "one or more individuals" for "one or more persons" and "death of the other individual or individuals" for "death of the other person or persons"; inserted "transfer-on-death designation affidavit" in (B); in (C), inserted "government" and substituted "political subdivision or instrumentality" for "political subdivision"; and deleted former (D), which read: "'Event' includes the death of another person."

151 v H 81, effective April 14, 2006, in (A), inserted "savings bank, credit union"; and made minor stylistic changes.

### RESEARCH REFERENCES AND PRACTICE AIDS

**Practice Guides**
Anderson's Ohio Probate Practice and Procedure § 17.03 Statute of descent and distribution; Revised Code § 2105.06

## § 2105.32 When person is deemed to have predeceased another person.

(A) Except as provided in section 2105.36 of the Revised Code, if title to property, the devolution of property, the right to elect an interest in property, or the right to exempt property, homestead, or allowance for support depends upon an individual's survivorship of the death of another individual, an individual who is not established by clear and convincing evidence to have survived the other individual by one hundred twenty hours is deemed to have predeceased the other individual.

(B) This section does not apply if its application would result in a taking of an intestate estate by the state.

**HISTORY:**
149 v H 242. Eff 5-16-2002; 2016 hb432, § 1, effective April 6, 2017.

**Editor's Notes**
See provisions, § 5 of HB 345 (149 v —) following RC § 2105.39.

**Amendment Notes**
The 2016 amendment by HB 432 rewrote the section.

### NOTES TO DECISIONS

**Interpretation**
Mother's estate was precluded from inheriting under the daughter's will because the mother did not survive the daughter by 120 hours as required by the Presumption of Death Statute, and the language used in the daughter's will was broad, general language designating beneficiaries, and not the explicit language required to override the presumption. In re Estate of Wall, 2017-Ohio-5713, 94 N.E.3d 104, 2017 Ohio App. LEXIS 2746 (Ohio Ct. App., Mahoning County 2017).

## § 2105.33 When person deemed to have predeceased specified event.

Except as provided in section 2105.36 of the Revised Code, an individual who is not established by clear and convincing evidence to have survived an event by one hundred twenty hours is deemed to have predeceased the event for purposes of a provision of a governing instrument that relates to the individual surviving an event, including the death of another individual.

**HISTORY:**
149 v H 242. Eff 5-16-2002; 2016 hb432, § 1, effective April 6, 2017.

**Editor's Notes**
See provisions, § 5 of HB 345 (149 v —) following RC § 2105.39.

**Amendment Notes**
The 2016 amendment by HB 432 substituted "an individual who is not established" for "a person who is not established," "to have survived an event" for "to have survived a specified event," and "relates to the individual surviving an event, including the death of another individual" for "relates to the person surviving an event."

## § 2105.34 Disposition where there are co-owners with right of survivorship.

Except as provided in section 2105.36 of the Revised Code, the following shall apply:

(A) If it is not established by clear and convincing evidence that one of two co-owners with right of survivorship survived the other co-owner by one hundred twenty hours, one-half of the property or account passes as if one co-owner had survived the other co-owner by one hundred twenty hours, and one-half of the property or account passes as if the other co-owner had survived the one co-owner by one hundred twenty hours.

(B) If there are more than two co-owners with right of survivorship and it is not established by clear and convincing evidence that at least one of the co-owners survived the others by one hundred twenty hours, the property or account passes in the proportion that one co-owner's ownership bears to the ownership of the whole number of co-owners.

**HISTORY:**
149 v H 242. Eff 5-16-2002; 2016 hb432, § 1, effective April 6, 2017.

**Editor's Notes**
See provisions, § 5 of HB 345 (149 v —) following RC § 2105.39.

**Amendment Notes**
The 2016 amendment by HB 432 rewrote the section.

### § 2105.35 Determination of death; evidence of death; presumption; evidence of survivorship.

In addition to any provisions of the Rules of Evidence, the following provisions relating to the determination of death and status apply:

(A)(1) An individual is dead if the individual has sustained either irreversible cessation of circulatory and respiratory functions or irreversible cessation of all functions of the brain, including the brain stem, as determined in accordance with accepted medical standards. If the respiratory and circulatory functions of an individual are being artificially sustained, under accepted medical standards a determination that death has occurred is made by a physician by observing and conducting a test to determine that the irreversible cessation of all functions of the brain has occurred.

(2) A physician who makes a determination of death in accordance with division (A) of this section and accepted medical standards is not liable for damages in any civil action or subject to prosecution in any criminal proceeding for the physician's acts or the acts of others based on that determination.

(3) Any person who acts in good faith and relies on a determination of death made by a physician in accordance with division (A) of this section and accepted medical standards is not liable for damages in any civil action or subject to prosecution in any criminal proceeding for the person's actions.

(B) A certified or authenticated copy of a death certificate purporting to be issued by an official or agency of the place where the death of an individual purportedly occurred is prima-facie evidence of the fact, place, date, and time of the individual's death and the identity of the decedent.

(C) A certified or authenticated copy of any record or report of a domestic or foreign governmental agency that an individual is missing, detained, dead, or alive is prima-facie evidence of the status and of the dates, circumstances, and places disclosed by the record or report.

(D) In the absence of prima-facie evidence of death under division (B) or (C) of this section, the fact of death may be established by clear and convincing evidence, including circumstantial evidence.

(E) Except as provided in division (F) of this section, a presumption of the death of an individual arises when either of the following applies:

(1) The individual has disappeared and has been continuously absent from the individual's place of last domicile for a five-year period without being heard from during the period;

(2) The individual has disappeared and has been continuously absent from the individual's place of last domicile without being heard from and was at the beginning of the individual's absence exposed to a specific peril of death, even though the absence has continued for less than a five-year period.

(F) When an individual who is on active duty in the armed services of the United States has been officially determined to be absent in a status of "missing" or "missing in action," a presumption of death arises when the head of the federal department concerned has made a finding of death pursuant to the "Federal Missing Persons Act," 80 Stat. 625 (1966), 37 U.S.C.A. 551, as amended.

(G) In the absence of evidence disputing the time of death stipulated on a document described in division (B) or (C) of this section, a document described in either of those divisions that stipulates a time of death of an individual one hundred twenty hours or more after the time of death of another individual, however the time of death of the other individual is determined, establishes by clear and convincing evidence that the individual survived the other individual by one hundred twenty hours.

**HISTORY:**
149 v H 242. Eff 5-16-2002; 152 v H 529, § 1, eff. 4-7-09; 2016 hb432, § 1, effective April 6, 2017.

**Editor's Notes**
See provisions, § 5 of HB 345 (149 v —) following RC § 2105.39.

**Amendment Notes**
The 2016 amendment by HB 432 rewrote the section.
152 v H 529, effective April 7, 2009, corrected internal references.

#### RESEARCH REFERENCES AND PRACTICE AIDS

**Practice Guides**
Anderson's Ohio Probate Practice and Procedure § 17.07 Effect of the order of death on intestate succession

### § 2105.36 Governing instrument provisions; effect of statute against perpetuities.

Survival by one hundred twenty hours is not required if any of the following applies:

(A) The governing instrument contains language dealing explicitly with simultaneous deaths or deaths in a common disaster, and that language is operable under the facts of the case.

(B) The governing instrument expressly indicates that an individual is not required to survive an event, including the death of another individual, by any specified period, or expressly requires the individual to survive the event for a specified period, but the survival of the event for the specified period shall be established by clear and convincing evidence.

(C) The imposition of a one-hundred-twenty-hour requirement of survival would cause a nonvested property interest or a power of appointment to be invalid under section 2131.08 of the Revised Code, but the survival shall be established by clear and convincing evidence.

(D) The application of a one-hundred-twenty-hour requirement of survival to multiple governing instruments would result in an unintended failure or duplication of a disposition, but the survival shall be established by clear and convincing evidence.

**HISTORY:**
149 v H 242. Eff 5-16-2002; 2016 hb432, § 1, effective April 6, 2017.

**Editor's Notes**
See provisions, § 5 of HB 345 (149 v —) following RC § 2105.39.

**Amendment Notes**
The 2016 amendment by HB 432 rewrote the section.

#### NOTES TO DECISIONS

**Interpretation**
Mother's estate was precluded from inheriting under the daughter's will because the mother did not survive the daughter by 120 hours as required by the Presumption of Death Statute, and the language used in the daughter's will was broad, general language designating beneficiaries, and not the explicit language required to override the presumption. In re Estate of Wall, 2017-Ohio-5713, 94 N.E.3d 104, 2017 Ohio App. LEXIS 2746 (Ohio Ct. App., Mahoning County 2017).

#### RESEARCH REFERENCES AND PRACTICE AIDS

**Practice Guides**
Anderson's Ohio Probate Practice and Procedure § 17.07 Effect of the order of death on intestate succession

### § 2105.37 Liability of payor or other third party; notice of claimed lack of entitlement.

(A) A payor or other third party is not liable for any of the following:

(1) Having made a payment or transferred an item of property or any other benefit to a person designated in a governing instrument who, under sections 2105.31 to 2105.40 of the Revised Code, is not entitled to the payment or item of property or other benefit, if the payment or transfer was made before the payor or other third party received written notice of a claimed lack of entitlement under those sections;

(2) Having taken any other action in good faith reliance on the person's apparent entitlement under the terms of the governing instrument before the payor or other third party received written notice of a claimed lack of entitlement under sections 2105.31 to 2105.40 of the Revised Code.

(B) A payor or other third party is liable for a payment, transfer, or other action taken after the payor or other third party receives written notice of a claimed lack of entitlement under sections 2105.31 to 2105.40 of the Revised Code.

(C) Written notice of a claimed lack of entitlement under division (A) or (B) of this section shall be mailed to the payor's or other third party's main office or home by registered or certified mail, return receipt requested, or served upon the payor or other third party in the same manner as a summons in a civil action. Upon receipt of written notice of a claimed lack of entitlement under sections 2105.31 to 2105.40 of the Revised Code, a payor or other third party may pay any amount owed or transfer or deposit any item of property held by it to or with the probate court that has jurisdiction over the decedent's estate. If no probate proceedings have been commenced, upon receipt of written notice of a claimed lack of entitlement under sections 2105.31 to 2105.40 of the Revised Code, a payor or other third party may pay any amount owed or transfer or deposit any item of property held by it to or with the probate court located in the county of the decedent's residence. The court shall hold the funds or items of property, and upon its determination under sections 2105.31 to 2105.40 of the Revised Code to whom the funds or items of property should be disbursed, shall order disbursement in accordance with its determination. Payments, transfers, or deposits made to or with the court discharge the payor or other third party from all claims for the value of amounts paid to or items of property transferred to or deposited with the court.

(D) A person who purchases property for value or receives a payment or other item of property or benefit in partial or full satisfaction of a legally enforceable obligation, and without notice that the person selling or transferring the property or benefit or making a payment is not entitled to the property or benefit under sections 2105.31 to 2105.40 of the Revised Code, is neither obligated under those sections to return the payment or item of property or benefit nor liable under those sections for the amount of the payment or the value of the item of property or benefit.

(E) A person who, not for value, receives a payment, item of property, or any other benefit to which the person is not entitled under sections 2105.31 to 2105.40 of the Revised Code is obligated to return the payment, item of property, or benefit, or is personally liable for the amount of the payment or the value of the item of property or benefit, to the person who is entitled to it under sections 2105.31 to 2105.40 of the Revised Code.

(F) If sections 2105.31 to 2105.40 of the Revised Code or any provision of those sections are preempted by federal law with respect to a payment, an item of property, or any other benefit covered by those sections, a person who, not for value, receives the payment, item of property, or other benefit to which the person is not entitled under sections 2105.31 to 2105.40 of the Revised Code is obligated to return the payment, item of property, or benefit, or is personally liable for the amount of the payment or the value of the item of property or benefit, to the person who would have been entitled to it were sections 2105.31 to 2105.40 of the Revised Code or any provision of those sections not preempted.

**HISTORY:**

149 v H 242. Eff 5-16-2002; 2016 hb432, § 1, effective April 6, 2017.

**Editor's Notes**

See provisions, § 5 of HB 345 (149 v —) following RC § 2105.39.

**Amendment Notes**

The 2016 amendment by HB 432 rewrote the section.

### § 2105.38 Bona fide purchaser or transferee for value; liability of other transferees; federal preemption. [Repealed]

**HISTORY:**

149 v H 242. Eff 5-16-2002; repealed by 2016 hb432, § 1, effective April 6, 2017.

### § 2105.38 Retroactive application of provisions; severability of provisions.

(A) Sections 2105.31 to 2105.40 of the Revised Code do not impair any act done in any proceeding, or any right that accrued, before the effective date of the amendment of this section. If a right is acquired, extinguished, or barred upon the expiration of a prescribed period of time that has commenced to run, prior to the effective date of the amendment of this section, under any provision of the Revised Code, the provision of the applicable section of the Revised Code applies with respect to that right.

(B) Any rule of construction regarding any provision of a governing instrument that is provided in sections 2105.31 to 2105.40 of the Revised Code applies to any governing instrument that is executed prior to the effective date of the amendment of this section, unless there is a clear indication of a contrary intent in the governing instrument.

**HISTORY:**

149 v H 242 (Eff 5-16-2002); 149 v H 345, § 3. Eff 5-16-2002; renumbered from § 2105.39 by 2016 hb432, § 1, effective April 6, 2017.

**Editor's Notes**

Former § 2105.38 [149 v H 242. Eff 5-16-2002], concerning bona fide purchaser or transferee for value, was repealed by 2016 HB 432, § 1 effective April 6, 2017.

**Amendment Notes**

The 2016 amendment by HB 432 rewrote the section.

### § 2105.39 Retroactive application of provisions; severability of provisions. [Renumbered]

**HISTORY:**

149 v H 242 (Eff 5-16-2002); 149 v H 345, § 3. Eff 5-16-2002; renumbered to § 2105.38 by 2016 hb432, § 1, effective April 6, 2017.

### § 2105.39 Law to be construed as uniform.

Sections 2105.31 to 2105.40 of the Revised Code shall be applied and construed to effectuate their general purpose to make uniform the law with respect to the subject of those sections among the states enacting the law.

**HISTORY:**

2016 hb432, § 1, effective April 6, 2017.

### § 2105.40 Cited as the Uniform Simultaneous Death Act.

Sections 2105.31 to 2105.40 of the Revised Code may be cited as the uniform simultaneous death act.

**HISTORY:**

2016 hb432, § 1, effective April 6, 2017.

# CHAPTER 2106

# RIGHTS OF SURVIVING SPOUSES

Election



Allowance for Support

# ELECTION

## § 2106.01 Election by surviving spouse.

(A) After the initial appointment of an administrator or executor of the estate, the probate court shall issue a citation to the surviving spouse, if any is living at the time of the issuance of the citation, to elect whether to exercise the surviving spouse's rights under Chapter 2106. of the Revised Code, including, after the probate of a will, the right to elect to take under the will or under section 2105.06 of the Revised Code.

A surviving spouse may waive the service of the citation required under this division by filing in the probate court a written waiver of the citation. The waiver shall include an acknowledgment of receipt of the description of the general rights of the surviving spouse required by division (B) of section 2106.02 of the Revised Code.

(B) If the surviving spouse elects to take under section 2105.06 of the Revised Code and if the value of the property that the surviving spouse is entitled to receive is equal to or greater than the value of the decedent's interest in the mansion house as determined under section 2106.10 of the Revised Code, the surviving spouse also is entitled to make an election pursuant to division (A) of section 2106.10 of the Revised Code.

(C) If the surviving spouse elects to take under section 2105.06 of the Revised Code, the surviving spouse shall take not to exceed one-half of the net estate, unless two or more of the decedent's children or their lineal descendants survive, in which case the surviving spouse shall take not to exceed one-third of the net estate.

For purposes of this division, the net estate shall be determined before payment of federal estate tax, estate taxes under Chapter 5731. of the Revised Code, or any other tax that is subject to apportionment under section 2113.86 or 2113.861 of the Revised Code.

(D) Unless the will expressly provides that in case of an election under division (A) of this section there shall be no acceleration of remainder or other interests bequeathed or devised by the will, the balance of the net estate shall be disposed of as though the surviving spouse had predeceased the testator. If there is a disposition by a will to an inter vivos trust that was created by the testator, if under the terms of the trust the surviving spouse is entitled to any interest in the trust or is granted any power or nomination with respect to the trust, and if the surviving spouse makes an election to take under section 2105.06 of the Revised Code, then, unless the trust instrument provides otherwise, the surviving spouse is considered for purposes of the trust to have predeceased the testator, and there shall be an acceleration of remainder or other interests in all property bequeathed or devised to the trust by the will, in all property held by the trustee at the time of the death of the decedent, and in all property that comes into the possession or under the control of the trustee by reason of the death of the decedent.

(E) The election of a surviving spouse to take under a will or under section 2105.06 of the Revised Code may be made at any time after the death of the decedent, but the surviving spouse shall not make the election later than five months from the date of the initial appointment of an administrator or executor of the estate. On a motion filed before the expiration of the five-month period, and for good cause shown, the court may allow further time for the making of the election. If no action is taken by the surviving spouse before the expiration of the five-month period, it is conclusively presumed that the surviving spouse elects to take under the will. The election shall be entered on the journal of the court.

When proceedings for advice or to contest the validity of a will are begun within the time allowed by this division for making the election, the election may be made within three months after the final disposition of the proceedings, if the will is not set aside.

(F) When a surviving spouse succeeds to the entire estate of the testator, having been named the sole devisee and legatee, it shall be presumed that the spouse elects to take under the will of the testator, unless the surviving spouse manifests a contrary intention.

**HISTORY:**

GC §§ 10504-55, 10504-58; 114 v 320(357); 116 v 385; 119 v 394; Bureau of Code Revision, RC § 2107.39, 10-1-53; 125 v 411 (Eff 10-16-53); 133 v S 185 (Eff 1-1-71); 135 v H 374 (Eff 10-31-73); 136 v S 145 (Eff 1-1-76); 138 v S 317 (Eff 3-23-81); 141 v H 139 (Eff 7-24-86); 141 v S 248 (Eff 12-17-86); 142 v S 228 (Eff 3-22-89); RC § 2106.01, 143 v H 346 (Eff 5-31-90); 149 v H 85. Eff 12-31-2001; 150 v H 51, § 1, eff. 4-8-04; 2011 SB 124, § 1, eff. Jan. 13, 2012.

**Editor's Notes**

Acts 2011, SB 124, § 3 provides: "The provisions of this act that relate to the estates of decedents apply to the estates of decedents who die on or after the effective date of this act."

The provisions of § 3, H.B. 51 (150 v —), as amended by H.B. 161 (150 v —), read as follows:

SECTION 3. (A) Sections 2106.01, 2106.02, and 2109.32 of the Revised Code, as amended by Am. Sub. H.B. 51 of the 125th General Assembly, apply to estates that are in existence or are initiated on or after April 8, 2004.

The provisions of § 5 of HB 85 (149 v —) read as follows:

SECTION 5. Sections 2106.01, 2106.02, 2106.13, 2107.19, 2107.76, 2109.07, 2109.09, 2109.18, 2109.24, 2109.30, 2109.31, 2109.32, 2113.25, 2113.28, 2113.53, 2113.64, 2115.09, and 2117.06 of the Revised Code, as amended by this act, and sections 2106.25 and 2109.301 of the Revised Code, as enacted by this act, apply only to estates of decedents who die on or after January 1, 2002.

**Amendment Notes**

The 2011 amendment, in the second sentence of (D), substituted "considered" for "deemed" and "possession or under the control" for "hands".

### NOTES TO DECISIONS

Analysis

Generally
Acceleration of remainder
Antenuptial agreement
Appeal
Applicability
Construction with other laws
Early election
Extension of time
Failure to make timely election
Gifts
Invalid election
Marital residence
Proceedings for advice
Right to contest election
Second spouse, burden of proof
Spousal election
Statutory allowance
Tax apportionment
Tax provision in will
Time period generally
Trusts

**Generally**

If a surviving spouse of a deceased testator elects, pursuant to former R.C. 2107.39, to take against the deceased spouse's will, the surviving spouse is entitled to that share of the decedent's estate as set forth in R.C. 2105.06, to the extent that it does not exceed one-half of the net estate or one-third of the decedent's net estate if there are two or more of decedent's children, or their lineal descendants, surviving: (decided under former analogous section) Winkelfoos v. Mann, 16 Ohio App. 3d 266, 475 N.E.2d 509, 1984 Ohio App. LEXIS 12376 (Ohio Ct. App., Huron County 1984).

Where a deceased husband, by his will, made a specific bequest of a certain number of shares of stock in a corporation for the creation of a trust for the benefit of one of his employees, and where the remaining portion of his estate is sufficient, after the payment of all debts and other obligations, to provide his relict, who elected not to take under the will, with the share of his net estate to which she is entitled under the provisions of R.C. 2105.06, the relict's share of the net estate is an undivided fractional interest in the real estate plus such additional amount of personal property not specifically bequeathed under the will, either in kind or in money, as shall make her total share of the net estate that amount to which she is entitled under the provisions of the statute: (decided under former analogous section) Winters Nat'l Bank & Trust Co. v. Riffe, 2 Ohio St. 2d 72, 31 Ohio Op. 2d 56, 206 N.E.2d 212, 1965 Ohio LEXIS 487 (Ohio 1965).

The election of a surviving spouse to renounce the provisions made for her under a will and take under the law does not destroy the efficacy of the entire will, and the provisions of such will other than those for such surviving spouse remain in full force and effect and must be administered as far as possible to effect the testator's intention: (decided under former analogous section) Union Commerce Bank v. Roth, 120 Ohio App. 349, 29 Ohio Op. 2d 199, 197 N.E.2d 216, 94 Ohio Law Abs. 408, 1964 Ohio App. LEXIS 583 (Ohio Ct. App., Cuyahoga County 1964).

Where a testator in his will directs the executor to sell all the property of his estate and to divide the proceeds from certain real property among his grandchildren and to divide the proceeds from the residue, consisting of other real property and the personal property, among his children, and the surviving spouse elects to take under the statute of descent and distribution, the surviving spouse is thereupon vested, as of the time of testator's death, with a fee simple title in an undivided one-third interest in all the real property owned by testator at the time of his death; is entitled to all the rents and profits from such undivided one-third interest in real property which was received after the date of testator's death and to an undivided one-third interest in all the personal property of the estate, including rents and profits received after testator's death from such personal property and from the other undivided two-thirds interest in real property; such share of the surviving spouse is a charge against all the remaining property of the estate, both real and personal, available to the executor; and the different classes of legatees bear an equitable, but not necessarily equal or proportionate, share of the reduction in the assets of the estate which was caused by the election of the surviving spouse to take under the statute of descent and distribution: (decided under former analogous section) Blackford v. Vermillion, 107 Ohio App. 26, 7 Ohio Op. 2d 350, 156 N.E.2d 339, 1958 Ohio App. LEXIS 699 (Ohio Ct. App., Hancock County 1958).

In the absence of a showing that the testator intends the effect of an election of a surviving spouse to take against the will should be borne to the contrary, when the election results in the executor being deprived of property, or interests in property, to such extent and in such manner, that the property, or interests in property, remaining available for distribution to different classes of legatees named in different items of the will would, if so distributed, cause the reduction resulting from said election to be borne equitably, but not necessarily equally or proportionately, between said classes, distribution shall be made accordingly without further adjustment or contribution between the classes: (decided under former analogous section) Blackford v. Vermillion, 107 Ohio App. 26, 7 Ohio Op. 2d 350, 156 N.E.2d 339, 1958 Ohio App. LEXIS 699 (Ohio Ct. App., Hancock County 1958).

Under this section the surviving spouse, not only of a testator who was domiciled in Ohio at the time of his death but also of a testator who was not domiciled in, but owned property in Ohio, and whose will has not previously been admitted to probate in any other county of Ohio or elsewhere, has the right to elect whether to take under the will or under the statute of descent and distribution: (decided under former analogous section) In re Estate of Gould, 1 Ohio Op. 2d 366, 140 N.E.2d 793, 75 Ohio Law Abs. 289, 1956 Ohio Misc. LEXIS 331 (Ohio P. Ct.), aff'd, 1 Ohio Op. 2d 372, 140 N.E.2d 801, 75 Ohio Law Abs. 298, 1956 Ohio App. LEXIS 790 (Ohio Ct. App., Hamilton County 1956).

The plain intent of former R.C. 2107.39 is that the election of the surviving spouse shall be made after the filing of the inventory and appraisement, at which time the explanation by the probate judge as to her rights under the will and under the law, as required by former R.C. 2107.43 can be made to such spouse: (decided under former analogous section) In re Estate of Bersin, 98 Ohio App. 432, 57 Ohio Op. 475, 129 N.E.2d 868, 1955 Ohio App. LEXIS 651 (Ohio Ct. App., Medina County 1955).

Elections under this section, involve choice and intelligent choice involves a knowledge of both the facts and the law applicable thereto and where such election is made by a widow, without full knowledge of the condition of the estate, and of her rights, but in ignorance of both, it cannot be asserted that she has made any choice or election: (decided under former analogous section) Smith v. First Nat'l Bank, 124 N.E.2d 851, 69 Ohio Law Abs. 102, 1954 Ohio Misc. LEXIS 364 (Ohio C.P. 1954).

The purpose of that part of this section, stating that in the event of election to take under the statute of descent and distribution "such spouse shall take not to exceed one-half of the net estate," is to limit a widow who declines to take the provision made by her husband to not more than one-half of the estate in lieu of the provision made for her in the rejected will, relates entirely to testamentary disposition of estates and does not limit the widow's rights to intestate property by virtue of GC § 10503-4 (R.C. 2105.06): (decided under former analogous section) Goodfellow v. Wilson, 32 Ohio Law Abs. 569, 1940 Ohio App. LEXIS 1041 (Ohio Ct. App., Clark County June 15, 1940).

The election by a surviving spouse to renounce the provisions of a will made for her and to take under the law, as provided by this section, does not destroy the efficacy of the testator's last will and testament as to other provisions, and the surviving spouse is not entitled to have her one-half of the net estate administered as though there were no will: (decided under former analogous section) In re Ellis' Estate, 66 Ohio App. 121, 19 Ohio Op. 392, 32 N.E.2d 23, 1940 Ohio App. LEXIS 985 (Ohio Ct. App., Lake County 1940).

The filing of the written election by the widow, which election had incorporated in it a statement to the effect that the antenuptial agreement was procured by fraud and was repudiated, did not present an issue on the validity of the agreement for determination by the court: (decided under former analogous section) Juhasz v. Juhasz, 134 Ohio St. 257, 12 Ohio Op. 57, 16 N.E.2d 328, 1938 Ohio LEXIS 294 (Ohio 1938).

In case of refusal to take under the will, the statutes do not contemplate a determination of contested rights upon an election whether it is made in person or by written instrument: (decided under former analogous section) Juhasz v. Juhasz, 134 Ohio St. 257, 12 Ohio Op. 57, 16 N.E.2d 328, 1938 Ohio LEXIS 294 (Ohio 1938).

If election is made in person the court is required to explain the provisions of the will and what the rights are under it as well as what the rights are by law: (decided under former analogous section) Juhasz v. Juhasz, 134 Ohio St. 257, 12 Ohio Op. 57, 16 N.E.2d 328, 1938 Ohio LEXIS 294 (Ohio 1938).

Under GC § 10504-55 (former R.C. 2107.39) et seq a citation may be issued to compel an election; but whether the citation is issued, the election of the surviving spouse may be made either in person in the probate court or by written instrument signed by the spouse and duly acknowledged and filed in the probate court within the time allowed for making an election: (decided under former analogous section) Juhasz v. Juhasz, 134 Ohio St. 257, 12 Ohio Op. 57, 16 N.E.2d 328, 1938 Ohio LEXIS 294 (Ohio 1938).

Where a testatrix devises one-half of her real estate to her spouse for life, remainder to be sold and the proceeds divided among devisees, and the other half to a devisee in fee, the surviving spouse electing not to take under the will and there being no surviving children or parents of the deceased, does not take the whole estate under the provisions of GC § 10503-4 (R.C. 2105.06), but is limited to one-half the net estate under the terms of this section: (decided under former analogous section) Shearn v. Shearn, 60 Ohio App. 317, 14 Ohio Op. 262, 21 N.E.2d 133, 1937 Ohio App. LEXIS 210 (Ohio Ct. App., Coshocton County 1937).

The actual taking of a share of such estate by such surviving spouse is under this section and GC § 10504-60 (former R.C. 2107.41); GC § 10503-5 (R.C. 2105.10), relating to the "descent" of an estate which came from a deceased spouse, has no application; therefore, upon the death of the surviving spouse intestate, his or her whole estate passes under GC § 10503-4 (R.C. 2105.06), pertaining to descent and distribution: (decided under former analogous section) Miller v. Miller, 129 Ohio St. 230, 2 Ohio Op. 45, 194 N.E. 450, 1935 Ohio LEXIS 362 (Ohio 1935).

A surviving spouse may make an election at and after the admittance of the will to probate, within the time limited, and need not wait until the schedule of debts is filed and citation issued: (decided under former analogous section) Davis v. Warner, 47 Ohio App. 495, 192 N.E. 270, 18 Ohio Law Abs. 26, 40 Ohio L. Rep. 384, 1933 Ohio App. LEXIS 305 (Ohio Ct. App., Morrow County 1933), writ of error dismissed, 127 Ohio St. 597, 190 N.E. 386, 39 Ohio L. Rep. 655, 1934 Ohio LEXIS 375 (Ohio 1934).

A widower, electing not to take under the will of his wife who died testate but leaving no children or their legal representatives, is entitled to take such portion of the personalty as though decedent had died intestate leaving children: (decided under former analogous section) Whyde v. Lunn, 15 Ohio App. 297, 32 Ohio C.A. 183, 32 Ohio C.C. (n.s.) 183, 1921 Ohio App. LEXIS 230 (Ohio Ct. App., Muskingum County 1921).].

A surviving spouse cannot be deprived, by the last will of the decedent, of the distributive share fixed by statute: (decided under former analogous section) Whyde v. Lunn, 15 Ohio App. 297, 32 Ohio C.A. 183, 32 Ohio C.C. (n.s.) 183, 1921 Ohio App. LEXIS 230 (Ohio Ct. App., Muskingum County 1921); State ex rel. Zollinger v. Sloane, 24 Ohio Dec. 119, 1912 Ohio Misc. LEXIS 82 (Ohio C.P. 1912).

A widow who elects not to take under the will of her deceased husband is entitled to only so much of the personalty belonging to the said estate as would have passed to her had her husband died intestate: (decided under former analogous section) Harbeson v. Mellinger, 2 Ohio App. 75, 25 Ohio Cir. Dec. 195, 18 Ohio C.A. 504, 18 Ohio C.C. (n.s.) 504, 1913 Ohio App. LEXIS 255 (Ohio Ct. App., Wayne County 1913).

A widow is not deprived of a distributive share of the personal estate of her deceased husband, by his leaving a will in which he disposed of all of it to others, without making any provision for her. As to her in such case, he is regarded as dying intestate: (decided under former analogous section) Doyle v. Doyle, 50 Ohio St. 330, 34 N.E. 166, 1893 Ohio LEXIS 132 (Ohio 1893).

**Acceleration of remainder**

The requirement for an expressed prohibition against acceleration is not satisfied by the creation of a contingent remainder. The provisions of the amended statute do not limit its application to vested remainders: (decided under former analogous section) Funkhouser v. Dorfmeier, 31 Ohio Op. 2d

42, 202 N.E.2d 226, 95 Ohio Law Abs. 140, 1963 Ohio Misc. LEXIS 200 (Ohio P. Ct. 1963).

In order to prevent the application of an acceleration of the remainder or other interest the testator must use words which anticipate the situation in which the spouse would elect to take against the will or at least must use words which prohibit the acceleration in any event: (decided under former analogous section) Funkhouser v. Dorfmeier, 31 Ohio Op. 2d 42, 202 N.E.2d 226, 95 Ohio Law Abs. 140, 1963 Ohio Misc. LEXIS 200 (Ohio P. Ct. 1963).

Where the widow elects to take under the law it is equivalent to her death and the remainders will be accelerated if that intent is warranted by a construction of the will as a whole, subject to the limitation that under certain circumstances where equity deems it right, the life estate will be sequestered to compensate disappointed legatees and acceleration will be denied: (decided under former analogous section) Blair v. Bouton, 15 Ohio Op. 2d 474, 176 N.E.2d 280, 1956 Ohio App. LEXIS 1337 (Ohio Ct. App., Knox County 1956).

**Antenuptial agreement**

Where an antenuptial agreement places restraints upon a testator and where such testator neglects to comply properly with such provisions in his will, and the widow, within nine months following the appointment of the executor, brings an action in a declaratory judgment proceeding to determine the validity of such antenuptial agreement and seeks the advice of the court, such declaratory judgment action is a "proceedings for advice" as is contemplated in former R.C. 2107.39: (decided under former analogous section) Barlup v. Holloway, 25 Ohio App. 2d 44, 54 Ohio Op. 2d 77, 266 N.E.2d 241, 1971 Ohio App. LEXIS 561 (Ohio Ct. App., Logan County 1971).

**Appeal**

Trial court's finding that the surviving spouse had been properly served and that the time to elect against the will had expired was a final appealable order. There was sufficient evidence that the surviving spouse was properly served where her son signed for the certified mail and had the authority to do so: In re Estate of Riley, 2006-Ohio-956, 165 Ohio App. 3d 471, 847 N.E.2d 22, 2006 Ohio App. LEXIS 898 (Ohio Ct. App., Scioto County 2006).

Probate court's decision to grant an estate executrix's motion to strike a surviving spouse's exercise of her elective share to take against the decedent's will pursuant to R.C. 2106.01(A) and 2105.06 was a final judgment which affected the spouse's substantial rights for purposes of R.C. 2505.02(B)(2), and the appellate court had jurisdiction to review the matter pursuant to Ohio Const. art. IV, § 3(B)(2). In re Estate of Riley, 2006-Ohio-956, 165 Ohio App. 3d 471, 847 N.E.2d 22, 2006 Ohio App. LEXIS 898 (Ohio Ct. App., Scioto County 2006).

**Applicability**

This section does not by its words apply only "after the probate of a will" in Ohio. The words, "In Ohio" do not appear in the statute: (decided under former analogous section) Pfau v. Moseley, 9 Ohio St. 2d 13, 38 Ohio Op. 2d 8, 222 N.E.2d 639, 1966 Ohio LEXIS 286 (Ohio 1966).

**Construction with other laws**

The words "net estate," as used in former R.C. 2107.39, describe the same property as do the words which describe the property to be distributed and to pass and descend according to R.C. 2105.06. (Weeks v. Vandeveer, 13 Ohio St. 2d 15, 42 Ohio Op. 2d 25, 233 N.E.2d 502, 1968 Ohio LEXIS 457 (Ohio 1968), and Campbell v. Lloyd, 162 Ohio St. 203, 55 Ohio Op. 102, 122 N.E.2d 695, 1954 Ohio LEXIS 458 (Ohio 1954), cert. denied, 349 U.S. 911, 75 S. Ct. 600, 99 L. Ed. 1246, 1955 U.S. LEXIS 933 (U.S. 1955).

Revised Code §§ 2105.06 and 2107.39 concern the devolution of a decedent's property; they are to be read in pari materia and construed together: (decided under former analogous section) Winkelfoos v. Mann, 16 Ohio App. 3d 266, 475 N.E.2d 509, 1984 Ohio App. LEXIS 12376 (Ohio Ct. App., Huron County 1984).

**Early election**

The probate court will permit an earlier election where the surviving spouse waives the right to have the inventory and appraisement and schedule of debts filed prior to making the election: (decided under former analogous section) In re Rogers' Estate, 10 Ohio Op. 2d 205, 160 N.E.2d 442, 81 Ohio Law Abs. 10, 1959 Ohio Misc. LEXIS 335 (Ohio P. Ct. 1959).

Under this section a surviving spouse cannot elect to take under a will or under the statute of descent and distribution until after the probate of the will: (decided under former analogous section) Raleigh v. Raleigh, 153 Ohio St. 160, 41 Ohio Op. 209, 91 N.E.2d 241, 1950 Ohio LEXIS 459 (Ohio 1950).

**Extension of time**

Because the probate court had failed to issue the mandatory R.C. 2106.01(A) citation to the surviving spouse following appointment of the estate's administrator, there was good cause for the probate court to grant the spouse's motion under R.C. 2106.25 to extend the time to make spousal elections. In re Estate of Weitzel, 2021-Ohio-1859, 2021 Ohio App. LEXIS 1817 (Ohio Ct. App., Warren County 2021).

**Failure to make timely election**

A surviving spouse who fails to make a timely election as to whether to take under the will is conclusively presumed to have elected to take under the will: In re Estate of Reddick, 102 Ohio App. 3d 488, 657 N.E.2d 531, 1995 Ohio App. LEXIS 1596 (Ohio Ct. App., Hancock County 1995).

**Gifts**

Where a testator devises certain property to his spouse and then makes an inter vivos gift of the property to her, such gift does not amount to an equitable advancement or ademption. If the surviving spouse then elects against the will, the property does not count against her statutory share: King v. King, 82 Ohio App. 3d 747, 613 N.E.2d 251, 1992 Ohio App. LEXIS 4823 (Ohio Ct. App., Montgomery County 1992).

But the husband may, by a gift inter vivos during his last illness, dispose of all his personalty to his daughter, that he might die intestate and thereby defeat his wife in sharing in the property. This is not a testamentary devise: (decided under former analogous section) Hickman v. Huntington & Co., 9 Ohio Dec. 503, 7 Ohio N.P. 79 (1898).

**Invalid election**

Court erred by finding the purported election to take against the will to be valid, because it was undisputed that the surviving spouse did not make an election in person before a probate judge, referee or commissioner as required by R.C. 2106.06, when the spouse signed an election form in his attorney's office and the space on the form provided for the signature of the probate judge was blank. In re Estate of Woods, 2011-Ohio-1831, 193 Ohio App. 3d 371, 951 N.E.2d 1120, 2011 Ohio App. LEXIS 1581 (Ohio Ct. App., Greene County 2011).

**Marital residence**

Where the decedent conveyed his one-half interest in the marital residence without his spouse's consent, she was entitled to both that dower interest and a statutory distributive share of the rest of his estate: Armstrong v. Armstrong, 128 Ohio App. 3d 393, 715 N.E.2d 207, 1998 Ohio App. LEXIS 2705 (Ohio Ct. App., Wayne County), dismissed, State v. Jackson, 83 Ohio St. 3d 1446, 700 N.E.2d 330, 1998 Ohio LEXIS 2829 (Ohio 1998).

**Proceedings for advice**

Where proceedings for advice are sought, the widow has three months after the final disposition of such declaratory judgment proceedings within which to make her election as to whether she will take under the statute of descent and distribution or whether she will take under the will: (decided under former analogous section) Barlup v. Holloway, 25 Ohio App. 2d 44, 54 Ohio Op. 2d 77, 266 N.E.2d 241, 1971 Ohio App. LEXIS 561 (Ohio Ct. App., Logan County 1971).

**Right to contest election**

Legatees under the will of a decedent have no legal interest in or right to contest an election of a surviving spouse made under this section, and are not properly appellees in an appeal by the guardian of the surviving spouse: (decided under former analogous section) In re Estate of Strauch, 11 Ohio App. 2d 173, 40 Ohio Op. 2d 331, 229 N.E.2d 95, 1967 Ohio App. LEXIS 426 (Ohio Ct. App., Franklin County 1967), aff'd, 15 Ohio St. 2d 192, 44 Ohio Op. 2d 158, 239 N.E.2d 43, 1968 Ohio LEXIS 394 (Ohio 1968).].

For the purpose of determining whether distribution should be made under the terms of a will or under the provisions of law when a surviving spouse has elected to take against a will, an executor has the right to object to the making of an election by such spouse: (decided under former analogous section) In re Estate of Gould, 1 Ohio Op. 2d 372, 140 N.E.2d 801, 75 Ohio Law Abs. 298, 1956 Ohio App. LEXIS 790 (Ohio Ct. App., Hamilton County 1956).

**Second spouse, burden of proof**

Where the decedent was married twice, the second wife had the burden of showing that the first marriage was properly terminated: Bajurczak v. Bajurczak, 139 Ohio App. 3d 78, 742 N.E.2d 1191, 2000 Ohio App. LEXIS 4696 (Ohio Ct. App., Lorain County 2000).

**Spousal election**

Even though the husband took some action to indicate he would elect to take against the will, he did not follow the statutory directives in place for preserving his elective right and nothing prevented him from moving to expedite the election process in light of the uncontested inventory prior to its approval. Estate Of Adams, 2013-Ohio-5824, 6 N.E.3d 673, 2013 Ohio App. LEXIS 6119 (Ohio Ct. App., Ashtabula County 2013).

Trial court erred when it extended the time frame for the husband to take against the will without being properly moved to do so because the limitation period set forth had passed without being properly extended and thus, the husband was bound to take under the will. Estate Of Adams,

2013-Ohio-5824, 6 N.E.3d 673, 2013 Ohio App. LEXIS 6119 (Ohio Ct. App., Ashtabula County 2013).

Where a certified letter which notified a surviving spouse of her right to make an election regarding her deceased husband's will was properly served pursuant to Civ.R. 4.1(A) and 73(E)(3) when it was clearly delivered to the correct address and the spouse's son signed for the letter, the five-month statutory period to make such an election pursuant to R.C. 2105.06 and 2106.01(E) began to run; as the spouse made an election to take against her deceased husband's will beyond that five-month period, the probate court properly granted the executrix's motion to strike the election and the spouse was presumed to have elected to take pursuant to the will. In re Estate of Riley, 2006-Ohio-956, 165 Ohio App. 3d 471, 847 N.E.2d 22, 2006 Ohio App. LEXIS 898 (Ohio Ct. App., Scioto County 2006).



**Statutory allowance**

Where a decedent's widow was not provided for in his Last Will and Testament, which he had executed the year before their marriage, and she obtained her spousal election under R.C. 2106.01 from the estate, she achieved her fair equity, such that her claims for unjust enrichment and subrogation rights against the estate administrator upon his rejection of her claim for hospital bills that were incurred by the decedent prior to his death was proper. The widow had obtained a financial aid forgiveness of the debt from the hospital, for which she had personally contracted to obligate herself, and although the estate was "enriched" by her actions, it was not unjustly enriched. Phillips v. Campbell, 2007-Ohio-4022, 2007 Ohio App. LEXIS 3641 (Ohio Ct. App., Ashland County 2007).

A surviving spouse taking against a will of a deceased spouse under former R.C. 2107.39 is entitled to the $5,000 statutory allowance under former R.C. 2117.20 unless specifically barred by the will: (decided under former analogous section) In re Estate of Green, 63 Ohio Misc. 44, 17 Ohio Op. 3d 388, 410 N.E.2d 812, 1980 Ohio Misc. LEXIS 53 (Ohio P. Ct. 1980).

**Tax apportionment**

When a surviving spouse elects to take against the will of a decedent spouse, the federal estate tax is to be apportioned to the estate prior to determining the interest of the surviving spouse. The enactment of R.C. 2113.86 and 2113.88 effective March 23, 1981 does not change this result: (decided under former analogous section) In re Estate of McVicker, 23 Ohio Misc. 2d 43, 492 N.E.2d 491, 1985 Ohio Misc. LEXIS 98 (Ohio C.P. 1985).

**Tax provision in will**

The presence or absence of a tax provision in the will of a testator does not alter the statutory share of a surviving spouse electing to take against the will as provided in this section: (decided under former analogous section) Weeks v. Vandeveer, 13 Ohio St. 2d 15, 42 Ohio Op. 2d 25, 233 N.E.2d 502, 1968 Ohio LEXIS 457 (Ohio 1968).

**Time period generally**

Underlying claims of the executrix of the decedent's estate were properly dismissed because of the failure of the executrix to comply with the statutory deadlines under R.C. 2106.01(E) to elect against the will, to request an extension of time, or to contest the will. Mays v. Carl L. Mays Trust, 2012-Ohio-618, 2012 Ohio App. LEXIS 553 (Ohio Ct. App., Huron County 2012).

The period of time prescribed by this section within which a surviving spouse may make an election to take under the will of a decedent or under the statute of descent and distribution is not extended by the filing after the termination of such period of an action alleging that an election made during the period is void and praying that it be held void: (decided under former analogous section) In re Estate of Wolfel, 3 Ohio App. 2d 11, 32 Ohio Op. 2d 75, 209 N.E.2d 594, 1965 Ohio App. LEXIS 528 (Ohio Ct. App., Marion County 1965).

**Trusts**

The revocable living trust executed by the husband and accompanied by the wife's waiver of rights was effective to waive her statutory rights as surviving spouse: Miller v. Miller, 139 Ohio App. 3d 512, 744 N.E.2d 778, 2000 Ohio App. LEXIS 3751 (Ohio Ct. App., Cuyahoga County 2000), dismissed, 91 Ohio St. 3d 1445, 742 N.E.2d 143, 2001 Ohio LEXIS 379 (Ohio 2001).

A valid, nontestamentary trust executed by a settlor and in existence at the time of his or her death bars the settlor's spouse from claiming a distributive share in the trust assets under the statutes of descent and distribution, even though the settlor is the trustee, derives all income from the trust, and reserves the rights to revoke or amend the trust and to withdraw and deposit assets: Dumas v. Estate of Dumas, 1994-Ohio-312, 68 Ohio St. 3d 405, 627 N.E.2d 978, 1994 Ohio LEXIS 498 (Ohio 1994).

A surviving spouse, electing to take against her husband's will under former R.C. 2107.39, retains her beneficial life income interests in all assets of an inter vivos trust, including those amounts added to the trust from the decedent's estate via a residuary clause of the will: (decided under former analogous section) Carnahan v. Stallman, 29 Ohio App. 3d 293, 504 N.E.2d 1218, 1986 Ohio App. LEXIS 10013 (Ohio Ct. App., Franklin County 1986).

Where the settlor exercises continued dominion and control over the property in a revocable inter vivos trust and the trustee continually yields to the will of the settlor, a mere agency or custodianship results, which is revoked upon the death of the so-called settlor and the property passes either under a will or pursuant to the intestate laws: (decided under former analogous section) Osborn v. Osborn, 10 Ohio Misc. 171, 39 Ohio Op. 2d 275, 226 N.E.2d 814, 1966 Ohio Misc. LEXIS 226 (Ohio C.P. 1966), aff'd, 18 Ohio St. 2d 144, 47 Ohio Op. 2d 310, 248 N.E.2d 191, 1969 Ohio LEXIS 390 (Ohio 1969).].

A valid voluntary trust in praesenti, formally executed by a husband and existing at the time of his death, in which he reserved to himself the income therefrom during life, coupled with an absolute power to revoke the trust in whole or in part, as well as the right to modify the terms of the settlement and to control investments, bars the wife, upon the death of the settlor, from a claimed right to a distributive share of the property in the trust upon her election to take under the statutes of descent and distribution: (decided under former analogous section) Smyth v. Cleveland Trust Co., 172 Ohio St. 489, 18 Ohio Op. 2d 42, 179 N.E.2d 60, 1961 Ohio LEXIS 619 (Ohio 1961).

## RESEARCH REFERENCES AND PRACTICE AIDS

**Cross-References to Related Sections**

Apportionment of taxes, RC § 2113.86.
Citation to make the election, RC § 2106.02.
Commission issued to take election of spouse, RC § 2106.07.
Complaint; construction of will, RC § 2106.03.
Distribution of assets of estate, RC § 2113.53.
Application of legatee or distributee, RC § 2113.54.
Election made by one under legal disability, RC § 2106.08.
Failure to make election; presumption, RC § 2106.04.
Proceedings to admit foreign will to record, RC § 2129.07.
Property devised, bequeathed or appointed to trustee of existing trust, RC § 2107.63.
Time limit for exercising rights of surviving spouse, RC § 2106.25.

**Practice Manuals and Treatises**

Anderson's Ohio Elder Law Practice Manual § 6.5 Elective Share, Disclaimer
Anderson's The Simple Will in Ohio § 5.7 Right to Take Against Will
Anderson's The Simple Will in Ohio § 5.22 Exemption of Spouse's Share
Anderson's Ohio Probate Practice and Procedure Form 15.14 Commissioner's report
Anderson's Ohio Probate Practice and Procedure Form 15.19 Election of surviving spouse to receive mansion house
Anderson's Ohio Probate Practice and Procedure Standard Probate Form 8.0 Citation to Surviving Spouse to Exercise Elective Rights
Anderson's Ohio Probate Practice and Procedure Standard Probate Form 8.2 Election of Surviving Spouse to Take Against Will
Anderson's Ohio Probate Practice and Procedure Outline No. § 39 Distribution-requirement by legatee or distributee
Anderson's Ohio Probate Practice and Procedure Outline No. § 43 Election by spouse under will-by citation
Anderson's Ohio Probate Practice and Procedure Outline No. § 44 Election by spouse under will-commission issued
Anderson's Ohio Probate Practice and Procedure Outline No. § 45 Election by spouse under will-under legal disability
Anderson's Ohio Probate Practice and Procedure Outline No. § 74 Probate of will-will made in foreign country

**Practice Guides**

Anderson's Ohio Probate Practice and Procedure § 6.02 Who may bring action
Anderson's Ohio Probate Practice and Procedure § 15.01 General
Anderson's Ohio Probate Practice and Procedure § 15.05 Election to take the testamentary share or to take against the will
Anderson's Ohio Probate Practice and Procedure § 15.06 Election to receive the mansion house as part of intestate share and family allowance
Anderson's Ohio Probate Practice and Procedure § 18.08 Afterborn and pretermitted heirs
Anderson's Ohio Probate Practice and Procedure § 23.10 Apportionment of taxes among beneficiaries
Anderson's Ohio Probate Practice and Procedure § 26.06 Circumstances that may prevent relief from administration
Anderson's Ohio Probate Practice and Procedure § 48.02 Revocable inter vivos trusts

**Practice Forms**

Citation to Surviving Spouse to Elect to Take Under or Against Will, Couse's Ohio Form Book Form SPF 8.0
Entry Dispensing with Citation to Surviving Spouse, Couse's Ohio Form Book Form SPF 8.02
SUMMARY OF GENERAL RIGHTS OF SURVIVING SPOUSE, Couse's Ohio Form Book Form SPF 8.3

Agreement Waiving Spouse's Elective Share, Ohio Transaction Guide: Estate Planning Law & Forms § 2.221

Standard Probate Form 8.0 1 —Citation to Surviving Spouse to Exercise Elective Rights 2, 12 OH Forms of Pleading & Practice — Probate Form 14:21

Standard Probate Form 8.2 1 —Election of Surviving Spouse to Take Against Will 2, 12 OH Forms of Pleading & Practice — Probate Form 14:23

## § 2106.02 Citation to make election.

(A) The citation to make the election referred to in section 2106.01 of the Revised Code shall be served on the surviving spouse pursuant to Civil Rule 73. Notice that the citation has been issued by the court shall be given to the administrator or executor of the estate of the deceased spouse.

(B) The citation shall be accompanied by a general description of the effect of the election to take under the will or under section 2105.06 of the Revised Code and the general rights of the surviving spouse under Chapter 2106. of the Revised Code. The description shall include a specific reference to the procedures available to the surviving spouse under section 2106.03 of the Revised Code and to the presumption that arises if the surviving spouse does not make the election in accordance with division (E) of section 2106.01 of the Revised Code. The description of the general rights of the surviving spouse under Chapter 2106. of the Revised Code shall include a specific reference to the presumption that arises if the surviving spouse does not exercise the rights under Chapter 2106. of the Revised Code within the time period specified by section 2106.25 of the Revised Code. The description of the effect of the election and of the general rights of the surviving spouse need not relate to the nature of any particular estate.

(C) A surviving spouse electing to take under the will may manifest the election in writing within the times described in division (E) of section 2106.01 of the Revised Code.

**HISTORY:**

RC § 2107.39.1, 136 v S 145 (Eff 1-1-76); 136 v S 466 (Eff 5-26-76); RC § 2106.02, 143 v H 346 (Eff 5-31-90); 149 v H 85. Eff 12-31-2001; 150 v H 51, § 1, eff. 4-8-04.

**Editor's Notes**

The provisions of § 3, H.B. 51 (150 v —), as amended by H.B. 161 (150 v —), read as follows:

SECTION 3. (A) Sections 2106.01, 2106.02, and 2109.32 of the Revised Code, as amended by Am. Sub. H.B. 51 of the 125th General Assembly, apply to estates that are in existence or are initiated on or after April 8, 2004.

See provisions, § 5 of HB 85 (149 v —), following RC § 2106.01.

### NOTES TO DECISIONS

Analysis

Appeal
Defects in mailing notice

**Appeal**

Trial court's finding that the surviving spouse had been properly served and that the time to elect against the will had expired was a final appealable order. There was sufficient evidence that the surviving spouse was properly served where her son signed for the certified mail and had the authority to do so: In re Estate of Riley, 2006-Ohio-956, 165 Ohio App. 3d 471, 847 N.E.2d 22, 2006 Ohio App. LEXIS 898 (Ohio Ct. App., Scioto County 2006).

**Defects in mailing notice**

Where the evidence establishes that the surviving spouse effectively received notice of her right to elect against the will, any technical defects with regard to mailing the notice will be ignored: (decided under former analogous section) Hutton v. Rygalski, 62 Ohio App. 3d 125, 574 N.E.2d 1128, 1989 Ohio App. LEXIS 1078 (Ohio Ct. App., Lucas County 1989).

### RESEARCH REFERENCES AND PRACTICE AIDS

**Cross-References to Related Sections**

Proceedings to admit foreign will to record, RC § 2129.07.

**Practice Manuals and Treatises**

Anderson's Ohio Probate Practice and Procedure Standard Probate Form 8.0 Citation to Surviving Spouse to Exercise Elective Rights

Anderson's Ohio Probate Practice and Procedure Standard Probate Form 8.3 Summary of General Rights of Surviving Spouse

Anderson's Ohio Probate Practice and Procedure Standard Probate Form 8.4 Certificate of Service and Notice of Citation to Surviving Spouse to Exercise Elective Rights

Anderson's Ohio Probate Practice and Procedure Outline No. § 43 Election by spouse under will-by citation

**Practice Guides**

Anderson's Ohio Probate Practice and Procedure § 15.05 Election to take the testamentary share or to take against the will

**Practice Forms**

Citation to Surviving Spouse to Elect to Take Under or Against Will, Couse's Ohio Form Book Form SPF 8.0

Entry Dispensing with Citation to Surviving Spouse, Couse's Ohio Form Book Form SPF 8.02

Summary of General Rights of Surviving Spouse, Couse's Ohio Form Book Form SPF 8.3

Return for Certificate of Service of Citation to Surviving Spouse to Exercise Elective Rights, Couse's Ohio Form Book Form SPF 8.5

Standard Probate Form 8.0 1 —Citation to Surviving Spouse to Exercise Elective Rights 2, 12 OH Forms of Pleading & Practice — Probate Form 14:21

Standard Probate Form 8.3—Summary of General Rights of Surviving Spouse 1, 12 OH Forms of Pleading & Practice — Probate Form 14:23A



## § 2106.03 Complaint; construction of will.

Within the times described in division (E) of section 2106.01 of the Revised Code for making an election, the surviving spouse may file a complaint in the probate court making all persons interested in the will defendants, that requests a construction of the will in favor of the surviving spouse and for the court to render a judgment to that effect.

**HISTORY:**

GC § 10504-57; 114 v 320(357); 118 v 78; Bureau of Code Revision, RC § 2107.40, 10-1-53; 136 v S 145 (Eff 1-1-76); RC § 2106.03, 143 v H 346. Eff 5-31-90.

### NOTES TO DECISIONS

Analysis

Generally
Appeal
Parties

**Generally**

Where property specifically devised must be taken for payment of testator's debts, his widow is entitled to be judicially advised whether, if she accepts the provisions made for her by the will, she will be obliged to contribute her proportion of the loss to the person from whom the property so devised is taken: (decided under former analogous section) Allen v. Tressenrider, 72 Ohio St. 77, 73 N.E. 1015, 2 Ohio L. Rep. 495, 1905 Ohio LEXIS 143 (Ohio 1905).

**Appeal**

From the construction placed on the provisions of a will, at the suit of a widow under this section, error may be prosecuted to the supreme court from the judgment of the circuit court for reversal of the same: (decided under former analogous section) Davis v. Coffman, 55 Ohio St. 556, 45 N.E. 707, 1897 Ohio LEXIS 209 (Ohio 1897), [for report of this case on merits, see 39 Weekly L. Bull. 307.].

**Parties**

All persons interested in the will must be made defendants in an action by the widow for the construction thereof. This rule is followed in federal courts: (decided under former analogous section) Stevens v. Smith, 126 F. 706, 1903 U.S. App. LEXIS 4356 (6th Cir. Ohio 1903), cert. denied, 193 U.S. 671, 24 S. Ct. 853, 48 L. Ed. 841, 1904 U.S. LEXIS 941 (U.S. 1904).].

### RESEARCH REFERENCES AND PRACTICE AIDS

**Cross-References to Related Sections**

Citation to make the election, RC § 2106.02.

Proceedings to admit foreign will to record, RC § 2129.07.

**Practice Manuals and Treatises**

Anderson's Ohio Probate Practice and Procedure Outline No. § 29 Construction of will

**Practice Guides**

Anderson's Ohio Probate Practice and Procedure § 18.02 Methods of construing the will

**Practice Forms**

Complaint by Surviving Spouse for Construction of Will 1, 11 OH Forms of Pleading & Practice — Probate Form 8:2

Complaint by Surviving Spouse for Construction of Will 1, 12 OH Forms of Pleading & Practice — Probate Form 14:25

### § 2106.04 Failure to make election; presumption.



If the surviving spouse dies before probate of the will, or, having survived the probate, thereafter either fails to make the election provided by section 2106.01 of the Revised Code or dies without having made an election within the times described in division (E) of that section, the surviving spouse shall be conclusively presumed to have elected to take under the will, and the surviving spouse and the heirs, devisees, and legatees of the surviving spouse, and those claiming through or under them, shall be bound by the conclusive presumption, and persons may deal with the property of the decedent accordingly; provided that, if applicable, the provisions of sections 2105.31 to 2105.39 of the Revised Code shall prevail over the provisions relating to the right of election of a surviving spouse.

**HISTORY:**

GC § 10504-60; 114 v 320(357); 116 v 385; 122 v 498; Bureau of Code Revision, RC § 2107.41, 10-1-53; 125 v 411 (Eff 10-16-53); RC § 2106.04, 143 v H 346 (Eff 5-31-90); 149 v H 242. Eff 5-16-2002.

**Editor's Notes**

See provisions, § 5 of HB 345 (149 v —) following RC § 2105.39.

#### NOTES TO DECISIONS

Analysis

Generally
Death of surviving spouse
Invalid election
Mental illness of surviving spouse

**Generally**

A surviving spouse who fails to make a timely election as to whether to take under the will is conclusively presumed to have elected to take under the will: In re Estate of Reddick, 102 Ohio App. 3d 488, 657 N.E.2d 531, 1995 Ohio App. LEXIS 1596 (Ohio Ct. App., Hancock County 1995).

The right of a surviving spouse to elect against the will, granted pursuant to former R.C. 2107.39, is personal to such surviving spouse and does not survive his or her death, and that right may not be exercised in favor of the surviving spouse's estate: (decided under former analogous section) In re Estate of La Spina, 60 Ohio St. 2d 101, 14 Ohio Op. 3d 336, 397 N.E.2d 1196, 1979 Ohio LEXIS 508 (Ohio 1979).

A void election, as contrasted with a voidable one, is void ab initio, and if no valid election is made thereafter within nine months after the appointment of the executor, and nothing has occurred or failed to occur which would operate to extend such nine month period, the surviving spouse shall be conclusively presumed to have elected to take under the will of the decedent, as provided by this section: (decided under former analogous section) In re Estate of Wolfel, 3 Ohio App. 2d 11, 32 Ohio Op. 2d 75, 209 N.E.2d 594, 1965 Ohio App. LEXIS 528 (Ohio Ct. App., Marion County 1965).

If a surviving spouse remains alive and competent and, within nine months after the appointment of the first fiduciary charged with the administration of the estate under the will of the deceased spouse, no citation is issued and served upon him to elect whether to take under the will or under R.C. 2105.06 and within such nine-month period he also fails voluntarily so to elect, he will be conclusively presumed to have elected to take under the will, regardless of whether or not the inventory, appraisement and schedule of debts are filed: (decided under former analogous section) In re Estate of Witteman, 3 Ohio St. 2d 66, 32 Ohio Op. 2d 49, 209 N.E.2d 427, 1965 Ohio LEXIS 593 (Ohio 1965).

Under this section, as amended 116 v 116, if the surviving spouse fails to make an election, or dies at any time before the expiration of the time limit provided by law without having elected, the spouse "shall be conclusively presumed to have elected to take under the will": (decided under former analogous section) Price v. Herbert, 11 Ohio Op. 138, 33 N.E.2d 398, 26 Ohio Law Abs. 330, 1937 Ohio Misc. LEXIS 897 (Ohio Ct. App., Delaware County 1937).

**Death of surviving spouse**

This section is not applicable if the surviving spouse referred to therein dies before the probate of the will of his spouse, and, in such case, after the probate of the will of the latter and the filing of the inventory, appraisement and schedule of debts thereunder, the probate court is authorized to make an election for the estate of the deceased surviving spouse as will be most advantageous to that estate: (decided under former analogous section) Raleigh v. Raleigh, 153 Ohio St. 160, 41 Ohio Op. 209, 91 N.E.2d 241, 1950 Ohio LEXIS 459 (Ohio 1950).

Where the surviving spouse of a testator dies before the expiration of the time for making election, she shall be conclusively presumed to have elected to take under the will notwithstanding that during the period between the testator's death and her death she was continuously insane and incapable of making an election: (decided under former analogous section) In re Knofler's Estate, 143 Ohio St. 294, 28 Ohio Op. 203, 55 N.E.2d 262, 1944 Ohio LEXIS 409 (Ohio 1944).].

This section, which provides, inter alia, that if a surviving spouse dies before the expiration of the time limit provided by law without having made an election, such spouse shall be conclusively presumed to have elected to take under the will, does not by such provision deny due process of law and is constitutional: (decided under former analogous section) In re Knofler's Estate, 143 Ohio St. 294, 28 Ohio Op. 203, 55 N.E.2d 262, 1944 Ohio LEXIS 409 (Ohio 1944).].

**Invalid election**

Court erred by finding the purported election to take against the will to be valid, because it was undisputed that the surviving spouse did not make an election in person before a probate judge, referee or commissioner as required by R.C. 2106.06, when the spouse signed an election form in his attorney's office and the space on the form provided for the signature of the probate judge was blank. In re Estate of Woods, 2011-Ohio-1831, 193 Ohio App. 3d 371, 951 N.E.2d 1120, 2011 Ohio App. LEXIS 1581 (Ohio Ct. App., Greene County 2011).

**Mental illness of surviving spouse**

This section, providing for a conclusive presumption of election, is not violative of due process, where the surviving spouse fails to elect by reason of continued insanity, and his guardian fails to make application for a commission to elect, within the time provided by GC § 10504-55 (R.C. 2107.39): (decided under former analogous section) In re Iwinski's Estate, 83 Ohio App. 463, 38 Ohio Op. 491, 77 N.E.2d 375, 49 Ohio Law Abs. 609, 1947 Ohio App. LEXIS 592 (Ohio Ct. App., Cuyahoga County 1947).

The provisions of former GC § 10571 (see now R.C. 2107.39, 2107.43) that if the widow or widower fails to make an election within the time specified, it shall be deemed that she or he has elected to take under the will, have no application in a case where the widow was mentally incompetent at the time of the death of the testator and continued in such condition until her death two months later, during which period no action was taken by the probate court: (decided under former analogous section) Ambrose v. Rugg, 123 Ohio St. 433, 175 N.E. 691, 9 Ohio Law Abs. 477, 1931 Ohio LEXIS 359 (Ohio 1931).

#### RESEARCH REFERENCES AND PRACTICE AIDS

**Cross-References to Related Sections**

Proceedings to admit foreign will to record, RC § 2129.07.

**Practice Manuals and Treatises**

Anderson's Ohio Probate Practice and Procedure Standard Probate Form 8.1 Election of Surviving Spouse to Take Under Will

**Practice Forms**

Election of Surviving Spouse to Take Under Will, Couse's Ohio Form Book Form SPF 8.1

### § 2106.05 Election to take under the will; effect.

If a surviving spouse elects to take under the will, the surviving spouse shall be barred of all right to an intestate share of the property passing under the will and shall take under the will alone, unless it plainly appears from the will that the provision for the surviving spouse was intended to be in addition to an intestate share. An election to take under the will does not bar the right of the surviving spouse to an intestate share of that portion of the estate as to which the decedent dies intestate. Unless the will expressly otherwise directs, an election to take under the will does not bar the right of the surviving spouse to remain in the mansion house, and does not bar the right of the surviving spouse to receive the allowance for the support provided by section 2106.13 of the Revised Code.

**HISTORY:**

GC § 10504-61; 114 v 320(357); 116 v 385; 119 v 394; Bureau of Code Revision, RC § 2107.42, 10-1-53; 136 v S 145 (Eff 1-1-76); RC § 2106.05, 143 v H 346. Eff 5-31-90.

**NOTES TO DECISIONS**

Analysis

Generally
Allowance for support
Intestate share of decedent's estate

**Generally**

Where the will of a husband, after making certain provisions for his wife, recites that "the foregoing devises and bequests to my said wife. . . shall be in lieu of her dower and all other interest which she may have in my estate," if the wife elects to take under the husband's will, such election shall bar her of her year's allowance and money exemption; and where, in such will, household goods are specifically bequeathed to the wife, such election shall bar the wife of her right under GC § 10509-54 (R.C. 2115.13 [repealed]) to select such household goods as property exempt from administration: (decided under former analogous section) Atwood v. Miller, 24 Ohio Op. 398 (Ohio P. Ct. 1942).

Under the provisions of this section, if a surviving spouse elects to take under a will, such spouse shall be barred of all rights to an intestate share of the estate, and shall take under the will alone, unless it plainly appears from the will that the provision therein for the spouse was intended to be in addition to an intestate share: (decided under former analogous section) Jones v. Webster, 133 Ohio St. 492, 11 Ohio Op. 184, 14 N.E.2d 928, 1938 Ohio LEXIS 361 (Ohio 1938).

The exemption allowed to a surviving spouse by the provisions of GC § 10509-54 (former R.C. 2115.13) of the articles enumerated therein or a proper amount of cash in lieu thereof, must be allowed, if the selection allowed by the statute is made by such spouse even though such spouse later elects to take under a will conditioned that the surviving spouse be barred of all claims against the estate in order to take thereunder: (decided under former analogous section) Landfear v. Scharkofsky, 50 Ohio App. 213, 3 Ohio Op. 48, 197 N.E. 810 (1935).

A widower electing to take under will of his wife is not barred of his right to statutory allowance of personal property not deemed assets of estate of wife, unless will expressly provides that provisions made for him are in lieu thereof (former GC § 10572): (decided under former analogous section) In re Guthrie, 28 Ohio N.P. 447 (1931); Brown v. Routzahn, 63 F.2d 914 (6th Cir. 1933), reversing 58 F.2d 329.].

**Allowance for support**

Under this section, a testator may, by express direction in his will, bar the right of his widow to receive one year's allowance for the support of herself and children if she elects to take under the will: (decided under former analogous section) Bolles v. Toledo Trust Co., 144 Ohio St. 195, 29 Ohio Op. 376, 58 N.E.2d 381, 1944 Ohio LEXIS 355 (Ohio 1944), overruled, Smyth v. Cleveland Trust Co., 172 Ohio St. 489, 18 Ohio Op. 2d 42, 179 N.E.2d 60, 1961 Ohio LEXIS 619 (Ohio 1961).].

**Intestate share of decedent's estate**

When the surviving spouse elects to take under the will, she is entitled to an intestate share of that portion of the estate as to which the decedent dies intestate: (decided under former analogous section) Abram v. Wilson, 8 Ohio Misc. 420, 37 Ohio Op. 2d 288, 220 N.E.2d 739, 1966 Ohio Misc. LEXIS 402 (Ohio P. Ct. 1966).

**RESEARCH REFERENCES AND PRACTICE AIDS**

**Cross-References to Related Sections**

Proceedings to admit foreign will to record, RC § 2129.07.

**Practice Manuals and Treatises**

Anderson's Ohio Elder Law Practice Manual § 6.5 Elective Share, Disclaimer

Anderson's Ohio Probate Practice and Procedure Standard Probate Form 8.1 Election of Surviving Spouse to Take Under Will

**Practice Forms**

Election of Surviving Spouse to Take Under Will, Couse's Ohio Form Book Form SPF 8.1

Election of Surviving Spouse to Take Against Will, Couse's Ohio Form Book Form SPF 8.2

Summary of General Rights of Surviving Spouse, Couse's Ohio Form Book Form SPF 8.3

Standard Probate Form 8.1 1 —Election of Surviving Spouse To Take Under Will 2, 12 OH Forms of Pleading & Practice — Probate Form 14:22

## § 2106.06 Election made in person.

The election of a surviving spouse to take under section 2105.06 of the Revised Code and thereby refusing to take under the will shall be made in person before the probate judge, or a deputy clerk who has been appointed to act as a referee, except as provided in sections 2106.07 and 2106.08 of the Revised Code.

When the election is made in person before the judge or referee, the judge or referee shall explain the will, the rights under the will, and the rights, by law, in the event of a refusal to take under the will.

**HISTORY:**

GC §§ 10504-56, 10504-59; 114 v 320(357); 122 v 498; Bureau of Code Revision, RC § 2107.43, 10-1-53; 125 v 411 (Eff 10-16-53); 136 v S 145 (Eff 1-1-76); 136 v S 466 (Eff 5-26-76); RC § 2106.06, 143 v H 346. Eff 5-31-90.

**NOTES TO DECISIONS**

Analysis

Constitutionality
Generally
Election not taken
Invalid election
Rescission of election

**Constitutionality**

The legislative requirement that a surviving spouse appear personally to elect against the will is rationally related to the general purpose of protecting the interest of surviving spouses and decedents, and is constitutional: (decided under former analogous section) Hutton v. Rygalski, 62 Ohio App. 3d 125, 574 N.E.2d 1128, 1989 Ohio App. LEXIS 1078 (Ohio Ct. App., Lucas County 1989).

**Generally**

While this section requires the judge or referee appointed by him to explain the will, the rights under such will and under the law, the right of the widow to elect to take under the law or under the will is an absolute right in the nature of a personal privilege which cannot be taken from her: (decided under former analogous section) In re Estate of Callan, 101 Ohio App. 114, 1 Ohio Op. 2d 64, 135 N.E.2d 464, 1956 Ohio App. LEXIS 686 (Ohio Ct. App., Cuyahoga County 1956).

**Election not taken**

Even though the husband took some action to indicate he would elect to take against the will, he did not follow the statutory directives in place for preserving his elective right and nothing prevented him from moving to expedite the election process in light of the uncontested inventory prior to its approval. Estate Of Adams, 2013-Ohio-5824, 6 N.E.3d 673, 2013 Ohio App. LEXIS 6119 (Ohio Ct. App., Ashtabula County 2013).

Trial court erred when it extended the time frame for the husband to take against the will without being properly moved to do so because the limitation period set forth had passed without being properly extended and thus, the husband was bound to take under the will. Estate Of Adams, 2013-Ohio-5824, 6 N.E.3d 673, 2013 Ohio App. LEXIS 6119 (Ohio Ct. App., Ashtabula County 2013).

**Invalid election**

Court erred by finding the purported election to take against the will to be valid, because it was undisputed that the surviving spouse did not make an election in person before a probate judge, referee or commissioner as required by R.C. 2106.06, when the spouse signed an election form in his attorney's office and the space on the form provided for the signature of the probate judge was blank. In re Estate of Woods, 2011-Ohio-1831, 193 Ohio App. 3d 371, 951 N.E.2d 1120, 2011 Ohio App. LEXIS 1581 (Ohio Ct. App., Greene County 2011).

**Rescission of election**

Where a surviving spouse, in making her election to take against the will, relied upon the erroneous advice of her counsel as to what she would receive under the will, or at law, to her detriment, and the probate judge did not make any further explanation of her rights as required by this section, a court of equity, where there were no intervening rights of third parties, will permit her to rescind such election: (decided under former analogous section) Smith v. First Nat'l Bank, 124 N.E.2d 851, 69 Ohio Law Abs. 102, 1954 Ohio Misc. LEXIS 364 (Ohio C.P. 1954).

**RESEARCH REFERENCES AND PRACTICE AIDS**

**Cross-References to Related Sections**

Proceedings to admit foreign will to record, RC § 2129.07.

**Practice Manuals and Treatises**

Anderson's Ohio Probate Practice and Procedure Standard Probate Form 8.2 Election of Surviving Spouse to Take Against Will

Anderson's Ohio Probate Practice and Procedure Outline No. § 36 Distribution-in general

**Practice Forms**

Election of Surviving Spouse to Take Against Will, Couse's Ohio Form Book Form SPF 8.2

Standard Probate Form 8.2 1 —Election of Surviving Spouse to Take Against Will 2, 12 OH Forms of Pleading & Practice — Probate Form 14:23

## § 2106.07 Commission issued to take election of spouse.



Upon the filing of an application on behalf of a surviving spouse, the probate court may issue a commission, with a copy of the will annexed, directed to any suitable person, to take the election of the surviving spouse as described in section 2106.01 of the Revised Code. In the commission, the court shall direct the suitable person to explain the rights of the surviving spouse under the will and under Chapter 2105. of the Revised Code.

**HISTORY:**

GC § 10504-62; 114 v 320(358); 122 v 498; Bureau of Code Revision, RC § 2107.44, 10-1-53; RC § 2106.07, 143 v H 346. Eff 5-31-90.

### NOTES TO DECISIONS

**Generally**

Former Revised Code § 2107.44 permits the election of a surviving spouse to be taken by a commissioner appointed by the court upon application on behalf of a surviving spouse: (decided under former analogous section) Baker v. Hutyera, 27 Ohio Misc. 19, 56 Ohio Op. 2d 230, 267 N.E.2d 604, 1971 Ohio Misc. LEXIS 240 (Ohio P. Ct. 1971).

Court erred by finding the purported election to take against the will to be valid, because it was undisputed that the surviving spouse did not make an election in person before a probate judge, referee or commissioner as required by R.C. 2106.06, when the spouse signed an election form in his attorney's office and the space on the form provided for the signature of the probate judge was blank. In re Estate of Woods, 2011-Ohio-1831, 193 Ohio App. 3d 371, 951 N.E.2d 1120, 2011 Ohio App. LEXIS 1581 (Ohio Ct. App., Greene County 2011).

### RESEARCH REFERENCES AND PRACTICE AIDS

**Cross-References to Related Sections**

Election made in person, RC § 2106.06.

Proceedings to admit foreign will to record, RC § 2129.07.

**Practice Manuals and Treatises**

Anderson's Ohio Probate Practice and Procedure Form 15.11 Application for appointment of commissioner to take election

Anderson's Ohio Probate Practice and Procedure Form 15.12 Entry appointing commissioner to take election

Anderson's Ohio Probate Practice and Procedure Form 15.13 Commission to take election of surviving spouse

Anderson's Ohio Probate Practice and Procedure Form 15.14 Commissioner's report

**Practice Forms**

Motion for Appointment of Commissioner To Take Election of Surviving Spouse Unable to Appear, 12 OH Forms of Pleading & Practice — Probate Form 14:28

## § 2106.08 Election made by one under legal disability.

If, because of a legal disability, a surviving spouse is unable to make an election as provided by section 2106.01 of the Revised Code, as soon as the facts come to the knowledge of the probate court, the probate court shall appoint some suitable person to ascertain the value of the provision made for the surviving spouse by the testator, the value of the rights of the surviving spouse in the estate of the testator under Chapter 2105. of the Revised Code, and the adequate support needs of the surviving spouse after taking into consideration the other available resources and the age, probable life expectancy, physical and mental condition, and present and reasonably anticipated future needs of the surviving spouse. The appointment by the court shall be made at any time within the times described in division (E) of section 2106.01 of the Revised Code for making an election under that section.

When the person so appointed returns the report of the person's investigation, the court may elect for the surviving spouse to take under section 2105.06 of the Revised Code only if it finds, after taking into consideration the other available resources and the age, probable life expectancy, physical and mental condition, and present and reasonably anticipated future needs of the surviving spouse, that the election to take under section 2105.06 of the Revised Code is necessary to provide adequate support for the surviving spouse during the surviving spouse's life expectancy.

After making its determination under this section, the court shall record upon its journal the election made for the surviving spouse. The election, when so entered, shall have the same effect as an election made by one not under legal disability.

**HISTORY:**

GC §§ 10504-63, 10504-64; 114 v 320(358); Bureau of Code Revision, RC § 2107.45, 10-1-53; 125 v 903(963) (Eff 10-1-53); 141 v S 248 (Eff 12-17-86); RC § 2106.08, 143 v H 346. Eff 5-31-90; 2011 SB 124, § 1, eff. Jan. 13, 2012.

**Editor's Notes**

Acts 2011, SB 124, § 3 provides: "The provisions of this act that relate to the estates of decedents apply to the estates of decedents who die on or after the effective date of this act."

**Amendment Notes**

The 2011 amendment made stylistic changes.

### NOTES TO DECISIONS

Analysis



**Generally**

The changes in R.C. 2106.08 from former R.C. 2107.45 are remedial or procedural in nature: In re Estate of Pendleton, 2001-Ohio-2413, 141 Ohio App. 3d 708, 753 N.E.2d 237, 2001 Ohio App. LEXIS 1160 (Ohio Ct. App., Highland County 2001).

Proceeding under R.C. 2107.45 (election by one under legal disability) (see now R.C. 2106.08) qualifies as trial for purposes of CivR 59: (decided under former analogous section) In re Estate of Gaines, 1990 Ohio App. LEXIS 2343 (Ohio Ct. App., Knox County June 6, 1990).

Where the court must make an election for or against the will on behalf of an incompetent surviving spouse, it should be the election which is better for the spouse: (decided under former analogous section) In re Estate of Hinklin, 66 Ohio App. 3d 676, 586 N.E.2d 130, 1989 Ohio App. LEXIS 2797 (Ohio Ct. App., Marion County 1989).

Revised Code § 2107.45 simply provides the basis for the reasoning to be exercised by a court performing functions for a spouse under legal disability: (decided under former analogous section) In re Estate of Hinklin, 66 Ohio App. 3d 676, 586 N.E.2d 130, 1989 Ohio App. LEXIS 2797 (Ohio Ct. App., Marion County 1989).

Where the surviving spouse is under a disability and the probate court must make an election to take under or against the will as provided in R.C. 2107.45, the probate court's discretion in making the election is limited to considering only the incompetent's interests: (decided under former analogous section) In re Estate of Cromley, 2 Ohio App. 3d 27, 440 N.E.2d 588, 1981 Ohio App. LEXIS 9897 (Ohio Ct. App., Pickaway County 1981).

The probate judge in determining in behalf of an incompetent widow whether to take under the will or under the law of intestacy must determine whether provision made by the testator for the surviving spouse in the will or provision under the law "is better for such spouse" and elect accordingly: (decided under former analogous section) In re Estate of Callan, 101 Ohio App. 114, 1 Ohio Op. 2d 64, 135 N.E.2d 464, 1956 Ohio App. LEXIS 686 (Ohio Ct. App., Cuyahoga County 1956).

The election by the probate judge made in behalf of an incompetent widow to take either under the law or under the will is made solely for the benefit of the incompetent spouse and not for the benefit of third parties: (decided under former analogous section) In re Estate of Callan, 101 Ohio App. 114, 1 Ohio Op. 2d 64, 135 N.E.2d 464, 1956 Ohio App. LEXIS 686 (Ohio Ct. App., Cuyahoga County 1956).

In making an election under GC §§ 10504-63 and 10504-64 (former R.C. 2107.45), for a surviving spouse because of incompetency, the probate court, having plenary power at law and in equity fully to dispose of the matter, should put itself in the place of the surviving spouse and assume that such surviving spouse is one having at least ordinary business ability, and in addition the qualities of fairness, loyalty and respect for the memory and good deeds of the deceased spouse: (decided under former analogous section) In re Estate of Morton, 6 Ohio Op. 343, 21 Ohio Law Abs. 438, 1936 Ohio Misc. LEXIS 1308 (Ohio P. Ct. 1936).

Where testator refers in his will to direct gifts made during his lifetime to his wife for her care, support and comfort, such reference may not be construed as a "provision in the will" under GC § 10504-64 (R.C. 2107.45), relative to the election by the probate court for such surviving spouse who is under legal disability because of incompetency: (decided under former analogous section) In re Estate of Morton, 6 Ohio Op. 343, 21 Ohio Law Abs. 438, 1936 Ohio Misc. LEXIS 1308 (Ohio P. Ct. 1936).

**Appeal**

An order made by a probate court in a special proceeding under GC §§ 10504-63 and 10504-64 (R.C. 2107.45), relative to the election by a surviving spouse under legal disability, determining whether the provision in the will or the provision by law is better for the spouse, and electing accordingly, is a final order affecting a substantial right in a special proceeding, and appealable under GC § 12223-2 (R.C. 2505.02): (decided under former analogous section) In re Knofler's Estate, 73 Ohio App. 383, 29 Ohio Op. 93, 52 N.E.2d 667, 39 Ohio Law Abs. 263, 1943 Ohio App. LEXIS 662 (Ohio Ct. App., Marion County 1943), aff'd, 143 Ohio St. 294, 28 Ohio Op. 203, 55 N.E.2d 262, 1944 Ohio LEXIS 409 (Ohio 1944).].

**Death of surviving spouse**

Death is not a "legal disability" within the meaning of R.C. 2107.45, which would require the probate court to make an election for the estate of a surviving spouse who dies having failed to elect against the will: (decided under former analogous section) In re Estate of La Spina, 60 Ohio St. 2d 101, 14 Ohio Op. 3d 336, 397 N.E.2d 1196, 1979 Ohio LEXIS 508 (Ohio 1979).

The death of an incompetent spouse within the time limit for making an election does not raise a presumption that she shall take under the will of her deceased husband: (decided under former analogous section) In re Estate of Jones, 15 Ohio Op. 250, 29 Ohio Law Abs. 148, 1939 Ohio Misc. LEXIS 1088 (Ohio P. Ct. 1939).

**Invalid election**

Court erred by finding the purported election to take against the will to be valid, because it was undisputed that the surviving spouse did not make an election in person before a probate judge, referee or commissioner as required by R.C. 2106.06, when the spouse signed an election form in his attorney's office and the space on the form provided for the signature of the probate judge was blank. In re Estate of Woods, 2011-Ohio-1831, 193 Ohio App. 3d 371, 951 N.E.2d 1120, 2011 Ohio App. LEXIS 1581 (Ohio Ct. App., Greene County 2011).

**Medicaid eligibility**

The probate court properly elected for the incompetent surviving spouse to take against the will in order to maintain her medicaid eligibility: In re Estate of Cross, 75 Ohio St. 3d 530, 664 N.E.2d 905, 1996 Ohio LEXIS 362 (Ohio 1996).

**Standing to contest election**

Only the guardian of such spouse or some other party acting on behalf of such spouse may question the court's determination: (decided under former analogous section) In re Estate of Cook, 19 Ohio St. 2d 121, 48 Ohio Op. 2d 113, 249 N.E.2d 799, 1969 Ohio LEXIS 343 (Ohio 1969).

The executor and testamentary trustee under a deceased husband's will, as well as a legatee under the will have interests which conflict with what is "better" for the incompetent widow and, therefore, they have no standing to contest the court's election on behalf of the spouse pursuant to the provisions of R.C. 2107.45: (decided under former analogous section) In re Estate of Cook, 19 Ohio St. 2d 121, 48 Ohio Op. 2d 113, 249 N.E.2d 799, 1969 Ohio LEXIS 343 (Ohio 1969).

Legatees under a will have no right to contest an election not to take under a will by the probate court on behalf of a surviving spouse who because of legal disability is unable to make such election on his own behalf: (decided under former analogous section) In re Estate of Strauch, 15 Ohio St. 2d 192, 44 Ohio Op. 2d 158, 239 N.E.2d 43, 1968 Ohio LEXIS 394 (Ohio 1968).].

When the probate judge, acting in pursuance of and in accordance with this section, has made election in behalf of an incompetent widow to take either under the will or under the law of intestacy, the election so made has the same effect as if made by one not under disability, and the widow's right thereby becomes absolute; and third parties are without right to complain: (decided under former analogous section) In re Estate of Callan, 101 Ohio App. 114, 1 Ohio Op. 2d 64, 135 N.E.2d 464, 1956 Ohio App. LEXIS 686 (Ohio Ct. App., Cuyahoga County 1956).

**Tax considerations**

Where the wills of a husband and wife were made in pursuance of a plan to minimize estate and inheritance taxes, and the wife's bequest of her entire estate directly to her children, rather than to her husband, was made to minimize the impact of federal estate taxes upon their joint estates, the probate court may properly make an election for the incompetent surviving husband to permit the wife's estate to pass directly to her legatees: (decided under former analogous section) In re Estate of Rieley, 28 Ohio Op. 2d 122, 194 N.E.2d 918, 92 Ohio Law Abs. 296, 1963 Ohio Misc. LEXIS 234 (Ohio P. Ct. 1963).

**Vacation of order**

An order of a probate court making an election for an incompetent surviving spouse under this section, is subject to the control of the court and may be vacated under R.C. 2101.33, within term time: (decided under former analogous section) In re Estate of Strauch, 11 Ohio App. 2d 173, 40 Ohio Op. 2d 331, 229 N.E.2d 95, 1967 Ohio App. LEXIS 426 (Ohio Ct. App., Franklin County 1967), aff'd, 15 Ohio St. 2d 192, 44 Ohio Op. 2d 158, 239 N.E.2d 43, 1968 Ohio LEXIS 394 (Ohio 1968).



## RESEARCH REFERENCES AND PRACTICE AIDS

**Cross-References to Related Sections**

Election made in person, RC § 2106.06.

Proceedings to admit foreign will to record, RC § 2129.07.

**Practice Manuals and Treatises**

Anderson's Ohio Elder Law Practice Manual § 2.8 Power to Elect to Take Under or Against a Will

Anderson's Ohio Probate Practice and Procedure Form 15.15 Application for appointment of commissioner where spouse is under disability

Anderson's Ohio Probate Practice and Procedure Form 15.16 Journal entry appointing commissioner to ascertain values

Anderson's Ohio Probate Practice and Procedure Form 15.17 Commission to ascertain value of provision for surviving spouse under legal disability under will and value of rights at law

Anderson's Ohio Probate Practice and Procedure Form 15.18 Journal entry making election for surviving spouse under legal disability

Anderson's Ohio Probate Practice and Procedure Outline No. § 45 Election by spouse under will-under legal disability

**Practice Forms**

Application for Appointment of Commissioner to Ascertain Value of Rights for Surviving Spouse Under a Disability 1, 12 OH Forms of Pleading & Practice — Probate Form 14:32

## § 2106.10 Election to receive mansion house.

(A) A surviving spouse may elect to receive, as part of the surviving spouse's share of an intestate estate under section 2105.06 of the Revised Code and the allowance for support under section 2106.13 of the Revised Code, the entire interest of the decedent spouse in the mansion house. The interest of the decedent spouse in the mansion house shall be valued at the appraised value with the deduction of that portion of all liens on the mansion house existing at the time of death and attributable to the decedent's interest in the mansion house.

(B) The election pursuant to division (A) of this section shall be made at or before the time a final account is rendered.

(C) If the spouse makes an election pursuant to division (A) of this section, the administrator or executor shall file, unless the election is one made under division (D) of this section, an application for a certificate of transfer as provided for in section 2113.61 of the Revised Code. The application also shall contain an inventory of the property and the allowance for support that the spouse is entitled to receive under sections 2105.06 and 2106.13 of the Revised Code. If the value of the property and the allowance for support that the spouse is entitled to receive is equal to or greater than the value of the decedent's interest in the mansion house, the court shall issue the certificate of transfer.

(D) The surviving spouse may make an election pursuant to division (A) of this section in an estate relieved from administration under section 2113.03 of the Revised Code or in an estate that is subject to an order granting a summary release from administration under section 2113.031 of the Revised Code. The election shall be made at the time of or prior to the entry of the order relieving the estate from administration or the order granting a summary release from administration. Either the surviving spouse or the applicant for the order shall file the application for the certificate of transfer under division (C) of this section.

(E) If the surviving spouse dies prior to making an election pursuant to division (A) of this section, the surviving spouse shall be conclusively presumed not to have made an election pursuant to that division. After the surviving spouse's death, no other person is authorized to make an election pursuant to that division on behalf of the estate of the surviving spouse.

(F) As used in this section, the mansion house includes the decedent's title in the parcel of land on which the house is situated and, at the option of the surviving spouse, the decedent's title in the household goods contained within the house and the lots or farmland adjacent to the house and used in conjunction with it as the home of the decedent.

Titles 11 — 37

**HISTORY:**

RC § 2105.06.2, 136 v S 145 (Eff 1-1-76); 136 v S 466 (Eff 5-26-76); 137 v H 1003 (Eff 9-25-78); 138 v S 317 (Eff 3-23-81); 141 v S 248 (Eff 12-17-86); RC § 2106.10, 143 v H 346 (Eff 5-31-90); 146 v H 391 (Eff 10-1-96); 148 v H 313. Eff 8-29-2000.

**NOTES TO DECISIONS**

**Jurisdiction**

Appellate court lacked jurisdiction over a surviving spouse's claim as it related to her statutory right to elect to receive the decedent's interest in the mansion house because the trial court's decision did not address the statute at all and did not completely foreclose the surviving spouse from exercising her substantial right to elect to receive the decedent's interest in the mansion house. Mayberry v. Chevalier, 2018-Ohio-781, 106 N.E.3d 89, 2018 Ohio App. LEXIS 819 (Ohio Ct. App., Hocking County 2018).

**RESEARCH REFERENCES AND PRACTICE AIDS**

**Cross-References to Related Sections**

Election by surviving spouse, RC § 2106.01.

Passing of real property subject to monetary charge of surviving spouse, RC § 2105.06.1.

Payment of specific monetary share to surviving spouse; charge on realty, RC § 2106.11.

**Practice Manuals and Treatises**

Anderson's The Simple Will in Ohio § 5.7 Right to Take Against Will

Anderson's Ohio Probate Practice and Procedure Form 15.19 Election of surviving spouse to receive mansion house

Anderson's Ohio Probate Practice and Procedure Outline No. § 42 Election of spouse to take property-real property

**Practice Guides**

Anderson's Ohio Probate Practice and Procedure § 13.01 General

Anderson's Ohio Probate Practice and Procedure § 15.06 Election to receive the mansion house as part of intestate share and family allowance

Anderson's Ohio Probate Practice and Procedure § 16.04 Certificate of transfer; unregistered land

Anderson's Ohio Probate Practice and Procedure § 17.07 Effect of the order of death on intestate succession

Anderson's Ohio Probate Practice and Procedure § 26.03 Surviving spouse

**Practice Forms**

Election of Surviving Spouse to Take Against Will, Couse's Ohio Form Book Form SPF 8.2

Summary of General Rights of Surviving Spouse, Couse's Ohio Form Book Form SPF 8.3

Election by Surviving Spouse to Take Entire Interest in Mansion House 1, 12 OH Forms of Pleading & Practice — Probate Form 14:6

Standard Probate Form 12.0 1 —Application for Certificate of Transfer [of Decedent's Interest in Real Estate, Including Mansion House and Realty Subject to a Charge in Favor of Surviving Spouse, Combined With Entry Issuing Certificate] 2(Cuyahoga County Form), 12 OH Forms of Pleading & Practice — Probate Form 14:7

### § 2106.11 Payment of specific monetary share to surviving spouse; charge on realty.

Subject to the right of the surviving spouse to elect to receive the decedent's interest in the mansion house pursuant to section 2106.10 of the Revised Code, the specific monetary share payable to a surviving spouse under division (B), (C), or (D) of section 2105.06 of the Revised Code shall be paid out of the tangible and intangible personal property in the intestate estate to the extent that the personal property is available for distribution. The personal property distributed to the surviving spouse, other than cash, shall be valued at the appraised value.

Before tangible and intangible personal property is transferred to the surviving spouse in payment or part payment of the specific monetary share, the administrator or executor shall file an application that includes an inventory of the personal property intended to be distributed in kind to the surviving spouse, together with a statement of the appraised value of each item of personal property included. The court shall examine the application and make a finding of the amount of personal property to be distributed to the surviving spouse, and shall order that the personal property be distributed to the surviving spouse. The court concurrently shall make a finding of the amount of money that remains due and payable to the surviving spouse in satisfaction of the specific monetary share to which the surviving spouse is entitled under division (B), (C), or (D) of section 2105.06 of the Revised Code. Any amount that remains due and payable shall be a charge on the title to any real property in the estate but the charge does not bear interest. This charge may be conveyed or released in the same manner as any other interest in real property and may be enforced by foreclosure or any other appropriate remedy.

**HISTORY:**

RC § 2105.06.3, 136 v S 466 (Eff 5-26-76); 141 v S 248 (Eff 12-17-86); RC § 2106.11, 143 v H 346 (Eff 5-31-90); 148 v S 152. Eff 3-22-2001; 2011 SB 124, § 1, eff. Jan. 13, 2012.

**Editor's Notes**

Acts 2011, SB 124, § 3 provides: "The provisions of this act that relate to the estates of decedents apply to the estates of decedents who die on or after the effective date of this act."

See provisions, § 3 of SB 152 (148 v —), following RC § 2105.06.

**Amendment Notes**

The 2011 amendment substituted "property" for "estate" in the last sentence of the second paragraph.

**RESEARCH REFERENCES AND PRACTICE AIDS**

**Practice Manuals and Treatises**

Anderson's Ohio Probate Practice and Procedure Form 21.08 Application for distribution of personal property to surviving spouse in satisfaction of specific monetary share

Anderson's Ohio Probate Practice and Procedure Form 21.09 Order of distribution of personal property to surviving spouse in satisfaction of specific monetary share

**Practice Guides**

Anderson's Ohio Probate Practice and Procedure § 13.01 General

**Practice Forms**

Application for Certificate of Transfer, Couse's Ohio Form Book Form SPF 12.0

Summary of General Rights of Surviving Spouse, Couse's Ohio Form Book Form SPF 8.3

Application by Administrator or Executor for Distribution of Personal Property in Kind to Surviving Spouse 1, 12 OH Forms of Pleading & Practice — Probate Form 14:10

## ALLOWANCE FOR SUPPORT

### § 2106.13 Allowance for support.

(A) If a person dies leaving a surviving spouse and no minor children, leaving a surviving spouse and minor children, or leaving minor children and no surviving spouse, the surviving spouse, minor children, or both shall be entitled to receive, subject to division (B) of this section, in money or property the sum of forty thousand dollars as an allowance for support. If the surviving spouse selected more than one automobile under section 2106.18 of the Revised Code, the allowance for support prescribed by this section shall be reduced by the value of the automobile having the lowest value of the automobiles so selected. The money or property set off as an allowance for support shall be considered estate assets.

(B) The probate court shall order the distribution of the allowance for support described in division (A) of this section as follows:

(1) If the person died leaving a surviving spouse and no minor children, one hundred per cent to the surviving spouse;

(2) If the person died leaving a surviving spouse and minor children, and if all of the minor children are the children of the surviving spouse, one hundred per cent to the surviving spouse;

(3) If the person died leaving a surviving spouse and minor children, and if not all of the minor children are children of the surviving spouse, in equitable shares, as fixed by the probate court in accordance with this division, to the surviving spouse and the minor children who are not the children of the surviving spouse. In determining equitable shares under this division, the probate court shall do all of the following:

(a) Consider the respective needs of the surviving spouse, the minor children who are children of the surviving spouse, and the minor children who are not children of the surviving spouse;

(b) Allocate to the surviving spouse, the share that is equitable in light of the needs of the surviving spouse and the minor children who are children of the surviving spouse;

(c) Allocate to the minor children who are not children of the surviving spouse, the share that is equitable in light of the needs of those minor children.

(4) If the person died leaving minor children and no surviving spouse, in equitable shares, as fixed by the probate court in accordance with this division, to the minor children. In determining equitable shares under this division, the probate court shall consider the respective needs of the minor children and allocate to each minor child the share that is equitable in light of the child's needs.

(C) If the surviving spouse selected more than one automobile under section 2106.18 of the Revised Code, the probate court, in considering the respective needs of the surviving spouse and the minor children when allocating an allowance for support under division (B)(3) of this section, shall consider the benefit derived by the surviving spouse from the transfer of the automobile having the lowest value of the automobiles so selected.

(D) If, pursuant to this section, the probate court must allocate the allowance for support, the administrator or executor, within five months of the initial appointment of an administrator or executor, shall file with the probate court an application to allocate the allowance for support.

(E) The administrator or executor shall pay the allowance for support unless a competent adult or a guardian with the consent of the court having jurisdiction over the guardianship waives the allowance for support to which the adult or the ward represented by the guardian is entitled.

(F) For the purposes of this section, the value of an automobile that a surviving spouse selects pursuant to section 2106.18 of the Revised Code is the value that the surviving spouse specifies for the automobile in the affidavit executed pursuant to division (B) of section 4505.10 of the Revised Code.

**HISTORY:**

RC § 2117.20, 136 v S 145 (Eff 1-1-76); RC § 2106.13, 143 v H 346 (Eff 5-31-90); 146 v H 156 (Eff 3-11-96); 147 v H 366 (Eff 3-18-99); 148 v H 313 (Eff 8-29-2000); 149 v H 85. Eff 12-31-2001; 2016 hb432, § 1, effective April 6, 2017; 2021 hb7, § 1, effective August 17, 2021.

**Editor's Notes**

See provisions, § 5 of HB 85 (149 v —), following RC § 2106.01.

**Amendment Notes**

The 2021 amendment by HB 7, in the second sentence of (A) and in (C), substituted "more than one automobile" for "one or more automobiles" and "of the automobiles" for "if more than one automobile is."

The 2016 amendment by HB 432, in the second sentence of (A) and in (C), substituted "one or more automobiles" for "two automobiles" and "having the lowest value if more than one automobile is so selected" for "having the lower value of the two automobiles so selected."

**NOTES TO DECISIONS**

Analysis



**Generally**

Pursuant to R.C. 2101.24(B)(1)(b) and 2721.05, the probate court had jurisdiction to order payment of the surviving spouse's statutory allowance from the assets of an inter vivos trust established by the decedent for his support. The trust specifically provided that, if the estate assets were insufficient, the trustee was to satisfy certain estate obligations, including the payment of statutory allowances: Zahn v. Nelson, 2007-Ohio-667, 170 Ohio App. 3d 111, 866 N.E.2d 58, 2007 Ohio App. LEXIS 601 (Ohio Ct. App., Highland County 2007).

Unless barred by an antenuptial agreement or "the will expressly directs otherwise" as required by R.C. 2107.42, a widow is entitled to her year's allowance, use of the mansion house and exemptions under R.C. 2117.20 and 2115.13 [repealed], even though she takes under the will, whether by her voluntary election or by operation of law: (decided under former analogous section) Jacobsen v. Cleveland Trust Co., 6 Ohio Misc. 173, 35 Ohio Op. 2d 366, 217 N.E.2d 262, 1965 Ohio Misc. LEXIS 278 (Ohio C.P. 1965).

A widow may not set aside as fraud a conveyance without consideration made by her husband of real estate which eliminates any assets from which to pay an allowance or year's support: (decided under former analogous section) Dick v. Bauman, 73 Ohio App. 107, 28 Ohio Op. 176, 55 N.E.2d 137, 1943 Ohio App. LEXIS 669 (Ohio Ct. App., Sandusky County 1943); In re Estate of Kusar, 5 Ohio Misc. 23, 34 Ohio Op. 2d 32, 211 N.E.2d 535, 1965 Ohio Misc. LEXIS 283 (Ohio P. Ct. 1965).

Acceptance by a widow as sole heir and devisee under the will of a transfer of all the assets of the estate effects a merger of all claims of the widow for allowance and reimbursement for funeral expenses: (decided under former analogous section) Kaczenski v. Kaczenski, 118 Ohio App. 225, 25 Ohio Op. 2d 68, 193 N.E.2d 731, 1962 Ohio App. LEXIS 556 (Ohio Ct. App., Trumbull County 1962).

Where the widow of a testator is bequeathed for life the income of a going business which is to be operated by a trustee, she is entitled to such income from the time of the death of the testator in the absence of anything in the will to the contrary, notwithstanding the fact that she is allowed an amount in money for support pursuant to GC § 10509-74 (R.C. 2117.20): (decided under former analogous section) Holmes v. Hrobon, 158 Ohio St. 508, 49 Ohio Op. 450, 110 N.E.2d 574, 1953 Ohio LEXIS 643 (Ohio 1953).

Rights to which a surviving spouse is entitled are contingent in the sense that they go to the survivor if not sold or given away prior to death: (decided under former analogous section) Neville v. Sawicki, 146 Ohio St. 539, 33 Ohio Op. 19, 67 N.E.2d 323, 1946 Ohio LEXIS 346 (Ohio 1946).

**Children out of wedlock**

An illegitimate child whose paternity has been established during the lifetime of the natural father is entitled to a year's allowance for support from the father's estate: (decided under former analogous section) In re Estate of Holley, 44 Ohio Misc. 78, 73 Ohio Op. 2d 265, 337 N.E.2d 675, 1975 Ohio Misc. LEXIS 99 (Ohio P. Ct. 1975).

**Deduction from gross estate**

The value of the statutory allowance taken under R.C. 2117.20 shall be deducted from the gross estate prior to computing a surviving spouse's interest under R.C. 2105.06: (decided under former analogous section) In re Estate of Green, 63 Ohio Misc. 44, 17 Ohio Op. 3d 388, 410 N.E.2d 812, 1980 Ohio Misc. LEXIS 53 (Ohio P. Ct. 1980).

**Desertion by surviving spouse**

The widow's year's allowance under this section, and the allowance given her under R.C. 2115.13 [repealed], as property exempt from administration, are preferred claims against her deceased husband's estate and even though a wife deserted her husband through her own fault and choosing and remained separate and apart from him for a long period of time, she is nevertheless entitled to such allowance if the marriage relationship existed at the time of the husband's death: (decided under former analogous section) In re Estate of Clark, 99 Ohio App. 458, 59 Ohio

Op. 244, 125 N.E.2d 917, 1955 Ohio App. LEXIS 640 (Ohio Ct. App., Darke County 1955).

**Election against will**

A surviving spouse taking against a will of a deceased spouse under former R.C. 2107.39 is entitled to the $5,000 statutory allowance under former R.C. 2117.20 unless specifically barred by the will: (decided under former analogous section) In re Estate of Green, 63 Ohio Misc. 44, 17 Ohio Op. 3d 388, 410 N.E.2d 812, 1980 Ohio Misc. LEXIS 53 (Ohio P. Ct. 1980).

**Fraudulent conveyance**

Although a husband may, by conveyance and trust agreement made during his lifetime, defeat his widow's interest as statutory heir and distributee, yet such conveyance and trust agreement will be constructively fraudulent to the extent of the wife's statutory right to an allowance for a year's support from the estate of the husband, and a lien for the amount of such allowance will be impressed on the real estate conveyed in the proportion that the value of such real estate bears to the total value of such real estate plus the value of the real estate of which the husband died seized: (decided under former analogous section) Routson v. Hovis, 60 Ohio App. 536, 15 Ohio Op. 38, 22 N.E.2d 209, 1938 Ohio App. LEXIS 347 (Ohio Ct. App., Hancock County 1938).



**Legal separation**

Probate court did not err in ruling that the ex-husband was not entitled to a family allowance as a surviving spouse under R.C. 2106.13 because his rights as a surviving spouse had been terminated by the legal separation decree awarded to the parties. In re Estate of Ramminger, 2003-Ohio-3697, 2003 Ohio App. LEXIS 3352 (Ohio Ct. App., Butler County 2003).

**Legally disabled adult child**

Given the lack of a definition of "legal disability" in R.C. 3109.01, the inclusion of guardianship in the definition of "legal disability" in R.C. 2131.02 was to be applied to the facts where the decedent's adult child was 19 years old and legally disabled. Because the decedent's adult child was legally disabled, the child had not reached the age of majority, and was therefore a minor for purposes of R.C. 2106.13, the family allowance section, and entitled to a portion of the family allowance. In re Estate of Davis, 2010-Ohio-2131, 2010 Ohio App. LEXIS 1757 (Ohio Ct. App., Greene County 2010).

**Legislative intent**

The legislative intent in providing a widow's allowance for her support for twelve months after the death of her husband was to hold sacred that amount against execution for her debts, other than for her necessary support during that period: (decided under former analogous section) Norwood-Hyde Park Bank & Trust Co. v. Howard, 32 Ohio N.P. 191 (1934).

**Marriage of child**

A daughter who was under the age of eighteen years at the time of her father's death and marries before the period of one year during which she was entitled, under this section to support from his estate, is thereby limited to an allowance for support which will end at the date of her marriage: (decided under former analogous section) In re Estate of Nixon, 5 Ohio Misc. 169, 34 Ohio Op. 2d 333, 214 N.E.2d 716, 1965 Ohio Misc. LEXIS 291 (Ohio P. Ct. 1965).

**Nonresident decedent**

This section and GC § 10509-75 (R.C. 2117.21) do not create a right in favor of a widow of a nonresident decedent to a year's allowance out of the personal property located in this state: (decided under former analogous section) In re McComb's Estate, 80 N.E.2d 573, 52 Ohio Law Abs. 353, 1948 Ohio Misc. LEXIS 247 (Ohio P. Ct. 1948).

**Postnuptial agreement**

A postnuptial agreement, providing that "I hereby agree to release all claims on anything belonging to him," does not bar a surviving widow of her right to property not deemed assets under GC § 10509-54 (R.C. 2115.13 [repealed]), and her right to an allowance for a year's support under the provisions of this section: (decided under former analogous section) In re Estate of Crabtree, 15 Ohio Op. 487, 30 Ohio Law Abs. 176, 1938 Ohio Misc. LEXIS 878 (Ohio P. Ct. 1938).

**Prenuptial agreement**

A widow can be barred from any part of her husband's estate where both have substantial amounts of land from a prior marriage and execute a valid pre-nuptial agreement: (decided under former analogous section) Troha v. Sneller, 169 Ohio St. 397, 8 Ohio Op. 2d 435, 159 N.E.2d 899, 1959 Ohio LEXIS 623 (Ohio 1959).

**Priority of claims**

The allowance to the surviving spouse is payable as a preferred claim against the estate, before distribution: In re Estate of Hudson, 82 Ohio App. 3d 422, 612 N.E.2d 506, 1993 Ohio App. LEXIS 697 (Ohio Ct. App., Licking County 1993).

The surviving spouse's exempt property and year's allowance take precedence over a claim from the Division of Aid for the Aged: (decided under former analogous section) Fultz v. Singer, 5 Ohio Op. 2d 433, 149 N.E.2d 270, 78 Ohio Law Abs. 177, 1958 Ohio Misc. LEXIS 343 (Ohio P. Ct. 1958).

The year's allowance given to a widow by this section is governed by GC § 10510-46 (R.C. 2115.07), so that the widow's claim is subject and subordinate to the claims of judgment lien creditors to the proceeds of the sale of real estate: (decided under former analogous section) Dillman v. Warner, 54 Ohio App. 170, 7 Ohio Op. 492, 6 N.E.2d 757, 20 Ohio Law Abs. 459, 1935 Ohio App. LEXIS 371 (Ohio Ct. App., Allen County 1935).

Where the payee of a promissory note, executed jointly by husband and wife, upon default and death of the husband, secured judgment against the widow, individually and as administratrix of the husband's estate, the widow's allowance for twelve months' support was not subject to levy by the payee in satisfaction of the judgment: (decided under former analogous section) Norwood-Hyde Park Bank & Trust Co. v. Howard, 32 Ohio N.P. 191 (1934).

**Rescission of contract**

A widow who freely enters into a contract with other beneficiaries before an inventory was made is not entitled to rescission of the contract when she discovers she has greater rights: (decided under former analogous section) Carnahan v. Carnahan, 109 Ohio App. 350, 11 Ohio Op. 2d 142, 159 N.E.2d 795, 1959 Ohio App. LEXIS 831 (Ohio Ct. App., Clinton County 1959).

**Separation agreement**

A surviving spouse may waive any right to her husband's estate by virtue of a separation agreement: (decided under former analogous section) Burlovic v. Farmer, 96 Ohio App. 403, 54 Ohio Op. 399, 115 N.E.2d 411, 1953 Ohio App. LEXIS 680 (Ohio Ct. App., Cuyahoga County 1953), aff'd, 162 Ohio St. 46, 54 Ohio Op. 5, 120 N.E.2d 705, 1954 Ohio LEXIS 433 (Ohio 1954).

**Spousal allowance**

Because the surviving spouse did not raise his intention to take the spousal allowance from the proceeds of the real property when he initially moved to sell it, the evidence supported the trial court's finding of waiver and that allowing him to receive priority distribution waiver and that allowing him to receive priority distribution based on the statute before the mortgage lien would create an unjust result. Severing v. Severing, 2015-Ohio-5236, 54 N.E.3d 724, 2015 Ohio App. LEXIS 5058 (Ohio Ct. App., Franklin County 2015).

**—Death of surviving spouse**

Probate court properly granted summary judgment for the decedent's wife because, upon receipt of the executor's request for sufficient funds to satisfy the wife's $ 40,000 statutory allowance, pursuant to R.C. 2106.13, the plain language of the inter vivos trust obligated the trustee to pay such sums to the estate. Zahn v. Nelson, 2007-Ohio-667, 170 Ohio App. 3d 111, 866 N.E.2d 58, 2007 Ohio App. LEXIS 601 (Ohio Ct. App., Highland County 2007).

The right of a widow to a year's allowance in the estate of her deceased husband vests immediately upon death and such debt survives as an asset of her estate if not contested by the children: (decided under former analogous section) In re Estate of Wreede, 106 Ohio App. 324, 7 Ohio Op. 2d 75, 154 N.E.2d 756, 1958 Ohio App. LEXIS 807 (Ohio Ct. App., Van Wert County 1958); Monger v. Jones, 91 Ohio App. 246, 48 Ohio Op. 347, 108 N.E.2d 116, 1949 Ohio App. LEXIS 564 (Ohio Ct. App., Jackson County 1949).

**—Prenuptial agreement**

Trial court properly found that deceased spouses' prenuptial agreement was invalid and unenforceable due to the husband's failure to have fully and fairly disclosed his finances and assets to the wife, such that the wife's estate's claim for the family allowance under R.C. 2106.13 was properly granted; there was no attachment to the agreement of a listing of the assets of the parties, and there was a lack of any other adequate proof that such disclosure had been properly made. Gearheart v. Cooper, 2007-Ohio-25, 2007 Ohio App. LEXIS 18 (Ohio Ct. App., Hamilton County 2007).

**—Waiver**

Trial court erred in holding that a decedent's spouse waived her statutory spousal allowance because she failed to open an estate for the decedent for 7 years, concealed the stock owned by the decedent, and fraudulently cashed dividend checks that were made payable to the decedent as it did not consider whether she knew about the statutory allowance or intended to waive it; there was no evidence that the spouse knew that she was entitled to a spousal allowance or that she intended to waive it. Estate of Kuzman, 2019-Ohio-4135, 146 N.E.3d 1181, 2019 Ohio App. LEXIS 4213 (Ohio Ct. App., Trumbull County 2019).

**Waiver generally**

When the evidence relating to exceptions to an inventory and final account shows that the surviving spouse has, on numerous occasions, counseled and directed the administratrix of her husband's estate to pay the bills of the estate, even if such payment would result in no money being left for distribution to the surviving spouse, stating as her reason that her husband never had any bills that weren't paid, and the surviving spouse has offered no evidence of probative value to the contrary, it is clearly apparent that she has waived the determination and payment or allowance to her of the year's allowance provided by R.C. 2117.20 and the property exempt from administration as provided by R.C. 2115.13 [repealed]: (decided under former analogous section) In re Estate of Burchett, 16 Ohio App. 2d 45, 45 Ohio Op. 2d 133, 241 N.E.2d 787, 1968 Ohio App. LEXIS 314 (Ohio Ct. App., Marion County 1968).

A delay of eight years in seeking her year's allowance, deprives a widow of her right to such: (decided under former analogous section) In re Estate of Gardner, 13 Ohio Op. 2d 293, 160 N.E.2d 20, 81 Ohio Law Abs. 250, 1959 Ohio Misc. LEXIS 326 (Ohio C.P.), aff'd, 112 Ohio App. 462, 16 Ohio Op. 2d 349, 176 N.E.2d 316, 1959 Ohio App. LEXIS 669 (Ohio Ct. App., Meigs County 1959).

## RESEARCH REFERENCES AND PRACTICE AIDS

**Cross-References to Related Sections**

Claims against estate; order in which debts to be paid, RC § 2117.25.
Election to receive mansion house, RC § 2106.10.
Election to take under the will; effect, RC § 2106.05.
Hearing on inventory; filing of exceptions, RC § 2115.16.
Mansion house, RC § 2106.15.
Release from administration, RC § 2113.03.
Sale of real property—
Payment of debts, RC § 2127.02.
Payment of legacies, RC § 2127.03.
Persons interested may give bond to prevent sale, RC § 2127.31.
Proceeds arising from partition of real estate may be reached by executor or administrator, RC § 2127.41.
Taxes are lien; dischargeable when, RC § 5731.37.
Deductions for expenses and debts, RC § 5731.16.

**Practice Manuals and Treatises**

Anderson's Ohio Elder Law Practice Manual § 6.5 Elective Share, Disclaimer
Anderson's Ohio Probate Practice and Procedure Standard Probate Form 1.0 Surviving Spouse, Children, Next of Kin, Legatees and Devisees
Anderson's Ohio Probate Practice and Procedure Standard Probate Form 7.0 Application for Family Allowance (Entry
Anderson's Ohio Probate Practice and Procedure Standard Probate Form 7.1 Application for Apportionment of Family Allowance (Entry Setting Hearing and Ordering Notice; Entry on Apportionment)
Anderson's Ohio Probate Practice and Procedure Outline No. § 79 Relief of estate from administration

**Practice Guides**

Anderson's Ohio Probate Practice and Procedure § 15.03 Allowance for support
Anderson's Ohio Probate Practice and Procedure § 15.04 Remaining in the mansion house
Anderson's Ohio Probate Practice and Procedure § 17.07 Effect of the order of death on intestate succession
Anderson's Ohio Probate Practice and Procedure § 19.02 Sales of personalty (statutory)
Anderson's Ohio Probate Practice and Procedure § 21.02 Timing of distributions
Anderson's Ohio Probate Practice and Procedure § 26.01 General
Anderson's Ohio Probate Practice and Procedure § 26.03 Surviving spouse
Anderson's Ohio Probate Practice and Procedure § 26.09 Summary release from administration

**Practice Forms**

Application for Family Allowance (Entry, Couse's Ohio Form Book Form SPF 7.1
Application for Apportionment of Family Allowance (Entry Setting Hearing and Ordering Notice; Entry on Apportionment), Couse's Ohio Form Book Form SPF 7.2
Summary of General Rights of Surviving Spouse, Couse's Ohio Form Book Form SPF 8.3
Surviving Spouse, Next of Kin, Legatees and Devisees, Couse's Ohio Form Book Form SPF 1.0
Standard Probate Form 7.1 1 —Application for Family Allowance 2, 12 OH Forms of Pleading & Practice — Probate Form 14:2
Exceptions to Inventory Relating to Allowance 1, 12 OH Forms of Pleading & Practice — Probate Form 14:3

## § 2106.15 Mansion house.

A surviving spouse may remain in the mansion house free of charge for one year, except that such real property may be sold within that time for the payment of debts of the decedent. If the real property is so sold, the surviving spouse shall be compensated from the estate to the extent of the fair rental value for the unexpired term, such compensation to have the same priority in payment of debts of estates as the allowance for support made to the surviving spouse, minor children, or surviving spouse and minor children of the decedent under section 2106.13 of the Revised Code.

**HISTORY:**

GC § 10509-79; 114 v 320(418); Bureau of Code Revision, RC § 2117.24, 10-1-53; 136 v S 466 (Eff 5-26-76); RC § 2106.15, 143 v H 346. Eff 5-31-90.

### NOTES TO DECISIONS

Analysis

Marital residence
Spousal allowance
Spousal election
—Waiver

**Marital residence**

Under former R.C. 2117.24, a surviving spouse who, immediately prior to her decedent's death, had not lived in the marital residence for eight months and was under a restraining order prohibiting her from being at the residence, is entitled to live in the mansion house for one year, or to receive a payment equal to the fair rental value of the mansion house for one year. Revised Code § 2117.24 was enacted to protect the surviving spouse, and its language, "may remain in the mansion house," does not limit its application to one who was a resident at the time of the decedent's death: (decided under former analogous section) In re Estate of Johnson, 14 Ohio App. 3d 235, 470 N.E.2d 492, 1984 Ohio App. LEXIS 11559 (Ohio Ct. App., Hancock County 1984).

A widow's right to live in the mansion house is not a vested right under Ohio law, and is therefore a terminable interest within the meaning of Internal Revenue Code § 2056, and as such, is not includible in the marital deduction: (decided under former analogous section) Miller v. United States, 71 Ohio Op. 2d 31 (F. D.C. Ohio 1974).

An antenuptial agreement signed by the deceased's spouse bars her from exempt property and year's allowance: (decided under former analogous section) Troha v. Sneller, 108 Ohio App. 153, 9 Ohio Op. 2d 195, 151 N.E.2d 595, 79 Ohio Law Abs. 74, 1958 Ohio App. LEXIS 667 (Ohio Ct. App., Cuyahoga County 1958), aff'd, 169 Ohio St. 397, 8 Ohio Op. 2d 435, 159 N.E.2d 899, 1959 Ohio LEXIS 623 (Ohio 1959).

Where there is a valid prenuptial agreement relinquishing all rights in the property of the other, the wife will be barred from all rights to the husband's estate: (decided under former analogous section) Troha v. Sneller, 108 Ohio App. 153, 9 Ohio Op. 2d 195, 151 N.E.2d 595, 79 Ohio Law Abs. 74, 1958 Ohio App. LEXIS 667 (Ohio Ct. App., Cuyahoga County 1958), aff'd, 169 Ohio St. 397, 8 Ohio Op. 2d 435, 159 N.E.2d 899, 1959 Ohio LEXIS 623 (Ohio 1959).

A surviving spouse is not entitled to money received from rental of apartment in mansion house under this section: (decided under former analogous section) Scobey v. Fair, 70 Ohio App. 51, 24 Ohio Op. 371, 45 N.E.2d 139, 1942 Ohio App. LEXIS 676 (Ohio Ct. App., Ashland County 1942).

This section, granting to the surviving spouse of a deceased consort the right to remain in the mansion house for one year free of charge, does not entitle a husband living separate and apart from his wife for twenty-five years to the occupancy of the mansion house for one year after the wife's death, where the husband never occupied the property after his separation from his wife and she continued to remain therein until her death: (decided under former analogous section) Lonz' Estate v. Glann, 66 Ohio App. 467, 20 Ohio Op. 430, 35 N.E.2d 153, 1940 Ohio App. LEXIS 807 (Ohio Ct. App., Lucas County 1940).

The right of the surviving spouse of a bankrupt to remain in the mansion house of the deceased consort free of charge for one year is recognized in the bankruptcy courts: (decided under former analogous section) In re Parschen, 13 Ohio Fed. 443, 119 F. 976 (N.D. Ohio 1902).

The right of a widow to remain in the mansion house of her deceased husband, as provided by statute, is not restricted to a personal continuance in the house merely, but she is entitled to a reasonable enjoyment of the possession of the premises, and may therefore either personally occupy them or she may rent them, as she may deem best promotive of her comfort: (decided under former analogous section) Conger v. Atwood, 28 Ohio St. 134, 1875 Ohio LEXIS 275 (Ohio 1875).

**Spousal allowance**

Devise in wills of "amount entitled to under state law" discussed in: (decided under former analogous section) Schardt v. Prexler, 67 N.E.2d 549, 45 Ohio Law Abs. 119, 1946 Ohio App. LEXIS 789 (Ohio Ct. App., Hamilton County 1946).

**Spousal election**

**—Waiver**

The revocable living trust executed by the husband and accompanied by the wife's waiver of rights was effective to waive her statutory rights as surviving spouse: Miller v. Miller, 139 Ohio App. 3d 512, 744 N.E.2d 778, 2000 Ohio App. LEXIS 3751 (Ohio Ct. App., Cuyahoga County 2000), dismissed, 91 Ohio St. 3d 1445, 742 N.E.2d 143, 2001 Ohio LEXIS 379 (Ohio 2001).

RESEARCH REFERENCES AND PRACTICE AIDS

**Cross-References to Related Sections**

Execution against property; dower, mansion house rights not impaired, RC § 2329.83.

**Practice Manuals and Treatises**

Anderson's The Simple Will in Ohio § 5.6 Right to Live in "Mansion House"

Anderson's Ohio Probate Practice and Procedure Form 15.22 Application to fix rental value due to surviving spouse

Anderson's Ohio Probate Practice and Procedure Form 15.23 Entry fixing rental value due to surviving spouse

**Practice Guides**

Anderson's Ohio Probate Practice and Procedure § 15.04 Remaining in the mansion house

**Practice Forms**

Summary of General Rights of Surviving Spouse, Couse's Ohio Form Book Form SPF 8.3

Application to Fix Rental Value for Mansion House Sold to Pay Claims of Estate 1, 12 OH Forms of Pleading & Practice — Probate Form 14:4

# SPOUSE TAKING AT APPRAISED VALUE

### § 2106.16 Purchase of property by surviving spouse.

A surviving spouse, even though acting as executor or administrator, may purchase the following property, if left by the decedent, and if not specifically devised or bequeathed:

(A) The decedent's interest in the mansion house, including the decedent's title in the parcel of land on which the mansion house is situated and lots or farm land adjacent to the mansion house and used in conjunction with it as the home of the decedent, and the decedent's title in the household goods contained in the mansion house, at the appraised value as fixed by the appraisers;

(B) Except for any automobile that passes to the surviving spouse of the decedent under division (A) of section 2106.18 of the Revised Code, any other real or personal property of the decedent not exceeding, with the decedent's interest in the mansion house and the decedent's title in the land used in conjunction with it, and the decedent's title in the household goods the spouse elects to purchase, one-third of the gross appraised value of the estate, at the appraised value as fixed by the appraisers.

A spouse desiring to exercise this right of purchase with respect to personal property shall file in the probate court an application setting forth an accurate description of the personal property and the election of the spouse to purchase it at the appraised value. No notice is required for the court to hear the application insofar as it pertains to household goods contained in the mansion house. If the application includes other personal property, the court shall cause a notice of the time and place of the hearing of the application with respect to the other personal property to be given to the executor or administrator, the heirs or beneficiaries interested in the estate, and to any other interested persons as the court determines.

A spouse desiring to exercise this right of purchase with respect to an interest in real property shall file in the court a petition containing an accurate description of the real property and naming as defendants the executor or administrator, the persons to whom the real property passes by inheritance or residuary devise, and all mortgagees and other lienholders whose claims affect the real property or any part of it. Spouses of defendants need not be made defendants. The petition shall set forth the election of the surviving spouse to purchase the interest in real property at the appraised value and shall contain a prayer accordingly. A summons upon that petition shall be issued and served on the defendants in the same manner as provided for service of summons in actions to sell real property to pay debts.

No hearing on the application or petition shall be held until the inventory is approved. On the hearing of the application or petition, the finding of the court shall be in favor of the surviving spouse, unless it appears that the appraisement was made as a result of collusion or fraud or that it is so manifestly inadequate that a sale at that price would unconscionably prejudice the rights of the parties in interest or creditors. The action of the court shall not be held to prejudice the rights of lienholders.

Upon a finding in favor of the surviving spouse, the court shall make an entry fixing the terms of payment to the executor or administrator for the property, having regard for the rights of creditors of the estate, and ordering the executor or administrator, or a commissioner who may be appointed and authorized for the purpose, to transfer and convey the property to the spouse upon compliance with the terms fixed by the court. If the court, having regard for the amount of property to be purchased, its appraised value, and the distribution to be made of the proceeds arising from the sale, finds that the original bond given by the executor or administrator is sufficient, the court may dispense with the giving of additional bonds. If the court finds that the original bond is insufficient, as a condition to transfer and conveyance, the court shall require the executor or administrator to execute an additional bond in an amount as the court may fix, with proper surety, conditioned and payable as provided in section 2127.27 of the Revised Code. This section does not prevent the court from ordering transfer and conveyance without bond in cases where the will of a testator provides that the executor need not give bond. The executor or administrator, or a commissioner, then shall execute and deliver to the surviving spouse a proper bill of sale or deed, as the case may be, for the property, and shall make a return to the court.

The death of the surviving spouse prior to the filing of the court's entry fixing the terms of payment for property elected to be purchased shall nullify the election. The real or personal property then shall be free of the right granted in this section.

The application or petition provided for in this section shall not be filed prior to filing the inventory required by section 2115.02 of the Revised Code or later than one month after the approval of that inventory. Failure to file an application or petition within that time nullifies the election with respect to the property required to be included, and the real or personal property then shall be free of the right granted in this section.

**HISTORY:**

GC § 10509-89; 114 v 320(420); 116 v 385(396); 119 v 394(406); 123 v 460; Bureau of Code Revision, RC § 2113.38, 10-1-53; 125 v 903(975) (Eff 10-1-53); 132 v S 398 (Eff 4-29-68); 136 v S 145 (Eff 1-1-76); 141 v S 248 (Eff 12-17-86); RC § 2106.16, 143 v H 346 (Eff 5-31-90); 146 v H 156. Eff 3-11-96.

NOTES TO DECISIONS

Analysis

**Generally**

Because the property of the decedent which the surviving spouse wished to purchase was not specifically devised or bequeathed, the surviving spouse was entitled, pursuant to R.C. 2106.16, to purchase the property at its appraised value. In re Estate of Campbell, 2013-Ohio-1356, 989 N.E.2d 1090, 2013 Ohio App. LEXIS 1266 (Ohio Ct. App., Wood County 2013).

Where a surviving spouse elected to take against the will and sought to purchase property of the estate pursuant to R.C. 2106.16, but failed to set forth specific, written exceptions to a final accounting, as required by R.C. 2109.33, and failed to object to the sale of the estate property, as required by R.C. 2127.04, the probate court properly dismissed her claimed exceptions; in addition, the spouse lacked standing under Civ.R. 17(A) to object to the division of the estate as it related to her daughter. In re Estate of Eyajan, 2005-Ohio-351, 2005 Ohio App. LEXIS 322 (Ohio Ct. App., Ashtabula County 2005).

Filing an objection to the inventory and appraisement is not a condition precedent to attacking the appraisement under R.C. 2113.38, nor a waiver of any rights: (decided under former analogous section) Bratanov v. Riemenschneider, 1 Ohio App. 3d 42, 439 N.E.2d 434, 1980 Ohio App. LEXIS 9752 (Ohio Ct. App., Summit County 1980).

If the evidence obtained from the adversary proceeding shows fraud, collusion or the manifest inadequacy of the price fixed in the inventory, the court shall order a reappraisal as provided in R.C. 2115.17. If these items are not shown, then the price fixed in the inventory is final: (decided under former analogous section) Bratanov v. Riemenschneider, 1 Ohio App. 3d 42, 439 N.E.2d 434, 1980 Ohio App. LEXIS 9752 (Ohio Ct. App., Summit County 1980).

Revised Code § 2113.38, which authorizes the surviving spouse to file a petition to purchase the "mansion house" at the appraised value, contemplates an adversary-type proceeding in which the defendants—the heirs, devisees, legatees, lienholders et al.—are given the opportunity to show the presence of fraud, collusion or the manifest inadequacy of the price fixed in the inventory: (decided under former analogous section) Bratanov v. Riemenschneider, 1 Ohio App. 3d 42, 439 N.E.2d 434, 1980 Ohio App. LEXIS 9752 (Ohio Ct. App., Summit County 1980).

The provision of this section that the probate court "shall make the entry fixing the terms of payment" for property selected to be purchased by a surviving spouse, does not authorize the court to require the surviving spouse to pay more than the appraised value for the property: (decided under former analogous section) In re Estate of Fouts, 103 Ohio App. 313, 3 Ohio Op. 2d 353, 145 N.E.2d 440, 1957 Ohio App. LEXIS 850 (Ohio Ct. App., Clark County 1957).

**Death of surviving spouse**

Where a valid judgment entry has been made in favor of the petition of a surviving spouse to purchase an interest in real estate pursuant to this section and fixing the terms of payment therefor, the subsequent death of that spouse will not nullify the right to purchase on those terms: (decided under former analogous section) In re Estate of Witteman, 21 Ohio St. 2d 3, 50 Ohio Op. 2d 2, 254 N.E.2d 345, 1969 Ohio LEXIS 284 (Ohio 1969).].

**Guardian of surviving spouse**

The right of election under this section, being a personal right, in the absence of express statutory authority, the guardian of an incompetent person cannot make such election, and such election must be made by or under the direction of a court having chancery jurisdiction over the person or estate of the incompetent, and this power in the court is an inherent power, independent of statute: (decided under former analogous section) Dorfmeier v. Dorfmeier, 123 N.E.2d 681, 69 Ohio Law Abs. 15, 1954 Ohio Misc. LEXIS 368 (Ohio P. Ct. 1954).

**Inventory motion to vacate**

Where, in the administration of an estate, a motion to vacate and set aside an order previously entered approving and confirming an inventory filed therein is timely filed by the surviving spouse, although not within one month after such order approving such inventory, and is subsequently found to be well taken, and an order is thereupon entered that such previously approved inventory be modified by the deletion therefrom of certain personal property and by increasing the amount of the widow's year's allowance, such order of modification does not constitute a vacation of the previous order of approval so as to reinstate in such surviving spouse the right of election to purchase the mansion house for the one-month period, provided in this section, from the date of such order of modification: (decided under former analogous section) In re Estate of Hrabnicky, 167 Ohio St. 507, 5 Ohio Op. 2d 181, 149 N.E.2d 909, 1958 Ohio LEXIS 531 (Ohio 1958).

**Mansion house appraisal**

When devisees, other than the surviving spouse, have added substantial value to the mansion house after the appraisement, the surviving spouse is not entitled to purchase the property at the appraisement price. Such a sale would unconscionably prejudice the rights of the parties in interest: (decided under former analogous section) Wobser v. Tanner, 60 Ohio St. 2d 28, 14 Ohio Op. 3d 195, 396 N.E.2d 753, 1979 Ohio LEXIS 492 (Ohio 1979).

**Mansion house generally**

Under this section providing that a surviving spouse may purchase "the mansion house, including the parcel of land on which such house is situated and lots or farm land adjacent thereto and used in conjunction therewith as the home of the decedent," such spouse may purchase at the appraised value the interest of the decedent in a farm which had been owned in common by the spouse and the decedent, jointly operated by them as a farm, and used by them as their residence, with all the parts of the farm being combined to make up the "farm home," and not as a business or commercial enterprise so as to deprive the spouse of such right, even though both husband and wife had outside employment: (decided under former analogous section) Young v. Young, 106 Ohio App. 206, 6 Ohio Op. 2d 458, 154 N.E.2d 19, 1958 Ohio App. LEXIS 795 (Ohio Ct. App., Madison County 1958).

The words and phrases describing the real property subject to purchase by the surviving spouse under this section, may, under proper circumstances, contemplate a larger amount of property than that which would ordinarily fall within the limits of the curtilage of common law: (decided under former analogous section) Nagel v. Wilcox, 104 Ohio App. 534, 5 Ohio Op. 2d 267, 150 N.E.2d 667, 1957 Ohio App. LEXIS 953 (Ohio Ct. App., Lorain County 1957).

A surviving spouse has the right, under this section which provides that a surviving spouse may purchase "the mansion house, including the parcel of land on which such house is situated and lots or farm land adjacent thereto and used in conjunction therewith as the home of the decedent," to purchase, at the appraised value, an entire farm, where such farm land and the buildings thereon were used in conjunction with the mansion house in establishing and maintaining a home for the decedent and his family: (decided under former analogous section) In re Estate of Clark, 102 Ohio App. 200, 2 Ohio Op. 2d 185, 141 N.E.2d 890, 1956 Ohio App. LEXIS 636 (Ohio Ct. App., Ross County 1956).].

The exercise of the absolute right in a surviving spouse to purchase the mansion house at the appraised value, under this section, deprives the common pleas court of any jurisdiction in partition: (decided under former analogous section) Strawser v. Stanton, 47 Ohio Op. 255, 103 N.E.2d 797, 66 Ohio Law Abs. 121, 1952 Ohio Misc. LEXIS 385 (Ohio C.P. 1952).

The surviving spouse is entitled to purchase the mansion house at the appraised value and either deduct from the purchase price the amount of the mortgage or pay the full purchase price and require the fiduciary to pay the amount of the unpaid mortgage: (decided under former analogous section) McAdams v. Bolsinger, 57 Ohio Op. 338, 129 N.E.2d 878, 71 Ohio Law Abs. 531, 1950 Ohio Misc. LEXIS 311 (Ohio P. Ct. 1950).

This section does not entitle a surviving spouse to purchase, at the appraised value, the entire lot on which the mansion house is situated, where there are located on the same lot two other buildings which are rented and used for business purposes, not in conjunction with the mansion house, but limits such spouse to the purchase, at the appraised value, of only that portion of the lot which is not occupied by such other two buildings: (decided under former analogous section) In re Burgoon's Estate, 80 Ohio App. 465, 36 Ohio Op. 200, 76 N.E.2d 310, 1946 Ohio App. LEXIS 642 (Ohio Ct. App., Henry County 1946).

**Nonresident surviving spouse**

Where a nonresident widow could not assert a right to purchase certain stock of her decedent at its appraised value under the law of the state of domicile, such law being substantive in nature, the probate court is without jurisdiction to approve the election under this section by virtue of which the widow sought to purchase such stock: (decided under former analogous section) In re McComb's Estate, 80 N.E.2d 573, 52 Ohio Law Abs. 353, 1948 Ohio Misc. LEXIS 247 (Ohio P. Ct. 1948).

**Specific legacy**

A specific legacy is a bequest of some particular thing or portion of a testator's estate which is so described by the will as to distinguish it from other articles of the same general nature in the estate: (decided under former analogous section) In re Mellott's Estate, 162 Ohio St. 113, 54 Ohio Op. 53, 121 N.E.2d 7, 1954 Ohio LEXIS 442 (Ohio 1954).].

Where the only asset in an estate was the home and the land on which it was located in the village of Donnelsville, Clark county, Ohio and testatrix's will stated "I give and devise all real estate located in the village of Donnelsville, Clark county, Ohio, that I may own at the time of my decease to my beloved husband. . . for and during the period of his lifetime, and at his death to my daughter. . . the same to be hers absolutely, and in fee simple," then the testatrix did specifically devise her home real estate to her husband for and during his lifetime, with a remainder in fee simple to her daughter: (decided under former analogous section) Reed, 114 N.E.2d 314, 65 Ohio Law Abs. 129, 1952 Ohio App. LEXIS 1381 (Ohio Ct. App., Clark County 1952).

**Time of application**

Probate court properly determined that this statute did not give a surviving spouse the right to purchase the decedent's interest in the mansion house because the surviving spouse was recognized as such in February 2016 but did not file her petition until May 2017, and, thus, the surviving spouse's petition fell outside the statutory one-month time limit.

Mayberry v. Chevalier, 2018-Ohio-781, 106 N.E.3d 89, 2018 Ohio App. LEXIS 819 (Ohio Ct. App., Hocking County 2018).

The provision of this section, giving a widow the exclusive privilege of purchasing at the appraised value any items listed in the inventory upon the filing of a proper application within one month of the approval of the inventory, is mandatory as to the time element: (decided under former analogous section) Palmer v. Smith, 28 Ohio Law Abs. 673, 1939 Ohio Misc. LEXIS 1111 (Ohio Ct. App., Cuyahoga County Mar. 27, 1939).

**Waiver**

Relief to which a widow would otherwise be entitled under GC §§ 10503-4, 10509-54 (R.C. 2105.06, 2115.13 [repealed]) and this section, will not be decreed where by contract she has agreed not to claim any other part of the estate than that given her by the contract: (decided under former analogous section) In re Schubert, 32 Ohio N.P. 169 (1939).



### RESEARCH REFERENCES AND PRACTICE AIDS

**Cross-References to Related Sections**

Auditor's fee not charged when transfer is made, RC § 319.54.

Transfer of automobile title, RC § 2106.18.

**Practice Manuals and Treatises**

Anderson's The Simple Will in Ohio § 5.6 Right to Live in "Mansion House"

Anderson's The Simple Will in Ohio § 5.8 Right To Purchase Mansion House and Other Property

Anderson's Ohio Civil Practice with Forms § 85.02 Procedure for Sale of Lands Valued at $3,000.00 or More

Anderson's Ohio Probate Practice and Procedure Form 15.01 Application to purchase property at appraised value

Anderson's Ohio Probate Practice and Procedure Form 15.02 Entry authorizing purchase at appraised value

Anderson's Ohio Probate Practice and Procedure Form 15.03 Complaint to purchase at appraised value

Anderson's Ohio Probate Practice and Procedure Form 15.04 Entry authorizing purchase at appraised value

Anderson's Ohio Probate Practice and Procedure Form 15.05 Return of sale to surviving spouse

Anderson's Ohio Probate Practice and Procedure Form 15.06 Entry confirming sale to surviving spouse

Anderson's Ohio Probate Practice and Procedure Form 15.19 Election of surviving spouse to receive mansion house

Anderson's Ohio Probate Practice and Procedure Outline No. § 41 Election of spouse to take property-personal property

Anderson's Ohio Probate Practice and Procedure Outline No. § 42 Election of spouse to take property-real property

**Practice Guides**

Anderson's Ohio Probate Practice and Procedure § 13.05 Notice of the taking of the inventory

Anderson's Ohio Probate Practice and Procedure § 13.11 Effect of the Court's approval of the inventory

Anderson's Ohio Probate Practice and Procedure § 15.04 Remaining in the mansion house

Anderson's Ohio Probate Practice and Procedure § 15.07 Right to purchase the mansion house and other property

Anderson's Ohio Probate Practice and Procedure § 19.03 Land sales (statutory)

Anderson's Ohio Probate Practice and Procedure § 26.06 Circumstances that may prevent relief from administration

**Practice Forms**

Summary of General Rights of Surviving Spouse, Couse's Ohio Form Book Form SPF 8.3

Entry Authorizing Sale of Personal Property, Couse's Ohio Form Book Form SPF 9.1

Notice of Sale of Personal Property, Couse's Ohio Form Book Form SPF 9.2

Application of Surviving Spouse to Purchase Personal Property at Appraised Value 1, 12 OH Forms of Pleading & Practice — Probate Form 14:15

## § 2106.17 Renumbered.

Renumbered RC § 2131.12 in 149 v H 345. Eff 7-23-2002.

## § 2106.18 Transfer of automobile titles.

(A) Upon the death of a married resident who owned at least one automobile at the time of death, the interest of the deceased spouse in one or more automobiles that are not transferred to the surviving spouse due to joint ownership with right of survivorship established under section 2131.12 of the Revised Code, that are not transferred to a transfer-on-death beneficiary or beneficiaries designated under section 2131.13 of the Revised Code, and that are not otherwise specifically disposed of by testamentary disposition may be selected by the surviving spouse. This interest shall immediately pass to the surviving spouse upon transfer of the title or titles in accordance with section 4505.10 of the Revised Code. The sum total of the values of the automobiles selected by a surviving spouse under this division, as specified in the affidavit that the surviving spouse executes pursuant to division (B) of section 4505.10 of the Revised Code, shall not exceed sixty-five thousand dollars. Each automobile that passes to a surviving spouse under this division shall not be considered an estate asset and shall not be included in the estate inventory.

(B) The executor or administrator, with the approval of the probate court, may transfer title to an automobile owned by the decedent to any of the following:

(1) The surviving spouse, when the automobile is purchased by the surviving spouse pursuant to section 2106.16 of the Revised Code;

(2) A distributee;

(3) A purchaser.

(C) The executor or administrator may transfer title to an automobile owned by the decedent without the approval of the probate court to any of the following:

(1) A legatee entitled to the automobile under the terms of the will;

(2) A distributee if the distribution of the automobile is made without court order pursuant to section 2113.55 of the Revised Code;

(3) A purchaser if the sale of the automobile is made pursuant to section 2113.39 of the Revised Code.

(D) As used in division (A) of this section, "automobile" includes a motorcycle and includes a truck if the truck was used as a method of conveyance by the deceased spouse or the deceased spouse's family when the deceased spouse was alive.

**HISTORY:**

RC § 2113.53.2, 133 v S 185 (Eff 1-1-71); 136 v S 145 (Eff 1-1-76); 136 v S 466 (Eff 5-26-76); 137 v S 277 (Eff 1-13-78); 139 v H 620 (Eff 9-9-82); 140 v S 260 (Eff 9-20-84); RC § 2106.18, 143 v H 346 (Eff 5-31-90); 145 v H 458 (Eff 7-20-94); 146 v H 156 (Eff 3-11-96); 148 v H 313 (Eff 8-29-2000); 149 v H 345. Eff 7-23-2002; 151 v H 246, § 1, eff. 3-29-06; 2016 hb432, § 1, effective April 6, 2017.

**Amendment Notes**

The 2016 amendment by HB 432, in (A), substituted "one or more automobiles that are not transferred to the surviving spouse" for "up to two automobiles that are not transferred to the surviving spouse" in the first sentence and "shall not exceed sixty-five thousand dollars" for "shall not exceed forty thousand dollars" in the second sentence.

151 v H 246, effective March 29, 2006, in (D), inserted "a motorcycle and includes".

### NOTES TO DECISIONS

**Generally**

Wife who declared joint bankruptcy with her husband under Chapter 7 of the Bankruptcy Code was not allowed to claim an exemption under Ohio Rev. Code Ann. § 2329.66 in a motor vehicle that was owned by her husband and titled solely in his name because she did not have a property interest in the vehicle; the fact that the wife had a right under Ohio Rev. Code Ann. § 2106.18 to obtain title to the vehicle if her husband predeceased her, still owned the vehicle and was an Ohio resident at the time he died, and the vehicle was not otherwise specifically disposed of by testamentary disposition, did not give the wife a property interest in the vehicle that could be exempted under § 2329.66. In re Whitt, 534 B.R. 320, 2015 Bankr. LEXIS 2457 (Bankr. N.D. Ohio 2015).

The value of an automobile taken under R.C. 2113.532 shall not be considered an asset of the estate in computing a surviving spouse's interest under R.C. 2105.06: (decided under former analogous section) In re Estate of Green, 63 Ohio Misc. 44, 17 Ohio Op. 3d 388, 410 N.E.2d 812, 1980 Ohio Misc. LEXIS 53 (Ohio P. Ct. 1980).

### ATTORNEY GENERAL OPINIONS

Pursuant to R.C. 2113.532, where the decedent left an automobile, a truck, and a motor home or any other type of motor vehicle, the surviving spouse is entitled to the automobile, but may not select from among the other vehicles: (decided under former analogous section) 1983 Ohio Op. Att'y Gen. No. 083 (1983).

"Automobile" as used in R.C. 2113.532 means a "passenger car," except when the decedent did not own a passenger car, in which case "automobile" includes a truck, if the truck was used as a method of conveyance by the deceased spouse or his family when the deceased spouse was alive: (decided under former analogous section) 1983 Ohio Op. Att'y Gen. No. 083 (1983).

### RESEARCH REFERENCES AND PRACTICE AIDS

**Cross-References to Related Sections**

Allowance for support, RC § 2106.13.

Certificate of title when ownership changed by operation of law, RC § 4505.10.

Purchase of property by surviving spouse, RC § 2106.16.

Transfer of title to watercraft or outboard motor, RC § 2106.19.

**Practice Manuals and Treatises**

Anderson's The Simple Will in Ohio § 5.4 Right to Automobile

Anderson's The Simple Will in Ohio § 5.7 Right to Take Against Will

Anderson's Ohio Probate Practice and Procedure § 13.13 Standard Probate Forms

Anderson's Ohio Probate Practice and Procedure Form 11.04 Affidavit

Anderson's Ohio Probate Practice and Procedure Form 21.20 Affidavit for transfer of vehicle(s) under will

Anderson's Ohio Probate Practice and Procedure Form 21.21 Application for authority to transfer motor vehicle(s)

Anderson's Ohio Probate Practice and Procedure Form 21.22 Entry directing transfer of motor vehicle(s)

Anderson's Ohio Probate Practice and Procedure Outline No. § 36 Distribution-in general

**Practice Guides**

Anderson's Ohio Probate Practice and Procedure § 11.08 Transfer of two automobiles

Anderson's Ohio Probate Practice and Procedure § 11.09 Transfer of watercraft

Anderson's Ohio Probate Practice and Procedure § 12.03 Non-probate assets

Anderson's Ohio Probate Practice and Procedure § 15.02 Right to automobiles and watercraft not specifically bequeathed

Anderson's Ohio Probate Practice and Procedure § 26.01 General

**Practice Forms**

Inventory and Appraisal (Appraiser's Certificate; Waiver of Notice of Taking of Inventory; Waiver of Notice of Hearing on Inventory; Entry Setting Hearing), Couse's Ohio Form Book Form SPF 6.0

Summary of General Rights of Surviving Spouse, Couse's Ohio Form Book Form SPF 8.3

Affidavit of Surviving Spouse to Obtain Title to Decedent's Automobile 1, 12 OH Forms of Pleading & Practice — Probate Form 14:1

## § 2106.19 Transfer of title to watercraft, watercraft trailer or outboard motor.

(A) Upon the death of a married resident who owned at least one watercraft, one watercraft trailer, one outboard motor, or one of each at the time of death, the interest of the deceased spouse in one watercraft, one watercraft trailer, one outboard motor, or one of each that is not otherwise specifically disposed of by testamentary disposition and that is selected by the surviving spouse immediately shall pass to the surviving spouse upon receipt by the clerk of the court of common pleas, or in the case of an untitled but registered watercraft trailer, upon receipt by the bureau of motor vehicles, of both of the following:

(1) The title executed by the surviving spouse, if titled;

(2) An affidavit sworn by the surviving spouse stating the date of the decedent's death, a description of the watercraft, watercraft trailer, or outboard motor, the approximate value, and that the watercraft, watercraft trailer, or outboard motor is not disposed of by testamentary disposition.

The watercraft, watercraft trailer, or outboard motor shall not be considered an estate asset and shall not be included and stated in the estate inventory.

Transfer of a decedent's interest under this division does not affect the existence of any lien against a watercraft, watercraft trailer, or outboard motor so transferred.

(B) Except for a watercraft, watercraft trailer, or outboard motor transferred as provided in division (A) of this section, the executor or administrator may transfer title to a watercraft, watercraft trailer, or outboard motor in the manner provided for transfer of an automobile under divisions (B) and (C) of section 2106.18 of the Revised Code.

(C) A watercraft trailer under this section only refers to one trailer used to transport the watercraft transferred under this section.

**HISTORY:**

145 v S 182. Eff 10-20-94; 2015 hb64, § 101.01, effective September 29, 2015.

**Amendment Notes**

The 2015 amendment by HB 64, rewrote (A); in (B), substituted "watercraft trailer, or outboard motor" for "outboard motor, or both" and inserted "watercraft trailer" following "to a watercraft"; and added (C).

### RESEARCH REFERENCES AND PRACTICE AIDS

**Cross-References to Related Sections**

Certificate of title when ownership changed by operation of law, RC § 1548.11.

**Practice Guides**

Anderson's Ohio Probate Practice and Procedure § 11.09 Transfer of watercraft

Anderson's Ohio Probate Practice and Procedure § 15.02 Right to automobiles and watercraft not specifically bequeathed

**Practice Forms**

Summary of General Rights of Surviving Spouse, Couse's Ohio Form Book Form SPF 8.3

## § 2106.20 Reimbursement for funeral expenses and burial after funeral.

A surviving spouse or a person with the right of disposition under section 2108.70 or 2108.81 of the Revised Code is entitled to a reimbursement from the estate of the decedent for funeral and burial expenses, if paid by the surviving spouse or person with the right of disposition, to the extent that the rights of other creditors of the estate will not be prejudiced by the reimbursement.

**HISTORY:**

GC § 10509-125; 114 v 320(429); Bureau of Code Revision, RC § 2117.26, 10-1-53; 129 v 1265 (Eff 8-4-61); RC § 2106.20, 143 v H 346. Eff 5-31-90; 151 v H 426, § 1, eff. 10-12-06.

**Amendment Notes**

151 v H 426, effective October 12, 2006, rewrote the section.

### NOTES TO DECISIONS

**Jurisdiction**

Probate court was not deprived of subject matter jurisdiction because there was not a sufficient rejection under R.C. 2117.11 that started the clock running on the time to bring an action on the funeral expenses claim under R.C. 2117.12. In re Estate of Liggons, 2010-Ohio-1624, 187 Ohio App. 3d 750, 933 N.E.2d 1118, 2010 Ohio App. LEXIS 1347 (Ohio Ct. App., Lucas County 2010).

### RESEARCH REFERENCES AND PRACTICE AIDS

**Practice Forms**

Summary of General Rights of Surviving Spouse, Couse's Ohio Form Book Form SPF 8.3

## § 2106.22 Action to set aside antenuptial or separation agreement.

Any antenuptial or separation agreement to which a decedent was a party is valid unless an action to set it aside is commenced within four months after the appointment of the executor or administrator of the estate of the decedent, or unless, within the four-month period, the validity of the agreement otherwise is attacked.

**HISTORY:**

GC § 10512-3; 114 v 320(469); Bureau of Code Revision, RC § 2131.03, 10-1-53; RC § 2106.22, 143 v H 346. Eff 5-31-90.

## NOTES TO DECISIONS

Analysis

Generally
Antenuptial agreement
Estate tax
Separation agreement
Time limitation

**Generally**

There must be the utmost good faith in the making of such agreements. Where the husband has misrepresented the value of his estate, the wife has the right to set the agreement aside after his death when the fraud is discovered. Such contracts are to be tested by the rules which determine the validity of contracts between persons standing in a confidential relation to each other: (decided under former analogous section) Duttenhofer v. Duttenhofer, 12 Ohio Dec. 736 (Ohio Cincinnati Super. Ct. 1902).

By the terms of GC § 8000 (R.C. 3103.06), a husband and wife may agree to an immediate separation and make provisions for the support of either of them and their children during the separation. Also it has been held that a reasonable antenuptial contract in bar of dower, if between parties of mature age, without imposition and in good faith, given full effect during life by the husband, will be enforced: (decided under former analogous section) Mintier v. Mintier, 28 Ohio St. 307, 1876 Ohio LEXIS 479 (Ohio 1876).



**Antenuptial agreement**

An antenuptial agreement waiving a spouse's interest in an individual retirement account controls over the beneficiary designation clause of an individual retirement account contract entered into prior to the antenuptial agreement: Kinkle v. Kinkle, 1998-Ohio-119, 83 Ohio St. 3d 150, 699 N.E.2d 41, 1998 Ohio LEXIS 2490 (Ohio 1998).

An antenuptial agreement will be upheld where the duty of full disclosure is met: Sasarak v. Sasarak, 66 Ohio App. 3d 744, 586 N.E.2d 172, 1990 Ohio App. LEXIS 2121 (Ohio Ct. App., Cuyahoga County 1990).

An antenuptial agreement will not be set aside unless the provision for the surviving spouse is wholly disproportionate to the amount she would receive under the law and such spouse was misled as to value of her spouse's property: (decided under former analogous section) Hook v. Hook, 69 Ohio St. 2d 234, 23 Ohio Op. 3d 239, 431 N.E.2d 667, 1982 Ohio LEXIS 562 (Ohio 1982).

Where an antenuptial agreement places restraints upon a testator and where such testator neglects to comply properly with such provisions in his will, and the widow, within nine months following the appointment of the executor, brings an action in a declaratory judgment proceeding to determine the validity of such antenuptial agreement and seeks the advice of the court, such declaratory judgment action is a "proceedings for advice" as is contemplated in former R.C. 2107.39: (decided under former analogous section) Barlup v. Holloway, 25 Ohio App. 2d 44, 54 Ohio Op. 2d 77, 266 N.E.2d 241, 1971 Ohio App. LEXIS 561 (Ohio Ct. App., Logan County 1971).

In an action by a wife seeking to share in her deceased husband's estate, contrary to the provisions of an antenuptial agreement, relief will be denied where there is a lack of proof of actual intent to impose or of a gross disproportion of her share under the agreement as compared to her share under the law, and where the parties were both of advanced age, the wife was an experienced businesswoman and knew of her prospective husband's desire that their marriage interfere as little as possible with the inheritance which his children would otherwise have received: (decided under former analogous section) Rocker v. Rocker, 13 Ohio Misc. 199, 42 Ohio Op. 2d 184, 232 N.E.2d 445, 1967 Ohio Misc. LEXIS 276 (Ohio P. Ct. 1967).

An antenuptial contract must be voluntarily entered into and the provisions for the wife must be fair and reasonable under all the surrounding facts and circumstances and an adult man and woman, each owning a substantial amount of property and each having grown children by prior marriages, may lawfully enter into a prenuptial agreement whereby each relinquishes every and all rights in the property of the other: (decided under former analogous section) Osborn v. Osborn, 10 Ohio Misc. 171, 39 Ohio Op. 2d 275, 226 N.E.2d 814, 1966 Ohio Misc. LEXIS 226 (Ohio C.P. 1966), aff'd, 18 Ohio St. 2d 144, 47 Ohio Op. 2d 310, 248 N.E.2d 191, 1969 Ohio LEXIS 390 (Ohio 1969).

Where no attack is made on an antenuptial agreement within six months from the appointment of the decedent's administrator, no evidence is admissible in support of the defenses that the agreement was void for failure of the decedent to disclose all pertinent facts in fraud of his wife's rights and was disproportionate to his property: (decided under former analogous section) Cantor v. Cantor, 15 Ohio Op. 2d 148, 174 N.E.2d 304, 86 Ohio Law Abs. 452, 1959 Ohio Misc. LEXIS 253 (Ohio P. Ct. 1959).

The filing of exceptions to an inventory and appraisement, on the ground that the appraisers failed to allow the statutory set-off and a year's support to the widow, did not constitute an attack upon an antenuptial agreement, under the provisions of this section: (decided under former analogous section) In re Thrush's Estate, 76 Ohio App. 411, 32 Ohio Op. 147, 64 N.E.2d 839, 1945 Ohio App. LEXIS 571 (Ohio Ct. App., Auglaize County 1945).

The probate court has jurisdiction to render a declaratory judgment determining the validity of an antenuptial contract entered into between a decedent and his widow, where the estate is in process of being settled and the widow is contending that the antenuptial contract is of no effect, while the heirs of decedent claim that it is a binding contract, and the executor cannot safely distribute assets of the estate until the question is determined: (decided under former analogous section) Pearson v. Pearson, 58 Ohio App. 503, 12 Ohio Op. 300, 16 N.E.2d 837, 26 Ohio Law Abs. 485, 1938 Ohio App. LEXIS 485, 1938 Ohio Misc. LEXIS 1244 (Ohio Ct. App., Miami County 1938).

Under this section an antenuptial agreement is deemed valid unless an action to set it aside is brought within six months after the appointment of the executor or administrator or unless the validity of the agreement is otherwise attacked within that period, and neither the filing of a written election to take under the law, in which is incorporated a statement that the widow repudiates "the prenuptial agreement, which was procured by fraud," nor the filing of exceptions to the inventory and appraisement on the ground that the appraisers failed to allow the statutory set-off and a year's support to the widow, constitutes an attack within the purview of the statute: (decided under former analogous section) Juhasz v. Juhasz, 134 Ohio St. 257, 12 Ohio Op. 57, 16 N.E.2d 328, 1938 Ohio LEXIS 294 (Ohio 1938).

An antenuptial contract cannot be avoided by the surviving husband, by proof of concealment of a fact that did not affect the interest of such survivor: (decided under former analogous section) Keever v. Brown, 36 Ohio App. 1, 172 N.E. 626, 9 Ohio Law Abs. 296, 1930 Ohio App. LEXIS 485 (Ohio Ct. App., Highland County 1930).

**Estate tax**

A succession tax is, under the provisions of R.C. 5731.01 et seq., levied upon the right to receive or to succeed to an estate upon death, which right arises and the tax attaches to the succession at the time of death, unaffected by any subsequent settlement agreement among the beneficiaries for a different distribution of the estate: (decided under former analogous section) Cantor v. Department of Taxation, 3 Ohio App. 2d 285, 32 Ohio Op. 2d 386, 210 N.E.2d 285, 1964 Ohio App. LEXIS 501 (Ohio Ct. App., Montgomery County 1964).

**Separation agreement**

here was no dispute that the administrator was appointed on May 14, 2018 and the former husband did not challenge the separation agreement until the February 7, 2019 hearing, approximately five months past the deadline; because the husband failed to timely challenge the separation agreement, it was presumed to be valid. In re Estate of Lodwick, 2019-Ohio-4559, 2019 Ohio App. LEXIS 4600 (Ohio Ct. App., Lawrence County 2019).

A collateral attack upon judgment of domestic relations division of court of common pleas under this section may not be entertained by the probate division of court of common pleas whether or not facts before rendering court warranted such attack. The latter court is bound by the divorce decree incorporating the terms of a separation agreement, which compelled conclusion that provisions for divorced wife in decedent's will had been revoked by implication: (decided under former analogous section) Davis v. Davis, 24 Ohio Misc. 17, 51 Ohio Op. 2d 388, 258 N.E.2d 277, 1970 Ohio Misc. LEXIS 234 (Ohio P. Ct. 1970).

The six-month limitation of this section, within which the validity of a separation agreement must be attacked by a surviving spouse after the appointment of the executor or administrator of the estate of his deceased spouse, applies to a surviving spouse notwithstanding he was an infant at the time of his marriage, at the time the separation agreement was executed, and during the entire period of limitation: (decided under former analogous section) Burlovic v. Farmer, 162 Ohio St. 46, 54 Ohio Op. 5, 120 N.E.2d 705, 1954 Ohio LEXIS 433 (Ohio 1954).

A statute which provides that, in the event of death of a husband or wife, where prior thereto a separation agreement had been entered into between them as provided by law, unless action is taken within six months of the appointment of the administrator of such deceased, seeking to set aside such agreement, it shall thereafter be valid, is appealable to a surviving spouse even though she was an infant at the time of her marriage, at the time the agreement was entered into and at the time of death of her husband and within the six months period after the appointment of the administrator: (decided under former analogous section) Burlovic v. Farmer, 96 Ohio App. 403, 54 Ohio Op. 399, 115 N.E.2d 411, 1953 Ohio App. LEXIS 680 (Ohio Ct. App., Cuyahoga County 1953), aff'd, 162 Ohio St. 46, 54 Ohio Op. 5, 120 N.E.2d 705, 1954 Ohio LEXIS 433 (Ohio 1954).

Where exceptions to an inventory of a decedent husband's estate states that, by a separation agreement between such decedent and his wife, the latter is barred from certain allowances set-off to her in the inventory, and the wife by reply to the exceptions pleads that she is entitled to such allowances because such agreement is null and void, such reply is an attack on the agreement, within the purview of this section, which provides that such an agreement is deemed valid unless its validity is attacked within the time stated in such section. In such a case, upon the filing of such reply to the exceptions it becomes incumbent upon the exceptor to prove that the agreement was fair, reasonable and just to the wife under the circumstances at the time of its execution: (decided under former analogous section) In re Estate of Shafer, 77 Ohio App. 105, 32 Ohio Op. 380, 65 N.E.2d 902, 1944 Ohio App. LEXIS 440 (Ohio Ct. App., Hancock County 1944).

**Time limitation**
Underlying claims of the executrix of the decedent's estate were properly dismissed because of the failure of the executrix to comply with the statutory deadlines under R.C. 2106.22 to set aside an antenuptial agreement or to challenge its validity. Mays v. Carl L. Mays Trust, 2012-Ohio-618, 2012 Ohio App. LEXIS 553 (Ohio Ct. App., Huron County 2012).

**RESEARCH REFERENCES AND PRACTICE AIDS**

**Practice Manuals and Treatises**
Anderson's Ohio Probate Practice and Procedure Form 17.07 Complaint to set aside antenuptial agreement
Anderson's Ohio Probate Practice and Procedure Form 17.08 Complaint to set aside separation agreement

**Practice Guides**
Anderson's Ohio Probate Practice and Procedure § 17.10 Modification of succession by contract
Anderson's Ohio Probate Practice and Procedure § 50.06 Actions to set aside antenuptial agreements and separation agreements

**Practice Forms**
Summary of General Rights of Surviving Spouse, Couse's Ohio Form Book Form SPF 8.3
Complaint to set aside separation agreement, Couse's Ohio Form Book Form 24.64

### § 2106.24 Additional rights of surviving spouse.

In addition to the rights provided in this chapter, a surviving spouse of a decedent who died testate or intestate is entitled to any other rights prescribed in other chapters of the Revised Code, including, but not limited to, any dower rights under Chapters 2103. and 5305. of the Revised Code.

**HISTORY:**
143 v H 346. Eff 5-31-90.

**RESEARCH REFERENCES AND PRACTICE AIDS**

**Practice Guides**
Anderson's Ohio Probate Practice and Procedure § 15.08 Miscellaneous rights

### § 2106.25 Time limit for exercising rights; motion for extension.

Unless otherwise specified by a provision of the Revised Code or this section, a surviving spouse shall exercise all rights under Chapter 2106. of the Revised Code within five months of the initial appointment of an executor or administrator of the estate. It is conclusively presumed that a surviving spouse has waived any right not exercised within that five-month period or within any longer period of time allowed by the court pursuant to this section. Upon the filing of a motion to extend the time for exercising a right under Chapter 2106. of the Revised Code and for good cause shown, the court may allow further time for exercising the right that is the subject of the motion.

**HISTORY:**
149 v H 85. Eff 10-31-2001.

**Editor's Notes**
See provisions, § 5 of HB 85 (149 v —), following RC § 2106.01.

**NOTES TO DECISIONS**

Analysis

Extension warranted
Preservation of right
Time expiration
Waiver

**Extension warranted**
Because the probate court had failed to issue the mandatory R.C. 2106.01(A) citation to the surviving spouse following appointment of the estate's administrator, there was good cause for the probate court to grant the spouse's motion under R.C. 2106.25 to extend the time to make spousal elections. In re Estate of Weitzel, 2021-Ohio-1859, 2021 Ohio App. LEXIS 1817 (Ohio Ct. App., Warren County 2021).

**Preservation of right**
Even though the husband took some action to indicate he would elect to take against the will, he did not follow the statutory directives in place for preserving his elective right and nothing prevented him from moving to expedite the election process in light of the uncontested inventory prior to its approval. Estate Of Adams, 2013-Ohio-5824, 6 N.E.3d 673, 2013 Ohio App. LEXIS 6119 (Ohio Ct. App., Ashtabula County 2013).

**Time expiration**
Trial court erred when it extended the time frame for the husband to take against the will without being properly moved to do so because the limitation period set forth had passed without being properly extended and thus, the husband was bound to take under the will. Estate Of Adams, 2013-Ohio-5824, 6 N.E.3d 673, 2013 Ohio App. LEXIS 6119 (Ohio Ct. App., Ashtabula County 2013).

**Waiver**
As a separation agreement evinced the parties' intention to fully and finally dispose of each party's prospective property rights in the property of the other, a surviving husband's right to elect to take against the deceased wife's will was deemed to have been relinquished; his timely election under R.C. 2106.25 was properly dismissed. Estate of Dragovich v. Dragovich, 2012-Ohio-4114, 976 N.E.2d 920, 2012 Ohio App. LEXIS 3616 (Ohio Ct. App., Mahoning County 2012).

**RESEARCH REFERENCES AND PRACTICE AIDS**

**Cross-References to Related Sections**
Citation to make election, RC § 2106.02.

**Practice Guides**
Anderson's Ohio Probate Practice and Procedure § 15.05 Election to take the testamentary share or to take against the will

**Practice Forms**
Summary of General Rights of Surviving Spouse, Couse's Ohio Form Book Form SPF 8.3
Motion for Extension of Time Within Which to Make Election 1, 12 OH Forms of Pleading & Practice — Probate Form 14:24

# CHAPTER 2107

# WILLS

Execution



Deposit



## EXECUTION

### § 2107.02 Who may make will.

A person who is eighteen years of age or older, of sound mind and memory, and not under restraint may make a will.

**HISTORY:**
GC § 10504-2; 114 v 320(346); Bureau of Code Revision, 10-1-53; 131 v 617. Eff 8-10-65; 2011 SB 124, § 1, eff. Jan. 13, 2012.

**Editor's Notes**
Acts 2011, SB 124, § 3 provides: "The provisions of this act that relate to the estates of decedents apply to the estates of decedents who die on or after the effective date of this act."

**Amendment Notes**

The 2011 amendment substituted "person who is eighteen years of age or older, of sound mind" for "person of the age eighteen years or over, sound mind".

## NOTES TO DECISIONS

Analysis



**Generally**

The contract law theory of no "meeting of the minds" did not apply to the trust agreement. There was no presumption of undue influence where the attorney who drafted the trust amendments was also the settlor's grandson. Despite conflicting evidence, there was sufficient proof of testamentary capacity: Lah v. Rogers, 125 Ohio App. 3d 164, 707 N.E.2d 1208, 1997 Ohio App. LEXIS 6039 (Ohio Ct. App., Lake County 1997).

In Ohio there is no inherent right to make a will. The right to dispose of property by will is given and the manner of exercising it is prescribed by statute: In re Miller's Estate, 160 Ohio St. 529, 52 Ohio Op. 437, 117 N.E.2d 598, 1954 Ohio LEXIS 624 (Ohio 1954); Lozier v. Lozier, 99 Ohio St. 254, 124 N.E. 167, 16 Ohio L. Rep. 536, 1919 Ohio LEXIS 218 (Ohio 1919); German Mut. Ins. Co. v. Lushey, 66 Ohio St. 233, 64 N.E. 120, 1902 Ohio LEXIS 171 (Ohio 1902); Sears v. Sears, 77 Ohio St. 104, 82 N.E. 1067, 5 Ohio L. Rep. 495, 1907 Ohio LEXIS 95 (Ohio 1907).

Whether a gift during the world war to the chancellor of the German empire in trust for needy German soldiers is valid or not, it does not render the rest of the will invalid: In re Will of Schrader, 20 Ohio N.P. (n.s.) 433, 1918 Ohio Misc. LEXIS 73 (Ohio P. Ct. Feb. 1, 1918).

A will is ambulatory in its nature, and takes effect only from the death of the testator: Reynolds v. Reynolds, 9 Ohio App. 337 (1918), motion to certify record overruled, Gott v. Reynolds, 16 Ohio L. 364, 63 Weekly L. Bull. 473.].

The testator may die testate as to part of his property and intestate as to the rest: Hess v. American Bible Soc., 28 Ohio Cir. Dec. 172, 26 Ohio C.C. (n.s.) 439 (1916), [following Goff v. Moore, 20 Ohio C.C. (n.s.) 224.].

If testator gives instructions for drawing his will and his will is drawn in accordance with such instructions, and the evidence shows that after it was written the testator looked at it "just a second or two" before he signed it, it is said that the evidence shows that testator had no knowledge of what the will contained and that a verdict sustaining such will is to be set aside: Koch v. Meyers, 7 Ohio App. 306, 30 Ohio Cir. Dec. 439, 29 Ohio C.A. 142, 29 Ohio C.C. (n.s.) 142, 1916 Ohio App. LEXIS 175 (Ohio Ct. App., Hamilton County 1916).

One to whom an executory interest is bequeathed, with a provision that if he dies before testator's widow it shall pass to his issue if he has any, and, if not, to the survivors, cannot bequeath such interest by will if he dies before the death of the testator's widow and before the time of distribution fixed by the will: Westwater v. Guitner, 30 Ohio Dec. 370, 18 Ohio N.P. (n.s.) 209, 1915 Ohio Misc. LEXIS 60 (Ohio C.P. 1915).

A testator has the right to dispose of his property by will as he pleases, without reference to moral obligations, or to the needs or merits of the different natural objects of testator's bounty: Sadler v. Sadler, 23 Ohio C.C. (n.s.) 353, 27 Ohio Cir. Dec. 445 (1915), motion to certify record overruled by the supreme court, 13 Ohio L. 420, 60 Weekly L. Bull. 432.].

A jury cannot set aside a will on the ground that they do not regard it as a fair and reasonable will: Gregg v. Moore, 23 Ohio Cir. Dec. 534, 14 Ohio C.C. (n.s.) 570, 1911 Ohio Misc. LEXIS 239 (Ohio Ct. App., Licking County Mar. 1, 1911).

An oral contract by which a legatee agrees with the testator to hold a legacy in trust for a third person is not affected by the statute of wills: Winder v. Scholey, 83 Ohio St. 204, 93 N.E. 1098 (1910), affirming circuit court, which affirmed Scholey v. Winder, 10 Ohio N.P. (n.s.) 642, 21 Ohio Dec. 59.].

No disposition of property can be made by will except the party has an interest therein. Where a husband provided, in his will, that his wife might dispose of the residue of his estate as she saw fit, and she made a will disposing of same, but the wife died before the husband, the husband died intestate as to such residue: Thomas v. Hobson, 20 Ohio Cir. Dec. 214, 10 Ohio C.C. (n.s.) 351, 1907 Ohio Misc. LEXIS 292 (Ohio Ct. App., Columbiana County Apr. 1, 1907).

The expressed wish of a testatrix that all of her property "shall go as the law directs with the following modifications," is a testamentary disposition of her property, and her heirs take nothing by descent: Huber v. Carew, 7 Ohio C.C. (n.s.) 609, 16 Ohio Cir. Dec. 389 (1904), affirming 2 Ohio N.P. (n.s.) 81, 14 Ohio Dec. 656, and affirmed, without opinion, 74 Ohio St. 469.].

As to early provisions in regard to the making of wills in Ohio: Jones v. Robinson, 17 Ohio St. 171, 1867 Ohio LEXIS 67 (Ohio 1867); Theobald v. Fugman, 64 Ohio St. 473, 60 N.E. 606, 1901 Ohio LEXIS 124 (Ohio 1901).

**Adoption**

Where a testator uses the term "heirs of the body" as a term of limitation in a class gift to exclude adopted beneficiaries, such term in the absence of contrary intent constitutes an express exclusion of adopted persons under R.C. 3107.15: Tootle v. Tootle, 22 Ohio St. 3d 244, 490 N.E.2d 878, 1986 Ohio LEXIS 585 (Ohio 1986).

**Attorney-client privilege**

In a proceeding to contest a will, a rule that communications by a client to an attorney are privileged, is not altered by the fact that the law partner of such attorney was a subscribing witness to the will: Haley v. Dempsey, 14 Ohio App. 326 (1921), motion to certify record overruled, Dempsey v. Haley, 19 Ohio L. 155; judgment on retrial sustaining will affirmed by court of appeals; motion to certify record overruled, Haley v. Dempsey, 21 Ohio L. Rep. 300 (Ohio Oct. 30, 1923).].

The testimony of an attorney is not competent to vary the terms of a written instrument prepared by him as such, and in a proceeding to construe a will the attorney who wrote the will, and with whom the testator consulted concerning it, is not competent to testify concerning a communication made to him by his client touching his estate, the objects of his bounty or the meaning and effect of provisions contained in the will: Knepper v. Knepper, 103 Ohio St. 529, 134 N.E. 476, 19 Ohio L. Rep. 462, 1921 Ohio LEXIS 160 (Ohio 1921).

Testator's attorney is competent to testify, if a subscribing witness: Knepper v. Knepper, 103 Ohio St. 529, 134 N.E. 476 (1921); Baird v. Detrick, 8 Ohio App. 198, 28 Ohio Ct. App. 257 (1917), affirming 20 Ohio N.P. (n.s.) 209, 28 Ohio Dec. 110; motion to certify record overruled, 15 Ohio L. Rep. 439.].

**Authority**

Trial court properly granted summary judgment to a church official in an action by a decedent's nephews and nieces, alleging that he engaged in negligence after he undertook a duty to remove the church pastor from the decedent's legal documents, including her healthcare power of attorney, as only the decedent had the authority to remove the pastor from the power of attorney and to designate the beneficiaries of her will pursuant to R.C. 1337.12(A)(1) and 2107.02. Kitchen v. Teeters, 2012-Ohio-4343, 2012 Ohio App. LEXIS 3802 (Ohio Ct. App., Clermont County 2012).

**Construction with other laws**

This section, permitting a testator to bequeath his property to any person he desires, is not repealed by GC § 10564 (see now R.C. 2107.34), but is limited thereby: German Mut. Ins. Co. v. Lushey, 20 Ohio C.C. 198, 11 Ohio Cir. Dec. 52 (1900), affirmed, German Mut. Ins. Co. v. Lushey, 66 Ohio St. 233.].

**Contingent will**

Ambiguous language in a will should be construed as to referring to the reason for making a will, rather than as a condition precedent to its taking effect: McMerriman v. Schiel, 108 Ohio St. 334, 140 N.E. 600, 1 Ohio Law Abs. 883, 1923 Ohio LEXIS 223 (Ohio 1923).

A testamentary clause in a will disposing of the testatrix's property after death, in case she does not recover, is a contingent will, and valid if recovery does not occur: Underwood v. Rutan, 101 Ohio St. 306, 128 N.E. 78, 1920 Ohio LEXIS 133 (Ohio 1920).

A will may be subject to a condition subsequent, such as the acceptance of a devise and of certain obligations therefor: Scott v. Kramer, 31 Ohio St. 295, 1877 Ohio LEXIS 409 (Ohio 1877).

**Evidence generally**

There was substantial evidence that the decedent's 2002 will was reduced to writing and signed by the decedent in the presence of the attorney who drew up the will and his former secretary because both the attorney and the secretary testified that they witnessed the signing of the 2002 will after the attorney drafted it and the secretary transcribed it; the secretary specifically recalled the decedent and testified that she signed the will after coming into the office with her granddaughter. In re L.M.W., 2020-Ohio-6856, 2020 Ohio App. LEXIS 4687 (Ohio Ct. App., Summit County 2020).

Declarations of a testator made either before, after, or at the time of the execution of the will are competent as evidence as tending to prove mental capacity of testator, but are not competent to prove undue influence nor, in most cases, to prove forgery: S. F. CHANEY, EX'R OF THE WILL OF LYNCH v. COULTER, 29 Ohio C.A. 177, 1918 Ohio Misc. LEXIS 101 (Ohio

Ct. App., Coshocton County May 1, 1918), motion to certify record overruled, Coulter v. Chaney, 16 Ohio L. 349, 63 Weekly L. Bull. 446.

Declarations of a subscribing witness, made after leaving the room in which the will was executed, cannot be admitted on the theory that they are part of the res gestae: Baird v. Detrick, 8 Ohio App. 198, 28 Ohio Ct. App. 257 (1917), affirming 20 Ohio N.P. (n.s.) 209, 28 Ohio Dec. 110; motion to certify record overruled, 15 Ohio L. Rep. 439.].

**Gift**

A gift without consideration, to take effect at death, passes no title unless there is a delivery: Flanders v. Blandy, 45 Ohio St. 108, 12 N.E. 321, 1887 Ohio LEXIS 101 (Ohio 1887).

**Joint wills**

Tenants in common may dispose of the property which they own in common by a single will which is not in the nature of a contract, and in the same will they may dispose of other personal property as long as no provision is made for a legacy which can be paid only from the personal property of both testators: Ballard v. Ballard, 5 Ohio App. 469, 27 Ohio Cir. Dec. 562, 26 Ohio C.A. 490, 26 Ohio C.C. (n.s.) 490, 1916 Ohio App. LEXIS 132 (Ohio Ct. App., Sandusky County 1916).

Where the will of a survivor to a compact to make mutual wills cannot be found after her death, its provisions will be carried out, if there is no question as to its exact contents, or as to the execution of mutual wills, or the adequacy of the consideration to the survivor: Minor v. Minor, 15 Ohio Dec. 264, 2 Ohio N.P. (n.s.) 439, 1904 Ohio Misc. LEXIS 104 (Ohio C.P. 1904).

Joint or mutual wills made and executed concurrently, in compliance with a contract between parties competent and free to act, supported by a sufficient consideration, and with mutuality pervading and running through every part of both wills, are upheld: Minor v. Minor, 15 Ohio Dec. 264, 2 Ohio N.P. (n.s.) 439, 1904 Ohio Misc. LEXIS 104 (Ohio C.P. 1904).

A joint will is not created by the execution of separate and distinct wills at different times, and the making of separate and distinct codicils to such wills at the same time, by husband and wife, wherein disposition is made of the separate property and estate of each (it not appearing that the wills were in the nature of a compact), although the will of each refers to the will and to the property and estate of the other, and the disposition in both is practically identical: Coghlin v. Coghlin, 16 Ohio Cir. Dec. 18, 4 Ohio C.C. (n.s.) 161, 1904 Ohio Misc. LEXIS 189 (Ohio Ct. App., Lucas County Jan. 25, 1904).

Joint wills, if they are not changed or revoked during the life of either testator, will be sustained, although executed and attested jointly in one paper: Coghlin v. Coghlin, 16 Ohio Cir. Dec. 18, 4 Ohio C.C. (n.s.) 161, 1904 Ohio Misc. LEXIS 189 (Ohio Ct. App., Lucas County Jan. 25, 1904).

Twin wills made by two persons (husband and wife here) are not irrevocable unless each is the consideration for the other, and this contract appears by the most clear and satisfactory evidence. A reciprocity must pervade both wills. If a power is reserved to one party to alter or revoke, the other cannot be held: Albery v. Sessions, 3 Ohio Dec. 330 (Ohio C.P. 1895).

Tenants in common of real estate, who are also owners, severally, of personal property, may dispose of same by will by uniting in a single instrument, where the bequests are severable and the instrument is not in the nature of a compact, but is, in effect, the will of each, revocable by him, and subject to probate as such several will: Betts v. Harper, 39 Ohio St. 639, 1884 Ohio LEXIS 421 (Ohio 1884).

A will by husband and wife where he owns all the property, and she signs merely in acceptance of its provisions, is not a joint will but a valid will of the husband: Kunnen v. Zurline, 13 Ohio Dec. Reprint 998, 2 Cin. Super. Ct. 440 (1873).

**Presumptions**

It will be presumed that a will was drawn in accordance with the wishes of testator: Morris v. Osborne, 27 Ohio Ct. App. 161, 29 Ohio Cir. Dec. 280 (1916), motion to certify record overruled, 61 Weekly L. Bull. 152]; Chaney v. Coulter, 29 Ohio Ct. App. 177, 35 Ohio Cir. Dec. 481 (1918), motion to certify record overruled, Coulter v. Chaney, 16 Ohio L. 349, 63 Weekly L. Bull. 446.].

**Restraint**

"Restraint," as used in R.C. 2107.02, includes undue influence. Poor physical health does not establish susceptibility. An application to probate a will is properly denied if uncontradicted evidence establishes that the testator was under restraint: In re Estate of Smith, 120 Ohio App. 3d 480, 698 N.E.2d 455, 1997 Ohio App. LEXIS 2499 (Ohio Ct. App., Ross County 1997).

**Tenant in common**

The estate of a tenant in common cannot be affected or his right to compel partition defeated, deferred or limited by the provisions of the will of his cotenant whereby he attempts to entail his estate including the lands owned as a cotenant: Lauer v. Green, 99 Ohio St. 20, 121 N.E. 821, 1918 Ohio LEXIS 152 (Ohio 1918).

**Testamentary capacity**

Affidavit of a decedent's friend did not rebut the presumptive validity of the decedent's will and the executor's evidence regarding the decedent's testamentary capacity because the statements in the affidavit constituted inadmissible hearsay and the affidavit was not be based on personal knowledge; the friend failed to offer any evidence to corroborate the allegations contained in her affidavit. Smith v. Gold-Kaplan, 2014-Ohio-1424, 2014 Ohio App. LEXIS 1340 (Ohio Ct. App., Cuyahoga County 2014).

Summary judgment was precluded on the will contestants' testamentary capacity claim, under R.C. 2107.02, because a triable question of fact existed as to the decedent's testamentary capacity at the time when the decedent executed the testamentary documents, in that the affidavits submitted for and against summary judgment provided competing inferences as to the decedent's capacity at the time when the decedent signed the decedent's will. Daubel v. Dineen, 2012-Ohio-5924, 2012 Ohio App. LEXIS 5107 (Ohio Ct. App., Lorain County 2012).

Trial court did not err in granting summary judgment to a decedent's son and his wife on a claim by the decedent's daughter that the decedent lacked testamentary capacity pursuant to R.C. 2107.02 to execute a handwritten will that left everything to the son, as she was deemed competent and aware, despite the onset of dementia/Alzheimer's disease. In re Estate of Marsh, 2011-Ohio-5554, 2011 Ohio App. LEXIS 4534 (Ohio Ct. App., Greene County 2011).

A directed verdict on the issue of testamentary capacity is error where the decedent suffered from senile dementia and failed to recognize the natural objects of his bounty: Doane College v. Nemic, 1993 Ohio App. LEXIS 3961 (Ohio Ct. App., Mahoning County Aug. 12, 1993).

Evidence of the testatrix' alcohol abuse does not by itself create an inference of testamentary incapacity. The evidence did not support the claim of undue influence: Doyle v. Schott, 65 Ohio App. 3d 92, 582 N.E.2d 1057, 1989 Ohio App. LEXIS 3935 (Ohio Ct. App., Hamilton County 1989).

A testator for whom a guardian of the person has been appointed is presumed to lack the testamentary capacity to write a valid will. This presumption may be rebutted by evidence which establishes that, at the time of the execution of the will, the testator had sufficient mind and memory (1) to understand the nature of what he was doing, (2) to comprehend, generally, the nature and extent of his property, (3) to hold in his mind the names and identity of those who had natural claims upon his bounty, and (4) to be able to appreciate his relation to the members of his family. However, a "high degree of proof" is not required: Taylor v. Garinger, 30 Ohio App. 3d 184, 507 N.E.2d 406, 1986 Ohio App. LEXIS 10066 (Ohio Ct. App., Fayette County 1986).

A testator's treating physician's opinion is competent in an action where the testator's mental strength and weakness are in issue; however, that opinion is not conclusive as a matter of law: Gannett v. Booher, 12 Ohio App. 3d 49, 465 N.E.2d 1326, 1983 Ohio App. LEXIS 11316 (Ohio Ct. App., Huron County 1983).

Expert opinion testimony is admissible as to an ultimate fact without infringing upon the function of the jury, if the determination of such ultimate fact requires the application of expert knowledge not within the common knowledge of the jury. This rule permits the giving of an expert opinion as to the mental capacity of the decedent and her competency to make a will. (EvR 704 applied): In re estate of Seelig, 2 Ohio App. 3d 223, 441 N.E.2d 598 (1981).

The testimony of a physician as to the issue of an individual's competency is not dispositive of that issue as a matter of law: Vetter v. Hampton, 54 Ohio St. 2d 227, 8 Ohio Op. 3d 198, 375 N.E.2d 804, 1978 Ohio LEXIS 549 (Ohio 1978).

The appointment of a guardian on the ground of physical incompetency does not imply a lack of testamentary capacity: Roderick v. Fisher, 97 Ohio App. 95, 54 Ohio Op. 264, 122 N.E.2d 475, 1954 Ohio App. LEXIS 694 (Ohio Ct. App., Franklin County 1954).

Requirement that testator shall be of sound mind and memory at time of executing will does not mean that one weakened by sickness is incapable of making a will, but only that he have sufficient memory and mental capacity to understand fully what he is doing: Fulkerson v. Fulkerson, 12 Ohio Law Abs. 324, 35 Ohio L. Rep. 478, 1932 Ohio App. LEXIS 499 (Ohio Ct. App., Fairfield County Sept. 25, 1932).

If testator was able to understand the nature of business, nature and extent of his property, the names of claimants on his bounty, his relationships and his ability to choose as to disposition of his property, it is sufficient: Phillips v. Board of Education, 21 Ohio App. 194, 153 N.E. 119, 1924 Ohio App. LEXIS 127 (Ohio Ct. App., Pickaway County 1924).

For elements of testamentary capacity: Brown v. Lane, 15 Ohio App. 321, 32 Ohio C.A. 305, 32 Ohio C.C. (n.s.) 305, 1921 Ohio App. LEXIS 229 (Ohio Ct. App., Fairfield County 1921); Ross v. Stewart, 15 Ohio App. 339, 32 Ohio C.A. 217, 32 Ohio C.C. (n.s.) 217, 1921 Ohio App. LEXIS 200 (Ohio Ct. App., Coshocton County 1921).

The opinion of a nonexpert witness that a testator was mentally unsound is admissible only after he has testified to some fact or circumstance indicating mental weakness or unsoundness in some degree, and must be confined to the opinion of the witness as to the mental condition of the testator at the time of observation: Kohl v. Kohl, 31 Ohio Dec. 27, 22 Ohio N.P. (n.s.) 171, 1919 Ohio Misc. LEXIS 51 (Ohio C.P. 1919).

An answer that witness "never did think" that testator was of sound mind, shows the opinion of the witness at the time of giving his answer and not at the time at which he had observed testator: Otte v. Bullock, 31 Ohio Dec. 177, 22 Ohio N.P. (n.s.) 305, 1919 Ohio Misc. LEXIS 62 (Ohio C.P. 1919).

Declarations of a testator made either before, after, or at the time of the execution of the will are competent as evidence where the mental capacity of the testator is in issue: Chaney v. Coulter, 29 Ohio Ct. App. 177, 35 Ohio Cir. Dec. 481 (1918), motion to certify record overruled, Coulter v. Chaney, 16 Ohio L. 349, 63 Weekly L. Bull. 446.].

It is assumed that an adjudication of insanity deprives such person of capacity to make a will: In re Murray, 20 Ohio N.P. 305 (1917).

One is not incapacitated to make and execute a will merely because of advanced years or illiteracy: Barlion v. Connor, 9 Ohio App. 72, 31 Ohio C.A. 463, 31 Ohio C.C. (n.s.) 463, 1917 Ohio App. LEXIS 334 (Ohio Ct. App., Hamilton County 1917).

Mental capacity to make a will requires ability to understand the nature of the act testator is performing, the general extent of property of which he is disposing, the relation which he holds to those who have claims upon him, and to appreciate his relation to the members of his family: Niemes v. Niemes, 97 Ohio St. 145, 119 N.E. 503, 1917 Ohio LEXIS 140 (Ohio 1917); Welsh Hills Baptist Church v. Wilson, 19 Ohio Cir. Dec. 391, 9 Ohio C.C. (n.s.) 611, 1905 Ohio Misc. LEXIS 310 (Ohio Ct. App., Licking County Mar. 1, 1905), aff'd, 75 Ohio St. 636, 80 N.E. 1135, 4 Ohio L. Rep. 664 (Ohio 1907), aff'd, Washer v. Iler, 75 Ohio St. 638, 80 N.E. 1134, 4 Ohio L. Rep. 664 (Ohio 1907); Quay v. Quay, 16 Ohio Dec. 435, 4 Ohio N.P. (n.s.) 529, 1906 Ohio Misc. LEXIS 19 (Ohio C.P. 1906).



A nonexpert witness, even though not a subscribing witness, may give an opinion as to testator's sanity if he has first testified to the facts on which he bases his opinion: Niemes v. Niemes, 97 Ohio St. 145, 119 N.E. 503 (1917), reversing 26 Ohio C.C. (n.s.) 513, 28 Ohio Cir. Dec. 61.].

If the evidence in a proceeding to contest a will shows that the testator was of sound mind and memory, of sufficient legal capacity and very methodical, and that the will was properly signed by testator and by the subscribing witnesses, it will be presumed in the absence of evidence to the contrary that testator knew the contents of such will before execution: Morris v. Osborne, 27 Ohio Ct. App. 161, 29 Ohio Cir. Dec. 280 (1916), motion to certify record overruled, Morris v. Osborne, 61 Weekly L. Bull. 152.].

A testator who is so lacking in mental capacity, and who is so controlled by delusion, that he cannot make a rational choice in determining the proper objects of his bounty, does not possess testamentary capacity: Kammann v. Kammann, 6 Ohio App. 455, 26 Ohio C.C. (n.s.) 60, 29 Ohio Cir. Dec. 349 (1916), dismissed, Kammann v. Kammann, 96 Ohio St. 600; motion to certify record overruled, 15 Ohio L. Rep. 238.].

While it is incorrect to hold that a photograph of testator is always inadmissible in evidence if the question of his capacity is raised, it is not reversible error for the trial court to exclude a photograph which was taken when testator was eighty-two years of age, if he did not execute his will until he was ninety-one years of age: Rogers v. Monroe, 29 Ohio Cir. Dec. 558, 26 Ohio C.C. 193 (1914).

It is competent for the physician of a testator to express an opinion as to the actual condition of his patient's mind, founded on his study and observation of the testator while in professional attendance on him at the time and prior to the date of the will, and whether he was capable of comprehending large and complicated business propositions or the distribution of a large estate: Bahl v. Byal, 90 Ohio St. 129, 106 N.E. 766, 11 Ohio L. Rep. 519, 1914 Ohio LEXIS 216 (Ohio 1914).

It is error to refuse to charge in a will case, that a person who attaches his name as a witness to a testamentary instrument impliedly certifies that the testator is of sound mind, and competent to make a will, and while the law will permit him to subsequently testify to the contrary, because the truth, if such it be, should be learned, yet the jury in weighing his testimony may consider the fact of such implied contradiction: Stark v. Cress, 4 Ohio App. 92, 22 Ohio C.C. (n.s.) 88, 28 Ohio Cir. Dec. 442 (1914), reversing Cress v. Stark, 14 Ohio N.P. (n.s.) 545.].

The opinions of nonexpert witnesses as to the sanity of a testator are incompetent, where such witnesses do not qualify by giving the facts coming under their observation upon which their opinions are based: Board of Foreign Missions v. Bevan, 2 Ohio App. 182, 24 Ohio Cir. Dec. 318, 17 Ohio C.A. 275, 17 Ohio C.C. (n.s.) 275, 1913 Ohio App. LEXIS 150 (Ohio Ct. App., Delaware County 1913), aff'd, 91 Ohio St. 395, 110 N.E. 1054, 12 Ohio L. Rep. 298 (Ohio 1914); Ross v. Stewart, 15 Ohio App. 339, 32 Ohio C.A. 217, 32 Ohio C.C. (n.s.) 217, 1921 Ohio App. LEXIS 200 (Ohio Ct. App., Coshocton County 1921); Gregg v. Moore, 23 Ohio Cir. Dec. 534, 14 Ohio C.C. (n.s.) 570, 1911 Ohio Misc. LEXIS 239 (Ohio Ct. App., Licking County Mar. 1, 1911).

In a proceeding to contest a will, the question, "I will ask you to state now upon that occasion whether, in your judgment, he (the testator) had sufficient mind and memory to form an intention and purpose to dispose of his property by will," calls for the present recollection or opinion of the witness as to the mental condition of the testator at the time that he signed the instrument. Accordingly, it is not error to permit such question to be asked. If the answer to such question is "at the time I signed the will I thought he was, as far as I was capable of judging," such answer is not responsive to the question; but if no objection is made to it, and no motion is made to strike it out, it is not error for the court to permit it to go to the jury: Dunlap v. Dunlap, 89 Ohio St. 28, 104 N.E. 1006, 1913 Ohio LEXIS 552 (Ohio 1913).

Lack of testamentary capacity is not shown by evidence of a religious conviction on the part of the testator upon the subject of foreign missions, where his delusion with reference thereto, if any existed, did not control the making of his will, but on the contrary, he disposed of his property without reference to foreign missions except and in the event of his son and only heir dying without issue: Board of Foreign Missions v. Bevan, 2 Ohio App. 182, 17 Ohio C.C. (n.s.) 275 (1913), sub nomine, Presbyterian Church v. Bevan, 24 Ohio Cir. Dec. 318; affirmed, without opinion, Board of Foreign Missions v. Bevan, 91 Ohio St. 395.].

The fact that the testator was afflicted with progressive locomotor ataxia and was for a number of years before his death physically unable to perform any task or to help himself in any way, is not sufficient ground for setting the will aside, where it appears that during all that time he directed in detail the operations on farms aggregating over three hundred acres, and with reference to the management of his said lands did all that could have been done by a person of a sound and active mind; and the only testimony tending to show mental incapacity was slight forgetfulness on certain occasions and failure to include in his will certain legacies which he had declared he intended to make: Gregg v. Moore, 23 Ohio Cir. Dec. 534, 14 Ohio C.C. (n.s.) 570, 1911 Ohio Misc. LEXIS 239 (Ohio Ct. App., Licking County Mar. 1, 1911).

The fact that testator was intoxicated when he returned home at night does not show that he was intoxicated when he executed his will some hours before: Gregg v. Moore, 23 Ohio Cir. Dec. 534, 14 Ohio C.C. (n.s.) 570, 1911 Ohio Misc. LEXIS 239 (Ohio Ct. App., Licking County Mar. 1, 1911).

An hypothetical question should not be permitted which calls for the opinion of a medical expert as to the capacity of testator to plan and express in technical language a long and complicated will. It is not necessary that testator should be able to express in apt language his wishes with reference to the creation, maintenance and operation of certain trusts. It is sufficient if he has sufficient mind and memory to dispose of his property by will: Walsh v. Walsh, 32 Ohio Cir. Dec. 617, 18 Ohio C.C. (n.s.) 91, 1910 Ohio Misc. LEXIS 351 (Ohio Ct. App., Cuyahoga County Dec. 30, 1910).

An expert may not be called upon to say whether one was competent to make a particular will, but only whether, in his opinion, his mental capacity was such as the law requires for the making of a valid will: Walsh v. Walsh, 32 Ohio Cir. Dec. 617, 18 Ohio C.C. (n.s.) 91, 1910 Ohio Misc. LEXIS 351 (Ohio Ct. App., Cuyahoga County Dec. 30, 1910).

Want of mental capacity on the part of a testator is not shown by a recital of circumstances and incidents which go no further than to indicate some physical weakness, or failure of memory, or mistake of an unimportant character, in connection with his business affairs; nor can an attack on a will be successfully maintained where the witnesses for the contestants seem to have reached the belief that the testator was incompetent to make a will because he did not make the kind of a will which they would have made or which they thought he ought to have made: Wilson v. Wilson, 14 Ohio C.C. (n.s.) 241, 22 Ohio Cir. Dec. 498, 56 Weekly L. Bull. 377 (1909), reversing 7 Ohio N.P. (n.s.) 435, 19 Ohio Dec. 188.].

Guardianship on the ground of intemperance does not raise the same presumption of testamentary capacity as would be the case if the guardianship rested upon the ground of insanity or imbecility: Fagan v. Welsh, 32 Ohio Cir. Dec. 409, 19 Ohio C.C. (n.s.) 177, 1909 Ohio Misc. LEXIS 439 (Ohio Ct. App., Cuyahoga County Jan. 25, 1909).

A testator's eccentricities, peculiarities or delusions must not affect either the natural or selected objects of his bounty or interfere with his testamentary capacity to make a will: Wadsworth v. Purdy, 21 Ohio Cir. Dec. 110, 12 Ohio C.C. (n.s.) 8, 1908 Ohio Misc. LEXIS 259 (Ohio Ct. App., Cuyahoga County June 30, 1908).

A charge that "capacity enough to attend to ordinary business, and to know and understand the business he was engaged in," lacks essential requisites of testamentary capacity to make a will, and is misleading and prejudicial: Wadsworth v. Purdy, 21 Ohio Cir. Dec. 110, 12 Ohio C.C. (n.s.) 8, 1908 Ohio Misc. LEXIS 259 (Ohio Ct. App., Cuyahoga County June 30, 1908).

Hypothetical questions as to testator's mental condition cannot be asked a witness who is not an expert, even upon cross-examination: Hathaway v. Farley, 22 Ohio C.C. (n.s.) 462, 33 Ohio Cir. Dec. 668 (1907), affirmed, without opinion, 76 Ohio St. 562.].

A delusion on the part of a testator does not constitute mental incapacity, unless it is an insane delusion: Moore v. Caldwell, 6 Ohio C.C. (n.s.) 484, 17 Ohio Cir. Dec. 449 (1904), petition in error dismissed by consent, Ross v. Caldwell, 50 Weekly L. Bull. 108.].

In determining whether a testator was suffering from an insane delusion at the time he made his will, the testimony of experts does not outweigh absolutely that of laymen who had known the testator for years, and had business transactions with him, and frequently met and conversed with him: Moore v. Caldwell, 6 Ohio C.C. (n.s.) 484, 17 Ohio Cir. Dec. 449 (1904), petition in error dismissed by consent, Ross v. Caldwell, 50 Weekly L. Bull. 108.].

Where testator, for twenty years after making his will, associated socially with men in general, bought lands and built and repaired houses, rented houses and collected the rents, bought bonds and sold them, and conducted a merchant tailoring business, made no bad bargains nor showed mental incapacity to cope with the men with whom he dealt, it was held that the evidence showed testamentary capacity, although testator was eccentric and excitable, occasionally became intoxicated, and during the latter years of his life allowed his business to become more or less run down: Kettemann v. Metzger, 13 Ohio Cir. Dec. 61, 3 Ohio C.C. (n.s.) 224, 1901 Ohio Misc. LEXIS 194 (Ohio Ct. App., Lucas County Nov. 1, 1901).

The expressions of a man standing upon the verge of eternity, with the grave yawning before him, with every indication of dissolution, cannot be said to be those of a man of sound mind and memory, and a will made under such conditions will not be admitted to probate: In re Estate of Burrows, 11 Ohio Dec. 229, 8 Ohio N.P. 358, 1900 Ohio Misc. LEXIS 146 (Ohio P. Ct. 1900).

There is a legal presumption in favor of a will, and in favor of the mental soundness and capacity of the testator: Beresford v. Stanley, 9 Ohio Dec. 134, 6 Ohio N.P. 38, 1898 Ohio Misc. LEXIS 182 (Ohio C.P. 1898).

**Undue influence**

Trial court erred in granting summary judgment to a decedent's son and his wife on a claim by the decedent's daughter that the decedent's handwritten will that left everything to the son was a product of undue influence pursuant to R.C. 2107.02, as the son and his wife had the opportunity to exert influence over the decedent, who was in a vulnerable state. In re Estate of Marsh, 2011-Ohio-5554, 2011 Ohio App. LEXIS 4534 (Ohio Ct. App., Greene County 2011).

Where a will is attacked on grounds of undue influence, a wide range of inquiry should be permitted to bring before the jury the facts and influences bearing upon the preparation of the will: Rich v. Quinn, 13 Ohio App. 3d 102, 468 N.E.2d 365, 1983 Ohio App. LEXIS 11387 (Ohio Ct. App., Warren County 1983).

In order to sustain allegations of undue influence in a will contest, a plaintiff must prove: (1) that the testator was "susceptible"; (2) another's opportunity to exert the influence; (3) the fact of improper influence exerted or attempted; and (4) the result showing the effect of such influence: Rich v. Quinn, 13 Ohio App. 3d 102, 468 N.E.2d 365, 1983 Ohio App. LEXIS 11387 (Ohio Ct. App., Warren County 1983).

Because undue influence is usually proved by circumstantial evidence and because a wide range of evidence is to be permitted to establish undue influence, it is error for a trial court to grant a motion in limine limiting the presentation of evidence to those events occurring within a specified time period before and after the execution of the contested will: Rich v. Quinn, 13 Ohio App. 3d 102, 468 N.E.2d 365, 1983 Ohio App. LEXIS 11387 (Ohio Ct. App., Warren County 1983).

The essential elements of undue influence are a susceptible testator, another's opportunity to exert it, the fact of improper influence exerted or attempted, and the result showing the effect of such influence: West v. Henry, 173 Ohio St. 498, 20 Ohio Op. 2d 119, 184 N.E.2d 200, 1962 Ohio LEXIS 668 (Ohio 1962).

A daughter may legally seek her mother's preference to the exclusion of her sisters, so long as she does not go to the extent of making her mother do something she does not want to do. Such conduct, of course, is reprehensible, but it is not illegal. It does not amount to undue influence: Meyer v. Geiger, 34 N.E.2d 581, 34 Ohio Law Abs. 1, 1938 Ohio Misc. LEXIS 942 (Ohio Ct. App., Hamilton County 1938).

The sole beneficiary under a purported will who procured the scrivener to draw the instrument and her own friends to witness it and who was the testator's landlady and a non-relative will be presumed to have unduly influenced the maker, if the maker is an old man who signed the instrument six days before he died in the home of the sole beneficiary away from his next of kin, while in a feeble condition: In re Maurer, 31 Ohio N.P. 247 (1933).

Exercise of undue influence in execution of will need not be shown by direct proof, but it may be inferred from circumstances: Raymond v. Hearon, 30 Ohio App. 184, 164 N.E. 644, 6 Ohio Law Abs. 548, 1928 Ohio App. LEXIS 506 (Ohio Ct. App., Hamilton County 1928).

"Undue influence," which will invalidate a deed, must be such as to control mental operations of grantor, overcome his power of resistance, and oblige him to adopt the will of another, thus producing disposition of property which he would not have made freely: Finney v. Morehouse, 27 Ohio App. 499, 161 N.E. 293, 6 Ohio Law Abs. 419, 1927 Ohio App. LEXIS 420 (Ohio Ct. App., Wood County 1927).

Evidence of inferior capacity, not amounting to incapacity, is admissible on the issue of undue influence: Board of Education v. Phillips, 103 Ohio St. 622, 134 N.E. 646, 19 Ohio L. Rep. 516, 1921 Ohio LEXIS 140 (Ohio 1921).

Evidence that testator was of advanced age and weak mentality, and that the beneficiary lived with testator on intimate terms and was also on intimate terms with the attorney who drew the will, is sufficient evidence of undue influence to require submission of the issue to the jury: Board of Education v. Phillips, 103 Ohio St. 622, 134 N.E. 646, 19 Ohio L. Rep. 516, 1921 Ohio LEXIS 140 (Ohio 1921).

When contestants of a will have produced evidence from which legitimate inferences could be drawn that a daughter had acquired a dominating influence over the testator five years preceding the will, declarations of the testator just preceding this period are not too remote to be admissible as material evidence of the last free exercise of his faculties and as showing his testamentary intentions: Otte v. Bullock, 31 Ohio Dec. 177, 22 Ohio N.P. (n.s.) 305, 1919 Ohio Misc. LEXIS 62 (Ohio C.P. 1919).

The fact that the will in question differs in some respects from prior wills is not sufficient to show an undue influence: Chaney v. Coulter, 29 Ohio Ct. App. 177, 35 Ohio Cir. Dec. 481 (1918), motion to certify record overruled, Coulter v. Chaney, 16 Ohio L. 349, 63 Weekly L. Bull. 446.].

The fact that testator makes an unequal and unfair distribution of his property does not raise the presumption of undue influence: Bahl v. Byal, 90 Ohio St. 129, 106 N.E. 766, 11 Ohio L. Rep. 519, 1914 Ohio LEXIS 216 (Ohio 1914).

Undue influence over a testator on the part of his second wife is not shown by the fact that the children of the second wife fared better than the contestant, a child of the first wife, where the second wife was not herself given an undue proportion of the estate: O'Rourke v. Kenny, 22 Ohio Dec. 56, 11 Ohio N.P. (n.s.) 602, 1911 Ohio Misc. LEXIS 46 (Ohio C.P. 1911).

The making of a change in a will, which there is reason to believe was done for reasons satisfactory to the testator, is not, where standing alone, a sufficient reason for setting the instrument aside on the ground of undue influence: Gregg v. Moore, 23 Ohio Cir. Dec. 534, 14 Ohio C.C. (n.s.) 570, 1911 Ohio Misc. LEXIS 239 (Ohio Ct. App., Licking County Mar. 1, 1911).

It is erroneous to charge a jury that undue influence "is coercion produced by importunity, or by a silent, resistless power, which the strong will often exercises over the weak and infirm, so that the motive was tantamount to force or fear": Gregg v. Moore, 23 Ohio Cir. Dec. 534, 14 Ohio C.C. (n.s.) 570, 1911 Ohio Misc. LEXIS 239 (Ohio Ct. App., Licking County Mar. 1, 1911).

The presence of a beneficiary at the place at which a will was executed, and the fact that he gave advice to the testator with reference to such will, is not sufficient to justify a verdict setting aside the will on the ground of undue influence: Wilson v. Wilson, 14 Ohio C.C. (n.s.) 241, 22 Ohio Cir. Dec. 498, 56 Weekly L. Bull. 377 (1909), reversing 7 Ohio N.P. (n.s.) 435, 19 Ohio Dec. 188.].

The relation of a ward, under guardianship for intemperance, to a person with whom she boards under an arrangement made by the guardian for her, though such person has received certain instructions from the guardian as to the care of the ward, is not the same as the relation of the ward to the guardian, and does not, of itself, raise a presumption of undue influence in an action to set aside a will under which such person is a beneficiary: Fagan v. Welsh, 32 Ohio Cir. Dec. 409, 19 Ohio C.C. (n.s.) 177, 1909 Ohio Misc. LEXIS 439 (Ohio Ct. App., Cuyahoga County Jan. 25, 1909).

The fact that a wife guides or even dominates her husband in the ordinary affairs of life, or has acquired an ascendency over him, does not render his will made in her favor invalid: Kornfield v. Kornfield, 33 Ohio Cir. Dec. 617, 22 Ohio C.C. (n.s.) 363, 1908 Ohio Misc. LEXIS 403 (Ohio Ct. App., Cuyahoga County Mar. 23, 1908).

In an action contesting a will, it is error to charge that the law scrutinizes with greater care the acts of a son or daughter who is remembered in a will to a larger extent than any others bearing the same kinship, if such son or daughter is in close relationship of trust or confidence, or upon whom a testatrix would implicitly rely, than it would on others bearing no such relationship: Hall v. Hall, 78 Ohio St. 415, 85 N.E. 1125, 6 Ohio L. Rep. 65, 6 Ohio L. Rep. 69 (Ohio 1908).

To invalidate a will for fraud or undue influence, it must appear that the fraud or influence complained of had some effect upon the testator in producing the very act of making his will: Monroe v. Barclay, 17 Ohio St. 302, 1867 Ohio LEXIS 82 (Ohio 1867); Kettemann v. Metzger, 13 Ohio Cir. Dec. 61, 3 Ohio C.C. (n.s.) 224, 1901 Ohio Misc. LEXIS 194 (Ohio Ct. App., Lucas County Nov. 1, 1901).

**—Presumptions**

The so-called presumption of undue influence arising from confidential relations between testator and beneficiary is a mere inference of fact and not a presumption of law regarding which the court should charge the jury: Haley v. Dempsey, 14 Ohio App. 326 (1921), motion to certify record overruled, Dempsey v. Haley, 19 Ohio L. 155; judgment on retrial sustained will affirmed by court of appeals; motion to certify record overruled, Haley v. Dempsey, 21 Ohio L. Rep. 300 (Ohio Oct. 30, 1923).].

## RESEARCH REFERENCES AND PRACTICE AIDS

**Cross-References to Related Sections**

Declaration of validity; procedure for revoking or modifying will, RC § 2107.084.

Petition for judgment declaring validity of will, RC § 2107.081.

Will ineffectual, RC § 2107.61.

**Comparative Legislation**

Execution of will by married woman:

CA—Cal Prob Code § 6100 et seq
FL—Fla. Stat. § 732.501
IL—755 Ill. Comp. Stat. § 5/4-1
IN—Burns Ind. Code Ann. § 29-1-5-1
KY—KRS § 394.020

MI—MCLS §§ 700.2501, 700.2502
NY—NY CLS EPTL § 3-1.1
PA—20 P.S. § 2501
Requisites to make will:
CA—Cal Prob Code § 6110 et seq
FL—Fla. Stat. § 732.502
IL—755 Ill. Comp. Stat. § 5/4-1
IN—Burns Ind. Code Ann. § 29-1-5-2
KY—KRS § 394.040
MI—MCLS § 700.2502
NY—NY CLS EPTL § 3-2.1
PA—20 P.S. § 2502
Testamentary capacity:
CA—Cal Prob Code § 6100 et seq
FL—Fla. Stat. § 732.501
IL—755 Ill. Comp. Stat. § 5/4-1
IN—Burns Ind. Code Ann. § 29-1-5-1
KY—KRS § 394.020
MI—MCLS § 700.2501
NY—NY CLS EPTL § 3-1.1
PA—20 P.S. § 2501



**Practice Manuals and Treatises**
Anderson's The Simple Will in Ohio § 6.1 Proper Execution

**Practice Guides**
Anderson's Ohio Probate Practice and Procedure § 6.01 Will contest action
Anderson's Ohio Probate Practice and Procedure § 8.01 General

## § 2107.03 Method of making will.

Except oral wills, every will shall be in writing, but may be handwritten or typewritten. The will shall be signed at the end by the testator or by some other person in the testator's conscious presence and at the testator's express direction. The will shall be attested and subscribed in the conscious presence of the testator, by two or more competent witnesses, who saw the testator subscribe, or heard the testator acknowledge the testator's signature.

For purposes of this section, "conscious presence" means within the range of any of the testator's senses, excluding the sense of sight or sound that is sensed by telephonic, electronic, or other distant communication.

**HISTORY:**
GC § 10504-3; 114 v 320(346); Bureau of Code Revision. Eff 10-1-53; 152 v S 302, § 1, eff. 9-11-08; 2011 SB 124, § 1, eff. Jan. 13, 2012.

**Editor's Notes**
Acts 2011, SB 124, § 3 provides: "The provisions of this act that relate to the estates of decedents apply to the estates of decedents who die on or after the effective date of this act."

**Amendment Notes**
The 2011 amendment, in the first paragraph, substituted "will" for "last will and testament" in the first sentence, deleted "making it" following "the testator' in the second sentence, and added "The will shall" to the beginning of the last sentence; and made a related change.

152 v S 302, effective September 11, 2008, rewrote the section.

### NOTES TO DECISIONS

Analysis

Generally
Acknowledgment of paternity
Affidavit of testator
Attestation
Attorney as witness
Attorney of testator, liability
Codicils
Common law
Contract by devisee
Copies of will
Evidence generally
Holographic instrument
Intention
Interested witnesses
Jury instructions generally
Parol evidence
Presumptions
Probate
Rehearing for probate
Retroactivity
Revocation of will
Signatures
Signed at the end
Subsequent will
Validity
Wills
—Execution

**Generally**

To rebut the presumption of validity created when a will is admitted to probate, a contestant must produce evidence which furnishes a reasonable basis for sustaining his claim. Burden of proof in determining testamentary capacity is on the party contesting the will. R.C. 2107.03 requires only that a will be attested to by two witnesses who saw the testator sign his name or acknowledge his signature. There is no requirement that there be an actual attestation clause, that the signatures of the witnesses be on the same sheet as the signature of the testator, that the pages be numbered, or that the attestation clause be dated. A probate court is not prevented from construing a will while it is also determining the validity of a will. Children can be completely disinherited by implication if a testator completely disposes of all of his property by will. That disposition overcomes the presumption against disinheritance: Estate of Snell v. Kilburn, 2005-Ohio-7076, 165 Ohio App. 3d 352, 846 N.E.2d 572, 2005 Ohio App. LEXIS 6382 (Ohio Ct. App., Monroe County 2005).

Testator's will complied with the testamentary formalities set forth in R.C. 2107.03, in that it was drafted by the attorney who was present at its execution, it was regular on its face, the attestation clause was signed by two witnesses and recited compliance with the statutory requirements, and all witnesses signed affidavits stating that the will was properly executed. Estate of Snell v. Kilburn, 2005-Ohio-7076, 165 Ohio App. 3d 352, 846 N.E.2d 572, 2005 Ohio App. LEXIS 6382 (Ohio Ct. App., Monroe County 2005).

A proponent of a purported will who is also a beneficiary thereof is not for that reason incompetent to testify as to the will's validity: In re Estate of Wachsmann, 55 Ohio App. 3d 265, 563 N.E.2d 734, 1988 Ohio App. LEXIS 4142 (Ohio Ct. App., Cuyahoga County 1988).

Though no specific statutory definition of the term "will" exists, case law and statutory language clearly demonstrate that a will must be in writing, executed with certain formalities and by its language illustrate, at the minimum, a testamentary intent, i.e., a disposition of property to take effect only at death: In re Estate of Ike, 7 Ohio App. 3d 87, 454 N.E.2d 577, 1982 Ohio App. LEXIS 11109 (Ohio Ct. App., Shelby County 1982).

General Code § 10504-3 (R.C. 2107.03) requires that, in order to be valid and effective, a will must comply with certain definite formalities. The reason for such formalities is to prevent the diversion of a decedent's estate from those who would take it under the statutes of descent and distribution except in instances where the decedent has clearly and deliberately expressed an intention to so divert it: Sherman v. Johnson, 159 Ohio St. 209, 50 Ohio Op. 257, 112 N.E.2d 326, 1953 Ohio LEXIS 564 (Ohio 1953).

The statutory requirements providing for the execution of wills must be complied with regardless of the apparent intention of the testator: In re Borgman's Estate, 105 N.E.2d 69, 61 Ohio Law Abs. 429, 1951 Ohio App. LEXIS 869 (Ohio Ct. App., Franklin County 1951).

The fact that one subscribing witness forgets the facts of execution, does not render a will invalid: Egbert v. Egbert, 10 Ohio App. 432, 29 Ohio Ct. App. 584 (1918), motion to certify record overruled, 16 Ohio L. 507, 64 Weekly L. Bull. 61.].

The object of requiring the execution of wills to conform to a statutory formula, in order to render them valid, is to prevent fraud upon heirs at law in the distribution of the estate of their ancestors, and courts in the construction of these provisions should have this object in mind, and should not place such a liberal construction, in order to sustain the execution, that the object of the statute would be destroyed: Slemmons v. Toland, 5 Ohio App. 201, 28 Ohio Cir. Dec. 455, 25 Ohio C.A. 485, 25 Ohio C.C. (n.s.) 485, 1916 Ohio App. LEXIS 173 (Ohio Ct. App., Harrison County 1916).

Where, in an action to contest a will, it is evident from the testimony that the will was not read either to or by the testator, that it was not acknowledged by him, and that he had no knowledge of what it contained, it can not be said that such will was executed by the testator in such a manner as to comply with the requirements of GC § 10505; and the verdict of a jury sustaining such a will is not sustained by the evidence and will be set aside: Koch v. Meyers, 7 Ohio App. 306, 30 Ohio Cir. Dec. 439, 29 Ohio C.A. 142, 29 Ohio C.C. (n.s.) 142, 1916 Ohio App. LEXIS 175 (Ohio Ct. App., Hamilton County 1916).

A power to dispose of lands by will must be executed with the same formalities as are necessary in a deed directly conveying the land: Boltz v. Riley, 18 Ohio C.C. (n.s.) 71, 24 Ohio Cir. Dec. 178 (1912), reversed, without opinion, Riley v. Boltz, 90 Ohio St. 447.].

A will is not invalidated by a space between dispositive and testimonium clauses, where it is signed directly after the testimonium clause and under this is the attesting clause and the signatures of the witnesses: Mader v.

Apple, 80 Ohio St. 691, 89 N.E. 37, 7 Ohio L. Rep. 117, 1909 Ohio LEXIS 108 (Ohio 1909); Crafts v. Wilber, 19 Ohio Dec. 421, 9 Ohio N.P. (n.s.) 161, 1909 Ohio Misc. LEXIS 6 (Ohio C.P. 1909).

Where the testator, before requesting witnesses to sign, had so folded the paper that they could not see that it contained any writing at all and one of them could see only the word "witness" and not testator's signature, execution is defective: Missionary Soc. of M. E. Church v. Ely, 61 Ohio St. 636, 57 N.E. 1133 (Ohio 1899), [without opinion; for argument, etc., see 42 Weekly L. Bull. 473.].

**Acknowledgment of paternity**

Civ.R. 12 dismissal of a putative son's will contest (of a father's will) for lack of standing was proper; the son could not prove under R.C. 2105.15 that he was a son and an R.C. 2107.71 "person interested" by being acknowledged by the father during the father's lifetime to be a son; a prior alleged will naming the son was not executed with the proper R.C. 2107.03, 2107.26 formalities to be prima facie proof that he was acknowledged. Estate of Okos v. Farley, 2004-Ohio-2882, 2004 Ohio App. LEXIS 2542 (Ohio Ct. App., Lucas County 2004).

**Affidavit of testator**

An affidavit of the testator, made contemporaneously with the will but not executed conformably to the wills act nor referred to in the will, cannot be employed to vary or add to the clear dispositive terms of the will: Leopold v. Weaver, 9 Ohio App. 379, 29 Ohio Ct. App. 567 (1918), motion to certify record overruled, Weaver v. Leopold, 16 Ohio L. 465, 64 Weekly L. Bull. 40.].

It is not necessary that the will be written on the same grade of paper or the same size sheets of paper: Chaney v. Coulter, 29 Ohio Ct. App. 177, 35 Ohio Cir. Dec. 481 (1918), motion to certify record overruled, Coulter v. Chaney, 16 Ohio L. 349, 63 Weekly L. Bull. 446.].

In Ohio the making, probating and contesting of wills is controlled by the statutes: Kelley v. Hazzard, 96 Ohio St. 19, 117 N.E. 182, 15 Ohio L. Rep. 55, 1917 Ohio LEXIS 227 (Ohio 1917); In re Murray, 20 Ohio N.P. 305 (1917).

A will may be partly written and partly printed: Sears v. Sears, 77 Ohio St. 104, 82 N.E. 1067, 5 Ohio L. Rep. 495, 1907 Ohio LEXIS 95 (Ohio 1907); Roush v. Wensel, 8 Ohio Cir. Dec. 141, 15 Ohio C.C. 133, 1897 Ohio Misc. LEXIS 473 (Ohio Ct. App., Wood County Oct. 1, 1897).

**Attestation**

Will's attestation clause was valid because the attorney who drafted the will reviewed it with the testator, witnessed the testator sign the will, and saw the witness sign the will, the attorney and the witness confirmed their signatures, and the witness's lack of memory as to the details of the execution did not create a triable issue. Ayer v. Morenz-Harbinger, 2020-Ohio-6861, 2020 Ohio App. LEXIS 4702 (Ohio Ct. App., Hamilton County 2020).

Because a purported codicil failed to comply with the attestation requirement of R.C. 2107.03, it was not valid as a will and, accordingly, was an invalid exercise of the power of appointment under the trust. Collins v. Hearty Inv. Trust, 2017-Ohio-1270, 2017 Ohio App. LEXIS 1267 (Ohio Ct. App., Summit County 2017).

Trial court did not err when it concluded that the decedent's will was not executed in compliance with R.C. 2107.03, and when it therefore revoked its prior order admitting the will to probate under R.C. 2107.18, because the subscribing witnesses to the decedent's will were not in the decedent's conscious presence when they signed their attestations to the will. Whitacre v. Crowe, 2012-Ohio-2981, 972 N.E.2d 659, 2012 Ohio App. LEXIS 2611 (Ohio Ct. App., Medina County 2012).

A will is properly subscribed by witnesses when they sign their names thereto in presence of testator, but it is not properly attested unless witnesses see testator sign his name, or hear him acknowledge either the paper as his will or his signature thereto: In re Pittis, 29 Ohio N.P. 41 (1930).

Attestation and subscription of witnesses to a will are two separate and distinct acts, and both are necessary in proper execution of a will: In re Pittis, 29 Ohio N.P. 41 (1930).

Proof that will was signed by testatrix and her signature was attested by two subscribing witnesses, is sufficient proof of due execution under former GC § 10505 (see now R.C. 2107.03). That section only required that subscribing witnesses see testatrix subscribe and did not require that testatrix make declaration of fact that it was her will: Glanz v. Bauer, 7 Ohio Law Abs. 165, 1929 Ohio Misc. LEXIS 1291 (Ohio Ct. App., Cuyahoga County Feb. 11, 1929).

"Attest" means to bear witness to, to certify, to affirm to be true or genuine: In re Reckard, 24 Ohio Dec. 609, 15 Ohio N.P. (n.s.) 465, 1914 Ohio Misc. LEXIS 20 (Ohio C.P. 1914).

**Attorney as witness**

Where a written will is signed by a testator and attested and subscribed in the presence of such testator by two witnesses who are attorneys practicing law as partners, one of whom prepared such will, and who are nominated in such will as executor and alternate executor, respectively, such witnesses are competent within the meaning of this section, requiring such will to be attested and subscribed to "by two or more competent witnesses," and such will, if otherwise valid, is not thereby invalidated: Blankner v. Lathrop, 169 Ohio St. 229, 8 Ohio Op. 2d 221, 159 N.E.2d 229, 1959 Ohio LEXIS 579 (Ohio 1959), overruled in part, Rogers v. Helmes, 69 Ohio St. 2d 323, 23 Ohio Op. 3d 301, 432 N.E.2d 186, 1982 Ohio LEXIS 578 (Ohio 1982).

While an attorney cannot testify as to confidential communications made to him by testator, he may, if he is a subscribing witness, testify as any other subscribing witness may: Collins v. Collins, 110 Ohio St. 105, 143 N.E. 561, 2 Ohio Law Abs. 260, 1924 Ohio LEXIS 370 (Ohio 1924).

General Code § 11494 (R.C. 2317.02) disqualifies an attorney from testifying "concerning a communication made to him by his client in that relation, or his advice to his client," except by the express consent of the client, and when a testator procures his attorney as a subscribing witness to his will he by that act expressly consents that the attorney may testify as fully as any other subscribing witness touching the capacity of the testator or any other fact affecting the validity of the will. The object of requesting a person to witness a will is to assure the legal execution of the will and preserve the evidence thereto: Knepper v. Knepper, 103 Ohio St. 529, 134 N.E. 476, 19 Ohio L. Rep. 462, 1921 Ohio LEXIS 160 (Ohio 1921).

**Attorney of testator, liability**

Beneficiary of a decedent's will may not maintain a negligence action against an attorney for the preparation of a deed that results in increased tax liability for the estate: Shoemaker v. Gindlesberger, 2008-Ohio-2012, 118 Ohio St. 3d 226, 887 N.E.2d 1167, 2008 Ohio LEXIS 1192 (Ohio 2008).

A decedent's attorney may not be sued by the intended beneficiaries and the court-appointed administrator for the attorney's negligence in failing to obtain the required signature of an attesting witness, which negligence results in denial of admission of the will to probate: Dykes v. Gayton, 139 Ohio App. 3d 395, 744 N.E.2d 199, 2000 Ohio App. LEXIS 2152 (Ohio Ct. App., Franklin County 2000).

**Codicils**

A writing designated a "Mutual Understanding" which was not executed as a codicil, but was signed by testator and his principal beneficiary later on the day his will was executed, and purported to bind the beneficiary to share her portion, with their sister, who was stated not to have been provided for in the will, was only an attempted contract between the signers. An attempted contract between a testator and a beneficiary under his previously executed will, by which the beneficiary agrees to share her portion of the estate with another, is invalid where not executed in the manner prescribed for the execution of wills: Pfahl v. Pfahl, 10 Ohio Misc. 234, 39 Ohio Op. 2d 348, 225 N.E.2d 305, 1967 Ohio Misc. LEXIS 341 (Ohio P. Ct. 1967).

Where a will and the codicil thereto are both legally executed, the fact that the codicil was written in the blank space between the last dispositive item and the testimonium clause does not invalidate the instrument: Clark v. Carpenter, 14 Ohio App. 278, 32 Ohio C.A. 87, 32 Ohio C.C. (n.s.) 87, 1921 Ohio App. LEXIS 276 (Ohio Ct. App., Morgan County 1921).

A codicil which is not executed in accordance with the requirements concerning a will is itself invalid: In re Murray, 20 Ohio N.P. 305 (1917).

In Ohio a will and a codicil are to be regarded as different parts of the same instrument; and a codicil may operate as a republication of a defectively executed will: Morris v. Osborne, 27 Ohio Ct. App. 161, 29 Ohio Cir. Dec. 280 (1916), motion to certify record overruled, 61 Weekly L. Bull. 152, and citing Mack v. Bonner, 3 Ohio St. 366, 1854 Ohio LEXIS 160 (Ohio 1854); Black v. Webb, 20 OHIO 304, 1851 Ohio LEXIS 86 (Ohio Dec. 1, 1851).].

Even if testator executes a will without knowing its contents, such will is rendered valid by the subsequent execution by testator of a valid codicil to such will after such will and codicil have been read over to him: Morris v. Osborne, 27 Ohio Ct. App. 161, 29 Ohio Cir. Dec. 280 (1916), motion to certify record overruled, 61 Weekly L. Bull. 152.].

Indorsements upon a will signed by the testator but not witnessed as provided by law are not codicils: Porterfield v. Porterfield, 17 Ohio Dec. 448, 4 Ohio N.P. (n.s.) 654, 1907 Ohio Misc. LEXIS 137 (Ohio C.P. 1907).

**Common law**

Unless modified by statute, the rule of the common law controls the competency of witnesses and the question of interest: Vrooman v. Powers, 47 Ohio St. 191, 24 N.E. 267, 1890 Ohio LEXIS 97 (Ohio 1890).

**Contract by devisee**

This section does not apply to a contract by a devisee to hold in trust for certain beneficiaries: Winder v. Scholey, 83 Ohio St. 204, 93 N.E. 1098 (1910), affirming circuit court, which affirmed Scholey v. Winder, 10 Ohio N.P. (n.s.) 642, 21 Ohio Dec. 59.].

**Copies of will**

Executed and attested carbon copies of a will cannot be admitted to probate in lieu of the original last will and testament: In re Estate of Steel, 8 Ohio Misc. 133, 37 Ohio Op. 2d 70, 219 N.E.2d 236, 1966 Ohio Misc. LEXIS 254 (Ohio P. Ct. 1966).

**Evidence generally**

Even though all who have apparently signed an instrument as attesting witnesses affirmatively testify that the instrument was not executed according to law, such execution and attestation may be established by other competent evidence: In re Estate of Lyons, 166 Ohio St. 207, 2 Ohio Op. 2d 26, 141 N.E.2d 151, 1957 Ohio LEXIS 378 (Ohio 1957).

In the absence of direct testimony that the provisions of R.C. 2107.03, relating to the method for the execution of wills, has been complied with as to signature and acknowledgment, there must be some evidence upon which an inference of implied acknowledgment can be based, and probate will be refused where the witnesses to the will testified not only that they neither saw testatrix sign the instrument nor heard her acknowledge it, but also that they at no time prior to probate saw testatrix's signature on the instrument, even though both witnesses were able to testify that the signature on the will was that of testatrix: In re Will of La Mar, 146 N.E.2d 472, 77 Ohio Law Abs. 140, 1957 Ohio Misc. LEXIS 255 (Ohio P. Ct. 1957).

A declaration made by a testator to the effect that he has made a will, or that he has revoked a will, is not independent evidence of such fact, and it is not admissible without some foundation of direct evidence or presumption as to the existence of such fact: Kornfield v. Kornfield, 33 Ohio Cir. Dec. 617, 22 Ohio C.C. (n.s.) 363, 1908 Ohio Misc. LEXIS 403 (Ohio Ct. App., Cuyahoga County Mar. 23, 1908).

**Holographic instrument**

Under the provisions of this section a holographic instrument is signed at the end by the party making it where the following appears at the end of all dispositive items: "I Clara M. Smith, have subscribed my name this the 28th day of August, 1940. Signed and acknowledged by Clara M. Smith as and for her last Will and Testament in her presence and in the presence of each other have subscribed our names as witnesses. John S. Leggett, Mrs. Olga M. Leggett," and the same is entitled to probate as a last will and testament: In re Smith, 27 Ohio Op. 520, 39 Ohio Law Abs. 637, 1944 Ohio Misc. LEXIS 190 (Ohio P. Ct. 1944).

**Intention**

Probate court erred in voiding a bequest to one who was a witness to the execution of a 2006 document that purported to be a will, as it was determined that the decedent intended the document to be his will, such that the purging statute was not applicable despite the failure to comply with the statutory formalities for it to be a will. In re Estate of Shaffer, 2019-Ohio-234, 2019 Ohio App. LEXIS 250 (Ohio Ct. App., Lucas County 2019), rev'd, 2020-Ohio-6672, 163 Ohio St. 3d 487, 171 N.E.3d 272, 2020 Ohio LEXIS 2788 (Ohio 2020), rev'd in part, 2020-Ohio-6973, 163 Ohio St. 3d 497, 171 N.E.3d 281, 2020 Ohio LEXIS 2976 (Ohio 2020).

**Interested witnesses**

Because R.C. 2107.15, which voids a will's devise to a witness if that witness was essential to establishing the validity of the will, applies equally to both wills executed in compliance with R.C. 2107.03 and nonconforming wills remediated pursuant to R.C. 2107.24, a handwritten note signed by the decedent naming his caretaker as a beneficiary was properly denied admission to probate. In re Estate of Shaffer, 2020-Ohio-6672, 163 Ohio St. 3d 487, 171 N.E.3d 272, 2020 Ohio LEXIS 2788 (Ohio), modified, 2020-Ohio-6973, 163 Ohio St. 3d 497, 171 N.E.3d 281, 2020 Ohio LEXIS 2976 (Ohio 2020).

Appellate court erred in ruling that probate court was required to admit testator's handwritten note to probate as a will despite the fact that the note's witness was a beneficiary under it because R.C. 2107.15 applied both to wills executed in compliance with the statute and those submitted pursuant to R.C. 2107.24, and the probate court had correctly applied 2107.15 and determined that the note witness and beneficiary could not be included in the list of estate beneficiaries. In re Estate of Shaffer, 2020-Ohio-6973, 163 Ohio St. 3d 497, 171 N.E.3d 281, 2020 Ohio LEXIS 2976 (Ohio 2020).

Interested witnesses to a written will are competent witnesses thereto if they otherwise meet the test of competency set forth in R.C. 2317.01: Rogers v. Helmes, 69 Ohio St. 2d 323, 23 Ohio Op. 3d 301, 432 N.E.2d 186, 1982 Ohio LEXIS 578 (Ohio 1982).

A witness is not incompetent as a subscribing witness to a will because he is also named as an executor or trustee: Fazekas v. Gobozy, 150 N.E.2d 319, 78 Ohio Law Abs. 258, 1958 Ohio App. LEXIS 873 (Ohio Ct. App., Cuyahoga County 1958).

An executor who is not also a legatee or devisee is competent to be one of the necessary witnesses: Blankner v. Lathrop, 154 N.E.2d 95, 79 Ohio Law Abs. 6, 1958 Ohio App. LEXIS 916 (Ohio Ct. App., Franklin County 1958), aff'd, 169 Ohio St. 229, 8 Ohio Op. 2d 221, 159 N.E.2d 229, 1959 Ohio LEXIS 579 (Ohio 1959).

**Jury instructions generally**

Request in will contest to charge that every will must be in writing and signature of testator and that of witnesses subscribed as one continuous transaction held properly refused as not correctly stating law: Scholl v. Sterkel, 46 Ohio App. 389, 189 N.E. 15, 16 Ohio Law Abs. 491, 40 Ohio L. Rep. 9, 1933 Ohio App. LEXIS 379 (Ohio Ct. App., Richland County 1933).

**Parol evidence**

A document purported to be a will must evidence requisite testamentary intent from the document itself and evidence of statements, circumstances, or events dehors the instrument may be used to clarify or resolve an ambiguity in meaning, but cannot be utilized to add something to the document which is not there: In re Estate of Ike, 7 Ohio App. 3d 87, 454 N.E.2d 577, 1982 Ohio App. LEXIS 11109 (Ohio Ct. App., Shelby County 1982).

**Presumptions**

There is no requirement in R.C. 2107.03 that there be an actual attestation clause, that the signatures of the witnesses be on the same sheet as signature of the testator, that the pages be numbered, or that the attestation clause be dated. While these things would certainly entitle the will to a greater presumption of validity, the lack of them does not negate the presumption. Estate of Snell v. Kilburn, 2005-Ohio-7076, 165 Ohio App. 3d 352, 846 N.E.2d 572, 2005 Ohio App. LEXIS 6382 (Ohio Ct. App., Monroe County 2005).

There is a strong presumption that a will drawn by an attorney who directed its execution and was present when it was executed was regularly executed: In re McGraw, 14 Ohio App. 2d 87, 43 Ohio Op. 2d 207, 236 N.E.2d 684 (1967).

The presumption that a will was duly executed can be overcome by other evidence, but not by the mere absence of evidence: In re McGraw, 14 Ohio App. 2d 87, 43 Ohio Op. 2d 207, 236 N.E.2d 684 (1967).

Where the proof of record shows testatrix was of full age, sound mind and memory, and not under any restraint, and the proffered will is typewritten, testamentary in character, with a testimonium clause and attestation clause reciting all essentials of due execution, and signed at the end by testatrix and attested by two subscribing witnesses, one of whom is deceased and the signature of the deceased witness, together with that of the testatrix and the surviving attesting witness are shown by substantial evidence to be genuine, a prima facie case in favor of the validity of the will is established, so that where the surviving attesting witness testifies in substance that testatrix requested her to witness what she stated to be her will, which was lying on the table, folded in such a manner that the witness could not see whether there was any other signature thereon other than that of the first subscribing attesting witness who was not present, and the surviving witness did not see the testatrix sign the will, nor did testatrix acknowledge her signature by spoken word, the probate court is required to disregard such testimony against the validity of the will and must admit the will to probate on the prima facie case of record, which includes an appraisal of all the surrounding facts and circumstances attending the execution of the will, and it is prejudicial error for the probate court to determine the ultimate issue of due execution of the will as on contest against the validity of the will, in the face of substantial evidence making a prima facie case in favor of the validity of the will: Roosa v. Wickward, 90 Ohio App. 213, 47 Ohio Op. 207, 105 N.E.2d 454, 1950 Ohio App. LEXIS 582 (Ohio Ct. App., Hamilton County 1950).

**Probate**

Probate court erred when it entered an interlocutory order denying appellant's application to probate a purported 2006 document as a will of an 87-year-old decedent after his will, executed in 1967, was already admitted to probate, as there was no need for such an order prior to a hearing, but the order did not prejudice appellant. In re Estate of Shaffer, 2019-Ohio-234, 2019 Ohio App. LEXIS 250 (Ohio Ct. App., Lucas County 2019), rev'd, 2020-Ohio-6672, 163 Ohio St. 3d 487, 171 N.E.3d 272, 2020 Ohio LEXIS 2788 (Ohio 2020), rev'd in part, 2020-Ohio-6973, 163 Ohio St. 3d 497, 171 N.E.3d 281, 2020 Ohio LEXIS 2976 (Ohio 2020).

Because a purported will was executed in compliance with R.C. 2107.03, the clear and convincing evidence standard was not required, and the will should have been admitted into probate. More than two competent witnesses, who signed the purported will, testified they were present, as was a notary public, when an aunt signed it. Jackson v. Estate of Henderson, 2010-Ohio-3084, 2010 Ohio App. LEXIS 2602 (Ohio Ct. App., Cuyahoga County 2010).

**Rehearing for probate**

While R.C. 2107.181 generally permits the court to receive evidence to determine if the will was executed in compliance with the law, the mere submission of such evidence does not supersede the specific requirement under R.C. 2107.03 that a will must be attested and subscribed by two witnesses in the presence of the testator in order to be eligible for probate: In re Estate of Weilert, 1998 Ohio App. LEXIS 5717 (Ohio Ct. App., Franklin County Dec. 3, 1998).

**Retroactivity**

A statute which changes the requirements of a valid will does not apply to wills already executed: Giddings v. Schmuck, 20 Ohio C.C. (n.s.) 142, 31 Ohio Cir. Dec. 238 (1912), affirmed, without opinion, 90 Ohio St. 465.].

**Revocation of will**

Uncorroborated allegations that a testator stated that she had executed a new will and intended to revoke an earlier one are not admissible in an action contesting admission of the "earlier" will to probate: Gockel v. Eble, 98 Ohio App. 3d 281, 648 N.E.2d 539, 1994 Ohio App. LEXIS 4570 (Ohio Ct. App., Cuyahoga County 1994).

Once a will is "made" in the manner provided in R.C. 2107.03, it remains a will unless and until it is revoked by one of the means provided in R.C. 2107.33: In re Will of Nash, 50 Ohio Misc. 4, 3 Ohio Op. 3d 347, 361 N.E.2d 558, 1976 Ohio Misc. LEXIS 53 (Ohio P. Ct. 1976).

The republication of a will which has been once revoked must be attended by the same formalities as were required to render valid its original execution: Crane v. Tunkey, 11 Ohio L. Rep. 454 (Ohio C.P. June 10, 1913).

**Signatures**

Will complied with the statute because, since the lawyer's assistant did not attempt to notarize the will, but, rather, she signed as a witness, there was no false notary acknowledgment in regard to the will. The affidavits submitted by the wife in support of her motion were properly before the trial court, and established that the date of March 25, 1997, contained on the last page of the will, was a typographical mistake and that the decedent, with presence of mind and on his own accord, signed the will. Black v. Watson, 2016-Ohio-1470, 2016 Ohio App. LEXIS 1364 (Ohio Ct. App., Cuyahoga County 2016).

Widow's application to admit her deceased husband's purported handwritten will to probate was properly denied because it was only signed by the husband and not by the witnesses, and there was not clear and convincing evidence that he intended for the document to constitute his will. Estate of Hand, 2016-Ohio-7437, 73 N.E.3d 880, 2016 Ohio App. LEXIS 4300 (Ohio Ct. App., Butler County 2016).

Trial court did not err in finding that the testimony failed to prove by clear and convincing evidence under R.C. 2107.24 that there were two witnesses who observed the decedent sign and execute the will in question, in accordance with the requirements of R.C. 2107.03, because, while the decedent's son, the son's wife, and the decedent's son-in-law all testified that they were in the room and saw the decedent sign the will, their testimony was suspect due to the facts that the son was the sole beneficiary under the will and that the son-in-law felt indebted to the son and his wife for all the help they had given him throughout the years. Moreover, the sole witness listed on the will, the only non-family member in the room at the time that the will was signed, testified that he was the only one in the room when the decedent signed the will. In re Estate of Pittson, 2009-Ohio-1862, 2009 Ohio App. LEXIS 1574 (Ohio Ct. App., Stark County 2009).

R.C. 2107.03 prescribed the requirements respecting signatures on wills, and, while requiring two or more competent persons to witness or hear a testator acknowledge his signature, § 2107.03 did not require that the signatures be notarized. Siggers v. Strother, 2006-Ohio-6372, 2006 Ohio App. LEXIS 6334 (Ohio Ct. App., Franklin County 2006).

It was not an abuse of discretion for a trial court to decline to re-examine a will, under R.C. 2107.18, when a son claimed one of its witnesses notarized witness signatures, because R.C. 2107.03 did not require notarization, so, even if the witness improperly notarized witness signatures, this did not render the will invalid, and no other basis for claiming the will's invalidity was alleged. Siggers v. Strother, 2006-Ohio-6372, 2006 Ohio App. LEXIS 6334 (Ohio Ct. App., Franklin County 2006).

Where testatrix made her mark in the presence of two persons whom she had asked to sign as witnesses, there was no statutory duty upon testatrix to acknowledge her mark or signature: Kemp v. Matthews, 183 N.E.2d 259, 89 Ohio Law Abs. 524, 1962 Ohio App. LEXIS 801 (Ohio Ct. App., Cuyahoga County 1962).

By virtue of this section, it is not necessary to the validity of a last will and testament that the attesting and subscribing witnesses thereto sign the same in the presence of each other: McFadden v. Thomas, 154 Ohio St. 405, 43 Ohio Op. 340, 96 N.E.2d 254, 1951 Ohio LEXIS 625 (Ohio 1951).

Where the witnesses to a will signed at the request of the testatrix who produced the instrument for the purpose of acknowledgment, all of the requirements of this section were complied with providing the testatrix had previously signed the will: In re Borgman's Estate, 105 N.E.2d 69, 61 Ohio Law Abs. 429, 1951 Ohio App. LEXIS 869 (Ohio Ct. App., Franklin County 1951).

A will may be admitted to probate where there is a mark consisting of a cross which the witnesses testified was put there by the testatrix with the assistance of one of the witnesses, although the name of the testatrix does not appear anywhere in the body of the will or at the end thereof: In re Ryan, 23 Ohio Op. 356, 36 Ohio Law Abs. 341, 1942 Ohio Misc. LEXIS 277 (Ohio P. Ct. 1942).

When a woman asked two friends to be witnesses to her will, and said to them "This is my will," and the witnesses, at the time, saw upon the instrument some writing and the only other writing on it was the signature of the testatrix, prima facie proof is made that she acknowledged her signature as required by this section: In re Fisher's Will, 67 Ohio App. 6, 21 Ohio Op. 44, 35 N.E.2d 784, 1941 Ohio App. LEXIS 807 (Ohio Ct. App., Lucas County 1941).

If the subscribing witnesses signed when testator had not signed, and four days later he signed in their presence, the court held that the will was valid since it was deemed to have been attested by the subscribing witnesses at the time of the testator's signature: Bloechle v. Davis, 132 Ohio St. 415, 8 Ohio Op. 249, 8 N.E.2d 247, 1937 Ohio LEXIS 233 (Ohio 1937).

Where a will was signed by the testator in one room and then taken into another room where at the request of testator it was signed by two witnesses, but no express acknowledgment by the testator of his signature which was visible to the witness or of the nature of the instrument was made, the requirements of this section, relative to the execution of wills, have been complied with, since the production of the instrument and the request that the witnesses sign, imported that the signature to be witnessed was that of the testator and that he acknowledged it to be his: Blagg v. Blagg, 55 Ohio App. 518, 9 Ohio Op. 180, 9 N.E.2d 991, 23 Ohio Law Abs. 286, 1936 Ohio App. LEXIS 245 (Ohio Ct. App., Montgomery County 1936).

A will is properly executed if it is signed at the end by the maker in the presence of two subscribing witnesses even though the witnesses have no knowledge that the instrument signed is a will: In re Maurer, 31 Ohio N.P. 247 (1933); In re Williamson, 6 Ohio N.P. 79, 8 Ohio Dec. 47 (1898), reversing In re Williamson, 5 Ohio N.P. 1, 6 Ohio Dec. 505.].

Where a witness to a will took part in the physical act of writing his name as a witness by holding pencil while name was written by another at his direction, at testator's request and in his presence, he was an effectual subscribing witness: In re Gatchel, 29 Ohio N.P. 207 (1932).

Where signature to will is by mark, it is presumed, in contest of will, in absence of contrary showing, that signature was made by express direction, and mark inserted by testator: Aston v. Hauck, 22 Ohio App. 430, 153 N.E. 277, 4 Ohio Law Abs. 319, 1926 Ohio App. LEXIS 558 (Ohio Ct. App., Hamilton County 1926).

In determining validity of will containing decedent's mark instead of signature, it was duty of court to pass on question whether will was lawfully attested and executed from face of instrument itself and evidence, and submission of question to jury was prejudicial error: Hayes v. Halle, 23 Ohio App. 522, 155 N.E. 493, 4 Ohio Law Abs. 170, 1925 Ohio App. LEXIS 168 (Ohio Ct. App., Cuyahoga County 1925).

A will is not properly signed by testator if, while he is unconscious, a pen is put in his hand and a mark is made therewith: West v. Lucas, 106 Ohio St. 255, 139 N.E. 859, 1 Ohio Law Abs. 72, 1922 Ohio LEXIS 243 (Ohio 1922).

If testator does not sign the will nor authorize another to sign his name in his presence, the will is not properly signed: West v. Lucas, 106 Ohio St. 255, 139 N.E. 859, 1 Ohio Law Abs. 72, 1922 Ohio LEXIS 243 (Ohio 1922).

If the subscribing witnesses signed before testator signed, and testator then signed in their presence at the same transaction, the will was held to be valid: Slemmons v. Toland, 5 Ohio App. 201, 28 Ohio Cir. Dec. 455, 25 Ohio C.A. 485, 25 Ohio C.C. (n.s.) 485, 1916 Ohio App. LEXIS 173 (Ohio Ct. App., Harrison County 1916).

The provision of this section which requires that a will must be signed by two or more competent witnesses, refers to the execution of the will, and not to the amount of testimony which must be offered at probate. The probate court may admit a will to probate although one subscribing witness testifies to facts which amount to a due execution of the will, even though the other subscribing witness testifies that the signature of the testator was not upon the will when he signed it as a witness and that he did not sign it in the presence of the testator. The questions as to the credibility of such witnesses are for the probate court: In re Will of Watts, 27 Ohio Dec. 87, 19 Ohio N.P. (n.s.) 225, 1916 Ohio Misc. LEXIS 37 (Ohio C.P. 1916).

One who signs testator's name to a will may also be a subscribing witness: Trembley v. Trembley, 5 Ohio Dec. 750, 4 Ohio L. Rep. 545, 1884 Ohio Misc. LEXIS 14 (Ohio 1884).

Where a will has been signed for the testator by another person, in his presence and by his express direction, in the absence of the attesting witnesses, the acknowledgment of the fact by the testator in the hearing of the witnesses, which is requisite, is not required to be made in any particular form of words, or in any specified manner; but, if by signs, motions, conduct or attending circumstances, the attesting witnesses are given to understand, by the testator, that he acknowledges the signature thereto as his, and the instrument itself as a will, it is sufficient: Haynes v. Haynes, 33 Ohio St. 598, 1878 Ohio LEXIS 226 (Ohio 1878).

**Signed at the end**

When a purported will contained, after the testator's signature, language stating the testator's unequivocal intent to disinherit his daughter, this language was a dispositive provision of the purported will, and, because it appeared after the testator's signature, the will was not "signed at the end," as required by R.C. 2107.03, so the will was invalid, and a prior will the testator had executed was enforced. In re Estate of Metz, 2006-Ohio-4809, 2006 Ohio App. LEXIS 4716 (Ohio Ct. App., Huron County 2006).

Will is signed at the end pursuant to R.C. 2107.03 where signature is within the testamentary clause, and where words following signature have no legal significance, do not affect other will provisions, and will not change the property distribution: Judy v. Wilson, 1994 Ohio App. LEXIS 3438 (Ohio Ct. App., Hocking County Aug. 1, 1994).

A probate court has no jurisdiction to admit to probate, as a will, an instrument which is not signed at the end thereof by the purported maker, and an order of a probate court admitting such an instrument is a nullity and may be collaterally attacked: In re Eakins' Will, 63 Ohio App. 265, 16

Ohio Op. 583, 26 N.E.2d 219, 1939 Ohio App. LEXIS 249 (Ohio Ct. App., Gallia County 1939).

Where a will is written on two sheets of paper which are continuous in sense even though in fastening them together the sheet containing testimonium clause and signature is placed on top, the will is signed at the end thereof as required by former GC § 10505 (now GC § 10504-3 [R.C. 2107.03]): Lyon v. Lyon, 16 Ohio Op. 2, 34 N.E.2d 281, 34 N.E. 281, 6 Ohio Law Abs. 346, 1928 Ohio Misc. LEXIS 1060 (Ohio Ct. App., Gallia County 1928).

If the only signature of testator appears in the testimonium clause, the will is not signed at the end: Schubert v. Christman, 16 Ohio App. 432, 1922 Ohio App. LEXIS 196 (Ohio Ct. App., Hamilton County 1922).

A will which is written on a double sheet of legal cap paper, to which a small sheet of paper is pinned, containing a dispositive clause added before execution, is said not to be signed at the end: Smith v. Ellis, 15 Ohio App. 38 (1921), motion to certify record overruled, Ellis v. Smith, 19 Ohio L. 512.].



A will is not signed at the end thereof, as required by the statute, where the testator's name and the words "his mark" appear, in the handwriting of the scrivener, on the line where the signature of the testator is customarily inserted at the end of the testimonium clause and the space between the words "his" and "mark" is blank, but an X appears between the given name and surname of the testator on the first line of the attestation clause: Herbster v. Pincombe, 10 Ohio App. 322, 31 Ohio Ct. App. 358 (1918), motion to certify record overruled, Pincombe v. Herbster, 16 Ohio L. 79, 63 Weekly L. Bull. 195.].

The end of the will is the blank line intended for his signature immediately after the testimonium clause, even if by mistake in transposing the different sheets on which the will is written, the sheet on which the testimonium clause and the signature of testator are found, is placed in front of a sheet of paper on which dispositive provisions are found: Chandler v. Dockman, 8 Ohio App. 113, 29 Ohio Cir. Dec. 405, 28 Ohio C.A. 297, 28 Ohio C.C. (n.s.) 297, 1917 Ohio App. LEXIS 209 (Ohio Ct. App., Madison County 1917).

A will is signed at the end thereof, as required by the statute, when the signature of the testator appears after the will, just below a line intended in a blank form for the signature and in a blank space in the attestation clause intended for the name of the testator as part thereof, said name also appearing in the attestation clause, in the handwriting of the scrivener of the will, just below the testator's signature in such position as to read as a part of said attestation clause: Giddings v. Schmuck, 20 Ohio C.C. (n.s.) 142, 31 Ohio Cir. Dec. 238 (1912), affirmed, without opinion, 90 Ohio St. 465; distinguishing Sears v. Sears, 77 Ohio St. 104, 82 N.E. 1067, 5 Ohio L. Rep. 495, 1907 Ohio LEXIS 95 (Ohio 1907) (see also Mauk v. Shellabarger, 84 Ohio St. 461, 95 N.E. 1152, 9 Ohio L. Rep. 21, 1911 Ohio LEXIS 137 (Ohio 1911)).].

Where the testator omitted to sign at the end of the testimonium clause, but did write his name in the attestation clause immediately following, it was held that the will was not signed at the end thereof: Sears v. Sears, 77 Ohio St. 104, 82 N.E. 1067, 5 Ohio L. Rep. 495, 1907 Ohio LEXIS 95 (Ohio 1907), [see also Mauk v. Shellabarger, 84 Ohio St. 461, 95 N.E. 1152, 9 Ohio L. Rep. 21, 1911 Ohio LEXIS 137 (Ohio 1911).].

Where there was written, on the left margin of a will, a dispositive clause extending lengthwise from the bottom to the top of the page, and not connected with the body of the instrument by any words or marks to show where it is to be read in relation to the other provisions, and the testimony shows that the marginal matter was written after all the other provisions, at the request of the testator and before he attached his signature, then such will is not signed at the end thereof and is invalid: Irwin v. Jacques, 71 Ohio St. 395, 73 N.E. 683, 2 Ohio L. Rep. 442, 1905 Ohio LEXIS 148 (Ohio 1905).

The words "the executrix is not required to give bond," added below the place of signing, do not avoid the rest of the will as not being signed at the end thereof: Baker v. Baker, 51 Ohio St. 217, 37 N.E. 125, 1894 Ohio LEXIS 132 (Ohio 1894).

**Subsequent will**

The testator's second will was invalid where it was subscribed by only one witness, even though two other witnesses testified that the testator told them he had executed that will. The second will was of no effect as to a previous will already admitted to probate: In re Estate of Carmedy, 95 Ohio App. 3d 572, 642 N.E.2d 1170, 1994 Ohio App. LEXIS 3656 (Ohio Ct. App., Franklin County 1994).

**Validity**

Executor made a prima facie showing that an Interim Will was valid as (1) the will was typewritten, (2) was signed at the end by the decedent, and (3) was signed by three witnesses that attested the decedent signed the will in their presence. Cook v. Everhart, 2019-Ohio-3044, 2019 Ohio App. LEXIS 3134 (Ohio Ct. App., Cuyahoga County 2019).

Trial court did not err in denying the son's motion for summary judgment because the notary testified that he witnessed the decedent sign the will and that the second signature was his wife's signature as the second witness. Because the conscious presence of the notary's wife at the time of execution was not an issue, the notary jurat demonstrated that the decedent acknowledged that he executed the 2005 will in the notary's presence, the burden rested with the disinherited son to demonstrate that the 2005 will was not executed pursuant to the requirements of Ohio law, which he failed to do. Estate of Harris v. Harris, 2016-Ohio-2615, 63 N.E.3d 744, 2016 Ohio App. LEXIS 1498 (Ohio Ct. App., Stark County 2016).

R.C. 2107.03 requires that to create a valid written will there must be a document that is signed at the end by the testator or the testator's agent, in the presence of two competent witnesses, who must observe the testator's signature or hear the testator acknowledge the testator's signature. Naple v. Bednarik, 2012-Ohio-5881, 2012 Ohio App. LEXIS 5069 (Ohio Ct. App., Mahoning County 2012).

Although there was an admitted false notary acknowledgement for a quitclaim deed and a will, there was no error in a will contest action where the jury considered the will, as a notary acknowledgement was not required under R.C. 2107.03 and the false acknowledgement accordingly did not affect the validity thereof. The deed was invalid due to the false notarization, as such an acknowledgement was required pursuant to R.C. 5301.01 and 147.53, such that the property had to pass through the decedent's estate rather than be transferred through deed or other separate document. Marshall v. Scalf, 2007-Ohio-3667, 2007 Ohio App. LEXIS 3373 (Ohio Ct. App., Cuyahoga County 2007).

**Wills**

**—Execution**

When a purported will contained, after the testator's signature, language stating the testator's unequivocal intent to disinherit his daughter, this language was a dispositive provision of the purported will, and, because it appeared after the testator's signature, the will was not "signed at the end," as required by R.C. 2107.03, so the will was invalid, and a prior will the testator had executed was enforced. In re Estate of Metz, 2006-Ohio-4809, 2006 Ohio App. LEXIS 4716 (Ohio Ct. App., Huron County 2006).

It was not an abuse of discretion for a trial court to decline to re-examine a will, under R.C. 2107.18, when a son claimed one of its witnesses notarized witness signatures, because R.C. 2107.03 did not require notarization, so, even if the witness improperly notarized witness signatures, this did not render the will invalid, and no other basis for claiming the will's invalidity was alleged. Siggers v. Strother, 2006-Ohio-6372, 2006 Ohio App. LEXIS 6334 (Ohio Ct. App., Franklin County 2006).

R.C. 2107.03 prescribed the requirements respecting signatures on wills, and, while requiring two or more competent persons to witness or hear a testator acknowledge his signature, § 2107.03 did not require that the signatures be notarized. Siggers v. Strother, 2006-Ohio-6372, 2006 Ohio App. LEXIS 6334 (Ohio Ct. App., Franklin County 2006).

Testator's will complied with the testamentary formalities set forth in R.C. 2107.03, in that it was drafted by the attorney who was present at its execution, it was regular on its face, the attestation clause was signed by two witnesses and recited compliance with the statutory requirements, and all witnesses signed affidavits stating that the will was properly executed. Estate of Snell v. Kilburn, 2005-Ohio-7076, 165 Ohio App. 3d 352, 846 N.E.2d 572, 2005 Ohio App. LEXIS 6382 (Ohio Ct. App., Monroe County 2005).

There is no requirement in R.C. 2107.03 that there be an actual attestation clause, that the signatures of the witnesses be on the same sheet as signature of the testator, that the pages be numbered, or that the attestation clause be dated. While these things would certainly entitle the will to a greater presumption of validity, the lack of them does not negate the presumption. Estate of Snell v. Kilburn, 2005-Ohio-7076, 165 Ohio App. 3d 352, 846 N.E.2d 572, 2005 Ohio App. LEXIS 6382 (Ohio Ct. App., Monroe County 2005).

## RESEARCH REFERENCES AND PRACTICE AIDS

**Cross-References to Related Sections**

Declaration of validity; procedure for revoking or modifying will, RC § 2107.084.

Petition for judgment declaring validity of will, RC § 2107.081.

Will ineffectual, RC § 2107.61.

**Comparative Legislation**

Manner of execution:

CA—Cal Prob Code § 6110
FL—Fla. Stat. § 732.502
IL—755 Ill. Comp. Stat. § 5/4-3
IN—Burns Ind. Code Ann. § 29-1-5-3
KY—KRS § 394.040
MI—MCLS § 700.2502
NY—NY CLS EPTL § 3-2.1
PA—20 P.S. § 2502

**Practice Manuals and Treatises**

Anderson's The Simple Will in Ohio § 6.1 Proper Execution

Anderson's Ohio Probate Practice and Procedure Form 8.14 Complaint for judgment declaring validity of will

Anderson's Ohio Probate Practice and Procedure Form 9.07 Testimony of witnesses

## § 2107.04 Agreement to make a will.

No agreement to make a will or to make a devise or bequest by will shall be enforceable unless it is in writing. The agreement shall be signed by the maker or by some other person at the maker's express direction. If signed by a person other than the maker, the instrument shall be subscribed by two or more competent witnesses who heard the maker acknowledge that it was signed at the maker's direction.

**HISTORY:**

GC § 10504-3a; 116 v 385(404), § 2; Bureau of Code Revision. Eff 10-1-53; 2011 SB 124, § 1, eff. Jan. 13, 2012.

**Editor's Notes**

Acts 2011, SB 124, § 3 provides: "The provisions of this act that relate to the estates of decedents apply to the estates of decedents who die on or after the effective date of this act."

**Amendment Notes**

The 2011 amendment made stylistic changes.

### NOTES TO DECISIONS

Analysis

Generally
Agreement to die intestate
Devise to class
Employment agreements
Enforceability
Evidence
Exceptions not applicable
Mutual wills
Oral promise
Partial performance
Personal services as consideration
Priority of agreement
Probating of will
Remedies for violation of agreement
Statute of frauds

**Generally**

Trial court did not err by granting summary judgment for the executor of the stepmother's estate because the oral promise to create a will was unenforceable. Although the stepchildren granted the stepmother the consideration she requested by refraining from contesting their father's will, they were never aware of the definite terms in the offer or the promise which they were accepting, and they were uncertain as to how the stepmother intended to accomplish the distribution; their testimony demonstrated that they did not expect the stepmother to distribute their shares of her and their father's estate until after the stepmother died. Lapoint v. Templeton, 2008-Ohio-1792, 2008 Ohio App. LEXIS 1515 (Ohio Ct. App., Fulton County 2008).

Where a will by which a decedent leaves his property to another person is executed the same day as a contract between the decedent and such other person, which contract contains no promise or agreement to make a will and which provides that "it is impossible to arrive at a definite figure. . . to be paid for the services to be rendered by" such other person and that such other person "will accept whatever" decedent "determines to be a just consideration for the services performed and to be performed," and the will makes no reference to the contract; neither the will nor the contract constitutes an enforceable contract entitling such other person to specific performance thereof, and such will is subject to revocation by a subsequently executed will: Stork v. Troeger, 103 Ohio App. 144, 3 Ohio Op. 2d 207, 144 N.E.2d 675, 1956 Ohio App. LEXIS 581 (Ohio Ct. App., Defiance County 1956).

In an action against the executor or administrator of a decedent's estate to subject the estate to the payment of a claim, where the petition alleges that there is an oral contract between the plaintiff and the decedent, and where the contract as alleged indicates that it created a monetary obligation of the decedent existing in his lifetime, although such obligation was not, by the terms of the contract, to be discharged until at or after the death of the decedent, such petition does not allege a contract to make a will, within the meaning of GC § 10504-3a (R.C. 2107.04), and states facts sufficient to show a cause of action: Moore v. Curtzweiler, 165 Ohio St. 194, 59 Ohio Op. 263, 134 N.E.2d 835, 1956 Ohio LEXIS 475 (Ohio 1956).

A writing consisting of a revoked will which does not contain words which can reasonably be construed as words of promise or agreement, or as an indication of any contract or agreement, cannot be a memorandum or note of any agreement within the meaning of R.C. 1335.05, or an agreement in writing within the meaning of R.C. 2107.04, providing that a contract to make a will must be in writing, and a petition which bases its cause of action upon such a writing, praying in the alternative for specific performance or a decree impressing a constructive trust, does not state facts constituting a cause of action and is subject to demurrer: Wilson v. Dunkle, 132 N.E.2d 483, 71 Ohio Law Abs. 483, 1955 Ohio Misc. LEXIS 308 (Ohio C.P. 1955).

By virtue of GC § 10504-3a (R.C. 2107.04), an agreement to make a will or to make a devise or bequest by will is not enforceable under any circumstances unless it is in writing: Sherman v. Johnson, 159 Ohio St. 209, 50 Ohio Op. 257, 112 N.E.2d 326, 1953 Ohio LEXIS 564 (Ohio 1953).

Where a writing does not contain words which can be reasonably construed as words of promise or agreement or as an indication of any contract or agreement, such writing cannot be a memorandum or note of any agreement within the meaning of GC § 8621 (R.C. 1335.05) or an agreement in writing within the meaning of GC § 10504-3a (R.C. 2107.04): Sherman v. Johnson, 159 Ohio St. 209, 50 Ohio Op. 257, 112 N.E.2d 326, 1953 Ohio LEXIS 564 (Ohio 1953).

An oral contract to make a will is unenforceable by virtue of this section, and payment of consideration by one in whose favor the contract is made, whether that payment consists of money or pecuniarily compensable services, will not remove such a contract from the operation of the section: Snyder v. Warde, 151 Ohio St. 426, 39 Ohio Op. 253, 86 N.E.2d 489, 1949 Ohio LEXIS 447 (Ohio 1949).

An action was instituted upon an oral contract made prior to the effective date of this section to make a bequest in consideration of the performance of services as a physician, during the remainder of the promisor's life. Performance of all conditions precedent was alleged. At the trial the plaintiff failed to prove that he was ready, willing and able to perform the services. For that reason he was not entitled to judgment: Heyn v. Kahn, 69 Ohio App. 274, 24 Ohio Op. 64, 39 N.E.2d 866 (1941), affirming 19 Ohio Op. 29 (CP); appeal dismissed, 140 Ohio St. 337.].

A promise to make a will in favor of a party, supported by sufficient consideration and in due form of law, is a valid contract and may be specifically enforced against the heirs of the promisor: Emery v. Darling, 50 Ohio St. 160, 33 N.E. 715, 1893 Ohio LEXIS 149 (Ohio 1893).

**Agreement to die intestate**

This section, providing that "no agreement to make a will or to make a devise or bequest by will shall be enforceable unless it is in writing," has no application to an oral agreement to not make a will but to die intestate: Frantz v. Maher, 106 Ohio App. 465, 7 Ohio Op. 2d 209, 155 N.E.2d 471, 1957 Ohio App. LEXIS 750 (Ohio Ct. App., Clark County 1957).

**Devise to class**

An agreement to devise a family farm to a specific class of individuals was met where the devise was made to a narrow subset of the broad class: Kretzer v. Brubaker, 1996-Ohio-178, 74 Ohio St. 3d 519, 660 N.E.2d 446, 1996 Ohio LEXIS 101 (Ohio 1996).

**Employment agreements**

Money damages were not awarded to an employee for the employer's anticipatory breach of an oral promise to leave a business to the employee in exchange for services that the employee provided: Gottfried-Smith v. Gottfried, 119 Ohio App. 3d 646, 695 N.E.2d 1229, 1997 Ohio App. LEXIS 2313 (Ohio Ct. App., Lucas County 1997).

**Enforceability**

Summary judgment was properly granted because the probate court correctly determined that 1993 Amended Agreement rendered the Family Agreement enforceable, since there was no evidence that the Family Agreement was revoked during the deceased husband's lifetime, and thus, the First Amended Trust was the controlling trust. The Family Agreement was enforceable because, under Ohio law it was enforceable upon execution since it was executed in accordance with the statute and under Florida law, the 1993 Amended Agreement validated it. Giffin v. Mull, 2015-Ohio-5440, 56 N.E.3d 270, 2015 Ohio App. LEXIS 5249 (Ohio Ct. App., Belmont County 2015).

**Evidence**

Lack of evidence of a written instrument transferring title or demonstrating the decedent's intent to transfer title barred the son's claim in probate court that the property was transferred to him via oral contract. Poling v. Poling, 2003-Ohio-5601, 2003 Ohio App. LEXIS 4988 (Ohio Ct. App., Hocking County 2003).

In an action for specific performance of an alleged contract to make mutual and irrevocable wills leaving all property to the plaintiff, testimony concerning conversations had by the witnesses with plaintiff's stepmother shortly after the death of plaintiff's father is inadmissible under the provisions of this section: McGlone v. Gompert, 112 F. Supp. 840, 52 Ohio Op. 77, 67 Ohio Law Abs. 76, 1953 U.S. Dist. LEXIS 2859 (D. Ohio 1953).

**Exceptions not applicable**

Under R.C. 2107.04, an agreement to make a will or to make a devise or bequest by will is not enforceable under any circumstances unless it is in writing. Thus, the doctrine of part performance and the "family exception doctrine" do not apply to R.C. 2107.04, and the trial court properly granted summary judgment against a married couple who claimed that the husband's mother had orally promised to make a will in their favor. Erwin v. Wanda E., 2013-Ohio-952, 2013 Ohio App. LEXIS 833 (Ohio Ct. App., Scioto County 2013).

**Mutual wills**

The mere fact that wills are executed concurrently, with full knowledge of their contents on the part of the testators, will not be sufficient to imply a contract to make mutual wills: McGlone v. Gompert, 112 F. Supp. 840, 52 Ohio Op. 77, 67 Ohio Law Abs. 76, 1953 U.S. Dist. LEXIS 2859 (D. Ohio 1953).

**Oral promise**

Trial court did not err by granting summary judgment for the executor of the stepmother's estate because the oral promise to create a will was unenforceable. Although the stepchildren granted the stepmother the consideration she requested by refraining from contesting their father's will, they were never aware of the definite terms in the offer or the promise which they were accepting, and they were uncertain as to how the stepmother intended to accomplish the distribution; their testimony demonstrated that they did not expect the stepmother to distribute their shares of her and their father's estate until after the stepmother died. Lapoint v. Templeton, 2008-Ohio-1792, 2008 Ohio App. LEXIS 1515 (Ohio Ct. App., Fulton County 2008).

**Partial performance**

The doctrine of partial performance may be applied in an action in equity to enforce the provisions of an oral contract to devise real estate by will, notwithstanding GC § 8621 (R.C. 1335.05) and this section: Emley v. Selepchak, 76 Ohio App. 257, 31 Ohio Op. 558, 63 N.E.2d 919, 1945 Ohio App. LEXIS 588 (Ohio Ct. App., Medina County 1945).

When an interest in a business is sold to two persons, by agreement in writing, and one of purchasers enters into a contemporaneous oral agreement to leave real estate to vendors by will, completed transfer of the business with payment of specified amount constitutes such part performance of contract as whole as takes the case out of both general statute of frauds, GC § 8621, and specific statute of frauds, this section: Ayres v. Cook, 140 Ohio St. 281, 23 Ohio Op. 491, 43 N.E.2d 287, 1942 Ohio LEXIS 443 (Ohio 1942), overruled, Sherman v. Johnson, 159 Ohio St. 209, 50 Ohio Op. 257, 112 N.E.2d 326, 1953 Ohio LEXIS 564 (Ohio 1953).

**Personal services as consideration**

A suit upon a contract to devise and bequeath all of an estate in consideration for personal services, which asks that the executor be ordered to pay over the residue of the personal property, and the heirs be ordered to convey the realty, is a suit for specific performance: Foltz v. Boone, 107 Ohio St. 562, 140 N.E. 761, 1 Ohio Law Abs. 421, 1 Ohio Law Abs. 864, 1923 Ohio LEXIS 254 (Ohio 1923).

The measure of damages for breach of a contract to make provision by will, without specifying the kind of property or amount of the money, is the value of services rendered under such contract: Schulte v. Hagemeyer, 16 Ohio App. 1 (1922), motion to certify record overruled, 20 Ohio L. 147.].

**Priority of agreement**

An agreement to make a will takes priority over any other later disposition of property made during the lifetime of any of the parties to the agreement: Fitch v. Oesch, 30 Ohio Misc. 15, 59 Ohio Op. 2d 16, 281 N.E.2d 206, 1971 Ohio Misc. LEXIS 201 (Ohio P. Ct. 1971).

**Probating of will**

Admitting a will to probate does not constitute a ruling by the probate court on the validity of the contents of the will and thus is not res judicata as to a subsequent action alleging breach of contract to make a will: Georgekopoulos v. Vasilopoulos, 26 Ohio App. 3d 43, 498 N.E.2d 165, 1984 Ohio App. LEXIS 12705 (Ohio Ct. App., Summit County 1984).

**Remedies for violation of agreement**

It is not the duty of the administrator of the estate to recover nonprobate assets which were disposed of in violation of an agreement to make a will, but the right of action is left with those parties who might be injured by not receiving their full amount under the agreement and the will: Fitch v. Oesch, 30 Ohio Misc. 15, 59 Ohio Op. 2d 16, 281 N.E.2d 206, 1971 Ohio Misc. LEXIS 201 (Ohio P. Ct. 1971).

**Statute of frauds**

Trial court did not err in dismissing appellant's cause of action for breach of contract to make a will as the alleged contract was not in writing, as required by R.C. 2107.04. Section 2107.04 was not the Statute of Frauds, and an agreement to make a will was not enforceable under any circumstances unless a written agreement existed. Hammond v. Perry, 2013-Ohio-3683, 2013 Ohio App. LEXIS 3806 (Ohio Ct. App., Hocking County 2013).

Where a decedent died in 1990 and left a will that devised certain properties to his widow, where the widow's attorney advised counsel for the decedent's children that she would devise the properties to them in her will if they did not challenge the decedent's will, and where the widow sold the property to third parties in 2008, summary judgment was properly granted in favor of the widow in the children's breach of contract action against her because there was no signed writing and no meeting of the minds; the correspondence between the parties' attorneys evidenced a lack of understanding as to the precise properties involved, and although the attorneys planned to meet to resolve the discrepancies, they failed to do so, and the issue was never resolved. Further, the initial writing of the stepmother's attorney was insufficient under R.C. 2107.04, which required that the writing be witnessed by two or more competent witnesses who heard the stepmother acknowledge that the writing was signed at her direction, and R.C. 1335.05 required that contracts for the transfer of real estate must be in writing Johannsen v. Ward, 2010-Ohio-4203, 2010 Ohio App. LEXIS 3574 (Ohio Ct. App., Huron County 2010).

An oral promise to convey realty and a business may be unenforceable under R.C. 1335.04 even if it is not deemed invalid under R.C. 2107.04: Brannan v. Fowler, 100 Ohio App. 3d 577, 654 N.E.2d 434, 1995 Ohio App. LEXIS 539 (Ohio Ct. App., Scioto County 1995).

### RESEARCH REFERENCES AND PRACTICE AIDS

**Comparative Legislation**

Contract to make will:
CA—Cal Prob Code § 21700
FL—Fla. Stat. § 732.701
IL—735 Ill. Comp. Stat. § 5/13-221
KY—KRS § 394.540
MI—MCLS § 700.2514
NY—NY CLS EPTL § 13-2.1

## § 2107.05 Incorporation by reference.

(A) An existing document, book, record, or memorandum may be incorporated in a will by reference, if referred to as being in existence at the time the will is executed. That document, book, record, or memorandum shall be deposited in the probate court when the will is probated or within thirty days after the will is probated, unless the court grants an extension of time for good cause shown. A copy may be substituted for the original document, book, record, or memorandum if the copy is certified to be correct by a person authorized to take acknowledgments.

(B) Notwithstanding division (A) of this section, if a will incorporates a trust instrument only in the event that a bequest or devise to the trust is ineffective, the trust instrument shall be deposited in the probate court not later than thirty days after the final determination that such bequest or devise is ineffective.

(C) If a testator intends to incorporate a trust instrument in a will, the testator's will shall manifest that intent through the use of the term "incorporate," "made a part of," or similar language. In the absence of such clear and express intent, a trust instrument shall not be incorporated into or made a part of the will. Any language in the testator's will that only identifies a trust shall not be sufficient to manifest an intent to incorporate that trust instrument by reference in the will.

(D) The amendment of this section by adding divisions (B) and (C) applies, and shall be construed as applying, to the wills of testators who die on or after the effective date of this amendment.

**HISTORY:**

GC § 10504-4; 114 v 320(346); Bureau of Code Revision. Eff 10-1-53; 2011 SB 124, § 1, eff. Jan. 13, 2012; 2018 hb595, § 1, effective March 22, 2019.

**Editor's Notes**

Acts 2011, SB 124, § 3 provides: "The provisions of this act that relate to the estates of decedents apply to the estates of decedents who die on or after the effective date of this act."

**Amendment Notes**

The 2018 amendment by HB 595, redesignated the former section as (A); and added (B) through (D).

The 2011 amendment deleted "on deeds" from the end of the last sentence; and made stylistic changes.

### NOTES TO DECISIONS

Analysis



**Generally**

Probate court properly granted a will proponent's motion to release a small estate from administration pursuant to R.C. 2113.03, and it also properly denied the will opponent's request to have the decedent's trust agreement admitted to the court in order to review it with the will, as the probate court determined that the trust had not been incorporated into the will pursuant to R.C. 2107.05, and further, there was no showing that the estate assets were beyond the statutory $35,000 limit or that the value of the assets of the estate had been misrepresented. In support of the request to release the estate administration, the will proponent had submitted a list of assets that did not exceed $19,000, and the opponent did not contest that figure or show other assets that were allegedly part of the estate. In re Estate of Marsico, 2006-Ohio-4413, 2006 Ohio App. LEXIS 4341 (Ohio Ct. App., Lorain County 2006).

In order to incorporate a document in a will, the will must refer to the document so as to show that it is in existence, it must identify it, and must show testator's intention to incorporate it; the document must in fact be in existence at the time of execution of the will, and it must correspond to the description: Miller v. Mackenzie, 31 Ohio Dec. 497, 1920 Ohio Misc. LEXIS 24 (Ohio C.P. 1920).

**Contract to make will**

Failure to deposit a contract to make a will within 30 days of the date the will was probated does not require a finding that the document was not properly incorporated into the will: Winkle v. United States, 381 F. Supp. 536, 1974 U.S. Dist. LEXIS 9479 (S.D. Ohio 1974).

**Deposit with probate court**

Although Trust and Amendment were not deposited with the probate court within the 30 days following the probate of the 2013 Will, there was evidence that appellants' had notice of the existence of the 2013 Trust and Amendment at least 23 days before the running of the statute of limitations for contesting the Will. The probate court did not err in finding that the purpose of the deposit requirement had been satisfied. Gehrke v. Senkiw, 2016-Ohio-2657, 63 N.E.3d 773, 2016 Ohio App. LEXIS 1517 (Ohio Ct. App., Montgomery County 2016).

A provision of a will incorporating an extrinsic writing into the will, pursuant to R.C. 2107.05, has no effect unless such extrinsic writing is deposited with the probate court within thirty days after the will is probated, unless the court grants an extension of time for good cause shown: Hirsch v. Hirsch, 32 Ohio App. 2d 200, 61 Ohio Op. 2d 212, 289 N.E.2d 386, 1972 Ohio App. LEXIS 373 (Ohio Ct. App., Franklin County 1972).

**Requirements not met**

Trial court did not err by finding that a will contest action was barred because a church did not come within the exception granted under R.C. 2107.71(B) to the bar arising from a 1992 final judgment in a testator's will validation proceeding. The requirements of R.C. 2107.05 were not met; even if they were, a declaration of trust did not operate to give a church the status of a beneficiary under the will. Hayes Mem. United Methodist Church v. Artz, 2011-Ohio-3847, 2011 Ohio App. LEXIS 3257 (Ohio Ct. App., Sandusky County 2011).

**Trusts**

Because the probate court did not err in concluding that Item II of the 2013 Will incorporated the 2013 Trust and Amendment into the will by reference, it did not err in holding that the nephew and his sisters could not contest the trust without also challenging the will. Gehrke v. Senkiw, 2016-Ohio-2657, 63 N.E.3d 773, 2016 Ohio App. LEXIS 1517 (Ohio Ct. App., Montgomery County 2016).

Provision in the will demonstrated a clear intent that the decedent's property go to the trustee of the inter vivos trust, and it could not be construed as intending to create a testamentary trust. Gehrke v. Senkiw, 2016-Ohio-2657, 63 N.E.3d 773, 2016 Ohio App. LEXIS 1517 (Ohio Ct. App., Montgomery County 2016).

Though an unfunded "pour over" trust is invalid under R.C. 2107.63, such a trust may be upheld as a document incorporated by reference into the will pursuant to R.C. 2107.05: Hageman v. Cleveland Trust Co., 45 Ohio St. 2d 178, 74 Ohio Op. 2d 295, 343 N.E.2d 121, 1976 Ohio LEXIS 556 (Ohio 1976).

A will which contains a provision attempting to "pour over" assets into an inter vivos trust which was not validly created, followed by language expressing that it was not the testator's intention to incorporate such trust agreement "as a probate trust" unless necessary to avoid his intestacy is thereby effective to incorporate such trust agreement by reference under this section: Knowles v. Knowles, 4 Ohio Misc. 153, 33 Ohio Op. 2d 218, 212 N.E.2d 88, 1965 Ohio Misc. LEXIS 313 (Ohio P. Ct. 1965).

An existing revocable and amendable living trust agreement, deed or settlement may be incorporated by reference in a will under this section: Bolles v. Toledo Trust Co., 144 Ohio St. 195, 29 Ohio Op. 376, 58 N.E.2d 381 (1944), overruled in part in Smyth v. Cleveland Trust Co., 172 Ohio St. 489, 18 Ohio Op. 2d 42, 179 N.E.2d 60].

Incorporated trust agreement and will must be read together: Shawan v. City Bank Farmers Trust Co., 6 Ohio Op. 309, 21 Ohio Law Abs. 432, 1936 Ohio Misc. LEXIS 1168 (Ohio P. Ct. 1936).

**Wills**

Probate court properly granted a will proponent's motion to release a small estate from administration pursuant to R.C. 2113.03, and it also properly denied the will opponent's request to have the decedent's trust agreement admitted to the court in order to review it with the will, as the probate court determined that the trust had not been incorporated into the will pursuant to R.C. 2107.05, and further, there was no showing that the estate assets were beyond the statutory $ 35,000 limit or that the value of the assets of the estate had been misrepresented; in support of the request to release the estate administration, the will proponent had submitted a list of assets that did not exceed $ 19,000, and the opponent did not contest that figure or show other assets that were allegedly part of the estate. In re Estate of Marsico, 2006-Ohio-4413, 2006 Ohio App. LEXIS 4341 (Ohio Ct. App., Lorain County 2006).



### RESEARCH REFERENCES AND PRACTICE AIDS

**Practice Manuals and Treatises**

Anderson's The Simple Will in Ohio § 2.3 In a Letter

Anderson's The Simple Will in Ohio § 5.1 Incorporation by Reference

Anderson's Ohio Probate Practice and Procedure Form 18.01 Bequest of personal property-letter incorporated by reference

**Practice Guides**

Anderson's Ohio Probate Practice and Procedure § 18.03 General rules of construction

Anderson's Ohio Probate Practice and Procedure § 48.02 Revocable inter vivos trusts

## § 2107.06 Age requirement for witnessing will.

No person under eighteen years of age shall witness a will executed pursuant to section 2107.03 of the Revised Code or an agreement to make a will or to make a devise or bequest by will pursuant to section 2107.04 of the Revised Code.

**HISTORY:**

149 v H 345. Eff 7-23-2002.

### RESEARCH REFERENCES AND PRACTICE AIDS

**Practice Guides**

Anderson's Ohio Probate Practice and Procedure § 9.03 Proper execution of will

# DEPOSIT

## § 2107.07 Deposit of will.

A will may be deposited by the testator, or by some person for the testator, in the office of the judge of the probate court in the county in which the testator lives, before or after the death of the testator, and if deposited after the death of the testator, with or without applying for its probate. Upon the payment of the fee of twenty-five dollars to the court, the judge shall receive, keep, and give a certificate of deposit for the will. That will shall be safely kept until delivered or disposed of as provided by section 2107.08 of the Revised Code. If the will is not delivered or disposed of as provided in that section within one hundred years after the date the will was deposited, the judge may dispose of the will in any manner the judge considers feasible. The judge shall retain an electronic copy of the will prior to its disposal after one hundred years under this section.

Every will that is so deposited shall be enclosed in a sealed envelope that shall be indorsed with the name of the testator. The judge shall indorse on the envelope the date of delivery and the person by whom the will was delivered. The envelope may be indorsed with the name of a person to whom it is to be delivered after the death of the testator. The will shall not be opened or read until delivered to a person entitled to receive it, until the testator files a complaint in the probate court for a declaratory judgment of the validity of the will pursuant to section 5817.02 of the Revised Code, or until otherwise disposed of as provided in section 2107.08 of the Revised Code. Subject to section 2107.08 of the Revised Code, the deposited will shall not be a public record until the time that an application is filed to probate it.

**HISTORY:**

GC §§ 10504-6, 10504-7; 114 v 320(346, 347); Bureau of Code Revision, 10-1-53; 137 v H 505. Eff 1-1-79; 2011 SB 124, § 1, eff. Jan. 13, 2012; 2016 hb432, § 1, effective April 6, 2017; 2018 hb595, § 1, effective March 22, 2019.



**Editor's Notes**

Acts 2011, SB 124, § 3 provides: "The provisions of this act that relate to the estates of decedents apply to the estates of decedents who die on or after the effective date of this act."

**Amendment Notes**

The 2018 amendment by HB 595, substituted "section 5817.02" for "section 2107.081" in the second to the last sentence of the second paragraph.

The 2016 amendment by HB 432, in the first paragraph, inserted "before or after the death of the testator, and if deposited after the death of the testator, with or without applying for its probate" in the first sentence, added the second and the second to the last sentences, and rewrote the last sentence, which formerly read: "The judge, on being paid the fee of five dollars, shall receive, keep, and give a certificate of deposit for the will"; and added the last sentence of the second paragraph.

The 2011 amendment, in the first paragraph, substituted "testator" for "maker" twice in the first sentence and substituted "five dollars" for "one dollar" in the last sentence; in the second paragraph, substituted "envelope" for "wrapper" in the first and third sentences, inserted "on the envelope" in the second sentence, and substituted "testator files a complaint in" for "maker petitions" in the last sentence; and made stylistic changes.

**NOTES TO DECISIONS**

Analysis

Expectancy of inheritance
Prior law

**Expectancy of inheritance**

A probate court lacks jurisdiction over a claim for intentional interference with expectancy of inheritance. Such a claim may not be pursued if adequate relief is available through probate procedures: Roll v. Edwards, 2004-Ohio-767, 156 Ohio App. 3d 227, 805 N.E.2d 162, 2004 Ohio App. LEXIS 719 (Ohio Ct. App., Ross County 2004).

**Prior law**

There being no statutory provisions governing the deposit of deeds in escrow with a probate judge, the deposit of a deed in escrow can not be received by the probate judge in his official capacity, and in the absence of such statutory provision there is no implied reservation in the person depositing the deeds in escrow with the probate judge to recall the same: Gordon v. Bartlett, 62 Ohio App. 295, 16 Ohio Op. 13, 23 N.E.2d 964, 28 Ohio Law Abs. 161, 1938 Ohio App. LEXIS 319 (Ohio Ct. App., Hardin County 1938).

**RESEARCH REFERENCES AND PRACTICE AIDS**

**Cross-References to Related Sections**

Delivery of will, RC § 2107.08.

**Ohio Rules**

Declaratory judgment, CivR 57.
Wills, SupR 59.

**Comparative Legislation**

Deposit of wills:
CA—Cal Prob Code § 8200
KY—KRS § 394.110
MI—MCLS § 700.2515
NY—NY CLS SCPA § 2507

**Practice Manuals and Treatises**

Anderson's Ohio Probate Practice and Procedure Form 8.01 Certificate of deposit of will

Anderson's Ohio Probate Practice and Procedure Form 8.02 Endorsement on wrapper

Anderson's Ohio Probate Practice and Procedure Outline No. § 15 Appointment of master commissioner, report, etc.

Anderson's Ohio Probate Practice and Procedure Checklist Checklist for the attorney for a personal representative

**Practice Guides**

Anderson's Ohio Probate Practice and Procedure § 8.05 Location of the will: custody of the Probate Court

Anderson's Ohio Probate Practice and Procedure § 9.09 Application to admit will to probate

**Practice Forms**

Certificate of Deposit of Will in Probate Court 1, 11 OH Forms of Pleading & Practice — Probate Form 4:1

## § 2107.08 Delivery of deposited will.

During the lifetime of a testator, the testator's will, deposited according to section 2107.07 of the Revised Code, shall be delivered only to the testator, to some person authorized by the testator by a written order, or to a probate court for a determination of its validity when the testator so requests. After the testator's death, the will shall be delivered to the person named in the indorsement on the envelope of the will, if there is a person named who demands it. If the testator has filed a complaint in the probate court for a judgment declaring the validity of the will pursuant to section 5817.02 of the Revised Code and a judgment is rendered pursuant to division (A)(1) of section 5817.10 of the Revised Code declaring the will valid, the judge of the court who rendered the judgment shall deliver the will to the proper probate court as determined under section 2107.11 of the Revised Code, upon the death of the testator, for probate.

If no person named in the indorsement demands the will and it is not one that has been declared valid pursuant to division (A)(1) of section 5817.10 of the Revised Code, it shall be publicly opened in the probate court within one month after notice of the testator's death and retained in the office of the probate judge until offered for probate. If the jurisdiction belongs to any other probate court, the will shall be delivered to the person entitled to its custody, to be presented for probate in the other court. If the probate judge who opens the will has jurisdiction of it, the probate judge immediately shall give notice of its existence to the executor named in the will or, if any, to the persons holding a power to nominate an executor as described in section 2107.65 of the Revised Code, or, if it is the case, to the executor named in the will and to the persons holding a power to nominate a coexecutor as described in that section. If no executor is named and no persons hold a power to nominate an executor as described in that section, the probate judge shall give notice to other persons immediately interested.

**HISTORY:**

GC §§ 10504-8, 10504-9; 114 v 320(347); Bureau of Code Revision, 10-1-53; 137 v H 505 (Eff 1-1-79); 140 v S 115 (Eff 10-14-83); 144 v H 427. Eff 10-8-92; 2011 SB 124, § 1, eff. Jan. 13, 2012; 2018 hb595, § 1, effective March 22, 2019.

**Editor's Notes**

Acts 2011, SB 124, § 3 provides: "The provisions of this act that relate to the estates of decedents apply to the estates of decedents who die on or after the effective date of this act."

**Amendment Notes**

The 2018 amendment by HB 595, substituted "section 5817.02 of the Revised Code and a judgment is rendered pursuant to division (A)(1) of section 5817.10 of the Revised Code declaring the will valid, the judge of the court who rendered the judgment shall deliver" for "section 2107.081 of the Revised Code and the court has rendered the judgment the probate judge with possession shall deliver" at the end of the first paragraph; and substituted "pursuant to division (A)(1) of section 5817.10" for "pursuant to section 2107.084" in the first sentence of the second paragraph.

The 2011 amendment, in the first paragraph, substituted "envelope" for "wrapper" in the second sentence and substituted "filed a complaint in" for "petitioned" in the last sentence; substituted "one month" for "two months" in the first sentence of the second paragraph; and made stylistic changes.

**RESEARCH REFERENCES AND PRACTICE AIDS**

**Cross-References to Related Sections**

Deposit of will, RC § 2107.07.

**Practice Manuals and Treatises**

Anderson's Ohio Probate Practice and Procedure Form 8.03 Order by testator for delivery of will

Anderson's Ohio Probate Practice and Procedure Form 8.04 Notice as to will on deposit

**Practice Guides**

Anderson's Ohio Probate Practice and Procedure § 8.05 Location of the will: custody of the Probate Court

Anderson's Ohio Probate Practice and Procedure § 9.05 When will is offered for probate

**Practice Forms**

Certificate of Deposit of Will in Probate Court 1, 11 OH Forms of Pleading & Practice — Probate Form 4:1

# CHAPTER 2108

# REVISED UNIFORM ANATOMICAL GIFT ACT

Section



**§ 2108.01 (UAGA 2) Definitions.**

As used in sections 2108.02 to 2108.35 of the Revised Code:

(A) "Adult" means an individual who is at least eighteen years of age.

(B) "Agent" means an individual who is either of the following:

(1) The principal's attorney in fact under a durable power of attorney for health care;

(2) Expressly authorized to make an anatomical gift on the principal's behalf by any other record signed by the principal.

(C) "Anatomical gift" means a donation of all or part of a human body to take effect after the donor's death for the purpose of transplantation, therapy, research, or education.

(D) "Decedent" means a deceased individual whose body or part is or may be the source of an anatomical gift. The term includes a stillborn infant and, subject to restrictions imposed by law other than sections 2108.01 to 2108.29 of the Revised Code, a fetus.

(E) "Disinterested witness" means a witness other than a spouse, child, parent, sibling, grandchild, grandparent, or guardian of the individual who makes an anatomical gift, or another adult who exhibited special care and concern for the individual. "Disinterested witness" does not include a person to which an anatomical gift could pass under section 2108.11 of the Revised Code.

(F) "Document of gift" means a donor card or other record used to make an anatomical gift. "Document of gift" includes a statement or symbol on a driver's license or identification card or in the donor registry.

(G) "Donor" means an individual whose body or part is the subject of an anatomical gift.

(H) "Donor registry" means a database that contains records of anatomical gifts and amendments to or revocations of anatomical gifts.

(I) "Driver's license" means a license or permit issued by the registrar of motor vehicles, or a deputy registrar, to operate a vehicle, whether or not conditions are attached to the license or permit and includes a driver's license, commercial driver's license, and a motorcycle operator's license or endorsement.

(J) "Durable power of attorney for health care" means a document created pursuant to sections 1337.11 to 1337.17 of the Revised Code.

(K) "Eye bank" means a person conducting operations in this state that is licensed, accredited, or regulated under federal or state law to engage in the recovery, screening, testing, processing, storage, or distribution of human eyes or portions of human eyes.

(L) "Guardian" means a person appointed by a court to make decisions regarding the support, care, education, health, or welfare of an individual. "Guardian" does not include a guardian ad litem.

(M) "Hospital" means a facility operated as a hospital under the laws of this or any other state or a facility operated as a hospital by the United States, this or any other state, or a subdivision of this or any other state.

(N) "Identification card" means an identification card issued by the registrar of motor vehicles or a deputy registrar.

(O) "Know" means to have actual knowledge.

(P) "Minor" means an individual who is under eighteen years of age.

(Q) "Organ procurement organization" means a person conducting operations in this state that is designated by the secretary of the United States department of health and human services as an organ procurement organization.

(R) "Parent" means a parent whose parental rights have not been terminated.

(S) "Part" means an organ, an eye, or tissue of a human being. "Part" does not include the whole body.

(T) "Person" means an individual, corporation, business trust, estate, trust, partnership, limited liability company, association, joint venture, public corporation, government or governmental subdivision, agency, or instrumentality, or any other legal or commercial entity.

(U) "Physician" means an individual authorized under Chapter 4731. of the Revised Code to practice medicine and surgery, osteopathic medicine and surgery, or podiatric medicine and surgery, or an individual authorized under the laws of any other state to practice medicine and surgery, osteopathic medicine and surgery, or podiatric medicine and surgery.

(V) "Procurement organization" means an eye bank, organ procurement organization, or tissue bank.

(W) "Prospective donor" means an individual who is dead or near death and has been determined by a procurement organization to have a part that could be medically suitable for transplantation, therapy, research, or education. "Prospective donor" does not include an individual who has made a refusal.

(X) "Reasonably available" means able to be contacted by a procurement organization without undue effort and willing and able to act in a timely manner consistent with existing medical criteria necessary for the making of an anatomical gift.

(Y) "Recipient" means an individual into whose body a decedent's part has been or is intended to be transplanted.

(Z) "Record" means information that is inscribed on a tangible medium or that is stored in an electronic or other medium and is retrievable in perceivable form.

(AA) "Refusal" means a record created under section 2108.07 of the Revised Code that expressly states an intent to bar other persons from making an anatomical gift of an individual's body or part.

(BB) "Sign" means to do either of the following with the present intent to authenticate or adopt a record:

(1) Execute or adopt a tangible symbol;

(2) Attach to or logically associate with the record an electronic symbol, sound, or process.

(CC) "Technician" means an individual determined to be qualified to remove or process parts by an appropriate organization that is licensed, accredited, or regulated under federal or state law. "Technician" includes an enucleator and an embalmer licensed pursuant to Chapter 4717. of the Revised Code who has completed a course in eye enucleation and has received a certificate of competency to that effect from a school of medicine recognized by the state medical board or from an eye bank that is a member of the eye bank association of America.

(DD) "Tissue" means a portion of the human body other than an organ or an eye. "Tissue" does not include blood unless the blood is donated for the purpose of research or education.

(EE) "Tissue bank" means a person conducting operations in this state that is licensed, accredited, or regulated under federal or state law to engage in the recovery, screening, testing, processing, storage, or distribution of tissue.

(FF) "Transplant hospital" means a hospital that furnishes organ transplants and other medical and surgical specialty services required for the care of transplant patients.

**HISTORY:**

152 v H 529, § 1, eff. 4-7-09.

**Official Comment**

Prefatory Note

As of January, 2006 there were over 92,000 individuals on the waiting list for organ transplantation, and the list keeps growing. It is estimated that approximately 5,000 individuals join the waiting list each year. *See* "Organ Donation: Opportunities for Action," Institute of Medicine of the National Academies (2006) www.nap.edu. Every hour another person in the United States dies because of the lack of an organ to provide a life saving organ transplant.

The lack of organs results from the lack of organ donors. For example, according to the Scientific Registry of Transplant Recipients in 2005 when there were about 90,000 people on the organ transplant waiting list, there were 13,091 individuals who died under the age of 70 using cardiac and brain death criteria and who were eligible to be organ donors. Of these, only 58% or 7,593 were actual donors who provided just over 23,000 organs. Living donors, primarily of kidneys, contributed about 6,800 more organs. Between them about 28,000 organs were transplanted into patients on the waiting list in 2005. (*See* www.optn.org).

The 2005 data on cadaveric organ donors suggests there were 5,498 individuals who died that year that could have been donors who weren't and that had they been organ donors there would have been approximately 17,000 additional organs potentially available for transplantation. (*See generally* , www.unos.org and www.ustransplant.org). However, these numbers to some extent are only estimates. First, they exclude individuals dying over the age of 70. Second, the data are self reported for eligible donors. Indicative of the absence of precision in this area is the report from the Institute of Medicine. According to the IOM, it has been estimated that donor-eligible deaths range between 10,500 and 16,800 per year. *See* Organ Donation: Opportunities for Action," Institute of Medicine of the National Academies (2006) at page 27. www.nap.edu Using the 2005 figures for deceased organ donors, this would suggest that between approximately 3,000 and 9,000 decedents could have been donors but weren't. Further, if one assumes an average of three solid organs recovered from each of them, there could be between 9,000 and 27,000 more organs that might have been available to transplant into individuals on the waiting list.

The data for eye and tissue is, however, more encouraging. On an annual basis there are approximately 50,000 eye donors and tissue donors and over 1,000,000 ocular and tissue transplants.

This Revised Uniform Anatomical Gift Act ("UAGA") is promulgated by the National Conference of Commissioners on Uniform State Laws ("NCCUSL") to address in part the critical organ shortage by providing additional ways for making organ, eye, and tissue donations. The original UAGA was promulgated by NCCUSL in 1968 and promptly enacted by all states. In 1987, the UAGA was revised and updated, but only 26 states adopted that version. Since 1987, many states have adopted non-uniform amendments to their anatomical gift acts. The law among the various states is no longer uniform and harmonious, and the diversity of law is an impediment to transplantation. Furthermore the federal government has been increasingly active in the organ transplant process.

Since 1987, there also have been substantial improvements in the technology and practice of organ, eye, and tissue transplantation and therapy. And, the need for organs, eyes, and tissue for research and education has increased to assure more successful transplantations and therapies. The improvements in technology and the growing needs of the research community have correspondingly increased the need for more donors.

This 2006 Revised UAGA is promulgated with the substantial and active participation of the major stakeholders representing donors, recipients, doctors, procurement organizations, regulators, and others affected. The Drafting Committee held four meetings with the stakeholders beginning on Friday morning and ending Sunday noon, reading and discussing each section of the drafts word by word (Chicago, December 3-5, 2004; Philadelphia, March 18-20, 2005; Chicago, November 2-4, 2005; and Detroit, April 21-23, 2006). The following stakeholders were actively engaged in the dialogue working for a consensus that could and should be adopted on a uniform basis to facilitate the anatomical gifts of human bodies and parts: American Bar Association, American Medical Association, American Lung Association, Association of Organ Procurement Organizations, American Association of Tissue Banks, Eye Bank Association of America, Health Law Institute and Center for Race and Bioethics, Life Alaska Donor Services, Musculoskeletal Transplant Foundation, National Association of Medical Examiners, National Disease Research Interchange, National Kidney Foundation, North American Transplant Coordinators Organization, RTI Donor Services, United Network for Organ Sharing (UNOS) and United States Department of Health & Human Services. In addition, there were many who contributed their views and comments by correspondence, including the Funeral Consumers Alliance, Inc. and Funeral Ethics Organization.

This [act] adheres to the significant policy determinations reflected in existing anatomical gift acts. First, the [act] is designed to encourage the making of anatomical gifts. Second, the [act] is designed to honor and respect the autonomy interest of individuals to make or not to make an anatomical gift of their body or parts. Third, the [act] preserves the current anatomical gift system founded upon altruism by requiring a positive affirmation of an intent to make a gift and prohibiting the sale and purchase of organs. This [act] includes a number of provisions, discussed below, that enhance these policies.

History of 1968 and 1987 Acts

The first reported medical transplant occurred in the third century. However, medical miracles flowing from transplants are truly a modern story beginning in the first decade of the twentieth century with the first successful transplant of a cornea. But, not until three events occurred in the twentieth century, in addition to the development of surgical techniques to effectuate a transplant, could transplants become a viable option to save and meaningfully extend lives.

The first event was the development in the late 1960s of the first set of neurological criteria for determining death. These criteria allowed persons to be declared dead upon the cessation of all brain activity. Ultimately these criteria, together with the historic measure of determining death by cessation of circulation and respiration, were incorporated into Section 1 of the Uniform Determination of Death Act providing that: "An individual who has sustained either (1) irreversible cessation of circulatory and respiratory function, or (2) irreversible cessation of all functions of the entire brain, including the brain stem, is dead."

The second event, following shortly after Dr. Christian Barnard's successful transplant of a heart in November, 1967, was this Conference's adoption of the first Uniform Anatomical Gift Act. In short order, every jurisdiction uniformly adopted the 1968 Act. The most significant contribution of the 1968 Act was to create a right to donate organs, eyes, and tissue. This right was not clearly recognized at common law. By creating this right, individuals became empowered to donate their parts or their loved one's parts to save or improve the lives of others.

The last event was the development of immunosuppressive drugs that prevented organ recipients from rejecting transplanted organs. This permitted many more successful organ transplants, thus contributing to the rapid growth in the demand for organs and the need for changes in the law to facilitate the making of anatomical gifts.

In 1987, a revised Uniform Anatomical Gift Act was promulgated to address changes in circumstances and in practice. Only 26 jurisdictions enacted the 1987 revision. Consequently, there is significant non-uniformity between states with the 1968 Act and those with the 1987 revisions. Neither of those acts comports with changes in federal law adopted subsequent to the 1987 Act relating to the role of hospitals and procurement organization in securing organs, eyes, and tissues for transplantation. And, both of them have impediments that are inconsistent with a policy to encourage donation.

The two previous anatomical gift acts, as well as this [act], adhere to an "opt in" principle as its default rule. Thus, an individual becomes a donor only if the donor or someone acting on the donor's behalf affirmatively makes an anatomical gift. The system universally adopted in this country is contrary to the system adopted in some countries, primarily in Europe, where an individual is deemed to be a donor unless the individual or another person acting on the individual's behalf "opts out." This other system is known as "presumed consent." While there are proponents of presumed consent who believe the concept of presumed consent could receive in the future a favorable reception in this country, the professional consensus appears to be not to replace the present opt-in principle at this time. *See* "Organ Donation: Opportunities in Action," Institute of Medicine of the National Academies (2006) at page 12.

Scope of the 2006 Revised Act

This [act] is limited in scope to donations from deceased donors as a result of gifts made before or after their deaths. Although recently there has been a significant increase in so-called "living donations," where a living donor immediately donates an organ (typically a kidney or a section of a liver) to a recipient, donations by living donors are not covered in this [act] because they raise distinct and difficult legal issues that are more appropriate for a separate act.

A majority of donors or prospective donors are candidates for donation of eyes or tissue, but only a small percentage of individuals die under circumstances that permit an anatomical gift of an organ. To procure an anatomical gift for transplantation, therapy, research, or education, a donor or prospective donor must be declared dead (see Uniform Determination of Death Act). In cases of potential organ donation, measures necessary to ensure the medical suitability of an organ for transplantation or therapy are administered to a patient who is dead or near death to determine if the patient could be a prospective donor.

Pursuant to federal law, when a donor or a patient who could be a prospective donor is dead or near death, a procurement organization, or a designee, must be notified. The organization begins to develop a medical and social history to determine whether the dying or deceased individual's body might be medically suitable for donation. If the body of a dying or deceased person might be medically suitable for donation, the procurement organization checks for evidence of a donation, if not otherwise known, and seeks consent to donation from authorized persons, if necessary. In the case of an organ, the organ procurement organization obtains from the Organ Procurement and Transplantation Network ("OPTN") a prioritized list of potential recipients from the national organ waiting list and takes the necessary steps to see that the organ finds its way to the appropriate recipient. If eye or tissue is donated, the appropriate procurement organization procures the eye or tissue and takes the necessary steps to screen, test, process, store, or distribute them as required for transplantation, therapy, research, or education. All must be done expeditiously.

Recent technological innovations have increased the types of organs that can be transplanted, the demand for organs, and the range of individuals who can donate or receive an organ, thereby increasing the number of organs available each year and the number of transplantations that occur each year. Nonetheless, the number of deaths for lack of available organs also has increased. While the Commissioners are under no illusion that any anatomical gift act can fully satisfy the need for organs, any change that could increase the supply of organs and thus save lies is an improvement.

Transplantation occurs across state boundaries and requires speed and efficiency if the organ is to be successfully transplanted into a recipient. There simply is no time for researching and conforming to variations of the laws among the states. Thus, uniformity of state law is highly desirable. Furthermore, the decision to be a donor is a highly personal decision of great generosity and deserves the highest respect from the law. Because current state anatomical gift laws are out of harmony with both federal procurement and allocation policies and do not fully respect the autonomy interests of donors, there is a need to harmonize state law with federal policy as well as to improve the manner in which anatomical gifts can be made and respected.

Summary of the Changes in the Revised Act

This revision retains the basic policy of the 1968 and 1987 anatomical gift acts by retaining and strengthening the "opt-in" system that honors the free choice of an individual to donate the individual's organ (a process known in the organ transplant community as "first person consent" or "donor designation"). This revision also preserves the right of other persons to make an anatomical gift of a decedent's organs if the decedent had not made a gift during life. And, it strengthens the right of an individual not to donate the individual's organs by signing a refusal that also bars others from making a gift of the individual's organs after the individual's death. This revision:

1. Honors the choice of an individual to be or not to be a donor and strengthens the language barring others from overriding a donor's decision to make an anatomical gift (Section 8);

2. Facilitates donations by expanding the list of those who may make an anatomical gift for another individual during that individual's lifetime to include health-care agents and, under certain circumstances, parents or guardians (Section 4);

3. Empowers a minor eligible under other law to apply for a driver's license to be a donor (Section 4);

4. Facilitates donations from a deceased individual who made no lifetime choice by adding to the list of persons who can make a gift of the deceased individual's body or parts the following persons: the person who was acting as the decedent's agent under a power of attorney for health care at the time of the decedent's death, the decedent's adult grandchildren, and an adult who exhibited special care and concern for the decedent (Section 9) and defines the meaning of "reasonably available" which is relevant to who can make an anatomical gift of a decedent's body or parts (Section 2(23));

5. Permits an anatomical gift by any member of a class where there is more than one person in the class so long as no objections by other class members are known and, if an objection is known, permits a majority of the members of the class who are reasonably available to make the gift without having to take account of a known objection by any class member who is not reasonably available (Section 9);

6. Creates numerous default rules for the interpretation of a document of gift that lacks specificity regarding either the persons to receive the gift or the purposes of the gift or both (Section 11);

7. Encourages and establishes standards for donor registries (Section 20);

8. Enables procurement organizations to gain access to documents of gifts in donor registries, medical records, and the records of a state motor vehicle department (Sections 14 and 20);

9. Resolves the tension between a health-care directive requesting the withholding or withdrawal of life support systems and anatomical gifts by permitting measures necessary to ensure the medical suitability of organs for intended transplantation or therapy to be administered (Sections 14 and 21);

10. Clarifies and expands the rules relating to cooperation and coordination between procurement organizations and coroners or medical examiners (Sections 22 and 23);

11. Recognizes anatomical gifts made under the laws of other jurisdictions (Section 19); and

12. Updates the [act] to allow for electronic records and signatures (Section 25).

In addition, Section 2 provides a number of new definitions that are used in the substantive provisions of the [act] to clarify and expand the opportunities for anatomical gifts. These include: adult, agent, custodian, disinterested witness, donee, donor registry, driver's license, eye bank, guardian, know, license, minor, organ procurement organization, parent, prospective donor, reasonably available, recipient, record, sign, tissue, tissue bank, and transplant hospital.

Section 4 authorizes individuals to make anatomical gifts of their bodies or parts. It also permits certain persons, other than donors, to make an anatomical gift on behalf of a donor during the donor's lifetime. The expanded list includes agents acting under a health-care power of attorney or other record, parents of unemancipated minors, and guardians. The section also recognizes that it is appropriate that minors who can apply for a driver's license be empowered to make anatomical gifts, but, under Section 8(g), either parent can revoke the gift if the minor dies under the age of 18.

Section 5 recognizes that, since the adoption of the previous versions of this [act], some states and many private organizations have created donor registries for the purpose of making anatomical gifts. Thus, in addition to evidencing a gift on a donor card or driver's license, this [act] allows for the making of anatomical gifts on donor registries. It also permits gifts to be made on state-issued identification cards and, under limited circumstances, to be made orally. Except for oral gifts, there is no witnessing requirement to make an anatomical gift.

Section 6 permits anatomical gifts to be amended or revoked by the execution of a later-executed record or by inconsistent documents of gifts. It also permits revocation by destruction of a document of gift and, under limited circumstances, permits oral revocations.

Section 7 permits an individual to sign a refusal that bars all other persons from making an anatomical gift of the individual's body or parts. A refusal generally can be made by a signed record, a will, or, under limited circumstances, orally. By permitting refusals, this [act] recognizes the autonomy interest of an individual either to be or not to be a donor. The section also recognizes that a refusal can be revoked.

Section 8 substantially strengthens the respect due a decision to make an anatomical gift. While the 1987 Act provided that a donor's anatomical gift was irrevocable (except by the donor), until quite recently it had been a common practice for procurement organizations to seek affirmation of the gift from the donor's family. This could result in unnecessary delays in the recovery of organs as well as a reversal of a donor's donation decision. Section 8 intentionally disempowers families from making or revoking anatomical gifts in contravention of a donor's wishes. Thus, under the strengthened language of this [act], if a donor had made an anatomical gift, there is no reason to seek consent from the donor's family as they have no right to give it legally. *See* Section 8(a). Of course, that would not bar, nor should it bar, a procurement organization from advising the donor's family of the donor's express wishes, but that conversation should focus more on what procedures will be followed to carry out the donor's wishes and on answering a family's questions about the process rather than on seeking approval of the donation. A limited exception applies if the donor is a minor at the time of death. In this case, either parent may amend or revoke the donor's anatomical gift. *See* Section 8(g).



Section 8 also recognizes that some decisions of a donor are inherently ambiguous, making it appropriate to adopt rules that favor the making of anatomical gifts. For example, a donor's revocation of a gift of a part is not to be construed as a refusal for others to make gifts of other parts. Likewise, a donor's gift of one part is not to be construed as a refusal that would bar others from making gifts of other parts absent an express, contrary intent.

Section 9 sets forth a prioritized list of classes of persons who can make an anatomical gift of a decedent's body or part if the decedent was neither a donor nor had signed a refusal. The list is more expansive than under previous versions of this [act]. It includes persons acting as agents at the decedent's death, adult grandchildren, and close friends.

Section 10 deals with the manner of making, amending, or revoking an anatomical gift following the decedent's death.

Section 11 deals with the passing of parts to named persons and more generally to eye banks, tissue banks, and organ procurement organizations. In part, the section is designed to harmonize this [act] with federal law, particularly with respect to organs donated for transplantation or therapy. The National Organ Transplant Act created the Organ Procurement and Transplantation Network ("OPTN") to facilitate the nationwide, equitable distribution of organs. Currently, United Network Organ Sharing ("UNOS") operates the OPTN under contract with the U.S. Department of Health and Human Services. When an organ donor dies, the donor's organs, barring the rare instance of a donation to a named individual, are recovered by the organ procurement organization for the service area in which the donor dies, as custodian of the organs, to be allocated by it either locally, regionally, or nationally in accordance with allocation policies established by the OPTN.

Section 11 includes two important improvements to previous versions of this [act]. First, it creates a priority for transplantation or therapy over research or education when an anatomical gift is made for all four purposes in a document of gift that fails to establish a priority.

Second, it specifies the person to whom a part passes when the document of gift merely expresses a "general intent" to be an "organ donor." This type of general designation is common on a driver's license. Under Section 11(f) a general statement of intent to be a donor results only in an anatomical gift of the donor's eyes, tissues, and organs (not the whole body) for transplantation or therapy. Since a general statement of intent to be an organ donor does not result in the making of an anatomical gift of the whole body, or any part, for research or education, more specific language is required to make such a gift.

Section 11(b) provides that, if an anatomical gift of the decedent's body or parts does not pass to a named person designated in a document of gift, it passes to a procurement organization typically for transplantation or therapy and possibly for research or education. Custody of a body or part that is the subject of an anatomical gift that cannot be used for any intended purpose passes to the "person under obligation to dispose of the body or parts." *See* Section 11(i).

Section 11(j) prohibits a person from accepting an anatomical gift if the person knows that the gift was not validly made. For this purpose, if a person knows that an anatomical gift was made on a document of gift, the person is deemed to know of a refusal to make a gift if the refusal is on the same document of gift.

Lastly, Section 11(k) clarifies that nothing in this [act] affects the allocation of organs for transplantation or therapy except to the extent there has been a gift to a named recipient. *See* Section 11(a)(2). The allocation of organs is administered exclusively under policies of the Organ Procurement and Transplantation Network.

In part, Section 14 has been redrafted to accord with controlling federal law when applicable. The federal rules require hospitals to notify an organ procurement organization or third party designated by the organ procurement organization of an individual whose death is imminent or who has died in the hospital to increase donation opportunity, and thus, transplantation. *See* 42 CFR § 482.45 (Medicare and Medicaid Programs: Conditions of Participation: Identification of Potential Organ, Tissue, and Eye Donors and Transplant Hospitals' Provision of Transplant-Related Data). The right of the procurement organization to inspect a patient's medical records in Section 14(e) does not violate HIPAA. *See* 45 CFR § 164.512(h) ("A covered entity may use or disclose protected health information to organ procurement organizations or other entities engaged in the procurement, banking, or transplantation of cadaveric organs, eyes, or tissue for the purpose of facilitating organ, eye, or tissue donation and transplantation"). Section 14(c) permits measures necessary to ensure the medical suitability of parts to be administered to a patient who is being evaluated to determine whether the patient has organs that are medically suitable for transplantation.

Section 17 and Section 18 deal with liability and immunity, respectively. (Section 16, dealing with the sale of parts, also provides for potential liabilities but is essentially the same as prior law). Section 17 includes a new provision establishing criminal sanctions for falsifying the making, amending, or revoking of an anatomical gift. Section 18, in substance, is the same as the 1987 Act providing immunity for "good faith" efforts to comply with this [act]. However, while the [act] contains no provisions relating to bad faith it is important to note that other laws of the state and federal governments may provide for further remedies and sanctions for bad faith, including those under regulatory rules, licensing requirements, Unfair and Deceptive Practices acts, and the common law.

Section 18(c) provides that in determining whether an individual has a right to make an anatomical gift under Section 9, a person, such as an organ procurement organization, may rely on the individual's representation regarding the individual's relationship to the donor or prospective donor.

Section 19 sets forth rules relating to the validity of documents of gift executed outside of the state while providing that any document of gift shall be interpreted in accordance with the laws of the state.

Section 20 authorizes an appropriate state agency to establish or contract for the establishment of a donor registry. It also provides that a registry can be established without a state contract. While this [act] does not specify in great detail what could or should be on a donor registry, it does mandate minimum requirements for all registries. First, the registry must provide a database that allows a donor or other person authorized to make an anatomical gift to include in the registry a statement or symbol that the donor has made a gift. Second, at or near the death of a donor or prospective donor, the registry must be accessible to all procurement organizations to obtain information relevant to determine whether the donor or prospective donor has made, amended, or revoked an anatomical gift. Lastly, the registry must be accessible on a twenty four hour, seven day a week basis.

Section 21 creates a default rule to adjust the tension that might exist between preserving organs to assure their medical suitability for transplantation or therapy and the expression of intent by a prospective donor in either a declaration or advance health-care directive not to have life prolonged by use of life support systems. The default rule under this [act] is that measures necessary to ensure the medical suitability of an organ for transplantation or therapy may not be withheld or withdrawn from the prospective donor. A prospective donor could expressly provide otherwise in the declaration or advance health-care directive.

Sections 22 and 23 represent a complete revision of the relationship of the [coroner] [medical examiner] to the anatomical gift process. Previous versions of this [act] permitted the [coroner] [medical examiner], under limited circumstances, to make anatomical gifts of the eyes of a decedent in the [coroner's] [medical examiner's] possession. In light of a series of Section 1983 lawsuits in which the [coroner's] [medical examiner's] actions were held to violate the property rights of surviving family members, *see, e.g.*, Brotherton v. Cleveland, 923 F.2d 477 (6th Cir. 1991), the authority of the [coroner] [medical examiner] to make anatomical gifts was deleted from this [act]. Parts, with the rare exception discussed in the comments to Section 9, can be recovered for the purpose of transplantation, therapy, research, or education from a decedent whose body is under the jurisdiction of the [coroner] [medical examiner] only if there was an anatomical gift of those parts under Section 5 or Section 10 of this [act].

This [act] includes a series of new provisions in Sections 22 and 23 relating to the relationship between the [coroner] [medical examiner] and procurement organizations. These provisions should encourage meaningful cooperation between these groups in hopes of increasing the number of anatomical gifts. Importantly, the section does not permit a [coroner] [medical examiner] to make an anatomical gift.

Uniform Anatomical Gift Act § 2.

"Agent" (paragraph (2)) is an individual who, under certain circumstances, can make an anatomical gift on the principal's behalf. An agent is empowered to make a gift if the agent is authorized by a power of attorney for health care to make health-care decisions on the principal's behalf. Thus, this [act], independent of any other law, empowers an agent acting under a power of attorney for health care to make an anatomical gift on the principal's behalf. It is unnecessary that states adopting this [act] amend their power of attorney for health care statutes to specifically empower agents to make anatomical gifts on behalf of principals. On the other hand, a state may choose to amend its health-care power of attorney statute in order that all of the agent's powers, including the power to make an anatomical gift, are located and visible in one place setting forth the powers of a health-care agent. Even though this [act] enables an agent acting under a power of attorney for health care to make an anatomical gift, if the principal prohibits the agent from making an anatomical gift of the principal's parts, the agent would have no authority to do so. See Section 4(2).

An agent also may be designated by a record, other than a power of attorney for health care, which authorizes the agent to make an anatomical gift. This would permit a principal to empower one individual to make health-care decisions and another individual to make anatomical gift decisions. In light of the definition of record, this authority could be expressed in a financial power of attorney.

"Anatomical gift" (paragraph (3)) means a gift that takes effect after the donor's death. Thus, an "anatomical gift" does not include a gift of an organ from a living donor to a living recipient.

"Decedent" (paragraph (4)) is defined as it was under prior versions of this [act] to include both stillborns and fetuses. A fetus, by definition, is not an embryo and nothing in this [act] allows for an anatomical gift of an embryo. Under other law fetuses can be used for research. *See* , 42 U.S. C. § 289g-1 & 289g-2; 42 CFR § 46.201.

By including stillborns and fetuses in the definition of "decedent," this [act] assures that stillborns and fetuses continue to receive the statutory protections conferred by this [act]; namely that their bodies or parts cannot be used for transplantation, therapy, research, or education without the same appropriate consents afforded other prospective donors. The definition of decedent does not broaden the scope of available transplant or research subjects or techniques. Although the needs of research and transplantation may have changed and expanded since the original 1968 Act was drafted, the scope of this [act] with regard to the definition of those who may be a source of an anatomical gift has neither changed nor expanded. By its terms, this [act] is silent on the issue of the use or donation of blastocytes and embryos, neither authorizing nor prohibiting their donation or use. Similarly, this [act] is silent on the nature of the research to be performed and provides no authorization or prohibition for somatic cell nuclear transfer or other specific research techniques. The complicated legal, scientific, moral, and ethical issues which may arise in the consideration of such research is, or should be, dealt with in separate statutes and policies. Thus, nothing in this [act] affects embryonic stem cell research. However, for jurisdictions that might prefer a more restrictive definition in the second sentence of the definition of "decedent," the following language is suggested: "The term does not include a blastocyst, embryo, or fetus that is the subject of an induced abortion."

"Disinterested witness" (paragraph (5)) means a witness other than those listed in the paragraph. Under Sections 5 and 6 anatomical gifts may be made or revoked. Under Section 7 a person may also make or revoke a refusal. In most circumstances these acts must be evidenced by a record. However, in limited circumstances they can be evidenced by oral statements to at least two adult witnesses. In those circumstances at least one of the witnesses must be a disinterested witness.

"Document of gift" (paragraph (6)) includes a donor card or any other record. It also includes a donor registry (paragraph (8)), a driver's license (paragraph (9)), and an identification card (paragraph (13)). While a donor card is a record, the reference to donor cards had been specifically retained because of the wide acceptance of that concept in our culture. Prior versions of this [act] also expressly referred to a will in the definition of a document of gift. The omission in this [act] of a will in the definition of a document of gift does not mean a will is not a document of gift. Rather, the "will" is subsumed in the word "record." Where there is a need in this [act] to specially treat wills as documents of gift, the will is singled out from other documents of gift.

A statement or symbol on a driver's license or donor registry is a document of gift; it is not merely an expression of intent to make a gift. Therefore, where there is such a statement or symbol, no other document of gift is necessary to evidence the making of an anatomical gift. Potential donors utilizing records other than a driver's license or a donor registry to make an anatomical gift should be strongly encouraged to make their gifts on a driver's license or donor registry, as gifts on a license or registry are more likely to be discovered when the donor is dead or near death.

Under Section 5(b) a donor can make an anatomical gift by authorizing the persons who maintains a donor registry to include on the registry a statement or symbol that the donor has made an anatomical gift. By adding a "donor registry" as a device for making an anatomical gift, this [act] recognizes the increasing use of donor registries to make anatomical gifts. The use of donor registries was not contemplated when the previous versions of this act were adopted. Today, however, they have assumed increased importance and in time may come to dominate how anatomical gifts are made. While the format of donor registries differ, generally they allow for the making of an anatomical gift of one or more parts and permit that gift to be made over the internet. No known donor registry provides for a refusal to make an anatomical gift, and this [act] does not require that they do so. The person who maintains a donor registry may, if it chooses, follow up an electronic registration by sending the donor a card to sign. However, that is not legally required by this [act] to make an effective anatomical gift.

"Donor" (paragraph (7)) means the individual whose body or part is the subject of an anatomical gift. Thus, an individual who signs a donor card or authorizes a symbol to be placed on a driver's license or donor registry evidencing an anatomical gift is a donor even though the part donated will not be removed from the donor until the donor dies. Likewise, if the family of a decedent who did not make an anatomical gift during life donates a part of the decedent, that decedent is a donor. Thus, "donor" refers to a living individual who made an anatomical gift or on whose behalf an anatomical gift was made to take effect in the future. The term also includes a decedent whose body or part is the subject of an anatomical gift. Anatomical gifts by a donor, as well as amendments, revocations, and refusals, may preclude the ability of others to make or revoke anatomical gifts on behalf of the donor. *See* Sections 7 and 8.

"Donor registry" (paragraph (8)) means a database containing records of anatomical gifts. The concept of the registry is new to this version of the anatomical gift act. Many states now have donor registries. Most of them are operated by private organizations, such as a procurement organization (paragraph (21)) while some are operated by the state. Section 20 of this [act] authorizes states to either establish or contract for the establishment of a donor registry. Donor registries, like driver's licenses, are very effective devices to record the making of an anatomical gift. The making of an anatomical gift by these devices assures that the evidence of a gift is always available, unlike the traditional donor card which can often be lost. Furthermore, they are easily accessible by procurement organizations.



"Driver's license" (paragraph (9)) includes both driver's licenses for which adults qualify, as well as licenses or permits issued to minors whether denoted "temporary permit," "permit," or "learner's permit," or something else. State laws vary widely on how young an individual under the age of 18 can be to obtain a driver's license. For example, it is not uncommon for a learner's permit to be issued to a 16-year-old individual. And, in some states licenses or permits can be issued to 14-year-olds for the purpose of driving only certain types of motorized vehicles, such as farm equipment. The definition of "driver's license" is broad enough to include all of these. Furthermore, under the definition, a condition, such as that the holder must be accompanied by an adult or the holder can drive only certain types of vehicles, does not prevent the license or permit from being considered a "driver's license" under this [act].

Under Section 4 if a minor is of an age that the minor would be entitled to obtain a driver's license, the minor can make an anatomical gift even though the minor does not actually apply for a license. Thus, a minor who could apply for a permit could make an anatomical gift by another means, such as a donor card or donor registry. Furthermore, if a minor acquires a license on which the minor has made an anatomical gift, the minor would not have to re-apply for a driver's license when attaining age 18 for the gift to be effective.

This [act], however, does not require that licenses provide space for a notation that the holder is a donor. That mandate, if it exists, is left to other law.

"Guardian" (paragraph (11)) means any person judicially appointed to make decisions for the support, care, education, health, or welfare of the ward. The intent is to exclude guardians ad litem or temporary guardians who would not have an expected long-term relationship to the ward.

"Identification card" (paragraph (13)) means an identification card issued by the [state department of motor vehicles]. Some individuals desire an identification card rather than a driver's license. These individuals could make an anatomical gift by authorizing a statement or symbol to be put on the card. While this [act] does not require that space be provided on the card for that purpose, it is anticipated that states will design these cards in ways to permit the making of an anatomical gift.

"Know" (paragraph (14)) means actual knowledge. Thus, it does not mean imputed knowledge. When imputed knowledge is relevant under any section of this [act], the section expressly so provides. *See, e.g.* , section 11(j).

"Parent" (paragraph (17)) means a parent whose parental rights have not been terminated. An adopting parent is a parent. On the other hand, a stepparent or judicially appointed guardian not otherwise by law designated as the child's parent is not a parent.

"Part" (paragraph (18)) means organ, eye, or tissue. This definition is shorter than the definition in the 1987 Act, which defined "part" as "organ, tissue, eye, bone, artery, blood, fluid, or other portion of a human body." Nonetheless, the definition is intended to be functionally the same because, according to the medical experts advising the drafting committee, all parts of the human body, including bones and fluids, are encompassed within the act's definition of part. Thus, blood, plasma, and sperm would be parts under this act because they are tissue. The definition excludes the whole body.

"Prospective donor" (paragraph (22)) means an individual who is dead or near death and has been determined to have one or more parts that could be medically suitable for transplantation, therapy, research, or education. The term includes an individual who made an anatomical gift during life and, therefore, is a donor. The term also includes a non-donor individual at or near the time of death with parts that are medically suitable for donation who could become a donor if the individual's family made an anatomical gift under Section 9. The term does not include an individual who made a refusal as the refusal bars other persons from making an anatomical gift on that individual's behalf.

"Reasonably available" (paragraph (23)) is defined in a manner similar to that in the Uniform Health-Care Decisions Act. A decision to make an anatomical gift, particularly of an organ, is extremely time sensitive. Life-saving organs may be forfeited if persons with a priority to make an anatomical gift under Section 9 cannot be located. Physical presence, however, is not required to be "reasonably available." An individual is "reasonably available" if the individual can be contacted without undue effort. Also, the concept assumes that an individual is willing to act in a timely manner to permit the successful recovery of organs. An individual who is unwilling to make a decision to either donate or refuse to donate in a timely manner is not considered to be "reasonably available."

"Tissue" (paragraph (30)), as defined in this act, includes bone. The definition excludes blood unless donated for research or education. Blood is not obtained from deceased persons for purposes of transplantation or therapy. Furthermore, blood banks are not treated as tissue banks under other law. Accordingly, it is appropriate to exclude blood from the operation of this [act] except when donated for purposes of research or education.





### RESEARCH REFERENCES AND PRACTICE AIDS

**Cross-References to Related Sections**

Disclosure of HIV test results or diagnosis, RC § 3701.243.

HIV test permitted on donated body parts, RC § 3701.242.

Superior rights of person to which part passes; acceptance or rejection of gift, RC § 2108.15.

**Comparative Legislation**

Uniform Anatomical Gift Act:

CA—Cal Health & Saf Code §§ 7150-7156.5
FL—Fla. Stat. §§ 765.510-765.522
IL—755 Ill. Comp. Stat. §§ 50/1-50/11
IN—Burns Ind. Code Ann. §§ 29-2-16-1—29-2-16-11
MI—MCLS §§ 333.10101-333.10109
NY—NY CLS Pub Health §§ 4300-4308
PA—20 P.S. §§ 8601-8607

**Practice Guides**

Anderson's Ohio Probate Practice and Procedure § 60.01 Who may make anatomical gift

## § 2108.02 Adoption of revised uniform act (2006).

Sections 2108.01 to 2108.29 of the Revised Code are enacted to adopt the Revised Uniform Anatomical Gift Act (2006), national conference of commissioners on uniform state laws.

**HISTORY:**

133 v H 51. Eff 11-6-69; 152 v H 529, § 1, eff. 4-7-09.

**Publisher's Note:**

This section was amended and renumbered from RC § 2108.09 by 152 v H 529, effective April 7, 2009.

**Amendment Notes**

152 v H 529, effective April 7, 2009, rewrote the section.

## § 2108.021 Repealed.

Repealed, 152 v H 529, § 2 [148 v H 283 (Eff 9-29-99); 148 v S 188. Eff 12-13-2000]. Eff 4-7-09.

**Editor's Notes**

This section concerned development of procurement protocol by hospitals.

## § 2108.022 Repealed.

Repealed, 148 v S 188, § 2 [148 v H 283]. Eff 12-13-2000.

**Editor's Notes**

This section concerned request to make anatomical gift.

## § 2108.03 (UAGA 3) Applicability.

Sections 2108.01 to 2108.29 of the Revised Code apply to an anatomical gift or amendment to, revocation of, or refusal to make an anatomical gift, whenever made.

**HISTORY:**

152 v H 529, § 1, eff. 4-7-09.

## § 2108.04 (UAGA 4) Who may make anatomical gift before donor's death.

Subject to section 2108.08 of the Revised Code, an anatomical gift of a donor's body or part may be made during the life of the donor for the purpose of transplantation, therapy, research, or education in the manner provided in section 2108.05 of the Revised Code by any of the following:

(A) The donor, if the donor is an adult or if the donor is a minor and either of the following applies:

(1) The donor is emancipated.

(2) The donor is authorized to apply for a temporary instruction permit issued under section 4507.05 of the Revised Code because the donor is at least fifteen years and six months of age.

(B) An agent of the donor, unless the durable power of attorney for health care or other record prohibits the agent from making an anatomical gift;

(C) A parent of the donor, if the donor is an unemancipated minor;

(D) The donor's guardian.

**HISTORY:**

152 v H 529, § 1, eff. 4-7-09.

**Official Comment**

Uniform Anatomical Gift Act § 4.

Structurally, this [act] includes within Sections 4 through 8 provisions that were included in Section 2 of the 1987 Act. Section 4 relates to who may make an anatomical gift before a donor dies, Section 5 to the manner in which an anatomical gift may be made, Section 6 to the amending and revoking of an anatomical gift, Section 7 to the refusal to make an anatomical gift, and Section 8 to the effect of gifts, amendments, and revocations on the ability of others to make an anatomical gift.

Like the predecessor acts, this [act] provides that an individual may make an anatomical gift of the individual's body or part if the individual is an adult. This [act], however, expands prior law in a number of ways.

In most states a minor, under limited circumstances, can apply for a driver's license. The minor might wish to be a donor. As a policy matter, if the minor is old enough to drive a vehicle the minor should be old enough to make an anatomical gift. Thus, this [act] provides that a minor who could obtain a driver's license is empowered to make an anatomical gift whether on a driver's license or other document of gift. On the other hand, if the minor donor dies under the age of 18, it seems appropriate that the minor's parents should be able to revoke the gift. *See* Section 8(g). Because the minor's parents cannot revoke the anatomical gift if the minor donor later dies over the age of 18, there is no necessity under this [act] for the minor donor to confirm that anatomical gift after reaching 18. Thus, in a state that provides that a license issued to a minor is good for five years and the minor applies for the license at age 17, the minor can make an anatomical gift on the driver's license and need not reaffirm the gift for another five years. Furthermore, once the minor reaches age 18, the minor's parents cannot revoke the gift.

Section 4 expands prior law in other important respects. It permits anatomical gifts by an emancipated minor. The act does not define "emancipated minor," although a common example would be a married minor. State laws vary regarding the definition of an emancipated minor. By not defining the phrase in this [act], the phrase is effectively defined by other law of the state.

Section 4 expressly empowers an anatomical gift to be made on behalf of an individual by that individual's agent or a parent, if that individual is an unemancipated minor, or by a guardian.

An anatomical gift by an agent, parent, or guardian remains in effect until such time as amended or revoked by an agent, parent, or guardian, or by the donor on whose behalf the gift was made. For example, if a parent makes an anatomical gift for a minor and the parent does not revoke that gift before the minor reaches age 18 or becomes emancipated, the anatomical gift remains in effect until such time as it is altered by the donor or by the donor's agent or guardian. While agents, parents, and guardians can make an anatomical gift, they can not sign a refusal under Section 7 on their principal's or ward's behalf. A refusal can only be made by that individual whose part or body might otherwise have been the subject of an anatomical gift.

As noted in the comments to the definitions, an agent acting under a power of attorney for health care is authorized merely by that designation to make an anatomical gift on the principal's behalf. If the principal does not wish to authorize the agent acting under a power of attorney for health care to make that decision, the power must include language to expressly negate that authority. *See* Section 4(2). Conversely, if the agent is acting under another record, such as a financial power of attorney, the agent would be empowered to make an anatomical gift only if that authority was expressly conferred in the record. *See* Section 2(2)(B).

Section 4 specifically delineates the four purposes for which an anatomical gift may be made, namely, transplantation, therapy, research or education. The terms "transplantation", "therapy", "research" and "education" are not defined in this [act]. Rather, they are defined by their common usage in the communities to which they apply. In general terms, transplantation refers to the removal and grafting of one individual's body part into the body of another individual. Research is a process of testing and observing, the goal of which is to obtain generalizable knowledge, while therapy involves the processing and use of a donated part to develop and provide amelioration or treatment for a disease or condition. Education posits the use of the whole body or parts to teach medical professionals and others about human anatomy and its characteristics.



## § 2108.05 Manner of making anatomical gift before donor's death [UAGA 5]. [Effective until October 1, 2022]

(A) A donor may make an anatomical gift by doing any of the following:

(1) Authorizing a statement or symbol to be imprinted on the donor's driver's license or identification card indicating that the donor has certified a willingness to make an anatomical gift;

(2) During a terminal illness or injury of the donor, communicating in any manner to a minimum of two adults, at least one of whom is a disinterested witness, that the donor intends to make an anatomical gift;

(3) Following the procedure in division (B) of this section.

(B) A donor or other person authorized to make an anatomical gift under section 2108.04 of the Revised Code may make a gift by a donor card or other record signed by the donor or other person making the gift or by authorizing that a statement or symbol indicating that the donor has certified a willingness to make an anatomical gift be included in a donor registry. If the donor or other person is physically unable to sign a record, the record may be signed by another individual at the direction of the donor or other person and shall do both of the following:

(1) Be witnessed by at least two adults, at least one of whom is a disinterested witness, who have signed at the request of the donor or the other person;

(2) State that it has been signed and witnessed as provided in division (B)(1) of this section.

(C) Once a donor has authorized a statement or symbol to be imprinted on the donor's driver's license or identification card indicating that the donor has certified a willingness to make an anatomical gift, the donor does not need to recertify the donor's willingness to make an anatomical gift upon renewal of the driver's license or identification card. The authorization shall remain in effect until the donor withdraws that authorization.

(D) Revocation, suspension, expiration, or cancellation of a driver's license or identification card upon which an anatomical gift is indicated does not invalidate the gift.

**HISTORY:**

152 v H 529, § 1, eff. 4-7-09; 2013 HB 59, § 101.01, eff. Sept. 29, 2013; 2021 hb7, § 1, effective August 17, 2021.

### Amendment Notes

The 2021 amendment by HB 7 deleted former (A)(2) and (A)(3), which read: "(2) Specifying in the donor's will an intent to make an anatomical gift; (3) Specifying an intent to make an anatomical gift in the donor's declaration as described in section 2133.16 of the Revised Code"; redesignated former (A)(4) and (A)(5) as (A)(2) and (A)(3); and deleted former (E), which read: "An anatomical gift made by will takes effect on the donor's death whether or not the will is probated. Invalidation of the will after the donor's death does not invalidate the gift."

The 2013 amendment inserted (C); and redesignated former (C) and (D) as (D) and (E).

**Official Comment**

Uniform Anatomical Gift Act § 5.

The execution formalities associated with the making of an anatomical gift generally remain the same as under the 1987 Act. However, in addition to the making of an anatomical gift by a donor card, will, or state-issued driver's license, an anatomical gift can also be made on a state-issued identification card or a donor registry.

Section 5(a) provides that a donor can make an anatomical gift by authorizing a statement or symbol to be imprinted on the donor's driver's license, in the donor's will, or during a terminal illness or injury, orally to at least two adult witnesses, at least one of whom is disinterested. Only a donor can make a gift under Section 5(a). A Section 5(a) gift cannot be made by an agent, parent, or guardian.

Under Section 5(a)(2) an anatomical gift can be made in a donor's will. The section is silent regarding who must sign the will. Statutes of Wills generally require wills to be signed by the testator, and under certain circumstances, permit wills to be signed by another individual acting on behalf of the testator at the testator's request and often in the testator's presence. *See* Uniform Probate Code 2-502. Thus, an anatomical gift can be made by the will of a donor whether the will is signed by a donor or a third party acting at the donor's request.

Typically an anatomical gift of a part for transplantation or therapy is not made by a will. In fact, donors are ill-advised to make an anatomical gift by will as the terms of the will may not be known in sufficient time to allow for successful recovery of the gifted parts. Individuals who make an anatomical gift of their parts in a will for transplantation or therapy should make their wishes known by other means as well. On the other hand, some individuals donate their bodies to medical science for research or education, and they may do so by a will. Subsection (d) provides that, if an anatomical gift is made by will, it takes effect at the donor's death. The gift is valid even though the will is not probated or is declared invalid. *See* Section 5(d).

Subsection (a)(3) permits an oral gift by a terminally ill or injured donor if the donor's communication is addressed to at least two adult witness, at least one of whom is a disinterested witness. This subsection is new to anatomical gift acts. The ability to make an oral gift parallels the ability to make oral revocations and refusals.

Section 5(b) permits an anatomical gift by a signed donor card or other record. The card or record can be signed by any person (donor, agent, parent, or guardian) authorized to make an anatomical gift under Section 4. If the person making the gift is physically unable to sign the card or record, the record can be signed by another individual acting at the direction of the donor or other person making the gift. In this case, the record must be witnessed by at least two adult witnesses, at least one of whom is a disinterested witness. Furthermore, the record must state that it was signed and witnessed at the request of the donor or other person.

A disinterested witness is a witness other than the spouse, child, parent, sibling, grandchild, grandparent, or guardian, of the individual who makes, amends, revokes, or refuses to make an anatomical gift, or another adult who exhibited special care and concern for that individual. A disinterested witness also does not include any person to whom an anatomical gift could pass under Section 11. *See* Section 2(5). For example, a terminally ill individual could make an anatomical gift by an oral communication to two unrelated neighbors or to one unrelated neighbor and one of the individual's adult children, but not to the individual's two adult children.

Section 5(b) also permits any person (donor, agent, parent, or guardian) authorized to make an anatomical gift under Section 4 to make that gift by authorizing that a statement or symbol indicating that the donor has made a gift be included on a donor registry. Donor registries were not contemplated by the prior versions of this [act]. Since the promulgation of those versions, numerous donor registries have been created under the auspices of states or private organizations. Over time donor registries may become the primary device by which anatomical gifts are made by donors. *See* Section 20 (creation of donor registry).

A decision was made in drafting this [act] not to include a specific form in the statute for the making of an anatomical gift. Rather, the drafting committee concluded that suggested forms consistent with this [act] be included in these comments. Three such forms follow:

DONOR CARD

I wish to donate my organs, eyes, and tissue. I give:

Any needed organs, ONLY the following organs,

eyes, and tissue eyes, and tissue:

..............................................................................

Date: .......... Donor's Signature ..........

DONOR CARD

I wish to donate my organs, eyes, and tissue. I wish to give (complete either Section A, B, or C):

Subject of Gift: Purpose of Gift:

Transplantation or therapy Research or Education

Both

Yes No

Section A

ALL of my organs, eyes, and tissue

Section B

My Organs

My Eyes

My Tissue
Section C
Special Instructions (If none of the above apply), I wish to give ONLY:
..........................................................................
Date: .......... Donor's Signature ..........

DONOR CARD

I give, upon my death, the following gifts for the purpose of ( *choose whichever applies* ): [ ] only transplantation and therapy, [ ] only research and education, [ ] transplantation, therapy, research, or education

For the purposes specified above, I give:
[ ] ALL needed organs, tissues, and eyes; or
(If you checked the box immediately above, you should not check specific boxes below).
[ ] Organs [ ] Tissues [ ] Eyes
If none of the above applies, I wish to give ONLY:
The following organs and tissues: ..........................................
Date: .......... Donor's Signature ..........





## § 2108.05 Manner of making anatomical gift before donor's death [UAGA 5]. [Effective October 1, 2022]

(A) A donor may make an anatomical gift by doing any of the following:

(1) Authorizing a statement or symbol to be imprinted on the donor's driver's license or identification card indicating that the donor has certified a willingness to make an anatomical gift;

(2) Specifying during an application for or renewal of a motor vehicle registration that the donor has certified a willingness to make an anatomical gift;

(3) During a terminal illness or injury of the donor, communicating in any manner to a minimum of two adults, at least one of whom is a disinterested witness, that the donor intends to make an anatomical gift;

(4) Following the procedure in division (B) of this section.

(B) A donor or other person authorized to make an anatomical gift under section 2108.04 of the Revised Code may make a gift by a donor card or other record signed by the donor or other person making the gift or by authorizing that a statement or symbol indicating that the donor has certified a willingness to make an anatomical gift be included in a donor registry. If the donor or other person is physically unable to sign a record, the record may be signed by another individual at the direction of the donor or other person and shall do both of the following:

(1) Be witnessed by at least two adults, at least one of whom is a disinterested witness, who have signed at the request of the donor or the other person;

(2) State that it has been signed and witnessed as provided in division (B)(1) of this section.

(C) Once a donor has certified a willingness to make an anatomical gift through either a symbol on the donor's driver's license or identification card or at the time of motor vehicle registration, the donor does not need to recertify the donor's willingness to make an anatomical gift upon renewal of the driver's license, identification card, or motor vehicle registration. The authorization shall remain in effect until the donor withdraws that authorization.

(D) Revocation, suspension, expiration, or cancellation of a driver's license or identification card upon which an anatomical gift is indicated does not invalidate the gift.

**HISTORY:**

152 v H 529, § 1, eff. 4-7-09; 2013 HB 59, § 101.01, eff. Sept. 29, 2013; 2021 hb7, § 1, effective August 17, 2021; 2021 hb21, § 1, effective October 1, 2022.

**Amendment Notes**

The 2021 amendment by HB 21 added (A)(2); redesignated former (A)(2) and (A)(3) as (A)(3) and (A)(4); and in the first sentence of (C), deleted "authorized a statement or symbol to be imprinted on the donor's driver's license or identification card indicating that the donor has" following "Once a donor has," added "through either a symbol on the donor's driver's license or identification card or at the time of motor vehicle registration" and substituted "license, identification card, or motor vehicle registration" for "license or identification card."

## § 2108.06 Amending or revoking anatomical gift before donor's death [UAGA 6].

(A) Subject to section 2108.08 of the Revised Code, an anatomical gift made under section 2108.04 of the Revised Code may be amended by any of the following means:

(1) By a record signed by the donor or other person authorized to make an anatomical gift under section 2108.04 of the Revised Code;

(2) Subject to division (C) of this section, by a record signed by another individual acting at the direction of the donor or other person authorized to make an anatomical gift under section 2108.04 of the Revised Code if the donor or other person is physically unable to sign;

(3) By a later-executed document of gift that amends a previous anatomical gift or portion of an anatomical gift, either expressly or by inconsistency;

(4) By any form of communication during a terminal illness or injury addressed to at least two adults;

(5) By a parent who is reasonably available, if the donor is an unemancipated minor who has died.

(B) Subject to section 2108.08 of the Revised Code, an anatomical gift made under section 2108.04 of the Revised Code may be revoked by any of the following means:

(1) By a record signed by the donor or other person authorized to make an anatomical gift under section 2108.04 of the Revised Code;

(2) Subject to division (C) of this section, by a record signed by another individual acting at the direction of the donor or other person authorized to make an anatomical gift under section 2108.04 of the Revised Code if the donor or other person is physically unable to sign;

(3) By a later-executed document of gift that revokes a previous anatomical gift or portion of an anatomical gift, either expressly or by inconsistency;

(4) By any form of communication during a terminal illness or injury addressed to at least two adults;

(5) By a parent who is reasonably available, if the donor is an unemancipated minor who has died;

(6) By the destruction or cancellation of the document of gift, or the portion of the document of gift, used to make the gift, with the intent to revoke the gift.

(C) A record signed pursuant to division (A)(2) or (B)(2) of this section shall do both of the following:

(1) Be witnessed by a minimum of two adults who have signed at the request of the donor or other person;

(2) State that it has been signed and witnessed as provided in division (C)(1) of this section.

**HISTORY:**

152 v H 529, § 1, eff. 4-7-09; 2021 hb7, § 1, effective August 17, 2021.

**Amendment Notes**

The 2021 amendment by HB 7 deleted former (A)(6), which read: "If made in a will, by the manner provided for amendment of wills or by any of the applicable means described in divisions (B)(1) to (5) of this section"; deleted former (B)(7), which read: "If made in a will, by the manner provided for revocation of wills or by any of the applicable means described in divisions (B)(1) to (6) of this section"; and made related changes.

**Official Comment**

Uniform Anatomical Gift Act § 6.

Section 6 largely mirrors the provisions in the prior acts. It applies to the amendment or revocation of an anatomical gift whether made by a donor or by another person acting on behalf of the donor.

Under Section 6(a)(1), an anatomical gift can be revoked or amended by a record signed by the donor or the other person authorized to make an anatomical gift under Section 4. If the donor or other person is physically unable to sign a record amending or revoking an anatomical gift, the record may be signed by another individual acting at the direction of the donor or other person so long as the record is witnessed by at least two adult witness, at least one of whom is a disinterested witness. In this case, the record must state that it was signed and witnessed at the request of the donor or other person.

Subsection (a)(2), borrowing from statutes dealing with the revocation of wills, contemplates revocations or amendments made by a later-executed document of gift either expressly or by inconsistency. For example, suppose a donor executes a will bequeathing her entire body to Medical School A for research or education. Later, the donor signs a document of gift donating a kidney for transplantation. Since the later-executed document of gift is only inconsistent with the prior document of gift to the extent of the donated kidney, the donor's kidney would, if medically suitable, pass to the appropriate procurement organization, and the donor's body without the kidney would pass to Medical School A. *See* Section 11.

A driver's license that makes no provision for the making of an anatomical gift is not a document of gift because a document of gift is defined to be a donor card or other record "used to make an anatomical gift." *See* Section 2(6). Therefore, a later-issued driver's license that is silent regarding the licensee's intent to make an anatomical gift would not be inconsistent with a prior driver's license on which the donor had made an anatomical gift. Thus, the gift on the prior license would still be effective. For donors using a driver's license to make an anatomical gift, however, it is wise to always make the gift on the most current license as motor vehicle departments may have expunged information on a previously issued license from their electronic databases.

There is no requirement under this [act] that documents of gift be dated. A "dating requirement" was purposely omitted to avoid invalidating documents of gift written without the advice of counsel that may not have included a date. That purposeful omission could result in some proof issues if a question arises whether one document of gift revokes another by inconsistency. There is little evidence to suggest that this would be a problem, but should it arise, the matter would have to be resolved by resort to any competent evidence. If the evidence is not available, a presumption should arise that the document of gift with the most comprehensive gift controls given the policy of this [act] to favor the making of anatomical gifts.

Under Section 6(c) an anatomical gift made by a document of gift also can be revoked by destruction of the document of gift if the destruction is done with the intent to revoke that gift. As a practical matter revocation by destruction is not possible for anatomical gifts made on a donor registry. A donor wishing to revoke anatomical gifts made on a donor registry should revise the registry. If an anatomical gift was evidenced by a written document that was destroyed inadvertently and cannot be found, there may be no effective Section 4 anatomical gift because no one may know of the anatomical gift. Inadvertent destruction of donor cards is common. A card may be lost when the donor decides to clean out a wallet or purse. Thus, donors are well advised to make their wishes known on documents of gift with greater permanency, such as a driver's license or a donor registry, in order to reduce the risk of inadvertent destruction.

The ability to revoke an anatomical gift is subject to the limitations in Section 8. For example, if a donor makes an anatomical gift of a kidney, all other persons are precluded from revoking that gift. Therefore, the donor's later-appointed guardian would not be empowered to revoke that anatomical gift under Section 6.

Under Section 6(d) an anatomical gift may also be amended or revoked by a donor with a terminal illness or injury by any form of communication that is addressed to at least two adult witnesses, at least one of whom must be a disinterested witness. If the donor cannot communicate orally, acceptable forms of communication, in addition to a record, could include a movement of the head or eye in response to specific questions.



## § 2108.07 Refusal to make anatomical gift; effect of refusal [UAGA 7].

(A) An individual may refuse to make an anatomical gift of the individual's body or part by doing any of the following:

(1) Indicating a refusal in a record signed by either of the following:

(a) The individual;

(b) Subject to division (B) of this section, another individual acting at the direction of the individual, if the individual is physically unable to sign.

(2) Indicating a refusal by any form of communication made by the individual during the individual's terminal illness or injury addressed to a minimum of two adults.

(B) A record signed pursuant to division (A)(1)(b) of this section shall do both of the following:

(1) Be witnessed by at least two adults who have signed at the request of the individual;

(2) State that it has been signed and witnessed as provided in division (B)(1) of this section.

(C) An individual who has made a refusal may amend or revoke the refusal by doing any of the following:

(1) Amending or revoking the refusal in the manner provided in division (A) of this section for making a refusal;

(2) Subsequently making an anatomical gift pursuant to section 2108.05 of the Revised Code that is inconsistent with the refusal;

(3) Destroying or canceling the record evidencing the refusal, or the portion of the record used to make the refusal, with the intent to revoke the refusal.

(D) Except as provided in division (E) of this section, in the absence of an express, contrary indication by the individual set forth in the refusal, an individual's unrevoked refusal to make an anatomical gift of the individual's body or part bars all other persons from making an anatomical gift of the individual's body or part.

(E) The parent of a deceased unemancipated minor who is reasonably available may revoke a refusal made by the minor.

**HISTORY:**

152 v H 529, § 1, eff. 4-7-09; 2021 hb7, § 1, effective August 17, 2021.

**Amendment Notes**

The 2021 amendment by HB 7 deleted former (A)(2), which read: "Indicating a refusal in the individual's will, whether or not the will is admitted to probate or invalidated after the individual's death"; and redesignated former (A)(3) as (A)(2).

**Official Comment**

Uniform Anatomical Gift Act § 7.

Section 7 honors the autonomy of an individual whose body or part might otherwise be the subject of an anatomical gift by empowering the individual to make a refusal. There is no age limitation for an individual to sign a refusal. An individual of any age can do so. (However, if a minor has made a refusal and dies under the age of 18, the refusal can be revoked by the minor's parents. *See* Section 8(h)).

A refusal can only be made by the individual whose parts are the subject of the refusal. Thus, an individual's agent, parent, or guardian cannot make a refusal for the individual under Section 7 even though the agent, parent, or guardian could have made a gift for the individual under Section 4.

Refusals typically are made by a signed record. If the individual who wants to sign a refusal cannot physically do so, the refusal can be signed by another individual acting at the request of the individual. If the refusal is signed by another individual acting at the request of the individual making the refusal, the refusal must be witnessed by at least two adults, at least one of whom is a disinterested witness. Furthermore, the record must state that it was signed and witnessed at the request of the individual. *See* Section 7(a)(1) and (b).

A refusal can also be made by the individual's will whether or not the will is admitted to probate or is later invalidated. Additionally, a refusal can be made by any form of communication by a terminally ill or injured individual addressed to at least two adults, at least one of whom is a disinterested witness. *See* Section 7(a)(3).

Subsection (c) provides for the amendment or revocation of a refusal. A refusal may be revoked by a signed record. It can also be revoked by a later-made anatomical gift that is inconsistent with the refusal. For example, suppose an individual signs a refusal to be an organ donor under Section 7. Later that individual signs a record stating only "I revoke the refusal." At this point that individual is neither a donor nor a refuser and upon the individual's death, an anatomical gift could be made by the person or persons listed in Section 9. On the other hand, suppose the individual who had signed a refusal later executed a document of gift donating "my eyes." Here there is an anatomical gift of the eyes and a refusal to be a donor of any other part. This would bar any person from revoking the anatomical gift of the eyes or making an anatomical gift of any other part. Similarly, suppose the individual had signed a refusal and later obtained a driver's license stating that the individual wanted to be an "organ donor." The driver's license would revoke the refusal to the extent inconsistent with the refusal, and there would be an anatomical gift of the donor's organs, eyes, and tissue. *See* Section 11(f). Lastly, under limited circumstances, a refusal can be revoked orally. *See* Section 7(c)(1).

Subsection (d) provides that an individual's unrevoked refusal to make an anatomical gift of the individual's body or part bars all others from later making an anatomical gift of the body or part. Thus, suppose an individual signs an unrevoked Section 7 refusal. No other person before or after that individual's death could make an anatomical gift for that individual. This section honors the autonomy of the individual to refuse to have his body or parts become the subject of an anatomical gift. It prevents families from making donations on behalf of decedents who, while living, had signed a refusal to make an anatomical gift unless there is evidence that the individual signing the refusal did not intend to have that refusal bind others after death.

An individual might sign a Section 7 refusal that expressly provides that it is not intended to affect the ability of others to make an anatomical gift following the individual's death. If that intent is expressly indicated in the refusal, or if the refusal were later revoked, then other persons listed in Section 9 can make an anatomical gift. For example, suppose an individual signs a Section 7 refusal barring the making of an anatomical gift of the individual's body and parts. If that person does not revoke the refusal, then neither that individual's agent nor guardian nor any person listed in Section 9 can make an anatomical gift of the individual's body or parts. However, it is possible that an individual might wish to bar the individual's guardian from making an anatomical gift under Section 5 but not the individual's family from making a gift under Section 10. If that intent is expressed in the refusal, it will be honored. The intent to make only a limited refusal must be set forth expressly in the Section 7 refusal. Extrinsic evidence would not be admissible to establish intent to limit the refusal as subsection (d) provides that a contrary indication be expressly set forth in the refusal.

An individual's refusal could be limited to a part. For example, an individual might sign a refusal to donate the individual's eyes. In the absence of an express, contrary indication, the refusal would not apply to the individual's other parts. Thus, following the individual's death, the persons listed in Section 9 could make an anatomical gift of the individual's other parts.

A simple form of refusal under this [act] could provide:

I, .............., refuse to make any anatomical gift of my body or any part.

.......... ..........

Date Signed: Signature of Declarant





### § 2108.071 Repealed.

Repealed, 152 v H 529, § 2 [135 v H 1242 (Eff 3-4-75); 143 v H 21. Eff 3-27-91]. Eff 4-7-09.

**Editor's Notes**

This section concerned eye enucleation by embalmer.

### § 2108.08 (UAGA 8) Preclusive effect of anatomical gift, amendment, or revocation.

(A) Subject to division (F) of this section, in the absence of an express, contrary indication by the donor, a person other than the donor shall be barred from making, amending, or revoking an anatomical gift of a donor's body or part if the donor made an anatomical gift of the donor's body or part under section 2108.05 of the Revised Code or an amendment to an anatomical gift of the donor's body or part under section 2108.06 of the Revised Code.

(B) A donor's revocation of an anatomical gift of the donor's body or part under section 2108.06 of the Revised Code is not a refusal and shall not bar another person specified in section 2108.04 or 2108.09 of the Revised Code from making an anatomical gift of the donor's body or part under section 2108.05 or 2108.10 of the Revised Code.

(C) If a person other than the donor makes an unrevoked anatomical gift of the donor's body or part under section 2108.05 of the Revised Code or an amendment to an anatomical gift of the donor's body or part under section 2108.06 of the Revised Code, another person shall not make, amend, or revoke the gift of the donor's body or part under section 2108.10 of the Revised Code.

(D) A revocation by a person other than the donor of an anatomical gift of a donor's body or part under section 2108.06 of the Revised Code shall not bar another person from making an anatomical gift of the body or part under section 2108.05 or 2108.10 of the Revised Code.

(E) In the absence of an express, contrary indication by the donor or other person authorized to make an anatomical gift under section 2108.04 of the Revised Code, an anatomical gift of a part is neither a refusal to give another part nor a limitation on the making of an anatomical gift of another part at a later time by the donor or another person.

(F) In the absence of an express, contrary indication by the donor or other person authorized to make an anatomical gift under section 2108.04 of the Revised Code, an anatomical gift of a part for one or more of the purposes set forth in section 2108.04 of the Revised Code shall not be a limitation on the making of an anatomical gift of the part for any of the other purposes by the donor or other person under section 2108.05 or 2108.10 of the Revised Code.

**HISTORY:**

152 v H 529, § 1, eff. 4-7-09.

**Official Comment**

Uniform Anatomical Gift Act § 8.

Section 2(h) of the 1987 Act provided that "an anatomical gift that is not revoked by the donor before death is irrevocable and does not require the consent or concurrence of any person after the donor's death." The intent of that section was to assure donation finality for anatomical gifts made by donors prior to death. For many years, however, it was the practice, albeit now changing, for procurement organizations to seek permission from donor families before parts could be recovered from deceased donors. This practice, however, is inconsistent both with the 1987 Act and, more importantly, the respect due to donors who have made anatomical gifts during their lives. Furthermore, that practice could result in unnecessary delays in the recovery of organs.

Section 8 is designed to state firmly the rule that a donor's autonomous decision regarding the making of an anatomical gift is to be honored and implemented and is not subject to change by others. Section 8 not only continues the policy of making lifetime donations irrevocable but also is restated to take away from families the power, right, or authority to consent to, amend, or revoke donations made by donors during their lifetimes.

Section 8 addresses the possible tension between a donor's autonomous decision to be a donor with the interest of surviving family members to make that decision. It addresses this tension by favoring the decision of the donor over the desires of the family. Section 8(a) strips surviving family members of at least one stick in a bundle of property rights they might otherwise have under state law — the right to make, amend, or revoke an anatomical gift of a body or part if the donor made an anatomical gift or an amendment of the gift of the body or part. This section does not affect property rights families might otherwise have in a decedent's body under other law, such as the right to dispose of a decedent's body after the part that was the subject of the anatomical gift has been recovered. In fact, language in Section 11(h) confirms the family's right to dispose of the donor's body after the donor's parts have been recovered for transplantation, therapy, research, or education.

Section 8(a) provides that, if a donor has made an anatomical gift or has amended an anatomical gift, no other person can make, amend, or revoke that gift. For example, suppose a donor gifts the donor's organs for transplantation. By virtue of Section 8(a), no other person can amend or revoke that gift. In fact, because all other persons are barred from doing so, they have no legal authority or right to amend or revoke the anatomical gift. This section does not apply to bar the parents of an unemancipated minor donor who dies under the age of 18 from revoking the minor donor's gift. *See* Section 8(g).

Section 8(a) is subject to the provisions of subsection (f). Under subsection (f) the donor's gift of a part for one purpose does not preclude another person from expanding the gift to include another purpose under either Section 5 or 10. For example, suppose the donor signs a document of gift stating: "I give my kidney for transplantation." Following the donor's death, an individual listed in Section 9 could expand that gift to include research in the event the kidney was not medically suitable for transplantation. The right to expand the purposes of the gift can be restricted by the donor.

Section 8(b) provides that the donor's revocation of an anatomical gift (as distinguished from a refusal) bars no one from making an anatomical gift of the donor's body or parts. The difference between Section 8(a) and Section 8(b) is that a revocation is an ambiguous act respecting the donor's intention to bind others. A donor might want to bind others, but it is just as likely that a donor was ambivalent and was more than willing to leave the decision to donate to others. For example, suppose an individual who had donated a kidney by a donor card later destroys that card with the intent to revoke the anatomical gift. This revocation will not prevent another person acting under either Section 5 or 10 from making an anatomical gift. A donor who wishes both to revoke and bind others not to make a gift must sign a refusal.

Section 8(c) provides that a gift or an amendment of a gift by a person other than the donor under Section 5 or 6 bars other persons from making, amending, or revoking that gift under Section 10 only. For example, suppose the guardian of an adult makes a gift on the adult's behalf. At the adult's later death, the adult's surviving child could not amend or revoke that gift. On the other hand, suppose a donor's agent makes a gift during the donor's lifetime and later a guardian is appointed for the donor. The guardian would not be barred from amending that gift or revoking it. The difference is that the persons named in Section 4 are viewed as the donor's alter egos with power to control the donation decision up until the time of the donor's death. Of course, the donor could also amend or revoke the agent's gift.

Under Section 8(d) if a person other than the donor revokes an anatomical gift under Section 6, the revocation does not bar another person from making a gift under either Section 5 or Section 10. For example, suppose the donor's parent makes an anatomical gift. Twelve years later the donor's agent revokes that gift under Section 6. (Section 8(c) does not bar the agent from revoking the gift). Then, five years later a guardian is appointed for the principal. The guardian could make an anatomical gift for the principal under Section 5 because Section 8(d) does not bar the guardian from making the gift. Likewise, the revocation of an anatomical gift by an agent, parent, or guardian would not prevent the making of an anatomical gift under Section 10. For example, suppose an agent makes an anatomical gift for a donor which the agent revokes prior to the principal's death. The principal takes no further action to effectuate the anatomical gift and dies survived by a spouse and predeceased by the agent. The spouse could make an anatomical gift under Section 10 because the agent's revocation of the anatomical gift does not prevent the spouse from making the anatomical gift.

Section 8(e), consistent with prior law, provides that, absent express, contrary indications by the person making an anatomical gift, the gift of a part is neither a refusal to give other parts nor a limitation on the making of gifts of other parts. Thus, if a donor makes an anatomical gift of the donor's kidney, this gift does not bar the donor's family after the donor's death from making a gift of the donor's heart.

Anatomical gifts can only be made for four purposes — transplantation, therapy, research or education. *See* Sections 4 and 9. Section 8(f) provides that an anatomical gift of a part for one or more of the purposes of transplantation, therapy, research or education does not limit the ability to make a later gift of the part for other purposes by the donor or any other person under Section 5 or Section 10. For example, suppose a donor donates "all organs, eyes, and tissue for transplantation or therapy." That gift would not bar a gift under Section 10 of the organs, eyes, or tissue for research. The donor can bar an expansion of the gift's purposes by an express contrary direction. For example a donor's gift of "organs, eyes, and tissue only for transplantation" would bar others from expanding the purpose of the gift to include research.

Section 8(g) permits either parent of an unemancipated minor donor who dies under the age of 18 to revoke that gift. This subsection applies only if the child dies under the age of 18. It does not empower the parent of a living minor to revoke that minor's anatomical gift while the minor is living. In fact, Section 8(a) would preclude the parent from revoking the minor child's anatomical gift. A parent who does not wish the parent's minor child to make an anatomical gift should communicate the parent's desires to that child. Once the minor donor becomes an adult, neither parent has the right to revoke the gift.

Under Section 8(h) an unemancipated minor's refusal can also be revoked by the minor's parent if the minor dies under the age of 18. Like Section 8(g), a minor's refusal cannot be revoked by the minor's parent while the minor is alive.

Both Section 8(g) and 8(h) require the parent to be reasonably available to either revoke a gift or a refusal. If both parents are reasonably available, either one can revoke the gift or the refusal.



## § 2108.09 (UAGA 9) Who may make anatomical gift of decedent's body or part.

(A) Subject to divisions (B) and (C) of this section, and unless barred by section 2108.07 or 2108.08 of the Revised Code, an anatomical gift of a decedent's body or part for purpose of transplantation, therapy, research, or education may be made in the manner provided for under section 2108.10 of the Revised Code by any member of the following classes of persons who is reasonably available, in the following order of priority:

(1) An agent of the decedent at the time of death who could have made an anatomical gift under division (B) of section 2108.04 of the Revised Code immediately before the decedent's death;

(2) The decedent's surviving spouse;

(3) The decedent's surviving adult children;

(4) The decedent's surviving parent or parents;

(5) The decedent's surviving adult siblings;

(6) The decedent's surviving adult grandchildren;

(7) The decedent's surviving grandparent or grandparents;

(8) A surviving adult who exhibited special care and concern for the decedent;

(9) The persons who were acting as the guardians of the person of the decedent at the time of death;

(10) The persons, other than those in divisions (A)(1) to (9) of this section, to whom the right of disposition for the decedent's body has been assigned pursuant to section 2108.70 of the Revised Code or who have the right of disposition for the decedent's body as described in section 2108.81 of the Revised Code.

(B) If there is more than one member of a class listed in division (A)(1), (3), (4), (5), (6), (7), or (9) of this section entitled to make an anatomical gift, an anatomical gift may be made by a single member of the class unless that member or a person to which the gift may pass under section 2108.11 of the Revised Code knows of an objection by another member of the class. If an objection is known, the gift may be made only by a majority of the members of the class who are reasonably available.

(C) A person shall not make an anatomical gift if, at the time of the decedent's death, a person in a prior class under division (A) of this section is reasonably available to make or object to the making of an anatomical gift.

**HISTORY:**

152 v H 529, § 1, eff. 4-7-09.

**Official Comment**

Uniform Anatomical Gift Act § 9.

Section 9(a) empowers the persons listed in the section to make an anatomical gift of a decedent's body or parts unless they are otherwise barred from doing so under Section 7 or Section 8. Persons who can make an anatomical gift under Section 9 often will be consulted whether they would be willing to make a gift when the prospective donor is near death. *See also* Section 10, comment (last paragraph).

The list of persons who can make an anatomical gift on behalf of a decedent is slightly expanded from prior law. This list now includes that individual who at the time of the decedent's death was acting as an agent of the decedent, adult grandchildren of the decedent, and a close friend of the decedent.

This [act] does not extend the agency relationship beyond a principal's death. Under other law, an agent's power under a power of attorney for health care or any other power terminates when the principal dies. But, under this [act] and assuming that the agent was neither barred under Section 8 nor prohibited in the power of attorney for health care from making anatomical gifts, the person who had been acting as an agent at the time of the principal's death (even though death terminated the agency relationship) has the first priority to make an anatomical gift on behalf of the deceased principal.

Absent a donation by the decedent or the decedent's former agent, other persons or classes of person are empowered to make an anatomical gift in the following order: spouse of the decedent; adult children of the decedent; parents of the decedent; adult siblings of the decedent; adult grandchildren of the decedent; grandparents of the decedent; an adult who exhibited "special care and concern for the decedent;" and the person who was acting as guardian of the decedent at the time of the decedent's death. Lastly, "any other person having the authority to dispose of the decedent's body" can make the decision if no other persons are reasonably available. In those states that recognize domestic partners, the addition of the domestic partner to Section 9(a)(2) would be warranted. In states that do not recognize domestic partners, individuals with domestic partners who wish to be donors should make an anatomical gift before death or designate their domestic partners as agents to give them the first priority under this section.

To the extent that an individual is concerned that the person named in Section 9 may not take adequate account of the individual's personal preferences regarding anatomical gifts, the onus is on the individual to either make or bar the making of an anatomical gift.

In the absence of any person listed in paragraphs (1) through (9) to make an anatomical gift, the gift can be made by "any other person having the authority to dispose of the decedent's body." This [act], like its predecessors, does not specify what person has the authority to dispose of a decedent's body. Who that person is must be determined by law other than this [act]. One such person might be a coroner or medical examiner in possession of an unclaimed body who under law other than this [act] is authorized to dispose of the body after a certain period of time. Of course, in that case it is most unlikely that the decedent's organs could be donated as they are not likely to be medically suitable for transplantation or therapy given the amount of time that likely will pass before it can be determined that no one else will claim the body. But, the decedent's eyes or tissue might be medically suitable for donation. And, of course, the whole body could be the subject of an anatomical gift.

Subsection (a) permits any member of a class to make an anatomical gift. Under subsection (b), however, a class member cannot make an anatomical gift if the class member, or the person to which the gift could pass under Section 11, knows of any objection to the making of the gift by another member of the class. If an objection is known, the gift can only be made by a majority of the members of the same class who are reasonably available. If the class member wishing to make the gift is the only reasonably available member of the class, that class member alone can make the gift even though the class member knows of an objection by another class member who is not reasonably available. If more than one member of the class is reasonably available, the gift can be made only if a majority of them agree. To illustrate, suppose the decedent is survived by three children. The eldest, who is unaware of any objection by the other two, can make an anatomical gift. If, however, the eldest knows that one of the other siblings objects and that sibling is reasonably available, both must agree to make the gift if the third sibling is not reasonably available. If all three siblings are reasonably available, at least two would have to agree to make the gift.

This section departs from both the 1968 Act which required children to act by a majority and the 1987 Act which barred a class member from making a gift (and the donee from accepting the gift) if there was a known objection by another member of the class.

The rule of subsection (b) does not apply to adults who exhibited special care and concern for the decedent. If there is more than one such person, any one of them can make an anatomical gift.

A person cannot make an anatomical gift if, at the time of the decedent's death, a person in a prior class is reasonably available to either make or object to the making of an anatomical gift. *See* Section 9(c). The assumption here is that a person in a prior class is reasonably available but has not yet been contacted by a procurement organization. For example, suppose only the decedent's grandchildren are physically present at the hospital when the decedent dies, but the decedent's children are able to be contacted. For purposes of this [act], the children are reasonably available and, therefore, the grandchildren who are at the hospital cannot make an anatomical gift.

As highlighted above, known objections by persons not reasonably available do not bar persons who are reasonably available from making an anatomical gift whether the objections are held by a person in a prior class or the same class. This is purposeful. The policy choice here is essentially that only persons who are reasonably available can make or object to the making of an anatomical gift. That is because the known objection of a person who is not reasonably available may be based upon faulty information about the effects of a gift or other concerns that could have been ameliorated had the person been reasonably available to discuss the matter with a procurement organization or others.

The concept and definition of "reasonably available" is drawn from lessons learned in the drafting of the Uniform Health-Care Decisions Act and borrows from the language in Section 1(14) of that act. The making of an anatomical gift following a decedent's death is extremely time sensitive, and a decision to donate must be made within a relatively short period of time following death if the organs are to remain viable and human lives are to be saved. Reasonably available is not synonymous with physically present. The phrase (defined in Section 2 (23)) means able to be contacted without "undue effort and willing and able to act in a timely manner consistent with existing medical criteria necessary for the making of an anatomical gift." Thus, a sibling who can be easily contacted by telephone is reasonably available. Section 14(g) imposes on procurement organizations an obligation to make a reasonable search for persons with a priority to make an anatomical gift.

An individual with a higher priority to make an anatomical gift may be unwilling to make a decision, preferring it be made by others. For example, a decedent's spouse may be unwilling to make a decision to donate the decedent's organs, preferring that any decision be made by the decedent's children. Under this [act] the spouse, being unwilling to make a decision, is not reasonably available. There is some concern that an unwillingness to make a decision is equivalent to an objection and should have been treated as such under this [act]. But, this [act] reflects a judgment that the potential savings in human life justifies the position that the inability to express a decision is tantamount to not being available to make a decision. This policy choice was supported by the fact that procurement organizations are well-trained to work with family members when seeking an anatomical gift to distinguish between an objection and a true unwillingness to make a decision.



### § 2108.10 (UAGA 10) Manner of making, amending, or revoking anatomical gift of decedent's body or part.

(A) A person authorized to make an anatomical gift under section 2108.09 of the Revised Code may make an anatomical gift by a document of gift signed by the person making the gift or by that person's oral communication that is electronically recorded or is contemporaneously reduced to a record and signed by the individual receiving the oral communication.

(B) Subject to division (C) of this section, an anatomical gift made by a person authorized to make a gift under section 2108.09 of the Revised Code may be amended or revoked orally or in a record by any member of a prior class who is reasonably available. If more than one member of the prior class is reasonably available, the gift made by a person authorized to make a gift under section 2108.09 of the Revised Code may be amended if a majority of the reasonably available members agree to the amendment or revoked if at least half of the reasonably available members agree to the revocation.

(C) A revocation under division (B) of this section shall be effective only if the procurement organization, transplant hospital, physician, or technician knows of the revocation, before an incision has been made to remove a part from the donor's body or before invasive procedures have begun to prepare the recipient.

**HISTORY:**

152 v H 529, § 1, eff. 4-7-09.

**Official Comment**

Uniform Anatomical Gift Act § 10.

Section 10(a) provides that an anatomical gift by a person authorized to make the gift under Section 9 can be made by a document of gift that is signed by the person making the gift. The document of gift could be an e-mail. This might be a common form of a document of gift where the gift is made by a person named in Section 9 who is reasonably available but not physically present at the hospital where the donor died to deal in person with the procurement organization.

The person also may make the gift orally. An oral gift must be recorded or reduced to a record that is signed by the individual receiving the oral communication. For example, the decedent's spouse might consent to a gift over the telephone at the request of a procurement organization. The individual to whom the gift was communicated should then note that gift in a signed record.

In common with prior law, if a person makes an anatomical gift but there is a member of a prior class who becomes reasonably available, that member may revoke the gift. *See* Section 10(b)(2). If more than one member of the prior class becomes reasonably available, then the gift can be revoked only if the majority of the members of the prior class agree to revoke the gift or if they are equally divided. *See* Section 10(b)(2). For example, suppose an anatomical gift of a kidney is made by a parent of the decedent because none of the decedent's children are reasonably available to make the gift. However, before an incision is made to remove the kidney from the donor's body or invasive procedures have begun to prepare the recipient, a child of the decedent becomes reasonably available and purports to revoke the gift. If this child is the decedent's only reasonably available child, the gift is revoked. If, on the other hand, two children become reasonably available, the gift is revoked only if they agree to revoke or they are equally divided whether to revoke. And, if three children become reasonably available, the gift is revoked if at least two of the three agree to revoke the gift.

If a gift is made by a member of a more remote class, the gift can be amended by the members of the prior class who become reasonably available. *See* Section 10(b)(1). If more than one member becomes reasonably available, the gift can be amended only if a majority of them agree. *See* Section 10(b)(1). For example, a grandchild of the decedent makes an anatomical gift of the decedent's kidneys for transplant. Any reasonably available child or, if more than one, a majority of them can amend the gift to provide that if the kidney is not medically suitable for transplant, it can be used for research. Amendments are not subject to subsection (c) (requiring revocations to be made before the incision is made to remove a part from the body or before invasive procedures have begun to prepare the recipient) as amendments typically would involve extending the purpose of the gift rather than preventing the gift from being made at all.

This [act] is silent regarding whether a Section 10 gift can be made while a donor or prospective donor is near death or whether the gift can only be made after the donor or prospective donor has died. This is purposeful in order to allow procurement organizations and the person having the priority to make an anatomical gift under Section 9 some latitude as to when to sign a document of gift. Of course, no gift is effective unless the donor or prospective donor dies and at the time of death the person making the anatomical gift then had the priority to make the gift.



## RIGHT OF DISPOSITION OF PERSON'S REMAINS OR BODY PARTS

### § 2108.72 Contents of declaration; form; DD form 93, federal record of emergency data.

(A) The written declaration described in section 2108.70 of the Revised Code shall include all of the following:

(1) The declarant's legal name and present address;

(2) A statement that the declarant, an adult being of sound mind, willfully and voluntarily appoints a representative to have the declarant's right of disposition for the declarant's body upon the declarant's death;

(3) A statement that all decisions made by the declarant's representative with respect to the right of disposition are binding;

(4) The name, last known address, and last known telephone number of the representative or, if the representative is a group of persons, the name, last known address, and last known telephone number of each person in the group;

(5) If the declarant chooses to have a successor representative, a statement that if any person or group of persons named as the declarant's representative is disqualified from serving in such position as described in section 2108.75 of the Revised Code, the declarant appoints a successor representative;

(6) If applicable, the name, last known address, and last known telephone number of the successor representative or, if

the successor representative is a group of persons, the name, last known address, and last known telephone number of each person in the group;

(7) A space where the declarant may indicate the declarant's preferences regarding how the right of disposition should be exercised, including any religious observances the declarant wishes the person with the right of disposition to consider;

(8) A space where the declarant may indicate one or more sources of funds that may be used to pay for goods and services associated with the exercise of the right of disposition;

(9) A statement that the declarant's written declaration becomes effective on the declarant's death;

(10) A statement that the declarant revokes any written declaration that the declarant executed, in accordance with section 2108.70 of the Revised Code, prior to the execution of the present written declaration;

(11) A space where the declarant can sign and date the written declaration;

(12) A space where a notary public or two witnesses can sign and date the written declaration as described in section 2108.73 of the Revised Code.

(B) A written declaration may take the following form:

APPOINTMENT OF REPRESENTATIVE FOR DISPOSITION OF BODILY REMAINS, FUNERAL ARRANGEMENTS, AND BURIAL OR CREMATION GOODS AND SERVICES:

I, .............................. (legal name and present address of declarant), an adult being of sound mind, willfully and voluntarily appoint my representative, named below, to have the right of disposition, as defined in section 2108.70 of the Revised Code, for my body upon my death. All decisions made by my representative with respect to the right of disposition shall be binding.

REPRESENTATIVE:

(If the representative is a group of persons, indicate the name, last known address, and telephone number of each person in the group.)

Name(s):

Address(es):

Telephone Number(s):

SUCCESSOR REPRESENTATIVE:

If my representative is disqualified from serving as my representative as described in section 2108.75 of the Revised Code, then I hereby appoint the following person or group of persons to serve as my successor representative.

(If the successor representative is a group of persons, indicate the name, last known address, and telephone number of each person in the group.)

Name(s):

Address(es):

Telephone Number(s):

PREFERENCES REGARDING HOW THE RIGHT OF DISPOSITION SHOULD BE EXERCISED, INCLUDING ANY RELIGIOUS OBSERVANCES THE DECLARANT WISHES A REPRESENTATIVE OR A SUCCESSOR REPRESENTATIVE TO CONSIDER:

ONE OR MORE SOURCES OF FUNDS THAT COULD BE USED TO PAY FOR GOODS AND SERVICES ASSOCIATED WITH AN EXERCISE OF THE RIGHT OF DISPOSITION:

DURATION:

The appointment of my representative and, if applicable, successor representative, becomes effective upon my death.

PRIOR APPOINTMENTS REVOKED:

I hereby revoke any written declaration that I executed in accordance with section 2108.70 of the Ohio Revised Code prior to the date of execution of this written declaration indicated below.

AUTHORIZATION TO ACT:

I hereby agree that any of the following that receives a copy of this written declaration may act under it:

— Cemetery organization;
— Crematory operator;
— Business operating a columbarium;
— Funeral director;
— Embalmer;
— Funeral home;
— Any other person asked to assist with my funeral, burial, cremation, or other manner of final disposition.

MODIFICATION AND REVOCATION — WHEN EFFECTIVE:

Any modification or revocation of this written declaration is not effective as to any party until that party receives actual notice of the modification or revocation.

LIABILITY:

No person who acts in accordance with a properly executed copy of this written declaration shall be liable for damages of any kind associated with the person's reliance on this declaration.

Signed this ........... day of ........

(Signature of declarant)

ACKNOWLEDGMENT OF ASSUMPTION OF OBLIGATIONS AND COSTS:

By signing below, the representative, or successor representative, if applicable, acknowledges that he or she, as representative or successor representative, assumes the right of disposition as defined in section 2108.70 of the Revised Code, and understands that he or she is liable for the reasonable costs of exercising the right, including any goods and services that are purchased.

ACCEPTANCE (OPTIONAL):

The undersigned hereby accepts this appointment as representative or successor representative, as applicable, for the right of disposition as defined in section 2108.70 of the Revised Code.

Signed this ........... day of ........

Signature of representative
(if representative is a group of persons, each person in the group shall sign)

Signed this ........... day of .......

Signature of successor representative
(if successor representative is a group of persons, each person in the group shall sign)

WITNESSES:

I attest that the declarant signed or acknowledged this assignment of the right of disposition under section 2108.70 of the Revised Code in my presence and that the declarant is at least eighteen years of age and appears to be of sound mind and not under or subject to duress, fraud, or undue influence. I further attest that I am not the declarant's representative or successor representative, I am at least eighteen years of age, and I am not related to the declarant by blood, marriage, or adoption.

First witness:
Name (printed):
Residing at:
Signature:
Date:

Second witness:
Name (printed):
Residing at:
Signature:
Date:

OR

NOTARY ACKNOWLEDGMENT:

State of Ohio
County of ............... SS.

On ........, before me, the undersigned notary public, personally appeared ............, known to me or satisfactorily proven to be the person whose name is subscribed as the declarant, and who has acknowledged that he or she executed this written declaration under section 2108.70 of the Revised Code for the purposes expressed in that section. I attest that the declarant is at least eighteen years of age and appears to be of sound mind and not under or subject to duress, fraud, or undue influence.

Signature of notary public

My commission expires on:

(C) Completion of a federal Record of Emergency Data form, DD Form 93, or its successor form, by a member of the military, is sufficient to constitute a written declaration under section 2108.70 of the Revised Code if section 13a of DD Form 93, entitled "Person Authorized to Direct Disposition," has been properly completed by the member of the military who has subsequently died while under active duty orders as described in 10 U.S.C. 1481.

**HISTORY:**

151 v H 426, § 1, eff. 10-12-06; 153 v H 449, § 1, eff. 6-18-10.

**Amendment Notes**

153 v H 449, effective June 18, 2010, added (C).

### § 2108.73 Execution of declaration.

A written declaration executed by a declarant under section 2108.70 of the Revised Code shall be signed and dated by the declarant in the presence of one of the following:

(A) A notary public who shall make the certification described in section 147.53 of the Revised Code.

(B) Two witnesses who are adults and who are not related by blood, marriage, or adoption to the declarant.

(C) If the written declaration is a DD Form 93, Record of Emergency Data, by whomever the form requires.

**HISTORY:**

151 v H 426, § 1, eff. 10-12-06; 153 v H 449, § 1, eff. 6-18-10.

**Amendment Notes**

153 v H 449, effective June 18, 2010, added (C) and made related changes.

### § 2108.74 Declarant warrants truthfulness.

A declarant who executes a written declaration in accordance with section 2108.73 of the Revised Code warrants the truthfulness of the entire content of the declaration.

**HISTORY:**

151 v H 426, § 1, eff. 10-12-06.

### § 2108.75 Disqualification generally from serving as representative or having right of disposition.

(A) A person shall be disqualified from serving as a representative or successor representative, or from having the right of disposition for a deceased adult pursuant to section 2108.81 of the Revised Code, if any of the following occurs:

(1) The person dies.

(2) A probate court declares or determines that the person is incompetent.

(3) The person resigns or declines to exercise the right as described in section 2108.88 of the Revised Code.

(4) The person refuses to exercise the right within two days after notification of the declarant's death.

(5) The person cannot be located with reasonable effort.

(6) The person meets the criteria described in section 2108.76 or 2108.77 of the Revised Code.

(B) No owner, employee, or agent of a funeral home, cemetery, or crematory providing funeral, burial, or cremation services for a declarant shall serve as a representative or successor representative for the declarant unless the owner, employee, or agent is related to the declarant by blood, marriage, or adoption.

(C) Subject to divisions (C)(2) and (D)(2) of section 2108.70 of the Revised Code, if a person is disqualified from serving as the declarant's representative or successor representative, or from having the right of disposition for a deceased adult pursuant to section 2108.81 of the Revised Code, as described in division (A) of this section, the right is automatically reassigned to, and vests in, the next person who has the right pursuant to the declarant's written declaration or pursuant to the order of priority in section 2108.81 of the Revised Code.

**HISTORY:**

151 v H 426, § 1, eff. 10-12-06.

### § 2108.76 Disqualification of former spouse.

(A) Except as provided in division (B) of this section, if the person named as the declarant's representative or successor representative in a written declaration was the declarant's spouse at the time the declaration was executed, but is not the declarant's spouse at the time of the declarant's death, the former spouse shall no longer be qualified to serve as the declarant's representative or successor representative.

(B) Division (A) of this section shall not apply and a former spouse is qualified to serve as a declarant's representative or successor representative if the declarant signs and dates, after the termination of the marriage, a document stating the declarant's intent that the former spouse be the declarant's representative or successor representative. The document must be notarized or witnessed in accordance with the procedures described in section 2108.73 of the Revised Code.

**HISTORY:**

151 v H 426, § 1, eff. 10-12-06.

### § 2108.77 Disqualification based on homicide, domestic violence, pending action for termination of marriage, or estrangement of spouses.

If the person named as the declarant's representative or successor representative in a written declaration, or the person who has a deceased adult's right of disposition pursuant to section 2108.81 of the Revised Code, meets any of the following criteria, the person shall be disqualified from serving as the representative or successor representative, or from having the right:

(A)(1) Subject to division (A)(2) of this section, the person has been charged with murder, aggravated murder, or voluntary manslaughter.

(2) If the charges against the person described in division (A)(1) of this section are dismissed or if the person is acquitted of such charges, the right is restored to the person.

(B)(1) Subject to division (B)(2) of this section, the person has been charged with an act of domestic violence under section 2919.25 of the Revised Code and it has been alleged in the charging instrument or accompanying papers that the act resulted in or contributed to the declarant's death.

(2) If the charges against the person described in division (B)(1) of this section are dismissed or if the person is acquitted of such charges, the right is restored to the person.

(C) The person and the declarant or deceased adult are spouses and an action to terminate the marriage pursuant to Chapter 3105. of the Revised Code was pending at the time of the declarant's or deceased adult's death.

(D) The person and the declarant or deceased adult are spouses and a probate court, on the motion of any other person or its own motion, determines that the declarant's or deceased adult's spouse and the declarant were estranged at the time of the declarant's or deceased adult's death. As used in this division, "estranged" means that a declarant's or a deceased adult's spouse and the declarant or deceased adult were physically and emotionally separated from each other, at the time of the declarant's or deceased adult's death, and had been separated for a period of time that clearly demonstrates an absence of due affection, trust, and regard between spouse and the declarant of deceased adult.

**HISTORY:**

151 v H 426, § 1, eff. 10-12-06.

### § 2108.78 Effect of anatomical gifts.

If a declarant or deceased adult has made an anatomical gift under sections 2108.01 to 2108.29 of the Revised Code, any person to whom the declarant has assigned the right of disposition under section 2108.70 of the Revised Code, or who has the right as described in section 2108.81 of the Revised Code, is bound by the anatomical gift and must follow the instructions associated with the gift before making any decisions or taking any other actions associated with the right.

**HISTORY:**

151 v H 426, § 1, eff. 10-12-06; 152 v H 529, § 1, eff. 4-7-09.

**Amendment Notes**

152 v H 529, effective April 7, 2009, deleted "a valid declaration of" following "adult has made" and "declaration of the" following "bound by the", and substituted "under sections 2108.01 to 2108.29" for "by will or any other document or means described in section 2108.04".

### § 2108.79 Disagreement among group representatives or class with right of disposition.

(A) Subject to divisions (B) and (C) of this section, if a declarant's representative or successor representative is a group of people in whom the right of disposition has vested as described in section 2108.71 of the Revised Code, or if a class of persons has the right as described in section 2108.81 of the Revised Code, and the persons in the group or class disagree regarding how the right is to be exercised, the decisions of the majority of the persons in the group or class shall prevail.

(B) If, after reasonable efforts, less than all of the persons in a group or class described in division (A) of this section have been located, the decisions of the majority of the persons in the group or class who have been located prevail.

(C) If a majority of persons cannot reach a decision under division (A) or (B) of this section, the probate court of the county in which the declarant or deceased person resided at the time of death shall make the decision in accordance with the criteria set forth in division (B) of section 2108.82 of the Revised Code.

**HISTORY:**

151 v H 426, § 1, eff. 10-12-06.

### § 2108.80 Revocation of declaration.

A declarant may revoke a written declaration executed under section 2108.70 of the Revised Code by indicating the declarant's desire to revoke the declaration in a document signed and dated by the declarant in the presence of either of the following:

(A) A notary public who shall make the certification described in section 147.53 of the Revised Code.

(B) Two witnesses who are adults and are not related by blood, marriage, or adoption to the declarant.

**HISTORY:**

151 v H 426, § 1, eff. 10-12-06.

### § 2108.81 Statutory right of disposition in absence of valid declaration or qualified representative.

(A) If either of the following is true, division (B) of this section shall apply:

(1) An adult has not executed a written declaration pursuant to sections 2108.70 to 2108.73 of the Revised Code that remains in force at the time of the adult's death.

(2) Each person to whom the right of disposition has been assigned or reassigned pursuant to a written declaration is disqualified from exercising the right as described in section 2108.75 of the Revised Code.

(B) Subject to division (A) of this section and sections 2108.75 and 2108.79 of the Revised Code, the right of disposition is assigned to the following persons, if mentally competent adults who can be located with reasonable effort, in the order of priority stated:

(1) The deceased person's surviving spouse;

(2) The sole surviving child of the deceased person or, if there is more than one surviving child, all of the surviving children, collectively.

(3) The deceased person's surviving parent or parents;

(4) The deceased person's surviving sibling, whether of the whole or of the half blood or, if there is more than one sibling of the whole or of the half blood, all of the surviving siblings, collectively;

(5) The deceased person's surviving grandparent or grandparents;

(6) The deceased person's surviving grandchild, or if there is more than one surviving grandchild, all of the surviving grandchildren collectively;

(7) The lineal descendants of the deceased person's grandparents, as described in division (I) of section 2105.06 of the Revised Code;

(8) The person who was the deceased person's guardian at the time of the deceased person's death, if a guardian had been appointed;

(9) Any other person willing to assume the right of disposition, including the personal representative of the deceased person's estate or the licensed funeral director with custody of the deceased person's body, after attesting in writing that a good faith effort has been made to locate the persons in divisions (B)(1) to (8) of this section.

(10) If the deceased person was an indigent person or other person the final disposition of whose body is the financial and statutory responsibility of the state or a political subdivision of this state, the public officer or employee responsible for arranging the final disposition of the remains of the deceased person.

**HISTORY:**

151 v H 426, § 1, eff. 10-12-06; 152 v S 196, § 1, eff. 7-7-09.

**Amendment Notes**

152 v S 196, effective July 7, 2009, inserted (B)(6) and redesignated the remaining subdivisions accordingly; and added (B)(10).

**NOTES TO DECISIONS**

**Disinterment**

Right of disposition did not preclude the probate court from granting the application for disinterment since the equities weighed in favor of doing so. In re Disinterment of Swing, 2014-Ohio-5454, 26 N.E.3d 827, 2014 Ohio App. LEXIS 5284 (Ohio Ct. App., Lucas County 2014).



### § 2108.82 Authority of probate court to assign right of disposition.

(A) Notwithstanding section 2108.81 of the Revised Code and in accordance with division (B) of this section, the probate court for the county in which the declarant or deceased person resided at the time of death may, on its own motion or the motion of another person, assign to any person the right of disposition for a declarant or deceased person.

(B) In making a determination for purposes of division (A) of this section and division (C) of section 2108.79 of the Revised Code, the court shall consider the following:

(1) Whether evidence presented to, or in the possession of the court, demonstrates that the person who is the subject of the motion and the declarant or deceased person had a close personal relationship;

(2) The reasonableness and practicality of any plans that the person who is the subject of the motion may have for the declarant's or deceased person's funeral, burial, cremation, or final disposition, including the degree to which such plans allow maximum participation by all persons who wish to pay their final respects to the deceased person;

(3) The willingness of the person who is the subject of the motion to assume the responsibility to pay for the declarant's or deceased person's funeral, burial, cremation, or final disposition and the desires of that person;

(4) The convenience and needs of other families and friends wishing to pay their final respects to the declarant or deceased person;

(5) The express written desires of the declarant or deceased person.

(C) Except to the extent considered under division (B)(3) of this section, the following persons do not have a greater claim to the right of disposition than such persons otherwise have pursuant to law:

(1) A person who is willing to assume the responsibility to pay for the declarant's or deceased person's funeral, burial, cremation, or final disposition;

(2) The personal representative of the declarant or deceased person.

**HISTORY:**

151 v H 426, § 1, eff. 10-12-06.

### § 2108.83 Rights and immunities of funeral home or other person assisting in final disposition in cases of disputed disposition.

In the event of a dispute regarding the right of disposition, a funeral home, funeral director, crematory operator, cemetery operator, cemetery organization, or other person asked to assist with a declarant's or deceased person's funeral, burial, cremation, or other manner of final disposition shall not be liable for damages of any kind for refusing to accept the remains, refusing to inter, cremate, or otherwise dispose of the remains, or refusing to complete funeral or other arrangements pertaining to final disposition until such funeral home, funeral director, crematory operator, cemetery operator, cemetery organization, or other person receives a court order or a written document that is executed by a person that the funeral home, funeral director, crematory operator, cemetery operator, cemetery organization, or other person reasonably believes has the right of disposition and that clearly expresses how the right of disposition is to be exercised.

**HISTORY:**
151 v H 426, § 1, eff. 10-12-06.



NOTES TO DECISIONS

**Provisional remedy.**
In disinterment suit, the cemetery association's appeal of the denial of its motion to quash third-party subpoena was allowed to proceed because it satisfied the standards for a provisional remedy; appealed entry was thus a final order that may be appealed. The cemetery association had plausibly alleged, or made a colorable claim that this provision applied, and it would not be afforded meaningful review of appealed entry if it had to wait for final judgment to appeal. In re Disinterment of Marion J. Glass, 2021-Ohio-4645, 182 N.E.3d 22, 2021 Ohio App. LEXIS 4603 (Ohio Ct. App., Montgomery County 2021).

### § 2108.84 Embalming, refrigeration, and sheltering of remains while dispute is pending.

If a funeral home, funeral director, crematory operator, or other person asked to assist with a declarant's or deceased person's funeral, burial, cremation, or other manner of final disposition is in possession of a declarant's or deceased person's remains while a dispute described in section 2108.83 of the Revised Code is pending, the funeral home, funeral director, crematory operator, or other person may embalm or refrigerate and shelter the remains to preserve them and may add the cost of embalming, refrigeration, and sheltering to the final disposition costs to be charged.

**HISTORY:**
151 v H 426, § 1, eff. 10-12-06.

### § 2108.85 Right of funeral home or other person bringing legal action to reimbursement for fees and costs.

(A) If a funeral home, funeral director, crematory operator, cemetery operator, cemetery organization, or other person asked to assist with a declarant's or deceased person's funeral, burial, cremation, or other manner of final disposition brings a legal action for purposes of section 2108.83 or 2108.84 of the Revised Code, the funeral home, funeral director, crematory operator, cemetery operator, cemetery organization, or other person may add to the costs the person charges for the goods and services the person provided the legal fees, if reasonable, and the court costs that the person incurred.

(B) The right created by division (A) of this section shall neither be construed to require, nor impose a duty on, a funeral home, funeral director, crematory operator, cemetery operator, cemetery organization, or other person asked to assist with a declarant's or deceased person's funeral, burial, cremation, or other manner of final disposition, to bring a legal action and such person shall not be held criminally or civilly liable for not bringing an action.

**HISTORY:**
151 v H 426, § 1, eff. 10-12-06.

### § 2108.86 Right of funeral home or other person to rely on written declaration and instructions of person believed to have right of disposition.

(A) A funeral home, funeral director, crematory operator, cemetery operator, cemetery organization, or other person asked to assist with a declarant's funeral, burial, cremation, or other manner of final disposition has the right to rely on the content of a written declaration and the instructions of the person or group of persons whom the funeral home, funeral director, crematory operator, cemetery operator, cemetery organization, or other person reasonably believes has the right of disposition.

(B) If the circumstances described in division (A) of section 2108.81 of the Revised Code apply, a funeral home, funeral director, crematory operator, cemetery operator, cemetery organization, or other person asked to assist with a deceased person's funeral, burial, cremation, or other manner of final disposition has the right to rely on the instructions of the person or group of persons the funeral home, funeral director, crematory operator, cemetery operator, cemetery organization, or other person reasonably believes has the right of disposition pursuant to section 2108.81 of the Revised Code.

(C) No funeral home, funeral director, crematory operator, cemetery operator, cemetery organization, or other person asked to assist with a deceased person's funeral, burial, cremation, or other manner of final disposition, who relies, pursuant to divisions (A) and (B) of this section, in good faith on the contents of a written declaration or the instructions of the person or group of persons the funeral home, funeral director, crematory operator, cemetery operator, cemetery organization, or other person reasonably believes has the right of disposition, shall be subject to criminal or civil liability or subject to disciplinary action for taking an action or not taking an action in reliance on such contents or instructions and for otherwise complying with sections 2108.70 to 2108.90 of the Revised Code.

**HISTORY:**
151 v H 426, § 1, eff. 10-12-06.

### § 2108.87 Independent investigation by funeral home or other person.

(A) A funeral home, funeral director, crematory operator, cemetery operator, cemetery organization, or other person asked to assist with a deceased person's funeral, burial, cremation, or other manner of final disposition may independently investigate the existence of, or locate or contact, the following persons:

(1) A representative or successor representative named in a written declaration;

(2) A person listed in section 2108.81 of the Revised Code.

(B) In no circumstances shall a funeral home, funeral director, crematory operator, cemetery operator, cemetery organization, or other person asked to assist with a deceased person's funeral, burial, cremation, or other manner of final disposition have a duty to independently investigate the existence of, or locate or contact, the persons described in division (A) of this section.

**HISTORY:**
151 v H 426, § 1, eff. 10-12-06.

### § 2108.88 Resignation or refusal to serve as representative.

(A) A person to whom a declarant's or deceased person's right of disposition has been assigned or reassigned pursuant to section 2108.70 or 2108.81 of the Revised Code may decline to exercise the right or resign after beginning to exercise the right.

(B) A person described in division (A) of this section who resigns after beginning to exercise the right shall be subject to section 2108.89 of the Revised Code.

**HISTORY:**
151 v H 426, § 1, eff. 10-12-06.

### § 2108.89 Liability of representative for cost of goods and services.

The following persons shall be liable for the reasonable costs of any goods or services purchased in connection with the exercise of the right of disposition for a declarant or deceased person:

(A) A representative or successor who assumes liability for the cost of such goods and services by signing a written declaration that states that such an assumption is made;

(B) A person to whom the right of disposition is assigned pursuant to section 2108.81 of the Revised Code and who has purchased goods or services associated with an exercise of the right.

**HISTORY:**
151 v H 426, § 1, eff. 10-12-06.

### § 2108.90 Jurisdiction of probate court.

Pursuant to division (A) of section 2101.24 of the Revised Code, the probate court for the county in which the declarant or deceased person resided at the time of death or the county in which a living person whose post-death arrangements are the subject of dispute resides shall have exclusive jurisdiction over any action that results from sections 2108.70 to 2108.89 of the Revised Code.

**HISTORY:**
151 v H 426, § 1, eff. 10-12-06.

# CHAPTER 2111
# GUARDIANS; CONSERVATORSHIPS



### § 2111.01 Definitions.

As used in Chapters 2101. to 2131. of the Revised Code:

(A) "Guardian," other than a guardian under sections 5905.01 to 5905.19 of the Revised Code, means any person, association, or corporation appointed by the probate court to have the care and management of the person, the estate, or both of an incompetent or minor. When applicable, "guardian" includes, but is not limited to, a limited guardian, an interim guardian, a standby guardian, and an emergency guardian appointed pursuant to division (B) of section 2111.02 of the Revised Code. "Guardian" also includes an agency under contract with the department of developmental disabilities for the provision of protective service under sections 5123.55 to 5123.59 of the Revised Code when appointed by the probate court to have the care and management of the person of an incompetent.

(B) "Ward" means any person for whom a guardian is acting or for whom the probate court is acting pursuant to section 2111.50 of the Revised Code.

(C) "Resident guardian" means a guardian appointed by a probate court to have the care and management of property in this state that belongs to a nonresident ward.

(D) "Incompetent" means either of the following:

(1) Any person who is so mentally impaired, as a result of a mental or physical illness or disability, as a result of intellectual disability, or as a result of chronic substance abuse, that the person is incapable of taking proper care of the person's self or property or fails to provide for the person's family or other persons for whom the person is charged by law to provide;

(2) Any person confined to a correctional institution within this state.

(E) "Next of kin" means any person who would be entitled to inherit from a ward under Chapter 2105. of the Revised Code if the ward dies intestate.

(F) "Conservator" means a conservator appointed by the probate court in an order of conservatorship issued pursuant to section 2111.021 of the Revised Code.

(G) "Parent" means a natural parent or adoptive parent of a minor child whose parental rights and responsibilities have not been terminated by a juvenile court or another court.

(H) "Financial harm" means impairment of an individual's financial assets by unlawfully obtaining or exerting control over the individual's real or personal property in any of the following ways:

(1) Without the consent of the individual or the person authorized to give consent on the individual's behalf;

(2) Beyond the scope of the express or implied consent of the individual or the person authorized to give consent on the individual's behalf;

(3) By deception;

(4) By threat;

(5) By intimidation;

(6) By fraud;

(7) By undue influence.

**HISTORY:**
GC § 10507-1; 114 v 320(382); Bureau of Code Revision, 10-1-53; 129 v 1448 (Eff 10-25-61); 133 v H 688 (Eff 11-21-69); 134 v H 290 (Eff 3-23-72); 136 v H 244 (Eff 8-26-76); 137 v S 415 (Eff 7-20-78); 138 v H 900 (Eff 7-1-80); 141 v S 322 (Eff 4-4-86); 143 v S 46 (Eff 1-1-90); 145 v H 571 (Eff 10-6-94); 146 v H 288. Eff 1-14-97; 153 v S 79, § 1, eff. 10-6-09; 2012 HB 27, § 1, eff. Mar. 22, 2013; 2016 hb158, § 1, effective October 12, 2016.

**Editor's Notes**
The provisions of § 3 of SB 46 (143 v —) read as follows:
SECTION 3. The amendments to the definition of an incompetent in section 2111.01 of the Revised Code that are made by this act do not affect any guardianship of the person, the estate, or the person and estate of an incompetent that was established prior to the effective date of this act and that was based upon advanced age, chronic alcoholism, or physical disability or infirmity.

**Amendment Notes**
The 2016 amendment by HB 158 substituted "as a result of intellectual disability" for "or mental retardation" in (D)(1); and made stylistic changes.
The 2012 amendment added (H).
153 v S 79, effective October 6, 2009, deleted "mental retardation and" preceding "developmental disabilities" throughout.



#### NOTES TO DECISIONS

Analysis



**Administrator**
Where a woman who is divorced dies survived by her four minor children, her former husband may be appointed administrator of her estate provided he is a "suitable person" as set forth in R.C. 2113.06: In re Estate of Robertson, 26 Ohio App. 3d 64, 498 N.E.2d 206, 1985 Ohio App. LEXIS 10225 (Ohio Ct. App., Cuyahoga County 1985).

**Application by agency**
When an agency sought appointment as guardian of a person's estate and person, while it was inappropriate for the same agency that sought such an appointment, for which it would receive a fee, to perform the initial investigation into whether the person needed a guardian, the person did not present any evidence of a less restrictive alternative, and it could not be said that the evidence did not authorize the trial court to find, by clear and convincing evidence, that it was necessary to appoint a guardian for the person and her estate or that such an appointment was in her best interest. In re Vanko, 2006-Ohio-4068, 2006 Ohio App. LEXIS 4018 (Ohio Ct. App., Stark County 2006).

**Appointment of guardian**
Appointment of a guardian was not against the manifest weight of the evidence as: (1) the ward had been diagnosed with a mental illness; (2) she was confused and combative at the hearings, claimed the bank was embezzling funds and accused the nursing home and the court of kidnapping her; (3) the ward did not have water or utility service at her home and was a hoarder; (4) she had fallen at home, could not get up, and was discovered several days later with serious injuries; (5) at the nursing home, she had fallen four or five times with injury; and (6) she refused to take medication, insulted the staff and could not remember whether she had eaten or taken her medication without the help of the nursing home staff. In re Guardianship of Hoffman, 2017-Ohio-8023, 2017 Ohio App. LEXIS 4375 (Ohio Ct. App., Marion County 2017).

**Authority of ward**
A person who is adjudicated incompetent and who is voluntarily admitted by his guardian to a mental hospital does not lose, by the adjudication of incompetency, his right to request his release from the mental hospital

pursuant to R.C. 5122.03: Lippmann v. Johnson, 68 Ohio App. 2d 233, 22 Ohio Op. 3d 393, 429 N.E.2d 167, 1980 Ohio App. LEXIS 9670 (Ohio Ct. App., Lucas County 1980).

Ward did not have the capacity to bind his own guardianship estate without his guardian's consent; an agreed judgment entry signed by an inmate but not the guardian did not bind any party, did not affect any substantial right, was not a final order, and was not appealable. Sovak v. Spivey, 2003-Ohio-6717, 155 Ohio App. 3d 479, 801 N.E.2d 896, 2003 Ohio App. LEXIS 6027 (Ohio Ct. App., Mahoning County 2003).

**Death of ward**

Death of a ward terminates all powers of the guardian, and the guardian has no authority to bring an action on the ward's behalf after the ward's death: Whitley v. River's Bend Health Care, 2009-Ohio-3366, 183 Ohio App. 3d 145, 916 N.E.2d 515, 2009 Ohio App. LEXIS 2911 (Ohio Ct. App., Lawrence County 2009).



**History**

For history of this section, see State ex rel. Connor v. Lamneck, 133 Ohio St. 257, 10 Ohio Op. 342, 13 N.E.2d 127, 1938 Ohio LEXIS 412 (Ohio 1938).

**Incompetency**

Defendant was found competent to stand trial, which included competency to enter a plea, and he was given a full hearing in compliance with Crim.R. 11(C) before entering his plea; the trial court conducted an extensive inquiry of defendant to ensure he understood the charges against him and all of the penalties he faced, the effect of his guilty plea, and the rights he was waiving by pleading guilty, and defendant also denied being coerced or promised anything in exchange for his guilty plea. State v. Bush, 2016-Ohio-551, 2016 Ohio App. LEXIS 474 (Ohio Ct. App., Clermont County 2016).

Petitioner did not provide clear and convincing proof to indicate that the petitioner's parent was incompetent, as defined in R.C. 2111.01. The testimony and reports of two psychologists, the parent's family doctor, and the court appointed guardian ad litem, in addition to an in camera interview of the parent by the court, showed that, while the parent may have needed help, this need seemed to arise from the pressure from the constant fighting of the parent's children over who was to be in charge of the parent and the parent's money, which was putting the parent under tremendous stress that affected the parent's memory and the parent's ability to handle the parent's own affairs. In re Guardianship of Miller, 2010-Ohio-2159, 187 Ohio App. 3d 445, 932 N.E.2d 420, 2010 Ohio App. LEXIS 1767 (Ohio Ct. App., Logan County 2010).

Appellant's contention that he was entitled to relief from judgment because the trial court entered summary judgment against him when appellant was under a "legal disability" because of his imprisonment and was entitled to the appointment of counsel was without merit since inmates were not considered either incompetent or under a legal disability under Civ.R. 17(B) or R.C. 2111.01(D) for purposes of defending a lawsuit; thus, the trial court did not err in failing to appoint counsel for appellant. Cincinnati Ins. Co. v. Schaub, 2008-Ohio-4729, 2008 Ohio App. LEXIS 3986 (Ohio Ct. App., Montgomery County 2008).

Evidence received from two medical experts supported a finding that appellant, an alleged incompetent, was in fact incompetent. The incompetent's psychiatrist testified that the incompetent was non-compliant in taking medication for her acknowledged mental illness and that when off medication, the incompetent did bizarre things, and the second expert reported that the incompetent was unable to make decisions concerning issues of daily living or to manage her own finances. In re Guardianship of Guill, 2008-Ohio-696, 2008 Ohio App. LEXIS 582 (Ohio Ct. App., Richland County 2008).

Evidence that a ward was a paranoid schizophrenic, that he was unable to independently provide for his basic needs, and that he had been arrested 21 times during a two-and-a-half-year period on various criminal charges, including disorderly conduct for urinating in public places and criminal trespass, constituted sufficient evidence to support the trial court's finding that the ward was incompetent under R.C. 2111.01(D) by clear and convincing evidence, as required by R.C. 2111.02(B). In re Crawford, 2007-Ohio-2179, 2007 Ohio App. LEXIS 2043 (Ohio Ct. App., Richland County 2007).

When the guardian of an applicant for Medicaid assistance, who was in a nursing home, initiated proceedings to evict the applicant's son from the applicant's real property so that the property could be sold to render the applicant eligible for such assistance, it was unnecessary to stay these proceedings pending a determination of whether the father would be returning to the property because this issue was determined by the probate court, under R.C. 2111.01 et seq., which had already decided that the father could not return to his home. Barnick v. Barnick, 2007-Ohio-635, 2007 Ohio App. LEXIS 572 (Ohio Ct. App., Cuyahoga County 2007).

There was clear and convincing evidence which supported a probate court's adoption of a magistrate's determination that an individual was incompetent and required the appointment of a guardian over her person and property, pursuant to R.C. 2111.02(C)(3) and 2111.01(D), as the individual suffered from multiple sclerosis, dementia, and organic mood disorder, and she was not able to walk, feed, dress, or bathe herself, and was not capable of making decisions concerning medical treatment and diet. In re Poliksa, 2006-Ohio-2617, 2006 Ohio App. LEXIS 2464 (Ohio Ct. App., Hamilton County 2006).

There was sufficient evidence to support a probate court's denial of an incompetent's motion to terminate a guardianship pursuant to R.C. 2111.47, as she suffered from Parkinson's Disease and dementia and there was evidence from treating doctors and others that the incompetent, who fit into that definition under R.C. 2111.01(D), was unable to care for herself, could not handle all of her physical responsibilities, was not clear in her thinking, acted impulsively, and could not manage to take her medications regularly without assistance. In re Guardianship of Morton, 2006-Ohio-1139, 2006 Ohio App. LEXIS 1028 (Ohio Ct. App., Miami County 2006).

Summary judgment in application for guardianship of father was reversed and remanded after the probate court failed to hold a hearing; although a doctor and the court investigator concluded that the father was not mentally impaired, the child's affidavit alleging that the father withdrew funds from bank accounts with nothing to show for it raised a genuine issue of material fact under R.C. 2111.01(D). In re McClintock, 2003-Ohio-5147, 2003 Ohio App. LEXIS 4662 (Ohio Ct. App., Harrison County 2003).

Under R.C. 2111.01(D) as amended in January, 1990, a person cannot be found to be incompetent solely on the basis of a physical disability. There must also be proof of mental impairment: In re Bolander, 88 Ohio App. 3d 498, 624 N.E.2d 322, 1993 Ohio App. LEXIS 3363 (Ohio Ct. App., Lake County 1993).

This statute treats incompetency resulting from drunkenness in the same way that it treats incapacity resulting from mental disability: Murphy v. Murphy, 85 Ohio App. 392, 40 Ohio Op. 254, 87 N.E.2d 102, 54 Ohio Law Abs. 116, 1948 Ohio App. LEXIS 655 (Ohio Ct. App., Hamilton County 1948).

**—Evidence sufficient**

There was clear and convincing evidence that a ward was incompetent and that a guardian of the person was warranted as doctor one diagnosed her with schizophrenia and doctor two diagnosed her with paranoid psychosis; the doctors indicated that the ward's paranoid psychosis was affecting her judgment and personal care and that she had stopped taking her psychotropic medication, was frequently agitated, paranoid and suspicious of staff, had delusions about being impregnated and visual hallucinations about people traveling through walls, threw food, refused to wear clothes at times, and was unwilling to accept assistance with her hygiene and dressing. In re Rose, 2017-Ohio-694, 85 N.E.3d 498, 2017 Ohio App. LEXIS 704 (Ohio Ct. App., Champaign County 2017).

Trial court's determination that an individual was incompetent was not against the manifest weight of the evidence because the trial court based its decision on the evaluation of the individual by the individual's doctor of ten years, the testimony before the court at the hearing, and the court's ability to observe the individual in the courtroom and to hear the individual's responses to specific questions. In re Sauber, 2017-Ohio-1317, 2017 Ohio App. LEXIS 1337 (Ohio Ct. App., Seneca County 2017).

Probate court did not abuse its discretion by appointing a guardian for the ward because clear and convincing evidence supported the conclusion that the ward was no longer competent to manage his own business and personal affairs and a guardianship was necessary. Based on diminished capacity and the risk of abuse at the hands of third parties and with the extreme risk from inability to reliably administer medication, the guardianship was appropriate. In re Guardianship of Schwarzbach, 2017-Ohio-7299, 2017 Ohio App. LEXIS 3590 (Ohio Ct. App., Franklin County 2017).

Wife's motion to terminate the guardianship of her husband, who was suffering from Alzheimer's, was properly denied because the probate court determined that the husband was not competent, the powers of attorney that he had signed before losing his competency were not as effective for managing his care as a full guardianship, and he required a guardian due to his incompetency. In re Nauth, 2016-Ohio-5089, 2016 Ohio App. LEXIS 2974 (Ohio Ct. App., Medina County 2016).

Probate court properly adopted a magistrate's decision to appoint a guardian over the person of an allegedly incompetent person (IP) because the determination was based on relevant information, including the IP's mental impairment and other physical ailments, and his conduct. In re Guardianship of Al Bani, 2014-Ohio-5783, 2014 Ohio App. LEXIS 5595 (Ohio Ct. App., Summit County 2014).

Adoption of a magistrate's decision to appoint a guardian over the person of an allegedly incompetent person (IP) was supported by the weight of the evidence, as there was testimony from multiple health care providers and others that the IP was not capable of taking proper care of himself or his property. In re Guardianship of Al Bani, 2014-Ohio-5783, 2014 Ohio App. LEXIS 5595 (Ohio Ct. App., Summit County 2014).

Probate court did not abuse its discretion in granting the guardianship over the ward,because there was evidence that the ward suffered from a mental impairment or disability and was incapable of properly caring for himself or his property. In re Guardianship of Kalan, 2014-Ohio-4159, 2014 Ohio App. LEXIS 4075 (Ohio Ct. App., Mahoning County 2014).

Trial court's finding of respondent's incompetency was not against the manifest weight of the evidence, as the disarray in respondent's home, the fact that respondent had waited for days to seek medical attention for a fractured hip, respondent's refusal of physical therapy, and respondent's refusals to take prescribed mental health medications supported the conclusion that respondent could not be relied upon to take proper care of herself. In re Guardianship of Waters, 2013-Ohio-4132, 2013 Ohio App. LEXIS 4323 (Ohio Ct. App., Warren County 2013).

There was credible evidence that appellant was incompetent, as two expert doctor evaluations and a report from a court investigator all concluded appellant was incapable of making decisions concerning appellant's medical treatment and finances because of appellant's mental illness. In re Guardianship of Jung, 2012-Ohio-1873, 2012 Ohio App. LEXIS 1640 (Ohio Ct. App., Ottawa County 2012).

Evidence that a ward was a paranoid schizophrenic, that he was unable to independently provide for his basic needs, and that he had been arrested 21 times during a two-and-a-half-year period on various criminal charges, including disorderly conduct for urinating in public places and criminal trespass, constituted sufficient evidence to support the trial court's finding that the ward was incompetent under R.C. 2111.01(D) by clear and convincing evidence, as required by R.C. 2111.02(B). In re Crawford, 2007-Ohio-2179, 2007 Ohio App. LEXIS 2043 (Ohio Ct. App., Richland County 2007).

**Jury service**

The general rule that a party is deemed to have waived the disqualification of a juror unless he is able to show upon hearing that with the exercise of reasonable diligence he could not have objected to the seating of such juror at his impaneling thereof, applies to a juror who is an incompetent person under this section, and by reason of advanced age and mental and physical disability and infirmity is incapable of caring for his person and estate: Cottman v. Federman Co., 71 Ohio App. 89, 25 Ohio Op. 435, 47 N.E.2d 1009, 1942 Ohio App. LEXIS 571 (Ohio Ct. App., Summit County 1942).

**Limited guardian**

Probate court did not abuse its discretion where it denied an incompetent adult's motion to stay proceedings involving the appointment of a limited guardian pursuant to R.C. 2111.01(B)(1) for the purpose of assuring that the incompetent received a full psychiatric evaluation, as there was sufficient notice given, there was insufficient evidence to show that the incompetent had established her residence in Alabama instead of Ohio, and she was given the opportunity to present witnesses. In re Lipford, 2007-Ohio-3527, 2007 Ohio App. LEXIS 3260 (Ohio Ct. App., Cuyahoga County 2007).

**Standard of proof**

A motion for granting an order for removal of a respirator from a terminally ill individual is a civil matter and the criminal standard of proof — beyond a reasonable doubt — cannot be applied: Leach v. Akron General Medical Center, 68 Ohio Misc. 1, 22 Ohio Op. 3d 49, 426 N.E.2d 809, 1980 Ohio Misc. LEXIS 67 (Ohio C.P. 1980).

### NOTES TO UNPUBLISHED DECISIONS

**Incompetency**

*Unpublished decision:* Bankruptcy court was not in a position to declare a debtor incompetent because the materials supplied showed more of a physical disability; it suggested a possibility of lessened cognitive function. The record did not leave the court with the firm conviction that the debtor met the definition of incompetency, thereby warranting appointment of a next friend. In re Burchell, 2014 Bankr. LEXIS 1336 (Bankr. N.D. Ohio Mar. 31, 2014).

### ATTORNEY GENERAL OPINIONS

The Ohio Department of Mental Retardation and Developmental Disabilities may delegate to an agency providing protective services under contract with the Department the duty of filing, pursuant to R.C. 5123.58, applications in probate courts for appointment as a guardian or trustee: 1984 Ohio Op. Att'y Gen. No. 015 (1984).

A member of the state teachers retirement system who has the requisite age and years of service to qualify for superannuation retirement is not disqualified for such form of retirement merely by reason of his mental incompetency, and the guardian of the estate of the member may apply for the retirement allowance which is payable throughout the life of the member: 1956 OAG No. 6553 (1956).

A guardian merely by virtue of his office is without authority to select a superannuation retirement payment option for his ward under R.C. 3307.50, which would provide a lesser allowance of equivalent actuarial value to the ward for his lifetime and payments after the ward's death to a beneficiary designated by the guardian. Before the state teachers retirement board honors the selection of such an option, it should require adequate proof that a probate court has ordered or authorized the guardian to select such option: 1956 OAG No. 6553 (1956).

A student who has reached the age of 18 is entitled to attend school free in the district of his parents' or guardian's actual residence, or, if he works to support himself by his own labor, in the district in which he is employed. For purposes of R.C. 3313.64, the term "guardian" must be given a liberal construction, and can include a person who stands in loco parentis to an adult student: 1974 Ohio Op. Att'y Gen. No. 076 (1974).

### RESEARCH REFERENCES AND PRACTICE AIDS

**Cross-References to Related Sections**

Fiduciary defined, RC § 2109.01.
Gifts or transfers to minors, RC § 1339.31 et seq.
Legal disability defined, RC § 2131.02.
Mental incompetent; guardian's authority as to consent, RC § 5126.043.
Mentally retarded minors, guardianship of, RC § 5123.93.
Payment of reparations to person under age eighteen, RC § 2743.66.
Physically infirm adult may petition for conservatorship, RC § 2111.021.
Rules and procedure of court of common pleas to govern, RC § 2101.32.
Will construed, RC § 2107.01.

**Practice Guides**

Anderson's Ohio Probate Practice and Procedure § 28.01 General
Anderson's Ohio Probate Practice and Procedure § 37.01 General

**Practice Forms**

Application for Appointment of Guardian of Alleged Incompetent, Couse's Ohio Form Book Form SPF 17.0

Statement of Expert Evaluation, Couse's Ohio Form Book Form SPF 17.1

Investigator's Report, Couse's Ohio Form Book Form SPF 17.8

Standard Probate Form 17.1 (Guardianship) 1 Statement of Expert Evaluation 2(Cuyahoga County Form), 14 OH Forms of Pleading & Practice — Probate Form 33:17



## § 2111.021 Physically infirm adult may petition for conservatorship.

A competent adult who is physically infirm may petition the probate court of the county in which the petitioner resides, to place, for a definite or indefinite period of time, the petitioner's person, any or all of the petitioner's real or personal property, or both under a conservatorship with the court. A petitioner either may grant specific powers to the conservator or court or may limit any powers granted by law to the conservator or court, except that the petitioner may not limit the powers granted to the court by this section and may not limit the requirement for bond as determined by the court. The petition shall state whether the person of the competent adult will be placed under the conservatorship, shall state with particularity all real and personal property that will be placed under the conservatorship, shall state the powers granted and any limitation upon the powers of the conservator or court, and shall state the name of a proposed suitable conservator.

After a hearing, if the court finds that the petition was voluntarily filed and that the proposed conservator is suitable, the court shall issue an order of conservatorship. Upon issuance of the order, all sections of the Revised Code governing a guardianship of the person, the estate, or both, whichever is involved, except those sections the application of which specifically is limited by the petitioner, and all rules and procedures governing a guardianship of the person, the estate, or both, shall apply to the conservatorship, including, but not limited to, applicable bond and accounting requirements.

A conservatorship shall terminate upon a judicial determination of incompetency, the death of the petitioner, the order of the probate court, or the execution of a written termination notice by the petitioner. A termination notice shall take effect upon execution by the petitioner, and shall be filed with the court and served upon the conservator. A termination notice executed by a petitioner relative to a conservatorship of the estate and the termination of a conservatorship of the estate based upon a termination notice are void unless the termination notice is filed with the court within fourteen days after its execution. Modification of the powers of a conservator or the court may be made by the petitioner upon motion to the court at any time during the conservatorship. Neither the establishment of a conservatorship nor the filing of a petition for conservatorship with the probate court shall be considered as evidence of mental impairment under section 2111.01 of the Revised Code.

Upon motion to the probate court and a showing of good cause, the court may make confidential, or remove from confidential status, any file, record, petition, motion, account, or paper, except for an index, docket, or journal, that pertains to a conservatorship and that is in the possession of the court.

**HISTORY:**
143 v S 46. Eff 1-1-90; 2011 SB 124, § 1, eff. Jan. 13, 2012.

**Editor's Notes**
Acts 2011, SB 124, § 3 provides: "The provisions of this act that relate to the estates of decedents apply to the estates of decedents who die on or after the effective date of this act."

**Amendment Notes**
The 2011 amendment inserted "of the person, the estate, or both" in the second sentence of the second paragraph; and made stylistic changes.



### NOTES TO DECISIONS

Analysis

Generally
Attorney fees
Capacity to sue
Less restrictive alternative
Physical disability, former law

**Generally**
As an individual was found to be mentally incompetent, she could not have a conservatorship under R.C. 2111.021 and accordingly, the appointment of a guardian over the individual's person and property was the least restrictive alternative pursuant to R.C. 2111.02(C)(5). In re Poliksa, 2006-Ohio-2617, 2006 Ohio App. LEXIS 2464 (Ohio Ct. App., Hamilton County 2006).

The conservatorship statute, R.C § 2111.021(A), merely states that one may petition the probate court of the county in which he resides; a trial court had proper subject matter jurisdiction to impose a conservatorship over the effects of a prison inmate, convicted of killing his wife and four others, because the issue that gave rise to the conservatorship took place in the same county as the court. In re Conservatorship of Ahmed, 2003-Ohio-3272, 2003 Ohio App. LEXIS 2938 (Ohio Ct. App., Belmont County 2003).

A competent ward may request or authorize transactions that fall under a conservatorship, including expenditures that benefit the conservator: Miebach v. Mathias, 91 Ohio Misc. 2d 72, 697 N.E.2d 297, 1998 Ohio Misc. LEXIS 10 (Ohio Ct. App., Licking County 1998).

Revised Code § 2111.02.1, which was enacted on the same date that the present versions of R.C. 2111.01 and 2111.02 were last amended, sets forth a procedure under which an adult who is physically infirm, can petition the probate court to place his real or personal property under a conservatorship. However, in order to invoke this procedure, the adult must be competent: In re Bolander, 88 Ohio App. 3d 498, 624 N.E.2d 322, 1993 Ohio App. LEXIS 3363 (Ohio Ct. App., Lake County 1993).

**Attorney fees**
Although the conservatorship petition limited the powers of the probate court under R.C. 2111.021, it could not limit its powers over the accounting, which included a determination did reasonable attorney fees. The petition's limiting language over "all property" did not dispose of the probate court's authority to determine reasonable attorney fees. In re Conservatorship of: Adamosky, 2011 Ohio 3166, 2011 Ohio App. LEXIS 2672 (June 21, 2011).

**Capacity to sue**
In a medical malpractice suit, plaintiff, as the disabled patient's conservator, had standing to sue on behalf of the patient, by court order, by statute, and by Civ.R. 17(A) as the real party in interest. Moore v. Mount Carmel Health Sys., 2018-Ohio-2831, 117 N.E.3d 89, 2018 Ohio App. LEXIS 3056 (Ohio Ct. App., Franklin County 2018), rev'd, 2020-Ohio-4113, 162 Ohio St. 3d 106, 164 N.E.3d 376, 2020 Ohio LEXIS 1898 (Ohio 2020).

**Less restrictive alternative**
As an individual was found to be mentally incompetent, she could not have a conservatorship under R.C. 2111.021 and accordingly, the appointment of a guardian over the individual's person and property was the least restrictive alternative pursuant to R.C. 2111.02(C)(5). In re Poliksa, 2006-Ohio-2617, 2006 Ohio App. LEXIS 2464 (Ohio Ct. App., Hamilton County 2006).

**Physical disability, former law**
The spirit and purpose of the provision of R.C. 2111.02 that "if a person is incompetent due to physical disability, the consent of the incompetent must first be obtained before the appointment of a guardian for him" requires that the "consent" should be in writing or made in open court by the proposed ward who is mentally competent: In re Guardianship of Gallagher, 2 Ohio App. 3d 218, 441 N.E.2d 593, 1981 Ohio App. LEXIS 9949 (Ohio Ct. App., Madison County 1981).

When one, due to physical disability, has voluntarily consented to the appointment of a guardian under the statutes providing for such appointment and the court has acted upon the matter and made the appointment, the ward cannot terminate the guardianship by merely withdrawing her consent: In re Guardianship of Barr, 156 N.E.2d 357, 80 Ohio Law Abs. 488, 1958 Ohio Misc. LEXIS 301 (Ohio P. Ct. 1958).

The question of consent, as required by the statute, to the appointment of a guardian is an issue of fact to be established by the evidence and not one affecting the court's jurisdiction: In re Gerstenek, 139 N.E.2d 64, 76 Ohio Law Abs. 280, 1956 Ohio App. LEXIS 771 (Ohio Ct. App., Cuyahoga County 1956).

There is no legal distinction between a guardian for a mentally incompetent person and a person incompetent by reason of physical disability or infirmity, except that specified in this section, which requires that a person for whom a guardian is to be appointed for reason of physical disability or infirmity must consent to the appointment of a guardian: In re Tillman, 137 N.E.2d 172, 73 Ohio Law Abs. 534, 1956 Ohio Misc. LEXIS 333 (Ohio P. Ct. 1956), [See also In re Guardianship of Tillman, 100 Ohio App. 291, 60 Ohio Op. 254, 136 N.E.2d 291, 1955 Ohio App. LEXIS 586 (Ohio Ct. App., Darke County 1955).].

The practical effect of paragraph two of this section, regarding consent of the ward, is to place in the hands of the ward the power to select a guardian, because at any time before the appointment the applicant can withdraw the consent: In re Luft's Guardianship, 91 Ohio App. 409, 45 Ohio Op. 333, 97 N.E.2d 561, 59 Ohio Law Abs. 33, 1950 Ohio App. LEXIS 566 (Ohio Ct. App., Franklin County 1950).

The spirit and purpose of the provision of this section, "that if the incompetency" of an incompetent "be due to physical disability or infirmity the consent of the incompetent" to the appointment of a guardian "must first be obtained," require that "the consent" should be in writing or made in open court by the proposed ward who is mentally competent: In re Irvine's Guardianship, 72 Ohio App. 405, 27 Ohio Op. 332, 52 N.E.2d 536, 1943 Ohio App. LEXIS 719 (Ohio Ct. App., Knox County 1943).

The appointment of a guardian for an alleged incompetent can be made, under the provisions of this section, only upon the basis of mental disability or infirmity when the incompetent does not consent but in fact opposes the appointment: Jacobs v. Porter, 73 Ohio App. 286, 28 Ohio Op. 449, 43 N.E.2d 879, 36 Ohio Law Abs. 282, 1941 Ohio App. LEXIS 723 (Ohio Ct. App., Franklin County 1941).

### RESEARCH REFERENCES AND PRACTICE AIDS

**Ohio Administrative Code**
Department of mental retardation and developmental disabilities—Protective services: petition for conservatorship. OAC 5123-15-01.

**Practice Manuals and Treatises**
Anderson's Ohio Probate Practice and Procedure Standard Probate Form 20.0 Application for Appointment of Conservator
Anderson's Ohio Probate Practice and Procedure Standard Probate Form 20.1 Judgment Entry—Appointment of Conservator
Anderson's Ohio Probate Practice and Procedure Outline No. § 13-3 Appointment of guardian-conservatorship

**Practice Guides**
Anderson's Ohio Probate Practice and Procedure § 28.04 Conservatorships

**Practice Forms**
Application for Appointment of Conservator, Couse's Ohio Form Book Form SPF 20.0
Judgment Entry—Appointment of Conservator, Couse's Ohio Form Book Form SPF 20.1

# CHAPTER 2112
# ADULT GUARDIANSHIP AND PROTECTIVE PROCEEDINGS JURISDICTION ACT

Section

### § 2112.01 Definitions.

As used in this chapter:

(A) "Adult" means an individual who is eighteen years of age or older.

(B) "Guardian" has the same meaning as in section 2111.01 of the Revised Code.

(C) "Guardian of the person" means a person appointed by the court to make decisions regarding the support, care, education, health, and welfare of a ward. "Guardian of the person" does not include a guardian ad litem.

(D) "Guardian of the estate" means a person appointed by the court to administer the estate of a ward.

(E) "Ward" means any adult who has been adjudicated incompetent and for whom a guardian is acting or for whom the probate court is acting pursuant to section 2111.50 of the Revised Code.

(F) "Emergency" means a circumstance that makes it reasonably certain that immediate action is required to prevent significant injury to a respondent's health, safety, welfare, or property and for which the appointment of a guardian or issuance of a protective order is necessary because no other person has authority and is willing to act on the respondent's behalf.

(G) "Guardianship order" means an order appointing a guardian.

(H) "Guardianship proceeding" means a judicial proceeding in which an order for the appointment of a guardian is sought or has been issued.

(I) "Home state" means the state in which the respondent was physically present, including any period of temporary absence, for at least six consecutive months immediately before the filing of an application for appointment of a guardian or the issuance of a protective order or, if none, the state in which the respondent was physically present, including any period of temporary absence, for at least six consecutive months ending within the six months prior to the filing of the application.

(J) "Party" means the respondent, applicant, guardian, or other person allowed by the court to participate in a guardianship or protective proceeding.

(K) "Person," except in the terms guardian of the person and protected person, means an individual, parent, corporation, business trust, estate, trust, partnership, limited liability company, association, joint venture, government, governmental agency or instrumentality, public corporation, or other legal or commercial entity.

(L) "Protected person" means an adult for whom a protective order has been issued.

(M) "Protective order" means an order appointing a guardian or other order under division (B)(3) of section 2111.02 of the Revised Code related to the management of an adult's person, property, or both or an order under section 2111.022 of the Revised Code related to the management of an individual's property.

(N) "Protective proceeding" means a judicial proceeding in which a protective order is sought or has been issued.

(O) "Record" means information that is inscribed on a tangible medium or that is stored in an electronic or other medium and is retrievable in perceivable form.

(P) "Respondent" means an adult for whom a protective order or the appointment of a guardian is sought.

(Q) "Significant-connection state" means a state, other than the home state, with which a respondent has a significant connection other than mere physical presence and in which substantial evidence concerning the respondent is available.

(R) "Incompetent" has the same meaning as in section 2111.01 of the Revised Code.

(S) "State" means a state of the United States, the District of Columbia, Puerto Rico, the United States Virgin Islands, or any territory or insular possession subject to the jurisdiction of the United States. "State" includes an Indian tribe or band that is recognized by federal law or formally acknowledged by a state.

**HISTORY:**
2012 HB 27, § 1, eff. Mar. 22, 2013.

**Editor's Notes**
Acts 2012, HB 27, § 3 provides: "Sections 2112.01, 2112.011, 2112.02, 2112.03, 2112.04, 2112.05, 2112.31, 2112.32, 2112.41, 2112.42, and 2112.43 of the Revised Code, as enacted by this act, apply to guardianship and protective proceedings begun before the effective date of this act, regardless of whether a guardianship or protective order has been issued pursuant to those proceedings."

### § 2112.011 Chapter title.

Chapter 2112. of the Revised Code may be cited as the Adult Guardianship and Protective Proceedings Jurisdiction Act.

**HISTORY:**
2012 HB 27, § 1, eff. Mar. 22, 2013.

**Editor's Notes**
Acts 2012, HB 27, § 3 provides: "Sections 2112.01, 2112.011, 2112.02, 2112.03, 2112.04, 2112.05, 2112.31, 2112.32, 2112.41, 2112.42, and 2112.43 of the Revised Code, as enacted by this act, apply to guardianship and protective proceedings begun before the effective date of this act, regardless of whether a guardianship or protective order has been issued pursuant to those proceedings."

### § 2112.02 Application of chapter on foreign country.

A probate court of this state may treat a foreign country as if it were a state for the purpose of applying this chapter.

**HISTORY:**
2012 HB 27, § 1, eff. Mar. 22, 2013.

**Editor's Notes**
Acts 2012, HB 27, § 3 provides: "Sections 2112.01, 2112.011, 2112.02, 2112.03, 2112.04, 2112.05, 2112.31, 2112.32, 2112.41, 2112.42, and 2112.43 of the Revised Code, as enacted by this act, apply to guardianship and protective proceedings begun before the effective date of this act, regardless of whether a guardianship or protective order has been issued pursuant to those proceedings."

### § 2112.03 Communication with other state courts.

(A) A probate court of this state may communicate with a court in another state concerning a proceeding arising under this chapter. The probate court may allow the parties to participate in the communication. Except as otherwise provided in division (B) of this section, the probate court shall make a record of the communication. The record may be limited to the fact that the communication occurred.

(B) Probate courts may communicate concerning schedules, calendars, court records, and other administrative matters without making a record.

**HISTORY:**
2012 HB 27, § 1, eff. Mar. 22, 2013.

**Editor's Notes**
Acts 2012, HB 27, § 3 provides: "Sections 2112.01, 2112.011, 2112.02, 2112.03, 2112.04, 2112.05, 2112.31, 2112.32, 2112.41, 2112.42, and 2112.43 of the Revised Code, as enacted by this act, apply to guardianship and protective proceedings begun before the effective date of this act, regardless of whether a guardianship or protective order has been issued pursuant to those proceedings."

### § 2112.04 Requests of other state courts.

(A) In a guardianship or protective proceeding in this state, a probate court of this state may request the appropriate court of another state to do any of the following:

(1) Hold an evidentiary hearing;

(2) Order a person in that state to produce evidence or give testimony pursuant to the procedures of that state;

(3) Order that an evaluation or assessment be made of the respondent;

(4) Order any appropriate investigation of a person involved in the proceeding;

(5) Forward to the probate court of this state a certified copy of the transcript or other record of a hearing under division (A)(1) of this section or any other proceeding, any evidence otherwise produced under division (A)(2) of this section, and any evaluation or assessment prepared in compliance with an order under division (A)(3) or (4) of this section;

(6) Issue any order necessary to assure the appearance in the proceeding of a person whose presence is necessary for the probate court to make a determination, including the respondent, ward, or a protected person;

(7) Issue an order authorizing the release of medical, financial, criminal, or other relevant information in that state, including protected health information as authorized in 45 C.F.R. 164.504, as amended.

(B) If a court of another state in which a guardianship or protective proceeding is pending requests assistance of the kind provided in division (A) of this section, a probate court of this state has jurisdiction for the limited purpose of granting the request or making reasonable efforts to comply with the request. A probate court of this state may require an advance deposit for costs in an amount sufficient to obtain or provide the requested assistance.

**HISTORY:**

2012 HB 27, § 1, eff. Mar. 22, 2013.

**Editor's Notes**

Acts 2012, HB 27, § 3 provides: "Sections 2112.01, 2112.011, 2112.02, 2112.03, 2112.04, 2112.05, 2112.31, 2112.32, 2112.41, 2112.42, and 2112.43 of the Revised Code, as enacted by this act, apply to guardianship and protective proceedings begun before the effective date of this act, regardless of whether a guardianship or protective order has been issued pursuant to those proceedings."

### § 2112.05 Testimony of witness in another state; documentary evidence transmitted from another state; adoptions of local rules of practice.

(A) In a guardianship proceeding or protective proceeding, in addition to other procedures that may be available, the testimony of a witness who is located in another state may be offered by deposition or other means allowable in this state for testimony taken in another state. The probate court on the court's own motion may order that the testimony of a witness be taken in another state and may prescribe the manner in which and the terms upon which the testimony is to be taken.

(B) In a guardianship or protective proceeding, a probate court in this state may permit a witness located in another state to be deposed or to testify by telephone, audiovisual, or other electronic means. A probate court of this state shall cooperate with the court of the other state in designating an appropriate location for the deposition or testimony.

(C) Documentary evidence transmitted from another state to a probate court of this state by technological means that do not produce an original writing may not be excluded from evidence on an objection based on the best evidence rule.

(D) A probate court of this state may adopt local rules of practice that promote the use of any device or procedure to facilitate the expeditious disposition of the cases.

**HISTORY:**

2012 HB 27, § 1, eff. Mar. 22, 2013.

**Editor's Notes**

Acts 2012, HB 27, § 3 provides: "Sections 2112.01, 2112.011, 2112.02, 2112.03, 2112.04, 2112.05, 2112.31, 2112.32, 2112.41, 2112.42, and 2112.43 of the Revised Code, as enacted by this act, apply to guardianship and protective proceedings begun before the effective date of this act, regardless of whether a guardianship or protective order has been issued pursuant to those proceedings."

### § 2112.21 Jurisdiction to appoint guardian.

(A) A probate court of this state has jurisdiction to appoint a guardian or issue a protective order for a respondent if any of the following applies:

(1) This state is the respondent's home state.

(2) On the date that the application is filed, this state is a significant-connection state, and either of the following applies:

(a) The respondent does not have a home state, or a court of the respondent's home state has declined to exercise jurisdiction because this state is a more appropriate forum.

(b) The respondent has a home state, a petition for an appointment or order is not pending in a court of that state or another significant-connection state, and before the probate court makes the appointment or issues the order all of the following apply:

(i) An application for an appointment or order is not filed in the respondent's home state.

(ii) An objection to the probate court's jurisdiction is not filed by a person required to be notified of the proceeding.

(iii) The probate court in this state concludes that the probate court is an appropriate forum under the factors set forth in section 2112.24 of the Revised Code.

(3) This state does not have jurisdiction under division (A) or (B) of this section, the respondent's home state and all significant-connection states have declined to exercise jurisdiction because this state is the more appropriate forum, and jurisdiction in this state is consistent with the constitutions of this state and the United States.

(4) The requirements for special jurisdiction under section 2112.22 of the Revised Code are met.

(B) In determining whether a respondent has a significant connection with a particular state for purposes of this section, the probate court may consider any of the following:

(1) The location of the respondent's family and other persons required to be notified of the guardianship or protective proceeding;

(2) The length of time the respondent at any time was physically present in the state and the duration of any absence;

(3) The location of the respondent's property;

(4) The extent to which the respondent has ties to the state, including, but not limited to, voting registration, state or local tax return filing, vehicle registration, driver's license, social relationships, and receipt of services.

**HISTORY:**

2012 HB 27, § 1, eff. Mar. 22, 2013.

### § 2112.22 Special jurisdiction of court.

(A) A probate court of this state lacking jurisdiction under section 2112.21 of the Revised Code has special jurisdiction to do any of the following:

(1) Appoint a guardian in an emergency for a respondent who is physically present in this state;

(2) Issue a protective order in an emergency with respect to the adult or to the real or tangible personal property located in this state;

(3) Appoint a guardian for a ward or protected person for whom a provisional order to transfer the proceeding from another state has been issued under procedures similar to section 2112.31 of the Revised Code.

(B) If an application for the appointment of a guardian in an emergency is brought in this state and this state was not the respondent's home state on the date that the application was filed, the probate court shall dismiss the proceeding at the request of the court of the home state, if any, whether dismissal is requested before or after the emergency appointment.

**HISTORY:**

2012 HB 27, § 1, eff. Mar. 22, 2013.

**§ 2112.23 Exclusive and continuing jurisdiction.**

Except as otherwise provided in section 2112.22 of the Revised Code, a probate court that has appointed a guardian or issued a protective order consistent with this chapter has exclusive and continuing jurisdiction over the proceeding until it is terminated by the probate court or the appointment or order expires by the appointment's or order's own terms.

**HISTORY:**

2012 HB 27, § 1, eff. Mar. 22, 2013.

**§ 2112.24 Court may decline to exercise jurisdiction when court of another state more appropriate forum.**

(A) A probate court of this state having jurisdiction under section 2112.21 of the Revised Code to appoint a guardian or issue a protective order may decline to exercise the court's jurisdiction if the probate court determines at any time that a court of another state is a more appropriate forum.

(B) If a probate court of this state declines to exercise the court's jurisdiction under division (A) of this section, the probate court shall either dismiss or stay the proceeding. The probate court may impose any condition that the probate court considers just and proper, including the condition that an application for the appointment of a guardian or issuance of a protective order be filed promptly in another state.

(C) In determining whether it is an appropriate forum, the probate court shall consider all relevant factors, including, but not limited to, the following:

(1) Any expressed preference of the respondent;

(2) Whether abuse, neglect, or exploitation of the respondent has occurred or is likely to occur and which state could best protect the respondent from the abuse, neglect, or exploitation;

(3) The length of time the respondent was physically present in or was a legal resident of this or another state;

(4) The distance of the respondent from the court in each state;

(5) The financial circumstances of the respondent's estate;

(6) The nature and location of the evidence;

(7) The ability of the court in each state to decide the issue expeditiously and the procedures necessary to present evidence;

(8) The familiarity of the court of each state with the facts and issues in the proceeding;

(9) The probate court's ability, if an appointment were made, to monitor the conduct of the guardian;

(10) Any other factors that the probate court considers relevant.

**HISTORY:**

2012 HB 27, § 1, eff. Mar. 22, 2013.

**§ 2112.25 Actions by court when jurisdiction acquired because of unjustifiable conduct.**

(A) If at any time a probate court of this state determines that the probate court has acquired jurisdiction to appoint a guardian or issue a protective order because of unjustifiable conduct, the probate court may do any of the following:

(1) Decline to exercise jurisdiction;

(2) Exercise jurisdiction for the limited purpose of fashioning an appropriate remedy to ensure the health, safety, and welfare of the respondent or the protection of the respondent's property or to prevent a repetition of the unjustifiable conduct, including staying the proceeding until an application for the appointment of a guardian or issuance of a protective order is filed in a court of another state having jurisdiction;

(3) Continue to exercise jurisdiction after considering all of the following:

(a) The extent to which the respondent and all persons required to be notified of the proceedings have acquiesced in the exercise of the probate court's jurisdiction;

(b) Whether the probate court is a more appropriate forum than the court of any other state under the factors set forth in division (C) of section 2112.24 of the Revised Code;

(c) Whether the court of any other state would have jurisdiction under factual circumstances in substantial conformity with the jurisdictional standards of section 2112.21 of the Revised Code.

(B) If a probate court of this state determines that the probate court has acquired jurisdiction to appoint a guardian or issue a protective order because a party seeking to invoke the court's jurisdiction engaged in unjustifiable conduct, the probate court may assess against that party necessary and reasonable expenses, including, but not limited to, attorney's fees, investigative fees, court costs, communication expenses, witness fees and expenses, and travel expenses. Except as otherwise provided by any provision of the Revised Code, the probate court may not assess fees, costs, or expenses of any kind against this state or a governmental subdivision, agency, or instrumentality of this state.

(C) As used in this section, "unjustifiable conduct" includes, but is not limited to, conduct by a person that attempts to create jurisdiction in this state by removing the adult from the adult's home state, secreting the adult, retaining the adult, or restraining or otherwise preventing the adult from returning to the adult's home state in order to prevent or deprive a court of the adult's home state from taking jurisdiction.

**HISTORY:**

2012 HB 27, § 1, eff. Mar. 22, 2013.

**§ 2112.26 Required notice.**

If an application for the appointment of a guardian or issuance of a protective order is brought in this state and this state was not the respondent's home state on the date that the application was filed, in addition to complying with the notice requirements of this state, the applicant shall give notice of the application to those persons who would be entitled to notice of the application if a proceeding were brought in the respondent's home state. The notice must be given in the same manner as notice is required to be given in this state.

**HISTORY:**

2012 HB 27, § 1, eff. Mar. 22, 2013.

**§ 2112.27 Application for appointment of guardian filed in multiple states.**

Except for an application for the appointment of a guardian in an emergency or issuance of a protective order in an emergency, if an application for the appointment of a guardian or issuance of a protective order is filed in this state and in another state and neither application has been dismissed or withdrawn, the following rules apply:

(A) If the probate court in this state has jurisdiction under section 2112.21 of the Revised Code, the probate court may proceed with the case unless a court in another state acquires jurisdiction under provisions similar to section 2112.21 of the Revised Code before the appointment or issuance of the order.

(B) If the probate court in this state does not have jurisdiction under section 2112.21 of the Revised Code, whether at the time the application is filed or at any time before the appointment or issuance of the order, the probate court shall stay the proceeding and communicate with the court in the other state. If the court in the other state has jurisdiction, the probate court in this state shall dismiss the application unless the court in the other state determines that the probate court in this state is a more appropriate forum.

**HISTORY:**

2012 HB 27, § 1, eff. Mar. 22, 2013.

**§ 2112.31 Petition to transfer guardianship to another state.**

(A) A guardian appointed in this state may petition the probate court to transfer the guardianship to another state.

(B) Notice of a petition under division (A) of this section must be given by the guardian to the persons that would be entitled to notice of an application in this state for the appointment of a guardian.

(C) On the probate court's own motion or on request of the guardian, ward, protected person, or other person required to be notified of the petition, the probate court shall hold a hearing on a petition filed pursuant to division (A) of this section.

(D) The probate court shall issue a provisional order granting a petition to transfer a guardianship of the person and shall direct the guardian to petition for guardianship in the other state if the probate court is satisfied that the guardianship will be accepted by the court in the other state, and the probate court finds all of the following:

(1) The ward is physically present in or is reasonably expected to move permanently to the other state.

(2) An objection to the transfer has not been made, or, if an objection has been made, the objector has not established that the transfer would be contrary to the interests of the ward.

(3) Plans for care and services for the ward in the other state are reasonable and sufficient.

(E) The probate court shall issue a provisional order granting a petition to transfer a guardianship of the estate and shall direct the guardian to petition for a guardianship of the estate in the other state if the probate court is satisfied that the guardianship of the estate will be accepted by the court of the other state, and the probate court finds all of the following:

(1) The ward is physically present in or is reasonably expected to move permanently to the other state, or the ward has a significant connection to the other state and meets the requirements of division (A)(2) of section 2112.21 of the Revised Code.

(2) An objection to the transfer has not been made, or, if an objection has been made, the objector has not established that the transfer would be contrary to the interests of the protected person.

(3) Adequate arrangements will be made for management of the ward's property.

(F) The probate court shall issue a final order confirming the transfer and terminating the guardianship upon the probate court's receipt of both of the following:

(1) A provisional order accepting the proceeding from the court to which the proceeding is to be transferred and that is issued under provisions similar to section 2112.32 of the Revised Code;

(2) The documents required to terminate a guardianship in this state.

(G) In determining whether a respondent has a significant connection with a particular state for purposes of this section, the probate court may consider any of the following:

(1) The location of the respondent's family and other persons required to be notified of the guardianship or protective proceeding;

(2) The length of time the respondent at any time was physically present in the state and the duration of any absence;

(3) The location of the respondent's property;

(4) The extent to which the respondent has ties to the state, including, but not limited to, voting registration, state or local tax return filing, vehicle registration, driver's license, social relationships, and receipt of services.

**HISTORY:**

2012 HB 27, § 1, eff. Mar. 22, 2013.

**Editor's Notes**

Acts 2012, HB 27, § 3 provides: "Sections 2112.01, 2112.011, 2112.02, 2112.03, 2112.04, 2112.05, 2112.31, 2112.32, 2112.41, 2112.42, and 2112.43 of the Revised Code, as enacted by this act, apply to guardianship and protective proceedings begun before the effective date of this act, regardless of whether a guardianship or protective order has been issued pursuant to those proceedings."

**NOTES TO DECISIONS**

**Appeal**

Provisional order transferring guardianship of an adult ward was not a final order under 2505.02(B)(1), as it did not affect a substantial right, determine the action, and prevent further judgment, or under R.C. 2505.02(B)(4), as the appellant was not foreclosed from appropriate relief in the future because appellate relief would be available upon appeal from the trial court's final order confirming the transfer and terminating the guardianship pursuant to R.C. 2112.31(F). Guardianship of Basista, 2015-Ohio-4831, 2015 Ohio App. LEXIS 4719 (Ohio Ct. App., Geauga County 2015).

## § 2112.32 Confirmation of guardianship transfer.

(A) To confirm transfer of a guardianship transferred to this state under provisions similar to section 2112.31 of the Revised Code, the guardian shall petition the probate court in this state to accept the guardianship of the person, guardianship of the estate, or both. The petition must include a certified copy of the other state's provisional order of transfer.

(B) Notice of a petition under division (A) of this section must be given by the guardian to those persons that would be entitled to notice if the petition were an application for the appointment of a guardian or issuance of a protective order in both the transferring state and this state. The notice must be given in the same manner as notice is required to be given in this state.

(C) On the probate court's own motion or on the request of the guardian, ward, protected person, or other person required to be notified of the proceeding, the probate court shall hold a hearing on a petition filed pursuant to division (A) of this section.

(D) The probate court shall issue a provisional order granting a petition filed under division (A) of this section unless either of the following applies:

(1) An objection is made, and the objector establishes that transfer of the proceeding would be contrary to the interests of the ward or protected person.

(2) The guardian is ineligible for appointment in this state.

(E) The probate court shall issue a final order accepting the proceeding and appointing the guardian as a guardian in this state upon the probate court's receipt from the court from which the proceeding is being transferred of a final order transferring the proceedings to this state issued under provisions similar to section 2112.31 of the Revised Code.

(F) In granting a petition under this section, the probate court shall recognize a guardianship order from the other state, including the determination of the incompetence of the ward and the appointment of the guardian. Nothing in this section shall limit the probate court's authority under Chapter 2111. of the Revised Code.

(G) The denial by a probate court of this state of a petition to accept a guardianship transferred from another state does not affect the ability of the guardian to seek appointment as a guardian in this state under section 2111.02 of the Revised Code if the probate court has jurisdiction to make an appointment other than by reason of the provisional order of transfer.

**HISTORY:**

2012 HB 27, § 1, eff. Mar. 22, 2013.

**Editor's Notes**

Acts 2012, HB 27, § 3 provides: "Sections 2112.01, 2112.011, 2112.02, 2112.03, 2112.04, 2112.05, 2112.31, 2112.32, 2112.41, 2112.42, and 2112.43 of the Revised Code, as enacted by this act, apply to guardianship and protective proceedings begun before the effective date of this act, regardless of whether a guardianship or protective order has been issued pursuant to those proceedings."

## § 2112.41 Registration of guardianship order in foreign jurisdiction.

If a guardian has been appointed in another state and an application for the appointment of a guardian of the person is not pending in this state, the guardian appointed in the other state, after giving notice to the appointing court of an intent to register, may register the guardianship order in this state by filing as a foreign judgment in a probate court, in any appropriate county of this state, certified copies of the order and letters of office.

**HISTORY:**

2012 HB 27, § 1, eff. Mar. 22, 2013.

**Editor's Notes**

Acts 2012, HB 27, § 3 provides: "Sections 2112.01, 2112.011, 2112.02, 2112.03, 2112.04, 2112.05, 2112.31, 2112.32, 2112.41, 2112.42, and 2112.43

of the Revised Code, as enacted by this act, apply to guardianship and protective proceedings begun before the effective date of this act, regardless of whether a guardianship or protective order has been issued pursuant to those proceedings."

### § 2112.42 Registration of protective order from foreign jurisdiction.

If a guardian of the estate has been appointed in another state and an application for the appointment of a guardian of the estate is not pending in this state, the guardian of the estate appointed in the other state, after giving notice to the appointing court of an intent to register, may register a protective order or guardianship in this state by filing as a foreign judgment in a probate court of this state, in any county in which property belonging to the ward or protected person is located, certified copies of the order and letters of office and of any bond.

**HISTORY:**

2012 HB 27, § 1, eff. Mar. 22, 2013.

**Editor's Notes**

Acts 2012, HB 27, § 3 provides: "Sections 2112.01, 2112.011, 2112.02, 2112.03, 2112.04, 2112.05, 2112.31, 2112.32, 2112.41, 2112.42, and 2112.43 of the Revised Code, as enacted by this act, apply to guardianship and protective proceedings begun before the effective date of this act, regardless of whether a guardianship or protective order has been issued pursuant to those proceedings."

### § 2112.43 Guardian may exercise powers authorized in order of appointment.

(A) Upon the registration of a guardianship or protective order from another state, the guardian may exercise in this state all powers authorized in the order of appointment except as prohibited under the laws of this state, including maintaining actions and proceedings in this state and, if the guardian is not a resident of this state, subject to any conditions imposed upon nonresident parties.

(B) A probate court of this state may grant any relief available under the Revised Code to enforce a registered order.

**HISTORY:**

2012 HB 27, § 1, eff. Mar. 22, 2013.

**Editor's Notes**

Acts 2012, HB 27, § 3 provides: "Sections 2112.01, 2112.011, 2112.02, 2112.03, 2112.04, 2112.05, 2112.31, 2112.32, 2112.41, 2112.42, and 2112.43 of the Revised Code, as enacted by this act, apply to guardianship and protective proceedings begun before the effective date of this act, regardless of whether a guardianship or protective order has been issued pursuant to those proceedings."

# CHAPTER 2131

# MISCELLANEOUS

Statute of Perpetuities



## STATUTE OF PERPETUITIES

### § 2131.08 Statute against perpetuities.

(A) Subject to sections 1746.14, 1747.09, and 2131.09 of the Revised Code, no interest in real or personal property shall be good unless it must vest, if at all, not later than twenty-one years after a life or lives in being at the creation of the interest. All estates given in tail, by deed or will, in real property lying within this state shall be and remain an absolute estate in fee simple to the issue of the first donee in tail. It is the intention by the adoption of this section to make effective in this state what is generally known as the common law rule against perpetuities, except as set forth in divisions (B) and (C) of this section.

(B) For the purposes of this section and subject to sections 1746.14, 1747.09, and 2131.09 of the Revised Code, the time of the creation of an interest in real or personal property subject to a power reserved by the grantor to revoke or terminate the interest shall be the time at which the reserved power expires by reason of the death of the grantor, by release of the power, or otherwise.

(C) Any interest in real or personal property that would violate the rule against perpetuities under division (A) of this section shall be reformed, within the limits of the rule, to approximate most closely the intention of the creator of the interest. In determining whether an interest would violate the rule and in reforming an interest, the period of perpetuities shall be measured by actual rather than possible events.

(D) For purposes of this section and subject to sections 1746.14, 1747.09, and 2131.09 of the Revised Code, the following apply:

(1) The time of the creation of an interest in real or personal property resulting from the exercise of a general power of appointment exercisable in a nonfiduciary capacity by deed, whether or not also exercisable by will, shall be the time at which that power of appointment is exercised.

(2) The time of the creation of an interest in real or personal property resulting from the termination, without exercise, of a general power of appointment exercisable in a nonfiduciary capacity by deed, whether or not also exercisable by will, shall be the time at which that power of appointment terminates by reason of the death of the power holder, by release of the power, or otherwise.

(E) Divisions (B) and (C) of this section shall be effective with respect to interests in real or personal property created by wills of decedents dying after December 31, 1967, with respect to interests in real or personal property created by inter vivos instruments executed after December 31, 1967, and with respect to interests in real or personal property created by inter vivos instruments executed on or before December 31, 1967, that by reason of division (B) of this section will be treated as interests created after December 31, 1967. Divisions (B) and (C) of this section shall be effective with respect to interests in real or personal property created by the exercise of a power of appointment if divisions (B) and (C) of this section apply to the instrument that exercises the power, whether or not divisions (B) and (C) of this section apply to the instrument that creates the power.

(F) Divisions (D) and (G) of this section are intended to be a statement of the common law of this state and shall be effective with respect to interests in real or personal property whenever created.

(G) For purposes of this section:

(1) "General power of appointment" has the same meaning as in section 2131.09 of the Revised Code.

(2) "Exercisable by deed" in reference to a power of appointment means a power that can be exercised during the power holder's lifetime by an instrument that takes effect immediately.

**HISTORY:**

GC § 10512-8; 114 v 320(470); Bureau of Code Revision, 10-1-53; 132 v S 13 (Eff 10-24-67); 138 v S 317 (Eff 3-23-81); 147 v H 701. Eff 3-22-99; 2011 SB 124, § 1, eff. Jan. 13, 2012; 2012 HB 479, § 1, eff. Mar. 27, 2013.

**Editor's Notes**

Acts 2011, SB 124, § 3 provides: "The provisions of this act that relate to the estates of decedents apply to the estates of decedents who die on or after the effective date of this act."

**Amendment Notes**

The 2012 amendment inserted (D); redesignated former (D) as (E); and added (F) and (G).

The 2011 amendment substituted "real property" for "lands or tenements" in the second sentence of (A).

**NOTES TO DECISIONS**

Analysis

Generally
Applicability

Titles 11 — 37

**Generally**

Where the testator left property to one of his children for life, with the remainder to be divided among his grandchildren, the widow of one of the grandchildren was entitled to the share which had vested in her husband. Where life estates in other property were left to other children of the testator, with the remainder to the heirs of their bodies, and those children died without heirs, the remainder went equally to the widow and to the surviving grandchildren: Peters v. Allison, 2004-Ohio-4143, 158 Ohio App. 3d 223, 814 N.E.2d 568, 2004 Ohio App. LEXIS 3784 (Ohio Ct. App., Sandusky County 2004).

Pursuant to R.C. 2131.08 (C), the period of perpetuities shall be measured by actual rather than possible events: Bd. of County Comm'rs v. City of Cincinnati, 2003-Ohio-5089, 154 Ohio App. 3d 504, 797 N.E.2d 1027, 2003 Ohio App. LEXIS 4592 (Ohio Ct. App., Hamilton County 2003).

A deed restriction granting a right of first refusal to adjoining landowners was a property interest which violated the rule against perpetuities: Schafer v. Deszcz, 120 Ohio App. 3d 410, 698 N.E.2d 60, 1997 Ohio App. LEXIS 1846 (Ohio Ct. App., Ottawa County 1997).

Where there are two possible constructions of an instrument, one which renders it valid under the rule against perpetuities and the other which renders it invalid, preference will be accorded to the construction which upholds its validity: Stratman v. Sheetz, 60 Ohio App. 3d 71, 573 N.E.2d 776, 1989 Ohio App. LEXIS 3259 (Ohio Ct. App., Hamilton County 1989).

If a preemptive right to purchase is personal to the grantee and does not extend beyond his lifetime, the rule against perpetuities (R.C. 2131.08) is not violated. To determine if a preemptive right is personal to either the grantee or the grantor, the court must look exclusively to the language of the contract and focus on whether the language states that the right extends to the heirs or assigns of either party, or otherwise indicates that the parties intended the contract to be binding beyond either of their lives. Absent such language, the preemptive right is deemed to be personal: Stratman v. Sheetz, 60 Ohio App. 3d 71, 573 N.E.2d 776, 1989 Ohio App. LEXIS 3259 (Ohio Ct. App., Hamilton County 1989).

The establishment of an annual harness horse stake race "in memory of my daughter," under the terms of a will is neither for a charitable purpose nor a community benefit purpose and thus does not create a valid and enforceable charitable trust. In such a case the doctrine of cy-pres does not apply and there not being a valid charitable trust, the provision in the will violates R.C. 2131.08, the rule against perpetuities: Barton v. Parrott, 25 Ohio Misc. 2d 8, 495 N.E.2d 973, 1984 Ohio Misc. LEXIS 222 (Ohio C.P. 1984).

When land is conveyed in trust, to terminate upon the occurrence of a limiting event and then to "x, y and z, the heirs of their body and assigns forever, if any, and if none, to the survivor or survivors of them," said grantees become the owners of estates in fee tail and the natural issue of each grantee who survives any of such donees prior to the occurrence of the limiting event, take the expectant estate of the deceased donee as heirs of his body and become vested in interest, although not in possession, of such estate: Eisenmann v. Eisenmann, 52 Ohio Misc. 119, 6 Ohio Op. 3d 449, 370 N.E.2d 788, 1976 Ohio Misc. LEXIS 56 (Ohio C.P. 1976).

Common law fee tail estate exists in Ohio; R.C. 2131.08 converting fee tail estate into fee simple absolute in issue of first donee in tail does not change nature of estate in donee in tail from inheritable estate to life estate but merely restricts entailment to immediate issue of such donee: Long v. Long, 45 Ohio St. 2d 165, 74 Ohio Op. 2d 287, 343 N.E.2d 100, 1976 Ohio LEXIS 555 (Ohio 1976).

There remains in the grantor of a fee tail estate a reversion in fee simple expectant upon the failure of a stated condition, which reversion is a descendible, devisable and alienable estate, which, if otherwise undisposed of, passes upon the death of the grantor by descent to his heirs then living: Long v. Long, 45 Ohio St. 2d 165, 74 Ohio Op. 2d 287, 343 N.E.2d 100, 1976 Ohio LEXIS 555 (Ohio 1976).

A land purchase option which is appurtenant to a mineral estate and is limited to the necessary and reasonable use of the overlying surface estate for the exercise of mining rights, is a vested part of the mineral estate and is not void as a restraint upon alienation, although unlimited in time: Quarto Mining Co. v. Litman, 42 Ohio St. 2d 73, 71 Ohio Op. 2d 58, 326 N.E.2d 676, 1975 Ohio LEXIS 464 (Ohio), cert. denied, 423 U.S. 866, 96 S. Ct. 128, 46 L. Ed. 2d 96, 1975 U.S. LEXIS 2771 (U.S. 1975).

The last sentence of paragraph (D) of R.C. 2131.08 applies only to the effective date of the 1967 amendment and its purpose was not to establish a general starting time for all powers of appointment; it does not change the Ohio common law rule that the perpetuities period of an interest derived from the exercise of a general testamentary power of appointment is measured from the time of the creation of the power and not from its exercise: Dollar Sav. & Trust Co. v. First Nat'l Bank, 32 Ohio Misc. 81, 61 Ohio Op. 2d 134, 285 N.E.2d 768, 1972 Ohio Misc. LEXIS 177 (Ohio C.P. 1972).

In applying the rule against perpetuities, the test of vesting is not whether the beneficial enjoyment of the proceeds of the estate will arise within the period of the lives in being plus twenty-one years, but, whether, within such period it becomes certain that the interest is unconditional and will reach fruition in the future: Third Nat'l Bank & Trust Co. v. Eaton, 33 Ohio App. 2d 264, 62 Ohio Op. 2d 379, 294 N.E.2d 247, 1972 Ohio App. LEXIS 344 (Ohio Ct. App., Montgomery County 1972).

The rule against perpetuities applies to property interests, not to contractual obligations: (decided under former analogous section) Doyle v. Massachusetts Mut. Life Ins. Co., 377 F.2d 19, 41 Ohio Op. 2d 348, 1967 U.S. App. LEXIS 6666 (6th Cir. Ky. 1967).

A provision in a will that the testamentary trust should terminate on the day the youngest living child of testator's son, in being on the date of the testator's death, attains the age of twenty-five, does not violate the rule against perpetuities: (decided under former analogous section) Green v. Green, 9 Ohio Misc. 15, 37 Ohio Op. 2d 394, 221 N.E.2d 388, 1966 Ohio Misc. LEXIS 233 (Ohio P. Ct. 1966).

A future interest must vest, if at all, within the period of the rule against perpetuities; where the testamentary trust shall terminate the day the youngest living child of the son of the testator, in being on the date of the testator's death, attains twenty-five years of age, the rule is not violated: (decided under former analogous section) Green v. Green, 9 Ohio Misc. 15, 37 Ohio Op. 2d 394, 221 N.E.2d 388, 1966 Ohio Misc. LEXIS 233 (Ohio P. Ct. 1966).

Under this section, the twenty-one year period must follow, not precede, the lives in being by which the period of the rule is measured, and the measuring lives must be lives in being at the creation of the interest, i.e., in the case of a testamentary trust, at the death of the testator: (decided under former analogous section) Thomas v. Harrison, 24 Ohio Op. 2d 148, 191 N.E.2d 862, 92 Ohio Law Abs. 175, 1962 Ohio Misc. LEXIS 284 (Ohio P. Ct. 1962).

If there is any possibility that the interests will not vest within lives in being plus twenty-one years, then the interests are void ab initio: (decided under former analogous section) Thomas v. Harrison, 24 Ohio Op. 2d 148, 191 N.E.2d 862, 92 Ohio Law Abs. 175, 1962 Ohio Misc. LEXIS 284 (Ohio P. Ct. 1962).

If a power of appointment can be exercised at a time beyond the limits of the rule against perpetuities, the estate or interest to be appointed is too remote: (decided under former analogous section) Thomas v. Harrison, 24 Ohio Op. 2d 148, 191 N.E.2d 862, 92 Ohio Law Abs. 175, 1962 Ohio Misc. LEXIS 284 (Ohio P. Ct. 1962).

The remoteness of interests appointed under a special power of appointment is measured from the time of the creation of the power, not from the time of its exercise: (decided under former analogous section) Thomas v. Harrison, 24 Ohio Op. 2d 148, 191 N.E.2d 862, 92 Ohio Law Abs. 175, 1962 Ohio Misc. LEXIS 284 (Ohio P. Ct. 1962).

Where property is deeded by a mother to her son for life, and then to the heirs of his body, and if he dies without heirs of his body, the remainder to revert to the grantor, if living, and if not living, then the remainder to the grantor's heirs at law, it is incumbent upon the widow of the grantee-son, in an action to have quieted her title to such premises, to prove by a preponderance of the evidence that upon the death of the grantee-son without having had issue he had an absolute estate in fee simple in such premises which could pass to her as his heir or which could pass to her under the provisions of his will, i.e., that the grantor-mother had not successfully conveyed or devised away the reversion: (decided under former analogous section) Kohler v. Ichler, 116 Ohio App. 16, 21 Ohio Op. 2d 221, 186 N.E.2d 202, 1961 Ohio App. LEXIS 544 (Ohio Ct. App., Hardin County 1961).

Where identical bequests to each of the testator's sons are payable out of the same testamentary trust fund the legal title to which is in the same trustee, but the gifts to the sons are not a gift to a class, the gifts must be considered separate and distinct from one another in applying the rule against perpetuities: (decided under former analogous section) Gwinner v. Schoeny, 111 Ohio App. 177, 13 Ohio Op. 2d 389, 171 N.E.2d 728, 1960 Ohio App. LEXIS 721 (Ohio Ct. App., Hamilton County 1960).

The question of remoteness is to be determined from the time of testator's death, and not of his will: (decided under former analogous section) Large v. National City Bank, 14 Ohio Op. 2d 100, 170 N.E.2d 309, 85 Ohio Law Abs. 11, 1960 Ohio Misc. LEXIS 235 (Ohio P. Ct. 1960).

In such case, each of the testator's living and after-born grandchildren had a life estate in the undivided interest of his father, which must vest upon the instant of his father's death, and therefore vests within a life in being and twenty-one years thereafter as required by the rule: (decided under former analogous section) Gwinner v. Schoeny, 111 Ohio App. 177, 13 Ohio Op. 2d 389, 171 N.E.2d 728, 1960 Ohio App. LEXIS 721 (Ohio Ct. App., Hamilton County 1960).

A will by which a testatrix left her estate to a designated person in trust with almost unlimited power to manage, control and dispose of both income and principal, and to pay or expend from time to time such sums as she deems necessary for the benefit of certain named beneficiaries, "until my grandson, M., shall, or would if he lived so long, attain the age of thirty years"; and upon disposition of the principal the trust to that extent to terminate; and in case the trust shall not be wholly disposed of under the foregoing provisions, such part not disposed of shall vest in equal shares in such of certain named beneficiaries "as shall be living when my grandson, M., shall, or would if he lived so long, attain the age of thirty years and the trust shall cease and determine," does not violate the rule against perpetuities as codified in this section: (decided under former analogous section) Finkbeiner v. Finkbeiner, 111 Ohio App. 64, 13 Ohio Op. 2d 424, 165 N.E.2d 825, 1959 Ohio App. LEXIS 678 (Ohio Ct. App., Hamilton County 1959).

While the possibility of reversion on failure of issue remaining in the donor is not an estate, there is authority to the effect that the donor can release it to the person holding the intermediate estate, the first donee in tail. But this does not have the effect of converting the estate tail into an estate in fee simple in the hands of the first donee in tail so as to enable him to alien it in fee simple to a third person and thereby defeat the heirs of his body from acquiring it by descent upon his death. The only probable effect of an original donor's release of his reversion expectancy to the donee in tail would be to defeat donor's possibility of reversion in event the donee should die without issue and thereby vest the estate in the donee's general heirs in fee simple: (decided under former analogous section) Guida v. Thompson, 160 N.E.2d 153, 80 Ohio Law Abs. 148, 1957 Ohio Misc. LEXIS 261 (Ohio C.P. 1957).

In applying the rule against perpetuities to litigation involving the validity of appointments made under a general power to appoint by will lodged in a donee of the power by virtue of an inter vivos indenture of trust, the period of time permitted for the vesting of interests given by the donee of the power in his will must be computed from the time of the creation of the power and not from the exercise thereof: (decided under former analogous section) Cleveland Trust Co. v. McQuade, 106 Ohio App. 237, 6 Ohio Op. 2d 493, 142 N.E.2d 249, 76 Ohio Law Abs. 324, 1957 Ohio App. LEXIS 741 (Ohio Ct. App., Cuyahoga County 1957).

Where the first donee in tail purports to reconvey the property in fee simple to the donor, the effect of such conveyance is to create a defeasible fee in such donor which vests absolutely in the donor in the event the donee in tail dies without issue: (decided under former analogous section) Hoppes v. American Nat'l Red Cross, 128 N.E.2d 851, 71 Ohio Law Abs. 259, 1955 Ohio Misc. LEXIS 342 (Ohio C.P. 1955).

A granting clause in a deed from a father to a son who had no children "for the term of his natural life, then to the heirs of his body their heirs and assigns forever" creates an estate in fee tail in the son: (decided under former analogous section) Hoppes v. American Nat'l Red Cross, 128 N.E.2d 851, 71 Ohio Law Abs. 259, 1955 Ohio Misc. LEXIS 342 (Ohio C.P. 1955).

A will provided that after all debts, funeral and administration expenses, and the year's allowance for the support of the widow were paid, the executor should select one-half of the inventory value of the property without deducting any taxes, and that only such assets should be selected as qualified to marital deduction under the federal estate tax law, and on making such selection the assets so selected should be delivered to a named trustee in trust for the testator's widow for life, with power in the trustee to pay to her the income and such of the principal as his widow might deem necessary for her comfortable support and welfare, and upon her death to dispose of the remaining assets as she might direct by will, and in the absence of such direction to the testator's daughters. The residue of the estate was placed in trust to pay the income to the widow and upon her death the principal and any accumulated income was payable to the daughters. Held: The estate vested within the period required by the rule against perpetuities: (decided under former analogous section) Braun v. Central Trust Co., 92 Ohio App. 110, 49 Ohio Op. 249, 109 N.E.2d 476, 1952 Ohio App. LEXIS 695 (Ohio Ct. App., Hamilton County 1952).

Where a testator in his will gives, devises and bequeaths to a trustee property to be selected by the executor in order to qualify for the marital deduction of the federal estate tax, the title of the trustee to the property vests immediately upon the death of the testator and the rule against perpetuities does not apply: (decided under former analogous section) Braun v. Central Trust Co., 46 Ohio Op. 198, 104 N.E.2d 480, 62 Ohio Law Abs. 127, 1951 Ohio Misc. LEXIS 366 (Ohio C.P. 1951), aff'd, 92 Ohio App. 110, 49 Ohio Op. 249, 109 N.E.2d 476, 1952 Ohio App. LEXIS 695 (Ohio Ct. App., Hamilton County 1952).

The state of Ohio, by virtue of this section, limits all estates given in tail by deed or will in lands or tenements lying within the state to be an absolute state in fee simple to the issue of the first donee in tail: (decided under former analogous section) In re Jones' Estate, 64 N.E.2d 609, 44 Ohio Law Abs. 339, 1943 Ohio App. LEXIS 822 (Ohio Ct. App., Van Wert County 1943).

Under devise to issue of daughter (a life tenant) and their heirs, grandchildren and two children jointly of deceased grandchild of daughter take per capita as daughter's immediate descendants, within former GC § 8622 (see now R.C. 2131.08): (decided under former analogous section) Von Overbeck v. Dahlgren, 28 F.2d 936, 1928 U.S. App. LEXIS 2499 (6th Cir. Ohio 1928).

Will providing for distribution after deaths of life tenants to their bodily heirs in fee simple held not to create an estate tail in that words in fee simple are inconsistent with usual form of limitation in estate tail to bodily heirs: (decided under former analogous section) Pollock v. Brayton, 28 Ohio App. 172, 162 N.E. 608, 6 Ohio Law Abs. 616, 1924 Ohio App. LEXIS 110 (Ohio Ct. App., Hamilton County 1924).

A testamentary disposition is not affected by the provision that possession by the grandchildren is postponed until they reach the age of thirty years, and then only on condition that they qualify as distributees to a designated standard of character and habits of life. The interest of grandchildren, then in being and who might be thereafter born, vested at the death of the testator, subject to divestment in the case of any who might fail to qualify as distributees: (decided under former analogous section) Sager v. Byrer, 24 Ohio N.P. 129 (CP 1921).

If A devises an estate tail to B, and B dies without issue surviving, such realty reverts to the heirs of A: (decided under former analogous section) Evangelical Lutheran St. Pauls Congregational Unaltered Augsbierian Confession v. Sheffield, 90 Ohio St. 467, 108 N.E. 1119, 12 Ohio L. Rep. 97 (Ohio 1914).

The recital of the consideration of one dollar is sufficient to support a deed, but it is insufficient to make such deed enforceable in equity as a contract if it is inoperative at law, because given by the child of a donee in tail during the lifetime of such donee, when the grantor had no interest in such realty, but had merely the hope of inheriting it: (decided under former analogous section) Carter v. Grossnickle, 22 Ohio Dec. 680, 11 Ohio N.P. (n.s.) 465, 1911 Ohio Misc. LEXIS 75 (Ohio C.P. 1911), aff'd, 88 Ohio St. 577, 106 N.E. 1059, 11 Ohio L. Rep. 55, 1913 Ohio LEXIS 1214 (Ohio 1913).].

Under a devise of certain real estate to a son "to have and to hold the said property for his life, and the remainder over at his death to the heirs of his body, their heirs and assigns forever, share and share alike," the children of said son take the fee and not an estate tail: (decided under former analogous section) Poor v. Hart, 21 Ohio Dec. 260, 11 Ohio N.P. (n.s.) 49, 1910 Ohio Misc. LEXIS 19 (Ohio C.P. 1910), aff'd, (Ohio C.P. 1910), aff'd, 84 Ohio St. 489, 95 N.E. 1149, 9 Ohio L. Rep. 96 (Ohio 1911).].

During the life of the first donee in tail, the issue of such donee has no estate or interest in the lands entailed which he can alienate; and a deed given by such issue during the life of the first donee in tail passes no interest where such issue die before the death of the first donee in tail, themselves leaving issue surviving: (decided under former analogous section) Dungan v. Kline, 81 Ohio St. 371, 90 N.E. 938, 7 Ohio L. Rep. 578, 1910 Ohio LEXIS 151 (Ohio 1910); In re Youtsey, 260 F. 423, 15 Ohio L. Rep. 125, 1916 U.S. Dist. LEXIS 1774 (S.D. Ohio 1916).

This section forbids gifts to any persons except those who are in being or the immediate issue or descendants thereof at the time of testator's death: (decided under former analogous section) Phillips v. Herron, 55 Ohio St. 478, 45 N.E. 720, 1896 Ohio LEXIS 104 (Ohio 1896).

This section does not reduce the interest of the first donee from an estate tail to a life estate; and accordingly the surviving spouse of the first donee in tail is entitled to dower or curtesy in accordance with the statutes then in force: (decided under former analogous section) Harkness v. Corning, 24 Ohio St. 416, 1873 Ohio LEXIS 137 (Ohio 1873).

**Applicability**

Trial court erred in incorporating appellee's contractual right of first refusal into its order concerning the parties' settlement agreement because the right in question was unlimited in time and therefore violated the rule against perpetuities. Hanahan v. DPA Dev., LLC, 2021-Ohio-1212, 171 N.E.3d 462, 2021 Ohio App. LEXIS 1204 (Ohio Ct. App., Montgomery County 2021).

Where conveyances were made in 1900 and 1901, the validity of the limitations over to a municipal corporation is governed by GC § 8622 (see now R.C. 2131.08), in effect at that time, and not by the law in effect when the purpose is abandoned, or by the common law rule against perpetuities: (decided under former analogous section) Joseph Schonthal Co. v. Sylvania, 60 Ohio App. 407, 14 Ohio Op. 471, 21 N.E.2d 1008, 1938 Ohio App. LEXIS 346 (Ohio Ct. App., Lucas County 1938).

The rule against perpetuities applies to trust estates as well as to legal estates: (decided under former analogous section) Hoopert v. Gugel, 25 Ohio N.P. 516 (CP 1924).

The provisions of former GC § 8622 (see now R.C. 2131.08) do not apply to a bequest of the income from lands and tenements devised in trust, nor the payment of such income to the child of a grandson born after testator's death: (decided under former analogous section) Dahlgren v. Pierce, 270 F. 507, 1921 U.S. App. LEXIS 2435 (6th Cir. Ohio), cert. denied, 256 U.S. 692, 41 S. Ct. 534, 65 L. Ed. 1174, 1921 U.S. LEXIS 1674 (U.S. 1921).

**Care of animal**

A bequest of money for the care of a dog does not, by the terms of the creating instrument, violate the rule against perpetuities: (decided under former analogous section) In re Searight's Estate, 87 Ohio App. 417, 43 Ohio Op. 169, 95 N.E.2d 779, 1950 Ohio App. LEXIS 701 (Ohio Ct. App., Wayne County 1950).

**Charitable bequests**

Where a testator bequeaths money in trust for a charitable corporation to be organized after his death for the purpose of accomplishing certain charitable purposes, the gift is valid although it is possible that the corporation might not be organized within the period of the rule against perpetuities. In such a case there is an immediate gift for charitable purposes, and the court will direct that the property be conveyed to the corporation if it is organized within a reasonable time, and if not so organized, will frame a scheme for the application of the property to the designated charitable purposes and direct that it be administered under the doctrine of cy-pres: Rice v. Stanley, 42 Ohio St. 2d 209, 71 Ohio Op. 2d 205, 327 N.E.2d 774, 1975 Ohio LEXIS 482 (Ohio 1975).

Where a charitable gift vests, a direction for accumulation, being for the management of the fund and not of the essence of the gift, will not, even if invalid, affect the validity of the gift: Third Nat'l Bank & Trust Co. v. Eaton, 33 Ohio App. 2d 264, 62 Ohio Op. 2d 379, 294 N.E.2d 247, 1972 Ohio App. LEXIS 344 (Ohio Ct. App., Montgomery County 1972).

Forty-five-year-old restrictions in a deed to a church congregation forbidding the use of musical instruments and any practice unauthorized in the New Testament on the premises and providing that in the event of a breach the property is to revert to those in the congregation who object to the breach will not be enforced to prevent the sale of the premises by the corporate successor of the congregation: (decided under former analogous section) Church of Christ v. Ezzell, 31 Ohio Op. 2d 224, 202 N.E.2d 212, 95 Ohio Law Abs. 89, 1964 Ohio Misc. LEXIS 279 (Ohio C.P. 1964).



Where a will creates a trust for the benefit of one person for life, then for the use of others until their marriage or death, and then "the trust to be continued and one-half of the annual income of said trust fund" to be paid to a charity, the gift to the charity does not violate the rule against perpetuities as the equitable estate vests in the charity immediately upon the transfer of the legal title to the trustee: (decided under former analogous section) Schreiner v. Cincinnati Altenheim, 61 Ohio App. 344, 15 Ohio Op. 228, 22 N.E.2d 587, 29 Ohio Law Abs. 249, 1939 Ohio App. LEXIS 449 (Ohio Ct. App., Hamilton County 1939).

**Class gifts**

If there is any possibility that the gift to a class will not vest in every possible member of the class within the rule, the gift must fail: (decided under former analogous section) Abram v. Wilson, 8 Ohio Misc. 420, 37 Ohio Op. 2d 288, 220 N.E.2d 739, 1966 Ohio Misc. LEXIS 402 (Ohio P. Ct. 1966).

**Common law**

This statute abrogated the common law rule under the statute de bonis, although generally speaking many of the common law attributes were retained through interpretation: (decided under former analogous section) Guida v. Thompson, 160 N.E.2d 153, 80 Ohio Law Abs. 148, 1957 Ohio Misc. LEXIS 261 (Ohio C.P. 1957).

The legislature of Ohio specifically adopted the common law rule against perpetuities in the year 1932 (now codified at R.C. 2131.08), although the rule had existed as a part of the common law of the state of Ohio for generations prior thereto: (decided under former analogous section) Cleveland Trust Co. v. McQuade, 106 Ohio App. 237, 6 Ohio Op. 2d 493, 142 N.E.2d 249, 76 Ohio Law Abs. 324, 1957 Ohio App. LEXIS 741 (Ohio Ct. App., Cuyahoga County 1957).

The common-law rule against perpetuities applies only to indestructible contingent interests, which the rule renders invalid at the time of their creation if at that time it is possible that they may remain contingent longer than lives then in being and twenty-one years thereafter: (decided under former analogous section) Braun v. Central Trust Co., 46 Ohio Op. 198, 104 N.E.2d 480, 62 Ohio Law Abs. 127, 1951 Ohio Misc. LEXIS 366 (Ohio C.P. 1951), aff'd, 92 Ohio App. 110, 49 Ohio Op. 249, 109 N.E.2d 476, 1952 Ohio App. LEXIS 695 (Ohio Ct. App., Hamilton County 1952).

This section has supplanted the common law rule that a bequest for the permanent care of the settlor's cemetery grave or family lot violated the rule against perpetuities, and under the statute such trusts are valid: (decided under former analogous section) Heinlein v. Elyria Sav. & Trust Co., 75 Ohio App. 353, 31 Ohio Op. 123, 62 N.E.2d 284, 1945 Ohio App. LEXIS 1125 (Ohio Ct. App., Lorain County 1945).

The common law rule against perpetuities was abrogated in Ohio in 1812 (10 v 7; RS § 4200; GC § 8622; repealed 114 v 745), and was not effective from that time until the enactment of this section in 1932, which readopted the rule. General Code § 8622 (see now R.C. 2131.08) applied to municipal corporations as well as to persons: (decided under former analogous section) Joseph Schonthal Co. v. Sylvania, 60 Ohio App. 407, 14 Ohio Op. 471, 21 N.E.2d 1008, 1938 Ohio App. LEXIS 346 (Ohio Ct. App., Lucas County 1938).

**Contingent interest**

"A contingent interest is one in which there is no present fixed right of either present or future employment; but in which a fixed right will arise in the future under certain specified contingencies. Where, under the terms of the gift of remainder, there is no ascertained person in being who could take if the particular estate were at once to determine, or where the remainderman is ascertained by the terms of the gift but he cannot take upon the determination of the particular estate, unless some other or further event occurs before such determination, the remainder is contingent." 3 Page on Wills (Lifetime Ed.) § 1257, quoted in: (decided under former analogous section) Cleveland Trust Co. v. McQuade, 106 Ohio App. 237, 6 Ohio Op. 2d 493, 142 N.E.2d 249, 76 Ohio Law Abs. 324, 1957 Ohio App. LEXIS 741 (Ohio Ct. App., Cuyahoga County 1957).

**Partial invalidity**

When part of an attempted disposition fails as a direct consequence of the rule against perpetuities the effect, if any, of this partial invalidity upon the balance of the attempted disposition is determined by judicially ascertaining whether the conveyor, if he had known of this partial invalidity, would have preferred that (a) all the balance of the attempted disposition take effect, in accordance with its terms; or that (b) certain parts of the balance of the attempted disposition fail, but the rest thereof take effect in accordance with its terms; or that (c) all the balance of the attempted disposition fail: (decided under former analogous section) Gwinner v. Schoeny, 111 Ohio App. 177, 13 Ohio Op. 2d 389, 171 N.E.2d 728, 1960 Ohio App. LEXIS 721 (Ohio Ct. App., Hamilton County 1960).

The invalidity of a part of a will by reason of this section does not necessarily make other gifts invalid, if the will does not show the intention of testator that the gifts must stand or fall as a whole: (decided under former analogous section) Hatch v. Hatch, 1 Ohio Dec. 270 (Ohio C.P. 1894).

**Purpose**

The immediate purpose of the rule against perpetuities is to prevent the creation of interests which may vest too remotely: (decided under former analogous section) Thomas v. Harrison, 24 Ohio Op. 2d 148, 191 N.E.2d 862, 92 Ohio Law Abs. 175, 1962 Ohio Misc. LEXIS 284 (Ohio P. Ct. 1962).

The rule against perpetuities applies only to the vesting of interests, and it applies to equitable as well as legal interests: (decided under former analogous section) Thomas v. Harrison, 24 Ohio Op. 2d 148, 191 N.E.2d 862, 92 Ohio Law Abs. 175, 1962 Ohio Misc. LEXIS 284 (Ohio P. Ct. 1962).

An interest is not vested if, in order for it to come into possession, the fulfillment of some condition precedent other than the determination of the preceding estate is necessary: (decided under former analogous section) Thomas v. Harrison, 24 Ohio Op. 2d 148, 191 N.E.2d 862, 92 Ohio Law Abs. 175, 1962 Ohio Misc. LEXIS 284 (Ohio P. Ct. 1962).

The intent clearly expressed by the language of this section is that it is the vesting of the title that is the concern of the legislature: (decided under former analogous section) Gwinner v. Schoeny, 111 Ohio App. 177, 13 Ohio Op. 2d 389, 171 N.E.2d 728, 1960 Ohio App. LEXIS 721 (Ohio Ct. App., Hamilton County 1960).

In such case, each great-grandchild in actual or potential existence at the time of testator's death also had a vested life estate which will come into enjoyment after both his parent and grandparent of the testator's blood have died: (decided under former analogous section) Gwinner v. Schoeny, 111 Ohio App. 177, 13 Ohio Op. 2d 389, 171 N.E.2d 728, 1960 Ohio App. LEXIS 721 (Ohio Ct. App., Hamilton County 1960).

Where the testator created a testamentary trust and directed his trustee to pay each month the sum of two hundred dollars to each of his five sons during each son's lifetime and after the son's death to continue to pay such sum to the deceased son's issue per stirpes, until the trust fund had been exhausted, each son had a vested life estate which became vested immediately upon the testator's death: (decided under former analogous section) Gwinner v. Schoeny, 111 Ohio App. 177, 13 Ohio Op. 2d 389, 171 N.E.2d 728, 1960 Ohio App. LEXIS 721 (Ohio Ct. App., Hamilton County 1960).

The purpose of the rule against perpetuities is to prevent the tying up of land and its removal from commerce for long periods of time by the creation of future estates which would prevent the alienation of lands; the application of the rule has been extended by the common law and statute to personal property: (decided under former analogous section) Warner & Swasey Co. v. Rusterholz, 41 F. Supp. 498, 22 Ohio Op. 114, 1941 U.S. Dist. LEXIS 2710 (D. Minn. 1941).

**Retroactivity**

R.C. 2131.08, as amended effective October 24, 1967, does not apply to authorize reform of any inter vivos conveyance (deed) executed before December 31, 1967 (invalid as not within the rule against perpetuities), except those wherein the grantor reserved a power to revoke or terminate such interest or such a power expired "by reason of the death of the grantor or by release of the power or otherwise." R.C. 2131.08(B) and (D): Eisenmann v. Eisenmann, 52 Ohio Misc. 119, 6 Ohio Op. 3d 449, 370 N.E.2d 788, 1976 Ohio Misc. LEXIS 56 (Ohio C.P. 1976).

A deed dated November 30, 1962, purporting to convey land in trust "for and during the natural lifetime of the Grantor herein or until December 1, 1990, whichever later occurs" is invalid to create any expectant estates in said land because not within the rule against perpetuities (R.C. 2131.08 as in effect in 1962): Eisenmann v. Eisenmann, 52 Ohio Misc. 119, 6 Ohio Op. 3d 449, 370 N.E.2d 788, 1976 Ohio Misc. LEXIS 56 (Ohio C.P. 1976).

There is no constitutional prohibition against applying the 1967 statute against perpetuities, R.C. 2131.08, to a power of appointment granted before that date. This statute is not regarded as operating retroactively merely because it relates to antecedent events, since it does not take away or impair vested rights: Dollar Sav. & Trust Co. v. First Nat'l Bank, 32 Ohio Misc. 81, 61 Ohio Op. 2d 134, 285 N.E.2d 768, 1972 Ohio Misc. LEXIS 177 (Ohio C.P. 1972).

**Vested interest**

Deed restriction for a subdivision lot, which granted contractors who originally sold the lot, the present and future right to build a house on the lot, was already vested. Accordingly, whether the deed restriction was viewed as conveying a property right or a contractual right, the rule against perpetuities was not violated. Marinelli v. Prete, 2010-Ohio-2257, 2010 Ohio App. LEXIS 1855 (Ohio Ct. App., Erie County 2010).

A vested interest is not subject to the rule against perpetuities: (decided under former analogous section) Cleveland Trust Co. v. McQuade, 106 Ohio App. 237, 6 Ohio Op. 2d 493, 142 N.E.2d 249, 76 Ohio Law Abs. 324, 1957 Ohio App. LEXIS 741 (Ohio Ct. App., Cuyahoga County 1957).

**Will contest**

Where by the terms of a will, lands are entailed to a son and the heirs of his body, and the son brings suit to contest such will, his children then in being are "interested persons" within the meaning of GC § 12080 (R.C. 2741.02), and such children as survive their father will not be bound by a judgment setting such will aside in a proceeding to which they were not parties: (decided under former analogous section) Harris v. Maholm, 28 Ohio Dec. 228, 20 Ohio N.P. (n.s.) 439, 1918 Ohio Misc. LEXIS 3 (Ohio C.P. 1918).

### RESEARCH REFERENCES AND PRACTICE AIDS

**Cross-References to Related Sections**

Exemption of certain trusts, RC § 2131.09.

**Comparative Legislation**

Estates tail:
- CA—Cal Civ Code § 763
- FL—Fla. Stat. § 689.14
- IL—765 Ill. Comp. Stat. § 5/6
- IN—Burns Ind. Code Ann. § 32-1-2-33
- KY—KRS § 381.070
- MI—MCLS § 554.3
- NY—NY CLS EPTL § 6-1.2
- PA—20 P.S. § 6116

Rule against perpetuities:
- CA—Cal Prob Code §§ 21200-21231
- FL—Fla. Stat. § 689.225
- IL—765 Ill. Comp. Stat. § 315/1
- IN—Burns Ind. Code Ann. § 32-1-4.5-5
- KY—KRS § 381.215
- MI—MCLS §§ 554.71-554.78
- NY—NY CLS EPTL § 9-1.1
- PA—20 P.S. § 6104

**Practice Guides**

Anderson's Ohio Probate Practice and Procedure § 18.03 General rules of construction

Anderson's Ohio Probate Practice and Procedure § 21.07 Void bequests

Anderson's Ohio Probate Practice and Procedure § 44.01 Explanation of provisions of rule

Anderson's Ohio Probate Practice and Procedure § 44.02 Exceptions to rule

Anderson's Ohio Probate Practice and Procedure § 44.03 Brief history of rule

Anderson's Ohio Probate Practice and Procedure § 45.01 Statutory provisions for modification of trusts

## § 2131.10 Deposit payable on death.

A natural person, adult or minor, referred to in sections 2131.10 and 2131.11 of the Revised Code as the owner, may enter into a written contract with any bank, building and loan or savings and loan association, credit union, or society for savings, authorized to receive money on an investment share certificate, share account, deposit, or stock deposit, and transacting business in this state, whereby the proceeds of the owner's investment share certificate, share account, deposit, or stock deposit may be made payable on the death of the owner to another person or to any entity or organization, referred to in such sections as the beneficiary, notwithstanding any provisions to the contrary in Chapter 2107. of the Revised Code. In creating such accounts, "payable on death" or "payable on the death of" may be abbreviated to "P.O.D."

Every contract of an investment share certificate, share account, deposit, or stock deposit authorized by this section shall be deemed to contain a right on the part of the owner during the owner's lifetime both to withdraw the proceeds of such investment share certificate, share account, deposit, or stock deposit, in whole or in part, as though no beneficiary has been named, and to designate a change in beneficiary. The interest of the beneficiary shall be deemed not to vest until the death of the owner.

No change in the designation of the beneficiary shall be valid unless executed in the form and manner prescribed by the bank, building and loan or savings and loan association, credit union, or society for savings.

**HISTORY:**

129 v 245 (Eff 7-25-61); 130 v 619 (Eff 1-23-63); 140 v H 348 (Eff 9-20-84); 148 v H 313. Eff 8-29-2000.

### NOTES TO DECISIONS

Analysis





**Generally**

A valid P.O.D. account may be established despite the lack of the decedent's signature on the signature card. A party seeking to void a P.O.D. account due to lack of mental capacity has the burden of proof by clear and convincing evidence: Giurbino v. Giurbino, 89 Ohio App. 3d 646, 626 N.E.2d 1017, 1993 Ohio App. LEXIS 3654 (Ohio Ct. App., Cuyahoga County 1993).

The 1984 amendment to R.C. 2131.10 permits artificial persons to be named as beneficiaries of P.O.D. accounts: Estate of Kinsey v. Janes, 82 Ohio App. 3d 822, 613 N.E.2d 686, 1992 Ohio App. LEXIS 5220 (Ohio Ct. App., Franklin County 1992).

Although a P.O.D. account is contractual in nature, it has a special purpose. It allows a person to make a testamentary disposition of assets without following the formalities of the Statute of Wills. One of the basic requirements of the Statute of Wills cannot be ignored, that is, the requirement of a writing signed by the testator evidencing his intent. Such a P.O.D. account is testamentary in nature; it follows that the term "written contract" means a writing signed by the owner of the funds showing the intent to dispose of property in contravention of his or her will or the statutes of descent and distribution: Witt v. Ward, 60 Ohio App. 3d 21, 573 N.E.2d 201, 1989 Ohio App. LEXIS 439 (Ohio Ct. App., Preble County 1989).

When R.C. 1107.08(B), 2131.10 and 2131.11 are read in pari materia, it is clear that the General Assembly intended that only natural persons may be designated as the beneficiaries of "P.O.D." (payable on death) accounts; hence, a corporation may not be a beneficiary of a "P.O.D." account: Powell v. City Nat'l Bank & Trust Co., 2 Ohio App. 3d 1, 440 N.E.2d 560, 1981 Ohio App. LEXIS 9888 (Ohio Ct. App., Franklin County 1981).

Under the Ohio rules of statutory construction the singular includes the plural and the plural includes the singular. Where there is no evidence that such a construction is out of context with the language of a statute, that construction should be used. "Person" and "beneficiary" in R.C. 2131.10 include both the singular and the plural; therefore, multiple beneficiaries for a "payable on death" account are legally permissible: Wingate v. Hordge, 60 Ohio St. 2d 55, 14 Ohio Op. 3d 212, 396 N.E.2d 770, 1979 Ohio LEXIS 496 (Ohio 1979).

A payable on death (P.O.D.) account created under R.C. 2131.10 is one where funds are made payable upon the death of the owner to another without the documents having complied with the formalities of the statute of wills. The funds involved do not become part of the decedent's estate. In a P.O.D. account the owner retains sole ownership of the account and only he may withdraw the proceeds or change the beneficiary during his lifetime. The beneficiary's interest does not vest until the death of the owner: Eger v. Eger, 39 Ohio App. 2d 14, 68 Ohio Op. 2d 150, 314 N.E.2d 394, 1974 Ohio App. LEXIS 2670 (Ohio Ct. App., Cuyahoga County 1974).

Where a natural adult person enters into a contract with his bank, as provided for by this section, depositing therein various sums of money in savings accounts, payable on death to certain named individuals, such savings accounts, upon the death of the depositor, are, by such statute, expressly exempt from the statute of wills: In re Estate of Tonsic, 13 Ohio App. 2d 195, 42 Ohio Op. 2d 341, 235 N.E.2d 239, 1968 Ohio App. LEXIS 414 (Ohio Ct. App., Summit County 1968).

**Authority of guardian**

Where the father owned a certificate of deposit that was payable on death to the son, but the daughter, as guardian of the father's person and estate, deleted the payable-on-death clause from the certificate, the daughter had the authority to do so: Estate of Strang v. Strang, 2004-Ohio-3677, 2004 Ohio App. LEXIS 3312 (Ohio Ct. App., Ashland County 2004).

Where appellant mother on behalf of her children sued appellee executor, guardian, and bank for wrongful and negligent liquidation of payable on death certificates, and the evidence showed that (1) the mother's children were named as beneficiaries on two payable on death (P.O.D.) bank accounts, (2) the owner of the accounts became incompetent and the owner's guardian closed the accounts and used the money for the owner, (3) later, the owner died and the mother filed creditor's claims in the owner's probate estate, but the claims were denied, summary judgment and judgment on the pleadings were proper because the guardian had a duty to take care of the owner and acted within her powers as guardian in closing the P.O.D. accounts under R.C. 2111.13, 2111.14. Ferguson v. Walsh, 2003-Ohio-4504, 2003 Ohio App. LEXIS 3994 (Ohio Ct. App., Franklin County 2003).

Guardians do not have the authority to change the names of beneficiaries of P.O.D. and joint and survivorship accounts, giving one guardian a personal interest in the accounts when such a change does not relate to managing or preserving the ward's estate and, when it is not in the best interest of the ward: Witt v. Ward, 60 Ohio App. 3d 21, 573 N.E.2d 201, 1989 Ohio App. LEXIS 439 (Ohio Ct. App., Preble County 1989).

A change of beneficiary on a payable on death account is not a sale, gift, conveyance, or encumbrance of such account within the meaning of R.C. 2111.04: Ogilvie v. Kehr, 39 Ohio App. 3d 170, 530 N.E.2d 957, 1988 Ohio App. LEXIS 809 (Ohio Ct. App., Fairfield County 1988).

A guardian cannot, as a matter of law, revoke an inter vivos trust established by her ward prior to the ward's being declared incompetent without first obtaining court approval for the revocation: Friedrich v. BancOhio Nat'l Bank, 14 Ohio App. 3d 247, 470 N.E.2d 467, 1984 Ohio App. LEXIS 11561 (Ohio Ct. App., Madison County 1984).

The depositor of a payable-on-death (P.O.D.) account retains her rights to ownership and full control of such account during her lifetime. Following a finding of incompetency by the Probate Court, the depositor's ownership rights pass to the legally appointed guardian of her estate, including the right to designate a change in the registration of such account: Miller v. Peoples Federal Sav. & Loan Ass'n, 68 Ohio St. 2d 175, 22 Ohio Op. 3d 406, 429 N.E.2d 439, 1981 Ohio LEXIS 638 (Ohio 1981).

**Challenge by former beneficiary**

Trial court did not err in granting the executor of a decedent's estate and a bank summary judgment in heirs' action seeking a declaration that they were the designated pay-on-death beneficiaries on a bank account the decedent opened because the account signature card revealed no ambiguities as to its final pay-on-death and beneficiary terms under R.C. 2131.10; the instruction removing the pay-on-death designation of the account, by itself, implicitly deleted any existing beneficiaries. Olds v. Jones, 2012-Ohio-4941, 2012 Ohio App. LEXIS 4325 (Ohio Ct. App., Cuyahoga County 2012).

A former beneficiary of a P.O.D. account may challenge the action of the savings institution with respect to changing the registration of such account only by complying with the provisions of R.C. 1151.192: Miller v. Peoples Federal Sav. & Loan Ass'n, 68 Ohio St. 2d 175, 22 Ohio Op. 3d 406, 429 N.E.2d 439, 1981 Ohio LEXIS 638 (Ohio 1981).

**Construction**

Under R.C. 2131.10, the term "owner" and "natural person" are one and the same. In other words, owner is simply another means of referring in the statute to the person entitled to enter into a payable on death. Hillier v. Fifth Third Bank, 2020-Ohio-3679, 154 N.E.3d 1266, 2020 Ohio App. LEXIS 2623 (Ohio Ct. App., Miami County 2020).

**Creditors' rights**

After a taxpayer with a federal income tax liability gave money to his spouse, the IRS properly levied on bank accounts containing those funds. The spouse testified that the money was not hers; the IRS created a lien on the taxpayer's property as of the date of the tax assessment under 26 U.S.C.S. §§ 6321-6322; and under R.C. 2131.10, the spouse, as the taxpayer's beneficiary, was not the owner of the money. Hawthorne v. United States, 523 F. Supp. 2d 621, 2007 U.S. Dist. LEXIS 93237 (N.D. Ohio 2007).

Where a lifetime owner of a payable-on-death certificate of deposit ("P.O.D. C.D.") signs a demand note and security agreement pledging the certificate to a bank as collateral for a loan, then dies with the loan outstanding, the bank has an immediate right to satisfy the debt from the proceeds of the P.O.D. C.D. without first seeking payment from the decedent's estate, and the beneficiary of the P.O.D. C.D. is entitled only to the surplus. The lifetime owner of a payable-on-death certificate of deposit ("P.O.D. C.D.") has a complete present interest in the account, and may withdraw its proceeds, change the beneficiary, or pledge the P.O.D. C.D. as collateral for a loan. Upon the owner's death, the beneficiary's interest vests and, if the owner has pledged the P.O.D. C.D. as collateral, the beneficiary is entitled to only an encumbered interest in the P.O.D. C.D. proceeds: Jamison v. Society Nat'l Bank, 66 Ohio St. 3d 201, 611 N.E.2d 307, 1993 Ohio LEXIS 955 (Ohio 1993).

Payable on death funds pledged as collateral and assigned to a bank by the lifetime owner may be taken in satisfaction of decedent's debt to the bank and the surplus paid to the beneficiary: In re Estate of Gullett, 36 Ohio Misc. 2d 8, 521 N.E.2d 14, 1987 Ohio Misc. LEXIS 165 (Ohio C.P. 1987).

Where the trustee/grantor of a savings account trust retains full control over the trust, including the power to revoke the trust completely, that fact establishes the right of creditors of the trustee to reach the funds on deposit in the account: Prestige Vacations, Inc. v. Kozak, 471 F. Supp. 410, 13 Ohio Op. 3d 409, 1979 U.S. Dist. LEXIS 11915 (N.D. Ohio 1979).

**Liability of financial institution**

Trial court erred in rendering summary judgment in favor of the bank on the contract and conversion claims because, under the unambiguous terms of the contract between the decedent and the bank, his accounts were not payable on death (POD) accounts and should have been paid instead to the decedent's estate for distribution under his will. To establish the existence of POD beneficiaries, both R.C. 1109.07(B) and R.C. 2131.10 required a written contract signed by the account owner and the bank could not produce a written signature card, and its internal records were insufficient to substitute for the statutory requirements. Hillier v. Fifth Third Bank, 2020-Ohio-3679, 154 N.E.3d 1266, 2020 Ohio App. LEXIS 2623 (Ohio Ct. App., Miami County 2020).

A bank's failure to discover that plaintiff was a beneficiary to a payable-on-death account and, therefore, entitled to the proceeds raises a genuine issue of fact whether the bank violated its duty of good faith and reasonable care when it paid the account proceeds to an estate creditor, even though the bank relied on a facially valid probate court order. Although material to the question of the bank's adherence to its duty to act in good faith and exercise reasonable care, the probate court order does not wholly absolve the bank from liability: Taylor v. First Nat'l Bank, 31 Ohio App. 3d 49, 508 N.E.2d 1006, 1986 Ohio App. LEXIS 10110 (Ohio Ct. App., Hamilton County 1986).

A beneficiary to a payable-on-death account has a vested interest in the proceeds of the account and, as a third-party beneficiary to the agreement between a defendant-bank and the decedent-depositor, has a right to enforce this interest. Thus, where the bank pays the account proceeds to an estate creditor, a genuine issue of material fact exists as to whether the bank breached its contract with the depositor to pay the proceeds to the beneficiary upon the depositor's death: Taylor v. First Nat'l Bank, 31 Ohio App. 3d 49, 508 N.E.2d 1006, 1986 Ohio App. LEXIS 10110 (Ohio Ct. App., Hamilton County 1986).

**Safe deposit box**

A lease agreement executed by two parties as co-lessees for a safe deposit box, which agreement provides that such co-lessees are joint tenants with right of survivorship, is a contract vesting inter vivos a present and equal joint interest in such co-lessees, and where the evidence of decedent's intention confirms the written provisions of the contract, then upon the death of one of the co-lessees the survivor becomes the absolute owner of the entire contents of the box by operative provisions of that contract: Steinhauser v. Repko, 30 Ohio St. 2d 262, 59 Ohio Op. 2d 334, 285 N.E.2d 55, 1972 Ohio LEXIS 434 (Ohio 1972).

Where the decedent placed currency in a safe deposit box which was rented from the bank pursuant to a lease agreement signed by the decedent and his sister-in-law as "joint tenants with right of survivorship," which agreement also recited that all property placed in such box was declared to be the joint property of both lessees and upon the death of either passes to the survivor, and the only testimony concerning the statements of the decedent made at the time such arrangement was made confirmed his intention to establish a right of survivorship, it is effective to vest title in such survivor upon his death: Steinhauser v. Repko, 28 Ohio App. 2d 251, 57 Ohio Op. 2d 374, 277 N.E.2d 73, 1971 Ohio App. LEXIS 469 (Ohio Ct. App., Mahoning County 1971), aff'd, 30 Ohio St. 2d 262, 59 Ohio Op. 2d 334, 285 N.E.2d 55, 1972 Ohio LEXIS 434 (Ohio 1972).

### RESEARCH REFERENCES AND PRACTICE AIDS

**Cross-References to Related Sections**

Joint bank accounts payable on death, RC §§ 1109.07, 1151.19.

**Practice Guides**

Anderson's Ohio Probate Practice and Procedure § 12.03 Non-probate assets

Anderson's Ohio Probate Practice and Procedure § 21.05 Distributing personal property

## § 2131.12 Joint ownership with right of survivorship in motor vehicle, watercraft or outboard motor.

(A) As used in this section:

(1) "Motor vehicle" has the same meaning as in section 4505.01 of the Revised Code.

(2) "Joint ownership with right of survivorship" means a form of ownership of a motor vehicle, all-purpose vehicle, off-highway motorcycle, watercraft, or outboard motor that is established pursuant to this section and pursuant to which the entire interest in the motor vehicle, all-purpose vehicle, off-highway motorcycle, watercraft, or outboard motor is held by

two persons for their joint lives and thereafter by the survivor of them.

(3) "Watercraft" has the same meaning as in division (A) of section 1548.01 of the Revised Code.

(4) "All-purpose vehicle" has the same meaning as in section 4519.01 of the Revised Code.

(5) "Off-highway motorcycle" has the same meaning as in section 4519.01 of the Revised Code.

(B)(1) Any two persons may establish in accordance with this section joint ownership with right of survivorship in a motor vehicle, an all-purpose vehicle, an off-highway motorcycle, a watercraft, or an outboard motor for which a certificate of title is required under Chapter 1548., 4505., or 4519. of the Revised Code.

(2) If two persons wish to establish joint ownership with right of survivorship in a motor vehicle, an all-purpose vehicle, an off-highway motorcycle, a watercraft, or an outboard motor that is required to be titled under Chapter 1548., 4505., or 4519. of the Revised Code, they may make a joint application for a certificate of title under section 1548.07, 4505.06, or 4519.55 of the Revised Code, as applicable.

(C) If two persons have established in a certificate of title joint ownership with right of survivorship in a motor vehicle, an all-purpose vehicle, an off-highway motorcycle, a watercraft, or an outboard motor that is required to be titled under Chapter 1548., 4505., or 4519. of the Revised Code, and if one of those persons dies, the interest of the deceased person in the motor vehicle, all-purpose vehicle, off-highway motorcycle, watercraft, or outboard motor shall pass to the survivor of them upon transfer of title to the motor vehicle, all-purpose vehicle, off-highway motorcycle, watercraft, or outboard motor in accordance with section 1548.11, 4505.10, or 4519.60 of the Revised Code. The motor vehicle, all-purpose vehicle, off-highway motorcycle, watercraft, or outboard motor shall not be considered an estate asset and shall not be included and stated in the estate inventory.

**HISTORY:**

RC § 2106.17, 145 v H 458 (Eff 7-20-94); RC § 2131.12, 149 v H 345. Eff 7-23-2002; 2021 hb74, § 101.01, effective June 30, 2021.

**Amendment Notes**

The 2021 amendment by HB 74 added "all-purpose vehicle, off- highway motorcycle" twice in (A)(2) and in the second sentence of (C); added (A)(4) and (A)(5); in (B)(1), substituted "an all-purpose vehicle, an off-highway motorcycle, a watercraft, or an" for "or in a watercraft or" and added "4505., or 4519."; in (B)(2), substituted "an all-purpose vehicle, an off-highway motorcycle, a watercraft, or an outboard" for "or in a watercraft or," added ", 4505., or 4519." and substituted "1548.07, 4505.06, or 4519.55" for "4505.06 or 1548.07"; and in the first sentence of (C), substituted "an all-purpose vehicle, an off-highway motorcycle, a watercraft, or an" for "or a watercraft," added "4505., or 4519.," and substituted "deceased person in the motor vehicle, all-purpose vehicle, off-highway motorcycle" for "deceased person in the motor vehicle," "title to the motor vehicle, all-purpose vehicle, off-highway motorcycle, watercraft, or" for "title to the motor vehicle or watercraft or" and "section 1548.11, 4505.10, or 4519.60" for "section 4505.10 or 1548.11."

# CHAPTER 2133

# MODIFIED UNIFORM RIGHTS OF THE TERMINALLY ILL ACT AND THE DNR IDENTIFICATION AND DO-NOT-RESUSCITATE ORDER LAW





## § 2133.01 Definitions.

Unless the context otherwise requires, as used in sections 2133.01 to 2133.15 of the Revised Code:

(A) "Adult" means an individual who is eighteen years of age or older.

(B) "Attending physician" means the physician to whom a declarant or other patient, or the family of a declarant or other patient, has assigned primary responsibility for the treatment or care of the declarant or other patient, or, if the responsibility has not been assigned, the physician who has accepted that responsibility.

(C) "Comfort care" means any of the following:

(1) Nutrition when administered to diminish the pain or discomfort of a declarant or other patient, but not to postpone the declarant's or other patient's death;

(2) Hydration when administered to diminish the pain or discomfort of a declarant or other patient, but not to postpone the declarant's or other patient's death;

(3) Any other medical or nursing procedure, treatment, intervention, or other measure that is taken to diminish the pain or discomfort of a declarant or other patient, but not to postpone the declarant's or other patient's death.

(D) "Consulting physician" means a physician who, in conjunction with the attending physician of a declarant or other patient, makes one or more determinations that are required to be made by the attending physician, or to be made by the attending physician and one other physician, by an applicable provision of this chapter, to a reasonable degree of medical certainty and in accordance with reasonable medical standards.

(E) "Declarant" means any adult who has executed a declaration in accordance with section 2133.02 of the Revised Code.

(F) "Declaration" means a written document executed in accordance with section 2133.02 of the Revised Code.

(G) "Durable power of attorney for health care" means a document created pursuant to sections 1337.11 to 1337.17 of the Revised Code.

(H) "Guardian" means a person appointed by a probate court pursuant to Chapter 2111. of the Revised Code to have the care and management of the person of an incompetent.

(I) "Health care facility" means any of the following:

(1) A hospital;

(2) A hospice care program, pediatric respite care program, or other institution that specializes in comfort care of patients in a terminal condition or in a permanently unconscious state;

(3) A nursing home or residential care facility, as defined in section 3721.01 of the Revised Code;

(4) A home health agency and any residential facility where a person is receiving care under the direction of a home health agency;

(5) An intermediate care facility for individuals with intellectual disabilities.

(J) "Health care personnel" means physicians, nurses, physician assistants, emergency medical technicians-basic, emergency medical technicians-intermediate, emergency medical technicians-paramedic, medical technicians, dietitians, other authorized persons acting under the direction of an attending physician, and administrators of health care facilities.

(K) "Home health agency" has the same meaning as in section 3740.01 of the Revised Code.

(L) "Hospice care program" and "pediatric respite care program" have the same meanings as in section 3712.01 of the Revised Code.

(M) "Hospital" has the same meanings as in sections 3701.01, 3727.01, and 5122.01 of the Revised Code.

(N) "Hydration" means fluids that are artificially or technologically administered.

(O) "Incompetent" has the same meaning as in section 2111.01 of the Revised Code.

(P) "Intermediate care facility for the individuals with intellectual disabilities" has the same meaning as in section 5124.01 of the Revised Code.

(Q) "Life-sustaining treatment" means any medical procedure, treatment, intervention, or other measure that, when administered to a qualified patient or other patient, will serve principally to prolong the process of dying.

(R) "Nurse" means a person who is licensed to practice nursing as a registered nurse or to practice practical nursing as a licensed practical nurse pursuant to Chapter 4723. of the Revised Code.

(S) "Nursing home" has the same meaning as in section 3721.01 of the Revised Code.

(T) "Nutrition" means sustenance that is artificially or technologically administered.

(U) "Permanently unconscious state" means a state of permanent unconsciousness in a declarant or other patient that, to a reasonable degree of medical certainty as determined in accordance with reasonable medical standards by the declarant's or other patient's attending physician and one other physician who has examined the declarant or other patient, is characterized by both of the following:

(1) Irreversible unawareness of one's being and environment.

(2) Total loss of cerebral cortical functioning, resulting in the declarant or other patient having no capacity to experience pain or suffering.

(V) "Person" has the same meaning as in section 1.59 of the Revised Code and additionally includes political subdivisions and governmental agencies, boards, commissions, departments, institutions, offices, and other instrumentalities.

(W) "Physician" means a person who is authorized under Chapter 4731. of the Revised Code to practice medicine and surgery or osteopathic medicine and surgery.

(X) "Political subdivision" and "state" have the same meanings as in section 2744.01 of the Revised Code.

(Y) "Professional disciplinary action" means action taken by the board or other entity that regulates the professional conduct of health care personnel, including the state medical board and the board of nursing.

(Z) "Qualified patient" means an adult who has executed a declaration and has been determined to be in a terminal condition or in a permanently unconscious state.

(AA) "Terminal condition" means an irreversible, incurable, and untreatable condition caused by disease, illness, or injury from which, to a reasonable degree of medical certainty as determined in accordance with reasonable medical standards by a declarant's or other patient's attending physician and one other physician who has examined the declarant or other patient, both of the following apply:

(1) There can be no recovery.

(2) Death is likely to occur within a relatively short time if life-sustaining treatment is not administered.

(BB) "Tort action" means a civil action for damages for injury, death, or loss to person or property, other than a civil action for damages for breach of a contract or another agreement between persons.

**HISTORY:**

144 v S 1 (Eff 10-10-91); 146 v S 150 (Eff 11-24-95); 146 v S 143 (Eff 3-5-96); 147 v H 354. Eff 7-9-98; 150 v H 95, § 1, eff. 9-26-03; 152 v H 529, § 1, eff. 4-7-09; 2012 HB 303, § 1, eff. Mar. 20, 2013; 2013 HB 59, § 101.01, eff. Sept. 29, 2013; 2021 hb110, § 101.01, effective September 30, 2021.

**Editor's Notes**

The provisions of §§ 3, 4 of HB 354 (147 v —) read as follows:

SECTION 3. That Section 3 of Am. Sub. S.B. 1 of the 119th General Assembly be amended to read as follows:

"Sec. 3. Chapter 2133. of the Revised Code, as amended by this act, shall be entitled the Modified Uniform Rights of the Terminally Ill Act and the DNR Identification and Do-Not-Resuscitate Order Law."

SECTION 4. That existing Section 3 of Am. Sub. S.B. 1 of the 119th General Assembly is hereby repealed.

**Amendment Notes**

The 2021 amendment by HB 110 substituted "section 3740.01" for "section 3701.881" in (K).

The 2013 amendment substituted "individuals with intellectual disabilities" for "the mentally retarded" in (I)(5); and in (P), substituted "individuals with intellectual disabilities" for "mentally retarded" and "section 5124.01" for "section 5111.20".

The 2012 amendment inserted "pediatric respite care program" in (I)(2); substituted "and 'pediatric respite care program' have" for "has" in (L); and made a stylistic change.

152 v H 529, effective April 7, 2009, corrected internal references.

## NOTES TO DECISIONS

**Professional disciplinary action**

As used in R.C. 2133.11 and defined in R.C. 2133.01(Y), the term "professional disciplinary action" is susceptible of reasonable interpretation to encompass the disciplinary sanctions authorized by R.C. 4731.22(A) and (B) or to encompass the entire disciplinary process; the term is ambiguous and subject to statutory interpretation. State ex rel. Gelesh v. State Med. Bd., 2007-Ohio-3328, 172 Ohio App. 3d 365, 874 N.E.2d 1256, 2007 Ohio App. LEXIS 3053 (Ohio Ct. App., Franklin County 2007).

## ATTORNEY GENERAL OPINIONS

Existing statutes and case law do not expressly authorize a member of a rescue squad, acting in an emergency situation and without direction of a physician, to honor the request of a relative of a resident of a rest home to provide no extraordinary care to the resident: 1993 Ohio Op. Att'y Gen. No. 062 (1993).

The statutes governing living wills and durable powers of attorney for health care do not provide for the application of those documents when a rescue squad is acting in an emergency situation and without the direction of an individual's attending physician: 1993 Ohio Op. Att'y Gen. No. 062 (1993).

## RESEARCH REFERENCES AND PRACTICE AIDS

**Cross-References to Related Sections**

Application may indicate whether applicant executed a declaration re life-sustaining treatment—

Commercial driver's license, RC § 4506.07

Driver's or motorcycle operator's license, RC § 4507.06.

Identification card, RC § 4507.51.

**Ohio Administrative Code**

Department of health—

Do not resuscitate (DNR) protocol. OAC ch. 3701-62.

Definitions. OAC 3701-62-01.

**Practice Manuals and Treatises**

Ohio Transaction Guide: Family Law & Forms § 1.22 Planning for Illness or Death

Anderson's Ohio Elder Law Practice Manual § 8.4 Persistent Vegetative State and Terminal Condition

Anderson's Ohio Elder Law Practice Manual § 10.2 Ohio Statute

Anderson's Ohio Probate Practice and Procedure Form 59.01 Living will declaration (Acknowledged)

Anderson's Ohio Probate Practice and Procedure Form 59.02 Living will declaration (Witnessed)

**Practice Guides**

Anderson's Ohio Probate Practice and Procedure § 59.01 Living will

### § 2133.02 Declaration governing use or continuation, or withholding or withdrawal, of life-sustaining treatment; refusal to comply.

(A)(1) An adult who is of sound mind voluntarily may execute at any time a declaration governing the use or continuation, or the withholding or withdrawal, of life-sustaining treatment. The declaration shall be signed at the end by the declarant or by another individual at the direction of the declarant, state the date of its execution, and either be witnessed as described in division (B)(1) of this section or be acknowledged by the declarant in accordance with division (B)(2) of this section. The declaration may include a designation by the declarant of one or more persons who are to be notified by the declarant's attending physician at any time that life-sustaining treatment would be withheld or withdrawn pursuant to the declaration. The declaration may include a specific authorization for the use or continuation or the withholding or withdrawal of CPR, but the failure to include a specific authorization for the withholding or withdrawal of CPR does not preclude the withholding or withdrawal of CPR in accordance with sections 2133.01 to 2133.15 or sections 2133.21 to 2133.26 of the Revised Code.

(2) Depending upon whether the declarant intends the declaration to apply when the declarant is in a terminal condition, in a permanently unconscious state, or in either a terminal condition or a permanently unconscious state, the declarant's declaration shall use either or both of the terms "terminal condition" and "permanently unconscious state" and shall define or otherwise explain those terms in a manner that is substantially consistent with the provisions of section 2133.01 of the Revised Code.

(3)(a) If a declarant who has authorized the withholding or withdrawal of life-sustaining treatment intends that the declarant's attending physician withhold or withdraw nutrition or hydration when the declarant is in a permanently unconscious state and when the nutrition and hydration will not or no longer will serve to provide comfort to the declarant or alleviate the declarant's pain, then the declarant shall authorize the declarant's attending physician to withhold or withdraw nutrition or hydration when the declarant is in the permanently unconscious state by doing both of the following in the declaration:

(i) Including a statement in capital letters or other conspicuous type, including, but not limited to, a different font, bigger type, or boldface type, that the declarant's attending physician may withhold or withdraw nutrition and hydration if the declarant is in a permanently unconscious state and if the declarant's attending physician and at least one other physician who has examined the declarant determine, to a reasonable degree of medical certainty and in accordance with reasonable medical standards, that nutrition or hydration will not or no longer will serve to provide comfort to the declarant or alleviate the declarant's pain, or checking or otherwise marking a box or line that is adjacent to a similar statement on a printed form of a declaration;

(ii) Placing the declarant's initials or signature underneath or adjacent to the statement, check, or other mark described in division (A)(3)(a)(i) of this section.

(b) Division (A)(3)(a) of this section does not apply to the extent that a declaration authorizes the withholding or withdrawal of life-sustaining treatment when a declarant is in a terminal condition. The provisions of division (E) of section 2133.12 of the Revised Code pertaining to comfort care shall apply to a declarant in a terminal condition.

(B)(1) If witnessed for purposes of division (A) of this section, a declaration shall be witnessed by two individuals as described in this division in whose presence the declarant, or another individual at the direction of the declarant, signed the declaration. The witnesses to a declaration shall be adults who are not related to the declarant by blood, marriage, or adoption, who are not the attending physician of the declarant, and who are not the administrator of any nursing home in which the declarant is receiving care. Each witness shall subscribe the witness' signature after the signature of the declarant or other individual at the direction of the declarant and, by doing so, attest to the witness' belief that the declarant appears to be of sound mind and not under or subject to duress, fraud, or undue influence. The signatures of the declarant or other individual at the direction of the declarant under division (A) of this section and of the witnesses under this division are not required to appear on the same page of the declaration.

(2) If acknowledged for purposes of division (A) of this section, a declaration shall be acknowledged before a notary public, who shall make the certification described in section 147.53 of the Revised Code and also shall attest that the declarant appears to be of sound mind and not under or subject to duress, fraud, or undue influence.

(C) An attending physician, or other health care personnel acting under the direction of an attending physician, who is furnished a copy of a declaration shall make it a part of the declarant's medical record and, when section 2133.05 of the Revised Code is applicable, also shall comply with that section.

(D)(1) Subject to division (D)(2) of this section, an attending physician of a declarant or a health care facility in which a declarant is confined may refuse to comply or allow compliance with the declarant's declaration on the basis of a matter of conscience or on another basis. An employee or agent of an attending physician of a declarant or of a health care facility in which a declarant is confined may refuse to comply with the declarant's declaration on the basis of a matter of conscience.

(2) If an attending physician of a declarant or a health care facility in which a declarant is confined is not willing or not able to comply or allow compliance with the declarant's declaration, the physician or facility promptly shall so advise the declarant and comply with the provisions of section 2133.10 of the Revised Code, or, if the declaration has become operative as described in division (A) of section 2133.03 of the Revised Code, shall comply with the provisions of section 2133.10 of the Revised Code.

(E) As used in this section, "CPR" has the same meaning as in section 2133.21 of the Revised Code.

**HISTORY:**

144 v S 1 (Eff 10-10-91); 147 v H 354 (Eff 7-9-98); 148 v H 494 Eff 3-15-2001.

**Editor's Notes**

The provisions of § 3(B) of HB 494 (148 v —) read as follows:

SECTION 3. * * *

(B) The amendments made by this act to section 2133.02 of the Revised Code do not invalidate an otherwise valid declaration governing the use or continuation, or the withholding or withdrawal, of life-sustaining treatment that was executed prior to the effective date of this act in conformity with that section as it existed on the date of the execution of the declaration.

## NOTES TO DECISIONS

Analysis

Generally
Patient's expressed intentions
Wrongful administration of life-prolonging medical treatment

**Generally**

Removal of nutrition and hydration from persons in a persistent vegetative state is rapidly becoming a legally accepted practice in the United States. The test to be applied by the probate court is the best interests of such a person. The twelve-month wait provided by R.C. 2133.09(B)(2) is unreasonable and not binding: In re Guardianship of Myers, 62 Ohio Misc. 2d 763, 610 N.E.2d 663, 1993 Ohio Misc. LEXIS 5 (Ohio C.P. 1993).

In the absence of advance directives, the administration or withdrawal of life-sustaining treatment should be based on medical expertise, consistent with the patient's wishes, as they are expressed by family members: In re Guardianship of McInnis, 61 Ohio Misc. 2d 790, 584 N.E.2d 1389, 1991 Ohio Misc. LEXIS 41 (Ohio P. Ct. 1991).

**Patient's expressed intentions**

Termination of life-sustaining treatment for a terminal patient was in accord with the patient's previously expressed intentions: Carpenter v.

Mason, 2003-Ohio-6490, 126 Ohio Misc. 2d 17, 800 N.E.2d 404, 2003 Ohio Misc. LEXIS 42 (Ohio C.P. 2003).

**Wrongful administration of life-prolonging medical treatment**

Damages were not recoverable on a claim of wrongful prolongation of life. Unwanted medical care did not constitute a battery: Allore v. Flower Hosp., 121 Ohio App. 3d 229, 699 N.E.2d 560, 1997 Ohio App. LEXIS 2753 (Ohio Ct. App., Lucas County 1997).

Ohio does not recognize a claim for wrongful administration of life-prolonging medical treatment. Any damages must be based on negligence or battery: Anderson v. St. Francis-St. George Hosp., 77 Ohio St. 3d 82, 671 N.E.2d 225, 1996 Ohio LEXIS 1693 (Ohio 1996).



### RESEARCH REFERENCES AND PRACTICE AIDS

**Cross-References to Related Sections**

Application to document executed prior to effective date of provisions, RC § 2133.15.

Certain persons may consent to withholding or withdrawing life-sustaining treatment from patient, RC § 2133.08.

Conditions for withholding or withdrawing nutrition and hydration from patient, RC § 2133.09.

Duties of attending physician when declaration becomes operative, RC § 2133.05.

Fees for recording, RC § 317.32.

Records to be kept by county recorder, RC § 317.08.

Use of printed form, RC § 2133.07.

**Ohio Administrative Code**

Department of health—

Do not resuscitate (DNR) protocol. OAC ch. 3701-62.

Individual rights not abrogated. OAC 3701-62-13.

**Practice Manuals and Treatises**

Anderson's Ohio Elder Law Practice Manual § 8.3 Nutrition and Hydration

Anderson's Ohio Elder Law Practice Manual § 8.9 Prolonging Care

Anderson's Ohio Elder Law Practice Manual § 10.2 Ohio Statute

Anderson's Ohio Elder Law Practice Manual § 10.6 Common Provisions

Anderson's Ohio Probate Practice and Procedure Form 59.01 Living will declaration (Acknowledged)

Anderson's Ohio Probate Practice and Procedure Form 59.02 Living will declaration (Witnessed)

**Practice Guides**

Anderson's Ohio Probate Practice and Procedure § 59.01 Living will

Anderson's Ohio Probate Practice and Procedure § 59.02 Nondeclarants; written consent

Anderson's Ohio Probate Practice and Procedure § 60.03 Ways to make anatomical gift

## § 2133.03 When declaration becomes operative; declaration supersedes general consent to treatment, DNR identification or durable power of attorney for health care.

(A)(1) A declaration becomes operative when it is communicated to the attending physician of the declarant, the attending physician and one other physician who examines the declarant determine that the declarant is in a terminal condition or in a permanently unconscious state, whichever is addressed in the declaration, the applicable requirements of divisions (A)(2) and (3) of this section are satisfied, and the attending physician determines that the declarant no longer is able to make informed decisions regarding the administration of life-sustaining treatment. When the declaration becomes operative, the attending physician and health care facilities shall act in accordance with its provisions or comply with the provisions of section 2133.10 of the Revised Code.

(2) In order for a declaration to become operative in connection with a declarant who is in a permanently unconscious state, the consulting physician associated with the determination that the declarant is in the permanently unconscious state shall be a physician who, by virtue of advanced education or training, of a practice limited to particular diseases, illnesses, injuries, therapies, or branches of medicine or surgery or osteopathic medicine and surgery, of certification as a specialist in a particular branch of medicine or surgery or osteopathic medicine and surgery, or of experience acquired in the practice of medicine or surgery or osteopathic medicine and surgery, is qualified to determine whether the declarant is in a permanently unconscious state.

(3) In order for a declaration to become operative in connection with a declarant who is in a terminal condition or in a permanently unconscious state, the attending physician of the declarant shall determine, in good faith, to a reasonable degree of medical certainty, and in accordance with reasonable medical standards, that there is no reasonable possibility that the declarant will regain the capacity to make informed decisions regarding the administration of life-sustaining treatment.

(B)(1)(a) A declaration supersedes any general consent to treatment form signed by or on behalf of the declarant prior to, upon, or after the declarant's admission to a health care facility to the extent there is a conflict between the declaration and the form, even if the form is signed after the execution of the declaration. To the extent that the provisions of a declaration and a general consent to treatment form do not conflict, both documents shall govern the use or continuation, or the withholding or withdrawal, of life-sustaining treatment and other medical or nursing procedures, treatments, interventions, or other measures in connection with the declarant. Division (B)(1)(a) of this section does not apply if a declaration is revoked pursuant to section 2133.04 of the Revised Code after the signing of a general consent to treatment form.

(b) A declaration supersedes a DNR identification, as defined in section 2133.21 of the Revised Code, of the declarant that is based upon a prior, inconsistent declaration of the declarant or that is based upon a do-not-resuscitate order, as defined in section 2133.21 of the Revised Code, that a physician has issued for the declarant and that is inconsistent with the declaration.

(2) If a declarant has both a valid durable power of attorney for health care and a valid declaration, the declaration supersedes the durable power of attorney for health care to the extent that the provisions of the documents would conflict if the declarant should be in a terminal condition or in a permanently unconscious state. Division (B)(2) of this section does not apply if the declarant revokes the declaration pursuant to section 2133.04 of the Revised Code.

**HISTORY:**

144 v S 1 (Eff 10-10-91); 147 v H 354. Eff 7-9-98.

### RESEARCH REFERENCES AND PRACTICE AIDS

**Cross-References to Related Sections**

Application to document executed prior to effective date of provisions, RC § 2133.15.

Durable power of attorney for health care, RC § 1337.12.

Refusal of physician to comply with declaration of terminally ill, RC § 2133.02.

**Ohio Administrative Code**

DNR identification. OAC 3701-62-04.

Relationship of DNR orders and identification with declarations and durable powers of attorney for health care. OAC 3701-62-10.

**Practice Manuals and Treatises**

Ohio Transaction Guide: Family Law & Forms § 1.22 Planning for Illness or Death

Anderson's Ohio Elder Law Practice Manual § 10.2 Ohio Statute

**Practice Guides**

Anderson's Ohio Probate Practice and Procedure § 59.01 Living will

## § 2133.04 Revocation of declaration.

(A) A declarant may revoke a declaration at any time and in any manner. The revocation shall be effective when the declarant expresses an intention to revoke the declaration, except that, if the declarant made the declarant's attending physician aware of the declaration, the revocation shall be effective upon its communication to the attending physician of the declarant by the declarant, a witness to the revocation, or other health care personnel to whom the revocation is communicated by that witness. Absent actual knowledge to the contrary, the attending physician of a declarant and other health care personnel who are informed of the revocation of a declaration by an alleged witness may rely on the information and act in accordance with the revocation.

(B) Upon the communication as described in division (A) of this section to the attending physician of a declarant of the fact that the declaration has been revoked, the attending physician or other health care personnel acting under the direction of the attending physician shall make the fact a part of the declarant's medical record.

(C) Unless a declaration provides otherwise, a declaration is revoked by a subsequent declaration.

**HISTORY:**

144 v S 1. Eff 10-10-91; 2011 SB 124, § 1, eff. Jan. 13, 2012; 2013 HB 126, § 1, eff. Mar. 20, 2014.

**Editor's Notes**

Acts 2011, SB 124, § 3 provides: "The provisions of this act that relate to the estates of decedents apply to the estates of decedents who die on or after the effective date of this act."

**Amendment Notes**

The 2013 amendment added (C).
The 2011 amendment made stylistic changes.

### RESEARCH REFERENCES AND PRACTICE AIDS

**Cross-References to Related Sections**

Declaration supersedes general consent to treatment or durable power of attorney for health care, RC § 2133.03.
DNR identification defined, RC § 2133.21.

**Ohio Administrative Code**

Revocation of DNR identification or DNR order. OAC 3701-62-06.

**Practice Manuals and Treatises**

Anderson's Ohio Elder Law Practice Manual § 10.6 Common Provisions

**Practice Guides**

Anderson's Ohio Probate Practice and Procedure § 59.01 Living will

## § 2133.05 Duties of attending physician when declaration becomes operative; notice to certain persons; complaint by objecting person.

(A) If the attending physician of a declarant and one other physician who examines the declarant determine that the declarant is in a terminal condition or in a permanently unconscious state, whichever is addressed in the declaration, if the attending physician additionally determines that the declarant no longer is able to make informed decisions regarding the administration of life-sustaining treatment for the declarant and that there is no reasonable possibility that the declarant will regain the capacity to make those informed decisions for the declarant, and if the attending physician is aware of the existence of the declarant's declaration, then the attending physician shall do all of the following:

(1) Record the determinations, together with the terms of the declaration or any copy of the declaration acquired as described in division (C) of section 2133.02 of the Revised Code, in the declarant's medical record;

(2)(a) Make a good faith effort, and use reasonable diligence, to notify either of the following of the determinations:

(i) If the declarant designated in the declarant's declaration one or more persons to be notified at any time that life-sustaining treatment would be withheld or withdrawn pursuant to the declaration, that person or those persons;

(ii) If division (A)(2)(a)(i) of this section is not applicable, the appropriate individual or individuals, in accordance with the following descending order of priority: if any, the guardian of the declarant, but this division does not permit or require, and shall not be construed as permitting or requiring, the appointment of a guardian for the declarant; the declarant's spouse; the declarant's adult children who are available within a reasonable period of time for consultation with the declarant's attending physician; the declarant's parents; or an adult sibling of the declarant or, if there is more than one adult sibling, a majority of the declarant's adult siblings who are available within a reasonable period of time for the consultation.

(b) The attending physician shall record in the declarant's medical record the names of the individual or individuals notified pursuant to division (A)(2)(a) of this section and the manner of notification.

(c) If, despite making a good faith effort, and despite using reasonable diligence, to notify the appropriate individual or individuals described in division (A)(2)(a) of this section, the attending physician cannot notify the individual or individuals of the determinations because the individual or individuals are deceased, cannot be located, or cannot be notified for some other reason, then the requirements of divisions (A)(2)(a) and (b) and (3) of this section and, except as provided in division (B)(1)(b) of this section, the provisions of division (B) of this section shall not apply in connection with the declarant and the declarant's declaration. However, the attending physician shall record in the declarant's medical record information pertaining to the reason for the failure to provide the requisite notices and information pertaining to the nature of the good faith effort and reasonable diligence used.

(3) Afford time for the individual or individuals notified in accordance with division (A)(2) of this section to object in the manner described in division (B)(1)(a) of this section.

(B)(1)(a) Within forty-eight hours after receipt of a notice pursuant to division (A)(2) of this section, any individual so notified shall advise the attending physician of the declarant whether the individual objects on a basis specified in division (B)(2)(c) of this section. If an objection as described in that division is communicated to the attending physician, then, within two business days after the communication, the individual shall file a complaint as described in division (B)(2) of this section in the probate court of the county in which the declarant is located. If the individual fails to so file a complaint or if the individual would not be competent to decide whether or not to consent to the withholding or withdrawing of life-sustaining treatment for any of the reasons described in division (C)(2) of section 2133.08 of the Revised Code, the individual's objections as described in division (B)(2)(c) of this section shall be considered to be void.

(b) Within forty-eight hours after a person described in division (A)(2)(a)(i) of this section or a priority individual or any member of a priority class of individuals described in division (A)(2)(a) (ii) of this section receives a notice pursuant to division (A)(2) of this section or within forty-eight hours after information pertaining to an unnotified person described in division (A)(2)(a)(i) of this section or an unnotified priority individual or unnotified priority class of individuals described in division (A)(2)(a)(ii) of this section is recorded in a declarant's medical record pursuant to division (A)(2)(c) of this section, either of the following shall advise the attending physician of the declarant whether there is an objection on a basis specified in division (B)(2)(c) of this section:

(i) If a person described in division (A)(2)(a)(i) of this section was notified pursuant to division (A)(2) of this section or was the subject of a recordation under division (A)(2)(c) of this section, then the objection shall be communicated by the individual or a majority of the individuals in either of the first two classes of individuals that pertain to the declarant in the descending order of priority set forth in division (A)(2)(a)(ii) of this section.

(ii) If an individual or individuals in the descending order of priority set forth in division (A) (2)(a)(ii) of this section were notified pursuant to division (A)(2) of this section or were the subject of a recordation under division (A)(2)(c) of this section, then the objection shall be communicated by the individual or a majority of the individuals in the next class of individuals that pertains to the declarant in the descending order of priority set forth in division (A)(2)(a)(ii) of this section.

If an objection as described in division (B)(2)(c) of this section is communicated to the attending physician in accordance with division (B)(1)(b)(i) or (ii) of this section, then, within two business days after the communication, the objecting individual or majority shall file a complaint as described in division (B)(2) of this section in the probate court of the county in which the declarant is located. If the objecting individual or majority fails to file a complaint or if the individual or a member of the majority would not be competent to decide whether or not to consent to the withholding or withdrawing of life-sustaining treatment for any of the reasons described in division (C)(2) of section 2133.08 of the Revised Code, the objections as described in division (B)(2)(c) of this section shall be considered to be void.

(2) A complaint of an individual that is filed in accordance with division (B)(1)(a) of this section or of an individual or majority of individuals that is filed in accordance with division (B)(1) (b) of this section shall satisfy all of the following:

(a) Name any health care facility in which the declarant is confined;

(b) Name the declarant, the declarant's attending physician, and the consulting physician associated with the determination that the declarant is in a terminal condition or in a permanently unconscious state, whichever is addressed in the declaration;

(c) Indicate whether the plaintiff or plaintiffs object on one or more of the following bases:

(i) To the attending physician's and consulting physician's determinations that the declarant is in a terminal condition or in a permanently unconscious state, whichever is addressed in the declaration;

(ii) To the attending physician's determination that the declarant no longer is able to make informed decisions regarding the administration of life-sustaining treatment;

(iii) To the attending physician's determination that there is no reasonable possibility that the declarant will regain the capacity to make informed decisions regarding the administration of life-sustaining treatment;

(iv) That the course of action proposed to be undertaken by the attending physician is not authorized by the declarant's declaration;

(v) That the declaration was executed when the declarant was not of sound mind or was under or subject to duress, fraud, or undue influence;

(vi) That the declaration otherwise does not substantially comply with this chapter.

(d) Request the probate court to issue one of the following types of orders:

(i) An order to the attending physician to reevaluate, in light of the court proceedings, the determination that the declarant is in a terminal condition or in a permanently unconscious state, whichever is addressed in the declaration, the determination that the declarant no longer is able to make informed decisions regarding the administration of life-sustaining treatment, the determination that there is no reasonable possibility that the declarant will regain the capacity to make those informed decisions, or the course of action proposed to be undertaken;

(ii) An order invalidating the declaration because it was executed when the declarant was not of sound mind or was under or subject to duress, fraud, or undue influence, or because it otherwise does not substantially comply with this chapter;

(e) Be accompanied by an affidavit of the plaintiff or plaintiffs that includes averments relative to whether the plaintiff is an individual or the plaintiffs are individuals as described in division (A)(2)(a)(i) or (ii) of this section and to the factual basis for the plaintiff's or the plaintiffs' objections;

(f) Name any individuals who were notified by the attending physician in accordance with division (A)(2)(a) of this section and who are not joining in the complaint as plaintiffs;

(g) Name, in the caption of the complaint, as defendants the attending physician of the declarant, the consulting physician associated with the determination that the declarant is in a terminal condition or in a permanently unconscious state, whichever is addressed in the declaration, any health care facility in which the declarant is confined, and any individuals who were notified by the attending physician in accordance with division (A)(2)(a) of this section and who are not joining in the complaint as plaintiffs.

(3) Notwithstanding any contrary provision of the Revised Code or of the Rules of Civil Procedure, the state and persons other than an objecting individual as described in division (B)(1)(a) of this section, other than an objecting individual or majority of individuals as described in division (B)(2)(b)(i) or (ii) of this section, and other than persons described in division (B)(2)(g) of this section are prohibited from commencing a civil action under this section and from joining or being joined as parties to an action commenced under this section, including joining by way of intervention.

(4)(a) A probate court in which a complaint as described in division (B)(2) of this section is filed within the period specified in division (B)(1)(a) or (b) of this section shall conduct a hearing on the complaint after a copy of the complaint and a notice of the hearing have been served upon the defendants. The clerk of the probate court in which the complaint is filed shall cause the complaint and the notice of the hearing to be so served in accordance with the Rules of Civil Procedure, which service shall be made, if possible, within three days after the filing of the complaint. The hearing shall be conducted at the earliest possible time, but no later than the third business day after the service has been completed. Immediately following the hearing, the court shall enter on its journal its determination whether a requested order will be issued.

(b) If the declarant's declaration authorized the use or continuation of life-sustaining treatment should the declarant be in a terminal condition or in a permanently unconscious state and if the plaintiff or plaintiffs requested a reevaluation order to the attending physician of the declarant as described in division (B)(2)(d)(i) of this section, the court shall issue the reevaluation order only if it finds that the plaintiff or plaintiffs have established a factual basis for the objection or objections involved by clear and convincing evidence, to a reasonable degree of medical certainty, and in accordance with reasonable medical standards.

(c) If the declarant's declaration authorized the withholding or withdrawal of life-sustaining treatment should the declarant be in a terminal condition or in a permanently unconscious state and if the plaintiff or plaintiffs requested a reevaluation order to the attending physician of the declarant as described in division (B)(2)(d)(i) of this section, the court shall issue the reevaluation order only if it finds that the plaintiff or plaintiffs have established a factual basis for the objection or objections involved by a preponderance of the evidence, to a reasonable degree of medical certainty, and in accordance with reasonable medical standards.

(d) If the plaintiff or plaintiffs requested an invalidation order as described in division (B)(2) (d)(ii) of this section, the court shall issue the order only if it finds that the plaintiff or plaintiffs have established a factual basis for the objection or objections involved by clear and convincing evidence.

(e) If the court issues a reevaluation order to the declarant's attending physician pursuant to division (B)(4)(b) or (c) of this section, then the attending physician shall make the requisite reevaluation. If, after doing so, the attending physician again determines that the declarant is in a terminal condition or in a permanently unconscious state, that the declarant no longer is able to make informed decisions regarding the administration of life-sustaining treatment, that there is no reasonable possibility that the declarant will regain the capacity to make those informed decisions, or that the attending physician would undertake the same proposed course of action, then the attending physician shall notify the court in writing of the determination and comply with the provisions of section 2133.10 of the Revised Code.

**HISTORY:**

144 v S 1. Eff 10-10-91; 2011 SB 124, § 1, eff. Jan. 13, 2012; 2016 hb451, § 1, effective April 6, 2017.

**Editor's Notes**

Acts 2011, SB 124, § 3 provides: "The provisions of this act that relate to the estates of decedents apply to the estates of decedents who die on or after the effective date of this act."

**Amendment Notes**

The 2016 amendment by HB 451 inserted "or if the individual would not be competent to decide whether or not to consent to the withholding or withdrawing of life-sustaining treatment for any of the reasons described in division (C)(2) of section 2133.08 of the Revised Code" in the third sentence of (B)(1)(a); and inserted "or if the individual or a member of the majority would not be competent to decide whether or not to consent to the withholding or withdrawing of life-sustaining treatment for any of the reasons described in division (C)(2) of section 2133.08 of the Revised Code" in the second sentence of the second paragraph of (B)(1)(b)(ii).

The 2011 amendment made stylistic changes.

**RESEARCH REFERENCES AND PRACTICE AIDS**

**Cross-References to Related Sections**

Comfort care continuation, RC § 2133.12.

Declaration governing use, continuation, withholding or withdrawal of life-sustaining treatment, RC § 2133.02.

Immunity from civil or criminal liability or professional disciplinary action, RC § 2133.11.

Jurisdiction of probate court, RC § 2101.24.

Transfer of patient to physician or facility willing to comply, RC § 2133.10.

**Ohio Rules**

Intervention, CivR 24.

**Practice Manuals and Treatises**

Anderson's Ohio Elder Law Practice Manual § 10.2 Ohio Statute

**Practice Guides**

Anderson's Ohio Probate Practice and Procedure § 59.01 Living will

Anderson's Ohio Probate Practice and Procedure § 2.01 Scope of jurisdiction

## § 2133.06 Patient may make decisions as long as able; effect of pregnancy.

(A) As long as a qualified patient is able to make informed decisions regarding the administration of life-sustaining treatment, the qualified patient may continue to do so.

(B) Life-sustaining treatment shall not be withheld or withdrawn from a declarant pursuant to a declaration if the declarant is pregnant and if the withholding or withdrawal of the treatment would terminate the pregnancy, unless the declarant's attending physician and one other physician who has examined the declarant determine, to a reasonable degree of medical certainty and in accordance with reasonable medical standards, that the fetus would not be born alive.

**HISTORY:**

144 v S 1. Eff 10-10-91; 2011 SB 124, § 1, eff. Jan. 13, 2012.

**Editor's Notes**

Acts 2011, SB 124, § 3 provides: "The provisions of this act that relate to the estates of decedents apply to the estates of decedents who die on or after the effective date of this act."

**Amendment Notes**

The 2011 amendment made stylistic changes.

## § 2133.07 Use of printed form.

(A) As used in this section, "DNR identification" has the same meaning as in section 2133.21 of the Revised Code.

(B) A printed form of a declaration may be sold or otherwise distributed in this state for use by adults who are not advised by an attorney. By use of a printed form of that nature, a declarant may authorize the use or continuation, or the withholding or withdrawal, of life-sustaining treatment should the declarant be in a terminal condition, a permanently unconscious state, or either a terminal condition or a permanently unconscious state, may authorize the withholding or withdrawal of nutrition or hydration should the declarant be in a permanently unconscious state as described in division (A)(3)(a) of section 2133.02 of the Revised Code, and may designate one or more persons who are to be notified by the declarant's attending physician at any time that life-sustaining treatment would be withheld or withdrawn pursuant to the declaration. The printed form shall not be used as an instrument for granting any other type of authority or for making any other type of designation, except that the printed form may be used as a DNR identification if the declarant specifies on the form that the declarant wishes to use it as a DNR identification.

(C)(1) A printed form of a declaration under division (B) of this section shall include, as a separate page or as a portion of a page that can be detached from the declaration, a donor registry enrollment form that permits the donor to be included in the donor registry created under section 2108.23 of the Revised Code.

(2) The donor registry enrollment form may be in any form that complies with the requirements of division (B) of section 2108.05 of the Revised Code. On completion, the form shall be forwarded to the bureau of motor vehicles.

**HISTORY:**

144 v S 1 (Eff 10-10-91); 147 v H 354. Eff 7-9-98; 150 v H 392, § 1, eff. 12-15-04; 152 v H 529, § 1, eff. 4-7-09; 2021 hb7, § 1, effective August 17, 2021.

**Editor's Notes**

The provisions of § 4, H.B. 392 (150 v —), read as follows:

SECTION 4. The amendments made by this act to section 2133.07 of the Revised Code do not affect an otherwise valid declaration governing the use, continuation, withholding, or withdrawal of life-sustaining treatment that was executed before the effective date of section 2133.07 of the Revised Code as amended by this act.

**Amendment Notes**

The 2021 amendment by HB 7 deleted former (A)(1); deleted the former (A)(2) designation; deleted "and except as provided in division (C) of this section" at the end of the last sentence of (B); deleted former (C); and redesignated former (D) as (C).

152 v H 529, effective April 7, 2009, added (A) and redesignated the remaining subsections accordingly; and rewrote present (D)(2).

**RESEARCH REFERENCES AND PRACTICE AIDS**

**Cross-References to Related Sections**

Free distribution of living will and durable power of attorney for health care forms, RC § 317.41.

**Ohio Administrative Code**

DNR identification. OAC 3701-62-04.

**Practice Manuals and Treatises**

Anderson's Ohio Elder Law Practice Manual § 10.2 Ohio Statute

**Practice Guides**

Anderson's Ohio Probate Practice and Procedure § 60.03 Ways to make anatomical gift

**Practice Forms**

Do not resuscitate (DNR) form, Couse's Ohio Form Book Form 32.44

## § 2133.08 Certain persons may consent to withholding or withdrawing life-sustaining treatment from patient; complaint by objecting person.

(A)(1) If written consent to the withholding or withdrawal of life-sustaining treatment, witnessed by two individuals who satisfy the witness eligibility criteria set forth in division (B)(1) of section 2133.02 of the Revised Code, is given by the appropriate individual or individuals as specified in division (B) of this section to the attending physician of a patient who is an adult, and if all of the following apply in connection with the patient, then, subject to section 2133.09 of the Revised Code, the patient's attending physician may withhold or withdraw the life-sustaining treatment:

(a) The attending physician and one other physician who examines the patient determine, in good faith, to a reasonable degree of medical certainty, and in accordance with reasonable medical standards, that the patient is in a terminal condition or the patient currently is and for at least the immediately preceding twelve months has been in a permanently unconscious state, and the attending physician additionally determines, in good faith, to a reasonable degree of medical certainty, and in accordance with reasonable medical standards, that the patient no longer is able to make informed decisions regarding the administration of life-sus-

Titles 11 — 37

taining treatment and that there is no reasonable possibility that the patient will regain the capacity to make those informed decisions.

(b) The patient does not have a declaration that addresses the patient's intent should the patient be determined to be in a terminal condition or in a permanently unconscious state, whichever applies, or a durable power of attorney for health care, or has a document that purports to be such a declaration or durable power of attorney for health care but that document is not legally effective.

(c) The consent of the appropriate individual or individuals is given after consultation with the patient's attending physician and after receipt of information from the patient's attending physician or a consulting physician that is sufficient to satisfy the requirements of informed consent.

(d) The appropriate individual or individuals who give a consent are of sound mind and voluntarily give the consent.

(e) If a consent would be given under division (B)(3) of this section, the attending physician made a good faith effort, and used reasonable diligence, to notify the patient's adult children who are available within a reasonable period of time for consultation as described in division (A)(1)(c) of this section.

(2) The consulting physician under division (A)(1)(a) of this section associated with a patient allegedly in a permanently unconscious state shall be a physician who, by virtue of advanced education or training, of a practice limited to particular diseases, illnesses, injuries, therapies, or branches of medicine or surgery or osteopathic medicine and surgery, of certification as a specialist in a particular branch of medicine or surgery or osteopathic medicine and surgery, or of experience acquired in the practice of medicine or surgery or osteopathic medicine and surgery, is qualified to determine whether the patient currently is and for at least the immediately preceding twelve months has been in a permanently unconscious state.

(B) For purposes of division (A) of this section and subject to division (C) of this section, a consent to withhold or withdraw life-sustaining treatment may be given by the appropriate individual or individuals, in accordance with the following descending order of priority:

(1) If any, the guardian of the patient. This division does not permit or require, and shall not be construed as permitting or requiring, the appointment of a guardian for the patient.

(2) The patient's spouse;

(3) An adult child of the patient or, if there is more than one adult child, a majority of the patient's adult children who are available within a reasonable period of time for consultation with the patient's attending physician;

(4) The patient's parents;

(5) An adult sibling of the patient or, if there is more than one adult sibling, a majority of the patient's adult siblings who are available within a reasonable period of time for that consultation;

(6) The nearest adult who is not described in divisions (B)(1) to (5) of this section, who is related to the patient by blood or adoption, and who is available within a reasonable period of time for that consultation.

(C)(1) If an appropriate individual or class of individuals entitled to decide under division (B) of this section whether or not to consent to the withholding or withdrawal of life-sustaining treatment for a patient is not available within a reasonable period of time for the consultation and competent to so decide, or declines to so decide, then the next priority individual or class of individuals specified in that division is authorized to make the decision. However, an equal division in a priority class of individuals under that division does not authorize the next class of individuals specified in that division to make the decision. If an equal division in a priority class of individuals under that division occurs, no written consent to the withholding or withdrawal of life-sustaining treatment from the patient can be given pursuant to this section.

(2)(a) If an appropriate individual entitled to decide under division (B) of this section whether or not to consent to the withholding or withdrawing of life-sustaining treatment for a patient and that patient are married and are the parties to a pending divorce, dissolution, legal separation, or annulment proceeding, the individual is not competent to so decide, and the next priority individual or class of individuals specified in that division is authorized to make the decision.

(b) If an appropriate individual entitled to decide under division (B) of this section whether or not to consent to the withholding or withdrawing of life-sustaining treatment for a patient is subject to a temporary protection order, civil protection order, or any other protection order issued by a court in this state or another state and the patient is the alleged victim, the individual is not competent to so decide, and the next priority individual or class of individuals specified in that division is authorized to make that decision.

(c) If a member of a class of individuals entitled to decide under division (B) of this section whether or not to consent to the withholding or withdrawal of life-sustaining treatment for a patient is subject to a temporary protection order, civil protection order, or any other protection order issued by a court in this state or another state and the patient is the alleged victim, the member is not competent to so decide, and the other members of the class of individuals are authorized to make the decision.

(d) If an appropriate individual entitled to decide under division (B) of this section whether or not to consent to the withholding or withdrawal of life-sustaining treatment for a patient has been charged with the offense of felonious assault under section 2903.11 of the Revised Code or the offense of aggravated assault under section 2903.12 of the Revised Code against the patient and the serious physical harm or physical harm suffered by the patient as a result of the offense directly caused the patient to be in a terminal condition, the individual is not competent to so decide, and the next priority individual or class of individuals specified in that division is authorized to make the decision.

(e) If a member of a class of individuals entitled to decide under division (B) of this section whether or not to consent to the withholding or withdrawal of life-sustaining treatment for a patient has been charged with the offense of felonious assault under section 2903.11 of the Revised Code or the offense of aggravated assault under section 2903.12 of the Revised Code against the patient and the serious physical harm or physical harm suffered by the patient as a result of the offense directly caused the patient to be in a terminal condition, that member is not competent to so decide, and the other members of the class of individuals are authorized to make the decision.

(D)(1) A decision to consent pursuant to this section to the use or continuation, or the withholding or withdrawal, of life-sustaining treatment for a patient shall be made in good faith.

(2) Except as provided in division (D)(4) of this section, if the patient previously expressed an intention with respect to the use or continuation, or the withholding or withdrawal, of life-sustaining treatment should the patient subsequently be in a terminal condition or in a permanently unconscious state, whichever applies, and no longer able to make informed decisions regarding the administration of life-sustaining treatment, a consent given pursuant to this section shall be valid only if it is consistent with that previously expressed intention.

(3) Except as provided in division (D)(4) of this section, if the patient did not previously express an intention with respect to the use or continuation, or the withholding or withdrawal, of life-sustaining treatment should the patient subsequently be in a terminal condition or in a permanently unconscious state, whichever applies, and no longer able to make informed decisions regarding the administration of life-sustaining treatment, a consent given pursuant to this section shall be valid only if it is consistent with the type of informed consent decision that the patient would have made if the patient previously had expressed an intention with respect to the use or continuation, or the withholding or withdrawal, of life-sustaining treatment should the patient subsequently be in a terminal condition or in a permanently unconscious state, whichever applies, and no longer able to make informed decisions regarding the administration of life-sustaining treatment, as inferred from the lifestyle and character of the patient, and from any other evidence of the desires of the patient, prior to the patient's becoming no longer able to make informed decisions regarding the administration of life-sustaining treat-

ment. The Rules of Evidence shall not be binding for purposes of this division.

(4)(a) The attending physician of the patient, and other health care personnel acting under the direction of the attending physician, who do not have actual knowledge of a previously expressed intention as described in division (D)(2) of this section or who do not have actual knowledge that the patient would have made a different type of informed consent decision under the circumstances described in division (D)(3) of this section, may rely on a consent given in accordance with this section unless a probate court decides differently under division (E) of this section.

(b) The immunity conferred by division (C)(1) of section 2133.11 of the Revised Code is not forfeited by an individual who gives a consent to the use or continuation, or the withholding or withdrawal, of life-sustaining treatment for a patient under division (B) of this section if the individual gives the consent in good faith and without actual knowledge, at the time of giving the consent, of either a contrary previously expressed intention of the patient, or a previously expressed intention of the patient, as described in division (D)(2) of this section, that is revealed to the individual subsequent to the time of giving the consent.

(E)(1) Within forty-eight hours after a priority individual or class of individuals gives a consent pursuant to this section to the use or continuation, or the withholding or withdrawal, of life-sustaining treatment and communicates the consent to the patient's attending physician, any individual described in divisions (B)(1) to (5) of this section, except an individual who is not competent to give consent under division (C)(2) of this section, who objects to the application of this section to the patient shall advise the attending physician of the grounds for the objection. If an objection is so communicated to the attending physician, then, within two business days after that communication, the objecting individual shall file a complaint against the priority individual or class of individuals, the patient's attending physician, and the consulting physician associated with the determination that the patient is in a terminal condition or that the patient currently is and for at least the immediately preceding twelve months has been in a permanently unconscious state, in the probate court of the county in which the patient is located for the issuance of an order reversing the consent of the priority individual or class of individuals. If the objecting individual fails to so file a complaint, the individual's objections shall be considered to be void.

A probate court in which a complaint is filed in accordance with this division shall conduct a hearing on the complaint after a copy of the complaint and a notice of the hearing have been served upon the defendants. The clerk of the probate court in which the complaint is filed shall cause the complaint and the notice of the hearing to be so served in accordance with the Rules of Civil Procedure, which service shall be made, if possible, within three days after the filing of the complaint. The hearing shall be conducted at the earliest possible time, but no later than the third business day after the service has been completed. Immediately following the hearing, the court shall enter on its journal its determination whether the decision of the priority individual or class of individuals to consent to the use or continuation, or the withholding or withdrawal, of life-sustaining treatment in connection with the patient will be confirmed or reversed.

(2) If the decision of the priority individual or class of individuals was to consent to the use or continuation of life-sustaining treatment in connection with the patient, the court only may reverse that consent if the objecting individual establishes, by clear and convincing evidence and, if applicable, to a reasonable degree of medical certainty and in accordance with reasonable medical standards, one or more of the following:

(a) The patient is able to make informed decisions regarding the administration of life-sustaining treatment.

(b) The patient has a legally effective declaration that addresses the patient's intent should the patient be determined to be in a terminal condition or in a permanently unconscious state, whichever applies, or a legally effective durable power of attorney for health care.

(c) The decision to use or continue life-sustaining treatment is not consistent with the previously expressed intention of the patient as described in division (D)(2) of this section.

(d) The decision to use or continue life-sustaining treatment is not consistent with the type of informed consent decision that the patient would have made if the patient previously had expressed an intention with respect to the use or continuation, or the withholding or withdrawal, of life-sustaining treatment should the patient subsequently be in a terminal condition or in a permanently unconscious state, whichever applies, and no longer able to make informed decisions regarding the administration of life-sustaining treatment as described in division (D)(3) of this section.

(e) The decision of the priority individual or class of individuals was not made after consultation with the patient's attending physician and after receipt of information from the patient's attending physician or a consulting physician that is sufficient to satisfy the requirements of informed consent.

(f) The priority individual, or any member of the priority class of individuals, who made the decision to use or continue life-sustaining treatment was not of sound mind or did not voluntarily make the decision.

(g) If the decision of a priority class of individuals under division (B)(3) of this section is involved, the patient's attending physician did not make a good faith effort, and use reasonable diligence, to notify the patient's adult children who were available within a reasonable period of time for consultation as described in division (A)(1)(c) of this section.

(h) The decision of the priority individual or class of individuals otherwise was made in a manner that does not comply with this section.

(3) If the decision of the priority individual or class of individuals was to consent to the withholding or withdrawal of life-sustaining treatment in connection with the patient, the court only may reverse that consent if the objecting individual establishes, by a preponderance of the evidence and, if applicable, to a reasonable degree of medical certainty and in accordance with reasonable medical standards, one or more of the following:

(a) The patient is not in a terminal condition, the patient is not in a permanently unconscious state, or the patient has not been in a permanently unconscious state for at least the immediately preceding twelve months.

(b) The patient is able to make informed decisions regarding the administration of life-sustaining treatment.

(c) There is a reasonable possibility that the patient will regain the capacity to make informed decisions regarding the administration of life-sustaining treatment.

(d) The patient has a legally effective declaration that addresses the patient's intent should the patient be determined to be in a terminal condition or in a permanently unconscious state, whichever applies, or a legally effective durable power of attorney for health care.

(e) The decision to withhold or withdraw life-sustaining treatment is not consistent with the previously expressed intention of the patient as described in division (D)(2) of this section.

(f) The decision to withhold or withdraw life-sustaining treatment is not consistent with the type of informed consent decision that the patient would have made if the patient previously had expressed an intention with respect to the use or continuation, or the withholding or withdrawal, of life-sustaining treatment should the patient subsequently be in a terminal condition or in a permanently unconscious state, whichever applies, and no longer able to make informed decisions regarding the administration of life-sustaining treatment as described in division (D)(3) of this section.

(g) The decision of the priority individual or class of individuals was not made after consultation with the patient's attending physician and after receipt of information from the patient's attending physician or a consulting physician that is sufficient to satisfy the requirements of informed consent.

(h) The priority individual, or any member of the priority class of individuals, who made the decision to withhold or withdraw life-sustaining treatment was not of sound mind, was not competent to make the decision under division (C)(2) of this section, or did not voluntarily make the decision.

(i) If the decision of a priority class of individuals under division (B)(3) of this section is involved, the patient's attending physician did not make a good faith effort, and use reasonable diligence, to notify the patient's adult children who were available within a reasonable period of time for consultation as described in division (A)(1)(c) of this section.

(j) The decision of the priority individual or class of individuals otherwise was made in a manner that does not comply with this section.

(4) Notwithstanding any contrary provision of the Revised Code or of the Rules of Civil Procedure, the state and persons other than individuals described in divisions (B)(1) to (5) of this section are prohibited from filing a complaint under division (E) of this section and from joining or being joined as parties to a hearing conducted under division (E) of this section, including joining by way of intervention.



(F) A valid consent given in accordance with this section supersedes any general consent to treatment form signed by or on behalf of the patient prior to, upon, or after the patient's admission to a health care facility to the extent there is a conflict between the consent and the form.

(G) Life-sustaining treatment shall not be withheld or withdrawn from a patient pursuant to a consent given in accordance with this section if the patient is pregnant and if the withholding or withdrawal of the treatment would terminate the pregnancy, unless the patient's attending physician and one other physician who has examined the patient determine, to a reasonable degree of medical certainty and in accordance with reasonable medical standards, that the fetus would not be born alive.

(H) As used in this section, "civil protection order" and "temporary protection order" have the same meanings as in section 2923.124 of the Revised Code.

**HISTORY:**

144 v S 1. Eff 10-10-91; 2011 SB 124, § 1, eff. Jan. 13, 2012; 2016 hb451, § 1, effective April 6, 2017.

**Editor's Notes**

Acts 2011, SB 124, § 3 provides: "The provisions of this act that relate to the estates of decedents apply to the estates of decedents who die on or after the effective date of this act."

**Amendment Notes**

The 2016 amendment by HB 451 inserted "and subject to division (C) of this section" in the introductory language of (B); inserted (C)(2)(a) through (C)(2)(e); redesignated former (C) as (C)(1); inserted "except an individual who is not competent to give consent under division (C)(2) of this section" in the first sentence of the first paragraph of (E)(1); inserted "was not competent to make the decision under division (C)(2) of this section" in (E)(3)(h); and added (H).

The 2011 amendment made stylistic changes.

### NOTES TO DECISIONS

Analysis

Generally
Minors
Patient's expressed intentions

**Generally**

Removal of nutrition and hydration from persons in a persistent vegetative state is rapidly becoming a legally accepted practice in the United States. The test to be applied by the probate court is the best interests of such a person. The twelve-month wait provided by R.C. 2133.09(B)(2) is unreasonable and not binding: In re Guardianship of Myers, 62 Ohio Misc. 2d 763, 610 N.E.2d 663, 1993 Ohio Misc. LEXIS 5 (Ohio C.P. 1993).

**Minors**

R.C. 2133.08 does not permit the withdrawal of life-sustaining treatment for a minor. The probate court exceeded its statutory authority in granting the guardian the power to withdraw life-supporting treatments before the parents' rights were permanently terminated: In re Guardianship of Stein, 2004-Ohio-7114, 105 Ohio St. 3d 30, 821 N.E.2d 1008, 2004 Ohio LEXIS 3072 (Ohio 2004).

**Patient's expressed intentions**

Termination of life-sustaining treatment for a terminal patient was in accord with the patient's previously expressed intentions: Carpenter v. Mason, 2003-Ohio-6490, 126 Ohio Misc. 2d 17, 800 N.E.2d 404, 2003 Ohio Misc. LEXIS 42 (Ohio C.P. 2003).

### RESEARCH REFERENCES AND PRACTICE AIDS

**Cross-References to Related Sections**

Application to document executed prior to effective date of provisions, RC § 2133.15.

Comfort care continuation, RC § 2133.12.

Conditions for withholding or withdrawing nutrition and hydration from patient, RC § 2133.09.

Immunity from civil or criminal liability or professional disciplinary action, RC § 2133.11.

Jurisdiction of probate court, RC § 2101.24.

Transfer of patient to physician or facility willing to comply, RC § 2133.10.

**Ohio Rules**

Intervention, CivR 24.

**Practice Manuals and Treatises**

Anderson's Ohio Elder Law Practice Manual § 8.4 Persistent Vegetative State and Terminal Condition

Anderson's Ohio Elder Law Practice Manual § 8.6 Family Consent Statutes

Anderson's Ohio Elder Law Practice Manual § 8.7 Court Hearings

**Practice Guides**

Anderson's Ohio Probate Practice and Procedure § 59.02 Nondeclarants; written consent

## § 2133.09 Conditions for withholding or withdrawing nutrition and hydration from patient who has been in a permanently unconscious state for at least twelve months.

(A) The attending physician of a patient who is an adult and who currently is and for at least the immediately preceding twelve months has been in a permanently unconscious state may withhold or withdraw nutrition and hydration in connection with the patient only if all of the following apply:

(1) Written consent to the withholding or withdrawal of life-sustaining treatment in connection with the patient has been given by an appropriate individual or individuals in accordance with section 2133.08 of the Revised Code, and divisions (A)(1)(a) to (e) and (2) of that section have been satisfied.

(2) A probate court has not reversed the consent to the withholding or withdrawal of life-sustaining treatment in connection with the patient pursuant to division (E) of section 2133.08 of the Revised Code.

(3) The attending physician of the patient and one other physician as described in division (A)(2) of section 2133.08 of the Revised Code who examines the patient determine, in good faith, to a reasonable degree of medical certainty, and in accordance with reasonable medical standards, that nutrition and hydration will not or no longer will provide comfort or alleviate pain in connection with the patient.

(4) Written consent to the withholding or withdrawal of nutrition and hydration in connection with the patient, witnessed by two individuals who satisfy the witness eligibility criteria set forth in division (B)(1) of section 2133.02 of the Revised Code, is given to the attending physician of the patient by an appropriate individual or individuals as specified in division (B) of section 2133.08 of the Revised Code.

(5) The written consent to the withholding or withdrawal of the nutrition and hydration in connection with the patient is given in accordance with division (B) of this section.

(6) The probate court of the county in which the patient is located issues an order to withhold or withdraw the nutrition and hydration in connection with the patient pursuant to division (C) of this section.

(B)(1) A decision to consent pursuant to this section to the withholding or withdrawal of nutrition and hydration in connection with a patient shall be made in good faith.

(2) Except as provided in division (B)(4) of this section, if the patient previously expressed an intention with respect to the use or continuation, or the withholding or withdrawal, of nutrition and hydration should the patient subsequently be in a permanently unconscious state and no longer able to make informed decisions regarding the administration of nutrition and hydration, a consent given pursuant to this section shall be valid only if it is consistent with that previously expressed intention.

(3) Except as provided in division (B)(4) of this section, if the patient did not previously express an intention with respect to the use or continuation, or the withholding or withdrawal, of nutrition and hydration should the patient subsequently be in a permanently unconscious state and no longer able to make informed decisions regarding the administration of nutrition and hydration, a consent given pursuant to this section shall be valid only if it is consistent with the type of informed consent decision that the patient would have made if the patient previously had expressed an intention with respect to the use or continuation, or the withholding or withdrawal, of nutrition and hydration should the patient subsequently be in a permanently unconscious state and no longer able to make informed decisions regarding the administration of nutrition and hydration, as inferred from the lifestyle and character of the patient, and from any other evidence of the desires of the patient, prior to the patient's becoming no longer able to make informed decisions regarding the administration of nutrition and hydration. The Rules of Evidence shall not be binding for purposes of this division.

(4)(a) The attending physician of the patient, and other health care personnel acting under the direction of the attending physician, who do not have actual knowledge of a previously expressed intention as described in division (B)(2) of this section or who do not have actual knowledge that the patient would have made a different type of informed consent decision under the circumstances described in division (B)(3) of this section, may rely on a consent given in accordance with this section unless a probate court decides differently under division (C) of this section.

(b) The immunity conferred by division (C)(2) of section 2133.11 of the Revised Code is not forfeited by an individual who gives a consent to the withholding or withdrawal of nutrition and hydration in connection with a patient under division (A)(4) of this section if the individual gives the consent in good faith and without actual knowledge, at the time of giving the consent, of either a contrary previously expressed intention of the patient, or a previously expressed intention of the patient, as described in division (B)(2) of this section, that is revealed to the individual subsequent to the time of giving the consent.

(C)(1) Prior to the withholding or withdrawal of nutrition and hydration in connection with a patient pursuant to this section, the priority individual or class of individuals that consented to the withholding or withdrawal of the nutrition and hydration shall apply to the probate court of the county in which the patient is located for the issuance of an order that authorizes the attending physician of the patient to commence the withholding or withdrawal of the nutrition and hydration in connection with the patient. Upon the filing of the application, the clerk of the probate court shall schedule a hearing on it and cause a copy of it and a notice of the hearing to be served in accordance with the Rules of Civil Procedure upon the applicant, the attending physician, the consulting physician associated with the determination that nutrition and hydration will not or no longer will provide comfort or alleviate pain in connection with the patient, and the individuals described in divisions (B)(1) to (5) of section 2133.08 of the Revised Code who are not applicants, which service shall be made, if possible, within three days after the filing of the application. The hearing shall be conducted at the earliest possible time, but no sooner than the thirtieth business day, and no later than the sixtieth business day, after the service has been completed.

At the hearing, any individual described in divisions (B)(1) to (5) of section 2133.08 of the Revised Code who is not an applicant, except an individual who is not competent under division (C)(2) of section 2133.08 of the Revised Code, and who disagrees with the decision of the priority individual or class of individuals to consent to the withholding or withdrawal of nutrition and hydration in connection with the patient shall be permitted to testify and present evidence relative to the use or continuation of nutrition and hydration in connection with the patient. Immediately following the hearing, the court shall enter on its journal its determination whether the requested order will be issued.

(2) The court shall issue an order that authorizes the patient's attending physician to commence the withholding or withdrawal of nutrition and hydration in connection with the patient only if the applicants establish, by clear and convincing evidence, to a reasonable degree of medical certainty, and in accordance with reasonable medical standards, all of the following:

(a) The patient currently is and for at least the immediately preceding twelve months has been in a permanently unconscious state.

(b) The patient no longer is able to make informed decisions regarding the administration of life-sustaining treatment.

(c) There is no reasonable possibility that the patient will regain the capacity to make informed decisions regarding the administration of life-sustaining treatment.

(d) The conditions specified in divisions (A)(1) to (4) of this section have been satisfied.

(e) The decision to withhold or withdraw nutrition and hydration in connection with the patient is consistent with the previously expressed intention of the patient as described in division (B) (2) of this section or is consistent with the type of informed consent decision that the patient would have made if the patient previously had expressed an intention with respect to the use or continuation, or the withholding or withdrawal, of nutrition and hydration should the patient subsequently be in a permanently unconscious state and no longer able to make informed decisions regarding the administration of nutrition and hydration as described in division (B)(3) of this section.

(3) Notwithstanding any contrary provision of the Revised Code or of the Rules of Civil Procedure, the state and persons other than individuals described in division (A)(4) of this section or in divisions (B)(1) to (5) of section 2133.08 of the Revised Code and other than the attending physician and consulting physician associated with the determination that nutrition and hydration will not or no longer will provide comfort or alleviate pain in connection with the patient are prohibited from filing an application under this division and from joining or being joined as parties to a hearing conducted under this division, including joining by way of intervention.

(D) A valid consent given in accordance with this section supersedes any general consent to treatment form signed by or on behalf of the patient prior to, upon, or after the patient's admission to a health care facility to the extent there is a conflict between the consent and the form.

**HISTORY:**

144 v S 1. Eff 10-10-91; 2011 SB 124, § 1, eff. Jan. 13, 2012; 2016 hb451, § 1, effective April 6, 2017.

**Editor's Notes**

Acts 2011, SB 124, § 3 provides: "The provisions of this act that relate to the estates of decedents apply to the estates of decedents who die on or after the effective date of this act."

**Amendment Notes**

The 2016 amendment by HB 451 inserted "except an individual who is not competent under division (C)(2) of section 2133.08 of the Revised Code" in the first sentence of the second paragraph of (C)(1).

The 2011 amendment made stylistic changes.

## NOTES TO DECISIONS

**Generally**

Removal of nutrition and hydration from persons in a persistent vegetative state is rapidly becoming a legally accepted practice in the

United States. The test to be applied by the probate court is the best interests of such a person. The twelve-month wait provided by R.C. 2133.09(B)(2) is unreasonable and not binding: In re Guardianship of Myers, 62 Ohio Misc. 2d 763, 610 N.E.2d 663, 1993 Ohio Misc. LEXIS 5 (Ohio C.P. 1993).

Under appropriate circumstances, a probate court may authorize withdrawal of nutrition and hydration from a permanently vegetative patient: In re Guardianship of Crum, 61 Ohio Misc. 2d 596, 580 N.E.2d 876, 1991 Ohio Misc. LEXIS 19 (Ohio P. Ct. 1991).



**RESEARCH REFERENCES AND PRACTICE AIDS**

**Cross-References to Related Sections**

Certain persons may consent to withholding or withdrawing life-sustaining treatment from patient, RC § 2133.08.

Immunity from civil or criminal liability or professional disciplinary action, RC § 2133.11.

Jurisdiction of probate court, RC § 2101.24.

Transfer of patient to physician or facility willing to comply, RC § 2133.10.

**Ohio Rules**

Intervention, CivR 24.

**Practice Manuals and Treatises**

Anderson's Ohio Elder Law Practice Manual § 8.6 Family Consent Statutes

Anderson's Ohio Elder Law Practice Manual § 8.7 Court Hearings

**Practice Guides**

Anderson's Ohio Probate Practice and Procedure § 59.02 Nondeclarants; written consent

## § 2133.10 Transfer of patient to physician or facility willing to comply.

(A) An attending physician who, or a health care facility in which a qualified patient or other patient is confined that, is not willing or is not able to comply or allow compliance with a declaration of a qualified patient, with a consent given in accordance with section 2133.08 or 2133.09 of the Revised Code, with any probate court order issued pursuant to section 2133.05, 2133.08, or 2133.09 of the Revised Code, or with any other applicable provision of sections 2133.01 to 2133.15 of the Revised Code shall not prevent or attempt to prevent, or unreasonably delay or attempt to unreasonably delay, the transfer of the qualified patient or other patient to the care of a physician who, or a health care facility that, is willing and able to so comply or allow compliance.

(B) If a declaration provides for the use or continuation of life-sustaining treatment should its declarant subsequently be in a terminal condition or in a permanently unconscious state, if a consent decision of a priority individual or class of individuals under section 2133.08 of the Revised Code is to use or continue life-sustaining treatment in connection with a patient described in that section, or if a probate court issues a reevaluation order pursuant to section 2133.05 or 2133.08 of the Revised Code that is intended to result in the use or continuation of life-sustaining treatment in connection with a qualified patient or other patient, then the attending physician of the qualified patient or other patient who, or health care facility in which the qualified patient or other patient is confined that, is not willing or is not able to comply or allow compliance with the declaration, consent decision, or reevaluation order shall use or continue the life-sustaining treatment or cause it to be used or continued until a transfer as described in division (A) of this section is made.

**HISTORY:**

144 v S 1 (Eff 10-10-91); 147 v H 354. Eff 7-9-98.

**RESEARCH REFERENCES AND PRACTICE AIDS**

**Cross-References to Related Sections**

Declaration becomes operative, when, RC § 2133.03.

Duties of attending physician, RC § 2133.05.

Refusal to comply with declaration of terminally ill, RC § 2133.02.

**Practice Manuals and Treatises**

Anderson's Ohio Elder Law Practice Manual § 10.6 Common Provisions

## § 2133.11 Immunity from civil or criminal liability or professional disciplinary action.

(A) Subject to division (D) of this section, an attending physician, consulting physician, health care facility, and health care personnel acting under the direction of an attending physician are not subject to criminal prosecution, are not liable in damages in a tort or other civil action, and are not subject to professional disciplinary action for any of the following:

(1) Giving effect to a declaration, if the physician, facility, or personnel gives effect to the declaration in good faith and does not have actual knowledge that the declaration has been revoked or does not substantially comply with this chapter;

(2) Giving effect to a consent under the circumstances described in section 2133.08 of the Revised Code, if the physician, facility, or personnel gives effect to the consent in good faith and does not have actual knowledge that the consent is invalid under that section and if a probate court has not issued an order reversing the consent pursuant to division (E) of that section;

(3) Giving effect to a consent under the circumstances described in section 2133.09 of the Revised Code, if the physician, facility, or personnel gives effect to the consent in good faith and does not have actual knowledge that the consent is invalid under that section and if the appropriate probate court has issued an order authorizing the withholding or withdrawal of nutrition and hydration in connection with the patient in question;

(4) Refusing to or not being able to comply or allow compliance with a declaration of a qualified patient, with a consent given in accordance with section 2133.08 or 2133.09 of the Revised Code, with a probate court order issued pursuant to section 2133.05, 2133.08, or 2133.09 of the Revised Code, or with another applicable provision of this chapter, if the refusal or inability to comply or allow compliance is in good faith, provided that, in the case of an attending physician or health care facility, whichever of the following apply are satisfied:

(a) The attending physician or health care facility does not prevent or attempt to prevent, or unreasonably delay or attempt to unreasonably delay, the transfer of the qualified patient or other patient to the care of a physician who, or a health care facility that, is willing and able to so comply or allow compliance.

(b) If the declaration of the qualified patient provided for the use or continuation of life-sustaining treatment should the declarant subsequently be in a terminal condition or in a permanently unconscious state, if the consent decision of a priority individual or class of individuals under section 2133.08 of the Revised Code was to use or continue life-sustaining treatment in connection with the patient described in that section, or if the probate court issued a reevaluation order pursuant to section 2133.05 or 2133.08 of the Revised Code that was intended to result in the use or continuation of life-sustaining treatment in connection with the qualified patient or other patient, the attending physician or health care facility used or continued the life-sustaining treatment or caused it to be used or continued until a transfer as described in division (A)(4)(a) of this section was made.

(5) Making determinations other than those described in division (B) of this section, or otherwise acting under this chapter, if the determinations or other actions are made in good faith and in accordance with reasonable medical standards;

(6) Prescribing, dispensing, administering, or causing to be administered any particular medical procedure, treatment, intervention, or other measure to a qualified patient or other patient, including, but not limited to, prescribing, personally furnishing, administering, or causing to be administered by judicious titration or in another manner any form of medication, for the purpose of diminishing the qualified patient's or other patient's pain or discomfort and not for the purpose of postponing or causing the qualified patient's or other patient's death, even though the medical procedure, treatment, intervention, or other measure may appear to hasten or increase the risk of the patient's death, if the attending physician so prescribing, dispensing, administering, or causing to be admin-

istered or the health care personnel acting under the direction of the attending physician so dispensing, administering, or causing to be administered are carrying out in good faith the responsibility to provide comfort care described in division (E)(1) of section 2133.12 of the Revised Code.

(B) Subject to division (D) of this section, an attending or consulting physician is not subject to criminal prosecution, is not liable in damages in a tort or other civil action, and is not subject to professional disciplinary action if the physician makes any of the following determinations in good faith, to a reasonable degree of medical certainty, and in accordance with reasonable medical standards:

(1) A determination that a declarant or a patient as described in section 2133.08 of the Revised Code is in a terminal condition;

(2) A determination that a declarant is in a permanently unconscious state;

(3) A determination that a patient as described in section 2133.08 of the Revised Code currently is and for at least the immediately preceding twelve months has been in a permanently unconscious state;

(4) A determination that a declarant or a patient as described in section 2133.08 of the Revised Code no longer is able to make informed decisions regarding the administration of life-sustaining treatment;

(5) A determination that there is no reasonable possibility that a declarant or a patient as described in section 2133.08 of the Revised Code will regain the capacity to make informed decisions regarding the administration of life-sustaining treatment;

(6) A determination that nutrition or hydration will not or no longer will provide comfort or alleviate pain in connection with a patient as described in section 2133.09 of the Revised Code.

(C)(1) Subject to division (D) of this section, an individual who is authorized to give a consent to the use or continuation, or the withholding or withdrawal, of life-sustaining treatment under division (B) of section 2133.08 of the Revised Code and who makes the decision in good faith is not subject to criminal prosecution, is not liable in damages in a tort or other civil action, and is not subject to professional disciplinary action in connection with that decision.

(2) Subject to division (D) of this section, an individual who is authorized to give a consent to the withholding or withdrawal of nutrition and hydration in connection with a patient under division (A)(4) of section 2133.09 of the Revised Code and who gives the consent in good faith is not subject to criminal prosecution, is not liable in damages in a tort or other civil action, and is not subject to professional disciplinary action in connection with that consent.

(D) This section does not grant an immunity from criminal or civil liability or from professional disciplinary action to health care personnel for actions that are outside the scope of their authority.

**HISTORY:**

144 v S 1 (Eff 10-10-91); 145 v H 343 (Eff 7-22-94); 147 v S 66. Eff 7-22-98.

### NOTES TO DECISIONS

Analysis

Construction
Immunity
Immunity determination
Medication error
State medical board
Wrongful administration of life-prolonging medical treatment

**Construction**

As used in R.C. 2133.11 and defined in R.C. 2133.01(Y), the term "professional disciplinary action" is susceptible of reasonable interpretation to encompass the disciplinary sanctions authorized by R.C. 4731.22(A) and (B) or to encompass the entire disciplinary process; the term is ambiguous and subject to statutory interpretation. State ex rel. Gelesh v. State Med. Bd., 2007-Ohio-3328, 172 Ohio App. 3d 365, 874 N.E.2d 1256, 2007 Ohio App. LEXIS 3053 (Ohio Ct. App., Franklin County 2007).

**Immunity**

There was no due process violation as the only violation found was that charged in the notice; thus, as a matter of law, under the requirements of R.C. 119.07, the doctor was provided with sufficient notice of the allegations against him regarding his medical license. Whether the doctor was rendering comfort care in good faith or intentionally hastening the demise of the patient became an issue once the doctor raised the affirmative defense of statutory immunity pursuant to R.C. 2133.11 and, thus, it was not unreasonable or outside the scope of the notice for the state medical board to examine the entire course of care for the patient. Gelesh v. State Med. Bd., 2010-Ohio-4378, 2010 Ohio App. LEXIS 3698 (Ohio Ct. App., Franklin County 2010).

**Immunity determination**

Contrary to the argument of a doctor who received a notice of opportunity for a hearing from the State Medical Board of Ohio, the "comfort care" immunity afforded to doctors under R.C. 2311.11 did not provide immunity from the entire disciplinary adjudication process; the statute provided immunity from damages, and it was the Board's responsibility to make the determination of whether the doctor was entitled to the immunity. State ex rel. Gelesh v. State Med. Bd., 2007-Ohio-3328, 172 Ohio App. 3d 365, 874 N.E.2d 1256, 2007 Ohio App. LEXIS 3053 (Ohio Ct. App., Franklin County 2007).

R.C. 2133.11 immunity does not preclude the State Medical Board of Ohio from determining the applicability of immunity in disciplinary proceedings under R.C. 4731.22 and R.C. ch. 119. State ex rel. Gelesh v. State Med. Bd., 2007-Ohio-3328, 172 Ohio App. 3d 365, 874 N.E.2d 1256, 2007 Ohio App. LEXIS 3053 (Ohio Ct. App., Franklin County 2007).

Titles 11 — 37

**Medication error**

Although the doctor was, in good faith, providing comfort care to an elderly woman on the verge of death, and thus, entitled to immunity up to and including the time when he was administering increasing doses of narcotics (particularly morphine) the administration of succinylcholine could not have been considered comfort care. It was a medication error and not in accordance with minimal standards of care; nor did the patient's do-not-resuscitate directive provide authority to administer succinylcholine under the circumstances, particularly with no respiratory support. Gelesh v. State Med. Bd., 2010-Ohio-4378, 2010 Ohio App. LEXIS 3698 (Ohio Ct. App., Franklin County 2010).

**State medical board**

R.C. 2133.11 immunity concerning terminally ill patients does not preclude the state medical board from determining the applicability of immunity in disciplinary proceedings under R.C. 4731.22 and R.C. Chapter 119: State ex rel. Gelesh v. State Med. Bd., 2007-Ohio-3328, 172 Ohio App. 3d 365, 874 N.E.2d 1256, 2007 Ohio App. LEXIS 3053 (Ohio Ct. App., Franklin County 2007).

**Wrongful administration of life-prolonging medical treatment**

Ohio does not recognize a claim for "wrongful living." However, nonconsensual medical treatment that prolongs a person's life may still be a battery: Anderson v. Saint Francis-Saint George Hosp., 83 Ohio App. 3d 221, 614 N.E.2d 841, 1992 Ohio App. LEXIS 5792 (Ohio Ct. App., Hamilton County 1992).

### RESEARCH REFERENCES AND PRACTICE AIDS

**Cross-References to Related Sections**

Certain persons may consent to withholding or withdrawing life-sustaining treatment from patient, RC § 2133.08.

Conditions for withholding or withdrawing nutrition and hydration from patient, RC § 2133.09.

**Ohio Administrative Code**

State medical board—

Drug treatment of intractable pain. OAC ch. 4731-21.

**Practice Manuals and Treatises**

Anderson's Ohio Elder Law Practice Manual § 10.6 Common Provisions

## § 2133.12 Death is not a suicide or homicide; health or life insurance or annuity rights not affected; no presumption created; limitations on effect of chapter; comfort care.

(A) The death of a qualified patient or other patient resulting from the withholding or withdrawal of life-sustaining treatment in accordance with sections 2133.01 to 2133.15 of the Revised Code does not constitute for any purpose a suicide, aggravated murder, murder, or any other homicide offense.

(B)(1) The execution of a declaration shall not do either of the following:

(a) Affect the sale, procurement, issuance, or renewal of any policy of life insurance or annuity, notwithstanding any term of a policy or annuity to the contrary;

(b) Be deemed to modify or invalidate the terms of any policy of life insurance or annuity that is in effect on October 10, 1991.

(2) Notwithstanding any term of a policy of life insurance or annuity to the contrary, the withholding or withdrawal of life-sustaining treatment from an insured, qualified patient or other patient in accordance with sections 2133.01 to 2133.15 of the Revised Code shall not impair or invalidate any policy of life insurance or annuity.

(3) Notwithstanding any term of a policy or plan to the contrary, the use or continuation, or the withholding or withdrawal, of life-sustaining treatment from an insured, qualified patient or other patient in accordance with sections 2133.01 to 2133.15 of the Revised Code shall not impair or invalidate any policy of health insurance or any health care benefit plan.

(4) No physician, health care facility, other health care provider, person authorized to engage in the business of insurance in this state under Title XXXIX of the Revised Code, health insuring corporation, other health care plan, legal entity that is self-insured and provides benefits to its employees or members, or other person shall require any individual to execute or refrain from executing a declaration, or shall require an individual to revoke or refrain from revoking a declaration, as a condition of being insured or of receiving health care benefits or services.



(C)(1) Sections 2133.01 to 2133.15 of the Revised Code do not create any presumption concerning the intention of an individual who has revoked or has not executed a declaration with respect to the use or continuation, or the withholding or withdrawal, of life-sustaining treatment if the individual should be in a terminal condition or in a permanently unconscious state at any time.

(2) Sections 2133.01 to 2133.15 of the Revised Code do not affect the right of a qualified patient or other patient to make informed decisions regarding the use or continuation, or the withholding or withdrawal, of life-sustaining treatment as long as the qualified patient or other patient is able to make those decisions.

(3) Sections 2133.01 to 2133.15 of the Revised Code do not require a physician, other health care personnel, or a health care facility to take action that is contrary to reasonable medical standards.

(4) Sections 2133.01 to 2133.15 of the Revised Code and, if applicable, a declaration do not affect or limit the authority of a physician or a health care facility to provide or not to provide life-sustaining treatment to a person in accordance with reasonable medical standards applicable in an emergency situation.

(D) Nothing in sections 2133.01 to 2133.15 of the Revised Code condones, authorizes, or approves of mercy killing, assisted suicide, or euthanasia.

(E)(1) Sections 2133.01 to 2133.15 of the Revised Code do not affect the responsibility of the attending physician of a qualified patient or other patient, or other health care personnel acting under the direction of the patient's attending physician, to provide comfort care to the patient. Nothing in sections 2133.01 to 2133.15 of the Revised Code precludes the attending physician of a qualified patient or other patient who carries out the responsibility to provide comfort care to the patient in good faith and while acting within the scope of the attending physician's authority from prescribing, dispensing, administering, or causing to be administered any particular medical procedure, treatment, intervention, or other measure to the patient, including, but not limited to, prescribing, personally furnishing, administering, or causing to be administered by judicious titration or in another manner any form of medication, for the purpose of diminishing the qualified patient's or other patient's pain or discomfort and not for the purpose of postponing or causing the qualified patient's or other patient's death, even though the medical procedure, treatment, intervention, or other measure may appear to hasten or increase the risk of the patient's death. Nothing in sections 2133.01 to 2133.15 of the Revised Code precludes health care personnel acting under the direction of the patient's attending physician who carry out the responsibility to provide comfort care to the patient in good faith and while acting within the scope of their authority from dispensing, administering, or causing to be administered any particular medical procedure, treatment, intervention, or other measure to the patient, including, but not limited to, personally furnishing, administering, or causing to be administered by judicious titration or in another manner any form of medication, for the purpose of diminishing the qualified patient's or other patient's pain or discomfort and not for the purpose of postponing or causing the qualified patient's or other patient's death, even though the medical procedure, treatment, intervention, or other measure may appear to hasten or increase the risk of the patient's death.

(2)(a) If, at any time, a person described in division (A)(2)(a)(i) of section 2133.05 of the Revised Code or the individual or a majority of the individuals in either of the first two classes of individuals that pertain to a declarant in the descending order of priority set forth in division (A)(2) (a)(ii) of section 2133.05 of the Revised Code believes in good faith that both of the following circumstances apply, the person or the individual or majority of individuals in either of the first two classes of individuals may commence an action in the probate court of the county in which a declarant who is in a terminal condition or permanently unconscious state is located for the issuance of an order mandating the use or continuation of comfort care in connection with the declarant in a manner that is consistent with division (E)(1) of this section:

(i) Comfort care is not being used or continued in connection with the declarant.

(ii) The withholding or withdrawal of the comfort care is contrary to division (E)(1) of this section.

(b) If a declarant did not designate in the declarant's declaration a person as described in division (A)(2)(a)(i) of section 2133.05 of the Revised Code and if, at any time, a priority individual or any member of a priority class of individuals under division (A)(2)(a)(ii) of section 2133.05 of the Revised Code or, at any time, the individual or a majority of the individuals in the next class of individuals that pertains to the declarant in the descending order of priority set forth in that division believes in good faith that both of the following circumstances apply, the priority individual, the member of the priority class of individuals, or the individual or majority of individuals in the next class of individuals that pertains to the declarant may commence an action in the probate court of the county in which a declarant who is in a terminal condition or permanently unconscious state is located for the issuance of an order mandating the use or continuation of comfort care in connection with the declarant in a manner that is consistent with division (E)(1) of this section:

(i) Comfort care is not being used or continued in connection with the declarant.

(ii) The withholding or withdrawal of the comfort care is contrary to division (E)(1) of this section.

(c) If, at any time, a priority individual or any member of a priority class of individuals under division (B) of section 2133.08 of the Revised Code or, at any time, the individual or a majority of the individuals in the next class of individuals that pertains to the patient in the descending order of priority set forth in that division believes in good faith that both of the following circumstances apply, the priority individual, the member of the priority class of individuals, or the individual or majority of individuals in the next class of individuals that pertains to the patient may commence an action in the probate court of the county in which a patient as described in division (A) of section 2133.08 of the Revised Code is located for the issuance of an order mandating the use or continuation of comfort care in connection with the patient in a manner that is consistent with division (E)(1) of this section, unless the individual is not competent under division (C)(2) of section 2133.08 of the Revised Code:

(i) Comfort care is not being used or continued in connection with the patient.

(ii) The withholding or withdrawal of the comfort care is contrary to division (E)(1) of this section.

**HISTORY:**

144 v S 1 (Eff 10-10-91); 145 v H 343 (Eff 7-22-94); 147 v S 67 (Eff 6-4-97); 147 v H 354 (Eff 7-9-98); 147 v S 66. Eff 7-22-98; 2016 hb451, § 1, effective April 6, 2017.

**Amendment Notes**

The 2016 amendment by HB 451 inserted "unless the individual is not competent under division (C)(2) of section 2133.08 of the Revised Code" in the introductory paragraph of (E)(2)(c).

**Comment, Legislative Service Commission**

Section 2133.12 of the Revised Code is amended by this act [Am. Sub. S.B. 66] and also by Sub. H.B. 354 of the 122nd General Assembly. * * * Comparison of these amendments in pursuance of section 1.52 of the Revised Code discloses that they are not irreconcilable so that they are required by that section to be harmonized to give effect to each amendment.

**NOTES TO DECISIONS**

**Immunity**

Although the doctor was, in good faith, providing comfort care to an elderly woman on the verge of death, and thus, entitled to immunity up to and including the time when he was administering increasing doses of narcotics (particularly morphine) the administration of succinlycholine could not have been considered comfort care. It was a medication error and not in accordance with minimal standards of care; nor did the patient's do-not-resuscitate directive provide authority to administer succinylcholine under the circumstances, particularly with no respiratory support. Gelesh v. State Med. Bd., 2010-Ohio-4378, 2010 Ohio App. LEXIS 3698 (Ohio Ct. App., Franklin County 2010).

**RESEARCH REFERENCES AND PRACTICE AIDS**

**Cross-References to Related Sections**

Declaration governing use, continuation, withholding or withdrawal of life-sustaining treatment, RC § 2133.02.

Immunity from civil or criminal liability or professional disciplinary action, RC § 2133.11.

Jurisdiction of probate court, RC § 2101.24.

**Ohio Administrative Code**

State medical board—

Drug treatment of intractable pain. OAC ch. 4731-21.

## § 2133.13 Assumption of validity of declaration.

In the absence of actual knowledge to the contrary and if acting in good faith, an attending or consulting physician, other health care personnel, and health care facilities may assume that a declaration complies with sections 2133.01 to 2133.15 of the Revised Code and is valid.

**HISTORY:**

144 v S 1 (Eff 10-10-91); 147 v H 354. Eff 7-9-98.

## § 2133.14 Out-of-state declaration valid.

A declaration executed under the law of another state in compliance with that law or in substantial compliance with sections 2133.01 to 2133.15 of the Revised Code shall be considered to be valid for purposes of sections 2133.01 to 2133.15 of the Revised Code.

**HISTORY:**

144 v S 1 (Eff 10-10-91); 147 v H 354. Eff 7-9-98.

## § 2133.15 Application to document executed prior to effective date of provisions.

(A) Sections 2133.01 to 2133.15 of the Revised Code apply to any written document that was executed anywhere prior to October 10, 1991, that voluntarily was so executed by an adult who was of sound mind, that was signed by the adult or by another individual at the direction of the adult, that was or was not witnessed or acknowledged before a notary public as described in division (B) of section 2133.02 of the Revised Code, and that specifies the adult's intention with respect to the use or continuation, or the withholding or withdrawal, of life-sustaining treatment if the adult is at any time in a terminal condition, in a permanently unconscious state, or in either a terminal condition or a permanently unconscious state, if the adult is at that time no longer able to make informed decisions regarding the administration of life-sustaining treatment, and if at that time there is no reasonable possibility that the adult will regain the capacity to make those informed decisions. The document shall be considered to be a declaration, shall be given effect as if it had been executed on or after October 10, 1991, in accordance with sections 2133.01 to 2133.15 of the Revised Code, and, except as otherwise provided in division (B) of this section, shall be subject to all provisions of sections 2133.01 to 2133.15 of the Revised Code pertaining to declarations.

(B)(1) If a declaration as described in division (A) of this section does not state that, or does not contain a checked or marked box or line adjacent to a statement indicating that, the declarant authorizes the declarant's attending physician to withhold or withdraw nutrition or hydration when the declarant is in a permanently unconscious state and when the declarant's attending physician and at least one other physician who has examined the declarant determine, to a reasonable degree of medical certainty and in accordance with reasonable medical standards, that nutrition or hydration will not or no longer will serve to provide comfort to the declarant or alleviate the declarant's pain, then, if the declaration becomes operative under section 2133.03 of the Revised Code because the declarant is in a permanently unconscious state, the attending physician of the declarant shall apply to the probate court of the county in which the declarant is located for the issuance of an order whether or not the attending physician is required to provide the declarant with nutrition and hydration for as long as the declarant is in the permanently unconscious state. Upon the filing of the application, the clerk of the probate court shall schedule a hearing on it and cause a copy of it and a notice of the hearing to be served in accordance with the Rules of Civil Procedure upon the attending physician and the individuals described in divisions (B)(1) to (5) of section 2133.08 of the Revised Code, which service shall be made, if possible, within three days after the filing of the application. The hearing shall be conducted at the earliest possible time, but no sooner than the thirtieth business day, and no later than the sixtieth business day, after that service has been completed.

(2) At the hearing, the attending physician and any individual described in divisions (B)(1) to (5) of section 2133.08 of the Revised Code shall be permitted to testify and present evidence relative to the use or continuation, or the withholding or withdrawal, of nutrition and hydration for as long as the declarant is in the permanently unconscious state. Immediately following the hearing, the court shall enter on its journal its determination, based on the evidence presented by all of the parties at the hearing on the application and subject to division (B)(3) of this section, whether or not the attending physician is required to provide the declarant with nutrition and hydration for as long as the declarant is in the permanently unconscious state.

(3) The court shall issue an order that authorizes the declarant's attending physician to commence the withholding or withdrawal of nutrition and hydration in connection with the declarant only if the applicant establishes, by clear and convincing evidence, that the order would be consistent with one of the following:

(a) The declarant's previously expressed intention with respect to the use or continuation, or the withholding or withdrawal, of nutrition and hydration should the declarant subsequently be in a permanently unconscious state and no longer able to make informed decisions regarding the administration of nutrition and hydration;

(b) In the absence of a previously expressed intention of that nature, the type of informed consent decision that the declarant would have made if the declarant had expressed the declarant's intention with respect to the use or continuation, or the withholding or withdrawal, of nutrition and hydration should the declarant subsequently be in a permanently unconscious state and no longer able to make informed decisions regarding the administration of nutrition and hydration, as inferred from the lifestyle and character of the declarant, and from any other evidence of the declarant's desires, prior to the declarant becoming no longer able to make informed decisions regarding the administration of nutrition and hydration. The Rules of Evidence shall not be binding for purposes of this division.

(4) Notwithstanding any contrary provision of the Revised Code or of the Rules of Civil Procedure, the state and persons other than individuals described in divisions (B)(1) to (5) of section 2133.08 of the Revised Code and other than the attending physician of the declarant are prohibited from filing an application under division (B) of this section and from joining or being joined as parties to a hearing conducted under division (B) of this section, including joining by way of intervention.

**HISTORY:**

144 v S 1 (Eff 10-10-91); 147 v H 354. Eff 7-9-98.

**RESEARCH REFERENCES AND PRACTICE AIDS**

**Cross-References to Related Sections**

Jurisdiction of probate court, RC § 2101.24.

**Ohio Rules**

Intervention, CivR 24.

### § 2133.16 Anatomical gift. [Repealed]

**HISTORY:**

150 v H 392, § 1, eff. 9-16-04; 152 v H 529, § 1, eff. 4-7-09; repealed by 2021 hb7, § 3, effective August 17, 2021.

## DNR IDENTIFICATION AND DO-NOT-RESUSCITATE ORDER LAW

### § 2133.21 Definitions.

As used in sections 2133.21 to 2133.26 of the Revised Code, unless the context clearly requires otherwise:

(A) "Attending physician" means the physician to whom a person, or the family of a person, has assigned primary responsibility for the treatment or care of the person or, if the person or the person's family has not assigned that responsibility, the physician who has accepted that responsibility.

(B) "Declaration," "health care facility," "life-sustaining treatment," "physician," "professional disciplinary action," and "tort action" have the same meanings as in section 2133.01 of the Revised Code.

(C) "DNR identification" means a standardized identification card, form, necklace, or bracelet that is of uniform size and design, that has been approved by the department of health pursuant to section 2133.25 of the Revised Code, and that signifies either of the following:

(1) That the person who is named on and possesses the card, form, necklace, or bracelet has executed a declaration that authorizes the withholding or withdrawal of CPR and that has not been revoked pursuant to section 2133.04 of the Revised Code;

(2) That the attending physician of the person who is named on and possesses the card, form, necklace, or bracelet has issued a current do-not-resuscitate order, in accordance with the do-not-resuscitate protocol adopted by the department of health pursuant to section 2133.25 of the Revised Code, for that person and has documented the grounds for the order in that person's medical record.

(D) "Do-not-resuscitate order" means a directive issued by a physician that identifies a person and specifies that CPR should not be administered to the person so identified.

(E) "Do-not-resuscitate protocol" means the standardized method of procedure for the withholding of CPR by physicians, emergency medical service personnel, and health care facilities that is adopted in the rules of the department of health pursuant to section 2133.25 of the Revised Code.

(F) "Emergency medical services personnel" means paid or volunteer firefighters, law enforcement officers, first responders, emergency medical technicians-basic, emergency medical technicians-intermediate, emergency medical technicians-paramedic, medical technicians, or other emergency services personnel acting within the ordinary course of their profession.

(G) "CPR" means cardiopulmonary resuscitation or a component of cardiopulmonary resuscitation, but it does not include clearing a person's airway for a purpose other than as a component of CPR.

**HISTORY:**

147 v H 354. Eff 7-9-98.

**NOTES TO DECISIONS**

Analysis

Emergency medical services personnel
Wrongful administration of life-prolonging medical treatment

**Emergency medical services personnel**

Sufficient evidence supported defendant's conviction for misconduct at an emergency because defendant knowingly prevented the paramedics from treating her sister during an emergency (the sister had severe abdominal pains) by interrupting the paramedics by asking repeated questions in a badgering manner, raising her voice over that of the paramedics, and being abusive and interfering. Due to her behavior, the police had to be called and the paramedics had to exit the apartment, leaving the sister unattended, and defendant delayed one of the paramedic's attempts to proceed back into the apartment. State v. Blocker, 2007-Ohio-144, 2007 Ohio App. LEXIS 131 (Ohio Ct. App., Franklin County 2007).

**Wrongful administration of life-prolonging medical treatment**

Damages were not recoverable on a claim of wrongful prolongation of life. Unwanted medical care did not constitute a battery: Allore v. Flower Hosp., 121 Ohio App. 3d 229, 699 N.E.2d 560, 1997 Ohio App. LEXIS 2753 (Ohio Ct. App., Lucas County 1997).

**RESEARCH REFERENCES AND PRACTICE AIDS**

**Cross-References to Related Sections**

Declaration governing use, continuation, withholding or withdrawal of life-sustaining treatment, RC § 2133.02.

**Ohio Administrative Code**

Department of health—
Do not resuscitate (DNR) protocol. OAC ch. 3701-62.
Definitions. OAC 3701-62-01.

### § 2133.211 Authority and immunity of nurses and physician assistants.

A person who holds a current, valid license issued under Chapter 4723. of the Revised Code to practice as an advanced practice registered nurse may take any action that may be taken by an attending physician under sections 2133.21 to 2133.26 of the Revised Code and has the immunity provided by section 2133.22 of the Revised Code if the action is taken pursuant to a standard care arrangement with a collaborating physician.

A person who holds a license to practice as a physician assistant issued under Chapter 4730. of the Revised Code may take any action that may be taken by an attending physician under sections 2133.21 to 2133.26 of the Revised Code and has the immunity provided by section 2133.22 of the Revised Code if the action is taken pursuant to a supervision agreement entered into under section 4730.19 of the Revised Code, including, if applicable, the policies of a health care facility in which the physician assistant is practicing.

**HISTORY:**

147 v H 354. Eff 7-9-98; 2012 HB 284, § 1, eff. Mar. 22, 2013; 2015 sb110, § 1, effective October 15, 2015; 2016 hb216, § 1, effective April 6, 2017.

**Amendment Notes**

The 2016 amendment by HB 216 in the first paragraph, substituted "current, valid license" for "certificate of authority as a certified nurse practitioner or clinical nurse specialist", and added "to practice as an advanced practice registered nurse" following "Chapter 4723. of the Revised Code".

The 2015 amendment, by SB 110, in the first paragraph, deleted "to practice" following "of authority" and substituted "Chapter 4723." for "section 4723.42"; and, in the second paragraph, substituted "license" for "certificate", "supervision agreement entered into under section 4730.19" for "physician supervisory plan approved pursuant to section 4730.17", and "including, if applicable" for "or".

The 2012 amendment added the second paragraph.

**RESEARCH REFERENCES AND PRACTICE AIDS**

**Ohio Administrative Code**

Authority of certified nurse practitioners and clinical nurse specialists. OAC 3701-62-02.

Authority of certified nurse practitioners and clinical nurse specialists. OAC 3701-62-02.

## § 2133.22 Immunity in connection with withholding, withdrawing or providing CPR.

(A)(1) None of the following are subject to criminal prosecution, to liability in damages in a tort or other civil action for injury, death, or loss to person or property, or to professional disciplinary action arising out of or relating to the withholding or withdrawal of CPR from a person after DNR identification is discovered in the person's possession and reasonable efforts have been made to determine that the person in possession of the DNR identification is the person named on the DNR identification:

(a) A physician who causes the withholding or withdrawal of CPR from the person possessing the DNR identification;

(b) A person who participates under the direction of or with the authorization of a physician in the withholding or withdrawal of CPR from the person possessing the DNR identification;

(c) Any emergency medical services personnel who cause or participate in the withholding or withdrawal of CPR from the person possessing the DNR identification.

(2) None of the following are subject to criminal prosecution, to liability in damages in a tort or other civil action for injury, death, or loss to person or property, or to professional disciplinary action arising out of or relating to the withholding or withdrawal of CPR from a person in a health care facility after DNR identification is discovered in the person's possession and reasonable efforts have been made to determine that the person in possession of the DNR identification is the person named on the DNR identification or a do-not-resuscitate order is issued for the person:

(a) The health care facility or the administrator of the health care facility;

(b) A physician who causes the withholding or withdrawal of CPR from the person possessing the DNR identification or for whom the do-not-resuscitate order has been issued;

(c) Any person who works for the health care facility as an employee, contractor, or volunteer and who participates under the direction of or with the authorization of a physician in the withholding or withdrawal of CPR from the person possessing the DNR identification;

(d) Any person who works for the health care facility as an employee, contractor, or volunteer and who participates under the direction of or with the authorization of a physician in the withholding or withdrawal of CPR from the person for whom the do-not-resuscitate order has been issued.

(3) If, after DNR identification is discovered in the possession of a person, the person makes an oral or written request to receive CPR, any person who provides CPR pursuant to the request, any health care facility in which CPR is provided, and the administrator of any health care facility in which CPR is provided are not subject to criminal prosecution as a result of the provision of the CPR, are not liable in damages in a tort or other civil action for injury, death, or loss to person or property that arises out of or is related to the provision of the CPR, and are not subject to professional disciplinary action as a result of the provision of the CPR.

(B) Divisions (A)(1), (A)(2), and (C) of this section do not apply when CPR is withheld or withdrawn from a person who possesses DNR identification or for whom a do-not-resuscitate order has been issued unless the withholding or withdrawal is in accordance with the do-not-resuscitate protocol.

(C) Any emergency medical services personnel who comply with a do-not-resuscitate order issued by a physician and any individuals who work for a health care facility as employees, contractors, or volunteers and who comply with a do-not-resuscitate order issued by a physician are not subject to liability in damages in a civil action for injury, death, or loss to person or property that arises out of or is related to compliance with the order, are not subject to criminal prosecution as a result of compliance with the order, and are not subject to professional disciplinary action as a result of compliance with the order.

In an emergency situation, emergency medical services personnel and emergency department personnel are not required to search a person to determine if the person possesses DNR identification. If a person possesses DNR identification, if emergency medical services personnel or emergency department personnel provide CPR to the person in an emergency situation, and if, at that time, the personnel do not know and do not have reasonable cause to believe that the person possesses DNR identification, the emergency medical services personnel and emergency department personnel are not subject to criminal prosecution as a result of the provision of the CPR, are not liable in damages in a tort or other civil action for injury, death, or loss to person or property that arises out of or is related to the provision of the CPR, and are not subject to professional disciplinary action as a result of the provision of the CPR.

(D) Nothing in sections 2133.21 to 2133.26 of the Revised Code or the do-not-resuscitate protocol grants immunity to a physician for issuing a do-not-resuscitate order that is contrary to reasonable medical standards or that the physician knows or has reason to know is contrary to the wishes of the patient or of a person who is lawfully authorized to make informed medical decisions on the patient's behalf.

**HISTORY:**

147 v H 354. Eff 7-9-98.

**RESEARCH REFERENCES AND PRACTICE AIDS**

**Cross-References to Related Sections**

Death from withholding or withdrawal of CPR is not homicide, RC § 2133.24.

Definitions, RC § 2133.21.

Immunity of qualified nurses, RC § 2133.211.

**Ohio Administrative Code**

Immunity from criminal prosecution, civil liability, and professional disciplinary action. OAC 3701-62-03.

## § 2133.23 Compliance with do-not-resuscitate protocol; transfer to physician or facility willing to comply.

(A) If emergency medical services personnel, other than physicians, are presented with DNR identification possessed by a person or are presented with a written do-not-resuscitate order for a person or if a physician directly issues to emergency medical services personnel, other than physicians, an oral do-not-resuscitate order for a person, the emergency medical services personnel shall comply with the do-not-resuscitate protocol for the person. If an oral do-not-resuscitate order is issued by a physician who is not present at the scene, the emergency medical services personnel shall verify the physician's identity.

(B) If a person possesses DNR identification and if the person's attending physician or the health care facility in which the person is located is unwilling or unable to comply with the do-not-resuscitate protocol for the person, the attending physician or the health care facility shall not prevent or attempt to prevent, or unreasonably delay or attempt to delay, the transfer of the person to a different physician who will follow the protocol or to a different health care facility in which the protocol will be followed.

(C) If a person who possesses DNR identification or for whom a current do-not-resuscitate order has been issued is being transferred from one health care facility to another, before or at the time of the transfer, the transferring health care facility shall notify the receiving health care facility and the persons transporting the person of the existence of the DNR identification or the order. If a current do-not-resuscitate order was issued orally, it shall be reduced to writing before the time of the transfer. The DNR identification or the order shall accompany the person to the receiving health care facility and shall remain in effect unless it is revoked or unless, in the case of a do-not-resuscitate order, the order no longer is current.

**HISTORY:**
147 v H 354. Eff 7-9-98.



**RESEARCH REFERENCES AND PRACTICE AIDS**

**Cross-References to Related Sections**
Death from withholding or withdrawal of CPR is not homicide, RC § 2133.24.
Definitions, RC § 2133.21.
Prohibition against delaying transfer, RC § 2133.26.

**Ohio Administrative Code**
Compliance with DNR protocol by —
Attending physician, or CNP or CNS, or health care facility. OAC 3701-62-08.
Emergency medical services personnel. OAC 3701-62-07.
Transfer of person between health care facilities; forwarding of DNR order. OAC 3701-62-09.

### § 2133.24 Death is not homicide; effect on insurance or annuity; effect of provisions generally.

(A) The death of a person resulting from the withholding or withdrawal of CPR for the person pursuant to the do-not-resuscitate protocol and in the circumstances described in section 2133.22 of the Revised Code or in accordance with division (A) of section 2133.23 of the Revised Code does not constitute for any purpose a suicide, aggravated murder, murder, or any other homicide.

(B)(1) If a person possesses DNR identification or if a current do-not-resuscitate order has been issued for a person, the possession or order shall not do either of the following:

(a) Affect in any manner the sale, procurement, issuance, or renewal of a policy of life insurance or annuity, notwithstanding any term of a policy or annuity to the contrary;

(b) Be deemed to modify in any manner or invalidate the terms of any policy of life insurance or annuity that is in effect on the effective date of this section.

(2) Notwithstanding any term of a policy of life insurance or annuity to the contrary, the withholding or withdrawal of CPR from a person who is insured or covered under the policy or annuity and who possesses DNR identification or for whom a current do-not-resuscitate order has been issued, in accordance with sections 2133.21 to 2133.26 of the Revised Code, shall not impair or invalidate any policy of life insurance or annuity.

(3) Notwithstanding any term of a policy or plan to the contrary, neither of the following shall impair or invalidate any policy of health insurance or other health care benefit plan:

(a) The withholding or withdrawal in accordance with sections 2133.21 to 2133.26 of the Revised Code of CPR from a person who is insured or covered under the policy or plan and who possesses DNR identification or for whom a current do-not-resuscitate order has been issued;

(b) The provision in accordance with sections 2133.21 to 2133.26 of the Revised Code of CPR to a person of the nature described in division (B)(3)(a) of this section.

(4) No physician, health care facility, other health care provider, person authorized to engage in the business of insurance in this state under Title XXXIX [39] of the Revised Code, health insuring corporation, other health care benefit plan, legal entity that is self-insured and provides benefits to its employees or members, or other person shall require an individual to possess DNR identification, or shall require an individual to revoke or refrain from possessing DNR identification, as a condition of being insured or of receiving health care benefits or services.

(C)(1) Sections 2133.21 to 2133.26 of the Revised Code do not create any presumption concerning the intent of an individual who does not possess DNR identification with respect to the use, withholding, or withdrawal of CPR.

(2) Sections 2133.21 to 2133.26 of the Revised Code do not affect the right of a person to make informed decisions regarding the use, withholding, or withdrawal of CPR for the person as long as the person is able to make those decisions.

(3) Sections 2133.21 to 2133.26 of the Revised Code are in addition to and independent of, and do not limit, impair, or supersede, any right or responsibility that a person has to effect the withholding or withdrawal of life-sustaining treatment to another pursuant to sections 2133.01 to 2133.15 of the Revised Code or in any other lawful manner.

(D) Nothing in sections 2133.21 to 2133.26 of the Revised Code condones, authorizes, or approves of mercy killing, assisted suicide, or euthanasia.

**HISTORY:**
147 v H 354. Eff 7-9-98.

**RESEARCH REFERENCES AND PRACTICE AIDS**

**Cross-References to Related Sections**
Definitions, RC § 2133.21.

**Ohio Administrative Code**
Compliance with DNR protocol not homicide or suicide. OAC 3701-62-11.
Effect of DNR identification or order on insurance. OAC 3701-62-12.

### § 2133.25 Standardized method for withholding CPR; rules; advisory committee.

(A) The department of health, by rule adopted pursuant to Chapter 119. of the Revised Code, shall adopt a standardized method of procedure for the withholding of CPR by physicians, emergency medical services personnel, and health care facilities in accordance with sections 2133.21 to 2133.26 of the Revised Code. The standardized method shall specify criteria for determining when a do-not-resuscitate order issued by a physician is current. The standardized method so adopted shall be the "do-not-resuscitate protocol" for purposes of sections 2133.21 to 2133.26 of the Revised Code. The department also shall approve one or more standard forms of DNR identification to be used throughout this state.

(B) The department of health shall adopt rules in accordance with Chapter 119. of the Revised Code for the administration of sections 2133.21 to 2133.26 of the Revised Code.

(C) The department of health shall appoint an advisory committee to advise the department in the development of rules under this section. The advisory committee shall include, but shall not be limited to, representatives of each of the following organizations:

(1) The association for hospitals and health systems (OHA);
(2) The Ohio state medical association;
(3) The Ohio chapter of the American college of emergency physicians;
(4) The Ohio hospice organization;
(5) The Ohio council for home care;
(6) The Ohio health care association;
(7) The Ohio ambulance association;
(8) The Ohio medical directors association;
(9) The Ohio association of emergency medical services;
(10) The bioethics network of Ohio;
(11) The Ohio nurses association;
(12) The Ohio academy of nursing homes;
(13) The Ohio association of professional firefighters;
(14) The department of developmental disabilities;
(15) The Ohio osteopathic association;
(16) The association of Ohio philanthropic homes, housing and services for the aging;
(17) The catholic conference of Ohio;
(18) The department of aging;
(19) The department of mental health and addiction services;
(20) The Ohio private residential association;
(21) The northern Ohio fire fighters association.

**HISTORY:**

147 v H 354. Eff 7-9-98; 153 v S 79, § 1, eff. 10-6-09; 2013 HB 59, § 101.01, eff. Sept. 29, 2013.

**Amendment Notes**

The 2013 amendment substituted "mental health and addiction services" for "mental health" in (C)(19).

153 v S 79, effective October 6, 2009, deleted "mental retardation and" preceding "developmental disabilities" throughout.

**RESEARCH REFERENCES AND PRACTICE AIDS**

**Cross-References to Related Sections**

DNR identification, do-not-resuscitate protocol defined, RC § 2133.21.

Immunity in connection with withholding, withdrawing or providing CPR, RC § 2133.22.

**Ohio Administrative Code**

Department of health—

Do not resuscitate (DNR) protocol. OAC ch. 3701-62.

Identification. OAC 3701-62-04; revocation of identification or order. OAC 3701-62-06.

Prohibitions. OAC 3701-62-14.

## § 2133.26 Prohibitions.

(A)(1) No physician shall purposely prevent or attempt to prevent, or delay or unreasonably attempt to delay, the transfer of a patient in violation of division (B) of section 2133.23 of the Revised Code.

(2) No person shall purposely conceal, cancel, deface, or obliterate the DNR identification of another person without the consent of the other person.

(3) No person shall purposely falsify or forge a revocation of a declaration that is the basis of the DNR identification of another person or purposely falsify or forge an order of a physician that purports to supersede a do-not-resuscitate order issued for another person.

(4) No person shall purposely falsify or forge the DNR identification of another person with the intent to cause the use, withholding, or withdrawal of CPR for the other person.

(5) No person who has personal knowledge that another person has revoked a declaration that is the basis of the other person's DNR identification or personal knowledge that a physician has issued an order that supersedes a do-not-resuscitate order that the physician issued for another person shall purposely conceal or withhold that personal knowledge with the intent to cause the use, withholding, or withdrawal of CPR for the other person.

(B)(1) Whoever violates division (A)(1) or (5) of this section is guilty of a misdemeanor of the third degree.

(2) Whoever violates division (A)(2), (3), or (4) of this section is guilty of a misdemeanor of the first degree.

**HISTORY:**

147 v H 354. Eff 7-9-98.

**RESEARCH REFERENCES AND PRACTICE AIDS**

**Cross-References to Related Sections**

Definitions, RC § 2133.21.

Immunity in connection with withholding, withdrawing or providing CPR, RC § 2133.22.

**Ohio Administrative Code**

Prohibitions. OAC 3701-62-14.

# TITLE 29

# CRIMES — PROCEDURE



# CHAPTER 2903

# HOMICIDE AND ASSAULT

Homicide



## HOMICIDE

### § 2903.10 Definitions: functionally impaired person; caretaker.

As used in sections 2903.13 and 2903.16 of the Revised Code:

(A) "Functionally impaired person" means any person who has a physical or mental impairment that prevents him from providing for his own care or protection or whose infirmities caused by aging prevent him from providing for his own care or protection.

(B) "Caretaker" means a person who assumes the duty to provide for the care and protection of a functionally impaired person on a voluntary basis, by contract, through receipt of payment for care and protection, as a result of a family relationship, or by order of a court of competent jurisdiction. "Caretaker" does not include a person who owns, operates, or administers, or who is an agent or employee of, a care facility, as defined in section 2903.33 of the Revised Code.

**HISTORY:**
142 v H 642. Eff 3-17-89.

NOTES TO DECISIONS

Analysis

Caretaker
Functionally impaired person

**Caretaker**

Officer possessed probable cause to conclude defendant was the victim's "caretaker" because defendant admitted that she agreed to care for the wheelchair-bound victim, her 79-year-old aunt, after the amputation of the aunt's left leg but could no longer "handle it," and defendant ignored the victim's pleas for help after she kicked the victim out of the house; thus, the officer had the requisite probable cause to arrest defendant for failure to provide for a functionally impaired person. State v. Kirkland, 2015-Ohio-1978, 2015 Ohio App. LEXIS 1912 (Ohio Ct. App., Montgomery County 2015).

Sufficient evidence supported defendant's conviction for assault because there was evidence defendant had assumed a duty to provide for the disabled student's care and protection, under her contract with the public school system, by reason of her having voluntarily interacted with the student or both. State v. Cox, 2014-Ohio-2201, 12 N.E.3d 466, 2014 Ohio App. LEXIS 2129 (Ohio Ct. App., Montgomery County 2014).

**Functionally impaired person**

Officer possessed probable cause to conclude the victim, defendant's aunt, was a functionally impaired person because, in response to a call of a "domestic disturbance," the officer discovered the wheelchair-bound 79-year-old victim sitting outside on a wet towel in below freezing temperatures wearing a light housecoat with only a thin blanket in her lap and pleading for help; the aunt was recovering from surgery to amputate her left leg. State v. Kirkland, 2015-Ohio-1978, 2015 Ohio App. LEXIS 1912 (Ohio Ct. App., Montgomery County 2015).

RESEARCH REFERENCES AND PRACTICE AIDS

**Practice Guides**

Anderson's Ohio Manual of Criminal Complaints and Indictments
§ 2903.10 Assault—definitions



## ASSAULT

### § 2903.13 Assault.

(A) No person shall knowingly cause or attempt to cause physical harm to another or to another's unborn.

(B) No person shall recklessly cause serious physical harm to another or to another's unborn.

(C)(1) Whoever violates this section is guilty of assault, and the court shall sentence the offender as provided in this division and divisions (C)(1), (2), (3), (4), (5), (6), (7), (8), (9), and (10) of this section. Except as otherwise provided in division (C)(2), (3), (4), (5), (6), (7), (8), or (9) of this section, assault is a misdemeanor of the first degree.

(2) Except as otherwise provided in this division, if the offense is committed by a caretaker against a functionally impaired person under the caretaker's care, assault is a felony of the fourth degree. If the offense is committed by a caretaker against a functionally impaired person under the caretaker's care, if the offender previously has been convicted of or pleaded guilty to a violation of this section or section 2903.11 or 2903.16 of the Revised Code, and if in relation to the previous conviction the offender was a caretaker and the victim was a functionally impaired person under the offender's care, assault is a felony of the third degree.

(3) If the offense occurs in or on the grounds of a state correctional institution or an institution of the department of youth services, the victim of the offense is an employee of the department of rehabilitation and correction or the department of youth services, and the offense is committed by a person incarcerated in the state correctional institution or by a person institutionalized in the department of youth services institution pursuant to a commitment to the department of youth services, assault is a felony of the third degree.

(4) If the offense is committed in any of the following circumstances, assault is a felony of the fifth degree:

(a) The offense occurs in or on the grounds of a local correctional facility, the victim of the offense is an employee of the local correctional facility or a probation department or is on the premises of the facility for business purposes or as a visitor, and the offense is committed by a person who is under custody in the facility subsequent to the person's arrest for any crime or delinquent act, subsequent to the person's being charged with or convicted of any crime, or subsequent to the person's being alleged to be or adjudicated a delinquent child.

(b) The offense occurs off the grounds of a state correctional institution and off the grounds of an institution of the department of youth services, the victim of the offense is an employee of the department of rehabilitation and correction, the department of youth services, or a probation department, the offense occurs during the employee's official work hours and while the employee is engaged in official work responsibilities, and the offense is committed by a person incarcerated in a state correctional institution or institutionalized in the department of youth services who temporarily is outside of the institution for any purpose, by a parolee, by an offender under transitional control, under a community control sanction, or on an escorted visit, by a person under post-release control, or by an offender under any other type of supervision by a government agency.

(c) The offense occurs off the grounds of a local correctional facility, the victim of the offense is an employee of the local correctional facility or a probation department, the offense occurs during the employee's official work hours and while the employee is engaged in official work responsibilities, and the offense is committed by a person who is under custody in the facility subsequent to the person's arrest for any crime or delinquent act, subsequent to the person being charged with or convicted of any crime, or subsequent to the person being alleged to be or adjudicated a delinquent child and who temporarily is outside of the facility for any purpose or by a parolee, by an offender under transitional control, under a community control sanction, or on an escorted visit, by a person under post-release control, or by an offender under any other type of supervision by a government agency.

(d) The victim of the offense is a school teacher or administrator or a school bus operator, and the offense occurs in a school, on school premises, in a school building, on a school bus, or while the victim is outside of school premises or a school bus and is engaged in duties or official responsibilities associated with the victim's employment or position as a school teacher or administrator or a school bus operator, including, but not limited to, driving, accompanying, or chaperoning students at or on class or field trips, athletic events, or other school extracurricular activities or functions outside of school premises.

(5) If the victim of the offense is a peace officer or an investigator of the bureau of criminal identification and investigation, a firefighter, or a person performing emergency medical service, while in the performance of their official duties, assault is a felony of the fourth degree.

(6) If the victim of the offense is a peace officer or an investigator of the bureau of criminal identification and investigation and if the victim suffered serious physical harm as a result of the commission of the offense, assault is a felony of the fourth degree, and the court, pursuant to division (F) of section 2929.13 of the Revised Code, shall impose as a mandatory prison term one of the prison terms prescribed for a felony of the fourth degree that is at least twelve months in duration.

(7) If the victim of the offense is an officer or employee of a public children services agency or a private child placing agency and the offense relates to the officer's or employee's performance or anticipated performance of official responsibilities or duties, assault is either a felony of the fifth degree or, if the offender previously has been convicted of or pleaded guilty to an offense of violence, the victim of that prior offense was an officer or employee of a public children services agency or private child placing agency, and that prior offense related to the officer's or employee's performance or anticipated performance of official responsibilities or duties, a felony of the fourth degree.

(8) If the victim of the offense is a health care professional of a hospital, a health care worker of a hospital, or a security officer of a hospital whom the offender knows or has reasonable cause to know is a health care professional of a hospital, a health care worker of a hospital, or a security officer of a hospital, if the victim is engaged in the performance of the victim's duties, and if the hospital offers de-escalation or crisis intervention training for such professionals, workers, or officers, assault is one of the following:

(a) Except as otherwise provided in division (C)(8)(b) of this section, assault committed in the specified circumstances is a misdemeanor of the first degree. Notwithstanding the fine specified in division (A)(2)(b) of section 2929.28 of the Revised Code for a misdemeanor of the first degree, in sentencing the offender under this division and if the court decides to impose a fine, the court may impose upon the offender a fine of not more than five thousand dollars.

(b) If the offender previously has been convicted of or pleaded guilty to one or more assault or homicide offenses committed against hospital personnel, assault committed in the specified circumstances is a felony of the fifth degree.

(9) If the victim of the offense is a judge, magistrate, prosecutor, or court official or employee whom the offender knows or has reasonable cause to know is a judge, magistrate, prosecutor, or court official or employee, and if the victim is engaged in the performance of the victim's duties, assault is one of the following:

(a) Except as otherwise provided in division (C)(8)(b) of this section, assault committed in the specified circumstances is a misdemeanor of the first degree. In sentencing the offender under this division, if the court decides to impose a fine, notwithstanding the fine specified in division (A)(2)(b) of section 2929.28 of the Revised Code for a misdemeanor of the first degree, the court may impose upon the offender a fine of not more than five thousand dollars.

(b) If the offender previously has been convicted of or pleaded guilty to one or more assault or homicide offenses committed against justice system personnel, assault committed in the specified circumstances is a felony of the fifth degree.

(10) If an offender who is convicted of or pleads guilty to assault when it is a misdemeanor also is convicted of or pleads guilty to a specification as described in section 2941.1423 of the Revised Code that was included in the indictment, count in the indictment, or information charging the offense, the court shall sentence the offender to a mandatory jail term as provided in division (G) of section 2929.24 of the Revised Code.

If an offender who is convicted of or pleads guilty to assault when it is a felony also is convicted of or pleads guilty to a specification as described in section 2941.1423 of the Revised Code that was included in the indictment, count in the indictment, or information charging the offense, except as otherwise provided in division (C)(6) of this section, the court shall sentence the offender to a mandatory prison term as provided in division (B)(8) of section 2929.14 of the Revised Code.

(D) As used in this section:

(1) "Peace officer" has the same meaning as in section 2935.01 of the Revised Code.

(2) "Firefighter" has the same meaning as in section 3937.41 of the Revised Code.

(3) "Emergency medical service" has the same meaning as in section 4765.01 of the Revised Code.

(4) "Local correctional facility" means a county, multicounty, municipal, municipal-county, or multicounty-municipal jail or workhouse, a minimum security jail established under section 341.23 or 753.21 of the Revised Code, or another county, multicounty, municipal, municipal-county, or multicounty-municipal facility used for the custody of persons arrested for any crime or delinquent act, persons charged with or convicted of any crime, or persons alleged to be or adjudicated a delinquent child.

(5) "Employee of a local correctional facility" means a person who is an employee of the political subdivision or of one or more of the affiliated political subdivisions that operates the local correctional facility and who operates or assists in the operation of the facility.

(6) "School teacher or administrator" means either of the following:

(a) A person who is employed in the public schools of the state under a contract described in section 3311.77 or 3319.08 of the Revised Code in a position in which the person is required to have a certificate issued pursuant to sections 3319.22 to 3319.311 of the Revised Code.

(b) A person who is employed by a nonpublic school for which the state board of education prescribes minimum standards under section 3301.07 of the Revised Code and who is certificated in accordance with section 3301.071 of the Revised Code.

(7) "Community control sanction" has the same meaning as in section 2929.01 of the Revised Code.

(8) "Escorted visit" means an escorted visit granted under section 2967.27 of the Revised Code.

(9) "Post-release control" and "transitional control" have the same meanings as in section 2967.01 of the Revised Code.

(10) "Investigator of the bureau of criminal identification and investigation" has the same meaning as in section 2903.11 of the Revised Code.

(11) "Health care professional" and "health care worker" have the same meanings as in section 2305.234 of the Revised Code.

(12) "Assault or homicide offense committed against hospital personnel" means a violation of this section or of section 2903.01, 2903.02, 2903.03, 2903.04, 2903.041, 2903.11, 2903.12, or 2903.14 of the Revised Code committed in circumstances in which all of the following apply:

(a) The victim of the offense was a health care professional of a hospital, a health care worker of a hospital, or a security officer of a hospital.

(b) The offender knew or had reasonable cause to know that the victim was a health care professional of a hospital, a health care worker of a hospital, or a security officer of a hospital.

(c) The victim was engaged in the performance of the victim's duties.

(d) The hospital offered de-escalation or crisis intervention training for such professionals, workers, or officers.

(13) "De-escalation or crisis intervention training" means de-escalation or crisis intervention training for health care professionals of a hospital, health care workers of a hospital, and security officers of a hospital to facilitate interaction with patients, members of a patient's family, and visitors, including those with mental impairments.

(14) "Assault or homicide offense committed against justice system personnel" means a violation of this section or of section 2903.01, 2903.02, 2903.03, 2903.04, 2903.041, 2903.11, 2903.12, or 2903.14 of the Revised Code committed in circumstances in which the victim of the offense was a judge, magistrate, prosecutor, or court official or employee whom the offender knew or had reasonable cause to know was a judge, magistrate, prosecutor, or court official or employee, and the victim was engaged in the performance of the victim's duties.

(15) "Court official or employee" means any official or employee of a court created under the constitution or statutes of this state or of a United States court located in this state.

(16) "Judge" means a judge of a court created under the constitution or statutes of this state or of a United States court located in this state.

(17) "Magistrate" means an individual who is appointed by a court of record of this state and who has the powers and may perform the functions specified in Civil Rule 53, Criminal Rule 19, or Juvenile Rule 40, or an individual who is appointed by a United States court located in this state who has similar powers and functions.

(18) "Prosecutor" has the same meaning as in section 2935.01 of the Revised Code.

(19)(a) "Hospital" means, subject to division (D)(19)(b) of this section, an institution classified as a hospital under section 3701.01 of the Revised Code in which are provided to patients diagnostic, medical, surgical, obstetrical, psychiatric, or rehabilitation care or a hospital operated by a health maintenance organization.

(b) "Hospital" does not include any of the following:

(i) A facility licensed under Chapter 3721. of the Revised Code, a health care facility operated by the department of mental health or the department of developmental disabilities, a health maintenance organization that does not operate a hospital, or the office of any private, licensed health care professional, whether organized for individual or group practice;

(ii) An institution for the sick that is operated exclusively for patients who use spiritual means for healing and for whom the acceptance of medical care is inconsistent with their religious beliefs, accredited by a national accrediting organization, exempt from federal income taxation under section 501 of the "Internal Revenue Code of 1986," 100 Stat. 2085, 26 U.S.C. 1, as amended, and providing twenty-four-hour nursing care pursuant to the exemption in division (E) of section 4723.32 of the Revised Code from the licensing requirements of Chapter 4723. of the Revised Code.

(20) "Health maintenance organization" has the same meaning as in section 3727.01 of the Revised Code.

**HISTORY:**

134 v H 511 (Eff 1-1-74); 142 v H 642 (Eff 3-17-89); 144 v H 561 (Eff 4-9-93); 145 v S 116 (Eff 9-29-94); 145 v H 571 (Eff 10-6-94); 146 v H 614 (Eff 6-16-96); 146 v S 2 (Eff 7-1-96); 146 v S 239 (Eff 9-6-96); 146 v H 480 (Eff 10-16-96); 147 v H 106 (Eff 11-21-97); 147 v S 111 (Eff 3-17-98); 148 v S 1 (Eff 8-6-99); 148 v S 142 (Eff 2-3-2000); 148 v H 412. Eff 4-10-2001; 149 v H 490, § 1, eff. 1-1-04; 151 v H 347, § 1, eff. 3-14-07; 152 v H 280, § 1, eff. 4-7-09; 2011 HB 86, § 1, eff. Sept. 30, 2011; 2012 HB 525, § 1, eff. Oct. 1, 2012; 2012 HB 62, § 1, eff. Mar. 22, 2013; 2013 HB 59, § 101.01, eff. Sept. 29, 2013.

**Editor's Notes**

Acts 2013, HB 59, § 815.10 provides: "The General Assembly, applying the principle stated in division (B) of section 1.52 of the Revised Code that amendments are to be harmonized if reasonably capable of simultaneous operation, finds that the following sections, presented in this act as composites of the sections as amended by the acts indicated, are the resulting versions of the sections in effect prior to the effective date of the sections as presented in this act:

"Section 2903.13 of the Revised Code as amended by both Sub. H.B. 525 and Am. Sub. H.B. 62 of the 129th General Assembly."

Governor Taft's veto of 2005 Ohio HB 347 was overridden by the Ohio General Assembly.

**Amendment Notes**

The 2013 amendment, in (C)(1), substituted "divisions (C)(1), (2), (3), (4), (5), (6), (7), (8), (9), and (10)" for "divisions (C)(1), (2), (3), (4), (5), (6), (7), (8), and (9)" in the first sentence and "division (C)(2), (3), (4), (5), (6), (7), (8), or (9)" for "division (C)(2), (3), (4), (5), (6), (7), or (8)" in the second sentence; inserted (C)(3); redesignated former (C)(3) through (C)(9) and (C)(4)(b) through (C)(4)(e) as (C)(4) through (C)(10) and (C)(4)(a) through (C)(4)(d); deleted (C)(4)(a); and made stylistic changes.

The 2012 amendment by HB 62, added the (C)(1) designation; redesignated former (C)(1) through (C)(6) as (C)(2) through (C)(6) and (C)(9); in present (C)(1), substituted "divisions (C)(1), (2), (3), (4), (5), (6), (7), (8), and (9)" for "divisions (C)(1), (2), (3), (4), (5), and (6)" in the first sentence and substituted "division (C), (2), (3), (4), (5), (6), (7), or (8)" for "division (C)(1), (2), (3), (4), or (5)" in the second sentence; inserted (C)(7) and (C)(8); added (D)(11) through (D)(20); and made a stylistic change.

The 2012 amendment by HB 525, substituted "section 3311.77 or 3319.08" for "section 3319.08" in (D)(6)(a).

The 2011 amendment substituted "division (B)(8)" for "division (D)(8)" in the second paragraph of (C)(6).

152 v H 280, effective April 7, 2009, in the introductory paragraph of (C), added the language beginning "and the court shall" to the end of the first sentence; and added (C)(6).

151 v H 347, effective March 14, 2007, inserted "or an investigator of the bureau of criminal identification and investigation" in (C)(3) and (4); and added (D)(10).

**1974 Committee Comment to H 511**

This section prohibits simple assault and simple battery in the traditional sense. It expands upon former law, however, by including within its purview reckless actions which result in serious physical harm to another.

Assault is a misdemeanor of the first degree.

## NOTES TO DECISIONS

Analysis

**Generally**

Defendant's conviction of improper discharge of a firearm into a habitation did not merge into his felonious assault or assault convictions; as the assault against the victim was complete and he had already run away when defendant shot into the house, defendant had more than one animus when he shot into the house and damaged another victim's property. State v. Williams, 2014-Ohio-4475, 2014 Ohio App. LEXIS 4389 (Ohio Ct. App., Cuyahoga County 2014).

First-degree misdemeanor assault, in violation of R.C. 2903.13, carries a maximum penalty of six months in jail, making it a petty offense under Crim.R. 2(C) and 2(D). Pierson v. Rion, 2010-Ohio-1793, 2010 Ohio App. LEXIS 1492 (Ohio Ct. App., Montgomery County 2010).

**Acquittal**

Trial court did not err in denying defendant's motion to acquit the assault conviction because the evidence was sufficient to support his conviction as there was testimony from the victim and her husband that defendant shoved her causing her to fall backwards. State v. Howard, 2019-Ohio-4274, 2019 Ohio App. LEXIS 4340 (Ohio Ct. App., Stark County 2019).

Acquittal motion under Crim.R. 29(A) was properly denied because a reasonable trier of fact could have found that all of the elements of the offenses of robbery, intimidation, and assault were proven beyond a reasonable doubt; inter alia, defendant attacked and threatened his drinking partners and threatened police. State v. Small, 2012-Ohio-149, 2012 Ohio App. LEXIS 114 (Ohio Ct. App., Licking County 2012).

**Allied offenses**

Trial court did not err in accepting appellant's guilty plea for the offense of kidnapping because the trial court was not required to determine whether a factual basis existed to support the plea prior to entering judgment. Further, by knowingly, intelligently, and voluntarily entering his guilty plea, appellant waived the right to require the State to prove each and every element of the offense of Kidnapping beyond a reasonable doubt. State v. Crew, 2022-Ohio-752, 2022 Ohio App. LEXIS 670 (Ohio Ct. App., Portage County 2022).

Trial court did not err in accepting appellant's guilty plea for the offense of kidnapping because the trial court was not required to determine whether a factual basis existed to support the plea prior to entering judgment. Further, by knowingly, intelligently, and voluntarily entering his guilty plea, appellant waived the right to require the State to prove each and every element of the offense of Kidnapping beyond a reasonable doubt. State v. Crew, 2022-Ohio-752, 2022 Ohio App. LEXIS 670 (Ohio Ct. App., Portage County 2022).

Offenses of attempted rape and attempted burglary were not allied offenses of similar import where the harm caused by defendant's assault of the victim was separate and identifiable from the harm caused by the aggravated burglary offense; once defendant was found to be trespassing in the victim's house, his purpose was to have sex with her and he ripped off her nightgown, threw it outside, pinned her to the wall, and took off his own clothes in an attempt to rape her, and as such, the aggravated burglary was completed by an attempt to forcibly have sexual intercourse with the victim before defendant committed the additional assault on the victim by pulling out her hair extensions and choking her. State v. Johnson, 2018-Ohio-3999, 121 N.E.3d 776, 2018 Ohio App. LEXIS 4320 (Ohio Ct. App., Cuyahoga County 2018).

Because the offenses of assault and obstruction of official business were committed against separate victims and with separate conduct, the trial court did not err by failing to merge the convictions. The assault convictions stemmed from defendant's physical confrontation with two deputies, while the obstruction conviction was based on defendant's initial interruption of court proceedings when he failed to comply with the deputy's order to remove his shoelaces. State v. Hendricks, 2015-Ohio-2268, 2015 Ohio App. LEXIS 2175 (Ohio Ct. App., Cuyahoga County 2015).

It was plain error for the trial court not to merge for sentencing defendant's convictions for resisting arrest and one of the assault charges, as they were allied offenses of similar import because they were the result of conduct committed by a single act with a single state of mind. State v. Johnson, 2014-Ohio-4253, 2014 Ohio App. LEXIS 4173 (Ohio Ct. App., Mahoning County 2014).

Trial court committed plain error by not merging a felonious assault count with a simple assault count, as the charges arose from the same conduct—defendant's knowingly causing serious physical harm to the victim with a deadly weapon—and were committed with a single animus. State v. Williams, 2014-Ohio-4475, 2014 Ohio App. LEXIS 4389 (Ohio Ct. App., Cuyahoga County 2014).

Trial court committed plain error in failing to conduct an allied offenses analysis prior to sentencing. Although it was possible to commit the offenses of gross sexual imposition and assault with the same conduct, the record did not reveal what conduct formed the basis for the assault conviction. State v. Frederick, 2014-Ohio-548, 2014 Ohio App. LEXIS 530 (Ohio Ct. App., Erie County 2014).

Defendant's convictions for assault and unlawful restraint did not merge as allied offenses of similar import because, although it was possible to commit the offenses with the same conduct, the offenses were committed as separate acts and defendant had a separate animus for each act. City of Lakewood v. Bretzfelder, 2013-Ohio-4477, 2013 Ohio App. LEXIS 4729 (Ohio Ct. App., Cuyahoga County 2013).

Trial court committed plain error in failing to merge defendant's domestic violence and assault convictions. State v. Blakely, 2012-Ohio-3841, 2012 Ohio App. LEXIS 3391 (Ohio Ct. App., Montgomery County 2012).

Trial court did not commit plain error by failing to merge defendant's convictions for assault on a peace officer and obstructing official business because the offenses arose from separate conduct. The assault conviction was based upon defendant kicking the officer, while her conviction for obstructing official business was based on her conduct in jerking, pulling away, "stutter stepping," and screaming while she was in custody. State v. Standifer, 2012-Ohio-3132, 2012 Ohio App. LEXIS 2758 (Ohio Ct. App., Warren County 2012).

Assault on a police officer and harassment with a bodily substance were not allied offenses of similar import under R.C. 2941.25 because the record described two completely different actions by defendant separated in time and committed against two different victims. State v. Irwin, 2012-Ohio-2720, 2012 Ohio App. LEXIS 2386 (Ohio Ct. App., Columbiana County 2012).

Trial court did not err by failing to merge the two offenses under R.C. 2941.25 because the aggravated menacing count was completed before defendant committed the simple assault. After the conduct giving rise to the aggravated menacing count was completed, the events escalated, and defendant later committed the simple assault by striking the victim. State v. Dowdell, 2012-Ohio-2063, 2012 Ohio App. LEXIS 1813 (Ohio Ct. App., Cuyahoga County 2012).

Since the felonious assault, assault, and domestic violence charges arose from the same conduct and defendant committed these offenses with a single animus, the trial court committed plain error by not merging the assault, felonious assault, and domestic violence counts for sentencing. While the State argued that the felonious assault count should not merge since defendant's gestures toward the victim with the knife constituted a separate act, this was not the State's theory at trial; instead, the State relied on defendant's use of a vase as a bludgeon to support his felonious assault conviction. State v. Carner, 2012-Ohio-1190, 2012 Ohio App. LEXIS 1046 (Ohio Ct. App., Cuyahoga County 2012).

Trial court did not violate R.C. 2941.25(A) by convicting defendant of both domestic violence and assault because, although it recited in the judgment entry that defendant was "convicted" of assault, it was clear that "convicted" meant no more than that defendant was adjudicated to be guilty of that offense; no sentence was imposed for it. State v. Tilton, 2011-Ohio-5564, 2011 Ohio App. LEXIS 4542 (Ohio Ct. App., Montgomery County 2011).

When defendant was charged with both felonious assault and simple assault of peace officers regarding defendant's actions toward the same two victims, it was error to convict defendant of both crimes because (1) the crimes were allied offenses of similar import, as simple assault was a lesser included offense of felonious assault, and (2) the charges arose from a single course of conduct, as the State did not prove more than one animus. State v. Anderson, 2009-Ohio-3900, 183 Ohio App. 3d 522, 917 N.E.2d 843, 2009 Ohio App. LEXIS 3323 (Ohio Ct. App., Cuyahoga County 2009).

When defendant was properly convicted of domestic violence, under R.C. 2919.25(A)(1), it was plain error, under Crim.R. 52(B), to also enter defendant's conviction for assault, under R.C. 2903.13(A), based on the same incident, because defendant's domestic violence conviction established at once that defendant was guilty of assault, so the two crimes were allied offenses of similar import, and defendant could not be convicted of both, under R.C. 2941.25(A). State v. Applegate, 2007-Ohio-6672, 2007 Ohio App. LEXIS 5848 (Ohio Ct. App., Montgomery County 2007).

Simple assault, under R.C. 2903.13(A), and aggravated menacing, under R.C. 2903.21(A), were not allied offenses of similar import, under R.C. 2941.25(A), for which only one sentence could be imposed, because, objectively, one could be committed without committing the other, as the aggravated menacing element of placing a victim in apprehension was not an element of assault. State v. Swanson, 2006-Ohio-4957, 2006 Ohio App. LEXIS 4901 (Ohio Ct. App., Mahoning County 2006).

Resisting arrest, as defined in R.C. 2921.33(B), and assault, as set forth in R.C. 2903.13(A), were not allied offenses of similar import, pursuant to R.C. 2941.25(A), because resisting arrest required proof of the additional element of resistance of a lawful arrest. Thus, the elements of the offenses did not correspond to such a degree that commission of one crime resulted in the commission of the other. City of Maple Heights v. Sweeney, 2005-Ohio-2820, 2005 Ohio App. LEXIS 2663 (Ohio Ct. App., Cuyahoga County 2005).

**Attempt**

Trial court committed plain error when it found defendant guilty of "attempted" assault because it was an offense which was not cognizable at law. Also, because the trial court failed to specifically inform defendant of its findings with respect to each count of the indictment, the trial court's decision affected defendant's "substantial rights." State v. McCornell, 2009-Ohio-1245, 2009 Ohio App. LEXIS 1050 (Ohio Ct. App., Cuyahoga County 2009).

**Caretaker**

Sufficient evidence supported defendant's conviction for assault because there was evidence defendant had assumed a duty to provide for the disabled student's care and protection, under her contract with the public school system, by reason of her having voluntarily interacted with the student or both. State v. Cox, 2014-Ohio-2201, 12 N.E.3d 466, 2014 Ohio App. LEXIS 2129 (Ohio Ct. App., Montgomery County 2014).

**Challenge to sufficiency of indictment**

Trial court did not, in fact, rule on defendant's Crim.R. 29 motion as its order was not based on a consideration of whether the State had presented sufficient evidence to support a conviction for assault on a police officer; rather, the trial court's decision was reached after reviewing the constitutionality of R.C. 2945.75(A) and analyzing whether the indictment was legally sufficient to charge defendant. It was error to address the sufficiency of the indictment in this manner. State v. Lee, 2009-Ohio-4617, 2009 Ohio App. LEXIS 3919 (Ohio Ct. App., Lorain County 2009).

**Correctional institutions**

Sufficient evidence supported defendant's convictions of assault on a corrections officer, as two officers testified that after defendant's request for a brownie was denied during dinner time while inmates were getting food, he attacked one officer and later threw a chair at the officers when the officers attempted to restrain him; both officers were hit by the chair. State v. Bloodworth, 2017-Ohio-9122, 2017 Ohio App. LEXIS 5559 (Ohio Ct. App., Richland County 2017).

Sufficient evidence supported defendant's conviction for assault on a corrections officer, in violation of R.C. 2903.13, because, based on the testimony of the victim and three additional witnesses, there was evidence that defendant knowingly caused physical harm to the corrections officer by punching him in the face. State v. Tyson, 2013-Ohio-3540, 2013 Ohio App. LEXIS 3633 (Ohio Ct. App., Ross County 2013).

Evidence that defendant caused injury to an elderly victim by defendant using defendant's body to prevent the victim from passing defendant in a condominium building hallway, grabbing the victim, throwing the victim into a wall, and restraining the victim against the wall until another person arrived and threatened to call the police supported defendant's conviction for assault. City of Lakewood v. Bretzfelder, 2013-Ohio-4477, 2013 Ohio App. LEXIS 4729 (Ohio Ct. App., Cuyahoga County 2013).

Sufficient evidence supported that defendant's assault conviction was a fifth-degree felony because it was proven that defendant was an inmate, he destroyed correctional facility property, and he attacked a corrections officer, who had been an employee of the department of rehabilitation and correction for over 16 years. Defendant angrily punched a hole in the shower door and, when officers tried to transport defendant to segregation for his property damage, he made it extremely difficult for them to handcuff him and kicked one of the officers, resulting in injury and loss of work. State v. Godfrey, 2011-Ohio-512, 2011 Ohio App. LEXIS 448 (Ohio Ct. App., Lorain County 2011).

In a prosecution for assault on a corrections officer, under R.C. 2903.13(A), it was not an abuse of discretion to exclude a psychologist's testimony about the officer's racial bias, under Evid.R. 403(A), because such testimony was not probative of whether a felonious assault occurred or whether the defendant had a valid defense, as nothing showed racial bias caused the underlying physical altercation between defendant and the victim. State v. Atkinson, 2010-Ohio-2825, 2010 Ohio App. LEXIS 2350 (Ohio Ct. App., Warren County 2010).

Because the evidence indicated that the assault occurred on the grounds of a correctional facility, and thus, the trial court properly convicted defendant in conformity with the evidence and the law; the special finding (occurring on the grounds of a correctional facility) set forth in R.C. 2903.13(B)(2)(b) only affected the punishment available upon conviction, and was not part of the crime of assault and thus, the finding was not an essential element of the offense. Also, since defendant was charged with felonious assault, he was put on notice that he could be found guilty of all lesser included offenses, together with any of the special, statutory findings dictated by the evidence. State v. McPherson, 2010-Ohio-64, 2010 Ohio App. LEXIS 49 (Ohio Ct. App., Cuyahoga County 2010).

Verdict form did not comply with R.C. 2945.75(A)(2) because it failed to set forth the degree of the assault offense or the additional elements required to make it a fifth-degree felony under R.C. 2903.13(C)(2)(a), that defendant was an inmate, in a correctional facility, and the victim was a correctional officer. State v. DiCarlo, 2010-Ohio-3759, 2010 Ohio App. LEXIS 3190 (Ohio Ct. App., Scioto County 2010).

Sufficient evidence supported defendant's convictions for assault on a corrections officer because the testimony revealed that defendant became noncompliant during a strip search when he came off the cell wall, threw his boxers in an officer's face, and then began resisting them by "donkey kicking" an officer in the face and striking another in the groin. It was not refuted that defendant was an inmate in a local correctional facility and that the victims were corrections officers of that facility performing their official duties. State v. Hilliard, 2007-Ohio-6193, 2007 Ohio App. LEXIS 5435 (Ohio Ct. App., Cuyahoga County 2007).

Trial court had subject matter jurisdiction to convict defendant and did not err when it found defendant guilty of both assaults, fifth-degree felonies, under R.C. 2903.13(C)(2)(a), because the indictment gave adequate notice when it referenced the degree of the offense; the State used language within the indictment that comported with Crim.R. 7(B) and R.C. 2945.75(A)(1). In addition, the State provided defendant with a bill of particulars that notified him of the enhancement element in more detail and the trial court gave an instruction to the jury regarding the enhancement element. State v. Fields, 2007-Ohio-4191, 2007 Ohio App. LEXIS 3779 (Ohio Ct. App., Scioto County 2007).

Trial court had subject matter jurisdiction to convict defendant and did not err when it found defendant guilty of both assaults, fifth-degree felonies, under R.C. 2903.13(C)(2)(a), because the indictment gave adequate notice when it referenced the degree of the offense; the State used language within the indictment that comported with Crim.R. 7(B) and R.C. 2945.75(A)(1). In addition, the State provided defendant with a bill of particulars that notified him of the enhancement element in more detail and the trial court gave an instruction to the jury regarding the enhancement element. State v. Fields, 2007-Ohio-4191, 2007 Ohio App. LEXIS 3779 (Ohio Ct. App., Scioto County 2007).

Sufficient evidence supported defendant's conviction for assault on a corrections officer on the grounds of a correctional facility, under R.C. 2903.13(A)(2)(a), and that conviction was not against the manifest weight of the evidence, because (1) the evidence showed defendant's victim was a corrections officer where defendant was an inmate, (2) defendant resisted the officer's attempt to handcuff defendant, after which defendant assaulted the officer, and (3) the jury clearly chose to accept the officer's version of the incident, as it was authorized to do, and this resolution of conflicts in the evidence did not create a manifest miscarriage of justice. State v. Talley, 2007-Ohio-2902, 2007 Ohio App. LEXIS 2671 (Ohio Ct. App., Richland County 2007).

Sufficient evidence showed defendant knowingly assaulted a corrections officer, under R.C. 2903.13(A) and 2901.22(B), because it showed (1) he was told he had to obey an order of a corrections officer, whether or not he agreed with it, (2) an officer ordered him to return to his bunk area, which he refused to do, (3) he, instead, went downstairs, which was also prohibited, as it was time for a count, when he was supposed to be standing by his bed, (4) he struck an officer who physically restrained him, after he refused to obey verbal orders, and (5) he acted knowingly, as he was presumed to know the result of his conduct, because he started a course of conduct which increased the likelihood of violence and injury. State v. Bailey, 2006-Ohio-5286, 2006 Ohio App. LEXIS 5270 (Ohio Ct. App., Lorain County 2006).



Defendant's conviction for failure to comply with an order or signal of a police officer, grand theft, assault, driving under an Ohio Financial Responsibility Act suspension, and resisting arrest was supported by sufficient evidence in light of a determination that the conviction was not against the manifest weight of the evidence. State v. Tate, 2005-Ohio-2156, 2005 Ohio App. LEXIS 2057 (Ohio Ct. App., Summit County 2005).

In a prosecution for harassment by an inmate in violation of R.C. 2921.38(A) and of assault in violation of R.C. 2903.13(C)(2)(a), testimony that defendant was an inmate at the time of the offense was properly admitted, as this was an element of both crimes, but admission of the details of the prior offense was error, as its prejudicial effect outweighed its probative value. However, there was no plain error due to the strength of the State's case, defendant's own testimony about her prior crime, and the trial court's limiting instruction. State v. Adkins, 2004-Ohio-4019, 2004 Ohio App. LEXIS 3641 (Ohio Ct. App., Union County 2004).

Witnesses testified that defendant, an inmate, took a swing toward a correctional officer's face while the officer was performing his duties; though the officer was not injured, the evidence was sufficient to prove that defendant acted knowingly because he should have known that he could have seriously injured the officer. State v. Varner, 2004-Ohio-2790, 2004 Ohio App. LEXIS 2455 (Ohio Ct. App., Ashtabula County 2004).

Where defendant was charged with assaulting a corrections officer, the trial court did not abuse its discretion by refusing to instruct the jury that if the State failed to prove that the contract under which the prison was operated failed to comply with the requirements of R.C. 9.06, then they should find defendant not guilty, because the trial court properly determined as a matter of law that the prison was a state correctional institution, despite its having been run privately under contract. State v. Varner, 2004-Ohio-2790, 2004 Ohio App. LEXIS 2455 (Ohio Ct. App., Ashtabula County 2004).

Convictions of assault of a peace officer pursuant to R.C. 2903.13 and intimidation pursuant to R.C. 2921.03 were not against the manifest weight of the evidence where the jury could find that defendant knowingly engaged in the unlawful conduct pursuant to RC. § 2901.22(B), as defendant's expert admitted on cross-examination that the conduct likely resulted from intoxication. State v. Hamad, 2003-Ohio-4401, 2003 Ohio App. LEXIS 3913 (Ohio Ct. App., Cuyahoga County 2003).

The elements for assault under R.C. 2903.13 were met through the testimony that defendant refused to comply with police orders and resisted, kicked, head-butted, shoulder-butted, and flailed about, conduct demonstrating knowledge that his actions would cause a certain result. State v. Jones, 2003-Ohio-3004, 2003 Ohio App. LEXIS 2696 (Ohio Ct. App., Cuyahoga County 2003).

Evidence that defendant forced her way into the complainant's apartment, threatened "to kick her ass," and knocked complainant into a wall, among other evidence, meant that convictions for assault, trespass, and aggravated menacing were not against the manifest weight of the evidence. State v. Burns, 2003-Ohio-2957, 2003 Ohio App. LEXIS 2675 (Ohio Ct. App., Montgomery County 2003).

Defendant's conviction for third-degree felony assault was not against manifest weight of evidence because the jury was presented with two conflicting versions of the events depicted in the video surveillance footage taken of the incident, one from the two victims, and one from defendant himself. Given its verdict, the jury clearly chose to believe victims' testimony and not the testimony offered by defendant; and such was well within jury's purview as the trier of fact and ultimate factfinder. State v. Simmons, 2021-Ohio-3563, 2021 Ohio App. LEXIS 3476 (Ohio Ct. App., Warren County 2021).

**Defenses**

Trial court did not abuse its discretion in preventing the admission of evidence of defendant's post-traumatic stress disorder (PTSD) or prior military service as a defense to the intent element of his charge because a partial defense of diminished capacity was not recognized in Ohio. Because defendant did not qualify for a not guilty by reason of insanity defense, he could not offer expert testimony to negate his capacity to form the specific mental state required for assault on a peace officer. State v. Napier, 2017-Ohio-246, 2017 Ohio App. LEXIS 248 (Ohio Ct. App., Clermont County 2017).

In defendant's criminal trial on charges of felonious assault and assault, in violation of R.C. 2903.11(A)(2) and 2903.13(A), the trial court properly instructed the jury to disregard medical evidence of possible metabolic derangement from an aspirin overdose with respect to defendant's mental state of acting "knowingly" to commit the crimes against police officers, as the defense of diminished capacity was not recognized in Ohio and there was no other relevance shown for that evidence; further, there was insufficient evidence to support a determination that defendant suffered from metabolic derangement at the time of the criminal incident. State v. Fulmer, 2008-Ohio-936, 117 Ohio St. 3d 319, 883 N.E.2d 1052, 2008 Ohio LEXIS 549 (Ohio 2008).

In defendant's prosecution for assault on a peace officer, under R.C. 2903.13, defendant did not show that defendant received ineffective assistance of counsel when counsel did not investigate whether an insanity defense should have been raised because no evidence in the record suggested that defendant was legally incompetent to stand trial, as a competency evaluation reached the opposite conclusion, and no evidence in the record indicated that defendant did not know, as a result of a severe mental disease or defect, the wrongfulness of defendant's acts, under R.C. 2901.01(A)(14). State v. Flesher, 2007-Ohio-4982, 2007 Ohio App. LEXIS 4406 (Ohio Ct. App., Monroe County 2007).

Defendant was not deprived of the effective assistance of counsel guaranteed by U.S. Const. amends. VI and XIV and Ohio Const. art. I, § 10 on the ground that his defense counsel advanced the theory of self-defense during defendant's trial on a charge of assault on a peace officer, in violation of R.C. 2903.13(A) and (C)(3), rather than challenging the legality of the arrest because, while the theory of self-defense, if established, was a complete defense to an assault charge, the fact that an arrest was unlawful was not a defense to a charge of assault on a peace officer, in that a lawful arrest was not an element of assault on a peace officer. State v. Newsome, 2005-Ohio-3775, 2005 Ohio App. LEXIS 3446 (Ohio Ct. App., Ashtabula County 2005).

**—Assumption of risk**

The defense of assumption of the risk is not available to a defendant who has committed an assault in violation of R.C. 2903.13: Johnson v. Hardnett, 62 Ohio App. 2d 165, 16 Ohio Op. 3d 345, 405 N.E.2d 324, 1978 Ohio App. LEXIS 7698 (Ohio Ct. App., Lucas County 1978).

**—Defense of another**

While defendant alleged in his prosecution for misdemeanor assault that he shoved the victim's head into a store's display rack because he was defending the victim's wife, who had been involved in a physical altercation with defendant, the trial court did not err in determining that the victim's wife was not in the store when defendant shoved the victim's head into a display rack and, thus, properly concluded that defendant was not acting in defense of another. State v. Sykes, 2006-Ohio-4523, 2006 Ohio App. LEXIS 4516 (Ohio Ct. App., Montgomery County 2006).

**—Defense of others**

In defendant's assault prosecution under R.C. 2903.13(A) and (C)(3), the evidence did not support a "defense of others" jury instruction as the evidence did not show that defendant believed that his brother was in imminent danger of death or bodily harm; instead, the testimony indicated that defendant was not acting in defense of his brother but was, in fact, the aggressor. State v. Abalos, 2011-Ohio-3489, 2011 Ohio App. LEXIS 2956 (Ohio Ct. App., Lucas County 2011).

In a prosecution for assaulting a police officer, since defendant failed to prove that a woman being handcuffed had a right to self-defense, she could not rely on the "defense of others" defense to justify her act of striking the police officer who was handcuffing the woman. The officer was attempting lawfully to arrest the woman, and absent an improper use of force, defendant had no justification to intervene. State v. Smith, 2008-Ohio-6402, 2008 Ohio App. LEXIS 5344 (Ohio Ct. App., Lucas County 2008).

**—Self-defense**

State met its burden of proof when it found defendant's act of punching the victim in the back of the head was a "cheap shot" that amounted to "assaultive behavior" in violation of the statute; the intent behind the self-defense law was to provide a legal justification for the use of force in circumstances where the person being defended would have been justified in using force to defend themselves. State v. Lewis, 2020-Ohio-3762, 156 N.E.3d 281, 2020 Ohio App. LEXIS 2689 (Ohio Ct. App., Butler County 2020).

Trial court erred by denying defendant's request for a self-defense instruction on the assault charge because there was evidence that could have supported a conclusion that defendant was not at fault in creating the situation that gave rise to his use of nondeadly force against his girlfriend's niece and defendant feared imminent bodily harm. State v. Sullivan, 2020-Ohio-1439, 2020 Ohio App. LEXIS 1410 (Ohio Ct. App., Lake County 2020).

Defendant's assault conviction was supported by sufficient evidence and was not against the manifest weight of the evidence because the evidence reasonably supported the conclusion that defendant was at fault in creating the situation giving rise to the altercation between her and the bailiff where jury reasonably credited the bailiff's testimony that, as he entered the home, defendant immediately punched him twice in the face, and he acted to defend himself, striking her back to "daze" her and gain control of the situation. State v. Robinson, 2020-Ohio-5214, 2020 Ohio App. LEXIS 4050 (Ohio Ct. App., Montgomery County 2020).

Defendant's conviction for assault was upheld as he was the initial aggressor in the physical altercation. Despite his probation status as a result of pleading guilty to assaulting the victim, he chose to interact with the victim and made derogatory remarks about the victim's wife. Evidence introduced showed that he attacked the victim first, causing him physical harm, grabbed him by the neck and kept assaulting him, that the victim had lacerations on his arm and ended up going to the hospital. State v. Clemmons, 2020-Ohio-5394, 2020 Ohio App. LEXIS 4246 (Ohio Ct. App., Butler County 2020).

Where defendant was convicted of assault and domestic violence after a bench trial, the court's finding that she failed to establish the affirmative defense of self-defense was not against the manifest weight of the evidence because the court did not credit her testimony that the victim slapped her, and that she sprayed him with mace because she had a reasonable belief that he was going to strike her again. State/City of Toledo v. Owens, 2019-Ohio-311, 2019 Ohio App. LEXIS 325 (Ohio Ct. App., Lucas County 2019).

Defendant's conviction for assault was not against the manifest weight of the evidence because defendant had hit the victim with the large ax handle in the head and leg three times and the evidence did not support a finding of self-defense; he committed an act of anger, was only person in the room with a weapon, and he offered no credible evidence that he was ever in fear for his safety. State v. Griffin, 2018-Ohio-3119, 2018 Ohio App. LEXIS 3351 (Ohio Ct. App., Clermont County 2018).

Trial court erred in convicting defendant of assaulting a man who had unlawfully entered defendant's home because the state did not rebut R.C. 2901.05(B)(1)'s self-defense presumption by proving that defendant's use of force was not reasonably necessary to repel the attack, as the testimony of the complainant and the other state witness was so impractical and illogical that it was not credible. State v. Montgomery, 2015-Ohio-4652, 48 N.E.3d 1042, 2015 Ohio App. LEXIS 4540 (Ohio Ct. App., Clermont County 2015).

Trial counsel did not act deficiently by failing to request a self-defense instruction because a self-defense jury instruction would have been improper since defendant failed to present sufficient evidence to raise the defense; self-defense was not defendant's theory of the case or trial strategy. The outcome of the proceeding would not have been different had a self-defense theory been pursued. State v. Oates, 2013-Ohio-2609, 993 N.E.2d 846, 2013 Ohio App. LEXIS 2588 (Ohio Ct. App., Hardin County 2013).

There was no showing of self defense under R.C. 2901.05(C), and the trial court's refusal to give a self-defense instruction in an assault trial was proper, because the situation arose through defendant's refusal to follow a direct order given by an officer and it was unreasonable for defendant to feel the need to retaliate from an officer's use of lawful force; defendant's testimony about his fear of attack contradicted his acknowledgement that, at the time, he realized the officer's intention was to grab him at the collar of his shirt. This was force meant to subdue defendant, not a physical attack. State v. Warner, 2001 Ohio App. LEXIS 6109 (Ohio Ct. App., Lorain County Sept. 21, 2001).

**—Voluntary intoxication**

Voluntary intoxication did not apply where an offense included a culpable mental state; therefore, defendant's voluntary intoxication was not a defense to his assault charge. State v. Koballa, 2014-Ohio-3592, 2014 Ohio App. LEXIS 3529 (Ohio Ct. App., Cuyahoga County 2014).

Defendant's claim that his intoxication prevented him from forming the intent necessary to have committed the crime of assaulting a police officer failed because under R.C. 2901.21(C) that defense was no longer available. State v. Melton, 2012-Ohio-2386, 2012 Ohio App. LEXIS 2098 (Ohio Ct. App., Cuyahoga County 2012).

Defendant failed to show that his intoxication acted to preclude the formation of intent for attempted assault of a police officer, under R.C. 2903.13(C)(3) and R.C. 2923.02, because, despite his intoxication, other testimony indicated that he acknowledged his inappropriate actions and apologized for them. He continually threatened the officers he came into contact with on the night of the incident, yet acknowledged that he was wrong; those actions did not indicate that his intoxication rose to such a level as to serve as a defense. State v. Fuote, 2007-Ohio-80, 2007 Ohio App. LEXIS 79 (Ohio Ct. App., Cuyahoga County 2007).

The mental state of recklessness does not involve a specific intent. Thus voluntary intoxication is not a defense to a crime requiring a mental state of recklessness: State v. Davis, 145 Ohio App. 3d 296, 762 N.E.2d 1027, 2001 Ohio App. LEXIS 3455 (Ohio Ct. App., Butler County 2001).

**Doctrine of transferred intent**

Trial court properly instructed a jury on the doctrine of transferred intent in defendant's trial on a charge of assault, in violation of R.C. 2903.13(A), arising from his attack of a peace officer in the performance of his official duties during a festival, as the attack by defendant was not incidental or accidental where he was aware of the officer's presence when he struck a punch; knowledge under R.C. 2901.22(B) that the victim was an officer was not required under § 2903.13(C)(3). State v. Kovacic, 2010-Ohio-5663, 2010 Ohio App. LEXIS 4804 (Ohio Ct. App., Lake County 2010).

Student who attempted to strike another student could not be convicted, under the doctrine of transferred intent, of striking a teacher who inserted herself between the students. The student did not "knowingly" strike a teacher, a more serious offense: In re A.C.T., 158 Ohio App. 3d 473, 2004 Ohio 4935, 816 N.E.2d 1098, Ohio App. LEXIS 4496 (2004).

**Double jeopardy**

Defendants' convictions for felonious assault and assault did not violate double jeopardy because they related to two separate incidents that occurred during the altercation at the victim's residence; defendant was struck by one defendant with a gun, injuring him and causing him to fall to the ground, and he was separately knocked down to his knee, injuring it, when struggling with the gun. State v. Mejia, 2020-Ohio-4883, 2020 Ohio App. LEXIS 3736 (Ohio Ct. App., Union County 2020), dismissed, 2022-Ohio-140, 165 Ohio St. 3d 1508, 179 N.E.3d 1268, 2022 Ohio LEXIS 132 (Ohio 2022), dismissed, 2022-Ohio-140, 165 Ohio St. 3d 1508, 179 N.E.3d 1268, 2022 Ohio LEXIS 136 (Ohio 2022).

Defendant's conviction for aggravated robbery, under R.C. 2911.01(A)(3), did not violate the Double Jeopardy Clause of the Fifth Amendment of the United States Constitution because the aggravated robbery and robbery (R.C. 2911.02(A)(2)) charges required an element that the misdemeanor assault charge, in violation of R.C. 2903.13(A), to which defendant had previously entered a guilty plea did not, i.e., the commission or attempted commission of a theft offense. Also, aggravated robbery and robbery both could have been completed by the "threat to inflict" harm, which was an element not required for assault; likewise the assault offense required a more heightened mental state, "knowingly," than either the aggravated robbery charge or the robbery charge, which only required a mens rea of "recklessness." State v. Patterson, 2006-Ohio-1902, 2006 Ohio App. LEXIS 1740 (Ohio Ct. App., Washington County 2006).

Because resisting arrest under R.C. 2921.33(B) and assault on a peace officer under R.C. 2903.13(A), (C)(3) had different elements and were not allied offenses, double jeopardy did not attach; consequently, defendant's trial counsel was not ineffective for failing to raise the issue. State v. Loomis, 2005-Ohio-1103, 2005 Ohio App. LEXIS 1072 (Ohio Ct. App., Ashtabula County 2005).

Because the elements of assault upon a peace officer required proof of an additional fact that disorderly conduct did not, defendant's protections against double jeopardy were not violated when defendant was convicted of the assault after his conviction for disorderly conduct. State v. Caesar, 2003-Ohio-6168, 2003 Ohio App. LEXIS 5542 (Ohio Ct. App., Cuyahoga County 2003).

Where a defendant is charged with assault (R.C. 2903.13(A)) and resisting arrest (R.C. 2921.33(A)) arising from the same incident, and where, upon trial, the jury acquits the defendant on the assault charge but is unable to reach a verdict on the resisting arrest charge, a second trial on the resisting arrest charge is not barred by the double jeopardy clause, for the two offenses each require proof of a fact which the other does not: State v. Rhinehart, 12 Ohio App. 3d 156, 467 N.E.2d 902, 1983 Ohio App. LEXIS 11359 (Ohio Ct. App., Summit County 1983).

**Elements**

Defendant met his burden of showing plain error as a manifest miscarriage of justice occurred due to the trial court's omission of the "by use of a deadly weapon or dangerous ordnance" element in the jury instructions on felonious assault, which resulted in the jury being instructed on assault, since whether defendant used a deadly weapon was disputed, and the failure to submit that element to the jury deprived defendant of his right to have the jury decide the issue; that the indictment charged defendant with felonious assault and specifically alleged the use of a dangerous weapon and that closing arguments centered on the felonious assault charge did not cure the error or prevent a manifest miscarriage of justice. State v. Bethel, 2014-Ohio-3861, 2014 Ohio App. LEXIS 3788 (Ohio Ct. App., Jackson County 2014).

Defendant met his burden of showing plain error as a manifest miscarriage of justice occurred due to the trial court's omission of the "by use of a deadly weapon or dangerous ordnance" element in the jury instructions on felonious assault, which resulted in the jury being instructed on assault, since whether defendant used a deadly weapon was disputed, and the failure to submit that element to the jury deprived defendant of his right to have the jury decide the issue; that the indictment charged defendant with felonious assault and specifically alleged the use of a dangerous weapon and that closing arguments centered on the felonious assault charge did not cure the error or prevent a manifest miscarriage of justice. State v. Bethel, 2014-Ohio-3861, 2014 Ohio App. LEXIS 3788 (Ohio Ct. App., Jackson County 2014).

Victim's statement to a police deputy was defendant's own statement being offered against him, such that the statement was admissible under

Evid.R. 801(D)(2)(a) and there was no prosecutorial misconduct; further, the statement was not offered to prove the truth of the matter asserted, but to show that the statement caused the victim to believe that defendant would cause him physical harm, which was an element of the charged offense of assault, in violation of R.C. 2903.13(A). State v. Junod, 2009-Ohio-2817, 2009 Ohio App. LEXIS 2381 (Ohio Ct. App., Auglaize County 2009).

Defendant's claim that the criminal complaint was deficient under Crim.R. 3 because it did not identify the victim by name lacked merit, as there was no such requirement where the identity of the victim was not an essential element of the crime; as defendant was charged with assault, in violation of R.C. 2903.13(A), the name of the victim was not required. State v. Givens, 2008-Ohio-3434, 2008 Ohio App. LEXIS 2898 (Ohio Ct. App., Columbiana County 2008).

When defendant was arrested for assault on a peace officer, under R.C. 2903.13(A) and (C)(3), defendant's lawful arrest was not an element of the crime, as it was defined as causing or attempting to cause physical harm to a peace officer while in the performance of official duties, and, unlike resisting arrest, a lawful arrest was not an element. State v. Martin, 2005-Ohio-3511, 2005 Ohio App. LEXIS 3265 (Ohio Ct. App., Madison County 2005).



**Emergency medical personnel**

Sufficient evidence supported crash victim defendant's R.C. 2903.13(A), (C)(3) knowing assault on emergency medical technician conviction. State v. Jamison, 2004-Ohio-2514, 2004 Ohio App. LEXIS 2232 (Ohio Ct. App., Medina County 2004).

**—Insufficient**

Trial court erred in overruling the Crim.R. 29(A) motion for acquittal as the State failed to prove beyond a reasonable doubt that defendant committed the assault, pursuant to R.C. 2903.13(A). Based on defendant's App.R. 9(C) statement (to which the State did not object), although the evidence established that defendant was at the pub and in the area where part of the assault occurred, there was no witness testimony that defendant was directly involved in the altercation. State v. Norwood, 2005-Ohio-3402, 2005 Ohio App. LEXIS 3159 (Ohio Ct. App., Lake County 2005).

**—Manifest weight**

Finding that defendant was a delinquent for committing complicity to commit assault and unlawful restraint was not against the manifest weight of the evidence because, standing alone, the victim's testimony, to the effect that defendant told his friends to perform "the bandit" on the victim and that he held the victim down while his friend performed "the bandit," which entailed his friend's insertion of two fingers into the victim's anal cavity, established defendant's guilt. A factfinder could conclude that defendant not only initiated the illegal act by his words of incitement and/or encouragement but also assisted in the commission of that offense by holding the victim down while his friend forcefully violated him. In re J.P., 2005-Ohio-3390, 2005 Ohio App. LEXIS 3168 (Ohio Ct. App., Cuyahoga County 2005).

Conviction for assault under R.C. 2903.13(A) was not against the manifest weight of the evidence because, while there was a conflict between the victim's statement given to police and his testimony at trial, the conflict presented an issue of credibility for the trier of fact to resolve. Further, the victim's testimony that defendant's punch induced pain was sufficient to satisfy the physical harm element of assault. State v. Hill, 2005-Ohio-3701, 2005 Ohio App. LEXIS 3400 (Ohio Ct. App., Montgomery County 2005).

Defendant's conviction for assault of a police officer was not against the manifest weight of the evidence as the jury did not have to credit defendant's testimony that he touched the detective's hand only to remove it from his mouth and nose so that he could breathe, nor was it required to discredit the testimony of the officers and the witness that the officers were identified as police officers and that defendant "dug three holes" into an officer's hand, causing it to bleed. State v. Fritz, 2005-Ohio-4736, 163 Ohio App. 3d 276, 837 N.E.2d 823, 2005 Ohio App. LEXIS 4233 (Ohio Ct. App., Montgomery County 2005).

**Evidence**

Defendant juvenile's adjudication of delinquency for aggravated burglary was supported by sufficient evidence because the State established that defendant trespassed in the victim's house, an occupied structure, with the purpose of committing the criminal offense of assault; the testimony of the victim and her mother sufficiently established that defendant did not have permission to come into a house, and the State's evidence established that he formed the intent to commit assault. In re A.T., 2021-Ohio-2934, 2021 Ohio App. LEXIS 2889 (Ohio Ct. App., Cuyahoga County 2021).

Defendant's assault conviction was not against the manifest weight of the evidence because notwithstanding the obvious issues of credibility and recollection with respect to witness, his testimony was unnecessary to satisfy the manifest weight of the evidence standard. State v. Landingham, 2021-Ohio-4258, 2021 Ohio App. LEXIS 4196 (Ohio Ct. App., Lake County 2021).

Sufficient evidence supported defendant's conviction for aggravated burglary and assault because he forced his way into his girlfriend's home without permission, he punched his girlfriend with a closed fist, and he choked her son and threatened to kill him. Ohio v. Allison, 2021-Ohio-3723, 2021 Ohio App. LEXIS 3629 (Ohio Ct. App., Stark County 2021).

In a prosecution for assault, the trial court did not abuse its discretion in excluding evidence that the victim's mother allegedly texted defendant's friend offering to make the charge "go away" in return for a payment, as such evidence did not tend prove defendant's innocence, and the court feared admitting the alleged bribery offer would confuse the jury as to the real issues, i.e., whether defendant knowingly caused physical harm to victim and whether defendant acted in self-defense. State v. Green, 2015-Ohio-1513, 2015 Ohio App. LEXIS 1462 (Ohio Ct. App., Franklin County 2015).

Although the failure of defense counsel to object to the admission of an assault victim's unsworn, signed domestic violence witness statement, given at the scene of the assault and admitted for the purpose of rebutting the victim's trial testimony that the physical contact made by defendant was "playful," was error, this error did not alter the outcome of the proceeding because the record contained much evidence implicating defendant in the assault. The officer who responded to the scene testified that defendant admitted that he struck the victim, and he also testified that he observed broken objects, arguing, and injuries that were consistent with an assault. State v. English, 2007-Ohio-5979, 2007 Ohio App. LEXIS 5272 (Ohio Ct. App., Montgomery County 2007).

**—Cross-examination**

Trial court's limitation under Evid.R. 611 on defendant's ability to cross-examine the victim's sister regarding a bank card dispute was within the trial court's discretion, as that dispute was not relevant to a criminal charge against defendant of assault, in violation of R.C. 2903.13, and the marginal probative value as to any impeachment of the sister was far outweighed by the danger of unfair prejudice and confusion of the issues under Evid.R. 403(A). State v. Baker, 2008-Ohio-3000, 2008 Ohio App. LEXIS 2515 (Ohio Ct. App., Montgomery County 2008).

**—Insufficient**

Defendant's conviction for assault was supported by weight and sufficiency of evidence, as it was established that victim was treated to immediately reinsert and prevent loss of tooth caused by punching victim multiple times in the head; he also received sutures for lacerations near his mouth. State v. Vugrinovich, 2020-Ohio-3541, 2020 Ohio App. LEXIS 2449 (Ohio Ct. App., Medina County 2020).

Evidence was insufficient to support defendant's conviction for assault because a video supported the finding defendant's contact with the victim was an attempt to block her from catching the dog rather than to cause her physical harm. The court determined defendant's intent was to block the victim so that he could accomplish his purpose which was so that the dog could get away so he could get it. State v. Lillie, 2018-Ohio-2714, 2018 Ohio App. LEXIS 2922 (Ohio Ct. App., Tuscarawas County 2018).

Sufficient evidence did not support defendant's conviction for assault on a person performing emergency medical service because reasonable minds could not have concluded that the woman who sat in the courtroom was the perpetrator of the assault on the emergency medical technician. The fact that defendant subsequently testified to being the patient in the ambulance was irrelevant, because that testimony would never have been offered if the acquittal motion had been granted at the close of the State's case. State v. Bailey, 2017-Ohio-2679, 2017 Ohio App. LEXIS 1709 (Ohio Ct. App., Montgomery County 2017).

Trial court erred in denying defendant's motion to an acquittal, on the charge of assaulting a police officer, because the evidence only established that defendant was resisting arrest when his hands struck the officer's face, not that defendant acting knowingly in causing physical harm to the officer. State v. Santiago-Dennis, 2014-Ohio-4204, 2014 Ohio App. LEXIS 4116 (Ohio Ct. App., Cuyahoga County 2014).

Trial court erred in denying defendant's motion to an acquittal, on the charge of assaulting a police officer, because the evidence only established that defendant was resisting arrest when his hands struck the officer's face, not that defendant acting knowingly in causing physical harm to the officer. State v. Santiago-Dennis, 2014-Ohio-4204, 2014 Ohio App. LEXIS 4116 (Ohio Ct. App., Cuyahoga County 2014).

Defendant's conviction for assault was not supported by sufficient evidence because the State did not present any evidence that defendant caused or attempted to cause physical harm to the named victim, such that it was plain error that the trial court did not grant defendant a judgment of acquittal. State v. Watson, 2014-Ohio-2395, 2014 Ohio App. LEXIS 2339 (Ohio Ct. App., Cuyahoga County 2014).

Although there was conflicting testimony as to whether defendant hit another individual with a shovel, as she was not named in the assault charge against him, the conviction could not stand on that alleged conduct. State v. Watson, 2014-Ohio-2395, 2014 Ohio App. LEXIS 2339 (Ohio Ct. App., Cuyahoga County 2014).

There was insufficient evidence to prove either count of assault on a police officer because there was no proof that defendant acted knowingly to cause physical harm to the officers. Defendant was plainly resisting arrest and the contact she made with the officers was part and parcel of that resistance; the State offered no evidence that her struggle with the officers contained a separate intent to knowingly cause or attempt to cause the officers physical harm. State v. Curlee-Jones, 2013-Ohio-1175, 2013 Ohio App. LEXIS 1069 (Ohio Ct. App., Cuyahoga County 2013).

There was insufficient evidence to support the assault conviction because there was no indication that defendant knowingly caused or attempted to cause physical harm when he placed his hands on his former girlfriend's shoulders to move her out of the way in order to retrieve items from the residence. When asked what physical harm she suffered as a result of the shoving, the girlfriend did not indicate that she suffered any physical harm. State v. Kemper, 2012-Ohio-5958, 983 N.E.2d 951, 2012 Ohio App. LEXIS 5114 (Ohio Ct. App., Butler County 2012).

Insufficient evidence supported defendant's conviction for assault on a police officer because the evidence did not show that he knowingly caused or attempted to cause physical harm to the officer. The officer's testimony did not establish that defendant caused the injury; the testimony merely established that somehow the car door closed and then he hurt his wrist as he placed defendant in the back seat of the police cruiser. State v. Fussell, 2011-Ohio-4815, 2011 Ohio App. LEXIS 3983 (Ohio Ct. App., Cuyahoga County 2011).

Juvenile's adjudication of delinquency by way of assault was not supported by sufficient evidence because there was no evidence that the juvenile's incidental contact with the officer during a few seconds of flailing, done as he attempted to enter the library to follow his older sister, might cause or attempt to cause physical harm. In re S. C. W., 2011-Ohio-3193, 2011 Ohio App. LEXIS 2687 (Ohio Ct. App., Summit County 2011).

Defendant's assault conviction involving his act of spitting on a peace officer was not supported by sufficient evidence as there was no evidence that the officer suffered physical harm. Nothing in the record suggested that defendant's saliva was tainted, that defendant carried or believed that he carried a disease that could have been transferred to the officer via bodily fluids, or that the officer sought treatment for injuries, although he did seek medical testing to see if there was a potential for injuries to develop. State v. Wyland, 2011-Ohio-455, 2011 Ohio App. LEXIS 393 (Ohio Ct. App., Cuyahoga County 2011).

In a juvenile proceeding, an Crim.R. 29 motion should have been granted because the State did not prove the elements of aggravated trespass, aggravated riot, criminal activity on school property, and assault beyond a reasonable doubt. Defendant was not identified as a person participating in a fight on school property, and, although he was originally on school property, he left when he was asked to do so; moreover, there was no intent to injure shown. In re L.R., 2010-Ohio-15, 2010 Ohio App. LEXIS 7 (Ohio Ct. App., Cuyahoga County 2010).

**—Manifest weight**

Appellant's convictions for felonious assault and assault was supported by sufficient evidence and was not against the manifest weight of the evidence because the officer's testimony established the appellant struck him multiple times in the face, causing a gash to his forehead, fractures to his nasal cavity and right orbital bone, and a concussion, the officer's injuries were serious. State v. Lee, 2022-Ohio-248, 2022 Ohio App. LEXIS 219 (Ohio Ct. App., Warren County 2022).

Defendant's convictions for assault stemming from separate physical confrontations were not against the manifest weight of evidence because even though the surveillance video did not show defendant grab the officer's genitals, it did not contradict the officer's testimony as the defendant claimed. Furthermore, the officer grabbed the defendant after he refused multiple orders to return to his cell, and what the defendant did with his hands after he grabbed the officer's genitals was irrelevant. State v. Bullock, 2022-Ohio-925, 2022 Ohio App. LEXIS 881 (Ohio Ct. App., Hamilton County 2022).

Trial court's conviction of defendant for assaulting peace officer was affirmed because court found that the jury did not lose its way so as to create a manifest injustice in finding defendant guilty as there was substantial evidence supporting each element; there was no dispute that deputy was a peace officer in the performance of duties at the time of incident, that defendant punched him in the eye, with pictures taken by fellow deputy that day. State v. Smallwood, 2021-Ohio-1103, 2021 Ohio App. LEXIS 1099 (Ohio Ct. App., Highland County 2021).

Jury was free to choose either the state or defendant's version of how the child received the injuries to her neck, and to the extent defendant contended the violation of his confrontation rights undermined his ability to challenge the child's credibility, there was no error in the trial court's admission of the challenged statements; the jury did not clearly lose its way in finding defendant guilty of the offenses beyond a reasonable doubt. State v. O.A.B., 2020-Ohio-547, 2020 Ohio App. LEXIS 509 (Ohio Ct. App., Franklin County 2020).

Verdict finding defendant guilty of assault was not against the weight of the evidence because the victim stated that defendant punched her in the ribs intentionally, and her testimony was uncontroverted by other evidence or testimony. State v. DiBattista, 2020-Ohio-3564, 2020 Ohio App. LEXIS 2486 (Ohio Ct. App., Portage County 2020).

Defendant's conviction for assault was not against the manifest weight of the evidence because the victim's testimony, if believed, was sufficient to establish each and every element of assault. The fact that the trial court believed the victim's testimony over that of defendant did not render defendant's conviction against the manifest weight of the evidence. State v. Baker, 2020-Ohio-2882, 2020 Ohio App. LEXIS 1843 (Ohio Ct. App., Butler County 2020).

Defendant's conviction of assault of a functionally impaired person was not against the manifest weight of the evidence given testimony that after defendant, a caretaker, was struck in the groin by the victim, defendant struck the victim on his arms or legs, pulled him from the couch, and finally dragged him to his bedroom by his ankles. State v. Grable, 2019-Ohio-4516, 2019 Ohio App. LEXIS 4568 (Ohio Ct. App., Ashtabula County 2019).

Defendant's convictions for domestic violence, assault, and disorderly conduct because, based upon testimony and the pictorial evidence of physical injuries, the jury reasonably concluded that defendant knowingly caused physical harm to the victim, his wife. Defendant admitted striking his wife once and the photographic evidence demonstrated that the wife had a black eye, redness around her neck, and a laceration inside her lip and she testified that defendant struck her more than one time. State v. Demint, 2018-Ohio-2091, 2018 Ohio App. LEXIS 2260 (Ohio Ct. App., Ross County 2018).

Defendant's convictions for assault and domestic violence were supported by the manifest weight of the evidence because the trial court specifically found that neither of the defense witnesses observed the entirety of the interactions between the victim and defendant. Thus, it could not be concluded that the trial court, acting as the trier of fact, lost its way and created a manifest miscarriage of justice by accepting the victim's testimony that defendant hit her and yanked her hair. State v. Allen, 2018-Ohio-3393, 2018 Ohio App. LEXIS 3670 (Ohio Ct. App., Montgomery County 2018)

Defendant's assault conviction was against the manifest weight of the evidence; defendant had to knowingly cause physical harm to the victim, but while she was intoxicated and belligerent and struggled when officers attempted to handcuff her, it could have been inferred that the victim was inadvertently struck during defendant's resistance. The record supported a conviction for disorderly conduct and the conviction was modified accordingly. State v. Fips, 2018-Ohio-2296, 2018 Ohio App. LEXIS 2485 (Ohio Ct. App., Cuyahoga County 2018), rev'd, 2020-Ohio-1449, 160 Ohio St. 3d 348, 157 N.E.3d 680, 2020 Ohio LEXIS 940 (Ohio 2020).

Defendant's conviction for assault was not against the manifest weight of the evidence; the State presented testimony from the victim and two witnesses that defendant grabbed the victim's throat with both hands and lifted him off the ground, plus there were red marks around the victim's neck, such that the trier of fact was entitled to find that defendant knowingly caused or attempted to the victim physical harm. State v. Anderson, 2018-Ohio-4262, 2018 Ohio App. LEXIS 4589 (Ohio Ct. App., Butler County 2018).

In connection with defendant's assault offense, he did not act in self-defense or in defense of another; although defendant presented evidence that the victim threatened to beat defendant and approached him with clenched fists, there was no credible evidence that defendant, at six inches taller and 50 pounds heavier than the victim, honestly believed the victim posed a threat of imminent bodily harm, and even if he did, defendant exceeded the degree of force necessary to repel any attack by choking the victim. State v. Anderson, 2018-Ohio-4262, 2018 Ohio App. LEXIS 4589 (Ohio Ct. App., Butler County 2018).

Defendant's conviction for assault was not against the manifest weight of the evidence because the evidence supported the finding that defendant was the individual who assaulted the victim. The victim identified defendant twice in open court and affirmed to the trial court that she had no doubt that defendant was her assailant and, because the victim and defendant conversed prior to and following the physical altercation, the victim had a clear view of her assailant and was in the best position to identify defendant as her attacker. State v. Henderson, 2018-Ohio-4550, 2018 Ohio App. LEXIS 4872 (Ohio Ct. App., Allen County 2018).

Defendant's convictions for aggravated menacing and assault were not against the manifest weight of the evidence, as the victim believed he would cause her serious physical harm based on his verbal and physical assault when she was conducting an investigation in his home. State v. Thomas, 2017-Ohio-957, 2017 Ohio App. LEXIS 964 (Ohio Ct. App., Cuyahoga County 2017).

Defendant's conviction for abduction of three victims and misdemeanor assault was not against the manifest weight of the evidence; inter alia, the minor inconsistencies between the victims' memories of an event that transpired over two years before the trial or the fact that some may have been intoxicated did not rise to the level of creating a manifest miscarriage of justice in the case. State v. Melton, 2016-Ohio-1227, 2016 Ohio App. LEXIS 1121 (Ohio Ct. App., Cuyahoga County 2016).

Defendant's felonious assault and assault convictions were supported by sufficient evidence and not against the manifest weight of the evidence because, while engaging in an altercation with police officers, defendant struck an officer's hand with a hammer fist and the "natural, foreseeable and probable consequence" of that voluntary act was to cause injury to the officer, whose hand became numb after defendant's strike. State v. Parker, 2016-Ohio-5663, 2016 Ohio App. LEXIS 3531 (Ohio Ct. App., Lorain County 2016).

Defendant's conviction for assault was not against the manifest weight of the evidence because, although the victim changed her story and described at least three versions of the assault, the trial court, as the trier of fact, did not lose its way by choosing to believe the version of the events set forth in her initial report to the police and in her written statement, which were consistent with one another. State v. Wilson, 2016-Ohio-7329, 2016 Ohio App. LEXIS 4176 (Ohio Ct. App., Montgomery County 2016).

Defendant's assault conviction was not against the manifest weight of the evidence based on a record that included testimony from the victim and her boyfriend as well as an admission by defendant that her hands might have come in contact with the victim's neck. Vill. of Grafton v. Ortiz, 2016-Ohio-7539, 2016 Ohio App. LEXIS 4401 (Ohio Ct. App., Lorain County 2016).

Defendant's robbery and assault convictions were not against the manifest weight of the evidence because defendant, who had smoked crack cocaine, had a dispute with the victim about money, punched the victim in the face and, after the victim fell to the ground, started kicking her in the head and stomach, and left the victim's house with her cell phone in his possession. State v. Binford, 2016-Ohio-7678, 2016 Ohio App. LEXIS 4545 (Ohio Ct. App., Summit County 2016).

Defendant inmate's conviction for assault was not against the manifest weight of the evidence because the victim, a corrections officer, ordered the inmate several times to get in the regular chow line, but he ignored her, he knocked the handcuffs out of her hand, she attempted to spray mace on the inmate, and the inmate then grabbed her by her shirt and the back of her head and threw her face-first into a guard rail; a supervising corrections officer witnessed the inmate throw punches at the victim's face, grab her and throw her into the guard rail, and then kick her; and a registered nurse at the correctional facility testified that the victim had bruising to her nose, knees, and under an eye, and redness on both sides of her neck. State v. Adams, 2016-Ohio-4946, 2016 Ohio App. LEXIS 2740 (Ohio Ct. App., Richland County 2016).

Defendant's conviction for assault was not against the manifest weight of the evidence, as the evidence indicated that defendant assaulted the victim by hitting her in the back with a wrench as she was attempting to exit his vehicle, and officers testified that the victim told them that defendant had done so. State v. Sims, 2015-Ohio-5454, 2015 Ohio App. LEXIS 5270 (Ohio Ct. App., Mahoning County 2015), vacated, different results reached on reconsid., 2016-Ohio-5316, 2016 Ohio App. LEXIS 3177 (Ohio Ct. App., Mahoning County 2016).

Defendant's complicity to commit assault conviction was not against the manifest weight of the evidence as while defendant testified that he was not present at the time of the altercation, the jury credited the bouncer's and the victim's version. State v. Fritz, 2015-Ohio-1496, 2015 Ohio App. LEXIS 1438 (Ohio Ct. App., Seneca County 2015).

Defendant's conviction was not against the manifest weight of the evidence, as the judge fairly and impartially decided the matter and neither lost his way nor created a miscarriage of justice. State v. Wolfe, 2015-Ohio-3455, 2015 Ohio App. LEXIS 3339 (Ohio Ct. App., Tuscarawas County 2015).

Defendant's convictions for misdemeanor assault were not against the manifest weight of the evidence, based on the strong force that defendant used on both victims by forcing one victim to the ground and fracturing the other victim's leg. State v. Taslitz, 2015-Ohio-3474, 2015 Ohio App. LEXIS 3360 (Ohio Ct. App., Cuyahoga County 2015).

Defendant's conviction for assault of a corrections officer was not against the manifest weight of the evidence because, whether defendant "head butted" the officer or engaged in some other type of physical contact with him, both witnesses testified consistently that defendant, unprovoked by any conduct by the officer, came at the officer and made physical contact with him. The officer further testified that, as a result of the altercation, he sustained a physical injury, i.e., a laceration to his forehead as well as a headache and dizziness. State v. May, 2015-Ohio-4275, 49 N.E.3d 736, 2015 Ohio App. LEXIS 4167 (Ohio Ct. App., Cuyahoga County 2015).

Defendant's convictions for domestic violence under R.C. 2919.25(A) and (C) and assault under R.C. 2903.13(A) were not against the manifest weight of the evidence because although the victim said that she did not feel anything after defendant slapped her, the responding officer saw no evidence of injury, and the victim's children were calm after the incident, the trial court was entitled to believe the victim after weighing her credibility and that of defendant. State v. Abbasov, 2015-Ohio-5379, 2015 Ohio App. LEXIS 5197 (Ohio Ct. App., Montgomery County 2015).

Defendant's complicity to commit assault conviction was not against the manifest weight of the evidence as while defendant testified that he was not present at the time of the altercation, the jury credited the bouncer's and the victim's version. State v. Fritz, 2015-Ohio-1496, 2015 Ohio App. LEXIS 1438 (Ohio Ct. App., Seneca County 2015).

Defendant's conviction for assault on a deputy was not against the manifest weight of the evidence as three eyewitnesses testified that defendant struck the deputy in the face with a closed fist, and defendant did not present any evidence to corroborate her claim that she struck the deputy accidentally. State v. Evans, 2015-Ohio-2298, 2015 Ohio App. LEXIS 2227 (Ohio Ct. App., Lake County 2015).

Although defendant testified that the victim attacked her with a brick and that she used the grilling fork to defend herself, defendant's misdemeanor assault and felonious assault convictions were not against the manifest weight of the evidence as she never reported the attack to the police, did not seek medical attention, and failed to offer any photographs of the alleged injuries to her head; and defendant violated a duty to avoid the fight and was equally responsible for creating the situation. State v. Smith, 2014-Ohio-828, 2014 Ohio App. LEXIS 801 (Ohio Ct. App., Cuyahoga County 2014).

Defendant's convictions for felonious assault and assault were not against the manifest weight of the evidence, as the jury was free to believe a victim's testimony that defendant threatened to kill him, the quality of the physical evidence was not dispositive, and three separate witnesses testified that they heard gunshots State v. Burns, 2014-Ohio-303, 2014 Ohio App. LEXIS 290 (Ohio Ct. App., Cuyahoga County 2014).

Defendant's claim that he should not have been convicted of assault because his intoxication made him unconscious and precluded him from acting voluntarily did not raise a sufficiency issue; the jury's finding that defendant's alcoholic stupor did not rise to the level of unconsciousness rendering his act of striking a firefighter involuntary was not against the manifest weight of the evidence as the witnesses variously testified he was flaring his arms, swearing, spitting, and at times loud and at times subdued, and defendant was the only one who testified that he was in a complete blackout. State v. Koballa, 2014-Ohio-3592, 2014 Ohio App. LEXIS 3529 (Ohio Ct. App., Cuyahoga County 2014).

Although defendant argued that he rather than the victim was the more credible witness at trial, his conviction was not against the manifest weight of the evidence, as there was no indication that the jury lost its way so as to create a manifest miscarriage of justice and warrant the reversal of his conviction of assault. State v. Crockett, 2014-Ohio-3512, 2014 Ohio App. LEXIS 3458 (Ohio Ct. App., Sandusky County 2014).

Defendant's convictions for rape, kidnapping, attempted rape, and assault were not against the manifest weight of the evidence as the jury did not lose its way simply because it chose to believe the testimony of the victim, who admitted to being a crack cocaine user for approximately 25 years and to using crack cocaine twice on the day of the incident, that defendant punched her, forced her to remain in his apartment after she tried to leave, anally raped her, and attempted to vaginally rape her; the victim specifically denied that she went with defendant to his apartment to trade sex for drugs; and the trauma nurse who examined the victim testified that her injuries were consistent with an individual who had been forcibly raped. State v. Smith, 2013-Ohio-5345, 2013 Ohio App. LEXIS 5562 (Ohio Ct. App., Montgomery County 2013).

Appellate court could not say that the trial court, in a bench trial, clearly lost its way and created such a manifest miscarriage of justice that the appellate court had to reverse defendant's conviction for assault, in violation of R.C. 2903.13(A), because the trial court could reasonably have returned a guilty verdict based on the State of Ohio's version of events. State v. Simmons, 2013-Ohio-2890, 2013 Ohio App. LEXIS 2935 (Ohio Ct. App., Highland County 2013).

There was no merit to defendant's argument that his conviction under R.C. 2903.13(C)(2)(b) was against the manifest weight of the evidence because the State failed to establish the requisite mens rea of "knowingly." A corrections officer testified that defendant tried to bite the officer when the officer tried to nudge him off his bed and that defendant continued his attempts to bite the officer until he was tased by other jail officials; the officer also suffered scratches on his forearm caused by defendant. State v. Fisher, 2013-Ohio-1045, 2013 Ohio App. LEXIS 935 (Ohio Ct. App., Delaware County 2013).

Convictions of domestic violence and misdemeanor assault were not against the manifest weight of the evidence. Defendant admitted to hitting the victim three times in the head and face area with a closed fist; thus, the jury was asked to resolve the conflicting testimony concerning whether defendant acted in the defense of her child, and it was free to find the State's witnesses to be more credible. State v. Martinez, 2013-Ohio-1025, 2013 Ohio App. LEXIS 913 (Ohio Ct. App., Cuyahoga County 2013).

Manifest weight of the evidence supported defendant's conviction of assault on a police officer, as a police sergeant testified that defendant kicked the sergeant on the left leg and described defendant as lifting defendant's left leg and kicking backwards, and another officer similarly testified to seeing defendant kick the sergeant in this fashion; video of the incident was consistent with the officers' testimony. State v. Galbraith, 2012-Ohio-5231, 2012 Ohio App. LEXIS 4582 (Ohio Ct. App., Marion County 2012).

Weight of the evidence supported defendant's convictions for assault and attempted felonious assault because, in one incident, defendant threatened to beat a corrections officer to death and, in a second incident, defendant pushed the corrections officer and, while pinning him against the railing, defendant put his arm around the officer's neck and tried to choke him and push him over the top of the railing. The officer testified that during the struggle his glasses were knocked off, part of his upper body was over the top of the railing, one of his feet was off the ground, and he was feeling light-headed from being choked. State v. Stewart, 2012-Ohio-4640, 2012 Ohio App. LEXIS 4076 (Ohio Ct. App., Butler County 2012).

Defendant's conviction of assault was not against the manifest weight of the evidence, as the victim testified that defendant suddenly attacked the victim, and a witness testified that defendant hit the victim in the head with a beer bottle. State v. Breneman, 2012-Ohio-3632, 2012 Ohio App. LEXIS 3210 (Ohio Ct. App., Wayne County 2012).

Defendant's conviction for assault was not against the weight of the evidence, as an officer observed a cut under the victim's left eye and that the victim's lip was swollen, injuries consistent with the victim's version of events that defendant struck the victim more than once. State v. Heydinger, 2011-Ohio-5022, 2011 Ohio App. LEXIS 4141 (Ohio Ct. App., Montgomery County 2011).

Defendant's assault conviction was not against the manifest weight of the evidence as the testimony of three witnesses was clear that defendant struck the victim in the eye on at least one occasion, and the testimony of these witnesses was not inherently incredible. State v. Olsen, 2011-Ohio-3420, 2011 Ohio App. LEXIS 2890 (Ohio Ct. App., Clark County 2011).

Convictions for assault and disorderly conduct were not against the manifest weight of the evidence because the jury was free to believe statements that defendant's girlfriend made previously about the origin of her facial injuries; the girlfriend had obvious injuries, and she made statements to police and to a medic that defendant had caused them. City of Columbus v. Nearhood, 2011-Ohio-905, 193 Ohio App. 3d 178, 951 N.E.2d 452, 2011 Ohio App. LEXIS 776 (Ohio Ct. App., Franklin County 2011).

Defendant's conviction for assault was not against the manifest weight of the evidence because the State presented substantial evidence through the testimony of the victim and a witness upon which the trial court could reasonably have concluded that all of the elements for an assault were proven beyond a reasonable doubt. The jury chose to believe the version of events as presented by the victim and the witness, that when they asked defendant to leave, defendant grabbed the victim by the throat and threw him up against the wall, rather than that presented by defendant. State v. Johnson, 2008-Ohio-1222, 2008 Ohio App. LEXIS 1052 (Ohio Ct. App., Highland County 2008).

**—Materially exculpatory**

Trial court erred when it overruled defendant's dismissal motion with respect to a charge of assault (peace officer) because a videotape of the incident was inadvertently erased by a police officer, it was materially exculpatory, and defendant could not obtain comparable evidence by other reasonably available means. State v. Blair, 2014-Ohio-1279, 2014 Ohio App. LEXIS 1215 (Ohio Ct. App., Montgomery County 2014).

**—Prior discipline**

There was no plain error in the trial court's exclusion of a mother's testimony regarding prior disciplinary problems with her 11-year-old son, who was the victim of defendant's alleged assault, as the defense admitted other evidence that non-corporal punishment had been tried unsuccessfully in the past, such that the outcome would not have been different. State v. Smith, 2019-Ohio-2467, 2019 Ohio App. LEXIS 2577 (Ohio Ct. App., Montgomery County 2019).

There was no plain error in the trial court's exclusion of a mother's testimony regarding prior disciplinary problems with her 11-year-old son, who was the victim of defendant's alleged assault, as the defense admitted other evidence that non-corporal punishment had been tried unsuccessfully in the past, such that the outcome would not have been different. State v. Smith, 2019-Ohio-2467, 2019 Ohio App. LEXIS 2577 (Ohio Ct. App., Montgomery County 2019).

**—Relevant**

As the issue of whether hospital emergency room personnel violated hospital policies and procedures was not relevant to the State's burden of proving whether defendant committed assaults under R.C. 2903.13(A) and 2901.05(A) on them while she was there, visiting a friend who was being treated, the trial court did not abuse its discretion in excluding such evidence from defendant's trial pursuant to Evid.R. 401 and 402. State v. Belcher, 2013-Ohio-1234, 2013 Ohio App. LEXIS 1133 (Ohio Ct. App., Montgomery County 2013).

**—Sufficient**

Appellant's convictions for felonious assault and assault was supported by sufficient evidence and was not against the manifest weight of the evidence because the officer's testimony established the appellant struck him multiple times in the face, causing a gash to his forehead, fractures to his nasal cavity and right orbital bone, and a concussion, the officer's injuries was serious. State v. Lee, 2022-Ohio-248, 2022 Ohio App. LEXIS 219 (Ohio Ct. App., Warren County 2022).

Evidence was sufficient to support convictions of assault and obstructing official business because at trial, evidence was presented that defendant had caused victim physical harm by dragging her off a couch and slamming her onto a dog cage; furthermore, evidence established essential elements of defendant's conviction for obstructing official business since officer had ordered defendant to stop at least twice, but defendant ignored him and ran. State v. Brown, 2022-Ohio-716, 2022 Ohio App. LEXIS 650 (Ohio Ct. App., Montgomery County 2022).

Conviction of defendant for assault was supported with sufficient evidence and was not against the manifest weight of the evidence because his cell-phone video recording was not pointed at the victim or the door throughout the entirety of the incident. It omitted the critical portion of the episode, and, therefore, it had limited probative value. State v. Johnson, 2021-Ohio-116, 2021 Ohio App. LEXIS 112 (Ohio Ct. App., Hamilton County 2021).

Defendant's conviction of assault was supported by the manifest weight of the evidence because evidence showed that she acted recklessly pursuant to R.C. 2901.22(C) where prior to injuring victim, defendant was aggressive, yelling and screaming, and victim's surgeon determined that victim needed surgery to heal. State v. Mack, 2021-Ohio-1102, 2021 Ohio App. LEXIS 1097 (Ohio Ct. App., Cuyahoga County 2021).

Defendant's convictions for unlawful restraint and assault were supported by sufficient evidence because victim testified that defendant's forceful actions when wrestling her cell phone from her caused her pain and injured her hand. The rational factfinder could have found the state had proved beyond a reasonable doubt every element of unlawful restraint and assault, including that he acted knowingly when he barricaded victim in his house preventing her from leaving and separately injured her hand. State v. Rouzier, 2021-Ohio-1466, 2021 Ohio App. LEXIS 1475 (Ohio Ct. App., Hamilton County 2021).

Sufficient evidence supported defendant's convictions for assault and domestic violence, because his girlfriend stated that he took her phone, questioned her about communications with another man, and then repeatedly beat her, punched her in the head, and kicked her. She had bruises on her face, chin, arms, side, and shoulder resulting from the assault. City of Columbus v. C.G., 2021-Ohio-71, 2021 Ohio App. LEXIS 63 (Ohio Ct. App., Franklin County 2021).

Sufficient evidence supported defendant's conviction for assaulting a peace officer where the officer testified that the defendant made eye contact and swore at the officer while kicking the officer in the throat; the officer's testimony constituted evidence of "knowingly." State v. Humphrey, 2021-Ohio-916, 2021 Ohio App. LEXIS 929 (Ohio Ct. App., Delaware County 2021).

Trial court did not err in denying defendant's motion for judgment of acquittal or in finding her guilty of assault where the evidence showed that she knowingly caused physical harm to the child during their interactions, and the state provided eyewitness testimony to the events that occurred in the gym and testimony as to visual observation of scratches and red marks on the child's person; the factfinder afforded more weight to the state witnesses' testimony and found it more credible than defendant's testimony. State v. Bell, 2021-Ohio-899, 2021 Ohio App. LEXIS 907 (Ohio Ct. App., Portage County 2021).

Evidence was sufficient to support defendant's assault conviction because the jury could infer that defendant was aware that her conduct of accelerating the vehicle while the sergeant was positioned in front of the car would probably cause the sergeant physical harm. The sergeant testified that defendant had to have seen him because he made eye contact with her and slapped the top of the car a couple of times and that once the passenger entered the vehicle the car went forward, striking his left arm and thumb. State v. Kreischer, 2021-Ohio-1235, 2021 Ohio App. LEXIS 1222 (Ohio Ct. App., Van Wert County 2021).

Evidence was sufficient to support defendant's conviction of assault because the record contained sufficient evidence to support the jury's finding that defendant was guilty of assault and that she was not acting in defense of her property, both beyond a reasonable doubt. The jury had sufficient evidence before it to conclude that defendant did not allow victim reasonable time to comply to leave property and that the force that she used to eject him was not reasonable under the circumstances. State v. Behnfeldt, 2021-Ohio-1915, 2021 Ohio App. LEXIS 1859 (Ohio Ct. App., Stark County 2021).

There was evidence that defendant knowingly caused physical harm to a household member, which was sufficient to uphold his convictions for domestic violence and assault and that he knowingly caused another to believe that he would cause serious physical harm to her, which was sufficient to uphold his conviction for aggravated menacing. The victim told an officer that a red mark on her cheek was from a slap by defendant and that a mark on her temple was from when he slammed her into a kitchen cabinet and she had told defendant's ex-wife that defendant was high on cocaine, that he had beaten her up throughout the day and that she suspected that defendant was going to try to kill her. State v. Varouh, 2020-Ohio-528, 2020 Ohio App. LEXIS 487 (Ohio Ct. App., Lorain County 2020).

Evidence that defendant kicked a deputy, headbutted an officer and pinned a sergeant's leg to the restraint chair while they were in the performance of their duties, and the officers' testimony that defendant acted with the requisite mental state, knowing that his actions would cause physical harm, was sufficient to support defendant's three convictions for assault on a peace officer. State v. Walker, 2020-Ohio-617, 2020 Ohio App. LEXIS 569 (Ohio Ct. App., Gallia County 2020).

There was ample proof that defendant knowingly possessed cocaine weighing between 20 and 27 grams and that he knowingly caused or attempted to cause physical harm to two peace officers while in performance of their official duties when defendant, who acted differently from other passengers in a stopped vehicle, struggled with officers attempting to cuff him and tossed aside a bag containing 24.6 grams of cocaine. State v.

Smith, 2020-Ohio-760, 2020 Ohio App. LEXIS 695 (Ohio Ct. App., Belmont County 2020).

Sufficient evidence supported defendant's assault conviction because no other evidence was presented to indicate that the child's injuries were caused by anything other than the force that defendant used, and the severity of the force was clearly disproportionate to the reason given for administering the punishment, namely, that the child had glared at defendant's fiancée that day during a trip to a waterpark. State v. Middleton, 2020-Ohio-1308, 2020 Ohio App. LEXIS 1239 (Ohio Ct. App., Greene County 2020).

Defendant's convictions of domestic violence and assault were not against the manifest weight and sufficiency of the evidence; defendant handled the victim in such a way that she could have been injured, as he grabbed her by her upper arms, picked her up off the ground, and slammed her against the car, then held the victim in a chokehold. The jury was free to reject defendant's self-serving testimony. State v. Spiess, 2020-Ohio-4376, 2020 Ohio App. LEXIS 3258 (Ohio Ct. App., Licking County 2020).

Evidence was sufficient to support defendants' convictions of assault and felonious assault with firearm specifications because the victim testified that two men pulled guns on him, he was struck by one of them with a gun, injuring him and causing him to fall to the ground, and he was separately knocked down to his knee, injuring it, when struggling with the gun. The victim identified defendants as the men who approached and spoke to him and his blood was found on one defendant's pants. State v. Mejia, 2020-Ohio-4883, 2020 Ohio App. LEXIS 3736 (Ohio Ct. App., Union County 2020), dismissed, 2022-Ohio-140, 165 Ohio St. 3d 1508, 179 N.E.3d 1268, 2022 Ohio LEXIS 132 (Ohio 2022), dismissed, 2022-Ohio-140, 165 Ohio St. 3d 1508, 179 N.E.3d 1268, 2022 Ohio LEXIS 136 (Ohio 2022).

Conviction of defendant of felonious assault and assault was proper since the evidence was sufficient to support that he knowingly caused serious physical harm to him. Lastly, the State's evidence that he swung at the other officer also demonstrated the culpable mental state required to convict him of assault and was sufficient to establish that he attempted to cause the officer physical harm. Thus, the court did not err in denying his motion for acquittal under Crim.R. 29(A). State v. Hendricks, 2020-Ohio-5218, 2020 Ohio App. LEXIS 4061 (Ohio Ct. App., Lucas County 2020).

Sufficient evidence supported trial court's guilty verdict and defendant's conviction for assault was not against manifest weight of the evidence because defendant assaulted victim, unprovoked, victim was injured during altercation and her injuries were consistent with being hit repeatedly in the head, face, and body, as well as being forcibly pushed into the gravel, and police officer observed injuries consistent with victim and witness' reports. State v. Packnett, 2020-Ohio-5276, 2020 Ohio App. LEXIS 4123 (Ohio Ct. App., Montgomery County 2020).

Evidence supported the delinquency adjudication for assault on a peace officer based on a finding that appellant had intentionally stomped on the officer's foot to inflict physical harm on the officer so that the officer would back up. Based on the cruiser camera footage, appellant lifted her right knee and stomped her foot down on the officer's foot. In re A.F., 2020-Ohio-5420, 2020 Ohio App. LEXIS 4296 (Ohio Ct. App., Hamilton County 2020).

Defendant's conviction for fourth-degree felony assault of a peace officer was supported by sufficient evidence and not against the manifest weight of the evidence because defendant, with a clear line of sight, kicked the officer in the left side of the face as the officer attempted to secure defendant's legs so paramedics to could tend to his injuries, and both responding officers testified that defendant had not made any similar kicking motions prior to kicking the officer in the face. State v. Erdmann, 2019-Ohio-261, 2019 Ohio App. LEXIS 263 (Ohio Ct. App., Clermont County 2019).

Defendant, a former sheriff's department sergeant, was properly convicted of assault, as it was not against the manifest weight of the evidence because the body camera video proved that he assaulted the victim and caused him serious injury. State v. Truckey, 2019-Ohio-407, 2019 Ohio App. LEXIS 442 (Ohio Ct. App., Ashtabula County 2019).

Evidence was sufficient as the testimony indicated there was a heated verbal exchange between defendant and an individual and during this exchange defendant punched another individual, the victim, in the face; both individuals believed defendant intended to punch the first person, but missed and hit the victim instead. State v. Lambert, 2019-Ohio-1226, 2019 Ohio App. LEXIS 1317 (Ohio Ct. App., Mahoning County 2019).

Defendant's conviction for assault was supported by the weight and sufficiency of the evidence, as it was established that defendant's actions in disciplining the victim, who was his girlfriend's 11-year-old son, for lying about school work were not reasonable and proper physical measures in the circumstances based on the degree of bruising on his buttocks and thighs from being struck by a belt multiple times, such that the injury and physical harm were not a legally protected interest. State v. Smith, 2019-Ohio-2467, 2019 Ohio App. LEXIS 2577 (Ohio Ct. App., Montgomery County 2019).

Defendant's convictions for felonious assault and assault were supported by the weight and sufficiency of the evidence, such that denial of his acquittal motion was not error, as it was established by witnesses that defendant kicked and stomped on one victim, who suffered broken bones and needed a spleen removal, and that he punched the other victim, such that he caused each the requisite harm, and inconsistencies in testimony were within the jury's province. State v. Loomis, 2019-Ohio-2576, 2019 Ohio App. LEXIS 2705 (Ohio Ct. App., Franklin County 2019).

Defendant's conviction for assault was supported by the weight and sufficiency of the evidence, as it was established that defendant's actions in disciplining the victim, who was his girlfriend's 11-year-old son, for lying about school work were not reasonable and proper physical measures in the circumstances based on the degree of bruising on his buttocks and thighs from being struck by a belt multiple times, such that the injury and physical harm were not a legally protected interest. State v. Smith, 2019-Ohio-2467, 2019 Ohio App. LEXIS 2577 (Ohio Ct. App., Montgomery County 2019).

Sufficient evidence supported defendant's conviction for assault on a peace officer because, although he may not have had the specific intent to harm the paramedics, there was testimony that he crashed into the two paramedics in an attempt to escape from the ambulance and that he continued to fight and struggle even after being ordered to stop. Defendant's actions were sufficient to demonstrate that he knew that his actions would "probably cause a certain result," i.e., an injury to the paramedics. State v. Warren, 2019-Ohio-2927, 2019 Ohio App. LEXIS 3011 (Ohio Ct. App., Fairfield County 2019).

Defendant's conviction for assault on a corrections officer was not against the manifest weight of the evidence, as there was testimony from officers involved in the altercation as well as other evidence that defendant, who was an inmate, refused to heed the officers' directives, knowingly punched one in the face, and then resisted their efforts to stop his conduct. State v. Lanier, 2019-Ohio-3213, 2019 Ohio App. LEXIS 3288 (Ohio Ct. App., Lucas County 2019).

Eyewitness's identification testimony was sufficient, if believed by the jury, to support the convictions for robbery and assault. Further, the jury did not lose its way in finding the witness's testimony credible as to the identification of defendant as one of the men involved in the assault and robbery of the victim because the jury was made aware of the inconsistencies between her testimony and the victim's testimony, the jury was aware she was charged as an accomplice in the incident, and defendant's counsel criticized her actions in running from the scene, failing to call the police, and refusing to talk to police until she was arrested for the crime. State v. Proctor, 2019-Ohio-3259, 2019 Ohio App. LEXIS 3349 (Ohio Ct. App., Stark County 2019).

Record presented sufficient, undisputed evidence that the peace officers were in the performance of their official duties at the time of the assault. Thus, the fact that defense counsel stipulated to that element of the assault offense had no determinative bearing on the verdict. State v. Buckley, 2019-Ohio-3991, 2019 Ohio App. LEXIS 4056 (Ohio Ct. App., Lake County 2019).

Defendant's conviction of assault was supported with sufficient evidence because the victim testified that she saw him look at her prior to assaulting her, and both she and the police officer on the scene testified regarding her injuries. Her testimony was sufficient evidence to support a conviction. And lastly, there was no need for her testimony to be corroborated. State v. Rainey, 2019-Ohio-4618, 2019 Ohio App. LEXIS 4649 (Ohio Ct. App., Lucas County 2019).

Evidence supported defendant's domestic violence and assault convictions because the victim, who was the child of defendant's paramour, testified that defendant grabbed the victim by the throat, lifted the victim by the neck, slammed the victim against an interior wall, slapped the victim in the face, and whipped the victim several times with a rubber-coated cord, striking the victim in the arms and legs. The State of Ohio also presented photographic exhibits of visible marks and bruising that the victim sustained and slight damage to the wall. State v. Faggs, 2018-Ohio-3643, 2018 Ohio App. LEXIS 3949 (Ohio Ct. App., Delaware County 2018), aff'd, 2020-Ohio-523, 159 Ohio St. 3d 420, 151 N.E.3d 593, 2020 Ohio LEXIS 453 (Ohio 2020).

Evidence supported defendant's convictions for assault because the video from a police officer's body camera showed that police officers had to struggle with defendant to place defendant in the back seat of a police car when defendant's hands were handcuffed in the front of defendant's body. Photos showed a scratch to the right side of one police officer's face and a bloody cut to the officer's right eyebrow, which the officer testified required stitches, and the bloody arm of another officer from where defendant bit the officer. State v. Howard, 2018-Ohio-973, 2018 Ohio App. LEXIS 1027 (Ohio Ct. App., Stark County 2018).

Defendant's conviction for assault was proper because the trial court reasonably rejected defendant's assertion that he acted in self-defense. The security officer and the cashier testified that the officer and defendant were involved in a physical altercation in front of the store and the officer testified to the progression of events and to defendant's resort to violence when the officer tried to escort defendant back into the store. State v. Coleman, 2018-Ohio-1951, 2018 Ohio App. LEXIS 2124 (Ohio Ct. App., Montgomery County 2018).

Defendant's conviction of Assault was supported with sufficient evidence because the record reflected that sufficient evidence was presented to the trial court, including the testimonies of the victim, the investigating police officer, and the victim's mother, which supported a finding that the visible injuries on the victim's forehead were inflicted by defendant's headbutting the victim, his daughter, subsequent to pressing his head up against her head in midst of a heated dispute. State/City of Toledo v. Pitts, 2018-Ohio-2031, 2018 Ohio App. LEXIS 2199 (Ohio Ct. App., Lucas County 2018); In re Adoption of X.A.F., 2018-Ohio-215, 2018 Ohio App. LEXIS 219 (Ohio Ct. App., Athens County 2018).

Defendant's conviction for assault on a police officer was supported by sufficient evidence and was not against the manifest weight of the evidence because the wife testified that all of the dogs were crated prior to the police arriving at the residence and that she advised the 911 dispatcher the dogs were crated but expressed her concern that defendant would let her dog loose because she knew her dog could be aggressive with strangers. A house mate testified that he heard defendant say the police were there, heard the dogs running in the hallway, heard defendant angrily calling the dog's name, and then heard banging doors opening, and finally a gunshot. State v. Schrader, 2018-Ohio-2634, 2018 Ohio App. LEXIS 2855 (Ohio Ct. App., Stark County 2018).

Defendant's conviction for assault was supported by the weight and the sufficiency of the evidence because she herself testified that she sought to discourage the four-year-old's inappropriate expectorations by intimidating him with the hot sauce bottle and telling him that the sauce would burn his mouth and expressed her belief that ingestion of hot sauce could harm him only if he were to swallow it or it came into contact with his eyes. The pain caused was sufficient to satisfy the "physical harm" element. State v. Taylor, 2018-Ohio-4048, 2018 Ohio App. LEXIS 4372 (Ohio Ct. App., Montgomery County 2018).

Defendant's convictions of assault and disorderly conduct were supported by sufficiency evident and not against the great weight of the evidence, as he approached the two victims in an aggressive and hostile manner, pushed both of them, then punched one of them in the face, and after being asked to stop his violent behavior prior to the assault, he continued his disorderly conduct and after the assault, grabbed a metal tire thumper out of his truck and was waiving it around at the one victim. State v. Gurley, 2018-Ohio-4152, 2018 Ohio App. LEXIS 4471 (Ohio Ct. App., Licking County 2018).

Weight and sufficiency of the evidence supported defendant's convictions for misdemeanor assault, as it was established by the State that he accidentally shot his minor niece and nephew in a reckless manner and caused them serious physical harm. State v. Curry, 2018-Ohio-4771, 2018 Ohio App. LEXIS 5089 (Ohio Ct. App., Cuyahoga County 2018).

Although there was testimony that defendant, a juvenile, did not intend to harm the victim and was merely attempting to free his arm when he hit the victim across the chin, evidence, including video, showing defendant struggling with the victim, making contact with her face, and violently pushing her towards to door was sufficient to support a conviction for assault. In re E.C., 2018-Ohio-5276, 2018 Ohio App. LEXIS 5567 (Ohio Ct. App., Clark County 2018).

Evidence was sufficient to support defendant's convictions for abduction, felonious assault, and having a weapon under disability because a rational trier of fact could have concluded that the State proved beyond a reasonable doubt that the gun found inside defendant's car was operable and that he knowingly shot the victim. State v. Robinson-Bey, 2018-Ohio-5224, 127 N.E.3d 417, 2018 Ohio App. LEXIS 5529 (Ohio Ct. App., Summit County 2018).

Sufficient evidence supported defendant's assault conviction because the neighbor testified that, when she was attempting to break up the fight between defendant and the first victim, defendant picked her up and threw her down on top of the first victim. She also stated that she was sore for days after the altercation. State v. Williams, 2017-Ohio-803, 2017 Ohio App. LEXIS 801 (Ohio Ct. App., Stark County 2017).

There was sufficient evidence establishing the elements of assault and the conviction was supported by the weight of the evidence because, although the victim denied that defendant hit him, several witnesses testified that defendant hit the victim. State v. Wauer, 2017-Ohio-1337, 2017 Ohio App. LEXIS 1357 (Ohio Ct. App., Trumbull County 2017).

Defendant's conviction for assault, in violation of R.C. 2903.13(A), was supported by the evidence because an officer testified that the victim, defendant's girlfriend, told him that defendant had pushed her out of his moving vehicle during an argument; when the officer encountered defendant in person, he admitted that he pushed the victim out of his vehicle. State v. Thomas, 2017-Ohio-5534, 2017 Ohio App. LEXIS 2592 (Ohio Ct. App., Franklin County 2017).

Evidence was sufficient to convict defendant of assault because the officer stated that he asked the victim to write out a statement; the officer stated that he did not prompt her to name defendant or tell her what to write on the form; the trial court heard and considered a recording of the victim's 911 call; and both the 911 call and the victim's written statement identified defendant as the person who knowingly caused physical harm to the victim. State v. Wilson, 2016-Ohio-7329, 2016 Ohio App. LEXIS 4176 (Ohio Ct. App., Montgomery County 2016).

Defendant's conviction for assault was proper because the State's evidence identifying defendant as the perpetrator of the assault, which consisted of the eyewitness testimony of a witness and the victim, as well as the testimony of two officers, was sufficient to overcome a motion for judgment of acquittal at the end of the State's case. In part, the physical injuries sustained by the victim were well documented by the evidence adduced at trial and the jury was free to discredit defendant's testimony that he acted in self-defense. State v. Stokes, 2016-Ohio-7520, 2016 Ohio App. LEXIS 4396 (Ohio Ct. App., Greene County 2016).

Sufficient evidence supported defendant's assault conviction, as surveillance video showed that when the victim exited a restroom defendant was in front of her, there was a struggle, the victim pushed past defendant to get away, and defendant then followed her and smacked her buttocks. State v. Wilson, 2016-Ohio-5895, 2016 Ohio App. LEXIS 3734 (Ohio Ct. App., Stark County 2016).

Trier of fact did not lose its way in finding that defendant committed the offense of assault on a peace officer where the officers testified that despite their warnings, defendant continually engaged in actions such as throwing his body to the ground, scratching, kicking, and contorting his body to make it extremely difficult for the officers; the trier of fact also heard evidence regarding the injuries the officers sustained as a result of defendant's behavior. State v. Whetstone, 2016-Ohio-6989, 2016 Ohio App. LEXIS 3841 (Ohio Ct. App., Lake County 2016).

Evidence supported defendant's assault conviction, such that it was not against the manifest weight of the evidence, as the State showed through testimony and surveillance video that she punched the victim in the face, which caused the victim physical harm that required stitches and dental surgery. State v. Jackson, 2016-Ohio-4835, 2016 Ohio App. LEXIS 2625 (Ohio Ct. App., Stark County 2016).

Defendant's assault conviction was not against the manifest weight of the evidence or supported by insufficient evidence because, by swinging at the police officer, defendant was trying to cause physical harm, even if no actual physical harm resulted. The testimony from the State's case supported the jury's verdict. State v. Protich, 2016-Ohio-1326, 2016 Ohio App. LEXIS 1209 (Ohio Ct. App., Franklin County 2016).

Defendant's assault conviction was proper because the evidence supported a finding that defendant knowingly caused harm to the officer. In part, an officer testified that defendant was verbally confrontational upon the officer's arrival at the apartment and the victim officer testified that defendant's foot connected solid with his head, causing a concussion. State v. Fort, 2016-Ohio-1242, 61 N.E.3d 864, 2016 Ohio App. LEXIS 1337 (Ohio Ct. App., Franklin County 2016).

Sufficient evidence supported defendant's assault conviction because there was evidence that the victim was the victim of an assault, defendant admitted to hitting the victim during his interview with the police, and defendant's girlfriend testified that defendant punched the victim hard enough to render him unconscious and then dragged the victim across the street. State v. Ashe, 2016-Ohio-136, 2016 Ohio App. LEXIS 117 (Ohio Ct. App., Montgomery County 2016).

Evidence was sufficient to support defendant's conviction for assault of a corrections officer based on evidence that while defendant was under custody at a county jail, he bit the corrections officer on the finger and caused him injury. State v. Penque, 2015-Ohio-4880, 2015 Ohio App. LEXIS 4737 (Ohio Ct. App., Lucas County 2015).

Defendant's assault conviction was not against the manifest weight of the evidence; while defendant told a different story, testimony from an eyewitness that defendant cursed at the severally disabled victim, sprayed air freshener in the victim's face, and pushed the victim backwards twice, pinning the victims legs backward established all of the elements of the crime. State v. Kiger, 2015-Ohio-3951, 2015 Ohio App. LEXIS 3821 (Ohio Ct. App., Belmont County 2015).

Defendant's convictions for assault and domestic violence were supported by sufficient evidence and not against the manifest weight of the evidence because the victim, who was defendant's sister, testified that defendant repeatedly punched her in the head, struck her with a bat, and pulled out her hair, photos that a police officer took after the incident show bruising the victim suffered, and the jury was entitled to believe the consistent testimony of the victim, the officer, and a witness. State v. Coffman, 2015-Ohio-3722, 2015 Ohio App. LEXIS 3625 (Ohio Ct. App., Lorain County 2015).

Defendant's conviction for misdemeanor assault was supported by the weight and sufficiency of the evidence, as there was credible and competent testimony from eyewitnesses who indicated that they observed defendant beating the victim. State v. Sherman, 2015-Ohio-3514, 2015 Ohio App. LEXIS 3418 (Ohio Ct. App., Licking County 2015).

There was sufficient evidence to support defendant's conviction for domestic violence, including the victim's testimony that defendant pushed her and she fell to the ground, causing her pain and leaving marks on her hands and legs. State v. Wolfe, 2015-Ohio-3455, 2015 Ohio App. LEXIS 3339 (Ohio Ct. App., Tuscarawas County 2015).

Evidence was sufficient to convict defendant of assault on a deputy and that defendant acted knowingly because, by punching the deputy in the face with a closed fist, defendant was aware her conduct would probably cause injury to the deputy. State v. Evans, 2015-Ohio-2298, 2015 Ohio App. LEXIS 2227 (Ohio Ct. App., Lake County 2015).

Evidence supported defendant's conviction for assault, as two law enforcement officers testified that defendant punched one of the officers in the head twice while defendant was struggling to resist arrest. State v. Bowlin, 2015-Ohio-1039, 2015 Ohio App. LEXIS 999 (Ohio Ct. App., Montgomery County 2015).

Defendant's conviction for assault on a corrections officer was supported by sufficient evidence because, while the trial court found that the evidence did not support the officer's testimony that he was brutally beaten, the trial court did conclude that the evidence was sufficient to demonstrate that defendant attempted to cause the officer physical harm. State v. Conner, 2015-Ohio-1860, 2015 Ohio App. LEXIS 1776 (Ohio Ct. App., Lucas County 2015).

Sufficient evidence supported defendant's complicity to commit assault conviction as: (1) he, an accomplice and the assailant (A) walked into a bar like they were going to get someone, defendant, A said something to the victim and the bar became tense and hostile; (2) the victim then tried to leave; (3) defendant, A, and the accomplice were outside, and defendant asked, "Who are we whooping?"; (4) A indicated the victim; and (5) defendant circled around the victim and said something, which drew the victim's attention, and then A punched the victim. State v. Fritz, 2015-Ohio-1496, 2015 Ohio App. LEXIS 1438 (Ohio Ct. App., Seneca County 2015).



Sufficient evidence supported defendant's conviction for assault based on testimony from various eyewitnesses to the incident, which was within the trial court's credibility determination. State v. Graham, 2014-Ohio-5174, 2014 Ohio App. LEXIS 5025 (Ohio Ct. App., Guernsey County 2014).

Evidence was sufficient to convict defendant of assault as defendant was apprehended immediately after the crime was committed, a "reverse track" by a police K-9 established that defendant had been near the victim's home, and the victim identified defendant as one of two perpetrators of the crime by his eyes, skin tone, height, clothes and hair. In re Q.E., 2014-Ohio-4445, 2014 Ohio App. LEXIS 4358 (Ohio Ct. App., Stark County 2014).

Evidence was sufficient to convict defendant of assault as defendant was apprehended immediately after the crime was committed, a "reverse track" by a police K-9 established that defendant had been near the victim's home, and the victim identified defendant as one of two perpetrators of the crime by his eyes, skin tone, height, clothes and hair. In re Q.E., 2014-Ohio-4445, 2014 Ohio App. LEXIS 4358 (Ohio Ct. App., Stark County 2014).

Sufficient evidence supported defendant's conviction for assault because the evidence permitted the jury reasonably to find that the teacher hit the victim's upper right chest, in the area of his shoulder, and the jury could reasonably have inferred that she intended to cause the victim physical harm in the form of pain. State v. Cox, 2014-Ohio-2201, 12 N.E.3d 466, 2014 Ohio App. LEXIS 2129 (Ohio Ct. App., Montgomery County 2014).

Evidence supported defendant's assault conviction, as he admitted he knowingly punched the victim in the mouth with his fist, and the State presented photographic evidence of the injuries; furthermore, both of the victim's roommates testified at trial and corroborated the victim's account of the incident. State v. Moses, 2014-Ohio-1748, 2014 Ohio App. LEXIS 1701 (Ohio Ct. App., Franklin County 2014).

There was sufficient evidence to support defendant's convictions for felonious assault and assault, as a reasonable jury could infer that the victims were "in the line of fire" when defendant discharged his weapon; moreover, defendant's act of pointing a gun at the victims, coupled with his threat, "I'm going to kill you," constituted sufficient evidence to convict him of felonious assault, regardless of whether he actually fired the weapon State v. Burns, 2014-Ohio-303, 2014 Ohio App. LEXIS 290 (Ohio Ct. App., Cuyahoga County 2014).

Where two eyewitnesses testified that defendant broke into a residence where his girlfriend was visiting a friend so that he could tell his girlfriend to go back home, both women were injured as a result of defendant's force. The evidence was sufficient to support his conviction for assault, because pictures of the victims' injuries were admitted into evidence. State v. Doyle, 2014-Ohio-285, 2014 Ohio App. LEXIS 274 (Ohio Ct. App., Fairfield County 2014).

Sufficient evidence supported defendant's conviction for assault because the victim testified that, during a scuffle, he was bitten multiple times and suffered some scratches, pictures of which were admitted into evidence, which satisfied the physical harm element of assault. There was also sufficient evidence that defendant acted knowingly because he never said that he felt unclear about what he was doing, nor did he testify to gaps in his memory or lack of control and, in fact, he claimed to have a clear plan as to why he went to his neighbor's household. State v. Martin, 2013-Ohio-5866, 2013 Ohio App. LEXIS 6163 (Ohio Ct. App., Mahoning County 2013).

Trial court did not lose its way or create a manifest miscarriage of injustice by finding defendant guilty of assault because the victim and three other bar patrons all testified that defendant struck the victim in the face with a beer glass and the trial court was in the best position to judge the credibility of the witnesses State v. Wolf, 2013-Ohio-5271, 2013 Ohio App. LEXIS 5472 (Ohio Ct. App., Butler County 2013).

Weight and sufficiency of the evidence supported defendant's conviction for assault because it was established through testimony from multiple witnesses that defendant and the victim were involved in a physical confrontation in a parking lot and that she sustained injuries as a result. State v. Jones, 2013-Ohio-5231, 2013 Ohio App. LEXIS 5442 (Ohio Ct. App., Montgomery County 2013).

Defendant's conviction for assault was supported by sufficient evidence showing that defendant acted knowingly given evidence that defendant was calling the victim a degrading ethnic slur when he smacked her, and there had been an earlier violent encounter between defendant and the victim and a history of "not peaceful" encounters between the two prior to the incident. State v. Pigg, 2013-Ohio-4722, 2013 Ohio App. LEXIS 4938 (Ohio Ct. App., Montgomery County 2013).

Defendant's convictions for assault, in violation of R.C. 2903.13(A), were not against the manifest weight of the evidence, as the evidence supported the determination that defendant assaulted two hospital employees, and that such actions were not accidental; the jury did not clearly lose its way and create a manifest miscarriage of justice. State v. Belcher, 2013-Ohio-1234, 2013 Ohio App. LEXIS 1133 (Ohio Ct. App., Montgomery County 2013).

Where the victim testified that after parking his vehicle, he and defendant began to argue when defendant made a disparaging comment about the victim parking in a handicap space, albeit legally, and after exiting separate stores, defendant continued his "tirade" and ultimately head-butted the victim, and two other witnesses corroborated the victim's testimony, there was sufficient evidence to convict defendant of assault. City of Berea v. McElroy, 2013-Ohio-1188, 2013 Ohio App. LEXIS 1084 (Ohio Ct. App., Cuyahoga County 2013).

Defendant's conviction for assault on a police officer was supported by the officer's testimony that he was sure that he had been punched in the face by defendant. State v. Lacy, 2013-Ohio-842, 2013 Ohio App. LEXIS 785 (Ohio Ct. App., Huron County 2013).

Sufficient evidence supported defendant's convictions for assault and resisting arrest because the evidence supported the finding that defendant knowingly attempted to cause physical harm to a police sergeant while in the performance of his official duties and that defendant recklessly or by force resisted his arrest. State v. Jones, 2013-Ohio-815, 2013 Ohio App. LEXIS 721 (Ohio Ct. App., Cuyahoga County 2013).

Assault conviction under R.C. 2903.13(A) was not against the manifest weight and sufficiency of the evidence when a neighbor saw defendant run out of the victim's house and through her gate before the victim called her to say defendant had beaten her; police found the victim's lip split open and blood throughout the house; and they noted that the gate was open. Furthermore, the jury was clearly able to give greater weight to some evidence, as defendant was found not guilty of a greater charge and of charges related to a previous incident. State v. Herring, 2012-Ohio-4788, 2012 Ohio App. LEXIS 4190 (Ohio Ct. App., Stark County 2012).

Defendant's convictions for assault, as well as for kidnapping and a firearm specification under R.C. 2905.01(A)(3) and 2941.145(A), were not against the manifest weight of the evidence, as there was testimony from the victim that defendant was argumentative and assaulted her, that he refused to let her leave the residence that they were in, and that he hit and punched her and threatened her life with both a gun and a machete. State v. Howell, 2012-Ohio-4349, 2012 Ohio App. LEXIS 3805 (Ohio Ct. App., Mahoning County 2012).

Sufficient evidence supported defendant's assault conviction because the evidence showed defendant knowingly kicked a police officer while trying to break free from the officer's grip. State v. Jackson, 2012-Ohio-4278, 2012 Ohio App. LEXIS 3755 (Ohio Ct. App., Cuyahoga County 2012).

State's evidence was sufficient to support defendant's convictions for domestic violence and assault as the recording of the 911 call in the case allowed the inference that the victim was stating that defendant had caused her injuries; the recording also contained defendant's statement that he threw the victim to the floor; and officers who responded to the scene observed a broken candle, overturned pottery in the kitchen, and blood on the top of a chair back. Although the court may not have given the same weight to the 911 tapes that the trial court did or may not have reached the same conclusions as the trial court about what was said therein, these issues were for the trier of fact to resolved. State v. Blakely, 2012-Ohio-3841, 2012 Ohio App. LEXIS 3391 (Ohio Ct. App., Montgomery County 2012).

Defendant's conviction for assault, in violation of R.C. 2903.13(A), was not against the weight of the evidence where the State's evidence demonstrated that defendant repeatedly punched and kicked the victim in the face, such that it showed that she knowingly caused him physical harm; the determination of the witnesses' credibility was within the jury's province. State v. Swindler, 2012-Ohio-3398, 2012 Ohio App. LEXIS 2988 (Ohio Ct. App., Clark County 2012).

Evidence was sufficient to support derfendant's convictions for aggravated assault, in violation of R.C. 2903.12, and assault on a school administrator, in violation of R.C. 2903.13(A), because testimony, by the victim and other eyewitnesses, was presented that defendant physically assaulted the athletic director of a high school during an argument after a basketball game. State v. Mundell, 2012-Ohio-3378, 2012 Ohio App. LEXIS 2975 (Ohio Ct. App., Delaware County 2012).

Sufficient evidence supported defendant's conviction for assault on a peace officer because the jury could have inferred from defendant's conduct and the surrounding circumstances that she "knowingly" kicked the officer. The officer and a paramedic testified that defendant leaned forward, raised her foot, and kicked the officer and the jury saw a videotape of the incident. State v. Standifer, 2012-Ohio-3132, 2012 Ohio App. LEXIS 2758 (Ohio Ct. App., Warren County 2012).

State's evidence was sufficient to prove that defendant committed domestic violence, assault, and unlawful restraint. The record showed that defendant pushed the victim onto the basement couch and held her down while he attempted to sexually assault her; that the victim's wrists, arms, hands, and legs were hurt by defendant's action; that the victim was scratched and sustained a rug burn during defendant's attack; and that defendant later wrestled her to the floor, held her arms so that she couldn't move, and sat on her until the police arrived. State v. Burns, 2012-Ohio-2536, 2012 Ohio App. LEXIS 2240 (Ohio Ct. App., Montgomery County 2012).

Defendant's conviction on a charge of assaulting a police officer was supported by the evidence and was not against the manifest weight of the evidence because a dashboard video camera showed defendant kicking a police officer. State v. Melton, 2012-Ohio-2386, 2012 Ohio App. LEXIS 2098 (Ohio Ct. App., Cuyahoga County 2012).

Juvenile court did not err because the 90-day sentence was imposed for the assault under R.C. 2903.13 and not for the parole violation in violation of R.C. 2152.02(F)(2). Appellant juvenile admitted to both the parole violation and the assault. In re K.T., 2012-Ohio-2228, 2012 Ohio App. LEXIS 1959 (Ohio Ct. App., Lucas County 2012).

Defendant's assault conviction was supported by sufficient evidence as the jury could find that defendant at least took a substantial step, pursuant to R.C. 2923.02(A), in a course of conduct planned to culminate in the commission of assault, in that witnesses testified that defendant angrily confronted the victim, backed her up against railing, and made contact with her throat. The evidence showed that defendant acted knowingly and that he attempted to cause physical harm to the victim had the deputy not intervened; thus, defendant's motion for acquittal was properly denied. State v. Blair, 2012-Ohio-1706, 2012 Ohio App. LEXIS 1499 (Ohio Ct. App., Stark County 2012).

Defendant did not show that the verdicts for two counts of assault, in violation of R.C. 2903.13, as lesser included offenses, and one count of retaliation, in violation of R.C. 2921.05(B), were against the manifest weight of the evidence because the victim, although the victim's testimony was inconsistent, and police officers testified as to domestic disputes between defendant and the victim, both of whom were mentally challenged, and the extent of the victim's injuries in the disputes, and photographs of the victim's injuries were entered into evidence. Furthermore, the trial court took into account the evidentiary conflicts and credibility issues, and it could not be said that the trial court lost its way in convicting defendant. State v. Poole, 2012-Ohio-1534, 2012 Ohio App. LEXIS 1347 (Ohio Ct. App., Cuyahoga County 2012).

State proved each and every element of the crime of assault because defendant conceded that he assaulted the victim by testifying at trial that he punched him three times and the victim's testimony that he was trying to close the door and start the car to get away undermined defendant's theory that he was reaching for a weapon and thus acted in self-defense. State v. Picklesimer, 2012-Ohio-1282, 2012 Ohio App. LEXIS 1104 (Ohio Ct. App., Pickaway County 2012).

State's evidence was sufficient to sustain defendant's conviction for R.C. 2903.13(A). The victim unequivocally testified that defendant confronted her in the hallway of the father's apartment building and struck her in the face and that defendant sprayed her with mace, which caused her to fall down. the victim testified that when she fell to the ground. State v. Peterson, 2012-Ohio-735, 2012 Ohio App. LEXIS 632 (Ohio Ct. App., Montgomery County 2012).

Sufficient evidence supported defendant's convictions because it established that defendant knowingly committed assault against a peace officer and forcefully resisted a lawful arrest. When a police officer attempted to stop defendant from charging her father, she cursed and spit at the officer and attempted to punch him, she continued to assault the officer as he tried to handcuff her, and, after being placed in handcuffs, she was spitting, kicking, and biting at the officers; photographs were introduced depicting saliva on the officer's uniform, a scratch on his neck, and bite marks on his arm. State v. Whitby, 2012-Ohio-264, 2012 Ohio App. LEXIS 210 (Ohio Ct. App., Cuyahoga County 2012).

There was insufficient evidence to support defendant's conviction for felonious assault because the State failed to present sufficient evidence that the victim suffered serious physical harm since evidence that the victim was bleeding from the head was not sufficient to prove he suffered serious physical harm, nor was testimony that he was bleeding and stumbling. However, there was sufficient evidence to support a conviction for the lesser included offense of simple assault. State v. Addison, 2012-Ohio-260, 2012 Ohio App. LEXIS 222 (Ohio Ct. App., Cuyahoga County 2012).

Although there was insufficient evidence to support defendant's conviction for felonious assault because the State failed to prove a causal nexus between a fight and the blunt force trauma that the State claimed was the result of that fight, there was sufficient evidence to support a conviction for the lesser included offense of simple assault. State v. Addison, 2012-Ohio-260, 2012 Ohio App. LEXIS 222 (Ohio Ct. App., Cuyahoga County 2012).

There was substantial evidence upon which a jury could reasonably have concluded, beyond a reasonable doubt, that defendant knowingly caused or attempted to cause physical harm to a victim where a witness heard the defendant and the victim arguing, the victim screamed, "stop it," and the victim had blood on her shirt when she exited the house. Thus, defendant's assault conviction was not against the manifest weight of the evidence. Accordingly, there was also sufficient evidence to support the conviction. State v. Roulette, 2011-Ohio-6993, 2011 Ohio App. LEXIS 5698 (Ohio Ct. App., Scioto County 2011).

Weight and sufficiency of the evidence supported defendant's conviction for assault on a peace officer, in violation of R.C. 2903.13(A) and (C)(3), as a police officer's testimony that defendant spit on him and kicked him in the head was deemed credible. City of Toledo v. Young, 2011-Ohio-2817, 2011 Ohio App. LEXIS 2403 (Ohio Ct. App., Lucas County 2011).

Evidence was sufficient to support defendant's convictions for assault of a peace officer, in violation of R.C. 2903.13(A), and obstructing official business, in violation of R.C. 2921.31(A), because, during a pretrial hearing in a criminal proceeding, defendant was found in contempt of court when defendant refused to follow an order of the trial judge and injured a deputy when the deputy attempted to place handcuffs on defendant and to remove defendant from the courtroom. State v. Birinyi, 2011-Ohio-6257, 2011 Ohio App. LEXIS 5134 (Ohio Ct. App., Cuyahoga County 2011).

Defendant's convictions for negligent homicide, negligent assault, assault, and failure to stop after an accident were not against the manifest weight of the evidence as the evidence showed that defendant admitted to smoking marijuana, taking Valium, and drinking alcohol on the night of the incident; that defendant admitted driving the truck with her boyfriend running alongside; and that defendant admitted to another witness that she had gotten into a fight with her boyfriend and that he was hanging onto the truck for two blocks before he fell off. State v. Zimmerman, 2011-Ohio-6156, 2011 Ohio App. LEXIS 5035 (Ohio Ct. App., Cuyahoga County 2011).

Sufficient evidence supported defendant's conviction for assault in violation of R.C. 2903.13(A) and resisting arrest in violation of R.C. 2921.33(A), because two police officers testified that defendant kicked one of the officers when they responded to a domestic violence call at defendant's home. State v. Chapple, 2011-Ohio-5670, 2011 Ohio App. LEXIS 4644 (Ohio Ct. App., Cuyahoga County 2011).

Defendant's assault conviction was supported by the evidence, as a deputy testified that in the process of serving a court order to remove the children from defendant's home, defendant lunged forward and hit the deputy with both hands and knocked him three feet back down the stairs of the porch; this testimony was sufficient to prove the elements of the offense. State v. Daniels, 2011-Ohio-5603, 2011 Ohio App. LEXIS 4575 (Ohio Ct. App., Scioto County 2011).

Defendant's conviction for assault of a police officer, in violation of R.C. 2903.13(A) and (C)(3), was not against the manifest weight of the evidence, as defendant punched a police officer who had repeatedly identified himself as such; further, his claim of self-defense did not absolve him of liability in the situation. State v. Evans, 2011-Ohio-5267, 2011 Ohio App. LEXIS 4335 (Ohio Ct. App., Cuyahoga County 2011).

Sufficient evidence supported appellant's assault conviction because there was evidence that could have convinced the average fact finder beyond a reasonable doubt that he knowingly caused or attempted to cause physical harm to the deputy. The deputy testified that, after he opened the door to the holding cell, appellant punched him in the face and that, after he pinned appellant to the wall, appellant continued punching him and tried to get his gun out of its holster. State v. Leaver, 2011-Ohio-4068, 2011 Ohio App. LEXIS 3409 (Ohio Ct. App., Summit County 2011).

Weight and sufficiency of the evidence supported defendant's conviction for assault on a peace officer, in violation of R.C. 2903.13(A) and (C)(3), as a police officer's testimony that defendant spit on him and kicked him in the head was deemed credible. City of Toledo v. Young, 2011-Ohio-2817, 2011 Ohio App. LEXIS 2403 (Ohio Ct. App., Lucas County 2011).

Defendant's misdemeanor assault conviction under R.C. 2903.13(A) was supported by evidence showing that defendant swung her arm toward the victim and scratched his neck, allowing a finding that she caused physical injury to the victim and that she acted knowingly given the nature in which she manipulated her arm around her boyfriend, who was standing in front of her, in the victim's direction. Thus, defendant's motion for acquittal was properly denied. State v. Cross-Necas, 2011-Ohio-2591, 2011 Ohio App. LEXIS 2212 (Ohio Ct. App., Portage County 2011).

Evidence was sufficient to sustain an assault conviction because the uniformed officer described an altercation in which defendant "came at" him multiple times and on one occasion slammed the officer to the floor, and the officer testified to suffering strains, sprains, and bruising from the altercation. The State showed beyond a reasonable doubt that defendant knowingly caused or attempted to cause physical harm to a peace officer in the performance of his official duties. State v. Bai, 2011-Ohio-2206, 2011 Ohio App. LEXIS 1887 (Ohio Ct. App., Butler County 2011).

Evidence supported defendant's conviction of assault on a peace officer in violation of R.C. 2903.13, as corrections officers testified that they suffered physical harm as a result of defendant knowingly hitting and kicking them during an altercation while removing defendant from defendant's cell. State v. Bernhart, 2011-Ohio-2139, 2011 Ohio App. LEXIS 1815 (Ohio Ct. App., Richland County 2011).

There was sufficient evidence that defendant recklessly caused serious physical harm to the two police officers for his assault on a peace officer convictions; because the officers were transported by ambulance to the hospital, where they were treated for their injuries, the jury could reasonably have inferred that the force exerted on the officers caused serious physical harm. The evidence demonstrates "some temporary, substantial incapacity" to satisfy the serious physical harm element. State

v. Littlejohn, 2011-Ohio-2035, 2011 Ohio App. LEXIS 1733 (Ohio Ct. App., Cuyahoga County 2011).

Weight of the evidence supported defendant's assault conviction because, based on the evidence, a reasonable jury could have found that defendant knowingly aided and abetted a group that intentionally caused harm to the victim. Defendant was identified by the victim as a member of the group that pushed their way into the victim's home and assaulted her, the victim testified that she was injured as a result of the group attack, and it was clear that the intention animating the actions of the group was to cause injury to the victim. State v. Greene, 2011-Ohio-1283, 2011 Ohio App. LEXIS 1113 (Ohio Ct. App., Montgomery County 2011).

Defendant's convictions for obstructing official business and assault were not against the manifest weight of the evidence because, while investigating a gas leak, defendant forcefully, with both hands, pushed a firefighter out of the kitchen and he suffered an abrasion to his head as a result of his fight with defendant. Several firefighters and police officers testified to the altercation that occurred in the hallway of the apartment complex between defendant and at least three firefighters. State v. Hunter, 2011-Ohio-1068, 2011 Ohio App. LEXIS 974 (Ohio Ct. App., Cuyahoga County 2011).

Evidence was sufficient to support defendant's convictions of assault on police officers because although there was evidence showing that defendant had been drinking prior to the assaults, the record did not support the conclusion that he was incapable of acting knowingly. The evidence showed that defendant was initially compliant with the officers' requests to go over the car and place his hands on the bumper bar and he told them about the knife; then, while the officer began to handcuff him, defendant suddenly became combative and broke away from the officers. State v. Millan, 2011-Ohio-331, 2011 Ohio App. LEXIS 271 (Ohio Ct. App., Cuyahoga County 2011).

Defendant's conviction for assault on a peace officer was supported by evidence showing that defendant knew that a police officer's hand was under an open window in her house when she slammed it shut and that she knew that hurting the officer's hand was a likely consequence of her slamming the window shut. State v. Cornette, 2010-Ohio-3647, 2010 Ohio App. LEXIS 3110 (Ohio Ct. App., Montgomery County 2010).

There was sufficient evidence regarding each element of the crime of assault because the victim's wife testified that she saw defendant punch her husband in the face repeatedly while he lay unconscious on the floor of the bar. The victim testified that he received injuries to his face and eyes from the beating. State v. Burnham, 2010-Ohio-3275, 2010 Ohio App. LEXIS 2777 (Ohio Ct. App., Mahoning County 2010).

Conviction for assault, in violation of R.C. 2903.13(A), was not against the manifest weight of the evidence as the fact finder could have reasonably concluded that defendant was not acting in self-defense when defendant, following an altercation in a parking lot with two people, rear-ended with defendant's car the car the other people were driving as defendant pursued them as they fled from the parking lot. State v. Gates, 2010-Ohio-2994, 2010 Ohio App. LEXIS 2490 (Ohio Ct. App., Summit County 2010).

Defendant's assault conviction under R.C. 2903.13(A) was not against the manifest weight of the evidence as the evidence sufficiently showed that defendant knowingly kicked the victim in the face and caused him physical harm, including swelling, bruising, and cuts requiring multiple stitches. The results of the polygraph examinations, showing no physiological indication of deception on the part of the victim while showing an indication of deception by defendant, corroborated the victim's testimony. State v. Bekelesky, 2010-Ohio-2198, 2010 Ohio App. LEXIS 1805 (Ohio Ct. App., Summit County 2010).

Delinquency adjudication of a juvenile was not against the manifest weight of the evidence because the juvenile acted knowingly, under R.C. 2901.22(B), in assaulting a sheriff's deputy, in violation of R.C. 2903.13(A) and 2903.13(C)(3), by kicking the deputy in the shin during a struggle in a courtroom between the juvenile and sheriff's deputies. The seventeen-year old juvenile would have been aware that a kick directed to the front part of another person's shin would probably have caused that person to experience significant pain; thus, even if, for whatever reason, the kick to the deputy's shin was not, in fact, painful, it was an intentional act likely to cause significant pain, and therefore constituted a knowing attempt to cause physical harm to the deputy. In re G.S., 2010-Ohio-2132, 2010 Ohio App. LEXIS 1762 (Ohio Ct. App., Montgomery County 2010).

Conviction for assault against a peace officer was not against the manifest weight of the evidence because (1) defendant was handcuffed and placed in the back of a police cruiser following a domestic disturbance; (2) defendant banging defendant's head against the glass partition separating the front seat of the cruiser from the passenger compartment; (3) a police detective leaned into the cruiser and placed the detective's hand on defendant's forearm to restrain defendant; (4) defendant banged defendant's head into the partition again, smashing the detective's hand against the glass; (5) defendant, who was wearing steel-towed work shoes, then leaned back on the seat and kicked both legs out, striking the detective in the chest and knocking the detective out of the door; (6) defendant got out of the cruiser; (7) the detective had to taser defendant twice and get assistance to restrain defendant; and (8) defendant was taken to a hospital for examination, but continued to struggle with the police and EMS technicians. State v. Miller, 2010-Ohio-2097, 2010 Ohio App. LEXIS 1714 (Ohio Ct. App., Cuyahoga County 2010).

Sufficient evidence supported defendant's conviction for assault on a peace officer because, while a coworker of defendant may have been motivated to share defendant's story with the police by his personal circumstances at the time, his account of events as reported to him by defendant were consistent with the patrolman's account of the incident. Further, the coworker was aware that defendant sold his four wheeler and purchased a small red and white minibike soon after the incident and, shortly thereafter, defendant was seen fleeing from the police on a red and white minibike; a police officer was able to identify defendant in court as the driver of the minibike. State v. Kienzle, 2010-Ohio-2045, 2010 Ohio App. LEXIS 1677 (Ohio Ct. App., Tuscarawas County 2010).

Defendant's conviction for assault was supported by evidence showing that defendant knowingly caused or attempted to cause physical harm to the victim, in that the evidence showed that thé victim reported to an emergency room nurse that, after defendant requested sex, he punched her in the left check and jaw, held her down, and pulled her hair. State v. Vanderhorst, 2010-Ohio-1856, 2010 Ohio App. LEXIS 1536 (Ohio Ct. App., Cuyahoga County 2010).

In a prosecution for assault, although defendant and the victim both testified at trial that defendant had not injured the victim, the State's evidence was sufficient to prove that defendant had, in fact, assaulted the victim in her car as the victim acknowledged that she was not injured prior to picking up defendant from a bar, that she had various injuries upon reaching her destination four blocks away, and that she had reported to the police and the prosecutor that defendant had assaulted her. State v. Cole, 2010-Ohio-1608, 2010 Ohio App. LEXIS 1339 (Ohio Ct. App., Miami County 2010).

In an assault case, a trial court did not err by denying defendant's motion for an acquittal under Crim.R. 29 because the State presented sufficient evidence from which a jury could have concluded, beyond a reasonable doubt, that defendant knowingly committed the offense of assault where he grabbed the victim's throat and pulled on the victim's arm hand during a dispute over entering a residence; moreover, the evidence established the injuries to the victim's wrist and back. Additionally, there was no testimony or evidence that defendant had reasonable grounds to believe and an honest belief, even though mistaken, that some force was necessary to defend himself against the imminent use of unlawful force by the elderly victim, the testimony of one witness was sufficient to prove a fact, and the trial court obviously found the victim to be more credible. State v. Wilson, 2010-Ohio-1394, 2010 Ohio App. LEXIS 1193 (Ohio Ct. App., Fairfield County 2010).

Defendant's convictions for assault and unlawful restraint as he forced the victim to get into his vehicle against her will, depriving her of her liberty. Moreover, defendant forced the victim to the vehicle by twisting her arm behind her back and dragging her to the vehicle by her hair. State v. Rohm, 2010-Ohio-1240, 2010 Ohio App. LEXIS 1030 (Ohio Ct. App., Greene County 2010).

Sufficient evidence supported defendant's conviction for assault on a peace officer because defendant punched the officer in the face, resulting in damage to the officer's eyeglasses and a scratch to his nose. It could have been inferred that, by punching the officer in the face, defendant knew that harm to the officer was a reasonably foreseeable result. State v. Totty, 2010-Ohio-1234, 2010 Ohio App. LEXIS 1029 (Ohio Ct. App., Montgomery County 2010).

Despite minor inconsistencies in the testimony of the State's witnesses, defendant's assault conviction was not against the manifest weight of evidence. The State's witnesses were consistent in their description of the assault perpetrated on the victim, and it was within the province of the trial court to determine whether their testimony was worthy of belief. State v. Hightower, 2010-Ohio-1055, 2010 Ohio App. LEXIS 863 (Ohio Ct. App., Cuyahoga County 2010).

There was sufficient evidence to support defendant's assault conviction because the neighbors observed defendant chasing the victim around the apartment building. One neighbor saw him grab the victim by the back of her neck and pull her down and the jury saw photographs depicting the injuries. State v. Poole, 2010-Ohio-460, 2010 Ohio App. LEXIS 370 (Ohio Ct. App., Stark County 2010).

Defendant's convictions for assault and involuntary manslaughter were supported by sufficient evidence as defendant admitted to punching the victim in the head, and he told detectives that he believed he knocked the victim out when he punched him. From this evidence, the jury could have reasonably found that defendant acted "knowingly," within the meaning of R.C. 2901.22, in that defendant was aware that punching the victim in the head could cause him harm. State v. Dykas, 2010-Ohio-359, 185 Ohio App. 3d 763, 925 N.E.2d 685, 2010 Ohio App. LEXIS 290 (Ohio Ct. App., Cuyahoga County 2010).

Evidence was sufficient to sustain a conviction for assault on the grounds of a correction facility because the victim testified that he went into defendant's cell at the county jail to talk with him. When the victim was leaving the cell, defendant came at him from the side and pushed him into the wall where he hit his head; the victim sustained a head injury, including a bruise on the brain, dizziness, and vertigo, and defendant admitted that he pushed and hit the victim. State v. McPherson, 2010-Ohio-64, 2010 Ohio App. LEXIS 49 (Ohio Ct. App., Cuyahoga County 2010).

Evidence was sufficient to convict defendant of assault of a police officer, because a rational trier of fact could have found beyond a reasonable doubt that defendant knowingly caused or attempted to cause physical harm to the officer, a rational trier of fact could have found beyond a reasonable doubt that the officer did not engage in the use of excessive or unnecessary force at the time he confronted defendant and attempted to stop the fight, and that defendant knew or had good reason to believe that the officer was an authorized police officer engaged in the performance of his duties at the time. State v. Prescott, 2010-Ohio-6048, 190 Ohio App. 3d 702, 943 N.E.2d 1092, 2010 Ohio App. LEXIS 5079 (Ohio Ct. App., Wood County 2010).

Weight and sufficiency of the evidence supported defendant's convictions for domestic violence and assault, in violation of R.C. 2919.25(A) and 2903.13(A), as she dug her fingernails into her husband's arm after he dropped their children off at defendant's home; the injuries were sufficient "physical harm" under R.C. 2901.01(A)(3), the husband was clearly a "family or household member," and her claim of self-defense was not deemed credible. State v. Foster-Jones, 2010-Ohio-5758, 2010 Ohio App. LEXIS 4851 (Ohio Ct. App., Montgomery County 2010).

Evidence was sufficient to convict defendant juvenile of assault upon a teacher, because circumstantial evidence supported the reasonable inference that defendant knowingly attempted to cause physical harm by pushing the teacher aside, and one could reasonably infer that defendant sought out a physical confrontation with the teacher, when before defendant pushed the teacher, there was a verbal confrontation that included profanities and very belligerent behavior. In re D.S., 2010-Ohio-5694, 2010 Ohio App. LEXIS 4789 (Ohio Ct. App., Adams County 2010).

Although the juvenile argued that his delinquency adjudication was against the manifest weight of the evidence, defendant was found delinquent for conduct which, if he were an adult, would constitute assault, in violation of R.C. 2903.13(A), and the court found that although the versions of exactly how the victim was injured varied somewhat, they were not materially inconsistent. The inconsistencies were minor, reconcilable, and, ultimately, not of any fundamental importance in the case, and in both versions, the victim and her mother could reasonably be determined to be in each other's view, to one extent or another; therefore, the appellate court could not say that the judge clearly lost his way or created such a manifest miscarriage of justice that defendant's adjudication of delinquency based on the offense of assault should have been reversed. In re T.T., 2010-Ohio-5649, 2010 Ohio App. LEXIS 4757 (Ohio Ct. App., Huron County 2010).

Evidence was sufficient to sustain assault convictions because defendant did not dispute that the officers were in uniform and were in performance of their official duties, and the officers clearly described how defendant resisted arrest, reacted combatively to the uniformed officers' presence, and proceeded to strike them. State v. Dixon, 2010-Ohio-5541, 2010 Ohio App. LEXIS 4671 (Ohio Ct. App., Stark County 2010).

Although the testimony by a clinical supervisor about events that occurred prior to 1994 should have been excluded as the events were too remote in time in time to the charged offenses to be relevant or admissible under either Evid.R. 404(B) or R.C. 2945.59, the error was harmless because there was sufficient evidence to convict defendant of assault and sexual imposition exclusive of the improper other acts testimony. The events to which the social worker testified had occurred only two years prior and, like the incident with the instant victim, involved defendant's spanking and inappropriate touching of young boys. City of Middleburg Heights v. Bunt, 2010-Ohio-5479, 2010 Ohio App. LEXIS 4596 (Ohio Ct. App., Cuyahoga County 2010).

Evidence supported defendant's conviction for assaulting a police officer, as two officers testified that defendant "head-butted" an officer, and the testimony from all the witnesses, including defendant and defendant's son, demonstrated defendant's belligerent behavior during the course of the incident. State v. Robinson, 2010-Ohio-5245, 2010 Ohio App. LEXIS 4429 (Ohio Ct. App., Cuyahoga County 2010).

Evidence was sufficient to sustain defendant's assault conviction because the victim testified that she and defendant got into an argument about the victim's smoking, defendant hit her twice, and the court found that the photos of the victim "absolutely showed injury" and demonstrated "striking," not "holding." State v. Marshall, 2010-Ohio-5160, 191 Ohio App. 3d 444, 946 N.E.2d 762, 2010 Ohio App. LEXIS 4357 (Ohio Ct. App., Montgomery County 2010).

Sufficient evidence supported defendant's assault conviction because the evidence showed that defendant, who weighed 250 pounds, forcefully slammed the victim, who was described as being of slight build, into a wall and held her there until someone else intervened and hit the victim during a "scuffle" over a child. A reasonable finder of fact could have inferred from the evidence regarding defendant's behavior that he acted knowingly—meaning, that he knew that his conduct would probably cause the victim injury or physiological impairment, regardless of its gravity or duration; the element of physical harm was also established. State v. Mustaine, 2010-Ohio-4922, 2010 Ohio App. LEXIS 4168 (Ohio Ct. App., Montgomery County 2010).

Defendant's assault conviction was supported by sufficient evidence as the victim testified that defendant punched her on her arm and chest with his fist, and a police officer observed a light scratch and a red mark on the victim's forearm and back. This evidence was sufficient to show that defendant knowingly caused physical harm to the victim. State v. White, 2010-Ohio-4537, 2010 Ohio App. LEXIS 3834 (Ohio Ct. App., Montgomery County 2010).

Definite testimony of two police officers that they observed defendant throwing water balloons was sufficient for any reasonable trier of fact to conclude that defendant was in fact throwing water balloons, in vioaltion of Athens, Ohio, City Code 13.02.01(A), a provision identical to R.C. 2903.13. State v. Weiss, 2010-Ohio-4509, 2010 Ohio App. LEXIS 3843 (Ohio Ct. App., Athens County 2010).

Evidence was sufficient to support defendant's conviction for assault, in violation of R.C. 2903.13(A) because defendant, who was a nurse at a hospital, admitted that defendant put defendant's hand on the jaw of the victim, who was a patient at the hospital, and pushed the victim backward. Additionally, witnesses saw a mark on the victim's neck as a result and heard the victim complain that defendant was choking the victim. City of Westlake v. Filiaggi, 2010-Ohio-4481, 2010 Ohio App. LEXIS 3778 (Ohio Ct. App., Cuyahoga County 2010).

Defendants' convictions for two counts of robbery, in violation of R.C. 2911.02(A)(2), and one count of assault, in violation of R.C. 2903.13, were affirmed, despite defendant's defense of mistaken identity, because one of the victims and an eyewitness testified that defendant, who was in a group of people who accosted the victims, punched the other victim in the face and fled on a bicycle which was taken from the victims. The guilty verdicts therefore were not against the manifest weight of the evidence because the fact-finder did not lose its way in determining that it was defendant who broke the nose of one of the victims and stole one of the bicycles. State v. Kimbro, 2010-Ohio-4111, 2010 Ohio App. LEXIS 3489 (Ohio Ct. App., Cuyahoga County 2010).

Defendant's convictions for assault and theft were supported by evidence showing that defendant ran up and started hitting the victim after defendant's brother tackled the victim, that the victim was visibly injured from the assault, that the victim observed his wallet in defendant's hand, and that money was taken from his wallet. While defendant argued that his motion for acquittal should have been granted because the witnesses who were present during the incident all had credibility issues, the determination of credibility was for the jury to decide. State v. Simpson, 2010-Ohio-4045, 2010 Ohio App. LEXIS 3416 (Ohio Ct. App., Montgomery County 2010).

Defendant's conviction for assault on a peace officer was not against the manifest weight of the evidence as the evidence sowed that, as the officer was trying to arrest defendant for disorderly conduct, defendant punched the officer in the side of the face and the chest and also kicked him in the leg. State v. Corbin, 2010-Ohio-3819, 2010 Ohio App. LEXIS 3237 (Ohio Ct. App., Fayette County 2010).

Conviction for misdemeanor assault, in violation of R.C. 2903.13(A), was affirmed because the evidence supported the conviction, despite defendant's claim of self-defense, as defendant pulled the victim, who was defendant's former girlfriend, from defendant's car when they arrived at defendant's home from a bar where they had been drinking, threw the victim to the ground, and repeatedly kicked the victim. Furthermore, the emergency room physician that examined the victim shortly after the incident, testified that the victim sustained numerous bruises to the victim's arms and torso, consistent with blunt force trauma. State v. Hamrick, 2010-Ohio-3796, 2010 Ohio App. LEXIS 3223 (Ohio Ct. App., Lorain County 2010).

In an assault case, the trial court did not err by denying defendant's motion for judgment of acquittal because the verdict was not against the manifest weight of the evidence; the victim testified that defendant caused her facial injuries in the manner alleged, and photographs of her facial injuries were admitted into evidence. The victim's testimony also established the knowing element of the assault offense, given that defendant repeatedly and deliberately stomped on her face during the altercation. City of Columbus v. McDaniel, 2010-Ohio-3744, 2010 Ohio App. LEXIS 3186 (Ohio Ct. App., Franklin County 2010).

Convictions for assault arising from an incident at a bar where defendant allegedly hit two victims were supported by sufficient evidence and were not against the manifest weight of the evidence; defendant's argument that the testimony of the State's witnesses was inconsistent and incredible was rejected because that determination was for the trier of fact. Moreover, the appellate court was unable say after reviewing the record that the trier of fact lost its way and created such a manifest miscarriage of justice that it was required to reverse the convictions and order a new trial. State v. Blair, 2010-Ohio-6310, 2010 Ohio App. LEXIS 5294 (Ohio Ct. App., Hamilton County 2010).

There was sufficient evidence to support defendant's convictions of involuntary manslaughter and assault. It was a foreseeable consequence for someone to fall to the ground after being punched in the head: State v. Dykas, 2010-Ohio-359, 185 Ohio App. 3d 763, 925 N.E.2d 685, 2010 Ohio App. LEXIS 290 (Ohio Ct. App., Cuyahoga County 2010).

Evidence supported defendant's convictions for assault, in violation of R.C. 2903.13(B), and domestic violence, in violation of R.C. 2919.25(A), because (1) defendant lived in the downstairs apartment of a duplex; (2) defendant's granddaughter and the granddaughter's baby were staying with the resident of the upstairs apartment; (3) when defendant's daughter, who was the granddaughter's mother, came to the duplex to pick up the granddaughter and the baby to take them to the daughter's house, the resident and the daughter began to argue; (4) defendant went upstairs, joined in the argument, and, according to the daughter and the granddaughter, pushed the daughter on the bed, punched the daughter, kneed the daughter, choked the daughter with a necklace, and punched the daughter in the eye; and (5) the daughter suffered a black eye, the right side of the daughter's face was swollen and bruised, the daughter's neck was scratched and sore, and the daughter had bruises on the daughter's thighs and buttocks. State v. Plemmons-Greene, 2010-Ohio-655, 2010 Ohio App. LEXIS 541 (Ohio Ct. App., Cuyahoga County 2010).

Conviction for assault of a peace officer, in violation of R.C. 2903.13(A), was not against the manifest weight of the evidence and was therefore supported by sufficient evidence because (1) an off duty sheriff's deputy heard defendant and a woman arguing on the sidewalk outside the deputy's apartment in the early morning hours; (2) the deputy left the apartment, wearing gym shorts, and showed the deputy's badge to defendant and the woman; and (3 ) when the deputy told defendant and the woman to quiet down and leave the area, defendant at first walked away and then turned and assaulted the deputy. State v. Ford, 2009-Ohio-6046, 2009 Ohio App. LEXIS 5072 (Ohio Ct. App., Butler County 2009).



Sufficient evidence supported defendant's conviction for assaulting a police officer because the evidence supported the finding that defendant caused serious physical harm to the officer, who suffered temporary, serious disfigurement to his lower lip and physical harm that involved any degree of prolonged pain. The officer testified that defendant struck him in the face with his fist, causing him to fall, that the other officers with him noticed that he was bleeding from the nose and mouth, and that he required three stitches to close a deep laceration that stretched the entire height of his inner lower lip. State v. Greene, 2009-Ohio-2518, 2009 Ohio App. LEXIS 2239 (Ohio Ct. App., Lorain County 2009).

Defendant's conviction for misdemeanor assault was not against the weight of the evidence as the victim clearly identified defendant at trial as the man who held onto his foot and twisted his leg while the others beat him. While defendant offered alibi testimony, the trier of fact was in the best position to weigh the credibility of witnesses, and the court could not conclude that the jury's verdict led to a manifest miscarriage of justice. State v. Chadwick, 2009-Ohio-2472, 2009 Ohio App. LEXIS 2086 (Ohio Ct. App., Knox County 2009).

Assault conviction under R.C. 2903.13 was supported by the evidence as evidence that defendant punched the victim up to five times, causing injuries to his head and arm, allowing a finding that defendant had caused physical harm to another within the meaning of R.C. 2901.01(A)(3). State v. Dawson, 2009-Ohio-2331, 2009 Ohio App. LEXIS 1980 (Ohio Ct. App., Licking County 2009).

Where defendant swung at a police officer who was trying to arrest him, such conduct demonstrated that defendant acted knowingly pursuant to R.C. 2901.22(B) for purposes of finding sufficient evidence to support his assault conviction, in violation of R.C. 2903.13(A); although the victim, a police officer, conceded that his broken finger could have been caused by falling or punching defendant, defendant's conduct still constituted an assault. State v. Smith, 2009-Ohio-2166, 2009 Ohio App. LEXIS 1816 (Ohio Ct. App., Franklin County 2009).

Defendant's assault conviction was not against the manifest weight of the evidence because the testimony at trial clearly showed that defendant tried to cause physical harm to the officers who were trying to arrest him by head butting them and by kicking them. The testimony clearly demonstrated all of the elements of assault on a police officer and thus, there was sufficient evidence. State v. Kegg, 2009-Ohio-2150, 2009 Ohio App. LEXIS 1803 (Ohio Ct. App., Franklin County 2009).

Defendant's convictions for assault on a peace officer and resisting arrest were not against the manifest weight of the evidence, as he was identified as the perpetrator of an assault on a train passenger by other passengers, witnesses observed him in a physical altercation with a transit officer who attempted to investigate the situation, and the jury's determination that defendant was the initial aggressor was one of credibility which was entitled to deference; the transit officer had a reasonable suspicion of criminal activity that justified the investigative stop of defendant. State v. McShane, 2009-Ohio-3455, 2009 Ohio App. LEXIS 2979 (Ohio Ct. App., Cuyahoga County 2009).

Defendant's assault conviction under R.C. 2903.13 and his aggravated menacing conviction under R.C. 2903.21 were not against the weight of the evidence as the victim's testimony showed that defendant tasered her leg and caused a bruise, that he sent message to her "myspace" page and threatened to kill her, and that he once held a gun to her head. State v. Fletcher, 2009-Ohio-3255, 2009 Ohio App. LEXIS 2787 (Ohio Ct. App., Lawrence County 2009).

Evidence sufficiently showed that defendant knowingly bit officer, thereby supporting conviction for assault on officer under R.C. 2903.13(A), as it showed that defendant refused to follow officer's commands, that he bit the officer's finger and refused to comply with officer's command to release his finger, and that officer had to use force to free his finger. Thus, the trial court properly denied defendant's Crim.R. 29 motion for acquittal. State v. Workman, 2009-Ohio-2995, 2009 Ohio App. LEXIS 2586 (Ohio Ct. App., Summit County 2009).

Defendant's conviction for assault, in violation of R.C. 2903.13(A), was not against the manifest weight of the evidence where there was testimony from multiple witnesses and police who responded to the scene that defendant assaulted the victim with a walking cane and threatened him because defendant believed that the victim had stolen money; defendant's claim of self-defense was not supported by the evidence and was not deemed credible by the jury. State v. Junod, 2009-Ohio-2817, 2009 Ohio App. LEXIS 2381 (Ohio Ct. App., Auglaize County 2009).

Conviction for assault under R.C. 2903.13(A) was supported by sufficient evidence and was not against the manifest weight of the evidence because a trial court was in the best position to determine the credibility of defendant and her boyfriend, who testified she did not attack the victim; the victim identified defendant as the perpetrator. State v. Ritchie, 2009-Ohio-5280, 2009 Ohio App. LEXIS 4464 (Ohio Ct. App., Butler County 2009).

Weight of the evidence supported defendant's conviction for assault because the evidence reasonably supported the conclusion that defendant intentionally sprayed the victim in the face with mace, pepper spray, or some other substance, causing her skin to burn and redden. The victim and her boyfriend both testified to that effect, and a police officer recalled seeing redness on the victim's face. State v. Wise, 2009-Ohio-5264, 2009 Ohio App. LEXIS 4457 (Ohio Ct. App., Lawrence County 2009).

Defendant's conviction for complicity to commit assault under R.C. 2903.13 and 2923.03(A)(2) was supported by evidence showing that defendant aided and abetted his wife in the wife's assault of the victim by not allowing anyone to intervene in the wife's attack on the victim or that he actively participated in the attack by pulling the victim out of her car before the wife attacked the victim. State v. Calvin, 2009-Ohio-4593, 2009 Ohio App. LEXIS 3869 (Ohio Ct. App., Lucas County 2009).

In a delinquency proceeding on two charges of assault on a school administrator, in violation of R.C. 2903.13(A) and (C)(2)(e), the trier of fact could have found the essential elements of delinquency proven as it could reasonably infer from the titles given to the principal and assistant principal that they had an obligation to ask students, present on or by school grounds, to attend classes as scheduled and to suppress a disturbance of a student on school grounds. In re T.C., 2009-Ohio-4325, 2009 Ohio App. LEXIS 3654 (Ohio Ct. App., Washington County 2009).

Defendant's convictions for assault and menacing were not against the manifest weight of the evidence, as the testimony of a public transportation passenger who claimed that defendant threatened her and beat her was deemed more credible than defendant's alibi defense offered by his grandmother. City of Cleveland v. Bello, 2009-Ohio-3899, 2009 Ohio App. LEXIS 3304 (Ohio Ct. App., Cuyahoga County 2009).

Denial of defendant's acquittal motion under Crim.R. 29(A) was proper, as the weight and sufficiency of the evidence supported defendant's multiple convictions, arising out of a physical altercation against his wife, as her claim that he made a falsified call because she was intoxicated and angry at defendant was not deemed credible and contradicted other evidence that showed that defendant attacked her; he was properly convicted of domestic violence, criminal damaging or endangering, and endangering children, in violation of R.C. 2919.25(A), 2909.06(A)(1), and 2919.22(A), as well as the lesser-included offenses of unlawful restraint and assault, in violation of R.C. 2905.03(A) and 2903.13.(A) State v. Swaby, 2009-Ohio-3690, 2009 Ohio App. LEXIS 3159 (Ohio Ct. App., Summit County 2009).

Defendant's assault conviction was not against the weight of the evidence, in that the victim described specific details surrounding the assault, which the police independently verified, including the victim's testimony that she and defendant were arguing and physically struggling outside the victim's apartment and that defendant hit the victim several times. While the medical records showed that the victim was intoxicated when she arrived at the hospital the following day, the victim's testimony that she had taken oxycodone shortly after she was punched and drank "shots of 151" for pain the next morning accounted for her high level of intoxication at the hospital. State v. Collins, 2009-Ohio-3290, 2009 Ohio App. LEXIS 2868 (Ohio Ct. App., Cuyahoga County 2009).

Defendant's assault conviction under R.C. 2903.13(A) was supported by evidence as a reasonable fact-finder could determine that defendant acted "knowingly" under R.C. 2901.22(B), in that he was aware that striking the victim in the face with a crowbar would probably cause physical harm to the victim. Defendant's conviction also was not against the manifest weight of the evidence as the victim's testimony was corroborated by that of his girlfriend and by the medical records showing the victim's injuries. State v. Lemmons, 2009-Ohio-862, 2009 Ohio App. LEXIS 727 (Ohio Ct. App., Cuyahoga County 2009).

Manifest weight of the evidence supported defendant's convictions on two counts of assault; although defendant testified that he had acted in self-defense, the trial court was privileged to credit the testimony from two neighbors that defendant had been the aggressor in a verbal incident that became physical after defendant drove his vehicle on the neighbor's property, jumped out of his car, and grabbed and kicked one of the neighbors. State v. Harpster, 2009-Ohio-823, 2009 Ohio App. LEXIS 671 (Ohio Ct. App., Ashland County 2009).

Defendant's assault conviction under R.C. 2903.13(A) was supported by sufficient evidence as the victim's testimony established that defendant grabbed her by her ponytail during a physical altercation between the victim and another woman and pulled the victim up off the other woman, allowing a clear shot for another assailant to kick the victim in the chest. While the defense witnesses and the other two State's witnesses did not observe defendant's act, this did not make the evidence insufficient; thus, defendant's motion for acquittal was properly denied. State v. Rhoden, 2008-Ohio-6590, 2008 Ohio App. LEXIS 5485 (Ohio Ct. App., Mahoning County 2008).

Weight of the evidence supported defendant's convictions for assaulting a police officer, resisting arrest, and obstruction of justice because multiple officers testified that defendant charged at one officer, grabbed him, fought with him, and pinned his legs down. Despite being told that he was under arrest, defendant not comply with their instructions, resisted their attempts to handcuff him, and even pushed them up off the ground. State v. Jordan, 2008-Ohio-6575, 2008 Ohio App. LEXIS 5481 (Ohio Ct. App., Lorain County 2008).

Defendant's conviction for assault of a police officer under R.C. 2903.13 was supported by sufficient evidence showing that defendant knowingly caused harm to the victim, who was a police officer in the course of her duties. While defendant contended that she lacked knowledge that the officer was a police officer, § 2903.13 did not require that the defendant knew that the victim was a police officer. State v. Smith, 2008-Ohio-6402, 2008 Ohio App. LEXIS 5344 (Ohio Ct. App., Lucas County 2008).

Defendant's conviction for assault, in violation of R.C. 2903.13(A), was not against the manifest weight of the evidence where he acted knowingly pursuant to R.C. 2901.22(B) when he forced the victim down on his lap by choking her with his forearm, which caused her "physical harm" as defined in R.C. 2901.01(A)(3). State v. Ellis, 2008-Ohio-6283, 2008 Ohio App. LEXIS 5243 (Ohio Ct. App., Cuyahoga County 2008), rev'd in part, 2010-Ohio-3753, 126 Ohio St. 3d 322, 933 N.E.2d 801, 2010 Ohio LEXIS 1931 (Ohio 2010).

Evidence that defendant turned toward a police deputy aggressively while being transferred to another unit, swinging at and fighting with the deputy, was sufficient to show that defendant knowingly attempted to cause harm to the deputy. Thus, defendant's motion for acquittal was properly overruled. State v. Ward, 2008-Ohio-6133, 2008 Ohio App. LEXIS 5145 (Ohio Ct. App., Summit County 2008).

There was enough credible evidence in the record to find that defendant's assault conviction was both supported by sufficient evidence and the manifest weight of the evidence because the testimony clearly established that there was an assault and that all of the elements of the charge of assault had been proven; defendant knowingly caused physical harm to the victim. State v. Damron, 2008-Ohio-6081, 2008 Ohio App. LEXIS 5100 (Ohio Ct. App., Franklin County 2008).

Adjudication of defendant as a delinquent for having committed an assault on a police officer, in violation of R.C. 2903.13, was not against the weight of the evidence as two police officers testified that defendant approached one of the officers and struck him in the face and chest. Though defendant presented testimony that he did not strike the officer, the witnesses were friends of defendant, and several of them acknowledged that they did not see the initial part of the interaction. In re B.S., 2008-Ohio-1712, 2008 Ohio App. LEXIS 1467 (Ohio Ct. App., Cuyahoga County 2008).

Defendant's constant pursuit of the victim during the altercation and the facts that he threw a frying pan at her and twisted her arms and legs displayed knowing acts of causing and/or attempting to cause physical harm to her and constituted sufficient evidence to support defendant's conviction for misdemeanor assault. State v. Pearce, 2008-Ohio-1527, 2008 Ohio App. LEXIS 1367 (Ohio Ct. App., Belmont County 2008).

Weight and sufficiency of the evidence supported a determination that defendant juvenile was delinquent for having committed robbery and assault, in violation of R.C. 2911.02(A)(2) and 2903.13(A), as defendant and a group of other teenage males surrounded two theater patrons as they left the theater, assaulted and attacked them, and robbed them of their wallets; defendant and another member of the group were positively identified by the victims shortly after the incident had occurred, and there was sufficient evidence to support the convictions based on aiding and abetting under R.C. 2923.03(A)(2). In re R.N., 2008-Ohio-1086, 2008 Ohio App. LEXIS 938 (Ohio Ct. App., Cuyahoga County 2008).

Defendant's conviction for assaulting a peace officer, under R.C. 2903.13(A)(3), was not against the manifest weight of the evidence because it was clear from the testimony of two deputies that defendant knowingly, under R.C. 2901.22(B), attempted to punch the deputies when attacking the deputies in an attempt to escape, despite defendant's denials, as defendant's testimony about defendant's numerous convictions for crimes of dishonesty put defendant's credibility in issue. State v. Davis, 2008-Ohio-999, 2008 Ohio App. LEXIS 876 (Ohio Ct. App., Medina County 2008).

Defendant's conviction for assaulting a police officer, in violation of R.C. 2903.13, was supported by sufficient evidence. Defendant's words threatening a police officer and his actions, engaging in a struggle with several officers and striking one officer in the face, established that he "knowingly" became combative under R.C. 2901.22(B) and assaulted the officers. State v. Ross, 2008-Ohio-902, 2008 Ohio App. LEXIS 757 (Ohio Ct. App., Stark County 2008).

Defendant's conviction for assault on a corrections officer, in violation of R.C. 2903.13(A), was supported by the weight and sufficiency of the evidence, as two officers testified to the altercation that defendant caused upon being taken from defendant's cell on information regarding an alleged gambling operation, and their testimony was deemed more credible than that of defendant; one officer was allegedly hit by defendant's elbow and bitten, which satisfied the physical injury element under R.C. 2901.01(A)(3), and it was determined that defendant acted knowingly under R.C. 2901.22(B). State v. Collier, 2008-Ohio-826, 2008 Ohio App. LEXIS 718 (Ohio Ct. App., Lorain County 2008).

Weight and sufficiency of the evidence supported defendant's convictions for felonious assault and assault, in violation of R.C. 2903.11(A)(2) and 2903.13(A), (C)(3), where defendant acted knowingly pursuant to R.C. 2901.22(B) in attacking police officers who were questioning and arresting defendant on an outstanding warrant, and defendant's conflicting version of events was not deemed credible; defendant came out of a vehicle upon an officer's request, but defendant held a handgun, pulled the trigger, and also physically attacked the officers while attempting to flee. State v. Dixon, 2008-Ohio-438, 2008 Ohio App. LEXIS 368 (Ohio Ct. App., Stark County 2008).

Defendant's assault conviction under R.C. 2903.13(A) was supported by evidence showing that defendant punched two victims. One could infer that defendant attempted to cause physical harm under R.C. 2901.01(A)(3) due to the fact that she aimed her punch at victim one's face and that she actually landed a full blow to victim two's shoulder. State v. Blake, 2008-Ohio-4728, 2008 Ohio App. LEXIS 3979 (Ohio Ct. App., Montgomery County 2008).

Assault conviction under R.C. 2903.13 was not against the weight of the evidence. The testimony of the victim that defendant threw her on the couch and put his fists on her neck and that he later struck her, along with the testimony of a police officer that the victim had a bump on her face and was visibly upset when the officer responded to the victim's call, was sufficient to allow a finding that defendant knowingly caused or attempted to cause physical harm to the victim. State v. Taylor, 2008-Ohio-4670, 2008 Ohio App. LEXIS 3929 (Ohio Ct. App., Ashtabula County 2008).

Defendant's convictions for gross sexual imposition, assault, and unlawful restraint, in violation of R.C. 2907.05(A)(1), 2903.13, and 2905.03, were not against the manifest weight of the evidence where defendant hit the victim about the face, threatened her with a knife, refused to let her leave the house that they were in, and improperly touched her sexually despite her protests; credibility determinations were within the trial court's discretion. State v. Rosario, 2008-Ohio-3804, 2008 Ohio App. LEXIS 3225 (Ohio Ct. App., Cuyahoga County 2008).

Defendant's conviction for assault was supported by sufficient evidence as evidence that defendant pushed, kicked, and punched police officers was sufficient for a jury to infer that defendant knowingly struck the officers. State v. Fulmer, 2008-Ohio-3730, 2008 Ohio App. LEXIS 3173 (Ohio Ct. App., Trumbull County 2008).

Weight and sufficiency of the evidence supported defendant's convictions for assault, kidnapping, intimidation, and retaliation, in violation of R.C. 2903.13, 2905.01(A)(2), 2921.04(B), and 2921.05(B), where defendant burst into the home of the victim, with whom defendant had been previously romantically involved, held the victim against her will and threatened to rape her, and then thereafter threatened her with harm if she informed the authorities about defendant's behavior; there was also compelling testimonial and physical evidence that defendant beat the victim and that he sexually assaulted her. State v. Smith, 2008-Ohio-3657, 2008 Ohio App. LEXIS 3118 (Ohio Ct. App., Cuyahoga County 2008).

Evidence was sufficient to support defendant's conviction for assault on a peace officer as defendant "knowingly" chose to engage in the physical altercation with a police officer, and thus, she was aware that her conduct would probably cause a certain result even though the State did not prove that she would cause any specific injury to the officer. The testimony regarding defendant's acts of kicking the officer and swinging her hands at him was sufficient to permit the trier of fact to find the essential elements of the crime proven beyond a reasonable doubt. State v. Sorrells-Johnson, 2008-Ohio-3469, 2008 Ohio App. LEXIS 2924 (Ohio Ct. App., Franklin County 2008).

Denial of defendant's acquittal motion under Crim.R. 29(A) was proper where the weight and sufficiency of the evidence supported defendant's conviction for assault, in violation of R.C. 2903.13(A), as there was testimony from defendant's girlfriend and a police officer who responded to the scene that the girlfriend was bruised and upset from the criminal incident; the girlfriend testified that defendant became angry with her while driving and that he hit her, threatened her, and then dragged her by her hair when they were out of the car. State v. Givens, 2008-Ohio-3434, 2008 Ohio App. LEXIS 2898 (Ohio Ct. App., Columbiana County 2008).

Defendant's conviction for assault on a police officer was not against the weight of the evidence as the officer's testimony showed that defendant fought with him when the officer tried to handcuff him and that the officer suffered several injuries when defendant punched and choked him. Though defendant and the female who was with him offered different testimony, the court could not say that the jury lost its way in finding the State's witnesses more credible than the testimony of defendant and the female, both of whom had addictions and multiple prior convictions. State v.

Newton, 2008-Ohio-3210, 2008 Ohio App. LEXIS 2729 (Ohio Ct. App., Lorain County 2008).

Defendant's conviction for assault on a corrections officer was not against the weight of the evidence. Though defendant and another inmate testified that the officer attacked defendant first, the officer offered contrary testimony, and in light of inconsistencies in the testimony of defendant and the inmate, the jury could discredit their testimony and believe the testimony of the officer that defendant instigated the altercation. State v. Dixon, 2008-Ohio-3184, 2008 Ohio App. LEXIS 2684 (Ohio Ct. App., Scioto County 2008).

Trial court's denial of defendant's acquittal motion under Crim.R. 29 was proper where the weight and sufficiency of the evidence showed that defendant committed an assault, in violation of R.C. 2903.13(A); the evidence showed that defendant acted knowingly pursuant to R.C. 2901.22(B) when defendant punched the victim in the forehead, and no visible injury on the victim was required to complete the offense. State v. Baker, 2008-Ohio-3000, 2008 Ohio App. LEXIS 2515 (Ohio Ct. App., Montgomery County 2008).

Defendant's convictions on three counts of assault on a peace officer in violation of R.C. 2903.13(A), (C)(3), were supported by the evidence, which established that defendant kicked and grabbed two sheriff's deputies and their sergeant, resulting in minor injuries to them, as they attempted to subdue and arrest defendant. State v. Broucker, 2008-Ohio-2946, 2008 Ohio App. LEXIS 2459 (Ohio Ct. App., Stark County 2008).

Defendant's conviction for assault, in violation of R.C. 2903.13, was supported by the weight and sufficiency of the evidence, as the jury reasonably found that defendant acted knowingly under R.C. 2901.22(B) when defendant attacked police officers after being pepper sprayed for non-compliance with their orders regarding relocation to a new jail cell. State v. Crowley, 2008-Ohio-2718, 2008 Ohio App. LEXIS 2281 (Ohio Ct. App., Clark County 2008).

Defendant's conviction for reckless assault on peace officer under R.C. 2903.13(B) was supported by the evidence as the testimony of various witnesses established that defendant was caught committing a felony and that, in an effort to evade arrest, defendant grabbed the officer's legs, and the two fell to the ground, resulting in multiple fractures to the officer's leg. Since, between defendant and the officer, they weighed 400 pounds, broken bones were a significant risk, and defendant's conduct constituted recklessness under R.C. 2901.22(C). State v. Crawford, 2008-Ohio-2568, 2008 Ohio App. LEXIS 2187 (Ohio Ct. App., Franklin County 2008).

Weight and sufficiency of the evidence supported defendant's conviction for assault, in violation of R.C. 2903.13, where defendant got out of the car that defendant was riding in and kicked, scratched, punched, and pulled the hair of the victim, who was the former stepdaughter of defendant's boyfriend; there was testimony from multiple witnesses regarding defendant's conduct, and there was no requirement that actual harm be proved. City of Alliance v. Kelly, 2008-Ohio-2475, 2008 Ohio App. LEXIS 2100 (Ohio Ct. App., Stark County 2008).

Any error in admitting a tape-recorded answering machine (on which defendant stated that she had hit the victim) was harmless because even without the tape recording, the remaining evidence supported the guilty verdict. The victim identified defendant as the individual who had thrown her into a cinder-block wall at a bar and testified that defendant verbally threatened her on the morning of the incident and a police officer testified as to the events that occurred at the bar. State v. Hutson, 2008-Ohio-2315, 2008 Ohio App. LEXIS 1968 (Ohio Ct. App., Portage County 2008).

Conviction for assault on peace officer under R.C. 2903.13(A) was not against the weight of evidence as the testimony showed that defendant attacked sheriff's deputies, stomping on one deputy's foot, wrapping his legs around the deputy's waist, and bending another deputy's fingers backwards. Though defendant denied attacking the deputies, the mere fact that the jury chose to believe the testimony of the State's witnesses did not render the verdict against the manifest weight; thus, defendant's motion for acquittal was properly denied. State v. Prieto, 2008-Ohio-1914, 2008 Ohio App. LEXIS 1640 (Ohio Ct. App., Summit County 2008).

Sufficient evidence supported defendant's convictions for domestic violence and assault because it was reasonable to have found that defendant purposely caused physical harm to the victim; purposeful conduct satisfied the requirement that a defendant acted "knowingly," pursuant to R.C. 2901.22(E). The evidence showed that defendant appeared angry when he entered the victim's workplace, that he approached the victim's cubicle, leaned over the barrier, called her a name, and flung a warehouse club card at her that struck her above the eye, causing a small cut. State v. Terrell, 2008-Ohio-1863, 2008 Ohio App. LEXIS 1594 (Ohio Ct. App., Montgomery County 2008).

Sufficient evidence supported defendant's convictions for domestic violence and assault because it was reasonable to have found that defendant purposely caused physical harm to the victim; purposeful conduct satisfied the requirement that a defendant acted "knowingly," pursuant to R.C. 2901.22(E). The evidence showed that defendant appeared angry when he entered the victim's workplace, that he approached the victim's cubicle, leaned over the barrier, called her a name, and flung a warehouse club card at her that struck her above the eye, causing a small cut. State v. Terrell, 2008-Ohio-1863, 2008 Ohio App. LEXIS 1594 (Ohio Ct. App., Montgomery County 2008).

Defendant's convictions for felonious assault and assault on a peace officer, in violation of R.C. 2903.11(A)(2) and 2903.13(A), (C)(3), were supported by evidence that defendant refused to heed officers' warnings to get out of the vehicle, and instead, defendant backed the vehicle into the officers' paths until defendant's vehicle was stopped because it struck a police car; the evidence supported a determination that defendant acted knowingly pursuant to R.C. 2901.22(B). State v. Franklin, 2008-Ohio-1089, 2008 Ohio App. LEXIS 949 (Ohio Ct. App., Cuyahoga County 2008).

Assault convictions under R.C. 2903.13(A) and (C)(3) were not against the manifest weight of the evidence. Although defendant claimed that he did not attempt to punch, kick, or otherwise harm police officers after he was arrested, the officers' testimony that one officer was kicked in the face during a struggle with defendant, along with photographic evidence of the officer's injuries, was enough to belie defendant's claim. State v. Battaia, 2007-Ohio-6729, 2007 Ohio App. LEXIS 5889 (Ohio Ct. App., Lake County 2007).

Defendant's convictions for misdemeanor assault were not against the manifest weight of the evidence because (1) defendant's claim that defendant established self-defense was not sustained as defendant's testimony indicated defendant did not feel threatened by defendant's victim and that defendant made no effort to retreat from defendant's encounter with the victims, and (2) the trial court which convicted defendant was authorized to find the testimony of defendant's victims more credible than the testimony of defendant and defendant's witness. State v. Andric, 2007-Ohio-6701, 2007 Ohio App. LEXIS 5856 (Ohio Ct. App., Columbiana County 2007).

In reviewing a trial court's findings made in a proceeding under R.C. 2945.39(A)(2), the court applied the civil manifest weight of the evidence review and concluded that defendant's convictions for aggravated burglary, assault, and attempted gross sexual imposition were not against the manifest weight of the evidence as the evidence showed that defendant entered the victim's room at night, without her permission; pulled her out of bed; pushed her onto the dresser; attempted to remove her sweatpants; and touched her crotch area. Though defendant attempted to discredit the victim's testimony, his arguments concerned matters regarding the weight of the evidence and the credibility of witnesses, which were matters for the trial court to decide State v. Sloan, 2007-Ohio-6558, 2007 Ohio App. LEXIS 5716 (Ohio Ct. App., Lake County 2007).

Defendant's assault conviction was supported by sufficient evidence as the evidence showed that defendant "knowingly" struck the victim, within the meaning of R.C. 2901.22(B), with his fists several times, causing injury. State v. Cunningham, 2007-Ohio-6431, 2007 Ohio App. LEXIS 5636 (Ohio Ct. App., Columbiana County 2007).

In an assault prosecution under R.C. 2903.13(A), the trial court did not err in denying defendant's motion for acquittal under Crim.R. 29(A) as the evidence showed that defendant went after the victim with a martial arts-type weapon and scratched the victim on the back, neck, and arm. State v. Mims, 2007-Ohio-6200, 2007 Ohio App. LEXIS 5444 (Ohio Ct. App., Cuyahoga County 2007).

Assault conviction under R.C. 2903.13(A) was not against the manifest weight of the evidence as the State presented the testimony of three sober individuals who observed defendant punch a bartender while defendant's testimony denying that she was even a participant in the fight was uncorroborated. The matter of the credibility of the witnesses was for the factfinder to decide. State v. Homan, 2007-Ohio-6162, 2007 Ohio App. LEXIS 5391 (Ohio Ct. App., Portage County 2007).

Defendant's conviction for assault on a peace officer, in violation of R.C. 2903.13(C)(3), was not against the manifest weight of the evidence, as the State offered multiple witnesses who testified that defendant kicked and pushed an officer who was trying to arrest defendant's brother. State v. Jankite, 2007-Ohio-5955, 2007 Ohio App. LEXIS 5223 (Ohio Ct. App., Cuyahoga County 2007).

Defendant's assault conviction under R.C. 2903.13(A) was supported by sufficient evidence as the evidence showed that defendant, while in the victim's house, attacked the victim. Though defendant claimed that he was acting in self-defense, the trial court did not err in rejecting the defense as the evidence was conflicting, and the trial court was free to discredit defendant's testimony. State v. Black, 2007-Ohio-5871, 2007 Ohio App. LEXIS 5159 (Ohio Ct. App., Hamilton County 2007).

Defendant's conviction for assault on a peace officer was supported by sufficient evidence because four police officers testified that defendant ran away from them when they arrived at his house and failed to comply with the injured officer's commands. When the injured officer grabbed defendant, he resisted and they both fell to the ground, where defendant continued to resist and had to be tasered several times; based on the scuffle, the officer was injured and received medical treatment for a broken hand. State v. Dumas, 2007-Ohio-5724, 2007 Ohio App. LEXIS 5016 (Ohio Ct. App., Cuyahoga County 2007).

Defendant's acquittal motion under Crim.R. 29 was properly denied by a trial court where the weight and sufficiency of the evidence supported his convictions for murder, assault, and felonious assault, in violation of R.C. 2903.02(A), 2903.13(A), and 2903.11(A)(1); the State presented 29 witnesses who testified that defendant had attacked women brutally and stomped on their heads multiple times, he had been positively identified, and he had made statements to friends that implicated him in the crimes.

State v. Markovanovich, 2007-Ohio-5676, 2007 Ohio App. LEXIS 5000 (Ohio Ct. App., Summit County 2007).

Sufficient evidence supported defendant's conviction for assault on a police officer because the officer testified that the felt a blow to his back, that defendant was the only person behind him, that defendant was within an arm's length of him, and that defendant was the person who struck him. Another officer also supported the assaulted officer's testimony of defendant's proximity when he testified that he observed the officer push defendant away. State v. Jiminez-Ortiz, 2007-Ohio-5496, 2007 Ohio App. LEXIS 4839 (Ohio Ct. App., Butler County 2007).

Jury did not lose its way in finding defendant guilty of assault. Given the testimony by a corrections officer that defendant charged at another corrections officer and knocked him to the floor, the jury could have inferred that the corrections officer sustained sufficient pain and discomfort from the attack to constitute physical harm, under R.C. 2901.01(A)(3). State v. Trikilis, 2007-Ohio-5475, 2007 Ohio App. LEXIS 4814 (Ohio Ct. App., Medina County 2007).

Although defendant claimed that he was defending himself from his former girlfriend's physical rage at him, her testimony that he punched her in the mouth and dragged her by her hair after he came to her home unannounced was deemed more credible by the trial court judge, such that defendant's conviction for assault, in violation of R.C. 2903.13, was not against the manifest weight of the evidence; photographs taken of the girlfriend showed that she had a swollen lip, which constituted the necessary "physical harm" pursuant to R.C. 2901.01(A)(3). City of E. Cleveland v. Arnett, 2007-Ohio-5075, 2007 Ohio App. LEXIS 4480 (Ohio Ct. App., Cuyahoga County 2007).

Defendant's assault conviction under R.C. 2903.13(A) was supported by evidence showing that defendant, during a verbal argument, got in the victim's face and started yelling at him while swinging her arms, scratching the victim, and pushing him down onto a couch, despite the attempt by the victim's mother to quell defendant. State v. Kelly, 2007-Ohio-4816, 2007 Ohio App. LEXIS 4340 (Ohio Ct. App., Stark County 2007).

Though there were minor inconsistencies between the testimony of the witnesses proffered by the State in defendant's prosecution for assault on a peace officer, the trier of fact was in the best position to take into account conflicting evidence and inconsistencies and to determine whether each witness's testimony was credible; thus, the reviewing court had to accord deference to the fact finder's credibility determinations. The evidence showed that a rational jury could have reasonably concluded that defendant knowingly caused and/or attempted to cause physical harm to a police officer as all three witnesses testified that defendant approached the police officer and punched the officer. State v. Hairston, 2007-Ohio-4457, 2007 Ohio App. LEXIS 4023 (Ohio Ct. App., Franklin County 2007).

Assault conviction under R.C. 2903.13 was not against the manifest weight of the evidence as defendant admitted during his testimony that he assaulted the victim, slapping her several times in an effort to get her to leave his house, and a forensic scientist testified that the victim's DNA was found in the blood stains on defendant's clothing. State v. Powers, 2007-Ohio-4420, 2007 Ohio App. LEXIS 3985 (Ohio Ct. App., Summit County 2007).

Where the State produced eyewitnesses who testified that during a physical altercation between defendant's teenage daughter and another individual, defendant struck the other individual, and defendant produced eyewitnesses to the altercation who testified that defendant was not involved in the altercation, the determination that defendant was guilty of assault, in violation of R.C. 2903.13(A), was within the province of the trial court judge as fact-finder, such that any claim on appeal regarding weight and sufficiency of the evidence lacked merit. State v. Horne, 2007-Ohio-4083, 2007 Ohio App. LEXIS 3717 (Ohio Ct. App., Darke County 2007).

Defendant's conviction for assault on a peace officer was supported by sufficient evidence because four police officers testified that defendant ran away from them when they arrived at his house and failed to comply with the injured officer's commands. When the injured officer grabbed defendant, he resisted and they both fell to the ground, where defendant continued to resist and had to be tasered several times; based on the scuffle, the officer was injured and received medical treatment for a broken hand. State v. Dumas, 2007-Ohio-5724, 2007 Ohio App. LEXIS 5016 (Ohio Ct. App., Cuyahoga County 2007).

Defendant's acquittal motion under Crim.R. 29 was properly denied by a trial court where the weight and sufficiency of the evidence supported his convictions for murder, assault, and felonious assault, in violation of R.C. 2903.02(A), 2903.13(A), and 2903.11(A)(1); the State presented 29 witnesses who testified that defendant had attacked women brutally and stomped on their heads multiple times, he had been positively identified, and he had made statements to friends that implicated him in the crimes. State v. Markovanovich, 2007-Ohio-5676, 2007 Ohio App. LEXIS 5000 (Ohio Ct. App., Summit County 2007).

Sufficient evidence supported defendant's conviction for assault on a police officer because the officer testified that the felt a blow to his back, that defendant was the only person behind him, that defendant was within an arm's length of him, and that defendant was the person who struck him. Another officer also supported the assaulted officer's testimony of defendant's proximity when he testified that he observed the officer push defendant away. State v. Jiminez-Ortiz, 2007-Ohio-5496, 2007 Ohio App. LEXIS 4839 (Ohio Ct. App., Butler County 2007).

Jury did not lose its way in finding defendant guilty of assault. Given the testimony by a corrections officer that defendant charged at another corrections officer and knocked him to the floor, the jury could have inferred that the corrections officer sustained sufficient pain and discomfort from the attack to constitute physical harm, under R.C. 2901.01(A)(3). State v. Trikilis, 2007-Ohio-5475, 2007 Ohio App. LEXIS 4814 (Ohio Ct. App., Medina County 2007).

Although defendant claimed that he was defending himself from his former girlfriend's physical rage at him, her testimony that he punched her in the mouth and dragged her by her hair after he came to her home unannounced was deemed more credible by the trial court judge, such that defendant's conviction for assault, in violation of R.C. 2903.13, was not against the manifest weight of the evidence; photographs taken of the girlfriend showed that she had a swollen lip, which constituted the necessary "physical harm" pursuant to R.C. 2901.01(A)(3). City of E. Cleveland v. Arnett, 2007-Ohio-5075, 2007 Ohio App. LEXIS 4480 (Ohio Ct. App., Cuyahoga County 2007).

Defendant's assault conviction under R.C. 2903.13(A) was supported by evidence showing that defendant, during a verbal argument, got in the victim's face and started yelling at him while swinging her arms, scratching the victim, and pushing him down onto a couch, despite the attempt by the victim's mother to quell defendant. State v. Kelly, 2007-Ohio-4816, 2007 Ohio App. LEXIS 4340 (Ohio Ct. App., Stark County 2007).

Though there were minor inconsistencies between the testimony of the witnesses proffered by the State in defendant's prosecution for assault on a peace officer, the trier of fact was in the best position to take into account conflicting evidence and inconsistencies and to determine whether each witness's testimony was credible; thus, the reviewing court had to accord deference to the fact finder's credibility determinations. The evidence showed that a rational jury could have reasonably concluded that defendant knowingly caused and/or attempted to cause physical harm to a police officer as all three witnesses testified that defendant approached the police officer and punched the officer. State v. Hairston, 2007-Ohio-4457, 2007 Ohio App. LEXIS 4023 (Ohio Ct. App., Franklin County 2007).

Assault conviction under R.C. 2903.13 was not against the manifest weight of the evidence as defendant admitted during his testimony that he assaulted the victim, slapping her several times in an effort to get her to leave his house, and a forensic scientist testified that the victim's DNA was found in the blood stains on defendant's clothing. State v. Powers, 2007-Ohio-4420, 2007 Ohio App. LEXIS 3985 (Ohio Ct. App., Summit County 2007).

Where the State produced eyewitnesses who testified that during a physical altercation between defendant's teenage daughter and another individual, defendant struck the other individual, and defendant produced eyewitnesses to the altercation who testified that defendant was not involved in the altercation, the determination that defendant was guilty of assault, in violation of R.C. 2903.13(A), was within the province of the trial court judge as fact-finder, such that any claim on appeal regarding weight and sufficiency of the evidence lacked merit. State v. Horne, 2007-Ohio-4083, 2007 Ohio App. LEXIS 3717 (Ohio Ct. App., Darke County 2007).

Defendant's convictions for criminal damaging and assault were supported by sufficient evidence because there was evidence that defendant knowingly jumped through a closed screen window to enter an apartment and then knowingly hit, kicked or otherwise "beat" the victim, causing a serious injury. During several telephone calls from the jail to family members and friends, defendant admitted that he went to the home and that, while he did not break a window, he knocked out a window screen when he jumped through the window; he also admitted during one phone call that he "beat up the guy." State v. McCloud, 2007-Ohio-368, 2007 Ohio App. LEXIS 329 (Ohio Ct. App., Summit County 2007).

Prosecution provided overwhelming evidence to support defendant's convictions for possession of cocaine, assault on a fireman, vandalism, making false alarms, and resisting arrest because a fireman testified that, responding to a fire alarm, he found defendant destroying property, defendant tried to hit him and later tried to strangle him, requiring four officers, the use of pepper spray, and the use of multiple tasers to stop him. Also, the State introduced video surveillance which clearly showed defendant damaging the property on multiple floors and, upon taking defendant to the hospital, a police officer found a rock of crack cocaine in the pocket of defendant's pants. State v. Purefoy, 2007-Ohio-371, 2007 Ohio App. LEXIS 327 (Ohio Ct. App., Summit County 2007).

Weight of the evidence supported defendant's convictions for burglary and assault because the victim testified that defendant pushed her way into the victim's home, grabbed her by her hair, threw her in the corner, and started hitting and punching her, which was sufficient for the force element of burglary. Also, both the victim and her friend testified that defendant, whom they independently identified in court and from a photo array, was the person that had attacked the victim and a polygraph examiner testified that when asked if she had assaulted anyone on the date of the incident, defendant was not truthful. State v. Thornton, 2007-Ohio-3743, 2007 Ohio App. LEXIS 3425 (Ohio Ct. App., Summit County 2007).

Sufficient evidence supported defendant's conviction for assault because both the victim and her boyfriend testified as to the events of the night in question, and did not waiver in their assertion that defendant struck the victim; evidence regarding the victim's medical injuries was also submitted to the jury for consideration. Additional evidence was presented to the jury, including the testimony of the bar owner, the investigating officer, and several bystanders, who were disinterested witnesses. State v. Schenker, 2007-Ohio-3732, 2007 Ohio App. LEXIS 3415 (Ohio Ct. App., Tuscarawas County 2007).

Assault conviction under R.C. 2903.13(A) was supported by sufficient evidence as the State's evidence showed that defendant, by biting a police officer's arm, clearly intended to cause physical harm to the officer. State v. McDuffie, 2007-Ohio-3421, 2007 Ohio App. LEXIS 3175 (Ohio Ct. App., Cuyahoga County 2007).

In defendant's prosecution for assault, evidence that one of the police officers involved in restraining defendant suffered a broken ulna, as a result of defendant's actions in punching the police officers trying to arrest him and swinging his arms and elbows during the arrest, satisfied the element of serious physical harm, within the meaning of R.C. 2901.01(A)(5)(c) and (e). State v. Latessa, 2007-Ohio-3373, 2007 Ohio App. LEXIS 3097 (Ohio Ct. App., Lake County 2007).

Testimony of the police officers involved in restraining defendant allowed a finding that defendant acted recklessly under R.C. 2901.22(C) by punching the officers and swinging his arms and elbows while the officers were trying to restrain him, thereby perversely disregarding the risk that his conduct was likely to cause an injury to an officer arriving on the scene to assist in arresting him. This evidence supported defendant's conviction for assault under R.C. 2903.13(B). State v. Latessa, 2007-Ohio-3373, 2007 Ohio App. LEXIS 3097 (Ohio Ct. App., Lake County 2007).



Defendant's conviction for assault of a peace officer under R.C. 2903.13(A) and (C)(3) was supported by evidence showing that defendant began kicking while a police officer was in close proximity to her attempting to place defendant in the back of a police car. This was sufficient to show that defendant acted with knowledge of the possible consequences of her actions under R.C. 2901.22(B). State v. Holland, 2007-Ohio-3149, 2007 Ohio App. LEXIS 2941 (Ohio Ct. App., Mahoning County 2007).

Defendant's convictions for kidnapping, under R.C. 2905.01(A)(4), rape, under R.C. 2907.02(A)(2), and assault, under R.C. 2903.13, were not against the manifest weight of the evidence when defendant and defendant's associates forced a victim to have sexual contact with defendant and defendant's associates because (1) the jury's apparent belief that one of defendant's associates did not have sexual contact with the victim did not dispose of the rape charge against defendant, (2) the jury's apparent belief that defendant's associate did not see the assault did not mean the assault did not happen, and (3) the victim's relatively minor physical injuries were not dispositive as a crime lab technician testified that the technician had seen rape cases where there were even fewer injuries. State v. Serva, 2007-Ohio-3060, 2007 Ohio App. LEXIS 2800 (Ohio Ct. App., Summit County 2007).

Police officer's testimony that defendant came running out of her bedroom, immediately recognized that he was a police officer, ran at him, pushed him several times, and was kicking and flailing at him was sufficient for the trier of fact to have found that defendant "knowingly" caused "physical harm" to the officer, as those terms are defined in R.C. 2901.22(B) and 2901.01(A)(3) respectively. Thus, the trial court did not commit plain error under Crim.R. 52(B) in finding defendant guilty of assault on a peace officer. State v. Dixon, 2007-Ohio-2989, 2007 Ohio App. LEXIS 2745 (Ohio Ct. App., Crawford County 2007).

Substantial, credible evidence supported defendant's convictions for involuntary manslaughter, under R.C. 2903.04, and assault, under R.C. 2903.13, because the jury had two versions of the cause of the victim's miscarriage, one non-specific and the other caused by "blunt force injury" to the placenta. The jury chose to follow the opinions of the coroner and the State's expert because those opinions were consistent with the testimony of the victim, that defendant had kicked her in the back multiple times. State v. Marshall, 2007-Ohio-1686, 2007 Ohio App. LEXIS 1538 (Ohio Ct. App., Muskingum County 2007).

Defendant did not show his assault conviction, under R.C. 2903.13(A), was against the manifest weight of the evidence because both the victim and a witness credibly testified about the assault, defendant did not show they lacked credibility, and their testimony showed defendant assaulted the victim, photographs showed the injuries inflicted by the assault, and an officer's testimony showed the victim was distraught shortly after the attack and still had visible injuries. State v. Dunlap, 2007-Ohio-1624, 2007 Ohio App. LEXIS 1498 (Ohio Ct. App., Lorain County 2007).

Defendant's convictions of the lesser-included offenses of involuntary manslaughter and misdemeanor assault, in violation of R.C. 2903.04 and 2903.13, were not against the manifest weight of the evidence, as he was identified by a number of witnesses as the assailant who punched and kicked a victim who later died from his injuries; although the witnesses were mainly partygoers who had used marijuana and alcohol, their credibility was an issue for the trier of fact. State v. Ferko, 2007-Ohio-1588, 2007 Ohio App. LEXIS 1464 (Ohio Ct. App., Cuyahoga County 2007), cert. denied, 552 U.S. 1245, 128 S. Ct. 1477, 170 L. Ed. 2d 301, 2008 U.S. LEXIS 2265 (U.S. 2008).

Sufficient evidence supported defendant's convictions for assault, in violation of Columbus, Ohio, Code § 2303.13, and domestic violence, in violation of R.C. 2919.25, because the victim, defendant's wife, had a bruise on her right eye and she testified that she and defendant were fighting about a gun when he struck her on the right side of her face. Although the victim did not see him hit her because she had bent over to check her daughter's wet pants, she testified that he was standing in the yard, approximately one foot to one-and-a-half feet away from her and then ran and entered the passenger seat of the vehicle and his girlfriend drove away. State v. Gray, 2007-Ohio-1504, 2007 Ohio App. LEXIS 1364 (Ohio Ct. App., Franklin County 2007).

Defendant's assault conviction, under R.C. 2903.13(A), was not against the manifest weight of the evidence because the trial court, as the trier of fact, could properly rely on the testimony of an independent, non-party, witness showing that defendant approached the victim from behind and knowingly struck her with a paint can, causing injury. State v. Andrews, 2007-Ohio-1056, 2007 Ohio App. LEXIS 1016 (Ohio Ct. App., Wayne County 2007).

Where defendant kicked at police officers who were trying to restrain him and who then attempted to use a hobble tie to restrain defendant further due to his continued physical struggle with them, he "knowingly" kicked the officer pursuant to R.C. 2901.22(B) for purposes of his conviction of assault of a police officer, in violation of R.C. 2903.13(A), (C)(3), such that the trial court properly denied defendant's acquittal motion under Crim.R. 29. State v. Coughlin, 2007-Ohio-897, 2007 Ohio App. LEXIS 803 (Ohio Ct. App., Ashtabula County 2007).

Defendant's assault conviction under R.C. 2903.13(A) was supported by sufficient evidence as both of State's witnesses testified that defendant grabbed a store's manager by the neck and pushed him into some soda coolers. Although the manager's neck did not hurt until a couple hours after incident, the trier of fact could easily conclude that defendant intended to cause physical harm to the manager. State v. Artemus, 2007-Ohio-864, 2007 Ohio App. LEXIS 772 (Ohio Ct. App., Montgomery County 2007).

Where defendant admitted that he was involved in a physical fight with two victims, and they testified that he punched each of them in the face and that they suffered injuries therefrom, there was sufficient evidence to support his conviction for two counts of assault, in violation of R.C. 2903.13(A); the jury's determination that defendant acted knowingly pursuant to R.C. 2901.22 was within its province, such that the convictions were not against the manifest weight of the evidence. State v. Myers, 2006-Ohio-7018, 2006 Ohio App. LEXIS 6970 (Ohio Ct. App., Stark County 2006).

Trial court's denial of defendant's acquittal motion under Crim.R. 29(A) was proper, as the evidence was sufficient to support defendant's convictions for assault against police officers, in violation of R.C. 2903.13(A) and (B), where the evidence established that defendant tried to inflict or actually inflicted physical harm to the officers who were arresting him when he kicked his feet out and attempted to connect with them as he was being led out of the hospital and placed in the police car for transport to the police station; the evidence sufficiently established that defendant acted "recklessly" and "knowingly" for purposes of R.C. 2901.22(C) and (B). State v. Deir, 2006-Ohio-6885, 2006 Ohio App. LEXIS 6786 (Ohio Ct. App., Lake County 2006).

Although defendant waived any challenge to the sufficiency of the evidence, the State presented sufficient evidence to find, beyond a reasonable doubt, that defendant assaulted the police officer. Based on testimony by the police officers, there was sufficient evidence to demonstrate that defendant knowingly attempted to cause physical harm to the officer because the testimony showed that defendant attacked the officer, even after she had dislodged his arm from her shoulder, and she kicked at both him and another officer; such actions indicated knowledge, or even desire, that injury would occur. State v. Fussell, 2006-Ohio-6438, 2006 Ohio App. LEXIS 6387 (Ohio Ct. App., Cuyahoga County 2006), cert. denied, 552 U.S. 992, 128 S. Ct. 508, 169 L. Ed. 2d 342, 2007 U.S. LEXIS 11864 (U.S. 2007).

Victim's testimony was not only sufficient to show that defendant, a juvenile, was the aggressor during the confrontation, but also established each element of assault because a videotape of the altercation showed that, by walking towards the victim, defendant forced her into a corner created by the wall and the back edge of the lockers, one of defendant's own witnesses testified that defendant had cornered the victim, and other evidence supported the finding that defendant had been the aggressor. The fact that the victim made a racial comment did not make her the aggressor who instigated the fight; nor did it justify a violent response. In re Britaini K., 2006-Ohio-6216, 2006 Ohio App. LEXIS 6187 (Ohio Ct. App., Stark County 2006).

Denial of defendant's acquittal motion under Crim.R. 29 was proper where the weight and sufficiency of the evidence supported his conviction for assault on a corrections officer, in violation of R.C. 2903.13(A), as defendant had refused to give a corrections officer his bed sheets while in a justice center and upon the officer's entry into defendant's cell to retrieve the sheets, defendant confronted the officer by intruding into his personal space, a physical altercation ensued, and defendant bit the officer's finger; the jury found that defendant's claim of self-defense, which was supported by the testimony of one witness, was not a credible version of events. State v. Bevins, 2006-Ohio-5455, 2006 Ohio App. LEXIS 5453 (Ohio Ct. App., Hamilton County 2006).

Conviction of assault was supported by sufficient evidence, and the conviction was not against the manifest weight of the evidence; a security guard testified that, after he asked defendant to leave the parking lot of a restaurant, defendant swung his arms at him and struck him on the cheek with his hand. A police officer also testified to seeing a red mark on the security guard's face. State v. Williams, 2006-Ohio-5401, 2006 Ohio App. LEXIS 5397 (Ohio Ct. App., Montgomery County 2006).

Misdemeanor assault conviction under R.C. 2903.13 was not against the manifest weight of the evidence. The trial court could have reasonably found that defendant knowingly attempted to cause physical harm by grabbing the victim from behind and shoving his head into a display rack for the express purpose of teaching him "a lesson" and was not required to accept defendant's testimony that the victim made an aggressive move and that defendant acted in self defense, merely intending to avoid being hit. State v. Sykes, 2006-Ohio-4523, 2006 Ohio App. LEXIS 4516 (Ohio Ct. App., Montgomery County 2006).

Defendant's conviction for assault on a police officer was not against the manifest weight of the evidence. The four police officers involved in the incident offered consistent and credible testimony that defendant kicked at them repeatedly while the officers were attempting to secure defendant during an arrest, and the jury did not lose its way in finding that defendant caused or attempted to cause physical harm to the four officers. State v. Pitts, 2006-Ohio-4517, 2006 Ohio App. LEXIS 4475 (Ohio Ct. App., Greene County 2006).

Defendant's conviction for felonious assault on a police officer, in violation of R.C. 2903.13, was supported by the weight and sufficiency of the evidence where the jury chose to believe the testimony of various police officers who presented a credible, consistent account of defendant engaging in punching of an officer who had attempted to detain him in order to conduct an investigatory stop regarding a possible drug deal that the officer observed, rather than finding defendant's self-serving version of events credible. State v. Antonio, 2006-Ohio-4107, 2006 Ohio App. LEXIS 4075 (Ohio Ct. App., Cuyahoga County 2006).

Evidence sufficiently supported the conclusion that defendant was, at the least, attempting to cause physical harm, as defined by R.C. 2901.01, to the police officers for assault, under R.C. 2903.13. Two officers testified that defendant pulled a gun on them, engaged in a physical altercation, and hit one of them in the torso causing him to suffer bumps and bruises. State v. Peyton, 2006-Ohio-3735, 2006 Ohio App. LEXIS 3694 (Ohio Ct. App., Cuyahoga County 2006).

There was ample evidence presented to allow the trial court to conclude that defendant "knowingly" caused physical harm to the victim, within the meaning of R.C. 2901.22(B), in that defendant was aware that his conduct would probably cause physical harm to the victim, in violation of R.C. 2903.13(A); thus, defendant's motion for acquittal under Crim.R. 29(A) was properly denied. The evidence showed that defendant bent the victim's wrist backward, that he pushed her, and that the two of them wound up on the floor with defendant on top of the victim. State v. Gesell, 2006-Ohio-3621, 2006 Ohio App. LEXIS 3580 (Ohio Ct. App., Butler County 2006).

Defendant's convictions for assault and failure to stop after an accident, in violation of R.C. 2903.13(A) and 4549.02(A), were supported by the weight and sufficiency of the evidence where defendant backed his vehicle into another driver's car, and he then slapped the other driver and spit on her before getting into his car and driving away; his actions towards the other driver supported a finding that he caused, or attempted to cause, her harm for purposes of the assault, the fact that defendant drove away after the accident and had to be tracked down by his license plate number supported the conviction under § 4549.02(A), the other driver's credibility was uncontroverted and corroborated by testimony of two police officers, and there was also physical damage to the other driver's car. State v. Skinner, 2006-Ohio-3486, 2006 Ohio App. LEXIS 3421 (Ohio Ct. App., Mahoning County 2006).

There was sufficient evidence of an assault by defendant, an inmate, on a corrections officer on the grounds of a correctional facility, pursuant to R.C. 2903.13(A)(2)(a), because when defendant questioned the corrections officer's authority to ask him to perform extra duty and, the officer tried to handcuff him, and defendant resisted. Defendant's argument regarding the corrections officer's "authority" was not valid because whether the officer had the authority to ask defendant to perform extra duty was separate and apart from the assault. State v. McCraney, 2006-Ohio-3460, 2006 Ohio App. LEXIS 3390 (Ohio Ct. App., Richland County 2006).

Sufficient evidence supported defendant's involuntary manslaughter and assault convictions because the jury could reasonably find his infliction of a blow to an approximately 14-month-old child with enough force to cause internal injuries was heedless indifference to the consequences of his act, his failure to seek medical care after the child had dark green-tinged vomitus related to her internal injuries disregarded a known risk, and the child's death was a foreseeable consequence within the scope of the risk created by his blow to her abdomen. State v. Tribett, 2006-Ohio-3437, 2006 Ohio App. LEXIS 3363 (Ohio Ct. App., Franklin County 2006), aff'd, 2007-Ohio-5551, 116 Ohio St. 3d 31, 876 N.E.2d 528, 2007 Ohio LEXIS 2567 (Ohio 2007).

Defendant's assault conviction under R.C. 2903.13(A) was supported by sufficient evidence and was not against the manifest weight of the evidence because the State presented evidence that defendant initiated a confrontation with the victim and subsequently struck the victim with his fist. The evidence did not reflect that defendant's actions were inadvertent or accidental, and as a result, one could draw the reasonable inference that defendant acted "knowingly" under R.C. 2903.22(B). State v. Harco, 2006-Ohio-3408, 2006 Ohio App. LEXIS 3357 (Ohio Ct. App., Ashtabula County 2006).

Appellant's adjudication as a delinquent child, due to committing assault, under R.C. 2903.13(A), was supported by sufficient evidence and was not against the manifest weight of the evidence because the victim of the assault testified that appellant struck him in the face, breaking his nose, after the victim approached him for throwing snowballs at the victim's car, and a detective testified that appellant admitted the victim did not actually strike him before he hit the victim. In re D.B., 2006-Ohio-3240, 2006 Ohio App. LEXIS 3147 (Ohio Ct. App., Butler County 2006).

Conviction of assault on a police officer against defendant was not against the manifest weight of the evidence, as the matter was tried to the bench, which had the discretion to determine the credibility of the witnesses, and there was no miscarriage of justice in its determinations, given that defendant's counsel had a thorough opportunity to cross-examine the police officers involved in order to bring out alleged inconsistencies in their version of events; the officers contended that while trying to arrest defendant for committing assaults against two women, he resisted and caused injury to the officers, whereas defendant claimed that he was never prosecuted for the underlying assaults, he was not lawfully arrested, and the testimony by the officers as to the events in question was not credible. State v. Ogletree, 2006-Ohio-2603, 2006 Ohio App. LEXIS 2449 (Ohio Ct. App., Cuyahoga County 2006).

There was sufficient evidence to support the convictions for assault on a peace officer, under R.C. 2903.13(A), because the record clearly showed that defendant knowingly assaulted two police officers. Defendant ran toward the officers, while screaming and swinging her arms at them, to prevent her son from being arrested; she acted knowingly when she approached the officers in a confrontational manner, trying to protect her son; and she knowingly interfered with the officers while they were attempting to perform their duties. State v. DeMurillo, 2006-Ohio-2569, 2006 Ohio App. LEXIS 2421 (Ohio Ct. App., Cuyahoga County 2006).

Conviction for assault on a peace officer under R.C. 2903.13 was supported by sufficient evidence because the police officers' testimony established that they were acting in their official capacities when defendant assaulted them, and their testimony further showed that defendant attempted to retrieve a knife during struggle and attempted to bite one officer. Since § 2903.13(A) only requires that an individual attempt to cause physical harm to another, the lack of physical evidence establishing the officers' injuries was not fatal to the State's case. State v. Frye, 2006-Ohio-1875, 2006 Ohio App. LEXIS 1727 (Ohio Ct. App., Ashtabula County 2006).

Trial court did not err in overruling defendant's Crim.R. 29(A) motion because the evidence presented was legally sufficient to sustain defendant's conviction; defendant admitted that she stabbed the victim, her neighbor, with a box cutter. Defendant did not prove by a preponderance of the evidence that she had acted in self-defense, pursuant to R.C. 2901.05(A), because the evidence regarding the elements of self-defense conflicted; Defendant maintained that the victim created the violent situation, while the victim testified that he was merely trying to console defendant's husband after a marital argument. State v. McClendon, 2006-Ohio-1846, 2006 Ohio App. LEXIS 1692 (Ohio Ct. App., Hamilton County 2006).

Defendant's conviction for assault, under Columbus, Ohio, Code 2303.13, was supported by sufficient evidence. Both security guards testified that defendant caused physical harm to one of the guards and thus, a reasonable trier of fact could have found that the act of defendant hitting the guard was conduct in which defendant knew, as defined by Columbus, Ohio, Code 2301.22(B), would probably cause injury to the guard. City of Columbus v. Peoples, 2006-Ohio-1718, 2006 Ohio App. LEXIS 1578 (Ohio Ct. App., Franklin County 2006).

Evidence was sufficient to support a conviction of assault on a local corrections officer, R.C. 2903.13(C)(2)(b), where defendant lunged toward a corrections officer with a utensil which had been sharpened so as to make it capable of penetrating the skin and causing serious injury. State v. Hunter, 2006-Ohio-1428, 2006 Ohio App. LEXIS 1320 (Ohio Ct. App., Champaign County 2006).

Defendant's conviction for assault on a peace officer under R.C. 2903.13(A) and (C)(3) was not against the manifest weight of the evidence because it could not say that the jury clearly lost its way or created a miscarriage of justice in finding each element of the offense, including knowledge (R.C. 2901.22(B)) and physical harm (R.C. 2901.01(A)(3)), to have been proven beyond a reasonable doubt. Proof of knowledge of the victim's status was not required because the finding that the victim was a peace officer simply enhanced the degree of the offense and potential penalty and the severity of the victim's injuries had no bearing on the case. State v. Jackson, 2006-Ohio-965, 2006 Ohio App. LEXIS 896 (Ohio Ct. App., Lucas County 2006).

Record contained sufficient evidence that defendant aided and abetted two others in the burglary (R.C. 2911.12), aggravated burglary (R.C. 2911.11), and assault (R.C. 2903.13) pursuant to the complicity statute,

R.C. 2923.03(A)(2), (F), because witness testimony established that defendant supported, encouraged, advised, and incited the other two in the commission of the crimes. His intent was fairly inferred from the circumstances in that he entered the apartment of his own volition, without permission, and proceeded to instruct and encourage the others to assault the victims. State v. Gibbs, 2006-Ohio-175, 2006 Ohio App. LEXIS 143 (Ohio Ct. App., Cuyahoga County 2006).

Where defendant's girlfriend, who was the victim of his crimes, recanted her statements regarding his criminal actions, the use of statements given by her to police officers, as well as the statements of police officers who processed the complaint and photographs of the victim's injuries supported the convictions for assault and felonious assault, in violation of R.C. 2903.13 and 2903.11, as her recantation was properly impeached by her prior inconsistent statements and by the photographs which showed her injuries, although the jury was cautioned not to use the evidence for purposes of substantive proof of the crimes charged; however, as there was no such evidence to impeach the victim's recantation with respect to charges against defendant of intimidation and abduction, in violation of R.C. 2921.03 and 2905.02, the trial court erred in denying his motion for acquittal under Crim.R. 29(A) as to those charges. State v. Kelly, 2006-Ohio-5902, 2006 Ohio App. LEXIS 5862 (Ohio Ct. App., Cuyahoga County 2006).



Defendant's conviction for assault was not against the manifest weight of the evidence which showed that while officers were arresting defendant for his involvement in a hit and run accident, defendant resisted and attempted to punch an officer in the face, that, instead of hitting the officer's face, defendant hit and scratched his neck, and that the officers were unable to get a firm grip on defendant and, ultimately, had to tackle him to restrain him. State v. Barnes, 2006-Ohio-5436, 2006 Ohio App. LEXIS 5428 (Ohio Ct. App., Cuyahoga County 2006).

Defendant was not entitled to acquittal, under Crim.R. 29(A), as to charges of felonious assault, under R.C. 2903.11(A)(2), or assault, under R.C. 2903.13(A) and/or (B), because his convictions for those offenses were not against the manifest weight of the evidence because (1) the weight of the evidence supported the conclusion that defendant used a knife to cut a victim's lip, causing physical harm, under R.C. 2901.01(A)(5), necessitating stiches, (2) that defendant incited his co-defendants, under R.C. 2923.03(A)(2), to violence and that he blocked the escape of victims who were stabbed or cut by the co-defendants, (3) that defendant knowingly, under R.C. 2901.22(B) caused serious physical harm to two victims and/or recklessly, under R.C. 2901.22(C), caused them serious physical harm. State v. Nguyen, 2006-Ohio-5064, 2006 Ohio App. LEXIS 4983 (Ohio Ct. App., Summit County 2006).

As defendant's girlfriend initially filed complaints against defendant arising from his domestic violence incidents against her, which resulted in criminal charges being filed against defendant, and she thereafter recanted her statements and repeatedly claimed that they were fabricated, only convictions for assault and felonious assault, in violation of R.C. 2903.11 and 2903.13, were sufficiently proved based on photographs of the victim's injuries and statements by the police, which were used only to impeach the victim's credibility but not as substantive evidence of the content thereof; however, convictions for abduction and intimidation, in violation of R.C. 2905.02 and 2921.03, could not stand without the victim's testimony, as there was no independent evidence to support the convictions and the victim's prior inconsistent statements to police could not be used as substantive evidence, and defendant's motion for acquittal as to those charges should have been granted under Crim.R. 29(A), based on judicial precedent, evidentiary rules, and the Confrontation Clause of U.S. Const. amend. VI. State v. Kelly, 2006-Ohio-4879, 970 N.E.2d 986, 2006 Ohio App. LEXIS 4800 (Ohio Ct. App., Cuyahoga County), sub. op., 2006-Ohio-5902, 2006 Ohio App. LEXIS 5862 (Ohio Ct. App., Cuyahoga County 2006).

There was sufficient evidence that defendant assaulted a peace officer, pursuant to R.C. 2903.13(A), because, according to the police officers, defendant became belligerent once they attempted to handcuff her; she attempted to break away from the officers, and when she and of the officers fell into the patrol car, defendant tried to kick him in the head. The State presented further evidence that the kick was so hard that the officer felt a breeze, and that defendant began yelling and shouting profanities. State v. Jones, 2006-Ohio-299, 2006 Ohio App. LEXIS 259 (Ohio Ct. App., Cuyahoga County 2006).

When defendant, who was handcuffed, ran toward an officer as if to kick him, there was sufficient evidence for a jury to find defendant guilty of assault on a peace officer, under R.C. 2903.13(A) and 2923.02(A), as two officers consistently testified that defendant tried to harm the officer by making an overt act that appeared to be an attempt to strike the officer with some part of her body. State v. McConkey, 2005-Ohio-6580, 2005 Ohio App. LEXIS 5892 (Ohio Ct. App., Ashtabula County 2005).

There was sufficient evidence to support all of the elements of defendant's conviction for assault, under R.C. 2903.13(A), as the victim clearly testified that defendant did strike her. Further, although the victim did state during her testimony that she had trouble remembering the things that happened that night because she was intoxicated, the evidence did not weight so heavily against conviction that the trial court's judgment had to be reversed. State v. Hamblett-Catt, 2005-Ohio-5894, 2005 Ohio App. LEXIS 5313 (Ohio Ct. App., Van Wert County 2005).

There was sufficient evidence to support the conviction for assault of a peace officer, R.C. 2903.13, because the evidence established that defendant knowingly (R.C. 2901.22(B)) caused or attempted to cause harm to a peace officer. Despite the inconsistencies in defendant's recollection of the events, it was apparent that she was aware that her actions would result in her fist making contact with the deputy because when the deputy placed his hand on her shoulder and asked her to stop, she immediately swung around with her arm extended and hand balled into a fist, and it was clear that defendant intended for her fist to make contact with the deputy and was aware that such contact would result. State v. Johnson, 2005-Ohio-5559, 2005 Ohio App. LEXIS 5018 (Ohio Ct. App., Cuyahoga County 2005).

Defendant's conviction for assault on a peace officer, R.C. 2903.13(A) and (C)(3), was not against the manifest weight of the evidence because the testimony of the officers established that after defendant was pulled over so that his girlfriend could retrieve her keys, defendant became belligerent and combative and would not take his hand out of his pocket. Three officers removed him from his vehicle, he fought them and repeatedly kicked one of the officers. State v. Walach, 2005-Ohio-5456, 2005 Ohio App. LEXIS 4929 (Ohio Ct. App., Lucas County 2005).

Weight and sufficiency of the evidence supported defendant's conviction for assault on a peace officer, in violation of R.C. 2903.13(A), (C)(3), where the jurors chose to believe the deputy's version of events over the conflicting version provided by defendant with respect to defendant's assault on a deputy while defendant was incarcerated in a county jail; defendant refused his lunch food tray, which defendant claimed was due to another inmate's having put his fingers in the food, and a physical altercation resulted between defendant and the deputy at the jail, resulting in injuries to the deputy, and accordingly, defendant's acquittal motion under Crim.R. 29 was properly denied. State v. Jones, 2005-Ohio-6930, 2005 Ohio App. LEXIS 6252 (Ohio Ct. App., Mahoning County 2005).

There was sufficient evidence for assault, under R.C. 2903.13(A), against the girlfriend's mother because the evidence demonstrated that her fingers were injured and she testified that defendant picked her up and threw her to the floor. Thus, the evidence showed that defendant knowingly caused or attempted to cause physical harm to the mother when he threw her to the floor. State v. Brown, 2005-Ohio-6731, 2005 Ohio App. LEXIS 6082 (Ohio Ct. App., Cuyahoga County 2005).

Defendant's conviction for assault of a police officer was supported by sufficient evidence as: (1) two officers were displaying their police badges when they approached defendant, (2) one officer testified that he identified them as police officers, (3) a witness supported the officer's testimony that two of the officers had their shields on a neck string around their necks, (4) the injured officer testified that he was attempting to arrest defendant when he "dug three holes" into the officer's hand, causing it to bleed, and (5) the injured officer stated that he had scars on his hand as a result of the injury. State v. Fritz, 2005-Ohio-4736, 163 Ohio App. 3d 276, 837 N.E.2d 823, 2005 Ohio App. LEXIS 4233 (Ohio Ct. App., Montgomery County 2005).

There was substantial evidence upon which the jury could reasonably have concluded that all of the elements of assault, under Cleveland, Ohio, Mun. Ordinance § 621.03 (similar to R.C. 2903.13), were proven beyond a reasonable doubt. Witnesses, including a customer, confirmed the victim's version of events that defendant, the building owner, struck the victim, the commercial lessee, in the face, which left an imprint. City of Cleveland v. Gonzalez, 2005-Ohio-4413, 2005 Ohio App. LEXIS 4001 (Ohio Ct. App., Cuyahoga County 2005).

Weight and sufficiency of the evidence supported defendant's convictions of misdemeanor assault, aggravated robbery, and kidnapping, in violation of R.C. 2903.13, 2911.01, and 2905.01, respectively, where he kicked in the door of the victim's house, attacked the victim, who was sitting on his bed, and forced the victim to remain in his bathroom; the victim was beaten by defendant when defendant caught him watching his movements, he was threatened, and certain valuables were missing from the victim's home. State v. Butler, 2005-Ohio-4122, 2005 Ohio App. LEXIS 3762 (Ohio Ct. App., Cuyahoga County 2005).

When the evidence showed that defendant and the victim engaged in a physical altercation in which defendant attempted to physically injure the victim, but was unsuccessful, the fact that defendant did not actually injure the victim did not mean that the trial court's judgment finding defendant guilty of a violation of R.C. 2903.13(A) was error, because the statute only required proof that defendant attempted to cause physical harm to the victim, and, under R.C. 2901.01(A)(3), physical harm was any injury, regardless of its gravity or duration. State v. Brown, 2005-Ohio-3871, 2005 Ohio App. LEXIS 3573 (Ohio Ct. App., Montgomery County 2005).

Trial court did not err in finding defendant guilty of assault in violation of R.C. 2903.13 because a finding of guilty upon the testimony of one witness, although it might be contradicted by another witness, was sufficient to support the finding if the trier of fact found that witness more credible; the trial court found the victim's testimony more credible than defendant's testimony. State v. Frazier, 2005-Ohio-3766, 2005 Ohio App. LEXIS 3476 (Ohio Ct. App., Delaware County 2005).

Defendant's assault conviction in violation of R.C. 2903.13(A) was not against the manifest weight of the evidence where there was evidence that all the elements of assault were proven beyond a reasonable doubt, and the record established that defendant was at the time and place where the assault occurred. State v. Rowland, 2005-Ohio-3756, 2005 Ohio App. LEXIS 3473 (Ohio Ct. App., Montgomery County 2005).

Defendant's conviction for assaulting a corrections officer, under R.C. 2903.13(C)(2), was not against the manifest weight of the evidence because his testimony was directly contradicted by his victims and the physician he presented could only testify that he had been injured and could not establish that the injury occurred when he assaulted his victims, so he did not prove self-defense by a preponderance of the evidence, as required by R.C. 2901.05(A). State v. Hill, 2005-Ohio-3569, 2005 Ohio App. LEXIS 3299 (Ohio Ct. App., Cuyahoga County 2005).

When evidence was presented that, when police responded to defendant's complaint that his girlfriend had damaged his property, he raised his hand as if to strike one of the officers, although defendant and his witnesses testified that defendant was only pointing out his girlfriend to the officers, defendant's conviction for assault on a peace officer, under R.C. 2903.13(C)(3), was not against the manifest weight of the evidence, which disposed of his claim that the conviction was not supported by sufficient evidence, so it was not error to deny his Crim.R. 29 motion for a judgment of acquittal. State v. Bray, 2005-Ohio-3297, 2005 Ohio App. LEXIS 3076 (Ohio Ct. App., Lorain County 2005).

Trial court properly denied defendant's motion for a judgment of acquittal, pursuant to Crim.R. 29(A), and convicted him of assault in violation of R.C. 2903.13(A), as the weight and sufficiency of the evidence supported the conviction where defendant went to his girlfriend's trailer and beat her up, verbally threatened her, and would not let her leave for more than an hour and a half; defendant's girlfriend testified that defendant repeatedly hit her, banged her head into a wall, threw her onto furniture, and punched her in the head, and the fact that there were no photographs of the injuries or that the girlfriend did not go to the hospital did not lessen the credibility of her story, as her testimony alone was sufficient to support the conviction. State v. Brown, 2005-Ohio-2879, 2005 Ohio App. LEXIS 2704 (Ohio Ct. App., Ashtabula County 2005).

Although R.C. 2935.03(A)(1) and 4506.23 may be pertinent in deciding whether a deputy had authority to stop, detain and arrest an appellant, they do not govern a court's analysis to determine whether he was in the performance of his official duties for purposes of R.C. 2903.13(C)(3); accordingly, a determination that defendant had committed such a violation was governed by the inquiry as to whether the peace officer was engaged in a duty imposed upon him by law, which was not limited to official duties occurring within one's territorial jurisdiction. State v. Dawson, 2005-Ohio-2276, 2005 Ohio App. LEXIS 2171 (Ohio Ct. App., Pickaway County 2005).

Trial court properly denied defendant's motion for a judgment of acquittal, pursuant to Crim.R. 29(A), and convicted him of assault in violation of R.C. 2903.13(A), as the weight and sufficiency of the evidence supported the conviction where defendant went to his girlfriend's trailer and beat her up, verbally threatened her, and would not let her leave for more than an hour and a half. Defendant's girlfriend testified that defendant repeatedly hit her, banged her head into a wall, threw her onto furniture, and punched her in the head, and the fact that there were no photographs of the injuries or that the girlfriend did not go to the hospital did not lessen the credibility of her story, as her testimony alone was sufficient to support the conviction. State v. Brown, 2005-Ohio-2879, 2005 Ohio App. LEXIS 2704 (Ohio Ct. App., Ashtabula County 2005).

Defendant's conviction for failure to comply with an order or signal of a police officer, grand theft, assault, driving under an Ohio Financial Responsibility Act suspension, and resisting arrest was not against the manifest weight of the evidence where: (1) defendant was "messing around" with the driver's side door before he entered the vehicle, (2) defendant sped away in the vehicle after the police officers activated their lights and sirens, (3) defendant continually punched an officer after he was apprehended, and (4) an inspection of the vehicle showed that no keys were in the vehicle, that the center column under the steering wheel was smashed, and that there was a screwdriver on the driver's side floorboard. State v. Tate, 2005-Ohio-2156, 2005 Ohio App. LEXIS 2057 (Ohio Ct. App., Summit County 2005).

Because the victim's trial testimony supported an inference that defendant knowingly struck the victim, as defined by R.C. 2901.22(B), the evidence was sufficient to support a conviction for assault. State v. Chatman, 2005-Ohio-1930, 2005 Ohio App. LEXIS 1845 (Ohio Ct. App., Montgomery County 2005).

There was legally sufficient evidence to support defendant's convictions for robbery, R.C. 2911.02(A)(2), and misdemeanor assault, R.C. 2903.13(A), because the evidence showed that, as defendant struggled with the victim, his former girlfriend, he attempted to take her car keys and, in fact, grabbed her purse from underneath her as she was lying on the ground. The evidence also showed that defendant repeatedly hit and kicked the victim, dragged her out of her car, ripped her hair weave from her head, caused multiple bruises all over her body, and broke several of her fingernails. State v. Haywood, 2005-Ohio-1856, 2005 Ohio App. LEXIS 1767 (Ohio Ct. App., Cuyahoga County 2005).

There was legally sufficient evidence for a jury to have found the elements of the crime of misdemeanor assault proven beyond a reasonable doubt since the victim's daughter saw defendant holding her mother (the victim) down and hitting her in the face, the victim gave a statement that defendant had hit her in the face several times, and the police officers observed red marks on the victim's face. State v. Quiles, 2005-Ohio-388, 2005 Ohio App. LEXIS 459 (Ohio Ct. App., Cuyahoga County 2005).

Trial court did not err in finding defendant guilty of assault in violation of R.C. 2903.13 because a finding of guilty upon the testimony of one witness, although it might be contradicted by another witness, was sufficient to support the finding if the trier of fact found that witness more credible; the trial court found the victim's testimony more credible than defendant's testimony. State v. Frazier, 2005-Ohio-3766, 2005 Ohio App. LEXIS 3476 (Ohio Ct. App., Delaware County 2005).

Defendant's assault conviction in violation of R.C. 2903.13(A) was not against the manifest weight of the evidence where there was evidence that all the elements of assault were proven beyond a reasonable doubt, and the record established that defendant was at the time and place where the assault occurred. State v. Rowland, 2005-Ohio-3756, 2005 Ohio App. LEXIS 3473 (Ohio Ct. App., Montgomery County 2005).

Conviction for assault under R.C. 2903.13(A) was not against the manifest weight of the evidence because, while there was a conflict between the victim's statement given to police and his testimony at trial, the conflict presented an issue of credibility for the trier of fact to resolve. Further, the victim's testimony that defendant's punch induced pain was sufficient to satisfy the physical harm element of assault. State v. Hill, 2005-Ohio-3701, 2005 Ohio App. LEXIS 3400 (Ohio Ct. App., Montgomery County 2005).

Finding that defendant was a delinquent for committing complicity to commit assault and unlawful restraint was not against the manifest weight of the evidence because, standing alone, the victim's testimony, to the effect that defendant told his friends to perform "the bandit" on the victim and that he held the victim down while his friend performed "the bandit," which entailed his friend's insertion of two fingers into the victim's anal cavity, established defendant's guilt. A factfinder could conclude that defendant not only initiated the illegal act by his words of incitement and/or encouragement but also assisted in the commission of that offense by holding the victim down while his friend forcefully violated him. In re J.P., 2005-Ohio-3390, 2005 Ohio App. LEXIS 3168 (Ohio Ct. App., Cuyahoga County 2005).

Defendant's conviction for assaulting a corrections officer, under R.C. 2903.13(C)(2), was not against the manifest weight of the evidence because his testimony was directly contradicted by his victims and the physician he presented could only testify that he had been injured and could not establish that the injury occurred when he assaulted his victims, so he did not prove self-defense by a preponderance of the evidence, as required by R.C. 2901.05(A). State v. Hill, 2005-Ohio-3569, 2005 Ohio App. LEXIS 3299 (Ohio Ct. App., Cuyahoga County 2005).

Defendant's assault conviction was supported by legally sufficient evidence. The testimony of the victim and the bar manager was sufficient to prove that defendant hit the victim in the face with a glass and it could reasonably have been inferred that she was aware that such conduct would probably result in physical harm. State v. Monie, 2004-Ohio-4515, 2004 Ohio App. LEXIS 4102 (Ohio Ct. App., Montgomery County 2004).

Defendant's conviction of assault in violation of R.C. 2903.13(C)(2)(a) was not against the manifest weight of the evidence, as the State admitted photos of the victim's injuries, defendant admitted physically attacking the victim, and the jury was entitled to disbelieve defendant's claim that she acted in self-defense. State v. Adkins, 2004-Ohio-4019, 2004 Ohio App. LEXIS 3641 (Ohio Ct. App., Union County 2004).

In light of the testimony of the victim, who testified that defendant hit him three times with a 10-pound tow-chain, certified medical records regarding the treatment the victim received, and photos of the victim's injuries, including one that showed the imprint of the chain on the victim's skin, defendant's conviction for assault in violation of R.C. 2903.13(A) was not against the manifest weight of the evidence. State v. Keene, 2004-Ohio-2344, 2004 Ohio App. LEXIS 2107 (Ohio Ct. App., Cuyahoga County 2004).

Where the victim and another witness testified that defendant shoved her to the ground, causing her to hit her head against a sidewalk, that other witnesses testified that defendant and the victim accidentally ran into each other and that the victim persuaded a witness to lie did not mean that defendant's assault conviction was against the weight of the evidence because the trial court found the State's witnesses more credible, as was its right. State v. Bates, 2004-Ohio-1370, 2004 Ohio App. LEXIS 1226 (Ohio Ct. App., Belmont County 2004).

Where defendant merely asserted the victim was the aggressor and the trial court could believe the victim's testimony over defendant's, the conviction for assault under R.C. 2903.13(A) was not against the manifest weight of the evidence. State v. Curtis, 2004-Ohio-660, 2004 Ohio App. LEXIS 649 (Ohio Ct. App., Montgomery County 2004).

There was sufficient evidence to support the finding of delinquency for committing assault and gross sexual imposition because the victim testified that defendant grabbed her and pulled her into the bathroom where he touched her through her clothes and hit her in the face. When confronted by the police, defendant admitted to grabbing the victim and pulling her into the boys' bathroom, but claimed the touching of her private area was an accident. State v. Yarnell, 2004-Ohio-447, 2004 Ohio App. LEXIS 402 (Ohio Ct. App., Stark County 2004).

There was sufficient evidence to find that defendant knowingly caused or attempted to cause physical harm to the victim, the mother of his baby, in violation of R.C. 2903.13(A); the victim's friend testified that she encountered defendant and the victim arguing and that, after they had been out of her site briefly, the victim was crying and had red marks on her neck. State v. Garrett, 2003-Ohio-5185, 2003 Ohio App. LEXIS 4725 (Ohio Ct. App., Erie County 2003).

Conviction for assault, under R.C. 2903.13, was not against the manifest weight of the evidence where the defendant failed to present any witness who saw the incident commence but the state presented two witnesses who testified that the victim was struck by the defendant. State v. Dietz, 2003-Ohio-3249, 2003 Ohio App. LEXIS 2886 (Ohio Ct. App., Cuyahoga County 2003).

Trial court did not err in denying defendant's acquittal motion pursuant to Crim.R. 29(A), as reasonable minds could have reached different conclusions regarding whether defendant proved each element of self-defense by a preponderance of the evidence in a trial against defendant on a charge of criminal assault, in violation of R.C. 2903.13(A); defendant was the only witness who claimed that he was forced to punch the victim in order to escape a chokehold that the victim had defendant in. State v. Fawcett, 2001-Ohio-2167, 2001 Ohio App. LEXIS 6104 (Ohio Ct. App., Seneca County 2001).



As the evidence supported defendant's conviction for assault, in violation of R.C. 2903.13(A), where the jury did not believe defendant's claim of self-defense, a trial court did not abuse its discretion by overruling defendant's new trial motion under Crim.R. 33(A)(4). State v. Fawcett, 2001-Ohio-2167, 2001 Ohio App. LEXIS 6104 (Ohio Ct. App., Seneca County 2001).

Evidence that defendant severely injured his child by violently shaking him was sufficient to support a conviction of assault: State v. Weeks, 64 Ohio App. 3d 595, 582 N.E.2d 614, 1989 Ohio App. LEXIS 3691 (Ohio Ct. App., Clermont County 1989).

Trial court had before it substantial evidence upon which it could reasonably have concluded that all of the elements of assault and public indecency had been proven beyond a reasonable doubt. The convictions were also not against the manifest weight of the evidence because, reviewing the entire record, the evidence and all reasonable inferences, considering the credibility of the witnesses, the appellate court determined that the jury in resolving conflicts in the evidence clearly did not lose its way or create such a manifest miscarriage of justice that the conviction had to be reversed and a new trial ordered. State v. Green, 1985 Ohio App. LEXIS 10452 (Ohio Ct. App., Hamilton County Oct. 30, 1985).

**Expungement**

Trial court did not err in ruling that defendant was not an eligible offender to have his criminal records sealed under under R.C. 2953.31(A)(1)(b) because he had a prior conviction for assault, which was an offense of violence under R.C. 2901.01(A)(9)(a). State v. J.B., 2021-Ohio-187, 2021 Ohio App. LEXIS 189 (Ohio Ct. App., Summit County 2021).

Because defendant was convicted of assault of a police officer under R.C. 2903.13, which was a crime of violence under R.C. 2901.01(A)(9)(a) and a fourth-degree felony, the exceptions set forth in R.C. 2953.36(A) did not apply, and defendant was not eligible for expungement of the conviction. State v. B.J., 2018-Ohio-5358, 2018 Ohio App. LEXIS 5671 (Ohio Ct. App., Cuyahoga County 2018).

Denial of defendant's application to expunge his misdemeanor assault conviction was inappropriate because a misdemeanor assault conviction was eligible for expungement consideration by the trial court since it was one of the specifically excluded offenses excepted from the application of R.C. 2953.36(C). State v. Klempay, 2011-Ohio-2643, 2011 Ohio App. LEXIS 2253 (Ohio Ct. App., Mahoning County 2011).

Defendant's application for expungement of his felony assault conviction was properly denied because R.C. 2953.36(C) removed from the "offense of violence" exception to the expungement procedures only misdemeanor assault convictions, not felony assault convictions. State v. Ventura, 2005-Ohio-5048, 2005 Ohio App. LEXIS 4560 (Ohio Ct. App., Butler County 2005).

**False arrest**

**—Probable cause**

Police officers could not be held liable on claims of false arrest and false imprisonment arising out of their arrest of appellant on a charge of domestic violence, occurring after the officers received reports from witnesses that appellant struck his girlfriend's son-in-law and that the son-in-law lived at appellant's home. Even if the officers did not have probable cause to arrest appellant for domestic violence, in that the son-in-law was not related to appellant, the officers did have probable cause to arrest appellant for assault. Frazier v. Clinton County Sheriff's Office, 2008-Ohio-6064, 2008 Ohio App. LEXIS 5071 (Ohio Ct. App., Clinton County 2008).

**Indictment**

Because the underlying offense in an aggravated burglary indictment did not have to be specified in the indictment, a trial court did not err in amending, prior to trial, the aggravated burglary charge against defendant to include assault as one of several crimes charged. The amendment inserting the underlying offense of assault was proper because the nature and identity of the offense charged, aggravated burglary, was not changed, and because defendant was on notice the State alleged an assault as one of the offenses it sought to prove at trial, given that violence was alleged as one of the offenses that he had the purpose to commit when he entered the home. State v. Kidd, 2020-Ohio-4994, 2020 Ohio App. LEXIS 3838 (Ohio Ct. App., Cuyahoga County 2020).

Indictment charging defendant with aggravated burglary was not defective for failing to inform defendant of the charge against him as the indictment tracked the statutory elements of aggravated burglary and, thus, did not need to allege the particular criminal offense that defendant intended to commit. Moreover, the bill of particulars requested by defendant and provided by the State notified defendant of the predicate offense of assault by its allegation that defendant was aware of the fact that entering the victim's home carrying a loaded gun would probably lead to a confrontation and physical harm or attempted physical harm to the occupants; thus, defendant's contention that he was denied the effective assistance of counsel by counsel's failure to object to the indictment prior to trial, as required by Crim.R. 12(C)(2), was without merit. State v. Woyan, 2007-Ohio-6376, 2007 Ohio App. LEXIS 5562 (Ohio Ct. App., Erie County 2007).

**Ineffective assistance of counsel**

In an appeal from a conviction for assault, defense counsel was not was ineffective in failing to raise objections to the portions of victim's testimony because counsel thoroughly cross-examined victim regarding; by obtaining victim's admission that she never reported defendant's behavior, defense counsel established a reasonable inference that victim was not bothered by defendant's behavior or that victim had been untruthful and exaggerated defendant's actions. State v. Terry, 2021-Ohio-2091, 2021 Ohio App. LEXIS 2053 (Ohio Ct. App., Hamilton County 2021).

Where defendant was convicted of assault and domestic violence, there was no merit to her claim that her attorney was ineffective for not calling corroborating witnesses; as she did not identify such witnesses or describe their testimony, she did not demonstrate that counsel's performance was deficient, or that a reasonable probability existed that the result of the proceedings would have been different. State/City of Toledo v. Owens, 2019-Ohio-311, 2019 Ohio App. LEXIS 325 (Ohio Ct. App., Lucas County 2019).

Defendant received effective assistance of counsel, despite counsel's failure to object to testimony regarding a prior uncharged incident that had occurred on the same date as the subject offense, because counsel established the victim was intoxicated, used the first uncharged incident to establish the victim slapped defendant, and argued self-defense in closing argument; there was no indication that the trial court was influenced by the testimony of the first uncharged incident. State v. Triona, 2016-Ohio-5163, 2016 Ohio App. LEXIS 3032 (Ohio Ct. App., Licking County 2016).

Defendant was denied the effective assistance of counsel as counsel failed to request an instruction on self-defense where: (1) under defendant's version of events, the officers were the aggressors and their actions caused him to believe that he was in imminent danger of bodily harm, (2) although defendant testified that the injury to an officer was not intentional, he specifically testified that he attempted to move the officer's hand from his face so that he could breathe, (3) the jury could have reasonably concluded that defendant purposefully used force to protect himself from his assailants, and (4) there was a reasonable probability that, but for counsel's errors, the result of the proceeding would have been different as the officers admitted that they punched defendant over 30 times. State v. Fritz, 2005-Ohio-4736, 163 Ohio App. 3d 276, 837 N.E.2d 823, 2005 Ohio App. LEXIS 4233 (Ohio Ct. App., Montgomery County 2005).

**Inferior degree offense**

Court did not err by failing to instruct on simple assault because the evidence presented at trial demonstrated that defendant struck the victim, resulting in pain and a broken nose, which caused her nose to shift out of place and left a wound that exposed the bone; no reasonable jury could have found that defendant did not knowingly cause serious physical harm to the victim. State v. Lanier, 2020-Ohio-3394, 2020 Ohio App. LEXIS 2327 (Ohio Ct. App., Ottawa County 2020).

**Instructions**

Trial court did not abuse its discretion in deciding not to charge the jury on reckless assault, as the testimony of the State's witnesses provided evidence that defendant acted knowingly, i.e., he was aware that punching the victim in the jaw with a closed fist would probably cause serious injury; moreover, there was no evidence that defendant acted recklessly. State v. Bolden, 2016-Ohio-4727, 2016 Ohio App. LEXIS 2530 (Ohio Ct. App., Lake County 2016).

Trial court did not err in declining to instruct the jury on disorderly conduct by engaging in fighting as a lesser included offense of assault, as defendant had only made an oral request, but he had not requested such an instruction in writing, as required. State v. McFadden, 2014-Ohio-5294, 2014 Ohio App. LEXIS 5118 (Ohio Ct. App., Washington County 2014).

In defendant's felonious assault case, the court did not err in failing to give a lesser-included jury instruction on simple assault because the evidence did not support an instruction on the lesser included offense of simple assault, as the harm done to the victim was indeed serious. The victim suffered a crushed eye socket, a broken nose, and various other facial fractures and contusions and was transferred to a different hospital due to possible blood on the brain. State v. Portillo, 2011-Ohio-52, 2011 Ohio App. LEXIS 35 (Ohio Ct. App., Tuscarawas County 2011).

Trial court's failure to sua sponte instruct the jury on assault was not plain error because the evidence of serious physical harm was overwhelming; the victim spent five days in the hospital with a broken nose, broken cheekbone, broken collarbone, dislocated shoulder, and fractured shin. While the victim remembered nothing after defendant punched him twice, there was no evidence in the record to support defendant's argument that the serious physical harm was inflicted by another man who entered the apartment with him, rather than by defendant. State v. Wells, 2010-Ohio-3126, 2010 Ohio App. LEXIS 2622 (Ohio Ct. App., Stark County 2010).

Defendant was unable to prove the elements of self-defense by a preponderance of the evidence as the evidence showed that defendant created the situation giving rise to the altercation, there was no evidence that defendant believed that she was in immediate danger of death or great bodily harm, and defendant presented no evidence suggesting avoidance of the alleged danger in any way. Any jury instruction on self-defense would have been futile; thus, trial counsel was not ineffective for failing to request an instruction on self-defense. State v. McDuffie, 2007-Ohio-3421, 2007 Ohio App. LEXIS 3175 (Ohio Ct. App., Cuyahoga County 2007).

In defendant's prosecution for assault, a self-defense instruction was not warranted because defendant's entire defense was predicated upon his denial of using force to resist his arrest. State v. Latessa, 2007-Ohio-3373, 2007 Ohio App. LEXIS 3097 (Ohio Ct. App., Lake County 2007).

Since disorderly conduct as a fourth degree misdemeanor required proof of an additional element, to wit: that the offender persisted after a request to desist, it was not a lesser-included offense of assault, and the trial court did not err in failing to instruct the jury on disorderly conduct as a fourth degree misdemeanor. State v. Latessa, 2007-Ohio-3373, 2007 Ohio App. LEXIS 3097 (Ohio Ct. App., Lake County 2007).

As defendant punched the victim twice in the face and the blows were so hard that the victim's tooth punctured his cheek, he suffered a fractured skull, and he had permanent disabilities from the incident, the trial court did not abuse its discretion in declining to instruct the jury on the lesser included offense of simple assault, in violation of R.C. 2903.13, rather than on the charged offense of felonious assault, in violation of R.C. 2903.11(A)(1), as defendant's actions could not have been viewed as "reckless" under R.C. 2901.22(C), which was the scienter needed for purposes of a simple assault conviction, and the victim clearly suffered "serious physical harm" pursuant to R.C. 2901.01(A)(5); rather, he was deemed to have acted knowingly pursuant to R.C. 2901.22(B) based on the circumstances of the situation. State v. Bennett, 2006-Ohio-3566, 2006 Ohio App. LEXIS 3519 (Ohio Ct. App., Mahoning County 2006).

It was not plain error, under Crim.R. 52(B), for a trial court to instruct a jury, in a prosecution for felonious assault on a peace officer, that defendant did not have to know the person assaulted was a peace officer because (1) defendant stated no objection to the instruction, under Crim.R. 30(A), (2) such an instruction had been specifically approved as to a charge of assault on a peace officer, under R.C. 2903.13, and (3) this logically extended to a charge of felonious assault on a peace officer. State v. Mundy, 2005-Ohio-6608, 2005 Ohio App. LEXIS 5948 (Ohio Ct. App., Medina County 2005).

Trial court properly refused to give defendant's requested involuntary manslaughter instruction with an underlying misdemeanor of aggravated menacing; defendant's claim that a simple assault instruction was implicit in her request was rejected as defendant was bound to identify the proper underlying misdemeanor that would support an involuntary manslaughter instruction. Defendant did not object to the jury instructions and waived all but an error that clearly would have changed the outcome of the trial; it could not be said that the outcome of the trial would have been otherwise had an involuntary manslaughter instruction with an underlying offense of simple assault been given. State v. Davis, 2005-Ohio-5783, 2005 Ohio App. LEXIS 5208 (Ohio Ct. App., Montgomery County 2005).

Failure to instruct the jury on self-defense, during the trial for assault on a peace officer under R.C. 2903.13(A) and (C)(3), did not constitute plain error because trial counsel did not request a jury instruction on the affirmative defense of self-defense, thereby effectively waiving any error on that issue, and because the facts of the case clearly did not support a finding that the outcome of the trial would have been otherwise had an instruction on self-defense been given. The police officers testified that, after defendant was pulled over, he became belligerent, combative, and he kicked one of the officers. State v. Walach, 2005-Ohio-5456, 2005 Ohio App. LEXIS 4929 (Ohio Ct. App., Lucas County 2005).

In defendant's felonious assault prosecution, a jury instruction on the lesser-included offense of assault under R.C. 2903.13(B) was properly denied because defendant denied kicking the victim, and the only testimony as to the contact came from the victim, who testified that defendant deliberately and forcefully kicked her head; thus, a jury instruction allowing a finding that defendant acted recklessly was not appropriate. State v. Fuller, 2005-Ohio-3696, 2005 Ohio App. LEXIS 3397 (Ohio Ct. App., Montgomery County 2005).

**—Lesser included offenses**

Trial court plainly erred in instructing a jury on misdemeanor assault as a lesser included offense of misdemeanor domestic violence because the inclusion of assault as a lesser included offense was improper where the domestic violence and assault charges were of the same degree. Defendant 's assault conviction was thus vacated. State v. Kidd, 2020-Ohio-4994, 2020 Ohio App. LEXIS 3838 (Ohio Ct. App., Cuyahoga County 2020).

Trial court did not err in not giving an instruction on simple assault because the evidence did not support such an instruction. Surveillance video of the fight clearly demonstrated that defendant's last punch rendered the victim unconscious, which constituted serious physical harm for felonious assault and there was no evidence that the victim's unconsciousness was due to anything other than defendant's punch. State v. Wimpey, 2019-Ohio-4823, 2019 Ohio App. LEXIS 4887 (Ohio Ct. App., Lucas County 2019).

**Insurance**

Where a couple was convicted of intentional assault, and their insurance policy contained an intentional acts exclusion provision, the insurer had no duty to them in an underlying lawsuit; as there was no duty to defend, a bad faith claim was moot. Westfield Ins. v. Barnett, 2003-Ohio-6278, 2003 Ohio App. LEXIS 5615 (Ohio Ct. App., Noble County 2003).

**Intentional conduct**

Defendant's conduct did not fall within the definition of assault by way of "recklessly" causing serious physical harm, rather than felonious assault with which he was charged, because defendant acted intentionally in twice punching the victim in the face. State v. Clark, 2016-Ohio-5143, 2016 Ohio App. LEXIS 3068 (Ohio Ct. App., Cuyahoga County 2016).

**Interference with arrest**

When defendant was arrested for assault on a peace officer, under R.C. 2903.13(A) and (C)(3), defendant's lawful arrest was not an element of the crime, as it was defined as causing or attempting to cause physical harm to a peace officer while in the performance of official duties, and, unlike resisting arrest, a lawful arrest was not an element. State v. Martin, 2005-Ohio-3511, 2005 Ohio App. LEXIS 3265 (Ohio Ct. App., Madison County 2005).

A third person has no right to volunteer assistance or interpose resistance when the person assisted is being lawfully arrested; and if the intervenor, in good faith, aggressively intervenes in a struggle between another person and a plain clothes officer, who is attempting to effectuate a lawful arrest, then the intervenor is guilty of an assault because he has no greater right to use force than the person whom he is endeavoring to protect: State v. Wenger, 58 Ohio St. 2d 336, 12 Ohio Op. 3d 309, 390 N.E.2d 801, 1979 Ohio LEXIS 439 (Ohio 1979).

**Jury instructions**

Trial court did not err by not giving an instruction on misdemeanor assault because the evidence did not reasonably support a conviction for assault and an acquittal on the indicted charge of felonious assault. Because of the stipulation that the victim suffered serious physical harm after being attacked by defendant and his codefendants, no jury could have reasonably found defendant not guilty of causing serious physical harm, but guilty of causing physical harm. State v. Koch, 2019-Ohio-4099, 146 N.E.3d 1238, 2019 Ohio App. LEXIS 4175 (Ohio Ct. App., Montgomery County 2019).

Trial court did not err by not giving an instruction on misdemeanor assault because the evidence did not reasonably support a conviction for assault and an acquittal on the indicted charge of felonious assault. Because of the stipulation that the victim suffered serious physical harm after being attacked by defendant and his codefendants, no jury could have reasonably found defendant not guilty of causing serious physical harm, but guilty of causing physical harm. State v. Koch, 2019-Ohio-4099, 146 N.E.3d 1238, 2019 Ohio App. LEXIS 4175 (Ohio Ct. App., Montgomery County 2019).

Even if the trial court's failure to give defendant's requested jury instructions on various assault charges was error, it was not reversible because defendant failed to show that he was prejudiced thereby. State v. Thompson, 2016-Ohio-4689, 2016 Ohio App. LEXIS 2511 (Ohio Ct. App., Wayne County 2016).

Trial court did not abuse its discretion in refusing to instruct the jury on self-defense or defense of others in defendant's criminal trial, as defendant did not raise sufficient evidence with regard to either of those defenses pursuant to R.C. 2901.05, such that the submission of the issue to the jury was unwarranted in defendant's trial on charges of assault, in violation of R.C. 2903.13(A). State v. Belcher, 2013-Ohio-1234, 2013 Ohio App. LEXIS 1133 (Ohio Ct. App., Montgomery County 2013).

In a felonious assault case, the court erred by failing instruct on the lesser included offense of simple assault because a juror could have believed defendant was the person who threw the initial punch, but did not stomp or kick the victim after he was on the ground, and therefore, did not knowingly cause serious physical harm. State v. Barker, 2012-Ohio-522, 2012 Ohio App. LEXIS 458 (Ohio Ct. App., Portage County 2012).

Defendant failed to establish that he received ineffective assistance of counsel; because resisting arrest was not a lesser-included offense of assault upon a peace officer, defendant was not entitled to an instruction on resisting arrest. Thus, counsel was not ineffective for having failed to request an instruction. State v. Totty, 2010-Ohio-1234, 2010 Ohio App. LEXIS 1029 (Ohio Ct. App., Montgomery County 2010).

Trial court did not commit plain error under Crim.R. 52(B) by failing to give jury instructions on the lesser included offenses of aggravated assault and simple assault, in violation of R.C. 2903.12(A)(1) and 2903.13(A) and (B), in defendant's criminal trial on a charge of felonious assault, in violation of R.C. 2903.11(A)(1), as the evidence did not support convictions under either of the lesser offenses; there was no provocation, and the jury could not have reasonably found that the laceration on the victim's head that required multiple stitches was not serious or that defendant merely acted recklessly. State v. Powell, 2009-Ohio-2822, 2009 Ohio App. LEXIS 2383 (Ohio Ct. App., Lake County 2009).

Trial court did not abuse its discretion in declining to give the requested instruction because the jury could not have reasonably acquitted defendant of felonious assault yet convicted him of assault. The greater offense of felonious assault could not have been committed without also committing the lesser offense of assault, except that felonious assault involved the use of a deadly weapon and defendant used a firearm to inflict physical harm on the victim. State v. Reese, 2009-Ohio-5046, 2009 Ohio App. LEXIS 4257 (Ohio Ct. App., Montgomery County 2009).

As the evidence did not support a finding that defendant committed an assault on a bar employee, in violation of R.C. 2903.13, and that he did not commit a felonious assault, in violation of R.C. 2903.11(A), the trial court properly refused to provide the jury with a lesser-included offense instruction on assault; the evidence show that defendant acted "knowingly" pursuant to R.C. 2901.22(B), but not that he acted "recklessly" under § 2901.22(C). State v. Krug, 2009-Ohio-3815, 2009 Ohio App. LEXIS 3253 (Ohio Ct. App., Lake County 2009).

Trial court did not err in declining to give a lesser included offense jury instruction on assault in defendant's criminal action on charges of felonious assault, in violation of R.C. 2903.11(A)(1) and (2), as defendant's assertions that he acted in defense of himself and of his son, and that he did not use his cane as a dangerous ordnance or instrument, were a complete defense to any degree of assault; further, the victim's severe injuries took the issue of assault as a lesser included offense out of consideration. State v. Foster, 2009-Ohio-3337, 2009 Ohio App. LEXIS 2878 (Ohio Ct. App., Richland County 2009).

When defendant was charged with felony murder, it was not error for a trial court to decline to instruct the jury on involuntary manslaughter or assault based on defendant's claim that defendant committed misdemeanor assault, because the felonious assault of which defendant was convicted established that defendant caused serious physical harm, not the lesser degree of harm required to establish misdemeanor assault or, as a result, involuntary manslaughter. State v. Nesbitt, 2009-Ohio-972, 2009 Ohio App. LEXIS 817 (Ohio Ct. App., Hamilton County 2009).

Evidence did not warrant a jury instruction on the lesser included offense of assault because under no reasonable view of the evidence could the jury have found that defendant did not act knowingly, but rather was merely reckless in aiding and abetting the girlfriend in causing serious physical harm to the victim. The jury could reasonably have inferred from the evidence that when defendant handed the gun to the girlfriend he was aware that she probably would use it to shoot the victim. State v. Wilson, 2009-Ohio-525, 2009 Ohio App. LEXIS 460 (Ohio Ct. App., Montgomery County 2009).

Trial court did not err in instructing the jury that, if it found that defendant had fled from the police, it could consider his flight as evidence of his consciousness of guilt because a reasonable juror could have found that defendant left the scene as police officers approached in order to avoid an encounter with the police. Defendant admitted that he heard police sirens, saw his friends disperse, and began walking south from the scene and the fact that defendant was in the vicinity of the assault was not dispositive because the jury could reasonably have concluded that he attempted to leave but failed to do so because of his injuries. State v. Babu, 2008-Ohio-5287, 2008 Ohio App. LEXIS 4429 (Ohio Ct. App., Athens County 2008).

Trial court did not err by failing to instruct the jury on the lesser included offense of assault because the jury could not have found defendant guilty of simple assault when all of the testimony adduced at trial demonstrated that defendant used a hard, blunt, metal object to hit the victim on the head in an attempt to cause serious injury to her. There was no evidence whatsoever that defendant was under extreme emotional stress brought on by substantial and adequate provocation caused by the victim; the evidence showed that it was an unprovoked attack on the victim by defendant. State v. Fayne, 2008-Ohio-3036, 2008 Ohio App. LEXIS 2535 (Ohio Ct. App., Cuyahoga County 2008).

In a felonious assault prosecution, under R.C. 2903.11(A)(1), it was not plain error not to instruct the jury on the lesser included offense of assault, under R.C. 2903.13(B), because a video of the assault showed defendant charge the victim and throw defendant's right forearm squarely into the right side of the face of the victim, who fell to the floor, unconscious, so the jury could not have reasonably found defendant acted recklessly rather than knowingly. State v. Mullins, 2008-Ohio-2892, 2008 Ohio App. LEXIS 2415 (Ohio Ct. App., Montgomery County 2008).

In defendant's prosecution for felonious assault, the trial court erred in refusing to instruct the jury on the lesser included offense of simple assault as the evidence allowed finding that the scissors defendant used to stab the victim were not capable of inflicting death and, thus, were not a "deadly weapon" under R.C. 2923.11(A). There was no testimony as to the length or sharpness of the scissors' blade, and the wound suffered by the victim was not deep enough to require stitches. State v. Smith, 2008-Ohio-2061, 2008 Ohio App. LEXIS 1765 (Ohio Ct. App., Athens County 2008).

There was no plain error in the jury instruction because defendant did not provide any authority for the claim that corporal punishment was an affirmative defense to assault, in violation of R.C. 2903.13. Moreover, a jury would likely have concluded that striking a child two times with a horse whip was not within the realm of permissible corporal punishment. State v. Wickard, 2006-Ohio-6088, 2006 Ohio App. LEXIS 6025 (Ohio Ct. App., Hancock County 2006).

In a felonious assault prosecution, it was not error for the trial court to refuse to instruct the jury on simple assault, negligent assault, reckless assault, or finding defendant not guilty if his actions were merely reckless because (1) the victim's severe injury precluded a finding of simple assault, (2) the jury was properly instructed that, to convict defendant, it had to find he acted knowingly, and a definition of "knowingly" was provided, and (3) there was no evidence defendant acted merely negligently or recklessly when he threw a tire iron at the vehicle in which the victim was a passenger. State v. Thornton, 2005-Ohio-3744, 2005 Ohio App. LEXIS 3472 (Ohio Ct. App., Montgomery County 2005).

**—Aggravated assault**

Defendant's conviction for felonious assault, as either the principal or an aider and abettor, was supported by sufficient evidence because he testified that he approached the confrontation that his cohort started and punched the complainant before fleeing with his cohort in a vehicle. The trial court did not err when it refused to give a jury instruction on the lesser included offense of aggravated assault because no one testified about the existence of the type of sudden rage or passion which was required for aggravated assault; he was not entitled to an instruction on misdemeanor assault, because the extent of the complainant's injuries and enduring pain established that he suffered serious physical harm and not non-serious physical harm. State v. Wright, 2019-Ohio-4803, 2019 Ohio App. LEXIS 4859 (Ohio Ct. App., Montgomery County 2019).

Trial court did not plainly err by refusing to instruct the jury on the lesser-included offenses of misdemeanor child endangering and misdemeanor assault because defendant paddled the 11-year-old victim on his clothed buttocks five times during one tutoring session, the abrasion caused by the paddling lasted over two weeks, and the victim testified that it hurt when defendant hit him with the paddle and when he sat down; thus, there was sufficient evidence to sustain the verdict. State v. Henderson, 2018-Ohio-2816, 2018 Ohio App. LEXIS 3047 (Ohio Ct. App., Mahoning County 2018).

**—Felonious assault**

When defendant was charged with felonious assault, the trial court did not err in declining to give a jury instruction for misdemeanor assault, as the evidence demonstrated that serious physical harm was inflicted upon the victim, not just physical harm State v. Mason, 2020 Ohio 4998, 2020 Ohio App. LEXIS 3834 (October 22, 2020).

Trial court did not err by giving an instruction for felonious assault, and not misdemeanor assault, because the jury instruction was given for the offense for which defendant was indicted and which was supported by the evidence. Given the extensive evidence as to the seriousness of the injury, a lesser-included-offense instruction was not warranted. State v. Wauer, 2017-Ohio-1337, 2017 Ohio App. LEXIS 1357 (Ohio Ct. App., Trumbull County 2017).

Because defendant clearly acted knowingly in causing the victim serious physical harm, the trial court did not err by failing to instruct the jury on the lesser included offense of assault. State v. Redman, 2016-Ohio-860, 2016 Ohio App. LEXIS 768 (Ohio Ct. App., Allen County 2016).

There was no error in the trial court's refusal to instruct the jury on the lesser included offense of assault in defendant's criminal trial because the corrections officer involved in defendant's altercation suffered a bone fracture, which constituted serious physical harm for purposes of felonious assault, such that no reasonable jury could have convicted him of the lesser offense. State v. Tolle, 2015-Ohio-1414, 2015 Ohio App. LEXIS 1380 (Ohio Ct. App., Clermont County 2015).

**—Lesser included offenses**

Trial court did not abuse its discretion by not giving jury instructions on the lesser included or inferior degree offenses because the evidence indicated that defendant punched officer in the nose followed by a struggle between the two until defendant was subdued with the assistance of a tavern patron and, as a result of the punch, the officer's nose sustained a large gash and loss of blood. Given the facts, the jury could not reasonably have found defendant not guilty of assault, but guilty of the lesser offense of disorderly conduct. State v. Napier, 2017-Ohio-246, 2017 Ohio App. LEXIS 248 (Ohio Ct. App., Clermont County 2017).

There was no plain error in the trial court's failure to instruct the jury on the lesser included offense of assault in his trial on a charge of felonious assault, as defendant inflicted injuries on the victim that including punching her in the face and resulted in a laceration that required stitches and a permanent scar, which were within the definition of "serious physical harm" and constituted "knowing" conduct for purposes of felonious assault. State v. Wynn, 2017-Ohio-4062, 2017 Ohio App. LEXIS 2111 (Ohio Ct. App., Cuyahoga County 2017).

Court did not err by refusing to give a lesser included instruction on misdemeanor assault because the video recording admitted in evidence showed defendant swinging his arm toward the victim's head, punching the victim in the face, then shoving the victim down to cause an impact with the hard floor; no reasonable jury could have found that defendant's infliction of serious physical harm was reckless, but not knowing. State v. Underwood, 2016-Ohio-1101, 2016 Ohio App. LEXIS 990 (Ohio Ct. App., Montgomery County 2016).

Because aggravated burglary, as statutorily defined, clearly can be committed without the commission of an assault offense, assault is not a lesser-included offense of aggravated burglary, and the trial court did not err in denying defendant's requested jury instruction for the offense of misdemeanor assault as a lesser included offense. State v. Trammel, 2013-Ohio-4354, 2013 Ohio App. LEXIS 4586 (Ohio Ct. App., Stark County 2013).

Trial court incorrectly determined that disorderly conduct was a lesser-included offense of assault because it was possible to knowingly cause or attempt to cause physical harm to another (assault) without causing inconvenience, annoyance, or alarm to another (disorderly conduct). State v. Conley, 2013-Ohio-3347, 2013 Ohio App. LEXIS 3419 (Ohio Ct. App., Summit County 2013).

Evidence did not reasonably support both an acquittal on felonious assault and a conviction on reckless assault because there was no evidence to support the inference that defendant merely "recklessly" caused the victim's injuries; instead, the evidence supported either the conclusion that defendant "knowingly" caused the victim's injuries or that he did not injure her at all. Thus, the trial court did not err in refusing a lesser included offense instruction on reckless assault. State v. Gatliff, 2013-Ohio-2862, 2013 Ohio App. LEXIS 2909 (Ohio Ct. App., Clermont County 2013).

Jury instruction on assault was not warranted as a lesser included offense of felonious assault under R.C. 2903.11(A)(1) as the State adduced evidence establishing that the son suffered serious physical harm under R.C. 2901.01(A)(5), and no version of the facts tended to establish mere physical harm. State v. Hamby, 2010-Ohio-4040, 2010 Ohio App. LEXIS 3437 (Ohio Ct. App., Montgomery County 2010).

Trial court did not err in refusing to instruct the jury on the lesser included offense of assault as the jury could not reasonably find defendant not guilty of felonious assault under R.C. 2903.11(A)(2) but convict him of assault as the State's evidence showed that defendant beat his sister and her son with a pipe, a deadly weapon under R.C. 2923.11(A), and that he stated that he intended to kill the son. Significantly, defendant admitted using the pipe but claimed that he did so in self defense. State v. Hamby, 2010-Ohio-4040, 2010 Ohio App. LEXIS 3437 (Ohio Ct. App., Montgomery County 2010).

Defendant failed to establish ineffective assistance of counsel because the trial court could not have found that defendant committed an assault without a deadly weapon or dangerous ordnance for assault as a lesser included offense of felonious assault. The consistent testimony of all witnesses who were outside at the time of the shooting was that the victim was struck in his calf with a bullet emanating from the gun that defendant had fired from the area of his residence in the victim's direction. State v. Perez, 2009-Ohio-959, 2009 Ohio App. LEXIS 839 (Ohio Ct. App., Cuyahoga County 2009).

Trial court did not error in failing to instruct the jury on the lesser included offense of assault, under R.C. 2903.13(B). Based on the victim's testimony and the nature of her injuries, the evidence did not support an acquittal on the offense of felonious assault, under R.C. 2903.11(A)(1), and a conviction on the offense of assault. State v. Burks, 2007-Ohio-3562, 2007 Ohio App. LEXIS 3270 (Ohio Ct. App., Lucas County 2007).

Trial court erred in finding defendant guilty of fourth-degree misdemeanor disorderly conduct (DC), in violation of R.C. 2917.11(A)(2), as a lesser-included offense of assault, in violation of R.C. 2903.13(A); rather, minor-misdemeanor DC was the lesser-included offense. City of Cincinnati v. Bell, 2007-Ohio-3091, 2007 Ohio App. LEXIS 2835 (Ohio Ct. App., Hamilton County 2007).

Since the "inconvenience, annoyance and alarm" elements of disorderly conduct, under R.C. 2917.11, were mental states, and not part of the concept of the physical harm element of assault, under R.C. 2903.13, disorderly conduct was not a lesser included offense of assault. State v. Sankey, 2006-Ohio-5316, 2006 Ohio App. LEXIS 5289 (Ohio Ct. App., Stark County 2006).

It was not plain error, under Crim.R. 52(B), for a trial court, in a prosecution for assault, under R.C. 2903.13, not to, sua sponte, give an instruction on disorderly conduct, under R.C. 2917.11, as a lesser included offense because the evidence that defendant repeatedly struck the victim about the head did not reasonably allow the jury to acquit defendant of assault and convict her of disorderly conduct. State v. Sankey, 2006-Ohio-5316, 2006 Ohio App. LEXIS 5289 (Ohio Ct. App., Stark County 2006).

As defendant's use of a belt to squeeze it around the victim's neck was clearly capable of inflicting death, the evidence would not have reasonably supported an acquittal on the charge of felonious assault, in violation of R.C. 2903.11(A)(2), and accordingly, an instruction on assault, in violation of R.C. 2903.13, as a lesser included offense was not warranted; the belt in this matter was not, in and of itself, a deadly weapon, as defined by R.C. 2923.11. State v. Breeden, 2005-Ohio-510, 2005 Ohio App. LEXIS 544 (Ohio Ct. App., Cuyahoga County 2005).

While the "serious physical harm" element of the crime of felonious assault encompasses mental injury and the crime of assault does not, where an indictment for attempted felonious assault was sufficiently narrow as to charge only a form of the offense of attempted felonious assault requiring bodily harm, then that definition, and not the broader definition set forth in the statute, was the starting point of analyzing what other offenses might constitute lesser included offenses under the facts of the case. Thus, the trial court erred in refusing to instruct the jury on the lesser included offense of assault in defendant's prosecution for attempted felonious assault arising out of an incident where defendant attacked a prison guard with a plastic fork because, under the facts of the case, the jury could have reasonably concluded that the evidence supported a conviction for attempted assault rather than for attempted felonious assault; although defendant had filed the fork handle so as to make it pointed, a reasonable jury could have concluded that such a device was not capable of inflicting or was not intended to inflict serious physical harm. State v. Hunter, 2005-Ohio-443, 2005 Ohio App. LEXIS 470 (Ohio Ct. App., Champaign County 2005).



Defendant's claim that he was entitled to an instruction on resisting arrest did not implicate his ineffective assistance of counsel claim as counsel requested such an instruction; further, defendant was not entitled to the instruction as defendant was not charged with resisting arrest and resisting arrest was not a lesser-included offense of assault on a police officer. State v. Fritz, 2005-Ohio-4736, 163 Ohio App. 3d 276, 837 N.E.2d 823, 2005 Ohio App. LEXIS 4233 (Ohio Ct. App., Montgomery County 2005).

There was no plain error in failing to give a jury instruction on the lesser offenses of aggravated assault or assault because defendant failed to demonstrate that he would have been acquitted of felonious assault, and convicted of aggravated assault or assault, had the instruction been given. The evidence did not begin to approach the level of serious provocation required to warrant an aggravated assault instruction because the victim's words and actions did not arouse the passions of an ordinary person beyond his ability to control himself and, because it was clear that defendant deliberately and knowingly punched the victim, the evidence also did not support an instruction on assault. State v. Owens, 2005-Ohio-4402, 2005 Ohio App. LEXIS 3997 (Ohio Ct. App., Richland County 2005).

In a felonious assault prosecution, it was not error for the trial court to refuse to instruct the jury on simple assault, negligent assault, reckless assault, or finding defendant not guilty if his actions were merely reckless because (1) the victim's severe injury precluded a finding of simple assault, (2) the jury was properly instructed that, to convict defendant, it had to find he acted knowingly, and a definition of "knowingly" was provided, and (3) there was no evidence defendant acted merely negligently or recklessly when he threw a tire iron at the vehicle in which the victim was a passenger. State v. Thornton, 2005-Ohio-3744, 2005 Ohio App. LEXIS 3472 (Ohio Ct. App., Montgomery County 2005).

In defendant's felonious assault prosecution, a jury instruction on the lesser-included offense of assault under R.C. 2903.13(B) was properly denied because defendant denied kicking the victim, and the only testimony as to the contact came from the victim, who testified that defendant deliberately and forcefully kicked her head; thus, a jury instruction allowing a finding that defendant acted recklessly was not appropriate. State v. Fuller, 2005-Ohio-3696, 2005 Ohio App. LEXIS 3397 (Ohio Ct. App., Montgomery County 2005).

In a prosecution for assault under R.C. 2903.13, the trial court's failure to sua sponte instruct the jury on the lesser-included offense of disorderly conduct was not plain error, as the trial evidence did not reasonably support both an acquittal on the assault charge and conviction of disorderly conduct. State v. Walton, 2003-Ohio-6514, 2003 Ohio App. LEXIS 5815 (Ohio Ct. App., Ross County 2003).

Defendant was not entitled to a sua sponte instruction on the lesser included offense of assault and was properly convicted of felonious assault for the extended beating of defendant's common-law spouse where the spouse suffered split lips, black eyes, a cut ear, a gashed cheek, skinned knees, and bruises because a jury could not have reasonably concluded that defendant was guilty only of the lesser included offense of assault, but not of the greater offense of felonious assault. State v. Nipper, 2003-Ohio-4449, 2003 Ohio App. LEXIS 3985 (Ohio Ct. App., Butler County 2003).

Where defendant was convicted of felonious assault under R.C. 2903.11(A)(2), the trial court erred in failing to give an instruction on the lesser included offense of assault under R.C. 2903.13(A); assault did not include the use of a deadly weapon while felonious assault did, and defendant testified that defendant did not use a breaker bar to beat the victim, which appeared to be corroborated by the lack of seriousness of the victim's injuries. State v. Cochran, 2003-Ohio-3980, 2003 Ohio App. LEXIS 3557 (Ohio Ct. App., Montgomery County 2003).

Where the only issue in a prosecution for felonious assault was essentially who attacked whom, the court should not have included an instruction on the lesser offenses of assault: State v. Hartman, 130 Ohio App. 3d 645, 720 N.E.2d 971, 1998 Ohio App. LEXIS 5753 (Ohio Ct. App., Hamilton County 1998), dismissed, 85 Ohio St. 3d 1455, 708 N.E.2d 1010, 1999 Ohio LEXIS 1217 (Ohio 1999).

**— —Aggravated assault**

In defendant's felonious assault prosecution, the trial court did not err in failing to instruct the jury on the lesser included offenses of aggravated assault and simple assault as there was no evidence that defendant was influenced by passion or rage or that defendant was provoked. Moreover, the evidence showed that defendant acted knowingly, not recklessly. State v. Andrews, 2010-Ohio-3864, 2010 Ohio App. LEXIS 3262 (Ohio Ct. App., Cuyahoga County 2010).



**— —Aggravated robbery**

R.C. 2903.13(B), assault, is a lesser included offense of R.C. 2911.01(A)(2), aggravated robbery: State v. Crawford, 10 Ohio App. 3d 207, 461 N.E.2d 312, 1983 Ohio App. LEXIS 11143 (Ohio Ct. App., Hamilton County 1983).

**— —Disorderly conduct**

Evidence overwhelmingly supported the jury's verdict finding defendant guilty of assault and there was no reason to believe that the verdict would have been different had a disorderly conduct instruction been given. The evidence presented at trial would not have reasonably supported an acquittal, as was necessary to require a lesser-included instruction. State v. Jevnikar, 2016-Ohio-8113, 2016 Ohio App. LEXIS 4976 (Ohio Ct. App., Lake County 2016).

Trial court did not err by including a lesser included offense instruction because the record reflected that, not only did defendant's trial counsel fail to object to the lesser included offense instruction, but counsel, in fact, requested it in writing and in open court. Regardless, disorderly conduct, as defined in Cleveland Heights, Ohio, City Ordinances 509.03, which was identical to disorderly conduct under R.C. 2917.11, was a lesser included offense of assault, as defined by R.C. 2903.13. State v. Lynch, 2011-Ohio-3062, 2011 Ohio App. LEXIS 2603 (Ohio Ct. App., Cuyahoga County 2011).

Defendant did not establish that trial counsel was ineffective based on a failure to request an instruction on disorderly conduct under R.C. 2917.11 as a lesser-included offense of assault on a peace officer because this was a matter of trial strategy; moreover, a decision to pursue a total acquittal, rather than requesting the instruction, was also a tactical choice. Trial counsel argued that defendant had resisted arrest, but that it did not rise to the level of an assault. State v. Gonzales, 2010-Ohio-22, 2010 Ohio App. LEXIS 14 (Ohio Ct. App., Wood County 2010).

Defendant's conviction for the lesser included offense to assault, under R.C. 2903.13(A), of disorderly conduct, under R.C. 2917.11(A)(1), was not in error because disorderly conduct was a lesser included offense of assault pursuant to Crim.R. 31(C) and R.C. 2945.74. State v. Breidenbach, 2010-Ohio-4335, 2010 Ohio App. LEXIS 3665 (Ohio Ct. App., Athens County 2010).

Trial court did not commit plain error because failure to charge the jury on the lesser included offense of disorderly conduct or persistent disorderly conduct (for assault) had no impact on the verdict. Defendant was clearly guilty of assault on a peace officer for attempting to harm the officers who were trying to arrest him for having pulled a knife on a third party. State v. Kegg, 2009-Ohio-2150, 2009 Ohio App. LEXIS 1803 (Ohio Ct. App., Franklin County 2009).

While the minor misdemeanor form of disorderly conduct is a lesser included offense of assault, the trial court did not err in refusing to instruct the jury on disorderly conduct because defendant did not present evidence that allowed a conclusion that he recklessly caused inconvenience or alarm by engaging in violent behavior; instead, the evidence showed that defendant engaged in a significant fight with police officers after he broke away from them, throwing each officer onto the floor and injuring both of them. State v. Keith, 2008-Ohio-6122, 2008 Ohio App. LEXIS 5115 (Ohio Ct. App., Franklin County 2008).

While disorderly conduct is a lesser included offense of assault, the trial court did not err in refusing to instruct the jury on disorderly conduct because defendant did not present evidence that allowed a conclusion that he recklessly caused inconvenience or alarm by engaging in violent behavior; instead, the evidence showed that defendant engaged in a significant fight with police officers after he broke away from them, throwing each officer onto the floor and injuring both of them. State v. Keith, 2008-Ohio-6122, 2008 Ohio App. LEXIS 5115 (Ohio Ct. App., Franklin County 2008).

Obstruction of official business, under R.C. 2921.31(A), was not a lesser included offense because it include an additional element—the intent to hinder a police officer in the performance of an officer's duties—that was not required for assault on a police officer, under R.C. 2903.13(A). Further, the trial court did not abuse its discretion in concluding that no reasonable finder of fact could have found defendant not guilty of assault upon an employee of a local correctional facility and assault on a police officer, but guilty of disorderly conduct, under R.C. 2917.11(A)(1). State v. Daniels, 2008-Ohio-2236, 2008 Ohio App. LEXIS 1924 (Ohio Ct. App., Greene County 2008).

Obstruction of official business, under R.C. 2921.31(A), was not a lesser included offense because it include an additional element—the intent to hinder a police officer in the performance of an officer's duties—that was not required for assault on a police officer, under R.C. 2903.13(A). Further, the trial court did not abuse its discretion in concluding that no reasonable finder of fact could have found defendant not guilty of assault upon an employee of a local correctional facility and assault on a police officer, but guilty of disorderly conduct, under R.C. 2917.11(A)(1). State v. Daniels, 2008-Ohio-2236, 2008 Ohio App. LEXIS 1924 (Ohio Ct. App., Greene County 2008).

Trial court erred in finding that minor misdemeanor disorderly conduct, under R.C. 2917.11(A), was a lesser included offense of assault, pursuant to R.C. 2903.13(A). Disorderly conduct required proof of inconvenience, annoyance, or alarm and, because annoyance and alarm were each mental states, they were not part of the concept of physical harm set forth in the assault statute. City of Uhrichsville v. Conrad, 2006-Ohio-1293, 2006 Ohio App. LEXIS 1192 (Ohio Ct. App., Tuscarawas County 2006).

In a prosecution for burglary and assault, a trial court did not have to instruct the jury on lesser included offenses of criminal trespass or disorderly conduct because the jury could not, under the evidence, have reasonably convicted defendant of the lesser offense while acquitting him of the greater offense. State v. Jones, 2005-Ohio-6859, 2005 Ohio App. LEXIS 6192 (Ohio Ct. App., Allen County 2005), rev'd in part, 2006-Ohio-2721, 109 Ohio St. 3d 509, 849 N.E.2d 284, 2006 Ohio LEXIS 1600 (Ohio 2006).

Disorderly conduct, under R.C. 2917.11, is not a lesser included offense of assault. State v. Brown, 2005-Ohio-3871, 2005 Ohio App. LEXIS 3573 (Ohio Ct. App., Montgomery County 2005).

Where defendant was found not guilty as charged of assault and of domestic violence, in violation of R.C. 2903.13(A) and 2919.25(A)(1), respectively, the trial court erred in convicting him of disorderly conduct in violation of R.C. 2917.11, as such offense was not a lesser included offense of the charged offenses. State v. Brack, 2005-Ohio-48, 2005 Ohio App. LEXIS 56 (Ohio Ct. App., Montgomery County 2005).

Trial court erred, in defendant's case involving assault on a peace officer, in concluding that disorderly conduct was a lesser-included offense of assault, as they were separate offenses, because the offense of assault, as statutorily defined, could be committed without having the lesser offense, disorderly conduct, also be committed. Accordingly, the trial court should not have instructed the jury that disorderly conduct was a lesser-included offense of assault. State v. Ocasio, 2003-Ohio-6240, 2003 Ohio App. LEXIS 5627 (Ohio Ct. App., Montgomery County 2003).

A fourth-degree misdemeanor offense of disorderly conduct requires, as an additional element, that the offender persisted in the conduct after a reasonable warning or request to desist. It is not a lesser included offense of assault: State v. Parker, 2002-Ohio-5536, 149 Ohio App. 3d 681, 778 N.E.2d 646, 2002 Ohio App. LEXIS 5543 (Ohio Ct. App., Clark County 2002), overruled in part, State v. Ocasio, 2003-Ohio-6240, 2003 Ohio App. LEXIS 5627 (Ohio Ct. App., Montgomery County 2003).

Assault is always a lesser-included offense of felonious assault. A court must give an instruction on a lesser-included offense, even if not requested by the defense, if the jury could reasonably find the defendant guilty of only the lesser offense: State v. Thrasher, 1994 Ohio App. LEXIS 172 (Ohio Ct. App., Clark County Jan. 21, 1994).

Disorderly conduct as a fourth-degree misdemeanor under R.C. 2917.11(E) is not a lesser included offense of assault, in view of the aggravating element requiring the persistence of proscribed behavior after a reasonable warning or request to desist: State v. Reynolds, 25 Ohio App. 3d 59, 495 N.E.2d 971, 1985 Ohio App. LEXIS 10207 (Ohio Ct. App., Hamilton County 1985).

Disorderly conduct as a minor misdemeanor under R.C. 2917.11(A)(1) is a lesser included offense of assault under R.C. 2903.13: State v. Reynolds, 25 Ohio App. 3d 59, 495 N.E.2d 971, 1985 Ohio App. LEXIS 10207 (Ohio Ct. App., Hamilton County 1985).

Disorderly conduct under R.C. 2917.11 (A)(1) is a lesser included offense of assault under R.C. 2903.13(A): State v. Roberts, 7 Ohio App. 3d 253, 455 N.E.2d 508, 1982 Ohio App. LEXIS 11153 (Ohio Ct. App., Hamilton County 1982).

**— —Domestic violence**

Assault under R.C. 2903.13 is not a lesser included offense of domestic violence because both offenses carry an identical maximum penalty. Since assault is not lesser included offense of domestic violence, defendant's assault conviction, imposed after the trial court ruled that defendant could not be convicted of domestic violence because the State failed to prove that the victim was a family or household member of defendant's, violated defendant's right to due process. State v. Daugherty, 2006-Ohio-1133, 166 Ohio App. 3d 551, 852 N.E.2d 202, 2006 Ohio App. LEXIS 1026 (Ohio Ct. App., Montgomery County 2006).

Assault is not a lesser included offense of misdemeanor domestic violence. State v. Daugherty, 2006-Ohio-1133, 166 Ohio App. 3d 551, 852 N.E.2d 202, 2006 Ohio App. LEXIS 1026 (Ohio Ct. App., Montgomery County 2006).

Defendant, who was charged with violence against his pregnant, former girlfriend, could be charged with both domestic violence and assault. City of Cleveland v. Sheldon, 2003-Ohio-6331, 2003 Ohio App. LEXIS 5679 (Ohio Ct. App., Cuyahoga County 2003).

**— —Felonious assault**

When defendant was charged with felonious assault, the trial court did not err in refusing to instruct the jury on the lesser included offense of simple assault, as no reasonable juror could have found that defendant acted recklessly rather than knowingly in assaulting the victim. State v. Fife, 2021-Ohio-2000, 2021 Ohio App. LEXIS 1976 (Ohio Ct. App., Franklin County 2021).

When defendant was charged with felonious assault, the trial court properly denied his request for a jury instruction on the lesser-included offense of simple assault , as the evidence presented at trial demonstrated that he knowingly caused serious physical harm when, while trying to flee in the car he was stealing from the victims, he drove over the unconscious first victim, causing her to die from blunt force trauma, despite having had room to exit the parking lot without striking her. State v. Preston, 2021-Ohio-2278, 2021 Ohio App. LEXIS 2241 (Ohio Ct. App., Cuyahoga County 2021).

Trial court did not abuse its discretion when it refused to instruct the jury on assault as a lesser offense of felonious assault because the jury could not reasonably find that the harm the victim suffered was not serious given her testimony that defendant choked her to the point that she lost consciousness, photos showing bruises on the victim's neck, and a doctor's testimony that the injuries were consistent with strangulation. State v. Conant, 2020-Ohio-4319, 2020 Ohio App. LEXIS 3204 (Ohio Ct. App., Adams County 2020).

Trial court did not err in refusing to instruct the jury on the lesser included offense of assault because it could not have been concluded that defendant was guilty only of the lesser included offense of assault, but not of the greater offense of felonious assault. It was clear from the victim's testimony, the testimony of the emergency room nurse and the police sergeant, and the photographs of the victim's injuries that she sustained serious physical harm as a result of defendant's attack. State v. Church, 2012-Ohio-3877, 2012 Ohio App. LEXIS 3421 (Ohio Ct. App., Butler County 2012).

Defendant's actions constituted felonious assault, rather than simple or aggravated assault, where defendant repeatedly kicked and stomped on the victim's head while the victim was on the ground in that the victim, who died from multiple blunt force injuries to the head and neck, suffered serious physical harm, not just physical harm and defendant's conduct reflected knowing, not reckless, conduct by defendant. State v. Kleekamp, 2010-Ohio-1906, 2010 Ohio App. LEXIS 1589 (Ohio Ct. App., Montgomery County 2010).

In defendant's felonious assault prosecution, the trial court properly refused to instruct the jury on the lesser included offense of assault as evidence that the victim sustained lacerations to his face, requiring up to 30 stitches and six staples in his head, and that he was presribed pain medication showed that the victim suffered incapacity, disfigurement, and prolonged pain and constituted evidence of "serious physical harm" under R.C. 2901.01(A)(5). State v. Caster, 2006-Ohio-6594, 2006 Ohio App. LEXIS 6535 (Ohio Ct. App., Cuyahoga County 2006).

**— —Negligent assault**

Trial court erred in convicting defendant of negligent assault under R.C. 2903.14(A) as negligent assault was not a lesser included offense of assault under R.C. 2903.13(A), in that negligent assault contained an element which assault did not, namely that the offense must be committed by means of a deadly weapon or dangerous ordnance. State v. Baker, 2013-Ohio-2507, 2013 Ohio App. LEXIS 2479 (Ohio Ct. App., Hamilton County 2013).

Negligent assault is not a lesser included offense of assault because it contains an additional element: State v. Evans, 2003-Ohio-3475, 153 Ohio App. 3d 226, 792 N.E.2d 757, 2003 Ohio App. LEXIS 3147 (Ohio Ct. App., Jefferson County 2003).

Negligent assault was a lesser-included offense of assault: City of Toledo v. Golis, 1994 Ohio App. LEXIS 4876 (Ohio Ct. App., Lucas County Oct. 28, 1994).

**— —Reckless assault**

Defendant, who was charged with felonious assault, was not entitled to a lesser included offense instruction on assault, as a jury could not have found that he acted recklessly instead of knowingly. His own testimony demonstrated that he knowingly introduced a knife into the situation as a weapon, and security camera footage showed him making deliberate slashing motions with his right arm, toward the victim's left arm, on two occasions. State v. Strong, 2014-Ohio-4206, 18 N.E.3d 1282, 2014 Ohio App. LEXIS 4121 (Ohio Ct. App., Cuyahoga County 2014), vacated, superseded, 2015-Ohio-169, 2015 Ohio App. LEXIS 144 (Ohio Ct. App., Cuyahoga County 2015).

Assault in violation of R.C. 2903.13(B) is a lesser included offense of a felonious assault in violation of R.C. 2903.11(A)(1). The State v. Ellis is overruled. State v. Turks, 2010-Ohio-5944, 2010 Ohio App. LEXIS 5001 (Ohio Ct. App., Allen County 2010).

Trial court did not err by failing to instruct the jury on assault under R.C. 2903.13(B) because, even though assault was a lesser-included offense of felonious assault under R.C. 2903.11(A)(1), the evidence at trial did not reasonably support both an acquittal on felonious assault and a conviction on assault, as the victim told her mother that defendant picked her up and threw her down to the ground, paralyzing her, and defendant consistently denied that he caused the victim's injuries. State v. Turks, 2010-Ohio-5944, 2010 Ohio App. LEXIS 5001 (Ohio Ct. App., Allen County 2010).

In defendant's prosecution for felonious assault, the trial court did not err in refusing to charge the jury on the lesser-included offense of reckless assault because defendant, who only offered testimony denying that he was ever at the scene where a shot was fired at another vehicle, had offered no evidence that the harm to the victim was caused by recklessness. Instead, the facts that the shot was fired from close range, and the location of the shot, entering the rear passenger side of an occupied vehicle, shattering the window and striking a post in close approximation to the head of the front seat passenger, did not support a conclusion that defendant's conduct was merely reckless or negligent. State v. Darrington, 2006-Ohio-5042, 2006 Ohio App. LEXIS 5183 (Ohio Ct. App., Franklin County 2006).

Reckless assault defined in R.C. 2903.13(B) cannot be a lesser included offense of felonious assault defined in R.C. 2903.11(A)(2): State v. Wong, 95 Ohio App. 3d 39, 641 N.E.2d 1137, 1994 Ohio App. LEXIS 2157 (Ohio Ct. App., Jackson County 1994).



**—Reckless assault**

Defendant was not entitled to a jury instruction under this statute because the victim suffered serious physical harm, not merely physical harm, and the record did not support a finding that defendant acted recklessly. State v. Shakhmanov, 2019-Ohio-4705, 2019 Ohio App. LEXIS 4770 (Ohio Ct. App., Montgomery County 2019).

Defendant, who was charged with felonious assault, was not entitled to a lesser included offense instruction on assault, as a jury could not have found that he acted recklessly instead of knowingly. His own testimony demonstrated that he knowingly introduced a knife into the situation as a weapon, and security camera footage showed him making deliberate slashing motions with his right arm, toward the victim's left arm, on two occasions. State v. Strong, 2014-Ohio-4206, 18 N.E.3d 1282, 2014 Ohio App. LEXIS 4121 (Ohio Ct. App., Cuyahoga County 2014), vacated, superseded, 2015-Ohio-169, 2015 Ohio App. LEXIS 144 (Ohio Ct. App., Cuyahoga County 2015).

**Jury trial**

While a criminal defendant's right to a jury trial was guaranteed in the Sixth and Fourteenth Amendments to the United States Constitution and Ohio Const. art. I, §§ 5 and 10, a defendant who was charged with charged with first-degree misdemeanor assault, in violation of R.C. 2903.13, did not have an absolute right to a jury trial. Rather, because the defendant was charged with a misdemeanor, the defendant waived the right to a jury trial unless the defendant made a timely written demand in accordance with Crim.R. 23(A). Pierson v. Rion, 2010-Ohio-1793, 2010 Ohio App. LEXIS 1492 (Ohio Ct. App., Montgomery County 2010).

**Knowingly**

Sufficient evidence supported defendant's conviction for assault because the evidence showed that defendant knowingly kicked the officer in the stomach, rather than it being an involuntary reflex due to having been tased. The video recording appeared to show that after being tased, rather than being paralyzed, defendant turned, climbed into the vehicle, tried to pull the door shut, and then intentionally kicked at the officer. State v. Brown, 2020-Ohio-1650, 2020 Ohio App. LEXIS 1632 (Ohio Ct. App., Lucas County 2020).

Defendant's convictions for felonious assault and assault were supported by sufficient evidence and were not against the manifest weight of the evidence because the jury could have reasonably concluded that defendant knowingly caused serious physical harm to the victim. According to the victim and his wife's testimony, defendant struck the victim with a 16-pound rock in the right side of his forehead after being punched very hard by the codefendant, to the extent he was in "tremendous" pain and feared his eyeball was actually out of the socket, and he sustained lacerations and a broken thumb. State v. Miller, 2019-Ohio-92, 2019 Ohio App. LEXIS 92 (Ohio Ct. App., Hocking County 2019).

Defendant's conviction for assault was not against the manifest weight of the evidence because the victim and a witness testified that defendant "swung" at the victim, defendant admitted as much to the patrolman and at trial, and the video showed the "swing." Thus, the evidence, if believed, was sufficient to demonstrate that defendant knowingly attempted to cause physical harm to the victim and it was noted that the swing was accompanied by a threat to break the victim's jaw, which defendant also admitted. State v. Buchar, 2017-Ohio-7601, 2017 Ohio App. LEXIS 3910 (Ohio Ct. App., Tuscarawas County 2017).

Defendant's conviction for assault was not against the sufficiency or the manifest weight of the evidence, as the evidence showed defendant knowingly attempted to cause physical harm to the victim based on defendant's actions in driving at the victim in a truck, among other evidence. City of Ashland v. Francis, 2017-Ohio-8525, 2017 Ohio App. LEXIS 4929 (Ohio Ct. App., Ashland County 2017).

There was no error in the trial court's refusal to instruct the jury on the lesser included offense of reckless assault in defendant's criminal trial because the evidence did not support a conviction for reckless assault, as defendant's conduct in striking the corrections officer with a tray was knowing rather than reckless. State v. Tolle, 2015-Ohio-1414, 2015 Ohio App. LEXIS 1380 (Ohio Ct. App., Clermont County 2015).

Sufficient evidence supported defendant's conviction for assault upon a peace officer because defendant's argument that he was accidentally flailing his arms after the officer grabbed his left arm was not sufficient to overcome that defendant knowingly struck the officer. Because both officers testified that defendant's strike to the officer was a deliberate action, his act of striking the officer was a reasonable and probable consequence of his own action. State v. Munoz, 2013-Ohio-4987, 2013 Ohio App. LEXIS 5190 (Ohio Ct. App., Franklin County 2013).



Delinquency complaint complied with the requirements of Ohio R. Juv. P. 10(B) and R.C. 2152.021(A)(1) by alleging a factual basis to determine delinquency based upon assault of a school teacher and by identifying the specific subsection of the assault statute upon which the claim in delinquency was to be prosecuted. The assault statute itself, by reference, identified "knowingly" as the applicable level of mens rea for the offense. In re M.H., 2010-Ohio-689, 186 Ohio App. 3d 513, 928 N.E.2d 1174, 2010 Ohio App. LEXIS 572 (Ohio Ct. App., Ottawa County 2010).

As the jury necessarily found that defendant acted knowingly pursuant to R.C. 2901.22(B) when he caused physical harm to a victim, as the jury convicted him of domestic violence and assault, in violation of R.C. 2919.25 and 2903.13(A), there was no error in the trial court's refusal to give an instruction on accident. State v. Juntunen, 2010-Ohio-5625, 2010 Ohio App. LEXIS 4741 (Ohio Ct. App., Franklin County 2010).

R.C. 2903.13(A) only required the State of Ohio to show that defendant knowingly caused or attempted to cause physical harm. Therefore, the use of sufficient force by defendant to leave a mark on the victim, as well as the victim's complaint that the victim was choking, were sufficient for the jury to conclude that defendant was aware that defendant's conduct would probably cause physical harm, that is, an injury or other physiological impairment, regardless of its gravity or duration, pursuant to R.C. 2901.22(B) and 2901.01(A)(3). City of Westlake v. Filiaggi, 2010-Ohio-4481, 2010 Ohio App. LEXIS 3778 (Ohio Ct. App., Cuyahoga County 2010).

Record contained substantial evidence to show that defendant had the criminal intent (knowingly) to commit an assault, as the underlying crime for aggravated burglary, because the victim testified that defendant kicked her in the head and was trying to kill her. The jury could have reasonably concluded that defendant went to the victim's apartment to punish her after being injured in a fist fight with her ex-husband or to punish her for banishing him from the apartment. State v. Wamsley, 2009-Ohio-1858, 2009 Ohio App. LEXIS 1552 (Ohio Ct. App., Columbiana County 2009).

Trial court properly found that defendant knowingly caused physical harm to the victim when it convicted him of assault under R.C. 2903.13(A). It appeared that the trial court was referring to defendant's whole course of conduct on the night and morning of the incident as being reckless when it found that defendant was intoxicated; he voluntarily fought with another individual; despite his injuries, he pursued the individuals associated with the fight in order to continue the altercation; and he participated in a group assault upon an individual that he could not say had attacked him. State v. Babu, 2008-Ohio-5287, 2008 Ohio App. LEXIS 4429 (Ohio Ct. App., Athens County 2008).

When, in a prosecution for felonious assault, under R.C. 2903.11(A)(2), and assault, under R.C. 2903.13(A), the trial court instructed the jury that it could not consider any evidence of defendant's alleged medical condition or low intelligence, because the defense of diminished capacity was not recognized in Ohio, it improperly removed evidence of defendant's medical condition from the jury's consideration, because this evidence was relevant to whether defendant was able to form the requisite intent of "knowingly," under R.C. 2901.22(B), so defendant was entitled to a new trial. State v. Fulmer, 2006-Ohio-7015, 2006 Ohio App. LEXIS 6956 (Ohio Ct. App., Lake County 2006), rev'd, 2008-Ohio-936, 117 Ohio St. 3d 319, 883 N.E.2d 1052, 2008 Ohio LEXIS 549 (Ohio 2008).

Defendant's conviction for assault under R.C. 2903.13 was not against the manifest weight of the evidence, in that, the testimony established that defendant attempted to strike his girlfriend but, instead, hit the victim, who was trying to break up the fight. Defendant's "knowing" assault was still an assault regardless of the victim. State v. Ehlermann, 2006-Ohio-3931, 2006 Ohio App. LEXIS 3890 (Ohio Ct. App., Licking County 2006).

Trial court did not "lose its way" in determining that a juvenile who was engaged in a shoving match with a victim acted "knowingly" rather than "recklessly" pursuant to R.C. 2901.22(B) and (C), for purposes of finding that, if he was an adult, he would have committed more than a simple assault in violation of R.C. 2903.13, as his actions were more akin to a felonious assault in violation of R.C. 2903.11 where he was engaged in the shoving match, left to retrieve the victim's shirt, and upon returning he continued to engage in the shoving on a raised deck, which ultimately resulted in the victim sustaining injury upon being pushed off the deck; the evidence supported a finding that the juvenile was aware that shoving the victim off of an elevated deck would probably cause serious physical injuries. In re Shane L. F., 2006-Ohio-3876, 2006 Ohio App. LEXIS 3825 (Ohio Ct. App., Huron County 2006).

In an assault case, the testimony of defendant's victim, viewed in the light most favorable to the State, showed defendant hit or shoved the victim in the chest with his open hand and that he knew, under R.C. 2901.22(B), that he would probably the victim physical harm, under R.C. 2901.01(A)(3), so sufficient evidence supported his assault conviction. State v. Lee, 2006-Ohio-2126, 2006 Ohio App. LEXIS 1966 (Ohio Ct. App., Montgomery County 2006).

Defendant's assault conviction could rest independently upon his having punched the victim, which a reasonable trier of fact could find to have been an act whereby defendant would have been aware that his conduct would probably cause injury, satisfying the culpability state of knowingly set forth in R.C. 2901.22(B). State v. Hill, 2005-Ohio-3701, 2005 Ohio App. LEXIS 3400 (Ohio Ct. App., Montgomery County 2005).

Defendant's assault conviction could rest independently upon his having punched the victim, which a reasonable trier of fact could find to have been an act whereby defendant would have been aware that his conduct would probably cause injury, satisfying the culpability state of knowingly set forth in R.C. 2901.22(B). State v. Hill, 2005-Ohio-3701, 2005 Ohio App. LEXIS 3400 (Ohio Ct. App., Montgomery County 2005).

There was no evidence that defendant "knowingly" caused harm to another where the court found that he did not attempt to cause the victim's injuries but that his actions resulted in the injuries: State v. Johnston, 1990 Ohio App. LEXIS 5382 (Ohio Ct. App., Mahoning County Dec. 6, 1990).

**Manifest weight of the evidence**

Defendant's conviction for assault was not against the manifest weight of the evidence because defendant punched the victim in the face, causing a knot on her forehead and black eyes, the victim also testified that defendant struck her side and stomach and bruised her arm. The officer testified that he observed and took photographs of the victim's facial injuries; victim and officer's testimony, if believed, was sufficient to establish that defendant knowingly caused physical harm to victim. State v. Webb, 2021-Ohio-1977, 2021 Ohio App. LEXIS 1937 (Ohio Ct. App., Montgomery County 2021).

Defendant's conviction for assault was not against the manifest weight of evidence because nothing suggested that the jury lost its way by rejecting defendant's claim for self-defense where the evidence established that defendant lost his temper and he knew that it was his neighbor that was approaching him that night in the rain. Moreover, his claim for fear of imminent danger was dubious considering his admission that moments earlier, he saw someone shining a flashlight toward him from his neighbor's porch. State v. Anthony, 2020-Ohio-861, 2020 Ohio App. LEXIS 791 (Ohio Ct. App., Ashtabula County 2020).

In an appeal from her conviction for one count of assault, there was no merit in the defendant's manifest-weight challenge because the trial court quite reasonably credited the testimony provided by the State's witnesses, applied said evidence and all reasonable inferences to the elements of the offense, and found her guilty of assault. Whether she used pepper spray during her attack on the victim was a question of fact for the trial court to decide. State v. Hill, 2020-Ohio-4235, 2020 Ohio App. LEXIS 3124 (Ohio Ct. App., Montgomery County 2020).

Defendant's convictions for assault and domestic violence were not against the manifest weight of the evidence, which showed that defendant struck the 12-year-old victim with a belt five or six times over the course of five or six minutes, resulting in welts, redness, and bruising to multiple areas of his body. State v. M.H., 2020-Ohio-4477, 2020 Ohio App. LEXIS 3343 (Ohio Ct. App., Franklin County 2020).

Conviction of defendant of felonious assault and assault was proper since the evidence was sufficient to support that he knowingly caused serious physical harm to him. Lastly, the State's evidence that he swung at the other officer also demonstrated the culpable mental state required to convict him of assault and was sufficient to establish that he attempted to cause the officer physical harm. Thus, the court did not err in denying his motion for acquittal under Crim.R. 29(A). State v. Hendricks, 2020-Ohio-5218, 2020 Ohio App. LEXIS 4061 (Ohio Ct. App., Lucas County 2020).

Trial court's decision convicting defendant of assault was not against the manifest weight of the evidence because the victim's and officer's testimony established that defendant grabbed the victim by her throat, threw her on the ground, and kicked her in the face; the officer testified that he observed several bruises and cuts on victim's face and head when he saw her minutes after the assault. State v. Nettles, 2019-Ohio-3682, 2019 Ohio App. LEXIS 3790 (Ohio Ct. App., Hamilton County 2019).

Defendant's conviction for assault was not against the manifest weight of the evidence because the State presented sufficient credible evidence that she knowingly harmed the victim, since she testified that she grabbed her arm, squeezed it hard enough to leave bruises, and then pulled her to the ground. Lastly, the witness's testimony was not essential to a finding of guilt since even without her testimony, there was ample evidence from which to find her guilty. State v. Sizemore, 2019-Ohio-4186, 2019 Ohio App. LEXIS 4259 (Ohio Ct. App., Montgomery County 2019).

Defendant's conviction for assault was not against the manifest weight of the evidence because the State presented sufficient credible evidence that she knowingly harmed the victim, since she testified that she grabbed her arm, squeezed it hard enough to leave bruises, and then pulled her to the ground. Lastly, the witness's testimony was not essential to a finding of guilt since even without her testimony, there was ample evidence from which to find her guilty. State v. Sizemore, 2019-Ohio-4186, 2019 Ohio App. LEXIS 4259 (Ohio Ct. App., Montgomery County 2019).

Defendant's conviction of assault on a peace officer was not against the great weight of the evidence simply because the trier of fact believed the testimony of the prosecution's witnesses. State v. Sergent, 2019-Ohio-4717, 2019 Ohio App. LEXIS 4793 (Ohio Ct. App., Seneca County 2019).

Evidence supported defendant's domestic violence and assault convictions because the victim, who was the child of defendant's paramour, testified that defendant grabbed the victim by the throat, lifted the victim by the neck, slammed the victim against an interior wall, slapped the victim in the face, and whipped the victim several times with a rubber-coated cord, striking the victim in the arms and legs. The State of Ohio also presented photographic exhibits of visible marks and bruising that the victim sustained and slight damage to the wall. State v. Faggs, 2018-Ohio-3643, 2018 Ohio App. LEXIS 3949 (Ohio Ct. App., Delaware County 2018), aff'd, 2020-Ohio-523, 159 Ohio St. 3d 420, 151 N.E.3d 593, 2020 Ohio LEXIS 453 (Ohio 2020).

In a prosecution for first-degree misdemeanor assault, the trial court's decision to reject defendant's self-defense claim was not against the manifest weight of the evidence, as the testimony of two witnesses was consistent with that of the victim that defendant was the primary aggressor, and a third witness acknowledged that she informed police that she did not see who "threw the first hit." State v. Allison, 2016-Ohio-5262, 2016 Ohio App. LEXIS 3124 (Ohio Ct. App., Montgomery County 2016).

Weight of the evidence supported defendant juvenile's adjudications of delinquency for aggravated burglary, assault, and criminal damaging because although there were some minor inconsistencies between the victim's initial statements to police and trial testimony, her statements and testimony were consistent in material respects; the victim's testimony was credible and consistent that defendant forcibly broke into a house through the back door without permission and grabbed her neck or throat. In re A.T., 2021-Ohio-2934, 2021 Ohio App. LEXIS 2889 (Ohio Ct. App., Cuyahoga County 2021).

**Mentally impaired victims**

Sufficient evidence existed to convict defendant of rape and assault of two mentally impaired individuals who resided at a residential treatment home where defendant worked as the witnesses were found to be competent to testify and one of the witnesses testified regarding the specifics of the rape and assault. State v. Swartsell, 2003-Ohio-4450, 2003 Ohio App. LEXIS 3971 (Ohio Ct. App., Butler County 2003).

Convictions for menacing, aggravated trespassing, and assault were supported by sufficient evidence as defendant admitted that he threatened and attempted to hit the mother and wanted to hit the mother's boyfriend when defendant went to the mother's residence claiming that her son had attempted to sell drugs to his sister. State v. Ellis, 2003-Ohio-3768, 2003 Ohio App. LEXIS 3417 (Ohio Ct. App., Greene County 2003).

**Mistrial**

In a prosecution for assault, the trial court did not abuse its discretion in not ordering a mistrial due to the State's and city's violation of Crim.R. 16 by their delay in providing summaries of witnesses' testimony, as defense counsel had the statements before he cross-examined the witnesses. State v. Green, 2015-Ohio-1513, 2015 Ohio App. LEXIS 1462 (Ohio Ct. App., Franklin County 2015).

**Motor vehicles**

Assaults, pursuant to R.C. 2903.13(B), may be effectuated through the operation of a motor vehicle: State v. Spencer, 1990 Ohio App. LEXIS 4808 (Ohio Ct. App., Portage County Nov. 2, 1990).

**Offense of moral turpitude**

When, as in the case of assault, a misdemeanor conviction cannot be determined as a matter of law to involve or not involve moral turpitude, it is permissible to consider the circumstances underlying the offense for which an EMT was convicted: Bivins v. Ohio State Bd. of Emergency Med. Servs., 2005-Ohio-5999, 165 Ohio App. 3d 390, 846 N.E.2d 881, 2005 Ohio App. LEXIS 5419 (Ohio Ct. App., Erie County 2005).

**Offense of violence**

Trial court erred in granting defendant's application to seal his criminal records because he was ineligible where offenses of violence were statutorily forbidden to be sealed, a conviction for assault was deemed an offense of violence, and defendant was convicted of assault. State v. Schoenberger, 2015-Ohio-4870, 2015 Ohio App. LEXIS 4732 (Ohio Ct. App., Franklin County 2015).

Trial court properly affirmed the Ohio State Board of Education's decision revoking a teacher's teaching license under R.C. 3319.31(B) because the record showed that the teacher had been convicted of misdemeanor assault and that the teacher had attended a high school dance smelling of alcohol and rubbed his hand across a student's buttocks. The teacher's assault conviction was an offense of violence and constituted grounds for revocation of the teacher's teaching license under § 3319.31(B)(2)(c). Contini v. Ohio State Bd. of Educ., 2008-Ohio-5710, 2008 Ohio App. LEXIS 4803 (Ohio Ct. App., Licking County 2008).

**Official duties**

There was sufficient evidence for a rational fact finder to find that the officer was a peace officer engaged in assisting the loss prevention officer in the apprehension of a shoplifter and enforcement of the laws of the state of Ohio and that, consequently, she was engaged in the performance of her official duties for a felony offense. State v. Davis, 2017 Ohio App. LEXIS 5642 (Ohio Ct. App., Licking County Dec. 20, 2017), rev'd, 2020-Ohio-309, 159 Ohio St. 3d 31, 146 N.E.3d 560, 2020 Ohio LEXIS 231 (Ohio 2020).

Trial court did not err in denying defendant's motion for acquittal on a charge of assault on a peace officer because evidence existed that a police chief was in the performance of his official duties under R.C. 2903.13(C)(3) when defendant drove his car towards him; although the chief received the complaint when he was off duty, he responded by putting on his uniform and going to investigate. State v. Kessinger, 2014-Ohio-2496, 2014 Ohio App. LEXIS 2429 (Ohio Ct. App., Highland County 2014).

Where a deputy sheriff was dispatched to investigate a vehicle in a ditch and a possible drunk driver, and upon finding none, he continued along the roadway and approximately one mile into the next county, he encountered defendant, who assaulted the sheriff, such activity fell within the sheriff's duty to render assistance to a disabled vehicle or stranded motorist, and as he was performing a recognized duty, he was "in the performance of his official duties" for purposes of finding that defendant assaulted a peace officer, in violation of R.C. 2903.13(C)(3); the fact that defendant was acting outside of his jurisdiction was not sufficient to find that he was not acting within the scope of his official duties. State v. Dawson, 2005-Ohio-2276, 2005 Ohio App. LEXIS 2171 (Ohio Ct. App., Pickaway County 2005).

**Other offenses**

**—Domestic violence**

Trial court committed plain error in allowing an amendment of defendant's domestic violence charge, a fourth-degree misdemeanor, to a charge of assault, a first-degree misdemeanor, because the amendment changed both the name of the offense as well as identity of the crime charged; however, the error was harmless because the charge was ultimately dismissed. State v. Williams, 2018-Ohio-1954, 2018 Ohio App. LEXIS 2125 (Ohio Ct. App., Lucas County 2018).

In defendant's criminal trial on a charge of domestic violence, in violation of R.C. 2919.25(A), arising from defendant's having beaten his stepson with a belt, the trial cout did not err in failing to give jury instructions on lesser included offenses of knowing, reckless, or negligent assault, in violation of R.C. 2903.13 and 2903.14, as there was no question that the victim was a family and household member of defendant's at the time of the offense; the jury would have had to ignore the undisputed evidence regarding the victim's relationship to defendant in order to acquit defendant of domestic violence and find him guilty of assault. State v. Moore, 2005-Ohio-4531, 163 Ohio App. 3d 23, 836 N.E.2d 18, 2005 Ohio App. LEXIS 4112 (Ohio Ct. App., Montgomery County 2005).

**Parental discipline**

Reasonable parental discipline was held to be an affirmative defense to a charge of domestic violence or assault, with the burden of proof resting with the accused; because the State was only required to show that defendant knowingly caused or attempted to cause physical harm to a household member, proof of unreasonable parental discipline was not a component of the physical-harm element. Since the only difference between the domestic-violence statute and the portion of the assault statute involved was the status of the victim (family or household member versus another), the reasonableness or unreasonableness of parental discipline was not a part of the physical-harm element of that offense either. State v. Faggs, 2020-Ohio-523, 159 Ohio St. 3d 420, 151 N.E.3d 593, 2020 Ohio LEXIS 453 (Ohio 2020).

**Peace officers**

Evidence that defendant kicked one officer in the groin and another officer in the arm was sufficient evidence of attempted harm; the juvenile court could have inferred that defendant was aware that kicking her legs in the direction of the officers would probably cause harm to the officers. In re M.H., 2021-Ohio-1041, 169 N.E.3d 971, 2021 Ohio App. LEXIS 1088 (Ohio Ct. App., Hamilton County 2021).

Evidence was sufficient to support defendant's conviction for assault on peace officer because when defendant struggled with peace officer and drove his body into officer forcing him up and against guardrail, he was aware his conduct would result in causing or attempting to cause physical harm to officer. State v. Chamberlain, 2020-Ohio-3583, 2020 Ohio App. LEXIS 2532 (Ohio Ct. App., Jefferson County 2020).

Sufficient evidence supported defendant's conviction for assault on an officer because the officers' testimony, in conjunction with the video of the incident, provided sufficient evidence for the jury to conclude that defendant acted knowingly to cause physical harm. The officer testified that defendant struck her twice and that she experienced pain and a twisted knee when he assaulted her. State v. Davis, 2017 Ohio App. LEXIS 5642 (Ohio Ct. App., Licking County Dec. 20, 2017), rev'd, 2020-Ohio-309, 159 Ohio St. 3d 31, 146 N.E.3d 560, 2020 Ohio LEXIS 231 (Ohio 2020).

Order adjudicating the juvenile a delinquent child was proper because the record supported his adjudication for assault on a police officer since voluntary intoxication was not a defense and the fact that the officer did not seek medical attention after the attack was immaterial. State v. K.W., 2016-Ohio-7365, 2016 Ohio App. LEXIS 4229 (Ohio Ct. App., Warren County 2016).



Sufficient evidence supported that defendant knowingly assaulted a peace officer because defendant stipulated to competency and he was aware that his kicking would cause injury as evidenced by his belligerent and aggressive behavior. The officers both testified that when they attempted to get defendant handcuffed and into the patrol wagon, defendant was continually struggling and kicked one officer in the face with his leg. State v. Wilson, 2014-Ohio-461, 2014 Ohio App. LEXIS 453 (Ohio Ct. App., Stark County 2014).

There was sufficient evidence that a sheriff's deputy working a special assignment on behalf of a power company to keep order at a job site met the definition of "peace officer" to support defendant's conviction for assault on a police officer, as the deputy and a sheriff both testified that the deputy was employed full-time by the county sheriff's department and the deputy was working at the power company's request; there was also testimony that the deputy was wearing an official uniform. State v. Ogle, 2013-Ohio-3420, 2013 Ohio App. LEXIS 3510 (Ohio Ct. App., Hocking County 2013), cert. denied, 574 U.S. 1011, 135 S. Ct. 674, 190 L. Ed. 2d 389, 2014 U.S. LEXIS 7669 (U.S. 2014).

Evidence supported defendant's conviction for assault on a police officer, as the officer's testimony confirmed that, in the officer's attempt to respond to a call for assistance due to an alleged theft and to escort defendant from a convenient store, defendant caused the officer physical harm by swinging defendant's arms, punching the officer in the face, and cutting the officer's lip. State v. Jackson, 2012-Ohio-2985, 2012 Ohio App. LEXIS 2626 (Ohio Ct. App., Franklin County 2012).

Defendant's conviction for assault on a peace officer under R.C. 2903.13(A) and (C)(3) was based on sufficient evidence because testimony from the trial indicated that on the night in question, the officer was acting in his official police duties, in uniform, when defendant charged at and struck the officer, causing physical injury to his face. State v. Kurek, 2012-Ohio-1993, 2012 Ohio App. LEXIS 1748 (Ohio Ct. App., Wood County 2012).

While it was possible for defendant to commit assault while committing obstruction of official business, in violation of R.C. 2903.13(A), (C)(3), and 2921.31(A), the two offenses arose from separate conduct; therefore, they were not allied offenses, subject to merger for sentencing under R.C. 2941.25. State v. Hight, 2011-Ohio-5013, 2011 Ohio App. LEXIS 4197 (Ohio Ct. App., Licking County 2011).

Conviction for assault on a police officer, in violation of R.C. 2903.13(A), was not against the manifest weight of the evidence, despite defendant's claim of self-defense, because two police officers testified that defendant was belligerent and confrontational during a booking process at a jail and surveillance video corroborated their testimony concerning defendant's conduct during the booking process which led to an altercation between defendant and an officer. State v. Radecki, 2010-Ohio-4108, 2010 Ohio App. LEXIS 3484 (Ohio Ct. App., Cuyahoga County 2010).

Conviction for assault on a peace officer was supported by sufficient evidence and was not against the manifest weight of the evidence where defendant spat at officers after telling them that he had hepatitis because the jury could have inferred that he intended to cause physical harm; because information regarding the fact that hepatitis could not have been transmitted through saliva was not in the record, it was not considered on appeal. State v. Morris, 2009-Ohio-6033, 2009 Ohio App. LEXIS 5091 (Ohio Ct. App., Trumbull County 2009).

When defendant was charged with felonious assault and assault of peace officers, in violation of R.C. 2903.11(A)(2) and 2903.13(A), the failure of the indictments and jury instructions to mention defendant's awareness that defendant's victims were peace officers did not cause reversible error because it was unnecessary to mention such a culpable mental state, as defendant's awareness that defendant's victims were peace officers was not an essential element of defendant's crimes, as the victims' status as peace officers merely enhanced the degree of defendant's crimes and the possible penalties, and (2) the general assembly intended to impose strict liability for this enhancement. State v. Anderson, 2009-Ohio-3900, 183 Ohio App. 3d 522, 917 N.E.2d 843, 2009 Ohio App. LEXIS 3323 (Ohio Ct. App., Cuyahoga County 2009).

Defendant could be convicted of felonious assault and assault of a peace officer under R.C. 2903.11 and R.C. 2903.13, regardless of whether he knew that the persons who were trying to stop his vehicle. There was sufficient evidence for conviction of felonious assault where the defendant attempted to harm the officers during a high speed chase. However, the defendant could be convicted of only one form of assault per victim where the convictions arose from a single course of conduct: State v. Anderson, 2009-Ohio-3900, 183 Ohio App. 3d 522, 917 N.E.2d 843, 2009 Ohio App. LEXIS 3323 (Ohio Ct. App., Cuyahoga County 2009).

Weight of the evidence supported defendant's convictions for assault upon an employee of a local correctional facility and assault on a police officer. The testimony of the victims, three sheriff's deputies, established that, as they were attempting to restrain defendant, as he charged at another officer, during a routine bi-monthly pat-down procedure at the jail, defendant punched one deputy several times, bit another on the hand, and elbowed the third in the mouth while he was on the ground, resulting in him suffering a split lip. State v. Daniels, 2008-Ohio-2236, 2008 Ohio App. LEXIS 1924 (Ohio Ct. App., Greene County 2008).

Defendant's convictions for felonious assault and assault on a peace officer, in violation of R.C. 2903.11(A)(2) and 2903.13(A), (C)(3), were supported by evidence that defendant refused to heed officers' warnings to get out of the vehicle, and instead, defendant backed the vehicle into the officers' paths until defendant's vehicle was stopped because it struck a police car; the evidence supported a determination that defendant acted knowingly pursuant to R.C. 2901.22(B). State v. Franklin, 2008-Ohio-1089, 2008 Ohio App. LEXIS 949 (Ohio Ct. App., Cuyahoga County 2008).

There was no constitutional violation sufficient to excuse defendant's conduct because, while defendant could have lawfully refused to consent to a warrantless entry, that right to refuse entry was limited. Even if the police officers has unlawfully entered defendant's private residence, defendant was not privileged to assault the officers after the unlawful entry; a lawful arrest was not an element of assault on a police officer. State v. Durham, 2007-Ohio-6262, 2007 Ohio App. LEXIS 5516 (Ohio Ct. App., Montgomery County 2007).

In defendant's prosecution for assault on a peace officer, under R.C. 2903.13, defendant did not show that defendant received ineffective assistance of counsel when counsel did not move to suppress evidence arising from an allegedly illegal entry and defendant's allegedly illegal arrest because, even if an officer illegally entered defendant's home to arrest defendant, this did not justify defendant's assault on the officer, so a motion to suppress would have been futile. State v. Flesher, 2007-Ohio-4982, 2007 Ohio App. LEXIS 4406 (Ohio Ct. App., Monroe County 2007).

Finding by a jury that the victim of an assault was a peace officer simply enhanced the degree of the offense of assault and the potential penalty, so proof of knowledge of the victim's status as a peace officer was not required under these circumstances, and the State was not required to demonstrate that the accused knew or was aware of the fact that the victim was a peace officer, in order to elevate the offense of assault from a misdemeanor to a fourth-degree felony under R.C. 2903.13(C), as the general assembly articulated the elements of R.C. 2903.13 with sufficient clarity to indicate that the victim's status as a peace officer elevated the criminal offense of assault from a misdemeanor of the first degree to a felony of the fourth degree regardless of whether or not the accused specifically knew of the victim's status as a peace officer. State v. Watson, 2007-Ohio-129, 2007 Ohio App. LEXIS 105 (Ohio Ct. App., Madison County 2007).

While R.C. 2903.13(C), regarding assault on a peace officer, did not specify a required culpable mental state, R.C. 2901.21 did not require a trial court to instruct a jury to find defendant was reckless as to the identity of his victim as a peace officer because there was no indication that the general assembly intended to impose anything other than strict liability for the peace-officer penalty enhancement in R.C. 2903.13(C), as R.C. 2935.01, defining a peace officer, did not suggest a mental state other than strict liability or conflict with other statutory definitions in a way that would call the relevant mental state in question. State v. Watson, 2007-Ohio-129, 2007 Ohio App. LEXIS 105 (Ohio Ct. App., Madison County 2007).

When defendant was charged with assault on a peace officer, in violation of R.C. 2903.13(C), it was not an abuse of discretion for the trial court to reject his tendered instruction on mistake of fact or to fail to instruct the jury that it had to find he was reckless regarding whether he perceived that his victim as a peace officer because the State did not have to prove he knew his victim was a peace officer or that he was reckless as to his victim's identity as a peace officer. State v. Watson, 2007-Ohio-129, 2007 Ohio App. LEXIS 105 (Ohio Ct. App., Madison County 2007).

There was sufficient evidence that defendant attempted to assault a police officer, under R.C. 2903.13(C)(3) and R.C. 2923.02, because testimony showed that defendant grabbed an officer's arm and placed it in a death grip, attempting to twist it. R.C. 2903.13 did not require serious physical harm, only that defendant caused or attempted to cause physical harm. State v. Fuote, 2007-Ohio-80, 2007 Ohio App. LEXIS 79 (Ohio Ct. App., Cuyahoga County 2007).

Defendant's conviction for assault on a police officer, under R.C. 2903.13(A) and 2901.01(A)(3) was not against the manifest weight of the evidence because the weight of the evidence supported the conclusion that defendant repeatedly hit an officer in the chest, as officers attempted to restrain defendant, and, while the officer did not seek medical attention, defendant's repeated punches were an attempt to cause physical harm to the officer. State v. Vandyke, 2007-Ohio-1356, 2007 Ohio App. LEXIS 1254 (Ohio Ct. App., Lorain County 2007).

Defendant's conviction of knowingly assaulting a police officer was supported by sufficient evidence and was not against the manifest weight of the evidence. Defendant was entitled to an instruction on self-defense where there was evidence that the officers used excessive or unnecessary force in subduing him: State v. Fritz, 2005-Ohio-4736, 163 Ohio App. 3d 276, 837 N.E.2d 823, 2005 Ohio App. LEXIS 4233 (Ohio Ct. App., Montgomery County 2005).

There was sufficient evidence to support defendant's conviction for assault because the police officer's testimony demonstrated that defendant knowingly attempted to cause physical harm to both officers thus meeting the elements of assault. When the officers attempted to arrest defendant, he was crouched on the floor and refused to get up, he then attempted to punch the officer, and even after the officers used pepper spray, defendant threw his elbow at the back of one officer's head. State v. Cossack, 2005-Ohio-965, 2005 Ohio App. LEXIS 999 (Ohio Ct. App., Mahoning County 2005).

Defendant's conviction for assault on a peace officer, in violation of R.C. 2903.13(C)(3) was supported by the weight and sufficiency of the evidence, as the record revealed that while defendant was being restrained by two grocery store employees who suspected defendant of attempting to steal meat from the store without paying for it, the officer arrived at the store and while attempting to handcuff defendant, defendant attempted to bite him. State v. Miller, 2005-Ohio-518, 2005 Ohio App. LEXIS 533 (Ohio Ct. App., Franklin County 2005).

Defendant's conviction for assault was upheld on appeal where a rational trier of fact could have found that defendant assaulted the police officer who had administered a breathalyzer test to him by knowingly causing or knowingly attempting to cause physical harm to the officer when defendant's shoulder struck the officer's stomach in an attempt to grab his gun as well as evidence from another officer, who witnessed defendant pinning the officer to the wall. State v. Veith, 2005-Ohio-422, 2005 Ohio App. LEXIS 465 (Ohio Ct. App., Marion County 2005).

Strict liability applies to the peace-officer penalty enhancement in R.C. 2903.13(C)(3). The state need not prove that the defendant knew that the victim was a police officer: State v. Wilcox, 2005-Ohio-1745, 160 Ohio App. 3d 468, 827 N.E.2d 832, 2005 Ohio App. LEXIS 1675 (Ohio Ct. App., Cuyahoga County 2005).

Defendant's conviction for assault on a police officer was not against the manifest weight of the evidence when the evidence showed that defendant charged at two police officers when they were standing in a doorway on a back porch, with little room to move or time to react, as it could be inferred that defendant knew, under R.C. 2901.22(B), his actions would likely knock one or both of them off the porch, and that their injury would likely result. State v. Nieves, 2004-Ohio-4334, 2004 Ohio App. LEXIS 3929 (Ohio Ct. App., Lorain County 2004).

Evidence was sufficient to support defendant's conviction for assaulting a police officer, as the evidence showed that defendant knew that when he threw the first officer to the ground quite forcefully, he was likely to cause physical harm to her. State v. Lester, 2004-Ohio-2909, 2004 Ohio App. LEXIS 2549 (Ohio Ct. App., Butler County 2004).

Sufficient evidence existed to sustain defendant's conviction for assaulting a police officer, in violation of R.C. 2903.13, where defendant resisted arrest while being ejected from a skating rink and, during the struggle, broke the officer's rib; jury was not required to accept defendant's claim that the officer was the aggressor or that defendant accidentally brushed against the officer while leaving. State v. Dixon, 2004-Ohio-2406, 2004 Ohio App. LEXIS 2141 (Ohio Ct. App., Cuyahoga County 2004).

Defendant's conviction for assaulting a police officer, in violation of R.C. 2903.13, was upheld where the trial court properly instructed the jury on the meaning of "knowingly" by capturing the applicable law as set forth in R.C. 2901.22(B) in charging that it was presumed defendant knew the result of his conduct since he initiated a course of conduct which increased the likelihood of violence and injury; the term "knowingly" does not require the offender to have the specific intent to cause a certain result and the State is not required to prove that defendant knew he would cause any specific injury to the officer. State v. Dixon, 2004-Ohio-2406, 2004 Ohio App. LEXIS 2141 (Ohio Ct. App., Cuyahoga County 2004).

Where the police officers testified that defendant attacked the officers by slamming them against a wall, slamming one the officers against a door or wall, attempting to take the weapon of one of the officers, and biting the finger of one of the officers, thereby cracking the rib of one of the officers and causing bruising and lacerations on both officers, there was sufficient evidence to convict defendant of assault in violation of R.C. 2903.13(A)(1) and of felonious assault in violation of R.C. 2903.11(A)(1). State v. Pearson, 2004-Ohio-1632, 2004 Ohio App. LEXIS 1456 (Ohio Ct. App., Stark County 2004).

Evidence that a deputy arrested defendant, handcuffed him, and had begun to lead him away when defendant kicked him twice and bit his hand, was sufficient to convict defendant of assault on a peace officer in violation of R.C. 2903.13(C)(3). State v. Glenn, 2004-Ohio-1489, 2004 Ohio App. LEXIS 1321 (Ohio Ct. App., Hamilton County 2004).

Actual physical harm was not required under R.C. 2903.13, but an attempt to commit physical harm sufficed; where police officers testified that a defendant repeatedly tried to elbow, kick, and head butt them, a rational trier of fact could have found that the defendant attempted to physically harm the officers, and assault convictions were affirmed. State v. Taylor, 2003-Ohio-7117, 2003 Ohio App. LEXIS 6451 (Ohio Ct. App., Seneca County 2003).

Where defendant was convicted of attempted retaliation in violation of R.C. 2923.02, 2921.05 and attempted assault on a police officer in violation of R.C. 2903.13, 2923.02, the trial court made the findings required by R.C. 2929.14(E)(4); in support the court pointed to the serious nature of the offenses, including a threat against a police officer, and to defendant's lengthy criminal record, including recent offenses. State v. Metcalf, 2003-Ohio-6782, 2003 Ohio App. LEXIS 6109 (Ohio Ct. App., Butler County 2003).

Conviction for assault on a police officer was upheld as not against the manifest weight of the evidence that, causing him to fall backward; even if the officer did not receive medical treatment, the act was an attempt to harm. State v. Clark, 2003-Ohio-6689, 2003 Ohio App. LEXIS 5942 (Ohio Ct. App., Ashtabula County 2003).

Defendant's conviction for assault on a police officer, as defined by R.C. 2903.13(A), was upheld, where the evidence showed that defendant, in attempting to flee and elude apprehension, struck an officer in the face. State v. Moore, 2003-Ohio-6255; 2003 Ohio App. LEXIS 5605 (Ohio Ct. App., Butler County 2003).

Pursuant to R.C. 2903.13, defendant's conviction for assaulting a police officer was not against the weight and sufficiency of the evidence that defendant kicked the arresting officer while being arrested for the disorderly conduct of raving and stomping around his mother's house. State v. Caesar, 2003-Ohio-6168, 2003 Ohio App. LEXIS 5542 (Ohio Ct. App., Cuyahoga County 2003).

Statute did not require the State to prove that defendant knew the assault victim, a police officer working as a security guard, was a police officer in order to elevate an assault from a misdemeanor to a fourth-degree felony. State v. Carter, 2003-Ohio-5042, 2003 Ohio App. LEXIS 4552 (Ohio Ct. App., Summit County 2003).

Where defendant punched a police officer in the face when the officer attempted to remove defendant's foot from the cell door and a fight ensued, such evidence supported the assault on a police officer conviction. State v. Beesler, 2003-Ohio-2815, 2003 Ohio App. LEXIS 2532 (Ohio Ct. App., Ashtabula County 2003).

A prison term longer than the shortest term authorized was proper where the defendant repeatedly assaulted several police officers: State v. Yontz, 135 Ohio App. 3d 530, 734 N.E.2d 882, 1999 Ohio App. LEXIS 6163 (Ohio Ct. App., Jefferson County 1999).

Off-duty police officer was performing official duties, for purposes of R.C. 2903.13(C)(3), when providing security at a school football game for which he was paid by the school system: State v. Duvall, 1997 Ohio App. LEXIS 2464 (Ohio Ct. App., Portage County June 6, 1997).

**Physical harm**

Defendant's assault conviction was proper as it was not against the manifest weight of the evidence because he knowingly caused physical harm when he admitted intentionally spraying victim in face, which caused pain and resulted in her eyes swelling. State v. Schooler, 2020-Ohio-4327, 2020 Ohio App. LEXIS 3214 (Ohio Ct. App., Montgomery County 2020).

Defendant's conviction for assault was not against the manifest weight of the evidence because the video clearly demonstrated that the woman in the white top, identified at trial by both the victim and her mother as defendant, punched the mother during the altercation. Defendant did not demonstrate that, due to inconsistencies in the evidence, "a miscarriage of justice" occurred or that the jury "lost its way" in finding her guilty of assault. State v. Davenport, 2019-Ohio-2297, 2019 Ohio App. LEXIS 2395 (Ohio Ct. App., Franklin County 2019).

In an aggravated assault prosecution, defendant's trial counsel was not ineffective in failing to request a jury instruction on the lesser offense of misdemeanor assault as the jurors would have properly found that the victim, who was hospitalized for more than a week and would likely suffer permanent incapacity and disfigurement, suffered serious physical harm, rather than simply physical harm, as a result of defendant's actions. State v. Black, 2012-Ohio-2874, 2012 Ohio App. LEXIS 2511 (Ohio Ct. App., Stark County 2012).

Weight of the evidence supported defendant's assault conviction because the victim testified that defendant hit him in the side of the face with a closed fist, which constituted an attempt to cause physical harm, regardless of the result of the blow. State v. Beach, 2012-Ohio-298, 2012 Ohio App. LEXIS 259 (Ohio Ct. App., Trumbull County 2012).

Evidence did not support a finding of assault, rather than felonious assault as the predicate offense for murder, because the coroner testified that the victim suffered extensive hemorrhaging under his scalp as a result of repeated blunt force injuries. Witnesses who observed the victim on the ground in the parking lot testified that the victim's face was swollen and covered in blood and that he had difficulty breathing; thus, the evidence established that the victim suffered "serious physical harm," not merely "physical harm," and the conduct reflected knowing, not reckless, conduct by defendant. State v. Hancher, 2010-Ohio-2507, 2010 Ohio App. LEXIS 2047 (Ohio Ct. App., Montgomery County 2010).

Person struck with a water balloon may satisfy the physical harm requirement of R.C. 2903.13(A) and, by extension, Athens, Ohio, City Code 13.02.01(A). State v. Weiss, 2010-Ohio-4509, 2010 Ohio App. LEXIS 3843 (Ohio Ct. App., Athens County 2010).

Sufficient evidence supported defendant's assault conviction because a reasonable person could have found beyond a reasonable doubt that defendant had caused physical harm to the victim. There was no dispute that defendant took the victim to the ground, grabbed him by the face and jaw, and put him in a headlock, and the victim testified that defendant hit him on the side of the head with some object; the victim's face was red, swollen, and bruised. State v. Hoopingarner, 2010-Ohio-6490, 2010 Ohio App. LEXIS 5379 (Ohio Ct. App., Tuscarawas County 2010).

In a prosecution for assault on a peace officer, the trial court's finding that a police officer, with whom defendant engaged in a physical confrontation, suffered no actual harm did not undermine the assault conviction as actual physical harm was not required; an attempt to commit physical harm sufficed. Defendant's act of kicking at the officer supported a finding that defendant attempted to cause harm to the officer. State v. Sorrells-Johnson, 2008-Ohio-3469, 2008 Ohio App. LEXIS 2924 (Ohio Ct. App., Franklin County 2008).

Trial court did not abuse its discretion by admitting the victim's medical records into evidence because they were relevant and their probative value outweighed their prejudicial effect; the records were cumulative of the victim's testimony and corroborated that he went to the hospital, had a dislocated shoulder, experienced pain, did not have a preexisting shoulder problem, and underwent surgery and physical therapy. The evidence supported the finding that defendant caused serious physical harm to the victim, an off-duty police officer. State v. Hidvegi, 2008-Ohio-2662, 2008 Ohio App. LEXIS 2235 (Ohio Ct. App., Cuyahoga County 2008).

Sufficient evidence supported the essential elements for assault because a forensic nurse substantiated the fact that the victim sustained physical harm after having vaginal, anal, and oral intercourse with defendant; the nurse described the victim's physical injuries as abrasions and swelling to her upper right lip; redness on her neck; bruising to her right ear; abrasions to the hairline; leg and knee contusions; lacerations and bruising to the anus; and redness and swelling of the vaginal area. The victim's own testimony and description of how defendant hit, kicked and beat her, and grabbed her head and how her body began shaking and went numb was further evidence that she sustained physical harm. State v. Egli, 2008-Ohio-2507, 2008 Ohio App. LEXIS 2121 (Ohio Ct. App., Portage County 2008).

In defendant's prosecution for, inter alia, felonious assault under R.C. 2903.11(A)(1) and (2) related to the shooting of a police officer in the face, defendant was not entitled to a lesser included offense instruction on assault under R.C. 2903.13 because serious physical harm was demonstrated under R.C. 2901.01(A)(5)(d) based on the necessity of plastic surgery to repair a laceration to the officer's face and the fact that glass shards from the officer's glasses had to be surgically removed from her eye; an instruction on negligent assault was also unnecessary because there was no evidentiary support for the claim that the shooting could have been an accident. State v. Person, 2007-Ohio-6869, 174 Ohio App. 3d 287, 881 N.E.2d 924, 2007 Ohio App. LEXIS 6039 (Ohio Ct. App., Hamilton County 2007), aff'd, 2008-Ohio-6250, 120 Ohio St. 3d 323, 898 N.E.2d 961, 2008 Ohio LEXIS 3480 (Ohio 2008).

Since defendant was charged with causing or attempting to cause physical harm to a peace officer, whether or not the officer, whom defendant kicked, actually suffered physical harm was of no consequence as there was no requirement that the officer suffer actual physical injury. State v. Holland, 2007-Ohio-3149, 2007 Ohio App. LEXIS 2941 (Ohio Ct. App., Mahoning County 2007).

In defendant's prosecution for assault, in violation of R.C. 2903.13, and patient abuse, in violation of R.C. 2903.34, the patient, who was mentally disabled, was unable to communicate verbally; however, a witness testified that, when defendant punched the patient and hit him with hanger, the patient began moaning and crying. This was sufficient to support a finding that the patient was physically injured under R.C. 2901.01(A)(3) even though the patient had no visible injuries after the incident. State v. Barnes, 2006-Ohio-5239, 2006 Ohio App. LEXIS 5233 (Ohio Ct. App., Cuyahoga County 2006).

Sufficient evidence supported a jury's findings that the victim's injuries constituted physical harm, as set forth in R.C. 2903.13(A). The State offered photos of red marks and bruises on the victim's neck, wrist, and leg occurring as a result of an incident in which defendant physically tried to prevent victim from leaving his house, and the victim testified that the injuries caused her pain. State v. Hawke, 2006-Ohio-3037, 2006 Ohio App. LEXIS 2914 (Ohio Ct. App., Montgomery County 2006).

"Serious physical harm" is not an element of assault; assault merely requires "physical harm," which is defined in R.C. 2901.01(A)(3). State v. Hill, 2005-Ohio-3701, 2005 Ohio App. LEXIS 3400 (Ohio Ct. App., Montgomery County 2005).

Because "serious physical harm," as defined in R.C. 2901.01(A)(5)(e), incorporates the concept of an injury that causes pain and suffering only, albeit acute, prolonged or intractable pain, and because "physical harm," as defined in § 2901.01(A)(3), includes any injury, regardless of its gravity or duration, a pain-inducing blow is sufficient to satisfy the "physical harm" element of assault. State v. Hill, 2005-Ohio-3701, 2005 Ohio App. LEXIS 3400 (Ohio Ct. App., Montgomery County 2005).

A minor welt near the victim's eye qualified as physical harm under R.C. 2901.01(A)(3): State v. Guidugli, 2004-Ohio-2871, 157 Ohio App. 3d 383, 811 N.E.2d 567, 2004 Ohio App. LEXIS 2529 (Ohio Ct. App., Hamilton County 2004).

Defendant juvenile's adjudication of delinquency for assault was supported by the evidence because the State sufficiently established that the victim suffered physical harm; there was sufficient evidence establishing that defendant caused a tangible injury or impairment, red bruising or scarring, to the victim's neck when he grabbed her. In re A.T., 2021-Ohio-2934, 2021 Ohio App. LEXIS 2889 (Ohio Ct. App., Cuyahoga County 2021).

**Plea withdrawal**

Trial court's judgment denying defendant's pre-sentence motion to withdraw his plea of no contest entered on a count of misdemeanor assault was inherently reasonable and supported by the record because defendant appeared with counsel and was given a complete and fair opportunity to be heard; he was afforded a full and thorough plea hearing where he knowingly, intelligently, and voluntarily waived his rights and was apprised of penalties he would face upon trial court's acceptance of his plea. State v. Martin, 2022-Ohio-758, 2022 Ohio App. LEXIS 676 (Ohio Ct. App., Portage County 2022).

Trial court did not abuse its discretion in denying defendant's presentence motion to withdraw his no contest plea to two counts of misdemeanor assault, because defendant was informed of the possible penalties he was facing and that by entering a no contest plea, he was waiving his right to a trial and all that entailed. Defendant's two-year delay in filing the motion to withdraw did not weigh in his favor, and he provided no evidence to support his self-defense claim. State v. Posey, 2014-Ohio-1994, 2014 Ohio App. LEXIS 1936 (Ohio Ct. App., Ottawa County 2014).

**Probable cause**

Police officers had probable cause to arrest the arrestee for criminal assault, and therefore the arrestee's malicious prosecution claim under the Federal Tort Claims Act was properly dismissed, because state prosecutors brought the assault charge against the arrestee in state court only after obtaining an indictment, which established prima facie evidence of probable cause. Harris v. United States, 422 F.3d 322, 2005 FED App. 0376P, 2005 U.S. App. LEXIS 19058 (6th Cir. Ohio 2005), amended, 2005 U.S. App. LEXIS 28860 (6th Cir. Dec. 1, 2005).

**Procedure**

Trial court erred when it found defendant guilty, instead of not guilty, upon his no contest plea to assault, under R.C. 2903.13, in the absence of an explanation of circumstances to support each element of the offense. That was plain error, in the sense that the result would clearly have been otherwise had the error not occurred, and defendant was entitled not merely to the reversal of his conviction, but to discharge. State v. Young, 2006-Ohio-6659, 2006 Ohio App. LEXIS 6558 (Ohio Ct. App., Montgomery County 2006).

State was not required to charge defendant with domestic violence, under R.C. 2903.13(A), or child endangering, under R.C. 2919.22(B)(1) or (B)(3), instead of assault, under R.C. 2903.13(A), for striking his foster child with a horse whip. Since neither domestic violence nor child endangering were allied offenses of similar import with assault, R.C. 1.51, regarding special provisions, did not apply; the commission of one offense could have occurred without the commission of the other. State v. Wickard, 2006-Ohio-6088, 2006 Ohio App. LEXIS 6025 (Ohio Ct. App., Hancock County 2006).

Where a trial court judge announced in his verdict that defendant was convicted of a fourth degree felony for having committed an assault on a police officer, in violation of R.C. 2903.13(C)(3), but the journal entry of conviction as well as the sentencing entry indicated that defendant was convicted of a third degree assault conviction, the trial court was directed to correct the journal entry of conviction to correctly reflect a fourth degree felony offense, and the sentence was reversed and remanded for resentencing. State v. Ogletree, 2006-Ohio-2603, 2006 Ohio App. LEXIS 2449 (Ohio Ct. App., Cuyahoga County 2006).

**Prosecutorial misconduct**

There was no prosecutorial misconduct in bringing charges against defendant of assault, carrying a concealed weapon, and menacing, in violation of R.C. 2903.13(A), 2923.12(A)(1), and 2903.22(A), despite the fact that the jury only found defendant guilty of the assault charge, as the facts supported the elements of the charges. State v. Junod, 2009-Ohio-2817, 2009 Ohio App. LEXIS 2381 (Ohio Ct. App., Auglaize County 2009).

Because the evidence was not overwhelming that defendant knowingly attempted to remove the police officer's weapon for aggravated robbery, R.C. 2911.01, or that the officer established control over defendant sufficient for an arrest to support a conviction for escape, under R.C. 2921.34, it could not be said that the prosecutor's comment regarding defendant's failure to testify was not harmless as to those convictions. But, because there was overwhelming evidence that defendant was guilty of assault, under R.C. 2903.13, since the officer testified that, after he pulled defendant's vehicle over, defendant grabbed him by the waist, shoved him backwards, and essentially wrestled him to the ground, among other things, the prosecutor's comments were harmless as to that conviction. State v. Askew, 2006-Ohio-4769, 2006 Ohio App. LEXIS 4670 (Ohio Ct. App., Ross County 2006).

Prosecutor's repeated interjection of his opinion as to the credibility of defendant, his opinion about the credibility of witnesses, and his opinion of defendant's guilt, including the use of the word "lies" or a derivative of it 19 times, was prosecutorial misconduct and constituted plain error as to defendant's assault conviction; the prosecutorial misconduct did not impact the underage possession conviction or the prohibited acts for possessing a fictitious driver's license identification conviction. State v. Baldev, 2005-Ohio-2369, 2005 Ohio App. LEXIS 2256 (Ohio Ct. App., Butler County 2005).

**Proximate cause**

Defendant's convictions for assault and involuntary manslaughter were not against the weight of the evidence. The assault was a proximate cause of the victim's death since, if defendant had not punched the victim in the head, the victim would not have fallen to the ground and struck his head on the sidewalk, and he would not have sustained the injuries that ultimately caused his death. State v. Dykas, 2010-Ohio-359, 185 Ohio App. 3d 763, 925 N.E.2d 685, 2010 Ohio App. LEXIS 290 (Ohio Ct. App., Cuyahoga County 2010).

**Restitution**

In defendant's assault prosecution, the trial court erred in ordering defendant to pay an unspecified amount of restitution as R.C. 2929.18(A)(1) required the trial court, at sentencing, to determine the amount of restitution to be made by the defendant. State v. Chadwick, 2009-Ohio-2472, 2009 Ohio App. LEXIS 2086 (Ohio Ct. App., Knox County 2009).

While the trial court could not order the restitution of a victim's medical expenses as part of a defendant's sentence for misdemeanor assault (R.C. 2903.13(B)), it properly ordered such restitution as a condition of his probation and suspended sentence under R.C. 2951.02 because the medical expenses were reasonably related to the offense for which he had been placed on probation. State v. Bates, 2004-Ohio-1370, 2004 Ohio App. LEXIS 1226 (Ohio Ct. App., Belmont County 2004).

**Retaliation**

Defendant's testimony that he kicked and hit the victim in retaliation for being punched was sufficient to support a conviction on an assault charge under R.C. 2903.13(A). State v. Norfleet, 2003-Ohio-5627, 2003 Ohio App. LEXIS 5006 (Ohio Ct. App., Coshocton County 2003).

**School personnel**

Victim of an assault was a school administrator engaging in the victim's official responsibilities at the time of the offense, pursuant to R.C. 2903.13(C)(2)(e), because the victim was the athletic director of a high school and was investigating a brawl in the parking lot of the high school after a basketball game. When the brawl broke up, the victim noticed that defendant's car was parked in a fire lane and an argument broke out between the victim and defendant in which the jury found that defendant assaulted the victim. State v. Mundell, 2012-Ohio-3378, 2012 Ohio App. LEXIS 2975 (Ohio Ct. App., Delaware County 2012).

Sufficient evidence existed to find that the victim of the assault, under R.C. 2903.13(C)(2)(e), was a school teacher because she was a person who was employed in the public schools at the time of the incident, while under a contract described in R.C. 3319.08, and in a position requiring a certificate issued pursuant to R.C. 3319.22. The victim, a special education teacher, testified that appellant, a juvenile, puncher her with her fist during the course of a dispute. In re M.H., 2010-Ohio-689, 186 Ohio App. 3d 513, 928 N.E.2d 1174, 2010 Ohio App. LEXIS 572 (Ohio Ct. App., Ottawa County 2010).

There was sufficient evidence that a special education teacher qualified as a "school teacher" for purposes of the assault statute. State v. Nelson, 2010-Ohio-5932, 2010 Ohio App. LEXIS 4984 (Ohio Ct. App., Portage County 2010).

As used in R.C. 2903.13(C), the term "school teacher" does not include educational assistants: In re Shafer, 145 Ohio App. 3d 53, 761 N.E.2d 1096, 2001 Ohio App. LEXIS 3241 (Ohio Ct. App., Miami County 2001).

In order to prove the crime of assault under R.C. 2903.13(A) by a school teacher, principal or administrator against a pupil, the prosecution must prove not only all of the elements of that offense beyond a reasonable doubt, but also that the corporal punishment inflicted was unreasonable and not rationally related to the maintenance of discipline and order. R.C. 3319.41 creates no affirmative defense placing the burden of proof on the defendant: State v. Hoover, 5 Ohio App. 3d 207, 450 N.E.2d 710, 1982 Ohio App. LEXIS 11055 (Ohio Ct. App., Ottawa County 1982).

**Self-defense**

Defendant's assault convictions were not against the manifest weight of the evidence because the trial court did not err in concluding that defendant did not act in self-defense where defendant was at fault for creating the situation as he was not privileged under the circumstances to resist the correctional officers' orders. State v. Williams, 2019-Ohio-5381, 2019 Ohio App. LEXIS 5448 (Ohio Ct. App., Allen County 2019).

Defendant's assault convictions were not against the manifest weight of the evidence because the trial court did not err in concluding that defendant did not act in self-defense where defendant was at fault for creating the situation as he was not privileged under the circumstances to resist the correctional officers' orders. State v. Williams, 2019-Ohio-5381, 2019 Ohio App. LEXIS 5448 (Ohio Ct. App., Allen County 2019).

While a trial court committed plain error under Crim.R. 52 in not instructing the jury in an assault trial as to the third element of self-defense, whether defendant violated a duty to retreat, the error did not affect defendant's substantial rights as, from the victim's testimony that defendant was the aggressor in a marital dispute, the jury could have found defendant was at fault in creating situation. Moreover, from the victim's testimony that defendant immediately got back into bed and went to sleep following the assault, the jury could reasonably conclude that defendant did not have a bona fide belief that she was in imminent danger of death or great bodily harm. State v. Parks, 2011-Ohio-4056, 2011 Ohio App. LEXIS 3401 (Ohio Ct. App., Franklin County 2011).

Weight of the evidence supported defendant's convictions for assault and disorderly conduct because defendant failed to prove all of the elements of the affirmative defense of self-defense. There was evidence to support a determination that defendant's actions during the child exchange gave rise to the altercation and he did not prove that he had both reasonable grounds to believe that he was in imminent danger of bodily harm and an honest belief, even though mistaken, that he was in imminent danger of bodily harm (from the 62-year-old victim) and his only means of protection was through the use of force not likely to cause death or great bodily harm. State v. DiFrancesca, 2011-Ohio-3087, 2011 Ohio App. LEXIS 2579 (Ohio Ct. App., Franklin County 2011).

Ineffective assistance of counsel claim was rejected in a case involving assault on a corrections officer because it was clear from statements made by defendant and his counsel that defendant knew that he was unable to claim self-defense if he did not take the stand. State v. Beckett, 2010-Ohio-755, 2010 Ohio App. LEXIS 618 (Ohio Ct. App., Noble County 2010).

In a prosecution on charges of assault and involuntary manslaughter, there was ample evidence presented to support the jury's findings that defendant failed to prove his self-defense claim as evidence that the victim did not block defendant's punch and did not use his body to break his fall supported the State's theory that the victim was not intending to assault defendant; thus, defendant was unable to show that he had a bona fide belief that he was in imminent danger. State v. Dykas, 2010-Ohio-359, 185 Ohio App. 3d 763, 925 N.E.2d 685, 2010 Ohio App. LEXIS 290 (Ohio Ct. App., Cuyahoga County 2010).

For purposes of self-defense, defendant did not establish that he had a bona fide belief that he was in imminent danger: State v. Dykas, 2010-Ohio-359, 185 Ohio App. 3d 763, 925 N.E.2d 685, 2010 Ohio App. LEXIS 290 (Ohio Ct. App., Cuyahoga County 2010).

In an assault prosecution, defendant's claim that he acted in self-defense when he punched the victim was properly rejected as the victim's testimony showed that defendant's attack was unprovoked. While the victim's girlfriend testified that the victim began swinging first and that defendant simply retaliated, this testimony contradicted her earlier written statement to the police, in which the girlfriend stated that defendant punched the victim without provocation, and the trial court did not err in finding the victim's testimony more credible. State v. Dawson, 2009-Ohio-2331, 2009 Ohio App. LEXIS 1980 (Ohio Ct. App., Licking County 2009).

Defendant did not receive ineffective assistance of counsel because there was no demonstrable basis for the defenses of self-defense or defense-of-family-member; because defendant did not see how her husband came by his injuries in the men's bathroom, but only saw him as he was lying on the floor, afterwards, it was too late for defendant to have come to the defense of her husband since he had already been injured. Also, defendant assaulted the victim before he did anything to which defendant could have claimed to have been reacting either in self-defense or in defense of her husband. State v. England, 2009-Ohio-4322, 2009 Ohio App. LEXIS 3633 (Ohio Ct. App., Montgomery County 2009).

Defendant's conviction for assault was against the manifest weight of the evidence as the evidence clearly showed that defendant was acting in self-defense when he punched the victim three times in the face after the victim picked up a metal tie bar in an attempt to strike defendant. Defendant was threatened with a reasonably serious amount of force, and he was entitled to act as he did in punching the victim three times until the victim fell to the ground; the proper inquiry was whether the force was reasonable, not whether the force was necessary. City of Struthers v. Williams, 2008-Ohio-6637, 2008 Ohio App. LEXIS 5538 (Ohio Ct. App., Mahoning County 2008).

In defendant's prosecution on two charges of assault, the trial court properly did not instruct the jury on self-defense because defendant never stated that he felt in fear of imminent danger during an altercation with police officers, an essential element of self-defense. State v. Keith, 2008-Ohio-6122, 2008 Ohio App. LEXIS 5115 (Ohio Ct. App., Franklin County 2008).

Weight of the evidence supported defendant's assault conviction because evidence that the victim put his hand on defendant's chest did not support defendant's claim that he reasonably believed it was necessary to punch the victim in the face in order to protect himself. Also, the victim's and the witness's testimony that defendant pushed the victim immediately after exiting the vehicle negated defendant's claim that he was not at fault in creating the situation that gave rise to his use of force against the victim. State v. Favor, 2008-Ohio-5371, 2008 Ohio App. LEXIS 4533 (Ohio Ct. App., Franklin County 2008).

Weight of the evidence supported defendant's conviction for misdemeanor assault because defendant did not demonstrate that he acted in self-defense; the evidence supported the conclusion that defendant did not believe that he was in imminent danger at the time of the attack on the victim. Defendant sought out a confrontation with the individual or individuals who assaulted him and several witnesses testified that defendant was standing among his friends watching the victim fight with another man before kicking the victim in the face; defendant admitted that all the victim did was look at him and did not testify that it would have been impossible for him to retreat. State v. Babu, 2008-Ohio-5287, 2008 Ohio App. LEXIS 4429 (Ohio Ct. App., Athens County 2008).



Trial court applied the proper standard to determine whether defendant's belief that he was in danger of bodily harm was reasonable and thus, properly rejected defendant's self-defense claim to assault; defendant's belief had to not only be honest, but reasonable. The trial court's conclusion that defendant "overreacted" was based upon the circumstances, which included: that defendant was six to eight inches taller than the victim; that there was no testimony that the victim actually swung at or threatened defendant; and that mere poking and pushing did not demonstrate a threat of imminent use of unlawful force. State v. Fink, 2008-Ohio-1503, 2008 Ohio App. LEXIS 1307 (Ohio Ct. App., Ashtabula County 2008).

Though defendant asserted that he acted in self-defense, as there were two plausible versions of events, one from defendant and one from the victim, the inconsistencies between the two versions raised a credibility question. The trial court specifically indicated that it found that the victim was more credible than defendant, and the appellate court had to defer to this finding. State v. Pearce, 2008-Ohio-1527, 2008 Ohio App. LEXIS 1367 (Ohio Ct. App., Belmont County 2008).

Cross-motions for summary judgment as to the nondischargeability, pursuant to 11 U.S.C.S. § 523(a)(6), of any judgment that a plaintiff subsequently was awarded in then-pending state court litigation arising out of debtor's having struck plaintiff on the head with a baseball bat and having pleaded no contest to charges under R.C. 2903.13(A) were denied. There were genuine issues of fact as to whether debtor had acted in self-defense, and a finding that debtor had acted in self-defense would negate malice with the result that the two elements required by § 523(a)(6) would not be shown. Smith v. Nitschke (In re Nitschke), 2008 Bankr. LEXIS 138 (Bankr. N.D. Ohio Jan. 11, 2008).

In a prosecution for assault, the trial court did not err in finding that defendant had not acted in self-defense when he struck the victim multiple times with his fists because, while the evidence revealed that the victim was agitating defendant, the evidence did not show that the victim created the violent nature of the situation. Defendant also never testified that he was in imminent danger of bodily harm and that his only means of escape was by use of force. State v. Cunningham, 2007-Ohio-6431, 2007 Ohio App. LEXIS 5636 (Ohio Ct. App., Columbiana County 2007).

In an assault prosecution, the trial court did not err in failing to give a self-defense instruction to the jury as defendant did not establish that he was not at fault in creating the confrontation because he approached the victim, and he did not establish that he had a bona fide belief that he was in imminent danger. The victim's act of raising his hands in the air toward defendant did not establish that the victim was trying to cause defendant harm. State v. Estep, 2007-Ohio-5516, 2007 Ohio App. LEXIS 4844 (Ohio Ct. App., Licking County 2007).

In an assault prosecution, the trial court did not err in failing to give a self-defense instruction to the jury as defendant did not establish that he was not at fault in creating the confrontation because he approached the victim, and he did not establish that he had a bona fide belief that he was in imminent danger. The victim's act of raising his hands in the air toward defendant did not establish that the victim was trying to cause defendant harm. State v. Estep, 2007-Ohio-5516, 2007 Ohio App. LEXIS 4844 (Ohio Ct. App., Licking County 2007).

Evidence that defendant grabbed the victim's buttocks two times and that defendant grabbed the victim's wrist and started pushing her, eventually forcing her to the floor, showed that defendant was the aggressor in the altercation; thus, defendant failed to meet his burden of proving the affirmative defense of self-defense by a preponderance of the evidence. State v. Gesell, 2006-Ohio-3621, 2006 Ohio App. LEXIS 3580 (Ohio Ct. App., Butler County 2006).

In a prosecution for assault, the trial court properly rejected defendant's affirmative defense of self-defense because defendant failed to establish the two elements of a valid self-defense claim applicable to the facts of the case, in that the testimony at trial showed that defendant was the aggressor since he came to the victim's house looking for his son and called the victim's daughter a "bitch"; thus, defendant failed to establish that he was not at fault in creating the situation. Further, defendant failed to prove that he possessed a bona fide belief that he was in imminent danger of bodily harm; instead, defendant's supposed fear that the victim was going to strike him was not genuine especially in light of the fact that defendant conceded that the victim swung at him but never touched him. State v. Johnson, 2006-Ohio-2380, 2006 Ohio App. LEXIS 2261 (Ohio Ct. App., Lake County 2006).

Because defendant unequivocally denied striking the hospital security guard by testifying at trial, defendant could not assert self-defense because self-defense effectively admits the facts asserted by the prosecution for the assault charge, under Columbus, Ohio, Code 2311.21. To hold both positions was logically and legally inconsistent because defendant could not claim absolute innocence and simultaneously avail himself of the affirmative defense of self-defense. City of Columbus v. Peoples, 2006-Ohio-1718, 2006 Ohio App. LEXIS 1578 (Ohio Ct. App., Franklin County 2006).

Trial court did not err by rejecting defendant's claim of self-defense where the record supported a finding that the defendant was at fault for creating the altercation between himself and the victim: City of Cleveland v. Welms, 2006-Ohio-6441, 169 Ohio App. 3d 600, 863 N.E.2d 1125, 2006 Ohio App. LEXIS 6391 (Ohio Ct. App., Cuyahoga County 2006).

Defendant was entitled to an instruction on self-defense where there was evidence that the officers used excessive or unnecessary force in subduing him: State v. Fritz, 2005-Ohio-4736, 163 Ohio App. 3d 276, 837 N.E.2d 823, 2005 Ohio App. LEXIS 4233 (Ohio Ct. App., Montgomery County 2005).

**Sentence**

Defendant's sentence was properly enhanced under sentencing guidelines because his prior Ohio convictions for felonious assault and aggravated robbery each qualified as crime of violence. United States v. Raymore, 965 F.3d 475, 2020 FED App. 211P, 2020 U.S. App. LEXIS 21625 (6th Cir. Ohio 2020), cert. denied, 141 S. Ct. 2814, 210 L. Ed. 2d 938, 2021 U.S. LEXIS 3244 (U.S. 2021), dismissed, 2022 U.S. Dist. LEXIS 38051 (N.D. Ohio Mar. 3, 2022).

Trial court's decision to impose the maximum term of one year on defendant's attempted assault conviction was supported by the facts that defendant was on probation at the time of his offense, that he had an extensive criminal history and failure to respond favorably to past sanctions, and he had a repeated pattern of the same activity giving rise to the underlying offense. State v. Johnson, 2012-Ohio-2508, 2012 Ohio App. LEXIS 2201 (Ohio Ct. App., Cuyahoga County 2012).

Trial court complied with the dictates of the newly amended R.C. 2929.14(C)(4) and made all the required findings to support the imposition of consecutive sentences upon defendant's convictions for attempted assault and harassment by inmate. The trial judge found that the imposition of consecutive sentences would not be disproportionate to the seriousness of defendant's conduct and to the danger that he posed to the public, especially since the trial judge emphasized that this was defendant's third case involving disrespect and violence toward a peace officer. State v. Johnson, 2012-Ohio-2508, 2012 Ohio App. LEXIS 2201 (Ohio Ct. App., Cuyahoga County 2012).

Imposition of consecutive sentences resulting in a nine-year prison sentence in a case involving robbery, assault, and intimidation was not erroneous because no judicial fact-finding was required before the imposition of the sentences; moreover, the sentences imposed were within the range provided for by R.C. 2929.14. State v. Small, 2012-Ohio-149, 2012 Ohio App. LEXIS 114 (Ohio Ct. App., Licking County 2012).

When appellant pleaded guilty to assault in violation of R.C. 2903.13 and aggravated burglary in violation of R.C. 2911.11 (A)(2), the trial court sentenced appellant to a prison term of four years for the aggravated burglary and he received a concurrent six-month sentence for the misdemeanor assault; the trial court erred by failing to impose post-release control under R.C. 2967.28(B), 2929.19. Because appellant did not appeal his convictions and had already served his prison terms, res judicata precluded a collateral attack to his conviction irrespective of the defects in the trial court's imposition of post-release control. State v. Turner, 2011-Ohio-2993, 2011 Ohio App. LEXIS 2536 (Ohio Ct. App., Ashtabula County 2011).

As to the State's assignment of error, that the trial court erred by imposing community control because it failed to make the required findings under R.C. 2929.13(D)(2)(a), (b) and failed to give adequate reasons for overcoming the presumption in favor of a prison term, the court found that the trial court followed the court's mandate on remand and made the appropriate findings necessary to grant community control in this case. The trial court found that: (1) defendant had already served 10 months in prison; (2) by providing defendant with mental health treatment and community supervision with family support, he was more likely to be rehabilitated successfully and have a much lower likelihood of recidivism; (3) the victim had relocated and there was no evidence that defendant knew where she lived; (4) defendant showed genuine remorse; and (5) it remained unclear whether defendant genuinely expected to physically harm the victim. State v. Martin, 2010-Ohio-5863, 2010 Ohio App. LEXIS 4931 (Ohio Ct. App., Franklin County 2010), modified, 2011-Ohio-951, 192 Ohio App. 3d 681, 950 N.E.2d 221, 2011 Ohio App. LEXIS 796 (Ohio Ct. App., Franklin County 2011).

Trial court's sentence of 180 days for the first-degree misdemeanor of assault was within the statutory sentencing ranges under R.C. 2929.24 and, as such, was proper. Further, the sentencing term was not unreasonable, arbitrary, or unconscionable. State v. Chadwick, 2009-Ohio-2472, 2009 Ohio App. LEXIS 2086 (Ohio Ct. App., Knox County 2009).

One hundred eighty day prison sentence and two years of intensive supervised probation, imposed on defendant upon his conviction on two counts of misdemeanor assault, was not inconsistent with the relevant sentencing considerations in R.C. 2929.22 as defendant repeatedly punched his cousin in front of two young children and as the condition of the victim, who was in the midst of recovering from a total abdominal hysterectomy, made her particularly vulnerable to the offense. State v. Best, 2009-Ohio-6806, 2009 Ohio App. LEXIS 5702 (Ohio Ct. App., Mahoning County 2009).

One hundred eighty day prison sentence and two years of intensive supervised probation, imposed on defendant upon his conviction on two counts of misdemeanor assault, were imposed after the trial court considered the purposes and principles of sentencing in R.C. 2929.21(A) and the relevant factors under R.C. 2929.22. The trial court noted that defendant assaulted his cousin in front of two children while his cousin was recovering from a total abdominal hysterectomy, that defendant did not seem to be remorseful, that he failed to seek help for his alcohol problem, and that he had a pattern of beating people when he became intoxicated. State v. Best, 2009-Ohio-6806, 2009 Ohio App. LEXIS 5702 (Ohio Ct. App., Mahoning County 2009).

Defendant's 120-day sentence, imposed upon his convictions for resisting arrest, obstruction of justice, and assault was proper as the terms were within their respective statutory ranges found in R.C. 2929.24(A)(1) and (2) and as it could be gleaned from the record that the trial court considered some of the sentencing factors in R.C. 2929.21 and 2929. 22, in that defendant requested the imposition of community control, and the trial court considered defendant's likelihood of recidivism under R.C. 2929.22(B). State v. Cossack, 2009-Ohio-3327, 2009 Ohio App. LEXIS 2946 (Ohio Ct. App., Mahoning County 2009).

Defendant's sentence was not disproportionate or inconsistent with his codefendant's sentence because the codefendant was convicted of a different offense. Also, the trial court imposed the mandatory minimum sentence that was allowed by law for assault of a peace officer; there was no lesser sentence that could possibly have been imposed as a result of defendant's conviction. State v. Hidvegi, 2008-Ohio-2662, 2008 Ohio App. LEXIS 2235 (Ohio Ct. App., Cuyahoga County 2008).

Defendant's post-Foster sentences—a maximum sentence for failure to comply with the order or signal of a police officer and non-minimum, non-maximum sentences on two counts of assault, all to be served consecutively—were not subject to reversal as they did not violate defendant's due process rights or the ex post facto clause. State v. Peterson, 2007-Ohio-6917, 2007 Ohio App. LEXIS 6068 (Ohio Ct. App., Mahoning County 2007).

Defendant's four-year sentence, imposed upon his convictions for failure to comply and assault, was proper as it was within the statutory range. The trial court properly considered under R.C. 2929.12 the fact that defendant had been diagnosed with major depression and the fact that defendant had violated a condition imposed earlier requiring defendant to remain law abiding. State v. Brown, 2007-Ohio-5994, 2007 Ohio App. LEXIS 5247 (Ohio Ct. App., Ottawa County 2007).

Defendant failed to overcome the presumption that the trial court considered the sentencing criteria in R.C. 2929.21 in imposing the maximum prison term on defendant upon his conviction for misdemeanor assault. The record showed that, during the sentencing hearing, the trial court referred to the fact that defendant had a criminal history and a pending charge for driving under the influence and that defendant explicitly told the trial court that he was not sorry for having committed the assault. State v. Black, 2007-Ohio-5871, 2007 Ohio App. LEXIS 5159 (Ohio Ct. App., Hamilton County 2007).

Defendant's resentencing for complicity in the commission of involuntary manslaughter and misdemeanor assault, pursuant to Foster, did not violate his rights to due process because (1) Apprendi had been decided when defendant committed his crimes, so that he had notice of a likely change in the sentencing laws, and (2) Foster did not change the sentencing ranges which applied to defendant's crimes, and he had notice of those ranges. State v. Cole, 2007-Ohio-4485, 2007 Ohio App. LEXIS 4052 (Ohio Ct. App., Defiance County 2007).

Defendant's sentences of three years for failure to comply with an order or signal of a police officer, under R.C. 2921.331(B), to be served consecutively to a sentence of one year for assault, under R.C. 2903.13(A), were not an abuse of discretion because the trial court stated that it considered the record, oral statements, any victim impact statement, a pre-sentence report and/or drug and alcohol evaluation, the principles and purposes of sentencing, and that it balanced seriousness and recidivism factors. State v. Haney, 2007-Ohio-3712, 2007 Ohio App. LEXIS 3394 (Ohio Ct. App., Lake County 2007).

Trial court's imposition of, inter alia, a jail term on defendant upon his conviction of simple assault, in violation of R.C. 2903.13, wherein the trial court indicated that defendant was to serve "180 days" and "a six-month term" was erroneous, as six months was not necessarily 180 days, and the maximum range that could be imposed on the first degree misdemeanor under R.C. 2929.24(A)(1) was 180 days. State v. DeSalvo, 2007-Ohio-1411, 2007 Ohio App. LEXIS 1288 (Ohio Ct. App., Mahoning County 2007).

Although the trial court cited incorrect sentencing statutes in its judgment entry, its comments at the sentencing hearing reflected its intention to sentence defendant to a period of three years pursuant to R.C. 2929.14(A)(1), and the only term of "mandatory" incarceration imposed at the sentencing hearing was the 12-month term for assault upon a police officer. There was no error in the nunc pro tunc correction because the sentencing hearing transcript and the judgment entry reflected that the appellation of "mandatory" to the three-year term instead of the 12-month term was mechanical in nature and apparent on the record. State v. Love, 2006-Ohio-2925, 2006 Ohio App. LEXIS 2798 (Ohio Ct. App., Lucas County 2006).

Since the trial court considered the factors of R.C. 2929.13(B) and determined that defendant caused physical harm to a police officer, committed the offenses as part of organized criminal activity, committed the offenses while under community control sanctions, that defendant was not amenable to an available community control sanction, and that the shortest prison terms would demean the seriousness of defendant's conduct and not adequately protect the public from future crime, it properly sentenced defendant to an aggregate sentence of 17 months for complicity to theft, assault on a police officer, and receiving stolen property. State v. Velotta, 2005-Ohio-6707, 2005 Ohio App. LEXIS 6025 (Ohio Ct. App., Lake County 2005), rev'd, 2006-Ohio-2109, 109 Ohio St. 3d 313, 847 N.E.2d 1174, 2006 Ohio LEXIS 1161 (Ohio 2006).

Trial court's imposition of the maximum term of imprisonment on defendant upon his conviction of assault on a peace officer, in violation of R.C. 2903.13(A), (C)(3), was supported by the requisite findings and reasons under R.C. 2929.14(C) where the trial court determined that it was concerned about protecting the public and law enforcement personnel and that the shortest sentence would demean the seriousness of the offense; the trial court also found that defendant posed a great likelihood of recidivism based on his prior assault conviction and his "very, very significant lack of remorse." State v. Jones, 2005-Ohio-6930, 2005 Ohio App. LEXIS 6252 (Ohio Ct. App., Mahoning County 2005).

Trial court complied with the statutory mandates of R.C. 2929.14(E)(4) and 2929.19(B)(2)(c) in imposing consecutive sentences on defendant upon his convictions for assault of a peace officer, drug trafficking, carrying a concealed weapon, and having a weapon while under a disability because it found that consecutive sentences were necessary to protect the public and punish defendant in light of defendant's lengthy criminal record, that consecutive sentences were not disproportionate to the seriousness of the offense, and that defendant committed the crimes while he was on post-release control. State v. Simmons, 2005-Ohio-3428, 2005 Ohio App. LEXIS 3194 (Ohio Ct. App., Cuyahoga County 2005).

**—Greater than minimum term**

Trial court complied with R.C. 2929.14(B)(2) in sentencing defendant, a first-time offender, to a greater than the minimum term for felonious assault where the trial court stated that "the shortest prison term (would) demean the seriousness of the offender's conduct and (would) not adequately protect the public." State v. Enebeli, 2005-Ohio-3998, 2005 Ohio App. LEXIS 3647 (Ohio Ct. App., Lucas County 2005).

**—Merger**

Resisting arrest, as defined in R.C. 2921.33(B), and assault, as set forth in R.C. 2903.13(A), were not allied offenses of similar import, pursuant to R.C. 2941.25(A), because resisting arrest required proof of the additional element of resistance of a lawful arrest. Thus, the elements of the offenses did not correspond to such a degree that commission of one crime resulted in the commission of the other. City of Maple Heights v. Sweeney, 2005-Ohio-2820, 2005 Ohio App. LEXIS 2663 (Ohio Ct. App., Cuyahoga County 2005).

**—Proper**

Defendant's 18-month sentence for assault was upheld because it fell within the statutory range, the trial court considered the applicable sentencing criteria, and the record supported the trial court's findings that defendant was likely to commit future crimes, given that she committed the offense while awaiting sentencing in another case, she had a significant history or criminal convictions, and she had a demonstrated pattern of drug and alcohol abuse. State v. Kreischer, 2021-Ohio-1235, 2021 Ohio App. LEXIS 1222 (Ohio Ct. App., Van Wert County 2021).

Trial court did not abuse its discretion in imposing 180-day jail sentence on defendant for misdemeanor assault because he tore victim's ear during altercation, and that defendant's actions caused the victim's earlobe to be torn apart. The trial court also considered the principles and purposes of misdemeanor sentencing as it fashioned defendant's sentence, and his 180-day jail sentence was within the statutory limits. State/City of Port Clinton v. Yates, 2020-Ohio-2659, 2020 Ohio App. LEXIS 1608 (Ohio Ct. App., Ottawa County 2020).

Imposition of maximum consecutive terms of imprisonment upon defendant's negotiated guilty plea to improperly handling a firearm in a motor vehicle and assault was proper, as the trial court considered the statutory factors and made the requisite findings which were supported by the record, and defendant failed to show clear and convincing evidence that there was a lack of support for those findings. State v. McGinnis, 2019-Ohio-3803, 2019 Ohio App. LEXIS 3870 (Ohio Ct. App., Greene County 2019).

In that defendant assaulted a corrections officer while serving time for a prior offense and had been convicted of assault on a peace officer, it could not clearly and convincing have been found that the record did not support the imposition of consecutive sentences. That defendant did not cause significant physical harm defendant not change the seriousness or proportionality. State v. McClenton, 2018-Ohio-5378, 2018 Ohio App. LEXIS 5701 (Ohio Ct. App., Ashtabula County 2018).

Sufficient evidence supported defendant's conviction for assaulting a peace officer while in the performance of official duties, because the officers' testimony indicated that defendant yelled obscenities after being pulled over for speeding; he then struck one of the officers several times, knocking him down. State v. Kepich, 2015-Ohio-1920, 2015 Ohio App. LEXIS 1847 (Ohio Ct. App., Summit County 2015).

Seventeen month sentence imposed on defendant after he pled guilty to assault on a peace officer proper as the record reflected that the trial court had considered the factors set forth in R.C. 2929.12, that the sentence was not based on the consideration of improper factors, was not unreasonable, arbitrary or unconscionable, and was not contrary to law. State v. France, 2015-Ohio-4930, 2015 Ohio App. LEXIS 4833 (Ohio Ct. App., Richland County 2015).

Trial court did not err in denying appellant's petition for post-conviction relief because it properly imposed separate sentences for appellant's convictions; appellant's convictions for aggravated robbery, felonious assault, and possession of different drugs were not of similar import, were dissimilar, or were based on separate conduct. State v. Ranson, 2013-Ohio-1874, 2013 Ohio App. LEXIS 1751 (Ohio Ct. App., Franklin County 2013).

Defendant's aggregate sentence of 14 years in prison, imposed upon his convictions on two counts of child endangering and one count of assault, was not contrary to law as the sentence fell within the statutory range for the offenses, the trial court properly applied postrelease control, and it considered the purposes and principles of sentencing in R.C. 2929.11 and balanced the seriousness and recidivism factors under R.C. 2929.12. The sentence was not an abuse of discretion as the trial court considered defendant's criminal record, the fact that he had abused all three children while on community control, and the seriousness of the injuries suffered by the young children. State v. Micomonaco, 2012-Ohio-5239, 2012 Ohio App. LEXIS 4566 (Ohio Ct. App., Butler County 2012).

Imposition of the maximum sentences on defendant for felonious assault and attempted assault on a police officer did not violate Blakely v. Washington, 542 U.S. 296 (2004) as the intermediate court had held that R.C. 2929.14(C) and (E) did not implicate the Sixth Amendment as construed in Blakely. State v. Brooks, 2005-Ohio-6015, 2005 Ohio App. LEXIS 5440 (Ohio Ct. App., Cuyahoga County 2005), rev'd in part, 2006-Ohio-2109, 109 Ohio St. 3d 313, 847 N.E.2d 1174, 2006 Ohio LEXIS 1161 (Ohio 2006).

Trial court engaged in the appropriate analysis when it imposed the maximum sentences upon defendant for felonious assault and attempted assault on a police officer where it reviewed defendant's history of mental illness, violence, and criminal conduct, considered the nature of the offenses and appropriately found that the maximum terms of incarceration were necessary to adequately protect the public, and sufficiently stated its reasons for making its findings. State v. Brooks, 2005-Ohio-6015, 2005 Ohio App. LEXIS 5440 (Ohio Ct. App., Cuyahoga County 2005), rev'd in part, 2006-Ohio-2109, 109 Ohio St. 3d 313, 847 N.E.2d 1174, 2006 Ohio LEXIS 1161 (Ohio 2006).

Trial court complied with the statutory mandates of R.C. 2929.14(E)(4) and 2929.19(B)(2)(c) in imposing consecutive sentences on defendant upon his convictions for assault of a peace officer, drug trafficking, carrying a concealed weapon, and having a weapon while under a disability because it found that consecutive sentences were necessary to protect the public and punish defendant in light of defendant's lengthy criminal record, that consecutive sentences were not disproportionate to the seriousness of the offense, and that defendant committed the crimes while he was on post-release control. State v. Simmons, 2005-Ohio-3428, 2005 Ohio App. LEXIS 3194 (Ohio Ct. App., Cuyahoga County 2005).

**Serious physical harm**

Since police officer suffered multiple fractures of his leg when defendant tackled him to the ground as the officer was trying to handcuff defendant, the evidence supported a finding that the officer suffered serious physical harm as defined in R.C. 2901.01(A)(5) and supported defendant's conviction for reckless assault of a peace officer. State v. Crawford, 2008-Ohio-2568, 2008 Ohio App. LEXIS 2187 (Ohio Ct. App., Franklin County 2008).

**Spitting**

Insufficient evidence supported defendant's conviction for assault because there was no testimony establishing physical harm or an attempt to cause physical harm, since the officers explicitly denied any evidence of harm or any contact from defendant's spit and neither police officer provided any testimony as to what kind of harm could have resulted or might have been intended from the spit had it connected with the patrolman. State v. Sepulveda, 2016-Ohio-7177, 71 N.E.3d 1240, 2016 Ohio App. LEXIS 4020 (Ohio Ct. App., Mercer County 2016).

Defendant's spitting on police officers did not constitute an assault: State v. Bailey, 83 Ohio App. 3d 544, 615 N.E.2d 322, 1992 Ohio App. LEXIS 5767 (Ohio Ct. App., Montgomery County 1992).

**Sports, recreation**

The doctrine of implied consent did not apply to a retaliatory punch thrown during a pause in play in an intramural basketball game: State v. Guidugli, 2004-Ohio-2871, 157 Ohio App. 3d 383, 811 N.E.2d 567, 2004 Ohio App. LEXIS 2529 (Ohio Ct. App., Hamilton County 2004).

**Sufficiency of indictment**

Since defendant did not challenge the sufficiency of the indictment prior to trial, as required by Crim.R. 12, he had forfeited all but plain error. The trial court did not properly find a showing of good cause to justify granting relief from the forfeiture; thus, since the motion challenging the sufficiency of the indictment was not properly before the trial court, the trial court erred in finding that the offenses charging defendant with assault on a police officer were not properly charged. State v. Lee, 2009-Ohio-4617, 2009 Ohio App. LEXIS 3919 (Ohio Ct. App., Lorain County 2009).

**Transferred intent**

Although the trial court properly relied on the doctrine of transferred intent when it convicted defendant of first-degree misdemeanor assault, the trial court erred as a matter of law when it refused to apply the strict liability corrections-officer penalty enhancement in conjunction with the doctrine of transferred intent to raise the penalty to a fifth-degree felony. State v. Calhoun, 2015-Ohio-5505, 57 N.E.3d 139, 2015 Ohio App. LEXIS 5318 (Ohio Ct. App., Clinton County 2015).

**Venue**

Sufficient evidence supported defendant's conviction for assault of a corrections officer charge because the State presented sufficient evidence of venue and the location of the offense for the case to be properly considered by the jury. It was not necessary for the State to specifically ask one of the witnesses if the jail was run by the state or the county. State v. May, 2015-Ohio-4275, 49 N.E.3d 736, 2015 Ohio App. LEXIS 4167 (Ohio Ct. App., Cuyahoga County 2015).

In defendant's prosecution for assaulting a peace officer, under R.C. 2903.13(A)(3), while it was not specifically stated at trial that the incident for which defendant was arrested occurred in the State of Ohio, venue was sufficiently demonstrated because (1) witnesses testified to the township and intersection where the incident occurred, (2) two officers testified that the officers were employed by the Medina County, Ohio, Sheriff's Department, and (3) the testimony mentioned two hospitals, both of which were located in Ohio. State v. Davis, 2008-Ohio-999, 2008 Ohio App. LEXIS 876 (Ohio Ct. App., Medina County 2008).

**Weight of the evidence**

In a conviction for assault and domestic violence, the court's judgment was supported by the weight and sufficiency of the evidence because the victim explained that she believed the threat had passed during that time because the defendant had apologized for Sunday's tirade. Additionally, once the violence resumed, she testified that she was afraid to seek help for fear of provoking the defendant further. State v. Johnson, 2021-Ohio-1321, 2021 Ohio App. LEXIS 1314 (Ohio Ct. App., Hamilton County 2021).

Defendant's conviction for assault was not against the manifest weight of the evidence because the victim's testimony, if believed, was sufficient to establish each and every element of assault in violation of R.C. 2903.13(A) and convince the trial court of his guilt beyond a reasonable doubt. State v. Lunsford, 2020-Ohio-965, 2020 Ohio App. LEXIS 893 (Ohio Ct. App., Butler County 2020).

Because the State produced competent and credible evidence as to all the elements of assault, and the trial court was in the best position to assess the credibility of each witness, the guilty verdict was not against the manifest weight of the evidence. Witnesses testified that, when defendant was placed in an ambulance to be checked out, he assaulted a paramedic by throwing her out of the ambulance, biting her arm, hitting her, and trying to light the hairs on her arm on fire with a lighter. State v. Wrona, 2018-Ohio-632, 107 N.E.3d 133, 2018 Ohio App. LEXIS 659 (Ohio Ct. App., Allen County 2018).

Defendant's assault conviction was not against the manifest weight of the evidence because defendant admitted to continuing to punch the victim in the face while the victim was restrained, and defendant posted a video to social media immediately following the attack in which he boasted about assaulting the victim. State v. Lipkins, 2017-Ohio-4085, 92 N.E.3d 82, 2017 Ohio App. LEXIS 2122 (Ohio Ct. App., Franklin County 2017).

Defendant's convictions for assault and domestic violence under R.C. 2903.13(A) and R.C. 2919.25(A)(1) were not against the manifest weight of the evidence, as the victim testified credibly that defendant pushed her, choked her, and hit her in the face after an argument, harming her in the process, and the trial court, which found the victim to be credible, was free to credit some, all, or none of the testimony of defendant and the victim.

State v. Mahe, 2017-Ohio-7516, 2017 Ohio App. LEXIS 3845 (Ohio Ct. App., Montgomery County 2017).

Defendant's conviction for assault was no against the manifest weight of the evidence because the record contained evidence from which the trial court could have found that defendant did knowingly cause or attempt to cause physical harm to the victim; the trier of fact was free to believe the victim's version of the events and the testimony of a police officer regarding the bruising on the victim's right leg and right arm. State v. Becks, 2015-Ohio-4431, 2015 Ohio App. LEXIS 4308 (Ohio Ct. App., Lake County 2015).

Defendant's conviction for assault on a peace officer was not against the weight of the evidence, as defendant's father testified that when an officer approached defendant, defendant got into a fighting stance and readied himself to fight, and the officer testified that defendant stood up from a couch, lunged at him, and then swung his right hand and struck him on the face. State v. Mitchell, 2015-Ohio-4379, 2015 Ohio App. LEXIS 4327 (Ohio Ct. App., Cuyahoga County 2015).

Defendant's assault conviction was not against the manifest weight of the evidence, because the witness testified that the victim's face was swollen, red and that his eye was red, and the witness and victim both testified that defendant initiated three separate confrontations. State v. Thoennes, 2014-Ohio-2524, 2014 Ohio App. LEXIS 2456 (Ohio Ct. App., Mahoning County 2014).

Defendant's conviction for assault of a peace officer, pursuant to R.C. 2903.13, was not against the manifest weight of the evidence because evidence that defendant charged at a police officer, who was in full dress uniform and on duty, was enough to show that defendant assaulted a peace officer. State v. Ervin, 2005-Ohio-3160, 2005 Ohio App. LEXIS 2948 (Ohio Ct. App., Cuyahoga County 2005).

## NOTES TO UNPUBLISHED DECISIONS

**Crime of violence under federal law**

*Unpublished decision:* In a case involving a felon in possession of a firearm, an enhancement under the Armed Career Criminal Act was properly applied because a 2004 assault conviction under Ohio law qualified as a violent felony since defendant pled guilty to knowingly causing or attempting to cause harm to a police officer. United States v. Price, 559 Fed. Appx. 496, 2014 FED App. 0230N, 2014 U.S. App. LEXIS 5830 (6th Cir. Ohio 2014).

## RESEARCH REFERENCES AND PRACTICE AIDS

**Cross-References to Related Sections**

Penalties for felony, RC § 2929.11 et seq.; misdemeanor, RC § 2929.21.
Amount of bail, RC § 2937.23.
Assault defined as offense of violence, RC § 2901.01.
Competency of spouse as witness, RC § 2945.42.
Conditions of probation, RC § 2951.02.
Criminal records check; employment of offenders prohibited —
Applicants for employment with PASSPORT agencies, RC § 109.572.
Certain persons having frequent contact with children, RC § 2151.86.
Child day-care employees, RC §§ 5104.013, 5104.09
County board of developmental disabilities employees, RC § 5126.0221, 5126.20 et seq.
Employees responsible for out-of-home child care and prospective adoptive or foster parents, RC § 2151.86.
Foster care givers, RC § 5103.0319.
Head start employees responsible for children, RC § 3301.32.
Home health agency employees, RC § 3701.881.
Criminal records check of applicants for employment; certain offenders ineligible, RC § 5123.081.
Preschool employees, RC § 3301.541.
Prospective employees providing direct care to older adult, RC §§ 3712.09, 3721.121.
Public children services agency employees, RC § 5153.111.
School employees, RC § 3319.39.
Investigative unit of department of public safety, RC § 5502.13.
Juvenile court —
Foster caregivers to receive information concerning certain delinquent children, RC § 2152.72.
Hearing on motion for permanent custody of child upon conviction of parent, RC § 2151.414.
Reasonable efforts to prevent removal of child not required, RC § 2151.419.
Knowingly defined, RC § 2901.22.
Legal abortions and acts or omissions of pregnant woman excepted, when, RC § 2903.09.
Limitation of criminal prosecutions, RC § 2901.13.
Motion for issuance of anti-stalking protection order, RC § 2903.213.
Offense of violence defined, RC § 2901.01.
Person defined, RC § 2901.01.
Prior conviction increases degree of felony —
Domestic violence, RC § 2919.25.
Considerations in setting bail, RC § 2919.251.
Motion for temporary protection order, RC § 2919.26.
Recklessly defined, RC § 2901.22.
School building defined, RC § 2901.01.
School bus defined, RC § 2901.01.
School premises defined, RC § 2901.01.

**Ohio Administrative Code**

Department of job and family services, division of social services—
Obtaining permanent custody of child: termination of parental rights upon conviction of certain offenses. OAC 5101:2-42-95.

**Comparative Legislation**

Assault:
18 USCS § 111
CA— Cal Pen Code § 240
FL— Fla. Stat. § 784.011
IL— 720 Ill. Comp. Stat. § 5/12-1
IN—Burns Ind. Code Ann. §§ 35-42-2-1
KY—KRS § 508.030
MI— MCLS § 750.81 et seq.
NY—NY CLS Penal § 120.00
PA—18 P.S. § 2701

**Practice Guides**

Anderson's Ohio Manual of Criminal Complaints and Indictments § 2903.13 Assault

**Practice Forms**

Motion for Temporary Protection Order; Domestic Violence 1, 18 Ohio Forms of Pleading and Practice Form 57:17

**Jury Instructions**

OJI-CV 429.01 Civil Assault [Rev. 12-11-05]



## § 2903.16 Failing to provide for a functionally impaired person.

(A) No caretaker shall knowingly fail to provide a functionally impaired person under the caretaker's care with any treatment, care, goods, or service that is necessary to maintain the health or safety of the functionally impaired person when this failure results in physical harm or serious physical harm to the functionally impaired person.

(B) No caretaker shall recklessly fail to provide a functionally impaired person under the caretaker's care with any treatment, care, goods, or service that is necessary to maintain the health or safety of the functionally impaired person when this failure results in serious physical harm to the functionally impaired person.

(C)(1) Whoever violates division (A) of this section is guilty of knowingly failing to provide for a functionally impaired person, a misdemeanor of the first degree. If the functionally impaired person under the offender's care suffers serious physical harm as a result of the violation of this section, a violation of division (A) of this section is a felony of the fourth degree.

(2) Whoever violates division (B) of this section is guilty of recklessly failing to provide for a functionally impaired person, a misdemeanor of the second degree. If the functionally impaired person under the offender's care suffers serious physical harm as a result of the violation of this section, a violation of division (B) of this section is a felony of the fourth degree.

**HISTORY:**

142 v H 642 (Eff 3-17-89); 146 v S 2. Eff 7-1-96.

## NOTES TO DECISIONS

Analysis

Allied offenses
Evidence sufficient
Jurisdiction
Manifest weight
No predicate offense
Probable cause

**Allied offenses**

Offenses of failure to provide for a functionally impaired person and failure to report child abuse or neglect were not allied offenses of similar import but, rather, were committed by distinct instances of failing to act, namely as the victim's case manager of her personal caretakers, and separately as a statutorily mandated reporter, which was buttressed by the fact that the failure to provide charge did not require defendant to make a report regarding the victim's abuse or neglect, while the failure to report charge mandated that she make such a report. One was an omission in rendering medical assistance, the other a crime of omission in not contacting the appropriate authorities. State v. Kilby, 2013-Ohio-5340, 2013 Ohio App. LEXIS 5559 (Ohio Ct. App., Montgomery County 2013).

Juvenile court erred in dismissing the charge of failure to report child abuse or neglect because defendant's previous conviction for failure to provide for a functionally impaired person and her failure to report charge were not allied offenses of similar import. As a result, double jeopardy protections were not implicated and a dismissal was not warranted. State v. Williams, 2013-Ohio-5335, 2013 Ohio App. LEXIS 5557 (Ohio Ct. App., Montgomery County 2013).



**Evidence sufficient**

Evidence was sufficient to convict defendant of Felonious Assault, Firearm Specification, Carrying a Concealed Weapon, and Illegal Handling of a Firearm in a Motor Vehicle because the witness testimony combined with the video footage which showed that he was seemingly pointing something at the victim were indicative of him having a firearm concealed while he was in the witness's motor vehicle and ultimately used it in the commission of the offense. State v. Jackson, 2019-Ohio-1697, 2019 Ohio App. LEXIS 1785 (Ohio Ct. App., Allen County 2019).

Sufficient evidence supported defendant's conviction for failure to provide for a functionally impaired person because defendant told the doctors that he was the victim's caregiver, that he made medical decisions for her, that he disagreed with the doctors and had stopped giving her the anti-seizure medication, and, although he was told to get the victim to a hospital immediately, defendant waited a few hours. State v. Debartolo, 2012-Ohio-3449, 2012 Ohio App. LEXIS 3055 (Ohio Ct. App., Cuyahoga County 2012).

**Jurisdiction**

Defendant's conviction for recklessly failing to provide for a functionally impaired person had to be vacated, because the trial court did not have subject matter jurisdiction to proceed with the case to the extent that defendant was charged with a felony, and the terms of this section did not set forth a misdemeanor offense. State v. Wooden, 2015-Ohio-2633, 2015 Ohio App. LEXIS 2606 (Ohio Ct. App., Summit County 2015).

**Manifest weight**

Defendant's convictions of Felonious Assault, Firearm Specification, Carrying a Concealed Weapon, and Illegal Handling of a Firearm in a Motor Vehicle were not against the manifest weight of the evidence because when combining all these pieces of evidence, the trial court did not clearly lose its way in convicting defendant of the charges. State v. Jackson, 2019-Ohio-1697, 2019 Ohio App. LEXIS 1785 (Ohio Ct. App., Allen County 2019).

**No predicate offense**

Because the failure to provide for a functionally impaired person statute did not identify a predicate offense, the trial court's statement that defendant's failure to report child abuse or neglect violation resulted in and formed the predicate offense of failure to provide for a functionally impaired person was made in error. State v. Williams, 2013-Ohio-5335, 2013 Ohio App. LEXIS 5557 (Ohio Ct. App., Montgomery County 2013).

Trial court erred in determining that defendant's failure to report child abuse and neglect resulted in and formed the predicate offense of her failure to provide for a functionally impaired person. State v. Kilby, 2013-Ohio-5340, 2013 Ohio App. LEXIS 5559 (Ohio Ct. App., Montgomery County 2013).

**Probable cause**

Officer possessed probable cause to conclude defendant was the victim's "caretaker" because defendant admitted that she agreed to care for the wheelchair-bound victim, her 79-year-old aunt, after the amputation of the aunt's left leg but could no longer "handle it," and defendant ignored the victim's pleas for help after she kicked the victim out of the house; thus, the officer had the requisite probable cause to arrest defendant for failure to provide for a functionally impaired person. State v. Kirkland, 2015-Ohio-1978, 2015 Ohio App. LEXIS 1912 (Ohio Ct. App., Montgomery County 2015).

### RESEARCH REFERENCES AND PRACTICE AIDS

**Cross-References to Related Sections**

Assault; prior conviction raises degree of felony, RC § 2903.13.
Caretaker defined, RC § 2903.10.
Criminal records check; employment of offenders prohibited —
Applicants for employment with PASSPORT agencies, RC § 109.572.
Certain persons having frequent contact with children, RC § 2151.86.
Child day-care employees, RC §§ 5104.013, 5104.09
Employees responsible for out-of-home child care and prospective adoptive or foster parents, RC § 2151.86.
Foster care givers, RC § 5103.0319.
Head start employees responsible for children, RC § 3301.32.
Home health agency employees, RC § 3701.881.
Criminal records check of applicants for employment; certain offenders ineligible, RC § 5123.081.
Preschool employees, RC § 3301.541.
Prospective employees providing direct care to older adult, RC §§ 3712.09, 3721.121.
Public children services agency employees, RC § 5153.111.
School employees, RC § 3319.39.
Juvenile court; hearing on motion for permanent custody of child upon conviction of parent, RC § 2151.414.
Knowingly defined, RC § 2901.22.
Recklessly defined, RC § 2901.22.

**Comparative Legislation**

Functionally impaired persons:
CA—Cal Wel & Inst Code § 9008
FL—Fla. Stat. § 415.102
IL—720 Ill. Comp. Stat. § 5/12-21
IN—Burns Ind. Code Ann. § 35-46-1-4
KY—KRS § 508.090 et seq.
MI—MCLS § 400.11a
NY—NY CLS Men Hyg § 31.19
PA—18 P.S. § 2713

**Practice Guides**

Anderson's Ohio Manual of Criminal Complaints and Indictments § 2903.16 Failing to provide for a functionally impaired person

## PATIENT ABUSE AND NEGLECT IN CARE FACILITIES

### § 2903.33 Definitions.

As used in sections 2903.33 to 2903.36 of the Revised Code:

(A) "Care facility" means any of the following:

(1) Any "home" as defined in section 3721.10 of the Revised Code;

(2) Any "residential facility" as defined in section 5123.19 of the Revised Code;

(3) Any institution or facility operated or provided by the department of mental health and addiction services or by the department of developmental disabilities pursuant to sections 5119.14 and 5123.03 of the Revised Code;

(4) Any "residential facility" as defined in section 5119.34 of the Revised Code;

(5) Any unit of any hospital, as defined in section 3701.01 of the Revised Code, that provides the same services as a nursing home, as defined in section 3721.01 of the Revised Code;

(6) Any institution, residence, or facility that provides, for a period of more than twenty-four hours, whether for a consideration or not, accommodations to one individual or two unrelated individuals who are dependent upon the services of others.

(B) "Abuse" means knowingly causing physical harm or recklessly causing serious physical harm to a person by physical contact with the person or by the inappropriate use of a physical or chemical restraint, medication, or isolation on the person.

(C)(1) "Gross neglect" means knowingly failing to provide a person with any treatment, care, goods, or service that is necessary to maintain the health or safety of the person when the failure results in physical harm or serious physical harm to the person.

(2) "Neglect" means recklessly failing to provide a person with any treatment, care, goods, or service that is necessary to maintain the health or safety of the person when the failure results in serious physical harm to the person.

(D) "Inappropriate use of a physical or chemical restraint, medication, or isolation" means the use of physical or chemical restraint, medication, or isolation as punishment, for staff convenience, excessively, as a substitute for treatment, or in quantities that preclude habilitation and treatment.

**HISTORY:**
141 v H 566 (Eff 9-17-86); 142 v S 156 (Eff 7-1-88); 143 v S 2 (Eff 11-1-89); 143 v H 253 (Eff 11-15-90); 145 v H 152 (Eff 7-1-93); 145 v S 21 (Eff 10-29-93); 146 v S 2. Eff 7-1-96; 153 v S 79, § 1, eff. 10-6-09; 153 v H 1, § 101.01, eff. 10-16-09; 2011 HB 153, § 101.01, eff. July 1, 2011; 2012 HB 487, § 101.01, eff. Sept. 10, 2012; 2013 HB 59, § 101.01, eff. Sept. 29, 2013.

**Editor's Notes**
Acts 2011, HB 153, § 815.20 provides: "The General Assembly, applying the principle stated in division (B) of section 1.52 of the Revised Code that amendments are to be harmonized if reasonably capable of simultaneous operation, finds that the following sections, presented in this act as composites of the sections as amended by the acts indicated, are the resulting versions of the sections in effect prior to the effective date of the sections as presented in this act:

"Section 2903.33 of the Revised Code as amended by Am. Sub. H.B. 1 and Sub. S.B. 79 of the 128th General Assembly."

The provisions of § 7 of SB 2 (146 v —) read as follows:

SECTION 7. * * * Section 2903.33 of the Revised Code is presented in this act as a composite of the section as amended by both Am. Sub. H.B. 152 and Am. Sub. S.B. 21 of the 120th General Assembly, with the new language of neither of the acts shown in capital letters. * * * This is in recognition of the principle stated in division (B) of section 1.52 of the Revised Code that such amendments are to be harmonized where not substantively irreconcilable and constitutes a legislative finding that such is the resulting version in effect prior to the effective date of this act.

**Amendment Notes**
The 2013 amendment substituted "section 3721.10" for "section 3721.10 or 5111.20" in (A)(1); in (A)(3), inserted "and addiction services" and substituted "sections 5119.14 and 5123.03" for "sections 5119.02 and 5123.03"; and substituted "section 5119.34" for "section 5119.22" in (A)(4).

The 2012 amendment deleted (A)(7) and (A)(8), which read: "(7) Any 'adult care facility' as defined in section 5119.70 of the Revised Code; (8) Any adult foster home certified under section 5119.692 of the Revised Code"; and made a related change.

The 2011 amendment substituted "section 5119.70" for "section 3722.01" in (A)(7); and substituted "under section 5119.692" for "by the department of aging or its designee under section 173.36" in (A)(8).

153 v H 1, effective October 16, 2009, deleted (A)(9), which read: "Any 'community alternative home' as defined in section 3724.01 of the Revised Code"; and made a related change.

153 v S 79, effective October 6, 2009, deleted "mental retardation and" preceding "developmental disabilities" throughout.

**Comment, Legislative Service Commission**
Section 2903.33 of the Revised Code is amended by Am. Sub. H.B. 1 and Sub. S.B. 79 of the 128th General Assembly. Comparison of these amendments in pursuance of section 1.52 of the Revised Code discloses that they are not irreconcilable so that they are required by that section to be harmonized to give effect to each amendment.

## NOTES TO DECISIONS

Analysis

Generally
Abuse
Care facility
Serious physical harm.

**Generally**
Defendant was properly convicted of patient abuse under R.C. 2903.34(A)(1), where evidence showed that defendant nursing home worker pushed a patient back into a chair, the patient's head snapped back, and the patient cried out. Actual intent to injure was not required as long as act (pushing the patient back into the chair) was committed knowingly and defendant was aware that the act might result in physical harm. State v. Lohr, 2004-Ohio-1609, 2004 Ohio App. LEXIS 1424 (Ohio Ct. App., Lorain County 2004).

R.C. 2903.33 and 2903.34 do not limit "abuse" to knowingly causing serious physical harm: State v. Curry, 76 Ohio App. 3d 175, 601 N.E.2d 176, 1991 Ohio App. LEXIS 5157 (Ohio Ct. App., Cuyahoga County 1991).

**Abuse**
Trial court had jurisdiction to consider defendant's application to seal the record of her conviction, because her conviction of attempted patient abuse was not an offense of violence. There was no evidence in the record indicating that it occurred knowingly rather than recklessly. State v. Evans, 2014-Ohio-2081, 2014 Ohio App. LEXIS 2020 (Ohio Ct. App., Franklin County 2014).

Because defendant pled guilty to seven counts of patient abuse, and "abuse" was, by definition, the causing of "physical harm" to the victim, the trial court did not act improperly in coming to the conclusion that the presentence investigation report was not entirely accurate in that it had concluded that the victim incurred no physical harm. Also, the State introduced into evidence a video that depicted some of the treatment the victim received at defendant's hands and, based upon that evidence, the trial court concluded that the victim certainly sustained some physical harm. State v. Caraballo, 2012-Ohio-5725, 2012 Ohio App. LEXIS 4923 (Ohio Ct. App., Cuyahoga County 2012).

Defendant's conviction for patient abuse under R.C. 2903.34 was supported by the evidence as the evidence showed that, contrary to defendant's contention, she taunted a patient in a nursing home and lured her into a secluded room where she engaged in physical abuse against the victim, as defined in R.C. 2903.33(B), causing the victim physical harm. State v. Simmons, 2011-Ohio-2068, 2011 Ohio App. LEXIS 1774 (Ohio Ct. App., Montgomery County 2011).

Sufficient evidence supported defendant's conviction for patient abuse, under R.C. 2903.34 because defendant, a mental health worker, used inappropriate physical restraint on the victim, a patient, and knowingly caused physical harm to her. Witnesses testified that defendant grabbed the victim around the neck, pushed her to the ground, straddled her, and started choking her; people were shouting and pushing at defendant for several minutes before he finally released his grip on the victim's neck. State v. Grimes, 2006-Ohio-4262, 2006 Ohio App. LEXIS 4189 (Ohio Ct. App., Cuyahoga County 2006).

**Care facility**
Sufficient evidence supported defendant's conviction for patient abuse, under R.C. 2903.34. Because the victim was involuntarily committed to the psychiatric care facility, she was dependent upon the services of others, which fell within the definition of care facility in R.C. 2903.33(A)(6). State v. Grimes, 2006-Ohio-4262, 2006 Ohio App. LEXIS 4189 (Ohio Ct. App., Cuyahoga County 2006).

**Serious physical harm.**
Conviction of defendant of patient-neglect under R.C. 2903.34(A)(3) and R.C. 2903.33(C)(2) was sustained since the State presented sufficient evidence that his reckless conduct was the actual and legal "cause" of the result the patient's serious physical harm. Further, the State presented the detective who testified that, because he did not review his aftercare instructions, he did not appear for his follow-up appointment as scheduled. State v. Goins, 2022-Ohio-985, 2022 Ohio App. LEXIS 888 (Ohio Ct. App., Allen County 2022).

## RESEARCH REFERENCES AND PRACTICE AIDS

**Comparative Legislation**
Patient abuse:
CA—Cal Pen Code § 368
FL—Fla. Stat. § 415.101
IL—720 Ill. Comp. Stat. § 5/12-19
KY—KRS § 508.090 et seq.

**Practice Guides**
Anderson's Ohio Manual of Criminal Complaints and Indictments § 2903.33 Patient abuse or neglect—definitions

## § 2903.34 Patient abuse; neglect.

(A) No person who owns, operates, or administers, or who is an agent or employee of, a care facility shall do any of the following:

(1) Commit abuse against a resident or patient of the facility;

(2) Commit gross neglect against a resident or patient of the facility;

(3) Commit neglect against a resident or patient of the facility.

(B)(1) A person who relies upon treatment by spiritual means through prayer alone, in accordance with the tenets of a recognized religious denomination, shall not be considered neglected under division (A)(3) of this section for that reason alone.

(2) It is an affirmative defense to a charge of gross neglect or neglect under this section that the actor's conduct was committed in good faith solely because the actor was ordered to commit the conduct by a person with supervisory authority over the actor.

(C) Whoever violates division (A)(1) of this section is guilty of patient abuse, a felony of the fourth degree. If the offender previously has been convicted of, or pleaded guilty to, any violation of this section, patient abuse is a felony of the third degree.

(D) Whoever violates division (A)(2) of this section is guilty of gross patient neglect, a misdemeanor of the first degree. If the offender previously has been convicted of, or pleaded guilty to, any violation of this section, gross patient neglect is a felony of the fifth degree.

(E) Whoever violates division (A)(3) of this section is guilty of patient neglect, a misdemeanor of the second degree. If the offender previously has been convicted of or pleaded guilty to any violation of this section, patient neglect is a felony of the fifth degree.

Titles 11 — 37

**HISTORY:**

141 v H 566 (Eff 9-17-86); 146 v S 2. Eff 7-1-96.

## NOTES TO DECISIONS

Analysis



**Abuse**

Evidence was insufficient to support a conviction of gross neglect of a patient under R.C. 2903.34(A)(2), as defendant could not have been reasonably found guilty under a theory of assault in that he was not charged under the "abuse" provision, and there was insufficient evidence that the patient's injuries resulted from an assault or that if they did, that defendant was the perpetrator. State v. Webster, 2018-Ohio-3698, 112 N.E.3d 587, 2018 Ohio App. LEXIS 3998 (Ohio Ct. App., Montgomery County 2018).

R.C. 2903.33 and 2903.34 do not limit "abuse" to knowingly causing serious physical harm: State v. Curry, 76 Ohio App. 3d 175, 601 N.E.2d 176, 1991 Ohio App. LEXIS 5157 (Ohio Ct. App., Cuyahoga County 1991).

**Competency of victim**

Despite defendant's contention that the trial court erred when it determined that the victim was competent to testify, nothing in the record supported her allegation that the victim suffered from dementia, as the victim was able to perceive, recall, and communicate accurately; thus, defendant's felonious assault and patient abuse convictions were upheld. State v. Murphy, 2004-Ohio-638, 2004 Ohio App. LEXIS 613 (Ohio Ct. App., Cuyahoga County 2004).

**Evidence sufficient**

Conviction of defendant of patient-neglect under R.C. 2903.34(A)(3) was sustained since the State presented sufficient evidence that his reckless conduct was the actual and legal "cause" of the result the patient's serious physical harm. Further, the State presented the detective who testified that, because he did not review his aftercare instructions, he did not appear for his follow-up appointment as scheduled. State v. Goins, 2022-Ohio-985, 2022 Ohio App. LEXIS 888 (Ohio Ct. App., Allen County 2022).

Sufficient evidence supported defendant's conviction for patient abuse because the State presented testimony from an eyewitness that defendant struck the patient with Downs Syndrome three times on the back with an open palm. Multiple employees testified to noticing marks on the victim and observed the victim uncharacteristically sad and angry on the day of the incident. State v. Buell, 2016-Ohio-5477, 2016 Ohio App. LEXIS 3365 (Ohio Ct. App., Warren County 2016).

Defendant's conviction for patient abuse under R.C. 2903.34 was supported by the evidence as the evidence showed that, contrary to defendant's contention, she taunted a patient in a nursing home and lured her into a secluded room where she engaged in physical abuse against the victim, as defined in R.C. 2903.33(B), causing the victim physical harm. State v. Simmons, 2011-Ohio-2068, 2011 Ohio App. LEXIS 1774 (Ohio Ct. App., Montgomery County 2011).

Sufficient evidence supported defendant's conviction for patient abuse, under R.C. 2903.34. Because the victim was involuntarily committed to the psychiatric care facility, she was dependent upon the services of others, which fell within the definition of care facility in R.C. 2903.33(A)(6). State v. Grimes, 2006-Ohio-4262, 2006 Ohio App. LEXIS 4189 (Ohio Ct. App., Cuyahoga County 2006).

**Expungement**

Trial court had jurisdiction to consider defendant's application to seal the record of her conviction, because her conviction of attempted patient abuse was not an offense of violence. There was no evidence in the record indicating that it occurred knowingly rather than recklessly. State v. Evans, 2014-Ohio-2081, 2014 Ohio App. LEXIS 2020 (Ohio Ct. App., Franklin County 2014).

**Gross neglect**

Evidence was insufficient to support a conviction of gross neglect of a patient. Even if defendant violated protocol by not checking on the patient as often as required, the record contained no evidence establishing when the patient became injured or proving that his injuries would not have occurred if defendant had made his rounds more frequently, and the State failed to present medical evidence that a delay in seeking treatment resulted in or caused the patient's swelling or bruising to be worse than if treatment had started an hour or so earlier. State v. Webster, 2018-Ohio-3698, 112 N.E.3d 587, 2018 Ohio App. LEXIS 3998 (Ohio Ct. App., Montgomery County 2018).

**Lesser included offenses**

There was no evidence presented that would have required the trial court to give an instruction on the lesser included offense of attempted patient abuse because three witnesses testified that defendant, a mental health worker, slammed the victim, a patient, to the floor and choked her and the victim testified that she lost consciousness for several minutes and sustained bruising on her neck. Defendant's argument that he was entitled to an instruction on the lesser included offense because the victim did not sustain "serious" physical harm was not supported by the record and "serious" harm was not required for patient abuse under R.C. 2903.34. State v. Grimes, 2006-Ohio-4262, 2006 Ohio App. LEXIS 4189 (Ohio Ct. App., Cuyahoga County 2006).

Attempted patient abuse is a lesser included offense of patient abuse, since the lesser offense does not require proof of actual serious harm to the patient: State v. Briscoe, 84 Ohio App. 3d 569, 617 N.E.2d 747, 1992 Ohio App. LEXIS 6363 (Ohio Ct. App., Cuyahoga County 1992), dismissed, 66 Ohio St. 3d 1485, 612 N.E.2d 1242, 1993 Ohio LEXIS 1073 (Ohio 1993).

**Physical harm**

Conviction of defendant of patient-neglect under R.C. 2903.34(A)(3) was not against the manifest weight of the evidence because the jury was able to compare the State's witnesses' testimony against the testimony that he presented in his defense (including his own testimony. The jury clearly did not loss its way in concluding that he recklessly failed to provide him treatment or care which resulted in his serious physical harm. State v. Goins, 2022-Ohio-985, 2022 Ohio App. LEXIS 888 (Ohio Ct. App., Allen County 2022).

Because defendant pled guilty to seven counts of patient abuse, and "abuse" was, by definition, the causing of "physical harm" to the victim, the trial court did not act improperly in coming to the conclusion that the presentence investigation report was not entirely accurate in that it had concluded that the victim incurred no physical harm. Also, the State introduced into evidence a video that depicted some of the treatment the victim received at defendant's hands and, based upon that evidence, the trial court concluded that the victim certainly sustained some physical harm. State v. Caraballo, 2012-Ohio-5725, 2012 Ohio App. LEXIS 4923 (Ohio Ct. App., Cuyahoga County 2012).

In defendant's prosecution for assault, in violation of R.C. 2903.13, and patient abuse, in violation of R.C. 2903.34, the patient, who was mentally disabled, was unable to communicate verbally; however, a witness testified that, when defendant punched the patient and hit him with hanger, the patient began moaning and crying. This was sufficient to support a finding that the patient was physically injured under R.C. 2901.01(A)(3) even though the patient had no visible injuries after the incident. State v. Barnes, 2006-Ohio-5239, 2006 Ohio App. LEXIS 5233 (Ohio Ct. App., Cuyahoga County 2006).

Sufficient evidence supported defendant's conviction for patient abuse, under R.C. 2903.34 because defendant, a mental health worker, used inappropriate physical restraint on the victim, a patient, and knowingly caused physical harm to her. Witnesses testified that defendant grabbed the victim around the neck, pushed her to the ground, straddled her, and started choking her; people were shouting and pushing at defendant for several minutes before he finally released his grip on the victim's neck. State v. Grimes, 2006-Ohio-4262, 2006 Ohio App. LEXIS 4189 (Ohio Ct. App., Cuyahoga County 2006).

Defendant was properly convicted of patient abuse under R.C. 2903.34(A)(1), where evidence showed that defendant nursing home worker pushed a patient back into a chair, the patient's head snapped back, and the patient cried out. Actual intent to injure was not required as long as act (pushing the patient back into the chair) was committed knowingly and defendant was aware that the act might result in physical harm. State v. Lohr, 2004-Ohio-1609, 2004 Ohio App. LEXIS 1424 (Ohio Ct. App., Lorain County 2004).

Defendant group home employee's neglect of patient clearly impaired patient's normal and healthy functioning and was therefore sufficient to establish the element of "physical harm" required to establish "gross neglect" as defined in R.C. 2903.33. Defendant's conviction of gross patient neglect under R.C. 2903.34(A)(2) was therefore proper: State v. Ruffin, 1997 Ohio App. LEXIS 5359 (Ohio Ct. App., Stark County Nov. 10, 1997).

There is sufficient evidence of "physical harm" for a conviction of patient abuse where a nursing home resident is slapped and reacts with a grimace and moan: State v. Hustead, 83 Ohio App. 3d 809, 615 N.E.2d 1081, 1992 Ohio App. LEXIS 5995 (Ohio Ct. App., Ross County 1992).

### RESEARCH REFERENCES AND PRACTICE AIDS

**Cross-References to Related Sections**

Penalties for felony, RC § 2929.11 et seq.; misdemeanor, RC § 2929.21.

Attorney general to investigate incidents of patient abuse, RC § 109.86.

Criminal records check; employment of offenders prohibited —

Applicants for employment with PASSPORT agencies, RC § 109.572.

Certain persons having frequent contact with children, RC § 2151.86.

Child day-care employees, RC §§ 5104.013, 5104.09

Employees responsible for out-of-home child care and prospective adoptive or foster parents, RC § 2151.86.

Foster care givers, RC § 5103.0319.

Head start employees responsible for children, RC § 3301.32.

Home health agency employees, RC § 3701.881.

Criminal records check of applicants for employment; certain offenders ineligible, RC § 5123.081.

Preschool employees, RC § 3301.541.

Prospective employees providing direct care to older adult, RC §§ 3712.09, 3721.121.

Public children services agency employees, RC § 5153.111.

School employees, RC § 3319.39.

Employee discrimination or retaliation prohibited, RC § 2903.36.

False patient abuse or neglect complaint, RC § 2903.35.

Juvenile court; hearing on motion for permanent custody of child upon conviction of parent, RC § 2151.414.

Report of abuse; adult protective services, RC § 5101.61 et seq.

Report of abused or neglected residents of supported living facility, RC § 5123.61.

Revocation of license upon conviction, RC § 2903.37.

**Ohio Administrative Code**

Department of aging, division of long-term care —

Background investigations by PASSPORT agencies. OAC 173-9-01.

Department of health—

Hiring of direct-care provider employees: personal character standards. OAC 3701-13-06.

Home health agencies. OAC 3701-60-07.

Department of mental health—

Incident reporting in the integrated behavioral healthcare system (IBHS). OAC 5122-3-13.

Department of developmental disabilities; —

Complaint resolution; major unusual incidents; special reporting provisions relative to abuse or neglect. OAC ch. 5123:2-17.

**Practice Guides**

Anderson's Ohio Manual of Criminal Complaints and Indictments § 2903.34 Patient abuse; neglect

Anderson's Ohio Manual of Criminal Complaints and Indictments § 2903.36 Discrimination; retaliation prohibited

## § 2903.341 Patient endangerment.

(A) As used in this section:

(1) "Developmental disabilities caretaker" means any developmental disabilities employee or any person who assumes the duty to provide for the care and protection of a person with a developmental disability on a voluntary basis, by contract, through receipt of payment for care and protection, as a result of a family relationship, or by order of a court of competent jurisdiction. "Developmental disabilities caretaker" includes a person who is an employee of a care facility and a person who is an employee of an entity under contract with a provider. "Developmental disabilities caretaker" does not include a person who owns, operates, or administers a care facility or who is an agent of a care facility unless that person also personally provides care to a person with a developmental disability.

(2) "Developmental disabilities employee" has the same meaning as in section 5123.50 of the Revised Code.

(3) "Developmental disability" has the same meaning as in section 5123.01 of the Revised Code.

(B) No developmental disabilities caretaker shall create a substantial risk to the health or safety of a person with a developmental disability. A developmental disabilities caretaker does not create a substantial risk to the health or safety of a person with a developmental disability under this division when the developmental disabilities caretaker treats a physical or mental illness or defect of the person with a developmental disability by spiritual means through prayer alone, in accordance with the tenets of a recognized religious body.

(C) No person who owns, operates, or administers a care facility or who is an agent of a care facility shall condone, or knowingly permit, any conduct by a developmental disabilities caretaker who is employed by or under the control of the owner, operator, administrator, or agent that is in violation of division (B) of this section and that involves a person with a developmental disability who is under the care of the owner, operator, administrator, or agent. A person who relies upon treatment by spiritual means through prayer alone, in accordance with the tenets of a recognized religious denomination, shall not be considered endangered under this division for that reason alone.

(D)(1) It is an affirmative defense to a charge of a violation of division (B) or (C) of this section that the actor's conduct was committed in good faith solely because the actor was ordered to commit the conduct by a person to whom one of the following applies:

(a) The person has supervisory authority over the actor.

(b) The person has authority over the actor's conduct pursuant to a contract for the provision of services.

(2) It is an affirmative defense to a charge of a violation of division (C) of this section that the person who owns, operates, or administers a care facility or who is an agent of a care facility and who is charged with the violation is following the individual service plan for the involved person with a developmental disability or that the admission, discharge, and transfer rule set forth in the Administrative Code is being followed.

(3) It is an affirmative defense to a charge of a violation of division (C) of this section that the actor did not have readily available a means to prevent either the harm to the person with a developmental disability or the death of such a person and the actor took reasonable steps to summon aid.

(E)(1) Except as provided in division (E)(2) or (E)(3) of this section, whoever violates division (B) or (C) of this section is guilty of patient endangerment, a misdemeanor of the first degree.

(2) If the offender previously has been convicted of, or pleaded guilty to, a violation of this section, patient endangerment is a felony of the fourth degree.

(3) If the violation results in serious physical harm to the person with a developmental disability, patient endangerment is a felony of the third degree.

**HISTORY:**

150 v S 178, § 1, eff. 1-30-04; 2016 hb158, § 1, effective October 12, 2016.

**Amendment Notes**

The 2016 amendment by HB 158 rewrote (A) and (B); substituted "a developmental disabilities" for "an MR/DD" in the first sentence of (C); substituted "person with a developmental disability" for "mentally retarded person or a developmentally disabled person" in the first sentence of (C), in (D)(2); and deleted "mental retardation or" following "person with" in (D)(3) and (E)(3).

### NOTES TO DECISIONS

Analysis

Culpable mental state
Evidence sufficient
Indictment

**Culpable mental state**

Indictment for patient endangerment failed to charge that defendant acted recklessly in creating a substantial risk to the health or safety of the patient, a mentally retarded/developmentally disabled person; that omission, of one of the essential elements of the crime, rendered the indictment defective. The State's line of questioning reflected the State's position that it was a strict liability offense: that defendant was paid to care for the patient, he was not receiving proper care, and the lack of proper care created a substantial risk to his health and well-being. State v. Rash, 2009-Ohio-2220, 2009 Ohio App. LEXIS 1864 (Ohio Ct. App., Stark County 2009).

**Evidence sufficient**

Defendant's claim that the State's evidence was insufficient to convict her of patient endangerment because the record showed that defendant was a MR/DD caretaker, that two of the women had mental retardation and that all four women in the group home had developmental disabilities, and evidence established that defendant in fact left the group home prior to the end of her scheduled shift without another staff to relieve her which created a substantial risk of harm to the residents. State v. Bagley, 2019-Ohio-3193, 2019 Ohio App. LEXIS 3282 (Ohio Ct. App., Montgomery County 2019).

Evidence offered a substantial basis upon which the jury could reasonably have concluded that those elements of R.C. 2903.341(B) were satisfied because the parties agreed that defendant was an MR/DD caretaker and that the victim was a mentally retarded person or a developmentally disabled person. Also, because two witnesses testified that they observed defendant push the victim, resulting in her fall to the floor, the jury could have reasonably determined that defendant's act of pushing the victim to the floor "recklessly" created a substantial risk to the health and safety of the victim. State v. McMillen, 2009-Ohio-210, 2009 Ohio App. LEXIS 186 (Ohio Ct. App., Stark County 2009).



**Indictment**

Defendant's indictment was not structurally defective and defendant failed to establish that, but for the error, the outcome of the trial clearly would have been otherwise. Defendant had notice through the arguments of counsel that recklessness was the mens rea for the crime charged, the State did not treat patient endangerment as a strict-liability offense, the trial court correctly informed the jury as to the definition of "recklessness," and defendant did not object. State v. McMillen, 2009-Ohio-210, 2009 Ohio App. LEXIS 186 (Ohio Ct. App., Stark County 2009).

### § 2903.35 Filing false patient abuse or neglect complaints.

(A) No person shall knowingly make a false statement, or knowingly swear or affirm the truth of a false statement previously made, alleging a violation of section 2903.34 of the Revised Code, when the statement is made with purpose to incriminate another.

(B) Whoever violates this section is guilty of filing a false patient abuse or neglect complaint, a misdemeanor of the first degree.

**HISTORY:**

141 v H 566. Eff 9-17-86.

#### RESEARCH REFERENCES AND PRACTICE AIDS

**Cross-References to Related Sections**

Penalties, RC § 2929.21.

Knowingly defined, RC § 2901.22.

Report of abuse; adult protective services, RC § 5101.61 et seq.

Report of abused or neglected residents of supported living facility, RC § 5123.61.

**Practice Guides**

Anderson's Ohio Manual of Criminal Complaints and Indictments § 2903.35 Filing false patient abuse or neglect complaints

### § 2903.36 Discrimination, retaliation prohibited.

No care facility shall discharge or in any manner discriminate or retaliate against any person solely because such person, in good faith, filed a complaint, affidavit, or other document alleging a violation of section 2903.34 of the Revised Code.

**HISTORY:**

141 v H 566. Eff 9-17-86.

#### NOTES TO DECISIONS

**Blood tests**

Although defendant's blood samples were not taken until seven hours after a one-car accident resulting in his passenger's death, the results should not have been suppressed under former R.C. 4511.19(D)(1) as defendant was charged with aggravated vehicular homicide under R.C. 2903.06(A)(1)(a) due to a violation of R.C. 4511.19(A), which was not a per se offense under § 4511.19; thus, the blood alcohol content test results would be admissible to prove that defendant under the influence of alcohol as proscribed by R.C. 4511.19(A)(1)(a) in the prosecution for a violation of R.C. 2903.06, provided that the administrative requirements of R.C. 4511.19(D) were substantially complied with and expert testimony was offered. State v. Hassler, 2007-Ohio-4947, 115 Ohio St. 3d 322, 875 N.E.2d 46, 2007 Ohio LEXIS 2232 (Ohio 2007).

#### RESEARCH REFERENCES AND PRACTICE AIDS

**Practice Guides**

Anderson's Ohio Manual of Criminal Complaints and Indictments § 2903.36 Discrimination; retaliation prohibited

### § 2903.37 License revocation.

Any individual, who owns, operates, or administers, or who is an agent or employee of, a care facility, who is convicted of a felony violation of section 2903.34 of the Revised Code, and who is required to be licensed under any law of this state, shall have his license revoked in accordance with Chapter 119. of the Revised Code.

**HISTORY:**

141 v H 566. Eff 9-17-86.

#### RESEARCH REFERENCES AND PRACTICE AIDS

**Practice Guides**

Anderson's Ohio Manual of Criminal Complaints and Indictments § 2903.37 License revocation

# CHAPTER 2913

# THEFT AND FRAUD

Theft



## THEFT

### § 2913.02 Theft.

(A) No person, with purpose to deprive the owner of property or services, shall knowingly obtain or exert control over either the property or services in any of the following ways:

(1) Without the consent of the owner or person authorized to give consent;

(2) Beyond the scope of the express or implied consent of the owner or person authorized to give consent;

(3) By deception;

(4) By threat;

(5) By intimidation.

(B)(1) Whoever violates this section is guilty of theft.

(2) Except as otherwise provided in this division or division (B)(3), (4), (5), (6), (7), (8), or (9) of this section, a violation of this section is petty theft, a misdemeanor of the first degree. If the value of the property or services stolen is one thousand dollars or more and is less than seven thousand five hundred dollars or if the property stolen is any of the property listed in section 2913.71 of the Revised Code, a violation of this section is theft, a felony of the fifth degree. If the value of the property or services stolen is seven thousand five hundred dollars or more and is less than one hundred fifty thousand dollars, a violation of this section is grand theft, a felony of the fourth degree. If the value of the property or services stolen is one hundred fifty thousand dollars or more and is less than seven hundred fifty thousand dollars, a violation of this section is aggravated theft, a felony of the third degree. If the value of the property or services is seven hundred fifty thousand dollars or more and is less than one million five hundred thousand dollars, a violation of this section is aggravated theft, a felony of the second degree. If the value of the property or services stolen is one million five hundred thousand dollars or more, a violation of this section is aggravated theft of one million five hundred thousand dollars or more, a felony of the first degree.

(3) Except as otherwise provided in division (B)(4), (5), (6), (7), (8), or (9) of this section, if the victim of the offense is an elderly person, disabled adult, active duty service member, or spouse of an active duty service member, a violation of this section is theft from a person in a protected class, and division

(B)(3) of this section applies. Except as otherwise provided in this division, theft from a person in a protected class is a felony of the fifth degree. If the value of the property or services stolen is one thousand dollars or more and is less than seven thousand five hundred dollars, theft from a person in a protected class is a felony of the fourth degree. If the value of the property or services stolen is seven thousand five hundred dollars or more and is less than thirty-seven thousand five hundred dollars, theft from a person in a protected class is a felony of the third degree. If the value of the property or services stolen is thirty-seven thousand five hundred dollars or more and is less than one hundred fifty thousand dollars, theft from a person in a protected class is a felony of the second degree. If the value of the property or services stolen is one hundred fifty thousand dollars or more, theft from a person in a protected class is a felony of the first degree. If the victim of the offense is an elderly person, in addition to any other penalty imposed for the offense, the offender shall be required to pay full restitution to the victim and to pay a fine of up to fifty thousand dollars. The clerk of court shall forward all fines collected under division (B)(3) of this section to the county department of job and family services to be used for the reporting and investigation of elder abuse, neglect, and exploitation or for the provision or arrangement of protective services under sections 5101.61 to 5101.71 of the Revised Code.

(4) If the property stolen is a firearm or dangerous ordnance, a violation of this section is grand theft. Except as otherwise provided in this division, grand theft when the property stolen is a firearm or dangerous ordnance is a felony of the third degree, and there is a presumption in favor of the court imposing a prison term for the offense. If the firearm or dangerous ordnance was stolen from a federally licensed firearms dealer, grand theft when the property stolen is a firearm or dangerous ordnance is a felony of the first degree. The offender shall serve a prison term imposed for grand theft when the property stolen is a firearm or dangerous ordnance consecutively to any other prison term or mandatory prison term previously or subsequently imposed upon the offender.

(5) If the property stolen is a motor vehicle, a violation of this section is grand theft of a motor vehicle, a felony of the fourth degree.

(6) If the property stolen is any dangerous drug, a violation of this section is theft of drugs, a felony of the fourth degree, or, if the offender previously has been convicted of a felony drug abuse offense, a felony of the third degree.

(7) If the property stolen is a police dog or horse or an assistance dog and the offender knows or should know that the property stolen is a police dog or horse or an assistance dog, a violation of this section is theft of a police dog or horse or an assistance dog, a felony of the third degree.

(8) If the property stolen is anhydrous ammonia, a violation of this section is theft of anhydrous ammonia, a felony of the third degree.

(9) Except as provided in division (B)(2) of this section with respect to property with a value of seven thousand five hundred dollars or more and division (B)(3) of this section with respect to property with a value of one thousand dollars or more, if the property stolen is a special purpose article as defined in section 4737.04 of the Revised Code or is a bulk merchandise container as defined in section 4737.012 of the Revised Code, a violation of this section is theft of a special purpose article or articles or theft of a bulk merchandise container or containers, a felony of the fifth degree.

(10) In addition to the penalties described in division (B)(2) of this section, if the offender committed the violation by causing a motor vehicle to leave the premises of an establishment at which gasoline is offered for retail sale without the offender making full payment for gasoline that was dispensed into the fuel tank of the motor vehicle or into another container, the court may do one of the following:

(a) Unless division (B)(10)(b) of this section applies, suspend for not more than six months the offender's driver's license, probationary driver's license, commercial driver's license, temporary instruction permit, or nonresident operating privilege;

(b) If the offender's driver's license, probationary driver's license, commercial driver's license, temporary instruction permit, or nonresident operating privilege has previously been suspended pursuant to division (B)(10)(a) of this section, impose a class seven suspension of the offender's license, permit, or privilege from the range specified in division (A)(7) of section 4510.02 of the Revised Code, provided that the suspension shall be for at least six months.

(c) The court, in lieu of suspending the offender's driver's or commercial driver's license, probationary driver's license, temporary instruction permit, or nonresident operating privilege pursuant to division (B)(10)(a) or (b) of this section, instead may require the offender to perform community service for a number of hours determined by the court.

(11) In addition to the penalties described in division (B)(2) of this section, if the offender committed the violation by stealing rented property or rental services, the court may order that the offender make restitution pursuant to section 2929.18 or 2929.28 of the Revised Code. Restitution may include, but is not limited to, the cost of repairing or replacing the stolen property, or the cost of repairing the stolen property and any loss of revenue resulting from deprivation of the property due to theft of rental services that is less than or equal to the actual value of the property at the time it was rented. Evidence of intent to commit theft of rented property or rental services shall be determined pursuant to the provisions of section 2913.72 of the Revised Code.

(C) The sentencing court that suspends an offender's license, permit, or nonresident operating privilege under division (B)(10) of this section may grant the offender limited driving privileges during the period of the suspension in accordance with Chapter 4510. of the Revised Code.



**HISTORY:**

134 v H 511 (Eff 1-1-74); 138 v S 191 (Eff 6-20-80); 139 v S 199 (Eff 1-1-83); 140 v H 632 (Eff 3-28-85); 141 v H 49 (Eff 6-26-86); 143 v H 347 (Eff 7-18-90); 143 v S 258 (Eff 11-20-90); 146 v H 4 (Eff 11-9-95); 146 v S 2 (Eff 7-1-96); 147 v S 66 (Eff 7-22-98); 148 v H 2. Eff 11-10-99; 150 v H 7, § 1, eff. 9-16-03; 150 v H 179, § 1, eff. 3-9-04; 150 v H 12, § 1, eff. 4-8-04; 150 v H 369, § 1, eff. 11-26-04; 150 v H 536, § 1, eff. 4-15-05; 151 v H 530, § 101.01, eff. 6-30-06; 151 v H 347, § 1, eff. 3-14-07; 152 v S 320, § 1, eff. 4-7-09; 2011 HB 86, § 1, eff. Sept. 30, 2011; 2012 SB 337, § 1, eff. Sept. 28, 2012; 2013 HB 51, § 101.01, eff. July 1, 2013; 2014 HB 488, § 1, eff. Sept. 16, 2014; 2018 sb158, § 1, effective March 20, 2019.

**Editor's Notes**

Acts 2013, HB 51, § 812.10 provides: "Except as otherwise provided in this act, the amendment, enactment, or repeal by this act of a section of law is subject to the referendum under Ohio Constitution, Article II, Section 1c and therefore takes effect on the ninety-first day after this act is filed with the Secretary of State or, if a later effective date is specified below, on that date."

Acts 2013, HB 51, § 806.10 provides: "The items of law contained in this act, and their applications, are severable. If any item of law contained in this act, or if any application of any item of law contained in this act, is held invalid, the invalidity does not affect other items of law contained in this act and their applications that can be given effect without the invalid item or application."

The provisions of § 4 of HB 86 read as follows:

"SECTION 4. The amendments to sections 926.99, 1333.99, 1707.99, 1716.99, 2909.03, 2909.05, 2909.11, 2913.02, 2913.03, 2913.04, 2913.11, 2913.21, 2913.31, 2913.32, 2913.34, 2913.40, 2913.401, 2913.42, 2913.421, 2913.43, 2913.45, 2913.46, 2913.47, 2913.48, 2913.49, 2913.51, 2913.61, 2915.05, 2917.21, 2917.31, 2917.32, 2921.13, 2921.41, 2923.31, and 2981.07, division (B) of section 2929.13, and division (A) of section 2929.14 of the Revised Code that are made in this act apply to a person who commits an offense specified or penalized under those sections on or after the effective date of this section and to a person to whom division (B) of section 1.58 of the Revised Code makes the amendments applicable.

"The provisions of sections 926.99, 1333.99, 1707.99, 1716.99, 2909.03, 2909.05, 2909.11, 2913.02, 2913.03, 2913.04, 2913.11, 2913.21, 2913.31, 2913.32, 2913.34, 2913.40, 2913.401, 2913.42, 2913.421, 2913.43, 2913.45, 2913.46, 2913.47, 2913.48, 2913.49, 2913.51, 2913.61, 2915.05, 2917.21, 2917.31, 2917.32, 2921.13, 2921.41, 2923.31, and 2981.07 of the Revised Code in existence prior to the effective date of this section shall apply to a person upon whom a court imposed sentence prior to the effective date of this section for an offense specified or penalized under those sections. The amendments to sections 926.99, 1333.99, 1707.99, 1716.99, 2909.03, 2909.05, 2909.11, 2913.02, 2913.03, 2913.04, 2913.11, 2913.21, 2913.31, 2913.32, 2913.34, 2913.40, 2913.401, 2913.42, 2913.421, 2913.43, 2913.45, 2913.46, 2913.47, 2913.48, 2913.49, 2913.51, 2913.61, 2915.05, 2917.21,

2917.31, 2917.32, 2921.13, 2921.41, 2923.31, and 2981.07 of the Revised Code that are made in this act do not apply to a person who upon whom a court imposed sentence prior to the effective date of this section for an offense specified or penalized under those sections."

Governor Taft's veto of HB 347 was overridden by the Ohio General Assembly.

The provisions of § 3 of H.B. 369 (150 v —) read as follows:

SECTION 3. Section 2913.02 of the Revised Code is presented in this act as a composite of the section as amended by Am. Sub. H.B. 7, Am. Sub. H.B. 12, and Sub. H.B. 179, all of the 125th General Assembly. The General Assembly, applying the principle stated in division (B) of section 1.52 of the Revised Code that amendments are to be harmonized if reasonably capable of simultaneous operation, finds that the composite is the resulting version of the section in effect prior to the effective date of the section as presented in this act.

The provisions of § 10, H.B. 12 (150 v —), read as follows:

SECTION 10. If any provision of sections 1547.69, 2911.21, 2913.02, 2921.13, 2923.12, 2923.121, 2923.123, 2923.16, 2929.14, 2953.32, and 4749.10 of the Revised Code, as amended by this act, any provision of sections 109.69, 109.731, 311.41, 311.42, 2923.124, 2923.125, 2923.126, 2923.127, 2923.128, 2923.129, 2923.1210, 2923.1211, 2923.1212, and 2923.1213 of the Revised Code, as enacted by this act, or the application of any provision of those sections to any person or circumstance is held invalid, the invalidity does not affect other provisions or applications of the particular section or related sections that can be given effect without the invalid provision or application, and to this end the provisions of the particular section are severable.

The provisions of § 3, H.B. 179 (150 v —), read as follows:

SECTION 3. The General Assembly declares that the sections of the Revised Code that regulate persons who leave the premises of establishments at which gasoline is offered for retail sale without the person making full payment for gasoline that was dispensed at that establishment, including section 2913.02 of the Revised Code, are general laws that completely fill the field of regulation of that nature. Any municipal ordinance that prohibits establishments at which gasoline is offered for retail sale from requiring the prepayment of gasoline is in conflict with those general laws.

**Amendment Notes**

The 2018 amendment by SB 158 added the last two sentences in (B)(3).

The 2014 amendment by HB 488, in (A)(3), substituted "a person in a protected class" for "an elderly person or disabled adult" throughout and inserted "active duty service member, or spouse of an active duty service member"; and made a related change.

The 2013 amendment substituted "(B)(3), (4), (5), (6), (7), (8), or (9)" for "(B)(3), (4), (5), (6), (7), or (8)" in the first sentence of (B)(2); substituted "(B)(4), (5), (6), (7), (8), or (9)" for "(B)(4), (5), (6), (7), or (8)" in the first sentence of (B)(3); inserted (B)(9); redesignated former (B)(9) and (B)(10) as (B)(10) and (B)(11); and made stylistic changes.

The 2012 amendment added (B)(9)(c).

The 2011 amendment substituted "one thousand dollars" for "five hundred dollars" in the second sentence of (B)(2) and the third sentence of (B)(3); substituted "seven thousand five hundred dollars" for "five thousand dollars" throughout (B)(2) and (B)(3); substituted "one hundred fifty thousand dollars" for "one hundred thousand dollars" in the third and fourth sentences of (B)(2) and the fifth and last sentences of (B)(3); in (B)(2), substituted "seven hundred fifty thousand dollars" for "five hundred thousand dollars" in the fourth and fifth sentences and substituted "one million five hundred thousand dollars" for "one million dollars" wherever it appears in the fifth and last sentences; and substituted "thirty-seven thousand five hundred dollars" for "twenty-five thousand dollars" in the fourth and fifth sentences of (B)(3).

152 v S 320, effective April 7, 2009, added (B)(10).

151 v H 347, effective March 14, 2007, rewrote (B)(4).

151 v H 530, effective June 30, 2006, in (B)(7), substituted "an assistance" for "service" three times.

**1974 Committee Comment to H 511**

This section covers a plethora of former offenses of which the gist was larceny, embezzlement, conversion, fraud, or false pretense. In addition, the section includes a "minor league" species of robbery, insofar as a threat may be an element of the offense.

Theft of services and real property, as well as theft of personal property, are within the purview of the section. At common law, only personal property could be the subject of larceny, although an older Ohio statute (Section 1.03 of the Revised Code) expands this to include money, goods, chattels, commercial paper, receipts, choses in action, severed crops and real property fixtures, and other things of value.

The section expands upon the common law requirement that the taking of property must occur simultaneously with a purpose to deprive the owner of the property. Formerly, a wrongful conversion or embezzlement could not constitute larceny, since the intent to deprive was formed after the property came into the offender's possession. *Berry v. State*, 31 Ohio St. 219, 27 Am. Rep. 506 (1877); *Porter v. State*, 8 OApp 231 (Scioto Co. App., 1917). Under the new section, the basic elements of the offense must still coincide, but conversion or embezzlement now constitutes theft, since the section defines theft as exerting control (as opposed to initially gaining control over property or services) beyond the scope of the owner's consent, and with purpose to deprive the owner of the same.

The section also includes theft by deception, formerly the subject of section 2907.21, larceny by trick, as well as a long list of former statutes of which some variety of fraud or false pretense was an element.

In addition, the section defines theft by threat, which may be a lesser included offense to robbery. The threat involved in theft is not restricted to the threat of personal harm, which is one of the distinguishing characteristics of robbery.

This section increases from $60 to $150 the point at which petty theft becomes grand theft, because in the twenty years or so since $60 was adopted as the breaking point, inflation rendered the former amount unrealistic. $150 is chosen because, statistically, there is less likelihood that whether the offender is liable to a relatively short spell in jail or a long sojourn in the penitentiary will turn on the difference of a penny in the value of stolen property. Also, a substantial number of thefts which formerly had to be tried in common pleas court may not be disposed of in lower courts.

The new section also makes stealing certain items grand theft, regardless of their value, because they are particularly subject to organized criminal activity, and because of the high risk that the ultimate harm flowing from their unlawful acquisition may far exceed the harm intrinsic in the theft itself. These items are listed in new section 2913.71, and in part in new section 2923.11 of the Revised Code.

Finally under the section, theft is grand theft (regardless of what is stolen or its worth) when the offender has previously been convicted of a theft offense.

Petty theft, which is the theft of property or services worth less than $150, is a misdemeanor of the first degree. Grand theft is a felony of the fourth degree, and any of the following constitutes grand theft: theft of property or services worth $150 or more; theft of any of the property listed in new section 2913.71 of the Revised Code; and theft, regardless of the nature of the property or services or their value, when the offender has previously been convicted of a theft offense.

## NOTES TO DECISIONS

Analysis

**Constitutionality**

Because defendant's conviction for theft of the elderly was supported by sufficient evidence, probable cause existed for the second officer to file a criminal charge. The statute was not so unclear (vague) that defendant could not reasonably understand that it prohibited the act in which he engaged, nor was it unconstitutional as applied to his conduct. State v. Burton, 2016-Ohio-5380, 2016 Ohio App. LEXIS 3289 (Ohio Ct. App., Delaware County 2016).

**Generally**

Trial court erred by denying a motion to seal an applicant's criminal record pursuant to R.C. 2953.32 without a full and fair hearing where the applicant's misdemeanor theft conviction under R.C. 2913.02(A)(1) was not an offense that was statutorily exempt from sealing and the record did not reveal whether the applicant was a "first offender" or had received a prior expungement. State v. Calderon, 2010-Ohio-2807, 2010 Ohio App. LEXIS 2342 (Ohio Ct. App., Medina County 2010).

When proving a violation of R.C. 2913.02(A)(2), (3), a defendant roofer was under no obligation to use the exact funds that a customer gave him to order materials for the customer's roof; the down payment was defendant's to use as he desired so long as he performed under the contract. State v. Coleman, 2003-Ohio-5724, 2003 Ohio App. LEXIS 5118 (Ohio Ct. App., Champaign County 2003).

When a customer at a gasoline service station mistakenly pumps his own gasoline from a full-service pump instead of a self-service pump, and pays at the lower self-service price, a conviction for theft cannot stand if based on a complaint for theft of "property" in the amount of the price difference, where the price difference represents only the value of services not rendered: State v. Lavandera, 34 Ohio App. 3d 83, 517 N.E.2d 251, 1986 Ohio App. LEXIS 10311 (Ohio Ct. App., Cuyahoga County 1986).

In enacting R.C. 2913.02(A), the General Assembly intended that the word "either" be used as a pronoun and that the four prepositional phrases be mutually exclusive and read in the disjunctive: State v. Dugger, 49 Ohio App. 2d 220, 3 Ohio Op. 3d 272, 360 N.E.2d 706, 1975 Ohio App. LEXIS 5912 (Ohio Ct. App., Summit County 1975).

**Abuse of process**

Summary judgment was properly granted on the rentee's abuse of process claim because R.C. 2913.72 provided support for the conclusion that criminal prosecution against the rentee for theft was valid under Ohio law. Although R.C. 2913.72 was an evidentiary statute, it supported the conclusion that the type of conduct engaged in by the rentee of not making the required rental payments, retaining the property, and ignoring the company's repeated efforts to recover the property, was subject to criminal prosecution under R.C. 2913.02. Pierson v. Aaron's Rental, 2010-Ohio-5443, 2010 Ohio App. LEXIS 4604 (Ohio Ct. App., Franklin County 2010).

**Accident**

Defendant was entitled to a jury instruction on the defense of accident to the theft charge where he claimed that the failure to pay for certain items was inadvertent: City of Mentor v. Hamercheck, 112 Ohio App. 3d 291, 678 N.E.2d 622, 1996 Ohio App. LEXIS 2732 (Ohio Ct. App., Lake County 1996).

**Aggregated offenses**

R.C. 2913.61(C)(1) was applicable because defendant committed a series of theft offenses against the same store with the same scheme or plan; defendant entered the store on several occasions under the guise of being a legitimate customer and left after stealing the same type of item, 29 copies of the same video game. As a business invitee, defendant had a relationship to the store sufficient to invoke § 2913.61(C). State v. Williams, 2009-Ohio-732, 2009 Ohio App. LEXIS 598 (Ohio Ct. App., Cuyahoga County 2009).

**Aggregation**

Trial court did not err by denying defendant's motion to dismiss because the statute did not limit the aggregation of theft offenses to theft offenses involving victims who were elderly persons, disabled adults, or military persons. State v. Pettus, 2019-Ohio-2023, 2019 Ohio App. LEXIS 2168 (Ohio Ct. App., Hamilton County 2019), aff'd, 2020-Ohio-4836, 163 Ohio St. 3d 55, 168 N.E.3d 406, 2020 Ohio LEXIS 2259 (Ohio 2020).

**Aiding and abetting**

Trial court properly denied defendant's motions for acquittal of aggravated robbery, aggravated burglary, and grand theft under R.C. 2911.01, 2911.11, and 2913.02 as there was sufficient evidence of aiding and abetting under R.C. 2923.03(A)(2) in that a codefendant testified that defendant stated that he wanted to rob somebody, that he drove the getaway van, and that he was excited about getting the victim's money and spoke of robbing him again. Furthermore, the convictions were not against the manifest weight of the evidence, as video surveillance undercut defendant's testimony that he had gone to the scene merely because a codefendant needed a ride and that he never got out of the car. State v. Larry, 2016-Ohio-829, 2016 Ohio App. LEXIS 741 (Ohio Ct. App., Holmes County 2016).

Defendant's conviction for petty theft, R.C. 2913.02(A)(1), for aiding and abetting her daughter in the commission of a theft was supported by the weight of the evidence as the trial court reasonably found the testimony of the store employees to be more credible. The risk-management worker's testimony supported that defendant's petty theft conviction was premised on an aiding and abetting theory. He testified that he saw defendant's daughter conceal two curling irons in her clothes while defendant appeared to act as a lookout. State v. Jackson, 2005-Ohio-4521, 2005 Ohio App. LEXIS 4088 (Ohio Ct. App., Montgomery County 2005).

A passenger in a stolen vehicle may be guilty of complicity for aiding and abetting the driver in possessing it: In re Straquadine, 1994 Ohio App. LEXIS 274 (Ohio Ct. App., Cuyahoga County Jan. 27, 1994).

**Allied offenses**

Trial court did not err by failing to merge grand theft of a motor vehicle and aggravated robber because the aggravated robbery was committed by the use of deadly force upon the victim to obtain the keys to the vehicle and, while it may have been necessary to obtain the keys to exercise control of the vehicle, the conduct relative to each action was distinct. The crime of aggravated robbery was completed when defendants obtained possession of the keys and the grand theft was not committed until defendants used the keys to exercise control over the vehicle itself. State v. Stanley, 2021-Ohio-108, 2021 Ohio App. LEXIS 96 (Ohio Ct. App., Lake County 2021).

Trial court did not err by failing to merge the theft and telecommunications fraud counts during sentencing as the offenses were not allied because defendant's separate conduct of downloading the gaming application and repeatedly making charges against the victim's debit card were committed separately, with a separate animus, and caused separate identifiable harm. State v. Burey, 2021-Ohio-943, 2021 Ohio App. LEXIS 959 (Ohio Ct. App., Cuyahoga County 2021).

Defendant's convictions for attempted murder, aggravated robbery, and grand theft of a motor vehicle were not allied offenses of similar import subject to merger for purposes of sentencing, as the grand theft of the victim's motor vehicle occurred at a different time and different location than the attempted murder and aggravated robbery and also involved conduct and harm separate and apart from the aggravated robbery and attempted murder; further, the purpose was to steal the car. State v. Spurrier, 2021-Ohio-1061, 2021 Ohio App. LEXIS 1058 (Ohio Ct. App., Lake County 2021).

Defendant's convictions were based on the theft of separate items - the grand theft pertained to the firearm, and the underlying theft in the aggravated robbery addressed the firearm and the money found on defendant and folded up in the driveway near defendant. Because each offense had a separate and identifiable harm, each was dissimilar in import and significance and not subject to merger. State v. Conrad, 2019-Ohio-263, 2019 Ohio App. LEXIS 265 (Ohio Ct. App., Hocking County 2019).

Trial court did not err by failing to merge the convictions for aggravated robbery, aggravated burglary, grand theft, and having weapons under disability into aggravated murder because defendant murdered (aggravated murder) the victim while invading his home (aggravated burglary), then stole money (aggravated robbery) and a gun (grand theft). For the offense of having weapons under disability, the victim was the state of Ohio, which was separate and identifiable from the harm caused to the victim. State v. Conrad, 2019-Ohio-263, 2019 Ohio App. LEXIS 265 (Ohio Ct. App., Hocking County 2019).

Because the offenses of forgery and theft were separate and distinct acts committed during a course of criminal conduct, the trial court did not err in failing to merge the offenses. The offenses of forgery were committed when defendant uttered the checks that he knew to have been forged and the offenses of theft were then subsequently committed when defendant made a cash withdrawal from his account. State v. Pettus, 2019-Ohio-2023, 2019 Ohio App. LEXIS 2168 (Ohio Ct. App., Hamilton County 2019), aff'd, 2020-Ohio-4836, 163 Ohio St. 3d 55, 168 N.E.3d 406, 2020 Ohio LEXIS 2259 (Ohio 2020).

Trial court erred by merging Counts 1 and 2 and Counts 3 through 7 because the grand theft offenses resulted in separate and identifiable harm. Additionally, each offense was committed with a separate animus or motivation: each stolen vehicle had to be removed from the building one at a time, and with regard to vehicles for which they did not have keys, the ignitions had to be individually "hotwired." State v. Dotson, 2019 Ohio 2393, 2019 Ohio App. LEXIS 2504 (June 17, 2019).

Trial court erred by not merging two of the three theft offenses because defendant's conduct victimized one person in a single event, and thus the harm was not separate and distinct. The trial judge said as much on the record, but ultimately the sentence did not reflect that conclusion. State v. Wright, 2018-Ohio-877, 2018 Ohio App. LEXIS 937 (Ohio Ct. App., Hamilton County 2018).

Trial court did not commit plain error by failing to merge defendant's convictions because, inter alia, the offense of aggravated robbery was complete when defendant hit the victim with a bat in order to take his gun, after knocking the victim out and taking his gun, defendant went to the closet and took other firearms thereby completing the grand theft offense, and at some point, defendant also took the victim's medication and completed the offense of theft of drugs. State v. Gray, 2018-Ohio-3326, 2018 Ohio App. LEXIS 3598 (Ohio Ct. App., Lake County 2018).

Trial court did not commit plain error by failing to merge defendant's convictions because, inter alia, the State established the harm resulting from each offense was separate and identifiable, including the victim suffering a severe laceration to his head, a broken orbital socket, and bleeding on the brain as a result of the aggravated robbery, the victim having to pay a pawn shop in order to retrieve the stolen shotgun, and the theft of drugs depriving the victim of his anxiety medication. State v. Gray, 2018-Ohio-3326, 2018 Ohio App. LEXIS 3598 (Ohio Ct. App., Lake County 2018).

Trial court erred by failing to merge the aggravated robbery and theft from an elderly person or disabled adult offenses because they were not dissimilar in import and, since defendant's conduct victimized one person in a single event, the harm was not separate and distinct. No temporal break occurred between the commission of the theft and aggravated-robbery offenses and the offenses were committed as part of the same course of conduct with a single state of mind because, after knocking the 87-year-old victim to the ground and beating him, defendant rifled through his pockets, took his wallet, grabbed his keys, and then drove away in his car. State v. Shelton, 2018-Ohio-3895, 2018 Ohio App. LEXIS 4216 (Ohio Ct. App., Hamilton County 2018).

Trial court did not err by failing at sentencing to merge a burglary count with a theft count because, when defendant entered the apartment without permission with the intent to commit a criminal offense, he committed the crime of burglary. It was not until later when he took the victim's gun that he committed the crime of grand theft of a firearm. State v. Redmyer, 2017-Ohio-572, 2017 Ohio App. LEXIS 588 (Ohio Ct. App., Medina County 2017).

Trial court did not err in not merging the offenses of aggravated burglary and theft for purposes of sentencing because the offenses were committed separately. Because the aggravated burglary was completed when defendant entered the apartment and threatened the victim, his theft offenses were committed separately, and the offenses were not allied offenses of similar import because the offenses involved separate victims. State v. Yancey, 2017-Ohio-1040, 2017 Ohio App. LEXIS 1013 (Ohio Ct. App., Cuyahoga County 2017).

Court did not err by failing to merge the telecommunications fraud conviction with the theft from an elderly person conviction and attempted theft from an elderly person conviction because, while defendant's constant telephone contact with the alleged victim furthered her overall scheme to scam the victim, defendant's act of using the telephone was separate from each theft count. State v. Stuward, 2017-Ohio-2918, 2017 Ohio App. LEXIS 1950 (Ohio Ct. App., Seneca County 2017).

Trial court's failure to inquire whether the convictions for Counts 18, 20, and 22 (unemployment benefits stolen from the state of Ohio) merged was not plain error because defendant's conduct resulted in three offenses of the same or similar kind, but each offense was based on a separate and distinct act, and each act had its own independent animus. State v. Minich, 2017-Ohio-9262, 2017 Ohio App. LEXIS 5736 (Ohio Ct. App., Lake County 2017).

Trial court erred by not merging all of the grand theft and theft counts, and the grand theft and theft counts should have been merged with the count of aggravated robbery, because it was a home invasion and the court was not required to treat the theft of separate items from the same situs as separate and identifiable offenses. State v. Lewis, 2016-Ohio-7002, 72 N.E.3d 48, 2016 Ohio App. LEXIS 3854 (Ohio Ct. App., Richland County 2016).

Trial court erred by not merging all of the grand theft and theft counts, and the grand theft and theft counts should have been merged with the count of aggravated robbery, because it was a home invasion and the court was not required to treat the theft of separate items from the same situs as separate and identifiable offenses. State v. Lewis, 2016-Ohio-7002, 72 N.E.3d 48, 2016 Ohio App. LEXIS 3854 (Ohio Ct. App., Richland County 2016).

Trial court did not err when it failed to merge defendant's conviction for grand theft of a motor vehicle with his conviction for aggravated murder because defendant committed the aggravated murder when he shot and killed the victim in his apartment and the grand theft conviction was based upon defendant's distinct conduct in stealing the victim's motor vehicle ostensibly after committing the murder. The harm suffered by the victim from having his car stolen is clearly separate and identifiable from the harm Turner suffered from being shot in the head and killed. State v. Wood, 2016-Ohio-143, 2016 Ohio App. LEXIS 130 (Ohio Ct. App., Montgomery County 2016).

Defendant's burglary conviction under R.C. 2911.12(A)(3) and his convictions of grand theft and theft under R.C. 2913.02(A)(1) were not allied offenses of similar import under R.C. 2941.25(B) as the burglary was committed separately from the theft offenses in that defendant broke the door jamb, entered the house, ran away upon hearing a loud noise, and then returned to commit the thefts. State v. Champada, 2016-Ohio-7291, 2016 Ohio App. LEXIS 4153 (Ohio Ct. App., Fulton County 2016).

Convictions of grand theft and theft under R.C. 2913.02(A)(1) were not allied offense of similar import under R.C. 2941.25(B) as the theft of the firearms created separate harm from the theft of other items in that defendant illegally sold the firearms, creating the risk of future harm. State v. Champada, 2016-Ohio-7291, 2016 Ohio App. LEXIS 4153 (Ohio Ct. App., Fulton County 2016).

Because defendant's animus in creating and uttering the fake stimulus checks was distinguishable from the collection of over $32,000 resulting in the theft count, the conviction for grand theft did not merge with the forgery convictions. State v. Walker, 2016-Ohio-8615, 2016 Ohio App. LEXIS 5431 (Ohio Ct. App., Richland County 2016).

Defendant's convictions for grand theft of a firearm and theft of drugs were not allied offenses of similar import subject to merger at sentencing because the victim of the grand theft of a firearm was defendant's former foster mother and the victim of the theft of drugs was identified as the foster mother's daughter, and, as such, each of defendant's thefts involved separate victims. State v. Ervin, 2015-Ohio-3688, 2015 Ohio App. LEXIS 3595 (Ohio Ct. App., Champaign County 2015).

Trial court did not commit plain error in imposing separate sentences for complicity to breaking and entering and complicity to theft because it could have inferred that he aided and abetted in the commission of breaking and entering, which resulted in damage to the store, and then aided and abetted in the commission of theft, which was the removal of the cartons of cigarettes from the store. State v. Harless, 2015-Ohio-4753, 2015 Ohio App. LEXIS 4658 (Ohio Ct. App., Ashland County 2015).

Defendant's three grand theft convictions did not merge because each act was separate and distinct since each charge included a different item stolen, one for stealing the utility truck, one for the dump truck, and the third for the stolen tools. Although defendant did not personally drive the red dump truck away from the business, he was complicit in its theft and the evidence supported the conclusion that he had organized the break in and thefts, that he had helped recruit people for the task, that he had assisted in loading the dump truck with tools, and that he helped the driver of the dump truck, after the driver had driven a short distance, to activate the headlights on the truck. State v. Choate, 2015-Ohio-4972, 2015 Ohio App. LEXIS 4809 (Ohio Ct. App., Summit County 2015).

Defendant's grand theft offenses did not merge with other offenses, as defendant's act of fabricating the work orders for his employer without authorization was separate from the act of receiving the brass supplies and reselling them at a local recycling center. State v. Russell, 2015-Ohio-2802, 2015 Ohio App. LEXIS 2716 (Ohio Ct. App., Lucas County 2015).

Defendant's convictions for solicitation fraud and theft, which arose from his fund-raising activities on behalf of a purported veteran's organization, were properly not merged for sentencing because they were not allied offenses of similar import, as the fraud constituted a sufficiently distinct act from the purposeful obtention of others' property that was part of the theft. State v. Hargrove, 2014-Ohio-1919, 2014 Ohio App. LEXIS 1867 (Ohio Ct. App., Franklin County 2014).

Evidence supported defendant's conviction for theft, as defendant and his co-defendants made plans to travel to various shopping areas, enter restaurants, and steal wallets from purses located near the back of chairs while the victim of the theft ate at the restaurant; the evidence demonstrated that defendant aided and abetted his co-defendants in the utilization of the stolen credit cards and all three received stolen property as a result of the transactions. State v. Mack, 2014-Ohio-4552, 2014 Ohio App. LEXIS 4457 (Ohio Ct. App., Delaware County 2014).

Defendant's conviction for petty theft was supported by sufficient evidence based on security camera footage of defendant and her sister as they went through a store, unpaid items in a bag after they left the store, and defendant's sister's admission that they were "stealing" from the store. State v. Poore, 2014-Ohio-3089, 2014 Ohio App. LEXIS 3022 (Ohio Ct. App., Wayne County 2014).

Evidence that defendant was authorized to remove the vehicle from the car dealership for 10 to 15 minutes to complete a test drive and that defendant failed to return the vehicle in the allotted time, the whereabouts of the vehicle were unknown until the vehicle was located five days later in a high crime area with the keys in the center console, and defendant did not inform the dealership of the vehicle's location supported defendant's conviction for theft of a motor vehicle. State v. Jackson, 2014-Ohio-3779, 2014 Ohio App. LEXIS 3711 (Ohio Ct. App., Butler County 2014).

Evidence that defendant was authorized to remove the vehicle from the car dealership for 10 to 15 minutes to complete a test drive and that defendant failed to return the vehicle in the allotted time, the whereabouts of the vehicle were unknown until the vehicle was located five days later in a high crime area with the keys in the center console, and defendant did not inform the dealership of the vehicle's location supported defendant's conviction for theft of a motor vehicle. State v. Jackson, 2014-Ohio-3779, 2014 Ohio App. LEXIS 3711 (Ohio Ct. App., Butler County 2014).

Since defendant presented a complete defense to the charge of theft of a motor vehicle, he was not entitled to a jury instruction on the lesser included offense of unauthorized use of a motor vehicle. State v. Jackson, 2014-Ohio-3779, 2014 Ohio App. LEXIS 3711 (Ohio Ct. App., Butler County 2014).

Sentence of 17 months was supported by consideration of factors in R.C. 2929.12, finding defendant was not amenable to community control, and fact that sentence was within the statutory range. State v. Jackson, 2014-Ohio-3779, 2014 Ohio App. LEXIS 3711 (Ohio Ct. App., Butler County 2014).

Sufficient evidence supported defendant's felony theft conviction because the State presented some evidence that the cost to replace the stolen property equaled or exceeded $1,000. The owner of the property testified that it would cost $1,000 to replace the plumbing stolen from the home and that the additional repairs to fix all the damage totaled over $3,500. State v. Washington, 2014-Ohio-4578, 2014 Ohio App. LEXIS 4476 (Ohio Ct. App., Cuyahoga County 2014).

Defendant's burglary offenses did not merge with each other or with the breaking and entering, vandalism, or theft offenses because once defendant entered the structure with an intent to commit a crime inside, the crime of burglary was complete and any crimes actually committed once defendant gained access were committed with separate conduct. Because the theft and vandalism acts themselves were not actually necessary to committing the burglary and breaking and entering crimes, it could not be said that the same conduct resulted in the commission of multiple crimes. State v. Washington, 2014-Ohio-4578, 2014 Ohio App. LEXIS 4476 (Ohio Ct. App., Cuyahoga County 2014).

There was no error in the failure to merge defendant's convictions for theft and forgery because they may have been part of a single course of conduct, but the conduct constituted multiple criminal acts, as the theft consisted of obtaining another's property and the forgery consisted of fabricating or creating spurious documents. State v. Smith, 2014-Ohio-5076, 2014 Ohio App. LEXIS 4952 (Ohio Ct. App., Geauga County 2014).

When defendant was convicted of theft and receiving stolen property, it was error not to merge the convictions for sentencing purposes because the crimes were allied offenses of similar import. State v. Schuttinger, 2013-Ohio-5793, 2013 Ohio App. LEXIS 6088 (Ohio Ct. App., Franklin County 2013).

Trial court erred by not conducting a Johnson conduct analysis to determine if defendant's convictions for extortion, burglary, and theft from the elderly, were allied offenses of similar import. Although the question was minimally discussed at sentencing, it appeared that the trial court relied upon the State's representation that the offenses were separate and there were insufficient facts in the record for the appellate court to make an allied offense determination. State v. Woolum, 2013-Ohio-5611, 2013 Ohio App. LEXIS 5866 (Ohio Ct. App., Athens County 2013).

Defendant's convictions for grand theft and tampering with government records were not required to be merged because, although they were similar offenses, they were committed at separate times. Defendant's conduct in signing the contracts and invoices was significantly separated in time from his conduct in receiving and cashing the checks from the county. State v. Trammell, 2013-Ohio-4615, 3 N.E.3d 260, 2013 Ohio App. LEXIS 4835 (Ohio Ct. App., Montgomery County 2013).

Trial court committed an obvious error when it failed to merge defendant's convictions for theft and burglary because they constituted allied offenses of similar import. It was clear that he committed the offenses as part of a single act and had the same animus for both crimes, i.e., to steal the victims' property while they were at a funeral. State v. Carsey, 2013-Ohio-4482, 2013 Ohio App. LEXIS 4709 (Ohio Ct. App., Athens County 2013).

Counsel was not ineffective for failing to argue merger of the remaining counts because defendant committed identity fraud, telecommunications fraud, and aggravated theft through separate and distinct conduct. Defendant made numerous telephone calls to two companies, utilized his father's personal information with the purpose to obtain disbursements from his father's annuities, signed his father's name to cause the monies to be dispersed and, then, after moving the funds between two banks, he withdrew and subsequently spent a large portion of the funds ($182,000) from the annuities. State v. Haney, 2013-Ohio-2823, 2013 Ohio App. LEXIS 2875 (Ohio Ct. App., Lake County 2013).

Because the offenses of grand theft and safecracking were allied offenses subject to merger, counsel was ineffective in failing to investigate and argue that those offenses should have been merged under R.C. 2941.25. The inmate's act of tampering with the safe and strong boxes by removing them was committed with the same act and animus as exerting control over the contents therein; his purpose in removing the safe was so that he could subsequently break into the safe, therefore exercising dominion and control over any potential valuables. State v. Newman, 2013-Ohio-2053, 2013 Ohio App. LEXIS 1948 (Ohio Ct. App., Fayette County 2013).

Because it was possible to commit the offenses of safecracking and grand theft with the same conduct, as a defendant who tampered with a safe, such as removing a safe from the owner's house, was also exerting control over the safe's contents without the consent of the owner, with the purpose to deprive the owner of his or her property, and there was no evidence that defendant committed the offenses with a separate animus as there was no evidence that he knew guns were inside the safe or that he opened the safe and removed the guns from the safe, defendant should not have been sentenced for both safecracking and grand theft. State v. Richardson, 2013-Ohio-1953, 2013 Ohio App. LEXIS 1834 (Ohio Ct. App., Clermont County 2013).

Defendant was properly convicted of and sentenced upon both robbery and felonious assault because defendant entered the car and put the knife to one victim's neck to force her to give up her money and personal items, and then continued to hold the knife against her neck to subdue her, to the extent that she tried to push it away, seriously cutting herself and slicing nerves in her hand. However, robbery and theft were allied offenses of similar import pursuant to R.C. 2941.25 under the circumstances, and should have merged for sentencing. State v. Boyd, 2013-Ohio-1333, 2013 Ohio App. LEXIS 1263 (Ohio Ct. App., Richland County 2013).

Defendant's theft and forgery were allied offenses of similar conduct, under R.C. 2941.25, because they occurred simultaneously, as a result of the same conduct, and arose from the same animus. Defendant committed the crime when he presented the check at the bank and received, in return, $300 of the victim's money; the passing (or "uttering") of the check was the forgery offense and his receipt of money was the theft offense. State v. Taylor, 2013-Ohio-472, 2013 Ohio App. LEXIS 409 (Ohio Ct. App., Hocking County 2013).

Defendant's possession of criminal tools under R.C. 2923.24 and theft under R.C. 2913.02(A)(1) offenses were allied offenses of similar import under R.C. 2941.25 as the only objects found on defendant were a flashlight and a wrench; the flashlight was undoubtedly used to locate the items to steal, and the wrench could have been used to disassemble the radiator, which was removed in pieces. State v. Ballard, 2013-Ohio-373, 2013 Ohio App. LEXIS 321 (Ohio Ct. App., Cuyahoga County 2013).

Defendant's theft offense under R.C. 2913.02(A)(1) and breaking and entering offense under R.C. 2911.13(A) were not allied offenses of similar import under R.C. 2941.25 as the offenses could not be committed with the same conduct since once defendant forced his way into the school with the purpose to steal scrap metal, the breaking and entering was complete; the theft was completed after he took control of the scrap metal with the purpose to deprive the owner of the scrap without the owner's consent, which was after the breaking and entering was complete. State v. Ballard, 2013-Ohio-373, 2013 Ohio App. LEXIS 321 (Ohio Ct. App., Cuyahoga County 2013).



Receiving stolen property and grand theft were allied offenses of similar import under R.C. 2941.25 because it was possible to commit theft and receiving stolen property with the same conduct and the counts both related to the principal offender's act of stealing guns from one residence. State v. Haller, 2012-Ohio-5233, 2012 Ohio App. LEXIS 4583 (Ohio Ct. App., Allen County 2012).

Complicity to commit burglary and grand theft were not committed with the same conduct, i.e., a single act, and therefore are not allied offenses because the principal offender testified that after the residents left the residence he broke in and proceeded to ransack the residence taking weapons, games, and movies. Thus, the burglary was complete upon entering the residence; it was not until the principal offender exerted control over the victim's guns, an act which undoubtedly occurred apart from the unlawful entry into the residence, that he committed grand theft. State v. Haller, 2012-Ohio-5233, 2012 Ohio App. LEXIS 4583 (Ohio Ct. App., Allen County 2012).

Nothing in the record supported defendant's assertion that in committing the unauthorized use of a vehicle, and in taking money, he committed a single act with a single state of mind, rather, it was clear that defendant took the car to purchase drugs with the victim's money. Furthermore, nothing supported a conclusion that the wallet containing cash was attached to the car keys, nor a finding that the theft of the cash and misuse of the vehicle were accomplished by the same conduct; thus, those offenses did not constitute allied offenses of similar import. State v. Robinson, 2012-Ohio-4976, 2012 Ohio App. LEXIS 4352 (Ohio Ct. App., Champaign County 2012).

Because defendant's breaking and entering, in violation of R.C. 2911.13(A) was complete before defendant stole the furniture at issue, in violation of R.C. 2913.02(A)(1), the two offenses were committed separately for purposes of R.C. 2941.25(B), notwithstanding their proximity in time and that one was committed in order to commit the other. State v. Sludder, 2012-Ohio-4014, 2012 Ohio App. LEXIS 3530 (Ohio Ct. App., Allen County 2012).

Trial court erred in failing to merge defendant's theft and robbery convictions into a single count for conviction prior to sentencing because the two offenses were committed by a single conduct with a single state of mind, involving a single victim. Defendant's taking merchandise without payment and using his upper body to push his way out of the store to prevent detainment by the store's employee was a single transaction with a single intention, to leave the store with unpaid merchandise; thus, the offenses were allied offenses of similar import under R.C. 2941.25 and should have been merged. State v. Muncy, 2012-Ohio-2830, 2012 Ohio App. LEXIS 2481 (Ohio Ct. App., Ashtabula County 2012).

Trial court properly sentenced defendant on both breaking and entering and theft because the circumstances surrounding the crimes, i.e., the length of time involved between the breaking and entry into the vehicle and the theft of the particular property therein, indicated that he had a separate animus for each crime. State v. Rogers, 2012-Ohio-2496, 2012 Ohio App. LEXIS 2191 (Ohio Ct. App., Cuyahoga County 2012).

Burglary and the grand theft committed should have been merged because they constituted the same conduct and/or a single act. However, receiving stolen property stood independent of the burglary/grand theft convictions because defendant's intention in depriving the victim of the guns (revenge) was distinguishable to his intention in selling the guns (profit) and the receiving and retention of the victim's guns associated with the burglary/grand theft was a distinct act, occurring in a different time and a different place, from the disposing of the guns by sale to defendant's brother. State v. Green, 2012-Ohio-2355, 2012 Ohio App. LEXIS 2081 (Ohio Ct. App., Lake County 2012).

State conceded that the charges associated with the burglary of the second victims' home should have been merged at sentencing with possessing criminal tools and petty theft. State v. Green, 2012-Ohio-2355, 2012 Ohio App. LEXIS 2081 (Ohio Ct. App., Lake County 2012).

Trial court erred by sentencing defendant on both offenses; because the conduct that qualified as the complicity to burglary also qualified as the theft they were allied offenses of similar import. Defendant's act of picking up and driving the principal offenders after the burglary constituted a single act with a single state of mind. State v. Congrove, 2012-Ohio-1159, 2012 Ohio App. LEXIS 1019 (Ohio Ct. App., Morrow County 2012).

Trial court should have merged defendant's burglary and theft convictions under R.C. 2941.25 as the charges stemmed from defendant's conduct of entering a garage to steal the items inside. Defendant committed both offenses through a single course of conduct and with a single state of mind; therefore, the charges were allied offenses and should have been merged. State v. James, 2012-Ohio-966, 2012 Ohio App. LEXIS 849 (Ohio Ct. App., Delaware County 2012).

Trial court erred by convicting and sentencing defendant on all of the charges because the offense of grand theft by deception under R.C. 2913.02(A)(3), carried out by way of a continuing course of conduct, and the offenses of three counts of passing bad checks under R.C. 2913.11 were allied offenses of similar import. Passing bad checks could have resulted in grand theft by deception, and the offense of grand theft by deception, carried out by way of a continuing course of conduct, was committed at the same time as, rather than separately from, the three offenses of passing bad checks. State v. Snyder, 2011-Ohio-6346, 2011 Ohio App. LEXIS 5216 (Ohio Ct. App., Butler County 2011), dismissed, 2012-Ohio-819, 131 Ohio St. 3d 1468, 962 N.E.2d 800, 2012 Ohio LEXIS 550 (Ohio 2012).

Trial court should have merged the offenses of theft and robbery under R.C. 2941.25 because defendant committed the acts against the same victim at the same time and with the same conduct. Defendant engaged in a single act with a single state of mind. State v. White, 2011-Ohio-5835, 2011 Ohio App. LEXIS 4741 (Ohio Ct. App., Cuyahoga County 2011).

Trial court did not err by not merging the convictions for forgery and theft of mortgage proceeds because the offenses were committed separately and with a separate animus. The forgery conviction stemmed from defendant's fraudulent creation of the 2002 purchase agreement, while his theft conviction stemmed from his obtaining a mortgage to which he was not entitled in 2004. State v. Rhodehamel, 2011-Ohio-5618, 2011 Ohio App. LEXIS 4595 (Ohio Ct. App., Franklin County 2011).

Because there was only one victim and one single continuous transaction, the trial court erred in not merging the kidnapping, aggravated robbery, and the theft charges. Defendant held the victim at gunpoint with the single purpose to rob him; the resultant kidnapping, aggravated robbery, and theft were all part of a single transaction with a single intention, to relieve the victim of his watch, ring, cell phone, and money. State v. Cook, 2011-Ohio-5156, 2011 Ohio App. LEXIS 4258 (Ohio Ct. App., Cuyahoga County 2011).

Because defendant's conviction for theft was not based on the same conduct as his aggravated burglary and robbery convictions, the theft offense was not an allied offense of similar import. The offenses of aggravated burglary and robbery were complete at the time the victim escaped from the residence; the theft offense was committed separately, at a different time than the aggravated burglary and robbery offenses, as well as in a different location, the upstairs bedroom versus the kitchen. State v. Wright, 2011-Ohio-4874, 2011 Ohio App. LEXIS 3965 (Ohio Ct. App., Montgomery County 2011).

Aggravated burglary and grand theft counts should have been merged because the theft of firearms and money was the purpose and grand incidence of the burglary, and only those items were taken from the residence. State v. Ruby, 2011-Ohio-4864, 2011 Ohio App. LEXIS 4010 (Ohio Ct. App., Sandusky County 2011).

Trial court did not err in not merging the sentences for the counts of theft of a firearm by deception and tampering with evidence because he committed separate and distinct crimes for which he had a separate animus. The animus for the tampering with records charge occurred when he manipulated the sales records to show cancelled class registrations followed by deposits made to his lay away account and the animus for the theft of a firearm by deception charge occurred when he physically removed the firearm from the premises. State v. Leach, 2011-Ohio-4745, 195 Ohio App. 3d 433, 960 N.E.2d 531, 2011 Ohio App. LEXIS 3921 (Ohio Ct. App., Delaware County 2011).

Failing to merge the aggravated robbery and grand theft convictions in the grocery store robbery was plain error because they were allied offenses of similar import. Defendant broke into the store, stealing $10,000, after ordering two employees to open the store safe at gunpoint, then fled in one of their vehicles. State v. Ayers, 2011-Ohio-4719, 2011 Ohio App. LEXIS 3919 (Ohio Ct. App., Warren County 2011).

Although the offenses of breaking and entering and grand theft were "intertwined" insomuch as it was necessary for defendant to break into the jewelry store before he could make off with the jewels, because the conduct required to commit one of the offenses would never result in the commission of the other, the trial court did not err by failing to merge these offenses for sentencing purposes. State v. Ayers, 2011-Ohio-4719, 2011 Ohio App. LEXIS 3919 (Ohio Ct. App., Warren County 2011).

Pursuant to R.C. 2941.25, a trial court should have merged the offenses of burglary, theft, and receiving stolen property because defendant committed all three crimes with a single act when he trespassed in a residence with the intent to steal a television, stole the television, and retained it. State v. Blackburn, 2011-Ohio-4624, 2011 Ohio App. LEXIS 3826 (Ohio Ct. App., Pickaway County 2011).

Considering defendant's conduct, the offenses of receiving stolen property and theft were allied offenses because each of the charges of receiving stolen property related to an item or items of property charged in the theft offenses. Having stolen the items, defendant also "received" the items within the definition of R.C. 2913.51 and, thus, he could not be sentenced separately on each count of theft and each count of receiving stolen property. State v. Fannin, 2011-Ohio-3211, 2011 Ohio App. LEXIS 2702 (Ohio Ct. App., Delaware County 2011).

Charges of aggravated robbery, aggravated burglary, and grand theft were allied offenses of similar import because all of the charges stemmed from defendant's conduct of entering the bank to conduct a robbery, threatening the employees with a firearm, demanding money, and leaving the bank with $8,218. The three counts should have been merged prior to sentencing. State v. Bridgeman, 2011-Ohio-2680, 2011 Ohio App. LEXIS 2291 (Ohio Ct. App., Champaign County 2011).

Trial court should have merged the robbery and theft convictions for sentencing because it was possible to commit the offenses of robbery and theft with the same conduct and the robbery and theft both stemmed from defendant having shoplifted the same items from the grocery store. State v. Jones, 2011-Ohio-2306, 2011 Ohio App. LEXIS 1969 (Ohio Ct. App., Licking County 2011).

Because the State conceded that robbery and theft constituted allied offenses of similar import under R.C. 2941.25, a determination by the trial court was needed as to whether defendant committed the offenses with a separate animus. State v. Reives-Bey, 2011-Ohio-1778, 2011 Ohio App. LEXIS 1539 (Ohio Ct. App., Summit County 2011).

Defendant's convictions for receiving stolen property and theft were allied offenses of similar import and should have merged for the purposes of sentencing because both offenses were committed by the same conduct. It was apparent from the testimony adduced at trial that the State relied on the same occurrence and the same conduct to convict defendant of both offenses. State v. Washington, 2011-Ohio-1149, 2011 Ohio App. LEXIS 985 (Ohio Ct. App., Lorain County 2011).

Because the commission of aggravated robbery necessarily resulted in the commission of theft, they were allied offenses of similar import. The crimes were not committed separately or with a separate animus because defendant entered a convenience store with an accomplice and demanded money from the store clerk at gun point; thus, the commission of the theft was subsumed within the commission of the aggravated robbery. State v. Washington, 2010-Ohio-3389, 2010 Ohio App. LEXIS 2908 (Ohio Ct. App., Summit County 2010).

Defendant's convictions for theft and breaking and entering, in violation of R.C. 2913.02(A)(1) and 2911.13(A), were not allied offenses of similar import under R.C. 2941.25, as one could commit a breaking and entering without committing a theft, as the purpose to commit any felony was sufficient, and similarly, one did not have to commit a breaking and entering to commit a theft; sentences imposed on defendant for both crimes were accordingly proper. State v. Raleigh, 2010-Ohio-2966, 2010 Ohio App. LEXIS 2457 (Ohio Ct. App., Clermont County 2010).

Defendant's convictions for theft and receiving stolen property, in violation of R.C. 2913.02(A)(1) and 2913.51(A), were allied offenses of similar import under R.C. 2941.25, as a theft was necessary in order to commit the offense of receiving stolen property, and the crimes were committed with a single animus; sentences imposed on defendant for both crimes were accordingly improper. State v. Raleigh, 2010-Ohio-2966, 2010 Ohio App. LEXIS 2457 (Ohio Ct. App., Clermont County 2010).

Under R.C. 2941.25, the offenses of theft and receiving stolen property were allied offenses of similar import because they were so similar that the commission of one offense would have necessarily resulted in the commission of the other offense. The merger analysis applied where defendant was convicted of stealing and receiving the same property. State v. Slager, 2010-Ohio-1797, 2010 Ohio App. LEXIS 1494 (Ohio Ct. App., Delaware County 2010).

Defendant's convictions for two counts of theft, in violation of R.C. 2913.02(A)(1), were not considered allied offenses of similar import under R.C. 2941.25 because the offenses were committed separately and with a separate animus, as different checks were involved in the commission of each crime. Defendant stole two social security checks made payable to the recipient from the home of the recipient, and then endorsed the recipient's name on both checks and also endorsed the checks with defendant's own name. State v. Bowlin, 2010-Ohio-1635, 2010 Ohio App. LEXIS 1358 (Ohio Ct. App., Butler County 2010).

Trial court committed plain error under Crim.R. 52(B) in failing to merge defendant's sentences for theft, in violation of R.C. 2913.02(A)(1), and receiving stolen property, in violation of R.C. 2913.51(A), because they were offenses of similar import under R.C. 2941.25. Defendant stole two social security checks made payable to the recipient from the home of the recipient, and then endorsed the recipient's name on both checks and also endorsed the checks with defendant's own name. State v. Bowlin, 2010-Ohio-1635, 2010 Ohio App. LEXIS 1358 (Ohio Ct. App., Butler County 2010).

When the owner of a title insurance agency withdrew funds from the agency's escrow accounts and deposited those funds into the agency's operating account, the owner's convictions for aggravated theft, under R.C. 2913.02(A)(2), money laundering, under R.C. 1315.55(A)(1) and (3), and engaging in a pattern of corrupt activity, under R.C. 2923.32(A)(1), did not merge for sentencing purposes because (1) aggravated theft and money laundering were not allied offenses of similar import, as aggravated theft required proof that an individual deprived an owner of property or services, in conjunction with obtaining or exerting control over the property beyond the express or implied consent of the owner, while neither money laundering statute contained those elements, (2) the two money laundering convictions were not allied offenses of similar import, as R.C. 1315.55(A)(1) required that an individual conduct a transaction knowing that the property involved was proceeds from some other unlawful activity, while R.C. 1315.55(A)(3) did not require that the transaction involve proceeds from an unlawful activity, and (3) the aggravated theft and money laundering convictions did not merge with the corrupt activity conviction as commission of engaging in a pattern of corrupt activity did not necessarily result in the commission of aggravated theft or money laundering, since a conviction for engaging in a pattern of corrupt activity could be based on two or more violations of numerous other criminal statutes, under R.C. 2923.31(I). State v. Clayton, 2009-Ohio-7040, 2009 Ohio App. LEXIS 5897 (Ohio Ct. App., Montgomery County 2009).

Although money laundering requires proceeds from an unlawful activity, that activity need not be a theft; therefore, the elements of money laundering and theft did not correspond to such a degree that the commission of one crime resulted in the commission of the other. As a result, the offenses were not allied offenses of similar import under R.C. 2941.25(A). State v. Noe, 2009-Ohio-6978, 2009 Ohio App. LEXIS 5825 (Ohio Ct. App., Lucas County 2009).

Trial court did not commit plain error by sentencing defendant to multiple sentences because the offenses of burglary and attempted grand theft of a motor vehicle were not allied offenses of similar import since the two offenses were not committed at the same time. The offense of burglary was complete at the time that defendant entered into the structure, and the theft offense was not necessary for the burglary conviction because the purpose to commit "any" criminal offense was sufficient; the attempted theft offense was complete when defendant attempted to exert control over the motor vehicle. State v. Fedele, 2009-Ohio-1916, 2009 Ohio App. LEXIS 1634 (Ohio Ct. App., Van Wert County 2009).

Trial court committed plain error when it failed to merge defendant's theft, under R.C. 2913.02(A)(1), and robbery, under R.C. 2911.02(A)(2), convictions pursuant to R.C. 2941.25 because they were allied offenses of similar import. Defense counsel was also ineffective for failing to object to the multiple sentences. State v. Curtis, 2009-Ohio-6740, 2009 Ohio App. LEXIS 5643 (Ohio Ct. App., Brown County 2009).

Defendant's forgery offenses did not merge with the theft offense, and the trial court did not commit error, let alone plain error, by separately convicting and sentencing defendant for forgery and theft. Forgery did not involve exerting control over property without the consent of the owner and theft did not involve a fraudulent writing. State v. Anderson, 2009-Ohio-6566, 2009 Ohio App. LEXIS 5514 (Ohio Ct. App., Franklin County 2009), aff'd, 2011-Ohio-228, 128 Ohio St. 3d 234, 943 N.E.2d 534, 2011 Ohio LEXIS 166 (Ohio 2011), writ denied, 2012-Ohio-3773, 2012 Ohio App. LEXIS 3332 (Ohio Ct. App., Franklin County 2012).

While defendant could have been properly charged with both theft by deception and workers' compensation fraud, the convictions had to merge such that defendant could only be sentenced for one offense. The charges arose from the same nucleus of facts and were committed with a single animus. State v. Urich-Feckler, 2009-Ohio-5965, 2009 Ohio App. LEXIS 5014 (Ohio Ct. App., Cuyahoga County 2009).

State presented evidence that defendant committed two separate acts when she aided and abetted theft and obstructed justice because the distraction of the store clerk while her accomplice removed the cartons of cigarettes from the storeroom completed the aiding and abetting theft offense and then defendant provided transportation to the accomplice in order to hinder the discovery, apprehension, prosecution, conviction or punishment of the accomplice. However, although receiving was technically not an included offense of theft, it was, under R.C. 2941.25, an allied offense of similar import; defendant's possession of the cigarettes was coincidental to her participation in the theft of the cigarettes. State v. Tubbs, 2009-Ohio-3263, 2009 Ohio App. LEXIS 2805 (Ohio Ct. App., Richland County 2009).

As defendant's commission of robbery, in violation of R.C. 2911.02(A)(3), necessarily included commission of theft, in violation of R.C. 2913.02(A)(1), the crimes were allied offenses of similar import under R.C. 2941.25; they were committed at the same time and with the same animus, such that it was error to convict defendant of two separate crimes. State v. Smith, 2009-Ohio-3258, 2009 Ohio App. LEXIS 2850 (Ohio Ct. App., Hamilton County 2009).

Because robbery and theft constituted allied offenses of similar import, and since defendant's conduct in the bank involved a single animus and a single course of conduct, the two convictions should have been merged for sentencing purposes under R.C. 2941.25(A). State v. Eckert, 2009-Ohio-3312, 2009 Ohio App. LEXIS 2837 (Ohio Ct. App., Clermont County 2009).

When defendant pled guilty to engaging in a pattern of corrupt activity, under R.C. 2923.32(A)(1), aggravated theft by deception, under R.C. 2913.02(A)(3), forgery, under R.C. 2913.31(A)(3), and tampering with records, under R.C. 2913.42(A)(2), defendant did not receive ineffective assistance of counsel when counsel did not advise defendant that the crimes to which defendant pled guilty were allied offenses of similar import because the crimes were not such offenses, as, viewed abstractly, committing one of the crimes did not necessarily result in committing one or more of the other crimes. State v. Edwards, 2009-Ohio-1408, 2009 Ohio App. LEXIS 1179 (Ohio Ct. App., Montgomery County 2009).

Theft by deception, forgery, and record tampering are not allied offenses of similar import because, comparing the elements of these offenses in the abstract, it was apparent that commission of one of them will not necessarily result in commission of another. Because a defendant need not engage in theft, forgery, or record tampering to commit the offense of engaging in a pattern of corrupt activity and vice versa, the crimes are not allied offenses of similar import. State v. Musselman, 2009-Ohio-424, 2009 Ohio App. LEXIS 348 (Ohio Ct. App., Montgomery County 2009).

Defendant's convictions for burglary and theft, in violation of R.C. 2911.12(A)(2), (3), and 2913.02(A)(1), were not allied offenses of similar import under R.C. 2941.25(A), as commission of one offense did not necessarily result in commission of the other offense. State v. Appenzeller, 2008-Ohio-7005, 2008 Ohio App. LEXIS 5889 (Ohio Ct. App., Lake County 2008).

Defendant was properly convicted of and sentenced for both telecommunications fraud, under R.C. 2913.05(A), and grand theft by deception, under R.C. 2913.02(A)(3), because, under R.C. 2941.25(A), the crimes were not allied offenses of similar import, as, comparing the elements of the crimes objectively, commission of one of the offenses did not necessarily include the commission of the other. State v. West, 2008-Ohio-368, 2008 Ohio App. LEXIS 326 (Ohio Ct. App., Wood County 2008).

Defendant's convictions for theft and forgery, in violation of R.C. 2913.02(A)(2) and 2913.31(A)(2), were not allied offenses of similar import, as the commission of one did not result in the commission of the other; the act of forgery was a separate and distinct act from the theft. State v. Taylor, 2008-Ohio-3777, 2008 Ohio App. LEXIS 3205 (Ohio Ct. App., Delaware County 2008).

Defendant's consecutive sentences imposed upon his convictions for burglary and theft did not violate the Double Jeopardy Clause of Ohio Const. art. I, § 10 because the offenses were not similar and allied offenses, in that the elements of the crimes did not correspond to such a degree that commission of one crime resulted in the commission of other. The law set forth in Rance applied. State v. Church, 2007-Ohio-6759, 2007 Ohio App. LEXIS 5926 (Ohio Ct. App., Guernsey County 2007).

Upon resentencing, the sentence for aggravated theft (R.C. 2913.02(A)(1)) was properly not merged with the conspiracy offenses (R.C. 2923.01(A)(1)) because aggravated theft was not an allied offense of conspiracy. Thus, because the crimes involved were not so similar that commission of one would have resulted in the commission of the other, they were not allied offenses of similar import. State v. Payne, 2007-Ohio-6740, 2007 Ohio App. LEXIS 5898 (Ohio Ct. App., Lake County 2007).

Elements of theft by deception, under R.C. 2913.02(A)(3), and passing bad checks, under R.C. 2913.11, do not correspond to such a degree that the commission of one crime will result in the commission of the other because passing bad checks requires that a negotiable instrument, such as a money order, be transferred or presented for payment knowing that it will be dishonored, and theft by deception requires obtaining control over property with the purpose of depriving the owner of the property. State v. Wilson, 2007-Ohio-5187, 2007 Ohio App. LEXIS 4574 (Ohio Ct. App., Clermont County 2007).

Defendant's convictions for theft by deception, under R.C. 2913.02(A)(3), and passing bad checks, under R.C. 2913.11, did not merge for purposes of sentencing, under R.C. 2941.25(A), because (1) the elements of those crimes did not correspond to the degree that the commission of one resulted in the commission of the other, and (2) defendant committed the two crimes separately and with separate animus because defendant committed theft by deception when defendant deposited a counterfeit money order into defendant's account, and defendant committed passing bad checks when defendant withdrew money, based on this deposit, from defendant's account 21 days later. State v. Wilson, 2007-Ohio-5187, 2007 Ohio App. LEXIS 4574 (Ohio Ct. App., Clermont County 2007).

Under the plain error standard of review pursuant to Crim.R. 52(B) due to defendant's failure to raise the issue at the trial court level, there was no error in the trial court's imposition of sentences for defendant's convictions of aggravated robbery and theft by threat, in violation of R.C. 2911.01(A)(1) and 2913.02(A)(4), as they were not allied offenses of similar import under R.C. 2941.25; the elements of each offense did not correspond to such a degree with the elements of the other that the commission of one crime would result in the commission of the other. State v. Shields, 2007-Ohio-462, 2007 Ohio App. LEXIS 422 (Ohio Ct. App., Marion County 2007).

Trial court did not err by convicting defendant of multiple offenses under R.C. 2941.25(B) because, although defendant was convicted of 11 counts of six different offenses (felonious assault, theft, kidnapping, abduction, aggravated robbery, and robbery), he was convicted of no more than three counts of any one offense; the victim testified to at least three separate segments of defendant attacking her: inside the house, outside on the street, and in the alley. Also, the trial court found that defendant stole $6,000 in cash from the victim, attempted to steal the contents of the victim's safe, and assaulted the victim with his fists, elbow, a stun gun, pillow, and knife multiple times throughout the incident, showing separate times and manners of animus. State v. Loparo, 2007-Ohio-2783, 2007 Ohio App. LEXIS 2572 (Ohio Ct. App., Cuyahoga County 2007).

Aggravated robbery and grand theft were not allied offenses of similar import because defendant committed aggravated robbery by taking the victim's purse after he killed her and he committed grand theft after he left the house and drove off in the victim's car. Thus, defendant's theft of the victim's purse was committed separately from his theft of her car. State v. Elmore, 2006-Ohio-6207, 111 Ohio St. 3d 515, 857 N.E.2d 547, 2006 Ohio LEXIS 3415 (Ohio 2006), cert. denied, 551 U.S. 1133, 127 S. Ct. 2974, 168 L. Ed. 2d 707, 2007 U.S. LEXIS 7771 (U.S. 2007).

Burglary and theft were not allied offenses of similar import because, although the two offenses did have some common elements in that burglary could involve the purpose to commit a theft offense, completion of the theft offense was not a necessary element because the purpose to commit any felony would have sufficed to supply the requisite intent. State v. Gonzalez, 2006-Ohio-6276, 2006 Ohio App. LEXIS 6255 (Ohio Ct. App., Cuyahoga County 2006).

As commission of an aggravated robbery in violation of R.C. 2911.01(A)(1) and commission of theft by threat in violation of R.C. 2913.02(A)(4) could each be done without committing the other offense, the crimes were not allied offenses of similar import under R.C. 2941.25, and accordingly, there was no plain error under Crim.R. 52(B) in the trial court's conviction of defendant for both offenses. As defendant had entered his guilty plea to the offenses under Crim.R. 11(B)(1) and he had failed to raise an argument regarding whether they were allied offenses at the trial court level, the plain error standard of review was employed. State v. Gooden, 2006-Ohio-5387, 2006 Ohio App. LEXIS 5378 (Ohio Ct. App., Marion County 2006).

Trial court did not commit any error, let alone plain error, when it convicted and sentenced defendant for both theft, under R.C. 2913.02, and uttering, under R.C. 2913.31, because the elements of the two crimes did not correspond. Therefore, they were not allied offenses of similar import and merger was inappropriate under R.C. 2941.25(A). State v. Storey, 2006-Ohio-3498, 2006 Ohio App. LEXIS 3441 (Ohio Ct. App., Cuyahoga County 2006).

The elements of uttering and theft by deception do not correspond to such a degree that the commission of either offense would result in the commission of the other offense: State v. Griffiths, 1993 Ohio App. LEXIS 1997 (Ohio Ct. App., Cuyahoga County Apr. 8, 1993).

Theft in office (R.C. 2921.41) and grand theft (R.C. 2913.02) may be allied offenses of similar import within the meaning of R.C. 2941.25 if they are committed with the same animus as part of one plan to abscond with government funds: State v. McGhee, 37 Ohio App. 3d 54, 523 N.E.2d 864, 1987 Ohio App. LEXIS 10570 (Ohio Ct. App., Cuyahoga County 1987).

Pursuant to R.C. 2941.25, the offenses of breaking and entering, grand theft, and possessing criminal tools are not allied offenses of similar import inasmuch as these offenses have elements which do not correspond to such a degree that the commission of one offense will result in the commission of the other. Accordingly, inquiry into whether the crimes were committed with separate animus as to each is unnecessary (State v. Mitchell, 6 Ohio St. 3d 416, 453 N.E.2d 593, 1983 Ohio LEXIS 846 (Ohio 1983).

Because the key element of the offense of breaking and entering is the risk of harm to persons, while that of theft is merely the nonconsensual taking of property by whatever means, theft and breaking and entering are dissimilar crimes under R.C. 2941.25 for which a criminal defendant may be separately punished: State v. Dunihue, 20 Ohio App. 3d 210, 485 N.E.2d 764, 1984 Ohio App. LEXIS 12569 (Ohio Ct. App., Clinton County 1984).

Where a theft by deception offense was necessarily dependent upon evidence showing that a forgery offense was an integral part of the single transaction, the two offenses, when taken together under such circumstances, were "allied offenses of similar import," under R.C. 2941.25(A), for which the defendant could be convicted of only one: State v. Wolfe, 10 Ohio App. 3d 324, 462 N.E.2d 455, 1983 Ohio App. LEXIS 11179 (Ohio Ct. App., Montgomery County 1983).

Forgery and grand theft are not allied offenses of similar import because each crime contains an element not possessed by the other, and because one is not wholly incidental to the other: State v. Hunter, 12 Ohio App. 3d 75, 466 N.E.2d 183, 1983 Ohio App. LEXIS 11323 (Ohio Ct. App., Cuyahoga County 1983).

The elements of aggravated burglary, R.C. 2911.11(A), and theft, R.C. 2913.02(A), do not correspond to such a degree as to constitute allied offenses of similar import under R.C. 2941.25(A): State v. Mitchell, 6 Ohio St. 3d 416, 453 N.E.2d 593, 1983 Ohio LEXIS 846 (Ohio 1983).

Theft is an allied offense of similar import to aggravated robbery, but not to aggravated burglary: State v. Parson, 6 Ohio St. 3d 442, 453 N.E.2d 689, 1983 Ohio LEXIS 852 (Ohio 1983).

Under R.C. 2941.25(B), aggravated burglary and grand theft are offenses of "dissimilar import" where conviction of grand theft is predicated upon a prior theft conviction, involving independent conduct and a separate animus from the aggravated burglary conviction at issue: State v. Brown, 3 Ohio App. 3d 131, 443 N.E.2d 1382, 1981 Ohio App. LEXIS 11621 (Ohio Ct. App., Cuyahoga County 1981).

Where it is charged in separate counts that the defendant, with purpose to commit theft, knowingly entered, forced an entrance into, tampered with, or inserted any part of an instrument into any coin machine, in violation of R.C. 2911.32, and that upon entry, theft of money or property contained therein was consummated by the defendant, in violation of R.C. 2913.02, the offenses together constitute "allied offenses of similar import" as to which the defendant may be indicted for both offenses but convicted of only one: State v. Baer, 67 Ohio St. 2d 220, 21 Ohio Op. 3d 138, 423 N.E.2d 432, 1981 Ohio LEXIS 569 (Ohio 1981).

Petty theft and robbery arising out of a single incident constitute the same offense for purposes of double jeopardy because petty theft does not require proof of any element not required to be proved for a conviction for robbery: State v. Nelson, 51 Ohio App. 2d 31, 5 Ohio Op. 3d 158, 365 N.E.2d 1268, 1977 Ohio App. LEXIS 6917 (Ohio Ct. App., Cuyahoga County 1977).

Theft and safecracking are not necessarily similar offenses for purposes of R.C. 2945.59: State v. Snowden, 49 Ohio App. 2d 7, 3 Ohio Op. 3d 92, 359 N.E.2d 87, 1976 Ohio App. LEXIS 5799 (Ohio Ct. App., Clermont County 1976).

**Amendment of indictment**

Where defendant was charged with theft of drugs in violation of R.C. 2913.02(A)(3) and (B)(6), the trial court did not err by allowing the state to amend the indictments to include the language in R.C. 2913.02(A)(2), i.e., that she knowingly obtained the property beyond the scope of the expressed or implied consent of the owner or person authorized to give consent, as the amendment did not change the name or identity of the theft offense. State v. Rhodus, 2016-Ohio-7292, 71 N.E.3d 1250, 2016 Ohio App. LEXIS 4148 (Ohio Ct. App., Lucas County 2016).

Although defendant committed a fifth degree felony violation of R.C. 2913.02, as he pled guilty and was sentenced after R.C. 2913.02 was amended by H.B. 86, Gen. Assem. (Ohio) he was entitled to sentencing on a first degree misdemeanor. However, he was not entitled to amendment of the fifth degree felony conviction to a first degree misdemeanor. State v. Saplak, 2012-Ohio-4281, 2012 Ohio App. LEXIS 3756 (Ohio Ct. App., Cuyahoga County 2012).

Since R.C. 2945.74 and Crim.R. 31(C) permitted the jury to reach a verdict on an inferior degree of the indicted offense, it followed that the State could amend the indictment (grand theft) to charge defendant with an inferior degree of the originally indicted offense (theft). Accordingly, the amendment to the theft indictment charging defendant with an inferior degree of the original, indicted offense did not violate Crim.R. 7(D). State v. Washington, 2010-Ohio-3389, 2010 Ohio App. LEXIS 2908 (Ohio Ct. App., Summit County 2010).

There was sufficient evidence to establish that defendant acted both "without consent" and "beyond the scope of the consent given" in embezzling funds, such that the trial court did not err in allowing the State to amend the indictment under Crim.R. 7(D) from a charge against defendant of theft, in violation of R.C. 2913.02(A)(1), to a charge under § 2913.02(A)(2); defendant was not misled or prejudiced by the amendment, and it did not change the name or identity or the crime charged. State v. Taylor, 2008-Ohio-3777, 2008 Ohio App. LEXIS 3205 (Ohio Ct. App., Delaware County 2008).

Where the evidence presented at trial established a theft offense under R.C. 2913.02(A)(2) but the appellant was indicted, tried and convicted under R.C. 2913.02(A)(1), the appellant must be discharged since a reviewing court may not amend an indictment to conform to the evidence: State v. Burrows, 80 Ohio App. 3d 404, 609 N.E.2d 571, 1992 Ohio App. LEXIS 2633 (Ohio Ct. App., Cuyahoga County), dismissed, 65 Ohio St. 3d 1430, 600 N.E.2d 675, 1992 Ohio LEXIS 2555 (Ohio 1992).

**Amendment of statute**

Trial court erred in finding defendant guilty of theft as a felony of the fifth degree. Applying R.C. 2913.02(B), as amended by Am. Sub. H.B. 86, Gen. Assem. (Ohio 2011), he should have been convicted of a misdemeanor of the first degree because the value of the stolen property (less than $1,000) was only relevant when determining the penalty for the offense. State v. Cornett, 2013-Ohio-2367, 2013 Ohio App. LEXIS 2314 (Ohio Ct. App., Wood County 2013).

Because the elements of theft and the classification as a misdemeanor or felony are separated in discrete subsections within R.C. 2913.02, the value of the stolen property is only relevant when determining the penalty for the offense. Thus, an increase in the felony-threshold from $500 to $1,000 amounts to a reduction in penalty, triggering the application of R.C. 1.58(B). State v. Cornett, 2013-Ohio-2367, 2013 Ohio App. LEXIS 2314 (Ohio Ct. App., Wood County 2013).

**Asportation**

In a prosecution for theft under R.C. 2913.02, the least removing of an item with an intent to deprive the owner of it is a sufficient asportation, though the property is not removed from the premises of the owner nor retained in the possession of the defendant: State v. Williams, 16 Ohio App. 3d 232, 475 N.E.2d 168, 1984 Ohio App. LEXIS 12352 (Ohio Ct. App., Montgomery County 1984).

**Bad checks**

Defendant's convictions for complicity to commit grand larceny, under R.C. 2913.02(A)(3) and 2923.03, were not against the manifest weight of the evidence because witnesses testified they opened bank accounts at defendant's request, gave him their checkbooks after opening the accounts or signed the checks and then gave the checks to defendant, showing defendant acted with purpose to steal money from the banks by orchestrating the commission of a crime, i.e. a check cashing scheme. State v. Higgins, 2007-Ohio-1261, 2007 Ohio App. LEXIS 1168 (Ohio Ct. App., Summit County 2007).

Since the jury was entitled to infer that defendant committed theft and passed a bad check, as it was in the ideal position to weigh the evidence and judge the various witnesses' credibility, the evidence was sufficient to convict defendant where he deposited a bad check and then withdrew all of the funds at several locations shortly thereafter. State v. Robinson, 2005-Ohio-4795, 2005 Ohio App. LEXIS 4330 (Ohio Ct. App., Summit County 2005).

Not every theft involving writing of a bad check must be charged under R.C. 2913.11: State v. Cooper, 112 Ohio Misc. 2d 52, 753 N.E.2d 289, 2001 Ohio Misc. LEXIS 13 (Ohio C.P. 2001).

Where the defendant wrote bad checks to her son, who then deposited the checks into his bank account, she received bad checks from her son written on the same account into which he had previously deposited her bad checks, and she withdrew funds from a second account before the checks from her son had cleared, these actions evinced an intent to deprive the banks of funds which supported a conviction of theft under R.C. 2913.02(A)(3): State v. Linn, 2000 Ohio App. LEXIS 528 (Ohio Ct. App., Summit County Feb. 16, 2000), dismissed, 89 Ohio St. 3d 1426, 729 N.E.2d 1197, 2000 Ohio LEXIS 1516 (Ohio 2000).

**Bailments**

The essential elements necessary to support a conviction for a violation of this section [former R.C. 2907.39] (making the conversion of property by a bailee a crime), are venue, and that such bailee, with intent to defraud, sold, converted to his own use, destroyed or otherwise disposed of personal property of another, which came into his possession by pledge, bailment, deposit, or purchase on installment or otherwise: (decided under former analogous section) Cincinnati v. Young, 20 Ohio App. 2d 92, 49 Ohio Op. 2d 113, 252 N.E.2d 173, 1969 Ohio App. LEXIS 503 (Ohio Ct. App., Hamilton County 1969).

**Bankruptcy proceedings**

Debtor was not entitled to summary judgment on a claim of a violation of the automatic stay or of the discharge injunction when the debtor was prosecuted and convicted of a violation of R.C. 2913.02 and ordered to pay restitution to a union because the debtor had not established that the prosecutor acted with an improper motive or bad faith in proceeding with the charge against the debtor or that the prosecutor pursued the claim only so the union could recover amounts owed to it after the debtor filed for bankruptcy. Justen v. Ohio (In re Justen), 2007 Bankr. LEXIS 4096 (Bankr. N.D. Ohio Dec. 5, 2007).

In an adversary proceeding filed by a Chapter 7 debtor against a bank and a county prosecutor, a bankruptcy court erred by ruling that a criminal prosecution for theft by deception under R.C. 2913.02 and passing bad checks under R.C. 2913.11 violated the automatic bankruptcy stay because 11 U.S.C.S. § 362(b)(1) stated that the stay did not preclude criminal proceedings against a debtor; the court refused to graft a bad faith exception onto the plain language statute. Dovell v. The Guernsey Bank, 2007 U.S. Dist. LEXIS 58312 (S.D. Ohio Aug. 9, 2007), dismissed, 2007 U.S. Dist. LEXIS 58196 (S.D. Ohio Aug. 9, 2007), amended, 373 B.R. 533, 2007 U.S. Dist. LEXIS 59358 (S.D. Ohio 2007).

**—Excepted from automatic stay**

In an adversary proceeding filed by a Chapter 7 debtor against a bank and a county prosecutor, a bankruptcy court erred by ruling that a criminal prosecution for theft by deception under R.C. 2913.02 and passing bad checks under R.C. 2913.11 violated the automatic bankruptcy stay because 11 U.S.C.S. § 362(b)(1) stated that the stay did not preclude criminal proceedings against a debtor; the court refused to graft a bad faith exception onto the plain language statute. Dovell v. The Guernsey Bank, 2007 U.S. Dist. LEXIS 58312 (S.D. Ohio Aug. 9, 2007), dismissed, 2007 U.S. Dist. LEXIS 58196 (S.D. Ohio Aug. 9, 2007), amended, 373 B.R. 533, 2007 U.S. Dist. LEXIS 59358 (S.D. Ohio 2007).

**Basis for robbery offense**

Evidence was sufficient to support defendant's robbery convictions as the evidence showed that defendant committed a theft offense under R.C. 2913.02(A) when he took the victim's purse with the purpose of depriving her of that property, that defendant inflicted or attempted to inflict physical harm on the victim, and that several items from the victim's purse were found in defendant's car. The testimony of other witnesses in the store at the time of the attack corroborated the victim's story. State v. Brown, 2007-Ohio-6542, 2007 Ohio App. LEXIS 5733 (Ohio Ct. App., Franklin County 2007).

**Bill of information**

Language within the bill of information closely tracked the language, and the elements, set forth in the theft statute and sufficiently apprised defendant of the charges against which he had to defend. Even if the bill of information was insufficient, defendant could have requested an amendment by the state or a bill of particulars and his failure to do so precluded him from establishing prejudice. Ohio v. Oliver, 2021-Ohio-2543, 2021 Ohio App. LEXIS 2504 (Ohio Ct. App., Clermont County 2021).

**Blackmail**

A defendant may be guilty of blackmail because of a demand for certain money, accompanied by a threat to the well-being of a person's family, and also be guilty of larceny by trick because he obtained possession of the same money with the consent of the person from whom it was obtained which was induced by a false or fraudulent representation [see now (4) of this section]: (decided under former analogous section) State v. Wilkinson, 17 Ohio St. 2d 9, 46 Ohio Op. 2d 114, 244 N.E.2d 480, 1969 Ohio LEXIS 405 (Ohio), cert. denied, 395 U.S. 946, 89 S. Ct. 2020, 23 L. Ed. 2d 465, 1969 U.S. LEXIS 1400 (U.S. 1969).

**Civil damages**

In a fee dispute, the first attorney was entitled to summary judgment on his theft/embezzlement/conversion claims because the second attorney initially legally had possession of the funds, but despite a court order to turn a portion of them over for the first attorney's compensation, refused to do so. Dickson & Campbell, L.L.C. v. Marshall, 2017-Ohio-1032, 2017 Ohio App. LEXIS 1008 (Ohio Ct. App., Cuyahoga County 2017).

Borrowers' counterclaim for theft against a mortgage servicer should not have been dismissed because it appeared that the criminal theft offense could apply, based on the servicer's conduct regarding the parties' loan modification agreement, for purposes of the civil cause of action arising from a theft, and there was no statutory requirement that a criminal conviction occur. Citimortgage, Inc. v. Rudzik, 2014-Ohio-1472, 2014 Ohio App. LEXIS 1403 (Ohio Ct. App., Mahoning County 2014).

When a provider of legal services sued an attorney for retaining the provider's share of the attorney's fees, the provider was not entitled to summary judgment as to the provider's claim, under R.C. 2307.60(A) and 2307.61, of the attorney's theft by deception, under R.C. 2913.02(A)(3), because, as to the fees, the trial court did not find that the attorney knowingly obtained or exerted control over the fees by deception, and, despite the attorney's admission that the attorney failed to pay the disputed fees to the provider, a genuine issue of fact remained because this admission did not prove the requisite mens rea for theft by deception, as, rather, the evidence demonstrated that the attorney believed a fee dispute existed between the parties due to the attorney's allegations of nonperformance by the provider, not that the attorney knowingly retained the funds by deception. Estate Planning Legal Servs., P.C. v. Cox, 2008-Ohio-2258, 2008 Ohio App. LEXIS 1942 (Ohio Ct. App., Warren County 2008).

When a provider of legal services sued an attorney for retaining the provider's share of the attorney's fees, the provider was not entitled to summary judgment as to the provider's claim, under R.C. 2307.60(A) and 2307.61, of the attorney's theft by deception, under R.C. 2913.02(A)(3), because the provider claimed, on appeal, that the attorney's theft was of the provider's marketing services and documents, but the provider did not show that the attorney deceptively requested marketing or document services with the purpose to deprive the provider of property or services so as to entitle the provider to judgment as a matter of law. Estate Planning Legal Servs., P.C. v. Cox, 2008-Ohio-2258, 2008 Ohio App. LEXIS 1942 (Ohio Ct. App., Warren County 2008).

When a provider of legal services sued an attorney for retaining the provider's share of the attorney's fees, the provider was not entitled to summary judgment as to the provider's claim, under R.C. 2307.60(A) and 2307.61, of the attorney's theft by deception, under R.C. 2913.02(A)(3), because, as to the fees, the trial court did not find that the attorney knowingly obtained or exerted control over the fees by deception, and, despite the attorney's admission that the attorney failed to pay the disputed fees to the provider, a genuine issue of fact remained because this admission did not prove the requisite mens rea for theft by deception, as, rather, the evidence demonstrated that the attorney believed a fee dispute existed between the parties due to the attorney's allegations of nonperformance by the provider, not that the attorney knowingly retained the funds by deception. Estate Planning Legal Servs., P.C. v. Cox, 2008-Ohio-2258, 2008 Ohio App. LEXIS 1942 (Ohio Ct. App., Warren County 2008).

When a provider of legal services sued an attorney for retaining the provider's share of the attorney's fees, the provider was not entitled to summary judgment as to the provider's claim, under R.C. 2307.60(A) and 2307.61, of the attorney's theft by deception, under R.C. 2913.02(A)(3), because the provider claimed, on appeal, that the attorney's theft was of the provider's marketing services and documents, but the provider did not show that the attorney deceptively requested marketing or document services with the purpose to deprive the provider of property or services so as to entitle the provider to judgment as a matter of law. Estate Planning Legal Servs., P.C. v. Cox, 2008-Ohio-2258, 2008 Ohio App. LEXIS 1942 (Ohio Ct. App., Warren County 2008).

R.C. 2307.60 and 2307.61 did not require a store to prove that a customer committed a theft before sending the customer a demand letter as: (1) § 2307.61(G)(1) provided that an owner had a right to recover damages regardless of whether the accused pleaded guilty to or had been convicted of a theft, (2) the statute provided recourse to a successful defendant, so there was no need for the store to prove prior to sending the demand letter that the recipient of the letter committed a criminal act, and (3) the removal of the cat treats without payment was sufficient evidence of theft for the store to allege a criminal violation under R.C. 2913.02. Riley v. Supervalu Holdings, Inc., 2005-Ohio-6996, 2005 Ohio App. LEXIS 6318 (Ohio Ct. App., Hamilton County 2005).

**Classification**

Trial court erred by failing to amend defendant's information and should have reduced his theft conviction from a fifth-degree felony to a first-degree misdemeanor. The reforms in Am. Sub. H.B. 86, Gen. Assem. (Ohio 2011), with respect to R.C. 2913.02 and the reclassification of theft offenses, applied retroactively under the narrow exception present, whereby defendant was entitled to a reduced penalty or punishment as a result of the amendments because the terms "penalty" and "punishment" meant two different things for purposes of R.C. 1.58 State v. Cefalo, 2012-Ohio-5594, 2012 Ohio App. LEXIS 4881 (Ohio Ct. App., Lake County 2012), aff'd, 2014-Ohio-1174, 138 Ohio St. 3d 526, 8 N.E.3d 932, 2014 Ohio LEXIS 775 (Ohio 2014).

Defendant was incorrectly convicted of a misdemeanor by applying the amendments to R.C. 2913.02(A) that did not become effective until after the date of the offense, but under R.C. 1.58(B), the trial court correctly gave defendant the benefit of the decreased penalty that was instituted between the date of the offense and the date of the sentencing; the reversal on the limited issue of retroactive application of the amended statute did not affect defendant as he remained convicted of a first-degree misdemeanor under R.C. 2945.67(A). State v. Taylor, 2012-Ohio-5403, 2012 Ohio App. LEXIS 4689 (Ohio Ct. App., Summit County 2012), rev'd, 2014-Ohio-460, 138 Ohio St. 3d 194, 5 N.E.3d 612, 2014 Ohio LEXIS 254 (Ohio 2014).

Amendments to R.C. 2913.02(A) regarding classification do not apply to defendants who committed crimes before the effective date of the amendments, but under R.C. 1.58(B), defendants who have not yet been sentenced are to receive the benefit of the reduced penalty provisions; the amendments to R.C. 2913.02 are not retroactive. State v. Taylor, 2012-Ohio-5403, 2012 Ohio App. LEXIS 4689 (Ohio Ct. App., Summit County 2012), rev'd, 2014-Ohio-460, 138 Ohio St. 3d 194, 5 N.E.3d 612, 2014 Ohio LEXIS 254 (Ohio 2014).

Trial court's sentencing journal entry was in error to the extent it reflected that defendant was convicted of a first degree felony theft rather than a felony of the fourth degree as defendant obtained $8,196.89 of merchandise and R.C. 2913.02(B)(2) provided that if the value of the property or services stolen was $5,000 or more and was less than $100,000, a violation of the section was grand theft, a felony of the fourth degree. Accordingly, the matter was remanded to the trial court with instructions to correct the error to properly reflect defendant's conviction for a fourth degree felony theft. State v. Colon, 2010-Ohio-361, 2010 Ohio App. LEXIS 292 (Ohio Ct. App., Cuyahoga County 2010).

**Complicity**

Sufficient evidence supported defendant's conviction for complicity to theft because the evidence showed that defendant had entered the store with his friend, had watched to see if they were being observed, and had taken clothing without paying for it, and an officer testified that both defendant and the friend were apprehended together shortly after leaving the store and that stolen clothing items were found with them. The State proved all elements of the charged crime beyond a reasonable doubt, including that defendant had aided and abetted his friend in committing a theft offense. State v. Jones, 2018-Ohio-4754, 124 N.E.3d 439, 2018 Ohio App. LEXIS 5084 (Ohio Ct. App., Hamilton County 2018), aff'd, 2020-Ohio-3051, 160 Ohio St. 3d 314, 156 N.E.3d 872, 2020 Ohio LEXIS 1282 (Ohio 2020).

Sufficient evidence supported defendant's conviction for complicity to commit theft because, in opening the undisclosed out-of-state bank account, defendant aided and abetted his mother in committing theft. It could have been found that the account was opened in anticipation of a receiver being appointed in order to establish a hidden account that would be available to funnel money from the company's incoming receipts without the knowledge of the receiver. State v. Pellin, 2012-Ohio-5342, 2012 Ohio App. LEXIS 4650 (Ohio Ct. App., Mahoning County 2012).

Trial court erred when it found defendant guilty of petty theft, in violation of R.C. 2913.02(A)(1), because there was no showing, pursuant to R.C. 2923.03(A)(2), that defendant aided or abetted defendant's sibling in committing the offense while acting with the kind of culpability required under R.C. 2901.22(A) for the commission of the offense. The evidence did not show that defendant, when defendant helped defendant's sibling remove property from the basement of a duplex where the sibling had previously lived and left property behind, acted with the purpose or specific intent to deprive the people who were then tenants of the duplex of their property. State v. Chessman, 2012-Ohio-1427, 2012 Ohio App. LEXIS 1223 (Ohio Ct. App., Montgomery County 2012).

Defendant's theft conviction was supported by sufficient evidence; even though the complaint charged defendant with theft and not complicity to commit theft, the trial court was free to consider whether she was an aider and abettor because the evidence reasonably supported a finding of aiding and abetting. Defendant's actions were sufficient to establish that she was a complicitor to theft because she helped to select the stolen items, concealed evidence of the theft, acted as a lookout while her daughter stashed the stolen items in her purse, and, in general, provided companionship during the commission of the crime; the security officer's testimony demonstrated that defendant was not "merely present" with her daughter during the shoplifting. State v. Gorayeb, 2010-Ohio-2535, 2010 Ohio App. LEXIS 2070 (Ohio Ct. App., Belmont County 2010).

Evidence supported defendant's conviction for complicity to commit theft, as security camera footage from a store clearly depicted defendant carrying a bag the police later found in defendant's car into the store and handing it to another individual, who used it to commit a theft. State v. Chatman, 2010-Ohio-4652, 2010 Ohio App. LEXIS 3926 (Ohio Ct. App., Summit County 2010).

Despite the defendant's alleged intoxication and claim that he was only riding in the vehicle with the principal offender, there was sufficient evidence to support his convictions of complicity in the illegal possession of chemicals for manufacturing drugs and of complicity to theft: State v. Gragg, 2007-Ohio-4731, 173 Ohio App. 3d 270, 878 N.E.2d 55, 2007 Ohio App. LEXIS 4276 (Ohio Ct. App., Fayette County 2007).

There was sufficient evidence to support defendant's conviction for complicity to theft because the state presented evidence that defendant knowingly aided and abetted his friend in obtaining or exerting control over the anhydrous ammonia without the owner's consent and with purpose to deprive the owner of the substance. Although defendant claimed to have been heavily intoxicated throughout the night, he was able to remember that no one talked about stealing anhydrous ammonia and was able to direct the driver back to the friend's house after the theft; defendant also testified that he could smell the anhydrous ammonia as they were driving and he testified as to his physical reactions to the substance. State v. Gragg, 2007-Ohio-4731, 173 Ohio App. 3d 270, 878 N.E.2d 55, 2007 Ohio App. LEXIS 4276 (Ohio Ct. App., Fayette County 2007).

Since the evidence at trial did not reasonably support a finding that defendant was an aider or abettor, the trial court committed plain error in giving a jury instruction on complicity to commit theft. While defendant clearly acted with terrible judgment, she did not support, assist, encourage, cooperate with, advise, or incite her son in the commission of the theft, the son completed the theft when he ran out of the store, and the evidence did not suggest that defendant knew what her son was planning to do when she dropped him off at the store. State v. Ratkovich, 2003-Ohio-7286, 2003 Ohio App. LEXIS 6576 (Ohio Ct. App., Jefferson County 2003).

There was sufficient evidence to prove complicity to aggravated robbery where appellant traveled in a car with the principal, entered the apartment and stood by while the principal brandished a gun and took items from their owners, and looked out the window frequently while talking and laughing: State v. Saunders, 1993 Ohio App. LEXIS 5956 (Ohio Ct. App., Ross County Dec. 1, 1993).

**Consent**

Trial court did not err in convicting defendant for theft because there was sufficient evidence to conclude that defendant stole electricity from service provider when he reconnected electrical services to account holder's house without consent and which bypassed the provider's disconnection of the services. State v. Hunt, 2019-Ohio-2352, 2019 Ohio App. LEXIS 2457 (Ohio Ct. App., Darke County 2019).

Defendant's conviction was not supported by sufficient evidence and was against the manifest weight of the evidence because she had consent to obtain and exert control over the funds in a joint and survivorship bank account she held with her mother; the mother's signature appeared to be on the credit union agreement, and there was no evidence that her signature was forged, that she was coerced into signing the agreement, or that defendant's withdrawal of money violated the account terms. State v. Woodburn, 2019-Ohio-2757, 140 N.E.3d 66, 2019 Ohio App. LEXIS 2873 (Ohio Ct. App., Pike County 2019).

Trial court's finding that defendant exceeded the scope of express or implied consent was not against the manifest weight of the evidence because defendant acknowledged the funds joint and survivorship bank account she held with her mother belonged to the mother and were for her use; the mother testified that she never authorized defendant to spend the money on herself. State v. Woodburn, 2019-Ohio-2757, 140 N.E.3d 66, 2019 Ohio App. LEXIS 2873 (Ohio Ct. App., Pike County 2019).

Trial court did not err in convicting defendant for theft because there was sufficient evidence to conclude that defendant stole electricity from service provider when he reconnected electrical services to account holder's house without consent and which bypassed the provider's disconnection of the services. State v. Hunt, 2019-Ohio-2352, 2019 Ohio App. LEXIS 2457 (Ohio Ct. App., Darke County 2019).

Because the facts as set forth by the prosecutor during a no contest plea hearing showed that defendant, in fact, received money with the victim's consent, the element of "without consent" in this statute was not established and the trial court erred in making a finding of guilt. State v. Williams, 2016-Ohio-7777, 2016 Ohio App. LEXIS 4637 (Ohio Ct. App., Cuyahoga County 2016).

Defendant's theft conviction under R.C. 2913.02(A)(1) was not against the manifest weight of the evidence as when defendant made check 2 payable to herself, she had been terminated as the victim's bookkeeper and the victim had implicitly revoked its consent to having defendant exert control over its checks. State v. Dobbins, 2011-Ohio-6777, 2011 Ohio App. LEXIS 5592 (Ohio Ct. App., Washington County 2011).

Defendant's theft conviction for check 1 based on R.C. 2913.02(A)(1) was against the manifest weight of the evidence as when defendant, the victim's bookkeeper, made check 1 payable to herself, she had the victim's permission to obtain and exert control over the check; she acted outside the scope of the consent and violated § 2913.02(A)(2), not § 2913.02(A)(1). State v. Dobbins, 2011-Ohio-6777, 2011 Ohio App. LEXIS 5592 (Ohio Ct. App., Washington County 2011).

In a theft prosecution, given an officer's testimony that she was a loss prevention officer for the store from which defendant had stolen property, and given the nature of a loss prevention officer's job, it was reasonable to infer that the officer was a person who was authorized to give consent to shoppers to leave the store with merchandise; thus, the officer's testimony that defendant was not given consent to take the items without paying for them was sufficient to support defendant's conviction. State v. Jeantine, 2009-Ohio-6775, 2009 Ohio App. LEXIS 5689 (Ohio Ct. App., Franklin County 2009).

Defendant's conviction of theft beyond the scope of consent (R.C. 2913.02(A)(2)) was proper as to a $4,000 check that defendant received, as defendant had not yet paid for any bricks, but represented to one of the victims that defendant had already purchased the bricks and other exterior supplies as part of a home renovation contract. State v. Wells, 2009-Ohio-908, 2009 Ohio App. LEXIS 751 (Ohio Ct. App., Champaign County 2009).

Trial court erred in denying defendant's motion for judgment of acquittal regarding his convictions on two counts of the theft of drugs pursuant to R.C. 2913.02(A)(1), which required a person to have exerted control over property without the owner's consent; in the instant case, defendant exerted control over the property, prescription drugs he was delivering, after the owner of the drugs knowingly permitted him to exert control over the drugs for the purpose of delivering them, and, thus, defendant should have been charged with exceeding the scope of the consent the owner gave him by stealing the drugs once they were in his possession, in violation of R.C. 2913.02(A)(2). State v. Martin, 2005-Ohio-688, 2005 Ohio App. LEXIS 691 (Ohio Ct. App., Lake County 2005).

When the owner of property, or his authorized agent, solicits, encourages or affirmatively assists in the taking of his own property, the owner has consented to the taking of his property and there is no indictable offense: State v. Troutman, 1994 Ohio App. LEXIS 2999 (Ohio Ct. App., Lorain County July 6, 1994), dismissed, 71 Ohio St. 3d 1411, 641 N.E.2d 1110, 1994 Ohio LEXIS 2654 (Ohio 1994).

The company bookkeeper could not be convicted of theft under R.C. 2913.02(A)(1) where she did not obtain control over the cash payments without consent of the owner, even though she could have been convicted under R.C. 2913.02(A)(2): State v. Burrows, 80 Ohio App. 3d 404, 609 N.E.2d 571, 1992 Ohio App. LEXIS 2633 (Ohio Ct. App., Cuyahoga County), dismissed, 65 Ohio St. 3d 1430, 600 N.E.2d 675, 1992 Ohio LEXIS 2555 (Ohio 1992).

A public agency does not "consent" to the theft of welfare benefits by failing to terminate them as soon as it becomes aware of the deception: State v. Clifton, 65 Ohio App. 3d 117, 583 N.E.2d 326, 1989 Ohio App. LEXIS 4008 (Ohio Ct. App., Clermont County 1989).

Where an employer originates a "sting" to test the honesty of its own security guards by staging a series of mock thefts, and the security guards cooperate with the purported thief, the employer has consented to the removal of its property, and the security guards cannot be convicted of theft, in violation of R.C. 2913.02(A)(1): State v. Mehozonek, 8 Ohio App. 3d 271, 456 N.E.2d 1353, 1983 Ohio App. LEXIS 10954 (Ohio Ct. App., Cuyahoga County 1983).

**Conviction not against manifest weight of evidence**

Conviction for theft was not against manifest weight of evidence because one of store employees requested witness to call 911 as defendant had just stolen merchandise from store, officer drove to keep an eye out for subject vehicle and observed defendant driving in a suspicious fashion, followed, engaged in high speed pursuit, eventually came face-to-face with defendant, the eyewitness in the parking lot, testified and definitively responded that he was absolutely confident of defendant's identity. State v. Marx, 2021-Ohio-984, 2021 Ohio App. LEXIS 990 (Ohio Ct. App., Wood County 2021).

Evidence was sufficient to support defendant's convictions of burglary and theft because circumstantial evidence showed that defendant stole victim's items after he forced his way to victim's apartment and defendant failed to demonstrate that his convictions were not supported by sufficient evidence or were against the manifest weight of the evidence. State v. Staten, 2018-Ohio-4681, 2018 Ohio App. LEXIS 5000 (Ohio Ct. App., Franklin County 2018).

Defendant's conviction for petty theft, a misdemeanor of the first degree, in violation of R.C. 2913.02(A)(1), was not against the manifest weight of the evidence where an officer at the company where defendant worked testified that the officer never gave defendant permission to take any scrap metal from the company. State v. Sanders, 2008-Ohio-1126, 2008 Ohio App. LEXIS 1039 (Ohio Ct. App., Lake County 2008).

**Corrupt activity**

Allegations made by an unencumbered asset trust to which a debtor's claims were transferred as part of a bankruptcy court-approved liquidation plan that an investment bank had violated the Ohio Corrupt Activities Act, R.C. 2923.31, were sufficient to survive a defense motion to dismiss because the trust adequately alleged the existence of an "enterprise" as well as the commission of sufficient predicate acts per R.C. 2923.34(A) including theft as defined by R.C. 2913.02(A) and securities fraud as defined by R.C. 1707.44. Unencumbered Assets Trust v. JP Morgan Chase Bank (In re Nat'l Century Fin. Enters.), 604 F. Supp. 2d 1128, 2009 U.S. Dist. LEXIS 35660 (S.D. Ohio 2009).

As the failure to pay back loans did not by itself support a finding of theft by deception under R.C. 2913.02(A)(3) claims under Ohio's civil RICO statute, R.C. 2923.32(A)(1), were properly dismissed by summary judgment pursuant to Civ.R. 56(C); and there was also a failure to show that defendants were part of an entity that was separate and apart from the borrowing companies as was required to overcome defendants' motions for summary judgment. Patton v. Wilson, 2003-Ohio-3379, 2003 Ohio App. LEXIS 3067 (Ohio Ct. App., Cuyahoga County 2003).



**Credit cards**

Defendant's indictment correctly indicated that the charges presented to the grand jury of receiving stolen property and theft constituted felony offenses because they involved the use of stolen credit cards. State v. Minite, 2011-Ohio-3585, 2011 Ohio App. LEXIS 3032 (Ohio Ct. App., Cuyahoga County 2011).

**Dangerous drugs**

Defendant's convictions for theft of drugs and receiving stolen property had to be reversed, because the jury did not receive an instruction for "dangerous drug," for purposes of those offenses. State v. Mockbee, 2013-Ohio-5504, 5 N.E.3d 50, 2013 Ohio App. LEXIS 5737 (Ohio Ct. App., Scioto County 2013).

Defendant's motion for acquittal was properly denied during his trial for attempt to commit theft of drugs under R.C. 2913.02(A)(1), (B)(6), 2923.02 and other offenses because there was sufficient evidence that when, as a prison inmate, he tried to break into a prison pharmacy where a drug safe was kept, the object of the theft was a dangerous drug as defined by R.C. 4729.01(F); there was testimony that controlled substances that had to be prescribed by a physician were kept in the drug safe, that the pharmacy was kept locked at all times, and that only the pharmacist had a key. State v. Bell, 2006-Ohio-6560, 2006 Ohio App. LEXIS 6485 (Ohio Ct. App., Fairfield County 2006).

**Deception**

Defendant's conviction for theft by deception was supported by sufficient evidence because the evidence presented by the state, specifically the officer's testimony, provided that defendant obtained possession of the cellphone through an act of deception, i.e., misrepresenting his status as the cellphone's owner, and that this act deprived decedent's father of possession of the cellphone. State v. Green, 2020-Ohio-500, 2020 Ohio App. LEXIS 483 (Ohio Ct. App., Hamilton County 2020).

Conviction of defendant for theft by deception was supported with sufficient evidence and was not against the manifest weight of the evidence because although he returned a portion of the money paid by the victims for the total cost of their window replacement, trial testimony indicated that he failed to repay the remaining money despite repeated promises to them, and failed to contact them for approximately two years thereafter. State v. Barnthouse, 2019-Ohio-5209, 2019 Ohio App. LEXIS 5297 (Ohio Ct. App., Hamilton County 2019).

Sufficient evidence supported defendant's convictions for grand theft because the jury could reasonably have concluded that she deprived the rental business of its property by acquiring it without the intention to return it after the rental period—or, indeed, at any point—which was beyond the scope of the consent given by the store manager and that she did so by providing a nonexistent business name and job location and by using a credit card that did not belong to her, actions that constituted deception. Given that she acknowledged that her actions were part of a "scam" during two separate telephone conversations, the jury could also reasonably have inferred that defendant was aware that her conduct constituted a theft. State v. Jones, 2019-Ohio-4216, 2019 Ohio App. LEXIS 4290 (Ohio Ct. App., Medina County 2019).

Sufficient evidence supported defendant's convictions for grand theft because the jury could reasonably have concluded that she deprived the rental business of its property by acquiring it without the intention to return it after the rental period—or, indeed, at any point—which was beyond the scope of the consent given by the store manager and that she did so by providing a nonexistent business name and job location and by using a credit card that did not belong to her, actions that constituted deception. Given that she acknowledged that her actions were part of a "scam" during two separate telephone conversations, the jury could also reasonably have inferred that defendant was aware that her conduct constituted a theft. State v. Jones, 2019-Ohio-4216, 2019 Ohio App. LEXIS 4290 (Ohio Ct. App., Medina County 2019).

Defendant's conviction for theft by deceit was not against the manifest weight nor based on insufficient evidence, as defendant and his co-defendant were observed collecting money donations in homemade tins for the alleged purpose of paying the funeral expenses for defendant's estranged granddaughter, but the State introduced a letter stating that no charges were due as the goods and services were donated. State v. McAllister, 2016-Ohio-8262, 2016 Ohio App. LEXIS 5101 (Ohio Ct. App., Stark County 2016).

Evidence supported defendant's convictions of theft by deception, as defendant never returned to begin work on any of the three home repair projects he contracted to perform, nor did he purchase and deliver the supplies and materials for which he received down payments. State v. Fasino, 2015-Ohio-2265, 2015 Ohio App. LEXIS 2178 (Ohio Ct. App., Cuyahoga County 2015).

There was sufficient evidence to find that defendant knowingly obtained control of money by deception by submitting false billing statements to the agency for services she did not provide. State v. Mahone, 2014-Ohio-1251, 2014 Ohio App. LEXIS 1128 (Ohio Ct. App., Franklin County 2014).

There was sufficient evidence for the jury to have inferred that defendant knowingly obtained control of monies by deception by submitting false Medicaid billing claims for overlapping periods of time because an investigation revealed a total of 19 separate occasions in which she submitted billing for overlapping services, totaling $1,127.56. State v. Mahone, 2014-Ohio-1251, 2014 Ohio App. LEXIS 1128 (Ohio Ct. App., Franklin County 2014).

Evidence was sufficient to prove the deception element for aggravated theft because defendant's mother, the victim, who was 87 years old, testified that she executed the power of attorney with an understanding that defendant would exercise the power to her use and benefit, not his own, and that she never authorized him to engage in the transfers which were the subject of the theft charges against him. State v. Haggerty, 2011-Ohio-6705, 2011 Ohio App. LEXIS 5519 (Ohio Ct. App., Montgomery County 2011).

Evidence was sufficient to prove theft by deception, as defendant acted deceptively by reporting to the Ohio Department of Job and Family Services or allowing them to believe that independent Medicaid providers were providing in-home health services for which defendant and her child were submitting timesheets and invoices while keeping payouts. State v. Moore, 2010-Ohio-4322, 2010 Ohio App. LEXIS 3646 (Ohio Ct. App., Franklin County 2010).

Defendant's conviction of theft by deception (R.C. 2913.02(A)(3)) was proper as to a $4,000 check that defendant received, as defendant had not yet paid for any bricks, but represented to one of the victims that defendant had already purchased the bricks and other exterior supplies as part of a home renovation contract. State v. Wells, 2009-Ohio-908, 2009 Ohio App. LEXIS 751 (Ohio Ct. App., Champaign County 2009).

Defendant's conviction for theft by deception, R.C. 2913.02(A)(3), was supported by the evidence, as defendant's failure to tell the part owner of a business that a radiator defendant brought in for repair was defendant's personal radiator rather than one belonging to defendant's former employer gave the business owner the impression that the radiator belonged to the former employer. In addition, defendant signed a job work order which listed the former employer as the party to be billed. State v. Butler, 2008-Ohio-781, 2008 Ohio App. LEXIS 678 (Ohio Ct. App., Summit County 2008).

There was sufficient evidence to support defendant's conviction for theft by deception because the evidence showed that defendant knowingly deceived his clients and that he had the purpose of permanently depriving them of their property at the time that he gained control of it. By obtaining quitclaim deeds, defendant deprived homeowners of their right of redemption and their interest in any overpayment remaining after satisfaction of the mortgage; he collected over $92,000 in processing fees and rent payments from his clients, many of them after their homes had been sold at auction. State v. Keith, 2008-Ohio-348, 2008 Ohio App. LEXIS 297 (Ohio Ct. App., Butler County 2008).

When an employee alleged the employee's public employer encouraged and facilitated the illegal accumulation of compensatory time by public employees for later use on political activities for the employer, and that the employee was terminated for insufficiently cooperating with this scheme, the employee sufficiently alleged the clarity element of a wrongful discharge in violation of public policy claim because the employer's activities invoked the public's interest, expressed in R.C. 2913.02(A)(3), barring theft by deception, in prohibiting public employers or employees from committing theft by using public funds, either directly or indirectly, to pay employees for activities unrelated to the employees' employment. Ripley v. Montgomery, 2007-Ohio-7151, 2007 Ohio App. LEXIS 6256 (Ohio Ct. App., Franklin County 2007).

When defendant was convicted of both theft by deception and receiving stolen property, regarding the same property, and the trial court, while recognizing that the crimes were allied offenses of similar import, sentenced defendant on each offense, reversal of defendant's sentence was required to allow the trial court to merge one offense into the other before imposing sentence. State v. Wilson, 2006-Ohio-2945, 2006 Ohio App. LEXIS 2823 (Ohio Ct. App., Clermont County 2006).

Criminal complaint and warrant to arrest defendant for receiving stolen property were supported by probable cause where defendant used deception regarding his credentials to receive the tainted vials, and theft element of the crime was satisfied by the theft by deception: United States v. Harris, 961 F. Supp. 1127, 1997 U.S. Dist. LEXIS 11769 (S.D. Ohio 1997).

R.C. 4705.07 did not preclude prosecution of a disbarred attorney for theft by deception because theft involved the additional element of taking money from clients: State v. Brown, 108 Ohio App. 3d 489, 671 N.E.2d 280, 1995 Ohio App. LEXIS 5509 (Ohio Ct. App., Cuyahoga County 1995), dismissed, 75 Ohio St. 3d 1484, 664 N.E.2d 536 (Ohio 1996).

The evidence did not support a conviction for theft by deception in performing house repairs. That defendant charged more for his work than someone else might have and did not perform it in accordance with the standards of the prosecution's expert witness did not establish intent to deceive: State v. Fyffe, 67 Ohio App. 3d 608, 588 N.E.2d 137, 1990 Ohio App. LEXIS 1810 (Ohio Ct. App., Franklin County 1990).

Defendant was properly convicted of theft by deception where she made false statements as to her available resources in order to obtain food stamps: State v. Patterson, 63 Ohio App. 3d 91, 577 N.E.2d 1165, 1989 Ohio App. LEXIS 1903 (Ohio Ct. App., Montgomery County), dismissed, 46 Ohio St. 3d 707, 545 N.E.2d 1280, 1989 Ohio LEXIS 2280 (Ohio 1989).

**Definitions**

Applicant's residential mortgage loan officer's license should have been granted because the plain language of R.C. 1322.041 showed that the Ohio General Assembly intended to bar those applicants convicted of theft from obtaining licenses; OAC 1301:8-7-01(K) was invalid because it conflicted with R.C. ch. 1322. Moreover, it was fundamentally unfair to apply the definition of "theft" used by the Division of Financial Institutions of the Ohio Department of Commerce in this applicant's case because he had been licensed since 2002, and his renewal was being denied based on 40-year-old convictions for breaking and entering. Holtz v. Ohio DOC, 2009-Ohio-6304, 2009 Ohio App. LEXIS 5292 (Ohio Ct. App., Cuyahoga County 2009).

Plain language of R.C. 1322.041 shows that the Ohio General Assembly intended to bar only those applicants previously convicted of "theft" from obtaining licenses; in contrast, the Superintendent of the Division of Financial Institutions of the Ohio Department of Commerce, through OAC 1301:8-7-01(K), bars applicants convicted of a variety of offenses from obtaining licenses. OAC 1301:8-7-01(K) conflicts with R.C. ch. 1322, so the Court of Appeals of Ohio, Eighth Appellate District, Cuyohoga County, finds the administrative rule invalid. Holtz v. Ohio DOC, 2009-Ohio-6304, 2009 Ohio App. LEXIS 5292 (Ohio Ct. App., Cuyahoga County 2009).

**Degree of offense**

Where defendant was convicted of theft, although the state failed to prove that the victim was an elderly person, it presented sufficient evidence of the theft offense and the value of the property being between $1,000 and $7,500 to enhance the degree of the offense from a fifth-degree felony to a felony of the fourth degree. State v. Lenard, 2018-Ohio-3365, 2018 Ohio App. LEXIS 3640 (Ohio Ct. App., Cuyahoga County 2018).

Trial court correctly concluded that the theft conviction under R.C. 2913.02 remained a fifth-degree felony because defendant committed the offense prior to the effective date of H.B. 86, Gen. Assem. (Ohio 2011). Since he was sentenced after the effective date, he was entitled to and received the reduced penalty for a first-degree misdemeanor based on R.C. 1.58 and H.B. 86's amendments to R.C. 2913.02. State v. Steinfurth, 2012-Ohio-3257, 2012 Ohio App. LEXIS 2859 (Ohio Ct. App., Cuyahoga County 2012).

Trial court erred in assuming that a theft charge against defendant, which the State moved to amend from a charge of burglary, was a fifth-degree felony rather than a first-degree misdemeanor as there was no explanation on the record as to how the amended charge qualified for enhanced treatment as a fifth-degree felony, and there was no indication in the record of the value or type of items underlying the charge. Additionally, the trial court erred in classifying defendant's plea to a charge of theft of money with the specification that the amount was less than $500 as the count was a first-degree misdemeanor. State v. Lindsey, 2012-Ohio-804, 2012 Ohio App. LEXIS 698 (Ohio Ct. App., Cuyahoga County 2012), overruled in part, State v. Rogers, 2013-Ohio-3235, 994 N.E.2d 499, 2013 Ohio App. LEXIS 3326 (Ohio Ct. App., Cuyahoga County 2013).

Discrepancy between the oral pronouncements made by the trial court at the conclusion of trial and sentencing, finding defendant not guilty of felony theft, and the journal entries, which referenced aggravated theft, was error. Thus, the trial court was directed to correct the journal entries. State v. McGowan, 2011-Ohio-6166, 2011 Ohio App. LEXIS 5040 (Ohio Ct. App., Cuyahoga County 2011).

Theft of a credit card conviction was not a felony of the fourth degree simply because the theft occurred from an elderly person as R.C. 2913.71 and 2913.02(B)(3) did not allow for stacking of the enhancements to elevate the crime to a fourth-degree felony. State v. McGowan, 2011-Ohio-6166, 2011 Ohio App. LEXIS 5040 (Ohio Ct. App., Cuyahoga County 2011).

Guilty verdict for the count alleging grand theft neither stated the degree of the offense nor indicated that any additional element or elements were present to enhance the offense level of the charge; the verdict form did not indicate that the property stolen was a motor vehicle or that the value of the property stolen was five thousand dollars or more and less than $1,000. State v. Horne, 2011-Ohio-1901, 2011 Ohio App. LEXIS 1625 (Ohio Ct. App., Summit County 2011).

Regarding the receiving stolen property and theft offenses, the jury's intent to convict defendant of felonies was clear from their findings on the verdict forms. The jury's additional findings that the value of the property or services was between $500 and $5,000 was all that was required pursuant to R.C. 2945.75 to elevate the degree of the offenses. State v. Nichols, 2010-Ohio-3104, 2010 Ohio App. LEXIS 2568 (Ohio Ct. App., Richland County 2010).

Trial court erred in entering a conviction for fifth-degree felonies on two theft counts because, as indicted under R.C. 2913.02(A)(3), they were first-degree misdemeanors. Although the trial court erred when it did not inform defendant of the range of sentence for a first-degree misdemeanor prior to accepting her plea, defendant failed to show that she was prejudiced. State v. Moulton, 2010-Ohio-4484, 2010 Ohio App. LEXIS 3782 (Ohio Ct. App., Cuyahoga County 2010).

**Disabled adult**

Where defendant pled no contest to theft, a furthermore enhancement of theft of a disabled adult was in error because the victim was not a disabled adult as defined by R.C. 2913.01(DD), since his Asperger's Syndrome was not considered a disability and did not prevent him from completing college and holding a job; defendant should have been found guilty of theft, a misdemeanor of the first degree, instead of the felony. State v. Miller, 2015-Ohio-3880, 2015 Ohio App. LEXIS 3757 (Ohio Ct. App., Cuyahoga County 2015).

There was sufficient evidence to prove that the victim was a "disabled adult," as defined by R.C. 2913.01(DD), for the furthermore clauses in the theft charges because testimony established that the victim functioned mentally at the level "of a second grader" and that, although over 50 years old, the victim could not live on his own because he could neither cook for himself, nor read or write. State v. McKissick, 2008-Ohio-4856, 2008 Ohio App. LEXIS 4076 (Ohio Ct. App., Cuyahoga County 2008).



**Disabled victim**

Weight of the evidence supported defendant's conviction for theft of a disabled adult because the victim, who was in a wheelchair, testified that she saw defendant's face when he snatched her purse and she identified him in a photo spread after the incident, at the preliminary hearing, and in court as the person who snatched her purse. A witness testified that he heard the victim yell for help and that he observed defendant trying to pull a purse from the victim's arms, when he caught defendant, the witness got a good look at defendant's face, and the witness also identified defendant in a photo spread and in court as the man who snatched the victim's purse. State v. Reynolds, 2007-Ohio-6903, 2007 Ohio App. LEXIS 6052 (Ohio Ct. App., Montgomery County 2007).

**Discovery**

Where defendant was convicted of theft in violation of R.C. 2913.02 and receiving stolen property in violation of R.C. 2913.51 following the theft of a motor vehicle and some items from the victim's garage, the trial court did not err in denying his motions to exclude the testimony of the State's forensic expert for discovery violations; defendant was indicted prior to the effective date of the newly enacted Crim.R. 16(K). Defendant was not prejudiced by the late disclosure of the State's exhibits and a correctional officer who testified, because defendant's presence at the crime scene was established by the fingerprints and his co-defendant's identification. State v. Viera, 2011-Ohio-5263, 2011 Ohio App. LEXIS 4352 (Ohio Ct. App., Delaware County 2011).

**Double jeopardy**

Because receiving stolen property was not a lesser included offense of either theft or unauthorized use of a motor vehicle, the Double Jeopardy Clause did not bar a successive prosecution for receiving stolen property. State v. Workman, 2015-Ohio-4483, 2015 Ohio App. LEXIS 4382 (Ohio Ct. App., Athens County 2015).

Double jeopardy did not apply to bar defendant's successive prosecutions for misuse of a credit card and theft, pursuant to R.C. 2913.02(A), because misuse of a credit card is not a lesser included offense of theft of a credit card. State v. Schrier, 2006-Ohio-974, 2006 Ohio App. LEXIS 889 (Ohio Ct. App., Wood County 2006).

Misuse of a credit card cannot be considered a lesser included offense of theft of a credit card, and theft of a credit card cannot be considered a lesser included offense of misuse of a credit card. Double jeopardy does not apply to bar a defendant's successive prosecutions for misuse of a credit card and theft of that credit card because theft of a credit card can be committed without misuse also being committed. State v. Schrier, 2006-Ohio-974, 2006 Ohio App. LEXIS 889 (Ohio Ct. App., Wood County 2006).

Where defendant was charged in a criminal matter with grand theft, in violation of R.C. 2913.02(A)(1), and the victim's insurer filed a subrogation claim in a civil matter against him, arising from the insurer's having paid the victim for her property loss, there was no cause to dismiss the criminal action under either civil principles of res judicata or double jeopardy principles under the Fifth Amendment; the State had only commenced one criminal action and it was not a party or a privity to a party in the civil action, and no case law prevented both pending actions from proceeding in the circumstances. State v. Taylor, 2005-Ohio-7141, 136 Ohio Misc. 2d 18, 846 N.E.2d 106, 2005 Ohio Misc. LEXIS 604 (Ohio C.P. 2005).

Where a conviction of grand theft in violation of R.C. 2913.02 does not require proof of any element not required to be proved for a conviction of robbery in violation of R.C. 2911.02, both are the same offense for purposes of double jeopardy: State v. Harris, 58 Ohio St. 2d 257, 12 Ohio Op. 3d 265, 389 N.E.2d 1121, 1979 Ohio LEXIS 426 (Ohio 1979).

**Elderly victims**

Sufficient evidence supported defendant's conviction for theft from the elderly because the victim testified that she was present when defendant asked to clean her grandmother's rings the second time, that he took the rings and made several statements that they were in the garage in "acid," the house and garage were thoroughly searched and the rings were not located, and when defendant was questioned about the rings by the detective, defendant stated that he had thrown them away. The rings had been appraised in 1984 and 1991 for a total of $5,000. State v. Gipson, 2016-Ohio-994, 2016 Ohio App. LEXIS 890 (Ohio Ct. App., Allen County 2016).

Because the State only presented sufficient evidence of the theft offense and of the value of the property, defendant's theft offense was a fifth-degree felony instead of a fourth-degree felony; although the victim testified that she owned her home for 50 years, that did not establish that she was at least 65 years old. State v. Jennings, 2013-Ohio-5428, 2013 Ohio App. LEXIS 5674 (Ohio Ct. App., Cuyahoga County 2013).

In an action charging defendant with theft from an elderly person, defendant was resentenced for first degree misdemeanor theft and fifth degree felony theft, as the State failed to present sufficient evidence that the victim qualified as an elderly person, was 65 years of age or older, a specification used to elevate the degree of a theft offense. State v. Roe, 2012-Ohio-4216, 2012 Ohio App. LEXIS 3702 (Ohio Ct. App., Noble County 2012).

Defendant was ineligible for drug treatment in lieu of conviction because the condition listed in R.C. 2951.041(B)(7), that the victim be under the age of 65, was unsatisfied; because the victims of the theft (the principal defendant's grandparents) were 65 years of age or older, the trial court had no discretion to grant defendant's motion for drug treatment in lieu of conviction. Pursuant to the indictment, defendant was charged under R.C. 2913.02(B)(3) with complicity in theft from an elderly person and R.C. 2913.01(CC) defined an "elderly person" as a person who was 65 years of age or older. State v. Duvall, 2009-Ohio-6580, 2009 Ohio App. LEXIS 5506 (Ohio Ct. App., Greene County 2009).

Sufficient evidence supported defendant's convictions for theft from an elderly person, under R.C. 2913.02(A)(2) and (B)(3), because the evidence showed that (1) defendant did not deny obtaining the victim's funds and using those funds for defendant's personal use, (2) defendant's acts exceeded the scope of defendant's authority pursuant to a power of attorney appointing defendant as the victim's attorney-in-fact, and (3) the victim's implied consent to defendant's acts was not shown. State v. Hanusosky, 2009-Ohio-3409, 2009 Ohio App. LEXIS 2942 (Ohio Ct. App., Lake County 2009).

In a prosecution for theft from an elderly person, under R.C. 2913.02(A)(2) and (B)(3), evidence of the victim's mental capacity before and after the victim executed a power of attorney used by the accused to perpetrate the crime was admissible, pursuant to Evid.R. 402, because the evidence was relevant, pursuant to Evid.R. 401, to determine whether the accused exceeded the scope of the victim's express or implied consent. State v. Hanusosky, 2009-Ohio-3409, 2009 Ohio App. LEXIS 2942 (Ohio Ct. App., Lake County 2009).

When defendant was charged with theft from her elderly great-great aunt, under R.C. 2913.02(A)(2), it was not ineffective assistance of counsel for her attorney not to call as a witness a physician who found the great-great aunt incompetent or to introduce his evaluation because the evaluation, which occurred after the relevant events in the case, did not show the victim was incompetent at the time of those events or when she testified at trial against defendant, and it could not be said that the result of the trial would have been different had the witness been called or the evaluation introduced. State v. Harris, 2006-Ohio-1396, 2006 Ohio App. LEXIS 1275 (Ohio Ct. App., Erie County 2006), different results reached on reconsid., 2007-Ohio-2397, 2007 Ohio App. LEXIS 2247 (Ohio Ct. App., Erie County 2007).

Defendant's convictions for stealing funds from an her great-great aunt, under R.C. 2913.02(A)(2), were supported by sufficient evidence, including evidence of defendant's intent, under R.C. 2901.22(A), because (1) while defendant's defense was that the victim gave her the funds, bank officials testified defendant told them the victim was ill and needed defendant to take her funds, which were in another state, to her, (2) defendant, rather than the victim, inquired at a bank about obtaining a power of attorney regarding the victim, (3) the victim testified she never gave defendant permission to take the money and had expressed concerns that defendant was using her for her money, and (4) after the victim was released from the hospital, defendant refused to return her personal property, including her purse and medication, to her, when she wanted to live with another relative. State v. Harris, 2006-Ohio-1396, 2006 Ohio App. LEXIS 1275 (Ohio Ct. App., Erie County 2006), different results reached on reconsid., 2007-Ohio-2397, 2007 Ohio App. LEXIS 2247 (Ohio Ct. App., Erie County 2007).

Defendant did not show the elderly victim from whom she stole funds, who testified against her, was incompetent, rendering her convictions under R.C. 2913.02(A)(2) against the manifest weight of the evidence because, under Evid.R. 601(A), the victim was presumed to be a competent witness, nothing in her trial testimony showed she was of unsound mind, and the weight of her testimony was for the jury to decide. State v. Harris, 2006-Ohio-1396, 2006 Ohio App. LEXIS 1275 (Ohio Ct. App., Erie County 2006), different results reached on reconsid., 2007-Ohio-2397, 2007 Ohio App. LEXIS 2247 (Ohio Ct. App., Erie County 2007).

**Elements**

Ex-wife never gave defendant permission to take the money where the ex-wife testified that she did not know defendant's name was still on the account; there was evidence that defendant knew the money in the savings account was the ex-wife's not his, and therefore, his withdrawal of the money showed an intent to deprive the owner of the money. State v. Nye, 2021-Ohio-2557, 2021 Ohio App. LEXIS 2517 (Ohio Ct. App., Wood County 2021).

Evidence showed even though defendant returned the merchandise, he took a substantial step toward committing a theft when he placed a can of body spray under his shirt for purposes of evading detection by store employees and exiting through the front door of the store beyond all points of purchase before returning the spray while standing in the store lobby. State v. Moore, 2016-Ohio-3506, 2016 Ohio App. LEXIS 2348 (Ohio Ct. App., Lucas County 2016)

Theft offense was established for purposes of defendant's conviction for aggravated robbery under R.C. 2911.01 by the victim's testimony that showed that defendant deprived the victim of his cell phone and cell phone accessories without the victim's consent when the victim in his car waiting to give defendant a ride. State v. Speaks, 2016-Ohio-522, 2016 Ohio App. LEXIS 450 (Ohio Ct. App., Clark County 2016).

Where the victim drove a co-worker (co-defendant) and the co-worker's boyfriend (defendant) to an after-hours bar, where co-defendant, while at the bar, said that she lost some money in the victim's car, where they returned to the car and the victim began looking for co-defendant's money, where defendant grabbed her neck from behind and demanded money and her car keys, and where defendant was convicted of robbery under R.C. 2911.02(A)(1), the court rejected defendant's contention that the evidence was insufficent to support his conviction on the basis that the victim's money and keys were never recovered and if he had been the perpetrator, they would have been in his possession when he was arrested less than 24 hours after the robbery because the victim testified that defendant took her car keys from her hand and her money from her brad. Those actions constituted obtaining the victim's property without her consent under R.C. 2913.02(A)(1); the fact that defendant did not have possession of those items at the time he was arrested was immaterial. State v. Secessions, 2011-Ohio-6066, 196 Ohio App. 3d 741, 965 N.E.2d 359, 2011 Ohio App. LEXIS 4951 (Ohio Ct. App., Summit County 2011).

Value of stolen property is not an essential element of the offense of theft but, rather, is a finding that enhances the penalty of the offense, so value is submitted to a factfinder for a special finding in order to determine the degree of the offense. State v. Smith, 2009-Ohio-787, 121 Ohio St. 3d 409, 905 N.E.2d 151, 2009 Ohio LEXIS 549 (Ohio 2009).

Evidence supported defendant's conviction for grand theft of a motor vehicle because the jury had sufficient evidence to rationally conclude that defendant acted with the requisite purpose to permanently deprive the car dealerships of the vehicles. Abandonment of the vehicle alone was not a sufficient basis upon which to determine that defendant did not intend to permanently deprive the owner of its property; defendant did not present evidence showing that he failed to return the vehicle because it ran out of gas as he argued on appeal or that he had any intent to return any of the vehicles to the dealerships. State v. Sidders, 2009-Ohio-409, 2009 Ohio App. LEXIS 319 (Ohio Ct. App., Union County 2009).

There was no abuse of discretion in a trial court's denial of defendant's second request for a continuance in two criminal matters, as there was no showing that additional investigation of the two theft incidents would have yielded exculpatory evidence that might have changed the outcome of the trial; even if a surveillance video in a store might have showed that defendant had not passed the last point of sale when a police officer apprehended defendant, the crime of petty theft, in violation of R.C. 2913.02, was already completed when defendant had shoved steaks into his pants. State v. Bean, 2007-Ohio-6132, 2007 Ohio App. LEXIS 6343 (Ohio Ct. App., Montgomery County 2007).

Defendant's robbery conviction, under R.C. 2911.02(A)(2), was not against the manifest evidence, even though defendant said he intended to give the property he admitted taking from the victim back to her, because the theft, under R.C. 2913.02(A), on which the robbery charge was based, did not require, under the definition of "deprive," in R.C. 2913.01(C)(3), that defendant intended to permanently deprive the victim of her property, so, even if the jury believed his claim that he intended to return the property, it was still clear that defendant appropriated the victim's property with purpose not to give proper consideration in return, without any justification for not giving such consideration. State v. Davis, 2007-Ohio-1131, 2007 Ohio App. LEXIS 1051 (Ohio Ct. App., Summit County 2007).

Amount of work defendant completed on an owner's garage was not sufficient to negate the finding that defendant acted with "purpose" to deprive the owner of his property, as defined in R.C. 2901.22(A), thereby constituting the offense of theft by deception under R.C. 2913.02(A)(3), because, while defendant admitted that he could have finished the garage in a week, he did not do so but, instead, asked for $1,000 more to finish the garage. The evidence was sufficient to show that, at the time he took the owner's money, he had no intent to repay the money or perform under the contract. State v. Smith, 2005-Ohio-6551, 2005 Ohio App. LEXIS 5899 (Ohio Ct. App., Butler County 2005).

Trial court did not err in permitting defendant to be tried both for theft from an elderly person and for engaging in a hearing aid business without a license; while R.C. 2941.25 protected against multiple punishments for the same criminal conduct, the statutorily defined elements of the offenses were not of similar import, such that the commission of one of the crimes resulted in the commission of the other. State v. Wright, 2005-Ohio-3907, 2005 Ohio App. LEXIS 3596 (Ohio Ct. App., Clermont County 2005), rev'd, 2006-Ohio-2109, 109 Ohio St. 3d 313, 847 N.E.2d 1174, 2006 Ohio LEXIS 1161 (Ohio 2006).

**—Deception**

Amount of work defendant completed on an owner's garage was not sufficient to negate the finding that defendant acted with "purpose" to deprive the owner of his property, as defined in R.C. 2901.22(A), thereby constituting the offense of theft by deception under R.C. 2913.02(A)(3), because, while defendant admitted that he could have finished the garage in week, he did not do so but, instead, asked for $1,000 more to finish the garage; thus, the evidence was sufficient to show that, at the time he took the owner's money, he had no intent to repay the money or perform under the contract. State v. Smith, 2005-Ohio-6551, 2005 Ohio App. LEXIS 5899 (Ohio Ct. App., Butler County 2005).

There was sufficient evidence to support the theft conviction, pursuant to R.C. 2913.02, as the evidence showed that defendant tried to "deceive," as defined by R.C. 2913.01(A), the hotel employees by continuously assuring them that he would pay for the theft conviction, under. Defendant had paid part of his bill and had agreed to meet with the hotel manager in regard to his account balance, but vacated the hotel without checking out when he still owed $2,563.26. State v. Sampson, 2005-Ohio-5692, 2005 Ohio App. LEXIS 5132 (Ohio Ct. App., Cuyahoga County 2005).

**—Intent**

Defendant's motion for acquittal was properly denied because adequate circumstantial evidence was presented to show that defendant knowingly exerted control over a microwave box containing DVDs with the purpose to deprive a store by means of deception, in that, while defendant did not pack the microwave box, which he purchased, with DVDs, the girlfriend of the man who did so testified that she retrieved the man from the store and took him to defendant's residence where defendant and the man conversed privately for a long time, and the loss prevention officer observed the man return to the store with defendant, lead defendant to the aisle where he had left the box and point out the box to defendant. This evidence was sufficient to show that defendant acted "knowingly," under R.C. 2901.22, and that he acted with deception, under R.C. 2913.01(A). State v. Thomas, 2005-Ohio-6570, 2005 Ohio App. LEXIS 5882 (Ohio Ct. App., Lake County 2005).

**—Manifest weight**

Based on the observations made by the store manager with regard to defendant placing the shirt in her cart, noticing that she did not pay for the shirt, and that the shirt was no longer in the cart, defendant's failure to give a credible explanation as to what she did with the shirt and the statement made to him by defendant before pulling the shirt out of her purse, her conviction was not against the manifest weight of the evidence. State v. Hager, 2019 Ohio App. LEXIS 4594 (Ohio Ct. App., Holmes County Oct. 17, 2019).

Defendant's convictions for petty theft were not against the manifest weight of the evidence where: (1) upon her arrest, defendant had items from four stores she had visited, (2) employees from each store stated that she had not purchased the items on the day in question, (3) the only items purchased by defendant were found in the same bag that contained items that she had not purchased that day, (4) an employee testified that she observed defendant place items in her purse that she had not purchased, and (5) an officer indicated that defendant had not been forthright during his initial questioning. State v. Smith, 2006-Ohio-1558, 2006 Ohio App. LEXIS 1491 (Ohio Ct. App., Wayne County 2006).

Defendant's convictions for aggravated robbery, robbery, and theft were not against the manifest weight of the evidence. While there were inconsistencies between the testimony of defendant and that of victim, their testimony was consistent in significant areas, including their testimony that defendant took possession of a gun belonging to defendant's fiancee without permission and maintained possession of the gun through the exertion of force and that defendant was angry, and it was the province of the jury to make determinations with respect to credibility. State v. Hairston, 2006-Ohio-1644, 2006 Ohio App. LEXIS 1423 (Ohio Ct. App., Franklin County 2006).

Defendant's theft conviction was not against the manifest weight of the evidence. While defendant's testimony, to the effect that he did not drive away without paying for gasoline, conflicted with the testimony offered by the State's witnesses, the weight to be given the evidence and the credibility of the witnesses are primarily for the trier of fact. State v. Brasty, 2006-Ohio-3752, 2006 Ohio App. LEXIS 3734 (Ohio Ct. App., Medina County 2006).

Defendant's theft conviction under R.C. 2913.02(A)(1) was not against the manifest weight of the evidence because the evidence showed that defendant took microwave/refrigerator units, which were located on the loading dock on a university's campus, and that defendant did not have permission to take the units. It was within the province of the jury to reject defendant's mistake of fact defense. State v. Crisp, 2006-Ohio-5041, 2006 Ohio App. LEXIS 5184 (Ohio Ct. App., Franklin County 2006).

Defendant's conviction for theft was not against the manifest weight of the evidence, although the victim was only 75-80 percent sure that defendant was the individual he confronted with his tools, as defendant admitted that he was one of the two men in the parking lot that had been confronted by the victim and that he had, at least temporarily, possession of the victim's toolbox; the only pertinent question was whether defendant was stealing the toolbox, or simply returning the toolbox that he claimed he found in the parking lot. State v. King, 2005-Ohio-4656, 2005 Ohio App. LEXIS 4184 (Ohio Ct. App., Lake County 2005).

**Evidence insufficient**

The trial court did not err in overruling defendant's motion for acquittal because there was sufficient evidence that defendant, with purpose to deprive the department store, knowingly obtained approximately 10 items without its consent and also by deception. Also, the store employee's testimony did not constitute inadmissible hearsay since the employee testified to her firsthand observation from the day of the incident. State v. Clinkscale, 2020-Ohio-4735, 2020 Ohio App. LEXIS 3611 (Ohio Ct. App., Mahoning County 2020).

Defendant's theft convictions, premised on defendant's removal of items from leased property the day before the lessor repossessed the premises, were not supported by the evidence as, pursuant to the terms of the lease, the lease terminated at the time that the lessor repossessed the premises, and the improvements or fixtures were to become the lessor's property upon termination of the lease. Even though the notice of default purported to terminate the lease immediately, the terms of the lease governed the parties' ownership rights, and it did not provide for termination until repossession occurred, which happened the following day; thus, since the lessor would not have become owner of the fixtures until the day after they were removed, the State presented insufficient evidence of theft. State v. Hardesty, 2013-Ohio-2120, 2013 Ohio App. LEXIS 2022 (Ohio Ct. App., Montgomery County 2013).

Record was devoid of sufficient evidence to support two separate theft convictions. The State presented sufficient evidence to support only one conviction of theft under R.C. 2913.02(A)(1) relating to defendant's theft of the victim's purse. State v. Brown, 2013-Ohio-1982, 2013 Ohio App. LEXIS 1871 (Ohio Ct. App., Cuyahoga County 2013).

Defendant's convictions of theft with regard to a remodeling contract defendant entered into with two homeowners were improper, as the State failed to establish that defendant had the purpose to deprive the homeowners of money either by deception or by exceeding the scope of their consent; the evidence established that he showed up to work on the project the day or two after the contract was signed, brought people to help, and continued to work from September until sometime in November 2009. State v. Chait, 2012-Ohio-6104, 2012 Ohio App. LEXIS 5268 (Ohio Ct. App., Medina County 2012).

Insufficient evidence existed to convict defendant of theft by deception, in violation of R.C. 2913.02(A)(3), because the State of Ohio failed to present evidence of the scope of express or implied consent. State v. Lusher, 2012-Ohio-5526, 982 N.E.2d 1290, 2012 Ohio App. LEXIS 4787 (Ohio Ct. App., Gallia County 2012).

Even assuming the check was forged, the State failed to introduce evidence that defendant possessed that knowledge or that he was deceptive when he uttered the writing. Thus, because the State failed to introduce sufficient evidence to reach the jury as a matter of law on the theft charge, the trial court committed reversible error by denying defendant's motion for acquittal. State v. Windle, 2011-Ohio-4171, 2011 Ohio App. LEXIS 3477 (Ohio Ct. App., Lake County 2011).

Sufficient evidence did not support defendant's conviction for theft by deception, as the evidence did not prove that defendant knew that documents a title company drafted and delivered to defendant's ex-husband as part of refinancing would extinguish the ex-husband's interest in a town home. State v. Soueidi, 2011-Ohio-3580, 2011 Ohio App. LEXIS 3019 (Ohio Ct. App., Cuyahoga County 2011).

State failed to present sufficient evidence to support defendant's conviction for theft without consent, based upon defendant's act of taking his car from a repair shop's lot without paying for the repairs that the shop had performed on the car, as the State did not present any evidence that the repair shop provided defendant with any written form or estimate prior to beginning repairs on his car, as required by OAC 109:4-3-13(A)(1). This failure violated the Ohio Consumer Sales Practices Act and negated the shop's right to retain a possessory lien over the car; thus, defendant's motion for acquittal was improperly denied. State v. Pawloski, 2010-Ohio-

3504, 188 Ohio App. 3d 267, 935 N.E.2d 111, 2010 Ohio App. LEXIS 2976 (Ohio Ct. App., Cuyahoga County 2010).

There was insufficient evidence to support the conclusion that defendant knowingly exerted control over the victim's coins without the victim's consent for defendant's theft conviction. Although the testimony of the victim, defendant's mother-in-law, provided some circumstantial evidence that defendant's husband had taken coins from the victim's home, there was no evidence that defendant knew the coins came from the victim's home or that her husband had taken them without the victim's permission. State v. Whiteaker, 2010-Ohio-3502, 188 Ohio App. 3d 489, 935 N.E.2d 934, 2010 Ohio App. LEXIS 2993 (Ohio Ct. App., Cuyahoga County 2010).

Juvenile court erred in adjudicating defendant a delinquent by reason of having committed robbery with a firearm in violation of R.C. 2911.02(A)(1) because the evidence presented by the State was insufficient as a matter of law to prove one of the essential elements of robbery: that defendant attempted or committed a theft offense in violation of R.C. 2913.02(A) and 2923.02(A); the evidence was sufficient to prove that defendant and his associates planned to commit a theft offense and left a residence with a gun and a bag in which to put money the offense produced, but the evidence was insufficient as a matter of law to prove that the conduct in which they in fact engaged involved knowingly obtaining or exerting control over property or services owned by another in violation of § 2913.02(A), or was conduct which, if successful, would have had that result. In re V.D., 2010-Ohio-4148, 2010 Ohio App. LEXIS 3535 (Ohio Ct. App., Montgomery County 2010).

Because the State did not prove the existence of a common-law lien, the evidence was insufficient to support the theft conviction. Absent proof that the truck repair services had been accepted by defendant with the purpose not to pay for them, and without proper justification for not paying, there was insufficient evidence to convict defendant of theft of services without consent. State v. Ames, 2009-Ohio-3509, 182 Ohio App. 3d 736, 914 N.E.2d 1118, 2009 Ohio App. LEXIS 3012 (Ohio Ct. App., Darke County 2009).

Defendant's conviction for theft of a motor vehicle was not supported by the evidence. While there was evidence that defendant exceeded the scope of the consent given to him by the car's owner to use the car, there was no evidence that he acted with a purpose to deprive the owner of her car in the context of a theft offense. State v. Bowden, 2009-Ohio-3598, 2009 Ohio App. LEXIS 3082 (Ohio Ct. App., Cuyahoga County 2009).

Although there was sufficient evidence that defendant committed a theft by taking the purse of defendant's grandmother without her permission, the weight and sufficiency of the evidence did not support elevating the crime of misdemeanor theft to felony theft under R.C. 2913.02(B)(2) and 2913.71(A) because the victim gave inconsistent testimony as to whether there were credit cards in her purse when it was stolen. State v. Jackson, 2008-Ohio-1078, 2008 Ohio App. LEXIS 951 (Ohio Ct. App., Cuyahoga County 2008).

State failed to prove each element of the crime of aggravated theft, in violation of R.C. 2913.02(A)(3) and (B)(2), where there was not sufficient evidence that defendant was involved in a scheme to cash counterfeit checks within the county within the relevant period of time that totalled at least $100,000; rather, the evidence showed that defendant was involved in counterfeit check-cashing that totalled approximately $12,000 with respect to the applicable county and timeframe. State v. Darrington, 2008-Ohio-3269, 2008 Ohio App. LEXIS 2767 (Ohio Ct. App., Wood County 2008).

Evidence was insufficient to support an aiding and abetting conviction because there was no evidence of an affirmative act by the second defendant to establish his participation in, or encouragement of, the first defendant's theft of the victim's ring. There was no evidence that the second defendant diverted the victim's attention, served as a lookout, helped the first defendant get the ring out of the house, or had possession of the ring himself. State v. Buelow, 2007-Ohio-5929, 2007 Ohio App. LEXIS 5196 (Ohio Ct. App., Franklin County 2007).

Defendant's conviction for theft, in violation of R.C. 2913:02(A)(3), was not supported by sufficient evidence, as it was based on the fact that defendant allegedly used her Medicaid card to purchase drugs that had been overprescribed due to defendant's deception to the treating doctors, and that the drugs were stolen from the State of Ohio; however, although the State offered evidence that defendant used her Medicaid card to pay for some part of the cost of the drugs, there was no evidence that ownership of the drugs was by the State of Ohio. State v. Zweifel, 2006-Ohio-4844, 2006 Ohio App. LEXIS 4726 (Ohio Ct. App., Union County 2006).

Evidence was insufficient to prove that defendant acted with the purpose to "deprive" owners of a van within the meaning of R.C. 2913.01(C)(1) since the evidence tended to show that defendant was returning to the party with the van when the accident occurred, and thus, the State failed to prove that defendant intended to withhold the owners' van permanently so as to constitute the offense of theft of a motor vehicle under R.C. 2913.02(A)(1). Since the evidence showed that defendant was guilty of the lesser-included offense of unauthorized use of a motor vehicle, the court modified the conviction, as it was authorized to do under App.R. 12(B), and remanded the case with instructions to the trial court to enter a conviction on the lesser-included offense. State v. Davis, 2006-Ohio-4599, 2006 Ohio App. LEXIS 4545 (Ohio Ct. App., Hamilton County 2006).

Even though defendant's behavior was ill-spirited and unacceptable, the City failed to meet its burden of producing sufficient evidence to support the charge of petty theft, under Brooklyn, Ohio, Ordinance 545.05 (which is substantially similar to R.C. 2913.02(A)(1)), because the City did not establish that when defendant took and then ate the restaurant's food he also had a purpose to deprive the restaurant of its property without paying. City of Brooklyn v. Fouche, 2006-Ohio-169, 2006 Ohio App. LEXIS 151 (Ohio Ct. App., Cuyahoga County 2006).

State did not meet its burden of establishing that the value of a ring allegedly stolen by defendant was over $500, pursuant to R.C. 2913.51(C) and 2913.61(D), for purposes of his conviction under R.C. 2913.02(A)(1), (B)(1), (2), as hearsay testimony regarding what the victim's deceased mother had told her years earlier regarding the value was inadmissible, a newspaper advertisement regarding the potential sale of the ring was unreliable self-serving hearsay upon hearsay under Evid.R. 801(C), and there was no other testimony regarding the value of the ring based on the stones in it or the fact that it was allegedly an heirloom; rather than reverse the conviction, the court reduced the charge to a first degree misdemeanor. State v. Reese, 2005-Ohio-7075, 165 Ohio App. 3d 21, 844 N.E.2d 873, 2005 Ohio App. LEXIS 6381 (Ohio Ct. App., Mahoning County 2005).

Appeals court vacated a judgment and discharged a juvenile after the juvenile was adjudicated delinquent for acts that would have been R.C. 2911.12 burglary and R.C. 2913.02 theft if committed by an adult; the State did not produce present sufficient evidence (no testimony from arresting officers, and insufficient identification testimony) to link the juvenile to the stolen items or the crime so the trial court should not have denied the juvenile's Crim.R. 29 motion for acquittal. In re C.L., 2004-Ohio-987, 2004 Ohio App. LEXIS 895 (Ohio Ct. App., Cuyahoga County 2004).

Although defendant was apparently picked up with the group of boys, there was no indication that he was with the boys at the time of the burglary, nor was any evidence presented that he had stolen possessions on his person implicating him in the crime, and there was nothing linking him to the actual crime; thus, the evidence was insufficient to support the trial court's finding him delinquent for committing the offenses of burglary and theft. In re C.S., 2004-Ohio-857, 2004 Ohio App. LEXIS 786 (Ohio Ct. App., Cuyahoga County), amended, 2004-Ohio-864, 2004 Ohio App. LEXIS 801 (Ohio Ct. App., Cuyahoga County 2004).

Pursuant to R.C. 2913.02(A)(2), defendant's conviction was against the manifest weight of the evidence where it showed that defendant took possession of a check which defendant was supposed to pay an advertising account and did not. State v. Bratton, 2004-Ohio-187, 2004 Ohio App. LEXIS 166 (Ohio Ct. App., Allen County 2004).

Pursuant to Crim.R. 29(A), the trial court abused its discretion in denying defendant's motion for acquittal from a charge of grand theft, in violation of R.C. 2913.02(A)(1), because the evidence demonstrated that there was testimony that a car dealer may have authorized an advertising agent to take a 15 percent commission. State v. Bratton, 2004-Ohio-187, 2004 Ohio App. LEXIS 166 (Ohio Ct. App., Allen County 2004).

Defendant could not be convicted under R.C. 2913.02(A)(1) where the bank permitted withdrawals prior to a deposited check clearing, but could have been convicted of theft by deception: State v. McGhee, 113 Ohio App. 3d 208, 680 N.E.2d 710, 1996 Ohio App. LEXIS 3267 (Ohio Ct. App., Summit County 1996).

Where a village board of public affairs adopts a bylaw requiring the president of the board to take action to collect delinquent accounts, the president's failure to do so constitutes dereliction of duty, but the president's receipt of unpaid for utility service does not constitute theft or theft in office: State v. Metheney, 87 Ohio App. 3d 562, 622 N.E.2d 730, 1993 Ohio App. LEXIS 2463 (Ohio Ct. App., Medina County 1993).

A conviction for grand theft by deception is not supported by sufficient evidence and must be vacated when there is no evidence that defendant did not intend to repay a loan or that the representation made which induced the loan was a lie: State v. Bakies, 71 Ohio App. 3d 810, 595 N.E.2d 449, 1991 Ohio App. LEXIS 1289 (Ohio Ct. App., Cuyahoga County), dismissed, 61 Ohio St. 3d 1428, 575 N.E.2d 216, 1991 Ohio LEXIS 2023 (Ohio 1991).

The evidence is legally insufficient to support a verdict of guilty for the offense of theft by deception where the amounts defendant allegedly stole were always recorded on the plaintiff's books and such records were always available to anyone who wished to examine them: State v. Baumgarden, 49 Ohio App. 3d 24, 550 N.E.2d 206, 1988 Ohio App. LEXIS 2498 (Ohio Ct. App., Warren County), dismissed, 39 Ohio St. 3d 707, 534 N.E.2d 78, 1988 Ohio LEXIS 986 (Ohio 1988).

There was insufficient evidence to find that attorney and companion had intent to rob store where they tried to collect debt from employee of business who pleaded poverty, but then took $50 from cash register belonging to business, not employee: Tipton v. Jago, 818 F.2d 1264, 1987 U.S. App. LEXIS 6278 (6th Cir. Ohio 1987).

**Evidence sufficient**

Defendant's conviction for theft was not against the manifest weight and sufficiency of the evidence because witness took a cell phone photograph of a man carrying a bag containing what was later determined to be stolen property and the officer confirmed the man in witness' photograph was defendant, the man they apprehended. State v. Flickinger, 2021-Ohio-3261, 2021 Ohio App. LEXIS 3165 (Ohio Ct. App., Tuscarawas County 2021).

In an appeal from a judgment of conviction for theft, the evidence supported that defendant knew she had improperly obtained various items from the trailer because she had moved into a fully furnished residence and left with the mattress and numerous kitchen items that were not hers; defendant knowingly obtained or exerted control over property beyond the scope of the express or implied consent of the owner with purpose to deprive the owner. State v. Love, 2021-Ohio-4470, 2021 Ohio App. LEXIS 4376 (Ohio Ct. App., Logan County 2021).

State presented sufficient evidence to support a finding of theft offenses because the security footage depicted defendant walking by the area where victim was gambling and defendant was seen stopping in that area and picking items up off the floor, eventually approaching casino employees and turning in the cellphone but not the wallet containing debit cards that could be used to withdraw cash from an ATM and/or make purchases. State v. Davis, 2021-Ohio-142, 2021 Ohio App. LEXIS 136 (Ohio Ct. App., Montgomery County 2021).

Sufficient evidence supported defendant's conviction for theft from a person in a protected class, a felony of the third degree because the owner of the stolen vehicle testified that he and his wife bought the vehicle for $27,000 although he was not sure exactly how much it had depreciated since he purchased it, he estimated that it was currently worth at least double or triple $7,500, which was around $20,000. State v. Hastings, 2021-Ohio-662, 2021 Ohio App. LEXIS 655 (Ohio Ct. App., Portage County 2021).

Sufficient evidence supported defendant's conviction for grand theft of a motor vehicle because the testimony established that defendant purposely deprived the owner of her vehicle without her consent. The owner called 9-1-1 and reported her vehicle had been stolen and also told the deputy that she tried to get the man in the driver's seat out of her vehicle, but he pushed her to the ground. State v. Drane, 2021-Ohio-730, 2021 Ohio App. LEXIS 739 (Ohio Ct. App., Montgomery County 2021).

Defendant was not deprived of due process under Fourteenth Amendment because his convictions under were not against the manifest weight and sufficiency of the evidence since in the bank's security video, he was seen removing the stolen check from his pocket and handing it to his companion, who signed the check and handed it to the teller. State v. Foggin, 2021-Ohio-830, 2021 Ohio App. LEXIS 824 (Ohio Ct. App., Muskingum County 2021).

For purposes of defendant's theft by deception and telecommunications fraud convictions, there was proof beyond a reasonable doubt as defendant used the victim's cell phone beyond the scope of consent by downloading a game app on the victim's phone; defendant made over $450 of unauthorized in-app purchases with the victim's debit card; even if the first transaction was a mistake, it was reasonable for the jury to believe that the other 12 purchases were deliberate; and defendant's attempt to fix his mistake after he was caught did not demonstrate that he did not act purposely. State v. Burey, 2021-Ohio-943, 2021 Ohio App. LEXIS 959 (Ohio Ct. App., Cuyahoga County 2021).

Sufficient evidence supported defendant's convictions for passing bad checks and theft, as the evidence demonstrated he wrote a check to the victim, the check remained unpaid, he received verbal and written notice from the victim and a detective that the check had been dishonored, and the check remained unpaid and was not discharged by payment or satisfaction within 10 days; the uncontroverted evidence further demonstrated that defendant knowingly deprived the victim of $15,000. State v. Newman, 2021-Ohio-2124, 2021 Ohio App. LEXIS 2083 (Ohio Ct. App., Fairfield County 2021).

Evidence was sufficient to sustain defendant's conviction for theft from an elderly person or disabled adult because several accounts of seniors were missing funds, some were short funds due to lateral transfers, some due to missing cash deposits, and others due to the issuance of improper checks signed by defendant. State v. Hulbert, 2021-Ohio-2298, 2021 Ohio App. LEXIS 2266 (Ohio Ct. App., Van Wert County 2021).

Evidence supported defendant's conviction for petty theft because the State of Ohio presented evidence indicating that defendant took the victim's package into defendant's apartment shortly after the package was delivered, opened the package, removed the contents, put the package in a trash bag, disposed of the trash bag in the community dumpster, kept the contents of the package inside of defendant's apartment, and made no effort to contact the victim or to return the contents of the package to the victim. State v. Perkins, 2021-Ohio-2630, 2021 Ohio App. LEXIS 2605 (Ohio Ct. App., Wayne County 2021).

Defendant's conviction for aggravated theft was supported by sufficient evidence, as defendant routed funds of a nonprofit organization totaling over $200,000 into an investment account and his girlfriend's personal bank accounts for his personal use, without prior approval of the organization's board of trustees and in a manner indicative of his awareness that he was not entitled to do so. Ohio v. Craig, 2021-Ohio-2790, 176 N.E.3d 395, 2021 Ohio App. LEXIS 2747 (Ohio Ct. App., Wood County 2021).

Sufficient evidence supported defendant's convictions for theft and misuse of a credit card of an elderly person because the credit card was stolen from the victim's locker while he worked out at the gym and video evidence taken from a store showed defendant using the credit card to make three separate purchases and an attempted fourth purchase, all within minutes of one another. State v. Green, 2020-Ohio-1552, 2020 Ohio App. LEXIS 1505 (Ohio Ct. App., Clermont County 2020).

Sufficient evidence supported defendant's theft conviction; a cashier testified that she saw defendant exiting the store with unbagged groceries, that customers confirmed they had not seen defendant use self-checkout, and that a co-worker confirmed that defendant did not come through the checkout line. State v. Glavic, 2020-Ohio-2789, 2020 Ohio App. LEXIS 1757 (Ohio Ct. App., Lake County 2020).

Sufficient evidence supported defendant's conviction for theft because the police found the stolen tractor, bucket loader and the trailer in defendant's possession and told the police that he had bought them at auction. He then provided documentation that had several items missing, including the seller's name, ad the Bureau of Motor Vehicles Power of Attorney they provided was blank of most of the important information. State v. Hodge, 2020-Ohio-3002, 154 N.E.3d 671, 2020 Ohio App. LEXIS 1945 (Ohio Ct. App., Fairfield County 2020).

Defendant's conviction for theft under R.C. 2913.02(A)(1) was supported by the evidence because both an asset protection officer for a store and a police officer testified that they observed defendant exert control over a car battery by placing it in an accomplice's purse; defendant and the accomplice left the store without paying for the battery. State v. Fornash, 2020-Ohio-3265, 2020 Ohio App. LEXIS 2191 (Ohio Ct. App., Stark County 2020).

Sufficient evidence supported defendant's convictions for two counts of grand theft, each fourth-degree felonies, and on one count of theft with an elderly specification, a third-degree felony because the evidence supported the conclusion that defendant, holding himself out to be a general contractor, intended to deprive his clients of their money when their contracts were entered into and knowingly acted with purpose to deprive the clients of their money by exerting control over such property beyond the scope of the owner's express or implied consent. State v. Delmonico, 2020-Ohio-3368, 2020 Ohio App. LEXIS 2306 (Ohio Ct. App., Cuyahoga County 2020).

Evidence supported defendant's conviction for theft because the complainant and defendant's former paramour testified that defendant held the complainant at gunpoint and demanded money from the complainant, that the complainant gave defendant a credit card, and that defendant told the complainant they were going to an ATM together. The complainant also testified that defendant held a gun to the complainant as they walked to the ATM and that defendant told the complainant that defendant would shoot the complainant if the complainant ran. State v. Cottingham, 2020-Ohio-4220, 2020 Ohio App. LEXIS 3106 (Ohio Ct. App., Cuyahoga County 2020).

Defendant juvenile was properly adjudicated delinquent because a reasonable juror could deduce that she committed petty theft; defendant took a phone from her classmate's zipped bookbag without the classmate's consent, and the factfinder could reasonably infer that defendant removed the phone's SIM card to enable her to use the phone as her own. In re A.M., 2019-Ohio-1843, 2019 Ohio App. LEXIS 1919 (Ohio Ct. App., Lake County 2019).

Sufficient evidence supported defendant's convictions for theft by deception and forgery because it established that defendant knowingly committed theft by deception and had, with the purpose to defraud, uttered checks that he knew to have been forged. Because the theft alleged in count eight of the indictment took place in both Ohio and another state, he was subject to prosecution in Ohio. State v. Pettus, 2019-Ohio-2023, 2019 Ohio App. LEXIS 2168 (Ohio Ct. App., Hamilton County 2019), aff'd, 2020-Ohio-4836, 163 Ohio St. 3d 55, 168 N.E.3d 406, 2020 Ohio LEXIS 2259 (Ohio 2020).

Sufficient evidence supported defendant's convictions for grand theft of a motor vehicle, attempted grand theft under, and breaking and entering because the trial court properly instructed the jury in accord with the statute regarding the testimony of the accomplice. Because defendant's girlfriend was not indicted on any charges and no evidence was presented that she was offered or received any favorable treatment in return for testifying on behalf of the prosecution, the trial court did not err in failing to include her in its jury instruction concerning accomplices. State v. Dotson, 2019-Ohio-2393, 139 N.E.3d 430, 2019 Ohio App. LEXIS 2504 (Ohio Ct. App., Trumbull County 2019).

Trial court did not err in convicting defendant for theft because there was sufficient evidence to conclude that defendant tampered with meter and stole electricity, including testimony from service provider's employees that someone twice bypassed the provider's disconnection by reconnecting electrical services to account holder's house, that he was the boyfriend of account holder's daughter, that he called provider to complain and that he acknowledged hooking up a generator to breaker box. State v. Hunt, 2019-Ohio-2352, 2019 Ohio App. LEXIS 2457 (Ohio Ct. App., Darke County 2019).

Trial court did not err by overruling defendant's motion for acquittal because evidence was sufficient to sustain defendant's conviction for theft by deception for funds received under a construction contract as defendant took the money paid by client as partial payment for the work to be performed and never returned to complete the work or refund any monies. State v. Hickey, 2019-Ohio-2640, 2019 Ohio App. LEXIS 2798 (Ohio Ct. App., Harrison County 2019).

Sufficient evidence supported defendant's convictions for grand theft of a motor vehicle, attempted grand theft under, and breaking and entering because the trial court properly instructed the jury in accord with the statute regarding the testimony of the accomplice. Because defendant's girlfriend was not indicted on any charges and no evidence was presented that she was offered or received any favorable treatment in return for testifying on behalf of the prosecution, the trial court did not err in failing to include her in its jury instruction concerning accomplices. State v. Dotson, 2019-Ohio-2393, 139 N.E.3d 430, 2019 Ohio App. LEXIS 2504 (Ohio Ct. App., Trumbull County 2019).

Trial court did not err in convicting defendant for theft because there was sufficient evidence to conclude that defendant tampered with meter and stole electricity, including testimony from service provider's employees that someone twice bypassed the provider's disconnection by reconnecting electrical services to account holder's house, that he was the boyfriend of account holder's daughter, that he called provider to complain and that he acknowledged hooking up a generator to breaker box. State v. Hunt, 2019-Ohio-2352, 2019 Ohio App. LEXIS 2457 (Ohio Ct. App., Darke County 2019).



Evidence was sufficient to support the defendant's conviction for one count of theft, because he exerted control of the bank's property beyond the scope of consent when he withdrew and failed to return $4,800 despite having an account balance of $41.74. State v. Harris, 2019-Ohio-3102, 2019 Ohio App. LEXIS 3187 (Ohio Ct. App., Cuyahoga County 2019).

Sufficient evidence supported defendant's conviction for petty theft because a rational trier of fact could have found that defendant knowingly exerted control over the victim's fishing reel without his consent with the purpose to deprive him of it. According to the victim, defendant presented the rod and reel to him after he returned to the lake, refused to give them back to him, and loaded it into her fiancé's van. State v. Black, 2019-Ohio-5017, 2019 Ohio App. LEXIS 5100 (Ohio Ct. App., Wayne County 2019).

Overwhelming weight of evidence, including all the machinations of defendant's criminal enterprise found in the basement office of his residence, demonstrated that his convictions for engaging in a pattern of corrupt activity, money laundering, conspiracy, forgery, theft, telecommunications fraud, and possession of criminal tools were supported by sufficient evidence. The evidence seized from defendant's home, testimony, and surveillance evidence of defendant driving with people or meeting people at various locations with banking institutions where fraudulent checks were cashed or attempts to cash checks were made at that time established his guilt. State v. Mock, 2018-Ohio-268, 106 N.E.3d 154, 2018 Ohio App. LEXIS 264 (Ohio Ct. App., Cuyahoga County 2018).

Sufficient evidence supported defendant's conviction for petty theft because the State was not required to demonstrate that defendant knew the identity of the owner of the property at issue, since the identity of the owner of the property was not an element of the offense. There was also evidence that he had the purpose to deprive the owner of property and knowingly obtained or exerted control over the property by deception because he agreed to assist his brother in stealing from someone (a confidential informant) who was trying to buy drugs, by providing fake drugs in exchange for $60. State v. Senz, 2018-Ohio-628, 107 N.E.3d 685, 2018 Ohio App. LEXIS 656 (Ohio Ct. App., Medina County 2018).

Evidence was sufficient to support defendant's conviction for theft because The State proved that victim owned the car and keys. The State introduced a copy of certificate of title that identified the victim as the owner of the car; although the victim testified that she had allowed defendant to use the car, the unrefuted evidence was that victim owned the car, and defendant refused to return the sole set of car keys. State v. Brogden, 2018-Ohio-722, 2018 Ohio App. LEXIS 758 (Ohio Ct. App., Hamilton County 2018).

Court could rationally view the circumstantial evidence as proving that defendant took the victim's car keys, as the victim had last seen his keys on a chair, near a pizza box, and the keys disappeared after defendant asked the victim if he could have a slice of pizza. State v. Mallory, 2018-Ohio-1846, 2018 Ohio App. LEXIS 1973 (Ohio Ct. App., Cuyahoga County 2018).

Sufficient evidence sustained defendant's robbery conviction because the state presented evidence of theft by showing that defendant ordered the victim to give him bag and evidence of force was shown by defendant's statement that he would "pull the hammer" if the victim did not turn it over. The conviction was not against the manifest weight of the evidence because the jury was in the best position to evaluate witness credibility, and the appellate court could not say that the jury lost its way. State v. Henry, 2018-Ohio-2174, 2018 Ohio App. LEXIS 2359 (Ohio Ct. App., Summit County 2018).

Sufficient evidence supported defendant's convictions for aggravated robbery, felonious assault, theft of an elderly person because, in addition to linking him to the vehicle at the scene, overwhelming evidence established that defendant was the victim's attacker including that searches of both the vehicle and defendant's apartment revealed items that had been stolen from the victim and a license plate for the victim's vehicle was found in the blue vehicle when defendant was arrested. State v. Shelton, 2018-Ohio-3895, 2018 Ohio App. LEXIS 4216 (Ohio Ct. App., Hamilton County 2018).

Defendant's conviction for grand theft by deception under R.C. 2913.02(A)(3) was supported by sufficient evidence when multiple witnesses testified as to how they determined that defendant, a courier, was billing for deliveries he did not make. State v. DeRemer, 2018-Ohio-3931, 120 N.E.3d 490, 2018 Ohio App. LEXIS 4254 (Ohio Ct. App., Summit County 2018).

Sufficient evidence supported defendant's theft conviction because defendant admitted to pawning the victim's property, the victim did not give permission to defendant to take the items, and the items went missing after the victim terminated defendant's employment; thus, defendant was not entitled to an acquittal on the charge. State v. Magri, 2018-Ohio-4275, 2018 Ohio App. LEXIS 4602 (Ohio Ct. App., Geauga County 2018).

Sufficient evidence supported defendant's convictions for burglary and theft because there was more than just eyewitness identification linking him to the first property since he and his codefendant were present at the city hall meeting where they attempted to defend their unlawful presence at the property. With respect to the second property, the testimony that defendant was ignorant to the status of the house did not show that defendant's conviction was supported by insufficient evidence. State v. Heaggans, 2018-Ohio-4328, 2018 Ohio App. LEXIS 4653 (Ohio Ct. App., Cuyahoga County 2018).

Defendant's convictions for misuse of credit cards and grand theft were supported by the weight and sufficiency of the evidence, as the State showed defendant's purposeful unauthorized use of the credit card for gas purchases beyond his company's required driving for work appointments, and while on vacation. State v. Luton, 2018-Ohio-4708, 2018 Ohio App. LEXIS 5028 (Ohio Ct. App., Cuyahoga County 2018).

Sufficient evidence supported defendant's theft conviction because defendant took money out of the developmentally disabled victim's wallet and told her "he needed it," the victim responded, "you can't have my money," and the victim got the money back by punching and kicking defendant; thus, defendant was not entitled to a Crim.R. 29 acquittal. State v. Moore, 2018-Ohio-4778, 2018 Ohio App. LEXIS 5120 (Ohio Ct. App., Cuyahoga County 2018).

There was sufficient evidence to convict defendant of burglary under R.C. 2911.12(A)(3) and grand theft under R.C. 2913.02(1), and the convictions were not against the manifest weight of the evidence, in light of the circumstantial evidence, including the presence of a phone near the victim's home with defendant's picture on the lockscreen, a neighbor's recognition of the man on the screen as the person he had seen carrying a television in the neighbor's backyard and his pointing out to police the home where defendant lived, the victim's testimony that defendant was always watching him from his porch when he returned home from work, the presence of stolen items in the bushes at defendant's residence, and defendant's fleeing and hiding from police when they approached him. State v. Jones, 2017-Ohio-288, 2017 Ohio App. LEXIS 285 (Ohio Ct. App., Cuyahoga County 2017).

Defendant's convictions for burglary, grand theft, and theft of drugs were proper because evidence was sufficient. When the victims came home from the store, they discovered that approximately $19,000 in cash, jewelry, and prescription medication was missing, defendant's son admitted to going into their home and taking the money and items at issue, and a reasonable juror could have concluded that defendant supported, assisted, encouraged, cooperated with, advised, or incited her son and shared his criminal intent. State v. Vanhorn, 2017-Ohio-704, 81 N.E.3d 15, 2017 Ohio App. LEXIS 696 (Ohio Ct. App., Ashtabula County 2017).

There was sufficient evidence to support a finding that defendant, a building contractor, committed the crime of theft from a person in a protected class; a building official testified that projects were left uncompleted and not done in a workmanlike manner at the victims' home, including new windows that were paid for by the victims but never ordered or installed. State v. Vertucci, 2017-Ohio-2838, 2017 Ohio App. LEXIS 1868 (Ohio Ct. App., Summit County 2017).

Sufficient evidence supported defendant's conviction for attempted theft because the State offered sufficient evidence, if believed, to support that defendant took a substantial step. Defendant solicited a woman to open a bank account, hired a driver to take them from downtown to the bank, and repeatedly instructed the woman about opening the account and the woman's testimony was corroborated by the bank employee. State v. Elahee, 2017-Ohio-7085, 2017 Ohio App. LEXIS 3214 (Ohio Ct. App., Hamilton County 2017).

Sufficient evidence supported defendant's conviction for theft from an elderly person (beyond the scope of consent) because the evidence showed that defendant, with purpose to deprive the victims, knowingly obtained or exerted control over their property beyond the scope of their consent. The amounts of the checks written by defendant, as well as the close relationships she had to the recipients of the checks, further supported a finding that she acted beyond the scope of the victims' consent. State v. Marcum, 2017-Ohio-7517, 2017 Ohio App. LEXIS 3848 (Ohio Ct. App., Montgomery County 2017).

Sufficient evidence supported defendant's conviction for theft of checks because the evidence showed that, with purpose to deprive the victims, she knowingly obtained the checks without their consent. Evidence reflected that an online order for checks in the victims' and defendant's names on the victims' bank account was placed on the date that defendant's powers of attorney were revoked and the checks were ordered to be sent to defendant at her home address. State v. Marcum, 2017-Ohio-7517, 2017 Ohio App. LEXIS 3848 (Ohio Ct. App., Montgomery County 2017).

Defendant's theft convictions were supported by sufficient evidence and were not against the manifest weight of the evidence, given the evidence that defendant used school funds for his personal expenses, which the jury could find more credible than defendant's claims. State v. Tucker, 2017-Ohio-7735, 97 N.E.3d 1056, 2017 Ohio App. LEXIS 4069 (Ohio Ct. App., Franklin County 2017).

There was sufficient evidence that defendant was complicit in aiding and abetting in a theft from a sporting goods store because defendant admitted that she was present in the car at the time the burglary was being committed and she helped close the trunk after the stolen goods were placed there, the stolen property was found in defendant's vehicle, and security video footage revealed that the item used to smash the store door was transported to the crime scene in defendant's vehicle. State v. King, 2017-Ohio-7731, 2017 Ohio App. LEXIS 4063 (Ohio Ct. App., Delaware County 2017).

Sufficient evidence supported defendant's convictions for theft, as surveillance videos captured the perpetrator's face and body, and after comparing these images to defendant's booking photo, a police officer identified defendant as the perpetrator of the thefts. State v. Prickett, 2017-Ohio-8128, 2017 Ohio App. LEXIS 4495 (Ohio Ct. App., Butler County 2017).

Evidence was sufficient to convict defendant of workers' compensation fraud and theft because it established that she worked at a pub in violation of the terms of the temporary total compensation she was receiving, and the circumstantial evidence belied her claim that she was unaware of her ineligibility for the benefits she received. State v. Fletcher, 2017-Ohio-9207, 2017 Ohio App. LEXIS 5646 (Ohio Ct. App., Delaware County 2017).

Convictions for theft and receiving stolen property were supported by sufficient evidence, including evidence that defendant's driver's licence was on record as having been photocopied in relation to the sale of a necklace that matched the description of the one reported stolen from the victim, defendant was still in possession of that license, and the karat weight of the gold and the size of the diamond matched the appraisal for the victim's stolen necklace. State v. Nichols, 2016-Ohio-567, 2016 Ohio App. LEXIS 501 (Ohio Ct. App., Delaware County 2016).

State set forth sufficient evidence of defendant juvenile's guilt on two counts of theft because the record demonstrated that defendant confessed to a detective in a written statement to the theft of the property at issue; the trial court properly considered the written statement. In re T.B., 2016-Ohio-575, 2016 Ohio App. LEXIS 503 (Ohio Ct. App., Tuscarawas County 2016).

Defendant's convictions for robbery and theft were supported by the weight and sufficiency of the evidence, as there was surveillance video and testimony showing defendant's complicity in the robbery of the store, and it was within the jury's province to find that her multiple, conflicting explanations for her hand gestures during the incident were not credible. State v. Moore, 2016-Ohio-1020, 2016 Ohio App. LEXIS 920 (Ohio Ct. App., Delaware County 2016).

Sufficient evidence supported defendant's theft conviction because the testimony did not require the trial court to stack inferences or rely on speculation. Instead, the prosecution presented credible evidence that defendant knowingly deceived the store by switching Universal Product Code (UPC) stickers on its property to obtain a TV wall mount for a lesser amount than it was actually priced. City of Brooklyn v. Woods, 2016-Ohio-1223, 2016 Ohio App. LEXIS 1122 (Ohio Ct. App., Cuyahoga County 2016).

Evidence supported defendant's convictions for felonious assault, kidnapping, and theft because eyewitness testimony placed him at the scene as the one who attacked the victim, the aunt of defendant's girlfriend testified that defendant told her that he stabbed the victim in self-defense, and the victim testified that defendant was the one who stabbed him. State v. Halstead, 2016-Ohio-290, 2016 Ohio App. LEXIS 262 (Ohio Ct. App., Cuyahoga County 2016).

Defendant's conviction for theft by deception was supported by the weight and sufficiency of the evidence, as the State established that defendant billed for in-home Medicaid services that she did not perform, and the credibility of the witnesses and of an investigator was within the trial court's province. State v. Sims, 2016-Ohio-4763, 2016 Ohio App. LEXIS 2557 (Ohio Ct. App., Franklin County 2016).

Defendant's conviction of theft based on her forging her employer's checks was supported by sufficient evidence and was not against the manifest weight of the evidence, as the evidence supported a finding that someone forged all of the disputed checks, defendant essentially admitted forging the few checks the general manager discovered before defendant was fired and a thorough investigation was launched, defendant was the only employee who benefitted from the forgery of the checks, and defendant was uniquely situated to enter the forged checks into the employer's accounting system as having been issued to bona fide vendors. State v. Blevins, 2016-Ohio-5049, 2016 Ohio App. LEXIS 2841 (Ohio Ct. App., Clark County 2016).

Sufficient evidence supported defendant's conviction for petty theft under Tallmadge, Ohio, Codified Ordinances 545.05, which was analogous to the instant statute, because a security employee testified that two women with large purses put merchandise into them, when he approached the women after they completed a transaction at the cash registers, they ran. The employee identified defendant as one of the two women, and records from the layaway transaction also identified her as the owner of the layaway account. City of Tallmadge v. Johnson, 2016-Ohio-5214, 2016 Ohio App. LEXIS 3089 (Ohio Ct. App., Summit County 2016).

There was sufficient evidence to support defendant's conviction of first-degree misdemeanor theft when an officer located a missing stove and refrigerator at defendant's residence, defendant admitted to moving the items, the victim testified that the stove and refrigerator were missing and identified the items in the officer's photographs as being his property, the victim testified that he did not give defendant consent to take his property, nor did defendant return the property, and the victim testified that the replacement cost for the stove and refrigerator was $850. State v. Wickwire, 2016-Ohio-5217, 2016 Ohio App. LEXIS 3092 (Ohio Ct. App., Summit County 2016).

Trial court properly convicted defendant of theft because the jury could infer that defendant had knowledge of a fraudulent return of goods at a store because of the involved role he played in driving the accomplice to the store and providing his identification to engage in the fraudulent return, the record did not reflect that a witness's in-court identification of defendant was erroneous, and video evidence of defendant completing the fraudulent return and the receipt from the transaction that was labelled with his name and address were provided for the jury. State v. Spencer, 2016-Ohio-5304, 2016 Ohio App. LEXIS 3158 (Ohio Ct. App., Stark County 2016).



Sufficient evidence supported defendant's theft conviction because it showed that, at the time he took the customer's money, defendant did not intend to perform the transmission work or refund the money. Even after a visit from the detective, defendant did no work on the transmission, nor did he refund the money. State v. Kuhar, 2016-Ohio-5280, 2016 Ohio App. LEXIS 3141 (Ohio Ct. App., Medina County 2016).

Sufficient evidence supported defendant's conviction for theft of an elderly person with purpose to deprive him of services because defendant agreed to clean up trees and brush piles in exchange for $800, which was paid to him in advance, but did not do any of the work. The jury could reasonably have inferred that defendant had no intent to repay the money or perform under the contract and that the misrepresentation actually caused the victim to transfer property to the accused. State v. Burton, 2016-Ohio-5380, 2016 Ohio App. LEXIS 3289 (Ohio Ct. App., Delaware County 2016).

Defendant's convictions for complicity to burglary and complicity to theft were supported by sufficient evidence, as the State established that defendant acted knowingly when he aided and abetted his codefendants in the theft and then resale of personal property from a residence because he was aware of their plan to take property from the residence without permission, and he drove them to and from the residence. State v. Wright, 2016-Ohio-5465, 2016 Ohio App. LEXIS 3349 (Ohio Ct. App., Hardin County 2016).

Sufficient evidence supported defendant's convictions for aggravated robbery, aggravated vehicular assault, failure to comply with an order or signal of a police officer, breaking and entering, and grand theft because the State showed that, after breaking into the maintenance area, defendant drove away from the golf club in the club's stolen truck, evaded the police officers that were pursuing him, and crashed the truck into a bar, injuring 13 people. Multiple witnesses testified that defendant was the only occupant of the truck when it crashed into the bar. State v. Pawlak, 2016-Ohio-5926, 2016 Ohio App. LEXIS 3779 (Ohio Ct. App., Cuyahoga County 2016).

Manifest weight and sufficient evidence supported defendant's theft conviction because defendant was not authorized to use a company credit card, defendant admitted to making the purchases with the company credit card including purchases of non-diesel gasoline and gift cards, and the jury found defendant's employer more credible with respect to whether defendant had permission to use the card. State v. Ferguson, 2016-Ohio-363, 2016 Ohio App. LEXIS 314 (Ohio Ct. App., Franklin County 2016).

Sufficient evidence supported defendant's convictions for aggravated murder, aggravated robbery, grand theft of a motor vehicle, and having a weapon while under disability because the evidence showed that defendant shot the victim in the back of the head in the victim's apartment, ransacked the apartment and stole items such as televisions, and then stole the victim's car. State v. Wood, 2016-Ohio-143, 2016 Ohio App. LEXIS 130 (Ohio Ct. App., Montgomery County 2016).

Defendant juvenile's adjudication of delinquent for committing theft was supported by the weight and sufficiency of the evidence, based on testimony that she exerted control over store items when she exited the store without paying for them, and that she did not have consent to do so. In re E.A., 2016-Ohio-7281, 2016 Ohio App. LEXIS 4139 (Ohio Ct. App., Summit County 2016).

State met its burden of production regarding each element of the crime of theft, and, accordingly, there was sufficient evidence to prove defendant's conviction; a receipt was generated that indicated there should be over $1,000 in a kiosk, but when the money was counted somewhere around $500-$700 was missing. State v. Andrews, 2016-Ohio-7389, 2016 Ohio App. LEXIS 4246 (Ohio Ct. App., Delaware County 2016).

Sufficient evidence supported defendant's theft conviction because, inter alia, defendant and co-defendant took a laptop, which belonged to neither of them, from the home of co-defendant's grandmother, defendant made several statements to the investigating sergeant that he knew the laptop was stolen, and defendant took the laptop inside the dealer's home, exchanged the laptop for drugs, returned to the grandmother's home, and consumed the drugs with co-defendant. State v. Octavio, 2016-Ohio-7661, 2016 Ohio App. LEXIS 4530 (Ohio Ct. App., Stark County 2016).

Evidence that defendant boxed up several pieces of the victim's property, loaded them in his van, left the premises, and did not have consent of the owner was sufficient to allow a finder of fact to find the elements of theft proven beyond a reasonable doubt. State v. Kraus, 2016-Ohio-8003, 74 N.E.3d 880, 2016 Ohio App. LEXIS 4877 (Ohio Ct. App., Ottawa County 2016).

Sufficient evidence supported defendant's conviction, in light of the magnitude of electronic benefits transfer (EBT) activity at defendant's convenience store; according to agents, the five stores it examined that were similar to defendant's store had EBT sales that normally ranged from $2,000 to $4,000 a month, but defendant's store had EBT sales that sometimes exceeded $100,000 in a month. State v. Byrd, 2016-Ohio-8135, 2016 Ohio App. LEXIS 4995 (Ohio Ct. App., Summit County 2016).

Defendant's convictions for theft and safecracking were supported by sufficient evidence because, although no direct evidence placed defendant in the safe room, the circumstantial evidence could have reasonably supported a finding that defendant was the person who took the money and the checks from the safe and left the checks in the men's restroom because the State showed that defendant was the only person who entered the business office area at the relevant times, money and checks were found missing from the area on Monday morning, and defendant was the only person who entered the men's restroom on Saturday where the checks were later found by the janitor. State v. Sexton, 2015-Ohio-934, 2015 Ohio App. LEXIS 913 (Ohio Ct. App., Union County 2015).

Evidence supported defendant's conviction for theft, as the evidence showed that defendant drove a getaway car, several witnesses identified his vehicle outside a store that was robbed, and defendant received a portion of the money obtained from the crime. State v. Peterson, 2015-Ohio-1013, 2015 Ohio App. LEXIS 959 (Ohio Ct. App., Cuyahoga County 2015).

There was sufficient evidence presented to convict defendant of grand theft because testimony demonstrated that defendant guaranteed the investment money for seven investors in his Ponzi scheme and many of the "receipts" or "invoices" defendant gave to the investors stated specific timelines for the return on their investment. Although a few of the investors gave some money to one investor to give to defendant, the evidence showed that defendant had received that money to "invest," but he did not as there was no work to invest in. State v. Sevitz, 2015-Ohio-5047, 2015 Ohio App. LEXIS 4892 (Ohio Ct. App., Allen County 2015).

Because the indictment clearly stated that the element of "beyond the scope of the express or implied consent" was present in the theft case, defendant's no contest plea to the indictment was properly accepted. Even if the State's factual narrative was deficient, and had it been required, the trial court specifically and explicitly stated it also considered the allegations in the indictment, which were sufficient to convict defendant. State v. Sevitz, 2015-Ohio-5047, 2015 Ohio App. LEXIS 4892 (Ohio Ct. App., Allen County 2015).

There was sufficient evidence to support defendant's convictions for breaking and entering and three counts of grand theft because it was demonstrated that a day after defendant was told he could not get his job back from his former employer, he robbed the business of a utility truck, a dump truck, multiple tools, and cash. The convictions were not against the manifest weight of the evidence because there was a video recording of a police interview where defendant told the officer that the reason he had taken the tools was because he wanted to start his own business. State v. Choate, 2015-Ohio-4972, 2015 Ohio App. LEXIS 4809 (Ohio Ct. App., Summit County 2015).

Evidence supported defendant's conviction of theft by deception, as the evidence indicated that induced his neighbor to sign a contract for roof repair and pay for additional work that he never commenced, and that defendant advised the neighbor that he spoke with her husband and that he approved the work and desired her to sign the contract; the court could infer that defendant had the purpose to deprive his neighbor of property when he kept and cashed a check. State v. Morrison, 2014-Ohio-5467, 2014 Ohio App. LEXIS 5301 (Ohio Ct. App., Ashtabula County 2014).

Evidence that defendant was authorized to remove the vehicle from the car dealership for 10 to 15 minutes to complete a test drive and that defendant failed to return the vehicle in the allotted time, the whereabouts of the vehicle were unknown until the vehicle was located five days later in a high crime area with the keys in the center console, and defendant did not inform the dealership of the vehicle's location supported defendant's conviction for theft of a motor vehicle. State v. Jackson, 2014-Ohio-3779, 2014 Ohio App. LEXIS 3711 (Ohio Ct. App., Butler County 2014).

Evidence that defendant sold the victim a fake baseball card via Craiglist, along with properly admitted evidence of similar sales of fake cards made by defendant on two prior occasions and that the victim received a call from a person saying he made fake baseball cards for defendant, was sufficient to support defendant's convictions for both forgery and theft. State v. Regan, 2014-Ohio-3797, 2014 Ohio App. LEXIS 3725 (Ohio Ct. App., Delaware County 2014).

Defendant's conviction for petty theft was supported by sufficient evidence based on security camera footage of defendant and her sister as they went through a store, unpaid items in a bag after they left the store, and defendant's sister's admission that they were "stealing" from the store. State v. Poore, 2014-Ohio-3089, 2014 Ohio App. LEXIS 3022 (Ohio Ct. App., Wayne County 2014).

Evidence supported defendant's petty theft conviction, as the State presented evidence from the victim's neighbors, who witnessed defendant walk behind her house, heard the sound of glass breaking, and then saw defendant and another male carrying out of the house a large item and a plastic bag that had wires coming out of it. State v. Smith, 2014-Ohio-3420, 2014 Ohio App. LEXIS 3356 (Ohio Ct. App., Cuyahoga County 2014).

Evidence that defendant was authorized to remove the vehicle from the car dealership for 10 to 15 minutes to complete a test drive and that defendant failed to return the vehicle in the allotted time, the whereabouts of the vehicle were unknown until the vehicle was located five days later in a high crime area with the keys in the center console, and defendant did not inform the dealership of the vehicle's location supported defendant's conviction for theft of a motor vehicle. State v. Jackson, 2014-Ohio-3779, 2014 Ohio App. LEXIS 3711 (Ohio Ct. App., Butler County 2014).

Evidence that defendant sold the victim a fake baseball card via Craiglist, along with properly admitted evidence of similar sales of fake cards made by defendant on two prior occasions and that the victim received a call from a person saying he made fake baseball cards for defendant, was sufficient to support defendant's convictions for both forgery and theft. State v. Regan, 2014-Ohio-3797, 2014 Ohio App. LEXIS 3725 (Ohio Ct. App., Delaware County 2014).

Defendant's convictions for aggravated robbery and theft were supported by the weight and sufficiency of the evidence, as there was testimony from the victim that he was beaten and that his car and wallet were stolen, and both codefendants testified about the incident. State v. Roth, 2014-Ohio-4273, 2014 Ohio App. LEXIS 4188 (Ohio Ct. App., Muskingum County 2014).

Evidence supported defendant's conviction of theft by deception, as the testimony of witnesses, combined with video and documentary evidence admitted at trial, if believed, established that defendant knowingly submitted false and fraudulent billing statements to the Ohio Bureau of Workers' Compensation, with the purpose or intent to deceive it, and that he obtained reimbursement in an amount greater than $7,500 for chiropractic services he did not perform. State v. Bliss, 2014-Ohio-4357, 2014 Ohio App. LEXIS 4262 (Ohio Ct. App., Franklin County 2014).

Defendant's conviction for theft of a credit card was supported by the evidence, which included a video surveillance tape showing defendant apparently picking the card up and then leaving the restaurant where he worked, statements made by defendant,and the testimony of a co-workers. State v. Turner, 2014-Ohio-4460, 2014 Ohio App. LEXIS 4371 (Ohio Ct. App., Summit County 2014).

Evidence supported defendant's conviction for theft, as defendant and his co-defendants made plans to travel to various shopping areas, enter restaurants, and steal wallets from purses located near the back of chairs while the victim of the theft ate at the restaurant; the evidence demonstrated that defendant aided and abetted his co-defendants in the utilization of the stolen credit cards and all three received stolen property as a result of the transactions. State v. Mack, 2014-Ohio-4552, 2014 Ohio App. LEXIS 4457 (Ohio Ct. App., Delaware County 2014).

Defendant's conviction for aiding and abetting theft was supported by the weight and sufficiency of the evidence because she tacitly admitted her identity as the perpetrator who activated a store's entrance doors, which allowed other perpetrators to leave with unpaid merchandise. State v. Ihinger, 2014-Ohio-5237, 2014 Ohio App. LEXIS 5074 (Ohio Ct. App., Coshocton County 2014).

Sufficient evidence supported defendant's convictions, as the perpetrators fled a store with possession of the victims' property, thereby demonstrating their intent to permanently withhold the property from each victim, and a detective testified that defendant admitted his role in the robbery and identified himself as the individual wearing a green-hooded sweatshirt during the incident. State v. Evans, 2020-Ohio-3968, 2020 Ohio App. LEXIS 2868 (Ohio Ct. App., Cuyahoga County 2020).

Sufficient evidence supported defendant's aggravated robbery conviction because both clerks testified that defendant entered their store and, upon displaying a knife, he demanded money from the clerks. His purpose to deprive the owners without their consent was clear in his actions and in his attempting to exit the stores with the money. State v. Russell, 2014-Ohio-2467, 2014 Ohio App. LEXIS 2408 (Ohio Ct. App., Columbiana County 2014).

Sufficient evidence supported defendant's conviction for theft by deception because he provided false information with the purpose not to give proper consideration; i.e., to pay for, the medical services that he received, and did so knowingly. Defendant lied about his identity to three hospital employees, failed to pay his bill, and he admitted to a detective — both orally and in a written statement — that he provided false information. State v. Cullins, 2014-Ohio-2202, 2014 Ohio App. LEXIS 2128 (Ohio Ct. App., Montgomery County 2014).

Sufficient evidence supported defendant's convictions for theft, theft in office, tampering with evidence, and falsification because a deputy sheriff testified that the stolen items were found on defendant's property and that defendant had worked security for the companies whose property was stolen. State v. Hughes, 2014-Ohio-2328, 2014 Ohio App. LEXIS 2278 (Ohio Ct. App., Morrow County 2014).

Evidence supported defendant's conviction of theft by deception, as the victim's testimony demonstrated that defendant initiated and completed a transaction for college basketball tickets with the victim, and that defendant provided the victim with two fake tickets in exchange for the victim's two valid tickets and $250. State v. Cargill, 2014-Ohio-2073, 2014 Ohio App. LEXIS 2012 (Ohio Ct. App., Franklin County 2014).

Sufficient evidence supported the delinquency adjudication for burglary, tampering with evidence, theft, and obstructing official business because appellant juvenile trespassed in the victim's house by stealth while she was home with purpose to commit a theft offense, knowingly obtained control over the victim's laptop without consent, hampered the officer's performance of his lawful duties, and attempted to dispose of the laptop. In re M.R., 2014-Ohio-1554, 2014 Ohio App. LEXIS 1505 (Ohio Ct. App., Erie County 2014).

Defendant's convictions for five counts of theft and one count of possession of criminal tools were not against the sufficiency or the manifest weight of the evidence, because the car that he owned was consistent with the vehicle involved in the drive-offs and defendant's interviews with the police showed inconsistencies in his explanation. The jury was shown the video of each incident, the clothing taken from defendant's home and photographs of his car. State v. Cheatham, 2014-Ohio-1547, 2014 Ohio App. LEXIS 1502 (Ohio Ct. App., Ashland County 2014).

Sufficient evidence supported defendant's conviction for five counts of theft and one count of possessing criminal tools for stealing gasoline from a gas station, because the jury was shown the video of each incident, the clothing taken from defendant's home and photographs of his car that matched the description of the vehicle involved in the drive-offs. Defendant's interviews with the police showed inconsistencies in his explanation, and his credibility was a matter for the jury to decide. State v. Cheatham, 2014-Ohio-1545, 2014 Ohio App. LEXIS 1498 (Ohio Ct. App., Ashland County 2014).

Sufficient evidence supported defendant's conviction for five counts of theft and one count of possessing criminal tools for stealing gasoline from a gas station, because the jury was shown the video of each incident, the clothing taken from defendant's home and photographs of his car that matched the description of the vehicle involved in the drive-offs. Defendant's interviews with the police showed inconsistencies in his explanation. State v. Cheatham, 2014-Ohio-1544, 2014 Ohio App. LEXIS 1497 (Ohio Ct. App., Ashland County 2014).

Reasonable jury could conclude that all the elements of theft were met as a reasonable jury could conclude that defendant purposefully deprived the first victim of a game system and that he exerted his control over the game system by taking it from the home without the first victim's consent. State v. Coker, 2014-Ohio-1210, 2014 Ohio App. LEXIS 1123 (Ohio Ct. App., Summit County 2014).

Defendant's conviction for robbery was supported by sufficient evidence that defendant committed a "theft offense" because defendant stole cash from a victim's wallet and then fled the scene. State v. DeBorde, 2014-Ohio-761, 2014 Ohio App. LEXIS 748 (Ohio Ct. App., Butler County 2014).

Sufficient evidence supported defendant's conviction for breaking and entering, because he admitted that he was trespassing, copper plumbing was stolen from the house, the back door had been kicked in, and his DNA matched the blood sample found in the kitchen. The jury concluded that defendant, by force or stealth, unlawfully entered the vacant home with the purpose to commit a theft offense. State v. Easley, 2014-Ohio-575, 2014 Ohio App. LEXIS 554 (Ohio Ct. App., Summit County 2014).

Sufficient evidence supported defendant's conviction for grand theft of a motor vehicle because defendant listed a vehicle for sale, the victim purchased the vehicle and paid defendant in cash, the victim received a signed title and a set of keys to the vehicle, at which point the victim became the owner and defendant no longer had a lawful right to possess the vehicle, but defendant deprived the victim of the vehicle by moving the vehicle to another location, without the victim's consent. State v. Plata, 2014-Ohio-449, 2014 Ohio App. LEXIS 450 (Ohio Ct. App., Warren County 2014).

State presented sufficient evidence to support defendant's convictions of breaking and entering and theft, as it was shown that the person who entered the property and took the vehicle did so without privilege, no one had given permission to take the vehicle and the property contained no trespassing signs, and given the short amount of time between the theft and defendant's apprehension in the vehicle, the jury could have inferred that the driver had stolen the vehicle. State v. Cole, 2014-Ohio-233, 2014 Ohio App. LEXIS 216 (Ohio Ct. App., Miami County 2014).

Sufficient evidence supported defendant's conviction for burglary, because officers found him inside an apartment belonging to the complainant without permission to be there; the physical evidence supported a finding that defendant gained entry to the residence by removing bolts from the security door and kicking open the front door. The complainant testified that copper wire were removed from the back of the stove; the State was not required to prove that defendant actually committed a theft offense inside the apartment — only that he had the intent to do so. State v. Smith, 2014-Ohio-94, 2014 Ohio App. LEXIS 81 (Ohio Ct. App., Franklin County 2014).

Defendant's theft conviction was supported by evidencethat defendant, once inside the dairy bar, exerted control over the owner's property, without her permission. State v. Tolle, 2013-Ohio-5568, 2013 Ohio App. LEXIS 5814 (Ohio Ct. App., Adams County 2013).

Evidence was sufficient to support defendant's conviction for theft because the State proved that defendant knowingly exerted control over the victim's property, without her consent, and with the purpose to deprive her of that property; the State presented evidence from the victim's neighbor that she saw defendant carrying a lamp out of the victim's home, and the police found several of the victim's things in the backyard of the house across the street. State v. Jennings, 2013-Ohio-5428, 2013 Ohio App. LEXIS 5674 (Ohio Ct. App., Cuyahoga County 2013).

Sufficient evidence supported defendant's conviction for theft because he was observed loading materials into a truck and it could have been inferred that he did not have the consent of the owner to remove scrap iron from the premises. State v. Hooper, 2013-Ohio-4898, 2013 Ohio App. LEXIS 5093 (Ohio Ct. App., Delaware County 2013).

Sufficiency and weight of the evidence supported defendant's convictions for breaking and entering, possessing criminal tools, and theft, as the State introduced evidence to establish each of the elements of the crimes, and it showed that defendant was the perpetrator through DNA evidence found on a water bottle that was recovered within the bag of criminal tools at the scene of the crime. State v. Merritt, 2013-Ohio-4834, 2013 Ohio App. LEXIS 5036 (Ohio Ct. App., Fulton County 2013).

Sufficient evidence supported defendant's convictions for grand theft, forgery, and tampering with government records because the State presented testimony indicating that defendant signed invoices containing false information, he entered into the contracts fraudulently from the very beginning because he never intended to comply with the contract, and he signed the contracts and purported that they were genuine, when he never intended to comply with the terms. State v. Trammell, 2013-Ohio-4615, 3 N.E.3d 260, 2013 Ohio App. LEXIS 4835 (Ohio Ct. App., Montgomery County 2013).

-Evidence that defendant pushed the shopping cart filled with items past the last point of sale without paying and began exiting the store, showing a lack of intent to turn around and move back into the store, was sufficient to support defendant's conviction for petty theft. State v. Csillag, 2013-Ohio-4608, 2013 Ohio App. LEXIS 4810 (Ohio Ct. App., Franklin County 2013).

Evidence was sufficient to support defendant's theft conviction, as the State presented evidence that defendant assisted an accomplice in loading television sets onto a shopping cart at a store, and a store asset protection associate's testimony that defendant distracted the store greeter near the exit as the accomplice pushed the shopping cart out of the store was corroborated by store security video. State v. Jordan, 2013-Ohio-4172, 2013 Ohio App. LEXIS 4369 (Ohio Ct. App., Summit County 2013).

Jury did not lose its way in returning a guilty verdict of aggravated robbery, kidnapping, and theft of drugs, as the victim's version of event supported the convictions and was corroborated by a 911 recording, and a witness would testified favorably for defendant was impeached. State v. Tackett, 2013-Ohio-4098, 2013 Ohio App. LEXIS 4285 (Ohio Ct. App., Lake County 2013).

Evidence supported defendant's theft conviction, as a store manager expressly stated that the manager saw defendant place DVDs inside defendant's jacket and then attempt to leave the store without paying for any of the items. State v. Grega, 2013-Ohio-4094, 2013 Ohio App. LEXIS 4288 (Ohio Ct. App., Ashtabula County 2013).

Sufficient evidence supported defendant's convictions for theft based on complicity and, as such, he was not entitled to an acquittal because defendant knew his acquaintance was a "booster," and defendant acted to conceal the activities of his acquaintance when they went to "open houses," by closely following or blocking the path of the realtors when they attempted to move from the area and engaging the realtors in conversation to divert attention from his acquaintance. State v. Shipley, 2013-Ohio-4055, 2013 Ohio App. LEXIS 4216 (Ohio Ct. App., Franklin County 2013).

Evidence supported defendant's theft conviction, as defendant only agreed to return the victims' stolen property if defendant received $70 as a reward, and there was testimony that the victims had never given permission to defendant to possess their property and that defendant kept changing defendant's story when interviewed by detectives. State v. Carter, 2013-Ohio-3787, 2013 Ohio App. LEXIS 3944 (Ohio Ct. App., Seneca County 2013).

Evidence that defendant and codefendant entered the store, immediately went to the frozen food section to select turkeys, secured deli meat, and promptly left the store without paying was sufficient to support defendant's theft conviction. City of Cuyahoga Falls v. Campanalie, 2013-Ohio-3509, 2013 Ohio App. LEXIS 3611 (Ohio Ct. App., Summit County 2013).

Defendant's conviction of theft of a dangerous drug was supported by the evidence, as defendant admitted on a tape recording that defendant took five pain pills, and testimony established that approximately half the victim's pills had gone missing. State v. Young, 2013-Ohio-3418, 2013 Ohio App. LEXIS 3508 (Ohio Ct. App., Washington County 2013).

Evidence was sufficient to convict defendant of theft, because testimony was offered that the victim's mental deficiencies were apparent in his physical condition, and the fact the victim nearly depleted his $400,000 savings, thereby jeopardizing his future, supported the trial court's conclusion that defendant knowingly deprived the victim of over $400,000 without the victim's consent State v. Arthurs, 2013-Ohio-3138, 2013 Ohio App. LEXIS 3183 (Ohio Ct. App., Cuyahoga County 2013).

Sufficient evidence supported defendant's convictions for identity fraud, telecommunications fraud, and aggravated theft because, although defendant claimed there was inadequate evidence to prove that he lacked consent to claim his portion of his father's inheritance, he failed to support or put forth a substantive argument in support of that conclusion. The evidence showed that defendant utilized his father's personal identifying information to obtain and cash monies ($182,000) from his father's annuities during the last months of his father's life. State v. Haney, 2013-Ohio-2823, 2013 Ohio App. LEXIS 2875 (Ohio Ct. App., Lake County 2013).

Sufficient evidence supported defendant's convictions because the testimony of the witnesses along with the DNA evidence was sufficient to establish defendant as one of the intruders of the home invasion robbery. That none of the victims could identify defendant as one of the masked intruders and that the DNA profile on the T-shirt had defendant's DNA as the major contributor and the DNA of at least two other, unidentified individuals, as minor contributors did not warrant overturning the convictions. State v. Brown, 2013-Ohio-2690, 2013 Ohio App. LEXIS 2679 (Ohio Ct. App., Cuyahoga County 2013).

Defendant's theft conviction, under R.C. 2913.02(A)(3), was supported by sufficient evidence and was not against the manifest weight of the evidence because the evidence established that defendant, by deception, received compensation from defendant's government employer for work which defendant did not perform. The evidence established that defendant purposely decided not to inform defendant's supervisors that, after losing a union election, that defendant was required to perform regular assigned work in the office and was no longer entitled to 100 percent official time so that defendant could receive 100 percent official time. State v. Davis, 2013-Ohio-2539, 2013 Ohio App. LEXIS 2511 (Ohio Ct. App., Cuyahoga County 2013).

State presented sufficient evidence to sustain defendant's theft conviction, as the victim testified that during a struggle defendant punched the victim in the shoulder and attempted to place the victim in a headlock; believing defendant could cause the victim further harm, the victim complied with defendant's demands and gave defendant $20. State v. Spraggins, 2013-Ohio-2537, 2013 Ohio App. LEXIS 2506 (Ohio Ct. App., Cuyahoga County 2013).

There was sufficient evidence for complicity to commit aggravated robbery, theft, and kidnapping because defendant's niece testified that she and defendant planned to rob the pharmacy, and that defendant aided the robbery by providing her with information concerning the pharmacy's layout, materials to facilitate the robbery, and transportation to and from the pharmacy. State v. Klein, 2013-Ohio-2387, 2013 Ohio App. LEXIS 2338 (Ohio Ct. App., Union County 2013), cert. denied, 573 U.S. 909, 134 S. Ct. 2735, 189 L. Ed. 2d 773, 2014 U.S. LEXIS 4072 (U.S. 2014).

There was sufficient evidence to have found that defendant, as treasurer, intended to purposefully deprive the little league of its property by knowingly exerting control over the league's funds in a way that was beyond the scope of the league's consent, in violation of R.C. 2902.13(A)(2), grand theft. The jury could have determined that many or all of the discrepant checks were utilized for defendant's personal purchases, and that the checks did not represent "reimbursements" because there was no evidence that defendant made any purchases on behalf of the league utilizing her personal funds. State v. Wingate, 2013-Ohio-2079, 2013 Ohio App. LEXIS 1979 (Ohio Ct. App., Summit County 2013).

Defendant's theft conviction was supported by sufficient evidence and was not against the manifest weight of the evidence as the evidence showed that defendant took the victim's purse, which contained her credit cards and checkbook. The evidence supported a finding that defendant had a purpose to knowingly deprive the victim of her credit cards and checkbook as defendant took the purse while the victim was sleeping nearby, he concealed the purse, he decided not to turn the purse into hospital personnel, and he delayed several weeks in returning the purse. State v. Smith, 2013-Ohio-1873, 2013 Ohio App. LEXIS 1753 (Ohio Ct. App., Franklin County 2013).

Defendant's convictions for theft, grand theft, aggravated robbery, and felonious assault were supported by sufficient evidence as the evidence showed that the two victims both identified defendant in a photo spread as being one of the two individuals involved in the theft of their respective dirt bikes; another witness who was present at the time of one of the crimes also identified defendant in a photo spread; the three witnesses also identified defendant in person at trial; the tread pattern on the boots found in defendant's closet matched one set of prints in the back of the second victim's truck, showing that defendant was the person who helped the victim remove the dirt bike from the truck bed before shooting the victim and stealing the bike; defendant was wearing clothing at the time of his arrest that matched the clothing worn by the victim's assailant; and defendant's cell phone showed multiple calls between his cell phone and the victims' respective phones just before the dirt bikes were stolen. State v. Simpson, 2013-Ohio-1696, 2013 Ohio App. LEXIS 1585 (Ohio Ct. App., Montgomery County 2013).

Where victim one identified defendant and codefendant as the two individuals who robbed him at gunpoint and saw defendants drag the second victim behind a building and then, after the second victim ran, heard gunshots and saw the victim fall in the street, and the second victim testified to being robbed at gunpoint and identified a photo of a male, who was defendant, wearing the victim's white "hoodie," there was sufficient evidence to convict defendant of kidnapping, felonious assault, aggravated robbery, theft, and having a weapon while under a disability. State v. Scott, 2013-Ohio-1559, 2013 Ohio App. LEXIS 1434 (Ohio Ct. App., Cuyahoga County 2013).

Evidence supported defendant's conviction for theft, as a surveillance videotape depicted the suspect, what the suspect was wearing, and items that were in the suspect's possession at the time of a break-in at a dental office, and defendant was arrested a week later with similar items which the State contended were the same items used in the break-in, including a hooded sweatshirt, gloves, a flashlight, and a crowbar. State v. Hughes, 2013-Ohio-1551, 2013 Ohio App. LEXIS 1440 (Ohio Ct. App., Cuyahoga County 2013).

Evidence supported defendant's theft conviction, based on defendant's identification on surveillance video; at the time of defendant's arrest defendant was caught with what appeared to be the same items used in surveillance videos during two break-ins. State v. Hughes, 2013-Ohio-1550, 2013 Ohio App. LEXIS 1441 (Ohio Ct. App., Cuyahoga County 2013).

Defendant's theft conviction under R.C. 2913.02 was supported by sufficient evidence showing that she acted knowingly when she failed to pay for certain items in her shopping cart. Though defendant contended that her failure to pay for the items was inadvertent, it was in the jury's province to believe the prosecution's witnesses over defendant and her mother. State v. Sturgeon, 2013-Ohio-1389, 2013 Ohio App. LEXIS 1307 (Ohio Ct. App., Marion County 2013).

Sufficient evidence supported defendant's convictions for aggravated burglary, theft, theft of a firearm, and kidnapping because the testimony of the victims, who were not able to specifically identify defendant but did provide a link to him because he dated their granddaughter, had been in their home, and was aware they had ready cash and firearms. The accomplices and the girl who drove them from the scene detailed the events the night of the home invasion and defendant's involvement therein; also, DNA consistent with defendant was found on a metal bar under the deck of the residence, found with a radio removed from the granddaughter's car and cell phone evidence implicated the accomplices, which led to defendant. State v. Riley, 2013-Ohio-1332, 2013 Ohio App. LEXIS 1260 (Ohio Ct. App., Muskingum County 2013).

Sufficient evidence supported defendant's convictions for burglary, theft, and vandalism because the circumstantial evidence adduced at trial, coupled with defendant's undisputed possession of the victim's recently stolen property, permitted the jury to conclude that he unlawfully entered the victim's residence and committed the alleged offenses once inside. State v. Calimeno, 2013-Ohio-1177, 2013 Ohio App. LEXIS 1066 (Ohio Ct. App., Cuyahoga County 2013).

Defendant's conviction for theft of a victim's Rolex watch was supported by sufficient evidence as it was reasonable for the jury to draw the conclusion that defendant stole the watch from the victim's house, where he had been working with a contractor, that he brought it to a seller, and that the seller immediately sold the watch to the pawn shop where the watch was later recovered. The evidence showed that defendant, the victim, and the contractor were the only people in the home during the time in question; that the contractor dropped defendant off at the seller's house after leaving the victim's house; and that the seller sold the victim's watch to a pawn shop that evening. State v. Trimacco, 2013-Ohio-1114, 2013 Ohio App. LEXIS 1000 (Ohio Ct. App., Columbiana County 2013).

Defendant's theft conviction under R.C. 2913.02(A)(1) was supported by evidence showed that, upon transferring passwords and log-in information for a company's billing clients onto her note cards, defendant caused the cards to become property of the company and its owner. The information on the cards constituted "data" as defined in R.C. 2901.01(A)(10). State v. Ramey, 2013-Ohio-665, 2013 Ohio App. LEXIS 592 (Ohio Ct. App., Delaware County 2013).

Evidence was sufficient to support defendant's theft conviction as the prosecution submitted videotape evidence of defendant entering into the back room of the store where the cigarettes were kept, the store's manager and assistant manager testified that twelve cartons of cigarettes worth over $600 were stolen, and they testified that defendant was not given permission to enter the back room or to obtain the cigarettes. State v. Crutchfield, 2013-Ohio-631, 2013 Ohio App. LEXIS 558 (Ohio Ct. App., Huron County 2013).

There was sufficient evidence to support defendant's convictions for theft, as defendant took money from customers with the intent to deprive them of their money by deceiving them into believing that good title to a vehicle would be transferred; one victim discovered that defendant's business never held title to a car the victim purchased from defendant. State v. Newman, 2013-Ohio-414, 2013 Ohio App. LEXIS 348 (Ohio Ct. App., Erie County 2013).

Sufficient evidence supported defendant's theft conviction (R.C. 2913.02) because the victim testified that the farm equipment was his property and that it had been taken without his knowledge or permission. Defendant was found at the scrap yard with the equipment in his truck, and he was trying to sell the property for scrap value. Thus, defendant knowingly exerted control over the property. State v. Tusing, 2012-Ohio-5945, 2012 Ohio App. LEXIS 5128 (Ohio Ct. App., Seneca County 2012).

Evidence supported a theft conviction under R.C. 2913.02(A)(1) because a market employee caught defendant, also an employee of the grocery market, in the act of stealing a box of spare ribs. The employee's testimony indicated that defendant did not have consent to exert control over the merchandise in the manner that he was doing when the employee caught him. State v. Knight, 2012-Ohio-5816, 2012 Ohio App. LEXIS 5012 (Ohio Ct. App., Lorain County 2012).

Sufficient evidence supported defendant's convictions because the testimony that defendant was on the victim's property maneuvering a screwdriver behind the electrical meter was sufficient to find the essential elements of possessing criminal tools and attempted theft proven beyond a reasonable doubt. Defendant's own testimony about his proximity to the meter called into question the credibility of the rest of his testimony denying any criminal motive and the presence of the screwdriver in his hand near the meter could have been seen as a substantial step towards removing the meter from the house. State v. Perry, 2012-Ohio-5574, 2012 Ohio App. LEXIS 4840 (Ohio Ct. App., Mahoning County 2012).

Sufficient evidence supported defendant's conviction for theft because the deposit of funds into and/or withdrawal of funds from the undisclosed out-of-state bank account was beyond the scope of the authority granted by the receiver or the bankruptcy court's order. Under the order, the receiver had the right to possess all cash, checks, and income, the out-of-state account was in the control of defendant because he opened it and remained a cosignatory and he knew of the order because he had filed objections to the magistrate's order, and, even if some authority had existed, the withdrawals were beyond the scope of that authority. State v. Pellin, 2012-Ohio-5342, 2012 Ohio App. LEXIS 4650 (Ohio Ct. App., Mahoning County 2012).

Defendant's conviction theft was proper, as the victim's testimony established that defendant committed theft by taking checks and money from the victim's account; defendant's handwriting was identified on the checks. State v. Hess, - Ohio App. 3d ", 2012 Ohio V. 4516, (Oct. 1, 2012).

Defendant's conviction for breaking and entering, safecracking, and theft were supported by sufficient evidence showing that defendant entered a bar by force, with the purpose to crack into an ATM and safe and steal the money inside and that the value of the properly stolen was at least $500. State v. Jackson, 2012-Ohio-4219, 2012 Ohio App. LEXIS 3705 (Ohio Ct. App., Butler County 2012).

Sufficient evidence supported defendant's convictions for aggravated burglary, domestic violence, aggravated menacing, theft, and criminal damaging because the State produced testimony and photographic evidence that supported its theory of the case. The prosecution did not rely on the victim's testimony alone, a neighbor testified that she heard someone knock on her door asking that she call the police, a police officer testified that, when the victim came to the police station to file a report, she had bruises around her neck and on her face, photographic evidence depicted the victim's injuries, and other photographic exhibits identified the victim's shattered television set, her torn clothing, clumps of her extensions that had been pulled out of her head, and the bloody towel. State v. Johnson, 2012-Ohio-3812, 2012 Ohio App. LEXIS 3368 (Ohio Ct. App., Cuyahoga County 2012).

Sufficient evidence supported defendant's convictions for grand theft and robbery because defendant took the truck by force, without the consent of the victims or the owner, and only drove to the police station after police officers gave chase and activated their cruiser's lights and sirens. State v. Floyd, 2012-Ohio-3551, 2012 Ohio App. LEXIS 3135 (Ohio Ct. App., Summit County 2012).

Based on defendant's apparent control over the victim's finances, a reasonable juror could have found that defendant used his access to the victim's account to commit theft. Although defendant claimed that the checks made out to him were repayment on a loan for a condominium, defendant wrote a letter to the victim's family stating that the victim had never owned any property and withdrawals from the victim's bank account continued after her death. State v. Debartolo, 2012-Ohio-3449, 2012 Ohio App. LEXIS 3055 (Ohio Ct. App., Cuyahoga County 2012).

Evidence supported defendant's theft conviction, as evidence was presented that defendant or a codefendant closed the victim's individual retirement account (IRA) and deposited the proceeds into a bank account; a subsequent check was then written from the bank account to the victim, after the victim's death, in the same amount that was deposited from the IRA. State v. Kerr, 2012-Ohio-3360, 2012 Ohio App. LEXIS 2953 (Ohio Ct. App., Cuyahoga County 2012).

Evidence was sufficient to prove the crimes of breaking and entering, theft, and criminal damaging as the victim's testimony showed that she saw defendant outside her apartment with the license plates from her vehicle and that, after defendant fled, she saw that the license plates were missing and that her car had been damaged. State v. Blackwell, 2012-Ohio-3253, 2012 Ohio App. LEXIS 2863 (Ohio Ct. App., Cuyahoga County 2012).

Defendant's conviction was not against the manifest weight of the evidence where, inter alia, a store clerk observed a man pump gas and then pull forward, when the clerk ran out to the man he said he would pay and then drove off, although the initial license plate number the clerk gave to the police did not match defendant's black Mercedes, the clerk obtained the correct license plate two months later when defendant returned to the store, that number was registered to defendant's vehicle, and when shown a picutre of defendant, the clerk identified him as the man who had not paid. State v. Cassell, 2012-Ohio-3061, 2012 Ohio App. LEXIS 2692 (Ohio Ct. App., Stark County 2012).

There was ample evidence from which to have found that defendant committed aggravated robbery against the two victims by brandishing a gun and threatening them with the weapon to accomplish the theft because the victims testified at trial that defendant was the man who committed the robberies and a witness to the robbery, who knew defendant by his nickname, saw defendant approach a car with a gun and lean inside the car while pointing the gun at the car's two occupants. State v. Stuart, 2012-Ohio-2961, 2012 Ohio App. LEXIS 2583 (Ohio Ct. App., Lucas County 2012).

Defendant's convictions of money laundering under R.C. 1315.55, theft under R.C. 2913.02(A), securing writings by deception under R.C. 2913.43(A), receiving stolen property under R.C. 2913.51(A), and tampering with records under R.C. 2913.42(A) were supported by sufficient evidence and by the manifest weight of the evidence. Both the State's witnesses and defendant's office manager testified that at the point when a face-to-face meeting with a loan officer took place, defendant knew that most of the loan officer's deals had "double" settlement statements. Defendant's title company nevertheless finished processing three of those deals prior to ceasing to do business with the loan officer. State v. Petti, 2012-Ohio-2761, 2012 Ohio App. LEXIS 2415 (Ohio Ct. App., Cuyahoga County 2012).

Evidence supported defendant's conviction for complicity to theft, pursuant to R.C. 2913.02(A)(1) and 2923.03, because, when three of defendant's friends entered the store where defendant was working, they filled up two carts with merchandise and defendant rang up the merchandise for less than its value. State v. Muntean, 2012-Ohio-2741, 2012 Ohio App. LEXIS 2395 (Ohio Ct. App., Stark County 2012).

There was sufficient evidence of the theft of watches from a house to sustain defendant's conviction for theft, as police officers testified to removing the watches from defendant, and the victim identified at least one of the watches as one belonging to a downstairs tenant. State v. Willis, 2012-Ohio-2623, 2012 Ohio App. LEXIS 2309 (Ohio Ct. App., Cuyahoga County 2012).

Amendment in Am. Sub. H.B. 86, Gen. Assem. (Ohio 2011) that raises the dollar value for misdemeanors from $500 to $1000 comes within the provisions of R.C. 1.58(B) regarding the effect of amendments on penalties and punishments. Thus, while defendant pled guilty to a charge of passing bad checks before the amendment, as his sentencing occurred after the amendment defendant should have been sentenced on a first degree misdemeanor, not a fifth degree felony. State v. Gillespie, 2012-Ohio-3485, 975 N.E.2d 492, 2012 Ohio App. LEXIS 3067 (Ohio Ct. App., Tuscarawas County 2012).

Sufficient evidence supported defendant's convictions for vandalism, possession of criminal tools, theft, breaking and entering, and receiving stolen because the trial court could reasonably have found defendant guilty of complicity to each of the five offenses. Defendant was in constructive possession of the bolt cutters and the stolen copper, evidence demonstrated that wire had been pulled from the ground at the utility substation, defendant was found in possession of wire which appeared to have been pulled from the ground, and evidence showed that he knew of and had active participation in the copper theft. State v. Collins, 2012-Ohio-2452, 2012 Ohio App. LEXIS 2164 (Ohio Ct. App., Delaware County 2012).

Defendant did not demonstrate that he received ineffective assistance of counsel because there was sufficient evidence to support his theft conviction. The evidence showed that defendant obtained or exerted control over the gasoline in a private gasoline pump because the vehicle was depicted on a security camera, the vehicle and defendant smelled of gasoline, and defendant's ex-girlfriend testified that defendant pumped gas into her vehicle using the private pump. State v. Moore, 2012-Ohio-2426, 2012 Ohio App. LEXIS 2135 (Ohio Ct. App., Wayne County 2012).

Defendant's conviction for theft was supported by the evidence, as a store's loss prevention officer testified to observing defendant grab items without checking for sizes or condition, and that defendant folded the items and placed them under defendant's purse, flattening the cloth purse on top of the items. State v. Coleman, 2012-Ohio-2399, 2012 Ohio App. LEXIS 2132 (Ohio Ct. App., Stark County 2012).

Evidence was sufficient to prove that defendant knowingly tried to steal the computer where a manager's testimony that he saw defendant place a computer in a cart, leave, come back with a receipt and try and leave with the unpaid-for computer, was supported by the video surveillance photos that showed where defendant and another man who purchased an identical computer were and at what times, and the only model of the particular computer that defendant tried to leave the store with, that was sold that day, was purchased when defendant was not in the store and the computer he had selected sat in an unattended shopping cart. State v. McLeod,

2012-Ohio-2366, 2012 Ohio App. LEXIS 2074 (Ohio Ct. App., Belmont County 2012).

Sufficient evidence supported defendant's convictions for burglary, possession of criminal tools, and petty theft because there was evidence in the record that defendant was looking for more than just coins, and that the burglary was interrupted by the arrival of the police. His accomplice testified that defendant had talked about stealing a gun from the victim because he had not paid him enough for a job and the victim described the bedroom as being in disarray caused by defendant searching through the drawers and closet. State v. Green, 2012-Ohio-2355, 2012 Ohio App. LEXIS 2081 (Ohio Ct. App., Lake County 2012).

Sufficient evidence supported defendant's theft conviction under R.C. 2913.02(A)(2). Defendant's intent, pursuant to R.C. 2913.72, to knowingly deprive a furniture rental center of its property could be inferred from her retention of the furniture without further payment and evidence establishing that she did not return it on demand, despite notice that the center sought return of the furniture. State v. Latham, 2012-Ohio-2106, 970 N.E.2d 1169, 2012 Ohio App. LEXIS 1846 (Ohio Ct. App., Montgomery County 2012).

Defendant's breaking and entering conviction was supported by substantial evidence as, in light of the victim's testimony that no one was permitted in his garage without supervision and that he generally kept the garage locked, a finding that defendant stole the items necessitated a finding that he also used some effort to open the door, which qualified as "force." Since the victim had not given defendant permission to be in the garage when he stole the items, the evidence showed that defendant was trespassing when he stole the items. State v. Alexander, 2012-Ohio-2041, 2012 Ohio App. LEXIS 1778 (Ohio Ct. App., Scioto County 2012).

Defendant's conviction for theft from an elderly person was supported by the victim's testimony that defendant admitted to taking tools from the vicitm's garage and offered to repay the victim for the items he no longer possessed. While defendant contended that he had impeached the victim, the jury obviously gave credence to the victim's testimony, which was within its province. State v. Alexander, 2012-Ohio-2041, 2012 Ohio App. LEXIS 1778 (Ohio Ct. App., Scioto County 2012).

Defendant's convictions of burglary and theft were supported by sufficient evidence where: (1) a witness saw two men walking across the street carrying the victim's property, and described the men and what each was wearing; (2) both men went into an apartment with the victim's belongings; (3) an officer stated that defendant wore tan khaki shorts, and was bald-headed and muscular; and (4) defendant also was wearing athletic shoes with treads that, in comparison to the digital photos, matched or came close to" the shoe print mark on the victim's door. State v. Grice, 2012-Ohio-1938, 2012 Ohio App. LEXIS 1704 (Ohio Ct. App., Cuyahoga County 2012).

Evidence was sufficient to sustain defendant's theft conviction because defendant's contract of employment with the law firm unequivocally stated that all clients were clients of the law firm, not of individual attorneys, and that all fees received from the practice of law belonged to, and were to be turned over to, the firm. Defendant provided no support for his contention that some of the fees he was alleged to have stolen were earned for work performed after he left the firm. State v. Slagle, 2012-Ohio-1575, 2012 Ohio App. LEXIS 1384 (Ohio Ct. App., Montgomery County 2012).

Evidence was sufficient to support defendant's conviction for complicity to theft as the evidence showed that proceeds from insurance payments, fraudulently submitted by defendant, were deposited in various accounts in the name of defendant's wife, the doctor at the clinic; thus, it was reasonable for the jury to infer that both the doctor and defendant exerted control over the funds received as a result of the fraudulent insurance claims State v. Davis, 2012-Ohio-1394, 2012 Ohio App. LEXIS 1205 (Ohio Ct. App., Wood County 2012).

Evidence was sufficient to support defendant's five theft convictions; as to each theft offense, the victim testified that the victim gave defendant a certain sum of money, that defendant promised to hold car/bike shows, that defendant promised the victim that the victim would receive all of the victim's money back, and that defendant never held the shows and never refunded the money. State v. Grillon, 2012-Ohio-893, 2012 Ohio App. LEXIS 773 (Ohio Ct. App., Columbiana County 2012).

There was sufficient circumstantial evidence that defendant purposely deprived a car's owner of her car without consent as the evidence showed that the owner's husband left defendant in the car while he went inside a house, that the car was gone when he came out of the house, that he saw defendant driving the car the following day, and that the husband never gave defendant permission to drive the car. State v. Kirkland, 2012-Ohio-792, 2012 Ohio App. LEXIS 688 (Ohio Ct. App., Summit County 2012).

Fifth-degree felony theft conviction under R.C. 2913.02(A)(1) was supported by sufficient evidence as the indictment, to which defendant stipulated by pleading no contest, alleged all the elements of the crime. Moreover, the State elaborated on the facts contained within the indictment, declaring that defendant entered a store, stole over $500 in merchandise, and that the evidence showed that he was the one who committed the theft through fingerprinting the receipts and identification of him as the offender through a photo lineup. State v. Newrones, 2012-Ohio-710, 2012 Ohio App. LEXIS 616 (Ohio Ct. App., Cuyahoga County 2012).

There was substantial evidence upon which the jury could have reasonably concluded that defendant aided or abetted his codefendant because the evidence demonstrated that defendant was not merely present, but assisted the codefendant in the commission of the crimes of aggravated robbery, kidnapping, and petty theft. Defendant made a statement that demonstrated that he knew what the codefendant was doing, defendant rushed into the house with the codefendant, who had a gun, and defendant blocked the front door to prevent the victim from escaping. State v. Jordan, 2012-Ohio-668, 2012 Ohio App. LEXIS 558 (Ohio Ct. App., Pickaway County 2012).

In a prosecution for theft of a firearm, although the State produced evidence that defendant stole a muzzle-loader, none of that evidence related to the muzzle-loader's operability, which was a required element of the crime; thus, insufficient evidence supported defendant's conviction for this offense. The evidence did demonstrate that defendant stole the muzzle-loader, though, so the court remanded the matter with instructions to the trial court to modify its judgment and enter a conviction for misdemeanor petty theft under R.C. 2913.02(A)(1). State v. Henry, 2012-Ohio-371, 2012 Ohio App. LEXIS 326 (Ohio Ct. App., Gallia County 2012).

Defendant's theft conviction was not against the manifest weight or sufficiency of the evidence because an assets protection associate testified that he saw defendant rip open a package, remove the mouse from the package, and conceal the mouse in his front pocket after going over to another aisle. While the associate did not see defendant throw the mouse into the recycling bin, he testified that he never had full control of defendant and that defendant was out of his grip a couple of times; the mouse was located in a recycling bin in a corner near where defendant had been. State v. Greenwalt, 2012-Ohio-341, 2012 Ohio App. LEXIS 289 (Ohio Ct. App., Guernsey County 2012).

There was sufficient evidence to support defendant's convictions for aggravated robbery, robbery, grand theft, and receiving stolen property because a reasonable jury could have determined that defendant cooperated with his two codefendants in the gun-point robbery of the victim, in the theft of the victim's van, shoes, and other belongings, and that defendant received or retained the victim's property, which he knew or had reason to know belonged to the victim. State v. Peterson, 2012-Ohio-250, 2012 Ohio App. LEXIS 198 (Ohio Ct. App., Summit County 2012).

Defendant's convictions for robbery and theft of an elderly or disabled person was not against the manifest weight of the evidence as the trier of fact's finding that defendant's alibi witnesses lacked credibility was appropriate as all were known drug offenders, they consistently refused to give precise details concerning the party that defendant was reportedly at during the time of the incident, and the details that were provided differed among all of the witnesses. While the victim was not perfectly consistent with the details of the incident either, he consistently told both his daughter and law enforcement that defendant attacked him and stole his money, and the State presented evidence that the victim's car ignition was broken, which was consistent with the way that the victim described the robbery. State v. Shane, 2012-Ohio-129, 2012 Ohio App. LEXIS 106 (Ohio Ct. App., Allen County 2012).

There was substantial evidence upon which a jury could reasonably have concluded, beyond a reasonable doubt, that defendant threatened to force a daughter into prostitution if her father did not pay him $600. There was also testimony that defendant threatened to kill the victim. Thus, defendant's attempted theft conviction was not against the manifest weight of the evidence. Accordingly, there was also sufficient evidence to support the conviction. State v. Roulette, 2011-Ohio-6993, 2011 Ohio App. LEXIS 5698 (Ohio Ct. App., Scioto County 2011).

Where the victim was 49, did not work, received a total of $494 at the beginning of each month from Social Security and SSI because he suffered from anxiety, was bipolar and a depressant schizophrenic, and he sometimes did "side jobs," resulting in earnings of $5 to $15 per job, there was sufficient evidence to convict defendant of theft from a disabled adult where defendant made false representations that he could withhold taxes from lottery winnings and that a lottery retailer was permitted to cash a lottery ticket in the amount of $1000. State v. Tabassum, 2011-Ohio-6790, 2011 Ohio App. LEXIS 5606 (Ohio Ct. App., Summit County 2011).

Sufficient evidence supported defendant's conviction for attempted grand theft in an amount in excess of $25,000 because defendant admitted that he contacted a credit union and an insurance company asking to close his elderly mother's accounts and to cut him a check for the money in the accounts (one account had $36,000 and the other had $42,967.22), after defendant was told by his mother's attorney that his power of attorney had been revoked. State v. Haggerty, 2011-Ohio-6705, 2011 Ohio App. LEXIS 5519 (Ohio Ct. App., Montgomery County 2011).

Conviction for theft was not against the manifest weight of the evidence because the trial court gave greater weight to the victim's testimony and the evidence showed that (1) the victim agreed to meet with codefendant, to sell the victim's car stereo equipment to codefendant's friend; (2) the victim went to the meeting with the victim's sibling; (3) defendant and another person were at the meeting; (4) defendant pulled out a gun, and demanded everything that the victim had; (4) the other person fled; (5) after cleaning out the victim's pockets, defendant and codefendant fled; (6) when the victim and the victim's sibling pursued, defendant turned around and fired a shot at the victim; (7) the victim and the victim's sibling identified defendant and codefendant; and (8) cell phone records showed that calls were made between the victim and codefendant at the time of the incident. State v. Orr, 2011-Ohio-6269, 2011 Ohio App. LEXIS 5139 (Ohio Ct. App., Cuyahoga County 2011).

Evidence supported defendant's conviction for theft, in violation of R.C. 2913.02(A)(1), because (1) circumstantial evidence was presented that defendant forcefully trespassed on the victim's premises by breaking the victim's window to gain entrance into the victim's residence; and (2) text messages between defendant and the victim circumstantially proved that defendant gained entrance into the victim's house and an inference could have been made that defendant subsequently removed the victim's missing property from the residence. State v. Roseberry, 2011-Ohio-5921, 197 Ohio App. 3d 256, 967 N.E.2d 233, 2011 Ohio App. LEXIS 4844 (Ohio Ct. App., Cuyahoga County 2011).

Sufficient evidence supported the theft by deception conviction because defendant derived personal gain by renting the homeowner's house to third parties without her permission. By renting the property to the tenants without permission and by holding himself out as the homeowner's legal agent, defendant exerted control over the property and deprived the homeowner of her ability to use or enjoy the property for her own purposes. State v. Burrell, 2011-Ohio-5655, 2011 Ohio App. LEXIS 4625 (Ohio Ct. App., Cuyahoga County 2011).

Sufficient evidence supported defendant's conviction for theft of the mortgage proceeds because he submitted a mortgage application, he lied to the bank by claiming that he acquired the company in 2002 and gave the bank a copy of the spurious 2002 purchase agreement. The bank was deprived of the mortgage proceeds it was deceived into giving defendant and it suffered deprivation when defendant defaulted on the mortgage. State v. Rhodehamel, 2011-Ohio-5618, 2011 Ohio App. LEXIS 4595 (Ohio Ct. App., Franklin County 2011).

Sufficient evidence supported defendant's conviction for theft of $50,000 because his employer sent a property activity statement indicating a disbursement of $250,000, but the company owner only received a check for $200,000. Given defendant's history and connection with that company, the jury could reasonably have inferred that defendant was engaging in another scheme to bilk that company by not disbursing the $50,000 that its property activity statement said it was entitled to and by leaving that money in the bank at his disposal. State v. Rhodehamel, 2011-Ohio-5618, 2011 Ohio App. LEXIS 4595 (Ohio Ct. App., Franklin County 2011).

Evidence was sufficient to support defendant's theft conviction under R.C. 2913.02(A) because it showed that he depleted the proceeds of the 2000 and 2002 property sales from the church's building fund, mortgaged the church building, and took out loans in the church's name without express or implied consent. In addition, defendant's misrepresentations about the proceeds and the building fund balance, as well as his creation and presentation of forged documents to obtain a 2005 loan, constituted evidence of defendant's purpose to deprive the church of its property. State v. Thompson, 2011-Ohio-5169, 2011 Ohio App. LEXIS 4279 (Ohio Ct. App., Franklin County 2011).

There was sufficient evidence to establish defendant as the perpetrator of the robbery because the victim testified that defendant had nothing covering his face, the robbery lasted three to five minutes, and that he had a clear view of defendant's face. The victim identified defendant in open court, which was corroborated by his immediate identification of defendant in a six-picture photo array. State v. Cook, 2011-Ohio-5156, 2011 Ohio App. LEXIS 4258 (Ohio Ct. App., Cuyahoga County 2011).

Evidence supported defendant's conviction for petty theft, as defendant's girlfriend testified that defendant, defendant's brother, and a friend talked about robbing a store and took certain items, and after a robbery at a market a blue sweatshirt, sunglasses, and a camouflage hat were found in an alley directly behind the market; defendant's girlfriend identified the property as belonging to the girlfriend. State v. Rouse, 2011-Ohio-5097, 2011 Ohio App. LEXIS 4212 (Ohio Ct. App., Tuscarawas County 2011).

Neither acquittal under Crim.R. 29(A) nor a new trial under Crim.R. 33(A)(4) were appropriate in an action alleging workers' compensation fraud and theft because the evidence was sufficient to show that defendant intended to commit the crimes when he obtained money from a bill in August 2007, despite having already been paid for a project; defendant accepted payment, despite an admonition that he was not entitled to it, and his billings were substantially higher than the amount billed by a company that eventually performed the work. The verdict was also not against the manifest weight of the evidence because defendant's testimony was not corroborated, he did not show that he intended to perform the work, and defendant was unable to justify the fraudulent means he used to obtain the money. State v. Brown, 2011-Ohio-4766, 2011 Ohio App. LEXIS 3937 (Ohio Ct. App., Franklin County 2011).

Sufficient evidence supported defendant's convictions for breaking and entering, aggravated robbery, grand theft, two counts of kidnapping, and grand theft of a motor vehicle for his role in the grocery store robbery because the State presented extensive uncontroverted evidence, albeit circumstantial, that clearly implicated defendant in the crimes. State v. Ayers, 2011-Ohio-4719, 2011 Ohio App. LEXIS 3919 (Ohio Ct. App., Warren County 2011).

Sufficient evidence supported defendant's theft conviction because the evidence showed that the cell phone that defendant threw out of the car window belonged to the victim; the paid the bills and exercised control over the phone at all times. State v. Clark, 2011-Ohio-4109, 2011 Ohio App. LEXIS 3447 (Ohio Ct. App., Cuyahoga County 2011).

There was sufficient evidence to support defendant's convictions as an aider and abettor based on his involvement in the aggravated robbery, felonious assault, and theft against the elderly victim because defendant took an active role in the commission of the crimes and was not merely present at the scene. Defendant admitted during a field interview that he drove the codefendant to the area with the knowledge that the codefendant intended to commit some type of theft offense so that the men could purchase heroin. State v. Perez, 2011-Ohio-3983, 2011 Ohio App. LEXIS 3338 (Ohio Ct. App., Cuyahoga County 2011).

Convictions for breaking and entering, safecracking, theft, petty theft, grand theft, and burglary under R.C. 2911.13, 2911.31, 2913.02, and 2911.12 were not against the manifest weight of the evidence based on defendant's admissions to others relating to the fact that a safe was acquired from the Amish; the statements were bolstered by parallel testimony regarding the opening, contents, and disposal of the safe. Moreover, defendant admitted to his girlfriend that he was involved in the taking of a lockbox from a residence; one witness, believed by a jury, was sufficient to establish a fact. State v. Lucas, 2011-Ohio-3935, 2011 Ohio App. LEXIS 3300 (Ohio Ct. App., Tuscarawas County 2011).

Conviction for theft was not against the manifest weight of the evidence because the State presented testimony, video recordings, and computer evidence that defendant, a store clerk, repeatedly failed to scan or scanned and voided merchandise at a register by a particular customer, thereby allowing him to take unpaid merchandise. State v. Turic, 2011-Ohio-3869, 2011 Ohio App. LEXIS 3268 (Ohio Ct. App., Greene County 2011).

Defendant's convictions for aggravated robbery and theft were not against the manifest weight of the evidence as the evidence showed that, after defendant robbed a car from the victim at gunpoint, police saw defendant exit from the stolen car and flee on foot, never losing sight of defendant during the entire foot chase, at the conclusion of which defendant was apprehended. State v. Glenn, 2011-Ohio-3684, 2011 Ohio App. LEXIS 3171 (Ohio Ct. App., Cuyahoga County 2011).

Sufficient evidence supported defendant's convictions for aggravated burglary, aggravated robbery, kidnapping, theft, and having a weapon while under disability because both defendant's girlfriend and one of the codefendants identified defendant as the other gunman, and testified that defendant aided his cousin in committing the home invasion and the robbery of the men present in the apartment. State v. Smith, 2011-Ohio-3581, 2011 Ohio App. LEXIS 3022 (Ohio Ct. App., Cuyahoga County 2011).

Appellant inmate's request for a new trial under Crim.R. 33(A)(6) was properly denied with respect to his conviction for grand theft, in violation of R.C. 2913.02, as whether his employer owed him back wages was not dispositive of the charges; he did not show that he was authorized to engage in self-help measures in order to take the employer's money as wage payments. State v. Baldwin, 2011-Ohio-3205, 2011 Ohio App. LEXIS 2697 (Ohio Ct. App., Stark County 2011).

Conviction for theft by deception, pursuant to R.C. 2913.02(A)(3), was not clearly against the manifest weight of the evidence because defendant deceptively failed to notify defendant's employer or a health insurance company that defendant's ex-spouse and defendant's sibling were no longer eligible for defendant's employer provided insurance coverage and, thus, aided and abetted them in stealing health insurance coverage and benefits. State v. Balo, 2011-Ohio-3341, 2011 Ohio App. LEXIS 2828 (Ohio Ct. App., Allen County 2011).

Defendant's convictions for robbery under R.C. 2911.02(A)(2), (3) and theft under R.C. 2913.02 were not against the manifest weight of the evidence based on the testimony of a pharmacist that a man matching defendant's description demanded OxyContin and left the store with the pills. Defendant's accomplice testified he sat in the passenger's side of the vehicle while defendant went in to rob the pharmacy; the accomplice also identified defendant as the man in the surveillance video. State v. Taylor, 2011-Ohio-3162, 2011 Ohio App. LEXIS 2663 (Ohio Ct. App., Franklin County 2011).

State presented sufficient evidence that defendant was the perpetrator of the bank robbery because defendant's DNA was located on clothing that appeared to have been worn by the perpetrator, the dye pack from the robbery was located in the general area of defendant's residence, and defendant made statements to a police officer that indicated knowledge of the crime beyond the information known by the general public. State v. Bridgeman, 2011-Ohio-2680, 2011 Ohio App. LEXIS 2291 (Ohio Ct. App., Champaign County 2011).

Defendant's convictions for burglary, grand theft, and theft, arising out of his burglary of a victim's home, during which he stole money and firearms, were not against the weight of the evidence. In all instances, both witnesses' testimony consistently implicated defendant as the individual who committed the offenses for which he was convicted, and their only point of inconsistency related to their respective levels of involvement in the crimes. State v. Simons, 2011-Ohio-2071, 193 Ohio App. 3d 784, 954 N.E.2d 176, 2011 Ohio App. LEXIS 1768 (Ohio Ct. App., Champaign County 2011), aff'd, 2012-Ohio-3213, 132 Ohio St. 3d 411, 972 N.E.2d 594, 2012 Ohio LEXIS 1795 (Ohio 2012).

Defendant's convictions for breaking and entering and theft, involving defendant's break-in of a diner and his theft of money from the diner, were not against the weight of the evidence. Both witnesses, who were with defendant on the night of the break-in, testified regarding statements defendant made to them implicating himself in the crimes, and their only point of inconsistency related to their respective levels of involvement in the crimes. State v. Simons, 2011-Ohio-2071, 193 Ohio App. 3d 784, 954 N.E.2d 176, 2011 Ohio App. LEXIS 1768 (Ohio Ct. App., Champaign County 2011), aff'd, 2012-Ohio-3213, 132 Ohio St. 3d 411, 972 N.E.2d 594, 2012 Ohio LEXIS 1795 (Ohio 2012).

State presented sufficient evidence that defendant used deceptive practices to entice his victims to prepay for the mesotherapy treatments because, after taking the victims' money, the services were not completed as agreed, and defendant did not refund the money. State v. Annable, 2011-Ohio-2029, 194 Ohio App. 3d 336, 956 N.E.2d 341, 2011 Ohio App. LEXIS 1736 (Ohio Ct. App., Cuyahoga County 2011).

Misdemeanor theft conviction was not against the manifest weight of the evidence, because the complainant's testimony, if believed, was sufficient to sustain a conviction; the complainant testified that he made daily cash deposits, he had a cash deposit with him when he left work and the money was in his pants pocket when he went to sleep, the complainant and defendant were the only two in his apartment, and defendant and the cash were missing when he awoke. State v. Moore-Bennett, 2011-Ohio-1937, 2011 Ohio App. LEXIS 1651 (Ohio Ct. App., Cuyahoga County 2011).

Sufficient evidence supported defendant's convictions for aggravated robbery with a firearm specification, having a weapon while under a disability, and grand theft because the State presented evidence that the victim was robbed at gunpoint of his vehicle and the victim readily identified defendant as the perpetrator in a photo array. Also, the results of the stipulated polygraph examination indicated deception when defendant denied any involvement in the crimes and the State presented evidence of defendant's prior conviction for aggravated robbery and kidnapping. State v. Horne, 2011-Ohio-1901, 2011 Ohio App. LEXIS 1625 (Ohio Ct. App., Summit County 2011).

Sufficient evidence supported defendant's aggravated theft convictions because it was shown that defendant deceived four disabled adults into giving him money, either for goods that were not delivered or for goods that he misrepresented the condition or size of, or for food. Defense counsel stipulated to the fact that all four victims were "disabled adults" as defined by R.C. 2913.01(DD). State v. Terry, 2011-Ohio-1681, 2011 Ohio App. LEXIS 1453 (Ohio Ct. App., Cuyahoga County 2011).

Evidence was sufficient to support defendant's conviction of grand theft under R.C. 2913.02 after stealing from her employer because defendant was the only person responsible for calculating receipts, maintaining the cash records, creating daily account sheets, filling out bank deposit slips, and making the bank deposits. Fellow employees testified that the accounting system was examined in detail, and there had never been any problems with receipts and deposits balancing before or after defendant was responsible for those tasks. State v. Duncan, 2011-Ohio-1168, 2011 Ohio App. LEXIS 1019 (Ohio Ct. App., Allen County 2011).

There was sufficient evidence that defendant committed theft, R.C. 2913.02(B)(2), as an officer testified that the officer saw defendant driving away from a business and the owner testified that items found in defendant's car were stolen from the owner's business; the owner testified that the items were worth between $1,100 and $1,200. State v. Davis, 2011-Ohio-1510, 2011 Ohio App. LEXIS 1301 (Ohio Ct. App., Summit County 2011).

Evidence was sufficient to sustain defendant's theft conviction because witnesses testified that defendant committed the theft; both testified that defendant was underneath a car at the auto lot on the night of the theft, and an accomplice stated that defendant was in the process of stealing catalytic converters. State v. Merritt, 2011-Ohio-1468, 2011 Ohio App. LEXIS 1254 (Ohio Ct. App., Jefferson County 2011).

Defendant's conviction for theft, R.C. 2913.02(A)(1) was proper, as the jury did not lose its way when finding that defendant received cash payments from customers and ultimately stole them from defendant's employer; the employer's president stated that the president had witnessed a transaction where defendant received money that was not later deposited into the employer's bank account. State v. Urbancic, 2011-Ohio-1011, 2011 Ohio App. LEXIS 846 (Ohio Ct. App., Lake County 2011).

Evidence supported defendant's conviction for theft, R.C. 2913.02(A)(2)), as the victim had time to observe defendant when the victim turned around to see who had spoken to the victim, and the victim identified defendant in a photo array and during trial, testifying in detail about defendant's physical appearance and defendant's clothing at the time of defendant's attack on the victim. State v. Seales, 2011-Ohio-720, 2011 Ohio App. LEXIS 619 (Ohio Ct. App., Cuyahoga County 2011).

Evidence was sufficient to sustain a complicity to commit theft conviction because defendant was seen in the company of the accomplice who admitted to stealing, stolen merchandise was found in the car, he carried shoplifting tools, and the items were the type found in the electronics department where defendant spent much time. State v. Winters, 2011-Ohio-141, 2011 Ohio App. LEXIS 118 (Ohio Ct. App., Fulton County 2011).

Trial court did not err in denying defendant's motion for acquittal where the record contained sufficient evidence to support his convictions for robbery, felonious assault, and theft of a motor vehicle because the victim testified that defendant beat her and stole her car, and an independent witness testified that she observed defendant punching the victim before he pulled her from the car and drove away, leaving her in the middle of the street. State v. Givan, 2011-Ohio-100, 2011 Ohio App. LEXIS 86 (Ohio Ct. App., Cuyahoga County 2011).

Defendant's conviction for aggravated theft of instant lottery games from defendant's employer in violation of R.C. 2913.02(A)(1) was proper, as the evidence showed defendant knowingly printed game tickets with the intent of not paying for them; the employer's documentation showed that ticket sales consistently spiked during defendant's solo work shifts. State v. Thomas, 2011-Ohio-85, 2011 Ohio App. LEXIS 57 (Ohio Ct. App., Cuyahoga County 2011).

Documentary evidence showing that a liquor store had both inventory and cash shortages, along with circumstantial evidence pointing to defendant, the liquor store's manager, as the person responsible for the missing money, was sufficient to sustain defendant's conviction under R.C. 2913.02(A)(1). State v. Scimone, 2011-Ohio-75, 2011 Ohio App. LEXIS 55 (Ohio Ct. App., Cuyahoga County 2011).

Even if improper, the admission of the testimony about defendant's prior arrests did not rise to the level of plain error because the State presented sufficient evidence to find defendant guilty beyond a reasonable doubt of theft, even absent the evidence of her prior arrests. Defendant's employer erroneously overpaid defendant by approximately $10,000 but, instead of returning the money, defendant withdrew it from her account and, when questioned by the police about the missing money, defendant lied, stating she had no knowledge of the money, even though her credit union records demonstrated otherwise; thus, it was apparent that defendant committed theft by knowingly exerting control over the employer's money without its consent. State v. Tufts, 2011-Ohio-73, 2011 Ohio App. LEXIS 58 (Ohio Ct. App., Cuyahoga County 2011).

State presented sufficient evidence of theft by deception as the evidence showed that defendant came onto car repair shop's lot and took his car without making any attempt to pay his bill or speak with the owner and that defendant never returned the owner's subsequent phone calls. Thus, defendant's motion for acquittal was properly denied. State v. Pawloski, 2010-Ohio-3504, 188 Ohio App. 3d 267, 935 N.E.2d 111, 2010 Ohio App. LEXIS 2976 (Ohio Ct. App., Cuyahoga County 2010).

Theft conviction under R.C. 2913.02(A)(1) was supported by evidence showing that defendant did not have consent to take coins owned by his parents as defendant's mother gave unequivocal testimony that she did not give defendant consent to take the money. Even assuming that defendant's father had the capacity to grant consent despite his dementia, defendant's testimony did not conclusively show that the father consented to defendant taking the money, and in any event, defendant's use of the money for his own personal need was inconsistent with the directive given by his parents to remove the coins in the event that something happened to either the mother or the father. State v. Whiteaker, 2010-Ohio-3410, 2010 Ohio App. LEXIS 2919 (Ohio Ct. App., Cuyahoga County 2010).

Conviction for theft of a motor vehicle under R.C. 2913.02 was supported by sufficient evidence and was not against the manifest weight of the evidence where a teenager did not give anyone permission to take his all terrain vehicle (ATV) and not return it; the teenager felt threatened when he was asked to let three men borrow the ATV, and defendant was one of the men who drove off on the ATV. State v. Johnson, 2010-Ohio-3096, 2010 Ohio App. LEXIS 2555 (Ohio Ct. App., Stark County), vacated, sub. op., 2010-Ohio-5703, 2010 Ohio App. LEXIS 4799 (Ohio Ct. App., Stark County 2010).

Defendant's conviction for burglary and theft, in violation of R.C. 2911.12(A)(2) and 2913.02, was supported by the weight and sufficiency of the evidence, as defendant's criminal actions could be inferred from the fact that the victim's house was isolated and often left unlocked, defendant broke into other homes within the vicinity of his work as part of his modus operandi, the victim believed that the stolen rings were in his home, and defendant was found in possession of the rings; the "recency" requirement was satisfied with respect to defendant's possession of the stolen property. State v. Raleigh, 2010-Ohio-2966, 2010 Ohio App. LEXIS 2457 (Ohio Ct. App., Clermont County 2010).

Defendant's conviction for burglary, in violation of R.C. 2911.12(A)(2), was supported by the weight and sufficiency of the evidence where the jury heard testimony that defendant was standing in a home owner's doorway with the owner's dog, the dog had been in a locked cage in the home, and the door to the home had been closed before the owner left; accordingly, there was sufficient evidence to determine that defendant had committed a theft, in violation of R.C. 2913.02(A)(2), in that he intended to take the dog from the home. State v. Raleigh, 2010-Ohio-2966, 2010 Ohio App. LEXIS 2457 (Ohio Ct. App., Clermont County 2010).

Defendant nurse's convictions on four counts of theft in violation of R.C. 2913.02(A)(2) for stealing prescription pain medications from a hospital were supported by sufficient evidence and were not against the manifest weight of the evidence where investigators found multiple discrepancies between records from the hospital's drug dispensing machines and the medication administration records of defendant's patients. State v. Graham, 2010-Ohio-2907, 2010 Ohio App. LEXIS 2409 (Ohio Ct. App., Franklin County 2010).

Sufficient evidence supported defendant's conviction for theft from a disabled adult because, although the victim, a disabled adult, gave defendant $84,000 to build motorcycles, defendant used the funds for a different purpose, beyond the scope of the victim's express or implied consent. There was also evidence that defendant obtained the $84,000 by deceiving the victim about whether he had a motorcycle building business. State v. White, 2010-Ohio-2865, 2010 Ohio App. LEXIS 2372 (Ohio Ct. App., Summit County 2010).

Convictions for theft by deception, securing writings by deception, and falsification wree supported by sufficient evidence as the evidence demonstrated that defendant provided false information and documents to the lender in order to secure financing for the purchase of property, that he signed a document attesting that he obtained the information and documents from the buyer when, in fact, he had never had any contact with the buyer, that the lender would not have approved the loan if defendant had presented it with truthful information, and that defendant obtained his fee as a result of his actions. State v. Stevens, 2010-Ohio-2600, 2010 Ohio App. LEXIS 2141 (Ohio Ct. App., Cuyahoga County 2010).

Defendant's convictions for breaking and entering under R.C. 2911.13(A) and theft under R.C. 2913.02(A)(1) were supported by evidence showing that defendant was identified as the person on a surveillance tape who broke into a carry out store and stole items from the store, that most of the stolen items were found in the downstairs closet of the apartment where defendant spent the night, and that clothing similar to that worn by the individual on the surveillance tape was found in defendant's apartment. Thus, defendant's motion for acquittal was properly denied. State v. Hill, 2010-Ohio-2552, 2010 Ohio App. LEXIS 2106 (Ohio Ct. App., Highland County 2010).

Evidence supported a conviction of theft by deception because defendant, a licensed real estate agent and licensed appraiser, knowingly engaged in a mortgage fraud scheme in a real estate transaction involving the use of a fraudulent appraisal, doctored loan documents, inflated buyer's income, and fraudulent proof of repairs. The lender granted the loan and released the funds based upon this fraudulent information, and defendant received some of the funds on behalf of a contractor in which defendant had an interest. State v. Ivy, 2010-Ohio-2463, 2010 Ohio App. LEXIS 2015 (Ohio Ct. App., Cuyahoga County 2010).

Evidence was sufficient to support defendant's conviction for theft because (1) the State of Ohio presented evidence from two loss prevention employees at a retail store that defendant picked up merchandise, secreted it away in bags, and then left the store without paying for any of it; (2) the State presented surveillance videotape from the store showing defendant with store merchandise in defendant's possession, passing points of sale without paying, and exiting the store; and (3) the State presented sufficient evidence that the value of all items taken by defendant and an accomplice exceeded $500 so that, under a theory of aiding and abetting, the total value could be attributed to defendant. State v. Wagner, 2010-Ohio-2221, 2010 Ohio App. LEXIS 1821 (Ohio Ct. App., Cuyahoga County 2010).

Defendant's aggravated theft conviction was supported by evidence showing that the victim's credit cards were stolen from her purse; that her cards were used only a few hours later at a store; that the person using cards matched the description of defendant; and that defendant admitted that he would go into developments, break into cars, take credit cards, and use the cards as quickly as possible after the theft. Defendant also conceded to the detective that he had messed up in the incident. State v. Sturgill, 2010-Ohio-2090, 2010 Ohio App. LEXIS 1720 (Ohio Ct. App., Cuyahoga County 2010).

Defendant's theft conviction was not against the manifest weight of the evidence. While there were discrepancies in the testimony of witnesses concerning the description of the car driven by defendant during the theft, there was one consistency in the evidence adduced, namely that defendant was driving the car when it pulled up to a store and a man put a stolen television in it. State v. Pizzulo, 2010-Ohio-2048, 2010 Ohio App. LEXIS 1687 (Ohio Ct. App., Trumbull County 2010).

Sufficient evidence supported defendant's convictions for aggravated robbery, robbery, felonious assault, aggravated burglary, all with firearm specifications, and theft, because two witnesses testified regarding defendant's active criminal participation in the entirety of the offenses; one witness testified that defendant was contacted regarding the pending criminal plan, arrived with ski masks, traveled with the group of criminals to the premises where the crimes occurred, and went inside armed with a pistol and participated in the crimes. Also, the admissible plea allocution statement of defendant's brother was clearly further reflective of defendant's criminal conduct consistent with the offenses charged. State v. Jones, 2010-Ohio-1780, 2010 Ohio App. LEXIS 1478 (Ohio Ct. App., Sandusky County 2010).

Direct and circumstantial evidence presented were sufficient to establish all of the elements of breaking and entering and theft because the owner of the building that was broken into testified that the items seized from the residence of defendant's girlfriend belonged to him, a witness to the break-in saw two men carrying out the couch and another man carrying the weed eater, the building's front door glass was broken out and there was blood on the door, and, when appellant was arrested, there were cuts on his arms and elbows that appeared to be fresh. In defendant's own typed statement, he admitted to going into the building and taking the couch. State v. Scott, 2010-Ohio-1734, 2010 Ohio App. LEXIS 1446 (Ohio Ct. App., Guernsey County 2010).

Circumstantial evidence was sufficient to support defendant's convictions for theft, forgery, and receiving stolen property as the evidence showed that defendant was aware that a check he deposited was not his own to deposit, that it was forged, and that it was obtained through the commission of a theft offense. A reasonable juror could conclude that defendant's "job," which required little more than depositing a check and wiring some of the funds outside of the country, was not legitimate, and the documents purporting to establish defendant's employment arrangement were so suspect that a reasonable juror could conclude that not even defendant believed in their authenticity; thus, defendant's motion for acquittal was properly denied. State v. Terry, 2010-Ohio-1604, 186 Ohio App. 3d 670, 929 N.E.2d 1111, 2010 Ohio App. LEXIS 1309 (Ohio Ct. App., Athens County 2010).

Evidence supported a conviction for theft, under R.C. 2913.02(A)(1), because there was sufficient evidence to support the conviction and the conviction was not against the manifest weight of the evidence as defendant deposited a check into a bank, withdrew the entire balance of the check prior to the check being cleared, and did not make any effort to rectify the situation when defendant was informed that the check was counterfeit. State v. Dorsey, 2010-Ohio-1424, 2010 Ohio App. LEXIS 1211 (Ohio Ct. App., Cuyahoga County 2010).

Grand theft conviction under R.C. 2913.02(A)(2) was supported by sufficient evidence as the record contained evidence beyond mere nonpayment of contract for rental of forklift. The testimony of several witnesses that defendant knew that defendant's construction company was retaining the forklift without the equipment company's permission and without paying the forklift's monthly rental fee was sufficient to show that defendant purposely deprived the owner of the forklift. State v. Riley, 2010-Ohio-1350, 2010 Ohio App. LEXIS 1141 (Ohio Ct. App., Summit County 2010).

Defendant's theft conviction under R.C. 2913.02(A)(3) was supported by evidence showing that defendant acted knowingly to deprive the victim of money by deception, in that the evidence showed that the victim, at defendant's behest, provided blank checks to defendant so that defendant could buy properties in the victim's name and make improvements to resell the properties at a profit, that defendant continued to ask for additional checks, and that he never caused the victim to own any properties. State v. Judson, 2010-Ohio-1083, 2010 Ohio App. LEXIS 893 (Ohio Ct. App., Lorain County 2010).

Evidence supported defendant's conviction for theft because the victim, who was elderly, testified that defendant, the victim's niece, entered the victim's home and took an electric scooter and other items to hold until the victim paid a debt which the victim owed to defendant, and, after the victim reported the incident to the police, the next day, defendant returned, struck the victim in the head, kicked the victim in the sides, and took the victim's push wheelchair. Furthermore, under R.C. 2913.01(D), the victim was the owner of the scooter and the wheelchair for purposes of the conviction, regardless of whether the victim actually possessed title ownership. State v. Jones, 2010-Ohio-902, 2010 Ohio App. LEXIS 764 (Ohio Ct. App., Cuyahoga County 2010).

Defendant's conviction for theft by deception was not against the weight and sufficiency of the evidence because on each sheet, defendant signed her name, certifying that she was at work while the child care services were being provided, defendant was aware that she had to report changes in her employment, and defendant was not always at work when she was using the child care benefits. State v. Bowden, 2010-Ohio-758, 2010 Ohio App. LEXIS 628 (Ohio Ct. App., Summit County 2010).

Evidence was sufficient to sustain defendant's burglary, grand theft of checks, receiving stolen property, and engaging in a pattern of corrupt activity convictions because the victims' daughter testified that defendant and his friends never had permission to take anything from the house, jewelry, power tools, and a television were taken, at least four checks were missing, and the conduct occurred over the course of the victims' vacation, lasting a week. Reasonable minds could have concluded that those events were not so closely related that they constituted a single incident, but instead were repeated incidents so related that they constituted a pattern of corrupt activity. State v. Lightner, 2010-Ohio-483, 2010 Ohio App. LEXIS 393 (Ohio Ct. App., Hardin County 2010).

Defendant's convictions for aggravated murder, aggravated robbery, aggravated burglary, burglary, and grand theft of a motor vehicle were supported by evidence showing that the victim was found stabbed to death inside his apartment, that a bent kitchen knife was found outside defendant's apartment; that the knife was consistent with the victim's stab wounds; that a shoe print from the crime scene matched the make and model of shoe that defendant admitted to wearing on the night of the murder; that defendant was placed near the victim's apartment from the time the victim was last seen alive until his death later that day; and that defendant acted strangely on the night of the murder including an untimely change of clothing and his possession of the victim's keys, television, stereo equipment, and vehicle. The forensic testimony, including testimony regarding DNA evidence found at the crime scene, physical evidence, and the combined statements of witnesses describing defendant's suspicious behavior provided sufficient evidence to establish defendant's guilt. State v. O'Hara, 2010-Ohio-408, 2010 Ohio App. LEXIS 331 (Ohio Ct. App., Butler County 2010).

Given the detailed testimony by numerous eyewitnesses who were employees of a home improvement store, there was sufficient evidence of the fraudulent credit scheme employed by defendant in the purchase of merchandise at the store to support defendant's convictions for theft in violation of R.C. 2913.02(A)(3). Furthermore, the convictions were not against the manifest weight of the evidence. State v. Colon, 2010-Ohio-361, 2010 Ohio App. LEXIS 292 (Ohio Ct. App., Cuyahoga County 2010).

Defendant's conviction for theft was supported by evidence showing that defendant admitted that he had assisted in hooking an air tank up to a business's anhydrous tank, that the air tank's contents tested positive for the presence of anhydrous ammonia, and that defendant had implicated himself in the theft of the anhydrous during phone calls made following the theft. State v. Stamper, 2010-Ohio-330, 2010 Ohio App. LEXIS 261 (Ohio Ct. App., Fayette County 2010).

Evidence was sufficient to convict defendant of aggravated robbery, robbery, kidnapping and theft, because the jury carefully considered all the evidence, and where defendant presented credible, conflicting evidence, the jury disregarded the State's evidence, when the jury acquitted defendant of all charges relating to the presence of a gun, including the aggravated robbery by use of a deadly weapon, as well as the firearm specifications, and no one corroborated defendant's version of the events, including his girlfriend who testified against him. State v. Burst, 2010-Ohio-5773, 2010 Ohio App. LEXIS 4853 (Ohio Ct. App., Cuyahoga County 2010).

Because the State met its burden of production regarding attempting or committing a theft offense as required by R.C. 2913.02(A)(1), there was sufficient evidence to support defendant's conviction. The State presented evidence that defendant offered to sell the stolen guns and knives to a wide range of people at a flea market and evidence of cell phone usage was presented to the jury, placing defendant in the area of the shooting center at the time of the theft. State v. Wise, 2010-Ohio-5739, 2010 Ohio App. LEXIS 4818 (Ohio Ct. App., Delaware County 2010).

Evidence was sufficient to convict defendant of theft of a motor vehicle, because two witnesses testified that defendant and a second man got on the victim's ATV and drove it away, and the victim testified that he did not give anyone permission to take his ATV and not return it to him; while the victim testified that he did acquiesce to letting the men take his ATV, he did so only because he felt that he did not have a choice since he was a kid and the man requesting his ATV was a bigger adult. State v. Johnson, 2010-Ohio-5703, 2010 Ohio App. LEXIS 4799 (Ohio Ct. App., Stark County 2010).

Evidence was sufficient to sustain defendant's convictions for aggravated burglary and theft of motor vehicle because defendant and his son forced their way into the victim's apartment, held him down, assaulted him, and took his cash and car keys. The evidence also showed that defendant's vehicle was removed from his garage and was discovered in a junk yard; additionally, defendant and his son drove off in another vehicle without the owners' permission. State v. Huber, 2010-Ohio-5598, 2010 Ohio App. LEXIS 4723 (Ohio Ct. App., Cuyahoga County 2010).

Evidence was sufficient to support defendant's conviction of theft in violation of R.C. 2913.02 where there was the positive identification of defendant as being in the store at the time of the disappearance of the rib packages, rib packages with sensors ripped off were discovered in defendant's vehicle, and those rib packages were from the store. Clearly the jury chose to accept the account given by the store employees as opposed to defendant's claims. State v. Williams, 2010-Ohio-5536, 2010 Ohio App. LEXIS 4668 (Ohio Ct. App., Stark County 2010).

Evidence supported defendant's conviction for theft, R.C. 2913.02(A)(1), as defendant was identified as the man who had been standing outside the window of a store that had been broken into with a two-wheel dolly containing paintings stolen from an apartment building. State v. Grant, 2010-Ohio-5483, 2010 Ohio App. LEXIS 4592 (Ohio Ct. App., Cuyahoga County 2010).

Sufficient evidence supported defendant's theft conviction because the State provided sufficient evidence that defendant knowingly deprived the store of the photographs that she printed in their photo department and then placed in her purse without paying for them. State v. Thompson, 2010-Ohio-5331, 2010 Ohio App. LEXIS 4494 (Ohio Ct. App., Guernsey County 2010).

Evidence supported defendant's conviction for theft of a motor vehicle, as both victims had an opportunity to view defendant; thus, the victims' identification of defendant was not merely based on a co-defendant's identification, but was based on their own observations when defendant robbed the victims. State v. Royal, 2010-Ohio-5235, 2010 Ohio App. LEXIS 4400 (Ohio Ct. App., Cuyahoga County 2010).

Although none of the witnesses could testify that he or she had personal knowledge that defendant had reconnected defendant's electrical service to defendant's apartment, in violation of R.C. 2913.02(A)(2), the verdict was against the manifest weight of the evidence because a large amount of circumstantial evidence supported this conclusion. Testimony was heard (1) that defendant was the responsible party for the utilities at defendant's apartment; (2) that defendant was mailed a disconnection notice and a bill; (3) that defendant's electricity was disconnected; (4) that defendant lived alone; (5) that a reading of the meter revealed electricity had been consumed at the apartment after the disconnection; (6) that the meter was running, the seal had been broken, and the boots had been removed; (7) that it was not difficult for a layperson to reconnect electricity after it had been disconnected; (8) that defendant told a police officer that defendant did not have electricity because defendant did not pay the bill; (9) that the officer informed defendant that defendant was responsible for the meter and was receiving electricity illegally, which defendant stated defendant understood; (10) that defendant went to the police department and asked them to drop the charges if defendant paid the bill; and (11) that defendant told the trial court judge defendant wanted to plead guilty because defendant knew what defendant did. State v. Fisher, 2010-Ohio-5192, 2010 Ohio App. LEXIS 4376 (Ohio Ct. App., Auglaize County 2010).

Defendant's multiple convictions for aggravated theft by deception, securing writings by deception, falsification, and telecommunications fraud, in violation of R.C. 2913.02(A)(3), 2913.43, 2921.13, and 2913.05(A), were not against the manifest weight of the evidence, as there was sufficient evidence that defendant was the mastermind behind a complicated mortgage fraud scheme involving others who were participants or innocent victims. State v. Holman, 2010-Ohio-4886, 2010 Ohio App. LEXIS 4134 (Ohio Ct. App., Cuyahoga County 2010).

Defendant's conviction of grand theft (R.C. 2913.02(A)(1) & (B(2)) was proper; defendant's testimony was contradicted by the testimony of the buyer of a vehicle who never received a promised payment and other evidence; there was sufficient evidence of each element of the offenses to find defendant guilty. State v. O'Black, 2010-Ohio-4812, 2010 Ohio App. LEXIS 4072 (Ohio Ct. App., Allen County 2010).

Theft conviction was supported by sufficient evidence since defendant admitted that he did not return rented equipment on the due date and that it was later destroyed during a demolition project. State v. Meyer, 2010-Ohio-4804, 189 Ohio App. 3d 628, 939 N.E.2d 944, 2010 Ohio App. LEXIS 4079 (Ohio Ct. App., Clermont County 2010).

There was sufficient evidence to prove theft by deception because 46 separate Medicaid checks, totaling $57,333.60, were processed through defendant's bank accounts. Defendant deprived the State of the use of the money acted with deception by, at very least, allowing the Ohio Department of Job and Family Services to believe that the named Medicaid providers were providing the in-home specified health services for which defendant had received payments. State v. Frazier, 2010-Ohio-4440, 2010 Ohio App. LEXIS 3736 (Ohio Ct. App., Franklin County 2010).

Defendant's conviction was not against the manifest weight of the evidence even though there was conflicting evidence, including the testimony of two alibi witnesses who placed defendant at a family gathering at the time that a theft occurred; it was in the purview of the jury to not believe the alibi witnesses, and the State presented evidence that defendant was the only person at the victim's apartment who was capable of removing and transporting a shotgun and crossbow away from the victim's apartment without raising suspicion, that defendant's roommate had observed defendant place the shotgun and crossbow in a closet and that defendant told her he had just robbed someone. State v. Townsend, 2010-Ohio-4417, 2010 Ohio App. LEXIS 3718 (Ohio Ct. App., Delaware County 2010).

Defendant's convictions for assault and theft were supported by evidence showing that defendant ran up and started hitting the victim after defendant's brother tackled the victim, that the victim was visibly injured from the assault, that the victim observed his wallet in defendant's hand, and that money was taken from his wallet. While defendant argued that his motion for acquittal should have been granted because the witnesses who were present during the incident all had credibility issues, the determination of credibility was for the jury to decide. State v. Simpson, 2010-Ohio-4045, 2010 Ohio App. LEXIS 3416 (Ohio Ct. App., Montgomery County 2010).

Burglary and theft convictions were not against the weight of the evidence. While defendant challenged his girlfriend's testimony that defendant had told her that he had taken money from his grandmother's home, the trial court was entitled to believe the girlfriend's testimony even though the girlfriend admitted to having lied to the police in the past, and the testimony of the victim and defendant's aunt established that defendant had the oportunity to commit the crime. State v. Park, 2010-Ohio-3943, 2010 Ohio App. LEXIS 3336 (Ohio Ct. App., Lorain County 2010).

Defendant's conviction for theft under R.C. 2913.02(A)(1) was supported by sufficient evidence as the evidence showed that defendant, the victim's landlord, knew that the furniture in the victim's apartment belonged to the victim and that he took the furniture from her apartment without her consent while she was away from the apartment. State v. Boyce, 2010-Ohio-3870, 2010 Ohio App. LEXIS 3271 (Ohio Ct. App., Cuyahoga County 2010).

Convictions for aggravated robbery, three amended counts of kidnapping, and grand theft were affirmed because the convictions were not against the manifest weight of the evidence as circumstantial evidence showed that defendant robbed a restaurant, where defendant had previously worked, at gun point and tied up three employees in the process. The circumstantial evidence consisted of (1) a witness giving the police a description and a partial license plate number of a car which was parked near the restaurant at the time of the robbery that matched that of defendant's car; (2) money which was in a floor safe and on a desk were taken from the restaurant, but money which was locked in a desk because the lock on the safe had only recently broken was not taken; (3) cell phone records showed that defendant placed two cell phone calls from near the restaurant on the night of the robbery; (4) after the robbery, defendant, who had very little income, purchased an engagement ring; (5) defendant's cousin testified that defendant confessed to the cousin that defendant had committed the robbery and asked that the cousin lie to the police; and (6) defendant changed defendant's story during questioning by a police investigator as to defendant's whereabouts during the robbery. State v. Babyak, 2010-Ohio-3820, 2010 Ohio App. LEXIS 3235 (Ohio Ct. App., Madison County 2010).

Sufficient evidence supported defendant's conviction for grand theft because defendant aided and abetted her brother in committing theft by deception when she signed the loan application as the owner of the restaurant for the purpose of obtaining money without the consent of the investing partner. The loan proceeds were transferred to a bank account, where defendant used the proceeds to pay for renovation expenses for her cabin in the amount of $6,500. State v. Jones, 2011-Ohio-4440, 2010 Ohio App. LEXIS 5541 (Ohio Ct. App., Stark County 2010).

Evidence was sufficient to find the elements of complicity to commit robbery proven beyond a reasonable doubt because the victim testified that his clothes, wallet and cell phone were taken from him. The jury clearly believed that when the victim was abandoned in a ditch, tied up and wearing only his underwear after suffering physical harm, it was unlikely he would recover his clothing or other possessions. State v. Conner, 2010-Ohio-6500, 2010 Ohio App. LEXIS 5453 (Ohio Ct. App., Lucas County 2010).

Defendant's conviction for grand theft was based upon sufficient evidence, and not against the manifest weight of the evidence, because a detective testified that he interviewed defendant following his arrest and that defendant acknowledged that the firearm was stolen. Defendant specifically told the detective that the only thing he had done wrong was selling a stolen firearm; that statement was not ambiguous. State v. Botan, 2010-Ohio-6414, 2010 Ohio App. LEXIS 5341 (Ohio Ct. App., Licking County 2010).

Adjudication of a juvenile as a delinquent child for receiving stolen property was not against the manifest weight of the evidence because (1) the juvenile received American money from a wallet which was found by two other juveniles at their school; (2) the wallet contained pictures of the foreign exchange student who owned the wallet and a card with the local address of the student's American host parents; (3) the juvenile was present when an announcement was made over the loudspeaker at school the next day informing the student body that a student had lost a wallet with a large amount of money and requesting anyone with information regarding the wallet to see school officials; and (4) the juvenile participated in a plan to exchange foreign money that was in the wallet at a bank. Therefore, the juvenile finder knowingly exerted control over the property with the purpose of depriving the owner of the property pursuant to R.C. 2913.02(A)(1). In re B.C., 2010-Ohio-6377, 191 Ohio App. 3d 739, 947 N.E.2d 724, 2010 Ohio App. LEXIS 5319 (Ohio Ct. App., Logan County 2010).

Defendant's theft convictions were supported by sufficient evidence as the State provided ample evidence demonstrating that the Bureau of Workers' Compensation (BWC) had, at minimum, an "interest," as contemplated under R.C. 2913.01(D), in coin funds, which were established by defendant and in which the BWC invested heavily, in that defendant was limited in his role as funds manager by the terms of the operating agreements, he was specifically prohibited from using the funds of the company in any manner except for the benefit of the company in furtherance of its business purposes. Taking money from the funds for personal use with no evidence of a note and overt attempts at concealment was contrary to the best interest of the coin funds. State v. Noe, 2009-Ohio-6978, 2009 Ohio App. LEXIS 5825 (Ohio Ct. App., Lucas County 2009).

Sufficient evidence supported defendant's convictions for grand theft and records tampering because testimony established that defendant, the cash control supervisor of the amusement park stole money and then used a check from a vendor to cover up the missing $75,000 park receipts previously generated. Defendant personally wrote a check for $10.55 to make up the variance. State v. Powers, 2009-Ohio-2625, 2009 Ohio App. LEXIS 2243 (Ohio Ct. App., Warren County 2009).

Defendant's robbery and theft convictions were not against the manifest weight of the evidence as the clerk of a convenience store identified defendant as the man who held her at gunpoint, took money out of her cash register, and rode away on a bicycle; the bicycle in question was found parked outside the house of defendant's stepmother; and defendant's stepbrother testified that someone had used his bike and that he had found his sweatshirt, which matched the one worn by the perpetrator of the robbery, laying on the floor of his bedroom. State v. Porter, 2009-Ohio-990, 2009 Ohio App. LEXIS 803 (Ohio Ct. App., Huron County 2009).

Evidence was sufficient to support defendant's conviction for theft by deception, in violation of R.C. 2913.02(A)(3), based on his participation in a foreclosure rescue scheme that deprived a victim of the equity in her house and turned her into a tenant; defendant's conduct deceived the victim into believing that she could regain title to her house and he failed to inform her that she was selling the house when she signed papers he presented to her. State v. Quick, 2009-Ohio-2124, 2009 Ohio App. LEXIS 1778 (Ohio Ct. App., Cuyahoga County 2009).

Defendant's convictions for theft of items from a store, under R.C. 2913.02(A)(1), were not against the manifest weight of the evidence because (1) defendant was videotaped concealing store merchandise and leaving the store on a certain date, (2) defendant was videotaped carrying empty bags and otherwise looking suspicious on another date, and (3) three officers testified that the officers detained defendant after defendant left the store on these two dates, and found defendant with no proof of purchase for the store merchandise defendant possessed. State v. Carson, 2009-Ohio-2122, 2009 Ohio App. LEXIS 1769 (Ohio Ct. App., Cuyahoga County 2009).

Sufficient evidence supported defendant's convictions for theft of items from a store, under R.C. 2913.02(A)(1), because (1) defendant was identified in videotapes of defendant's crimes and as the person officers detained after being contacted by store security personnel, and (2) price tags showed the value of the items defendant stole. State v. Carson, 2009-Ohio-2122, 2009 Ohio App. LEXIS 1769 (Ohio Ct. App., Cuyahoga County 2009).

Sufficient evidence supported defendant's convictions for breaking and entering, criminal trespass, and receiving stolen property because defendant created a living space in a vacant store (located in a mall), as evidenced by his flight from the area, his fingerprint, and the personal items that he left in the store, including a receipts. The store was filled with numerous items that were taken from other stores, and those items were taken at night when the mall was unoccupied. State v. Shawhan, 2009-Ohio-1986, 2009 Ohio App. LEXIS 1703 (Ohio Ct. App., Summit County 2009).

Evidence was sufficient to support defendant's conviction for theft of more than $25,000 and less than $100,000 from an elderly person, in violation of R.C. 2913.02(A), because the State of Ohio submitted evidence that defendant knowingly exerted control over the finances of the victim, defendant's mother, without the victim's express consent and exceeded the victim's express and implied consent to make financial decisions. State v. Estright, 2009-Ohio-5676, 2009 Ohio App. LEXIS 4779 (Ohio Ct. App., Summit County 2009).

Based on the evidence of defendant's collecting payment for hours that she neither worked nor were authorized for her to take paid leave, the theft conviction was supported by the evidence. The only evidence to support defendant's claim that her supervisor altered her time submission was defendant's own self-serving testimony. State v. Sancho, 2009-Ohio-5478, 2009 Ohio App. LEXIS 4616 (Ohio Ct. App., Cuyahoga County 2009).

Defendant's convictions for theft by deception and securing writings by deception were supported by evidence showing that defendant falsely represented on a loan application that loan applicant was providing his own funds for downpayment. By presenting downpayment on property in the applicant's place, defendant used deception to secure loan, to deprive the lender of loan proceeds, and to exert control over the loan proceeds. Moreover, the evidence showed that defendant arranged to make the downpayment on the property look as though it came from the applicant's bank account when, in reality, it did not. State v. Huff, 2009-Ohio-5368, 2009 Ohio App. LEXIS 4527 (Ohio Ct. App., Cuyahoga County 2009).

Defendant's convictions for grand theft and passing bad checks were supported by sufficient evidence as the evidence showed that defendant obtained a loan from the victim using an accounts receivable from a purchase order (PO) as collateral, that the PO was a sham, and that the checks defendant gave to the victim as repayment for the loan could not be cashed due to insufficient funds. State v. Shanklin, 2009-Ohio-6843, 185 Ohio App. 3d 603, 925 N.E.2d 161, 2009 Ohio App. LEXIS 5732 (Ohio Ct. App., Licking County 2009).

Defendant's theft conviction was supported by sufficient evidence since, in addition to defendant's testimony, wherein she did not deny that she left a grocery store with unpaid items, the jury also had before it the testimony of three store managers, each of whom testified as to the chronology of events. Since defendant had just made an issue with the store's customer service of requesting that she be given many of these additional items for which she had not paid, it was unlikely that she could have immediately forgotten that she had them in her cart, as she claimed. State v. Butts, 2009-Ohio-6561, 2009 Ohio App. LEXIS 5499 (Ohio Ct. App., Stark County 2009).

Defendant's convictions for breaking and entering and petty theft were supported by sufficient evidence as the State presented two witnesses, who both viewed the store's surveillance video and testified that suspect who broke into store looked up at the video camera, and the store's owner identified defendant as the culprit, having known defendant as a frequent customer and as someone who had done work for the owner in the past. State v. Milton, 2009-Ohio-6312, 2009 Ohio App. LEXIS 5287 (Ohio Ct. App., Cuyahoga County 2009).

Evidence was sufficient to sustain defendant's convictions for theft, securing writings by deception, and receiving stolen property because defendant conceded that as an acting escrow officer at a closing agent it was her responsibility to disburse funds at the direction of the lender, and defendant conceded that the loan transactions did not contain reference to the use of a third-party company on the buyer's HUD statement, which was the only portion that was sent to the lender. State v. Foster, 2009-Ohio-6213, 185 Ohio App. 3d 117, 923 N.E.2d 227, 2009 Ohio App. LEXIS 5213 (Ohio Ct. App., Cuyahoga County 2009).

Weight of the evidence supported defendant's convictions for theft and robbery because the evidence demonstrated that defendant was identified in a photo array and on surveillance videos as the perpetrator of the thefts. A store clerk testified at trial that she witnessed defendant leave the store without paying for two cases of beer, that she followed him into the parking lot, and that defendant threatened her with a knife. State v. Pruitt, 2009-Ohio-6119, 2009 Ohio App. LEXIS 5129 (Ohio Ct. App., Stark County 2009).

In a theft case under R.C. 2913.02(A)(1), a trial court did not err by denying defendant's Crim.R. 29 motion because defendant's contention that he could not have stolen money by cashing checks made payable to a mortgage company was rejected; even if he believed the money was his, this belief became unreasonable when he was told to return the money, and defendant's subsequent refusal to return the funds led to the inference that his purpose was to deprive the mortgage company of funds that he knew did not belong to him and that he held the funds without consent of the owner. Therefore, the evidence was sufficient to support the conviction. State v. Arnold, 2009-Ohio-6077, 2009 Ohio App. LEXIS 5105 (Ohio Ct. App., Summit County 2009).



Defendant's theft conviction was supported by sufficient evidence because, had defendant not been prevented from leaving the store with the television by the assistant manager, defendant would have left the store with a television he did not pay for. Defendant was not authorized to leave the store with the television without paying for it, he ignored requests by store employees to come back in the store, and he never offered an explanation for his behavior. State v. Morgan, 2009-Ohio-6050, 2009 Ohio App. LEXIS 5070 (Ohio Ct. App., Clinton County 2009).

Sufficient evidence supported defendant's convictions for workers' compensation fraud and theft by deception because defendant worked at two bird stores. Tapes showed her waiting on customers, lifting objects, bending and moving about, and operating the cash register and defendant admitted placing orders and overseeing deliveries, which was confirmed by other evidence received from vendors; while defendant was not paid a salary or wage, all the evidence and her own testimony established that she owned the store, which was a family business. State v. Urich-Feckler, 2009-Ohio-5965, 2009 Ohio App. LEXIS 5014 (Ohio Ct. App., Cuyahoga County 2009).

Weight and sufficiency of the evidence supported defendant's conviction for theft, in violation of R.C. 2913.02, as the jury could reasonably have found that defendant knew, or probably knew, that a section of railroad railing that he took belonged to the nearby railroad due to the proximity of the railing to an active railroad line and information received from a nearby business owner. State v. Blackshear, 2009-Ohio-3270, 2009 Ohio App. LEXIS 2788 (Ohio Ct. App., Stark County 2009).

Defendant's convictions for robbery and petty theft were supported by the evidence because a security guard and two employees of the pharmacy testified that when the guard confronted defendant after he put some deodorant in his pocket, defendant stated that he had a gun. The security guard let defendant go (so that he would not get shot) but followed him out of the store and got the license plate number of defendant's vehicle. State v. Martinez, 2009-Ohio-3218, 2009 Ohio App. LEXIS 2723 (Ohio Ct. App., Lucas County 2009).

Sufficient evidence supported defendant's conviction for theft because, by accepting payment in full, performing minimally on the repair contract, and avoiding contact with the victim, it was reasonable to have inferred that defendant intended to deprive the victim of her money by deception and/or beyond the scope of her consent. State v. Dalton, 2009-Ohio-3149, 2009 Ohio App. LEXIS 2679 (Ohio Ct. App., Portage County 2009).

Defendant's claim that his counsel was ineffective for failing to object to testimony by a victim regarding the value of items that defendant allegedly took from her for purposes of a charge against him of theft, in violation of R.C. 2913.02, lacked merit, as the victim's testimony was sufficient to establish the value thereof and the admission of her testimony was within the trial court's discretion. State v. Bartolomeo, 2009-Ohio-3086, 2009 Ohio App. LEXIS 2571 (Ohio Ct. App., Franklin County 2009).

Even if a trial court did abuse its discretion when it qualified as an expert witness an individual offering shoe identification testimony, any such error would be harmless in light of the overwhelming circumstantial evidence of identification in the case. Multiple police officers testified that they observed shoeprints with the same distinct tread pattern outside of numerous establishments that had been broken into; the jury observed for itself the photographs of the shoeprints located in the snow; and it had viewed the treads on the shoe that defendant was wearing when he was arrested, enabling it to connect defendant's shoeprint to the shoeprints found on the ground around the establishments that had been broken into. State v. Davis, 2009-Ohio-2527, 2009 Ohio App. LEXIS 2298 (Ohio Ct. App., Allen County 2009).

When defendant persuaded victims to contribute substantial funds to a foreign foundation defendant controlled, in purported compliance with the victims' directive to preserve those funds, defendant's aggravated theft conviction was not against the manifest weight of the evidence because circumstantial evidence demonstrated that the foundation was defendant's alter ego. State v. Olcese, 2009-Ohio-5057, 2009 Ohio App. LEXIS 4314 (Ohio Ct. App., Portage County 2009).

When defendant persuaded victims to contribute substantial funds to a foreign foundation defendant controlled, in purported compliance with the victims' directive to preserve those funds, sufficient evidence supported defendant's aggravated theft conviction because (1) the evidence showed defendant exerted control over the victims' funds beyond the victims' express or implied consent, under R.C. 2913.02(A)(2), and (2) defendant created false impressions to achieve defendant's goals of controlling the victims' funds, under R.C. 2913.02(A)(3). State v. Olcese, 2009-Ohio-5057, 2009 Ohio App. LEXIS 4314 (Ohio Ct. App., Portage County 2009).

There was sufficient evidence to support defendant's theft conviction because defendant was seen on the surveillance video hurriedly grabbing the totes of drugs in his arms after the room was cleared of employees and running out of the back door of the pharmacy. State v. Smith, 2009-Ohio-5010, 2009 Ohio App. LEXIS 4248 (Ohio Ct. App., Cuyahoga County 2009).

Defendant's conviction for theft, in violation of R.C. 2913.02(A)(2), was supported by the weight and sufficiency of the evidence, as witnesses who were deemed credible testified that he removed scrap metal from his employer's facility and received cash for it, which was not the usual and proper work procedure for selling the scrap metal; venue under R.C. 2901.12(A) was properly established and the determination regarding credibility was within the jury's province, such that denial of acquittal under Crim.R. 29 was proper. State v. Straubhaar, 2009-Ohio-4757, 2009 Ohio App. LEXIS 4025 (Ohio Ct. App., Stark County 2009).

Evidence that a lender lent money to unqualified individuals based on deceptive down-payments and fraudulent information in loan applications prepared by defendant was sufficient to support defendant's convictions for theft and receiving stolen property; whether or not the lender suffered any loss was irrelevant. State v. Wells, 2009-Ohio-4712, 2009 Ohio App. LEXIS 3985 (Ohio Ct. App., Cuyahoga County 2009).

Defendant's multiple convictions were supported by circumstantial evidence, such that denial of his acquittal motion under Crim.R. 29 was proper, as there was testimony from an eyewitness and others that supported the determination that defendant was one of the perpetrators of multiple break-ins to commercial establishments; defendant's alibi was not deemed credible, and break-in tools were found in the co-defendant's vehicle, such that the convictions for breaking and entering, theft, safecracking, and possessing criminal tools, in violation of R.C. 2911.13(A), 2913.02(A)(1), 2911.31(A), and 2923.24(A), survived a challenge on appeal. State v. Bice, 2009-Ohio-4672, 2009 Ohio App. LEXIS 3976 (Ohio Ct. App., Clermont County 2009).

Sufficient evidence supported defendant's convictions for aggravated murder, aggravated robbery, kidnapping, aggravated burglary, theft, and tampering with evidence because there was overwhelming evidence to prove that defendant not only actively participated in robbing the victim, but that she also wielded one of the knives used to kill him and then helped conceal her knife in a dumpster. Defendant, along with her brother and his friend, attacked and killed the victim in his motel room by binding his arms and legs with duct tape and stabbing him 11 times; they scrounged through the victim's pockets, took his credit cards and cell phones, and proceeded to engage in an all out shopping spree; and they cut up the victim's credit cards, broke his cell phones into a number of pieces, and tossed their murder weapons into a dumpster. State v. Rodriguez, 2009-Ohio-4460, 2009 Ohio App. LEXIS 3746 (Ohio Ct. App., Butler County 2009).

Defendant's conviction for theft of a car from a dealership was supported by evidence showing that defendant obtained the car from the dealership through deception and that, while the dealership held a title to the car in defendant's name, it never transferred physical possession of the title to defendant; instead, it held onto the title pending payment. Defendant never owned the car, and he deceived the dealership by giving it bad checks that had been written on accounts that he knew were closed. State v. Baker, 2009-Ohio-4188, 2009 Ohio App. LEXIS 3574 (Ohio Ct. App., Hamilton County 2009).

Defendant's theft convictions were supported by evidence showing that defendant obtained money from the two female victims by deception. Defendant could not have had the requisite intent to repay the money or to perform because there was no reasonable expectation that he would make any legitimate money; defendant regularly and systematically deceived people to obtain money and made outlandish promises that he could not have reasonably expected to fulfill. State v. Baker, 2009-Ohio-4188, 2009 Ohio App. LEXIS 3574 (Ohio Ct. App., Hamilton County 2009).

Defendant's theft conviction was supported by the victim's testimony that defendant saw the victim put the victim's bankcard in the victim's purse, that defendant had the opportunity to take the card shortly thereafter, that defendant knew the victim's PIN, and that defendant later left the victim. Moreover, a surveillance videotape from ATM location revealed the victim using the ATM on the date in question. State v. Shields, 2009-Ohio-3545, 2009 Ohio App. LEXIS 3056 (Ohio Ct. App., Stark County 2009).

Denial of defendant's acquittal motion under Crim.R. 29(A) was proper, as the weight and sufficiency of the evidence supported the convictions for robbery and theft, in violation of R.C. 2911.02(A)(3) and 2913.02(A)(1), based on testimony from a co-defendant and a victim regarding defendant's actions; defendant posed as an insurance agent to enter the victim's home, and when the victim took out his cash-filled wallet to show his identification, defendant grabbed the wallet and the cash and then threw the

80-year-old victim against the wall. State v. Smith, 2009-Ohio-3258, 2009 Ohio App. LEXIS 2850 (Ohio Ct. App., Hamilton County 2009).

Evidence supported defendant's theft conviction under because the evidence showed that defendant used deception with the purpose to deprive the store of seven multimeters; defendant took merchandise from a hardware department, concealed it in his outer clothing, and left the store. Since the store inventory provided information concerning the units placed on the shelf, which ones had been sold, and which ones had been removed from the "peg hooks" during defendant's store visit when the plastic securing the items to the hooks was cut, sufficient evidence existed that the value of the stolen items exceeded $500. State v. Klepatzki, 2009-Ohio-3288, 2009 Ohio App. LEXIS 2828 (Ohio Ct. App., Cuyahoga County 2009).

Defendant's conviction for aggravated theft (R.C. 2913.02(A)(3)) was proper, as the victim testified that the victim gave defendant $2,200 for equipment the victim purchased, which included a $1,500 oven that was never received. There was also evidence that defendant cashed the victim's check, did not return calls, and eventually sold the oven to someone else. State v. Hughes, 2009-Ohio-1246, 2009 Ohio App. LEXIS 1048 (Ohio Ct. App., Cuyahoga County 2009).

Weight and sufficiency of the evidence supported defendant's conviction for theft, in violation of R.C. 2913.02(A)(1), where he was seen on a surveillance video entering an office for a long enough period of time to have taken cash that was in an unlocked drawer; the only other person who entered the office during the time that the cash was in the drawer was not there long enough to have taken the money. State v. Moorer, 2009-Ohio-736, 2009 Ohio App. LEXIS 618 (Ohio Ct. App., Cuyahoga County 2009).

Defendant's R.C. 2913.02(A)(1) theft conviction was supported by sufficient evidence as the evidence showed that televisions were taken from a store without the store's consent and that defendant was present at the time. While defendant argued that he did not know that his father, who was with him, had not paid for the televisions, it was jury's province to determine credibility of witnesses. State v. McIntyre, 2009-Ohio-709, 2009 Ohio App. LEXIS 592 (Ohio Ct. App., Stark County 2009).

Evidence supported defendant's conviction for theft, based on the testimony of individuals who worked in the retail industry and evidence that defendant lived in a house where police recovered massive amounts of merchandise, boxes of blank price tags, ticketing guns and plastic fasteners, various credit cards, and over $50,000 in cash. State v. Neff, 2009-Ohio-459, 2009 Ohio App. LEXIS 396 (Ohio Ct. App., Cuyahoga County 2009).

Denial of defendant's acquittal motion under Crim.R. 29 was proper, as there was sufficient circumstantial evidence, based upon inferences and facts, which supported defendant's conviction for theft, in violation of R.C. 2913.02; defendant had withdrawn funds and converted bonds of an elderly, somewhat demented victim who was in defendant's care, and facts surrounding the incidents, including the victim's frugal habits and her spending needs, supported a finding of guilty. State v. Kalman, 2009-Ohio-222, 2009 Ohio App. LEXIS 195 (Ohio Ct. App., Cuyahoga County 2009).

Weight of the evidence supported defendant's convictions for burglary and theft were not against the manifest weight of the evidence because the testimony established that, after helping the victim move his belongings into a mobile home, defendant showed three other men the mobile home and told them that there were guns to steal. Defendant waited in the vehicle with one of the men while the other two entered the mobile home and stole six guns and two bows. State v. Wittmer, 2009-Ohio-72, 2009 Ohio App. LEXIS 81 (Ohio Ct. App., Wayne County 2009).

Defendant's convictions for burglary, theft, and attempted burglary, in violation of R.C. 2911.12(A)(2), (3), 2913.02(A)(1), and 2923.02, were not against the manifest weight of the evidence where there was physical evidence, eyewitness testimony, and defendant's statements to a fellow inmate that tied him to commission of the multiple crimes; defendant's conduct was in conformity with one who had perpetrated the crimes, defendant was seen leaving a burglarized apartment by an eyewitness, and defendant was seen at a coin machine after loose change was discovered missing from burglarized apartments. State v. Appenzeller, 2008-Ohio-7005, 2008 Ohio App. LEXIS 5889 (Ohio Ct. App., Lake County 2008).

Defendant's convictions for theft by deception from the elderly, under R.C. 2913.02(A)(3) and (B)(3), misuse of a credit card, under R.C. 2913.21(B)(2), grand theft by deception from the elderly, under R.C. 2913.02(A)(2) and (A)(3), and theft by deception from the elderly, under R.C. 2913.02(A)(3), for taking money from elderly victims for work defendant did not perform, were not against the manifest weight of the evidence, despite defendant's contention that defendant intended to do the work, because (1) a reasonable person could find defendant committed the crimes beyond a reasonable doubt, and (2) a jury could accept or reject any evidence and assess witness credibility. State v. Snyder, 2008-Ohio-6709, 2008 Ohio App. LEXIS 5623 (Ohio Ct. App., Licking County 2008).

Defendant's conviction of theft for false billings to the Ohio Medicaid program was supported by the evidence, as Ohio Attorney General special agents testified that defendant admitted to billing for services defendant did not provide, and defendant's conduct allowed for an inference that defendant engaged in false billings. The parent of one of the children defendant cared for as a nurse testified that defendant revealed an intention to bill for a day that defendant did not care for the child State v. McKinney, 2008-Ohio-6522, 2008 Ohio App. LEXIS 5398 (Ohio Ct. App., Franklin County 2008).

Weight and sufficiency of the evidence supported defendant's convictions for theft and receiving stolen property, in violation of R.C. 2913.02(A)(1) and 2913.51(A), where the State showed that defendant knowingly removed copper wire from a barn with the purpose of depriving the owner of it, and he then sold it to a scrap metal yard; there was testimony from witnesses who were qualified as experts that the value of the property taken was in excess of $500. State v. Schandel, 2008-Ohio-6359, 2008 Ohio App. LEXIS 5320 (Ohio Ct. App., Carroll County 2008).

Defendant's convictions for theft (R.C. 2913.02(A)) were not against the manifest weight of the evidence, as the fact-finder could conclude that defendant knew state tax refunds were being generated illegally, and participated in the scheme. Although defendant testified that defendant thought defendant was simply receiving unclaimed funds, there was ample evidence to establish that checks were being generated based on amended tax returns, not unclaimed funds; variance letters so indicating were mailed to defendant. State v. Burt, 2008-Ohio-6129, 2008 Ohio App. LEXIS 5147 (Ohio Ct. App., Summit County 2008).

Weight and sufficiency of the evidence supported defendant's convictions for theft and misuse of credit cards, in violation of R.C. 2913.02(B)(2) and 2913.21(D)(3), where an elderly victim testified that defendant withdrew money from her account by use of the victim's bank card without the victim's permission, and that defendant did not give her the money or items purchased with the money; defendant's claim that the money represented gifts or loans was not deemed credible, and there was sufficient testimony as to the value thereof for purposes of finding that the values exceeded $500. State v. Hoover, 2008-Ohio-6136, 2008 Ohio App. LEXIS 5146 (Ohio Ct. App., Scioto County 2008).

Sufficient evidence supported defendant's petty theft conviction because the evidence established that a television set was taken from a university campus building through a little-used back entrance and that the television was placed into a vehicle that was registered to defendant's father. Because police officers were able to identify the vehicle based on the license plate information provided by two witnesses, and the two passengers in the vehicle acknowledged that defendant had driven them to the campus, it was reasonable to have inferred that defendant had driven away from the university with the television in the car. State v. Hill, 2008-Ohio-6040, 2008 Ohio App. LEXIS 5055 (Ohio Ct. App., Champaign County 2008).

Evidence was sufficient for the jury to find that defendant knowingly deprived the hotel of services by deception for his grand theft conviction because the jury could have properly inferred from defendant's completion of the direct billing request, including the listing of a bank in which he had never deposited any money and an entity with which he had never had an account, that he never intended to pay for the rooms that he and his employees used for a month. State v. Keiner, 2008-Ohio-5849, 2008 Ohio App. LEXIS 4959 (Ohio Ct. App., Summit County 2008).

Defendant's theft conviction was not against the manifest weight of the evidence where the State presented evidence, including testimony from the victim, that established each of the elements of theft; while the witnesses at trial provided differing accounts of the events in question, the jury was in a better position to determine the credibility of the witnesses and the weight of the evidence. State v. Miller, 2008-Ohio-5661, 2008 Ohio App. LEXIS 4771 (Ohio Ct. App., Butler County 2008).

Appellant juvenile's adjudication as delinquent for committing burglary and theft, in violation of R.C. 2911.12(A)(2) and 2913.02, was supported by the weight and sufficiency of the evidence where the juvenile was seen riding on another minor's bicycle, when asked why the juvenile had the bicycle, the juvenile did not provide a response but instead, left the scene, and the bicycle had been left in the minor's unlocked home, where the juvenile was seen earlier peering through the windows; the circumstantial evidence created an inference that the juvenile had committed the crimes charged. In re A.F., 2008-Ohio-5479, 2008 Ohio App. LEXIS 4607 (Ohio Ct. App., Cuyahoga County 2008).

Weight and sufficiency of the evidence supported defendant's convictions for theft and forgery, in violation of R.C. 2913.02(A)(3) and 2913.31(A)(1), as the circumstantial evidence supported a finding that she signed a countercheck for an elderly bank customer without the customer's knowledge, and she withdrew funds from the customer's account and retained them for herself. State v. Stout, 2008-Ohio-1366, 2008 Ohio App. LEXIS 5906 (Ohio Ct. App., Gallia County 2008).

Trial court did not err in convicting defendant of robbery, in violation of R.C. 2911.02(A)(2) because defendant used force in an attempt to deprive a motel of its property, either without the consent of the owner or its agent, in violation of R.C. 2913.02(A)(1), or beyond the scope of the express or implied consent of the owner or its agent, in violation of R.C. 2913.02(A)(2); a refund had not been consummated and defendant's belief that the motel owed defendant money was immaterial. State v. Padgett, 2008-Ohio-1166, 2008 Ohio App. LEXIS 1011 (Ohio Ct. App., Montgomery County 2008).

Defendant's convictions for theft and possession of criminal tools were not against the manifest weight of the evidence, as defendant was seen with a co-defendant pushing a generator down the back alley of a hardware store, the generator belonged to the store and there was no permission given to defendant to take it, and defendant was just attempting to load it into a truck when defendant was stopped by police. State v. Neal,

2008-Ohio-1077, 2008 Ohio App. LEXIS 947 (Ohio Ct. App., Cuyahoga County 2008).

Defendant's conviction for theft, in violation of R.C. 2913.02, was not against the manifest weight of the evidence where defendant admitted to taking the purse of the victim, defendant's grandmother, and other witnesses also testified to observing that action; defendant's alleged justification that defendant believed that the grandmother had taken a government check that belonged to defendant did not change the fact that defendant took the purse and exerted knowing control over it without permission. State v. Jackson, 2008-Ohio-1078, 2008 Ohio App. LEXIS 951 (Ohio Ct. App., Cuyahoga County 2008).

Weight of the evidence supported defendant's theft conviction because the testimony of the arresting officer and the owner was sufficient to establish the existence and ownership of the stolen item; the testimony established that the cement mixer was locked up, that defendant was found removing the cement mixer without permission, that he did not own the cement mixer, that he returned the cement mixer to the lot after he was caught driving away with it, and that the lock and chain were removed. Further, the owner's testimony that the cement mixer was worth $2000 in its current condition was uncontradicted and sufficient to establish the value of the cement mixer. State v. Rhodes, 2008-Ohio-1037, 2008 Ohio App. LEXIS 908 (Ohio Ct. App., Columbiana County 2008).



Defendant's conviction for grand theft motor vehicle under R.C. 2913.02 was supported by sufficient evidence, in that the eyewitness testimony of the employees of a rental car company showed that defendant, without permission, got behind the wheel of a rental car and drove it around the security gate on the rental car lot and off the lot. State v. Nash, 2008-Ohio-914, 2008 Ohio App. LEXIS 798 (Ohio Ct. App., Cuyahoga County 2008).

Sufficient evidence supported defendant's conviction for complicity in the commission of theft, in violation of R.C. 2913.02(A)(1) and 2923.03, because sufficient evidence let a rational trier of fact find defendant knowingly aided and abetted a co-defendant to obtain or exert control over a substance without the consent of the substance's owner and with the purpose to deprive the owner of it. State v. Howland, 2008-Ohio-521, 2008 Ohio App. LEXIS 453 (Ohio Ct. App., Fayette County 2008).

Weight and sufficiency of the evidence supported defendant's convictions for aggravated burglary and aggravated robbery, in violation of R.C. 2911.11(A)(2) and 2911.01(A)(1), where defendant and another kicked in the victims' apartment door, demanded money from the victims at gunpoint, and took one victim's coat; although neither victim had seen defendant or the other perpetrator take anything from the apartment during the criminal incident, the evidence supported a determination that defendant had committed a theft, in violation of R.C. 2913.02, where the victims later saw defendant wearing one of their coats and neither had given defendant permission to have it. State v. Sanford, 2008-Ohio-472, 2008 Ohio App. LEXIS 415 (Ohio Ct. App., Lucas County 2008).

Although circumstantial, the evidence did not weigh heavily in favor of the conclusion that someone other than defendant committed the crimes of aggravated robbery with a firearm specification, robbery, failure to comply with an order or signal of a police officer, possession of a weapon under a disability, grand theft, carrying a concealed weapon, felonious assault, and vandalism. Instead, the timeline of events leading to defendant's arrest after fleeing the victim's vehicle on foot supported the conclusion that defendant robbed the victim, stole her car, and was in possession of it until he was apprehended after a high speed chase; the victim's purse and belongings were found in her vehicle, along with an operable firearm. State v. Gibson, 2008-Ohio-410, 2008 Ohio App. LEXIS 358 (Ohio Ct. App., Summit County 2008).

Defendant's motion for acquittal, under Crim.R. 29(A), was properly denied as to a charge of grand theft by deception, under R.C. 2913.02(A)(3), because sufficient evidence supported defendant's conviction, when defendant sold football tickets defendant did not possess by eBay, as a jury could find beyond a reasonable doubt that defendant intended to accept customers' money without giving proper consideration in return when defendant accepted customers' money for tickets defendant did not possess and then used that money for personal expenses, instead of to acquire the tickets, so, with purpose to deprive customers of the customers' property, defendant knowingly obtained that property by deception. State v. West, 2008-Ohio-368, 2008 Ohio App. LEXIS 326 (Ohio Ct. App., Wood County 2008).

Weight of the evidence supported defendant's convictions for burglary theft and of having weapons under a disability because a witness testified that defendant entered the victim's home and took several guns, and that he carried the guns from the home and subsequently into an apartment. A detective testified that another witness gave him a cell phone number to call to attempt to purchase the guns and that defendant answered the phone. The detective testified that defendant was in the targeted vehicle that arrived to sell the guns. State v. Evans, 2008-Ohio-5000, 2008 Ohio App. LEXIS 4203 (Ohio Ct. App., Wayne County 2008).

Evidence was sufficient to support defendant's conviction for aggravated robbery, in violation of R.C. 2911.01(A)(3), where defendant ransacked a victim's home and left it in disarray, with possible items of value missing, such that the attempted theft offense pursuant to R.C. 2913.02 was committed; State v. Young, 2008-Ohio-4752, 2008 Ohio App. LEXIS 4002 (Ohio Ct. App., Scioto County 2008).

Defendant's motion under Crim.R. 29 for a judgment of acquittal was properly denied, as the evidence was sufficient to support defendant's conviction for theft, in violation of R.C. 2913.02(A)(1); defendant acted without the employer's consent when defendant failed to return a cellular phone upon being terminated from employment. State v. Frezgi, 2008-Ohio-4732, 2008 Ohio App. LEXIS 3988 (Ohio Ct. App., Montgomery County 2008).

Defendant's theft conviction under R.C. 2913.02(A)(1) was not against the weight of the evidence. A teacher identified defendant as the man she had seen opening door of victim's vehicle to take victim's wallet, the license plate number given by the victim matched defendant's license plate number, and the description of the suspect's vehicle also matched defendant's vehicle. State v. Moman, 2008-Ohio-4563, 2008 Ohio App. LEXIS 3826 (Ohio Ct. App., Delaware County 2008).

Sufficient evidence supported defendant's convictions for burglary and theft because the individual pieces of evidence offered supported the making of parallel inferences from which the jury could have concluded that defendant was the person who entered the victim's apartment and removed his property. The evidence showed that: tracks could be seen in the wet grass between the victim's apartment and defendant's apartment; defendant was seen pushing a wheeled trash can from the area behind the victim's apartment; the trash can was filled nearly to the top; and entry to the victim's apartment was made by a key, rather than by force, and defendant at one time had access to a key to the victim's apartment. State v. Moore, 2008-Ohio-4546, 2008 Ohio App. LEXIS 3818 (Ohio Ct. App., Franklin County 2008).

Sufficient evidence supported defendant's conviction for theft by obtaining control of property beyond the scope of the consent of the owner because it was reasonable to have found that defendant obtained the money upon the understanding that he would perform remodeling work for the victim, and then, without making any meaningful effort to do so, kept the $800, beyond the victim's consent in surrendering the check to defendant. State v. Sears, 2008-Ohio-4531, 2008 Ohio App. LEXIS 3808 (Ohio Ct. App., Montgomery County 2008).

Defendant's conviction for theft under R.C. 2913.02 was supported by sufficient evidence. While defendant contended that he was unable to deprive the owner of her property because he was unable to move her car, any rational trier of fact could have found that breaking the car's door lock and disabling the steering column was exerting control over the victim's car; thus, defendant's Crim.R. 29 motion was properly denied. State v. Littlefield, 2008-Ohio-4356, 2008 Ohio App. LEXIS 3678 (Ohio Ct. App., Franklin County 2008).

Defendant's convictions for identity fraud under R.C. 2913.49(B), forgery under R.C. 2913.31(A)(1), and theft under R.C. 2913.02(A)(3) were supported by sufficient evidence as the assistant manager of a store identified defendant as the person who appeared in the store, identified himself as the victim, signed the victim's name to a credit application, and obtained tires and an oil change totaling almost $700. State v. Mann, 2008-Ohio-3762, 2008 Ohio App. LEXIS 3186 (Ohio Ct. App., Stark County 2008).

Defendant's conviction of theft of childcare benefits from the Ohio Department of Job and Family Services, R.C. 2913.02(A)(2), was not against the manifest weight of the evidence, as a caseworker maintained that defendant did not tell the caseworker about defendant's maternity leave until it was time for her to return to work and add her newborn baby to the childcare case. State v. Travis, 2008-Ohio-3638, 2008 Ohio App. LEXIS 3072 (Ohio Ct. App., Summit County 2008).

Defendant's theft conviction under R.C. 2913.02(A)(3) was supported by evidence showing that, though defendant did not leave a store with any contraband, he exerted control over power tools that were hidden inside a vanity that he had placed on a cart and wheeled toward the checkout and that he had the intent to deprive the store of its merchandise. State v. Cadle, 2008-Ohio-3639, 2008 Ohio App. LEXIS 3073 (Ohio Ct. App., Summit County 2008).

Sufficient evidence supported theft and receiving stolen property because the victim's credit card number and name were found on defendant's computer in connection with internet purchases. Sufficient evidence also supported the tampering with evidence conviction; in throwing the credit card into the river because defendant did not want to have anything to do with the card, the jury could have reasonably inferred that defendant knew that an official proceeding or investigation was likely to be instituted. State v. Hicks, 2008-Ohio-3600, 2008 Ohio App. LEXIS 3031 (Ohio Ct. App., Union County 2008).

Sufficient evidence supported defendant's convictions for burglary, receiving stolen property, and theft because defendant was stopped driving the victim's stolen car loaded with items taken from burglary victim's apartment; a security camera across the street from the burglary victim's apartment showed a man in a white t-shirt taking items from the apartment and putting them into a dark colored car; defendant was wearing a white t-shirt, and was the sole occupant of the car at the time it was stopped; and the burglary victim's white car had been damaged and had purple paint streaks on it, and the other victim's purple car had damage to it as well. State v. Jones, 2008-Ohio-3565, 2008 Ohio App. LEXIS 2989 (Ohio Ct. App., Franklin County 2008).

Sufficient evidence supported defendant's conviction for attempted theft because defendant attempted to deceive a check store clerk by presenting a forged check as an authentic check. The representation was false and misleading because the payor did not issue the check to defendant and defendant withheld that information from the check store. State v. Parker, 2008-Ohio-3538, 2008 Ohio App. LEXIS 2983 (Ohio Ct. App., Cuyahoga County 2008).

Evidence was sufficient to support a determination that appellant juvenile was a delinquent for having committed the offense of theft, in violation of R.C. 2913.02, as the evidence showed that the juvenile acted knowingly pursuant to R.C. 2901.22(B) when the juvenile took the victim's work van without the victim's consent. In re C.C., 2008-Ohio-2803, 2008 Ohio App. LEXIS 2346 (Ohio Ct. App., Franklin County 2008).

Jury's verdict convicting defendant of breaking and entering under R.C. 2911.13(A) and/or (B), felony vandalism under R.C. 2909.05(B)(2), and felony theft under R.C. 2913.02(A)(1) was not against the weight of the evidence. The testimony of the school's principal and defendant's probation officer, identifying defendant as one of the individuals appearing on the surveillance tape that captured the break-in and vandalism of a high school, supported the jury's conclusion that defendant was one of the perpetrators of the crimes. State v. Reading, 2008-Ohio-2748, 2008 Ohio App. LEXIS 2299 (Ohio Ct. App., Licking County 2008).

Defendant's convictions for theft and receiving stolen property, in violation of R.C. 2913.02(A)(1), (B)(2), and 2913.51(A) and (C), were supported by sufficient direct and circumstantial evidence, including photographs and video clips from surveillance cameras in the store where defendant stole laptop computers, and testimony from store employees; defendant had removed the computers from a glass display case which later bore defendant's fingerprints, put the unboxed computers in another box that had contained an unassembled chair, and left the store after paying for the "chair." State v. Gillman, 2008-Ohio-2606, 2008 Ohio App. LEXIS 2192 (Ohio Ct. App., Union County 2008).

Finding that defendant, a juvenile, was delinquent by reason of committing a theft offense which would be a first-degree misdemeanor if committed by an adult was not against the manifest weight of the evidence. The testimony of defendant's friends involved in the theft and the testimony of the victim's mother as to the value of the tools stolen from the victim provided competent, credible evidence to establish that defendant committed the offense of theft and to establish that the value of the property was under $500, therefore warranting a conviction of misdemeanor theft. In re Miller, 2008-Ohio-2399, 2008 Ohio App. LEXIS 2053 (Ohio Ct. App., Licking County 2008).

Evidence was sufficient to sustain the jury's verdict convicting defendant of complicity to theft under R.C. 2923.03(A)(2) and 2913.02(A)(3) as the evidence showed that defendant acted suspiciously upon entering the store, that she was continuously looking at the surveillance camera, and that she used her body to shield her friend's actions in removing earrings from a rounder and placing them in her purse from the surveillance camera. State v. Murchison, 2008-Ohio-2327, 2008 Ohio App. LEXIS 1970 (Ohio Ct. App., Lake County 2008).

Defendant's conviction for theft from a disabled adult was supported by the State's presentation of still pictures from a store's surveillance camera showing defendant using the victim's gift card. Circumstantial evidence also showed that defendant was a "disabled adult" under R.C. 2913.01(DD) as the victim's testimony showed that she was unable to hold substantially remunerative employment, in that she had multiple sclerosis, that she was confined to a wheelchair, and that she needed assistance getting dressed and using the restroom. State v. Davis, 2008-Ohio-2326, 2008 Ohio App. LEXIS 1966 (Ohio Ct. App., Lake County 2008).

Defendant's conviction for grand theft of a motor vehicle under R.C. 2913.02(A)(1) was not against the manifest weight of the evidence because the evidence placed defendant at the scene of the theft and behind the wheel of the stolen vehicle within few minutes and a few miles of its having been reported stolen. The State's failure to show that defendant was driving the car was unimportant. State v. LeMasters, 2008-Ohio-2139, 2008 Ohio App. LEXIS 1834 (Ohio Ct. App., Lake County 2008).

Because the elements of theft could have been found beyond a reasonable doubt, sufficient evidence supported defendant's robbery conviction; although defendant claimed that his purpose was not to maintain control over the money he took, but to get someone to call the police, because the act was a crime, a good motive or purpose was not a defense. Also, there was ample evidence from which to find that defendant was, in fact, exerting control over the property of another with the intent to deprive that person of the property; on several occasions, defendant referred to the money as "my money," and, upon being approached by an off-duty police officer, defendant did not surrender the money. State v. McArthur, 2007-Ohio-7133, 2007 Ohio App. LEXIS 6235 (Ohio Ct. App., Lake County 2007).

Evidence was sufficient to find appellant, a juvenile, delinquent of aggravated robbery as the evidence showed that the threat made by appellant and his cohorts that they would continue the attack against the victim if the victim refused to pay them a dollar constituted an attempt to commit a theft offense and that appellant was one of the four people who kicked the victim before the stabbing. Evidence that the victim was unable to work for six weeks after the attack and that he injured his back was sufficient to show that the victim suffered serious physical harm under R.C. 2901.01(A)(5). In re I.A., 2007-Ohio-6992, 2007 Ohio App. LEXIS 6128 (Ohio Ct. App., Cuyahoga County 2007).

Evidence was sufficient to support defendant's conviction for theft by deception as the evidence showed that the victim appointed defendant as her power of attorney so that defendant could act as the victim's agent in selling the victim's home and that defendant refused to return the money collected from the potential buyers as defendant had promised to do, showing that defendant had the intent to keep the money even though defendant had no permission to do so and constituting "deception," within the meaning of R.C. 2913.01(A). State v. Farmer, 2007-Ohio-6810, 2007 Ohio App. LEXIS 5978 (Ohio Ct. App., Cuyahoga County 2007).

Sufficient evidence supported defendant's convictions for complicity to commit attempted murder under R.C. 2903.02(A), 2923.02(A), and 2923.03(A)(2) and complicity to commit aggravated robbery under R.C. 2911.01(A)(1), 2913.02(A)(1), and 2923.03(A)(2) because, though defendant testified that he was not at the convenience store at the time that his codefendant shot at the two victims, one of the two victims testified that he had seen defendant at the scene. It was reasonable for the jury to believe that defendant was in the vehicle when his codefendant committed the aggravated robbery and when the vehicle was seen following the two victims to the hospital, especially in light of the fact that defendant himself testified that he and the codefendant had joined forces to sell drugs around the city, and the shooting at issue arose during an attempted drug transaction with one of the victims. State v. Wade, 2007-Ohio-6611, 2007 Ohio App. LEXIS 5785 (Ohio Ct. App., Clark County 2007).

Sufficient evidence supported defendant's convictions for burglary, theft, failure to comply with the order of a police officer, safe cracking, and receiving stolen property as the evidence showed that defendant was identified as the intruder seen at one victim's home and the individual caught after a high-speed chase with deputies, that defendant refused to comply with officers' orders to stop, that defendant led officers on a high-speed chase, that items stolen from two victims' residences were found in defendant's car, that a safe at one of the vicitm's homes was found "cracked open," and that a credit card stolen from a third victim was found on defendant's person. State v. Evans, 2007-Ohio-6575, 2007 Ohio App. LEXIS 5756 (Ohio Ct. App., Pickaway County 2007).

Defendant's convictions for breaking and entering and theft, in violation of R.C. 2911.13(A) and 2913.02, were supported by sufficient evidence where defendant informed a security guard on premises that were being demolished that defendant had consent to be there and to remove scrap metal when in fact there was conflicting testimony that defendant lacked such authority and consent to be on the premises and to remove the property; denial of defendant's acquittal motions under Crim.R. 29(A) were proper. State v. Wade, 2007-Ohio-6490, 2007 Ohio App. LEXIS 5684 (Ohio Ct. App., Cuyahoga County 2007).

State presented sufficient evidence to allow a rational trier of fact to find defendant guilty of theft as the evidence showed that the $1.00 secretary fee that defendant, the secretary of two bowling leagues, charged was beyond the bowling leagues' express or implied consent, in that the testimony of several bowling league officers and several other league bowlers established that defendant had never been authorized to collect such a fee. Further, the jury was reasonable in not believing defendant's testimony that the money had been stolen given the fact that defendant had lied several times during the course of the investigation; thus, defendant's Crim.R. 29(A) motion for acquittal was properly denied. State v. Fisher, 2007-Ohio-6421, 2007 Ohio App. LEXIS 5623 (Ohio Ct. App., Auglaize County 2007).

Sufficient evidence supported defendant's conviction for theft by deception because the evidence showed that defendant negotiated the entire sale of the tractors and assured the buyer that they were not stolen, that he had the authority to sell them, and that the proceeds were to go to his accomplice's boyfriend in jail; defendant spent the money on himself. Thus, the evidence was sufficient to support an inference that defendant knew that he did not have permission to deal with the property, and that, in fact, he intended to deprive the owner of the property. State v. Hall, 2007-Ohio-6352, 2007 Ohio App. LEXIS 5606 (Ohio Ct. App., Montgomery County 2007).

Defendant's convictions for theft and failure to comply with the order or signal of a police officer were not against the manifest weight of the evidence as three officers identified defendant as the person who was driving the stolen vehicle at the time that the officers tried to stop the vehicle. State v. Flynn, 2007-Ohio-6210, 2007 Ohio App. LEXIS 5461 (Ohio Ct. App., Medina County 2007).

Sufficient evidence to support defendant's theft conviction because the trial court reasonably inferred his guilt from the presence of the ring when the victim left the room, his close proximity to the ring, his movement within the kitchen, the ring's absence when the victim returned, and his unusually hurried departure. State v. Buelow, 2007-Ohio-5929, 2007 Ohio App. LEXIS 5196 (Ohio Ct. App., Franklin County 2007).

Evidence that, as defendant was running away from police officers who were trying to stop him to investigate defendant's possible shoplifting, defendant was seen throwing seven packs of cigarettes from his pockets, all of which still had the sensor strips on them from the store, was sufficient to support defendant's theft conviction. State v. Odd, 2007-Ohio-5813, 2007 Ohio App. LEXIS 5114 (Ohio Ct. App., Stark County 2007).

There was sufficient evidence that defendant committed theft by obtaining the property of the murder victims without their consent to support his aggravated murder and aggravated robbery convictions; a witness had given the police an accurate description of defendant and she picked defendant from a photo array. Also, the witness testified that she saw the perpetrator run from the scene with a bag that contained something; an officer testified the trunk and the right rear door of the victims' car were open, which the jury could have reasonably interpreted to demonstrate that defendant had taken money and/or drugs from inside the vehicle or trunk; there was substantial evidence that the victims were in Ohio to sell a large quantity of drugs and had the drugs in their possession; and defendant had a great deal of money following the murder. State v. Covington, 2007-Ohio-5008, 2007 Ohio App. LEXIS 4919 (Ohio Ct. App., Franklin County 2007).



Weight of the evidence supported defendant's theft conviction because the evidence showed that defendant purposely deprived the victim of his retirement money. Testimony revealed that the victim, who was in prison, gave defendant his retirement check for the purpose of paying the victim's relatives, court costs, and attorneys; the check was not a gift that defendant could use for his own personal expenses; when the police asked defendant about the money, he told them it had been garnished by the IRS, but the IRS had not done so; and, when the victim's relatives asked defendant about the money, he told them there was a holder on it from the victim's divorce, but the court had not done so. State v. Davis, 2007-Ohio-4741, 2007 Ohio App. LEXIS 4284 (Ohio Ct. App., Marion County 2007).

In a theft prosecution under R.C. 2913.02(A)(1), the evidence sufficiently showed that defendant took monies from the cash register without his employer's consent. Defendant's permission to control the monies from the store's cash register was limited to counting the money, placing it in an envelope, and putting the envelope in box; thus, his act of placing the money in his pocket instead constituted deception as it clearly went beyond the scope of his employer's consent. State v. Slone, 2007-Ohio-4748, 2007 Ohio App. LEXIS 4277 (Ohio Ct. App., Delaware County 2007).

Sufficient evidence supported defendant's convictions for kidnapping and theft because one of the two victims identified defendant as the perpetrator and testified that defendant held a small handgun to his head, participated in restraining him with dog leashes, and then broke into his safe and took $750, his cellular phone, and a video game. Additionally, when the police arrested defendant, they confiscated a small black firearm; thus, there was ample evidence that defendant used a gun. State v. Williams, 2007-Ohio-4581, 2007 Ohio App. LEXIS 4130 (Ohio Ct. App., Cuyahoga County 2007).

Grand theft conviction under R.C. 2913.02(A)(3) was supported by evidence showing that defendant, an inn's manager, had no authority to withdraw money from the inn's bank account, that various bank tellers had cashed the inn's checks for defendant, and that defendant was the only person who came into the bank to handle the inn's business during the period in question. This testimony not only established defendant's identity as the person cashing the checks but also established the element of deception, as defined in R.C. 2913.01(A), showing that defendant's actions and omissions misled the bank into believing that he had the authority to withdraw those funds. State v. Ahmad, 2007-Ohio-4567, 2007 Ohio App. LEXIS 4095 (Ohio Ct. App., Adams County 2007).

Adjudication of defendant as a delinquent under R.C. 2152.01(F) for committing attempted grand theft of a motor vehicle under R.C. 2913.02(A)(1) and (5) and R.C. 2923.02(A) was supported by evidence that defendant and another man were seen walking through the parking lot in the same area where the car that was broken into was parked and that the other man admitted responsibility for breaking into the vehicle. The evidence was sufficient to give rise to a reasonable inference that defendant, under R.C. 2923.03(A)(2), aided and abetted the other man in attempting to steal the car. In re J.B., 2007-Ohio-4335, 2007 Ohio App. LEXIS 3874 (Ohio Ct. App., Montgomery County 2007).

There was sufficient evidence to find that defendant committed burglary and theft beyond a reasonable doubt, either as the principal offender or by aiding and abetting the accomplices, because after a neighbor called the police, defendant and two accomplices fled the scene but were apprehended; the victim described the items taken from his home, including cash from a recent garage sale, a video game system, jewelry, and a pair of sunglasses, and stated that they had a value greater than $500.00. Although there was no physical evidence that put defendant in the victim's residence, his flight was admissible as evidence showing consciousness of guilt. State v. Blackburn, 2007-Ohio-4282, 2007 Ohio App. LEXIS 3829 (Ohio Ct. App., Guernsey County 2007).

Sufficient evidence supported defendant's convictions for theft and forgery because the testimony at trial from defendant's accomplice and the victim's internal audit manager, demonstrated that defendant and the accomplice submitted invoices to the accomplice's employer for work that was never done, totaling over $100,000. State v. Alexander, 2007-Ohio-4177, 2007 Ohio App. LEXIS 3767 (Ohio Ct. App., Franklin County 2007).

Evidence was sufficient to support defendant's conviction for theft by deception as evidence that defendant attempted to utilize a lifetime, nontransferable warranty on struts, which was in his deceased mother's name, in order to receive free parts for his car was sufficient to establish that defendant intended to deprive the service station of property and services by deception. The evidence also established that defendant obtained goods and services from the station as defendant was not charged for the struts because they were under the warranty, and he had not paid any part of the $1,300 bill for the work performed on his vehicle. State v. Hess, 2007-Ohio-4099, 2007 Ohio App. LEXIS 3722 (Ohio Ct. App., Montgomery County 2007).

Undisputed evidence that defendant sold defendant's employer's property to an investigator on an internet auction site, that a search of defendant's home revealed more such property, and defendant's admission, at trial, to making other sales of the employer's property on the site sufficiently supported defendant's convictions for theft and receiving stolen property. State v. Goerndt, 2007-Ohio-4067, 2007 Ohio App. LEXIS 3699 (Ohio Ct. App., Cuyahoga County 2007).

Sufficient evidence supported defendant's convictions for theft and receiving stolen property because a rational trier of fact could have found that defendant was acting in complicity with his friends; all of the actions of defendant and his two friends, who went to a superstore and stole expensive items, including a computer, a printer, a television, and a DVD player, were captured on videotape. Also, there was testimony that, although the items that defendant alone took equaled $246.72, the total of the items that all three took equaled $3,012.40. State v. Schuster, 2007-Ohio-3977, 2007 Ohio App. LEXIS 3595 (Ohio Ct. App., Union County 2007).

Sufficient evidence supported the conviction for aggravated theft by deception, under R.C. 2913.02(A)(3) and (B)(2), because defendant, as comptroller, stole funds from his corporate employer in an amount of $186,276.84. The record showed voluminous documentation establishing that defendant engaged in a clear pattern of issuing and executing thousands of dollars in payments from the corporate accounts for unauthorized personal benefit; he tapped corporate accounts to pay off his many personal credit cards, took unauthorized salary increases, cash payouts, and tuition reimbursements. State v. Walsh, 2007-Ohio-103, 2007 Ohio App. LEXIS 93 (Ohio Ct. App., Lucas County 2007).

There was sufficient circumstantial evidence to establish that defendant committed the crimes of theft, grand theft, aggravated burglary, aggravated robbery, and two counts of kidnapping because DNA evidence was obtained from the tee shirt lost by the suspect as he fled the authorities, which matched a known standard from defendant. Also, among other things, the ATM surveillance photo showed a man in dark clothes and mask pull up to the ATM, wearing large, black eyeglasses above the mask, which were identical to the eyeglasses found inside the discarded backpack found along the suspect's escape route, and close scrutiny of the ATM surveillance photo revealed that the interior of the suspect's vehicle was identical to the interior of the victim's van, as depicted in photographs taken of the van by the police. State v. Smith, 2007-Ohio-51, 2007 Ohio App. LEXIS 37 (Ohio Ct. App., Summit County 2007).

Weight and sufficiency of the evidence supported defendant's convictions for aggravated burglary, kidnapping, theft of a motor vehicle, and receiving stolen property, in violation of R.C. 2911.11(A)(1), 2905.01(A)(2), 2913.02, and 2913.51, where the State offered sufficient proof on every element of the offenses; based on testimony from the victim of the crimes, it was established that defendant and another man were allowed into the victim's home to use his telephone, they attacked him, dragged him into his basement where he was bound and beaten about the head, and they took the victim's van and certain of the possessions in his home. State v. Sheppard, 2007-Ohio-24, 2007 Ohio App. LEXIS 17 (Ohio Ct. App., Hamilton County 2007).

Evidence was sufficient to support defendant's conviction for complicity to grand theft, in violation of R.C. 2913.02(A)(3) and 2923.03(A)(2), based on his having removed heavy machinery from a victim's real property without the victim's consent; there was adequate proof of valuation with respect to the replacement value of the property pursuant to R.C. 2913.61(A), and defendant's assistance to another individual in removing the property made him liable in an aiding and abetting capacity. State v. Pesec, 2007-Ohio-3846, 2007 Ohio App. LEXIS 3487 (Ohio Ct. App., Portage County 2007).

Defendant's conviction for grand theft from defendant's employer, under R.C. 2913.02(A)(1), and/or (2) and/or (3), was not against the manifest weight of the evidence because (1) defendant never denied processing the employer's credit card charge backs for defendant's personal benefit, (2) defendant's supervisors denied that the charge backs were authorized, (3) once confronted, defendant attempted to set up some sort of restitution, (4) defendant tried to extort a dismissal by threatening to sue the employer, and (5) defendant admitted making the charge backs. State v. Baldwin, 2007-Ohio-3511, 2007 Ohio App. LEXIS 3211 (Ohio Ct. App., Stark County 2007).

Even though defendant's friend, not defendant, was the one who physically carried stolen merchandise out of the store, the State introduced sufficient evidence to show that defendant "knowingly" had actual or constructive possession of the stolen merchandise, under R.C. 2901.22(B), and, thus, purposely deprived the store of property so as to constitute the offense of theft as the evidence showed that defendant and his friend exited the store with a bag of stolen merchandise without stopping at a cash register, that defendant fled the scene with the stolen merchandise in his car, and that the merchandise was later found in defendant's car. Thus, defendant's motion for acquittal was properly denied. State v. McKinney,

2007-Ohio-3389, 2007 Ohio App. LEXIS 3115 (Ohio Ct. App., Lake County 2007).

Weight and sufficiency of the evidence supported defendant's convictions for engaging in a pattern of corrupt activity, burglary, grand theft, theft, breaking and entering, and conspiracy to commit burglary, in violation of R.C. 2923.32(A)(1), 2911.12, 2913.02, 2911.13, and 2923.01, as there was sufficient testimony from witnesses and accomplices, as well as physical evidence, to support the determination that defendant had engaged in 12 instances of criminal activity involving residences and a business over a two-month period, wherein he had taken cash, jewelry, weapons, vehicles, and other items of personal property from the premises which were broken into; defendant and a group of other individuals conducted and participated in an enterprise of corrupt activity, as defined by R.C. 2923.31, and the testimony that supported the convictions was deemed credible despite any potential biases that existed. State v. Dioneff, 2007-Ohio-3387, 2007 Ohio App. LEXIS 3112 (Ohio Ct. App., Ashtabula County 2007).

Sufficient evidence supported that defendant knowingly stole the delivery truck for grand theft of a motor vehicle (and denial of the motion for acquittal) because defendant's fingerprints were found on a soda bottle inside, and on the exterior of the driver's side windows, of the stolen delivery truck; defendant was in the area of the truck on the night that it was stolen; and the former employee testified that he did not know defendant, did not ask him to move furniture, and did not drive the delivery truck on the day it was stolen. Defendant admitted that his fingerprints would be on the soda bottle and on the exterior of the driver's side window. State v. Mossburg, 2007-Ohio-3343, 2007 Ohio App. LEXIS 3070 (Ohio Ct. App., Van Wert County 2007).

Defendant failed to show that his counsel provided ineffective assistance in violation of U.S. Const. amend. VI and Ohio Const. art. I, § 10 where his counsel failed to object to testimony by a police officer that marks on bolt cutters in defendant's possession were consistent with use to cut a padlock, as his counsel cross-examined the officer on that issue and no prejudice was shown; the evidence apart from the officer's testimony was sufficient to support defendant's convictions for theft and possession of criminal tools, in violation of R.C. 2913.02 and 2923.24, and he was acquitted of criminal damaging, which was most dependent on that testimony. State v. Maksem, 2007-Ohio-3288, 2007 Ohio App. LEXIS 3019 (Ohio Ct. App., Franklin County 2007).

Weight and sufficiency of the evidence supported defendant's convictions for breaking and entering, theft, criminal damaging, safecracking and possession of criminal tools, in violation of R.C. 2911.13, 2913.02, 2909.06, 2911.31, and 2923.24, where there was testimony from defendant and many others regarding defendant's conduct, his admissions to having committed those offenses, and his possession of various items that further supported his convictions; some of the witnesses had been participants in the criminal conduct and testified as to defendant's actions in the criminal incidents that the charges were based on. State v. Nichols, 2007-Ohio-3257, 2007 Ohio App. LEXIS 2999 (Ohio Ct. App., Richland County 2007).

Weight and sufficiency of the evidence supported defendant's conviction for theft, in violation of R.C. 2913.02(A)(2), where she had refused to turn in her weekly receipts from her employment despite the requirement to do so prior to receiving her commission thereon, which conduct constituted theft of the employer's property; there was sufficient evidence to establish that she had retained approximately $2,000 from the employer pursuant to R.C. 2913.61(A), and the trial court acted within its discretion in finding that her conflicting version of events lacked credibility. State v. Bartunek, 2007-Ohio-3247, 2007 Ohio App. LEXIS 2983 (Ohio Ct. App., Stark County 2007).

There was sufficient evidence to prove the elements of felonious assault, theft, kidnapping, abduction, aggravated robbery, and robbery beyond a reasonable doubt because the victim testified that defendant cut her in the neck with a knife and used a stun gun on her and eyewitness testimony and medical records from the victim's emergency room treatment corroborated the story. What the medical records showed was that the victim reported being robbed and assaulted with a stun gun and a knife by a man she knew, and that she was treated for a laceration on her neck and the trial court found the medical records, as well as the victim's and eyewitnesses' stories, more credible than defendant's testimony that the victim provoked the incident as a scorned lover. State v. Loparo, 2007-Ohio-2783, 2007 Ohio App. LEXIS 2572 (Ohio Ct. App., Cuyahoga County 2007).

Weight and sufficiency of the evidence supported defendant's conviction for theft where a store clerk and a customer noticed that defendant's actions while in the store indicated conduct that appeared to be a concealment of something under his jacket, he walked out of the store without paying for anything, and a pair of jeans with the tickets still on them dropped out of his jacket and onto the ground while he was walking to his car, whereupon he picked it up and got into the car; the customer, a former police officer, followed the car and called up the police, who searched the vehicle defendant was in and found four pairs of jeans with all of the tickets and the security tags still on them. State v. Carter, 2007-Ohio-2532, 2007 Ohio App. LEXIS 2363 (Ohio Ct. App., Pickaway County 2007).

Convictions for breaking and entering, in violation of R.C. 2911.13; safecracking, in violation of R.C. 2911.31; felony theft, in violation of R.C. 2913.02; and misdemeanor theft were supported by sufficient evidence as the evidence showed that the three automotive retail stores that were burglarized were burglarized in the hours after defendant was terminated from his employment with the chain of automotive retail stores, that none of the stores showed any signs of forced entry, that defendant was the only person known to possess keys to all three of the locations that were burglarized, that defendant knew the location of the keys to the safes located in each store, and that defendant was seen at two of the three burglarized locations in the evening hours after his employment was terminated. Thus, defendant's Crim.R. 29(A) motion for acquittal was properly denied. State v. Abdul-Rahman, 2007-Ohio-2386, 2007 Ohio App. LEXIS 2217 (Ohio Ct. App., Franklin County 2007).

Evidence was sufficient to convict defendant of theft. With respect to defendant's challenges to the State's eyewitness testimony, the eyewitnesses identified defendant as the perpetrator of the crime, they both immediately recognized defendant as their former middle school and high school classmate, their identification of defendant occurred during daylight hours and from a distance of only approximately four feet away, and they picked defendant out of a lineup and also identified him in court during trial. State v. Burton, 2007-Ohio-2320, 2007 Ohio App. LEXIS 2140 (Ohio Ct. App., Ross County 2007).

Defendant's grand theft conviction, under R.C. 2913.02(A)(2) and (B)(2), was supported by sufficient evidence and was not against the manifest weight of the evidence because it was shown that she and her husband deposited $5,000 belonging to the organization for which she was treasurer into their personal account and defendant could not verify that she was entitled to any of that money. State v. Eppard, 2007-Ohio-2257, 2007 Ohio App. LEXIS 2110 (Ohio Ct. App., Lucas County 2007).

Theft conviction under R.C. 2913.02 was not against the manifest weight of the evidence as the jury had the opportunity to watch a videotape that showed defendant taking actions that seemed inconsistent with his job duties and exercising control over the merchandise of the store where he worked, consistent with the admission of defendant's co-worker that he and defendant planned to steal the merchandise. State v. Willis, 2007-Ohio-2120, 2007 Ohio App. LEXIS 1984 (Ohio Ct. App., Cuyahoga County 2007).

Sufficient evidence supported defendant's convictions for theft and breaking and entering because defendant admitted that he was the man that the victim found in her van; the victim testified that she grabbed the man's arm as he fled and that she found her wallet, in which she kept her wedding ring, open in the van. Thus, it could have been found that defendant took the ring from the wallet, and dropped it as he fled, which was all the control required to commit theft, and it was reasonable to conclude that defendant discovered the ring while rifling through the victim's wallet, and determined to take it at that instant, which was all the intent required for breaking and entering. State v. Leavitt, 2007-Ohio-2057, 2007 Ohio App. LEXIS 1925 (Ohio Ct. App., Lake County 2007).

Defendant's convictions for breaking and entering under R.C. 2911.13(B), grand theft under R.C. 2913.02(A)(1), and theft under § 2913.02(A)(1) were not against the manifest weight of the evidence as the two codefendants unambiguously gave testimony disclosing defendant's participation in the theft of computers and cartons of cigarettes, the latter occurring after one of the perpetrators broke out a side window in order to gain entry into the building. While defendant attacked the codefendants' credibility, the attack was based purely upon supposition and innuendo. State v. Curns, 2007-Ohio-2029, 2007 Ohio App. LEXIS 1839 (Ohio Ct. App., Lucas County 2007).

Convictions for aggravated robbery under R.C. 2911.01, theft of a motor vehicle under R.C. 2913.02, and having weapons while under disability under R.C. 2923.13 were supported by sufficient evidence as evidence showed that defendant was found driving the stolen vehicle, that individuals who were riding with defendant in the vehicle indicated that defendant had been driving the car for the last couple of days, and that the victim identified defendant in an unbiased photo array as the perpetrator who had brandished the gun during the robbery. Thus, defendant's Crim.R. 29(A) motion for acquittal was properly denied. State v. Crawford, 2007-Ohio-1854, 2007 Ohio App. LEXIS 1688 (Ohio Ct. App., Cuyahoga County 2007).

Sufficient evidence supported defendant's conviction for theft of a vehicle because his accomplice testified that defendant drove the stolen vehicle off of the car lot. A witness identified defendant as one of the men with the vehicle in the creek after it got stuck and the president of the car dealership identified the vehicle as the one was stolen from his used car lot. State v. Beatty, 2007-Ohio-1392, 2007 Ohio App. LEXIS 1289 (Ohio Ct. App., Jefferson County 2007).

Defendant's convictions for theft and uttering, in violation of R.C. 2913.02 and 2913.31, were supported by sufficient evidence where defendant indicated that she had received a check from her son's friend that was made payable to her from a company that she did not know, that she deposited it into her bank account and thereafter withdrew the sum, and later it was determined that the check was written from a closed account; the State sufficiently showed that defendant acted "knowingly" pursuant to R.C. 2901.22(B). State v. McClain, 2007-Ohio-1293, 2007 Ohio App. LEXIS 1180 (Ohio Ct. App., Cuyahoga County 2007).

Evidence supporting defendant's conviction for grand theft, under R.C. 2913.02 was sufficient because it showed that, over eight years while she was a club's treasurer, she wrote checks to herself and family members totalling over $60,000 and concealed them on the club's ledger by recording them as (1) written to others, (2) not written, or (3) void, and she recorded the checks as having been written in smaller amounts than they were, and accounted for them on the ledger by recording checks written to legitimate payees as being for sums greater than the checks, so she was not entitled to acquittal, under Crim.R. 29(A). State v. Gregg, 2007-Ohio-1201, 2007 Ohio App. LEXIS 1135 (Ohio Ct. App., Ashtabula County 2007).

Weight of the evidence supported defendant's conviction for theft because a police officer in the attic of a store saw defendant put a vase in her jacket and subsequently exit the store without putting the vase down, the police chief saw her open the car door, and later, the police chief found the vase in her car. The owner of the property testified that defendant had not been authorized to take it. State v. Stone, 2007-Ohio-752, 2007 Ohio App. LEXIS 686 (Ohio Ct. App., Sandusky County 2007).

Evidence was sufficient to support defendant's conviction for aggravated murder, in violation of R.C. 2903.01, based on an underlying felony of aggravated robbery in volation of R.C. 2911.01, as well as on the capital specification under R.C. 2929.04(A)(7) of aggravated robbery in connection with aggravated murder, as the killing of the victim was associated with the aggravated robbery of his keys and car as part of one continuous occurred; there was physical and testimonial evidence that defendant and her boyfriend planned to kill, and did in fact kill, defendant's former husband and then they took the husband's vehicle after his death, and the fact that the car was not kept but merely driven to a new location and then abandoned with the keys inside was not dispositive on the fact of the theft based on the purposefulness of the act under R.C. 2913.02(A). State v. Roberts, 2006-Ohio-3665, 110 Ohio St. 3d 71, 850 N.E.2d 1168, 2006 Ohio LEXIS 2174 (Ohio 2006).



Defendant's conviction for theft, in violation of R.C. 2913.02(A)(1); robbery, in violation of R.C. 2911.02(A)(1); and aggravated robbery in violation of R.C. 2911.01(A)(1) was not against the manifest weight of the evidence. While defendant contended that the victim had misidentified him, the court could not say that the jury lost its way in convicting defendant because the victim was present to testify at trial and was subjected to cross-examination by defendant's counsel; the State supported the victim's testimony with the testimony of other witnesses; and the trial court instructed the jury as to its role in evaluating the credibility of each witness. State v. Spikes, '2006-Ohio-1822, 2006 Ohio App. LEXIS 1673 (Ohio Ct. App., Lorain County 2006).

Sufficient evidence supported defendant's theft conviction under R.C. 2913.02(A)(1) and his vandalism conviction under R.C. 2909.05(B)(1)(a), and thus, his motion for acquittal was properly denied. Eyewitnesses' testimony sufficiently showed that they were able to identify defendant as the perpetrator of the theft of siding from a house because one eyewitness testified that he looked right at defendant's face during the incident in question and saw defendant get into a truck filled with siding and the second eyewitness testified that he recognized defendant because he had talked with defendant on prior occasions. State v. McGraw, 2006-Ohio-1598, 2006 Ohio App. LEXIS 1502 (Ohio Ct. App., Cuyahoga County 2006).

Evidence supported defendant's conviction for attempted theft under R.C. 2913.02(A)(1) as the evidence showed that defendant, a man on the run from police offices, saw an officer exit his personal vehicle; that he ran for the vehicle, hoping that the officer left his keys in the ignition; and that he continued his flight when he found out the keys were not there. State v. Green, 2006-Ohio-7074, 2006 Ohio App. LEXIS 7002 (Ohio Ct. App., Belmont County 2006).

Defendant's theft conviction was supported by evidence showing that defendant purchased a home theater system and three DVD players; that he left the items in the sporting goods department; that he obtained identical items and used the receipt from his original purchase to leave the store with these items; and that he reentered the store, retrieved the items he originally bought, and returned them for a cash refund. The testimony of the clerk who processed defendant's original purchase, a sheriff who observed defendant walk out of the store with the items in the cart and later observed defendant walking inside the store with the same items taken out of the store, and the cashier who provided the refunds to defendant all showed that defendant purposely deprived the store of its property without the store's consent and without paying for the items. State v. Smith, 2006-Ohio-6979, 2006 Ohio App. LEXIS 6939 (Ohio Ct. App., Hamilton County 2006).

Essential elements of aggravated robbery and grand theft motor vehicle were proven beyond a reasonable doubt because the victim testified that he knew defendant, he provided his name and a description to the police, and that he would not have abandoned the car but for defendant pointing a gun at him. Also the car was reported stolen and there was testimony that it was being driven that evening by someone other than the owner or the victim and thus, the jury viewing the record as whole, could have found that the victim's testimony was credible. State v. York, 2006-Ohio-6934, 2006 Ohio App. LEXIS 6840 (Ohio Ct. App., Cuyahoga County 2006).

Defendant's motion for acquittal was properly denied during his trial for attempt to commit burglary under R.C. 2911.12(A)(1), 2923.02, attempt to commit theft of drugs under R.C. 2913.02(A)(1), (B)(6), 2923.02, and possession of criminal tools under R.C. 2923.24 and his convictions were not against the manifest weight or sufficiency of the evidence because there was sufficient evidence that he was the perpetrator of all three offenses; there was testimony that he was found standing on a desk in a room in a prison infirmary where a hole in the wall was later found, that he was overheard stating that he had tried to break into the infirmary before to steal drugs and that he had plans to break into the pharmacy, and during the investigation, a piece of the chair on which he was standing was found to be broken off, cement pieces were found in a shop vac, and raised ceiling tiles were found in the room. State v. Bell, 2006-Ohio-6560, 2006 Ohio App. LEXIS 6485 (Ohio Ct. App., Fairfield County 2006).

There was sufficient evidence to find that defendant intended to deprive the State of Ohio of the patrol vehicle because a police officer testified that, while he was trying to arrest the driver of the motorcycle, the passenger, defendant, drove away in his patrol car. The passenger testified that she took the vehicle, drove it a short distance down the road, then threw the keys in a ditch on the side of the road; the fact that she traveled a mere eighth of a mile did not negate the fact that when she entered the police cruiser, she intended to deprive the officer of it. State v. Watkins, 2006-Ohio-6380, 2006 Ohio App. LEXIS 6337 (Ohio Ct. App., Summit County 2006).

Defendant's theft convictions under R.C. 2913.02(A)(1) and (3) were not against the manifest weight of the evidence because: (1) the State proved that defendant had no ownership interest in silos that he removed from property after selling them to the victim at an auction, as the evidence showed that the property owner gave the victim permission to leave the silos on the property beyond the time period in the auction's terms and conditions, and even if the silos were left on the property for longer than was permissible, the ownership of the silos reverted to the auction company, not defendant; (2) the State offered evidence that defendant was not authorized to remove the silos as two witnesses testified that they informed defendant that he was not permitted to remove the silos from the property; and (3) defendant conceded that he purposely removed the silos and sold them to a third party. State v. Woosnam, 2006-Ohio-6327, 2006 Ohio App. LEXIS 6297 (Ohio Ct. App., Medina County 2006).

There was sufficient evidence to support the convictions for burglary, theft, and having a weapon while under a disability because there was direct witness testimony that clearly incriminated defendant and evidence linking guns and ammunition found in defendant's possession with the guns and ammunition reported stolen from the victim. There was also clear evidence that defendant was in a position to have an opportunity to commit the crimes for which he was convicted. State v. Gonzalez, 2006-Ohio-6276, 2006 Ohio App. LEXIS 6255 (Ohio Ct. App., Cuyahoga County 2006).

Defendant's convictions for theft with an elderly specification and tampering with evidence, in violation of R.C. 2913.02, 2913.01(CC), and 2921.12, were supported by the weight and sufficiency of the evidence where she was one of three individuals who delivered food trays to the residents of a nursing home, one of the residents alleged that the breakfast tray delivery person had taken a large amount of cash from his room, defendant exhibited suspicious behavior and initially admitted to police officers that she committed the crime, and although she later denied having done so, she was seen removing cash from her car and placing it on the ground, where much of it was retrieved as it blew around the parking lot; the State offered sufficient evidence that the victim's age was clearly over 65 and its case against defendant was based on more than mere speculation, such that denial of her acquittal motion under Crim.R. 29(A) on all aspects except as to the value of the money taken was proper. State v. Washington, 2006-Ohio-6027, 2006 Ohio App. LEXIS 5974 (Ohio Ct. App., Cuyahoga County 2006).

Defendant's conviction for aggravated robbery under R.C. 2911.01(A) was not against the manifest weight of evidence because the evidence showed that the victim was robbed at gunpoint. The evidence showed that defendant committed a theft offense because, while the victim left his jacket behind in order to escape from the gun that defendant was holding to the victim's side, defendant took the jacket to his car, and the $350 in the jacket was never returned. State v. Lewis, 2006-Ohio-5929, 2006 Ohio App. LEXIS 5891 (Ohio Ct. App., Cuyahoga County 2006).

Sufficient evidence supported defendant's convictions for aggravated robbery, under R.C. 2911.01(A)(3), and theft from the elderly, under R.C. 2913.02(B)(3), because the evidence, including surveillance cameras, showed that, after selling the 65-year-old victim some meat in his apartment, defendant returned and beat and punched the victim, tied him up, and stole money from his wallet. State v. Robinson, 2006-Ohio-5879, 2006 Ohio App. LEXIS 5820 (Ohio Ct. App., Summit County 2006).

Weight and sufficiency of the evidence supported defendant's conviction for theft, in violation of R.C. 2913.02, where he assisted a beauty salon owner in leasing financial processing business machines, such as a credit card processor and a check reader, but he thereafter indicated to the owner that the lease on the machines was cancelled and he removed the credit card processor without her consent and failed to return it despite her repeated requests for same; the credibility determinations by the jury regarding their acceptance of the testimony by the owner and the State's other witnesses, including defendant's employer's claim that defendant's conduct was not in line with his employment responsibilities, was within the jury's discretion. State v. Bedell, 2006-Ohio-5746, 2006 Ohio App. LEXIS 5705 (Ohio Ct. App., Franklin County 2006).

Sufficient evidence supported defendant's burglary conviction, under R.C. 2911.12(A)(1), and his theft conviction, under R.C. 2913.02(A)(1), because the evidence showed (1) the victims' home was broken into while they were temporarily absent, (2) the intruder broke a window to gain entry into the home, (3) defendant's fingerprints were on the broken glass, (4) those fingerprints had no reason for being there, and (5) personal property was removed from the home without the victims' permission. State v. Young, 2006-Ohio-5723, 2006 Ohio App. LEXIS 5716 (Ohio Ct. App., Cuyahoga County 2006).

Weight and sufficiency of the evidence supported defendant's convictions for theft, in violation of R.C. 2913.02(A)(2) and (3), where she worked as a supervisor in a city parking garage and she had failed to make the necessary deposits to the city's bank account of garage funds and had also provided counterfeit deposit slips; the evidence established, based on her position of employment, that she acted beyond the scope of the express or implied permission of her employer and the city by her actions, and that she had exerted control over the city's funds by deception. State v. Bohache, 2006-Ohio-5560, 2006 Ohio App. LEXIS 5556 (Ohio Ct. App., Montgomery County 2006).

Weight and sufficiency of the evidence supported defendant's convictions for aggravated robbery with a firearm specification and grand theft of a motor vehicle, in violation of R.C. 2911.01, 2941.145, and 2913.02, where he broke the steering column of a van and drive it away from where the owner had parked it, drove to a bank, while wearing latex gloves, a mask, and armed with a gun, he exited the van and was apprehended; based on the direct and circumstantial evidence, including the description of the van and its condition by the van owner, defendant's appearance near the bank, and the fact that he was shot by an apprehending officer due to defendant having wielded a gun toward that officer, the evidence supported the convictions. State v. Ivery, 2006-Ohio-5548, 2006 Ohio App. LEXIS 5524 (Ohio Ct. App., Stark County 2006).

When, in a robbery prosecution, there were some inconsistencies in the testimony of some witnesses, this did not render the evidence insufficient to support defendant's convictions for aggravated robbery, under R.C. 2911.01(A)(1), robbery, under R.C. 2911.02(A)(1), theft, under R.C. 2913.02, kidnapping, under R.C. 2905.01(A)(1), or abduction, under R.C. 2905.02(A)(2), because defense counsel cross-examined the witnesses as to these inconsistencies, and the jury, as the fact finders, had the best view of the demeanor and credibility of the witnesses. State v. Ayers, 2006-Ohio-5533, 2006 Ohio App. LEXIS 5508 (Ohio Ct. App., Guernsey County 2006).

Defendant's convictions for theft with an elderly specification, uttering, and tampering with records, in violation of R.C. 2913.02, 2913.01(CC), 2913.31, and 2913.42 were not against the manifest weight of the evidence, as he obtained ownership of real property from adult children of a former grantor of the property, although defendant was aware that the children were not the true owners of the property but instead, that the grantor's sister had been quit-claimed the property at an earlier point in time; further, defendant did not reveal the true owner of the property and he benefitted from his actions. State v. Azir, 2006-Ohio-5449, 2006 Ohio App. LEXIS 5441 (Ohio Ct. App., Cuyahoga County 2006).

During defendant's trial for complicity to attempted grand theft in violation of R.C. 2923.03(A)(2), R.C. 2923.02(A), 2913.02(A)(1), his motions for acquittal under Crim.R. 29 were properly denied; under the three statutes taken together, the State had the burden to produce evidence showing that he knowingly aided and abetted another in an attempt to commit a theft, and a shopping mall customer's testimony that she saw defendant appearing to pretend to read a sales flyer while blocking from view another man who was using a screwdriver to try to break into a display case that contained jewelry worth over $19,000 was sufficient, when viewed in a light most favorable to the State, to establish each element of the crime and allow the case to go to the jury. State v. Higgins, 2006-Ohio-5372, 2006 Ohio App. LEXIS 5381 (Ohio Ct. App., Lake County 2006).

Defendant's theft conviction under R.C. 2913.02(A)(1) was supported by sufficient evidence, in that the evidence showed that defendant removed some microwave/refrigerator units from a loading dock on a university campus and that the university did not intend to throw out the units. The record was also devoid of any evidence that defendant had permission to take the units. State v. Crisp, 2006-Ohio-5041, 2006 Ohio App. LEXIS 5184 (Ohio Ct. App., Franklin County 2006).

Defendant's theft conviction under R.C. 2913.02 was supported by sufficient evidence; thus, defendant's motion for a judgment of acquittal was properly denied. While a store manager testified that the merchandise in the stolen boxes was defective, her testimony still established that similar unblemished merchandise would have been worth $1,100, more than double the base amount of $500 for the charged offense, and it was in jury's province to weigh evidence. State v. Collins, 2006-Ohio-4898, 2006 Ohio App. LEXIS 4816 (Ohio Ct. App., Cuyahoga County 2006).

Sufficient evidence supported the finding that defendant obtained control over various items that belonged to his 71-year-old mother, without her consent or authorization, for theft, under R.C. 2913.02. with an elderly specification, (as elderly was defined under R.C. 2913.01) because the mother testified that only she and defendant had access to her apartment and that defendant did not have permission to work on her car or to sell, destroy, throw away, or move any of her property. She identified the large number of items that disappeared from her apartment soon after defendant had access to her house and a neighbor testified that defendant offered to sell him the mother's computer. State v. Brelo, 2006-Ohio-4767, 2006 Ohio App. LEXIS 4690 (Ohio Ct. App., Cuyahoga County 2006).

Sufficient evidence supported defendant's petty theft conviction, under R.C. 2913.02(A)(1), because the evidence showed he removed merchandise from a store that was closed, and his claim that he intended to return the next day to pay for it did not defeat the conviction because his intent to permanently deprive the store of its property did not have to be proved, so evidence that he deprived the store of its merchandise on the day he removed it was sufficient, without regard for what he might have intended to do the next day. State v. Haney, 2006-Ohio-4687, 2006 Ohio App. LEXIS 4600 (Ohio Ct. App., Mahoning County 2006).

Defendant's aggravated theft conviction was not against the manifest weight of the evidence, as the jury was informed that the victim had a criminal history and they made a credibility determination that the victim's version of events as to the criminal incident was more credible than that of defendant, who claimed that the victim was framing him because he owed the victim money for drugs; defendant's claim that he had been assaulted by the victim was not supported by the evidence, as police testimony and photographs did not indicate any bruises or cuts to defendant's face. State v. Zanders, 2006-Ohio-4491, 2006 Ohio App. LEXIS 4409 (Ohio Ct. App., Cuyahoga County 2006).

There was sufficient evidence to support defendant's convictions for aggravated robbery and theft because defendant's accomplice signed a sworn statement that defendant robbed the store, using a knife, and witnesses testified that they knew defendant and that he had robbed the store, one had even gone to the police. The bandanas worn in the robbery were found in the accomplice's home and a friend had turned over a dark grey hoodie, dark grey sweat pants, and a bandanna (articles of clothing worn in the robber) to the police that had been kept at her house. State v. Bromagen, 2006-Ohio-4429, 2006 Ohio App. LEXIS 4353 (Ohio Ct. App., Clermont County 2006).

There was sufficient evidence as to the value of copper piping that defendant removed from a vacant house which was the subject of foreclosure proceedings for purposes of supporting his conviction of theft, in violation of R.C. 2913.02, which was based on the material costs as well as the labor and repair work estimates to restore the home; denial of his acquittal motion under Crim.R. 29(A) was proper. State v. Turner, 2006-Ohio-4098, 2006 Ohio App. LEXIS 4069 (Ohio Ct. App., Cuyahoga County 2006).

Defendant's conviction for theft under R.C. 2913.02(A)(1) was not against the manifest weight of evidence. The evidence showed that the store's loss prevention officer observed defendant conceal five DVD players in his shopping cart, that the officer saw defendant proceed to the store's lawn and garden department, and that an assistant manager saw someone pass five DVD players to the outside under a temporary wall. State v. Mays, 2006-Ohio-4039, 2006 Ohio App. LEXIS 3980 (Ohio Ct. App., Trumbull County 2006).

Trial court properly concluded that defendant's clients were theft victims and that the thefts were tied to defendant, a personal injury attorney, because 10 clients testified that they did not receive all of their due settlement money from defendant; some received none of the settlement money, in some instances, subrogation liens went unpaid, and, in some instances, the clients received a check in an amount to cover a portion of the settlement, but the check did not clear due to insufficient funds. Although the clients were not receiving their money, most, if not all, of the clients' funds disappeared from the law firm's general trust account soon after each deposit of the funds. State v. Silverman, 2006-Ohio-3826, 2006 Ohio App. LEXIS 3791 (Ohio Ct. App., Franklin County 2006), aff'd, 2007-Ohio-5551, 116 Ohio St. 3d 31, 876 N.E.2d 528, 2007 Ohio LEXIS 2567 (Ohio 2007).

In a case in which defendant was convicted of breaking and entering, under R.C. 2911.13, theft and grand theft, under R.C. 2913.02, and burglary, under R.C. 2911.12, with a firearm specification, his motion for a judgment of acquittal, under Crim.R. 29(A), was properly denied because, at the scene of the breaking and entering, a print matching the slipper he was wearing when he was arrested was found, and, at the scene of the other crimes, his fingerprints were found on broken glass, allowing a jury to find he broke a window there to enter the victim's apartment. State v. Crouse, 2006-Ohio-3776, 2006 Ohio App. LEXIS 3740 (Ohio Ct. App., Lake County 2006).

When defendant was prosecuted for complicity to commit aggravated robbery, under R.C. 2911.01(A)(1) and complicity to commit theft, under R.C. 2913.02, as well as R.C. 2923.03(A)(2), on complicity, and R.C. 2901.22(A) and (B), regarding requisite mental states for theft, based on the testimony of his accomplice that defendant instructed the accomplice in how to carry out a robbery and theft and drove the getaway car, and corroborating testimony placing defendant at the scene of the crime, as the jury was properly instructed under R.C. 2923.03(D), to view the accomplice's testimony with caution, so defendant's motion for a judgment of acquittal, under Crim.R. 29(A), was properly denied. State v. Gaines, 2006-Ohio-3750, 2006 Ohio App. LEXIS 3737 (Ohio Ct. App., Wayne County 2006).

There was sufficient evidence to support the convictions for theft, under R.C. 2913.02(A)(1), forgery, and uttering because the State showed that defendant had stolen nearly $240,000 from her employer; without permission to do so, defendant, the company office manager, appropriated company funds for her own benefit. Defendant admitted to the police that she stole $24,000; the disposition of stolen property was not a listed element of the offense that the State had to prove; she wrote checks and forged her employer's signature and even got a loan from the bank by falsely notarizing documents. State v. Curtis, 2006-Ohio-3724, 2006 Ohio App. LEXIS 3688 (Ohio Ct. App., Cuyahoga County 2006).

Theft conviction, under R.C. 2913.02(A)(2), was supported by sufficient evidence because the State's evidence demonstrated that defendant obtained and kept the car owner's money, $700, for the repair of the car's transmission without performing the job. Although defendant spoke with a gas station owner about the transmission repair, the evidence indicated that defendant ultimately failed to find a transmission for the vehicle, did not return the owner's money, and failed to return her calls; the vehicle was ultimately impounded. State v. Halczysak, 2006-Ohio-3734, 2006 Ohio App. LEXIS 3692 (Ohio Ct. App., Cuyahoga County 2006).

Defendant's convictions for breaking and entering, under R.C. 2911.13, and theft, under R.C. 2913.02, were not against the manifest weight of the evidence because the State presented overwhelming evidence of his guilt. A neighbor, who knew him, saw him carrying boxes out of the apartment building and loading them onto a truck; he did not have permission to be on the property or to exercise control over the approximate $4,000 worth of supplies and tools; and entry was gained into the building by force; the back door had kick marks on it and a basement window was broken out and the alarm wire had been cut. State v. Johnson, 2006-Ohio-3685, 2006 Ohio App. LEXIS 3648 (Ohio Ct. App., Cuyahoga County 2006).

Convictions of passing bad checks and theft based on a transaction involving the purchase of a washer and a dryer from an appliance store were not against the weight of the evidence and were supported by sufficient evidence that defendant submitted a check in her name to the appliance store delivery driver in payment for the washer and dryer purchased, knowing that her checking account was closed; further, the driver testified that he was certain that defendant was the exact same person to whom he delivered the washer and dryer. Finally, the offenses were not allied offenses of similar import under R.C. 2941.25 because the commission of one offense did not automatically result in the commission of the other when reviewed in the abstract. State v. Ransby, 2006-Ohio-3596, 2006 Ohio App. LEXIS 3535 (Ohio Ct. App., Cuyahoga County 2006).

Conviction for aggravated theft, under R.C. 2913.02(A)(1) and (B)(3), was supported by sufficient evidence as defendant exerted control over the 84-year-old victim's property, in excess of $100,000, without his consent. After rerouting the victim's mail, defendant deposited large checks from the sale of his stocks into her own personal bank account; the victim testified that he did not give defendant permission to take or keep his money; and defendant cashed a number of personal checks from the victim to herself during her employment with him. State v. Dyer, 2006-Ohio-3537, 2006 Ohio App. LEXIS 3486 (Ohio Ct. App., Butler County 2006).

There was sufficient evidence to support defendant's convictions for theft, under R.C. 2913.02, and uttering, under R.C. 2913.31, because the victim, defendant's ex-wife testified that she had not known of the deed's existence, that the signature on the deed was not hers, and that she had not given anyone permission to transfer the property. Defendant admitted that he prepared the deed, but neither version of his account of how he obtained the victim's signature was corroborated, he obtained an improper notarization of the victim's signature, and neither of his accounts explained how the deed could have been signed, notarized, and recorded on the same day. State v. Storey, 2006-Ohio-3498, 2006 Ohio App. LEXIS 3441 (Ohio Ct. App., Cuyahoga County 2006).

Evidence was sufficient to support defendant's conviction for grand theft of a motor vehicle, in violation of R.C. 2913.02(A)(1) and (B)(5), because a witness testified that he saw defendant behind the wheel of the victim's car, approached him, after which defendant fled, and pursued him until police arrived, and another witness testified that she saw defendant being pursued by the victim, and that defendant tried to flee by placing himself on her car, so it was shown that defendant exerted control over the victim's vehicle and tried to remove it without the victim's consent, and defendant's motion for a judgment of acquittal, under Crim.R. 29, was properly denied. State v. McMillion, 2006-Ohio-3229, 2006 Ohio App. LEXIS 3121 (Ohio Ct. App., Ashtabula County 2006).

Evidence that defendant never told the owners of the company for which she worked that the checks she had written from the company's account were payable to her own home equity account and that she transferred other money from the company's account into her home equity account without the knowledge or consent of the owners was sufficient to allow a rational trier of fact to find that defendant, within the meaning of R.C. 2901.22(B), "knowingly" obtained or exerted control over the company's money by deception with the purpose to deprive the company of its money. State v. Wilson, 2006-Ohio-3103, 2006 Ohio App. LEXIS 2968 (Ohio Ct. App., Franklin County 2006).

Defendant's convictions for burglary, under R.C. 2911.12(A)(2), and theft, under R.C. 2913.02(A), were not against the manifest weight of the evidence because his two accomplices testified against him, the jury was properly instructed, under R.C. 2923.03(D), to view their testimony with "grave suspicion" and "great caution," and the fact that the victims' neighbor, who said she was familiar with defendant, testified that she did not see him at the scene of the crime around the time it was committed did not demonstrate otherwise because the jury was authorized to determine the weight to give each witness's testimony. State v. Williams, 2006-Ohio-3084, 2006 Ohio App. LEXIS 2971 (Ohio Ct. App., Fayette County 2006).

Sufficient evidence showed that defendant deprived the victim of her property under R.C. 2913.01(C)(1) and supported defendant's conviction for theft under R.C. 2913.02(A)(1). The victim testified that she asked defendant to return her cell phone that he had taken from her during an argument and that she tried unsuccessfully for a couple of weeks to get her phone back from defendant before she gave up and bought a new phone. State v. Hawke, 2006-Ohio-3037, 2006 Ohio App. LEXIS 2914 (Ohio Ct. App., Montgomery County 2006).

Sufficient evidence was presented to support defendant's conviction for petty theft because, during the store loss prevention manager's investigation of the matter, defendant gave a written statement admitting that she stole items and cash from her employer and her confession was admitted into evidence at trial. State v. Duffy, 2006-Ohio-2724, 2006 Ohio App. LEXIS 2578 (Ohio Ct. App., Knox County 2006).

Convictions against defendants for theft of property and vandalism, in violation of R.C. 2913.02 and 2909.05, were supported by sufficient circumstantial evidence where defendants had rented premises and upon vacating the premises, an inspection revealed that the property had been destroyed structurally in many ways, items were removed and appliances were taken, and garbage was strewn about the premises; there was no sign of a forced entry, defendants had made threats against the owner if he served them with an eviction, no one else had access to the premises, and they had the time, opportunity, and motive to have committed the crimes. State v. Kiley, 2006-Ohio-2469, 2006 Ohio App. LEXIS 2335 (Ohio Ct. App., Cuyahoga County 2006).

Sufficient evidence supported defendant's conviction for theft, under R.C. 2913.02. There was sufficient circumstantial evidence to prove beyond a reasonable doubt that defendant took the envelope of money from her employer (a fast food restaurant) or conspired with the employee from the security company to take the money because defendant gave conflicting accounts of who took the money and admitted to receiving some of the stolen money. State v. Berry, 2006-Ohio-2086, 2006 Ohio App. LEXIS 1933 (Ohio Ct. App., Cuyahoga County 2006).

Defendant's convictions for aggravated robbery; in violation of R.C. 2911.01; robbery, in violation of R.C. 2911.02; and theft, in violation of R.C. 2913.02 were not against the manifest weight of the evidence because, while there were inconsistencies between the testimony of defendant's co-defendant and that of the victim, their testimony was consistent in significant areas, including their testimony that the best friend took possession of a gun belonging to the victim's fiancee with the help of defendant, and it was the province of the jury to make determinations with respect to credibility. The jury's verdict was also supported by sufficient evidence since, while the co-defendant testified that defendant did not possess a weapon during the incident, the jury could have found that defendant still assisted the co-defendant in the robbery. State v. Chandler, 2006-Ohio-2070, 2006 Ohio App. LEXIS 1913 (Ohio Ct. App., Franklin County 2006).

Evidence that a box on which defendant's fingerprints were found in a burglarized home was moved during the burglary; that the fingerprint lifted from the box matched defendant's fingerprints; that there was no other possible source for the fingerprints, in that the box had never been taken outside the apartment and no other persons had access to the box; that defendant did not have access to the victims' residence prior to the break-in; and that the fingerprint from the box was, at the most, two weeks old was sufficient to support defendant's convictions for burglary under R.C. 2911.12 and theft under R.C. 2913.02. State v. Williams, 2006-Ohio-1524, 2006 Ohio App. LEXIS 1390 (Ohio Ct. App., Franklin County 2006).

Weight and sufficiency of the evidence supported defendant's conviction of theft by deception, in violation of R.C. 2913.02(A)(3), where he contracted to do home renovation work for the victim, repeatedly induced her to give him more money for labor and materials, but he did not do any of the work, did not purchase any of the materials, and there was evidence that at the time he took the money, he had no intent to repay the victim or to do the work; defendant's intent was to deprive the victim of her money by deception, pursuant to R.C. 2913.01(A) and 2901.22(A) and (B). State v. Capone, 2006-Ohio-1537, 2006 Ohio App. LEXIS 1413 (Ohio Ct. App., Cuyahoga County 2006).

Where defendant's co-worker saw defendant take money from a purse in an apartment where they were working and then leave the premises, and defendant left the State for a few days thereafter, the verdict convicting him of theft in violation of R.C. 2913.02(A)(1) was not against the manifest weight of the evidence; the eyewitness testimony remained consistent, unlike defendant's version of events, which varied in his statements to the police and to the jury. State v. McElroy, 2006-Ohio-1453, 2006 Ohio App. LEXIS 1284 (Ohio Ct. App., Lake County 2006).

Trial court's adjudication of defendant as a delinquent child for theft of a gun, under R.C. 2913.02(A)(1), with a firearm specification, pursuant to R.C. 2941.141, and violation of probation, ungovernable, under R.C. 2152.02, were supported by sufficient evidence. The codefendants testified that they, along with defendant, stole items from the victim's house, including a gun, some jewelry, and electronic equipment, with the help of the victim's daughters and defendant stipulated to the fact that he was on probation for purposes of the violation of probation, ungovernable charge. In re R.T., 2006-Ohio-1311, 2006 Ohio App. LEXIS 1199 (Ohio Ct. App., Lorain County 2006).

Based on testimony and a videotape, there was substantial direct and circumstantial evidence to support defendant's conviction for complicity to commit grand theft, in violation of R.C. 2923.03, and R.C. 2913.02(A)(1) and (B)(5), under the theory that she knowingly served as a lookout, diverted the attention of the store clerk, or both while her male companion stole the store owner's vehicle. State v. Hill, 2006-Ohio-1166, 2006 Ohio App. LEXIS 1056 (Ohio Ct. App., Ashtabula County 2006).

There was sufficient evidence to support defendant's theft conviction (R.C. 2913.02(A)(1)) of the nickel from his employer because a witness testified that defendant acknowledged that he was aware that the boxes of nickel in his vehicle were stolen and defendant was informed, a week prior to driving his co-defendant to the scrap yard, that their supervisor suspected that someone was stealing nickel from the plant and that employees involved in the theft would be prosecuted. That evidence, coupled with the testimony of four witnesses that defendant admitted to transporting the co-defendant and two boxes from the plant to a scrap yard and receiving $40 for his assistance, sufficiently established defendant's knowledge of the theft. State v. Ferguson, 2006-Ohio-799, 2006 Ohio App. LEXIS 718 (Ohio Ct. App., Cuyahoga County 2006).

Defendant's conviction was not against the manifest weight or the sufficiency of the evidence. The testimony showed that the store manager saw defendant exit his store with a shopping cart full of 212 items, that defendant's girlfriend never showed up to pay for the items as defendant had said that she would despite the fact that she was paged, and that defendant had no money on him. State v. Higinbotham, 2006-Ohio-635, 2006 Ohio App. LEXIS 569 (Ohio Ct. App., Stark County 2006).

Trial court properly denied defendant's motion for acquittal pursuant to Crim.R. 29(A), as the evidence was sufficient to support defendant's conviction for theft, in violation of R.C. 2913.02(A), based on a theory that he was complicit with others in committing the offense, pursuant to R.C. 2923.03(A); the evidence supported the finding that defendant approached another, asked her to deposit a check into her account and then withdraw funds therefrom and give them to him, and that he had no legitimate right to the check. State v. Lee, 2006-Ohio-455, 2006 Ohio App. LEXIS 390 (Ohio Ct. App., Cuyahoga County 2006).

Defendant's conviction for theft, in violation of R.C. 2913.02(A)(1), was supported by sufficient evidence, as there was testimony and some videotaped evidence that defendant and others entered a retail store, defendant purchased a television set, he then gave the receipt to a co-defendant who walked through the cashier line and out the door with an unpaid-for television set with defendant's receipt on it, and thereafter defendant attempted to leave the store with the television that he had purchased, which was lacking the receipt. State v. Beamer, 2006 Ohio App. LEXIS 278 (Ohio Ct. App., Tuscarawas County Jan. 24, 2006).

Defendant's conviction for aggravated robbery was supported by sufficient evidence of a theft offense where: (1) a witness testified that she left the victim alone in his house and defendant then walked into the house, (2) a passenger in the same car as defendant heard gunshots while defendant was in the victim's house, and the victim was later found shot to death, (3) the victim normally wore a chain with a cross on it and a watch that was not on his body or in the house after he was murdered and the victim's cousin drew pictures of that jewelry, (4) the passenger testified that defendant had a chain with a cross on it and a watch in his possession after he saw defendant leave the victim's house, and (5) the passenger also drew pictures of the jewelry, which was strikingly similar to the drawings and descriptions of the jewelry given by the cousin. State v. Johnson, 2006-Ohio-209, 2006 Ohio App. LEXIS 139 (Ohio Ct. App., Franklin County 2006).

Defendant's convictions of theft and criminal damage, in violation of R.C. 2913.02(A)(1) and 2909.06(A)(1), respectively, were not against the manifest weight of the evidence, as defendant was seen in a telephone store in the mall, using a demo phone and speaking in a loud and vulgar manner into it, and then he ran out of the store, and an immediate inspection of the area where defendant was indicated that the demo phone was missing and the phone terminal had been damaged; although the phone was not recovered, the evidence was sufficient to support the conviction based on testimony from employees who observed defendant's conduct in the store. State v. Williams, 2006-Ohio-73, 2006 Ohio App. LEXIS 56 (Ohio Ct. App., Summit County 2006).

Identification evidence, coupled with other evidence, was sufficient to support defendant's conviction for robbery and grand theft of a motor vehicle and the convictions were not against the manifest weight of the evidence where: (1) defendant generally fit one of the descriptions that the victim had given to the police, (2) the victim unequivocally identified defendant at trial as one of the two men with whom he had struggled before his car was taken and testified that he had seen defendant driving his car later that night, (3) two other witnesses identified defendant as the man who was driving the victim's vehicle, and (4) defendant was arrested just outside the car a short while later, having been observed by the same witnesses getting out of the car. State v. Longs, 2005-Ohio-6677, 2005 Ohio App. LEXIS 6002 (Ohio Ct. App., Montgomery County 2005).

In defendant's prosecution for theft by deception, while the State's evidence was circumstantial in nature and directly conflicted with the statement given by defendant to the police, to the effect that he did not know that the microwave box, which he purchased, was stuffed full of DVDs, there was nothing to indicate that the testimony of the State's witnesses lacked fundamental credibility. Thus, the verdict was not against the manifest weight of the evidence. State v. Thomas, 2005-Ohio-6570, 2005 Ohio App. LEXIS 5882 (Ohio Ct. App., Lake County 2005).

Defendant's convictions for aggravated robbery, in violation of R.C. 2911.01, aggravated burglary, in violation of R.C. 2911.11, kidnapping, in violation of R.C. 2905.01, felonious assault, in violation of R.C. 2903.11, all with firearm specifications, in violation of R.C. 2941.141, conspiracy to commit aggravated robbery, in violation of R.C. 2911.01 and 2923.01, conspiracy to commit aggravated burglarly, in violation of R.C. 2911.11 and 2923.01, conspiracy to commit kidnapping, in violation of R.C. 2905.01 and 2923.01, and aggravated theft, in violation of R.C. 2913.02 were not against the manifest weight of the evidence, despite the victim's erroneous statement of which of two perpetrators made an inculpatory statement during the crime, as she was distraught when she made the statement, another had said he drove defendant to the crime scene, and defendant made a somewhat inculpatory statement by saying "it was not all him." State v. Hickenbottom, 2005-Ohio-6569, 2005 Ohio App. LEXIS 5881 (Ohio Ct. App., Lake County 2005).

Sufficient evidence supported defendant's convictions for complicity to commit theft and complicity to commit breaking and entering because the State presented evidence that a person matching his description was seen in the vicinity of the crimes at about the time the occurred, his wallet was found in the possession of one of the others involved in the crime, and he admitted to a jail inmate that he committed the crimes, giving details not made available to the public. State v. Ankrom, 2005-Ohio-6568, 2005 Ohio App. LEXIS 5880 (Ohio Ct. App., Lake County 2005), rev'd, 2006-Ohio-2109, 109 Ohio St. 3d 313, 847 N.E.2d 1174, 2006 Ohio LEXIS 1161 (Ohio 2006).

Evidence was sufficient for a jury to find that defendant exerted control over merchandise with the intent to deprive the store to which the merchandise belonged and that defendant was guilty of theft, pursuant to R.C. 2913.02(A)(1); thus, defendant's motion for acquittal pursuant to Crim.R. 29 was properly denied. The State's evidence showed that defendant hurriedly placed merchandise into her cart and stuffed duffle bags with merchandise, that defendant pushed the shopping cart past the check out points toward the exit doorway, that defendant turned the cart around when she observed a police officer speaking with her companion and began unloading merchandise from the bags onto the store's floor, and that price tags had been torn off from some of the merchandise. State v. Peak, 2005-Ohio-6422, 2005 Ohio App. LEXIS 5774 (Ohio Ct. App., Lake County 2005).

There was sufficient evidence to support the convictions for kidnapping (R.C. 2905.01(A)), felonious assault (R.C. 2903.11(A)(1)), and grand theft (R.C. 2913.02(A)) because defendant forcibly restrained the victim's liberty and removed her from the place where she was found to terrorize and inflict serious physical harm on her. Defendant forced the victim (the mother of his children) into the back seat of her car and restrained her liberty by sitting on top of her; after he was pulled off of her, he forced his way into car, pushing the victim from the driver's seat to the passenger's seat, and drove away with the victim, refusing to let her go; and, as he drove, he continually beat on the victim, bit her severely, insulted and attacked her character, and drove recklessly at an excessive rate of speed. State v. Marshall, 2005-Ohio-5947, 2005 Ohio App. LEXIS 5366 (Ohio Ct. App., Summit County 2005).

Weight and sufficiency of the evidence supported defendant's conviction for multiple counts of theft by deception, in violation of R.C. 2913.02, where, as president of a home remodeling company, he entered into numerous remodeling projects with homeowners, but then failed to either commence them, complete them, or to pay back the funds that he had collected from the homeowners, and he engaged subcontractors to perform work on the projects and failed to pay them for their services; based on defendant's conduct, there was adequate evidence that his actions "deprived" the homeowners, as that term was defined in R.C. 2913.01(C)(1)-(3), and that he did so either "purposely" or "knowingly," pursuant to R.C. 2901.22(A), (B). State v. Piesciuk, 2005-Ohio-5767, 2005 Ohio App. LEXIS 5187 (Ohio Ct. App., Butler County 2005).

Weight and sufficiency of the evidence supported defendant's conviction for theft, in violation of R.C. 2913.02(A)(2), where he rented a stereo and a dryer from a rental store, and he failed to either make further rental payments or to return the items to the store, despite repeated requests and demands to do so; the State proved that the offense occurred on a date reasonably near to the time period charged in the indictment, that defendant acted knowingly under R.C. 2901.22(B), and it was inferred that defendant intended to deprive the owner of its property. State v. Marshall, 2005-Ohio-5585, 2005 Ohio App. LEXIS 5054 (Ohio Ct. App., Montgomery County 2005).

Where defendant, a juvenile, stole a vehicle that belonged to another, drove it until he collided with his friend's car, and then immediately drove off and abandoned the vehicle, his conviction for felony theft of a motor vehicle, in violation of R.C. 2913.02(A)(1), was supported by the weight of the evidence, as was his adjudication of delinquency; there was testimony from the friend and from an investigating detective that supported the conviction. In re Travis L. H., 2005-Ohio-5571, 2005 Ohio App. LEXIS 5032 (Ohio Ct. App., Huron County 2005).

Evidence sufficiently demonstrated that defendant knowingly (R.C. 2901.22(B)) deprived the victim of his wood for the theft conviction, under R.C. 2913.02(A)(1), because defendant was aware that the victim's wood had been moved to a part of his property and that giving another man permission to bulldoze that area would result in the victim being deprived of his wood. Moreover, the jury could have found that defendant knowingly and purposely intended to deprive the victim of his wood from defendant's statement that he "got rid" of the wood and the evidence that the wood was not, in fact, bad. State v. Boyle, 2005-Ohio-5493, 2005 Ohio App. LEXIS 4959 (Ohio Ct. App., Portage County 2005).

There was sufficient evidence to support the theft conviction through the victim's testimony (that defendant had come over to his house, they had fallen asleep, and defendant had taken $1,000 from a drawer) because there were various factors that corroborated the victim's version of events, including his knowledge of defendant's recent pregnancy, the location of her home, and the phone number of her family members and there was testimony that the family members observed defendant spending a lot of money during the time in question. State v. Wring, 2005-Ohio-5443, 2005 Ohio App. LEXIS 4932 (Ohio Ct. App., Cuyahoga County 2005).

Aggravated robbery, theft, and kidnapping convictions were not against the manifest weight of the evidence where, inter alia, defendant's car was found in the parking lot of a store on the night the store was robbed, where, inside the car were remnants of tape which were associated to the tape used to bind the store employees, where a DNA analysis of cigarette butts established the co-defendant's presence in defendant's car, where the co-defendant and defendant were linked via cell phone numbers found in the car, and where evidence in a bag found near the store was connected to defendant, and the contents of the bag were linked to the robbery as there was money in an amount close to the amount stolen, the tape that was used to bind the employees, and a ski mask which was matched to defendant by a hair sample. State v. Banks, 2005-Ohio-5286, 2005 Ohio App. LEXIS 4766 (Ohio Ct. App., Ashtabula County 2005).

Evidence was sufficient to support defendant's theft conviction for stealing a car because he admitted stealing the car. State v. Hanson, 2005-Ohio-4185, 2005 Ohio App. LEXIS 3825 (Ohio Ct. App., Marion County 2005).

Weight of the evidence supported defendant's convictions for murder, aggravated robbery, and robbery, in violation of R.C. 2903.02, 2911.01, and 2911.02, respectively, where there was sufficient evidence that defendant committed or attempted to commit the underlying crime of theft, in violation of R.C. 2913.02; defendant was seen by eyewitnesses getting into the victim's car, driving it away while the victim hung on to the outside of it, and when the car collided with another vehicle, the victim flew through the air and landed on the street, which resulted in his death. State v. Charley, 2005-Ohio-4116, 2005 Ohio App. LEXIS 3761 (Ohio Ct. App., Cuyahoga County 2005).

Weight and sufficiency of the evidence supported defendant's conviction for theft, in violation of R.C. 2913.02, where there was surveillance video from a variety of branches of a home supply store which showed that defendant and a few other men routinely went into the store, shopped independently or in pairs for an extended period of time without acknowledging each other, that some of the men stayed in the garden area and eventually left empty-handed, and that others in the group took the same particular item and put it in the shopping cart, covered it with a coat or a sign, and eventually, the cart was found next to a hole in the fence of the garden section, with the items missing from it; although the evidence against defendant was mostly circumstantial, it still had probative value and supported the conviction. State v. Whitlow, 2005-Ohio-4005, 2005 Ohio App. LEXIS 3657 (Ohio Ct. App., Cuyahoga County 2005).

There was sufficient evidence to support defendant's conviction for grand theft, under R.C. 2913.02(A)(1), because, although the evidence did not directly implicate defendant, the overwhelming amount of circumstantial evidence showed that defendant and a friend stole aluminum castings and machine parts and put them into a woman's garage. Defendant's pants were wet and covered in buds and his socks covered in dark soil from traversing the path between the garage and the aluminum company; the friend's shirt was covered in what the police officer termed casting dust; a jacket with a name patch bearing the friend's name was found near the company's fence; laundry bins in the garage contained company property coated in a dust similar to the dust on the friend's shirt; one bin was also covered in dirt, scratches, and grass as if it had been dragged; and the drag marks along the path between the company and the garage were the same size as the bin. State v. Wells, 2005-Ohio-3904, 2005 Ohio App. LEXIS 3581 (Ohio Ct. App., Butler County 2005).

There was sufficient evidence supporting defendant's conviction for grand theft of a motor vehicle, pursuant to R.C. 2913.02(A)(1), because the evidence presented showed that defendant confessed that he took the vehicle; he was not authorized to possess the vehicle; he was seen driving the vehicle; the keys were found on defendant; and his fingerprints were on items retrieved from the vehicle. State v. Thomas, 2005-Ohio-3418, 2005 Ohio App. LEXIS 3177 (Ohio Ct. App., Cuyahoga County 2005).

When a car dealer promised consumers that he would assume the debt on their present car if they bought a new car from him, but did not apply the proceeds from his sale of their present car to the debt on it, there was sufficient evidence of a violation of the Consumer Sales Practices Act, R.C. 1345.01 et seq. and of theft by deception, under R.C. 2913.02(A)(3), because the consumers would not have bought the new car but for the dealer's false promise, and his sale of their present car without applying the proceeds to its debt showed his intent to defraud. Gonzalez v. Spofford, 2005-Ohio-3415, 2005 Ohio App. LEXIS 3182 (Ohio Ct. App., Cuyahoga County 2005).

Defendant's conviction for petty theft, in violation of R.C. 2913.02(B)(2), was supported by the weight and sufficiency of the evidence, based on the eyewitness testimony of a store employee who saw defendant switch retail price stickers on various items in a store before checking out with the switched stickers, as well as photocopies of the items; there was no requirement that the actual items with the switched stickers be introduced into evidence for purposes of sufficiency of the Evidence City of Alliance v. Yin, 2005-Ohio-2989, 2005 Ohio App. LEXIS 2788 (Ohio Ct. App., Stark County 2005).

There was sufficient evidence to support the convictions for breaking and entering (R.C. 2911.13(A)) and theft (R.C. 2913.02) because, for the first theft, the DNA evidence established that defendant had been inside the first victim's garage, there was testimony from an auctioneer who stated he had purchased the stolen sleigh runners from defendant, and defendant did not have the victim's permission to enter his garage or take items therein. For the second theft, the property owner and her son testified that defendant was the man they encountered in their barn, the son saw items from the barn in the back of defendant's truck, and the license plate number that the owner wrote down that night turned out to be registered to defendant's son. State v. Lawhorn, 2005-Ohio-2776, 2005 Ohio App. LEXIS 2617 (Ohio Ct. App., Paulding County 2005).

Weight and sufficiency of the evidence supported defendant's convictions for burglary and theft, in violation of R.C. 2911.12(A)(3) and 2913.02(A)(1), respectively, where homeowners testified that the back door of their house was kicked in while they were out and that items of property were stolen, defendant and his friends were seen driving around the neighborhood and parked near the owners' home, they were all dressed in black, and stolen property was recovered which was linked to one of the individuals that defendant admitted having been with that night; although there was no direct evidence that linked defendant to the crimes, there was sufficient circumstantial evidence to support the jury's verdict. State v. Patton, 2005-Ohio-2721, 2005 Ohio App. LEXIS 2555 (Ohio Ct. App., Jefferson County 2005).

Evidence was sufficient to support defendant's conviction for theft from the elderly because he took advantage of the victim's deteriorating mental state to persuade her to take out two mortgages she could not afford to repay, one of which directly benefitted defendant, and, to obtain this second mortgage, he misrepresented the victim's income and the appraised value of her house to a mortgage broker, Sufficiently demonstrating deception, under R.C. 2913.01(A). State v. Mamounis, 2005-Ohio-2654, 2005 Ohio App. LEXIS 2502 (Ohio Ct. App., Trumbull County 2005).

Evidence was sufficient to support defendant's conviction for theft, in violation of R.C. 2913.02(A)(2), where defendant had been a bookkeeper for a company that had a high sales volume but was losing money, prompting the company president to have a former bookkeeper conduct an investigation of the books, whereupon it was determined that 38 checks had been misidentified as being paid to company vendors when, in fact, they were paid to "cash," to defendant's husband, or to defendant's personal credit card companies; defendant's claims were not credible, and the jury did not clearly lose its way in finding that defendant had stolen funds from the company. State v. Derrickson, 2005-Ohio-2565, 2005 Ohio App. LEXIS 2438 (Ohio Ct. App., Wayne County 2005).

There was sufficient evidence to support defendant's conviction for aggravated theft, under R.C. 2913.02(A)(1) and (B)(2), because defendant had a purpose to deprive the victim of her property, and it came into his hands, giving him control over it. The victim testified that she did not consent to the theft of her property, further testified that the value of the stolen property was close to $1,000,000, and an appraisal showed that one ring was worth at least $300,000 by itself. State v. Payne, 2005-Ohio-7043, 2005 Ohio App. LEXIS 6355 (Ohio Ct. App., Lake County 2005).

Defendant's convictions for aggravated robbery, robbery, and theft and kidnapping, all with firearm specifications, were not against the manifest weight of the evidence because (1) the victim identified defendant as one of two men who approached him on the night in question, (2) defendant looked through the victim's pockets and took his wallet, containing cash, and beer, (3) the wallet, a sweatshirt worn by the accomplice, and the beer were found in the vehicle in which defendant was riding, and (4) the driver of this vehicle said she drove another to the apartments where the crime occurred, and, when he returned to the car, defendant and the accomplice were with him and were whispering about what to do with a weapon and the wallet. State v. Wheat, 2005-Ohio-6958, 2005 Ohio App. LEXIS 6278 (Ohio Ct. App., Franklin County 2005).

Defendant's convictions for theft of a dangerous drug, in violation of R.C. 2913.02(A)(1), (B)(6) and trafficking in drugs, in violation of R.C. 2925.03(A)(1), (C)(1)(b), was not the against manifest weight of evidence. During his initial appearance, defendant admitted to stealing MS Contin from his grandmother's medicine cabinet, defendant's friend testified that defendant had given him some of the pills, the officer who investigated the incident testified that he found the prescription pill bottle near where defendant had been hiding when the officer arrived to conduct the initial investigation, and defendant's grandmother testified that she had never given defendant permission to take her prescription medication. State v. Sawmiller, 2005-Ohio-6863, 2005 Ohio App. LEXIS 6195 (Ohio Ct. App., Auglaize County 2005).

Evidence was sufficient to support defendant's conviction for theft, in violation of R.C. 2913.02(A)(1), where he was given the keys to an owner's vehicle in order to repair it, various individuals testified that defendant was aware that he was not authorized to remove the vehicle from the garage facility and that the facility's power and water were in working order that day, defendant's claim that he needed to remove the vehicle from the garage in order to fix it was contradicted in many aspects by other witnesses' testimony, and defendant failed to return the vehicle until the following day, at which time it was filthy on the interior and was extensively damaged. State v. Jenkins, 2005-Ohio-2824, 2005 Ohio App. LEXIS 2668 (Ohio Ct. App., Cuyahoga County 2005), rev'd in part, 2006-Ohio-2109, 109 Ohio St. 3d 313, 847 N.E.2d 1174, 2006 Ohio LEXIS 1161 (Ohio 2006).

Defendant's conviction for failure to comply with an order or signal of a police officer, grand theft, assault, driving under an Ohio Financial Responsibility Act suspension, and resisting arrest was not against the manifest weight of the evidence where: (1) defendant was "messing around" with the driver's side door before he entered the vehicle, (2) defendant sped away in the vehicle after the police officers activated their lights and sirens, (3) defendant continually punched an officer after he was apprehended, and (4) an inspection of the vehicle showed that no keys were in the vehicle, that the center column under the steering wheel was smashed, and that there was a screwdriver on the driver's side floorboard. State v. Tate, 2005-Ohio-2156, 2005 Ohio App. LEXIS 2057 (Ohio Ct. App., Summit County 2005).

Defendant's conviction for failure to comply with an order or signal of a police officer, grand theft, assault, driving under an Ohio Financial Responsibility Act suspension, and resisting arrest was supported by sufficient evidence in light of a determination that the conviction was not against the manifest weight of the evidence. State v. Tate, 2005-Ohio-2156, 2005 Ohio App. LEXIS 2057 (Ohio Ct. App., Summit County 2005).

Evidence was sufficient to support his convictions for theft, receiving stolen property, and possession of criminal tools. Defendant was observed in the area before and after the theft, in the company of his co-defendant he walked up to a witness and asked for a screwdriver, and defendant was caught by the police while in possession of the stolen property. A jury could infer from the testimony of a police officer and defendant's possession of the stolen property that defendant was complicit in the crime. State v. Sykes, 2005-Ohio-1813, 2005 Ohio App. LEXIS 1725 (Ohio Ct. App., Franklin County 2005).

When the evidence showed that defendant and his co-defendants had a common scheme of entering the victim's stores, after which one of them would place several of a certain item in a shopping cart, conceal the fact that the items were in the shopping cart, then eventually go to the store's garden department, after which they left the store without merchandise, but the items that were in the cart were missing and a hole had been cut in the garden department's fence allowed a jury to infer that defendant intended to permanently deprive the store of the items placed in the shopping cart, which was sufficient for a theft conviction, under R.C. 2913.02(A). State v. Owens, 2005-Ohio-1166, 2005 Ohio App. LEXIS 1150 (Ohio Ct. App., Cuyahoga County 2005).

Evidence supported defendant's conviction for theft, in violation of R.C. 2913.02(A)(1), where he was seen leaving a bar, a van loaded with Christmas presents that was idling across the street from the bar was stolen, the police followed it in a car chase, and then followed footprints from the vehicle left in the snow to a house where defendant was found; there was also evidence tying defendant to a wet sock, shoes that made the foot prints, and witnesses who saw various parts of the incident. State v. Mayle, 2005-Ohio-1346, 2005 Ohio App. LEXIS 1294 (Ohio Ct. App., Carroll County 2005).

Defendant's conviction for grand theft for stealing a van was not against the manifest weight of the evidence, as an accomplice testified that she and defendant stole the van, a stipulation was entered that defendant did not own the van and did not have consent from the owner to remove it from the owner's property, and that defendant had been on the owner's property shortly before the van was reported missing. State v. Siney, 2005-Ohio-1081, 2005 Ohio App. LEXIS 1106 (Ohio Ct. App., Warren County 2005).

There was sufficient evidence to support defendant's conviction for theft, under R.C. 2913.02(B)(2) and 2913.61(A) because, according to witness testimony the value of a single hard plastic kit was $499 plus tax and defendant admitted he was involved in the theft of at least three or four kits. State v. Miller, 2005-Ohio-771, 2005 Ohio App. LEXIS 743 (Ohio Ct. App., Cuyahoga County 2005), aff'd, 2006-Ohio-2109, 109 Ohio St. 3d 313, 847 N.E.2d 1174, 2006 Ohio LEXIS 1161 (Ohio 2006).

Evidence was sufficient to support defendant's conviction of theft, as he took money from an informant and an undercover agent under an agreement that he would sell them one ounce of cocaine, he went into his grandmother's house, and he never reappeared, nor did he answer calls on his phone; the state was entitled to an inference that defendant intended to take the money and run. State v. Burkhart, 2005-Ohio-502, 2005 Ohio App. LEXIS 536 (Ohio Ct. App., Cuyahoga County 2005).

There were sufficient facts to support the charge that defendant, with purpose to deprive the victim of her car, knowingly obtained and exerted control over the car without the victim's consent; the victim testified she and defendant were planning to attend a banquet for her grandson, that she asked defendant to go out to the driveway to clean out the car and within moments, both the car and defendant were gone, that the victim never gave permission to defendant to use her car, and that defendant never showed up at the banquet that night, nor did she hear from him. State v. Davis, 2005-Ohio-289, 2005 Ohio App. LEXIS 259 (Ohio Ct. App., Cuyahoga County 2005).

Defendant's conviction for robbery and theft was not against the manifest weight of the evidence due to inconsistencies in a store employee's testimony as inconsistent evidence did not make a conviction against the manifest weight of the evidence and the employee testified that he had no doubt that defendant had a knife and took cigarettes. State v. Haynes, 2005-Ohio-256, 2005 Ohio App. LEXIS 229 (Ohio Ct. App., Franklin County 2005).

Defendant took substantial steps toward the completion of a theft offense and did not voluntarily abandon his plan where: (1) he entered a store with the intention of stealing cigarettes, (2) he hid cigarettes in a cabinet in order to retrieve them later, (3) he kept two packs in his hand with the intention of paying for them if someone noticed him, (4) he was confronted, left the two packs on the floor, and left the store, and (5) a store employee testified that defendant hid many packs of cigarettes in his pants and took them out of the store when he left. State v. Haynes, 2005-Ohio-256, 2005 Ohio App. LEXIS 229 (Ohio Ct. App., Franklin County 2005).

Jury was not required to accept the defendant's explanation conduct as innocent where the circumstances indicated an attempted theft. State v. Morris, 2005-Ohio-962, 159 Ohio App. 3d 775, 825 N.E.2d 637, 2005 Ohio App. LEXIS 961 (Ohio Ct. App., Pickaway County 2005).

Sufficient evidence existed to convict defendant of felonious assault, kidnapping, aggravated burglary, and theft, where defendant kept the victim in his bedroom at knife-point and suffocated the victim to quiet his screams for help. In addition, there were photographs of a torn coat and a cut on the victim's hand which corroborated the victim's testimony that defendant, who was a neighbor, was the perpetrator of the crimes; thus, the trial court properly declined to acquit defendant as to those charges. State v. Miller, 2004-Ohio-2549, 2004 Ohio App. LEXIS 2266 (Ohio Ct. App., Cuyahoga County 2004).

Evidence was sufficient to convict defendant of grand theft, in violation of R.C. 2913.02(A)(1), as he was identified as the person who accelerated a vehicle backwards out of a driveway while the victim was standing in the open driver's side door with his hand on the steering wheel, dragging the victim, and he was later found bleeding near the abandoned vehicle. State v. Norris, 2004-Ohio-2516, 2004 Ohio App. LEXIS 2241 (Ohio Ct. App., Summit County 2004).

Evidence was sufficient to convict defendant, who was aided by two other women, of complicity to commit theft from two stores, in violation of R.C. 2913.02(A)(1), where store employees testified that (1) bags the women carried appeared fuller when they left the store than when they entered; (2) they acted suspiciously; (3) security tags that had been removed from merchandise were found in areas where the women had been; (4) one of the women triggered a security sensor while leaving, and the others helped her escape; and (5) merchandise recovered from the women's getaway car came from the two stores, but the women had not paid for the items. State v. Mingo, 2004-Ohio-2247, 2004 Ohio App. LEXIS 2000 (Ohio Ct. App., Medina County 2004).

Where several witnesses testified as to the value of stolen property, and the maximum values testified to totalled $943, the State offered sufficient evidence to establish that the stolen property had a value of at least $500, pursuant to R.C. 2913.02(B)(2); therefore, the trial court properly overruled defendant's motion for acquittal. State v. Mingo, 2004-Ohio-2247, 2004 Ohio App. LEXIS 2000 (Ohio Ct. App., Medina County 2004).

Evidence that (1) a girl matching appellant's description was seen at a burglarized home near the time of the crime with a boy and the victim's daughter, (2) appellant told two witnesses she and the daughter had burglarized the home, and (3) she admitted the boy paid for a motel room the three shared using money that the daughter had given him, was sufficient to support her adjudication as a delinquent for committing the crime of theft in violation of R.C. 2913.02(A)(1). In re Kadri, 2004-Ohio-2253, 2004 Ohio App. LEXIS 2010 (Ohio Ct. App., Tuscarawas County 2004).

Defendant's conviction for theft was not against the sufficiency of the evidence because the State produced evidence at trial in the form of letters written by defendant, taped telephone conversations and witness testimony, and in much of the State's evidence, defendant incriminated herself by her very own spoken and written words; specifically, the evidence showed that defendant answered advertisements from the elderly victims while in prison, misrepresenting her incarceration status, or the circumstances therein, and certain personal information in order to entice the victims into sending her money. State v. Weiss, 2004-Ohio-1948, 2004 Ohio App. LEXIS 1697 (Ohio Ct. App., Union County 2004).

Evidence was sufficient to support a prisoner's conviction of aggravated robbery under R.C. 2911.01(A) and 2913.02, where a witness testified that the prisoner admitted to her that he killed his victim for her ATM card; the prosecution introduced evidence that the prisoner had the victim's ATM card, that the card was used twice after her death, and that the prisoner tossed it to the ground as police approached to arrest him; and the prosecution introduced evidence that a pocket on the victim's coat, which was found floating in a river, was turned inside out. The prisoner's own testimony established that he was out of work and implied that he was in need of money to support his drug habit. Benge v. Johnson, 312 F. Supp. 2d 978, 2004 U.S. Dist. LEXIS 6029 (S.D. Ohio 2004), amended, 2004 U.S. Dist. LEXIS 30294 (S.D. Ohio July 7, 2004), aff'd, 474 F.3d 236, 2007 FED App. 0017P, 2007 U.S. App. LEXIS 856 (6th Cir. Ohio 2007).

Trial court properly denied defendant's motion for judgment of acquittal pursuant to Crim.R. 29(A), as there was sufficient evidence to support defendant's conviction for receiving stolen property in violation of R.C. 2913.51(A) where he was observed sitting in a stolen vehicle in a high crime and high drug activity area, and it was determined that he had reasonable cause to believe that the person who had initially obtained the car had done so through theft; the court found that defendant had deprived the owner of the property without having obtained consent, pursuant to R.C. 2913.02(A)(1) and 2913.01(C)(3), and that even though title ownership pursuant to R.C. 2913.01(D) was not a necessary element of the offense, there was sufficient evidence as to who the title owner of the car was. State v. Edwards, 2004-Ohio-1595, 2004 Ohio App. LEXIS 1412 (Ohio Ct. App., Summit County 2004).



Defendant's conviction for theft by deception was not against the manifest weight of the evidence where defendant contracted to refurbish the victim's barn, accepted a down payment, cashed the check, and then never did the work. State v. Belt, 2004-Ohio-1511, 2004 Ohio App. LEXIS 1341 (Ohio Ct. App., Union County 2004).

There was sufficient evidence to support defendant's convictions for breaking and entering and theft. Defendant broke into the store's secured storage area by cutting a chain and then took merchandise valued at $1,637.21. When stopped by the police in the middle of the night, defendant was discovered driving a truck and trailer containing the missing merchandise, and, although defendant testified that he was hired to transfer the merchandise from one store to another, merchandise was never transferred in such a manner. State v. Caldwell, 2004-Ohio-1567, 2004 Ohio App. LEXIS 1392 (Ohio Ct. App., Stark County 2004).

Where defendant, after taking the victim's deposit, failed to ever start the remodeling job, never contacted the victim about failing to start the project, and was indifferent about retaining the victim's deposit for over a year, this left an implication that defendant had no intention of completing any work for the victim, and the jury could have found that defendant took the victim's $1,900 deposit with no intention of providing consideration for that money pursuant to R.C. 2913.01(A), (C), 2901.22(A), (B). There was sufficient evidence, pursuant to Crim.R. 29(A), to convict defendant of theft against the elderly in violation of R.C. 2913.02(A)(3). State v. Lewis, 2004-Ohio-1233, 2004 Ohio App. LEXIS 1084 (Ohio Ct. App., Summit County 2004).

There was sufficient circumstantial evidence for a jury to conclude that items taken—a box of jewelry, money, and several other items made of gold (the jewelry consisting of 13 or 14 rings made of gold and set with rubies, diamonds, and sapphires)—were worth over $500, but under $5,000. State v. Bradford, 2004-Ohio-769, 2004 Ohio App. LEXIS 714 (Ohio Ct. App., Greene County 2004).

There was sufficient evidence to support defendant's convictions for grand theft and a motor vehicle title offense because the testimony established that after defendant received the total payment of $52,000 from the victim for the car, he used the car as collateral on a loan, which he defaulted on resulting in repossession of the car. State v. Simpson, 2004-Ohio-602, 2004 Ohio App. LEXIS 567 (Ohio Ct. App., Summit County 2004).

There was sufficient evidence to support defendant's conviction for theft because the owner testified that after she secured her new puppy's collar and properly latched the gate in her neighbor's yard, someone removed the puppy from the yard; defendant was observed in the area around the time the puppy was reported missing, he was later seen with the puppy, and the puppy eventually was found at his home. State v. Sova, 2004-Ohio-604, 2004 Ohio App. LEXIS 572 (Ohio Ct. App., Highland County 2004).

State presented evidence that (1) an employee of the motorcycle dealership that owned the motorcycle told defendant to get off it and did not give defendant permission to drive it, and (2) that immediately upon being told to get off it, defendant drove it from the owner's property at a high rate of speed, drove it some distance away, failed to stop it for the police who were in pursuit, and only relinquished control of it after he crashed it into a parked truck and was apprehended by the police. That evidence was sufficient evidence as to each element of the offense of R.C. 2913.02(A)(1), theft beyond a reasonable doubt. State v. Fowler, 2004-Ohio-349, 2004 Ohio App. LEXIS 299 (Ohio Ct. App., Franklin County 2004).

Pursuant to Crim.R. 29(A), the trial court did not abuse its discretion in denying defendant's motion for acquittal from a charge of grand theft, in violation of R.C. 2913.02(A)(2), because the evidence demonstrated that defendant exceeded his authority in taking possession of a payment check that defendant was supposed to use to pay a newspaper advertising account. State v. Bratton, 2004-Ohio-187, 2004 Ohio App. LEXIS 166 (Ohio Ct. App., Allen County 2004).

Defendant's conviction for engaging in a pattern of corrupt activity in violation of R.C. 2923.32(A)(1) was supported by substantial evidence, as the evidence established: (1) 21 specific incidents of thefts of property by deception with a value exceeding $500, (2) the activities were related to defendant's construction business, (3) the bulk of the contracts were entered into on a monthly basis over six months, and (4) the thefts spanned at least six months, 21 locations, eight counties, and three states. State v. Hicks, 2003-Ohio-7210, 2003 Ohio App. LEXIS 6490 (Ohio Ct. App., Butler County 2003).

As defendant was in the vicinity of the break-in and theft, it was clear an individual of his physical description was seen in a stolen motor home, and berry-type stains on the seat of the motor home and defendant's jeans were consistent, there was sufficient evidence to support his conviction for theft. State v. Tanner, 2003-Ohio-6866, 2003 Ohio App. LEXIS 6203 (Ohio Ct. App., Muskingum County 2003).

Evidence that the manager of the electronics store observed the items in defendant's purse, the alarm sounded when defendant left the store, and that the security guard observed defendant's license plate number was sufficient for a jury to find defendant guilty of theft pursuant to R.C. 2913.02(A)(1) State v. Groce-Hopson, 2003-Ohio-6735, 2003 Ohio App. LEXIS 5992 (Ohio Ct. App., Lake County 2003).

In a prosecution for uttering, receiving stolen property, grand theft, and possessing criminal tools, where the evidence showed that defendant used the victim's check to buy a car, and the victim testified she had not given defendant the check, signed it, or authorized him to buy a car, the jury could have inferred that defendant knew the check was forged and used it for criminal purposes. State v. King, 2003-Ohio-6489, 2003 Ohio App. LEXIS 5797 (Ohio Ct. App., Cuyahoga County 2003), rev'd, 2004-Ohio-6403, 104 Ohio St. 3d 262, 819 N.E.2d 283, 2004 Ohio LEXIS 2871 (Ohio 2004).

Defendant's conviction for burglary and theft was not against the manifest weight of the evidence, where testimony showed, inter alia, that defendant was the last person in the victim's home, saw that the victim was drunk, and would have known that he would be in an alcohol-induced sleep; that a ring and his wallet and were in plain view while defendant was over; that defendant had the victim's toolbox in his closet; and that he told his accomplice that he had the victim's credit cards and that he went on a spending spree with them. State v. Boergert, 2003-Ohio-6492, 2003 Ohio App. LEXIS 5790 (Ohio Ct. App., Cuyahoga County 2003).

Defendant's conviction of misdemeanor theft, R.C. 2913.02, was supported by sufficient evidence, because defendant admitted at trial that he gave the victim a worthless check in exchange for gaming chips; upon review pursuant to Ohio Const. art. IV, § 3(B)(3), the conviction was determined not to be against the manifest weight of the evidence, as the trial court did not lose its way so as to create a manifest miscarriage of justice. State v. Farah, 2003-Ohio-5936, 2003 Ohio App. LEXIS 5282 (Ohio Ct. App., Cuyahoga County 2003).

Evidence that defendant deposited into his own banking account a check sent to a former resident at his address was sufficient to support the theft conviction. State v. Hughley, 2003-Ohio-5656, 2003 Ohio App. LEXIS 5051 (Ohio Ct. App., Cuyahoga County 2003).

Where defendant continued to take orders for new homes and accept money from customers knowing that the homes would not be delivered due to circumstances related to defendant's financial problems, defendant's conviction for theft by deception under R.C. 2913.02(A)(3) was not against the manifest weight of the evidence. State v. Gates, 2003-Ohio-5186, 2003 Ohio App. LEXIS 4724 (Ohio Ct. App., Wood County 2003).

Appellate court could not conclude that the jury lost its way in finding defendant guilty on the grand theft counts where defendant never explained why he did not immediately send checks to the materials suppliers when the money was available. State v. Hemsley, 2003-Ohio-5192, 2003 Ohio App. LEXIS 4701 (Ohio Ct. App., Williams County 2003).

Conviction of theft in violation of R.C. 2913.02 was affirmed because any rational trier of fact could have found the essential elements of theft where defendant, in a romantic relationship with the victim, threatened her at knifepoint and stole her jewelry, cash, and rental car; minor inconsistencies in the victim's testimony did not undermine the victim's testimony on whether a theft took place. State v. McCall, 2003-Ohio-5034, 2003 Ohio App. LEXIS 4520 (Ohio Ct. App., Franklin County 2003).

Trial court did not err in denying defendant's Crim.R. 29 motion for acquittal, as there was sufficient evidence to support defendant's conviction of theft of a motor vehicle under R.C. 2913.02(A)(1); the vehicle owner and his father testified that they did not give defendant permission to take the vehicle to the junkyard and the police officer testified that defendant admitted to the officer that defendant had neither title nor permission to take the vehicle to the junkyard. State v. Hunt, 2003-Ohio-4525, 2003 Ohio App. LEXIS 4022 (Ohio Ct. App., Lorain County 2003).

Where evidence from the state included testimony that a desk valued at over $500 was stored in the basement of the duplex; that defendant was told that he could not have or use the desk; that the victim and her son saw the desk in defendant's apartment; and that the desk could not be found after defendant vacated the premises, the evidence supported conviction for theft. State v. Williams, 2003-Ohio-4453, 2003 Ohio App. LEXIS 3975 (Ohio Ct. App., Butler County 2003).

Evidence was sufficient to show that defendant knowingly participated in an aggravated robbery under R.C. 2911.01(A) and 2913.02(A), even though he did not get out of the vehicle in which he and his codefendants were traveling, because the evidence showed he aided and abetted his codefendants, as they all talked about robbing someone, defendant was the mastermind of the crime, he was driving the vehicle when he suggested robbing the victims, and his codefendant's plea bargain did not render his conviction contrary to the manifest weight of the evidence. State v. Lewis, 2003-Ohio-3673, 2003 Ohio App. LEXIS 3319 (Ohio Ct. App., Cuyahoga County 2003).

Evidence that two men, posing as police, ransacked a woman's home, detained her while they stole her money and property, ripped her phone from the wall, and that defendant's fingerprints were found at the victim's homes, was sufficient to support defendant's conviction for theft and impersonating a police officer. State v. Johnson, 2003-Ohio-3241, 2003 Ohio App. LEXIS 2903 (Ohio Ct. App., Cuyahoga County 2003).

Defendant's convictions for grand theft, perjury, and engaging in a pattern of corrupt activity, were all upheld, as defendant was unanimously convicted of three acts which satisfied the requirements of R.C. 2923.32, he was unable to show that his substantial rights were impaired, plain error was not shown, and other acts testimony was more probative than prejudicial; further, where defendant misstated his testimony to the grand jury, despite his claims of innocent mistake, confusion, and nervousness, it was within the jury's province to believe that he knowingly made said statements. State v. Saxton, 2003-Ohio-3158, 2003 Ohio App. LEXIS 2831 (Ohio Ct. App., Lorain County 2003).

Where a jury was free to accept or reject the witnesses' testimony that defendant took money from the victim, the evidence was sufficient to support the guilty verdict of misdemeanor theft. State v. Degraffinreed, 2003-Ohio-3081, 2003 Ohio App. LEXIS 2760 (Ohio Ct. App., Stark County 2003).

Where some of the more incriminating evidence that the state presented included the following: (1) the defendants entered the store together, (2) presented the forged contracts together, and (3) left with the misappropriated cellular phones together and the defendant's own car was used to leave the crime scene, a motion for acquittal was properly denied. State v. Lee, 2003-Ohio-2737, 2003 Ohio App. LEXIS 2486 (Ohio Ct. App., Cuyahoga County 2003).

Based on the statutory definitions of "purposely" and "deprive", the trial court's decision finding the defendant guilty of theft was not against the manifest weight and sufficiency of the evidence where he clearly exerted control over the cash beyond the scope of the customer's express consent in that he never returned the money, repaired the vehicle, or tendered the repair parts which should have been purchased with the money: State v. Schultz, 2000 Ohio App. LEXIS 1506 (Ohio Ct. App., Tuscarawas County Apr. 3, 2000).

Where appellant walked into victim's home, threatened him, demanded money, took his pager, and departed with $560 in cash, there was sufficient evidence indicating that appellant had committed theft, in violation of R.C. 2913.02(A)(4): State v. Jackson, 1998 Ohio App. LEXIS 2769 (Ohio Ct. App., Lake County June 19, 1998).

The defendant was properly convicted of theft by deception for misrepresentations made in connection with sales of puppies, even though a different price for a puppy was set in a related civil case: State v. Barker, 128 Ohio App. 3d 233, 714 N.E.2d 447, 1998 Ohio App. LEXIS 2369 (Ohio Ct. App., Fulton County 1998).

A provider who is charged with medicaid fraud and theft by deception may properly be convicted of the latter offense where knowingly false billings are submitted and paid: State v. Brown, 99 Ohio App. 3d 604, 651 N.E.2d 470, 1994 Ohio App. LEXIS 6056 (Ohio Ct. App., Franklin County 1994).

Appellant was properly convicted of grand theft of a motor vehicle where he contacted rental agency pretending to be an insurance agent who needed a car for his client, rode to the rental agency with an agency employee, and signed the rental agreement and took delivery of the car without paying any deposit: State v. Jenkins, 1993 Ohio App. LEXIS 5921 (Ohio Ct. App., Lake County Dec. 10, 1993).

A police officer can be properly convicted of theft by deception where, after answering a police call, he takes advantage of the person's senile dementia to acquire large sums of money from the person: State v. Lewis, 85 Ohio App. 3d 29, 619 N.E.2d 57, 1993 Ohio App. LEXIS 170 (Ohio Ct. App., Allen County 1993), dismissed, 66 Ohio St. 3d 1494, 613 N.E.2d 236, 1993 Ohio LEXIS 1160 (Ohio 1993), cert. denied, 510 U.S. 1041, 114 S. Ct. 685, 126 L. Ed. 2d 652, 1994 U.S. LEXIS 80 (U.S. 1994).

A contractor may be convicted of theft where he enters into home remodeling contracts with an intention not to complete them: State v. Karns, 80 Ohio App. 3d 199, 608 N.E.2d 1145, 1992 Ohio App. LEXIS 2566 (Ohio Ct. App., Hamilton County 1992).

Defendant contractor was properly convicted of theft where he accepted money from the city for rehabilitating the houses but had not actually done the work: State v. Jacobozzi, 6 Ohio St. 3d 86, 451 N.E.2d 749, 1983 Ohio LEXIS 784 (Ohio 1983).

**Federal preemption**

State theft laws are not preempted by the social security act: State v. Wallace, 2005-Ohio-1746, 160 Ohio App. 3d 528, 828 N.E.2d 125, 2005 Ohio App. LEXIS 1673 (Ohio Ct. App., Cuyahoga County 2005).

**Felony**

Trial court did not err in convicting defendant of felony theft offenses rather than misdemeanors because the there was ample evidence from which to conclude that the value of the stolen goods was greater than the amount that the codefendant was able to procure when he sold the items for scrap. The $1,000 loss from the business met the threshold amount for felony theft, and the $4,000 loss from the vacant house exceeded that threshold amount. State v. Oren, 2013-Ohio-531, 2013 Ohio App. LEXIS 464 (Ohio Ct. App., Madison County 2013).

**Firearm theft**

Trial court erred in denying defendant's Crim.R. 29 motion for judgment of acquittal because even in viewing the evidence in a light most favorable to the prosecution, the State failed to present sufficient evidence that the stolen firearms met the definition of "firearms" under R.C. 2923.11(B)(1). Therefore, there was also insufficient evidence presented to find him guilty of third-degree felony theft of a firearm. State v. Ihinger, 2019-Ohio-1881, 2019 Ohio App. LEXIS 1952 (Ohio Ct. App., Muskingum County 2019).

Evidence was sufficient to convict defendant of gun theft and receiving stolen property because the victim testified that he specifically informed her that the muzzleloader was a pistol when she inquired about it. Also, there was no indication in the record that she was given any reason to believe the gun was not operable before she took it from the victim's apartment. And, he testified that the gun was operable, as he fired it on a previous occasion. State v. Idler, 2019-Ohio-2159, 2019 Ohio App. LEXIS 2245 (Ohio Ct. App., Brown County 2019).

Trial court erred in finding defendant guilty of third-degree felony theft of a firearm and of the firearm specification because the State presented insufficient evidence that the guns were operable, and thus it failed to demonstrate that the guns were firearms as that term had been defined. There was no testimony as to whether the guns were loaded or unloaded or whether any of the ammunition recovered was of a caliber such that it could be used in any of the guns and, while the names of the weapons were mentioned at trial, that was insufficient to demonstrate operability. State v. Johnson, 2016-Ohio-872, 2016 Ohio App. LEXIS 778 (Ohio Ct. App., Lorain County 2016).

Defendant was not punished twice for a firearm specification and for grand theft of the guns that formed the basis of the specification, because a firearm specification is not a criminal offense but a sentence enhancement, and penalties for a specification and its predicate offense do not merge under R.C. 2941.25. State v. Wilson, 2012-Ohio-3567, 2012 Ohio App. LEXIS 3154 (Ohio Ct. App., Cuyahoga County 2012).

In a prosecution for theft of a firearm, although the State produced evidence that defendant stole a muzzle-loader, none of that evidence related to the muzzle-loader's operability, which was a required element of the crime; thus, insufficient evidence supported defendant's conviction for this offense. Ohio courts had rejected the notion that, without additional evidence, operability could be inferred from the name used to describe an alleged firearm. State v. Henry, 2012-Ohio-371, 2012 Ohio App. LEXIS 326 (Ohio Ct. App., Gallia County 2012).

Sufficient evidence supported defendant's conviction for theft by deception of a firearm from a federally licensed firearms dealer because his actions fell squarely within the definition of deception. The scheme was for the purpose of making it appear that he had paid for the firearms so that he could remove them from the firearms store where he worked; no cash was actually stolen or removed from the store. State v. Leach, 2011-Ohio-4745, 195 Ohio App. 3d 433, 960 N.E.2d 531, 2011 Ohio App. LEXIS 3921 (Ohio Ct. App., Delaware County 2011).

There was sufficient evidence to support defendant's conviction for theft of a firearm because the State produced evidence that the serial number on the gun in its possession matched the serial number of the gun that was found on the roof and the identification of the gun by the store manager and police personnel was also undisputed. Further, the circumstantial evidence was more than sufficient to establish that defendant exerted control over the gun and intended to deprive the owner of it without the owner's consent because the store manager stated that the gun was always kept in a cubbyhole about five or six feet away from the cash register, the gun was never allowed to leave the store and was there when the manager closed the store before the burglary, the gun was missing when the manager arrived at the store the night of the burglary. State v. Mobley, 2008-Ohio-4641, 2008 Ohio App. LEXIS 3892 (Ohio Ct. App., Montgomery County 2008).

Sufficient evidence was presented to establish the operability of the two stolen firearms for defendant's convictions for grand theft and having a weapon while under a disability. The state presented evidence that the victim was a gun collector and had held a federal firearms license; the two different types of ammunition that could be used in one of the firearms;

that the purpose of the scope on the other firearm was for target practice or hunting; that the victim had taken steps to hide the weapons in her home; and that defendant stole the firearms to get back into "gunrunning." State v. Comsa, 2007-Ohio-5561, 2007 Ohio App. LEXIS 4898 (Ohio Ct. App., Washington County 2007).

**Grand theft**

Evidence was insufficient to sustain a conviction for grand theft because defendant was known by and had a relationship with the person from whom the vehicle was taken, and nothing in the record suggested that he tried to conceal the fact that he took the vehicle. State v. Piskac, 2022-Ohio-1209, 2022 Ohio App. LEXIS 1106 (Ohio Ct. App., Portage County 2022).

Court overruled defendant's assignment of error and affirmed the findings of guilt but reversed the judgment of conviction because state presented legally sufficient evidence for a reasonable jury to find that defendant purposely deprived Ohio Department of Medicaid of funds in excess of the $7,500.00 threshold for grand theft. State v. Bamonte, 2022-Ohio-1331, 2022 Ohio App. LEXIS 1220 (Ohio Ct. App., Franklin County 2022).

Sufficient evidence supported defendant's conviction for grand theft because police officers observed a camper trailer matching the tip for a stolen trailer and a truck with lights on top and a toolbox mounted directly behind the cab with no truck bed on defendant's property. Defendant claimed that his friend loaned him the camper but the stolen the trailer was confirmed by comparing the serial number. State v. Hodge, 2020-Ohio-3002, 154 N.E.3d 671, 2020 Ohio App. LEXIS 1945 (Ohio Ct. App., Fairfield County 2020).

Defendant's convictions for attempted grand theft and breaking and entering were supported by sufficient evidence and were not against the manifest weight of the evidence because after entering into federally licensed firearms dealer through a window he had broken, proceeded to the area of the store where the firearms were kept, removed two rifles from their shelf, and attempted to pry open the handgun display case. State v. Robinson, 2020-Ohio-6978, 2020 Ohio App. LEXIS 4793 (Ohio Ct. App., Sandusky County 2020).

Evidence was sufficient to support defendant's conviction for grand theft under R.C. 2913.02(A)(2) based on circumstantial evidence of her use of a bank card that was meant to be used in her role as director for a peewee cheerleading organization for her personal purchases, including alcohol, groceries, and livestock supplies. State v. Allgeyer, 2018-Ohio-1893, 112 N.E.3d 27, 2018 Ohio App. LEXIS 2036 (Ohio Ct. App., Clinton County 2018).

Evidence supported defendant's grand theft conviction, as a bullet matching the type used by the victim was found in defendant's pocket, and a notebook was found, in a different town than from where it was taken, alongside footprints matching defendant's shoes. State v. Johnson, 2014-Ohio-1305, 2014 Ohio App. LEXIS 1285 (Ohio Ct. App., Fulton County 2014).

Trial court properly denied defendant's application for expungement; he was not an eligible offender, because the second offense of grand theft of a motor vehicle occurred beyond the three-month statutory time period. The two offenses could not be counted as one conviction on the basis that they violated the same statute, as the crimes involved two separate vehicles, taken from two separate locations and from two separate victims. State v. Mullin, 2014-Ohio-764, 2014 Ohio App. LEXIS 746 (Ohio Ct. App., Clermont County 2014).

There was sufficient evidence to find that defendant "knowingly" committed grand theft by failing to report that her fiance resided in her household for the purpose of her continued receipt of food stamps. Although defendant was informed that she needed to disclose anyone else living in the residence at that time and in the future, and signed documents stating that no one other than herself and her two children were residing in her home and that she understood her duty to disclose any changes, a fraud investigator testified that he determined that the fiance was living in defendant's home. State v. Fairchild, 2013-Ohio-2382, 2013 Ohio App. LEXIS 2330 (Ohio Ct. App., Hardin County 2013).

Trial court erred by convicting defendant of one of the counts of grand theft because, while defendant clearly exerted control over $4,210, there was no evidence that he exerted control over the $1,100 (which was paid directly to defendant's cousin) absent prosecution for complicity. The State did not argue a theory of complicity with respect to that charge. State v. Keith, 2008-Ohio-348, 2008 Ohio App. LEXIS 297 (Ohio Ct. App., Butler County 2008).

Defendant's conviction for grand theft was vacated because evidence of construction contract indicated that he did not voluntarily abandon the project and thus negated the inference that he failed to complete the complainants' project with the intent to deprive the them of their $41,000. Rather, the evidence of surrounding facts and circumstances established that he intended to perform the agreed-upon work in Phase II, but could not do so as a result of financial difficulties with his business. State v. O'Donnell, 2021-Ohio-3253, 2021 Ohio App. LEXIS 3169 (Ohio Ct. App., Champaign County 2021).

**Grand theft of a motor vehicle**

Trial court properly convicted defendant of grand theft of a motor vehicle because, even assuming the prosecutor's comments regarding the missing rear view mirror were improper, they did not prejudicially affect the outcome of the trial and defendant was not denied a fair trial inasmuch as the missing mirror was not the only evidence the prosecution used to establish that defendant acted with a purpose to deprive the owner of her motor vehicle. State v. Patton, 2019-Ohio-2769, 2019 Ohio App. LEXIS 2883 (Ohio Ct. App., Highland County 2019).

Evidence was sufficient to support a grand theft of a motor vehicle conviction because, although defendant claimed an ownership interest by providing some money for a down payment and lease payments, the victim was named on the lease and maintained insurance on the vehicle. She stated that on the day of the incident, because she would not drive defendant home and would not give him the car keys, he took them from her and took the vehicle without her consent. State v. Williamson, 2019-Ohio-4380, 2019 Ohio App. LEXIS 4443 (Ohio Ct. App., Wood County 2019).

Evidence was sufficient to support a grand theft of a motor vehicle conviction because, although defendant claimed an ownership interest by providing some money for a down payment and lease payments, the victim was named on the lease and maintained insurance on the vehicle. She stated that on the day of the incident, because she would not drive defendant home and would not give him the car keys, he took them from her and took the vehicle without her consent. State v. Williamson, 2019-Ohio-4380, 2019 Ohio App. LEXIS 4443 (Ohio Ct. App., Wood County 2019).

Prior to pleading guilty to grand theft defendant was well-aware that he was charged with a fourth-degree felony, to wit, theft of a motor vehicle and, by pleading guilty to grand theft of a motor vehicle as a felony of the fourth-degree, he waived the issue for appeal. The record contained no information from which to conclude that the trial court erred in determining that the all-terrain vehicle stolen by defendant was a "motor vehicle." State v. Penwell, 2017-Ohio-7465, 2017 Ohio App. LEXIS 3781 (Ohio Ct. App., Fayette County 2017).

Sufficient evidence supported defendant's conviction for grand theft auto because, after concluding the sale of the tractors that he did not own, defendant hurriedly drove off in the owner's truck, leaving his accomplice behind, and later abandoned the truck after it broke down, leaving it in a driveway where the police recovered and impounded it. That evidence was sufficient to support an inference that defendant knew that he did not have permission to take the vehicle. State v. Hall, 2007-Ohio-6352, 2007 Ohio App. LEXIS 5606 (Ohio Ct. App., Montgomery County 2007).

**Guilty plea**

Trial court properly denied defendant's motion to withdraw her guilty plea to theft from an elderly or disabled person on the ground that defendant had had a mere change of heart. Defendant did not contribute any money to the bank accounts she and her mother had together and thus could not raise a viable defense that the existence of the joint and survivorship accounts permitted her to spend the money during the mother's lifetime as a co-owner; as for her gift defense, defendant was aware of the factual basis for it when she pleaded guilty and was presumed to have taken it into consideration when she chose to plead guilty. State v. Warrix, 2015-Ohio-5390, 2015 Ohio App. LEXIS 5199 (Ohio Ct. App., Montgomery County 2015).

When defendant pleaded guilty to fourth-degree felony theft under R.C. 2913.02(A)(1), and did not contend that his plea was not knowing, intelligent, or voluntary, he could not argue on appeal that the value of the ring in question did not support a fourth-degree felony charge. The record was clear that defendant understood he was pleading guilty to a fourth-degree felony. State v. Phillips, 2012-Ohio-4823, 2012 Ohio App. LEXIS 4214 (Ohio Ct. App., Cuyahoga County 2012).

Based on the court's compliance with use Crim.R. 11(C)(2), defendant entered his plea to theft of firearms in violation of R.C. 2913.02(A)(1), (B)(1)(4) knowingly, voluntarily, and intelligently. Defendant's sentence of four years was within the statutory range set forth for a third-degree felony under R.C. 2929.14(A)(3). State v. Tusin, 2011-Ohio-2629, 2011 Ohio App. LEXIS 2251 (Ohio Ct. App., Mahoning County 2011).

As defendant entered a guilty plea that was counseled and voluntary pursuant to Crim.R. 11(B)(1) to theft, in violation of R.C. 2913.02(A)(1), defendant was precluded from arguing on appeal that the conviction was not supported by the weight and sufficiency of the evidence; entry of the plea constituted an admission of the factual guilt of the crime. State v. Heard, 2008-Ohio-4639, 2008 Ohio App. LEXIS 3886 (Ohio Ct. App., Montgomery County 2008).

A guilty plea admits the facts set forth in the indictment, not the facts set forth at the plea hearing. However, the court did not determine whether the defendant fully understood the elements of the offense of automobile theft to which he was pleading: State v. Greathouse, 2004-Ohio-3402, 158 Ohio App. 3d 135, 814 N.E.2d 502, 2004 Ohio App. LEXIS 3050 (Ohio Ct. App., Greene County 2004).

**Harmless error**

Even if admission of calibration records was made in error, such error was harmless because the victim's employee was a qualified person to testify about, at the very least, the grinder, which was purchased for $2,500 and listed by a pawn shop for $1,300, and evidence establishing the grinder theft alone would have justified defendant's fifth-degree felony theft conviction. State v. Magri, 2018-Ohio-4275, 2018 Ohio App. LEXIS 4602 (Ohio Ct. App., Geauga County 2018).

Although a neighbor who witnessed defendant steal the victim's car testified to the amount of damage done to her car when defendant hit it while making his escape in the stolen car in defendant's criminal trial on a charge of violating R.C. 2913.02(A)(1), which information was provided without the prompting of a question, any error in the admission thereof was harmless under Crim.R. 52 and Evid.R. 103(A) because the evidence of defendant's guilty was substantial and defendant failed to show how he was prejudiced by the admission thereof State v. Thompson, 2005-Ohio-6792, 2005 Ohio App. LEXIS 6115 (Ohio Ct. App., Jefferson County 2005).

**Identity**

Defendant's convictions of aggravated robbery, kidnapping, theft, possessing criminal tools and having weapons while under a disability were based on sufficient evidence, as a rational trier of fact could have found that defendant was the person who committed the offenses based upon the testimony of nine witnesses. State v. Morrissey, 2021-Ohio-4471, 2021 Ohio App. LEXIS 4383 (Ohio Ct. App., Hardin County 2021).

Sufficient evidence supported defendant's convictions for murder, aggravated robbery, aggravated burglary, trespass in a habitation, felonious assault, grand theft, having weapons while under disability, and carrying concealed weapons because the jury had the opportunity to consider the issues as they related to credibility of the witnesses'; testimony implicating or identifying defendant and defendant's argument regarding the absence of forensic evidence failed to present a challenge to the sufficiency of the evidence. State v. Turner, 2018-Ohio-3898, 2018 Ohio App. LEXIS 4204 (Ohio Ct. App., Summit County 2018).

**Indictment**

Because petty theft under Parma, Ohio, Codified Ordinances 642.02 and R.C. 2913.02 were the same, and there was no error in terms of notice to defendant of the crimes of which she was charged; the jury found her guilty of theft, without notation as to whether it was under the city's ordinances or the Ohio Revised Code. City of Parma v. Schrader, 2014-Ohio-2060, 2014 Ohio App. LEXIS 2000 (Ohio Ct. App., Cuyahoga County 2014).

Indictment properly charged defendant with fourth-degree felony theft offenses because the indictment informed him that he was being charged with the fourth-degree felony offenses. Although the amount required to prove the offenses for grand theft increased after it was amended, it did not change defendant's degree of crime because the amounts at issue ($38,000) substantially exceeded the amount necessary to establish a fourth-degree felony under either the former or current version of the statute. State v. Trammell, 2013-Ohio-4615, 3 N.E.3d 260, 2013 Ohio App. LEXIS 4835 (Ohio Ct. App., Montgomery County 2013).

Trial court did not commit plain error in amending the indictment from R.C. 2913.02(A)(2) to § 2913.02(A)(1): Defendant was not prejudiced by the amendment because he clearly had notice that the State was proceeding under (A)(1), in that the body of the indictment and the bill of particulars notified defendant that the State alleged he took property without the consent of the owner in violation of § 2913.02(A)(1) and because there was no evidence to show that the victim gave defendant permission to use the guns and that defendant simply went beyond the scope of that consent. State v. Stodgel, 2013-Ohio-1109, 2013 Ohio App. LEXIS 1004 (Ohio Ct. App., Fayette County 2013).

State of Ohio's amended indictment for theft by deception, pursuant to R.C. 2913.02(A)(3), instead of insurance fraud, pursuant to R.C. 2913.47(B)(1), was proper because defendant was accused of having deceptively failed to notify defendant's employer or a health insurance company that defendant ex-spouse and/or sibling were no longer eligible for defendant's employer provided insurance coverage and, in doing so, defendant aided and abetted them in stealing health insurance coverage and benefits. Defendant did not present, prepare, or make a written or oral statement to the insurer as required by R.C. 2913.47. State v. Balo, 2011-Ohio-3341, 2011 Ohio App. LEXIS 2828 (Ohio Ct. App., Allen County 2011).

Complaint for theft of electricity was sufficient because the complaint tracked the language of the charging statute, R.C. 2913.02(A)(2), the complaint contained all essential and material elements of the offense, and the complaint was not required to further narrow the offense. Moreover, the record did not reflect that defendant ever requested a bill of particulars or was denied the same. State v. Fisher, 2010-Ohio-5192, 2010 Ohio App. LEXIS 4376 (Ohio Ct. App., Auglaize County 2010).

Because both of defendant's aggravated robbery counts tracked the language of R.C. 2911.01(A)(2) and specified that he committed aggravated robbery when he used a deadly weapon in attempting to commit or in committing theft, in violation of R.C. 2913.02, the indictment was not defective for failure to identify a culpable mental state. The statute itself failed to specify a mental state. State v. Brown, 2010-Ohio-4453, 2010 Ohio App. LEXIS 3756 (Ohio Ct. App., Summit County 2010).

Defendant's theft convictions, under R.C. 2913.02(A)(1), were not reversed when defendant's original robbery indictment, under R.C. 2911.02(A)(3), did not include a culpable mental state, because defendant was not convicted of robbery, and defendant was properly indicted for theft, as the required mental state for theft was expressly stated in the statute to which the indictment referred. State v. Carson, 2009-Ohio-2122, 2009 Ohio App. LEXIS 1769 (Ohio Ct. App., Cuyahoga County 2009).

Defendant was properly convicted of fifth-degree felony theft, pursuant to R.C. 2913.02(B)(2), because (1) the value of the property stolen was not an element of the crime, so the indictment did not have to allege the value, and (2) defendant's indictment for robbery provided defendant with notice, pursuant to Crim.R. 7(B), of the lesser-included offense of theft. State v. Smith, 2009-Ohio-787, 121 Ohio St. 3d 409, 905 N.E.2d 151, 2009 Ohio LEXIS 549 (Ohio 2009).

There was no plain error under Crim.R. 52(B) in an indictment that charged defendant with aggravated robbery, in violation of R.C. 2911.01(A)(1), as it was a strict liability offense that required no mens rea beyond that contained in the theft offense statute under R.C. 2913.02(A); further, as a charge of felony murder, in violation of R.C. 2903.02(B), was predicated on the aggravated robbery charge, no additional mens rea was needed and the indictment against defendant was not defective. State v. Mason, 2008-Ohio-5034, 2008 Ohio App. LEXIS 4239 (Ohio Ct. App., Lucas County 2008).

Indictment was not defective because defendant was alleged to have acted with the purpose to commit theft as the predicate offense for burglary; both the indictment for theft and the jury instructions included the mens rea necessary for a conviction on a charge of theft, which required that defendant acted knowingly. Also, the indictment for burglary tracked the language of R.C. 2911.12, including the identification of trespassing as a predicate offense. State v. Moore, 2008-Ohio-4546, 2008 Ohio App. LEXIS 3818 (Ohio Ct. App., Franklin County 2008).

Indictment sufficiently charged defendant with the "knowingly" element of aggravated robbery, under Crim.R. 7(B), as (1) the indictment charged defendant with attempting or committing a theft offense, as defined in R.C. 2913.01, and (2) R.C. 2913.01(K)(1) defined a theft offense as including a violation of R.C. 2913.02, which contained the element of knowingly. State v. McCoy, 2006-Ohio-56, 2006 Ohio App. LEXIS 37 (Ohio Ct. App., Licking County 2006).

An indictment for violating R.C. 2913.02(A)(3) is defective where it does not allege essential facts showing the element of deception: State v. Luna, 96 Ohio App. 3d 207, 644 N.E.2d 1056, 1994 Ohio App. LEXIS 3265 (Ohio Ct. App., Huron County 1994).

**Instructions**

Trial court did not abuse its discretion by declining to instruct the jury on the affirmative defense of mistake of fact because defendant categorically denied she removed the bedding from the laundromat, explicitly denied taking the bedding by mistake, and further confirmed she did not own bedding matching the description of the victim's bedding. State v. Reeves, 2020-Ohio-5565, 2020 Ohio App. LEXIS 4435 (Ohio Ct. App., Clermont County 2020).

Trial court's error in failing to properly instruct the jury as to all the elements of theft, as an underlying element of robbery, did not clearly and substantially affect the outcome of the trial because did not dispute that a theft occurred. State v. Moorer, 2016-Ohio-5216, 2016 Ohio App. LEXIS 3088 (Ohio Ct. App., Summit County 2016).

Trial court did not err when it instructed the jury on who the victim was, as the specific victim of theft was not an element of theft to be found by a jury, and, pursuant to the bill of particulars, defendant was on trial for theft of that person's property. State v. Kraus, 2016-Ohio-8003, 74 N.E.3d 880, 2016 Ohio App. LEXIS 4877 (Ohio Ct. App., Ottawa County 2016).

In defendant's criminal trial on a charge of, inter alia, aggravated robbery (use of deadly weapon), the trial court properly overruled defendant's request to instruct the jury on the lesser-included offense of theft because the evidence did not support that charge. State v. Dover, 2014-Ohio-2303, 2014 Ohio App. LEXIS 2244 (Ohio Ct. App., Clark County 2014).

Since defendant presented a complete defense to the charge of theft of a motor vehicle, he was not entitled to a jury instruction on the lesser included offense of unauthorized use of a motor vehicle. State v. Jackson, 2014-Ohio-3779, 2014 Ohio App. LEXIS 3711 (Ohio Ct. App., Butler County 2014).

According to defendant, he owned the bridges and sold them in 2005, and thus he was not acting under a mistake of fact concerning the ownership of the bridges, and his concern that he could not be found guilty of vandalism and theft if he was mistaken about ownership was adequately addressed by other jury instructions, such that the trial court did not abuse its discretion in failing to give a mistake instruction. State v. Taylor, 2013-Ohio-5751, 2013 Ohio App. LEXIS 6030 (Ohio Ct. App., Holmes County 2013).

Trial court did not commit plain error in not instructing the jury on the lesser included offense of theft under R.C. 2913.02(A) because there was insufficient evidence in the record that would justify the use of an instruction on the lesser included offense of theft on the aggravated robbery charge. All of the evidence indicated that there was a box cutter and there was no evidence to the contrary. State v. Freeman, 2012-Ohio-2244, 2012 Ohio App. LEXIS 1984 (Ohio Ct. App., Trumbull County 2012).

In a theft by deception prosecution, the trial court did not err in its jury instruction relating to the reimbursement requirements for ambulette services in the Ohio Administrative Code as the trial court's instruction was based on Ohio Admin. Code 5101:3-15-03(B)(2)(b) and (e). State v. Kimkhe, 2012-Ohio-1964, 2012 Ohio App. LEXIS 1730 (Ohio Ct. App., Franklin County 2012).

Defendant's theft convictions under R.C. 2913.02(A)(2) and 2913.02(A)(3) were reversed as plain error because the jury was not instructed on those offenses. State v. Dobbins, 2011-Ohio-6777, 2011 Ohio App. LEXIS 5592 (Ohio Ct. App., Washington County 2011).

Because the evidence did not support an acquittal on the crime of robbery, as charged, because the State proved all the elements of robbery by force, the trial court was not required to give the instruction on the lesser included offense of theft by threat. State v. Palmer, 2010-Ohio-4628, 2010 Ohio App. LEXIS 3910 (Ohio Ct. App., Richland County 2010).

Trial court did not err in failing to give a jury instruction on theft by threat in defendant's robbery trial because there was testimony that defendant threatened the use of immediate force or bodily harm and led at least some of his victims to believe that he had a gun. The implied threats dealt with inflicting physical harm or the use of force. State v. Gloss, 2010-Ohio-4059, 2010 Ohio App. LEXIS 3432 (Ohio Ct. App., Stark County 2010).

In a theft prosecution, the trial court did not abuse its discretion when it refused to give corporate law jury instructions based on his defense that coin funds, which defendant established and in which the Bureau of Workers' Compensation (BWC) heavily invested, were the owners of the money, not the BWC, and that the funds were able to consent to defendant's use of the money. Even assuming that the coin funds were the owners of the money, there was no evidence to suggest that the operating agreements or any other agreement between the parties permitted personal use of the funds by defendant. State v. Noe, 2009-Ohio-6978, 2009 Ohio App. LEXIS 5825 (Ohio Ct. App., Lucas County 2009).

Trial court did not abuse its discretion in failing to give the exact definition of the word "implied" as defendant proposed regarding R.C. 2913.02(A). Furthermore, the trial court did not abuse its discretion by declining to instruct the jury, as defendant requested, on R.C. 1109.07, which concerned deposits in the name of two or more persons and deposits payable on death, because the statute was inapplicable. State v. Estright, 2009-Ohio-5676, 2009 Ohio App. LEXIS 4779 (Ohio Ct. App., Summit County 2009).

In defendant's prosecution for grand theft motor vehicle and receiving stolen property, since defendant testified in his own defense, the trial court did not violate defendant's Fifth Amendment right to remain silent in instructing the jury that defendant's flight, if it were not satisfactorily explained, tended to show consciousness of guilt. State v. Nash, 2008-Ohio-914, 2008 Ohio App. LEXIS 798 (Ohio Ct. App., Cuyahoga County 2008).

In defendant's prosecution for theft, the trial court did not commit plain error in failing to give a jury instruction on attempted theft as defendant's actions were sufficient to constitute a completed theft, in that the evidence showed that, though defendant did not leave store with any contraband, he exerted control over power tools that were hidden inside a vanity that he had placed on a cart and wheeled toward the checkout and that he had the intent to deprive the store of its merchandise. Thus, an instruction on attempted theft was not required because the evidence did not support the conclusion that defendant was unsuccessful in committing the offense of theft. State v. Cadle, 2008-Ohio-3639, 2008 Ohio App. LEXIS 3073 (Ohio Ct. App., Summit County 2008).

In defendant's prosecution on a charge of grand theft of a motor vehicle, the trial court did not abuse its discretion in allowing a jury instruction on the issue of defendant's flight as the evidence showed that defendant fled, running from the scene of the accident, that he was found some distance away, and that he he ignored the officer's requests for him to stop and turn around. State v. Meeks, 2007-Ohio-6559, 2007 Ohio App. LEXIS 5719 (Ohio Ct. App., Lake County 2007).

Because the concepts of petty theft and theft as given by the trial court were sufficiently different, it could have been said that an essential element of the offense was omitted from the instruction on petty theft, which required reversal. The trial court instructed on petty theft first, theft thereafter; the petty theft instruction did not include the proviso that the control sought to be exerted over another's property was without that person's consent, while the theft instruction did. State v. Cochran, 2007-Ohio-345, 2007 Ohio App. LEXIS 291 (Ohio Ct. App., Geauga County 2007).

Trial court did not err by failing to instruct the jury as to theft as a lesser included offense because a reasonable jury would not have acquitted defendant of robbery; the uncontroverted evidence indicated that defendant threatened the victims by stating that he was going to "pop" them, which provided a sufficient basis for the jury to find that defendant threatened to inflict physical harm. In addition, defendant's hands were concealed in a bundled sweatshirt that he was carrying and thus, the victims believed that defendant could have been concealing a gun and testified to feeling threatened and scared that defendant was going to shoot them. State v. Thomas, 2007-Ohio-3522, 2007 Ohio App. LEXIS 3254 (Ohio Ct. App., Cuyahoga County 2007).

As defendant, a dentist, admitted at trial that he was aware that he was under a Medicaid exclusion, which meant that he could not treat Medicaid patients and he could not be reimbursed for the rendering of any services to them, his trial counsel did not act ineffectively in violation of defendant's rights under U.S. Const. amend. VI and Ohio Const. art. I, § 10 when he failed to seek a jury instruction on mistake of fact in defendant's criminal matter on charges of Medicaid fraud and grand theft, in violation of R.C. 2913.40(B) and 2913.02, as such an instruction was not warranted under the evidence; knowingly, pursuant to R.C. 2901.22, was an element of each offense, and the evidence did not support a defense that defendant acted without intent to violate the law or that he acted under a mistake of fact. State v. DiNozzi, 2007 Ohio App. LEXIS 1579 (Ohio Ct. App., Licking County Apr. 6, 2007).

Even though jury instruction did not explicitly inform jury that one element of theft is that the act be undertaken without the consent of the owner, instruction on elements of theft was sufficiently clear: Mira v. Marshall, 806 F.2d 636, 1986 U.S. App. LEXIS 34162 (6th Cir. Ohio 1986).

**Insurance coverage**

For purposes of insurance coverage for theft, a conviction for a theft offense was not required: Columbiana County Bd. of Comm'rs v. Nationwide Ins. Co., 130 Ohio App. 3d 8, 719 N.E.2d 561, 1998 Ohio App. LEXIS 4399 (Ohio Ct. App., Columbiana County 1998).

**Intent**

Defendant's conviction for theft was not supported by sufficient evidence because she found her neighbor's dog, gave it a bath because it was flea infested and had blood on it, called the dog warden and posted photos on lost/found pet websites. The evidence did not establish that defendant had intent to deprive the owner of his dog because there was no evidence indicating that she tried to alter the dog's appearance before posting the pictures, or that she posted the pictures in an attempt to sell the dog, thus further depriving the owner. State v. Brown, 2019-Ohio-4663, 2019 Ohio App. LEXIS 4711 (Ohio Ct. App., Adams County 2019).

Defendant juvenile was properly adjudicated as delinquent for committing theft, as although she did not have a phone to fit the phone case that she took, and she did not wear clip-on earrings because her ears were pierced, that did not negate her intent to deprive the store of those items. In re E.A., 2016-Ohio-7281, 2016 Ohio App. LEXIS 4139 (Ohio Ct. App., Summit County 2016).

Conviction for theft of a motor vehicle was not against the manifest weight of the evidence because defendant acted with the purpose to deprive his ex-wife of the vehicle without her consent when he stabbed her nine times, left her covered with blood, and abandoned the vehicle in a deserted, dead-end alley. The finding regarding the manifest weight of the evidence was dispositive of defendant's sufficiency argument as well. State v. McGraw, 2010-Ohio-3949, 2010 Ohio App. LEXIS 3346 (Ohio Ct. App., Fayette County 2010).

As the State failed to show defendant acted with the necessary intent to commit the crime, defendant's conviction for theft by deception in violation of R.C. 2913.02(A)(3) was improper. It was not a case in which defendant accepted the victim's money and was never heard from again; rather, defendant returned to discuss the subject home remodeling work with the alleged victim. State v. Waiters, 2009-Ohio-1251, 2009 Ohio App. LEXIS 1049 (Ohio Ct. App., Cuyahoga County 2009).

Evidence was sufficient to prove that appellant juvenile intended to deprive the victim of his property for theft because the ATV was not returned to the victim's property; there was no evidence of any intention or effort to return the ATV, and the ATV was left in a location where it was unlikely that the victim, double amputee could recover it. It was not necessary that the pictures depicted the modifications to the ATV which allowed the victim to identify the ATV as his because he testified that he took the pictures and that they represented his ATV; moreover, appellant's stepbrother identified the ATV in the pictures as the one taken from the victim's barn. In re Moff, 2008-Ohio-1656, 2008 Ohio App. LEXIS 1424 (Ohio Ct. App., Portage County 2008).

Since a trial court specifically found that defendant had no purpose to commit a theft but intended only to play with a cashier when he told the cashier that he was "fixing to rob" him and put his hand in his pocket to represent that he had a concealed gun, the evidence was insufficient to sustain defendant's robbery conviction. The State failed to convince the trier of fact that defendant had an intent to deprive the cashier of his property, a necessary element of a theft offense. State v. Johnson, 2008-Ohio-4013, 2008 Ohio App. LEXIS 3397 (Ohio Ct. App., Montgomery County 2008).

Sufficient evidence supported defendant's theft conviction because there was ample evidence that defendant knowingly exerted control over the landlord's personal property without her consent and with a purpose to deprive the landlord of the property. The landlord gave defendant permission to use the items for only so long as the landlord chose to loan them to defendant; defendant's refusal to return the items, and her asportation of the items to another home after her eviction from the landlord's property, despite the request for their return, demonstrated defendant's clear and unambiguous intent to deprive the landlord of her property. State v. Smidt-Walker, 2008-Ohio-3034, 2008 Ohio App. LEXIS 2540 (Ohio Ct. App., Cuyahoga County 2008).

Trial court's determination that a juvenile was a delinquent minor due to his commission of two offenses was supported by the weight and sufficiency of the evidence, as there was sufficient proof that the juvenile took his girlfriend's car knowingly and without her authorization or permission, and as such, that act supported his conviction for receiving stolen property in violation of R.C. 2913.51(A) and (C); the evidence established the juvenile's intent to deprive the girlfriend of her property, such that his actions amounted to a theft offense under R.C. 2913.02. In re M.T., 2006-Ohio-3613, 2006 Ohio App. LEXIS 3522 (Ohio Ct. App., Franklin County 2006).

Statute on theft, R.C. 2913.02(A)(1), required the State to establish, beyond a reasonable doubt, defendant's intent to deprive "at the time" property was taken, but the intent to deprive did not have to be an intent to permanently deprive. State v. Haney, 2006-Ohio-4687, 2006 Ohio App. LEXIS 4600 (Ohio Ct. App., Mahoning County 2006).

Defendant was properly convicted of unauthorized use of a motor vehicle, under R.C. 2913.03, rather than grand theft of a motor vehicle, under R.C. 2913.02, as charged, as there was an issue as to whether he intended to permanently deprive the owner of the rented vehicle, as he testified he believed he was entitled to use the vehicle during its rental period. State v. Vrazalica, 2005-Ohio-1164, 2005 Ohio App. LEXIS 1148 (Ohio Ct. App., Cuyahoga County 2005).

Appellate court rejected defendant's argument that because he had no mens rea the State could not prosecute him for theft, in violation of R.C. 2913.02, and failure to maintain an endowment-care fund while operating a cemetery, in violation of R.C. 1721.21, on the basis of evidence which showed that he allowed the balance in the fund to fall below $50,000 and used money he withdrew for personal expenses. State v. Merkle, 2004-Ohio-1913, 2004 Ohio App. LEXIS 1666 (Ohio Ct. App., Hamilton County 2004).

When proving a violation of R.C. 2913.02(A)(2), (3), nonpayment alone is not sufficient to prove a party's intent not to pay. State v. Coleman, 2003-Ohio-5724, 2003 Ohio App. LEXIS 5118 (Ohio Ct. App., Champaign County 2003).

To prove a violation of R.C. 2913.02(A)(2), the State must show that at the time the defendant exceeds the scope of consent of the money's owner, defendant has the intent to deprive the owner of the money. State v. Coleman, 2003-Ohio-5724, 2003 Ohio App. LEXIS 5118 (Ohio Ct. App., Champaign County 2003).

**Introduction of stolen property into evidence**

In a prosecution for theft of several blouses in violation of R.C. 2913.02, it is not essential for conviction that the state introduce the blouses into evidence: State v. Williams, 16 Ohio App. 3d 232, 475 N.E.2d 168, 1984 Ohio App. LEXIS 12352 (Ohio Ct. App., Montgomery County 1984).

**Judgment entry**

Any oral mention by the trial court of alternate forms of theft was harmless because in the judgment entry, defendant was found guilty of theft by deception, which was the charge contained in the indictment. State v. Sims, 2016-Ohio-4763, 2016 Ohio App. LEXIS 2557 (Ohio Ct. App., Franklin County 2016).

Defendant was convicted of theft under R.C. 2913.02, not unauthorized use of property. While handwritten notations appeared on the journal entry, crossing out the phrase "Theft" and writing "Unauth Use Prop," since the notations were not immediately accompanied by the judge's signature or date and since there was no mention of unauthorized use of property during trial or sentencing, the notations were of no legal import. City of Cincinnati v. Walker, 2008-Ohio-4473, 2008 Ohio App. LEXIS 3779 (Ohio Ct. App., Hamilton County 2008).

**Larceny by trick**

The offense of larceny by trick, forbidden by this section, is not committed by causing a creditor to include false information in the statement of a lawful indebtedness, where the only result is to conceal a defendant's duty to reimburse the debtor who pays the obligation. In such case there is no larceny by trick of the sum paid: (decided under former analogous section) State v. Curtis, 2 Ohio App. 2d 31, 31 Ohio Op. 2d 72, 206 N.E.2d 217, 1965 Ohio App. LEXIS 571 (Ohio Ct. App., Miami County 1965).

Because theft is a lesser included offense of robbery, an indictment for robbery necessarily includes all the elements of all lesser included offenses, together with any of the special, statutory findings dictated by the evidence produced in the case. When an indictment charges a defendant with robbery, the defendant may be convicted of theft as a lesser included offense of robbery, and the degree of the offense will depend on the special finding of the value of the property stolen: State v. Smith, 2009-Ohio-787, 121 Ohio St. 3d 409, 905 N.E.2d 151, 2009 Ohio LEXIS 549 (Ohio 2009).

**Lesser included offenses**

Because there was evidence from which a reasonable inference could be drawn that the theft was committed without the use of force and that the jury could acquit on the charge of robbery, a jury instruction on the lesser included offense of theft was warranted, and it was error for the trial court to refuse to instruct the jury on the lesser included offense of theft. State v. Coker, 2014-Ohio-1210, 2014 Ohio App. LEXIS 1123 (Ohio Ct. App., Summit County 2014).

In a grand theft of a motor vehicle case, the court did not err in refusing to instruct on the lesser included offense of unauthorized use of a motor vehicle because defendant drove the motorcycle, which he took from the owner's front porch, 25-30 miles, while driving 110 miles per hour; defendant did not know the owner prior to taking the motorcycle. State v. Whitman, 2013-Ohio-5822, 2013 Ohio App. LEXIS 6123 (Ohio Ct. App., Ashtabula County 2013).

Where defendant was convicted by a jury of robbery, in violation of R.C. 2911.02(A)(2), as a lesser included offense of the original charge of aggravated robbery, the affirmative act by defendant of reaching into a car and ordering the victim to surrender the victim's money contained an implied threat of potential harm to the victim if the victim did not comply with the order. Thus, the trial court could rationally have found that the evidence did not support an instruction on the lesser included offense of mere theft, under R.C. 2913.02. State v. Cooper, 2012-Ohio-355, 2012 Ohio App. LEXIS 315 (Ohio Ct. App., Cuyahoga County 2012).

Defendant, charged with burglary, was not entitled to a lesser included offense instruction on criminal trespass, because a jury could not reasonably find defendant not guilty of burglary, as (1) the evidence showed defendant entered a house that was for sale, wherein defendant consumed candy and pop left out for people attending an open house showing, and (2) defendant did not have implied consent to consume the candy or pop, since defendant was not attending an open house showing when defendant consumed the items, so defendant committed a theft offense while in the house. State v. Benit, 2011-Ohio-6832, 2011 Ohio App. LEXIS 5649 (Ohio Ct. App., Franklin County 2011).

In a robbery case, a trial court did not err by refusing to instruct the jury on the lesser included offense of theft where the jury heard evidence that physical harm was inflicted in the course of a theft from a cab driver, and the jury heard evidence that no harm was inflicted from appellant. Because the case rested largely on the credibility of the witnesses, an appellate court was unable say that the jury would have reasonably rejected the greater offense of robbery. State v. Kunz, 2011-Ohio-3115, 2011 Ohio App. LEXIS 2636 (Ohio Ct. App., Wood County 2011).

As a jury could not reasonably have found defendant guilty of theft, in violation of R.C. 2913.02(A), but not guilty of robbery, in violation of R.C. 2911.02(A)(2), there was no error in the trial court's failure to give the jury a lesser included offense instruction on theft; defendant threatened one store clerk while demanding money, and he showed his gun to another store clerk in a second robbery, which also constituted a threat of physical harm. State v. Malloy, 2011-Ohio-30, 2011 Ohio App. LEXIS 20 (Ohio Ct. App., Clark County 2011).

Court did not commit plain error by failing to sua sponte instruct the jury on the lesser included offense of unauthorized use of a motor vehicle in defendant's trial for theft of a motor vehicle, because the evidence simply did not support an instruction on unauthorized use of a motor vehicle, as the ATV was never returned to the victim. State v. Johnson, 2010-Ohio-5703, 2010 Ohio App. LEXIS 4799 (Ohio Ct. App., Stark County 2010).

In a case involving theft of a motor vehicle under R.C. 2913.02, a trial court did not commit plain error by refusing to instruct the jury on the lesser included offense of unauthorized use of a motor vehicle because an all terrain vehicle was not returned to a teenager after it was borrowed by defendant and others. State v. Johnson, 2010-Ohio-3096, 2010 Ohio App. LEXIS 2555 (Ohio Ct. App., Stark County), vacated, sub. op., 2010-Ohio-5703, 2010 Ohio App. LEXIS 4799 (Ohio Ct. App., Stark County 2010).

Trial court did not err by failing to instruct the jury on the lesser-included offense of theft because the evidence did not support both an acquittal on the charged offense of aggravated robbery and a conviction on the lesser-included offense of theft. There was no testimony or other suggestion that the theft was committed, but that defendant did not have a gun at the time of the theft. State v. Smith, 2008-Ohio-6998, 2008 Ohio App. LEXIS 5855 (Ohio Ct. App., Trumbull County 2008).

Because robbery may be committed by either committing a theft or attempting to commit a theft, there are two possible ways to commit the offense: robbery by theft or robbery by attempted theft, and, if these two alternatives are essentially treated as separate offenses, then fifth-degree felony theft is a lesser included offense of robbery as statutorily defined in the alternative of robbery by theft, because it would impossible to ever commit a robbery by theft without also committing a theft. State v. Smith, 2008-Ohio-1260, 117 Ohio St. 3d 447, 884 N.E.2d 595, 2008 Ohio LEXIS 717 (Ohio 2008).

Theft, as defined in R.C. 2913.02, is a lesser included offense of robbery, as defined in R.C. 2911.02. State v. Smith, 2008-Ohio-1260, 117 Ohio St. 3d 447, 884 N.E.2d 595, 2008 Ohio LEXIS 717 (Ohio 2008).

Defendant was properly convicted of fifth-degree felony theft as a lesser included offense of robbery because it was necessary to clarify the test used to determine if one offense was a lesser included offense of another to provide that, when there were alternative ways to commit the greater crime, each alternative had to be compared to the lesser crime, and, applying this test to the crimes of robbery and theft, it was possible to commit robbery by either theft or attempted theft, and it was objectively impossible to commit robbery by theft without also committing theft. State v. Smith, 2008-Ohio-1260, 117 Ohio St. 3d 447, 884 N.E.2d 595, 2008 Ohio LEXIS 717 (Ohio 2008).

Trial court did not err in refusing to instruct the jury on the offense of theft as a lesser included offense of robbery because no reasonable juror could have rejected the robbery charge and concluded that the taking of the box from the victim was without force or the immediate threat of force, as defined by R.C. 2901.01(A). The victim testified that while he was trying to deliver a package, defendant grabbed it from him and shoved his shoulder into him in an attempt to get the victim to release the package. State v. Lancaster, 2008-Ohio-1247, 2008 Ohio App. LEXIS 1083 (Ohio Ct. App., Stark County 2008).

Trial court did not err in failing to instruct a jury in defendant's criminal trial on charges of robbery, in violation of R.C. 2911.02(A)(2) and (3), on the lesser included offense of theft, in violation of R.C. 2913.02, as robbery could be committed in the course of an attempted theft, in violation of R.C. 2913.02 and 2923.02, such that theft was not actually a lesser-included offense of robbery. State v. Lucky, 2008-Ohio-331, 2008 Ohio App. LEXIS 287 (Ohio Ct. App., Delaware County 2008).

In determining whether an offense is a lesser included offense of another when a statute sets forth mutually exclusive ways of committing the greater offense, a court is required to apply the second part of the test established in State v. Deem (1988), 40 Ohio St. 3d 205, 533 NE2d 294, paragraph three of the syllabus, to each alternative method of committing the greater offense. Theft, as defined in R.C. 2913.02, is a lesser included offense of robbery, as defined in R.C. 2911.02: State v. Smith, 2008-Ohio-1260, 117 Ohio St. 3d 447, 884 N.E.2d 595, 2008 Ohio LEXIS 717 (Ohio 2008).

In defendant's prosecution on a charge of grand theft of a motor vehicle, the trial court did not commit plain error in failing to instruct the jury on the lesser included offense of unauthorized use of a motor vehicle because the evidence revealed that defendant went to a car dealership, knowing that he had a suspended driver's license, told the co-owner of the dealership a fabricated story, and asked to test drive a vehicle with the intent to deprive the dealership of the vehicle. This was not a case of someone using a motor vehicle simply without the consent of the owner; instead, the evidence clearly showed that defendant took the motor vehicle through deceit and subterfuge with the intent to permanently deprive the dealership of its vehicle. State v. Meeks, 2007-Ohio-6559, 2007 Ohio App. LEXIS 5719 (Ohio Ct. App., Lake County 2007).

Trial court's refusal to give the jury an instruction on the lesser included offense of attempted theft, in violation of R.C. 2913.02(A) and 2923.02, was proper in defendant's criminal trial on a charge of, inter alia, theft, as the State successfully proved the elements of theft where defendant successfully exercised control over property from department stores when he left without paying for the items; as the evidence did not support the elements of attempt because defendant's failure to escape with the property did not prove that he made only an "attempt" at the theft, no such instruction was required. State v. Lee, 2007-Ohio-288, 2007 Ohio App. LEXIS 273 (Ohio Ct. App., Cuyahoga County 2007).

Defendant's conviction for theft under R.C. 2913.02 as a lesser-included offense of robbery was proper. While the offense of robbery, which does not include as an element the value of the property obtained, can be committed without the lesser offense of theft, which does require proof of the value of property, also being committed, the Ohio Supreme Court's decision in State v. Davis had earlier held that theft by threat is a lesser-included offense of robbery; thus, the court was constrained to adhere to the supreme court's decision. State v. Smith, 2006-Ohio-6980, 2006 Ohio App. LEXIS 6937 (Ohio Ct. App., Hamilton County 2006), aff'd, 2008-Ohio-1260, 117 Ohio St. 3d 447, 884 N.E.2d 595, 2008 Ohio LEXIS 717 (Ohio 2008).

Sufficient evidence supported defendant's robbery conviction because a reasonable jury could have found all of the elements of the offense of robbery, pursuant to R.C. 2911.02(A)(3), including the identification of defendant as the perpetrator, beyond a reasonable doubt. A neighbor of the gas station and the clerk testified that they identified defendant from a photo array provided by the police and police officers testified that the neighbor and clerk separately chose defendant's photograph from a photo array. State v. Accord, 2006-Ohio-2250, 2006 Ohio App. LEXIS 2088 (Ohio Ct. App., Fayette County 2006).

Defendant's conviction for theft under R.C. 2913.02 as a lesser-included offense of robbery was proper. While the offense of robbery, which does not include as an element the value of the property obtained, can be committed without the lesser offense of theft, which does require proof of the value of property, also being committed, the Ohio Supreme Court's decision in State v. Davis had earlier held that theft by threat is a lesser-included offense of robbery; thus, the court was constrained to adhere to the supreme court's decision. State v. Smith, 2006-Ohio-6980, 2006 Ohio App. LEXIS 6937 (Ohio Ct. App., Hamilton County 2006), aff'd, 2008-Ohio-1260, 117 Ohio St. 3d 447, 884 N.E.2d 595, 2008 Ohio LEXIS 717 (Ohio 2008).

Where defendant was on trial for theft, in violation of R.C. 2913.02, the trial court did not err in failing to give an instruction on the lesser-included offense of unauthorized use of a vehicle, in violation of R.C. 2913.03, as there was no evidence that defendant had any intent to return the van that he stole, which would have possibly supported such a lesser-included offense instruction pursuant to Crim.R. 31(C) and R.C. 2945.74; the jury could not have reasonably concluded that defendant did not have the purpose to deprive the victim of the van, based on the evidence. State v. Mayle, 2005-Ohio-1346, 2005 Ohio App. LEXIS 1294 (Ohio Ct. App., Carroll County 2005).

Theft is not a lesser included offense of aggravated robbery: State v. Bozeman, 1994 Ohio App. LEXIS 1747 (Ohio Ct. App., Montgomery County Apr. 20, 1994), dismissed, 71 Ohio St. 3d 1404, 641 N.E.2d 202, 1994 Ohio LEXIS 2530 (Ohio 1994).

Unauthorized use of property is not a lesser included offense to a charge of petty theft: State v. Canellos, 91 Ohio App. 3d 701, 633 N.E.2d 591, 1993 Ohio App. LEXIS 5604 (Ohio Ct. App., Butler County 1993).

Attempted theft by threat, as defined in R.C. 2913.02(A)(4) and 2923.02(A), may be a lesser included offense of robbery as defined in R.C. 2911.02(A) since (1) it is a crime of a lesser degree than robbery; (2) the greater offense of robbery cannot be committed without attempted theft by threat also having been committed; and (3) attempted theft by threat consists entirely of some, but not all, the elements of robbery: State v. Gates, 2 Ohio App. 3d 485, 442 N.E.2d 1321, 1981 Ohio App. LEXIS 10006 (Ohio Ct. App., Franklin County 1981).

**Liens**

Generally, the criminal laws should not be used to enforce an artisan's lien. A garageman's possessory lien is lost when he voluntarily relinquishes possession of a repaired vehicle back to the owner: State v. Vitale, 96 Ohio App. 3d 695, 645 N.E.2d 1277, 1994 Ohio App. LEXIS 3322 (Ohio Ct. App., Cuyahoga County 1994), dismissed, 71 Ohio St. 3d 1443, 644 N.E.2d 406, 1995 Ohio LEXIS 18 (Ohio 1995).

**Malicious prosecution**

Summary judgment was properly granted as the rentee did not establish her claim of malicious prosecution as the evidence established that the rentee was seven months in arrears on her payments and had ignored the company's efforts to recover the property. There existed probable cause to believe that the rentee acted with the requisite intent to commit theft of the merchandise she rented; the failure of the company and its general manager to comply with R.C. 2913.72(B) did not vitiate the existence of probable cause for a complaint for theft. Pierson v. Aaron's Rental, 2010-Ohio-5443, 2010 Ohio App. LEXIS 4604 (Ohio Ct. App., Franklin County 2010).

**Manifest weight of evidence**

Defendant's convictions for workers' compensation fraud and grand theft were not against manifest weight of evidence because forms, May 16, 2018 letter, and documentation related to defendant's enrollment in electronic benefits transfer and electronic funds transfer programs constituted persuasive, credible evidence that defendant was aware that he could not simultaneously work and receive temporary total disability benefits and, in doing so, intended to defraud Bureau of Workers' Compensation. State v. Doerschuk, 2021-Ohio-3686, 178 N.E.3d 1026, 2021 Ohio App. LEXIS 3586 (Ohio Ct. App., Franklin County 2021).

Defendant's conviction for theft was not against the manifest weight of evidence because she took the purse and placed it in the vehicle. Both officers testified that defendant did not immediately tell them she mistakenly thought she won the purse, and that defendant was not cooperative in identifying the purse in her vehicle. State v. Stone, 2020-Ohio-502, 2020 Ohio App. LEXIS 470 (Ohio Ct. App., Adams County 2020).

Manifest weight of the evidence supported defendant's conviction, as the victim's testimony was credible and consistent that defendant was the man who jumped in her car and robbed her at gunpoint. State v. Padgette, 2020-Ohio-672, 152 N.E.3d 504, 2020 Ohio App. LEXIS 607 (Ohio Ct. App., Cuyahoga County 2020).

Defendant's conviction of theft was not against the manifest weight of the evidence, because while the State did not produce physical or photographic evidence of the bank card defendant was charged with stealing, the victim testified that it had been inside the wallet recovered from defendant's car and a police officer testified that the card was added to the evidence log, photographed, and then returned to the victim. State v. Armocida, 2020-Ohio-3621, 2020 Ohio App. LEXIS 2572 (Ohio Ct. App., Mahoning County 2020).

Defendant's conviction for petty theft was not against the manifest weight of the evidence; a witness testified he observed defendant rolling up clothing items from the men's apparel department and placing the items in her shopping cart next to her purse, then inside her purse, and when she checked out, she did not pay for those items. State v. Haven, 2019-Ohio-973, 2019 Ohio App. LEXIS 1028 (Ohio Ct. App., Ashland County 2019).

Defendant's conviction for theft was not against the manifest weight of the evidence since the asset testified that he picked up DVDs and used a cutting device to remove a cell phone box from the store's prepaid phone wall. He also identified these items fell from his clothes as the ones taken from the store. And, since the officers found a pair of scissors in his pocket, the jury reasonably could have inferred that he used it to cut the cell phone box from its peg hook. State v. Seidowsky, 2019-Ohio-2610, 2019 Ohio App. LEXIS 2732 (Ohio Ct. App., Medina County 2019).

Manifest weight of the evidence supported defendant's conviction for attempted grand theft, as on surveillance video, defendant pulled his mother's minivan up next to an ATM and defendant's accomplice could be seen bending over and moving around the base of the ATM before standing back as the minivan lurched forward multiple times; an examination revealed that the ATM's mounting had been loosened, and it appeared as though a chain had been wrapped around it. State v. Dayton, 2019-Ohio-2635, 2019 Ohio App. LEXIS 2751 (Ohio Ct. App., Seneca County 2019).

Defendant's conviction on the second count of grand theft was not against the manifest weight of the evidence because the evidence supported the conclusion that he had no intent to purchase the kitchen cabinets with the money he solicited from the homeowner and that the money was instead used to remedy his construction company's overdrawn bank account. Defendant continued to deceive and mislead the homeowner as to the status of her cabinets for a series of months. State v. Burns, 2019-Ohio-2663, 2019 Ohio App. LEXIS 2779 (Ohio Ct. App., Portage County 2019).

Defendant's grand theft conviction was against the manifest weight of the evidence because the evidence did not support the conclusion that, at the time he was given the money, defendant had no intention to purchase kitchen cabinets and intended to permanently deprive the homeowner of the funds. The lack of evasiveness and refusal to continue performing before the fallout weigh against the prosecution in proving beyond a reasonable doubt that defendant intended to commit theft at the time he received the kitchen cabinet money. State v. Burns, 2019-Ohio-2663, 2019 Ohio App. LEXIS 2779 (Ohio Ct. App., Portage County 2019).

Defendant's conviction of theft from a person in a protected class, and attempt to commit an offense were not against the manifest weight of evidence, based upon the witness's testimony, the jury concluded that she was an owner of the account, the person responsible for control of the account on owner's behalf. The bank records supplemented her testimony regarding ownership of account and defendant had offered no evidence to contradict the conclusion that she was an owner or the person controlling the account. State v. Flanagan, 2019-Ohio-4665, 2019 Ohio App. LEXIS 4710 (Ohio Ct. App., Stark County 2019).

Defendant's conviction of robbery was not against the manifest weight of the evidence; although defendant claimed the theft of money was not credible because the initial police report did not indicate that money was stolen, a report from days after the incident did indicate that money was stolen, plus the victim and two police officers testified and it was for the jury to determine witness credibility. State v. Leasock, 2018-Ohio-1774, 2018 Ohio App. LEXIS 1894 (Ohio Ct. App., Trumbull County 2018).

Defendant's conviction for grand theft by deception under R.C. 2913.02(A)(3) was not against the manifest weight of the evidence, because while witnesses testified to some omissions in checking records, other evidence supported the conviction. State v. DeRemer, 2018-Ohio-3931, 120 N.E.3d 490, 2018 Ohio App. LEXIS 4254 (Ohio Ct. App., Summit County 2018).

Defendant's conviction was supported by the manifest weight of the evidence, as police officers observed defendant in the driveway of the victims' residence within minutes of a burglary, defendant was found in possession of the type of tool that effectuated the forced entry into the residence, and his DNA was found on the door of the victims' residence. State v. Frye, 2017-Ohio-7733, 2017 Ohio App. LEXIS 4066 (Ohio Ct. App., Richland County 2017).

Defendant's conviction for theft of a motor vehicle under R.C. 2913.02(A)(1), as opposed to the lesser included offense of unauthorized use of a motor vehicle under R.C. 2913.03, was not against the manifest weight of the evidence. The essential difference between the two offenses was the purpose to deprive the owner of property, and the evidence here that the vehicle was missing overnight and later found parked behind a house with defendant sleeping inside established that the vehicle was hidden behind a house to deprive the owner of his property State v. Emler, 2016-Ohio-5162, 2016 Ohio App. LEXIS 3031 (Ohio Ct. App., Coshocton County 2016).

Defendant's convictions for complicity to burglary and complicity to theft were not against the manifest weight of the evidence, although there was a conflict between the two co-defendants' version of events regarding whether defendant had knowledge of their actions in taking personal property from a house, as his overt acts of driving the getaway car amounted to aiding and abetting, and the credibility of the co-defendants was within the jury's province. State v. Wright, 2016-Ohio-5465, 2016 Ohio App. LEXIS 3349 (Ohio Ct. App., Hardin County 2016).

Manifest weight of the evidence supported defendant's conviction for theft, as the State presented substantial evidence that defendant was one of the perpetrators of a theft at a gas station; the jury could reasonably conclude based on surveillance videos, witness testimony, and scientific evidence establishing that defendant was the major contributor to DNA found on gloves dropped during the police pursuit, that defendant was one of the men seen on surveillance video who participated in the theft. State v. Littlejohn, 2015-Ohio-875, 2015 Ohio App. LEXIS 829 (Ohio Ct. App., Cuyahoga County 2015).

Defendant's convictions for theft, criminal damaging, and burglary were not against the manifest weight of the evidence when it was undisputed that the saliva on a cigarette butt found in a decedent's house matched defendant's, the decedent's daughter testified that she neither knew defendant nor gave him permission to enter the house, photographs corroborated the daughter's testimony, and the daughter testified that the house's contents were undisturbed prior to the break-in and the discovery of the cigarette butt. State v. Bell, 2015-Ohio-1294, 2015 Ohio App. LEXIS 1224 (Ohio Ct. App., Cuyahoga County 2015).

While it may have been true that defendant did not receive "more" or "better" treatment from the hospital than was required under federal law, no provision of federal law required the hospital to refrain from attempting to collect payment for those services. Because the trial court could reasonably have inferred that defendant had, as at least one of his purposes for having provided false identifying information, the purpose to avoid having to pay for the services he received from the hospital, the theft by deception was supported by the weight of the evidence. State v. Cullins, 2014-Ohio-2202, 2014 Ohio App. LEXIS 2128 (Ohio Ct. App., Montgomery County 2014).

Defendant's convictions for five counts of theft and one count of possessing criminal tools were not against the sufficiency or the manifest weight of the evidence because, although no witness was able to identify defendant as having been the perpetrator of any of the offenses, evidence was submitted to tie him to the crimes. The car that defendant owned and drove was consistent with the vehicle involved in the gas station drive-offs. State v. Cheatham, 2014-Ohio-1548, 2014 Ohio App. LEXIS 1500 (Ohio Ct. App., Ashland County 2014).

Defendant's convictions for five counts of theft and one count of possessing criminal tools were not against the sufficiency or the manifest weight of the evidence because, although no witness was able to identify defendant as having been the perpetrator of any of the offenses, evidence was submitted to tie him to the crimes. The car that defendant owned and drove was consistent with the vehicle involved in the gas station drive-offs. State v. Cheatham, 2014-Ohio-1546, 2014 Ohio App. LEXIS 1499 (Ohio Ct. App., Ashland County 2014).

Defendant's convictions for aggravated robbery with a firearm specification, felonious assault, and grand theft were not against the manifest weight of the evidence because the evidence showed that defendant hit the victim in the head with a gun, resulting in hospitalization, and the victim's estranged wife, having known him prior to the incident, identified defendant as the assailant. Additionally, a drop of blood from the victim was found on defendant's shoe, defendant's shoes matched a distinctive shoe print from the scene, and items from the robbery were found abandoned with the shirt that defendant had been wearing. State v. Palmer, 2014-Ohio-5491, 2014 Ohio App. LEXIS 5322 (Ohio Ct. App., Butler County 2014).

Defendant's conviction of attempted theft from a store was not against the manifest weight of the evidence, as there was testimony that defendant took a "substantial step" toward the commission of theft; defendant stuffed underwear into her purse even though she had nothing else in her hands. State v. Radcliff, 2014-Ohio-3981, 2014 Ohio App. LEXIS 3898 (Ohio Ct. App., Shelby County 2014).

Defendant's theft conviction was not against the manifest weight of the evidence because (1) defendant gave no notice, under Crim.R. 12.1, of an alleged alibi, nor did defendant seek a jury instruction on the alleged alibi or so testify, and the evidence did not support the alibi, and (2) compelling circumstantial evidence showed defendant's guilt. State v. Schuttinger, 2013-Ohio-5793, 2013 Ohio App. LEXIS 6088 (Ohio Ct. App., Franklin County 2013).

Defendant's theft conviction was not against the manifest weight of the evidence because the victim's neighbor saw defendant taking things out of the victim's home, and the police found many of the victim's in the backyard of the neighbor, exactly where he saw defendant walking with items from the victim's house. State v. Jennings, 2013-Ohio-5428, 2013 Ohio App. LEXIS 5674 (Ohio Ct. App., Cuyahoga County 2013).

While there was contrasting testimony by defendant and a store loss prevention specialist, the trier of fact's determination that defendant was guilty of petty theft was not against the manifest weight of the evidence. State v. Csillag, 2013-Ohio-4608, 2013 Ohio App. LEXIS 4810 (Ohio Ct. App., Franklin County 2013).

Defendant's theft convictions were not against the manifest weight of the evidence because five realtors testified that defendant told them he brought an acquaintance to look at houses because she was upset over the death of a relative and he actively distracted the realtors away from the acquaintance by either the use of conversation or by physically placing himself in their lines of sight, obstructing their view of the acquaintance as she stole items from the homes. State v. Shipley, 2013-Ohio-4055, 2013 Ohio App. LEXIS 4216 (Ohio Ct. App., Franklin County 2013).

While there was conflicting evidence presented at trial, defendant's conviction was not against the manifest weight of the evidence, as the trier of fact was in the best position to evaluate the credibility of the witnesses. City of Cuyahoga Falls v. Campanalie, 2013-Ohio-3509, 2013 Ohio App. LEXIS 3611 (Ohio Ct. App., Summit County 2013).

Defendant's conviction for theft of drugs was not against the manifest weight of the evidence, as an individual in a red shirt identified as defendant was seen breaking a window on the door of a residence, and the individual in the red shirt was seen coming from the back of the residence with a full backpack. State v. Troche, 2013-Ohio-3110, 2013 Ohio App. LEXIS 3159 (Ohio Ct. App., Richland County 2013).

In a prosecution on charges of having weapons while under disability, grand theft, safecracking, and possessing criminal tools, the manifest weight of the evidence showed that defendant possessed the firearms, safes, and criminal tools, in that his codefendant initially implicated defendant in the crimes, one victim explained that several items that were stolen from him were heavy and would require two people to lift them, and a sheriff testified that defendant was driving a van with the stolen goods inside. State v. Stodgel, 2013-Ohio-1109, 2013 Ohio App. LEXIS 1004 (Ohio Ct. App., Fayette County 2013).

In a prosecution on charges of having weapons while under disability and grand theft, the manifest weight of the evidence showed that the firearms were operable at the time defendant possessed them as the victim testified that several guns were stolen from his home and that, after he received these guns from police, he successfully fired every firearm. Additionally, the victim stated that several of the firearms fired successfully a few months before the burglary. State v. Stodgel, 2013-Ohio-1109, 2013 Ohio App. LEXIS 1004 (Ohio Ct. App., Fayette County 2013).



Manifest weight of the evidence supported defendant's guilt for attempted theft and tampering with records because, with knowledge of his client's diminished mental capacity, defendant took valid will and trust documents, altered them on his work computer to make himself the sole beneficiary of the trust, and had the client sign them. Defendant's false statement to the notary, his failure to disclose to his employer that he was now the sole beneficiary of the trust, and his attempts to deny any knowledge about the transaction, demonstrated that de knew of the client's diminished mental capacity and took advantage of her condition for his own financial gain. State v. Dilley, 2012-Ohio-5288, 2012 Ohio App. LEXIS 4617 (Ohio Ct. App., Cuyahoga County 2012), writ denied, 2017-Ohio-9184, 2017 Ohio App. LEXIS 5699 (Ohio Ct. App., Cuyahoga County 2017).

Weight of the evidence supported the finding that appellant was delinquent for having committed theft and receiving stolen property because the juvenile court found that no evidence existed to show that appellant really texted anyone and that the entire attempt was a poor effort to reduce appellant's culpability. Also, the village chief testified that appellant had initially confessed, that there was blood on the stolen dirt bike and appellant was covered with road rash, and that the witness who had already been sentenced for his involvement in the offenses had nothing to gain by testifying against appellant. In re Cory P., 2012-Ohio-5453, 2012 Ohio App. LEXIS 4742 (Ohio Ct. App., Tuscarawas County 2012).

Convictions for burglary and theft from an elderly person was not against the manifest weight of evidence. No evidence indicated that anyone other than defendant was in the victim's home the day the guitar went missing, the victim testified that defendant inquired about his guitar and knew that it would be unattended while the victim napped, another witness saw defendant leave the victim's driveway with a guitar case, and a different witness testified that defendant tried to sell him the guitar. Moreover, defendant gave different versions of what happened. State v. Stapleton, 2012-Ohio-4964, 2012 Ohio App. LEXIS 4341 (Ohio Ct. App., Scioto County 2012).

Defendant's conviction for theft with an elderly specification was not against the manifest weight of the evidence, as two police officers testified that they saw defendant exit through a window of a house prior to defendant's apprehension and arrest; they identified defendant by defendant's face, not by defendant's clothing. State v. Townsend, 2012-Ohio-4400, 2012 Ohio App. LEXIS 3866 (Ohio Ct. App., Cuyahoga County 2012).

Defendants' convictions of burglary, theft, grand theft, and firearm specifications were not against the manifest weight of the evidence, as 1) an unidentified 911 caller stated he saw two men enter a house and one man acting as a lookout; 2) an officer testified that he saw three men near the residence exchanging bags, that two fled, and that defendant was caught; 3) bags containing items taken from the residence, including guns, were found within 10 feet of defendant; and 4) other stolen items were found inside the police cruiser where defendant was secured. State v. Wilson, 2012-Ohio-3567, 2012 Ohio App. LEXIS 3154 (Ohio Ct. App., Cuyahoga County 2012).

Guilty verdict finding defendant guilty of theft by deception was not against the manifest weight of the evidence as, based on the testimony of defendant's employee and a special agent, the jury could have reasonably believed that defendant knew that ambulette clients had to be transported in wheelchairs, in that the employee testified that, when she addressed to defendant her concerns that clients were not being transported in wheelchairs, defendant told her it was none of her business, and defendant told the agent, during his recorded interview, that he knew that ambulette patients had to be transported in a wheelchair, that he could only bill for services provided, and that various patients were not transported in the ambulette in a wheelchair. State v. Kimkhe, 2012-Ohio-1964, 2012 Ohio App. LEXIS 1730 (Ohio Ct. App., Franklin County 2012).

Defendant's convictions of burglary and theft were not against the manifest weight of the evidence where: (1) defendant stated he did not see who brought the TV and its stand into the unit because he had been there only a short time, but admitted he was wearing cream-colored cargo shorts that night; (2) although the witness testified the other of the two men carrying the victim's items wore blue jean shorts, and although the officer testified the accomplice was wearing jean shorts, defendant stated he thought that the accomplice was wearing black pants; (3) defendant did not remember the accomplice raising his hand to state that he committed the crimes, but the resident did; (4) the resident could not recall anything about the man who helped the accomplice bring the items inside; and (5) the jury could determine that the witness and the officer presented credible versions of events that were corroborated by the victim, another officer, and the photos, and that defendant's evidence was unpersuasive and self-serving. State v. Grice, 2012-Ohio-1938, 2012 Ohio App. LEXIS 1704 (Ohio Ct. App., Cuyahoga County 2012).

Convictions for robbery, theft, and felonious assault were not against the manifest weight of the evidence based on the fact that a hospital victim was initially unsure of her identification of defendant as the perpetrator; the victim saw the picture of defendant shortly after being released from the hospital, the jury could have reasonably attributed any initial uncertainty to nervousness and the effects of pain medication, and the victim was 100 percent certain at trial that defendant was her attacker. State v. Colley, 2010-Ohio-4834, 2010 Ohio App. LEXIS 4050 (Ohio Ct. App., Scioto County 2010).

Convictions for theft, vandalism, possessing criminal tools, and receiving stolen property were supported by the manifest weight of the evidence where the evidence showed that a retail store employee observed someone taking spools of electrical wiring, defendant was found in possession of those items after a traffic stop, and he was in possession of distinctive bolt cutters. Moreover, after his arrest and the impounding of his vehicle, defendant's vehicle was stolen from the impound lot, he was later found driving a vehicle with the stolen vehicle's plates, and he was again found in possession of bolt cutters with a distinctive mark. State v. Hundley, 2010-Ohio-4640, 2010 Ohio App. LEXIS 4001 (Ohio Ct. App., Hamilton County 2010).

Conviction for theft under R.C. 2913.02 was not against the manifest weight of the evidence because, even though an appellate court reviewed credibility when considering such a challenge, the credibility of the witnesses was primarily for the trier of fact; a judge was in the best position to view the witnesses and observe their demeanor. A victim stated that defendant stole money out of her purse when he entered her residence to retrieve a cigarette, but defendant denied coming to the house to request a cigarette, and he stated that the victim's testimony was not credible due to a relationship between the victim, her daughter, and the mother of defendant's child. State v. Benson, 2009-Ohio-6741, 2009 Ohio App. LEXIS 5672 (Ohio Ct. App., Butler County 2009).

In a theft case under R.C. 2913.02(A)(1), a conviction was not against the manifest weight of the evidence because the jury did not lose its way in believing the testimony of the State's witnesses and disbelieving defendant's testimony. Although defendant testified that his cashing checks made payable to a mortgage company was in line with company procedure, the State's witnesses testified to the contrary; moreover, defendant's own testimony could have led the jury to believe that he knew the checks were the property of the mortgage company, and his refusal to return the money when asked to do so led to the inference that defendant intended to deprive the mortgage company of its funds. State v. Arnold, 2009-Ohio-6077, 2009 Ohio App. LEXIS 5105 (Ohio Ct. App., Summit County 2009).

Conviction for theft under R.C. 2913.02(A)(1), (2) was not against the manifest weight of the evidence because there was no evidence that anyone other than defendant was in possession of a set of earrings after a jewelry store employee placed them on a store counter; moreover, the employee's credibility was not challenged during her testimony. State v. Anderson, 2009-Ohio-5136, 2009 Ohio App. LEXIS 4340 (Ohio Ct. App., Delaware County 2009).

**Mental status**

In a case in which defendant stole items from a grocery store, the trial court did not err by not allowing the defense to argue the effect of defendant's medication on her mental status during closing argument, where there was not sufficient evidence for the defense to argue an affirmative defense. Moreover, there was sufficient evidence to show that defendant had her faculties about her while in the store. State v. Peters, 2011-Ohio-3132, 2011 Ohio App. LEXIS 2650 (Ohio Ct. App., Ashland County 2011).

**Merger**

Defendant had not established the trial court committed plain error in failing to merge theft and receiving stolen property offenses, as the same facts were not used to convict him of both offenses, and each offense relied on different episodes of conduct; the theft was committed after he set up a meeting on Facebook posing as a buyer, met with the seller, and snatched a ring from the seller, while the receiving stolen property offense was based upon his conduct of selling the ring at a pawn shop. State v. Green, 2021-Ohio-2412, 2021 Ohio App. LEXIS 2377 (Ohio Ct. App., Mahoning County 2021).

Trial court properly declined to merge defendant's robbery and theft convictions because the two convictions arose out of a single incident involving theft and threats made against two victims, a pharmacist and another store employee, and thus, there was separate, identifiable harm caused by the separate threats made during the separate theft offenses. State v. Parcher, 2020-Ohio-293, 2020 Ohio App. LEXIS 258 (Ohio Ct. App., Lucas County 2020).

Counts of grand theft and burglary did not merge for the purpose of sentencing because the offenses were committed separately, and thus, they were not allied offenses of similar import; the burglary offense, while occurring on the same date as the grand theft offense, occurred at a different home than the grand theft, and although the homes of the victims were in the same complex, they were not the same apartments. State v. Rose, 2017-Ohio-8435, 2017 Ohio App. LEXIS 4836 (Ohio Ct. App., Hardin County 2017).

Defendant's burglary and theft convictions did not merge because the victim explained that their sense of privacy had been invaded, which related to the harm that resulted from the burglary offenses, and that she suffered economic damage from the theft offenses, and, as such, the harm from each offense was separate and identifiable. State v. Gillman, 2015-Ohio-4421, 46 N.E.3d 130, 2015 Ohio App. LEXIS 4303 (Ohio Ct. App., Vinton County 2015).

Trial court committed plain err by failing to merge the theft offenses for purposes of sentencing because defendant committed the theft offenses based upon her relationship to the agency as a Medicaid service provider. Thus, the thefts were committed while she was in the same employment, capacity, or relationship to the agency. State v. Mahone, 2014-Ohio-1251, 2014 Ohio App. LEXIS 1128 (Ohio Ct. App., Franklin County 2014).

Although convictions of theft and passing bad checks were allied offenses of similar import, merger was avoided per R.C. 2941.25(B) because defendant's conduct in stealing a payroll check was not the same conduct in which defendant engaged when he cashed it. The two offenses were therefore committed separately. State v. Rogers, 2012-Ohio-4451, 2012 Ohio App. LEXIS 3913 (Ohio Ct. App., Greene County 2012).

Trial court did not err by failing to merge defendant's conviction for possession of criminal tools in violation of R.C. 2923.24(A) with his conviction for theft in violation of R.C. 2913.02(A)(1) because defendant possessed the criminal tools with an animus separate from the theft offense; concealing one's identity and preventing one's subsequent apprehension are distinct and separate purposes or motives (animus) from committing the theft offense, itself. State v. Brewer, 2012-Ohio-3899, 2012 Ohio App. LEXIS 3438 (Ohio Ct. App., Wyandot County 2012).

Trial court did not err by failing to merge defendant's convictions for theft and breaking and entering because the offenses were not allied offenses under R.C. 2941.25(A); theft in violation of R.C. 2913.02(A)(1) and breaking and entering in violation of R.C. 2911.13(A) cannot be committed with the same conduct. State v. Brewer, 2012-Ohio-3899, 2012 Ohio App. LEXIS 3438 (Ohio Ct. App., Wyandot County 2012).

Trial court erred in refusing to merge the theft and possession of criminal tools offenses for which defendant was convicted and sentenced, as they were allied offenses of similar import subject to merger under R.C. 2941.25 since it was undisputed that the tools used during the commission of the theft, namely, the drill, wrench, pipe and wire cutters, were also the subject of the possession of criminal tools charge and that he used those tools in removing the air conditioning unit from the church premises, the subject of the theft charge, thus, both offenses were committed with the same animus. State v. Simmonds, 2012-Ohio-1479, 2012 Ohio App. LEXIS 1275 (Ohio Ct. App., Clermont County 2012).

Where defendant was charged with removing government funds from disabled persons' accounts, he pleaded guilty to 15 counts of theft under R.C. 2913.02(A)(1) and one count of forgery under R.C. 2913.31(A)(2) in four different cases; the trial court did not err by failing to merge all of the counts for sentencing. Because defendant committed ten different acts of theft against ten different victims in the first case, these offenses were not allied under R.C. 2941.25(A) and could be separately punished. State v. Snuffer, 2011-Ohio-6430, 2011 Ohio App. LEXIS 5287 (Ohio Ct. App., Cuyahoga County 2011), overruled in part, State v. Rogers, 2013-Ohio-3235, 994 N.E.2d 499, 2013 Ohio App. LEXIS 3326 (Ohio Ct. App., Cuyahoga County 2013).

Trial court did not err in imposing consecutive sentences because aggravated burglary under R.C. 2911.12(A)(1), safecracking under R.C. 2911.31(A), and grand theft under R.C. 2913.02(A) were not allied offenses of similar import subject to merger under R.C. 2941.25(A) in that each required a separate and distinct animus. Theft involved knowingly obtaining property of another with the intent to deprive the owner thereof, while safecracking involved entry into a safe with the purpose to commit an offense; because the issue of control was distinct and separate from the issue of entry, defendant could be convicted of safecracking without being guilty of a theft as long as he had the purpose to commit an offense. Similarly, defendant committed burglary with different conduct and a separate animus from safecracking and grand theft because, in order to violate R.C. 2911.12(A)(1), defendant had to, by force, stealth, or deception, trespass in an occupied structure intending to commit a criminal offense. State v. Crosby, 2011-Ohio-4907, 2011 Ohio App. LEXIS 4039 (Ohio Ct. App., Clermont County 2011).

Where defendant was convicted of eight counts of robbery in violation of R.C. 2911.02(A)(2), (3) and four counts of theft under R.C. 2913.02 arising out of his robbery of four pharmacies, the offenses should have been merged under R.C. 2941.25 prior to sentencing because the robbery and theft charges arising from each robbery stemmed from the same conduct as they involved the same items and the same victim. State v. Taylor, 2011-Ohio-3162, 2011 Ohio App. LEXIS 2663 (Ohio Ct. App., Franklin County 2011).

**Method of payment**

Record reflects that the victim borrowed money from family members in order to be able to pay defendant. The fact that some of the payments were made directly to defendant by the family member on the victim's behalf was inconsequential to defendant's conviction for grand theft. State v. Keith, 2008-Ohio-348, 2008 Ohio App. LEXIS 297 (Ohio Ct. App., Butler County 2008).

**Mistake of fact defense**

Appeal from a theft conviction based on defendant's Medicaid billing practices was found to have no merit because defendant did not show that she received ineffective assistance of counsel under U.S. Const. amend. VI based on a failure to present former R.C. 5111.02 (See now R.C. § 5164.02), 42 C.F.R. § 410.78, or R.C. 5111.026 in support of a mistake of fact defense; R.C. 5111.026 had never been enacted, R.C. 5111.02 was not helpful to the defense since it did not relate to reimbursement for the machines at issue in this case, and 42 C.F.R. § 410.78 related to Medicare's coverage for "telehealth" services. Moreover, defense counsel was not ineffective due to a failure to call certain witnesses because defendant did not explain what testimony would have been provided to support her mistake of fact defense, and nothing in the record showed what the witnesses would have testified to. State v. Cooper, 2009-Ohio-6275, 2009 Ohio App. LEXIS 5264 (Ohio Ct. App., Franklin County 2009).

In defendant's criminal trial on a charge of theft and receiving stolen property, in violation of R.C. 2913.02(A)(1) and 2913.51(A), where defendant had admitted that he transferred title to his boat and trailer to his daughter prior to the theft of those items, the trial court properly denied his request for an instruction on "mistake of fact"; defendant's claim that he hired two "street guys" to get the items back for him did not support a mistake of fact defense and instruction where he knew he no longer held title to them. State v. Feltner, 2007-Ohio-866, 2007 Ohio App. LEXIS 773 (Ohio Ct. App., Greene County 2007).



**Motion for acquittal**

Defendant's claim that the trial court erred by denying his motion for acquittal was without merit because the record showed that defendant systematically withdrew, without the victim's knowledge or consent, amounts of money from the victim's bank account vastly in excess of the amount that the victim had requested to be withdrawn; moreover, defendant capitalized on the victim's trust and disability in order to take cash and personal property from the victim. State v. Barton, 2018-Ohio-1877, 2018 Ohio App. LEXIS 2008 (Ohio Ct. App., Wood County 2018).

Defendant's motion for acquittal was properly denied as reasonable minds could have reached different conclusions as to the material elements of the crime of theft and there was an abundance of evidence that defendant was caught in the act of exerting control over the property of another with the intent to deprive that person of the property; an eyewitness confirmed that the victim had not given anyone permission to touch his tools, and that it appeared to be simple theft. State v. King, 2005-Ohio-4656, 2005 Ohio App. LEXIS 4184 (Ohio Ct. App., Lake County 2005).

**Motor vehicle repairs**

There was insufficient evidence to support a conviction concerning an alleged theft of services without consent where the defendant regained possession of his vehicle without paying for repairs: State v. Majid, 2009-Ohio-3075, 182 Ohio App. 3d 730, 914 N.E.2d 1113, 2009 Ohio App. LEXIS 2584 (Ohio Ct. App., Cuyahoga County 2009).

**Motor vehicles**

Trial court did not commit plain error in not defining the term "vehicle" in instructing the jury on the theft of a motor vehicle crime, relating to defendant's theft of an ATV, as, pursuant to R.C. 4501.01(B), "motor vehicle" included an ATV. State v. Henry, 2012-Ohio-371, 2012 Ohio App. LEXIS 326 (Ohio Ct. App., Gallia County 2012).

Sufficient evidence supported the aggravated robbery conviction; the object of the underlying theft offense, the motor vehicle, did simultaneously satisfy the element of being a deadly weapon because defendant could have stolen the car without using it as a weapon, distinguishing the aggravated robbery from the theft offense. State v. Quinonez, 2011-Ohio-3064, 2011 Ohio App. LEXIS 2601 (Ohio Ct. App., Cuyahoga County 2011).

Defendant's convictions for robbery, felonious assault, and theft of a motor vehicle were not against the manifest weight of the evidence where witnesses' testimony contradicted defendant's testimony and corroborated the victim's version of the incident. An independent witness testified that she observed defendant punching the victim before he pulled the victim from the car and drove away, leaving the victim in the middle of the street, and, contrary to defendant's testimony that the victim crashed the car and deployed the airbags before leaving the car, the responding police officer testified that he did not observe any debris or evidence of a car accident at the scene. State v. Givan, 2011-Ohio-100, 2011 Ohio App. LEXIS 86 (Ohio Ct. App., Cuyahoga County 2011).

Defendant, having taken the victim's vehicle, was properly convicted of grand theft of a motor vehicle because, while defendant argued that his motive in taking the car was to conceal evidence of the murder, and not to deprive the victim of the vehicle, the method that he chose to accomplish that was by stealing the vehicle and moving it to a different location without the consent of the owner (the owner's body was in the trunk). It was abundantly clear that, in taking the vehicle and moving it to another location, defendant's purpose, by implication, was to deprive the victim of his property pursuant to the language of the statute, and the evidence suggested that defendant was in possession of the firearm when he moved the vehicle, and the jury was free to make that finding and convict on the firearm specification attendant to the grand theft of a motor vehicle. State v. Russell, 2007-Ohio-137, 2007 Ohio App. LEXIS 129 (Ohio Ct. App., Montgomery County 2007).

A defendant "knowingly obtain(s) or exert(s) control over" a motor vehicle, for purposes of committing a theft offense under R.C. 2913.02, when the defendant has rendered the vehicle immediately capable of movement: State v. Hope, 9 Ohio App. 3d 65, 458 N.E.2d 414, 1983 Ohio App. LEXIS 11009 (Ohio Ct. App., Cuyahoga County 1983).



**Multiple counts**

Sufficient evidence supported defendant's kidnapping conviction because the evidence revealed that defendant and his brother, after binding the two victims with cords and dog leashes, defendant stole $750, a video game player, 23 video games, and a cellular phone. Because inconsistent verdicts on different counts of a multi-count indictment did not justify overturning a verdict of guilt, defendant's conviction for kidnapping was not required to be overturned based on the jury finding him guilty of misdemeanor theft instead of felony theft. State v. Williams, 2007-Ohio-4577, 2007 Ohio App. LEXIS 4127 (Ohio Ct. App., Cuyahoga County 2007).

In affirming convictions, appeals court decided grand theft of auto under R.C. 2913.02(A)(2), (B)(5) and unauthorized use of auto under R.C. 2913.03(B) were not allied offences of similar import requiring a sentence merger under R.C. 2941.25; grand theft required proof of intent to deprive, while unauthorized use did not. State v. Whited, 2003-Ohio-5747, 2003 Ohio App. LEXIS 5114 (Ohio Ct. App., Champaign County 2003).

The elements of theft under R.C. 2913.02(A)(1) and safecracking under R.C. 2911.31(A) do not correspond to such a degree that the commission of one offense necessarily results in the commission of the other, since each includes a distinctive element not included in the other: State v. Metcalf, 1998 Ohio App. LEXIS 1098 (Ohio Ct. App., Highland County Mar. 23, 1998).

Where defendant in one act steals money from two purses, each belonging to a different person but left in the same automobile, it is error for the trial court to sentence defendant for two separate theft offenses, as the thefts constituted a single act with a singular intent and should have merged under R.C. 2941.25(A): State v. Coffman, 16 Ohio App. 3d 200, 475 N.E.2d 139, 1984 Ohio App. LEXIS 12340 (Ohio Ct. App., Franklin County 1984).

The act of stealing a motor vehicle containing personal property constitutes one offense and a defendant may not be additionally convicted of stealing the personalty: State v. Fischer, 52 Ohio App. 2d 53, 6 Ohio Op. 3d 40, 368 N.E.2d 332, 1977 Ohio App. LEXIS 6938 (Ohio Ct. App., Clermont County 1977).

Under R.C. 2941.25(A) a thief may be charged with both theft and receiving stolen goods, but he may be convicted of only one: Maumee v. Geiger, 45 Ohio St. 2d 238, 74 Ohio Op. 2d 380, 344 N.E.2d 133, 1976 Ohio LEXIS 567 (Ohio 1976).

**Multiple offenses**

Defendant may be tried both for theft from an elderly person and for engaging in a hearing aid business without a license; while R.C. 2941.25 protects against multiple punishments for the same criminal conduct, the statutorily defined elements of the offenses are not of similar import, such that the commission of one of the crimes results in the commission of the other. State v. Wright, 2005-Ohio-3907, 2005 Ohio App. LEXIS 3596 (Ohio Ct. App., Clermont County 2005), rev'd, 2006-Ohio-2109, 109 Ohio St. 3d 313, 847 N.E.2d 1174, 2006 Ohio LEXIS 1161 (Ohio 2006).

**No contest plea**

Insufficient evidence supported defendant's conviction for the no contest plea to three counts of petty theft because at no point did the State indicate that defendant removed the items from the store without payment or indicate that the items were "taken" from the store with the purpose to deprive, nor did it state that he obtained the items without the consent or beyond the scope of consent of the owner, by deception, threat, or intimidation. State v. Jenkins, 2016-Ohio-1428, 2016 Ohio App. LEXIS 1307 (Ohio Ct. App., Hancock County 2016).

Trial court erred in making a finding of defendant's guilt after defendant pleaded no contest to misdemeanor theft because the trial court did not make statutorily required explanation of circumstances, and neither the trial court's reliance, in part, on its earlier review of the complaint nor the trial court's consideration of defendant's plea as a basis for the finding of guilt was sufficient to satisfy the statutorily required explanation of circumstances. State v. Horvath, 2015-Ohio-4729, 49 N.E.3d 847, 2015 Ohio App. LEXIS 4606 (Ohio Ct. App., Seneca County 2015).

After the entry of a no contest plea, a trial court was obligated to find appellant guilty as charged where he did not object to the information after the reading of the statement of facts; the indictment and the statement of facts recited the necessary elements of grand theft. The plea of no contest waived alleged errors at trial, including due process and prosecutorial misconduct claims. State v. Bullard, 2013-Ohio-3313, 2013 Ohio App. LEXIS 3382 (Ohio Ct. App., Clermont County 2013).

Defendant's entry of a no contest plea pursuant to Crim.R. 11(B)(2) to a charge of theft by deception, in violation of R.C. 2913.02(A)(2), based on her having stopped payment on post-dated checks that she had provided to a lender under a payday loan agreement, precluded her from asserting on appeal that the conviction was erroneous due to an alleged lack of proof that she had acted deceptively; her plea constituted an admission to the allegations contained in the charging instrument. State v. Widener, 2007-Ohio-429, 2007 Ohio App. LEXIS 381 (Ohio Ct. App., Darke County 2007).

**Nonprofit corporation**

A nonprofit corporation was properly convicted of grand theft where its officers agreed, essentially, to steal money that was mistakenly wired to the organization's account: State v. Black on Black Crime, Inc., 136 Ohio App. 3d 436, 736 N.E.2d 962, 1999 Ohio App. LEXIS 6360 (Ohio Ct. App., Cuyahoga County 1999).

**—Aggravated robbery**

Defendant's claim that theft could not be a lesser included offense of aggravated robbery was rejected as defendant negotiated a plea bargain to a reduced charge of theft and waived any right to claim that the theft offense had not been indicted by a grand jury; further, any error was barred by the doctrine of invited errors. State v. Steele, 2005-Ohio-4786, 2005 Ohio App. LEXIS 4289 (Ohio Ct. App., Franklin County 2005).

**Other offenses**

**—Hearing aid business**

Defendant may be tried both for theft from an elderly person and for engaging in a hearing aid business without a license; while R.C. 2941.25 protects against multiple punishments for the same criminal conduct, the statutorily defined elements of the offenses are not of similar import, such that the commission of one of the crimes results in the commission of the other. State v. Wright, 2005-Ohio-3907, 2005 Ohio App. LEXIS 3596 (Ohio Ct. App., Clermont County 2005), rev'd, 2006-Ohio-2109, 109 Ohio St. 3d 313, 847 N.E.2d 1174, 2006 Ohio LEXIS 1161 (Ohio 2006).

Trial court did not err in permitting defendant to be tried both for theft from an elderly person and for engaging in a hearing aid business without a license; while R.C. 2941.25 protected against multiple punishments for the same criminal conduct, the statutorily defined elements of the offenses were not of similar import, such that the commission of one of the crimes resulted in the commission of the other. State v. Wright, 2005-Ohio-3907, 2005 Ohio App. LEXIS 3596 (Ohio Ct. App., Clermont County 2005), rev'd, 2006-Ohio-2109, 109 Ohio St. 3d 313, 847 N.E.2d 1174, 2006 Ohio LEXIS 1161 (Ohio 2006).

**—Racketeering**

Where a chiropractor, workers' compensation specialist, and a hospital and its parent company were never charged with or convicted of theft by threat or deception, in violation of R.C. 2913.02(A)(3) and (4), based on the fact that the specialist recommended to an injured hospital employee that she could seek chiropractic care with the particular chiropractor rather than previously recommended physical therapy, and that such chiropractic care led to injuries that continually caused the employee pain, the employee's claim that the parties were engaged in a pattern of corrupt activity by threatening and/or deceiving her into receiving such treatment, in violation of R.C. 2923.32 and 2923.21, completely lacked merit. Wilson v. Marino, 2005-Ohio-6521, 164 Ohio App. 3d 662, 843 N.E.2d 849, 2005 Ohio App. LEXIS 5853 (Ohio Ct. App., Lucas County 2005).

**—Robbery**

Sufficient evidence supported defendant's aggravated robbery conviction, as the facts established defendant committed a theft; the fact that defendant put a phone in his pocket and never returned it to the victim demonstrated the intent to deprive the victim of her property, and while defendant's father testified he returned the victim's phone to her after defendant fled, witnesses testified the father had returned her shoe, not her phone. State v. Jenkins, 2021-Ohio-1978, 2021 Ohio App. LEXIS 1942 (Ohio Ct. App., Richland County 2021).

Sufficient evidence supported defendant's convictions for aggravated burglary and aggravated robbery because, although the victim originally gave defendant permission to be in the home, his privilege to remain in the home terminated the moment he commenced his assault. Because defendant's blood was found in the living room and in the hallway outside the bedroom where the money was located, a reasonable inference from the facts was that defendant was aware, after his permission to be on the premises had terminated, that a theft had been committed and he did not need to be the principal offender in order to be found guilty of the crime. State v. Gray, 2016-Ohio-1419, 2016 Ohio App. LEXIS 1286 (Ohio Ct. App., Montgomery County 2016).

Although the State established that defendant juvenile committed an assault on the victim, the evidence did not support the conclusion that she or the other vehicle occupants had the purpose to deprive the victim of her property, such that the culpable mental state for a theft offense was not satisfied and accordingly, the finding of true to a charge of robbery was erroneous and required vacatur. In re K.E.W., 2016-Ohio-7844, 2016 Ohio App. LEXIS 4718 (Ohio Ct. App., Lake County 2016).

State was not required to prove that defendant "recklessly" used force while committing or attempting to commit a robbery because the robbery statute defined every robbery to include the culpable mental states of the predicate theft offense, and, as such, the statutory strict-liability and read-in-recklessness rules did not apply; the statutory strict-liability and read-in-recklessness rules only applied to statutes not specifying any degree of culpability. State v. Tolliver, 2014-Ohio-3744, 140 Ohio St. 3d 420, 19 N.E.3d 870, 2014 Ohio LEXIS 2070 (Ohio 2014).

In a case in which a co-defendant snatched the victim's moneybag, the jury did not lose its way in convicting defendant of grand theft. Although defendant did not want to be involved in actually taking the money from the victim, he provided inside information to the co-defendant concerning the victim's depositing procedures that was essential to completing the robbery. State v. Pellegrini, 2013-Ohio-141, 2013 Ohio App. LEXIS 116 (Ohio Ct. App., Allen County 2013).

Because it was reasonable to conclude that defendant's threats to the store clerk constituted a threat of the immediate use of force, for the purpose of robbery under R.C. 2911.02(A), and not just a threat of disagreeable consequence, the trial court was not required to give a jury instruction on the lesser included offense of theft by threat, R.C. 2913.02(A)(4). Only jury instructions which were correct and pertinent had to be included in substance in the general charge to the jury. State v. Delany, 2005-Ohio-4067, 2005 Ohio App. LEXIS 3712 (Ohio Ct. App., Franklin County 2005).

**Ownership**

Trial court's finding that defendant's mother owned a portion of the funds the State alleged had been stolen from a joint and survivorship bank account was not against the manifest weight of the evidence because defendant acknowledged the money belonged to the mother and was deposited for the mother. State v. Woodburn, 2019-Ohio-2757, 140 N.E.3d 66, 2019 Ohio App. LEXIS 2873 (Ohio Ct. App., Pike County 2019).

Sufficient evidence supported defendant's theft conviction because the definition in R.C. 2913.01(D) resulted in a conclusion that the receiver was considered an "owner" because he was any person, other than the actor, who had possession or control, or who had any license or interest in property or services. Thus, the receiver was not only a "person authorized to give consent," but he was also considered an owner that could be deprived and an owner whose consent was breached beyond its scope. State v. Pellin, 2012-Ohio-5342, 2012 Ohio App. LEXIS 4650 (Ohio Ct. App., Mahoning County 2012).

Contrary to defendant's contention, the State, in a theft prosecution, was not required to prove who owned the items that defendant stole; the State merely had to show that defendant did not have a lawful right to possession. Merchandise in a store was in the possession of that store until someone had paid for the merchandise, and the evidence was sufficient to demonstrate that the store possessed or controlled the property in question. State v. Jeantine, 2009-Ohio-6775, 2009 Ohio App. LEXIS 5689 (Ohio Ct. App., Franklin County 2009).

Trial court did not err in convicting defendant of robbery, in violation of R.C. 2911.02(A)(2) because defendant used force in an attempt to deprive a motel of its property, either without the consent of the owner or its agent, in violation of R.C. 2913.02(A)(1), or beyond the scope of the express or implied consent of the owner or its agent, in violation of R.C. 2913.02(A)(2); a refund had not been consummated and defendant's belief that the motel owed defendant money was immaterial. State v. Padgett, 2008-Ohio-1166, 2008 Ohio App. LEXIS 1011 (Ohio Ct. App., Montgomery County 2008).

There was substantial direct and circumstantial evidence from which to conclude that the victim was the "owner" of the computer for the purposes of R.C. 2913.02, regardless of whether she actually possessed title ownership (she was renting the computer), and it could have been inferred that defendant, with purpose to deprive the victim of her possession and control of the computer, knowingly exerted possession and control over the computer. Defendant did not deny taking certain undisclosed items from the apartment because he claimed that they were his. State v. Grayson, 2007-Ohio-1772, 2007 Ohio App. LEXIS 1629 (Ohio Ct. App., Lake County 2007).

Evidence showed that the company was the "owner" of the funds she removed from the company's account under the definition of "owner" in R.C. 2913.01(D) because, once defendant deposited money into the company's account, the company took possession and control of those funds, and the company became the owner of that property for purposes of R.C. 2913.02 regardless of whether the company was obligated to repay the loans made by defendant. Consequently, when defendant transferred money or wrote checks from the company's account to her home equity account without the consent of the company's owners, she deprived the company of money that it owned. State v. Wilson, 2006-Ohio-3103, 2006 Ohio App. LEXIS 2968 (Ohio Ct. App., Franklin County 2006).

In a prosecution for theft of a motor vehicle under R.C. 2913.02, R.C. 4505.04 does not mandate that a certificate of title be produced by the prosecution to demonstrate that the person deprived of the motor vehicle is the "owner" of the motor vehicle within the meaning of R.C. 2913.01(D): State v. Rhodes, 2 Ohio St. 3d 74, 442 N.E.2d 1299, 1982 Ohio LEXIS 763 (Ohio 1982).

**—Partnership property**

A partner who is authorized by the partnership to transfer title to partnership property cannot be held criminally liable for theft of that property, even assuming he embezzled the proceeds or the transferee did not pay for the property: State v. King, 10 Ohio App. 3d 93, 460 N.E.2d 1143, 1983 Ohio App. LEXIS 11106 (Ohio Ct. App., Franklin County 1983).

**Permissive use**

Defendant was afforded the benefit of having the jury consider the issue of his allegedly permissive use of the vehicle in the context of whether he had the requisite knowledge or intent to use the vehicle without consent, without having to sustain the burden of proof imposed upon affirmative defenses; therefore, any error was harmless as a matter of law. Also, the defense of reasonable belief that defendant was authorized to use or operate the property was not provided as an affirmative defense to a charge of grand theft of a motor vehicle, under R.C. 2913.02. State v. Hall, 2007-Ohio-6352, 2007 Ohio App. LEXIS 5606 (Ohio Ct. App., Montgomery County 2007).

**Possession of stolen property**

Evidence was sufficient to support defendant's conviction for receiving stolen property in violation of R.C. 2913.51, and his conviction was not against the manifest weight of the evidence, because, according to defendant's testimony, he had only paid a lessee to rent the vehicle in question through November, and he was arrested in December; thus, his own evidence showed that he retained possession of the car clearly beyond the scope authorized by the lessee, thereby constituting "theft" under R.C. 2913.02. State v. Asberry, 2005-Ohio-4547, 2005 Ohio App. LEXIS 4056 (Ohio Ct. App., Franklin County 2005).

The unexplained possession by a defendant of recently stolen property may give rise to a permissive inference from which a jury may conclude, beyond a reasonable doubt, that the accused is guilty of the theft: State v. McAllister, 53 Ohio App. 2d 176, 7 Ohio Op. 3d 247, 372 N.E.2d 1341, 1977 Ohio App. LEXIS 6984 (Ohio Ct. App., Cuyahoga County 1977).

**Prior convictions**

Where defendant, who was not a first-time offender, was found guilty of theft in violation of R.C. 2913.02 and the trial court advised defendant that a violation of community control would result in a sentence of up to 12 months pursuant to R.C. 2929.14(A)(5), the trial court did not have to set forth the law and rationale that supported the sentence in excess of the minimum under R.C. 2929.14(B)(1) when defendant subsequently violated the community control. State v. Westerman, 2004-Ohio-2467, 2004 Ohio App. LEXIS 2195 (Ohio Ct. App., Sandusky County 2004).

For purposes of R.C. 2913.02(B), a prior conviction is an element of grand theft which must be proved beyond a reasonable doubt: State v. Mitchell, 1996 Ohio App. LEXIS 5454 (Ohio Ct. App., Cuyahoga County Dec. 5, 1996).

The defendant could not be convicted of felony theft when the offense used to elevate the degree of the instant offense occurred after the instant offense: State v. Johnson, 101 Ohio App. 3d 129, 655 N.E.2d 208, 1994 Ohio App. LEXIS 5969 (Ohio Ct. App., Trumbull County 1995).

Where an indictment complies with Crim.R. 7(B) and gives the accused adequate notice that the state will seek to prove the accused previously had been convicted of prior theft offenses, the indictment does not need to allege that the accused was, at a certain stated time, in a certain stated court, convicted of a certain stated offense: State v. Larsen, 89 Ohio App. 3d 371, 624 N.E.2d 766, 1993 Ohio App. LEXIS 3925 (Ohio Ct. App., Lawrence County 1993).

Where questions arise concerning a prior conviction, a reviewing court must presume all underlying proceedings were conducted in accordance with the rules of law and a defendant must introduce evidence to the contrary in order to establish a prima-facie showing of constitutional infirmity: State v. Brandon, 45 Ohio St. 3d 85, 543 N.E.2d 501, 1989 Ohio LEXIS 202 (Ohio 1989).

Evidence of a defendant's prior adjudications of delinquency predicated on petit theft, otherwise not admissible under R.C. 2151.358(H), is admissible as prior convictions to enhance the degree of a theft offense to grand theft for the purposes of disposition. The prior adjudications become an element of the present offense and must be proved by the state beyond a reasonable doubt (In re Russell, 12 Ohio St. 3d 304, 466 N.E.2d 553, 1984 Ohio LEXIS 1215 (Ohio 1984).

A prior adjudication of delinquency based on a theft offense constitutes a previous conviction of a theft offense under R.C. 2913.02 for purposes of disposition of the minor: In re Russell, 12 Ohio St. 3d 304, 466 N.E.2d 553, 1984 Ohio LEXIS 1215 (Ohio 1984).

The recidivist clause found in R.C. 2913.02(B) which enables the state to indict a once-convicted theft offender for grand theft upon the individual's commission of a second theft offense, does not constitute cruel and unusual punishment in violation of the United States and Ohio Constitutions: State v. Oher, 9 Ohio App. 3d 348, 460 N.E.2d 320, 1983 Ohio App. LEXIS 11084 (Ohio Ct. App., Cuyahoga County 1983).

Mere compliance with R.C. 2945.75(B) is insufficient, without the state's affirmative proof that defendant's previous conviction was either counseled or that defendant knowingly and intelligently waived counsel, to sustain a conviction of grand theft under R.C. 2913.02(A)(1): State v. Elling, 11 Ohio Misc. 2d 13, 463 N.E.2d 668, 1983 Ohio Misc. LEXIS 428 (Ohio C.P. 1983).

An uncounseled misdemeanor conviction for theft may be used under the enhancement provision of R.C. 2913.02(B) to convert the subsequent misdemeanor into a felony when no actual imprisonment results: State v. Gerwin, 69 Ohio St. 2d 488, 23 Ohio Op. 3d 420, 432 N.E.2d 828, 1982 Ohio LEXIS 604 (Ohio 1982).

The provision in R.C. 2913.02(B) providing that "if the offender has previously been convicted of a theft offense, then violation of this section is grand theft, a felony of the fourth degree" does not violate the Eighth and Fourteenth Amendments to the U. S. Constitution: State v. Green, 2 Ohio App. 3d 38, 440 N.E.2d 615, 1981 Ohio App. LEXIS 9901 (Ohio Ct. App., Hamilton County 1981).

Where an accused has entered a plea of guilty to a theft offense but has not been sentenced by the court on that charge, such offender has not been previously convicted of a theft offense within the meaning of R.C. 2913.02(B): State v. Henderson, 58 Ohio St. 2d 171, 12 Ohio Op. 3d 177, 389 N.E.2d 494, 1979 Ohio LEXIS 408 (Ohio 1979), limited, State v. Allen, 29 Ohio St. 3d 53, 506 N.E.2d 199, 1987 Ohio LEXIS 244 (Ohio 1987).

A plea of guilty is not rendered involuntary because the defendant is not apprised that subsequent similar criminal conduct will subject him to additional criminal liability under a repeat offender statute: State v. Porter, 49 Ohio App. 2d 227, 3 Ohio Op. 3d 276, 360 N.E.2d 759, 1976 Ohio App. LEXIS 5816 (Ohio Ct. App., Summit County 1976).

It is proper to submit the question of a previous conviction to a jury for their determination: State v. Alexander, 50 Ohio App. 2d 55, 4 Ohio Op. 3d 39, 361 N.E.2d 459, 1975 Ohio App. LEXIS 5918 (Ohio Ct. App., Lorain County 1975).



**Procedure**

Trial court erred in refusing to reduce defendant's theft conviction due to an error in the verdict form because the verdict form did not mention the degree of the theft offense, nor did it mention the aggravating element, namely, the value of the property taken. State v. Simmonds, 2012-Ohio-1479, 2012 Ohio App. LEXIS 1275 (Ohio Ct. App., Clermont County 2012).

When defendant was charged with grand theft, under R.C. 2913.02(A)(2) and (B)(2), for misappropriating funds belonging to the organization for which defendant was treasurer, the trial court did not violate defendant's right to due process when it refused to appoint a forensic accountant at state expense because defendant did not show how the appointment of such an expert would benefit defendant's defense, as the case was a relatively simple matter of defendant's inability to show that defendant was entitled to funds defendant paid to defendant, which a forensic accountant would not be able to explain, so no required particularized showing was made that the requested expert assistance would aid the defense or that denial of it would result in an unfair trial. State v. Eppard, 2007-Ohio-2257, 2007 Ohio App. LEXIS 2110 (Ohio Ct. App., Lucas County 2007).

**—Accomplice**

The principal offender's prior convictions cannot be imputed to an accomplice for purposes of enhancing the degree of an offense: State v. Jackson, 90 Ohio App. 3d 702, 630 N.E.2d 414, 1993 Ohio App. LEXIS 4636 (Ohio Ct. App., Lucas County 1993).

**Public assistance**

The value of property stolen in welfare theft cases is the total amount of benefits received regardless of whether the government suffers a loss: State v. Woods, 145 Ohio App. 3d 751, 764 N.E.2d 485, 2001 Ohio App. LEXIS 3947 (Ohio Ct. App., Montgomery County 2001).

Where an applicant for public assistance committed theft by deception in obtaining a greater amount of benefits than the amount to which she was entitled, the correct valuation of the benefits stolen was the entire amount received: State v. Edmondson, 2001-Ohio-210, 92 Ohio St. 3d 393, 750 N.E.2d 587, 2001 Ohio LEXIS 1885 (Ohio 2001).

Where R.C. 2913.46 concerns the fraudulent use of food stamps, and that section has previously been held to constitute an unconstitutional delegation of legislative power to a federal administrative agency, allegations of the fraudulent use of food stamps may be brought under the general theft statute, R.C. 2913.02: State v. Diehl, 1991 Ohio App. LEXIS 1402 (Ohio Ct. App., Union County Mar. 25, 1991).

The state may charge a defendant under the general theft statute rather than under the falsification statute for making a false statement in order to obtain welfare benefits: State v. Cooper, 66 Ohio App. 3d 551, 585 N.E.2d 868, 1990 Ohio App. LEXIS 2516 (Ohio Ct. App., Ross County), dismissed, 55 Ohio St. 3d 720, 564 N.E.2d 496, 1990 Ohio LEXIS 1582 (Ohio 1990).

**Religious beliefs**

It is not a defense to a prosecution under former R.C. 2911.16 that the accused is a member of a religious society, and that the representation made, alleged to constitute the offense, was a part of his religious belief: (decided under former analogous section) Davis v. State, 118 Ohio St. 25, 160 N.E. 473, 6 Ohio Law Abs. 61, 1928 Ohio LEXIS 370 (Ohio), writ of error dismissed, 277 U.S. 571, 48 S. Ct. 432, 72 L. Ed. 993, 1928 U.S. LEXIS 700 (U.S. 1928).

**Rental property**

A defendant who rents personal property pursuant to a rental agreement, and who retains possession of the rental property after failing to pay the rent required by the agreement, is not guilty of theft under R.C. 2913.02(A), where the rental property is not an automobile and where the defendant has not absconded with the property, concealed its whereabouts, or acted to prevent its repossession by the creditor: State v. Glenn, 56 Ohio Misc. 2d 1, 564 N.E.2d 1149, 1990 Ohio Misc. LEXIS 9 (Ohio Mun. Ct. 1990).

**Res judicata**

Trial court did not err in denying defendant's motion to vacate sentence because his arguments were barred by res judicata; and, even considering his arguments, the General Assembly's enactment of Am. Sub. H.B. 86, Gen. Assem. 2011 reviving the judicial fact-finding requirement prior to imposing consecutive sentences was not retroactive. State v. Hilton, 2019-Ohio-3037, 2019 Ohio App. LEXIS 3132 (Ohio Ct. App., Cuyahoga County 2019).

Defendant's claim in her post conviction petition that her grand theft conivction was against the manifest weight of the evidence was rejected as she raised the same claim in her direct appeal, when she claimed that the trial court erred by failing to grant her Crim.R. 29 motion for acquittal; the claim was barred by the doctrine of res judicata. State v. Sanders, 2005-Ohio-4267, 2005 Ohio App. LEXIS 3867 (Ohio Ct. App., Summit County 2005), cert. denied, 549 U.S. 850, 127 S. Ct. 116, 166 L. Ed. 2d 87, 2006 U.S. LEXIS 6657 (U.S. 2006).

**Restitution**

Amount of restitution that defendant was ordered to pay the victim of her theft offense improperly included more than "economic loss," as the costs of investigating the loss were not a direct and proximate result of the theft but instead, were consequential costs incurred for valuing the property taken which were not properly part of the restitution award. State v. Cook, 2017-Ohio-1503, 2017 Ohio App. LEXIS 1515 (Ohio Ct. App., Fairfield County 2017).

Where defendant pleaded guilty to felony theft and possession of criminal tools, the total amount of victim's economic loss could be ordered as restitution even though the amount of the theft charge was $4,999 under the law in effect at the time of the crime. However, the trial court erred by failing to hold a restitution hearing because defendant objected to $53,000 as the amount of restitution imposed at sentencing. State v. Mendez, 2014-Ohio-2601, 2014 Ohio App. LEXIS 2544 (Ohio Ct. App., Mahoning County 2014).

Order of restitution that was imposed on defendant upon her guilty plea to grand theft was not excessive because it was supported by the victim's testimony as to the value of the stolen goods, which the trial court deemed credible. State v. Lyons, 2014-Ohio-2239, 2014 Ohio App. LEXIS 2181 (Ohio Ct. App., Warren County 2014), overruled in part, State v. Collins, 2015-Ohio-3710, 41 N.E.3d 899, 2015 Ohio App. LEXIS 3609 (Ohio Ct. App., Warren County 2015).

Trial court did not err in ordering defendant to pay restitution to the victim because there was some evidence in the record that the trial court considered defendant's present and future ability to pay the restitution, and the fact that he was indigent was not a bar to the imposition of restitution; the trial court based the amount of restitution on an amount recommended by the theft victim. State v. Jennings, 2013-Ohio-5428, 2013 Ohio App. LEXIS 5674 (Ohio Ct. App., Cuyahoga County 2013).

Trial court committed plain error in imposing restitution, pursuant to R.C. 2929.18(A)(1), because the $76,424 amount which the court ordered to be paid exceeded the monetary parameters of the theft offense. Because defendant pleaded guilty under the former RC. 2913.02(B)(3) to the theft of property valued at $5,000 or more, but less than $25,000, the trial court could not order defendant to pay restitution of $25,000 or more. State v. Ford, 2012-Ohio-1327, 2012 Ohio App. LEXIS 1155 (Ohio Ct. App., Summit County 2012).

Where defendant entered a no-contest plea to aggravated theft, a third degree felony under former R.C. 2913.02, the trial court did not abuse its discretion in determining that her restitution obligation exceeded $100,000 because a witness testified that $111,000 was missing from the condominium association's reserve fund that should have been deposited while defendant was employed as the property manager. Based on the testimony of six witnesses, the trial court found defendant owed the association $206,545.35 in restitution. State v. Jackson, 2012-Ohio-288, 2012 Ohio App. LEXIS 240 (Ohio Ct. App., Montgomery County 2012).

Award of restitution in the amount of $60,900 was proper, because the award was supported by the evidence adduced at the restitution hearing, and the amount of the award did not exceed the amount corresponding to the degree of the theft offense, theft of copper wiring, of which defendant was convicted; the trial court's consideration of defendant's ability to pay was presumed from the trial court's statement that it considered the pre-sentence investigation report in the case, which contained information bearing upon defendant's present and future ability to pay a restitution award. State v. Littler, 2012-Ohio-210, 2012 Ohio App. LEXIS 166 (Ohio Ct. App., Montgomery County 2012).

Defendant was indicted for felony theft in violation of R.C. 2913.02(A)(1) for stealing more than $500 but less than $5,000 worth of property, but agreed to plead guilty to misdemeanor theft; because the plea agreement provided that defendant would pay restitution in connection with the dismissed count, he could not be ordered to pay more than $5,000 in restitution. The trial court erred when it ordered defendant to pay $10,637.21 in restitution to the victim and $20,254.69 to the insurance company, because it exceeded the amount of restitution permitted by the plea agreement; the portion of the restitution order requiring payment to an insurance company violated R.C. 2929.18(A)(1) as revised in 2004. State v. Wickline, 2011-Ohio-3004, 2011 Ohio App. LEXIS 2543 (Ohio Ct. App., Logan County 2011).

Court committed an error in law with respect to the restitution order, because there was clearly an inconsistency between the amount of restitution ordered and the court's decision to impose a misdemeanor conviction, when the court ordered defendant to pay restitution in an amount exceeding the value of property for a misdemeanor theft offense under R.C. 2913.02(B)(2); defendant was ordered to pay restitution in the amount of $2,061.72, and misdemeanor theft required that the value of the property or services stolen must be less than $500. State v. Moore-Bennett, 2011-Ohio-1937, 2011 Ohio App. LEXIS 1651 (Ohio Ct. App., Cuyahoga County 2011).

Court erred in ordering restitution in the amount of $10,000, because the indictment for theft from an elderly person affirmatively stated the value of the property taken was less than $500. It was undisputed that defendant returned the victim's ring as requested by the State to secure a recommendation of community control. State v. Amburgey, 2011-Ohio-748, 2011 Ohio App. LEXIS 649 (Ohio Ct. App., Greene County 2011).

In a misdemeanor theft case, restitution ordered by a trial court was improper to the extent that it exceeded the amount of $500; for a person to be convicted of misdemeanor theft, the value of the property or services deprived had to be less than $500. State v. Henry, 2010-Ohio-4571, 2010 Ohio App. LEXIS 3847 (Ohio Ct. App., Clermont County 2010).

Imposition of an order of restitution pursuant to R.C. 2929.18(A)(1) on defendant upon her conviction for theft, in violation of R.C. 2913.02(A)(2), was error because the trial court failed to hold an evidentiary hearing despite defendant's dispute as to the amount of restitution; further, the trial court failed to consider defendant's present and future ability to pay the restitution under R.C. 2929.19(B)(6). State v. Broud, 2009-Ohio-2922, 2009 Ohio App. LEXIS 2468 (Ohio Ct. App., Wood County 2009).

Costs were properly imposed upon a defendant convicted of violating R.C. 2913.02(A)(1), (B)(2) and 2913.49(B)(1), (I)(2) as the trial court was required to impose costs under R.C. 2947.23 regardless of defendant's indigent status, and the presentencing investigation provided sufficient evidence of defendant's educational background and finances to support the award. State v. Shaffer, 2009-Ohio-4804, 2009 Ohio App. LEXIS 4066 (Ohio Ct. App., Union County 2009).

As defendant's conviction for theft under R.C. 2913.02 was a fifth-degree felony under § 2913.02(B)(2), a restitution order under R.C. 2929.18 in the amount of $5,000 was error because fifth-degree felony theft involved property valued at less than $5,000. State v. Miller, 2008-Ohio-5661, 2008 Ohio App. LEXIS 4771 (Ohio Ct. App., Butler County 2008).

Trial court erred in ordering defendant to pay restitution in the amount of $167,940.89 as part of defendant's sentence for theft in violation of R.C. 2913.02(A)(3) because a hearing on restitution was required by R.C. 2929.18(A)(1) where restitution was disputed, and both the parties and the trial court recognized that restitution was disputed. State v. Sanner, 2008-Ohio-1168, 2008 Ohio App. LEXIS 1041 (Ohio Ct. App., Greene County 2008).

Because the State did not prove that defendant obtained or exerted control over the money paid directly by defendant's clients to defendant's cousin, the restitution orders with respect to three counts of grand theft were in error. However, with respect to the count whereby defendant was given money by his client, which defendant directed to his cousin, defendant obtained control over that money and, when a client paid money to the cousin under direct instructions from defendant, defendant exerted control over the money such that both supported the restitution awards. State v. Keith, 2008-Ohio-348, 2008 Ohio App. LEXIS 297 (Ohio Ct. App., Butler County 2008).

Defendant's claim that he should have been given an opportunity to make restitution to the victims before he was indicted for theft from an elderly person was rejected as the crime was complete once defendant deprived the victims of their money by deception; the State was permitted to prosecute defendant for his crimes even if he made restitution. State v. Wright, 2005-Ohio-3907, 2005 Ohio App. LEXIS 3596 (Ohio Ct. App., Clermont County 2005), rev'd, 2006-Ohio-2109, 109 Ohio St. 3d 313, 847 N.E.2d 1174, 2006 Ohio LEXIS 1161 (Ohio 2006).

Where defendant argued that in sentencing defendant for misdemeanor assault under R.C. 2903.13, the trial court violated former R.C. 2929.21(E) when it ordered defendant's probationary period on the assault charge to be served under the same terms as defendant's community control sanction for grand theft auto in violation of R.C. 2913.02(A) and ordered defendant to pay reparations for both offenses; the trial court only ordered defendant to pay restitution on the grand theft auto offense, and given that defendant was properly ordered to pay restitution on that offense, defendant was not prejudiced if, indeed, an error had occurred. State v. Riegsecker, 2004-Ohio-3808, 2004 Ohio App. LEXIS 3414 (Ohio Ct. App., Fulton County 2004).

**Return of property**

As an inmate's motion to return personal property to him pursuant to R.C. 4510.41, which property was allegedly seized in a municipal court after the inmate was convicted of theft, in violation of R.C. 2913.02, was already ruled upon by a municipal court judge, the inmate's complaint, seeking to compel the judge to rule thereon through a writ of mandamus under R.C. 2731.01, was dismissed; the court did not have the authority to release the property, including motor vehicles, to the inmate. State ex rel. Mace v. Lanzo, 2010-Ohio-611, 2010 Ohio App. LEXIS 506 (Ohio Ct. App., Mahoning County 2010).

**Right to possession**

When the owner of a title insurance agency withdrew funds from the agency's escrow accounts and deposited those funds into the agency's operating account, sufficient evidence supported the owner's conviction for aggravated theft, under R.C. 2913.02(A)(2), because (1) the funds in the escrow accounts did not belong to the owner, pursuant to R.C. 3953.23(B), as the owner was merely allowed to maintain the funds in the accounts until the funds were needed for real estate closings, and (2) the owner did not return all of the funds that were withdrawn from the escrow accounts. State v. Clayton, 2009-Ohio-7040, 2009 Ohio App. LEXIS 5897 (Ohio Ct. App., Montgomery County 2009).

A defendant may be convicted of theft of a motor vehicle where he did not have any legal right to its possession, regardless of the status of the legal title: State v. Montes, 92 Ohio App. 3d 539, 636 N.E.2d 378, 1993 Ohio App. LEXIS 5729 (Ohio Ct. App., Cuyahoga County 1993).

**Robbery**

State presented sufficient direct and circumstantial evidence to identify defendant as having been involved in both the theft and robbery incidents because one man showed a gun to the driver before he and a second man unloaded cigarettes from the truck into a car; approximately 88 cartons of cigarettes were stolen and that delivery truck driver identified defendant as the man who loaded cigarettes into the car with the gunman involved in the Cleveland Incident. State v. Fields, 2022-Ohio-620, 2022 Ohio App. LEXIS 538 (Ohio Ct. App., Cuyahoga County 2022).

Sufficient evidence supported defendant's conviction for robbery because defendant's action of taking the phone and fleeing after he beat her prevented the victim from using her phone to call for help at a critical and potentially life-threatening time and did not return the phone until after he became aware that a neighbor called 9-1-1 and that the victim had spoken to the police. State v. Singleton, 2020-Ohio-2920, 2020 Ohio App. LEXIS 1874 (Ohio Ct. App., Summit County 2020).

Sufficient evidence sustained defendant's robbery conviction because the state presented evidence of theft by showing that defendant ordered the victim to give him bag and evidence of force was shown by defendant's statement that he would "pull the hammer" if the victim did not turn it over. The conviction was not against the manifest weight of the evidence because the jury was in the best position to evaluate witness credibility, and the appellate court could not say that the jury lost its way. State v. Henry, 2018-Ohio-2174, 2018 Ohio App. LEXIS 2359 (Ohio Ct. App., Summit County 2018).

Sufficient evidence supported defendant's robbery conviction because the victim testified that she and defendant engaged in a struggle wherein defendant attempted to gain possession of her phone. Thus, the State offered sufficient evidence of an attempted theft offense to support the conviction for robbery. State v. Catney, 2017-Ohio-90, 2017 Ohio App. LEXIS 76 (Ohio Ct. App., Cuyahoga County 2017).

Defendant's conviction for robbery was supported by the weight and sufficiency of the evidence because it was shown, through testimony and a store surveillance video, that she committed theft when she took items from a store and placed them in her purse without paying for them, she had the requisite purposeful intent, and that she threatened the store clerk with a box cutter upon being confronted. State v. Campbell, 2016-Ohio-598, 2016 Ohio App. LEXIS 530 (Ohio Ct. App., Montgomery County 2016).

Sufficient evidence supported defendant's conviction for because defendant got his mother's purse, took her debit card and her keys and then grabbed the cell phone out of her hand and he did not have permission to take her mother's things. The evidence was sufficient to establish that the mother suffered physical harm when defendant twisted her hand until she dropped her cell phone, because she testified that when defendant was attempting to get her cell phone out of her hand, he twisted her hand until she let go of the phone and that it hurt "a little." State v. Stanton, 2015-Ohio-3031, 2015 Ohio App. LEXIS 2938 (Ohio Ct. App., Cuyahoga County 2015).

**—Lesser included offense**

Insufficient evidence supported defendant's robbery conviction because the State failed to support the "use or threaten use of force" element, since the State had to prove that defendant committed theft with the use, or threat of immediate use, of force against the "victim," not the victim's cell phone. However, there was sufficient evidence to support the lesser included offense of theft because defendant reached through the victim's car window and grabbed the cell phone from his hand and then threatened to smash the phone to the ground unless he gave him money. State v. Evans, 2015-Ohio-3032, 2015 Ohio App. LEXIS 2939 (Ohio Ct. App., Cuyahoga County 2015).

**Search warrants**

Search warrant that permitted police to search the contents of defendant's cellphone for evidence of the crime of theft was sufficiently particular; it was not necessary to limit the search to a review of text messages because defendant admitted to conducting an online scam using the cellphone, and it was entirely possible that evidence of the theft offense could have been preserved in other areas of the cellphone, not limited to the text messages. State v. Chebegwen, 2020-Ohio-3297, 2020 Ohio App. LEXIS 2232 (Ohio Ct. App., Montgomery County 2020).



**Sentence**

Trial court's sentencing of community control was contrary to law because the trial court did not specify whether it considered the presumption in favor of a prison term, and defendant's conviction for grand theft of a firearm included a presumption of prison; the offense was not included in R.C. 2929.13(D), but the trial court applied it and did not make any finding that the presumption of prison term was rebutted. State v. Coleman, 2016-Ohio-7264, 2016 Ohio App. LEXIS 4123 (Ohio Ct. App., Clermont County 2016).

Sentence of 12 months for fifth-degree felony theft was not clearly and convincingly contrary to law as it was within the statutory range provided in R.C. 2929.14 and due to defendant's criminal history he was not required to receive a community control sanction under R.C. 2929.13, nor was it an abuse of discretion given the facts surrounding the crime and defendant's criminal history. State v. Kerr, 2014-Ohio-2031, 2014 Ohio App. LEXIS 1969 (Ohio Ct. App., Ashland County 2014).

After defendant pleaded guilty to grand theft and identity fraud, the trial court acted within its discretion by imposing a nine-month prison term rather than a community control sanction because defendant committed a violation of a condition of her bond by failing to report to the county clerk, thereby entitling the trial court to impose a prison term. State v. Hughes, 2014-Ohio-1320, 2014 Ohio App. LEXIS 1237 (Ohio Ct. App., Butler County 2014).

Sentence of 17 months was supported by consideration of factors in R.C. 2929.12, finding defendant was not amenable to community control, and fact that sentence was within the statutory range. State v. Jackson, 2014-Ohio-3779, 2014 Ohio App. LEXIS 3711 (Ohio Ct. App., Butler County 2014).

Defendant pleaded guilty to forgery and theft based on allegations that he used money from his company's expense account for his own personal use and forged signatures on a purported contract. The trial court's denial of his request for intervention in lieu of conviction was not an abuse of discretion; defendant was sentenced to a community control sanction. State v. Cebula, 2014-Ohio-3276, 2014 Ohio App. LEXIS 3199 (Ohio Ct. App., Lake County 2014).

Sentence of 17 months was supported by consideration of factors in R.C. 2929.12, finding defendant was not amenable to community control, and fact that sentence was within the statutory range. State v. Jackson, 2014-Ohio-3779, 2014 Ohio App. LEXIS 3711 (Ohio Ct. App., Butler County 2014).

Where defendant pleaded guilty to attempted theft for acting in concert with his brother and wife to steal a winning $10,000 lottery ticket from an individual they believed to be a customer of defendant's convenience store, the trial court's sentence of 20 days in jail and 4 years of community control was not an abuse of discretion because it was within the statutory range for a first-degree misdemeanor offense. There was nothing indicating the trial court failed to consider the proper factors. State v. Fahmawi, 2014-Ohio-4162, 2014 Ohio App. LEXIS 4079 (Ohio Ct. App., Columbiana County 2014).

Defendant's 12-month sentence after being convicted of theft of a credit card could not stand because the trial court's statements both before the trial and at the sentencing hearing created the appearance that the court sentenced defendant to prison, rather than community control, because he chose to proceed to trial rather than accept a plea offer. State v. Turner, 2014-Ohio-4460, 2014 Ohio App. LEXIS 4371 (Ohio Ct. App., Summit County 2014).

Without a complete record of the hearing, the court presumed the omitted hearings supported the decision and the sentencing complied with applicable statutes; the 30-day jail sentence, one year of house arrest, restitution, a fine, probation, and community service for vandalism and theft was within the range, the trial court considered factors, so the sentence was not clearly contrary to law, and while defendant could disagree with the weight given the statutory factors, the sentence could not be said to be an abuse of discretion. State v. Taylor, 2013-Ohio-5751, 2013 Ohio App. LEXIS 6030 (Ohio Ct. App., Holmes County 2013).

Trial court did not err when it sentenced defendant for theft because the sentence was consistent with sentences imposed for similar crimes committed by similar offenders, and the trial court properly considered the statutory factors and guidelines before imposing defendant's sentence; the trial court indicated why defendant and some of his co-defendants were not similar offenders, finding that defendant had an "extremely significant" role in the fraud. State v. Murphy, 2013-Ohio-5599, 2013 Ohio App. LEXIS 5828 (Ohio Ct. App., Franklin County 2013).

Trial court properly ordered defendant to pay restitution as part of her sentence for theft because the restitution contemplated the retail replacement cost of the television, such that she was not entitled to credit for rental payments made for it, and it appeared that she had the ability to pay restitution based on information in the pre-sentence investigation report. State v. Franklin, 2013-Ohio-5164, 2013 Ohio App. LEXIS 5381 (Ohio Ct. App., Montgomery County 2013).

Sentence of 11 months' imprisonment on defendant's conviction for theft was proper because it was within the statutory range, the trial court considered the applicable statutory factors, it properly notified defendant that he could be subject to a period of postrelease control, and the term imposed was not an abuse of discretion in the circumstances. State v. Gibbs, 2013-Ohio-4252, 2013 Ohio App. LEXIS 4457 (Ohio Ct. App., Washington County 2013).

Because defendant had completed his sentence and there was no issue as to the validity of the underlying conviction, there was no relief which could be granted. An appeal in his favor on the issue of maximum sentence pursuant to R.C. 2913.02(A)(1) and R.C. 2929.22(C) would have granted him no relief because he had already been released from incarceration on the charge. State v. McKinnon, 2013-Ohio-2324, 2013 Ohio App. LEXIS 2248 (Ohio Ct. App., Ross County 2013).

Defendant's one-year sentence for fifth-degree felony theft under R.C. 2913.02(A)(3) was not contrary to law. It was within the range allowed by R.C. 2929.14; the trial court considered the factors in R.C. 2929.11 and 2929.12; and the trial court considered defendant's history of similar offenses and her failure to take responsibility for her actions. State v. Morrow, 2013-Ohio-841, 2013 Ohio App. LEXIS 784 (Ohio Ct. App., Sandusky County 2013).

Because defendant pled guilty and was sentenced on a fifth degree felony after amendments to the theft statute reduced the penalty for defendant's crime to a first degree misdemeanor, defendant was entitled to resentencing. His original sentence included a period of post-release control, which only applied to felonies. State v. Saplak, 2012-Ohio-4281, 2012 Ohio App. LEXIS 3756 (Ohio Ct. App., Cuyahoga County 2012).

Defendant's four year theft sentence was proper because defendant stole at least $500,000 from the law firm in which he was a shareholder, trusted by his colleagues; that was the maximum amount corresponding to the degree of his offense, a third-degree felony. Before defendant was sentenced, he had been convicted in two cases for stealing money from clients out of settlements they had won, and defendant showed no remorse. State v. Slagle, 2012-Ohio-1575, 2012 Ohio App. LEXIS 1384 (Ohio Ct. App., Montgomery County 2012).

Defendant's four-year sentence, imposed upon her aggravated theft conviction, was not contrary to law as it was within the applicable statutory range in R.C. 2929.14(A)(3), and the trial court stated at the sentencing hearing and in its judgment entry that it considered the principles and purposes of sentencing pursuant to R.C. 2929.11 and that it balanced the seriousness and recidivism factors in R.C. 2929.12. Likewise, the trial court did not abuse its discretion in sentencing defendant, in that the trial court noted the serious economic harm caused by defendant's theft, the position of trust held by defendant with the victim, and how she used that to facilitate the offense and also noted that the money was stolen over a long period of time, essentially constituting serial theft offenses. State v. Chance, 2012-Ohio-1266, 2012 Ohio App. LEXIS 1102 (Ohio Ct. App., Mahoning County 2012).

There was no abuse of discretion in sentencing defendant to twelve years in prison for aggravated robbery, having weapons while under disability and grand theft of a motor vehicle, because the court observed that the victim suffered serious physical harm, was struck in the face with a gun and required hospital care and treatment, and the court emphasized that defendant had a high risk of recidivism since he had been incarcerated several times for theft and robbery related offenses and committed the present offense while awaiting sentencing on separate charges. State v. Davis, 2011-Ohio-5435, 2011 Ohio App. LEXIS 4468 (Ohio Ct. App., Lake County 2011).

Trial court was aware that it had discretion with regard to sentencing on the theft offenses and it used its discretion to order the sentences to be served consecutively. The trial court considered the sentencing factors and found that defendant held a position of trust that facilitated the offense, that he had no remorse, and that recidivism was likely. State v. Leach, 2011-Ohio-4745, 195 Ohio App. 3d 433, 960 N.E.2d 531, 2011 Ohio App. LEXIS 3921 (Ohio Ct. App., Delaware County 2011).

Nine consecutive sentences for a total of 15 years, which were imposed for theft from an elderly person, securities prohibitions, grand theft, and passing bad checks, were not clearly and convincingly contrary to law where R.C. 2929.11 and R.C. 2929.12 were considered, and the sentences were within the statutory range; moreover, there was no abuse of discretion based on the trial court's weight of the sentencing factors. The trial court considered the presentence report, along with the record, oral statements, and victim impact statements; defendant's actions were not the result of an addiction, but rather to maintain an extravagant lifestyle, defendant had no genuine remorse and did not have the intent of repaying the victims, and defendant preyed on the elderly and disabled and took their life savings out of greed. State v. Kirchoff, 2011-Ohio-4718, 2011 Ohio App. LEXIS 3917 (Ohio Ct. App., Clermont County 2011).

In imposing sentence following defendant's conviction on his guilty plea of theft from the elderly person under R.C. 2913.02(A)(1), the trial court did not abuse its discretion in imposing the maximum term of imprisonment and requiring defendant to serve the sentence consecutive to a term he was serving at the time of the sentencing hearing despite defendant's contention that he committed the theft as a result of drug addiction but was prepared to overcome his addiction and start his life anew because addiction, while a factor in considering defendant's motive, was neither an excuse nor a justification for the commission of the offense. Morever, the record demonstrated that, shortly after defendant was placed on probation for a previous theft offense, he committed the current offense. State v. Kozel, 2011-Ohio-4306, 2011 Ohio App. LEXIS 3579 (Ohio Ct. App., Lake County 2011).

Trial court's imposition of maximum consecutive sentences for theft and drug possession was not clearly and convincingly contrary to law because they were within the statutory range in R.C. 2929.14(A)(5), the trial court considered the principals and factors contained in R.C. 2929.11 and R.C. 2929.12, defendant was afforded his allocution rights under Crim.R. 32(A)(1), and he was properly notified about post-release control. A deviation from the jointly recommended sentence did not constitute an abuse of discretion where defendant was forewarned about the penalties for his crimes, including the possibility that he could have received a greater sentence than recommended; moreover, the sentence was reasonable under the totality of the circumstances because the trial court could have reasonably concluded that defendant was not amenable to community control, and the factors contained in R.C. 2929.12(D) demonstrated a high likelihood of recidivism. State v. Little, 2011-Ohio-4256, 2011 Ohio App. LEXIS 3545 (Ohio Ct. App., Mahoning County 2011).

In a case involving theft from an elderly person, a one-year sentence was not contrary to law because the appellate court was unable to determine if the trial court failed to comply with R.C. 2930.14(B). Even if there was a failure to comply, the sentence was within the statutory range, the trial court properly imposed postrelease control, and the principals of felony sentences were considered; moreover, the trial court was unable to find an abuse of discretion since it could not review a presentence investigation report. State v. Sheppard, 2011-Ohio-3516, 2011 Ohio App. LEXIS 2981 (Ohio Ct. App., Medina County 2011).

After a revocation of community control, a trial court did not abuse its discretion by imposing the maximum sentence for theft; because the findings requirement under R.C. 2929.14(C)(2) was severed by the decision in State v. Foster, 109 Ohio St.3d 1, 2006 Ohio 856, the trial court could have imposed a prison term within the appropriate range without making findings for imposing the maximum sentence. The trial court considered the appropriate factors, the sentence was within the permissible range, and there was nothing to suggest that the decision was unreasonable, unconscionable, or arbitrary. State v. Sherouse, 2011-Ohio-3421, 2011 Ohio App. LEXIS 2898 (Ohio Ct. App., Montgomery County 2011).

Defendant's sentence was not clearly and convincingly contrary to law and the appellate court could not find an abuse of discretion related to defendant's individual sentences or cumulative sentence, because defendant's total combined sentence of 10 years for multiple offenses was within the statutory range for his various crimes, and the trial court explained its reasons for imposing, with respect to some of the counts, maximum and consecutive prison sentences; two year sentence for theft from an elderly person was within the statutory range. State v. Slagle, 2011-Ohio-1463, 2011 Ohio App. LEXIS 1252 (Ohio Ct. App., Highland County), overruled in part, State v. Pierce, 2011-Ohio-5353, 2011 Ohio App. LEXIS 4387 (Ohio Ct. App., Meigs County 2011).

Defendant's sentence was not clearly and convincingly contrary to law and the appellate court could not find an abuse of discretion related to defendant's individual sentences or cumulative sentence, because defendant's total combined sentence of 10 years for multiple offenses was within the statutory range for his various crimes, and the trial court explained its reasons for imposing, with respect to some of the counts, maximum and consecutive prison sentences; term of twelve months and two eighteen month sentences for three counts of grand theft were within the statutory range. State v. Slagle, 2011-Ohio-1463, 2011 Ohio App. LEXIS 1252 (Ohio Ct. App., Highland County), overruled in part, State v. Pierce, 2011-Ohio-5353, 2011 Ohio App. LEXIS 4387 (Ohio Ct. App., Meigs County 2011).

Defendant's sentence was not clearly and convincingly contrary to law and the appellate court could not find an abuse of discretion related to defendant's individual sentences or cumulative sentence, because defendant's total combined sentence of 10 years for multiple offenses was within the statutory range for his various crimes, and the trial court explained its reasons for imposing, with respect to some of the counts, maximum and consecutive prison sentences; the three year prison term for aggravated theft was within the statutory range. State v. Slagle, 2011-Ohio-1463, 2011 Ohio App. LEXIS 1252 (Ohio Ct. App., Highland County), overruled in part, State v. Pierce, 2011-Ohio-5353, 2011 Ohio App. LEXIS 4387 (Ohio Ct. App., Meigs County 2011).

Defendant's sentence for two counts of theft was not contrary to law because the trial court stated that it had fully considered the information contained in the presentence investigation report, the information presented at the hearing, the record, and the statutory factors. Also, the trial court did not abuse its discretion in imposing maximum sentences because it could have reasonably found that the victims suffered serious economic harm, that defendant held a position of trust in the community (he was an attorney), his professional reputation or occupation was used to facilitate the offenses, his relationship with the victims facilitated the offense, and that his previous position as a prosecutor increased the seriousness of these offenses. State v. Saunders, 2011-Ohio-391, 2011 Ohio App. LEXIS 334 (Ohio Ct. App., Greene County 2011).

In a case where defendant entered an Alford plea to grand theft and forgery, a trial court did not abuse its discretion by imposing a 24 month sentence; the trial court considered the record as well as the principles and purposes of sentencing under R.C. 2929.11 and balanced the seriousness and recidivism factors under R.C. 2929.12 before imposing sentence. Moreover, the sentences imposed were within the statutory ranges for the crimes, and there was no abuse of discretion in imposing the sentences. State v. Bielek, 2010-Ohio-5402, 2010 Ohio App. LEXIS 4565 (Ohio Ct. App., Lake County 2010).

Trial court properly imposed upon defendant five 12-month sentences upon jury verdicts finding him guilty of theft, vandalism, possessing criminal tools, and receiving stolen property; the court was not required to make specific factual findings before imposing consecutive sentences. Moreover, the sentences were within the statutory guidelines, and there was no abuse of discretion. State v. Hundley, 2010-Ohio-4640, 2010 Ohio App. LEXIS 4001 (Ohio Ct. App., Hamilton County 2010).

Trial court erred by imposing a six-month jail sentence for misdemeanor theft under R.C. 2913.02, which exceeded by two days the maximum 180-day sentence specified in R.C. 2929.24(A)(1). State v. Au, 2010-Ohio-4418, 2010 Ohio App. LEXIS 3716 (Ohio Ct. App., Delaware County 2010).

Trial court did not abuse its discretion in sentencing defendant to the 180-day maximum jail sentence after defendant was convicted of first degree misdemeanor theft; the trial court considered all of the factors in R.C. 2929.22 including defendant's lack of a prior record but believed that defendant had shown no remorse at trial and sentenced him to 180 days to punish him, to make him serve as an example to others, and to dissuade him from committing similar crimes. State v. Townsend, 2010-Ohio-4417, 2010 Ohio App. LEXIS 3718 (Ohio Ct. App., Delaware County 2010).

Trial court acted within its discretion when it sentenced defendant to 18 years in prison based upon his convictions for engaging in a pattern of corrupt activity, aggravated theft, money laundering, forgery, and tampering with records since, before imposing sentence, the trial court stated that it had reviewed the presentence investigation report and the sentencing memoranda prepared by the parties, that it had considered the principles and purposes of sentencing under R.C. 2929.11 and the seriousness and recidivism factors in R.C. 2929.12, that defendant had engaged in a substantial degree of premeditation in an elaborate scheme of theft that continued for six years, that defendant manipulated records and presented tampered records in order to continue the deception, and that defendant was in a position of trust and used the position to facilitate the offense. State v. Noe, 2009-Ohio-6978, 2009 Ohio App. LEXIS 5825 (Ohio Ct. App., Lucas County 2009).

As defendant completely served and satisfied the sentence imposed on his conviction for misdemeanor theft, in violation of R.C. 2913.02(A)(3), and he did not assert a civil disability or loss of civil rights that he might suffer as a result of that conviction, any appeal therefrom was rendered moot. State v. Cicerchi, 2009-Ohio-2249, 182 Ohio App. 3d 753, 915 N.E.2d 350, 2009 Ohio App. LEXIS 1923 (Ohio Ct. App., Cuyahoga County 2009).

Trial court did not err in sentencing defendant to a non-minimum consecutive sentence because the court's imposition of a one-year term of incarceration for felony theft consecutive to an additional one-year term of incarceration for committing that felony while out on post-release control was not an abuse of discretion. Given defendant's substantial and serious criminal history, pattern of violations while out on parole, and commission of the underlying offense in the case while out on parole, the record unequivocally demonstrated that the trial court's imposition of a one-year term of incarceration for felony theft consecutive to an additional one-year term of incarceration for committing that felony while out on post-release control was within the statutory range and the discretion of the trial court in sentencing defendant and was not arbitrary, unreasonable, or unconscionable. State v. Wallerstein, 2009-Ohio-6685, 2009 Ohio App. LEXIS 5611 (Ohio Ct. App., Lucas County 2009).

Sentence of two-years' imprisonment imposed for theft, by deception, from an elderly person, in violation of R.C. 2913.02(A)(3) and 2913.02(B)(3), was affirmed because defendant made no showing that the sentence was grossly disproportionate under R.C. 2929.11(B). State v. Webb, 2009-Ohio-6127, 2009 Ohio App. LEXIS 5144 (Ohio Ct. App., Darke County 2009).

Trial court did not violate the purposes and principles of sentencing under R.C. 2929.11 and 2929.12 in sentencing defendant to serve maximum sentences, consecutively, on his convictions for fifth-degree felony theft under R.C. 2913.02(A) and (B)(2), theft from an elderly person or disabled adult under § 2913.02(A)(3) and (B)(3), and petty theft as the sentence imposed was in the permissible range and was not clearly and convincingly contrary to law. The trial court gave substantial consideration to the relevant statutory factors, considering the nature of the offenses, the fact that defendant was a repeat offender, and that he violated the terms of his community control on more than one occasion. State v. Walters, 2009-Ohio-3198, 2009 Ohio App. LEXIS 2726 (Ohio Ct. App., Lucas County 2009).

In a case involving consecutive sentences, plain error under Crim.R. 52 was not shown because a 60-month sentence for breaking and entering, theft, and vandalism was not contrary to law, and the trial court considered R.C. 2929.11 and R.C. 2929.12; moreover, the trial court considered the nature of the offenses, the impact on the victims, the lack of remorse, and defendant's criminal history. Defendant waived a Blakely challenge by failing to object to the sentence on that ground; therefore, only a plain error review was available. State v. Montgomery, 2009-Ohio-5073, 2009 Ohio App. LEXIS 4298 (Ohio Ct. App., Clermont County 2009).

Defendant's maximum sentence for theft, under R.C. 2913.02(A)(1), was not improper, even though a codefendant received a lesser sentence, because the codefendant admitted guilt and cooperated by testifying against defendant, while defendant denied guilt and testified falsely, which were factors that could be taken into account in imposing defendant's sentence. State v. Bean, 2009-Ohio-5037, 2009 Ohio App. LEXIS 4264 (Ohio Ct. App., Montgomery County 2009).

Maximum, consecutive sentences imposed upon defendant's theft and drug possession convictions were not clearly and convincingly contrary to law as they were within the statutory range for fifth-degree felonies and as the trial court considered the factors in R.C. 2929.11 and 2929.12. The trial court did not abuse its discretion in imposing the sentences as the trial court considered the factors in §§ 2929.11 and 2929.12, taking particular note of the fact that defendant had 17 prior adult criminal convictions, which supported the findings that defendant was more likely to recidivate, that maximum and consecutive sentences were necessary to protect the public, and that maximum and consecutive sentences were necessary to punish and rehabilitate defendant. State v. Voycik, 2009-Ohio-3669, 2009 Ohio App. LEXIS 3142 (Ohio Ct. App., Washington County 2009).

Trial court did not err by finding defendant, a nurse, eligible for intervention in lieu of conviction (ILC) following defendant's guilty plea to theft of drugs under R.C. 2913.02, because the legislature intended for nurses and other licensed medical professionals to be eligible for ILC. The phrase "position of trust" in R.C. 2929.13(B)(1)(d), the community control statute, was meant to apply predominantly to the offender's public standing and, because R.C. 4723.28(B)(1)(5) specifically allowed the board of nursing to impose sanctions for a judicial finding of eligibility for intervention in lieu of conviction for violating any municipal, state, county, or federal drug law, the legislature intended ILC to apply to medical professionals. State v. Massien, 2009-Ohio-1521, 2009 Ohio App. LEXIS 1340 (Ohio Ct. App., Summit County 2009), aff'd, 2010-Ohio-1864, 125 Ohio St. 3d 204, 926 N.E.2d 1282, 2010 Ohio LEXIS 1043 (Ohio 2010).

It was no abuse of discretion for a trial court to impose consecutive prison terms for defendant's fifth degree felonies of breaking and entering, under R.C. 2911.13(A), and theft, under R.C. 2913.02(A)(1), because (1) prison was required, under R.C. 2929.13(B)(2)(a), due to defendant's prior incarceration and a finding that defendant was not amenable to community control, and (2) the terms imposed were the minimum allowed for a fifth degree felony, under R.C. 2929.14(A)(5). State v. Jones, 2009-Ohio-694, 2009 Ohio App. LEXIS 561 (Ohio Ct. App., Greene County 2009).

As defendant's conviction for theft, in violation of R.C. 2913.02(A)(2), was a third-degree felony, a sentence imposed on her of four years' imprisonment was not excessive because it was within the statutory range pursuant to R.C. 2929.14(A)(3); the sentence could not be disturbed where there was no showing that it was clearly and convincingly not supported by the record or otherwise contrary to law pursuant to R.C. 2953.08(G)(2). State v. Preztak, 2009-Ohio-621, 181 Ohio App. 3d 106, 907 N.E.2d 1254, 2009 Ohio App. LEXIS 539 (Ohio Ct. App., Cuyahoga County 2009).

Defendant's consecutive sentences for various theft crimes against elderly victims were not erroneous because the sentences were not clearly and convincingly contrary to law, as (1) the sentences were within the statutory ranges specified by R.C. 2929.14, (2) the trial court considered the purposes and principles of sentencing in R.C. 2929.11 in imposing the sentences, as well as the seriousness and recidivism factors in R.C. 2929.12, and (3) the court advised defendant of post release control, and the sentences were not an abuse of discretion because the court considered defendant's criminal record, each victim's vulnerability, and the harm caused by defendant's acts, and no sentence was selected arbitrarily or based on impermissible factors, pertinent factors were considered, without giving unreasonable weight to one factor, and no sentence was based on an arbitrary distinction contrary to due process. State v. Snyder, 2008-Ohio-6709, 2008 Ohio App. LEXIS 5623 (Ohio Ct. App., Licking County 2008).

Court rejected defendant's contention that his 14-year prison sentence, imposed upon his convictions for robbery, domestic violence, intimidation of a crime victim or witness, failure to comply with the order or signal of a police officer, grand theft, driving under suspension, and three misdemeanor traffic violations, was grossly disproportionate to his crimes because, while the State had originally offered defendant a five-year sentence, which defendant had rejected, this fact did not show that defendant's sentence was disproportionate. The trial court considered the facts that defendant had committed two prior domestic violence offenses against the victim, that the purpose of sentencing was to protect the public and punish the offender, and that the trial court considered the presentence investigation report, and defendant pointed to no evidence that the trial court failed to properly consider the factors in R.C. 2929.11 and 2929.12 in his sentencing. State v. Banks, 2008-Ohio-6432, 2008 Ohio App. LEXIS 5381 (Ohio Ct. App., Summit County 2008).

Consecutive 9-month prison sentences for the possession of cocaine under R.C. 2925.11(A), (C)(4)(a) and theft under R.C. 2913.02 were appropriate as both charges were felonies of the fifth degree punishable by up to 12 months in prison under R.C. 2929.14(A)(5) and the trial court had the discretion to impose a sentence within the statutory range. State v. Hinkle, 2008-Ohio-6344, 2008 Ohio App. LEXIS 5278 (Ohio Ct. App., Licking County 2008).

Since a trial court followed the statutory process for felony sentencing, considered the overriding purposes of felony sentence in R.C. 2929.11, the sentence imposed was within the statutory range for defendant's convictions, and the record was devoid of any evidence of inconsistency or disproportionality, defendant's maximum sentence, imposed upon her convictions on one count of theft with elderly victim specification attached and ten counts of forgery with elderly victim specifications attached, was supported by the record and was not contrary to law. State v. Hicks, 2008-Ohio-6284, 2008 Ohio App. LEXIS 5249 (Ohio Ct. App., Cuyahoga County 2008).

Trial court did not abuse its discretion by imposing a more than minimum sentence on defendant upon his convictions on two counts of theft and one count of breaking and entering because, contrary to defendant's contention, the trial court considered the R.C. 2929.12(E) factors. Specifically, the trial court considered defendant's criminal history, noting its awareness of defendant's lengthy experience with the criminal justice system; defendant's acknowledgement of his substance abuse and defendant's desire to obtain treatment, noting that defendant had failed to seek out any treatment on his own; and whether defendant's remorse was genuine. State v. Plaisted, 2008-Ohio-1337, 2008 Ohio App. LEXIS 1183 (Ohio Ct. App., Lake County 2008).

Defendant's maximum sentence for theft, under R.C. 2913.02(A)(1), was not an abuse of discretion because (1) the trial court stated that the court considered the purposes and principles of sentencing, in R.C. 2929.11, as well as seriousness and recidivism factors in R.C. 2929.12, (2) the sentence was within the statutory range for defendant's crime, and (3) defendant's request for drug treatment was properly denied given defendant's prior squandered opportunities for such treatment. State v. Fortune, 2008-Ohio-3741, 2008 Ohio App. LEXIS 3168 (Ohio Ct. App., Geauga County 2008).

Trial court's imposition of a recommended, non-minimum term of imprisonment on defendant was proper where defendant was convicted of fifth-degree felony theft, in violation of R.C. 2913.02(A)(2), as the trial court considered the statutory factors under R.C. 2929.11 and 2929.12, it acted within the Foster decision by not engaging in judicial fact-finding, and the sentence was within the allowable statutory range under R.C. 2929.14(A)(5). State v. Long, 2007-Ohio-6921, 2007 Ohio App. LEXIS 6072 (Ohio Ct. App., Columbiana County 2007).

As defendant entered a no contest plea to attempted theft, in violation of R.C. 2913.02 and 2923.02, based on the value of property that was $500 or more and less than $5,000, he was convicted of a first-degree misdemeanor offense; the imposition of a one-year sentence of incarceration by the trial court exceeded the maximum allowable term of 180 days under R.C. 2929.24(A)(1), such that the sentence imposed was erroneous. State v. Smith, 2007-Ohio-3420, 2007 Ohio App. LEXIS 3173 (Ohio Ct. App., Cuyahoga County 2007).

Because the court modified defendant's theft conviction from a fifth degree felony to a first degree misdemeanor, it had to vacate that portion of defendant's sentence that ordered him to serve six months in prison for the theft conviction and remand for resentencing on the modified petty theft conviction. Pursuant to R.C. 2929.24(A), convictions for misdemeanors are punishable by a "jail term" not a "prison term." State v. Russell, 2006-Ohio-6764, 2006 Ohio App. LEXIS 6681 (Ohio Ct. App., Cuyahoga County 2006).

Trial court did not err in sentencing defendant to an additional three years for the firearm specification, under R.C. 2941.145, on the theft of a firearm charge, under R.C. 2913.02(A)(1), even though possession of a firearm was an element of both the offense and the specification, because more than mere possession was required to be found guilty. The jury specifically found that defendant not only possessed the firearm but also that he indicated that he possessed the firearm. State v. Mosley, 2006-Ohio-1756, 166 Ohio App. 3d 71, 849 N.E.2d 73, 2006 Ohio App. LEXIS 1628 (Ohio Ct. App., Delaware County 2006).

Trial court did not abuse its discretion in sentencing defendant to a fine and 90 days in jail for four petty theft convictions as: (1) defendant did not support her claim that a presentence investigation was required, (2) the trial court considered the R.C. 2929.22 factors, including defendant's mental illness as defendant was ordered to undergo mental health counseling, and (3) defendant's § 2929.22(E) claim lacked merit as

§ 2929.22(E) had been removed. State v. Smith, 2006-Ohio-1558, 2006 Ohio App. LEXIS 1491 (Ohio Ct. App., Wayne County 2006).

In imposing the maximum sentences for grand theft and forgery, the court properly found that defendant posed the greatest likelihood of committing future crimes and committed the worst forms of the offense where defendant defrauded a hospital of almost $40,000. State v. Weiss, 2005-Ohio-6704, 2005 Ohio App. LEXIS 6031 (Ohio Ct. App., Lake County 2005).

While the trial court had complied with R.C. 2929.14(B) and made the required findings before imposing more than the shortest prison term for a third-degree felony, and a two-year prison term did not seem excessive based on the seriousness of defendant's conduct of stealing $435,049 from her employer, the trial court could not elevate the shortest sentence for her since she had not previously served a prison term by consideration of the more serious factors under R.C. 2929.12(B) alone, even if they were admitted by defendant. State v. Weber, 2005-Ohio-4854, 2005 Ohio App. LEXIS 4376 (Ohio Ct. App., Hamilton County 2005), aff'd in part and rev'd in part, 2006-Ohio-2394, 109 Ohio St. 3d 411, 848 N.E.2d 809, 2006 Ohio LEXIS 1395 (Ohio 2006).

Imposing non-minimum sentences for theft from an elderly person and engaging in a hearing aid business without a license did not violate Blakely v. Washngton, 542 U.S. 296 (2004), because the findings made in imposing maximum or non-minimum sentences limited the sentence that the sentencing court could impose within the statutory range authorized in R.C. 2929.14(A). State v. Wright, 2005-Ohio-3907, 2005 Ohio App. LEXIS 3596 (Ohio Ct. App., Clermont County 2005), rev'd, 2006-Ohio-2109, 109 Ohio St. 3d 313, 847 N.E.2d 1174, 2006 Ohio LEXIS 1161 (Ohio 2006).

Trial court did not err in imposing a term of local incarceration as part of a community control sentence upon defendant's felony theft conviction, where defendant participated in a scheme to obtain, by deception, more than $5,000 dollars from her employer, while she was employed in a position of trust further, the trial court was not required to explicitly state on the record that it considered a financial sanction or a community service sanction as the sole sanction for the offense. State v. Jordan, 2004-Ohio-2111, 2004 Ohio App. LEXIS 1831 (Ohio Ct. App., Scioto County 2004).

Where the trial court failed to find that consecutive sentences were necessary to protect the public from future crime or to punish the offender, and that said sentence was not disproportionate to the seriousness of the offender's conduct and to the danger the offender posed to the public, the consecutive sentence imposed was reversed. State v. Wallace, 2004-Ohio-1694, 2004 Ohio App. LEXIS 1490 (Ohio Ct. App., Delaware County 2004).

Maximum sentence imposed against defendant upon his grand theft conviction was upheld where the trial court sufficiently met the mandates set forth in R.C. 2929.14(C), finding that defendant was not amenable to community control and posed the greatest likelihood of recidivism; further, the sentence was not against the manifest weight of the evidence and contrary to law where defendant failed to include the pre-sentence investigation reports or any of the victim impact statements as part of the record, contrary to App.R. 9. State v. Wallace, 2004-Ohio-1694, 2004 Ohio App. LEXIS 1490 (Ohio Ct. App., Delaware County 2004).

Where a trial court did not find at a sentencing hearing that defendant committed the worst form of theft (in violation of R.C. 2913.02), posed a likelihood of reoffending, or was a major drug or repeat violent offender as required by R.C. 2929.14(C), the trial court erred by imposing a maximum sentence. State v. Lint, 2003-Ohio-6020, 2003 Ohio App. LEXIS 5349 (Ohio Ct. App., Stark County 2003).

Trial court did not point to specific reasons contained in the record on which it relied and why it relied on them to impose consecutive sentences; it named aggravating factors (including, permissibly, aggravating factors which were specific elements of the crimes charged, such as the age of the victim, under R.C. 2913.02(A)(3) (theft from an elderly person)), but did not indicate the relationship of those factors to its specific conclusions as required by R.C. 2929.14. State v. Wilson, 2003-Ohio-4599, 2003 Ohio App. LEXIS 4091 (Ohio Ct. App., Lake County 2003).

Appeals court reversed the sentences imposed for R.C. 2911.12(A)(2) (burglary) and R.C. 2913.02(A)(3) (theft from an elderly person), to run consecutively with a sentence a defendant was presently serving, because the trial court (1) did not fully comply with the consecutive sentencing statute, R.C. 2929.14(E)(4), by not making the requisite proportionality analysis, and (2) did not provide sufficient supporting reasons for imposing consecutive sentences. State v. Wilson, 2003-Ohio-4599, 2003 Ohio App. LEXIS 4091 (Ohio Ct. App., Lake County 2003).

**—Consecutive sentences**

Trial court did not err in imposing consecutive sentences on defendant, amounting to 102 months, after she pleaded guilty to three counts of theft and one count of money laundering; although the trial court did not recite the statute verbatim, it could be gleaned from the language that the trial court carefully considered the statutory factors, plus the sentence was not disproportionate to defendant's conduct, and the financial and mental harm to multiple victims was great. State v. Whitman, 2019-Ohio-2718, 2019 Ohio App. LEXIS 2820 (Ohio Ct. App., Columbiana County 2019).

Defendant's sentence of 54 months in prison for theft of drugs and aggravated possession of drugs was proper because the trial court considered R.C. 2929.11 in sentencing defendant and considered his extensive criminal history, his failure to respond to previous attempts at community control, and the need to protect the public. State v. Dildine, 2018-Ohio-1771, 2018 Ohio App. LEXIS 1903 (Ohio Ct. App., Logan County 2018).

Trial court made the required findings to support the imposition of a consecutive sentence where the trial court found: (1) that consecutive sentences were necessary to protect the public from future crime by defendant and to punish defendant, (2) that consecutive sentences were not disproportionate to the seriousness of defendant's conduct and to the danger he posed to the public, and (3) that defendant's history of criminal conduct demonstrated that consecutive sentences were necessary to protect the public from future crime by him, which was based upon the fact that he posed the maximum likelihood of recidivism. State v. Agostini, 2005-Ohio-5371, 2005 Ohio App. LEXIS 4874 (Ohio Ct. App., Clermont County 2005).

**—Maximum sentence**

Trial court did not abuse its discretion in imposing a jail term of 180 days for defendant's theft conviction because the sentence was designed to punish defendant and, since he had been sanctioned multiple times before, the sentence was necessary to protect the public from future crime. The trial court did not base its determination of the maximum sentence based upon the "worst form" of the offense, but upon defendant's conduct and response to his prior criminal convictions and sanctions and the necessity to deter appellant from committing a future crime, given his lengthy criminal history. State v. Taylor, 2018-Ohio-827, 2018 Ohio App. LEXIS 873 (Ohio Ct. App., Muskingum County 2018).

Where defendant entered a guilty plea, the trial court did not abuse its discretion by imposing the maximum 12 month sentence in prison for theft, 18 months for safecracking, and 18 months for burglary, to be served consecutively; the sentence was within the proper range and the trial court carefully considered the statutory factors. The fact that defendant committed the offenses so that he could obtain money to purchase illegal drugs was a factor supporting a more severe penalty. State v. Pyles, 2014-Ohio-4146, 2014 Ohio App. LEXIS 4063 (Ohio Ct. App., Belmont County 2014).

Trial court made the required findings to support the imposition of the maximum sentence for grand theft and gave its reasons for doing so where the trial court read into the record parts of defendant's lengthy criminal record, which included over 40 arrests; the trial court also noted the probation department's assessment that defendant had never taken responsibility for his actions, and noted that it seemed like a "fair assessment." State v. Agostini, 2005-Ohio-5371, 2005 Ohio App. LEXIS 4874 (Ohio Ct. App., Clermont County 2005).

Where the judge found that consecutive sentences were necessary to protect the public and punish the offender, the sentences were not disproportionate to the seriousness of defendant's conduct, and defendant was under post release control at the time for a similar offense, and the court complied with R.C. 2929.19(B) and 2929.14(C) by stating its reasons for imposing maximum sentences, the maximum and consecutive sentences for theft and passing bad checks were not contrary to law. State v. Robinson, 2005-Ohio-4795, 2005 Ohio App. LEXIS 4330 (Ohio Ct. App., Summit County 2005).

Trial court did not abuse its discretion in giving defendant the maximum sentence for theft where the trial court found that defendant had a long history of criminal convictions and had served five different prison terms for a variety of offenses, that there had been a failure of rehabilitation, and that the likelihood of recidivism was very high; further, the trial court stated its reasons for finding that defendant posed the greatest likelihood of recidivism, and those reasons were supported by the record. State v. King, 2005-Ohio-4656, 2005 Ohio App. LEXIS 4184 (Ohio Ct. App., Lake County 2005).

**—Motion to reconsider**

Defendant's appeal from the denial of his nunc pro tunc filing was dismissed as his nunc pro tunc filing was, in effect, a motion seeking reconsideration of a valid final judgment sentencing him to three years for theft pursuant to a plea bargain, which the trial court had no jurisdiction to reconsider; the nunc pro tunc filing was a nullity. State v. Steele, 2005-Ohio-4786, 2005 Ohio App. LEXIS 4289 (Ohio Ct. App., Franklin County 2005).

**—Non-minimum**

Imposing non-minimum sentences for theft from an elderly person and engaging in a hearing aid business without a license did not violate Blakely v. Washngton, 542 U.S. 296 (2004), because the findings made in imposing maximum or non-minimum sentences limited the sentence that the sentencing court could impose within the statutory range authorized in R.C. 2929.14(A). State v. Wright, 2005-Ohio-3907, 2005 Ohio App. LEXIS 3596 (Ohio Ct. App., Clermont County 2005), rev'd, 2006-Ohio-2109, 109 Ohio St. 3d 313, 847 N.E.2d 1174, 2006 Ohio LEXIS 1161 (Ohio 2006).

**—Statutory amendment**

Because defendant was sentenced more than six months after the effective date of Am. Sub. H.B. 86, Gen. Assem. (Ohio 2011), he was entitled to have been sentenced under its provisions. Thus, in each count of the indictment, the bill of particulars, the trial court's jury charge, and the verdict forms signed by the jury, the value of the properties stolen was erroneously categorized under the pre-H.B. 86 threshold values, making the offenses of more serious degree, resulting in sentences that exceeded the maximum. State v. Johnson, 2016-Ohio-781, 60 N.E.3d 661, 2016 Ohio App. LEXIS 699 (Ohio Ct. App., Hamilton County 2016).

Trial court did not err in following the mandates of H.B. 86, Gen. Assem. (Ohio) and R.C. 1.58(B), and reducing defendant's charges to first-degree misdemeanors pursuant to the amended valuation thresholds established in H.B. 86, because the amended valuation thresholds of R.C. 2913.02 and 2913.11, became effective on September 30, 2011 before sentencing. State v. David, 2012-Ohio-3984, 2012 Ohio App. LEXIS 3516 (Ohio Ct. App., Licking County 2012).



**Sentence proper**

In a case in which defendant was convicted of theft and telecommunications fraud, defendant's request to vacate, modify, or decrease his sentence based on his arguments that the victim allowed defendant to use his phone and that he mistakenly charged the victim's debit card and attempted to correct the mistake was unsupported by the record. State v. Burey, 2021-Ohio-943, 2021 Ohio App. LEXIS 959 (Ohio Ct. App., Cuyahoga County 2021).

Trial court imposed upon defendant an indefinite prison term with a minimum of six years and a maximum of nine years for each of the three second-degree felony burglary offenses, 30-months for third-degree felony identity fraud, and 18-months for fourth-degree felony grand theft offense; these prison terms were within the appropriate statutory range and the trial court considered the sentencing factors, such that the sentences were not clearly contrary to law. State v. Reed, 2021-Ohio-1623, 2021 Ohio App. LEXIS 1577 (Ohio Ct. App., Union County 2021).

Although court maintained that defendant's aggregate 65-year sentence was disproportionate to her conduct and shocked the court's conscience, each of defendant's individual sentences for 17 counts of second-degree burglary, 4 counts of third-degree theft, 10 counts of fourth-degree theft, and 15 misdemeanor counts of receiving stolen property were within the range authorized and thus they did not constitute cruel and unusual punishment. State v. Gwynne, 2021-Ohio-2378, 173 N.E.3d 603, 2021 Ohio App. LEXIS 2353 (Ohio Ct. App., Delaware County 2021).

Defendant's assertion that he "needed treatment" did not suffice to establish that the trial court committed legal error by sentencing him to a prison term; the 11-month sentence imposed by the trial court was within the permissible sentencing range and the trial court opined that defendant's extensive history of prior theft offenses made him an inappropriate candidate for alternatives to imprisonment. State v. Waggoner, 2020-Ohio-212, 2020 Ohio App. LEXIS 180 (Ohio Ct. App., Montgomery County 2020).

Trial court did not err in not sentencing defendant similarly to his codefendant and in imposing a greater sentence upon defendant, for four counts of grand theft and two counts of theft, which arose from a home improvement business scam, because the fact that he was sentenced to greater sentence did not in itself violate the consistency requirement; trial court found that defendant's home improvement scam was one of the worst forms of the offense because of the large amount of money involved. State v. Dishong, 2020-Ohio-4049, 2020 Ohio App. LEXIS 2938 (Ohio Ct. App., Stark County 2020).

Trial court did not abuse its discretion in sentencing defendant to the maximum jail term of 90 days after he pleaded guilty to attempted theft; there was nothing in the record that affirmatively indicated that the trial court failed to consider the proper factors, and given the information in the presentence investigation report, the trial court could have found that the maximum jail sentence was necessary to deter defendant from committing future crime in light of his conduct and response to prior sanctions. State v. Moore, 2019-Ohio-2267, 2019 Ohio App. LEXIS 2360 (Ohio Ct. App., Medina County 2019).

Upon entering guilty pleas to two fourth degree theft offenses, arising from a scheme in which defendant defrauded elderly victims, the trial court acted within its discretion in imposing a sentence of imprisonment on him, as the community control presumption was inapplicable because he pleaded guilty to more than one nonviolent felony of the fourth or fifth degree. State v. Boswell, 2019-Ohio-2949, 2019 Ohio App. LEXIS 3038 (Ohio Ct. App., Erie County 2019).

Defendant's 18-month sentence for grand theft was not contrary to law, even though the State recommended that defendant be sentenced to community control sanctions as agreed in the plea negotiations, as the sentence was within the range for a third degree felony, and defendant had been informed at the plea hearing that he could be sentenced to either community control sanctions or a prison term. State v. Heinlein, 2017-Ohio-7425, 2017 Ohio App. LEXIS 3740 (Ohio Ct. App., Greene County 2017).

Evidence supported defendant's 18-month sentence for grand theft, even though defendant was 46 and this was his first felony conviction, as: (1) he had been convicted of traffic violations, passing bad checks, theft and criminal trespass; (2) the pre-sentence report indicated that defendant was not candid concerning his involvement in the theft offense, that he did not consider his daily heroin use to be a problem, and that he did not complete an ordered drug and alcohol assessment; and (3) defendant did not show remorse. State v. Heinlein, 2017-Ohio-7425, 2017 Ohio App. LEXIS 3740 (Ohio Ct. App., Greene County 2017).

Trial court did not err when ordering defendant to serve his grand theft of firearm sentence consecutively to his theft of drugs sentence because consecutive sentences were mandatory for defendant's theft offenses since one of his offenses was grand theft of a firearm, and, thus, the trial court was not required to make certain statutory findings. State v. Ervin, 2015-Ohio-3688, 2015 Ohio App. LEXIS 3595 (Ohio Ct. App., Champaign County 2015).

After defendant pleaded guilty to theft charge, the trial court's imposition of an 11-month sentence was not contrary to law because, inter alia, the sentence was within the statutory range, and defendant committed the offense while under community control sanctions, admitted to causing serious physical harm to an individual during the events leading to the theft charge, had a history of criminal convictions, and was under the influence of drugs at his presentence investigation interview. State v. Lewis, 2015-Ohio-4629, 2015 Ohio App. LEXIS 4517 (Ohio Ct. App., Wood County 2015).

Sentence imposed for defendant's conviction of fifth-degree felony theft was appropriate because at the time of his plea entry, defendant understood that he was pleading guilty to fifth-degree felony theft. State v. Smith, 2014-Ohio-5076, 2014 Ohio App. LEXIS 4952 (Ohio Ct. App., Geauga County 2014).

**Series of offenses**

Trial court was not statutorily required to aggregate a series of forgery offenses with a count of theft from an elderly person or disabled adult, which was already an aggregation of multiple theft offenses, because they were two separate series of offenses. State v. Gibson, 2014-Ohio-136, 2014 Ohio App. LEXIS 126 (Ohio Ct. App., Champaign County 2014).

Because R.C. 2913.61(C) does not identify Medicaid fraud under R.C. 2913.40 as a series of offenses committed by a defendant in his or her employment involving a common course of conduct to defraud multiple victims under R.C. 2913.02 or as a theft offense under R.C. 2913.01(K) authorized to be prosecuted as a single offense, the State cannot prosecute any defendant for a series of Medicaid fraud offenses as a single offense; defendant could not be prosecuted for acts committed over an 11-month period as a single offense, which qualified as a fourth-degree felony, based on an aggregation of the value of the funds but was instead found guilty of Medicaid fraud as a first-degree misdemeanor. State v. McGhee, 2007-Ohio-6537, 2007 Ohio App. LEXIS 5729 (Ohio Ct. App., Franklin County 2007).

**Series of thefts**

Defendant's dismissal motion based on the alleged expiration of the statute of limitations on a charge against her of theft, in violation of R.C. 2913.02(A)(2), was properly denied, as her multiple thefts had to be aggregated under R.C. 2913.61(C)(1), as they all involved taking money from her employer, such that the limitations period on defendant's continuing course of conduct did not being to run until the final theft was committed pursuant to R.C. 2901.13(D) State v. Preztak, 2009-Ohio-621, 181 Ohio App. 3d 106, 907 N.E.2d 1254, 2009 Ohio App. LEXIS 539 (Ohio Ct. App., Cuyahoga County 2009).

**Shoplifting**

Weight of the evidence supported defendant's robbery conviction because his actions, as shown on the security DVD and through the testimony of loss prevention officer, in putting on and wearing store clothes, placing merchandise in his pockets, and then proceeding through the door without paying supported the jury's finding that defendant took store property without consent, evidencing the use of force while attempting or committing a theft offense. State v. Taylor, 2011-Ohio-6493, 2011 Ohio App. LEXIS 5362 (Ohio Ct. App., Stark County 2011).

Trial court did not err by overruling defendant's motion for acquittal in a complicity to theft prosecution. While defendant could have been indicted under R.C. 2913.02(A)(1) for shoplifting, the State was allowed, instead, to indict her on complicity to theft by deception because the evidence supported a finding that defendant committed "deception" under R.C. 2913.01(A), and a prosecutor could bring charges against a defendant under any statute that proscribed the criminal behavior. State v. Murchison, 2008-Ohio-2327, 2008 Ohio App. LEXIS 1970 (Ohio Ct. App., Lake County 2008).

R.C. 2913.02(A)(1) is the proper subsection for a prosecution for shoplifting: State v. Phillips, 84 Ohio App. 3d 836, 619 N.E.2d 29, 1993 Ohio App. LEXIS 6506 (Ohio Ct. App., Lake County 1993).

**Statute of limitations**

Because the indictment clearly stated that the element of "beyond the scope of the express or implied consent" was present in the theft case, defendant's no contest plea to the indictment was properly accepted. Even if the State's factual narrative was deficient, and had it been required, the trial court specifically and explicitly stated it also considered the allegations in the indictment, which were sufficient to convict defendant. State v. Sevitz, 2015-Ohio-5047, 2015 Ohio App. LEXIS 4892 (Ohio Ct. App., Allen County 2015).

Because R.C. 2913.61(C)(1) required that the employee's thefts from the employer be aggregated, which evidenced the fact that the employee engaged in a continuing course of conduct, the statute of limitations did not begin to run until the thefts were discovered: State v. Preztak, 2009-Ohio-621, 181 Ohio App. 3d 106, 907 N.E.2d 1254, 2009 Ohio App. LEXIS 539 (Ohio Ct. App., Cuyahoga County 2009).

**Theft from protected class**

Sufficient evidence supported defendant's conviction for theft of a person in a protected class because, even without the brief testimony of the casino employee, the State was able to prove that defendant knowingly exerted control over the 89-year-old victim's credit union account without his consent, with purpose to deprive him of funds in the amount of $37,500 or more and less than $150,000. A rational juror could have found that defendant's testimony regarding the source of her gambling funds was not credible. State v. McKee, 2019-Ohio-4307, 2019 Ohio App. LEXIS 4378 (Ohio Ct. App., Logan County 2019).

**Theft in office**

Trial court's omission of the additional elements of theft in the jury instruction did not to the level of plain error because the omission of the specific instruction that the jury needed to find deception for the theft in office charge did not deprive defendant of a fair trial or result in a manifest miscarriage of justice because the theft was predicated upon deception. The jury, finding him guilty of theft, inherently found that he deceived the school district. State v. Burns, 2011-Ohio-4230, 2011 Ohio App. LEXIS 3572 (Ohio Ct. App., Cuyahoga County 2011).

Under R.C. 2913.02 and 2921.41, lawful seizure of property by law enforcement authorities is not an element of crime of theft in office, which is a crime against actual possession and not ownership or lawful possession: Payne v. Janasz, 711 F.2d 1305, 1983 U.S. App. LEXIS 26515 (6th Cir. Ohio), cert. denied, 464 U.S. 1019, 104 S. Ct. 552, 78 L. Ed. 2d 726, 1983 U.S. LEXIS 2757 (U.S. 1983).

**Theft offense**

Court concluded that sufficient evidence supported the grand theft of a motor vehicle convictions although no one witnessed him take his mother's van, there was circumstantial evidence that he knowingly obtained or exerted control over it on two occasions without her consent and with purpose to deprive her of it as there was evidence that officer saw a man in the van who had some of the same features, and a trooper caught him driving the van though he never had permission to use it. State v. Dettwiller, 2022-Ohio-134, 2022 Ohio App. LEXIS 116 (Ohio Ct. App., Highland County 2022).

Sufficient evidence was presented that defendant was involved in the theft of cigarettes because defendant's phone records indicated that his phone pinged off of a cellphone tower less than one and one-half miles away from the road nine minutes before the theft occurred. Further, the driver of the cigarette truck testified that defendant looked similar to one of the men involved in the incident. State v. Fields, 2022-Ohio-620, 2022 Ohio App. LEXIS 538 (Ohio Ct. App., Cuyahoga County 2022).

Evidence was sufficient to convict defendant for theft because testimony was sufficient to establish that she specifically intended to deprive the store of its property by knowingly exerting control over merchandise that was not scanned or paid for without store's consent. State v. Champion, 2021-Ohio-4002, 2021 Ohio App. LEXIS 3915 (Ohio Ct. App., Hamilton County 2021).

Evidence was sufficient to convict defendant of theft because the State presented three witnesses to testify regarding the theft, and the investigation into the theft, including the amount and value of the missing cigarettes, and how the perpetrator was ultimately identified. And, it introduced the shelf labels and the training receipt which were used to calculate the amount and value of the stolen cigarettes. State v. Kanable, 2020-Ohio-4335, 2020 Ohio App. LEXIS 3223 (Ohio Ct. App., Wood County 2020).

Evidence was sufficient to support defendant's conviction of first degree theft as when viewing the evidence in the light most favorable to prosecution, a rational trier of fact could find the elements of misdemeanor theft offense proven beyond a reasonable doubt; record reflected the hotel washing machines were not in front, or immediately adjacent to, the hotel dumpsters, so as to arguably indicate they had been discarded and were available to be taken free of charge on a unilateral basis. State v. Taylor, 2020-Ohio-4852, 2020 Ohio App. LEXIS 3696 (Ohio Ct. App., Wood County 2020).

Defendant's claim that the finding of his guilt for misdemeanor theft was against the manifest weight of evidence was without merit because the record showed that although defendant testified that he did not know his friend was going to steal the phone of the victim, when he saw what his friend did, defendant kept the money of the victim and ran away to the same house that his friend ran to. State v. Allen, 2019-Ohio-1995, 2019 Ohio App. LEXIS 2059 (Ohio Ct. App., Cuyahoga County 2019).

Defendant's conviction for theft and possession of criminal tools was supported with sufficient evidence since the asset testified that he picked up DVDs and used a cutting device to remove a cell phone box from the store's prepaid phone wall. He also identified these items fell from his clothes as the ones taken from the store. And, since the officers found a pair of scissors in his pocket, the jury reasonably could have inferred that he used it to cut the cell phone box from its peg hook. State v. Seidowsky, 2019-Ohio-2610, 2019 Ohio App. LEXIS 2732 (Ohio Ct. App., Medina County 2019).

**Threat**

There was sufficient evidence to prove that defendant made a "threat," an essential element of the theft by threat charge and for extortion because the victim testified that defendant told him that if he did not give her money for an abortion, he would suffer some "disagreeable consequences," including that he would lose his job of 30 years and that, in view of his limitations, he would not be able to find another one. Also, defendant told the victim's father that if she did not get the money, she would tell the police that the victim raped her. State v. McKissick, 2008-Ohio-4856, 2008 Ohio App. LEXIS 4076 (Ohio Ct. App., Cuyahoga County 2008).

Where evidence could be viewed in such a way that the jury could find that defendant's conduct did not constitute threat of immediate force but amounted only to a threat of disagreeable consequences that did not involve the immediate use of force, court should have instructed the jury on theft by threat in addition to instructing on robbery, aggravated robbery and theft without consent: State v. Stone, 1996 Ohio App. LEXIS 254 (Ohio Ct. App., Hamilton County Jan. 31, 1996).

**Theft offense**

Defendant received over $13,000.00 in childcare cash assistance benefits and she did not commit the crime of illegal use of supplemental nutrition assistance program benefits or WIC program benefits in violation of R.C. 2913.46(B) until she exercised dominion and control over the benefits; defendant did not consummate the theft offense until she knowingly obtained or exerted control over the childcare cash assistance benefits. State v. Atkins, 2013-Ohio-2326, 2013 Ohio App. LEXIS 2251 (Ohio Ct. App., Fairfield County 2013).

**Underlying offense**

Sufficient evidence supported defendant's robbery conviction because the testimony established that defendant took the victim's wallet and disposed of it after strewing the contents around the floor. The victim had to search for the contents of his wallet, and ultimately never recovered the $60 that was in his wallet. State v. Gatewood, 2012-Ohio-3756, 2012 Ohio App. LEXIS 3312 (Ohio Ct. App., Fayette County 2012).

Any rational trier of fact could have found the essential elements, including serious physical harm, of both counts of aggravated robbery beyond a reasonable doubt because defendant attempted to commit a theft offense by entering a delicatessen to deprive the owner of his cash, without the owner's consent. Furthermore, defendant used a .25 caliber firearm against the owner and in doing so caused serious physical harm by inflicting three gunshot wounds that not only carried a substantial risk of death, but actually caused the owner's death. State v. Clark, 2008-Ohio-1404, 2008 Ohio App. LEXIS 1224 (Ohio Ct. App., Cuyahoga County 2008).

Weight of the evidence demonstrated that defendant aided and abetted the burglary of the victim's apartment (with the underlying offense being theft) because before the burglary, defendant directed his friends to follow the victim in order to discover where he lived so that they could rob his home; he gave them a key to the apartment; and told them to go to the apartment and search it for marijuana and money. State v. Hudson, 2007-Ohio-3227, 2007 Ohio App. LEXIS 2972 (Ohio Ct. App., Franklin County 2007).

**Use of false name**

The mere use of a false name in returning merchandise to a department store in exchange for a refund slip which was cashed, without a showing that either the merchandise or refund slip was obtained by a fraudulent representation or pretense whereby the alleged victim parted with any property or suffered any loss, does not constitute the crime of larceny by trick: (decided under former analogous section) Cincinnati v. Woodruff, 4 Ohio App. 2d 253, 33 Ohio Op. 2d 291, 211 N.E.2d 890, 1965 Ohio App. LEXIS 508 (Ohio Ct. App., Hamilton County 1965).

**Value of property**

Defendant implied the investigation of the theft was defective or incomplete, but as the police officer testified, defendant admitted to the theft and was clearly caught on video committing the offense; the service manager and parts manager of the Toyota dealership created a service quote for replacement of the radio premised upon the car's VIN number, and it was difficult to discern how a better estimate of fair market value could be arrived at. State v. Emerick, 2020-Ohio-3510, 2020 Ohio App. LEXIS 2442 (Ohio Ct. App., Licking County 2020).

Because the testimony of defendant's former fiancé valuing the ATV at $2,000 was probative of its fair market value under, his testimony, if believed, was sufficient to support a finding by the jury that the value of the stolen ATV was at least $1,000, thereby elevating the theft offense to a fifth-degree felony. State v. McKee, 2019-Ohio-4307, 2019 Ohio App. LEXIS 4378 (Ohio Ct. App., Logan County 2019).

Expert testimony was not required to establish the value of the victim's stolen property because the victim's testimony as to the value of her extensive collection of jewelry was sufficient to support the jury's finding that the value of the stolen property was greater than $37,500, but less than $150,000, which enhanced the offense to a second degree felony under this statute. State v. Chudzinski, 2018-Ohio-39, 2018 Ohio App. LEXIS 40 (Ohio Ct. App., Ottawa County 2018).

Trial court erred by sentencing defendant for the crime of theft as a fifth-degree felony. Because the value statute did not provide for rental fees when ascertaining the value of a stolen piece of business equipment, the trial court should not have included the rental fees in its calculation, only its replacement value. State v. Kuhns, 2016-Ohio-5312, 2016 Ohio App. LEXIS 3171 (Ohio Ct. App., Summit County 2016).

Testimony that the State presented was sufficient evidence that defendant stole in excess of $7,500 from the widow's savings account for theft from an elderly person because ATM security photos all depicted defendant making withdrawals from the widow's savings account, the widow testified that she only withdrew money from her savings account to pay her taxes, and that any other withdrawal that she made was taken solely from her checking account, and defendant admitted to the deputy that he stole approximately $9,000 from the widow. State v. Vigilante, 2015-Ohio-4221, 2015 Ohio App. LEXIS 4110 (Ohio Ct. App., Medina County 2015).

Victim's testimony, if believed, was sufficient to support the jury's finding the aggregate value of the stolen property involved was $1,000 or more, thereby elevating defendant's convictions for receiving stolen property and theft to fifth-degree felonies. the victim testified the value of the stolen property involved was approximately $2,100 to $2,200, which included the replacement value of approximately 350 fence posts at $1,400 to $1,575. State v. Gray, 2015-Ohio-3174, 2015 Ohio App. LEXIS 3091 (Ohio Ct. App., Brown County 2015).

Even though appellant, a juvenile, committed the offense of theft, the evidence was insufficient to support an adjudication for theft as a fourth-degree felony because the State failed to prove that the value of the property stolen was between $7,500 and $150,000; a victim's testimony was insufficient as he did not have firsthand knowledge of how much money was in a bag. The State presented evidence showing that the bag contained $1,600 when it was recovered; therefore, appellant should have been adjudicated delinquent for committing theft as a fifth-degree felony. In re D.L., 2015-Ohio-4747, 2015 Ohio App. LEXIS 4682 (Ohio Ct. App., Hamilton County 2015).

Sufficient evidence supported defendant's felony theft conviction because the State presented some evidence that the cost to replace the stolen property equaled or exceeded $1,000. The owner of the property testified that it would cost $1,000 to replace the plumbing stolen from the home and that the additional repairs to fix all the damage totaled over $3,500. State v. Washington, 2014-Ohio-4578, 2014 Ohio App. LEXIS 4476 (Ohio Ct. App., Cuyahoga County 2014).

There was no error in the trial court's use of the replacement value of bridges as the measure of damages to determine the level of the offenses, as the bridges were severed and sold as scrap, the property was purchased with the intent to use the bridges, and the trail could not be completed without replacing them; alternatively, the evidence was uncontroverted that the bridges were sold for scrap at a price over $20,000, which value exceeded the minimum threshold. State v. Taylor, 2013-Ohio-5751, 2013 Ohio App. LEXIS 6030 (Ohio Ct. App., Holmes County 2013).

Each offense, vandalism and theft, requires the State to present evidence of the value in order to substantiate the level of the offense. State v. Taylor, 2013-Ohio-5751, 2013 Ohio App. LEXIS 6030 (Ohio Ct. App., Holmes County 2013).

Even assuming it was error to admit a witness's opinion, it was harmless error because it was undisputed that the actual scrap value for the bridges was over $20,000 and the verdict forms indicated that the jury found the value of the property more than $7,500 and less than $150,000, which is the threshold requirement for a theft and vandalism felony of the fourth-degree. State v. Taylor, 2013-Ohio-5751, 2013 Ohio App. LEXIS 6030 (Ohio Ct. App., Holmes County 2013).

State proved the value of the property taken because it introduced numerous photos of the victim's home and property, and the victim testified that she obtained an estimate as to what it would cost to replace and fix everything in her home State v. Jennings, 2013-Ohio-5428, 2013 Ohio App. LEXIS 5674 (Ohio Ct. App., Cuyahoga County 2013).

Sufficient evidence supported defendant's theft conviction because there was prima facie evidence of their value under R.C. 2913.61(E)(1) (2000). The store's asset protection officer testified about the "sticker price" of both items involved in the theft and explained that the store computer system listed the items for sale at those prices. State v. Holter, 2012-Ohio-3784, 2012 Ohio App. LEXIS 3345 (Ohio Ct. App., Summit County 2012).

Evidence was sufficient to prove that the articles stolen were property belonging to another with a value in excess of $100,000 for the aggravated theft conviction under because the total value of the stolen property was determined to be approximately $204,249.55, consisting of checks, gold coins, and a condominium. Because defendant had returned most of the stolen property prior to trial, the value of his mother's net "economic loss" for purposes of restitution was not determinative of the value of her property that defendant stole. State v. Haggerty, 2011-Ohio-6705, 2011 Ohio App. LEXIS 5519 (Ohio Ct. App., Montgomery County 2011).

Defendant's conviction for felony theft had to be modified to first-degree misdemeanor theft as the victim never provided his age, was not retired, and provided no dollar amount from which the jury could determine the cost of the items which defendant attempted to steal. State v. Bronczyk, 2011-Ohio-5924, 2011 Ohio App. LEXIS 4852 (Ohio Ct. App., Cuyahoga County 2011), writ denied, 2016-Ohio-5335, 2016 Ohio App. LEXIS 3280 (Ohio Ct. App., Cuyahoga County 2016).

Defendant's conviction for theft, in violation of R.C. 2913.02(A), was properly deemed a fifth-degree felony where the value of the property taken from homeowners was deemed to be more than $500; there was testimony from one homeowner regarding the value of one of two rings taken as well as the amount that a stolen coin jar held, and the other owner provided testimony and evidence regarding the value of tools and equipment taken. State v. Raleigh, 2010-Ohio-2966, 2010 Ohio App. LEXIS 2457 (Ohio Ct. App., Clermont County 2010).

Victim's testimony was insufficient to establish the value of stolen paintings in order to elevate defendant's theft conviction from a first-degree misdemeanor to a fifth-degree felony; the testimony that the paintings were worth anywhere from $700 to $2,000 each, depending on the painting, was sufficient to prove the value was more than $500 but less than $5,000 as required for the felony theft conviction. State v. Grant, 2010-Ohio-5483, 2010 Ohio App. LEXIS 4592 (Ohio Ct. App., Cuyahoga County 2010).

Sufficient evidence supported defendant's first-degree felony theft conviction under R.C. 2913.02(B)(2) because he did not just obtain and exercise control over the $180,476.55 in proceeds that he retained from the mortgages, he engaged in the mortgage fraud scheme to obtain and exercise control over the mortgages in their entirety, and that amount exceeded $1 million. State v. Anderson, 2009-Ohio-6566, 2009 Ohio App. LEXIS 5514 (Ohio Ct. App., Franklin County 2009), aff'd, 2011-Ohio-228, 128 Ohio St. 3d 234, 943 N.E.2d 534, 2011 Ohio LEXIS 166 (Ohio 2011), writ denied, 2012-Ohio-3773, 2012 Ohio App. LEXIS 3332 (Ohio Ct. App., Franklin County 2012).

Trial court erred by finding defendant guilty of theft as a fifth degree felony because the victim's testimony failed to establish the fair market value of the property that was stolen under the criteria in R.C. 2913.61(D)(3); the cost of replacing stolen property did not demonstrate what a willing buyer would have given and a willing seller would have taken for it. Although the detective's testimony that the scrap value on the street of a catalytic converter was up to $150 dollars, that amount was less than the minimum value of $500 that R.C. 2913.02(B)(2) established as a basis to increase a misdemeanor theft offense to a fifth degree felony. State v. Hanke, 2009-Ohio-3023, 2009 Ohio App. LEXIS 2565 (Ohio Ct. App., Clark County 2009).

State proved beyond a reasonable doubt that defendant stole $258,941.34 from four retail stores and a government agency. Therefore, the trial court could have found that theft of over $100,000 had occurred. State v. Hall, 2009-Ohio-462, 2009 Ohio App. LEXIS 395 (Ohio Ct. App., Cuyahoga County), writ denied, 2009-Ohio-1356, 2009 Ohio App. LEXIS 1129 (Ohio Ct. App., Cuyahoga County 2009).

Juvenile court erred in adjudicating appellant juvenile delinquent for felony theft in violation of R.C. 2913.51 because a loss-prevention officer's testimony recounting what a department store manager had determined the value of stolen clothing to be was inadmissible hearsay pursuant to Evid.R. 801, and since there was no other evidence of the value of the clothing (R.C. 2913.61), the admission of the officer's value testimony clearly affected appellant's substantial rights and it should have been stricken pursuant to Evid.R. 103 and 802. In re Wells, 2008-Ohio-6688, 2008 Ohio App. LEXIS 5583 (Ohio Ct. App., Hamilton County 2008).

Sufficient evidence supported defendant's conviction for breaking and entering because the evidence supported the trespass element in that the rims found in the bed of a truck were taken from inside a locked van, which was inside a barbed wire fence and an eyewitness watched as two men threw what appeared to be rims over the fence that surrounded a tire store and carried the rims toward the truck. Also, defendant was riding in a truck matching the description of the suspect vehicle that was operating without headlights, the police observed this truck shortly after being notified of the criminal activity, the stolen items were in plain view inside the bed of the truck, and the store owner testified that the value of the stolen items exceeded $500. State v. McBride, 2008-Ohio-5888, 2008 Ohio App. LEXIS 4952 (Ohio Ct. App., Stark County 2008).

In a prosecution for theft, the trial court properly admitted an ice cream machine owner's testimony regarding the replacement value of the compressor removed from the machine by defendant as the owner testified as to his years of involvement with the ice cream business, with ice cream machines, and with purchasing and maintaining those machines. State v. Gordon, 2008-Ohio-3003, 2008 Ohio App. LEXIS 2512 (Ohio Ct. App., Montgomery County 2008).

In a prosecution for theft, the trial court correctly applied R.C. 2913.61(D)(2) in order to value the amount of property stolen by defendant as the owner of the property testified that he used the ice cream machine stolen by defendant for its parts and that the parts from the stolen machine had been usable. State v. Gordon, 2008-Ohio-3003, 2008 Ohio App. LEXIS 2512 (Ohio Ct. App., Montgomery County 2008).

Trial court erred in convicting defendant of a fourth-degree felony theft offense, in violation of R.C. 2913.02, where there was inadequate evidence to establish that the value of stolen racehorses was between $5,000 and $100,000 pursuant to R.C. 2913.61(D)(3); rather, the value was established for a fifth degree felony theft offense. State v. Burneson, 2007-Ohio-4037, 2007 Ohio App. LEXIS 3675 (Ohio Ct. App., Cuyahoga County 2007).

Although there was sufficient evidence that defendant took race horses from their owner without the owner's consent for purposes of defendant's conviction of fourth-degree felony theft, in violation of R.C. 2913.02, there was insufficient evidence as to the value of the horses for purposes of that degree of the offense; rather, the value established pursuant to R.C. 2913.61(D) showed that the race horses were worth $500, which made the offense one of the fifth degree. State v. Queen, 2007-Ohio-4042, 2007 Ohio App. LEXIS 3676 (Ohio Ct. App., Cuyahoga County 2007).

Evidence failed to establish that the stolen laptop's replacement cost exceeded $500 for the theft conviction and the fifth-degree felony was reduced to a first-degree misdemeanor. The State failed to present direct evidence of replacement cost and instead relied solely upon the laptop's purchase price, specifying neither the status of the laptop's technology, the devaluation rate, nor other details essential to allow the trial court to ascertain the laptop's replacement cost nine months after the purchase of such rapidly depreciating technology. State v. Parsons, 2007-Ohio-1204, 2007 Ohio App. LEXIS 1025 (Ohio Ct. App., Franklin County 2007).

Trial court erred in convicting defendant of a fourth-degree felony theft offense, in violation of R.C. 2913.02, where there was inadequate evidence to establish that the value of stolen racehorses was between $5,000 and $100,000 pursuant to R.C. 2913.61(D)(3); rather, the value was established for a fifth degree felony theft offense. State v. Burneson, 2007-Ohio-4037, 2007 Ohio App. LEXIS 3675 (Ohio Ct. App., Cuyahoga County 2007).

Although there was sufficient evidence that defendant took race horses from their owner without the owner's consent for purposes of defendant's conviction of fourth-degree felony theft, in violation of R.C. 2913.02, there was insufficient evidence as to the value of the horses for purposes of that degree of the offense. The value established pursuant to R.C. 2913.61(D) showed that the race horses were worth $500, which made the offense one of the fifth degree. State v. Queen, 2007-Ohio-4042, 2007 Ohio App. LEXIS 3676 (Ohio Ct. App., Cuyahoga County 2007).

Trial court erred in denying defendant's motion for acquittal because there was insufficient evidence to prove a theft over $500 in value. There was no evidence beyond the trial judge's statement at sentencing that he inferred that the stolen coat was worth more than $500 and the State conceded that the trial court received no evidence regarding the actual value of the fur coat in question. State v. Turner, 2007-Ohio-2776, 2007 Ohio App. LEXIS 2575 (Ohio Ct. App., Cuyahoga County 2007).

Jury instruction regarding the value of property taken by defendant in her criminal trial on charges of theft and unauthorized use of property, in violation of R.C. 2913.02(A)(1) and 2913.04(A), was not an abuse of discretion, as some of the craft items taken still had a price tag and accordingly, use of the value under R.C. 2913.61(D)(3) rather than under § 2913.61(D)(2) was proper. There was direct and circumstantial evidence that supported the value determination and the convictions against defendant, including an inventory list of the items taken and testimony. State v. Reid, 2007-Ohio-2139, 2007 Ohio App. LEXIS 1994 (Ohio Ct. App., Greene County 2007).

Trial court did not abuse its discretion when it allowed the State to reopen its case after the State had rested and defendant had moved for on Crim.R. 29 judgment of acquittal because, although the State failed to present specific evidence on the value of the merchandise that defendant attempted to steal, which determined the degree of the offense of theft, the State had the evidence in its possession, prior to the presentation of any witness testimony. It was a case of mere oversight by the State which had already obtained the necessary evidence through its prior investigation of the incident and preparation for trial and there was no claim of surprise or prejudice on the part of defendant due to the nature or content of the additional testimony. State v. Roberson, 2007-Ohio-1981, 2007 Ohio App. LEXIS 1829 (Ohio Ct. App., Cuyahoga County 2007).

Since the value of property stolen from the victim's purse was only $40, the evidence did not support defendant's aggravated theft conviction but, instead, supported only a petty theft conviction. State v. Russell, 2006-Ohio-6764, 2006 Ohio App. LEXIS 6681 (Ohio Ct. App., Cuyahoga County 2006).

Although the verdict forms in defendant's criminal action on charges of theft over $100,000, in violation of R.C. 2913.02(A)(2) and (3), did not require the jury to determine the value of the property involved in the crimes, as required by R.C. 2913.61(A), the jury's finding of aggravated theft satisfied the requirement, as aggravated theft was defined as involving a value over $100,000, and the jury instruction also specified a value of that amount or above. State v. Bohache, 2006-Ohio-5560, 2006 Ohio App. LEXIS 5556 (Ohio Ct. App., Montgomery County 2006).

Defendant's conviction for complicity to attempted grand theft in violation of R.C. 2923.03(A)(2), .02(A), 2913.02(A)(1), for aiding and abetting another man in trying to break into a shopping mall jewelry display case was not against the manifest weight of the evidence on the ground that, because individual items of jewelry in the case varied in price from $100 to $5499, there was no way to prove that defendant intended to steal items worth more than $5,000. There was evidence that the total value of the jewelry in the case was over $19,000, and the jury could reasonably have inferred from the circumstantial evidence that defendant intended to steal all of the rings in the case. State v. Higgins, 2006-Ohio-5372, 2006 Ohio App. LEXIS 5381 (Ohio Ct. App., Lake County 2006).

Defendant's conviction for breaking and entering, in violation of R.C. 2911.13(B), was not against the manifest weight of the evidence in light of evidence that defendant stated that he stole sheets of plywood to sell them for money; that defendant had access to 28 sheets of wood at the construction site where he had been seen and where his truck was located; that the total value of the sheets at the site was $700, which was more than the amount required to constitute a felony theft offense under R.C. 2913.02(B)(2); and that defendant had the means to transport all the sheets. While defendant testified that he did not intend to steal more than a misdemeanor's value of wood, given defendant's criminal history, the trial court was within its discretion to not believe defendant's testimony; thus, defendant's motion for acquittal under Crim.R. 29(A) was properly denied. State v. Dula, 2006-Ohio-1238, 2006 Ohio App. LEXIS 1105 (Ohio Ct. App., Lucas County 2006).

Trial court erred in admitting testimony regarding the value of a ring that was allegedly stolen by defendant, in violation of R.C. 2913.02(A)(1), (B)(1), (2), as the trial court's admission of the testimony of the victim as to what her deceased mother had previously told her about the value of the ring was not the type of evidence that was within the hearsay exception of Evid.R. 804(B)(4); as there was no other evidence to establish the value of the stolen property, the error was not harmless, necessitating a reduction in the charge to a lesser degree of the offense. State v. Reese, 2005-Ohio-7075, 165 Ohio App. 3d 21, 844 N.E.2d 873, 2005 Ohio App. LEXIS 6381 (Ohio Ct. App., Mahoning County 2005).

State failed to meet its burden of proving that the stolen ring was worth more than $500. Neither a hearsay statement by the victim's mother nor a newspaper ad constituted admissible proof of value: State v. Reese, 2005-Ohio-7075, 165 Ohio App. 3d 21, 844 N.E.2d 873, 2005 Ohio App. LEXIS 6381 (Ohio Ct. App., Mahoning County 2005).

Where the jury found defendant guilty of robbery, without making the finding of value under R.C. 2913.61(A), but the conviction was remanded for sentencing for theft, the trial court could not find the defendant guilty of grand theft: State v. Furlow, 90 Ohio App. 3d 699, 630 N.E.2d 413, 1993 Ohio App. LEXIS 4684 (Ohio Ct. App., Montgomery County 1993).

The price listed on a sales tag, including any applicable discounts, is prima facie proof of the item's value: State v. Cunningham, 67 Ohio App. 3d 366, 587 N.E.2d 310, 1990 Ohio App. LEXIS 1525 (Ohio Ct. App., Montgomery County 1990).

The amendment to R.C. 2913.02, raising from $150 to $300 the value of property or services stolen which constitutes the offense of theft, relates only to the penalty imposed and therefore comes within the provisions of R.C. 1.58(B), requiring that the penalty be imposed according to the amendment in cases where the offense occurred prior to, but sentencing occurred after, the effective date of the amendment: State v. Collier, 22 Ohio App. 3d 25, 488 N.E.2d 887, 1984 Ohio App. LEXIS 12687 (Ohio Ct. App., Shelby County 1984).

A dog shown to be worth an appreciable amount, whether listed for taxation or not, is a thing of value, subject to larceny within the meaning and intendment of this section: (decided under former analogous section) State v. Weekly, 146 Ohio St. 277, 32 Ohio Op. 337, 65 N.E.2d 856, 1946 Ohio LEXIS 322 (Ohio 1946).

**Venue**

State presented sufficient evidence to establish Cuyahoga County as the proper venue for charges against defendant of misuse of credit cards (MCC) and grand theft, as there was testimony that the employer's card was used by defendant improperly at gas stations in that County to steal money from his employer, as well as for establishing the course of criminal conduct venue provision. State v. Luton, 2018-Ohio-4708, 2018 Ohio App. LEXIS 5028 (Ohio Ct. App., Cuyahoga County 2018).

Trial court did not err by granting defendant's motion for acquittal on the charges of passing bad checks and theft because venue was not proven. The elements of the offenses were committed in another county, the checks were negotiated, issued, and delivered in the other county, were deposited in a bank in the other county, all negotiations involving the purchase of the 300 basketball tickets in exchange for court time before the game occurred in the other county and the acts of deception used to obtain control over the tickets and court time occurred in the other county. State v. Untied, 2014-Ohio-3920, 2014 Ohio App. LEXIS 3848 (Ohio Ct. App., Cuyahoga County 2014).

Trial court could rationally have found that the facts supported venue in the county for complicity to commit theft because a reasonable person could have found, under the facts and circumstances, that the purpose to deprive the receiver arose before the checks were received; thus when the checks were received in the county, the purpose already existed. It could also have been concluded that defendant opened the account with purpose to eventually deprive a receiver that was likely to be appointed soon. State v.

Pellin, 2012-Ohio-5342, 2012 Ohio App. LEXIS 4650 (Ohio Ct. App., Mahoning County 2012).

In defendant's prosecution on charges of engaging in a pattern of corrupt activity, theft, possession of criminal tools, and forgery, the State, pursuant to R.C. 2901.12(A), established venue in Licking County as the evidence demonstrated that, while defendant was not directly involved in counterfeit check cashing in Licking County, her association with the counterfeit check cashing enterprise extended into Licking County by virtue of her activities. State v. Yates, 2009-Ohio-6622, 2009 Ohio App. LEXIS 5543 (Ohio Ct. App., Licking County 2009).

**Verdict form**

While the trial court properly instructed the jury that it had to find that the stolen property was a dangerous drug in order to convict defendant of a fourth degree felony theft offense, it did not excuse the failure to comply with R.C. 2945.75(A)(2), because the verdict form did not include either the degree of the offense (i.e., a fourth degree felony) or the aggravating element (i.e., that the property stolen was a dangerous drug). State v. Klein, 2013-Ohio-2387, 2013 Ohio App. LEXIS 2338 (Ohio Ct. App., Union County 2013), cert. denied, 573 U.S. 909, 134 S. Ct. 2735, 189 L. Ed. 2d 773, 2014 U.S. LEXIS 4072 (U.S. 2014).

As the verdict form stated that the jury found defendant guilty of theft of a motor vehicle violation of R.C. 2913.02(A)(1)/(B)(5), the jury found the presence of an aggravating element, theft involving a motor vehicle; accordingly, the requirements of R.C. 2945.75(A)(2) were met. State v. Markins, 2013-Ohio-602, 2013 Ohio App. LEXIS 530 (Ohio Ct. App., Scioto County 2013).

Although there was ample evidence of value to find that defendant committed felony degrees of theft and misuse of credit cards, in violation of R.C. 2913.02(B)(2) and 2913.21(D)(3), as the verdict forms did not specifically set forth either the degree of the crimes or the amount of money involved in the offenses, pursuant to R.C. 2945.75(A)(2) only the misdemeanor degree of offenses could be imposed. State v. Hoover, 2008-Ohio-6136, 2008 Ohio App. LEXIS 5146 (Ohio Ct. App., Scioto County 2008).

Verdict forms in the counts alleging tampering with documents did not support an entry of conviction for tampering with records with the specification that the records were kept by a government entity. Therefore, according to R.C. 2945.75(A)(2), defendant could only be convicted of the least degree of the offense charged. State v. Keith, 2008-Ohio-348, 2008 Ohio App. LEXIS 297 (Ohio Ct. App., Butler County 2008).

**Verdicts**

**—Inconsistent verdicts**

Verdicts were not inconsistent because, although the jury found defendant not guilty of the theft offense as it related specifically to the $60, that finding did not foreclose the jury from finding that defendant deprived the first victim of his wallet and used force to do so. State v. Gatewood, 2012-Ohio-3756, 2012 Ohio App. LEXIS 3312 (Ohio Ct. App., Fayette County 2012).

**Weight and sufficiency of the evidence**

In an appeal from a judgment of conviction for theft, the evidence supported that defendant knew she had improperly obtained various items from the trailer because she had moved into a fully furnished residence and left with the mattress and numerous kitchen items that were not hers; defendant knowingly obtained or exerted control over property beyond the scope of the express or implied consent of the owner with purpose to deprive the owner. State v. Love, 2021-Ohio-4470, 2021 Ohio App. LEXIS 4376 (Ohio Ct. App., Logan County 2021).

Defendant's convictions for theft and telecommunications fraud were not against the manifest weight of the evidence because the fact that the victim refused to give defendant his cell phone again to fix the so-called mistake in downloading a game app on the victim's phone and making $450 of unauthorized in-app purchases with the victim's debit card and to transfer the charges to defendant's own phone or credit card was not grounds to reverse his convictions. State v. Burey, 2021-Ohio-943, 2021 Ohio App. LEXIS 959 (Ohio Ct. App., Cuyahoga County 2021).

Defendant's conviction was not against the manifest weight of the evidence because the jury heard testimony from five witnesses, evaluated the evidence, and was convinced of defendant's guilt; defendant's counsel highlighted the issues of credibility and inconsistencies during cross-examination and closing argument, and the jury chose to believe the version of events presented by the prosecutor's witnesses. State v. Durham, 2020-Ohio-4758, 2020 Ohio App. LEXIS 3569 (Ohio Ct. App., Delaware County 2020).

Defendant's claim that the finding of guilt of grand theft was against the manifest weight of evidence was without merit because the record showed that the trial court found defendant guilty of grand theft based on defendant exerting control over the victim's truck without the victim's consent. State v. Randall, 2019-Ohio-1358, 2019 Ohio App. LEXIS 1462 (Ohio Ct. App., Cuyahoga County 2019).

Denial of defendant's motion for acquittal under Crim.R. 29(A) was proper because her conviction for theft was supported with sufficient evidence, since there was competent, credible evidence indicating that she placed the shirts on top of her purse in the cart and that she later looked around before placing them in her purse just prior to leaving the store. State v. Crabtree, 2019-Ohio-3686, 2019 Ohio App. LEXIS 3772 (Ohio Ct. App., Champaign County 2019).

Denial of defendant's motion for acquittal under Crim.R. 29(A) was proper because her conviction for theft was not against the manifest weight of the evidence, since the jury did not lose their way in concluding that she intended to take the shirts without paying for them. State v. Crabtree, 2019-Ohio-3686, 2019 Ohio App. LEXIS 3772 (Ohio Ct. App., Champaign County 2019).

Conviction of defendant for theft involving a person in a protected class was supported with sufficient evidence and was not against the manifest weight of the evidence because the jury accordingly had before it sufficient evidence that enabled it to conclude that the victim, was an owner of the checking account and over the age of 65 at the time of the incident. State v. Barnthouse, 2019-Ohio-5209, 2019 Ohio App. LEXIS 5297 (Ohio Ct. App., Hamilton County 2019).

Defendant's conviction for grand theft was not against the manifest weight of the evidence; circumstantial evidence showed, inter alia, that the victim, a police officer, returned home to find that the home had been broken into, that when apprehended in the vicinity of the home, defendant had cuts on his hands, and that defendant provided the location of a duffle bag containing a gun and other items stolen from the victim's home. State v. Coleman, 2016-Ohio-297, 2016 Ohio App. LEXIS 263 (Ohio Ct. App., Cuyahoga County 2016).

Theft conviction was supported by legally sufficient evidence and was not against the manifest weight of the evidence, because a reasonable jury could conclude that defendant in fact signed for the order and knowingly deceived the store by taking possession of merchandise for which she had not legally paid. State v. Williams, 2014-Ohio-2438, 2014 Ohio App. LEXIS 2366 (Ohio Ct. App., Wood County 2014).

Evidence was sufficient to support defendant's conviction for grand theft where: (1) defendant persuaded his victims to give him $60,000 to purchase two modular homes for later delivery, (2) defendant never delivered the homes, (3) a victim received one home after he arranged to have it delivered by a third party and apparently had access to the second home, (4) the fact that the victims' losses were limited was not due to anything defendant did, and (5) the victims lost $5,000 in moving expenses; for the same reasons, the conviction was not against the manifest weight of the evidence. State v. Agostini, 2005-Ohio-5371, 2005 Ohio App. LEXIS 4874 (Ohio Ct. App., Clermont County 2005).

**Wrongful discharge in violation of public policy**

When an employee alleged the employee was wrongfully discharged in violation of the public policies expressed in R.C. 2913.02(A)(3), prohibiting theft by deception, and R.C. 3517.092, prohibiting the solicitation of campaign contributions from public employees engaged in official duties, the employee did not sufficiently allege the jeopardy element of such a claim because the employee did not show recognition of a tort claim for wrongful discharge in violation of these public policies was necessary to protect these policies, since significant criminal and civil penalties already existed to protect them, and the employee's allegations further indicated that an employer's alleged scheme encouraging and facilitating the illegal accumulation of compensatory time by public employees for later use on political activities was a conspiracy/corrupt activity violation under R.C. 2923.01 and a violation of Ohio's RICO statute, R.C. 2923.32(A)(1), for which additional civil and criminal penalties were available. Ripley v. Montgomery, 2007-Ohio-7151, 2007 Ohio App. LEXIS 6256 (Ohio Ct. App., Franklin County 2007).

## RESEARCH REFERENCES AND PRACTICE AIDS

**Cross-References to Related Sections**

Penalties for felony, RC § 2929.11 et seq.; misdemeanor, RC § 2929.21.

Aggregating value involved in a course of conduct to determine degree of offense, RC § 2913.49.

Compounding a crime, RC § 2921.21.

Corrupt activity defined, RC § 2923.31.

Criminal records check; employment of offenders prohibited —

Applicants for employment with PASSPORT agencies, RC § 109.572.

Certain persons having frequent contact with children, RC § 2151.86.

Home health agency employees, RC § 3701.881.

Prospective employees providing direct care to older adult, RC §§ 3712.09, 3721.121.

Degree of offense when certain property involved, RC § 2913.71.

Detention and arrest of shoplifters, RC § 2935.041.

Falsification; in theft offense, RC § 2921.13.

Fraudulent viatical settlement acts, RC § 3916.99.

Knowingly defined, RC § 2901.22.

Misrepresenting oneself as owning or operating minority business enterprise; theft by deception, RC §§ 122.83, 123.151, 125.081, 340.13, 5126.071.

Organized criminal activity, RC § 177.01.

Prior conviction —

Pleading, RC § 2941.11.

Proof, RC § 2945.75.
Property defined, RC § 2901.01.
Property owner may recover for willful damage or theft, RC § 2307.61.
Release of confidential specific identity of a chemical not theft, RC §§ 3750.09, 3751.04.
Ski area operator's liability to violators of theft statute, RC § 4169.10.
Reward for information re offense involving school property, RC § 3313.173.
Taking the identity of another, RC § 2913.49.
Theft of drugs is drug abuse offense, RC § 2925.01.
Theft of utility service; notice to customers, RC § 4933.19.
Value of stolen property, RC § 2913.61.
Wire or oral communications, interception of, RC § 2933.51.

**Ohio Administrative Code**

Misrepresentation for purpose of obtaining contract, loan or public assistance considered a theft offense —

Department of administrative services, division of EEO for construction —

Application for certification as minority business enterprise. OAC 123:2-15-01.

Department of job and family services, division of public assistance—

Application for replacement warrant for aid payments. OAC 5101:1-2-55.

Ohio instructional grant program —

False statement on unemployment affidavit. OAC 3351-2-02.

**Comparative Legislation**

Theft:
CA—Cal Pen Code § 484
FL—Fla. Stat. § 812.014
IL—720 Ill. Comp. Stat. § 5/16-1
IN—Burns Ind. Code Ann. § 35-43-4-2
KY—KRS §§ 514.020-514.090
MI—MCLS § 750.356
NY—NY CLS Penal § 155.05
PA—18 P.S. §§ 3901, 3921

**Practice Manuals and Treatises**

Ohio Transaction Guide: Family Law & Forms § 7.03 Legal Background

**Practice Guides**

Anderson's Ohio Manual of Criminal Complaints and Indictments § 2913.02 Theft

**Practice Forms**

Affidavit for Search Warrant?Receiving Stolen Property?College Campus, Anderson's Ohio Search Warrant Manual Form 43

Motion and Supporting Memorandum To Dismiss Indictment for Failure To State the Offense of Grand Theft, or To Allege the Requisite Intent 1, 15 Ohio Forms of Pleading and Practice Form 7:4A

# TITLE 31

# DOMESTIC RELATIONS — CHILDREN



## CHAPTER 3109

## CHILDREN



### § 3109.05 Child support.

(A)(1) In a divorce, dissolution of marriage, legal separation, or child support proceeding, the court may order either or both parents to support or help support their children, without regard to marital misconduct. In determining the amount reasonable or necessary for child support, including the medical needs of the child, the court shall comply with Chapter 3119. of the Revised Code.

(2) The court, in accordance with Chapter 3119. of the Revised Code, shall include in each support order made under this section the requirement that one or both of the parents provide for the health care needs of the child to the satisfaction of the court, and the court shall include in the support order a requirement that all support payments be made through the office of child support in the department of job and family services.

(3) The court shall comply with Chapters 3119., 3121., 3123., and 3125. of the Revised Code when it makes or modifies an order for child support under this section.

(B) The juvenile court has exclusive jurisdiction to enter the orders in any case certified to it from another court.

(C) If any person required to pay child support under an order made under division (A) of this section on or after April 15, 1985, or modified on or after December 1, 1986, is found in contempt of court for failure to make support payments under the order, the court that makes the finding, in addition to any other penalty or remedy imposed, shall assess all court costs arising out of the contempt proceeding against the person and require the person to pay any reasonable attorney's fees of any adverse party, as determined by the court, that arose in relation to the act of contempt and, on or after July 1, 1992, shall assess interest on any unpaid amount of child support pursuant to section 3123.17 of the Revised Code.

(D) The court shall not authorize or permit the escrowing, impoundment, or withholding of any child support payment ordered under this section or any other section of the Revised Code because of a denial of or interference with a right of parenting time granted to a parent in an order issued under this section or section 3109.051 or 3109.12 of the Revised Code or companionship or visitation granted in an order issued under this section, section 3109.051, 3109.11, 3109.12, or any other section of the Revised Code, or as a method of enforcing the specific provisions of any such order dealing with parenting time or visitation.

**HISTORY:**

RS § 3140-1; 90 v 186; GC § 8005-5; 100 v 97; 121 v 557; 124 v 178(195); Bureau of Code Revision, 10-1-53; 134 v H 544 (Eff 1-20-72); 134 v H 163 (Eff 2-17-72); 135 v H 233 (Eff 9-23-74); 139 v H 71 (Eff 8-27-81); 139 v H 694 (Eff 11-15-81); 140 v H 614 (Eff 4-10-85); 141 v H 509 (Eff 12-1-86); 142 v H 231 (Eff 10-5-87); 142 v H 708 (Eff 4-19-88); 143 v H 15 (Eff 5-31-90); 143 v H 591 (Eff 4-12-90); 143 v H 514 (Eff 1-1-91); 143 v S 3 (Eff 4-11-91); 144 v S 10 (Eff 7-15-92); 145 v S 115 (Eff 10-12-93); 145 v H 173 (Eff 12-31-93); 147 v H 352 (Eff 1-1-98); 148 v H 471 (Eff 7-1-2000); 148 v S 180. Eff 3-22-2001.

#### NOTES TO DECISIONS

Analysis

**Constitutionality**

Because the parties entered into an agreement finding the obligor in contempt for unpaid medical expenses, the obligor was required under the contempt statute to pay the reasonable attorney fees the obligee incurred in the prosecution of her motion, and the magistrate had sufficient evidence to determine that the fees were reasonable. 2014 Ohio 4813, 2013 Ohio App. LEXIS 6258.

Former R.C. 3113.215(B)(6)(a) withstood the father's constitutional challenges because the father's initial premise was incorrect in that he claimed that former R.C. 3113.215 contained a presumption that in shared parenting cases, only one parent was presumed to pay child support. The statute contained no express language to support that premise. Tonti v. Tonti, 2007-Ohio-2658, 2007 Ohio App. LEXIS 2466 (Ohio Ct. App., Franklin County 2007).

**Generally**

The 1992 amendments to R.C. 3103.03 and 3109.05 require support orders to continue until the child ceases to attend high school and apply to prior support orders: Smith v. Smith, 119 Ohio App. 3d 15, 694 N.E.2d 476, 1997 Ohio App. LEXIS 1139 (Ohio Ct. App., Butler County 1997).

The amount necessary for child support is that amount necessary to maintain for the children the standard of living they would have enjoyed had the marriage continued. The amount reasonable for child support includes consideration of other factors including the financial resources and needs of both the custodial and noncustodial parent: Birath v. Birath, 53 Ohio App. 3d 31, 558 N.E.2d 63, 1988 Ohio App. LEXIS 3033 (Ohio Ct. App., Franklin County 1988).

A parent cannot be totally excused from paying child support without any showing of good faith in making some type of payment: Allen v. Allen, 59 Ohio App. 3d 54, 571 N.E.2d 139, 1988 Ohio App. LEXIS 2915 (Ohio Ct. App., Columbiana County 1988).

Voluntary payments made by a noncustodial parent, where the child is not living with the noncustodial parent, are not to be considered payments in lieu of support where the divorce decree orders that support payments shall be made through the court or directly to the custodial parent: Evans v. Brown, 23 Ohio App. 3d 97, 491 N.E.2d 384, 1985 Ohio App. LEXIS 10111 (Ohio Ct. App., Franklin County 1985).

A custodial parent is not entitled to reimbursement for child support from the non-custodial parent where no support order is made or requested at the time custody is awarded (Pretzinger v. Pretzinger [1887], 45 OS 452, and McDaniel v. Rucker [1948], 150 OS 261, 37 OO 495, overruled to the extent inconsistent herewith: Meyer v. Meyer, 17 Ohio St. 3d 222, 17 Ohio B. 455, 478 N.E.2d 806 (1985).

When a noncustodial parent obtains custody of his child in accordance with a judgment entry which both parties consent to, he is not obligated to make support payments to his former wife while he has custody of their child and is directly supporting the child during such time. When the wife regains physical custody of the child, the noncustodial parent is responsible to make the necessary support payments required by the original separation agreement: Flynn v. Flynn, 15 Ohio App. 3d 34, 472 N.E.2d 388, 1984 Ohio App. LEXIS 11946 (Ohio Ct. App., Madison County 1984).

The only duty upon the father in a divorce action in the absence of an agreement on his part to continue support of his children is to support the children until eighteen years of age or so long as the child continuously attends on a full-time basis any recognized and accredited high school: Verplatse v. Verplatse, 17 Ohio App. 3d 99, 477 N.E.2d 648, 1984 Ohio App. LEXIS 12441 (Ohio Ct. App., Hancock County 1984).

Although consideration of all relevant factors is mandated by R.C. 3109.05, none of the factors is ranked as being more decisive or conclusive than the others. Their relative importance and persuasiveness to the trier of facts will depend upon the circumstances. Factors as to which neither party produces relevant evidence may be disregarded: Zacek v. Zacek, 11 Ohio App. 3d 91, 463 N.E.2d 391, 1983 Ohio App. LEXIS 11249 (Ohio Ct. App., Franklin County 1983).

The burden of going forward with evidence of factors necessary for a determination of support under R.C. 3109.05 may vary depending upon the circumstances of the case, but generally each party must bear the responsibility of bringing forth evidence as to his or her needs. Factors as to which neither party adduces evidence may be deemed by the trial court to be of no significance: Cheek v. Cheek, 2 Ohio App. 3d 86, 440 N.E.2d 831, 1982 Ohio App. LEXIS 10879 (Ohio Ct. App., Franklin County 1982).

In determining the amount of child support which is reasonable and necessary to support the child under R.C. 3109.05(A), the first concern of the trial court is to determine the needs of the child. This determination is to be guided by consideration of all relevant factors, including those listed in R.C. 3109.05(A). The determination of the amount "necessary for child support" must then be tempered by ascertaining the amount of child support which is "reasonable" in view of the overall financial picture of the parents and the child: Bright v. Collins, 2 Ohio App. 3d 421, 442 N.E.2d 822, 1982 Ohio App. LEXIS 10899 (Ohio Ct. App., Franklin County 1982).

In order to determine child support, first there should be established the monetary amount necessary for the support of the children in a standard of living commensurate with the incomes of their parents. Then, there should be determined the proportionate share of the child support so established that each parent equitably should bear: In re Machmer, 2 Ohio App. 3d 84, 440 N.E.2d 829, 1981 Ohio App. LEXIS 9915 (Ohio Ct. App., Franklin County 1981).

Where a husband and wife are divorced, a wife may be required to assume some financial support for her minor children who are in the custody of the husband: Hacker v. Hacker, 5 Ohio App. 3d 46, 448 N.E.2d 831, 1981 Ohio App. LEXIS 10089 (Ohio Ct. App., Fairfield County 1981).

Where a husband and wife are divorced, the duty to support a minor child is governed by R.C. 3109.05 (child support; visitation rights) and not R.C. 3103.03 (duty of husband to support family), so that a wife may be required to assume the support of her child which is in the custody of another: Hill v. Hill, 40 Ohio App. 2d 1, 69 Ohio Op. 2d 1, 317 N.E.2d 250, 1973 Ohio App. LEXIS 1480 (Ohio Ct. App., Hamilton County 1973).

This section does not apply to others than parents: Kay v. Kay, 51 Ohio Op. 434, 112 N.E.2d 562, 65 Ohio Law Abs. 472, 1953 Ohio Misc. LEXIS 374 (Ohio C.P. 1953).

The mere fact that the father failed to contribute to the support of his minor child, when the person having custody neither expected nor claimed compensation for the care and support of such child, does not amount to an abandonment as a matter of law: In re Duffy, 78 Ohio App. 16, 33 Ohio Op. 381, 68 N.E.2d 842, 46 Ohio Law Abs. 558, 1946 Ohio App. LEXIS 638 (Ohio Ct. App., Franklin County 1946).

**Ability to pay**

In its calculation of a former husband's child support obligation, the trial court did not err in failing to reduce the husband's income by $30,000 to reflect the annual interest expense that the father would incur due to his inability to pay the amounts awarded to the former wife in the judgment. The husband's assignment of error was based on a faulty factual premise since both the trial court and the court of appeals determined that the father was capable of paying the judgment. Meeks v. Meeks, 2008-Ohio-2015, 2008 Ohio App. LEXIS 1718 (Ohio Ct. App., Franklin County 2008).

**Adoption**

Since a biological father of two children had a statutory duty to support them from the time of their birth until the date on which the probate court issued the final decrees of adoption in favor of the stepfather, the biological father was properly ordered to pay child support until that date. G.A. v. G.L., 2009-Ohio-5184, 2009 Ohio App. LEXIS 4358 (Ohio Ct. App., Erie County 2009).

**Adoption, consent to**

Agreement between biological parents to exchange a consent to adoption for forgiveness of child support arrearages is an enforceable agreement: Eckliff v. Walters, 2006-Ohio-4817, 168 Ohio App. 3d 727, 861 N.E.2d 843, 2006 Ohio App. LEXIS 4722 (Ohio Ct. App., Lake County 2006).

Parties' "contract," relieving the father's obligations to pay future child support in exchange for his consent to the stepparent adoption and termination of his visitation rights, was unenforceable. The parties failed to obtain court approval and failed to have the trial court confirm that the agreement comported with the Ohio Child Support Guidelines. Day v. Bloom, 2006-Ohio-6957, 2006 Ohio App. LEXIS 6921 (Ohio Ct. App., Medina County 2006).

The father's signed consent to adoption of the children by the mother's second husband, which adoption never happened, did not relieve him of the duty to make future child support payments: Przylepa v. Przylepa, 77 Ohio App. 3d 808, 603 N.E.2d 1083, 1991 Ohio App. LEXIS 5032 (Ohio Ct. App., Hancock County 1991).

Where the wife agrees to waive child support payments in exchange for the father's consent to an adoption by her present husband, such agreement is valid between the parties, even though the adoption never actually occurred. Thus where an action for the arrearage is brought after the child is emancipated, and no longer a beneficiary of the support order, the action is barred: Lawhorn v. Lawhorn, 1990 Ohio App. LEXIS 3880 (Ohio Ct. App., Montgomery County Sept. 7, 1990).

**Appeal**

Because the mother did not comply with the specificity requirements of Civ.R. 53(D)(3)(b)(ii) or Summit County, Ohio, Ct. C.P. Dom. Rel. Div. R.12.03(B), her objection to the standard visitation order, the child support calculations, and the tax exemption had no factual or legal support. Stanley v. Stanley, 2007-Ohio-2740, 2007 Ohio App. LEXIS 2528 (Ohio Ct. App., Summit County 2007).

The court's reduction of a child support obligation was not a final appealable order where the custody issue remained unresolved: Koroshazi v. Koroshazi, 110 Ohio App. 3d 637, 674 N.E.2d 1266, 1996 Ohio App. LEXIS 1784 (Ohio Ct. App., Summit County 1996).

**Arbitration**

In a domestic relations case, matters of temporary or permanent spousal and/or child support may, by mutual consent of marriage partners, be made subject to an agreement to arbitrate. R.C. Title 31 and Civ.R. 75, read in conjunction with R.C. Chapter 2711., allow a trial court to intervene and oversee that arbitration of matters of spousal and/or child support, whether of a temporary or permanent nature, is accomplished in an expeditious, efficient, and reasonable manner: Kelm v. Kelm, 1993-Ohio-56, 68 Ohio St. 3d 26, 623 N.E.2d 39, 1993 Ohio LEXIS 2526 (Ohio 1993).

**Arrearages**

There was no error in the award of a child support arrearage because it was an acceptable arrearage which occurred due to a time lapse between when an issue was submitted and the trial court could journalize its order on the issue. The fact the financial needs of the child were met during the pendency of the divorce did not mean that the child is not entitled to support from both parents. Davis v. Evans, 2012-Ohio-1664, 2012 Ohio App. LEXIS 1464 (Ohio Ct. App., Franklin County 2012).

In light of the income disparity between the parties, the trial court did not err in rejecting the mother's request to require the father to pay a greater amount toward his child support arrearage. The decision to decrease the father's monthly payment on his child support arrearage to $64.20 was in keeping with the rebuttable presumption established by R.C. 3123.21(A), since the amount was at least 20 percent of the father's current monthly child support payment, which the trial court had decreased to $321.03. York v. York, 2011-Ohio-5872, 2011 Ohio App. LEXIS 4791 (Ohio Ct. App., Clermont County 2011).

Trial court abused its discretion by refusing to allow the father to voluntarily withdraw his motion to determine support arrearages after it placed the significant burden of proof on him to prove whether the mother should have been given credit for unpaid daycare expenses. The trial court essentially converted the motion to determine support arrearages into a motion to modify child support; no exigent circumstances existed that warranted modifying child support back to 1997. Reinhard v. Reinhard, 2011-Ohio-343, 2011 Ohio App. LEXIS 279 (Ohio Ct. App., Cuyahoga County 2011).

Because the father did not appeal the issues, he was precluded from challenging the award of support and the collection of arrearages; the trial court's judgment granting the adoption of the father's children did not terminate the father's obligation to support his children prior to their adoption, did not terminate the award of spousal support, and did not terminate the amount of child support previously owed in the 1984 divorce action. The agency was not only entitled to collect the support arrearages, it was required by law to do so. Lyons v. Lyons, 2009-Ohio-6868, 2009 Ohio App. LEXIS 5771 (Ohio Ct. App., Crawford County 2009).

Record supported the magistrate's finding that the parents had mutually agreed to direct payments of child support and that the husband had an arrearage in support because the wife's exhibits regarding the husband's temporary child support payments were more orderly and, therefore, more credible. Miller v. Miller, 2008-Ohio-4297, 2008 Ohio App. LEXIS 3618 (Ohio Ct. App., Wayne County 2008).

Although a magistrate subtracted a former husband's previous payments for child support arrearages, the magistrate ordered that he pay interest on the entire principal amount, because payment in full had not been made, causing interest to accrue at the same rate as though the entire principal amount was still outstanding. Because of the former husband's repeated failure to pay and the consistent rate of interest that continued to accrue, the magistrate's calculation was appropriate. Belkin v. Belkin, 2007-Ohio-2378, 2007 Ohio App. LEXIS 2221 (Ohio Ct. App., Cuyahoga County 2007).

Arrearage amount was incorrect because it should have been calculated from the time of the motion for child support. As to the specific directives of the contempt purge order, the amount of arrearage should have been calculated from the date that a request was made for a hearing on arrearages. Pickenpaugh v. Pickenpaugh, 2007-Ohio-1438, 2007 Ohio App. LEXIS 1300 (Ohio Ct. App., Muskingum County 2007).

There was no abuse of discretion in refusing to award interest on the underpayment of child support because the trial court reasonably concluded that the husband did not act willfully, pursuant to R.C. 3123.17(A). The record did not show that the husband willfully ceased or miscalculated payments; rather it showed that he did not pay the proper amount pursuant to the mathematical formula set forth in the divorce decree, which did not indicate a willful failure to provide support for his children. Toensing v. Toensing, 2006-Ohio-3320, 2006 Ohio App. LEXIS 3236 (Ohio Ct. App., Cuyahoga County 2006).

Trial court abused its discretion in failing to determine the issue of the husband's child support arrearage; the Child Support Enforcement Agency did not perform an audit of the arrears owed by the husband as required by R.C. 3109.05 and as instructed by the trial court. Poptic v. Poptic, 2003-Ohio-7211, 2003 Ohio App. LEXIS 6493 (Ohio Ct. App., Butler County 2003).

Magistrate's decision to award the mother $12,481.35 in child support arrearage did not constitute an abuse of discretion. The magistrate did not misapply the doctrine of laches because the father did not demonstrate that he was prejudiced by the delay in collecting back child support or that he sold his business in reliance on the mother's inaction, and he failed to establish the first two elements necessary for application of laches, unreasonable delay or lapse of time in asserting a right and absence of an excuse for a delay. Marcum v. Marcum, 2003-Ohio-7012, 2003 Ohio App. LEXIS 6394 (Ohio Ct. App., Columbiana County 2003).

Father was liable for child support arrearages during the time the maternal grandmother had custody as there was no evidence of an agreement absolving the father of his responsibility or that the grandmother was guilty of laches; the court-ordered child support could not be waived, and the father should have known that no adoption occurred. Porter v. Ferrall, 2003-Ohio-6685, 2003 Ohio App. LEXIS 5944 (Ohio Ct. App., Portage County 2003).

A trial court must calculate a child support arrearage on the basis of the express language of the most recent court entry relating to the issue of child support. This allows a court to change a per-child order to an in-gross order or vice versa. A court lacks jurisdiction to modify an in-gross order retroactively: Lytle v. Lytle, 130 Ohio App. 3d 697, 720 N.E.2d 1007, 1998 Ohio App. LEXIS 6160 (Ohio Ct. App., Franklin County 1998), dismissed, 85 Ohio St. 3d 1464, 709 N.E.2d 171, 1999 Ohio LEXIS 1334 (Ohio 1999).

Arrearages in child support which have not been reduced to a lump-sum judgment are not subject to the interest provisions of R.C. 1343.03. The enactment of former R.C. 3113.21.9 and the amendment of R.C. 3109.05 (C) providing for interest on delinquent support, apply only to support orders issued or modified on or after July 1, 1992: Dunbar v. Dunbar, 1994-Ohio-509, 68 Ohio St. 3d 369, 627 N.E.2d 532, 1994 Ohio LEXIS 371 (Ohio 1994).

For purposes of liability for an arrearage, an obligor is not relieved of a duty to make child support payments by the custodial party's indication that he need not make them: Wise v. Wise, 86 Ohio App. 3d 702, 621 N.E.2d 1213, 1993 Ohio App. LEXIS 1442 (Ohio Ct. App., Butler County 1993).

Aid to dependent children payments are exempt from execution, and a court may not order payment of child support arrearages from such source. After the children of a marriage have attained the age of majority, the trial court cannot enforce a prior order for child support by exercising the power of contempt; however, the party entitled to child support payments has the right to collect any arrearage in support by garnishment, attachment, or execution on the lump sum judgments previously granted: Crigger v. Crigger, 71 Ohio App. 3d 410, 594 N.E.2d 67, 1991 Ohio App. LEXIS 1215 (Ohio Ct. App., Franklin County 1991).

Laches is not a defense in an action to enforce a child support order where the obligor does not show any prejudice resulting from the passage of time: Johnson v. Johnson, 71 Ohio App. 3d 713, 595 N.E.2d 388, 1991 Ohio App. LEXIS 1498 (Ohio Ct. App., Portage County 1991).

Trial court did not clearly err in finding that the defense of laches was not established as to the child support arrearage: Kinney v. Mathias, 10 Ohio St. 3d 72, 461 N.E.2d 901, 1984 Ohio LEXIS 1067 (Ohio 1984).

**—Calculation**

Trial court's child support arrearage calculation based only on the statements by the father's counsel was not supported by competent, credible evidence because the mother's testimony, that the father moved out of their home in March of 2011, was the only evidence. Shendel v. Graham, 2017-Ohio-4236, 92 N.E.3d 43, 2017 Ohio App. LEXIS 2303 (Ohio Ct. App., Lake County 2017).

Trial court did not abuse its discretion in determining that the husband underpaid his child support obligation in the amount of $7,273.98. The wife's calculation included bonus income with respect to spousal support, which was not contemplated in the divorce decree, and to which the wife did not object, and any actual miscalculation would have been de minimis. Toensing v. Toensing, 2006-Ohio-3320, 2006 Ohio App. LEXIS 3236 (Ohio Ct. App., Cuyahoga County 2006).

**—Commencement date**

Trial court's order for retroactive child support of $500 per month for 14 months prior to the trial was without a solid legal foundation. The ruling that a "temporary order" or order pendente lite should be entered in the decree of divorce and judgment granted for an arrearage based upon that "temporary order" was inconsistent with the applicable rules of civil procedure. Young v. Young, 2013-Ohio-2568, 2013 Ohio App. LEXIS 2533 (Ohio Ct. App., Franklin County 2013).

Arrearage amount was incorrect because it should have been calculated from the time of the motion for child support. As to the specific directives of the contempt purge order, the amount of arrearage should have been calculated from the date that a request was made for a hearing on arrearages. Pickenpaugh v. Pickenpaugh, 2007-Ohio-1438, 2007 Ohio App. LEXIS 1300 (Ohio Ct. App., Muskingum County 2007).

**—Emancipated beneficiary**

The existence of a child support arrearage upon the beneficiary's emancipation and the death of a custodial parent establishes a prima facie case that the emancipated child has been denied the standard of living to which he or she was entitled. When the statutory beneficiary of child support is found to have been so denied the benefits of a child support award, he or she has a superior claim to the arrearages. This presumption applies only in those cases where the custodial parent has died and only when there is an emancipated beneficiary: Janowiecki v. Lucas County Child Support Enforcement Agency (In re Estate of Antkowiak), 95 Ohio App. 3d 546, 642 N.E.2d 1154, 1994 Ohio App. LEXIS 2714 (Ohio Ct. App., Lucas County 1994).



**—Interest**

Although a magistrate subtracted a former husband's previous payments for child support arrearages, the magistrate ordered that he pay interest on the entire principal amount, because payment in full had not been made, causing interest to accrue at the same rate as though the entire principal amount was still outstanding. Because of the former husband's repeated failure to pay and the consistent rate of interest that continued to accrue, the magistrate's calculation was appropriate. Belkin v. Belkin, 2007-Ohio-2378, 2007 Ohio App. LEXIS 2221 (Ohio Ct. App., Cuyahoga County 2007).

There was no abuse of discretion in refusing to award interest on the underpayment of child support because the trial court reasonably concluded that the husband did not act willfully, pursuant to R.C. 3123.17(A). The record did not show that the husband willfully ceased or miscalculated payments; rather it showed that he did not pay the proper amount pursuant to the mathematical formula set forth in the divorce decree, which did not indicate a willful failure to provide support for his children. Toensing v. Toensing, 2006-Ohio-3320, 2006 Ohio App. LEXIS 3236 (Ohio Ct. App., Cuyahoga County 2006).

In the absence of factors making it inequitable, a right to interest under R.C. 1343.03(A) on unpaid child support accrues on the date each installment becomes due, and runs until paid. Such interest may be included in a lump-sum judgment for arrearages in child support: In re Hammond, 78 Ohio App. 3d 170, 604 N.E.2d 197, 1992 Ohio App. LEXIS 277 (Ohio Ct. App., Hamilton County 1992).

In the absence of factors making it inequitable, a right to interest under R.C. 1343.03(A) on unpaid child support accrues on the date each installment becomes due, and runs until paid. Such interest may be included in a lump-sum judgment for child support arrearages: Allen v. Allen, 62 Ohio App. 3d 621, 577 N.E.2d 126, 1990 Ohio App. LEXIS 1876 (Ohio Ct. App., Summit County 1990).

Arrearages in child support which have not been reduced to a lump-sum judgment are not subject to the interest provisions of R.C. 1343.03: Krause v. Krause, 35 Ohio App. 3d 18, 518 N.E.2d 1221, 1987 Ohio App. LEXIS 10482 (Ohio Ct. App., Butler County 1987).

**—Majority**

After a child has attained the age of majority and child support money yet unpaid is reduced to a lump-sum judgment during a civil proceeding, the judgment becomes a debt, and imprisonment for that debt is precluded under Ohio Const. art I, § 15. R.C. 2705.03.1 is only constitutional to the extent it applies to criminal contempt proceedings and as a punishment for a contumacious individual who refused to pay a court ordered support obligation: Martin v. Martin, 76 Ohio App. 3d 638, 602 N.E.2d 772, 1992 Ohio App. LEXIS 830 (Ohio Ct. App., Franklin County 1992).

**—Offset**

Trial court properly ordered that the husband's share of the money that he had paid for the children's medical expenses be used to offset his child support arrearages. Poitinger v. Poitinger, 2005-Ohio-2680, 2005 Ohio App. LEXIS 2535 (Ohio Ct. App., Summit County 2005).

**—Setoff**

A father who is ordered to pay a support order arrearage may not claim an offset for support he could have requested earlier for a child who chose to live with him: Wilmer v. Wilmer, 66 Ohio App. 3d 713, 586 N.E.2d 153, 1990 Ohio App. LEXIS 2295 (Ohio Ct. App., Montgomery County 1990).

Generally speaking, a father is not entitled to credit against arrearages for overpayments in support money which he made to the mother. Whether or not he is entitled to credit for medical expenses, or other necessities, depends to a large degree on the particular circumstances surrounding each case: Ferrere v. Ferrere, 20 Ohio App. 3d 82, 484 N.E.2d 753, 1984 Ohio App. LEXIS 12544 (Ohio Ct. App., Cuyahoga County 1984).

**Attorney fees**

Trial court, in accordance with the statutes, ordered the husband to pay the wife's attorney fees because he was found in contempt of court; the trial court was not required to consider the wife's ability to pay, and only awarded attorney fees for the time spent litigating the motion to show cause. T.R.H. v. A.D.H., 2021-Ohio-3036, 2021 Ohio App. LEXIS 2975 (Ohio Ct. App., Cuyahoga County 2021).

Mother was not entitled to recover her attorney fees under this statute because the father's obligation to contribute to the cost of the child's college education was not "child support," and the trial court properly refused to hold the father in contempt for his failure to pay his share of the child's college expenses. Vail v. String, 2019-Ohio-984, 2019 Ohio App. LEXIS 1091 (Ohio Ct. App., Cuyahoga County 2019).

Mother had the burden to establish her inability to pay the attorney fees, and she failed to establish her inability to pay the purge order with sufficient evidence, as she did not provide evidence of her income or employment. Colagiovanni v. Hayden, 2018-Ohio-4951, 2018 Ohio App. LEXIS 5266 (Ohio Ct. App., Lake County 2018).

Trial court properly awarded attorney fees to a mother in her proceeding, wherein the father was held in contempt for failure to make certain child support payments, because the father's conduct was deemed contemptuous and the fees were reasonable. Seaman v. Sloan, 2016-Ohio-5432, 60 N.E.3d 1270, 2016 Ohio App. LEXIS 3306 (Ohio Ct. App., Lucas County 2016).

In parties' divorce action, the trial court erred when it failed to impose all court costs and the wife's reasonable attorney fees arising out of the contempt proceeding against the husband because it sustained the wife's objection to the magistrate's failure to find him in contempt. Durisala v. Durisala, 2014-Ohio-5229, 2014 Ohio App. LEXIS 5131 (Ohio Ct. App., Hamilton County 2014).

Because the parties entered into an agreement finding the obligor in contempt for unpaid medical expenses, the obligor was required under the contempt statute to pay the reasonable attorney fees the obligee incurred in the prosecution of her motion, and the magistrate had sufficient evidence to determine that the fees were reasonable. 2014 Ohio 4813, 2013 Ohio App. LEXIS 6258.

There was no plain error because, even though the trial court should have awarded the father attorney fees in connection with his contempt motion, the error did not seriously affect the basic fairness, integrity, or public reputation of the judicial process. Jacobs v. Jacobs, 2012-Ohio-5815, 2012 Ohio App. LEXIS 5008 (Ohio Ct. App., Wayne County 2012).

Pursuant to R.C. 3109.05(C), although a magistrate properly awarded a wife attorney fees in her post-divorce decree proceedings, there were errors in the calculation of the fees, which were not supported by the record; the record contained no documentation in conformance with Cuyahoga County, Ohio, Ct. C.P. Dom. Rel. Div. R. 21(B)(1). Radford v. Radford, 2011-Ohio-6263, 2011 Ohio App. LEXIS 5144 (Ohio Ct. App., Cuyahoga County 2011).

Pursuant to R.C. 3109.05(C), a magistrate provided an analysis and reasoning on its award of attorney fees and litigation expenses to a wife in post-divorce decree proceedings, such that the trial court's adoption thereof was not an abuse of discretion. Radford v. Radford, 2011-Ohio-6263, 2011 Ohio App. LEXIS 5144 (Ohio Ct. App., Cuyahoga County 2011).

Trial court violated the law of the case doctrine when it refused to award a child support enforcement agency attorney fees under R.C. 3109.05(C) after a father was found in contempt; in a prior appeal, an appellate court had already determined that the agency was entitled to some fees, and it was the trial court's sole duty to determine the amount of reasonable fees to award. Roush v. Brown, 2010-Ohio-1520, 2010 Ohio App. LEXIS 1262 (Ohio Ct. App., Butler County 2010).

When a child support enforcement agency brought an action to have a father found in contempt for failing to comply with an order to pay child support, and the father was found to be in contempt, the trial court was not required to award the agency $500 in attorney's fees, pursuant to Butler County, Ohio, Ct. C.P. Dom. Rel. Div. R. 31(C)(5), because local rules could not determine substantive rights, but the court was required, on remand, to determine what the agency's reasonable attorney's fee was, because the agency was entitled to a fee award, pursuant to R.C. 3109.05(C), since the father was found in contempt and the agency was an adverse party. Roush v. Brown, 2009-Ohio-2446, 2009 Ohio App. LEXIS 2036 (Ohio Ct. App., Butler County 2009).

When a child support enforcement agency brought an action to have a father found in contempt for failing to comply with an order to pay child support, the agency was entitled to an award of attorney's fees, pursuant to R.C. 3109.05(C), because (1) the agency was a proper party to the action, pursuant to R.C. 2705.031(B)(1), (2) the father was found in contempt, which required the father to pay an adverse party's reasonable attorney's fee, and (3) the agency was such an adverse party, as the agency's interests were in opposition to those of the father. Roush v. Brown, 2009-Ohio-2446, 2009 Ohio App. LEXIS 2036 (Ohio Ct. App., Butler County 2009).

Lower court did not abuse its discretion when it reduced the award of attorney's fees, pursuant to R.C. 3109.05(C), because the magistrate's award of attorney's fees included all fees for the motion to modify, the wife's motion to continue, and her subsequent motion to reconsider her motion to continue, not just the motion for contempt. The wife's need did not outweigh the husband's ability to pay. Goldberg v. Goldberg, 2006-Ohio-1948, 2006 Ohio App. LEXIS 1796 (Ohio Ct. App., Cuyahoga County 2006).

Trial court's award for father to pay attorney fees to mother was proper; attorney fees assessment was automatic in child support contempt proceeding under R.C. 3109.05(C) and did not require findings of father's ability to pay or mother's ability to prosecute as was required in R.C.

3105.18(H), which did not apply. Bergman v. Bergman, 2004-Ohio-584, 2004 Ohio App. LEXIS 555 (Ohio Ct. App., Franklin County 2004).

Where a trial court held that a husband showed a substantial change in circumstances to justify a modification of support, and it was unable to determine the wife's need since she had not complied with discovery requests, it did not abuse its discretion in only awarding the wife a portion of the attorney fees requested, as the husband's ability to pay attorney fees was diminished; further, the trial court was not required to impose attorney fees on the husband for the prosecution of the wife's contempt motion, as R.C. 3109.05(C) only required the imposition of fees on one who was found in contempt. Norris v. Norris, 2004-Ohio-4072, 2004 Ohio App. LEXIS 3710 (Ohio Ct. App., Cuyahoga County 2004).

Trial court was required to award attorney fees pursuant to R.C. 3109.05(C) against father in contempt of court for failing to pay child support and medical bills; furthermore, since the mother's attorney complied with Cuyahoga County, Ohio, Ct. C.P. Dom. Rel. Div. R. 21, the court did not err in awarding the mother a reasonable amount of her requested attorney fees. Oleksy v. Oleksy, 2003-Ohio-5657, 2003 Ohio App. LEXIS 5048 (Ohio Ct. App., Cuyahoga County 2003).

Where the trial court found that the father was in contempt for failure to pay child support, the trial court erred in failing to award attorney fees, as attorney fees were mandated under R.C. 3109.05(C). Sinnott v. Sinnott, 2003-Ohio-4571, 2003 Ohio App. LEXIS 4058 (Ohio Ct. App., Franklin County 2003).

A trial court has jurisdiction to award appellate attorney fees relating to a prior appeal: Rhoades v. Rhoades, 1991 Ohio App. LEXIS 1122 (Ohio Ct. App., Wyandot County Feb. 28, 1991).

Where a party is found in contempt for failure to make child support payments, R.C. 3109.05 and 3111.13(F) require the court to award costs and attorney fees. A court is not required to issue findings of fact and conclusions of law in a contempt proceeding for the nonpayment of support: Miller v. Barker, 64 Ohio App. 3d 649, 582 N.E.2d 647, 1989 Ohio App. LEXIS 5222 (Ohio Ct. App., Cuyahoga County 1989).

A trial court does not abuse its discretion in awarding reasonable attorney fees to a divorced spouse in a successful appeal to enforce a former spouse's legal obligations: Evans v. Brown, 34 Ohio App. 3d 56, 516 N.E.2d 1289, 1986 Ohio App. LEXIS 10330 (Ohio Ct. App., Franklin County 1986).

A trial court has authority, after entry of a divorce decree, to enter an order requiring the divorced husband to pay reasonable expense money to his former wife to enable her to pay attorney fees incurred in post decree proceedings relative to the support of the minor children of the marriage (R.C. 3103.03, former 3105.06.1, former 3105.14 and 3109.05 construed and applied): Blum v. Blum, 9 Ohio St. 2d 92, 38 Ohio Op. 2d 224, 223 N.E.2d 819, 1967 Ohio LEXIS 421 (Ohio 1967).

**—Bankruptcy**

Where a state court judgment mandated the payment of attorney fees to enforce debtor's child support obligations, the attorney fee award was clearly intertwined with the litigation by debtor's former spouse to obtain child support and was entitled to priority treatment under 11 U.S.C.S. § 507(a)(7)(B). In re McLaughlin, 320 B.R. 661, 2005 Bankr. LEXIS 234 (Bankr. N.D. Ohio 2005).

Attorney fees and travel expenses incurred in enforcing an obligation to pay a child's medical expenses and health insurance costs also constitute "support" under the bankruptcy law. Forgiveness of debt by creditors of an ex-spouse does not affect the obligation to the ex-spouse: Bratton v. Frederick, 109 Ohio App. 3d 13, 671 N.E.2d 1030, 1996 Ohio App. LEXIS 326 (Ohio Ct. App., Defiance County 1996).

**Attorney-client liability**

An attorney who represents a spouse in the negotiation of a separation agreement relative to a marriage dissolution action does not simultaneously, automatically represent the interests of a minor child of the marriage: Scholler v. Scholler, 10 Ohio St. 3d 98, 462 N.E.2d 158, 1984 Ohio LEXIS 1072 (Ohio 1984).

**Award proper**

Trial court awarded the child support in accord with the worksheet and thus, did not abuse its discretion by following the mandates of R.C. 3119.022. The husband's independent agreement for tuition did not automatically result in a deviation from the figure generated through use of the child support worksheet. Scherer v. Scherer, 2011-Ohio-6822, 2011 Ohio App. LEXIS 5640 (Ohio Ct. App., Franklin County 2011).

Trial court properly calculated a father's child support obligation at $884 per month based on the father's gross annual salary of $103,000, giving the father credit for his annual $2,400 insurance premiums for the child. Pellettiere v. Pellettiere, 2009-Ohio-5407, 2009 Ohio App. LEXIS 4557 (Ohio Ct. App., Montgomery County 2009).

**Bond forfeiture**

Trial court properly ordered that an ex-husband's bond be forfeited, pursuant to R.C. 2937.35 and Crim.R. 46, for his failure to appear in a timely fashion at a contempt hearing due to the husband's continued failure to pay child support, pursuant to R.C. 3109.05; the record revealed that the husband had continually failed to appear at scheduled hearings, had diverted funds in order to avoid the support order, and had failed to provide documentation as to his alleged disabilities. Stuber v. Stuber, 2003-Ohio-1795, 2003 Ohio App. LEXIS 1719 (Ohio Ct. App., Allen County 2003).

**Calculation**

As the parties contemplated, in their shared parenting plan, that child care expenses would be included in the child support calculation, the trial court did not abuse its discretion in including such expense when calculating the father's child support obligation. Kaethow v. Kaethow, 2013-Ohio-2354, 2013 Ohio App. LEXIS 2305 (Ohio Ct. App., Licking County 2013).

In parties' contested divorce, wherein the husband was awarded full custody of their child, the trial court erred when it failed to include the wife's income when computing the amount of child support that she currently owed. Bergman v. Bergman, 2013-Ohio-715, 2013 Ohio App. LEXIS 634 (Ohio Ct. App., Montgomery County 2013).

Trial court did not err in determining that it was appropriate to use the 2007 information to perform the 2007 child support calculations because, given that the child support award was intended to cover the time period for 2007, it was appropriate for the magistrate to consider documentation related to that time period, rather than current data. Further, the trial court did not abuse its discretion in choosing to make the child-support modification retroactive to the date the shared parenting terminated or in selecting $2,450 as an appropriate downward deviation. Kemp v. Kemp, 2009-Ohio-6089, 2009 Ohio App. LEXIS 5100 (Ohio Ct. App., Stark County 2009).



**Change of circumstances**

Since a father did not submit a signed statement of evidence on appeal, the court could not say that the trial court committed an error of law in determining that the father had failed to submit any evidence of a substantial change in circumstances that would warrant a decrease in his child support obligation. Since the inception of the case, the father sold or depleted his assets and rental properties, refused to file income taxes for several years, and continued to be unemployed while, at the same time, judgment creditors had been paid ahead of his child support obligation; thus, nothing had changed since the initial child support order in which the trial court determined that the father was capable of employment but remained voluntarily unemployed. In re Cunningham, 2008-Ohio-3737, 2008 Ohio App. LEXIS 3171 (Ohio Ct. App., Trumbull County 2008).

Trial court did not err in ordering the amount of child support because the "more than 10-percent difference" requirement was only for a modification in the amount of child support. It did not apply to the change of circumstance as to the zero-support order. Powers v. Powers, 2008-Ohio-3159, 2008 Ohio App. LEXIS 2674 (Ohio Ct. App., Hamilton County 2008).

Trial court did not err in finding that changes of circumstances existed, pursuant to R.C. 3109.05(E)(1)(a), because the findings were supported by the record. Although the magistrate failed to determine that the factors had an adverse effect on the child, the trial court addressed that issue and found that maintaining the mother as the residential parent would have subjected the child to instability and uncertainty which would materially and adversely effect any child. Orians v. Orians, 2006-Ohio-1142, 2006 Ohio App. LEXIS 1042 (Ohio Ct. App., Wyandot County 2006).

**—Incarceration**

Because the father violated his community control, resulting in his incarceration, and his violations were not based upon his disability, the trial court did not abuse its discretion when it denied the father's motion to modify the child support order. Dreher v. Stevens, 2006-Ohio-351, 2006 Ohio App. LEXIS 309 (Ohio Ct. App., Defiance County 2006).

**Commencement date**

Trial court erred in its award of child support because the trial court, in granting a parent's motion for child support, should have selected the date when that parent first made a request in a pleading for child support as the date when the other parent's obligation commenced. Gajarsky v. Kottler, 2012-Ohio-1817, 2012 Ohio App. LEXIS 1595 (Ohio Ct. App., Summit County 2012).

Because no reason supporting the June 2006 date appeared of record, the trial court abused its discretion in fixing the effective date of the child-support obligation. Powers v. Powers, 2008-Ohio-3159, 2008 Ohio App. LEXIS 2674 (Ohio Ct. App., Hamilton County 2008).

As a trial court's child support and spousal support orders were reversed on remand for failure to have used a child support worksheet, those orders were void and the trial court's new orders entered after the worksheet was relied upon should have been effective from the original date rather than a later time; accordingly, the trial court erred in modifying the support awards from a time later than the original order. Raff v. Raff, 2007-Ohio-737, 2007 Ohio App. LEXIS 671 (Ohio Ct. App., Stark County 2007).

Trial court did not abuse its discretion in ordering a mother of a minor child to pay child support, which modification was retroactive to the date that the child was placed in the father's home for custody purposes, as that was a significant date in the case and the mother had been put on notice when the father filed his complaint that he was seeking "such further relief," which encompassed child support. In re Smith, 2007-Ohio-893, 2007 Ohio App. LEXIS 812 (Ohio Ct. App., Ashtabula County 2007).

It was not an abuse of discretion for a trial court to adopt a magistrate's recommendation requiring a wife to pay child support retroactive to the date the wife had moved the magistrate to modify temporary orders because (1) the wife's motion had raised the issue of child support, and (2) the wife did not object to the magistrate's order requiring the wife to pay child support retroactive to the date of this motion. Yarnell v. Yarnell, 2006-Ohio-3929, 2006 Ohio App. LEXIS 3886 (Ohio Ct. App., Delaware County 2006).

In light of the mother's admission that the son began residing with his father in May, 2002, there was nothing arbitrary, unreasonable, or unconscionable in ordering her to pay child support effective the following month. Dadosky v. Dadosky, 2005-Ohio-3496, 2005 Ohio App. LEXIS 3242 (Ohio Ct. App., Pike County 2005).

When a wife's motion to vacate a trial court's judgment ordering her to pay child support was denied, the fact that she was not ordered to pay child support when primary custody of one of the parties' children was originally placed with the husband under a shared parenting agreement did not bar the trial court from ordering the wife to pay future support. Baddam-Reddy v. Baddam-Reddy, 2005-Ohio-3432, 2005 Ohio App. LEXIS 3165 (Ohio Ct. App., Cuyahoga County 2005).



**Contempt**

Trial court did not abuse its discretion in awarding the mother attorney fees because once the trial court found that the father was in contempt for failing to comply with the court's cash medical support order, the court was required to order father to pay mother's attorney fees. In re I.L.J., 2020-Ohio-5434, 2020 Ohio App. LEXIS 4283 (Ohio Ct. App., Cuyahoga County 2020).

Appellate court did not have a final appealable order with respect to the mother's motion to show cause because while the trial court granted the mother's motion to show cause and ordered the father to pay $398.07, the trial court did not make a finding of contempt or impose a penalty or sanction for the contempt and did not include a purge order, and the trial court's award of attorney fees related to the motion was not a penalty or sanction for the contempt. In re I.L.J., 2019-Ohio-5241, 2019 Ohio App. LEXIS 5303 (Ohio Ct. App., Cuyahoga County 2019).

Because the trial court found the husband in contempt for failing to comply with the temporary support orders, an award of attorney fees was mandated. The trial court considered the evidence, assessed the reasonableness of the attorney fees, and determined that the fees were associated with the husband's act of contempt. Allan v. Allan, 2015-Ohio-2037, 2015 Ohio App. LEXIS 1971 (Ohio Ct. App., Cuyahoga County 2015).

Trial court's determination that the mother was in contempt for not complying with the child support order was supported by the evidence because the mother stated that she chose to stop making monthly payments. Jacobs v. Jacobs, 2012-Ohio-5815, 2012 Ohio App. LEXIS 5008 (Ohio Ct. App., Wayne County 2012).

Trial court abused its discretion in finding a father in contempt as, in significantly reducing the father's child support obligation, the trial court implied that the father's ability to earn income had been drastically affected by his mental health issues, and the father had attempted to pay some child support over the years, albeit in greatly reduced payments. These factors supported the father's defense of an inability to pay the previously ordered child support amount. E.W. v. T.P., 2012-Ohio-5805, 2012 Ohio App. LEXIS 4988 (Ohio Ct. App., Lucas County 2012).

Since there was no evidence in the record that a father ever attempted to discover and pay day care expenses as ordered in the divorce decree, the trial court was within its discretion to find the father in contempt for failure to pay one-half of the day care expenses. The day care expenses were in the nature of child support and were, thus, subject to the provisions of R.C. 3109.05(C), as they qualified as "necessaries" under R.C. 3103.03, in that they were a necessity for the care of the child while the mother worked and as they were included in that portion of the original decree establishing the father's child support obligation; thus, the father's contempt for failure to pay one-half of the day care expenses fell under the purview of § 3109.05(C), and the trial court was required to order attorney fees related to the contempt. Shirvani v. Momeni, 2010-Ohio-2975, 2010 Ohio App. LEXIS 2471 (Ohio Ct. App., Franklin County 2010).

Trial court did not abuse its discretion for failing to find a father in contempt during the time when the issue of his child support obligation was pending before the court; both parties collectively filed numerous motions to change custody, to modify the father's child support obligation, and for contempt, and the issues were not resolved until 2008. Likewise, the trial court did not abuse its discretion by failing to order the father to pay the mother's attorney fees for these proceedings. Onyshko v. Onyshko, 2010-Ohio-969, 2010 Ohio App. LEXIS 831 (Ohio Ct. App., Portage County 2010).

There was no abuse of discretion by a trial court's determination that a husband in a divorce proceeding was in criminal contempt pursuant to R.C. 3105.18(G) and 3109.05(C) due to his failure to make various court-ordered payments to the wife, as the sanction was authorized as a penalty against the husband for his repeated and blatant disregard of court orders. Deacon v. Deacon, 2009-Ohio-2491, 2009 Ohio App. LEXIS 2075 (Ohio Ct. App., Cuyahoga County 2009).

Trial court did not err in finding a father in contempt of its prior order requiring the father to pay monthly child support because the record showed that the father failed to meet his monthly obligation during 23 months of the 14-year period at issue and that he failed to pay any child support during 75 months of the same period. Even if tax intercept payments met the father's support obligations for some of the months at issue, the record revealed that the father still owed a substantial amount of money in support arrearages. Campbell v. Clark, 2006-Ohio-6482, 2006 Ohio App. LEXIS 6435 (Ohio Ct. App., Crawford County 2006).

Father was properly held in contempt for failing to pay child support because he failed to purge himself, in that he did not pay the current support obligation but simply paid an amount each month in a sum sufficient to meet the monthly arrearage installment, thereby requiring the child support collection agency to apply the payments first toward the current support obligations and, then, toward arrears, as mandated by OAC 5101:1-31-14. The father's alleged belief that he could purge the contempt order by merely paying on the arrearage was unreasonable. Slagle v. Slagle, 2005-Ohio-4330, 2005 Ohio App. LEXIS 3930 (Ohio Ct. App., Lake County 2005).

Evidence that a father was on notice of the amount of child support due, admitted that he had not paid it, and faced an unambiguous order supported a finding of contempt. Kershner v. Kershner, 2003-Ohio-6780, 2003 Ohio App. LEXIS 6107 (Ohio Ct. App., Butler County 2003).

An obligation to pay child support is not a "debt" within the meaning of that term in Ohio Const. art I, § 15. Because this obligation does not fall within the scope of Ohio Const. art I, § 15, an order to pay child support may be enforced by means of imprisonment through contempt proceedings even after the child who is the subject of the order is emancipated: Cramer v. Petrie, 1994-Ohio-404, 70 Ohio St. 3d 131, 637 N.E.2d 882, 1994 Ohio LEXIS 1842 (Ohio 1994).

A civil contempt order suspending punishment on condition that the contemnor comply in the future with the terms of a pre-existing child support order does not properly allow for purging: Tucker v. Tucker, 10 Ohio App. 3d 251, 461 N.E.2d 1337, 1983 Ohio App. LEXIS 11157 (Ohio Ct. App., Franklin County 1983).

**—Burden of proof**

In a case of contempt against a parent who has not made child support payments due to physical disabilities and failure to find employment, the burden is on the parent to prove his or her inability to pay the support and thus comply with the court's support order (State ex rel. Cook v. Cook [1902], 66 OS 566, 64 NE 567, paragraph one of the syllabus, and Pugh v. Pugh, 15 Ohio St. 3d 136, 472 N.E.2d 1085, 1984 Ohio LEXIS 1280 (Ohio 1984).

**Costs and expenses**

Trial court's child support guidelines computation sheet listed the wife's child care expenses as $5,910 and the husband's child care expenses as $19,700, which was plainly error because the amount allocated to the husband constituted the entire amount of child care expenses, instead of the husband's 70 percent share. The error caused the husband's support obligation to be understated and thus, had the obligation been correctly computed, the trial court might not have found the downward deviation of the child support guidelines to be appropriate. Brokaw v. Brokaw, 2010-Ohio-1053, 2010 Ohio App. LEXIS 864 (Ohio Ct. App., Cuyahoga County 2010).

Trial court did not err by adding the annual child-care expense that the father paid to his mother as an adjustment to his income and then reduced the mother's actual annual support obligation by the full amount. Powers v. Powers, 2008-Ohio-3159, 2008 Ohio App. LEXIS 2674 (Ohio Ct. App., Hamilton County 2008).

In post-divorce decree motion proceedings, it is not an abuse of discretion for the trial court to award the wife accommodation, travel and legal expenses incurred in defending the husband's motion to modify child support payments and in prosecuting her own motion for contempt for failure to pay existing child support obligations: Harpole v. Harpole, 27 Ohio App. 3d 289, 500 N.E.2d 915, 1986 Ohio App. LEXIS 9444 (Ohio Ct. App., Medina County 1986).

**Credit**

Trial court did not err in granting the father a credit toward his child support obligation, finding that checks totaling $2,450 that the father gave the mother after he moved out of her house were for child support, as the father testified that he made the payments for the child's benefit, and the mother also testified that the checks were for the child for support. R.C. 3121.44, which required child support payments to be made to the office of child support, did not apply as there was no support order in effect at the time the payments were made. Knouff v. Walsh-Stewart, 2010-Ohio-4063, 2010 Ohio App. LEXIS 3452 (Ohio Ct. App., Wayne County 2010).

**Custody**

Although guardianship applications over adult children were within the exclusive jurisdiction of a probate court except as provided by law, pursuant to R.C. 2101.24(A)(1)(e), where a domestic relations court which handled parents' divorce and ancillary custody issues over their mentally impaired autistic son continued to exercise jurisdiction in that area, the probate court declined jurisdiction over the guardianship applications of the parents; the domestic relations court had the first opportunity to decide whether to exercise or decline jurisdiction due to the continuing nature of its jurisdiction under R.C. 3105.011 and 3109.05. In re Guardianship of Campbell, 2006-Ohio-1764, 2006 Ohio App. LEXIS 1614 (Ohio Ct. App., Mahoning County 2006).

**Day care expenses**

Trial court did not abuse its discretion in calculating the child support amount because, in light of its decision excluding the email exhibit and its failure to include any childcare expenses on the worksheet, it evidently found that the mother's $100 per week babysitting expense was either unreasonable or lacking in credibility. Shendel v. Graham, 2017-Ohio-4236, 92 N.E.3d 43, 2017 Ohio App. LEXIS 2303 (Ohio Ct. App., Lake County 2017).

Trial court's award fell within the bounds of reasonable day care expenses presented by the mother; although the trial court did not outline the exact reasons underlying its decision to award $15,000 in day care expenses, in the absence of a proper Civ.R. 52 request for findings of fact and conclusions of law, it had no independent duty to do so. The mother never asked the trial court to make separate findings of fact or conclusions of law pursuant to Civ.R. 52. O'Brien v. O'Brien, 2010-Ohio-3258, 2010 Ohio App. LEXIS 2760 (Ohio Ct. App., Butler County 2010).

**Denial or interference with visitation, etc.**

Trial court properly vacated an order that stayed child support disbursement to a mother due to her failure to comply with visitation issues, as such was not in accord with R.C. 3109.05(D) because escrowing of support payments, which were for the benefit of the child, was improper as a means of enforcement of visitation issues. The trial court retained continuing jurisdiction over the issues pursuant to R.C. 3111.16 for puposes of vacating or modifying the order. CSEA ex rel. Spencer v. Gatten, 2007-Ohio-4071, 2007 Ohio App. LEXIS 3684 (Ohio Ct. App., Cuyahoga County 2007).

Trial court did not abuse its discretion in finding a minor child's father and his parents in contempt for failing to abide by the court's orders regarding visitation time with the child's maternal grandparents, which resulted in the grandparents being required to engage in prolonged and costly litigation in order to ensure their rights to be with the child; accordingly, the trial court's imposition of payment of all costs and fees to the father and his parents was reasonable and necessary, and proper in the circumstances due to their bad faith pursuant to R.C. 3109.05 and 2705.05. Smith v. Quigg, 2006-Ohio-1495, 2006 Ohio App. LEXIS 1368 (Ohio Ct. App., Fairfield County 2006).

Competent and credible evidence existed to support the trial court's decision to terminate the child support effective January 21, 2001, rather than October 1999, because the father had continuously denied the mother her right to parenting time with the children as required by the shared parenting plan and the interim visitation agreement. The fact that their son chose not to follow the shared parenting visitation schedule and that the father did not enforce the schedule did not warrant the termination of the child support obligation in October 1999. Difranco v. Difranco, 2006-Ohio-5010, 2006 Ohio App. LEXIS 4959 (Ohio Ct. App., Cuyahoga County 2006).

The fact that a non-custodial parent failed to comply with a mandatory support order of the court does not, in itself, justify the denial or suspension of visitation; denial or suspension of visitation is only appropriate where it can be demonstrated that particularly egregious conduct by the non-custodial parent would result in harm to the children: Leasure v. Leasure, 1998 Ohio App. LEXIS 987 (Ohio Ct. App., Cuyahoga County Mar. 12, 1998).

A court may not impound support payments as a sanction for interference with visitation rights: Logan v. Vice, 79 Ohio App. 3d 838, 608 N.E.2d 786, 1992 Ohio App. LEXIS 2439 (Ohio Ct. App., Adams County 1992).

Modification of a custody order is not among the available sanctions listed under R.C. 2705.05(A) as punishment for contempt. Suspension of a child support obligation pending compliance with a visitation order exceeds the authority of the court for punishment of contempt: Fry v. Fry, 64 Ohio App. 3d 519, 582 N.E.2d 11, 1989 Ohio App. LEXIS 3662 (Ohio Ct. App., Paulding County 1989).

A court has inherent power to order that support payments be impounded in order to enforce compliance with its visitation orders: Rodriguez v. Rodriguez, 61 Ohio Misc. 2d 112, 575 N.E.2d 519, 1988 Ohio Misc. LEXIS 50 (Ohio C.P. 1988).

A trial court exceeds its authority under R.C. 2705.05 in modifying visitation and support payments as a sanction for contempt of a visitation order. Modification of visitation or support may be accomplished only after notice and hearing upon motion to invoke the continuing jurisdiction of the trial court: Andrulis v. Andrulis, 26 Ohio App. 3d 164, 498 N.E.2d 1380, 1985 Ohio App. LEXIS 10252 (Ohio Ct. App., Summit County 1985).

When a noncustodial parent is denied visitation rights, he shall obtain an appropriate remedy through proper legal channels rather than refusing to make support payments: Flynn v. Flynn, 15 Ohio App. 3d 34, 472 N.E.2d 388, 1984 Ohio App. LEXIS 11946 (Ohio Ct. App., Madison County 1984).

There is no authority, either in R.C. 3115.21 or in R.C. 3109.05, for the suspension of a support order because of the denial or interference with visitation rights: Brown v. Brown, 16 Ohio App. 3d 26, 474 N.E.2d 613, 1984 Ohio App. LEXIS 12297 (Ohio Ct. App., Warren County 1984).

A finding of contempt based on a custodial parent's interference with the visitation rights of the other parent must include an opportunity for the offending parent to purge himself of contempt: Smith v. Smith, 70 Ohio App. 2d 87, 24 Ohio Op. 3d 100, 434 N.E.2d 749, 1980 Ohio App. LEXIS 9714 (Ohio Ct. App., Franklin County 1980).

Where circumstances indicate an inability on the part of the noncustodial parent to pay child support, such parent cannot be deprived of his right of visitation solely by reason of his inability to pay: Johnson v. Johnson, 52 Ohio App. 2d 180, 6 Ohio Op. 3d 170, 368 N.E.2d 1273, 1977 Ohio App. LEXIS 6951 (Ohio Ct. App., Summit County 1977).

R.C. 3109.05 does not permit an automatic termination of support if visitation privileges are denied without cause, but requires a determination based upon evidence as to what, if any, modification of support is just, which necessarily includes an evaluation of the needs of a child for support against the right of a parent to visit with such child and a balancing of the equities involved: Foster v. Foster, 40 Ohio App. 2d 257, 69 Ohio Op. 2d 250, 319 N.E.2d 395, 1974 Ohio App. LEXIS 2638 (Ohio Ct. App., Franklin County 1974).

**—Arrearages**

The equitable powers of a domestic relations court permit it to suspend a child support order where the custodial parent takes the children to a foreign country and then in effect severs all contact between the children and the obligor. A court may set off against an arrearage the obligor's expenses in attempting to obtain visitation: Miller v. Miller, 92 Ohio App. 3d 340, 635 N.E.2d 384, 1993 Ohio App. LEXIS 5588 (Ohio Ct. App., Erie County 1993).

The doctrine of laches is applicable to an eighteen-year-old claim for unpaid child support where the obligor demonstrates material prejudice in that he was denied a relationship with the child for that period of time: Ferree v. Sparks, 77 Ohio App. 3d 185, 601 N.E.2d 568, 1991 Ohio App. LEXIS 4319 (Ohio Ct. App., Warren County 1991).

**Disability, child with**

The court reasonably retained jurisdiction for a possible future support order where an adult child of the parties was presently self-supporting, but had a severe reading disability: Shaffer v. Shaffer, 109 Ohio App. 3d 205, 671 N.E.2d 1317, 1996 Ohio App. LEXIS 534 (Ohio Ct. App., Crawford County 1996).

Whether a child with a disability is emancipated depends on the circumstances of the particular case: Powell v. Powell, 111 Ohio App. 3d 418, 676 N.E.2d 556, 1996 Ohio App. LEXIS 2339 (Ohio Ct. App., Athens County 1996).

A handicapped child does not necessarily become emancipated as a result of leaving his mother's home and enlisting in the Job Corps: In re Owens, 96 Ohio App. 3d 429, 645 N.E.2d 130, 1994 Ohio App. LEXIS 3462 (Ohio Ct. App., Clark County 1994).

To continue a child support order beyond the age of majority on the basis of the child's mental or physical disabilities, a court must find a causal connection between the disability and the inability to be self-supporting: Ulery v. Ulery, 86 Ohio App. 3d 290, 620 N.E.2d 933, 1993 Ohio App. LEXIS 757 (Ohio Ct. App., Summit County 1993).

Where the father reaches an agreement during the proceedings with the custodial mother to provide support for their incompetent adult child, the domestic relations court may incorporate the agreement into decree and give the agreement the force of law: O'Connor v. O'Connor, 71 Ohio App. 3d 541, 594 N.E.2d 1081, 1991 Ohio App. LEXIS 1330 (Ohio Ct. App., Franklin County 1991).

A father has no duty to provide support for his child, disabled from epilepsy, after the child becomes emancipated and is capable of self-support: Cooksey v. Cooksey, 55 Ohio App. 3d 135, 562 N.E.2d 934, 1988 Ohio App. LEXIS 4467 (Ohio Ct. App., Erie County 1988).

There is no authority in Ohio for a court to compel a divorced husband to continue to provide support for his disabled child past the age of majority: Maphet v. Heiselman, 13 Ohio App. 3d 278, 469 N.E.2d 92, 1984 Ohio App. LEXIS 10769 (Ohio Ct. App., Clermont County 1984).

**Education expenses**

Trial court abused its discretion by ordering the father to pay one-half of the child's college expenses for the third and fourth years of college in monthly installments of $600 until the total judgment, which moreover did not include interest, was paid in full. The mother presented evidence that she had paid $121,988.80 for the child's college expenses and that the father had only paid $18,100 at the time of the hearing. In addition, the evidence established that the father had not paid any of those expenses contemporaneously with their accrual. Carter v. Carter, 2012-Ohio-2475, 2012 Ohio App. LEXIS 2176 (Ohio Ct. App., Summit County 2012).

Weight of the evidence supported the conclusion that the mother was entitled to judgment in an amount which included the accumulated interest on the father's unpaid balance for the child's college expenses for the first two years. The trial court's order, which reiterated the father's obligation to continue to make installment payments for his share of the first two years of college expenses until they were paid in full, necessarily included the accumulated interest. Carter v. Carter, 2012-Ohio-2475, 2012 Ohio App. LEXIS 2176 (Ohio Ct. App., Summit County 2012).

There was no abuse of discretion in the trial court's denial of the wife's motion to show cause and for attorney fees because there was competent and credible evidence to support the conclusion that the husband provided his children with a college education to the extent that he was then able, as required by the agreed divorce decree, and thus, there was no abuse of discretion in the trial court's denial of the wife's request for attorney fees, pursuant to R.C. 3105.73. Toensing v. Toensing, 2006-Ohio-3320, 2006 Ohio App. LEXIS 3236 (Ohio Ct. App., Cuyahoga County 2006).



Because parent either knew or should have known about the provision in the modification of the separation agreement requiring that that parent pay for the child's college education, the other parent's delay in asserting a reimbursement claim did not materially prejudice the obligor parent: Gilvin v. Gilvin, 1997 Ohio App. LEXIS 2918 (Ohio Ct. App., Montgomery County July 3, 1997).

The separation agreement provision that the children's CDS and other sources of funds be first exhausted to pay college costs was a condition precedent to the father's obligation to pay them: Troha v. Troha, 105 Ohio App. 3d 327, 663 N.E.2d 1319, 1995 Ohio App. LEXIS 2784 (Ohio Ct. App., Greene County 1995).

The parties may enter into an agreement which modifies their obligations under a separation agreement which has been incorporated into a decree of divorce or dissolution, including a provision for college expenses. A domestic relations court has jurisdiction to enforce such agreement: In re Dunn, 101 Ohio App. 3d 1, 654 N.E.2d 1303, 1995 Ohio App. LEXIS 403 (Ohio Ct. App., Clinton County 1995).

A court cannot order an obligor to set aside money for a child's college education unless the parties agreed to it in a separation agreement: Pratt v. McCullough, 100 Ohio App. 3d 479, 654 N.E.2d 372, 1995 Ohio App. LEXIS 276 (Ohio Ct. App., Warren County 1995).

A court may not place limitations on a parent's obligation to pay for educational expenses where the decree does not contain such limitations: Wesselman v. Wesselman, 88 Ohio App. 3d 338, 623 N.E.2d 1300, 1993 Ohio App. LEXIS 3144 (Ohio Ct. App., Butler County 1993).

R.C. 3109.05 requires the court to consider the financial resources of the child, including a savings account for later educational expenses: Frost v. Frost, 84 Ohio App. 3d 699, 618 N.E.2d 198, 1992 Ohio App. LEXIS 6731 (Ohio Ct. App., Franklin County 1992).

In the absence of any express or implied limitation in a divorce decree and separation agreement concerning the "college education" of children, the term "college education" is unambiguous and should be read and interpreted in its broadest sense, subject only to the ability to pay: Forstner v. Forstner, 68 Ohio App. 3d 367, 588 N.E.2d 285, 1990 Ohio App. LEXIS 5376 (Ohio Ct. App., Lake County 1990).

As used in the separation agreement, the term "tuition" included the university's general fee: Baker v. Baker, 68 Ohio App. 3d 402, 588 N.E.2d 944, 1990 Ohio App. LEXIS 2616 (Ohio Ct. App., Wood County 1990).

Where public schools are available and in the absence of a requirement in the divorce decree, tuition payments for children's attendance at parochial schools are not necessary for their support: Mihna v. Mihna, 48 Ohio App. 3d 303, 549 N.E.2d 558, 1989 Ohio App. LEXIS 548 (Ohio Ct. App., Cuyahoga County 1989).

A provision in a separation agreement defining "college costs" as including such items as tuition, fees and books cannot be extended to include room and board: Uram v. Uram, 65 Ohio App. 3d 96, 582 N.E.2d 1060, 1989 Ohio App. LEXIS 3944 (Ohio Ct. App., Summit County 1989).

The custodial parent may choose the school to be attended by a minor child and the parent with the obligation to pay tuition must pay said tuition even where a different school is identified in the separation agreement or divorce decree, provided that if the custodial parent selects a school having tuition costs different from the school specified in the separation agreement or divorce decree, then the parent obligated to pay tuition shall not be required to pay additional amounts beyond what it would have cost to send the child to the school specified in the separation agreement or divorce decree: Evans v. Brown, 23 Ohio App. 3d 97, 491 N.E.2d 384, 1985 Ohio App. LEXIS 10111 (Ohio Ct. App., Franklin County 1985).

Judicial enforcement of a separation agreement requiring a noncustodial parent to pay tuition for his children's education at a religiously oriented school does not constitute unconstitutional state support of such religiously oriented school under the establishment clause or the free exercise clause of USConst amend I, nor the religious freedom provision of the Ohio Constitution: In re Landis, 5 Ohio App. 3d 22, 448 N.E.2d 845, 1982 Ohio App. LEXIS 11018 (Ohio Ct. App., Franklin County 1982).

**Effective date**

Trial court erred in failing to clarify its reasons for making a modified child support obligation effective as of the date that the shared parenting agreement was amended and not as of the date that the father filed the modification motion, which was the presumptive effective date. The trial court did not provide an adequate basis for rejecting the retroactive modification. Sandel v. Choma, 2012-Ohio-3781, 2012 Ohio App. LEXIS 3350 (Ohio Ct. App., Summit County 2012).

Trial court abused its discretion by setting an effective date for paying child support because it did not pick the date that a mother had requested child support or any other date that was significant to the litigation. The trial court did not disclose it reasons for picking the date or any special circumstances leading to the decision. In re P.J.H., 2011-Ohio-5970, 196 Ohio App. 3d 122, 962 N.E.2d 389, 2011 Ohio App. LEXIS 4876 (Ohio Ct. App., Miami County 2011).

**Emancipation**

Trial court's determination that the oldest child became emancipated on June 1, 2009 was unsupported by the record and inconsistent with the trial court's previous orders. The trial court had adopted the Child Support Enforcement Agency's recommendation to reduce the support due to the child's emancipation, effective May 25, 2008. Carpenter v. Carpenter, 2010-Ohio-6601, 2010 Ohio App. LEXIS 5523 (Ohio Ct. App., Noble County 2010).

"Emancipation" and "majority" are not synonymous. Emancipation generally discharges a parent's duty to pay child support. If a child is emancipated for purposes of visitation, the child is likewise emancipated for purposes of child support: Risser v. Risser, 2007-Ohio-4936, 173 Ohio App. 3d 430, 878 N.E.2d 1073, 2007 Ohio App. LEXIS 4624 (Ohio Ct. App., Hardin County 2007).

Seventeen-year-old high school student who stayed several days a week in a continuing sexual relationship at the home of a friend was properly held, for purposes of R.C. 3109.05(E), to be an unemancipated minor child currently unable to provide financial self-support: Siefker v. Siefker, 1997 Ohio App. LEXIS 5048 (Ohio Ct. App., Putnam County Oct. 23, 1997).

The child did not become "emancipated" by his enrollment at the Coast Guard Academy where he still considered his mother's residence as his home and received financial assistance from her. A child's receipt of a scholarship or other assistance does not relieve a parent of a duty of support: Howard v. Howard, 80 Ohio App. 3d 832, 610 N.E.2d 1152, 1992 Ohio App. LEXIS 3979 (Ohio Ct. App., Clermont County 1992).

Duty to plead emancipation as a defense in a support enforcement proceeding depends on the language of the support order and the age of the child: Hidey v. Tope, 1990 Ohio App. LEXIS 5703 (Ohio Ct. App., Tuscarawas County Dec. 19, 1990).

The question as to when a child is emancipated so as to relieve a parent from the obligation of support depends upon the particular facts and circumstances of each case: Price v. Price, 12 Ohio App. 3d 42, 465 N.E.2d 922, 1983 Ohio App. LEXIS 11313 (Ohio Ct. App., Darke County 1983).

Emancipation by induction into the armed services of the United States is not automatic, but is determined from the circumstances in each case by whether the minor ceases to be dependent upon the parent: Omohundro v. Omohundro, 8 Ohio App. 3d 318, 457 N.E.2d 324, 1982 Ohio App. LEXIS 11272 (Ohio Ct. App., Franklin County 1982).

**Enforcement**

Trial court properly vacated an order that stayed child support disbursement to a mother due to her failure to comply with visitation issues, as such was not in accord with R.C. 3109.05(D) because escrowing of support payments, which were for the benefit of the child, was improper as a means of enforcement of visitation issues; the trial court retained continuing jurisdiction over the issues pursuant to R.C. 3111.16 for puposes of vacating or modifying the order. CSEA ex rel. Spencer v. Gatten, 2007-Ohio-4071, 2007 Ohio App. LEXIS 3684 (Ohio Ct. App., Cuyahoga County 2007).

**—Contempt**

Trial court did not abuse its discretion in finding a minor child's father and his parents in contempt for failing to abide by the court's orders regarding visitation time with the child's maternal grandparents, which resulted in the grandparents being required to engage in prolonged and costly litigation in order to ensure their rights to be with the child; accordingly, the trial court's imposition of payment of all costs and fees to the father and his parents was reasonable and necessary, and proper in the circumstances due to their bad faith pursuant to R.C. 3109.05 and 2705.05. Smith v. Quigg, 2006-Ohio-1495, 2006 Ohio App. LEXIS 1368 (Ohio Ct. App., Fairfield County 2006).

**—Arrearages**

Trial court did not err in finding a father in contempt of its prior order requiring the father to pay monthly child support because the record showed that the father failed to meet his monthly obligation during 23 months of the 14-year period at issue and that he failed to pay any child support during 75 months of the same period. Even if tax intercept payments met the father's support obligations for some of the months at issue, the record revealed that the father still owed a substantial amount of money in support arrearages. Campbell v. Clark, 2006-Ohio-6482, 2006 Ohio App. LEXIS 6435 (Ohio Ct. App., Crawford County 2006).

Father was properly held in contempt for failing to pay child support because he failed to purge himself, in that he did not pay the current support obligation but simply paid an amount each month in a sum sufficient to meet the monthly arrearage installment, thereby requiring the child support collection agency to apply the payments first toward the current support obligations and, then, toward arrears, as mandated by OAC 5101:1-31-14. The father's alleged belief that he could purge the contempt order by merely paying on the arrearage was unreasonable. Slagle v. Slagle, 2005-Ohio-4330, 2005 Ohio App. LEXIS 3930 (Ohio Ct. App., Lake County 2005).

**Escrow of parent's funds**

Trial court properly reversed the magistrate's ruling that the money the mother agreed to pay the father for the sale of the marital estate was to be placed in escrow due to the father's failure to pay proper child support. Duncan v. Duncan, 2004-Ohio-326, 2004 Ohio App. LEXIS 281 (Ohio Ct. App., Summit County 2004).

**Evidence**

Trial court erred in ordering a mother to pay a certain child support award to a father who was awarded the designation as residential parent of the parties' child upon a custody modification, as there was no evidence to support a determination that the mother owed an arrearage, nor was there evidence to support the income determined by the trial court for the mother on the child support computation worksheet. Kimbler v. Kimbler, 2006-Ohio-2695, 2006 Ohio App. LEXIS 2516 (Ohio Ct. App., Scioto County 2006).

**—Generally**

There was no error in the finding that the husband had failed to provide sufficient credible evidence that he paid child support to the wife because the husband testified at trial that he paid the wife child support directly rather than pursuant to income withholding as required by the administrative order, and he testified that he had made the payments on the support order but did not provide supporting documentation that those payments had been made. Kilpatrick v. Kilpatrick, 2011-Ohio-443, 2011 Ohio App. LEXIS 383 (Ohio Ct. App., Delaware County 2011).

Trial court's judgment entry did not determine the issue of support, but merely continued the temporary order in effect until the magistrate determined the final support obligation. The magistrate's decision contained the support computation worksheet required by R.C. 3119.022 and was based on the consideration of all the relevant evidence regarding the parties' income and lifestyle. Sweet v. Sweet, 2009-Ohio-1924, 2009 Ohio App. LEXIS 1607 (Ohio Ct. App., Ashtabula County 2009).

Trial court erred in ordering a mother to pay a certain child support award to a father who was awarded the designation as residential parent of the parties' child upon a custody modification, as there was no evidence to support a determination that the mother owed an arrearage, nor was there evidence to support the income determined by the trial court for the mother on the child support computation worksheet. Kimbler v. Kimbler, 2006-Ohio-2695, 2006 Ohio App. LEXIS 2516 (Ohio Ct. App., Scioto County 2006).

Although there was conflicting information concerning the wife's financial circumstances, at the hearing, the husband could not convincingly explain that the wife earned more than $ 9,000 in 2002. Accordingly, under the circumstances, the husband failed to show that the child support calculated by the trial court was against the manifest weight of the evidence. Ricciardella v. Ricciardella, 2004-Ohio-1184, 2004 Ohio App. LEXIS 1032 (Ohio Ct. App., Portage County 2004).

Under Evid.R. 404(B), providing that "[e]vidence of other crimes, wrongs, or acts is not admissible to prove the character of a person in order to show that he acted in conformity therewith," evidence that a former husband allegedly did not comply with pendente lite orders in a divorce proceeding is not admissible in a post-decree proceeding to show that the husband did not generally comply with court orders: Ferguson v. Owens, 27 Ohio App. 3d 155, 500 N.E.2d 396, 1985 Ohio App. LEXIS 10309 (Ohio Ct. App., Hamilton County 1985).

**—Insufficient**

Trial court erred when it imposed a variety of conditions on a husband in a divorce proceeding that varied from the terms of the parties' settlement agreement that had been read into the record at the final hearing, as there was no other evidence in the record upon which the varied terms could have been based; the court failed to consider passive gain on the nonmarital portion of the parties' retirement accounts rather than by division pursuant to R.C. 3105.82(D)(2), and it imposed an order of child support although there was none in the agreement. Asbury v. Asbury, 2008-Ohio-2609, 2008 Ohio App. LEXIS 2197 (Ohio Ct. App., Paulding County 2008).

**Extracurricular activities**

Trial court's failure to include the "agreement" regarding extracurricular activities in its child support order was not an abuse of discretion because it was too indefinite to be enforceable. While the parties agreed to share in their son's varying extracurricular activities, they nevertheless did not agree on the record which sports or activities they would be willing to pay for. Shendel v. Graham, 2017-Ohio-4236, 92 N.E.3d 43, 2017 Ohio App. LEXIS 2303 (Ohio Ct. App., Lake County 2017).

**Findings**

Trial court adequately set forth the basis for the child support order because it utilized the same basis for the calculation of each parties' support obligation and attached a child support worksheet indicating how the support was calculated. There was no need for the trial court to further extrapolate how it determined the amount of the father's child support obligation. Halliday v. Halliday, 2010-Ohio-3194, 2010 Ohio App. LEXIS 2665 (Ohio Ct. App., Cuyahoga County 2010).

**Fraud**

Where the obligor fraudulently and substantially misstated his income on the child support worksheet, the court had authority to modify the amount of support ordered to the amount that should have been ordered. To prevent the obligor from profiting from the fraud, the court properly made the change retroactive to the date of the original support order: Osborne v. Osborne, 81 Ohio App. 3d 666, 611 N.E.2d 1003, 1992 Ohio App. LEXIS 3542 (Ohio Ct. App., Meigs County 1992).

**Full faith and credit**

Orders for child support, payable in installments and subject to modification under the laws of the rendering state, made in a divorce or dissolution in that state, are not entitled to full faith and credit in the courts of a sister state because they are not considered to be sufficiently final. Thus the fact that the duty to pay support survives the obligor's death under Indiana law does not require Ohio courts to enforce such claims: Barnett v. Barnett, 85 Ohio App. 3d 1, 619 N.E.2d 38, 1993 Ohio App. LEXIS 46 (Ohio Ct. App., Lorain County 1993).

Where a child, the original custody of whom was determined by an out of state court, presently resides in Ohio, a court of this state has jurisdiction to determine whether it is in the best interests of the child to give full faith and credit to the out of state order: Purcell v. Purcell, 47 Ohio App. 2d 258, 1 Ohio Op. 3d 316, 353 N.E.2d 882, 1975 Ohio App. LEXIS 5878 (Ohio Ct. App., Hamilton County 1975).

**Graduation from high school**

The father's support obligation under the separation agreement did not terminate until the child turned eighteen, despite her graduation from high school a month earlier: Dudziak v. Dudziak, 81 Ohio App. 3d 361, 611 N.E.2d 337, 1992 Ohio App. LEXIS 2829 (Ohio Ct. App., Cuyahoga County 1992).

**Gross income**

While the magistrate expressly agreed that the father's income should not be reduced by his depreciation expenses for child support purposes, it allowed his other business expenses identified on his returns to reduce his income without any evidence that they were ordinary, necessary, or were actual cash expenditures made in the year claimed. Thus, the trial court erred by reducing his income for the purpose of his child support obligation based on any of his business expenses since he failed to satisfy his burden of proof. Shendel v. Graham, 2017-Ohio-4236, 92 N.E.3d 43, 2017 Ohio App. LEXIS 2303 (Ohio Ct. App., Lake County 2017).

Pursuant to the statutory exception, the trial court did not abuse its discretion in excluding the father's onetime withdrawal from his retirement accounts that he used to pay off a designated debt since it was specifically excluded as gross income under the statute. It was neither recurring nor sustainable income. Shendel v. Graham, 2017-Ohio-4236, 92 N.E.3d 43, 2017 Ohio App. LEXIS 2303 (Ohio Ct. App., Lake County 2017).

Trial court's gross income calculation for child support was short by $4,000 and was not supported by competent, credible evidence because, based on its inclusion of the father's depreciation expenses as income, his income was $39,166 since $62,069 minus his lump sum $32,930 equaled $29,139 and $29,139 plus his depreciation expenses of $1,743 and $8,284 equaled $39,166. Shendel v. Graham, 2017-Ohio-4236, 92 N.E.3d 43, 2017 Ohio App. LEXIS 2303 (Ohio Ct. App., Lake County 2017).

In drawing the conclusion that the husband spent $23,165 on gambling and in adding that figure to his gross income for child support purposes, the trial court did not abuse its discretion as it based its decision on the evidence. Thus, based upon the husband's testimony as to his spending habits, the magistrate concluded that he had a gross income of at least $96,113.00 that he could use to cover the costs of his personal expenses. Siferd v. Siferd, 2017-Ohio-8624, 100 N.E.3d 915, 2017 Ohio App. LEXIS 5048 (Ohio Ct. App., Hancock County 2017).

Trial court erred when it calculated the mother's gross income for of child support because it included phantom income from and nothing in the record so much as hinted that the trial court imputed, or intended to impute, income to the mother. Despite the mother's uncontroverted testimony that she ceased her employment at the retail store in 2005, the trial court inexplicably found the mother's employment there current. Mangan v. Mangan, 2008-Ohio-3622, 2008 Ohio App. LEXIS 3059 (Ohio Ct. App., Greene County 2008).

**Guardianship**

The domestic relations court had implicit authority under R.C. 3105.011 and 3105.21 to establish a guardianship to facilitate child support payments. That court also properly reduced arrearages to a lump sum. The probate court exercised its authority as superior guardian when it denied the request to distribute funds in a lump sum: In re Derakhshan, 110 Ohio App. 3d 190, 673 N.E.2d 954, 1996 Ohio App. LEXIS 1227 (Ohio Ct. App., Lake County 1996).

**Health care coverage**

Trial court did require the father to provide the child's health insurance, albeit in less than clear terms, because the inclusion of the father's health care related expenses on the child support worksheet and the fathers testimony at the hearing regarding his employer's health care coverage made it clear that he was responsible for the minor's health care coverage as long as he has employer provided coverage available. Shendel v. Graham, 2017-Ohio-4236, 92 N.E.3d 43, 2017 Ohio App. LEXIS 2303 (Ohio Ct. App., Lake County 2017).

**Hearing**

Trial court did not err in declining to conduct a de novo hearing regarding modification of child and spousal support because the mother did not demonstrate that she could not have presented that evidence to the magistrate and the evidence she did present included her allegations and documents regarding the father's employment status. Dibble v. Dibble, 2011-Ohio-5803, 2011 Ohio App. LEXIS 4786 (Ohio Ct. App., Stark County 2011).

**Imputed income**

Trial court did not plainly err by finding the wife was voluntarily unemployed and imputing income to her for child support purposes in the amount of $16,536 because the wife: (1) had been a stay at home mother since 1993, which reduced her earning ability; (2) had not looked for employment; and (3) could enter the work force, earning entry-level wages, while she obtained further vocational training. Ortega v. Ortega, 2017-Ohio-7346, 2017 Ohio App. LEXIS 3638 (Ohio Ct. App., Fairfield County 2017).

Given the mother's employment history, her physical limitations, and the lack of evidence indicating she was not working to her full potential, the trial court did not err when it overruled the father's objection to the magistrate's decision to impute $7,124 of income to the mother. King v. King, 2012-Ohio-5219, 2012 Ohio App. LEXIS 4565 (Ohio Ct. App., Medina County 2012).

Trial court did not abuse its discretion because there was evidence to support the finding that the father's 2009 income was an aberration and the decision not to use the father's 2009 income and to impute annual income to him of $32,705 was rational and based on a sound reasoning process. The $32,705 imputed to the father was more than he had earned in his entire employment history except for 2008 and 2009. York v. York, 2011-Ohio-5872, 2011 Ohio App. LEXIS 4791 (Ohio Ct. App., Clermont County 2011).

Trial court did not state any reason for deviating from the parties' child support agreement, and there was no evidence that the shared parenting plan was entered into by fraud, duress, overreaching or undue influence. Because the child support obligation was determined by the parties' agreement, the parties did not offer evidence regarding the husband's salary or earning potential, sufficient to impute $62,000 in income to him. Flynn v. Flynn, 2011-Ohio-4714, 196 Ohio App. 3d 93, 962 N.E.2d 368, 2011 Ohio App. LEXIS 3914 (Ohio Ct. App., Butler County 2011).

Trial court did not err in failing to impute income to a mother on the ground that she was voluntarily underemployed as, while, after the child was born, the mother left a job in which she was earning $75,732 to work two part-time jobs in which she earned only $47,625, there was evidence that the mother's change in employment was to the child's advantage, in that the mother would have less travel and child care expenses and would be able to spend more time caring for the child. Knouff v. Walsh-Stewart, 2010-Ohio-4063, 2010 Ohio App. LEXIS 3452 (Ohio Ct. App., Wayne County 2010).

In calculating a father's child support obligation, the trial court did not err in not awarding to the father a credit to cover visitation travel expenses. While the trial court had given the mother such a credit when the father had custody of the child and the mother was forced to travel from Virginia to Ohio for visitation, given the disparity in income between the two parties, the father was in the best position to bear the travel costs associated with the new visitation order. Pellettiere v. Pellettiere, 2009-Ohio-5407, 2009 Ohio App. LEXIS 4557 (Ohio Ct. App., Montgomery County 2009).

While a mother possessed two bachelors' degrees and a master's degree, this was insufficient to impute additional income to her for the purpose of calculating the father's child support obligation in light of the fact that the father had provided no evidence that the mother was underemployed as a preschool teacher earning $20,000 annually. Pellettiere v. Pellettiere, 2009-Ohio-5407, 2009 Ohio App. LEXIS 4557 (Ohio Ct. App., Montgomery County 2009).

Trial cout did not abuse its discretion in denying child support to either party in a divorce action, as they had agreed to a shared parenting arrangement and based upon imputed income to each party as well as the spousal support to be paid to the wife, the parties would have approximately the same income. Meyer v. Meyer, 2008-Ohio-436, 2008 Ohio App. LEXIS 367 (Ohio Ct. App., Licking County 2008).

Trial court did not abuse its discretion by imputing $40,000 in income to the wife for purposes of child support because, although the wife had suffered from cancer, she had been without a recurrence for six years and, although she had been diagnosed as suffering from a form of bipolar disorder, she had been responsive to treatment. Further, a vocational counselor testified that the wife could return to work immediately and find a position in the biological sciences paying between $30,000 and $40,000 per year. Miller v. Miller, 2008-Ohio-4297, 2008 Ohio App. LEXIS 3618 (Ohio Ct. App., Wayne County 2008).

Trial court's finding that a mother was voluntarily underemployed and, thus, should have income imputed to her in determining the father's child support obligation was supported by evidence that the mother worked only when it did not interfere with school matters for her children and that the mother's employment was voluntarily less than full-time employment. Holcomb v. Holcomb, 2007-Ohio-478, 2007 Ohio App. LEXIS 429 (Ohio Ct. App., Delaware County 2007).

Trial court did not abuse its discretion in failing to impute income to a mother for spousal and child support purposes as the mother had the primary responsibility of providing day-to-day care for the parties' children and her job allowed her to minimize daycare costs and to maximize the time that she could spend with the children. Daugherty v. Daugherty, 2005-Ohio-4056, 2005 Ohio App. LEXIS 3705 (Ohio Ct. App., Butler County 2005).

Trial court did not abuse its discretion in failing to impute income to a mother for spousal and child support purposes as the mother had the primary responsibility of providing day-to-day care for the parties' children and her job allowed her to minimize daycare costs and to maximize the time that she could spend with the children. Daugherty v. Daugherty, 2005-Ohio-4056, 2005 Ohio App. LEXIS 3705 (Ohio Ct. App., Butler County 2005).

It was not error for a trial court to impute income to a father, when considering the issue of child support, as his health did not prevent him from working full time, he had worked as a veterinarian at various locations, his Ohio veterinary license was currently in good standing, he admitted having more than $50,000 in a bank account, the "trusts" to which the father said his assets had been assigned were shams, and the father could earn $72,800 as a full-time veterinarian. Temple v. Temple, 2005-Ohio-92, 2005 Ohio App. LEXIS 69 (Ohio Ct. App., Cuyahoga County 2005).

When, in a divorce, a father testified that he previously earned $75,000 a year, that two weeks before trial he was offered a job paying $80,000 a year with benefits, which he turned down but expected to be offered again, that once the divorce was over he expected to earn about $75,000 again, and he voluntarily quit his job to start his own company and spend more time with his children, the trial court could reasonably impute income of $75,000 to him, as he said he would make at least that much. Caceres v. Caceres, 2005-Ohio-1915, 2005 Ohio App. LEXIS 1826 (Ohio Ct. App., Marion County 2005).

Where a father did not ask the trial court to impute income to the mother, who was voluntarily unemployed, when the court determined child support obligations he waived the issue and it would not be considered on appeal; nevertheless, since the father did not raise the issue the trial court did not abuse its discretion when it did not impute income to the mother . Chirico v. Chirico, 2003-Ohio-3238, 2003 Ohio App. LEXIS 2894 (Ohio Ct. App., Montgomery County 2003).

**In general**

Imposed on each biological or adoptive parent is the duty to support their minor child, regardless of the parent's gender or marital status. This obligation is owed to the State of Ohio as well as to the child. State ex rel. Browning v. Browning, 2012-Ohio-2158, 2012 Ohio App. LEXIS 1903 (Ohio Ct. App., Muskingum County 2012).

**Incarceration**

Trial court properly ordered an inmate to pay child support, under R.C. 3109.05, because his incarceration was due to a voluntary act causing him to voluntarily reduce his earning ability, and he was held to the same standard as any other parent who voluntarily reduced his income, and his incarceration did not relieve him of his duty of support. Abel v. Renicker, 2008-Ohio-3281, 2008 Ohio App. LEXIS 2698 (Ohio Ct. App., Tuscarawas County 2008).

**Income**

Trial court did not err by failing to find that the definition of income included trust income because the father's trust disbursements were discretionary funds and not potential cash flow under the definition of gross income. Since the trust income of $3,500 to $4,000 was less than the state minimum wage income, the trial court properly imputed minimum wage income to the father. In re R.H., 2016-Ohio-6961, 71 N.E.3d 751, 2016 Ohio App. LEXIS 3821 (Ohio Ct. App., Montgomery County 2016).

Trial court's ruling as to the wife's income level for child support purposes did not constitute an abuse of discretion because the trial court determined that there had been a substantial drop in real estate sales and that the husband offered no evidence to the contrary. Also, the wife provided in-court testimony on the issue of child care expenses, against which she was cross-examined. by the husband's counsel, and she provided an exhibit detailing unpaid or unreimbursed costs pertaining to the parties' child. Jackson v. Jackson, 2013-Ohio-1422, 2013 Ohio App. LEXIS 1338 (Ohio Ct. App., Morrow County 2013).

Because a trial court based a parent's child support calculation upon erroneous income figures, the matter was remanded for the trial court to recalculate that parent's obligation using the correct income figures for both parties. Gajarsky v. Kottler, 2012-Ohio-1817, 2012 Ohio App. LEXIS 1595 (Ohio Ct. App., Summit County 2012).

Review of the transcript supported the trial court's refusal to offset the $600 that the mother received in rent with the expenses she allegedly incurred as a result of renting space in her house to her roommate for child support purposes because the transcript showed that the mother failed to present sufficient evidence showing what her expenses actually were. York v. York, 2011-Ohio-5872, 2011 Ohio App. LEXIS 4791 (Ohio Ct. App., Clermont County 2011).

Trial court erred by not including in the mother's gross income the social security income from her minor child from another marriage. However, the trial court did not fail to take into account and apply the deviation factors set forth in R.C. 3119.24 because it explicitly considered the 50/50 time allocation between the parties, as well as other factors such as the difference in the parties' resources and incomes. Epitropoulos v. Epitropoulos, 2011-Ohio-3701, 2011 Ohio App. LEXIS 3123 (Ohio Ct. App., Franklin County 2011).

There was no abuse of discretion in the trial court's calculations of parental income for child support purposes because the trial court elected to extrapolate the husband's 2010 income at $55,525 based on documentary evidence that he had grossed $24,559 approximately 23 weeks into the year. Rowan v. Kemery, 2011-Ohio-2307, 2011 Ohio App. LEXIS 1971 (Ohio Ct. App., Licking County 2011).

Trial court was reasonable in calculating the father's gross income for his child support obligation using the limited verified information it had before it because, despite the father's promises to provide verification of his income as ordered by the trial court, he never did so, and failed to appear for an additional hearing on the matter; throughout the proceedings, the father was evasive regarding his income. The trial court did not impute income to the father; rather, it extrapolated his annual gross income from the limited verified financial data it had before it, i.e., his commissions from the first four months of 2007. In re Massey v. Lambert, 2011-Ohio-1341, 2011 Ohio App. LEXIS 1178 (Ohio Ct. App., Columbiana County 2011).

Without documentation of a substantial reduction in income, the trial court did not err by utilizing the income figure originally provided by the husband when calculating his child support obligation. Brewer v. Brewer, 2011-Ohio-1275, 2011 Ohio App. LEXIS 1102 (Ohio Ct. App., Darke County 2011).

Trial court did not abuse its discretion by denying the father's request for an evidentiary hearing and additional discovery; because the father was given ample opportunity to depose the mother regarding her income, an additional hearing was not necessary. The trial court obviously believed that the documents satisfied the purge order as no jail time was ordered for the mother and, given that it was a case that involved years of discovery and litigation and involved a 33-day trial, the trial court did not abuse its discretion in refusing to unnecessarily reopen issues. Halliday v. Halliday, 2010-Ohio-3194, 2010 Ohio App. LEXIS 2665 (Ohio Ct. App., Cuyahoga County 2010).

Since a father did not object to any finding as to the amount of his child support obligation, he waived, pursuant to Civ.R. 53(D)(3)(b)(iv), the right to assign as error the amount of his obligation based on the lack of any evidence regarding his income. Even if the argument was not waived, the trial court properly determined the father's child support obligation as the mother presented unrebutted evidence of the father's income. Daniels v. O'Dell, 2010-Ohio-1341, 2010 Ohio App. LEXIS 1127 (Ohio Ct. App., Summit County 2010).

In a child support dispute, a trial court did not abuse its discretion by concluding that the most appropriate figure to represent a father's income was $52,000 per year in light of the variable incomes of the father and the lack of evidence before the trial court. This was the same figure used at the time of an original divorce decree. Onyshko v. Onyshko, 2010-Ohio-969, 2010 Ohio App. LEXIS 831 (Ohio Ct. App., Portage County 2010).

Trial court did not err by modifying a magistrate's decision and ordering a father to pay more child support based on a significant income disparity; only a slight deviation from the child support worksheet was warranted. Even though a mother only requested a formal hearing, the trial court was permitted to adopt the magistrate's decision in whole or in part, with or without modification, under Civ.R. 53(D)(4)(b). Peskind v. Peskind, 2010-Ohio-5146, 2010 Ohio App. LEXIS 4332 (Ohio Ct. App., Cuyahoga County 2010).

It was within the trial court's discretion to choose not to deduct the losses from the farming operation from the father's gross income for child support purposes because he failed to show that the cattle operation was anything more than a hobby. According to the father, his son raised pigs for the fair and his daily chores included feeding the cattle after school, the father was vague about the extent of his cattle business, and, although the father claimed to have made a profit on the farm sometime in the past, he could point to no specific year. Carpenter v. Carpenter, 2010-Ohio-6601, 2010 Ohio App. LEXIS 5523 (Ohio Ct. App., Noble County 2010).

Trial court's determination that the husband's income was $150,000 for purposes of child support was supported by the evidence because, in his trial brief, the husband stated that the evidence would show that his income was approximately $150,000 per year. It was reasonable for the magistrate to find that, if the husband's shareholder distributions remained equal from 2004 to 2005, the combined total of his salary and shareholder distributions would have exceeded $150,000; the husband also failed to establish that his business had to borrow money so that he could meet his temporary support obligations. Miller v. Miller, 2008-Ohio-4297, 2008 Ohio App. LEXIS 3618 (Ohio Ct. App., Wayne County 2008).

Trial court used an incorrect income figure of $8,522 for the mother in calculating child support because the mother testified that she worked an average of 34 hours per week at $9.50 an hour, which equaled $16,796. Further, because the matter was remanded with respect to child support, the trial court had to reconsider, on remand, its award of spousal support to the mother, pursuant to R.C. 3105.18(C)(1)(i); the trial court was required to consider an award of child support as a factor when crafting a spousal support award. Ewart v. Ewart, 2007-Ohio-4750, 2007 Ohio App. LEXIS 4278 (Ohio Ct. App., Muskingum County 2007).

Trial court used an incorrect income figure of $8,522 for the mother in calculating child support because the mother testified that she worked an average of 34 hours per week at $9.50 an hour, which equaled $16,796. Further, because the matter was remanded with respect to child support, the trial court had to reconsider, on remand, its award of spousal support to the mother, pursuant to R.C. 3105.18(C)(1)(i); the trial court was required to consider an award of child support as a factor when crafting a spousal support award. Ewart v. Ewart, 2007-Ohio-4750, 2007 Ohio App. LEXIS 4278 (Ohio Ct. App., Muskingum County 2007).

Trial court did not abuse its discretion in calculating the husband's income for child support purposes because it was thoughtful and thorough in its explanation of the income valuation and it noted that the husband's income was $191,169, which included the $45,219 of pass-through income from his corporation. There was also no error in calculating the husband's income due to the impact of the new Medicaid rules which would significantly impact future income for the dentistry practice, and the trial court retained jurisdiction over the support order, so the parties could seek modification of the order in future due to a change in circumstances. El-Badewi v. El-Badewi, 2007-Ohio-3800, 2007 Ohio App. LEXIS 3460 (Ohio Ct. App., Stark County 2007).

Trial court did not abuse its discretion in calculating the husband's income for child support purposes because it was thoughtful and thorough in its explanation of the income valuation and it noted that the husband's income was $191,169, which included the $ 45,219 of pass-through income from his corporation. There was also no error in calculating the husband's income due to the impact of the new Medicaid rules which would significantly impact future income for the dentistry practice, and the trial court retained jurisdiction over the support order, so the parties could seek modification of the order in the future due to a change in circumstances. El-Badewi v. El-Badewi, 2007-Ohio-3800, 2007 Ohio App. LEXIS 3460 (Ohio Ct. App., Stark County 2007).

Trial court's spousal support award under R.C. 3105.18 and its child support order were unreasonable and arbitrary because they were based on a mistaken figure used for the wife's income. Thus, one of the factors considered by the trial court was incorrect, and the trial court's decision was an abuse of discretion. Davis v. Davis, 2006-Ohio-6391, 2006 Ohio App. LEXIS 6343 (Ohio Ct. App., Perry County 2006).

Trial court's spousal support award under R.C. 3105.18 and its child support order were unreasonable and arbitrary because they were based on a mistaken figure used for the wife's income. Thus, one of the factors considered by the trial court was incorrect, and the trial court's decision was an abuse of discretion. Davis v. Davis, 2006-Ohio-6391, 2006 Ohio App. LEXIS 6343 (Ohio Ct. App., Perry County 2006).

Although the trial court used a correct approach in requiring the father either to produce records and submit to an expert evaluation of his businesses or to accept the income figures the magistrate used, in abandoning that approach and in failing to properly verify income, the trial court abused its discretion. The father's gross income was likely higher than what the magistrate calculated. In re Custody of Harris, 2006-Ohio-3649, 168 Ohio App. 3d 1, 857 N.E.2d 1235, 2006 Ohio App. LEXIS 3597 (Ohio Ct. App., Champaign County 2006).

Trial court erred in averaging a father's income to determine his child support obligation as the father's income did not fluctuate but, instead, decreased. Johnson v. Huddle, 2004-Ohio-410, 2004 Ohio App. LEXIS 370 (Ohio Ct. App., Lawrence County 2004).

A court should not include any portion of retained earnings in a closely held corporation as part of a parent's gross income when calculating his child support payments, at least where the earnings are not retained as a subterfuge: Riepenhoff v. Riepenhoff, 64 Ohio App. 3d 135, 580 N.E.2d 846, 1990 Ohio App. LEXIS 392 (Ohio Ct. App., Jackson County 1990).

Under the Child Support Guidelines, amounts for depreciation and other non-cash deductible items allowable by the Internal Revenue Service are not deducted from the gross revenue of a person who is self-employed, and significant amounts of reimbursements and in-kind payments received by a self-employed parent are to be counted as income. Therefore, the court's taking into consideration amounts on the self-employed parent's tax returns which do not affect cash flow and the fact that he receives a residence and use of an automobile from his business as additional compensation is not arbitrary, unreasonable or unconscionable: Pruden-Wilgus v. Wilgus, 46 Ohio App. 3d 13, 545 N.E.2d 647, 1988 Ohio App. LEXIS 4944 (Ohio Ct. App., Lucas County 1988).

Where a separation agreement, incorporated into a decree of dissolution, provides that child support shall be increased annually by "an amount equal to the percentage increase in husband's net income as shown by the previous year's income tax return," but said agreement fails to define "net income," then the proper definition of that term is gross income less the expenses in realizing that income, minus taxes. Under such circumstances, the husband may not deduct a $25,000 stock loss from his gross income in arriving at "net income" since the stock loss is not an expense incurred in producing his gross income: Chaney v. Chaney, 24 Ohio App. 3d 169, 493 N.E.2d 997, 1985 Ohio App. LEXIS 10167 (Ohio Ct. App., Franklin County 1985).

**Insurance**

Although the trial court could properly have ordered the husband to secure the property division payment and his child support obligation with a life insurance policy, it was improper for the trial court to require him no name the wife as the beneficiary to the extent that the policy secured his child support obligation. Zaccardelli v. Zaccardelli, 2013-Ohio-1878, 2013 Ohio App. LEXIS 1765 (Ohio Ct. App., Summit County 2013).

Although a trial court appropriately calculated a child's healthcare expense for the period of August 1, 2008 to 2009, the trial court abused its discretion in ordering the father to pay increased health care insurance amounts before August 1, 2008, because there was no evidence that the amount of the child's health insurance changed until the child was added to the stepfather's health insurance plan in August 2008. In re M.L.H., 2013-Ohio-1668, 2013 Ohio App. LEXIS 1560 (Ohio Ct. App., Cuyahoga County 2013).

Trial court did not err when it refused to modify a father's obligation to provide health insurance for his minor child. Given the fact that the father could insure the child for less than $70 per month, the cost of insuring the child was reasonable. Maxwell v. Maxwell, 2008-Ohio-1324, 2008 Ohio App. LEXIS 1170 (Ohio Ct. App., Wayne County 2008).

**Jurisdiction**

As the parties' child, who had physical and developmental disabilities, was 38 at the time the final judgment of divorce was entered, the trial court had no jurisdiction over him and therefore no authority to order the husband to pay child support or to enter orders regarding custody and visitation. Geygan v. Geygan, 2012-Ohio-1965, 973 N.E.2d 276, 2012 Ohio App. LEXIS 1733 (Ohio Ct. App., Franklin County 2012).

Trial court did not its discretion in overruling the father's objections to the magistrate's decision because the language of the divorce decree was clear. The divorce decree specifically mentioned direct payments and did not state that it reserved jurisdiction to consider in-kind payments as the father alleged. Lurz v. Lurz, 2010-Ohio-910, 2010 Ohio App. LEXIS 748 (Ohio Ct. App., Cuyahoga County 2010).

Husband failed to cite to any authority in support of his claim that a common pleas court lacked subject matter jurisdiction over the issue of child support for an adult-aged mentally retarded daughter, such that his claim failed under App.R. 16(A)(7); further, pursuant to R.C. 2101.24(D), 3109.05(A)(1), and 3105.011, the common pleas court had jurisdiction over the child support issue despite the fact that the parents had been appointed as guardians over the daughter. In re Edgell, 2010-Ohio-6435, 2010 Ohio App. LEXIS 5325 (Ohio Ct. App., Lake County 2010).

As Ohio was a child's home state within six months of the filing by the father of a motion for a change of custody and other relief, the juvenile court in Ohio had jurisdiction over the matter pursuant to R.C. 3721.15(A)(1); further, as there was a prior juvenile court order that required the father to pay child support, the juvenile court had continuing jurisdiction over the matter pursuant to R.C. 2151.23(F)(1), (2), 3109.04, 3109.05, 3105.21, and Civ.R. 75(J). In re A.D.M., 2009-Ohio-1951, 183 Ohio App. 3d 802, 919 N.E.2d 224, 2009 Ohio App. LEXIS 1669 (Ohio Ct. App., Montgomery County 2009).

Since the trial court's judgment entry did not constitute a final order, the trial court was not deprived of jurisdiction to determine the husband's child support obligation. That the support order continued in the final decree of divorce was only a temporary order was further evidenced by the fact that the magistrate's child support order was made retroactive to July 2004, when the temporary support order became effective. Sweet v. Sweet, 2009-Ohio-1924, 2009 Ohio App. LEXIS 1607 (Ohio Ct. App., Ashtabula County 2009).

Juvenile court erred in modifying a father's child support pursuant to R.C. 3105.21, 3109.05 because service on the mother had to be by personal service pursuant to Civ.R 4.1(A) where the father requested personal service; the residential service effected was inadequate for notice because the mother had moved from the residence. Any failure by the mother to notify the juvenile court promptly of any change in her address could not justify ineffective service of process when the juvenile court's continuing jurisdiction was invoked, because those service requirements were rooted in the mother's constitutional due process right to notice and an opportunity to be heard. In re Alexander-Segar, 2008-Ohio-1580, 2008 Ohio App. LEXIS 1325 (Ohio Ct. App., Montgomery County 2008).

Failure to support a mandamus petition with an affidavit as required by Ohio Eighth Dist. Ct. App. R. 45(B)(1)(a) made the petition fatally defective; a judge did not have a clear legal duty to hear a mother's motion for child custody and support because a different court had jurisdiction over those issues. State ex rel. Allen v. Burney, 2003-Ohio-5253, 2003 Ohio App. LEXIS 4750 (Ohio Ct. App., Cuyahoga County 2003).

The court which granted the dissolution, finding no children born or expected, did not have continuing jurisdiction to later enter a child support order: Bailey v. Bailey, 109 Ohio App. 3d 569, 672 N.E.2d 747, 1996 Ohio App. LEXIS 823 (Ohio Ct. App., Lawrence County 1996).

A nonresident custodial parent has a right to pursue an action for child support against the noncustodial parent in a court of competent jurisdiction in this state when the noncustodial parent is a resident of Ohio and the parties' foreign divorce decree and child custody order do not address the issue of support: Haskins v. Bronzetti, 1992-Ohio-140, 64 Ohio St. 3d 202, 594 N.E.2d 582, 1992 Ohio LEXIS 1567 (Ohio 1992).

A failure to support one's minor children constitutes a tortious act or omission in Ohio conferring in personam jurisdiction under Civ.R 4.3(A)(3): Wayne County Bureau of Support v. Wolfe, 71 Ohio App. 3d 765, 595 N.E.2d 421, 1991 Ohio App. LEXIS 1521 (Ohio Ct. App., Wayne County 1991).

The court which enters a decree for child support has full power to enforce its decree and retains jurisdiction over all matters of custody and child support-even in the case where the obligor has died and his estate is now obligated to pay child support: Gilford v. Wurster, 24 Ohio App. 3d 77, 493 N.E.2d 258, 1983 Ohio App. LEXIS 16063 (Ohio Ct. App., Lorain County 1983).

Out-of-state service of a motion and notice of a hearing on the issue of indirect civil contempt for failure to comply with court-ordered visitation need not be made personally but may be accomplished by certified mail pursuant to Civ.R. 4.3(B)(1): McGill v. McGill, 3 Ohio App. 3d 455, 445 N.E.2d 1163, 1982 Ohio App. LEXIS 10941 (Ohio Ct. App., Montgomery County 1982).

**—Service of process**

Juvenile court erred in modifying a father's child support pursuant to R.C. 3105.21, 3109.05 because service on the mother had to be by personal service pursuant to Civ.R. 4.1(A) where the father requested personal service; the residential service effected was inadequate for notice because the mother had moved from the residence. Any failure by the mother to notify the juvenile court promptly of any change in her address could not justify ineffective service of process when the juvenile court's continuing jurisdiction was invoked, because those service requirements were rooted in the mother's constitutional due process right to notice and an opportunity to be heard. In re Alexander-Segar, 2008-Ohio-1580, 2008 Ohio App. LEXIS 1325 (Ohio Ct. App., Montgomery County 2008).

**Laches**

Trial court properly rejected a father's defense, asserting that a mother was barred by laches from seeking child support pursuant to the first motion for support filed by the mother, as the mother did not fail to assert her rights for an unreasonable and unexplained length of time; instead, if anything, the father's failure to prosecute his motion for modification of parental rights caused the delay in the mother's motion. Moreover, the father failed to show how he was materially prejudiced by the delay. Howell v. Howell, 2008-Ohio-6639, 2008 Ohio App. LEXIS 5536 (Ohio Ct. App., Columbiana County 2008).

Mother's attempt to obtain child support 17 years after she rejected support from the child's father was barred by the doctrine of laches. Equity favored a ruling in favor of the father on the issue of support because (1) the mother sought child support only after she released custody of the child, who was approaching emancipation, to the child's maternal grandmother; (2) the father had offered to marry the mother and provide her with financial support when he learned that the mother was pregnant; (3) the father had abided by the mother's wishes and had remained outside the child's life; and (4) the mother's delay in seeking child support prejudiced the father as he could not go back and have involvement in the child's upbringing. Barker v. Jarrell, 2007-Ohio-7024, 2007 Ohio App. LEXIS 6182 (Ohio Ct. App., Lorain County 2007).

**Law of the case**

Trial court did not err in affirming the magistrate's calculations pursuant to the law of the case doctrine. While the issues of day-care and child support were before the appellate court, the trial court lacked jurisdiction to receive additional evidence or to modify its decision. Thus, the trial court's second judgment entry was void and it did not err in failing to use its computations from its void order. Dario v. Colliver, 2011-Ohio-4342, 2011 Ohio App. LEXIS 3597 (Ohio Ct. App., Butler County 2011).

**Life insurance**

A domestic relations court has the implied and inherent authority to order the parent to designate the child as the beneficiary on the parent's life insurance policy so as to ensure that a child receive the support that he or she is entitled to during his or her minority: Webb v. Webb, 1997 Ohio App. LEXIS 5968 (Ohio Ct. App., Montgomery County Dec. 31, 1997).

Where a separation agreement embodied in a divorce decree mandates insurance coverage and unambiguously designates a purpose for which insurance proceeds are to be used by certain beneficiaries, a constructive trust for that designated purpose is the appropriate remedy to ensure that the proceeds are used for the purpose intended under the agreement: Aetna Life Ins. Co. v. Hussey, 63 Ohio St. 3d 640, 590 N.E.2d 724, 1992 Ohio LEXIS 934 (Ohio 1992).

Where the decree provides that the children are to receive the proceeds of the father's life insurance, they are not thereby entitled to an additional amount provided for accidental death. General division of the court of common pleas lacked jurisdiction over insurer's interpleader action where the domestic relations order concerning insurance was in the nature of child support: Nalesnik v. Nalesnik, 1990 Ohio App. LEXIS 1368 (Ohio Ct. App., Cuyahoga County Apr. 5, 1990).

Where the separation agreement obligates the husband to maintain life insurance with the child as irrevocable beneficiary, and no monetary amount or time limit is specified in the agreement, the child's recovery of the proceeds is not limited to the value of the policy at the time of the divorce. Equitable considerations compel the conclusion that the child is entitled to the amount of proceeds payable at the time of the husband's death: Thomas v. Studley, 59 Ohio App. 3d 76, 571 N.E.2d 454, 1989 Ohio App. LEXIS 171 (Ohio Ct. App., Cuyahoga County 1989).

Where the separation agreement provides that the husband "shall keep or cause to be kept" a life insurance policy with his child as "primary, irrevocable beneficiary," the right of the child to the policy proceeds is thereby vested. This right is enforceable in equity, and cannot be defeated by the husband's failure to maintain the policy as required: Thomas v. Studley, 59 Ohio App. 3d 76, 571 N.E.2d 454, 1989 Ohio App. LEXIS 171 (Ohio Ct. App., Cuyahoga County 1989).

A constructive trust is the appropriate remedy to ensure that insurance proceeds are paid to those who were to be named beneficiaries of an insurance policy by the terms of a separation agreement embodied in a divorce decree: Kelly v. Medical Life Ins. Co., 31 Ohio St. 3d 130, 509 N.E.2d 411, 1987 Ohio LEXIS 302 (Ohio 1987).

Where a divorce decree provided that a parent was required to purchase and maintain a certain amount of life insurance for the benefit of his children, a court may impose a constructive trust where another beneficiary was in fact named: Ferguson v. Owens, 9 Ohio St. 3d 223, 459 N.E.2d 1293, 1984 Ohio LEXIS 1047 (Ohio 1984).

**Magistrate's decision on appeal**

In a child support case, a trial court should not have adjusted the parties' income figures and recalculated a father's support obligation based on those new figures since neither party supported their objection to a magistrate's decision by providing a transcript, pursuant to Civ.R. 53(D)(3)(b)(iii). Moreover, no new hearing was held. Veal v. Dilauro, 2009-Ohio-5675, 2009 Ohio App. LEXIS 4778 (Ohio Ct. App., Summit County 2009).

**Majority**

Trial court did not abuse its discretion when it ordered a father's duty of support to continue beyond the age of the child's majority because the record showed significant defects in the young man relative to the needs imposed by his self-sufficient life even compared to young persons of the child's age; in addition, the trial court did not lack jurisdiction to proceed on the mother's claim for continued child support since the trial court interpreted the mother's letter to be an Civ.R. 60(B) motion, but the trial court should not have emancipated the child without holding an evidentiary hearing to determine if the child was disabled. Blacker v. Blacker, 2004-Ohio-2193, 2004 Ohio App. LEXIS 1950 (Ohio Ct. App., Montgomery County 2004).

Where the parties' child was twenty-five at the time of the divorce and was disabled since birth, the court had jurisdiction to enter a subsequent support order: Abbas v. Abbas, 128 Ohio App. 3d 513, 715 N.E.2d 613, 1998 Ohio App. LEXIS 3261 (Ohio Ct. App., Mahoning County 1998).

If a child does not continuously attend high school on a full-time basis after turning eighteen, the duty to provide support ends: Gleason v. Gleason, 129 Ohio App. 3d 563, 718 N.E.2d 512, 1998 Ohio App. LEXIS 4156 (Ohio Ct. App., Ross County 1998).

Whether a support obligation in a pre-1974 decree was altered by the lowering of the age of majority depends on whether the decree, explicitly or implicitly, enumerated the duration of the obligation: Cox v. Cox, 130 Ohio App. 3d 609, 720 N.E.2d 946, 1998 Ohio App. LEXIS 5758 (Ohio Ct. App., Hamilton County 1998).

The plain and unambiguous language of a court-entered separation agreement ending support obligations of a child upon reaching eighteen controls over R.C. 3103.03, even where the child still attends high school: Richardson v. Richardson, 1991 Ohio App. LEXIS 2555 (Ohio Ct. App., Butler County June 3, 1991).

Once a child of the parties to a divorce proceeding reaches the age of majority, the court that granted the divorce is without jurisdiction of the subject matter to provide for the support of such child: Maphet v. Heiselman, 13 Ohio App. 3d 278, 469 N.E.2d 92, 1984 Ohio App. LEXIS 10769 (Ohio Ct. App., Clermont County 1984).

**Medical expenses**

Trial court erred by not providing for the division of the child's unreimbursed and out-of-pocket medical expenses and co-pays in the child support order because the statutory language was mandatory. Shendel v. Graham, 2017-Ohio-4236, 92 N.E.3d 43, 2017 Ohio App. LEXIS 2303 (Ohio Ct. App., Lake County 2017).

Testimony and supporting documentation presented at the hearing by the mother was competent, credible evidence that supported the juvenile court's finding that the father owed $10,005.13 for unpaid medical expenses for his children. In re S.B., 2012-Ohio-1228, 2012 Ohio App. LEXIS 1079 (Ohio Ct. App., Montgomery County 2012).

Trial court did not err by ordering the father to pay only 30 percent of the child's uninsured medical expense because the decision was consistent with the ratio of the parties' individual incomes to the parties' total income, as set forth in the child support worksheet. York v. York, 2011-Ohio-5872, 2011 Ohio App. LEXIS 4791 (Ohio Ct. App., Clermont County 2011).

Trial court did not abuse its discretion by failing to order a father to reimburse a mother for medical expenses because she did not provide sufficient documentation; moreover, he was not required to reimburse her for one-half of the cost of a child's orthodontia expenses because there was no finding by the trial court that the treatment was medically necessary, which was required under the terms of a divorce decree. Onyshko v. Onyshko, 2010-Ohio-969, 2010 Ohio App. LEXIS 831 (Ohio Ct. App., Portage County 2010).

Trial court did not abuse its discretion in ordering a father to continue to pay child support for his emancipated daughter until the day that medical treatment for her brain tumor came to an end: Blaner v. Blaner, 2004-Ohio-3678, 2004 Ohio App. LEXIS 3316 (Ohio Ct. App., Trumbull County 2004).

Where a separation agreement required the father to pay the children's medical expenses over a certain minimum, the father's liability was not reduced by the amount paid by insurance. Interest accrued from the date the bills should have been paid: Stracker v. Stracker, 94 Ohio App. 3d 261, 640 N.E.2d 611, 1994 Ohio App. LEXIS 1562 (Ohio Ct. App., Lorain County 1994).

A motion for child support, or modification of child support, necessarily includes the medical need portion of child support and raises that issue for consideration of the court; accordingly, such a motion need not contain a specific request relating to medical need in order to place the issue before the court: Gorman v. Gorman, 28 Ohio App. 3d 85, 501 N.E.2d 1234, 1986 Ohio App. LEXIS 9976 (Ohio Ct. App., Franklin County 1986).

Where the emancipation of a child has been determined to have occurred upon that child giving birth to her own child, the parent's responsibility, pursuant to an order of support, for the medical expenses incurred in delivering the child includes all reasonable post-delivery expenses incident to giving birth, such as a reasonable period of hospitalization after delivery: Nuckols v. Nuckols, 12 Ohio App. 3d 94, 467 N.E.2d 259, 1983 Ohio App. LEXIS 11330 (Ohio Ct. App., Wood County 1983).

A third party cannot hold a noncustodial parent liable for an elective abortion performed on a minor child where there was no showing that such parent had refused or neglected to provide for the minor child's support or medical care: Akron City Hospital v. Anderson, 68 Ohio Misc. 14, 22 Ohio Op. 3d 238, 428 N.E.2d 472, 1981 Ohio Misc. LEXIS 50 (Ohio Mun. Ct. 1981).

In an action by a hospital against the parents of a minor child for medical treatment provided to the minor child by the hospital, the mother of the child may not absolve herself of liability to the hospital, a third party, by reason of a provision in the divorce decree requiring the father of the child to pay all medical expenses incurred by the child: Children's Hospital of Akron v. Johnson, 68 Ohio App. 2d 17, 22 Ohio Op. 3d 11, 426 N.E.2d 515, 1980 Ohio App. LEXIS 9630 (Ohio Ct. App., Summit County 1980).

The obligee (the state) can collect only in accordance with R.C. Chapter 5121.; and, when both parents are obligated under R.C. Chapter 5121., the question of what share each of two divorced parents will pay is a matter to be determined from the divorce decree: Dept. of Mental Health & Mental Retardation v. Wiedemann, 1 Ohio App. 3d 27, 437 N.E.2d 1212 (1980).

**Modification**

There was nothing in the record to suggest that the trial court's decision to modify the father's child support obligation was the product of any fraud, bias, impartiality, pecuniary interest or any other conflict of interest on the part of the magistrate or the trial court judge. Story v. Story, 2021-Ohio-2439, 2021 Ohio App. LEXIS 2397 (Ohio Ct. App., Cuyahoga County 2021).

Assuming that the action of the trial court constituted a child support modification rather than enforcement of a pre-existing agreement, the father was in no way prejudiced because he agreed to pay $2,375 per month after the house sold. Whether it was allocated 100 percent to child support or zero percent to child support, there was no difference in the amount that he was contractually obligated to pay; regardless, the trial court did nothing more than affirm the enforcement of the 2004 separation agreement as incorporated into the divorce decree. Yodzis v. Savercool, 2012-Ohio-5558, 2012 Ohio App. LEXIS 4821 (Ohio Ct. App., Lucas County 2012).

Trial court did not err in denying a father's motion to reduce his support obligation. The father's proof of changed circumstances depended upon his testimony, which the trial court reasonably found not to be credible; thus, the trial court's finding of a failure of proof of changed circumstances was not against the manifest weight of the evidence. Barclay v. Barclay, 2012-Ohio-1974, 2012 Ohio App. LEXIS 1736 (Ohio Ct. App., Montgomery County 2012).

Trial court did not abuse its discretion by failing to consider a motion to modify child support because there was a lack of evidence presented regarding the needs of several children and their standard of living, pursuant to R.C. 3119.04(B); assuming that the trial court could have presumed the amount contained in the worksheets was appropriate or extrapolated some other amount, the court was not required to do so. The only definite change in the standard of living was that two of the four children had to attend public school, and there was no evidence or indicate of the children's other needs. Strimbu v. Strimbu, 2011-Ohio-3629, 2011 Ohio App. LEXIS 3066 (Ohio Ct. App., Trumbull County 2011).

In a child support modification case, a trial court did not err by finding that a husband's potential income under R.C. 3119.01(C)(5)(b) was $90,000 because that was the last income attributable to the husband prior to his criminal actions, which resulted in the suspension of his law license and subsequent incarceration; although the husband's incarceration did not warrant a change in circumstances, the wife's increase in income did. However, the husband could not have been held in contempt for failure to pay the support while he was incarcerated since an inability to pay child support was an affirmative defense to a criminal non-support charge, pursuant to R.C. 2919.21(D). L.B. v. T.B., 2011-Ohio-3418, 2011 Ohio App. LEXIS 2901 (Ohio Ct. App., Montgomery County 2011).

Trial court properly denied a father's motion to modify child support and to vacate previous child support orders and arrearages because he was unable to utilize Civ.R. 60 as a substitute for failed appeals, a fraud allegation was not filed within the one-year time limit in Civ.R. 60(B)(3), his motion was not made within a reasonable time, and the issue of the father's child support obligation had been decided twice previously. Moreover, the father's motion was barred by res judicata since he raised no new issues in his motion; even if new issues had been raised, res judicata was used to prevent relitigation of issues already decided by a court or matters that should have been brought as part of a previous action. Nolan v. Nolan, 2010-Ohio-1447, 2010 Ohio App. LEXIS 1225 (Ohio Ct. App., Geauga County 2010).

Trial court did not abuse its discretion by making a support modification order effective March 1, 2003, because, with the exception of an eight-day period in April 2003, there was a motion pending before the trial court on the issue of child support from April 2002 until the trial court's final judgment in March 2007; moreover, both parties were on notice, as of April 2002, that the trial court was going to revisit the issue of child support, thereby satisfying the requirements contained in R.C. 3119.84. In addition, the father sought a change of custody in April 2003, and there was evidence that the father's two eldest children were living with him during that time period. Onyshko v. Onyshko, 2010-Ohio-969, 2010 Ohio App. LEXIS 831 (Ohio Ct. App., Portage County 2010).

In a child support case, because a father failed to appeal from a trial court's decision regarding the modification or elimination of his child support obligation based on his alleged support of a mother and two children during the time that the parties had reconciled, he was foreclosed from advancing this argument in the present appeal. Jones v. Jones, 2010-Ohio-744, 2010 Ohio App. LEXIS 611 (Ohio Ct. App., Champaign County 2010).

In a child support case, because a trial court properly ordered a father to request that two children voluntarily submit to genetic testing prior to a hearing, pursuant to R.C. 3119.961, any decision to modify an arrearage owed by the father was premature until the genetic testing was performed. Jones v. Jones, 2010-Ohio-744, 2010 Ohio App. LEXIS 611 (Ohio Ct. App., Champaign County 2010).

With regard to the decision to require the mother to pay child support to the father, the mother was clearly on notice that the issue of child support would be revisited after the child moved in with the father. Schumann v. Schumann, 2010-Ohio-5472, 190 Ohio App. 3d 824, 944 N.E.2d 705, 2010 Ohio App. LEXIS 4625 (Ohio Ct. App., Cuyahoga County 2010).

Father's objections to a child support order failed as the trial court did not abuse its discretion in adopting a child support calculation based on the father as the obligor, the order was properly made retroactive to the date the father filed objections to an administrative support recommendation that support be ordered, and the zero support order in the original divorce decree could be modified as any other support order. Laubacher v. Laubacher, 2010-Ohio-5335, 2010 Ohio App. LEXIS 4496 (Ohio Ct. App., Stark County 2010).

Trial court did not give a reason for using March 16, 2009 as the effective date for the first modification; although an appeal from the final decree was pending at that time, the amount of child support ordered was not at issue, and thus the administrative modification proceedings did not conflict with the appellate court's jurisdiction. Thus, under R.C. 3119.71(B) the trial court should have made the first modification effective March 1, 2008. Carpenter v. Carpenter, 2010-Ohio-6601, 2010 Ohio App. LEXIS 5523 (Ohio Ct. App., Noble County 2010).

Trial court did not abuse its discretion in finding there was no change of circumstances warranting the modification of the existing custody order. The evidence did not show that the mother was cohabiting and, because no evidence was presented that the relationship between the mother and her boyfriend had an adverse impact on the child, the trial court properly denied the father's motions for custody of the child and to terminate his child support obligation. Cravens v. Cravens, 2009-Ohio-1733, 2009 Ohio App. LEXIS 1470 (Ohio Ct. App., Warren County 2009).

Because the arguments raised in a mother's motion to dismiss were identical to the arguments raised in a prior motion to dismiss, which was denied and dismissed for want of prosecution, an order of child support was not void as the trial court retained jurisdiction over the matter and its decision was not inconsistent with a juvenile court's orders. Reda v. Reda, 2009-Ohio-5248, 2009 Ohio App. LEXIS 4429 (Ohio Ct. App., Delaware County 2009).

Denial of a former spouse's second motion to modify spousal support was proper, based on the doctrine of res judicata. The former spouse did not appeal the denial of the first motion for modification, and it was represented that the only difference in the motions was that the former spouse's previous counsel had not presented any evidence in support of the first motion. Carlisle v. Carlisle, 2009-Ohio-215, 180 Ohio App. 3d 569, 906 N.E.2d 483, 2009 Ohio App. LEXIS 191 (Ohio Ct. App., Lawrence County 2009).

Trial court's decision to modify child support, and making the order retroactive to the time the motion to modify was originally filed was not an abuse of discretion, because the mother testified that she claimed the maximum daycare expenses allowed by the IRS, but that her expense was much higher due to her child's extensive needs as a handicapped child and that the child needed constant care. The mother also introduced a signed statement from the children's daycare provider indicating that the expenses were for work-related daycare and introduced documentation demonstrating extraordinary mileage and clothing due to trips to the child's medical specialists. Fugitt v. Fugitt, 2007-Ohio-6514, 2007 Ohio App. LEXIS 5693 (Ohio Ct. App., Fairfield County 2007).

As a trial court had declared that neither party owed the other child support in a post-divorce proceeding, and the mother's subsequent request for modification of child support was denied because no support order existed to modify, she was barred by res judicata from later arguing that she was entitled to modification based on a "zero support" order. Flanagan v. Flanagan, 2007-Ohio-6209, 174 Ohio App. 3d 77, 880 N.E.2d 962, 2007 Ohio App. LEXIS 5471 (Ohio Ct. App., Lorain County 2007).

Trial court's determination that a former husband's child support obligation should not be modified was proper, as the child support was properly calculated, the trial court specifically addressed the issue in its written decision, and there was no basis shown for such a modification; the husband failed to sustain his burden of showing a change in circumstances that warranted modification of the support order. Travis v. Travis, 2007-Ohio-4077, 2007 Ohio App. LEXIS 3665 (Ohio Ct. App., Clark County 2007).

Trial court's determination that a former husband's child support obligation should not be modified was proper, as the child support was properly calculated, the trial court specifically addressed the issue in its written decision, and there was no basis shown for such a modification; the husband failed to sustain his burden of showing a change in circumstances that warranted modification of the support order. Travis v. Travis, 2007-Ohio-4077, 2007 Ohio App. LEXIS 3665 (Ohio Ct. App., Clark County 2007).

Husband was not entitled to a modification of his child support obligation because (1) he did not show the future cost to treat his medical condition differed from the past cost, so he did not show a change in circumstances due to his medical treatment, (2) he sought modification eight months after it was ordered, even though he had his condition for 20 years, (3) he said he had been fired, but there was evidence that he had been negotiating a buy out from his employer for months before voluntarily leaving his job, and (4) any claims that he could not work due to his medical condition were undermined by the large salaries he earned which suffering from the condition and his active pursuit of employment. Reynolds v. Reynolds, 2007-Ohio-1263, 2007 Ohio App. LEXIS 1169 (Ohio Ct. App., Summit County 2007).

Trial court did not abuse its discretion in ordering a mother of a minor child to pay child support, which modification was retroactive to the date that the child was placed in the father's home for custody purposes, as that was a significant date in the case and the mother had been put on notice when the father filed his complaint that he was seeking "such further relief," which encompassed child support. In re Smith, 2007-Ohio-893, 2007 Ohio App. LEXIS 812 (Ohio Ct. App., Ashtabula County 2007).

Husband was not entitled to a modification of his child support obligation because (1) he did not show the future cost to treat his medical condition differed from the past cost, so he did not show a change in circumstances due to his medical treatment, (2) he sought modification eight months after it was ordered, even though he had his condition for 20 years, (3) he said he had been fired, but there was evidence that he had been negotiating a buy out from his employer for months before voluntarily leaving his job, and (4) any claims that he could not work due to his medical condition were undermined by the large salaries he earned which suffering from the condition and his active pursuit of employment. Reynolds v. Reynolds, 2007-Ohio-1263, 2007 Ohio App. LEXIS 1169 (Ohio Ct. App., Summit County 2007).

Trial court erred when it ordered a modification retroactive to its previous temporary order of child support. The final divorce decree essentially created an obligation on the husband to pay an additional sum of money, after the fact, and then penalized him for not having paid it. Ostmann v. Ostmann, 2006-Ohio-3617, 168 Ohio App. 3d 59, 858 N.E.2d 831, 2006 Ohio App. LEXIS 3578 (Ohio Ct. App., Medina County 2006).

Where a trial court denied a father's motion for a modification of child support, it was not required to include a child support worksheet; further, although the parties' incomes were briefly mentioned, the father failed to present any argument or to submit any evidence with respect to his request for a modification and accordingly, it was not an abuse of discretion to deny modification of the support order. Gordon v. Liberty, 2005-Ohio-2884, 2005 Ohio App. LEXIS 2700 (Ohio Ct. App., Portage County 2005).

Father could not collaterally attack the child support modification through Civ.R. 60(B), because the terms of the original decree relieving the father of a duty to pay child support did not insulate him from modification of the child support obligation, pursuant to R.C. 3109.05. Layne-Burnett v. Burnett, 2005-Ohio-2510, 2005 Ohio App. LEXIS 2403 (Ohio Ct. App., Montgomery County 2005).

Where a trial court denied a father's motion for a modification of child support, it was not required to include a child support worksheet; further, although the parties' incomes were briefly mentioned, the father failed to present any argument or to submit any evidence with respect to his request for a modification and accordingly, it was not an abuse of discretion to deny modification of the support order. Gordon v. Liberty, 2005-Ohio-2884, 2005 Ohio App. LEXIS 2700 (Ohio Ct. App., Portage County 2005).

Prior to commencing an R.C. 3119.66 hearing to review a father's child support obligation, the trial court granted the mother's pending motion to dismiss; the trial court met the requirement of § 3119.66, and did not abuse its discretion in granting the motion to dismiss, based upon the father's R.C. 3119.68 discovery violations and also based upon the father's failure to timely object under Civ.R. 53(E)(1)-(3), to a magistrate's decision. Dexter v. Dexter, 2004-Ohio-983, 2004 Ohio App. LEXIS 878 (Ohio Ct. App., Muskingum County 2004).

There was no abuse of discretion in denying an obligor parent's motion to modify the amount of child support because the parent's voluntary acts of pleading guilty to Medicaid fraud and agreeing to a suspension of a dental license did not constitute a change in circumstances. Pushkin v. Pushkin, 2003-Ohio-6109, 2003 Ohio App. LEXIS 5463 (Ohio Ct. App., Franklin County 2003).

A court may, but need not, make a support increase retroactive to the date of filing of the motion: Pacurar v. Pacurar, 132 Ohio App. 3d 787, 726 N.E.2d 552, 1999 Ohio App. LEXIS 1204 (Ohio Ct. App., Mahoning County 1999).

**Need**

In a child support dispute, a trial court did not abuse its discretion by failing to credit a father with an amount that he paid for his daughter to take a trip to Europe because there was no evidence that the three-week trip to Europe constituted a need of the parties' child. Onyshko v. Onyshko, 2010-Ohio-969, 2010 Ohio App. LEXIS 831 (Ohio Ct. App., Portage County 2010).

**Order to seek employment**

The trial court abused its discretion by issuing a sua sponte seek employment order against the custodial parent: Smith v. Smith, 75 Ohio App. 3d 679, 600 N.E.2d 396, 1991 Ohio App. LEXIS 4073 (Ohio Ct. App., Scioto County 1991).

**Overpayment**

Because it could not be determined whether the trial court concluded that a child support overage did (or did not) exist, or whether, alternatively, the trial court sought additional information prior to making the factual determination, the trial court's self-contradicting decision was arbitrary and unreasonable. Dario v. Colliver, 2011-Ohio-4342, 2011 Ohio App. LEXIS 3597 (Ohio Ct. App., Butler County 2011).

Father was not entitled to judgment interest because the child support credit that the father was entitled to had not been reduced to a judgment entry, and the father had not moved the trial court for a judgment entry. Further, the issue of interest under R.C. 1343.03 had never been before the trial court. Marder v. Marder, 2009-Ohio-3420, 2009 Ohio App. LEXIS 2958 (Ohio Ct. App., Clermont County 2009).

Trial court improperly refused to give the father the $18,576 overpayment due to child support credit that he was entitled to and improperly held it into abeyance instead. The appellate court's earlier decision did not condition the father's right to collect his $18,576 child support credit on further proceedings or the resolution of pleadings already filed or to be filed. Marder v. Marder, 2009-Ohio-3420, 2009 Ohio App. LEXIS 2958 (Ohio Ct. App., Clermont County 2009).

A court has continuing jurisdiction to enforce a child support order by reducing an overpayment of support to a judgment or by granting a credit in favor of the obligor: Jefferies v. Stanzak, 135 Ohio App. 3d 176, 733 N.E.2d 305, 1999 Ohio App. LEXIS 4864 (Ohio Ct. App., Butler County 1999).

Where the custodial parent does not notify the court of the emancipation of the child, the payor spouse may be awarded a lump sum judgment for the amount of any overpayment of support: Pearson v. Pearson, 1991 Ohio App. LEXIS 155 (Ohio Ct. App., Erie County Jan. 18, 1991), dismissed, 61 Ohio St. 3d 1409, 574 N.E.2d 1073, 1991 Ohio LEXIS 1683 (Ohio 1991).

**Parent's death**

A parent may agree to extend his or her obligation to support a child beyond the parent's death, in which case the support obligation becomes a charge against the estate: Gilford v. Wurster, 24 Ohio App. 3d 77, 493 N.E.2d 258, 1983 Ohio App. LEXIS 16063 (Ohio Ct. App., Lorain County 1983).

**Parental contract relieving obligations**

Although the parties had a no-child-support agreement, because the agreement could have been in the best interests of the parents, but not of the child, the trial court did not abuse its discretion when it adopted the magistrate's decision invalidating the agreement and ordering child support after completion of a child-support worksheet. Powers v. Powers, 2008-Ohio-3159, 2008 Ohio App. LEXIS 2674 (Ohio Ct. App., Hamilton County 2008).

Parties' "contract," relieving the father's obligations to pay future child support in exchange for his consent to the stepparent adoption and termination of his visitation rights, was unenforceable. The parties failed to obtain court approval and failed to have the trial court confirm that the agreement comported with the Ohio Child Support Guidelines. Day v. Bloom, 2006-Ohio-6957, 2006 Ohio App. LEXIS 6921 (Ohio Ct. App., Medina County 2006).

**Paternity**

Where a father failed to appear at two hearing dates on his motions to modify a prior child support order, to vacate the prior order, and to have genetic testing regarding his parentage, the trial court properly set the date that arrears on child support were due until and the date that the child support terminated as of the filing of the third set of motions, which resulted in the father's appearance; upon the trial court then ordering genetic testing, it was determined that the father was not in fact the parent of the child at issue, but the date was proper as to the support payment orders, based on the father's own failure to earlier appear. Patricia E. v. Wayne S., 2006-Ohio-28, 2006 Ohio App. LEXIS 21 (Ohio Ct. App., Lucas County 2006).

Where a father failed to appear at two hearing dates on his motions to modify a prior child support order, to vacate the prior order, and to have genetic testing regarding his parentage, the trial court properly set the date that arrears on child support were due until and the date that the child support terminated as of the filing of the third set of motions, which resulted in the father's appearance. When the trial court ordered genetic testing, it was determined that the father was not in fact the parent of the child at issue, but the date was proper as to the support payment orders, based on the father's own failure to earlier appear. Patricia E. v. Wayne S., 2006-Ohio-28, 2006 Ohio App. LEXIS 21 (Ohio Ct. App., Lucas County 2006).

Relief from a child support order may be proper under Civ.R. 60(B)(4) where the obligor subsequently learns through testing that he is not the father of the child: Dunkle v. Dunkle, 135 Ohio App. 3d 669, 735 N.E.2d 469, 1999 Ohio App. LEXIS 5434 (Ohio Ct. App., Hocking County 1999).

The trial court did not err by refusing to vacate the divorce decree and child support order on the basis of the husband's claim that he may not have been the actual father of the children: Weber v. Weber, 74 Ohio App. 3d 396, 599 N.E.2d 288, 1991 Ohio App. LEXIS 2536 (Ohio Ct. App., Fulton County 1991).

The court properly vacated a support order where a subsequent HLA test proved that the husband was not the father of the child the wife was expecting at the time of the marriage: Carson v. Carson, 62 Ohio App. 3d 670, 577 N.E.2d 391, 1989 Ohio App. LEXIS 1567 (Ohio Ct. App., Brown County 1989), limited, Emery v. Emery, 101 Ohio App. 3d 559, 656 N.E.2d 5, 1995 Ohio App. LEXIS 801 (Ohio Ct. App., Brown County 1995).

A man who marries a woman knowing her to be pregnant is conclusively presumed in law to be the father of the child born without formal acknowledgment because he is deemed to have contractually consented to being considered the father of the child regardless of whether he is the biological father: Zaperach v. Beaver, 6 Ohio App. 3d 17, 451 N.E.2d 1249, 1982 Ohio App. LEXIS 11073 (Ohio Ct. App., Franklin County 1982).

Although a man, after marrying a child's mother, signs a declaration of paternity indicating he is the father of such child and a birth certificate is issued reflecting this contention, he obtains no rights to custody or visitation after a decree of divorce has been entered, where it is undisputed that another is the biological father: Chatman v. Chatman, 54 Ohio App. 2d 6, 8 Ohio Op. 3d 24, 374 N.E.2d 433, 1977 Ohio App. LEXIS 7007 (Ohio Ct. App., Franklin County 1977).

**Practice and procedure**

Trial court erred by ordering a continuation of the 2005 temporary child support order without completing a new and revised worksheet. The children deserved support commensurate with their parents' current income and expenses. Wigal v. Wigal, 2008-Ohio-747, 2008 Ohio App. LEXIS 646 (Ohio Ct. App., Washington County 2008).

**Relief from judgment**

Trial court did not abuse its discretion by denying the mother Civ.R. 60(B) relief because the judgment entry was consistent with proceedings on the record; the agreed order was binding and enforceable, did not need the mother's signature, and was consistent with the material terms of the agreement read into the record. Although the parties' agreement did not explicitly call for the 2008 child-support order to be vacated, the parties clearly and explicitly agreed that any support arrearage before June,1, 2009 was to be eliminated. Digiorgio v. Digiorgio, 2013-Ohio-807, 2013 Ohio App. LEXIS 708 (Ohio Ct. App., Greene County 2013).

In a child support case, an appellate court presumed that a trial court's determination that a father had been served by certified mail was valid because the father did not provide a transcript of a hearing; the appellate court was unable to determine whether the father's statement that he never received service was truly uncontradicted. Therefore, the trial court had personal jurisdiction over the case, and the denial of a motion for relief was proper since the request was untimely; more than 20 years elapsed between the entry of a default judgment and the father's act of seeking relief. Eisel v. Austin, 2010-Ohio-816, 2010 Ohio App. LEXIS 690 (Ohio Ct. App., Lorain County 2010).

**Religion**

Judicial enforcement of a separation agreement, incorporated into a divorce decree, which requires a noncustodial parent to pay tuition for his child's religious education, does not offend Ohio Const. art I, § 7 (the religious freedom provision): Rand v. Rand, 18 Ohio St. 3d 356, 481 N.E.2d 609, 1985 Ohio LEXIS 460 (Ohio 1985).

**Retroactive support**

Trial court's order making child support effective as of the first day of the trial of the divorce case was appropriate because it carefully computed the mother's income for purposes of the child support guidelines, considered the desires of the two minor daughters of the parties to spend more time with their mother than with their father, and did not accept the father's request that child support be deviated downward or the mother's request that support be deviated upward. Young v. Young, 2013-Ohio-2568, 2013 Ohio App. LEXIS 2533 (Ohio Ct. App., Franklin County 2013).

Trial court erred by computing the husband's retroactive child support because, although the trial court made the child support order retroactive to December 1, 2007, it failed to use the husband's higher income during the period from December 2007 through October 2008. The child support computation worksheet appended to the divorce decree listed the husband's annual gross income as $120,000, even though he earned $185,000 annually during the period from December 2007 through October 2008. Brokaw v. Brokaw, 2010-Ohio-1053, 2010 Ohio App. LEXIS 864 (Ohio Ct. App., Cuyahoga County 2010).

Trial court did not abuse its discretion by not making the child support order retroactive to the date of the father's motion to terminate the shared parenting plan because the date chosen instead marked the first time the trial court ordered either party to pay child support, and also took into consideration the impending birth of the father's child with his new wife. The trial court's order was also the first time that the father was designated as the child's sole residential and legal custodian, which gave rise to the mother's obligation to pay child support for the child. Caldwell v. Caldwell, 2009-Ohio-2201, 2009 Ohio App. LEXIS 1964 (Ohio Ct. App., Clermont County 2009).

Trial court erred by failing to apply the doctrine of res judicata to bar a request for retroactive child support as the evidence showed that the child's mother and father entered into an agreement resulting in teh dismissal of the mother's initial child support complaint. This existing final judgment between the parties was conclusive as to all claims which were or might have been litigated in a first lawsuit. Mullins-Nessle v. Cardin, 2009-Ohio-6748, 2009 Ohio App. LEXIS 5657 (Ohio Ct. App., Clermont County 2009).

Trial court erred in establishing the payment of retroactive child support. The trial court's entry was in direct opposition to the parties' prior agreement, pursuant to which the mother agreed to dismiss the child support complaint if the father agreed to consent to the adoption of the child by the mother's fiance, and there was no evidence that the agreement was unreasonable, made under duress, or otherwise flawed. Mullins-Nessle v. Cardin, 2009-Ohio-6748, 2009 Ohio App. LEXIS 5657 (Ohio Ct. App., Clermont County 2009).

Trial court did not violate a father's right to due process when it granted a mother's motion for child support as the father had notice of the motion and an opportunity to present evidence in opposition thereto. The record did not support the father's contention that the mother had voluntarily dismissed her support motion and was, thus, not entitled to retroactive support; instead, nothing in the trial court's docket indicated that the mother ever voluntarily dismissed her motion for support. Howell v. Howell, 2008-Ohio-6639, 2008 Ohio App. LEXIS 5536 (Ohio Ct. App., Columbiana County 2008).

Trial court properly ordered a father to pay child support retroactive to the date that the mother filed her first motion for child support since it was proper practice for a trial court to order the payment of child support retroactive to the date of the filing of the motion for support. The record did not support the father's contention that the mother had voluntarily dismissed her support motion and was, thus, not entitled to retroactive support; instead, nothing in the trial court's docket indicated that the mother ever voluntarily dismissed her motion for support. Howell v. Howell, 2008-Ohio-6639, 2008 Ohio App. LEXIS 5536 (Ohio Ct. App., Columbiana County 2008).

While the mother materially prejudiced the father in denying him a role in his son's first nine years of life, for that same time period the father waived his rights as a father by failing to assert them so while laches barred the mother's claim for retroactive child support, there was no such bar for the child's claim for support; since paternity had already been established and admitted, the issue of whether specific administrative procedures were required by former R.C. 3111.22 was immaterial, the trial court had jurisdiction in regard to the child support action. State ex rel. Jackson County Child Support Enforcement Agency v. Long, 2004-Ohio-2184, 2004 Ohio App. LEXIS 1947 (Ohio Ct. App., Jackson County 2004).

An order establishing retroactive child support obligations ancillary to a divorce proceeding is invalid: Trump v. Trump, 136 Ohio App. 3d 123, 736 N.E.2d 39, 1999 Ohio App. LEXIS 5413 (Ohio Ct. App., Summit County 1999).

**Retroactivity**

When a wife's motion to vacate a trial court's judgment ordering her to pay child support was denied, the fact that she was not ordered to pay child support when primary custody of one of the parties' children was originally placed with the husband under a shared parenting agreement did not bar the trial court from ordering the wife to pay future support. Baddam-Reddy v. Baddam-Reddy, 2005-Ohio-3432, 2005 Ohio App. LEXIS 3165 (Ohio Ct. App., Cuyahoga County 2005).

**Savings account established by court**

The court abused its discretion by setting up a savings account for the child to be disbursed as the court might later order: Bailey v. Mitchell, 67 Ohio App. 3d 441, 587 N.E.2d 358, 1990 Ohio App. LEXIS 1450 (Ohio Ct. App., Cuyahoga County 1990).

**Setoff**

Once a trial court determined the individual expenses for which the parents were responsible upon remand, one parent was entitled to a set off by any expenses for which the parent was responsible during the retroactive period of child support. The expenses were to be deducted from that parent's retroactive obligation to pay full child support Gajarsky v. Kottler, 2012-Ohio-1817, 2012 Ohio App. LEXIS 1595 (Ohio Ct. App., Summit County 2012).

Given that the appellate court's prior decision only addressed the trial court's refusal to give the father child support credit for the years 2001-2004, neither the magistrate nor the trial court erred in refusing to give the father credit for the January-February 2005 period. Marder v. Marder, 2009-Ohio-3420, 2009 Ohio App. LEXIS 2958 (Ohio Ct. App., Clermont County 2009).

Because there was no prohibition against a trial court's ordering a child support enforcement agency to submit a proposed judgment entry for approval and supplemental security income benefits under 42 U.S.C.S. § 1382a(b)(9) and adoption subsidies for each child under R.C. 5101.141 did not diminish the disabled children's need for support, the trial court did not err by failing to off-set the parents' support obligations by the amount of the subsidies. In re Caravano, 2005-Ohio-1110, 2005 Ohio App. LEXIS 1114 (Ohio Ct. App., Fairfield County 2005).

The father was entitled to a setoff against his child support obligation where he was supposed to receive half the proceeds of the sale of the marital residence and the mother sold it in exchange for monthly payments: Schneider v. Schneider, 83 Ohio App. 3d 423, 615 N.E.2d 244, 1992 Ohio App. LEXIS 5528 (Ohio Ct. App., Clermont County 1992).

Court may uphold the parties' agreement that the husband's equity in the marital residence be transferred to the wife in lieu of child support: Charlton v. Charlton, 1990 Ohio App. LEXIS 5834 (Ohio Ct. App., Lake County Dec. 28, 1990).

**Social security**

Trial court did not err in crediting the father for the payments made and in applying future credits to both of the father's child support and cash medical account obligations. The Social Security payments were tantamount to earnings by the father and the payment of the benefits directly to the child's mother instead of directly to the agency did not change the fulfillment of the obligation. Whaley v. Hancock, 2013-Ohio-1648, 2013 Ohio App. LEXIS 1528 (Ohio Ct. App., Stark County 2013).

Trial court erred by not including Social Security benefits as part of a husband's annual income for purposes of determining the parties' child support obligations, as Social Security payments were deemed income for the disabled parent that enured to the benefit of the child. Alexander v. Alexander, 2009-Ohio-5856, 2009 Ohio App. LEXIS 4919 (Ohio Ct. App., Franklin County 2009).

Trial court properly credited children's Social Security benefits against a husband's child support obligation without ordering that the wife directly receive a portion of those benefits, as the benefits were directed solely to the benefit of the children although the husband remained the representative payee. Alexander v. Alexander, 2009-Ohio-5856, 2009 Ohio App. LEXIS 4919 (Ohio Ct. App., Franklin County 2009).

There was no competent, credible evidence supporting a trial court's conclusion that a father's only payment of child support was a sum secured by a child support enforcement agency from sums owed to him for workers' compensation; there was testimony that a substantial additional payment was made from the father's personal Social Security benefits. M.D. v. C.W., 2009-Ohio-6676, 2009 Ohio App. LEXIS 5616 (Ohio Ct. App., Wood County 2009).

Set-off for the children's derivative benefits should be deducted before an obligor's own intercepted social security disability check is applied to child support arrearages: Rice v. Rice, 2008-Ohio-3518, 177 Ohio App. 3d 476, 895 N.E.2d 198, 2008 Ohio App. LEXIS 2965 (Ohio Ct. App., Stark County 2008).

Regarding credit for child support arrearages based on Social Security Disability derivative benefits, because the record was not fully developed and there was no evidence as to what months the father was disabled, it was unclear to which months the derivative benefits credits applied, or even how many months were included. That information was crucial to the starting point of computing the accrued arrearages. Rice v. Rice, 2008-Ohio-3518, 177 Ohio App. 3d 476, 895 N.E.2d 198, 2008 Ohio App. LEXIS 2965 (Ohio Ct. App., Stark County 2008).

Receipt of a lump-sum payment of retroactive Social Security benefits by the child of a disabled parent ordered to pay child support for the child could not be used to offset arrearages, as this rule was premised on the importance of meeting the current needs of children, thereby protecting their right to regular and uninterrupted support, and enforcement of the rule eliminated the disincentive which obligors would otherwise have to suspend their support payments pending application for disability benefits. Filon v. Green, 2006-Ohio-4868, 2006 Ohio App. LEXIS 4779 (Ohio Ct. App., Summit County 2006).

When the child of child support obligor became eligible for Social Security benefits, due to her father's disability, in an amount exceeding his child support obligation, and the parties agreed that those payments would satisfy that obligation, after which the child received a retroactive lump-sum payment of benefits covering a period prior to the period covered by the parties' agreement, denying the father's request for reimbursement of the support he paid during that prior period, under the facts, did not place him in a less desirable position than a support obligor who did not pay support. Filon v. Green, 2006-Ohio-4868, 2006 Ohio App. LEXIS 4779 (Ohio Ct. App., Summit County 2006).

When the child of child support obligor became eligible for Social Security benefits, due to her father's disability, in an amount exceeding his child support obligation, and the parties agreed that those payments would satisfy that obligation, after which the child received a retroactive lump-sum payment of benefits covering a period prior to the period covered by the parties' agreement, denying the father's request for reimbursement of the support he paid during that prior period, under the facts, did not place him in a less desirable position than a support obligor who did not pay support. Filon v. Green, 2006-Ohio-4868, 2006 Ohio App. LEXIS 4779 (Ohio Ct. App., Summit County 2006).

Social security payments received by a child as a result of a parent's disability may be credited toward the parent's support obligation commencing at such time as the benefit is received and not exceeding the monthly support obligation: Young v. Young, 105 Ohio App. 3d 701, 664 N.E.2d 1323, 1995 Ohio App. LEXIS 3596 (Ohio Ct. App., Stark County 1995).

Social security payments for the benefit of the child must be considered in connection with child support payments ordered to be made by the parent whose retirement triggers the social security payments for the benefit of the minor child. However, under current law, this does not justify crediting the entire amount of the monthly benefit as attributable solely to the child support required to be paid by either parent: McNeal v. Cofield, 78 Ohio App. 3d 35, 603 N.E.2d 436, 1992 Ohio App. LEXIS 4545 (Ohio Ct. App., Franklin County 1992).

A domestic relations court does not abuse its discretion in ordering a representative payee to place Social Security funds in trust for the benefit of a minor child where the evidence indicates that the representative payee was not using such funds for the child's current maintenance: Catlett v. Catlett, 55 Ohio App. 3d 1, 561 N.E.2d 948, 1988 Ohio App. LEXIS 3079 (Ohio Ct. App., Clermont County 1988).

Social security payments received on behalf of a minor child as a result of a parent's disability may be credited toward that parent's support obligation commencing at such time as the benefit is received and not exceeding the monthly support obligation set forth in the decree of divorce. Such credit does not constitute a retroactive modification of a child support order, but is merely a credit against the arrearage: Pride v. Nolan, 31 Ohio App. 3d 261, 511 N.E.2d 408, 1987 Ohio App. LEXIS 8281 (Ohio Ct. App., Hamilton County 1987).

Social security death benefits may be used to offset the obligation of an estate for child support: Gilford v. Wurster, 24 Ohio App. 3d 77, 493 N.E.2d 258, 1983 Ohio App. LEXIS 16063 (Ohio Ct. App., Lorain County 1983).

Social Security benefits which a handicapped child receives under the Supplemental Security Income Program provided in Title 42, U.S. Code, § 1381 et seq. neither alter the father's obligation for his support nor constitute a change of circumstances warranting a modification of the support order for such child entered in a divorce action: Oatley v. Oatley, 57 Ohio App. 2d 226, 11 Ohio Op. 3d 260, 387 N.E.2d 245, 1977 Ohio App. LEXIS 7099 (Ohio Ct. App., Lucas County 1977).

Social Security benefits, payable to a mother for the support of her minor children due to the disability of the father, may not be credited toward arrearages of child support payments accrued by the father's violation of his then existing obligation of support: Fuller v. Fuller, 49 Ohio App. 2d 223, 3 Ohio Op. 3d 273, 360 N.E.2d 357, 1976 Ohio App. LEXIS 5815 (Ohio Ct. App., Summit County 1976).



**Stepparent, payment to**

Where a divorced and remarried custodial parent leaves a child in the actual custody of the stepparent, the child support obligor may be required to make support payments directly to the stepparent: Palmer v. Harrold, 101 Ohio App. 3d 732, 656 N.E.2d 708, 656 N.E.2d 732, 1995 Ohio App. LEXIS 998 (Ohio Ct. App., Greene County 1995).

**Stipulation**

Where the parties voluntarily entered into an agreement to modify the father's child support from $719.47 a month to $1,100 a month, it was not an abuse of discretion for the trial court to issue a child support order including an upward deviation in the father's support obligation. As the father freely, voluntarily, and with counsel, entered into the agreement, he stipulated to the amount of support he was obligated to pay. Spicer v. Spicer, 2015-Ohio-799, 2015 Ohio App. LEXIS 778 (Ohio Ct. App., Erie County 2015).

In light of the joint exhibit as well as the statements of the attorneys made on the record, the parties stipulated to the fact that the husband had satisfied his child support obligation with the exception of two payments totaling $781. The trial court attempted to incorporate the stipulated agreement between the parties in its journal entry but misstated several terms and the parties had also stipulated to an overpayment based upon the facts before them at the time of the hearing. Vengrow v. Vengrow, 2010-Ohio-2568, 2010 Ohio App. LEXIS 2109 (Ohio Ct. App., Summit County 2010).

Obligor could not challenge the child support award where he stipulated that the temporary support order would become the permanent support order: Kestner v. Kestner, 2007-Ohio-6222, 173 Ohio App. 3d 632, 879 N.E.2d 849, 2007 Ohio App. LEXIS 5459 (Ohio Ct. App., Columbiana County 2007).

**—Arrearages**

Where a trial court record was devoid of any evidence indicating that a former husband was in arrears on his spousal support obligation, a trial court abused its discretion in refusing to consider the issue of child support, which the husband had requested be reviewed due to the emancipation of one of the parties' children, where the court indicated that it would not consider that issue until the spousal support arrearages were at zero; further, the appropriateness of refusing to enter the child support order due to potential spousal support arrears was questionable. Cassidy v. Cassidy, 2005-Ohio-3199, 2005 Ohio App. LEXIS 2990 (Ohio Ct. App., Pike County 2005).

**Support**

Trial court did not err by affirming the notice to withhold income for child and spousal support because, in three different locations in the separation agreement, it was clearly stated that, on the sale of the house, the father was to have a total child and spousal support obligation of $2,375 per month. That amount was to be paid irrespective of whether spousal support was terminated and irrespective of the number of children who had been emancipated. Yodzis v. Savercool, 2012-Ohio-5558, 2012 Ohio App. LEXIS 4821 (Ohio Ct. App., Lucas County 2012).

**—Gross income**

There was no abuse of discretion in the calculation of the husband's gross as R.C. 3105.18 was silent as to whether to include "phantom income" in the husband's gross income for the purpose of calculating spousal support for the purpose of modification and he failed to cite to any authority in support of his argument with respect to calculation for spousal or child support. Thus, the husband failed to establish that the trial court abused its discretion by including the $32,171 (which was a shareholder's share of income which he claimed that he did not actually receive) in his gross income for the year 2000. Poitinger v. Poitinger, 2005-Ohio-2680, 2005 Ohio App. LEXIS 2535 (Ohio Ct. App., Summit County 2005).

**—Income verification**

Although the trial court used a correct approach in requiring the father either to produce records and submit to an expert evaluation of his businesses or to accept the income figures the magistrate used, in abandoning that approach and in failing to properly verify income, the trial court abused its discretion. The father's gross income was likely higher than what the magistrate calculated. In re Custody of Harris, 2006-Ohio-3649, 168 Ohio App. 3d 1, 857 N.E.2d 1235, 2006 Ohio App. LEXIS 3597 (Ohio Ct. App., Champaign County 2006).

**—Retroactivity**

Trial court erred when it ordered a modification retroactive to its previous temporary order of child support. The final divorce decree essentially created an obligation on the husband to pay an additional sum of money, after the fact, and then penalized him for not having paid it. Ostmann v. Ostmann, 2006-Ohio-3617, 168 Ohio App. 3d 59, 858 N.E.2d 831, 2006 Ohio App. LEXIS 3578 (Ohio Ct. App., Medina County 2006).



**—Termination**

Competent and credible evidence existed to support the trial court's decision to terminate the child support effective January 21, 2001, rather than October 1999, because the father had continuously denied the mother her right to parenting time with the children as required by the shared parenting plan and the interim visitation agreement. The fact that their son chose not to follow the shared parenting visitation schedule and that the father did not enforce the schedule did not warrant the termination of the child support obligation in October 1999. Difranco v. Difranco, 2006-Ohio-5010, 2006 Ohio App. LEXIS 4959 (Ohio Ct. App., Cuyahoga County 2006).

**Supported by record**

Trial court did not abuse its discretion by continuing the father's child support obligation or by increasing the child support award from $216 to $300 because the trial court provided sound reasons for its decisions, which were supported by evidence in the record. Contrary to the father's argument, the fact that he was the designated as the residential parent for school purposes under the modified shared parenting plan and may have had the child for more time than the mother did not necessarily mean that the mother should have been the obligor of child support. Kilgore v. Kilgore, 2008-Ohio-5858, 2008 Ohio App. LEXIS 4914 (Ohio Ct. App., Ashtabula County 2008).

**Temporary orders**

Trial court did not abuse its discretion and acted properly in modifying the temporary child support order, and regarding the assessment of arrearages and contempt of court. The temporary order remained unmodified until the judgment entry of divorce and thus, the trial court had the jurisdiction to modify the temporary support order at the final hearing, pursuant to a properly filed Civ.R. 75(N) motion by the husband. Schumann v. Schumann, 2005-Ohio-91, 2005 Ohio App. LEXIS 72 (Ohio Ct. App., Cuyahoga County 2005).

Order for a mother to pay child support while the children were temporarily in their father's care while a motion for modification of a shared parenting plan was pending was proper, and was affirmed, where the order specifically stated that the mother was to pay temporary support in amount to be determined in the future. Tate v. Wells, 2004-Ohio-4161, 2004 Ohio App. LEXIS 3791 (Ohio Ct. App., Van Wert County 2004).

The doctrine of merger precludes seeking payment of arrearages under a temporary support order where they are not incorporated into the final decree of divorce: Brooks v. Brooks, 117 Ohio App. 3d 19, 689 N.E.2d 987, 1996 Ohio App. LEXIS 5844 (Ohio Ct. App., Franklin County 1996).

**Termination**

Although a mother claimed support for the parties' child should continue past the child's nineteenth birthday due to his disability, R.C. 3119.86, the mother failed to demonstrate she was entitled to relief under Civ.R. 60(B) regarding the termination of child support because the mother did not put forth any operative facts that the child was unable to support himself or live independently due to his disability. In re R.B., 2013-Ohio-2392, 2013 Ohio App. LEXIS 2347 (Ohio Ct. App., Butler County 2013).

Mother failed to prove mistake with regard to her failure to object to the termination of child support because the county child support enforcement agency's recommendation and the trial court's order provided full and adequate notice and warning to the mother concerning her rights to a hearing regarding the termination of child support and the mother's failure to act upon the warnings was not a "mistake" as contemplated under Civ.R. 60(B)(1); the parties' child had reached the age of nineteen. In re R.B., 2013-Ohio-2392, 2013 Ohio App. LEXIS 2347 (Ohio Ct. App., Butler County 2013).

Trial court did not by terminating the father's child support obligation as of August 24, 2004 because the child support order of $4,000 per month was premised, in part upon the child attending a particular school, and she did not attend that school subsequent to June 2004. Schumann v. Schumann, 2010-Ohio-5472, 190 Ohio App. 3d 824, 944 N.E.2d 705, 2010 Ohio App. LEXIS 4625 (Ohio Ct. App., Cuyahoga County 2010).

**Third-party rights**

The state of Ohio has no authority to intervene in a divorce action and to file a motion to increase child support: De Long v. Stark County Dep't of Human Services, 36 Ohio App. 3d 103, 521 N.E.2d 463, 1986 Ohio App. LEXIS 10363 (Ohio Ct. App., Stark County 1986).

**Voluntary unemployment**

Magistrate's language that a father was deemed voluntarily unemployed was an express finding of voluntary unemployment. Therefore, the trial court made the required preliminary finding of voluntary unemployment before it imputed income to the father in its determination of child support. Daniels v. O'Dell, 2010-Ohio-1341, 2010 Ohio App. LEXIS 1127 (Ohio Ct. App., Summit County 2010).

**Waiver of support**

Parents may orally agree to suspend a court ordered child support obligation: Crow v. Crow, 1990 Ohio App. LEXIS 1460 (Ohio Ct. App., Butler County Apr. 16, 1990).

Court-ordered support is for the benefit of the children rather than the custodial parent and, consequently, cannot be waived by a parent. A mother can "forgive" the father for part arrearages by agreement, but she cannot summarily dispense with his future obligations in the same manner: Nelson v. Nelson, 65 Ohio App. 3d 800, 585 N.E.2d 502, 1989 Ohio App. LEXIS 4881 (Ohio Ct. App., Lake County 1989).

**Worksheets**

Trial court erred in omitting a spousal support award as income to the wife and as a reduction in income to the husband on the child support worksheet for purposes of determining the proper award of child support in the parties' divorce action; although the husband prepared the worksheet, it was not invited error because the trial court had the responsibility to make sure there were no omissions when it adopted the proposed worksheet. Raff v. Raff, 2007-Ohio-737, 2007 Ohio App. LEXIS 671 (Ohio Ct. App., Stark County 2007).

Trial court could not have included the mother's employment-related benefits as income for the purposes of calculating child support because the evidence demonstrated that the mother was employed by a corporation and, thus, R.C. 3119.01(C)(13), defining self-generated income, did not apply to her. The trial court calculated Katina's total income from both employers to be $40,430.84, the amount listed on the first line of the child support computation worksheet. Michael's claim that the trial court erred by not including Katina's aerobics-related income is factually incorrect. Spier v. Spier, 2006-Ohio-1289, 2006 Ohio App. LEXIS 1181 (Ohio Ct. App., Mahoning County 2006).

## RESEARCH REFERENCES AND PRACTICE AIDS

**Cross-References to Related Sections**

Additional fees for divorce or dissolution filings, RC § 3109.14.

Allocation of parental rights and responsibilities for care of children; shared parenting, RC § 3109.04.

Interfering with action to issue or modify support order, RC § 2919.231.

Juvenile court jurisdiction of child support matters, RC § 2151.23.

Nonsupport of dependents as misdemeanor of first degree; court costs and attorney fees may be imposed upon conviction of failure to obey certain support orders, RC § 2919.21.

**Ohio Rules**

Allowance of spousal support, child support, and custody pendente lite, Civ.R 75(N).

**Ohio Administrative Code**

Department of job and family services, division of public assistance—

Child support enforcement agency (CSEA): administrative rules. OAC ch. 5101:1-31.

Support payments collected and disbursed—

By the CSEA. OAC 5101:1-31-13.

Ohio works first (OWF). OAC ch. 5101:1-3.

Child support requirement. OAC 5101:1-3-10.

Title IV-D program: support collection; paternity services. OAC ch. 5101:1-29.

Authority of CSEA to petition court for support independent of divorce or custody action. OAC 5101:1-29-01.

Medical support payments; health insurance. OAC 5101:1-29-35 et seq.

**Comparative Legislation**

Child support guidelines:

CA—Cal Fam Code § 4053

FL—Fla. Stat. § 61.30

IL—750 Ill. Comp. Stat. § 5/505

KY—KRS § 405.430

MI—MCLS § 552.16

NY—NY CLS Family Ct Act § 413

PA—23 P.S. § 4322 et seq

**Practice Manuals and Treatises**

Anderson's Ohio Civil Practice with Forms § 52.08 Child Custody

**Practice Manuals & Treatises**

Anderson's Domestic Relations Practice in Ohio § 2.6 Allocation of Parental Rights and Responsibilities

Anderson's Domestic Relations Practice in Ohio § 5.1 Modification of Child Support

**Practice Forms**

Motion to modify support, Couse's Ohio Form Book Form 24.70

## § 3109.11 Companionship or visitation rights where parent is deceased.

If either the father or mother of an unmarried minor child is deceased, the court of common pleas of the county in which the minor child resides may grant the parents and other relatives of the deceased father or mother reasonable companionship or visitation rights with respect to the minor child during the child's minority if the parent or other relative files a complaint requesting reasonable companionship or visitation rights and if the court determines that the granting of the companionship or visitation rights is in the best interest of the minor child. In determining whether to grant any person reasonable companionship or visitation rights with respect to any child, the court shall consider all relevant factors, including, but not limited to, the factors set forth in division (D) of section 3109.051 of the Revised Code. Divisions (C), (K), and (L) of section 3109.051 of the Revised Code apply to the determination of reasonable companionship or visitation rights under this section and to any order granting any such rights that is issued under this section.

The remarriage of the surviving parent of the child or the adoption of the child by the spouse of the surviving parent of the child does not affect the authority of the court under this section to grant reasonable companionship or visitation rights with respect to the child to a parent or other relative of the child's deceased father or mother.

If the court denies a request for reasonable companionship or visitation rights made pursuant to this section and the complainant files a written request for findings of fact and conclusions of law, the court shall state in writing its findings of fact and conclusions of law in accordance with Civil Rule 52.

Except as provided in division (E)(6) of section 3113.31 of the Revised Code, if the court, pursuant to this section, grants any person companionship or visitation rights with respect to any child, it shall not require the public children services agency to provide supervision of or other services related to that person's exercise of companionship or visitation rights with respect to the child. This section does not limit the power of a juvenile court pursuant to Chapter 2151. of the Revised Code to issue orders with respect to children who are alleged to be abused, neglected, or dependent children or to make dispositions of children who are adjudicated abused, neglected, or dependent children or of a common pleas court to issue orders pursuant to section 3113.31 of the Revised Code.

**HISTORY:**

134 v H 163 (Eff 2-17-72); 143 v H 15 (Eff 5-31-90); 143 v S 3 (Eff 4-11-91); 146 v H 274 (Eff 8-8-96); 148 v S 180. Eff 3-22-2001.

### NOTES TO DECISIONS

Analysis

- Constitutionality
- Adoption of child
- Applicability
- Best interest of child
- Grandparents
- Other state's laws
- Relatives, generally
- Reviewability
- Visitation
- —Death of parent
- —Grandparents
- —Nonparents

**Constitutionality**

This statute was not unconstitutional as applied because a trial court's finding that visitation with their paternal grandparents would be in the children's best interest was not an abuse of discretion, and its minimal visitation order (twice monthly video visits for as little as 15 minutes) was narrowly tailored to serve that compelling interest; the trial court found that visitation with the grandparents would be in the children's best interest after considering the fact that they never first requested visitation from the mother, but it might have concluded, as the grandmother testified, that such a request would have been fruitless. Wentz v. Wideman, 2021-Ohio-2257, 2021 Ohio App. LEXIS 2224 (Ohio Ct. App., Wood County 2021).

Father met his burden of showing that, under the existing facts, the trial court unconstitutionally applied this section to him, because the trial court failed to weigh the father's opposition to the grandparents' visitation. In re I.R.H., 2014-Ohio-1180, 9 N.E.3d 529, 2014 Ohio App. LEXIS 1090 (Ohio Ct. App., Mahoning County 2014).

Although a mother argued that the grandparent visitation statute, R.C. 3109.11, was unconstitutional as applied to the facts of this case, the appellate court concluded that appellant could not complain that the trial court unconstitutionally failed to give special weight to her wishes in determining the best interests of her children. In re E.C., 2014-Ohio-4340, 2014 Ohio App. LEXIS 4251 (Ohio Ct. App., Lucas County 2014).

Court refused defendant's request that it reconsider and overrule the state supreme court's decision in Harrold v. Collier, 107 Ohio St.3d 44, 2005 Ohio 5334, 836 N.E.2d 1165, and find R.C. 3109.051(D) and 3109.11 unconstitutional. An intermediate appellate court had no authority to overrule controlling supreme court authority. Bauman v. Faught, 2008-Ohio-166, 2008 Ohio App. LEXIS 130 (Ohio Ct. App., Clermont County 2008), cert. denied, 556 U.S. 1208, 129 S. Ct. 2054, 173 L. Ed. 2d 1133, 2009 U.S. LEXIS 3122 (U.S. 2009).

State has a compelling interest in protecting a child's best interest, and Ohio's nonparental visitation statutes are narrowly tailored to serve that compelling interest; therefore, they are not unconstitutional under Troxel v. Granville. Since there exists a set of circumstances under which the statutes are valid, R.C. 3109.11, 3109.12 and 3109.051(D) are constitutional on their face. Harrold v. Collier, 2005-Ohio-5334, 107 Ohio St. 3d 44, 836 N.E.2d 1165, 2005 Ohio LEXIS 2241 (Ohio 2005), cert. denied, 547 U.S. 1004, 126 S. Ct. 1474, 164 L. Ed. 2d 248, 2006 U.S. LEXIS 2052 (U.S. 2006).

Ohio courts are obligated to afford some special weight to the wishes of parents of minor children when considering petitions for nonparental visitation made pursuant to R.C. 3109.11 or 3109.12. The state has a compelling interest in protecting a child's best interest, and Ohio's nonparental-visitation statutes are narrowly tailored to serve that compelling interest: Harrold v. Collier, 2005-Ohio-5334, 107 Ohio St. 3d 44, 836 N.E.2d 1165, 2005 Ohio LEXIS 2241 (Ohio 2005), cert. denied, 547 U.S. 1004, 126 S. Ct. 1474, 164 L. Ed. 2d 248, 2006 U.S. LEXIS 2052 (U.S. 2006).

Courts of Ohio are in agreement in concluding that R.C. 3109.11 and 3109.051 are constitutional; accordingly, an award of visitation of a father's two children to their maternal grandmother after the death of their mother was proper, as it was based on consideration of the best interests of the children, and "special weight" was accorded to the wishes of the father. Crigger v. Crigger, 2005-Ohio-519, 2005 Ohio App. LEXIS 532 (Ohio Ct. App., Franklin County), aff'd, 2005-Ohio-5975, 107 Ohio St. 3d 100, 836 N.E.2d 1221, 2005 Ohio LEXIS 2697 (Ohio 2005).

R.C. 3109.11, providing for visitation between a grandparent and the child of a deceased parent, does not violate dicta of Troxel v. Granville because the statute provides for the wishes of the parents to be considered as well as the best interests of the child. In re Talkington, 2004-Ohio-4215, 2004 Ohio App. LEXIS 3811 (Ohio Ct. App., Stark County 2004).

A Washington state statute which permitted "any person" to petition for visitation rights "at any time" and authorized a court to grant such visitation rights whenever "visitation may serve the best interest of the child" violated a mother's USConst amend XIV due process right to make decisions concerning the care, custody, and control of her daughters; grandparents' visitation petition denied: Troxel v. Granville, 530 U.S. 57, 120 S. Ct. 2054, 147 L. Ed. 2d 49, 2000 U.S. LEXIS 3767 (U.S. 2000).

**Adoption of child**

A stepparent's adoption of a child terminates any grandparent visitation rights: Foor v. Foor, 133 Ohio App. 3d 250, 727 N.E.2d 618, 1999 Ohio App. LEXIS 1885 (Ohio Ct. App., Preble County 1999).

The stepparent adoption divested the parents of the child's deceased natural father of any visitation rights: Beard v. Pannell, 110 Ohio App. 3d 572, 674 N.E.2d 1225, 1996 Ohio App. LEXIS 1668 (Ohio Ct. App., Sandusky County 1996).

Maternal grandparents may be granted visitation with their grandchildren where the grandchildren are adopted by a paternal grandmother and her husband. R.C. 3109.11 permits the court to grant such visitation on a case-by-case basis, considering all relevant facts and taking the best interests of the children as the guiding principle: In re Pennington, 55 Ohio App. 3d 99, 562 N.E.2d 905, 1988 Ohio App. LEXIS 3316 (Ohio Ct. App., Scioto County 1988).

A visitation order granting visitation rights to the maternal grandparents of a child, whose mother has died and who has been adopted by his stepmother, must be accompanied by an express determination that visitation is in the best interests of the child: In re Thornton, 24 Ohio App. 3d 152, 493 N.E.2d 977, 1985 Ohio App. LEXIS 10163 (Ohio Ct. App., Franklin County 1985).

An adoption of a child by a stepparent does not terminate the power of the court to determine visitation rights of grandparents under R.C. 3109.05, where, but for the adoption, the court finds such visitation to be in the best interests of the child: Welsh v. Laffey, 16 Ohio App. 3d 110, 474 N.E.2d 681, 1984 Ohio App. LEXIS 12315 (Ohio Ct. App., Butler County 1984).

**Applicability**

Juvenile court erred when it adopted a magistrate's award to a maternal grandmother of visitation with one of her grandchildren who was born after her parents' marriage, as there was no statutory authority that permitted the juvenile court to make such an award. In re K.M.-B., 2015-Ohio-4626, 48 N.E.3d 998, 2015 Ohio App. LEXIS 4520 (Ohio Ct. App., Lucas County 2015).

In visitation proceedings in which a step-grandmother sought to intervene, R.C. 3109.11 did not apply because the minor child's biological parents were both still living. McFall v. Watson, 2008-Ohio-5204, 178 Ohio App. 3d 540, 899 N.E.2d 158, 2008 Ohio App. LEXIS 4374 (Ohio Ct. App., Vinton County 2008).



**Best interest of child**

Award of reasonable visitation to child aunt under R.C. 3109.11 was proper, given that evidence showed that the child had lived with the aunt for three years, that the aunt had helped the child learn to speak English, that aunt had spent a significant amount of time with the child, and that aunt often attended child's school and sporting events. Adam v. Kovitch, 2013-Ohio-1020, 2013 Ohio App. LEXIS 903 (Ohio Ct. App., Summit County 2013).

The companionship and visitation rights vested by R.C. 3109.11 are neither absolute nor unqualified but are conditioned upon the finding by the proper court that such rights are in the best interest of the child: Graziano v. Davis, 50 Ohio App. 2d 83, 4 Ohio Op. 3d 55, 361 N.E.2d 525, 1976 Ohio App. LEXIS 5850 (Ohio Ct. App., Mahoning County 1976).

The companionship and visitation rights vested by R.C. 3109.11 are neither absolute nor unqualified but are conditioned upon the finding by a court of competent jurisdiction that such rights are in the best interests of the child: In re Griffiths, 47 Ohio App. 2d 238, 1 Ohio Op. 3d 307, 353 N.E.2d 884, 1975 Ohio App. LEXIS 5876 (Ohio Ct. App., Mahoning County 1975).

The companionship and visitation rights of relatives granted in R.C. 3109.11 are subservient to the best interest of the minor child: In re Griffiths, 47 Ohio App. 2d 238, 1 Ohio Op. 3d 307, 353 N.E.2d 884, 1975 Ohio App. LEXIS 5876 (Ohio Ct. App., Mahoning County 1975).

**Grandparents**

Juvenile court complied with the statute by considering each best-interest factor under the statute; because the grandparents did not argue or submit any evidence that the mother was an unfit parent, the court properly indicated that it would give special weight to the mother's wish not to allow visitation while also considering the remaining factors. In re P.R.P., 2018-Ohio-216, 104 N.E.3d 827, 2018 Ohio App. LEXIS 231 (Ohio Ct. App., Butler County 2018).

Trial court lacked jurisdiction to determine visitation and companionship rights and to issue a visitation schedule because a judgment entry determining visitation issues was based upon an improper exercise of subject matter jurisdiction, and the orders contained therein exceeded its authority; the complaint seeking custody was the only pleading ever filed, and at no point in the proceedings had the paternal grandparents ever filed a pleading or otherwise invoked the trial court's jurisdiction. In re C.W., 2018-Ohio-5265, 2018 Ohio App. LEXIS 5576 (Ohio Ct. App., Lorain County 2018).

Trial court gave the required special weight to the father's wishes regarding nonparent visitation, as the trial court evaluated the requisite factors, including the father's wishes and it noted his concerns regarding visitation with the maternal relatives and took those concerns into account when evaluating the other best-interest factors and crafting a relatively narrow visitation order; thus, the maternal grandmother was properly awarded one week of visitation. In re F.D., 2009-Ohio-4788, 2009 Ohio App. LEXIS 4052 (Ohio Ct. App., Montgomery County 2009).

Grandparents are not required to produce clear and convincing evidence that visitation is in the child's best interest before they may be granted visitation under R.C. 3109.11: Wiseman v. Wiseman, 1994 Ohio App. LEXIS 1261 (Ohio Ct. App., Logan County Mar. 24, 1994), dismissed, 70 Ohio St. 3d 1425, 638 N.E.2d 87, 1994 Ohio LEXIS 1887 (Ohio 1994).

The court did not err in terminating grandparent visitation rights pursuant to R.C. 3109.11 where the grandparent was so unrelentingly hostile to the surviving parent that it frightened the children: In re Skinner, 1994 Ohio App. LEXIS 1323 (Ohio Ct. App., Adams County Mar. 23, 1994).

In general, grandparent visitation is in a child's best interest. A criminal conviction from years ago does not necessarily preclude visitation rights: Holley v. Higgins, 86 Ohio App. 3d 240, 620 N.E.2d 251, 1993 Ohio App. LEXIS 769 (Ohio Ct. App., Franklin County 1993).

In determining whether to grant visitation rights to a child's grandparent, a court must ascertain whether such visitation is in the child's best interests. A trial court does not abuse its discretion in refusing to grant visitation rights to a grandparent where the record shows that the grandparent is likely to have close contact with the child's father, who has subjected the child to traumatic scenes of extreme violence directed against the child's mother and who has threatened violence to the child, and where the grandparent has allowed the father to be alone with the child despite an agreement with the mother not to do so: Drennen v. Drennen, 52 Ohio App. 3d 121, 557 N.E.2d 149, 1988 Ohio App. LEXIS 3456 (Ohio Ct. App., Erie County 1988).

Grandparents may be granted visitation rights under R.C. 3109.05(B) and 3109.11 if the trial court finds that such visitation is in the child's best interest: In re Whitaker, 36 Ohio St. 3d 213, 522 N.E.2d 563, 1988 Ohio LEXIS 125 (Ohio 1988).

In general, the visitation and companionship of a child's grandparents are in a child's best interests: In re Griffiths, 47 Ohio App. 2d 238, 1 Ohio Op. 3d 307, 353 N.E.2d 884, 1975 Ohio App. LEXIS 5876 (Ohio Ct. App., Mahoning County 1975).

**Other state's laws**

Indiana's grandparent visitation statute does not unconstitutionally interfere with parental rights. R.C. 3127.23 had no application to the Indiana decree and order that the grandparent sought to register pursuant to R.C. 3127.35: Reynolds v. Spicer, 2006-Ohio-1817, 166 Ohio App. 3d 485, 851 N.E.2d 527, 2006 Ohio App. LEXIS 1656 (Ohio Ct. App., Clark County 2006).

**Relatives, generally**

Juvenile court properly granted the stepfather's request to have a set schedule of visitation with the child after the child's mother died, because the stepfather had standing to move for visitation, when the stepfather was related by affinity, as the spouse of the child's mother. In re K.P.R., 2011-Ohio-6114, 197 Ohio App. 3d 193, 966 N.E.2d 952, 2011 Ohio App. LEXIS 4997 (Ohio Ct. App., Warren County 2011).

Trial court erred in determining that the widower lost his status as a "relative" when he remarried and therefore erred in determining that he lacked standing to pursue visitation under R.C. 3109.11 because the mother's death did not serve to sever the widower's relationship by affinity with her. The child lived with the widower for the first 11 years of his life, undoubtedly creating a very strong bond and thus, permitting the widower, as the surviving stepparent to pursue visitation, would have fulfilled the intent expressed in R.C. 3109.11 of providing for the child's best interests. Goeller v. Lorence, 2006-Ohio-5807, 2006 Ohio App. LEXIS 5786 (Ohio Ct. App., Lorain County 2006).

**Reviewability**

Trial court's order was reviewable by the appellate court because the trial court construed the action to be seeking companionship or visitation rights where the parent was deceased, which was a proceeding created by statute, prior to 1853 such an action was denoted as an action at law or a suit in equity, and, therefore, the action constituted a special proceeding. Davis v. Nathaniel, 2020-Ohio-6858, 2020 Ohio App. LEXIS 4683 (Ohio Ct. App., Summit County 2020).

**Visitation**

Trial court properly found a father in contempt of court because, while his child's stepmother allegedly was the cause of the child's missed visitations with his maternal relatives, the stepmother's adoption of the child did not excuse the father's failure to abide by the court-ordered visitation schedule. In re P.P., 2013-Ohio-4988, 2013 Ohio App. LEXIS 5191 (Ohio Ct. App., Franklin County 2013).

**—Death of parent**

Trial court erred in determining that the maternal aunt had standing to pursue companionship rights with the adopted children of married parents, one of whom was the aunt's sister because although the children, who were the children of the parties' deceased sister, were not adopted by strangers, an award of visitation contained a potential to introduce significant stress into the new parental relationship and threatened confusion and disruption for the new adoptive family relationship. Davis v. Nathaniel, 2020-Ohio-6858, 2020 Ohio App. LEXIS 4683 (Ohio Ct. App., Summit County 2020).

Trial court erred in determining that the widower lost his status as a "relative" when he remarried and therefore erred in determining that he lacked standing to pursue visitation under R.C. 3109.11 because the mother's death did not serve to sever the widower's relationship by affinity with her. The child lived with the widower for the first 11 years of his life, undoubtedly creating a very strong bond and thus, permitting the widower, as the surviving stepparent to pursue visitation, would have fulfilled the intent expressed in R.C. 3109.11 of providing for the child's best interests. Goeller v. Lorence, 2006-Ohio-5807, 2006 Ohio App. LEXIS 5786 (Ohio Ct. App., Lorain County 2006).

In a custody dispute between a deceased mother's husband and her child's natural father, under R.C. 2151.23(A)(2), it was not error for the trial court to decline to rule on the husband's request for visitation with the child because the husband, even though he was the child's relative, did not follow the procedure required by R.C. 3109.11 to seek such visitation by filing a complaint or motion for such relief. Lorence v. Goeller, 2005-Ohio-2678, 2005 Ohio App. LEXIS 2528 (Ohio Ct. App., Lorain County 2005).

**—Grandparents**

Trial court abused its discretion in determining grandmother's visitation for two-week periods with the transportation costs as her responsibility considering that the evidence in the record established that the child's father failed to cooperate with both visitation and phone calls, and the father was found to be unsuitable parent. In re D.M.W., 2021-Ohio-4657, 2021 Ohio App. LEXIS 4588 (Ohio Ct. App., Belmont County 2021).

Trial court did not abuse its discretion in awarding visitation to the maternal grandparents (MGP) because, despite two significant periods of intergenerational estrangement in the child's young life and consideration of the father's wishes, the MGP had been part of the child's life in the past, did not pose any health or safety concerns to the child, and did not present with any criminal or child protective services history or mental health issues. Rownd v. Marcelli, 2016-Ohio-7142, 2016 Ohio App. LEXIS 3969 (Ohio Ct. App., Stark County 2016).

In awarding limited visitation to two children's paternal grandparents, a trial court did not misapply the governing statutes and precedent because it appropriately gave special weight to the mother's wishes, and its order of minimal video visits addressed her concerns that the children did not know the grandparents and her concerns with the facility at which the magistrate had ordered visitation to take place. Moreover, the trial court did not shift the burden of proof to the mother, and the grandparents' lack of contact for over a year prior to the children's father's death was not a disqualifying fact but was properly considered as a factor in determining what was in the children's best interest. Wentz v. Wideman, 2021-Ohio-2257, 175 N.E.3d 628, 2021 Ohio App. LEXIS 2224 (Ohio Ct. App., Wood County 2021).

Trial court's order granting a child's grandfather and great-grandmother visitation with the child was not an abuse of discretion because, inter alia, a magistrate's finding that, given the child's long, secure and loving relationship with the grandfather and great-grandmother, it was in the child's best interest to be assured of continued contact with the child's extended family with whom the child had resided for extended periods, showed the trial court considered the child's best interest and did not abuse the court's discretion when the court found visitation with the grandfather and great-grandmother was in furtherance of the child's best interest. Jared S. v. Ashley G., 2008-Ohio-1297, 2008 Ohio App. LEXIS 1099 (Ohio Ct. App., Williams County 2008).

Trial court's order granting a child's grandfather and great-grandmother visitation with the child was not an abuse of discretion because, inter alia, it was apparent that the wishes of the child's parents were not ignored, and, apparently, the testimony on behalf of the grandfather and great-grandmother was found to be more credible than that presented on behalf of the child's parents. Jared S. v. Ashley G., 2008-Ohio-1297, 2008 Ohio App. LEXIS 1099 (Ohio Ct. App., Williams County 2008).

Trial court did not err by setting a visitation schedule for the maternal grandparents of a father's two children, granting the grandparents extended summer visitation, allowing the grandparents to arrange time with the father of the children's half-brother, and requiring the children's father to provide activity schedules. The trial court's decision adequately considered the necessary factors in light of the facts of the case, including the best interests of the children and the father's wishes and concerns as a parent, and it actually modified the magistrate's decision, awarding less visitation to the grandparents and allowing the father flexibility to determine the dates that the children would be available for extended visitation with the grandparents in the summer. Bauman v. Faught, 2008-Ohio-166, 2008 Ohio App. LEXIS 130 (Ohio Ct. App., Clermont County 2008), cert. denied, 556 U.S. 1208, 129 S. Ct. 2054, 173 L. Ed. 2d 1133, 2009 U.S. LEXIS 3122 (U.S. 2009).

Trial court properly considered the best interests of the child in granting the grandparents visitation and the father's wishes were afforded the proper weight under Ohio law because the grandparents functioned as the child's residential parents for nearly three years after the natural mother died and the father deprived them of any visitation with the child, in willful violation of court orders. Estate of Harrold v. Collier, 2006-Ohio-5634, 2006 Ohio App. LEXIS 5661 (Ohio Ct. App., Wayne County 2006).

While Ohio courts are obligated to afford special weight to the wishes of parents of minor children when considering petitions for non-parental visitation made pursuant to R.C. 3109.11 or 3109.12, those statutes do not unconstitutionally infringe on a parent's fundamental right under U.S. Const. amend. XIV to make decisions concerning the care, custody, and control of his or her child. The statutes limit the parties who can petition for visitation, limit the application of the statutes to cases where there is a specified predicate event or condition, and expressly identify the parents' wishes and concerns regarding visitation as a factor the court must consider in making its determination. Harrold v. Collier, 2005-Ohio-5334, 107 Ohio St. 3d 44, 836 N.E.2d 1165, 2005 Ohio LEXIS 2241 (Ohio 2005), cert. denied, 547 U.S. 1004, 126 S. Ct. 1474, 164 L. Ed. 2d 248, 2006 U.S. LEXIS 2052 (U.S. 2006).

**—Nonparents**

Juvenile court did not abuse its discretion in declining to grant companionship or visitation with the minor children to the non-parents because the non-parents had engaged in a pattern of disregard of the court's instructions and other conduct which were intended to, or had the effect of, interfering with the children's ability to have free and comfortable interaction with the children's father during court-ordered companionship. In re H.L.S., 2019-Ohio-2376, 2019 Ohio App. LEXIS 2511 (Ohio Ct. App., Columbiana County 2019).

Ohio courts are obligated to afford "special weight" to the wishes of the parents of minor children concerning non-parental visitation, but, while a court is required to consider the wishes of the parents regarding the requested visitation, nothing suggests that a parent's wishes should be placed before the child's best interest. Jared S. v. Ashley G., 2008-Ohio-1297, 2008 Ohio App. LEXIS 1099 (Ohio Ct. App., Williams County 2008).

### RESEARCH REFERENCES AND PRACTICE AIDS

**Cross-References to Related Sections**

Child support; interference with visitation, RC § 3109.05.

Contempt action for failure to comply with visitation order, RC § 2705.031.

Duties of public children services agency as to children in need of public care or protective services, RC § 5153.16.

Effect of adoption, RC § 3107.15.

Supervision of parenting time or visitation or companionship rights, RC § 3113.31.

Support order to include specific provisions for different time periods, RC § 3119.08.

Visitation or companionship rights, RC § 3109.051.

**Ohio Administrative Code**

Department of job and family services, division of social services—

School child day care centers: parental access to child and facility; limitations. OAC 5101:2-17-39.

**Comparative Legislation**

Visitation rights of relatives:

CA—Cal Fam Code §§ 3102-3103
IL—755 Ill. Comp. Stat. § 5/11-7.1
IN—Burns Ind. Code Ann. § 31-17-5-1 et seq
KY—KRS § 405.021
MI—MCLS § 722.27
NY—NY CLS Dom Rel § 72
PA—23 P.S. § 5301 et seq

## § 3109.12 Parenting time, companionship or visitation rights where mother is unmarried.

(A) If a child is born to an unmarried woman, the parents of the woman and any relative of the woman may file a complaint requesting the court of common pleas of the county in which the child resides to grant them reasonable companionship or visitation rights with the child. If a child is born to an unmarried woman and if the father of the child has acknowledged the child and that acknowledgment has become final pursuant to section 2151.232, 3111.25, or 3111.821 of the Revised Code or has been determined in an action under Chapter 3111. of the Revised Code to be the father of the child, the father may file a complaint requesting that the court of appropriate jurisdiction of the county in which the child resides grant him reasonable parenting time rights with the child and the parents of the father and any relative of the father may file a complaint requesting that the court grant them reasonable companionship or visitation rights with the child.

(B) The court may grant the parenting time rights or companionship or visitation rights requested under division (A) of this section, if it determines that the granting of the parenting time rights or companionship or visitation rights is in the best interest of the child. In determining whether to grant reasonable parenting time rights or reasonable companionship or visitation rights with respect to any child, the court shall consider all relevant factors, including, but not limited to, the factors set forth in division (D) of section 3109.051 of the Revised Code. Divisions (C), (K), and (L) of section 3109.051 of the Revised Code apply to the determination of reasonable parenting time rights or reasonable companionship or visitation rights under this section and to any order granting any such rights that is issued under this section.

The marriage or remarriage of the mother or father of a child does not affect the authority of the court under this section to grant the natural father reasonable parenting time rights or the parents or relatives of the natural father or the parents or relatives of the mother of the child reasonable companionship or visitation rights with respect to the child.

If the court denies a request for reasonable parenting time rights or reasonable companionship or visitation rights made pursuant to division (A) of this section and the complainant files a written request for findings of fact and conclusions of law, the court shall state in writing its findings of fact and conclusions of law in accordance with Civil Rule 52.

Except as provided in division (E)(6) of section 3113.31 of the Revised Code, if the court, pursuant to this section, grants parenting time rights or companionship or visitation rights with respect to any child, it shall not require the public children services agency to provide supervision of or other services related to that parent's exercise of parenting time rights with the child or that person's exercise of companionship or visitation rights with the child. This section does not limit the power of a juvenile court pursuant to Chapter 2151. of the Revised Code to issue orders with respect to children who are alleged to be abused, neglected, or dependent children or to make dispositions of children who are adjudicated abused, neglected, or dependent children or of a common pleas court to issue orders pursuant to section 3113.31 of the Revised Code.



**HISTORY:**

143 v H 15 (Eff 5-31-90); 143 v S 3 (Eff 4-11-91); 146 v H 274 (Eff 8-8-96); 147 v H 352 (Eff 1-1-98); 148 v S 180. Eff 3-22-2001.

## NOTES TO DECISIONS

Analysis



**Constitutionality**

Because the parents of the child married each other during the pendency of the grandmother's visitation complaint, there was no rational basis for differentiating married parents who were unmarried at the time of the complaint's filing from those who were married at that time; the was unconstitutional as applied to the facts of the case. Santos v. Parks, 2018-Ohio-3111, 105 N.E.3d 1283, 2018 Ohio App. LEXIS 3344 (Ohio Ct. App., Ashland County 2018).

Juvenile court lacked jurisdiction to award visitation to a maternal grandmother with respect to a child who was born several months before his parents' marriage, as the jurisdictional statute was unconstitutional as applied based on a strict scrutiny equal protection review because there was no significant disruptive event which justified the State's interference with the parents' autonomy interests. In re K.M.-B., 2015-Ohio-4626, 48 N.E.3d 998, 2015 Ohio App. LEXIS 4520 (Ohio Ct. App., Lucas County 2015).

With respect to a grandmother's request for visitation with her grandchildren, as her statutory visitation right was an infringement upon the parents' fundamental liberty interest regarding the care, custody, and control of their children, a strict scrutiny standard of review applied to an equal protection challenge. In re K.M.-B., 2015-Ohio-4626, 48 N.E.3d 998, 2015 Ohio App. LEXIS 4520 (Ohio Ct. App., Lucas County 2015).

R.C. 3109.12 was unconstitutional as applied to the particular facts and circumstances of the case and violated the Equal Protection Clause. Because the parents had married each other during the pendency of the grandmother's visitation complaint, there was no rational basis for differentiating married parents who were unmarried at the time of the complaint's filing from those who were married at that time. Rugola-Dye v. Dye, 2009-Ohio-2471, 2009 Ohio App. LEXIS 2082 (Ohio Ct. App., Delaware County 2009).

State has a compelling interest in protecting a child's best interest, and Ohio's nonparental visitation statutes are narrowly tailored to serve that compelling interest; therefore, they are not unconstitutional under Troxel v. Granville. Since there exists a set of circumstances under which the statutes are valid, R.C. 3109.11, 3109.12 and 3109.051(D) are constitutional on their face. Harrold v. Collier, 2005-Ohio-5334, 107 Ohio St. 3d 44, 836 N.E.2d 1165, 2005 Ohio LEXIS 2241 (Ohio 2005), cert. denied, 547 U.S. 1004, 126 S. Ct. 1474, 164 L. Ed. 2d 248, 2006 U.S. LEXIS 2052 (U.S. 2006).

Ohio courts are obligated to afford some special weight to the wishes of parents of minor children when considering petitions for nonparental visitation made pursuant to R.C. 3109.11 or 3109.12. The state has a compelling interest in protecting a child's best interest, and Ohio's nonparental-visitation statutes are narrowly tailored to serve that compelling interest: Harrold v. Collier, 2005-Ohio-5334, 107 Ohio St. 3d 44, 836 N.E.2d 1165, 2005 Ohio LEXIS 2241 (Ohio 2005), cert. denied, 547 U.S. 1004, 126 S. Ct. 1474, 164 L. Ed. 2d 248, 2006 U.S. LEXIS 2052 (U.S. 2006).

**Generally**

Court of Appeals of Ohio, Twelfth Appellate District, Clermont County, Ohio, will no longer follow In the Matter of Nichols, 1998 Ohio App. LEXIS 2539 (1998), to the extent that its language and holdings are inconsistent with statutory law dealing with a father seeking parenting time with the child of an unmarried woman. In re P.G., 2009-Ohio-6747, 2009 Ohio App. LEXIS 5655 (Ohio Ct. App., Clermont County 2009).

Pursuant to R.C. 3109.051(D)(15), the trial court gave "special weight" to the wishes and concerns of a minor child's parents that a maternal step-grandparent's request for unsupervised visitation with the child under R.C. 3109.12 was not in the child's best interest due to fear of inappropriate contact. The grandfather did not provide evidence that such visitation was in the child's best interest or that it was a compelling interest that overrode the parents' objections. In re Sadie Elizabeth S., 2006-Ohio-2928, 2006 Ohio App. LEXIS 2800 (Ohio Ct. App., Fulton County 2006).

Because neither parent was deceased, the mother was married when the child was born, and the relatives, a great aunt and uncle, sought visitation rights in a dependency action, the relatives were not entitled to visitation under R.C. 3109.11, 3109.12(A), 3109.051(B)(1); consequently, the trial court did not err in dismissing their motion for visitation rights. In re E. H., 2005-Ohio-1952, 2005 Ohio App. LEXIS 1854 (Ohio Ct. App., Lorain County 2005).

A strict-scrutiny analysis must be applied to a nonparental-visitation statute and to the method in which the statute is applied. The "special weight" requirement means the deference provided to a parent's wishes will be overcome only by some compelling governmental interest and overwhelmingly clear circumstances supporting that governmental interest: Oliver v. Feldner, 2002-Ohio-3209, 149 Ohio App. 3d 114, 776 N.E.2d 499, 2002 Ohio App. LEXIS 3401 (Ohio Ct. App., Noble County 2002).

**Abandonment of rights**

In a custody dispute, the trial court abused its discretion in awarding the father the right to relocation notice under R.C. 3109.051 as well as access to the child's records, daycare centers, and student activities since the father expressly abandoned his request for such rights. Pursuant to R.C. 3109.12, R.C. 3111.13, and R.C. 3111.26, the mere filing of a parentage action by an unwed mother did not automatically entitle the acknowledged father to parenting time rights after the father specifically abandoned his requests for those rights. J.V.C.-N. v. M.P.D., 2012-Ohio-1418, 2012 Ohio App. LEXIS 1261 (Ohio Ct. App., Franklin County 2012).

**Abuse, dependency, and neglect**

There is no bar to the filing of an R.C. 3109.12 action when an R.C. 2151.353 action is pending. Therefore, an aunt's companionship case was improperly dismissed because it was a permissible legal route to take after her request for joinder was denied in the Stark County Department of Job and Family Services' abuse, neglect, and dependency case. Brunner v. Stark County Dep't of Job & Family Servs., 2011-Ohio-271, 2011 Ohio App. LEXIS 226 (Ohio Ct. App., Stark County 2011).

**Appeal**

Although the trial court did not abuse its discretion in choosing to limit, restrict, or even eliminate the father's parenting time, it did abuse its discretion in the manner in which it set up the reunification counseling. The judgment provided for no periodic reviews to address the status of the reunification counseling, nor did it seek recommendations from the counselor to inform the trial court's decision-making process, leaving the expansion of the father's parenting time entirely in the hands of the reunification professional. Morrow v. Becker, 2018-Ohio-3316, 118 N.E.3d 1077, 2018 Ohio App. LEXIS 3591 (Ohio Ct. App., Medina County 2018).

Where a juvenile court found that as applied, R.C. 3109.12 violated the Equal Protection Clause of U.S. Const. amend. XIV and Ohio Const. art. I, § 2, and temporary custodians' arguments on appeal pursuant to App.R. 16(A)(7) did not address that issue at all, the arguments were irrelevant;

accordingly, their appeal lacked merit. In re A.Z., 2011-Ohio-6739, 2011 Ohio App. LEXIS 5556 (Ohio Ct. App., Meigs County 2011).

Where a complaint seeking grandparent visitation was filed pursuant to R.C. 3109.12, rather than R.C. 3109.051, denial of a motion to dismiss or for judgment on the pleadings was not a final appealable order: Digiantonio v. Turnmire, 2007-Ohio-6178, 173 Ohio App. 3d 665, 880 N.E.2d 109, 2007 Ohio App. LEXIS 5424 (Ohio Ct. App., Stark County 2007).

**Costs**

Mother failed to point to anything evidencing that the trial court's imposition of part of the costs associated with the father's visitation constituted an abuse of discretion. The father remained responsible for 75 percent of his visitation costs, and he testified in detail about the cost of each visit that included an 11-hour drive each way and a one-night stay at a hotel when the child was with him on his return trip, and which parent initially moved away from the child was not determinative. Shendel v. Graham, 2017-Ohio-4236, 92 N.E.3d 43, 2017 Ohio App. LEXIS 2303 (Ohio Ct. App., Lake County 2017).

**Criminal cases**

For purposes of extortion, the plain language of the phrase "any valuable thing or valuable benefit" in R.C. 2905.11 includes parenting time with a minor child to which a defendant has no right; the extortion statute is not void for vagueness. State v. Kopras, 2018-Ohio-2774, 2018 Ohio App. LEXIS 2989 (Ohio Ct. App., Jefferson County 2018).

Where defendant threatened to send out links to a sex tape involving the complainant unless she gave in to his demand for child visitation, his plea of guilty to extortion was not involuntary due to a misinterpretation or misapplication of the extortion statute; the evidence showed defendant did not have a court-ordered right to parental time when he committed his crime. He admitted that he acted with the purpose to coerce the victim into providing immediate access to his child to which he had no right. State v. Kopras, 2018-Ohio-2774, 2018 Ohio App. LEXIS 2989 (Ohio Ct. App., Jefferson County 2018).

**Denial of request overruled**

Trial court erred by dismissing the father's emergency motion for visitation, because the magistrate decision made no finding regarding the best interest factors, whether it considered them, or which factors were applicable in the case. In re K.S., 2014-Ohio-1347, 2014 Ohio App. LEXIS 1243 (Ohio Ct. App., Ashtabula County 2014).

Magistrate's denial of a father's request for parenting time in a case involving an unmarried mother was erroneous because the magistrate's decision did not mention the applicable law in R.C. 3109.12 nor did it appear to consider any of the best interest factors under R.C. 3109.051(D). In re P.G., 2009-Ohio-6747, 2009 Ohio App. LEXIS 5655 (Ohio Ct. App., Clermont County 2009).

**Grandparents**

Juvenile court erred in dismissing a paternal grandfather's (PGF's) complaint for visitation based on the pendency of the dependency action because the PGF satisfied the requirements for seeking visitation, intervention in the dependency action was not the exclusive means by which the PGF could seek visitation, the PGF filed his complaint for visitation in the same court in which the dependency action was pending, and the court could consolidate the two actions so that conflicts did not arise. In re N.M., 2017-Ohio-1288, 88 N.E.3d 548, 2017 Ohio App. LEXIS 1320 (Ohio Ct. App., Cuyahoga County 2017).

Because the trial court properly reviewed and discussed the statutory factors when analyzing the best interests of the children, its finding that it was in the best interests of the children to have visitation with their paternal grandparents was not an abuse of discretion. Brown v. Heitman, 2017-Ohio-4032, 2017 Ohio App. LEXIS 2073 (Ohio Ct. App., Logan County 2017).

As to a child who was born out of wedlock to parents who never married, the award of visitation to the maternal grandmother was improper because the juvenile court failed to give adequate deference and weight to the mother's decision to limit the grandmother's visitation, and the presumption that the mother's decision was in the child's best interest had not been refuted. In re K.M.-B., 2015-Ohio-4626, 48 N.E.3d 998, 2015 Ohio App. LEXIS 4520 (Ohio Ct. App., Lucas County 2015).

Trial court did not abuse its discretion by awarding the maternal grandmother of a child born to an unmarried mother visitation one weekend per month and one week each summer, because the court found visitation with the grandmother to be in the child's best interest despite the mother's wishes to the contrary. The evidence was clear that the grandmother had an ongoing and substantial relationship with the child, cared for the child almost daily when she lived with her, and provided financial support for the child and mother. In re H.A., 2013-Ohio-5457, 2013 Ohio App. LEXIS 5699 (Ohio Ct. App., Montgomery County 2013).

Trial court's order granting a child's grandfather and great-grandmother visitation with the child was not an abuse of discretion because, inter alia, a magistrate's finding that, given the child's long, secure and loving relationship with the grandfather and great-grandmother, it was in the child's best interest to be assured of continued contact with the child's extended family with whom the child had resided for extended periods, showed the trial court considered the child's best interest and did not abuse the court's discretion when the court found visitation with the grandfather and great-grandmother was in furtherance of the child's best interest. Jared S. v. Ashley G., 2008-Ohio-1297, 2008 Ohio App. LEXIS 1099 (Ohio Ct. App., Williams County 2008).

**Incarceration**

Visitation between a child and an incarcerated parent should be granted only where it is demonstrated that such visitation is in the best interests of the child: In re Hall, 65 Ohio App. 3d 88, 582 N.E.2d 1055, 1989 Ohio App. LEXIS 3970 (Ohio Ct. App., Franklin County 1989).

**Jurisdiction**

Juvenile court lacked the authority to issue any orders arising out of the grandmother's request for grandparent visitation because the juvenile court proceeded in the absence of subject matter jurisdiction and, as such, all orders emanating out of the case were void ab initio. In re R.G., 2021-Ohio-93, 2021 Ohio App. LEXIS 101 (Ohio Ct. App., Wayne County 2021).

In a grandparent visitation case, the trial court had subject matter jurisdiction under R.C. 3109.051(B)(1), as this was a divorce proceeding that involved a child in which a grandparent sought visitation, and R.C. 3109.12 applied as well because the mother was unmarried when she gave birth and there was a divorce proceeding that involved a child. Furthermore, there was no requirement in either R.C. 3109.051(B)(1) or R.C. 3109.12 that one section apply to the exclusion of the other; the standard of review, the best interest standard, was the same under both statutes; and R.C. 3109.12 did not require that the complaint be brought in juvenile court. Doughty v. Doughty, 2019-Ohio-974, 2019 Ohio App. LEXIS 1027 (Ohio Ct. App., Delaware County 2019).

Trial court lacked jurisdiction to determine visitation and companionship rights and to issue a visitation schedule because a judgment entry determining visitation issues was based upon an improper exercise of subject matter jurisdiction, and the orders contained therein exceeded its authority; the complaint seeking custody was the only pleading ever filed, and at no point in the proceedings had the paternal grandparents ever filed a pleading or otherwise invoked the trial court's jurisdiction. In re C.W., 2018-Ohio-5265, 2018 Ohio App. LEXIS 5576 (Ohio Ct. App., Lorain County 2018).

Mother's argument that the trial court lacked jurisdiction to order grandparent visitation was without merit because a journal entry simply memorialized the entire agreement of the parties; the trial court did not order grandparent visitation pursuant to the statute, but rather, the journal entry was an agreement between the parties to resolve the litigation, and it did not involve the trial court rendering a judgment or adjudicating the merits of any claims. In re C.W., 2018-Ohio-5265, 2018 Ohio App. LEXIS 5576 (Ohio Ct. App., Lorain County 2018).

Juvenile court erred when it adopted a magistrate's award to a maternal grandmother of visitation with one of her grandchildren who was born after her parents' marriage, as there was no statutory authority that permitted the juvenile court to make such an award. In re K.M.-B., 2015-Ohio-4626, 48 N.E.3d 998, 2015 Ohio App. LEXIS 4520 (Ohio Ct. App., Lucas County 2015).

Where a mother appealed the trial court's order that granted the child's biological father visitation during the following summer, the trial court had jurisdiction to enter a subsequent visitation order since that order did not interfere with and was not inconsistent with the appellate court's jurisdiction to address the prior visitation order. Tarajcak v. Petkovic, 2015-Ohio-5459, 2015 Ohio App. LEXIS 5282 (Ohio Ct. App., Geauga County 2015).

Writs of prohibition and mandamus were denied because the juvenile court judges and magistrate did not patently and unambiguously lack jurisdiction to determine child custody matters in the underlying case: Nationwide Mut. Fire Ins. Co. v. Delacruz, 2010-Ohio-6068, 2010 Ohio App. LEXIS 5113 (Ohio Ct. App., Hancock County 2010).

Doctrine of parental autonomy did not override the application of R.C. 3109.12(B) and thus, the trial court had subject matter jurisdiction to address the complaint for grandparent visitation. Although there was an equal protection violation in the case, technically speaking, the trial court did not err in concluding it had subject matter jurisdiction to proceed on the complaint. Rugola-Dye v. Dye, 2009-Ohio-2471, 2009 Ohio App. LEXIS 2082 (Ohio Ct. App., Delaware County 2009).

The court lacked jurisdiction under R.C. 3109.05.1, 3109.12 or 3111.13(C) to grant grandparent visitation rights: Borkosky v. Mihailoff, 132 Ohio App. 3d 508, 725 N.E.2d 694, 1999 Ohio App. LEXIS 960 (Ohio Ct. App., Wyandot County 1999).

The complaint of a grandparent seeking only visitation with the grandchild may not be determined by the juvenile court pursuant to its authority to determine the "custody" of children under R.C. 2151.23(A)(2): In re Gibson, 61 Ohio St. 3d 168, 573 N.E.2d 1074, 1991 Ohio LEXIS 1749 (Ohio 1991).

**Parenting time properly granted**

Trial court did not abuse its discretion in ordering one visit with an autistic child's biological father and deferring future visitation until the guardian ad litem (GAL) made recommendations, as the GAL and a counselor reported that prior visits had gone well, the GAL recommended that regular visitation and telephone contact continue under the counselor's supervision, and the record supported the trial court's finding that a major cause of the child's breakdown was his mother and stepfather's sudden move to Maryland. Tarajcak v. Petkovic, 2015-Ohio-5459, 2015 Ohio App. LEXIS 5282 (Ohio Ct. App., Geauga County 2015).

Trial court acted within its discretion in granting a father standard parenting time with his daughter under R.C. 3109.12(A) as the evidence showed that father supported the daughter for an extended period of time following the daughter's birth by adding the child to his health insurance plan and providing her with clothing, food, and money. While the mother was given an ample opportunity to present evidence during the hearing, she declined to do so. Otten v. Tuttle, 2009-Ohio-3158, 2009 Ohio App. LEXIS 2816 (Ohio Ct. App., Clermont County 2009).



**Parents of father**

Trial court's denial of a child's grandparents' request for visitation with the child was reversed because the record did not show that, in denying the request, the trial court balanced the opposition of the child's mother to visitation with the other factors specified in R.C. 3109.051(D) to determine whether such visitation was in the child's best interests. Estep v. Celek, 2009-Ohio-4990, 2009 Ohio App. LEXIS 4267 (Ohio Ct. App., Hamilton County 2009).

The parents of the natural father of a child are not qualified to seek visitation rights under R.C. 3109.12 until paternity is established by one of the methods provided for in the statute: In re Martin, 1994-Ohio-506, 68 Ohio St. 3d 250, 626 N.E.2d 82, 1994 Ohio LEXIS 47 (Ohio 1994).

**—Grandparents**

Juvenile court abused its discretion when it summarily dismissed a paternal grandmother's motion for visitation with her grandson without holding a hearing, without addressing the factors listed in R.C. 3109.051(D), and without determining whether granting visitation to the grandmother was in the child's best interest, in violation of R.C. 3109.051 and 3109.12, as the summary dismissal was in derogation of the statutes. In re Cassidy v. Wagner, 2011-Ohio-5868, 2011 Ohio App. LEXIS 4795 (Ohio Ct. App., Brown County 2011).

Sufficient evidence supported a magistrate's decision granting grandparent visitation to the paternal grandmother of a mother's children under R.C. 3109.12. The decision was a nine-page opinion and showed that the magistrate considered the factors in R.C. 3109.051(D) and specifically considered the fact that the grandmother and the children had a significant relationship before the mother ceased visitation. In re Newsome, 2008-Ohio-2132, 2008 Ohio App. LEXIS 1842 (Ohio Ct. App., Ashtabula County 2008).

**Review**

"Extraordinary circumstances" standard set forth and applied in Pettry v. Pettry, 486 N.E.2d 213 (8th Dist. 1984), and its progeny has been superseded by R.C. 3109.12 and 3109.051 and no longer applies when determining parental visitation rights; thus, the juvenile court erred in applying the "extraordinary circumstances" standard in determining whether to grant parenting time to the father, who never married the child's mother. In re L.R.M., 2015-Ohio-4445, 89 Ohio App. 3d 37, 42 N.E.3d 799, 2015 Ohio App. LEXIS 4351 (Ohio Ct. App., Butler County 2015).

There was no plain error in denying the grandmother visitation, because if the grandmother wanted to object to any of the magistrate's factual findings or the magistrate's decision to deny her application for visitation, it was incumbent upon her to file objections and support those objections with evidence, e.g., the transcript of the magistrate's hearing. In re S.H., 2014-Ohio-4476, 2014 Ohio App. LEXIS 4384 (Ohio Ct. App., Cuyahoga County 2014).

**Standing**

Juvenile court lacked subject matter jurisdiction to consider a petition for grandparent visitation by the maternal grandmother and her then-boyfriend because the boyfriend did not have the requisite legal interest at the time the action was initiated and, as such, the boyfriend lacked standing; once the boyfriend married the grandmother, he did not seek to become a party. In re R.G., 2021-Ohio-93, 2021 Ohio App. LEXIS 101 (Ohio Ct. App., Wayne County 2021).

Juvenile court's dismissal of a paternal grandmother's motion for visitation with her grandson was error where the mother was unmarried at the time of the child's birth, and the father's paternity was thereafter established; accordingly, the grandmother had standing under R.C. 3109.12(A) to seek visitation. In re Cassidy v. Wagner, 2011-Ohio-5868, 2011 Ohio App. LEXIS 4795 (Ohio Ct. App., Brown County 2011).

**Supervised visitation**

Trial court did not deny a father any parenting time with the children because there was currently no order for supervised visitation between the father and the children, but the parties were still under the agreed interim order that required the parties to follow all recommendations of the therapist selected by the father, and the therapist recommended that supervised visitation was not warranted at that time. Trent v. Taylor, 2017-Ohio-7189, 2017 Ohio App. LEXIS 3314 (Ohio Ct. App., Franklin County 2017).

All of the reasons that supported the trial court's finding of unsuitability supported its decision that requiring the father to have supervised, limited visitation with his daughter was in the best interest of the child. In re T.P., 2015-Ohio-1628, 2015 Ohio App. LEXIS 1570 (Ohio Ct. App., Summit County 2015).

**Unsupervised visitation**

Trial court exercised proper discretion when it ordered that father be allowed unsupervised visitation with parties' child because there was no evidence that he posed a danger to child, his visits with child had been appropriate and his communication with child had improved over time. Also, child had support of two counselors to assist with her transition to unsupervised visitation, and child had no trouble communicating freely with her counselors if any problems with supervised visits arose. Roderick v. Phillips, 2020-Ohio-3350, 2020 Ohio App. LEXIS 2280 (Ohio Ct. App., Summit County 2020).

It was an abuse of discretion for a trial court to grant a father unsupervised visitation with the father's child, under R.C. 3109.051(D)(7), (9), and (11), because (1) a non-party confirmed that the child, with whom the father had been having unsupervised visitation, had suffered trauma from abuse, and (2) it was revealed that the father had been diagnosed with substantial mental health disorders for which the father was not being treated, but it appeared that this factor was not considered. Morehart v. Snider, 2009-Ohio-5674, 2009 Ohio App. LEXIS 4776 (Ohio Ct. App., Summit County 2009).

**Visitation**

Evidence presented at the hearing supported the trial court's determination that it was in the child's best interest to grant the father additional parenting time as the father had successfully been granted additional parenting time during the duration of the proceedings; father's visitation time with child was positive and occurred without any adverse harmful incidents; and the parties live within close vicinity, making increased visitation with father convenient and undisruptive. Wilburn v. Ferguson, 2021-Ohio-4256, 2021 Ohio App. LEXIS 4143 (Ohio Ct. App., Lawrence County 2021).

**—Brother**

Because the record did not support the conclusion that the trial court considered the statutory factors in reaching its ultimate determination regarding visitation, it could not be determined whether it abused its discretion. The trial court made no reference to the statutory factors and did not give any indication as to why it did not award the mother the additional time associated with its standard order, particularly when she had been awarded that time on a temporary basis throughout the proceedings, and did not give any indication why it chose to reject the guardian ad litem's recommendation that the boys visit with each parent for a full week each month. Harrison v. Lewis, 2017-Ohio-275, 2017 Ohio App. LEXIS 274 (Ohio Ct. App., Summit County 2017).

**—Grandparents**

Trial court properly granted visitation rights to a child's maternal grandparents, as it was in the child's best interests based on the statutory factors that included the child's residential history, her relationships with family, her age, and family members' work obligations, and the visitation schedule was reasonable, not arbitrary, and consistent with the findings of fact. Boling v. Thacker, 2019-Ohio-3683, 2019 Ohio App. LEXIS 3768 (Ohio Ct. App., Clark County 2019).

Nothing in other cases suggested that grandparents were similarly situated to parents, and a child's parents must be afforded special consideration in determining the care and custody of the child; the trial court determined that the grandfather's unwillingness to address the mother's concerns about interactions between her child and another relative was the main obstacle in preventing the grandparents' contact with the child. Jenkins v. Jenkins, 2019-Ohio-4909, 2019 Ohio App. LEXIS 4962 (Ohio Ct. App., Lorain County 2019).

Trial court did not err by granting grandmother's motion to intervene in order to prosecute her motion for visitation with the children because the parties stipulated that the mother was deceased and that she was never married and as the evidence demonstrated that the grandmother had a colorable claim of a right to visitation. In re J.L.M., 2018-Ohio-2175, 114 N.E.3d 658, 2018 Ohio App. LEXIS 2362 (Ohio Ct. App., Summit County 2018).

Trial court did not abuse its discretion when it overruled the father's objections to the magistrate's decision related to parenting time because the record showed he never filed a complaint seeking a determination of parenting time. Consequently, a parenting time schedule had never been ordered in this case and he did not raise the issue at any time during the administrative proceedings nor did he raise at the hearing before the magistrate where evidence on the issue could have been submitted.

Mohammed Habib v. Hawa Shikur, 2018-Ohio-2955, 2018 Ohio App. LEXIS 3186 (Ohio Ct. App., Franklin County 2018).

Juvenile court did not abuse its discretion when it determined it was in the parties' children's best interest to award one of the father's two monthly weekends to the maternal grandmother for companionship or visitation rights, as in addition to his one weekend per month, the juvenile court awarded the father extended parenting time with the children during portions of major holidays and spring break, and for six consecutive weeks during the summer vacation of the school district in which the children resided. King v. King, 2016-Ohio-2681, 2016 Ohio App. LEXIS 1553 (Ohio Ct. App., Madison County 2016).

There was competent and credible evidence to support the trial court's determination that contact with the father was not in the child's best interest because though the father testified he had a close bond with the child, he had not seen her since March of 2010 and the caseworker testified the child never mentioned the father and had no emotional attachment to the father. In re K.J., 2014-Ohio-3100, 2014 Ohio App. LEXIS 3032 (Ohio Ct. App., Richland County 2014).

Trial court did not abuse its discretion in granting supervised, rather than unsupervised, visitation to the grandfather as the trial court considered the facts as they related to the best interest factors within R.C. 3109.051(D). Specifically, the mother had been the child's sole caregiver her entire life; the child had a very close relationship with the mother; the grandfather's visits with the granddaughter had been sporadic; the mother lived 12 hours away from the grandfather; and the mother had numerous concerns about the grandfather's possession of pornographic materials, his display of nude artwork in his home, and the facts that he drank non-alcoholic beer in front of the child and kept his medication where the child could reach it. In re K.C., 2013 Ohio 949, 2013 Ohio App. LEXIS 1831 (May 13, 2013).

Trial court did not abuse its discretion when it deviated from the standard order of visitation under R.C. 3109.12, as the trial court considered the factors under R.C. 3109.051(D) although it did not explicitly refer to the statute; the court considered, inter alia, the familial situations of each parent, their place of residence, their relocation intent, work schedules, and the child's age. Evangelista v. Horton, 2011-Ohio-1472, 2011 Ohio App. LEXIS 1256 (Ohio Ct. App., Mahoning County 2011).

Court's visitation award to a father was proper because the testimony indicated that the mother and the father lived within blocks of each other on the same street, the mother's grandmother, who acted as the point of custody exchange between the parties, lived next-door to the father, and therefore, transportation to facilitate the parties exercising their parenting time was not an issue of concern. In addition, the mother expressed her concern about extending the father's overnight visits during the week while the child was still very young. Pahl v. Haugh, 2011-Ohio-1302, 2011 Ohio App. LEXIS 1140 (Ohio Ct. App., Hancock County 2011).

R.C. 3109.051(G)(1) did not require a trial court's magistrate to provide an incarcerated father with the current address of the father's child, when the father's request for visitation with the child was granted, because, while R.C. 3109.12, which governed the father's situation when the father acknowledged paternity of the child as a result of genetic testing, incorporated certain parts of R.C. 3109.051, R.C. 3109.12 did not incorporate R.C. 3109.051(G) into a trial court's considerations when granting parenting time to unwed fathers. In re Brown, 2009-Ohio-2192, 2009 Ohio App. LEXIS 1840 (Ohio Ct. App., Seneca County 2009).

R.C. 3109.03 did not require a trial court's magistrate to provide an incarcerated father with the current address of the father's child, when the father's request for visitation with the child was granted, because (1) the father acknowledged the father's paternity as a result of genetic testing, so the statute did not apply, and (2) R.C. 3109.12 applied specifically to the father's situation. In re Brown, 2009-Ohio-2192, 2009 Ohio App. LEXIS 1840 (Ohio Ct. App., Seneca County 2009).

Ohio courts are obligated to afford "special weight" to the wishes of the parents of minor children concerning non-parental visitation, but, while a court is required to consider the wishes of the parents regarding the requested visitation, nothing suggests that a parent's wishes should be placed before the child's best interest. Jared S. v. Ashley G., 2008-Ohio-1297, 2008 Ohio App. LEXIS 1099 (Ohio Ct. App., Williams County 2008).

Trial court's order granting a child's grandfather and great-grandmother visitation with the child was not an abuse of discretion because, inter alia, it was apparent that the wishes of the child's parents were not ignored, and, apparently, the testimony on behalf of the grandfather and great-grandmother was found to be more credible than that presented on behalf of the child's parents. Jared S. v. Ashley G., 2008-Ohio-1297, 2008 Ohio App. LEXIS 1099 (Ohio Ct. App., Williams County 2008).

Pursuant to R.C. 3109.051(D)(15), the trial court gave "special weight" to the wishes and concerns of a minor child's parents that a maternal step-grandparent's request for unsupervised visitation with the child under R.C. 3109.12 was not in the child's best interest due to fear of inappropriate contact; the grandfather did not provide evidence that such visitation was in the child's best interest or that it was a compelling interest that overrode the parents' objections. In re Sadie Elizabeth S., 2006-Ohio-2928, 2006 Ohio App. LEXIS 2800 (Ohio Ct. App., Fulton County 2006).

While Ohio courts are obligated to afford special weight to the wishes of parents of minor children when considering petitions for non-parental visitation made pursuant to R.C. 3109.11 or 3109.12, those statutes do not unconstitutionally infringe on a parent's fundamental right under U.S. Const. amend. XIV to make decisions concerning the care, custody, and control of his or her child. The statutes limit the parties who can petition for visitation, limit the application of the statutes to cases where there is a specified predicate event or condition, and expressly identify the parents' wishes and concerns regarding visitation as a factor the court must consider in making its determination. Harrold v. Collier, 2005-Ohio-5334, 107 Ohio St. 3d 44, 836 N.E.2d 1165, 2005 Ohio LEXIS 2241 (Ohio 2005), cert. denied, 547 U.S. 1004, 126 S. Ct. 1474, 164 L. Ed. 2d 248, 2006 U.S. LEXIS 2052 (U.S. 2006).

It was clear from both the magistrate's decision and the trial court's entry adopting the decision, that the court considered both the mother's and maternal grandmother's proposed visitation schedules before entering its decision, in addition to its thorough analysis under R.C. 3109.051(D). The juvenile court specifically noted that it had reviewed both the mother and grandmother's visitation wishes and the report submitted by the child's guardian ad litem. In re J. F., 2005-Ohio-4816, 2005 Ohio App. LEXIS 4361 (Ohio Ct. App., Cuyahoga County 2005).

Juvenile court did not abuse its discretion in awarding visitation rights to the grandmother and the decision was supported by ample evidence. In accordance with R.C. 3109.051(D), in addition to several other findings, the magistrate noted the grandmother's strong, positive bond with her grandson and her daily care of the child since his birth and also noted that the guardian ad litem recommended that the child's best interests would be served by an award of visitation rights to his grandmother. In re J. F., 2005-Ohio-4816, 2005 Ohio App. LEXIS 4361 (Ohio Ct. App., Cuyahoga County 2005).

Trial court erred in awarding grandparent visitation upon a father's motion for contempt of a consent agreement as the grandparents did not file a motion for grandparent visitation and the consent order merely provided that if a mother failed to cooperate in allowing the grandparents babysitting time, the grandparents could file a motion for visitation. In re Street, 2005-Ohio-4469, 2005 Ohio App. LEXIS 4046 (Ohio Ct. App., Belmont County 2005).

**—Nonparents**

Trial court's decision to dismiss a husband's complaint for child visitation due to lack of standing was error because, pursuant to R.C. 3109.12, the husband had standing to seek visitation with the child where the child's mother was unmarried at the time of the child's birth and the husband was a relative of the child's mother by affinity. McFall v. Watson, 2008-Ohio-5205, 2008 Ohio App. LEXIS 4373 (Ohio Ct. App., Vinton County 2008).

Trial court's adoption of a magistrate's decision to grant a child's great-aunt specific visitation with the child was against the manifest weight of the evidence, as there was no "special weight" accorded to the mother's wishes to deny the visitation request, and the mother's reasons for such denial were reasonably objective in the circumstances; the deference due to the mother's wishes, based on her due process rights under U.S. Const. amend. XIV, was not provided by following the magistrate's bare bones findings. In re Madison C., 2007-Ohio-5983, 2007 Ohio App. LEXIS 5263 (Ohio Ct. App., Montgomery County 2007).

**—Relative of the mother**

As a child's maternal great aunt did not file a motion for visitation in a legal custody proceeding, that was not at issue, although the parties agreed that she would have specific visitation weekly with the child. D.T. v. Turner, 2015-Ohio-2333, 2015 Ohio App. LEXIS 2250 (Ohio Ct. App., Jefferson County 2015).

Leave to intervene in visitation proceedings was improperly denied to a step-grandmother for lack of standing because pursuant to R.C. 3109.12, since the mother was unwed when the child was born, any relative of the mother could seek visitation rights; based on the case law interpretation of step-relations as relatives for the purposes of non-parental visitation statutes, the step-grandmother had standing based on her relationship to the mother after her marriage to the stepfather, who was the step-grandmother's son. McFall v. Watson, 2008-Ohio-5204, 178 Ohio App. 3d 540, 899 N.E.2d 158, 2008 Ohio App. LEXIS 4374 (Ohio Ct. App., Vinton County 2008).

## RESEARCH REFERENCES AND PRACTICE AIDS

**Cross-References to Related Sections**

Child support, RC § 3109.05.

Contempt action for failure to comply with visitation order, RC § 2705.031.

Duties of public children services agency as to children in need of public care or protective services, RC § 5153.16.

Effect of granting relief on parenting time, companionship or visitation rights and on arrearages, RC § 3119.964.

Effects of final and enforceable acknowledgment, RC § 3111.26.

Form for acknowledgment of paternity affidavit, RC § 3111.31.

Judgment determining existence of parent and child relationship, RC § 3111.13.

Supervision of parenting time or visitation or companionship rights, RC § 3113.31.

Support order to include specific provisions for different time periods, RC § 3119.08.

Visitation or companionship rights, RC § 3109.051.

**Ohio Administrative Code**

Department of job and family services, division of social services—

School child day care centers: parental access to child and facility; limitations. OAC 5101:2-17-39.

**Practice Manuals and Treatises**

Ohio Transaction Guide: Family Law & Forms § 9.21 Rights of Cohabiting Couples

# TITLE 33

# EDUCATION — LIBRARIES



## CHAPTER 3345

## STATE UNIVERSITIES — GENERAL POWERS



### § 3345.27 Senior citizens to attend classes on a nontuition, noncredit, space available basis; tuition or fee for receiving credit.

(A) Each state university or college shall permit any person who is sixty years of age or older and who has resided in the state for at least one year to attend its courses and classes without charging that person a tuition or matriculation fee, provided the attendance is on a noncredit basis, is in courses where classroom space is available, and is approved by the instructors of the courses involved. The university or college may require payment of special fees, including any laboratory fees, if the fees are required of all students taking a course. Each university or college shall issue rules for determining the availability of classroom space and may issue such other rules as it considers necessary to implement this section, including rules exempting from the requirements of this section courses or classes for which special course or training prerequisites apply, in which physical demands upon students are inappropriate for imposition upon persons sixty years of age or older, or in which the number of participating regular students is insufficient to cover the university's or college's course-related expenses. A university or college also may extend to persons attending its courses and classes under this section any other student rights or privileges it considers appropriate.

(B) A state university or college may permit a person to attend its courses and classes and to receive credit for a course taken under the conditions set forth in division (A) of this section if that person's family income is less than two hundred per cent of the federal poverty guideline, as revised annually by the United States secretary of health and human services in accordance with section 673 of the "Community Services Block Grant Act," 95 Stat. 511 (1981) 42 U.S.C.A. 9902, as amended, for a family size equal to the size of the family of the person whose income is being determined. However, a person receiving credit for attending courses or classes under this division may be charged a tuition or matriculation fee in an amount no greater than the amount of any part-time student instructional grant awarded to that person by the state university or college in its discretion.

(C) For the purposes of this section, "state university or college" means any of the following:

(1) State universities referred to in section 3345.011 of the Revised Code;

(2) Community colleges created pursuant to Chapter 3354. of the Revised Code;

(3) University branches created pursuant to Chapter 3355. of the Revised Code;

(4) Technical colleges created pursuant to Chapter 3357. of the Revised Code;

(5) State community colleges created pursuant to Chapter 3358. of the Revised Code;

(6) Municipal educational institutions serving as affiliated units pursuant to section 3349.31 of the Revised Code.

**HISTORY:**

136 v S 497 (Eff 8-11-76); 139 v H 1 (Eff 8-5-81); 147 v H 147. Eff 3-30-99.

Titles 11 — 37

# TITLE 37

# HEALTH — SAFETY — MORALS



# CHAPTER 3701

# DEPARTMENT OF HEALTH

Miscellaneous



School Health and Safety Network



## MISCELLANEOUS

**§ 3701.74 Patient, personal representative or authorized person may request access to medical record.**

(A) As used in this section and section 3701.741 of the Revised Code:

(1) "Ambulatory care facility" means a facility that provides medical, diagnostic, or surgical treatment to patients who do not require hospitalization, including a dialysis center, ambulatory surgical facility, cardiac catheterization facility, diagnostic imaging center, extracorporeal shock wave lithotripsy center, home health agency, inpatient hospice, birthing center, radiation therapy center, emergency facility, and an urgent care center. "Ambulatory care facility" does not include the private office of a physician or dentist, whether the office is for an individual or group practice.

(2) "Chiropractor" means an individual licensed under Chapter 4734. of the Revised Code to practice chiropractic.

(3) "Emergency facility" means a hospital emergency department or any other facility that provides emergency medical services.

(4) "Health care practitioner" means all of the following:

(a) A dentist or dental hygienist licensed under Chapter 4715. of the Revised Code;

(b) A registered or licensed practical nurse licensed under Chapter 4723. of the Revised Code;

(c) An optometrist licensed under Chapter 4725. of the Revised Code;

(d) A dispensing optician, spectacle dispensing optician, contact lens dispensing optician, or spectacle-contact lens dispensing optician licensed under Chapter 4725. of the Revised Code;

(e) A pharmacist licensed under Chapter 4729. of the Revised Code;

(f) A physician;

(g) A physician assistant authorized under Chapter 4730. of the Revised Code to practice as a physician assistant;

(h) A practitioner of a limited branch of medicine issued a certificate under Chapter 4731. of the Revised Code;

(i) A psychologist licensed under Chapter 4732. of the Revised Code;

(j) A chiropractor;

(k) A hearing aid dealer or fitter licensed under Chapter 4747. of the Revised Code;

(*l*) A speech-language pathologist or audiologist licensed under Chapter 4753. of the Revised Code;

(m) An occupational therapist or occupational therapy assistant licensed under Chapter 4755. of the Revised Code;

(n) A physical therapist or physical therapy assistant licensed under Chapter 4755. of the Revised Code;

(o) A licensed professional clinical counselor, licensed professional counselor, social worker, independent social worker, independent marriage and family therapist, or marriage and family therapist licensed, or a social work assistant registered, under Chapter 4757. of the Revised Code;

(p) A dietitian licensed under Chapter 4759. of the Revised Code;

(q) A respiratory care professional licensed under Chapter 4761. of the Revised Code;

(r) An emergency medical technician-basic, emergency medical technician-intermediate, or emergency medical technician-paramedic certified under Chapter 4765. of the Revised Code.

(5) "Health care provider" means a hospital, ambulatory care facility, long-term care facility, pharmacy, emergency facility, or health care practitioner.

(6) "Hospital" has the same meaning as in section 3727.01 of the Revised Code.

(7) "Long-term care facility" means a nursing home, residential care facility, or home for the aging, as those terms are defined in section 3721.01 of the Revised Code; a residential facility licensed under section 5119.34 of the Revised Code that provides accommodations, supervision, and personal care services for three to sixteen unrelated adults; a nursing facility, as defined in section 5165.01 of the Revised Code; a skilled nursing facility, as defined in section 5165.01 of the Revised Code; and an intermediate care facility for individuals with intellectual disabilities, as defined in section 5124.01 of the Revised Code.

(8) "Medical record" means data in any form that pertains to a patient's medical history, diagnosis, prognosis, or medical condition and that is generated and maintained by a health care provider in the process of the patient's health care treatment.

(9) "Medical records company" means a person who stores, locates, or copies medical records for a health care provider, or is compensated for doing so by a health care provider, and charges a fee for providing medical records to a patient or patient's representative.

(10) "Patient" means either of the following:

(a) An individual who received health care treatment from a health care provider;

(b) A guardian, as defined in section 1337.11 of the Revised Code, of an individual described in division (A)(10)(a) of this section.

(11) "Patient's personal representative" means a minor patient's parent or other person acting in loco parentis, a court-appointed guardian, or a person with durable power of attorney for health care for a patient, the executor or administrator of the patient's estate, or the person responsible for the patient's estate if it is not to be probated. "Patient's personal representative" does not include an insurer authorized under Title XXXIX of the Revised Code to do the business of sickness and accident insurance in this state, a health insuring corporation holding a certificate of authority under Chapter 1751. of the Revised Code, or any other person not named in this division.

(12) "Pharmacy" has the same meaning as in section 4729.01 of the Revised Code.

(13) "Physician" means a person authorized under Chapter 4731. of the Revised Code to practice medicine and surgery, osteopathic medicine and surgery, or podiatric medicine and surgery.

(14) "Authorized person" means a person to whom a patient has given written authorization to act on the patient's behalf regarding the patient's medical record.

(B) A patient, a patient's personal representative, or an authorized person who wishes to examine or obtain a copy of part or all of a medical record shall submit to the health care provider a written request signed by the patient, personal representative, or authorized person dated not more than one year before the date on which it is submitted. The request shall indicate whether the copy is to be sent to the requestor, physician or chiropractor, or held for the requestor at the office of the health care provider. Within a reasonable time after receiving a request that meets the requirements of this division and includes sufficient information to identify the record requested, a health care provider that has the patient's medical records shall permit the patient to examine the record during regular business hours without charge or, on request, shall provide a copy of the record in accordance with section 3701.741 of the Revised Code, except that if a physician, psychologist, licensed professional clinical counselor, licensed professional counselor, independent social worker, social worker, independent marriage and family therapist, marriage and family therapist, or chiropractor who has treated the patient determines for clearly stated treatment reasons that disclosure of the requested record is likely to have an adverse effect on the patient, the health care provider shall provide the record to a physician, psychologist, licensed professional clinical counselor, licensed professional counselor, independent social worker, social worker, independent marriage and family therapist, marriage and family therapist, or chiropractor designated by the patient. The health care provider shall take reasonable steps to establish the identity of the person making the request to examine or obtain a copy of the patient's record.

(C) If a health care provider fails to furnish a medical record as required by division (B) of this section, the patient, personal representative, or authorized person who requested the record may bring a civil action to enforce the patient's right of access to the record.

(D)(1) This section does not apply to medical records whose release is covered by section 173.20 or 3721.13 of the Revised Code, by Chapter 1347., 5119., or 5122. of the Revised Code, by 42 C.F.R. part 2, "Confidentiality of Alcohol and Drug Abuse Patient Records," or by 42 C.F.R. 483.10.

(2) Nothing in this section is intended to supersede the confidentiality provisions of sections 2305.24, 2305.25, 2305.251, and 2305.252 of the Revised Code.

**HISTORY:**

140 v H 433 (Eff 3-28-85); 148 v H 508 (Eff 3-22-2001); 148 v H 506 (Eff 4-10-2001); 149 v S 179. Eff 4-9-2003; 150 v H 331, § 1, eff. 12-21-04; 152 v H 119, § 101.01, eff. 9-29-07; 2011 HB 153, § 101.01, eff. July 1, 2011; 2012 HB 487, § 101.01, eff. Sept. 10, 2012; 2013 HB 59, § 101.01, eff. Sept. 29, 2013; 2014 HB 232, § 1, eff. July 10, 2014; 2014 HB 483, § 101.01, eff. Sept. 15, 2014.

**Editor's Notes**

The provisions of § 3 of SB 179 (149 v S 179) read as follows:

SECTION 3. Section 3701.74 of the Revised Code is presented in this act as a composite of the section as amended by both Am. Sub. H.B. 508 and Sub. H.B. 506 of the 123rd General Assembly. The General Assembly, applying the principle stated in division (B) of section 1.52 of the Revised Code that amendments are to be harmonized if reasonably capable of simultaneous operation, finds that the composite is the resulting version of the section in effect prior to the effective date of the section as presented in this act.

**Amendment Notes**

The 2014 amendment by HB 232, in (A)(4)(o), inserted "licensed" preceding "professional" twice and inserted "independent marriage and family therapist, or marriage and family therapist"; inserted "psychologist, licensed professional clinical counselor, licensed professional counselor, independent social worker, social worker, independent marriage and family therapist, marriage and family therapist" twice in the third sentence of (B); and made related and stylistic changes.

The 2013 amendment, in (A)(7), substituted "section 5119.34" for "section 5119.22," "as defined in section 5165.01" for "or intermediate care facility for the mentally retarded, as those terms are defined in section 5111.20," and "as defined in section 5165.01 of the Revised Code; and an intermediate care facility for individuals with intellectual disabilities, as defined in section 5124.01 of the Revised Code" for "under Title XVIII of the 'Social Security Act,' 49 Stat. 286 (1965), 42 U.S.C.A. 1395, as amended".

The 2012 amendment, in (A)(7), substituted "a residential facility licensed under section 5119.22" for "an adult care facility, as defined in section 5119.70" and inserted "that provides accommodations, supervision, and personal care services for three to sixteen unrelated adults".

The 2011 amendment substituted "section 5119.70" for "section 3722.01" in (A)(7).

152 v H 119, effective September 29, 2007, in (B), substituted "one year" for "sixty days".

The 2014 amendment by HB 483 substituted "Chapter 1347., 5119., or 5122." for "Chapter 1347. or 5122." in (D)(1).

## NOTES TO DECISIONS

Analysis



**Failure to provide**

Dentist failed to demonstrate a patient's claim, seeking his dental casts, impressions, and molds was moot, and, as such, the dentist was not entitled to summary judgment because there was a genuine issue of material fact as to whether the dentist possessed cast/models and refused to provide them to the patient. Johnson v. Barbosa, 2018-Ohio-2558, 2018 Ohio App. LEXIS 2833 (Ohio Ct. App., Summit County 2018).

Patient's claim for failure to provide medical records was improperly dismissed by the trial court because, although the records were provided, it was after the lawsuit was filed and ignored the cost of counsel in pursuing the claim. Further, the patient was unable to review the records in contemplation of the action and should not have been obligated to file a lawsuit to obtain her medical records. S.S. v. Ruddock, 2014-Ohio-2270, 2014 Ohio App. LEXIS 2210 (Ohio Ct. App., Cuyahoga County 2014), dismissed, 2015 Ohio Misc. LEXIS 16270 (Ohio C.P. Oct. 19, 2015).

**Medical record**

Trial court properly awarded summary judgment to defendant hospital regarding plaintiff law firm's request for copies of plaintiff client's medical billing and the fees charged because a billing record was not generated and maintained by the health care provider in the process of a patient's health care treatment, and, thus, billing records were not medical records and not subject to the statutory pricing requirements. Fuller v. Univ. Hosps. Med. Group, Inc., 2021-Ohio-2518, 175 N.E.3d 962, 2021 Ohio App. LEXIS 2480 (Ohio Ct. App., Cuyahoga County 2021).

Because the Ohio General Assembly did not limit the definition of "medical record" in this statute to data in a medical-records department, the physical location of the data is not relevant to the determination whether that data qualifies as a medical record; thus, the appellate court erred in holding that the medical record sought by plaintiff consisted only of information maintained by the medical-records department. Griffith v. Aultman Hosp., 2016-Ohio-1138, 146 Ohio St. 3d 196, 54 N.E.3d 1196, 2016 Ohio LEXIS 759 (Ohio 2016).

For purposes of this statute, "maintain" means that a healthcare provided has made a decision to keep or preserve data; thus, the location where that data was kept was not the focus when deciding whether data was part of a medical record. Griffith v. Aultman Hosp., 2016-Ohio-1138, 146 Ohio St. 3d 196, 54 N.E.3d 1196, 2016 Ohio LEXIS 759 (Ohio 2016).

There was no genuine issue of material fact as to whether a hospital had produced a decedent's entire medical record, as information that a provider decides not to maintain is not part of the medical record and nothing indicates that the statute, the purpose of which is to enable a patient to obtain his file, was intended to be used as a broad discovery device. Gene'a Griffith v. Aultman Hosp., 2014-Ohio-1218, 2014 Ohio App. LEXIS 1147 (Ohio Ct. App., Stark County 2014), rev'd, 2016-Ohio-1138, 146 Ohio St. 3d 196, 54 N.E.3d 1196, 2016 Ohio LEXIS 759 (Ohio 2016).

**Prisoners**

Prisoner who admitted receipt of the requested documents had no private cause of action against an individual under R.C. 3701.74; in addition, where no judicial disqualification proceeding was pending and R.C. 2701.03(B)(1) met the requirements of due process and was constitutional, a hospital records custodian was entitled to summary judgment. Talley v. Springfield, 2003-Ohio-3979, 2003 Ohio App. LEXIS 3556 (Ohio Ct. App., Montgomery County 2003).

**Release**

Trial court erred by applying the release to preclude the patient's claims and by finding that she had breached the agreement by filing the action because the release did not manifest an intent to release the doctor from liability concerning violations of Ohio's informed consent law, medical record release laws, fraud and misrepresentation claims regarding the pregnancy itself, or spoliation of evidence claims. S.S. v. Ruddock, 2014-Ohio-2270, 2014 Ohio App. LEXIS 2210 (Ohio Ct. App., Cuyahoga County 2014), dismissed, 2015 Ohio Misc. LEXIS 16270 (Ohio C.P. Oct. 19, 2015).

RESEARCH REFERENCES AND PRACTICE AIDS

**Cross-References to Related Sections**

Hospitalization of the mentally ill, RC § 5122.01 et seq.

Information disclosed to hospital utilization review committee, RC § 2305.24.

Personal information systems, RC § 1347.01 et seq.

**Practice Forms**

Authorization for Release of Information in Medical Records, Ohio Transaction Guide: Family Law & Forms § 6.220

## § 3701.741 Maximum allowable fees for providing copies of medical records; certain copies to be provided without charge.

(A) Each health care provider and medical records company shall provide copies of medical records in accordance with this section.

(B) Except as provided in divisions (C) and (E) of this section, a health care provider or medical records company that receives a request for a copy of a patient's medical record shall charge not more than the amounts set forth in this section.

(1) If the request is made by the patient or the patient's personal representative, total costs for copies and all services related to those copies shall not exceed the sum of the following:

(a) Except as provided in division (B)(1)(b) of this section, with respect to data recorded on paper or electronically, the following amounts adjusted in accordance with section 3701.742 of the Revised Code:

(i) Two dollars and seventy-four cents per page for the first ten pages;

(ii) Fifty-seven cents per page for pages eleven through fifty;

(iii) Twenty-three cents per page for pages fifty-one and higher;

(b) With respect to data resulting from an x-ray, magnetic resonance imaging (MRI), or computed axial tomography (CAT) scan and recorded on paper or film, one dollar and eighty-seven cents per page;

(c) The actual cost of any related postage incurred by the health care provider or medical records company.

(2) If the request is made other than by the patient or the patient's personal representative, total costs for copies and all services related to those copies shall not exceed the sum of the following:

(a) An initial fee of sixteen dollars and eighty-four cents adjusted in accordance with section 3701.742 of the Revised Code, which shall compensate for the records search;

(b) Except as provided in division (B)(2)(c) of this section, with respect to data recorded on paper or electronically, the following amounts adjusted in accordance with section 3701.742 of the Revised Code:

(i) One dollar and eleven cents per page for the first ten pages;

(ii) Fifty-seven cents per page for pages eleven through fifty;

(iii) Twenty-three cents per page for pages fifty-one and higher.

(c) With respect to data resulting from an x-ray, magnetic resonance imaging (MRI), or computed axial tomography (CAT) scan and recorded on paper or film, one dollar and eighty-seven cents per page;

(d) The actual cost of any related postage incurred by the health care provider or medical records company.

(C)(1) On request, a health care provider or medical records company shall provide one copy of the patient's medical record and one copy of any records regarding treatment performed subsequent to the original request, not including copies of records already provided, without charge to the following:

(a) The bureau of workers' compensation, in accordance with Chapters 4121. and 4123. of the Revised Code and the rules adopted under those chapters;

(b) The industrial commission, in accordance with Chapters 4121. and 4123. of the Revised Code and the rules adopted under those chapters;

(c) The department of medicaid or a county department of job and family services, in accordance with Chapters 5160., 5161., 5162., 5163., 5164., 5165., 5166., and 5167. of the Revised Code and the rules adopted under those chapters;

(d) The attorney general, in accordance with sections 2743.51 to 2743.72 of the Revised Code and any rules that may be adopted under those sections;

(e) A patient, patient's personal representative, or authorized person if the medical record is necessary to support a claim under Title II or Title XVI of the "Social Security Act," 49 Stat. 620 (1935), 42 U.S.C.A. 401 and 1381, as amended, and the request is accompanied by documentation that a claim has been filed.

(2) Nothing in division (C)(1) of this section requires a health care provider or medical records company to provide a copy without charge to any person or entity not listed in division (C)(1) of this section.

(D) Division (C) of this section shall not be construed to supersede any rule of the bureau of workers' compensation, the industrial commission, or the department of medicaid.

(E) A health care provider or medical records company may enter into a contract with either of the following for the copying of medical records at a fee other than as provided in division (B) of this section:

(1) A patient, a patient's personal representative, or an authorized person;

(2) An insurer authorized under Title XXXIX of the Revised Code to do the business of sickness and accident insurance in this state or health insuring corporations holding a certificate of authority under Chapter 1751. of the Revised Code.

(F) This section does not apply to medical records the copying of which is covered by section 173.20 of the Revised Code or by 42 C.F.R. 483.10.

**HISTORY:**

148 v H 508. Eff 3-22-2001; 150 v H 95, § 1, eff. 6-26-03; 150 v H 331, § 1, eff. 12-21-04; 152 v H 119, § 101.01, eff. 9-29-07; 152 v H 125, § 1, eff. 6-25-08; 2013 HB 59, § 101.01, eff. Sept. 29, 2013.

**Editor's Notes**

The provisions of § 177 of H.B. 95 (150 v H 95) read as follows:

SECTION 177. Sections 2743.51, 2743.60, 2743.65, and 3701.741 of the Revised Code, as amended by Section 1 of this act, apply to claims filed under section 2743.56 of the Revised Code that are based on criminally injurious conduct occuring on and after July 1, 2003.

**Amendment Notes**

The 2013 amendment added "adjusted in accordance with section 3701.742 of the Revised Code" in the introductory language of (B)(1)(a) and (B)(2)(a) and (B)(2)(a); substituted "medicaid" for "job and family services" in (C)(1)(c) and (D); and substituted "Chapters 5160., 5161., 5162., 5163., 5164., 5165., 5166., and 5167." for "Chapters 5101. and 5111." in (C)(1)(c).

152 v H 125, effective June 25, 2008, rewrote the section.

152 v H 119, effective September 29, 2007, in (C)(1)(c), substituted "or a county department of job and family services, in accordance with Chapter 5101." for "in accordance with Chapters 5101. and 5111."

NOTES TO DECISIONS

**Amount charged for medical records**

Trial court properly awarded summary judgment to a hospital regarding a law firm's request for copies of a client's medical billing and the fees charged for the copies because a billing record was not generated and maintained by the health care provider in the process of a patient's health care treatment, and, thus, billing records were not medical records and not subject to the statutory pricing requirements. Fuller v. Univ. Hosps. Med. Group, Inc., 2021-Ohio-2518, 175 N.E.3d 962, 2021 Ohio App. LEXIS 2480 (Ohio Ct. App., Cuyahoga County 2021).

Medical records company's motion to dismiss plaintiff's complaint was granted because the company was authorized to contract at different rates for copies of medical records for use in litigation pursuant to R.C. 3701.741(E) and was not bound by the charges listed in R.C. 3701.741(B)(2). Bergmoser v. Smart Document Solutions, LLC, 2007 U.S. Dist. LEXIS 12224 (N.D. Ohio Feb. 22, 2007), aff'd, 268 Fed. Appx. 392, 2008 FED App. 0133N, 2008 U.S. App. LEXIS 6581 (6th Cir. Ohio 2008).

Medical records company's motion to dismiss plaintiff's complaint was granted because the company was authorized to contract at different rates for copies of medical records for use in litigation pursuant to R.C. 3701.741(E) and was not bound by the charges listed in R.C. 3701.741(B)(2). Bergmoser v. Smart Document Solutions, LLC, 2007 U.S.

Dist. LEXIS 12224 (N.D. Ohio Feb. 22, 2007), aff'd, 268 Fed. Appx. 392, 2008 FED App. 0133N, 2008 U.S. App. LEXIS 6581 (6th Cir. Ohio 2008).

### NOTES TO UNPUBLISHED DECISIONS

**Amount charged for medical records**

*Unpublished decision:* District court properly granted Fed. R. Civ. P. 12(b)(6) dismissal of an action by consumers who alleged that medical records processing companies violated the Ohio Consumer Sales Practice Act (OCSPA), R.C. 1345.01 et seq., by charging consumers more than the actual cost for shipping the requested medical records; because the parties entered into contracts that were expressly authorized by the Medical Records Statute, R.C. 3701.741(E), the transactions were outside the scope of the OCSPA pursuant to R.C. 1345.12(A) and outside the schedule of charges set forth in § 3701.741(B).Bergmoser v. Smart Document Solutions, LLC, 268 Fed. Appx. 392, 2008 FED App. 0133N, 2008 U.S. App. LEXIS 6581 (6th Cir. Ohio 2008).

Titles 11 — 37

### ATTORNEY GENERAL OPINIONS

A county department of job and family services is not included within the language "[t]he department of job and family services, in accordance with [R.C. Chapter 5101] and the rules adopted under those chapters," as used in R.C. 3701.741(C)(1)(c). 2005 Ohio Op. Att'y Gen. No. 039 (2005).

## § 3701.742 Consumer price index adjustment to fees for providing medical records.

The amounts specified in division (B) of section 3701.741 of the Revised Code shall be adjusted annually in accordance with this section. These amounts plus any amounts previously computed by annual adjustments made under this section shall be increased or decreased by the average percentage of increase or decrease in the consumer price index for all urban consumers (United States city average, all items), prepared by the United States department of labor, bureau of labor statistics, for the immediately preceding calendar year over the calendar year immediately preceding that year, as reported by the bureau. The director of health shall make this determination and adjust the amounts accordingly. The director shall make a list of the adjusted amounts available to the public on the internet web site maintained by the department of health.

**HISTORY:**

148 v H 508. Eff 3-22-2001; 150 v H 331, § 1, eff. 12-21-04; 2013 HB 59, § 101.01, eff. Sept. 29, 2013.

**Amendment Notes**

The 2013 amendment, in the first sentence, deleted "Not later than January 31, 2006" from the beginning and substituted "shall be adjusted annually in accordance with this section" for "and, not later than the first day of January of each year thereafter"; in the second sentence, substituted "These amounts plus any amounts previously computed by annual" for "any amounts computed by" and "immediately preceding calendar year over the calendar year immediately preceding that year" for "twelve-calendar-month period prior to the immediately preceding first day of January over the immediately preceding twelve-calendar-month period"; rewrote the last sentence, which formerly read: "The director shall provide a list of the adjusted amounts to any party upon request and the department of health shall make the list available to the public on its internet web site"; and made related and stylistic changes.

# SCHOOL HEALTH AND SAFETY NETWORK

## § 3701.94 Establishment of patient centered medical home program.

There is hereby established the patient centered medical home program in the department of health. The patient centered medical home model of care is an advanced model of primary care in which care teams attend to the multifaceted needs of patients, providing whole person comprehensive and coordinated patient centered care.

**HISTORY:**

2013 HB 59, § 101.01, eff. Sept. 29, 2013.

**Editor's Notes**

This section concerned handling sources of radiation.

Former § 3701.94 [128 v 728], was repealed by 140 v H 29, § 2, effective March 28, 1985.

## § 3701.941 Certification of providers of medical home care program.

(A) As part of the patient centered medical home program established under section 3701.94 of the Revised Code, the department of health shall establish a voluntary patient centered medical home certification program.

(B) Each primary care practice, that seeks a patient centered medical home certificate shall submit an application on a form prepared by the department. The department may require an application fee and annual renewal fee as determined by the department. If the department establishes a fee under this section, the fee shall be in an amount that is sufficient to cover the cost of any on-site evaluations conducted by the department or an entity under contract with the department pursuant to section 3701.942 of the Revised Code.

(C) A practice certified under this section shall do all of the following:

(1) Meet any standards developed by national independent accrediting and medical home organizations, as determined by the department;

(2) Develop a systematic follow-up procedure for patients, including the use of health information technology and patient registries;

(3) Implement and maintain health information technology that meets the requirements of 42 U.S.C. 300jj;

(4) Comply with the reporting requirements of section 3701.942 of the Revised Code;

(5) Meet any process, outcome, and quality standards specified by the department of health;

(6) Meet any other requirements established by the department.

(D) The department shall seek to do all of the following through the certification of patient centered medical homes:

(1) Expand, enhance, and encourage the use of primary care providers, including primary care physicians, advanced practice registered nurses, and physician assistants, as personal clinicians;

(2) Develop a focus on delivering high-quality, efficient, and effective health care services;

(3) Encourage patient centered care and the provision of care that is appropriate for a patient's race, ethnicity, and language;

(4) Encourage the education and active participation of patients and patients' families or legal guardians, as appropriate, in decision making and care plan development;

(5) Provide patients with consistent, ongoing contact with a personal clinician or team of clinical professionals to ensure continuous and appropriate care;

(6) Ensure that patient centered medical homes develop and maintain appropriate comprehensive care plans for patients with complex or chronic conditions, including an assessment of health risks and chronic conditions;

(7) Ensure that patient centered medical homes plan for transition of care from youth to adult to senior;

(8) Enable and encourage use of a range of qualified health care professionals, including dedicated care coordinators, in a manner that enables those professionals to practice to the fullest extent of their professional licenses.

**HISTORY:**

2013 HB 59, § 101.01, eff. Sept. 29, 2013.

## § 3701.942 Compliance with certification standards.

(A) Each certified patient centered medical home shall report health care quality and performance information to the department of health, including any data necessary for monitoring compliance with certification standards and for evaluating the impact of patient centered medical homes on health care quality, cost, and outcomes.

(B) The department may contract with a private entity to evaluate the effectiveness of certified patient centered medical homes. The department may provide the entity with data collected under division (A) of this section.

(C) The department may contract with national independent accrediting and medical home organizations to provide on-site evaluation of primary care practices and verification of data collected under division (A) of this section.

(D) Data collected under this section is not a public record under section 149.43 of the Revised Code.

**HISTORY:**

2013 HB 59, § 101.01, eff. Sept. 29, 2013.

### § 3701.943 Program reporting requirements.

(A) The department of health shall submit a report to the governor and, in accordance with section 101.68 of the Revised Code, the general assembly, evaluating the patient centered medical home program not later than three years after rules adopted pursuant to section 3701.944 of the Revised Code first become effective. The department shall submit a second report not later than five years after those rules first become effective.

(B) The reports submitted under division (A) of this section shall include all of the following:

(1) The number of patients receiving primary care services from certified patient centered medical homes and the number and characteristics of those patients with complex or chronic conditions. To the extent available, information regarding the income, race, ethnicity, and language of patients shall be included in the reports;

(2) The number and geographic distribution of certified patient centered medical homes;

(3) Performance of and quality of care measures implemented by certified patient centered medical homes;

(4) Preventive care measures implemented by certified patient centered medical homes;

(5) Payment arrangements of certified patient centered medical homes;

(6) Costs related to implementation of the patient centered medical home program and payment of care coordination fees;

(7) The estimated effect of certified patient centered medical homes on health disparities;

(8) The estimated savings from establishing the patient centered medical home program, as those savings apply to the fee for service, managed care, and state-based purchasing sectors.

**HISTORY:**

2013 HB 59, § 101.01, eff. Sept. 29, 2013.

### § 3701.944 Adoption of rules for patient centered medical homes.

The department of health shall adopt rules in accordance with Chapter 119. of the Revised Code to do all of the following:

(A) Considering the goals set forth in section 3701.941 of the Revised Code, establish standards and procedures for certifying a primary care practice as a patient centered medical home;

(B) Specify the types of medical practices that constitute primary care practices for the purpose of certifying patient centered medical homes;

(C) Specify the health care quality and performance information that certified patient centered medical homes must report to the department pursuant to section 3701.942 of the Revised Code.

**HISTORY:**

2013 HB 59, § 101.01, eff. Sept. 29, 2013.

# CHAPTER 3721

# NURSING HOMES; RESIDENTIAL CARE FACILITIES

Section



Residents' Rights



Abuse, Neglect or Misappropriation of Resident's Property At Long-Term Care Facility



Training, Competency Evaluation of Nurse Aides

### § 3721.01 Definitions and classifications; treatment by prayer or spiritual means.

(A) As used in sections 3721.01 to 3721.09 and 3721.99 of the Revised Code:

(1)(a) "Home" means an institution, residence, or facility that provides, for a period of more than twenty-four hours, whether for a consideration or not, accommodations to three or more unrelated individuals who are dependent upon the services of others, including a nursing home, residential care facility, home for the aging, and a veterans' home operated under Chapter 5907. of the Revised Code.

(b) "Home" also means both of the following:

(i) Any facility that a person, as defined in section 3702.51 of the Revised Code, proposes for certification as a skilled nursing facility or nursing facility under Title XVIII or XIX of the "Social Security Act," 49 Stat. 620 (1935), 42 U.S.C.A. 301, as amended, and for which a certificate of need, other than a certificate to recategorize hospital beds as described in section 3702.521 of the Revised Code or division (R)(7)(d) of the version of section 3702.51 of the Revised Code in effect immediately prior to April 20, 1995, has been granted to the person under sections 3702.51 to 3702.62 of the Revised Code after August 5, 1989;

(ii) A county home or district home that is or has been licensed as a residential care facility.

(c) "Home" does not mean any of the following:

(i) Except as provided in division (A)(1)(b) of this section, a public hospital or hospital as defined in section 3701.01 or 5122.01 of the Revised Code;

(ii) A residential facility as defined in section 5119.34 of the Revised Code;

(iii) A residential facility as defined in section 5123.19 of the Revised Code;

(iv) A community addiction services provider as defined in section 5119.01 of the Revised Code;

(v) A facility licensed under section 5119.37 of the Revised Code to operate an opioid treatment program;

(vi) A facility providing services under contract with the department of developmental disabilities under section 5123.18 of the Revised Code;

(vii) A facility operated by a hospice care program licensed under section 3712.04 of the Revised Code that is used exclusively for care of hospice patients;

(viii) A facility operated by a pediatric respite care program licensed under section 3712.041 of the Revised Code that is used exclusively for care of pediatric respite care patients;

(ix) A facility, infirmary, or other entity that is operated by a religious order, provides care exclusively to members of religious orders who take vows of celibacy and live by virtue of their vows within the orders as if related, and does not participate in the medicare program or the medicaid program if on January 1, 1994, the facility, infirmary, or entity was providing care exclusively to members of the religious order;

(x) A county home or district home that has never been licensed as a residential care facility.

(2) "Unrelated individual" means one who is not related to the owner or operator of a home or to the spouse of the owner or operator as a parent, grandparent, child, grandchild, brother, sister, niece, nephew, aunt, uncle, or as the child of an aunt or uncle.

(3) "Mental impairment" does not mean mental illness, as defined in section 5122.01 of the Revised Code, or developmental disability, as defined in section 5123.01 of the Revised Code.

(4) "Skilled nursing care" means procedures that require technical skills and knowledge beyond those the untrained person possesses and that are commonly employed in providing for the physical, mental, and emotional needs of the ill or otherwise incapacitated. "Skilled nursing care" includes, but is not limited to, the following:

(a) Irrigations, catheterizations, application of dressings, and supervision of special diets;

(b) Objective observation of changes in the patient's condition as a means of analyzing and determining the nursing care required and the need for further medical diagnosis and treatment;

(c) Special procedures contributing to rehabilitation;

(d) Administration of medication by any method ordered by a physician, such as hypodermically, rectally, or orally, including observation of the patient after receipt of the medication;

(e) Carrying out other treatments prescribed by the physician that involve a similar level of complexity and skill in administration.

(5)(a) "Personal care services" means services including, but not limited to, the following:

(i) Assisting residents with activities of daily living;

(ii) Assisting residents with self-administration of medication, in accordance with rules adopted under section 3721.04 of the Revised Code;

(iii) Preparing special diets, other than complex therapeutic diets, for residents pursuant to the instructions of a physician or a licensed dietitian, in accordance with rules adopted under section 3721.04 of the Revised Code.

(b) "Personal care services" does not include "skilled nursing care" as defined in division (A) (4) of this section. A facility need not provide more than one of the services listed in division (A)(5) (a) of this section to be considered to be providing personal care services.

(6) "Nursing home" means a home used for the reception and care of individuals who by reason of illness or physical or mental impairment require skilled nursing care and of individuals who require personal care services but not skilled nursing care. A nursing home is licensed to provide personal care services and skilled nursing care.

(7) "Residential care facility" means a home that provides either of the following:

(a) Accommodations for seventeen or more unrelated individuals and supervision and personal care services for three or more of those individuals who are dependent on the services of others by reason of age or physical or mental impairment;

(b) Accommodations for three or more unrelated individuals, supervision and personal care services for at least three of those individuals who are dependent on the services of others by reason of age or physical or mental impairment, and, to at least one of those individuals, any of the skilled nursing care authorized by section 3721.011 of the Revised Code.

(8) "Home for the aging" means a home that provides services as a residential care facility and a nursing home, except that the home provides its services only to individuals who are dependent on the services of others by reason of both age and physical or mental impairment.

The part or unit of a home for the aging that provides services only as a residential care facility is licensed as a residential care facility. The part or unit that may provide skilled nursing care beyond the extent authorized by section 3721.011 of the Revised Code is licensed as a nursing home.

(9) "County home" and "district home" mean a county home or district home operated under Chapter 5155. of the Revised Code.

(B) The director of health may further classify homes. For the purposes of this chapter, any residence, institution, hotel, congregate housing project, or similar facility that meets the definition of a home under this section is such a home regardless of how the facility holds itself out to the public.

(C) For purposes of this chapter, personal care services or skilled nursing care shall be considered to be provided by a facility if they are provided by a person employed by or associated with the facility or by another person pursuant to an agreement to which neither the resident who receives the services nor the resident's sponsor is a party.

(D) Nothing in division (A)(4) of this section shall be construed to permit skilled nursing care to be imposed on an individual who does not require skilled nursing care.

Nothing in division (A)(5) of this section shall be construed to permit personal care services to be imposed on an individual who is capable of performing the activity in question without assistance.

(E) Division (A)(1)(c)(ix) of this section does not prohibit a facility, infirmary, or other entity described in that division from seeking licensure under sections 3721.01 to 3721.09 of the Revised Code or certification under Title XVIII or XIX of the "Social Security Act." However, such a facility, infirmary, or entity that applies for licensure or certification must meet the requirements of those sections or titles and the rules adopted under them and obtain a certificate of need from the director of health under section 3702.52 of the Revised Code.

(F) Nothing in this chapter, or rules adopted pursuant to it, shall be construed as authorizing the supervision, regulation, or control of the spiritual care or treatment of residents or patients in any home who rely upon treatment by prayer or spiritual means in accordance with the creed or tenets of any recognized church or religious denomination.

**HISTORY:**

128 v 645 (Eff 9-7-59); 131 v 887 (Eff 10-20-65); 132 v H 1 (Eff 2-21-67); 137 v H 1 (Eff 8-26-77); 137 v H 870 (Eff 9-25-78); 137 v H 600 (Eff 1-9-79); 137 v H 1084 (Eff 1-5-79); 137 v H 704 (Eff 7-1-79); 139 v H 1 (Eff 8-5-81); 139 v H 694 (Eff 11-15-81); 140 v H 660 (Eff 7-26-84); 142 v H 499 (Eff 6-30-87); 142 v S 156 (Eff 7-1-88); 143 v S 2 (Eff 11-1-89); 143 v H 332, §§ 1, 3 (Eff 8-5-89); 143 v H 253 (Eff 11-15-90); 144 v S 132 (Eff 7-22-91); 144 v H 298 (Eff 7-26-91); 144 v S 233 (Eff 11-15-91); 144 v S 124 (Eff 4-16-93); 145 v H 152 (Eff 7-1-93); 145 v S 201 (Eff 11-15-93); 145 v H 715 (Eff 7-22-94); 145 v S 301 (Eff 11-23-94); 146 v S 50 (Eff 4-20-95); 146 v H 117 (Eff 9-29-95); 146 v S 310 (Eff 9-19-96); 148 v S 178 (Eff 7-21-2000); 149 v H 675. Eff 3-14-2003; 151 v H 66, § 101.01, eff. 7-1-05; 153 v S 79, § 1, eff. 10-6-09; 153 v H 1, § 101.01, eff. 10-16-09; 2011 HB 153, § 101.01, eff. Sept. 29, 2011; 2012 HB 487, § 101.01, eff. Sept. 10, 2012; 2012 HB 303, § 1, eff. Mar. 20, 2013; 2013 HB 59, § 101.01, eff. Sept. 29, 2013; 2016 hb158, § 1, effective October 12, 2016; 2018 hb111, § 1, effective June 29, 2019.

**Editor's Notes**

Acts 2011, HB 153, § 815.20 provides: "The General Assembly, applying the principle stated in division (B) of section 1.52 of the Revised Code that amendments are to be harmonized if reasonably capable of simultaneous operation, finds that the following sections, presented in this act as composites of the sections as amended by the acts indicated, are the resulting versions of the sections in effect prior to the effective date of the sections as presented in this act:

**Amendment Notes**

The 2018 amendment by HB 111, in (A)(1)(c)(v), deleted "to provide methadone treatment" following "facility licensed" and substituted "section 5119.37 of the Revised Code to operate an opioid treatment program" for "section 5119.391 of the Revised Code".

The 2016 amendment by HB 158, substituted "developmental disability" for "mental retardation" in (A)(3); and made related changes.

The 2013 amendment substituted "section 5119.34" for "section 5119.22" in (A)(1)(c)(ii); in (A)(1)(c)(iv), susbtiuted "A community addiction services provider" for "An alcohol or drug addiction program" and "section 5119.01" for "section 3793.01"; substituted "section 5119.39" for "section 3793.11" in (A)(1)(c)(v); and substituted "or the Medicaid program" for "Title XVIII of the 'Social Security Act' or the medical assistance program established under Chapter 5111. of the Revised Code and Title XIX of the 'Social Security Act'" in (A)(1)(c)(ix).

The 2012 amendment by HB 303, inserted (A)(1)(c)(viii); redesignated former (A)(1)(c)(viii) and (A)(1)(c)(ix) as (A)(1)(c)(ix) and (A)(1)(c)(x); and made a stylistic change.

The 2012 amendment by HB 487, substituted "section 3702.521" for "section 3702.522" in (A)(1)(b)(i); deleted "for mentally ill persons" following "residential facility" in (A)(1)(c)(ii); deleted (A)(1)(c)(iv), which read: "An adult care facility as defined in section 5119.70 of the Revised Code"; redesignated former (A)(1)(c)(v) through (A)(1)(c)(x) as (A)(1)(c)(iv) through (A)(1)(c)(ix); deleted "unless section 5123.192 of the Revised Code makes the facility subject to the requirements of this chapter" from the end of present (A)(1)(c)(vi); substituted "director of health" for "public health council" in the first sentence of (B); and made stylistic changes.

The 2011 amendment substituted "section 5119.70" for "section 3722.01" in (A)(1)(c)(iv); and added "unless section 5123.192 of the Revised Code makes the facility subject to the requirements of this chapter" to the end of (A)(1)(c)(vii).

153 v H 1, effective October 16, 2009, deleted (A)(1)(c)(iv), which read: "A community alternative home as defined in former section 3724.01 of the Revised Code" and redesignated the remaining subdivisions accordingly; and made a stylistic change.

153 v S 79, effective October 6, 2009, deleted "mental retardation and" preceding "developmental disabilities" throughout.

151 v H 66, effective July 1, 2005, deleted (A)(1)(c)(iv), pertaining to habilitation centers, and redesignated the remaining subdivisions accordingly; and corrected internal references in (E).

**NOTES TO DECISIONS**

Analysis



**Arbitration**

Arbitration agreement voluntarily executed by a nursing home resident upon her admission and not as a precondition to admission is not rendered procedurally unconscionable solely by virtue of the resident's age. An arbitration agreement voluntarily executed by a nursing home resident and not as a precondition to admission that waives the right to trial and the right to seek punitive damages and attorney fees is not substantively unconscionable. Hayes v. Oakridge Home, 2009-Ohio-2054, 122 Ohio St. 3d 63, 908 N.E.2d 408, 2009 Ohio LEXIS 1218 (Ohio 2009).

**Causation**

Trial court properly granted summary judgment to corporate entities related to a nursing home in an action by a deceased resident's daughter, arising from the decedent's fall and ultimate death, as although the entities were not nursing homes, the non-medical claims were not supported by evidence establishing causation. Chalmers v. HCR ManorCare, Inc., 2017-Ohio-5678, 93 N.E.3d 1237, 2017 Ohio App. LEXIS 2753 (Ohio Ct. App., Lucas County), dismissed, 2017-Ohio-8241, 151 Ohio St. 3d 1401, 84 N.E.3d 1042, 2017 Ohio LEXIS 2147 (Ohio 2017).

**Consumer sales practices act**

The consumer sales practices act applies to billing practices of a residential care facility. Elder v. Fischer, 129 Ohio App. 3d 209, 717 N.E.2d 730, 1998 Ohio App. LEXIS 3385 (Ohio Ct. App., Hamilton County), dismissed, 84 Ohio St. 3d 1434, 702 N.E.2d 1213, 1998 Ohio LEXIS 3475 (Ohio 1998).

Titles 11 — 37

**County homes**

Ohio Supreme Court holds that R.C. 3721.17(I)(1) specifically abrogates governmental immunity and grants a cause of action to residents of unlicensed county nursing homes against a political subdivision for violations of R.C. 3721.10 through 3721.17, the Ohio Nursing Home Patients' Bill of Rights, as the Ohio General Assembly clearly expressed its intent to give to all county nursing-home residents the rights set forth in the Bill of Rights by including "county homes" in the definition of home under R.C. 3721.01; accordingly, a claim by a deceased county home resident's estate administrator against the county home and the county board of commissioners fell under the exception to immunity in R.C. 2744.02(B)(5), although punitive damages could not be awarded against a political subdivision like the county pursuant to R.C. 2744.05(A). Cramer v. Auglaize Acres, 2007-Ohio-1946, 113 Ohio St. 3d 266, 865 N.E.2d 9, 2007 Ohio LEXIS 1130 (Ohio 2007).

**Former law**

For discussion and application of definitions of rest home, home for the aging, and nursing home under R.C. 3721.01 prior to amendment, see. Box v. Cleveland Board of Bldg. Standards, etc., 15 Ohio Misc. 17, 43 Ohio Op. 2d 143, 238 N.E.2d 578, 1968 Ohio Misc. LEXIS 279 (Ohio C.P. 1968).

**Injunction against unlicensed operation**

In an action by the director of health to enjoin the operation of an unlicensed nursing home pursuant to R.C. 3721.08, an injunction shall be granted where it is undisputed that the evidence shows that the facility is a nursing home pursuant to R.C. 3721.01, that the nursing home is unlicensed and that the home is unlicensed because it does not comply with essential licensing requirements. Ackerman v. Tri-City Geriatric & Health Care, Inc., 55 Ohio St. 2d 51, 9 Ohio Op. 3d 62, 378 N.E.2d 145, 1978 Ohio LEXIS 614 (Ohio 1978).

**Malpractice**

A nursing home which does not perform functions of a hospital cannot be guilty of malpractice. Morris v. Monterey Yorkshire Nursing Inn, Inc., 29 Ohio App. 2d 98, 58 Ohio Op. 2d 123, 278 N.E.2d 686, 1971 Ohio App. LEXIS 442 (Ohio Ct. App., Franklin County 1971).

**Relationship to insurance policies**

Under a convalescent care policy, an insurer was not required to cover services rendered to its insured in an assisted living facility because the policy clearly covered only services rendered in a skilled or intermediate nursing facility; the assisted living facility was a residential care facility whose main purpose was accommodation as defined by OAC 3701-17-50(A)(7); it was not licensed as a nursing facility under R.C. 3721.01(A)(6). Michel v. Am. Family Life Assur. Co., 481 F. Supp. 2d 887, 2007 U.S. Dist. LEXIS 25801 (N.D. Ohio 2007).

**Residents' rights**

Determining the type of health care facility involved is crucial to establishing the applicable standard of care. A cause of action under the nursing home residents' rights statutes will survive the death of the resident if the action is one for mesne profits, injuries to person or property, or deceit or fraud. Richards v. Broadview Heights Harborside Healthcare, 2002-Ohio-6491, 150 Ohio App. 3d 537, 782 N.E.2d 609, 2002 Ohio App. LEXIS 6378 (Ohio Ct. App., Cuyahoga County 2002).

A facility that meets the statutory definition of "home" is subject to the patients' bill of rights regardless of whether the department of health allows it to operate unlicensed. Peskin v. Seasons Health Care L.P., 141 Ohio App. 3d 436, 751 N.E.2d 546, 2001 Ohio App. LEXIS 993 (Ohio Ct. App., Hamilton County), dismissed, 92 Ohio St. 3d 1430, 749 N.E.2d 757, 2001 Ohio LEXIS 1758 (Ohio 2001).

**Termination of provider agreement**

A dispute concerning the termination of a provider agreement between a private nursing home and the Ohio Department of Public Welfare does not involve constitutional questions, but pertains to contractual responsibilities only. Crestwood Nursing Home v. White, 52 Ohio App. 2d 274, 6 Ohio Op. 3d 282, 369 N.E.2d 804, 1977 Ohio App. LEXIS 6950 (Ohio Ct. App., Franklin County 1977).

**Use of private property**

Where an individual, either for profit or otherwise, uses his private property for a humane and lawful purpose, and where the regulating authority makes no initial and conclusive showing that such use adversely affects the public welfare, no grounds of enforcement by such regulatory authority exists. State v. Picciochi, 16 Ohio Misc. 196, 45 Ohio Op. 2d 147, 241 N.E.2d 407, 1968 Ohio Misc. LEXIS 262 (Ohio C.P. 1968).

## ATTORNEY GENERAL OPINIONS

Neither R.C. Chapter 3721. nor the Ohio Fire Code are applicable to county homes and county nursing homes (1970 OAG No. 70-164 approved and followed): 1974 Ohio Op. Att'y Gen. No. 008 (1974).

## RESEARCH REFERENCES AND PRACTICE AIDS

**Cross-References to Related Sections**

County nursing homes; closing and subsequent care of residents, RC § 5155.31.
Enforcement; revocation of license, RC § 3721.03.
Medicaid investigations, RC § 109.85.
Nursing care agreements, RC § 140.04.
Nursing home administrator defined, RC § 4751.01.
Patient abuse and neglect, RC § 2903.33.
Records of home may be qualified as authentic evidence, RC § 2317.422.
Uniform rules for operation of homes; standards, RC § 3721.04.

**Ohio Administrative Code**

Department of health, public health council—
Definitions—
Nursing home. OAC 3701-17-01.
State board of examiners of nursing home administrators. OAC ch. 4751-1.

**Comparative Legislation**

Nursing homes:
CA—Cal Health & Saf Code § 1417 et seq
FL—Fla. Stat. § 400.011 et seq
IN—Burns Ind. Code Ann. § 12-10-6-1 et seq
KY—KRS § 216.510 et seq
MI—MCLS § 333.21701 et seq
NY—NY CLS Pub Health § 2850 et seq
PA—63 P.S. § 1102 et seq

## § 3721.011 Provision of skilled nursing care by residential care facility; administration of medication; admission or retention of hospice patients.

(A) In addition to providing accommodations, supervision, and personal care services to its residents, a residential care facility may do the following:

(1) Provide the following skilled nursing care to its residents:

(a) Supervision of special diets;

(b) Application of dressings, in accordance with rules adopted under section 3721.04 of the Revised Code;

(c) Subject to division (B)(1) of this section, administration of medication.

(2) Subject to division (C) of this section, provide other skilled nursing care on a part-time, intermittent basis for not more than a total of one hundred twenty days in a twelve-month period;

(3) Provide skilled nursing care for more than one hundred twenty days in a twelve-month period to a resident when the requirements of division (D) of this section are met.

A residential care facility may not admit or retain an individual requiring skilled nursing care that is not authorized by this section. A residential care facility may not provide skilled nursing care beyond the limits established by this section.

(B)(1) A residential care facility may admit or retain an individual requiring medication, including biologicals, only if the individual's personal physician has determined in writing that the individual is capable of self-administering the medication or the facility provides for the medication to be administered to the individual by a home health agency certified under Title XVIII of the "Social Security Act," 79 Stat. 620 (1965), 42 U.S.C. 1395, as amended; a hospice care program licensed under Chapter 3712. of the Revised Code; or a member of the staff of the residential care facility who is qualified to perform medication administration. Medication may be administered in a residential care facility only by the following persons authorized by law to administer medication:

(a) A registered nurse licensed under Chapter 4723. of the Revised Code;

(b) A licensed practical nurse licensed under Chapter 4723. of the Revised Code who holds proof of successful completion of a course in medication administration approved by the board of nursing and who administers the medication only at the direction of a registered nurse or a physician authorized under Chapter 4731. of the Revised Code to practice medicine and surgery or osteopathic medicine and surgery;

(c) A medication aide certified under Chapter 4723. of the Revised Code;

(d) A physician authorized under Chapter 4731. of the Revised Code to practice medicine and surgery or osteopathic medicine and surgery.

(2) In assisting a resident with self-administration of medication, any member of the staff of a residential care facility may do the following:

(a) Remind a resident when to take medication and watch to ensure that the resident follows the directions on the container;

(b) Assist a resident by taking the medication from the locked area where it is stored, in accordance with rules adopted pursuant to section 3721.04 of the Revised Code, and handing it to the resident. If the resident is physically unable to open the container, a staff member may open the container for the resident.

(c) Assist a physically impaired but mentally alert resident, such as a resident with arthritis, cerebral palsy, or Parkinson's disease, in removing oral or topical medication from containers and in consuming or applying the medication, upon request by or with the consent of the resident. If a resident is physically unable to place a dose of medicine to the resident's mouth without spilling it, a staff member may place the dose in a container and place the container to the mouth of the resident.

(C) Except as provided in division (D) of this section, a residential care facility may admit or retain individuals who require skilled nursing care beyond the supervision of special diets, application of dressings, or administration of medication, only if the care will be provided on a part-time, intermittent basis for not more than a total of one hundred twenty days in any twelve-month period. In accordance with Chapter 119. of the Revised Code, the director of health shall adopt rules specifying what constitutes the need for skilled nursing care on a part-time, intermittent basis. The director shall adopt rules that are consistent with rules pertaining to home health care adopted by the medicaid director for the medicaid program. Skilled nursing care provided pursuant to this division may be provided by a home health agency certified for participation in the medicare program, a hospice care program licensed under Chapter 3712. of the Revised Code, or a member of the staff of a residential care facility who is qualified to perform skilled nursing care.

A residential care facility that provides skilled nursing care pursuant to this division shall do both of the following:

(1) Evaluate each resident receiving the skilled nursing care at least once every seven days to determine whether the resident should be transferred to a nursing home;

(2) Meet the skilled nursing care needs of each resident receiving the care.

(D)(1) A residential care facility may admit or retain an individual who requires skilled nursing care for more than one hundred twenty days in any twelve-month period only if the facility has entered into a written agreement with each of the following:

(a) The individual or individual's sponsor;

(b) The individual's personal physician;

(c) Unless the individual's personal physician oversees the skilled nursing care, the provider of the skilled nursing care;

(d) If the individual is a hospice patient as defined in section 3712.01 of the Revised Code, a hospice care program licensed under Chapter 3712. of the Revised Code.

(2) The agreement required by division (D)(1) of this section shall include all of the following provisions:

(a) That the individual will be provided skilled nursing care in the facility only if a determination has been made that the individual's needs can be met at the facility;

(b) That the individual will be retained in the facility only if periodic redeterminations are made that the individual's needs are being met at the facility;

(c) That the redeterminations will be made according to a schedule specified in the agreement;

(d) If the individual is a hospice patient, that the individual has been given an opportunity to choose the hospice care program that best meets the individual's needs;

(e) Unless the individual is a hospice patient, that the individual's personal physician has determined that the skilled nursing care the individual needs is routine.

(E) Notwithstanding any other provision of this chapter, a residential care facility in which residents receive skilled nursing care pursuant to this section is not a nursing home.



**HISTORY:**

143 v H 253 (Eff 11-15-90); 145 v H 152 (Eff 7-1-93); 146 v H 117 (Eff 9-29-95); 146 v S 310 (Eff 6-20-96); 148 v H 471. Eff 7-1-2000; 151 v H 66, § 101.01, eff. 6-30-05; 151 v S 87, § 1, eff. 4-14-06; 2011 HB 153, § 101.01, eff. Sept. 29, 2011; 2012 HB 487, § 101.01, eff. Sept. 10, 2012; 2013 HB 59, § 101.01, eff. Sept. 29, 2013.

**Amendment Notes**

The 2013 amendment, in the first paragraph of (C), in the second sentence, substituted "medicaid director" for "director of job and family services" and deleted "established under Chapter 5111. of the Revised Code" from the end and substituted "for participation in the medicare program" for "under Title XVIII of the 'Social Security Act'" in the third sentence.

The 2012 amendment, in the first paragraph of (C), substituted "director of health" for "public health council" in the second sentence and substituted "director" for "council" preceding "shall adopt" in the third sentence.

The 2011 amendment added the (A)(1) designation; redesignated former (A)(1) through (A)(5) as (A)(1)(a) through (A)(1)(c), (2), and (3); in the first paragraph of present (A)(3), deleted "Subject to division (D) of this section" from the beginning and substituted "resident when the requirements of division (D) of this section are met" for "hospice patient, as defined in section 3712.01 of the Revised Code"; substituted "42 U.S.C.A. 1395" for "42 U.S.C. 1395" in the first sentence of (B)(1); in the first paragraph of (C), added the exception to the beginning of the first sentence and substituted "medicaid" for "medical assistance" in the third sentence; rewrote (D); and made related and stylistic changes.

151 v S 87, effective April 14, 2006, rewrote (A); in the introductory language of (B)(1), substituted "79 Stat. 620 (1965), 42 U.S.C.A. 1395" for "49 Stat. 620 (1935), 42 U.S.C.A. 301"; in the first paragraph of (C), deleted "49 Stat. 620 (1935), 42 U.S.C.A. 301" following " 'Social Security Act' "; and inserted (D) and redesignated former (D) as (E).

151 v H 66, effective June 30, 2005, inserted (B)(1)(c) and redesignated former (B)(1)(c) as (d).

## NOTES TO DECISIONS

Analysis



**Discharge of nurse aides**

The rest home did not wrongfully discharge nurse aides who refused to participate in the administration of medications in the mistaken belief that they were prohibited from doing so. Smith v. Justarr, Inc., 102 Ohio App. 3d 506, 657 N.E.2d 542, 1995 Ohio App. LEXIS 1508 (Ohio Ct. App., Hamilton County 1995).

**Nursing home**

Residential care facility (RCF) did not breach the standard of care to admit and retain a resident based on the assessment of the resident's treating physician because there was no evidence the physician's assessment of "nursing home" was a prescription for a higher level of care, and there was evidence that the RCF was capable of meeting the resident's needs; even if the resident required skilled nursing, the RCF could admit the resident because she was at the RCF for less than 120 days. McFarren v. Emeritus at Canton, 2018-Ohio-1593, 111 N.E.3d 87, 2018 Ohio App. LEXIS 1729 (Ohio Ct. App., Stark County 2018).

#### RESEARCH REFERENCES AND PRACTICE AIDS

**Cross-References to Related Sections**

Classification of rest home, RC § 3721.01.

Uniform rules for operation of homes; standards, RC § 3721.04.

**Ohio Administrative Code**

Drugs and medications—

Nursing home. OAC 3701-17-17.

Food and nutrition; dietary services—

Nursing home. OAC 3701-17-18.

Personnel requirements—

Nursing home. OAC 3701-17-07 et seq.

Training and evaluation for nurse aides. OAC 3701-17-07.1.



### § 3721.012 Risk agreement with resident or sponsor.

A residential care facility may enter into a risk agreement with a resident or the resident's sponsor. Under a risk agreement, the resident or sponsor and the facility agree to share responsibility for making and implementing decisions affecting the scope and quantity of services provided by the facility to the resident. The facility also agrees to identify the risks inherent in a decision made by a resident or sponsor not to receive a service provided by the facility. A risk agreement is valid only if it is made in writing.

**HISTORY:**

145 v H 152 (Eff 7-1-93); 146 v H 117. Eff 9-29-95.

#### RESEARCH REFERENCES AND PRACTICE AIDS

**Cross-References to Related Sections**

Notice of home's nonparticipation in state assistance program; risk agreements, RC § 3721.19.

### § 3721.02 Inspection and licensing of homes; fees.

(A) As used in this section, "residential facility" means a residential facility licensed under section 5119.34 of the Revised Code that provides accommodations, supervision, and personal care services for three to sixteen unrelated adults.

(B)(1) The director of health shall license homes and establish procedures to be followed in inspecting and licensing homes. The director may inspect a home at any time. The director may enter at any time, for the purposes of investigation, any institution, residence, facility, or other structure that has been reported to the director or that the director has reasonable cause to believe is operating as a nursing home, residential care facility, or home for the aging without a valid license required by section 3721.05 of the Revised Code or, in the case of a county home or district home, is operating despite the revocation of its residential care facility license. The director may delegate the director's authority and duties under this chapter to any division, bureau, agency, or official of the department of health.

(2)(a) Except as provided in division (B)(2)(b) of this section, prior to the issuance of a license, each home shall be inspected by the director and the state fire marshal or a township, municipal, or other legally constituted fire department approved by the marshal.

(b) The inspections set forth in division (B)(2)(a) of this section are not required prior to the issuance of a license if ownership of the home is assigned or transferred to a different person and the home was licensed under this chapter immediately prior to the assignment or transfer.

(3) After issuance of a license by the director, each home shall be inspected as follows:

(a) By the director at least once every fifteen months except that a home that is a residential care facility, or part of a home for the aging that is licensed as a residential care facility, may, at the discretion of the director, be inspected at least once every thirty months if all of the following apply:

(i) During the two most recent consecutive inspections that occurred at least once every fifteen months, there were no substantiated violations against the residential care facility;

(ii) During the time period of the inspections referred to in division (B)(4)(a) of this section, there were no substantiated violations against the residential care facility from any other inspections or from any investigations of complaints;

(iii) The residential care facility does not have any outstanding violations from any previous inspections or investigations.

(b) By the state fire marshal or a township, municipal, or other legally constituted fire department approved by the marshal at least once every fifteen months.

(4) A nursing home does not need to be inspected before the director increases the nursing home's licensed capacity if the beds being added to the nursing home are placed in resident rooms that were inspected, as part of the most recent previous inspection of the nursing home, for the same number of residents proposed to be placed in a room after the capacity increase.

(5)(a) The inspection procedures established under division (B) of this section shall include a process for conducting expedited licensing inspections. An expedited licensing inspection may be requested by an applicant seeking a license for a new home or, in the case of an existing home, an applicant seeking approval to increase or decrease the home's licensed capacity or to make any other change for which the director requires a licensing inspection to be conducted.

If an applicant submits a complete request for an expedited licensing inspection and the request is submitted in a manner and form approved by the director, the director shall commence the inspection of the home not later than ten business days after receiving the complete request.

Any rules adopted by the director pursuant to section 3721.04 of the Revised Code to implement the requirements described in division (B)(5)(a) of this section are not subject to the requirements of division (F) of section 121.95 of the Revised Code.

(b) The director may charge a fee for an expedited licensing inspection that is adequate to cover the expense of expediting the inspection. The fee shall be deposited in the state treasury to the credit of the general operations fund created in section 3701.83 of the Revised Code and used solely for expediting inspections.

(C) A single facility may be licensed both as a nursing home pursuant to this chapter and as a residential facility pursuant to section 5119.34 of the Revised Code if the director determines that the part or unit to be licensed as a nursing home can be maintained separate and discrete from the part or unit to be licensed as a residential facility.

(D) In determining the number of residents in a home for the purpose of licensing, the director shall consider all the individuals for whom the home provides accommodations as one group unless one of the following is the case:

(1) The home is a home for the aging, in which case all the individuals in the part or unit licensed as a nursing home shall be considered as one group, and all the individuals in the part or unit licensed as a residential care facility shall be considered as another group.

(2) The home is both a nursing home and a residential facility. In that case, all the individuals in the part or unit licensed as a nursing home shall be considered as one group, and all the individuals in the part or unit licensed as an residential facility shall be considered as another group.

(3) The home maintains, in addition to a nursing home or residential care facility, a separate and discrete part or unit that provides accommodations to individuals who do not require or receive skilled nursing care and do not receive personal care services from the home, in which case the individuals in the separate and discrete part or unit shall not be considered in determining the number of residents in the home if the separate and discrete part or unit is in compliance with the Ohio basic building code established by the board of building standards under Chapters 3781. and 3791. of the Revised Code and the home permits the director, on request, to inspect the separate and discrete part or unit and speak with the individu-

als residing there, if they consent, to determine whether the separate and discrete part or unit meets the requirements of this division.

(E)(1) The director of health shall charge the following application fee and annual renewal licensing and inspection fee for each fifty persons or part thereof of a home's licensed capacity:

(a) For state fiscal year 2010, two hundred twenty dollars;

(b) For state fiscal year 2011, two hundred seventy dollars;

(c) For each state fiscal year thereafter, three hundred twenty dollars. (2) All fees collected by the director for the issuance or renewal of licenses shall be deposited into the state treasury to the credit of the general operations fund created in section 3701.83 of the Revised Code for use only in administering and enforcing this chapter and rules adopted under it.

(F)(1) Except as otherwise provided in this section, the results of an inspection or investigation of a home that is conducted under this section, including any statement of deficiencies and all findings and deficiencies cited in the statement on the basis of the inspection or investigation, shall be used solely to determine the home's compliance with this chapter or another chapter of the Revised Code in any action or proceeding other than an action commenced under division (I) of section 3721.17 of the Revised Code. Those results of an inspection or investigation, that statement of deficiencies, and the findings and deficiencies cited in that statement shall not be used in either of the following:

(a) Any court or in any action or proceeding that is pending in any court and are not admissible in evidence in any action or proceeding unless that action or proceeding is an appeal of an action by the department of health under this chapter or is an action by any department or agency of the state to enforce this chapter or another chapter of the Revised Code;

(b) An advertisement, unless the advertisement includes all of the following:

(i) The date the inspection or investigation was conducted;

(ii) A statement that the director of health inspects all homes at least once every fifteen months or, if applicable under this section, at least once every thirty months;

(iii) If a finding or deficiency cited in the statement of deficiencies has been substantially corrected, a statement that the finding or deficiency has been substantially corrected and the date that the finding or deficiency was substantially corrected;

(iv) The number of findings and deficiencies cited in the statement of deficiencies on the basis of the inspection or investigation;

(v) The average number of findings and deficiencies cited in a statement of deficiencies on the basis of an inspection or investigation conducted under this section during the same calendar year as the inspection or investigation used in the advertisement;

(vi) A statement that the advertisement is neither authorized nor endorsed by the department of health or any other government agency.

(2) Nothing in division (F)(1) of this section prohibits the results of an inspection or investigation conducted under this section from being used in a criminal investigation or prosecution.

**HISTORY:**

131 v 889 (Eff 10-20-65); 134 v H 1086 (Eff 12-30-72); 139 v H 694 (Eff 11-15-81); 142 v S 386 (Eff 3-29-88); 143 v H 253 (Eff 11-15-90); 144 v H 298 (Eff 7-26-91); 144 v H 904 (Eff 12-22-92); 145 v H 152 (Eff 7-1-93); 146 v H 117 (Eff 9-29-95); 148 v S 178 (Eff 7-21-2000); 149 v H 412. Eff 11-7-2002; 150 v H 95, § 1, eff. 6-26-03; 151 v H 66, § 101.01, eff. 9-29-05; 153 v H 1, § 101.01, eff. 7-17-09; 2011 HB 153, § 101.01, eff. July 1, 2011; 2012 HB 487, § 101.01, eff. Sept. 10, 2012; 2013 HB 59, § 101.01, eff. Sept. 29, 2013; 2014 HB 483, § 101.01, eff. Sept. 15, 2014; 2014 hb290, § 1, effective March 23, 2015; 2017 hb49, § 101.01, effective September 29, 2017; 2021 hb110, § 101.01, effective September 30, 2021.

**Editor's Notes**

The provisions of § 4 of HB 412 (149 v H 412) read as follows:

SECTION 4. If any provision of section 2305.11, 2315.21, 3721.02, or 3721.17 of the Revised Code, as amended by this act, any provision of section 5111.411 of the Revised Code, as enacted by this act, or the application of any provision of those sections to any person or circumstance is held invalid, the invalidity does not affect other provisions or applications of the particular section or related sections that can be given effect without the invalid provision or application, and to this end the provisions of the particular section are severable.

**Amendment Notes**

The 2021 amendment by HB 110 rewrote (B); substituted "residential care facility" for "rest home" in (D)(1); substituted "residential facility" for "adult care facility" in the second sentence of (D)(2); and added "or, if applicable under this section, at least once every thirty months" in (F)(1)(b)(ii).

The 2017 amendment by HB 49 added the sixth sentence in (B)(1).

The 2014 amendment by HB 290, added "either of the following" to the end of the introductory language of (F)(1); added the (F)(1)(a) designation; added (F)(1)(b); and made a related change.

The 2014 amendment by HB 483 added (B)(2); and substituted "division (F)(1)" for "division (E)(1)" in (F)(2).

The 2013 amendment substituted "section 5119.34" for "section 5119.22" in (A) and (C).

The 2012 amendment added (A); redesignated former (A) through (E) as (B) through (F); substituted "a residential" for "an adult care" wherever it appears in present (C) and the first sentence of present (D)(2); and substituted "section 5119.22" for "Chapter 5119." in present (C).

The 2011 amendment substituted "Chapter 5119" for "Chapter 3722" in (B).

153 v H 1, effective July 17, 2009, rewrote (D).

151 v H 66, effective September 29, 2005, in (D), substituted "seventy" for "five".



## NOTES TO DECISIONS

Analysis



**Applicability**

Trial court did not err in finding the nursing facility survey documents inadmissible at trial because one statute was inapplicable and the documents were inadmissible pursuant to the other statute, since the documents proffered were in compliance with the Revised Code Chapter. The documents proffered were not related to the licensing of the nursing home; instead, they were related to the facility's compliance with Medicare and Medicaid requirements. Sliwinski v. Vill. of St. Edwards, 2014-Ohio-4655, 2014 Ohio App. LEXIS 4539 (Ohio Ct. App., Summit County 2014).

**Discovery of inspection reports**

Nursing home's contention that R.C. 3721.02(E)(1) conferred a complete statutory privilege on inspection reports prepared by the Ohio Department of Health and therefore the documents ordered to be produced were not discoverable was rejected because R.C. 3721.02(E)(1) did not create a privilege, but only prevented the admission of Department of Health licensing inspection reports into evidence in a trial. Licensing reports were discoverable to the extent allowed by the Civil Rules. Large v. Heartland-Lansing of Bridgeport Ohio, LLC, 2013-Ohio-2877, 995 N.E.2d 872, 2013 Ohio App. LEXIS 2923 (Ohio Ct. App., Belmont County 2013).

**Jurisdiction**

Revised Code § 2743.02(A), of the court of claims act, states, "* * * To the extent that the state has previously consented to be sued, this chapter has no applicability." A remedy for one wrongfully denied a nursing home license is provided by R.C. 119.01 et seq, the Administrative Procedure Act. Thus the court of claims lacks jurisdiction over such a claim. Marshall Nursing Home v. Ackerman, 3 Ohio Op. 3d 143 (Ohio Ct. App., Franklin County 1976).

**Liability of nursing home**

A nursing home may be liable for negligently failing to use nonintrusive methods of restraint in order to prevent a resident from falling. Gray v. Jefferson Geriatric & Rehabilitation Center, 76 Ohio App. 3d 499, 602 N.E.2d 396, 1991 Ohio App. LEXIS 5795 (Ohio Ct. App., Ashtabula County 1991).

**Liability of state**

Fire inspector employed by the Ohio Department of Commerce (ODC) did not exceed his statutory duties and assume an affirmative duty to act when he informed a residential care facility's maintenance supervisor that the facility was not permitted to utilize a delayed egress lock on a door. As no special relationship existed between the facility's operators and the state, the ODC was entitled to statutory immunity on the operators' third party-complaint, which was filed after the operators were sued by the co-executors of a resident who died after exiting the facility through an unlocked door. Lawrence v. Meridian Senior Living, L.L.C., 2016-Ohio-8500, 79 N.E.3d 1158, 2016 Ohio App. LEXIS 5340 (Ohio Ct. App., Franklin County 2016).

A nursing home may be liable for negligently failing to use nonintrusive methods of restraint in order to prevent a resident from falling. Gray v. Jefferson Geriatric & Rehabilitation Center, 76 Ohio App. 3d 499, 602 N.E.2d 396, 1991 Ohio App. LEXIS 5795 (Ohio Ct. App., Ashtabula County 1991).

The state's provisions for inspection and licensing of nursing homes do not make the state liable for the alleged negligence of nursing home employees. Lewis v. Ohio Dep't of Health, 66 Ohio App. 3d 761, 586 N.E.2d 182, 1990 Ohio App. LEXIS 2452 (Ohio Ct. App., Franklin County 1990).



**Social security Act**

Subchapter XIX of the Social Security Act does not authorize the summary decertification of a nursing home indirectly receiving benefits under its provisions, and where payments are discontinued without a hearing through the action of a state agency during the term of an existing agreement, between the state and the home, establishing the conditions pursuant to which the payments are made, such action is invalid. Shady Acres Nursing Home, Inc. v. Canary, 39 Ohio App. 2d 47, 68 Ohio Op. 2d 210, 316 N.E.2d 481, 1973 Ohio App. LEXIS 1495 (Ohio Ct. App., Franklin County 1973), (Motion to certify overruled Feb. 22, 1974).

**Transfer of license**

A license to operate a nursing home is made specifically non-transferable by a valid regulation of the public health council. Thus an attempted transferee is not entitled to the procedural due process of R.C. Chapter 119. when the director of health revokes the license of the original licensee. The state is not estopped by its acquiescence for a time in the continued operation of the home by the attempted transferee. Adams v. Ohio Dep't of Health, 5 Ohio Op. 3d 148, 356 N.E.2d 324, 1976 Ohio Misc. LEXIS 60 (Ohio C.P. 1976).

### RESEARCH REFERENCES AND PRACTICE AIDS

**Cross-References to Related Sections**

Additional penalties for failing to cease activity or using equipment or facility involved in violation, RC § 3702.55.

Conditions for issuing license; renewal; appeals, RC § 3721.07.

Criteria for qualifying as home for the aged, definitions, RC § 5701.13.

Duties of home administrator concerning residents' rights; grievance procedure, RC § 3721.12.

Enforcement; revocation of license, RC § 3721.03.

Definitions, RC § 5168.40.

Exemptions from fees, RC § 3721.511.

General operations fund, RC § 3701.83.

Inspection reports to be available for review by prospective residents and associated persons, RC § 3721.021.

Local regulation, RC § 3721.09.

Residential facilities; licensing; inspection; operation, RC § 5123.19.

Rule-making authority of public health council, RC § 3721.04.

**Ohio Administrative Code**

Department of job and family services, division of medical assistance —

Identification of nursing facility (NF) and hospital beds subject to the franchise permit fee (FPF). OAC 5101:3-3-49.2.

Nursing home—

Building and sanitation requirements; temperature. OAC 3701-17-22 et seq.

License application; fee; issuance; revocation. OAC 3701-17-03.

Prohibitions; open for inspection. OAC 3701-17-05.

Residential care facility—

Building, plumbing requirements; temperature. OAC 3701-17-63 et seq.

## § 3721.021 Documents to be available for review by prospective residents and associated persons.

Every person who operates a home, as defined in section 3721.01 of the Revised Code, and each county home and district home licensed as a residential care facility shall have available in the home for review by prospective patients and residents, their guardians, or other persons assisting in their placement, each inspection report completed pursuant to section 3721.02 of the Revised Code and each statement of deficiencies and plan of correction completed and made available to the public under Titles XVIII and XIX of the "Social Security Act," 49 Stat. 620 (1935), 42 U.S.C. 301, as amended, and any rules promulgated under Titles XVIII and XIX, including such reports that result from life safety code and health inspections during the preceding three years, and shall post prominently within the home a notice of this requirement.

**HISTORY:**

137 v H 600 (Eff 4-9-79); 148 v S 178. Eff 7-21-2000.

### RESEARCH REFERENCES AND PRACTICE AIDS

**Cross-References to Related Sections**

Penalties, RC § 3721.99.

Duties of home administrator concerning residents' rights, RC § 3721.12.

Enforcement; revocation of license, RC § 3721.03.

Rule-making authority of public health council, RC § 3721.04.

**Ohio Administrative Code**

Records and reports—

Nursing home. OAC 3701-17-19.

Responsibility of operator and nursing home administrator; quality assurance committee. OAC 3701-17-06.

## § 3721.022 Administration of survey and certification requirements for facilities; review of cited deficiencies.

(A) As used in this section:

(1) "Nursing facility" has the same meaning as in section 5165.01 of the Revised Code.

(2) "Deficiency" and "survey" have the same meanings as in section 5165.60 of the Revised Code.

(3) "Title XIX" and "Title XVIII" have the same meanings as in section 5165.01 of the Revised Code.

(B) The department of health is hereby designated the state agency responsible for establishing and maintaining health standards and serving as the state survey agency for the purposes of Title XVIII and Title XIX. The department shall carry out these functions in accordance with the regulations, guidelines, and procedures issued under Title XVIII and Title XIX by the United States secretary of health and human services and with sections 5165.60 to 5165.89 of the Revised Code. The director of health shall enter into agreements with regard to these functions with the department of medicaid and the United States department of health and human services. The director may also enter into agreements with the department of medicaid under which the department of health is designated to perform functions under sections 5165.60 to 5165.89 of the Revised Code.

The director, in accordance with Chapter 119. of the Revised Code, shall adopt rules necessary to implement the survey and certification requirements for skilled nursing facilities and nursing facilities established by the United States secretary of health and human services under Title XVIII and Title XIX and the survey requirements established under sections 5165.60 to 5165.89 of the Revised Code. The rules shall include an informal process by which a facility may obtain up to two reviews of any deficiencies that have been cited on a statement of deficiencies made by the department of health under 42 C.F.R. Part 488 and cause the facility to be in noncompliance as defined in 42 C.F.R. 488.301. The first review shall be conducted by an employee of the department who did not participate in and was not otherwise involved in any way with the survey. A facility that is not satisfied with the results of a first review may receive a second review on payment of a fee to the department. The amount of the fee shall be specified in rules adopted under this section. The fee shall be deposited into the state treasury to the credit of the general operations fund created in section 3701.83 of the Revised Code for use in the implementation of this section. The second review shall be conducted by either of the following as selected by the facility: a hearing officer employed by the department or a hearing officer included on a list the department shall provide the facility. A final determination that any deficiency citation is unjustified shall be reflected clearly in all records relating to the survey.

The director need not adopt as rules any of the regulations, guidelines, or procedures issued under Title XVIII and Title XIX by the United States secretary of health and human services.

**HISTORY:**

143 v H 822 (Eff 12-13-90); 148 v H 471. Eff 7-1-2000; 2011 HB 153, § 101.01, eff. Sept. 29, 2011; 2013 HB 59, § 101.01, eff. Sept. 29, 2013.

**Amendment Notes**

The 2013 amendment substituted "section 5165.01" for "section 5111.20" in (A)(1); substituted "section 5165.60" for "section 5111.35" in (A)(2); added (A)(3); and, in (B), in the first paragraph, substituted "Title XVIII and Title XIX" for "Titles XVIII and XIX of the 'Social Security Act,' 49 Stat. 620 (1935), 42 U.S.C.A. 301, as amended" in the first sentence, substituted "Title XVIII and Title XIX" for "Titles XVIII and XIX" in the second sentence, and substituted "medicaid" for "job and family services" in the last two sentences, substituted "sections 5165.60 to 5165.89" for "sections 5111.35 to 5111.62" in the second and last sentences of the first paragraph and the first sentence of the second paragraph, and substituted "Title XVIII and Title XIX" for "Titles XVIII and XIX of the 'Social Security Act'" in the first sentence of the second paragraph and in the last paragraph.

The 2011 amendment, in the second paragraph of (B), in the second sentence, substituted "up to two reviews of any" for "a review of" and "42 C.F.R. Part 488 and cause the facility to be in noncompliance as defined in 42 C.F.R. 488.301" for "section 5111.42 of the Revised Code", inserted "first" in the third sentence, inserted the fourth through seventh sentences, and, in the present last sentence, substituted "A final determination" for "If the employee conducting the review determines" and deleted "that determination" following "unjustified".

## RESEARCH REFERENCES AND PRACTICE AIDS

**Cross-References to Related Sections**

Surveys of every nursing facility, RC § 5165.64.

**Ohio Administrative Code**

Department of health, director of—

Appeal of denial of long-term care facility certification. OAC ch. 3701-63.

### § 3721.023 Party deemed sole owner of business on premises leased on or before 1-1-70.

Where a nursing home licensed under this Chapter is operated in a building that was leased pursuant to a written lease agreement entered into on or before January 1, 1970, and where the lease agreement does not expressly determine or state the identity of the party that owns the nursing home business, operating rights, certificate of need, or legal rights associated with ownership and operation of the nursing home beds located in the leased building and does not provide that the lessor retains any rights to the nursing home business that is operated in the leased building, the party identified in the nursing home license in existence on the effective date of this section shall be deemed the sole owner of the nursing home business, operating rights, certificate of need, and legal rights associated with ownership and operation of the nursing home beds and may relocate the nursing home business, beds, or operating rights without the consent of the owner of the real estate in or on which the nursing home is operated. Where a court having jurisdiction over a nursing home has determined prior to July 1, 1993, that the lessee or person in possession of and operating the nursing home owns the operating rights of the nursing home and there is no written lease agreement between the owner of the real estate and the person in possession and operating the nursing home, the director of health shall not grant a certificate of need under sections 3702.51 to 3702.62 of the Revised Code to relocate any of the nursing facility beds or the license from the owner's real estate in or on which the beds are located unless the lessee or person in possession of the facility obtains the voluntary written consent of the owner or sublessor of the real estate to such relocation and meets all other requirements for the relocation of beds as specified in this chapter and the rules adopted under it.

**HISTORY:**

145 v S 131. Eff 10-29-93.

### § 3721.024 Nursing facility recognition program.

As used in this section, "nursing facility" has the same meaning as in section 5165.01 of the Revised Code.

The department of health may establish a program of recognition of nursing facilities that provide the highest quality care to residents who are medicaid recipients. The program may be funded with public funds appropriated by the general assembly for the purpose of the program or any funds appropriated for nursing home licensure.

**HISTORY:**

146 v H 167. Eff 11-15-95; 2013 HB 59, § 101.01, eff. Sept. 29, 2013.

**Amendment Notes**

The 2013 amendment substituted "section 5165.01" for "section 5111.20" in the first paragraph; and substituted "medicaid recipients" for "recipients of medical assistance under Chapter 5111. of the Revised Code" in the first sentence of the second paragraph.

### § 3721.026 Transfer of operation of a nursing home.

(A) If the operation of a nursing home is assigned or transferred to a different person, the person to whom the operation is assigned or transferred must, before the director of health may issue a license authorizing the person to operate the nursing home, submit to the director documentation showing that the person meets all of the following requirements:

(1) Unless the assignment or transfer is in the form of a lease of the nursing home, the person has financial resources that the director determines are sufficient to cover any reasonably anticipated revenue shortfall for at least twelve months after the assignment or transfer.

(2) If the assignment or transfer is in the form of a lease of the nursing home, either of the following applies to the person:

(a) The person has obtained a bond that has a term of at least twelve months, has an annual renewal, and is for an amount not less than one million dollars.

(b) If the person is unable to obtain a bond that meets the requirements of division (A)(2)(a) of this section at a cost the director determines to be reasonable or operates other nursing homes in this state, the person has financial resources that the director determines are sufficient to cover any reasonably anticipated revenue shortfall for at least twelve months after the assignment or transfer.

(3) The person has at least five years of experience as an operator, manager, or administrator of a nursing home.

(4) The person has plans for quality assurance and risk management for the nursing home.

(5) The person has general and professional liability insurance coverage that provides coverage of at least one million dollars per occurrence and three million dollars aggregate.

(B) The documentation required by divisions (A)(1) and (2)(b) of this section shall include projected financial statements for the nursing home for the twelve-month period after the assignment or transfer of the operation of the nursing home.

The documentation required by division (A)(3) of this section shall include a list of each currently or previously licensed nursing home located in this or another state in which the person has or previously had any percentage of ownership. The percentage of ownership may have been in the operation, real property, or both of the nursing home.

(C) The requirements established by this section are in addition to the other requirements established by this chapter and the rules adopted under it for a license to operate a nursing home.

**HISTORY:**

2019 hb166, § 101.01, effective October 17, 2019.

### § 3721.027 Investigation of valid, unresolved complaints.

(A) As used in this section, "survey" has the same meaning as in section 5165.60 of the Revised Code.

(B) The department of health shall investigate within ten working days after referral, in accordance with procedures and criteria to be established by the department of health and the department of aging, any unresolved complaint that the office of the state long-term care ombudsman has investigated and found to be valid and refers to the department of health. This requirement does not supersede federal requirements for survey agency complaint investigations.

**HISTORY:**

148 v H 403. Eff 7-1-2000; 2013 HB 59, § 101.01, eff. Sept. 29, 2013.

**Amendment Notes**

The 2013 amendment added (A); redesignated the former provision as (B); and substituted "ombudsman" for "ombudsperson" in the first sentence of present (B).

Titles 11 — 37

RESEARCH REFERENCES AND PRACTICE AIDS

**Ohio Administrative Code**
Department of aging —
State long-term care ombudsman. OAC ch. 173-14.
Complaint handling protocol; referrals. OAC 173-14-15 et seq.

### § 3721.03 Enforcement; revocation of license.

(A) As used in this section, "person" has the same meaning as in section 1.59 of the Revised Code.

(B) The director of health shall enforce the provisions of sections 3721.01 to 3721.13 and 3721.99 of the Revised Code and may issue orders to secure compliance with the provisions of these sections and the rules adopted under them. The director may hold hearings, issue subpoenas, compel testimony, and make adjudications.

The director may issue an order revoking a license in the event the director finds, upon hearing or opportunity afforded pursuant to Chapter 119. of the Revised Code, that any of the following apply to a person, county home, or district home licensed under section 3721.07 of the Revised Code:

(1) Has violated any of the provisions of Chapter 3721. of the Revised Code or rules adopted by the director under it;

(2) Has violated any order issued by the director;

(3) Is not, or any of its principals are not suitable, morally or financially to operate such an institution;

(4) Is not furnishing humane, kind, and adequate treatment and care;

(5) Has had a long-standing pattern of violations of this chapter or the rules adopted under it that has caused physical, emotional, mental, or psychosocial harm to one or more residents.

Upon the issuance of any order of revocation, the person whose license is revoked, or the county home or district home that has its license revoked, may appeal in accordance with Chapter 119. of the Revised Code.

(C) Once the director notifies a person, county home, or district home licensed to operate a home that the license may be revoked or issues any order under this section, the person, county home, or district home shall not assign or transfer to another person or entity the right to operate the home, unless the notice or order is issued solely because the home has already closed or ceased operations. This prohibition shall remain in effect until proceedings under Chapter 119. of the Revised Code concerning the order or license revocation have been concluded or the director notifies the person, county home, or district home that the prohibition has been lifted.

If a license is revoked under this section, the former license holder shall not assign or transfer or consent to assignment or transfer of the right to operate the home. Any attempted assignment or transfer to another person or entity is void.

On revocation of a license, the former licensee shall take all necessary steps to cease operation of the home.

The director of health shall not accept a certificate of need application under section 3702.52 of the Revised Code regarding a home if the license to operate the home has been revoked under this section.

**HISTORY:**

128 v 645 (Eff 9-7-59); 129 v 582(816) (Eff 1-10-61); 131 v 890 (Eff 10-20-65); 134 v H 1086 (Eff 12-30-72); 145 v H 152 (Eff 7-1-93); 148 v S 178. Eff 7-21-2000; 151 v H 66, § 101.01, eff. 6-30-05; 2012 HB 487, § 101.01, eff. Sept. 10, 2012; 2015 hb340, § 101.01, effective December 22, 2015.

**Amendment Notes**

The 2015 amendment by HB 340, added "unless the notice or order is issued solely because the home has already closed or ceased operations" to the end of the first sentence of the first paragraph of (C).

The 2012 amendment substituted "director" for "public health council" in (B)(1).

151 v H 66, effective June 30, 2005, rewrote the section.

NOTES TO DECISIONS

**Exhaustion of administrative remedies**

Trial court properly dismissed a nursing home's declaratory judgment action, which a declaration that employees of the Ohio Department of Health violated its rights to due course of law and equal protection under the Ohio Constitution, because the nursing home failed to exhaust administrative remedies; all of the complaints against the employees were subject to administrative review, and until and when that review was complete, there was no justiciable claim or subject matter jurisdiction. Autumn Health Care of Zanesville, Inc. v. Todd, 2014-Ohio-5851, 2014 Ohio App. LEXIS 5688 (Ohio Ct. App., Muskingum County 2014).

RESEARCH REFERENCES AND PRACTICE AIDS

**Cross-References to Related Sections**
Local regulation, RC § 3721.09.

**Ohio Administrative Code**
Department of commerce—
Board of building standards—
Ohio building code. OAC ch. 4101:1-1 et seq.
Division of state fire marshal —
Ohio fire code. OAC ch. 1301:7-7 et seq.
Department of health, public health council—
Fire safety and building requirements—
Nursing home. OAC 3701-17-22 et seq.

### § 3721.031 Investigation of complaint concerning home; confidentiality of information.

(A) The director of health may investigate any complaint the director receives concerning a home.

(1) Except as required by court order, as necessary for the administration or enforcement of any statute relating to homes, or as provided in division (C) of this section, the director and any employee of the department of health shall not release any of the following information without the permission of the individual or of the individual's legal representative:

(a) The identity of any patient or resident;

(b) The identity of any individual who submits a complaint about a home;

(c) The identity of any individual who provides the director with information about a home and has requested confidentiality;

(d) Any information that reasonably would tend to disclose the identity of any individual described in division (A)(1)(a) to (c) of this section.

(2) An agency or individual to whom the director is required, by court order or for the administration or enforcement of a statute relating to homes, to release information described in division (A)(1) of this section shall not release the information without the permission of the individual who would be or would reasonably tend to be identified, or of the individual's legal representative, unless the agency or individual is required to release it by division (C) of this section, by court order, or for the administration or enforcement of a statute relating to homes.

(B) Except as provided in division (C) of this section, any record that identifies an individual described in division (A)(1)(a) to (c) of this section or that reasonably would tend to identify such an individual is not a public record for the purposes of section 149.43 of the Revised Code, and is not subject to inspection and copying under section 1347.08 of the Revised Code.

(C)(1) If the director, or an agency or individual to whom the director is required by court order or for administration or enforcement of a statute relating to homes to release information described in division (A)(1) of this section, uses information in any administrative or judicial proceeding against a home that reasonably would tend to identify an individual described in division (A)(1)(a) to (c) of this section, the director, agency, or individual shall disclose that information to the home. However, the director, agency, or individual shall not disclose information that directly identifies an individual described in divisions (A)(1)(a) to (c) of this section, unless the individual is to testify in the proceedings.

(2)(a) On the request of the director of aging or the director's designee and subject to division (C)(2)(b) of this section, the director of health may release to the department of aging the identity of a patient or resident of a home who receives assisted living services pursuant to sections 173.54 to 173.548 of the Revised Code.

(b) The department of aging shall not use information obtained under division (C)(2)(a) for any purpose other than monitoring the well-being of patients or residents who receive assisted living services.

(D) No person shall knowingly register a false complaint about a home with the director, or knowingly swear or affirm the truth of a false complaint, when the complaint is made for the purpose of incriminating another.

(E) An individual who in good faith submits a complaint under this section or any other provision of the Revised Code regarding a violation of this chapter, or participates in any investigation, administrative proceeding, or judicial proceeding resulting from the complaint, has the full protection against retaliatory action provided by sections 4113.51 to 4113.53 of the Revised Code.

**HISTORY:**

143 v H 822 (Eff 12-13-90); 148 v H 511. Eff 4-10-2001; 2017 hb49, § 101.01, effective September 29, 2017.

**Amendment Notes**

The 2017 amendment by HB 49 redesignated former (C) as (C)(1); and added (C)(2).

**NOTES TO DECISIONS**

**Letters of complaint**

Letters of complaint received by the Ohio department of health in regard to a particular nursing home are not records required to be kept and are thus not subject to inspection under R.C. 149.43. Additionally, there is a need to preserve the confidentiality of complaints and the identity of the complainants against nursing home operations both to encourage the giving of such information to the director of health and to protect the complainants against possible retaliation: Wayside Farms, Inc. v. State, 50 Ohio Misc. 13, 4 Ohio Op. 3d 364, 364 N.E.2d 297, 1977 Ohio Misc. LEXIS 88 (Ohio C.P. 1977).

**RESEARCH REFERENCES AND PRACTICE AIDS**

**Cross-References to Related Sections**

Penalties, RC § 3721.99.

Inspection of personal information maintained, exceptions, RC § 1347.08.

**Ohio Administrative Code**

Changes in residents' health status; incidents; injury, death—Nursing home. OAC 3701-17-12.

### § 3721.032 Fire safety in homes.

The state fire marshal shall enforce all statutes and rules pertaining to fire safety in homes and shall adopt rules pertaining to fire safety in homes as the marshal determines necessary. The rules adopted by the marshal shall be in addition to those fire safety rules that the board of building standards and the director of health are empowered to adopt. In the event of a dispute between the marshal and another officer having responsibilities under sections 3721.01 to 3721.09 of the Revised Code with respect to the interpretation or application of a specific fire safety statute or rule, the interpretation of the marshal shall prevail.

**HISTORY:**

151 v H 66, § 101.01, eff. 6-30-05; 2012 HB 487, § 101.01, eff. Sept. 10, 2012.

**Amendment Notes**

The 2012 amendment substituted "director of health" for "public health council" in the second sentence.

**NOTES TO DECISIONS**

**Former law**

Requirements by the Board of Building Standards that sprinkler systems be installed throughout nursing homes prevail over similar requirements of the State Fire Marshal, are valid and pertain to areas free of noncombustible materials as well as all other areas. In re Milcrest Nursing Home, 59 Ohio App. 2d 116, 13 Ohio Op. 3d 168, 392 N.E.2d 1097, 1978 Ohio App. LEXIS 7586 (Ohio Ct. App., Union County 1978).

### § 3721.04 Uniform rules for operation of homes; standards.

(A) The director of health shall adopt and publish rules governing the operation of homes, which shall have uniform application throughout the state, and shall prescribe standards for homes with respect to, but not limited to, the following matters:

(1) The minimum space requirements for occupants and equipping of the buildings in which homes are housed so as to ensure healthful, safe, sanitary, and comfortable conditions for all residents, so long as they are not inconsistent with Chapters 3781. and 3791. of the Revised Code or with any rules adopted by the board of building standards and by the state fire marshal;

(2) The number and qualifications of personnel, including management and nursing staff, for each class of home, and the qualifications of nurse aides, as defined in section 3721.21 of the Revised Code, used by long-term care facilities, as defined in that section;

(3) The medical, rehabilitative, and recreational services to be provided by each class of home;

(4) Dietetic services, including but not limited to sanitation, nutritional adequacy, and palatability of food;

(5) The personal and social services to be provided by each class of home;

(6) The business and accounting practices to be followed and the type of patient and business records to be kept by such homes;

(7) The operation of adult day-care programs provided by and on the same site as homes licensed under this chapter;

(8) The standards and procedures to be followed by residential care facilities in admitting and retaining a resident who requires the application of dressings, including requirements for charting and evaluating on a weekly basis;

(9) The requirements for conducting weekly evaluations of residents receiving skilled nursing care in residential care facilities.

(B) The director may adopt whatever additional rules are necessary to carry out or enforce the provisions of sections 3721.01 to 3721.09 and 3721.99 of the Revised Code.

(C) The following apply to the director when adopting rules under division (A)(1) of this section regarding the equipping of the buildings in which homes are housed:

(1) The rules shall not require that each resident sleeping room, or a percentage of the resident sleeping rooms, have a bathtub or shower that is directly accessible from or exclusively for the room.

(2) The rules shall require that the privacy and dignity of residents be protected when the residents are transported to and from bathing facilities, prepare for bathing, and bathe.

(D) The following apply to the director when adopting rules under division (A)(2) of this section regarding the number and qualifications of personnel in homes:

(1) When adopting rules applicable to residential care facilities, the director shall take into consideration the effect that the following may have on the number of personnel needed:

(a) Provision of personal care services;

(b) Provision of part-time, intermittent skilled nursing care pursuant to division (C) of section 3721.011 of the Revised Code;

(c) Provision of skilled nursing care to residents pursuant to division (D) of section 3721.011 of the Revised Code.

(2) When adopting rules applicable to nursing homes, the director shall require each nursing home to do both of the following:

(a) Have sufficient direct care staff on each shift to meet the needs of the residents in an appropriate and timely manner;

(b) Have the following individuals provide a minimum daily average of two and one-half hours of direct care per resident:

(i) Registered nurses, including registered nurses who perform administrative and supervisory duties;

(ii) Licensed practical nurses, including licensed practical nurses who perform administrative and supervisory duties;

(iii) Nurse aides.

(3) The rules prescribing qualifications of nurse aides used by long-term care facilities, as those terms are defined in section 3721.21 of the Revised Code, shall be no less stringent

than the requirements, guidelines, and procedures established by the United States secretary of health and human services under section 1819 of the "Social Security Act," 101 Stat. 1330-160 ( 1987 ), 42 U.S.C. 1395i-3, as amended, and section 1919 of the "Social Security Act," 101 Stat. 1330-182 (1987), 42 U.S.C. 1396r, as amended.

(E) The following apply to the director when adopting rules under division (A)(2) of this section regarding the number and qualifications of personnel in nursing homes or rules under division (A)(5) of this section regarding social services to be provided by nursing homes:

(1) The rules shall not prescribe the number of individuals licensed as social workers under Chapter 4757. of the Revised Code that a nursing home with one hundred twenty or fewer beds must employ.

(2) The rules shall require each nursing home with more than one hundred twenty beds to employ on a full-time basis one individual licensed as a social worker under Chapter 4757. of the Revised Code.

(3) The rules shall require each nursing home to offer its residents medically related social services that assist the residents in attaining or maintaining their highest practicable physical, mental, and psychosocial well-being.



**HISTORY:**

128 v 645 (Eff 9-7-59); 131 v 890 (Eff 10-20-65); 132 v H 1 (Eff 2-21-67); 134 v H 1086 (Eff 12-30-72); 137 v H 234 (Eff 10-25-78); 139 v H 694 (Eff 11-15-81); 143 v H 253 (Eff 11-15-90); 143 v H 359 (Eff 3-13-90); 143 v H 822 (Eff 12-13-90); 145 v H 152 (Eff 7-1-93); 146 v H 117 (Eff 9-29-95); 146 v S 310. Eff 6-20-96; 151 v S 87, § 1, eff. 4-14-06; 2011 HB 153, § 101.01, eff. Sept. 29, 2011; 2012 HB 487, § 101.01, eff. Sept. 10, 2012.

**Amendment Notes**

The 2012 amendment substituted "director of health" for "public health council" in the introductory language of (A); substituted "director" for "public health council" wherever it appears in (B) through (D); in (D)(3), substituted "section 1819" for "sections 1819 and 1919", substituted "101 Stat. 1330-160 (1987), 42 U.S.C. 1395i-3" for "49 Stat. 620 (1935), 42 U.S.C. 301", and added "and section 1919 of the 'Social Security Act,' 101 Stat. 1330-182 (1987), 42 U.S.C. 1396r, as amended" to the end; and added (E).

The 2011 amendment inserted (C) and (D)(2); redesignated former (C) and (D)(2) as (D) and (D)(3); substituted "residents" for "hospice patients" in present (D)(1)(c); and substituted "42 U.S.C. 301" for "42 U.S.C.A. 301" in present (D)(3).

151 v S 87, effective April 14, 2006, rewrote (C)(1).

## RESEARCH REFERENCES AND PRACTICE AIDS

**Cross-References to Related Sections**

Criminal records check for prospective employees providing direct care to older adult, RC § 3721.121.

Duties of superintendent of the bureau of criminal identification and investigation re employees of nursing homes, RC § 109.57.

Enforcement; revocation of license, RC § 3721.03.

Local regulation, RC § 3721.09.

Special diets, administration of medication to rest home residents; admission or retention of person needing skilled nursing care, RC § 3721.011.

**Ohio Administrative Code**

Nursing homes. OAC ch. 3701-17.

Activities; chaplain services; visiting hours; laundry; pets; mail—
Nursing home. OAC 3701-17-09.

Personnel requirements—
Nursing home. OAC 3701-17-07 et seq.

Resident assessments; medical supervision—
Nursing home. OAC 3701-17-10 et seq.

Space requirements—
Nursing home. OAC 3701-17-23.

Variances—
Nursing home. OAC 3701-17-34.

### § 3721.041 Vaccinations against influenza and pneumonia.

(A) As used in this section:

(1) "Advisory committee" means the advisory committee on immunization practices of the United States centers for disease control and prevention or a successor committee or agency.

(2) "Home" has the same meaning as in section 3721.01 of the Revised Code.

(3) "Physician" means an individual authorized under Chapter 4731. of the Revised Code to practice medicine and surgery or osteopathic medicine and surgery.

(B)(1) Each home shall, on an annual basis, offer to each resident, in accordance with guidelines issued by the advisory committee, vaccination against influenza, unless a physician has determined that vaccination of the resident is medically inappropriate. The vaccine shall be of a form approved by the advisory committee for that calendar year. A resident may refuse vaccination.

(2) Each home shall obtain the influenza vaccine information sheet described in section 3701.138 of the Revised Code and post the sheet in a conspicuous location that is accessible to all residents, employees, and visitors. Not later than the first day of August each year, the home shall determine whether the information sheet it has posted is the most recent version available. If it is not, the home shall replace the information sheet with the updated version. Nothing in this division requires an older adult to be vaccinated against influenza.

Failure to comply with the requirement to post the information sheet shall not be taken into account when any survey or inspection of the home is conducted and shall not be used as the basis for imposing any penalty against the home.

(C) Each home shall offer to each resident, in accordance with guidelines issued by the advisory committee, vaccination against pneumococcal pneumonia, unless the resident has already received such vaccination or a physician has determined that vaccination of the resident is medically inappropriate. Each vaccine shall be of a form approved by the advisory committee for that calendar year. A resident may refuse vaccination.

(D) The director of health may adopt rules under Chapter 119. of the Revised Code as the director considers appropriate to implement this section.

**HISTORY:**

151 v H 257, § 1, eff. 6-15-06; 2016 sb311, § 1, effective March 21, 2017.

**Amendment Notes**

The 2016 amendment by SB 311 inserted present (A)(2) and redesignated former (A)(2) as (A)(3); redesignated former (B) as (B)(1) and added (B)(2).

### § 3721.042 Denial of license based on noncompliance with requirements regarding toilet rooms and dining and recreational areas.

The director of health may not deny a nursing home license to a facility seeking a license under this chapter as a nursing home on the grounds that the facility does not satisfy a requirement established in rules adopted under section 3721.04 of the Revised Code regarding the toilet rooms and dining and recreational areas of nursing homes if all of the following requirements are met:

(A) The facility seeks a license under this chapter because it is a county home or district home being sold under section 5155.31 of the Revised Code to a person who may not operate the facility without a nursing home license under this chapter.

(B) The requirement would not have applied to the facility had the facility been a nursing home first licensed under this chapter before October 20, 2001.

(C) The facility was a nursing facility, as defined in section 5165.01 of the Revised Code, on the date immediately preceding the date the facility is sold to the person seeking the license.

**HISTORY:**

152 v H 125, § 1, eff. 6-25-08; 2013 HB 59, § 101.01, eff. Sept. 29, 2013.

**Amendment Notes**

The 2013 amendment substituted "section 5165.01" for "section 5111.20" in (C).

### § 3721.05 License required; prohibitions.

No person, firm, partnership, association, or corporation shall:

(A) Operate a home as defined in section 3721.01 of the Revised Code without obtaining a license from the director of health;

(B) Violate any of the conditions or requirements necessary for licensing after the license has been issued;

(C) Operate a home after the license for such has been revoked by the director of health;

(D) Interfere with the inspection of a licensed home by any state or local official when he is performing duties required of him by Chapter 3721. of the Revised Code. All licensed homes shall be open for inspection.

(E) Violate any of the provisions of Chapter 3721. of the Revised Code or any rules and regulations adopted pursuant thereto.

**HISTORY:**
128 v 645 (Eff 9-7-59); 131 v 891 (Eff 10-20-65); 146 v H 117. Eff 6-30-95.

#### NOTES TO DECISIONS

Analysis

Evidence sufficient for revocation
Transfer of license

**Evidence sufficient for revocation**
While the violation of a single public health regulation might be insufficient to justify the revocation of a license to operate a nursing home, multiple violations, taken together, establish a practice which justifies such a revocation. Erie Care Center, Inc. v. Ackerman, 5 Ohio App. 3d 102, 449 N.E.2d 486, 1982 Ohio App. LEXIS 11024 (Ohio Ct. App., Erie County 1982).

**Transfer of license**
A license to use premises for a specific purpose does not create a property right within the constitutional meaning of the term, nor even a contract, but only permission to engage in the specified business. Therefore the public health council may provide by valid regulation that a license to operate a nursing home is non-transferable. Adams v. Ohio Dep't of Health, 5 Ohio Op. 3d 148, 356 N.E.2d 324, 1976 Ohio Misc. LEXIS 60 (Ohio C.P. 1976).

#### ATTORNEY GENERAL OPINIONS

A "county home" is not necessarily a "nursing home operated by a governmental agency," which would require the licensing of the superintendent as a nursing home administrator, as provided by R.C. Chapter 4751. When a county operates a separate facility, or a distinct portion of a county home, as a nursing home, the superintendent or person charged with the general administration of the facility shall be licensed as provided in R.C. Chapter 4751.: 1970 Ohio Op. Att'y Gen. No. 164.

#### RESEARCH REFERENCES AND PRACTICE AIDS

**Cross-References to Related Sections**
Penalty, RC § 3721.99.
Conditions for issuing license, RC § 3721.07.
Enforcement; revocation of license, RC § 3721.03.
Inspection and licensing of homes; fees, RC § 3721.02.
Local regulation, RC § 3721.09.
Practice of environmental health defined, RC § 4736.01.

**Ohio Administrative Code**
Department of health—
Licensure application and renewal—
Nursing home. OAC 3701-17-03.
Prohibitions—
Nursing home. OAC 3701-17-05.

### § 3721.051 Prohibitions.

No county home or district home licensed under section 3721.07 of the Revised Code shall do any of the following:

(A) Violate any of the conditions or requirements necessary for licensing after the license has been issued;

(B) Continue operation after its license has been revoked by the director of health;

(C) Fail to be open for an inspection, or interfere with an inspection, by a state or local official performing inspection duties under Chapter 3721. of the Revised Code;

(D) Violate any of the provisions of this chapter or any rules adopted thereunder.

**HISTORY:**
148 v S 178. Eff 7-21-2000.

#### RESEARCH REFERENCES AND PRACTICE AIDS

**Cross-References to Related Sections**
Penalties, RC § 3721.99.
Local regulations, RC § 3721.09.

**Ohio Administrative Code**
Prohibitions—
Nursing home. OAC 3701-17-05.

### § 3721.06 Placement in unlicensed institution.

No public official or employee shall place any person in, or recommend that any person be placed in, or directly or indirectly cause any person to be placed in any home as defined in section 3721.01 of the Revised Code which is being operated without a license from the director of health or from a political subdivision certified pursuant to section 3721.09 of the Revised Code.

**HISTORY:**
128 v 645 (Eff 9-7-59); 131 v 892. Eff 10-20-65.

#### RESEARCH REFERENCES AND PRACTICE AIDS

**Cross-References to Related Sections**
Penalty, RC § 3721.99.
Enforcement; revocation of license, RC § 3721.03.
Rule-making authority of public health council, RC § 3721.04.

### § 3721.07 Conditions for issuing license; renewal; appeals.

Every person desiring to operate a home and the superintendent or administrator of each county home or district home for which a license as a residential care facility is sought shall apply for a license to the director of health. The director shall issue a license for the home, if after investigation of the applicant and, if required by section 3721.02 of the Revised Code, inspection of the home, the following requirements or conditions are satisfied or complied with:

(A) The applicant has not been convicted of a felony or a crime involving moral turpitude;

(B) The applicant is not violating any of the rules adopted by the director of health or any order issued by the director;

(C) The applicant has not had a license to operate the home revoked pursuant to section 3721.03 of the Revised Code because of any act or omission that jeopardized a resident's health, welfare, or safety nor has the applicant had a long-standing pattern of violations of this chapter or rules adopted under it that caused physical, emotional, mental, or psychosocial harm to one or more residents.

(D) The buildings in which the home is housed have been approved by the state fire marshal or a township, municipal, or other legally constituted fire department approved by the marshal. In the approval of a home such agencies shall apply standards prescribed by the board of building standards, and by the state fire marshal, and by section 3721.071 of the Revised Code.

(E) The applicant, if it is an individual, or the principal participants, if it is an association or a corporation, is or are suitable financially and morally to operate a home;

(F) The applicant is equipped to furnish humane, kind, and adequate treatment and care;

(G) The home does not maintain or contain:

(1) Facilities for the performance of major surgical procedures;

(2) Facilities for providing therapeutic radiation;

(3) An emergency ward;

(4) A clinical laboratory unless it is under the supervision of a clinical pathologist who is a licensed physician in this state;

(5) Facilities for radiological examinations unless such examinations are performed only by a person licensed to practice medicine, surgery, or dentistry in this state.

Titles 11 — 37

(H) The home does not accept or treat outpatients, except upon the written orders of a physician licensed in this state, maternity cases, boarding children, and does not house transient guests, other than participants in an adult day-care program, for twenty-four hours or less;

(I) The home is in compliance with sections 3721.28 and 3721.29 of the Revised Code.

When the director issues a license, the license shall remain in effect until revoked by the director or voided at the request of the applicant; provided, there shall be an annual renewal fee payable during the month of January of each calendar year. Any licensed home that does not pay its renewal fee in January shall pay, beginning the first day of February, a late fee of one hundred dollars for each week or part thereof that the renewal fee is not paid. If either the renewal fee or the late fee is not paid by the fifteenth day of February, the director may, in accordance with Chapter 119. of the Revised Code, revoke the home's license.

If, under division (B)(5) of section 3721.03 of the Revised Code, the license of a person has been revoked or the license of a county home or district home to operate as a residential care facility has been revoked, the director of health shall not issue a license to the person or home at any time. A person whose license is revoked, and a county home or district home that has its license as a residential care facility revoked other than under division (B)(5) of section 3721.03 of the Revised Code, for any reason other than nonpayment of the license renewal fee or late fees shall not be issued a new license under this chapter until a period of one year following the date of revocation has elapsed.

Any applicant who is denied a license may appeal in accordance with Chapter 119. of the Revised Code.

**HISTORY:**

128 v 645 (Eff 9-7-59); 131 v 892 (Eff 10-20-65); 134 v H 1086 (Eff 12-30-72); 136 v S 55 (Eff 11-14-75); 142 v S 386 (Eff 3-29-88); 143 v H 112 (Eff 2-16-89); 143 v H 822 (Eff 12-13-90); 145 v H 152 (Eff 7-1-93); 146 v H 117 (Eff 6-30-95); 148 v S 178. Eff 7-21-2000; 151 v H 66, § 101.01, eff. 6-30-05; 2012 HB 487, § 101.01, eff. Sept. 10, 2012.

**Amendment Notes**

The 2012 amendment, in (B), substituted "adopted by the director of health" for "made by the public health council" and deleted "of health" from the end.

151 v H 66, effective June 30, 2005, inserted (C) and redesignated the remaining subsections accordingly; and rewrote the third paragraph in (I).

### RESEARCH REFERENCES AND PRACTICE AIDS

**Cross-References to Related Sections**

Annual license required; prohibitions, RC § 3721.05.
Enforcement; revocation of license, RC § 3721.03.
Local regulation, RC § 3721.09.
Prohibitions, RC § 3721.051.
Rule-making authority of public health council, RC § 3721.04.

**Ohio Administrative Code**

Department of health, director of—
Appeal of denial of long-term care facility certification. OAC ch. 3701-63.
Licensure application and renewal; revocation—
Nursing home. OAC 3701-17-03.

## § 3721.071 Automatic fire alarm and extinguishing systems.

The buildings in which a home is housed shall be equipped with both an automatic fire extinguishing system and fire alarm system. Such systems shall conform to standards set forth in the regulations of the board of building standards and the state fire marshal.

The time for compliance with the requirements imposed by this section shall be January 1, 1975, except that the date for compliance with the automatic fire extinguishing requirements is extended to January 1, 1976, provided the buildings of the home are otherwise in compliance with fire safety laws and regulations and:

(A) The home within thirty days after August 4, 1975, files a written plan with the state fire marshal's office that:

(1) Outlines the interim safety procedures which shall be carried out to reduce the possibility of a fire;

(2) Provides evidence that the home has entered into an agreement for a fire safety inspection to be conducted not less than monthly by a qualified independent safety engineer consultant or a township, municipal, or other legally constituted fire department, or by a township or municipal fire prevention officer;

(3) Provides verification that the home has entered into a valid contract for the installation of an automatic fire extinguishing system or fire alarm system, or both, as required to comply with this section;

(4) Includes a statement regarding the expected date for the completion of the fire extinguishing system or fire alarm system, or both.

(B) Inspections by a qualified independent safety engineer consultant or a township, municipal, or other legally constituted fire department, or by a township or municipal fire prevention officer are initiated no later than sixty days after August 4, 1975, and are conducted no less than monthly thereafter, and reports of the consultant, fire department, or fire prevention officer identifying existing hazards and recommended corrective actions are submitted to the state fire marshal, the division of industrial compliance in the department of commerce, and the department of health.

It is the express intent of the general assembly that the department of medicaid shall terminate the medicaid provider agreements of those homes that do not comply with the requirements of this section for the submission of a written fire safety plan and the deadline for entering into contracts for the installation of systems.

**HISTORY:**

134 v H 1086 (Eff 12-30-72); 136 v S 14 (Eff 8-4-75); 141 v H 428 (Eff 12-23-86); 146 v S 162 (Eff 10-29-95); 148 v H 471. Eff 7-1-2000; 153 v H 1, § 101.01, eff. 10-16-09; 2012 HB 487, § 101.01, eff. Sept. 10, 2012; 2013 HB 59, § 101.01, eff. Sept. 29, 2013.

**Amendment Notes**

The 2013 amendment substituted "medicaid shall terminate the medicaid provider agreements of" for "job and family services shall terminate payments under Title XIX of the 'Social Security Act,' 49 Stat. 620 (1935), 42 U.S.C. 301, as amended, to" in the second paragraph of (B); and made a stylistic change.

The 2012 amendment substituted "industrial compliance" for "labor" in the first paragraph of (B).

153 v H 1, effective October 16, 2009, substituted "division of labor" for "division of industrial compliance" in the first paragraph of (B).

### NOTES TO DECISIONS

**Authority of board of building standards**

Nursing homes must comply with the board of building standards regulation requiring sprinklers throughout the home. In re Milcrest Nursing Home, 59 Ohio App. 2d 116, 13 Ohio Op. 3d 168, 392 N.E.2d 1097, 1978 Ohio App. LEXIS 7586 (Ohio Ct. App., Union County 1978).

### RESEARCH REFERENCES AND PRACTICE AIDS

**Cross-References to Related Sections**

Conditions for issuance of license, RC § 3721.07.
Enforcement; revocation of license, RC § 3721.03.
Rule-making authority of public health council, RC § 3721.04.

**Ohio Administrative Code**

Department of commerce—
Board of building standards—
Ohio building code. OAC ch. 4101:1-1 et seq.
Department of health, public health council—
Fire safety and disaster preparedness—
Nursing home. OAC 3701-17-25.

## § 3721.072 Nursing home quality improvement projects.

(A) As used in this section:

(1) "Advance care planning" means providing an opportunity to discuss the goals that may be met through the care provided by a nursing home.

(2) "Overhead paging" means sending audible announcements through an electronic sound amplification and distribution system throughout part or all of a nursing home to staff, residents, residents' families, or others.

(B) Beginning July 1, 2013, each nursing home shall participate every two years in at least one of the quality improvement projects included on the list made available by the department of aging under the nursing home quality initiative established under section 173.60 of the Revised Code.

(C) Beginning July 1, 2015, each nursing home shall participate in advance care planning with each resident or the resident's sponsor if the resident is unable to participate. For each resident, the advance care planning shall be provided on admission to the nursing home or, in the case of an individual residing in a nursing home on July 1, 2015, as soon as practicable. Thereafter, for each resident, the advance care planning shall be provided quarterly each year.

(D) Beginning July 1, 2015, each nursing home shall prohibit the use of overhead paging within the nursing home, except that the nursing home may permit the use of overhead paging for matters of urgent public safety or urgent clinical operations. The nursing home shall develop a written policy regarding its use of overhead paging and make the policy available to staff, residents, and residents' families.

**HISTORY:**

2013 HB 59, § 101.01, eff. Sept. 29, 2013.

### § 3721.08 Injunction against operation without license; elimination of real and present danger; notice to home prior to action; special master; on-site monitors.

(A) As used in this section, "real and present danger" means imminent danger of serious physical or life-threatening harm to one or more occupants of a home.

(B) The director of health may petition the court of common pleas of the county in which the home is located for an order enjoining any person from operating a home without a license or enjoining a county home or district home that has had its license revoked from continuing to operate. The court shall have jurisdiction to grant such injunctive relief upon a showing that the respondent named in the petition is operating a home without a license or that the county home or district home named in the petition is operating despite the revocation of its license. The court shall have jurisdiction to grant such injunctive relief against the operation of a home without a valid license regardless of whether the home meets essential licensing requirements.

(C) Unless the department of medicaid or contracting agency has taken action under section 5165.77 of the Revised Code to appoint a temporary manager or seek injunctive relief, if, in the judgment of the director of health, real and present danger exists at any home, the director may petition the court of common pleas of the county in which the home is located for such injunctive relief as is necessary to close the home, transfer one or more occupants to other homes or other appropriate care settings, or otherwise eliminate the real and present danger. The court shall have the jurisdiction to grant such injunctive relief upon a showing that there is real and present danger.

(D)(1) If the director determines that real and present danger exists at a home and elects not to immediately seek injunctive relief under division (C) of this section, the director may give written notice of proposed action to the home. The notice shall specify all of the following:

(a) The nature of the conditions giving rise to the real and present danger;

(b) The measures that the director determines the home must take to respond to the conditions;

(c) The date on which the director intends to seek injunctive relief under division (C) of this section if the director determines that real and present danger exists at the home.

(2) If the home notifies the director, within the time specified pursuant to division (D)(1)(c) of this section, that it believes the conditions giving rise to the real and present danger have been substantially corrected, the director shall conduct an inspection to determine whether real and present danger exists. If the director determines on the basis of the inspection that real and present danger exists, the director may petition under division (C) of this section for injunctive relief.

(E)(1) If in the judgment of the director of health conditions exist at a home that will give rise to real and present danger if not corrected, the director shall give written notice of proposed action to the home. The notice shall specify all of the following:

(a) The nature of the conditions giving rise to the director's judgment;

(b) The measures that the director determines the home must take to respond to the conditions;

(c) The date, which shall be no less than ten days after the notice is delivered, on which the director intends to seek injunctive relief under division (C) of this section if the conditions are not substantially corrected and the director determines that a real and present danger exists.

(2) If the home notifies the director, within the period of time specified pursuant to division (E)(1)(c) of this section, that the conditions giving rise to the director's determination have been substantially corrected, the director shall conduct an inspection. If the director determines on the basis of the inspection that the conditions have not been corrected and a real and present danger exists, the director may petition under division (C) of this section for injunctive relief.

(F)(1) A court that grants injunctive relief under division (C) of this section may also appoint a special master who, subject to division (F)(2) of this section, shall have such powers and authority over the home and length of appointment as the court considers necessary. Subject to division (F)(2) of this section, the salary of a special master and any costs incurred by a special master shall be the obligation of the home.

(2) No special master shall enter into any employment contract on behalf of a home, or purchase with the home's funds any capital goods totaling more than ten thousand dollars, unless the special master has obtained approval for the contract or purchase from the home's operator or the court.

(G) If the director takes action under division (C), (D), or (E) of this section, the director may also appoint employees of the department of health to conduct on-site monitoring of the home. Appointment of monitors is not subject to appeal under Chapter 119. or any other section of the Revised Code. No employee of a home for which monitors are appointed, no person employed by the home within the previous two years, and no person who currently has a consulting contract with the department or a home, shall be appointed under this division. Every monitor shall have the professional qualifications necessary to monitor correction of the conditions that give rise to or, in the director's judgment, will give rise to real and present danger. The number of monitors present at a home at any given time shall not exceed one for every fifty residents, or fraction thereof.

(H) On finding that the real and present danger for which injunctive relief was granted under division (C) of this section has been eliminated and that the home's operator has demonstrated the capacity to prevent the real and present danger from recurring, the court shall terminate its jurisdiction over the home and return control and management of the home to the operator. If the real and present danger cannot be eliminated practicably within a reasonable time following appointment of a special master, the court may order the special master to close the home and transfer all residents to other homes or other appropriate care settings.

(I) The director of health shall give notice of proposed action under divisions (D) and (E) of this section to both of the following:

(1) The home's administrator;

(2) If the home is operated by an organization described in subsection 501(c)(3) and tax exempt under subsection 501(a) of the "Internal Revenue Code of 1986," 100 Stat. 2085, 26 U.S.C.A. 1, as amended, the board of trustees of the organization; or, if the home is not operated by such an organization, the owner of the home.

Notices shall be delivered by certified mail or hand delivery. If notices are mailed, they shall be addressed to the persons specified in divisions (I)(1) and (2) of this section, as indicated in the department of health's records. If they are hand delivered, they shall be delivered to persons who would reasonably appear to the average prudent person to have authority to accept them.

(J) If ownership of a home is assigned or transferred to a different person, the new owner is responsible and liable for compliance with any notice of proposed action or order issued under this section prior to the effective date of the assignment or transfer.

**HISTORY:**

131 v 894 (Eff 10-20-65); 134 v H 1086 (Eff 12-30-72); 143 v H 822 (Eff 12-13-90); 145 v H 152 (Eff 7-1-93); 148 v H 471 (Eff 7-1-2000); 148 v S 178, §§ 1, 3. Eff 7-21-2000.; 2013 HB 59, § 101.01, eff. Sept. 29, 2013.

**Editor's Notes**

The effective date of section 3 of SB 178 (148 v S 178) differs from the effective date set for the section by section 5 of the act. See the provisions of Ohio Const. art II, §§ 1c and 1d.

The provisions of § 5 of SB 178 (148 v S 178) read as follows:

SECTION 5. Sections 3 and 4 of this act shall take effect on July 1, 2000.

**Amendment Notes**

The 2013 amendment, in the first sentence of (C), substituted "medicaid" for "job and family services" and "section 5165.77" for "section 5111.51".

## NOTES TO DECISIONS

**Injunction against operation**

In an action by the director of health to enjoin the operation of an unlicensed nursing home pursuant to R.C. 3721.08, an injunction shall be granted where it is undisputed that the evidence shows that the facility is a nursing home pursuant to R.C. 3721.01, that the nursing home is unlicensed and that the home is unlicensed because it does not comply with essential licensing requirements. Ackerman v. Tri-City Geriatric & Health Care, Inc., 55 Ohio St. 2d 51, 9 Ohio Op. 3d 62, 378 N.E.2d 145, 1978 Ohio LEXIS 614 (Ohio 1978).

## RESEARCH REFERENCES AND PRACTICE AIDS

**Cross-References to Related Sections**

Enforcement; revocation of license, RC § 3721.03.
Local regulation, RC § 3721.09.
Residents' rights, RC § 3721.13.
Residents' rights concerning transfer or discharge, RC § 3721.16.

**Ohio Rules**

Injunctions, CivR 65.

## § 3721.081 Actions by director to protect resident health or safety; possible orders; compliance by resident home; hearings.

(A) Notwithstanding any action the director of health may take under section 3721.08 of the Revised Code, if the director determines immediate action is necessary to protect resident health or safety because a home has neglected or refused to act with sufficient promptness or efficiency to protect resident health or safety, the director may do either or both of the following before a home is provided notice and an opportunity for a hearing under Chapter 119. of the Revised Code:

(1) Issue orders, including specifying actions that a home must take immediately to address resident health and safety;

(2) Take direct action to protect resident health or safety if the home fails to act on an order issued pursuant to division (A)(1) of this section.

(B)(1) Subject to divisions (B)(2) and (3) of this section, orders that may be issued and direct action that may be taken under this section include all of the following:

(a) Removing a threat to resident health or safety;

(b) Transferring residents to another home or appropriate care setting until a threat to resident health or safety is resolved;

(c) Appointing a temporary administrator for a home for the duration of an order;

(d) Issuing any other order or taking any other action as necessary to protect the health or safety of residents of a home.

(2) The director shall not enter a home pursuant to this section unless the director provides the operator with notice at least twenty-four hours in advance.

(3) The director's authority to transfer residents under this section is subject to both of the following:

(a) If the reason for the transfer is due to an environmental condition affecting the home, the director may transfer only those residents directly affected by the environmental condition.

(b) If the reason for the transfer is due to a clinical condition that affects the entire home, the director may transfer all residents for the lesser of thirty calendar days or until the date that the condition is no longer affecting the home. If the condition persists longer than thirty calendar days, the director shall provide the home a notice regarding the reason for determining that the condition is still affecting the home. The home may request a hearing regarding the notice in accordance with this section.

(C) Any expenses incurred by a home to comply with an order issued under this section shall be borne by the home.

If a hearing is conducted in accordance with this section and the director is found to have acted in violation of this section, all reasonable expenses incurred by the home as a result of the director's action shall be reimbursed to the home by the department of health within ninety days after the date that the final adjudication order is issued.

(D) If a home fails to comply with an order issued under this section, the director shall issue an order imposing a fine of not more than one hundred thousand dollars for each instance of noncompliance. Any fine imposed shall be reasonably commensurate to the harm caused by the home, and the home may request a hearing as to the fine's reasonableness in accordance with this section.

(E) All fines collected under this section shall be deposited in the state treasury to the credit of the general operations fund created by section 3701.83 of the Revised Code.

(F) A home subject to an order or action under this section may request a hearing under Chapter 119. of the Revised Code. The request must be received by the director within fifteen days after the notice of the order was mailed. If the home timely requests a hearing, the date set for the hearing shall be within ten days after the home requested the hearing, unless otherwise agreed to by both the director and the home.

An order issued under this section shall remain in effect, unless reversed by the director, until a final adjudication order issued by the director pursuant to this section and Chapter 119. of the Revised Code becomes effective. The director shall issue the final adjudication order not later than thirty days after completion of the hearing.

A home may appeal a final adjudication order in accordance with Chapter 119. of the Revised Code.

**HISTORY:**

2021 hb110, § 101.01, effective September 30, 2021.

## § 3721.09 Local regulation.

Sections 3721.02, 3721.03, 3721.04, 3721.05, 3721.051, 3721.07, and 3721.08 of the Revised Code and the regulations adopted pursuant thereto are not applicable in political subdivisions which the director of health, by annual certification, determines have adopted and are enforcing their own standards which are equal to or greater in the requirements than those of sections 3721.02, 3721.03, 3721.04, 3721.05, 3721.051, 3721.07, and 3721.08 of the Revised Code and the regulations adopted pursuant thereto. Officials of political subdivisions shall cooperate fully with the director and provide the director with information which the director finds necessary in order to make a determination.

**HISTORY:**

131 v 894 (Eff 10-20-65); 148 v S 178. Eff 7-21-2000.

## RESEARCH REFERENCES AND PRACTICE AIDS

**Cross-References to Related Sections**

Additional penalties for failing to cease activity or using equipment or facility involved in violation, RC § 3702.55.
Enforcement; revocation of license, RC § 3721.03.
Exemptions from fees, RC § 3721.511.
Franchise permit fees for funding of home and community-based services for elderly and disabled persons, RC § 5168.42.
Placement in unlicensed institution, RC § 3721.06.
Uniform rules for operation of homes; standards, RC § 3721.04.

# RESIDENTS' RIGHTS

## § 3721.10 Definitions.

As used in sections 3721.10 to 3721.18 of the Revised Code:

(A) "Home" means all of the following:

(1) A home as defined in section 3721.01 of the Revised Code;

(2) Any facility or part of a facility not defined as a home under section 3721.01 of the Revised Code that is a skilled nursing facility or nursing facility, both as defined in section 5165.01 of the Revised Code;

(3) A county home or district home operated pursuant to Chapter 5155. of the Revised Code.

(B) "Resident" means a resident or a patient of a home.

(C) "Administrator" means all of the following:

(1) With respect to a home as defined in section 3721.01 of the Revised Code, a nursing home administrator as defined in section 4751.01 of the Revised Code;

(2) With respect to a facility or part of a facility not defined as a home in section 3721.01 of the Revised Code that is authorized to provide skilled nursing facility or nursing facility services, the administrator of the facility or part of a facility;

(3) With respect to a county home or district home, the superintendent or administrator appointed or selected under Chapter 5155. of the Revised Code.

(D) "Sponsor" means an adult relative, friend, or guardian of a resident who has an interest or responsibility in the resident's welfare.

(E) "Residents' rights advocate" means:

(1) An employee or representative of any state or local government entity that has a responsibility regarding residents and that has registered with the department of health under division (B) of section 3701.07 of the Revised Code;

(2) An employee or representative of any private nonprofit corporation or association that qualifies for tax-exempt status under section 501(a) of the "Internal Revenue Code of 1986," 100 Stat. 2085, 26 U.S.C.A. 1, as amended, and that has registered with the department of health under division (B) of section 3701.07 of the Revised Code and whose purposes include educating and counseling residents, assisting residents in resolving problems and complaints concerning their care and treatment, and assisting them in securing adequate services to meet their needs;

(3) A member of the general assembly.

(F) "Physical restraint" means, but is not limited to, any article, device, or garment that interferes with the free movement of the resident and that the resident is unable to remove easily, a geriatric chair, or a locked room door.

(G) "Chemical restraint" means any medication bearing the American hospital formulary service therapeutic class 4:00, 28:16:08, 28:24:08, or 28:24:92 that alters the functioning of the central nervous system in a manner that limits physical and cognitive functioning to the degree that the resident cannot attain the resident's highest practicable physical, mental, and psychosocial well-being.

(H) "Ancillary service" means, but is not limited to, podiatry, dental, hearing, vision, physical therapy, occupational therapy, speech therapy, and psychological and social services.

(I) "Facility" means a facility, or part of a facility, certified as a nursing facility or skilled nursing facility, both as defined in section 5165.01 of the Revised Code. "Facility" does not include an intermediate care facility for individuals with intellectual disabilities, as defined in section 5124.01 of the Revised Code.

### HISTORY:

137 v H 600 (Eff 4-9-79); 143 v H 822 (Eff 12-13-90); 149 v H 94. Eff 9-5-2001; 2013 HB 59, § 101.01, eff. Sept. 29, 2013; 2016 hb290, § 1, effective April 6, 2017.

### Amendment Notes

The 2016 amendment by HB 290 inserted "or administrator" and "or selected" in (C)(3).

The 2013 amendment, in (A)(2), deleted "certified as" preceding "a skilled nursing", substituted "or nursing facility, both" for "under Title XVIII of the 'Social Security Act,' 79 Stat. 286 (1965), 42 U.S.C.A. 1395 and 1396, as amended, or as a nursing facility", and substituted "section 5165.01" for "section 5111.20"; substituted "class 4.00" for "class 4:00"; in (I), substituted "both as defined in section 5165.01 of the Revised Code" for "under Title XVIII or Title XIX of the 'Social Security Act'", "individuals with intellectual disabilities" for "the mentally retarded", and "section 5124.01" for "section 5111.20"; and deleted (J) and (K), which read: "(J) 'Medicare' means the program established by Title XVIII of the 'Social Security Act.' (K) 'Medicaid' means the program established by Title XIX of the 'Social Security Act' and Chapter 5111. of the Revised Code."

### NOTES TO DECISIONS

Analysis

Arbitration
Immunity
Liability
Standing
Unlicensed facility
Waiting list

#### Arbitration

There was no language in the Bill of Rights for Nursing Home Patients providing that simply being a "resident sponsor" for the purpose of enforcing the resident's rights provided a representative with the authority to sign an arbitration agreement when a health care power of attorney specifically set forth the conditions under which an agent could make health care decisions on behalf of the principal. McFarren v. Emeritus at Canton, 2013-Ohio-3900, 997 N.E.2d 1254, 2013 Ohio App. LEXIS 4058 (Ohio Ct. App., Stark County 2013).

Arbitration agreement voluntarily executed by a nursing home resident upon her admission and not as a precondition to admission is not rendered procedurally unconscionable solely by virtue of the resident's age. An arbitration agreement voluntarily executed by a nursing home resident and not as a precondition to admission that waives the right to trial and the right to seek punitive damages and attorney fees is not substantively unconscionable. Hayes v. Oakridge Home, 2009-Ohio-2054, 122 Ohio St. 3d 63, 908 N.E.2d 408, 2009 Ohio LEXIS 1218 (Ohio 2009).

#### Immunity

Former R.C. 3721.17(I)(1) specifically abrogates governmental immunity and grants a cause of action to residents of unlicensed county nursing homes against a political subdivision for violations of R.C. § § 3721.10 through 3721.17, the Ohio Nursing Home Patients' Bill of Rights. Cramer v. Auglaize Acres, 2007-Ohio-1946, 113 Ohio St. 3d 266, 865 N.E.2d 9, 2007 Ohio LEXIS 1130 (Ohio 2007).

Trial court erred in denying a county's summary judgment motion insofar as an administrator's claims alleged intentional torts where the administrator claimed that two county employees in a county home had intentionally deprived a decedent of proper medical care and intentionally falsified the decedent's medical records in an attempt to cover up his injury and that these actions violated the Ohio Nursing Home Patients' Bill of Rights, R.C. 3721.10 et seq. Cramer v. Auglaize Acres, 2005-Ohio-3609, 2005 Ohio App. LEXIS 3332 (Ohio Ct. App., Auglaize County 2005), aff'd in part and rev'd in part, 2007-Ohio-1946, 113 Ohio St. 3d 266, 865 N.E.2d 9, 2007 Ohio LEXIS 1130 (Ohio 2007).

#### Liability

A nursing home may be liable for negligently failing to use nonintrusive methods of restraint in order to prevent a resident from falling. Gray v. Jefferson Geriatric & Rehabilitation Center, 76 Ohio App. 3d 499, 602 N.E.2d 396, 1991 Ohio App. LEXIS 5795 (Ohio Ct. App., Ashtabula County 1991).

#### Standing

When a deceased nursing home resident's guardian sued the nursing home on the resident's behalf for alleged violations of the "Nursing Home Patient Bill of Rights," R.C. 3721.10 et seq., the guardian was not authorized to file suit as the resident's "sponsor," pursuant to R.C. 3721.10(D), because that provision had been repealed. Whitley v. River's Bend Health Care, 2009-Ohio-3366, 183 Ohio App. 3d 145, 916 N.E.2d 515, 2009 Ohio App. LEXIS 2911 (Ohio Ct. App., Lawrence County 2009).

When a deceased nursing home resident's guardian sued the nursing home on the resident's behalf for alleged violations of the "Nursing Home Patient Bill of Rights," R.C. 3721.10 et seq., it was not error to find that the guardian had no authority to file suit because, while the resident was unable to sue, R.C. 3721.17(I)(1)(b) required a showing that the resident's estate's legal representative, which was the co-administrators of the resident's decedent's estate, could not sue, and no such showing was made. Whitley v. River's Bend Health Care, 2009-Ohio-3366, 183 Ohio App. 3d 145, 916 N.E.2d 515, 2009 Ohio App. LEXIS 2911 (Ohio Ct. App., Lawrence County 2009).

Daughter had standing because she qualified to bring this action in her capacity as a sponsor for her mother under R.C. 3721.10(D) and 3721.13(B). Shelton v. LTC Mgmt. Servs., 2004-Ohio-507, 2004 Ohio App. LEXIS 469 (Ohio Ct. App., Highland County 2004).

**Unlicensed facility**

A facility that meets the statutory definition of "home" is subject to the patients' bill of rights regardless of whether the department of health allows it to operate unlicensed. Peskin v. Seasons Health Care L.P., 141 Ohio App. 3d 436, 751 N.E.2d 546, 2001 Ohio App. LEXIS 993 (Ohio Ct. App., Hamilton County), dismissed, 92 Ohio St. 3d 1430, 749 N.E.2d 757, 2001 Ohio LEXIS 1758 (Ohio 2001).

**Waiting list**

Rights under R.C. 3721.10 and related federal regulations are limited to residents of a home and do not include applicants who are placed on a waiting list. Rothstein v. Montefiore Home, 116 Ohio App. 3d 775, 689 N.E.2d 108, 1996 Ohio App. LEXIS 5611 (Ohio Ct. App., Cuyahoga County 1996).

**RESEARCH REFERENCES AND PRACTICE AIDS**

**Cross-References to Related Sections**

Duties of department of aging, RC § 173.01.

Patient abuse and neglect in care facilities, RC § 2903.33.

Recategorization of hospital beds to skilled nursing beds; nursing home placement clearinghouses, RC § 3702.521.

Registration of residents' rights advocates, RC § 3701.07.

State long-term care ombudsperson program; investigation and resolution of complaints, RC § 173.19.

Access to records of resident, recipient or provider; subpoenas; injunction; referral of complaints, RC § 173.20.

Toll-free patient safety telephone line, RC § 3701.91.

**Ohio Administrative Code**

Department of health, director of—

Nursing home residents' rights. OAC ch. 3701-61.

Definitions. OAC 3701-61-01.

**Practice Manuals and Treatises**

Ohio Transaction Guide: Family Law & Forms § 6.32 Patient's Rights Regulations

Ohio Transaction Guide: Family Law & Forms § 6.22 Financial Options Available to Healthcare Recipients

Ohio Transaction Guide: Family Law & Forms § 6.33 Consent to Medical Treatment

**Practice Forms**

Admission Agreement to Health Care Facility, Ohio Transaction Guide: Family Law & Forms § 6.201

## § 3721.11 Director to adopt rules.

(A) The director of the department of health shall adopt rules under Chapter 119. of the Revised Code to govern procedures for the implementation of sections 3721.10 to 3721.17 of the Revised Code.

(B) The director may adopt, amend, and repeal substantive rules under Chapter 119. of the Revised Code defining with reasonable specificity acts that violate division (A) of section 3721.13 of the Revised Code.

**HISTORY:**

137 v H 600. Eff 1-9-79.

**RESEARCH REFERENCES AND PRACTICE AIDS**

**Cross-References to Related Sections**

Criminal records check for prospective employees providing direct care to older adult, RC § 3721.121.

Definitions, RC § 3721.10.

Residents' rights, RC § 3721.13.

Rules of administrative procedure, RC § 119.01 et seq.

**Ohio Administrative Code**

Department of health, director of—

Nursing home residents' rights. OAC ch. 3701-61.

## § 3721.12 Duties of home administrator concerning residents' rights; grievance procedure.

(A) The administrator of a home shall:

(1) With the advice of residents, their sponsors, or both, establish and review at least annually, written policies regarding the applicability and implementation of residents' rights under sections 3721.10 to 3721.17 of the Revised Code, the responsibilities of residents regarding the rights, and the home's grievance procedure established under division (A)(2) of this section. The administrator is responsible for the development of, and adherence to, procedures implementing the policies.

(2) Establish a grievance committee for review of complaints by residents. The grievance committee shall be comprised of the home's staff and residents, sponsors, or outside representatives in a ratio of not more than one staff member to every two residents, sponsors, or outside representatives.

(3) Furnish to each resident and sponsor prior to or at the time of admission, and to each member of the home's staff, at least one of each of the following:

(a) A copy of the rights established under sections 3721.10 to 3721.17 of the Revised Code;

(b) A written explanation of the provisions of sections 3721.16 to 3721.162 of the Revised Code;

(c) A copy of the home's policies and procedures established under this section;

(d) A copy of the home's rules;

(e) A copy of the addresses and telephone numbers of the board of health of the health district of the county in which the home is located, the county department of job and family services of the county in which the home is located, the state departments of health and medicaid, the state and local offices of the department of aging, and any Ohio nursing home ombudsman program.

(B) Written acknowledgment of the receipt of copies of the materials listed in this section shall be made part of the resident's record and the staff member's personnel record.

(C) The administrator shall post all of the following prominently within the home:

(1) A copy of the rights of residents as listed in division (A) of section 3721.13 of the Revised Code;

(2) A copy of the home's rules and its policies and procedures regarding the rights and responsibilities of residents;

(3) A notice that a copy of this chapter, rules of the department of health applicable to the home, and federal regulations adopted under the medicare and medicaid programs, and the materials required to be available in the home under section 3721.021 of the Revised Code, are available for inspection in the home at reasonable hours;

(4) A list of residents' rights advocates;

(5) A notice that the following are available in a place readily accessible to residents:

(a) If the home is licensed under section 3721.02 of the Revised Code, a copy of the most recent licensure inspection report prepared for the home under that section;

(b) If the home is a facility, a copy of the most recent statement of deficiencies issued to the home under section 5165.68 of the Revised Code.

(D) The administrator of a home may, with the advice of residents, their sponsors, or both, establish written policies regarding the applicability and administration of any additional residents' rights beyond those set forth in sections 3721.10 to 3721.17 of the Revised Code, and the responsibilities of residents regarding the rights. Policies established under this division shall be reviewed, and procedures developed and adhered to as in division (A)(1) of this section.

**HISTORY:**

137 v H 600 (Eff 4-9-79); 140 v H 660 (Eff 7-26-84); 141 v H 428 (Eff 12-23-86); 143 v H 822 (Eff 12-13-90); 145 v H 152 (Eff 7-1-93); 148 v H 471 (Eff 7-1-2000); 149 v H 94. Eff 9-5-2001; 2013 HB 59, § 101.01, eff. Sept. 29, 2013.

**Amendment Notes**

The 2013 amendment, in (A)(3)(e), substituted "medicaid" for "job and family services" and "ombudsman" for "ombudsperson"; and substituted "section 5165.68" for "section 5111.42" in (C)(5)(b).

**NOTES TO DECISIONS**

**Arbitration agreement**

Arbitration agreement between a nursing home and a resident did not violate the statutory non-waiver language in the Bill of Rights because the statute did not reveal "non-waiver" language, but instead set forth the duties of the nursing home administrator concerning the residents' rights and the procedure for grievances, and there was no evidence the resident was not provided with the rights or that the nursing home failed to prominently display the rights. Harrison v. Winchester Place Nursing & Rehab. Ctr., 2013-Ohio-3163, 996 N.E.2d 1001, 2013 Ohio App. LEXIS 3205 (Ohio Ct. App., Franklin County 2013).

### RESEARCH REFERENCES AND PRACTICE AIDS

**Cross-References to Related Sections**

Definitions, RC § 3721.10.
Director to adopt rules, RC § 3721.11.
Resident may file grievance; procedures; prohibition, RC § 3721.17.

**Ohio Administrative Code**

Department of aging —
State long-term care ombudsman. OAC ch. 173-14.
Department of health—
Responsibility of operator and nursing home administrator; quality assurance committee. OAC 3701-17-06.

## § 3721.121 Criminal records check for prospective employees providing direct care to older adult.

(A) As used in this section:

(1) "Adult day-care program" means a program operated pursuant to rules adopted by the director of health under section 3721.04 of the Revised Code and provided by and on the same site as homes licensed under this chapter.

(2) "Applicant" means a person who is under final consideration for employment with a home or adult day-care program in a full-time, part-time, or temporary position that involves providing direct care to an older adult. "Applicant" does not include a person who provides direct care as a volunteer without receiving or expecting to receive any form of remuneration other than reimbursement for actual expenses.

(3) "Community-based long-term care services provider" means a provider as defined in section 173.39 of the Revised Code.

(4) "Criminal records check" has the same meaning as in section 109.572 of the Revised Code.

(5) "Home" means a home as defined in section 3721.10 of the Revised Code.

(6) "Older adult" means a person age sixty or older.

(B)(1) Except as provided in division (I) of this section, the chief administrator of a home or adult day-care program shall request that the superintendent of the bureau of criminal identification and investigation conduct a criminal records check of each applicant. If an applicant for whom a criminal records check request is required under this division does not present proof of having been a resident of this state for the five-year period immediately prior to the date the criminal records check is requested or provide evidence that within that five-year period the superintendent has requested information about the applicant from the federal bureau of investigation in a criminal records check, the chief administrator shall request that the superintendent obtain information from the federal bureau of investigation as part of the criminal records check of the applicant. Even if an applicant for whom a criminal records check request is required under this division presents proof of having been a resident of this state for the five-year period, the chief administrator may request that the superintendent include information from the federal bureau of investigation in the criminal records check.

(2) A person required by division (B)(1) of this section to request a criminal records check shall do both of the following:

(a) Provide to each applicant for whom a criminal records check request is required under that division a copy of the form prescribed pursuant to division (C)(1) of section 109.572 of the Revised Code and a standard fingerprint impression sheet prescribed pursuant to division (C)(2) of that section, and obtain the completed form and impression sheet from the applicant;

(b) Forward the completed form and impression sheet to the superintendent of the bureau of criminal identification and investigation.

(3) An applicant provided the form and fingerprint impression sheet under division (B)(2)(a) of this section who fails to complete the form or provide fingerprint impressions shall not be employed in any position for which a criminal records check is required by this section.

(C)(1) Except as provided in rules adopted by the director of health in accordance with division (F) of this section and subject to division (C)(2) of this section, no home or adult day-care program shall employ a person in a position that involves providing direct care to an older adult if the person has been convicted of or pleaded guilty to any of the following:

(a) A violation of section 2903.01, 2903.02, 2903.03, 2903.04, 2903.11, 2903.12, 2903.13, 2903.16, 2903.21, 2903.34, 2905.01, 2905.02, 2905.11, 2905.12, 2907.02, 2907.03, 2907.05, 2907.06, 2907.07, 2907.08, 2907.09, 2907.12, 2907.25, 2907.31, 2907.32, 2907.321, 2907.322, 2907.323, 2911.01, 2911.02, 2911.11, 2911.12, 2911.13, 2913.02, 2913.03, 2913.04, 2913.11, 2913.21, 2913.31, 2913.40, 2913.43, 2913.47, 2913.51, 2919.25, 2921.36, 2923.12, 2923.13, 2923.161, 2925.02, 2925.03, 2925.11, 2925.13, 2925.22, 2925.23, or 3716.11 of the Revised Code.

(b) A violation of an existing or former law of this state, any other state, or the United States that is substantially equivalent to any of the offenses listed in division (C)(1)(a) of this section.

(2)(a) A home or an adult day-care program may employ conditionally an applicant for whom a criminal records check request is required under division (B) of this section prior to obtaining the results of a criminal records check regarding the individual, provided that the home or program shall request a criminal records check regarding the individual in accordance with division (B)(1) of this section not later than five business days after the individual begins conditional employment. In the circumstances described in division (I)(2) of this section, a home or adult day-care program may employ conditionally an applicant who has been referred to the home or adult day-care program by an employment service that supplies full-time, part-time, or temporary staff for positions involving the direct care of older adults and for whom, pursuant to that division, a criminal records check is not required under division (B) of this section.

(b) A home or adult day-care program that employs an individual conditionally under authority of division (C)(2)(a) of this section shall terminate the individual's employment if the results of the criminal records check requested under division (B) of this section or described in division (I)(2) of this section, other than the results of any request for information from the federal bureau of investigation, are not obtained within the period ending thirty days after the date the request is made. Regardless of when the results of the criminal records check are obtained, if the results indicate that the individual has been convicted of or pleaded guilty to any of the offenses listed or described in division (C)(1) of this section, the home or program shall terminate the individual's employment unless the home or program chooses to employ the individual pursuant to division (F) of this section. Termination of employment under this division shall be considered just cause for discharge for purposes of division (D)(2) of section 4141.29 of the Revised Code if the individual makes any attempt to deceive the home or program about the individual's criminal record.

(D)(1) Each home or adult day-care program shall pay to the bureau of criminal identification and investigation the fee prescribed pursuant to division (C)(3) of section 109.572 of the Revised Code for each criminal records check conducted pursuant to a request made under division (B) of this section.

(2) A home or adult day-care program may charge an applicant a fee not exceeding the amount the home or program pays under division (D)(1) of this section. A home or program may collect a fee only if both of the following apply:

(a) The home or program notifies the person at the time of initial application for employment of the amount of the fee and that, unless the fee is paid, the person will not be considered for employment;

(b) The medicaid program does not reimburse the home or program the fee it pays under division (D)(1) of this section.

(E) The report of any criminal records check conducted pursuant to a request made under this section is not a public record for the purposes of section 149.43 of the Revised Code and shall not be made available to any person other than the following:

(1) The individual who is the subject of the criminal records check or the individual's representative;

(2) The chief administrator of the home or program requesting the criminal records check or the administrator's representative;

(3) The administrator of any other facility, agency, or program that provides direct care to older adults that is owned or operated by the same entity that owns or operates the home or program;

(4) A court, hearing officer, or other necessary individual involved in a case dealing with a denial of employment of the applicant or dealing with employment or unemployment benefits of the applicant;

(5) Any person to whom the report is provided pursuant to, and in accordance with, division (I)(1) or (2) of this section;

(6) The board of nursing for purposes of accepting and processing an application for a medication aide certificate issued under Chapter 4723. of the Revised Code;

(7) The director of aging or the director's designee if the criminal records check is requested by the chief administrator of a home that is also a community-based long-term care services provider.

(F) In accordance with section 3721.11 of the Revised Code, the director of health shall adopt rules to implement this section. The rules shall specify circumstances under which a home or adult day-care program may employ a person who has been convicted of or pleaded guilty to an offense listed or described in division (C)(1) of this section but meets personal character standards set by the director.

(G) The chief administrator of a home or adult day-care program shall inform each individual, at the time of initial application for a position that involves providing direct care to an older adult, that the individual is required to provide a set of fingerprint impressions and that a criminal records check is required to be conducted if the individual comes under final consideration for employment.

(H) In a tort or other civil action for damages that is brought as the result of an injury, death, or loss to person or property caused by an individual who a home or adult day-care program employs in a position that involves providing direct care to older adults, all of the following shall apply:

(1) If the home or program employed the individual in good faith and reasonable reliance on the report of a criminal records check requested under this section, the home or program shall not be found negligent solely because of its reliance on the report, even if the information in the report is determined later to have been incomplete or inaccurate;

(2) If the home or program employed the individual in good faith on a conditional basis pursuant to division (C)(2) of this section, the home or program shall not be found negligent solely because it employed the individual prior to receiving the report of a criminal records check requested under this section;

(3) If the home or program in good faith employed the individual according to the personal character standards established in rules adopted under division (F) of this section, the home or program shall not be found negligent solely because the individual prior to being employed had been convicted of or pleaded guilty to an offense listed or described in division (C)(1) of this section.

(I)(1) The chief administrator of a home or adult day-care program is not required to request that the superintendent of the bureau of criminal identification and investigation conduct a criminal records check of an applicant if the applicant has been referred to the home or program by an employment service that supplies full-time, part-time, or temporary staff for positions involving the direct care of older adults and both of the following apply:

(a) The chief administrator receives from the employment service or the applicant a report of the results of a criminal records check regarding the applicant that has been conducted by the superintendent within the one-year period immediately preceding the applicant's referral;

(b) The report of the criminal records check demonstrates that the person has not been convicted of or pleaded guilty to an offense listed or described in division (C)(1) of this section, or the report demonstrates that the person has been convicted of or pleaded guilty to one or more of those offenses, but the home or adult day-care program chooses to employ the individual pursuant to division (F) of this section.

(2) The chief administrator of a home or adult day-care program is not required to request that the superintendent of the bureau of criminal identification and investigation conduct a criminal records check of an applicant and may employ the applicant conditionally as described in this division, if the applicant has been referred to the home or program by an employment service that supplies full-time, part-time, or temporary staff for positions involving the direct care of older adults and if the chief administrator receives from the employment service or the applicant a letter from the employment service that is on the letterhead of the employment service, dated, and signed by a supervisor or another designated official of the employment service and that states that the employment service has requested the superintendent to conduct a criminal records check regarding the applicant, that the requested criminal records check will include a determination of whether the applicant has been convicted of or pleaded guilty to any offense listed or described in division (C)(1) of this section, that, as of the date set forth on the letter, the employment service had not received the results of the criminal records check, and that, when the employment service receives the results of the criminal records check, it promptly will send a copy of the results to the home or adult day-care program. If a home or adult day-care program employs an applicant conditionally in accordance with this division, the employment service, upon its receipt of the results of the criminal records check, promptly shall send a copy of the results to the home or adult day-care program, and division (C)(2)(b) of this section applies regarding the conditional employment.

**HISTORY:**

146 v S 160 (Eff 1-27-97); 147 v S 96 (Eff 6-11-97); 147 v H 18. Eff 1-30-98; 150 v H 95, § 1, eff. 9-26-03; 151 v H 66, § 101.01, eff. 6-30-05; 2012 HB 487, § 101.01, eff. Sept. 10, 2012; 2013 HB 59, § 101.01, eff. Sept. 29, 2013.

**Editor's Notes**

Acts 2012, HB 487, § 812.12 provides: "**Sections subject to referendum: mixed effective dates.** The sections listed in the left-hand column of the following table combine amendments by this act that take effect either on the ninety-first day after this act is filed with the Secretary of State or January 1, 2013. The middle column identifies amendments to the listed sections that take effect on the ninety-first day after this act is filed with the Secretary of State. The right-hand column identifies amendments to the listed sections that take effect January 1, 2013."

| "Section of law | Amendments that take effect on the ninety-first day after this act is filed with the Secretary of State | Amendments that take effect January 1, 2013 |
|---|---|---|
| "109.57 | The amendment in division (G) | All except as described in the middle column |

| | | |
|---|---|---|
| "109.572 | The amendment in relettered division (A)(2) striking the second comma, inserting "or", and striking ", 5119.693, or 5119.85", the amendment in relettered division (A)(12), the amendments in the first paragraph of division (B) and divisions (C)(1), (C)(2), and (C)(3) striking "5119.85," the amendment in division (B)(1) striking "5119.693, 5119.85,", and the amendment in division (C)(3) inserting "2151.33, 2151.412," | All except as described in the middle column |
| "3712.09 | The amendment in divisions (C)(1) and (F) | |
| "3721.121 | The amendment in divisions (A)(1) | |
| "5123.033 | All except as described in the right-hand column | The amendment striking '5123.169' and inserting '5123.1610' |
| "5123.081 | The amendment in relettered division (I)(1)(e)(ii) | All except as described in the middle column |
| "5123.166 | The amendment in division (D)(1)(c)(ii) | All except as described in the middle column" |

**Amendment Notes**

The 2013 amendment inserted (A)(3); redesignated former (A)(3) through (A)(5) as (A)(4) through (A)(6); and substituted "medicaid program" for "medical assistance program established under Chapter 5111. of the Revised Code" in (D)(2)(b); added (E)(7); and made a related change.

The 2012 amendment substituted "director of health" for "public health council" in (A)(1); deleted "and 'older adult'" following "Criminal records check" in (A)(3); added (A)(5); substituted "of each applicant" for "with respect to each applicant" in the first sentence of (B)(1); and made stylistic changes.

151 v H 66, effective June 30, 2005, added (E)(6); and, in (I)(2), substituted "adult day-care" for "adult-care".

## NOTES TO DECISIONS

**No statutory privilege**

Trial court properly ordered a nursing home to submit their employee criminal background checks to an executor in a negligent supervision case; construing this section in pari materia, there is no statutory privilege for criminal records checks because the statute contemplates the possibility that such records may be introduced to demonstrate their incompleteness or inaccuracy in the course of a tort or other civil action brought against a nursing home. Talani v. Manorcare, Inc., 2013-Ohio-4295, 2013 Ohio App. LEXIS 4518 (Ohio Ct. App., Lake County 2013).

## RESEARCH REFERENCES AND PRACTICE AIDS

**Cross-References to Related Sections**

Duties of superintendent of the bureau of criminal identification and investigation, RC § 109.57.

Criminal records check and fingerprinting of certain persons having contact with children, mentally retarded persons or older adults, RC § 109.572.

**Ohio Administrative Code**

Department of health—

Hiring of direct-care provider employees. OAC ch. 3701-13.

Requirements for criminal records check. OAC 3701-13-03.

Nursing home residents' rights. OAC ch. 3701-61.

Criminal records check; personal character standards. OAC 3701-61-07.

Nursing homes. OAC ch. 3701-17.

Qualifications and health of personnel. OAC 3701-17-07.

### § 3721.122 Sex offender admittance as a resident.

Before an individual is admitted as a resident to a home, the home's administrator shall search for the individual's name in the internet-based sex offender and child-victim offender database established under division (A)(11) of section 2950.13 of the Revised Code. If the search results identify the individual as a sex offender and the individual is admitted as a resident to the home, the administrator shall provide for the home to do all of the following:

(A) Develop a plan of care to protect the other residents' rights to a safe environment and to be free from abuse;

(B) Notify all of the home's other residents and their sponsors that a sex offender has been admitted as a resident to the home and include in the notice a description of the plan of care developed under division (A) of this section;

(C) Direct the individual in updating the individual's address under section 2950.05 of the Revised Code and, if the individual is unable to do so without assistance, provide the assistance the individual needs to update the individual's address under that section.

**HISTORY:**

2014 HB 483, § 101.01, eff. Sept. 15, 2014.



### § 3721.13 Residents' rights; sponsor may protect rights.

(A) The rights of residents of a home shall include, but are not limited to, the following:

(1) The right to a safe and clean living environment pursuant to the medicare and medicaid programs and applicable state laws and rules adopted by the director of health;

(2) The right to be free from physical, verbal, mental, and emotional abuse and to be treated at all times with courtesy, respect, and full recognition of dignity and individuality;

(3) Upon admission and thereafter, the right to adequate and appropriate medical treatment and nursing care and to other ancillary services that comprise necessary and appropriate care consistent with the program for which the resident contracted. This care shall be provided without regard to considerations such as race, color, religion, national origin, age, or source of payment for care.

(4) The right to have all reasonable requests and inquiries responded to promptly;

(5) The right to have clothes and bed sheets changed as the need arises, to ensure the resident's comfort or sanitation;

(6) The right to obtain from the home, upon request, the name and any specialty of any physician or other person responsible for the resident's care or for the coordination of care;

(7) The right, upon request, to be assigned, within the capacity of the home to make the assignment, to the staff physician of the resident's choice, and the right, in accordance with the rules and written policies and procedures of the home, to select as the attending physician a physician who is not on the staff of the home. If the cost of a physician's services is to be met under a federally supported program, the physician shall meet the federal laws and regulations governing such services.

(8) The right to participate in decisions that affect the resident's life, including the right to communicate with the physician and employees of the home in planning the resident's treatment or care and to obtain from the attending physician complete and current information concerning medical condition, prognosis, and treatment plan, in terms the resident can reasonably be expected to understand; the right of access to all information in the resident's medical record; and the right to give or withhold informed consent for treatment after the consequences of that choice have been carefully explained. When the attending physician finds that it is not medically advisable to give the information to the resident, the information shall be made available to the resident's sponsor on the resident's behalf, if the sponsor has a legal interest or is authorized by the resident to receive the information. The home is not liable for a violation of this division if the violation is found to be the result of an act or omission on the part of a physician selected by the resident who is not otherwise affiliated with the home.

(9) The right to withhold payment for physician visitation if the physician did not visit the resident;

(10) The right to confidential treatment of personal and medical records, and the right to approve or refuse the release of these records to any individual outside the home, except in case of transfer to another home, hospital, or health care system, as required by law or rule, or as required by a third-party payment contract;

(11) The right to privacy during medical examination or treatment and in the care of personal or bodily needs;

(12) The right to refuse, without jeopardizing access to appropriate medical care, to serve as a medical research subject;

(13) The right to be free from physical or chemical restraints or prolonged isolation except to the minimum extent necessary to protect the resident from injury to self, others, or to property and except as authorized in writing by the attending physician for a specified and limited period of time and documented in the resident's medical record. Prior to authorizing the use of a physical or chemical restraint on any resident, the attending physician shall make a personal examination of the resident and an individualized determination of the need to use the restraint on that resident.

Physical or chemical restraints or isolation may be used in an emergency situation without authorization of the attending physician only to protect the resident from injury to self or others. Use of the physical or chemical restraints or isolation shall not be continued for more than twelve hours after the onset of the emergency without personal examination and authorization by the attending physician. The attending physician or a staff physician may authorize continued use of physical or chemical restraints for a period not to exceed thirty days, and at the end of this period and any subsequent period may extend the authorization for an additional period of not more than thirty days. The use of physical or chemical restraints shall not be continued without a personal examination of the resident and the written authorization of the attending physician stating the reasons for continuing the restraint.

If physical or chemical restraints are used under this division, the home shall ensure that the restrained resident receives a proper diet. In no event shall physical or chemical restraints or isolation be used for punishment, incentive, or convenience.

(14) The right to the pharmacist of the resident's choice and the right to receive pharmaceutical supplies and services at reasonable prices not exceeding applicable and normally accepted prices for comparably packaged pharmaceutical supplies and services within the community;

(15) The right to exercise all civil rights, unless the resident has been adjudicated incompetent pursuant to Chapter 2111. of the Revised Code and has not been restored to legal capacity, as well as the right to the cooperation of the home's administrator in making arrangements for the exercise of the right to vote;

(16) The right of access to opportunities that enable the resident, at the resident's own expense or at the expense of a third-party payer, to achieve the resident's fullest potential, including educational, vocational, social, recreational, and habilitation programs;

(17) The right to consume a reasonable amount of alcoholic beverages at the resident's own expense, unless not medically advisable as documented in the resident's medical record by the attending physician or unless contradictory to written admission policies;

(18) The right to use tobacco at the resident's own expense under the home's safety rules and under applicable laws and rules of the state, unless not medically advisable as documented in the resident's medical record by the attending physician or unless contradictory to written admission policies;

(19) The right to retire and rise in accordance with the resident's reasonable requests, if the resident does not disturb others or the posted meal schedules and upon the home's request remains in a supervised area, unless not medically advisable as documented by the attending physician;

(20) The right to observe religious obligations and participate in religious activities; the right to maintain individual and cultural identity; and the right to meet with and participate in activities of social and community groups at the resident's or the group's initiative;

(21) The right upon reasonable request to private and unrestricted communications with the resident's family, social worker, and any other person, unless not medically advisable as documented in the resident's medical record by the attending physician, except that communications with public officials or with the resident's attorney or physician shall not be restricted. Private and unrestricted communications shall include, but are not limited to, the right to:

(a) Receive, send, and mail sealed, unopened correspondence;

(b) Reasonable access to a telephone for private communications;

(c) Private visits at any reasonable hour.

(22) The right to assured privacy for visits by the spouse, or if both are residents of the same home, the right to share a room within the capacity of the home, unless not medically advisable as documented in the resident's medical record by the attending physician;

(23) The right upon reasonable request to have room doors closed and to have them not opened without knocking, except in the case of an emergency or unless not medically advisable as documented in the resident's medical record by the attending physician;

(24) The right to retain and use personal clothing and a reasonable amount of possessions, in a reasonably secure manner, unless to do so would infringe on the rights of other residents or would not be medically advisable as documented in the resident's medical record by the attending physician;

(25) The right to be fully informed, prior to or at the time of admission and during the resident's stay, in writing, of the basic rate charged by the home, of services available in the home, and of any additional charges related to such services, including charges for services not covered under the medicare or medicaid program. The basic rate shall not be changed unless thirty days' notice is given to the resident or, if the resident is unable to understand this information, to the resident's sponsor.

(26) The right of the resident and person paying for the care to examine and receive a bill at least monthly for the resident's care from the home that itemizes charges not included in the basic rates;

(27)(a) The right to be free from financial exploitation;

(b) The right to manage the resident's own personal financial affairs, or, if the resident has delegated this responsibility in writing to the home, to receive upon written request at least a quarterly accounting statement of financial transactions made on the resident's behalf. The statement shall include:

(i) A complete record of all funds, personal property, or possessions of a resident from any source whatsoever, that have been deposited for safekeeping with the home for use by the resident or the resident's sponsor;

(ii) A listing of all deposits and withdrawals transacted, which shall be substantiated by receipts which shall be available for inspection and copying by the resident or sponsor.

(28) The right of the resident to be allowed unrestricted access to the resident's property on deposit at reasonable hours, unless requests for access to property on deposit are so persistent, continuous, and unreasonable that they constitute a nuisance;

(29) The right to receive reasonable notice before the resident's room or roommate is changed, including an explanation of the reason for either change.

(30) The right not to be transferred or discharged from the home unless the transfer is necessary because of one of the following:

(a) The welfare and needs of the resident cannot be met in the home.

(b) The resident's health has improved sufficiently so that the resident no longer needs the services provided by the home.

(c) The safety of individuals in the home is endangered.

(d) The health of individuals in the home would otherwise be endangered.

(e) The resident has failed, after reasonable and appropriate notice, to pay or to have the medicare or medicaid program pay on the resident's behalf, for the care provided by the home. A resident shall not be considered to have failed to have the resident's care paid for if the resident has applied for medicaid, unless both of the following are the case:

(i) The resident's application, or a substantially similar previous application, has been denied.

(ii) If the resident appealed the denial, the denial was upheld.

(f) The home's license has been revoked, the home is being closed pursuant to section 3721.08, sections 5165.60 to 5165.89, or section 5155.31 of the Revised Code, or the home otherwise ceases to operate.

(g) The resident is a recipient of medicaid, and the home's participation in the medicaid program is involuntarily terminated or denied.

(h) The resident is a beneficiary under the medicare program, and the home's participation in the medicare program is involuntarily terminated or denied.

(31) The right to voice grievances and recommend changes in policies and services to the home's staff, to employees of the department of health, or to other persons not associated with the operation of the home, of the resident's choice, free from restraint, interference, coercion, discrimination, or reprisal. This right includes access to a residents' rights advocate, and the right to be a member of, to be active in, and to associate with persons who are active in organizations of relatives and friends of nursing home residents and other organizations engaged in assisting residents.

(32) The right to have any significant change in the resident's health status reported to the resident's sponsor. As soon as such a change is known to the home's staff, the home shall make a reasonable effort to notify the sponsor within twelve hours.

(33) The right, if the resident has requested the care and services of a hospice care program, to choose a hospice care program licensed under Chapter 3712. of the Revised Code that best meets the resident's needs.

(B) A sponsor may act on a resident's behalf to assure that the home does not deny the residents' rights under sections 3721.10 to 3721.17 of the Revised Code.

(C) Any attempted waiver of the rights listed in division (A) of this section is void.

**HISTORY:**

137 v H 600 (Eff 4-9-79); 143 v H 822 (Eff 12-13-90); 149 v H 94. Eff 9-5-2001; 2012 HB 487, § 101.01, eff. Sept. 10, 2012; 2013 HB 59, § 101.01, eff. Sept. 29, 2013; 2019 hb166, § 101.01, effective October 17, 2019.

**Amendment Notes**

The 2019 amendment by HB 166 added (A)(33).

The 2013 amendment deleted "by the county department of job and family services" from the end of (A)(30)(e)(i); substituted "the denial was upheld" for "pursuant to division (C) of section 5101.35 of the Revised Code, the director of job and family services has upheld the denial" in (A)(30)(e)(ii); and substituted "sections 5165.60 to 5165.89" for "sections 5111.35 to 5111.62" in (A)(30)(f).

The 2012 amendment substituted "rules adopted by the director of health" for "regulations prescribed by the public health council" in (A)(1); and made a stylistic change.

## NOTES TO DECISIONS

Analysis



**Generally**

Under the circumstances, the court lawfully required the nursing home to allow a resident to smoke under regulated conditions. Meade v. Beverly Enterprises-Ohio, Inc., 2003-Ohio-5231, 154 Ohio App. 3d 521, 797 N.E.2d 1040, 2003 Ohio App. LEXIS 4711 (Ohio Ct. App., Lake County 2003).

A nursing home does not have a duty to make an unsolicited investigation into the financial standing of a patient's family or to give advice as to medicaid eligibility. Mraz v. Taft, 85 Ohio App. 3d 200, 619 N.E.2d 483, 1993 Ohio App. LEXIS 92 (Ohio Ct. App., Cuyahoga County 1993).

**Applicability**

Statute was inapplicable to the facts of the case because the unambiguous language of the statute stated that a resident of a home shall have the right not to be transferred or discharged from the home unless the transfer was necessary. The executor was arguing that the nursing home should have transferred the decedent. McFarren v. Emeritus at Canton, 2016-Ohio-484, 59 N.E.3d 652, 2016 Ohio App. LEXIS 412 (Ohio Ct. App., Stark County 2016).

**Consumer sales practices act**

The consumer sales practices act applies to billing practices of a residential care facility. Elder v. Fischer, 129 Ohio App. 3d 209, 717 N.E.2d 730, 1998 Ohio App. LEXIS 3385 (Ohio Ct. App., Hamilton County), dismissed, 84 Ohio St. 3d 1434, 702 N.E.2d 1213, 1998 Ohio LEXIS 3475 (Ohio 1998).

**Criminal trespass**

A labor organizer is not guilty of criminal trespass when he visits a nursing home, during normal visiting hours, at the invitation of some of its residents and while there he talks to some of the nursing home's employees and invites them to a union meeting. State v. Hohman, 14 Ohio App. 3d 142, 470 N.E.2d 162, 1983 Ohio App. LEXIS 11455 (Ohio Ct. App., Clermont County 1983).

**Disclosure**

Resident's Rights statute, R.C. 3721.13, did not include the denial of access to the names and addresses of potential material witnesses in a lawsuit pursuant to § 3721.13(A)(10), such that a trial court properly granted a motion to compel a nursing home to disclose the names and addresses of a deceased nursing home resident's roommates in a wrongful death and negligence action against the facility. May v. Northern Health Facilities, Inc., 2009-Ohio-1442, 2009 Ohio App. LEXIS 1195 (Ohio Ct. App., Portage County 2009).

**Erroneous denial of request to discharge a patient due to non-payment**

When a nursing home sought permission to discharge a patient due to non-payment of the costs of the patient's care, it was error for a hearing officer to deny the request on the grounds that, while the patient had not paid for the patient's care, the nursing home was equitably estopped from discharging the patient because the nursing home was complicit in allowing the past due charges for the patient's care to accrue, because this imposed an equitable layer of proof which the applicable statute, R.C. 3721.13(A)(30), and the applicable regulation, OAC 3701-61-02, did not contemplate, so it was an abuse of discretion, under R.C. 119.12, for a trial court to affirm the hearing officer. Dayspring of Miami Valley v. Shepherd, 2007-Ohio-2589, 2007 Ohio App. LEXIS 2416 (Ohio Ct. App., Clark County 2007).

**Liability**

Where the estate of a patient filed an action against a county nursing home, alleging negligence, wrongful death, and violations of the Ohio Nursing Home Patients' Bill of Rights, a trial court erred in granting summary judgment for the county home based on its finding that it was protected from liability by political subdivision immunity, as there was a genuine issue of material fact concerning whether the nursing staff exercised its discretion in a manner that was reckless, thus negating its immunity. Estate of Fleenor v. Cty. of Ottawa, 2021-Ohio-2251, 2021 Ohio App. LEXIS 2225 (Ohio Ct. App., Ottawa County 2021).

Resolving a conflict between this statute and R.C. 2305.51, the immunity afforded to mental health professionals and organizations does not apply to nursing homes; thus, a nursing home could not assert immunity in a wrongful death action arising out of the death of a resident resulting from an attack by another resident. Overholt v. United Church Homes, Inc., 2013 Ohio Misc. LEXIS 214 (Ohio C.P. June 28, 2013), dismissed without prejudice, 2013 Ohio Misc. LEXIS 213 (Ohio C.P. Dec. 13, 2013).

In a medical employer's action against an employee, alleging that he violated the parties' noncompetition covenant, it was proper to allow the employee to present evidence that he treated only those patients who had requested his services pursuant to their rights under R.C. 3721.13(A)(7); further, there was no error where the jury determined that although the employee breached the covenant, the employer suffered no damages as a

Titles 11 — 37

result thereof. General Med., P.C. v. Manolache, 2011-Ohio-340, 2011 Ohio App. LEXIS 281 (Ohio Ct. App., Cuyahoga County 2011).

A nursing home may be liable for negligently failing to use nonintrusive methods of restraint in order to prevent a resident from falling. Gray v. Jefferson Geriatric & Rehabilitation Center, 76 Ohio App. 3d 499, 602 N.E.2d 396, 1991 Ohio App. LEXIS 5795 (Ohio Ct. App., Ashtabula County 1991).

**Mail**

R.C. 3721.13(A)(21)(a) plainly and unambiguously requires a resident to request to receive sealed, unopened mail. However, it excepts communications from a resident's attorney, physician, or a public official from this requirement. Washington County Home v. Ohio Dep't of Health, 2008-Ohio-4342, 178 Ohio App. 3d 78, 896 N.E.2d 1011, 2008 Ohio App. LEXIS 3651 (Ohio Ct. App., Washington County 2008).



**Medical claims**

Where plaintiff executor alleged defendant was negligent and violated the Ohio Nursing Home Patients' Bill of Rights, as the complaint did not contain enough factual detail to characterize certain claims as medical claims, the trial court erred in dismissing them as time-barred under former R.C. 2305.113(E)(3) for not having been filed within one year of accrual. Lerner v. Broadview NH, LLC, 2017-Ohio-8001, 98 N.E.3d 1014, 2017 Ohio App. LEXIS 4327 (Ohio Ct. App., Franklin County 2017).

Where plaintiff alleged defendant was negligent and violated the Ohio Nursing Home Patients' Bill of Rights, as plaintiff failed to attach an affidavit of merit to his complaint or move to extend the time to file one, the court correctly dismissed the medical claims under Civ.R. 12(b)(6) but erred in dismissing those claims that did not contain enough factual detail to characterize as medical claims. Lerner v. Broadview NH, LLC, 2017-Ohio-8001, 98 N.E.3d 1014, 2017 Ohio App. LEXIS 4327 (Ohio Ct. App., Franklin County 2017).

**Pharmacies**

An agreement between a pharmacy and a nursing home that residents use that pharmacy whenever possible did not violate R.C. 1331.01 et seq. where it recognized the right to use other pharmacies. Lee v. United Church Homes, 115 Ohio App. 3d 705, 686 N.E.2d 288, 1996 Ohio App. LEXIS 5287 (Ohio Ct. App., Wyandot County 1996).

**Private visitation rights**

Whereas R.C. 3721.13(A)(20(c) grants residents of a nursing home certain rights, including that of private visits at reasonable times, the statute clearly limits a resident's private unrestricted visitation right to situations where a "reasonable request" has first been made. This requirement enables the nursing home official to consult with a resident's physician prior to granting the request if there is any question regarding the medical advisability of the visit. State v. Otten, 33 Ohio App. 3d 339, 515 N.E.2d 1009, 1986 Ohio App. LEXIS 10283 (Ohio Ct. App., Wayne County 1986).

**Request to discharge a patient**

While R.C. 3721.13(A)(30) does provide some protection for nursing home residents, in that it only permits transfer or discharge under certain circumstances, it specifically permits discharge for non-payment, and it does not refer to any equitable defenses nor does it cite any factors to be considered in determining whether discharge is appropriate. and the Ohio Administrative Code provides that in order to transfer or discharge a resident, a nursing home facility need only present evidence demonstrating compliance with § 3721.13(A)(30). Dayspring of Miami Valley v. Shepherd, 2007-Ohio-2589, 2007 Ohio App. LEXIS 2416 (Ohio Ct. App., Clark County 2007).

R.C. 3721.13(A)(30) does not require that a nursing facility seeking to discharge a resident for non-payment, in addition to demonstrating the existence of one of the factors set forth in § 3721.13(A)(30), also offer additional proof that the factor made discharge necessary, because it states that necessity is shown merely by demonstration of the existence of one of the factors. Dayspring of Miami Valley v. Shepherd, 2007-Ohio-2589, 2007 Ohio App. LEXIS 2416 (Ohio Ct. App., Clark County 2007).

While R.C. 3721.13(A)(30) does provide some protection for nursing home residents, in that it only permits transfer or discharge under certain circumstances, it specifically permits discharge for non-payment, and it does not refer to any equitable defenses nor does it cite any factors to be considered in determining whether discharge is appropriate. and the Ohio Administrative Code provides that in order to transfer or discharge a resident, a nursing home facility need only present evidence demonstrating compliance with § 3721.13(A)(30). Dayspring of Miami Valley v. Shepherd, 2007-Ohio-2589, 2007 Ohio App. LEXIS 2416 (Ohio Ct. App., Clark County 2007).

**Standing**

Daughter had standing because she qualified to bring this action in her capacity as a sponsor for her mother under R.C. 3721.10(D) and 3721.13(B). Shelton v. LTC Mgmt. Servs., 2004-Ohio-507, 2004 Ohio App. LEXIS 469 (Ohio Ct. App., Highland County 2004).

**Statute of limitations**

Plaintiff executor's claims that defendant was negligent and violated the Ohio Nursing Home Patients' Bill of Rights because its employees failed to ensure the decedent's nasal cannula stayed in place, to deliver pain medication, and to alleviate her physical injury were medical claims because they arose from the medical diagnosis, care, or treatment of the decedent; therefore, they were properly dismissed as time-barred because the action had not been filed within one year of the accrual of those claims. Lerner v. Broadview NH, LLC, 2017-Ohio-8001, 98 N.E.3d 1014, 2017 Ohio App. LEXIS 4327 (Ohio Ct. App., Franklin County 2017).

Where the daughter's action for personal or bodily injury suffered by her mother while under the care of a long-term nursing care facility was not an action created by statute, it was barred by the two-year statute of limitations; R.C. 3721.13(A)(1),(2),(3),(5) did not provide a cause of action that would not have existed but for the statute because the same action existed at common law. Shelton v. LTC Mgmt. Servs., 2004-Ohio-507, 2004 Ohio App. LEXIS 469 (Ohio Ct. App., Highland County 2004).

**Visiting hours**

Ohio Administrative Code 3701-17-10 is not in conflict with R.C. 3721.13, and provides guidance as to reasonable visiting hours. Belinky v. Drake Ctr., 117 Ohio App. 3d 497, 690 N.E.2d 1302, 1996 Ohio App. LEXIS 5891 (Ohio Ct. App., Hamilton County 1996), dismissed, 78 Ohio St. 3d 1495, 678 N.E.2d 1231, 1997 Ohio LEXIS 1593 (Ohio 1997).

## NOTES TO UNPUBLISHED DECISIONS

**Relation to other laws**

*Unpublished decision:* Where an employer fired an employee for circulating a petition criticizing work conditions at an assisted living facility and planning a one-day work stoppage, the National Labor Relations Board's conclusion that the employer violated § 8(a)(1) of the National Labor Relations Act, 29 U.S.C.S. § 158(a)(1), was upheld because (1) the employee's actions were protected under 29 U.S.C.S. § 157 in that were they were directed at challenging work conditions; (2) the employee did not pressure other aides in a manner that would have taken her actions outside the protection of the Act; (3) R.C. 3721.13, which did not compel the employer to fire the employee for planning a strike, did not provide a legitimate business reason for the employer's conduct; and (4) the Board's conclusion that the employee's discredited testimony did not amount to a malicious abuse of the Board's processes was not arbitrary and capricious. Thus, the Board's order requiring the employer to reinstate the employee with back pay was enforced pursuant to 29 U.S.C.S. § 160(e).Sunrise Senior Living, Inc. v. NLRB, 2006 U.S. App. LEXIS 13494 (May 31, 2006).

## RESEARCH REFERENCES AND PRACTICE AIDS

**Cross-References to Related Sections**

Authorization to handle resident's financial affairs, RC § 3721.15.
Definitions, RC § 3721.10.
Determination concerning transfer or discharge; appeals, RC § 3721.162.
Director to adopt rules, RC § 3721.11.
Duties of home administrator concerning residents' rights, RC § 3721.12.
Duties of home to implement rights, RC § 3721.14.
Resident may file grievance; procedures; prohibition, RC § 3721.17.
Resident or sponsor may request hearing challenging proposed transfer or discharge, RC § 3721.161.

**Ohio Administrative Code**

Department of aging —
State long-term care ombudsman. OAC ch. 173-14.
Department of health—
Nursing home residents' rights—
Right to challenge transfer or discharge. OAC 3701-61-02 et seq.
Nursing homes and residential care facilities—
Restraints. OAC 3701-17-15.

**Comparative Legislation**

Residents' rights:
CA—Cal Health & Saf Code § 1599 et seq
FL—Fla. Stat. § 400.022
KY—KRS § 216.515 et seq
MI—MCLS §§ 333.21741, 333.21763 et seq
NY—NY CLS Pub Health § 2803-c

**Practice Manuals and Treatises**

Ohio Transaction Guide: Family Law & Forms § 6.22 Financial Options Available to Healthcare Recipients
Ohio Transaction Guide: Family Law & Forms § 6.31 Standard of Care Owed by Health Care Providers
Ohio Transaction Guide: Family Law & Forms § 6.32 Patient's Rights Regulations

Ohio Transaction Guide: Family Law & Forms § 6.33 Consent to Medical Treatment

**Practice Forms**

Admission Agreement to Health Care Facility, Ohio Transaction Guide: Family Law & Forms § 6.201

### § 3721.14 Duties of home to implement rights; certain persons to have access to home.

To assist in the implementation of the rights granted in division (A) of section 3721.13 of the Revised Code, each home shall provide:

(A) Appropriate staff training to implement each resident's rights under division (A) of section 3721.13 of the Revised Code, including, but not limited to, explaining:

(1) The resident's rights and the staff's responsibility in the implementation of the rights;

(2) The staff's obligation to provide all residents who have similar needs with comparable service.

(B) Arrangements for a resident's needed ancillary services;

(C) Protected areas outside the home for residents to enjoy outdoor activity, within the capacity of the facility, consistent with applicable laws and rules;

(D) Adequate indoor space, which need not be dedicated to that purpose, for families of residents to meet privately with families of other residents;

(E) Access to the following persons to enter the home during reasonable hours, except where such access would interfere with resident care or the privacy of residents:

(1) Employees of the department of health, department of mental health and addiction services, department of developmental disabilities, department of aging, department of job and family services, and county departments of job and family services;

(2) Prospective residents and their sponsors;

(3) A resident's sponsors;

(4) Residents' rights advocates;

(5) A resident's attorney;

(6) A minister, priest, rabbi, or other person ministering to a resident's religious needs.

(F) In writing, a description of the home's grievance procedures.

**HISTORY:**

137 v H 600 (Eff 1-9-79); 140 v H 660 (Eff 7-26-84); 141 v H 428 (Eff 12-23-86); 143 v H 822 (Eff 12-13-90); 148 v H 471. Eff 7-1-2000; 153 v S 79, § 1, eff. 10-6-09; 2013 HB 59, § 101.01, eff. Sept. 29, 2013.

**Amendment Notes**

The 2013 amendment substituted "department of mental health and addiction services" for "department of mental health" in (E)(1).

153 v S 79, effective October 6, 2009, deleted "mental retardation and" preceding "developmental disabilities" throughout.

#### RESEARCH REFERENCES AND PRACTICE AIDS

**Cross-References to Related Sections**

Definitions, RC § 3721.10.

Director to adopt rules, RC § 3721.11.

Duties of home administrator concerning residents' rights, RC § 3721.12.

Resident may file grievance; procedures; prohibition, RC § 3721.17.

Residents' rights; sponsor may protect rights, RC § 3721.13.

### § 3721.15 Authorization to handle residents' financial affairs; accounts; return of funds.

(A) Authorization from a resident or a sponsor with a power of attorney for a home to manage the resident's financial affairs shall be in writing and shall be attested to by a witness who is not connected in any manner whatsoever with the home or its administrator. The home shall maintain accounts pursuant to division (A)(27) of section 3721.13 of the Revised Code. Upon the resident's transfer, discharge, or death, the account shall be closed and a final accounting made. All remaining funds shall be returned to the resident or resident's sponsor, except in the case of death, when all remaining funds shall be transferred or used in accordance with section 5162.22 of the Revised Code.

(B) A home that manages a resident's financial affairs shall deposit the resident's funds in excess of one thousand dollars, and may deposit the resident's funds that are one thousand dollars or less, in an interest-bearing account separate from any of the home's operating accounts. Interest earned on the resident's funds shall be credited to the resident's account. A resident's funds that are one thousand dollars or less and have not been deposited in an interest-bearing account may be deposited in a noninterest-bearing account or petty cash fund.

(C) Each resident whose financial affairs are managed by a home shall be promptly notified by the home when the total of the amount of funds in the resident's accounts and the petty cash fund plus other nonexempt resources reaches two hundred dollars less than the maximum amount permitted a recipient of medicaid. The notice shall include an explanation of the potential effect on the resident's eligibility for medicaid if the amount in the resident's accounts and the petty cash fund, plus the value of other nonexempt resources, exceeds the maximum assets a medicaid recipient may retain.

(D) Except as otherwise provided in section 3.061 of the Revised Code, each home that manages the financial affairs of residents shall purchase a surety bond or otherwise provide assurance satisfactory to the director of health, or, in the case of a home that participates in the medicaid program, to the medicaid director, to assure the security of all residents' funds managed by the home.

**HISTORY:**

137 v H 600 (Eff 4-9-79); 143 v H 822 (Eff 12-13-90); 146 v H 117 (Eff 9-29-95); 146 v H 167 (Eff 11-15-95); 148 v H 471 (Eff 7-1-2000); 149 v H 94. Eff 9-5-2001; 151 v H 66, § 101.01, eff. 6-30-05; 2013 HB 59, § 101.01, eff. Sept. 29, 2013; 2020 hb444, § 1, effective April 12, 2021.

**Amendment Notes**

The 2020 amendment by HB 444 added "Except as otherwise provided in section 3.061 of the Revised Code" at the beginning of (D).

The 2013 amendment substituted "section 5162.22" for "section 5111.113" in the last sentence of (A); substituted "one thousand dollars" for "one hundred thousand dollars" throughout (B); and substituted "medicaid director" for "director of job and family services" in (D).

151 v H 66, effective June 30, 2005, corrected internal references in (A).

#### NOTES TO DECISIONS

**Jurisdiction**

As Ohio was a child's home state within six months of the filing by the father of a motion for a change of custody and other relief, the juvenile court in Ohio had jurisdiction over the matter pursuant to R.C. 3721.15(A)(1); further, as there was a prior juvenile court order that required the father to pay child support, the juvenile court had continuing jurisdiction over the matter pursuant to R.C. 2151.23(F)(1), (2), 3109.04, 3109.05, 3105.21, and Ohio R. Civ. P. 75(J). In re A.D.M., 2009-Ohio-1951, 183 Ohio App. 3d 802, 919 N.E.2d 224, 2009 Ohio App. LEXIS 1669 (Ohio Ct. App., Montgomery County 2009).

#### RESEARCH REFERENCES AND PRACTICE AIDS

**Cross-References to Related Sections**

Definitions, RC § 3721.10.

Director to adopt rules, RC § 3721.11.

Duties of home administrator concerning residents' rights, RC § 3721.12.

Resident may file grievance; procedures; prohibition, RC § 3721.17.

### § 3721.16 Residents' rights concerning transfer or discharge.

For each resident of a home, notice of a proposed transfer or discharge shall be in accordance with this section.

(A)(1) The administrator of a home shall notify a resident in writing, and the resident's sponsor in writing by certified mail, return receipt requested, in advance of any proposed transfer or discharge from the home. The administrator shall send a copy of the notice to the state department of health. The notice shall be provided at least thirty days in advance of the proposed transfer or discharge, unless any of the following applies:

(a) The resident's health has improved sufficiently to allow a more immediate discharge or transfer to a less skilled level of care;

(b) The resident has resided in the home less than thirty days;

(c) An emergency arises in which the safety of individuals in the home is endangered;

(d) An emergency arises in which the health of individuals in the home would otherwise be endangered;

(e) An emergency arises in which the resident's urgent medical needs necessitate a more immediate transfer or discharge.

In any of the circumstances described in divisions (A)(1)(a) to (e) of this section, the notice shall be provided as many days in advance of the proposed transfer or discharge as is practicable.

(2) The notice required under division (A)(1) of this section shall include all of the following:

(a) The reasons for the proposed transfer or discharge;

(b) The proposed date the resident is to be transferred or discharged;

(c) Subject to division (A)(3) of this section, a proposed location to which the resident may relocate and a notice that the resident and resident's sponsor may choose another location to which the resident will relocate;

(d) Notice of the right of the resident and the resident's sponsor to an impartial hearing at the home on the proposed transfer or discharge, and of the manner in which and the time within which the resident or sponsor may request a hearing pursuant to section 3721.161 of the Revised Code;

(e) A statement that the resident will not be transferred or discharged before the date specified in the notice unless the home and the resident or, if the resident is not competent to make a decision, the home and the resident's sponsor, agree to an earlier date;

(f) The address of the legal services office of the department of health;

(g) The name, address, and telephone number of a representative of the state long-term care ombudsman program and, if the resident or patient has a developmental disability or mental illness, the name, address, and telephone number of the Ohio protection and advocacy system.

(3) The proposed location to which a resident may relocate as specified pursuant to division (A)(2)(c) of this section in the proposed transfer or discharge notice shall be capable of meeting the resident's health-care and safety needs. The proposed location for relocation need not have accepted the resident at the time the notice is issued to the resident and resident's sponsor.

(B) No home shall transfer or discharge a resident before the date specified in the notice required by division (A) of this section unless the home and the resident or, if the resident is not competent to make a decision, the home and the resident's sponsor, agree to an earlier date.

(C) Transfer or discharge actions shall be documented in the resident's medical record by the home if there is a medical basis for the action.

(D) A resident or resident's sponsor may challenge a transfer or discharge by requesting an impartial hearing pursuant to section 3721.161 of the Revised Code, unless the transfer or discharge is required because of one of the following reasons:

(1) The home's license has been revoked under this chapter;

(2) The home is being closed pursuant to section 3721.08, sections 5165.60 to 5165.89, or section 5155.31 of the Revised Code;

(3) The resident is a recipient of medicaid and the home's participation in the medicaid program has been involuntarily terminated or denied by the federal government;

(4) The resident is a beneficiary under the medicare program and the home's certification under the medicare program has been involuntarily terminated or denied by the federal government.

(E) If a resident is transferred or discharged pursuant to this section, the home from which the resident is being transferred or discharged shall provide the resident with adequate preparation prior to the transfer or discharge to ensure a safe and orderly transfer or discharge from the home, and the home or alternative setting to which the resident is to be transferred or discharged shall have accepted the resident for transfer or discharge.

(F) At the time of a transfer or discharge of a resident who is a recipient of medicaid from a home to a hospital or for therapeutic leave, the home shall provide notice in writing to the resident and in writing by certified mail, return receipt requested, to the resident's sponsor, specifying the number of days, if any, during which the resident will be permitted under the medicaid program to return and resume residence in the home and specifying the medicaid program's coverage of the days during which the resident is absent from the home. An individual who is absent from a home for more than the number of days specified in the notice and continues to require the services provided by the facility shall be given priority for the first available bed in a semi-private room.

**HISTORY:**

137 v H 600 (Eff 4-9-79); 143 v H 822 (Eff 12-13-90); 149 v H 94. Eff 9-5-2001; 2011 HB 153, § 101.01, eff. Sept. 29, 2011; 2011 HB 153, § 120.20, eff. Oct. 1, 2012; 2013 HB 59, § 101.01, eff. Sept. 29, 2013.

**Amendment Notes**

The 2013 amendment substituted "ombudsman" for "ombudsperson" in (A)(2)(g); and substituted "sections 5165.60 to 5165.89" for "sections 5111.35 to 5111.62" in (D)(2).

The 2011 amendment by HB 153 § 120.20 substituted "Ohio protection and advocacy system" for "Ohio legal rights service" in (A)(2)(g).

The 2011 amendment by HB 153 § 101.01, in (A)(2)(c), added "Subject to division (A)(3) of this section" to the beginning and substituted "may relocate and a notice that the resident and resident's sponsor may choose another location to which the resident will relocate" for "is to be transferred or discharged"; added (A)(3); and made a stylistic change.

The 2011 amendment, in (A)(2)(c), added "Subject to division (A)(3) of this section" to the beginning and substituted "may relocate and a notice that the resident and resident's sponsor may choose another location to which the resident will relocate" for "is to be transferred or discharged"; added (A)(3); and made a stylistic change.

**RESEARCH REFERENCES AND PRACTICE AIDS**

**Cross-References to Related Sections**

Closing of home and subsequent care of residents, RC § 5155.31.

Definitions, RC § 3721.10.

Director to adopt rules, RC § 3721.11.

Duties of home administrator concerning residents' rights, RC § 3721.12.

Resident may file grievance; procedures; prohibition, RC § 3721.17.

Resident or sponsor may request hearing challenging proposed transfer or discharge, RC § 3721.161.

**Ohio Administrative Code**

Nursing home residents' rights. OAC ch. 3701-61.

Right to challenge transfer or discharge. OAC 3701-61-02.

Transfer and discharge responsibilities of the home. OAC 3701-61-05.

### § 3721.161 Resident or sponsor may request hearing challenging proposed transfer or discharge.

(A) Not later than thirty days after the date a resident or the resident's sponsor receives notice of a proposed transfer or discharge, whichever is later, the resident or resident's sponsor may challenge the proposed transfer or discharge by submitting a written request for a hearing to the state department of health. On receiving the request, the department shall conduct a hearing in accordance with section 3721.162 of the Revised Code to determine whether the proposed transfer or discharge complies with division (A)(30) of section 3721.13 of the Revised Code.

(B) Except in the circumstances described in divisions (A)(1)(a) to (e) of section 3721.16 of the Revised Code, if a resident or resident's sponsor submits a written hearing request not later than ten days after the resident or the resident's sponsor received notice of the proposed transfer or discharge, whichever is later, the home shall not transfer or discharge the resident unless the department determines after the hearing that the transfer or discharge complies with division (A)(30) of section 3721.13 of the Revised Code or the department's determination to the contrary is reversed on appeal.

(C) If a resident or resident's sponsor does not request a hearing pursuant to division (A) of this section, the home may transfer or discharge the resident on the date specified in the notice required by division (A) of section 3721.16 of the Revised Code or thereafter, unless the home and the resident or, if the resident is not competent to make a decision, the home and the resident's sponsor, agree to an earlier date.

(D) If the resident or resident's sponsor requests a hearing in writing pursuant to division (A) of this section and the home transfers or discharges the resident before the department issues a hearing decision, the home shall readmit the resident in the first available bed if the department determines after the hearing that the transfer or discharge does not comply with division (A)(30) of section 3721.13 of the Revised Code or the department's determination to the contrary is reversed on appeal.

**HISTORY:**
149 v H 94. Eff 9-5-2001.

### RESEARCH REFERENCES AND PRACTICE AIDS

**Cross-References to Related Sections**
Determination concerning transfer or discharge; appeals, RC § 3721.162.
Residents' rights concerning transfer or discharge, RC § 3721.16.

**Ohio Administrative Code**
Nursing home residents' rights. OAC ch. 3701-61.
Impartial hearing by the department of health. OAC 3701-61-03.

## § 3721.162 Determination concerning transfer or discharge; appeals.

(A) On receiving a request pursuant to section 3721.161 of the Revised Code, the department of health shall conduct hearings under this section in accordance with 42 C.F.R. 431, subpart E, to determine whether the proposed transfer or discharge complies with division (A)(30) of section 3721.13 of the Revised Code.

(B) The department shall employ or contract with an attorney to serve as hearing officer. The hearing officer shall conduct a hearing in the home not later than ten days after the date the department receives a request pursuant to section 3721.161 of the Revised Code, unless the resident and the home or, if the resident is not competent to make a decision, the resident's sponsor and the home, agree otherwise. The hearing shall be recorded on audiotape, but neither the recording nor a transcript of the recording shall be part of the official record of the hearing. A hearing conducted under this section is not subject to section 121.22 of the Revised Code.

(C) Unless the parties otherwise agree, the hearing officer shall issue a decision within five days of the date the hearing concludes. In all cases, a decision shall be issued not later than thirty days after the department receives a request pursuant to section 3721.161 of the Revised Code. The hearing officer's decision shall be served on the resident or resident's sponsor and the home by certified mail. The hearing officer's decision shall be considered the final decision of the department.

(D) A resident, resident's sponsor, or home may appeal the decision of the department to the court of common pleas pursuant to section 119.12 of the Revised Code. The appeal shall be governed by section 119.12 of the Revised Code, except for all of the following:

(1) The resident, resident's sponsor, or home shall file the appeal in the court of common pleas of the county in which the home is located.

(2) The resident or resident's sponsor may apply to the court for designation as an indigent and, if the court grants the application, the resident or resident's sponsor shall not be required to furnish the costs of the appeal.

(3) The appeal shall be filed with the department and the court within thirty days after the hearing officer's decision is served. The appealing party shall serve the opposing party a copy of the notice of appeal by hand-delivery or certified mail, return receipt requested. If the home is the appealing party, it shall provide a copy of the notice of appeal to both the resident and the resident's sponsor or attorney, if known.

(4) The department shall not file a transcript of the hearing with the court unless the court orders it to do so. The court shall issue such an order only if it finds that the parties are unable to stipulate to the facts of the case and that the transcript is essential to the determination of the appeal. If the court orders the department to file the transcript, the department shall do so not later than thirty days after the day the court issues the order.

(E) The court shall not require an appellant to pay a bond as a condition of issuing a stay pending its decision.

(F) The resident, resident's sponsor, home, or department may commence a civil action in the court of common pleas of the county in which the home is located to enforce the decision of the department or the court. If the court finds that the resident or home has not complied with the decision, it shall enjoin the violation and order other appropriate relief, including attorney's fees.

**HISTORY:**
149 v H 94. Eff 9-5-2001.



### NOTES TO DECISIONS

Analysis



**Service of notice of appeal**
Although the certificate of service on the notice of appeal did not indicate service on the Department of Health, the notice filed with the trial court had a stamp reading: "Received, ODH/Personnel 04 Dec 13 AM 11:05;" this stamp was evidence that the notice of appeal was properly filed with the Department of Health as required, and the trial court erred in dismissing the appeal. Dayspring of Miami Valley v. Shepherd, 2006-Ohio-241, 2006 Ohio App. LEXIS 202 (Ohio Ct. App., Clark County 2006).

Although the certificate of service on the notice of appeal did not indicate service on the Department of Health, the notice filed with the trial court had a stamp reading: "Received, ODH/Personnel 04 Dec 13 AM 11:05;" this stamp was evidence that the notice of appeal was properly filed with the Department of Health as required, and the trial court erred in dismissing the appeal. Dayspring of Miami Valley v. Shepherd, 2006-Ohio-241, 2006 Ohio App. LEXIS 202 (Ohio Ct. App., Clark County 2006).

**Transcript**
Trial court acted arbitrarily in dismissing the nursing home resident's appeal, regarding the proposed transfer/discharge from the home, when the absence of the record was neither his fault nor responsibility. Because the resident complied with the statutory requirements for filing the administrative appeal, R.C. 119.12 required the Ohio Department of Health to submit a certified copy of the record within 30 days of the resident filing his notice of appeal. Miller v. Austinburg Nursing & Rehab. Ctr., 2008-Ohio-4298, 2008 Ohio App. LEXIS 3621 (Ohio Ct. App., Ashtabula County 2008).

### RESEARCH REFERENCES AND PRACTICE AIDS

**Cross-References to Related Sections**
Duties of home administrator concerning residents' rights; grievance procedure, RC § 3721.12.
Resident may file grievance; procedure upon complaint to department of health; retaliation prohibited, RC § 3721.17.
Resident or sponsor may request hearing challenging proposed transfer or discharge, RC § 3721.161.

**Ohio Administrative Code**
Nursing home residents' rights. OAC ch. 3701-61.
Written order as to advisable action. OAC 3701-61-04.

## § 3721.17 Resident may file grievance; procedure upon complaint to department of health; retaliation prohibited; cause of action for violation.

(A) Any resident who believes that the resident's rights under sections 3721.10 to 3721.17 of the Revised Code have been violated may file a grievance under procedures adopted pursuant to division (A)(2) of section 3721.12 of the Revised Code.

When the grievance committee determines a violation of sections 3721.10 to 3721.17 of the Revised Code has occurred, it shall notify the administrator of the home. If the violation cannot be corrected within ten days, or if ten days have elapsed without correction of the violation, the grievance committee shall refer the matter to the department of health.

(B) Any person who believes that a resident's rights under sections 3721.10 to 3721.17 of the Revised Code have been violated may report or cause reports to be made of the information directly to the department of health. No person who files a report is liable for civil damages resulting from the report.

(C)(1) Within thirty days of receiving a complaint under this section, the department of health shall investigate any complaint referred to it by a home's grievance committee and any complaint from any source that alleges that the home provided substantially less than adequate care or treatment, or substantially unsafe conditions, or, within seven days of receiving a complaint, refer it to the attorney general, if the attorney general agrees to investigate within thirty days.



(2) Within thirty days of receiving a complaint under this section, the department of health may investigate any alleged violation of sections 3721.10 to 3721.17 of the Revised Code, or of rules, policies, or procedures adopted pursuant to those sections, not covered by division (C)(1) of this section, or it may, within seven days of receiving a complaint, refer the complaint to the grievance committee at the home where the alleged violation occurred, or to the attorney general if the attorney general agrees to investigate within thirty days.

(D) If, after an investigation, the department of health finds probable cause to believe that a violation of sections 3721.10 to 3721.17 of the Revised Code, or of rules, policies, or procedures adopted pursuant to those sections, has occurred at a home that is certified under the medicare or medicaid program, it shall cite one or more findings or deficiencies under sections 5165.60 to 5165.89 of the Revised Code. If the home is not so certified, the department shall hold an adjudicative hearing within thirty days under Chapter 119. of the Revised Code.

(E) Upon a finding at an adjudicative hearing under division (D) of this section that a violation of sections 3721.10 to 3721.17 of the Revised Code, or of rules, policies, or procedures adopted pursuant thereto, has occurred, the department of health shall make an order for compliance, set a reasonable time for compliance, and assess a fine pursuant to division (F) of this section. The fine shall be paid to the general revenue fund only if compliance with the order is not shown to have been made within the reasonable time set in the order. The department of health may issue an order prohibiting the continuation of any violation of sections 3721.10 to 3721.17 of the Revised Code.

Findings at the hearings conducted under this section may be appealed pursuant to Chapter 119. of the Revised Code, except that an appeal may be made to the court of common pleas of the county in which the home is located.

The department of health shall initiate proceedings in court to collect any fine assessed under this section that is unpaid thirty days after the violator's final appeal is exhausted.

(F) Any home found, pursuant to an adjudication hearing under division (D) of this section, to have violated sections 3721.10 to 3721.17 of the Revised Code, or rules, policies, or procedures adopted pursuant to those sections may be fined not less than one hundred nor more than five hundred dollars for a first offense. For each subsequent offense, the home may be fined not less than two hundred nor more than one thousand dollars.

A violation of sections 3721.10 to 3721.17 of the Revised Code is a separate offense for each day of the violation and for each resident who claims the violation.

(G) No home or employee of a home shall retaliate against any person who:

(1) Exercises any right set forth in sections 3721.10 to 3721.17 of the Revised Code, including, but not limited to, filing a complaint with the home's grievance committee or reporting an alleged violation to the department of health;

(2) Appears as a witness in any hearing conducted under this section or section 3721.162 of the Revised Code;

(3) Files a civil action alleging a violation of sections 3721.10 to 3721.17 of the Revised Code, or notifies a county prosecuting attorney or the attorney general of a possible violation of sections 3721.10 to 3721.17 of the Revised Code.

If, under the procedures outlined in this section, a home or its employee is found to have retaliated, the violator may be fined up to one thousand dollars.

(H) When legal action is indicated, any evidence of criminal activity found in an investigation under division (C) of this section shall be given to the prosecuting attorney in the county in which the home is located for investigation.

(I)(1)(a) Any resident whose rights under sections 3721.10 to 3721.17 of the Revised Code are violated has a cause of action against any person or home committing the violation.

(b) An action under division (I)(1)(a) of this section may be commenced by the resident or by the resident's legal guardian or other legally authorized representative on behalf of the resident or the resident's estate. If the resident or the resident's legal guardian or other legally authorized representative is unable to commence an action under that division on behalf of the resident, the following persons in the following order of priority have the right to and may commence an action under that division on behalf of the resident or the resident's estate:

(i) The resident's spouse;

(ii) The resident's parent or adult child;

(iii) The resident's guardian if the resident is a minor child;

(iv) The resident's brother or sister;

(v) The resident's niece, nephew, aunt, or uncle.

(c) Notwithstanding any law as to priority of persons entitled to commence an action, if more than one eligible person within the same level of priority seeks to commence an action on behalf of a resident or the resident's estate, the court shall determine, in the best interest of the resident or the resident's estate, the individual to commence the action. A court's determination under this division as to the person to commence an action on behalf of a resident or the resident's estate shall bar another person from commencing the action on behalf of the resident or the resident's estate.

(d) The result of an action commenced pursuant to division (I)(1)(a) of this section by a person authorized under division (I)(1)(b) of this section shall bind the resident or the resident's estate that is the subject of the action.

(e) A cause of action under division (I)(1)(a) of this section shall accrue, and the statute of limitations applicable to that cause of action shall begin to run, based upon the violation of a resident's rights under sections 3721.10 to 3721.17 of the Revised Code, regardless of the party commencing the action on behalf of the resident or the resident's estate as authorized under divisions (I)(1)(b) and (c) of this section.

(2)(a) The plaintiff in an action filed under division (I)(1) of this section may obtain injunctive relief against the violation of the resident's rights. The plaintiff also may recover compensatory damages based upon a showing, by a preponderance of the evidence, that the violation of the resident's rights resulted from a negligent act or omission of the person or home and that the violation was the proximate cause of the resident's injury, death, or loss to person or property.

(b) If compensatory damages are awarded for a violation of the resident's rights, section 2315.21 of the Revised Code shall apply to an award of punitive or exemplary damages for the violation.

(c) The court, in a case in which only injunctive relief is granted, may award to the prevailing party reasonable attorney's fees limited to the work reasonably performed.

(3) Division (I)(2)(b) of this section shall be considered to be purely remedial in operation and shall be applied in a remedial manner in any civil action in which this section is relevant, whether the action is pending in court or commenced on or after July 9, 1998.

(4) Within thirty days after the filing of a complaint in an action for damages brought against a home under division (I)(1)(a) of this section by or on behalf of a resident or former resident of the home, the plaintiff or plaintiffs counsel shall send written notice of the filing of the complaint to the department of medicaid if the department has a right of recovery under section 5160.37 of the Revised Code against the

liability of the home for the cost of medicaid services arising out of injury, disease, or disability of the resident or former resident.

**HISTORY:**
137 v H 600 (Eff 4-9-79); 140 v H 660 (Eff 7-26-84); 143 v H 822 (Eff 12-13-90); 147 v H 354 (Eff 7-9-98); 149 v H 94 (Eff 9-5-2001); 149 v H 412. Eff 11-7-2002; 2013 HB 59, § 101.01, eff. Sept. 29, 2013.

**Editor's Notes**
See provisions, § 4 of HB 412 (149 v H 412) following RC § 3721.02.

**Amendment Notes**
The 2013 amendment substituted "sections 5165.60 to 5165.89" for "sections 5111.35 to 5111.62" in the first sentence of (D); and, in (I)(4), substituted "department of medicaid" for "department of job and family services", "section 5160.37" for "section 5101.58", and "medicaid services" for "medical services and care".

## NOTES TO DECISIONS

Analysis

Generally
Authority to sue
Child of deceased resident
Consumer sales practices act
County employees
Damages generally
Employees
Immunity
Jury instruction
Legislative intent
Medical claims
Punitive damages
Standing
Unlicensed facility
Wrongful discharge

**Generally**
It was error to dismiss wrongful death and medical malpractice claims against a nursing home under R.C. 3721.17 and to award it attorney fees and costs pursuant to R.C. 2323.42 because the claims were reasonably based on law and fact where the patient's estate presented expert medical testimony opining that the nursing home's failure to adequately document the patient's dehydration stemming from diabetes medicine led to the patient's preventable death. Sliwinski v. Vill. at St. Edward, 2010-Ohio-3006, 2010 Ohio App. LEXIS 2495 (Ohio Ct. App., Summit County 2010).

Determining the type of health care facility involved is crucial to establishing the applicable standard of care. A cause of action under the nursing home residents' rights statutes will survive the death of the resident if the action is one for mesne profits, injuries to person or property, or deceit or fraud. Richards v. Broadview Heights Harborside Healthcare, 2002-Ohio-6491, 150 Ohio App. 3d 537, 782 N.E.2d 609, 2002 Ohio App. LEXIS 6378 (Ohio Ct. App., Cuyahoga County 2002).

**Authority to sue**
Arbitration agreement between a nursing home and a resident did not violate the statutory right to pursue a cause of action in the Bill of Rights because the statute did not forbid a claim from being arbitrated. Harrison v. Winchester Place Nursing & Rehab. Ctr., 2013-Ohio-3163, 996 N.E.2d 1001, 2013 Ohio App. LEXIS 3205 (Ohio Ct. App., Franklin County 2013).

When a deceased nursing home resident's guardian sued the nursing home on the resident's behalf for alleged violations of the "Nursing Home Patient Bill of Rights," R.C. 3721.10 et seq., it was not error to find that the guardian had no authority to file suit because, while the resident was unable to sue, R.C. 3721.17(I)(1)(b) required a showing that the resident's estate's legal representative, which was the co-administrators of the resident's decedent's estate, could not sue, and no such showing was made. Whitley v. River's Bend Health Care, 2009-Ohio-3366, 183 Ohio App. 3d 145, 916 N.E.2d 515, 2009 Ohio App. LEXIS 2911 (Ohio Ct. App., Lawrence County 2009).

**Child of deceased resident**
Adult child of a deceased resident had no authority to bring an action under R.C. 3721.17 where there was no showing that the estate representatives were unable to commence the action. Whitley v. River's Bend Health Care, 2009-Ohio-3366, 183 Ohio App. 3d 145, 916 N.E.2d 515, 2009 Ohio App. LEXIS 2911 (Ohio Ct. App., Lawrence County 2009).

**Consumer sales practices act**
The consumer sales practices act applies to billing practices of a residential care facility. Elder v. Fischer, 129 Ohio App. 3d 209, 717 N.E.2d 730, 1998 Ohio App. LEXIS 3385 (Ohio Ct. App., Hamilton County), dismissed, 84 Ohio St. 3d 1434, 702 N.E.2d 1213, 1998 Ohio LEXIS 3475 (Ohio 1998).

**County employees**
Ohio Supreme Court holds that R.C. 3721.17(I)(1) does not expressly impose liability on the employees of a county nursing home within the meaning of R.C. 2744.03(A)(6)(a), as the use of the term "person" in R.C. 3721.17(I)(1) is too general to expressly impose liability on an employee of a political subdivision; accordingly, an estate administrator for a deceased county home resident had no cause of action against nurses of a county home under the Ohio Patients' Bill of Rights, R.C. 3721.10 through 3721.17. Cramer v. Auglaize Acres, 2007-Ohio-1946, 113 Ohio St. 3d 266, 865 N.E.2d 9, 2007 Ohio LEXIS 1130 (Ohio 2007).

**Damages generally**
A party seeking relief pursuant to R.C. 3721.17(I) on a claim alleging a violation of a nursing home resident's rights is not entitled to an award of nominal damages upon a showing of a violation; in view of the precise terms used in the statute, it is clear that the legislature intended to permit the recovery only of actual damages and punitive damages. Silver Circle v. Thomas, 1995 Ohio App. LEXIS 5193 (Ohio Ct. App., Hamilton County Nov. 29, 1995).

**Employees**
Trial court erred in finding that R.C. 3721.17(I)(1)(a) expressly created a right of action against two employees of a county home as § 3721.17(I)(1)(a) imposed liability upon "homes" and all persons in general, but not employees; as there was no statute expressly imposing liability upon the employees, R.C. 2744.01(A)(6)(c) did not abrogate their immunity. Cramer v. Auglaize Acres, 2005-Ohio-3609, 2005 Ohio App. LEXIS 3332 (Ohio Ct. App., Auglaize County 2005), aff'd in part and rev'd in part, 2007-Ohio-1946, 113 Ohio St. 3d 266, 865 N.E.2d 9, 2007 Ohio LEXIS 1130 (Ohio 2007).

**Immunity**
Resolving a conflict between this statute and R.C. 2305.51, the immunity afforded to mental health professionals and organizations does not apply to nursing homes; thus, a nursing home could not assert immunity in a wrongful death action arising out of the death of a resident resulting from an attack by another resident. Overholt v. United Church Homes, Inc., 2013 Ohio Misc. LEXIS 214 (Ohio C.P. June 28, 2013), dismissed without prejudice, 2013 Ohio Misc. LEXIS 213 (Ohio C.P. Dec. 13, 2013).

Ohio Supreme Court holds that R.C. 3721.17(I)(1) specifically abrogates governmental immunity and grants a cause of action to residents of unlicensed county nursing homes against a political subdivision for violations of R.C. 3721.10 through 3721.17, the Ohio Nursing Home Patients' Bill of Rights, as the Ohio General Assembly clearly expressed its intent to give to all county nursing-home residents the rights set forth in the Bill of Rights by including "county homes" in the definition of home under R.C. 3721.01; accordingly, a claim by a deceased county home resident's estate administrator against the county home and the county board of commissioners fell under the exception to immunity in R.C. 2744.02(B)(5), although punitive damages could not be awarded against a political subdivision like the county pursuant to R.C. 2744.05(A). Cramer v. Auglaize Acres, 2007-Ohio-1946, 113 Ohio St. 3d 266, 865 N.E.2d 9, 2007 Ohio LEXIS 1130 (Ohio 2007).

Former R.C. 3721.17(I)(1) specifically abrogates governmental immunity and grants a cause of action to residents of unlicensed county nursing homes against a political subdivision for violations of R.C. § § 3721.10 through 3721.17, the Ohio Nursing Home Patients' Bill of Rights. Cramer v. Auglaize Acres, 2007-Ohio-1946, 113 Ohio St. 3d 266, 865 N.E.2d 9, 2007 Ohio LEXIS 1130 (Ohio 2007).

**Jury instruction**
Trial court did not err in instructing the jury. Because its instruction contained language nearly identical to the language of the statute, regarding violation of the nursing facility resident's rights, the trial court's instruction was a correct statement of the law. Altercare of Mayfield Vill., Inc. v. Berner, 2017-Ohio-958, 86 N.E.3d 649, 2017 Ohio App. LEXIS 970 (Ohio Ct. App., Cuyahoga County 2017).

**Legislative intent**
Although H.B. 357 clearly indicates the general assembly's intent that the amendment to R.C. 3721.17(I)(3) be applied retroactively, this amendment is substantive rather than remedial, because it imposes a new, more difficult burden of proof upon a plaintiff attempting to recover punitive damages under R.C. 3721.17(I)(2)(a); since this amendment limits a substantive right, its retroactive application is prohibited by Ohio Const. art II, § 28. Blancett v. Nationwide Care, 1998 Ohio App. LEXIS 6504 (Ohio Ct. App., Guernsey County Dec. 16, 1998), dismissed, 85 Ohio St. 3d 1464, 709 N.E.2d 171, 1999 Ohio LEXIS 1338 (Ohio 1999).

**Medical claims**
Trial court did not err in granting a nursing home's motion to dismiss a resident's action alleging that it violated her rights under R.C. 3721.13

because the claims concerning the resident's rights were medical "medical claims" as defined in R.C. 2305.113(E)(3) and subject to its one-year statute of limitations; claims brought under R.C. chapter 3721 are also "medical claims" if the action arises from the individual's medical diagnosis, care, or treatment. Barley v. Hearth & Care of Greenfield, LLC, 2013-Ohio-279, 2013 Ohio App. LEXIS 201 (Ohio Ct. App., Highland County 2013).

**Punitive damages**

District court found that the record was replete with evidence from which a reasonable jury could find for the plaintiff on punitive damages where (1) the record reflected that multiple medication errors occurred prior to the one at issue; (2) because only 2 licensed practical nurses were responsible to care for 80 residents, the nurses were very rushed; (3) as a result of their haste, the nurses regularly engaged in the unsafe practice of pre-pouring residents' medications; (4) the medication cart was "a mess" most of the time with the wrong pills were found in the medication trays; (5) the nurses would borrow medication from one resident and give it to another; (6) at the time of her death, over 50 of decedent's pills were missing; (7) testimony indicated that medical records were routinely falsified or doctored, and on one described occasion, a supervisor altered the records to cover up a medication error; and (8) staff, including the supervisor, would routinely retroactively fill in "holes" in the residents' medication administration records at the end of the month. Punitive damages were appropriate to punish and deter such conduct. Freudeman v. Landing of Canton, 702 F.3d 318, 2012 FED App. 0413P, 2012 U.S. App. LEXIS 25850 (6th Cir. Ohio 2012).

Although the defendants argued in their motion that the plaintiff presented no evidence to the jury that the defendants' conduct could be characterized by the conscious disregard for the rights and safety of other persons that had a great probability of causing substantial harm, and therefore judgment as a matter of law was warranted on plaintiffs claims for punitive damages under R.C. 2315.21 and R.C. 3721.17 and attorney fees, the record was replete with evidence from which a reasonable jury could find for the plaintiff on punitive damages; that evidence included but was not limited to testimony from multiple witnesses that medication errors had occurred in the past, the medication cart was disorderly, the residents' medications could be found in other residents' compartment on the medication cart, when a resident's medication ran out the medication would be borrowed from other residents, nurses were understaffed and rushed to distribute medications on time, medications were pre-poured to save time, medication administration records were not completed contemporaneously with the administration of medication, and that under such circumstances medication errors could, and did, occur. Based on the evidence in the record, a reasonable jury could find that the defendants' practices regarding the administration of medication, which included giving a resident another resident's medication, could be characterized as a conscious disregard for the rights and safety of other persons with a great probability of causing substantial harm if a resident received the wrong medication. Freudeman v. Landing of Canton, 2011 U.S. Dist. LEXIS 150023 (N.D. Ohio Dec. 30, 2011), aff'd in part, rev'd, 702 F.3d 318, 2012 FED App. 0413P, 2012 U.S. App. LEXIS 25850 (6th Cir. Ohio 2012).

Revised Code § 3721.17 does not require a finding of malice to support an award of punitive damages. Belinky v. Drake Ctr., 117 Ohio App. 3d 497, 690 N.E.2d 1302, 1996 Ohio App. LEXIS 5891 (Ohio Ct. App., Hamilton County 1996), dismissed, 78 Ohio St. 3d 1495, 678 N.E.2d 1231, 1997 Ohio LEXIS 1593 (Ohio 1997).

Revised Code § 3721.17 expressly provides that punitive damages may be awarded for violation of the rights of a nursing home resident under R.C. 3721.10 to 3721.19. Pursuant to R.C. 2315.21(D)(1), R.C. 3721.17 controls. Sprosty v. Pearlview, Inc., 106 Ohio App. 3d 679, 666 N.E.2d 1180, 1995 Ohio App. LEXIS 4068 (Ohio Ct. App., Cuyahoga County 1995), dismissed, 75 Ohio St. 3d 1402, 661 N.E.2d 754, 1996 Ohio LEXIS 3857 (Ohio 1996).

**Standing**

Decedent's grandchildren had no standing, under R.C. 3721.17(I)(1)(b), to bring a claim alleging a violation of the decedent's rights as a nursing home resident because (1) the grandchildren were not the legal representatives of the decedent's estate, (2) there was no evidence that the person who was that representative was unable to bring this claim on behalf of the decedent's estate, and (3) had there been such evidence, the grandchildren were not included in the list in § 3721.17(I)(1)(b) stating those individuals who were authorized to file suit on behalf of the decedent's estate. Treadway v. Free Pentecostal Pater Ave. Church of God, Inc., 2008-Ohio-1663, 2008 Ohio App. LEXIS 1433 (Ohio Ct. App., Butler County 2008).

Decedent's grandchildren had no standing, under R.C. 3721.17(I)(1)(b), to bring a claim alleging a violation of the decedent's rights as a nursing home resident because (1) the grandchildren were not the legal representatives of the decedent's estate, (2) there was no evidence that the person who was that representative was unable to bring this claim on behalf of the decedent's estate, and (3) had there been such evidence, the grandchildren were not included in the list in § 3721.17(I)(1)(b) stating those individuals who were authorized to file suit on behalf of the decedent's estate. Treadway v. Free Pentecostal Pater Ave. Church of God, Inc., 2008-Ohio-1663, 2008 Ohio App. LEXIS 1433 (Ohio Ct. App., Butler County 2008).

**Unlicensed facility**

A facility that meets the statutory definition of "home" is subject to the patients' bill of rights regardless of whether the department of health allows it to operate unlicensed. Peskin v. Seasons Health Care L.P., 141 Ohio App. 3d 436, 751 N.E.2d 546, 2001 Ohio App. LEXIS 993 (Ohio Ct. App., Hamilton County), dismissed, 92 Ohio St. 3d 1430, 749 N.E.2d 757, 2001 Ohio LEXIS 1758 (Ohio 2001).

**Wrongful discharge**

A nurse could not recover on a wrongful discharge claim where the public policy involved was based on reporting abuse in a nursing home. R.C. 3721.24 provided the appropriate remedy. Dolan v. St. Mary's Mem'l Home, 2003-Ohio-3383, 153 Ohio App. 3d 441, 794 N.E.2d 716, 2003 Ohio App. LEXIS 3076 (Ohio Ct. App., Hamilton County 2003).

Revised Code § 3721.17(G), which provides that "[n]o home or employee of a home shall retaliate against any person who: (1) * * * report[s] an alleged violation to the Ohio commission on aging," is administrative and does not create a cause of action by an employee against an employer for a retaliatory termination of employment. Welch v. Brown's Nursing Home, 20 Ohio App. 3d 15, 484 N.E.2d 178, 1984 Ohio App. LEXIS 12524 (Ohio Ct. App., Hamilton County 1984).

### RESEARCH REFERENCES AND PRACTICE AIDS

**Cross-References to Related Sections**

Definitions, RC § 3721.10.
Determination of whether actions, practices, situations or incidents can be justified; declaration and citing of findings, RC § 5165.66.
Duties of home administrator concerning residents' rights, RC § 3721.12.
Investigations of alleged violations by department of aging, RC § 173.01.
Recategorization of hospital beds to skilled nursing beds; nursing home placement clearinghouses, RC § 3702.521.
Residents' rights; sponsor may protect rights, RC § 3721.13.
State long-term care ombudsperson program; investigation and resolution of complaints, RC § 173.19.
Access to records of resident, recipient or provider; subpoenas; injunction; referral of complaints, RC § 173.20.
Protection of employees of provider; residents and recipients from retaliation, RC § 173.24.

**Ohio Administrative Code**

Department of aging —
State long-term care ombudsman. OAC ch. 173-14.
Department of health—
Nursing home residents' rights. OAC ch. 3701-61.
Complaint investigations; adjudications; penalties. OAC 3701-61-06.
Nursing homes. OAC ch. 3701-17.

## § 3721.18 Attorney general may investigate violations; referral to prosecuting attorney.

The attorney general may investigate alleged violations of Chapter 3721. of the Revised Code or rules, policies, or procedures adopted thereunder. When it appears, as the result of the investigation, that there is cause to prosecute for the commission of a crime, the attorney general shall refer the evidence to the prosecuting attorney having jurisdiction in the matter.

**HISTORY:**

137 v H 600. Eff 4-9-79.

### RESEARCH REFERENCES AND PRACTICE AIDS

**Cross-References to Related Sections**

Definitions, RC § 3721.10.
Resident may file grievance; procedures; prohibition, RC § 3721.17.

## § 3721.19 Notice of home's nonparticipation in state assistance program; action for violation.

(A) As used in this section:

(1) "Home" and "residential care facility" have the same meanings as in section 3721.01 of the Revised Code;

(2) "Provider agreement" has the same meaning as in section 5165.01 of the Revised Code.

(3) "Sponsor" and "residents' rights advocate" have the same meanings as in section 3721.10 of the Revised Code.

A home licensed under this chapter that is not a party to a provider agreement shall provide each prospective resident, before admission, with the following information, orally and in a separate written notice on which is printed in a conspicuous manner: "This home is not a participant in the medicaid program administered by the Ohio department of medicaid. Consequently, you may be discharged from this home if you are unable to pay for the services provided by this home."

If the prospective resident has a sponsor whose identity is made known to the home, the home shall also inform the sponsor, before admission of the resident, of the home's status relative to the medicaid program. Written acknowledgement of the receipt of the information shall be provided by the resident and, if the prospective resident has a sponsor who has been identified to the home, by the sponsor. The written acknowledgement shall be made part of the resident's record by the home.

No home shall terminate its provider agreement unless it has complied with section 5165.50 of the Revised Code and, at least ninety days prior to such termination, provided written notice to the residents of the home and their sponsors of such action. This requirement shall not apply in cases where the department of medicaid terminates a home's provider agreement or provider status.

(B) A home licensed under this chapter as a residential care facility shall provide notice to each prospective resident or the individual's sponsor of the services offered by the facility and the types of skilled nursing care that the facility may provide. A residential care facility that, pursuant to section 3721.012 of the Revised Code, has a policy of entering into risk agreements with residents or their sponsors shall provide each prospective resident or the individual's sponsor a written explanation of the policy and the provisions that may be contained in a risk agreement. At the time the information is provided, the facility shall obtain a statement signed by the individual receiving the information acknowledging that the individual received the information. The facility shall maintain on file the individual's signed statement.

(C) A resident has a cause of action against a home for breach of any duty imposed by this section. The action may be commenced by the resident, or on the resident's behalf by the resident's sponsor or a residents' rights advocate, by the filing of a civil action in the court of common pleas of the county in which the home is located, or in the court of common pleas of Franklin county.

If the court finds that a breach of any duty imposed by this section has occurred, the court shall enjoin the home from discharging the resident from the home until arrangements satisfactory to the court are made for the orderly transfer of the resident to another mode of health care including, but not limited to, another home, and may award the resident and a person or public agency that brings an action on behalf of a resident reasonable attorney's fees. If a home discharges a resident to whom or to whose sponsor information concerning its status relative to the medicaid program was not provided as required under this section, the court shall grant any appropriate relief including, but not limited to, actual damages, reasonable attorney's fees, and costs.

**HISTORY:**

138 v H 176 (Eff 7-1-80); 141 v H 428 (Eff 12-23-86); 146 v H 117 (Eff 9-29-95); 148 v H 471. Eff 7-1-2000; 151 v H 66, § 101.01, eff. 7-1-05; 2013 HB 59, § 101.01, eff. Sept. 29, 2013.

**Amendment Notes**

The 2013 amendment inserted (A)(2); redesignated former (A)(2) as (A)(3); deleted "as defined in section 5111.20 of the Revised Code" following "agreement" in the first sentence of the second paragraph of (A); substituted "medicaid program" for "medical assistance program" in the first sentence of the second and third paragraphs of (A) and the second sentence of the second paragraph of (C); substituted "of medicaid" for "of job and family services" in the first sentence of the first paragraph of (A) and the second sentence of the last paragraph of (A); in the first sentence of the last paragraph of (A), substituted "provider agreement" for "status as a provider under the medicaid program" and "section 5165.50" for "section 5111.66".

151 v H 66, effective July 1, 2005, in the final paragraph of (A), substituted "medicaid" for "medical assistance", inserted "complied with section 5111.66 of the Revised Code and", and deleted "department of job and family services and" preceding "residents of the home".

### § 3721.20 Repealed.

Repealed, 138 v H 204, § 270 [137 v H 276; 138 v H 204]. Eff 9-1-79.

### § 3721.20 Compassionate care visits permitted in long-term care facilities. [Effective July 21, 2022]

(A) As used in this section:

(1) "Compassionate caregiver" means an individual who provides in-person visitation to a long-term care facility resident in compassionate care situations in accordance with this section.

(2) "Long-term care facility" means a home, as defined in section 3721.01 of the Revised Code.

"Long-term care facility" does not include any federal facility operated in this state, including a facility operated by the United States department of veterans affairs.

(3) "Transmission-based precautions" mean precautions that are used when the route of infection transmission is not completely interrupted using standard precautions alone. Transmission-based precautions are precautions used in addition to standard precautions.

(B)(1) During an epidemic, pandemic, or other state of emergency, a long-term care facility shall permit a compassionate caregiver to enter the facility to provide in-person visitation to a resident in compassionate care situations, which does not refer exclusively to end of life situations. Compassionate care situations include, but are not limited to, any of the following situations:

(a) The resident's end of life;

(b) The resident was recently admitted to the facility and is struggling with the change in environment and lack of physical family support;

(c) The resident is grieving after a friend or family member has recently passed away;

(d) The resident is experiencing weight loss or dehydration and needs cueing and encouragement when eating or drinking;

(e) The resident is experiencing emotional distress from isolation as demonstrated by behavioral changes such as rarely speaking or crying more frequently;

(f) The resident is in transmission-based precautions for a disease or illness.

(2) A long-term care facility shall use a person-centered approach in working with residents, family members, caregivers, personal representatives, and, as appropriate, the state long-term care ombudsman program to identify residents who are in need of visits by a compassionate caregiver for a compassionate care situation under division (B)(1) of this section.

(C)(1) When visiting a long-term care facility resident in a long-term care facility that is governed by United States centers for medicare and medicaid services regulations, the compassionate caregiver shall comply with all regulations and guidance issued by the centers for medicare and medicaid services, as well as the facility's visitor policy established under division (D) of this section. When visiting a resident in a long-term care facility that is not governed by centers for medicare and medicaid services regulations, the compassionate caregiver shall comply with the facility's visitor policy established under division (D) of this section.

(2) Before entering a long-term care facility, all compassionate caregivers and health care workers shall do both of the following:

(a) Undergo screening as the facility determines reasonably necessary to ascertain any exposure to a contagious disease or illness and disclose any symptoms, as defined by the facility;

(b) Produce valid federal or state identification and use all appropriate personal protective equipment. Except in an emergency, each individual shall provide the facility with the individual's current telephone number and address. The facility shall log each visitor, including the individual's telephone number and address, and retain the log in accordance with state and federal record retention requirements.

(D) Not later than thirty days after the effective date of this section, each long-term care facility shall develop and implement a visitation policy regulating compassionate care visits during an epidemic, pandemic, or other state of emergency. The policy shall do all of the following:

(1) Permit visitation at any time to accommodate the schedules of a compassionate caregiver and resident;

(2) Require a compassionate caregiver to provide support to the resident in the resident's room or designated visitor space and to limit movement throughout the facility;

(3) Reasonably provide hand sanitizing stations and alcohol-based hand sanitizer in accessible locations;

(4) Permit at least two visitors per resident for a minimum of two hours in the case of a resident who displays a substantial change of condition indicating that end of life is approaching, or longer if death is imminent.

(5) Require the facility to educate compassionate caregivers, family members, and other interested persons, about the right to contact the office of the state long-term care ombudsman program established under section 173.15 of the Revised Code with concerns about access to the facility and its residents;

(6) Require the facility to communicate to compassionate caregivers and residents its visitation policy established under this section;

(7) Require compassionate caregivers to comply with the screening requirements of division (C)(2) of this section;

(8) Specify whether compassionate caregivers must schedule compassionate care visits, other than end of life visits, with the facility in advance.

(E) The policies developed and implemented under division (D) of this section shall be the least restrictive possible and provide maximum access to the resident.

(F) During an epidemic, pandemic, or other state of emergency, a long-term care facility shall permit health care and other workers to enter the facility who are not employees of the facility but provide direct care to facility residents or essential services to the facility, including hospice care program and home health agency workers, emergency medical services personnel, dialysis technicians, clinical laboratory technicians, radiology technicians, social workers, clergy members, hair salon personnel, and contractors conducting critical on-site maintenance. A facility may, however, restrict such an individual from providing services in the facility if the individual is subject to a work exclusion due to direct exposure to a contagious disease or illness or shows symptoms of a contagious disease or illness when being screened before entering the facility. The health care and other workers shall adhere to the core principles of infection prevention and comply with testing requirements as applicable.

(G)(1) The screening and testing requirements of division (F) of this section do not apply in exigent circumstances, such as to emergency medical personnel, first responders, or other similarly situated individuals, in response to an emergency.

(2) Personnel who are providing nonemergency medical transportation, such as for scheduled medical appointments and who are considered to be providing services under arrangement with the facility shall be tested at a frequency consistent with the routine testing frequency applicable to the facility, if any.

(H) This section shall not be construed or implemented in such a way as to conflict with federal regulatory guidance regarding long-term care facility visitation, such as guidance issued by the centers for medicare and medicaid services or the centers for disease control and prevention.

(I) Beginning thirty days after the effective date of this section, a long-term care facility shall not fail to comply with this section.

**HISTORY:**

2022 hb120, § 1, effective July 21, 2022.

# ABUSE, NEGLECT OR MISAPPROPRIATION OF RESIDENT'S PROPERTY AT LONG-TERM CARE FACILITY

## § 3721.21 Definitions.

As used in sections 3721.21 to 3721.34 of the Revised Code:

(A) "Long-term care facility" means either of the following:

(1) A nursing home as defined in section 3721.01 of the Revised Code;

(2) A facility or part of a facility that is certified as a skilled nursing facility or a nursing facility under Title XVIII or XIX of the "Social Security Act."

(B) "Residential care facility" has the same meaning as in section 3721.01 of the Revised Code.

(C) "Abuse" means any of the following:

(1) Physical abuse;

(2) Psychological abuse;

(3) Sexual abuse.

(D) "Neglect" means recklessly failing to provide a resident with any treatment, care, goods, or service necessary to maintain the health or safety of the resident when the failure results in serious physical harm to the resident. "Neglect" does not include allowing a resident, at the resident's option, to receive only treatment by spiritual means through prayer in accordance with the tenets of a recognized religious denomination.

(E) "Exploitation" means taking advantage of a resident, regardless of whether the action was for personal gain, whether the resident knew of the action, or whether the resident was harmed.

(F) "Misappropriation" means depriving, defrauding, or otherwise obtaining the real or personal property of a resident by any means prohibited by the Revised Code, including violations of Chapter 2911. or 2913. of the Revised Code.

(G) "Resident" includes a resident, patient, former resident or patient, or deceased resident or patient of a long-term care facility or a residential care facility.

(H) "Physical abuse" means knowingly causing physical harm or recklessly causing serious physical harm to a resident through either of the following:

(1) Physical contact with the resident;

(2) The use of physical restraint, chemical restraint, medication that does not constitute a chemical restraint, or isolation, if the restraint, medication, or isolation is excessive, for punishment, for staff convenience, a substitute for treatment, or in an amount that precludes habilitation and treatment.

(I) "Psychological abuse" means knowingly or recklessly causing psychological harm to a resident, whether verbally or by action.

(J) "Sexual abuse" means sexual conduct or sexual contact with a resident, as those terms are defined in section 2907.01 of the Revised Code.

(K) "Physical restraint" has the same meaning as in section 3721.10 of the Revised Code.

(L) "Chemical restraint" has the same meaning as in section 3721.10 of the Revised Code.

(M) "Nursing and nursing-related services" means the personal care services and other services not constituting skilled nursing care that are specified in rules the director of health shall adopt in accordance with Chapter 119. of the Revised Code.

(N) "Personal care services" has the same meaning as in section 3721.01 of the Revised Code.

(O)(1) Except as provided in division (O)(2) of this section, "nurse aide" means an individual who provides nursing and nursing-related services to residents in a long-term care facility, either as a member of the staff of the facility for monetary compensation or as a volunteer without monetary compensation.

(2) "Nurse aide" does not include either of the following:

(a) A licensed health professional practicing within the scope of the professional's license;

(b) An individual providing nursing and nursing-related services in a religious nonmedical health care institution, if the individual has been trained in the principles of nonmedical care and is recognized by the institution as being competent in the administration of care within the religious tenets practiced by the residents of the institution.

(P) "Licensed health professional" means all of the following:

(1) An occupational therapist or occupational therapy assistant licensed under Chapter 4755. of the Revised Code;

(2) A physical therapist or physical therapy assistant licensed under Chapter 4755. of the Revised Code;

(3) A physician authorized under Chapter 4731. of the Revised Code to practice medicine and surgery, osteopathic medicine and surgery, or podiatric medicine and surgery;

(4) A physician assistant authorized under Chapter 4730. of the Revised Code to practice as a physician assistant;

(5) A registered nurse or licensed practical nurse licensed under Chapter 4723. of the Revised Code;

(6) A social worker or independent social worker licensed under Chapter 4757. of the Revised Code or a social work assistant registered under that chapter;

(7) A speech-language pathologist or audiologist licensed under Chapter 4753. of the Revised Code;

(8) A dentist or dental hygienist licensed under Chapter 4715. of the Revised Code;

(9) An optometrist licensed under Chapter 4725. of the Revised Code;

(10) A pharmacist licensed under Chapter 4729. of the Revised Code;

(11) A psychologist licensed under Chapter 4732. of the Revised Code;

(12) A chiropractor licensed under Chapter 4734. of the Revised Code;

(13) A nursing home administrator licensed or temporarily licensed under Chapter 4751. of the Revised Code;

(14) A licensed professional counselor or licensed professional clinical counselor licensed under Chapter 4757. of the Revised Code;

(15) A marriage and family therapist or independent marriage and family therapist licensed under Chapter 4757. of the Revised Code.

(Q) "Religious nonmedical health care institution" means an institution that meets or exceeds the conditions to receive payment under the medicare program established under Title XVIII of the "Social Security Act" for inpatient hospital services or post-hospital extended care services furnished to an individual in a religious nonmedical health care institution, as defined in section 1861(ss)(1) of the "Social Security Act," 79 Stat. 286 (1965), 42 U.S.C. 1395x(ss)(1), as amended.

(R) "Competency evaluation program" means a program through which the competency of a nurse aide to provide nursing and nursing-related services is evaluated.

(S) "Training and competency evaluation program" means a program of nurse aide training and evaluation of competency to provide nursing and nursing-related services.

**HISTORY:**

RC § 3721.27, 143 v H 112 (Eff 2-16-89); 143 v H 359 (Eff 3-13-90); RC § 3721.21, 143 v H 822 (Eff 12-13-90); 146 v H 117 (Eff 9-29-95); 146 v S 143 (Eff 3-5-96); 146 v S 223 (Eff 3-18-97); 148 v H 403. Eff 9-27-2000; 151 v H 66, § 101.01, eff. 6-30-05; 2012 HB 487, § 101.01, eff. Sept. 10, 2012; 2014 HB 232, § 1, eff. July 10, 2014; 2017 hb49, § 101.01, effective September 29, 2017.

**Amendment Notes**

The 2017 amendment by HB 49 rewrote (C), which formerly read: "Abuse' means knowingly causing physical harm or recklessly causing serious physical harm to resident by physical contact with the resident or by use of physical or chemical restraint, medication, or isolation as punishment, for staff convenience, excessively, as a substituted for treatment, or in amounts that preclude habilitation and treatment"; added (C)(1), (C)(2) and (C)(3); added (E); redesignated former (E) and (F) as (F) and (G); added (H) through (J); redesignated former (G) through (O) as (K) through (S); substituted "division (O)(2)" for "division (K)(2)" in (O)(1); and substituted "podiatric medicine and surgery" for "podiatry" in (P)(3).

The 2014 amendment by HB 232 inserted "licensed" preceding "professional" twice in (L)(14); added (L)(15); and made a related change.

The 2012 amendment deleted "other than a nursing home or part of a nursing home certified as an intermediate care facility for the mentally retarded under Title XIX of the 'Social Security Act,' 49 Stat. 620 (1935), 42 U.S.C.A. 301, as amended" from the end of (A)(1); and substituted "director of health" for "public health council" in (I).

151 v H 66, effective June 30, 2005, rewrote (K); and inserted (M) and redesignated the remaining subsections accordingly.

Titles 11 — 37

### NOTES TO DECISIONS

**Judicial review**

No statutory authority existed to grant the trial court jurisdiction to hear the State Tested Nurse Aide's request for a further appeal from the neglect determination because the legislature explicitly precluded the hearing at issue from being subject to judicial review and thus, there was no implicit right to judicial review of her administrative neglect determination. The record indicated that the notice and hearing provisions provided for within the statutory framework were adhered to and none of her constitutional rights were adversely affected. Biser v. Ohio Dep't of Health, 2020-Ohio-6836, 2020 Ohio App. LEXIS 4678 (Ohio Ct. App., Mahoning County 2020).

### RESEARCH REFERENCES AND PRACTICE AIDS

**Cross-References to Related Sections**

Recategorization of hospital beds to skilled nursing beds; nursing home placement clearinghouses, RC § 3702.521.

Rules to implement provisions, RC § 3721.26.

Uniform rules for operation of homes; standards, RC § 3721.04.

**Ohio Administrative Code**

Department of health, director of—

Abuse or neglect in long-term care facilities. OAC ch. 3701-64.

Definitions. OAC 3701-64-01.

State board of examiners of nursing home administrators. OAC ch. 4751-1.

## § 3721.22 Report of abuse or neglect of resident or misappropriation of property.

(A)(1) No person identified in division (P)(1) to (12), (14), or (15) of section 3721.21 of the Revised Code who knows or suspects that a resident has been abused, neglected, or exploited, or that a resident's property has been misappropriated, by any individual used by a long-term care facility or residential care facility to provide services to residents, shall fail to report that knowledge or suspicion to the facility.

(2) No nursing home administrator licensed or temporarily licensed under Chapter 4751. of the Revised Code, and no administrator of a residential care facility, who knows or suspects that a resident has been abused, neglected, or exploited, or that a resident's property has been misappropriated, by any individual used by a long-term care facility or residential care facility to provide services to residents, shall fail to report that knowledge or suspicion to the director of health.

(B) Any person, including a resident, who knows or suspects that a resident has been abused, neglected, or exploited, or that a resident's property has been misappropriated, by any individual used by a long-term care facility or residential care facility to provide services to residents, may report that knowledge or suspicion to the director of health.

(C) Any person who in good faith reports suspected abuse, neglect, exploitation, or misappropriation to a facility or the director of health, provides information during an investigation of suspected abuse, neglect, exploitation, or misappropriation conducted by the director, or participates in a hearing conducted under section 3721.23 of the Revised Code is not subject to criminal prosecution, liable in damages in a tort or other civil action, or subject to professional disciplinary action because of injury or loss to person or property allegedly arising from the making of the report, provision of information, or participation in the hearing.

(D) If the director has reason to believe that a violation of division (A) of this section has occurred, the director may report the suspected violation to the appropriate professional licensing authority and to the attorney general, county prosecutor, or other appropriate law enforcement official.

(E) No person shall knowingly make a false allegation of abuse, neglect, or exploitation of a resident or misappropriation of a resident's property, or knowingly swear or affirm the truth of a false allegation, when the allegation is made for the purpose of incriminating another.



**HISTORY:**

143 v H 822 (Eff 12-13-90); 146 v H 117. Eff 9-29-95; 2017 hb49, § 101.01, effective September 29, 2017.

**Amendment Notes**

The 2017 amendment by HB 49 redesignated former (A) as (A)(1); in (A)(1), substituted "person identified in division (P)(1) to (12), (14), or (15) of section 3721.21 of the Revised Code" for "licensed health professional," "neglected, or exploited" for "or, neglected" and "suspicion to the facility" for "suspicion to the director of health"; added (A)(2); substituted "neglected, or exploited" for "or, neglected" in (B); in (C), added "exploitation" twice and "a facility or"; and substituted "neglect, or exploitation" for "or, neglect" in (E).

## NOTES TO DECISIONS

Analysis

Relationship to other provisions
Reporting requirements

**Relationship to other provisions**

Plaintiff was not entitled to amend her complaint with leave of court, as the statutes regarding reporting of abuse in long-term care facilities and reporting abuse of persons with development disabilities were not so similar that an action under one could be substituted for the other and the trial court properly found that allowing plaintiff to amend her complaint on the day before trial to pursue an action under one provision instead of another would not have given defendant a fair opportunity to address the allegations in the amendment. Mayo v. Bethesda Lutheran Cmtys., 2014-Ohio-3499, 2014 Ohio App. LEXIS 3426 (Ohio Ct. App., Cuyahoga County 2014).

**Reporting requirements**

Employee or other person used to perform work or services who reports or indicates an intention to report suspected abuse or neglect of a long-term-care-facility or a residential-care-facility resident is not required to report or indicate an intent to report the suspected abuse or neglect to the Ohio director of health in order to state a claim for retaliatory discharge as the requirement that abuse be reported to the director of health contained in R.C. 3721.22 and the absence of that requirement in R.C. 3721.24 is presumably intentional; a nurse's reporting the suspected abuse or neglect of the resident to the nursing facility and to the resident's children triggered the protection of R.C. 3721.24. Hulsmeyer v. Hospice of Southwest Ohio, Inc., 2014-Ohio-5511, 142 Ohio St. 3d 236, 29 N.E.3d 903, 2014 Ohio LEXIS 3158 (Ohio 2014).

## RESEARCH REFERENCES AND PRACTICE AIDS

**Cross-References to Related Sections**

Penalties, RC § 3721.99.

Definitions, RC § 3721.21.

Duty of director of health to investigate allegations and conduct hearings, RC § 3721.23.

**Ohio Administrative Code**

Abuse or neglect in long-term care facilities. OAC ch. 3701-64.

Investigations of abuse and neglect of residents or misappropriation of property; notice of hearing rights. OAC 3701-64-02.

## § 3721.23 Duty of director of health to investigate allegations and notify proper authorities.

(A) The director of health shall receive, review, and investigate allegations of abuse, neglect, or exploitation of a resident or misappropriation of the property of a resident by any individual used by a long-term care facility or residential care facility to provide services to residents.

(B) The director shall make findings regarding alleged abuse, neglect, exploitation, or misappropriation of property after doing both of the following:

(1) Investigating the allegation and determining that there is a reasonable basis for it;

(2) Giving notice to the individual named in the allegation and affording the individual a reasonable opportunity for a hearing.

Notice to the person named in an allegation shall be given and the hearing shall be conducted pursuant to rules adopted by the director under section 3721.26 of the Revised Code. For purposes of conducting a hearing under this section, the director may issue subpoenas compelling attendance of witnesses or production of documents. The subpoenas shall be served in the same manner as subpoenas and subpoenas duces tecum issued for a trial of a civil action in a court of common pleas. If a person who is served a subpoena fails to attend a hearing or to produce documents, or refuses to be sworn or to answer any questions, the director may apply to the common pleas court of the county in which the person resides, or the county in which the long-term care facility or residential care facility is located, for a contempt order, as in the case of a failure of a person who is served a subpoena issued by the court to attend or to produce documents or a refusal of such person to testify.

(C)(1) If the director finds that an individual used by a long-term care facility or residential care facility has abused, neglected, or exploited a resident or misappropriated property of a resident, the director shall do both of the following:

(a) Notify the individual, the facility using the individual, the attorney general, county prosecutor, or other appropriate law enforcement official, and, if applicable, the appropriate professional licensing authority established under Title XLVII of the Revised Code;

(b) In accordance with section 3721.32 of the Revised Code, include in the nurse aide registry established under that section a statement detailing the findings pertaining to the individual.

(2) An individual about whom a statement is required by this division to be included in the nurse aide registry may provide the director with a statement disputing the director's findings and explaining the circumstances of the allegation. The statement shall be included in the nurse aide registry with the director's findings.

(D)(1) If the director finds that alleged abuse, neglect, or exploitation of a resident or misappropriation of property of a resident cannot be substantiated, the director shall notify the individual and expunge all files and records of the investigation and the hearing by doing all of the following:

(a) Removing and destroying the files and records, originals and copies, and deleting all index references;

(b) Reporting to the individual the nature and extent of any information about the individual transmitted to any other person or government entity by the director of health;

(c) Otherwise ensuring that any examination of files and records in question show no record whatever with respect to the individual.

(2)(a) If, in accordance with division (C)(1) of this section, the director includes in the nurse aide registry a statement of a finding of neglect, the individual found to have neglected a resident may, not earlier than one year after the date of the finding, petition the director to rescind the finding and remove the statement and any accompanying information from the nurse aide registry. The director shall consider the petition. If, in the judgment of the director, the neglect was a singular occurrence and the employment and personal history of the individual does not evidence abuse, exploitation, or any other incident of neglect of residents, the director shall notify the individual and remove the statement and any accompanying information from the nurse aide registry. The director shall expunge all files and records of the investigation and the hearing, except the petition for rescission of the finding of neglect and the director's notice that the rescission has been approved.

(b) A petition for rescission of a finding of neglect and the director's notice that the rescission has been approved are not public records for the purposes of section 149.43 of the Revised Code.

(3) When files and records have been expunged under division (D)(1) or (2) of this section, all rights and privileges are

restored, and the individual, the director, and any other person or government entity may properly reply to an inquiry that no such record exists as to the matter expunged.

**HISTORY:**

143 v H 822 (Eff 12-13-90); 146 v H 117. Eff 9-29-95; 153 v H 1, § 101.01, eff. 10-16-09; 2017 hb49, § 101.01, effective September 29, 2017.

**Amendment Notes**

The 2017 amendment by HB 49 substituted "neglect, or exploitation" for "or, neglect" in (A); added "exploitation" in the introductory language of (B); rewrote (C); substituted "abuse, neglect, or exploitation" for "neglect, or abuse" in the introductory language of (D); and, in (D)(2)(a), substituted "division (C)(1)" for "division (C)(1)(a) or (c)" in the first sentence and added "exploitation" in the third sentence.

153 v H 1, effective October 16, 2009, inserted (D)(2), and redesignated former (D)(2) as (3); and, in present (D)(3), inserted "or (2)".

### RESEARCH REFERENCES AND PRACTICE AIDS

**Cross-References to Related Sections**

Confidentiality of information concerning reports of abuse, neglect or misappropriation, RC § 3721.25.

Definitions, RC § 3721.21.

Report of abuse or neglect of resident or misappropriation of property, RC § 3721.22.

Retaliatory actions prohibited, RC § 3721.24.

Rules to implement provisions, RC § 3721.26.

State nurse aide registry, RC § 3721.32.

**Ohio Rules**

Subpoena, CivR 45.

**Ohio Administrative Code**

Findings of director. OAC 3701-64-05.

Investigations; notice of hearing rights. OAC 3701-64-02.

## § 3721.24 Retaliatory actions prohibited.

(A) No person or government entity shall retaliate against an employee or another individual used by the person or government entity to perform any work or services who, in good faith, makes or causes to be made a report of suspected abuse, neglect, or exploitation of a resident or misappropriation of the property of a resident; indicates an intention to make such a report; provides information during an investigation of suspected abuse, neglect, exploitation, or misappropriation conducted by the director of health; or participates in a hearing conducted under section 3721.23 of the Revised Code or in any other administrative or judicial proceedings pertaining to the suspected abuse, neglect, exploitation, or misappropriation. For purposes of this division, retaliatory actions include discharging, demoting, or transferring the employee or other person, preparing a negative work performance evaluation of the employee or other person, reducing the benefits, pay, or work privileges of the employee or other person, and any other action intended to retaliate against the employee or other person.

(B)(1) No person or government entity shall retaliate against a resident who reports or causes to be reported suspected abuse, neglect, exploitation, or misappropriation; indicates an intention to make such a report; provides information during an investigation of alleged abuse, neglect, exploitation, or misappropriation conducted by the director; or participates in a hearing under section 3721.23 of the Revised Code or in any other administrative or judicial proceeding pertaining to the suspected abuse, neglect, exploitation, or misappropriation; or on whose behalf any other person or government entity takes any of those actions.

(2) No person or government entity shall retaliate against a resident whose family member, guardian, sponsor, or personal representative reports or causes to be reported suspected abuse, neglect, exploitation, or misappropriation; indicates an intention to make such a report; provides information during an investigation of alleged abuse, neglect, exploitation, or misappropriation conducted by the director; or participates in a hearing under section 3721.23 of the Revised Code or in any other administrative or judicial proceeding pertaining to the suspected abuse, neglect, exploitation, or misappropriation; or on whose behalf any other person or government entity takes any of those actions.

(3) For purposes of divisions (B)(1) and (2) of this section, retaliatory actions include abuse, verbal threats or other harsh language, change of room assignment, withholding of services, failure to provide care in a timely manner, and any other action intended to retaliate against the resident.

(C) Any person has a cause of action against a person or government entity for harm resulting from violation of division (A) or (B) of this section. If it finds that a violation has occurred, the court may award damages and order injunctive relief. The court may award court costs and reasonable attorney's fees to the prevailing party.

**HISTORY:**

143 v H 822. Eff 12-13-90; 2017 hb49, § 101.01, effective September 29, 2017.

**Amendment Notes**

The 2017 amendment by HB 49, in the first sentence of (A), added "exploitation" three times and "or causes to be made"; redesignated the former first sentence of (B) as (B)(1); in (B)(1), added "or causes to be reported" and "exploitation" three times; added (B)(2); redesignated the former second sentence of (B) as (B)(3); and substituted "divisions (B)(1) and (2) of this section" for "this division" in (B)(3).



### NOTES TO DECISIONS

Analysis

Evidence insufficient
Remedies
Reporting requirements
Scope and effect

**Evidence insufficient**

Trial court properly granted summary judgment because the nurse failed to create a triable issue that her discharge was retaliatory. While the nurse created an inference of causation, she did not produce evidence to show that the employer was aware of her telephone report to the Ohio Department of Health and the employer cited legitimate reasons for the termination of her employment: her extensive history of disciplinary issues before she engaged in the protected activity and her inappropriate conduct after the bed-rail incident. O'Malley-Donegan v. Metrohealth Sys., 2017-Ohio-1362, 89 N.E.3d 113, 2017 Ohio App. LEXIS 1374 (Ohio Ct. App., Cuyahoga County 2017).

**Remedies**

Trial court erred in dismissing a nurse's claim for retaliation under the statute because she was not required to report suspected abuse or neglect of a nursing home patient to the Ohio Director of Health in order to state a claim for retaliation. Hulsmeyer v. Hospice of Southwest Ohio, Inc., 2013-Ohio-4147, 998 N.E.2d 517, 2013 Ohio App. LEXIS 4363 (Ohio Ct. App., Hamilton County 2013), aff'd, 2014-Ohio-5511, 142 Ohio St. 3d 236, 29 N.E.3d 903, 2014 Ohio LEXIS 3158 (Ohio 2014).

A nurse could not recover on a wrongful discharge claim where the public policy involved was based on reporting abuse in a nursing home. R.C. 3721.24 provided the appropriate remedy. Dolan v. St. Mary's Mem'l Home, 2003-Ohio-3383, 153 Ohio App. 3d 441, 794 N.E.2d 716, 2003 Ohio App. LEXIS 3076 (Ohio Ct. App., Hamilton County 2003).

**Reporting requirements**

Employee or other person used to perform work or services who reports or indicates an intention to report suspected abuse or neglect of a long-term-care-facility or a residential-care-facility resident is not required to report or indicate an intent to report the suspected abuse or neglect to the Ohio director of health in order to state a claim for retaliatory discharge as the requirement that abuse be reported to the director of health contained in R.C. 3721.22 and the absence of that requirement in R.C. 3721.24 is presumably intentional; a nurse's reporting the suspected abuse or neglect of the resident to the nursing facility and to the resident's children triggered the protection of R.C. 3721.24. Hulsmeyer v. Hospice of Southwest Ohio, Inc., 2014-Ohio-5511, 142 Ohio St. 3d 236, 29 N.E.3d 903, 2014 Ohio LEXIS 3158 (Ohio 2014).

**Scope and effect**

Where an employee allegedly was disciplined and terminated in retaliation for speaking with Ohio Department of Health investigators following the death of a nursing-home resident, and the employer contended that the termination was justified by its progressive discipline policy due to disciplinary action reports the employee received based on work rule violations, the employee's retaliation claim failed because the employee did not show pretext. Tingle v. Arbors at Hilliard, 692 F.3d 523, 2012 FED App. 0291P, 2012 U.S. App. LEXIS 18315 (6th Cir. Ohio 2012).

When a nursing home employee allegedly told a patient's daughter that the home would not properly handle a report that the patient had been sexually abused, and the employee was fired, it did not have to be shown that the employee actually made the statements, as the employer's good faith belief that she had made the statements, when it decided to fire her, was sufficient to avoid a violation of R.C. 3721.24. Thompson v. Merriman CCRC, Inc., 2006-Ohio-6008, 2006 Ohio App. LEXIS 5958 (Ohio Ct. App., Summit County 2006).

If a terminated nursing home employee demonstrated a prima facie case of retaliation, under R.C. 3721.24, her employer demonstrated a legitimate business reason for firing her because it had a good faith belief that the employee made statements to a patient's daughter that the home would not properly handle a report that her mother had been sexually abused at the home, disparaging the home's reputation. Thompson v. Merriman CCRC, Inc., 2006-Ohio-6008, 2006 Ohio App. LEXIS 5958 (Ohio Ct. App., Summit County 2006).



When a nursing home administrator said he decided to fire one of the nursing home's employees before she began cooperating with an investigation of a report of a patient's sexual abuse, the administrator was not required to suspend his decision to fire the employee because of her cooperation. Thompson v. Merriman CCRC, Inc., 2006-Ohio-6008, 2006 Ohio App. LEXIS 5958 (Ohio Ct. App., Summit County 2006).

When a nursing home being investigated for a patient's sexual abuse said it fired one of its employees for telling the patient's daughter the home would not properly handle the report of abuse, any such statements the employee made were not protected activity within the ambit of R.C. 3721.24. Thompson v. Merriman CCRC, Inc., 2006-Ohio-6008, 2006 Ohio App. LEXIS 5958 (Ohio Ct. App., Summit County 2006).

Nursing home employee did not establish a genuine issue of material fact as to whether she was fired for cooperating with an investigation of the home regarding a patient's sexual abuse because she could not show that the employer knew she had reported the abuse when it decided to fire her, as such reports were confidential. Thompson v. Merriman CCRC, Inc., 2006-Ohio-6008, 2006 Ohio App. LEXIS 5958 (Ohio Ct. App., Summit County 2006).

When a nursing home employee allegedly told a patient's daughter that the home would not properly handle a report that the patient had been sexually abused, and the employee was fired, it did not have to be shown that the employee actually made the statements, as the employer's good faith belief that she had made the statements, when it decided to fire her, was sufficient to avoid a violation of R.C. 3721.24. Thompson v. Merriman CCRC, Inc., 2006-Ohio-6008, 2006 Ohio App. LEXIS 5958 (Ohio Ct. App., Summit County 2006).

Revised Code § 3721.24 only forbids retaliation for reports, whether obligatory or voluntary, made to the director of health pursuant to R.C. 3721.22; any reports to others, such as to the plaintiff's employer, of suspected resident abuse or neglect do not qualify for protection under R.C. 3721.24(A). Arsham-Brenner v. Grande Point Health Care Community, 2000 Ohio App. LEXIS 3164 (Ohio Ct. App., Cuyahoga County July 13, 2000).

### NOTES TO UNPUBLISHED DECISIONS

**Scope and effect**

*Unpublished decision:* Because R.C. 3721.24(A) required the employee to report instances of abuse in nursing homes to the Ohio Director of Health and the employee's motion to amend did not state that she reported (or intended to report) the alleged abuse to public authorities, the motion was futile and accordingly was properly dismissed. Davis v. Marriott Int'l, Inc., 2005 FED App. 0812N, 2005 U.S. App. LEXIS 21789 (6th Cir. Ohio Oct. 4, 2005).

*Unpublished decision:* United States Court of Appeals for the Sixth Circuit holds that R.C. 3721.24(A) requires a plaintiff to report instances of abuse in nursing homes to the Ohio Director of Health. Davis v. Marriott Int'l, Inc., 2005 FED App. 0812N, 2005 U.S. App. LEXIS 21789 (6th Cir. Ohio Oct. 4, 2005).

### RESEARCH REFERENCES AND PRACTICE AIDS

**Cross-References to Related Sections**

Penalties, RC § 3721.99.

Duty of director of health to investigate allegations and notify proper authorities, RC § 3721.23.

## § 3721.25 Confidentiality of information concerning reports of abuse, neglect or misappropriation.

(A)(1) Except as required by court order, as necessary for the administration or enforcement of any statute or rule relating to long-term care facilities or residential care facilities, or as provided in division (D) of this section, the director of health shall not disclose any of the following without the consent of the individual or the individual's legal representative:

(a) The name of an individual who reports suspected abuse, neglect, or exploitation of a resident or misappropriation of a resident's property to the facility or director;

(b) The name of an individual who provides information during an investigation of suspected abuse, neglect, exploitation, or misappropriation conducted by the director;

(c) Any information that would tend to disclose the identity of an individual described in division (A)(1)(a) or (b) of this section.

(2) An agency or individual to whom the director is required, by court order or for the administration or enforcement of a statute relating to long-term care facilities or residential care facilities, to release information described in division (A)(1) of this section shall not release the information without the permission of the individual who would be or would reasonably tend to be identified, or of the individual's legal representative, unless the agency or individual is required to release it by division (D) of this section, by court order, or for the administration or enforcement of a statute relating to long-term care facilities or residential care facilities.

(B) Except as provided in division (D) of this section, any record that identifies an individual described in division (A)(1)(a) or (b) of this section, or that would tend to disclose the identity of such an individual, is not a public record for the purposes of section 149.43 of the Revised Code, and is not subject to inspection or copying under section 1347.08 of the Revised Code.

(C) Except as provided in division (B) of this section and division (D) of section 3721.23 of the Revised Code, the records of a hearing conducted under section 3721.23 of the Revised Code are public records for the purposes of section 149.43 of the Revised Code and are subject to inspection and copying under section 1347.08 of the Revised Code.

(D) If the director, or an agency or individual to whom the director is required by court order or for administration or enforcement of a statute relating to long-term care facilities or residential care facilities to release information described in division (A)(1) of this section, uses information in any administrative or judicial proceeding against a long-term care facility or residential care facility that reasonably would tend to identify an individual described in division (A)(1)(a) or (b) of this section, the director, agency, or individual shall disclose that information to the facility. However, the director, agency, or individual shall not disclose information that directly identifies an individual described in division (A)(1)(a) or (b) of this section, unless the individual is to testify in the proceedings.

**HISTORY:**

143 v H 822 (Eff 12-13-90); 146 v H 117. Eff 9-29-95; 2017 hb49, § 101.01, effective September 29, 2017.

**Amendment Notes**

The 2017 amendment by HB 49, in (A)(1)(a), added "or exploitation" and "facility or"; added "exploitation" in (A)(1)(b); and made a related change.

### RESEARCH REFERENCES AND PRACTICE AIDS

**Cross-References to Related Sections**

Availability of public records, RC § 149.43.

Inspection of personal information maintained, RC § 1347.08.

Rules to implement provisions, RC § 3721.26.

## § 3721.26 Rules to implement provisions.

The director of health shall adopt rules pursuant to Chapter 119. of the Revised Code to implement sections 3721.21 to 3721.25 of the Revised Code, including rules prescribing requirements for the notice and hearing required under section 3721.23 of the Revised Code. The notice and hearing required under section 3721.23 of the Revised Code are not subject to Chapter 119. of the Revised Code; however, the rules may provide for the notice to be provided and the hearing to be conducted in accordance with that chapter. Rules adopted under this section shall be no less stringent than the requirements, guidelines, and procedures established by the United States secretary of health and human services under sections 1819 and 1919 of the "Social Security Act," 49 Stat. 620 (1935), 42 U.S.C.A. 301, as amended.

**HISTORY:**
143 v H 822. Eff 12-13-90.

**RESEARCH REFERENCES AND PRACTICE AIDS**

**Cross-References to Related Sections**

Duty of director of health to investigate allegations and notify proper authorities, RC § 3721.23.

Rules of administrative procedure, RC § 119.01 et seq.

**Ohio Administrative Code**

Department of health, director of—

Abuse or neglect in long-term care facilities. OAC ch. 3701-64.

Hearing procedure. OAC 3701-64-04.

Request for hearing; scheduling hearing. OAC 3701-64-03.

Nursing home residents' rights. OAC ch. 3701-61.

### § 3721.261 Renumbered.

Amended and renumbered RC § 3721.42 in 143 v H 822. Eff 12-13-90.

### § 3721.27 Renumbered.

Amended and renumbered RC § 3721.21 in 143 v H 822. Eff 12-13-90.

### § 3721.271 Renumbered.

Amended and renumbered RC § 3721.35 in H 822. Eff 12-13-90.

## TRAINING, COMPETENCY EVALUATION OF NURSE AIDES

### § 3721.28 Training and competency evaluation programs for nurse aides; conditions for use of nurse aides.

(A)(1) Each nurse aide used by a long-term care facility on a full-time, temporary, per diem, or other basis on July 1, 1989, shall be provided by the facility a competency evaluation program approved by the director of health under division (A) of section 3721.31 of the Revised Code or conducted by the director under division (C) of that section. Each long-term care facility using a nurse aide on July 1, 1989, shall provide the nurse aide the preparation necessary to complete the competency evaluation program by January 1, 1990.

(2) Each nurse aide used by a long-term care facility on a full-time, temporary, per diem, or other basis on January 1, 1990, who either was not used by the facility on July 1, 1989, or was used by the facility on July 1, 1989, but had not successfully completed a competency evaluation program by January 1, 1990, shall be provided by the facility a competency evaluation program approved by the director under division (A) of section 3721.31 of the Revised Code or conducted by the director under division (C) of that section. Each long-term care facility using a nurse aide described in division (A)(2) of this section shall provide the nurse aide the preparation necessary to complete the competency evaluation program by October 1, 1990, and shall assist the nurse aide in registering for the program.

(B) Effective June 1, 1990, no long-term care facility shall use an individual as a nurse aide for more than four months unless the individual is competent to provide the services the individual is to provide, the facility has received from the nurse aide registry established under section 3721.32 of the Revised Code the information concerning the individual provided through the registry, and one of the following is the case:

(1) The individual was used by a facility as a nurse aide on a full-time, temporary, per diem, or other basis at any time during the period commencing July 1, 1989, and ending January 1, 1990, and successfully completed, not later than October 1, 1990, a competency evaluation program approved by the director under division (A) of section 3721.31 of the Revised Code or conducted by the director under division (C) of that section.

(2) The individual has successfully completed a training and competency evaluation program approved by the director under division (A) of section 3721.31 of the Revised Code or conducted by the director under division (C) of that section or has met the conditions specified in division (F)(1) or (2) of this section and, in addition, if the training and competency evaluation program or the training, instruction, or education the individual completed in meeting the conditions specified in division (F)(1) or (2) of this section was conducted by or in a long-term care facility, or if the director pursuant to division (E) of section 3721.31 of the Revised Code so requires, the individual has successfully completed a competency evaluation program conducted by the director.

(3) Prior to July 1, 1989, if the long-term care facility is certified as a skilled nursing facility or a nursing facility under Title XVIII or XIX of the "Social Security Act," 49 Stat. 620 (1935), 42 U.S.C.A. 301, as amended, or prior to January 1, 1990, if the facility is not so certified, the individual completed a program that the director determines included a competency evaluation component no less stringent than the competency evaluation programs approved by the director under division (A) of section 3721.31 of the Revised Code or conducted by the director under division (C) of that section, and was otherwise comparable to the training and competency evaluation programs being approved by the director under division (A) of that section.

(4) The individual is listed in a nurse aide registry maintained by another state and that state certifies that its program for training and evaluation of competency of nurse aides complies with Titles XVIII and XIX of the "Social Security Act" and regulations adopted thereunder.

(5) Prior to July 1, 1989, the individual was found competent to serve as a nurse aide after the completion of a course of nurse aide training of at least one hundred hours' duration.

(6) The individual is enrolled in a prelicensure program of nursing education approved by the board of nursing or by an agency of another state that regulates nursing education, has provided the long-term care facility with a certificate from the program indicating that the individual has successfully completed the courses that teach basic nursing skills including infection control, safety and emergency procedures, and personal care, and has successfully completed a competency evaluation program conducted by the director under division (C) of section 3721.31 of the Revised Code.

(7) The individual has the equivalent of twelve months or more of full-time employment in the preceding five years as a hospital aide or orderly and has successfully completed a competency evaluation program conducted by the director under division (C) of section 3721.31 of the Revised Code.

(C) Effective June 1, 1990, no long-term care facility shall continue for longer than four months to use as a nurse aide an individual who previously met the requirements of division (B) of this section but since most recently doing so has not performed nursing and nursing-related services for monetary compensation for twenty-four consecutive months, unless the individual successfully completes additional training and competency evaluation by complying with divisions (C)(1) and (2) of this section:

(1) Doing one of the following:

(a) Successfully completing a training and competency evaluation program approved by the director under division (A) of section 3721.31 of the Revised Code or conducted by the director under division (C) of that section;

(b) Successfully completing a training and competency evaluation program described in division (B)(4) of this section;

(c) Meeting the requirements specified in division (B)(6) or (7) of this section.

(2) If the training and competency evaluation program completed under division (C)(1)(a) of this section was conducted by or in a long-term care facility, or if the director pursuant to division (E) of section 3721.31 of the Revised Code so requires, successfully completing a competency evaluation program conducted by the director.

(D)(1) The four-month periods provided for in divisions (B) and (C) of this section include any time, on or after June 1, 1990, that an individual is used as a nurse aide on a full-time, temporary, per diem, or any other basis by the facility or any other long-term care facility.

(2) During the four-month period provided for in division (B) of this section, during which a long-term care facility may, subject to division (E) of this section, use as a nurse aide an individual who does not have the qualifications specified in divisions (B)(1) to (7) of this section, a facility shall require the individual to comply with divisions (D)(2)(a) and (b) of this section:

(a) Participate in one of the following:

(i) If the individual has successfully completed a training and competency evaluation program approved by the director under division (A) of section 3721.31 of the Revised Code, and the program was conducted by or in a long-term care facility, or the director pursuant to division (E) of section 3721.31 of the Revised Code so requires, a competency evaluation program conducted by the director;

(ii) If the individual is enrolled in a prelicensure program of nursing education described in division (B)(6) of this section and has completed or is working toward completion of the courses described in that division, or the individual has the experience described in division (B)(7) of this section, a competency evaluation program conducted by the director;

(iii) A training and competency evaluation program approved by the director under division (A) of section 3721.31 of the Revised Code or conducted by the director under division (C) of that section.

(b) If the individual participates in or has successfully completed a training and competency evaluation program under division (D)(2)(a)(iii) of this section that is conducted by or in a long-term care facility, or the director pursuant to division (E) of section 3721.31 of the Revised Code so requires, participate in a competency evaluation program conducted by the director.

(3) During the four-month period provided for in division (C) of this section, during which a long-term care facility may, subject to division (E) of this section, use as a nurse aide an individual who does not have the qualifications specified in divisions (C)(1) and (2) of this section, a facility shall require the individual to comply with divisions (D)(3)(a) and (b) of this section:

(a) Participate in one of the following:

(i) If the individual has successfully completed a training and competency evaluation program approved by the director, and the program was conducted by or in a long-term care facility, or the director pursuant to division (E) of section 3721.31 of the Revised Code so requires, a competency evaluation program conducted by the director;

(ii) If the individual is enrolled in a prelicensure program of nursing education described in division (B)(6) of this section and has completed or is working toward completion of the courses described in that division, or the individual has the experience described in division (B)(7) of this section, a competency evaluation program conducted by the director;

(iii) A training and competency evaluation program approved or conducted by the director.

(b) If the individual participates in or has successfully completed a training and competency evaluation program under division (D)(3)(a)(iii) of this section that is conducted by or in a long-term care facility, or the director pursuant to division (E) of section 3721.31 of the Revised Code so requires, participate in a competency evaluation program conducted by the director.

(E) A long-term care facility shall not permit an individual used by the facility as a nurse aide while participating in a training and competency evaluation program to provide nursing and nursing-related services unless both of the following are the case:

(1) The individual has completed the number of hours of training that must be completed prior to providing services to residents as prescribed by rules that shall be adopted by the director in accordance with Chapter 119. of the Revised Code;

(2) The individual is under the personal supervision of a registered or licensed practical nurse licensed under Chapter 4723. of the Revised Code.

(F) An individual shall be considered to have satisfied the requirement, under division (B)(2) of this section, of having successfully completed a training and competency evaluation program conducted or approved by the director, if either of the following apply:

(1) The individual, as of July 1, 1989, met both of the following conditions:

(a) Completed at least sixty hours divided between skills training and classroom instruction in the topic areas described in divisions (B)(1) to (8) of section 3721.30 of the Revised Code;

(b) Received at least the difference between seventy-five hours and the number of hours actually spent in training and competency evaluation in supervised practical nurse aide training or regular in-service nurse aide education.

(2) The individual meets both of the following conditions:

(a) Has completed during the COVID-19 public health emergency declared by the United States secretary of health and human services a minimum of seventy-five hours of training that occurs in a long-term care facility setting, includes on-site observation and work as a nurse aide under a COVID-19 pandemic waiver issued by the federal centers for medicare and medicaid services, and addresses all of the required areas specified in 42 C.F.R. 483.152(b), except that if gaps in on-site training are identified, the individual also must complete supplemental training;

(b) Has successfully completed the competency evaluation conducted by the director of health under section 3721.31 of the Revised Code.

(G) The director shall adopt rules in accordance with Chapter 119. of the Revised Code specifying persons, in addition to the director, who may establish competence of nurse aides under division (B)(5) of this section, and establishing criteria for determining whether an individual meets the conditions specified in division (F)(1) of this section.

(H) The rules adopted pursuant to divisions (E)(1) and (G) of this section shall be no less stringent than the requirements, guidelines, and procedures established by the United States secretary of health and human services under sections 1819 and 1919 of the "Social Security Act."

**HISTORY:**

143 v H 112 (Eff 2-16-89); 143 v H 359 (Eff 3-13-90); 143 v H 822 (Eff 12-13-90); 144 v H 298. Eff 7-26-91; 2012 HB 487, § 101.01, eff. Sept. 10, 2012; 2021 sb6, § 1, effective September 30, 2021.

**Amendment Notes**

The 2021 amendment by SB 6 substituted "(F)(1) or (2)" for "(F)" twice in (B)(2); rewrote (F); and substituted "(F)(1)" for "(F)" in (G).

The 2012 amendment substituted "director" for "public health council" preceding "shall adopt" in (G); and made stylistic changes.

## RESEARCH REFERENCES AND PRACTICE AIDS

**Cross-References to Related Sections**

Conditions for issuing license; renewal; appeal, RC § 3721.07.

Director may advise, consult or cooperate with other agencies or persons; agreements to implement provisions, RC § 3721.34.

Director of health to approve competency evaluation programs, RC § 3721.31.

Fees to be deposited in nurse aide training fund, RC § 3721.33.

State nurse aide registry, RC § 3721.32.

Structure of competency evaluation programs, RC § 3721.30.

Unauthorized practice of nursing not sanctioned, RC § 3721.35.

**Ohio Administrative Code**

Required training and competency evaluation for nurse aides working in long-term care facilities. OAC 3701-17-07.1.

Training and competency evaluation programs; train-the-trainer programs. OAC ch. 3701-18.

Definitions. OAC 3701-18-01.

State-administered competency evaluation program. OAC 3701-18-22 et seq.

### § 3721.29 Orientation program; performance review; in-service education.

In addition to competency evaluation programs and training and competency evaluation programs required by this chapter, each long-term care facility shall provide both of the following to each nurse aide it uses:

(A) An orientation program that includes at least an explanation of the organizational structure of the facility, its policies and procedures, its philosophy of care, a description of its resident population, and an enumeration of its employee rules;

(B) Regular performance review and in-service education to assure that individuals working in the facility as nurse aides are competent to perform the nursing and nursing-related services they perform. In-service education shall include training for nurse aides providing nursing and nursing-related services to residents and patients with cognitive impairments.

The director of health shall adopt rules to implement the purposes of this section. The rules shall be no less stringent than the requirements, guidelines, and procedures established by the United States secretary of health and human services under sections 1819 and 1919 of the "Social Security Act," 49 Stat. 620 (1935), 42 U.S.C.A. 301, as amended.

**HISTORY:**

143 v H 112 (Eff 2-16-89); 143 v H 359. Eff 3-13-90; 2012 HB 487, § 101.01, eff. Sept. 10, 2012.

**Amendment Notes**

The 2012 amendment substituted "director of health" for "public health council" in the first sentence of the second paragraph.

**RESEARCH REFERENCES AND PRACTICE AIDS**

**Cross-References to Related Sections**

Conditions for issuing license; renewal; appeal, RC § 3721.07.

Director of health to approve competency evaluation programs, RC § 3721.31.

Fees to be deposited in nurse aide training fund, RC § 3721.33.

Structure of competency evaluation programs, RC § 3721.30.

Unauthorized practice of nursing not sanctioned, RC § 3721.35.

### § 3721.30 Contents of evaluation programs; rules for approval; prohibited charges.

(A)(1) A competency evaluation program approved by the director of health under division (A) of section 3721.31 of the Revised Code or conducted by the director under division (C) of that section shall evaluate the competency of a nurse aide in the following areas:

(a) Basic nursing skills;

(b) Personal care skills;

(c) Recognition of mental health and social service needs;

(d) Care of cognitively impaired residents;

(e) Basic restorative services;

(f) Residents' rights;

(g) Any other area specified by rule of the director.

(2) Any competency evaluation program approved or conducted by the director may include a written examination, but shall permit a nurse aide, at the nurse aide's option, to establish competency in another manner approved by the director. A nurse aide shall be permitted to have the competency evaluation conducted at the long-term care facility at which the nurse aide is or will be employed, unless the facility has been determined by the director or the United States secretary of health and human services to have been out of compliance with the requirements of subsection (b), (c), or (d) of section 1819 or 1919 of the "Social Security Act," 49 Stat. 620 (1935), 42 U.S.C.A. 301, as amended, within the previous two years.

(B) A training and competency evaluation program approved or conducted by the director under section 3721.31 of the Revised Code shall consist of training and competency evaluation specified by the director in rules adopted under division (C) of this section, including a minimum of seventy-five hours divided between skills training and classroom instruction in the following topic areas:

(1) Basic nursing skills;

(2) Personal care skills;

(3) Recognition of mental health and social service needs;

(4) Care of cognitively impaired residents;

(5) Basic restorative services;

(6) Residents' rights;

(7) Needs of various groups of long-term care facility residents and patients;

(8) Other topic areas specified by rule of the director.

(C) In accordance with Chapter 119. of the Revised Code, the director shall adopt rules establishing procedures and criteria for approval of competency evaluation programs and training and competency evaluation programs. The requirements established by rules shall be no less stringent than the requirements, guidelines, and procedures established by the United States secretary of health and human services under sections 1819 and 1919 of the "Social Security Act." The director also shall adopt rules governing all of the following:

(1) Procedures for determination of an individual's competency to perform services as a nurse aide;

(2) The curriculum of training and competency evaluation programs;

(3) The clinical supervision and physical facilities used for competency evaluation programs and training and competency evaluation programs;

(4) The number of hours of training required in training and competency evaluation programs;

(5) The qualifications for instructors, coordinators, and evaluators of competency evaluation programs and training and competency evaluation programs;

(6) Requirements that approved competency evaluation programs and training and competency evaluation programs must meet to retain approval;

(7) Standards for successful completion of a competency evaluation program or training and competency evaluation program;

(8) Procedures and criteria for review and reapproval of competency evaluation programs and training and competency evaluation programs;

(9) Fees for application for approval or reapproval of competency evaluation programs, training and competency evaluation programs, and programs to train instructors and coordinators for training and competency evaluation programs and evaluators for competency evaluation programs;

(10) Fees for participation in any competency evaluation program, training and competency evaluation program, or other program conducted by the director under section 3721.31 of the Revised Code;

(11) Procedures for reporting to the nurse aide registry established under section 3721.32 of the Revised Code whether or not individuals participating in competency evaluation programs and training and competency evaluation programs have successfully completed the programs.

(D) In accordance with Chapter 119. of the Revised Code, the director may adopt rules prescribing criteria and procedures for approval of training programs for instructors and coordinators for training and competency evaluation programs, and for evaluators for competency evaluation programs. The director may adopt other rules that he considers necessary for the administration and enforcement of sections 3721.28 to 3721.34 of the Revised Code or for compliance with requirements, guidelines, or procedures issued by the United States secretary of health and human services for implementation of section 1819 or 1919 of the "Social Security Act."

(E) No person or government entity shall impose on a nurse aide any charge for participation in any competency evaluation program or training and competency evaluation program approved or conducted by the director under section 3721.31 of the Revised Code, including any charge for textbooks, other required course materials, or a competency evaluation.

(F) No person or government entity shall require that an individual used by the person or government entity as a nurse aide or seeking employment as a nurse aide pay or repay, either before or while the individual is employed by the person or government entity or when the individual leaves the person or government entity's employ, any costs associated with the individual's participation in a competency evaluation program or training and competency evaluation program approved or conducted by the director.

**HISTORY:**

143 v H 112 (Eff 2-16-89); 143 v H 359 (Eff 3-13-90); 143 v H 822 (Eff 12-13-90); 146 v H 117. Eff 6-30-95.

**RESEARCH REFERENCES AND PRACTICE AIDS**

**Cross-References to Related Sections**

Penalties, RC § 3721.99.
Conditions for use of nurse aides, RC § 3721.28.
Director may advise, consult, cooperate or enter into agreements to implement provisions concerning nurse aide training, RC § 3721.34.
Director of health to approve competency evaluation programs, RC § 3721.31.
Fees to be deposited in nurse aide training fund, RC § 3721.33.
State nurse aide registry, RC § 3721.32.
Unauthorized practice of nursing not sanctioned, RC § 3721.35.



**Ohio Administrative Code**

Curriculum criteria—
Training and competency evaluation program. OAC 3701-18-12 et seq.
Train-the-trainer program. OAC 3701-18-21.
Personnel requirements—
Training and competency evaluation program. OAC 3701-18-09.
Train-the-trainer program. OAC 3701-18-18.
Physical facilities requirements—
Training and competency evaluation program. OAC 3701-18-10.
Train-the-trainer program. OAC 3701-18-19.
Recordkeeping requirements—
Training and competency evaluation program. OAC 3701-18-11.
Train-the-trainer program. OAC 3701-18-20.

### § 3721.31 Approval or rejection of programs; periodic review, reapproval; director may conduct programs; fees.

(A)(1) Except as provided in division (E) of this section, the director of health shall approve competency evaluation programs and training and competency evaluation programs in accordance with rules adopted under section 3721.30 of the Revised Code and shall periodically review and reapprove programs approved under this section.

(2) Except as otherwise provided in division (A)(3) of this section, the director may approve and reapprove programs conducted by or in long-term care facilities, or by any government agency or person, including an employee organization.

(3) The director shall not approve or reapprove a competency evaluation program or training and competency evaluation program conducted by or in a long-term care facility that was determined by the director or the United States secretary of health and human services to have been out of compliance with the requirements of subsection (b), (c), or (d) of section 1819 or 1919 of the "Social Security Act," 49 Stat. 620 (1935), 42 U.S.C.A. 301, as amended, within a two-year period prior to making application for approval or reapproval and shall revoke the approval or reapproval of a program conducted by or in a facility for which such a determination is made.

(4) A long-term care facility, employee organization, person, or government entity seeking approval or reapproval of a competency evaluation program or training and competency evaluation program shall make an application to the director for approval or reapproval of the program and shall provide any documentation requested by the director.

(5) The director may conduct inspections and examinations of approved competency evaluation programs and training and competency evaluation programs, competency evaluation programs and training and competency evaluation programs for which an application for approval has been submitted under division (A)(4) of this section, and the sites at which they are or will be conducted. The director may conduct inspections of long-term care facilities in which individuals who have participated in approved competency evaluation programs and training and competency evaluation programs are being used as nurse aides.

(B) In accordance with Chapter 119. of the Revised Code, the director may do the following:

(1) Deny, suspend, or revoke approval or reapproval of any of the following that is not in compliance with this section and section 3721.30 of the Revised Code and rules adopted thereunder:

(a) A competency evaluation program;

(b) A training and competency evaluation program;

(c) A training program for instructors or coordinators for training and competency evaluation programs;

(d) A training program for evaluators for competency evaluation programs.

(2) Deny a request that the director determine any of the following for the purposes of division (B) of section 3721.28 of the Revised Code:

(a) That a program completed prior to the dates specified in division (B)(3) of section 3721.28 of the Revised Code included a competency evaluation component no less stringent than the competency evaluation programs approved or conducted by the director under this section, and was otherwise comparable to the training and competency evaluation programs being approved under this section;

(b) That an individual satisfies division (B)(5) of section 3721.28 of the Revised Code;

(c) That an individual meets the conditions specified in division (F)(1) or (2) of section 3721.28 of the Revised Code.

(C) The director may develop and conduct a competency evaluation program for individuals used by long-term care facilities as nurse aides at any time during the period commencing July 1, 1989, and ending January 1, 1990, and individuals who participate in training and competency evaluation programs conducted in or by long-term care facilities. The director also may conduct other competency evaluation programs and training and competency evaluation programs. When conducting competency evaluation programs and training and competency evaluation programs, the director may use a nurse aide competency evaluation prepared by a testing service, and may contract with the service to administer the evaluation pursuant to section 3701.044 of the Revised Code.

(D) The director may approve or conduct programs to train instructors and coordinators for training and competency evaluation programs and evaluators for competency evaluation programs. The director may conduct inspections and examinations of those programs that have been approved by the director or for which an application for approval has been submitted, and the sites at which the programs are or will be conducted.

(E) Notwithstanding division (A) of this section and division (C) of section 3721.30 of the Revised Code, the director, in the director's discretion, may decline to approve any competency evaluation programs. The director may require all individuals used by long-term care facilities as nurse aides after June 1, 1990, who have completed a training and competency evaluation program approved by the director under division (A) of this section or who have met the conditions specified in division (F)(1) or (2) of section 3721.28 of the Revised Code to complete a competency evaluation program conducted by the director under division (C) of this section. The director also may require all individuals used as nurse aides by long-term care facilities after June 1, 1990, who were used by a facility at any time during the period commencing July 1, 1989, and ending January 1, 1990, to complete a competency evaluation program conducted by the director under division (C) of this section rather than a competency evaluation program approved by the director under division (A) of this section.

(F) The test materials, examinations, or evaluation tools used in any competency evaluation program or training and competency evaluation program that the director conducts or approves under this section are subject to the confidentiality provisions of section 3701.044 of the Revised Code.

(G) The director shall impose fees prescribed by rules adopted under section 3721.30 of the Revised Code for both of the following:

(1) Making application for approval or reapproval of either of the following:

(a) A competency evaluation program or a training and competency evaluation program;

(b) A training program for instructors or coordinators for training and competency evaluation programs, or evaluators for competency evaluation programs;

(2) Participation in any competency evaluation program, training and competency evaluation program, or other program conducted by the director under this section.

**HISTORY:**

143 v H 112 (Eff 2-16-89); 143 v H 359 (Eff 3-13-90); 143 v H 822 (Eff 12-13-90); 144 v H 298 (Eff 7-26-91); 148 v H 283. Eff 9-29-99; 2021 sb6, § 1, effective September 30, 2021.

**Amendment Notes**

The 2021 amendment by SB 6 substituted "(F)(1) or (2)" for "(F)" in (B)(2)(c) and in the second sentence of (C); and made stylistic changes.

### RESEARCH REFERENCES AND PRACTICE AIDS

**Cross-References to Related Sections**

Director may advise, consult, cooperate or enter into agreements to implement provisions concerning nurse aide training, RC § 3721.34.

Fees to be deposited in nurse aide training fund, RC § 3721.33.

Requirements for competency testing of personnel in long-term care facility, RC § 3721.28.

State nurse aide registry, RC § 3721.32.

Structure of competency evaluation programs, RC § 3721.30.

Unauthorized practice of nursing not sanctioned, RC § 3721.35.

**Ohio Administrative Code**

Application requirements for approval and reapproval of programs—

Training and competency evaluation program. OAC 3701-18-04 to 3701-18-08.

Train-the-trainer program. OAC 3701-18-14 to 3701-18-17.

Inspections; revocation or suspension of programs—

Training and competency evaluation program. OAC 3701-18-03.

Train-the-trainer program. OAC 3701-18-03.

Required training and competency evaluation for nurse aides working in long-term care facilities. OAC 3701-17-07.1.

State-administered test and competency evaluation program. OAC 3701-18-22 et seq.

## § 3721.32 State nurse aide registry.

(A) The director of health shall establish a state nurse aide registry listing all individuals who have done any of the following:

(1) Were used by a long-term care facility as nurse aides on a full-time, temporary, per diem, or other basis at any time during the period commencing July 1, 1989, and ending January 1, 1990, and successfully completed, not later than October 1, 1990, a competency evaluation program approved by the director under division (A) of section 3721.31 of the Revised Code or conducted by the director under division (C) of that section;

(2) Successfully completed a training and competency evaluation program approved by the director under division (A) of section 3721.31 of the Revised Code or met the conditions specified in division (F)(1) or (2) of section 3721.28 of the Revised Code, and, if the training and competency evaluation program or the training, instruction, or education the individual completed in meeting the conditions specified in division (F)(1) of section 3721.28 of the Revised Code was conducted in or by a long-term care facility, or if the director so required pursuant to division (E) of section 3721.31 of the Revised Code, has successfully completed a competency evaluation program conducted by the director;

(3) Successfully completed a training and competency evaluation program conducted by the director under division (C) of section 3721.31 of the Revised Code;

(4) Successfully completed, prior to July 1, 1989, a program that the director has determined under division (B)(3) of section 3721.28 of the Revised Code included a competency evaluation component no less stringent than the competency evaluation programs approved or conducted by the director under section 3721.31 of the Revised Code, and was otherwise comparable to the training and competency evaluation program being approved by the director under section 3721.31 of the Revised Code;

(5) Are listed in a nurse aide registry maintained by another state that certifies that its program for training and evaluation of competency of nurse aides complies with Titles XVIII and XIX of the "Social Security Act," 49 Stat. 620 (1935), 42 U.S.C.A. 301, as amended, or regulations adopted thereunder;

(6) Were found competent, as provided in division (B)(5) of section 3721.28 of the Revised Code, prior to July 1, 1989, after the completion of a course of nurse aide training of at least one hundred hours' duration;

(7) Are enrolled in a prelicensure program of nursing education approved by the board of nursing or by an agency of another state that regulates nursing education, have provided the long-term care facility with a certificate from the program indicating that the individual has successfully completed the courses that teach basic nursing skills including infection control, safety and emergency procedures, and personal care, and have successfully completed a competency evaluation program conducted by the director under division (A) of section 3721.31 of the Revised Code;

(8) Have the equivalent of twelve months or more of full-time employment in the five years preceding listing in the registry as a hospital aide or orderly and have successfully completed a competency evaluation program conducted by the director under division (C) of section 3721.31 of the Revised Code.

(B) In addition to the list of individuals required by division (A) of this section, the registry shall include both of the following:

(1) The statement required by section 3721.23 of the Revised Code detailing findings by the director under that section regarding alleged abuse, neglect, or exploitation of a resident or misappropriation of resident property;

(2) Any statement provided by an individual under section 3721.23 of the Revised Code disputing the director's findings.

Whenever an inquiry is received as to the information contained in the registry concerning an individual about whom a statement required by section 3721.23 of the Revised Code is included in the registry, the director shall disclose the statement or a summary of the statement together with any statement provided by the individual under section 3721.23 or a clear and accurate summary of that statement.

(C) The director may by rule specify additional information that must be provided to the registry by long-term care facilities and persons or government agencies conducting approved competency evaluation programs and training and competency evaluation programs.

(D) Information contained in the registry is a public record for the purposes of section 149.43 of the Revised Code, and is subject to inspection and copying under section 1347.08 of the Revised Code.

**HISTORY:**

143 v H 112 (Eff 2-16-89); 143 v H 359 (Eff 3-13-90); 143 v H 822 (Eff 12-13-90); 144 v H 298 (Eff 7-26-91); 146 v H 117. Eff 9-29-95; 2017 hb49, § 101.01, effective September 29, 2017; 2021 sb6, § 1, effective September 30, 2021.

**Amendment Notes**

The 2021 amendment by SB 6, in (A)(2), substituted "division (F)(1) or (2)" for "division (F)" and "meeting the conditions specified in division (F)(1)" for "meeting the conditions specified in division (F)."

The 2017 amendment by HB 49 added "In addition to the list of individuals required by division (A) of this section" in the introductory language of (B); added "or exploitation" in (B)(1); substituted "to the registry" for "the registry" in (C); and made a related change.

### RESEARCH REFERENCES AND PRACTICE AIDS

**Cross-References to Related Sections**

Director of health to approve competency evaluation programs, RC § 3721.31.

Duty of director of health to investigate allegations and notify proper authorities, RC § 3721.23.

Fees to be deposited in nurse aide training fund, RC § 3721.33.

Requirements for competency testing of personnel in long-term care facility, RC § 3721.28.

Structure of competency evaluation programs, RC § 3721.30.

Unauthorized practice of nursing not sanctioned, RC § 3721.35.

**Ohio Administrative Code**

Investigations of abuse and neglect in long-term care facilities; report of findings. OAC 3701-64-02.

Required training and competency evaluation for nurse aides working in long-term care facilities. OAC 3701-17-07.1.

State-administered test and competency evaluation program. OAC 3701-18-22 et seq.

### § 3721.33 Nurse aide training fund.

Except for any fee collected and retained by a testing service under contract pursuant to division (C) of section 3721.31 of the Revised Code, all fees collected under section 3721.31 of the Revised Code shall be deposited in the state treasury to the credit of the nurse aide training fund, which is hereby created. The moneys in the fund shall be used solely for the purposes set forth in sections 3721.28 to 3721.32 of the Revised Code and rules adopted thereunder.

**HISTORY:**
143 v H 112 (Eff 2-16-89); 143 v H 822 (Eff 12-13-90); 148 v H 283. Eff 9-29-99.

RESEARCH REFERENCES AND PRACTICE AIDS

**Cross-References to Related Sections**
Director may advise, consult, cooperate or enter into agreements to implement provisions concerning nurse aide training, RC § 3721.34.
Director of health to approve competency evaluation programs, RC § 3721.31.
Structure of competency evaluation programs, RC § 3721.30.
Unauthorized practice of nursing not sanctioned, RC § 3721.35.

### § 3721.34 Director may advise, consult or cooperate with other agencies or persons; agreements to implement provisions.

For purposes of implementing sections 3721.28 to 3721.33 of the Revised Code, the director of health may advise, consult or cooperate with, or enter into agreements with state agencies, political subdivisions, the federal government, or any person. The director may enter into agreements that provide for a state agency to do any of the following:

(A) Approve or reapprove, in accordance with division (A) of section 3721.31 of the Revised Code and the rules adopted by the director under section 3721.30 of the Revised Code, competency evaluation programs and training and competency evaluation programs, or, in accordance with rules adopted by the director under section 3721.30 of the Revised Code, programs to train instructors and coordinators for training and competency evaluation programs and evaluators for competency evaluation programs, and to perform any functions related to approval and reapproval of those programs including any of the following:

(1) Conduct adjudications under Chapter 119. of the Revised Code;

(2) Conduct the inspections and examinations described in division (A)(5) or (D) of section 3721.31 of the Revised Code;

(3) Deny, suspend, or revoke approval or reapproval, in accordance with Chapter 119. of the Revised Code, of programs that are not in compliance with sections 3721.30 and 3721.31 of the Revised Code and the rules adopted thereunder;

(4) Collect the fees described in division (G) of section 3721.31 of the Revised Code in the amounts prescribed in rules adopted by the director of health under section 3721.30 of the Revised Code and deposit them into the nurse aide training fund created by section 3721.33 of the Revised Code.

(B) Approve or deny, in accordance with Chapter 119. of the Revised Code, the requests described in division (B)(2) of section 3721.31 of the Revised Code.

**HISTORY:**
143 v H 822 (Eff 12-13-90); 144 v H 298 (Eff 7-26-91); 148 v H 511. Eff 4-10-2001.

RESEARCH REFERENCES AND PRACTICE AIDS

**Cross-References to Related Sections**
Director of health to approve competency evaluation programs, RC § 3721.31.
Recategorization of hospital beds to skilled nursing beds; nursing home placement clearinghouses, RC § 3702.521.
Structure of competency evaluation programs, RC § 3721.30.
Unauthorized practice of nursing not sanctioned, RC § 3721.35.

**Ohio Administrative Code**
Department of health, public health council—
Training and competency evaluation programs; train-the-trainer programs. OAC ch. 3701-18.

### § 3721.35 Unauthorized practice of nursing not sanctioned.

Nothing in sections 3721.28 to 3721.34 of the Revised Code shall be construed to permit any individual to engage in the practice of nursing as a registered nurse or the practice of nursing as a licensed practical nurse if the individual does not hold a valid license issued under Chapter 4723. of the Revised Code.

**HISTORY:**
RC § 3721.27.1, 143 v H 112 (Eff 2-16-89); 143 v H 359 (Eff 3-13-90); RC § 3721.35, 143 v H 822. Eff 12-13-90.

## EMPLOYEE TRAINING CENTERS

### § 3721.41 Area training centers for employees of nursing homes. [Repealed]

**HISTORY:**
RC § 3721.26, 139 v H 694 (Eff 11-15-81); RC § 3721.41, 143 v H 822. Eff 12-13-90; repealed by 2019 hb166, § 105.01, effective October 17, 2019.

### § 3721.42 Supervisor of training center. [Repealed]

**HISTORY:**
RC § 3721.26.1, 139 v H 694 (Eff 11-15-81); RC § 3721.42, 143 v H 822. Eff 12-13-90; repealed by 2019 hb166, § 105.01, effective October 17, 2019.

## FRANCHISE PERMIT FEE

### § 3721.50 Definitions [Renumbered].

**Editor's Notes**
This section was renumbered as RC § 5168.40 by 2013 HB 59, § 101.01, effective September 29, 2013.

### § 3721.51 Annual franchise permit fee [Renumbered].

**Editor's Notes**
This section was renumbered as RC § 5168.42 by 2013 HB 59, § 101.01, effective September 29, 2013.

### § 3721.511 Redetermining nursing homes' and hospitals' franchise permit fees [Renumbered].

**Editor's Notes**
This section was renumbered as RC § 5168.43 by 2013 HB 59, § 101.01, effective September 29, 2013.

### § 3721.512 Proceedings after approval of waiver [Renumbered].

**Editor's Notes**
This section was renumbered as RC § 5168.44 by 2013 HB 59, § 101.01, effective September 29, 2013.

### § 3721.513 Increase in fee after waiver [Renumbered].

**Editor's Notes**
This section was renumbered as RC § 5168.45 by 2013 HB 59, § 101.01, effective September 29, 2013.

### § 3721.52 Annual report of number of licensed beds in each facility [Renumbered].

**Editor's Notes**
This section was renumbered as RC § 5168.46 by 2013 HB 59, § 101.01, effective September 29, 2013.

**§ 3721.53 Determination and payment of annual fee [Renumbered].**

**Editor's Notes**

This section was renumbered as RC § 5168.47 by 2013 HB 59, § 101.01, effective September 29, 2013.

**§ 3721.531 Redetermining nursing homes' and hospitals' franchise permit fees [Renumbered].**

**Editor's Notes**

This section was renumbered as RC § 5168.48 by 2013 HB 59, § 101.01, effective September 29, 2013.

**§ 3721.532 Franchise permit fee when nursing home or hospital undergoes change of operator [Renumbered].**

**Editor's Notes**

This section was renumbered as RC § 5168.49 by 2013 HB 59, § 101.01, effective September 29, 2013.

**§ 3721.533 Franchise permit fee not to be passed through to residents [Renumbered].**

**Editor's Notes**

This section was renumbered as RC § 5168.50 by 2013 HB 59, § 101.01, effective September 29, 2013.

**§ 3721.54 Penalty for overdue installments [Renumbered].**

**Editor's Notes**

This section was renumbered as RC § 5168.51 by 2013 HB 59, § 101.01, effective September 29, 2013.

**§ 3721.541 Additional sanctions for failing to pay required installment [Renumbered].**

**Editor's Notes**

This section was renumbered as RC § 5168.52 by 2013 HB 59, § 101.01, effective September 29, 2013.

**§ 3721.55 Appeal of amount of fee [Renumbered].**

**Editor's Notes**

This section was renumbered as RC § 5168.53 by 2013 HB 59, § 101.01, effective September 29, 2013.

**§ 3721.56 Nursing home franchise permit fee fund [Renumbered].**

**Editor's Notes**

This section was renumbered as RC § 5168.54 by 2013 HB 59, § 101.01, effective September 29, 2013.

**§ 3721.561 Nursing facility stabilization fund [Renumbered].**

**Editor's Notes**

This section was renumbered as RC § 3721.56 by 2011 HB 153, § 101.01, effective July 1, 2011.

**§ 3721.57 Investigations; enforcement actions [Renumbered].**

**Editor's Notes**

This section was renumbered as RC § 5168.55 by 2013 HB 59, § 101.01, effective September 29, 2013.

**§ 3721.58 Rules for implementation or ceasing implementation of provisions and for distributing moneys [Renumbered].**

**Editor's Notes**

This section was renumbered as RC § 5168.56 by 2013 HB 59, § 101.01, effective September 29, 2013.

**§ 3721.60 Definitions.**

As used in sections 3721.60 to 3721.67 of the Revised Code:

(A) "Attorney in fact" means a person designated as such by a durable power of attorney for health care executed pursuant to sections 1337.11 to 1337.17 of the Revised Code.

(B) "Electronic monitoring device" means a surveillance instrument with a fixed position video camera or an audio recording device, or a combination thereof, that is installed in a resident's room and broadcasts or records activities or sounds occurring in the room.

(C) "Guardian" has the same meaning as in section 2111.01 of the Revised Code.

(D) "Long-term care facility" has the same meaning as in section 3721.21 of the Revised Code.

(E) "Resident" means an individual who resides in a long-term care facility.

**HISTORY:**

2021 sb58, § 1, effective March 23, 2022.



**§ 3721.61 Installation and use of electronic monitoring devices in long-term care facilities; withdrawal of authorization.**

(A) Subject to section 3721.62 of the Revised Code, a resident or a resident's guardian or attorney in fact may authorize the installation and use of an electronic monitoring device in the resident's room in a long-term care facility.

(B) The installation and use of an electronic monitoring device may be authorized only if both of the following conditions are met:

(1) If a long-term care facility has prescribed a form described in section 3721.63 of the Revised Code, the resident or resident's guardian or attorney in fact completes the form and submits it to the facility.

(2) The cost of the device and the cost of installing, maintaining, and removing the device, other than the cost of electricity for the device, is paid for by the resident or the resident's guardian or attorney in fact.

(C) A resident who has authorized the installation and use of an electronic monitoring device may withdraw that authorization at any time.

**HISTORY:**

2021 sb58, § 1, effective March 23, 2022.

**§ 3721.62 Permission to monitor resident granted by resident's roommate; completion of form; reasonable accommodations; withdrawal of consent.**

(A) If a resident wishing to conduct authorized electronic monitoring of the resident's room lives with another resident in a long-term care facility, the consent of the other resident or the other resident's guardian or attorney in fact to the installation and use of an electronic monitoring device in the room is required before any installation or use of such a device may occur. If the long-term care facility has prescribed a form described in section 3721.63 of the Revised Code, the other resident or other resident's guardian or attorney in fact shall consent by completing the relevant part of the form.

(B)(1) If a resident living in a room with another resident wishes to conduct authorized electronic monitoring of the resident's room, but the other resident or other resident's guardian or attorney in fact refuses to consent to the installation and use of an electronic monitoring device, the facility shall make a reasonable attempt to accommodate the resident wishing to conduct authorized electronic monitoring by moving either resident to another available room with the consent of the resident being moved or resident's guardian or attorney in fact.

(2) In the case of a resident living in a room with another resident, the other resident or other resident's guardian or attorney in fact may place conditions on any consent to the installation and use of an electronic monitoring device, including conditions such as pointing the device away from the other resident or limiting or prohibiting the use of certain devices. If

conditions are placed on consent, the device shall be installed and used according to those conditions.

(C) A resident whose consent is required under this section may withdraw that consent at any time.

**HISTORY:**
2021 sb58, § 1, effective March 23, 2022.

### § 3721.63 Authorization form; items included.

A long-term care facility may prescribe a form for use by a resident or resident's guardian or attorney in fact seeking to authorize the installation and use of an electronic monitoring device in the resident's room in a long-term care facility. If a long-term care facility prescribes a form, it shall, at a minimum, include all of the following:

(A) An explanation of sections 3721.60 to 3721.67 of the Revised Code;

(B) An acknowledgment that the resident or resident's guardian or attorney in fact has consented to the installation and use of the device in the resident's room;

(C) In the case of a resident who lives in a room with another resident, an acknowledgment that the other resident or other resident's guardian or attorney in fact has consented to the installation and use of the device and a description of any conditions placed on that consent pursuant to division (B)(2) of section 3721.62 of the Revised Code;

(D) A section for providing the facility with information regarding the type, function, and use of the device to be installed and used;

(E) A section stating that the facility is released from liability in any civil or criminal action or administrative proceeding for a violation of the resident's right to privacy in connection with using the device.

**HISTORY:**
2021 sb58, § 1, effective March 23, 2022.

### § 3721.64 Posting notice of monitoring device in use.

A long-term care facility may post a notice in a conspicuous place at the entrance to a resident's room with an electronic monitoring device stating that an electronic monitoring device is in use in that room.

**HISTORY:**
2021 sb58, § 1, effective March 23, 2022.

### § 3721.65 No retaliation or discrimination against users of monitoring devices.

No person or resident shall be denied admission to or discharged from a long-term care facility or otherwise discriminated or retaliated against because of the decision to authorize the installation and use of an electronic monitoring device in a resident's room in the facility.

**HISTORY:**
2021 sb58, § 1, effective March 23, 2022.

### § 3721.66 Interference with monitoring devices prohibited; viewing of images on device; additional authorized viewing.

(A) No person other than the resident or resident's guardian or attorney in fact who authorized the installation and use of an electronic monitoring device in the resident's room in a long-term care facility shall intentionally obstruct, tamper with, or destroy the device or a recording made by the device.

(B) Except as provided in division (C) of this section, no person other than the following shall intentionally view or listen to the images displayed or sounds recorded by an electronic monitoring device installed in a resident's room:

(1) The resident;

(2) The resident's guardian or attorney in fact;

(3) Law enforcement personnel.

(C) A resident or resident's guardian or attorney in fact may authorize a person to view or listen to the images displayed or sounds recorded by an electronic monitoring device installed in a resident's room.

**HISTORY:**
2021 sb58, § 1, effective March 23, 2022.

### § 3721.67 Adoption of implementation rules.

The director of health may adopt rules in accordance with Chapter 119. of the Revised Code as necessary to implement sections 3721.60 to 3721.66 of the Revised Code.

**HISTORY:**
2021 sb58, § 1, effective March 23, 2022.

### § 3721.68 Sections inapplicable to devices installed by law enforcement agency.

Sections 3721.60 to 3721.67 of the Revised Code do not apply if an electronic monitoring device is installed by a law enforcement agency and used solely for a bona fide law enforcement purpose.

**HISTORY:**
2021 sb58, § 1, effective March 23, 2022.

### § 3721.69 Video-conference visitation option for residents of long-term care facilities.

(A) As used in this section, "long-term care facility" means all of the following:

(1) A home, as defined in section 3721.10 of the Revised Code;

(2) A residential facility licensed by the department of mental health and addiction services under section 5119.34 of the Revised Code;

(3) A residential facility licensed by the department of developmental disabilities under section 5123.19 of the Revised Code;

(4) A facility operated by a hospice care program licensed by the department of health under Chapter 3712. of the Revised Code that is used exclusively for care of hospice patients or any other facility in which a hospice care program provides care for hospice patients.

(B) During any declared disaster, epidemic, pandemic, public health emergency, or public safety emergency, each long-term care facility shall provide residents and their families with a video-conference visitation option if the governor, the director of health, other government official or entity, or the long-term care facility determines that allowing in-person visits at the facility would create a risk to the health of the residents.

**HISTORY:**
2021 hb122, § 1, effective March 23, 2022.

**Editor's Notes**
This section was enacted as RC 3721.60 by Acts 2021, SB 166 but was renumbered as RC 3721.69 to avoid conflicting enactments.

### § 3721.99 Penalties.

(A) Whoever violates section 3721.021, division (B), (D), or (E) of section 3721.05, division (A), (C), or (D) of section 3721.051, section 3721.06, division (A) of section 3721.22, division (A) or (B) of section 3721.24, or division (E) or (F) of section 3721.30, or section 3721.65 of the Revised Code shall be fined one hundred dollars for a first offense. For each subsequent offense, the violator shall be fined five hundred dollars.

(B) Whoever violates division (A) or (C) of section 3721.05 or division (B) of section 3721.051 of the Revised Code shall be fined five thousand dollars for a first offense. For each subsequent offense, the violator shall be fined ten thousand dollars.

(C) Whoever violates division (D) of section 3721.031 or division (E) of section 3721.22 of the Revised Code is guilty of registering a false complaint, a misdemeanor of the first degree.

(D) Whoever violates section 3721.66 of the Revised Code is guilty of tampering with an electronic monitoring device, a misdemeanor of the first degree.

**HISTORY:**

131 v 894 (Eff 10-20-65); 137 v H 600 (Eff 1-9-79); 143 v H 253 (Eff 11-15-90); 143 v H 359 (Eff 3-13-90); 143 v H 822 (Eff 12-13-90); 148 v S 178. Eff 7-21-2000; 2021 sb58, § 1, effective March 23, 2022.

**Amendment Notes**

The 2021 amendment by SB 58 added "or section 3721.65" in (A); added (D); and made a related change.

## ATTORNEY GENERAL OPINIONS

Revised Code § 3721.99 imposes a duty upon the attorney general to see that a proper affidavit is filed in a court of competent jurisdiction in all cases where evidence is received by him indicating a violation of R.C. 3721.02, 3721.05 or 3721.06: 1961 OAG No. 2279 (1961).

## RESEARCH REFERENCES AND PRACTICE AIDS

**Cross-References to Related Sections**

Penalty for misdemeanor, RC § 2929.21 et. seq.

Enforcement; revocation of license, RC § 3721.03.

Rule-making authority of public health council, RC § 3721.04.

# TITLE 39

# INSURANCE



## CHAPTER 3923

## SICKNESS AND ACCIDENT INSURANCE



### § 3923.121 Association of group sickness and accident insurers; coverage for residents 65 years of age or older; powers of superintendent.

(A) As used in this section:

(1) "Association" means a voluntary unincorporated association of insurers formed for the sole purpose of enabling cooperative action to provide sickness and accident insurance in accordance with this section.

(2) "Insurer" means any insurance company authorized to do the business of sickness and accident insurance in this state.

(3) "Insured" means a person covered under a group policy issued pursuant to this section.

(B) Any insurer may join with one or more other insurers, in an association, to offer, sell, and issue to a policyholder selected by the association a policy of group insurance against major financial loss from sickness and accident covering residents of this state who are sixty-five years of age or older and the spouses of such residents. The insurance shall be offered, issued, and administered in the name of the association. Membership in the association shall be open to any insurer and each insurer which participates shall be liable for a specified percentage of the risks. The policy may be executed on behalf of the association by a duly authorized person and need not be countersigned by an agent.

(C) The persons eligible for coverage under the policy shall be all residents of this state who are sixty-five years of age or older and their spouses, subject to reasonable underwriting restrictions to be set forth in the plan of the association. The policy may provide basic hospital and surgical coverage, basic medical coverage, major medical coverage, and any combination of these; provided that it shall not be required as a condition for obtaining major medical coverage that any basic coverage be taken.

(D) The association shall file with the superintendent of insurance any policy, contract, certificate, or other evidence of insurance, application, or other forms pertaining to such insurance together with the premium rates to be charged therefor. The superintendent may approve, disapprove, and withdraw approval of the forms in accordance with section 3923.02 of the Revised Code, or the premium rates if by reasonable assumptions such rates are excessive in relation to the benefits provided. In determining whether such rates by reasonable assumptions are excessive in relation to the benefits provided the superintendent shall give due consideration to past and prospective claim experience, within and outside this state, and to fluctuations in such claim experience, to a reasonable risk charge, to contribution to surplus and contingency funds, to past and prospective expenses, both within and outside this state, and to all other relevant factors within and outside this state, including any differing operating methods of the insurers joining in the issuance of the policy. In reviewing the forms the superintendent shall not be bound by the requirements of sections 3923.04 to 3923.07 of the Revised Code with respect to standard provisions to be included in sickness and accident policies or forms.

(E) The association may enroll eligible persons for coverage under the policy through any insurance agent licensed to sell sickness and accident insurance pursuant to Chapter 3905. of the Revised Code or section 3941.02 of the Revised Code.

(F) The association shall file annually with the superintendent on such date and in such form as the superintendent may prescribe, a financial summary of its operations.

(G) The association may sue and be sued in its associate name and for such purposes only shall be treated as a domestic corporation. Service of process against the association made upon a managing agent, any member thereof, or any agent authorized by appointment to receive service of process, shall have the same force and effect as if the service had been made upon all members of the association.

(H) Under any policy issued as provided in this section, the policyholder, or such person as the policyholder shall designate, shall alone be a member of each domestic mutual insurance company joining in the issue of the policy and shall be entitled to one vote by virtue of such policy at the meetings of each such mutual insurance company. Notice of the annual meetings of each such mutual insurance company may be given by written notice to the policyholder or as otherwise prescribed in the policy.

**HISTORY:**
130 v 905 (Eff 9-2-63); 146 v S 269 (Eff 7-1-96); 146 v S 259 (Eff 11-6-96); 147 v S 154 (Eff 6-30-98); 149 v S 129. Eff 9-1-2002.

**Editor's Notes**

The provisions of § 11 of SB 259 (146 v —) read as follows:

SECTION 11. Sections * * * 3923.121, 3931.11, and 3941.02 of the Revised Code are amended for similar purposes by this act (SB 259) and also by Am. Sub. S.B. 269 of the 121st General Assembly. Notwithstanding the rules of construction in section 1.52 of the Revised Code, it is the intention of the General Assembly that if both these acts become law, the amendments by this act (SB 259) to sections * * * 3923.121, 3931.11, and 3941.02 of the Revised Code supersede those of Am. Sub. S.B. 269 to the same sections.

**RESEARCH REFERENCES AND PRACTICE AIDS**

**Cross-References to Related Sections**

Policy of sickness and accident insurance defined, RC § 3923.01.
Policy terms defined, RC § 3923.011.

Validity of nonconforming policy, RC § 3923.09.

**Ohio Rules**
Process; who may be served, CivR 4.2.

# MEDICARE SUPPLEMENT POLICIES

## § 3923.33 Definitions.

As used in section 3923.33 and sections 3923.331 to 3923.339 of the Revised Code:

(A) "Applicant" means:

(1) In the case of an individual medicare supplement policy, the person who seeks to contract for insurance benefits; and

(2) In the case of a group medicare supplement policy, the proposed certificate holder.

(B) "Certificate" means, for purposes of section 3923.33 and sections 3923.331 to 3923.339 of the Revised Code, any certificate delivered or issued for delivery in this state under a group medicare supplement policy.

(C) "Certificate form" means the form on which the certificate is delivered or issued for delivery by the issuer.

(D) "Direct response insurance policy" means a medicare supplement policy or certificate marketed without the direct involvement of an insurance agent.

(E) "Issuer" includes insurance companies, fraternal benefit societies, health insuring corporations, and any other entities delivering or issuing for delivery in this state medicare supplement policies or certificates.

(F) "Medicare" means the "Health Insurance for the Aged Act," Title XVIII of the Social Security Amendments of 1965, 79 Stat. 291, 42 U.S.C.A. 1395, as then constituted or later amended.

(G) "Medicare supplement policy" means a group or individual policy of sickness and accident insurance or a subscriber contract of health insuring corporations or any other issuers, other than a policy issued pursuant to a contract under section 1876 of the "Social Security Act," 49 Stat. 620 (1935), 42 U.S.C.A., 1395mm, as amended, or an issued policy under any demonstration project specified in 42 U.S.C.A. 1395ss(g)(1), which is advertised, marketed, or designed primarily as a supplement to reimbursements under medicare for the hospital, medical, or surgical expenses of persons eligible for medicare.

(H) "Policy form" means the form on which the policy is delivered or issued for delivery by the issuer.

**HISTORY:**
139 v H 597 (Eff 3-15-82); 142 v S 124 (Eff 10-1-87); 144 v H 490 (Eff 1-31-92); 146 v H 374 (Eff 3-3-96); 147 v S 67. Eff 6-4-97.

**RESEARCH REFERENCES AND PRACTICE AIDS**

**Cross-References to Related Sections**
Additional remedies for violations, RC § 3923.338.
Application of provisions, RC § 3923.331.
Procedure for adopting rules, RC § 3923.337.
Severability of provisions, RC § 3923.339.
Standards of medicare supplement policy provisions, RC § 3923.332.

**Ohio Administrative Code**
Medicare supplement policies. OAC 3901-1-41.

**Practice Manuals and Treatises**
Anderson's Ohio Elder Law Practice Manual § 7.9 Medigap Overview

## § 3923.331 Application of provisions.

(A) Except as otherwise provided in the Revised Code, section 3923.33 and sections 3923.331 to 3923.339 of the Revised Code shall apply to:

(1) All medicare supplement policies delivered or issued for delivery in this state on or after the effective date of this amendment; and

(2) All certificates issued under group medicare supplement policies, which certificates are delivered or issued for delivery in this state on or after the effective date of this amendment.

(B) Section 3923.33 and sections 3923.331 to 3923.339 of the Revised Code shall not apply to a policy of one or more employers or labor organizations, or of the trustees of a fund established by one or more employers or labor organizations, or a combination thereof, for employees or former employees, or a combination thereof, or for members or former members, or a combination thereof, of the labor organizations.

(C) Except as otherwise provided in division (D) of section 3923.334 of the Revised Code, section 3923.33 and sections 3923.331 to 3923.339 of the Revised Code are not intended to prohibit or apply to insurance policies or health care benefit plans, including group conversion policies, provided to medicare eligible persons, which policies are not marketed or held to be medicare supplement policies or benefit plans.

**HISTORY:**
144 v H 490 (Eff 1-31-92); 146 v H 374. Eff 3-3-96.

**RESEARCH REFERENCES AND PRACTICE AIDS**

**Cross-References to Related Sections**
Additional remedies for violations, RC § 3923.338.
Definitions, RC § 3923.33.
Procedure for adopting rules, RC § 3923.337.
Severability of provisions, RC § 3923.339.
Standards of medicare supplement policy provisions, RC § 3923.332.

**Ohio Administrative Code**
Medicare supplement policies. OAC 3901-1-41.

## § 3923.332 Prohibited policy provisions; standards; rules.

(A) No medicare supplement policy or certificate in force in this state shall contain benefits that duplicate benefits provided by medicare.

(B) Notwithstanding section 3923.04 of the Revised Code or any other provision of law of this state, a medicare supplement policy or certificate shall not exclude or limit benefits for losses incurred more than six months from the effective date of coverage because it involved a preexisting condition. The policy or certificate shall not define a preexisting condition more restrictively than a condition for which medical advice was given or treatment was recommended by or received from a physician within six months before the effective date of coverage.

(C) The superintendent of insurance shall adopt reasonable rules to establish specific standards for policy provisions of medicare supplement policies and certificates. The standards shall be in addition to and in accordance with applicable laws of this state, including sections 3923.03 to 3923.09 of the Revised Code. No requirement in Title XVII [17] or XXXIX [39] of the Revised Code relating to minimum required policy benefits, other than the minimum standards contained in section 3923.33 and sections 3923.331 to 3923.339 of the Revised Code, shall apply to medicare supplement policies and certificates. The standards may cover, but are not limited to:

(1) Terms of renewability;
(2) Initial and subsequent conditions of eligibility;
(3) Nonduplication of coverage;
(4) Probationary periods;
(5) Benefit limitations, exceptions, and reductions;
(6) Elimination periods;
(7) Requirements for replacement;
(8) Recurrent conditions; and
(9) Definitions of terms.

(D) The superintendent shall adopt reasonable rules to establish minimum standards for benefits, claims payment, advertising and marketing practices and compensation arrangements, and reporting practices, for medicare supplement policies and certificates.

(E) The superintendent may adopt from time to time such reasonable rules as are necessary to conform medicare supplement policies and certificates to the requirements of federal law and regulations promulgated thereunder, including but not limited to:

(1) Requiring refunds or credits if the policies or certificates do not meet loss ratio requirements;

(2) Establishing a uniform methodology for calculating and reporting loss ratios;

(3) Assuring public access to policies, premiums, and loss ratio information of issuers of medicare supplement insurance;

(4) Establishing a process for approving or disapproving policy forms and certificate forms and proposed premium increases;

(5) Establishing a policy for holding public hearings prior to approval of premium increases; and

(6) Establishing standards for medicare select policies and certificates.

(F) The superintendent may adopt reasonable rules that specify prohibited policy provisions not otherwise specifically authorized by any provision in the Revised Code that, in the opinion of the superintendent, are unjust, unfair, or unfairly discriminatory to any person insured or proposed to be insured under a medicare supplement policy or certificate.

**HISTORY:**
144 v H 490. Eff 1-31-92.

**RESEARCH REFERENCES AND PRACTICE AIDS**

**Cross-References to Related Sections**
Definitions, RC § 3923.33.

**Ohio Administrative Code**
Medicare supplement policies. OAC 3901-1-41.

**Practice Manuals and Treatises**
Anderson's Ohio Elder Law Practice Manual § 7.9 Medigap Overview
Anderson's Ohio Elder Law Practice Manual § 7.10 Eligibility

## § 3923.333 Benefits paid to be reasonable in relation to charges.

Medicare supplement policies shall return to policyholders benefits that are reasonable in relation to the premium charged. The superintendent of insurance shall issue reasonable rules to establish minimum standards for loss ratios of medicare supplement policies on the basis of incurred claims experience, or incurred health care expenses where coverage is provided by a health insuring corporation on a service rather than reimbursement basis, and earned premiums in accordance with accepted actuarial principles and practices.

**HISTORY:**
144 v H 490 (Eff 1-31-92); 147 v S 67. Eff 6-4-97.

**RESEARCH REFERENCES AND PRACTICE AIDS**

**Cross-References to Related Sections**
Application of provisions, RC § 3923.331.
Definitions, RC § 3923.33.

## § 3923.334 Outline of coverage to be delivered at time of application; informational brochure; disclosures by insurers.

(A) In order to provide for full and fair disclosure in the sale of medicare supplement policies, no medicare supplement policy or certificate shall be delivered in this state, unless an outline of coverage is delivered to the applicant at the time application is made.

(B) The superintendent of insurance shall prescribe the format and content of the outline of coverage required by division (A) of this section. For purposes of this section, "format" means style, arrangements and overall appearance, including such items as the size, color and prominence of type, and arrangement of text and captions. The outline of coverage shall include:

(1) A description of the principal benefits and coverage provided in the policy;

(2) A statement of the renewal provisions, including any reservation by the issuer of a right to change premiums, and disclosure of the existence of any automatic renewal premium increases based on the age of the policyholder or certificate holder;

(3) A statement that the outline of coverage is a summary of the policy issued or applied for and that the policy should be consulted to determine governing contractual provisions.

(C) The superintendent may prescribe by rule a standard form and the contents of an informational brochure for persons eligible for medicare, which is intended to improve the buyer's ability to select the most appropriate coverage and improve the buyer's understanding of medicare. Except in the case of direct response insurance policies, the superintendent may require by rule that the informational brochure be provided to any prospective insureds eligible for medicare concurrently with delivery of the outline of coverage. With respect to direct response insurance policies, the superintendent may require by rule that the prescribed brochure be provided upon request to any prospective insureds eligible for medicare, but in no event later than the time of policy delivery.

(D) The superintendent may adopt rules for captions or notice requirements, determined to be in the public interest and designed to inform prospective insureds that particular insurance coverages are not medicare supplement coverages, for all sickness and accident insurance policies and subscriber contracts sold to persons eligible for medicare, other than:

(1) Medicare supplement policies; or

(2) Disability income policies.

(E) The superintendent may adopt reasonable rules to govern the full and fair disclosure of information in connection with the replacement of sickness and accident insurance policies, subscriber contracts, or certificates by persons eligible for medicare.

**HISTORY:**
144 v H 490 (Eff 1-31-92); 146 v H 374. Eff 3-3-96.

**RESEARCH REFERENCES AND PRACTICE AIDS**

**Cross-References to Related Sections**
Application of provisions, RC § 3923.331.
Definitions, RC § 3923.33.

**Ohio Administrative Code**
Medicare supplement policies. OAC 3901-1-41.

## § 3923.335 Notice of right to return policy and receive refund.

Medicare supplement policies and certificates shall have a notice prominently printed on the first page of the policy or certificate or attached thereto stating in substance that the applicant shall have the right to return the policy or certificate within thirty days of its delivery and to have the premium refunded if, after examination of the policy or certificate, the applicant is not satisfied for any reason. Any refund made pursuant to this section shall be paid directly to the applicant by the issuer in a timely manner.

**HISTORY:**
144 v H 490. Eff 1-31-92.

**RESEARCH REFERENCES AND PRACTICE AIDS**

**Cross-References to Related Sections**
Definitions, RC § 3923.33.

## § 3923.336 Prior review and approval of advertising.

(A) Each issuer of medicare supplement policies or certificates in this state shall provide a copy of any medicare supplement advertisement intended for use in this state, whether through written or electronic media, to the superintendent of insurance for review and approval.

(B) The superintendent shall adopt rules to carry out the purposes of this section.

**HISTORY:**
144 v H 490. Eff 1-31-92.

RESEARCH REFERENCES AND PRACTICE AIDS

**Cross-References to Related Sections**
Definitions, RC § 3923.33.

**Ohio Administrative Code**
Medicare supplement policies. OAC 3901-1-41.

### § 3923.337 Procedure for adopting rules.

All rules adopted pursuant to section 3923.33 and sections 3923.331 to 3923.339 of the Revised Code shall be subject to Chapter 119. of the Revised Code.

**HISTORY:**
144 v H 490. Eff 1-31-92.

RESEARCH REFERENCES AND PRACTICE AIDS

**Cross-References to Related Sections**
Definitions, RC § 3923.33.

**Ohio Administrative Code**
Medicare supplement policies. OAC 3901-1-41.



### § 3923.338 Additional remedies for violations.

In addition to any other applicable penalties for violations of Title XVII [17] or XXXIX [39] of the Revised Code, the superintendent of insurance, pursuant to an adjudication conducted in accordance with Chapter 119. of the Revised Code, may issue an order requiring issuers violating any provision of section 3923.33 or sections 3923.331 to 3923.339 of the Revised Code or rules adopted pursuant to those sections to do either or both of the following:

(A) Cease marketing any medicare supplement policy or certificate in this state that is related directly or indirectly to the violation;

(B) Take such actions as are necessary to comply with section 3923.33 and sections 3923.331 to 3923.339 of the Revised Code.

**HISTORY:**
144 v H 490. Eff 1-31-92.

RESEARCH REFERENCES AND PRACTICE AIDS

**Cross-References to Related Sections**
Definitions, RC § 3923.33.

### § 3923.339 Severability of provisions.

If any provision of section 3923.33 or sections 3923.331 to 3923.339 of the Revised Code or the application thereof to any person or circumstances is for any reason held to be invalid, the remainder of section 3923.33 and sections 3923.331 to 3923.339 of the Revised Code and the application of such remainder to other persons or circumstances shall not be affected thereby.

**HISTORY:**
144 v H 490. Eff 1-31-92.

RESEARCH REFERENCES AND PRACTICE AIDS

**Cross-References to Related Sections**
Definitions, RC § 3923.33.

### § 3923.39 Consolidated corporation may cancel individual policy for nonpayment; unnecessary services; medicare supplements.

(A) As used in this section:

(1) "Consolidated corporation" means any mutual insurance company that merged or consolidated with a hospital service association.

(2) "Individual policy" means a policy other than a policy issued pursuant to section 3923.11, 3923.12, or 3923.13 of the Revised Code.

(3) "Individual policyholder" means a person who is an insured under an individual policy.

(4) "Cancel" means any cancellation, denial of renewal, lapse, or other termination of coverage of an individual policyholder of a consolidated corporation on the ground of nonpayment of a policy payment.

(5) "Notice of cancellation" means a notice by a consolidated corporation of an intention to cancel an individual policy on the ground of nonpayment of a policy payment.

(6) "Extenuating circumstances" means circumstances that excuse an individual policyholder's failure to pay a policy payment after the mailing of a notice of cancellation under this section and include, but are not limited to, any of the following:

(a) Hospitalization;

(b) Incapacity or incompetency;

(c) Continuous absence from the address to which the notice was addressed for a period of time, including the date on which the notice was delivered to the address, of not more than sixty days from the date on which the notice was mailed.

(7) "Medicare supplement policy" has the same meaning as in section 3923.33 of the Revised Code.

(B) If a consolidated corporation does not receive a policy payment due from a policyholder on an individual policy on or before the due date shown on a billing mailed to the policyholder, the consolidated corporation may cancel the policyholder's coverage by mailing a notice of cancellation to the policyholder at his last known address.

No cancellation for nonpayment of a policy payment shall take effect until not less than fifteen days have passed since the date of mailing of a notice of cancellation.

An individual policyholder whose coverage is terminated for nonpayment may apply for reinstatement of coverage within sixty days after the date the notice of cancellation is mailed. The consolidated corporation shall reinstate the coverage, continuous from the date of cancellation, if it determines that the policyholder's failure to pay was due to extenuating circumstances, and the policyholder pays the payment required for reinstatement of coverage. A consolidated corporation shall establish an appeals procedure that will enable the policyholder to present the reasons why the consolidated corporation should reconsider the cancellation and reinstate the coverage.

The notice of cancellation shall advise the policyholder of the policyholder's rights to appeal the cancellation of coverage and of the amount of payment that will be required to reinstate the coverage.

(C) No individual policyholder of a consolidated corporation shall be billed either by a hospital or the consolidated corporation for rendered health care services adjudged unnecessary by a utilization review mechanism recognized by the consolidated corporation or the hospital, provided such individual policyholder has acted in good faith. The contract between the consolidated corporation and the hospital may specify the conditions under which the consolidated corporation or the hospital shall sustain the loss of revenue.

(D) Notwithstanding the provisions of section 3941.47 of the Revised Code, a medicare supplement policy issued or renewed by a consolidated corporation to an individual policyholder may not provide for the denial or reduction of benefits under such policy when services are provided at or by a hospital which does not have a contractual relationship with such consolidated corporation.

**HISTORY:**
142 v S 124. Eff 10-1-87.

RESEARCH REFERENCES AND PRACTICE AIDS

**Ohio Administrative Code**
Medicare supplement policies. OAC 3901-1-41.

## LONG-TERM CARE INSURANCE

### § 3923.41 Definitions.

As used in sections 3923.41 to 3923.48 of the Revised Code:

(A) "Long-term care insurance" means any insurance policy or rider advertised, marketed, offered, or designed to provide coverage for not less than one year for each covered person on an expense incurred, indemnity, prepaid, or other basis, for one or more necessary or medically necessary diagnostic, preventive, therapeutic, rehabilitative, maintenance, or personal care services, provided in a setting other than an acute care unit of a hospital. "Long-term care insurance" includes group and individual annuities and life insurance policies or riders that provide directly or supplement long-term care benefits, and policies or riders that provide for payment of benefits based on cognitive impairment or the loss of functional capacity. "Long-term care insurance" includes group and individual policies or riders whether issued by insurers, fraternal benefit societies, or health insuring corporations. "Long-term care insurance" includes qualified long-term care insurance contracts. "Long-term care insurance" does not include any insurance policy that is offered primarily to provide basic medicare supplement coverage, basic hospital expense coverage, basic medical-surgical expense coverage, hospital confinement indemnity coverage, major medical expense coverage, disability income protection coverage, accident only coverage, specified disease or specified accident coverage, or limited benefit health coverage.

With regard to life insurance, "long-term care insurance" does not include life insurance policies that accelerate the death benefits specifically for one or more of the qualifying events of terminal illness, medical conditions requiring extraordinary medical intervention, or permanent institutional confinement; that provide the option of a lump sum payment for those benefits; and in which neither the benefits nor the eligibility for the benefits is conditioned upon the receipt of long-term care.

Notwithstanding any other provision contained in sections 3923.41 to 3923.48 of the Revised Code, any product advertised, marketed, or offered as long-term care insurance shall be subject to sections 3923.41 to 3923.48 of the Revised Code.

(B) "Applicant" means either of the following:

(1) In the case of an individual long-term care insurance policy, the person who seeks to contract for benefits;

(2) In the case of a group long-term care insurance policy, the proposed certificate holder.

(C) "Certificate" means any certificate issued under a group long-term care insurance policy that has been delivered, issued for delivery, or used in or outside this state.

(D) "Group long-term care insurance" means a long-term care insurance policy that is delivered or issued for delivery in this state to any of the following:

(1) One or more employers or labor organizations, or a trust or the trustees of a fund established by one or more employers or labor organizations, or a combination thereof, established for either of the following:

(a) Employees or former employees or a combination thereof;

(b) Members of the labor organization, or former members of the labor organization, or a combination thereof.

(2) Any professional, trade, or occupational association for its members or former or retired members, or a combination thereof, if the association satisfies both of the following requirements:

(a) It is composed of individuals all of whom are or were actively engaged in the same profession, trade, or occupation.

(b) It is maintained in good faith for purposes other than obtaining insurance.

(3) An association or trust of the trustees of a fund established, created, or maintained for the benefit of members of one or more associations that meets the requirements of section 3923.43 of the Revised Code;

(4) A group other than as described in divisions (D)(1), (2), and (3) of this section about whom the superintendent of insurance finds that all of the following are true:

(a) The issuance of the group policy is not contrary to the best interest of the public.

(b) The issuance of the group policy would result in economies of acquisition or administration.

(c) The benefits of the group policy are reasonable in relation to the premiums charged.

(E) "Policy" means any policy, contract, rider, or endorsement delivered, issued for delivery, or used in or outside this state by an insurer, fraternal benefit society, or health insuring corporation.

(F)(1) "Qualified long-term care insurance contract" or "federally tax-qualified long-term care insurance contract" means an individual or group insurance contract of which all of the following are true pursuant to division (b) of section 7702B of the "Internal Revenue Code of 1986," 26 U.S.C. 7702B, as amended:

(a) The only insurance protection provided under the contract is coverage of qualified long-term care services including payments made on a per diem or other periodic basis without regard to the expenses incurred during the period to which the payments relate.

(b) The contract does not pay or reimburse expenses incurred for services or items to the extent that the expenses are reimbursable under Title XVIII of the "Social Security Act," 42 U.S.C. 1395 et seq., as amended, or would be so reimbursable but for the application of a deductible or coinsurance amount. The contract may pay or reimburse expenses that are reimbursable under Title XVIII of the Social Security Act as a secondary payer. A contract may allow payments to be made on a per diem or other periodic basis without regard to the expenses incurred during the period to which the payments relate.

(c) The contract is guaranteed renewable, within the meaning of division (b)(1)(C) of section 7702B of the "Internal Revenue Code of 1986," 26 U.S.C. 7702B, as amended.

(d) The contract does not provide for a cash surrender value or other money that can be paid, assigned, pledged as collateral for a loan, or borrowed except as provided in division (F)(1)(e) of this section.

(e) All refunds of premiums, and all policy holder dividends or similar amounts, under the contract shall be applied to a reduction in future premiums or to increase future benefits, except that a refund in the event of death of the insured or in the event of a complete surrender or cancellation of the contract shall not exceed the aggregate premiums paid under the contract.

(f) The contract meets the consumer protection provisions set forth in division (g) of section 7702B of the "Internal Revenue Code of 1986," 26 U.S.C. 7702B, as amended.

(2) "Qualified long-term care insurance contract" or "federally tax-qualified long-term care insurance contract" also means the portion of a life insurance contract that provides long-term care insurance coverage by a rider or as part of the contract and that satisfies the requirements of divisions (b) and (e) of section 7702B of the Internal Revenue Code of 1986, 26 U.S.C 7702B, as amended.

(G) "State long-term care partnership program" or "partnership program" means a program established under division (b) of section 1917 of the "Social Security Act," 42 U.S.C. 1396p, as amended.

(H) "Insurance agent" or "agent" means a person licensed under Chapter 3905. of the Revised Code to sell, solicit, or negotiate insurance.

(I) "Insurer" means any person authorized under Title XXXIX of the Revised Code to engage in the business of insurance in this state or any health insuring corporation authorized under Chapter 1751. of the Revised Code to do business in this state that issues long-term care insurance policies or certificates.

**HISTORY:**

142 v H 611 (Eff 9-14-88); 144 v H 216 (Eff 8-14-92); 147 v S 67. Eff 6-4-97; 152 v H 100, § 101.01, eff. 9-10-07.

**Amendment Notes**

152 v H 100, effective September 10, 2007, in the first paragraph of (A), inserted the fourth sentence; rewrote (D); and added (F) through (I).

RESEARCH REFERENCES AND PRACTICE AIDS

**Cross-References to Related Sections**

Application of provisions, RC § 3923.42.
Long-term care insurance—
Health insuring corporation, RC § 1751.63.
Pension, benefit or allowance recipients, RC § 145.581.
Political subdivision employees and officials, RC § 124.841.
State employees and officials, RC § 124.84.
Notice to job and family services department of policies meeting requirements; rules for qualification, RC § 3923.50.
Prohibition, RC § 3923.44.
Rules, RC § 3923.47.

**Ohio Administrative Code**

Long-term care insurance. OAC ch. 3901-4.

**Practice Manuals and Treatises**

Anderson's Ohio Elder Law Practice Manual § 7.1 Overview
Anderson's Ohio Elder Law Practice Manual § 7.8 Accelerated Benefits and Viatical Settlements

### § 3923.42 Citation of act; application of provisions.

(A) Sections 3923.41 to 3923.48 of the Revised Code may be cited as the "long-term care insurance act."

(B) Sections 3923.41 to 3923.48 of the Revised Code do not supersede the obligations of entities subject to these sections to comply with the substance of other applicable insurance laws insofar as they do not conflict with these sections, except that section 3923.33 and sections 3923.331 to 3923.339 of the Revised Code and rules intended to apply to medicare supplement insurance policies do not apply to long-term care insurance. A policy that is not advertised, marketed, or offered as long-term care insurance need not meet the requirements of sections 3923.41 to 3923.48 of the Revised Code.

Titles 39 — 57

**HISTORY:**

142 v H 611 (Eff 9-14-88); 144 v H 490. Eff 1-31-92.

RESEARCH REFERENCES AND PRACTICE AIDS

**Cross-References to Related Sections**

Definitions, RC § 3923.41.
Prohibition, RC § 3923.44.
Superintendent of insurance to adopt rules, RC § 3923.47.

**Ohio Administrative Code**

Long-term care insurance. OAC ch. 3901-4.

### § 3923.43 Evidence to be filed by association or insurer of association.

(A) Prior to advertising, marketing, or offering a policy within this state, the association or the insurer of the association described in division (D)(3) of section 3923.41 of the Revised Code, shall file evidence with the superintendent of insurance that the association has at the outset a minimum of one hundred persons and has been organized and maintained in good faith for purposes other than that of obtaining insurance, has been in active existence for at least one year, and has a constitution and bylaws that provide all of the following:

(1) The association holds regular meetings not less than annually to further the purposes of the members;

(2) Except for credit unions, the association collects dues or solicits contributions from members;

(3) The association's members have voting privileges and representation on the governing board and committees of the association.

(B) Thirty days after the evidence filing, the association is deemed to satisfy the organizational requirements listed in division (A) of this section unless the superintendent makes a specific finding that the association does not satisfy the organizational requirements.

**HISTORY:**

152 v H 100, § 101.01, eff. 9-10-07.

**Editor's Notes**

Not analogous to former RC § 3923.43 (142 v H 611), repealed 144 v H 216, § 2, eff 8-14-92.

### § 3923.44 Rules for sale of long-term care insurance; policy requirements; outline of coverage; disclosure form; inflation protection requirements.

(A) The superintendent of insurance, pursuant to Chapter 119. of the Revised Code, may adopt rules that include standards for full and fair disclosure setting forth the manner, content, and required disclosures for the sale of long-term care insurance policies, terms of renewability, initial and subsequent conditions of eligibility, nonduplication of coverage provisions, coverage of dependents, preexisting conditions, termination of coverage, continuation or conversion, probationary periods, limitations, exceptions, reductions, elimination periods, requirements for replacement, recurrent conditions, and definitions of terms. Such rules may include provisions related to the state long-term care partnership program, including, but not limited to, requirements related to offers to exchange partnership program policies for previously issued policies and for consumer disclosures related to the state long-term care partnership program.

(B) No long-term care insurance policy shall:

(1) Be canceled, nonrenewed, or otherwise terminated on the grounds of the age or the deterioration of the mental or physical health of the insured individual or certificate holder;

(2) Contain a provision establishing a new waiting period if existing coverage is converted to or replaced by a new or other form within the same company, except with respect to an increase in benefits voluntarily selected by the insured individual or group policyholder;

(3) Provide coverage for skilled nursing care only or provide significantly more coverage for skilled care in a facility than coverage for lower levels of care;

(4) Use a definition of "preexisting condition" that is more restrictive than the following: "Preexisting condition" means a condition for which medical advice or treatment was recommended by, or received from, a provider of health care services, within six months preceding the effective date of coverage of an insured person.

(5) Exclude coverage for a loss or confinement that is the result of a preexisting condition unless the loss or confinement begins within six months following the effective date of coverage of an insured person.

(C) The superintendent may extend the limitation periods set forth in divisions (B)(4) and (5) of this section as to specific age group categories in specific policy forms upon findings that the extension is in the best interest of the public.

(D) "Preexisting condition" does not prohibit an insurer from using an application form designed to elicit the complete health history of an applicant, and, on the basis of the answers on that application, from underwriting in accordance with that insurer's established underwriting standards. Unless otherwise provided in the policy or certificate, a preexisting condition, regardless of whether it is disclosed on the application, need not be covered until the waiting period described in division (B)(5) of this section expires. No long-term care insurance policy or certificate may exclude or use waivers or riders of any kind to exclude, limit, or reduce coverage or benefits for specifically named or described preexisting diseases or physical conditions beyond the waiting period described in division (B)(5) of this section.

(E)(1) No long-term care insurance policy shall do any of the following:

(a) Condition eligibility for any institutional benefits on a requirement of prior hospitalization;

(b) Condition eligibility for benefits provided in an institutional care setting on the receipt of a higher level of institutional care;

(c) Condition eligibility for any institutional benefits, other than waiver of premium or post-confinement, post-acute care, or recuperative benefits, on a requirement of prior institutionalization.

(2) Every long-term care insurance policy that conditions eligibility for noninstitutional benefits on the prior receipt of institutional care is subject to both of the following:

(a) The policy shall not require a prior institutional stay of more than thirty days.

(b) The policy shall provide that eligibility for noninstitutional benefits shall be established by the alternative of a period of hospitalization of not more than three days.

(3) No long-term care insurance policy, except for the policy described in division (E)(2) of this section, shall condition eligibility for noninstitutional benefits on the requirement of prior hospitalization.

(4) No long-term care insurance policy that provides benefits only following institutionalization shall condition the benefits upon admission to a facility for the same or related conditions within a period of less than thirty days after discharge from the institution.

(F) A long-term care insurance policy that provides post-confinement, post-acute care, or recuperative benefits shall state any limitations or conditions on eligibility for benefits, including any required period of prior institutionalization as permitted in division (E)(1)(c) of this section, in a separate paragraph of the policy or certificate and shall label that paragraph "Limitations or Conditions on Eligibility for Benefits."

(G) The superintendent, pursuant to Chapter 119. of the Revised Code, may adopt rules establishing loss ratio standards for long-term care insurance policies provided that a specific reference to long-term care insurance policies is contained in the rule.

(H)(1) A person insured under a long-term care insurance policy may return the policy or certificate in accordance with the procedures and requirements provided for individual policyholders under section 3923.31 of the Revised Code, except that the person has thirty days from the date of delivery to return the policy or certificate and have the premium refunded.

(2) A notice of the policyholder's or certificate holder's rights under division (H)(1) of this section and section 3923.31 of the Revised Code shall be printed prominently on the first page of the policy or certificate or attached to the policy or certificate.

(I) Except as provided in division (M) of this section, an outline of coverage and a notice that consumer information is available from the department of insurance under section 3923.49 of the Revised Code shall be delivered to a prospective applicant for long-term care insurance at the time of the initial solicitation through means that prominently direct the attention of the prospective applicant to the outline of coverage, the purpose of the outline of coverage, and the notice. In the case of agent solicitations, the agent shall deliver the outline of coverage and notice prior to the presentation of an application or enrollment form. In the case of direct response solicitations, the insurer shall deliver the outline of coverage and notice in conjunction with any application or enrollment form. The superintendent shall prescribe by rule the content and format of the outline of coverage and notice, including the style, overall appearance, size, color and prominence of type, and the arrangement of text and captions. The outline of coverage shall include all of the following:

(1) A description of the principal benefits and coverage provided in the policy;

(2) A statement of the principal exclusions, reductions, and limitations contained in the policy;

(3) A statement of the terms under which the individual policy or certificate or the group policy or certificate may be renewed and the terms under which cancellation is permitted, including any reservation in the policy of a right to change premiums. Continuation or conversion provisions of group long-term care insurance shall be specifically described.

(4) A description of the terms under which the policy or certificate may be returned and the premium refunded;

(5) A brief description of the relationship of the cost of care and benefits;

(6) A statement that the outline of coverage is a summary of the policy issued or applied for, and that the policy or group master policy should be consulted to determine governing contractual provisions;

(7) A statement that discloses to the policyholder or certificate holder whether the policy is intended to be a federally tax-qualified long-term care insurance contract.

(J) A certificate issued pursuant to a group long-term care insurance policy that is delivered, issued for delivery, or used in or outside this state shall include all of the following:

(1) A description of the principal benefits and coverage provided in the policy;

(2) A statement of the principal exclusions, reductions, and limitations contained in the policy;

(3) A statement that the group master policy determines governing contractual provisions.

(K) If an individual life insurance policy provides long-term care benefits within the policy or by rider, a policy summary shall be delivered to an applicant for the policy at the time of policy delivery. In the case of direct response solicitations, the insurer shall deliver the policy summary to the applicant upon the applicant's request. If no such request is made, the insurer shall deliver the policy summary no later than at the time of policy delivery. In addition to any other information required by this section, the policy summary shall include all of the following:

(1) A statement that explains how the terms of the policy that provide benefits for long-term care insurance affect the other terms of the policy, including how the payment of these benefits would reduce the death benefits payable by the policy;

(2) A description of the amount of benefits for long-term care insurance that is available under the policy, the length of time these benefits could be paid by the policy, and any guaranteed lifetime benefits provided by the policy, for each insured under the policy;

(3) A statement of the exclusions, reductions, and limitations on benefits for long-term care insurance that are contained in the policy;

(4) A statement of the effects of exercising other rights under the policy;

(5) A statement of the guarantees, if any, with respect to the policy costs of providing benefits for long-term care insurance;

(6) A statement of all current and projected maximum lifetime benefits;

(7) A statement of whether long-term care inflation protection is available under the policy.

(L) During the time when a long-term care benefit, funded through a life insurance vehicle by the acceleration of the death benefit, is in benefit payment status, the insurer shall provide a monthly report to the policyholder. The report shall include all of the following:

(1) A description of all benefits for long-term care insurance that were paid by the policy during that month;

(2) An explanation of any changes in the policy, including death benefits or cash values due to the payout of long-term care benefits;

(3) A statement of the amount of benefits for long-term care insurance that is still available under the policy.

(M) In case of a policy issued to a group defined in division (D)(1) of section 3923.41 of the Revised Code, an outline of coverage shall not be required to be delivered, provided that the information described in division (I) of this section is contained in other materials relating to enrollment and, upon request, these other materials are made available to the superintendent.

(N)(1) Policies that are intended to qualify under the state long-term care partnership program shall comply with all state and federal requirements applicable to policies issued in connection with the state long-term care partnership program.

(2)(a) For policies intended to qualify under the state long-term care partnership program, the agent or insurer shall deliver to the applicant a long-term care partnership policy disclosure form along with the outline of coverage specified in division (I) of this section.

(b) In the case of a policy issued to a group where an outline of coverage is not delivered, the long-term care partnership policy disclosure form is delivered with enrollment forms.

(c) In the case of a life insurance policy that offers long-term care insurance within the policy or as a rider, the disclosure form is provided with the policy summary.

(O) No insurer shall issue a policy intended to qualify as a state partnership program policy that fails to satisfy the following inflation protection requirements:

(1) For a person who is less than sixty-one years of age as of the date of purchase of the policy, the policy provides annual inflation protection of at least three per cent compounded

annually per year or a rate, compounded annually, that is equal to the annual consumer price index.

(2) For a person who is at least sixty-one years of age but less than seventy-six years of age as of the date of purchase of the policy, the policy provides annual inflation protection of at least three per cent simple or a rate equal to the annual consumer price index.

(3) For a person who is at least seventy-six years of age as of the date of purchase of the policy, the policy may provide inflation protection.

(P) As used in this section, "consumer price index" means consumer price index for all urban consumers, U.S. city average, all items, as determined by the bureau of labor statistics of the United States department of labor.

(Q) For purposes of division (O) of this section, the superintendent may approve an alternative index to be used in place of the consumer price index.

(R) The superintendent shall prescribe by rule pursuant to Chapter 119. of the Revised Code the content and format of the state long-term care partnership program policy disclosure form required by division (N)(2) of this section.

(S) No policy may be advertised, marketed, or offered as long-term care insurance unless it complies with sections 3923.41 to 3923.48 of the Revised Code.

(T) The superintendent may adopt rules in accordance with Chapter 119. of the Revised Code to establish minimum standards for marketing practices, agent compensation, agent testing, and reporting practices for long-term care insurance.



**HISTORY:**

142 v H 611 (Eff 9-14-88); 144 v S 16 (Eff 7-16-91); 144 v H 216 (Eff 8-14-92); 145 v H 152. Eff 7-1-93; 152 v H 100, § 101.01, eff. 9-10-07.

**Amendment Notes**

152 v H 100, effective September 10, 2007, added the last sentence to (A); added the exception to the beginning of the introductory language of (I); added (I)(7) and (K)(7); rewrote (L); and inserted (M) through (R) and redesignated the remaining subsections accordingly.

**RESEARCH REFERENCES AND PRACTICE AIDS**

**Cross-References to Related Sections**

Application of provisions, RC § 3923.42.
Definitions, RC § 3923.41.
Superintendent of insurance to adopt rules, RC § 3923.47.
Violations deemed unfair and deceptive practice, RC § 3923.48.

**Ohio Administrative Code**

Long-term care insurance. OAC ch. 3901-4.

**Practice Manuals and Treatises**

Anderson's Ohio Elder Law Practice Manual § 7.1 Overview
Anderson's Ohio Elder Law Practice Manual § 7.3 Eligibility
Anderson's Ohio Elder Law Practice Manual § 7.5 Basic Benefits
Anderson's Ohio Elder Law Practice Manual § 7.6 Future Benefits

### § 3923.441 Rescission of contract or denial of claim based on misrepresentation.

(A) Except as otherwise provided in division (C) of this section and notwithstanding division (B) of section 3923.04 of the Revised Code, no insurer shall rescind a long-term care insurance policy or certificate or deny an otherwise valid claim based upon a misrepresentation by the applicant without adhering to one of the following:

(1) For a policy or certificate that has been in force for less than six months, an insurer may rescind a long-term care insurance policy or certificate or deny an otherwise valid long-term care insurance claim if the insurer can demonstrate that the insured misrepresented facts that were material to the insurer's offer of coverage to the insured.

(2) For a policy or certificate that has been in force for at least six months but less than two years, an insurer may rescind a long-term care insurance policy or certificate or deny an otherwise valid long-term care insurance claim if the insurer can demonstrate that the insured misrepresented facts that were both material to the insurer's offer of coverage to the insured and that pertain to the condition for which the insured sought benefits.

(3) After a policy or certificate has been in force for at least two years, an insurer may rescind a long-term care insurance policy or certificate or deny an otherwise valid long-term care insurance claim if the insurer can demonstrate that the insured knowingly and intentionally misrepresented relevant facts relating to the insured's health in the insured's application for the policy.

(B) No insurer shall recover from the insured benefits that were paid under a long-term care insurance policy or certificate prior to the rescission of the policy or certificate pursuant to this section.

(C) In the event of the death of the insured, the remaining death benefits under a life insurance policy that accelerates benefits for long-term care are governed by section 3923.04 of the Revised Code.

**HISTORY:**

152 v H 100, § 101.01, eff. 9-10-07.

### § 3923.442 Option of purchasing nonforfeiture benefit.

(A)(1) Except as provided in division (B) of this section, no insurer shall deliver or issue for delivery a long-term care insurance policy or certificate in this state without offering the policyholder or certificate holder the option of purchasing a nonforfeiture benefit.

(2) An insurer's offer of a nonforfeiture benefit pursuant to this section may be in the form of a rider that is attached to the policy.

(3) If the policyholder or certificate holder declines the nonforfeiture benefit offered pursuant to this section, the insurer shall provide a contingent benefit upon lapse that shall be available for a period of time specified in the policy or certificate following a substantial increase in premium rates.

(B)(1) For a group long-term care insurance policy, the insurer shall make the offer required by division (A) of this section to the group policyholder.

(2) For a group long-term care insurance policy as defined by division (D)(4) of section 3923.41 of the Revised Code, other than to a continuing care retirement community or other similar entity, the insurer shall make the offer required by division (A) of this section to each proposed certificate holder.

(C) The superintendent of insurance may adopt rules specifying the type of nonforfeiture benefits insurers may offer as part of long-term care insurance policies and certificates, the standards for nonforfeiture benefits, and the rules regarding contingent benefit upon lapse, including a determination of the specified period of time during which a contingent benefit upon lapse will be available and the substantial premium rate increase that triggers a contingent benefit upon lapse as described in division (A) of this section.

**HISTORY:**

152 v H 100, § 101.01, eff. 9-10-07.

### § 3923.443 Agent training course and continuing education.

(A)(1) No agent shall sell, solicit, or negotiate long-term care insurance on or after September 1, 2008, without completing an initial eight-hour partnership program training course as described in division (B) of this section.

(2)(a) Any agent that sells, solicits, or negotiates any long-term care insurance shall complete at least four hours of continuing education in every twenty-four-month period commencing on the first day of January of the year immediately following the year of the issuance of the agent's license.

(b) No agent shall fail to complete the continuing education requirements in division (A)(2)(a) of this section in the twenty-four-month period described in that division.

(B) The initial training course and continuing education required under division (A) of this section may be approved by the superintendent of insurance as continuing education courses under sections 3905.481 to 3905.486 of the Revised Code and shall consist of combined topics related to long-term care insurance, long-term care services, and state long-term care insurance partnership programs, including all of the following:

(1) State and federal regulations and requirements and the relationship between state long-term care insurance partnership programs and other public and private coverage of long-term care services, including medicaid;

(2) Available long-term care services and providers;

(3) Changes or improvements in long-term care services or providers;

(4) Alternatives to the purchase of private long-term care insurance;

(5) The effect of inflation on benefits and the importance of inflation protection;

(6) Consumer suitability standards and guidelines;

(7) Any other topics required by the superintendent.

(C) The initial training and continuing education required by division (A) of this section shall not include training that is specific to a particular insurer or company product or that includes any sales or marketing information, materials, or training other than those required by state or federal law.

(D) A resident agent shall satisfy the training and continuing education required by division (A) of this section by completing long-term care courses that are approved by the superintendent. A nonresident agent may satisfy the training and continuing education required by division (A) of this section by completing the training requirements in any other state, provided that the course is approved for credit by the insurance department of that state prior to the agent taking the course.

(E) Each insurer shall obtain records of the initial training and continuing education completed by agents of that insurer pursuant to division (A) of this section as well as the training completed by the insurer's agents concerning the distribution of the insurer's partnership program policies and shall make those records available to the superintendent upon request.

(F) Each insurer shall maintain records with respect to the training of its agents concerning the distribution of the insurer's partnership program policies. Each insurer shall provide documentation to the superintendent that will allow the superintendent to provide assurance to the medicaid director that agents have received the training required by this section and that agents have demonstrated an understanding of the partnership program policies and their relationship to public and private coverage of long-term care in this state, including medicaid. The superintendent may audit each insurer's records annually to verify that the insurer is maintaining the records required by this division. The superintendent shall make the records provided to the superintendent pursuant to division (E) of this section available to the director.

**HISTORY:**

152 v H 100, § 101.01, eff. 9-10-07; 152 v H 562, § 101.01, eff. 9-23-08; 2013 HB 59, § 101.01, eff. Sept. 29, 2013.

**Amendment Notes**

The 2013 amendment substituted "medicaid director" for "director of job and family services" in the second sentence of (F).

152 v H 562, effective September 23, 2008, rewrote (D) and (F); and, in (E), substituted "obtain records" for "maintain records".

### § 3923.444 Field issuing of policy or certificate.

(A) No agent or third-party administrator shall field issue a long-term care insurance policy or certificate if the compensation to the agent or third-party administrator is not based on the number of policies or certificates issued.

(B) As used in this section, "field issue" means to issue a policy or certificate pursuant to the underwriting authority granted to an agent or third-party administrator by an insurer using the insurer's underwriting guidelines.

**HISTORY:**

152 v H 100, § 101.01, eff. 9-10-07.

### § 3923.45 Forms.

The form of all long-term care insurance policies and applications shall be filed and approved in accordance with section 3923.02 of the Revised Code.

**HISTORY:**

142 v H 611. Eff 9-14-88.

**RESEARCH REFERENCES AND PRACTICE AIDS**

**Cross-References to Related Sections**

Application of provisions, RC § 3923.42.
Definitions, RC § 3923.41.
Prohibition, RC § 3923.44.
Superintendent of insurance to adopt rules, RC § 3923.47.
Violations deemed unfair and deceptive practice, RC § 3923.48.

### § 3923.46 Individual rates.

Premium rates for any individual policy of long-term care insurance shall be filed in accordance with section 3923.021 of the Revised Code.

**HISTORY:**

142 v H 611. Eff 9-14-88.

**RESEARCH REFERENCES AND PRACTICE AIDS**

**Cross-References to Related Sections**

Application of provisions, RC § 3923.42.
Definitions, RC § 3923.41.
Prohibition, RC § 3923.44.
Superintendent of insurance to adopt rules, RC § 3923.47.
Violations deemed unfair and deceptive practice, RC § 3923.48.

### § 3923.47 Rules.

The superintendent of insurance shall, pursuant to Chapter 119. of the Revised Code, adopt rules to carry out the purposes of sections 3923.41 to 3923.48 of the Revised Code including rules related to the state long-term care partnership program.

**HISTORY:**

142 v H 611. Eff 9-14-88; 152 v H 100, § 101.01, eff. 9-10-07.

**Amendment Notes**

152 v H 100, effective September 10, 2007, added "including rules related to the state long-term care partnership program" to the end.

**RESEARCH REFERENCES AND PRACTICE AIDS**

**Cross-References to Related Sections**

Application of provisions, RC § 3923.42.
Definitions, RC § 3923.41.
Notice to job and family services department of policies meeting requirements; rules for qualification, RC § 3923.50.
Prohibition, RC § 3923.44.

**Ohio Administrative Code**

Long-term care insurance. OAC ch. 3901-4.

### § 3923.48 Violations.

Any violation of sections 3923.44 to 3923.46 of the Revised Code is an unfair and deceptive insurance practice under sections 3901.19 to 3901.23 of the Revised Code.

**HISTORY:**

142 v H 611 (Eff 8-14-92); 144 v H 216. Eff 8-14-92.

**RESEARCH REFERENCES AND PRACTICE AIDS**

**Cross-References to Related Sections**

Application of provisions, RC § 3923.42.
Definitions, RC § 3923.41.
Prohibition, RC § 3923.44.

### § 3923.49 Outreach program to educate consumers about long-term care insurance.

The department of insurance shall establish an outreach program to educate consumers about the following:

(A) The need for long-term care insurance;

(B) Mechanisms for financing long-term care;

(C) The availability of long-term care insurance;

(D) The resource protection provided by the Ohio long-term care insurance program under section 5164.86 of the Revised Code;

(E) That a consumer who purchased a long-term care insurance policy that does not meet the requirements of section 3923.50 of the Revised Code may purchase a policy that meets those requirements.

The department shall develop and make available to consumers information to assist them in choosing long-term care insurance coverage.

**HISTORY:**

145 v H 152. Eff 7-1-93; 2013 HB 59, § 101.01, eff. Sept. 29, 2013.

**Amendment Notes**

The 2013 amendment substituted "section 5164.86" for "section 5111.18" in (D).

**RESEARCH REFERENCES AND PRACTICE AIDS**

**Cross-References to Related Sections**

Rules for sale of long-term care insurance; outline of coverage, RC § 3923.44.



### § 3923.50 Notice to department of job and family services of policies meeting requirements; rules for qualification.

For the purposes of the Ohio long-term care insurance program established under section 5164.86 of the Revised Code, the department of insurance shall notify the department of medicaid of all long-term care insurance policies that meet all of the following requirements:

(A) Comply with sections 3923.41 to 3923.48 of the Revised Code and the rules adopted under section 3923.47 of the Revised Code;

(B) Provide benefits for home and community-based services in addition to nursing home care;

(C) Include case management services in its coverage of home and community-based services;

(D) Provide five per cent inflation protection compounded annually;

(E) Provide for the keeping of records and explanation-of-benefit reports on insurance payments that count toward resource exclusion for the medicaid program;

(F) Provide the information the medicaid director determines is necessary to document the extent of resource exclusion and to evaluate the Ohio long-term care insurance program;

(G) Comply with other requirements established in rules adopted under this section.

The superintendent of insurance shall adopt rules in accordance with Chapter 119. of the Revised Code establishing requirements under division (G) of this section that policies must meet to qualify under the Ohio long-term care insurance program. The superintendent shall consult with the departments of aging and medicaid in adopting those rules.

**HISTORY:**

145 v H 152 (Eff 7-1-93); 148 v H 471. Eff 7-1-2000; 2013 HB 59, § 101.01, eff. Sept. 29, 2013.

**Amendment Notes**

The 2013 amendment substituted "section 5164.86" for "section 5111.18" in the introductory language; substituted "medicaid" for "job and family services" in the introductory language and the second sentence of the second paragraph of (G); substituted "medicaid" for "medical assistance" in (E); and substituted "medicaid director" for "director of job and family services" in (F).

**RESEARCH REFERENCES AND PRACTICE AIDS**

**Cross-References to Related Sections**

Medical assistance program; long-term care insurance, RC § 5164.86.

Outreach program to educate consumers about long-term care insurance, RC § 3923.49.

# CHAPTER 3924

# SMALL EMPLOYER HEALTH BENEFIT PLANS; PROVISION OF HEALTH CARE COVERAGE

Medical Savings Accounts



## MEDICAL SAVINGS ACCOUNTS

### § 3924.69 Provisions for account holder's death.

(A) An account holder may designate a beneficiary or beneficiaries of the account holder's medical savings account.

(B) Any funds remaining in a medical savings account upon the death of an account holder shall be distributed to the decedent's estate and shall be subject to taxation as part of the decedent's estate under Chapter 5731. of the Revised Code.

**HISTORY:**

146 v H 179. Eff 10-1-96.

**RESEARCH REFERENCES AND PRACTICE AIDS**

**Cross-References to Related Sections**

Definitions, RC § 3924.61.

# TITLE 41
# LABOR AND INDUSTRY



# CHAPTER 4112
# CIVIL RIGHTS COMMISSION



### § 4112.02 Unlawful discriminatory practices.

It shall be an unlawful discriminatory practice:

(A) For any employer, because of the race, color, religion, sex, military status, national origin, disability, age, or ancestry of any person, to discharge without just cause, to refuse to hire, or otherwise to discriminate against that person with respect to hire, tenure, terms, conditions, or privileges of employment, or any matter directly or indirectly related to employment.

(B) For an employment agency or personnel placement service, because of race, color, religion, sex, military status, national origin, disability, age, or ancestry, to do any of the following:

(1) Refuse or fail to accept, register, classify properly, or refer for employment, or otherwise discriminate against any person;

(2) Comply with a request from an employer for referral of applicants for employment if the request directly or indirectly indicates that the employer fails to comply with the provisions of sections 4112.01 to 4112.07 of the Revised Code.

(C) For any labor organization to do any of the following:

(1) Limit or classify its membership on the basis of race, color, religion, sex, military status, national origin, disability, age, or ancestry;

(2) Discriminate against, limit the employment opportunities of, or otherwise adversely affect the employment status, wages, hours, or employment conditions of any person as an employee because of race, color, religion, sex, military status, national origin, disability, age, or ancestry.

(D) For any employer, labor organization, or joint labor-management committee controlling apprentice training programs to discriminate against any person because of race, color, religion, sex, military status, national origin, disability, or ancestry in admission to, or employment in, any program established to provide apprentice training.

(E) Except where based on a bona fide occupational qualification certified in advance by the commission, for any employer, employment agency, personnel placement service, or labor organization, prior to employment or admission to membership, to do any of the following:

(1) Elicit or attempt to elicit any information concerning the race, color, religion, sex, military status, national origin, disability, age, or ancestry of an applicant for employment or membership;

(2) Make or keep a record of the race, color, religion, sex, military status, national origin, disability, age, or ancestry of any applicant for employment or membership;

(3) Use any form of application for employment, or personnel or membership blank, seeking to elicit information regarding race, color, religion, sex, military status, national origin, disability, age, or ancestry; but an employer holding a contract containing a nondiscrimination clause with the government of the United States, or any department or agency of that government, may require an employee or applicant for employment to furnish documentary proof of United States citizenship and may retain that proof in the employer's personnel records and may use photographic or fingerprint identification for security purposes;

(4) Print or publish or cause to be printed or published any notice or advertisement relating to employment or membership indicating any preference, limitation, specification, or discrimination, based upon race, color, religion, sex, military status, national origin, disability, age, or ancestry;

(5) Announce or follow a policy of denying or limiting, through a quota system or otherwise, employment or membership opportunities of any group because of the race, color, religion, sex, military status, national origin, disability, age, or ancestry of that group;

(6) Utilize in the recruitment or hiring of persons any employment agency, personnel placement service, training school or center, labor organization, or any other employee-referring source known to discriminate against persons because of their race, color, religion, sex, military status, national origin, disability, age, or ancestry.

(F) For any person seeking employment to publish or cause to be published any advertisement that specifies or in any manner indicates that person's race, color, religion, sex, military status, national origin, disability, age, or ancestry, or expresses a limitation or preference as to the race, color, religion, sex, military status, national origin, disability, age, or ancestry of any prospective employer.

(G) For any proprietor or any employee, keeper, or manager of a place of public accommodation to deny to any person, except for reasons applicable alike to all persons regardless of race, color, religion, sex, military status, national origin, disability, age, or ancestry, the full enjoyment of the accommodations, advantages, facilities, or privileges of the place of public accommodation.

(H) Subject to section 4112.024 of the Revised Code, for any person to do any of the following:

(1) Refuse to sell, transfer, assign, rent, lease, sublease, or finance housing accommodations, refuse to negotiate for the sale or rental of housing accommodations, or otherwise deny or make unavailable housing accommodations because of race, color, religion, sex, military status, familial status, ancestry, disability, or national origin;

(2) Represent to any person that housing accommodations are not available for inspection, sale, or rental, when in fact they are available, because of race, color, religion, sex, military status, familial status, ancestry, disability, or national origin;

(3) Discriminate against any person in the making or purchasing of loans or the provision of other financial assistance for the acquisition, construction, rehabilitation, repair, or maintenance of housing accommodations, or any person in the making or purchasing of loans or the provision of other financial assistance that is secured by residential real estate, because of race, color, religion, sex, military status, familial status, ancestry, disability, or national origin or because of the racial composition of the neighborhood in which the housing accommodations are located, provided that the person, whether an individual, corporation, or association of any type, lends money as one of the principal aspects or incident to the person's principal business and not only as a part of the purchase price of an owner-occupied residence the person is selling nor merely casually or occasionally to a relative or friend;

(4) Discriminate against any person in the terms or conditions of selling, transferring, assigning, renting, leasing, or subleasing any housing accommodations or in furnishing facilities, services, or privileges in connection with the ownership, occupancy, or use of any housing accommodations, including the sale of fire, extended coverage, or homeowners insurance, because of race, color, religion, sex, military status, familial status, ancestry, disability, or national origin or

because of the racial composition of the neighborhood in which the housing accommodations are located;

(5) Discriminate against any person in the terms or conditions of any loan of money, whether or not secured by mortgage or otherwise, for the acquisition, construction, rehabilitation, repair, or maintenance of housing accommodations because of race, color, religion, sex, military status, familial status, ancestry, disability, or national origin or because of the racial composition of the neighborhood in which the housing accommodations are located;

(6) Refuse to consider without prejudice the combined income of both husband and wife for the purpose of extending mortgage credit to a married couple or either member of a married couple;

(7) Print, publish, or circulate any statement or advertisement, or make or cause to be made any statement or advertisement, relating to the sale, transfer, assignment, rental, lease, sublease, or acquisition of any housing accommodations, or relating to the loan of money, whether or not secured by mortgage or otherwise, for the acquisition, construction, rehabilitation, repair, or maintenance of housing accommodations, that indicates any preference, limitation, specification, or discrimination based upon race, color, religion, sex, military status, familial status, ancestry, disability, or national origin, or an intention to make any such preference, limitation, specification, or discrimination;

(8) Except as otherwise provided in division (H)(8) or (17) of this section, make any inquiry, elicit any information, make or keep any record, or use any form of application containing questions or entries concerning race, color, religion, sex, military status, familial status, ancestry, disability, or national origin in connection with the sale or lease of any housing accommodations or the loan of any money, whether or not secured by mortgage or otherwise, for the acquisition, construction, rehabilitation, repair, or maintenance of housing accommodations. Any person may make inquiries, and make and keep records, concerning race, color, religion, sex, military status, familial status, ancestry, disability, or national origin for the purpose of monitoring compliance with this chapter.

(9) Include in any transfer, rental, or lease of housing accommodations any restrictive covenant, or honor or exercise, or attempt to honor or exercise, any restrictive covenant;

(10) Induce or solicit, or attempt to induce or solicit, a housing accommodations listing, sale, or transaction by representing that a change has occurred or may occur with respect to the racial, religious, sexual, military status, familial status, or ethnic composition of the block, neighborhood, or other area in which the housing accommodations are located, or induce or solicit, or attempt to induce or solicit, a housing accommodations listing, sale, or transaction by representing that the presence or anticipated presence of persons of any race, color, religion, sex, military status, familial status, ancestry, disability, or national origin, in the block, neighborhood, or other area will or may have results including, but not limited to, the following:

(a) The lowering of property values;

(b) A change in the racial, religious, sexual, military status, familial status, or ethnic composition of the block, neighborhood, or other area;

(c) An increase in criminal or antisocial behavior in the block, neighborhood, or other area;

(d) A decline in the quality of the schools serving the block, neighborhood, or other area.

(11) Deny any person access to or membership or participation in any multiple-listing service, real estate brokers' organization, or other service, organization, or facility relating to the business of selling or renting housing accommodations, or discriminate against any person in the terms or conditions of that access, membership, or participation, on account of race, color, religion, sex, military status, familial status, national origin, disability, or ancestry;

(12) Coerce, intimidate, threaten, or interfere with any person in the exercise or enjoyment of, or on account of that person's having exercised or enjoyed or having aided or encouraged any other person in the exercise or enjoyment of, any right granted or protected by division (H) of this section;

(13) Discourage or attempt to discourage the purchase by a prospective purchaser of housing accommodations, by representing that any block, neighborhood, or other area has undergone or might undergo a change with respect to its religious, racial, sexual, military status, familial status, or ethnic composition;

(14) Refuse to sell, transfer, assign, rent, lease, sublease, or finance, or otherwise deny or withhold, a burial lot from any person because of the race, color, sex, military status, familial status, age, ancestry, disability, or national origin of any prospective owner or user of the lot;

(15) Discriminate in the sale or rental of, or otherwise make unavailable or deny, housing accommodations to any buyer or renter because of a disability of any of the following:

(a) The buyer or renter;

(b) A person residing in or intending to reside in the housing accommodations after they are sold, rented, or made available;

(c) Any individual associated with the person described in division (H)(15)(b) of this section.

(16) Discriminate in the terms, conditions, or privileges of the sale or rental of housing accommodations to any person or in the provision of services or facilities to any person in connection with the housing accommodations because of a disability of any of the following:

(a) That person;

(b) A person residing in or intending to reside in the housing accommodations after they are sold, rented, or made available;

(c) Any individual associated with the person described in division (H)(16)(b) of this section.

(17) Except as otherwise provided in division (H)(17) of this section, make an inquiry to determine whether an applicant for the sale or rental of housing accommodations, a person residing in or intending to reside in the housing accommodations after they are sold, rented, or made available, or any individual associated with that person has a disability, or make an inquiry to determine the nature or severity of a disability of the applicant or such a person or individual. The following inquiries may be made of all applicants for the sale or rental of housing accommodations, regardless of whether they have disabilities:

(a) An inquiry into an applicant's ability to meet the requirements of ownership or tenancy;

(b) An inquiry to determine whether an applicant is qualified for housing accommodations available only to persons with disabilities or persons with a particular type of disability;

(c) An inquiry to determine whether an applicant is qualified for a priority available to persons with disabilities or persons with a particular type of disability;

(d) An inquiry to determine whether an applicant currently uses a controlled substance in violation of section 2925.11 of the Revised Code or a substantively comparable municipal ordinance;

(e) An inquiry to determine whether an applicant at any time has been convicted of or pleaded guilty to any offense, an element of which is the illegal sale, offer to sell, cultivation, manufacture, other production, shipment, transportation, delivery, or other distribution of a controlled substance.

(18)(a) Refuse to permit, at the expense of a person with a disability, reasonable modifications of existing housing accommodations that are occupied or to be occupied by the person with a disability, if the modifications may be necessary to afford the person with a disability full enjoyment of the housing accommodations. This division does not preclude a landlord of housing accommodations that are rented or to be rented to a disabled tenant from conditioning permission for a proposed modification upon the disabled tenant's doing one or more of the following:

(i) Providing a reasonable description of the proposed modification and reasonable assurances that the proposed modification will be made in a workerlike manner and that any required building permits will be obtained prior to the commencement of the proposed modification;

(ii) Agreeing to restore at the end of the tenancy the interior of the housing accommodations to the condition they were in prior to the proposed modification, but subject to reasonable wear and tear during the period of occupancy, if it is reasonable for the landlord to condition permission for the proposed modification upon the agreement;

(iii) Paying into an interest-bearing escrow account that is in the landlord's name, over a reasonable period of time, a reasonable amount of money not to exceed the projected costs at the end of the tenancy of the restoration of the interior of the housing accommodations to the condition they were in prior to the proposed modification, but subject to reasonable wear and tear during the period of occupancy, if the landlord finds the account reasonably necessary to ensure the availability of funds for the restoration work. The interest earned in connection with an escrow account described in this division shall accrue to the benefit of the disabled tenant who makes payments into the account.

(b) A landlord shall not condition permission for a proposed modification upon a disabled tenant's payment of a security deposit that exceeds the customarily required security deposit of all tenants of the particular housing accommodations.

(19) Refuse to make reasonable accommodations in rules, policies, practices, or services when necessary to afford a person with a disability equal opportunity to use and enjoy a dwelling unit, including associated public and common use areas;

(20) Fail to comply with the standards and rules adopted under division (A) of section 3781.111 of the Revised Code;

(21) Discriminate against any person in the selling, brokering, or appraising of real property because of race, color, religion, sex, military status, familial status, ancestry, disability, or national origin;

(22) Fail to design and construct covered multifamily dwellings for first occupancy on or after June 30, 1992, in accordance with the following conditions:

(a) The dwellings shall have at least one building entrance on an accessible route, unless it is impractical to do so because of the terrain or unusual characteristics of the site.

(b) With respect to dwellings that have a building entrance on an accessible route, all of the following apply:

(i) The public use areas and common use areas of the dwellings shall be readily accessible to and usable by persons with a disability.

(ii) All the doors designed to allow passage into and within all premises shall be sufficiently wide to allow passage by persons with a disability who are in wheelchairs.

(iii) All premises within covered multifamily dwelling units shall contain an accessible route into and through the dwelling; all light switches, electrical outlets, thermostats, and other environmental controls within such units shall be in accessible locations; the bathroom walls within such units shall contain reinforcements to allow later installation of grab bars; and the kitchens and bathrooms within such units shall be designed and constructed in a manner that enables an individual in a wheelchair to maneuver about such rooms.

For purposes of division (H)(22) of this section, "covered multifamily dwellings" means buildings consisting of four or more units if such buildings have one or more elevators and ground floor units in other buildings consisting of four or more units.

(I) For any person to discriminate in any manner against any other person because that person has opposed any unlawful discriminatory practice defined in this section or because that person has made a charge, testified, assisted, or participated in any manner in any investigation, proceeding, or hearing under sections 4112.01 to 4112.07 of the Revised Code.

(J) For any person to aid, abet, incite, compel, or coerce the doing of any act declared by this section to be an unlawful discriminatory practice, to obstruct or prevent any person from complying with this chapter or any order issued under it, or to attempt directly or indirectly to commit any act declared by this section to be an unlawful discriminatory practice.

(K) Nothing in divisions (A) to (E) of this section shall be construed to require a person with a disability to be employed or trained under circumstances that would significantly increase the occupational hazards affecting either the person with a disability, other employees, the general public, or the facilities in which the work is to be performed, or to require the employment or training of a person with a disability in a job that requires the person with a disability routinely to undertake any task, the performance of which is substantially and inherently impaired by the person's disability.

(L) With regard to age, it shall not be an unlawful discriminatory practice and it shall not constitute a violation of division (A) of section 4112.14 of the Revised Code for any employer, employment agency, joint labor-management committee controlling apprenticeship training programs, or labor organization to do any of the following:

(1) Establish bona fide employment qualifications reasonably related to the particular business or occupation that may include standards for skill, aptitude, physical capability, intelligence, education, maturation, and experience;

(2) Observe the terms of a bona fide seniority system or any bona fide employee benefit plan, including, but not limited to, a retirement, pension, or insurance plan, that is not a subterfuge to evade the purposes of this section. However, no such employee benefit plan shall excuse the failure to hire any individual, and no such seniority system or employee benefit plan shall require or permit the involuntary retirement of any individual, because of the individual's age except as provided for in the "Age Discrimination in Employment Act Amendment of 1978," 92 Stat. 189, 29 U.S.C.A. 623, as amended by the "Age Discrimination in Employment Act Amendments of 1986," 100 Stat. 3342, 29 U.S.C.A. 623, as amended.

(3) Retire an employee who has attained sixty-five years of age who, for the two-year period immediately before retirement, is employed in a bona fide executive or a high policymaking position, if the employee is entitled to an immediate nonforfeitable annual retirement benefit from a pension, profit-sharing, savings, or deferred compensation plan, or any combination of those plans, of the employer of the employee, which equals, in the aggregate, at least forty-four thousand dollars, in accordance with the conditions of the "Age Discrimination in Employment Act Amendment of 1978," 92 Stat. 189, 29 U.S.C.A. 631, as amended by the "Age Discrimination in Employment Act Amendments of 1986," 100 Stat. 3342, 29 U.S.C.A. 631, as amended;

(4) Observe the terms of any bona fide apprenticeship program if the program is registered with the Ohio apprenticeship council pursuant to sections 4139.01 to 4139.06 of the Revised Code and is approved by the federal committee on apprenticeship of the United States department of labor.

(M) Nothing in this chapter prohibiting age discrimination and nothing in division (A) of section 4112.14 of the Revised Code shall be construed to prohibit the following:

(1) The designation of uniform age the attainment of which is necessary for public employees to receive pension or other retirement benefits pursuant to Chapter 145., 742., 3307., 3309., or 5505. of the Revised Code;

(2) The mandatory retirement of uniformed patrol officers of the state highway patrol as provided in section 5505.16 of the Revised Code;

(3) The maximum age requirements for appointment as a patrol officer in the state highway patrol established by section 5503.01 of the Revised Code;

(4) The maximum age requirements established for original appointment to a police department or fire department in sections 124.41 and 124.42 of the Revised Code;

(5) Any maximum age not in conflict with federal law that may be established by a municipal charter, municipal ordinance, or resolution of a board of township trustees for original appointment as a police officer or firefighter;

(6) Any mandatory retirement provision not in conflict with federal law of a municipal charter, municipal ordinance, or resolution of a board of township trustees pertaining to police officers and firefighters;

(7) Until January 1, 1994, the mandatory retirement of any employee who has attained seventy years of age and who is serving under a contract of unlimited tenure, or similar arrangement providing for unlimited tenure, at an institution of higher education as defined in the "Education Amendments of 1980," 94 Stat. 1503, 20 U.S.C.A. 1141(a).

(N)(1)(a) Except as provided in division (N)(1)(b) of this section, for purposes of divisions (A) to (E) of this section, a disability does not include any physiological disorder or condition, mental or psychological disorder, or disease or condition caused by an illegal use of any controlled substance by an employee, applicant, or other person, if an employer, employment agency, personnel placement service, labor organization, or joint labor-management committee acts on the basis of that illegal use.

(b) Division (N)(1)(a) of this section does not apply to an employee, applicant, or other person who satisfies any of the following:

(i) The employee, applicant, or other person has successfully completed a supervised drug rehabilitation program and no longer is engaging in the illegal use of any controlled substance, or the employee, applicant, or other person otherwise successfully has been rehabilitated and no longer is engaging in that illegal use.

(ii) The employee, applicant, or other person is participating in a supervised drug rehabilitation program and no longer is engaging in the illegal use of any controlled substance.

(iii) The employee, applicant, or other person is erroneously regarded as engaging in the illegal use of any controlled substance, but the employee, applicant, or other person is not engaging in that illegal use.

(2) Divisions (A) to (E) of this section do not prohibit an employer, employment agency, personnel placement service, labor organization, or joint labor-management committee from doing any of the following:

(a) Adopting or administering reasonable policies or procedures, including, but not limited to, testing for the illegal use of any controlled substance, that are designed to ensure that an individual described in division (N)(1)(b)(i) or (ii) of this section no longer is engaging in the illegal use of any controlled substance;

(b) Prohibiting the illegal use of controlled substances and the use of alcohol at the workplace by all employees;

(c) Requiring that employees not be under the influence of alcohol or not be engaged in the illegal use of any controlled substance at the workplace;

(d) Requiring that employees behave in conformance with the requirements established under "The Drug-Free Workplace Act of 1988," 102 Stat. 4304, 41 U.S.C.A. 701, as amended;

(e) Holding an employee who engages in the illegal use of any controlled substance or who is an alcoholic to the same qualification standards for employment or job performance, and the same behavior, to which the employer, employment agency, personnel placement service, labor organization, or joint labor-management committee holds other employees, even if any unsatisfactory performance or behavior is related to an employee's illegal use of a controlled substance or alcoholism;

(f) Exercising other authority recognized in the "Americans with Disabilities Act of 1990," 104 Stat. 327, 42 U.S.C.A. 12101, as amended, including, but not limited to, requiring employees to comply with any applicable federal standards.

(3) For purposes of this chapter, a test to determine the illegal use of any controlled substance does not include a medical examination.

(4) Division (N) of this section does not encourage, prohibit, or authorize, and shall not be construed as encouraging, prohibiting, or authorizing, the conduct of testing for the illegal use of any controlled substance by employees, applicants, or other persons, or the making of employment decisions based on the results of that type of testing.

(O) This section does not apply to a religious corporation, association, educational institution, or society with respect to the employment of an individual of a particular religion to perform work connected with the carrying on by that religious corporation, association, educational institution, or society of its activities.

The unlawful discriminatory practices defined in this section do not make it unlawful for a person or an appointing authority administering an examination under section 124.23 of the Revised Code to obtain information about an applicant's military status for the purpose of determining if the applicant is eligible for the additional credit that is available under that section.



**HISTORY:**

128 v 12 (Eff 7-29-59); 129 v 1694 (Eff 10-24-61); 131 v 982 (Eff 10-30-65); 133 v H 47 (Eff 10-24-69); 133 v H 432 (Eff 11-12-69); 135 v H 610 (Eff 12-19-73); 136 v H 151 (Eff 1-14-76); 136 v S 162 (Eff 7-23-76); 138 v H 230 (Eff 11-13-79); 138 v S 367 (Eff 3-23-81); 142 v H 5 (Eff 9-28-87); 143 v H 314 (Eff 5-31-90); 144 v H 321 (Eff 6-30-92); 146 v S 162 (Eff 10-29-95); 146 v S 2 (Eff 7-1-96); 146 v H 350 (Eff 1-27-97); 148 v H 264 (Eff 3-17-2000); 148 v H 471 (Eff 7-1-2000); 149 v S 108, § 2.01. Eff 7-6-2001; 152 v H 372, § 1, eff. 3-24-08; 2013 HB 59, § 101.01, eff. Sept. 29, 2013; 2020 hb352, § 1, effective April 15, 2021.

**Publisher's Note:**

Section 2.02(A) of SB 108 (149 v —) repeals the existing version and section 3(A)(1) amends this SB 108 version to remove HB 350 matter or revive matter removed by HB 350.

**Editor's Notes**

The provisions of § 8 of SB 108 (149 v —) read as follows:

SECTION 8. * * * Section 4112.02 of the Revised Code is presented in this act as a composite of the section as amended by both Am. H.B. 264 and H.B. 471 of the 123rd General Assembly. The General Assembly, applying the principle stated in division (B) of section 1.52 of the Revised Code that amendments are to be harmonized if reasonably capable of simultaneous operation, finds that the composites are the resulting version of the sections in effect prior to the effective date of the sections as presented in this act.

**Amendment Notes**

The 2020 amendment by HB 352 deleted former (L), which read: "An aggrieved individual may enforce the individual's rights relative to discrimination on the basis of age as provided for in this section by instituting a civil action, within one hundred eighty days after the alleged unlawful discriminatory practice occurred, in any court with jurisdiction for any legal or equitable relief that will effectuate the individual's rights. A person who files a civil action under this division is barred, with respect to the practices complained of, from instituting a civil action under section 4112.14 of the Revised Code and from filing a charge with the commission under section 4112.05 of the Revised Code"; redesignated former (M) through (P) as (L) through (O); substituted "division (N)(1)(b)" for "division (O)(1)(b)" in (N)(1)(a); substituted "division (N)(1)(a)" for "division (O)(1)(a)" in (N)(1)(b); substituted "division (N)(1)(b)(i)" for "division (O)(1)(b)(i)" in (N)(2)(a); and substituted "division (N)" for "division (O)" in (N)(4).

The 2016 amendment by HB 463 rewrote this section.

The 2013 amendment added (R).

152 v H 372, effective March 24, 2008, inserted "military status" throughout the section.

## NOTES TO DECISIONS

Analysis

**Constitutionality**

Amended Substitute HB No. 350 violates the one-subject provision of Ohio Const. art II, § 15(D) and is unconstitutional in toto: State ex rel. Ohio Academy of Trial Lawyers v. Sheward, 1999-Ohio-123, 86 Ohio St. 3d 451, 715 N.E.2d 1062, 1999 Ohio LEXIS 2580 (Ohio 1999).

R.C. 4112.02(G) which makes unlawful certain discriminatory practices, is a lawful exercise of legislative power and is constitutional: Gegner v. Graham, 1 Ohio App. 2d 442, 30 Ohio Op. 2d 442, 205 N.E.2d 69, 1964 Ohio App. LEXIS 558 (Ohio Ct. App., Greene County 1964).

**Generally**

Ohio courts examine state employment discrimination claims under federal case law interpreting Title VII of the Civil Rights Act of 1964, 42 U.S.C.S. § 2000 et seq. Fearn v. Longaberger Co., 2010-Ohio-1736, 2010 Ohio App. LEXIS 1445 (Ohio Ct. App., Muskingum County 2010).

Evidence that supported a finding of discrimination under Title VII of the Civil Rights Act of 1964, 42 U.S.C.S. § 2000(e) et seq., was required before a violation of the Ohio Fair Employment Practices Act (OFEPA), R.C. 4112.02(A), could be found; the scope of the OFEPA was identical to that of the federal legislation. Brown v. Dover Corp., 2007-Ohio-2128, 2007 Ohio App. LEXIS 2010 (Ohio Ct. App., Hamilton County 2007).

District court properly granted summary judgment to a former employer in a case brought under Title VII of the Civil Rights Act, 42 U.S.C.S. § 2000e, and under R.C. 4112.02 because the employee failed to meet make out a prima facie case as he did not show that he was treated differently than similarly situated employees who were not members of a protected class. Each employee who was discovered to have lied about past criminal history on his application was terminated; the fact that two were reinstated was unavailing as they, unlike plaintiff employee, were union members and were reinstated as part of the grievance process. Elgabi v. Toledo Area Reg'l Transit Auth., 228 Fed. Appx. 537, 2007 FED App. 0266N, 2007 U.S. App. LEXIS 8528 (6th Cir. Ohio 2007).

Employee's burden in demonstrating discrimination is heavier when a reduction in force is required by economic necessity. Employer had a legitimate reason for requiring employees in plaintiff's category to have a commercial driver's license and did not discriminate against her on the basis of gender: Hamilton v. SYSCO Food Servs. of Cleveland, Inc., 2006-Ohio-6419, 170 Ohio App. 3d 203, 866 N.E.2d 559, 2006 Ohio App. LEXIS 6369 (Ohio Ct. App., Cuyahoga County 2006).

Right to oppose discrimination does not entail a right to engage in conduct that interferes with the attainment of the employer's goals, violates legitimate workplace rules, or disrupts the work environment. Evidence established that the employee was terminated due to her profane language and unprofessional conduct, rather than disability discrimination: Proctor v. Ohio Civ. Rights Comm'n, 2006-Ohio-6007, 169 Ohio App. 3d 527, 863 N.E.2d 1069, 2006 Ohio App. LEXIS 5956 (Ohio Ct. App., Summit County 2006).

R.C. 4112.99 is a remedial statute and is subject to R.C. 2305.07's six-year statute of limitations. Race and disability discrimination claims were not precluded where a party filed prior administrative proceedings. "Prima facie case" requirement is an evidentiary standard, not a pleading standard: Jackson v. Int'l Fiber, 2006-Ohio-5799, 169 Ohio App. 3d 395, 863 N.E.2d 189, 2006 Ohio App. LEXIS 5750 (Ohio Ct. App., Champaign County 2006).

In an employment discrimination action, an employer's motion for partial judgment on the pleadings was granted because the employee's R.C. 4112.02(A), (N) claim was barred by R.C. 4112.08 due to his filing of a complaint with the Ohio Civil Rights Commission (OCRC) under R.C. 4112.05(B)(1). The pleadings and attached exhibits were devoid of any indication that the employee preserved his rights in a separate writing filed along with the OCR.C. charge, and the employee had not otherwise indicated that such a writing existed. Further, the action was time-barred pursuant to R.C. 4112.02(N) because he filed it more than a year after he resigned his employment, which was outside of the 180-day statutory requirement. Huston v. Mittal Steel USA, 2006 U.S. Dist. LEXIS 67323 (S.D. Ohio Sept. 20, 2006).

Episodes of harassment identified by two employees could not constitute pervasive harassment in the absence of other, ongoing misconduct about which the employer failed to act. Their claims under Title VII of the Civil Rights Act of 1964, 42 U.S.C.S. § 2000e et seq., 42 U.S.C.S. § 1981, and R.C. 4112.02 were properly dismissed on a motion for summary judgment. Long v. Ford Motor Co., 193 Fed. Appx. 497, 2006 FED App. 0634N, 2006 U.S. App. LEXIS 21893 (6th Cir. Ohio 2006).

R.C. 4112.02 is generally to be interpreted in accordance with interpretations of federal anti-discrimination laws including Title VII of the Civil Rights Act of 1964, 42 U.S.C.S. § 2000e-2 and the Age Discrimination in Employment Act, 29 U.S.C.S. § 621 et seq. Thus, in order to establish a prima facie case of discriminatory discharge under R.C. 4112.02, a plaintiff must prove the following: (1) that she was a member of the protected class when her employment was terminated; (2) that her employment was terminated; (3) that she was qualified to perform the job from which she was dismissed; and (4) that she was replaced by a man or, in the case of an age discrimination claim, by a substantially younger employee. Soliday v. Fluor Fernald, Inc., 2006 U.S. Dist. LEXIS 1504 (S.D. Ohio Jan. 18, 2006).

Where a 50-year old male, working as a newspaper music critic, alleged age and gender discrimination under R.C. 4112.02, the newspaper was denied summary judgment because there was a material question of disputed fact as to whether the male was replaced by a female who was outside of the protected age group, and there was evidence that the employer sought to achieve its goal of appealing to younger, female readers by replacing plaintiff with a young, female columnist. Nager v. The Cincinnati Enquirer, 2005 U.S. Dist. LEXIS 22770 (S.D. Ohio Oct. 6, 2005).

The trial court properly disregarded the general verdict for the plaintiff based on a finding that the defendants discriminated against plaintiff on the claim of wrongful discharge where the jury indicated in its answers to interrogatories that it found no discrimination on any of the three alleged bases, and there was a lack of evidence supporting a finding of discrimination: Bicudo v. Lexford Props., 2004-Ohio-3202, 157 Ohio App. 3d 509, 812 N.E.2d 315, 2004 Ohio App. LEXIS 2880 (Ohio Ct. App., Mahoning County 2004).

Pursuant to R.C. 4112.02(A). It is unlawful in Ohio for any employer, because of the sex of any person, to discharge without just cause, or otherwise to discriminate against that person with respect to hire, tenure, terms, conditions, or privileges of employment, or any matter directly or indirectly related to employment; the Ohio Supreme Court has held that the scope of § 4112.02(A) is identical to that of federal anti-discrimination statutes, so evidence sufficient to support a finding of discrimination under Title VII of the Civil Rights Act of 1964 is necessary before a violation of § 4112.02(A) can be found. Kimble v. Intermetro Indus., 288 F. Supp. 2d 876, 2003 U.S. Dist. LEXIS 19151 (N.D. Ohio 2003).

Non-supervisory employees are not subject to liability under R.C. Chapter 4112. There are subject to liability under § 1981. Appellant's inability to work cooperatively within a group medical practice constituted a legitimate nondiscriminatory reason for not renewing her contracts. Any rudeness by the staff or other annoyances did not rise to the level of adverse employment actions: Samadder v. DMF of Ohio, Inc., 2003-Ohio-5340, 154 Ohio App. 3d 770, 798 N.E.2d 1141, 2003 Ohio App. LEXIS 4798 (Ohio Ct. App., Franklin County 2003).

Ohio's requirements for civil rights claims such as those under R.C. 4112.02 and R.C. 4112.99 are the same as those of Title VII of the Civil Rights Act of 1964, 42 U.S.C.S. § 2000e — 2000e-17. Carter v. Univ. of Toledo, 349 F.3d 269, 2003 FED App. 0401P, 2003 U.S. App. LEXIS 23054 (6th Cir. Ohio 2003).

Federal case law interpreting Title VII of the Civil Rights Act of 1964, 42 U.S.C.S. § 2000e et seq., is applicable to cases involving R.C. 4112. Schwab v. Delphi Packard Elec. Sys., 2003-Ohio-4868, 2003 Ohio App. LEXIS 4387 (Ohio Ct. App., Trumbull County 2003).

To establish a prima facie case under R.C. 4112.02, an employee must meet essentially the same requirements of a prima facie case under Title VII of the Civil Rights Act of 1964, 42 U.S.C.S. §§ 2000e to 2000e-17. Gettings v. Bldg. Laborers Local 310 Fringe Bens. Fund, 349 F.3d 300, 2003 FED App. 0402P, 2003 U.S. App. LEXIS 23120 (6th Cir. Ohio 2003).

The employer did not present evidence that tied the employee's confrontational style to the decision to terminate her. The employer did not establish a legitimate, nondiscriminatory reason for termination that would entitle it to summary judgment: Blanton v. Cuyahoga County Bd.of Elections, 2002-Ohio-6044, 150 Ohio App. 3d 61, 779 N.E.2d 788, 2002 Ohio App. LEXIS 5867 (Ohio Ct. App., Cuyahoga County 2002).

Court of Claims properly denied an employee's claim that she was the victim of racial and handicap discrimination due to her employer's termination of her employment, where it was found that the employee was terminated due to her failure to cooperate with a disciplinary investigation; the court found no evidence of a racial animus on the part of the employer when it instituted disciplinary action against her and she accordingly failed to meet her burden of showing a prima facie case of discrimination indirectly, nor did she show that the employer considered her unable to carry out her daily duties especially in light of the results of a psychological examination which indicated that she was capable of performing her job. Peters v. Ohio Dep't of Natural Res., 2003-Ohio-5895, 2003 Ohio App. LEXIS 5239 (Ohio Ct. App., Franklin County 2003).

Discharged employee did not establish racial or religious discrimination where no other employee engaged in comparable misuse of the employer's computer and telephone systems: Obu v. Ohio Dep't of the Aging, 2002-Ohio-4141, 119 Ohio Misc. 2d 131, 774 N.E.2d 812, 2002 Ohio Misc. LEXIS 24 (Ohio Ct. Cl. 2002).

In determining whether a defendant's conduct is sufficiently extreme and outrageous, a factfinder may consider the context or environment in which the acts occur. The factfinder may also consider the plaintiff's role in creating or participating in that environment: Strausbaugh v. Ohio DOT, 2002-Ohio-6627, 150 Ohio App. 3d 438, 782 N.E.2d 92, 2002 Ohio App. LEXIS 6433 (Ohio Ct. App., Franklin County 2002).

An employee did not show age or gender discrimination where his position was eliminated as part of a reduction in force: Whitt v. Lockheed Martin Util. Servs., 209 F. Supp. 2d 787, 2002 U.S. Dist. LEXIS 18280 (S.D. Ohio 2002).

The intermediate level supervisors who allegedly made discriminatory remarks were "meaningfully involved" in the termination decision. In mixed motive cases where a defendant asserts an alternative justification for its employment decision or conduct, that justification becomes an affirmative defense: Williams v. United Dairy Farmers, 20 F. Supp. 2d 1193, 1998 U.S. Dist. LEXIS 14671 (S.D. Ohio 1998).

The plaintiff failed to show that his firing was unlawful under R.C. 4112.02(I) where he was fired for helping a deadbeat customer to re-acquire cable services by applying under a false name; prohibiting the fraudulent acquisition of cable services by deadbeat customers was not equivalent to denying female customers credit because of their sex or marital status: Williams v. Time Warner Cable, 1998 Ohio App. LEXIS 2793 (Ohio Ct. App., Summit County June 24, 1998).

Admonishing an employee for frequent tardiness and absenteeism and for wasting supplies and making costly mistakes does not constitute sexual or racial harassment: Bell v. Cuyahoga Community College, 129 Ohio App. 3d 461, 717 N.E.2d 1189, 1998 Ohio App. LEXIS 3741 (Ohio Ct. App., Cuyahoga County 1998).

Stray remarks in the workplace when unrelated to the decision-making process are insufficient to establish a prima facie case of discrimination: Brewer v. Cleveland City Schs.Bd. of Educ., 122 Ohio App. 3d 378, 701 N.E.2d 1023, 1997 Ohio App. LEXIS 3008 (Ohio 1997).

A cause of action exists for plaintiffs who can show discrimination based on sex and age: Myers v. Goodwill Indus., 122 Ohio App. 3d 294, 701 N.E.2d 738, 1997 Ohio App. LEXIS 3475 (Ohio Ct. App., Summit County 1997).

There was sufficient evidence that the employee was denied compensation and benefits that were given to similarly situated male employees. The fact that an employee remains on the job for a considerable time after the discrimination does not preclude a claim of constructive discharge. Front pay is appropriate to the extent that new employment does not make the employee whole: Sutherland v. Nationwide Gen. Ins. Co., 96 Ohio App. 3d 793, 645 N.E.2d 1338, 1994 Ohio App. LEXIS 4834 (Ohio Ct. App., Franklin County 1994).

Summary judgment for the employer was proper where it articulated legitimate, nondiscriminatory reasons for not renewing the employee and the employee did not produce substantial evidence to support the claims of gender, age and religious discrimination: Doerter v. Bluffton College, 98 Ohio App. 3d 95, 647 N.E.2d 876, 1994 Ohio App. LEXIS 5661 (Ohio Ct. App., Allen County 1994).

The McDonnell Douglas/Burdine formula is the evidentiary framework applicable to claims brought under Title VII, but also to claims of discrimination under Ohio state law: Mitchell v. Toledo Hosp., 964 F.2d 577, 1992 U.S. App. LEXIS 11505 (6th Cir. Ohio 1992).

To establish a prima facie case of discrimination, plaintiff must prove by a preponderance that she applied for an available position for which she was qualified, but was rejected under circumstances which give rise to an inference of unlawful discrimination: Mercy Hosp. Assn. v. Ohio Civ. Rights Comm., 65 Ohio App. 3d 613, 584 N.E.2d 1287 (1989).

**Adverse employment action**

Plaintiff, who alleged discrimination based upon race and national origin, had not shown that he was constructively discharged, and thus had not established an adverse employment action, as a claim that he was referred to as "Tony the African" was not substantiated, and although plaintiff believed that he was disciplined more harshly than others, defendant followed the progressive discipline grid when it issued corrective action; furthermore, he had not produced sufficient evidence that defendant intentionally discriminated against him. Moody v. Ohio Dep't of Mental Health & Addiction Servs., 2021-Ohio-1525, 2021 Ohio Misc. LEXIS 31 (Ohio Ct. Cl. 2021).

With respect to plaintiff's claim of disability discrimination, she pointed to no evidence suggesting that she was subjected to any materially adverse consequences due to defendant having merely initiated the involuntary disability separation process where, after plaintiff received the notice from defendant, she obtained a certification from her podiatrist that she was fit for duty and she returned to work, whereupon the involuntary disability separation process ended without the need for a hearing. That being the case, the notice issued to plaintiff did not rise to the level of an adverse employment action. Blashak v. Ohio Dep't of Youth Servs., 2019-Ohio-509, 2019 Ohio Misc. LEXIS 11 (Ohio Ct. Cl. 2019).

With respect to plaintiff's claim of disability discrimination, denying her request for vacation leave in lieu of sick leave was not an adverse employment action, as it did not represent a denial or material change of plaintiff's benefits. Blashak v. Ohio Dep't of Youth Servs., 2019-Ohio-509, 2019 Ohio Misc. LEXIS 11 (Ohio Ct. Cl. 2019).

With respect to plaintiff's claim of disability discrimination, her placement on desk duty pending defendant's investigation into a complaint about her was not an adverse employment action, as plaintiff did not identify evidence showing that this involved any financial or other materially adverse consequences. Blashak v. Ohio Dep't of Youth Servs., 2019-Ohio-509, 2019 Ohio Misc. LEXIS 11 (Ohio Ct. Cl. 2019).

University was entitled to summary judgment on a professor's retaliation claim because her "appeal" letter to the university president did not oppose or identify any unlawful or discriminatory practice, and she failed to show a causal connection between the review of her grant management and her letter. Min You v. Northeast Ohio Med. Univ., 2017-Ohio-4461, 2017 Ohio Misc. LEXIS 1787 (Ohio Ct. Cl. 2017).

With respect to plaintiff's claim of disability discrimination, a written reprimand she received for being late to a training session was not an adverse employment action, as it was ultimately removed from her personnel file after she filed a grievance through her union, and there was no evidence that it caused plaintiff to lose any pay or endure any other materially adverse consequence. State v. Smith, 2016-Ohio-8043, 2016 Ohio App. LEXIS 4919 (Ohio Ct. App., Cuyahoga County 2016).

While a demotion itself could also be an adverse employment action for purposes of R.C. Chapter 4112, the Ohio Department of Rehabilitation and Correction (ODRC) presented evidence that the employee was demoted for just cause, and the employee submitted no Civ.R. 56(C) evidence to contest ODRC's evidence. Thus, the employee had not shown that ODRC took adverse employment action in part because of the employee's disability. Hardgrow v. Dep't of Rehab. & Corr., 2012-Ohio-2731, 2012 Ohio App. LEXIS 2407 (Ohio Ct. App., Franklin County 2012).

In an action in which plaintiff, a former union secretary, alleged that defendant union violated R.C. 4112.02 and 42 U.S.C.S. § 2000e-3(a) by retaliating against her for filing a discrimination lawsuit, defendant was not entitled to summary judgment because there were genuine disputes as to whether defendant's conversion counterclaim was filed in bad faith, whether defendant invited union members to verbally attack plaintiff, and whether defendant's alleged conduct rose to the level of adverse action. Kendel v. Local 17-A UFCW, 835 F. Supp. 2d 421, 2011 U.S. Dist. LEXIS 139466 (N.D. Ohio 2011).

There was no error in the trial court's conclusion that the employee failed to demonstrate a prima facie case for discrimination under R.C. 4112.02, the Americans with Disabilities Act of 1990 (ADA), and the Rehabilitation Act of 1973 because the employee was unable to show that an adverse employment action occurred or that she was constructively discharged. There was no evidence that her tense professional relationships made her work conditions so intolerable that a reasonable person would have felt compelled to resign. Taylor v. Ohio Dep't of Job & Family Servs., 2011-Ohio-6060, 2011 Ohio App. LEXIS 4931 (Ohio Ct. App., Franklin County 2011).

Denial of a 64-year-old firefighter's request for a lateral transfer into a position with increased prestige but no increased benefits or pay could constitute an adverse employment action. Campolieti v. City of Cleveland, 2009-Ohio-5224, 184 Ohio App. 3d 419, 921 N.E.2d 286, 2009 Ohio App. LEXIS 4417 (Ohio Ct. App., Cuyahoga County 2009).

Grant of summary judgment to an employer was proper in an employee's action, alleging claims of, inter alia, racial discrimination in violation of R.C. 4112.02, as most of the complained-of actions by the employee were not adverse employment actions, and the denial of a pay raise to him was based on his poor performance rating, whereas a fellow employee who did get a raise had a better rating; there was no evidence to support the employee's claim of racial discrimination. Canady v. Rekau & Rekau, Inc., 2009-Ohio-4974, 2009 Ohio App. LEXIS 4211 (Ohio Ct. App., Franklin County 2009).

Denial of a transfer into a position of increased prestige, at least in the eyes of some employees, could constitute an adverse employment action even though the new position would not have entitled the employee to greater pay, benefits, or rank: Campolieti v. City of Cleveland, 2009-Ohio-5224, 184 Ohio App. 3d 419, 921 N.E.2d 286, 2009 Ohio App. LEXIS 4417 (Ohio Ct. App., Cuyahoga County 2009).

Employee did not meet the burden of showing a prima facie case of race discrimination under R.C. 4112.02(A) where the denial of overtime without prior approval was not an adverse employment action because there was no proof that the employee was actually denied such overtime; further, although the employee was disciplined regarding time-clock usage, there was no showing of how the employee was adversely affected thereby. Valentine v. Westshore Primary Care Assoc., 2008-Ohio-4450, 2008 Ohio App. LEXIS 3756 (Ohio Ct. App., Cuyahoga County 2008).

Employee failed to present evidence sufficient to establish her claim of disability discrimination as there was no evidence to show that the employer took an adverse treatment because the employee was disabled. Though the employee argued that the adverse employment action taken by the employer was the failure to rehire the employee after an indefinite leave, the employer was not required to hold her position open on an indefinite basis until after the employee returned from her treatment for esophageal cancer, and there was no evidence to support the employee's argument that a position was guaranteed to the employee upon her return. Hammercheck v. Coldwell Banker First Place Real Estate, 2007-Ohio-7127, 2007 Ohio App. LEXIS 6232 (Ohio Ct. App., Trumbull County 2007).

District court found that an employee failed to state a claim for relief under 29 U.S.C.S. § 185 when he filed a hybrid claim against a union and a corporation, alleging that the union and its representatives breached their duty of fair representation, and that the corporation and its representative breached a collective bargaining agreement, when they negotiated an agreement which allowed the corporation to remove a reprimand from his file in exchange for an admission that he acted inappropriately when he used the term "Jew Boy" while talking about a fellow employee. The court also found that the employee did not state a valid claim alleging a violation of R.C. 4112.02 when he claimed he was the victim of discrimination, and that the facts did not show that union representatives or the corporation's representative committed intentional infliction of emotional distress. Courie v. Alcoa Wheel & Forged Prods., 2007 U.S. Dist. LEXIS 90460 (N.D. Ohio Oct. 31, 2007), aff'd, 577 F.3d 625, 2009 FED App. 0295P, 2009 U.S. App. LEXIS 18561 (6th Cir. Ohio 2009).

When an employee alleged that the employee was the victim of racial discrimination when the employee was placed on involuntary disability separation, the employee did not demonstrate a prima facie case of employment discrimination, even though the employee was a member of a protected class and qualified for the employee's job, because it was arguable that the involuntary disability separation was not an adverse employment action. Carter v. Dep't of Rehab. & Corr., 2007-Ohio-3872, 2007 Ohio Misc. LEXIS 250 (Ohio Ct. Cl. 2007).

Trial court's grant of summary judgment to an employer in an employee's racial discrimination claim under R.C. 4112.02(A) of the Ohio Fair Employment Practices Act was proper, as the employee failed to show that she was subject to an adverse employment action for purposes of her prima facie disparate treatment claim; her claim that she was denied benefits granted to Caucasians failed because she ultimately received the benefits, and any temporary inconveniences did not cause a materially adverse change in the terms and conditions of employment. Brown v. Dover Corp., 2007-Ohio-2128, 2007 Ohio App. LEXIS 2010 (Ohio Ct. App., Hamilton County 2007).

When an employee alleged that the employee was the victim of racial discrimination when the employee was placed on involuntary disability separation, the employee did not demonstrate a prima facie case of employment discrimination, even though the employee was a member of a protected class and qualified for the employee's job, because it was arguable that the involuntary disability separation was not an adverse employment action. Carter v. Dep't of Rehab. & Corr., 2007-Ohio-3872, 2007 Ohio Misc. LEXIS 250 (Ohio Ct. Cl. 2007).

Former employee could not maintain an age discrimination case under R.C. 4412.02 and 4112.99, which claims were scrutinized under the same standard as claims under the Age Discrimination in Employment Act, because he did not present circumstantial or direct evidence of discrimination; statements made by co-workers did not constitute direct evidence as co-workers were not decision-makers with regard to the employee's job, and the employee did not establish an adverse employment decision. Because of the failure to establish an adverse employment decision, the employee's retaliation claim under R.C. 4112.02(I) and public policy violation claim also failed. Zivkovic v. Juniper Networks, Inc., 450 F. Supp. 2d 815, 2006 U.S. Dist. LEXIS 63785 (N.D. Ohio 2006).

Teacher claiming that he experienced an adverse employment action due to constructive discharge, because he was referred to an intervention program to improve his performance, did not support his claim because it was not reasonable for him to feel compelled to resign, under these circumstances, as the school district's actions did not indicate that his termination was imminent, as the referral explained in detail the areas in which the teacher needed to improve, which could have been helpful to him in the coming school year. Farris v. Port Clinton City Sch. Dist., 2006-Ohio-1864, 2006 Ohio App. LEXIS 1701 (Ohio Ct. App., Ottawa County 2006).

Teacher claiming that he experienced an adverse employment action due to constructive discharge, because of racial slurs from students, did not support his claim because he did not show that a reasonable person in his position would have felt compelled to resign. Farris v. Port Clinton City Sch. Dist., 2006-Ohio-1864, 2006 Ohio App. LEXIS 1701 (Ohio Ct. App., Ottawa County 2006).

Teacher claiming that he experienced an adverse employment action due to constructive discharge, because he was not hired for certain coaching jobs, did not support his claim because he was hired, during the course of his employment, for 25 coaching jobs, six of which he resigned from, and his primary employment was as a teacher, as to which he experienced no adverse employment action. Farris v. Port Clinton City Sch. Dist., 2006-Ohio-1864, 2006 Ohio App. LEXIS 1701 (Ohio Ct. App., Ottawa County 2006).

Summary judgment was properly granted, dismissing a Caucasian employee's racial discrimination claim brought under R.C. 4112.02 against her African-American supervisor and the city which employed her, because the employee was unable to demonstrate any adverse action, in that, while the supervisor submitted a negative appraisal of the employee's job performance, the appraisal did not affect the terms or conditions of her employment. While termination of the employee's probationary employment was initially recommended, the request was later rescinded, and the employee's employment continued. Mowery v. City of Columbus, 2006-Ohio-1153, 2006 Ohio App. LEXIS 1051 (Ohio Ct. App., Franklin County 2006).

Grant of summary judgment to county defendants in a racial discrimination action by a county employee, based on "adverse employment action," was proper, as the employee did not establish a prima facie case of discrimination as to one position which was awarded to a member of the same protected class as the employee, and as to another position, the employee was not qualified because he lacked the requisite licensure. Rice v. Cuyahoga County DOJ, 2005-Ohio-5337, 970 N.E.2d 470, 2005 Ohio App. LEXIS 4848 (Ohio Ct. App., Cuyahoga County 2005).

Employer's refusal to assign an employee to a position in its apprenticeship office, because she had filed a charge of discrimination, constituted an adverse employment action and, thus, retaliation in violation of the Americans with Disabilities Act, 42 U.S.C.S. § 12101 et seq., and R.C. ch. 4112; accordingly, the employer's motion for summary judgment as it related to the employee's claims of retaliation was overruled. Benge v. GMC, 267 F. Supp. 2d 794, 2003 U.S. Dist. LEXIS 10353 (S.D. Ohio 2003).

An employee did not show that she suffered an adverse employment action where her sales territory reassignment meant she had to spend more time in an adjacent state, but did not involve any other negative aspects: Policastro v. Northwest Airlines, Inc., 297 F.3d 535, 2002 FED App. 0254P, 2002 U.S. App. LEXIS 15116 (6th Cir. Ohio 2002).

**Age discrimination**

In a case of age discrimination claim, summary judgment was granted in favor of employer because there was no genuine issue of material fact that employee was replaced by someone substantially younger than her since there was no evidence to support her theory regarding replacement. She provided no evidence contradicting employer's indication that the costs associated with the in-house position outweighed its benefits. Cunningham v. Perry & Assocs., 2021-Ohio-4295, 2021 Ohio App. LEXIS 4230 (Ohio Ct. App., Belmont County 2021).

*Unpublished decision:* Employee had not demonstrated that genuine issues of material fact existed sufficient to support a finding that age was the "but-for" cause of her termination where the employee had not pointed to anything so irregular in the employment history scoring that it would give rise to an inference of discrimination. Lopez v. Am. Family Ins. Co., 618 Fed. Appx. 794, 2015 FED App. 0474N, 2015 U.S. App. LEXIS 11020 (6th Cir. Ohio 2015).

*Unpublished decision:* Where an employee was terminated for inappropriately submitting leads, his age discrimination claims under the ADEA and Ohio law failed because, inter alia, circumstantial evidence regarding perceived social slights and his performance did not suggest that his age was the "but-for" cause of his termination; contract and defamation claims failed. Green v. Fid. Invs., 374 Fed. Appx. 573, 2010 FED App. 0158N, 2010 U.S. App. LEXIS 5318 (6th Cir. Ohio), cert. denied, 562 U.S. 1044, 131 S. Ct. 598, 178 L. Ed. 2d 435, 2010 U.S. LEXIS 8874 (U.S. 2010).

*Unpublished decision:* Where an employee was terminated for violating cash handling rules, the employee's age discrimination claims failed because the employee was unable to show that the employee was replaced by a younger worker or that a similarly situated employee was treated more favorably; misappropriation of funds and marrying alcohol were different circumstances involving distinguishable conduct. Balding-Margolis v. Cleveland Arcade, 352 Fed. Appx. 35, 2009 FED App. 0732N, 2009 U.S. App. LEXIS 24604 (6th Cir. Ohio 2009).

In an age discrimination and retaliation action brought by a graduate student, the university was entitled to summary judgment because the adverse decision to, inter alia, change his grade on an exam from pass to fail related to his studies and not conditions of employment as a teaching assistant. The retaliation claim failed because the claim of protected conduct related exclusively to discriminatory practices in the academic setting that had only a tangential effect on his status as an employee. Grubach v. Univ. of Akron, 2020-Ohio-3467, 2020 Ohio App. LEXIS 2411 (Ohio Ct. App., Franklin County 2020).

When a search committee chairman's discriminatory remarks were combined with appellant's evidence regarding his qualifications for a university instructor position relative to another candidate, a reasonable trier of fact could conclude that the university's proffered reasons for denying him the position were merely pretextual and that the true reason was his age. Ceglia v. Youngstown State Univ., 2015-Ohio-2125, 38 N.E.3d 1222, 2015 Ohio App. LEXIS 2045 (Ohio Ct. App., Franklin County 2015).

Court of Claims erred in granting summary judgment to a university in a part-time instructor's age discrimination claim because the search committee chairman's comments that the committee, in seeking a full-time instructor, was focused on "mid-career" candidates who had not "been around a long time" permitted an inference that age was a motivating factor and the instructor produced evidence that he was as qualified for the position if not more qualified than the much younger successful applicant. Ceglia v. Youngstown State Univ., 2015-Ohio-2125, 38 N.E.3d 1222, 2015 Ohio App. LEXIS 2045 (Ohio Ct. App., Franklin County 2015).

With respect to plaintiff patrolman's claim that he was precluded from returning to work prior to receiving multiple fitness for duty evaluations, defendants, a city, a police department, and a police chief, were not entitled to summary judgment on age discrimination claims brought under the Age Discrimination in Employment Act of 1967, 29 U.S.C.S. § 623(a), and R.C. 4112.02 because defendants did not provide a legitimate, non-discriminatory reason for why a similarly situated, non-protected employee was subject to less stringent standards for returning to work after taking medical leave. Hodges v. City of Milford, 918 F. Supp. 2d 721, 2013 U.S. Dist. LEXIS 7779 (S.D. Ohio 2013).

Pursuant to R.C. 4112.02(A), the employee failed to establish her age discrimination claim by the direct method of proof because her own deposition testimony established that the hiring manager did not inquire about her age or retirement intentions until after she made the decision to hire the other candidate. Dautartas v. Abbott Labs., 2012-Ohio-1709, 2012 Ohio App. LEXIS 1495 (Ohio Ct. App., Franklin County 2012).

Former employee's R.C. 4112.02(A) complaint, which alleged that the employer repeatedly and relentlessly badgered the employee to retire, contained sufficient factual matter to state a claim to relief consistent with Fed. R. Civ. P. 8(a) because, so long as the employee could come forward with evidence that the employer used "retirement" as a proxy for "age," the retirement-related comments could plausibly support a claim of age discrimination based on direct evidence. Franks v. Vill. of Bolivar, 2011 U.S. Dist. LEXIS 133740 (N.D. Ohio Nov. 18, 2011).

Trial court erred by dismissing a former employee's age discrimination claim under R.C. 4112.02(A) and 4112.14(A) for failure to state a claim under Civ. R. 12(B)(6) because the court improperly required the employee to plead age was the "but-for" cause of the employee's termination. Morrissette v. DFS Servs., LLC, 2011-Ohio-2369, 2011 Ohio App. LEXIS 2023 (Ohio Ct. App., Franklin County 2011).

In a disparate impact discrimination case, a city was not entitled to a new trial on the ground that claims under both R.C. 4112.14 and R.C. 4112.02 should not have been presented to the jury because, although the statutes required plaintiffs to select under which statute an age discrimination claim would be pursued, the proofs of disparate impact under both statutes were substantially the same. Howe v. City of Akron, 789 F. Supp. 2d 786, 2010 U.S. Dist. LEXIS 137344 (N.D. Ohio 2010).

Employee did not establish a prima facie case of age discrimination because he presented no evidence that the employer's reason for the transfer was pretextual and did not demonstrate a genuine issue of material fact regarding the employer's legitimate, non-discriminatory reasons for promoting younger employees. The employee did not show that his termination was a pretext for impermissible age discrimination. Horsley v. Burton, 2010-Ohio-6315, 2010 Ohio App. LEXIS 5277 (Ohio Ct. App., Scioto County 2010).

Where an employee was terminated for inappropriately submitting leads, his age discrimination claims under the ADEA and Ohio law failed because, inter alia, circumstantial evidence regarding perceived social slights and his performance did not suggest that his age was the "but-for" cause of his termination; contract and defamation claims failed. Green v. Fid. Invs., 374 Fed. Appx. 573, 2010 FED App. 0158N, 2010 U.S. App. LEXIS 5318 (6th Cir. Ohio), cert. denied, 562 U.S. 1044, 131 S. Ct. 598, 178 L. Ed. 2d 435, 2010 U.S. LEXIS 8874 (U.S. 2010).

Trial court erred in dismissing on summary judgment an employee's age discrimination claim under R.C. 4112.02(A) as the testimony of the employee, to the effect that his manager harassed and humiliated him with comments relating to the employee's advanced age, created a genuine issue of material fact as to whether the employer harassed and humiliated the employee on account of his age, creating a hostile work environment and causing the employee's constructive discharge from his employment. Hidy Motors, Inc. v. Sheaffer, 2009-Ohio-3763, 183 Ohio App. 3d 316, 916 N.E.2d 1122, 2009 Ohio App. LEXIS 3210 (Ohio Ct. App., Greene County 2009).

Employer was not entitled to summary judgment on a claim of age-related harassment where the employee provided evidence of alleged abusive and humiliating language by the employer: Hidy Motors, Inc. v. Sheaffer, 2009-Ohio-3763, 183 Ohio App. 3d 316, 916 N.E.2d 1122, 2009 Ohio App. LEXIS 3210 (Ohio Ct. App., Greene County 2009).

Age discrimination claim brought pursuant to R.C. 4112.99 is subject to the substantive provisions of R.C. 4112.02 and 4112.14. Pursuant to R.C. 4112.14(C), when the discharge of an employee has been arbitrated and the discharge has been found to be for just cause, the discharged employee is barred from pursuing an action for age discrimination: Meyer v. UPS, 2009-Ohio-2463, 122 Ohio St. 3d 104, 909 N.E.2d 106, 2009 Ohio LEXIS 1598 (Ohio 2009).

In an appeal by a state university from an order of the Ohio Civil Rights Commission, finding that the university engaged in intentional age discrimination in violation of R.C. 4112.02(A) when it declined to grant an assistant professor's application for promotion and tenure, the trial court applied the proper standard of review under R.C. 4112.06(E) where it reviewed the record evidence and determined that the Commission drew improper inferences therefrom; the trial court reviewed the matter to determine whether there was reliable, probative, and substantial evidence under § 4112.06(E) to support the Commission's decision. Ohio Univ. v. Ohio Civ. Rights Comm'n, 2008-Ohio-1034, 175 Ohio App. 3d 414, 887 N.E.2d 403, 2008 Ohio App. LEXIS 888 (Ohio Ct. App., Athens County 2008).

Court granted summary judgment in favor of an insurance company in an insurance agent's allegation that the company had discriminated against him based on age when it terminated his employment; the court had found that the agent was an independent contractor, and not an employee, and therefore was not covered under R.C. 4112.02(A). Averill v. Gleaner Life Ins. Soc'y, 2008 U.S. Dist. LEXIS 10073 (N.D. Ohio Jan. 29, 2008).

There was no age discrimination because the employer, the Adult Parole Authority, provided articulated a legitimate, nondiscriminatory reason for the parole officers' rejection for a promotion in favor of a younger, female employee who was qualified for the position. The older employee's failure to complete the Ohio Civil Service Application was a legitimate, nondiscriminatory reason why for he was not offered an interview; although the officer testified that he submitted a resume with his application to serve as his required "criteria sheet," the application packet did not reflect that a resume was submitted. Bogdas v. Ohio Dep't of Rehab. & Corr., 2008-Ohio-3409, 2008 Ohio Misc. LEXIS 113 (Ohio Ct. Cl. 2008).

In a former employee's claim of age discrimination in violation of R.C. 4112.02(A), 4112.99 the trial court erred in granting summary judgment in favor of the former employer and two employees, as there was sufficient evidence from which reasonable minds could disbelieve the proffered reason for removing the former employee from the former employee's position as managing director; all evidence suggested the former employee was successfully performing in that position. Coryell v. Bank One Trust Co., N.A., 2008-Ohio-2698, 2008 Ohio App. LEXIS 2323 (Ohio Ct. App., Franklin County 2008).

Employee's age discrimination suit under R.C. 4112.99 was properly dismissed on summary judgment as the 51-year-old employee could not show that the reasons proffered by the employer for hiring a 21-year-old individual, not the employee, were pretextual. he younger individual was hired because she had more recent relevant business experience and because the younger individual viewed the position with long-term interest, while the employee indicated that she was interested in using the job as a stepping stone for a better accounting position. Dabney-Hall v. Cleveland Clinic Found., 2008-Ohio-1080, 2008 Ohio App. LEXIS 945 (Ohio Ct. App., Cuyahoga County 2008).

Where it was determined that an employer laid off all the hourly employees at its plant pursuant to a reduction-in-force provision contained in the collective bargaining agreement, the employees had to offer evidence that indicated they were singled out based on their age, which the workers were not able to accomplish under the Age Discrimination in Employment Act, 29 U.S.C.S. § 623 or R.C. 4112.02. Campbell v. PMI Food Equip.

Group, Inc., 509 F.3d 776, 2007 FED App. 0484P, 2007 U.S. App. LEXIS 28889 (6th Cir. Ohio 2007).

Employee's age discrimination claim was properly dismissed because the employee failed to demonstrate that he was replaced by, or that the employer retained, a person of substantially younger age as a result of the employee's discharge. While the employee presented evidence that showed that two substantially younger drivers had accidents but, unlike him, were not discharged, there was no evidence indicating that these two younger drivers took over the employee's route or that the employee's discharge allowed the younger men to remain drivers. Murphy v. Penske Logistics, 2007-Ohio-6407, 2007 Ohio App. LEXIS 5612 (Ohio Ct. App., Geauga County 2007).

Terminated employee's claim for age discrimination was dismissed, because she was only 32 years old when she was discharged and thus was not a member of a statutorily protected class under R.C. 4112.02. Huisjack v. Medco Health Solutions, Inc., 496 F. Supp. 2d 859, 2007 U.S. Dist. LEXIS 47833 (S.D. Ohio 2007).

Employee's age discrimination claim under R.C. 4112.02 was subject to summary judgment because while the employee established a prima facie case as his former client's account was given to a 35 year old, the employer established that ongoing service problems created a perception that the employee, who had ultimate responsibility for the account, was ineffective; no pretext was shown as the client had asked for a change on the account, although not specifically that the employee be removed. Walter v. ADT Sec. Sys., 2007-Ohio-3324, 2007 Ohio App. LEXIS 3051 (Ohio Ct. App., Franklin County 2007).

Common law tort claim for wrongful discharge based on Ohio's public policy against age discrimination does not exist, because the remedies in R.C. Chapter 4112 provide complete relief for a statutory claim for age discrimination: Leininger v. Pioneer Nat'l Latex, 2007-Ohio-4921, 115 Ohio St. 3d 311, 875 N.E.2d 36, 2007 Ohio LEXIS 2229 (Ohio 2007).

When the employee filed her age discrimination claim in federal court, she clearly elected to pursue the remedies available under R.C. 4112.14. Once the employee instituted her federal suit, she could not seek administrative remedies. That did not change merely because the federal action was voluntarily dismissed. Employee's dismissal was not a pretext for age discrimination where undisputed evidence showed that her behavior had been a consistent distraction in the workplace and the employer had tried resolving the issue in different ways to no avail: Dunn v. Bruzzese, 2007-Ohio-3500, 172 Ohio App. 3d 320, 874 N.E.2d 1221, 2007 Ohio App. LEXIS 3222 (Ohio Ct. App., Jefferson County 2007).

Employee's age discrimination claim under R.C. 4112.02 was subject to summary judgment because while the employee established a prima facie case as his former client's account was given to a 35 year old, the employer established that ongoing service problems created a perception that the employee, who had ultimate responsibility for the account, was ineffective. No pretext was shown as the client had asked for a change on the account, although not specifically that the employee be removed. Walter v. ADT Sec. Sys., 2007-Ohio-3324, 2007 Ohio App. LEXIS 3051 (Ohio Ct. App., Franklin County 2007).

State employee failed to prove by a preponderance of the evidence that he was the victim of age discrimination, in violation of R.C. 4112.02(A), where he failed to show that he was replaced by a substantially younger person, he failed to assert that any statements regarding his age were ever directed at him or mentioned in his presence, and even assuming that he presented his prima facie case, he did not successfully show that the reasons put forth by the employer for the termination were a mere pretext for discrimination. Swoger v. Wright State Univ., 2007-Ohio-2751, 2007 Ohio Misc. LEXIS 184 (Ohio Ct. Cl. 2007).

Trial court properly granted summary judgment to an employer and two supervisors in a former employee's age discrimination claim pursuant to R.C. 4112.02, as the employer was involved in a reduction in force due to a customer's decision to change its policy of outsourcing a great deal of work to the employer to a policy of insourcing that work. The employee failed to show a genuine issue of material fact existed as to whether the employer and supervisors' proffered non-discriminatory reasons for his termination were a pretext for age discrimination where he was terminated and another person in his position was retained. Kundtz v. AT&T Solutions, Inc., 2007-Ohio-1462, 2007 Ohio App. LEXIS 1318 (Ohio Ct. App., Franklin County 2007).

In an employment discrimination action, an employer's motion for partial judgment on the pleadings was granted because the employee's R.C. 4112.02(A), (N) claim was barred by R.C. 4112.08 due to his filing of a complaint with the Ohio Civil Rights Commission (OCRC) under R.C. 4112.05(B)(1); the pleadings and attached exhibits were devoid of any indication that the employee preserved his rights in a separate writing filed along with the OCR.C. charge, and the employee had not otherwise indicated that such a writing existed. Further, the action was time-barred pursuant to R.C. 4112.02(N) because he filed it more than a year after he resigned his employment, which was outside of the 180-day statutory requirement. Huston v. Mittal Steel USA, 2006 U.S. Dist. LEXIS 67323 (S.D. Ohio Sept. 20, 2006).

District court was bound by the United States Court of Appeals for the Sixth Circuit's holding in Carrasco and agreed with other courts in the Sixth Circuit that the broad scope of remedies that were available under R.C. ch. 4112 was sufficient to vindicate Ohio's public policy against age discrimination and thus foreclosed a separate cause of action for violation of public policy. Rusnak v. Dollar Gen. Corp., 2006 U.S. Dist. LEXIS 67319 (S.D. Ohio Sept. 20, 2006).

Former employee who was over 40 could not succeed on his action against his former employer under the Age Discrimination in Employment Act, 29 U.S.C.S. §§ 623, 631, R.C. 4112.02, 4112.99, and Ohio public policy because the employer showed a legitimate nondiscriminatory reason for the employee's termination; the employer had hired the employee to increase its sales, and the employee had not increased sales. Shiffman v. Thermal Indus., Inc., 2006 U.S. Dist. LEXIS 64351 (S.D. Ohio Sept. 8, 2006).

In order to establish a prima facie case of age discrimination in an employment discharge action, an employee had to demonstrate (1) that he or she was a member of the statutorily protected class, (2) that he or she was discharged, (3) that he or she was qualified for the position, and (4) that he or she was replaced by, or that the discharge permitted the retention of, a person not belonging to the protected class. Burrows v. Licking County, 2006-Ohio-4057, 2006 Ohio App. LEXIS 4029 (Ohio Ct. App., Licking County 2006).

Employee did not show his termination was the result of age discrimination, in violation of R.C. 4112.02, because, even though he was age 60 when he was hired, and was thus a member of a protected class, the evidence showed his termination was based on the employer's belief that the employee was intoxicated on the job, rather than on the employee's age. Burrows v. Licking County, 2006-Ohio-4057, 2006 Ohio App. LEXIS 4029 (Ohio Ct. App., Licking County 2006).

Employer's reasons for discharging the plaintiff were not a pretext for age discrimination where the employer believed that it would eliminate costs in the division and jump start the sales department: Chandler v. Dunn Hardware, Inc., 2006-Ohio-4376, 168 Ohio App. 3d 496, 860 N.E.2d 1042, 2006 Ohio App. LEXIS 4293 (Ohio Ct. App., Cuyahoga County 2006).

Plaintiff did not establish indirect evidence of age discrimination where he was not replaced. Age-related comments that are isolated, vague, or ambiguous, or that refer to other employees, cannot support a finding of age discrimination: Abrams v. Am. Computer Tech., 2006-Ohio-4032, 168 Ohio App. 3d 362, 860 N.E.2d 123, 2006 Ohio App. LEXIS 3973 (Ohio Ct. App., Hamilton County 2006).

District court was bound by the United States Court of Appeals for the Sixth Circuit's holding in Carrasco and agreed with other courts in the Sixth Circuit that the broad scope of remedies that were available under R.C. ch. 4112 was sufficient to vindicate Ohio's public policy against age discrimination and thus foreclosed a separate cause of action for violation of public policy. Rusnak v. Dollar Gen. Corp., 2006 U.S. Dist. LEXIS 67319 (S.D. Ohio Sept. 20, 2006).

Former employee who was over 40 could not succeed on his action against his former employer under the Age Discrimination in Employment Act, 29 U.S.C.S. §§ 623, 631, R.C. 4112.02, 4112.99, and Ohio public policy because the employer showed a legitimate non-discriminatory reason for the employee's termination. The employer had hired the employee to increase its sales, and the employee had not increased sales. Shiffman v. Thermal Indus., Inc., 2006 U.S. Dist. LEXIS 64351 (S.D. Ohio Sept. 8, 2006).

Employee did not show his termination was the result of age discrimination, in violation of R.C. 4112.02, because, even though he was age 60 when he was hired, and was thus a member of a protected class, the evidence showed his termination was based on the employer's belief that the employee was intoxicated on the job, rather than on the employee's age. Burrows v. Licking County, 2006-Ohio-4057, 2006 Ohio App. LEXIS 4029 (Ohio Ct. App., Licking County 2006).

Trial court's grant of summary judgment to former employers in an age discrimination claim under R.C. 4112.02 was appropriate where the former employee only satisfied the burden of proof as to the first three parts of the McDonnell Douglas test, but he failed to show that a substantially younger person was hired to replace him. Isolated, vague, and ambiguous comments by supervisors of the employer that were age-related or that referred to other employees did not constitute direct evidence of discrimination or discriminatory intent. Abrams v. Am. Computer Tech., 2006-Ohio-4032, 168 Ohio App. 3d 362, 860 N.E.2d 123, 2006 Ohio App. LEXIS 3973 (Ohio Ct. App., Hamilton County 2006).

Remark made by the employer's president that an employee was too old, and would never change, made in the context of a suggestion that a new management team should place their differences aside was insufficient to sustain the employee's age discrimination claim under R.C. 4112.02 as there was no evidence of a nexus between the comment and the employee's discharge. The employee was not "replaced" within the meaning of Ohio law, since the employer reassigned his responsibilities to a different worker. Langlois v. W.P. Hickman Sys., 2006-Ohio-3737, 2006 Ohio App. LEXIS 3693 (Ohio Ct. App., Cuyahoga County 2006).

Trial court properly granted summary judgment to a county, as employer, in an action by an employee, asserting claims of age discrimination pursuant to R.C. 4112.02, as the employee failed to establish a prima facie case of discrimination where he could not show that he was replaced or discharged by the county's decision to hire someone else to a position that the employee never held; further, the county had presented legitimate reasons for selecting the two top applicants for the job, although they were outside of the protected class. Smith v. Bd. of Cuyahoga County Comm'rs, 2006-Ohio-1073, 2006 Ohio App. LEXIS 978 (Ohio Ct. App., Cuyahoga County 2006).

When an employee claimed that his employer's failure to promote him and its termination of his employment was due to age discrimination, he proved (1) that he was over 40 years of age; (2) that he was subjected to an adverse employment action, both by being fired and by not being promoted; and (3) that he was qualified both for the job he held and for the job he sought, but he did not prove the age of the person who received the job he wanted, nor did he prove the age of anyone who was hired to replace him, so his age discrimination claim failed. Buckholz v. Bowling Green State Univ., 2006-Ohio-624, 2006 Ohio Misc. LEXIS 29 (Ohio Ct. Cl. 2006).

Former employee could not maintain an age discrimination case under R.C. 4412.02 and 4112.99, which claims were scrutinized under the same standard as claims under the Age Discrimination in Employment Act, because he did not present circumstantial or direct evidence of discrimination. Statements made by co-workers did not constitute direct evidence as co-workers were not decision-makers with regard to the employee's job, and the employee did not establish an adverse employment decision. Because of the failure to establish an adverse employment decision, the employee's retaliation claim under R.C. 4112.02(I) and public policy violation claim also failed. Zivkovic v. Juniper Networks, Inc., 450 F. Supp. 2d 815, 2006 U.S. Dist. LEXIS 63785 (N.D. Ohio 2006).

Student did not show a genuine issue of material fact as to whether she was dismissed from an instructional program at a college due to her age, because (1) the only remark the coordinator of clinical education allegedly made about the student's age was made after the student had already received a failing grade in the program, and (2) whatever remark the coordinator made on that subject was only made after the student raised the subject by saying she was too old to start over. McCrobie v. Stark State College of Tech., 2006-Ohio-2055, 2006 Ohio App. LEXIS 1885 (Ohio Ct. App., Stark County 2006).

Trial court's grant of summary judgment to an employer in an age discrimination action by an employee pursuant to R.C. 4112.02(A) and 4112.14(A) was proper, as the employer's claim that the employee was terminated for financial reasons was a legitimate, nondiscriminatory reason, and the employee failed to show that it was a mere pretext. Chandler v. Dunn Hardware, Inc., 2006-Ohio-4376, 168 Ohio App. 3d 496, 860 N.E.2d 1042, 2006 Ohio App. LEXIS 4293 (Ohio Ct. App., Cuyahoga County 2006).

Former employee established a prima facie case of age discrimination and the employer articulated a number of legitimate, non-discriminatory reasons for the employee's termination including the failure to meet sales and marketing expenses goals, the failure to increase sales, and the failure to establish overall profitability. The employee did not dispute that the employer's articulated reasons for the employee's termination were legitimate and non-discriminatory and in the light of the hard financial facts proffered by the employer, the employee's argument that the employer's justification for the employee's termination was insufficient was without merit. Bozsan v. Tradewinds Bev. Co., 2005 U.S. Dist. LEXIS 23032 (S.D. Ohio Sept. 21, 2005).

Trial court erred in granting defendants' motion for JNOV on an age discrimination claim. Jelinek v. Abbott Labs., 2005-Ohio-5696, 164 Ohio App. 3d 607, 843 N.E.2d 807, 2005 Ohio App. LEXIS 5122 (Ohio Ct. App., Franklin County 2005).

Granting of the employer's motion for summary judgment in the employee's action for age discrimination and retaliation pursuant to the Age Discrimination in Employment Act, 29 U.S.C.S. §§ 623, et seq., and R.C. 4112.02(I) and 4112.14. was proper where a former employee's statement of opinion could not be considered a statement of the party opponent for purposes of Fed. R. Evid. 801(d)(2)(D) because that employee had left the company. Further, the employee failed to identify evidence suggesting that the employer's articulated reason for the alleged adverse actions was mere pretext. Rufo v. Dave & Busters, Inc., 2005 U.S. Dist. LEXIS 33395 (S.D. Ohio Dec. 16, 2005), aff'd, 2007 FED App. 0075N, 2007 U.S. App. LEXIS 2366 (6th Cir. Ohio Jan. 31, 2007).

Trial court properly granted summary judgment to a judge in an age discrimination action under R.C. 4112.02(A) and 4112.14(A) by deputy clerks who were terminated when the judge took office in a county probate judge capacity, as the clerks did not show direct evidence of the discrimination. Statements by a co-worker were not evidence, as she had no decisionmaking authority and accordingly, the statements were not reflective of the judge's discriminatory intent, and as the clerks were unaware of the ages of those who replaced them, there was no statistical evidence to support their claims. Molnar v. Klammer, 2005-Ohio-6905, 2005 Ohio App. LEXIS 6227 (Ohio Ct. App., Lake County 2005).

Trial court properly granted summary judgment to an employer and co-workers of an employee in his age discrimination action pursuant to R.C. 4112.02(A) and 4112.99, as the employee's prima facie case of age discrimination was offset by the showing that his poor job performance and poor behavior were legitimate, nondiscriminatory reasons for the termination. The employee did not meet his burden under any of the Manzer factors of showing that the reasons for the discharge were pretextual. Sweet v. Abbott Foods, 2005-Ohio-6880, 2005 Ohio App. LEXIS 6216 (Ohio Ct. App., Franklin County 2005).

Trial court properly granted summary judgment to a country club on an employee's age discrimination claim as the country club dismissed the employee after two female employees alleged that the employee sexually harassed them. The employee failed to show that the country club's reason for his discharge was pretextual as the employee offered no additional evidence of age discrimination other than what he relied on to make his prima facie case, presented no evidence that the country club's explanations were factually false, or showed that other, but younger, employees were not fired even though they engaged in the same type of behavior. Wilson v. Rosemont Country Club, 2005-Ohio-6606, 2005 Ohio App. LEXIS 5953 (Ohio Ct. App., Summit County 2005).

Genuine issues of material fact remained as to whether an employer had a legitimate nondiscriminatory reason for terminating an employee, who had made a prima facie case of age discrimination, as the employer's financial problems did not explain why the employee, age 60, was discharged, while a retained employee, age 23, was not. Further, there was evidence that the proffered reasons were a mere pretext as they did not actually motivate the employee's discharge or were insufficient to motivate her discharge. Hoffman v. CHSHO, Inc., 2005-Ohio-3909, 2005 Ohio App. LEXIS 3597 (Ohio Ct. App., Clermont County 2005).

Former employee produced evidence to show that he was over 40; he was objectively qualified for his position; he was terminated; and he was replaced by an individual outside of the protected classes. His former employers articulated a legitimate, nondiscriminatory reason for the employee's termination in that they claimed he was terminated for poor management. Imwalle v. Reliance Med. Prods., 2005 U.S. Dist. LEXIS 27882 (S.D. Ohio Nov. 15, 2005).

Employer was denied summary judgment on the age discrimination claim because there were disputed issues of fact as to whether the employee was performing at a level comparable to or higher than her younger counterparts and whether employees outside of the protected classes with performance problems similar to the employee's alleged performance issues were treated more favorably and were not terminated. Hicks v. Novartis Pharms. Corp., 457 F. Supp. 2d 814, 2005 U.S. Dist. LEXIS 26495 (S.D. Ohio 2005).

Summary judgment was properly granted, dismissing an age discrimination claim, under R.C. 4112.02(N) and 4112.99, brought by a former employee and his wife against the employee's former employer and various managers, because plaintiffs' claim was not filed until more than 180 days after the employee's employment was terminated. Even if plaintiffs could bring suit pursuant to R.C. 4112.02(N) and 4112.99, defendants were entitled to summary judgment because the evidence showed that the work that the employee would have received was distributed among the retained workers, several of which were in the protected class; further, defendants offered a legitimate, non-discriminatory reason for the employee's discharge, a reduction in force, and plaintiffs failed to prove that defendants' work force reduction explanation was a pretext for age discrimination. Vickers v. Wren Indus., 2005-Ohio-3656, 2005 Ohio App. LEXIS 3366 (Ohio Ct. App., Montgomery County 2005).

Employee failed to establish that there was a genuine issue of material fact on the question of whether someone under the age of 40 was treated more favorably than he; although the employee pointed to a number of such individuals, none was a comparable. Bruce v. Office Depot, Inc., 2005 U.S. Dist. LEXIS 13418 (S.D. Ohio July 5, 2005).

Fact that the employer hired another account manager more than 11 months after the employee was discharged did not cause the court to conclude that the evidence raised a genuine issue of material fact concerning the fourth element of the employee's prima facie case of age discrimination, which requires a showing either that the plaintiff was replaced by someone outside the protected class or that a nonprotected similarly situated person was treated better. Bruce v. Office Depot, Inc., 2005 U.S. Dist. LEXIS 13418 (S.D. Ohio July 5, 2005).

Employer articulated a number of legitimate, non-discriminatory reasons for the employee's termination including the failure to meet sales and marketing expenses goals, the failure to increase sales, and the failure to establish overall profitability; employee did not dispute that the employer's articulated reasons for the employee's termination were legitimate and non-discriminatory and in the light of the hard financial facts proffered by the employer, the employee's argument that the employer's justification for the employee's termination was insufficient was without merit. Bozsan v. Tradewinds Bev. Co., 2005 U.S. Dist. LEXIS 23032 (S.D. Ohio Sept. 21, 2005).

In an action in which a former employee filed suit against his former employer alleging claims of age discrimination by way of having been replaced by a substantially younger individual, the employer was granted summary judgment where (1) the employee was not replaced as two already employed individuals absorbed all the functions of the department while continuing to perform the duties they previously performed; and (2) the employer asserted a legitimate, non-discriminatory reason for the employee's termination, i.e., his poor performance as a supervisor. Fabec v. STERIS Corp., 2005 U.S. Dist. LEXIS 20608 (N.D. Ohio Sept. 21, 2005).

Even if the employee had been able to establish a prima facie case for age discrimination, the employer established a nondiscriminatory intent for the employee's demotion through the same actor inference because the same two supervisors that hired him, later demoted him. Further, the employee's ability to establish a prima facie case of discrimination was called into question through the evidence submitted to the trial court because the employee's position was only taken away after he himself expressed his inability to do the job and it was ultimately given to a person that was older than the employee. Pirsil v. Int'l Steel Group - Cleveland, 2005-Ohio-3013, 2005 Ohio App. LEXIS 2815 (Ohio Ct. App., Cuyahoga County 2005).

Because an employee's statutory age discrimination claims failed, the employee's corresponding claim that the employee was terminated in violation of Ohio's public policy against age discrimination likewise failed. Weller v. Titanium Metals Corp., 361 F. Supp. 2d 712, 2005 U.S. Dist. LEXIS 8373 (S.D. Ohio 2005).

Summary judgment was properly granted in favor of a former employer in a former employee's suit alleging age discrimination in violation of R.C. 4112.02; that the employee's two co-workers, both of whom were younger than the 52-year old employee, were not subject to the reduction in force was not, by itself, sufficient for purposes of a prima facie case to indicate that the employee was discharged due to his age. Adams v. Proto Plastics, Inc., 151 Fed. Appx. 468, 2005 FED App. 0869N, 2005 U.S. App. LEXIS 23285 (6th Cir. Ohio 2005).

Deputy clerks who were discharged when a new county probate judge took office did not show indirect evidence of age discrimination under R.C. 4112.04(A) and 4112.14(A) in order to avoid summary judgment to the judge, although they offered sufficient evidence of the first three factors of the four-part Coryell test, as they were unable to show that the persons who replaced them were "substantially younger" in two out of the three clerks' cases, and as to the third, the judge's claim that the replacement was due to a reorganization of the court and issues of loyalty represented a legitimate, nondiscriminatory reason, which was not shown to be pretextual. Molnar v. Klammer, 2005-Ohio-6905, 2005 Ohio App. LEXIS 6227 (Ohio Ct. App., Lake County 2005).

Where a 60-year-old employee was terminated for poor performance due to a supervisor's evaluations and was replaced by a 47-year-old and a 40-year-old, the employee's age discrimination claims failed to survive summary judgment because the employer articulated a legitimate, nondiscriminatory reason for the employee's discharge and the employee could not show pretext based solely upon replacement by significantly younger persons. Weller v. Titanium Metals Corp., 361 F. Supp. 2d 712, 2005 U.S. Dist. LEXIS 8373 (S.D. Ohio 2005).

Parochial school teacher who entered into a marriage that was invalid under church doctrine, in violation of her contract, did not produce proof of age discrimination: Potts v. Catholic Diocese, 2004-Ohio-6816, 159 Ohio App. 3d 315, 823 N.E.2d 917, 2004 Ohio App. LEXIS 6319 (Ohio Ct. App., Mahoning County 2004).

Employee did not establish a prima facie case of age discrimination where his termination was part of a companywide reduction in force and his position was not refilled: Cassel v. Schuster Elecs., Inc., 2004-Ohio-6276, 159 Ohio App. 3d 224, 823 N.E.2d 519, 2004 Ohio App. LEXIS 5713 (Ohio Ct. App., Summit County 2004).

City employee alleged a prima facie case of constructive discharge based on age discrimination and that his retirement was not voluntary: Gessner v. City of Union, 2004-Ohio-5770, 159 Ohio App. 3d 43, 823 N.E.2d 1, 2004 Ohio App. LEXIS 5206 (Ohio Ct. App., Montgomery County 2004).

In reversing and remanding judgment against plaintiff under R.C. 4112.02, 4112.14(A), the Ohio Supreme Court held that a dismissed employee could plead a prima facie case of age discrimination by alleging that he was replaced by substantially younger person even if that person was inside the protected class of those over age 40. Coryell v. Bank One Trust Co. N.A., 2004-Ohio-723, 101 Ohio St. 3d 175, 803 N.E.2d 781, 2004 Ohio LEXIS 337 (Ohio 2004).

In cases of termination due to economic necessity, an age discrimination plaintiff carries a greater burden of supporting allegations of discrimination by coming forward with additional evidence, be it direct, circumstantial, or statistical to establish that age was a factor in the termination: Dahl v. Battelle Mem. Inst., 2004-Ohio-3884, 2004 Ohio App. LEXIS 3504 (Ohio Ct. App., Franklin County 2004).

Former employee failed to prove an age discrimination claim against a university pursuant to R.C. 4112.02, as ample evidence of legitimate, professional reasons for changes in the employee's role with the university had been presented. The employee's inability to work well with another physician, in and of itself, was a legally sufficient justification for the university's actions. Bhat v. Univ. of Cincinnati, 2003-Ohio-5623, 2003 Ohio Misc. LEXIS 93 (Ohio Ct. Cl. 2003).

Summary judgment against employee's age discrimination claim was proper because, inter alia, his employer's voluntary separation plan was not discriminatory because it counted age and length of service, remaining younger co-workers had different job classifications from the employee, and an over-50 co-employee with the same classification was retained. Howard v. Contech Constr. Prods., 2003-Ohio-6547, 2003 Ohio App. LEXIS 5848 (Ohio Ct. App., Butler County 2003).

District court's grant of summary judgment to defendant employer was affirmed on the alternative basis that the employee failed to make his prima facie case of age discrimination under R.C. 4112.02 because the person who replaced him was not significantly younger than he. Grosjean v. First Energy Corp., 349 F.3d 332, 2003 FED App. 0404P, 2003 U.S. App. LEXIS 23122 (6th Cir. Ohio 2003), cert. denied, 541 U.S. 1010, 124 S. Ct. 2069, 158 L. Ed. 2d 620, 2004 U.S. LEXIS 3082 (U.S. 2004).

Job applicant claiming to have been denied employment due to her age denied herself the ability to pursue almost all age discrimination claims under R.C. 4112 et seq. by filing a charge with the Ohio Civil Rights Commission and the Equal Employment Opportunity Commission rather than an R.C. 4112.99 claim based on R.C. 4112.02(A). Sterry v. Safe Auto Ins. Co., 2003 U.S. Dist. LEXIS 17363 (S.D. Ohio Aug. 25, 2003).

Defendants' motion for summary judgment was granted where an employee failed to establish a prima facie case of age discrimination because the employee's termination was due to a safety infraction and because the employee's replacement was only two years younger. Bolander v. BP Oil Co., 2003 U.S. Dist. LEXIS 15350 (N.D. Ohio Aug. 6, 2003), aff'd, 128 Fed. Appx. 412, 2005 U.S. App. LEXIS 2281 (6th Cir. Ohio 2005).

While an employee had a cause of action against individual defendants because they were supervisors and managers of the employee, the employee's state age discrimination claims were either barred, or lacked merit and were dismissed on summary judgment. Williams v. GE, 269 F. Supp. 2d 958, 2003 U.S. Dist. LEXIS 16658 (S.D. Ohio 2003), aff'd, 145 Fed. Appx. 535, 2005 FED App. 0695N, 2005 U.S. App. LEXIS 16937 (6th Cir. Ohio 2005).

Employer was not entitled to summary judgment on a former employee's claims for age discrimination in violation of R.C. 4112 et seq. and Ohio public policy, as there was evidence of age-related animus on the part of the employee's supervisor, who was involved in the employee's discharge, and there were fact questions as to the legitimacy of the employer's claim that the employee was fired for poor performance given, inter alia, that the employee had received a performance award two years before being fired. Chitwood v. Dunbar Armored, Inc., 267 F. Supp. 2d 751, 2003 U.S. Dist. LEXIS 10463 (S.D. Ohio 2003).

An employer's multiple references to negative, age-related stereotypes may be evidence of discriminatory intent. Although an absence of discrimination may be inferred where the same individual hired and fired an employee, such inference is not required: Wexler v. White's Fine Furniture, Inc., 317 F.3d 564, 2003 FED App. 0029P, 2003 U.S. App. LEXIS 1223 (6th Cir. Ohio 2003).

The evidence established that plaintiff left employment due to personality conflicts with managers and due to job reorganizations, not age discrimination: Manis v. Hoxworth Blood Ctr., 2002-Ohio-5496, 120 Ohio Misc. 2d 43, 777 N.E.2d 918, 2002 Ohio Misc. LEXIS 36 (Ohio Ct. Cl. 2002).

Plaintiff did not establish age discrimination where he was discharged based on a plausible claim of sexual misconduct. Age-related comments were not severe or pervasive enough to create an objectively hostile environment: Surry v. Cuyahoga Cmty. College, 2002-Ohio-5356, 149 Ohio App. 3d 528, 778 N.E.2d 91, 2002 Ohio App. LEXIS 5361 (Ohio Ct. App., Cuyahoga County 2002).

For purposes of age discrimination claims, the fact that younger employees assumed the plaintiff's duties is not sufficient to constitute replacement. Plaintiff did not show that his termination permitted promotion or retention of a younger employee: Gunthorpe v. DaimlerChrysler Corp., 205 F. Supp. 2d 820, 2002 U.S. Dist. LEXIS 11052 (N.D. Ohio 2002), aff'd in part and rev'd in part, 90 Fed. Appx. 877, 2004 U.S. App. LEXIS 1765 (6th Cir. Ohio 2004).

The plaintiff established a prima facie case of age discrimination. He did not rebut the employer's proffered business reasons for its action. What may have satisfied one management regime does not necessarily satisfy its successor: Peters v. Lincoln Elec. Co., 285 F.3d 456, 2002 FED App. 0097P, 2002 U.S. App. LEXIS 4463 (6th Cir. Ohio 2002).

Plaintiff did not establish a prima facie case of age discrimination where her alleged replacement was 42, also within the protected class: Keener v. Legacy Health Servs., 2001-Ohio-4384, 148 Ohio App. 3d 321, 773 N.E.2d 555, 2001 Ohio App. LEXIS 3021 (Ohio Ct. App., Cuyahoga County 2001).

There was sufficient evidence to support the finding that enforcement of the attendance policy was a pretext for age discrimination, but not to support an award of punitive damages: Pelletier v. Rumpke Container Serv., 142 Ohio App. 3d 54, 753 N.E.2d 958, 2001 Ohio App. LEXIS 1473 (Ohio Ct. App., Hamilton County 2001).

To establish a prima facie case of age discrimination, the employee must show that (1) he is a member of a protected class under R.C. 4112.02 or 4112.14; (2) he was subject to an adverse employment decision; (3) he is qualified for the position; and (4) he was replaced by, or his discharge permitted retention of, a person of comparable qualifications outside the protected class: Bullock v. Totes, Inc., 2000 Ohio App. LEXIS 6058 (Ohio Ct. App., Hamilton County Dec. 22, 2000), dismissed, 91 Ohio St. 3d 1514, 746 N.E.2d 615, 2001 Ohio LEXIS 1224 (Ohio 2001).

There is no reasonable relationship between the absolute age of an individual who assumes a plaintiff's duties with respect to the protected class and the potential for violations of R.C. 4112.02(A); thus, the appropriate inquiry in age discrimination cases arising pursuant to R.C. 4112.02(A) and 4112.14 is whether the plaintiff was replaced by a "substantially younger" individual (following O'Connor v. Consolidated Coin Caterers Corporation (1996), 517 US 308): Outzen v. Continental Gen. Tire,

Inc., 2000 Ohio App. LEXIS 287 (Ohio Ct. App., Summit County Feb. 2, 2000).

To establish a prima facie case of age discrimination, a plaintiff need not prove that he or she was replaced by a person under forty: Ahern v. Ameritech Corp., 137 Ohio App. 3d 754, 739 N.E.2d 1184, 2000 Ohio App. LEXIS 2015 (Ohio Ct. App., Cuyahoga County), dismissed, 90 Ohio St. 3d 1413, 735 N.E.2d 453, 2000 Ohio LEXIS 2341 (Ohio 2000).

A small number of ageist comments did not establish age discrimination: McCafferty v. Cleveland Bd. of Educ., 133 Ohio App. 3d 692, 729 N.E.2d 797, 1999 Ohio App. LEXIS 2431 (Ohio Ct. App., Cuyahoga County 1999).

Age discrimination was not established where the employer provided legitimate reasons for terminating the employee. Unlawful retaliation was also not established: Ricker v. John Deere Ins. Co., 133 Ohio App. 3d 759, 729 N.E.2d 1202, 1998 Ohio App. LEXIS 4680 (Ohio Ct. App., Franklin County 1998).

Plaintiff's age discrimination claim should be dismissed where he failed to check the box for age discrimination in his filings with the EEOC and OCRC: Metzenbaum v. John Carroll Univ., 987 F. Supp. 610, 1997 U.S. Dist. LEXIS 17340 (N.D. Ohio 1997).

Age discrimination action failed where plaintiff could not prove that he was replaced by an employee outside of the protected class and that he was meeting his employer's legitimate expectations at the time of his discharge: Pasko v. American Nat'l Can Co., 998 F. Supp. 807, 1998 U.S. Dist. LEXIS 3623 (N.D. Ohio 1998).

The direct, circumstantial and statistical evidence did not prove age discrimination: Sobolewski v. Manoir Electroalloys Corp., 120 Ohio App. 3d 225, 697 N.E.2d 688, 1997 Ohio App. LEXIS 2511 (Ohio Ct. App., Lorain County 1997).

Age discrimination may be established where a discharged employee's duties are transferred to another person already employed by the defendant: Cruz v. South Dayton Urological Assocs., 121 Ohio App. 3d 655, 700 N.E.2d 675, 1997 Ohio App. LEXIS 3652 (Ohio Ct. App., Montgomery County 1997).

Employee's age discrimination claim was time barred where the alleged discriminatory act occurred on August 11, 1995, and employee did not file her complaint until September 26, 1996: Wallace v. Trumbull Mem. Hosp., 970 F. Supp. 618, 1997 U.S. Dist. LEXIS 11544 (N.D. Ohio 1997).

Plaintiff failed to prove a case of age discrimination under R.C. 4112.02 under the direct evidence standard where he attempted to prove defendants' discriminatory attitude through testimony of remarks such as "it is time for the next generation," where those remarks were neither said to or about plaintiff and were distant in time and fact to plaintiff's termination: Smith v. E.G. Baldwin & Assocs., 119 Ohio App. 3d 410, 695 N.E.2d 349, 1997 Ohio App. LEXIS 1763 (Ohio Ct. App., Franklin County 1997).

Due to a reduction-in-force and reorganization of job duties, an age discrimination plaintiff was no longer qualified for the position. A causal connection between the adverse action and the sexual harassment complaint was not established where they were thirteen years apart: Mack v. B.F. Goodrich Co., 121 Ohio App. 3d 99, 699 N.E.2d 97, 1997 Ohio App. LEXIS 2112 (Ohio Ct. App., Cuyahoga County 1997).

An employee alleging age discrimination must prove a causal link or nexus between evidence of a discriminatory statement or conduct and that employee: Byrnes v. LCI Communs. Holdings, 1996-Ohio-307, 77 Ohio St. 3d 125, 672 N.E.2d 145, 1996 Ohio LEXIS 1837 (Ohio 1996), cert. denied, 521 U.S. 1104, 117 S. Ct. 2480, 138 L. Ed. 2d 989, 1997 U.S. LEXIS 3885 (U.S. 1997).

Where plaintiffs had a different department head than did comparison employees, evidence that male employees, only one of whom was younger than all three plaintiffs, were offered greater assistance by their department head in obtaining alternative employment with employer after reduction in force did not establish prima facie case of age discrimination: Creech v. Ohio Cas. Ins. Co., 944 F. Supp. 1347, 1996 U.S. Dist. LEXIS 16177 (S.D. Ohio 1996).

Plaintiffs age discrimination claims were precluded where evidence showed that younger applicants had superior educational backgrounds and/or superior relevant experience: Creech v. Ohio Cas. Ins. Co., 944 F. Supp. 1347, 1996 U.S. Dist. LEXIS 16177 (S.D. Ohio 1996).

An employer's use of records containing an employee's age is not proof of discrimination. Age-related statements about other employees do not constitute direct proof of discrimination: Miller v. Loral Defense Sys., 109 Ohio App. 3d 379, 672 N.E.2d 227, 1996 Ohio App. LEXIS 479 (Ohio Ct. App., Summit County 1996).

An isolated, ambiguous reference to plaintiffs age was not direct evidence of discrimination. Retained employees were not similarly qualified. The statistical evidence was flawed: Stair v. Phoenix Presentations, 116 Ohio App. 3d 500, 688 N.E.2d 582, 1996 Ohio App. LEXIS 5781 (Ohio Ct. App., Butler County 1996).

The factfinder's disbelief of the employer's reasons for the adverse employment action, especially if that disbelief is coupled with a suspicion of duplicity, may, along with the elements of a prima facie case, be sufficient to demonstrate intentional age discrimination: Atkinson v. International Technegroup, 106 Ohio App. 3d 349, 666 N.E.2d 257, 1995 Ohio App. LEXIS 3933 (Ohio Ct. App., Hamilton County 1995).

The employer's alleged statement concerning older employees, made three years prior to the discharge, did not constitute direct evidence of age discrimination: Street v. Gerstenslager Co., 103 Ohio App. 3d 156, 658 N.E.2d 1105, 1995 Ohio App. LEXIS 1855 (Ohio Ct. App., Wayne County 1995).

To prove that he was "qualified" for a position, a plaintiff alleging age discrimination must not only show that he was capable of doing the work but also that he was meeting the employer's legitimate expectations in performing the work: Neubauer v. A.M. McGregor Home Corp., 1994 Ohio App. LEXIS 2153 (Ohio Ct. App., Cuyahoga County May 19, 1994).

Plaintiff who had filed age discrimination charge with the Ohio Civil Rights Commission for the sole purpose of meeting the requirements of a suit under federal law could pursue state remedies in federal court even though Ohio law requires an election of remedies: Baker v. Siemens Energy & Automation, 838 F. Supp. 1227, 1993 U.S. Dist. LEXIS 16769 (S.D. Ohio 1993).

Protection against age discrimination is provided under Ohio law by three statutory sections: (1) R.C. 4101.17(B), which permits a civil action for violation of subsection (A) of that section; (2) R.C. 4112.02(N), which permits a civil action to be brought against those who violate the other subsections of that section; and (3) R.C. 4112.05, which permits a complaint to be brought with the Ohio Civil Rights Commission for violations of R.C. 4112.02 and 4112.021. Each of these statutory remedies is exclusive—the choice of one remedy precludes recourse to other remedies: Pozzobon v. Parts for Plastics, 770 F. Supp. 376, 1991 U.S. Dist. LEXIS 11655 (N.D. Ohio 1991).

Plaintiff alleged facts sufficient to state a prima facie case of discharge and employment by a younger person under both federal and Ohio law where she alleged facts supporting a claim of constructive discharge, and where she alleged that her duties were assumed in part by persons outside the protected class: Crawford v. ITT Consumer Financial Corp., 653 F. Supp. 1184, 1986 U.S. Dist. LEXIS 19155 (S.D. Ohio 1986).

The federal statute which requires federal firefighters to retire at age 55 does not serve to establish age 55 as a bona fide occupational qualification for all firemen within the meaning of the Age Discrimination in Employment Act: Johnson v. Baltimore, 472 U.S. 353, 105 S. Ct. 2717, 86 L. Ed. 2d 286, 1985 U.S. LEXIS 105 (U.S. 1985).

R.C. 4112.02(N) permits only those individuals allegedly discriminated against because of their age to proceed directly to court. All other plaintiffs alleging discriminatory discharge, including those with a claim for retaliatory discharge, must first exhaust administrative proceedings: Merkel v. Scovill, Inc., 570 F. Supp. 133, 1983 U.S. Dist. LEXIS 18632 (S.D. Ohio 1983).

**—Burden of proof**

Appellant failed to establish a prima facie case of age discrimination because he failed to establish that the allegedly younger managers were treated more favorably than he was for similar paid time off (PTO) issues as appellant had at least 20 violations where he was absent from work but did not submit PTO, but the other managers only had one to four days where they were absent from work and did not submit PTO. Sullivan v. Ikea, 2020-Ohio-6661, 2020 Ohio App. LEXIS 4526 (Ohio Ct. App., Butler County 2020).

In a graduate student's action against a university following his dismissal from the PhD program, his age discrimination claim failed because he could not prove discriminatory intent through either direct or indirect evidence, and his retaliation claim failed because he failed to show he was engaged in protected opposition activity where, inter alia, letters from his attorney fell into the category of a vague charge of discrimination in an internal letter or memorandum. Grubach v. Univ. of Akron, 2019-Ohio-2370, 2019 Ohio Misc. LEXIS 205 (Ohio Ct. Cl. 2019), aff'd in part, rev'd, 2020-Ohio-3467, 2020 Ohio App. LEXIS 2411 (Ohio Ct. App., Franklin County 2020).

In an action stemming from termination of employment, a grant of summary judgment in favor of the employer and president (employer) was proper because the employee's arguments for claiming that the employer's proffered reason was insufficient to motivate her termination lacked support in the record. The employee did not provide evidence that a similarly situated comparator was treated more favorably for engaging in similar conduct and failed to demonstrate pretext with regard to gender and age discrimination. Housden v. Wilke Global, Inc., 2018-Ohio-3959, 111 N.E.3d 1264, 2018 Ohio App. LEXIS 4330 (Ohio Ct. App., Franklin County 2018).

Employee failed to meet her burden of proving by a preponderance of the evidence that an employer terminated her because of her age because the employer articulated a legitimate non-discriminatory reason for terminating her, that her students performed at an inadequate level on an exam; there was no evidence that the music department chair's dislike for the employee was related to her age, and the employee did not establish that her replacement was less qualified. Pla v. Cleveland State Univ., 2016-Ohio-3150, 2016 Ohio Misc. LEXIS 62 (Ohio Ct. Cl.), aff'd, 2016-Ohio-8165, 2016 Ohio App. LEXIS 5020 (Ohio Ct. App., Franklin County 2016).

Grant of summary judgment to the employer on the employee's claims for age discrimination was proper because he failed to meet his burden of proof. His affidavit was insufficient to create a material dispute of fact of this issue insofar as it contradicted his deposition testimony; further, the fact that he could perform certain daily functions of life was insufficient to create a material dispute of fact in light of his statements that he could not perform the functions of his job. Drogell v. Westfield Group, 2013-Ohio-5262, 2013 Ohio App. LEXIS 5470 (Ohio Ct. App., Medina County 2013).

Retention of two younger accountants while the employee was terminated was sufficient for the employee to meet his burden of proving a prima face case of discrimination; there was sufficient evidence to create a dispute of material fact over each of the proffered justifications for the employee's termination as the argument that the employee was a temporary employee was belied by the employer's own employee manual and similar inconsistencies plagued the employer's argument that there was no more work for him to do once his initial projects were completed. Although there was evidence in the record of dissatisfaction with the employee's work, there was the fact that this justification was never raised by the employer until well into the litigation. Gaglioti v. Levin Group, Inc., 508 Fed. Appx. 476, 2012 FED App. 1288N, 2012 U.S. App. LEXIS 25625 (6th Cir. Ohio 2012).

*Unpublished decision:* Former employee's age discrimination claim in violation of R.C. 4112.02 survived a motion to dismiss because the employee's pleading of express statements indicating an unlawful and discriminatory use of age satisfied the plausibility requirement because the employee's allegations, if true, could have constituted direct discrimination and discovery might have uncovered such direct evidence. Rhodes v. R&L Carriers, Inc., 491 Fed. Appx. 579, 2012 FED App. 0841N, 2012 U.S. App. LEXIS 16534 (6th Cir. Ohio 2012).

*Unpublished decision:* District court properly granted summary judgment in favor of a successor corporation in an action under 29 U.S.C.S. § 623 of the Age Discrimination in Employment Act, 29 U.S.C.S. § 621 et seq., and under R.C. 4112.02, which was filed by 38 former employees who were not rehired after their employer sold its paper mill to the successor; the employees failed to establish a genuine issue of material fact regarding whether the successor's asserted reasons for declining to rehire the employees were pretextual. The successor asserted that it did not rehire the employees due to poor ratings by former managers and supervisors and due to a poor attendance record, and the employees provided no evidence suggesting that the successor's rating system and rehiring process were based on ageist factors. Campbell v. Int'l Paper Co., 138 Fed. Appx. 794, 2005 FED App. 0596N, 2005 U.S. App. LEXIS 14264 (6th Cir. Ohio 2005).

Although the driver met the requirements for establishing a prima facie case of age discrimination and raised a rebuttable presumption of discrimination, he failed to satisfy his burden of proving that the employer's nondiscriminatory reason for terminating him (violation of the employer's drug and alcohol policy) was merely pretext. Stookey v. South Shore Transp. Co., 2012-Ohio-3184, 2012 Ohio App. LEXIS 2811 (Ohio Ct. App., Erie County 2012).

Trial court did not err in finding that the employee failed to present a prima facie case of age discrimination through the indirect method of proof because the person hired was not substantially younger than the employee, since the employee was 50 and the person hired was 48. Dautartas v. Abbott Labs., 2012-Ohio-1709, 2012 Ohio App. LEXIS 1495 (Ohio Ct. App., Franklin County 2012).

Although it was undisputed that the plaintiff was over 40 years of age, was terminated, and was qualified for his job as a sales consultant, the magistrate judge correctly recommended that the plaintiff had not shown that he was replaced, much less that he was replaced by a substantially younger employee; moreover, although the plaintiff contended that some younger employees were hired at various times in 2008, those employees were hired before the plaintiff was terminated for cause for various policy violations. Further, the plaintiff and another employee were not similarly-situated as they worked in different departments and committed different acts; finally, the plaintiff had not shown that the employer's legitimate non-discriminatory reason for his termination, multiple violations of company policies, was merely a pretext for age discrimination. Green v. Schaeffer's Inv. Research, Inc., 2012 U.S. Dist. LEXIS 26136 (S.D. Ohio Feb. 29, 2012).

Employee had not pointed to any age-based comments that might amount to direct evidence of age discrimination under the Age Discrimination in Employment Act, 29 U.S.C.S. § 621 et seq., or the R.C. 4112.02, and moreover, the employer's vice-president testified that, in her duties with respect to terminating employees, she had not been told that age was a criteria, much less heard any such comments. Further, in urging that the attendant circumstances were purportedly sufficient to establish a prima facie case, the employee essentially rehashed the same arguments and evidence already found insufficient at step four of the McDonnell Douglas framework. Green v. Schaeffer's Inv. Research, Inc., 2012 U.S. Dist. LEXIS 26136 (S.D. Ohio Feb. 29, 2012).

To the extent his argument could have been construed as one contending that the employer's failure to subject him to progressive discipline implied that its motive for discharging him was age discrimination, that argument also failed. There was no evidence that required the employer to use progressive discipline prior to termination of employment and the employer provided evidence that disciplinary action for a first time offense could indeed consist of employment termination. Crase v. Shasta Bevs., Inc., 2012-Ohio-326, 2012 Ohio App. LEXIS 277 (Ohio Ct. App., Franklin County 2012).

Trial court did not err in granting summary judgment on the employee's claim for age discrimination because there was no evidence of pretext. The employee failed to discredit the legitimate, nondiscriminatory reason appellees offered for his employment termination, which was his removal of an oxygen unit from the plant. Crase v. Shasta Bevs., Inc., 2012-Ohio-326, 2012 Ohio App. LEXIS 277 (Ohio Ct. App., Franklin County 2012).

Where an employee who was terminated from employment for bringing a knife to work in violation of the employer's weapons policy showed that younger employees brought in knives and were not terminated or disciplined, she met the four prong test of McDonell-Douglas, such that she was entitled to a trial on the age discrimination claim under R.C. 4112.02(A) and 4112.14. Cittadini v. Southwest Gen. Health Sys., 2011-Ohio-6464, 2011 Ohio App. LEXIS 5335 (Ohio Ct. App., Cuyahoga County 2011).

Employee did not establish a prima facie case of age discrimination under R.C. 4112.14(A) and R.C. 4112.02(A) because the evidence presented at a deposition did not show that the employee was replaced by a substantially younger person or whether an employer was able to retain such a person due to the employee's discharge. Gradisher v. Barberton Citizens Hosp., 2011-Ohio-6243, 2011 Ohio App. LEXIS 5119 (Ohio Ct. App., Summit County 2011).

There was no direct evidence of age discrimination under R.C. 4112.02(A) in an employee's action against his employer following the employee's termination due to an alleged reduction in force, as language used by the employer regarding an employee's "anticipated future benefit" was used to indicate which employees the employer believed would be the most productive in the future and did not hinge on an age consideration. Southworth v. N. Trust Sec., Inc., 2011-Ohio-3467, 195 Ohio App. 3d 357, 960 N.E.2d 473, 2011 Ohio App. LEXIS 2936 (Ohio Ct. App., Cuyahoga County 2011).

Remarks made against an employee by a supervisor did not constitute direct evidence of age discrimination under R.C. 4112.02(A) where they were made approximately 18 months before the employee was terminated; accordingly, they were too remote in time to support the claim. Southworth v. N. Trust Sec., Inc., 2011-Ohio-3467, 195 Ohio App. 3d 357, 960 N.E.2d 473, 2011 Ohio App. LEXIS 2936 (Ohio Ct. App., Cuyahoga County 2011).

State university employee's age discrimination claim under R.C. 4112.02(A) failed with respect to indirect evidence, as a reduction in force was valid in that the employee's position was abolished and he was not replaced, and further, it was not shown that age was a factor in his termination. Wise v. Ohio State Univ., 2011-Ohio-1433, 2011 Ohio Misc. LEXIS 47 (Ohio Ct. Cl.), aff'd, 2011-Ohio-6566, 2011 Ohio App. LEXIS 5403 (Ohio Ct. App., Franklin County 2011).

State university employee failed to show by direct evidence that his termination from employment was due to age discrimination under R.C. 4112.02(A) rather than from abolishment of position due to a reduction in force from state budget cuts; he did not show that comments regarding age were made by a decision maker, were related to the decision-making process, or that they were proximate in time to the act of alleged discrimination. Wise v. Ohio State Univ., 2011-Ohio-1433, 2011 Ohio Misc. LEXIS 47 (Ohio Ct. Cl.), aff'd, 2011-Ohio-6566, 2011 Ohio App. LEXIS 5403 (Ohio Ct. App., Franklin County 2011).

Former employee's prima facie case for age discrimination, under R.C. 4112.02(A) and 29 U.S.C.S. § 623(a), failed because, despite the employee's perception of unfair treatment with regard to overtime, such perception had no genuine basis in fact because the employee actually received more overtime hours than his younger colleague. Patrick v. Ferguson Enters., 2011 U.S. Dist. LEXIS 10418 (S.D. Ohio Feb. 2, 2011).

In his age discrimination suit, a former employee offered sufficient evidence to show that an issue of fact existed as to whether the employer created the situation for the employee to underperform with respect to his sales goals, given the size of the accounts, which generated about 20 times more revenue than his other accounts, taken away from him prior to his termination. Pattison v. W.W. Grainger, Inc., 2010-Ohio-2484, 2010 Ohio App. LEXIS 2021 (Ohio Ct. App., Cuyahoga County 2010).

Employer and supervisors were entitled to summary judgment on a former employee's claim of age discrimination, in violation of R.C. 4112.02(A) and 4112.99, because multiple legitimate, nondiscriminatory reasons were asserted for terminating the employee's employment, and the employee failed to discredit the reasons that were offered as being a mere pretext. The multiple legitimate, nondiscriminatory reasons that were asserted for terminating the 51 year old employee's employment and, apparently, replacing the employee with a 43 year old employee included: (1) the employee hoarded relevant information; (2) the employee resisted change; (3) the employee's negative attitude and behavior towards co-workers; and (4) the employee's difficulty in responding to stressful situations. Wigglesworth v. Mettler Toledo Int'l, Inc., 2010-Ohio-1019, 2010 Ohio App. LEXIS 843 (Ohio Ct. App., Franklin County 2010).

Defendant was denied summary judgment on the claims for age discrimination under the Age Discrimination in Employment Act and Ohio law because (1) the comments were made by the decision maker in plaintiffs case and related in time to his termination; and (2) although defendant articulated a legitimate, nondiscriminatory reason for plaintiff's discharge, the record was replete with disputed facts that bore on the issue of pretext and precluded a determination on summary judgment as to whether defendant's reason for discharging plaintiff was a pretext for age discrimination. Mauer v. Deloitte & Touche, LLP, 752 F. Supp. 2d 819, 2010 U.S. Dist. LEXIS 113628 (S.D. Ohio 2010).

University was entitled to summary judgment in a former employee's wrongful discharge case because the employee could not prove age discrimination under R.C. 4112.02(A) and 4112.99 as there was no evidence that the employee was replaced by, or the discharge permitted the retention of, a person of substantially younger age. Pursuant to a reduction of force as part of a necessary cost cutting by the university, the duties of the employee were divided among three employees who were retained, including a younger employee who only did a part of the employee's work. Woods v. Capital Univ., 2009-Ohio-5672, 2009 Ohio App. LEXIS 4770 (Ohio Ct. App., Franklin County 2009).

Under either the federal Age Discrimination in Employment Act, 28 U.S.C.S. § 623(a)(1), or R.C. 4112.02(A), a fire department lieutenant failed to make out a prima facie case of age discrimination against the township fire department for promoting a colleague to a captain position rather than promoting the lieutenant, as the lieutenant and the promoted colleague were both within the protected class of being over 40 years of age. Sheridan v. Jackson Twp. Div. of Fire, 2009-Ohio-1267, 2009 Ohio App. LEXIS 1073 (Ohio Ct. App., Franklin County 2009).

Where a former employee's testimony about the retaliatory atmosphere he experienced following his complaints, and the relatively short period of time between the employee's EEOC complaint and his removal as president supported an inference of retaliation, the appellate court upheld the denial of the former employer's motion for judgment as a matter of law in the employee's action that alleged age and national-origin discrimination after the employee was terminated from his employment with the employer as president. Imwalle v. Reliance Med. Prods., 515 F.3d 531, 2004 FED App. 0066P, 2008 U.S. App. LEXIS 2810 (6th Cir. Ohio 2008).

There was a lack of reliable, probative, and substantial evidence to support an order by the Ohio Civil Rights Commission which determined that a state university had committed intentional age discrimination under R.C. 4112.02(A) against an assistant professor who was denied promotion and tenure, as the Commission drew improper inferences when it determined that the university's proffered reason of inadequate research was false because the assistant professor had received a variety of awards; there was no evidence that the same criteria was used to determine qualification for the awards and for tenure. Ohio Univ. v. Ohio Civ. Rights Comm'n, 2008-Ohio-1034, 175 Ohio App. 3d 414, 887 N.E.2d 403, 2008 Ohio App. LEXIS 888 (Ohio Ct. App., Athens County 2008).

Trial court properly reversed an order by the Ohio Civil Rights Commission, which determined that a state university had committed intentional age discrimination under R.C. 4112.02(A) against an assistant professor who was denied promotion and tenure, as the Commission drew improper inferences from a comparison of others who were granted tenure and concluded that the assistant professor's lack of research was a pretextual reason; rather, the compared professors were all judged by different committees and all had differing strengths and qualifications that were evaluated in making the tenure decision for each one. Ohio Univ. v. Ohio Civ. Rights Comm'n, 2008-Ohio-1034, 175 Ohio App. 3d 414, 887 N.E.2d 403, 2008 Ohio App. LEXIS 888 (Ohio Ct. App., Athens County 2008).

State employee failed to prove by a preponderance of the evidence that he was the victim of age discrimination, in violation of R.C. 4112.02(A), where he failed to show that he was replaced by a substantially younger person, he failed to assert that any statements regarding his age were ever directed at him or mentioned in his presence, and even assuming that he presented his prima facie case, he did not successfully show that the reasons put forth by the employer for the termination were a mere pretext for discrimination. Swoger v. Wright State Univ., 2007-Ohio-2751, 2007 Ohio Misc. LEXIS 184 (Ohio Ct. Cl. 2007).

In an action in which a former employee filed suit against her former employer alleging violations of the Age Discrimination in Employment Act, 29 U.S.C.S. § 621 et seq., Title VII of the Civil Rights Act of 1964, and R.C. 4112, the employer was denied summary judgment on the age and gender discrimination claims; there were disputed issues of fact as to whether the employee was performing at a level comparable to or higher than her male and/or younger counterparts and whether employees outside of the protected classes with performance problems similar to the employee's alleged performance issues were treated more favorably and were not terminated. Hicks v. Novartis Pharms. Corp., 457 F. Supp. 2d 814, 2005 U.S. Dist. LEXIS 26495 (S.D. Ohio 2005).

Trial court properly granted summary judgment to an employer and co-workers of an employee in his age discrimination action pursuant to R.C. 4112.02(A) and 4112.99, as the employee's prima facie case of age discrimination was offset by the showing that his poor job performance and poor behavior were legitimate, nondiscriminatory reasons for the termination; the employee did not meet his burden under any of the Manzer factors of showing that the reasons for the discharge were pretextual. Sweet v. Abbott Foods, 2005-Ohio-6880, 2005 Ohio App. LEXIS 6216 (Ohio Ct. App., Franklin County 2005).

In an action in which a former employee filed suit against his former employer alleging claims of age discrimination in violation of Ohio and federal law, the employer wsa granted summary judgment where (1) the employee was not replaced as two individuals absorbed all the functions of the department while continuing to perform the duties they previously performed; and (2) the employer asserted a legitimate, non-discriminatory reason for the employee's termination, i.e., his poor performance as a supervisor. The employee failed to show that this was a pretext for age discrimination. Fabec v. STERIS Corp., 2005 U.S. Dist. LEXIS 20608 (N.D. Ohio Sept. 21, 2005).

Trial court's grant of summary judgment to an employer in an employee's age discrimination action, based on alleged violations of public policy and of R.C. 4112.02(A) and 4112.14(A), was proper, as the employee failed to meet his burden of either directly or indirectly establishing a prima facie case of discrimination, as he was laid off due to a general work force reduction, and there was no showing that he was singled out for impermissible reasons or that the employer had a discriminatory intent. Ramacciato v. Argo-Tech Corp., 2005-Ohio-506, 2005 Ohio App. LEXIS 541 (Ohio Ct. App., Cuyahoga County 2005).

Where an employee over the age of 40 was terminated from a receptionist position in a one-person reduction in force and the employer retained another receptionist who was over 40 and was less than six years younger than the employee, the employee's age discrimination claims failed to survive summary judgment because the employee did not provide any evidence that a similarly situated younger employee received more favorable treatment than the employee. Van Diest v. Deloitte & Touche, LLP, 2005 U.S. Dist. LEXIS 22106 (N.D. Ohio Sept. 30, 2005).

Evidence that the employee's duties were redistributed to other stockbrokers of the employer who had already been performing related work failed to raise a genuine issue of material fact on the fourth element of the employee's prima facie case of age discrimination under R.C. 4112.02(A). Hoover v. Rice Prudential Sec., 2003 U.S. Dist. LEXIS 27470 (S.D. Ohio Sept. 22, 2003).

Where a terminated employee met his burden of showing a prima facie case of age discrimination, under R.C. 4112.02(A), where he was a member of the statutorily protected class, he was qualified for the position, was replaced by a substantially younger employee, and was forced to accept retirement as he was told that he had virtually no chance of being re-hired to his position which constituted a constructive discharge, a fact issue was raised which should have been heard by a jury on the issue of whether the employer's proffered nondiscriminatory reasons for the termination were mere pretext. Oleksiak v. John Carroll Univ., 2005-Ohio-886, 2005 Ohio App. LEXIS 912 (Ohio Ct. App., Cuyahoga County 2005).

Absent direct evidence of age discrimination, proof of discriminatory intent is subject to a burden-shifting analysis established by the U.S. Supreme Court in McDonnell Douglas Corp. v. Green (1973), 411 US 792; the purpose for shifting burdens of proof in discrimination claims is to assure that the employee has a day in court despite the unavailability of direct evidence: Bullock v. Totes, Inc., 2000 Ohio App. LEXIS 6058 (Ohio Ct. App., Hamilton County Dec. 22, 2000), dismissed, 91 Ohio St. 3d 1514, 746 N.E.2d 615, 2001 Ohio LEXIS 1224 (Ohio 2001).

Plaintiff produced no evidence of age discrimination other than being replaced by an employee under forty: Beauchamp v. CompuServe, Inc., 126 Ohio App. 3d 17, 709 N.E.2d 863, 1998 Ohio App. LEXIS 1482 (Ohio Ct. App., Franklin County 1998).

Plaintiff failed to establish a prima facie case of "replacement" under R.C. 4112.02 in the context of a reduction in force discharge where his alleged younger replacement assumed only one of the ten duties that encompassed plaintiff's primary job responsibilities and assumed several duties which were not performed by plaintiff; assumption of the same job title was not sufficient: Gordon v. Universal Elecs., 1997 Ohio App. LEXIS 4426 (Ohio Ct. App., Summit County Oct. 1, 1997).

A claim of age discrimination was properly held to fail as a matter of law when it was raised in an effort to obfuscate the parties' real dispute over the payment of post-employment commissions, when the mere hiring of a younger employee in the same protected class did not create an inference of discrimination, and when there was nothing to support the plaintiff's assertion that the hiring of a replacement seven years his junior could reasonably be said to reflect discriminatory conduct: Weiper v. W.A. Hill & Assocs., 104 Ohio App. 3d 250, 661 N.E.2d 796, 1995 Ohio App. LEXIS 2202 (Ohio Ct. App., Hamilton County 1995).

Where an employer implements a plan to reduce the work force due to economic necessity, an employee's burden of establishing a prima facie case of age discrimination is somewhat heavier: Wang v. Goodyear Tire & Rubber Co., 68 Ohio App. 3d 13, 587 N.E.2d 387, 1990 Ohio App. LEXIS 2356 (Ohio Ct. App., Summit County 1990).

**— —Replacement**

Trial court did not err by granting the employer summary judgment on the employee's age discrimination claim because she failed to show that she was replaced, as she admitted that tasks related to grants was only a portion of her job, the new employee was hired to do data entry for the new accounting system which was not part of the employee's job, there was no evidence that the new employee assumed any or all of the job responsibilities of the business retention and expansion coordinator, which was the employee's job title at the time of her termination, and the employee's responsibilities as manger of finance and administration were absorbed by multiple employees. Ksiazek v. Columbiana Cty. Port Auth., 2021-Ohio-1267, 171 N.E.3d 394, 2021 Ohio App. LEXIS 1251 (Ohio Ct. App., Columbiana County 2021).

In a former employee's suit for age discrimination, the employer's motion for summary judgment was denied because the former employee set forth a prima facie case based on the evidence that he was discharged from his job and replaced by a younger person. Wind v. Walgreen Co., 2011 U.S. Dist. LEXIS 154972 (S.D. Ohio June 22, 2011).

**—Collective bargaining agreement**

Trial court erred when it granted the employer's motion to dismiss under Civ.R. 12(B)(1) and (6) because the employee was not required to exhaust his administrative remedies before filing a lawsuit based on age discrimination; in his grievance, he alleged that he did not agree with the discipline imposed and thus, his grievance concerned his contractual rights but, in his lawsuit, he alleged age discrimination under R.C. 4112.02(A), a statutory right. His statutory rights under R.C. ch. 4112 were distinct from any right conferred from the collective bargaining agreement and were therefore independent of the arbitration process and the collective bargaining agreement, while mentioning that the employer could not discriminate based on age, did not contain a clear and unmistakable agreement to arbitrate statutory claims. Haynes v. Ohio Tpk. Comm'n, 2008-Ohio-133, 177 Ohio App. 3d 1, 893 N.E.2d 850, 2008 Ohio App. LEXIS 121 (Ohio Ct. App., Cuyahoga County 2008).

**—Evidence**

There was a genuine issue of material fact precluding summary judgment as to appellant's age discrimination claim, as a decision-maker told a human resources employee who scheduled interviews that appellant was "close to retirement age"; the comment dealt with age and was said to be made in the context of explaining why the decision-maker was not willing to interview and hire appellant, and was direct evidence of age discrimination. Sciaretta v. Refractory Specialties, Inc., 2018-Ohio-1141, 2018 Ohio App. LEXIS 1225 (Ohio Ct. App., Mahoning County 2018).

*Unpublished decision:* Jury could reasonably have concluded that the employer chose the employee for the reduction in force at least, in part, to satisfy the expressed desire to "go after" older employees and stop losing young ones, and another's expressed belief that the company should look "young and aggressive" and not employ "old, tired programmers;" six of the seven RIF'd employees were over 40 years old, with plaintiff the oldest at 55. Coburn v. Rockwell Automation, Inc., 238 Fed. Appx. 112, 2007 FED App. 0467N, 2007 U.S. App. LEXIS 16632 (6th Cir. Ohio 2007).

Although the nurse was a member of a statutorily protected class (she was 50 years old) and she was discharged, she failed to provide evidence that she was qualified for the job as a heart catheter lab registered nurse and, thus, failed to establish a prima facie case of age discrimination. When asked during her deposition whether, at the time of her termination, she was capable of handling the workload of a heart catheter lab R.N., she responded that she was not (she was terminated for making three medical mistakes in three consecutive days) and she also failed to produce evidence that she was replaced by, or that her discharge permitted the retention of, a person outside of the protected class. Guy v. Q.H.G. of Massillon, Inc., 2007 Ohio App. LEXIS 394 (Ohio Ct. App., Stark County Jan. 29, 2007).

In a case of age discrimination, it must be shown that age was the motivating factor for an adverse employment action, and, generally, the denial of a promotion is an adverse employment action. Buckholz v. Bowling Green State Univ., 2006-Ohio-624, 2006 Ohio Misc. LEXIS 29 (Ohio Ct. Cl. 2006).

When an employee claimed that his employer's failure to promote him and its termination of his employment was due to age discrimination, he proved (1) that he was over 40 years of age; (2) that he was subjected to an adverse employment action, both by being fired and by not being promoted; and (3) that he was qualified both for the job he held and for the job he sought, but he did not prove the age of the person who received the job he wanted, nor did he prove the age of anyone who was hired to replace him, so his age discrimination claim failed. Buckholz v. Bowling Green State Univ., 2006-Ohio-624, 2006 Ohio Misc. LEXIS 29 (Ohio Ct. Cl. 2006).

Granting of the employer's motion for summary judgment in the employee's action for age discrimination and retaliation pursuant to the Age Discrimination in Employment Act, 29 U.S.C.S. §§ 623, et seq., and R.C. 4112.02(I) and 4112.14. was proper where a former employee's statement of opinion could not be considered a statement of the party opponent for purposes of Fed. R. Evid. 801(d)(2)(D) because that employee had left the company. Further, the employee failed to identify evidence suggesting that the employer's articulated reason for the alleged adverse actions was mere pretext. Rufo v. Dave & Busters, Inc., 2005 U.S. Dist. LEXIS 33395 (S.D. Ohio Dec. 16, 2005), aff'd, 2007 FED App. 0075N, 2007 U.S. App. LEXIS 2366 (6th Cir. Ohio Jan. 31, 2007).

Trial court properly granted summary judgment to a country club on an employee's age discrimination claim as the country club dismissed the employee after two female employees alleged that the employee sexually harassed them; the employee failed to show that the country club's reason for his discharge was pretextual as the employee offered no additional evidence of age discrimination other than what he relied on to make his prima facie case, presented no evidence that the country club's explanations were factually false, or showed that other, but younger, employees were not fired even though they engaged in the same type of behavior. Wilson v. Rosemont Country Club, 2005-Ohio-6606, 2005 Ohio App. LEXIS 5953 (Ohio Ct. App., Summit County 2005).

There was sufficient evidence to support a jury's determination that an employee discriminated against a 53-year-old employee on the basis of his age, in violation of R.C. 4112.02(A) and 4112.99, where the employee's manager position was eliminated due to downsizing, and the new position offered to the employee was not in a competitive area and constituted a demotion in the sales hierarchy; further, the position that the employee could have been offered was given to a person who was younger and who did not have the seniority with the employer that the employee had, such that the trial court's grant of a judgment notwithstanding the verdict in favor of the employer and others, pursuant to Civ.R. 50(B), was error. Jelinek v. Abbott Labs., 2005-Ohio-5696, 164 Ohio App. 3d 607, 843 N.E.2d 807, 2005 Ohio App. LEXIS 5122 (Ohio Ct. App., Franklin County 2005).

Trial court properly granted summary judgment to a judge in an age discrimination action under R.C. 4112.02(A) and 4112.14(A) by deputy clerks who were terminated when the judge took office in a county probate judge capacity, as the clerks did not show direct evidence of the discrimination; statements by a co-worker were not evidence, as she had no decisionmaking authority and accordingly, the statements were not reflective of the judge's discriminatory intent, and as the clerks were unaware of the ages of those who replaced them, there was no statistical evidence to support their claims. Molnar v. Klammer, 2005-Ohio-6905, 2005 Ohio App. LEXIS 6227 (Ohio Ct. App., Lake County 2005).

Where an employee over the age of 40 was terminated from a receptionist position in a one-person reduction in force and the employer retained another receptionist who was over 40 and was less than six years younger than the employee, the employee's age discrimination claims failed to survive summary judgment because the employee did not provide any evidence that a similarly situated younger employee received more favorable treatment than the employee. Van Diest v. Deloitte & Touche, LLP, 2005 U.S. Dist. LEXIS 22106 (N.D. Ohio Sept. 30, 2005).

Where a 60-year-old employee was terminated for poor performance due to a supervisor's evaluations and was replaced by a 47-year-old and a 40-year-old, the employee's age discrimination claims failed to survive summary judgment because the employer articulated a legitimate, nondiscriminatory reason for the employee's discharge and the employee could not show pretext based solely upon replacement by significantly younger persons. Weller v. Titanium Metals Corp., 361 F. Supp. 2d 712, 2005 U.S. Dist. LEXIS 8373 (S.D. Ohio 2005).

**—Evidence insufficient**

Employee's race and age discrimination claims arising from the employer's failure to promote her failed, where although she had established a prima facie case, the employer's explanation that another candidate performed better in the interview process provided a legitimate, nondiscriminatory reason for not promoting the employee, and the employee offered no additional evidence that the determination that the other candidate's sociology degree met the minimum educational requirements for an interview was pretextual. Drummond v. Ohio Dep't of Rehab. & Corr., 2021-Ohio-2408, 2021 Ohio Misc. LEXIS 86 (Ohio Ct. Cl. 2021), aff'd, 2022-Ohio-1096, 2022 Ohio App. LEXIS 985 (Ohio Ct. App., Franklin County 2022).

Employee failed to establish a prima facie case of age discrimination because the employee failed to present evidence that the employee was replaced in the employee's position with a city by a younger person as an older person was hired and resigned before a younger person was hired. The employee also failed to prove that the city's proffered reason for terminating the employee, namely, the employee's outside employment on city time and the employee's failure to disclose such work during the city's investigations, was merely a pretext. Collins v. City of Mason, 2020-Ohio-1186, 153 N.E.3d 484, 2020 Ohio App. LEXIS 1109 (Ohio Ct. App., Warren County 2020).

Trial court did not err by granting summary judgment for the employer on the former nursing home administrator's age discrimination claim because he failed to produce sufficient evidence from which a reasonable jury could have rejected as pretextual the employer's legitimate nondiscriminatory reasons for termination of poor and substandard work performance. Brehm v. Macintosh Co., 2019-Ohio-5322, 2019 Ohio App. LEXIS 5396 (Ohio Ct. App., Franklin County 2019).

Employee's statistical data was insufficient to establish discriminatory intent because it did not confirm the employee's belief that the employer's music department chair regularly hired younger employees and fired older employees; two non-renewals out of approximately 200 employment decisions over a time period of approximately two years was statistically significant evidence of age discrimination. Pla v. Cleveland State Univ., 2016-Ohio-3150, 2016 Ohio Misc. LEXIS 62 (Ohio Ct. Cl.), aff'd, 2016-Ohio-8165, 2016 Ohio App. LEXIS 5020 (Ohio Ct. App., Franklin County 2016).

When a hospital terminated an employee there was no evidence that two related companies controlled the decision, or that the companies aided or assisted in the alleged age discrimination; further, the hospital could not aid or abet itself. Sampson v. Sisters of Mercy of Willard, 2015 U.S. Dist. LEXIS 84108 (N.D. Ohio June 29, 2015), dismissed in part, 2016 U.S. Dist. LEXIS 19753 (N.D. Ohio Feb. 18, 2016).

*Unpublished decision:* Employee's age discrimination claims based on circumstantial evidence failed because, inter alia, the employee claimed that the employer assigned the employee more difficult jobs than younger employees, but admitted that an employee with the employee's training and experience could better handle more difficult jobs, and the employee did not show pretext. Sloban v. Mahoning Youngstown Cmty. Action P'ship, 604 Fed. Appx. 407, 2015 FED App. 0184N, 2015 U.S. App. LEXIS 3928 (6th Cir. Ohio 2015).

Trial court properly granted summary judgment to a village and one of its employees in a former employee's age discrimination action, as she failed to establish a prima facie case of age discrimination, and her inferior qualifications were a legitimate, nondiscriminatory reason for not hiring her as a full-time clerk. McCarthy v. Vill. of Lordstown, 2015-Ohio-955, 2015 Ohio App. LEXIS 906 (Ohio Ct. App., Trumbull County 2015).

Where a terminated employee was not hired for an open position, the employee's disparate impact claim failed because the employee offered no evidence of any statistical disparities caused by the program through which a younger applicant was hired, and the employee did not offer any statistical evidence of any kind. Lawroski v. Nationwide Mut. INS. Co., 2013 U.S. Dist. LEXIS 157151 (S.D. Ohio Nov. 1, 2013).

Summary judgment was properly granted to an employer and another in an employee's age discrimination action because the employer provided legitimate, non-discriminatory reasons for termination of the employee from his job due to improper workplace conduct, and the employee failed to show that the reasons were merely pretextual and that age was the "but for" cause of termination. Morrissette v. DFS Servs., LLC, 2013-Ohio-4336, 2013 Ohio App. LEXIS 4570 (Ohio Ct. App., Franklin County 2013).

Medical center's motion for summary judgment was granted in a nurse's suit against it for age discrimination, in violation of the Age Discrimination and Employment Act, 29 U.S.C.S. § 623, and the Age Discrimination in Employment Act, R.C. 4112.02(A) and R.C. 4112.14, because the nurse failed to demonstrate the existence of a genuine dispute over the fact that the medical center had a reasonably-held belief about her work-performance problems based on two work performance plans she had been placed on and an email listing reasons for her termination, thus, the nurse failed to show that the medical center did not reasonably rely on the existence of those sources for terminating her employment. Fischbach v. Cmty. Mercy Health Partners, 2012 U.S. Dist. LEXIS 139019 (S.D. Ohio Sept. 27, 2012).

As an employee failed to set forth a prima facie case of age discrimination under R.C. 4112.02(A) because she could not demonstrate that she was replaced by a substantially younger person or that she was treated differently from a substantially similar individual, summary judgment was properly granted to the employer; she and another person who committed the same error were not similarly situated due, in part, to their different experience levels. Borad v. April Enters., 2012-Ohio-5096, 2012 Ohio App. LEXIS 4460 (Ohio Ct. App., Montgomery County 2012).

Summary judgment was properly granted for the corporation on the age discrimination claim because the corporation's president, the person who took the position, was the same age as the former vice president and he had legitimate, non-discriminatory reasons for taking the position in that he wanted to facilitate the integration of the two new business entities that the corporation had purchased. Hoyt v. Nationwide Mut. Ins. Co., 2005-Ohio-6367, 2005 Ohio App. LEXIS 5700 (Ohio Ct. App., Franklin County 2005).

Even if the employee established a prima facie case sufficient to raise a presumption of age discrimination, summary judgment in favor of the employer and the human resources manager was appropriate because they submitted evidentiary material sufficient to show a legitimate nondiscriminatory basis for termination and shifted the burden to the employee. The employee did not present any evidence that created a genuine issue regarding whether that reason was pretextual and the evidence only supported the conclusion that the employee was discharged because of her poor performance and her poor attitude, not because of her age. McGlumphy v. Cnty. Fire Prot., Inc., 2016-Ohio-8114, 74 N.E.3d 986, 2016 Ohio App. LEXIS 4977 (Ohio Ct. App., Portage County 2016).

**—Failure to hire**

In an appeal against a grant of summary judgment on claimant's claims for race and age discrimination, claimant had established a prima facie case of race and age discrimination because despite having the qualifications for the applied position, a white woman who was substantially younger than claimant was hired since she was African American and was 55 years old; therefore, she was a member of protected race and age classes. Defendant did not dispute that she was qualified for the position. Drummond v. Ohio Dep't of Rehab. & Corr., 2022-Ohio-1096, 2022 Ohio App. LEXIS 985 (Ohio Ct. App., Franklin County 2022).

In this Age Discrimination in Employment Act of 1967 and R.C. 4112.02(A) action, defendant was granted summary judgment because plaintiff never applied for a full-time position or explicitly informed defendant or management that he sought permanent employment and defendant had no reason a discriminatory qualification standard was being used to offer temporary employees full-time positions. Pate v. MetoKote Corp., 2012 U.S. Dist. LEXIS 162032 (S.D. Ohio Nov. 13, 2012).

Court of claims' judgment in favor of an employer on an employee's age discrimination claim was not against the manifest weight of the evidence as there was a lack of evidence that the employer made a discriminatory decision when it failed to hire him for a position; rather, the evidence was convincing that the employee did not possess the computer, model-building, and 3-D imaging skills important to the position, and the two employees hired did. In addition, there was evidence that the employee lacked other important qualities desired for the position. Knepper v. Ohio State Univ., 2011-Ohio-6054, 2011 Ohio App. LEXIS 4943 (Ohio Ct. App., Franklin County 2011).

In an age discrimination claim by a former high school counselor who was passed over for the counselor's own vacant position, the trial court improperly granted summary judgment to the school board and a school superintendent, as there was a genuine issue of material fact regarding whether the reason the superintendent gave for recommending the hired candidate was the true reason; testimony indicated the hiring committee was not unanimous. Welch v. Norton City Sch. Dist. Bd. of Educ., 2010-Ohio-6131, 2010 Ohio App. LEXIS 5157 (Ohio Ct. App., Summit County 2010).

Summary judgment in favor of an employer in an age discrimination case was affirmed because the employee failed to demonstrated that the reason given for failing to hire the employee into the newly-structured organization—that he had a negative attitude toward management and his negativity affected co-workers—was mere pretext. Miller v. Potash Corp. of Sask., Inc., 2010-Ohio-4291, 2010 Ohio App. LEXIS 3625 (Ohio Ct. App., Allen County 2010).

Job applicant did not present any direct evidence of age discrimination because the applicant failed to prove by a preponderance of the evidence that he was discriminated against on the basis of his age, that he was treated less favorably as a result of his age, or that the decision not to hire him was motivated by his age. According to the testimony, the applicant was not hired because he lacked both the necessary computer skills and experience in managing complex projects and thus, the interviewers articulated legitimate, nondiscriminatory reasons for not hiring the applicant. Knepper v. Ohio State Univ., 2010-Ohio-5914, 2010 Ohio Misc. LEXIS 349 (Ohio Ct. Cl. 2010), aff'd, 2011-Ohio-6054, 2011 Ohio App. LEXIS 4943 (Ohio Ct. App., Franklin County 2011).

In an age discrimination case, non-discriminatory reasons for rejecting appellants for the position and hiring a younger person existed because the philosophy of the employer began to shift away from a law enforcement approach that focused upon apprehension of parole violators to a community re-entry social work approach that focused upon keeping offenders out of prison, and the successful applicant had the type of educational background and work experience to supervise the unit in accordance with the new philosophy. Bogdas v. Ohio Dep't of Rehab. & Corr., 2009-Ohio-6327, 2009 Ohio App. LEXIS 5307 (Ohio Ct. App., Franklin County 2009).

Although an applicant, who was not hired after interviewing for either of two entry-level academic advisor positions with a community college district, presented a prima facie case of age discrimination, as two younger people were hired for the positions, the employer was entitled to summary judgment because the employer offered legitimate nondiscriminatory reasons for its hiring decisions, which were not rebutted. The people on the employer's committee which made the hiring decisions were concerned that the applicant was overqualified for the entry level positions and that the younger people who were hired were more suited for the positions. Silberstein v. Montgomery County Cmty. College Dist., 2009-Ohio-6138, 2009 Ohio App. LEXIS 5154 (Ohio Ct. App., Montgomery County 2009).

Employee's age discrimination suit under R.C. 4112.99 was properly dismissed on summary judgment as the 51-year-old employee could not show that the reasons proffered by the employer for hiring a 21-year-old individual, not the employee, were pretextual. he younger individual was hired because she had more recent relevant business experience and because the younger individual viewed the position with long-term interest, while the employee indicated that she was interested in using the job as a stepping stone for a better accounting position. Dabney-Hall v. Cleveland Clinic Found., 2008-Ohio-1080, 2008 Ohio App. LEXIS 945 (Ohio Ct. App., Cuyahoga County 2008).

*Unpublished decision:* Summary judgment in favor of a former employer on a former employee's age discrimination claim in violation of the Age Discrimination in Employment Act and Ohion law was affirmed where the school board's stated reasons for not considering the employee for the open position were legitimate and nondiscriminatory, and were unrefuted. Especially significant was that the employee's own deposition testimony demonstrated that she was interested in continuing to work only on a part-time basis and that she never told anyone with decision-making authority that she was specifically interested in the new full-time position. Herbick v. Salem City Sch. Dist. Bd. of Educ., 151 Fed. Appx. 463, 2005 FED App. 0870N, 2005 U.S. App. LEXIS 23286 (6th Cir. Ohio 2005).

Former employer's failure to hire a former worker, which it had recently terminated, for a subsequent position was an alleged discrete discriminatory act and actionable under Ohio's age discrimination statute. Yovanno v. Ryder Sys., 2003-Ohio-6824, 2003 Ohio App. LEXIS 6159 (Ohio Ct. App., Summit County 2003).

A school district's failure to hire a tutor as a classroom teacher is not age discrimination where another candidate is definitely better qualified: Twinsburg City Sch. v. Ohio Civil Rights Comm'n, 86 Ohio App. 3d 527, 621 N.E.2d 591, 1993 Ohio App. LEXIS 1195 (Ohio Ct. App., Summit County 1993).

**—Intent**

Appellant failed to offer any evidence tending to show discriminatory intent by appellant's former employer, precluding the showing of a prima facie case of age discrimination, as the former employer faced challenges including the loss of clients, a client's bankruptcy, and the departure of one of its shareholders; in light of these conditions, it took a number of measures to improve efficiency and cut costs, and appellant failed to offer any evidence tending to show discriminatory intent in appellant's dismissal. Karsnak v. Chess Fin. Corp., 2012-Ohio-1359, 2012 Ohio App. LEXIS 1181 (Ohio Ct. App., Cuyahoga County 2012).

There was no nexus between the defendants' general remarks concerning age and plaintiff's discharge. Where a former employee's duties are assumed by a variety of people, at least one of whom is in the age-protected class, discriminatory intent is not established indirectly: Smith v. E.G. Baldwin & Assocs., 119 Ohio App. 3d 410, 695 N.E.2d 349, 1997 Ohio App. LEXIS 1763 (Ohio Ct. App., Franklin County 1997).

**—Jury instruction**

Trial court abused its discretion by providing the jurors with an incomplete instruction on a former employee's claim of age discrimination because the trial court's instruction only informed the jurors of one of the two alternative ways to prove age discrimination, replacement, but not the retention of a younger employee. Fearn v. Longaberger Co., 2010-Ohio-1736, 2010 Ohio App. LEXIS 1445 (Ohio Ct. App., Muskingum County 2010).

**—Legitimate termination**

Discharged employee failed to create a genuine issue of material fact in support of his claim of age discrimination because, although the trial court erroneously found that the employee failed to establish a prima facie case of discrimination, it properly found that he was terminated for a legitimate, non-discriminatory reason. The employer presented evidence that between 2013 and 2015, he was given three corrective action notices, was placed on two performance improvement plans, and received below-average ratings on his 2015 performance evaluations. Beckloff v. Amcor Rigid Plastics USA, LLC, 2017-Ohio-4467, 93 N.E.3d 329, 2017 Ohio App. LEXIS 2525 (Ohio Ct. App., Sandusky County 2017).

**—Pretext**

Where a terminated employee was not hired for an open position, the employee's disparate treatment claim failed because the employer stated that the employee was terminated for lack of work and cost savings and that the employee was not re-hired because the employee was ranked the lowest of the five applicants, which were legitimate, nondiscriminatory reasons, and the employee did not show pretext. Lawroski v. Nationwide Mut. INS. Co., 2013 U.S. Dist. LEXIS 157151 (S.D. Ohio Nov. 1, 2013).

Former employee's age discrimination suit was properly dismissed on summary judgment because, although the employee established a prima facie case of discrimination, the employer articulated a legitimate, nondiscriminatory reason for the employee's termination, his violation of a known directive ordering him to cease communicating with other employees regarding a complaint, and the employee failed to establish that the employer's reason was pretextual. Vossman v. AirNet Sys., 2013-Ohio-4675, 2013 Ohio App. LEXIS 4894 (Ohio Ct. App., Franklin County 2013).

Genuine issues of material fact remained as to whether an employer had a legitimate nondiscriminatory reason for terminating an employee, who had made a prima facie case of age discrimination, as the employer's financial problems did not explain why the employee, age 60, was discharged, while a retained employee, age 23, was not; further, there was evidence that the proffered reasons were a mere pretext as they did not actually motivate the employee's discharge or were insufficient to motivate her discharge. Hoffman v. CHSHO, Inc., 2005-Ohio-3909, 2005 Ohio App. LEXIS 3597 (Ohio Ct. App., Clermont County 2005).

**—Prima facie case**

Trial court properly granted summary judgment on the age discrimination claim under Civ.R. 56(C) because the employee did not argue or establish a nexus between the township asking when she would retire and any of the events she claimed were adverse employment actions. Fonce v. Champion Twp., 2022-Ohio-1278, 2022 Ohio App. LEXIS 1173 (Ohio Ct. App., Trumbull County 2022).

Trial court properly granted summary judgment for the city because the former employee failed to establish a prima facie case of age discrimination. The former employee failed to establish the fourth element of either prima facie case, as he failed to present evidence indicating that he was replaced by a substantially younger person, that a comparable non-protected employee was treated better, or that other reasonable evidence existed to raise an inference that the city refused to rehire him because of his age. Tilley v. City of Dublin, 2013-Ohio-4930, 2013 Ohio App. LEXIS 5130 (Ohio Ct. App., Franklin County 2013).

Because the employee raised a genuine issue of material fact as to whether a substantially younger, similarly-situated co-worker was treated more favorably despite engaging in substantially similar conduct, the employee demonstrated that the reason for his termination was insufficient. Bowditch v. Mettler Toledo Int'l, Inc., 2013-Ohio-4206, 2013 Ohio App. LEXIS 4380 (Ohio Ct. App., Franklin County 2013).

Trial court erred by granting summary judgment for the employer and the human resources leader. Because reasonable minds could have differed as to whether similarly-situated employees were treated more favorably than the employee, he established the fourth element of his prima facie case for age discrimination. Bowditch v. Mettler Toledo Int'l, Inc., 2013-Ohio-4206, 2013 Ohio App. LEXIS 4380 (Ohio Ct. App., Franklin County 2013).

Employee had not identified evidence which a reasonable juror could conclude was direct evidence of age discrimination in violation of the Age Discrimination in Employment Act, 29 U.S.C.S. § 623 or R.C. 4112.02; in addition, the employee had not identified evidence from which a reasonable juror could conclude that the employee satisfied the fourth element of a prima facie case of age, national origin or race discrimination under Title VII of the Civil Rights Act of 1964, 42 U.S.C.S. § 2000e-2 or R.C. 4112.02, that he was replaced by someone outside the protected class or that he was treated differently than a similarly-situated, non-protected employee. Moreover, the employer showed a legitimate, nondiscriminatory reason for terminating the employee's employment, his poor performance over several years, and the employee had not identified evidence from which a reasonable juror could conclude that the employer's reason was a pretext for discrimination. Kumar v. Aldrich Chem. Co., 911 F. Supp. 2d 571, 2012 U.S. Dist. LEXIS 166354 (S.D. Ohio 2012).

Employee failed to raise a prima facie case of age discrimination under R.C. 4112.02(A) where: (1) although an office worker about 44 years younger than the employee hired after the employee was discharged replicated some, if not many, of the duties formerly handled by the employee, the employer testified that the officer worker and a co-worker jointly became responsible for handling the insurance after the employee's termination and that all were to a great extent handling patient accounts; (2) the employer made clear that the officer worker was not considered the new office manager of the practice; and (3) reasonable minds could only conclude that the office worker was utilized upon her hiring as part of a shared-duty approach to the dental practice's office work and that the employee's admitted position as office manager was never re-filled. Grimsley v. Cain DDS, LLC, 2012-Ohio-5273, 2012 Ohio App. LEXIS 4613 (Ohio Ct. App., Stark County 2012).

Employee established the "somewhat heightened" prima facie case for her age discrimination case, applicable to reduction in force cases, where: (1) the employee was 60 years old at the time of her discharge and was a member of a statutorily-protected class, (2) the employee was terminated from her position as a nurse aide scheduler, (3) the employee was qualified for that position, (4) her discharge permitted her employer to retain an employee who was not a member of a statutorily-protected class (retained employee), and (5) the employee's professional experience dwarfed that of the retained employee. Hoffman v. CHSHO, Inc., 2005-Ohio-3909, 2005 Ohio App. LEXIS 3597 (Ohio Ct. App., Clermont County 2005).

**—Proof of motivation**

In his age discrimination suit, a former employee offered sufficient evidence to allow a conclusion that age discrimination motivated the employer's decision to fire him as the evidence showed that only one of the employees holding the same sales position as the employee met the sales goals, that the employee's sales numbers consistently ranked in the mid-range of the other sales employees, and that at least five substantially younger employees whose sales numbers were below the employee's were neither disciplined nor terminated. Moreover, the employee's evidence showed that the false reason given for his termination masked the employer's discriminatory animus as the record showed that the employer had no written or verbal policy about the number of years an employee could fail to meet goals before being terminated. Pattison v. W.W. Grainger, Inc., 2010-Ohio-2484, 2010 Ohio App. LEXIS 2021 (Ohio Ct. App., Cuyahoga County 2010).

**—Proof of qualification for position**

In his age discrimination suit, a former employee offered sufficient evidence for a reasonable jury to find that he was qualified for his position as his proof showed that, prior to his termination, he generated $3.5 million in revenue, that he was responsible for 2400 accounts, and that several of his customers spoke highly of his qualifications and dependability. Pattison v. W.W. Grainger, Inc., 2010-Ohio-2484, 2010 Ohio App. LEXIS 2021 (Ohio Ct. App., Cuyahoga County 2010).

**—Punitive damages**

The employees established a prima facie case of age discrimination. The employer's conduct supported an award of punitive damages: Srail v. RJF Int'l Corp., 126 Ohio App. 3d 689, 711 N.E.2d 264, 1998 Ohio App. LEXIS 862 (Ohio Ct. App., Cuyahoga County), dismissed, 82 Ohio St. 3d 1473, 696 N.E.2d 602, 1998 Ohio LEXIS 1991 (Ohio 1998).

**—Reduction of work force**

Trial court properly found that the employee's discharge was pursuant to a reduction in force. Since the employee's argument focused exclusively on the proximity between the employer's loss of business and its decision to terminate his position, he failed to demonstrate that the employer was not entitled to judgment on his age discrimination claim. Weisfeld v. PASCO, Inc., 2013-Ohio-1528, 2013 Ohio App. LEXIS 1415 (Ohio Ct. App., Summit County 2013).

Where an employer contended that an employee was selected for termination in a reduction-in-force (RIF) because two other substantially younger workers had more experience and were more proficient in using advanced purchasing software, the employer was entitled to summary judgment on the employee's age discrimination claims because the informal nature of the plan to carry out the RIF was insufficient to support an inference that the employee was terminated because of his age. Trapp v. TSS Techs., Inc., 2011 U.S. Dist. LEXIS 86 (S.D. Ohio Jan. 3, 2011), aff'd, 485 Fed. Appx. 757, 2012 FED App. 0655N, 2012 U.S. App. LEXIS 12876 (6th Cir. Ohio 2012).

Former employee did not present evidence of age-related discrimination, in violation of R.C. 4112.02(A) and 4112.14, because a valid work force reduction occurred as the employee's position was abolished, the employee was not replaced, and the employee's duties were redistributed to other employees in the employee's unit at work, in addition to their existing duties. Wise v. Ohio State Univ., 2011-Ohio-6566, 2011 Ohio App. LEXIS 5403 (Ohio Ct. App., Franklin County 2011).

Trial court erred when it granted summary judgment to a terminated employee in his age discrimination matter under R.C. 4112.02(A), as he made out a prima facie case of age discrimination, and he also provided evidence that the employer's stated reason for his termination pursuant to a reduction in force was a mere pretext for purposeful age discrimination. Southworth v. N. Trust Sec., Inc., 2011-Ohio-3467, 195 Ohio App. 3d 357, 960 N.E.2d 473, 2011 Ohio App. LEXIS 2936 (Ohio Ct. App., Cuyahoga County 2011).

Trial court did not err by granting summary judgment for the employer on the age discrimination claim because the employee failed to present evidence demonstrating genuine issues of material fact at each stage of the McDonnell-Douglas burden shifting inquiry; the employer clearly reduced its work force when it eliminated the employee's position by discharging him and not replacing him. Freshour v. TK Constructors, Inc., 2011-Ohio-2163, 2011 Ohio App. LEXIS 1839 (Ohio Ct. App., Franklin County 2011).

**—Remark**

No inference of age bias would be drawn from a question the employer's music department chair posed to an employee about her retirement because there was no evidence that the question was related to the department chair's decision not to renew the employee's contract; the singular isolated comment was also made approximately two years before the department chair decided not to renew her contract. Pla v. Cleveland State Univ., 2016-Ohio-3150, 2016 Ohio Misc. LEXIS 62 (Ohio Ct. Cl.), aff'd, 2016-Ohio-8165, 2016 Ohio App. LEXIS 5020 (Ohio Ct. App., Franklin County 2016).

*Unpublished decision:* Where an employee alleged that the employee overheard a conversation between a director, an assistant director, and another individual involving age-related comments, the employee's age discrimination claims based on direct evidence failed because the comments were not direct evidence of discrimination attributable to the employee's supervisor and there was no evidence that the comments caused or were related to the employee's discharge. Sloban v. Mahoning Youngstown Cmty. Action P'ship, 604 Fed. Appx. 407, 2015 FED App. 0184N, 2015 U.S. App. LEXIS 3928 (6th Cir. Ohio 2015).

Remark made by the employer's president that an employee was too old, and would never change, made in the context of a suggestion that a new management team should place their differences aside was insufficient to sustain the employee's age discrimination claim under R.C. 4112.02 as there was no evidence of a nexus between the comment and the employee's discharge; further, the employee was not "replaced" within the meaning of Ohio law, since the employer reassigned his responsibilities to a different worker. Langlois v. W.P. Hickman Sys., 2006-Ohio-3737, 2006 Ohio App. LEXIS 3693 (Ohio Ct. App., Cuyahoga County 2006).

Student did not show a genuine issue of material fact as to whether she was dismissed from an instructional program at a college due to her age, because (1) the only remark the coordinator of clinical education allegedly made about the student's age was made after the student had already received a failing grade in the program, and (2) whatever remark the coordinator made on that subject was only made after the student raised the subject by saying she was too old to start over. McCrobie v. Stark State College of Tech., 2006-Ohio-2055, 2006 Ohio App. LEXIS 1885 (Ohio Ct. App., Stark County 2006).

**—Reorganization**

Summary judgment was properly granted, dismissing an age discrimination claim, under R.C. 4112.02(N) and 4112.99, brought by a former employee and his wife against the employee's former employer and various managers, because plaintiffs' claim was not filed until more than 180 days after the employee's employment was terminated. Even if plaintiffs could bring suit pursuant to R.C. 4112.02(N) and 4112.99, defendants were entitled to summary judgment because the evidence showed that the work that the employee would have received was distributed among the retained workers, several of which were in the protected class; further, defendants offered a legitimate, non-discriminatory reason for the employee's discharge, a reduction in force, and plaintiffs failed to prove that defendants' work force reduction explanation was a pretext for age discrimination. Vickers v. Wren Indus., 2005-Ohio-3656, 2005 Ohio App. LEXIS 3366 (Ohio Ct. App., Montgomery County 2005).

**—Replacement**

There were no genuine issues of material fact regarding the former employee's age discrimination claim because he failed to establish that he was replaced by an employee of a substantially younger age who was not a member of the protected class and failed to meet his burden of showing that the employer's reasons for the adverse employment action were a pretext for unlawful age discrimination. The employee was hired at the age of 52 and terminated at the age of 53 and the person who replaced him was only seven years younger. Brown v. O'Reilly Auto. Stores, Inc., 2015-Ohio-5146, 54 N.E.3d 638, 2015 Ohio App. LEXIS 5125 (Ohio Ct. App., Cuyahoga County 2015).

Summary judgment was properly granted for the employer because the employee failed to establish that a genuine issue of material fact existed regarding whether he was replaced by another worker. It was the network coordinator who took over almost all of the duties that the employee had as director of technology and that position was being held by a 60-year-old individual. Weisfeld v. PASCO, Inc., 2013-Ohio-1528, 2013 Ohio App. LEXIS 1415 (Ohio Ct. App., Summit County 2013).

Where a former employee alleged age discrimination in employment in violation of the Age Discrimination in Employment Act, 29 U.S.C.S. § 621 et seq., and R.C. 4112.02(A), (N), an alleged statement that he was being replaced by his German counterpart, when his company acquired a German manufacturing company, because he was 55-years old was not direct evidence, but he established a prima facie case via circumstantial evidence. The statement did not necessarily require a conclusion that the employer's decision was motivated by unlawful discrimination; however, the employee was qualified, the case was not a classic workforce reduction case, and the employee, who was not required, therefore, to meet a heightened pleading duty, clearly met the classic prima facie case as he fell within a protected class, suffered an adverse employment action, was qualified, and was replaced by a younger person; moreover, the employee raised a genuine issue of material fact regarding pretext as a reasonable jury could conclude that the employee's replacement was not better qualified than he, and that the employer would not have made the same decision absent age discrimination, given that he had successfully managed the company with profit while the replacement had not. Siemer v. Comet N. Am., 467 F. Supp. 2d 781, 2006 U.S. Dist. LEXIS 86898 (S.D. Ohio 2006).

Trial court's grant of summary judgment to former employers in an age discrimination claim under R.C. 4112.02 was appropriate where the former employee only satisfied the burden of proof as to the first three parts of the McDonnell Douglas test, but he failed to show that a substantially younger person was hired to replace him; further, isolated, vague, and ambiguous comments by supervisors of the employer that were age-related or that referred to other employees did not constitute direct evidence of discrimination or discriminatory intent. Abrams v. Am. Computer Tech., 2006-Ohio-4032, 168 Ohio App. 3d 362, 860 N.E.2d 123, 2006 Ohio App. LEXIS 3973 (Ohio Ct. App., Hamilton County 2006).

Where a 50-year old male, working as a newspaper music critic, alleged age and gender discrimination under R.C. 4112.02, the newspaper was denied summary judgment because there was a material question of disputed fact as to whether the male was replaced by a female who was outside of the protected age group, and there was evidence that the employer sought to achieve its goal of appealing to younger, female readers by replacing plaintiff with a young, female columnist. Nager v. The Cincinnati Enquirer, 2005 U.S. Dist. LEXIS 22770 (S.D. Ohio Oct. 6, 2005).

Trial court properly found that appellant failed to satisfy the fourth prong of the McDonnell Douglas and Coryell tests and, therefore, could not establish directly or indirectly a prima facie case of age discrimination; another individual assumed one relatively minor aspect of appellant's former job duties, and the balance of her functions were eliminated with the departure of appellant's supervisor. Wasserstrom v. Battelle Mem. Inst., 2016-Ohio-7943, 74 N.E.3d 827, 2016 Ohio App. LEXIS 4818 (Ohio Ct. App., Franklin County 2016).

**—Same actor inference**

Even if the employee had been able to establish a prima facie case for age discrimination, the employer established a nondiscriminatory intent for the employee's demotion through the same actor inference because the same two supervisors that hired him, later demoted him. Further, the employee's ability to establish a prima facie case of discrimination was called into question through the evidence submitted to the trial court because the employee's position was only taken away after he himself expressed his inability to do the job and it was ultimately given to a person that was older than the employee. Pirsil v. Int'l Steel Group - Cleveland, 2005-Ohio-3013, 2005 Ohio App. LEXIS 2815 (Ohio Ct. App., Cuyahoga County 2005).

**—Standard of proof**

Trial court properly granted summary judgment to a county, as employer, in an action by an employee, asserting claims of age discrimination pursuant to R.C. 4112.02, as the employee failed to establish a prima facie case of discrimination where he could not show that he was replaced or discharged by the county's decision to hire someone else to a position that the employee never held; further, the county had presented legitimate reasons for selecting the two top applicants for the job, although they were outside of the protected class. Smith v. Bd. of Cuyahoga County Comm'rs, 2006-Ohio-1073, 2006 Ohio App. LEXIS 978 (Ohio Ct. App., Cuyahoga County 2006).

**—Subject matter jurisdiction**

Trial court properly dismissed the school principal's age-discrimination claim for lack of subject-matter jurisdiction because he elected to pursue an administrative remedy by filing an Ohio Civil Rights Commission (OCRC) charge, even though it was later withdrawn. The charge and the complaint alleged the same discriminatory practices. Spitulski v. Bd. of Educ. of the Toledo City Sch. Dist., 2018-Ohio-3984, 121 N.E.3d 41, 2018 Ohio App. LEXIS 4311 (Ohio Ct. App., Lucas County 2018).

**Aiding and abetting**

Summary judgment was properly granted to a hockey facility and related coaches and individuals in parents' aiding and abetting claim with respect to alleged retaliatory and sexually harassing conduct, arising from complaints regarding their son's playing time in a youth hockey league, as they could not prove that claim where their underlying assertions of harassment and retaliation lacked merit. Pittman v. Parillo, 2017-Ohio-1477, 2017 Ohio App. LEXIS 1482 (Ohio Ct. App., Lucas County 2017).

**AIDS, HIV**

A hospital emergency room may not refuse to treat HIV-positive patients and merely refer them to another hospital: Fiske v. Rooney, 105 Ohio App. 3d 269, 663 N.E.2d 1014, 1995 Ohio App. LEXIS 3157 (Ohio Ct. App., Scioto County 1995).

In an action alleging housing discrimination against a person with AIDS, in violation of the Toledo Municipal Code, dismissal in favor of the defendant innkeeper was error: Phillips v. Mufleh, 95 Ohio App. 3d 289, 642 N.E.2d 411, 1994 Ohio App. LEXIS 2298 (Ohio Ct. App., Lucas County 1994).

**Alternative justification**

University was entitled to summary judgment on a professor's discrimination claim, based on termination of her administrative appointments, because she failed to show that comparable, nonprotected persons were treated more favorably, and her insubordination and failure to follow the chain of command gave the university legitimate, non-discriminatory reasons for the termination. Min You v. Northeast Ohio Med. Univ., 2017-Ohio-4461, 2017 Ohio Misc. LEXIS 1787 (Ohio Ct. Cl. 2017).

There was no error in granting summary judgment for the employer on the employee's retaliatory discharge claim because, given the time span between his complaints about his coworkers' use of swear words and denigration of women and his ultimate dismissal, the two events were not related. Even if the employee had been able to establish a prima facie case of retaliation, the employer provided a legitimate reason for its action in that the employee was terminated for his medical condition and narcotic use for pain management. Norton v. FirstEnergy Corp., 2006-Ohio-892, 2006 Ohio App. LEXIS 807 (Ohio Ct. App., Jefferson County 2006).

**Amendment of complaint**

Trial court properly denied a former employee's request to file an amended complaint, alleging discriminatory employment practices by the employer, as he did not have a right to amend due to lack of timeliness, and the trial court determined that the amendment would be futile because it would not cure the pleading deficiencies in the original complaint. Martin v. Block Communs., 2017-Ohio-1474, 2017 Ohio App. LEXIS 1480 (Ohio Ct. App., Lucas County 2017).

**Ancestry harassment**

Trial court did not err in granting summary judgment to an employer on the employee's hostile environment ancestry harassment claim as the employee had failed to show that the harassment was based on ancestry, in that there was extensive testimony that the employee's supervisor was verbally abusive to the other employees on his crew who were not Greek, was pushy and difficult to work with and was condescending; and there was evidence that the employee's workplace behavior and his work performance explained his being singled out by the supervisor and that the employee himself regularly insulted co-workers and/or supervisors. Moreover, the employee could not establish that the alleged ancestry harassment was severe or pervasive as the comments made by the supervisor were off-hand, isolated comments occurring over a brief period of time, which failed to alter any term or condition of the employee's employment. Gatsios v. Timken Co., 2012-Ohio-2875, 2012 Ohio App. LEXIS 2512 (Ohio Ct. App., Stark County 2012).

**Antidating policy**

Employees who violated an alleged antidating policy were not similarly situated where one was a supervisor and the other was not. The employer could lawfully choose to discipline only the supervisory employee: Koski v. Willowwood Care Ctr. Of Brunswick, 158 Ohio App. 3d 248, 2004 Ohio 2668, 814 N.E.2d 1235, Ohio App. LEXIS 2367 (2004).

**Applicability**

Summary judgment was properly granted to private outside counsel in parents' sexual harassment claim under the public accommodations statute, alleging that the mother was sexually harassed by hockey facility coaches and others while their son played in a youth hockey league, as counsel were not covered by the statute. Pittman v. Parillo, 2017-Ohio-1477, 2017 Ohio App. LEXIS 1482 (Ohio Ct. App., Lucas County 2017).

**Arbitration**

Where a former employee signed an arbitration agreement with his then-employer, his assertion that he could not be compelled to arbitrate his race discrimination and retaliation claims against the employer was without merit because the claims fell with the scope of the arbitration agreement. Thomas v. Hyundai of Bedford, 2020-Ohio-3030, 154 N.E.3d 701, 2020 Ohio App. LEXIS 1965 (Ohio Ct. App., Cuyahoga County 2020).

Summary judgment was properly granted to a former employer in an age discrimination case because a former employee's challenge of his discharge in a step four grievance procedure set forth in a collective bargaining agreement between the employer and a local union was the functional equivalent of arbitration under R.C. 4112.14(C). Tatman v. Kaiser Aluminum Corp., 2010-Ohio-6402, 2010 Ohio App. LEXIS 5355 (Ohio Ct. App., Licking County 2010).

District court properly dismissed a former employee's age discrimination claims under R.C. 4112.02 and the Age Discrimination in Employment Act, 29 U.S.C.S. § 621 et seq., on the ground that the claims were subject to an enforceable arbitration agreement; although the district court properly severed a cost-shifting provision from the arbitration agreement, it erred in severing an evidentiary provision because the provision could have been interpreted by the arbitrator in such a way as to avoid infringing the employee's rights. Scovill v. WSYX/ABC, Sinclair Broadcast Group, Inc., 425 F.3d 1012, 2005 FED App. 0409P, 2005 U.S. App. LEXIS 21612 (6th Cir. Ohio 2005).

District court properly dismissed a former employee's age discrimination claims under R.C. 4112.02 and the Age Discrimination in Employment Act, 29 U.S.C.S. § 621 et seq., on the ground that the claims were subject to an enforceable arbitration agreement; although the district court properly severed a cost-shifting provision from the arbitration agreement, it erred in severing an evidentiary provision because the provision could have been interpreted by the arbitrator in such a way as to avoid infringing the employee's rights. Scovill v. WSYX/ABC, Sinclair Broadcast Group, Inc., 425 F.3d 1012, 2005 FED App. 0409P, 2005 U.S. App. LEXIS 21612 (6th Cir. Ohio 2005).

The collective bargaining agreement did not require plaintiff to submit claims under R.C. 4112.02 to arbitration: O'Hara v. Mt. Vernon Bd. of Educ., 16 F. Supp. 2d 868, 1998 U.S. Dist. LEXIS 13289 (S.D. Ohio 1998).

An employment agreement requiring arbitration for "any controversy or claim arising out of or relating to this contract or the employment created hereby" covered not only an employee's breach-of-contract claims but also various tort claims asserted for assault, sex discrimination, sexual harassment, intentional infliction of emotional distress, and loss of consortium: Gaffney v. Powell, 107 Ohio App. 3d 315, 668 N.E.2d 951, 1995 Ohio App. LEXIS 4931 (Ohio Ct. App., Hamilton County 1995).

**Associational**

Because the employee's disability claim was "associational" in nature and because Ohio's disability-discrimination statute did not provide for such a claim, the district court correctly ruled that the employee could not assert it under state law. Kepreos v. Alcon Labs., Inc., 520 Fed. Appx. 375, 2013 FED App. 0326N, 2013 U.S. App. LEXIS 6856 (6th Cir. Ohio 2013).

**Attorney fees**

Trial court did not abuse its discretion when it found a tenant's discrimination cause of action under the Fair Housing Act could have been brought by a reasonable attorney and was not filed for any purpose identified in R.C. 2323.51(A)(2)(a)(i)-(iv) because the discrimination claim was warranted under existing law; the executed affidavits of the tenant and her brother attesting to a property owner's discriminatory behavior served as direct evidence of the owner's alleged discrimination. Walters v. Carter, 2020-Ohio-807, 2020 Ohio App. LEXIS 723 (Ohio Ct. App., Cuyahoga County 2020).

In an action in which employees asserted an unsuccessful U.S. Const. amend. XIV equal protection claim under 42 U.S.C.S. § 1983 and unsuccessful discrimination claims under R.C. 4112.02 against their employer, the district court did not abuse its discretion by imposing attorney fees against the employees under 42 U.S.C.S. § 1988 and by imposing an attorney fee sanction against the employees' attorney under 28 U.S.C.S. § 1927 for maintaining frivolous claims long after those claims had clearly become groundless; the district court erred, however, by imposing joint and several liability when the claims did not share a common factual nexis and by failing to address the salary information that was offered as proof of inability to pay. Garner v. Cuyahoga County Juvenile Court, 554 F.3d 624, 2009 FED App. 0023P, 2009 U.S. App. LEXIS 1289 (6th Cir. Ohio 2009).

**Authority of Civil Rights Commission**

Employee's claims that the Ohio Civil Rights Commission (OCRC) ignored a contract between the employee's union and a school district that the employer breached was rejected as under R.C. 4112.02,, the OCRC was not charged with enforcing contractual obligations Freeman v. Ohio Civ. Rights Comm'n, 2012-Ohio-4825, 2012 Ohio App. LEXIS 4217 (Ohio Ct. App., Cuyahoga County 2012).

Ohio Civil Rights Commission erred when it determined that a state university's proffered reason of inadequate research for denying an assistant professor promotion and tenure was false where the Commission independently evaluated the professor's research dossier and reached its own decision regarding the quality of the publications and the qualification for promotion and tenure; the Commission went beyond its authority in drawing that improper inference in the professor's age discrimination action under R.C. 4112.02(A), as such determination was within the university committee's authority. Ohio Univ. v. Ohio Civ. Rights Comm'n, 2008-Ohio-1034, 175 Ohio App. 3d 414, 887 N.E.2d 403, 2008 Ohio App. LEXIS 888 (Ohio Ct. App., Athens County 2008).

A court of common pleas must affirm the commission's finding of a lack of probable cause where such finding is not unlawful, irrational, arbitrary or capricious: Coleman v. Warner, 82 Ohio App. 3d 263, 611 N.E.2d 878, 1992 Ohio App. LEXIS 4592 (Ohio Ct. App., Lucas County 1992), dismissed, 66 Ohio St. 3d 1402, 605 N.E.2d 1260, 1993 Ohio LEXIS 268 (Ohio 1993).

The commission established a prima facie case of handicap discrimination by adducing sufficient evidence that the employee could safely and substantially perform the essential functions of his job: Asplundh Tree Expert Co. v. Ohio Civil Rights Comm'n, 68 Ohio App. 3d 550, 589 N.E.2d 102, 1991 Ohio App. LEXIS 1622 (Ohio Ct. App., Franklin County 1991).

The trial court did not abuse its discretion by reversing the Ohio Civil Rights Commission's determination that a company had sexually discriminated against an employee when pregnancy and maternity leave interfered with the employee's job performance, because the record did not establish that the employee was subjected to a higher standard of performance or commitment than that of other employees, male or female: United Parcel Serv. v. Ohio Civil Rights Comm'n, 71 Ohio App. 3d 146, 593 N.E.2d 87, 1991 Ohio App. LEXIS 2461 (Ohio Ct. App., Hamilton County 1991).

**Availability**

Dismissal of an assistant principal's request for punitive damages and attorney fees against a board of education, arising from discipline imposed against her, was warranted because they were not expressly authorized by statute. Speller v. Toledo Pub. Sch. Dist. Bd. of Educ., 2015-Ohio-2672, 38 N.E.3d 509, 2015 Ohio App. LEXIS 2562 (Ohio Ct. App., Lucas County 2015).

**Bona fide occupational qualification**

A BFOQ established for the women's quarters of a rehabilitation center stating that all positions "will be" filled by females operated in a preemployment situation by virtue of its perspective application, and was thus in violation of R.C. 4112.02(E)(2), since it was not certified in advance by the commission: Harden v. Dayton Human Rehabilitation Center, 520 F. Supp. 769, 1981 U.S. Dist. LEXIS 14142 (S.D. Ohio 1981), aff'd, 779 F.2d 50, 1985 U.S. App. LEXIS 14012 (6th Cir. Ohio 1985).

**Burden of proof**

Since a former employee failed to establish a prima facie case of disparate-treatment discrimination, the burden did not shift to the former employer to articulate a legitimate, nondiscriminatory reason for the adverse employment action, and the employee was not required to establish that the employer's reason for implementing its prior conviction standard was a pretext from some other discriminatory purpose. Chisholm v. Cleveland Clinic Found., 2019-Ohio-3369, 141 N.E.3d 674, 2019 Ohio App. LEXIS 3452 (Ohio Ct. App., Cuyahoga County 2019).

In the terminated university employee's action against her former university employer, the university was entitled to summary judgment on discrimination and retaliation claims because the employee failed to demonstrate discriminatory intent under the McDonnell Douglas framework where there was evidence she had been terminated for insubordination, and she failed to demonstrate retaliation where she failed to show her opposition to any unlawful discriminatory practice. You v. Ne. Ohio Med. Univ., 2018-Ohio-4838, 2018 Ohio App. LEXIS 5161 (Ohio Ct. App., Franklin County 2018).

Employer's motion for summary judgment was granted on race discrimination claim because the employee failed to produce sufficient evidence for a reasonable jury to conclude that the seating arrangement significantly changed her employment status. Rather, the evidence reflected that there was no isolation of employees and that all of the team members sat in the same general vicinity. McDaniel v. PNC Bank, 2013 U.S. Dist. LEXIS 8762 (S.D. Ohio Jan. 2, 2013).

Although a former employee alleged that the employee's employer discriminated against the employee on the basis of age and disability, in violation of R.C. 4112.02, by forcing the employee to retire early due to the disposition of the employee's Family and Medical Leave Act of 1993, 29 U.S.C.S. § 2601 et seq., and sick leave benefits, the employee could not prove a prima facie case of employment discrimination because the employee provided no evidence that would have compelled a reasonable person in the employee's position to resign. Furthermore, the employee provided no evidence that the employee was subjected to a hostile work environment, and, in fact, testimony was presented that at all times the employee was treated courteously, respectfully, and without regard for the employee's age or disability. Stanchina v. Wright State Univ., 2012-Ohio-1249, 2012 Ohio Misc. LEXIS 36 (Ohio Ct. Cl. 2012).

State university employee's claim of disability discrimination under R.C. 4112.01(A)(13) and 4112.02 failed where concerns with the employee's job performance constituted a legitimate, nondiscriminatory reason for her termination from employment; further, the employee failed to provide convincing evidence to show that the stated basis for her termination was a pretext. Warren v. Cent. State Univ., 2011-Ohio-5953, 2011 Ohio Misc. LEXIS 538 (Ohio Ct. Cl. 2011).

Employee failed to demonstrate in her disability discrimination claim that the employer's legitimate, nondiscriminatory reason for terminating the employee was a mere pretext; the employee was fired because the owner believed that she had been involved in the attempted theft. Turner v. Shahed Enters., 2011-Ohio-4654, 2011 Ohio App. LEXIS 3851 (Ohio Ct. App., Franklin County 2011).

To prove qualification for a position under the third element of the prima facie McDonnell Douglas test, a plaintiff need only show that he or she satisfied the objective criteria necessary for employment in the position; if an employer's subjective assessment of an employee could defeat the prima facie case, then the inquiry into possible discrimination would end without affording the employee the opportunity to challenge the subjective assessment as a pretext for discrimination. Consequently, whether an employee possesses a subjective quality, such as a superior's confidence and trust in his performance, is a consideration better left to the later stages of the McDonnell Douglas analysis; during the prima facie stage, the court should focus on criteria such as the plaintiff's education, experience in the relevant industry, and demonstrated possession of the required general skills. Boyd v. Ohio Dep't of Mental Health, 2011-Ohio-3596, 2011 Ohio App. LEXIS 3037 (Ohio Ct. App., Franklin County 2011).

Employee failed to show that the trial court erred in granting summary judgment in favor of the county on the employee's wrongful termination claim, because the employee failed to exhaust his administrative remedies by filing the instant action without first appealing the State Personnel Board of Review dismissal of his appeal, and an analysis of the merits of the employee's discrimination claim revealed he was not wrongfully terminated, when the employee could not establish a prima facie case of unlawful discrimination since convicted felons were not identified as a protected class. Tomko v. Cuyahoga County Bd. of Comm'rs, 2011-Ohio-1575, 2011 Ohio App. LEXIS 1357 (Ohio Ct. App., Cuyahoga County 2011).

There was no error in granting summary judgment for the employer because the employee failed to establish a prima facie case of race and/or age discrimination; although he was a member of two protected classes (age and race) and was terminated, he did not show that he was qualified for the position he held or that he was either replaced by someone outside the protected class or was treated less favorably than a similarly situated employee not in the protected class. The employee received eight Employee Warning Notices indicating that his work was defective and that he was careless and was also disciplined for engaging in altercations with other employees. Steadman v. Sterilite Corp., 2010-Ohio-3391, 2010 Ohio App. LEXIS 2876 (Ohio Ct. App., Stark County 2010).

Ohio courts examine state employment discrimination claims under federal case law interpreting Title VII of the Civil Rights Act of 1964, 42 U.S.C.S. § 2000 et seq. Title VII jurisprudence imposes upon a plaintiff the initial burden of establishing a prima facie case of discrimination. Fearn v. Longaberger Co., 2010-Ohio-1736, 2010 Ohio App. LEXIS 1445 (Ohio Ct. App., Muskingum County 2010).

Employee failed to prove racial discrimination because the employee offered no evidence, other than the fact that the employee was terminated, to support the employee's claim of discrimination in violation of R.C. 4112.02 and the employee brought forth no credible evidence that the stated reason by the employee's supervisor for the employee's termination was a pretext for discrimination. Boyd v. Ohio Dep't of Mental Health, 2010-Ohio-4306, 2010 Ohio Misc. LEXIS 219 (Ohio Ct. Cl. 2010), aff'd, 2011-Ohio-3596, 2011 Ohio App. LEXIS 3037 (Ohio Ct. App., Franklin County 2011).

Part-time doctor failed in her prima facie burden of proving racial or gender discrimination under R.C. 4112.02 against her employers, as she failed to meet her reciprocal burden of presenting evidence that the other perinatologists who worked for the hospital were similarly situated to her; she was an African-American female and they were Caucasian males, some of whom had supervisory or administrative duties and who differed from her in other employment characteristics. Lindsay v. Children's Hosp. Med. Ctr. of Akron, 2009-Ohio-1216, 2009 Ohio App. LEXIS 1044 (Ohio Ct. App., Summit County 2009).

Although an employee was a 57-year-old female at the time of her termination from employment, she failed to show age or gender discrimination under R.C. 4112.02 and 4112.14 where she was fired for poor performance and someone who was already working in the department assumed her duties; she failed to show that the employer's reason for firing her was a mere pretext. Goodyear v. Waco Holdings, Inc., 2009-Ohio-619, 2009 Ohio App. LEXIS 546 (Ohio Ct. App., Cuyahoga County 2009).

Although an employee made a prima facie showing under R.C. 4112.02(A) that she was discriminated against by an employer where the employee was the only individual in the department that did not get a performance review and a pay raise, the employer met its burden of showing that the employee was not disparately treated where it set forth evidence of a legitimate, non-discriminatory reason for its actions and the employee did not show that the reason was a mere pretext; the employer did not review the employee's work performance due to the very short time that the review was conducted after the employee's hiring date, and it did not raise the employee's pay because the employee's initial wages were higher than the usual entry level pay for that position. Valentine v. Westshore Primary Care Assoc., 2008-Ohio-4450, 2008 Ohio App. LEXIS 3756 (Ohio Ct. App., Cuyahoga County 2008).

Parks employee's claim of gender discrimination under R.C. 4112.02(A) was properly resolved summary judgment to county parks and others with respect to her claim that she was disciplined more harshly than her male counterparts, as the employee failed to show other employees who were similarly situated and who were treated more favorably than she was; she had been disciplined for her failure to have properly recorded her working hours, and other employees who were not disciplined had not committed the same type of misconduct. Fox v. Lorain County, 2007-Ohio-6143, 2007 Ohio App. LEXIS 5412 (Ohio Ct. App., Lorain County 2007).

As a state employee failed to prove that persons who were treated more favorably than he was were similarly situated to him in all relevant respects, he failed to meet his burden of proof under R.C. 4112.02(A) for his sex discrimination claim, arising from his termination from employment; one of the other employees did not work for the same supervisor and the other did not engage in the same conduct as the employee. Swoger v. Wright State Univ., 2007-Ohio-2751, 2007 Ohio Misc. LEXIS 184 (Ohio Ct. Cl. 2007).

Evidence that supported a finding of discrimination under Title VII of the Civil Rights Act of 1964, 42 U.S.C.S. § 2000(e) et seq., was required before a violation of the Ohio Fair Employment Practices Act (OFEPA), R.C. 4112.02(A), could be found; the scope of the OFEPA was identical to that of the federal legislation. Brown v. Dover Corp., 2007-Ohio-2128, 2007 Ohio App. LEXIS 2010 (Ohio Ct. App., Hamilton County 2007).

Employee met his burden of showing that he could have returned to his job as an inspector in his employer's plant with reasonable accommodation for his foot injury for purposes of his disability discrimination claim under R.C. 4112.02(A)(2), as there was testimony that the essential job functions were not walking and lifting but instead, inspecting and measuring, the latter of which the employee could perform without restriction; further, the employee had requested an accommodation of being allowed a few minutes to rest his foot and re-adjust his boot when his foot hurt, which was feasible in the circumstances, and the medical evidence, although conflicting, indicated that the employee could physically handle the job with the accommodation. Sicklesmith v. Hoist, 2006-Ohio-6137, 169 Ohio App. 3d 470, 863 N.E.2d 677, 2006 Ohio App. LEXIS 6103 (Ohio Ct. App., Columbiana County 2006).

Trial court's grant of summary judgment to an employer in an action by an employee who was terminated, alleging racial and religious discrimination, was proper where the employee met her burden of showing a prima facie case of discrimination, the employer then met its burden of providing legitimate nondiscriminatory reasons for the termination based on the employee's failure to work collaboratively with others, and the employee failed in her burden of showing that the reasons were pretextual; she did not establish a material issue of fact on the last step of the burden-shifting analysis. Smith v. Children's Aid Soc'y, 2006-Ohio-4754, 2006 Ohio App. LEXIS 4677 (Ohio Ct. App., Cuyahoga County 2006).

Trial court's grant of a directed verdict pursuant to Civ.R. 50 to an employer in an employee's racial discrimination action under R.C. 4112.02(A) was proper under a disparate impact theory, as the employee failed to identify and/or present evidence as to a specific facially neutral employment promotion practice that disparately impacted him as a member of a protected class; he also failed to show sufficient statistical data to support such a claim. Brown v. Worthington Steel, Inc., 2005-Ohio-4571, 2005 Ohio App. LEXIS 4136 (Ohio Ct. App., Franklin County 2005).

The employer's burden regarding the legitimate nondiscriminating rationale is one of production only. Once an explanation "legally sufficient to justify judgment" for the employer is presented, the plaintiff then bears the burden of persuasion upon the ultimate question of wrongful discrimination: Manofsky v. Goodyear Tire & Rubber Co., 69 Ohio App. 3d 663, 591 N.E.2d 752, 1990 Ohio App. LEXIS 4434 (Ohio Ct. App., Summit County 1990).

To establish employment discrimination as prohibited by R.C. 4112.02(A), the plaintiff must present a prima facie case of discrimination. The burden then shifts to the employer to show a reasonable nondiscriminatory rationale for the challenged action. The plaintiff must then demonstrate by a preponderance of the evidence that the stated rationale is a pretext for discrimination: In re Brantley, 34 Ohio App. 3d 320, 518 N.E.2d 602, 1987 Ohio App. LEXIS 10520 (Ohio Ct. App., Franklin County 1987).

**Business necessity**

Where the plaintiff failed to rebut the defendant's contention that he was dismissed for business necessity, he was not entitled to relief: Bellios v. Victor Balata Belting Co., 724 F. Supp. 514, 1989 U.S. Dist. LEXIS 12865 (S.D. Ohio 1989).

**Civil liability**

R.C. 4112.02(G) did not expressly impose civil liability on a political subdivision for a violation of R.C. 4112.02(G). Instead, R.C. 4112.05 set forth the procedure to be followed in charging such persons with such unlawful discriminatory practices. Horen v. Bd. of Educ. of Toledo Pub. Schs, 2010-Ohio-3631, 2010 Ohio App. LEXIS 3089 (Ohio Ct. App., Lucas County 2010).

**Collective bargaining agreements**

Because the statutory claim did exist independent of the contract, the teacher was not required to exhaust her contract remedies prior to pursuing her statutory claims. Also, since the statutory claim was independent and the contract did not address statutory claims, the statutory discrimination claims were not "related to" the collective bargaining agreement because the "related to" language in the settlement agreement was not specific enough to settle the statutory claims and thus, the settlement did not foreclose the teacher from pursuing the statutory discrimination claims. Janiszewski v. Belmont Career Ctr., 2017-Ohio-855, 86 N.E.3d 613, 2017 Ohio App. LEXIS 830 (Ohio Ct. App., Belmont County 2017).

Labor Management Relations Act, 29 U.S.C.S. § 185, preempted employees' racial discrimination claims that (1) persons outside a protected class were treated more favorably, (2) an employee did not receive proper call-back priority, and (3) the employees received disparate treatment regarding incentive pay and training opportunities, because these claims were controlled by the employees' collective bargaining agreement. Hargrette v. RMI Titanium Co., 2010-Ohio-406, 2010 Ohio App. LEXIS 325 (Ohio Ct. App., Trumbull County 2010).

Firefighter did not have to exhaust all administrative remedies contained in his collective-bargaining agreement (CBA) before filing an age discrimination suit, as he was attempting to enforce his statutory rights under R.C. 4112.02, and the CBA did not encompass the relinquishment of these rights. Campolieti v. City of Cleveland, 2009-Ohio-5224, 184 Ohio App. 3d 419, 921 N.E.2d 286, 2009 Ohio App. LEXIS 4417 (Ohio Ct. App., Cuyahoga County 2009).

Collective bargaining agreement did not require an employee to exhaust administrative remedies before pursuing a statutory age discrimination claim where the agreement contained no reference to discrimination claims: Campolieti v. City of Cleveland, 2009-Ohio-5224, 184 Ohio App. 3d 419, 921 N.E.2d 286, 2009 Ohio App. LEXIS 4417 (Ohio Ct. App., Cuyahoga County 2009).

Collective bargaining agreement, even if it contains an antidiscrimination clause, does not supersede an employee's rights under R.C. Chapter 4112: Haynes v. Ohio Tpk. Comm'n, 2008-Ohio-133, 177 Ohio App. 3d 1, 893 N.E.2d 850, 2008 Ohio App. LEXIS 121 (Ohio Ct. App., Cuyahoga County 2008).

**Colleges and universities**

State university was entitled to summary judgment in a professor's claim of race discrimination because the university followed a three-tiered tenure process and provided documentation that it denied the professor tenure because of the professor's failure to achieve excellence in teaching, a requirement for tenure. Hall v. Ohio State Univ. College of Humanities, 2011-Ohio-6842, 2011 Ohio Misc. LEXIS 599 (Ohio Ct. Cl. 2011), aff'd, 2012-Ohio-5036, 2012 Ohio App. LEXIS 4411 (Ohio Ct. App., Franklin County 2012).

Ohio Civil Rights Commission erred when it relied on circumstantial evidence to support its determination that a state university's actual reason to deny an assistant professor promotion and tenure was age for purposes of the professor's age discrimination claim, in violation of Ohio Code Ann. § 4112.02(A), as a comparison of others who were younger when they were given tenure was improper because the decision to grant tenure was made by different committees and based on a host of qualifications and abilities; further, age-related comments were "stray remarks" that were not made at the time of the promotion and tenure application, and they did not relate to the decisional process, Ohio Univ. v. Ohio Civ. Rights Comm'n, 2008-Ohio-1034, 175 Ohio App. 3d 414, 887 N.E.2d 403, 2008 Ohio App. LEXIS 888 (Ohio Ct. App., Athens County 2008).

Trial court properly found a lack of reliable, probative, and substantial evidence to support an order by the Ohio Civil Rights Commission which determined that a state university had committed intentional age discrimination under R.C. 4112.02(A) against an assistant professor who was denied promotion and tenure, as the Commission drew improper inferences from the assistant professor's merit raise when it concluded that the basis for the raise was the same as the basis for granting tenure; there was no evidence to show that the same standards were used for determining merit raises and tenure. Ohio Univ. v. Ohio Civ. Rights Comm'n, 2008-Ohio-1034, 175 Ohio App. 3d 414, 887 N.E.2d 403, 2008 Ohio App. LEXIS 888 (Ohio Ct. App., Athens County 2008).

Where reasonable minds could disagree as to whether the promotion and tenure committee established that its denial of tenure was based on research inadequacies, the trial court did not abuse its discretion by reversing the commission's finding that the denial was due to age discrimination. For age-related remarks to constitute circumstantial evidence of age discrimination, a nexus must exist between the remarks and the adverse employment action: Ohio Univ. v. Ohio Civ. Rights Comm'n, 2008-Ohio-1034, 175 Ohio App. 3d 414, 887 N.E.2d 403, 2008 Ohio App. LEXIS 888 (Ohio Ct. App., Athens County 2008).

University and university officials were entitled to summary judgment on a former employee's claims of race discrimination, retaliation, and civil conspiracy because (1) although the employee met three elements of a prima facie case of discrimination under Title VII, 42 U.S.C.S. § 1981, and R.C. ch. 4112 as he was a member of a protected class, suffered adverse employment action, and was qualified for his job, he failed to identify a non-protected, similarly-situated person whom the university treated better than himself; (2) although the employee established three elements of a prima facie case of retaliation as he engaged in protected action, which defendants knew about, and was subsequently terminated, he did not show a causal connection between the filing of this Title VII action and his termination as he did not show that temporal proximity existed between his protected action and his termination; (3) without an unlawful action causing injury, there was no support for a conspiracy claim under 42 U.S.C.S. § 1985. Giles v. Univ. of Toledo, 478 F. Supp. 2d 942, 2007 U.S. Dist. LEXIS 17892 (N.D. Ohio 2007), aff'd, 286 Fed. Appx. 295, 2008 FED App. 0422N, 2008 U.S. App. LEXIS 15216 (6th Cir. Ohio 2008).

District court erred by granting summary judgment to defendant university in a professor's discrimination suit under Title VII of the Civil Rights Act of 1964, 42 U.S.C.S. §§ 2000e — 2000e-17; R.C. 4112.02; and R.C. 4112.99; administrator's comments that a department head was racist and trying to "whitewash" the department, though not direct evidence of discrimination, were evidence of pretext and were not "isolated" because they were a response to the professor's inquiry. Carter v. Univ. of Toledo, 349 F.3d 269, 2003 FED App. 0401P, 2003 U.S. App. LEXIS 23054 (6th Cir. Ohio 2003).

An assistant college coach did not show race or gender discrimination where she intentionally violated a NCAA rule and did not report it: McKenzie v. Wright State Univ., 114 Ohio App. 3d 437, 683 N.E.2d 381, 1996 Ohio App. LEXIS 4294 (Ohio Ct. App., Franklin County 1996).

In deciding whether to grant tenure to faculty members, an educational institution may lawfully consider collegial relationships, unless such a criterion is shown to be a facade for discrimination prohibited by R.C. 4112.02(A): In re Brantley, 34 Ohio App. 3d 320, 518 N.E.2d 602, 1987 Ohio App. LEXIS 10520 (Ohio Ct. App., Franklin County 1987).

**Common law**

Former employee alleging discriminatory demotion and discharge in violation of the Ohio Unlawful Discriminatory Practices law was not entitled to common law relief beyond his statutory claims: Wyckoff v. Forest City Auto Parts Co., 916 F. Supp. 683, 1996 U.S. Dist. LEXIS 4942 (N.D. Ohio 1996).

**Comparable protected classes**

Inasmuch as women and African-Americans are in comparable protected classes, a white woman did not have a superior right to a promotion over a black male based on her higher test ranking: Bobash v. City of Toledo, 129 Ohio App. 3d 202, 717 N.E.2d 725, 1998 Ohio App. LEXIS 3368 (Ohio Ct. App., Lucas County 1998).

**Comparators**

In a reverse race and sex discrimination case, a black female co-worker was not a valid comparator to plaintiff, as their responsibilities differed, nothing suggested that she had any authority over plaintiff or over the marketing department in which they worked as a whole, and plaintiff was the only employee in the department's number two position and was paid considerably more than the other marketing assistant vice presidents. McGinty v. Ohio State Univ., 2020-Ohio-4315, 2020 Ohio Misc. LEXIS 125 (Ohio Ct. Cl. 2020).

**Complaint**

Where an employee sufficiently pleaded the elements of his claims for race and disability discrimination under R.C. 4112.02(A) and 4112.99, he met the pleading requirements of Civ.R. 8(A) and the trial court erred in granting the employer's motion to dismiss the complaint for failure to state a claim. The "prima facie case" requirement was an evidentiary standard for purposes of R.C. 4112.02(A) and not a pleading standard. Jackson v. Int'l Fiber, 2006-Ohio-5799, 169 Ohio App. 3d 395, 863 N.E.2d 189, 2006 Ohio App. LEXIS 5750 (Ohio Ct. App., Champaign County 2006).

**Complaint sufficient**

Where an employee sufficiently pleaded the elements of his claims for race and disability discrimination under R.C. 4112.02(A) and 4112.99, he met the pleading requirements of Civ.R. 8(A) and the trial court erred in granting the employer's motion to dismiss the complaint for failure to state a claim; the "prima facie case" requirement was an evidentiary standard for purposes of R.C. 4112.02(A) and not a pleading standard. Jackson v. Int'l Fiber, 2006-Ohio-5799, 169 Ohio App. 3d 395, 863 N.E.2d 189, 2006 Ohio App. LEXIS 5750 (Ohio Ct. App., Champaign County 2006).

**Conflict of laws**

The court properly applied the law of Texas to plaintiff's claim of discrimination by his former employer in that state: Sholes v. Agency Rent-A-Car, Inc., 76 Ohio App. 3d 349, 601 N.E.2d 634, 1991 Ohio App. LEXIS 5490 (Ohio Ct. App., Cuyahoga County 1991).

**Conspiracy**

As parents' claims of unlawful discrimination failed with respect to statutory claims of harassment, retaliation, and public accommodations, they could not assert an actionable claim of civil conspiracy. Pittman v. Parillo, 2017-Ohio-1477, 2017 Ohio App. LEXIS 1482 (Ohio Ct. App., Lucas County 2017).

**Constructive discharge**

Trial court erred in granting summary judgment to a school district, superintendent, and high school principal in a teacher's suit alleging they engaged in disability discrimination because there was an issue of fact as to whether they took an adverse employment action against the teacher based on her disability in the form of a constructive discharge; one could infer the denial of additional accommodation made the teacher's working conditions intolerable and that she was compelled to resign. Caldwell v. Niles City Schs, 2021-Ohio-1543, 2021 Ohio App. LEXIS 1506 (Ohio Ct. App., Trumbull County 2021).

Former employee failed to show that she was constructively discharged because the incidents did not create objectively intolerable working conditions that would have compelled a reasonable person in the employee's shoes to resign. Gosbin v. Jefferson Cty. Comm'rs, 725 Fed. Appx. 377, 2018 FED App. 0088N, 2018 U.S. App. LEXIS 4360 (6th Cir. Ohio 2018).

Ethnic Arab-American employee met his burden of proof in response to the employer's summary judgment motion with respect to his claim of disparate treatment and retaliatory discharge under 42 U.S.C.S. § 2000e-2(a) of Title VII of the Civil Rights Act of 1964, as amended, 42 U.S.C.S. § 2000e et seq., and R.C. 4112.02(A) and 4112.99 of the Ohio Civil Rights Act, R.C. 4112.01 et seq., as he established a genuine issue of material fact regarding an adverse employment action by his constructive discharge, evidence that the employer created conditions with the intention of forcing the employee to resign, and that the employer's explanation was a mere pretext. Mohanna v. Jake Sweeney Auto., 2012 U.S. Dist. LEXIS 97413 (S.D. Ohio July 13, 2012).

Employee's claim of disability discrimination was properly dismissed on summary judgment as the employee failed to present evidence creating a genuine issue of material fact for a prima facie case of disability discrimination, in that he failed to prove that ODRC took adverse employment action in part because of his disability. ODRC presented evidence indicating that the only change in the employee's work environment was the employee's demotion, which was precipitated by an altercation the employee had at work, and the employee did not respond with any evidence suggesting that his work environment was intolerable; thus, he did not prove that his demotion was really a constructive discharge. Hardgrow v. Dep't of Rehab. & Corr., 2012-Ohio-2731, 2012 Ohio App. LEXIS 2407 (Ohio Ct. App., Franklin County 2012).

Summary judgment for the former employer was appropriate as to the claim of constructive termination (due to a hostile work environment) because the employee did not offer any evidence, either from her affidavit or from her deposition, that she was either replaced by a person outside her protected class or that a similarly situated non-protected person was treated more favorably. McGraw v. Pilot Travel Ctrs., LLC, 2012-Ohio-1076, 2012 Ohio App. LEXIS 922 (Ohio Ct. App., Franklin County 2012).

Former employee's discrimination claim, which was premised on the basis of the employee's alleged constructive discharge because of the employee's disability and race, was found to be without merit in that the employee resigned from the employee's position at a correctional institution after the employee was reduced in rank for disciplinary reasons when the employee physically shoved a subordinate employee into a chair during a confrontation. Hardgrow v. Dep't of Rehab. & Corr., 2011-Ohio-5956, 2011 Ohio Misc. LEXIS 556 (Ohio Ct. Cl. 2011), aff'd, 2012-Ohio-2731, 2012 Ohio App. LEXIS 2407 (Ohio Ct. App., Franklin County 2012).

When an employee sued an employer for, inter alia, constructive discharge, as well as hostile environment race harassment, under R.C. 4112.02, and a jury found in the employee's favor, the trial court properly granted the employer judgment notwithstanding the verdict, under Civ.R. 50(B), because the jury also found the employee did not show that the harassment the employee suffered was based on race, so the employee did not prove hostile environment race harassment, and, as a result, the employee could not prevail on a constructive discharge claim since harassment required only a showing that conditions were severe and pervasive enough to affect working conditions, while constructive discharge required proof that the employer's actions made working conditions so intolerable that a reasonable person would have felt compelled to resign, requiring a showing of more adverse conditions than did the hostile environment harassment claim. Williams v. Spitzer Auto World, 2008-Ohio-1467, 2008 Ohio App. LEXIS 1288 (Ohio Ct. App., Lorain County 2008).

When an employee sued an employer for, inter alia, constructive discharge, as well as hostile environment race harassment, under R.C. 4112.02, and a jury found in the employee's favor, the trial court properly granted the employer judgment notwithstanding the verdict, under CivR 50(B), because the jury also found the employee did not show that the harassment the employee suffered was based on race, so the employee did not prove hostile environment race harassment, and, as a result, the employee could not prevail on a constructive discharge claim since harassment required only a showing that conditions were severe and pervasive enough to affect working conditions, while constructive discharge required proof that the employer's actions made working conditions so intolerable that a reasonable person would have felt compelled to resign, requiring a showing of more adverse conditions than did the hostile environment harassment claim. Williams v. Spitzer Auto World, 2008-Ohio-1467, 2008 Ohio App. LEXIS 1288 (Ohio Ct. App., Lorain County 2008).

Employee failed to meet her burden of showing a prima facie case of racial discrimination, in violation of R.C. 4112.02, where she alleged that she had to involuntarily terminate her working situation due to adverse employment actions by her supervisor, who allegedly acted in a discriminatory manner towards her; however, the employee failed to show that working conditions were so intolerable that a reasonable person would have felt compelled to resign for purposes of constructive discharge or that she was treated differently from other employees. Simmons-Means v. Cuyahoga County Dep't of Justice Affairs, 2006-Ohio-4123, 2006 Ohio App. LEXIS 4057 (Ohio Ct. App., Cuyahoga County 2006).

Summary judgment was properly granted, dismissing a Caucasian employee's constructive discharge claim brought against her African-American supervisor and the city which employed her, because, assuming that the employee was the only employee required to sign a time-sheet, limit her lunch break to a half-hour, and report for work on time, such conditions, while arguably unfair, are not so intolerable that a reasonable person would have felt compelled to resign because of them. Moreover, reasonable minds could not conclude that the employee's working conditions at the time of her resignation were so intolerable that a reasonable person would have felt compelled to resign in light of the fact that, for approximately two months before the employee left, she had a new supervisor who treated her cordially and responded to her complaints of racial comments, and no supervisory employees raised their voices to the employee or commented on her race. Mowery v. City of Columbus, 2006-Ohio-1153, 2006 Ohio App. LEXIS 1051 (Ohio Ct. App., Franklin County 2006).

Employer was granted summary judgment on a female employee's gender discrimination claim because she failed to come forward with sufficient evidence to establish a constructive discharge, and therefore she was unable to show an adverse employment action, because: (1) the primary incident giving rise to the employee's alleged constructive discharge was not attributable to the employer; rather it was the coworker's outburst and accusations that largely precipitated the employee's decision to resign; (2) the employee did not allege that the coworker behaved inappropriately toward her or that he disparaged her in front of others after the initial incident; (3) the employee did not allege any acts or omissions by the employer's managers after the coworker's outburst that may have contributed to an intolerable work situation; and (4) there was no evidence that the employee gave the employer an opportunity to remedy the situation before she quit. Helms v. Fischer Mgmt., 2005 U.S. Dist. LEXIS 27259 (S.D. Ohio Nov. 10, 2005).

Summary judgment was properly entered for an employer on a minor employee's claim for wrongful discharge as the employer's conduct, in seeking to remedy the minor employee's problems with another employee by offering the minor employee a job transfer, did not constitute egregious behavior sufficient to support a constructive discharge claim. Jackson v. Saturn of Chapel Hill, Inc., 2005-Ohio-5302, 2005 Ohio App. LEXIS 4821 (Ohio Ct. App., Stark County 2005).

Employer was entitled to summary judgment in an action by a former employee who took a "stress leave" and who alleged wrongful discharge in violation of public policy based on R.C. 4112.02(A); although the employee contended that the employer forced her from her job by failing to provide a safe working environment, there was no evidence that a reasonable person in the employee's position would have felt compelled to resign or would have thought that termination was imminent. The employee unreasonably determined that her workplace was intolerably unsafe based on the fact that a co-worker had falsely reported rumors of physical threats to the employee. Langley v. DaimlerChrysler Corp., 407 F. Supp. 2d 897, 2005 U.S. Dist. LEXIS 36332 (N.D. Ohio 2005), aff'd, 502 F.3d 475, 2007 FED App. 0379P, 2007 U.S. App. LEXIS 22211 (6th Cir. Ohio 2007).

When an employee complained that a co-employee engaged in sex acts in her presence, she could not show that she was constructively discharged from her employment because she was fired for excessive absenteeism, rather than resigning due to intolerable working conditions. Collins v. Flowers, 2005-Ohio-3797, 2005 Ohio App. LEXIS 3498 (Ohio Ct. App., Lorain County 2005).

Before a claim of constructive discharge can be submitted to the jury, the plaintiff must prove that her working conditions were so difficult or unpleasant that a reasonable person would have felt compelled to resign. To present a prima facie case of employment discrimination, the employee must establish: (1) she is within a protected "suspect" class, e.g., handicapped; (2) she was qualified for the job that she was performing and satisfied the normal requirements of the work; (3) she was in fact discharged; (4) she was discharged although other nonhandicapped employees were retained or not disciplined for similar conduct that resulted in the charging party's discharge. A retaliatory discharge claim cannot prevail if it appears from the evidence that the employer would have made the same decision regardless of plaintiff's participation in the protected activity: Neal v. Hamilton County, 87 Ohio App. 3d 670, 622 N.E.2d 1130, 1993 Ohio App. LEXIS 2470 (Ohio Ct. App., Hamilton County 1993).

**Contractual relationship**

Summary judgment was properly granted; because the doctor was not in a contractual relationship with an employee of, or denied any services by, the hospital, he failed to establish a prima facie case of discrimination under R.C. 4112.02 and, since there was no contractual relationship, there was no 42 U.S.C.S. 1981 claim. Bansal v. Mount Carmel Health Sys., 2011-Ohio-3827, 2011 Ohio App. LEXIS 3241 (Ohio Ct. App., Franklin County 2011).

**Criticism by party other than employer**

Where a client complained throughout the course of the employee's employment and demanded that she be replaced or the employer would lose its contract, the criticisms led to her termination and were legitimate, nondiscriminatory reasons for the employee's discharge, and the employee failed to demonstrate that these reasons were pretextual. Zelnik v. CB Richard Ellis, Inc., 2005 U.S. Dist. LEXIS 19611 (S.D. Ohio Sept. 9, 2005).

**Damages**

Trial court did not err by not ordering the supervisor to pay damages because, although the trial court erred by finding that the former employee's sexual harassment claims could not be brought against the supervisor individually since it was undisputed that he was her supervisor during the relevant times of her employment, she failed to establish that her terms, conditions and/or privileges of employment were affected by the supervisor's behavior. Osborne v. Douglas, 2013-Ohio-5072, 2013 Ohio App. LEXIS 5271 (Ohio Ct. App., Lucas County 2013).

In this Title VII of the Civil Rights Act of 1964 action, the record supported a compensatory award of $195,000, and as that amount was well within the Ohio statutory cap, no prejudice resulted from the district court's design of the jury interrogatories. Mengelkamp v. Lake Metro. Hous. Auth., 549 Fed. Appx. 323, 2013 FED App. 0949N, 2013 U.S. App. LEXIS 22771 (6th Cir. Ohio 2013).

Where a tenant filed suit against her former landlord, claiming sexual harassment, housing discrimination, and unlawful coercion or intimidation under R.C. 4112.02(H)(1), (4), and (12) after he made crude sexual comments and offered to pay her for sex and where the jury returned a verdict in favor of the tenant, the trial court erred in denying the landlord's motion for a new trial under Civ. R. 59(A) because the damages awarded were excessive in that the evidence was insufficient to support compensatory damages in the amount of $150,000. The alleged harassing remarks, while crude, took place on only two days, and on one of those days, the tenant returned to the landlord's dwelling of her own volition for the sole purpose of recording the landlord, and a number of her comments appeared designed to elicit further inappropriate remarks from the landlord. McDonald v. Burton, 2011-Ohio-6178, 2011 Ohio App. LEXIS 5067 (Ohio Ct. App., Montgomery County 2011).

Trial court properly denied an employer and general manager's motion for a directed verdict pursuant to Civ.R. 50(A)(4) on the issue of punitive damages in an employee's disability discrimination action brought under R.C. 4112.02(A)(2), as there was sufficient evidence of actual malice displayed towards the employee in not accepting him back to his employment position, not entertaining the concept of a reasonable accommodation for him, and in taunting him with how much his disability payments through workers' compensation had cost his fellow employees and the employer. Sicklesmith v. Hoist, 2006-Ohio-6137, 169 Ohio App. 3d 470, 863 N.E.2d 677, 2006 Ohio App. LEXIS 6103 (Ohio Ct. App., Columbiana County 2006).

There was sufficient evidence of how much an employee was earning at the time of his injury and how much he would have been earning eight years later had he remained in the same employment position, and such was sufficient for the trial court to submit the issues of front pay and back pay to the jury in the employee's disability discrimination claim under R.C. 4112.02(A)(2); accordingly, awards made for those types of damages in favor of the employee were proper and supported by the evidence. Sicklesmith v. Hoist, 2006-Ohio-6137, 169 Ohio App. 3d 470, 863 N.E.2d 677, 2006 Ohio App. LEXIS 6103 (Ohio Ct. App., Columbiana County 2006).

Front pay is an equitable remedy designed to compensate an employee where reinstatement would be impractical or inadequate. It is within the trial court's discretion to determine whether front pay is appropriate under the circumstances. The purpose of back pay is to make wrongfully terminated employees whole and to put them in the position they would have been in had their employment not been terminated: Sicklesmith v. Hoist, 2006-Ohio-6137, 169 Ohio App. 3d 470, 863 N.E.2d 677, 2006 Ohio App. LEXIS 6103 (Ohio Ct. App., Columbiana County 2006).

Even if a discrimination victim accepts a demotion, a different position, or enters into another line of work, the employer continues to be liable for back pay unless the discrimination victim accepts or rejects a job substantially similar to the one he was denied. Prejudgment interest is routinely awarded in back pay cases to restore victims of discrimination to the economic position they would have enjoyed had the discrimination not occurred: Little Forest Medical Ctr. v. Ohio Civil Rights Comm'n, 91 Ohio App. 3d 76, 631 N.E.2d 1068, 1993 Ohio App. LEXIS 4886 (Ohio Ct. App., Summit County 1993).

Compensatory and punitive damages are available under R.C. 4112.02(N): Crawford v. ITT Consumer Financial Corp., 653 F. Supp. 1184, 1986 U.S. Dist. LEXIS 19155 (S.D. Ohio 1986).

**—Mitigation**

Trial court did not abuse its discretion in failing to find that the employee had not mitigated his damages because the employer did not meet its burden. It introduced no evidence of any substantially-equivalent positions that had been available at the time that the employee had been looking for employment. Stallworth v. Wal-Mart Stores E., L.P., 2016-Ohio-2620, 50 N.E.3d 27, 2016 Ohio App. LEXIS 1511 (Ohio Ct. App., Hamilton County 2016).

**Dangerous employee**

In this Americans with Disabilities Act of 1990 action, a material factual dispute precluded summary judgment on the direct threat defense where the employer's defense was predicated on the same disputed factual contentions as its arguments that the employee was not qualified, given his deafness, to work as a Shipper or Pickle Line Processing Technician. Siewertsen v. Worthington Steel Co., 134 F. Supp. 3d 1091, 2015 U.S. Dist. LEXIS 129455 (N.D. Ohio 2015).

An employee is not perceived as mentally impaired merely because the employer believes that the employee's behavior poses a substantial danger, where an evaluating psychiatrist is unable to diagnose an actual impairment. Posing a substantial risk to other employees is a legitimate reason for discharge: Cochran v. Columbia Gas of Ohio, Inc., 138 Ohio App. 3d 888, 742 N.E.2d 734, 2000 Ohio App. LEXIS 4389 (Ohio Ct. App., Franklin County 2000).

**Directed verdict**

Trial court correctly granted a directed verdict because the employee failed to establish his claim of direct evidence of discrimination. The employee did not establish a causal link between the general manager's comment about the "old" company and the employee's eventual termination from the company. Peters v. Rock-Tenn Co., 2011-Ohio-3949, 2011 Ohio App. LEXIS 3319 (Ohio Ct. App., Delaware County 2011).

Trial court erred when it refused to admit a city-employer's affirmative action plan into evidence or consider it in an employee's racial and gender discrimination action under R.C. 4112.02 and with respect to the employer's directed verdict motion pursuant to Civ.R. 50, as the plan was in effect at the time that the employee alleged that he was passed over numerous times for a superintendent position and it was relevant pursuant to Evid.R. 401 and 402; further, there was sufficient evidence of "background circumstances" to support a prima facie case of reverse discrimination, the trial court overlooked the fact that there were racial as well as gender discrimination allegations, and the employee's further application for the position would have been clearly futile. Mitchell v. Lemmie, 2007-Ohio-5757, 2007 Ohio App. LEXIS 5060 (Ohio Ct. App., Montgomery County 2007).

Trial court erred when it refused to admit a city-employer's affirmative action plan into evidence or consider it in an employee's racial and gender discrimination action under R.C. 4112.02 and with respect to the employer's directed verdict motion pursuant to Civ.R. 50, as the plan was in effect at the time that the employee alleged that he was passed over numerous times for a superintendent position and it was relevant pursuant to Evid.R. 401 and 402; further, there was sufficient evidence of "background circumstances" to support a prima facie case of reverse discrimination, the trial court overlooked the fact that there were racial as well as gender discrimination allegations, and the employee's further application for the position would have been clearly futile. Mitchell v. Lemmie, 2007-Ohio-5757, 2007 Ohio App. LEXIS 5060 (Ohio Ct. App., Montgomery County 2007).

In appeals of cases in which racial discrimination in employment is alleged, the suggestion that a reviewing court should not revisit a prima facie case of discrimination once a verdict is rendered is consistent with federal practice, which provides that when a trial court denies a motion for judgment as a matter of law at the close of plaintiff's evidence, a renewed motion at the close of all evidence will be considered on the record as it stands at that time, but, unlike federal practice, Ohio practice permits an appellate court to reexamine the sufficiency of just the plaintiff's evidence in determining whether the trial court erred in denying a defendant's motion for a directed verdict at the close of plaintiff's case, even though the case has been tried to conclusion. Williams v. City of Akron, 2005-Ohio-6268, 107 Ohio St. 3d 203, 837 N.E.2d 1169, 2005 Ohio LEXIS 2836 (Ohio 2005).

In an employment discrimination case, under R.C. 4112.02, in which the trial court had denied the employer's motions for a directed verdict, under Civ.R. 50(A), at the close of the employee's evidence and at the close of all evidence, the employer did not waive appellate review of whether its motion at the close of the employee's evidence should have been denied by presenting evidence, contrary to federal practice, as this would foreclose appellate review of whether the employee met his threshold burden of proof, and it was the practice in all other Ohio civil cases, and there was no reason to make an exception for discrimination cases. Williams v. City of Akron, 2005-Ohio-6268, 107 Ohio St. 3d 203, 837 N.E.2d 1169, 2005 Ohio LEXIS 2836 (Ohio 2005).

Appellate court, in determining whether the trial court erred in denying a motion for a directed verdict at the close of a plaintiff's case, can review a plaintiff's case-in-chief, including, in a discrimination case, plaintiff's prima facie evidence of discrimination, if the defendant has properly preserved the issue for appeal by renewing the motion for a directed verdict at the close of all the evidence: Williams v. City of Akron, 2005-Ohio-6268, 107 Ohio St. 3d 203, 837 N.E.2d 1169, 2005 Ohio LEXIS 2836 (Ohio 2005).

A directed verdict for the defendant-employer was error where it was based on the court's interpretation of the evidence in the defendant's favor: Glover v. Boehm Pressed Steel Co., 122 Ohio App. 3d 702, 702 N.E.2d 929, 1997 Ohio App. LEXIS 3853 (Ohio Ct. App., Cuyahoga County 1997).

**Disability**

Summary judgment was properly granted to an employer in an employee's disability discrimination action under the Ohio Civil Rights Act, arising from the termination of his employment due to the employee's inability to fulfill the duties of his job without accommodation following an injury, as it was undisputed that there was no actual disability. Carnahan v. Morton Bldgs., Inc., 2015-Ohio-3528, 41 N.E.3d 239, 2015 Ohio App. LEXIS 3445 (Ohio Ct. App., Paulding County 2015).

Employee failed to state a prima facie case of discriminatory discharge under R.C. 4112.02(A) because even defining the term broadly, the employee failed to present sufficient evidence from which it could reasonably be concluded her impairment substantially limited any of her major life activities under R.C. 4112.01(A)(13). Physician imposed lifting restrictions, such as the one imposed on the employee did not, in and of themselves, constitute substantially limiting physical impairments; accordingly, the employee had not shown she has a legally cognizable disability. Bare v. Fed. Express Corp., 886 F. Supp. 2d 600, 2012 U.S. Dist. LEXIS 116095 (N.D. Ohio 2012).

Employee failed to prove by a preponderance of the evidence that he had either a legally cognizable disability that resulted in his four-day absence or that he had provided defendant with notice of such disability for a disability discrimination claim. The employee failed to ask for any reasonable accommodation until after he had been absent from work for four days without any explanation. Barnett v. Ohio State Univ. Med. Ctr., 2007-Ohio-5424, 2007 Ohio Misc. LEXIS 391 (Ohio Ct. Cl. 2007).

Employee failed to prove by a preponderance of the evidence that he had either a legally cognizable disability that resulted in his four-day absence or that he had provided defendant with notice of such disability for a disability discrimination claim. The employee failed to ask for any reasonable accommodation until after he had been absent from work for four days without any explanation. Barnett v. Ohio State Univ. Med. Ctr., 2007-Ohio-5424, 2007 Ohio Misc. LEXIS 391 (Ohio Ct. Cl. 2007).

For purposes of an employee's disability discrimination claim pursuant to R.C. 4112.02(A)(2), there was sufficient evidence to establish that he was "disabled," as that term was defined in R.C. 4112.01(A)(13) and (A)(16)(a)(ii), where his foot was run over by a forklift in a work accident and he suffered from an orthopedic condition as a result thereof and he still wore a brace on his foot; there was evidence from doctors and therapists regarding the employee's condition, the treatment he had received, and the physical therapy he had undergone, and there was testimony that the injury affected his day-to-day life activity of walking. Sicklesmith v. Hoist, 2006-Ohio-6137, 169 Ohio App. 3d 470, 863 N.E.2d 677, 2006 Ohio App. LEXIS 6103 (Ohio Ct. App., Columbiana County 2006).

**Disability discrimination**

Supervisor was not entitled to summary judgment on a former employee's disability discrimination claim because genuine issues of material fact remained with respect to whether repeated heavy lifting was an essential function of a sales specialist job at the employer's lumber yard and whether the employee could perform either the yard worker job or the sales specialist job with reasonable accommodation. 2015 Ohio 1522, 2015 Ohio App. LEXIS 1468.

It was error to grant summary judgment to a school district, superintendent, and principal in a teacher's suit alleging disability discrimination because there was a genuine issue of fact as to whether they made a good faith effort to assist the teacher in seeking an additional accommodation; since there was a genuine issue as to whether the teacher voluntarily resigned or was constructively discharged, there was a genuine issue as to whether she terminated the interactive process by resigning. Caldwell v. Niles City Schs, 2021-Ohio-1543, 2021 Ohio App. LEXIS 1506 (Ohio Ct. App., Trumbull County 2021).

Jury's verdict finding the employer liable for disability discrimination was not against the manifest weight of the evidence because the evidence showed that the employer terminated the doctor's employment because they perceived him as disabled. From the evidence, the jury could have concluded that the employer failed to establish that the fitness-for-duty examination was legitimately job-related and consistent with business necessity. Amesse v. Wright State Physicians, Inc., 2018-Ohio-416, 105

N.E.3d 612, 2018 Ohio App. LEXIS 431 (Ohio Ct. App., Montgomery County 2018).

In this Americans with Disabilities Act of 1990 action, summary judgment was unwarranted on individualized-inquiry issue because while it appeared managers may not have given adequate consideration to employee's past operation of forklifts and cranes, that omission, reasonable jury could find, only affected rigor of their individualized inquiry, and did not show managers failed adequately to undertake such inquiry in first place. Siewertsen v. Worthington Steel Co., 134 F. Supp. 3d 1091, 2015 U.S. Dist. LEXIS 129455 (N.D. Ohio 2015).

In this Americans with Disabilities Act of 1990 action, a reasonable jury could reach different conclusions as to whether the totality of the evidence established the abilities to communicate audibly, and to hear the audible communications of others, were truly essential job functions. Siewertsen v. Worthington Steel Co., 134 F. Supp. 3d 1091, 2015 U.S. Dist. LEXIS 129455 (N.D. Ohio 2015).

Court of Claims properly granted summary judgment to a university in a part-time instructor's action for disability discrimination because the instructor presented no evidence upon which it could be inferred that the search committee considered his disability in the decision-making process or that his disability was the true reason for denying him a full-time position. Ceglia v. Youngstown State Univ., 2015-Ohio-2125, 38 N.E.3d 1222, 2015 Ohio App. LEXIS 2045 (Ohio Ct. App., Franklin County 2015).

In light of the plaintiff's use of excerpts of testimony from various depositions to show inconsistency in the defendants' explanations for terminating the doctor, there was enough evidence from which a jury could conclude that the doctor was terminated because of his disability in violation of 42 U.S.C.S. § 12112 and R.C. 4112.02(A). Bligh-Glover v. Rizzo, 2012 U.S. Dist. LEXIS 141512 (N.D. Ohio Sept. 30, 2012).

In a case in alleging discrimination and disparate treatment under the Americans with Disabilities Act (ADA), 42 U.S.C.S. § 12101 et seq., and R.C. 4112.02 et seq., in which a district court entered summary judgment in favor of the employer, finding that the employee was not a qualified individual under the ADA, the employee, who was born without a left hand, was training to be a school bus driver, and the district court erred in finding that she was not a qualified individual because she did not have a commercial driver's license (CDL). The ADA covered discrimination on the basis of disability during job training, and a CDL was not needed for the employee to perform the essential functions of her bus driver training position. Rosebrough v. Buckeye Valley High Sch., 690 F.3d 427, 2012 FED App. 0255P, 2012 U.S. App. LEXIS 16434 (6th Cir. Ohio 2012).

Employer's motion for summary judgment was granted on the employee's disability discrimination claim under the Americans with Disabilities Act, 42 U.S.C.S. § 12112 and R.C. 4112.02 because the sole decision-maker was unaware of the employee's disability when he made the decision to terminate him. The Human Resource Department's knowledge of any protected activity could not be transferred to the decisionmaker on the limited showing the employee offered; moreover, to expect the decision-maker to be on notice that the employee suffered from a covered disability because the employee took several weeks leave due to sickness was unreasonable. Nilles v. Givaudan Flavors Corp., 2012 U.S. Dist. LEXIS 60551 (S.D. Ohio May 1, 2012), aff'd, 521 Fed. Appx. 364, 2013 FED App. 0314N, 2013 U.S. App. LEXIS 6416 (6th Cir. Ohio 2013).

Defendant was granted summary judgment on the disability discrimination under R.C. 4112.02(A) because a jury could conclude that defendant had a reasonable belief that plaintiff was being dishonest and that she could be terminated in accordance with company policy. Marks v. Ohio Bell Tel. Co., 2011 U.S. Dist. LEXIS 84508 (N.D. Ohio Aug. 2, 2011), aff'd, 2012 U.S. App. LEXIS 26891 (6th Cir. Ohio July 19, 2012).

In a case in which a former anesthesiology resident asserted that a hospital violated the Americans with Disabilities Act, 42 U.S.C.S. §§ 12101-12213, and R.C. 4112.01-4112.99 by not reinstating him after he receiving treatment for a corticosteroid addiction, his evidence that the hospital's proffered reasons for not reinstating him amounted to nothing more than speculation. His certificate of good standing was issued before he diverted drugs for his personal use, it was solely his unethical conduct —diverting a drug, in particular—that prompted a supervisor's negative opinion of him and the adverse recommendation, and the rejection letter, however awkwardly phrased, did not suggest that the hospital never even considered his application. Hall v. Ohiohealth Corp. Doctor's Hosp., 436 Fed. Appx. 430, 2011 FED App. 0521N, 2011 U.S. App. LEXIS 15565 (6th Cir. Ohio 2011).

When plaintiff nurse was terminated because she falsified her medical history on her employment application, the trial court properly granted summary judgment for defendants, a hospital and a medical center, in her action for wrongful termination. Plaintiff failed to establish a prima facie case of disability discrimination under R.C. 4112.02(A), because she did not point to any evidence to show that she was terminated based on a disability. Wagner v. Reg'l Med. Ctr., 2011-Ohio-2991, 194 Ohio App. 3d 589, 957 N.E.2d 351, 2011 Ohio App. LEXIS 2532 (Ohio Ct. App., Lorain County 2011).

Employer was entitled to summary judgment in a former employee's employment discrimination claim because, although the employee's chronic obstructive pulmonary disease and back problems qualified as physical impairments under R.C. 4112.01(A)(16)(a)(iii), the employee was not disabled as these impairments did not substantially affect one or more major life activities in that (1) the employee's slight discomfort in bathing did not rise to the level of substantially limiting the life activity of caring for oneself; (2)the employee's difficulties in cleaning the employee's home were mild and did not rise to the level of substantially limiting the life activity of performing manual tasks; and (3) the employee's walking difficulties were not substantially limiting. Hull v. Astro Shapes, Inc., 2011-Ohio-1656, 2011 Ohio App. LEXIS 1434 (Ohio Ct. App., Mahoning County 2011).

In an employee's disability discrimination suit, a directed verdict was properly awarded to the employee's former employer as the employee, who had sleep apnea and fell asleep on numerous occasions while at work, failed to establish that he could perform the essential functions of the job as staying awake was an essential job function. Medlin v. Springfield Metro. Hous. Auth., 2010-Ohio-3654, 2010 Ohio App. LEXIS 3105 (Ohio Ct. App., Clark County 2010).

Employee's complaint, alleging violation of R.C. 4112.02 for failure to transfer her to vacant position to accommodate her disability was rightly dismissed on summary judgment Employee's request for reassignment as a reasonable accommodation for her disability was not reasonable since the reassignment would have violated another employee's collective bargaining rights, in that the position the employee sought was a bargaining unit position and had to be filled by promotion before it could be filled by a lateral transfer; thus, since the movement to the vacant position would constitute a lateral transfer for the employee and a promotion for the employee who was eventually given the position, giving the position to the complaining employee would have violated the other employee's rights under the collective bargaining agreement. Rector v. Ohio Bureau of Workers' Comp., 2010-Ohio-2104, 2010 Ohio App. LEXIS 1734 (Ohio Ct. App., Franklin County 2010).

Employee failed to establish a prima facie case of disability discrimination under R.C. 4112.02(A) as, assuming that the employee's claimed condition, multiple chemical sensitivity, qualified as a "physical or mental impairment," the employee failed to present evidence that the board treated it as substantially limiting a major life activity. At most, the evidence supported the conclusion that the board treated the condition as disqualifying the employee from only one particular job — being a secretary at an elementary school; however, the inability to perform a single, particular job did not constitute a substantial limitation in the major life activity of working. Ogilbee v. Bd. of Educ. of Dayton Pub. Schs, 2010-Ohio-1913, 2010 Ohio App. LEXIS 1583 (Ohio Ct. App., Montgomery County 2010).

In a case alleging a failure to accommodate a disability under R.C. 4112.02 and R.C. 4112.99, an appellate court was unable to determine if proposed jury instructions on the interactive process an employer and an employee had to engage in to find a reasonable accommodation of a disability contained a correct statement of the law applicable to the facts of the case because they were not in the record; the case was reviewed under a plain error standard because a former employee did not object to the magistrate's handling of the jury trial. Even absent the proposed instructions, there was no plain error committed because the instruction given by the magistrate generally conformed to prevailing Ohio law. Ziadeh v. City of Columbus, 2010-Ohio-1323, 2010 Ohio App. LEXIS 1103 (Ohio Ct. App., Franklin County 2010).

Because defendants considered plaintiff's proposed accommodations, informed him why they were unreasonable, offered assistance in finding a new pathology residency (a position that involved less patient contact), and never hindered the process along the way, defendants participated in the interactive accommodation process in good faith, and were entitled to summary judgment on plaintiff's claim that they failed to accommodate his Asperger's Disorder. Jakubowski v. Christ Hosp., Inc., 627 F.3d 195, 2010 FED App. 0369P, 2010 U.S. App. LEXIS 24997 (6th Cir. Ohio 2010), cert. denied, 564 U.S. 1039, 131 S. Ct. 3071, 180 L. Ed. 2d 889, 2011 U.S. LEXIS 4937 (U.S. 2011).

Because communicating with professional colleagues and patients in ways that ensured patient safety was an essential function that plaintiff admittedly had difficulty performing, whether plaintiff was a qualified individual depended on whether he proposed a reasonable accommodation to account for his disability; plaintiff proposed "knowledge and understanding" of the hospital physicians and staff, but did not address how that accommodation would have improved his communication and interaction with patients, which were parts of the essential function of a family practice resident, but because the accommodation did not address a key obstacle preventing him from performing a necessary function of a medical resident, plaintiff had not met his burden of proving he was an otherwise qualified individual for the position. Jakubowski v. Christ Hosp., Inc., 627 F.3d 195, 2010 FED App. 0369P, 2010 U.S. App. LEXIS 24997 (6th Cir. Ohio 2010), cert. denied, 564 U.S. 1039, 131 S. Ct. 3071, 180 L. Ed. 2d 889, 2011 U.S. LEXIS 4937 (U.S. 2011).

Employee's disability discrimination claim under R.C. 4112.02 and 4112.99 failed because the employee failed to introduce sufficient evidence to establish a genuine issue of material fact on the question of whether he was disabled for purposes of such where: (1) with respect to the employee's assertion that his sexual impotence constituted a disability to support his claim, the employer correctly pointed out that there was no evidence in the record that the employer was in any way aware of this purported disability at the time of termination, and since the disability had to be known to the employer at the time of an adverse job action, that physical condition could not support his § 4112.02 claim; and (2) the employee was unable to safely and substantially perform the essential functions of the job in question since his medical limitations prevented the employee from safely and substantially performing the work required by his former position. Niles v. Nat'l Vendor Servs., 2010-Ohio-4610, 2010 Ohio App. LEXIS 3885 (Ohio Ct. App., Franklin County 2010).

Daughter failed to demonstrate a genuine issue of material fact with regard to her housing discrimination claims; the evidence did not support a disparate treatment claim because the daughter was not currently being treated differently than any similarly situated individuals. There was no evidence indicating that any of the daughter's siblings were residing rent free at the father's properties, such that the daughter was being treated differently than her non-disabled siblings; the evidence merely showed that the father had a history of providing housing to his children. Reid v. Plainsboro Partners, III, 2010-Ohio-4373, 2010 Ohio App. LEXIS 3694 (Ohio Ct. App., Franklin County 2010).

Summary judgment was properly granted on an employee's disability discrimination claim as no reasonable juror could find that the employee had a "disability," in that, while the evidence established that the employee had physical impairments, it did not establish that these impairments substantially limited one of the employee's major life activities, within the meaning of R.C. 4112.01(A)(13). Wallace v. Mantych Metalworking, 2010-Ohio-3765, 189 Ohio App. 3d 25, 937 N.E.2d 177, 2010 Ohio App. LEXIS 3207 (Ohio Ct. App., Montgomery County 2010).

Trial court properly granted a directed verdict to a former employer in a former employee's R.C. 4112.02 disability discrimination suit because reasonable minds could only find that the employee's extended periods of sleep while on the job far exceeded the employer's permission to take naps as necessary; thus, the employee failed to establish that he could safely and adequately perform his job of a security officer while on his medication and that allowing the employee to sleep for several hours while on the job was required as a reasonable accommodation under OAC 4112:5-08. Rongers v. Univ. Hosps. of Cleveland, Inc., 2009-Ohio-2137, 2009 Ohio App. LEXIS 1825 (Ohio Ct. App., Cuyahoga County 2009).

Trial court properly granted a directed verdict to a former employer in a former employee's R.C. 4112.02 disability discrimination suit because the employee had not established that his heart condition, controlled by medication, constituted a disability under R.C. 4112.01(A)(13). The medication, which made the employee drowsy, was not disabling because it improved the employee's heart condition and allowed him to work, and the employee's testimony showed that he was able to perform his job without restrictions and perform the same work at home that he did before he suffered his heart condition. Rongers v. Univ. Hosps. of Cleveland, Inc., 2009-Ohio-2137, 2009 Ohio App. LEXIS 1825 (Ohio Ct. App., Cuyahoga County 2009).

Trial court properly granted summary judgment to a former employee's employer and various personnel on the employee's disability discrimination claim because, while the employee claimed that she was disabled due to her permanent inability to reproduce or bear children, there was no evidence that the employee was discriminated against based on her inability to reproduce as she never requested any time off directly related to her inability to reproduce. Even assuming that the employee could establish a prima facie claim of discrimination, the employer offered a legitimate non-discriminatory reason for the employee's termination: the employee's tardiness and poor work history. King v. Aultman Health Found., 2009-Ohio-6277, 2009 Ohio App. LEXIS 5271 (Ohio Ct. App., Stark County 2009).

It was error to grant an employer's summary judgment motion dismissing an employee's disability discrimination claim because the facts that the employer (1) was aware of both the employee's medical restrictions regarding lifting and the employee's physical pain and (2) perceived the employee to be limited in the employee's ability to perform the tasks required in the employee's position, and believed the employee's limitations to be significant enough to terminate the employee's employment and qualify the employee for long-term disability, created a genuine fact issue as to whether the employer regarded the employee as disabled. Eifert v. Sample Machining, Inc., 2009-Ohio-6012, 2009 Ohio App. LEXIS 5043 (Ohio Ct. App., Montgomery County 2009).

It was error to grant an employer's summary judgment motion dismissing an employee's disability discrimination claim because, (1) while the evidence showed the employee was now not substantially limited in performing a major life activity, a jury could reasonably find that the employee was substantially impaired in performing the major life activity of lifting, and (2) a jury could also find that, despite the removal of the employee's medical restrictions, the employee continued to suffer sharp pains and numbness that substantially limited the employee from performing that major life activity. Eifert v. Sample Machining, Inc., 2009-Ohio-6012, 2009 Ohio App. LEXIS 5043 (Ohio Ct. App., Montgomery County 2009).

Where an employee alleged that he was ready to return to work, but that the employer refused to discuss identifying a reasonable accommodation that would allow him to continue his employment, and turned him away, the employee stated prima facie claims for disability discrimination under R.C. 4112.02(A) and retaliation. Lee v. Univ. Hosps. Health Sys., 2009 U.S. Dist. LEXIS 25816 (N.D. Ohio Mar. 27, 2009).

Summary judgment for a township fire department in a disability discrimination action by a fire department lieutenant who was not promoted to a captain position was proper, as the lieutenant's difficulty in standing or walking due to several foot and ankle surgeries was not a substantial limitation on the major life activity of walking that impaired his job duties under the Americans with Disabilities Act and R.C. 4112.02; rather, the lieutenant was able to perform his occupational duties of fighting fires. Sheridan v. Jackson Twp. Div. of Fire, 2009-Ohio-1267, 2009 Ohio App. LEXIS 1073 (Ohio Ct. App., Franklin County 2009).

Where an employee suffered from asthma, which limited his activity of breathing, could otherwise perform his job functions with reasonable accommodation, and the employee was arguably terminated at least in part because of his disability, he made out a prima facie case of discrimination in violation of R.C. 4112.02(A). Russell v. Nat'l Amusements, Inc., 2009 U.S. Dist. LEXIS 11598 (N.D. Ohio Feb. 4, 2009).

Employee did not prove that she was "disabled," as defined under R.C. 4112.01(A)(13) for her disability discrimination claim because the employee testified that she was capable of performing work that did not require lifting over 10 pounds. The employee also failed to prove that, despite her disability, she could safely and substantially perform the essential functions of the job in question since she conceded that after her surgery, she could no longer perform the duties of the job, and failed to demonstrate that the employer did not make a good faith effort to assist her in seeking an accommodation or that she could have been reasonably accommodated but for the employer's lack of good faith because her suggestion of simply performing the paperwork part of her job was not an objectively reasonable accommodation. Cioroch v. Ohio Dep't of Mental Retardation & Developmental Disabilities, 2008-Ohio-5725, 2008 Ohio Misc. LEXIS 241 (Ohio Ct. Cl. 2008).

Although the employee's fatigue caused by sleep-related impairments did not demonstrate that she was disabled under 42 U.S.C.S. § 12102(2)(A) based on the letter sent by the employer regarding her request for 40 work week, the employer regarded her as disabled for Americans with Disabilities Act (ADA) and state law purposes. Furthermore, the employer did not dispute that the employee was an otherwise qualified individual and genuine issues of fact existed as to the employer could accommodate her disability by limiting her work week to 40 hours. Geiger v. Pfizer, Inc., 2008 U.S. Dist. LEXIS 89238 (S.D. Ohio Sept. 18, 2008).

Evidence showed, at most, that the employer believed that the employee's back condition and current medication levels precluded him from performing the dangerous machinery functions required of the particular job of maintenance technician at the employer's, but did not regard him as unable to perform a broad class or range of jobs in the maintenance field or other categories of employment. Such evidence did not suffice to establish a prima facie regarded-as-disabled discrimination claim under the Americans with Disabilities Act, 42 U.S.C.S. § 12101 et seq., and the Ohio Civil Rights Act that implicated the major life activity of working. Daugherty v. Sajar Plastics, Inc., 544 F.3d 696, 2008 FED App. 0379P, 2008 U.S. App. LEXIS 21574 (6th Cir. Ohio 2008).

Parole officer did not establish a prima facie case for disability discrimination, perceived or otherwise, because the parole officer did not specify what "major life activity" his supervisors believed that he was incapable of performing. The stray comment that the parole officer had been diagnosed with cancer two years prior did not prove that the administrator perceived the parole officer as limited in a substantial life activity. Bogdas v. Ohio Dep't of Rehab. & Corr., 2008-Ohio-3409, 2008 Ohio Misc. LEXIS 113 (Ohio Ct. Cl. 2008).

Employee's R.C. 4112.02 disability discrimination claim was properly dismissed on summary judgment because the employee failed to show that his impairment, sinus cancer, rose to the level of a disability by substantially limiting a major life activity. The employee's own testimony established that, after surgery and treatment, the claimant could climb, grasp, lift, walk, eat, breathe, swallow, and sleep without difficulty. Slane v. MetaMateria Ptnrs, LLC, 2008-Ohio-2426, 176 Ohio App. 3d 459, 892 N.E.2d 498, 2008 Ohio App. LEXIS 2064 (Ohio Ct. App., Franklin County 2008).

Employer was entitled to summary judgment in a former employee's disability discrimination action under R.C. 4112.02(A) because the employee's inability to return to work after having had several surgeries showed an inability to perform the essential function of the job of regular attendance without a reasonable accommodation, such that the employee did not make out a prima facie case of disability discrimination. Foster v. Jackson County Broad., Inc., 2008-Ohio-70, 2008 Ohio App. LEXIS 57 (Ohio Ct. App., Jackson County 2008).

Cancer survivor who did not suffer from any substantially limiting impairment of a significant duration was not disabled for purposes of R.C. Chapter 4112: Slane v. MetaMateria Ptnrs, LLC, 2008-Ohio-2426, 176 Ohio App. 3d 459, 892 N.E.2d 498, 2008 Ohio App. LEXIS 2064 (Ohio Ct. App., Franklin County 2008).

Employer was entitled to summary judgment on a claim that the plaintiff was discharged due to a perceived disability: Cunningham v.

Steubenville Orthopedics & Sports Med., Inc., 2008-Ohio-1172, 175 Ohio App. 3d 627, 888 N.E.2d 499, 2008 Ohio App. LEXIS 983 (Ohio Ct. App., Jefferson County 2008).

In order to survive summary judgment on a statutory claim for disability discrimination pursuant to R.C. 4112.02(A), a plaintiff must set forth a prima facie case of disability discrimination by showing (1) that the plaintiff was disabled, (2) that the plaintiffs employer took adverse employment action motivated at least in part by the plaintiff's disability, and (3) that the plaintiff, even with the plaintiffs disability, can safely and substantially perform the essential functions of the plaintiff's job with or without reasonable accommodation. Davis v. Johnson, 2007-Ohio-6567, 2007 Ohio App. LEXIS 5739 (Ohio Ct. App., Richland County 2007).

Employee's claim of disability discrimination under R.C. 4112.02 failed where he was unable to show that his temporary back injury was within the definition of disability under R.C. 4112.01(A)(13). Young v. Stelter & Brinck, Ltd., 2007-Ohio-6510, 174 Ohio App. 3d 221, 881 N.E.2d 874, 2007 Ohio App. LEXIS 5688 (Ohio Ct. App., Hamilton County 2007).

Defendant was not wrongfully termination due to his epilepsy disability. Although it was undisputed that the employee suffered from epilepsy, because he testified that he did not have any seizure activity for the period during which he was absent from work, the employee's epilepsy was not the cause of his unexcused absence nor did the epilepsy condition impair his ability to give notice of his intent to take leave. Barnett v. Ohio State Univ. Med. Ctr., 2007-Ohio-5424, 2007 Ohio Misc. LEXIS 391 (Ohio Ct. Cl. 2007).

Defendants' did not violate 29 U.S.C.S. § 794 or R.C. 4112.02(G) because the disabled student was expelled because he admitted that he accepted the marijuana and violated the school's drug policy and plaintiffs failed to show pretext because other students involved in the drug incident had been expelled. Benedict v. Cent. Catholic High Sch., 511 F. Supp. 2d 854, 2007 U.S. Dist. LEXIS 69645 (N.D. Ohio 2007).

Former employee had stated a disability discrimination claim under R.C. 4112.02 and a wrongful discharge claim in violation of the public policy embodied in § 4112.02 sufficient to survive an Civ.R. 12(B)(6) challenge, in that the employee alleged in his complaint that he suffered from "spinal stenosis," depression, and diabetes, which qualified as disabilities under R.C. 4112.01(A)(13); that the employee was fired on the basis of his disabilities, specifying that the allegation that he had been observed lifting a jet ski off a sandbar was "false"; and that, during the course of his employment, he performed his assigned work duties in a manner satisfactory to the employer. Goss v. Kmart Corp., 2007-Ohio-3200, 2007 Ohio App. LEXIS 2923 (Ohio Ct. App., Trumbull County 2007).

As the record was devoid of evidence of the employee's alleged disability under R.C. 4112.01(A)(13), he failed to produce any statistical or expert evidence related to his employment opportunities, and he did not show that the employer took an adverse employment action against him, his discrimination claim under R.C. 4112.02(A) failed. Weitzman v. ISG Cleveland Works Ry. Co., 2007-Ohio-2918, 2007 Ohio App. LEXIS 2697 (Ohio Ct. App., Cuyahoga County 2007).

Employer was not entitled to Fed. R. Civ. P. 12(b)(6) dismissal of a discharged employee's action alleging disability discrimination in violation of 42 U.S.C.S. § 12112 of the Americans with Disabilities Act, 42 U.S.C.S. § 12101 et seq., and R.C. 4112.02(A); although the employee was discharged for violation of a zero tolerance policy related to sexual harassment and threats of violence, the employee's allegations could show that he was an individual with a disability under 42 U.S.C.S. § 12111(8), that he was otherwise qualified for his position, and that he was excluded from the position under circumstances that raised a reasonable inference of unlawful discrimination. The employee alleged that he had a mental disability in the form of depression, that the employer was aware of the disability by virtue of medical information furnished to the employer, and that when the employer became aware of the employee's depression, supervisors, coworkers, and union officials called the employee derogatory names in reference to his mental condition, vandalized his locker, and painted his name in graffiti on the walls. Bradshaw v. Goodyear Tire & Rubber Co., 485 F. Supp. 2d 821, 2007 U.S. Dist. LEXIS 35142 (N.D. Ohio 2007).

Employer was entitled to summary judgment on a former employee's claims under the American with Disabilities Act, 42 U.S.C.S. § 12101 et seq., and under R.C. 4112.02; the employee, who suffered severe head injuries in an off-the-job accident, failed to present sufficient evidence for a reasonable jury to conclude that he was qualified for an open position with the employer for purposes of 42 U.S.C.S. § 12112(a). Therefore, the employee could not show that the employer either failed to offer him a reasonable accommodation for, or terminated him because of, his disability. Kleiber v. Honda of Am. Mfg., 485 F.3d 862, 2007 FED App. 0155P, 2007 U.S. App. LEXIS 10326 (6th Cir. Ohio 2007).

Employer was entitled to summary judgment on a former employee's claims under the American with Disabilities Act, 42 U.S.C.S. § 12101 et seq., and under R.C. 4112.02. The employee, who suffered severe head injuries in an off-the-job accident, failed to present any evidence of lack of good faith on the employer's part and thus failed to establish a genuine issue of material fact as to whether the employer failed to participate in the interactive process required to identify a suitable reasonable accommodation and, as a result, denied him the reasonable accommodation of transferring him to a different job for purposes of 42 U.S.C.S. §§ 12111(9), 12112(b) Kleiber v. Honda of Am. Mfg., 485 F.3d 862, 2007 FED App. 0155P, 2007 U.S. App. LEXIS 10326 (6th Cir. Ohio 2007).

In an action in which a former employee filed suit against his former employer alleging violations of the Americans With Disabilities Act, 42 U.S.C.S. § 12101 et seq., and R.C. 4112.02(A), the employer was entitled to summary judgment on the termination claim where (1) the employee failed to present sufficient evidence to create a genuine issue of fact on the issue of whether he was "otherwise qualified" to perform any production position at the employer; and (2) the employer produced evidence that the employee's employment was terminated in accordance with its associate service policy, which stated that separation from employment would result in cases where the employee was not actively employed for any reason for twelve (12) consecutive months unless the employee was on approved leave of absence due to an occupational injury or illness, serving in the armed forces, on an educational leave, or laid off. Kleiber v. Honda of Am. Mfg., 420 F. Supp. 2d 809, 2006 U.S. Dist. LEXIS 7378 (S.D. Ohio 2006), aff'd, 485 F.3d 862, 2007 FED App. 0155P, 2007 U.S. App. LEXIS 10326 (6th Cir. Ohio 2007).

Employee met his burden of showing that he was terminated from his employment due to being disabled for purposes of one of the elements of his disability discrimination claim under R.C. 4112.02(A)(2), as his general manager testified that the employee could not perform his job as an inspector because he lacked the mobility to move around the employer's plant and he was unable to meet the lifting requirements of the job due to a foot injury that occurred previously at work. Sicklesmith v. Hoist, 2006-Ohio-6137, 169 Ohio App. 3d 470, 863 N.E.2d 677, 2006 Ohio App. LEXIS 6103 (Ohio Ct. App., Columbiana County 2006).

When an employee became hostile with her supervisors for asking her to provide medical documentation supporting her request for a different king of chair, as she had recently had hip replacement surgery, and she was fired, it was not arbitrary, capricious or irrational for the Ohio Civil Rights Commission to find that she was fired for violating workplace rules requiring certain workplace behavior, rather than because of her disability or for seeking an accomodation for it. Proctor v. Ohio Civ. Rights Comm'n, 2006-Ohio-6007, 169 Ohio App. 3d 527, 863 N.E.2d 1069, 2006 Ohio App. LEXIS 5956 (Ohio Ct. App., Summit County 2006).

Employer was entitled to summary judgment in a former employee's action alleging failure to accommodate his disability of having Hepatitis C, disparate treatment on the basis of the disability, and wrongful termination due to the disability in violation of R.C. 4112.02(A) and in violation of 42 U.S.C.S. § 12112(a) of the Americans with Disabilities Act, 42 U.S.C.S. § 12101 et seq.; the employee failed to meet his burden of establishing a prima facie case of discrimination because he could not establish that the requested accommodation, namely an undetermined amount of medical leave after his previous eight-month medical leave, was objectively reasonable. Further, the employee was not a "qualified individual" within the meaning of 42 U.S.C.S. § 12111(8) because he was unable to show that he was qualified to perform the essential functions of his position. Conners v. Spectrasite Communs., Inc., 465 F. Supp. 2d 834, 2006 U.S. Dist. LEXIS 76582 (S.D. Ohio 2006).

In an action in which a former employee filed suit against defendants, former employer, union, and a counselor for the employee assistance program, alleging claims of disability discrimination in violation of the Americans with Disabilities Act of 1990 and R.C. 4112.02, defendants were granted summary judgment where (1) there was no evidence from which a jury could conclude that the labor relations supervisor thought the employee was restricted in her ability to perform a class of jobs or a broad range of jobs; and (2) the supervisor's opinion that the employee had "mental problems" did not amount to proof that the supervisor or the employer perceived the employee as being substantially limited in her ability to perform a major life activity. Jaques v. Herbert, 447 F. Supp. 2d 858, 2006 U.S. Dist. LEXIS 59655 (N.D. Ohio 2006).

Mere conjecture that an employer's explanation for prima facie discrimination was a pretext for intentional discrimination was an insufficient basis for denial of summary judgment, as to show pretext, one had to produce evidence that the employer's stated reasons were factually untrue. Stembridge v. Summit Acad. Mgmt., 2006-Ohio-4076, 2006 Ohio App. LEXIS 4034 (Ohio Ct. App., Summit County 2006).

Insubordination on the part of an employee claiming discrimination was a legitimate, nondiscriminatory reason for termination. Stembridge v. Summit Acad. Mgmt., 2006-Ohio-4076, 2006 Ohio App. LEXIS 4034 (Ohio Ct. App., Summit County 2006).

To establish a prima facie disability wrongful discharge violation of R.C. 4112.02(A), a plaintiff had to show that 1) he was disabled; 2) he suffered an adverse employment action at least in part due to his handicap; and 3) that he could safely and substantially perform all essential functions of the job, and once the prima facie case was established, the burden shifted to the defendant to offer a legitimate, nondiscriminatory reason for its action, and, if said reason was offered, the burden shifted back to the plaintiff to demonstrate that the reason was actually pretext for impermissible discrimination. Stembridge v. Summit Acad. Mgmt., 2006-Ohio-4076, 2006 Ohio App. LEXIS 4034 (Ohio Ct. App., Summit County 2006).

When an employee claimed his employment was terminated as a result of disability discrimination, summary judgment was properly granted to his employer because, even if the employee stated a prima facie case of discrimination, the employer offered the employee's insubordination as its reason for firing him, because the employee did not return to a required program when he was told to, and the employee did not offer any evidence, other than his own self-serving assertions, that this reason was a pretext for discrimination, so the employee did not meet his burden of proof. Stembridge v. Summit Acad. Mgmt., 2006-Ohio-4076, 2006 Ohio App. LEXIS 4034 (Ohio Ct. App., Summit County 2006).

There was a distinction between taking an adverse job action for unacceptable misconduct and taking such action solely because of a disability, even if the misconduct was "caused" by the disability, as the Americans with Disabilities Act, 42 U.S.C.S. § 12101 et seq., protected recovering alcoholics, but did not protect a worker from his own bad judgment in drinking on the job. Burrows v. Licking County, 2006-Ohio-4057, 2006 Ohio App. LEXIS 4029 (Ohio Ct. App., Licking County 2006).

In order to establish a prima facie case of disability discrimination in an employment discharge action, the person seeking relief had to demonstrate (1) that he or she was handicapped, (2) that an adverse employment action was taken by an employer, at least in part, because the individual was handicapped, and (3) that the person, though handicapped, could safely and substantially perform the essential functions of the job in question. Burrows v. Licking County, 2006-Ohio-4057, 2006 Ohio App. LEXIS 4029 (Ohio Ct. App., Licking County 2006).

Employee did not show his termination was the result of disability discrimination, in violation of R.C. 4112.02, because (1) he did not show his employer was aware of the fact that he was a recovering alcoholic, as he had only mentioned it in confidence to other employees, and an employee who said she saw him intoxicated at work referred to him as an "old drunk," and (2) the evidence showed his termination was based on the employer's belief of a witness's statement that the employee was intoxicated on the job, rather than on the employee's disability. Burrows v. Licking County, 2006-Ohio-4057, 2006 Ohio App. LEXIS 4029 (Ohio Ct. App., Licking County 2006).

Employer was entitled to judgment as a matter of law on the handicap discrimination claim, under R.C. 4112.02, because it provided numerous accommodations for the employee but she did not return to work and was eventually terminated simply for exhausting her leave. Bowers v. Swagelok Co., 2006-Ohio-3605, 2006 Ohio App. LEXIS 3550 (Ohio Ct. App., Cuyahoga County 2006).

Employee did not meet her burden of establishing a prima facie case of disability discrimination where she only showed that she suffered from psychological disorders that rendered her disabled, but she failed to show that her voluntary resignation from her employment position due to stress was an adverse employment action and the fact that she was not offered a part-time position was not a constructive discharge, as there were no part-time positions available in the employee's work position; accordingly, summary judgment for the employer was proper. Swann v. Cardiology Assocs. of Cincinnati, 2006-Ohio-2758, 2006 Ohio App. LEXIS 2596 (Ohio Ct. App., Hamilton County 2006).

There was no evidence that a sole proprietor suffered disability discrimination under R.C. 4112.02(A) where he was initially promised salvage work but then the decision to allow him to do the work was revoked, as even if he had been allowed to do the work, the parties that he named as defendants would not have been his "employer" pursuant to R.C. 4112.01(A)(2) and accordingly, summary judgment against his claim was proper. Cooper v. Jones, 2006-Ohio-1770, 2006 Ohio App. LEXIS 1606 (Ohio Ct. App., Jackson County 2006).

Employer was not entitled to summary judgment on an employee's disability discrimination claims where there were issues of fact as to whether the employer considered the employee disabled or unable to perform the functions of his job, whether the employee's perceived disability limited his ability to work, and whether the employer discriminated against the employee as a result of the perceived disability. Allen v. Deerfield Mfg., 424 F. Supp. 2d 987, 2006 U.S. Dist. LEXIS 13870 (S.D. Ohio 2006).

Employee failed to state a claim under the Ohio Civil Rights Act, R.C. 4112.02 because she did not have an impairment that substantially limited a major life activity. Edwards v. Dialysis Clinic, Inc., 423 F. Supp. 2d 789, 2006 U.S. Dist. LEXIS 11911 (S.D. Ohio 2006).

Summary judgment was properly granted for the employer on the employee's claim for disability discrimination and employee liability because the evidence did not establish that the employee had a disability; the evidence failed to show that her condition met the threshold requirement of a substantial limitation of a major life activity, i.e., hearing or working, as set forth in R.C. 4112.01(A)(13). There was no evidence in the record to show that the employer's proffered reason for terminating the employee, unacceptable quality and production of work, was false or a pretext for disability discrimination. Northern v. Medical Mut. of Ohio, 2006-Ohio-1075, 2006 Ohio App. LEXIS 1001 (Ohio Ct. App., Cuyahoga County 2006).

When an employee became hostile with her supervisors for asking her to provide medical documentation supporting her request for a different kind of chair, as she had recently had hip replacement surgery, and she was fired, it was not arbitrary, capricious or irrational for the Ohio Civil Rights Commission to find that she was fired for violating workplace rules requiring certain workplace behavior, rather than because of her disability or for seeking an accomodation for it. Proctor v. Ohio Civ. Rights Comm'n, 2006-Ohio-6007, 169 Ohio App. 3d 527, 863 N.E.2d 1069, 2006 Ohio App. LEXIS 5956 (Ohio Ct. App., Summit County 2006).

Employer was entitled to summary judgment in a former employee's action alleging failure to accommodate his disability of having Hepatitis C, disparate treatment on the basis of the disability, and wrongful termination due to the disability in violation of R.C. 4112.02(A) and in violation of 42 U.S.C.S. § 12112(a) of the Americans with Disabilities Act, 42 U.S.C.S. § 12101 et seq.; the employee failed to meet his burden of establishing a prima facie case of discrimination because he could not establish that the requested accommodation, namely an undetermined amount of medical leave after his previous eight-month medical leave, was objectively reasonable. Further, the employee was not a "qualified individual" within the meaning of 42 U.S.C.S. § 12111(8) because he was unable to show that he was qualified to perform the essential functions of his position. Conners v. Spectrasite Communs., Inc., 465 F. Supp. 2d 834, 2006 U.S. Dist. LEXIS 76582 (S.D. Ohio 2006).

In an action in which a former employee filed suit against defendants, former employer, union, and a counselor for the employee assistance program, alleging claims of disability discrimination in violation of the Americans with Disabilities Act of 1990 and R.C. 4112.02, defendants were granted summary judgment where (1) there was no evidence from which a jury could conclude that the labor relations supervisor thought the employee was restricted in her ability to perform a class of jobs or a broad range of jobs; and (2) the supervisor's opinion that the employee had "mental problems" did not amount to proof that the supervisor or the employer perceived the employee as being substantially limited in her ability to perform a major life activity. Jaques v. Herbert, 447 F. Supp. 2d 858, 2006 U.S. Dist. LEXIS 59655 (N.D. Ohio 2006).

When an employee claimed his employment was terminated as a result of disability discrimination, summary judgment was properly granted to his employer because, even if the employee stated a prima facie case of discrimination, the employer offered the employee's insubordination as its reason for firing him, because the employee did not return to a required program when he was told to, and the employee did not offer any evidence, other than his own self-serving assertions, that this reason was a pretext for discrimination, so the employee did not meet his burden of proof. Stembridge v. Summit Acad. Mgmt., 2006-Ohio-4076, 2006 Ohio App. LEXIS 4034 (Ohio Ct. App., Summit County 2006).

Employer was entitled to judgment as a matter of law on the handicap discrimination claim, under R.C. 4112.02, because it provided numerous accommodations for the employee but she did not return to work and was eventually terminated simply for exhausting her leave. Bowers v. Swagelok Co., 2006-Ohio-3605, 2006 Ohio App. LEXIS 3550 (Ohio Ct. App., Cuyahoga County 2006).

Employee did not meet her burden of establishing a prima facie case of disability discrimination where she only showed that she suffered from psychological disorders that rendered her disabled, but she failed to show that her voluntary resignation from her employment position due to stress was an adverse employment action and the fact that she was not offered a part-time position was not a constructive discharge, as there were no part-time positions available in the employee's work position; accordingly, summary judgment for the employer was proper. Swann v. Cardiology Assocs. of Cincinnati, 2006-Ohio-2758, 2006 Ohio App. LEXIS 2596 (Ohio Ct. App., Hamilton County 2006).

Employer was not entitled to summary judgment on an employee's disability discrimination claims where there were issues of fact as to whether the employer considered the employee disabled or unable to perform the functions of his job, whether the employee's perceived disability limited his ability to work, and whether the employer discriminated against the employee as a result of the perceived disability. Allen v. Deerfield Mfg., 424 F. Supp. 2d 987, 2006 U.S. Dist. LEXIS 13870 (S.D. Ohio 2006).

There was no evidence that a sole proprietor suffered disability discrimination under R.C. 4112.02(A) where he was initially promised salvage work but then the decision to allow him to do the work was revoked, as even if he had been allowed to do the work, the parties that he named as defendants would not have been his "employer" pursuant to R.C. 4112.01(A)(2) and accordingly, summary judgment against his claim was proper. Cooper v. Jones, 2006-Ohio-1770, 2006 Ohio App. LEXIS 1606 (Ohio Ct. App., Jackson County 2006).

Employee failed to state a claim under the Ohio Civil Rights Act, R.C. 4112.02 because she did not have an impairment that substantially limited a major life activity. Edwards v. Dialysis Clinic, Inc., 423 F. Supp. 2d 789, 2006 U.S. Dist. LEXIS 11911 (S.D. Ohio 2006).

Summary judgment was properly granted for the employer on the employee's claim for disability discrimination and employee liability because the evidence did not establish that the employee had a disability. The evidence failed to show that her condition met the threshold requirement of a substantial limitation of a major life activity, i.e., hearing or working, as set forth in R.C. 4112.01(A)(13). There was no evidence in the record to show that the employer's proffered reason for terminating the employee, unacceptable quality and production of work, was false or a pretext for disability discrimination. Northern v. Medical Mut. of Ohio, 2006-Ohio-1075, 2006 Ohio App. LEXIS 1001 (Ohio Ct. App., Cuyahoga County 2006).

Accommodations for disabled workers are unreasonable only if they place an undue hardship on the employer. The employer carries the burden of showing undue hardship. The instructions, as a whole, provided the jury with the proper law regarding burdens of proof. Sicklesmith v. Hoist, 2006-Ohio-6137, 169 Ohio App. 3d 470, 863 N.E.2d 677, 2006 Ohio App. LEXIS 6103 (Ohio Ct. App., Columbiana County 2006).

When an employee sought special seating due to her recent hip replacement surgery, her employer could have an office furnishings policy even if fire regulations did not require restrictions on the seating the employee sought, and it was not discriminatory for the employer to ask her to provide medical documentation of her need for such an accommodation. Proctor v. Ohio Civ. Rights Comm'n, 2006-Ohio-6007, 169 Ohio App. 3d 527, 863 N.E.2d 1069, 2006 Ohio App. LEXIS 5956 (Ohio Ct. App., Summit County 2006).

Because the employee failed to demonstrate that the alleged harassment was sufficiently severe or pervasive to create an abusive working environment, she could not establish a hostile work environment claim, under R.C. 4112.02. Northern v. Medical Mut. of Ohio, 2006-Ohio-1075, 2006 Ohio App. LEXIS 1001 (Ohio Ct. App., Cuyahoga County 2006).

In an action in which a former employee filed suit against her former employer alleging violations of the American with Disabilities Act, 42 U.S.C.S. § 12101 et seq., and R.C. 4112, the employer was denied summary judgment on the disability discrimination claims where there were genuine issues of material fact as to whether the employer regarded the employee as an individual with a disability on account of her diabetes and whether the employer took an adverse employment action against the employee because it perceived her to be disabled. Hicks v. Novartis Pharms. Corp., 457 F. Supp. 2d 814, 2005 U.S. Dist. LEXIS 26495 (S.D. Ohio 2005).

Plaintiff former employee's response of yes to a narrow question of whether his depression impaired his work did not preclude the employee's argument that his ability to sleep was also impaired and thus, defendant employer's motion for summary judgment on the employee's disability discrimination claim under R.C. 4112 .02(A) was denied. Dage v. Time Warner Cable, 395 F. Supp. 2d 668, 2005 U.S. Dist. LEXIS 25361 (S.D. Ohio 2005).

Employer was entitled to summary judgment in an action by a former employee who took a "stress leave" and who alleged disability discrimination in violation of R.C. 4112.02(A); because the employee presented no evidence that her ability to work in a broad class of jobs was restricted, no jury could find her "disabled" within the meaning of R.C. 4112.01(A)(13). Further, the employee presented no evidence of an adverse employment action related to the employer's failure to transfer a co-worker who was allegedly causing the employee's stress because the employee never asked for such transfer as an accommodation. Langley v. DaimlerChrysler Corp., 407 F. Supp. 2d 897, 2005 U.S. Dist. LEXIS 36332 (N.D. Ohio 2005), aff'd, 502 F.3d 475, 2007 FED App. 0379P, 2007 U.S. App. LEXIS 22211 (6th Cir. Ohio 2007).

Where an employee was terminated from a receptionist position in a reduction in force and there was a reference in a performance evaluation indicating that the employee needed to speak louder when using the paging system, the disability discrimination claim failed because this single comment fell far short of creating a genuine issue of material fact as to whether the employee was terminated due to an actual or perceived disability. Van Diest v. Deloitte & Touche, LLP, 2005 U.S. Dist. LEXIS 22106 (N.D. Ohio Sept. 30, 2005).

Former employee's depression constituted a handicap under Ohio law because it eliminated him from an entire class of jobs; also, given the short amount of time between his disability leave and his termination, and the extensive efforts undertaken by him to return to work, the evidence was such that a reasonable jury could determine that he was terminated, at least in part, because of his disability. Furthermore, the jury could infer that the former employer's and the former supervisor's reason for terminating him was not based on a legitimate, non-discriminatory reason, but on his handicap, and that they did not attempt to accommodate him; thus, the employer and the supervisor's motion for summary judgment on the employee's discrimination claim under state law was denied. Francis v. UPS of Am., Inc., 2005 U.S. Dist. LEXIS 21225 (S.D. Ohio Aug. 29, 2005).

Employer was properly granted summary judgment in an action by a terminated employee, as the employee failed to show that she had a record of a disability or that the employer "regarded her" as disabled pursuant to her Americans with Disabilities Act claim under 42 U.S.C.S. § 12102(2), and further, the employer offered a legitimate explanation for the termination due to the employee's poor job performance, which she was unwilling to possibly remedy by taking other employment positions or shifts offered by the employer during job performance discussions; based on the failure of the federal statutory claims, the employee's claims under R.C. 4112.02 and for common law wrongful discharge also failed. Cox v. Kettering Med. Ctr., 2005-Ohio-5003, 2005 Ohio App. LEXIS 4526 (Ohio Ct. App., Montgomery County 2005).

Because a doctor's report failed to state whether stress caused plaintiff former employee to be significantly restricted in his ability to sleep compared to an average person, the employee's claims under the Americans with Disabilities Act of 1990, 42 U.S.C.S. § 12101 et seq., and R.C. 4112.01(A)(13), 4112.02, failed. McConnell v. Swifty Transp., Inc., 2005 U.S. Dist. LEXIS 15565 (S.D. Ohio July 29, 2005), aff'd, 198 Fed. Appx. 438, 2006 FED App. 0638N, 2006 U.S. App. LEXIS 21900 (6th Cir. Ohio 2006).

Summary judgment was properly granted, dismissing a disability discrimination claim, under R.C. 4112.02(A), brought by a former employee and his wife against the employee's former employer and various managers, because plaintiffs were unable to prove that the employee had a qualifying disability under R.C. 4112.01(A)(13), in that the employee's inability to lift and carry 100 pounds of steel did not constitute a significant restriction on his ability to work since the employee stated that 95 percent of his job was completed from his desk and that his bench helpers did the heavy lifting at work, and plaintiffs were unable to prove that the employer perceived the employee's cancer as substantially limiting his ability to perform the major life activity of working. Further, even if plaintiffs could have established a prima facie case of disability discrimination, they failed to demonstrate that defendants' proffered legitimate reasons for the employee's termination, a reduction in force, were a pretext for discrimination. Vickers v. Wren Indus., 2005-Ohio-3656, 2005 Ohio App. LEXIS 3366 (Ohio Ct. App., Montgomery County 2005).

Summary judgment was granted with respect to the Americans with Disabilities Act of 1990 (ADA), 42 U.S.C.S. § 12101 et seq., and R.C. 4112.02 claims because the deaf employee failed to prove that she was a qualified employee because it was undisputed that the employee did not completely understand written English and that she failed to meet the speed and accuracy requirements as Evidenced by the numerous counseling sessions and written warning provided to the employee. Dillbeck v. Huntington Nat'l Bank, 2005 U.S. Dist. LEXIS 10273 (S.D. Ohio May 26, 2005).

Employee who alleged that she was terminated because of walking limitations caused by a stress fracture in her toe failed to establish a prima facie case under the Americans with Disabilities Act, 42 U.S.C.S. § 12101 et seq., and R.C. 4112.02 because the employee did not use a cane or walker and was able to ride a bike without discomfort; thus, the walking limitations were not substantial enough to qualify as a disability under 42 U.S.C.S. § 12102(2). Martin v. Licking County Common Pleas Court Juvenile Div., 2005 U.S. Dist. LEXIS 9013 (S.D. Ohio Apr. 22, 2005).

Employer was entitled to summary judgment in an action by a former employee who took a "stress leave" and who alleged disability discrimination in violation of R.C. 4112.02(A); because the employee presented no evidence that her ability to work in a broad class of jobs was restricted, no jury could find her "disabled" within the meaning of R.C. 4112.01(A)(13). Further, the employee presented no evidence of an adverse employment action related to the employer's failure to transfer a co-worker who was allegedly causing the employee's stress because the employee never asked for such transfer as an accommodation. Langley v. DaimlerChrysler Corp., 407 F. Supp. 2d 897, 2005 U.S. Dist. LEXIS 36332 (N.D. Ohio 2005), aff'd, 502 F.3d 475, 2007 FED App. 0379P, 2007 U.S. App. LEXIS 22211 (6th Cir. Ohio 2007).

Where an employee suffered an injury to her foot, which caused her to be unable to perform her job duties as a corrections officer and resulted in her involuntary disability separation from work, even assuming that her injury was a "substantial impairment," she did not establish that she was a "qualified individual" and accordingly, she failed in her burden of establishing a prima facie case of disability discrimination, in violation of R.C. 4112.02(A); summary judgment was properly granted to the employer. Batiste v. Cuyahoga County Sheriff's Dep't, 2005-Ohio-6230, 2005 Ohio App. LEXIS 5617 (Ohio Ct. App., Cuyahoga County 2005).

Because a doctor's report failed to state whether stress caused plaintiff former employee to be significantly restricted in his ability to sleep compared to an average person, the employee's claims under the Americans with Disabilities Act of 1990, 42 U.S.C.S. § 12101 et seq., and R.C. 4112.01(A)(13), 4112.02, failed. McConnell v. Swifty Transp., Inc., 2005 U.S. Dist. LEXIS 15565 (S.D. Ohio July 29, 2005), aff'd, 198 Fed. Appx. 438, 2006 FED App. 0638N, 2006 U.S. App. LEXIS 21900 (6th Cir. Ohio 2006).

Employer was denied summary judgment on the disability discrimination claim where there were genuine issues of material fact as to whether the employer regarded the employee as an individual with a disability on account of her diabetes and whether the employer took an adverse employment action against the employee because it perceived her to be disabled. Hicks v. Novartis Pharms. Corp., 457 F. Supp. 2d 814, 2005 U.S. Dist. LEXIS 26495 (S.D. Ohio 2005).

In a disability discrimination action claiming violation of Ohio law, an employer's motion to dismiss was denied for several reasons: (1) the employer sought to hold the employee to a summary judgment standard of proof when the employee was only required to plead the elements of the direct evidence standard in order to survive a motion to dismiss under Fed. R. Civ. P. 12(b)(6); (2) the employer's reliance upon the McDonnell Douglas burden shifting analysis was inappropriate on a motion to dismiss because Fed. R. Civ. P. 8(a)(2) only required the employee to furnish a short and plain statement of her claim, which she did; and (3) the facts alleged were adequate to meet Ohio's test for disability discrimination under R.C. 4112.02(a), namely, that she was disabled by lung cancer, that she requested an accommodation that the employer refused, and that her employment was later terminated. Witte v. Rippe & Kingston Sys., 358 F. Supp. 2d 658, 2005 U.S. Dist. LEXIS 2865 (S.D. Ohio 2005).

Summary judgment was properly granted in favor of defendants, the employer and the supervisor, based on wrongful termination because the employee failed to offer any evidence that the employer's economic rationale, whether for layoff or arguably for termination, was a pretext for disability discrimination. Alam v. Chemstress Consultant Co., 2005-Ohio-272, 2005 Ohio App. LEXIS 244 (Ohio Ct. App., Summit County 2005).

There was no evidence that the employee's impaired vision was a reason for his termination. Desanzo v. Titanium Metals Corp., 351 F. Supp. 2d 769, 2005 U.S. Dist. LEXIS 653 (S.D. Ohio 2005).

Where a maintenance repair worker had permanent work restrictions due to his back injury, which impeded his ability to perform his job, such that he received an involuntary separation notice, his disability discrimination claim under R.C. 4112.02 failed, as he did not show that he was disabled under R.C. 4112.01(A)(13) and he did not show that he had requested an accommodation from his employer. Although he failed to exhaust his administrative remedies, such did not impede his ability to bring the discrimination action, based on the liberal construction given to the remedial law, pursuant to R.C. 4112.99, but the fact that he could not lift more than 50 pounds and could not twist, bend, or stoop was not sufficient to demonstrate a disability that allowed consideration of recovery to him. McClenaghan v. Ohio DOC, 2005-Ohio-1284, 2005 Ohio Misc. LEXIS 101 (Ohio Ct. Cl. 2005).

Employee who alleged that she was terminated because of walking limitations caused by a stress fracture in her toe failed to establish a prima facie case under the Americans with Disabilities Act, 42 U.S.C.S. § 12101 et seq., and R.C. 4112.02 because the employee did not use a cane or walker and was able to ride a bike without discomfort; thus, the walking limitations were not substantial enough to qualify as a disability under 42 U.S.C.S. § 12102(2). Martin v. Licking County Common Pleas Court Juvenile Div., 2005 U.S. Dist. LEXIS 9013 (S.D. Ohio Apr. 22, 2005).

The employee did not establish a prima facie case of disability discrimination: Grooms v. Supporting Council of Preventative Effort, 2004-Ohio-2034, 157 Ohio App. 3d 55, 809 N.E.2d 42, 2004 Ohio App. LEXIS 1774 (Ohio Ct. App., Montgomery County 2004).

As former employee's replacement suffered from multiple sclerosis which was a disability under the meaning of the Americans with Disabilities Act, the employee failed to make his prima facie case of discrimination based on disability. Bozsan v. Tradewinds Bev. Co., 2005 U.S. Dist. LEXIS 23032 (S.D. Ohio Sept. 21, 2005).

Employee could not satisfy the "regarded as" inquiry because he had not demonstrated that the employer held any mistaken belief where: (a) it sent him for fitness for duty examinations on at least two occasions as a result of his threats of severe violence in the workplace, (b) while the employee was returned to work, he was diagnosed with several mental conditions, (c) he began seeing his own psychologist in 1995, and (d) a doctor signed several requests for leave of absence on plaintiff's behalf for his chronic mental health condition and personality disorder. There was also no evidence that he was treated differently because the employer mistakenly regarded him as disabled. Palmer v. Ford Motor Co., 2004 U.S. Dist. LEXIS 28073 (N.D. Ohio Apr. 22, 2004), aff'd, 134 Fed. Appx. 887, 2005 U.S. App. LEXIS 10480 (6th Cir. Ohio 2005).

Employer was granted summary judgment on an employee's disability discrimination claims under 42 U.S.C.S. § 12102 and R.C. 4112.02(A) because he failed to adduce sufficient evidence to show that the employer regarded him as disabled. Simmons v. Wal-Mart Assocs. Inc., 2005 U.S. Dist. LEXIS 21772 (S.D. Ohio July 19, 2005).

Employer was entitled to summary judgment on an employee's claims of disability discrimination under R.C. 4112.02 because the employee failed to show that she was disabled or handicapped. While the employee complained of flare-ups of Polycystic Kidney Disease (PKD), there was no evidence that the PKD prevented her from performing her job or any particular class of jobs. Fink v. Ohio Health Corp., 2004 U.S. Dist. LEXIS 28567 (S.D. Ohio Aug. 25, 2004), aff'd, 139 Fed. Appx. 667, 2005 FED App. 0578N, 2005 U.S. App. LEXIS 13668 (6th Cir. Ohio 2005).

Employee could not satisfy the "regarded as" inquiry because he had not demonstrated that the employer held any mistaken belief where: (a) it sent him for fitness for duty examinations on at least two occasions as a result of his threats of severe violence in the workplace, (b) while the employee was returned to work, he was diagnosed with several mental conditions, (c) he began seeing his own psychologist in 1995, and (d) a doctor signed several requests for leave of absence on plaintiff's behalf for his chronic mental health condition and personality disorder. There was also no evidence that he was treated differently because the employer mistakenly regarded him as disabled. Palmer v. Ford Motor Co., 2004 U.S. Dist. LEXIS 28073 (N.D. Ohio Apr. 22, 2004), aff'd, 134 Fed. Appx. 887, 2005 U.S. App. LEXIS 10480 (6th Cir. Ohio 2005).

Trial court properly found that a doctor failed to substantiate a claim that the Ohio State Medical Board, in revoking the doctor's license to practice medicine and surgery, discriminated against the doctor in so revoking his license. The doctor claimed that his HIV Encephalopathy, a condition diagnosed after his license was revoked, caused him to delay filing his claim for discrimination, but failed to present any evidence to substantiate his reasons for the delay. Hosseinipour v. State Med. Bd., 2004-Ohio-1220, 2004 Ohio App. LEXIS 1065 (Ohio Ct. App., Franklin County 2004).

Lifting, kneeling, and sitting are major life activities. The test in establishing a disability is whether an impairment severely restricts the individual from doing activities that are of central importance to most people's daily lives. An employee's inability to perform her job duties for an indefinite, extended duration represents a nondiscriminatory reason for termination: House v. Kirtland Capital Ptnrs, 2004-Ohio-3688, 158 Ohio App. 3d 68, 814 N.E.2d 65, 2004 Ohio App. LEXIS 3330 (Ohio Ct. App., Lake County 2004).

Whether a condition such as sleep apnea constitutes a disability must be determined on a case-by-case basis. The ability to work overtime may be an essential function of certain jobs: Sanders v. FirstEnergy Corp., 2004-Ohio-3214, 157 Ohio App. 3d 826, 813 N.E.2d 932, 2004 Ohio App. LEXIS 2893 (Ohio Ct. App., Jefferson County 2004).

Summary judgment was properly granted in favor of employers as a former employee, who was an at-will employee, failed to provide any evidence that she was wrongfully discharged in violation of a public policy since she failed to show she was discharged based on her alleged disability. Tripp v. Beverly Enters.-Ohio, Inc., 2003-Ohio-6821, 2003 Ohio App. LEXIS 6158 (Ohio Ct. App., Summit County 2003).

Employee with loin pain hematuria syndrome was not substantially limited in the major life activity of walking, so he had not established the first prong of his prima facie case, i.e., that he was disabled for purposes of the Americans with Disabilities Act of 1990 (ADA), 42 U.S.C.S. § 12101 et seq. Neither one "episodic" manifestation nor an impairment of two and a half weeks could suffice to support a finding of disability under the ADA, and the employee simply had not presented sufficient evidence that the substantial impairment of his ability to walk was anything other than temporary. Brown v. BKW Drywall Supply, Inc., 305 F. Supp. 2d 814, 2004 U.S. Dist. LEXIS 2831 (S.D. Ohio 2004).

Trial court erred in granting summary judgment in favor of a former employer who was terminated by her employer after she was diagnosed with multiple sclerosis because, while the employee was not disabled, there was a genuine issue of material fact regarding whether the employer regarded the former employee as disabled and whether that disability was a factor in its employment decisions. Fitzmaurice v. Great Lakes Computer Corp., 2004-Ohio-235, 155 Ohio App. 3d 724, 803 N.E.2d 854, 2004 Ohio App. LEXIS 218 (Ohio Ct. App., Cuyahoga County 2004).

Trial court did not err in granting summary judgment pursuant to Civ.R. 56(C) to a former employer and supervisor in a former employee's claims for employment discrimination on the basis of a disability under the handicap discrimination statute, R.C. 4112.02, because the employee's sinusitis, which required that he be off from work for a week because he could not perform his job as a truck driver while taking narcotics, was not a "disability" within the meaning of R.C. 4112.01(A)(13). The employee's short-term upper respiratory infection and temporary work restrictions did not constitute a physical impairment which "substantially limited" a major life activity as required by R.C. 4112.01(A)(13), nor was he "disabled" for purposes of R.C. 4112.02(A) because his employer and supervisor allegedly perceived him as such. Jurczak v. J&R Schugel Trucking Co., 2003-Ohio-7039, 2003 Ohio App. LEXIS 6362 (Ohio Ct. App., Franklin County 2003).

Employer was granted summary judgment on employee's claims of disability discrimination in violation of R.C. 4112.02(A), as the employee failed to establish that narcolepsy caused him to be disabled under § 4112.02(A) or that the employer perceived him to be disabled; having a serious health condition as defined by the Family and Medical Leave Act, 29 U.S.C.S. § 2601 et seq. did not establish disability. Manns v. ArvinMeritor, Inc., 291 F. Supp. 2d 655, 2003 U.S. Dist. LEXIS 20776 (N.D. Ohio 2003).

Because an employee failed to raise a genuine issue of material fact regarding whether he was disabled, he could not raise a genuine issue of material fact as to whether the employer's actions would jeopardize Ohio's public policy against disability discrimination. Brock v. United Grinding Techs., Inc., 257 F. Supp. 2d 1089, 2003 U.S. Dist. LEXIS 12342 (S.D. Ohio 2003).

Whether a plaintiff is substantially limited in a major life activity is generally a question of fact not amenable to summary judgment: Ferguson v. Lear Corp., 2003-Ohio-7261, 155 Ohio App. 3d 677, 802 N.E.2d 1141, 2003 Ohio App. LEXIS 6551 (Ohio Ct. App., Erie County 2003).

An employer's duty to participate in an interactive process is triggered by a request for a reasonable accommodation by an employee with a disability: DeCesare v. Niles City Sch. Dist. Bd. of Educ., 2003-Ohio-5349, 154 Ohio App. 3d 644, 798 N.E.2d 655, 2003 Ohio App. LEXIS 4811 (Ohio Ct. App., Trumbull County 2003).

Trial court properly granted summary judgment to the county auditor and commissioners on the employee's claim that he was terminated based in part on his disabilities; he did not present a prima facie case of disability discrimination, and thus did not show that a material question of fact existed. Continenza v. Tablack, 2003-Ohio-6719, 2003 Ohio App. LEXIS 6026 (Ohio Ct. App., Mahoning County 2003).

Trial court erred in granting summary judgment to defendant in an employee's disability discrimination suit filed under R.C. 4112 et seq. where material fact issues remained as to whether the employee was mistakenly believed to be disabled, his ischemia was non-limiting, he suffered an adverse employment action as a result of his alleged impairment, and he could perform his job safely. Pierson v. Norfork S. Corp.,

2003-Ohio-6682, 2003 Ohio App. LEXIS 5931 (Ohio Ct. App., Ashtabula County 2003).

An employer's subjective perception that a 17-year disability absence provides grounds for treating an employee differently than an absence of fewer years is exactly the sort of stereotypical thinking which the ADA seeks to prohibit: Pollitt v. Roadway Express, Inc., 228 F. Supp. 2d 854, 2002 U.S. Dist. LEXIS 20005 (S.D. Ohio 2002).

The employer provided credible reasons that the discharge was due to job performance, rather than a perceived mental impairment: Detzel v. Wellman, 141 Ohio App. 3d 474, 751 N.E.2d 1067, 2001 Ohio App. LEXIS 448 (Ohio Ct. App., Ottawa County 2001).

An employer is not obligated to provide an accommodation that would eliminate an essential function of a job: Debolt v. Eastman Kodak Co., 2001-Ohio-3996, 146 Ohio App. 3d 474, 766 N.E.2d 1040, 2001 Ohio App. LEXIS 5276 (Ohio Ct. App., Franklin County 2001).

There was insufficient evidence that the employer perceived the employee as having a disability. The employee failed to show that he could safely and substantially perform the essential functions of the job: Miller v. Premier Indus. Corp., 136 Ohio App. 3d 662, 737 N.E.2d 594, 2000 Ohio App. LEXIS 1034 (Ohio Ct. App., Cuyahoga County 2000).

The employer was not required to place a handicapped employee on an indefinite leave of absence during which a position for which she might be qualified might become available: Scott v. University of Toledo, 137 Ohio App. 3d 538, 739 N.E.2d 351, 2000 Ohio App. LEXIS 851 (Ohio Ct. App., Franklin County 2000).

The employee failed to establish even a prima facie case of handicap discrimination: Markham v. Earle M. Jorgensen Co., 138 Ohio App. 3d 484, 741 N.E.2d 618, 2000 Ohio App. LEXIS 3752 (Ohio Ct. App., Cuyahoga County 2000).

Plaintiff's back injury did not rise to the level of a "handicap" as contemplated in R.C. 4112.02(A)(13), since at the time he was terminated, his injury did not have such permanent or long term impact as to render him substantially limited in performing routine labor duties: Rauhuff v. American Fan Co., 1999 Ohio App. LEXIS 2857 (Ohio Ct. App., Butler County June 21, 1999).

Plaintiff presented a prima facie case of handicap discrimination, precluding summary judgment for the defendants: McCafferty v. Cleveland Bd. of Educ., 133 Ohio App. 3d 692, 729 N.E.2d 797, 1999 Ohio App. LEXIS 2431 (Ohio Ct. App., Cuyahoga County 1999).

Employer's failure to enforce smoking ban did not constitute grounds for liability for handicap discrimination in employment conditions of employee suffering from asthma where employee failed to show that employer refused to enforce the ban because of the employee's disability: Holt v. Olmsted Twp. Bd. of Trustees, 43 F. Supp. 2d 812, 1998 U.S. Dist. LEXIS 22308 (N.D. Ohio 1998).



A mentally retarded applicant was qualified where she could perform the essential functions of the job and other employees were available to perform the other functions. Temporary job coaching by a social service agency may be a reasonable accommodation. A test must measure the applicant's ability to perform the essential functions of the particular job. Ohio law and the ADA do not require preferential hiring of handicapped persons: Miami Univ. v. Ohio Civ. Rights Comm'n, 133 Ohio App. 3d 28, 726 N.E.2d 1032, 1999 Ohio App. LEXIS 1478 (Ohio Ct. App., Butler County 1999).

That the employer regarded the prospective employee's physical limitations as unsuited for the specific job and subjectively believed that the specific duties associated with the job would potentially cause a recurrence of the employee's back injury was insufficient to support a finding that the employer regarded the employee as substantially limited in a major life activity: Kemo v. City of St. Clairsville, 128 Ohio App. 3d 178, 714 N.E.2d 412, 1998 Ohio App. LEXIS 2656 (Ohio Ct. App., Belmont County 1998).

The employer presented sufficient evidence that the layoff was due to a reduction in force and the employee's low ranking, rather than to the employee's handicap: Brock v. GE, 125 Ohio App. 3d 403, 708 N.E.2d 777, 1998 Ohio App. LEXIS 251 (Ohio Ct. App., Hamilton County), dismissed, 82 Ohio St. 3d 1411, 694 N.E.2d 75, 1998 Ohio LEXIS 1429 (Ohio 1998).

There was no evidence that the employee was terminated based on his handicap: Thatcher v. Goodwill Indus., 117 Ohio App. 3d 525, 690 N.E.2d 1320, 1997 Ohio App. LEXIS 6 (Ohio Ct. App., Summit County 1997).

The employer did not discriminate on the basis of the vision impairment. Placing the employee on paid leave until medical tests were concluded was reasonable. The employee voluntarily participated in the workplace jokes: Howard v. Ohio DOT, 91 Ohio Misc. 2d 48, 697 N.E.2d 281, 1997 Ohio Misc. LEXIS 320 (Ohio Ct. Cl. 1997).

A transitory back injury, with no residual effects, is not a handicap for purposes of R.C. 4112.02 or the ADA: Maloney v. Barberton Citizens Hosp., 109 Ohio App. 3d 372, 672 N.E.2d 223, 1996 Ohio App. LEXIS 480 (Ohio Ct. App., Summit County 1996).

In order to establish a prima facie case of handicap discrimination, the person seeking relief must demonstrate (1) that he or she was handicapped, (2) that an adverse employment action was taken by an employer, at least in part, because the individual was handicapped, and (3) that the person, though handicapped, can safely and substantially perform the essential functions of the job in question: Hood v. Diamond Prods., 1996-Ohio-259, 74 Ohio St. 3d 298, 658 N.E.2d 738, 1996 Ohio LEXIS 43 (Ohio 1996).

Employee did not establish prima facie case of handicap discrimination where she was suspended and ultimately discharged when she could not safely and substantially perform essential functions of any job at her employer's facility: Blankenship v. Martin Marietta Energy Sys., 83 F.3d 153, 1996 FED App. 0137P, 1996 U.S. App. LEXIS 10896 (6th Cir. Ohio 1996).

In order to establish a prima facie case of a "hostile work environment" based on a handicap pursuant to R.C. 4112.02, plaintiff must establish: (1) that he had a protected handicap; (2) that he was subjected to unwelcomed verbal or physical conduct; (3) that he was harassed by such unwelcomed verbal or physical conduct; (4) that the alleged harassment had the effect of unreasonably interfering with his work performance and created an intimidating, hostile, or offensive environment; and (5) that respondeat superior liability exists: Betosky v. Abbott Lab., 1996 Ohio App. LEXIS 4056 (Ohio Ct. App., Franklin County Sept. 19, 1996).

Handicap discrimination is not limited to wrongful discharge. Nonrenewal of a teacher's contract on a discriminatory basis is also prohibited: Csejpes v. Cleveland Catholic Diocese, 109 Ohio App. 3d 533, 672 N.E.2d 724, 1996 Ohio App. LEXIS 495 (Ohio Ct. App., Cuyahoga County 1996).

Summary judgment for defendants was error where there was evidence that a trade school discriminated on the basis of a student's speech impediment: Bryans v. English Nanny & Governess Sch., 117 Ohio App. 3d 303, 690 N.E.2d 582, 1996 Ohio App. LEXIS 5773 (Ohio Ct. App., Cuyahoga County 1996).

Summary judgment for the employer on a handicap discrimination claim is error where there are questions of fact as to reasonable accommodation and the existence of a legitimate business reason for termination: Degnan v. Goodwill Indus., 104 Ohio App. 3d 589, 662 N.E.2d 894, 1995 Ohio App. LEXIS 2655 (Ohio Ct. App., Lucas County 1995).

In order to succeed in a claim against an employer for handicap discrimination, a plaintiff must show that though handicapped, he could safely and substantially perform essential functions of the job in question, but was discharged, at least in part, because he was handicapped: Ali v. Chelsea Catering, 910 F. Supp. 338, 1995 U.S. Dist. LEXIS 20658 (N.D. Ohio 1995).

Ohio law does not require an employer to continue the employment of a disabled employee who is unable to perform his duties as a result of a work-related injury: Ali v. Chelsea Catering, 910 F. Supp. 338, 1995 U.S. Dist. LEXIS 20658 (N.D. Ohio 1995).

"Handicapped person" includes a person who is regarded as handicapped by the employer. Front pay is available for handicap discrimination where reinstatement is inappropriate. Punitive damages are available for a handicap discrimination claim under R.C. 4112.99: Potocnik v. Sifco Indus., 103 Ohio App. 3d 560, 660 N.E.2d 510, 1995 Ohio App. LEXIS 964 (Ohio Ct. App., Cuyahoga County 1995).

Ohio Administrative Code 4112-5-02(H) prohibits discrimination against not only those persons with functional disabilities, but also against those persons who are perceived by the employer as being handicapped: City of Cleveland v. Ohio Civil Rights Comm'n, 98 Ohio App. 3d 243, 648 N.E.2d 516, 1994 Ohio App. LEXIS 3908 (Ohio Ct. App., Cuyahoga County 1994).

A lumbrosacral sprain may constitute a "handicap" under R.C. 4112.01. The Americans with Disabilities Act does not create a right to a promotion as an accommodation or require the employer to make accommodations which the employee can make: Lillback v. Metropolitan Life Ins. Co., 94 Ohio App. 3d 100, 640 N.E.2d 250, 1994 Ohio App. LEXIS 1377 (Ohio Ct. App., Montgomery County 1994).

Summary judgment for the employer on the issue of handicap discrimination was improper where there was a question of fact as to whether the employee's seizures were a basis for termination. Summary judgment for the employer was error where there was a question of fact as to whether the employee's gender was a basis for termination: Cox v. Commercial Parts & Serv., 96 Ohio App. 3d 417, 645 N.E.2d 123, 1994 Ohio App. LEXIS 3531 (Ohio Ct. App., Franklin County 1994).

Reasonable accommodation of an employee's handicap may include reassignment to a vacant position for which the employee is qualified: Wooten v. City of Columbus, 91 Ohio App. 3d 326, 632 N.E.2d 605, 1993 Ohio App. LEXIS 5832 (Ohio Ct. App., Franklin County 1993).

An aggrieved party may, pursuant to R.C. 4112.99, institute an independent civil action to seek redress for discrimination on the basis of physical disability: Elek v. Huntington Nat'l Bank, 60 Ohio St. 3d 135, 573 N.E.2d 1056, 1991 Ohio LEXIS 1335 (Ohio 1991).

The public policy of Ohio proscribing discrimination against persons with physical handicaps does not extend so far as to require an employer to continue the employment of a disabled employee who is unable to perform his job duties as a result of a work-related injury (R.C. 4112.02[A] and [L], applied.): Barker v. Dayton Walther Corp., 56 Ohio App. 3d 1, 564 N.E.2d 738, 1989 Ohio App. LEXIS 1541 (Ohio Ct. App., Montgomery County 1989).

Even though handicapped, an employee has the responsibility of performing his job safely and satisfactorily, while complying with all reasonable work rules. Should the handicapped employee fail to fulfill all job requirements, the employer is within its rights to subject the handicapped employee to the full range of disciplinary proceedings up to and including discharge: Greater Cleveland Regional Transit Auth. v. Ohio Civil Rights Comm., 58 Ohio App. 3d 20, 567 N.E.2d 1325 (1989).

Where an employee, who is handicapped within the meaning of R.C. 4112.01(A)(13), is discharged from his employment for just cause and not on the basis of his or her handicap, the employer does not need to make any showing that it was unable to reasonably accommodate the handicap of its employee: Salazar v. Ohio Civil Rights Comm'n, 39 Ohio App. 3d 26, 528 N.E.2d 1303, 1987 Ohio App. LEXIS 10673 (Ohio Ct. App., Lucas County 1987).

**—Burden of proof**

Court of Claims did not err by granting summary judgment for the employer because the employee did not establish discrimination based on her disability. The employee failed to present direct evidence of disability discrimination because, in the absence of knowledge on the part of interim acting general counsel of the employee's disabilities, her comment that the employee was acting paranoid and crazy did not constitute direct evidence of disability discrimination. Ray v. Ohio Dep't of Health, 2018-Ohio-2163, 114 N.E.3d 297, 2018 Ohio App. LEXIS 2353 (Ohio Ct. App., Franklin County 2018).

Court of Claims did not err by granting summary judgment for the employer because, when the burden of production shifted to the employer to demonstrate a legitimate, non-discriminatory reason for the adverse employment action (termination), the employer produced evidence of multiple coworkers' complaints regarding the employee's aggressive and unprofessional behavior. Ray v. Ohio Dep't of Health, 2018-Ohio-2163, 114 N.E.3d 297, 2018 Ohio App. LEXIS 2353 (Ohio Ct. App., Franklin County 2018).

Court of Claims did not err by granting summary judgment for the employer because the employee did not demonstrate that the incidents cited as the basis for her termination were pretextual reasons. The employer presented evidence that it terminated her employment due to her unprofessional conduct, embarrassing conduct, and inability to work with colleagues/program staff. Ray v. Ohio Dep't of Health, 2018-Ohio-2163, 114 N.E.3d 297, 2018 Ohio App. LEXIS 2353 (Ohio Ct. App., Franklin County 2018).

Summary judgment was improperly granted to the former employer on the former employee's disability discrimination claims as the employee presented medical evidence that created a genuine issue of material fact as to whether she was disabled because it was inconsequential that she never received a definitive diagnosis as the record established that, at the time of her leave from the employer, the employee was experiencing severe pain in her hands and wrists; the employee testified that the pain left her depressed, unable to care for her child, unable to sleep and, often times, bedridden; and there was medical testimony that depression could cause physical symptoms and pain. Anderson v. Ohio Bell Tel. Co., 2017-Ohio-7318, 2017 Ohio App. LEXIS 3617 (Ohio Ct. App., Cuyahoga County 2017).

Trial court did not err by granting summary judgment on the racial discrimination claim because the employee failed to show that there was a genuine issue of material fact as to whether or not he was discriminated against on the basis of face and that the employer had articulated a non-discriminatory reason for not promoting him. None of the witnesses stated exactly how the employee was treated unfairly or that any unfair treatment was due to his race and they did not identify the job openings or related duties or explain how he was qualified for the same, but rather made generic allegations. Edwards v. Perry Twp. Bd. of Trs., 2016 Ohio App. LEXIS 3000 (Ohio Ct. App., Stark County July 25, 2016).

Employee failed to provide evidence of racial discrimination because, inter alia, the employee did not show that white employees were not disciplined for violations or were permitted to violate rules and company policy without sanction, and the employee was also unable to point to any evidence that his supervisor treated him differently than white employees in regard to discipline or judging work performance. English v. AK Steel Corp., 2016-Ohio-5287, 2016 Ohio App. LEXIS 3136 (Ohio Ct. App., Butler County 2016).

Summary judgment was improperly granted on employee's race discrimination claim under Title VII and Ohio law because the employee made out prima facie case for 2009 and 2010 and could establish inference of discrimination, and she presented genuine dispute of material fact about whether employer took materially adverse actions against her because of her protected activity in filing employment discrimination charge. Henry v. Abbott Labs., 651 Fed. Appx. 494, 2016 FED App. 0318N, 2016 U.S. App. LEXIS 10604 (6th Cir. Ohio 2016).

Employee failed to demonstrate pretext on his claim of disability discrimination sufficient to survive summary judgment; the employee could not show that the reason given for his termination from employment, his dishonesty, was false, or that it was not the actual motivation for termination or that it was insufficient to warrant termination. Mattessich v. Weathersfield Twp., 2016-Ohio-458, 59 N.E.3d 629, 2016 Ohio App. LEXIS 392 (Ohio Ct. App., Trumbull County 2016).

Employee could establish a prima facie case of discrimination "because of" disability where (1) the employee suffered from back pain that was acute enough for her to miss work; (2) the temporal proximity between the employee's accommodation requests, the employer's alleged failure to comply with the requests, and her termination gave rise to an inference of causation; and (3) the employee's lengthy tenure with the employer showed she could safely and substantially perform the essential functions of the job in question. Jones v. Honda of Am. Mfg., 2015 U.S. Dist. LEXIS 28682 (S.D. Ohio Mar. 9, 2015).

Employee demonstrated sufficient pretext to avoid summary judgment on her claim based on discrimination "because of" disability where a jury, and not the court, should weigh the persuasiveness of the employer's reason for firing the employee against the inferences that arose from the Associate Relations representative's statements. Jones v. Honda of Am. Mfg., 2015 U.S. Dist. LEXIS 28682 (S.D. Ohio Mar. 9, 2015).

**—Not shown**

Employer was entitled to summary judgment as a matter of law on plaintiff's claims of disability discrimination under R.C. 4112.02 because it articulated a legitimate, non-discriminatory reason for plaintiff's termination, specifically, plaintiff's behavior during a verbal altercation with another employee in the employer's lobby. Rivard v. Ohio State Univ., 2021-Ohio-4284, 2021 Ohio Misc. LEXIS 866 (Ohio Ct. Cl. 2021).

In a complaint against employer alleging that employee had been discriminated against due to his disability, the district court did not err in granting summary judgment in favor of the employer because employee failed to set forth a prima facie case of disability discrimination since employee was not able to adequately perform the essential functions of his employment with employee. Coco v. Beyesly's Rest., 2021-Ohio-4201, 2021 Ohio App. LEXIS 4101 (Ohio Ct. App., Stark County 2021).

Employee failed to satisfy the third element of his prima facie claim for disability discrimination, and thus the trial court did not err in awarding summary judgment on this claim to the employer because the employee provided no evidence that he could safely and substantially perform the essential functions of the job in question. Musil v. Gerken Materials, Inc., 2020-Ohio-3548, 2020 Ohio App. LEXIS 2497 (Ohio Ct. App., Lucas County 2020).

Employee failed to state a prima facie claim for disability discrimination because she did not establish that she suffered an adverse employment action since there was no evidence her employment terms, conditions, or privileges were altered; the employee did not suffer a reduction in pay, a demotion, or lose any material benefits as a result of the actions taken by the employer because her rate of pay increased. Toland v. Dep't of Mental Health & Addiction Servs., 2020-Ohio-3864, 2020 Ohio Misc. LEXIS 116 (Ohio Ct. Cl. 2020).

Trial court properly awarded summary judgment to an employer in an employee's disability discrimination case because the employee did not present any evidence, either direct or circumstantial, showing that the employer's decision to not retain him as a permanent employee was related to either a disability or a perceived disability, and there was no evidence that the employer had even the slightest inclination that the employee had cancer during the course of his employment. Davis v. Cinnamon Lake Ass'n, 2020-Ohio-5374, 2020 Ohio App. LEXIS 4219 (Ohio Ct. App., Wayne County 2020).

Employee's disability discrimination suit failed because he was not able to perform the essential functions of his job at the time of an initial medical evaluation and he did not show that the employer's reliance on two medical opinions to this effect was a pretext for unlawful disability discrimination. Stanley v. Bp Prods. N. Am., 753 Fed. Appx. 378, 2018 FED App. 0610N, 2018 U.S. App. LEXIS 34073 (6th Cir. Ohio 2018).

School principal's disability discrimination claim was properly dismissed because he failed to offer proper summary-judgment quality evidence in support of his assertion that similarly-situated non-class members were treated more favorably. Spitulski v. Bd. of Educ. of the Toledo City Sch. Dist., 2018-Ohio-3984, 121 N.E.3d 41, 2018 Ohio App. LEXIS 4311 (Ohio Ct. App., Lucas County 2018).

Employer was entitled to summary judgment on employee's claim of disability discrimination because employee was on a last chance agreement when he committed performance track infractions of sleeping on duty and leaving the work area/post/facility without the permission of a supervisor. Geter v. Ohio Dep't of Rehab. & Corr., 2018-Ohio-4148, 2018 Ohio Misc. LEXIS 1951 (Ohio Ct. Cl. 2018).

Summary judgment was properly granted for the board of education and others on the disability discrimination claim because the teacher was not qualified for the position, having missed the license renewal deadline. The teacher did not request an accommodation to perform her teaching duties, despite her injuries, instead she argued that she was discriminated against because she was not given an accommodation so she could qualify for the job. Janiszewski v. Belmont Career Ctr., 2017-Ohio-855, 86 N.E.3d 613, 2017 Ohio App. LEXIS 830 (Ohio Ct. App., Belmont County 2017).

In an employment termination case, the trial court properly granted summary judgment in favor of appellees because, for purposes of appellant's disability discrimination claim, she was not medically released by her physician until long after her Family Medical Leave Act leave had been exhausted; and, until that time, she was unable to perform an essential function of her former position; and because, for purposes of her failure to accommodate claim, appellant failed to show that despite her disability she could perform the essential function of her former position with reasonable accommodations as she was not released to perform any work until after her July 2013 termination; and she did not talk to anyone about a reasonable accommodation. Stewart v. Bear Mgmt., 2017-Ohio-7895, 98 N.E.3d 900, 2017 Ohio App. LEXIS 4234 (Ohio Ct. App., Stark County 2017).

Under R.C. 4112.02(A), an employee's termination from her job as assistant legal counsel was not based upon her mental disability, which consisted of ADHD and depression, but was based on multiple complaints from co-workers and a vendor regarding her aggressive and unprofessional behavior and the stress that it caused in the workplace. Ray v. Ohio Dep't of Health, 2017-Ohio-6960, 2017 Ohio Misc. LEXIS 2697 (Ohio Ct. Cl. 2017).

Summary judgment for the employer was appropriate on the disability discrimination claim because the former employee pointed to no evidence, other than her own self-serving assertions, to show that the reasons proffered by the employer had no basis in fact, did not actually motivate her termination, or were insufficient to warrant her termination. Roberson v. Ohio Dep't of Developmental Disabilities, 2017-Ohio-7541, 2017 Ohio Misc. LEXIS 3284 (Ohio Ct. Cl. 2017).

Assuming without deciding that the employee established a prima facie retaliation case, she presented no evidence that her position was abolished, or that she was not rehired, in retaliation for complaints of sex discrimination. Dewalt v. Harrison Cnty. Comm'rs, 654 Fed. Appx. 770, 2016 FED App. 0362N, 2016 U.S. App. LEXIS 12189 (6th Cir. Ohio 2016).

Defendants, an employer, its officer, and a supervisor, were properly granted summary judgment on plaintiff's retaliation claim, which was based on her protected activity of complaining to the officer about her supervisor's allegedly discriminatory comments, because it was the officer who terminated her and she conceded that he was not retaliating against her. Weber v. Ferrellgas, Inc., 2016-Ohio-4738, 68 N.E.3d 207, 2016 Ohio App. LEXIS 2728 (Ohio Ct. App., Trumbull County 2016).

Summary judgment was properly granted for the employer on the retaliation claim because the record establishes that he was involved in a number of preventable accidents with the result that work equipment was damaged and, thus, by the time he was subject to the last chance agreement, the rule violation and final accident were sufficient reason to terminate his employment. The employee presented no facts to demonstrate pretext. Hartman v. Ohio DOT, 2016-Ohio-5208, 68 N.E.3d 1266, 2016 Ohio App. LEXIS 3079 (Ohio Ct. App., Franklin County 2016).

Trial court did not err by granting summary judgment for the employer on the disability discrimination claim because the employee could not show that the employer's reason for terminating his employment was a pretext. His job was terminated for the express reason that he was involved in a preventable traffic accident while on a last chance agreement and partial hearing loss in one ear did not result in the employee repeatedly backing into silent, visible stationary objects or in deciding to violate a rule against crossing the highway on a mower without a supporting vehicle. Hartman v. Ohio DOT, 2016-Ohio-5208, 68 N.E.3d 1266, 2016 Ohio App. LEXIS 3079 (Ohio Ct. App., Franklin County 2016).

Firefighter failed to show a prima facie case of "regarded as disabled" disability discrimination in order to avoid summary judgment for the city and fire chief, as he had been diagnosed with Parkinson's Disease and there was evidence that his condition had deteriorated to the point that he could no longer safely perform his duties, based on monitoring his functioning and physical examinations. Crutchfield, Inc. v. Testa, 2015-Ohio-1871, 142 Ohio St. 3d 1460, 30 N.E.3d 970, 2015 Ohio LEXIS 1205 (Ohio 2015).

Village and city manager were entitled to judgment on the pleadings on the former police chief's disability-discrimination claim because the effect of Ohio Civ. Serv. R. 14.01 was to convert his termination into a resignation and to protect his retirement benefits. Thus, he could not claim that the village wrongfully terminated him' actually or constructively when he elected to resign, even though he had the opportunity to contest his firing. Daudistel v. Vill. of Silverton, 2014-Ohio-5731, 2014 Ohio App. LEXIS 5550 (Ohio Ct. App., Hamilton County 2014).

Trial court did not err by granting summary judgment in favor of the employer, a bank, on the former employee's claims alleging discrimination based on age, national origin, and perceived disability because the bank presented evidence that she received progressive discipline and multiple warnings and directives to cease her deficient and nonconforming activities. The employee did not present any evidence that the bank's concerns for complying with law and meeting customer service satisfaction did not motivate her discharge or was insufficient to support her discharge. Jaber v. FirstMerit Corp., 2017-Ohio-277, 81 N.E.3d 879, 2017 Ohio App. LEXIS 276 (Ohio Ct. App., Summit County 2017).

Trial court did not err by granting summary judgment in favor of the district manager, branch manager, and assistant branch manager on claims of discrimination based on age, national origin, and perceived disability because there was no genuine issue of material fact as to the individual managers' liability. The former employee failed to present evidence to rebut the evidence of legitimate, nondiscriminatory reasons and failed to create a genuine issue of material fact with regard to pretext. Jaber v. FirstMerit Corp., 2017-Ohio-277, 81 N.E.3d 879, 2017 Ohio App. LEXIS 276 (Ohio Ct. App., Summit County 2017).

Plaintiff failed to establish a prima facie case of disability discrimination by his former employer based on his alleged alcoholism, because 1)there was no expert testimony that he was an alcoholic; 2) there was no evidence that his alcohol use substantially limited a major life activity; and 3) even if his alcoholism were a disability, he was terminated pursuant to the terms of the collective bargaining agreement for failure to maintain a commercial drivers license. Hilbert v. Ohio DOT, 2016-Ohio-1256, 2016 Ohio Misc. LEXIS 42 (Ohio Ct. Cl. 2016), rev'd, 2017-Ohio-488, 84 N.E.3d 301, 2017 Ohio App. LEXIS 475 (Ohio Ct. App., Franklin County 2017).

Because doctor's mental illness rendered her unable to practice medicine and surgery according to acceptable and prevailing standards of care, State Medical Board of Ohio's order taking action against her license did not violate Americans With Disabilities Act or Ohio's discrimination statute, since doctor was not qualified individual with disability, and Board did not unlawfully discriminate against her on basis of disability. Flynn v. State Med. Bd. of Ohio, 2016-Ohio-5903, 62 N.E.3d 212, 2016 Ohio App. LEXIS 3754 (Ohio Ct. App., Franklin County 2016).

**—Perceived disability**

Trial court applied the wrong legal standard, evaluating the employee's perceived disability discrimination claim as a disability discrimination claim. Since the employee raised a perceived disability discrimination claim, she did not have to point to evidence that she actually had a qualifying disability in order to defeat summary judgment on the issue. Nance v. Lima Auto Mall, Inc., 2020-Ohio-3419, 2020 Ohio App. LEXIS 2352 (Ohio Ct. App., Allen County 2020).

**Disability discrimination; —Not shown.**

In a case filed raising claims of Workers' Compensation Discrimination and Violation of the Ohio Civil Rights Act, the trial court did not err in granting summary judgment to defendants as to plaintiffs' claim for disability discrimination because plaintiffs failed to raise a genuine issue of material fact as to whether defendant terminated plaintiff at least in part, because of her disability and/or whether defendant regarded her as having a physical impairment. Jones v. Natural Essentials, Inc., 2022-Ohio-1010, 2022 Ohio App. LEXIS 906 (Ohio Ct. App., Portage County 2022).

**Disabled**

Summary judgment was properly granted for the employer on the disability discrimination claim because the employee did not establish that she fit the definition of disabled, since the five-hour-per-day restriction did not rise to the level of a significant restriction on her work life. In fact, although she was restricted to five hours per day, the physician's note made no restriction as to the number of days worked per week. Barber v. Chestnut Land Co., 2016-Ohio-2926, 63 N.E.3d 609, 2016 Ohio App. LEXIS 1788 (Ohio Ct. App., Mahoning County 2016).

Nurse was not disabled within the meaning of 42 U.S.C.S. § 12102(1) and R.C. 4112.02(A) because the nurse's claim that she was unable to perform major life activities was unsustainable in light of her admissions that she could fix her hair, dress herself, do laundry, go grocery shopping, rake leaves, cut the grass, and perform other various activities, and the fact that the nurse had to be careful with her arm did not rise to the level of a cognizable disability. Overfield v. H.B. Magruder Mem. Hosp., Inc., 2012 U.S. Dist. LEXIS 8814 (N.D. Ohio Jan. 25, 2012).

Whether recurring ulcers and infection in the bones rose to the level of a disability was a question best suited for a jury as was deciding if the injury was long-term or permanent, considering the claim that the doctor did not regain his full abilities after his injury. Although the use of the wheelchair was not permanent while the doctor was still employed, the use of the chair or any aiding device was not necessary to prove a physical impairment; therefore, the claim of having a disability under 42 U.S.C.S § 12112 and R.C. 4112.02 survived summary judgment. Bligh-Glover v. Rizzo, 2012 U.S. Dist. LEXIS 141512 (N.D. Ohio Sept. 30, 2012).

For purposes of an employee's claims under 42 U.S.C.S. § 12112(a) of the Americans with Disabilities Act and R.C. 4112.02 of the Ohio Civil Rights Act, the employee's claim that he suffered from diabetes mellitus type 1 did not establish that he was "disabled" under 42 U.S.C.S. § 12102(1); a medical diagnosis, without more, was insufficient to establish a disability for purposes of the statutory provisions. Steele v. Oasis Turf & Tree, Inc., 2012 U.S. Dist. LEXIS 103722 (S.D. Ohio July 25, 2012).

Employer was granted summary judgment in a former employee's disability discrimination suit under R.C. 4112.02(A) because he failed to show that he had a statutorily recognized disability since when he returned from leave, he had no disability and was authorized to return to work without restrictions. Blosser v. AK Steel Corp., 2012 U.S. Dist. LEXIS 106777 (S.D. Ohio July 31, 2012), aff'd, 520 Fed. Appx. 359, 2013 FED App. 0324N, 2013 U.S. App. LEXIS 6845 (6th Cir. Ohio 2013).

In a customer's suit under the Americans with Disabilities Act, 42 U.S.C.S § 12182(a) and R.C. 4112.02(G), alleging discrimination after she was ordered out of a gas station/convenience store with her service dog and assaulted by an employee, a federal district court denied the motion for summary judgment filed by the gas station/convenience store, its owners, operators, and lessees (defendants), because genuine issues of material fact existed as to whether actual or apparent agency existed between defendants since reasonable jurors could differ as to whether the franchise agreement caused the owners to retain control over important aspects of the operation of sublicensees. Cooley v. Valero Energy Corp., 2012 U.S. Dist. LEXIS 40291 (S.D. Ohio Mar. 20, 2012).

Trial court erred by granting summary judgment on the teacher's disability discrimination claim because a genuine issue of material fact existed as to whether the teacher was disabled; the physician chosen by the district to examine the teacher, twice concluded that her case was "fairly complex and unusual," that she suffered from a "disability" under the Americans with Disabilities Act, and that her disability posed a direct threat of harm to her. Evidence also existed from two other doctors that the teacher was permanently disabled and that the district was well aware of the teacher's circumstance. Johnson v. Cleveland City Sch. Dist., 2011-Ohio-2778, 2011 Ohio App. LEXIS 2384 (Ohio Ct. App., Cuyahoga County 2011).

Employee's disability discrimination suit was properly dismissed on summary judgment as the employee had not met her burden of demonstrating that the employer regarded her as disabled. The employer's concerns were not about the employee's ability to work in general but about her ability to perform the specific job duties of a custodian due to the employee's inability to lift to the degree required by the position and the potential that she might re-injure herself in the course of doing the custodian job. McClain v. City of Shaker Heights, 2011-Ohio-4418, 2011 Ohio App. LEXIS 3660 (Ohio Ct. App., Cuyahoga County 2011).

Discrimination action by a former employee, who suffered from multiple sclerosis, against a state agency, for violation of R.C. 4112.02, failed because, even if the employee had a disability under R.C. 4112.01(A)(13) and 4112.01(A)(16)(a)(iii), the employee could not show that the employee's employment was terminated at least, in part, for the employee being disabled. The employee, who had a prior disciplinary offense, was terminated because of the property damage which the employee caused to an agency van in an auto accident. Winkfield v. Ohio Dep't of Developmental Disabilities, 2011-Ohio-4854, 2011 Ohio Misc. LEXIS 425 (Ohio Ct. Cl. 2011).

Trial court erred by granting summary judgment on the teacher's disability discrimination claim because a genuine issue of material fact existed as to whether the teacher was disabled; the physician chosen by the district to examine the teacher, twice concluded that her case was "fairly complex and unusual," that she suffered from a "disability" under the Americans with Disabilities Act, and that her disability posed a direct threat of harm to her. Evidence also existed from two other doctors that the teacher was permanently disabled and that the district was well aware of the teacher's circumstance. Johnson v. Cleveland City Sch. Dist., 2011-Ohio-2778, 2011 Ohio App. LEXIS 2384 (Ohio Ct. App., Cuyahoga County 2011).

**—Not shown**

Former employee failed to establish a prima facie case of disability discrimination under state law because his affidavit did not show that his fibromyalgia substantially limited his ability to complete a major life activity. Blank v. Nationwide Corp., 2021 FED App. 381N, 2021 U.S. App. LEXIS 23463 (6th Cir. Ohio Aug. 6, 2021).

Where an employee suffered from sleeping problems and was terminated, the employee's discriminatory discharge claims failed because the employee did not qualify as "disabled" since the employee was unable to establish that the employee suffered from a "physical or mental impairment" that caused the employee's sleeping problems, the employee was not diagnosed with sleep apnea, and the employee failed to show that the employee's sleep problems substantially limited a major life activity. Neely v. Benchmark Family Servs., 640 Fed. Appx. 429, 2016 FED App. 0048N, 2016 U.S. App. LEXIS 1391 (6th Cir. Ohio 2016).

Appellant did not show that appellee's reasons for reassigning and terminating her were pretextual to support her disability discrimination claim as: (1) fact issues remained as to the reasons appellant was relieved of administering exams; (2) the supervisor testified that he had appellant begin reporting directly to him based on her conflict with a co-worker; (3) the new duties appellant performed for the supervisor and a new manager were due to her having a new supervisor; (4) appellant was reassigned to a manager because her supervisor became executive director and no one filled his position; and (5) appellant was terminated because the supervisor believed her job duties were not essential. Ressler v. AG, 2015-Ohio-777, 2015 Ohio App. LEXIS 722 (Ohio Ct. App., Franklin County 2015).

No reasonable jury would have found a viable disability discrimination claim because (1) the former employee had not shown that her common variable immunodeficiency (CVID) had any relationship to her termination; (2) the employee had not shown she was replaced by anyone who was not disabled, and even if she had been, she had not shown the workforce reduction to be pretext; and (3) the record showed that the city made efforts to accommodate the employee's CVID. Sutherland v. City of Cincinnati, 2014 U.S. Dist. LEXIS 59237 (S.D. Ohio Apr. 29, 2014).

Where an applicant born without a left hand alleged that a school prevented the applicant from becoming employed as a bus driver for the school, the disability discrimination claims failed because the applicant did not suffer an adverse employment action since the applicant's abandonment of the commercial driver's license test could not be attributed to the school since it was the applicant's decision not to reschedule the test; the applicant's delay in obtaining a waiver and beginning training could not be causally linked to the school. Rosebrough v. Buckeye Valley High Sch., 582 Fed. Appx. 647, 2014 FED App. 0769N, 2014 U.S. App. LEXIS 19375 (6th Cir. Ohio 2014), cert. denied, 577 U.S. 816, 136 S. Ct. 38, 193 L. Ed. 2d 26, 2015 U.S. LEXIS 5127 (U.S. 2015).

Trial court properly granted summary judgment for the city on the paramedic's disability discrimination claim under R.C. 4112.02(A) because there were clear, meaningful distinctions between the paramedic and the two firefighters he identified as having received more favorable treatment; thus, they were not similarly situated. The paramedic was a supervisor and lieutenant when he was charged with multiple felonies, whereas the other employees were in nonsupervisory roles as firefighters, and he was still in his 90-day probationary period as a lieutenant. Chiancone v. City of Akron, 2014-Ohio-1500, 2014 Ohio App. LEXIS 1447 (Ohio Ct. App., Summit County 2014).

Grant of summary judgment to the employer on the employee's claims for disability and age discrimination was proper because there was no material dispute of fact that he was not qualified for his position since even he acknowledged that he could no longer perform it with or without accommodation. Drogell v. Westfield Group, 2013-Ohio-5262, 2013 Ohio App. LEXIS 5470 (Ohio Ct. App., Medina County 2013).

Employer was entitled to judgment on an employee's claim of disability discrimination because the employee could not establish one of the elements necessary for a prima facie showing of disability discrimination; the employee's inability to maintain regular, consistent attendance meant that he could not substantially perform an essential function of the job under the Americans with Disabilities Act. Evert v. Ohio State Univ., 2013-Ohio-5942, 2013 Ohio Misc. LEXIS 101 (Ohio Ct. Cl. 2013).

Community college was entitled to judgment on the disability discrimination claim because the former dean's heart attack, standing alone, did not constitute a disability since the dean did not provide evidence of how his heart attack substantially limited any major life activities compared with people in the general population. Randolph v. Terra State Cmty. College, 2013-Ohio-5929, 2013 Ohio Misc. LEXIS 93 (Ohio Ct. Cl. 2013).

Medical center's motion for summary judgment was granted in a nurse's suit against it for disability discrimination because the nurse failed to show that her knee impairment was anything more than a temporary impairment at or near the time of her termination. Fischbach v. Cmty. Mercy Health Partners, 2012 U.S. Dist. LEXIS 139019 (S.D. Ohio Sept. 27, 2012).

Former government employee's claims of disability discrimination failed because, although the employee alleged that the employee was overworked in the employee's position due to the employee's disability of anxiety and stress, the employee also testified that the employee's treating psychologist had released the employee to work in the position with no restrictions. Furthermore, with regard to the employee's walking impairment, the government employer responded to the employee's request to secure a nearby parking location by providing the employee with possible parking alternatives. Peaks v. Supreme Court of Ohio, 2012-Ohio-6321, 2012 Ohio Misc. LEXIS 201 (Ohio Ct. Cl. 2012).

Employer's motion for summary judgment was granted as to a former employee's claim for disability discrimination, in violation of R.C. 4112.02(A), because the complaint failed to set forth any evidence of a physical or mental impairment that substantially limited a major life activity or any record of such impairment to establish that he was disabled but merely stated that he was disabled. Wind v. Walgreen Co., 2011 U.S. Dist. LEXIS 154972 (S.D. Ohio June 22, 2011).

Employee's termination was not discrimination under R.C. 4112.02; the employee returned from knee surgery to a modified job program meant to return her to her prior nursing job, but when the employee's work restrictions became permanent, the purpose of the program was thwarted, the position the employee wanted in medical records was not available due to a partial hiring freeze, and the employee did not apply for other positions she was notified of. Feldkamp v. Viau, 2007-Ohio-6474, 2007 Ohio App. LEXIS 5660 (Ohio Ct. App., Richland County 2007).

**—Reasonable accommodation**

Court of Claims did not err by granting summary judgment for the employer because, assuming the employee's request constituted a reasonable accommodation (to be taken off the contracts to relieve her stress) as defined in the Americans with Disabilities Act (ADA), the interim director had already made the decision to terminate the employee before her request for an accommodation was made. The employer, therefore, was not required to consider the request for an accommodation. Ray v. Ohio Dep't of Health, 2018-Ohio-2163, 114 N.E.3d 297, 2018 Ohio App. LEXIS 2353 (Ohio Ct. App., Franklin County 2018).

There was a genuine issue of material fact as to whether the employer accommodated the employee's disability because although the employer asserted that the employee could have used her non-restricted foot to operate the pedal, the court believed that the employee's testimony to the contrary demonstrated a genuine issue of material fact regarding the employer's accommodation. Jones v. Honda of Am. Mfg., 2015 U.S. Dist. LEXIS 28682 (S.D. Ohio Mar. 9, 2015).

Defendant was not entitled to summary judgment on the plaintiff's claim that she was subjected to an adverse employment action when the defendant denied her a reasonable accommodation of a short period of leave for her chronic hypertension, in violation of the Americans with

Disabilities Act (ADA), 42 U.S.C.S. § 12112(b)(5)(A) and R.C. 4112.02 because it was clear that the defendant knew the plaintiff was suffering from a disability, and the defendant knew the plaintiff was precluded from working due to that disability until August 27, 2010. Accordingly, the plaintiff was subjected to an adverse employment action, suspension or termination, when the defendant denied her a reasonable accommodation for her preeclampsia in violation of the ADA. Alexander v. Trilogy Health Servs., LLC, 2012 U.S. Dist. LEXIS 152079 (S.D. Ohio Oct. 23, 2012).

Plaintiff's claim of disability discrimination under R.C. 4112.02 was subject to dismissal because the plaintiff had not alleged that she was denied an accommodation for her own disability. Moreover, there was no associational disability cause of action under Ohio law. Nelson v. Clermont County Veterans' Serv. Comm'n, 2012 U.S. Dist. LEXIS 78736 (S.D. Ohio June 6, 2012).

Notwithstanding the employee's failure to request an accommodation from the employer, the employee contended she subsequently requested a reasonable accommodation when she asked her manager to transfer her to an open position at the employer's wholly owned subsidiary. However, the employee conceded that the employer could not have forced its wholly owned subsidiary to hire the employee and that the employer and its wholly owned subsidiary were legally separate entities; therefore, the employer was under no legal obligation to place the employee at the separate subsidiary, and the employee had not met her burden in establishing a failure to accommodate under R.C. 4112.02. Bare v. Fed. Express Corp., 886 F. Supp. 2d 600, 2012 U.S. Dist. LEXIS 116095 (N.D. Ohio 2012).

Employer was entitled to summary judgment on the employee's failure to accommodate claims under R.C. 4112.02 and 42 U.S.C.S. § 12112 because to the extent there was a breakdown in the interactive process, it was not caused by the employer failing to act in good faith since the employer repeatedly communicated with the employee regarding his restrictions, and it developed accommodations that were reasonably consistent with the medical evidence that the employee had submitted, including his treating physician's assessment of his limitations. There was no evidence, however, that the employee attempted to limit his breaks to the five provided, by proactively emptying his bladder, or at least attempting to empty his bladder, at every provided break; in other words, the employee did not give the facially reasonable accommodation proposal a chance, which was fatal to his failure to accommodate claim. Linebarger v. Honda of America Mfg., 870 F. Supp. 2d 513, 2012 U.S. Dist. LEXIS 64229 (S.D. Ohio 2012).



Former employee, who suffered depression after the disappearance of the employee's child, did not show that a former employer, a medical center, discriminated against the employee, in violation of R.C. 4112.02, by terminating the employee instead of accommodating the employee's disability because the employer acted in good faith when making the modest request that the employee, who was a nurse, telephone a charge nurse and submit an application for leave as a condition for using the employee's leave under the Family and Medical Leave Act of 1993, 29 U.S.C.S. § 2601 et seq. However, the employee failed to comply with this request. Mowery v. Ohio State Univ. Med. Ctr., 2012-Ohio-1246, 2012 Ohio Misc. LEXIS 31 (Ohio Ct. Cl. 2012).

Defendant was granted summary judgment on the failure to accommodate claim because plaintiff failed to request an accommodation; plaintiff had been approved for intermittent Family and Medical Leave Act of 1993 (FMLA) leave, which she had been taking for several years, but the record did not indicate that plaintiff requested further accommodation beyond the intermittent FMLA leave she had already been utilizing. Marks v. Ohio Bell Tel. Co., 2011 U.S. Dist. LEXIS 84508 (N.D. Ohio Aug. 2, 2011), aff'd, 2012 U.S. App. LEXIS 26891 (6th Cir. Ohio July 19, 2012).

Trial court erred in granting the district's summary judgment motion on the failure to accommodate claim because a genuine issue of material fact existed as to both whether the district reasonably accommodated the teacher and whether the teacher rejected the job offered to her. Johnson v. Cleveland City Sch. Dist., 2011-Ohio-2778, 2011 Ohio App. LEXIS 2384 (Ohio Ct. App., Cuyahoga County 2011).

In an employee's disability discrimination suit, a directed verdict was properly awarded to the employee's former employer as the employee, who had sleep apnea and fell asleep on numerous occasions while at work, failed to ask for a reasonable accommodation for his alleged disability under OAC 4112-5-08(E)(1). There was no showing that the employer failed to act in good faith by giving the employee to option to resign or be fired for sleeping on the job, particularly when the employee had never asked for an accommodation. Medlin v. Springfield Metro. Hous. Auth., 2010-Ohio-3654, 2010 Ohio App. LEXIS 3105 (Ohio Ct. App., Clark County 2010).

**—Regarded as having a disability**

Where an employee suffered from sleeping problems and was terminated, the employee's discriminatory discharge claims failed because the employee did not establish that the employee was regarded as having an impairment since, inter alia, the employee admitted that the employee's sleep issues did not affect the employee's ability to work. Neely v. Benchmark Family Servs., 640 Fed. Appx. 429, 2016 FED App. 0048N, 2016 U.S. App. LEXIS 1391 (6th Cir. Ohio 2016).

Employee could not establish that she was regarded as disabled, and therefore could not meet the first prong of a prima facie case alleging indirect evidence of disability discrimination; three independent medical examinations were sought because her employer believed that the employee had exhibited behavior that made her potentially dangerous or lethal in the workplace, and were ordered in response to her behavior, not a perceived disability. Ames v. Ohio Dep't of Rehab. & Corr., 2014-Ohio-4774, 23 N.E.3d 162, 2014 Ohio App. LEXIS 4659 (Ohio Ct. App., Franklin County 2014), writ denied, 2019-Ohio-1003, 2019 Ohio App. LEXIS 1065 (Ohio Ct. App., Franklin County 2019).

Employee's disability discrimination suit was properly dismissed on summary judgment as the employee had failed to establish a genuine issue of material fact as to whether the employer regarded her as disabled under § 4112.01(A)(13). There was nothing in the record that showed that the employer had any knowledge that the employee suffered from alcoholism or any mental disorder, the record establishes that any transfer or reassignment of territories occurred prior to the employer learning that the employee was hospitalized or that she was having a "nervous breakdown," and that the employee was not terminated from employment with the employer until after the employee continued to perform unsatisfactorily in her new "smaller" territory. Field v. MedLab Ohio, Inc., 2012-Ohio-5068, 2012 Ohio App. LEXIS 4432 (Ohio Ct. App., Cuyahoga County 2012).

When an employee claimed the employee was discharged by a physician and the physician's practice because the employee was regarded as having a disability, the physician and practice were entitled to summary judgment because the employee did not show that the employee's perceived disability, which was lower back pain, substantially limited any major life activity. Cunningham v. Steubenville Orthopedics & Sports Med., Inc., 2008-Ohio-1172, 175 Ohio App. 3d 627, 888 N.E.2d 499, 2008 Ohio App. LEXIS 983 (Ohio Ct. App., Jefferson County 2008).

When an employee claimed the employee was discharged by a physician and the physician's practice because the employee was regarded as having a disability, the physician and practice were entitled to summary judgment because the employee did not show that the physician regarded the employee as having a disability since the employee did not show the physician regarded the employee as being unable to perform any job, as was required to support such a claim. Cunningham v. Steubenville Orthopedics & Sports Med., Inc., 2008-Ohio-1172, 175 Ohio App. 3d 627, 888 N.E.2d 499, 2008 Ohio App. LEXIS 983 (Ohio Ct. App., Jefferson County 2008).

**—Sick building syndrome**

Where the employee's handicap was a result of "sick building syndrome," reassignment of the employee to a different location was a reasonable accommodation even though the employee had a longer commute: Martinez v. Ohio Dep't of Admin. Servs., 118 Ohio App. 3d 687, 693 N.E.2d 1152, 1997 Ohio App. LEXIS 894 (Ohio Ct. App., Franklin County 1997).

**—Transitory and minor**

Trial court did not err by granting a directed verdict for the employer on the disability discrimination case because, as a matter of law, the employee's injury was transitory and minor since her injury (two broken hands) had an actual or expected duration of six months or less. The employee testified that her broken bones "pretty much healed after six weeks," she agreed that upon her return from medical leave, she was not prevented from working in any way, and it was undisputed that the return-to-work authorization issued by her doctor contained no physical limitations or restrictions. Thomas v. PNC Bank, N.A., 2018-Ohio-4000, 2018 Ohio App. LEXIS 4324 (Ohio Ct. App., Cuyahoga County 2018).

**Discovery**

There was no compelling reason not to allow the discovery regarding the employer's net worth as the employee had requested punitive damages for violations of this section, but a protective order preventing the employee from divulging any information regarding the employer's net worth to third parties without prior authorization from the court was required. Smith v. Tech. House, Ltd., 2019-Ohio-2670, 2019 Ohio App. LEXIS 2780 (Ohio Ct. App., Portage County 2019).

**Disparate treatment**

Summary judgment was properly granted for the board of education and others on the disparate treatment claim because the male that was hired was not similarly situated to the teacher. Since he was not seeking renewal under the contract, he was not required to renew his teaching license by the April 15 deadline as was the teacher. Janiszewski v. Belmont Career Ctr., 2017-Ohio-855, 86 N.E.3d 613, 2017 Ohio App. LEXIS 830 (Ohio Ct. App., Belmont County 2017).

**Driving occupations**

Employer (Department of Transportation) was entitled to summary judgment in an employee's action for disability discrimination and retaliation and violation of the Family and Medical Leave Act (FMLA), because there was no inference of causation where the employee entered into a last chance agreement with the employer as a result of incidents that occurred well before he submitted his FMLA leave request, he clearly violated the last chance agreement by being involved in a serious injury accident while operating a mowing tractor on a highway, and he admitted that the accident was not attributable to hearing loss or any other health concern. Hartman v. Ohio DOT, 2016-Ohio-1254, 2016 Ohio Misc. LEXIS 41 (Ohio Ct. Cl.), aff'd, 2016-Ohio-5208, 68 N.E.3d 1266, 2016 Ohio App. LEXIS 3079 (Ohio Ct. App., Franklin County 2016).

In an employee's disability discrimination action under R.C. 4112.02(A), a trial court properly granted summary judgment to the former employer, as the employee could not perform the essential function of his job as a commercial truck driver because under 49 C.F.R. 391.43 and 391.11(a) as well as R.C. 4506.01(G)(3), he was precluded from driving trucks due to the implantation of an electronic defibrillator in his chest to combat a heart condition. Tibbs v. Ernst Enters., 2009-Ohio-3042, 2009 Ohio App. LEXIS 2544 (Ohio Ct. App., Montgomery County 2009).

Terminated driver failed to make a prima facie case of discrimination under Title VII by showing similarly situated employees were treated differently since two drivers were not similarly situated due to their union status and other employees who were not terminated had only traffic violations, not both criminal and traffic convictions. Elgabi v. Toledo Area Reg'l Transit Auth., 2006 U.S. Dist. LEXIS 33910 (N.D. Ohio May 26, 2006), aff'd, 228 Fed. Appx. 537, 2007 FED App. 0266N, 2007 U.S. App. LEXIS 8528 (6th Cir. Ohio 2007).

Discrimination complaint of a Hispanic auto sales consultant applicant was dismissed because he failed to meet his burden with regard to the third element of a prima facie case, namely, that he was qualified for the position in question, where his driving record was too poor for him to be insured under the motor company's insurance policy. Sanabria v. Germain Motor Co., 2005 U.S. Dist. LEXIS 20683 (S.D. Ohio Sept. 21, 2005).

**—Employer liability**

Appellant's counterclaim again appellee for violation of the Fair Housing Act and Ohio Civil Rights Act, based on vicarious liability, was properly dismissed for failure to state a claim because the alleged sexual assault appellant suffered at the hands of a maintenance worker of the apartment were the intentional and criminal actions of the employee and, as a matter of law, in no way facilitated or promoted appellee's business interests. Kingston Mound Manor I v. Keeton, 2019-Ohio-3260, 2019 Ohio App. LEXIS 3350 (Ohio Ct. App., Pickaway County 2019).

**—Gender discrimination**

Grant of summary judgment to employer was affirmed because employee did not establish that employer's legitimate non-discriminatory reasons had no basis in fact, did not actually motivate, or were insufficient to motivate, elimination of her position and decision not to rehire her as part-time dog warden. Dewalt v. Harrison Cnty. Comm'rs, 654 Fed. Appx. 770, 2016 FED App. 0362N, 2016 U.S. App. LEXIS 12189 (6th Cir. Ohio 2016).

Defendants were properly granted summary judgment on plaintiff's gender discrimination claim, because her claim of employment discrimination based on "familial status" was not cognizable under this section; she failed to establish a genuine issue of material fact as to whether she experienced an adverse employment action; and she produced no evidence that, after her termination, she was replaced by a male. Weber v. Ferrellgas, Inc., 2016-Ohio-4738, 68 N.E.3d 207, 2016 Ohio App. LEXIS 2728 (Ohio Ct. App., Trumbull County 2016).

**Disability harassment**

Former employee's claim for disability harassment under R.C. 4112.02 was properly dismissed as the employee was unable to prove that he had a disability. Wallace v. Mantych Metalworking, 2010-Ohio-3765, 189 Ohio App. 3d 25, 937 N.E.2d 177, 2010 Ohio App. LEXIS 3207 (Ohio Ct. App., Montgomery County 2010).

**Discovery**

City that firefighter had sued for age discrimination filed a motion to compel discovery of his medical records for the past 10 years. The request was properly denied, because unlimited access to his medical records for the limited purpose of determining the amount of his damages was inappropriate. Campolieti v. City of Cleveland, 2009-Ohio-5224, 184 Ohio App. 3d 419, 921 N.E.2d 286, 2009 Ohio App. LEXIS 4417 (Ohio Ct. App., Cuyahoga County 2009).

In an employment discrimination case alleging violations of 42 U.S.C.S. §§ 1981, 1985, and 2000e-5 and R.C. 4112.02 and 4112.99 in which the former employee had failed to comply with his discovery obligations, had not complied with court orders, and had already been sanctioned, the court determined that any sanction other than dismissal would be ineffective and granted defendants' Fed. R. Civ. P. 36(b)(2)(C) and Fed. R. Civ. P. 41(b) motion to dismiss. Moses v. Sterling Commerce, 2003 U.S. Dist. LEXIS 13390 (S.D. Ohio July 1, 2003), aff'd, 122 Fed. Appx. 177, 2005 U.S. App. LEXIS 19 (6th Cir. Ohio 2005).

**Dismissal, generally**

Franchisor was entitled to dismissal of the claimants' suit, because the claimants failed to cross the line from the possibility to the plausibility that the franchisor was their employer for purposes of their Title VII of the Civil Rights Act of 1964, 42 U.S.C.S. § 2000e-5 et seq., and state statutory or common law claims, when the claimants failed to include any factual allegations supporting their claim that the franchisor was or could be deemed to have been their employer. Bricker v. R & A Pizza, Inc., 804 F. Supp. 2d 615, 2011 U.S. Dist. LEXIS 39017 (S.D. Ohio 2011).

Motion to dismiss, pursuant to Civ.R. 12(B)(6), filed by a former employee's former employer and her former supervisor was improperly granted on the employee's wrongful discharge claim because, even though the employee did not allege a statutory claim for wrongful discharge, the trial court should have first determined whether she had stated such a claim pursuant to R.C. 4112.02(A) since it found that the employee's common law claim was untenable only because there already existed a statutory remedy. Springer v. Fitton Ctr. for Creative Arts, 2005-Ohio-3624, 2005 Ohio App. LEXIS 3347 (Ohio Ct. App., Butler County 2005).

**Dismissal, voluntary**

Employee was not entitled to dismissal under Fed. R. Civ. P. 41(a)(2) of her sex and age discrimination claims against her employer under R.C. 4112.02. The employer had already conducted discovery and filed a motion for summary judgment regarding the sex and age discrimination claims; the employee failed to present any evidence or argument in response to the motion for summary judgment and failed to provide any explanation for her request to dismiss those claims. Langley v. DaimlerChrysler Corp., 407 F. Supp. 2d 897, 2005 U.S. Dist. LEXIS 36332 (N.D. Ohio 2005), aff'd, 502 F.3d 475, 2007 FED App. 0379P, 2007 U.S. App. LEXIS 22211 (6th Cir. Ohio 2007).

**Disparate treatment**

Community college was entitled to summary judgment as to the disparate treatment discrimination claims for age and sex discrimination because the former dean failed to present any evidence that the college's reasons for reorganization had no basis in fact, did not actually motivate the reorganization, or were insufficient to warrant the reorganization. Randolph v. Terra State Cmty. College, 2013-Ohio-5929, 2013 Ohio Misc. LEXIS 93 (Ohio Ct. Cl. 2013).

Employee did not set forth sufficient evidence to create a genuine issue of material fact, as to whether the non-protected individuals with whom he sought to compare his treatment were similarly situated, with regard to any of his claims except the allegation that the employer passed over him for temporary job reassignments, when he was not available during the job reassignment session, while holding open reassignments for unidentified white employees who were not present; as to the claim pertaining to holding open temporarily vacant job reassignments for white co-workers, the employee did not point to sufficient evidence to demonstrate that this was an adverse employment action. Berryman v. SuperValu Holdings, Inc., — F. Supp. 2d —, 2010 U.S. Dist. LEXIS 32525 (S.D. Ohio Mar. 31, 2010), affirmed by 669 F.3d 714, 2012 U.S. App. LEXIS 3823, 2012 FED App. 53P (6th Cir.), 2012 FED App. 053P (6th Cir.), 95 Empl. Prac. Dec. (CCH) P44429, 114 Fair Empl. Prac. Cas. (BNA) 808 (6th Cir. Ohio 2012)supra.

Employee did not identify an allegedly similarly situated non-protected co-worker or, in the three instances where he identified such a co-worker, did not demonstrate that all of the relevant aspects of his employment situation were nearly identical to those of the non-protected co-worker's employment situation, as was required. Berryman v. SuperValu Holdings, Inc., 2010 U.S. Dist. LEXIS 32522 (S.D. Ohio Mar. 31, 2010).

African American employee failed to prove her racial discrimination claim under former R.C. 4112.02, arising out of her termination from employment as a claims examiner after she performed work on her husband's workers' compensation claim, as she failed to prove her claim that a comparable non-protected person also worked on a relative's workers' compensation claim but was not terminated. Even so, the employer had a legitimate nondiscriminatory reason for its action: the employee's violation of the code of ethics. Jennings v. Indus. Comm'n of Ohio, 2009-Ohio-2350, 2009 Ohio Misc. LEXIS 36 (Ohio Ct. Cl. 2009).

When an employee sued an employer for, inter alia, disparate treatment, as well as hostile environment race harassment, under R.C. 4112.02, and a jury found in the employee's favor, the trial court improperly granted the employer judgment notwithstanding the verdict, under Civ.R. 50(B), because it was error for the court to find that the employee had to show that the employer's actions were based exclusively on race for the employee to prevail, as the correct standard was that race was "a" determining factor. Williams v. Spitzer Auto World, 2008-Ohio-1467, 2008 Ohio App. LEXIS 1288 (Ohio Ct. App., Lorain County 2008).

Employee's age discrimination claim was properly dismissed because the employee failed to create a genuine issue of material fact regarding a claim for disparate treatment. Though the employee showed that two substantially younger drivers had accidents but, unlike him, were not discharged, the younger drivers' accident were deemed minor preventable accidents, in contrast to the employee's major preventable accident. Murphy v. Penske Logistics, 2007-Ohio-6407, 2007 Ohio App. LEXIS 5612 (Ohio Ct. App., Geauga County 2007).

Parks employee's claim of gender discrimination under R.C. 4112.02(A) was properly resolved by a grant of summary judgment to county parks and others with respect to her disparate treatment claim, arising from the failure of the county parks to have accepted her revocation of resignation from employment, as the employee's claim that another employee's revocation of resignation had been accepted was prior to amendments to the collective bargaining agreement that controlled the parties' relationship; further, the employee did not show that she and the other employee were similarly situated. Fox v. Lorain County, 2007-Ohio-6143, 2007 Ohio App. LEXIS 5412 (Ohio Ct. App., Lorain County 2007).

Trial court properly granted a directed verdict, pursuant to Civ.R. 50, to an employer in an employee's racial discrimination claim under R.C. 4112.02(A), based on a theory of disparate treatment, as the employee only showed that he was a member of a protected class due to his race; however, he did not satisfy any of the other elements necessary to prove such a claim, as he failed to show that he applied for any position and that he was denied promotion due to his race. Brown v. Worthington Steel, Inc., 2005-Ohio-4571, 2005 Ohio App. LEXIS 4136 (Ohio Ct. App., Franklin County 2005).

As in Title VII cases, the employee claiming disparate treatment must compare himself to those co-employees receiving punishment who are "similarly situated in all respects;" a consensual, extramarital sexual relationship and a violation of an employer's drug policy are not comparable to violations of an employer's sexual-harassment policy with the attendant consequences of supervisor liability under R.C. 4112.02: Bullock v. Totes, Inc., 2000 Ohio App. LEXIS 6058 (Ohio Ct. App., Hamilton County Dec. 22, 2000), dismissed, 91 Ohio St. 3d 1514, 746 N.E.2d 615, 2001 Ohio LEXIS 1224 (Ohio 2001).

Plaintiff presented a prima facie case of age or gender discrimination where comparable non-protected employees were accorded more favorable treatment: Bucher v. Sibcy Cline, Inc., 137 Ohio App. 3d 230, 738 N.E.2d 435, 2000 Ohio App. LEXIS 321 (Ohio Ct. App., Hamilton County 2000).

Disparate impact analysis may apply where persons employed in different job classifications, one largely male and the female, are given unequal access to overtime: Albaugh v. City of Columbus, 132 Ohio App. 3d 545, 725 N.E.2d 719, 1999 Ohio App. LEXIS 1425 (Ohio Ct. App., Franklin County 1999).

Summary judgment was proper where the employee could not establish a prima facie case by showing that a comparable nonprotected employee was treated more favorably. The lapse of time precluded a claim of retaliation for protected activity: Baker v. Buschman Co., 127 Ohio App. 3d 561, 713 N.E.2d 487, 1998 Ohio App. LEXIS 2185 (Ohio Ct. App., Butler County 1998).

To make a prima facie showing of discriminatory discharge under disparate treatment theory, plaintiff must prove that she is a member of a protected minority group, that she was discharged, and that there was a causal connection between her protected status and discharge. Where plaintiff is replaced by someone also within her protected class she can not make such a prima facie showing: Brown v. Herman's Furniture, 772 F. Supp. 350, 1990 U.S. Dist. LEXIS 19199 (N.D. Ohio 1990), aff'd, 941 F.2d 1209, 1991 U.S. App. LEXIS 24180 (6th Cir. Ohio 1991).



**Drug or alcohol abuse**

Summary judgment was properly granted because there was no adverse employment action; it was neither a violation of the Americans With Disabilities Act nor of R.C. 4112.02 for the employer require drug testing, after the employee admitted to having convictions for drug use, to ensure that the employee was no longer using drugs prior to employment. Turner v. Shahed Enters., 2011-Ohio-4654, 2011 Ohio App. LEXIS 3851 (Ohio Ct. App., Franklin County 2011).

Even if the employee could have established a prima facie case of disability discrimination based upon his condition of alcoholism, the burden would then have shifted to the employer to set forth some legitimate, nondiscriminatory reason for the termination of the employee's employment; because the employee failed to follow the call-in procedures, and his failure caused him to be a "no-call, no-show" employee for four consecutive days, the employee's four-day unexcused absence was a legitimate, nondiscriminatory reason for his termination. The employee did not provide any evidence to prove that the stated basis for his termination was a pretext. Barnett v. Ohio State Univ. Med. Ctr., 2007-Ohio-5424, 2007 Ohio Misc. LEXIS 391 (Ohio Ct. Cl. 2007).

Even if the employee could have established a prima facie case of disability discrimination based upon his condition of alcoholism, the burden would then have shifted to the employer to set forth some legitimate, nondiscriminatory reason for the termination of the employee's employment; because the employee failed to follow the call-in procedures, and his failure caused him to be a "no-call, no-show" employee for four consecutive days, the employee's four-day unexcused absence was a legitimate, nondiscriminatory reason for his termination. The employee did not provide any evidence to prove that the stated basis for his termination was a pretext. Barnett v. Ohio State Univ. Med. Ctr., 2007-Ohio-5424, 2007 Ohio Misc. LEXIS 391 (Ohio Ct. Cl. 2007).

There was a distinction between taking an adverse job action for unacceptable misconduct and taking such action solely because of a disability, even if the misconduct was "caused" by the disability, as the Americans with Disabilities Act, 42 U.S.C.S. § 12101 et seq., protected recovering alcoholics, but did not protect a worker from his own bad judgment in drinking on the job. Burrows v. Licking County, 2006-Ohio-4057, 2006 Ohio App. LEXIS 4029 (Ohio Ct. App., Licking County 2006).

Employee who was addicted to prescription painkillers and fired for repeated absences did not state a claim for hostile work environment; he claimed that co-workers harassed him by calling him "brain dead" and "our token recovering addict," and that a supervisor told him he did not get a position he bid for because he was in a substance abuse program, but his complaint contained no evidence linking any failure to promote or workplace harassment to his termination. Gardull v. Perstorp Polyols, Inc., 382 F. Supp. 2d 960, 2005 U.S. Dist. LEXIS 17250 (N.D. Ohio 2005).

Employer was granted summary judgment on an employee's disability discrimination claim where the employee failed to establish a prima facie case because he failed to show that his alcoholism substantially limited one or more major life activities. The employee admitted that despite his alcoholism he was able to engage in basic daily activities and that it had never interfered with his work prior to the day he arrived at work under the influence. O'Neal v. Johns Manville Int'l, 2005 U.S. Dist. LEXIS 10114 (N.D. Ohio May 20, 2005).

Employer was denied summary judgment on an African-American employee's race discrimination claim because the employee presented evidence that could show that the employer's reason for terminating him was pretextual. The employee presented evidence that non-minority employees were not required to take drug and alcohol tests even though they were caught in possession of alcohol or drugs on company premises or under the influence during work hours, and that one non-minority employee was permitted to return to work after a suspension even though he never took a drug and alcohol test. O'Neal v. Johns Manville Int'l, 2005 U.S. Dist. LEXIS 10114 (N.D. Ohio May 20, 2005).

The employee was not protected under the Rehabilitation Act of 1973 or the ADA because he was a current drug user not participating in a supervised rehabilitation program: Corrections Corp. of Am. v. Human Rels. Comm'n, 139 Ohio App. 3d 58, 742 N.E.2d 1177, 2000 Ohio App. LEXIS 4379 (Ohio Ct. App., Mahoning County 2000).

An employee was not able to avail himself of the safe-harbor protections of R.C. 4112.02 where the evidence concretely established that he was not abstaining from the illegal use of drugs at the time of his termination: Hall v. Jewish Hosp. of Cincinnati, 2000 Ohio App. LEXIS 2312 (Ohio Ct. App., Hamilton County June 2, 2000).

Given the short interval between her illegal use of drugs and her termination, appellant was not drug-free for a sufficient period to come within the class of persons protected under the "safe-harbor" provision of R.C. 4112.02(Q)(1)(b); since her illegal use of drugs occurred recently enough to justify the reasonable belief that her involvement with illegal drugs was an on-going problem, she could not establish a prima facie case of handicap discrimination: Starr v. Delta Air Lines, 1995 Ohio App. LEXIS 5778 (Ohio Ct. App., Hamilton County Dec. 29, 1995), dismissed, 76 Ohio St. 3d 1405, 666 N.E.2d 566, 1996 Ohio LEXIS 688 (Ohio 1996).

Summary judgment against a black employee was error where he claimed that he was offered a choice of resigning or undergoing the disciplinary process after his job-related drug use, but that white employees were offered the option of rehabilitation. Summary judgment on the breach of contract and promissory estoppel claims was proper, since the drug use constituted just cause for discharge: Neely v. Franklin County Auditor, 97 Ohio App. 3d 771, 647 N.E.2d 557, 1994 Ohio App. LEXIS 5346 (Ohio Ct. App., Franklin County 1994).

Although chemical dependency and depression are handicaps under R.C. Chapter 4112., an employee may be discharged where chemical dependency adversely affects job performance, such as through chronic unexcused absence: Hayes v. Cleveland Pneumatic Co., 92 Ohio App. 3d 36, 634 N.E.2d 228, 1993 Ohio App. LEXIS 4843 (Ohio Ct. App., Cuyahoga County 1993), dismissed, 69 Ohio St. 3d 1415, 630 N.E.2d 376, 1994 Ohio LEXIS 837 (Ohio 1994).

Evidence that an employee has numerous drunk driving convictions is not, by itself, sufficient proof of the handicap of alcoholism. Where a handicapped employee is discharged for just cause, such as not having a required driver's license, the employer has no duty to accommodate the handicap: Sizemore v. Department of Rehabilitation & Corrections, 63 Ohio Misc. 2d 319, 629 N.E.2d 1096, 1992 Ohio Misc. LEXIS 83 (Ohio Ct. Cl. 1992).

Misconduct or absenteeism of a prospective employee, even if attributable to alcoholism, may be considered by an employer in making its hiring decision, so long as the same neutral criteria are applied to handicapped and nonhandicapped persons alike: Cleveland Civil Service Com. v. Ohio Civil Rights Com., 57 Ohio St. 3d 62, 565 N.E.2d 579, 1991 Ohio LEXIS 29 (Ohio 1991).

R.C. 4112.02(A), which prohibits an alcoholic employee from being discharged without just cause because of his alcoholism, is an exception to the at-will employment doctrine: Brandenburger v. Hilti, Inc., 52 Ohio App. 3d 21, 556 N.E.2d 212, 1989 Ohio App. LEXIS 904 (Ohio Ct. App., Cuyahoga County 1989).

An employer in not required to retain a high risk alcoholic employee and expose itself to civil and criminal liability when the alcoholic employee works in a dangerous work environment and is provided three opportunities to rehabilitate himself over a two-year period. Such an employee may be discharged for just cause as a matter of law: Brandenburger v. Hilti, Inc., 52 Ohio App. 3d 21, 556 N.E.2d 212, 1989 Ohio App. LEXIS 904 (Ohio Ct. App., Cuyahoga County 1989).

An employer has an obligation to take steps to avoid any occupational hazards involved in retaining an alcoholic employee through "reasonable accommodation" pursuant to OAC 4112-5-08(D) and (E). This obligation is not fulfilled when an employer unreasonably refuses to allow an alcoholic employee a second chance at rehabilitation through an alcohol addiction recovery program: Greater Cleveland Regional Transit Auth. v. Ohio Civil Rights Comm., 58 Ohio App. 3d 20, 567 N.E.2d 1325 (1989).

Claim of failure to hire on the basis of the handicap of alcoholism remanded for reconsideration under the holding in Hazlett v. Martin Chevrolet, Inc. that alcoholism is a handicap as defined in R.C. 4112.01(A)(13): 31 Ohio St. 3d 222, 510 N.E.2d 368.

**Election of remedies**

Former employee was barred under R.C. 4112.08 from bringing a civil action for age discrimination under R.C. 4112.02 and R.C. 4112.99 because the employee elected to pursue a charge of age discrimination in an administrative action with the Ohio Civil Rights Commission, and there was no evidence to suggest that the limited exception to the election of remedies doctrine applied. Moore v. Dep't of Rehab. & Corr., 2010-Ohio-3739, 2010 Ohio Misc. LEXIS 157 (Ohio Ct. Cl. 2010), aff'd, 2011-Ohio-1607, 2011 Ohio App. LEXIS 1376 (Ohio Ct. App., Franklin County 2011).

Summary judgment was properly granted because the nurse's assistant was barred from bringing a private age discrimination claim under R.C. 4112.02 and 4112.99. Because the nurse's assistant filed a charge with the Equal Employment Opportunity Commission (EEOC) and never indicated that she would forego an investigation (and was filing for technical purposes only), her charge to the EEOC was likewise deemed filed with the Ohio Civil Rights Commission. Neal v. Franklin Plaza Nursing Home, 2009-Ohio-2034, 2009 Ohio App. LEXIS 1724 (Ohio Ct. App., Cuyahoga County 2009).

Summary judgment was properly granted to an employer on a job applicant's age discrimination claim under R.C. 4112.02, .99 because the applicant elected to pursue an administrative remedy that precluded her from filing a civil action; before filing the civil action, she filed charges with the Ohio Civil Rights Commission and the United States Equal Employment Opportunity Commission, no exception to the election of remedies requirement was shown to exist, and the requirement applied to claims under both R.C. 4112.02 and R.C. 4112.99. McNeely v. Ross Corr. Inst., 2006-Ohio-5414, 2006 Ohio App. LEXIS 5408 (Ohio Ct. App., Franklin County 2006).

Employee's age discrimination claim under R.C. 4112.02 was dismissed as it was filed 260 days after the alleged discrimination, well outside of the 180-day statute of limitations found in § 4112.02(N); however, his decision to first file with the Equal Employment Opportunity Commission did not amount to an election to pursue a state administrative remedy under R.C. 4112.05(B)(1), precluding him from filing his civil action. Spengler v. Worthington Cylinders, 438 F. Supp. 2d 805, 2006 U.S. Dist. LEXIS 40022 (S.D. Ohio 2006).

The election of remedies requirement does not apply to claims of sex discrimination: Noday v. Mahoning County Sheriff, 2002-Ohio-609, 147 Ohio App. 3d 38, 768 N.E.2d 726, 2002 Ohio App. LEXIS 596 (Ohio Ct. App., Mahoning County 2002).

R.C. 4112.02 does not mandate an election of administrative or court remedies for claimants pursuing discrimination claims other than age discrimination claims: Bourquin v. KeyBank, 138 Ohio App. 3d 435, 741 N.E.2d 584, 2000 Ohio App. LEXIS 2881 (Ohio Ct. App., Lucas County 2000).

A union cannot prospectively waive the individual right of a member to select a judicial forum for resolution of the member's federal and state statutory claims: Thomas v. GE Co., 131 Ohio App. 3d 825, 723 N.E.2d 1139, 1999 Ohio App. LEXIS 301 (Ohio Ct. App., Hamilton County 1999).

The plaintiff was barred from bringing an age discrimination claim pursuant to R.C. 4112.14 where he earlier filed a charge with OCR.C. pursuant to R.C. 4112.05 without stating that the administrative charge was filed for the sole purpose of perfecting an ADEA claim: Fowler v. Hudson Foods, 96 Ohio Misc. 2d 19, 708 N.E.2d 792, 1998 Ohio Misc. LEXIS 57 (Ohio C.P. 1998).

An age discrimination plaintiff who files with the OCR.C. for the sole purpose of fulfilling the requirements of the federal age discrimination in employment act may elect to pursue state judicial remedies under R.C. 4112.02(N) and 4112.99, but only in federal court by appending the state claims to those under federal law, and not in a complaint under state law filed in an Ohio court: Crawford v. Medina Gen. Hosp., 1997 Ohio App. LEXIS 3744 (Ohio Ct. App., Medina County Aug. 20, 1997).

The 1987 amendment to R.C. 4112.99 did not alter the election of remedies requirement as to age discrimination claims: Balent v. National Revenue Corp., 93 Ohio App. 3d 419, 638 N.E.2d 1064, 1994 Ohio App. LEXIS 935 (Ohio Ct. App., Franklin County 1994).

Pursuant to OAC 4112-3-01(D), a charge filed with EEOC is deemed filed with Ohio's civil rights commission, precluding a private right of action under R.C. 4112.99: Schwartz v. Comcorp, Inc., 91 Ohio App. 3d 639, 633 N.E.2d 551, 1993 Ohio App. LEXIS 89 (Ohio Ct. App., Cuyahoga County 1993).

Even though R.C. 4112.02(N) and 4101.17 each preclude filing of age discrimination claims under both provisions, a court should not simply dismiss an action alleging both. The special provision of R.C. 4112.02(N) prevails over the general relief afforded by R.C. 4112.99: Giambrone v. Spalding & Evenflo Co., 79 Ohio App. 3d 308, 607 N.E.2d 106, 1992 Ohio App. LEXIS 2070 (Ohio Ct. App., Miami County 1992).

A party who has potential remedies for alleged age discrimination under R.C. 4101.17, 4112.02 and 4112.99 may not pursue an administrative action under R.C. 4112.05, fail to appeal an adverse determination and then bring an action under R.C. 4112.99: Gallant v. Toledo Pub. Sch., 84 Ohio App. 3d 378, 616 N.E.2d 1156, 1992 Ohio App. LEXIS 6324 (Ohio Ct. App., Lucas County 1992).

Public employees do not have a private cause of civil action against their employer to redress alleged violations by their employer of policies embodied in the Ohio Constitution when it is determined that there are other reasonably satisfactory remedies provided by statutory enactment and administrative process: Provens v. Stark County Bd. of Mental Retardation & Developmental Disabilities, 1992-Ohio-35, 64 Ohio St. 3d 252, 594 N.E.2d 959, 1992 Ohio LEXIS 1677 (Ohio 1992).

R.C. 4101.17, 4112.02 and 4112.05 are exclusive and once an action is brought under one of these sections a plaintiff is barred from bringing an action under either of the other two provisions: Pater v. Health Care & Retirement Corp., 808 F. Supp. 573, 1992 U.S. Dist. LEXIS 20568 (S.D. Ohio 1992).

The Ohio legislature has not manifested an intent to require a plaintiff alleging sex discrimination to elect between various remedies: Larkins v. G.D. Searle & Co., 68 Ohio App. 3d 746, 589 N.E.2d 488, 1991 Ohio App. LEXIS 3669 (Ohio Ct. App., Franklin County 1991).

Simply because Ohio's age discrimination law has the effect of requiring a litigant to choose between his or her state and federal remedies does not invalidate that law or require the court to construe the terms of that law inconsistently with its plain meaning: Keister v. Delco Products, 680 F. Supp. 281, 1987 U.S. Dist. LEXIS 13098 (S.D. Ohio 1987).

A plaintiff who files a charge of age discrimination with the OCR.C. under R.C. 4112.05 seeking administrative enforcement of the right against age discrimination is barred from bringing a civil action under R.C. 4101.17 or 4112.02(N): Smith v. L.M. Berry & Co., 654 F. Supp. 11, 1986 U.S. Dist. LEXIS 21317 (S.D. Ohio 1986).

A claimant who has previously filed an age discrimination action under R.C. 4101.17 is not barred from filing a claim with the Ohio Civil Rights Commission pursuant to R.C. 4112.05 in order to satisfy the mandatory prerequisite to an action under the federal Age Discrimination in Employment Act: Morris v. Kaiser Engineers, Inc., 14 Ohio St. 3d 45, 471 N.E.2d 471, 1984 Ohio LEXIS 1240 (Ohio 1984).

An action involving age discrimination is not foreclosed by the plaintiff's choice to sue under Ohio as well as federal law: Bailey v. Container Corp. of America, 594 F. Supp. 629, 1984 U.S. Dist. LEXIS 23120 (S.D. Ohio 1984), vacated in part, 594 F. Supp. 629, 1985 U.S. Dist. LEXIS 24066 (S.D. Ohio 1985), limited, Adleta v. GE (S.D. Ohio 1996).

A plaintiff who files a charge with the Ohio Civil Rights Commission before bringing a civil action in federal court pursuant to the Age Discrimination in Employment Act and either R.C. 4101.17 or 4112.02(N) is barred by state law from pursuing his state judicial remedy, and accordingly his pendent state claim must be dismissed: Merkel v. Scovill, Inc., 570 F. Supp. 133, 1983 U.S. Dist. LEXIS 18632 (S.D. Ohio 1983).

A plaintiff who brings an action in federal court pursuant to the Age Discrimination in Employment Act and R.C. 4101.17 or 4112.02(N), and who subsequently files a charge with the Ohio Civil Rights Commission pursuant to R.C. 4112.05 to satisfy the ADEA's requirement that a plaintiff commence state proceedings, may proceed with both his federal and state claims if the court finds it appropriate to retain the pendent claim: Merkel v. Scovill, Inc., 570 F. Supp. 133, 1983 U.S. Dist. LEXIS 18632 (S.D. Ohio 1983).

**Eleventh amendment**

State correctional department's dismissal motion was granted because U.S. Const. amend. XI barred a terminated employee from prosecuting his state tort and R.C. ch. 4112 claims against the department; the employee failed to present any evidence showing that the State of Ohio had waived its immunity or consented to be sue by the employee as to his state law claims. Gilbert v. Ohio Dep't of Rehab. & Corr., 2005 U.S. Dist. LEXIS 12073 (S.D. Ohio June 17, 2005), dismissed in part, 2005 U.S. Dist. LEXIS 59833 (S.D. Ohio June 20, 2005).

The eleventh amendment barred plaintiff's suit against state in federal court for violations of the Ohio statutes prohibiting employment discrimination: Williams v. Ohio Dep't of Mental Health, 960 F. Supp. 1276, 1997 U.S. Dist. LEXIS 5429 (S.D. Ohio 1997).

**Employee handbook**

Company's credo and employee handbook provisions were not specific promises of job security or continued employment that would support a breach of implied contract agreement action: Allen v. Ethicon, 919 F. Supp. 1093, 1996 U.S. Dist. LEXIS 8135 (S.D. Ohio 1996).

**Employer**

Where plaintiff, a male employee of a hospital, was forced to resigned after having sexual contact with a female co-worker who was not terminated, the trial court did not err in dismissing his sexual discrimination and unlawful retaliations claims against individual defendants who were employed by the hospital as they were not "employers" within the meaning of R.C. 4112.01(A)(2) and could not be held liable. The only "employer" who made the decision to terminate plaintiff was the director of human resources. Caiazza v. Mercy Med. Ctr., 2014-Ohio-2290, 2014 Ohio App. LEXIS 2232 (Ohio Ct. App., Stark County 2014).

In former law school professor's discrimination suit, the law school dean was not an employer because he was not an employee of the university before or during the time that the university decided not to renew the professor's contract. Han v. Univ. of Dayton, 541 Fed. Appx. 622, 2013 FED App. 0954N, 2013 U.S. App. LEXIS 22788 (6th Cir. Ohio 2013), cert. denied, 572 U.S. 1150, 134 S. Ct. 2699, 189 L. Ed. 2d 741, 2014 U.S. LEXIS 3856 (U.S. 2014).

Law school faculty members of a promotion, retention and tenure committee were not individually liable because they were former professor's colleagues or coworkers and not his supervisors or managers. Han v. Univ. of Dayton, 541 Fed. Appx. 622, 2013 FED App. 0954N, 2013 U.S. App. LEXIS 22788 (6th Cir. Ohio 2013), cert. denied, 572 U.S. 1150, 134 S. Ct. 2699, 189 L. Ed. 2d 741, 2014 U.S. LEXIS 3856 (U.S. 2014).

Trial court did not err in denying an employer's motion for judgment notwithstanding the verdict pursuant to Civ.R. 50 in an employee's sexual harassment claim based on her supervisor's allegedly improper conduct towards her, as her settlement with the supervisor did not preclude a finding of liability on the part of the employer; the supervisor was subject to liability because he met the definition of an employer pursuant to R.C. 4112.01(A)(2), and as the supervisor and employer were jointly and severally liable pursuant to R.C. 4112.02(A) and 4112.99, the settlement of the supervisor did not relieve the employer from potential vicarious liability. Edwards v. Ohio Inst. of Cardiac Care, 2007-Ohio-1333, 170 Ohio App. 3d 619, 868 N.E.2d 721, 2007 Ohio App. LEXIS 1214 (Ohio Ct. App., Greene County 2007).



For purposes of an employee's disability discrimination claim under R.C. 4112.02(A)(2), there was sufficient evidence to find that the general manager for the employer's plan was liable along with the employer under the definition of "employer" pursuant to R.C. 4112.01(A)(2), as the manager was the individual to whom the employee requested a return to work with an accommodation, the manager had examined all accommodations and concluded that there were no reasonable ones, he was the one who reviewed the employee's medical evidence, and he was the one who utlimately fired the employee from his employment position. Sicklesmith v. Hoist, 2006-Ohio-6137, 169 Ohio App. 3d 470, 863 N.E.2d 677, 2006 Ohio App. LEXIS 6103 (Ohio Ct. App., Columbiana County 2006).

Former employee waived his right to raise his arguments on appeal regarding his age discrimination and retaliation claims on which the district court entered judgment as a matter of law because the defendants were not "employers" under Ohio's civil rights statute; the employee had not raised his arguments- -that there need not be more than four employees in the state for managers and supervisors to be liable and that the prohibition against retaliation under R.C. 4112.02(I) was not limited to "employers" but to "any person"- -before the district court in arguing against the employers' motion for judgment as a matter of law, and thus, he could not raise them on appeal. Kusens v. Pascal Co., 448 F.3d 349, 2006 FED App. 0154P, 2006 U.S. App. LEXIS 11430 (6th Cir. Ohio 2006).

When an employee sued a school district and an assistant superintendent for race and gender discrimination and retaliation for not hiring the employee for a supervisory position, the assistant superintendent was not entitled to judgment on the pleadings, under Civ.R. 12(C), based on the theory that the assistant superintendent was immune, under R.C. 2744.03, because, under R.C. 2744.03(A)(6)(c), the employee's allegations regarding the assistant superintendent's responsibilities were sufficient to survive a motion for judgment on the pleadings on the question of whether the assistant superintendent was the employee's supervisor or manager, who, as a result, could be liable under R.C. ch. 4112. Senu-Oke v. Bd. of Educ., 2005-Ohio-5239, 2005 Ohio App. LEXIS 4744 (Ohio Ct. App., Montgomery County 2005).

**Employer, generally**

Employee was not employed by a bank's holding company, and as a result, the employee had no claim against the company for employment discrimination or retaliatory discharge. The employee's entire compensation came from the bank, she was appointed to her position by the bank's board of directors, and the employee served in an operational capacity for the bank, not for the company. Boesch v. Champaign Nat'l Bank, 2008-Ohio-3282, 2008 Ohio App. LEXIS 2771 (Ohio Ct. App., Summit County 2008).

Former employee waived his right to raise his arguments on appeal regarding his age discrimination and retaliation claims on which the district court entered judgment as a matter of law because the defendants were not "employers" under Ohio's civil rights statute. The employee had not raised his arguments- -that there need not be more than four employees in the state for managers and supervisors to be liable and that the prohibition against retaliation under R.C. 4112.02(I) was not limited to "employers" but to "any person"- -before the district court in arguing against the employers' motion for judgment as a matter of law, and thus, he could not raise them on appeal. Kusens v. Pascal Co., 448 F.3d 349, 2006 FED App. 0154P, 2006 U.S. App. LEXIS 11430 (6th Cir. Ohio 2006).

**Employment at will**

There is no need to carve out an exception to the employment-at-will doctrine to recognize a cause of action for wrongful discharge in violation of public policy because, the legislature has already carved out the exception by enacting R.C. 4101.17, 4112.02(N), 4112.05, and 4112.99: Napier v. VGC Corp., 797 F. Supp. 602, 1992 U.S. Dist. LEXIS 12914 (S.D. Ohio 1992).

Unless otherwise agreed, either party to an oral employment-at-will employment agreement may terminate the employment relationship for any reason which is not contrary to law: Mers v. Dispatch Printing Co., 19 Ohio St. 3d 100, 483 N.E.2d 150, 1985 Ohio LEXIS 521 (Ohio 1985).

**Employment not shown**

In a racial discrimination case, a magistrate's recommendation was not erroneous where it found that a student was not an employee of a university based on an internship because the evidence and testimony made it clear that any work performed by the student was at the direction of a federation for community planning and was paid for by it. Lewis v. Cleveland State Univ., 2010-Ohio-2654, 2010 Ohio Misc. LEXIS 101 (Ohio Ct. Cl. 2010), aff'd, 2011-Ohio-1192, 2011 Ohio App. LEXIS 1029 (Ohio Ct. App., Franklin County 2011).

**Estoppel**

Trial court erred by finding the employee was precluded from litigating his disability discrimination claim against the supervisor on the basis of issue preclusion because the supervisor was not in privity with the company owner. The employee had no opportunity to litigate his claims against the supervisor in his individual capacity. Price v. Carter Lumber Co., 2012-Ohio-6109, 985 N.E.2d 236, 2012 Ohio App. LEXIS 5275 (Ohio Ct. App., Summit County 2012), aff'd in part and rev'd in part, 2015-Ohio-1522, 2015 Ohio App. LEXIS 1468 (Ohio Ct. App., Summit County 2015).

Receipt of temporary total disability compensation does not judicially estop an employee from claiming handicap discrimination: Smith v. Dillard Dep't Stores, Inc., 139 Ohio App. 3d 525, 744 N.E.2d 1198, 2000 Ohio App. LEXIS 1659 (Ohio Ct. App., Cuyahoga County 2000).

A plaintiff's assertion in a social security or workers' compensation proceeding that he or she is "totally disabled" is not conclusive as to an ADA or R.C. 4112.02 claim: Dawson v. Qube Corp., 6 F. Supp. 2d 677, 1998 U.S. Dist. LEXIS 7958 (N.D. Ohio 1998).

Since R.C. 4112.02 is to be construed in accordance with interpretations of Title VII, and employee's federal discrimination claims were defeated, employee's discrimination claim against supervisor under Ohio law was also defeated: Blankenship v. BMI Refractories, 966 F. Supp. 555, 1997 U.S. Dist. LEXIS 8631 (S.D. Ohio 1997).

**Evidence**

Because competent, credible evidence showed that a hospital did not discriminate against plaintiff in violation of R.C. 4112.02, a judgment finding no liability on the hospital's part was proper; the hospital had discretion to choose among equally qualified candidates, and both candidates for a position had four years of management experience and both undisputedly had a strong understanding of imaging equipment and systems. Refaei v. Ohio State Univ. Hosp., 2011-Ohio-6727, 2011 Ohio App. LEXIS 5545 (Ohio Ct. App., Franklin County 2011).

Although the employee alleged discrimination and retaliation under a variety of state and federal statutes, the employer articulated a legitimate, nondiscriminatory reason for the termination of the employee's employment, namely, it received numerous customer complaints about the employee's services in less than two months; the employee failed to set forth sufficient evidence creating a genuine dispute of material fact as to whether the employer discharged her in retaliation for taking Family Medical Leave Act leave or for any other discriminatory reason. Diaz v. Mitchell's Salon & Day Spa, Inc., 2011 U.S. Dist. LEXIS 9878 (S.D. Ohio Feb. 2, 2011).

Summary judgment dismissal of the race and age discrimination and harassment suit was proper, because the meetings to review and correct the employee's work deficiencies were not adverse actions, the employee did not dispute the supervisor's dissatisfaction with his job performance or with his disregard of the rules for vacation leave, and the employee failed to either show that the supervisor's actions unreasonably interfered with his work performance or that the conduct of the maintenance staff was so hostile, abusive or extreme as to constitute a discriminatory change in the terms or conditions of employment. Perez v. Theller, 2011-Ohio-2176, 2011 Ohio App. LEXIS 1853 (Ohio Ct. App., Sandusky County 2011).

Employee was disciplined for three incidents: hitting a coworker with a crane, hitting a coworker with a tool, and putting a hammer in another employee's face. However, his employer's motion for summary judgment was granted because the employee did not establish that other individuals were similarly-situated, i.e., he failed to establish that they reported to his supervisor or that they engaged in similar acts. Johnson v. GMC, 2008 U.S. Dist. LEXIS 7981 (N.D. Ohio Feb. 4, 2008).

Employee failed to proffer evidence to demonstrate that the employee was replaced by a younger person; the younger person's job duties did not change after the employee was terminated. Thus, the younger person did not "replace" the employee within the meaning of Ohio law, and because the employee was not replaced, the employee could not establish indirectly a prima facie case of age discrimination under R.C. 4112.02. Mazzitti v. Garden City Group, Inc., 2007-Ohio-3285, 2007 Ohio App. LEXIS 3026 (Ohio Ct. App., Franklin County 2007).

In a Caucasian employee's racial discrimination suit brought against the city which employed her and her African-American supervisor, the trial court properly excluded from evidence under Evid.R. 403 a report issued by the city's Equal Employment Opportunity office because, while the statements contained in the report fell within the scope of the employment of the two representatives issuing the report and, thus, constituted an admission of a party-opponent pursuant to Evid.R. 801(D)(2)(d), the potential for unfair prejudice to the city and the supervisor and confusion of the issues before the jury substantially outweighed its probative value. The report contained lengthy discussions of and conclusions regarding claims of disparate treatment and retaliation, which were not before the jury, and it presented a substantial danger of jury confusion based on the interplay of the report's conclusion of probable cause and the jury's responsibility to independently evaluate the evidence under the trial court's instructions of law to determine whether the evidence demonstrated a violation of R.C. ch. 4112. Mowery v. City of Columbus, 2006-Ohio-1153, 2006 Ohio App. LEXIS 1051 (Ohio Ct. App., Franklin County 2006).

**—Admissibility**

Trial court did not abuse its discretion in affirming the administrative law judge's ruling on the use of Exhibit A, a letter from the Ohio Civil Rights Commission, in the retaliation case because the relevance of the statement attributed to the employee was not established, and reasonable, legitimate concerns were raised about holding the employee accountable for a hearsay statement in an agency's document by allowing the employer to "impeach" her with such a statement. Little York Tavern v. Lane, 2017-Ohio-850, 86 N.E.3d 715, 2017 Ohio App. LEXIS 848 (Ohio Ct. App., Montgomery County 2017).

**—Committee recommendations**

District court's reliance on defendant city's hiring committee recommendation in analyzing plaintiff employee's R.C. 4112.02(A) failure to promote claim and her pretext argument was not error merely because the letterhead incorrectly referred to a prior human resources director because the use of old letterhead alone was insufficient to create fact issues on authenticity. Sigall-Drakulich v. City of Columbus, 156 Fed. Appx. 791, 2005 FED App. 0965N, 2005 U.S. App. LEXIS 27772 (6th Cir. Ohio 2005).

**—Equal employment opportunity report**

In a Caucasian employee's racial discrimination suit brought against the city which employed her and her African-American supervisor, the trial court properly excluded from evidence under Evid.R. 403 a report issued by the city's Equal Employment Opportunity office because, while the statements contained in the report fell within the scope of the employment of the two representatives issuing the report and, thus, constituted an admission of a party-opponent pursuant to Evid.R. 801(D)(2)(d), the potential for unfair prejudice to the city and the supervisor and confusion of the issues before the jury substantially outweighed its probative value. The report contained lengthy discussions of and conclusions regarding claims of disparate treatment and retaliation, which were not before the jury, and it presented a substantial danger of jury confusion based on the interplay of the report's conclusion of probable cause and the jury's responsibility to independently evaluate the evidence under the trial court's instructions of law to determine whether the evidence demonstrated a violation of R.C. ch. 4112. Mowery v. City of Columbus, 2006-Ohio-1153, 2006 Ohio App. LEXIS 1051 (Ohio Ct. App., Franklin County 2006).

**—Insufficient**

Grant of summary judgment to appellees was affirmed because the district court did not err in finding the statistics insufficient to establish similarly-situated comparables where the employees' proffered spreadsheet had serious infirmities that greatly undermined its credibility as it did not address all of the "relevant" aspects of the employees' employment situation. O'Donnell v. City of Cleveland, 838 F.3d 718, 2016 FED App. 0240P, 2016 U.S. App. LEXIS 17379 (6th Cir. Ohio 2016), cert. denied, 137 S. Ct. 1206, 197 L. Ed. 2d 247, 2017 U.S. LEXIS 1457 (U.S. 2017).

In an employee's action, arising from being laid off from her job, the employee failed to establish a prima facie case of retaliatory discrimination, as the reduction in force by the employer was a valid, non-discriminatory reason for the employee's layoff, and her filing of a grievance unrelated to the employer's alleged discriminatory activity was not a protected activity. Bryan v. Valley Care Health Sys. of Ohio Ohio Northside, 2016-Ohio-7156, 2016 Ohio App. LEXIS 4057 (Ohio Ct. App., Trumbull County 2016).

*Unpublished decision:* While it was error for the district court to conclude that the cat's paw was inapplicable, the instant court took no issue with the district court's dismissal of the discrimination claim where the employee failed to show discriminatory animus. Voltz v. Erie County, 617 Fed. Appx. 417, 2015 FED App. 0451N, 2015 U.S. App. LEXIS 10309 (6th Cir. Ohio 2015).

Plaintiff's race discrimination claim under R.C. 4112.02(A), arising from his termination from employment, was resolved in favor of defendant where, although plaintiff established a prima facie case, defendant presented legitimate, nondiscriminatory reasons for its actions; further, they were not a mere pretext. Green v. Ohio Lottery Comm'n, 2012-Ohio-3647, 2012 Ohio Misc. LEXIS 91 (Ohio Ct. Cl. 2012).

Trial court's grant of summary judgment to an employer in an age discrimination action by an employee pursuant to R.C. 4112.02(A) and 4112.14(A) was proper, as the employer's claim that the employee was terminated for financial reasons was a legitimate, nondiscriminatory reason, and the employee failed to show that it was a mere pretext. Chandler v. Dunn Hardware, Inc., 2006-Ohio-4376, 168 Ohio App. 3d 496, 860 N.E.2d 1042, 2006 Ohio App. LEXIS 4293 (Ohio Ct. App., Cuyahoga County 2006).

Where an employee was unable to prove her claim of racial discrimination in violation of R.C. 4112.02, as she failed to show that she had a valid reason for "involuntarily terminating" her work relationship because any adverse employment action that she alleged occurred did not rise to the level that would have caused a constructive discharge, nor did she show that she was treated differently on the basis of race, her claims that she was wrongfully discharged in violation of public policy under Greeley also necessarily failed. Simmons-Means v. Cuyahoga County Dep't of Justice Affairs, 2006-Ohio-4123, 2006 Ohio App. LEXIS 4057 (Ohio Ct. App., Cuyahoga County 2006).

Employee was not entitled to dismissal under Fed. R. Civ. P. 41(a)(2) of her sex and age discrimination claims against her employer under R.C. 4112.02. The employer had already conducted discovery and filed a motion for summary judgment regarding the sex and age discrimination claims; the employee failed to present any evidence or argument in response to the motion for summary judgment and failed to provide any explanation for her request to dismiss those claims. Langley v. DaimlerChrysler Corp., 407 F. Supp. 2d 897, 2005 U.S. Dist. LEXIS 36332 (N.D. Ohio 2005), aff'd, 502 F.3d 475, 2007 FED App. 0379P, 2007 U.S. App. LEXIS 22211 (6th Cir. Ohio 2007).

**—Replacement**

If an employee's involuntary disability separation was an adverse employment action, for purposes of the employee's claim of racial discrimination, the employee still did not present a prima facie case of racial discrimination in employment because the employee did not show who replaced the employee or that an employee who was not a member of a protected class received more favorable treatment. Carter v. Dep't of Rehab. & Corr., 2007-Ohio-3872, 2007 Ohio Misc. LEXIS 250 (Ohio Ct. Cl. 2007).

Employee failed to proffer evidence to demonstrate that the employee was replaced by a younger person; the younger person's job duties did not change after the employee was terminated. Thus, the younger person did not "replace" the employee within the meaning of Ohio law, and because the employee was not replaced, the employee could not establish indirectly a prima facie case of age discrimination under R.C. 4112.02. Mazzitti v. Garden City Group, Inc., 2007-Ohio-3285, 2007 Ohio App. LEXIS 3026 (Ohio Ct. App., Franklin County 2007).

**—Sufficient**

Given the obvious anatomical and biological differences between men and women and the unique hygienic needs of women, including those during menstrual cycles, the practice of requiring women to urinate off the side of a crane in lieu of restroom breaks, if true, would have had a significant discriminatory impact on women. Johnson v. AK Steel Corp., 2008 U.S. Dist. LEXIS 41573 (S.D. Ohio May 22, 2008).

Because evidence that a progressive-discipline policy asserted as a rationale for an employee's termination was not uniformly applied was evidence of pretext, the court found that the employee had satisfied the third prong of the McDonnell Douglas test by providing evidence that the employer's asserted legitimate reason was a mere pretext for discrimination, in violation of 42 U.S.C.S. § 2000e et seq. Lamer v. Metaldyne Co. LLC, 240 Fed. Appx. 22, 2007 FED App. 0435N, 2007 U.S. App. LEXIS 15274 (6th Cir. Ohio 2007).

**Evidence insufficient**

Relocation of a professor's office space to a different building as a faculty member of a college was not direct evidence of discrimination. Jiashin Wu v. Northeast Ohio Med. Univ., 2019-Ohio-2530, 140 N.E.3d 100, 2019 Ohio App. LEXIS 2635 (Ohio Ct. App., Franklin County 2019).

Finding against a university employee was proper because he failed to prove that the reasons given for not hiring him were false, and that age discrimination was the real reason for not hiring him. Rather, the greater weight of the evidence shows that the university followed the standard hiring process with regard to the reorganized positions and that the employee was considered on his merits, along with his past performance in his prior duties at the university. Russell v. Cleveland State Univ., 2015 Ohio Misc. LEXIS 159 (Ohio Ct. Cl. Sept. 17, 2015).

Finding against the university employees was proper because, although the employees asserted that the university engaged in a pattern and practice of making employment decisions on the basis of age, an adverse effect on a single employee, or even a few employees, was not sufficient to establish disparate impact. Russell v. Cleveland State Univ., 2015 Ohio Misc. LEXIS 159 (Ohio Ct. Cl. Sept. 17, 2015).

**Exhaustion of state remedies**

A claimant under the federal age discrimination act must first exhaust his state administrative remedies: Colina v. McGraw Constr. Co., 69 Ohio App. 3d 422, 590 N.E.2d 1308, 1990 Ohio App. LEXIS 4059 (Ohio Ct. App., Butler County 1990).

**Failure to follow directions**

Failure to follow directions is a legitimate reason for discharge: Allen v. Totes/Isotoner Corp., 2009-Ohio-4231, 123 Ohio St. 3d 216, 915 N.E.2d 622, 2009 Ohio LEXIS 2284 (Ohio 2009).

**Failure to promote**

Defendant was entitled to summary judgment on the plaintiff's claim that the defendant failed to promote him based on his race because the record established that the defendant repeatedly promoted the plaintiff, and as to the five promotions denied the plaintiff, the defendant awarded two of those positions, one of which would be a lateral move for the plaintiff, to minority males. Moreover, the defendant established that it selected candidates who were more qualified than the plaintiff or who performed better during interviews; accordingly, the record established that the defendant selected other applicants for those positions for legitimate, nondiscriminatory reasons. Rush v. E.I.duPont De Nemours & Co., 911 F. Supp. 2d 545, 2012 U.S. Dist. LEXIS 166356 (S.D. Ohio 2012).

Where an employee at a residential care facility alleged reverse gender discrimination relating to employment opportunities, the claim survived summary judgment because a genuine issue of material fact existed regarding whether the employee was qualified for a position and whether the employee refused, or was even asked, to take a computer proficiency test. Turner v. Grande Pointe Healthcare Cmty., 631 F. Supp. 2d 896, 2007 U.S. Dist. LEXIS 66711 (N.D. Ohio 2007).

Employer was entitled to summary judgment on an employee's claim that a failure to promote her was due to sex discrimination in violation of R.C. 4112.02 because the employee was not qualified for the position and required more training than the male worker who was offered the position. Johnson v. Ohio Valley Elec. Corp., 2002 U.S. Dist. LEXIS 26493 (S.D. Ohio Mar. 26, 2002).



**Failure to state a claim**

Where plaintiff was terminated for using vulgar language in the workplace, she failed to establish a prima facie case of sex discrimination in violation of R.C. 4112.02 because she did not establish that she was treated more harshly than similarly-situated male employees or that she was replaced by a male employee. Plaintiff presented no direct evidence that defendant was motivated by discriminatory intent. Eschborn v. Ohio DOT, 2019-Ohio-1753, 2019 Ohio Misc. LEXIS 145 (Ohio Ct. Cl. 2019).

Former employee's reverse discrimination complaint warranted dismissal because he failed to satisfy the McDonnell Douglas elements, as the complaint lacked operative facts to support an inference of discriminatory intent because he did not allege that the employer unlawfully considered his race when it refused his scheduling requests, disciplined him, or terminated him. Martin v. Block Communs., 2017-Ohio-1474, 2017 Ohio App. LEXIS 1480 (Ohio Ct. App., Lucas County 2017).

Ohio Civil Rights Commission's claims against a resident of a multi-unit housing structure were properly dismissed for failure to state a claim, as allegations that the resident committed discriminatory conduct against a disabled neighbor were not within certain sections of the Ohio Fair Housing Act because those provisions were directed to the availability, not habitability, of the housing. Ohio Civ. Rights Comm'n v. Myers, 2014-Ohio-144, 2014 Ohio App. LEXIS 131 (Ohio Ct. App., Montgomery County 2014).

**Familial status**

Plaintiff was not entitled to partial summary judgment as to defendant's liability under the Fair Housing Act, 42 U.S.C.S. § 3604(c), and under R.C. 4112.02(H) because the three rental advertisements at issue were not facially discriminatory on the basis of familial status under 42 U.S.C.S. § 3602(k) and sex as they contained no express preferences or limitations, and thus, they did not constitute per se violations of § 3604(c), and genuine issues of material fact remained as to whether an ordinary reader would find that the three advertisements suggested that a person in a particular class was preferred or disfavored for the housing in question. Miami Valley Fair Hous. Ctr., Inc. v. Connor Group, 805 F. Supp. 2d 396, 2011 U.S. Dist. LEXIS 81896 (S.D. Ohio 2011).

Employer was properly granted summary judgment in an employee's wrongful termination suit, where: (1) discrimination based on status as a parent was not actionable under R.C. 4112.02, even under the sex-plus rationale; (2) the employee failed to demonstrate that comparable, non-protected persons were treated more favorably or that her termination for scheduling conflicts was merely pretextual; and (3) the employee was unable to show that she was discriminated against solely because of her gender. Mustard v. Timothy J. O'Reilly Co., 2004-Ohio-425, 2004 Ohio App. LEXIS 387 (Ohio Ct. App., Warren County 2004).

The civil rights commission was not liable for pursuing a charge of housing discrimination based on familial status where the lease provided a reasonable basis for the charge: Tomsu v. Ohio Civ. Rights Comm'n, 116 Ohio Misc. 2d 24, 764 N.E.2d 516, 2001 Ohio Misc. LEXIS 32 (Ohio C.P. 2001).

**Federal preemption**

Employee's disability discrimination and retaliation claims under R.C. 4112.02 were not completely preempted by the Labor Management Relations Act, 29 U.S.C.S. § 185(a), because the complaint asserted exclusively state law claims and did not invoke rights or procedures under a collective bargaining agreement (CBA); the employer's invocation of the CBA's terms as a defense was insufficient to trigger preemption, and the claims were only tangentially related to the terms of the CBA. Paul v. Kaiser Found. Health Plan of Ohio, 701 F.3d 514, 2012 FED App. 0404P, 2012 U.S. App. LEXIS 25247 (6th Cir. Ohio 2012).

Employee's disability discrimination claim under R.C. 4112.02 was preempted by the Railway Labor Act, 45 U.S.C.S. § 151 et seq., because proof of the employee's disability claim required an interpretation of the applicable collective bargaining agreements (CBA). The employee's theory of disability discrimination was that the union's general chairman and the employer's director of labor relations incorrectly interpreted the applicable CBAs; accordingly, the employee's success on his disability claim was contingent on an interpretation of the CBAs favored by the employee. Emswiler v. CSX Transp., Inc., 2011 U.S. Dist. LEXIS 60505 (S.D. Ohio Apr. 27, 2011), aff'd, 691 F.3d 782, 2012 FED App. 0223P, 2012 U.S. App. LEXIS 14884 (6th Cir. Ohio 2012).

Action was properly remanded because (1) ERISA did not preempt plaintiff's age discrimination claim pursuant to 29 U.S.C.S. § 1144(a) because plaintiff maintained that he was not seeking to recover benefits due to him under the terms of his plan, to enforce his rights under the terms of the plan, or to clarify his rights to future benefits under the terms of the plan pursuant to 29 U.S.C.S. § 1132(a)(1)(B), and it was not clear from the complaint whether plaintiff was attempting to vindicate his rights under 29 U.S.C.S. § 1140 or whether he was simply including a loss of benefits under an ERISA-based plan as part of his damages; and (2) the court did not have diversity jurisdiction under 28 U.S.C.S. § 1441(b) because defendants failed to establish that non-diverse defendants were fraudulently joined as Ohio law recognized a claim for aiding and abetting discrimination pursuant to R.C. 4112.02(J), so it was not clear that there could be no recovery under the law of the state on the cause alleged or on the facts in view of the law. Crase v. Shasta Bevs., Inc., 2011 U.S. Dist. LEXIS 1926 (S.D. Ohio Jan. 10, 2011).

Doctrine of federal preemption under U.S. Const. art. VI, cl. 2 did not preclude an employee's state law claim under R.C. 4112.02, alleging disability discrimination arising from his termination of employment at a nuclear power plant, as the claim did not deal with radiological hazards and safety considerations pursuant to 42 U.S.C.S. § 2021(k), the state law being relied upon did not directly and substantially impact the federal laws, and there was no express or implied intent by Congress to have preempted the field to the extent of precluding such a claim. Minshall v. Cleveland Illuminating Co., 2006-Ohio-2241, 2006 Ohio App. LEXIS 2095 (Ohio Ct. App., Lake County 2006).

None of the elements necessary to establish a hostile working environment claim in Ohio were remotely covered by the provisions of the collective bargaining agreement. Consequently, the claim was not preempted by the Labor Management Relations Act (LMRA): Dalton v. Jefferson Smurfit Corp. (U.S.), 979 F. Supp. 1187, 1997 U.S. Dist. LEXIS 15506 (S.D. Ohio 1997).

The federal reserve act does not preempt state employment discrimination claims against federal reserve banks: White v. Federal Reserve Bank, 103 Ohio App. 3d 534, 660 N.E.2d 493, 1995 Ohio App. LEXIS 1720 (Ohio Ct. App., Cuyahoga County), dismissed, 74 Ohio St. 3d 1416, 655 N.E.2d 737, 1995 Ohio LEXIS 2742 (Ohio 1995).

The Labor Management Relations Act did not preempt a handicap discrimination claim under R.C. 4112.02 where the collective bargaining agreement does not establish safety requirements or "essential job functions" applicable to plaintiff's position: DiPuccio v. United Parcel Serv., 890 F. Supp. 688, 1995 U.S. Dist. LEXIS 14791 (N.D. Ohio 1995).

**Gender discrimination**

In an action claiming race, gender, and gender identity discrimination, because the employee's claims under Ohio Rev. Code Ann. § 4117.17 were sufficiently pled, she could also bring claims under this statute that the employer paid her less than male counterparts because of her gender, and because she did not conform to male gender stereotype. Cummings v. Greater Cleveland Reg'l Transit Auth., 88 F. Supp. 3d 812, 2015 U.S. Dist. LEXIS 10569 (N.D. Ohio 2015), dismissed, 2018 U.S. Dist. LEXIS 7475 (N.D. Ohio Jan. 17, 2018).

Trial court did not err in granting a directed verdict in favor of the village because, even if it had been assumed that the former mayor was an "employee" for the purpose of her gender discrimination claim, she failed to show that she was replaced by, or her discharge permitted the retention of, a person of comparable qualifications outside the protected class, i.e. a male, as required. Mender v. Vill. of Chauncey, 2015-Ohio-4105, 41 N.E.3d 1289, 2015 Ohio App. LEXIS 3933 (Ohio Ct. App., Athens County 2015).

Applicant's hybrid sex-plus-age claim based on failure to hire failed because affidavits from interview panel members stated that they did not believe the applicant was one of the most qualified candidates for the position based on how the applicant conducted herself during the interview, and the applicant did not show pretext since the applicant could not prove that the applicant's qualifications rendered the applicant plainly superior to the comparators, and the subjective nature of the decision did not create a question of fact. Thompson v. City of Columbus, 2014 U.S. Dist. LEXIS 63119 (S.D. Ohio May 7, 2014).

Trial court did not err in dismissing the employee's gender discrimination claim under R.C. 4112.02(A) as the employee had not presented indirect evidence of discrimination; instead, the evidence showed that the employee was treated more favorably than males in the work place as she was not terminated even though she failed to pass required tests for over a year, and her request for further training was accommodated. Pitts-Baad v. Valvoline Instant Oil Change, 2012-Ohio-4811, 2012 Ohio App. LEXIS 4227 (Ohio Ct. App., Stark County 2012).

Trial court did not err in dismissing the employee's gender discrimination claim under R.C. 4112.02(A) as the employee had not established gender discrimination either by direct evidence or by indirect evidence. While the employee alleged gender discrimination by the employer's failure to accommodate her breastfeeding, there was no gender discrimination cause of action for an employer's failure to accommodate a breastfeeding employee. Pitts-Baad v. Valvoline Instant Oil Change, 2012-Ohio-4811, 2012 Ohio App. LEXIS 4227 (Ohio Ct. App., Stark County 2012).

Trial court did not err in dismissing the employee's gender discrimination claim under R.C. 4112.02(A) as the employee had not established gender discrimination either by direct evidence or by indirect evidence. While the employee alleged that a manager refused to order her new uniform pants when she was pregnant, this did not constitute direct evidence of gender discrimination as the employee's own testimony revealed that there was no evidence that the employer's initial refusal to buy her another pair of pants was motivated by the employee's gender. Pitts-Baad v. Valvoline Instant Oil Change, 2012-Ohio-4811, 2012 Ohio App. LEXIS 4227 (Ohio Ct. App., Stark County 2012).

Although the employee established an indirect evidence prima facie case, the employer presented a legitimate, nondiscriminatory basis for the employee's termination by asserting that the employee failed to meet her sales goals for 2007, 2008, and 2009, and had an awful start to 2010. The employee failed to demonstrate that the employer's stated reason for her termination had no basis in fact and was actually a pretext for gender discrimination where the employee admitted at deposition that she failed to meet her sales goals in 2007, 2008, and 2009, and it was undisputed that the employee received progressive discipline in the form of warnings and that she was terminated following her failure to meet the expectations issued in the final warning. Radzanowski v. Principal Fin. Group, 2012 U.S. Dist. LEXIS 38148 (N.D. Ohio Mar. 21, 2012).

Employer was entitled to summary judgment on the employee's claim of gender discrimination under 42 U.S.C.S. § 2000e-2 and R.C. 4112.02 because the employee was a male and therefore was not a member of any category protected by Title VII of the Civil Rights Act of 1964, and the employee failed to present any evidence which supported a suspicion that the employer was the rare employer who discriminated against the majority. Nilles v. Givaudan Flavors Corp., 2012 U.S. Dist. LEXIS 60551 (S.D. Ohio May 1, 2012), aff'd, 521 Fed. Appx. 364, 2013 FED App. 0314N, 2013 U.S. App. LEXIS 6416 (6th Cir. Ohio 2013).

Female employee did not establish a prima facie case of gender discrimination under R.C. 4112.02(A) where she failed to present evidence that she suffered an adverse employment action. To the extent that the employee claimed that her former employer's business-casual dress requirement constituted an adverse employment action, such a claim would fail because the employee was aware of the dress code when she previously accepted an administrative assistant position. Veal v. Upreach LLC, 2011-Ohio-5406, 2011 Ohio App. LEXIS 4415 (Ohio Ct. App., Franklin County 2011).

Employee's gender discrimination claim was properly dismissed because the employee did not show that the employee was treated less favorably than similarly situated coworkers who were not members of the employee's protected class, as (1) the employee's job was not unique, since a coworker who was a member of the employee's protected class performed the same job at another location, and (2) coworkers who were not members of the employee's protected class with whom the employee compared herself were not similarly situated, as they performed different jobs and/or had different supervisors, nor was it shown that the coworkers were treated differently than the employee for the same or similar conduct. Putney v. Contract Bldg. Components, 2009-Ohio-6718, 2009 Ohio App. LEXIS 5634 (Ohio Ct. App., Union County 2009).

In a reverse gender discrimination case, a manager's hiring procedures, although inconsistent with some of the employer's guidelines, were not corrupted by gender discrimination because legitimate, non-discriminatory reasons existed for hiring the successful applicant as she had 13 years of experience, counseling experience, was a manager at a halfway house, and had a positive attitude. Bogdas v. Ohio Dep't of Rehab. & Corr., 2009-Ohio-6327, 2009 Ohio App. LEXIS 5307 (Ohio Ct. App., Franklin County 2009).

Former employee failed to show that she was terminated due to her gender because she did not provide any evidence of any similarly situated male employees, who had the same tardiness issues and a "needs improvement" evaluation during the first three months of employment. Trout v. FirstEnergy Generation Corp., 339 Fed. Appx. 560, 2009 FED App. 0524N, 2009 U.S. App. LEXIS 16954 (6th Cir. Ohio 2009).

Summary judgment on employee's claims brought under Equal Pay Act (EPA), 29 U.S.C.S. § 206 (d)(1), and R.C. 4111.17, 4112.02 and 4112.99 was denied because although a comparison of the work performed by the employee to the work performed by the male co-workers, during the relevant time-period, led the court to conclude that the employee's positions did not require equal effort and responsibility, the court was unable to conclude that the evidence presented by the employee was such that a reasonable jury could not return a verdict for the employee. Gonzalez v. Abercrombie & Fitch Co., 2008 U.S. Dist. LEXIS 52171 (S.D. Ohio July 7, 2008).

Trial court erred in granting summary judgment to a probate court and a presiding probate court judge in an action by a probate court magistrate, alleging a claim of wage-based sex discrimination under R.C. 4112.02(A) of the Ohio Civil Rights Act, R.C. Chapter 4112, as genuine issues of material fact existed regarding whether the magistrate established a prima facie case of discrimination based on direct evidence that consisted of comments made by the judge during a meeting regarding the wage disparity between male and female magistrates; a genuine issue of material fact also precluded summary judgment with respect to whether there was adequate proof to rebut the alleged discrimination showing. Birch v. Cuyahoga County Probate Court, 2007-Ohio-6189, 173 Ohio App. 3d 696, 880 N.E.2d 132, 2007 Ohio App. LEXIS 5436 (Ohio Ct. App., Cuyahoga County 2007).

Trial court's grant of summary judgment to county parks and others in a parks employee's gender discrimination action under R.C. 4112.02(A) was proper, as the employee's claims that she was not promoted due to such discrimination were not supported by the evidence; in one instance where she sought a promotion, no one was hired for the job due to lack of sufficient qualifications, and in another instance, the person who was hired was a more qualified male candidate and the employee failed to show that such reasoning was merely pretextual. Fox v. Lorain County, 2007-Ohio-6143, 2007 Ohio App. LEXIS 5412 (Ohio Ct. App., Lorain County 2007).

Where an employee at a residential care facility alleged reverse gender discrimination relating to unequal pay, the claim failed because the employer met its burden of proof on an affirmative defense since the employer's interest in controlling attrition was a factor other than sex, and the employee could not show that the employer's affirmative defense was pretext. Turner v. Grande Pointe Healthcare Cmty., 631 F. Supp. 2d 896, 2007 U.S. Dist. LEXIS 66711 (N.D. Ohio 2007).

Male nurse could not support his claim of sex discrimination because the female nurse who engaged in similar conduct as the male nurse but, unlike the male nurse, retained her job, was not similarly situated as the male nurse presented no evidence that the female nurse had a similar pattern of reprimands comparable to the male nurse's own record. Moreover, the hospital presented undisputed evidence concerning legitimate reasons for the male nurse's termination. Clark v. Christ Hosp., 2007-Ohio-4317, 2007 Ohio App. LEXIS 3864 (Ohio Ct. App., Hamilton County 2007).

Police officer's claims of pregnancy discrimination under Title VII, 42 U.S.C.S. §§ 2000e-2(a)(1), 2000e(k), and R.C. 4112.02(A), 4112.99 need not have also been evaluated as sex discrimination claims where her complaint, which contained two counts, each alleging "pregnancy discrimination, a form of sex discrimination," did not allege sex discrimination apart from pregnancy discrimination; the officer's allegations regarding the city police department's refusal to grant her a position in a detective bureau or a position processing impound lot vehicles were included as support for her claims that the department wrongfully failed to accommodate her pregnancy, not to substantiate separate sex discrimination claims. Moreover, the claims would not be evaluated under separate standards, and, the merits of such claims were fatally undercut by the officer's acknowledgement that the opening she applied for was really not an opening. Tysinger v. Police Dep't, 463 F.3d 569, 2006 FED App. 0363P, 2006 U.S. App. LEXIS 24144 (6th Cir. Ohio 2006).

In an action in which a former employee filed suit against defendants, former employer, union, and a counselor for the employee assistance program, alleging claims of sex discrimination in violation of Title VII of the Civil Rights Act of 1964, 42 U.S.C.S. § 2000e et seq., and R.C. 4112.02, defendants were granted summary judgment where the employee had not shown that any of the "comparables" were fired for gross misconduct or that they had similar workmanship histories. Jaques v. Herbert, 447 F. Supp. 2d 858, 2006 U.S. Dist. LEXIS 59655 (N.D. Ohio 2006).

Court could not say as a matter of law that a former employer did not discriminate against a former employee on the basis of her gender in violation of 42 U.S.C.S. § 2000e-2 and R.C. 4112.02, even though the employee could not provide direct evidence of the alleged discrimination, because she adduced evidence that a male co-worker in the same position was paid more, received her referrals, was career-coached by their supervisors, and generally favored over her and because several questions of fact existed as to the employer's claim that it terminated the employee merely because it was planning to exit the market and close its department. Klaus

v. Hilb, Rogal & Hamilton Co. of Ohio, 437 F. Supp. 2d 706, 2006 U.S. Dist. LEXIS 46619 (S.D. Ohio 2006).

Employee could not maintain her action for sex discrimination in violation of Title VII of the Civil Rights Act of 1964, 42 U.S.C.S. § 2000e-2, and R.C. 4112.02 when she was not promoted and her position was not reclassified as other positions were because she had not applied for the promotion, similarly situated men were not treated differently, and there was no evidence that the employer's decision not to reclassify her position was a pretext for sexual discrimination. Johannes v. Monday Cmty. Corr. Inst., 434 F. Supp. 2d 509, 2006 U.S. Dist. LEXIS 43220 (S.D. Ohio 2006).

In an action in which a former employee filed suit against her former employer alleging violations of the Age Discrimination in Employment Act, 29 U.S.C.S. § 621 et seq., Title VII of the Civil Rights Act of 1964, and R.C. 4112, the employer was denied summary judgment on the age and gender discrimination claims; there were disputed issues of fact as to whether the employee was performing at a level comparable to or higher than her male and/or younger counterparts and whether employees outside of the protected classes with performance problems similar to the employee's alleged performance issues were treated more favorably and were not terminated. Hicks v. Novartis Pharms. Corp., 457 F. Supp. 2d 814, 2005 U.S. Dist. LEXIS 26495 (S.D. Ohio 2005).

In an action in which former employees filed suit against their former employer alleging that the employer fired them because of their gender in violation of 42 U.S.C.S. § 2000e et seq., R.C. 4112, the employe's motion for summary judgment was denied where (1) the employees were qualified for their jobs as both employees received favorable evaluations and were promoted twice; and (2) a genuine issue of material fact existed as to who participated in the decision to terminate the employees. Buckley v. Dollar Gen. Corp., 2005 U.S. Dist. LEXIS 25344 (S.D. Ohio Oct. 21, 2005).

Employee's sex discrimination claim failed because the employee, who was replaced by another female, could not establish a prima facie case. Zelnik v. CB Richard Ellis, Inc., 2005 U.S. Dist. LEXIS 19611 (S.D. Ohio Sept. 9, 2005).

Summary judgment was properly granted, dismissing a deputy's gender discrimination claim against a sheriff's department, because, while the deputy was similarly situated to two of the male employees involved in the same criminal investigation in which the deputy was involved relating to the falsification of reports, the deputy was not treated differently from the two men for the same conduct, in that the deputy was placed on administrative leave when she failed to obey an order from her superiors, and while the two male employees were never accused of disobeying an order, the department placed them on administrative leave after they were indicted. Further, even if the deputy had established a prima facie case of disparate treatment, the department provided a legitimate, nondiscriminatory reason for the disparate treatment, the desire to rid the department of all of the employees who participated in corrupt activities. Noday v. Mahoning County Sheriff's Dep't, 2005-Ohio-4682, 2005 Ohio App. LEXIS 4281 (Ohio Ct. App., Mahoning County 2005).

Where a female jail corrections officer was discharged in part for allegedly refusing to turn over a tape recorder used to record conversations at the jail, and the officer alleged that male co-workers were not asked to turn over their recorders, the officer was unable to show that the discharge was based on gender discrimination; although it appeared that the male co-workers were treated more favorably in not being asked to turn over their recorders, the discharge was based on the officer's insubordinate refusal to turn over her recorder and the co-workers were not shown to have engaged in similar insubordination. Hendricks v. Office of the Clermont County Sheriff, 415 F. Supp. 2d 782, 2005 U.S. Dist. LEXIS 13017 (S.D. Ohio 2005).

Where a female jail corrections officer was discharged in part for allegedly failing to come forward with information concerning an alleged rape of a jail inmate, the officer was unable to show that the discharge was based on gender discrimination since the amnesty offered to co-workers for previous failures to come forward with similar information was directed to both male and female co-workers. Hendricks v. Office of the Clermont County Sheriff, 415 F. Supp. 2d 782, 2005 U.S. Dist. LEXIS 13017 (S.D. Ohio 2005).

When a former employee sued her former employer for gender discrimination, under R.C. 4112.02(A), it was unnecessary to decide if she proved a prima facie case of discrimination because, after she applied to the employer for a truck-driving job, shortly before taking maternity leave, she effectively withdrew the application by announcing to her former co-workers that she did not intend to return to work, and, when she later inquired about a driving job, she was ineligible for it due to multiple moving violations and a suspension of her driving privilege. Yoho-Smith v. Santmyer Oil Co., 2005-Ohio-3295, 2005 Ohio App. LEXIS 3077 (Ohio Ct. App., Wayne County 2005).

**—Generally**

In a gender discrimination action, the employer was properly granted summary judgment because the female employee failed to establish a prima facie case, as she was replaced by a woman and she failed to show that employees outside the protected class were treated better. Brogan v. Family Video Movie Club, Inc., 2015-Ohio-70, 2015 Ohio App. LEXIS 66 (Ohio Ct. App., Lucas County 2015).

Employer was entitled to summary judgment on the employee's claims of race and gender discrimination under Title VII and R.C. 4112.02 because there was no evidence that the director was aware of another employee who submitted false mileage reports but did nothing about it. With respect to the vacation requests, although the employee claimed that a jury could infer the denial of her vacation request was racially motivated, the employee could not explain why the director approved the seven other vacation requests the employee made in 2009, if the denial of the most recent request was somehow racially motivated; further, there was no evidence of a comparable administrator who requested leave for the critical weeks leading up to the school year, and in the past 10 years no certificated employee had ever been AWOL for 5 days without being terminated. Senu-Oke v. Dayton Pub. Schs, 2012 U.S. Dist. LEXIS 105428 (S.D. Ohio July 30, 2012).

Employer was not entitled to summary judgment on a claim of gender-based discrimination in salaries where the employee produced evidence of gender-related statements by the employer that created issues of fact: Birch v. Cuyahoga County Probate Court, 2007-Ohio-6189, 173 Ohio App. 3d 696, 880 N.E.2d 132, 2007 Ohio App. LEXIS 5436 (Ohio Ct. App., Cuyahoga County 2007).

As a state employee failed to prove that persons who were treated more favorably than he was were similarly situated to him in all relevant respects, he failed to meet his burden of proof under R.C. 4112.02(A) for his sex discrimination claim, arising from his termination from employment; one of the other employees did not work for the same supervisor and the other did not engage in the same conduct as the employee. Swoger v. Wright State Univ., 2007-Ohio-2751, 2007 Ohio Misc. LEXIS 184 (Ohio Ct. Cl. 2007).

In an action in which a former employee filed suit against defendants, former employer, union, and a counselor for the employee assistance program, alleging claims of sex discrimination in violation of Title VII of the Civil Rights Act of 1964, 42 U.S.C.S. § 2000e et seq., and R.C. 4112.02, defendants were granted summary judgment where the employee had not shown that any of the "comparables" were fired for gross misconduct or that they had similar workmanship histories. Jaques v. Herbert, 447 F. Supp. 2d 858, 2006 U.S. Dist. LEXIS 59655 (N.D. Ohio 2006).

Court could not say as a matter of law that a former employer did not discriminate against a former employee on the basis of her gender in violation of 42 U.S.C.S. § 2000e-2 and R.C. 4112.02, even though the employee could not provide direct evidence of the alleged discrimination, because she adduced evidence that a male co-worker in the same position was paid more, received her referrals, was career-coached by their supervisors, and generally favored over her and because several questions of fact existed as to the employer's claim that it terminated the employee merely because it was planning to exit the market and close its department. Klaus v. Hilb, Rogal & Hamilton Co. of Ohio, 437 F. Supp. 2d 706, 2006 U.S. Dist. LEXIS 46619 (S.D. Ohio 2006).

Employee could not maintain her action for sex discrimination in violation of Title VII of the Civil Rights Act of 1964, 42 U.S.C.S. § 2000e-2, and R.C. 4112.02 when she was not promoted and her position was not reclassified as other positions were because she had not applied for the promotion, similarly situated men were not treated differently, and there was no evidence that the employer's decision not to reclassify her position was a pretext for sexual discrimination. Johannes v. Monday Cmty. Corr. Inst., 434 F. Supp. 2d 509, 2006 U.S. Dist. LEXIS 43220 (S.D. Ohio 2006).

Reasonable jury could not find in a gender discrimination case that the isolated incident with the employer, embarrassing though it was for plaintiff, together with the employer's handling of the incident would have compelled a reasonable individual to resign her employment several months later. Helms v. Fischer Mgmt., 2005 U.S. Dist. LEXIS 27259 (S.D. Ohio Nov. 10, 2005).

Employer was denied summary judgment on the gender discrimination claim because there were disputed issues of fact as to whether the employee was performing at a level comparable to or higher than her male counterparts and whether employees outside of the protected classes with performance problems similar to the employee's alleged performance issues were treated more favorably and were not terminated. Hicks v. Novartis Pharms. Corp., 457 F. Supp. 2d 814, 2005 U.S. Dist. LEXIS 26495 (S.D. Ohio 2005).

Where a female jail corrections officer was discharged in part for allegedly spreading disparaging rumors about the jail's investigation of an alleged rape of an inmate, the officer was unable to show that the discharge was based on gender discrimination since co-workers who also spread similar rumors and were not disciplined included both male and female co-workers. Hendricks v. Office of the Clermont County Sheriff, 415 F. Supp. 2d 782, 2005 U.S. Dist. LEXIS 13017 (S.D. Ohio 2005).

Where a female jail corrections officer was discharged in part for allegedly refusing to turn over a tape recorder used to record conversations at the jail, and the officer alleged that male co-workers were not asked to turn over their recorders, the officer was unable to show that the discharge was based on gender discrimination; although it appeared that the male co-workers were treated more favorably in not being asked to turn over their recorders, the discharge was based on the officer's insubordinate refusal to turn over her recorder and the co-workers were not shown to have engaged in similar insubordination. Hendricks v. Office of the

Clermont County Sheriff, 415 F. Supp. 2d 782, 2005 U.S. Dist. LEXIS 13017 (S.D. Ohio 2005).

Where a female jail corrections officer was discharged in part for allegedly failing to come forward with information concerning an alleged rape of a jail inmate, the officer was unable to show that the discharge was based on gender discrimination since the amnesty offered to co-workers for previous failures to come forward with similar information was directed to both male and female co-workers. Hendricks v. Office of the Clermont County Sheriff, 415 F. Supp. 2d 782, 2005 U.S. Dist. LEXIS 13017 (S.D. Ohio 2005).

In an action in which former employees filed suit against their former employer alleging that the employer fired them because of their gender in violation of 42 U.S.C.S. § 2000e et seq., R.C. 4112, the employe's motion for summary judgment was denied where (1) the employees were qualified for their jobs as both employees received favorable evaluations and were promoted twice; and (2) a genuine issue of material fact existed as to who participated in the decision to terminate the employees. Buckley v. Dollar Gen. Corp., 2005 U.S. Dist. LEXIS 25344 (S.D. Ohio Oct. 21, 2005).

Employee's sex discrimination claim failed because the employee, who was replaced by another female, could not establish a prima facie case. Zelnik v. CB Richard Ellis, Inc., 2005 U.S. Dist. LEXIS 19611 (S.D. Ohio Sept. 9, 2005).

Employee failed to establish a prima facie case of gender discrimination: Knox v. Neaton Auto Prods. Mfg., 375 F.3d 451, 2004 FED App. 0218P, 2004 U.S. App. LEXIS 14171 (6th Cir. Ohio 2004).

Employer was entitled to summary judgment on a sex discrimination claim where it had a legitimate business reason for terminating the employee, a manager, because she failed to pay required overtime, and because the alleged conduct was merely offensive, but not actionable: Timbers v. Sears, Roebuck & Co., 2004-Ohio-3469, 2004 Ohio App. LEXIS 3129 (Ohio Ct. App., Cuyahoga County 2004).

Restrictions on breast-feeding do not amount to discrimination based on sex: Derungs v. Wal-Mart Stores, Inc., 374 F.3d 428, 2004 FED App. 0203P, 2004 U.S. App. LEXIS 13439 (6th Cir. Ohio 2004).

Court applied the appropriate standard of review to find that the Ohio Civil Rights Commission (OCRC) properly dismissed the worker's sex discrimination claim where she was not denied overtime or subject to a demotion based on her sex. Gammon v. Ohio Civil Rights Comm'n, 2003-Ohio-5418, 2003 Ohio App. LEXIS 4874 (Ohio Ct. App., Lucas County 2003).

Summary judgment was proper where the employee failed to show discrimination based on his sex as the evidence confirmed that management warned both the employee and his female companion that any further physical displays of affection would not be tolerated; it was the employee's physical displays of affection in the workplace that were inappropriate, not management's subsequent actions. Schwab v. Delphi Packard Elec. Sys., 2003-Ohio-4868, 2003 Ohio App. LEXIS 4387 (Ohio Ct. App., Trumbull County 2003).

Summary judgment on the issue of sexual and/or gender discrimination was appropriate where the employee failed to establish all the prima facie elements of a discrimination claim and the employer articulated legitimate, non-discriminatory reasons to terminate her employment, including numerous incidents regarding her conduct and dress. Daniels v. Vienna Twp. Bd. of Trs., 2003-Ohio-3877, 2003 Ohio App. LEXIS 3477 (Ohio Ct. App., Trumbull County 2003).

The employer was not entitled to a directed verdict in a gender discrimination case where the employee presented sufficient evidence that comparable male employees were "similarly situated" in all relevant respects: Kroh v. Cont'l Gen. Tire, Inc., 2001-Ohio-59, 92 Ohio St. 3d 30, 748 N.E.2d 36, 2001 Ohio LEXIS 1527 (Ohio 2001).

An employer may be found to have committed gender discrimination where male and female violators of a rule against employee fraternization are disciplined differently: Russell v. UPS, 110 Ohio App. 3d 95, 673 N.E.2d 659, 1996 Ohio App. LEXIS 1309 (Ohio Ct. App., Franklin County 1996).

Remarks at work based on sex stereotypes do not inevitably prove that gender played a part in a particular employment decision. A plaintiff must show that the employer actually relied on gender in making a decision: Wall v. Firelands Radiology, 106 Ohio App. 3d 313, 666 N.E.2d 235, 1995 Ohio App. LEXIS 3785 (Ohio Ct. App., Huron County 1995).

Where, in an action brought pursuant to R.C. Chapter 4112. challenging alleged facially discriminatory employment practices, the employer seeks to justify gender-specific hiring criteria on the basis that such criteria constitute a bona fide occupational qualification, the burden is upon the employer to prove (1) that the gender-based criteria involve the essence of the employer's business, and (2) either that (a) all or substantially all members of the gender excluded by the employer are incapable of performing the job safely and efficiently, or (b) it is impossible or impractical to make determinations of each applicant's qualifications in a nondiscriminatory manner: Little Forest Medical Center v. Ohio Civil Rights Com., 61 Ohio St. 3d 607, 575 N.E.2d 1164, 1991 Ohio LEXIS 2124 (Ohio 1991), cert. denied, 503 U.S. 906, 112 S. Ct. 1263, 117 L. Ed. 2d 491, 1992 U.S. LEXIS 1405 (U.S. 1992).

**—Direct evidence**

Employee failed to show gender discrimination under R.C. 4112.02(A) where reasonable minds could only conclude that the employer's brief references to her husband assisting the dental practice following the employee's termination were not direct evidence of gender discrimination. Grimsley v. Cain DDS, LLC, 2012-Ohio-5273, 2012 Ohio App. LEXIS 4613 (Ohio Ct. App., Stark County 2012).

**—Hostile work environment**

Trial court did not err in granting summary judgment as to the sexual harassment claim because the former employee failed to meet her burden of establishing the existence of a genuine issue of material fact as to the essential condition of a sexual harassment case, i.e., harassment because of sex. There was no evidence as to how the mandatory use of the unisex locker room discriminated against her based on her gender and, instead, the testimony established that the locker room policy did not single out either gender as it applied to all medical personnel, male and female. Messer v. Summa Health Sys., 2018-Ohio-372, 105 N.E.3d 550, 2018 Ohio App. LEXIS 378 (Ohio Ct. App., Summit County 2018).

Employee failed to prove the existence of a hostile work environment because, while the employee was a member of a protected class, there was no indication the employee personally observed or encountered written or verbal racial slurs and no evidence that any rude treatment by supervisors, if such truly occurred, was based on the employee's race. English v. AK Steel Corp., 2016-Ohio-5287, 2016 Ohio App. LEXIS 3136 (Ohio Ct. App., Butler County 2016).

**—Insurance**

Trial court properly dismissed an employee's action against the State Teachers Retirement System because the employee failed to state a claim under the statute; the statute makes several discriminatory practices unlawful, but it does not bar the denial or limitation of health insurance coverage because of a person's race, color, religion, sex, military status, national origin, disability, age, or ancestry. Orders v. State Teachers Ret. Sys. of Ohio, 2016-Ohio-3345, 2016 Ohio App. LEXIS 2202 (Ohio Ct. App., Franklin County 2016).

**—Not shown**

Former employee had not made out a prima facie case of gender discrimination based on her suspension because she failed to identify a similarly-situated male who was treated differently, and, whether deserved or not, there was no proof that the suspension was based on the employee's gender. Even if the employee had made out a prima facie case, she had not shown that the Board of County Commissioners' reason for suspending her had no basis in fact, was not the actual reason, or was insufficient to explain the Board's action. Moody v. Ohio Dep't of Mental Health & Addiction Servs., 2021-Ohio-4578, 183 N.E.3d 21, 2021 Ohio App. LEXIS 4503 (Ohio Ct. App., Franklin County 2021).

Plaintiff failed to meet her prima facie case for gender discrimination, because she failed to demonstrate that male employees were treated differently than the females employees for cell phone usage. Therefore, the trial court did not err by granting the employer's motion for summary judgment. Khalia Ra v. Swagelok Mfg. Co., L.L.C., 2021-Ohio-1657, 2021 Ohio App. LEXIS 1621 (Ohio Ct. App., Cuyahoga County 2021).

Trial court did not err in granting the employer's motion for summary judgment because the employee failed to demonstrate that she was treated less favorably than her male coworkers after engaging in the same type of conduct and, in the absence of such a showing, she could not establish a prima facie case for gender discrimination. Further, the employer was able to produce evidence of legitimate, nondiscriminatory reasons for her termination and the employee was not able to demonstrate that the nondiscriminatory reasons for her termination were pretextual by producing evidence that they either were factually untrue or were insufficient grounds for her discharge. Nance v. Lima Auto Mall, Inc., 2020-Ohio-3419, 2020 Ohio App. LEXIS 2352 (Ohio Ct. App., Allen County 2020).

In plaintiff's complaint alleging age and gender discrimination against her employer and other employees, because there was no evidence that two other employees were involved in the decision to terminate plaintiff under the reduction in force, and her belief that a third employee's selection of plaintiff for termination was influenced by other employees was unsupported by evidence, liability against them could not attach to those employees under this statute. Witzigreuter v. Cent. Hosp. Servs., 2020-Ohio-5088, 2020 Ohio App. LEXIS 3930 (Ohio Ct. App., Cuyahoga County 2020).

Where a city and a foreman moved for summary judgment as to an employee's retaliation claim, because the employee had not established that he engaged in protected activity, his retaliation claim failed. Laughlin v. City of Cleveland, 102 F. Supp. 3d 944, 2015 U.S. Dist. LEXIS 45284 (N.D. Ohio), aff'd, 633 Fed. Appx. 312, 2015 FED App. 0800N, 2015 U.S. App. LEXIS 21468 (6th Cir. Ohio 2015).

Where a city and a foreman moved for summary judgment as to an employee's retaliation claim, evidence supported the position of the foreman and the city that even if the employee engaged in protected activity by complaining about discrimination, it was not the reason he was given bad reviews or fired; the evidence did not permit the inference that impermissible retaliation was the sole motivating factor in the city's decision to fire the employee. Laughlin v. City of Cleveland, 102 F. Supp. 3d 944, 2015 U.S.

Dist. LEXIS 45284 (N.D. Ohio), aff'd, 633 Fed. Appx. 312, 2015 FED App. 0800N, 2015 U.S. App. LEXIS 21468 (6th Cir. Ohio 2015).

**—Other discriminatory acts**

Because the employee only pled termination as the manner in which the terms, conditions, or privileges of employment was affected, it was proper for the employer to move for summary judgment and the trial court to decide gender discrimination based upon termination and not the other alleged discriminatory acts. Lehmier v. W. Reserve Chem. Corp., 2018-Ohio-3351, 2018 Ohio App. LEXIS 3623 (Ohio Ct. App., Summit County 2018).

**—Pregnancy discrimination**

Reliable, probative, and substantial evidence supported the administrative law judge's finding of discrimination based on pregnancy because the evidence, including the proximity of the employee's termination to her announcement that she was pregnant, the fact that the employer began treating the employee differently once the pregnancy was announced, and statements made by the employer to others indicated she intended to fire the employee due to her pregnancy, showed that the employer's proffered reason for the employee's termination was pretext. Hambuechen v. 221 Mkt. North, Inc., 2016-Ohio-3156, 66 N.E.3d 70, 2016 Ohio App. LEXIS 1992 (Ohio Ct. App., Stark County 2016).

**—Pretext**

Trial court did not err in granting the employer's summary judgment on the gender discrimination claim. The employee failed to put forth evidence creating a genuine issue of material fact that she was terminated based upon her gender because she failed to create a genuine issue of material fact that the employer's proffered reason for her termination was pretext. Lehmier v. W. Reserve Chem. Corp., 2018-Ohio-3351, 2018 Ohio App. LEXIS 3623 (Ohio Ct. App., Summit County 2018).

**—Punitive damages**

District court held that the former employee adduced sufficient evidence of actual malice at trial because her evidence suggested that the employer relied upon acceptable or routinely tolerated behavior to support its decision to terminate her employment, and this decision came within weeks of her written report of alleged sexual harassment. The court agreed with the district court that such evidence provided sufficient basis on which the jury could find, by clear and convincing evidence, that the employer acted with actual malice when it terminated the employee's employment. Braun v. Ultimate Jetcharters, LLC, 828 F.3d 501, 2016 FED App. 0159P, 2016 U.S. App. LEXIS 12559 (6th Cir. Ohio 2016).

**—Qualified for position**

In an action for gender discrimination, the record supported the employer's argument that the employee was not qualified for the position of police officer at the completion of the Police Training Officer (PTO) program, as the employee's performance during the PTO program showed that she did not meet the employer's legitimate expectations of a police officer. McGuire v. City of Newark, 2020-Ohio-4226, 2020 Ohio App. LEXIS 3114 (Ohio Ct. App., Licking County 2020).

**—Reverse discrimination**

Where plaintiff, a male employee of a hospital, was forced to resigned after having sexual contact with a female co-worker who was not terminated, the trial court erred in granting summary judgment to the employer on the sexual discrimination claim because there was a clear disparity of treatment between plaintiff and a female employee. Caiazza v. Mercy Med. Ctr., 2014-Ohio-2290, 2014 Ohio App. LEXIS 2232 (Ohio Ct. App., Stark County 2014).

Where a 50-year old male, working as a newspaper music critic, alleged age and gender discrimination under R.C. 4112.02, the newspaper was denied summary judgment because there was a material question of disputed fact as to whether the male was replaced by a female who was outside of the protected age group, and there was evidence that the employer sought to achieve its goal of appealing to younger, female readers by replacing plaintiff with a young, female columnist. Nager v. The Cincinnati Enquirer, 2005 U.S. Dist. LEXIS 22770 (S.D. Ohio Oct. 6, 2005).

**—Similarly situated**

As to sex discrimination, the evidence did not suffice to eliminate any genuine dispute of material fact regarding whether plaintiff was similarly situated to one or more of three male comparators identified in her complaint, as each was disciplined at least once for a "Group 2" violation, yet plaintiff received a significantly more severe sanction for her first Group 2 violation than they received for their first Group 2 violations. Saunders v. Greater Dayton Reg'l Transit Auth., 2021-Ohio-3052, 2021 Ohio App. LEXIS 2990 (Ohio Ct. App., Montgomery County 2021).

As to sex discrimination, the evidence did not suffice to eliminate any genuine dispute of material fact regarding whether plaintiff was similarly situated to one or more of three male comparators identified in her complaint, as each was disciplined at least once for a "Group 2" violation, yet plaintiff received a significantly more severe sanction for her first Group 2 violation than they received for their first Group 2 violations. Saunders v. Greater Dayton Reg'l Transit Auth., 2021-Ohio-3052, 2021 Ohio App. LEXIS 2990 (Ohio Ct. App., Montgomery County 2021).

Plaintiff's complaint alleging age and gender discrimination against her employer and other employees failed because she did not present evidence that she was treated less favorably than a younger, male employee during the reduction in force as she and the co-worker's jobs were not nearly identical and reasonable minds could not view them as similarly situated; the titles for their positions reflected a director-level position and a manager-level position; the imbalance in their salaries supported a conclusion that they held different roles from one another; and plaintiff did not introduce any evidence that her skill set was more beneficial to the employer. Witzigreuter v. Cent. Hosp. Servs., 2020-Ohio-5088, 2020 Ohio App. LEXIS 3930 (Ohio Ct. App., Cuyahoga County 2020).

In a gender discrimination action by two terminated part-time EMTs, the trial court did not err in finding that the EMTs failed to demonstrate "relevant similarity" to another employee in order to establish a prima facie case; because a paramedic was a full-time paramedic licensed in Ohio and West Virginia and a union member, he was not a similarly-situated male employee. Gast v. City of Martins Ferry, 2019-Ohio-1147, 129 N.E.3d 507, 2019 Ohio App. LEXIS 1245 (Ohio Ct. App., Belmont County 2019).

Where an employee was terminated for repeatedly failing to timely arrive to work and to properly punch the time card, the employee's sex and age discrimination claims failed because the comparators were not similarly situated, and the employee did not show pretext since the employee failed to punch the time card six times in less than two months, even after having received counseling. Budy v. Fed. Express Corp., 2015 U.S. Dist. LEXIS 158665 (N.D. Ohio Nov. 24, 2015).

Employee could not state a prima facie case of sex discrimination where there was no indication in the record that either male worker on the production line ever engaged in the same conduct as the employee that led to her termination, such as using profanity and creating a hostile work environment, without suffering any resulting adverse action. Jones v. Honda of Am. Mfg., 2015 U.S. Dist. LEXIS 28682 (S.D. Ohio Mar. 9, 2015).

Employer was granted summary judgment on the gender discrimination claim under Ohio state law where the evidence did not show that the employer's decisional process was unworthy of credence, that any of the male comparators were proper, or that the sheer weight of the evidence suggested that the employer's proffered reasons were a cover-up for discrimination. Hale v. Mercy Health Partners, 20 F. Supp. 3d 620, 2014 U.S. Dist. LEXIS 67564 (S.D. Ohio 2014), aff'd, 617 Fed. Appx. 395, 2015 FED App. 270N, 2015 U.S. App. LEXIS 6283 (6th Cir. Ohio 2015).

Defendants were granted summary judgment on plaintiff's gender discrimination claim because she did not attempt to show that she was replaced by a male or that a similarly situated male employee was treated differently, and even assuming the existence of a prima facie case of gender discrimination, plaintiff failed to show that the non-discriminatory reason for her termination proffered by defendant was a pretext for gender discrimination. Kendrick v. Walgreen Co., 2012 U.S. Dist. LEXIS 164869 (S.D. Ohio Nov. 19, 2012).

Summary judgment was properly granted, dismissing an employee's gender discrimination claim arising out of his termination for sexual harassment, because the employee failed to show that he and his female coworker were similarly situated. The evidence showed that the employee had committed past acts of sexual harassment and, unlike the coworker, was on notice that there was a problem with his conduct. Rainieri v. Land O'Lakes, Inc., 2006-Ohio-1791, 2006 Ohio App. LEXIS 1630 (Ohio Ct. App., Portage County 2006).

**—Termination**

Employer was granted summary judgment in an employee's action alleging gender discrimination because the employer articulated legitimate, nondiscriminatory reasons for the employee's termination, and the employee did not produce sufficient evidence to support an inference that its reasons were a pretext for gender discrimination; the evidence the employee submitted did not permit a reasonable inference that the employer's reasons for her non-renewal were insufficient for her termination. Kastner v. Kent State Univ., 2015 Ohio Misc. LEXIS 374 (Ohio Ct. Cl. Nov. 20, 2015).

**Handicap discrimination**

District court properly granted the former employer summary judgment on the former employee's wrongful-termination claim, under the Americans with Disabilities Act, the Rehabilitation Act, and the Ohio Civil Rights Act, because the employer maintained that it terminated the employee for violating the contractual leave-of-absence policy included in her collective bargaining agreement, and there was no evidence undercutting the employer's proffered non-discriminatory rationale for the employee's termination. Wheat v. Columbus Bd. of Educ., 644 Fed. Appx. 427, 2016 FED App. 0148P, 2016 U.S. App. LEXIS 4988 (6th Cir. Ohio 2016).

Former employee's failure-to-accommodate claim failed because the employee never asked the employer to accommodate her physical disabilities within the two-year time frame, and, when she demanded to return to work some seven months after the two-year limit expired, the employer was not obliged to exempt her from its contractual leave policy. Wheat v.

Columbus Bd. of Educ., 644 Fed. Appx. 427, 2016 FED App. 0148P, 2016 U.S. App. LEXIS 4988 (6th Cir. Ohio 2016).

When an employee was terminated and signed a release form upon his receipt of severance pay, that release waived any claim he might have had against the employer based on the fact that he was married to a disabled person arising from the fact that the employer had paid health insurance benefits for his wife because the release was a valid contract and the employee offered no authority for the proposition that the release did not encompass any claims the employee had under R.C. 4112.02(A). Cole v. Temple Israel, 2007-Ohio-245, 2007 Ohio App. LEXIS 224 (Ohio Ct. App., Summit County 2007).

As former employee's replacement suffered from multiple sclerosis which was a disability under the meaning of the Americans with Disabilities Act, the employee failed to make his prima facie case of discrimination based on disability. Bozsan v. Tradewinds Bev. Co., 2005 U.S. Dist. LEXIS 23032 (S.D. Ohio Sept. 21, 2005).

Former employee failed to establish a prima facie case of disability discrimination under § 4112.02 because although the employee suffered from an impaired medical condition, the employee's anxiety was controllable by medication and was not more than a short-term or temporary mental impairment having no long term residual effects. Because he never requested accommodations and was able to work around his disability, the employee's physical impairment did not substantially limit a major life activity and did not constitute a disability as defined under § 4112.01(A)(13). Curtis v. Dixon Ticonderoga Co., 2005 U.S. Dist. LEXIS 10272 (N.D. Ohio May 26, 2005).

**—Alcoholism**

Employer was granted summary judgment on an employee's disability discrimination claim where the employee failed to establish a prima facie case because he failed to show that his alcoholism substantially limited one or more major life activities. The employee admitted that despite his alcoholism he was able to engage in basic daily activities and that it had never interfered with his work prior to the day he arrived at work under the influence. O'Neal v. Johns Manville Int'l, 2005 U.S. Dist. LEXIS 10114 (N.D. Ohio May 20, 2005).

**—Hostile work environment**

Employee who was addicted to prescription painkillers and fired for repeated absences did not state a claim for hostile work environment; he claimed that co-workers harassed him by calling him "brain dead" and "our token recovering addict," and that a supervisor told him he did not get a position he bid for because he was in a substance abuse program, but his complaint contained no evidence linking any failure to promote or workplace harassment to his termination. Gardull v. Perstorp Polyols, Inc., 382 F. Supp. 2d 960, 2005 U.S. Dist. LEXIS 17250 (N.D. Ohio 2005).

**—Perception by employer**

District court erred in granting summary judgment in favor of an employer in a former employee's action alleging disability discrimination in violation of R.C. 4112.02; the district court erred in finding that the employee did not establish that the employer regarded her as disabled with respect to a neck condition and drug dependency for purposes of R.C. 4112.01(A)(13). Wysong v. Dow Chem. Co., 503 F.3d 441, 2007 FED App. 0402P, 2007 U.S. App. LEXIS 22975 (6th Cir. Ohio 2007).

Employer was granted summary judgment on an employee's disability discrimination claims under 42 U.S.C.S. § 12102 and R.C. 4112.02(A) because he failed to adduce sufficient evidence to show that the employer regarded him as disabled. There was no indication that the employee's medical condition had anything to do with the supervisor's decision, as neither he nor the employee made any reference to the employee's medical condition during their conversation. Simmons v. Wal-Mart Assocs. Inc., 2005 U.S. Dist. LEXIS 21772 (S.D. Ohio July 19, 2005).

**—Reasonable accommodation**

Employer was entitled to summary judgment on a former employee's claims under the American with Disabilities Act, 42 U.S.C.S. § 12101 et seq., and under R.C. 4112.02; the employee, who suffered severe head injuries in an off-the-job accident, failed to present any evidence of lack of good faith on the employer's part and thus failed to establish a genuine issue of material fact as to whether the employer failed to participate in the interactive process required to identify a suitable reasonable accommodation and, as a result, denied him the reasonable accommodation of transferring him to a different job for purposes of 42 U.S.C.S. §§ 12111(9), 12112(b) Kleiber v. Honda of Am. Mfg., 485 F.3d 862, 2007 FED App. 0155P, 2007 U.S. App. LEXIS 10326 (6th Cir. Ohio 2007).

When an employee sought special seating due to her recent hip replacement surgery, her employer could have an office furnishings policy even if fire regulations did not require restrictions on the seating the employee sought, and it was not discriminatory for the employer to ask her to provide medical documentation of her need for such an accommodation. Proctor v. Ohio Civ. Rights Comm'n, 2006-Ohio-6007, 169 Ohio App. 3d 527, 863 N.E.2d 1069, 2006 Ohio App. LEXIS 5956 (Ohio Ct. App., Summit County 2006).

In an action in which a former employee filed suit against his former employer alleging violations of the Americans With Disabilities Act, 42 U.S.C.S. § 12101 et seq., and R.C. 4112.02(A), the employer was entitled to summary judgment on the failure to accommodate claim where (1) the employer offered uncontroverted evidence that there were no vacant production associate positions in the fall of 2000, when the employee sought to return to the employer; and (2) the evidence indicated that the employer engaged in the interactive process by meeting with the Bureau of Vocational Rehabilitation personnel assisting the employee, by obtaining information concerning the employee's condition, by utilizing trained employees to identify and investigate possible positions for the employee, and by carefully considering and weighing the requirements of those positions against the employee's limitations. Kleiber v. Honda of Am. Mfg., 420 F. Supp. 2d 809, 2006 U.S. Dist. LEXIS 7378 (S.D. Ohio 2006), aff'd, 485 F.3d 862, 2007 FED App. 0155P, 2007 U.S. App. LEXIS 10326 (6th Cir. Ohio 2007).

**—Termination**

In an action in which a former employee filed suit against his former employer alleging violations of the Americans With Disabilities Act, 42 U.S.C.S. § 12101 et seq., and R.C. 4112.02(A), the employer was entitled to summary judgment on the termination claim where (1) the employee failed to present sufficient evidence to create a genuine issue of fact on the issue of whether he was "otherwise qualified" to perform any production position at the employer; and (2) the employer produced evidence that the employee's employment was terminated in accordance with its associate service policy, which stated that separation from employment would result in cases where the employee was not actively employed for any reason for twelve (12) consecutive months unless the employee was on approved leave of absence due to an occupational injury or illness, serving in the armed forces, on an educational leave, or laid off. Kleiber v. Honda of Am. Mfg., 420 F. Supp. 2d 809, 2006 U.S. Dist. LEXIS 7378 (S.D. Ohio 2006), aff'd, 485 F.3d 862, 2007 FED App. 0155P, 2007 U.S. App. LEXIS 10326 (6th Cir. Ohio 2007).

**—Violation of public policy**

In an action in which a former employee filed suit against his former employer alleging violations of the Americans With Disabilities Act, 42 U.S.C.S. § 12101 et seq., and R.C. 4112.02(A), the employer was entitled to summary judgment on the claim of public policy under Ohio law, referring to R.C. 4112.02(A), where the employee had not produced evidence sufficient to raise a genuine issue of fact as to whether he was "otherwise qualified" for a vacant position at the employer, or whether the employer attempted to accommodate his disability in good faith. Kleiber v. Honda of Am. Mfg., 420 F. Supp. 2d 809, 2006 U.S. Dist. LEXIS 7378 (S.D. Ohio 2006), aff'd, 485 F.3d 862, 2007 FED App. 0155P, 2007 U.S. App. LEXIS 10326 (6th Cir. Ohio 2007).

**Hostile work environment**

Plaintiff's complaint failed to state a claim of a hostile work environment theory of sexual harassment failed because she was not defendant's employee at the time of the alleged harassment. Sheppard v. Ohio Bd. of Regents, 2016-Ohio-3477, 2016 Ohio Misc. LEXIS 67 (Ohio Ct. Cl. 2016).

Trial court did not err in granting judgment on the pleading on the hostile-work-environment claim because he failed to allege "severe and pervasive" harassment. The unsuccessful attempt to change the terms and conditions of employment through proper legal channels and the recitation of the procedural steps that the village and the city manager took to terminate the former police chief prior to his conversion of the termination into a voluntary retirement did not state a claim for a hostile work environment. Daudistel v. Vill. of Silverton, 2014-Ohio-5731, 2014 Ohio App. LEXIS 5550 (Ohio Ct. App., Hamilton County 2014).

Where plaintiff filed suit against her employer, a state university, for racial and gender discrimination, the court held that she failed to state a prima facie claim of harassment based upon a hostile work environment. Plaintiff failed to present evidence that she endured intimidation, ridicule, or insult that was based upon any protected trait; i.e., her race or sex. McClair v. Univ. of Toledo, 2013-Ohio-5938, 2013 Ohio Misc. LEXIS 94 (Ohio Ct. Cl. 2013).

In an action in which a patrolman contended that a police chief attempted to place him on medical leave and did not allow him to park in a certain parking lot, even if the alleged incidents were based on age, the hostile work environment claims that the patrolman brought under 29 U.S.C.S. § 623(a) and R.C. 4112.02 could not survive a motion for summary judgment because the two isolated incidents did not amount to severe or pervasive conduct and there was no evidence tending to show that the incidents interfered with the patrolman's work performance or created an objectively intimidating, hostile, or offensive work environment. Hodges v. City of Milford, 918 F. Supp. 2d 721, 2013 U.S. Dist. LEXIS 7779 (S.D. Ohio 2013).

Hostile work environment claim under R.C. 4112.02(A) did not survive summary judgment where: (1) an employee claimed that he was subjected to unwelcome verbal conduct and harassment, was repeatedly denied a promotion when those less qualified were promoted over him, and was told to get a bachelor's degree when younger persons were promoted without one; (2) a reasonable person would not have found the conduct hostile or abusive, and it was not severe or pervasive; (3) there was no evidence that the employee was harassed based on his age; and (4) the employer explained its refusal to deem the employee a viable candidate for promotion with evidence of his performance and communication issues. Nemcek v. Northeast Ohio Reg'l Sewer Dist., 2012-Ohio-5516, 2012 Ohio App. LEXIS 4785 (Ohio Ct. App., Cuyahoga County 2012).

Summary judgment was properly granted for the employer on the hostile work environment claim because there was no evidence to establish that the person who told the employee that he knew that the employee had suffered racism at work and was sorry had personal firsthand knowledge that the people who committed the harassment events did so because of the employee's race, for lay opinion under Evid.R. 701. The circumstances of the incidents did not suggest that the employee was targeted by his coworkers because of his race. Jenkins v. Giesecke & Devrient Am., Inc., 2012-Ohio-4136, 985 N.E.2d 176, 2012 Ohio App. LEXIS 3646 (Ohio Ct. App., Summit County 2012).

Trial court correctly granted summary judgment to the employer on the employee's hostile-work-environment claim because the employee failed to establish that there was a genuine issue of material fact regarding whether he had been subjected to a hostile work environment because of his race. The two events were not severe or pervasive because the first racially-based incident occurred in 2002 and the other incident was in 2010 and neither incident was physically humiliating or threatening to the employee; they both involved mere offensive utterances. Jenkins v. Giesecke & Devrient Am., Inc., 2012-Ohio-4136, 985 N.E.2d 176, 2012 Ohio App. LEXIS 3646 (Ohio Ct. App., Summit County 2012).

Summary judgment was precluded in a township employee's sexual harassment hostile work environment claim against a township and others, arising from her termination from employment following an alcohol-related incident, as she had been subjected to a pornographic magazine in the company of male officers and her supervisor commented on his perception of the employee's agility, which was also in the presence of male coworkers; genuine issues of material fact existed as to whether the supervisor's conduct rose to the level of severe or pervasive conduct. Johnson v. Olmsted Twp., 2007-Ohio-6487, 2007 Ohio App. LEXIS 5680 (Ohio Ct. App., Cuyahoga County 2007).

Trial court did not err in granting summary judgment on the nurse's hostile work environment claim because the alleged conduct of the doctor was not sufficiently severe or pervasive to establish a claim for hostile work environment; the comments were limited in both time and number and another nurse and the nurse supervisor testified that they did not hear the doctor use foul language in the heart catheter lab. The nurse claimed that the doctor had ranted and raved and was abusive, that he had called her and other nurses derogatory and foul names, and that he had told dirty jokes, which had not been directed at her. Guy v. Q.H.G. of Massillon, Inc., 2007 Ohio App. LEXIS 394 (Ohio Ct. App., Stark County Jan. 29, 2007).

Trial court properly granted summary judgment to an employer in an employee's sexual harassment claim based on a hostile work environment under R.C. 4112.02(A), as the actions of a co-worker toward her were "odd and creepy," but they were not so severe or pervasive to have created a hostile work environment; the co-worker glared meanly at the employee, made harassing phone calls, and made her feel uncomfortable, but his actions in making additional calls and death threats to her after he was terminated from employment could not be attributed to the employer, and the employer had taken appropriate remedial action when it was informed about the co-worker's conduct. Kilgore v. Ethicon Endo-Surgery, Inc., 2007-Ohio-2952, 172 Ohio App. 3d 387, 875 N.E.2d 113, 2007 Ohio App. LEXIS 2719 (Ohio Ct. App., Hamilton County 2007).

State university employee failed to meet his burden of showing that he was a victim of hostile work environment sexual harassment, in violation of R.C. 4112.02(A), where he failed to show that his discharge from employment was based on a discriminatory animus; there was no showing of any acts by a supervisor that were offensive or harassing. Swoger v. Wright State Univ., 2007-Ohio-2751, 2007 Ohio Misc. LEXIS 184 (Ohio Ct. Cl. 2007).

Employee failed to show that she was subjected to a hostile work environment in her racial discrimination claim under R.C. 4112.02(A) of the Ohio Fair Employment Practices Act, as any perceived inconveniences in obtaining benefits, heightened scrutiny by her supervisor, racially offensive pictures, and the presence of a noose did not, as a matter of law, establish an actionable hostile-work-environment claim; rather, the incidents were isolated and the management for the employer immediately took proper remedial action upon being informed of them, such that summary judgment for the employer was proper. Brown v. Dover Corp., 2007-Ohio-2128, 2007 Ohio App. LEXIS 2010 (Ohio Ct. App., Hamilton County 2007).

Standard for a constructive discharge claim was whether an employer's actions made working conditions so intolerable that a reasonable person under the circumstances would have felt compelled to resign, requiring a showing of more adverse conditions than did a hostile environment race harassment claim, because the latter required only a showing that the conditions were severe and pervasive enough to affect working conditions, and, logically, working conditions could be affected without an employee's feeling compelled to resign, so the principle that a party's failure to support a claim for hostile environment race harassment necessarily resulted in the failure of an attendant claim of constructive discharge was expressly adopted. White v. Bay Mech. & Elec. Corp., 2007-Ohio-1752, 2007 Ohio App. LEXIS 1608 (Ohio Ct. App., Lorain County 2007).

When an employee claimed both that he was subjected to hostile environment race harassment and that he was constructively discharged, but he could not sufficiently support his harassment claim, he could not show constructive discharge because constructive discharge required him to show that working conditions were so intolerable that a reasonable person would feel compelled to resign, while his harassment claim only required him to show that working conditions were affected. White v. Bay Mech. & Elec. Corp., 2007-Ohio-1752, 2007 Ohio App. LEXIS 1608 (Ohio Ct. App., Lorain County 2007).

Factors that had to be considered in determining whether a workplace was a racially hostile environment included the frequency of the discriminatory conduct; its severity; whether it was physically threatening or humiliating, or a mere offensive utterance; and whether it unreasonably interfered with an employee's work performance. White v. Bay Mech. & Elec. Corp., 2007-Ohio-1752, 2007 Ohio App. LEXIS 1608 (Ohio Ct. App., Lorain County 2007).

When an employee claimed hostile environment race harassment, simple teasing, offhand comments, and isolated incidents (unless extremely serious) would not amount to discriminatory changes in the terms and conditions of employment, as a hostile work environment occurred when the workplace was permeated with discriminatory intimidation, ridicule, and insult that was sufficiently severe or pervasive to alter the conditions of the victim's employment and create an abusive working environment. White v. Bay Mech. & Elec. Corp., 2007-Ohio-1752, 2007 Ohio App. LEXIS 1608 (Ohio Ct. App., Lorain County 2007).

In order to support a claim for hostile environment race harassment, a party had to prove that (1) the harassment was unwelcome, (2) the harassment was based on race, (3) the harassing conduct was sufficiently severe or pervasive to affect the terms, conditions, or privileges of employment, or any matter directly or indirectly related to employment, and (4) either (a) the harassment was committed by a supervisor, or (b) the employer, through its agents or supervisory personnel, knew or should have known of the harassment and failed to take immediate and appropriate corrective action. White v. Bay Mech. & Elec. Corp., 2007-Ohio-1752, 2007 Ohio App. LEXIS 1608 (Ohio Ct. App., Lorain County 2007).

Employee did not sufficiently support his claim that he was subjected to hostile environment race harassment because (1) his pay was competitive within the employer's company, given the employee's documented attendance and motivation problems, and (2) the handful of racially-motivated comments he cited over the course of ten years of employment did not create an environment of severe and pervasive harassment affecting the terms and conditions of employment, and most comments were made about two years before he resigned. White v. Bay Mech. & Elec. Corp., 2007-Ohio-1752, 2007 Ohio App. LEXIS 1608 (Ohio Ct. App., Lorain County 2007).

Trial court's grant of summary judgment to an employer in an employee's sexual harassment claim based on a hostile work environment was proper, as she failed to establish a prima facie case under either R.C. 4112.02(A) or under Title VII for purposes of a common law claim, in that many of the derogatory comments allegedly made by a co-worker were not based on the employee's personal knowledge but upon statements of others, the employee failed to report the incidents for a period of time and after doing so, she indicated that a separation in work environment from her co-worker was unnecessary; the employee was also offered a promotion which would have allowed her to work apart from the co-worker and she turned it down. Cerett v. Timken Co., 2006-Ohio-5892, 2006 Ohio App. LEXIS 5837 (Ohio Ct. App., Stark County 2006).

Episodes of harassment identified by two employees could not constitute pervasive harassment in the absence of other, ongoing misconduct about which the employer failed to act. Their claims under Title VII of the Civil Rights Act of 1964, 42 U.S.C.S. § 2000e et seq., 42 U.S.C.S. § 1981, and R.C. 4112.02 were properly dismissed on a motion for summary judgment. Long v. Ford Motor Co., 193 Fed. Appx. 497, 2006 FED App. 0634N, 2006 U.S. App. LEXIS 21893 (6th Cir. Ohio 2006).

Employee failed to show that her workplace was permeated with discriminatory intimidation, ridicule, and insult which was sufficiently severe or pervasive to alter the conditions of the victim's employment and create an abusive working environment for purposes of her hostile work environment claim based on alleged racial discrimination from her new supervisor; there was conflict between the two individuals but it did not rise to an actionable level, there was no indication of racially biased behavior, and "abruptness" by the supervisor was how all employees were treated regardless of race. Simmons-Means v. Cuyahoga County Dep't of Justice Affairs, 2006-Ohio-4123, 2006 Ohio App. LEXIS 4057 (Ohio Ct. App., Cuyahoga County 2006).

Teacher did not show he was subjected to a hostile work environment, due to racial slurs from students and others, because he did not show that the slurs he testified to were severe or pervasive enough to alter the conditions of his employment. Farris v. Port Clinton City Sch. Dist., 2006-Ohio-1864, 2006 Ohio App. LEXIS 1701 (Ohio Ct. App., Ottawa County 2006).

Because the employee failed to demonstrate that the alleged harassment was sufficiently severe or pervasive to create an abusive working environment, she could not establish a hostile work environment claim, under R.C. 4112.02. Northern v. Medical Mut. of Ohio, 2006-Ohio-1075, 2006 Ohio App. LEXIS 1001 (Ohio Ct. App., Cuyahoga County 2006).

Summary judgment was properly granted on the former vice president's claim for a hostile work environment because he failed to establish that the conduct was sufficiently severe or pervasive to create a hostile working environment and he was not employed by the corporation at the time. His bruised ego over the perceived slights to him (he was not offered the position that he had expected after his company was purchased) was insufficient to constitute a hostile work environment. Hoyt v. Nationwide Mut. Ins. Co., 2005-Ohio-6367, 2005 Ohio App. LEXIS 5700 (Ohio Ct. App., Franklin County 2005).

Police dispatcher's allegations of a sexually hostile work environment under the Equal Protection Clause; Title VII of the Civil Rights Act of 1964, 42 U.S.C.S. § 2000e et seq.; and R.C. 4112.02 failed on their merits because the conduct at issue was isolated and sporadic, not ongoing. Kohler v. City of Wapakoneta, 381 F. Supp. 2d 692, 2005 U.S. Dist. LEXIS 16671 (N.D. Ohio 2005).

Trial court did not err by granting summary judgment for the board of education and others on the hostile work environment based on sex because the teacher did not demonstrate that the actions, even when viewed in her favor, were not severe and pervasive as to affect employment. Janiszewski v. Belmont Career Ctr., 2017-Ohio-855, 86 N.E.3d 613, 2017 Ohio App. LEXIS 830 (Ohio Ct. App., Belmont County 2017).

**—Sexual harassment**

Employee's hostile work environment claim survived summary judgment because reasonable minds could only conclude that the comments and actions towards the employee such as calling her a "pork chop," which refers to a younger woman dating an older man; attempting to kiss her; asking her on a date; and telling her she might get on a bar and start dancing would be unwelcome and the male police officers who made the comments and committed the actions towards the employee was because of her female gender. McGuire v. City of Newark, 2020-Ohio-4226, 2020 Ohio App. LEXIS 3114 (Ohio Ct. App., Licking County 2020).

Trial court erred by granting summary judgment for the manager and employer because genuine issues of material fact remained as to whether the manager's comments and actions created a hostile work environment based upon sexual harassment. The employee presented evidence that an objectively hostile work environment existed and that she subjectively perceived the environment to be abusive based on the manager's continuous preoccupation with sex talk and his unwelcome advances was objectively severe, degrading, offensive, and humiliating and resulted in an abusive and hostile work environment. Ellis v. Jungle Jim's Mkt., Inc., 2015-Ohio-4226, 44 N.E.3d 1034, 2015 Ohio App. LEXIS 4118 (Ohio Ct. App., Butler County 2015).

**Housing discrimination**

In a landlord's forcible entry and detainer action pursuant to R.C. 1923.02, the tenant's claim that the landlord engaged in unlawful discriminatory conduct in violation of R.C. 4112.02(H)(1) and (4) of the Ohio Fair Housing Act lacked merit as a valid defense, as he failed to provide evidence that he was refused holdover because he was a member of a protected category under the Act. Olympic Realty v. Zaleski, 2013-Ohio-1245, 2013 Ohio App. LEXIS 1143 (Ohio Ct. App., Franklin County 2013).

Borrower had not shown that the lender adopted a discriminatory policy and a description of one allegedly improper loan was not sufficient evidence of a discriminatory policy. There were no statistics supporting the claim that the lender made a higher percentage of "high cost" loans in African-American communities than in a similarly situated, non-minority community. Ohio Civ. Rights Comm'n v. Wells Fargo Bank, N.A., 2012 U.S. Dist. LEXIS 52829 (N.D. Ohio Apr. 16, 2012).

Where a tenant filed suit against her former landlord, claiming sexual harassment, housing discrimination, and unlawful coercion or intimidation under R.C. 4112.02(H)(1), (4), and (12) after he made crude sexual comments and offered to pay her for sex and where the jury returned a verdict in favor of the tenant, the trial court erred in failing to grant the landlord's motion for judgment notwithstanding the verdict on the housing harassment claim because there was no evidence of quid pro quo sexual harassment in that the landlord never told the tenant that he would evict her if she refused to have sex with him. McDonald v. Burton, 2011-Ohio-6178, 2011 Ohio App. LEXIS 5067 (Ohio Ct. App., Montgomery County 2011).

Because the record was devoid of any evidence to support the Ohio Civil Rights Commission's claim that the client was turned away from the residential care facility based on any of his purported disabilities, or on his alleged need for a "service animal," in violation of Ohio's Fair Housing Act, R.C. 4112.02, the trial court did not err by adopting the magistrate's decision granting judgment in the facility owner's favor. Had the client provided the facility staff with the necessary vaccination records, the client, as well as his dog, would have been admitted into the residential care facility. Ohio Civ. Rights Comm'n v. Mellon Ridge, Inc., 2009-Ohio-5807, 2009 Ohio App. LEXIS 4869 (Ohio Ct. App., Warren County 2009).

The duty required in an Ohio negligence claim can be based on a violation of the Fair Housing Act and Ohio's statutory counterpart, R.C. 4112.02(H). Overlook Mut. Homes, Inc. v. Spencer, 666 F. Supp. 2d 850, 2009 U.S. Dist. LEXIS 105100 (S.D. Ohio 2009).

Plaintiff potential buyers alleging housing discrimination under 42 U.S.C.S. §§ 1981, 1982, the Fair Housing Act, 42 U.S.C.S. § 3604, and R.C. 4112.01(H)(1), were not required to show the property had not "remained available" after the contract was terminated since the termination of the contract two days after defendant owners discovered the buyers were African Americans was additional evidence to infer discrimination; summary judgment to the owners was reversed. Lindsay v. Yates, 578 F.3d 407, 2009 FED App. 0301P, 2009 U.S. App. LEXIS 18849 (6th Cir. Ohio 2009).

In accord with the federal law on the subject, R.C. 4112.052 authorizes the Ohio Civil Rights Commission (OCRC) to commence a civil action, through the Ohio Attorney General, whenever OCR.C. has reasonable cause to believe that any group of persons has been denied any of the rights R.C. 4112.02(H) grants, and the denial raises an issue of public importance. Ohio Civ. Rights Comm'n v. Fairmark Dev., Inc., 2008-Ohio-6511, 2008 Ohio App. LEXIS 5400 (Ohio Ct. App., Franklin County 2008).

When the Ohio Civil Rights Commission (OCRC) filed a complaint alleging a claim under R.C. 4112.052, due to the builders of an apartment complex allegedly violating state and federal handicap accessibility requirements, it was error to fail to recognize the complaint's assertion of a claim based on a denial of rights under R.C. 4112.02(H) raising an issue of public importance because R.C. 4112.052 authorized OCR.C. to commence such a claim, through the Attorney General, whenever OCR.C. had reasonable cause to believe that any group of persons had been denied any of the rights R.C. 4112.02(H) granted, and the denial raised an issue of public importance. Ohio Civ. Rights Comm'n v. Fairmark Dev., Inc., 2008-Ohio-6511, 2008 Ohio App. LEXIS 5400 (Ohio Ct. App., Franklin County 2008).

Landlord could not be held liable under R.C. 4112.02(H)(4) for failing to take corrective action against a tenant whose racial harassment of another tenant created a hostile housing environment, as there was no agency relationship or requisite amount of control by the landlord over the tenant, and precedents did not support such a cause of action. Ohio Civ. Rights Comm'n v. Akron Metro. Hous. Auth., 2008-Ohio-3320, 119 Ohio St. 3d 77, 892 N.E.2d 415, 2008 Ohio LEXIS 1770 (Ohio 2008).

Landlord may not be held liable under R.C. 4112.02(H)(4) for failing to take corrective action against a tenant whose racial harassment of another tenant created a hostile housing environment: Ohio Civ. Rights Comm'n v. Akron Metro. Hous. Auth., 2008-Ohio-3320, 119 Ohio St. 3d 77, 892 N.E.2d 415, 2008 Ohio LEXIS 1770 (Ohio 2008).

Ohio Civil Rights Commission's motion to remand its housing discrimination claims brought pursuant to R.C. 4112.02(H) against an apartment complex and its management company was granted where the initial pleading was based solely on state law claims of housing discrimination, those claims were raised by the Commission on behalf of itself and the administrative complainant, a fair housing advocacy association, no federal claims were asserted until several months later when the association was permitted to file an intervening complaint, and the claims asserted by the association were not truly separate and independent within the meaning of 28 U.S.C.S. § 1441(c), since they were intimately related to and dependent upon the state law claims asserted by the Commission. Ohio Civ. Rights Comm'n v. SH-91 L.P., 2005 U.S. Dist. LEXIS 13430 (N.D. Ohio July 5, 2005).

Ohio Civil Rights Commission's motion to remand its housing discrimination claims brought pursuant to R.C. 4112.02(H) against an apartment complex and its management company was granted where the initial pleading was based solely on state law claims of housing discrimination, those claims were raised by the Commission on behalf of itself and the administrative complainant, a fair housing advocacy association, no federal claims were asserted until several months later when the association was permitted to file an intervening complaint, and the claims asserted by the association were not truly separate and independent within the meaning of 28 U.S.C.S. § 1441(c), since they were intimately related to and dependent upon the state law claims asserted by the Commission. Ohio Civ. Rights Comm'n v. SH-91 L.P., 2005 U.S. Dist. LEXIS 13430 (N.D. Ohio July 5, 2005).

The city did not violate fair housing laws by refusing to grant the multiple, substantial variances needed to permit transitional housing for homeless mentally ill persons on property zoned for semi-industrial use: Eppler v. Cleveland, 142 Ohio App. 3d 91, 753 N.E.2d 986, 2001 Ohio App. LEXIS 1344 (Ohio Ct. App., Cuyahoga County 2001).

Mere use of the words "mature adults only" in a housing rental advertisement did not constitute a per se violation of R.C. 4112.02(H): Ohio Civ. Rights Comm'n v. Harlett, 132 Ohio App. 3d 341, 724 N.E.2d 1242, 1999 Ohio App. LEXIS 565 (Ohio Ct. App., Wood County 1999).

The tenant's counterclaim based on alleged racial discrimination was properly raised in an eviction action for nonpayment of rent: Lable & Co. v. Flowers, 104 Ohio App. 3d 227, 661 N.E.2d 782, 1995 Ohio App. LEXIS 2295 (Ohio Ct. App., Lorain County 1995).

A complaint alleging "redlining" of minority neighborhoods was not subject to dismissal: Toledo Fair Hous. Ctr. v. Nationwide Mut. Ins. Co., 94

Ohio Misc. 2d 14, 703 N.E.2d 338, 1993 Ohio Misc. LEXIS 118 (Ohio C.P. 1993).

R.C. 4112.021(H)(1) applies only to discriminatory practices in the transfer of housing rights and not to the misconduct of other tenants in the same housing: Graves v. Van Buskirk, 1991 Ohio App. LEXIS 759 (Ohio Ct. App., Summit County Feb. 20, 1991).

A restaurant does not violate R.C. 4112.02(G) by enforcing its dress code and refusing to serve a patron wearing a motorcycle jacket: Yee v. Zappone, 65 Ohio App. 3d 696, 585 N.E.2d 436, 1989 Ohio App. LEXIS 4983 (Ohio Ct. App., Cuyahoga County 1989).

Where a tenant regulation which prohibits the wearing of "cut-offs" in the swimming pool of an apartment complex is applicable to all tenants, the enforcement of the regulation against a handicapped person is not a discriminatory practice under the Ohio Civil Rights Act: McIntyre v. Northern Ohio Properties, 64 Ohio App. 2d 179, 18 Ohio Op. 3d 139, 412 N.E.2d 434, 1979 Ohio App. LEXIS 8430 (Ohio Ct. App., Cuyahoga County 1979).

A city may discourage blockbusting by prohibiting real estate salesmen from contacting homeowners who have put their names on a no-solicitation list: Cleveland Heights v. Lindsay, 65 Ohio App. 2d 215, 19 Ohio Op. 3d 162, 417 N.E.2d 1019, 1979 Ohio App. LEXIS 8474 (Ohio Ct. App., Cuyahoga County 1979).

The Civil Rights Act of 1968, the decision of the United States Supreme Court in Jones v. Alfred H. Mayer Co., 47 OO2d 43, and Ohio R.C. Chapter 4112., relating to open housing, were not intended to pre-empt local housing ordinances or provide rights and remedies which were effective substitutes for a municipal ordinance: Hunter v. Erickson, 393 U.S. 385, 89 S. Ct. 557, 21 L. Ed. 2d 616, 1969 U.S. LEXIS 2782 (U.S. 1969).

**—Not shown**

Assuming that the tenant was making a "reasonable accommodation" argument, the trial court properly granted summary judgment for the property manager, finding that he failed to establish that he suffered from a disability. The tenant did not provide any evidence to support a disability and did not even file an affidavit in opposition to the motion for summary judgment. Winkle v. Co, 2016-Ohio-6957, 2016 Ohio App. LEXIS 3812 (Ohio Ct. App., Montgomery County 2016).

Similar to a finding that an apartment manager's internet advertisement for a "bachelor pad" apartment did not violate the Fair Housing Act under an ordinary reader standard, a directed verdict was not warranted under the Ohio fair housing statute because an ordinary reader could find multiple ways to interpret the advertisement as it related to Ohio's statutory non-specification requirement. Miami Valley Fair Hous. Ctr., Inc. v. Connor Group, 725 F.3d 571, 2013 FED App. 0207P, 2013 U.S. App. LEXIS 16077 (6th Cir. Ohio 2013).

**—Shown**

Ohio Civil Rights Commission's allegations that a resident of a multi-unit housing structure harassed and intimidated a disabled neighbor, such that she eventually moved, were properly within the coverage of the Ohio Fair Housing Act because liability existed for conduct that interfered with the exercise or enjoyment of the neighbor's fair housing right, and the allegations addressed more than a mere quarrel between neighbors. Ohio Civ. Rights Comm'n v. Myers, 2014-Ohio-144, 2014 Ohio App. LEXIS 131 (Ohio Ct. App., Montgomery County 2014).

**Immunity**

Summary judgment should have been granted in favor of a current mayor in a discrimination case because liability was not predicated upon the continuing violation doctrine; the doctrine could not have been used to establish discriminatory conduct on the part of a subsequently elected or appointed official who played no role in the original decision. Because there was no evidence or even any allegation in an amended complaint that the current mayor engaged in discriminatory conduct in relation to individuals appointed to a police department by a former mayor, the current mayor was immune from any award that might have been issued by the trial court in this action. State ex rel. Conroy v. Williams, 2009-Ohio-6040, 185 Ohio App. 3d 69, 923 N.E.2d 191, 2009 Ohio App. LEXIS 5069 (Ohio Ct. App., Mahoning County 2009).

In a discrimination case, summary judgment was properly denied as to a former mayor; because R.C. ch. 4112 had been interpreted to include supervisory and managerial employees in the statutory definition of "employer," the general immunity provided in R.C. 2744.02(A) did not apply to the former mayor since civil liability was imposed by R.C. 4112.02(A) for discriminatory hiring practices. It was possible for the former mayor to be held personally liable for damages resulting from his hiring decision, even though he was engaged in a governmental function when he appointed several others to the police department. State ex rel. Conroy v. Williams, 2009-Ohio-6040, 185 Ohio App. 3d 69, 923 N.E.2d 191, 2009 Ohio App. LEXIS 5069 (Ohio Ct. App., Mahoning County 2009).

**Independent contractor**

Plaintiff was owner of a company that provided housing and transportation for the elderly and special needs individuals. She was an independent contractor and not an employee of the Ohio District 5 Area Agency on Aging, where, inter alia, (i) she made no allegations that the Agency retained any control over how she carried out her transportation assignments or the routes she took, and (ii) there was no indication that the Agency provided her with a car or other vehicle to conduct her transportation duties or that the Agency held her out as being an employee. Williams v. Richland County Children Servs., 861 F. Supp. 2d 874, 2011 U.S. Dist. LEXIS 113762 (N.D. Ohio 2011), aff'd, 489 Fed. Appx. 848, 2012 FED App. 764N, 2012 U.S. App. LEXIS 14702 (6th Cir. Ohio 2012).

Court granted summary judgment in favor of an insurance company in an insurance agent's allegation that the company had discriminated against him based on age when it terminated his employment; the court had found that the agent was an independent contractor, and not an employee, and therefore was not covered under R.C. 4112.02(A). Averill v. Gleaner Life Ins. Soc'y, 2008 U.S. Dist. LEXIS 10073 (N.D. Ohio Jan. 29, 2008).

When a blind contractor who had a contract to operate a bait shop at a city reservoir raised various tort claims against city employees when that contract was terminated, the contractor could not also claim disability discrimination, under R.C. 4112.02(A), because the contractor had no standing to raise such a claim, as the contractor did not have an employment relationship with the city or its employees, but was an independent contractor. Davis v. Johnson, 2007-Ohio-6567, 2007 Ohio App. LEXIS 5739 (Ohio Ct. App., Richland County 2007).

R.C. 4112.02 does not apply to a sales director who works as an independent contractor for a national cosmetics company where company did not control director's work in any significant way: Eyerman v. Mary Kay Cosmetics, Inc., 967 F.2d 213, 1992 U.S. App. LEXIS 13378 (6th Cir. Ohio 1992).

**Individual liability**

Resident of a multi-unit housing structure was an "individual" under the Ohio Fair Housing Act's definition of "person" in his role as a neighbor or otherwise, and further, the statutory definition of "person" applied to individuals or entities beyond the context of a transaction in which the transfer of real estate was involved. Ohio Civ. Rights Comm'n v. Myers, 2014-Ohio-144, 2014 Ohio App. LEXIS 131 (Ohio Ct. App., Montgomery County 2014).

Sheriff was not entitled to immunity on the former nurse's harassment and retaliation claims because R.C. 2744.03(A)(6)(c) operated to withdraw immunity from the sheriff, as R.C. 4112.02(A) and (I) expressly imposed liability on the sheriff for such actions. Satterfield v. Karnes, 736 F. Supp. 2d 1138, 2010 U.S. Dist. LEXIS 86398 (S.D. Ohio 2010).

Firefighter sued a city and a chief of fire for age discrimination. As the actions of the chief were within the scope of his official responsibilities and were not done maliciously, in bad faith, or in a wanton or reckless manner, he was immune from liability under R.C. 2744.03. Campolieti v. City of Cleveland, 2009-Ohio-5224, 184 Ohio App. 3d 419, 921 N.E.2d 286, 2009 Ohio App. LEXIS 4417 (Ohio Ct. App., Cuyahoga County 2009).

Supervisors and managers may be held individually liable for unlawful discriminatory acts: Wallace v. Henderson, 138 F. Supp. 2d 980, 2000 U.S. Dist. LEXIS 20378 (S.D. Ohio 2000).

Liability under R.C. 4112.02 is not limited to employers: Vandiver v. Morgan Adhesive Co., 126 Ohio App. 3d 634, 710 N.E.2d 1219, 1998 Ohio App. LEXIS 1035 (Ohio Ct. App., Summit County 1998).

There is no basis for individual liability under R.C. 4112.02: Osman v. Isotec, Inc., 960 F. Supp. 118, 1997 U.S. Dist. LEXIS 4926 (S.D. Ohio 1997).

There is no basis for individual liability under R.C. 4112.02: Dalton v. Jefferson Smurfit Corp. (U.S.), 979 F. Supp. 1187, 1997 U.S. Dist. LEXIS 15506 (S.D. Ohio 1997).

**Insurance**

Police department's insurer was obligated to defend the chief of police in an action alleging sexual harassment. An insurer's duty to defend is broader than its duty to indemnify. An insurer must defend its insured in an action when the allegations state a claim that potentially or arguably falls within the insurance coverage: Ohio Gov't Risk Mgmt. Plan v. Harrison, 2007-Ohio-4948, 115 Ohio St. 3d 241, 874 N.E.2d 1155, 2007 Ohio LEXIS 2226 (Ohio 2007).

Intentional tort exclusion, shielding the insurers from a duty to defend, did not apply where a business and its employee were sued for sexual harassment and sexual battery of an adult co-employee: GNFH, Inc. v. W. Am. Ins. Co., 2007-Ohio-2722, 172 Ohio App. 3d 127, 873 N.E.2d 345, 2007 Ohio App. LEXIS 3630 (Ohio Ct. App., Miami County 2007).

The disparate-impact approach does not unduly undermine the business of selling insurance. Although R.C. 3901.21(M) makes it an unfair trade practice to engage in unfair discrimination in offering insurance, it does not deal with the specific situation of race discrimination in offering homeowner's insurance: Toledo Fair Hous. Ctr. v. Nationwide Mut. Ins. Co., 94 Ohio Misc. 2d 151, 704 N.E.2d 667, 1997 Ohio Misc. LEXIS 355 (Ohio C.P. 1997).

**Intent**

The trial court did not abuse its discretion by finding that the employer's failure to comply strictly with posted qualification requirements did not conclusively prove discriminatory animus: Omobien v. Ohio Civil Rights

Comm'n, 89 Ohio App. 3d 100, 623 N.E.2d 634, 1993 Ohio App. LEXIS 4170 (Ohio Ct. App., Summit County 1993).

Discrimination is prohibited by R.C. 4112.02(H) when it is made because of, on account of, or based upon race, color, religion, sex, ancestry, handicap, or national origin. When the ultimate issue in a case is defendants' intent, genuine issues of material fact exist with respect to whether defendants' articulated reasons were either the true reason or the motivating reason for their actions. Therefore, defendants are not entitled to judgment as a matter of law: Aloqaili v. National Housing Corp., 743 F. Supp. 1264, 1990 U.S. Dist. LEXIS 10408 (N.D. Ohio 1990).

**Intentional infliction of emotional distress**

Temporary worker failed to meet her burden to present evidence establishing either the causation or the severity of her claimed injuries because the record contained no evidence, other than the worker's uncorroborated testimony, to establish that she experienced severe emotional distress as a result of the supervisor's behavior. Gorajewski v. Douglas, 2014-Ohio-1296, 2014 Ohio App. LEXIS 1287 (Ohio Ct. App., Lucas County 2014).

Summary judgment was properly granted, dismissing a Caucasian employee's intentional infliction of emotional distress claim brought against her African-American supervisor and the city which employed her, because, while the coworkers' racial comments, jokes, criticism, and distribution of racially volatile literature were no doubt offensive to the employee and inappropriate for the workplace, the evidence failed to demonstrate conduct that was so extreme and outrageous to go beyond all bounds of human decency Mowery v. City of Columbus, 2006-Ohio-1153, 2006 Ohio App. LEXIS 1051 (Ohio Ct. App., Franklin County 2006).

Summary judgment was properly entered for an employer on a minor employee's claim for intentional infliction of emotional distress as the employer's actions, as distinguished from another employee's actions, did not rise to the level of extreme and outrageous conduct required for the tort as the employer, once notified of the minor employee's situation, proposed a reasonable remedy in accordance with the employer's stated prohibition against harassment in the workplace. Jackson v. Saturn of Chapel Hill, Inc., 2005-Ohio-5302, 2005 Ohio App. LEXIS 4821 (Ohio Ct. App., Stark County 2005).

Plaintiff's action for intentional infliction of emotional distress could be maintained against employer even though the actions of her supervisor were not calculated to promote the employer's business: Crihfield v. Monsanto Co., 844 F. Supp. 371, 1994 U.S. Dist. LEXIS 2614 (S.D. Ohio 1994).

**Joint and several liability**

For purposes of R.C. 4112.02, a supervisor/manager may be held jointly and/or severally liable with her/his employer for discriminatory conduct of the supervisor/manager in violation of R.C. Chapter 4112.: 1999 Ohio 352, 84 Ohio St. 3d 293, 703 N.E.2d 782, 1999 Ohio LEXIS 6.

**Jurisdiction**

In a customer's suit under the Americans with Disabilities Act, 42 U.S.C.S § 12182(a) and R.C. 4112.02(G), alleging discrimination after she was ordered out of a gas station/convenience store with her service dog and assaulted by an employee, a federal district court denied the motion for summary judgment filed by the gas station/convenience store, its owners, operators, and lessees (defendants) based on lack of personal jurisdiction because the customer made a prima facie showing that the actions of the employee occurred in Ohio and created a tortuous injury there; therefore, the customer made a prima facie showing of personal jurisdiction under Ohio's long-arm statute, R.C. 2307.382, under an apparent agency theory. Cooley v. Valero Energy Corp., 2012 U.S. Dist. LEXIS 40291 (S.D. Ohio Mar. 20, 2012).

Trial court's grant of a church's motion under Civ.R. 12(B)(1) to dismiss an action by terminated church employees against it, based on their claims that their terminations were wrongful as against public policy and in violation of R.C. 4112.02(I), was proper based on the ministerial exception to a secular court's ability to review an employment decision by a religious organization such as the church; there was competent, credible evidence to support the trial court's independent determination that the employees were ministers, such that the trial court lacked subject matter jurisdiction over the claims. Horine v. Vineyard Cmty. Church, 2006-Ohio-6620, 2006 Ohio App. LEXIS 6542 (Ohio Ct. App., Hamilton County 2006).

Trial court erred in granting an employer's motion to dismiss an employee's racial discrimination claims due to a finding of lack of subject matter jurisdiction, as the employee alleged that he performed 80 percent of his work for the employer in Ohio, that the employer conducted business in Ohio, and that he was only hired to help the employer meet minority quotas and he was terminated when the employer no longer contractually was required to employ a specific number of minority employees; there was jurisdiction under R.C. 4112.02(A)(2). Wilkerson v. Howell Contrs., Inc., 2005-Ohio-4418, 163 Ohio App. 3d 38, 836 N.E.2d 29, 2005 Ohio App. LEXIS 4005 (Ohio Ct. App., Hamilton County 2005).

Where the employee worked in both Ohio and Kentucky, the trial court erred in dismissing the state and federal discrimination claims on the basis of lack of subject matter jurisdiction: Wilkerson v. Howell Contrs., Inc., 2005-Ohio-4418, 163 Ohio App. 3d 38, 836 N.E.2d 29, 2005 Ohio App. LEXIS 4005 (Ohio Ct. App., Hamilton County 2005).

**—Court of claims**

A state employee may bring an action in the court of claims alleging age discrimination under R.C. 4101.17 (See now R.C. 4112.14) by a state agency: Harris v. Ohio Dept. of Adm. Serv., 63 Ohio App. 3d 115, 577 N.E.2d 1180 (1989).

**—Subject-matter**

Magistrate properly distinguished an employee's Americans with Disabilities Act, R.C. 4112.02, and Family and Medical Leave Act, 5 U.S.C.S. § 6381 et seq., claims from the employee's "unfair labor practices" claims, which were subject to the exclusive jurisdiction of State Employment Relations Board; further, the trial court properly held that it lacked subject-matter jurisdiction over the "unfair labor practices" claims. Baddour v. Rehab. Servs. Comm'n, 2005-Ohio-5698, 2005 Ohio App. LEXIS 5123 (Ohio Ct. App., Franklin County 2005).

**Jury trial**

A plaintiff may demand jury trial on claims under R.C. 4112.99 where the gravamen of the claims is discrimination on the basis of sex: Taylor v. National Group of Cos., 1992-Ohio-68, 65 Ohio St. 3d 482, 605 N.E.2d 45, 1992 Ohio LEXIS 3130 (Ohio 1992).

**Limitations period**

Retiree's R.C. 4112.02(A) and 4112.99 claim alleging racial discrimination was pre-empted by federal law and was time-barred under 29 U.S.C.S. § 160(b) even though it was originally based upon state law, as the claim was based on the Special Attrition Plan, which was an agreement directly resulting from the collective bargaining process between an employer and the union, and it was necessary to construe the plan in order to decide if a violation of R.C. ch. 4112 had occurred; the six-year limitations period under R.C. 2305.07 did not apply. Gordon v. GMC, 2012-Ohio-863, 2012 Ohio App. LEXIS 759 (Ohio Ct. App., Trumbull County 2012).

**Military status**

In this Uniformed Services Employment and Reemployment Rights Act and R.C. 4112.02(A) action, defendant was granted summary judgment because plaintiff provided no evidence of an adverse employment action connected to his prior military service; defendant's call to the police for a "no trespass" order that prevented plaintiff from returning to the property did not qualify as an employment action. Pate v. MetoKote Corp., 2012 U.S. Dist. LEXIS 162032 (S.D. Ohio Nov. 13, 2012).

**Motion to dismiss**

Motion to dismiss, pursuant to Civ.R. 12(B)(6), filed by a former employee's former employer and her former supervisor was improperly granted on the employee's wrongful discharge claim because, even though the employee did not allege a statutory claim for wrongful discharge, the trial court should have first determined whether she had stated such a claim pursuant to R.C. 4112.02(A) since it found that the employee's common law claim was untenable only because there already existed a statutory remedy. Springer v. Fitton Ctr. for Creative Arts, 2005-Ohio-3624, 2005 Ohio App. LEXIS 3347 (Ohio Ct. App., Butler County 2005).

**Municipal employer**

Nothing in the text of R.C. 4112.02, barring discriminatory employment practices, suggests that the general assembly meant to treat employees subject to civil service commission rules (or any other disciplinary procedure) differently than non-civil service employees, as R.C. 4112.01(A)(2) includes within the definition of "employer" any political subdivision of the state, and an "employee" is defined as an individual employed by any employer, so it makes no distinction between public and private employers or their employees. Dworning v. City of Euclid, 2006-Ohio-6772, 2006 Ohio App. LEXIS 6685 (Ohio Ct. App., Cuyahoga County 2006), aff'd, 2008-Ohio-3318, 119 Ohio St. 3d 83, 892 N.E.2d 420, 2008 Ohio LEXIS 1768 (Ohio 2008).

**National origin discrimination**

Employer was entitled to summary judgment dismissing an employee's national origin discrimination claim, when the employee was terminated for violating the employer's workplace violence policy, because the employee did not show the employee was treated differently in a relevant manner from similarly-situated, non-protected, employees who were accused of violating the employer's workplace violence policy, as the other workplace violence incidents the employee cited were factually dissimilar from the incident leading to the employee's termination. Ignatenkov v. U.S. Foodservice, Inc., 2012 U.S. Dist. LEXIS 99553 (S.D. Ohio July 18, 2012).

In this 42 U.S.C.S. § 1981 discrimination action, defendants were granted summary judgment because defendants provided a legitimate justification for their decision to terminate plaintiff: plaintiff's lack of clinical competence, described as a combination of knowledge and application of that knowledge to the patient at hand. Vechvitvarakul v. Health

Alliance of Greater Cincinnati, 2012 U.S. Dist. LEXIS 17674 (S.D. Ohio Feb. 13, 2012).

As a former employee's prior claims of national origin discrimination that were initially brought to the Equal Employment Opportunity Commission were beyond the six-year limitations period of R.C. 2305.07, they were time-barred and summary judgment for the employer on a national origin discrimination claim under R.C. 4112.02 was proper; moreover, the record supported the determination that the employee was terminated due to failure to wear a required headset at work and failure to call in and provide medical documentation for repeated absences. Kiraly v. Office Max, Inc., 2009-Ohio-863, 2009 Ohio App. LEXIS 731 (Ohio Ct. App., Cuyahoga County 2009).

Employee had not put forth sufficient evidence for a jury reasonably to conclude that the employer did not have an honest belief that he performed his job duties poorly. The fact that employees discussed the Iraq war during their lunch breaks did not make it more likely than not that he was fired in violation of Title VII because he was Iraqi. Abdulnour v. Campbell Soup Supply Co., LLC, 502 F.3d 496, 2007 FED App. 0382P, 2007 U.S. App. LEXIS 22302 (6th Cir. Ohio 2007).

Where several supervisors and several long-term hourly workers had reported to managers that an employee was uncommunicative, demeaning to employees, and "not engaged with the production process" of his unit, and a manager reportedly had seen the employee ignore a light indicating that a production line in his unit was down on five to ten occasions, the employee failed to establish that defendants' proffered reason for firing him—poor job performance—was a pretext for discrimination based on national origin in violation of Title VII of the Civil Rights Act of 1964, 42 U.S.C.S. § 2000e-2 et seq., and R.C. 4112.02(A) and (J). Abdulnour v. Campbell Soup Supply Co., L.L.C., 464 F. Supp. 2d 711, 2006 U.S. Dist. LEXIS 79313 (N.D. Ohio 2006), aff'd, 502 F.3d 496, 2007 FED App. 0382P, 2007 U.S. App. LEXIS 22302 (6th Cir. Ohio 2007).

Former employee produced evidence to show that he was an American; he was objectively qualified for his position; he was terminated; and he was replaced by an individual outside of the protected classes. His former employers, a Swiss company and its American subsidiaries, articulated a legitimate, nondiscriminatory reason for the employee's termination in that they claimed he was terminated for poor management. Imwalle v. Reliance Med. Prods., 2005 U.S. Dist. LEXIS 27882 (S.D. Ohio Nov. 15, 2005).

Polish doctor's language difficulties constituted a legitimate, nondiscriminatory reason for a decision to place her on academic probation and deny her course credit; the doctor failed to show that a university's motives were motivated by discriminatory reasons. Sarach-Kozlowska v. Univ. of Cincinnati College of Med., 2004-Ohio-1926, 2004 Ohio Misc. LEXIS 142 (Ohio Ct. Cl. 2004).

Other employees were similarly situated where they were in the same department at the same level and subject to the same superiors and review standards. There was sufficient evidence plaintiff was treated differently based on national origin: Ohio Civil Rights Comm'n v. Kent State Univ., 129 Ohio App. 3d 231, 717 N.E.2d 745, 1998 Ohio App. LEXIS 3514 (Ohio Ct. App., Portage County), cert. denied, Ohio Civ. Rights Comm. v. Kent State Univ., 84 Ohio St. 3d 1439, 702 N.E.2d 1215, 1998 Ohio LEXIS 3551 (Ohio 1998).

Appellee failed to adduce sufficient evidence that he had a reasonable or good-faith belief that appellant had engaged in a discriminatory employment practice by terminating him based on national origin where the employee had been hired on that basis; it was implausible that appellant would fail to discriminate against appellee while hiring him and then discriminate against him in his termination: Pulver v. Rookwood Highland Tower Invs., 1997 Ohio App. LEXIS 1153 (Ohio Ct. App., Hamilton County Mar. 26, 1997), dismissed, 79 Ohio St. 3d 1482, 683 N.E.2d 787, 1997 Ohio LEXIS 2274 (Ohio 1997).

An employer engages in an unlawful discriminatory practice where it is aware that an employee is being harassed on the basis of national origin, but takes no action to stop it: Manbeck Nurseries v. Ohio Civil Rights Comm'n, 93 Ohio App. 3d 809, 639 N.E.2d 1247, 1994 Ohio App. LEXIS 1520 (Ohio Ct. App., Auglaize County 1994).

Defendant could not establish national origin discrimination where he was not replaced, his plant was closed, and the alleged replacement at new plant was not shown to not be British: Francis v. Gaylord Container Corp., 837 F. Supp. 858, 1992 U.S. Dist. LEXIS 22045 (S.D. Ohio 1992).

**Negligent retention**

The employer was entitled to summary judgment on the negligent retention claim: Myers v. Goodwill Indus. of Akron, 130 Ohio App. 3d 722, 721 N.E.2d 130, 1998 Ohio App. LEXIS 6087 (Ohio Ct. App., Summit County 1998).

**Not shown**

Even if the records could constitute a record of impairment for purposes of a cause of action under R.C. 4112.02, there was also evidence that appellant's doctor released her to return to work on April 13 on a full-time basis without restrictions, home health care services were no longer needed, and the jury determined appellant failed to prove she was impaired. Bailey v. Providence Healthcare Mgmt., Inc., 2019-Ohio-5461, 2019 Ohio App. LEXIS 5523 (Ohio Ct. App., Columbiana County 2019).

Trial court's decision to deny the motions for JNOV and new trial in a wrongful discharge case were affirmed because the testimony and evidence presented conflicting evidence as to whether appellant had an actual disability and the jury was free to believe some, all or none of the witness? testimony, including that merely having the colectomy and having a stoma and waste bag did not mean that appellant was disabled. Bailey v. Providence Healthcare Mgmt., Inc., 2019-Ohio-5461, 2019 Ohio App. LEXIS 5523 (Ohio Ct. App., Columbiana County 2019).

Employee failed to establish whether she was disabled because the limitation on her ability to walk, even if it could be considered to have been substantial on a temporary basis, was not permanent or long-term, as the employee admitted that the knee injury has not caused any limitations on her ability to walk in the time since she left the employer. Giffin v. Provider Servs., 2011 U.S. Dist. LEXIS 32689 (S.D. Ohio Mar. 15, 2011).

**Not similarly situated**

Employee, who was an African-American woman employed as a sheriff's deputy, was unable to establish a prima facie case for race or gender discrimination arising out of her discharge from employment as she was unable to establish that a similarly situated, non-protected employee was treated more favorably during a disciplinary action, in that, while another deputy, a white male employee, was suspended for five days after he downloaded and viewed pornography on a computer at work, the deputy, unlike the employee, did not engage in any further inappropriate conduct during his probationary period. Thus, the employee was not similarly situated to the deputy. Smith v. Kelly, 2012-Ohio-2547, 2012 Ohio App. LEXIS 2235 (Ohio Ct. App., Clark County 2012).

**Perceived disability discrimination**

Former employee, a psychologist, failed to establish a prima facie case of perceived disability discrimination because merely sending him to an independent medical examination did not amount to evidence that the employer perceived the employee as disabled. Dalton v. Ohio Dep't of Rehab. & Corr., 2014-Ohio-2658, 2014 Ohio App. LEXIS 2598 (Ohio Ct. App., Franklin County 2014).

**Plain error**

**—None found**

In a landlord's forcible entry and detainer action pursuant to R.C. 1923.02, there was no plain error in the trial court's failure to recognize that R.C. 4112.02(H)(1) and (4) of the Ohio Fair Housing Act, R.C. Chapter 4112, applied to non-renewal of a lease, as there was no manifest miscarriage of justice. Olympic Realty v. Zaleski, 2013-Ohio-1245, 2013 Ohio App. LEXIS 1143 (Ohio Ct. App., Franklin County 2013).

**Police officers, firefighters**

Summary judgment to a city was properly granted in a hostile environment sexual harassment claim by a police dispatcher and her husband, in violation of R.C. 4112.02(A) and 4112.99, as they failed to satisfy two of the three necessary elements of the claim where there was no showing that the alleged harassment by a police chief to the dispatcher was unwelcome, and that the harassing conduct was sufficiently severe or pervasive to affect the terms, conditions, or privileges of employment, or any matter directly or indirectly related to employment. Armaly v. City of Wapakoneta, 2006-Ohio-3629, 2006 Ohio App. LEXIS 3562 (Ohio Ct. App., Auglaize County 2006).

Trial court erred by not granting a city's motion for a directed verdict in a police officer's employment discrimination action because the officer, who had been discharged upon pleading guilty to a charge of aggravated menacing in connection with a domestic violence incident in which he broke his wife's jaw and rendered her unconscious, did not offer evidence that he was replaced by a person outside of the protected classification and while the other officers who he offered as "comparables" may not have been exemplary officers, their offenses, which ranged from time sheet falsification to domestic violence resulting in lesser physical harm than that inflicted by the officer, did not make them "similarly situated." Williams v. City of Akron, 2003-Ohio-7197, 2003 Ohio App. LEXIS 6648 (Ohio Ct. App., Summit County 2003), aff'd, 2005-Ohio-6268, 107 Ohio St. 3d 203, 837 N.E.2d 1169, 2005 Ohio LEXIS 2836 (Ohio 2005).

Police officer was not able to establish a prima facie case on her claims of retaliation and sex discrimination since she was not able to show that she suffered an adverse employment action: Hann v. Perkins Twp., 2004-Ohio-3445, 2004 Ohio App. LEXIS 3059 (Ohio Ct. App., Erie County 2004).

In a case in which 16 police officers alleged employment discrimination in violation of 42 U.S.C.S. §§ 1983 and 2000e-2(a) and R.C. 4112.02 and 4112.99, the court denied defendants' motion for judgment on the pleadings because the allegations in the complaint permitted the officers to offer direct evidence of the discrimination complained of, and even if the McDonnell Douglas prima face case standard was applicable, that standard did not apply to the standard the officers had to satisfy to survive the motion for judgment on the pleadings. Grizzell v. City of Columbus, 2003 U.S. Dist. LEXIS 13393 (S.D. Ohio July 8, 2003).

Titles 39 — 57

Blanket exclusion of persons with insulin-dependent diabetes from employment as police officers violates the Ohio civil rights act: Bombrys v. City of Toledo, 849 F. Supp. 1210, 1993 U.S. Dist. LEXIS 20178 (N.D. Ohio 1993).

An occupational hazard to employment is not established where a firefighter candidate has a severe stutter, but his work history proves that he does not stutter in fire fighting situations. An oral employment interview cannot be used to disqualify such a candidate: City of Columbus v. Liebhart, 86 Ohio App. 3d 469, 621 N.E.2d 554, 1993 Ohio App. LEXIS 1186 (Ohio Ct. App., Franklin County 1993).

In raising a challenge to a city's visual acuity test for police officers, the relevant theories for requirements which constitute bona fide occupational qualifications demand that the employer demonstrate that the job qualifications in question are reasonably necessary, and also that the employer has reasonable cause to believe, based upon a factual reason, that all or substantially all of the protected class involved would be unable to perform safely and efficiently the duties of the job; or that some members of this class possess a trait precluding safe and efficient job performance; or that the employer has a rational basis in fact to believe that the elimination of its practice would increase the likelihood of risk to the public: City of Columbus v. Ohio Civil Rights Com., 23 Ohio App. 3d 178, 492 N.E.2d 482, 1985 Ohio App. LEXIS 10128 (Ohio Ct. App., Franklin County 1985).

R.C. 124.37 states that layoffs in police or fire departments shall be in order of seniority. Defendant city entered into a consent decree, in settlement of a discrimination suit, by which it bound itself to hire a greater percentage of minority applicants for positions in its fire department. In the absence of express agreement to the contrary in the consent decree, the city is not prohibited from basing its layoffs due to economic necessity on seniority: Youngblood v. Dalzell, 568 F.2d 506, 8 Ohio Op. 3d 146, 1978 U.S. App. LEXIS 13118 (6th Cir. Ohio 1978).

**Political subdivisions**

Employment-discrimination provisions in R.C. 4112.01(A)(2) and 4112.02(A) did not expressly impose civil liability on political-subdivision employees but imposed vicarious liability on the political-subdivision itself; just as respondeat superior refers only to the vicarious liability of an employer, R.C. 4112.01(A)(2) refers to the vicarious liability of a political-subdivision employer when the question is whether that statute "expressly" imposes liability on political-subdivision employees. Hauser v. City of Dayton Police Dep't, 2014-Ohio-3636, 140 Ohio St. 3d 268, 17 N.E.3d 554, 2014 Ohio LEXIS 2040 (Ohio 2014), limited, Johnson-Newberry v. Cuyahoga Cty., 2019-Ohio-3655, 2019 Ohio App. LEXIS 3750 (Ohio Ct. App., Cuyahoga County 2019).

R.C. 4112.01(A)(2) and 4112.02(A) do not expressly impose civil liability on political-subdivision employees so as to exempt them from immunity under R.C. 2744.03(A)(6)(c) but rather subject a political-subdivision employer to vicarious liability for the discriminatory acts of its employees; an individual political-subdivision employee still faces liability under other provisions of R.C. 4112.02 that expressly impose liability, including the aiding-and-abetting provision in R.C. 4112.02(J). Hauser v. City of Dayton Police Dep't, 2014-Ohio-3636, 140 Ohio St. 3d 268, 17 N.E.3d 554, 2014 Ohio LEXIS 2040 (Ohio 2014), limited, Johnson-Newberry v. Cuyahoga Cty., 2019-Ohio-3655, 2019 Ohio App. LEXIS 3750 (Ohio Ct. App., Cuyahoga County 2019).

R.C. 2744.03(A)(6)(c) excepts political subdivision employees from statutory immunity for employment discrimination claims. It was possible for the former mayor to be held personally liable for damages resulting from his hiring decision even though he was engaged in a governmental function when he appointed persons to the police department: State ex rel. Conroy v. Williams, 2009-Ohio-6040, 185 Ohio App. 3d 69, 923 N.E.2d 191, 2009 Ohio App. LEXIS 5069 (Ohio Ct. App., Mahoning County 2009).

Public employee alleging employment discrimination in violation of R.C. Chapter 4112 need not exhaust the administrative remedy of appeal to a civil service commission before pursuing the civil action allowed in R.C. 4112.99: Dworning v. City of Euclid, 2008-Ohio-3318, 119 Ohio St. 3d 83, 892 N.E.2d 420, 2008 Ohio LEXIS 1768 (Ohio 2008).

Nothing in the text of R.C. 4112.02, barring discriminatory employment practices, suggests that the general assembly meant to treat employees subject to civil service commission rules (or any other disciplinary procedure) differently than non-civil service employees. R.C. 4112.01(A)(2) includes within the definition of "employer" any political subdivision of the state, and an "employee" is defined as an individual employed by any employer, so it makes no distinction between public and private employers or their employees. Dworning v. City of Euclid, 2006-Ohio-6772, 2006 Ohio App. LEXIS 6685 (Ohio Ct. App., Cuyahoga County 2006), aff'd, 2008-Ohio-3318, 119 Ohio St. 3d 83, 892 N.E.2d 420, 2008 Ohio LEXIS 1768 (Ohio 2008).

District court's reliance on defendant city's hiring committee recommendation in analyzing plaintiff employee's R.C. 4112.02(A) failure to promote claim and her pretext argument was not error merely because the letterhead incorrectly referred to a prior human resources director because the use of old letterhead alone was insufficient to create fact issues on authenticity. Sigall-Drakulich v. City of Columbus, 156 Fed. Appx. 791, 2005 FED App. 0965N, 2005 U.S. App. LEXIS 27772 (6th Cir. Ohio 2005).

R.C. ch. 2744 immunity did not apply to the employee's allegations of sexual harassment under the Equal Protection Clause, Title VII, and R.C. 4112.02 against the city, former police chief, mayor, and safety director because her allegations related to the conditions of her employment and therefore were exempt from municipal immunity under R.C. 2744.09(C). Kohler v. City of Wapakoneta, 381 F. Supp. 2d 692, 2005 U.S. Dist. LEXIS 16671 (N.D. Ohio 2005).

Pursuant to R.C. 2744.03(A)(6), the mayor and the city safety director were immune from a police dispatcher's intentional tort claims of invasion of privacy and intentional infliction of emotional distress, which arose from the former police chief's alleged sexual harassment of her. When the mayor and safety director learned of the dispatcher's allegations against the chief, they referred the matter to the state Bureau of Criminal Investigation for an investigation and accepted the chief's letter of retirement, and nothing in the record showed that they acted outside the scope of their employment or acted maliciously or in bad faith; moreover, the sexual harassment statute, R.C. 4112.02(A), did not expressly impose liability on them. Kohler v. City of Wapakoneta, 381 F. Supp. 2d 692, 2005 U.S. Dist. LEXIS 16671 (N.D. Ohio 2005).

Where a jail corrections officer reported sexual harassment by a co-worker, but the jail allegedly took no corrective action until the officer filed criminal charges against the co-worker for assault and the jail's investigation of the incident resulted in the resignation of the co-worker, the jail's investigation of the assault did not preclude liability of the jail for failing to remediate the prior harassing conduct. Hendricks v. Office of the Clermont County Sheriff, 415 F. Supp. 2d 782, 2005 U.S. Dist. LEXIS 13017 (S.D. Ohio 2005).

All of an employee's state law claims brought pursuant to R.C. 4112.02(a) against a city and supervisor for sex-based disparate treatment, hostile work environment, and retaliation, which were construed using the same evidentiary framework as her claims brought under Title VII of the Civil Rights Act of 1964, 42 U.S.C.S. § 2000(e) et seq., survived summary judgment, including her claim against the supervisor for individual liability, because although the supervisor could not be individually liable under Title VII, he could be liable in his individual capacity under Ohio law. Dunnom v. Bennett, 290 F. Supp. 2d 860, 2003 U.S. Dist. LEXIS 20096 (S.D. Ohio 2003).

Since the county board of mental retardation does not fall within the ambit of the definition of an "employment agency" in R.C. 4112.02(A)(5), appellant improperly brought a cause of action against the board and its employees based on an alleged violation of R.C. 4112.02(B)(1): Albert v. Trumbull County Bd. of Mental Retardation/Developmental Disabilities, 1999 Ohio App. LEXIS 4136 (Ohio Ct. App., Trumbull County Sept. 3, 1999).

The city was not plaintiff's "employer" where it merely provided most of the funding for the organization that contracted with him. R.C. 4112.02 does not require that the employee be fired or demoted: Berge v. Columbus Community Cable Access, 136 Ohio App. 3d 281, 736 N.E.2d 517, 1999 Ohio App. LEXIS 6455 (Ohio Ct. App., Franklin County 1999).

Plaintiff municipal employee could not recover on her claim of quid pro quo harassment where her probationary period was extended as a result of her initial failure of the state firearm proficiency test: Washington v. City of Cleveland, 948 F. Supp. 1301, 1996 U.S. Dist. LEXIS 20586 (N.D. Ohio 1996).

**Preemption**

Trial court properly found that the employment discrimination and retaliation provisions of R.C. Chapter 4112 were in conflict with, and therefore preempted by, the National Bank Act's provision in 12 U.S.C.S. § 24, Fifth, that national banks had the power to appoint and dismiss its officers "at pleasure." Boesch v. Champaign Nat'l Bank, 2008-Ohio-3282, 2008 Ohio App. LEXIS 2771 (Ohio Ct. App., Summit County 2008).

Summary judgment was properly granted to a bank on its former employee's claim for employment discrimination occurring during the course of her employment prior to her termination from the bank because the bank showed that the employee was appointed to the position of a banking officer and was employed as a bank "officer" within the meaning of the National Bank Act (NBA), 12 U.S.C.S. § 24, Fifth; thus, the NBA preempted the employee's state law discrimination claim relating to the time in which she was actively engaged as a bank employee. Boesch v. Champaign Nat'l Bank, 2008-Ohio-3282, 2008 Ohio App. LEXIS 2771 (Ohio Ct. App., Summit County 2008).

**Pregnancy**

Because an employer's uniform minimum-length-of-service leave policy treated all employees the same and was "pregnancy-blind", an employee fired for taking leave before the employee reached the minimum length of service for complications in the employee's pregnancy failed to make a prima facie case of sex discrimination; the Supreme Court of Ohio held that such policy was not direct evidence of a violation of R.C. 4112.02(A). McFee v. Nursing Care Mgmt. of Am., Inc., 2010-Ohio-2744, 126 Ohio St. 3d 183, 931 N.E.2d 1069, 2010 Ohio LEXIS 1418 (Ohio 2010).

Defendants were granted summary judgment on a former employee's common law tort for a public policy violation because the public policy at issue, pregnancy discrimination, was already protected by an available and adequate remedy found in R.C. 4112.02, and the jeopardy element therefore could not be met. Pizzimenti v. Oldcastle Glass, Inc., 666 F. Supp. 2d 839, 2009 U.S. Dist. LEXIS 104018 (N.D. Ohio 2009).

Defendants were denied summary judgment on a former employee's pregnancy discrimination claim under R.C. 4112.02 because there was a genuine issue of material fact regarding whether the employee freely resigned or was pressured into resignation by defendants and whether defendants' rationale for terminating the employee was pretext for discriminatory motive. Pizzimenti v. Oldcastle Glass, Inc., 666 F. Supp. 2d 839, 2009 U.S. Dist. LEXIS 104018 (N.D. Ohio 2009).

Employer was entitled to summary judgment in a former employee's action alleging sex discrimination in violation of R.C. 4112.02 and OAC 4112-5-05(G) based on her termination upon return from her maternity leave under the Family and Medical Leave Act, 29 U.S.C.S. § 2601 et seq.; the employee returned to work one week later than expected and the employer was within its rights to terminate the employee in accordance with its attendance policy. There was no evidence that the employer's termination of the employee constituted unlawful discrimination. Morr v. Kamco Indus., 548 F. Supp. 2d 472, 2008 U.S. Dist. LEXIS 30908 (N.D. Ohio 2008).

Police officer's claims of pregnancy discrimination under Title VII, 42 U.S.C.S. §§ 2000e-2(a)(1), 2000e(k), and R.C. 4112.02(A), 4112.99 failed because, even assuming that she made out a prima facie case, the officer failed to rebut a city's legitimate and nondiscriminatory reason for not granting her request for a restricted duty assignment, that it had a policy prohibiting such assignment, by showing it to be a pretext for unlawful discrimination. The officer presented no evidence refuting the police chief's position that the city had a policy of no light duty, and, thus, she failed to demonstrate the falsity of the city's reason for not accommodating her condition. Tysinger v. Police Dep't, 463 F.3d 569, 2006 FED App. 0363P, 2006 U.S. App. LEXIS 24144 (6th Cir. Ohio 2006).

Plaintiff produced sufficient evidence to support the finding of discrimination on the basis of pregnancy. The employee was in a particularly vulnerable state when the employer engaged in discriminatory conduct, and vulnerability is relevant in determining damages. To recover punitive damages under Title VII, a plaintiff must prove by a preponderance of the evidence that the employer's intentional discrimination was the result of malice or reckless indifference to the federally protected rights of the aggrieved individual: Hollingsworth v. Time Warner Cable, 2006-Ohio-4903, 168 Ohio App. 3d 658, 861 N.E.2d 580, 2006 Ohio App. LEXIS 4833 (Ohio Ct. App., Hamilton County 2006).



After reviewing evidence presented, the court found that a nursing student had presented sufficient evidence to establish a prima facie case of pregnancy discrimination. It was undisputed that she was pregnant when she was subjected to an adverse employment decision, and evidence was submitted that the student was qualified for the job that she was seeking, and therefore the court denied the nursing facility's motion for summary judgment pursuant to Fed. R. Civ. P. 56. Davis v. E. Galbraith Health Care Ctr., 2005 U.S. Dist. LEXIS 33574 (S.D. Ohio July 11, 2005).

Nursing home terminated an employee during her pregnancy, in violation of R.C. 4112.02(A), because the termination was under the guise of not being able to lift 25 pounds, however, nothing indicated that such a requirement was actually part of the employee's job; specifically, she was not allowed to lift any of the patients, and her housekeeping duties did not involve lifting, and at the time that she was terminated, notes of the meeting did not refer to any alleged insufficiency of the doctor's note the employee provided, nor did they mention any statutory or administrative mandate that she be medically certified to perform her job duties as was contended by the nursing home. Voiers Enters. v. Ohio Civ. Rights Comm'n, 2004-Ohio-738, 156 Ohio App. 3d 195, 805 N.E.2d 138, 2004 Ohio App. LEXIS 685 (Ohio Ct. App., Scioto County 2004).

R.C. 4112.02(L) did not permit the employer to discharge a pregnant employee where her duties did not in fact require heavy lifting: Voiers Enters. v. Ohio Civ. Rights Comm'n, 2004-Ohio-738, 156 Ohio App. 3d 195, 805 N.E.2d 138, 2004 Ohio App. LEXIS 685 (Ohio Ct. App., Scioto County 2004).

The employer was not entitled to summary judgment where the employee produced sufficient evidence that the nondiscriminatory reasons for termination were pretextual. The employee presented a prima facie case of retaliation against her rights under pregnancy protection laws and right to consult an attorney: Hollingsworth v. Time Warner Cable, 2004-Ohio-3130, 157 Ohio App. 3d 539, 812 N.E.2d 976, 2004 Ohio App. LEXIS 2810 (Ohio Ct. App., Hamilton County 2004).

Nurse's aide failed to show that the court erred excluding rebuttal testimony which would have shown that the reason the employer proffered for not hiring her was not true and a pretext for discrimination on the basis of her pregnancy. Cominsky v. Madison Health Care, 2003-Ohio-6745, 2003 Ohio App. LEXIS 5981 (Ohio Ct. App., Lake County 2003).

Employee failed to establish a prima facie case of discrimination based on pregnancy where she was terminated because she was unable to comply with the employer's time clock and work station procedures. Birchard v. Marc Glassman, Inc., 2003-Ohio-4073, 2003 Ohio App. LEXIS 3634 (Ohio Ct. App., Cuyahoga County 2003).

Evidence that a company ignored discrimination complaints and promoted men over the employee, a pregnant woman, was insufficient to show that her termination for leaving money unsecured against company policy was a pretext for gender and pregnancy discrimination. Gover v. Speedway Super Am., LLC, 284 F. Supp. 2d 858, 2003 U.S. Dist. LEXIS 17310 (S.D. Ohio 2003).

The employee presented a prima facie case of pregnancy discrimination where a nonpregnant employee was afforded better disability leave benefits. An employer's compliance with the FMLA does not relieve it of an obligation to provide reasonable leave on account of childbearing: McConaughy v. Boswell Oil Co., 126 Ohio App. 3d 820, 711 N.E.2d 719, 1998 Ohio App. LEXIS 1179 (Ohio Ct. App., Hamilton County 1998).

The pregnancy discrimination act does not require an employer to make accommodations for pregnant employees unless it has made accommodations for similarly situated nonpregnant employees: Priest v. TFH-EB, Inc., 127 Ohio App. 3d 159, 711 N.E.2d 1070, 1998 Ohio App. LEXIS 1384 (Ohio Ct. App., Franklin County), dismissed, 82 Ohio St. 3d 1480, 696 N.E.2d 1087, 1998 Ohio LEXIS 2082 (Ohio 1998).

The employee established a prima facie case of discrimination based on pregnancy. Where the employer produced plausible, nondiscriminatory reasons for discharge, the employee had the burden of proving that they were pretextual: Frantz v. Beechmont Pet Hosp., 117 Ohio App. 3d 351, 690 N.E.2d 897, 1996 Ohio App. LEXIS 5897 (Ohio Ct. App., Hamilton County 1996).

Affirmance of civil rights commission's order to reinstate manager who was demoted after pregnancy leave not an abuse of discretion: Morse v. Sudan, Inc., 1994 Ohio App. LEXIS 3480 (Ohio Ct. App., Cuyahoga County Aug. 11, 1994).

Denial of maternity leave mandated by OAC 4112-5-05(G)(6) is, in effect, terminating the employee due to her pregnancy: Marvel Consultants v. Ohio Civil Rights Comm'n, 93 Ohio App. 3d 838, 639 N.E.2d 1265, 1994 Ohio App. LEXIS 2049 (Ohio Ct. App., Cuyahoga County 1994).

The employee presented sufficient evidence of discrimination based on her pregnancy: El Grande Steak House v. Ohio Civil Rights Comm'n, 99 Ohio App. 3d 557, 651 N.E.2d 440, 1994 Ohio App. LEXIS 5961 (Ohio Ct. App., Ashtabula County 1994).

Failure to make leave available to a pregnant employee in lieu of terminating her is not discriminatory unless it is shown that such employee was terminated because of, or on the basis of, sex, including pregnancy: Frank v. Toledo Hosp., 84 Ohio App. 3d 610, 617 N.E.2d 774, 1992 Ohio App. LEXIS 6556 (Ohio Ct. App., Lucas County 1992).

Where a teacher alleges her contract was not renewed based on her pregnancy by artificial insemination and her status as an unwed mother, a genuine issue of material fact exists precluding summary judgment on her sexual discrimination claim: Cameron v. Board of Educ., 795 F. Supp. 228, 1991 U.S. Dist. LEXIS 20245 (S.D. Ohio 1991).

**—Seniority**

A board of education's refusal to grant seniority to a teacher who had taken a maternity leave under a policy subsequently determined to be discriminatory but which she did not timely challenge and who failed to allege that the seniority policy discriminated against women who had been required to take maternity leaves did not constitute a present violation of her rights: White v. Columbus Bd. of Education, 2 Ohio App. 3d 178, 441 N.E.2d 303, 1982 Ohio App. LEXIS 10883 (Ohio Ct. App., Franklin County 1982).

**Pregnancy discrimination**

In a terminated employee's sex discrimination action, the trial court's grant of the employer's judgment on the pleadings was error because it improperly construed the material facts in the complaint in favor of the employer instead of the employee as the nonmoving party; the employee alleged sufficient facts to support her assertion that she was terminated due to her pregnancy. Toman v. Humility of Mary Health Partners, 2014-Ohio-4417, 2014 Ohio App. LEXIS 4335 (Ohio Ct. App., Mahoning County 2014), dismissed, 2015 Ohio Misc. LEXIS 10956 (Ohio C.P. Apr. 30, 2015).

Defendant's motion for summary judgment on the employee's pregnancy discrimination claim was denied because the plaintiff stated a prima facie case of pregnancy discrimination under 42 U.S.C.S. § 2000e(k) and R.C. 4112.02 where the plaintiff showed a nexus between her pregnancy and the adverse employment action since she was suspended three months after she told her employer that she was pregnant, and the plaintiff was the subject of three performance based disciplinary actions in the span of one month; moreover, the assistant director's comments constituted evidence of a motivation to discipline the plaintiff because of her pregnancy, and the defendant terminated two pregnant employees in two months. Although the defendant maintained that it terminated the plaintiff because she provided poor care and had multiple attendance violations, the defendant's director testified that the plaintiff had not accumulated enough occurrences under the defendant's attendance policy to warrant any discipline, much less suspension or termination. Alexander v. Trilogy Health Servs., LLC, 2012 U.S. Dist. LEXIS 152079 (S.D. Ohio Oct. 23, 2012).

Without offering any evidence that her employer replaced her with similarly-situated, non-pregnant flight attendants or other evidence that the employer retaliated for her exercise of pregnancy leave two years before, the employee could not state a prima facie case of pregnancy discrimination. Staunch v. Cont'l Airlines, Inc., 2007 U.S. Dist. LEXIS 5767 (N.D. Ohio Jan. 26, 2007), aff'd, 511 F.3d 625, 2008 FED App. 0004P, 2008 U.S. App. LEXIS 196 (6th Cir. Ohio 2008).

**Pretext for discrimination**

As plaintiff failed to demonstrate a genuine issue of material fact existed regarding pretext, summary judgment in favor of defendant was proper on plaintiff's claims of race discrimination; although plaintiff argued that he had a master's degree and the individual selected for the position did not, the job posting showed that a master's degree was a desired qualification, not a minimum qualification. Hughes v. Youngstown State Univ., 2020-Ohio-611, 2020 Ohio Misc. LEXIS 8 (Ohio Ct. Cl. 2020), aff'd, 2021-Ohio-2079, 2021 Ohio App. LEXIS 2045 (Ohio Ct. App., Franklin County 2021).

Even if an employee had proven a prima facie case for race or gender discrimination, the employee failed to put forward sufficient evidence to support a reasonable inference that the employer's proffered non-discriminatory grounds for her discharge were a pretext for race or gender discrimination. Thus, the employee's suit alleging claims of discrimination was properly dismissed on summary judgment. Smith v. Kelly, 2012-Ohio-2547, 2012 Ohio App. LEXIS 2235 (Ohio Ct. App., Clark County 2012).

Fact that airline chose to give the flight attendant a final reprieve was strong evidence that it's final decision to terminate her employment in April 2004 for flying with a non-compliant safety manual was not a pretext for pregnancy discrimination. Thus, she failed to present any evidence to create a genuine issue that its legitimate, non-discriminatory reason for her termination was insufficient to warrant the action. Staunch v. Cont'l Airlines, Inc., 511 F.3d 625, 2008 FED App. 0004P, 2008 U.S. App. LEXIS 196 (6th Cir. Ohio), cert. denied, 555 U.S. 883, 129 S. Ct. 223, 172 L. Ed. 2d 143, 2008 U.S. LEXIS 5461 (U.S. 2008).

If an employee's involuntary disability separation was an adverse employment action, for purposes of the employee's claim of racial discrimination, the employee's employer rebutted any presumption of discrimination because the employer showed the employer had a legitimate, non-discriminatory, reason for the employer's action, based on the employee's frequent absences and inability to do the employee's job, and the employee did not show this reason was a mere pretext. Carter v. Dep't of Rehab. & Corr., 2007-Ohio-3872, 2007 Ohio Misc. LEXIS 250 (Ohio Ct. Cl. 2007).

**Prima facie case**

Employee did not establish a prima facie case of racial discrimination in employment because the employee did not establish that the employee was treated less favorably than an employee who was not a member of the employee's protected class since a white employee submitted by the terminated employee as establishing this element, because both employees had been disciplined for sleeping on the job, did not establish the element because the two employees were not similarly situated since the employees did not have similar records, as the white employee had been disciplined over a number of years, while the terminated employee had been disciplined over 12 months. Isbell v. Johns Manville, Inc., 2007-Ohio-5355, 2007 Ohio App. LEXIS 4716 (Ohio Ct. App., Lucas County 2007).

Employee did not establish a prima facie case of racial discrimination in employment because the employee did not establish that the employee was qualified for the employee's job as the employee did not produce proper evidence to rebut or contradict the employee's employer's history of of dissatisfaction with the employee's performance due to the employee sleeping on the job and failing to wear required protective equipment. Isbell v. Johns Manville, Inc., 2007-Ohio-5355, 2007 Ohio App. LEXIS 4716 (Ohio Ct. App., Lucas County 2007).

Employee did not establish a prima facie case of racial discrimination in employment because the employee did not establish that the employee was treated less favorably than an employee who was not a member of the employee's protected class since a white employee submitted by the terminated employee as establishing this element, because both employees had been disciplined for sleeping on the job, did not establish the element because the two employees were not similarly situated since the employees did not have similar records, as the white employee had been disciplined over a number of years, while the terminated employee had been disciplined over 12 months. Isbell v. Johns Manville, Inc., 2007-Ohio-5355, 2007 Ohio App. LEXIS 4716 (Ohio Ct. App., Lucas County 2007).

Employee did not establish a prima facie case of racial discrimination in employment because the employee did not establish that the employee was qualified for the employee's job as the employee did not produce proper evidence to rebut or contradict the employee's employer's history of of dissatisfaction with the employee's performance due to the employee sleeping on the job and failing to wear required protective equipment. Isbell v. Johns Manville, Inc., 2007-Ohio-5355, 2007 Ohio App. LEXIS 4716 (Ohio Ct. App., Lucas County 2007).

District court properly granted summary judgment to a former employer in a case brought under Title VII of the Civil Rights Act, 42 U.S.C.S. § 2000e, and under R.C. 4112.02 because the employee failed to meet make out a prima facie case as he did not show that he was treated differently than similarly situated employees who were not members of a protected class. Each employee who was discovered to have lied about past criminal history on his application was terminated; the fact that two were reinstated was unavailing as they, unlike plaintiff employee, were union members and were reinstated as part of the grievance process. Elgabi v. Toledo Area Reg'l Transit Auth., 228 Fed. Appx. 537, 2007 FED App. 0266N, 2007 U.S. App. LEXIS 8528 (6th Cir. Ohio 2007).

University and university officials were entitled to summary judgment on a former employee's claims of race discrimination, retaliation, and civil conspiracy because (1) although the employee met three elements of a prima facie case of discrimination under Title VII, 42 U.S.C.S. § 1981, and R.C. ch. 4112 as he was a member of a protected class, suffered adverse employment action, and was qualified for his job, he failed to identify a non-protected, similarly-situated person whom the university treated better than himself; (2) although the employee established three elements of a prima facie case of retaliation as he engaged in protected action, which defendants knew about, and was subsequently terminated, he did not show a causal connection between the filing of this Title VII action and his termination as he did not show that temporal proximity existed between his protected action and his termination; (3) without an unlawful action causing injury, there was no support for a conspiracy claim under 42 U.S.C.S. § 1985. Giles v. Univ. of Toledo, 478 F. Supp. 2d 942, 2007 U.S. Dist. LEXIS 17892 (N.D. Ohio 2007), aff'd, 286 Fed. Appx. 295, 2008 FED App. 0422N, 2008 U.S. App. LEXIS 15216 (6th Cir. Ohio 2008).

Police officer's claims of pregnancy discrimination under Title VII, 42 U.S.C.S. §§ 2000e-2(a)(1), 2000e(k), and R.C. 4112.02(A), 4112.99 failed because she did not show a causal connection between the adverse action and the fact that her infirmity was the result of pregnancy; she could have continued working if able, but her doctor prescribed her light duty, which was unavailable. Further, the employees that she presented as comparable were not similarly situated in that, while they also suffered from temporary infirmities, they presented themselves as willing and able to continue working. Tysinger v. Police Dep't, 463 F.3d 569, 2006 FED App. 0363P, 2006 U.S. App. LEXIS 24144 (6th Cir. Ohio 2006).

Police officer's claims of pregnancy discrimination under Title VII, 42 U.S.C.S. §§ 2000e-2(a)(1), 2000e(k), and R.C. 4112.02(A), 4112.99 failed because, inter alia, even under a mixed motive analysis, she did not demonstrate that pregnancy discrimination was a motivating factor in the decision to deny her an accommodating restricted duty assignment. The police chief's statement that pregnancy was not a disability that the city was required to accommodate did not indicate unlawful discriminatory animus but, rather, was entirely consistent with the law; moreover, even if the chief's testimony was construed as potentially revealing a personal bias, it was undisputed that the decision to deny the officer a restricted duty assignment was consistent with the city's policy prohibiting light duty assignments, a policy that even the chief had no authority to alter or circumvent. Tysinger v. Police Dep't, 463 F.3d 569, 2006 FED App. 0363P, 2006 U.S. App. LEXIS 24144 (6th Cir. Ohio 2006).

On a retaliation claim a terminated employee failed to demonstrate a casual connection between his protected activities and his termination; he also failed to point to sufficient evidence to raise even an inference that his failure to pass a drug test was not the true reason for his discharge. There was no sufficient inference that the employer discharged the employee with a discriminatory animus. Counts v. Kraton Polymers U.S. LLC, 2006 U.S. Dist. LEXIS 65312 (S.D. Ohio Sept. 13, 2006), aff'd, 260 Fed. Appx. 825, 2008 FED App. 0064N, 2008 U.S. App. LEXIS 2187 (6th Cir. Ohio 2008).

Terminated driver failed to make a prima facie case of discrimination under Title VII by showing similarly situated employees were treated differently since two drivers were not similarly situated due to their union status and other employees who were not terminated had only traffic violations, not both criminal and traffic convictions. Elgabi v. Toledo Area Reg'l Transit Auth., 2006 U.S. Dist. LEXIS 33910 (N.D. Ohio May 26, 2006), aff'd, 228 Fed. Appx. 537, 2007 FED App. 0266N, 2007 U.S. App. LEXIS 8528 (6th Cir. Ohio 2007).

R.C. 4112.02 is generally to be interpreted in accordance with interpretations of federal anti-discrimination laws including Title VII of the Civil Rights Act of 1964, 42 U.S.C.S. § 2000e-2 and the Age Discrimination in Employment Act, 29 U.S.C.S. § 621 et seq. Thus, in order to establish a prima facie case of discriminatory discharge under R.C. 4112.02, a plaintiff must prove the following: (1) that she was a member of the protected class when her employment was terminated; (2) that her employment was terminated; (3) that she was qualified to perform the job from which she was dismissed; and (4) that she was replaced by a man or, in the case of an age discrimination claim, by a substantially younger employee. Soliday v. Fluor Fernald, Inc., 2006 U.S. Dist. LEXIS 1504 (S.D. Ohio Jan. 18, 2006).

Although former employer asserted in support of its summary judgment motion that the former employee's admission that he failed to meet his specific goals for sales and promotional expenses in 2000, 2001, and 2002, and that the employee acknowledged that he bore at least some responsibility for the losses the employer sustained in 2000, 2001, and 2002, precluded him from establishing a prima facie case for age discrimination, the focus at the instant stage of litigation was on the employee's objective qualifications, such as his experience in the industry and his demonstrated possession of the required general skills. Drawing all reasonable inferences in favor of the employee, the facts showed the employee was qualified for his position. Bozsan v. Tradewinds Bev. Co., 2005 U.S. Dist. LEXIS 23032 (S.D. Ohio Sept. 21, 2005).

When an employee alleged that a school district's non-competitive appointment of individuals to a supervisory position the employee eventually applied unsuccessfully for was racial and gender discrimination, the employee showed a prima facie case of discrimination because (1) the employee's failure, initially, to apply for the position was not dispositive as the position was not posted, so there was no mechanism to apply for the position, relieving her of the burden of showing she suffered an adverse employment action and was qualified for the position, (2) there was no dispute that she belonged to a protected class, and (3) the person who was appointed was not a member of the protected class. Senu-Oke v. Bd. of Educ., 2005-Ohio-5239, 2005 Ohio App. LEXIS 4744 (Ohio Ct. App., Montgomery County 2005).

Discrimination complaint of a Hispanic auto sales consultant applicant was dismissed because he failed to meet his burden with regard to the third element of a prima facie case, namely, that he was qualified for the position in question, where his driving record was too poor for him to be insured under the motor company's insurance policy. His state law claim, like his federal claims, could not survive summary judgment because he was not qualified for the position due to his poor driving record. Sanabria v. Germain Motor Co., 2005 U.S. Dist. LEXIS 20683 (S.D. Ohio Sept. 21, 2005).

**Public accommodation**

Co-worker's claim against her fellow worker was sufficient to survive dismissal, arising from her report to her employer against the fellow worker for his alleged sexually harassing conduct to her and other co-workers, as the parties worked at a county community college which was a place of public accommodation under R.C. 4112.01(A)(9), and the claim fit within R.C. 4112.02(G) for purposes of unlawful discriminatory practice. Hughes v. Miller, 2009-Ohio-963, 181 Ohio App. 3d 440, 909 N.E.2d 642, 2009 Ohio App. LEXIS 836 (Ohio Ct. App., Cuyahoga County 2009).

When applicants for membership in an all-male club claimed gender discrimination, and the jury found in favor of the club, the applicants did not show, under Civ.R. 50(A)(4), that the applicants were entitled to judgment notwithstanding the verdict because it could not be said that reasonable minds could not disagree as to whether the club was a public accommodation governed by R.C. 4112.02(G). Wilson v. United Fellowship Club, 2007-Ohio-2089, 2007 Ohio App. LEXIS 1949 (Ohio Ct. App., Summit County 2007).

When applicants for membership in an all-male club claimed gender discrimination, and the jury found in favor of the club, the applicants did not show, under Civ.R. 50(A)(4), that the applicants were entitled to judgment notwithstanding the verdict because it could not be said that reasonable minds could not disagree as to whether the club was a public accommodation governed by R.C. 4112.02(G). Wilson v. United Fellowship Club, 2007-Ohio-2089, 2007 Ohio App. LEXIS 1949 (Ohio Ct. App., Summit County 2007).



The city was not the proprietor, manager or keeper of an organization's building for purposes of a claim of handicap discrimination where the city merely paid the organization to run a cable access channel. The building was a place of public accommodation: Berge v. Columbus Community Cable Access, 136 Ohio App. 3d 281, 736 N.E.2d 517, 1999 Ohio App. LEXIS 6455 (Ohio Ct. App., Franklin County 1999).

When determining whether there has been unlawful discrimination under R.C. 4112.02(G), the test is simply whether the proprietor, keeper, manager or employee of a place of public accommodation has denied to any person the full enjoyment of such place for reasons not applicable alike to all persons, irrespective of race, color, religion, national origin or ancestry: Ohio Civil Rights Comm. v. Lysyj, 38 Ohio St. 2d 217, 221,, 67 Ohio Op. 2d 287, 313 N.E.2d 3 (1974).

A barbershop is a place of "public accommodation" within the meaning of that term as used in R.C. 4112.02. The classification contained in R.C. Chapter 4112. of a barbershop as a "place of public accommodation," is reasonable and valid: Gegner v. Graham, 1 Ohio App. 2d 442, 30 Ohio Op. 2d 442, 205 N.E.2d 69, 1964 Ohio App. LEXIS 558 (Ohio Ct. App., Greene County 1964).

**Public contracts**

**—Assurance of nondiscrimination**

A bidder for a construction contract to be awarded by a public body of this state may be required to assure nondiscrimination in employment in the entire performance of such contract, by appropriate promises contained in contract provisions or related instruments: Weiner v. Cuyahoga Community College Dist., 19 Ohio St. 2d 35, 48 Ohio Op. 2d 48, 249 N.E.2d 907, 1969 Ohio LEXIS 332 (Ohio 1969), cert. denied, 396 U.S. 1004, 90 S. Ct. 554, 24 L. Ed. 2d 495, 1970 U.S. LEXIS 3295 (U.S. 1970).

**Public policy claim**

Since the employee did not explain the conflict between his deposition testimony and his affidavit about having stated that he was going to contact an attorney, the trial court was correct in disregarding the conflicting statement made in the affidavit. Thus, because the employee did not present credible evidence that he ever told the human resources administrator and the company president that he planned to obtain legal counsel, he could not establish that his dismissal was motivated by conduct relating to a public policy. Robinson v. Quasar Energy Group LLC, 2014-Ohio-4218, 2014 Ohio App. LEXIS 4129 (Ohio Ct. App., Cuyahoga County 2014).

Availability of statutory remedies under the Family and Medical Leave Act, 29 U.S.C.S. § 2615 and R.C. 4112.02 barred the plaintiff's claim of retaliation in violation of public policy. Rush v. E.I.duPont De Nemours & Co., 911 F. Supp. 2d 545, 2012 U.S. Dist. LEXIS 166356 (S.D. Ohio 2012).

No genuine issue of material fact was demonstrated as to an employee's claim that the employee was discharged in violation of the public policy against racial discrimination, as a matter of law, because the employee did not demonstrate a genuine issue of material fact as to whether the employee's dismissal was motivated by conduct related to this public policy, so the causation element of the employee's claim was not satisfied. Fitch v. United States Foodservice Corp., 2008-Ohio-282, 2008 Ohio App. LEXIS 241 (Ohio Ct. App., Butler County 2008).

Employee could not assert a claim that the employee's termination violated the public policy against age discrimination because the Ohio Supreme Court had determined that such a tort could not be claimed, since the protections in R.C. ch. 4112 adequately protected that public policy. Craddock v. Flood Co., 2008-Ohio-112, 2008 Ohio App. LEXIS 102 (Ohio Ct. App., Summit County 2008).

It is unnecessary to recognize a common-law claim for the tort of wrongful discharge in violation of public policy when remedy provisions are an essential part of the statutes upon which a plaintiff depends for the public policy claim and when those remedies adequately protect society's interest by discouraging the wrongful conduct. Leininger v. Pioneer Nat'l Latex, 2007-Ohio-4921, 115 Ohio St. 3d 311, 875 N.E.2d 36, 2007 Ohio LEXIS 2229 (Ohio 2007).

When a statutory scheme contains a full array of remedies for a wrongful termination, the underlying public policy will not be jeopardized if a common-law claim for wrongful discharge is not recognized based on that policy. Leininger v. Pioneer Nat'l Latex, 2007-Ohio-4921, 115 Ohio St. 3d 311, 875 N.E.2d 36, 2007 Ohio LEXIS 2229 (Ohio 2007).

There is no need to recognize a common-law action for wrongful discharge if there already exists a statutory remedy that adequately protects society's interests. Leininger v. Pioneer Nat'l Latex, 2007-Ohio-4921, 115 Ohio St. 3d 311, 875 N.E.2d 36, 2007 Ohio LEXIS 2229 (Ohio 2007).

Employee asserting the tort of wrongful discharge in violation of the public policy against age discrimination had to prove the jeopardy element, meaning that without a common-law tort claim for wrongful discharge based on age, Ohio's clear policy against age discrimination would be compromised. Leininger v. Pioneer Nat'l Latex, 2007-Ohio-4921, 115 Ohio St. 3d 311, 875 N.E.2d 36, 2007 Ohio LEXIS 2229 (Ohio 2007).

Tort claim for wrongful discharge in violation of the public policy against age discrimination did not exist because the jeopardy element of such a tort could not be established as Ohio Rev. Code ch. 4112 protected the policy through the remedies it offered in (1) R.C. 4112.02(N), allowing for any legal or equitable relief that would effectuate an individual's rights, (2) R.C. 4112.05(G), allowing enforcement actions by the Ohio Civil Rights Commission, (3) R.C. 4112.14(B), allowing "an appropriate remedy," which could include damages and injunctive relief, and (4) R.C. 4112.99, which subjected violators to a civil action for damages, injunctive relief, or other appropriate relief. Leininger v. Pioneer Nat'l Latex, 2007-Ohio-4921, 115 Ohio St. 3d 311, 875 N.E.2d 36, 2007 Ohio LEXIS 2229 (Ohio 2007).

It is unnecessary to recognize a common-law claim for the tort of wrongful discharge in violation of public policy when remedy provisions are an essential part of the statutes upon which a plaintiff depends for the public policy claim and when those remedies adequately protect society's interest by discouraging the wrongful conduct. Leininger v. Pioneer Nat'l Latex, 2007-Ohio-4921, 115 Ohio St. 3d 311, 875 N.E.2d 36, 2007 Ohio LEXIS 2229 (Ohio 2007).

When a statutory scheme contains a full array of remedies for a wrongful termination, the underlying public policy will not be jeopardized if a common-law claim for wrongful discharge is not recognized based on that policy. Leininger v. Pioneer Nat'l Latex, 2007-Ohio-4921, 115 Ohio St. 3d 311, 875 N.E.2d 36, 2007 Ohio LEXIS 2229 (Ohio 2007).

There is no need to recognize a common-law action for wrongful discharge if there already exists a statutory remedy that adequately protects society's interests. Leininger v. Pioneer Nat'l Latex, 2007-Ohio-4921, 115 Ohio St. 3d 311, 875 N.E.2d 36, 2007 Ohio LEXIS 2229 (Ohio 2007).

Employee asserting the tort of wrongful discharge in violation of the public policy against age discrimination had to prove the jeopardy element, meaning that without a common-law tort claim for wrongful discharge based on age, Ohio's clear policy against age discrimination would be compromised. Leininger v. Pioneer Nat'l Latex, 2007-Ohio-4921, 115 Ohio St. 3d 311, 875 N.E.2d 36, 2007 Ohio LEXIS 2229 (Ohio 2007).

Tort claim for wrongful discharge in violation of the public policy against age discrimination did not exist because the jeopardy element of such a tort could not be established as Ohio Rev. Code ch. 4112 protected the policy through the remedies it offered in (1) R.C. 4112.02(N), allowing for any legal or equitable relief that would effectuate an individual's rights, (2) R.C. 4112.05(G), allowing enforcement actions by the Ohio Civil Rights Commission, (3) R.C. 4112.14(B), allowing "an appropriate remedy," which could include damages and injunctive relief, and (4) R.C. 4112.99, which subjected violators to a civil action for damages, injunctive relief, or other appropriate relief. Leininger v. Pioneer Nat'l Latex, 2007-Ohio-4921, 115 Ohio St. 3d 311, 875 N.E.2d 36, 2007 Ohio LEXIS 2229 (Ohio 2007).

Trial court did not err in granting summary judgment to the hospital because, since the nurse failed to establish that she was discriminated against or retaliated against based on either her age or sex, she had no footing upon which to support a finding that the decision to terminate her employment was motivated by her age in violation of public policy. The hospital set forth a legitimate business justification in terminating the nurse due to the serious medical errors she admittedly made; thus, the hospital terminated the nurse for purposes of patient safety. Guy v. Q.H.G. of Massillon, Inc., 2007 Ohio App. LEXIS 394 (Ohio Ct. App., Stark County Jan. 29, 2007).

When an employee who was placed on involuntary disability separation claimed the employee was a victim of wrongful termination in violation of public policy, the employee did not meet the employee's burden of showing a prima facie case because, while the employee showed a public policy under R.C. 4112.02 and that putting an employee on disability separation for discriminatory reasons would jeopardize that policy, the employee did not show the employee's separation was racially motivated of that the separation lacked an overriding justification, when the separation was based on the employee's frequent absences and the employee's inability to do the employee's job. Carter v. Dep't of Rehab. & Corr., 2007-Ohio-3872, 2007 Ohio Misc. LEXIS 250 (Ohio Ct. Cl. 2007).

Where a former employee alleged that the employer's co-owner sexually harassed her, the claim of wrongful discharge in violation of public policy failed to survive summary judgment because the Greeley claim did not satisfy the jeopardy requirement since the Ohio Civil Rights Act contained a sufficient remedy. Hollar v. RJ Coffey Cup, LLC, 505 F. Supp. 2d 439, 2007 U.S. Dist. LEXIS 52630 (N.D. Ohio 2007).

After citing a laundry list of case law in support, the employer argued that virtually every Ohio court had refused to recognize public policy claims premised on Ohio R.C. ch. 4112; the district court acknowledged that the Sixth Circuit Court of Appeals had often address public policy claims related to ch. 4112 by finding them necessarily invalid based on the circumstances in particular cases. Miller v. Burrows Paper Corp., 2007 U.S. Dist. LEXIS 27140 (S.D. Ohio Apr. 12, 2007).

Because the trial court properly determined that the employer was entitled to judgment as a matter of law on the employee's claims pursuant to R.C. 4123.90 and R.C. 4112.02, the employee could not establish that the discharge was motivated by conduct related to the public policies behind those statutes. Bowers v. Swagelok Co., 2006-Ohio-3605, 2006 Ohio App. LEXIS 3550 (Ohio Ct. App., Cuyahoga County 2006).

**Public policy, generally**

State university employee's claim of wrongful discharge in violation of public policy failed, as his claim was based on alleged retaliation, which was protected under R.C. 4112.02(I). Kellogg v. Ohio State Univ., 2011-Ohio-4848, 2011 Ohio Misc. LEXIS 411 (Ohio Ct. Cl. 2011).

Employer did not engage in unlawful religious discrimination in violation of public policy when it discharged a former employee after the employee refused to sign a form stating that he had received and acknowledged the employee handbook on the basis that signing the form would violate his firmly held religious beliefs and would require him to give his stamp of approval to the employer's anti-discrimination policy on the basis of sexual orientation. None of the proposed accommodations submitted by the employee resolved the root issue concerning the employee's refusal to abide by the employer's non-discrimination policy. Johnson v. SK Tech, Inc., 2010-Ohio-3449, 2010 Ohio App. LEXIS 2958 (Ohio Ct. App., Montgomery County 2010).

Daughter's public policy claim failed because R.C. ch. 4112 and R.C. ch. 5321 adequately protect society's interests in attempting to prevent the retaliation by her father, her landlord, that the daughter allegedly suffered. Reid v. Plainsboro Partners, III, 2010-Ohio-4373, 2010 Ohio App. LEXIS 3694 (Ohio Ct. App., Franklin County 2010).

Employer was entitled to summary judgment on a former employee's claim of wrongful discharge because it was based entirely on the employee's unsuccessful claims that the employer violated the Family and Medical Leave Act, 29 U.S.C.S. § 2601 et seq., and discriminated against her on the basis of sex in violation of R.C. 4112.02; the employee could not maintain a separate wrongful discharge claim because her allegations concerned actions prohibited by federal and state employment law statutes which provided adequate remedies. Morr v. Kamco Indus., 548 F. Supp. 2d 472, 2008 U.S. Dist. LEXIS 30908 (N.D. Ohio 2008).

After citing a laundry list of case law in support, the employer argued that virtually every Ohio court had refused to recognize public policy claims premised on Ohio R.C. ch. 4112. The district court acknowledged that the Sixth Circuit Court of Appeals had often address public policy claims related to ch. 4112 by finding them necessarily invalid based on the circumstances in particular cases. Miller v. Burrows Paper Corp., 2007 U.S. Dist. LEXIS 27140 (S.D. Ohio Apr. 12, 2007).

Because the trial court properly determined that the employer was entitled to judgment as a matter of law on the employee's claims pursuant to R.C. 4123.90 and R.C. 4112.02, the employee could not establish that the discharge was motivated by conduct related to the public policies behind those statutes. Bowers v. Swagelok Co., 2006-Ohio-3605, 2006 Ohio App. LEXIS 3550 (Ohio Ct. App., Cuyahoga County 2006).

**Punitive damages**

$10,000,000 punitive damages award for age discrimination for violation of R.C. 4112.02 was vacated because it was excessive and did not comport with due process. The district court was ordered to enter an order of remittitur on remand in an amount not to exceed the $6,000,000 award of compensatory damages. Morgan v. New York Life Ins. Co., 559 F.3d 425, 2009 FED App. 0096P, 2009 U.S. App. LEXIS 5088 (6th Cir. Ohio 2009).

Appellate court was unable to conclude that a punitive damages award in an age discrimination case violated Ohio law because the record included evidence that the employer consciously disregarded the employee's right to be free from age discrimination. Morgan v. New York Life Ins. Co., 559 F.3d 425, 2009 FED App. 0096P, 2009 U.S. App. LEXIS 5088 (6th Cir. Ohio 2009).

Judgment notwithstanding the verdict was properly denied; because R.C. ch. 2744 did not apply to the officer's causes of action (gender-based discrimination, hostile work environment, and retaliation) because they were causally connected to her employment, R.C. 2744.05 could not be applied to prevent the imposition of punitive damages. However, since there was no language in R.C. 4112.02 or R.C. 4112.99 expressly authorizing an award of punitive damages against a political subdivision, the officer could not recover punitive damages against the board of trustees. Henderhan v. Jackson Twp. Police Dep't, 2009-Ohio-949, 2009 Ohio App. LEXIS 794 (Ohio Ct. App., Stark County 2009).

Punitive damages were properly awarded to a terminated employee on her claims of defamation and retaliation under R.C. 4112.02(I) where there was clear and convincing evidence of actual malice by an employer and some of its board members regarding the desire to hire a younger individual to replace the employee, and the discouragement to others of offering the employee a position. Lynch v. Studebaker, 2007-Ohio-4014, 2007 Ohio App. LEXIS 3651 (Ohio Ct. App., Cuyahoga County 2007).

Punitive damages were properly awarded to a terminated employee on her claims of defamation and retaliation under R.C. 4112.02(I) where there was clear and convincing evidence of actual malice by an employer and some of its board members regarding the desire to hire a younger individual to replace the employee, and the discouragement to others of offering the employee a position. Lynch v. Studebaker, 2007-Ohio-4014, 2007 Ohio App. LEXIS 3651 (Ohio Ct. App., Cuyahoga County 2007).

Punitive damages were properly awarded to a terminated employee on her claims of defamation and retaliation under R.C. 4112.02(I) where there was clear and convincing evidence of actual malice by an employer and some of its board members regarding the desire to hire a younger individual to replace the employee, and the discouragement to others of offering the employee a position. Lynch v. Studebaker, 2007-Ohio-4014, 2007 Ohio App. LEXIS 3651 (Ohio Ct. App., Cuyahoga County 2007).

**Race discrimination**

In this Title VII of the Civil Rights Act of 1964 and Ohio Civil Rights Act action, defendant was granted summary judgment on the race discrimination claim because in the absence of any evidence from plaintiff suggesting that the other nurses present at the incident were non-white, or that they were sufficiently similarly-situated State Tested Nurse Aides, no reasonable jury could find that plaintiff satisfied the disparate treatment requirement of her prima facie case. Peacock v. Altercare of Canal Winchester Post-Acute Rehab. Ctr., Inc., 2011 U.S. Dist. LEXIS 124216 (S.D. Ohio Oct. 26, 2011).

Trial court did not err when it dismissed a student's claim of racial discrimination against a school because, other than his bare assertion that the school "might be playing racial/minorities discrimination," the student provided no factual basis for his claim. Ihenacho v. Ohio Inst. of Photography & Tech., 2011-Ohio-3730, 2011 Ohio App. LEXIS 3169 (Ohio Ct. App., Montgomery County 2011).

Former employee's race discrimination claim under R.C. 4112.02(A) was dismissed for failure to state a claim under Civ. R. 12(B)(6) because the employee failed to state a claim of reverse race discrimination. The employee alleged that (1) an African-American coworker made unsubstantiated and untruthful claims accusing the employee, a Caucasian, of using racially derogatory and improper language; (2) the employer, through the actions of its African-American human resources manager, then involuntarily terminated the employee from the employee's employment; and (3) similar action was not taken regarding other employees. Morrissette v. DFS Servs., LLC, 2011-Ohio-2369, 2011 Ohio App. LEXIS 2023 (Ohio Ct. App., Franklin County 2011).

Because plaintiff former employee's alleged comparators had corrected their expense reports immediately, while the employee never offered an explanation, never returned the money, and had not reminded his supervisor of an alleged prior conversation in which the employee allegedly notified the supervisor of the error, the employee's race discrimination claim under Ohio law against defendant former employer failed. Carson v. Patterson Cos., 423 Fed. Appx. 510, 2011 FED App. 0313N, 2011 U.S. App. LEXIS 9868 (6th Cir. Ohio 2011).

Employee could not assert race discrimination claims under R.C. 4112.02 and R.C. 4112.99 against the U.S. Postal Service because Title VII of the Civil Rights Act of 1964, 42 U.S.C.S. § 2000e et seq., provided the exclusive remedy for discrimination against federal employees. Williams v. United States Postal Serv., 2011 U.S. Dist. LEXIS 69396 (S.D. Ohio June 28, 2011).

Breach of contract and promissory estoppel action against a former employer was properly dismissed under Civ.R. 41(B)(2) because race discrimination was not shown; there was ample evidence that a former classified civil servant was not performing her job duties, and she failed to show that the persons whom she alleged were treated more favorably were similar to her in all relevant respects. Lindsey v. Ohio State Univ. Med. Ctr., 2010-Ohio-2656, 2010 Ohio Misc. LEXIS 109 (Ohio Ct. Cl. 2010).

Court sustained defendants' motion for summary judgment on an African-American employee's hostile work environment claims brought under 42 U.S.C.S. § 1981 and R.C. 4112.02, 4112.99 because the employee's allegations of five incidents of misconduct over an approximate seven year period and of seeing a racial epithet written on bathroom walls at least once a year for about 20 years, while reprehensible, was not sufficiently severe and pervasive, as a matter of law, to be said to have altered the conditions of the employee's employment, and regardless of whether the employee subjectively found that the alleged incidents created a hostile work environment, he failed to set forth sufficient facts to create a genuine issue of material fact as to the objective component of the third prong of his prima facie case of race-based harassment. Berryman v. Supervalu Holdings, Inc., — F. Supp. 2d —, 2010 U.S. Dist. LEXIS 32969 (S.D. Ohio Mar. 31, 2010), affirmed by 669 F.3d 714, 2012 U.S. App. LEXIS 3823, 2012 FED App. 53P (6th Cir.), 2012 FED App. 053P (6th Cir.), 95 Empl. Prac. Dec. (CCH) P44429, 114 Fair Empl. Prac. Cas. (BNA) 808 (6th Cir. Ohio 2012)supra.

Court sustained defendants' motion for summary judgment with regard to an African-American employee's racial discrimination claims based on disparate treatment under Title VII, 42 U.S.C.S. § 1981 and R.C. 4112.02, 4112.99 because the employee had not set forth sufficient evidence to create a genuine issue of material fact as to whether the individuals with whom he sought to compare his treatment were similarly situated with regard to his claims of less favorable job assignments and drug testing, and while the employee had met his burden with regard to his breakroom discipline claim, the breakroom reprimands did not constitute adverse employment actions as the reprimand did not constitute a significant change in employment status, such as hiring, firing, failing to promote, reassignment with significantly different responsibilities, or a decision causing a significant change in benefits. Berryman v. Supervalu Holdings, Inc., — F. Supp. 2d —, 2010 U.S. Dist. LEXIS 32969 (S.D. Ohio Mar. 31, 2010), affirmed by 669 F.3d 714, 2012 U.S. App. LEXIS 3823, 2012 FED App. 53P (6th Cir.), 2012 FED App. 053P (6th Cir.), 95 Empl. Prac. Dec. (CCH) P44429, 114 Fair Empl. Prac. Cas. (BNA) 808 (6th Cir. Ohio 2012)supra.



Court sustained defendants' motion for summary judgment on an African-American employee's hostile work environment claims brought under 42 U.S.C.S. § 1981 and R.C. 4112.02, 4112.99 because the employee allegations of being called a racially offensive name on two occasions between 1989-1991, seeing racially discriminatory graffiti on approximately 13 occasions between 2000-2005, learning that his coworkers had made a racially offensive statement in 2002-2003, and hearing a racially discriminatory word over his computerized system in approximately 2004, while reprehensible, was sufficiently not sufficiently severe and pervasive, as a matter of law, to be said to have altered the conditions of the employee's employment, and further, the employee also failed to satisfy his burden to set forth evidence indicating that the employer knew about the harassment but failed to take appropriate remedial action. Berryman v. SuperValu Holdings, Inc., 2010 U.S. Dist. LEXIS 32968 (S.D. Ohio Mar. 31, 2010), aff'd, 669 F.3d 714, 2012 FED App. 0053P, 2012 U.S. App. LEXIS 3823 (6th Cir. Ohio 2012).

Court sustained defendants' motion for summary judgment with regard to an African-American employee's racial discrimination based on disparate treatment claims under Title VII, 42 U.S.C.S. § 1981 and R.C. 4112.02, 4112.99 because the employee failed to create a genuine issue of material fact as to whether the individuals with whom he sought to compare his treatment were similarly situated with regard to any of his claims except the claim pertaining to a supervisor initially writing up the employee for being out of his work area when he was on his lunch break, while not writing up white coworker, and the employee failed to show that being written up and then having the write-up rescinded constituted an adverse employment action as it did not constitute a significant change in employment status, such as hiring, firing, failing to promote, reassignment with significantly different responsibilities, or a decision causing a significant change in benefits. Berryman v. SuperValu Holdings, Inc., 2010 U.S. Dist. LEXIS 32968 (S.D. Ohio Mar. 31, 2010), aff'd, 669 F.3d 714, 2012 FED App. 0053P, 2012 U.S. App. LEXIS 3823 (6th Cir. Ohio 2012).

Court sustained defendants' motion for summary judgment on an African-American employee's hostile work environment claims brought under 42 U.S.C.S. § 1981 and R.C. 4112.02, 4112.99 because (1) the facts did not indicate any racial connotation associated with the leave of absence incidents; (2) the seven instances of harassment occurred over a period that spanned greater than 20 years, and while the conduct was reprehensible, it was not sufficiently severe and pervasive to be said to have altered the conditions of the employee's employment; and (3) the employee had not satisfied his burden to set forth evidence indicating that the employer knew about the harassment but failed to take appropriate remedial action. Berryman v. SuperValu Holdings, Inc., — F. Supp. 2d —, 2010 U.S. Dist. LEXIS 32960 (S.D. Ohio Mar. 31, 2010), affirmed by 669 F.3d 714, 2012 U.S. App. LEXIS 3823, 2012 FED App. 53P (6th Cir.), 2012 FED App. 053P (6th Cir.), 95 Empl. Prac. Dec. (CCH) P44429, 114 Fair Empl. Prac. Cas. (BNA) 808 (6th Cir. Ohio 2012)supra.

Regardless of whether the employee subjectively found that one alleged incident created a hostile work environment, he failed to set forth sufficient facts to create a genuine issue of material fact as to the objective component of the third prong of his prima facie case of race-based harassment—the incident was not severe enough to alter the terms and conditions of his employment. Berryman v. SuperValu Holdings, Inc., — F. Supp. 2d —, 2010 U.S. Dist. LEXIS 32525 (S.D. Ohio Mar. 31, 2010), affirmed by 669 F.3d 714, 2012 U.S. App. LEXIS 3823, 2012 FED App. 53P (6th Cir.), 2012 FED App. 053P (6th Cir.), 95 Empl. Prac. Dec. (CCH) P44429, 114 Fair Empl. Prac. Cas. (BNA) 808 (6th Cir. Ohio 2012)supra.

Employee did not identify an allegedly similarly situated non-protected co-worker or, in the three instances where he identified such a co-worker, did not demonstrate that all of the relevant aspects of his employment situation were nearly identical to those of the non-protected co-worker's employment situation, as was required. Berryman v. SuperValu Holdings, Inc., 2010 U.S. Dist. LEXIS 32522 (S.D. Ohio Mar. 31, 2010).

Employees alleging racial discrimination did not show a hostile work environment because (1) nothing showed a supervisor allowed a noose to remain in place for any period of time, and (2) another employee's inappropriate comment appeared to be an isolated incident. Hargrette v. RMI Titanium Co., 2010-Ohio-406, 2010 Ohio App. LEXIS 325 (Ohio Ct. App., Trumbull County 2010).

Job applicant failed to prove his claim of employment discrimination based on his race because, regardless of whether the applicant misunderstood the senior director and the administrative director when they offered him the position, or if the parties simply failed to reach mutually agreeable terms of compensation, the hospital did not reject the applicant for the position. Rather, the applicant failed to obtain the position because he did not accept any of the hospital's offers. Refaei v. Ohio State Univ. Hosp., 2010-Ohio-5911, 2010 Ohio Misc. LEXIS 346 (Ohio Ct. Cl. 2010), aff'd, 2011-Ohio-6727, 2011 Ohio App. LEXIS 5545 (Ohio Ct. App., Franklin County 2011).

Job applicant failed to prove his claim of employment discrimination based on his race because he did not meet his burden of proving that the hospital's stated reasons for not offering him the position were a pretext for discrimination. The applicant failed to prove that the senior director was untruthful in testifying that the chosen applicant's experience in performing computed tomography (CT) scans made him a more preferable candidate than the applicant and did not prove that discrimination was the reason for his not being hired. Refaei v. Ohio State Univ. Hosp., 2010-Ohio-5911, 2010 Ohio Misc. LEXIS 346 (Ohio Ct. Cl. 2010), aff'd, 2011-Ohio-6727, 2011 Ohio App. LEXIS 5545 (Ohio Ct. App., Franklin County 2011).

Where an African-American employee's position was eliminated and a white male was hired to fill a new position, summary judgment was inappropriate as to the employee's race discrimination claims because (1) a question of fact existed regarding whether the newly-hired chef replaced the employee, and (2) regarding pretext, defendants' failure to alert the employee to the impending termination or of the chef 1 vacancy created an inference that they were intentionally attempting to get rid of the employee, and the employee offered evidence of a pattern of discrimination. Thompson v. UHHS Richmond Heights Hosp., Inc., 372 Fed. Appx. 620, 2010 FED App. 0225N, 2010 U.S. App. LEXIS 7439 (6th Cir. Ohio 2010).

Summary judgment was properly granted because the employee's bare assertions were not enough to make a prima facie case of discrimination; the employer proffered a legitimate, nondiscriminatory reason for the discharge—that the employee was terminated for violating company rules. Although the employee offered a different account of the events, he admitted using profanities; the employee did not present any evidence establishing that the employer discharged him for any reason other than having violated company rules. Harris v. Greater Cleveland Reg'l Transit Auth., 2008-Ohio-676, 2008 Ohio App. LEXIS 591 (Ohio Ct. App., Cuyahoga County 2008).

Summary judgment was properly granted in favor of a city and three supervisors sued by an African-American employee for racial discrimination because the employee gave few details about white employees the employee thought were treated more favorably, and the employee admitted that those employees' situations were not similar to the employee's, so the employee did not meet the employee's burden to show that similarly situated nonprotected employees were treated more favorably than the employee. Greene v. City of Cincinnati, 2008-Ohio-4908, 2008 Ohio App. LEXIS 4121 (Ohio Ct. App., Hamilton County 2008).

When an employee complained that he was terminated for reporting racial harassment by another employee, summary judgment was properly granted to the former employer because, while the employee demonstrated that he had engaged in protected activity and that he had been subjected to an adverse employment action, the employee did not show a genuine issue of material fact as to whether those who made the decision to discharge him knew that the employee had complained of racial harassment, nor did the employee show that the supervisor to whom he complained of the harassment, or any other mid-level supervisor, made any racially disparaging comments, nor did the employee show that this supervisor was "meaningfully involved" in the decision to terminate the employee, so no causal link between the employee's complaint and the employee's termination was shown. Fitch v. United States Foodservice Corp., 2008-Ohio-282, 2008 Ohio App. LEXIS 241 (Ohio Ct. App., Butler County 2008).

Employer was entitled to summary judgment in a race discrimination case under both 42 U.S.C.S. § 2000e-2 and R.C. 4112.02 because the employee showed no direct evidence of discrimination and his circumstantial evidence failed as he did not show that a similarly-situated individual outside of the protected class was treated more favorably. The employee set forth no evidence that the employer's reasons for reducing his pay were mere pretext for discriminatory action. The employer merely followed its established evaluation practice, which the court would not second guess. Chang v. Univ. of Toledo, 480 F. Supp. 2d 1009, 2007 U.S. Dist. LEXIS 22077 (N.D. Ohio 2007).

Trial court's grant of summary judgment to an employer in an employee's racial discrimination claim under R.C. 4112.02(A) of the Ohio Fair Employment Practices Act was proper, as the employee failed to show that she was subject to an adverse employment action for purposes of her prima facie disparate treatment claim. Her claim that she was denied benefits granted to Caucasians failed because she ultimately received the benefits, and any temporary inconveniences did not cause a materially adverse change in the terms and conditions of employment. Brown v. Dover Corp., 2007-Ohio-2128, 2007 Ohio App. LEXIS 2010 (Ohio Ct. App., Hamilton County 2007).

Employee failed to show that she was subjected to a hostile work environment in her racial discrimination claim under R.C. 4112.02(A) of the Ohio Fair Employment Practices Act, as any perceived inconveniences in obtaining benefits, heightened scrutiny by her supervisor, racially offensive pictures, and the presence of a noose did not, as a matter of law, establish an actionable hostile-work-environment claim. The incidents were isolated and the management for the employer immediately took proper remedial action upon being informed of them, such that summary judgment for the employer was proper. Brown v. Dover Corp., 2007-Ohio-2128, 2007 Ohio App. LEXIS 2010 (Ohio Ct. App., Hamilton County 2007).

Standard for a constructive discharge claim was whether an employer's actions made working conditions so intolerable that a reasonable person under the circumstances would have felt compelled to resign, requiring a showing of more adverse conditions than did a hostile environment race harassment claim, because the latter required only a showing that the conditions were severe and pervasive enough to affect working conditions, and, logically, working conditions could be affected without an employee's feeling compelled to resign, so the principle that a party's failure to support a claim for hostile environment race harassment necessarily resulted in the failure of an attendant claim of constructive discharge was expressly adopted. White v. Bay Mech. & Elec. Corp., 2007-Ohio-1752, 2007 Ohio App. LEXIS 1608 (Ohio Ct. App., Lorain County 2007).

Court rejected an employee's argument that an employer's disciplinary policy was selectively enforced based on race, which let to his termination under the guise of excessive violations. Although the employee successfully established a prima facie case of race discrimination, he failed to provide evidence of similarly situated employees who were treated differently. Thomas v. Ametech, 464 F. Supp. 2d 688, 2006 U.S. Dist. LEXIS 79318 (N.D. Ohio 2006).

Trial court properly granted summary judgment to an employer in an employee's racial discrimination claim under R.C. 4112.02, as the evidence indicated that due to psychological disorders suffered by the employee and the stress that she felt from her work situation, she voluntarily resigned from employment when there were no part-time positions available for her to transfer into from her full-time position; there was no showing that she was subject to an adverse employment action and the Caucasian employees who worked part-time were not in positions comparable to that of the employee. Swann v. Cardiology Assocs. of Cincinnati, 2006-Ohio-2758, 2006 Ohio App. LEXIS 2596 (Ohio Ct. App., Hamilton County 2006).

Trial court's affirmance of a decision by an administrative law judge (ALJ) for the Ohio Civil Rights Commission, finding that an employer had racially discriminated against two terminated employees in violation of R.C. 4112.02(A), was proper where it found that the administrative decision was supported by reliable, probative, and substantial evidence; the fact that an initial ALJ had heard the matter and that a successor ALJ had rendered the findings of fact, conclusions of law, and recommendation was not an impropriety or procedural deficiency which merited summary judgment in favor of the employer in the petition for review, as the successor ALJ had carefully reviewed the voluminous record of the administrative proceeding and such constituted "meaningful review" for purposes of due process under Ohio Const. art. I, § 16. Aircraft Braking Sys. Corp. v. Ohio Civil Rights Comm'n, 2006-Ohio-1304, 2006 Ohio App. LEXIS 1207 (Ohio Ct. App., Summit County 2006).

When a former teacher brought a race discrimination action against a public school district and certain of its administrators under federal law and R.C. 4112.02, 4112.99, and 4113.52, the teacher's inability to make a prima facie case of race discrimination under federal law resulted in summary judgment on his state law claims as well because the standard for the state law claims was the same as the standard for the federal claims. Pittman v. Cuyahoga Valley Career Ctr., 451 F. Supp. 2d 905, 2006 U.S. Dist. LEXIS 60411 (N.D. Ohio 2006).

Employer was not entitled to summary judgment on an employee's racial discrimination claim where a reasonable jury could have found that the employer thwarted his attempts to submit an application, thereby committing racial discrimination. Allen v. Deerfield Mfg., 424 F. Supp. 2d 987, 2006 U.S. Dist. LEXIS 13870 (S.D. Ohio 2006).

Jury verdict rendered for an African American supervisor and the city which employed the supervisor, in a Caucasian employee's hostile work environment harassment claim brought under R.C. 4112.02, was not against the manifest weight of the evidence because, on the evidence presented at trial, the jury reasonably could have concluded that the city addressed any harassing conduct when informed, followed up, and had no reason to believe that the harassment was continuing. Further, the jury could also have concluded that any harassment that the employee suffered, including racial comments made by her coworkers and her supervisor's allegedly discriminatory treatment of her, was not severe or pervasive enough to warrant relief. Mowery v. City of Columbus, 2006-Ohio-1153, 2006 Ohio App. LEXIS 1051 (Ohio Ct. App., Franklin County 2006).

High school principal, who was an African-American, whose contract was not renewed, did not prove racial discrimination through the use of "comparables" because he produced no evidence that he was treated differently from any other administrators in the district. Atkinson v. Akron Bd. of Educ., 2006-Ohio-1032, 2006 Ohio App. LEXIS 947 (Ohio Ct. App., Summit County 2006).

When a high school principal, who was an African-American, could not show, after the school board declined to renew his contract, that he was replaced by a person who was not a member of a protected class, because he was replaced by another African-American, he did not produce indirect evidence of racial discrimination. Atkinson v. Akron Bd. of Educ., 2006-Ohio-1032, 2006 Ohio App. LEXIS 947 (Ohio Ct. App., Summit County 2006).

Employer was properly granted summary judgment on an African-American employee's race discrimination claim because the employee failed to show that the employer's legitimate, non-discriminatory reason for terminating the employee, namely her failure to meet sales goals, was pretextual: (1) the evidence reflected that, although the sales goals program was likely an example of bad policy, it was not in anyway racially discriminatory, and the employer did not enforce it in a discriminatory manner; (2) the employee underachieved in her position in 2002 and 2003 pursuant to the sales goals and was terminated as a result; (3) because of the employer's elaborate four-step disciplinary process, the employee was provided with several opportunities to correct her behavior; (4) in addition, although the employee complained about her termination, she elected termination in lieu of a demotion; and (5) the employee's deposition testimony reflected that rather than directly accusing her supervisor of racial discrimination, she believed that the supervisor's suggestions for improvement were genuine. Brown v. Bank One, N.A., 168 Fed. Appx. 46, 2006 FED App. 0122N, 2006 U.S. App. LEXIS 3711 (6th Cir. Ohio 2006).

Employer was not entitled to summary judgment on a claim of race discrimination where a black employee was terminated for triggering a fire alarm and a white employee was not disciplined for the same possible offense, and the evidence did not necessarily support the differing treatment: Holbrook v. Lexis-Nexis, 2006-Ohio-5762, 169 Ohio App. 3d 345, 862 N.E.2d 892, 2006 Ohio App. LEXIS 5747 (Ohio Ct. App., Montgomery County 2006).

Trial court properly granted summary judgment to an employer in an employee's racial discrimination claim under R.C. 4112.02, as the evidence indicated that due to psychological disorders suffered by the employee and the stress that she felt from her work situation, she voluntarily resigned from employment when there were no part-time positions available for her to transfer into from her full-time position. There was no showing that she was subject to an adverse employment action and the Caucasian employees who worked part-time were not in positions comparable to that of the employee. Swann v. Cardiology Assocs. of Cincinnati, 2006-Ohio-2758, 2006 Ohio App. LEXIS 2596 (Ohio Ct. App., Hamilton County 2006).

Trial court's affirmance of a decision by an administrative law judge (ALJ) for the Ohio Civil Rights Commission, finding that an employer had racially discriminated against two terminated employees in violation of R.C. 4112.02(A), was proper where it found that the administrative decision was supported by reliable, probative, and substantial evidence. The fact that an initial ALJ had heard the matter and that a successor ALJ had rendered the findings of fact, conclusions of law, and recommendation was not an impropriety or procedural deficiency which merited summary judgment in favor of the employer in the petition for review, as the successor ALJ had carefully reviewed the voluminous record of the administrative proceeding and such constituted "meaningful review" for purposes of due process under Ohio Const. art. I, § 16. Aircraft Braking Sys. Corp. v. Ohio Civil Rights Comm'n, 2006-Ohio-1304, 2006 Ohio App. LEXIS 1207 (Ohio Ct. App., Summit County 2006).

Where an employee was unable to prove her claim of racial discrimination in violation of R.C. 4112.02, as she failed to show that she had a valid reason for "involuntarily terminating" her work relationship because any adverse employment action that she alleged occurred did not rise to the level that would have caused a constructive discharge, nor did she show that she was treated differently on the basis of race, her claims that she was wrongfully discharged in violation of public policy under Greeley also necessarily failed. Simmons-Means v. Cuyahoga County Dep't of Justice Affairs, 2006-Ohio-4123, 2006 Ohio App. LEXIS 4057 (Ohio Ct. App., Cuyahoga County 2006).

Employee failed to show that her workplace was permeated with discriminatory intimidation, ridicule, and insult which was sufficiently severe or pervasive to alter the conditions of the victim's employment and create an abusive working environment for purposes of her hostile work environment claim based on alleged racial discrimination from her new supervisor. There was conflict between the two individuals but it did not rise to an actionable level, there was no indication of racially biased behavior, and "abruptness" by the supervisor was how all employees were treated regardless of race. Simmons-Means v. Cuyahoga County Dep't of Justice Affairs, 2006-Ohio-4123, 2006 Ohio App. LEXIS 4057 (Ohio Ct. App., Cuyahoga County 2006).

Teacher did not show he was subjected to a hostile work environment, due to racial slurs from students and others, because he did not show that the slurs he testified to were severe or pervasive enough to alter the conditions of his employment. Farris v. Port Clinton City Sch. Dist., 2006-Ohio-1864, 2006 Ohio App. LEXIS 1701 (Ohio Ct. App., Ottawa County 2006).

State correctional department's dismissal motion was granted because U.S. Const. amend. XI barred a terminated employee from prosecuting his state tort and R.C. ch. 4112 claims against the department; the employee failed to present any evidence showing that the State of Ohio had waived its immunity or consented to be sued by the employee as to his state law claims. Gilbert v. Ohio Dep't of Rehab. & Corr., 2005 U.S. Dist. LEXIS 12073 (S.D. Ohio June 17, 2005), dismissed in part, 2005 U.S. Dist. LEXIS 59833 (S.D. Ohio June 20, 2005).



When a former teacher brought a race discrimination action against a public school district and certain of its administrators under federal law and R.C. 4112.02, 4112.99, and 4113.52, the teacher's inability to make a prima facie case of race discrimination under federal law resulted in summary judgment on his state law claims as well because the standard for the state law claims was the same as the standard for the federal claims. Pittman v. Cuyahoga Valley Career Ctr., 451 F. Supp. 2d 905, 2006 U.S. Dist. LEXIS 60411 (N.D. Ohio 2006).

Employer was not entitled to summary judgment on an employee's racial discrimination claim where a reasonable jury could have found that the employer thwarted his attempts to submit an application, thereby committing racial discrimination. Allen v. Deerfield Mfg., 424 F. Supp. 2d 987, 2006 U.S. Dist. LEXIS 13870 (S.D. Ohio 2006).

Employee's alleged, inter alia, that he was subjected to daily harassment by him and others, including his union representative, for not filing grievances; the evidence before the court, when viewed either separately or cumulatively, amounted to mere generalized complaints against the union. Thus the employee's allegations under either 42 U.S.C.S. § 2000e-2 or R.C. 4112.02(A) were insufficient to survive summary judgment. Patterson v. USW, Local 9, 2005 U.S. Dist. LEXIS 13019 (N.D. Ohio June 30, 2005).

African American employee's disparate treatment claim survived summary judgment because, while the employer contended that the employee crossed off her name for a position that was filled by a less senior white person, the employee raised a genuine issue of material fact that she was led to believe by her supervisor that she should cross her name off the intent sheet in order to obtain another position. Then the supervisor prevented her from applying for the other position and from re-signing her name on the intent sheet for the original position. Clay v. UPS, 2005 U.S. Dist. LEXIS 13016 (N.D. Ohio June 30, 2005), aff'd in part and rev'd in part, 501 F.3d 695, 2007 FED App. 0354P, 2007 U.S. App. LEXIS 20945 (6th Cir. Ohio 2007).

African American employee's disparate treatment claim failed on summary judgment because, while the employee alleged that she was denied a position for which she was qualified and the most senior, and the position was filled by a white employee, the position was posted for the required period of time, albeit earlier than normal in relation to the time of the opening, and the employee failed to sign her name to the intent sheet. The employee showed no knowledge on behalf of management that she was interested in the job and no unique disadvantage on her part, given that several others who might have been eligible were subject to the same job posting schedule. Clay v. UPS, 2005 U.S. Dist. LEXIS 13016 (N.D. Ohio June 30, 2005), aff'd in part and rev'd in part, 501 F.3d 695, 2007 FED App. 0354P, 2007 U.S. App. LEXIS 20945 (6th Cir. Ohio 2007).

African American employee's disparate treatment claim that alleged a failure to train did not survive summary judgment because, while the employee alleged that he was denied certain training that had been promised to him, there was no issue of fact that similarly situated employees were treated more favorably. Notably, the employee's initial grievance regarding this matter was brought on behalf of himself and a group of white employees. Clay v. UPS, 2005 U.S. Dist. LEXIS 13016 (N.D. Ohio June 30, 2005), aff'd in part and rev'd in part, 501 F.3d 695, 2007 FED App. 0354P, 2007 U.S. App. LEXIS 20945 (6th Cir. Ohio 2007).

Employee's hostile work environment claim failed on summary judgment because, while the employee alleged that her supervisor berated her for minor conduct such as eating a donut on work time, there was insufficient evidence that the employee was harassed back on race. Also, the treatment was not so severe or pervasive as to unreasonably interfere with the employee's work performance. Clay v. UPS, 2005 U.S. Dist. LEXIS 13016 (N.D. Ohio June 30, 2005), aff'd in part and rev'd in part, 501 F.3d 695, 2007 FED App. 0354P, 2007 U.S. App. LEXIS 20945 (6th Cir. Ohio 2007).

Employee's hostile work environment claim failed on summary judgment because, while the employee alleged that her supervisor berated her for minor conduct such as eating a donut on work time, there was insufficient evidence that the employee was harassed back on race. Also, the treatment was not so severe or pervasive as to unreasonably interfere with the employee's work performance. Clay v. UPS, 2005 U.S. Dist. LEXIS 13016 (N.D. Ohio June 30, 2005), aff'd in part and rev'd in part, 501 F.3d 695, 2007 FED App. 0354P, 2007 U.S. App. LEXIS 20945 (6th Cir. Ohio 2007).

African American employee failed to make a prima facie case of retaliation where he filed a grievance some 15 months prior to being terminated. He also failed to rebut the employer's non-discriminatory reason for his termination, which included that employer's inability to reach the employee during extended absences on the cell phone number provided by the employee. Clay v. UPS, 2005 U.S. Dist. LEXIS 13016 (N.D. Ohio June 30, 2005), aff'd in part and rev'd in part, 501 F.3d 695, 2007 FED App. 0354P, 2007 U.S. App. LEXIS 20945 (6th Cir. Ohio 2007).

African American employee failed to make a prima facie case of retaliation where he failed to allege facts to show that the adverse employment action, his termination, was caused by his filing of a discrimination charge some six months prior. Clay v. UPS, 2005 U.S. Dist. LEXIS 13016 (N.D. Ohio June 30, 2005), aff'd in part and rev'd in part, 501 F.3d 695, 2007 FED App. 0354P, 2007 U.S. App. LEXIS 20945 (6th Cir. Ohio 2007).

African American employee's disparate treatment claim failed on summary judgment because, while the employee alleged that he was suspended and eventually terminated due to an unequal application of policies, the employee could not make out a prima facie case because the employer did not make the suspension and termination decisions. Instead, the decisions were made by a joint labor management committee and the employer could not be held responsible. Clay v. UPS, 2005 U.S. Dist. LEXIS 13016 (N.D. Ohio June 30, 2005), aff'd in part and rev'd in part, 501 F.3d 695, 2007 FED App. 0354P, 2007 U.S. App. LEXIS 20945 (6th Cir. Ohio 2007).

Employee's racial discrimination claim under R.C. 4112.02 was without merit because, even if the employee was able to demonstrate a prima facie case of racial discrimination, the employer had rebutted the presumption of discrimination by its legitimate reasons for the employee's discharge, including the fact that the employee had lashed out at her supervisor and had refused to comply with an administrative investigation into charges that the employee had left a harassing voicemail message on her supervisor's voicemail, and the employee had produced no evidence that the employer's reasons for termination lacked a factual basis, were motivated by her race, or were insufficient to warrant her discharge. Glen v. Northcoast Behavioral Healthcare Sys., 2005-Ohio-3338, 2005 Ohio Misc. LEXIS 281 (Ohio Ct. Cl. 2005).

Employer was denied summary judgment on an African-American employee's race discrimination claim because the employee presented evidence that could show that the employer's reason for terminating him was pretextual. The employee presented evidence that non-minority employees were not required to take drug and alcohol tests even though they were caught in possession of alcohol or drugs on company premises or under the influence during work hours, and that one non-minority employee was permitted to return to work after a suspension even though he never took a drug and alcohol test. O'Neal v. Johns Manville Int'l, 2005 U.S. Dist. LEXIS 10114 (N.D. Ohio May 20, 2005).

Judge terminated an African American court employee due to the employee's record of four similar complaints of inappropriate conduct, made over the course of ten years by females working in his crews and the employee brought discrimination claims. Because the African-American court employee was replaced by an African-American male, he could not meet the required burden of proof under 42 U.S.C.S. § 1981 or R.C. 4112.02. James v. Lucas County Admin. Judge, 2005 U.S. Dist. LEXIS 35494 (N.D. Ohio Dec. 23, 2005).

Employee's alleged, inter alia, that he was subjected to daily harassment by him and others, including his union representative, for not filing grievances; the evidence before the court, when viewed either separately or cumulatively, amounted to mere generalized complaints against the union. Thus the employee's allegations under either 42 U.S.C.S. § 2000e-2 or R.C. 4112.02(A) were insufficient to survive summary judgment. Patterson v. USW, Local 9, 2005 U.S. Dist. LEXIS 13019 (N.D. Ohio June 30, 2005).

African American employee's disparate treatment claim survived summary judgment because, while the employer contended that the employee crossed off her name for a position that was filled by a less senior white person, the employee raised a genuine issue of material fact that she was led to believe by her supervisor that she should cross her name off the intent sheet in order to obtain another position. Then the supervisor prevented her from applying for the other position and from re-signing her name on the intent sheet for the original position. Clay v. UPS, 2005 U.S. Dist. LEXIS 13016 (N.D. Ohio June 30, 2005), aff'd in part and rev'd in part, 501 F.3d 695, 2007 FED App. 0354P, 2007 U.S. App. LEXIS 20945 (6th Cir. Ohio 2007).

African American employee's disparate treatment claim that alleged a failure to train did not survive summary judgment because, while the employee alleged that he was denied certain training that had been promised to him, there was no issue of fact that similarly situated employees were treated more favorably. Notably, the employee's initial grievance regarding this matter was brought on behalf of himself and a group of white employees. Clay v. UPS, 2005 U.S. Dist. LEXIS 13016 (N.D. Ohio June 30, 2005), aff'd in part and rev'd in part, 501 F.3d 695, 2007 FED App. 0354P, 2007 U.S. App. LEXIS 20945 (6th Cir. Ohio 2007).

Employee's hostile work environment claim failed on summary judgment because, while the employee alleged that her supervisor berated her for minor conduct such as eating a donut on work time, there was insufficient evidence that the employee was harassed back on race. Also, the treatment was not so severe or pervasive as to unreasonably interfere with the employee's work performance. Clay v. UPS, 2005 U.S. Dist. LEXIS 13016 (N.D. Ohio June 30, 2005), aff'd in part and rev'd in part, 501 F.3d 695, 2007 FED App. 0354P, 2007 U.S. App. LEXIS 20945 (6th Cir. Ohio 2007).

Former employers were entitled to summary judgment on a former employee's hostile work environment claim under 42 U.S.C.S. § 1981 and R.C. 4112.02 because no reasonable jury could find that the employee was subject to the harassment that she alleged, as the only physical evidence in the case either gave no support to the employee's account or squarely contradicted it. White v. Drs. Camm & Golian, D.D.S., Inc., 2005 U.S. Dist. LEXIS 19763 (N.D. Ohio Sept. 12, 2005).

The court found that the employee had failed to produce evidence that suggested a discriminatory animus by the employer, and the employer was entitled to summary judgment as a matter of law on the claims of race discrimination. Gregg v. SBC/Ameritech, 2005 U.S. Dist. LEXIS 12577 (S.D. Ohio June 24, 2005), aff'd, 321 Fed. Appx. 442, 2009 FED App. 0283N, 2009 U.S. App. LEXIS 8029 (6th Cir. Ohio 2009).

Employer was not entitled to summary judgment on a race discrimination claim by a black employee where the evidence was conflicting as to whether the employee was assigned a greater workload than white employees: Jones v. Swagelok Co., 2004-Ohio-3876, 2004 Ohio App. LEXIS 3499 (Ohio Ct. App., Cuyahoga County 2004).

Trial court's grant of summary judgment, pursuant to Civ.R. 56(C), to a police lieutenant's employer, a county housing authority, in the lieutenant's action under R.C. 4112.02(A) alleging that he was terminated due to racial discrimination, was proper where the lieutenant did not meet his burden of establishing a prima facie case of racial discrimination; the lieutenant was unable to show the authority's disparate treatment of someone who was directly comparable to him in all material respects, as his attempts to compare himself to sergeants who were terminated failed because they were not the same level as he was, nor were their actions anywhere near as egregious as his were. McGowan v. Cuyahoga Metro. Hous. Auth., 2004-Ohio-4070, 2004 Ohio App. LEXIS 3715 (Ohio Ct. App., Cuyahoga County 2004).

Where defendants' explanations for refusing to sell property to a buyer after she had accepted defendants' counteroffer to purchase the property were "beyond belief"—because, for example, defendants failed to produce the original of an alleged, unrecorded lease and the copy produced was not signed and notarized—their explanations appeared to be a cover for, and supported an inference of, discrimination in violation of the Fair Housing Act, 42 U.S.C.S. § 3601 et seq.; 42 U.S.C.S. § 1981 and 42 U.S.C.S. § 1982; and R.C. 4112.02(H). Following a bench trial, the court found discrimination and awarded the would-be buyer damages, although the court declined to award punitive damages and attorney fees under 42 U.S.C.S. § 3613(C)(2). Cleveland v. Ibrahim, 2003 U.S. Dist. LEXIS 26348 (N.D. Ohio May 29, 2003).

Former employee's race discrimination claim was properly dismissed on summary judgment because he failed to show that the employer's nondiscriminatory reason for terminating him — to cut costs by reducing its workforce — was a mere pretext. Howard v. Contech Constr. Prods., 2003-Ohio-6547, 2003 Ohio App. LEXIS 5848 (Ohio Ct. App., Butler County 2003).

Trial court properly granted summary judgment for an employer on an employee's claim of race discrimination after the employee failed to produce evidence showing that the employer's decision to discharge the employee because the employee made threatening and intimidating behavior towards a fellow employee on company property, was pretextual. Marbley v. Metaldyne Co., 2003-Ohio-2851, 2003 Ohio App. LEXIS 2548 (Ohio Ct. App., Summit County 2003).

On a claim of racial discrimination, the scope of the employee's medical restrictions was material as to whether other nonprotected employees were similarly situated and, therefore, valid comparables: Ferguson v. Lear Corp., 2003-Ohio-7261, 155 Ohio App. 3d 677, 802 N.E.2d 1141, 2003 Ohio App. LEXIS 6551 (Ohio Ct. App., Erie County 2003).

Employer was entitled to summary judgment on claim that it created a racially hostile work environment and of disparate impact, but not on certain claims of failure to promote: Ulmer v. Dana Corp., 200 F. Supp. 2d 804, 2002 U.S. Dist. LEXIS 8115 (N.D. Ohio 2002), aff'd, 115 Fed. Appx. 787, 2004 U.S. App. LEXIS 21311 (6th Cir. Ohio 2004).

African-American employees who were discharged for refusing overtime work did not present a prima facie case of discrimination where they did not produce evidence that they were replaced by workers who were not African-American: Vaughn v. Watkins Motor Lines, Inc., 291 F.3d 900, 2002 FED App. 0189P, 2002 U.S. App. LEXIS 10177 (6th Cir. Ohio 2002).

Dishonesty, per se, is insufficient to render an individual unqualified, as a matter of law, to hold a position as a park ranger where there is evidence that it was a pretextual basis for racial discrimination: Smith v. Five Rivers Metroparks, 134 Ohio App. 3d 754, 732 N.E.2d 422, 1999 Ohio App. LEXIS 4286 (Ohio Ct. App., Montgomery County 1999).

Plaintiff established a prima facie case of racial discrimination where he showed that he was a member of a protected class, he was discharged, there was no dispute he was qualified for the position, and he was replaced by a person outside the protected class; however, the presumption raised in the prima facie case was rebutted and dropped from the case once the defendant articulated a legitimate, non-discriminatory reason for the discharge: Sivarajan v. Nationwide Life Ins. Co., 1998 Ohio App. LEXIS 2665 (Ohio Ct. App., Franklin County June 16, 1998).

Plaintiff established a prima facie case of racial discrimination where he showed that he was a member of a protected class, he was discharged, there was no dispute he was qualified for the position, and he was replaced by a person outside the protected class; however, the presumption raised in the prima facie case was rebutted and dropped from the case once the defendant articulated a legitimate, non-discriminatory reason for the discharge: Sivarajan v. Nationwide Life Ins. Co., 1998 Ohio App. LEXIS 2665 (Ohio Ct. App., Franklin County June 16, 1998).

The plaintiff established a prima facie case of disparate treatment based on race and that the employer's reason for termination was a pretext. The fact that plaintiff was temporarily replaced by another black woman was not dispositive: Smith v. Goodwill Indus., 130 Ohio App. 3d 437, 720 N.E.2d 203, 1998 Ohio App. LEXIS 5045 (Ohio Ct. App., Miami County 1998), dismissed, 85 Ohio St. 3d 1424, 707 N.E.2d 515, 1999 Ohio LEXIS 728 (Ohio 1999).



Plaintiff did not establish racial discrimination where he had a lengthy record of misconduct and agreed to termination in a settlement agreement after being charged with numerous counts of sexual imposition on fellow employees: Newton v. Ohio Dep't of Mental Health, 83 Ohio Misc. 2d 67, 679 N.E.2d 750, 1997 Ohio Misc. LEXIS 255 (Ohio Ct. Cl. 1997).

Discharging an employee on the basis of his criminal convictions did not constitute racial discrimination: Ekunsumi v. Cincinnati Restoration, 120 Ohio App. 3d 557, 698 N.E.2d 503, 1997 Ohio App. LEXIS 2735 (Ohio Ct. App., Hamilton County 1997).

Assistant store director's remark that plaintiff was "a lazy black bitch" was a stray remark and was insufficient to sway the burden of persuasion to the employer in the racial discrimination case: Coleman v. Toys "R" Us, 976 F. Supp. 713, 1997 U.S. Dist. LEXIS 13077 (N.D. Ohio 1997), aff'd, 172 F.3d 872, 1999 U.S. App. LEXIS 11714 (6th Cir. Ohio 1999).

Plaintiff did not prove that he was disciplined differently from a nonminority employee: Henderson v. Cincinnati Bell Long Distance, 113 Ohio App. 3d 793, 682 N.E.2d 41, 1996 Ohio App. LEXIS 3898 (Ohio Ct. App., Hamilton County 1996).

For one to be guilty of an unlawful discriminatory act under R.C. Chapter 4112., it need only be proved that the race of the complainant was one factor, rather than the sole basis, of a discriminatory practice: Miller Properties v. Ohio Civil Rights Comm., 34 Ohio App. 2d 113, 63 Ohio Op. 2d 169, 296 N.E.2d 300, 1972 Ohio App. LEXIS 316 (Ohio Ct. App., Franklin County 1972).

In an action claiming race, gender, and gender identity discrimination, the employee's claims that the employer paid her less than a similarly situated white employee because she is black were viable; whether a demoted, Caucasian male subordinate, who she alleged to have been paid more, was similarly situated was a fact-bound inquiry not proper for a motion to dismiss, and job titles were not dispositive to this inquiry. Cummings v. Greater Cleveland Reg'l Transit Auth., 88 F. Supp. 3d 812, 2015 U.S. Dist. LEXIS 10569 (N.D. Ohio 2015), dismissed, 2018 U.S. Dist. LEXIS 7475 (N.D. Ohio Jan. 17, 2018).

In an action claiming race, gender, and gender identity discrimination, the employee's claims that the employer paid her less than a similarly situated white employee because she is black were viable; whether a demoted, Caucasian male subordinate, who she alleged to have been paid more, was similarly situated was a fact-bound inquiry not proper for a motion to dismiss, and job titles were not dispositive to this inquiry. Cummings v. Greater Cleveland Reg'l Transit Auth., 88 F. Supp. 3d 812, 2015 U.S. Dist. LEXIS 10569 (N.D. Ohio 2015), dismissed, 2018 U.S. Dist. LEXIS 7475 (N.D. Ohio Jan. 17, 2018).

**—Association**

R.C. 4112.02 prohibits an employer from engaging in discriminatory practices based upon an employee's association with persons of a particular race; therefore, a white woman stated a claim against her employer under this statute when she alleged that her supervisor ridiculed her, reduced her work hours, and ultimately discharged her as a result of her associations with African-Americans: Cole v. Seafare Enters., 1996 Ohio App. LEXIS 440 (Ohio Ct. App., Hamilton County Feb. 14, 1996).

**—Burden of proof**

Medical resident failed to present any evidence of the fourth requirement under McDonnell Douglas — that he was treated less favorably than a similarly-situated individual outside the protected class. Because the resident did not establish a prima facie case through the McDonnell Douglas test, the burden did not shift to the employer to articulate a nondiscriminatory reason for its actions. Glemaud v. Metrohealth Sys., 2018-Ohio-4024, 2018 Ohio App. LEXIS 4358 (Ohio Ct. App., Cuyahoga County 2018).

Employee did not establish that comparable non-protected persons were treated more favorably as required by the McDonnell Douglas framework on both his race and gender claim because the woman who replaced him came in under a different title and spent more than 50 percent of her time performing the duties that the employee never performed. Nelson v. Univ. of Cincinnati, 2016-Ohio-1278, 2016 Ohio Misc. LEXIS 44 (Ohio Ct. Cl. 2016), aff'd, 2017-Ohio-514, 75 N.E.3d 1304, 2017 Ohio App. LEXIS 508 (Ohio Ct. App., Franklin County 2017).

Summary judgment was properly granted to a former employer and supervisor in an employee's action, alleging disparate treatment race discrimination, because the employee failed to show background circumstances that supported the inference that they were the unusual employers who discriminated against non-minority employees, and he failed to show that he suffered an adverse employment action. Butler v. Lubrizol Corp., 2015-Ohio-1216, 2015 Ohio App. LEXIS 1253 (Ohio Ct. App., Lake County 2015).

Summary judgment was properly granted to a former employer and supervisor in an employee's action, alleging disparate treatment race discrimination, because the employee failed to show any direct evidence of reverse race discrimination, as the failure of the supervisor to directly address the accusation did not amount to the truth thereof. Butler v. Lubrizol Corp., 2015-Ohio-1216, 2015 Ohio App. LEXIS 1253 (Ohio Ct. App., Lake County 2015).



Construing the evidence most strongly in a former African-American employee's favor, the employee failed to prove racial discrimination because the fellow employee whom the employee used as a comparable employee was not in a comparable position to the employee. Moreover, the employee's claim that the employee did not receive a promotion failed because the employee did not apply for the position, even though the employee's supervisor encouraged the employee to apply for the position. Peaks v. Supreme Court of Ohio, 2012-Ohio-6321, 2012 Ohio Misc. LEXIS 201 (Ohio Ct. Cl. 2012).

Plaintiff could not establish a prima facie case of race discrimination based on discipline related to his attendance infractions since the written warning given to the plaintiff did not constitute adverse actions sufficient to establish a prima facie case of discrimination. Moreover, the plaintiff had not identified similarly situated comparators who were treated more favorably than he. Rush v. E.I.duPont De Nemours & Co., 911 F. Supp. 2d 545, 2012 U.S. Dist. LEXIS 166356 (S.D. Ohio 2012).

Defendants were granted summary judgment on plaintiff's race discrimination claim because plaintiff failed to identify a similarly situated employee, and even if plaintiff could satisfy her burden of establishing a prima facie case of discrimination on the basis of race, defendant offered a non-discriminatory reason for plaintiff's termination, i.e., absenteeism, and plaintiff failed to show pretext. Kendrick v. Walgreen Co., 2012 U.S. Dist. LEXIS 164869 (S.D. Ohio Nov. 19, 2012).

Employee failed to prove by a preponderance of the evidence a prima facie case of racial discrimination, either by direct or by indirect evidence, where the employee alleged that the employee's supervisor called the employee "boy" and "nigger," the supervisor denied the allegations, and investigators for the employer were unable to substantiate the allegations. Furthermore, to the extent that the employee alleged that the employee was discriminated against based upon the employee's race because the employee received discipline for sleeping at the employee's desk, while two other employees who were found sleeping at their desks were not disciplined, the employee did not present sufficient evidence regarding those employees' attendance records or accrued leave balances to show that they were similarly-situated, or that the employee's supervisor supervised either of those employees. Miller v. Ohio Dep't of Ins., 2009-Ohio-5313, 2009 Ohio Misc. LEXIS 222 (Ohio Ct. Cl. 2009).

Where an employer had offered a legitimate, non-discriminatory reson for the challenge major employment actions, that the employee had repeatedly violated at least one company policy, despite having been informed of that policy and specifically warned of the consequences of a repeated policy infraction, and where the employee did not contest that the facts underlying the misconduct, the court found that the employee had failed to produce evidence that suggested a discriminatory animus by the employer, and the employer was entitled to summary judgment as a matter of law on the claims of race discrimination. Gregg v. SBC/Ameritech, 2005 U.S. Dist. LEXIS 12577 (S.D. Ohio June 24, 2005), aff'd, 321 Fed. Appx. 442, 2009 FED App. 0283N, 2009 U.S. App. LEXIS 8029 (6th Cir. Ohio 2009).

Employer was entitled to summary judgment in a race discrimination case under both 42 U.S.C.S. § 2000e-2 and R.C. 4112.02 because the employee showed no direct evidence of discrimination and his circumstantial evidence failed as he did not show that a similarly-situated individual outside of the protected class was treated more favorably; further, the employee set forth no evidence that the employer's reasons for reducing his pay were mere pretext for discriminatory action. The employer merely followed its established evaluation practice, which the court would not second guess. Chang v. Univ. of Toledo, 480 F. Supp. 2d 1009, 2007 U.S. Dist. LEXIS 22077 (N.D. Ohio 2007).

Employer was properly granted summary judgment on an African-American employee's race discrimination claim because the employee failed to show that the employer's legitimate, non-discriminatory reason for terminating the employee, namely her failure to meet sales goals, was pretextual: (1) the evidence reflected that, although the sales goals program was likely an example of bad policy, it was not in anyway racially discriminatory, and the employer did not enforce it in a discriminatory manner; (2) the employee underachieved in her position in 2002 and 2003 pursuant to the sales goals and was terminated as a result; (3) because of the employer's elaborate four-step disciplinary process, the employee was provided with several opportunities to correct her behavior; (4) in addition, although the employee complained about her termination, she elected termination in lieu of a demotion; and (5) the employee's deposition testimony reflected that rather than directly accusing her supervisor of racial discrimination, she believed that the supervisor's suggestions for improvement were genuine. Brown v. Bank One, N.A., 168 Fed. Appx. 46, 2006 FED App. 0122N, 2006 U.S. App. LEXIS 3711 (6th Cir. Ohio 2006).

Trial court did not err in granting summary judgment to county defendants in a county employee's action, alleging inter alia, racial discrimination based on a hostile work environment, in violation of R.C. 4112.02(A), as the employee failed to show that his workplace was permeated with "discriminatory intimidation, ridicule, and insult" which was sufficiently severe or pervasive to alter the conditions of the employment and create an abusive working environment where he only proved that two supervisory employees had a personal conflict with him, but there was no evidence that it was based on his race; further, the employee failed to establish a connection between alleged occurrences involving other employees and his own claims. Rice v. Cuyahoga County DOJ, 2005-Ohio-5337, 970 N.E.2d 470, 2005 Ohio App. LEXIS 4848 (Ohio Ct. App., Cuyahoga County 2005).

Judge terminated an African American court employee due to the employee's record of four similar complaints of inappropriate conduct, made over the course of ten years by females working in his crews and the employee brought discrimination claims. Because the African American court employee was replaced by an African-American male, he could not meet the required burden of proof under 42 U.S.C.S. § 1981 or R.C. 4112.02. James v. Lucas County Admin. Judge, 2005 U.S. Dist. LEXIS 35494 (N.D. Ohio Dec. 23, 2005).

In an action in which a former employee filed suit against defendant former employer alleging race discrimination in violation of 42 U.S.C.S. § 1981 and R.C. 4112.02, the employer was denied summary judgment where (1) the employee had shown that there was an issue of fact as to whether he received field training inferior to that provided to white employees; (2) if the jury found that the employer discriminated against the employee in his field training, the jury could reasonably determine that racial discrimination affected the employee's work performance, and therefore tainted the employer's determination of the amount of the employee's raise; and (3) the employer's use of the employee's work performance to determine whether he would be laid off, where that work performance was potentially tainted by race-based discrimination in training, created an issue of fact as to whether race was a motivating factor in the decision. Guy v. Cent. Locating Serv., Ltd., 389 F. Supp. 2d 843, 2005 U.S. Dist. LEXIS 21401 (N.D. Ohio 2005).

**—Cat's paw**

Trial court did not abuse its discretion by failing to find that there was no evidence to support the Ohio Civil Rights Commission's finding of "cat's paw" liability as the decision to ultimately terminate his employment was based on the supervisor's allegation, motivated by a racial animus and found by the administrative law judge to be false, that the employee had used profanity and had been insubordinate. Stallworth v. Wal-Mart Stores E., L.P., 2016-Ohio-2620, 50 N.E.3d 27, 2016 Ohio App. LEXIS 1511 (Ohio Ct. App., Hamilton County 2016).

**—Demotion**

Trial court did not err by granting the employer summary judgment because the employee failed to prove that he was demoted based on racial animus on the ground that only African-American custodial employees were the subject of video surveillance because the employee was not replaced by a non-protected person, as the employee was not replaced by the substitute custodian, as he had no supervisory authority and did not order supplies, and the employee was eventually replaced by an African-American man. The employee was not similarly situated to a custodian who was later accused of abusing the employer's break policy because: (1) the employee was the custodian's supervisor and in a position of authority and trust; (2) the custodian was not accused of taking breaks of two, three, and four hour durations, but rather he admitted to returning to work 10 to 15 minutes late twice; (3) there was no evidence that the employer knew of the allegations against the custodian at the time the surveillance cameras were installed; and (4) there was no evidence that the employee was treated differently from the custodian. Blake v. Beachwood City Schs. Bd. of Educ., 2011-Ohio-1099, 2011 Ohio App. LEXIS 944 (Ohio Ct. App., Cuyahoga County 2011).

**—Discharge**

University's reason for terminating the assistant dean was for making the call to the vice chancellor for finance at the Ohio Board of Regents and not for any discriminatory reason. Because the call was unauthorized and inappropriate, and regardless of the content of the call or whether the information was conveyed incorrectly, the employee failed to show that the university's articulated reason for his termination was merely pretext. Nelson v. Univ. of Cincinnati, 2016-Ohio-1278, 2016 Ohio Misc. LEXIS 44 (Ohio Ct. Cl. 2016), aff'd, 2017-Ohio-514, 75 N.E.3d 1304, 2017 Ohio App. LEXIS 508 (Ohio Ct. App., Franklin County 2017).

Because the record contained reliable, probative and substantial evidence that the employee had been treated differently and had been subjected to different conditions of employment than similarly-situated Caucasian overnight stockers, the trial court did not abuse its discretion in finding that he had established a prima facie case of discrimination. Stallworth v. Wal-Mart Stores E., L.P., 2016-Ohio-2620, 50 N.E.3d 27, 2016 Ohio App. LEXIS 1511 (Ohio Ct. App., Hamilton County 2016).

Trial court erred by granting judgment notwithstanding the verdict for the employer on the racial discrimination claim because there was direct evidence that the employer was motivated by discriminatory animus in its decision to layoff the employee because the supervisor used the n-word directly to the employee, both staff and management commonly used the n-word at work with little or no reprimand, the supervisor used a gun to intimidate African-American employees, and he was involved in the decision to lay off the employee. Smith v. Superior Prod., LLC, 2014-Ohio-1961, 13 N.E.3d 664, 2014 Ohio App. LEXIS 1895 (Ohio Ct. App., Franklin County 2014).

Former state trooper could not prevail on the trooper's claim that the trooper was discharged from the trooper's position because of racial discrimination because, although the trooper asserted that the animosity of the trooper's supervisor toward the trooper was based upon the trooper's race, the court found that the trooper failed to prove that the supervisor's proffered reasons for the discharge had no basis in fact, that the proffered reasons did not actually motivate the discharge, or that they were insufficient to motivate the discharge. Smith v. Ohio Dep't of Pub. Safety, 2012-Ohio-6358, 2012 Ohio Misc. LEXIS 239 (Ohio Ct. Cl. 2012), aff'd, 2013-Ohio-4210, 997 N.E.2d 597, 2013 Ohio App. LEXIS 4384 (Ohio Ct. App., Franklin County 2013).

In an action in which a former employee filed suit against his former employer alleging race discrimination in violation of Title VII, 42 U.S.C.S. § 2000e et seq., and Ohio's civil rights statute, R.C. 4112.02/4112.99; hostile work environment; wrongful discharge; and retaliation in violation of R.C. 4112.02(I), 4112.99, the employer's motion for summary judgment was denied on the race discrimination claim; a reasonable juror could conclude that the reason given for his termination was a pretext for discrimination because it had no basis in fact, did not motivate his discharge, and was insufficient to warrant his discharge. The court reasoned in part that the employee presented evidence that the employer's substance abuse policy did not require termination for a violation. Satterwhite v. Faurecia Exhaust Sys., 2005 U.S. Dist. LEXIS 10282 (S.D. Ohio May 31, 2005).

**—Employer liability**

Employer was not liable on the claim of hostile environment based on race because, even if there were supervisors who were aware that the quality control manager (determined to be a coworker) had made some comments to the employee, there was no evidence that the employee asked the supervisors to take action against the manager or that an official complaint was lodged which would have alerted the employer to the specific problem. Chapa v. Genpak, LLC, 2014-Ohio-897, 2014 Ohio App. LEXIS 846 (Ohio Ct. App., Franklin County 2014).

Defendant was entitled to summary judgment as a matter of law as to plaintiffs claim for race discrimination, as she presented no evidence other than general statements in her self-serving affidavit to show that defendant's decision to abolish her position was motivated by her race. The evidence indicated that defendant abolished plaintiff's position for budgetary reasons, plaintiff was not entitled to be called back into another position because it entailed more responsibilities and was in a higher pay range, and a co-worker had more seniority than plaintiff had. McClair v. Univ. of Toledo, 2013-Ohio-5938, 2013 Ohio Misc. LEXIS 94 (Ohio Ct. Cl. 2013).

**—Hostile work environment**

Trial court did not err in granting summary judgment for the employer and the labor relations analyst on the hostile work environment claim because the employees' work environment was not sufficiently hostile and abusive so as to constitute a racially hostile work environment. When the black coworker's alleged threats were corroborated by other employees, the employer, in accordance with its company policy, effectively and adequately handled complaints regarding the same by suspending him. Johnson v. GMC, 2001-Ohio-1673, 2001 Ohio App. LEXIS 6113 (Ohio Ct. App., Richland County 2001).

Trial court erred by granting judgment notwithstanding the verdict for the employer on the hostile work environment claim because reasonable minds could easily have concluded that the supervisor's use of the n-word, directly to the employee, while on the production floor, at the same time telling him to go home, was humiliating. The trial court also disregarded the other testimony, including testimony about laying a cocked firearm on the desk when the supervisor talked to the employee. Smith v. Superior Prod., LLC, 2014-Ohio-1961, 13 N.E.3d 664, 2014 Ohio App. LEXIS 1895 (Ohio Ct. App., Franklin County 2014).

Trial court did not err by granting summary judgment for the employer and the quality control manager. The employee did not establish his hostile working environment based on race claim because he failed to demonstrate that the alleged conduct was so severe or pervasive as to create an environment that was hostile pursuant to both a subjective and objective analysis. Chapa v. Genpak, LLC, 2014-Ohio-897, 2014 Ohio App. LEXIS 846 (Ohio Ct. App., Franklin County 2014).

Although the trial court erred in failing to consider a hostile work environment claim, the claimed harassment was neither severe nor pervasive. There was no evidence that the individuals who made the alleged remarks were supervisors, that their alleged actions were committed within the scope of their agency from the employer, or that the remarks were physically threatening. Clinton v. Faurecia Exhaust Sys., 2012-Ohio-4618, 2012 Ohio App. LEXIS 4059 (Ohio Ct. App., Miami County 2012).

Jury verdict rendered for an African American supervisor and the city which employed the supervisor, in a Caucasian employee's hostile work environment harassment claim brought under R.C. 4112.02, was not against the manifest weight of the evidence because, on the evidence presented at trial, the jury reasonably could have concluded that the city addressed any harassing conduct when informed, followed up, and had no reason to believe that the harassment was continuing. Further, the jury could also have concluded that any harassment that the employee suffered, including racial comments made by her coworkers and her supervisor's allegedly discriminatory treatment of her, was not severe or pervasive enough to warrant relief. Mowery v. City of Columbus, 2006-Ohio-1153, 2006 Ohio App. LEXIS 1051 (Ohio Ct. App., Franklin County 2006).

In an action in which a former employee filed suit against defendant former employer alleging race discrimination in violation of 42 U.S.C.S. § 1981 and R.C. 4112.02, the employer was granted summary judgment on the hostile work environment claim where (1) the employee failed to present evidence showing several incidents occurred because of his race; and (2) several incidents were not physically threatening or humiliating, but were mere "offensive utterances." Guy v. Cent. Locating Serv., Ltd., 389 F. Supp. 2d 843, 2005 U.S. Dist. LEXIS 21401 (N.D. Ohio 2005).

Former employers were entitled to summary judgment on a former employee's hostile work environment claim under 42 U.S.C.S. § 1981 and R.C. 4112.02 because no reasonable jury could find that the employee was subject to the harassment that she alleged, as the only physical evidence in the case either gave no support to the employee's account or squarely contradicted it. White v. Drs. Camm & Golian, D.D.S., Inc., 2005 U.S. Dist. LEXIS 19763 (N.D. Ohio Sept. 12, 2005).

Former employee's race and national original claims under Ohio Rev. Code Ann. § 4112.02 were dismissed where the employee alleged only a single incident of discriminatory harassment. Longoria v. Autoneum North America, Inc., 2015 U.S. Dist. LEXIS 147613 (N.D. Ohio Oct. 30, 2015).

**—Not shown**

Employee did not establish that a supervisor's reliance on the check in and out violation as a basis for the suspension was a pretext for racial discrimination because there was no indication that the employee's failure to check in or out had no basis in fact, was not the actual reason the suspension was upheld, or was insufficient to explain the suspension. Tanksley v. Howell, 2020-Ohio-4278, 2020 Ohio App. LEXIS 3172 (Ohio Ct. App., Franklin County 2020).

Where a Health Information Technician (HIT) was hired by a company, which paid her wages and benefits, and placed her at a state correctional facility, the HIT's race discrimination claim failed because she did not suffer an adverse employment action since the correctional facility did not provide the company notice of the event, the HIT's e-mail stated that it would be her "last day anyway" and the HIT requested a letter stating that she voluntarily left the correctional facility, and in any event, she did not provide evidence of a similarly situated Caucasian person being treated differently. Brown v. Corr. Reception Ctr., 2019-Ohio-1067, 2019 Ohio Misc. LEXIS 22 (Ohio Ct. Cl. 2019), rev'd in part, 2020-Ohio-684, 146 N.E.3d 621, 2020 Ohio App. LEXIS 629 (Ohio Ct. App., Franklin County 2020).

Former employee could not establish a prima facie case of disparate-treatment discrimination because she could not demonstrate the "similarly situated" element of the disparate treatment test; the employee, who was African-American, was replaced by an African-American employee, and thus, she was replaced by an individual of the same race. Chisholm v.

Titles 39 — 57

Cleveland Clinic Found., 2019-Ohio-3369, 141 N.E.3d 674, 2019 Ohio App. LEXIS 3452 (Ohio Ct. App., Cuyahoga County 2019).

Former employee failed to support her claim of disparate-impact discrimination with significant statistical evidence because she did not present statistical evidence that could support a finding that the two felony disqualifications that occurred were due to the individuals' race rather than random chance or some other variable; the employee was the only employee whose employment was adversely affected by the former employer's felony-conviction standard. Chisholm v. Cleveland Clinic Found., 2019-Ohio-3369, 141 N.E.3d 674, 2019 Ohio App. LEXIS 3452 (Ohio Ct. App., Cuyahoga County 2019).

Trial court properly granted summary judgment for the employer because the employee, a medical resident, did not show that the employer was more likely than not motivated by discriminatory animus and thus did not present sufficient direct evidence of racial discrimination. His supervisor doctors had serious concerns with the resident's performance as a resident and his care of patients as well as his anger issues. Glemaud v. Metrohealth Sys., 2018-Ohio-4024, 2018 Ohio App. LEXIS 4358 (Ohio Ct. App., Cuyahoga County 2018).

There was no error in finding that discriminatory intent on the basis of race and gender was not the actual reason for the employee's termination because he failed to carry his ultimate burden of demonstrating that the adverse employment action resulted from unlawful discrimination. He was terminated for making the call to the vice chancellor of finance and data management at the Ohio Board of Regents and not for any discriminatory reason. Nelson v. Univ. of Cincinnati, 2017-Ohio-514, 75 N.E.3d 1304, 2017 Ohio App. LEXIS 508 (Ohio Ct. App., Franklin County 2017).

Plaintiffs complaint failed to state a claim of race discrimination; even if she could establish she suffered an adverse employment action, the complaint did not support an inference that comparable, non-protected persons were treated more favorably, as it stated that defendant hired African Americans for the position plaintiff sought. Sheppard v. Ohio Bd. of Regents, 2016-Ohio-3477, 2016 Ohio Misc. LEXIS 67 (Ohio Ct. Cl. 2016).



**—Promotion**

Employee failed to properly present either direct or indirect evidence to support his claim for racial discrimination in his failure to promote action because the quality control manager was not the person who decided whether or not the employee was promoted, nor was his recommendation on the subject sought. Also, because the comments were not made close in time with respect to the 2000/2001 and 2002 promotion denials, the comments could not be used as direct evidence. Chapa v. Genpak, LLC, 2014-Ohio-897, 2014 Ohio App. LEXIS 846 (Ohio Ct. App., Franklin County 2014).

African-American employee failed to present a prima facie case of racial discrimination under R.C. 4112.02(A) because although she claimed that she was unfairly denied a promotion to a project manager position, she failed to present evidence that she had applied for the project manager position-or that such a position was even available at the time. The employee also failed to satisfy the McDonnell Douglas analysis because she did not present evidence that she was qualified for the position, and she presented nothing to show that three Caucasian employees were similarly situated employees. Veal v. Upreach LLC, 2011-Ohio-5406, 2011 Ohio App. LEXIS 4415 (Ohio Ct. App., Franklin County 2011).

Employee of a state university did not show that he was similarly situated to non-protected employees in all relevant respects for purposes of his claim of indirect racial discrimination due to the denial of tenure, such that his claim failed. Saha v. Ohio State Univ., 2011-Ohio-3824, 2011 Ohio App. LEXIS 3245 (Ohio Ct. App., Franklin County 2011).

Employee of a state university did present sufficient evidence that he possessed the minimum objective criteria for employment within the relevant field of research for purposes of his claim of indirect racial discrimination due to the denial of tenure; the finding that his research productivity and grant funding did not meet the expectations of the department, college, or university was a different standard. Saha v. Ohio State Univ., 2011-Ohio-3824, 2011 Ohio App. LEXIS 3245 (Ohio Ct. App., Franklin County 2011).

In a racial discrimination suit, an African-American teacher's contention that the school district's articulated reason for hiring the other candidate instead of him to the position of assistant principal, that the other candidate was more qualified, was a pretext for discrimination was rejected as the search committee, the superintendent, and the board of education all determined that the other candidate was better qualified for the position after reviewing the application materials, asking both the teacher and the other candidate the same questions, and considering the strengths and concerns related to the teacher and the other candidate. Collins v. Orange City Sch. Dist. Bd. of Educ., 2010-Ohio-3195, 2010 Ohio App. LEXIS 2673 (Ohio Ct. App., Cuyahoga County 2010).

While an African-American teacher presented a prima facie case of discrimination by proof that he was a member of a protected class, that he was not promoted to the position of assistant principal, that the assistant principal position was filled by a person outside the protected class, and that the teacher met the initial qualifications, the school district demonstrated a legitimate, nondiscriminatory reason for its decision to promote the other candidate to the assistant principal position over the teacher: the other candidate was better qualified. Collins v. Orange City Sch. Dist. Bd. of Educ., 2010-Ohio-3195, 2010 Ohio App. LEXIS 2673 (Ohio Ct. App., Cuyahoga County 2010).

Employee failed to establish a prima facie case of failure to promote based on race where the employee never applied for new positions that were created after a company restructure, and the new positions did not include a pay raise, or adversely affect employment. Bolls v. South-Western Thomson Learning, 311 F. Supp. 2d 643, 2003 U.S. Dist. LEXIS 25071 (S.D. Ohio 2003).

**—Reverse discrimination**

Trial court properly awarded summary judgment to defendant on plaintiffs reverse race discrimination claim because there was no admissible evidence that the school principal ever made the purportedly discriminatory comments. Martcheva v. Dayton Bd. of Educ., 2021-Ohio-3524, 179 N.E.3d 687, 2021 Ohio App. LEXIS 3433 (Ohio Ct. App., Montgomery County 2021).

Employee did not establish a prima facie case of reverse race discrimination; the employee, who was still in her probationary period, was terminated for leaving the unit where she worked to socialize with former co-workers in another area of the prison compound, and she failed to record her absence in a log book in which employees were required to document when they entered or left the unit. Osborne v. Ohio Reformatory for Women, 2019-Ohio-5467, 2019 Ohio Misc. LEXIS 345 (Ohio Ct. Cl. 2019), aff'd, 2021-Ohio-1036, 2021 Ohio App. LEXIS 1047 (Ohio Ct. App., Franklin County 2021).

Trial court properly granted summary judgment to the employer and the labor relations analyst on the reverse discrimination claim because the employees failed to demonstrate that they had been treated differently than similarly-situated employees who were not members of the protected group. While they maintained that the employer treated a black coworker in a more lenient manner than it would treat white employees, who engaged in the same type of misconduct, they presented no evidence regarding white employees who had threatened black employees or the discipline, or lack thereof, that such white employees received. Johnson v. GMC, 2001-Ohio-1673, 2001 Ohio App. LEXIS 6113 (Ohio Ct. App., Richland County 2001).

**—Salary**

While an employee allegedly received a lower salary raise in comparison to other coworkers and claimed that the lower raise was retaliation for filing a complaint of race discrimination, the evidence established that the difference in pay raises was not statistically significant and was explained by performance issues and the fact that the employee's overall salary was already above market norms. Bolls v. South-Western Thomson Learning, 311 F. Supp. 2d 643, 2003 U.S. Dist. LEXIS 25071 (S.D. Ohio 2003).

While an employee claimed race discrimination based upon receiving a lower salary raise in comparison to other coworkers, the evidence established that the difference in pay raises was not statistically significant and was explained by performance issues and the fact that the employee's overall salary was already above market norms. Bolls v. South-Western Thomson Learning, 311 F. Supp. 2d 643, 2003 U.S. Dist. LEXIS 25071 (S.D. Ohio 2003).

**—Standard of proof**

High school principal, who was an African-American, whose contract was not renewed, did not prove racial discrimination through the use of "comparables" because he produced no evidence that he was treated differently from any other administrators in the district. Atkinson v. Akron Bd. of Educ., 2006-Ohio-1032, 2006 Ohio App. LEXIS 947 (Ohio Ct. App., Summit County 2006).

When a high school principal, who was an African-American, could not show, after the school board declined to renew his contract, that he was replaced by a person who was not a member of a protected class, because he was replaced by another African-American, he did not produce indirect evidence of racial discrimination. Atkinson v. Akron Bd. of Educ., 2006-Ohio-1032, 2006 Ohio App. LEXIS 947 (Ohio Ct. App., Summit County 2006).

When a high school principal, who was an African-American, produced no evidence of any remark or act on the part of any member of the school board or other supervisory personnel indicating that the nonrenewal of his contract was racially motivated, he did not show he was subjected to direct racial discrimination. Atkinson v. Akron Bd. of Educ., 2006-Ohio-1032, 2006 Ohio App. LEXIS 947 (Ohio Ct. App., Summit County 2006).

**—Retaliation**

Trial court erred in granting an employer summary judgment on an employee's retaliation claim because the employee produced evidence sufficient to demonstrate a genuine issue of material fact as to whether she engaged in a protected activity and whether she was subjected to an adverse action as a result of the protected activity; the employee testified that she complained to her supervisor that she was being discriminated against, and her transfer occurred after her complaints. Vogt v. Total Renal Care, Inc., 2016-Ohio-4955, 2016 Ohio App. LEXIS 2751 (Ohio Ct. App., Cuyahoga County 2016).

**—Work rules**

Although an employee set forth a prima facie case of race discrimination under 42 U.S.C.S. § 2000e-2(a)(1) and R.C. 4112.02(A), a court granted employer's motion for summary judgment because the employer offered a legitimate, non-discriminatory reason for termination, namely that the employee had violated an unwritten work policy that was known to the employee. Quintanilla v. AK Tube LLC, 477 F. Supp. 2d 828, 2007 U.S. Dist. LEXIS 17475 (N.D. Ohio 2007).

**Racial discrimination**

District court erred in granting summary judgment in favor of defendants, a city and supervisor, on an employee's unlawful discrimination claim, as a race-based shift change amounted to discrimination with respect to the terms and privileges of employment under Title VII and under the Ohio Civil Rights Act. Threat v. City of Cleveland, 2021 FED App. 168P, 2021 U.S. App. LEXIS 22076 (6th Cir. Ohio July 26, 2021).

**—Burdens of proof**

Plaintiff failed to present evidence to show that she was discriminated when the City of Akron hired a Caucasian male instead of her because she showed no evidence that the choice was racially motivated and she was not so plainly superior to the one hired as to rebut the factual basis behind the City's reasons. Harris v. City of Akron, 836 Fed. Appx. 415, 2020 FED App. 694N, 2020 U.S. App. LEXIS 39222 (6th Cir. Ohio 2020).

**Racial discrimination**

Trial court erred by granting of a new trial as to liability on the discrimination, retaliation, and hostile work environment claims because the employee was demoted after being racially demeaned, despite his 20 years of service to the company, he was one of first employees to be laid-off, and the employee and other African-American employees were demeaned and intimidated by having a loaded firearm placed in front of them and cocked when conversations were held with a white member of the management team. Smith v. Superior Prod., LLC, 2014-Ohio-1961, 13 N.E.3d 664, 2014 Ohio App. LEXIS 1895 (Ohio Ct. App., Franklin County 2014).

**Reasonable accommodation**

In this Americans with Disabilities Act of 1990 action, whether the accommodations were, in fact, reasonable, and whether they would enable the employee to perform the essential functions of the Shipper and Pickle Line Process Technician position, would be for the jury to decide. Siewertsen v. Worthington Steel Co., 134 F. Supp. 3d 1091, 2015 U.S. Dist. LEXIS 129455 (N.D. Ohio 2015).

**Reduction in force**

In a workforce reduction case, the former employee failed to adduce circumstantial evidence of intentional age and sex discrimination because the former employer established a legitimate, non-pretextual basis for her termination because the employer's managers thought they were complying with the collective bargaining agreement when they terminated the employee's position, and the employee had not identified any evidence suggesting that the employer singled her out or that its proffered reason for terminating her position was pretextual. McCarthy v. Ameritech Publ., Inc., 763 F.3d 469, 2014 FED App. 0181P, 2014 U.S. App. LEXIS 15517 (6th Cir. Ohio 2014).

Trial court properly granted summary judgment to an employer and two supervisors in a former employee's age discrimination claim pursuant to R.C. 4112.02, as the employer was involved in a reduction in force due to a customer's decision to change its policy of outsourcing a great deal of work to the employer to a policy of insourcing that work; the employee failed to show a genuine issue of material fact existed as to whether the employer and supervisors' proffered non-discriminatory reasons for his termination were a pretext for age discrimination where he was terminated and another person in his position was retained. Kundtz v. AT&T Solutions, Inc., 2007-Ohio-1462, 2007 Ohio App. LEXIS 1318 (Ohio Ct. App., Franklin County 2007).

**Regarded as having a disability**

As there were genuine issues of material fact as to whether an employer perceived the employee as having a neurological impairment following an accident, and whether the employee was terminated as a result thereof, summary judgment for the employer on the perceived disability discrimination claim was error. Carnahan v. Morton Bldgs., Inc., 2015-Ohio-3528, 41 N.E.3d 239, 2015 Ohio App. LEXIS 3445 (Ohio Ct. App., Paulding County 2015).

There was sufficient evidence to allow the jury to conclude that the nurse was perceived as disabled within the statutory meaning because she was taking measures (prescription medication) to correct or mitigate an underlying physical condition injuries caused by one or more auto accidents. Cavins v. S&B Health Care, Inc., 2015-Ohio-4119, 39 N.E.3d 1287, 2015 Ohio App. LEXIS 4072 (Ohio Ct. App., Montgomery County 2015).

**Release**

Trial court properly granted summary judgment to an employer in a former employee's action alleging claims of sex discrimination under R.C. 4112.02(A) and the Family and Medical Leave Act as the employee's claim that the employer's vice-president had verbally misrepresented that the position held by the employee was being eliminated was an allegation of fraud in the inducement, and the employee had not alleged any claims of fraud in her complaint in accordance with the provisions in Civ.R. 9(B); thus, the employee waived the defense that enforcement of the release signed by the employee agreeing to release all claims against the employer in exchange for severance pay was barred by fraud. As a result, the agreement signed by the employee barred her claims against the employer. Turner v. Salvagnini Am., Inc., 2008-Ohio-3596, 2008 Ohio App. LEXIS 3036 (Ohio Ct. App., Butler County 2008).

**Religion**

Where couple's federal religious discrimination claim failed, so did their state religious discrimination claim because R.C. 4112 et seq. track federal law under 42 U.S.C.S. § 2000e-5. Goldmeier v. Allstate Ins. Co., 337 F.3d 629, 2003 FED App. 0246P, 2003 U.S. App. LEXIS 14736 (6th Cir. Ohio 2003), cert. denied, 540 U.S. 1106, 124 S. Ct. 1052, 157 L. Ed. 2d 891, 2004 U.S. LEXIS 74 (U.S. 2004).

It was not reasonable to require a bank to waive its security procedures concerning check cashing in order to accommodate the alleged religious beliefs of an individual: Yeager v. Ohio Civ. Rights Comm'n, 2002-Ohio-3383, 148 Ohio App. 3d 459, 773 N.E.2d 1097, 2002 Ohio App. LEXIS 3391 (Ohio Ct. App., Trumbull County 2002), cert. denied, 537 U.S. 1113, 123 S. Ct. 928, 154 L. Ed. 2d 787, 2003 U.S. LEXIS 704 (U.S. 2003).

The fact that the employees' conduct violated tenets of the employing church provided a sufficient, nondiscriminatory justification for termination: Basinger v. Pilarczky, 137 Ohio App. 3d 325, 738 N.E.2d 814, 2000 Ohio App. LEXIS 1357 (Ohio Ct. App., Hamilton County), dismissed, 89 Ohio St. 3d 1466, 732 N.E.2d 998, 2000 Ohio LEXIS 1916 (Ohio 2000).

Deliberate failure to disclose a known religious conflict in response to direct questioning in an initial job interview calls into question the extent to which a religious belief is sincerely held. The employee established a prima facie case of religious discrimination: Franks v. National Lime & Stone Co., 2000-Ohio-1880, 138 Ohio App. 3d 124, 740 N.E.2d 694, 2000 Ohio App. LEXIS 2522 (Ohio Ct. App., Hancock County 2000).

The Title VII exemption of religious organizations from religious discrimination claims does not apply to a claim under R.C. 4112.02: Ward v. Hengle, 124 Ohio App. 3d 396, 706 N.E.2d 392, 1997 Ohio App. LEXIS 5472 (Ohio Ct. App., Summit County 1997), dismissed, 81 Ohio St. 3d 1510, 692 N.E.2d 617, 1998 Ohio LEXIS 1088 (Ohio 1998), cert. denied, 525 U.S. 878, 119 S. Ct. 183, 142 L. Ed. 2d 149, 1998 U.S. LEXIS 5723 (U.S. 1998).

Plaintiff did not directly or indirectly establish a prima facie case of religious discrimination: Seale v. City of Springfield, 113 Ohio App. 3d 384, 680 N.E.2d 1286, 1996 Ohio App. LEXIS 3317 (Ohio Ct. App., Clark County 1996).

It is an unlawful employment practice in Ohio for an employer to discharge an employee because of his or her religion. R.C. 4112.02(A): South Wind Motel v. Ohio Civil Rights Com., 24 Ohio App. 3d 209, 494 N.E.2d 1158, 1985 Ohio App. LEXIS 10182 (Ohio Ct. App., Franklin County 1985).

The provisions of R.C. 4112.02(E) do not apply to church-member relationships protected by USConst amend I: Dayton Christian Schools v. Ohio Civil Rights Commission, 578 F. Supp. 1004 (S.D. 1984), rev'd on other grounds, 766 F.2d 932, rev'd and remanded 477 U.S. 619.].

Since religious institutions are specifically exempted from the provisions of R.C. 4112.02(K), relating to discrimination in housing, it is clear that the legislature intended the other provisions of the statute to apply to religious educational institutions: Dayton Christian Schools v. Ohio Civil Rights Commission, 578 F. Supp. 1004 (S.D. 1984), rev'd on other grounds, 766 F.2d 932, rev'd and remanded 477 U.S. 619.].

**Religious discrimination**

Fitness club was entitled to summary judgment on Muslim member's discrimination claim brought under Title II of Civil Rights Act of 1964 and Ohio state law because he failed to establish that he had been prohibited or restricted from using or enjoying any of the club's services, facilities, privileges, advantages, and accommodations, because of his religion; neither Title II, nor its Ohio counterpart, required the club to allow the member to pray in the location he preferred. Fall v. LA Fitness, 161 F. Supp. 3d 601, 2016 U.S. Dist. LEXIS 17023 (S.D. Ohio 2016).

Accommodations proposed by a former employee, who refused to sign a form stating that he had received and acknowledged the employee handbook on the basis that signing the form would violate his firmly held religious beliefs and would require him to give his stamp of approval on the anti-discrimination policy on the basis of sexual orientation, were not reasonable as a matter of law because they did not address the core issue: his admitted refusal to abide by the non-discrimination policy in the company handbook as signified by his unwillingness to sign the form. Thus, the court rejected the employee's argument that his termination constituted religious discrimination. Johnson v. SK Tech, Inc., 2010-Ohio-3449, 2010 Ohio App. LEXIS 2958 (Ohio Ct. App., Montgomery County 2010).

**Remedies**

As parents' claims of unlawful discrimination failed with respect to statutory claims of harassment, retaliation, and public accommodations, they were not entitled to a preliminary injunction or declaratory relief with respect to the same allegations. Pittman v. Parillo, 2017-Ohio-1477, 2017 Ohio App. LEXIS 1482 (Ohio Ct. App., Lucas County 2017).

**Removal to federal court**

The use of the phrase "equal pay for equal work" in an amended complaint in a sex discrimination claim did not convert the Ohio claim to a federal claim: Butts v. Guardian Indus. Corp, 981 F. Supp. 1062, 1997 U.S. Dist. LEXIS 17338 (N.D. Ohio 1997).

In a removal action, former employer met its burden of showing that the amount-in-controversy exceeded the $50,000 jurisdictional minimum for removing the action to a federal court on diversity grounds: Szalay v. Yellow Freight Sys., 999 F. Supp. 972, 1996 U.S. Dist. LEXIS 22128 (N.D. Ohio 1996).

While the argument, that plaintiff filed complaint with Ohio Civil Rights Commission only in order to comply with Age Discrimination in Employment Act, 29 USC § 621 et seq., and did not intend to pursue state administrative remedy, points out inconsistency between state statutory scheme and federal statute, it does not keep plaintiff from being barred from bringing a claim under R.C. 4112.08: Keister v. Delco Products, 680 F. Supp. 281, 1987 U.S. Dist. LEXIS 13098 (S.D. Ohio 1987).

**Replacement of employee**

In a professor's action for discrimination, a judgment granting summary judgment to a university was proper, as the university submitted evidence demonstrating that a faculty member did not replace plaintiff; plaintiff was not a tenure-track faculty member and his area of expertise, cardiovascular research, was different. Jiashin Wu v. Northeast Ohio Med. Univ., 2019 Ohio 2530, 2019 Ohio App. LEXIS 2635 (June 25, 2019).

Former employee's age discrimination suit was properly dismissed on summary judgment as the 64-year-old employee was not "replaced" by a 28-year-old employee; instead, the younger employee was hired three years before the employee was discharged, and the employee's discharge did not permit the younger employee's retention as he was transferred to a different position two years earlier. Kowach v. Ohio Presbyterian Ret. Servs., 2010-Ohio-4428, 2010 Ohio App. LEXIS 3771 (Ohio Ct. App., Trumbull County 2010).

Employee did not meet the burden of showing a prima facie case of race discrimination under R.C. 4112.02(A) with respect to allegedly being terminated and replaced by a Caucasian individual, as there was no evidence that a similarly situated, non-protected employee was treated more favorably or that, in fact, a Caucasian was hired as a replacement; rather, other employees took over some of the terminated employee's job duties. Valentine v. Westshore Primary Care Assoc., 2008-Ohio-4450, 2008 Ohio App. LEXIS 3756 (Ohio Ct. App., Cuyahoga County 2008).

Employer was entitled to summary judgment on age and gender discrimination claims where the employee was not "replaced" by a male or by a younger person. A person is not replaced when another employee is assigned to perform the plaintiffs duties in addition to other duties or when the work is redistributed among other existing employees already performing related work: Mendlovic v. Life Line Screening of Am., Ltd., 2007-Ohio-4674, 173 Ohio App. 3d 46, 877 N.E.2d 377, 2007 Ohio App. LEXIS 4219 (Ohio Ct. App., Cuyahoga County 2007).

**Res judicata**

Teacher's disability discrimination claim was not barred under either the claim preclusion or issue preclusion portions of the doctrine of res judicata because there was no final judgment on the merits in the federal action as to the state claims, the teacher asserted her state claims in the federal action, and the federal court specifically declined to exercise jurisdiction over them. Johnson v. Cleveland City Sch. Dist., 2011-Ohio-2778, 2011 Ohio App. LEXIS 2384 (Ohio Ct. App., Cuyahoga County 2011).

Supervisors cannot invoke res judicata in a civil rights action in federal court after the plaintiff has prosecuted a state civil rights claim because, under R.C. 4112.02, supervisors do not fall within the scope of the term "employers" and, therefore, could not have been parties to the state proceeding; similarly, the plaintiff cannot extend the Ohio Civil Rights Commission liability finding to the supervisors through collateral estoppel because the supervisors never had a full and fair opportunity to litigate that issue: Foulks v. Ohio Dep't of Rehabilitation & Correction, 713 F.2d 1229, 1983 U.S. App. LEXIS 25191 (6th Cir. Ohio 1983).

**Respondeat superior**

There was no respondeat superior liability on the employer's part, and no liability for the alleged workplace harassment, because the employee did not suffer an adverse employment action due to the alleged harassment. His employment ended, not because of discrimination on the part of the employer, but because he could not physically perform his job due to an injury. Clinton v. Faurecia Exhaust Sys., 2012-Ohio-4618, 2012 Ohio App. LEXIS 4059 (Ohio Ct. App., Miami County 2012).

**Retaliation**

District court properly dismissed retaliation claims under Title VII and the Ohio Civil Rights Act, as third-party retaliation did not apply to a claim by employees based on an unfair-labor-practice charged filed by the city against the union. Threat v. City of Cleveland, 6 F.4th 672, 2021 FED App. 168P, 2021 U.S. App. LEXIS 22076 (6th Cir. Ohio 2021).

Former employee's voluntary resignation did not bar her sexual harassment and retaliation claims because a finder of fact could determine that the employee resigned under duress, notwithstanding the language of the resignation, as she was only given the options to be fired; to accept a demotion, execute a full release of her claims, and agree to remain silent about her complaints of harassment; or to resign; and she was precluded from receiving legal advice and forced her to make a decision without taking additional time to consider the matter. Jackson v. Northfield Park Assocs., LLC, 2020 Ohio Misc. LEXIS 46 (Ohio C.P. Apr. 6, 2020).

Summary judgment was denied as to the former employer on the former employee's retaliation claim against a supervisor because a reasonable jury could find that the supervisor's behavior in slapping her on her bottom and increasing his criticism of her work was retaliatory and dissuaded the employee, both subjectively and objectively, against reporting the behavior, particularly in light of the response to her earlier complaint; and the supervisor offered no legitimate reason for the stepped-up harassment and other retaliatory conduct. Jackson v. Northfield Park Assocs., LLC, 2020 Ohio Misc. LEXIS 46 (Ohio C.P. Apr. 6, 2020).

Because the employer never asserted an argument under the burden shifting analysis of a legitimate business reason as to the retaliation claim, the trial court incorrectly applied its legitimate business reason argument in the retaliation claim and improperly awarded summary judgment based on an argument that was not presented by the employer. Lehmier v. W. Reserve Chem. Corp., 2018-Ohio-3351, 2018 Ohio App. LEXIS 3623 (Ohio Ct. App., Summit County 2018).

Where an employee suffered from sleeping problems and was terminated, the employee's retaliation claim failed because the employee did not qualify as disabled, never requested an accommodation, and did not file a formal charge against the employee's supervisor before the employee was terminated. Neely v. Benchmark Family Servs., 640 Fed. Appx. 429, 2016 FED App. 0048N, 2016 U.S. App. LEXIS 1391 (6th Cir. Ohio 2016).

Summary judgment was granted in error because the employee presented evidence raising a genuine issue of material fact as to whether the employer's proffered reason for removing her from the seafood department was mere pretext since, although its claims that it removed the employee in order to protect her from the manager's actions. A jury could have determined that she was removed as a way of penalizing her for complaining about being sexually harassed. Ellis v. Jungle Jim's Mkt., Inc., 2015-Ohio-4226, 44 N.E.3d 1034, 2015 Ohio App. LEXIS 4118 (Ohio Ct. App., Butler County 2015).

Former employee failed to make out a prima facie case of retaliation and failed to establish that he engaged in activity protected by the statute. While the employee asked the chief operating officer (COO) one question insinuating that he had spoke down to him because he was black, the evidence demonstrated that the employee subsequently denied, both orally and in writing, that the COO had engaged in any racial discrimination and thus, charge was, at best, vague. Robinson v. Quasar Energy Group LLC, 2014-Ohio-4218, 2014 Ohio App. LEXIS 4129 (Ohio Ct. App., Cuyahoga County 2014).

Where plaintiff filed suit against her employer, a state university, for employment discrimination, the court held that she failed to state a prima facie claim of relatiation under Ohio law. Because plaintiff never made a formal or informal complaint of racial discrimination or harassment while she was employed at the state university, plaintiff did not engage in a protected activity that gave rise to a claim for retaliation. McClair v. Univ. of Toledo, 2013-Ohio-5938, 2013 Ohio Misc. LEXIS 94 (Ohio Ct. Cl. 2013).

As an employer never filed a motion for summary judgment with respect to the employee's claim for discriminatory retaliation under R.C. 4112.02(I), the trial court erred in granting summary judgment to the employer. Rivers v. Cashland Fin. Servs., 2013-Ohio-1225, 2013 Ohio App. LEXIS 1125 (Ohio Ct. App., Summit County 2013).

Insofar as plaintiff patrolman's retaliation claim was based on a failure to promote plaintiff, defendants, a city, a police department, and a police chief, were not entitled to summary judgment because defendants had changed their explanation as to why plaintiff was not promoted to sergeant and there was a genuine dispute as to whether the failure to promote plaintiff was based on a budgetary crisis. Hodges v. City of Milford, 918 F. Supp. 2d 721, 2013 U.S. Dist. LEXIS 7779 (S.D. Ohio 2013).

In this Age Discrimination in Employment Act of 1967 and R.C. 4112.02(I) action, defendant was granted summary judgment on the retaliation claim because plaintiff could not prove that defendant took any adverse employment action against him for opposing discriminatory employment practices; the record provided no evidence that defendant even knew that plaintiff suspected age discrimination until his discussion with the branch manager. Pate v. MetoKote Corp., 2012 U.S. Dist. LEXIS 162032 (S.D. Ohio Nov. 13, 2012).

Plaintiff former employee failed to establish a prima facie case of retaliation under the Age Discrimination in Employment Act or Ohio law because assuming that communications to defendant employer constituted protected activity, plaintiff failed to establish a causal connection between the communications, all of which took place in 2006, and the termination of her employment in 2008. Blizzard v. Marion Tech. College, 698 F.3d 275, 2012 FED App. 0362P, 2012 U.S. App. LEXIS 21846 (6th Cir. Ohio 2012), cert. denied, 569 U.S. 975, 133 S. Ct. 2359, 185 L. Ed. 2d 1068, 2013 U.S. LEXIS 3626 (U.S. 2013).

Employee's claim for retaliation was properly dismissed on summary judgment as appellees set forth a legitimate nondiscriminatory reason for terminating the employee: her failure to follow the employer's procedures, deviating from those procedures in a manner that she knew was improper. Pitts-Baad v. Valvoline Instant Oil Change, 2012-Ohio-4811, 2012 Ohio App. LEXIS 4227 (Ohio Ct. App., Stark County 2012).

Trial court did not err in rending summary judgment on the employee's claims under R.C. 4112.02 because he failed to present any evidence about a "mixed-motive" for his discharge; the employer did not cause the employee's injury, it simply responded to a situation that the employee created by becoming injured and being unable to perform his duties. Because there was no evidence that the employer did anything other than follow its normal procedures following injury to a temporary worker, there is no evidence of either retaliation or wrongful discharge. Clinton v. Faurecia Exhaust Sys., 2012-Ohio-4618, 2012 Ohio App. LEXIS 4059 (Ohio Ct. App., Miami County 2012).

For purposes of an employee's retaliation claims under 42 U.S.C.S. § 12203(a) of the Americans with Disabilities Act and R.C. 4112.02(I) of the Ohio Civil Rights Act, he failed to establish a prima facie case where his claim that he was fired the same day that he requested accommodations for his diabetic condition was not sufficient to show a causal connection with his termination; there was evidence of multiple complaints about the employee's job performance. Steele v. Oasis Turf & Tree, Inc., 2012 U.S. Dist. LEXIS 103722 (S.D. Ohio July 25, 2012).

Employer was entitled to summary judgment on the employee's retaliation claim because the employee failed to allege or proffer any evidence of a protected activity. Moreover, even if the employee did allege or proffer evidence of a protected activity, it was the Board of Education that made the ultimate decision to terminate the employee's contract, not the special education director, the human resources director or the superintendent; therefore, the employee failed to establish that a causal link existed between the protected activity and the adverse action. Senu-Oke v. Dayton Pub. Schs, 2012 U.S. Dist. LEXIS 105428 (S.D. Ohio July 30, 2012).

Employer was entitled to summary judgment on the employee's retaliation claim under R.C. 4112.02 because the undisputed facts demonstrated that the employer placed the employee on medical leave based on its determinations that the employee was effectively requesting unlimited restroom breaks, and that this circumstance could not be accommodated. To attribute that decision to animosity was simply not based on evidence or fact. Linebarger v. Honda of America Mfg., 870 F. Supp. 2d 513, 2012 U.S. Dist. LEXIS 64229 (S.D. Ohio 2012).

Employee's claim of retaliation was properly dismissed on summary judgment as there was no evidence that the employee was terminated, demoted, or reassigned with different responsibilities. While the employee argued that the employer retaliated against him by denying him help, occurring when an individual who had been his part-time helper transferred out of the department of his own accord, the lack of help was not caused by the employer. Gatsios v. Timken Co., 2012-Ohio-2875, 2012 Ohio App. LEXIS 2512 (Ohio Ct. App., Stark County 2012).

Summary judgment was properly granted on the retaliation claim, pursuant to R.C. 4112.02(I), because the employee failed to establish that a genuine issue of material fact existed regarding whether she engaged in a protected activity. Even assuming that the intern's actions constituted harassment, it was as likely that his conduct was motivated by a personality conflict or other non-discriminatory reasons as it was that it was motivated by prejudice. Pintagro v. Sagamore Hills Twp., 2012-Ohio-2284, 2012 Ohio App. LEXIS 2003 (Ohio Ct. App., Summit County 2012).

Civ.R. 60(B)(2) relief motion was properly denied because, even if the "newly discovered" evidence had been considered, it would not have affected the outcome since it had already been determined that the former employee failed to establish a prima facie case of retaliation (postemployment retaliation) under R.C. 4112.02(I). The lapse of 12-24 months from the alleged protected activity to the subsequent adverse employment action did not create an inference of a causal connection and, without additional evidence of retaliatory conduct, the employee could not rely simply on an inference of causation. Healey v. Goodyear Tire & Rubber Co., 2012-Ohio-2170, 2012 Ohio App. LEXIS 1913 (Ohio Ct. App., Summit County 2012).

In the absence of any direct proof of retaliatory intent and given the lapse of time between the purported protected activity and the adverse employment actions, the employee failed to establish the necessary causal connection to support the fourth element of her prima facie case for retaliation. Dautartas v. Abbott Labs., 2012-Ohio-1709, 2012 Ohio App. LEXIS 1495 (Ohio Ct. App., Franklin County 2012).

Trial court properly granted summary judgment on the retaliation claim because the former employee failed to demonstrate that she would not have been placed on the performance plan and would not have terminated but for her participation in protected activity (her sexual harassment claims). Because any employee who submitted an unauthentic signature would face termination, the former employee failed to establish that the reason given for her termination was a pretext for discrimination. Brandner v. Innovex, Inc., 2012-Ohio-462, 970 N.E.2d 1067, 2012 Ohio App. LEXIS 441 (Ohio Ct. App., Hamilton County 2012).

Employer was entitled to summary judgment on an employee's retaliation claim because the employee did not show that any decisionmaker was aware of the employee's complaint about age discrimination or that there was a causal connection between the employee's discrimination complaint and any adverse action. Blizzard v. Marion Tech. College, 2011 U.S. Dist. LEXIS 35460 (N.D. Ohio Mar. 30, 2011), aff'd, 698 F.3d 275, 2012 FED App. 0362P, 2012 U.S. App. LEXIS 21846 (6th Cir. Ohio 2012).

Trial court erred by granting summary judgment on the teacher's retaliation claim because a genuine issue of material fact remained as to whether a causal link existed between the protected activity and the adverse action; the record demonstrated that the teacher engaged in the protected activity of requesting a reasonable accommodation, and that the district knew of her participation in the protected activity. The teacher also suffered an adverse employment action, i.e., termination. Johnson v. Cleveland City Sch. Dist., 2011-Ohio-2778, 2011 Ohio App. LEXIS 2384 (Ohio Ct. App., Cuyahoga County 2011).

Court of claims properly granted summary judgment to an employer and dismissed the employee's retaliation claim as there was insufficient evidence of a causal connection between the employee's letter to the employer alleging discrimination and the employer's decision not to re-hire him. The decision not to re-hire the employee was 19 months after the employee sent the letter, and the employee had not submitted additional evidence of discriminatory intent. Knepper v. Ohio State Univ., 2011-Ohio-6054, 2011 Ohio App. LEXIS 4943 (Ohio Ct. App., Franklin County 2011).

Former employee failed to establish a prima facie case of retaliation under R.C. 4112.02(I) where she presented no evidence that she opposed an unlawful discriminatory practice or participated in an investigation, proceeding, or hearing under R.C. 4112.01 to 4112.07. She did not specifically allege or present evidence establishing that she was engaged in a protected activity under § 4112.02(I). Veal v. Upreach LLC, 2011-Ohio-5406, 2011 Ohio App. LEXIS 4415 (Ohio Ct. App., Franklin County 2011).

Employee failed to prove her claims of disparate treatment and retaliation under R.C. 4112.02, as her filing of an administrative complaint, wherein she alleged that demeaning and harassing conduct was experienced by both men and women, was not a protected activity. Parson v. Dep't of Youth Servs., 2011-Ohio-5322, 2011 Ohio Misc. LEXIS 478 (Ohio Ct. Cl. 2011).

State university employee's retaliation claim under R.C. 4112.02(I) failed, as he failed to show that he engaged in a protected activity where he was merely "concerned" for the health or safety of a fellow employee due to her having seizures in the workplace; there was no evidence that he actively opposed an unlawful discriminatory practice or engaged in other protected conduct. Kellogg v. Ohio State Univ., 2011-Ohio-4848, 2011 Ohio Misc. LEXIS 411 (Ohio Ct. Cl. 2011).

Employee failed to establish a prima facie case of retaliation under R.C. 4112.02(I), as the employee did not present evidence of a causal link between the protected activity and the employee's termination; even according to the employee, after January 2007 when the protected activity occurred, the employer's conduct, if anything, was favorable to the employee, not retaliatory, as the employee received a 3.5 percent merit raise in April 2007. Meyers v. Goodrich Corp., 2011-Ohio-3261, 2011 Ohio App. LEXIS 2746 (Ohio Ct. App., Cuyahoga County 2011).

Summary judgment was properly awarded on the retaliation issue because the teacher failed to establish a retaliatory causal link between her previous complaint and the action of the interview team. One member knew of the complaint but denied ever informing the rest of the members and the interview question preface (asserting that staff decisions were being protested by some teachers) was simply too ambiguous to support the teacher's conclusion that the member's knowledge of her protected activity could have been imputed to the full interview team which actually made the hiring recommendation. Warnsley v. Toledo Bd. of Educ., 2011-Ohio-3134, 2011 Ohio App. LEXIS 2646 (Ohio Ct. App., Lucas County 2011).

Trial court erred by granting summary judgment on the teacher's retaliation claim because a genuine issue of material fact remained as to whether a causal link existed between the protected activity and the adverse action; the record demonstrated that the teacher engaged in the protected activity of requesting a reasonable accommodation, and that the district knew of her participation in the protected activity. The teacher also suffered an adverse employment action, i.e., termination. Johnson v. Cleveland City Sch. Dist., 2011-Ohio-2778, 2011 Ohio App. LEXIS 2384 (Ohio Ct. App., Cuyahoga County 2011).

As the clerk of a city council had not established a causal connection between the clerk's protected activity of reporting allegations of sexual harassment against a councilman and the clerk's termination, a decision granting summary judgment to a city on the clerk's retaliation claim pursuant to R.C. 4112.02(I) was proper; the only instance where the clerk engaged in a protected activity to the knowledge of at least some of the clerk's employers was approximately five years before the clerk's firing. Bahar v. City of Youngstown, 2011-Ohio-1000, 2011 Ohio App. LEXIS 862 (Ohio Ct. App., Mahoning County 2011).

Defendants were granted summary judgment on an African-American employee's claim for retaliation under Title VII and/or R.C. 4112.02, 4112.99 because the employee conceded that he experienced no retaliation for engaging in activity protected by Title VII, and the employee made no argument and presented no facts in support of his retaliation claim.

Berryman v. SuperValu Holdings, Inc., 2010 U.S. Dist. LEXIS 32968 (S.D. Ohio Mar. 31, 2010), aff'd, 669 F.3d 714, 2012 FED App. 0053P, 2012 U.S. App. LEXIS 3823 (6th Cir. Ohio 2012).

Given the absence of a causal connection between any protected activity and the nurse's reassignment to a different shift, as well as the director of nursing's lack of knowledge that the nurse had made any sexual harassment complaints, the nurse failed to prove retaliation. Ballard v. Cmty. Support Network, 2010-Ohio-200, 2010 Ohio Misc. LEXIS 1 (Ohio Ct. Cl.), aff'd, 2010-Ohio-4742, 2010 Ohio App. LEXIS 4008 (Ohio Ct. App., Franklin County 2010).

Pursuant to R.C. 4112.02(I), denial of an employee's retaliation claim was proper, as the employee failed to demonstrate a causal link existed between her alleged reporting of her supervisor's sexual harassment and her reassignment to the second shift; due to such reassignment, she was forced to resign because she could not work those hours. Ballard v. Cmty. Support Network, 2010-Ohio-4742, 2010 Ohio App. LEXIS 4008 (Ohio Ct. App., Franklin County 2010).

Because a reasonable jury could have conclude that appellees retaliated against the daughter for attempting to assert her rights, genuine issues of material fact existed with regard to her R.C. 4112.02(I) retaliation claim because there was direct evidence that, if believed, demonstrated that unlawful retaliation may have served as a motivating factor in appellees' decision to charge rent and seek eviction. According to the record, the father threatened to evict the daughter if she and her sister did not stop complaining to government agencies and city inspectors regarding disability discrimination. Reid v. Plainsboro Partners, III, 2010-Ohio-4373, 2010 Ohio App. LEXIS 3694 (Ohio Ct. App., Franklin County 2010).

Trial court erred by granting summary judgment to the father on the doctrine of res judicata; because there was no final judgment rendered by a court of competent jurisdiction with regard to the daughter's retaliation claim under R.C. 4112.02(I), the first element of the res judicata analysis was lacking. The bankruptcy court never submitted to the district court proposed findings of fact and conclusions of law with regard to the daughter's retaliation counterclaim. Reid v. Plainsboro Partners, III, 2010-Ohio-4373, 2010 Ohio App. LEXIS 3694 (Ohio Ct. App., Franklin County 2010).



Defendant was denied summary judgment on the claims for retaliation under the Age Discrimination in Employment Act and Ohio law where a notes reflected that days before plaintiff's termination, members of defendant's management had discussed the fact that plaintiff and another employee had retained the same attorney, plaintiff had told some individuals that he was going to sue defendant, and the Deputy Regional Managing Partner and Regional Managing Partner wanted to terminate plaintiff because they considered him to be "disruptive." Mauer v. Deloitte & Touche, LLP, 752 F. Supp. 2d 819, 2010 U.S. Dist. LEXIS 113628 (S.D. Ohio 2010).

State trooper could not state a prima facie cause of retaliation, pursuant to R.C. 4112.02(I), based on his claim that he was terminated following his action in writing a letter in support of his union, which helped to reinstate him following his termination, as the alleged retaliatory action did not follow the trooper's participation in the protected activity sufficiently close in time to warrant an inference of retaliatory motivation. The trooper wrote the letter in the fall of 2006 but was not terminated until March 2008. Lajoye v. Ohio Highway Patrol, 2009-Ohio-7028, 2009 Ohio Misc. LEXIS 368 (Ohio Ct. Cl. 2009).

University was entitled to summary judgment in a former employee's retaliation claim under R.C. 4112.02(I) because the employee did not offer evidence establishing all the elements of a prima facie case of retaliation. Specifically, because approximately two months elapsed between the university's learning that the employee had engaged in a protected activity, a notice by letter of the employee's retention of an attorney to pursue a wrongful discharge claim against the university, and the adverse action, a statement by the university's attorney to a newspaper that job performance issues played a role in the employee's discharge, the temporal proximity was not so close that the employee could have relied upon timing alone to establish a causal connection. Woods v. Capital Univ., 2009-Ohio-5672, 2009 Ohio App. LEXIS 4770 (Ohio Ct. App., Franklin County 2009).

Employee's retaliation claim was properly dismissed because temporal proximity between the employee's protected activity of reporting a safety violation to the appropriate authorities and various adverse employment actions, including negative evaluations, suspension, and termination, did not show a causal connection, as a decision to discipline the employee was made before the employee engaged in the activity. Putney v. Contract Bldg. Components, 2009-Ohio-6718, 2009 Ohio App. LEXIS 5634 (Ohio Ct. App., Union County 2009).

Employee failed to prove that the employee was disciplined in retaliation both for complaining about alleged racial epithets that the employee's supervisor made and for filing a grievance about the supervisor. The employee failed to prove any causal link between the protected activities and the adverse employment action as the action occurred months after the alleged protected conduct, the employer brought forth a legitimate, nondiscriminatory reason for the disability separation of the employee, and the employee brought forth no credible evidence to demonstrate that the employer's stated reason for the disability separation was a pretext for discrimination. Miller v. Ohio Dep't of Ins., 2009-Ohio-5313, 2009 Ohio Misc. LEXIS 222 (Ohio Ct. Cl. 2009).

Employer was not liable to an employee for retaliation, under R.C. 4112.02(I), because, while the employee showed that the employee engaged in protected activity by filing a discrimination complaint with the Equal Employment Opportunity Commission, and arguably showed the employer was aware that the employee engaged in the protected activity, the employee did not prove that the employee was subjected to retaliatory conduct or that the employee suffered an adverse employment action, as the employee was never demoted, the employee's salary remained the same, and any change in the employee's duties resulted from the employer's legitimate business concerns. Chantana Kung v. Ohio Dep't of Ins., 2009-Ohio-5328, 2009 Ohio Misc. LEXIS 209 (Ohio Ct. Cl. 2009).

Part-time doctor's retaliation claims under R.C. 4112.02(I) against her employers, wherein she alleged that their disparaging remarks to prospective employers caused her not to be hired, failed, as she did not show any causal connection between the employers' comments and the decision by the prospective employers not to pursue her candidacy; further, the remarks made by the former employers contained comments and criticisms based on a fair evaluation of the doctor's work performance. Lindsay v. Children's Hosp. Med. Ctr. of Akron, 2009-Ohio-1216, 2009 Ohio App. LEXIS 1044 (Ohio Ct. App., Summit County 2009).

Part-time doctor's retaliation claims under R.C. 4112.02(I) against her employers failed, as her charge against them of discrimination and retaliation with the Ohio Civil Rights Commission was made after the employers had decided to terminate her, such that there was no causal link between her protected activities and her termination; further, the employers supported the termination decision with numerous legitimate business reasons due to the ongoing performance issues. Lindsay v. Children's Hosp. Med. Ctr. of Akron, 2009-Ohio-1216, 2009 Ohio App. LEXIS 1044 (Ohio Ct. App., Summit County 2009).

Based on the liberal notice pleading of Civ.R. 8(A) and the liberal construction required by R.C. 4112.08, a trial court erred in sua sponte dismissing a co-worker's claim under the opposition clause of R.C. 4112.02(I) against her fellow worker, who sued her for defamation action after she reported that he had engaged in sexually harassing conduct to her and other co-workers, as her complaint raised a claim as to whether her employer's corrective action against the fellow worker was immediate and appropriate, or whether it was an unlawful discriminatory practice. Hughes v. Miller, 2009-Ohio-963, 181 Ohio App. 3d 440, 909 N.E.2d 642, 2009 Ohio App. LEXIS 836 (Ohio Ct. App., Cuyahoga County 2009).

Where an employee filed an internal claim of sexual harassment against another employee and that employee subsequently filed a defamation claim against the complainant, the trial court erred by dismissing the complainant's counterclaim alleging retaliation for participating in protected activity: Hughes v. Miller, 2009-Ohio-963, 181 Ohio App. 3d 440, 909 N.E.2d 642, 2009 Ohio App. LEXIS 836 (Ohio Ct. App., Cuyahoga County 2009).

Corrections officer who did not request an investigation into any action on the part of the Ohio Department of Rehabilitation and Correction relating to the officer's race, color, religion, sex, or national origin failed to engage in a protected activity for purposes of a retaliation claim under R.C. 4112.02(I) or 42 U.S.C.S. § 2000e-3(a), such that the claim did not withstand challenge under Civ.R. 12(C); the matter arose after the officer was injured while breaking up an altercation between two inmates. Felts v. Ohio Dep't of Rehab. & Corr., 2008-Ohio-4797, 2008 Ohio Misc. LEXIS 208 (Ohio Ct. Cl. 2008).

State university was entitled to summary judgment on an employee's retaliation claim under R.C. 4112.02(I), wherein the employee had asserted that he informed the university that he felt he was not being rehired due to his age after his original position was abolished, as the employee failed to show that the letter written to the university that expressed his beliefs was a protected activity, and that there was a causal connection between the expression of his beliefs and the university's decision not to rehire him. Knepper v. Ohio State Univ., 2008-Ohio-4796, 2008 Ohio Misc. LEXIS 207 (Ohio Ct. Cl. 2008), aff'd, 2011-Ohio-6054, 2011 Ohio App. LEXIS 4943 (Ohio Ct. App., Franklin County 2011).

Employee failed to establish that she engaged in a protected activity for purposes of a retaliation claim under R.C. 4112.02(I) where the employee's complaint to a supervisor did not indicate anything about race discrimination but rather, the complaint was about concerns generally. Valentine v. Westshore Primary Care Assoc., 2008-Ohio-4450, 2008 Ohio App. LEXIS 3756 (Ohio Ct. App., Cuyahoga County 2008).

As a state employee conceded that a knee injury which resulted in surgery did not constitute a "disability" as defined under the Americans with Disabilities Act and R.C. 4112.02(L), the employee's claim for retaliation arising from a discharge from employment for a state agency failed; further, the agency provided the employee with a transfer to another team as a reasonable accommodation, the employee was not engaged in a protected activity at the time of termination, and the termination was based on the employee's illegal disclosure of confidential information. Frakes v. Ohio Rehab. Servs. Comm'n, 2008-Ohio-4220, 2008 Ohio Misc. LEXIS 177 (Ohio Ct. Cl. 2008).

Substantial, reliable, and probative evidence supported a trial court's affirmance of a finding by the Ohio Civil Rights Commission that an employer's reasons for terminating an employee were merely pretextual, such that it engaged in retaliation, in violation of R.C. 4112.02(I), after the employee had advised an African-American worker that the worker should obtain health care coverage from the employer because many other workers received such coverage; the employee had been offered a partnership in the business on a recent occasion prior to the incident, the employer was aware that the employee had motivated the worker to seek the health care coverage, and its claim that the employee's work performance had decreased were not supported by any evidence or explanations. HLS Bonding v. Ohio Civ. Rights Comm'n, 2008-Ohio-4107, 2008 Ohio App. LEXIS 3474 (Ohio Ct. App., Franklin County 2008).

Substantial, reliable, and probative evidence under R.C. 4112.06(E) supported a trial court's affirmance of a determination by the Ohio Civil Rights Commission that an employer had retaliated against an employee who had engaged in a protected activity, in violation of R.C. 4112.02(I), such that a prima face case of retaliation was presented; the employee had advised an African-American worker that he should seek health care benefits because other workers were receiving them, shortly after which the employee was demoted and ultimately terminated from employment. HLS Bonding v. Ohio Civ. Rights Comm'n, 2008-Ohio-4107, 2008 Ohio App. LEXIS 3474 (Ohio Ct. App., Franklin County 2008).

Retaliation claim under 42 U.S.C.S. § 2000e-3 and R.C. 4112.02 failed for a lack of a causal connection between the adverse employment action and the employee's protected activity; there was no evidence that the decision to terminate the employee was tainted by racial enimus or as a result of the employee's protected activities. Fuelling v. New Vision Med. Labs. LLC, 284 Fed. Appx. 247, 2008 FED App. 0384N, 2008 U.S. App. LEXIS 13915 (6th Cir. Ohio 2008).

To establish a causal connection between an employee's adverse employment action and a protected activity, to show retaliation, under R.C. 4112.02(I), an employee must produce sufficient evidence from which an inference can be drawn that the adverse action would not have been taken had the employee not engaged in the protectec activity, and a causal connection may be shown by direct evidence or by evidence of the employer's knowledge of the activity coupled with a closeness in time sufficient to create an inference of causation, but, in the absence of other compelling evidence, temporal proximity alone does not support a claim of retaliation. Motley v. Ohio Civ. Rights Comm'n, 2008-Ohio-2306, 2008 Ohio App. LEXIS 1958 (Ohio Ct. App., Franklin County 2008).

Filing of a union grievance that does not raise Title VII issues (e.g., discrimination) does not constitute "protected activity," for purposes of a claim of retaliation, under R.C. 4112.02(I). Motley v. Ohio Civ. Rights Comm'n, 2008-Ohio-2306, 2008 Ohio App. LEXIS 1958 (Ohio Ct. App., Franklin County 2008).

Employer was entitled to summary judgment as to an employee's retaliation claim, under R.C. 4112.02(I), because, inter alia, the employee did not show a causal link between the employer's termination of the employee's employment and the alleged protected activity in which the employee engaged, which was the successful pursuit of a union grievance against the employer, as the approximately three and one-half years between the grievance and the latest termination of the employee's employment was too long to infer temporal proximity and a retaliatory motive, absent any direct proof of the employer's retaliatory intent, which was not offered. Motley v. Ohio Civ. Rights Comm'n, 2008-Ohio-2306, 2008 Ohio App. LEXIS 1958 (Ohio Ct. App., Franklin County 2008).

Employer was entitled to summary judgment as to an employee's retaliation claim, under R.C. 4112.02(I), because, inter alia, the employee did not show that the employee engaged in a protected activity, as the employee said the employee was retaliated against for successfully pursuing a union grievance against the employer, but the employee did not allege that the employment termination which the grievance concerned was done because of the employee's race, color, religion, sex or national origin, so no evidence showed the employee engaged in a protected activity with respect to the grievance. Motley v. Ohio Civ. Rights Comm'n, 2008-Ohio-2306, 2008 Ohio App. LEXIS 1958 (Ohio Ct. App., Franklin County 2008).

When an employer sues an employee who has alleged discrimination by the employee, and the employee alleges that this constitutes retaliation, the employer's claim for punitive damages can support a finding of retaliation, but, just as the filing of the employer's lawsuit is not per se retaliatory, the inclusion of a punitive damages demand does not equal per se retaliatory animus, and, rather, when punitive damages are authorized under R.C. 2315.21 for the employer's claims, the punitive damages claim should be analyzed within the context of the entire lawsuit. Greer-Burger v. Temesi, 2007-Ohio-6442, 116 Ohio St. 3d 324, 879 N.E.2d 174, 2007 Ohio LEXIS 3049 (Ohio 2007).

When an employee claims an employer's suit against the employee for suing the employer for discrimination is retaliation, it is more prudent to permit the employer the opportunity to demonstrate that the employer's suit is not objectively baseless, rather than finding the employer's suit is retaliatory per se, and in determining whether the employer's action has an objective basis, an Ohio Civil Rights Commission (OCRC) administrative law judge should review the employer's lawsuit pursuant to the standard for rendering summary judgment, so the employer needs to show the employer's lawsuit raises genuine issues of material fact, and, if the employer satisfies this standard, the suit does not fall under the definition of sham litigation and shall proceed in court while proceedings before the OCR.C. are stayed, falling within the jurisdiction of the OCR.C. as provided for in R.C. 4112.04 and promoting judicial economy because the employer's lawsuit will not have to be fully litigated in the trial court before the OCR.C. can make its determination as to the reasonableness of the suit, so the OCR.C. essentially vets the action to ensure it is not sham litigation, and merely filing a suit is insufficient evidence of an employer's retaliatory motive. Greer-Burger v. Temesi, 2007-Ohio-6442, 116 Ohio St. 3d 324, 879 N.E.2d 174, 2007 Ohio LEXIS 3049 (Ohio 2007).

Under R.C. 4112.02(I), it is an unlawful discriminatory practice for any person to discriminate in any manner against any other person because that person has opposed any unlawful discriminatory practice defined in R.C. 4112.02 or because that person has made a charge, testified, assisted, or participated in any manner in any investigation, proceeding, or hearing under R.C. 4112.01 to 4112.07, and to establish a case of retaliation, a claimant must prove that (1) the claimant engaged in a protected activity, (2) the defending party was aware that the claimant had engaged in that activity, (3) the defending party took an adverse employment action against the employee, and (4) there is a causal connection between the protected activity and adverse action. Greer-Burger v. Temesi, 2007-Ohio-6442, 116 Ohio St. 3d 324, 879 N.E.2d 174, 2007 Ohio LEXIS 3049 (Ohio 2007).

When an employee unsuccessfully sued an employer for sexual harassment, and the employer then sued the employee, it was error for the Ohio Civil Rights Commission to find that the employer's suit was retaliation, under R.C. 4112.02(I), per se, because (1) the employer had to be given an opportunity to show that the employer's suit had an objective basis, even if the employee was able to demonstrate a prima facie case of retaliation, and (2) a per se standard would impermissibly undermine the employer's constitutional right to seek redress of grievances. Greer-Burger v. Temesi, 2007-Ohio-6442, 116 Ohio St. 3d 324, 879 N.E.2d 174, 2007 Ohio LEXIS 3049 (Ohio 2007).

Genuine issues of material fact precluded summary judgment to an employer and others in an employee's claim of retaliation under R.C. 4112.02(I), as the employee was engaged in a protected activity when she claimed that her supervisor engaged in sexual harassment and discrimination against her, and she was thereafter terminated, which was an adverse employment action; there was a dispute regarding whether a causal relationship existed between the employee's allegations and her termination. Johnson v. Olmsted Twp., 2007-Ohio-6487, 2007 Ohio App. LEXIS 5680 (Ohio Ct. App., Cuyahoga County 2007).

As there was no causal connection shown between an employee's protected activity of filing of a discrimination lawsuit and the employer's adverse employment action of filing allegedly retaliatory counterclaims, and there was scant evidence of a retaliatory motive by the employer for filing the counterclaims, damages awarded to the employee under her statutory retaliation claim pursuant to R.C. 4112.02(I) were properly stricken pursuant to a motion for judgment notwithstanding the verdict under Civ.R. 50(A)(4). Lynch v. Studebaker, 2007-Ohio-4014, 2007 Ohio App. LEXIS 3651 (Ohio Ct. App., Cuyahoga County 2007).

Evidence supported a trial court's conclusion that there was substantial evidence of retaliation and constructive discharge presented against an employer as the evidence showed that, after confronting the employer regarding his harassment, the employee was subjected to such egregious treatment that she left the workplace. Jordan v. Ohio Civ. Rights Comm'n, 2007-Ohio-3830, 173 Ohio App. 3d 87, 877 N.E.2d 693, 2007 Ohio App. LEXIS 3503 (Ohio Ct. App., Fayette County 2007).

Terminated employee's retaliation claim was dismissed for failing to allege any facts upon which to establish the necessary elements for retaliation. Specifically, he had not alleged when in his employment he engaged in protected activity, whether or if a decision-maker had knowledge of his complaints, or any facts giving rise to an inference of causation between a putative filing of a complaint and his termination. Rachells v. Cingular Wireless Emple. Servs., LLC, 483 F. Supp. 2d 583, 2007 U.S. Dist. LEXIS 25897 (N.D. Ohio 2007).

Filing of a lawsuit by an employer against an employee or former employee who has engaged in a protected activity is not per se retaliatory. If an employer can demonstrate that a lawsuit against an employee who has engaged in a protected activity is not objectively baseless, the suit shall be allowed to proceed, and the proceedings before the Ohio Civil Rights Commission are stayed: Greer-Burger v. Temesi, 2007-Ohio-6442, 116 Ohio St. 3d 324, 879 N.E.2d 174, 2007 Ohio LEXIS 3049 (Ohio 2007).

Right to oppose discrimination, as contemplated by R.C. 4112.02(I), did not entail a right to engage in conduct that interfered with the attainment of the employer's goals, violated the employer's legitimate workplace rules, or disrupted the work environment. Proctor v. Ohio Civ. Rights Comm'n, 2006-Ohio-6007, 169 Ohio App. 3d 527, 863 N.E.2d 1069, 2006 Ohio App. LEXIS 5956 (Ohio Ct. App., Summit County 2006).

When considering a retaliation claim, adverse employment action required a materially adverse change in the terms and conditions of employment, and, in considering whether an employment action was materially adverse, a court could consider whether employment was terminated, whether the employee was demoted, received a decrease in wage or salary, a less distinguished title, a material loss of benefits, significantly diminished material responsibilities, or other indices that might be unique to a particular situation. Brock v. Eaton Corp., 2006-Ohio-5580, 2006 Ohio App. LEXIS 5571 (Ohio Ct. App., Cuyahoga County 2006).

Employee claiming hostile work environment sexual harassment, under R.C. 4112.02(A), did not show that her employer retaliated against her when the co-worker whose sexual harassment she alleged dropped several of her grievances, as union president, because this did not show any action by the employer, nor did it materially adversely change the terms and conditions of her employment, as she did not show she suffered any loss of benefits, wages, change of title, or change of duties. Brock v. Eaton Corp., 2006-Ohio-5580, 2006 Ohio App. LEXIS 5571 (Ohio Ct. App., Cuyahoga County 2006).

Employee claiming hostile work environment sexual harassment, under R.C. 4112.02(A), did not show that her employer retaliated against her for pursuing this claim because, while her pursuit of a sexual harassment claim was protected activity, she did not show that her employer subected her to any adverse employment action, as she did not show a materially adverse change in the terms and conditions of her employment because her job description did not change, she was not demoted, and she was still employed by the employer. Brock v. Eaton Corp., 2006-Ohio-5580, 2006 Ohio App. LEXIS 5571 (Ohio Ct. App., Cuyahoga County 2006).

Former employee's R.C. 4112.02 and 42 U.S.C.S. § 1983 discrimination claims alleging retaliation were not summarily dismissed as they established a prima facie case by alleging the same elements that were required of a Title VII claim pursuant to 42 U.S.C.S. § 2000e-2(a)(1). Rice v. Cuyahoga County DOJ Affairs, 2006 U.S. Dist. LEXIS 76403 (N.D. Ohio Oct. 20, 2006), amended, 2006 U.S. Dist. LEXIS 91546 (N.D. Ohio Dec. 19, 2006).

Dismissal of a former employee's R.C. 4112.02 and 42 U.S.C.S. § 1983 discrimination claims alleging retaliation was granted to a county justice department as no government policy was alleged as a source of injury; it was denied as to department employees, though, as claim preclusion and qualified immunity defenses failed and constructive discharge was an adverse employment action. Rice v. Cuyahoga County DOJ Affairs, 2006 U.S. Dist. LEXIS 76403 (N.D. Ohio Oct. 20, 2006), amended, 2006 U.S. Dist. LEXIS 91546 (N.D. Ohio Dec. 19, 2006).



In an action in which a former employee filed suit against defendants, former employer, union, and a counselor for the employee assistance program, alleging claims of retaliation in violation of Title VII and R.C. 4112.02, defendants were granted summary judgment; Even if attempting to "engineer" the membership vote was an adverse employment action, the employee's evidence failed to show that any defendant undertook such an action. Jaques v. Herbert, 447 F. Supp. 2d 858, 2006 U.S. Dist. LEXIS 59655 (N.D. Ohio 2006).

Trial court properly granted summary judgment to an employer in a former employee's action, alleging retaliation in violation of R.C. 4112.02(I), as the delay by the employer in following its own policy for purposes of investigating the employee's complaints about her supervisor regarding racial discrimination was not retaliatory where there was no showing that such retaliation or prejudice resulted from the delay, there was no evidence in the record to support the employee's claims, and there was no causal link established between the employee having been written up by the supervisor for an employment violation after she had become the subject of a complaint by the employee. Simmons-Means v. Cuyahoga County Dep't of Justice Affairs, 2006-Ohio-4123, 2006 Ohio App. LEXIS 4057 (Ohio Ct. App., Cuyahoga County 2006).

Employee could not maintain her action for retaliation in violation of Title VII of the Civil Rights Act of 1964, 42 U.S.C.S. § 2000e-3, and R.C. 4112.02 when she was terminated three months after she filed a sex discrimination action because the three-month gap was insufficient to establish retaliation without further evidence that the termination was pretextual, and the employee offered no such evidence. Johannes v. Monday Cmty. Corr. Inst., 434 F. Supp. 2d 509, 2006 U.S. Dist. LEXIS 43220 (S.D. Ohio 2006).

Summary judgment was granted in favor of the employer with regard to the employee's claim of retaliation in violation of R.C. 4112.02 et seq., because the employer had proffered a legitimate, non-retaliatory business reason for refusing to let the employee return to work: namely, its concerns that the employee, who was diagnosed as a schizophrenic, paranoid type, was a safety threat to himself and co-workers and the employee failed to show that the employer's articulated reason was a pretext or that it was based on an improper desire to retaliate against him for filing a race discrimination lawsuit. Reid v. Rexam Bev. Can Co., 434 F. Supp. 2d 500, 2006 U.S. Dist. LEXIS 36360 (N.D. Ohio 2006).

Employee's claim that he was improperly discharged in retaliation for his complaints of discrimination failed under R.C. 4112.02(I), as the employee only complained about discriminatory conduct by his coworkers, and he neither opposed any unlawful dicriminatory practice by his employer, nor did he make a charge, testify, assist, or participate in an investigation, hearing or proceeding under R.C. ch. 4112; accordingly, summary judgment for the employer was properly granted. Osaze v. City of Strongsville, 2006-Ohio-1089, 2006 Ohio App. LEXIS 983 (Ohio Ct. App., Cuyahoga County 2006).

When an employee, who worked for a university as an architect, said he was fired in retaliation for complaining that his employer did not follow correct procedures for obtaining building permits before starting work on a project, while this was a protected activity and he was subjected to an adverse employment action, he did not show a causal link between his complaints and his firing because there was a significant lapse of time between the two events. Buckholz v. Bowling Green State Univ., 2006-Ohio-624, 2006 Ohio Misc. LEXIS 29 (Ohio Ct. Cl. 2006).

When an employee, who worked for a university as an architect, said he was fired in retaliation for suits filed by contractors involved in a project he worked on, he did not show, in support of his retaliation claim, that he had been engaged in a protected activity under federal or Ohio law, so his claim failed. Buckholz v. Bowling Green State Univ., 2006-Ohio-624, 2006 Ohio Misc. LEXIS 29 (Ohio Ct. Cl. 2006).

Right to oppose discrimination, as contemplated by R.C. 4112.02(I), did not entail a right to engage in conduct that interfered with the attainment of the employer's goals, violated the employer's legitimate workplace rules, or disrupted the work environment. Proctor v. Ohio Civ. Rights Comm'n, 2006-Ohio-6007, 169 Ohio App. 3d 527, 863 N.E.2d 1069, 2006 Ohio App. LEXIS 5956 (Ohio Ct. App., Summit County 2006).

When considering a retaliation claim, adverse employment action required a materially adverse change in the terms and conditions of employment, and, in considering whether an employment action was materially adverse, a court could consider whether employment was terminated, whether the employee was demoted, received a decrease in wage or salary, a less distinguished title, a material loss of benefits, significantly diminished material responsibilities, or other indices that might be unique to a particular situation. Brock v. Eaton Corp., 2006-Ohio-5580, 2006 Ohio App. LEXIS 5571 (Ohio Ct. App., Cuyahoga County 2006).

Employee claiming hostile work environment sexual harassment, under R.C. 4112.02(A), did not show that her employer retaliated against her for pursuing this claim because, while her pursuit of a sexual harassment claim was protected activity, she did not show that her employer subjected her to any adverse employment action, as she did not show a materially adverse change in the terms and conditions of her employment because her job description did not change, she was not demoted, and she was still employed by the employer. Brock v. Eaton Corp., 2006-Ohio-5580, 2006 Ohio App. LEXIS 5571 (Ohio Ct. App., Cuyahoga County 2006).

Former employee's R.C. 4112.02 and 42 U.S.C.S. § 1983 discrimination claims alleging retaliation were not summarily dismissed as they established a prima facie case by alleging the same elements that were required of a Title VII claim pursuant to 42 U.S.C.S. § 2000e-2(a)(1). Rice v. Cuyahoga County DOJ Affairs, 2006 U.S. Dist. LEXIS 76403 (N.D. Ohio Oct. 20, 2006), amended, 2006 U.S. Dist. LEXIS 91546 (N.D. Ohio Dec. 19, 2006).

Dismissal of a former employee's R.C. 4112.02 and 42 U.S.C.S. § 1983 discrimination claims alleging retaliation was granted to a county justice department as no government policy was alleged as a source of injury. It was denied as to department employees, though, as claim preclusion and qualified immunity defenses failed and constructive discharge was an adverse employment action. Rice v. Cuyahoga County DOJ Affairs, 2006 U.S. Dist. LEXIS 76403 (N.D. Ohio Oct. 20, 2006), amended, 2006 U.S. Dist. LEXIS 91546 (N.D. Ohio Dec. 19, 2006).

In an action in which a former employee filed suit against defendants, former employer, union, and a counselor for the employee assistance program, alleging claims of retaliation in violation of Title VII and R.C. 4112.02, defendants were granted summary judgment; Even if attempting to "engineer" the membership vote was an adverse employment action, the employee's evidence failed to show that any defendant undertook such an action. Jaques v. Herbert, 447 F. Supp. 2d 858, 2006 U.S. Dist. LEXIS 59655 (N.D. Ohio 2006).

Employee could not maintain her action for retaliation in violation of Title VII of the Civil Rights Act of 1964, 42 U.S.C.S. § 2000e-3, and R.C. 4112.02 when she was terminated three months after she filed a sex discrimination action because the three-month gap was insufficient to establish retaliation without further evidence that the termination was pretextual, and the employee offered no such evidence. Johannes v. Monday Cmty. Corr. Inst., 434 F. Supp. 2d 509, 2006 U.S. Dist. LEXIS 43220 (S.D. Ohio 2006).

Summary judgment was granted in favor of the employer with regard to the employee's claim of retaliation in violation of R.C. 4112.02 et seq., because the employer had proffered a legitimate, non-retaliatory business reason for refusing to let the employee return to work: namely, its concerns that the employee, who was diagnosed as a schizophrenic, paranoid type, was a safety threat to himself and co-workers and the employee failed to show that the employer's articulated reason was a pretext or that it was based on an improper desire to retaliate against him for filing a race discrimination lawsuit. Reid v. Rexam Bev. Can Co., 434 F. Supp. 2d 500, 2006 U.S. Dist. LEXIS 36360 (N.D. Ohio 2006).

Summary judgment was properly granted, dismissing a Caucasian employee's retaliation claim brought against her African-American supervisor and the city which employed her, because the supervisor's negative appraisal of her job performance did not constitute an adverse employment action, in that the employee did not demonstrate that the appraisal affected the terms or conditions of her employment. While termination of the employee's probationary employment was initially recommended, the request was later rescinded, and the employee's employment continued.

Mowery v. City of Columbus, 2006-Ohio-1153, 2006 Ohio App. LEXIS 1051 (Ohio Ct. App., Franklin County 2006).

Employee's claim that he was improperly discharged in retaliation for his complaints of discrimination failed under R.C. 4112.02(I), as the employee only complained about discriminatory conduct by his coworkers, and he neither opposed any unlawful dicriminatory practice by his employer, nor did he make a charge, testify, assist, or participate in an investigation, hearing or proceeding under R.C. ch. 4112; accordingly, summary judgment for the employer was properly granted. Osaze v. City of Strongsville, 2006-Ohio-1089, 2006 Ohio App. LEXIS 983 (Ohio Ct. App., Cuyahoga County 2006).

When an employee, who worked for a university as an architect, said he was fired in retaliation for complaining that his employer did not follow correct procedures for obtaining building permits before starting work on a project, while this was a protected activity and he was subjected to an adverse employment action, he did not show a causal link between his complaints and his firing because there was a significant lapse of time between the two events. Buckholz v. Bowling Green State Univ., 2006-Ohio-624, 2006 Ohio Misc. LEXIS 29 (Ohio Ct. Cl. 2006).

Applicant's act of prosecuting an age discrimination lawsuit against his former employer constituted a protected activity for purposes of a retaliation claim under the Age Discrimination in Employment Act (ADEA), 29 U.S.C.S. § 623(d), even though the applicant only pursued Ohio state law claims in his suit, because the applicant was opposing a practice made unlawful by the ADEA. Leib v. Atlas Capital Servs., 2005 U.S. Dist. LEXIS 31571 (S.D. Ohio May 25, 2005).

Despite close temporal proximity, summary judgment was granted to a former employer in a case alleging wrongful termination based on retaliation under R.C. 4112.02(I) because there was no causal link between protected activity and the adverse employment action since the reason for the termination, lying under oath at a workers' compensation hearing, was not pretextual; moreover, an employee was unable to prevail on a public policy violation of § 4112.02 as well. Sosby v. Miller Brewing Co., 415 F. Supp. 2d 809, 2005 U.S. Dist. LEXIS 23301 (S.D. Ohio 2005), aff'd, 211 Fed. Appx. 382, 2006 FED App. 0860N, 2006 U.S. App. LEXIS 29194 (6th Cir. Ohio 2006).

Where a 50-year old male, terminated from his job as a newspaper music critic, alleged retaliation under R.C. 4112.02 because he stated at a staff meeting that morale was low because of how a co-worker had been treated, the newspaper was granted summary judgment because there was no allegation that the treatment was unfair because it was discriminatory. Nager v. The Cincinnati Enquirer, 2005 U.S. Dist. LEXIS 22770 (S.D. Ohio Oct. 6, 2005).

Employee's retaliation claims failed to survive summary judgment because (1) the employee did not suffer an adverse action based upon job description changes, a falsification charge that did not result in any disciplinary action, and a poor evaluation, (2) the employee failed to establish a causal connection. Hurston v. Butler County Dep't of Jobs & Family Servs., 2005 U.S. Dist. LEXIS 22111 (S.D. Ohio Sept. 30, 2005).

Former employers were entitled to summary judgment on a former employee's retaliation claim under 42 U.S.C.S. § 1981 and R.C. 4112.02 because the employee failed to show that the employers' reason for firing her—that she abused the process for addressing legitimate grievances of racial discrimination by defaming her co-workers and disrupting their place of business—was pretextual. White v. Drs. Camm & Golian, D.D.S., Inc., 2005 U.S. Dist. LEXIS 19763 (N.D. Ohio Sept. 12, 2005).

Former employer and supervisors were entitled to summary judgment on a former employee's retaliation claim because the employer terminated the employee before the employer received the notice of the charge of discrimination from the U.S. Equal Employment Opportunity Commission regarding the age discrimination claim that the employee filed with the Commission. Further, the employee made no allegation that the employer was aware that the employee had filed a claim with the Commission when the employer terminated the employee. Macklin v. Turner, 2005 U.S. Dist. LEXIS 19616 (N.D. Ohio Sept. 9, 2005).

Trial court's grant of summary judgment pursuant to Civ.R. 56(C) to an employer in a retaliation claim, pursuant to R.C. 4112.02(I), by a union member who was laid off was proper, as the fact that the union member had advised another union member that she was given light duty work after she suffered injuries, although he was not, and they had discussed the possibility that a race issue was involved, was evaluated under the opposition clause because the conversation occurred prior to the other member filing a discrimination claim; the other member's discussion with their supervisor did not include any issue regarding race, and the supervisor gave a legitimate reason for the layoffs as being due to a decline in need, whereas the union member failed to then show that such was a mere pretext. Coch v. GEM Indus., 2005-Ohio-3045, 2005 Ohio App. LEXIS 2825 (Ohio Ct. App., Lucas County 2005).

Plaintiff produced sufficient evidence to withstand summary judgment on his retaliation claim. Plaintiff produced evidence to show that he engaged in protected activity by opposing defendants' alleged discrimination and by filing a charge with the EEOC; the exercise of his civil rights was known by defendants; defendants took an adverse employment action against plaintiff; and a reasonable fact-finder could draw an inference of a causal connection between the protected activity and the adverse employment action. Imwalle v. Reliance Med. Prods., 2005 U.S. Dist. LEXIS 27882 (S.D. Ohio Nov. 15, 2005).

Although an employee may have been involved in a protected activity that angered her supervisor, which allegedly caused him to retaliate against her, there were numerous legitimate business reasons for the employer's corrective actions and discipline against the employee, relating to her poor job performance, and as such, the employee failed to meet her burden of showing retaliatory discharge in violation of R.C. 4112.02(I). Wilson v. Northcoast Behavioral Healthcare Sys., 2005-Ohio-1291, 2005 Ohio Misc. LEXIS 108 (Ohio Ct. Cl. 2005).

Employee did not show she was retaliated against for complaining of sexual harassment by her employer's executive, under R.C. 4112.02(I), because, after she complained, her job description did not change, she received two pay raises, and her claims that she had to address superiors as "Mr." and knock on office doors before entering, while others did not, that she was retaliated against for opening a letter marked "confidential," and was admonished for inappropriate dress did not rise to the level of retaliation. Eakin v. Lakeland Glass Co., 2005-Ohio-266, 2005 Ohio App. LEXIS 231 (Ohio Ct. App., Lorain County 2005).

Applicant failed to make a prima facie case for retaliation where, even if some employees knew that he assisted a complainant in an administrative action against the employer, there was no other compelling evidence of discriminatory intent and more than one year lapsed between the applicant's assistance of the complainant and the employer's refusal to hire him; further, appellees articulated legitimate, non-discriminatory reasons for the hiring decision that the applicant failed to show were pretextual. Aycox v. Columbus Bd. of Educ., 2005-Ohio-69, 2005 Ohio App. LEXIS 59 (Ohio Ct. App., Franklin County 2005).

Where an employee alleged that he was fired for supporting a co-worker's sexual harassment case against his employer, the employer was entitled to summary judgment on the employee's retaliation claim under R.C. 4112.02(I) because the employee failed to offer any evidence linking the protected activity and the adverse employment action other than proximity in time. Thus, he failed to establish pretext. Pemberton v. DHL Worldwide Express, 2004 U.S. Dist. LEXIS 28722 (S.D. Ohio Sept. 15, 2004), aff'd, 145 Fed. Appx. 171, 2005 FED App. 0815N, 2005 U.S. App. LEXIS 21772 (6th Cir. Ohio 2005).

Where an employee alleged that he was fired for supporting a co-worker's sexual harassment case against his employer, the employer was entitled to summary judgment on the employee's retaliation claim under R.C. 4112.02(I) because the employee failed to identify any similar situated employees who received more favorable treatment. Thus, the employee failed to establish that his employer's reason for his termination was pretextual. Pemberton v. DHL Worldwide Express, 2004 U.S. Dist. LEXIS 28722 (S.D. Ohio Sept. 15, 2004), aff'd, 145 Fed. Appx. 171, 2005 FED App. 0815N, 2005 U.S. App. LEXIS 21772 (6th Cir. Ohio 2005).

In a suit for violation of R.C. 4112.02(I), where an employee alleged that he was fired for supporting a co-worker's sexual harassment case against his employer, the employee's conduct prior to the date of his deposition in the co-worker's suit was not protected because the employee did not participate in the investigation of the co-worker's claims, either in terms of offering testimony or otherwise supporting the co-worker's claim, until the date of his deposition. Pemberton v. DHL Worldwide Express, 2004 U.S. Dist. LEXIS 28722 (S.D. Ohio Sept. 15, 2004), aff'd, 145 Fed. Appx. 171, 2005 FED App. 0815N, 2005 U.S. App. LEXIS 21772 (6th Cir. Ohio 2005).

In a suit for violation of R.C. 4112.02(I), an employee's communication to his supervisor of the circumstances surrounding a co-worker's sexual harassment did not constitute protected conduct because it was nothing more than communication of the complaint to his superior rather than purported "opposition" to a company policy. Pemberton v. DHL Worldwide Express, 2004 U.S. Dist. LEXIS 28722 (S.D. Ohio Sept. 15, 2004), aff'd, 145 Fed. Appx. 171, 2005 FED App. 0815N, 2005 U.S. App. LEXIS 21772 (6th Cir. Ohio 2005).

In a suit for violation of R.C. 4112.02(I), an employee's communication to his supervisor of the circumstances surrounding a co-worker's sexual harassment did not constitute protected conduct because it was nothing more than communication of the complaint to his superior rather than purported "opposition" to a company policy. Pemberton v. DHL Worldwide Express, 2004 U.S. Dist. LEXIS 28722 (S.D. Ohio Sept. 15, 2004), aff'd, 145 Fed. Appx. 171, 2005 FED App. 0815N, 2005 U.S. App. LEXIS 21772 (6th Cir. Ohio 2005).

Employee did not establish that the employer's brief transfer of the employee to work at a restaurant where she held the title of "general manager" but performed mostly "crew work" that involved making and serving food, prior to the time she went on a pre-approved corporate sabbatical and, upon return, was made a restaurant manager at another one of the employer's restaurants, amounted to "retaliation" for the age discrimination suit she had filed earlier; the law distinguished between "permanent adverse employment actions" and those that were only temporary and her temporary adverse action meant she did not, as a matter of law, show "retaliation." Limberg v. Roosa, 2004-Ohio-1480, 2004 Ohio App. LEXIS 1319 (Ohio Ct. App., Montgomery County 2004).

A retaliation claim was not established where, in response to a threat of violence by the employee against his former department, the city issued a hazard poster: Pflanz v. City of Cincinnati, 2002-Ohio-5492, 149 Ohio App.

3d 743, 778 N.E.2d 1073, 2002 Ohio App. LEXIS 5506 (Ohio Ct. App., Hamilton County 2002).

District court improperly granted an employer summary judgment on an employee's retaliation claims brought pursuant to 42 U.S.C.S. § 2000e-3(a) and R.C. 4112.02 where the employee established that he engaged in protected activity when he notified a supervisor during an internal investigation of another employee's racial discrimination claim that he had witnessed the alleged discrimination and was willing to testify to that effect; the employee had established a causal connection between the protected activity and his termination by alleging that a supervisor told him that he was fired because he put his nose into other people's business and that the discrimination suit was the only thing with which he was involved, and the employee's testimony and that of another witness disputed the proffered reason for his termination, i.e., insubordination and threatening behavior. Abbott v. Crown Motor Co., 348 F.3d 537, 2003 FED App. 0388P, 2003 U.S. App. LEXIS 22559 (6th Cir. Ohio 2003).

Employer and a union were entitled to summary judgment on an employee's claims of race discrimination and retaliation arising out of the failure to transfer the employee to a clerical position or an apprenticeship program; clerical positions were awarded in accordance with contractual seniority requirements, and there was an insufficient showing of causation with respect to the retaliation claim. Hands v. DaimlerChrysler Corp., 282 F. Supp. 2d 645, 2003 U.S. Dist. LEXIS 15809 (N.D. Ohio 2003).

Employee's retaliatory discharge claim was properly disposed of by way of summary judgment because she failed to establish a causal connection between her sexual harassment complaint and her termination and did not dispute that she had violated her employer's attendance policy, of which she was aware. Doe v. Marker, 2003-Ohio-6230, 2003 Ohio App. LEXIS 5584 (Ohio Ct. App., Trumbull County 2003).

The employee did not show that there was retaliation for exercising her rights or that she was constructively discharged. The employee was not terminated by the employer's action where she declined to accept an extension of her probationary contract: Mittman v. Bahls, 2002-Ohio-2808, 148 Ohio App. 3d 109, 772 N.E.2d 181, 2002 Ohio App. LEXIS 2824 (Ohio Ct. App., Franklin County 2002).

The five month delay between filing of the discrimination claim and the disciplinary action rendered the connection too tenuous for purposes of a retaliation claim: McDonald v. Ford Motor Co., 208 F. Supp. 2d 837, 2002 U.S. Dist. LEXIS 12355 (N.D. Ohio 2002).

In order to establish a prima facie case of retaliation under R.C. 4112.02(I), an employee must prove the following elements: (1) the employee engaged in protected activity; (2) the employer knew of the employee's participation in the protected activity; (3) the employer engaged in retaliatory conduct; and (4) a causal link exists between the protected activity and the adverse action: Powers v. Pinkerton, Inc., 2001-Ohio-4119, 2001 Ohio App. LEXIS 138 (Ohio Ct. App., Cuyahoga County), dismissed, 91 Ohio St. 3d 1525, 747 N.E.2d 251, 2001 Ohio LEXIS 1418 (Ohio 2001).

The employer was entitled to summary judgment on the retaliatory discharge claim, but not on the sexual harassment claim: Brentlinger v. Highlights for Children, 142 Ohio App. 3d 25, 753 N.E.2d 937, 2001 Ohio App. LEXIS 1419 (Ohio Ct. App., Franklin County 2001).

Plaintiff was not collaterally estopped from bringing an action for retaliatory discharge where he did not have a full and fair opportunity to litigate the issue at the civil rights commission hearing: Doan v. S. Ohio Admin. Dist. Council, 145 Ohio App. 3d 482, 763 N.E.2d 639, 2001 Ohio App. LEXIS 3659 (Ohio Ct. App., Franklin County 2001).

Summary judgment for the employer was proper where the employee failed to offer sufficient evidence that all three justifications for his demotion were pretext, and failed to even raise an inference that retaliation actually motivated this decision: Powers v. Pinkerton, Inc., 2001-Ohio-4119, 2001 Ohio App. LEXIS 138 (Ohio Ct. App., Cuyahoga County), dismissed, 91 Ohio St. 3d 1525, 747 N.E.2d 251, 2001 Ohio LEXIS 1418 (Ohio 2001).

Plaintiff failed to prove a prima facie case of retaliation based on his complaint to the Ohio Psychology Board against a psychologist hired by his employer—plaintiff did not file a charge against the defendant as required by R.C. 4112.02: Metzenbaum v. John Carroll Univ., 987 F. Supp. 610, 1997 U.S. Dist. LEXIS 17340 (N.D. Ohio 1997).

Female employee established the "causal link" between her discharge and the filing of her complaint for sexual harassment and satisfied her burden of making prima facie showing of retaliation based solely on the fact that she was discharged less than one month after filing her claim: Dorricott v. Fairhill Ctr. for Aging, 2 F. Supp. 2d 982, 1998 U.S. Dist. LEXIS 14187 (N.D. Ohio 1998), aff'd, 187 F.3d 635, 1999 U.S. App. LEXIS 27676 (6th Cir. Ohio 1999).

For purposes of a claim of retaliatory discharge, opposing an employer's condoning of illegal discrimination is itself a protected activity: Thatcher v. Goodwill Indus., 117 Ohio App. 3d 525, 690 N.E.2d 1320, 1997 Ohio App. LEXIS 6 (Ohio Ct. App., Summit County 1997).

Appellant's claim based on alleged retaliation for filing a federal ADEA claim was not actionable under Ohio law; the fact that proof that plaintiff engaged in labor activity protected by law is a prima facie element of either a federal or Ohio retaliatory discrimination claim does not mean that engaging in a labor activity protected under federal law would suffice as proof in an Ohio retaliatory discrimination claim under R.C. 4112.02(I): Crawford v. Medina Gen. Hosp., 1997 Ohio App. LEXIS 3744 (Ohio Ct. App., Medina County Aug. 20, 1997).

Plaintiff's outbursts and uncooperativeness were not necessarily a valid cause for discharge where such conduct was common at the job site. There was sufficient evidence of wage discrimination even though the job status was downgraded before plaintiff accepted the position. There was sufficient evidence for a finding of a retaliatory discharge: Chandler v. Empire Chem., 99 Ohio App. 3d 396, 650 N.E.2d 950, 1994 Ohio App. LEXIS 5788 (Ohio Ct. App., Summit County 1994).

The employee did not produce any evidence that his failure to be recalled from a layoff was in retaliation for his age discrimination claim: Rudy v. Loral Defense Sys., 85 Ohio App. 3d 148, 619 N.E.2d 449, 1993 Ohio App. LEXIS 183 (Ohio Ct. App., Summit County 1993).

Even though physician was not an employee of hospital she could state a cause of action against hospital under R.C. 4112.02 for suspending and terminating her clinical staff privileges allegedly due to discrimination on the basis of sex and in retaliation for her participation in state civil rights administrative proceedings: LeMasters v. Christ Hosp., 777 F. Supp. 1378, 1991 U.S. Dist. LEXIS 11091 (S.D. Ohio 1991).

Whether an employee decides to assist the charging party, or refuses to assist the respondent employer, the employer may not retaliate against the employee, because this decision of the employee constitutes participation in an investigation or proceeding under Title VII, an activity specifically protected by both federal and state law (R.C. 4112.02(I)): Smith v. Columbus Metropolitan Housing Authority, 443 F. Supp. 61, 10 Ohio Op. 3d 169, 1977 U.S. Dist. LEXIS 15330 (S.D. Ohio 1977).

**—Cat's paw**

Former city employee failed to establish a prima facie case of retaliation for the employee's refusal to retire, despite a supervisor having asked the employee numerous times when the employee planned to retire, because the employee could not prevail under the cat's paw theory of liability as the evidence did not establish a causal connection between the employee's alleged protected activity and the employee's termination. Collins v. City of Mason, 2020-Ohio-1186, 153 N.E.3d 484, 2020 Ohio App. LEXIS 1109 (Ohio Ct. App., Warren County 2020).

In a retaliation case, a former employee failed to establish causation under a cat's paw theory because he failed to prove that his supervisors performed an act motivated by a retaliatory animus which was intended to cause an adverse employment action and the act was the but-for cause of the employee's discharge. There was no indication that the supervisors informed a vice-president of the employee's attempts to expense his personal trips and of the employee's falsified agenda and expenses reports because the employee had reported alleged sexual harassment, and the supervisors did not make false or grossly exaggerated reports of the employee's dishonesty. Nebozuk v. Abercrombie & Fitch Co., 2014-Ohio-1600, 2014 Ohio App. LEXIS 1543 (Ohio Ct. App., Franklin County 2014).

Former trooper could not prevail on the cat's paw theory of liability in his retaliation claim because the evidence failed to show that the post commander performed an act motivated by retaliatory animus that was intended to cause an adverse employment action and that that act was the but-for cause of the former trooper's discharge. Smith v. Ohio Dep't of Pub. Safety, 2013-Ohio-4210, 997 N.E.2d 597, 2013 Ohio App. LEXIS 4384 (Ohio Ct. App., Franklin County 2013).

**—Causation**

Employer did not retaliate against plaintiff by terminating her employment because, even if the court were to construe plaintiff's reporting of racist comments to her supervisor as a protected activity, plaintiff's termination two months following the incident was not close enough in time to be regarded as being causally related to her reporting of the comments. Rivard v. Ohio State Univ., 2021-Ohio-4284, 2021 Ohio Misc. LEXIS 866 (Ohio Ct. Cl. 2021).

With respect to plaintiff's claim of relation for filing an EEOC charge, the conduct she cited as adverse employment actions was insufficient to dissuade a reasonable person from making a charge of discrimination. Further, given that the protected activity and allegedly retaliatory actions were separated by more than a year-and-a-half, causality could not be shown by temporal proximity alone. Blashak v. Ohio Dep't of Youth Servs., 2019-Ohio-509, 2019 Ohio Misc. LEXIS 11 (Ohio Ct. Cl. 2019).

School principal's claim for retaliation was properly dismissed as he failed to demonstrate a causal connection between his termination and his engagement in protected activity and failed to show that the individual school board members knew of his most recent engagement in protected activity. Spitulski v. Bd. of Educ. of the Toledo City Sch. Dist., 2018-Ohio-3984, 121 N.E.3d 41, 2018 Ohio App. LEXIS 4311 (Ohio Ct. App., Lucas County 2018).

Ohio Rev. Code Ann. § 4112.02 retaliation claim against the individuals survived where the allegations of a positive record prior to reporting the incident and subsequent termination, the lack of involvement from a manager that spoke positively of work performance, and the failure to take action of the reported harassment created a reasonable inference of causation. Longoria v. Autoneum North America, Inc., 2015 U.S. Dist. LEXIS 147613 (N.D. Ohio Oct. 30, 2015).

No genuine issue of fact existed with respect to causation as the evidence pointed to the manager's termination being the direct result of the manager's absenteeism and his general dereliction of duty. Widmyer v. Steak 'n Shake Operations, Inc., 2014-Ohio-5413, 2014 Ohio App. LEXIS 5244 (Ohio Ct. App., Hamilton County 2014).

In a retaliation case, a dual causation principal from tort law was not applicable because this section required proof that the retaliation was the but-for cause of an adverse employment action. Nebozuk v. Abercrombie & Fitch Co., 2014-Ohio-1600, 2014 Ohio App. LEXIS 1543 (Ohio Ct. App., Franklin County 2014).

**—Evidence sufficient**

Jury's verdict finding the employer liable for retaliation was not against the manifest weight of the evidence; the jury was free to reject the employer's argument that the doctor's salary withholding had already been decided upon when he was first suspended because no evidence was adduced establishing that any other physician employed by the employer had ever been subject to having his entire salary withheld because of a departmental deficit. Additionally, the temporal proximity between the sending of the letters and the salary withholding was close enough in time to permit a reasonable inference that the two were causally connected. Amesse v. Wright State Physicians, Inc., 2018-Ohio-416, 105 N.E.3d 612, 2018 Ohio App. LEXIS 431 (Ohio Ct. App., Montgomery County 2018).

**—Knowledge of protected activity**

Trial court did not err in granting summary judgment as to the retaliatory discrimination claim because the former employee did not present any direct evidence and the circumstantial evidence upon which she relied was speculative and did not support the inference that the supervisor knew of her protected activity when she was terminated. Messer v. Summa Health Sys., 2018-Ohio-372, 105 N.E.3d 550, 2018 Ohio App. LEXIS 378 (Ohio Ct. App., Summit County 2018).

**—Legal standard**

Fact that the findings of fact did not change when the administrative law judge (ALJ) reviewed the applicable law did not demonstrate any shortcoming in the ALJ's handling of the retaliation case because the legal standard had no direct bearing on the ALJ's views with respect to the credibility of the witnesses. Likewise, although the ALJ applied a different, more stringent legal standard in its amended recommendation, it was not a clear indication of error that the ALJ reached the same legal conclusions. Little York Tavern v. Lane, 2017-Ohio-850, 86 N.E.3d 715, 2017 Ohio App. LEXIS 848 (Ohio Ct. App., Montgomery County 2017).

**—Not shown**

Trial court did not err by granting summary judgment in favor of the employer as to the retaliation claim because the employee could not demonstrate the first element of her retaliation claim under R.C. 4112.02(I), she could not demonstrate that a genuine triable issue of fact remained as to an essential element of her retaliation claim. Accordingly, no genuine issues of material fact exist regarding her retaliation claim. Hall v. Crawford Cnty. Job & Family Servs., 2022-Ohio-1358, 2022 Ohio App. LEXIS 1251 (Ohio Ct. App., Crawford County 2022).

Trial court properly awarded summary judgment to defendant on plaintiff's retaliation claim because even though plaintiff engaged in a protected activity and established a prima facie case, defendant had a legitimate, nondiscriminatory reason for terminating her contract, namely, plaintiff making inappropriate comments in the classroom, and plaintiff presented no evidence establishing pretext. Martcheva v. Dayton Bd. of Educ., 2021-Ohio-3524, 179 N.E.3d 687, 2021 Ohio App. LEXIS 3433 (Ohio Ct. App., Montgomery County 2021).

Trial court did not err by granting the employer summary judgment on the employee's relation claim because the employee's statement, about a coworker being hired in the manner she was while at the same time working for the county, was not a grievance alleging discrimination, but rather was about the legality of the situation. Ksiazek v. Columbiana Cty. Port Auth., 2021-Ohio-1267, 171 N.E.3d 394, 2021 Ohio App. LEXIS 1251 (Ohio Ct. App., Columbiana County 2021).

Defendant was entitled to summary judgment on plaintiff's retaliation claim, as it was undisputed that after an investigation initiated by plaintiff's complaints, it was found that plaintiff had failed to follow defendant's reporting policies, and plaintiff had not shown that the investigation and finding of good cause to recommend discipline had no basis in fact, did not actually motivate defendant's conduct, or was insufficient to warrant defendant's conduct. Moody v. Ohio Dep't of Mental Health & Addiction Servs., 2021-Ohio-1525, 2021 Ohio Misc. LEXIS 31 (Ohio Ct. Cl.), rev'd in part, aff'd, 2021-Ohio-4578, 183 N.E.3d 21, 2021 Ohio App. LEXIS 4503 (Ohio Ct. App., Franklin County 2021).

Because employee failed to satisfy the first element of his retaliation claim, summary judgment to the employer was appropriate where the employee's request for an accommodation was not participation in an investigation, proceeding, or hearing. Likewise, appellant's request for an accommodation was not opposition to an unlawful discriminatory practice. Musil v. Gerken Materials, Inc., 2020-Ohio-3548, 2020 Ohio App. LEXIS 2497 (Ohio Ct. App., Lucas County 2020).

Timing of plaintiff's Ohio Civil Rights Commission (OCRC) complaint defeated his claim of retaliation, as any protected activity that plaintiff engaged in occurred after he was notified by letter that his application for Chief of Police was not considered for the position; thus, he could not show a causal link existed between the protected activity (filing an OCRC charge) and the adverse employment action (not considering his application for the Chief of Police position). Hughes v. Youngstown State Univ., 2020-Ohio-611, 2020 Ohio Misc. LEXIS 8 (Ohio Ct. Cl. 2020), aff'd, 2021-Ohio-2079, 2021 Ohio App. LEXIS 2045 (Ohio Ct. App., Franklin County 2021).

Summary judgment was granted in favor of the former employer of the former employee's retaliation claim against a co-worker because there were no facts showing that the co-worker took any adverse employment action against the employee as, after the employee accused him of harassment, the co-worker did not step up his offending behavior; and the employee did not show a causal relationship between her protected activity and any adverse employment action the co-worker might have taken. Jackson v. Northfield Park Assocs., LLC, 2020 Ohio Misc. LEXIS 46 (Ohio C.P. Apr. 6, 2020).

Summary judgment was granted in favor of the former employer of the former employee's retaliation claim against a department manager because, although the facts showed that the manager took an adverse employment action against the employee after she reported a supervisor's harassing behavior, the manager offered a legitimate, non-retaliatory reason for the adverse employment action based on the inappropriate work conduct in which the employee engaged; and the employee did not present sufficient evidence that the reason for the adverse employment action was pretextual. Jackson v. Northfield Park Assocs., LLC, 2020 Ohio Misc. LEXIS 46 (Ohio C.P. Apr. 6, 2020).

Commercial truck driver's claim that his former employer retaliated against him due to his complaints about having to wear CPAP machine, in alleged violation of this statute, failed because the employer offered a legitimate, nondiscriminatory reason for its CPAP requirement and the employee failed to rebut that reason as pretextual. The employer's program of requiring drivers who had sleep apnea to wear a CPAP machine constituted a legitimate safety requirement and disability accommodation. Allman v. Walmart, Inc., 967 F.3d 566, 2020 FED App. 235P, 2020 U.S. App. LEXIS 24089 (6th Cir. Ohio 2020).

Employee failed to state a claim for retaliation because she was not overtime eligible and was not disciplined for an alleged HIPPA violation; a direct order, corrective action, and written reprimand all occurred because the employee did not reschedule a meeting that was to occur while she was on approved leave, and no further discipline resulted from that. Toland v. Dep't of Mental Health & Addiction Servs., 2020-Ohio-3864, 2020 Ohio Misc. LEXIS 116 (Ohio Ct. Cl. 2020).

Employee's retaliation claim failed to survive summary judgment because the timeline of the case did not establish that but for the employee's complaint, she would not have been terminated for her failure to pass the Police Training Officer (PTO) program. Reasonable minds could only conclude that the employee was terminated from the PTO program due to her failure to pass the program, as observed by her mid-term and final evaluations. McGuire v. City of Newark, 2020-Ohio-4226, 2020 Ohio App. LEXIS 3114 (Ohio Ct. App., Licking County 2020).

Supervisors A and B could not be liable on the employee's retaliation claim because while the employee's charge of unlawful discrimination before the Ohio Civil Rights Commission constituted protected activity, supervisor A issued the notice of policy violation two days before the employee filed the charge, and supervisor B did not possess any discretion regarding the decision to suspend the employee, and thus did not take an adverse employment action against the employee. Tanksley v. Howell, 2020-Ohio-4278, 2020 Ohio App. LEXIS 3172 (Ohio Ct. App., Franklin County 2020).

Where a Health Information Technician (HIT) was hired by a company and placed her at a state correctional facility, the HIT's HIT did not show a valid retaliation claim because she did not show that she engaged in any protected activity and a confrontation with a correctional facility supervisor was not close enough in time to have been causally related to an alleged protected activity of filing n incident report. Brown v. Corr. Reception Ctr., 2019-Ohio-1067, 2019 Ohio Misc. LEXIS 22 (Ohio Ct. Cl. 2019), rev'd in part, 2020-Ohio-684, 146 N.E.3d 621, 2020 Ohio App. LEXIS 629 (Ohio Ct. App., Franklin County 2020).

In an action against a university, a professor failed to make a prima facie showing of retaliation, as insofar as he claimed his wife's discrimination lawsuits constituted protected activities that were imputed to him, the filing of those lawsuits was not close in time to the issuance of a notice of non-reappointment to him. Jiashin Wu v. Northeast Ohio Med. Univ., 2019-Ohio-2530, 140 N.E.3d 100, 2019 Ohio App. LEXIS 2635 (Ohio Ct. App., Franklin County 2019).

Trial court did not err by granting summary judgment for the employer on the retaliation claim because the employee was terminated, not because he filed a racial and sexual discrimination case, but because he violated the Employee Security and Workplace Violence policy by making verbal threats of physical harm in the workplace. Further, the evidence was uncontested that the senior manager was unaware of the employee's earlier racial and sexual discrimination complaints when she approved the request to terminate him for the threats. Smith v. Allstate Ins. Co., 2019-Ohio-4557, 135 N.E.3d 828, 2019 Ohio App. LEXIS 4596 (Ohio Ct. App., Summit County 2019).

On review, it was not necessary to address the employee's arguments regarding the prima facie case because she failed to show pretext. In her brief on appeal, she merely reiterated the arguments she made regarding pretext for her wrongful termination claims and, as previously found in her argument regarding pretext for her termination to be without merit, she failed to demonstrate pretext with regard to her claim for retaliation. Housden v. Wilke Global, Inc., 2018-Ohio-3959, 111 N.E.3d 1264, 2018 Ohio App. LEXIS 4330 (Ohio Ct. App., Franklin County 2018).

Decision that appellant's employer terminated his employment for nondiscriminatory reasons was proper and his retaliation claim was not supported by the weight of the evidence, as a human resources manager described her intimidation during a meeting with appellant, that he became very agitated, that his hands were trembling, and that he was shaking; when he went to pull something out of his pocket, the manager was concerned that he might have a weapon. Rivenbark v. Disc. Drug Mart, 2018-Ohio-4072, 112 N.E.3d 947, 2018 Ohio App. LEXIS 4394 (Ohio Ct. App., Medina County 2018).

Plaintiff had not proven retaliation. His actions of redirecting discussions, suggesting reduced sanctions, and stating that his supervisor could not act a certain way because she could get sued were made pursuant to his role as a labor relations officer and did not constitute protected activity; he had not shown his alleged opposition to discriminatory behavior was the but-for cause of his termination seven months later, as he himself had pointed to media coverage about crimes committed against him as the cause; and defendant had stated a legitimate nondiscriminatory reason for his termination in that his supervisor testified that he continually argued and debated with her and was difficult to communicate with. Bentkowski v. Ohio Lottery Comm'n, 2016-Ohio-5222, 2016 Ohio Misc. LEXIS 87 (Ohio Ct. Cl. 2016).



Employer was entitled to judgment as a matter of law as to an employee's retaliation claim because, while the employee established a prima facie case of retaliation and that the termination of his position was an adverse employment action, the employer had legitimate, nondiscriminatory reasons for terminating the employee's position where the employee's supervisor was not aware that he had filed a complaint against him, there was no dispute that the changes in the employee's duties and office location began before he filed his internal complaint, an interval of nine months passed between the date that the employee filed his complaint and the date he was given notice that his position would be eliminated due to a budgetary reduction. Schiavone v. Univ. of Toledo, 2015-Ohio-5633, 2015 Ohio Misc. LEXIS 21378 (Ohio Ct. Cl. 2015).

Trial court did not err by granting summary judgment for the superintendent and the district board of education on the racial discrimination retaliation claim because the affidavits were sufficient to show, as a matter of low, that the superintendent recommended elimination of the student services supervisor's position at the end of the year, and that the board agreed to do so. The board was seeking to decrease expenses by the elimination of administrative positions and the fact that several other employment contracts were terminated at the same time as the supervisor's further served to corroborate the affidavit testimony. Crawford v. Notar, 2016-Ohio-3010, 2016 Ohio App. LEXIS 1867 (Ohio Ct. App., Trumbull County 2016).

Former employee failed to present any evidence tending to show how her termination was in retaliation for raising an issue of discrimination based on a perceived disability. As there was no genuine issue of material fact, the trial court did not err by granting summary judgment in favor of the employer on her retaliation claim for relief. Jaber v. FirstMerit Corp., 2017-Ohio-277, 81 N.E.3d 879, 2017 Ohio App. LEXIS 276 (Ohio Ct. App., Summit County 2017).

Summary judgment was properly granted to a hockey facility and related coaches and individuals in parents' retaliation claim, arising from alleged conduct towards them when they complained that their son was kept out of playing in a youth hockey league, as both under the particular circumstances and objectively the parents' safety and lifestyle were not implicated, and the actions were not materially adverse. Pittman v. Parillo, 2017-Ohio-1477, 2017 Ohio App. LEXIS 1482 (Ohio Ct. App., Lucas County 2017).

Summary judgment was properly granted to a city and fire chief on a firefighter's retaliation claim because his health change due to Parkinson's Disease was a valid reason to place him on leave and then seek his retirement, and his change of rank was justified by a lack of funds. Crutchfield, Inc. v. Testa, 2015-Ohio-1871, 142 Ohio St. 3d 1460, 30 N.E.3d 970, 2015 Ohio LEXIS 1205 (Ohio 2015).

Trial court did not err in granting summary judgment for the employer and the labor relations analyst on the retaliation claims because the employees were hopelessly vague as to the "oppositional activities" that they had taken to support a coworker in his litigation against the employer, and how it was that management was supposedly aware of such activities. The record did not support their contention that they engaged in "protected activity" because none of them testified that they informed the employer or anyone in its management of their alleged agreement to testify in support of the coworker. Johnson v. GMC, 2001-Ohio-1673, 2001 Ohio App. LEXIS 6113 (Ohio Ct. App., Richland County 2001).

**—Pretext**

Reliable, probative, and substantial evidence to support the Ohio Civil Rights Commission's order finding retaliation because, although the administrative law judge (ALJ) found that the employer had met its burden of production on the interim step of the McDonald-Douglass analysis, it was apparent that the ALJ was unpersuaded by the employer's claim that the employee was attempting to steal money on the day she was fired and that, rather, the alleged theft was a pretext for wrongful termination. Little York Tavern v. Lane, 2017-Ohio-850, 86 N.E.3d 715, 2017 Ohio App. LEXIS 848 (Ohio Ct. App., Montgomery County 2017).

There were no genuine issues of material fact regarding the former employee's retaliatory discharge claim because he failed to satisfy the causality element of the prima facie case for retaliatory discharge, and failed to meet his burden of showing that the employer's reasons for the adverse employment action were a pretext for unlawful retaliatory discharge. The employee was terminated based on performance. Brown v. O'Reilly Auto. Stores, Inc., 2015-Ohio-5146, 54 N.E.3d 638, 2015 Ohio App. LEXIS 5125 (Ohio Ct. App., Cuyahoga County 2015).

Summary judgment was improperly granted on employee's retaliation claim because employee's negative performance evaluation constituted materially adverse action as it affected her advancement potential, employee presented genuine dispute of material fact about whether employer took adverse actions against her because of her protected activity in filing employment discrimination charge, causation was established due to proximity between adverse actions and employee's filing of charge, and reasonable jury could infer that employer's proffered reasons for its adverse actions were pretext. Henry v. Abbott Labs., 651 Fed. Appx. 494, 2016 FED App. 0318N, 2016 U.S. App. LEXIS 10604 (6th Cir. Ohio 2016).

Trial court erred by granting judgment notwithstanding the verdict for the employer on the retaliation claim because the jury properly found that the employee engaged in protected activity of complaining about how he was treated because of his race, that, but-for the complaint, he would have been rehired, and that the employer's alternative reasoning for failure to rehire him was pretextual. Smith v. Superior Prod., LLC, 2014-Ohio-1961, 13 N.E.3d 664, 2014 Ohio App. LEXIS 1895 (Ohio Ct. App., Franklin County 2014).

Trial court did not err in finding that the trooper failed to show that the reasons for his discharge were a pretext for retaliation because the manifest weight of the evidence supported that finding. Since the State Highway Patrol extensively reviewed each incident, senior management could reasonably have relied on the particularized facts before it to decide what really happened. As senior management held an honest belief that the trooper was untruthful, the trooper could not establish pretext. Smith v. Ohio Dep't of Pub. Safety, 2013-Ohio-4210, 997 N.E.2d 597, 2013 Ohio App. LEXIS 4384 (Ohio Ct. App., Franklin County 2013).

**—Protected activity**

Summary judgment for defendant on a retaliation claim was inappropriate, as a private conversation in which plaintiff told a supervisor that he was being excessively critical of her work due to her standing up for someone of her same race, that he had engaged in a campaign to drive other black workers away, and that he was racist could constitute taking an overt stand against suspected illegal workplace discrimination and be protected opposition. Brown v. Corr. Reception Ctr., 2020-Ohio-684, 146 N.E.3d 621, 2020 Ohio App. LEXIS 629 (Ohio Ct. App., Franklin County 2020).

In a former employee's action for violation of R.C. 4112.02(I) stemming from his demotion and subsequent termination, the employer was not entitled to summary judgment because there was sufficient evidence of a good faith complaint of discrimination such that a reasonable jury could find that it was protected activity where the employee's e-mail gave examples of specific conduct where he felt a female co-worker was targeted based on her gender. Gamble v. Brown & Brown of Ky., Inc., 2020 Ohio Misc. LEXIS 29 (Ohio C.P. Jan. 31, 2020).

Employee's discussions with the employer's human resources department regarding his October 18, 2016 grievance did not alert the employer that unlawful discrimination was at issue, and, as such, the October 18, 2016 grievance did not amount to protected activity because while the employee possibly believed a supervisor's alleged favoritism was racially motivated, there was nothing indicating the employee communicated that belief to his employer. Tanksley v. Howell, 2020-Ohio-4278, 2020 Ohio App. LEXIS 3172 (Ohio Ct. App., Franklin County 2020).

Trial court erred in finding that appellant established the protected activity element of his retaliation claim because a manager's remark to appellant satisfied neither quid pro quo nor hostile-environment sexual harassment as the remark was not linked to the grant or denial of an employment benefit and it lacked the severity and pervasiveness necessary to affect the terms, conditions, or privileges of appellant's employment. Sullivan v. Ikea, 2020-Ohio-6661, 2020 Ohio App. LEXIS 4526 (Ohio Ct. App., Butler County 2020).

Trial court did not err by entering judgment for the employee doctor because, by stating in the letters that the employer's actions potentially violated the Americans With Disabilities Act (ADA), counsel was essentially arguing that the doctor was opposing the employer's discriminatory practices. Accordingly, the letters drafted by counsel and their contents constituted protected activity for the purposes of a claim for retaliation. Amesse v. Wright State Physicians, Inc., 2018-Ohio-416, 105 N.E.3d 612, 2018 Ohio App. LEXIS 431 (Ohio Ct. App., Montgomery County 2018).

**—Retaliatory discharge**

Employee's claim of retaliatory discrimination failed, as he did not show a "causal connection" between his complaints that another worker was receiving preferential treatment due to his race and the employee's subsequent termination, and there were intervening performance concerns related to his termination. Butler v. Lubrizol Corp., 2015-Ohio-1216, 2015 Ohio App. LEXIS 1253 (Ohio Ct. App., Lake County 2015).

Trial court erred in allowing a judgment on the retaliation claim because it did not meet the elements. No claim for "retaliation in violation of public policy" existed and there was no adverse employment action because the agent's employment terminated before she filed her complaint. Lucarell v. Nationwide Mut. Ins. Co., 2015-Ohio-5286, 44 N.E.3d 319, 2015 Ohio App. LEXIS 5110 (Ohio Ct. App., Mahoning County 2015), rev'd, 2018-Ohio-15, 152 Ohio St. 3d 453, 97 N.E.3d 458, 2018 Ohio LEXIS 16 (Ohio 2018).

Where plaintiff, a male employee of a hospital, was forced to resigned after having sexual contact with a female co-worker who was not terminated, the trial court did not err in granting summary judgment to the hospital on the unlawful retaliation claim because plaintiff's claim for sexual discrimination was not made until well after his termination date. Caiazza v. Mercy Med. Ctr., 2014-Ohio-2290, 2014 Ohio App. LEXIS 2232 (Ohio Ct. App., Stark County 2014).

Former state trooper did not prevail on the trooper's claim of retaliatory discharge, in violation of R.C. 4112.02(I), because the amount of time that passed between the alleged protected conduct and the trooper's discharge precluded the inference of a retaliatory motive on the part of the trooper's supervisor. Furthermore, the supervisor brought forth a legitimate, nondiscriminatory reason for the trooper's discharge. Smith v. Ohio Dep't of Pub. Safety, 2012-Ohio-6358, 2012 Ohio Misc. LEXIS 239 (Ohio Ct. Cl. 2012), aff'd, 2013-Ohio-4210, 997 N.E.2d 597, 2013 Ohio App. LEXIS 4384 (Ohio Ct. App., Franklin County 2013).

Employer was entitled to summary judgment dismissing an employee's claim that the employee was discharged for complaining about national origin discrimination because (1) the record amply supported the conclusion that the employer's ultimate decision maker had no knowledge that the employee had ever complained about national origin discrimination, so the employee could not show the termination was causally connected to a protected activity, and, (2) even if the employee could establish such a connection, the employer offered a legitimate justification for terminating the employee, since the employee violated the employer's workplace violence policy, and the employee could not show this justification was a pretext for discrimination, as the employee's denials of the facts found by the employer did not raise an inference that the employer did not honestly believe another employee's report of the underlying incident or that the proffered reason had no basis in fact, as the employee admitted the incident occurred and that the employee overreacted. Ignatenkov v. U.S. Foodservice, Inc., 2012 U.S. Dist. LEXIS 99553 (S.D. Ohio July 18, 2012).

It was not error to dismiss an employee's retaliation claim on summary judgment because, (1) after the employer gave a non-discriminatory reason for firing the employee, the employee made no pretext argument in the trial court, and (2) the employee did not explain on appeal how facts allegedly showing pretext demonstrated pretext. Camp v. Star Leasing Co., 2012-Ohio-3650, 2012 Ohio App. LEXIS 3236 (Ohio Ct. App., Franklin County 2012).

Former employee established a prima facie case of retaliation because (1) the former employer knew that the employee intended to raise questions regarding age discrimination; (2) a jury could have found that the employee's perception that he was being treated unfairly supported a good faith basis for a complaint; and (3) a jury might have found a causal connection between the employee's protected activity and his termination based on their temporal proximity. Patrick v. Ferguson Enters., 2011 U.S. Dist. LEXIS 10418 (S.D. Ohio Feb. 2, 2011).

Even assuming that an employee could establish a prima facie case of retaliation, the employee's claim against her employer failed as she could not establish that the employer's reasons for firing the employee were pretext where the employee's assertion of pretext were based on comments made by non decisionmakers who had no input into the employee's termination and on an affidavit regarding accommodations given to other employees who suffered injuries outside of work that lacked foundation. Garcia v. Whirlpool Corp., 2010 U.S. Dist. LEXIS 118409 (N.D. Ohio Nov. 5, 2010), aff'd, 468 Fed. Appx. 609, 2012 FED App. 393N, 2012 U.S. App. LEXIS 7327 (6th Cir. Ohio 2012).

Former employer was denied summary judgment on the employee's retaliation claims under R.C. 4112.02(I) and Title VII of the Civil Rights Act of 1964 where (1) the employee asserted that the manager had touched her in ways that went beyond normal professional behavior, and he had humiliated her by making sexual inferences in front of other employees; (2) there was evidence that the negative appraisals and performance plans supplied the necessary foundation for the employee's eventual separation; (3) because the employee had come forward with some evidence that she was treated differently after she engaged in protected activity, she had created a genuine issue of material fact as to causation; and (4) the evidence that the employee only started receiving frequent reprimands after she engaged in protected activity was sufficient to show that the employer's conduct was driven by a desire to retaliate. McBroom v. Barnes & Noble Booksellers, Inc., 747 F. Supp. 2d 906, 2010 U.S. Dist. LEXIS 107935 (N.D. Ohio 2010).

Sheriff was entitled to summary judgment on the former nurse's retaliation claim under 42 U.S.C.S. § 2000e-3(a) and R.C. 4112.02(I) because no reasonable jury could find that the sheriff's reason for terminating the nurse, namely her arrest for stealing from a grocery store, was pretextual, as the nurse failed to show that similarly situated individuals were treated more favorably, as two other nurses had also been terminated for theft. There was also no evidence that the sheriff condoned, tolerated, and encouraged the sexual harassment by the nurse's coworker. Satterfield v. Karnes, 736 F. Supp. 2d 1138, 2010 U.S. Dist. LEXIS 86398 (S.D. Ohio 2010).

Summary judgment was properly granted on a former employee's claim for retaliation under R.C. 4112.02(I) as there was no evidence that the employer was aware that the employee championed older workers' rights, and there was no showing of a causal connection between the protected activity and the adverse action taken by the employer against the employee. Wallace v. Mantych Metalworking, 2010-Ohio-3765, 189 Ohio App. 3d 25, 937 N.E.2d 177, 2010 Ohio App. LEXIS 3207 (Ohio Ct. App., Montgomery County 2010).

Employer was entitled to judgment as a matter of law on the whistleblower claim because the employee did not even allege that he complied with the requirements of R.C. 4113.52. Because the employee did not even claim that he properly notified his employers of the perceived violations, no reasonable mind could have found that he properly blew the whistle. Horsley v. Burton, 2010-Ohio-6315, 2010 Ohio App. LEXIS 5277 (Ohio Ct. App., Scioto County 2010).

African-American employee's retaliation claim failed because although there was a factual dispute as to whether the employee complained about perceived discrimination to a manager, there was no evidence to suggest that such complaints, whether or not they occurred, led to the employee's termination. Thompson v. UHHS Richmond Heights Hosp., Inc., 372 Fed. Appx. 620, 2010 FED App. 0225N, 2010 U.S. App. LEXIS 7439 (6th Cir. Ohio 2010).

When an employee complained that the employee was terminated for reporting another employee's racial harassment of the employee, summary judgment was properly granted to the employee's former employer because, while the employee demonstrated that the employee had engaged in protected activity and that the employee had been subjected to an adverse employment action, the employee did not show a genuine issue of material fact as to whether those who made the decision to discharge the employee knew that the employee had complained of racial harassment, nor did the employee show that the supervisor to whom the employee complained of the harassment, or any other mid-level supervisor, made any racially disparaging comments, nor did the employee show that this supervisor was "meaningfully involved" in the decision to terminate the employee, so no causal link between the employee's complaint and the employee's termination was shown. Fitch v. United States Foodservice Corp., 2008-Ohio-282, 2008 Ohio App. LEXIS 241 (Ohio Ct. App., Butler County 2008).

Summary judgment was properly granted in favor of a city and three supervisors sued by an African-American employee for retaliatory discharge because the employee showed no causal link between the employee's protected activity of filing discrimination complaints and adverse employment actions other than subjectively feeling those actions were retaliatory, and evidence that the employee filed complaints, many of which the employee's supervisors were unaware of, and was subjected to discipline, did not meet the employee's burden. Greene v. City of Cincinnati, 2008-Ohio-4908, 2008 Ohio App. LEXIS 4121 (Ohio Ct. App., Hamilton County 2008).

Summary judgment was properly granted in favor of an employer in an employee's wrongful discharge action based on retaliation in violation of public policy and in violation of R.C. 4112.02 and 4123.90, as the evidence showed that the employer had fired the employee for being dishonest in failing to report a non-work-related injury; the employee did not show that the proffered reason was a mere pretext, as the employer had a policy and a history of terminating employees for dishonesty. King v. Jewish Home, 2008-Ohio-4724, 178 Ohio App. 3d 387, 898 N.E.2d 56, 2008 Ohio App. LEXIS 3978 (Ohio Ct. App., Hamilton County 2008).

There was an issue of fact as to whether an employee's termination from her employment with a bank comported with the dismissal of a bank "officer" in the manner established by the National Bank Act, 12 U.S.C.S. § 24, Fifth; thus, the court could not conclude that summary judgment was warranted with respect to the employee's retaliatory discharge claim against the bank. Boesch v. Champaign Nat'l Bank, 2008-Ohio-3282, 2008 Ohio App. LEXIS 2771 (Ohio Ct. App., Summit County 2008).

Section 510 of the Employee Retirement Income Security Act of 1974 (ERISA), 29 U.S.C.S. § 1140, completely preempted a terminated employee's state law wrongful employment discharge-retaliation claim in violation of R.C. 4112.02(I) which alleged that she had been retaliated against for claiming or attempting to claim her right to receive long term disability (LTD) benefits under ERISA. Huisjack v. Medco Health Solutions, Inc., 496 F. Supp. 2d 859, 2007 U.S. Dist. LEXIS 47833 (S.D. Ohio 2007).

Terminated employee's claim for a wrongful employment discharge-retaliation claim in violation of R.C. 4112.02(I) was not dismissed, because the employee had sufficiently established her prima facie case. Namely, she alleged that her former employer terminated her employment because she sought long term disability (LTD) benefits under the employer's LTD benefits program. Huisjack v. Medco Health Solutions, Inc., 496 F. Supp. 2d 859, 2007 U.S. Dist. LEXIS 47833 (S.D. Ohio 2007).

There was no error in granting summary judgment for the employer on the employee's retaliatory discharge claim because, given the time span between his complaints about his coworkers' use of swear words and denigration of women and his ultimate dismissal, the two events were not related. Even if the employee had been able to establish a prima facie case of retaliation, the employer provided a legitimate reason for its action in that the employee was terminated for his medical condition and narcotic use for pain management. Norton v. FirstEnergy Corp., 2006-Ohio-892, 2006 Ohio App. LEXIS 807 (Ohio Ct. App., Jefferson County 2006).

On a retaliation claim a terminated employee failed to demonstrate a casual connection between his protected activities and his termination. He also failed to point to sufficient evidence to raise even an inference that his failure to pass a drug test was not the true reason for his discharge. There was no sufficient inference that the employer discharged the employee with a discriminatory animus. Counts v. Kraton Polymers U.S. LLC, 2006 U.S. Dist. LEXIS 65312 (S.D. Ohio Sept. 13, 2006), aff'd, 260 Fed. Appx. 825, 2008 FED App. 0064N, 2008 U.S. App. LEXIS 2187 (6th Cir. Ohio 2008).

**Retaliatory discharge**

Taken together, terminated employee's phone calls and email provided more than sufficient evidence of legally valid complaint of unlawful conduct; stated differently, evidence presented at trial sufficiently established that employer should have reasonably understood that employee was making complaint of sex discrimination in exercise of her rights under Ohio Rev. Code Ann. § 4112.02. Braun v. Ultimate Jetcharters, LLC, 828 F.3d 501, 2016 FED App. 0159P, 2016 U.S. App. LEXIS 12559 (6th Cir. Ohio 2016).

**—Burden of Proof**

In the terminated university employee's action against her former university employer, the university was entitled to summary judgment on discrimination and retaliation claims because the employee failed to demonstrate discriminatory intent under the McDonnell Douglas framework where there was evidence she had been terminated for insubordination, and she failed to demonstrate retaliation where she failed to show her opposition to any unlawful discriminatory practice. You v. Ne. Ohio Med. Univ., 2018-Ohio-4838, 2018 Ohio App. LEXIS 5161 (Ohio Ct. App., Franklin County 2018).

**—Disabled**

**—Burden of proof**

In a disability discrimination case in which an employer moved for summary judgment, since the employee failed to undergo the requested psychological independent medical examination, he could not establish the third prong of the prima facie case, that, despite his perceived disability, he could safely and substantially perform the essential functions of the job in question. Dalton v. Ohio Dep't of Rehab. & Corr., 2013-Ohio-5941, 2013 Ohio Misc. LEXIS 102 (Ohio Ct. Cl. 2013), aff'd, 2014-Ohio-2658, 2014 Ohio App. LEXIS 2598 (Ohio Ct. App., Franklin County 2014).

Employee's claim of disability discrimination under state law could not withstand challenge due to the similarity of the statutory language with the federal statute, and the determination that the allegations supporting the federal claim were not sufficient to survive challenge. Bracken v. Dasco Home Med. Equip., Inc., 2013 U.S. Dist. LEXIS 90628 (S.D. Ohio June 27, 2013), dismissed in part, 954 F. Supp. 2d 686, 2013 U.S. Dist. LEXIS 90629 (S.D. Ohio 2013), dismissed in part, 2014 U.S. Dist. LEXIS 123978 (S.D. Ohio Sept. 5, 2014).

Municipal employee's action brought under the Americans with Disabilities Act and Ohio's Fair Employment Practices Act would not be dismissed because the employee was not required to exhaust his administrative remedies prior to filing suit, and his failure to do so did not warrant dismissal of his claims, and the employee submitted sufficient evidence to create a genuine issue of material fact about whether he was qualified for his position. Brockmeier v. Greater Dayton Reg'l Transit Auth., 2013 U.S. Dist. LEXIS 124072 (S.D. Ohio Aug. 29, 2013), dismissed, 2016 U.S. Dist. LEXIS 90439 (S.D. Ohio July 12, 2016).

Employee's claim that she was fired from employment due to the employer's disability discrimination pursuant to R.C. 4112.02(A) should have survived challenge by the employer's summary judgment motion, as the employee raised a genuine issue of material fact as to whether, upon pursuing her permanent-partial disability claim, adverse employment action was taken against her at least in part due to her disability. Rivers v. Cashland Fin. Servs., 2013-Ohio-1225, 2013 Ohio App. LEXIS 1125 (Ohio Ct. App., Summit County 2013).

For purposes of an employee's claims under 42 U.S.C.S. § 12112(a) of the Americans with Disabilities Act and R.C. 4112.02 of the Ohio Civil Rights Act, the employee failed to show that he was treated "less favorably" due to his disabetes, as his subjective belief on that issue was unavailing. Steele v. Oasis Turf & Tree, Inc., 2012 U.S. Dist. LEXIS 103722 (S.D. Ohio July 25, 2012).

For purposes of an employee's claims under 42 U.S.C.S. § 12112(a) of the Americans with Disabilities Act and R.C. 4112.02 of the Ohio Civil Rights Act, the employee showed that he was a "qualified individual" under 42 U.S.C.S. § 12111(8), as he possessed the basic skills necessary to perform his job, and he received the requisite training and performed adequately for at least one season. Steele v. Oasis Turf & Tree, Inc., 2012 U.S. Dist. LEXIS 103722 (S.D. Ohio July 25, 2012).

Employee failed to prove that, though disabled, the employee could safely and substantially perform the essential functions of the employee's job; therefore, the employee failed to prove a prima facie case of disability discrimination. The employee received a letter from the employer's director of human resources notifying the employee that the employer was commencing an involuntary disability separation process based upon a doctor's report that the employee could no longer perform the employee's job duties due to the employee's sleep apnea and narcolepsy, but, when the employee was given the opportunity to rebut the doctor's findings at a hearing, the employee offered no rebuttal evidence. Miller v. Ohio Dep't of Ins., 2009-Ohio-5313, 2009 Ohio Misc. LEXIS 222 (Ohio Ct. Cl. 2009).

**—Common law**

It is an unlawful discriminatory practice for an employee to be discharged because of a handicap, and the employee may bring a common law wrongful discharge claim without seeking relief under R.C. Chapter 4112.: Clipson v. Schlessman, 89 Ohio App. 3d 230, 624 N.E.2d 220, 1993 Ohio App. LEXIS 2999 (Ohio Ct. App., Erie County 1993).

**—Depression**

Plaintiff's disability discrimination claim failed because although plaintiff suffered from depression and depression could be considered a disability entitled to protection under R.C. 4112.01, R.C. 4112.02, nothing in the record suggested that defendants knew or should have known that plaintiff suffered from depression. Kendrick v. Walgreen Co., 2012 U.S. Dist. LEXIS 164869 (S.D. Ohio Nov. 19, 2012).

It was not error to dismiss an employee's disability discrimination claim on summary judgment because the employee's depression did not manifest itself with sufficient frequency or in sufficient duration to qualify as a substantially limiting impairment. Camp v. Star Leasing Co., 2012-Ohio-3650, 2012 Ohio App. LEXIS 3236 (Ohio Ct. App., Franklin County 2012).

Plaintiff former employee's response of yes to a narrow question of whether his depression impaired his work did not preclude the employee's argument that his ability to sleep was also impaired and thus, defendant employer's motion for summary judgment on the employee's disability discrimination claim under R.C. 4112 .02(A) was denied. Dage v. Time Warner Cable, 395 F. Supp. 2d 668, 2005 U.S. Dist. LEXIS 25361 (S.D. Ohio 2005).

Employee's depression did not constitute a disability where there was no evidence that it caused any impairment of a life activity: Pattison v. Honda of Am. Mfg., 2004-Ohio-3788, 2004 Ohio App. LEXIS 3402 (Ohio Ct. App., Champaign County 2004).

Depression may qualify as a handicap under R.C. 4112.02. The reasonableness of an accommodation ordinarily presents a jury question: Mitnaul v. Fairmount Presbyterian Church, 2002-Ohio-5833, 149 Ohio App. 3d 769, 778 N.E.2d 1093, 2002 Ohio App. LEXIS 5670 (Ohio Ct. App., Cuyahoga County 2002).

Absent indications that one or more major life activities have been substantially limited, the experience of depression is insufficient to constitute a disability; thus, where a claimant was never diagnosed with depression and was substantially able to function on a day-to-day level, she failed to demonstrate that she suffered from a cognizable disability and did not state a prima facie case of disability discrimination: Cooke v. SGS Tool Co., 2000 Ohio App. LEXIS 1784 (Ohio Ct. App., Summit County Apr. 26, 2000).

Depression may qualify as a handicap. An employer's duty to make a reasonable accommodation also mandates that the employer interact with an employee in a good faith effort to seek a reasonable accommodation: Shaver v. Wolske & Blue, 138 Ohio App. 3d 653, 742 N.E.2d 164, 2000 Ohio App. LEXIS 3153 (Ohio Ct. App., Franklin County 2000).

Assuming the employee's depression constituted a handicap, there was no proof the employer knew or should have known of the handicap and resulting limitations. The employee's attitude and behavior constituted a legitimate, nondiscriminatory reason for the employer's actions: Beauchamp v. CompuServe, Inc., 126 Ohio App. 3d 17, 709 N.E.2d 863, 1998 Ohio App. LEXIS 1482 (Ohio Ct. App., Franklin County 1998).

R.C. 4112.02 was not violated by denying a position as hostage negotiator to appellant, who was handicapped because of her depression, where record supported a finding that appellant's work history included instances of her inability to remain calm and reason well in stressful situations, combativeness, criticizing others and being overly emotionally involved in her work: City of Columbus v. Lowe, 1995 Ohio App. LEXIS 2765 (Ohio Ct. App., Franklin County June 29, 1995).

**—Diabetes**

In a disability discrimination case under R.C. 4112.02(A), the employer's motion for summary judgment was granted; the employee could not make out a prima facie case because his diabetes was not inherently a qualifying disability, and the employee suffered no actual or expected long-term impairment or long-term impact related to his condition. Greer v. Cleveland Clinic Health Sys. East Region, 2011 U.S. Dist. LEXIS 13082 (N.D. Ohio Feb. 10, 2011), aff'd on other grounds in part, aff'd, 503 Fed. Appx. 422, 2012 FED App. 1124N, 2012 U.S. App. LEXIS 22594 (6th Cir. Ohio 2012).

**Reverse discrimination**

In a reverse race and sex discrimination case, magistrate properly concluded that the Chief Marketing Officer would have made the decision to terminate plaintiff absent any impermissible motive on her part, as there was sufficient evidence that plaintiff was not meeting her expectations and it was evident that once she determined plaintiff was not aligned with her vision, she made the decision to terminate him. McGinty v. Ohio State Univ., 2020-Ohio-4315, 2020 Ohio Misc. LEXIS 125 (Ohio Ct. Cl. 2020).

While an employer took an adverse action with respect to an employee's employment, by terminating the employee's employment, there was no evidence to support the employee's reverse race discrimination claim that the employer discriminated against non-minority employees and/or treated the employee disparately than other employees similarly situated as no other similarly situated, minority employee had two active suspensions, such as the employee had, nor did any other employee commit a dishonest act, such as the employee did. Hunter v. Bureau of Workers' Comp., 2016-Ohio-8577, 2016 Ohio Misc. LEXIS 131 (Ohio Ct. Cl. 2016).

Employee's reverse race discrimination claim failed as: (1) the employee did not show that the employer discriminated against non-minority employees; (2) the employee did not identify a similarly situated minority employee who was treated more favorably than the employee as his supervisor was not similarly situated and the differing penalties were imposed at different time periods; and (3) the employer's explanation for the employee's termination, a violation of the code of conduct, was not pretextual. Pohmer v. JPMorgan Chase Bank, N.A., 2015-Ohio-1229, 2015 Ohio App. LEXIS 1204 (Ohio Ct. App., Franklin County 2015).

Employee did not establish a prima facie case of reverse gender discrimination because he did not present evidence to demonstrate that the employer was the unusual employer that discriminated against males. A male received the promotion that the employee did not get. Horsley v. Burton, 2010-Ohio-6315, 2010 Ohio App. LEXIS 5277 (Ohio Ct. App., Scioto County 2010).

Male applicant, who was not hired after interviewing for either of two entry-level academic advisor positions with a community college district, failed to establish a prima facie case of sex discrimination, because the applicant's proof, even when viewed in a light most favorable to the applicant, did not meet the modified test applied in cases of reverse discrimination, which required applicants to demonstrate background circumstances supporting the suspicion that the employer discriminated against the majority, and that the employer treated differently employees who were similarly situated but were not members of the protected class. Silberstein v. Montgomery County Cmty. College Dist., 2009-Ohio-6138, 2009 Ohio App. LEXIS 5154 (Ohio Ct. App., Montgomery County 2009).

Where an employee alleged that union employees discriminated against the employee by failing to take the employee's grievance to arbitration and by settling it, and that another employee of the employer discriminated against the employee by settling the grievance, the claims failed because (1) the employee was a class of one and thus could not point to any "similarly-situated minority employees" who were warned and yet were not subject to the allegedly racist settlement agreement, and (2) the settlement agreement did not appear to be an "adverse action." Courie v. Alcoa Wheel & Forged Prods., 577 F.3d 625, 2009 FED App. 0295P, 2009 U.S. App. LEXIS 18561 (6th Cir. Ohio 2009).

Decision granting summary judgment in favor of an employer in a male employee's reverse sex discrimination action was proper. By the employee's own admissions, while the employer may not have consistently disciplined female employees for safety violations, it also did not uniformly enforce safety violations against its male employees. Tack v. PCC Airfoils, Inc., 2008-Ohio-6898, 2008 Ohio App. LEXIS 5758 (Ohio Ct. App., Stark County 2008).

Parole officers failed to make a prima facie case of reverse gender discrimination because they failed to present evidence that background circumstances supported the suspicion that the employer, the Adult Parole Authority, was that unusual employer who discriminated against the majority, or that it treated the parole officers differently than the successful applicants for a promotion. Bogdas v. Ohio Dep't of Rehab. & Corr., 2008-Ohio-3409, 2008 Ohio Misc. LEXIS 113 (Ohio Ct. Cl. 2008).

Prima facie case of reverse discrimination under 42 U.S.C.S. § 2000e-2 and R.C. 4112.02 failed as the employee, who was a Caucasian female, was replaced by a Caucasian female and because she failed to show that she was similarly situated to the employees who were purportedly treated better than she was; further, she failed to show that the employer's reason for terminating her, which was the filing of allegedly false reports against other employees, was pretext for discrimination. Fuelling v. New Vision Med. Labs. LLC, 284 Fed. Appx. 247, 2008 FED App. 0384N, 2008 U.S. App. LEXIS 13915 (6th Cir. Ohio 2008).

Trial court erred when it refused to admit a city-employer's affirmative action plan into evidence or consider it in an employee's racial and gender discrimination action R.C. 4112.02 and with respect to the employer's directed verdict motion, as the plan was in effect at the time that the employee alleged that he was passed over numerous times for a superintendent position and it was relevant pursuant to Evid.R. 401 and 402; further, there was sufficient evidence of "background circumstances" to support a prima facie case of reverse discrimination, the trial court overlooked the fact that there were racial as well as gender discrimination allegations, and the employee's further application for the position would have been clearly futile. Mitchell v. Lemmie, 2007-Ohio-5757, 2007 Ohio App. LEXIS 5060 (Ohio Ct. App., Montgomery County 2007).

Where a former employee was terminated from his position, his claim of reverse sex discrimination properly resulted in a grant of summary judgment for his employer and supervisors, as the employee did not meet his burden of showing that the employer was the unusual type that discriminated against the majority. The former employee was a white male and he was terminated due to a reduction in force, which was deemed a legitimate, non-discriminatory reason that was not shown to have been a mere pretext for the employer's discriminatory conduct. Kundtz v. AT&T Solutions, Inc., 2007-Ohio-1462, 2007 Ohio App. LEXIS 1318 (Ohio Ct. App., Franklin County 2007).

Plaintiff did not establish a prima facie case of reverse race discrimination: James v. Bob Ross Buick, Inc., 2006-Ohio-2638, 167 Ohio App. 3d 338, 855 N.E.2d 119, 2006 Ohio App. LEXIS 2490 (Ohio Ct. App., Montgomery County 2006).

In an action in which a former employee appealed a judgment of the district court granting summary judgment to her former employer and two supervisors on claims alleging violations of the Americans with Disabilities Act (ADA), Title VII, 42 U.S.C.S. § 1983, and R.C. 4112, the grant of summary judgment on the race discrimination claim was affirmed where (1) defendants claimed that the employee was terminated for failure of good behavior and discourteous treatment to the public after the employee committed many serious disciplinary offenses during the months prior to her removal; and (2) the employee had been unable to raise a genuine issue of material fact with respect to whether the proffered reason of her numerous disciplinary offenses was a pretext for unlawful reverse race discrimination. Myers v. Cuyahoga County, 182 Fed. Appx. 510, 2006 FED App. 0383N, 2006 U.S. App. LEXIS 13693 (6th Cir. Ohio), cert. denied, 549 U.S. 965, 127 S. Ct. 412, 166 L. Ed. 2d 292, 2006 U.S. LEXIS 7697 (U.S. 2006).

Summary judgment for an employer in employees' reverse race discrimination action was proper, as they failed to meet their burden under R.C. 4112.02(A) of showing a prima facie case of reverse race discrimination where there was no direct evidence that they were discharged from employment due to discrimination and there was no showing of a presumption of discrimination, as the employer allegedly terminated them due to a reduction-in-force, for which the employees failed to show additional direct, circumstantial, or statistical evidence of discrimination that others not in the protected class were treated more favorably; further, they failed to establish a claim for hostile work environment, which was notably not raised in their pleadings, sworn statements, or testimony, as the employer's conduct did not rise to the level necessary to establish that the employees were subjected to a racially hostile work environment. Hunt v. Trumbull Cmty. Action Program, 2006-Ohio-1698, 2006 Ohio App. LEXIS 1570 (Ohio Ct. App., Trumbull County 2006).

Police officer established reverse discrimination claims under 42 U.S.C.S. § 1981 and R.C. 4112 because a reasonable jury could conclude that his prolonged detail to gym duty and the filing of criminal and departmental charges were all based upon his race to alleviate public concern and thus were discriminatory. Lentz v. City of Cleveland, 410 F. Supp. 2d 673, 2006 U.S. Dist. LEXIS 1510 (N.D. Ohio 2006).

In an action in which a former employee appealed a judgment of the district court granting summary judgment to her former employer and two supervisors on claims alleging violations of the Americans with Disabilities Act (ADA), Title VII, 42 U.S.C.S. § 1983, and R.C. 4112, the grant of summary judgment on the race discrimination claim was affirmed where (1) defendants claimed that the employee was terminated for failure of good behavior and discourteous treatment to the public after the employee committed many serious disciplinary offenses during the months prior to her removal; and (2) the employee had been unable to raise a genuine issue of material fact with respect to whether the proffered reason of her numerous disciplinary offenses was a pretext for unlawful reverse race discrimination. Myers v. Cuyahoga County, 182 Fed. Appx. 510, 2006 FED App. 0383N, 2006 U.S. App. LEXIS 13693 (6th Cir. Ohio), cert. denied, 549 U.S. 965, 127 S. Ct. 412, 166 L. Ed. 2d 292, 2006 U.S. LEXIS 7697 (U.S. 2006).

Summary judgment for an employer in employees' reverse race discrimination action was proper, as they failed to meet their burden under R.C.

4112.02(A) of showing a prima facie case of reverse race discrimination where there was no direct evidence that they were discharged from employment due to discrimination and there was no showing of a presumption of discrimination, as the employer allegedly terminated them due to a reduction-in-force, for which the employees failed to show additional direct, circumstantial, or statistical evidence of discrimination that others not in the protected class were treated more favorably; further, they failed to establish a claim for hostile work environment, which was notably not raised in their pleadings, sworn statements, or testimony, as the employer's conduct did not rise to the level necessary to establish that the employees were subjected to a racially hostile work environment. Hunt v. Trumbull Cmty. Action Program, 2006-Ohio-1698, 2006 Ohio App. LEXIS 1570 (Ohio Ct. App., Trumbull County 2006).

Police officer established reverse discrimination claims under 42 U.S.C.S. § 1981 and R.C. 4112 because a reasonable jury could conclude that his prolonged detail to gym duty and the filing of criminal and departmental charges were all based upon his race to alleviate public concern and thus were discriminatory. Lentz v. City of Cleveland, 410 F. Supp. 2d 673, 2006 U.S. Dist. LEXIS 1510 (N.D. Ohio 2006).

Trial court properly granted summary judgment to an employer and a supervisor in a reverse racial discrimination claim by an employee under R.C. 4112.02(A), where the employee submitted supportive affidavits of co-workers which indicated that the employee was the only individual in the whole department who was disciplined for using a racial epithet against another co-worker; however, as the employee failed to show that he was treated disparately because he did not establish that he was singled out from co-workers of other races, he failed to make out a prima facie case of racial discrimination. Courie v. ALCOA, 2005-Ohio-3483, 162 Ohio App. 3d 133, 832 N.E.2d 1230, 2005 Ohio App. LEXIS 3232 (Ohio Ct. App., Cuyahoga County 2005).

Employee did not establish a claim of reverse race discrimination where he was the only employee reprimanded for use of a racially offensive nickname, despite the fact that other employees commonly used the same nickname: Courie v. ALCOA, 2005-Ohio-3483, 162 Ohio App. 3d 133, 832 N.E.2d 1230, 2005 Ohio App. LEXIS 3232 (Ohio Ct. App., Cuyahoga County 2005).



Trial court properly granted summary judgment to an employer and a supervisor in a terminated employee's reverse race discrimination claim, pursuant to R.C. 4112.02(A), where the employee failed to show, either through direct or indirect evidence, a prima facie case of such discrimination; there was no indirect showing of reverse race discrimination where the employee failed to establish background circumstances supporting the inference that the employer was the unusual employer who discriminated against white employees, and further, an African-American employee was treated in the same manner. Oleksiak v. John Carroll Univ., 2005-Ohio-886, 2005 Ohio App. LEXIS 912 (Ohio Ct. App., Cuyahoga County 2005).

The employee established a prima facie case of "reverse' racial discrimination based on his non-promotion and subsequent termination: Grooms v. Supporting Council of Preventative Effort, 2004-Ohio-2034, 157 Ohio App. 3d 55, 809 N.E.2d 42, 2004 Ohio App. LEXIS 1774 (Ohio Ct. App., Montgomery County 2004).

In the context of a reversed discrimination case brought under R.C. 4112.02(A), even assuming the former employee was able to make out a prima facie case of reverse discrimination, the employee could not show that similarly situated women employees were treated more favorably than he under equivalent circumstances; though the employee submitted affidavits from several female employees, none showed that women were not capable of operating all the presses, which the employee could not do. Kimble v. Intermetro Indus., 288 F. Supp. 2d 876, 2003 U.S. Dist. LEXIS 19151 (N.D. Ohio 2003).

The employee did not establish a prima facie case of reverse race discrimination or of retaliation: Ekstrom v. Cuyahoga County Cmty. College, 2002-Ohio-6228, 150 Ohio App. 3d 169, 779 N.E.2d 1067, 2002 Ohio App. LEXIS 6058 (Ohio Ct. App., Cuyahoga County 2002).

A white male failed to show that his employer was the unusual employer who discriminated against white males: Bellinger v. Weight Watchers Gourmet Food Co., 142 Ohio App. 3d 708, 756 N.E.2d 1251, 2001 Ohio App. LEXIS 2398 (Ohio Ct. App., Stark County 2001).

The employee was not required to exhaust her administrative remedies prior to filing an action under R.C. 4112.99 alleging reverse race and retaliatory discrimination. The employee failed to demonstrate a prima facie case on either claim: Carney v. Cleveland Heights - Univ. Heights City Sch. Dist., 143 Ohio App. 3d 415, 758 N.E.2d 234, 2001 Ohio App. LEXIS 2176 (Ohio Ct. App., Cuyahoga County), dismissed, 93 Ohio St. 3d 1427, 755 N.E.2d 351, 2001 Ohio LEXIS 2449 (Ohio 2001).

A white male did not establish a prima facie case of reverse employment discrimination where there was no evidence of background circumstances indicating a pattern of discrimination against white employees: Wagner v. Allied Steel & Tractor Co., 105 Ohio App. 3d 611, 664 N.E.2d 987, 1995 Ohio App. LEXIS 3159 (Ohio Ct. App., Cuyahoga County 1995).

To prove a prima facie case of reverse discrimination, an employee must show that the defendant is the unusual employer who discriminates against the majority and that other employees are treated more favorably: Bushman v. Mid-Ohio Regional Planning Comm'n, 107 Ohio App. 3d 654, 669 N.E.2d 305, 1995 Ohio App. LEXIS 5385 (Ohio Ct. App., Franklin County 1995).

**Seniority differences**

A black female employee did not show that similarly situated non-protected employees received preferential treatment. Employees are not similarly situated if they have different amounts of seniority: Homes-Naples v. Girard Bd. of Educ., 212 F. Supp. 2d 743, 2001 U.S. Dist. LEXIS 24597 (N.D. Ohio 2001), aff'd, Goodwin v. Barnhart, 195 F. Supp. 2d 1293, 2002 U.S. Dist. LEXIS 6515 (D. Kan. 2002).

**Settlement with supervisor**

Trial court did not err in denying an employer's motion for judgment notwithstanding the verdict pursuant to Civ.R. 50 in an employee's sexual harassment claim based on her supervisor's allegedly improper conduct towards her, as her settlement with the supervisor did not preclude a finding of liability on the part of the employer. The supervisor was subject to liability because he met the definition of an employer pursuant to R.C. 4112.01(A)(2), and as the supervisor and employer were jointly and severally liable pursuant to R.C. 4112.02(A) and 4112.99, the settlement of the supervisor did not relieve the employer from potential vicarious liability. Edwards v. Ohio Inst. of Cardiac Care, 2007-Ohio-1333, 170 Ohio App. 3d 619, 868 N.E.2d 721, 2007 Ohio App. LEXIS 1214 (Ohio Ct. App., Greene County 2007).

**Sexual harassment**

Summary judgment to a moving company owner and employee in an action by a former employee (FE), alleging sexual harassment and other claims as a result of the employer-owner's alleged actions, was error because the owner was within the statutory definition of "employer," he was a supervisor, the FE established his conduct that constituted sexual harassment, and he could be held individually liable. Retuerto v. Berea Moving Storage & Logistics, 2015-Ohio-2404, 38 N.E.3d 392, 2015 Ohio App. LEXIS 2448 (Ohio Ct. App., Cuyahoga County 2015).

Determination that an employee proved her quid pro quo sexual harassment claim pursuant to R.C. 4112.02(A) was not against the manifest weight of the evidence, as the employee provided examples in her testimony that evidenced a continuing course of conduct by her employer to have sexual relations with her, and that he ultimately terminated her employment position upon the realization that such relationship would never occur. West v. Curtis, 2009-Ohio-3050, 2009 Ohio App. LEXIS 2643 (Ohio Ct. App., Belmont County 2009).

Determining factor instruction was not erroneous in an employee's sexual harassment action based on a theory of quid pro quo under R.C. 4112.02(A), as the instruction was one of disparate treatment, which was based on the evidence in the matter. West v. Curtis, 2009-Ohio-3050, 2009 Ohio App. LEXIS 2643 (Ohio Ct. App., Belmont County 2009).

Jury verdict in favor of an employer and various individuals in claims by employees of sexual harassment involving a hostile work environment and constructive discharge was not against the manifest weight of the evidence, as the jury acted within its discretion in finding the employer's assertion that there was no inappropriate conduct or sexual innuendos in the workplace more credible than that of the employees; there was sufficient evidence to support the jury verdict. Conti v. Spitzer Auto World Amherst, 2008-Ohio-1320, 2008 Ohio App. LEXIS 1167 (Ohio Ct. App., Lorain County 2008).

Trial court improperly weighed the evidence in granting summary judgment for the defendants on claims of hostile environment sexual harassment: Stachura v. City of Toledo, 2008-Ohio-3581, 177 Ohio App. 3d 481, 895 N.E.2d 202, 2008 Ohio App. LEXIS 3017 (Ohio Ct. App., Lucas County 2008).

Insurer was required to defend a former city police chief in an employee's underlying R.C. 4112.02 sex discrimination action, alleging that the police chief, inter alia, used the department's computer system to display and distribute offensive and pornographic photographs and e-mails, because sexual harassment acts did not always fall outside the scope of employment in circumstances where an employee's ability to sexually harass another employee arose from authority or apparent authority vested in him by the employer. Ohio Gov't Risk Mgmt. Plan v. Harrison, 2007-Ohio-4948, 115 Ohio St. 3d 241, 874 N.E.2d 1155, 2007 Ohio LEXIS 2226 (Ohio 2007).

Insurer was required to defend a former city police chief in an employee's underlying R.C. 4112.02 sex discrimination action, alleging that the police chief, inter alia, used the department's computer system to display and distribute offensive and pornographic photographs and e-mails, because sexual harassment acts did not always fall outside the scope of employment in circumstances where an employee's ability to sexually harass another employee arose from authority or apparent authority vested in him by the employer. Ohio Gov't Risk Mgmt. Plan v. Harrison, 2007-Ohio-4948, 115 Ohio St. 3d 241, 874 N.E.2d 1155, 2007 Ohio LEXIS 2226 (Ohio 2007).

There was sufficient evidence to satisfy the "severe or pervasive" element of a claim or sexual harassment and to support the claims of retaliation and constructive discharge: Jordan v. Ohio Civ. Rights Comm'n, 2007-Ohio-3830, 173 Ohio App. 3d 87, 877 N.E.2d 693, 2007 Ohio App. LEXIS 3503 (Ohio Ct. App., Fayette County 2007).

Although the coworker's acts were odd and creepy and included staring at the plaintiff, they were not sufficiently severe or pervasive to create an objectively hostile working environment. The employer was not liable for the coworker's acts after it discharged him. Plaintiffs claims based on a common law duty to provide a safe work environment also did not survive summary judgment: Kilgore v. Ethicon Endo-Surgery, Inc., 2007-Ohio-2952, 172 Ohio App. 3d 387, 875 N.E.2d 113, 2007 Ohio App. LEXIS 2719 (Ohio Ct. App., Hamilton County 2007).

Employer was entitled to a jury instruction on its affirmative defense to a claim of hostile work environment sexual harassment by the plaintiffs supervisor; there was evidence that the employer had an effective policy against such harassment and that plaintiff failed to avail herself of the corrective measures. Because a supervisor who harasses an employee may be held personally liable for the harassment as a "co-employer," and thus is jointly liable with the employer, a release in favor of the supervisor does not extinguish the liability of the employer: Edwards v. Ohio Inst. of Cardiac Care, 2007-Ohio-1333, 170 Ohio App. 3d 619, 868 N.E.2d 721, 2007 Ohio App. LEXIS 1214 (Ohio Ct. App., Greene County 2007).

State university employee failed to meet his burden of showing that he was a victim of hostile work environment sexual harassment, in violation of R.C. 4112.02(A), where he failed to show that his discharge from employment was based on a discriminatory animus; there was no showing of any acts by a supervisor that were offensive or harassing. Swoger v. Wright State Univ., 2007-Ohio-2751, 2007 Ohio Misc. LEXIS 184 (Ohio Ct. Cl. 2007).

Employee claiming hostile work environment sexual harassment, under R.C. 4112.02(A), due to the conduct of a co-worker, did not show that her employer did not take immediate and appropriate action when the employee complained of the co-worker's conduct because (1) the employer told her to file a grievance with her union, (2) told the co-worker to minimize his contact with the employee, and (3) installed a curtain around the employee's work space to minimize contact between the employee and the co-worker. Brock v. Eaton Corp., 2006-Ohio-5580, 2006 Ohio App. LEXIS 5571 (Ohio Ct. App., Cuyahoga County 2006).

Employee did not show hostile work environment sexual harassment, under R.C. 4112.02(A), when a co-worker frequently walked by her work station and stared at her, because the co-worker's conduct was not severe or pervasive and did not unreasonably interfere with the employee's work performance. Brock v. Eaton Corp., 2006-Ohio-5580, 2006 Ohio App. LEXIS 5571 (Ohio Ct. App., Cuyahoga County 2006).

In an action in which a former employee filed suit against defendants, former employer, union, and a counselor for the employee assistance program, alleging claims of sexual harassment in violation of Title VII of the Civil Rights Act of 1964, 42 U.S.C.S. § 2000e et seq., and R.C. 4112.02, defendants were granted summary judgment on the employee's hostile work envirnonment claim where (1) the employee did not specify when the acts occurred and had not shown that any of them occurred within the relevant statutes of limitations; (2) the employee presented no evidence regarding the effect the incidents had on her work, other than to say that she sometimes laughed at them; and (3) the employee did not argue that the body shop harassment was unwelcome, nor did she present évidence that she indicated by her conduct that it was. Jaques v. Herbert, 447 F. Supp. 2d 858, 2006 U.S. Dist. LEXIS 59655 (N.D. Ohio 2006).

Summary judgment was error because the trial court effectively weighed the evidence and credibility of the employee's allegations and enforced its own factual conclusion regarding the evidence. The employee produced sufficient probative evidence to establish a genuine dispute over material facts in her quid pro quo sexual harassment case because she claimed that the third-assistant manager ordered her to show him her breasts, perform oral sex, and engage in sexual intercourse in the restaurant's office, or else he would have her fired and, believing her job to be in jeopardy, she complied. Scarvelli v. Melmont Holding Co., 2006-Ohio-4019, 2006 Ohio App. LEXIS 3986 (Ohio Ct. App., Lorain County 2006).

Trial court's grant of summary judgment to an employer in an employee's sexual harassment claim based on a hostile work environment was proper, as she failed to establish a prima facie case under either R.C. 4112.02(A) or under Title VII for purposes of a common law claim, in that many of the derogatory comments allegedly made by a co-worker were not based on the employee's personal knowledge but upon statements of others, the employee failed to report the incidents for a period of time and after doing so, she indicated that a separation in work environment from her co-worker was unnecessary; the employee was also offered a promotion which would have allowed her to work apart from the co-worker and she turned it down. Cerett v. Timken Co., 2006-Ohio-5892, 2006 Ohio App. LEXIS 5837 (Ohio Ct. App., Stark County 2006).

Pursuant to R.C. 2744.03(A)(6), the mayor and the city safety director were immune from a police dispatcher's intentional tort claims of invasion of privacy and intentional infliction of emotional distress, which arose from the former police chief's alleged sexual harassment of her. When the mayor and safety director learned of the dispatcher's allegations against the chief, they referred the matter to the state Bureau of Criminal Investigation for an investigation and accepted the chief's letter of retirement, and nothing in the record showed that they acted outside the scope of their employment or acted maliciously or in bad faith; moreover, the sexual harassment statute, R.C. 4112.02(A), did not expressly impose liability on them. Kohler v. City of Wapakoneta, 381 F. Supp. 2d 692, 2005 U.S. Dist. LEXIS 16671 (N.D. Ohio 2005).

Employer was not entitled to summary judgment on a claim of constructive discharge based on sexual harassment where the employer cooperated in sexual pranks by a nonemployee, including exposure of a penis or simulated penis: Radcliff v. Steen Elec., Inc., 2005-Ohio-5503, 164 Ohio App. 3d 161, 841 N.E.2d 794, 2005 Ohio App. LEXIS 4982 (Ohio Ct. App., Summit County 2005).

Employer was not entitled to summary judgment on the claims of sexual harassment, retaliatory discharge and negligent retention of the allegedly harassing co-worker. Among other remarks, the co-worker allegedly called the complainant a prostitute and offered her money for sex. Similar complaints concerning the co-worker put the employer on notice: Payton v. Receivables Outsourcing, Inc., 2005-Ohio-4978, 163 Ohio App. 3d 722, 840 N.E.2d 236, 2005 Ohio App. LEXIS 4515 (Ohio Ct. App., Cuyahoga County 2005).

When an employee complained that a co-employee engaged in sex acts in her presence, she could not show that her employer committed hostile work environment sexual harassment because there was no genuine issue that the employer responded immediately and reasonably to her complaint. Collins v. Flowers, 2005-Ohio-3797, 2005 Ohio App. LEXIS 3498 (Ohio Ct. App., Lorain County 2005).

Employer was liable for sexual harassment where it was made aware of the harassment by another employee, but did not take appropriate actions. McCombs v. Meijer, Inc., 395 F.3d 346, 2005 FED App. 0030P, 2005 U.S. App. LEXIS 949 (6th Cir. Ohio 2005).

Trial court properly granted summary judgment to the restaurant on the job applicant's claims against it for sex discrimination regarding the restaurant manager's alleged sexual advances and rubbing of her shoulders during her interview for a job with the restaurant, as the restaurant could not be held liable for the restaurant manager's alleged conduct, even if it occurred, because such conduct was a clear departure from his employment and there was no allegation that the restaurant facilitated or promoted the restaurant manager's alleged conduct. Paugh v. P.J. Snappers, 2005-Ohio-701, 2005 Ohio App. LEXIS 669 (Ohio Ct. App., Trumbull County 2005).

Police dispatcher's allegations of a sexually hostile work environment under the Equal Protection Clause; Title VII of the Civil Rights Act of 1964, 42 U.S.C.S. § 2000e et seq.; and R.C. 4112.02 failed on their merits because the conduct at issue was isolated and sporadic, not ongoing. Kohler v. City of Wapakoneta, 381 F. Supp. 2d 692, 2005 U.S. Dist. LEXIS 16671 (N.D. Ohio 2005).

Where a female jail corrections officer was allegedly told that she could not play on the jail's softball team because the team wanted to win, and that any sport a female plays is not a sport, the officer failed to show sexual harassment since the comment about winning was gender-neutral and another female was allowed to play softball and, while the comment concerning female sports was derogatory to females, it was no more than de minims harassment. Hendricks v. Office of the Clermont County Sheriff, 415 F. Supp. 2d 782, 2005 U.S. Dist. LEXIS 13017 (S.D. Ohio 2005).

Where a jail corrections officer alleged that a co-worker made sexual comments, propositioned the officer sexually, and grabbed the officer's genital area on the job, the officer sufficiently stated a prima facie case of sexual harassment which was more than de minimis, was severe and pervasive, and was offensive in the extreme, even to a person of average sensibilities. Hendricks v. Office of the Clermont County Sheriff, 415 F. Supp. 2d 782, 2005 U.S. Dist. LEXIS 13017 (S.D. Ohio 2005).

Employer was granted summary judgment with respect to the employee's claims of co-worker sexual harassment that were based on the four complaints that the supervisor admitted to receiving, as the human resources department's response to the complaints was reasonably calculated to end the alleged harassment where sexual harassment and hostile work environment training was recommended for employees. Thaman v. OhioHealth Corp., 2005 U.S. Dist. LEXIS 12872 (S.D. Ohio June 29, 2005).

Employee's allegations, taken as true when considering an employer's summary judgment motion, created a genuine issue of material fact as to whether she stated a claim for hostile work environment sexual harassment, under R.C. 4112.02(A), as she alleged an executive with her employer sent her inappropriate e-mails, made inappropriate sexual comments, and touched her inappropriately. Eakin v. Lakeland Glass Co., 2005-Ohio-266, 2005 Ohio App. LEXIS 231 (Ohio Ct. App., Lorain County 2005).

Trial court properly granted summary judgment to the restaurant on the job applicant's claims against it for quid pro quo sexual harassment or hostile environment sexual harassment, as she did not show that the restaurant manager ever indicated to her that she would be terminated unless she had sex with him or that the restaurant manager's alleged conduct of making advances at her or rubbing her shoulders at the restaurant qualified as sufficiently severe or pervasive to affect the terms, conditions, or privileges of her alleged employment; moreover, because she could not show that the restaurant had knowledge of the restaurant manager's alleged conduct toward her, it could not be said to have had a duty to protect her. Paugh v. P.J. Snappers, 2005-Ohio-701, 2005 Ohio App. LEXIS 669 (Ohio Ct. App., Trumbull County 2005).

Employee's quid pro quo sexual harassment claim failed because her supervisor's criticisms of her job performance, even if overlooked during the course of their affair, did not constitute a "tangible job detriment," and were only criticisms. Doe v. Marker, 2003-Ohio-6230, 2003 Ohio App. LEXIS 5584 (Ohio Ct. App., Trumbull County 2003).

Employee failed to establish a hostile work environment claim under R.C. 4112.02 because the employee failed to show that the incidents occurred because of her gender or that the environment resulted in tangible employment action or adversely affected her working conditions; defendant's motion for summary judgment was granted. Snyder v. Guardian Auto. Prods., 288 F. Supp. 2d 868, 2003 U.S. Dist. LEXIS 19153 (N.D. Ohio 2003).

Employer's motion for summary judgment on employee's Title VII harassment/hostile work environment claim was denied where the co-worker's offensive conduct went beyond staring at the employee and persisted despite warnings to stay away from her. Southerland v. Sycamore Cmty. Sch. Dist. Bd. of Educ., 277 F. Supp. 2d 807, 2003 U.S. Dist. LEXIS 14260 (S.D. Ohio 2003).

Evidence that company president told employee she could make more money if she accompanied him to a hotel, that another employee asked her out on dates 10 to 12 times, and that new president put his arm around her on several occasions was not enough to show sexual harassment in violation of R.C. 4112.02. Chamberlin v. Buick Youngstown Co., 2003-Ohio-3486, 2003 Ohio App. LEXIS 3185 (Ohio Ct. App., Mahoning County 2003).

Trial court erred in dismissing pursuant to Civ.R. 12(B)(6) for failure to state a claim upon which relief could be granted the employee's quid pro quo sexual harassment claim under R.C. 4112.02(A); the employee did not have to be an employee at the time of the harassment in order for the employee to state a quid pro quo sexual harassment claim. Kinnison v. Advance Stores Co., 2003-Ohio-3387, 2003 Ohio App. LEXIS 3055 (Ohio Ct. App., Richland County 2003).

Not all conduct in the employment context that can be construed as having sexual connotations can be classified as harassment in violation of R.C. 4112.02. Conduct that is offensive but is not severe or pervasive under the subjective and objective standard is not actionable: Vitatoe v. Lawrence Indus., 2003-Ohio-4187, 153 Ohio App. 3d 609, 795 N.E.2d 125, 2003 Ohio App. LEXIS 3727 (Ohio Ct. App., Cuyahoga County 2003).

For a single incident to constitute actionable sexual harassment, the conduct must be particularly egregious: Gliatta v. Tectum Inc., 211 F. Supp. 2d 992, 2002 U.S. Dist. LEXIS 14293 (S.D. Ohio 2002).

The employer was not entitled to summary judgment on a claim of hostile work environment sexual harassment: Hoschak v. Defiance County Eng'Rs, 218 F. Supp. 2d 917, 2002 U.S. Dist. LEXIS 17685 (N.D. Ohio 2002).

The defendants' conduct was not based on sex, but was a juvenile expression of provocation: Toth v. Ohio Dep't of Youth Servs., 113 Ohio Misc. 2d 1, 113 Misc. 2d 1, 754 N.E.2d 305, 2001 Ohio Misc. LEXIS 11 (Ohio Ct. Cl. 2001).

The employer was not entitled to summary judgment on all the claims of sex discrimination and sexual harassment: Starner v. Guardian Indus., 143 Ohio App. 3d 461, 758 N.E.2d 270, 2001 Ohio App. LEXIS 2437 (Ohio Ct. App., Franklin County 2001).

The employer was not entitled to summary judgment on claims of hostile environment sexual harassment, constructive discharge, and retaliation: Hogan v. Field Container Corp., 2001-Ohio-2204, 145 Ohio App. 3d 446, 763 N.E.2d 612, 2001 Ohio App. LEXIS 3575 (Ohio Ct. App., Marion County 2001).

A sexual harassment claim was sufficiently supported to withstand summary judgment: Bucher v. Sibcy Cline, Inc., 137 Ohio App. 3d 230, 738 N.E.2d 435, 2000 Ohio App. LEXIS 321 (Ohio Ct. App., Hamilton County 2000).

A plaintiff may establish a violation of R.C. 4112.02(A)'s prohibition of discrimination "because of . . . sex" by proving either of two types of sexual harassment: (1) "quid pro quo" harassment, i.e., harassment that is directly linked to the grant or denial of a tangible economic benefit, or (2) "hostile environment" harassment, i.e., harassment that, while not affecting economic benefits, has the purpose or effect of creating a hostile or abusive working environment. In order to establish a claim of hostile-environment sexual harassment, the plaintiff must show (1) that the harassment was unwelcome, (2) that the harassment was based on sex, (3) that the harassing conduct was sufficiently severe or pervasive to affect the "terms, conditions, or privileges of employment, or any matter directly or indirectly related to employment," and (4) that either (a) the harassment was committed by a supervisor, or (b) the employer, through its agents or supervisory personnel, knew or should have known of the harassment and failed to take immediate and appropriate corrective action. Harassing conduct that is simply abusive, with no sexual element, can support a claim for hostile-environment sexual harassment if it is directed at the plaintiff because of his or her sex. However, harassment is not automatically discrimination because of sex merely because the words used have sexual content or connotations. The social context in which particular behavior occurs and is experienced by its target is a relevant factor in judging the objective severity of harassment; however, sexual harassment that meets the statutory requirements is not excusable solely because it consists of conduct that is commonplace: Hampel v. Food Ingredients Specialties, 2000-Ohio-128, 89 Ohio St. 3d 169, 729 N.E.2d 726, 2000 Ohio LEXIS 1445 (Ohio 2000).

A manager's warning, without more, that an employee's clothing is inappropriate in the workplace is not sexual harassment: Courtney v. Landair Transp., Inc., 227 F.3d 559, 2000 FED App. 0285P, 2000 U.S. App. LEXIS 22135 (6th Cir. Ohio 2000).

Other than the bare fact of plaintiff's non-promotion to the position she desired, the evidence did not establish a pattern of inherently discriminatory conduct constituting a hostile work environment or an atmosphere of quid pro quo sexual harassment; a co-worker's romantic involvement with a supervisor does not by itself create a hostile work environment. Ohio has not recognized "sexual favoritism" as a form of sexual harassment: Asp v. Ohio Med. Transp., 1999 Ohio App. LEXIS 2991 (Ohio Ct. App., Franklin County June 29, 1999).

Summary judgment against a plaintiff claiming sexual harassment was error where there were questions of fact concerning the extent of unwelcome touching and comments and as to whether the harassment was by a "supervisor." Retaliation for reporting harassment may be found even where the employee suffers no decrease in salary or benefits: Peterson v. Buckeye Steel Casings, 133 Ohio App. 3d 715, 729 N.E.2d 813, 1999 Ohio App. LEXIS 2613 (Ohio Ct. App., Franklin County 1999).

The employer was not liable for sexual harassment by a nonsupervisory employee where it did not know of the employee's wrongful conduct and had no reason to suspect that he would engage in it: Steppe v. KMart Stores, 136 Ohio App. 3d 454, 737 N.E.2d 58, 1999 Ohio App. LEXIS 5449 (Ohio Ct. App., Cuyahoga County 1999).

Both the corporation and its owner and president could be held liable for sexual harassment by the president and other employees. The retaliation and constructive discharge claims were not subject to summary judgment: Wille v. Hunkar Lab., 132 Ohio App. 3d 92, 724 N.E.2d 492, 1998 Ohio App. LEXIS 6433 (Ohio Ct. App., Hamilton County 1998).

While the conduct and remarks of the employer, a plastic surgeon, concerning the plaintiff's and other women's appearance may have been in poor taste and sexually tinged, they did not constitute sexual harassment in view of the office atmosphere and the various surgeries performed by the doctor on the plaintiff: Takach v. American Med. Tech., 128 Ohio App. 3d 457, 715 N.E.2d 577, 1998 Ohio App. LEXIS 638 (Ohio Ct. App., Cuyahoga County 1998).

A hostile environment sexual harassment claim is not viable based solely on a supervisor's use of profanity where there is no speech or conduct of a sexual nature: Ciliotta v. Merrill Lynch, 121 Ohio App. 3d 324, 699 N.E.2d 997, 1997 Ohio App. LEXIS 3012 (Ohio Ct. App., Cuyahoga County 1997).

The employer was not entitled to summary judgment on a claim of quid pro quo sexual harassment: Harmon v. Belcan Eng'g Group, 119 Ohio App. 3d 435, 695 N.E.2d 783, 1997 Ohio App. LEXIS 1712 (Ohio Ct. App., Hamilton County 1997).

For a quid pro quo sexual harassment claim to be viable, the plaintiff must suffer an actual effect on the terms of employment, rather than mere threats: Schmitz v. Bob Evans Farms, 120 Ohio App. 3d 264, 697 N.E.2d 1037, 1997 Ohio App. LEXIS 1759 (Ohio Ct. App., Cuyahoga County 1997).

A genuine issue of material fact existed as to whether female municipal employee was subject to a hostile work environment based on her race and sex where there was some evidence that she was continuously propositioned and exposed to various unwelcome comments and touching: Washington v. City of Cleveland, 948 F. Supp. 1301, 1996 U.S. Dist. LEXIS 20586 (N.D. Ohio 1996).

Where employer did not know of employee's past history of sexual harassment he could not be held liable in hostile work environment statutory claim: Garcia v. ANR Freight Sys., 942 F. Supp. 351, 1996 U.S. Dist. LEXIS 19153 (N.D. Ohio 1996).

Appellant failed to set forth a prima facie case of hostile environment sexual harassment under R.C. 4112.02(A) because she failed to establish respondeat superior liability. Appellant was not excused from the duty to report incidents of sexual harassment as a condition of such liability by the fact that her alleged harassers were her supervisors where company policy specifically provided that such incidents were to be reported to the personnel manager: Thompson v. Western Auto Supply Co., 1996 Ohio App. LEXIS 3703 (Ohio Ct. App., Delaware County May 8, 1996).

In Ohio, a cause of action may be brought for wrongful discharge in violation of public policy based on sexual harassment/discrimination: Collins v. Rizkana, 1995 Ohio 135, 73 Ohio St. 3d 65, 652 N.E.2d 653, 1995 Ohio LEXIS 1762 (Ohio 1995).

Where plaintiffs bring a state claim for sexual harassment under Ohio R.C. Chapter 4112., their claims are subject to the same standards applied to federal harassment claims brought under Title VII: Blankenship v. Parke Care Ctrs., 913 F. Supp. 1045, 1995 U.S. Dist. LEXIS 20793 (S.D. Ohio 1995), aff'd, 123 F.3d 868, 1997 FED App. 0250P, 1997 U.S. App. LEXIS 22365 (6th Cir. Ohio 1997).

The mere fact that a fellow employee had not been previously accused of sexual harassment could not justify summary judgment for the defendants: Seiber v. Wilder, 1994 Ohio App. LEXIS 4609 (Ohio Ct. App., Greene County Oct. 12, 1994).

Coemployee supervisors may be sued in their individual capacity under R.C. 4112.02 for sexual harassment: Johnson v. University Surgical Group Assocs., 871 F. Supp. 979, 1994 U.S. Dist. LEXIS 18057 (S.D. Ohio 1994).

The following are the elements of a claim, brought under R.C. Chap. 4112. against an employer for "hostile work environment" sexual harassment: (1) the employee was a member of the protected class; (2) the employee was subjected to unwelcome harassment; (3) the harassment complained of was based upon sex; (4) the harassment had the purpose or effect of unreasonably interfering with the employee's work performance or creating an intimidating, hostile, or offensive work environment; and (5) the existence of respondeat superior liability: Delaney v. Skyline Lodge, 95 Ohio App. 3d 264, 642 N.E.2d 395, 1994 Ohio App. LEXIS 2110 (Ohio Ct. App., Hamilton County 1994), dismissed, 70 Ohio St. 3d 1465, 640 N.E.2d 527, 1994 Ohio LEXIS 2346 (Ohio 1994), cert. denied, 513 U.S. 1191, 115 S. Ct. 1253, 131 L. Ed. 2d 134, 1995 U.S. LEXIS 1691 (U.S. 1995).

Summary judgment for an employer is error in a sexual harassment case where there is evidence the employer was aware of prior harassment by an employee. A supervisor may be liable as an "employer" in such a case: Hart v. Justarr Corp., 98 Ohio App. 3d 673, 649 N.E.2d 316, 1994 Ohio App. LEXIS 5137 (Ohio Ct. App., Hamilton County 1994), dismissed, 71 Ohio St. 3d 1500, 646 N.E.2d 1125, 1995 Ohio LEXIS 769 (Ohio 1995).

Liability of the employer for "hostile environment" sexual harassment ordinarily presents a question of fact, and the employer is not insulated from liability merely because its supervisor's motivation was his own gratification: Davis v. Black, 70 Ohio App. 3d 359, 591 N.E.2d 11, 1991 Ohio App. LEXIS 5322 (Ohio Ct. App., Franklin County 1991).

A constructive discharge may be deemed to occur where a female employee is subjected to intolerable sexual harassment: Scandinavian Health Spa v. Ohio Civil Rights Comm'n, 64 Ohio App. 3d 480, 581 N.E.2d 1169, 1990 Ohio App. LEXIS 757 (Ohio Ct. App., Cuyahoga County 1990).

Revised Code Chapter 4112. was intended to add protections for victims of sexual harassment rather than reduce the protections and remedies for such conduct: Helmick v. Cincinnati Word Processing, Inc., 45 Ohio St. 3d 131, 543 N.E.2d 1212, 1989 Ohio LEXIS 205 (Ohio 1989).

**—Acts of third parties**

An employer may be liable for sexual harassment of an employee by a patient of the employer: Anania v. Daubenspeck Chiropractic, 129 Ohio App. 3d 516, 718 N.E.2d 480, 1998 Ohio App. LEXIS 3850 (Ohio Ct. App., Clark County 1998).

**—Based on sex**

Village's former emergency medical services captain could not prove that harassment was based on sex as every example of harassment recounted by the captain was suffered by all the fire department employees, both male and female. There was no evidence of differential treatment, that the harassment was directed at the captain because she was a woman, or that the harassment would not have occurred but for the fact that the captain was a woman; thus, her claim of sexual harassment was properly dismissed on summary judgment. Godsey-Marshall v. Vill. of Phillipsburg, 2010-Ohio-2266, 2010 Ohio App. LEXIS 1868 (Ohio Ct. App., Montgomery County 2010).

**—Employer liability**

No basis existed on which a village could be held liable for sexual harassment alleged by the village's emergency medical services captain as the record showed that the captain never complained about most of the harassment to the village council and that the village took immediate steps to end the problem when the captain did complain.. Godsey-Marshall v. Vill. of Phillipsburg, 2010-Ohio-2266, 2010 Ohio App. LEXIS 1868 (Ohio Ct. App., Montgomery County 2010).

**—Evidence insufficient**

Trial court did not err by finding that plaintiff did not satisfy her prima facie case for sexual harassment, because she demonstrated the romantic advances from her co-worker were unwelcomed but the employer investigated her complaints; and the employer's removal of him as plaintiff's trainer and his individual punishment halted the harassment. Khalia Ra v. Swagelok Mfg. Co., L.L.C., 2021-Ohio-1657, 2021 Ohio App. LEXIS 1621 (Ohio Ct. App., Cuyahoga County 2021).

Parents' claim of sexual harassment under the public accommodations statute was properly resolved by summary judgment against them, arising from allegations that a hockey facility and related coaches and individuals made sexual advances, flirted, and leered at the mother while her son was on a youth hockey league, as they did not establish unwelcome harassment and severe-or-pervasive harassing conduct. Pittman v. Parillo, 2017-Ohio-1477, 2017 Ohio App. LEXIS 1482 (Ohio Ct. App., Lucas County 2017).

Summary judgment was properly granted to a hockey facility and related coaches and individuals in parents' sexual harassment claim under the public accommodations statute, as there was no showing that the individuals did not satisfy their duty to take reasonable steps to ensure a safe and wholesome environment to the parents, whose son played in a youth hockey league, as well as to other patrons. Pittman v. Parillo, 2017-Ohio-1477, 2017 Ohio App. LEXIS 1482 (Ohio Ct. App., Lucas County 2017).

Coworker's conduct, while boorish and crass, was not outrageous or pervasive as to interfere with the manager's work performance, and his sexual harassment claim was without merit. Widmyer v. Steak 'n Shake Operations, Inc., 2014-Ohio-5413, 2014 Ohio App. LEXIS 5244 (Ohio Ct. App., Hamilton County 2014).

Employee failed to show that her supervisor's sexual harassment was sufficiently severe and pervasive as to alter the terms and conditions of her employment for purposes of her hostile work environment claim under R.C. 4112.02(A); she also failed to show that his conduct had a material impact on her job performance, as she managed to perform her job duties well despite his behavior towards her. Ballard v. Cmty. Support Network, 2010-Ohio-4742, 2010 Ohio App. LEXIS 4008 (Ohio Ct. App., Franklin County 2010).

Because New Jersey law applied, the former director could not assert an employment discrimination claim (sexual harassment) pursuant to R.C. 4112.02(A). Regardless, she would not have been able to establish her claim because she failed to show that the corporation's president made sexual advances or requests for sexual favors; failed to present any evidence demonstrating that her submission to the president's requests was an express or implied condition of employment with the corporation or that her refusal to submit to his requests resulted in a tangible job detriment; and her allegations of a hostile workplace simply did not rise to the level of severe and pervasive conduct necessary to support such a claim and she did not work for the corporation at the time. Hoyt v. Nationwide Mut. Ins. Co., 2005-Ohio-6367, 2005 Ohio App. LEXIS 5700 (Ohio Ct. App., Franklin County 2005).

**—Hostile work environment**

Former employee's sexual harassment claim did not fail as a matter of law as a jury could find that the evidence showed a hostile workplace, marked by sufficiently severe or pervasive sexualized conduct, including touching or slapping the employee's bottom, to violate the law and entitle plaintiff to a remedy, that the employer should have known of the harassing conditions, and that the employer failed to respond appropriately; and the court could not conclude that the department manager, a supervisor, and a co-worker could not be held jointly and severally liable along with their employer for their harassing conduct as they constituted "any person acting directly or indirectly in the interest of an employer." Jackson v. Northfield Park Assocs., LLC, 2020 Ohio Misc. LEXIS 46 (April 6, 2020).

Because the record did not demonstrate that the employee suffered a tangible employment detriment, the employer was entitled to assert the existence of a sexual harassment policy as an affirmative defense. The employee did not formally complain to management that she was harassed by the supervisor until one year after her employment was terminated, and she became aware that another employee had reported being sexually harassed, resulting in the supervisor's termination. Osborne v. Douglas, 2013-Ohio-5072, 2013 Ohio App. LEXIS 5271 (Ohio Ct. App., Lucas County 2013).

Trial court erred by granting summary judgment for the employers because genuine issues of material fact remained as to whether the conversations between the owner and the teenaged employee created a hostile work environment based upon sexual harassment. It could have been concluded that the owner's conduct toward the employee, while not frequent or physically threatening, was sufficiently severe to satisfy the claim because the 16-year-old employee was subjected to a thinly veiled solicitation for sex by a long-time, close family friend who was 32 years her senior. Ward v. Oakley, 2013-Ohio-4762, 2013 Ohio App. LEXIS 4968 (Ohio Ct. App., Butler County 2013).

Former government employee's claims of hostile work environment sexual harassment, as they related to the employee's supervisor failed as a matter of law, because the employee asserted in the employee's complaint that the employee was repeatedly harassed by the supervisor during the employee's employment, but, when the employee was asked in a deposition how the employee was harassed, the employee stated that the employee had a good working relationship with the supervisor. Moreover, the supervisor testified that although in an employment evaluation of the employee, the supervisor noted areas in which the employee needed to improve upon, the supervisor also recommended that the employee's title, classification, and salary were to be upgraded, and, soon thereafter, those changes were implemented. Peaks v. Supreme Court of Ohio, 2012-Ohio-6321, 2012 Ohio Misc. LEXIS 201 (Ohio Ct. Cl. 2012).

In showing that the doctor's treatment was unwelcome, disturbing and ongoing, the plaintiff established that it was sufficiently severe and pervasive to create a hostile work environment. The allegations that the doctor was ridiculed several times per week, that he found it hostile, abusive, threatening and humiliating, and that the physical contact, the touching and kissing on the forehead, were extremely humiliating, patently degrading and directed at him specifically because of his sex, provided enough evidence to create material questions of fact as to whether the doctor was subjected to a hostile work environment based on sex in violation of 42 U.S.C.S. § 2000e-2 and R.C. 4112.02. Bligh-Glover v. Rizzo, 2012 U.S. Dist. LEXIS 141512 (N.D. Ohio Sept. 30, 2012).

It was error to dismiss an employee's hostile-environment sexual harassment claim on summary judgment because fact issues existed as to whether (1) a supervisor mistreated the employee due to the employee's sex, (2) alleged harassing conduct was objectively severe or pervasive, (3) the employee subjectively felt the supervisor created a hostile and abusive working environment, and (4) the employee unreasonably failed to utilize the employer's complaint procedure and the employer failed to implement the employer's anti-harassment policy to reasonably correct harassment. Camp v. Star Leasing Co., 2012-Ohio-3650, 2012 Ohio App. LEXIS 3236 (Ohio Ct. App., Franklin County 2012).

Employees' claims of sexual harassment from a hostile work environment failed as a matter of law because they did not submit evidence of alleged harassment that was severe and pervasive to the point of altering the conditions of their work and creating an abusive or hostile environment. Many of the comments that the administrator allegedly made were not based upon sex; while the comments were sexually explicit and vulgar, they were offensive utterances, not discriminatory harassment specifically directed at women. Harter v. Chillicothe Long-Term Care, Inc., 2012-Ohio-2464, 2012 Ohio App. LEXIS 2153 (Ohio Ct. App., Ross County 2012).

Summary judgment for the former employer was appropriate as to the claim of a hostile work environment because the employee failed to prove that the employer was negligent in remedying the harassment after it was reported. McGraw v. Pilot Travel Ctrs., LLC, 2012-Ohio-1076, 2012 Ohio App. LEXIS 922 (Ohio Ct. App., Franklin County 2012).

Summary judgment for the former employer was appropriate as to the claim of a hostile work environment because the travel center's manager was not the employee's designated supervisor. Although he could direct actions when the employee was helping out on the travel center side, he could not significantly change her conditions of employment. McGraw v. Pilot Travel Ctrs., LLC, 2012-Ohio-1076, 2012 Ohio App. LEXIS 922 (Ohio Ct. App., Franklin County 2012).

Summary judgment for the pharmaceutical corporation on the hostile-work-environment claim was appropriate because the undisputed evidence showed that the allegedly harassing conduct occurred prior to the former employee's employment with the corporation. Brandner v. Innovex, Inc., 2012-Ohio-462, 970 N.E.2d 1067, 2012 Ohio App. LEXIS 441 (Ohio Ct. App., Hamilton County 2012).

Summary judgment was appropriate on the hostile-work-environment claim because the manager's boorish actions did not amount to severe or pervasive conduct that altered the terms and conditions of the employment and his conduct did not unreasonably interfere with the former employee's work performance such that her job became more difficult to perform. Brandner v. Innovex, Inc., 2012-Ohio-462, 970 N.E.2d 1067, 2012 Ohio App. LEXIS 441 (Ohio Ct. App., Hamilton County 2012).

Summary judgment was properly granted in favor of a former employer and coworkers in a hostile environment claim under R.C. 4112.02(A) because a former employee did not allege in a complaint or in a summary judgment response that he was a member of a protected class, was participating in a protected activity, or was protected by a clear public policy. Kimmel v. Lowe's, Inc., 2011-Ohio-28, 2011 Ohio App. LEXIS 12 (Ohio Ct. App., Montgomery County 2011).

Employee presented evidence of hostile-environment sexual harassment sufficient to overcome summary judgment as the employee's testimony showed that he was subjected to unwelcome sexual harassment by three female employees, that he reported the conduct to management, that no immediate and appropriate corrective action was taken, that he was made uncomfortable at work, and that he experienced stress and anxiety. Since the employee presented evidence of a tangible employment action, there were genuine issues of material fact in dispute that related to the affirmative defense to the hostile work environment claim asserted by the employer and a manager. Foster v. Ohio Bell Tel. Co., 2009-Ohio-6465, 2009 Ohio App. LEXIS 5412 (Ohio Ct. App., Cuyahoga County 2009).

Employee's claim of sexual harassment resulting in a hostile work environment was sustained because, inter alia, it was undisputed that the person who harassed the employee was the employee's supervisor. Tod v. Cincinnati State Tech. & Cmty. College, 2009-Ohio-3700, 2009 Ohio Misc. LEXIS 111 (Ohio Ct. Cl. 2009).

Employee's claim of sexual harassment resulting in a hostile work environment was sustained because, inter alia, the employee proved that throughout most or all of the employee's employment, the employee experienced frequent, and often intimidating, harassment by a supervisor, much of which occurred in the presence of the employee's co-workers, which, according to the employee, caused the employee great embarrassment and humiliation, and the supervisor's behavior impeded the employee's ability to carry out the employee's job responsibilities, as evidenced by the employee's efforts to report the supervisor to the employer's administrators, and, according to the employee, the harassment ultimately caused the employee to suffer a diagnosed anxiety disorder that was severe enough that the employee could no longer work. Tod v. Cincinnati State Tech. & Cmty. College, 2009-Ohio-3700, 2009 Ohio Misc. LEXIS 111 (Ohio Ct. Cl. 2009).

Employee's claim of sexual harassment resulting in a hostile work environment was sustained because, inter alia, the employee proved that the employee's harassment by a supervisor was based on sex, as the supervisor's harassment of the employee was permeated with gender-specific, derogatory remarks, and the supervisor did not similarly harass other employees, regardless of gender, so it was shown that the harassment would not have occurred but for the employee's gender. Tod v. Cincinnati State Tech. & Cmty. College, 2009-Ohio-3700, 2009 Ohio Misc. LEXIS 111 (Ohio Ct. Cl. 2009).

Employee's claim of sexual harassment resulting in a hostile work environment was sustained because, inter alia, the employee proved that a supervisor's harassing conduct was unwelcome, as the employee testified that the supervisor's conduct offended the employee, and there was no evidence to suggest that the employee solicited or invited such conduct, as the employee made numerous reports to the employee's employer's administrators informing the administrators of the supervisor's offensive conduct and requesting corrective action against the supervisor. Tod v. Cincinnati State Tech. & Cmty. College, 2009-Ohio-3700, 2009 Ohio Misc. LEXIS 111 (Ohio Ct. Cl. 2009).

Trial court did not abuse its discretion in finding that there was substantial evidence to support the "severe or pervasive" element of hostile environment sexual harassment as the evidence showed that the employee's period of employment included numerous and escalating instances of sexual harassment by the employer, involving the employer making sexually-oriented comments toward the employee, grabbing the employee from behind and pulling her against himself, and telling patients that the employee used to work in a strip club, all of which was unwelcome and constantly rebuffed by the employee. Jordan v. Ohio Civ. Rights Comm'n, 2007-Ohio-3830, 173 Ohio App. 3d 87, 877 N.E.2d 693, 2007 Ohio App. LEXIS 3503 (Ohio Ct. App., Fayette County 2007).

Where a former employee alleged that the employer's co-owner frequently rubbed his body against hers, frequently made inappropriate sexual comments, and stuck his tongue down her throat on one occasion, the hostile work environment claim survived summary judgment because the employee presented sufficient evidence indicating that the co-owner's conduct was both objectively and subjectively hostile since, inter alia, he allegedly made numerous offensive and intimidating remarks to her which made her feel uncomfortable. Hollar v. RJ Coffey Cup, LLC, 505 F. Supp. 2d 439, 2007 U.S. Dist. LEXIS 52630 (N.D. Ohio 2007).

Employee claiming hostile work environment sexual harassment, under R.C. 4112.02(A), due to the conduct of a co-worker, did not show that her employer did not take immediate and appropriate action when the employee complained of the co-worker's conduct because (1) the employer told her to file a grievance with her union, (2) told the co-worker to minimize his contact with the employee, and (3) installed a curtain around the employee's work space to minimize contact between the employee and the co-worker. Brock v. Eaton Corp., 2006-Ohio-5580, 2006 Ohio App. LEXIS 5571 (Ohio Ct. App., Cuyahoga County 2006).

Employee did not show hostile work environment sexual harassment, under R.C. 4112.02(A), when a co-worker frequently walked by her work station and stared at her, because the co-worker's conduct was not severe or pervasive and did not unreasonably interfere with the employee's work performance. Brock v. Eaton Corp., 2006-Ohio-5580, 2006 Ohio App. LEXIS 5571 (Ohio Ct. App., Cuyahoga County 2006).

In an action in which a former employee filed suit against defendants, former employer, union, and a counselor for the employee assistance program, alleging claims of sexual harassment in violation of Title VII of the Civil Rights Act of 1964, 42 U.S.C.S. § 2000e et seq., and R.C. 4112.02, defendants were granted summary judgment on the employee's hostile work envirnonment claim where (1) the employee did not specify when the acts occurred and had not shown that any of them occurred within the relevant statutes of limitations; (2) the employee presented no evidence regarding the effect the incidents had on her work, other than to say that she sometimes laughed at them; and (3) the employee did not argue that the body shop harassment was unwelcome, nor did she present evidence that she indicated by her conduct that it was. Jaques v. Herbert, 447 F. Supp. 2d 858, 2006 U.S. Dist. LEXIS 59655 (N.D. Ohio 2006).

It was error to grant summary judgment dismissing an employee's claim of constructive discharge based on hostile work environment sexual harassment, after a friend of her employers exposed or pretended to expose himself to her at her workplace, with the employers' collaboration, because she showed genuine fact issues as to (1) the unwelcome nature of the conduct, (2) whether the harassment was based on sex, (3) whether the conduct was sufficiently severe fo affect any matter relating to the employee's employment, and (4) whether the harassment was committed by her supervisors. Radcliff v. Steen Elec., Inc., 2005-Ohio-5503, 164 Ohio App. 3d 161, 841 N.E.2d 794, 2005 Ohio App. LEXIS 4982 (Ohio Ct. App., Summit County 2005).

It was error to grant summary judgment dismissing an employee's claim of constructive discharge based on hostile work environment sexual harassment, after a friend of her employers exposed or pretended to expose himself to her at her workplace, with the employers' collaboration, because (1) their collaboration showed a fact issue as to their discriminatory intent, (2) a reasonable employer would have foreseen that the employee would resign, after such conduct, (3) the employee showed the working conditions were so intolerable as to compel a reasonable person to resign, and (4) the employee was not required to allow the employers to apologize, where they participated in the conduct. Radcliff v. Steen Elec., Inc., 2005-Ohio-5503, 164 Ohio App. 3d 161, 841 N.E.2d 794, 2005 Ohio App. LEXIS 4982 (Ohio Ct. App., Summit County 2005).

Summary judgment was properly entered for an employer on a minor employee's claim for hostile work environment sexual harassment as the employer exercised reasonable care in preventing sexual harassment at the dealership via its training and reporting policies; the minor employee unreasonably refused to take corrective measures by not reporting his complaints as per the handbook prior to his walk-off and thereafter declining, via his mother, a lateral transfer opportunity. Jackson v. Saturn of Chapel Hill, Inc., 2005-Ohio-5302, 2005 Ohio App. LEXIS 4821 (Ohio Ct. App., Stark County 2005).

Trial court erred in granting summary judgment to an employer in an employee's sexual harassment claim under R.C. 4112.02(A), based on her claim of a hostile work environment arising from several acts by a co-employee and most notably, one such act where he called the employee a "strawberry" and offered her money for sex which prompted her to leave her employment that day, for which she was fired upon her return; she met her burden of proof of showing all of the prongs necessary to establish her claim where she showed that she was harassed, it was based on sex, it was sufficiently severe or pervasive, and the employer should have known about it and failed to take corrective action. Payton v. Receivables Outsourcing, Inc., 2005-Ohio-4978, 163 Ohio App. 3d 722, 840 N.E.2d 236, 2005 Ohio App. LEXIS 4515 (Ohio Ct. App., Cuyahoga County 2005).

When an employee complained that a co-employee engaged in sex acts in her presence, she could not show that her employer committed hostile work environment sexual harassment because there was no genuine issue that the employer responded immediately and reasonably to her complaint. Collins v. Flowers, 2005-Ohio-3797, 2005 Ohio App. LEXIS 3498 (Ohio Ct. App., Lorain County 2005).

Where a female jail corrections officer was allegedly told that she could not play on the jail's softball team because the team wanted to win, and that any sport a female plays is not a sport, the officer failed to show sexual harassment since the comment about winning was gender-neutral and another female was allowed to play softball and, while the comment concerning female sports was derogatory to females, it was no more than de minimis harassment. Hendricks v. Office of the Clermont County Sheriff, 415 F. Supp. 2d 782, 2005 U.S. Dist. LEXIS 13017 (S.D. Ohio 2005).

Where a jail corrections officer reported sexual harassment by a co-worker, but the jail allegedly took no corrective action until the officer filed criminal charges against the co-worker for assault and the jail's investigation of the incident resulted in the resignation of the co-worker, the jail's investigation of the assault did not preclude liability of the jail for failing to remediate the prior harassing conduct. Hendricks v. Office of the Clermont County Sheriff, 415 F. Supp. 2d 782, 2005 U.S. Dist. LEXIS 13017 (S.D. Ohio 2005).

Where a jail corrections officer alleged that a co-worker made sexual comments, propositioned the officer sexually, and grabbed the officer's genital area on the job, the officer Sufficiently stated a prima facie case of sexual harassment which was more than de minimis, was severe and pervasive, and was offensive in the extreme, even to a person of average sensibilities. Hendricks v. Office of the Clermont County Sheriff, 415 F. Supp. 2d 782, 2005 U.S. Dist. LEXIS 13017 (S.D. Ohio 2005).

In an action in which a former employee filed suit against her former employer alleging claims of sexual harassment hostile work environment in violation of Title VII of the Civil Rights Act of 1964 and R.C. 4112.02, the employer was granted summary judgment with respect to the employee's claims of co-worker sexual harassment that were based on the four complaints that the supervisor admitted to receiving; the human resources department's response to the complaints was reasonably calculated to end the alleged harassment where sexual harassment and hostile work environment training was recommended for employees. Thaman v. OhioHealth Corp., 2005 U.S. Dist. LEXIS 12872 (S.D. Ohio June 29, 2005).

Employee's former supervisor was liable for hostile work environment sexual harassment where the supervisor, among other things, repeatedly tried to kiss the employee, threatened her employment when she refused to go out with him, grabbed her breast, physically accosted her, harassed her on the telephone, and interfered with her relationship with her husband. The supervisor's conduct was unwelcome, based on sex, severe, and pervasive. Boggs v. Fernald, 2005 U.S. Dist. LEXIS 9876 (S.D. Ohio May 24, 2005).

**—Immunity**

R.C. ch. 2744 immunity did not apply to the employee's allegations of sexual harassment under the Equal Protection Clause, Title VII, and R.C. 4112.02 against the city, former police chief, mayor, and safety director because her allegations related to the conditions of her employment and therefore were exempt from municipal immunity under R.C. 2744.09(C). Kohler v. City of Wapakoneta, 381 F. Supp. 2d 692, 2005 U.S. Dist. LEXIS 16671 (N.D. Ohio 2005).

**—Intentional infliction of emotional distress**

It was error to grant summary judgment dismissing an employee's claim against her employers of intentional infliction of emotional distress, after a friend of her employers exposed or pretended to expose himself to her at her workplace, with the employers' collaboration, because (1) the employers knew about the conduct their friend intended to engage in, (2) it was not unreasonable to believe they knew it would involve sexual overtones, (3) they knew the employee would witness the conduct, (4) as a matter of law, actual or simulated self-exposure in the workplace was extreme and outrageous conduct, (5) the employers' sanctioning of this behavior was intolerable in a civilized community, and (6) the employee showed that she suffered mental anguish as a result of the conduct. Radcliff v. Steen Elec., Inc., 2005-Ohio-5503, 164 Ohio App. 3d 161, 841 N.E.2d 794, 2005 Ohio App. LEXIS 4982 (Ohio Ct. App., Summit County 2005).

Sexual harassment on the job is undoubtedly an intentional infliction of emotional distress. Such claims are subject to the statute of limitations for R.C. 4112.99: Johnson v. Cox, 1997 Ohio App. LEXIS 1346 (Ohio Ct. App., Adams County Mar. 28, 1997).

**—Minor**

Sexual relations between an employee and a supervisor do not constitute sexual harassment per se, even if the employee is a minor. There must still be evidence of damages: Bock v. Hamilton County Bd. of Park Comm'rs, 132 Ohio App. 3d 726, 726 N.E.2d 509, 1999 Ohio App. LEXIS 877 (Ohio Ct. App., Hamilton County), dismissed, 86 Ohio St. 3d 1415, 711 N.E.2d 1010, 1999 Ohio LEXIS 2212 (Ohio 1999).

**—Plaintiff's behavior**

Evidence that plaintiff discussed nude photographs of herself at work, danced on tables at parties and dressed provocatively was relevant as to whether any sexual advances by the employer were "unwelcome": Drawl v. Cleveland Orthopedic Ctr., 107 Ohio App. 3d 272, 668 N.E.2d 924, 1995 Ohio App. LEXIS 4896 (Ohio Ct. App., Lake County 1995).

**—Quid pro quo**

Plaintiff's complaint failed to state a claim of sex discrimination by a university based on "quid pro quo" harassment; even if her feet allegedly being touched by a department chairman could be construed as an unwelcome advance, the complaint did not support an inference that the chairman conditioned a job benefit on plaintiff's submission to the advance. Sheppard v. Ohio Bd. of Regents, 2016-Ohio-3477, 2016 Ohio Misc. LEXIS 67 (Ohio Ct. Cl. 2016).

Record did not contain evidence to support the temporary worker's claim of quid pro quo harassment because the record contained no admissible evidence to demonstrate that the worker suffered an adverse employment action that was legally sufficient to deprive her of a tangible employment benefit; even assuming that the supervisor made inappropriate and/or demeaning comments to or about the worker, the record did not establish a causal connection between such actions and the worker's ability or inability to obtain permanent employment at the employer; and the record did not show that the worker's sudden decision to quit working at the employer was based on anything other than her own subjective feelings. Gorajewski v. Douglas, 2014-Ohio-1296, 2014 Ohio App. LEXIS 1287 (Ohio Ct. App., Lucas County 2014).

Former employee did not establish a claim of quid pro quo sexual harassment because, in spite of her allegation that she was fired because the supervisor "set her up" in retaliation for not succumbing to his advances, there was no evidence that the employer was made aware of the supervisor's behavior, nor was there evidence that the employee was terminated for any reason other than her admitted decision to state that she was on time for work on two separate occasions when she was actually late. Osborne v. Douglas, 2013-Ohio-5072, 2013 Ohio App. LEXIS 5271 (Ohio Ct. App., Lucas County 2013).

Employee presented evidence of quid pro quo sexual harassment sufficient to withstand summary judgment by proof that a manager had a significant influence on the decision not to offer the employee the sales coach position as seen by the fact that the manager's job duties included staffing the position the employee sought, that she evaluated the candidates she interviewed, and that the employee was told that the manager was deciding who would be hired. An issue of fact existed as to whether there was a causal nexus between the employee's refusal of the manager's alleged advances and his failure to be offered the sales coach position, which the employee sought. Foster v. Ohio Bell Tel. Co., 2009-Ohio-6465, 2009 Ohio App. LEXIS 5412 (Ohio Ct. App., Cuyahoga County 2009).

Where a former employee alleged that the employer's co-owner frequently rubbed his body against hers, frequently made inappropriate sexual comments, and stuck his tongue down her throat on one occasion, the quid pro quo sexual harassment claim survived summary judgment because a reasonable jury could find that the employee suffered a tangible job detriment since she had no choice but to resign. Hollar v. RJ Coffey Cup, LLC, 505 F. Supp. 2d 439, 2007 U.S. Dist. LEXIS 52630 (N.D. Ohio 2007).

In an action in which a former employee filed suit against defendants, former employer, union, and a counselor for the employee assistance program, alleging claims of sexual harassment in violation of Title VII of the Civil Rights Act of 1964, 42 U.S.C.S. § 2000e et seq., and R.C. 4112.02, defendants were granted summary judgment on the employee's quid pro quo sexual harassment claim where (1) the employee could not show that the counselor's advances were unwelcome; (2) the record contained some evidence showing that the employee solicited or invited at least some of the counselor's advances; and (3) the employee could not show that her submission to the counselor's advances was a condition for receiving job benefits or the ending of her relationship with the counselor led to company management's failure to reinstate her. Jaques v. Herbert, 447 F. Supp. 2d 858, 2006 U.S. Dist. LEXIS 59655 (N.D. Ohio 2006).

Summary judgment was error because the trial court effectively weighed the evidence and credibility of the employee's allegations and enforced its own factual conclusion regarding the evidence. The employee produced sufficient probative evidence to establish a genuine dispute over material facts in her quid pro quo sexual harassment case because she claimed that the third-assistant manager ordered her to show him her breasts, perform oral sex, and engage in sexual intercourse in the restaurant's office, or else he would have her fired and, believing her job to be in jeopardy, she complied. Scarvelli v. Melmont Holding Co., 2006-Ohio-4019, 2006 Ohio App. LEXIS 3986 (Ohio Ct. App., Lorain County 2006).

Summary judgment was properly entered for an employer on a minor employee's claim for quid pro quo sexual harassment as even if another employee's actions towards the minor employee were considered gender-based sexual advances or requests, submission thereto was not a condition for benefits; the minor employee's refusal did not lead to a tangible job detriment as he was not disciplined, demoted, or given a cut in pay or hours. The other employee's threat that if the minor employee ever opened his mouth about his treatment, the other employee would "take him behind the garbage bin" in the parking lot did not reach the level of a condition for benefits or an indication of a tangible job detriment on the employer's part. Jackson v. Saturn of Chapel Hill, Inc., 2005-Ohio-5302, 2005 Ohio App. LEXIS 4821 (Ohio Ct. App., Stark County 2005).

When an employee complained that a co-employee engaged in sex acts in her presence, she could not show that her employer committed quid pro quo sexual harassment because the co-employee had no supervisory authority over her, nor did she allege that her actual supervisor engaged in any such acts. Collins v. Flowers, 2005-Ohio-3797, 2005 Ohio App. LEXIS 3498 (Ohio Ct. App., Lorain County 2005).

**—Refusal to interact**

A supervisor's refusal to interact with a worker he supervises could conceivably in itself constitute sexual harassment under a hostile work environment theory: Cechowski v. Goodwill Indus., 1997 Ohio App. LEXIS 2032 (Ohio Ct. App., Summit County May 14, 1997).

**—Same-sex**

Summary judgment was properly granted to a supervisor and an employer in a former employee's sexual harassment claim, as there was insufficient evidence to establish the supervisor's conduct was directed toward the employee because of his sex; the trial court found that there was no evidence to establish the supervisor was homosexual, that his acts were motivated by sexual desire for the employee, or that the supervisor was hostile to the presence of men in the workplace. Persichillo v. Motor Carrier Serv., 2004-Ohio-1042, 156 Ohio App. 3d 383, 806 N.E.2d 181, 2004 Ohio App. LEXIS 923 (Ohio Ct. App., Wood County 2004).

Same-gender sexual harassment is actionable under R.C. 4112.02. A corporate officer with knowledge of the harassment may be individually liable: Tarver v. Calex Corp., 125 Ohio App. 3d 468, 708 N.E.2d 1041, 1998 Ohio App. LEXIS 591 (Ohio Ct. App., Mahoning County 1998).

**—Severe and pervasive**

Triable issue of fact existed as to whether the harassment was severe or pervasive where the employee presented the court with numerous sexual comments, remarks, and at least one invitation the supervisor made directly to the employee or in the employee's presence over the course of at least four months. Rinehart v. PNC Bank, N.A., 219 F. Supp. 3d 682, 2016 U.S. Dist. LEXIS 155577 (S.D. Ohio 2016).

In an action for sexual harassment, the jury's finding that the employer's harassing behavior was sufficiently severe or pervasive to affect the employee's employment was not against the manifest weight of the evidence; the employee's testimony was consistent with several witnesses affirming that the employer frequently engaged in a variety of conduct ranging from inappropriate discussions to groping women. Roberts v. Mike's Trucking, Ltd., 2014-Ohio-766, 9 N.E.3d 483, 2014 Ohio App. LEXIS 751 (Ohio Ct. App., Madison County 2014), aff'd, 2014 Ohio Misc. LEXIS 7977 (Ohio C.P. May 27, 2014).

Nurse failed to prove her claim for hostile work environment sexual harassment because she failed to demonstrate that the director's harassment of her was sufficiently severe and pervasive as to alter the terms and conditions of her employment. The nurse described several ways in which the director harassed her early in her tenure with the company, but she testified that the director's behavior did not impede her from performing her job well during that time; there was no evidence that the nurse suffered psychological harm as a result of the harassment. Ballard v. Cmty. Support Network, 2010-Ohio-200, 2010 Ohio Misc. LEXIS 1 (Ohio Ct. Cl.), aff'd, 2010-Ohio-4742, 2010 Ohio App. LEXIS 4008 (Ohio Ct. App., Franklin County 2010).

Sexual harassment claim filed by village's former emergency medical services captain was properly dismissed on summary judgment as the harassment was not severe or pervasive as the harassment recounted by the captain was infrequent, relatively moderate, not physically threatening or humiliating, and did not interfere with the captain's work performance. Godsey-Marshall v. Vill. of Phillipsburg, 2010-Ohio-2266, 2010 Ohio App. LEXIS 1868 (Ohio Ct. App., Montgomery County 2010).

**—Sexual remarks**

Summary judgment was properly granted to a former employer in a sexual harassment case under R.C. 4112.02(A) based on a hostile work environment because, although remarks made by co-workers had sexual content or connotations, they were simply expressions of personal animosity or juvenile provocation. The comments were not harassment motivated by gender. Bowman v. AK Steel Corp., 2010-Ohio-6433, 2010 Ohio App. LEXIS 5403 (Ohio Ct. App., Butler County 2010).

**—Termination for**

Summary judgment was properly granted, dismissing an employee's gender discrimination claim arising out of his termination for sexual harassment, because the employee failed to show that he and his female coworker were similarly situated. The evidence showed that the employee had committed past acts of sexual harassment and, unlike the coworker, was on notice that there was a problem with his conduct. Rainieri v. Land O'Lakes, Inc., 2006-Ohio-1791, 2006 Ohio App. LEXIS 1630 (Ohio Ct. App., Portage County 2006).

**—Violation of public policy**

In an action in which a former employee filed suit against her former employer alleging violations of Ohio's public policy based on Title VII of the Civil Rights Act of 1964 and R.C. 4112.02, the employer was granted summary judgment where (1) there was no need to recognize an action for wrongful discharge in violation of public policy when a statute existed that adequately protected that public policy; and (2) the court could not conclude that the public policy of Ohio would be in jeopardy if the employee's Greeley claim was not recognized. Thaman v. OhioHealth Corp., 2005 U.S. Dist. LEXIS 12872 (S.D. Ohio June 29, 2005).

**Sexual orientation**

Even if there was a legal basis for a sexual orientation discrimination under Ohio law, the employee did not allege facts that suggested that she suffered adverse employment action because of her sexual orientation. In her deposition, she agreed that her manager (who was her father) was aware of her sexual orientation at the time that she was hired, was accepting of her lifestyle, and had never expressed displeasure that she was married to a woman. Nance v. Lima Auto Mall, Inc., 2020-Ohio-3419, 2020 Ohio App. LEXIS 2352 (Ohio Ct. App., Allen County 2020).

Trial court did not err by dismissing the student's claims for sex discrimination, sexual harassment, and retaliation where, under R.C. 4112.02(A), the term "sex" did not encompass sexual orientation; the student could not show that public policy prohibited discrimination based on sexual orientation, and she failed to state a claim upon which relief could be granted. Burns v. Ohio State Univ. College of Veterinary Med., 2014-Ohio-1190, 2014 Ohio App. LEXIS 1101 (Ohio Ct. App., Franklin County 2014).

An allegation of discrimination because of sexual orientation alone is not actionable under R.C. 4112.02(A). Inskeep v. Western Reserve Transit Auth., 2013-Ohio-897, 2013 Ohio App. LEXIS 798 (Ohio Ct. App., Mahoning County 2013).

In an action in which a former employee appealed a judgment of the district court granting summary judgment to her former employer and two supervisors on claims alleging violations of the Americans with Disabilities Act (ADA), Title VII, 42 U.S.C.S. § 1983, and R.C. 4112, the grant of summary judgment on the sex discrimination claim was affirmed where (1) the employee argued that the supervisors sought her termination because she did not conform to their sex and gender stereotypes; (2) defendants claimed that the employee was terminated for failure of good behavior and discourteous treatment to the public after the employee committed many serious disciplinary offenses during the months prior to her removal; and (3) the employee had been unable to show either that the employer's articulated reason of her disciplinary offenses had no basis in fact, that the disciplinary offenses did not actually motivate the employer's decision to discharge her, or that the disciplinary infractions were insufficient to motivate her discharge. Myers v. Cuyahoga County, 182 Fed. Appx. 510, 2006 FED App. 0383N, 2006 U.S. App. LEXIS 13693 (6th Cir. Ohio), cert. denied, 549 U.S. 965, 127 S. Ct. 412, 166 L. Ed. 2d 292, 2006 U.S. LEXIS 7697 (U.S. 2006).

Although same-sex harassment may be actionable under R.C. 4112.02 to the extent claimants can demonstrate that the harassment occurred because of their sex, the prohibitions of R.C. 4112.02(A) do not extend to sexual orientation; thus plaintiff's claim was properly dismissed where nothing in the record established a connection between her sex and any alleged harassment that occurred during her employment: Cooke v. SGS Tool Co., 2000 Ohio App. LEXIS 1784 (Ohio Ct. App., Summit County Apr. 26, 2000).

Plaintiff did not prove that his coworkers violated R.C. 4112.02 by alleging that he had AIDS. R.C. 4112.02 does not include sexual orientation: Retterer v. Whirlpool Corp., 111 Ohio App. 3d 847, 677 N.E.2d 417, 1996 Ohio App. LEXIS 3646 (Ohio Ct. App., Marion County 1996).

R.C. 4112.02 does not include sexual orientation: Greenwood v. Taft, Stettinius & Hollister, 105 Ohio App. 3d 295, 663 N.E.2d 1030, 1995 Ohio App. LEXIS 3932 (Ohio Ct. App., Hamilton County 1995).

**Sham lawsuit**

Plaintiff was entitled to summary judgment on the defendant's counterclaim for violation of Ohio's antidiscrimination statute, R.C. 4112.02, because the plaintiff's action against the defendant on a loan agreement and promissory note was protected by the First Amendment right to petition as it was not a sham lawsuit. Friel v. Swartz, 2012-Ohio-2405, 2012 Ohio App. LEXIS 2117 (Ohio Ct. App., Franklin County 2012).

**State employees**

Where a corrections officer's racial and sexual discrimination claim, based on her termination, was brought against a correctional institution and alleged a claim under R.C. 4112.02(A) and 4112.99, the two-year limitations period of R.C. 2743.16(A) was applicable and barred the complaint. As R.C. 4112.99 was not amended to provide that the State had "consented to be sued" for such a claim prior to the enactment of the Court of Claims Act, for purposes of R.C. 2743.02, the two-year period was applicable. McCoy v. Toledo Corr. Inst., 2005-Ohio-1848, 2005 Ohio App. LEXIS 1753 (Ohio Ct. App., Franklin County 2005).

**Statute of limitations**

Because an employee requested an accommodation in June 2016, and that request for accommodation was effectively denied at that time as she was placed on disability leave rather than accommodated, her failure to accommodate claim was barred by the statute of limitations. Toland v. Dep't of Mental Health & Addiction Servs., 2020-Ohio-3864, 2020 Ohio Misc. LEXIS 116 (Ohio Ct. Cl. 2020).

Former employee's discrimination complaint, as amended, was not timely filed under R.C. 2743.16 because, construing the evidence most strongly in the employee's favor, the only reasonable conclusion was that the employee was unequivocally informed of the termination of the employee's employment by correspondence, and that the employee was excluded from the participation in, denied the benefits of, or was subjected to discrimination or activity when the employee was informed of the employee's termination. Stevens v. Ohio Dep't of Mental Health, 2012-Ohio-6354, 2012 Ohio Misc. LEXIS 231 (Ohio Ct. Cl. 2012), aff'd, 2013-Ohio-3014, 2013 Ohio App. LEXIS 3059 (Ohio Ct. App., Franklin County 2013).

Plaintiff alleged that the discriminatory pay disparity between the plaintiff and similarly situated white employees continued throughout his employment with the defendants and as the pay raises he received were based on percentages of his original salary, the raise did not mitigate the discriminatory rate; any standardized raise he received was based on a salary that was $5,000 lower than a similarly situated white employee would have been paid. That was exactly the kind of situation that Congress intended to protect under the Fair Pay Act, 42 U.S.C.S. 2000e-5(e), and thus, the plaintiff's claim was not time-barred under either Title VII of the Civil Rights Act of 1964 or Ohio's wage discrimination statute, R.C. 4112.01 et seq. Greenleaf v. DTG Operations, Inc., 2011 U.S. Dist. LEXIS 24808 (S.D. Ohio Mar. 11, 2011).

Plaintiff did not support his claim of a "glass ceiling" with statistical evidence detailing relative promotional rates and he did not provide evidence that other African-American employees had experiences that were similar to his; accordingly, the plaintiff was not able to establish a claim of systemic continuing violations. While the "other practice" language of the Fair Pay Act, Pub. L. No. 111-2 § 3(A), 123 Stat. 5 extended beyond the act of determining pay, it did not encompass the failure to promote, retaliation, or termination claims at issue in the instant case, and the plaintiff was unable to establish that his claims for race discrimination and retaliation were tolled under the serial continuing violations theory or the systemic continuing violations theory, or encompassed by the "other practice" language of the Fair Pay Act; therefore, any discriminatory acts that occurred outside of the 300-day period were time-barred under Title VII, 42 U.S.C.S. § 2000e-5 and any acts that occurred outside of the six-year period were time-barred under the R.C. 4112.02. Greenleaf v. DTG Operations, Inc., 2011 U.S. Dist. LEXIS 24808 (S.D. Ohio Mar. 11, 2011).

Pursuant to R.C. 4112.051(A)(2), any action brought under R.C. 4112.02(H) must be brought within one year of the alleged discriminatory activity. The appraisal of the plaintiff's home occurred in March, 2006, the plaintiff closed on the mortgage loan in April, 2006, and the plaintiff's claim, filed February 20, 2008, was filed too late; therefore, the plaintiff's claims under 42 U.S.C.S. §§ 1981 and 1982 against the defendant were time-barred. Price v. Taylor, 2011 U.S. Dist. LEXIS 97378 (N.D. Ohio Aug. 30, 2011).

Claims asserted by a Department of Correction and Rehabilitation employee of racial discrimination under R.C. 4112.02(A) which fell outside the two-year limitations period of R.C. 2743.16(A) were barred. Campbell v. Dep't of Rehab. & Corr., 2011-Ohio-3897, 2011 Ohio Misc. LEXIS 281 (Ohio Ct. Cl. 2011).

Former employee failed to show that the six-year statute of limitation in R.C. 2305.07, which was applicable to claims brought under R.C. 4112.99 for violations of R.C. ch. 4112.02(I), governed the employee's common law claims of wrongful discharge and retaliation against two former supervisors. Therefore, the four-year statute of limitations under R.C. 2305.09(D), which provided the general limitation period for tort actions not specifically covered by other statutory sections, applied to the employee's common law claims. Davenport v. Big Bros. & Big Sisters of the Greater Miami Valley, Inc., 2010-Ohio-2503, 2010 Ohio App. LEXIS 2046 (Ohio Ct. App., Montgomery County 2010).

Former county employee's age discrimination claims were barred by the limitations periods of 29 U.S.C.S. § 626(d)(1)(B) and R.C. 4112.02(N) because the employee never asserted a claim that a six-year limitation period applied under R.C. 4112.14 and there was an insufficient basis for tolling of the limitations period. Wood v. Summit County Fiscal Office, 377 Fed. Appx. 512, 2010 FED App. 0301N, 2010 U.S. App. LEXIS 9999 (6th Cir. Ohio 2010).

Former employee's age discrimination claim under R.C. 4112.02 was not timely filed pursuant to R.C. 2743.16 and R.C. 4112.02(N) because the employee filed the employee's complaint more than 180 days after the termination of the employee from the employee's employment. Moore v. Dep't of Rehab. & Corr., 2010-Ohio-3739, 2010 Ohio Misc. LEXIS 157 (Ohio Ct. Cl. 2010), aff'd, 2011-Ohio-1607, 2011 Ohio App. LEXIS 1376 (Ohio Ct. App., Franklin County 2011).

Summary judgment was denied as to an African-American employee's 42 U.S.C.S. § 1981 and the Ohio Civil Rights Act claims that he suffered from a hostile work environment over 16 years of employment because fact issues existed about whether the employer knew of pervasive racial harassment in its warehouse or took effective steps to deal with it. Although certain acts that allegedly comprised the hostile environment occurred outside of the statutory limitations period, they could still be considered for purposes of determining the employer's liability as long as one of the acts occurred within the limitations period. Chancellor v. Coca-Cola Enters., 675 F. Supp. 2d 771, 2009 U.S. Dist. LEXIS 113348 (S.D. Ohio 2009).

Employer's motion to dismiss was granted because the employee's claim of age discrimination under R.C. 4112.99 was barred by R.C. 4112.05's age discrimination election of remedies scheme and the employee failed to file her age discrimination claim within the applicable statute of limitations under R.C. 4112.02(N). Hillery v. Fifth Third Bank, 2009 U.S. Dist. LEXIS 39658 (S.D. Ohio May 11, 2009).

As an employee failed to file her age discrimination claims pursuant to R.C. 4112.02 and 4112.99 within the 180-day statute of limitations, they were properly dismissed pursuant to Civ.R. 12(B)(6). Goodyear v. Waco Holdings, Inc., 2009-Ohio-619, 2009 Ohio App. LEXIS 546 (Ohio Ct. App., Cuyahoga County 2009).

Plaintiffs were time-barred from bringing their hostile work environment claims under R.C. 4112,02 and 4112.99. The period of tolling on plaintiffs' state law claims under Ohio law ended when the state court issued its final order denying class certification on the damages claims in the class action which plaintiffs were members. Chancellor v. Coca-Cola Enters., 2008 U.S. Dist. LEXIS 111430 (S.D. Ohio Aug. 7, 2008).

When the Ohio Civil Rights Commission (OCRC) filed a complaint alleging a claim under R.C. 4112.052, due to the builders of an apartment complex allegedly violating state and federal handicap accessibility requirements, the claim was not barred by a statute of limitations because (1) the statute authorized the Attorney General to seek any preventive relief considered necessary to ensure the full enjoyment of rights granted by R.C. 4112.02(H), including a permanent or temporary injunction or temporary restraining order, and, in granting such authority, R.C. 4112.052 set forth no time limitations on OCRC's ability to seek the authorized relief, (2) it was unnecessary to use the in pari materia rule of statutory construction to apply a limitations period to this statute because a cause of action under § 4112.052 was distinct from other causes of action under R.C. ch. 4112 in that R.C. 4112.052 was primarily designed to redress public wrongs, unlike other provisions in the chapter that were primarily designed to redress individual wrongs, and (3) OCR.C. was exempt from the operation of general statutes of limitation absent an express statutory provision to the contrary, which was absent. Ohio Civ. Rights Comm'n v. Fairmark Dev., Inc., 2008-Ohio-6511, 2008 Ohio App. LEXIS 5400 (Ohio Ct. App., Franklin County 2008).

As an employer and others waived their statute of limitations defense pursuant to R.C. 4112.02(N) to a terminated employee's age discrimination in violation of Ohio law claim in exchange for her dismissal of her claim of age discrimination in violation of public policy, it was irrelevant when the employee was informed of her termination for purposes of the limitation period. Lynch v. Studebaker, 2007-Ohio-4014, 2007 Ohio App. LEXIS 3651 (Ohio Ct. App., Cuyahoga County 2007).

Employee's state law claims under R.C. 4112.02 and 4112.99, alleging disability discrimination by the state agency that employed her, were time-barred pursuant to R.C. 2743.16(A), as she failed to commence her state action within the two-year period after she was "unequivocally informed" of the alleged adverse action underlying the complaint. Longstreet v. Indus. Comm'n of Ohio, 2007-Ohio-1883, 2007 Ohio Misc. LEXIS 79 (Ohio Ct. Cl. 2007).

When the Ohio Civil Rights Commission (OCRC) alleged that the builders and designers of certain apartments committed an unlawful discriminatory practice, under R.C. 4112.02(H)(20) and (22), because the apartments were not sufficiently accessible to the disabled, and a trial court found that its claims were barred by the statute of limitations in R.C. 4112.05(B)(1), the OCR.C. could not allege, on appeal, that a continuing violation theory extended the statute of limitations based on the theory that the apartments' failure to comply with accessibility requirements in R.C. 3781.111 was a continuing violation, because the OCRC's complaint only alleged a violation based on the actual construction and design of the apartments. Ohio Civ. Rights Comm'n v. Triangle Real Estate Servs., 2007-Ohio-1809, 2007 Ohio App. LEXIS 1639 (Ohio Ct. App., Franklin County 2007).

As an employer and others waived their statute of limitations defense pursuant to R.C. 4112.02(N) to a terminated employee's age discrimination in violation of Ohio law claim in exchange for her dismissal of her claim of age discrimination in violation of public policy, it was irrelevant when the employee was informed of her termination for purposes of the limitation period. Lynch v. Studebaker, 2007-Ohio-4014, 2007 Ohio App. LEXIS 3651 (Ohio Ct. App., Cuyahoga County 2007).

Employee's state law claims under R.C. 4112.02 and 4112.99, alleging disability discrimination by the state agency that employed her, were time-barred pursuant to R.C. 2743.16(A), as she failed to commence her state action within the two-year period after she was "unequivocally informed" of the alleged adverse action underlying the complaint. Longstreet v. Indus. Comm'n of Ohio, 2007-Ohio-1883, 2007 Ohio Misc. LEXIS 79 (Ohio Ct. Cl. 2007).

When the Ohio Civil Rights Commission (OCRC) alleged that the builders and designers of certain apartments committed an unlawful discriminatory practice, under R.C. 4112.02(H)(20) and (22), because the apartments were not sufficiently accessible to the disabled, and a trial court found that its claims were barred by the statute of limitations in R.C. 4112.05(B)(1), the OCR.C. could not allege, on appeal, that a continuing violation theory extended the statute of limitations based on the theory that the apartments' failure to comply with accessibility requirements in R.C. 3781.111 was a continuing violation, because the OCRC's complaint only alleged a violation based on the actual construction and design of the apartments. Ohio Civ. Rights Comm'n v. Triangle Real Estate Servs., 2007-Ohio-1809, 2007 Ohio App. LEXIS 1639 (Ohio Ct. App., Franklin County 2007).



Job applicant's age discrimination claim under R.C. 4112.02, .99 against her employer, an Ohio correctional institution, which she originally filed in federal court, voluntarily dismissed for lack of jurisdiction, and refiled in state court four months later, was properly dismissed as untimely because it was not filed within the 180-day limitations period of R.C. 4112.02(N); the doctrine of equitable tolling did not save the claims because the applicant did not show why she did not file the claim originally in state court or why it took her four months to refile it in state court after the voluntary dismissal of the federal claim, nor did she claim that she somehow was misled or tricked into filing the claim originally in the wrong court. McNeely v. Ross Corr. Inst., 2006-Ohio-5414, 2006 Ohio App. LEXIS 5408 (Ohio Ct. App., Franklin County 2006).

Because 42 U.S.C.S. §§ 1981 and 1982 did not include any limitation on the time period within which an action could be brought, the court had to turn to R.C. 4112. 051. Because the renters' claims under §§ 1981 and 1982 were filed more than one year after last date of alleged racially discriminatory behavior, the claims were untimely. Johnson v. GSM Mgmt. Co., 2006 U.S. Dist. LEXIS 70452 (N.D. Ohio Sept. 28, 2006).

When a retired member of a law firm said the other members of the firm discriminated against him due to his age when he signed two agreements regarding when firm members would retire, and he had to retire pursuant to those agreements, his claim was time-barred, under R.C. 4112.02(N), because he alleged two discrete discriminatory acts, which were pressuring him into signing the two retirement agreements, those acts occurred more than 180 days before suit was filed, and the subsequent issuance of checks to the retired member pursuant to those agreements were not discriminatory acts beginning new limitations periods, as they were mere ministerial acts. Tablack v. Wellman, 2006-Ohio-4688, 2006 Ohio App. LEXIS 4609 (Ohio Ct. App., Mahoning County 2006).

Job applicant's age discrimination claim under R.C. 4112.02, .99 against her employer, an Ohio correctional institution, which she originally filed in federal court, voluntarily dismissed for lack of jurisdiction, and refiled in state court four months later, was properly dismissed as untimely because it was not filed within the 180-day limitations period of R.C. 4112.02(N). The doctrine of equitable tolling did not save the claims because the applicant did not show why she did not file the claim originally in state court or why it took her four months to refile it in state court after the voluntary dismissal of the federal claim, nor did she claim that she somehow was misled or tricked into filing the claim originally in the wrong court. McNeely v. Ross Corr. Inst., 2006-Ohio-5414, 2006 Ohio App. LEXIS 5408 (Ohio Ct. App., Franklin County 2006).

Because 42 U.S.C.S. §§ 1981 and 1982 did not include any limitation on the time period within which an action could be brought, the court had to turn to R.C. 4112. 051. Because the renters' claims under §§ 1981 and 1982 were filed more than one year after last date of alleged racially discriminatory behavior, the claims were untimely. Johnson v. GSM Mgmt. Co., 2006 U.S. Dist. LEXIS 70452 (N.D. Ohio Sept. 28, 2006).

When a retired member of a law firm said the other members of the firm discriminated against him due to his age when he signed two agreements regarding when firm members would retire, and he had to retire pursuant to those agreements, his claim was time-barred, under R.C. 4112.02(N), because he alleged two discrete discriminatory acts, which were pressuring him into signing the two retirement agreements, those acts occurred more than 180 days before suit was filed, and the subsequent issuance of checks to the retired member pursuant to those agreements were not discriminatory acts beginning new limitations periods, as they were mere ministerial acts. Tablack v. Wellman, 2006-Ohio-4688, 2006 Ohio App. LEXIS 4609 (Ohio Ct. App., Mahoning County 2006).

Employee's age discrimination claim, filed over nine months after her termination, was barred by the applicable statute of limitations under R.C. 4112.02(N), which required the employee to file her complaint within 180 days of the alleged wrongful termination. Zelnik v. CB Richard Ellis, Inc., 2005 U.S. Dist. LEXIS 19611 (S.D. Ohio Sept. 9, 2005).

Age discrimination claim was untimely where the employee failed to file the claim within 180 days of suffering an adverse employment action, his removal from a position as a regional sales manger and replacement by a much younger employee with less relevant experience, as required by R.C. 4112.02(N); fact that the employee remained employed by the employer for an additional 13 months did not toll the statute of limitations. Williams v. GE, 145 Fed. Appx. 535, 2005 FED App. 0695N, 2005 U.S. App. LEXIS 16937 (6th Cir. Ohio 2005).

Trial court properly granted summary judgment to an employer in a terminated employee's age discrimination action, pursuant to R.C. 4112.02(A), as the 180-day limitations period of R.C. 4112.02(N) had expired prior to the commencement of the employee's action; the period of limitations began to run on the date that the employee was terminated from his position, although he was retained and did some of those same duties in a new capacity as part of a retention plan in order to allow him to stay on until his pension vested. Kozma v. AEP Energy Servs., 2005-Ohio-1157, 2005 Ohio App. LEXIS 1137 (Ohio Ct. App., Franklin County 2005).

180-day limitations period applied because the employee's R.C. 4112.99 claim could not fairly be read as based on R.C. 4112.14. Kaltenmark v. K-Mart, Inc., 2005 U.S. Dist. LEXIS 21699 (N.D. Ohio Sept. 28, 2005).

Former employee's age discrimination claim against her former employer was time-barred by the 180-day time limit of R.C. 4112.02(N), as the employee's filing a claim of age discrimination with the U.S. Equal Employment Opportunity Commission did not toll the running of the statute of limitations. Macklin v. Turner, 2005 U.S. Dist. LEXIS 19616 (N.D. Ohio Sept. 9, 2005).

Trial court did not err in granting the employer's motion to dismiss the terminated employee's age discrimination claim against the employer, as she could not show that the 180-day statute of limitations for filing the age discrimination claim violated either the state or federal constitution's equal protection clause; thus, her age-discrimination claim filed nearly one year after she was terminated was properly dismissed on the employer's motion to dismiss. Schamer v. W. & S. Life Ins. Co., 2004-Ohio-4249, 2004 Ohio App. LEXIS 3858 (Ohio Ct. App., Hamilton County 2004).

Former worker's age discrimination action met the statute of limitations requirement as the time began to run when the former employer made the decision not to hire the former worker and instead hire a younger worker. Yovanno v. Ryder Sys., 2003-Ohio-6824, 2003 Ohio App. LEXIS 6159 (Ohio Ct. App., Summit County 2003).

The limitations period applicable to R.C. 4112.14 age-discrimination claims is six years. Ohio law recognizes a claim for tortious wrongful termination in violation of public policy based on age discrimination: Ferraro v. B.F. Goodrich Co., 2002-Ohio-4398, 149 Ohio App. 3d 301, 777 N.E.2d 282, 2002 Ohio App. LEXIS 4549 (Ohio Ct. App., Lorain County 2002).

R.C. 2305.19, the saving statute, applies to claims filed pursuant to R.C. Chapter 4112.: Osborne v. AK Steel/Armco Steel Co., 2002-Ohio-4846, 96 Ohio St. 3d 368, 775 N.E.2d 483, 2002 Ohio LEXIS 2406 (Ohio 2002).

Age discrimination claim pursuant to O.RC§ 4112.02(A), (N) was not timely where it was filed approximately 15 months after plaintiff was terminated. Snay v. Ameriwood Indus., 2002 U.S. Dist. LEXIS 27188 (N.D. Ohio Dec. 5, 2002).

The statute of limitations period applicable to age discrimination claims brought under R.C. Chapter 4112. begins to run on the date of the employee-plaintiff's termination from the defendant-employer: Oker v. Ameritech Corp., 2000-Ohio-139, 89 Ohio St. 3d 223, 729 N.E.2d 1177, 2000 Ohio LEXIS 1587 (Ohio 2000).

An age discrimination claim, pursuant to R.C. 4112.02(A), accrues, and the 180-day limitation period under R.C. 4112.02(N) commences, when the discriminatory act or practice occurs, not when adverse consequences or other facts resulting therefrom manifest themselves: McCray v. City of Springboro, 1998 Ohio App. LEXIS 3208 (Ohio Ct. App., Warren County July 13, 1998).

The 180-day limitations period is applicable to age based discrimination claims under R.C. 4112.02 and 4112.99 not the six-year statute of limitations under R.C. 2305.07: Dunn v. Medina Gen. Hosp., 917 F. Supp. 1185, 1996 U.S. Dist. LEXIS 6311 (N.D. Ohio 1996).

Special provision of R.C. 4112.02(N) imposing a 180-day limit on claims of age discrimination prevails over the general relief afforded by R.C. 4112.99: Napier v. VGC Corp., 797 F. Supp. 602, 1992 U.S. Dist. LEXIS 12914 (S.D. Ohio 1992).

A homeowner's 1983 action charging city and various officials and employees thereof with discriminatory enforcement of local ordinances based on race, is controlled by the four-year statute governing actions on rights not otherwise enumerated or six-year period to bring action on liability created by statute other than a forfeiture or penalty. Neither Ohio's 180-day limitation statute for actions under Fair Housing Act nor one-year limitation action for false imprisonment, including false arrest, are applicable: Banks v. Forest Park, 599 F. Supp. 465, 1984 U.S. Dist. LEXIS 22940 (S.D. Ohio 1984).

As a consequence of the amendment of R.C. 4112.02(A) to include age as a category protected by the state's employment discrimination laws, Ohio is now a "deferral state" under 29 USC § 633(b). Thus, the 300-day statutory period would apply in determining the timeliness of the plaintiff ADEA claim: 590 F. Supp. 428.

**—Continuing violation doctrine**

"Continuing violation" doctrine was not applicable because an employee presented no evidence of a long-standing policy of discrimination, and she was aware of the alleged discriminatory acts at the time they occurred. Toland v. Dep't of Mental Health & Addiction Servs., 2020-Ohio-3864, 2020 Ohio Misc. LEXIS 116 (Ohio Ct. Cl. 2020).

Because the denial of a promotion was a discrete act, meaning it was easy to identify, the "continuing violation" theory was not applicable to the racial discrimination claim and thus the claim was time-barred. Even if the continuing violation doctrine were applicable, because the employee did not identify in his brief the promotion denials that were racially discriminatory in the six-year time period prior to the filing of the lawsuit, he did not identify the "continuing" violations that would have permitted inclusion of the 2000/2001 and 2002 claims. Chapa v. Genpak, LLC, 2014-Ohio-897, 2014 Ohio App. LEXIS 846 (Ohio Ct. App., Franklin County 2014).

**Summary judgment**

Trial court did not err in granting defendants summary judgment on plaintiff's claim that defendants failed to participate in the interactive process to determine the appropriate accommodation for her alleged disability because she never requested a reasonable accommodation, so defendants' obligation to participate in the interactive process never arose. Anderson v. Bright Horizons Children's Ctrs., LLC, 2022-Ohio-1031, 2022 Ohio App. LEXIS 931 (Ohio Ct. App., Franklin County 2022).

In a retaliation case, there was a genuine issue of material fact as to whether plaintiff was terminated, making summary judgment inappropriate, as her actions and her supervisor's after he allegedly told her to "get out" were consistent with the supervisor having terminated plaintiff and simultaneously believing he had no need to formally terminate her because plaintiff was not intending to return. Brown v. Corr. Reception Ctr., 2020-Ohio-684, 146 N.E.3d 621, 2020 Ohio App. LEXIS 629 (Ohio Ct. App., Franklin County 2020).

Decision granting summary judgment to a city and its Director of Public Utilities on a terminated African-American employee's claims for discrimination and retaliation was improper, as a material fact existed as to why the employee's position was kept open for nine months before the Director and the city hired someone to replace him who was not a member of a protected class. Love v. City of Columbus, 2019-Ohio-620, 2019 Ohio App. LEXIS 653 (Ohio Ct. App., Franklin County 2019).

Where appellant worked as a trauma surgeon and medical director, the trial court properly granted summary judgment for appellees on his claim of retaliation because the record demonstrated that the non-renewal of his contract was due to appellees' concerns about his leadership and communication issues prior to his sexual harassment. The pervasiveness of the complaints indicated that appellant's supervisor had an honest belief that he was not an effective leader of the trauma team. Ferguson v. ProMedica Cent. Physicians, LLC, 2018-Ohio-4358, 114 N.E.3d 429, 2018 Ohio App. LEXIS 4693 (Ohio Ct. App., Lucas County 2018).

Summary judgment was properly granted to a hockey facility and related individuals in an action by parents of a minor youth hockey league player, alleging sexual-harassment and sexual-discrimination by coaching staff and others towards the player's mother, as there was no evidence offered by the parents to raise a genuine issue of material fact as to allegations of flirting, leering, or attempts at sexual advances. Pittman v. Parillo, 2017-Ohio-1477, 2017 Ohio App. LEXIS 1482 (Ohio Ct. App., Lucas County 2017).

Where an employee was terminated following a workplace altercation with a coworker, the employee's race discrimination claims survived summary judgment because, inter alia, the employee created at least a genuine dispute of fact over whether the employee and the coworker performed sufficiently similar job functions to be considered similarly situated, a genuine factual dispute existed regarding the employee's status as the aggressor in the confrontation, and the employee showed pretext. Wheat v. Fifth Third Bank, 785 F.3d 230, 2015 FED App. 0084P, 2015 U.S. App. LEXIS 7532 (6th Cir. Ohio 2015).

In a gender discrimination action by two employees, the employer was properly granted summary judgment because its termination of their employment was based on the employees' disciplinary issues, which were legitimate, non-discriminatory reasons that were not shown to have been merely pretextual. Brogan v. Family Video Movie Club, Inc., 2015-Ohio-70, 2015 Ohio App. LEXIS 66 (Ohio Ct. App., Lucas County 2015).

Summary judgment was properly granted to an employer in an employee's claim of wrongful discharge in violation of public policy, as she had statutory remedies available to her for violations of R.C. 4112.02(A) and 4123.90, such that the common-law claim was not the proper avenue for relief. Rivers v. Cashland Fin. Servs., 2013-Ohio-1225, 2013 Ohio App. LEXIS 1125 (Ohio Ct. App., Summit County 2013).

Employee's challenge to the trial court's grant of summary judgment to the employer on the employee's claim of gender discrimination pursuant to R.C. 4112.02(A) lacked merit where she did not actually develop an argument, as required by App.R. 16(A)(7). Rivers v. Cashland Fin. Servs., 2013-Ohio-1225, 2013 Ohio App. LEXIS 1125 (Ohio Ct. App., Summit County 2013).

Employee's claim that she was fired from employment due to the employer's race discrimination pursuant to R.C. 4112.02(A) should have survived challenge by the employer's summary judgment motion, as the employee raised a genuine issue of material fact as to whether the reason articulated by the employer for the firing was merely pretextual. Rivers v. Cashland Fin. Servs., 2013-Ohio-1225, 2013 Ohio App. LEXIS 1125 (Ohio Ct. App., Summit County 2013).

In an action in which defendants, a county and a county auditor's office, contended that plaintiff employee was discharged for making three errors in performing her duties, defendants were entitled to summary judgment on plaintiff's gender and age discrimination claims because plaintiff could not show that defendants' legitimate, non-discriminatory reason for her termination was a pretext for discrimination, plaintiff's errors were directly related to the overall function of the auditor's office, and defendants had lost faith in plaintiff's ability to competently fulfill her duties. Foust v. Butler County, 2013 U.S. Dist. LEXIS 11653 (S.D. Ohio Jan. 25, 2013).

Decision granting summary judgment in favor of appellees on appellant's claims including sexual harassment and negligent hiring or retention was improper, as there was no dispute that a chiropractor behaved in the manner alleged by appellant and despite two serious complaints that had been registered, the chiropractor was retained. Silvey v. Wash. Square Chiropractic Clinic, 2012-Ohio-6214, 2012 Ohio App. LEXIS 5427 (Ohio Ct. App., Geauga County 2012).

Same actor inference allows one to infer a lack of discrimination from the fact that the same individual both hired and fired the employee; where the fact finder decides to draw the same-actor inference, it is insufficient to warrant summary judgment for the defendant if the employee has otherwise raised a genuine issue of material fact. Gaglioti v. Levin Group, Inc., 508 Fed. Appx. 476, 2012 FED App. 1288N, 2012 U.S. App. LEXIS 25625 (6th Cir. Ohio 2012).

For purposes of an employee's disability discrimination and retaliation claims under 42 U.S.C.S. §§ 12112 and 12203(a) of the Americans with Disabilities Act and R.C. 4112.02 of the Ohio Civil Rights Act, he failed to establish that the employer's termination of him was a mere pretext, as there was sufficient evidence to support the employer's claim that termination was due to the employee's poor job performance as well as numerous customer complaints. Steele v. Oasis Turf & Tree, Inc., 2012 U.S. Dist. LEXIS 103722 (S.D. Ohio July 25, 2012).

Ethnic Arab-American employee failed to meet his burden of proof in response to the employer's summary judgment motion with respect to his claim of hostile work environment under 42 U.S.C.S. § 2000e-2(a) of Title VII of the Civil Rights Act of 1964, as amended, 42 U.S.C.S. § 2000e et seq., and R.C. 4112.02(A) and 4112.99 of the Ohio Civil Rights Act, R.C. 4112.01 et seq., as to his damage claim for lost commissions and lost wages, as pursuant to Fed. R. Civ. P. 26 and 37, he failed to provide a calculation of those damages, and such failure was not substantially justified or harmless. Mohanna v. Jake Sweeney Auto., 2012 U.S. Dist. LEXIS 97413 (S.D. Ohio July 13, 2012).

Ethnic Arab-American employee failed to meet his burden of proof in response to the employer's summary judgment motion with respect to his claim of religious discrimination under 42 U.S.C.S. § 2000e-2(a) of Title VII of the Civil Rights Act of 1964, as amended, 42 U.S.C.S. § 2000e et seq., and R.C. 4112.02(A) and 4112.99 of the Ohio Civil Rights Act, R.C. 4112.01 et seq., as he failed to demonstrate a genuine issue of material fact on his failure to accommodate claims where he did not show that his constructive discharge related to his failure to comply with an employment requirement. Mohanna v. Jake Sweeney Auto., 2012 U.S. Dist. LEXIS 97413 (S.D. Ohio July 13, 2012).

Ethnic Arab-American employee met his burden of proof in response to the employer's summary judgment motion with respect to his claim of hostile work environment under 42 U.S.C.S. § 2000e-2(a) of Title VII of the Civil Rights Act of 1964, as amended, 42 U.S.C.S. § 2000e et seq., and R.C. 4112.02(A) and 4112.99 of the Ohio Civil Rights Act, R.C. 4112.01 et seq., as to his damage claim for emotional distress, as he provided evidence as to whether he was in a vulnerable state and he testified as to manifestations of emotional distress, which testimony was bolstered by the testimony of co-workers. Mohanna v. Jake Sweeney Auto., 2012 U.S. Dist. LEXIS 97413 (S.D. Ohio July 13, 2012).

In an action in which an employer contended that an employee was discharged due to her inadequate work performance and erratic behavior, the employer was entitled to summary judgment on national origin discrimination claims brought under R.C. 4112.02(A) and Title VII of the Civil Rights Act of 1964, 42 U.S.C.S. § 2000e-2(a)(1), because the employee admitted that she took notes over students' shoulders while working as a technology assistant in a middle school computer lab, the employee did not explain how allegedly derogatory statements influenced the decision to terminate her employment, and the employee did not show that the employer's articulated reason was a pretext for unlawful discrimination. Ndene v. Columbus Acad., 2011 U.S. Dist. LEXIS 21398 (S.D. Ohio Mar. 3, 2011).

Where an employer stated that an employee was discharged because she did not follow proper procedures in using new software systems, she was unaccountably absent from her work area, and she exhibited an unwillingness to attend training, the employer was entitled to summary judgment on the employee's age discrimination claim because the employer's stated reasons had a basis in fact and were not unreasonable and the employee's replacement seven months later by a worker who was six-and-a-half years younger did not show that the employer's reasons were pretextual. Blizzard v. Marion Tech. College, 2011 U.S. Dist. LEXIS 35460 (N.D. Ohio Mar. 30, 2011), aff'd, 698 F.3d 275, 2012 FED App. 0362P, 2012 U.S. App. LEXIS 21846 (6th Cir. Ohio 2012).

Employer was entitled to summary judgment on a gender discrimination claim that an employee brought pursuant to R.C. 4112.02(A) because the employer had a legitimate, nondiscriminatory reason for terminating the employee, the employee's failure to follow established bank procedures resulted in two major losses for the employer, the employee's deficient performance was well-documented, and there was no indication that the employee was terminated because she was female. Queer v. PNC Bank, 2011 U.S. Dist. LEXIS 140729 (N.D. Ohio Dec. 7, 2011).

Summary judgment in favor of the employer in the age discrimination suit was proper, because the employee's performance review did contain negative feedback, and the employee admitted in his deposition that he never submitted any cost-saving ideas, never took a welding class, and never passed the welding tests that the employer scheduled for him. Cozzuli v. Sandridge Food Corp., 2011-Ohio-4878, 2011 Ohio App. LEXIS 4035 (Ohio Ct. App., Medina County 2011).

Summary judgment was granted to the Department of Rehabilitation and Correction in an employee's reverse racial discrimination claim under R.C. 4112.02(A), as her conclusory assertions of harassment did not establish a prima facie case of either disparate treatment or a hostile work environment Campbell v. Dep't of Rehab. & Corr., 2011-Ohio-3897, 2011 Ohio Misc. LEXIS 281 (Ohio Ct. Cl. 2011).

Trial court properly granted summary judgment to a county agency and two of its supervisors on a county employee's claims of gender and racial discrimination under R.C. 4112.02(A), as he failed to establish even the first prong of a claim of gender discrimination where he did not show that the agency treated women more favorably than men; he also failed to show that he was qualified for a position after his driver's license was suspended and that he received disparate treatment in being demoted. Mosley v. Cuyahoga County Bd. of Mental Retardation, 2011-Ohio-3072, 2011 Ohio App. LEXIS 2615 (Ohio Ct. App., Cuyahoga County 2011).

Summary judgment in favor of an employer in an age discrimination case was affirmed because the employee failed to demonstrated that the reason given for failing to hire him into the newly-structured organization —that he was hard-headed, was unwilling to accept other views and suggestions, and enjoyed causing friction between his co-workers and their supervisors—was mere pretext. Frick v. Potash Corp. of Sask., Inc., 2010-Ohio-4292, 2010 Ohio App. LEXIS 3627 (Ohio Ct. App., Allen County 2010).

Vocational teacher established a prima facie case of sex discrimination to survive summary judgment because (1) the teacher was qualified to receive a master's pay when the teacher obtained a bachelor's degree; and (2) at least one of the members of the opposite sex who was excepted from an alleged settlement regarding pay for teachers was similarly situated to the vocational teacher. Zindroski v. Parma City Sch. Dist. Bd. of Educ., 2010-Ohio-3188, 2010 Ohio App. LEXIS 2659 (Ohio Ct. App., Cuyahoga County 2010).

Trial court erred by granting summary judgment to an employer in a sex discrimination case, brought under Ohio Code Rev. Ann. §§ 4112.02(A) and 4112.99, because a former employee introduced sufficient direct evidence of discrimination and sufficient evidence for summary judgment purposes that the reasons advanced by the employer for requesting the employee's resignation were pretextual. The employee presented evidence that board members of the employer stated they did not want a woman as head golf professional at the employer's golf course, that the employee knew that the president of the employer would have fired the employee if the employee had not resigned when requested, and that two of the employer's board members who voted to demand the employee's resignation were consistently hostile to the employee's employment on the basis of the employee's sex. Egli v. Congress Lake Club, 2010-Ohio-2444, 2010 Ohio App. LEXIS 2003 (Ohio Ct. App., Stark County 2010).

Where a former employee of a mental health hospital claimed that she was terminated because she complained about a discriminatory treatment environment, in violation of R.C. 4112.02(G), summary judgment for the employer was granted because the employee has a remedy under § 4112.02(I) if the employer terminated her because she opposed a discriminatory treatment environment at the hospital and she could not satisfy the jeopardy element necessary to assert a public policy claim. Mincy v. Cincinnati Children's Hosp. Med. Ctr., 2010 U.S. Dist. LEXIS 51803 (S.D. Ohio May 26, 2010).

Where a former employee of a mental health hospital claimed that she was terminated because she was regarded as being disabled, in violation of R.C. 4112.02(A), summary judgment for the employer was not warranted because a superior testified that she had concerns whether the employee's mental health condition adversely affected her ability to perform her job and discussed with the employee whether she needed to consider receiving social security or disability payments, in lieu of working. Mincy v. Cincinnati Children's Hosp. Med. Ctr., 2010 U.S. Dist. LEXIS 51803 (S.D. Ohio May 26, 2010).

Where a former employee of a mental health hospital claimed that patients and other staff members directed racial slurs at each other or used racially-offensive language, creating a hostile work environment, in violation of R.C. 4112.02, summary judgment for the employer was granted because patients or staff members did not direct racial slurs at the employee or physically threaten her in a racially-charged manner, and it was undisputed that management took remedial steps in response to certain racial incidents. Mincy v. Cincinnati Children's Hosp. Med. Ctr., 2010 U.S. Dist. LEXIS 51803 (S.D. Ohio May 26, 2010).

Summary judgment in favor of the employer and supervisor in the employment retaliation action was proper, because the employee failed to offer any non-hearsay evidence that the supervisor gave her bad references, and failed to present any evidence that a causal relationship existed between the alleged bad references and her gender discrimination complaints. Healey v. Goodyear Tire & Rubber Co., 2010-Ohio-5463, 2010 Ohio App. LEXIS 4607 (Ohio Ct. App., Summit County 2010).

In a former employee's disability discrimination suit, a trial court erred by granting summary judgment to his former supervisor based on determining that the former employee failed to state a separate claim against him because the definition of "employer" under R.C. 4112.01(A)(2) included supervisors in the definition of an employer and the complaint did state separate allegations against the former supervisor, including allegations of intentional infliction of emotional distress. However, the trial court properly granted summary judgment to the former employer based on claim preclusion because a federal jury's verdict in favor of the former employer disposed of all the claims against it, including the state claims. Price v. Carter Lumber Co., 2010-Ohio-4328, 2010 Ohio App. LEXIS 3658 (Ohio Ct. App., Summit County 2010).

Sheriff was entitled to summary judgment on the nurse's hostile work environment claim under 42 U.S.C.S. § 2000e-2(a)(1) and Ohio Rev. Stat. Ann. § 4112.02(A) because no reasonable jury could find that the sheriff's actions were not prompt and appropriate. The undisputed facts showed that the sheriff and his top officials took the matter very seriously from the moment they first learned of the complaint through the end of the investigation when the sheriff decided to fire the nurse's coworker, and that strong actions were taken in the interim, including ordering the coworker not to contact the nurse and moving the coworker, to protect against any further harassment. Satterfield v. Karnes, 736 F. Supp. 2d 1138, 2010 U.S. Dist. LEXIS 86398 (S.D. Ohio 2010).

City employee's wrongful termination action, alleging, inter alia, disability discrimination under R.C. 4112.02, failed where there was no evidence that the city regarded her as substantially limited in her ability to work or lift, such that it did not consider her disabled under R.C. 4112.01(A)(13). McClain v. City of Shaker Heights, 2010 Ohio Misc. LEXIS 570 (Ohio C.P. Nov. 19, 2010), aff'd, 2011-Ohio-4418, 2011 Ohio App. LEXIS 3660 (Ohio Ct. App., Cuyahoga County 2011).

City alleged its reason for denying a 64-year-old firefighter's application for a lateral transfer was that, as a transferee entering a position requiring specialized training, he needed to have at least five years in which to use such training, but he was obliged by ordinance to retire at age 65. Evidence that no request for an employment extension had been denied for several years established a genuine issue of material fact as to whether the city's alleged reason was pretextual; therefore, summary judgment for the city was inappropriate. Campolieti v. City of Cleveland, 2009-Ohio-5224, 184 Ohio App. 3d 419, 921 N.E.2d 286, 2009 Ohio App. LEXIS 4417 (Ohio Ct. App., Cuyahoga County 2009).

Summary judgment was properly granted to an employer in an employee's action, alleging claims of, inter alia, racial discrimination in violation of R.C. 4112.02, as the adverse employment action of termination of the employee from employment was based on the employer's legitimate, non-discrimination reason of not needing two workers in the employee's position, and there was no pretext shown; the other worker who had that same position had seniority and had gotten better performance reviews. Canady v. Rekau & Rekau, Inc., 2009-Ohio-4974, 2009 Ohio App. LEXIS 4211 (Ohio Ct. App., Franklin County 2009).

Grant of summary judgment to a parent corporation of a subsidiary that employed an employee was error in the employee's action, alleging, inter alia, sex discrimination under R.C. 4112.02, as there were genuine issues of material fact as to whether the subsidiary/employer was merely the parent corporation's alter-ego for purposes of piercing the corporate veil. Bacoccini v. Ice Indus., 2009-Ohio-3800, 2009 Ohio App. LEXIS 3213 (Ohio Ct. App., Lucas County 2009).

Employer was not entitled to summary judgment on an applicant's claims that the employer committed race discrimination, in violation of R.C. 4112.02(A), and retaliated against him, in violation of R.C. 4112.02(I). Although the employer claimed that it did not hire the applicant because he had felony convictions, evidence showed that the employer hired Caucasian applicants who had felony convictions, and that evidence raised genuine issues of material fact about whether the employer used the fact that the applicant had felony convictions as a pretext for rejecting his application because he was African-American. Barrow v. Terminix Int'l Co., L.P., 2009 U.S. Dist. LEXIS 6433 (S.D. Ohio Jan. 29, 2009).

Employer was entitled to summary judgment in a pro se action filed by a former employee who alleged sex discrimination in violation of R.C. 4112.02(A) and in violation of 42 U.S.C.S. § 2000e-2(a)(1) of Title VII of the Civil Rights Act of 1964, 42 U.S.C.S. § 2000e et seq.; the employee failed to establish a prima facie case of discrimination in relation to an alleged wrongful transfer because there was no evidence that individuals outside the protected class were given more favorable treatment. Rogers v. Daimlerchrysler Corp., 588 F. Supp. 2d 804, 2008 U.S. Dist. LEXIS 97487 (N.D. Ohio 2008).

There was a question of fact as to whether statements made by a deputy firefighter, and arguably ratified by the chief, evidenced an improper managerial motive; it would not be unreasonable to infer that this motive manifested itself in the treatment of which female firefighters complained, and it was also a question of fact as to whether that treatment was disparate from that received by male firefighters. Consequently, summary judgment was inappropriate on appellants' disparate treatment claim. Stachura v. City of Toledo, 2008-Ohio-3581, 177 Ohio App. 3d 481, 895 N.E.2d 202, 2008 Ohio App. LEXIS 3017 (Ohio Ct. App., Lucas County 2008).

Employer was entitled to summary judgment as to an employee's age discrimination claims because (1) the employee's affidavit, on which the employee relied to oppose the employer's summary judgment motion, contradicted the employee's prior deposition testimony on the issues of the reasons for the employee's discharge and whether the employee was replaced by younger workers, and the contradiction was not explained, and (2) a statement in the affidavit that the employee's discharge resulted in the retention of workers under 40 merely reiterated the employee's complaint, without elaboration, contrary to the requirements of Civ.R. 56(E). Craddock v. Flood Co., 2008-Ohio-112, 2008 Ohio App. LEXIS 102 (Ohio Ct. App., Summit County 2008).

Employer was not entitled to summary judgment on a claim of age discrimination where the employee established a prima facie case and the employer did not establish that the reasons for termination were a pretext: Peters v. Rock-Tenn Co., 2008-Ohio-6444, 180 Ohio App. 3d 10, 903 N.E.2d 1256, 2008 Ohio App. LEXIS 5384 (Ohio Ct. App., Delaware County 2008).

Summary judgment was precluded in a township employee's sex discrimination claim pursuant to R.C. 4112.02(A) against a township and others, arising from her termination from employment following an alcohol-related incident, as she showed that she was a woman, she was discharged, and she was qualified for the job, and there was disputed evidence from the parties regarding whether comparable males were treated more favorably than she was after being involved in alcohol-related incidents. Johnson v. Olmsted Twp., 2007-Ohio-6487, 2007 Ohio App. LEXIS 5680 (Ohio Ct. App., Cuyahoga County 2007).

Trial court's grant of summary judgment to county parks and others in a parks employee's gender discrimination action under R.C. 4112.02(A) was proper with respect to her claim that she was laterally transferred when a new assistant manager was hired, as there was no showing that such transfer was an adverse employment action because it afforded the employee more of the type of experience that she had requested, and she failed to identify any similarly situated person who was treated more favorably than she was; further, as she had been personally involved with the assistant manager, a transfer was deemed prudent in order to avoid a potential sexual harassment scenario, such that it was a legitimate, nondiscriminatory reason, and the employee failed to show that such reason was merely pretextual. Fox v. Lorain County, 2007-Ohio-6143, 2007 Ohio App. LEXIS 5412 (Ohio Ct. App., Lorain County 2007).

Although magistrate erred in concluding that a terminated employee failed to show a prima facie case of race discrimination in her action against a university and various officials under 42 U.S.C.S. §§ 1983, 1985 and R.C. 4112.02, the district court nevertheless adopted the magistrate's ultimate conclusion that the defendants were entitled to summary judgment; the defendants articulated a nondiscriminatory reason for terminating the employee, a nurse, because she improperly administered a drug to a patient and failed to comply with a physician's directive, and the evidence failed to support a finding of pretext. Russell v. Univ. of Toledo, 2007 U.S. Dist. LEXIS 47379 (N.D. Ohio June 29, 2007), aff'd, 537 F.3d 596, 2008 FED App. 0288P, 2008 U.S. App. LEXIS 17117 (6th Cir. Ohio 2008).

Terminated employee failed to meet her burden of proof under the McDonnell Douglas test to show a prima facie case of racial discrimination after she was terminated from employment for violating the employee handbook policy that prohibited two no-shows for work with less than two hours' notice, as she did not show that she was replaced by someone outside of the protected class; rather, the employer offered evidence that two out of four replacement employees were within the protected class, such that there were no genuine issues of dispute. Mosley v. Miami Shores of Moraine, LLC, 2007-Ohio-2138, 2007 Ohio App. LEXIS 1993 (Ohio Ct. App., Montgomery County 2007).

In order to survive a summary judgment when claiming disability discrimination, under R.C. 4112.02(A), an appellant must set forth a prima facie case of disability discrimination: (1) appellant was disabled; (2) her employer took adverse employment action motivated at least in part by her disability; and (3) appellant, even with her disability, can safely and substantially perform the essential functions of her job with or without reasonable accommodation. Miller v. Pond, 2007-Ohio-2084, 171 Ohio App. 3d 347, 870 N.E.2d 787, 2007 Ohio App. LEXIS 1937 (Ohio Ct. App., Stark County 2007).

It was not error to grant summary judgment in favor of an employee's employer, as to her disability discrimination claim under R.C. 4112.02(A), because her complaint did not allege all the elements of disability discrimination, nor did he brief in opposition to summary judgment, as she did not allege what her disability was, did not establish that she was qualified for the job she was performing, and did not establish that her termination was because of any alleged disability. Miller v. Pond, 2007-Ohio-2084, 171 Ohio App. 3d 347, 870 N.E.2d 787, 2007 Ohio App. LEXIS 1937 (Ohio Ct. App., Stark County 2007).

Where a former employee was terminated from his position, his claim of reverse sex discrimination properly resulted in a grant of summary judgment for his employer and supervisors, as the employee did not meet his burden of showing that the employer was the unusual type that discriminated against the majority; the former employee was a white male and he was terminated due to a reduction in force, which was deemed a legitimate, non-discriminatory reason that was not shown to have been a mere pretext for the employer's discriminatory conduct. Kundtz v. AT&T Solutions, Inc., 2007-Ohio-1462, 2007 Ohio App. LEXIS 1318 (Ohio Ct. App., Franklin County 2007).

Although magistrate erred in concluding that a terminated employee failed to show a prima facie case of race discrimination in her action against a university and various officials under 42 U.S.C.S. §§ 1983, 1985 and R.C. 4112.02, the district court nevertheless adopted the magistrate's ultimate conclusion that the defendants were entitled to summary judgment. The defendants articulated a nondiscriminatory reason for terminating the employee, a nurse, because she improperly administered a drug to a patient and failed to comply with a physician's directive, and the evidence failed to support a finding of pretext. Russell v. Univ. of Toledo, 2007 U.S. Dist. LEXIS 47379 (N.D. Ohio June 29, 2007), aff'd, 537 F.3d 596, 2008 FED App. 0288P, 2008 U.S. App. LEXIS 17117 (6th Cir. Ohio 2008).

Terminated employee failed to meet her burden of proof under the McDonnell Douglas test to show a prima facie case of racial discrimination after she was terminated from employment for violating the employee handbook policy that prohibited two no-shows for work with less than two hours' notice, as she did not show that she was replaced by someone outside of the protected class. The employer offered evidence that two out of four replacement employees were within the protected class, such that there were no genuine issues of dispute. Mosley v. Miami Shores of Moraine, LLC, 2007-Ohio-2138, 2007 Ohio App. LEXIS 1993 (Ohio Ct. App., Montgomery County 2007).

In order to survive a summary judgment when claiming disability discrimination, under R.C. 4112.02(A), an appellant must set forth a prima facie case of disability discrimination: (1) appellant was disabled; (2) her employer took adverse employment action motivated at least in part by her disability; and (3) appellant, even with her disability, can safely and substantially perform the essential functions of her job with or without reasonable accommodation. Miller v. Pond, 2007-Ohio-2084, 171 Ohio App. 3d 347, 870 N.E.2d 787, 2007 Ohio App. LEXIS 1937 (Ohio Ct. App., Stark County 2007).

Trial court erred in granting summary judgment to a former employer in an employee's racial discrimination claim brought under R.C. 4112.02(A), where the employee satisfied the four prongs of the McDonnell Douglas test by showing that he was fired from his job for having intentionally pulled a fire alarm in a stairwell that he was in when it went off although he adamantly denied having done so, a surveillance video of the area lacked clarity and depth, and a similarly situated non-protected employee who was also accused of having pulled a fire alarm was deemed to have done so accidentally and she was not disciplined; a genuine issue of material fact was raised as to discriminatory intent and pretext which precluded summary judgment in the circumstances. Holbrook v. LexisNexis, 2006-Ohio-5762, 169 Ohio App. 3d 345, 862 N.E.2d 892, 2006 Ohio App. LEXIS 5747 (Ohio Ct. App., Montgomery County 2006).

Youth softball league head coach applicant failed in her burden of proof in a motion for summary judgment by the league and officials thereof, wherein they claimed that the applicant's sexual discrimination claim under R.C. 4112.02(C) et seq. failed because the league was comprised wholly of volunteers, as the applicant did not offer proof that raised a genuine issue of fact as to whether she was involved in an employment relationship pursuant to R.C. 4112.01(2) and (3) for purposes of supporting the allegations of her claim; various responsive papers to the motion were not considered where leave for filing them was not properly obtained from the trial court pursuant to Summit County, Ohio, Ct. C.P. R. 7.14(C)(1), and the employee's attempt to amend her complaint to remove the allegation alluding to the employment relationship was presumed denied where the trial court had not ruled upon it. Koballa v. Twinsburg Youth Softball League, 2006-Ohio-4872, 2006 Ohio App. LEXIS 4783 (Ohio Ct. App., Summit County 2006).

Summary judgment in favor of an employer in an employee's retaliatory discharge claim under 42 U.S.C.S. § 2220e-3(a) and/or R.C. 4112.02(I), arising from her having filed a complaint with the Equal Employment Opportunity Commission, was proper where she failed to show the necessary connection between the filing of the complaint and her discharge from employment; it was noted that disciplinary action based on complaints about the employee's job performance had commenced prior to the time that she filed her complaint. Smith v. Children's Aid Soc'y, 2006-Ohio-4754, 2006 Ohio App. LEXIS 4677 (Ohio Ct. App., Cuyahoga County 2006).

Summary judgment to a city was properly granted in a hostile environment sexual harassment claim by a police dispatcher and her husband, in violation of R.C. 4112.02(A) and 4112.99, as they failed to satisfy two of the three necessary elements of the claim where there was no showing that the alleged harassment by a police chief to the dispatcher was unwelcome, and that the harassing conduct was sufficiently severe or pervasive to affect the terms, conditions, or privileges of employment, or any matter directly or indirectly related to employment. Armaly v. City of Wapakoneta, 2006-Ohio-3629, 2006 Ohio App. LEXIS 3562 (Ohio Ct. App., Auglaize County 2006).

Trial court's grant of summary judgment to a police chief in an action by a police dispatcher and her husband, alleging a variety of tort claims and work-related statutory claims in violation of R.C. 4112.02(A) and 4112.99, was proper as to the hostile environment sexual harassment claim against the chief, as he was not specifically included within that count of the complaint; rather, that form of discrimination was only alleged against the city and accordingly, the chief was properly granted summary judgment on that claim. Armaly v. City of Wapakoneta, 2006-Ohio-3629, 2006 Ohio App. LEXIS 3562 (Ohio Ct. App., Auglaize County 2006).

Employee's claim that he was the subject of age, race, and sex discrimination under R.C. 4112.02(A) properly resulted in a grant of summary judgment to the employer, as he did not make out a prima facie case where he did not show that he was subjected to an adverse employment action or that similarly-situated employees outside of his protected classes were treated more favorably than the employee; further, he failed to establish that he was constructively discharged and instead, his resignation was unreasonable in the circumstances, as his work environment went through a consolidation which affected many workers. Crable v. Nestle USA, Inc., 2006-Ohio-2887, 2006 Ohio App. LEXIS 2786 (Ohio Ct. App., Cuyahoga County 2006).

Trial court's grant of summary judgment to an employer and others in an employee's reverse racial discrimination and harassment action under R.C. 4112.02(A) was proper, as she failed to show that the employer exhibited discriminatory intent or that she suffered an adverse employment action where she was laterally moved in her position and relocated to another office following an altercation with a co-worker; she also did not show that she was treated differently from other similarly situated employees. Lennon v. Cuyahoga County Juvenile Court, 2006-Ohio-2587, 2006 Ohio App. LEXIS 2443 (Ohio Ct. App., Cuyahoga County 2006).

Where workers who omitted from their job applications only moving violations were not fired, while workers who omitted criminal convictions were fired, and the employee omitted both criminal convictions and moving violations, the employee failed to establish a prima facie case of discrimination in violation of Title VII of the Civil Rights Act of 1964, 42 U.S.C.S. § 2000e et seq., and the Ohio Civil Rights law, R.C. 4112.02; the employee failed to establsh that similarly situated workers were treated better than the employee. Thus, the curt granted summary judgment for the employer. Elgabi v. Toledo Area Reg'l Transit Auth., 2006 U.S. Dist. LEXIS 32833 (N.D. Ohio May 24, 2006), amended, 2006 U.S. Dist. LEXIS 33910 (N.D. Ohio May 26, 2006).

Trial court erred in granting summary judgment to a former employer in an employee's racial discrimination claim brought under R.C. 4112.02(A), where the employee satisfied the four prongs of the McDonnell Douglas test by showing that he was fired from his job for having intentionally pulled a fire alarm in a stairwell that he was in when it went off although he adamantly denied having done so, a surveillance video of the area lacked clarity and depth, and a similarly situated non-protected employee who was also accused of having pulled a fire alarm was deemed to have done so accidentally and she was not disciplined. A genuine issue of material fact was raised as to discriminatory intent and pretext which precluded summary judgment in the circumstances. Holbrook v. LexisNexis, 2006-Ohio-5762, 169 Ohio App. 3d 345, 862 N.E.2d 892, 2006 Ohio App. LEXIS 5747 (Ohio Ct. App., Montgomery County 2006).

Youth softball league head coach applicant failed in her burden of proof in a motion for summary judgment by the league and officials thereof, wherein they claimed that the applicant's sexual discrimination claim under R.C. 4112.02(C) et seq. failed because the league was comprised wholly of volunteers, as the applicant did not offer proof that raised a genuine issue of fact as to whether she was involved in an employment relationship pursuant to R.C. 4112.01(2) and (3) for purposes of supporting the allegations of her claim. Various responsive papers to the motion were not considered where leave for filing them was not properly obtained from the trial court pursuant to Summit County, Ohio, Ct. C.P. R. 7.14(C)(1), and the employee's attempt to amend her complaint to remove the allegation alluding to the employment relationship was presumed denied where the trial court had not ruled upon it. Koballa v. Twinsburg Youth Softball League, 2006-Ohio-4872, 2006 Ohio App. LEXIS 4783 (Ohio Ct. App., Summit County 2006).

Summary judgment in favor of an employer in an employee's retaliatory discharge claim under 42 U.S.C.S. § 2220e-3(a) and/or R.C. 4112.02(I), arising from her having filed a complaint with the Equal Employment Opportunity Commission, was proper where she failed to show the necessary connection between the filing of the complaint and her discharge from employment; it was noted that disciplinary action based on complaints about the employee's job performance had commenced prior to the time that she filed her complaint. Smith v. Children's Aid Soc'y, 2006-Ohio-4754, 2006 Ohio App. LEXIS 4677 (Ohio Ct. App., Cuyahoga County 2006).

Employee's claim that he was the subject of age, race, and sex discrimination under R.C. 4112.02(A) properly resulted in a grant of summary judgment to the employer, as he did not make out a prima facie case where he did not show that he was subjected to an adverse employment action or that similarly-situated employees outside of his protected classes were treated more favorably than the employee. He failed to establish that he was constructively discharged and instead, his resignation was unreasonable in the circumstances, as his work environment went through a consolidation which affected many workers. Crable v. Nestle USA, Inc., 2006-Ohio-2887, 2006 Ohio App. LEXIS 2786 (Ohio Ct. App., Cuyahoga County 2006).

Where workers who omitted from their job applications only moving violations were not fired, while workers who omitted criminal convictions were fired, and the employee omitted both criminal convictions and moving violations, the employee failed to establish a prima facie case of discrimination in violation of Title VII of the Civil Rights Act of 1964, 42 U.S.C.S. § 2000e et seq., and the Ohio Civil Rights law, R.C. 4112.02. The employee failed to establsh that similarly situated workers were treated better than the employee. Thus, the court granted summary judgment for the employer. Elgabi v. Toledo Area Reg'l Transit Auth., 2006 U.S. Dist. LEXIS 32833 (N.D. Ohio May 24, 2006), amended, 2006 U.S. Dist. LEXIS 33910 (N.D. Ohio May 26, 2006).

Trial court's grant of summary judgment to an employer and others in an employee's reverse racial discrimination and harassment action under R.C. 4112.02(A) was proper, as she failed to show that the employer exhibited discriminatory intent or that she suffered an adverse employment action where she was laterally moved in her position and relocated to another office following an altercation with a co-worker; she also did not show that she was treated differently from other similarly situated employees. Lennon v. Cuyahoga County Juvenile Court, 2006-Ohio-2587, 2006 Ohio App. LEXIS 2443 (Ohio Ct. App., Cuyahoga County 2006).

Trial court's grant of summary judgment to an employer in an action by an employee who was terminated, alleging racial and religious discrimination, was proper where the employee met her burden of showing a prima facie case of discrimination, the employer then met its burden of providing legitimate nondiscriminatory reasons for the termination based on the employee's failure to work collaboratively with others, and the employee failed in her burden of showing that the reasons were pretextual; she did not establish a material issue of fact on the last step of the burden-shifting analysis. Smith v. Children's Aid Soc'y, 2006-Ohio-4754, 2006 Ohio App. LEXIS 4677 (Ohio Ct. App., Cuyahoga County 2006).

Where an employee suffered an injury to her foot, which caused her to be unable to perform her job duties as a corrections officer and resulted in her involuntary disability separation from work, even assuming that her injury was a "substantial impairment," she did not establish that she was a "qualified individual" and accordingly, she failed in her burden of establishing a prima facie case of disability discrimination, in violation of R.C. 4112.02(A); summary judgment was properly granted to the employer. Batiste v. Cuyahoga County Sheriff's Dep't, 2005-Ohio-6230, 2005 Ohio App. LEXIS 5617 (Ohio Ct. App., Cuyahoga County 2005).

Former employee produced evidence to show that he was an American who was over the age of 40; he was objectively qualified for his position; he was terminated; and he was replaced by an individual outside of the protected classes, but his former employers, a Swiss company and its American subsidiaries, articulated a legitimate, nondiscriminatory reason for the employee's termination in that they claimed he was terminated for poor management, including inventory and consignment problems at one subsidiary which led to a $1 million write-off; the employee presented evidence that called into question whether the reason offered by the employers was pretextual, which included evidence that suggested that the employee was not responsible for the inventory and consignment problems and that a decision-maker made a comment regarding dismissing elderly employees under certain circumstances shortly before the employers sent the employee's purported replacement, who was substantially younger than the employee, to the United States. It was for the jury to weigh the evidence presented by the parties, make credibility determinations, and decide whether the reason offered by the employers was the true reason for the termination decision; accordingly, the district court denied the employers' motion for summary judgment as to the employee's age and national origin discrimination claims under 42 U.S.C.S. § 2000e-2(a)(1) of Title VII, R.C. 4112.01(A), and the Age Discrimination in Employment Act. Imwalle v. Reliance Med. Prods., 2005 U.S. Dist. LEXIS 27882 (S.D. Ohio Nov. 15, 2005).

When an employee alleged that a school district's non-competitive appointment of individuals to a supervisory position the employee eventually applied unsuccessfully for was racial and gender discrimination, the district was entitled to summary judgment because, while the employee showed a prima facie case of discrimination, the district's budgetary reasons for appointing someone, rather than going through a competitive hiring process, were not shown to be a pretext for discrimination. Senu-Oke v. Bd. of Educ., 2005-Ohio-5239, 2005 Ohio App. LEXIS 4744 (Ohio Ct. App., Montgomery County 2005).

Material fact disputes precluded summary judgment for an employer and a public official in an employee's gender discrimination lawsuit brought under 42 U.S.C.S. § 1983 for an alleged violation of the Equal Protection Clause of the Fourteenth Amendment and under R.C. 4112.02(A) and R.C. 4112.99. The employee offered sufficient evidence of pretext to create a triable issue: The employee proffered evidence that her successor was paid more than the employee for the same work and later was promoted to another managerial position over the employee; that while the successor had more budgeting experience than the employee, he had considerably less managerial experience in the public sector; that in addition to budgeting, managerial and supervisory tasks were primary components of the successor's positions while he worked for defendants; that, before posting the announcement for the position to which the successor was promoted, defendant official changed the job description for that position, apparently eliminating a requirement the successor did not meet; that the official expressed a preference for the successor during the hiring process; and that the official offered a different reason to the employee for not promoting her than was being offered in the instant lawsuit to justify that same decision. Herman v. Montgomery County Combined Health Dist., 2005 U.S. Dist. LEXIS 9333 (S.D. Ohio May 4, 2005).

Where an employer filled a manager's old job while the manger worked on a special project, but once the project ended, the employer offered the manager several positions, including one with same pay rate as the manager's former position, the manager's national origin discrimination claims under Title VII of the Civil Rights Act of 1964 and R.C. 4112.02 failed because the manager had not suffered an adverse employment action. The manager did not offer substantial evidence that the positions the employer offered him would result in a loss of pay, benefits, or reaponsibility; rather, the record showed that the employer made extensive efforts to find the manager a suitable position. Timmons v. Boehringer Ingelheim Corp., 132 Fed. Appx. 598, 2005 U.S. App. LEXIS 8983 (6th Cir. Ohio 2005).

Where an employer filled a manager's old job while the manger worked on a special project, but once the project ended, the employer offered the manager several positions, including one with same pay rate as the manager's former position, the manager's age discrimination claims under the Age Discrimination in Employment Act and R.C. 4112.02 failed because the manager had not suffered an adverse employment action. The manager did not offer substantial evidence that the positions the employer offered him would result in a loss of pay, benefits, or reaponsibility; rather, the record showed that the employer made extensive efforts to find the manager a suitable position. Timmons v. Boehringer Ingelheim Corp., 132 Fed. Appx. 598, 2005 U.S. App. LEXIS 8983 (6th Cir. Ohio 2005).

Former employer and supervisors were entitled to summary judgment on a former employee's retaliation claim because the employer terminated the employee before the employer received the notice of the charge of discrimination from the U.S. Equal Employment Opportunity Commission regarding the age discrimination claim that the employee filed with the Commission; further, the employee made no allegation that the employer was aware that the employee had filed a claim with the Commission when the employer terminated the employee. Macklin v. Turner, 2005 U.S. Dist. LEXIS 19616 (N.D. Ohio Sept. 9, 2005).

Conclusory allegations and self-serving statements by a charging party that he was denied a promotion on the basis of race are insufficient to withstand a motion for summary judgment by the employer: Hollowell v. Society Bank & Trust, 78 Ohio App. 3d 574, 605 N.E.2d 954, 1992 Ohio App. LEXIS 835 (Ohio Ct. App., Lucas County 1992).

Summary judgment for defendant was proper where plaintiff-employee's evidence failed, as a matter of law to establish racial or sexual harassment: Barney v. Chi Chi's, 84 Ohio App. 3d 40, 616 N.E.2d 269, 1992 Ohio App. LEXIS 5987 (Ohio Ct. App., Montgomery County 1992).

**Timeliness**

Employer's Fed. R. Civ. P. 12(c) motion was granted because 180-day limitations period applied because the employee's R.C. 4112.99 claim could not fairly be read as based on R.C. 4112.14. Because the employee filed an administrative action with the Equal Employment Opportunities Commission (EEOC) and the Ohio Civil Rights Commission he was precluded from later asserting a claim pursuant to any provision of R.C. 4112.14. Kaltenmark v. K-Mart, Inc., 2005 U.S. Dist. LEXIS 21699 (N.D. Ohio Sept. 28, 2005).

Former employee's age discrimination claim against her former employer was time-barred by the 180-day time limit of R.C. 4112.02(N), as the employee's filing a claim of age discrimination with the U.S. Equal Employment Opportunity Commission did not toll the running of the statute of limitations. Macklin v. Turner, 2005 U.S. Dist. LEXIS 19616 (N.D. Ohio Sept. 9, 2005).

**Union activities**

Trial court did not err by dismissing the masonry workers' complaints for failure to state a claim because a claim alleging discrimination in union membership could not be brought against a union representatives individually. Because the definition of labor organization in the statute did not extend liability to any person action directly or indirectly in the interest of a union, there was no legal authority for holding the union representative individually liable. Rivera v. Riggle, 2016-Ohio-8032, 74 N.E.3d 822, 2016 Ohio App. LEXIS 4908 (Ohio Ct. App., Mahoning County 2016).

Trial court correctly found that the workers' complaints failed to plead a claim of national origin discrimination because they did not allege what the application process was to join the union, that they submitted an application, that they were qualified for union membership, or that their applications were rejected. Rivera v. Riggle, 2016-Ohio-8032, 74 N.E.3d 822, 2016 Ohio App. LEXIS 4908 (Ohio Ct. App., Mahoning County 2016).

A job applicant claiming discrimination based on his father's union activities was not within a protected class: Murdock v. Village of Ottawa Hills, 134 Ohio App. 3d 470, 731 N.E.2d 284, 1999 Ohio App. LEXIS 4194 (Ohio Ct. App., Lucas County 1999).

**Union as employer**

Trial court did not err by granting summary judgment for the teacher's union on the R.C. 4112.02(A) claim because the union was not the teacher's employer, neither was it her supervisor or manager. As the duly recognized organization representing teachers in the public schools, the union had an interest independent from the school board in ensuring that its members were met with fairness in process and had an independent duty to ensure the selection of competent leadership from its ranks; the teacher set forth no evidence suggesting that it operated with any other purpose. Warnsley v. Toledo Bd. of Educ., 2011-Ohio-3134, 2011 Ohio App. LEXIS 2646 (Ohio Ct. App., Lucas County 2011).

**Unlawful discriminatory practices**

Lower court properly denied a plaintiff's appeal of a decision by the Ohio Civil Rights Commission denying the plaintiff's claims against a hospital for lack of probable cause because the plaintiff's claims—that the hospital invaded the plaintiff's privacy, violated the Health Insurance Portability & Accountability Act, and misused medical information—did not qualify under the definition of "Unlawful discriminatory practices" enumerated in R.C. 4112.02. Smart v. Ohio Civ. Rights Comm'n, 2012-Ohio-2899, 2012 Ohio App. LEXIS 2542 (Ohio Ct. App., Stark County 2012).

**Vicarious liability**

Trial court erred by granting summary judgment for the employer on the vicarious liability claim because the employee met her burden on summary judgment of introducing evidence creating issues of fact as to whether the employer thoroughly investigated her allegations and whether its actions were reasonably intended to prevent and correct the manager's sexually harassing behavior. There was also an issue of fact as to whether implementation of the employer's sexual harassment policy was effective in practice in reasonably preventing and correcting harassing behavior. Ellis v. Jungle Jim's Mkt., Inc., 2015-Ohio-4226, 44 N.E.3d 1034, 2015 Ohio App. LEXIS 4118 (Ohio Ct. App., Butler County 2015).

**Wrongful discharge**

Employee's claim of wrongful termination in violation of public policy failed because R.C. 4112.02 created a cause of action for wrongful discharge on account of a perceived or actual disability. Compton v. Swan Super Cleaners, Inc., 2008 U.S. Dist. LEXIS 39526 (S.D. Ohio Apr. 29, 2008).

Former employers were entitled to summary judgment on a former employee's claim for wrongful discharge in violation of public policy because the employee failed to establish a violation of R.C. 4112. White v. Drs. Camm & Golian, D.D.S., Inc., 2005 U.S. Dist. LEXIS 19763 (N.D. Ohio Sept. 12, 2005).

**—Sexual harassment**

In a same sex sexual harassment suit, trial court erred by granting summary judgment to the employer because a question of fact remained whether the shipping leader treated plaintiff the way he did because of plaintiff's sex, or whether the shipping leader subjected all employees to sexual comments and touching, regardless of gender. Fry v. Wheatland Tube, LLC, 2019-Ohio-1453, 135 N.E.3d 420, 2019 Ohio App. LEXIS 1536 (Ohio Ct. App., Guernsey County 2019).

In a same sex sexual harassment suit, the trial court properly found that the shipping leader was not plaintiff's supervisor as three co-workers testified that the shipping leader was not plaintiff's supervisor, therefore, no genuine issue of material fact existed on the issue. Fry v. Wheatland Tube, LLC, 2019-Ohio-1453, 135 N.E.3d 420, 2019 Ohio App. LEXIS 1536 (Ohio Ct. App., Guernsey County 2019).

Ohio Supreme Court has held that the harasser's words and conduct themselves may sometimes suffice to raise the inference of homosexuality or sexual desire circumstantially. Fry v. Wheatland Tube, LLC, 2019-Ohio-1453, 135 N.E.3d 420, 2019 Ohio App. LEXIS 1536 (Ohio Ct. App., Guernsey County 2019).

## NOTES TO UNPUBLISHED DECISIONS

Analysis



**Adverse employment action**

*Unpublished decision:* City employees' race discrimination claims failed because they did not suffer an adverse employment action based on investigations, media coverage, the loss of remote parking privileges, the requirement to complete time sheets, the presence of a union representative during interviews, and the use of tape-recording during interviews. Arnold v. City of Columbus, 515 Fed. Appx. 524, 2013 FED App. 0189N, 2013 U.S. App. LEXIS 3786 (6th Cir. Ohio), cert. denied, 571 U.S. 991, 134 S. Ct. 532, 187 L. Ed. 2d 370, 2013 U.S. LEXIS 7971 (U.S. 2013).

*Unpublished decision:* Human Resources Vice-President's (VP's) alleged conduct qualified as a materially adverse employment action because even though the district court characterized the encounter as an "occasional insult" or "stray comment," a disinterested witness to the incident, a temporary employee, perceived it quite differently. He confirmed that he heard the VP yell "of shit" at the employee, described the tone in the VP's voice as "one of extreme anger," characterized the look that the VP gave to the employee as "one of hate" and "very threatening," and stated that the VP's "demeanor and voice frightened me as I was not sure what he would do next."Wharton v. Gorman-Rupp Co., 309 Fed. Appx. 990, 2009 FED App. 0116N, 2009 U.S. App. LEXIS 2667 (6th Cir. Ohio 2009).

**Burden of proof**

*Unpublished decision:* Plaintiff, a female former employee, stated a prima facie claim for violations of the Equal Pay Act, 29 U.S.C.S. § 206(d), the Ohio Equal Pay Act, R.C. 4111.17, and R.C. 4112.02; she also showed that the defendant employer's stated reasons for her lower pay than similar male workers could be pretextual. Vehar v. Cole Nat'l Group, Inc., 251 Fed. Appx. 993, 2007 FED App. 0760N, 2007 U.S. App. LEXIS 25474 (6th Cir. Ohio 2007).

*Unpublished decision:* Employee failed to present a prima facie case of retaliation under R.C. 4112.02 because the fact that her termination occurred soon after she filed an Ohio Civil Rights Commission charge, standing alone, was insufficient to establish a causal connection. Sosby v. Miller Brewing Co., 211 Fed. Appx. 382, 2006 FED App. 0860N, 2006 U.S. App. LEXIS 29194 (6th Cir. Ohio 2006).

**Disability discrimination**

*Unpublished decision:* Even if a former employee established prima facie cases of retaliation under 29 U.S.C.S. § 2615(a) and disability discrimination under R.C. 4112.02(A) against a former employer, the claims failed because the employee could not demonstrate that the employer's proffered reason for the employee's termination, which was the employee's misrepresentations about the employee's absence from work, was pretextual; the employer made a reasonably informed and considered decision before terminating the employee for violating its code of business conduct, and the employee failed to present evidence calling into question its honest belief. Marks v. Ohio Bell Tel. Co., 2012 U.S. App. LEXIS 26891 (6th Cir. Ohio July 19, 2012).

**—Burden of proof**

*Unpublished decision:* Employee could not carry her burden of showing that she was able to safely and substantially perform the essential functions of her job, with or without reasonable accommodation where hiring a part-time aide would have violated the district's collective bargaining agreement with the teachers' union because the union was unwilling to provide its consent. Belasco v. Warrensville Heights City Sch. Dist., 634 Fed. Appx. 507, 2015 FED App. 0813N, 2015 U.S. App. LEXIS 21493 (6th Cir. Ohio 2015).

*Unpublished decision:* District court properly granted summary judgment to defendants on the employee's disability-discrimination claim where the District's stated reasons for terminating the employee—her failure to perform the essential functions of her job, her falsification of records, and the results of her fitness-for-duty tests—had an adequate basis in fact. Belasco v. Warrensville Heights City Sch. Dist., 634 Fed. Appx. 507, 2015 FED App. 0813N, 2015 U.S. App. LEXIS 21493 (6th Cir. Ohio 2015).

**—Diabetes**

*Unpublished decision:* Terminated employee's disability discrimination claim failed because the employee's diabetes was not a qualifying disability since, at most, the employee's diabetes caused a temporary limitation on a major life activity. Greer v. Cleveland Clinic Health Sys. - E. Region, 503 Fed. Appx. 422, 2012 FED App. 1124N, 2012 U.S. App. LEXIS 22594 (6th Cir. Ohio 2012).

**—Not shown**

*Unpublished decision:* Terminated employee's disability discrimination claim failed because the employee was excluded from statutory protection and failed to set forth a prima facie case for discrimination on the basis of perceived drug use since the employee was a "current" drug user at the time of the termination because the employee was engaged in illegal drug use approximately three months prior to the termination. Greer v. Cleveland Clinic Health Sys. - E. Region, 503 Fed. Appx. 422, 2012 FED App. 1124N, 2012 U.S. App. LEXIS 22594 (6th Cir. Ohio 2012).

**Dismissal, generally**

*Unpublished decision:* Summary judgment in favor of the employer with regard to employee's race discrimination and retaliation claims brought under Title VII of the Civil Rights Act of 1964, 42 U.S.C.S. § 2000e-2 et seq., 42 U.S.C.S. § 1981 and R.C. 4112.02 et seq., was affirmed because the employee failed to establish that he was similarly situated to other employees who were not terminated due to safety violations and the employee did not establish a causal link between his termination and the prior civil rights complaints he had filed. Gibson v. Shelly Co., 314 Fed. Appx. 760, 2008 FED App. 0507N, 2008 U.S. App. LEXIS 17799 (6th Cir. Ohio 2008).

**Employer**

*Unpublished decision:* Individual defendants could not be held personally liable under Title VII of the Civil Rights Act of 1964; thus, the Title VII and R.C. 4112.02 claims against the individual library workers and the former assistant chief of security were properly dismissed. Colston v. Cleveland Pub. Library, 522 Fed. Appx. 332, 2013 FED App. 0371N, 2013 U.S. App. LEXIS 7519 (6th Cir. Ohio), modified, 2013 FED App. 0377N, 2013 U.S. App. LEXIS 7690 (6th Cir. Ohio 2013).

**Federal preemption**

*Unpublished decision:* Labor Management Relations Act preempted employees' gender discrimination claims regarding the employer's failure to recall them from layoff, because resolution of each of the claims was dependent on an analysis of the collective bargaining agreement between the union and the employer. Diehl v. Int'l Truck & Engine Corp., 132 Fed. Appx. 590, 2005 U.S. App. LEXIS 8977 (6th Cir. Ohio 2005).

**Gender discrimination**

*Unpublished decision:* Employee's gender discrimination claim failed because the employee did not show that the supervisor's insults and profane language, and comments about employees' appearances, were based on gender or were only directed at females. Colston v. Cleveland Pub. Library, 522 Fed. Appx. 332, 2013 FED App. 0371N, 2013 U.S. App. LEXIS

7519 (6th Cir. Ohio), modified, 2013 FED App. 0377N, 2013 U.S. App. LEXIS 7690 (6th Cir. Ohio 2013).

*Unpublished decision:* Terminated employee's sex discrimination and retaliation claims failed because the employee presented evidence in support of an allegation that the employee's supervisor treated the employee unfairly due to the supervisor's jealousy of the employee's relationship with the employee's partner, but provided no evidence of discriminatory treatment due to the employee's gender. Blackshear v. Interstate Brands Corp., 495 Fed. Appx. 613, 2012 FED App. 0917N, 2012 U.S. App. LEXIS 17628 (6th Cir. Ohio 2012).

*Unpublished decision:* Because gender-related statements were not made by the decisionmaker or related to a termination decision, the alleged comparator was not similarly situated as he was plaintiff former employee's supervisor, and defendant former employer's reason for terminating the employee was department restructuring and aligning talents, the employee's gender discrimination claims failed. Mann v. Navicor Group, LLC, 488 Fed. Appx. 994, 2012 FED App. 0782N, 2012 U.S. App. LEXIS 14978 (6th Cir. Ohio 2012).

*Unpublished decision:* Employee, who worked as a coating and finishing mechanic, failed to make a prima facie case as to claims of sex discrimination because there was no evidence that similarly situated male employees received more overtime or training than she did. A group leader, who had a different job description and a higher rate of pay, was not similarly situated to the employee, and the employee did not identify which employees received training or what training similarly situated male employees received. Martin v. GE, 187 Fed. Appx. 553, 2006 FED App. 0466N, 2006 U.S. App. LEXIS 16810 (6th Cir. Ohio 2006).

**—Generally**

*Unpublished decision:* District court properly dismissed employee's gender discrimination claim because employee failed to allege any occasion where employer selected male employee over her for position of kitchen manager. Freeman v. Shaker Heights City Sch. Dist., 2012 U.S. App. LEXIS 27048 (6th Cir. Ohio Nov. 26, 2012).

*Unpublished decision:* District court properly granted summary judgment in favor of a city, as employer, in a hostile work environment suit filed under R.C. 4112.02 and 42 U.S.C.S. § 2000e-2(a)(1) of Title VII of the Civil Rights Act of 1964 by a terminated employee who admitted a share of blame in a massive wastewater spill at the city's water pollution control plant; the employee failed to establish that she was harassed in a sexually explicit manner or that the alleged harassment was motivated by any sort of sexual animus as opposed to personality conflicts. Conley v. City of Findlay, 266 Fed. Appx. 400, 2008 FED App. 0083N, 2008 U.S. App. LEXIS 2382 (6th Cir. Ohio 2008).

**—Similarly situated**

*Unpublished decision:* Employee's gender discrimination and hostile work environment claims under 42 U.S.C.S. § 2000e-2 and R.C. 4112.02 against an employer failed under summary judgment because the employee did not establish that the employee was treated differently than similarly situated male coworkers or that the employer did not take immediate and appropriate corrective action; retaliation claims against the employer that alleged the employer retaliated against the employee for complaining about perceived harassment and hostile work environment also failed under summary judgment because the employee did not establish a causal connection between each alleged adverse employment action and the employee's complaints to the employer. Colston v. Cleveland Pub. Library, 2013 FED App. 0377N, 2013 U.S. App. LEXIS 7690 (6th Cir. Ohio Apr. 15, 2013).

**Handicap discrimination**

*Unpublished decision:* In a Fair Housing Act case in which a non-profit fair housing advocacy organization appealed a district court's entry of judgment in favor of a property owner and his company on its claim that they made discriminatory statements based on handicap in connection with rental housing, the jury instructions were not a model of clarity. But as the jury had a basis from which to decide whether the owner's statements were discriminatory, any error was harmless. Fair Hous. Res. Ctr., Inc. v. Djm's 4 Reasons, LTD., 499 Fed. Appx. 414, 2012 FED App. 0981N, 2012 U.S. App. LEXIS 18894 (6th Cir. Ohio 2012).

**—Perception by employer**

*Unpublished decision:* Prospective employer was entitled to summary judgment in an action under R.C. 4112.02(A) and the Americans with Disabilities Act (ADA), 42 U.S.C.S. § 12101 et seq., by a job applicant who was denied employment as a machine repairman after a pre-employment medical examination showed that a prior knee injury might result in restrictions; the applicant failed to create a genuine issue of fact as to whether the employer regarded him as disabled under R.C. 4112.02(A) and under 42 U.S.C.S. § 12102(2) of the ADA. Therefore, the applicant was not a qualified individual with a disability for purposes of 42 U.S.C.S. § 12112(a) and R.C. 4112.02(A).Dunaway v. Ford Motor Co., 134 Fed. Appx. 872, 2005 U.S. App. LEXIS 10089 (6th Cir. Ohio 2005).

**—Reasonable accommodation**

*Unpublished decision:* District court properly granted summary judgment for the employer on the employees' reasonable modification claims under Americans with Disabilities Act, 42 U.S.C.S. § 12101 et seq., and R.C. 4112.02 because the employees did not specify the particular job modifications they sought, which made it impossible to determine whether such accommodations were reasonable or whether they would have resulted in the shifting of "essential" work tasks to other employees. Bingaman v. P&G, 2005 FED App. 0563N, 2005 U.S. App. LEXIS 13596 (6th Cir. Ohio July 6, 2005).

*Unpublished decision:* District court properly granted summary judgment for the employer on the employees' failure-to-transfer claims under Americans with Disabilities Act, 42 U.S.C.S. § 12101 et seq., and R.C. 4112.02 because the employees did not show, at the time their positions were terminated, that positions were available in other facilities for which they were qualified and which would have accommodated their restrictions. Bingaman v. P&G, 2005 FED App. 0563N, 2005 U.S. App. LEXIS 13596 (6th Cir. Ohio July 6, 2005).

**Hostile work environment**

*Unpublished decision:* Employee had not offered any evidence or arguments that the library did not take immediate and appropriate corrective action after her complaints, and therefore, her hostile work environment claim failed as a matter of law. Colston v. Cleveland Pub. Library, 522 Fed. Appx. 332, 2013 FED App. 0371N, 2013 U.S. App. LEXIS 7519 (6th Cir. Ohio), modified, 2013 FED App. 0377N, 2013 U.S. App. LEXIS 7690 (6th Cir. Ohio 2013).

*Unpublished decision:* City employees' hostile work environment claims failed because the alleged incidents, which included investigations and race-related comments, took place over a number of years and the employees did not show that they were sufficiently severe or pervasive to alter the conditions of their employment and create an abusive working environment. Arnold v. City of Columbus, 515 Fed. Appx. 524, 2013 FED App. 0189N, 2013 U.S. App. LEXIS 3786 (6th Cir. Ohio), cert. denied, 571 U.S. 991, 134 S. Ct. 532, 187 L. Ed. 2d 370, 2013 U.S. LEXIS 7971 (U.S. 2013).

*Unpublished decision:* District court properly granted summary judgment in favor of a city, as employer, in a hostile work environment suit filed under R.C. 4112.02 and 42 U.S.C.S. § 2000e-2(a)(1) of Title VII of the Civil Rights Act of 1964 by a terminated employee who admitted a share of blame in a massive wastewater spill at the city's water pollution control plant; the employee failed to establish that she was harassed in a sexually explicit manner or that the alleged harassment was motivated by any sort of sexual animus as opposed to personality conflicts. Conley v. City of Findlay, 266 Fed. Appx. 400, 2008 FED App. 0083N, 2008 U.S. App. LEXIS 2382 (6th Cir. Ohio 2008).

*Unpublished decision:* Employees failed to establish a prima facie case of a racially hostile work environment because they did not show workplace conduct that was sufficiently severe or pervasive to be actionable under 42 U.S.C.S. § 2000e-2(a)(1), 42 U.S.C.S. § 1981, or R.C. 4112. Although a coworker's alleged comments, if true, were offensive, she denied using a racial epithet, and the employer's investigation of her alleged statement did not corroborate the employees' complaints; the employer responded reasonably and appropriately to the employees' complaints while the employees contributed to the workplace tension by taking the offense at fellow employees' innocuous comments, gestures, or looks. Lovelace v. BP Prods. N. Am., Inc., 252 Fed. Appx. 33, 2007 FED App. 0749N, 2007 U.S. App. LEXIS 24807 (6th Cir. Ohio 2007).

*Unpublished decision:* While workplace conduct and comments were both inappropriate and racially insensitive, in the context of the joking workplace environment the conduct and comments were not severe or pervasive and did not affect the employees' ability to work. Woods v. FacilitySource, LLC, 640 Fed. Appx. 478, 2016 FED App. 0074N, 2016 U.S. App. LEXIS 1988 (6th Cir. Ohio 2016).

*Unpublished decision:* Reasonable jury could find that the executive chef's alleged assault on one employee was sufficiently severe by itself that it created a hostile work environment where (1) the employee could feel the chef's penis as he pressed against her, (2) the chef positioned himself in a way that prevented the employee from moving to escape the invasion, and (3) the chef failed to relent, despite repeated requests. Ault v. Oberlin Coll., 620 Fed. Appx. 395, 2015 FED App. 0527N, 2015 U.S. App. LEXIS 12904 (6th Cir. Ohio 2015).

**Housing discrimination**

*Unpublished decision:* Given that the law regarding companion animals was somewhat unclear at the time that plaintiff housing corporation sought a declaratory judgment, and given that defendants had the benefit of their pet's company while awaiting the outcome of the litigation, the corporation's failure to engage in a more constructive dialogue with defendants did not constitute a denial of their request for an accommodation. Overlook Mut. Homes, Inc. v. Spencer, 415 Fed. Appx. 617, 2011 FED App. 0061N, 2011 U.S. App. LEXIS 1949 (6th Cir. Ohio 2011).

**Joint and several liability**

*Unpublished decision:* District court properly granted summary judgment in favor of a labor union chairman in an employee's action alleging retaliation in violation of R.C. 4112.02(I); even assuming that the employee could show that the union chairman met the statutory definition of "employer" under R.C. 4112.01(A)(2), there was no liability to attach jointly or severally to the union chairman because neither the employer nor the union were found liable for the alleged retaliation. Garcia v. Daimler Chrysler Corp., 320 Fed. Appx. 356, 2009 FED App. 0266N, 2009 U.S. App. LEXIS 7391 (6th Cir. Ohio 2009).

**Jurisdiction**

*Unpublished decision:* When a district court properly granted summary judgment in favor of a company on an employee's claim against the company under the Americans with Disabilities Act, 42 U.S.C.S. § 12111 et seq., on the ground that the claim was time-barred under 42 U.S.C.S. § 12117(a), the district court also properly declined to exercise supplemental jurisdiction over the employee's state law claim under Ohio's handicap discrimination law, R.C. 4112.01 et seq., pursuant to 28 U.S.C.S. § 1367(c)(3). Certainly, if the federal claims are dismissed before trial, even though not insubstantial in a jurisdictional sense, the state claims should be dismissed as well. Hall v. Scotts Co., 211 Fed. Appx. 361, 2006 FED App. 0818N, 2006 U.S. App. LEXIS 27733 (6th Cir. Ohio 2006).

**Municipal employer**

*Unpublished decision:* Retaliation claims brought against town board members under R.C. 4112.02 failed because employee never made any board member aware of the alleged harassment he endured and township's policy specifically provided that the employee could bypass his supervisors if he felt that the supervisor was the source of the perceived misconduct. Anderson v. Ravenna Twp. Fire Dep't, 159 Fed. Appx. 619, 2005 FED App. 0882N, 2005 U.S. App. LEXIS 23917 (6th Cir. Ohio 2005).

**Not similarly situated**

*Unpublished decision:* Employer came forth with identical legitimate, nondiscriminatory reason for the employee's termination and refusal to rehire and reassign: a day prior to the employee's termination he was arrested on rape charge that would reasonably be made public and negatively impact the employer and none of the employees who the employee identified was identical to him. Voltz v. Erie County, 617 Fed. Appx. 417, 2015 FED App. 0451N, 2015 U.S. App. LEXIS 10309 (6th Cir. Ohio 2015).

**Police officers, firefighters**

*Unpublished decision:* Summary judgment in favor of a city was appropriate where a firefighter who voluntarily opted out of a paramedic training program had not raised a genuine issue as to whether the city's stated rationale for refusing him readmittance into the paramedic program was a pretext for unlawful discrimination or retaliation. Turner v. City of Akron, 324 Fed. Appx. 453, 2009 FED App. 0243N, 2009 U.S. App. LEXIS 6828 (6th Cir. Ohio 2009).

**Pretext for discrimination**

*Unpublished decision:* Former employee failed to show former employer's stated reasons for her termination were pretext for unlawful discrimination under the Age Discrimination in Employment Act of 1967, Title VII of the Civil Rights Act of 1964, and Ohio discrimination statute because the existence of differing opinions regarding sufficiency of the employee's performance did not create a genuine issue of material fact as to whether the employer's stated reasons for terminating her employment masked impermissible discrimination; the employer's legitimate business reason for terminating the employee was based on a supervisor losing confidence in the employee's leadership abilities. McKinley v. Skyline Chili, Inc., 534 Fed. Appx. 461, 2013 FED App. 0776N, 2013 U.S. App. LEXIS 17641 (6th Cir. Ohio 2013).

*Unpublished decision:* City employee's race discrimination claims failed because the city asserted that the employee was suspended for making false allegations against a lieutenant and that the employee's transfer was based in part on the false allegations, and the employee did not show pretext based on comments allegedly made before and during investigations or the city's continuous investigation of the employee and the fire prevention bureau. Arnold v. City of Columbus, 515 Fed. Appx. 524, 2013 FED App. 0189N, 2013 U.S. App. LEXIS 3786 (6th Cir. Ohio), cert. denied, 571 U.S. 991, 134 S. Ct. 532, 187 L. Ed. 2d 370, 2013 U.S. LEXIS 7971 (U.S. 2013).

*Unpublished decision:* Even assuming that plaintiff employee stated a prima facie case of race discrimination, her claim would have failed on summary judgment because she could not overcome defendant employer's reason for not promoting her, namely, that she was not pre-qualified prior to the election as required by the governing CBA. A reasonable jury could not have concluded that defendant's consistent enforcement of a specifically negotiated, plain and unambiguous requirement that it review team leader candidates before their election was a pretext for intentional racial discrimination. Wilson v. Ford Motor Co., 513 Fed. Appx. 585, 2013 FED App. 0137N, 2013 U.S. App. LEXIS 2671 (6th Cir. Ohio 2013).

*Unpublished decision:* District court properly granted summary judgment in favor of a city, as employer, in a sex discrimination suit filed under R.C. 4112.02 and 42 U.S.C.S. § 2000e-2(a)(1) of Title VII of the Civil Rights Act of 1964 by a terminated employee who admitted a share of blame in a massive wastewater spill at the city's water pollution control plant; the city's termination notice listed incompetence, nonfeasance, negligence, and dishonesty as the reasons for the termination, and the employee failed to rebut as pretextual the city's legitimate and nondiscriminatory reasons for terminating her employment. Conley v. City of Findlay, 266 Fed. Appx. 400, 2008 FED App. 0083N, 2008 U.S. App. LEXIS 2382 (6th Cir. Ohio 2008).

*Unpublished decision:* Former employer was entitled to summary judgment on a former employee's disability and race discrimination claims under the Americans with Disabilities Act, 42 U.S.C.S. § 12101 et seq., Title VII, 42 U.S.C.S. § 2000e et seq., and R.C. 4112.02, because the employee failed to show that the employer's proffered reason for her discharge—falsification of bank records—was a pretext for discrimination. Instead, the evidence showed that the employer had been equally unforgiving with many other employees when it came to similar falsification charges. Scott v. FirstMerit Corp., 167 Fed. Appx. 480, 2006 FED App. 0060N, 2006 U.S. App. LEXIS 1709 (6th Cir. Ohio 2006).

*Unpublished decision:* Where store employees, each over 50 years old, were fired for accepting plants from vendor who was going to throw them away, district court erred in granting summary judgment to employer because there were genuine issues of material fact regarding whether its proffered reason for discharging employees was pretext for age discrimination since employer did not have zero-tolerance rule for violations of gifts policy and employees were fired for what was at worst technica—and seemingly innocent—violation of gifts policy. Moffat v. Wal-Mart Stores, Inc., 620 Fed. Appx. 453, 2015 FED App. 0582N, 2015 U.S. App. LEXIS 14537 (6th Cir. Ohio 2015).

*Unpublished decision:* In this Age Discrimination in Employment Act action, the grant of summary judgment to the employer was affirmed because the employee failed to prove by a preponderance of the evidence that the employer's terminating his employment for failure to comply with the 2012 sales plan was a pretext for age discrimination. Moore v. AMPAC, 645 Fed. Appx. 495, 2016 FED App. 0276N, 2016 U.S. App. LEXIS 9326 (6th Cir. Ohio 2016).

**Prima facie case**

*Unpublished decision:* District court properly granted summary judgment for an employer in a former employee's action alleging discrimination based on race and sex in violation of 42 U.S.C.S. § 2000e-2 of Title VII of the Civil Rights Act of 1964, 42 U.S.C.S. § 2000e et seq., and in violation of R.C. 4112.02; the employee failed to make out a prima facie case of discrimination on a wrongful termination claim because she failed to demonstrate that she was treated differently than other employees to whom she was similarly situated. The employee failed to show that other employees exceeded their allotted short-term disability benefits, elected not to apply for long-term disability benefits, and were not subsequently terminated for failure to return to work. Sullivan v. Coca-Cola Bottling Co., 182 Fed. Appx. 473, 2006 FED App. 0360N, 2006 U.S. App. LEXIS 12390 (6th Cir. Ohio 2006).

*Unpublished decision:* Where store employees, each over 50 years old, were fired for accepting plants from a vendor who was going to throw them away, leaving the department staffed primarily by three significantly younger employees, and the employer hired two significantly younger employees as replacements, the former employees established a prima facie case of age discrimination. Moffat v. Wal-Mart Stores, Inc., 620 Fed. Appx. 453, 2015 FED App. 0582N, 2015 U.S. App. LEXIS 14537 (6th Cir. Ohio 2015).

**Race discrimination**

*Unpublished decision:* Terminated Caucasian employee's race discrimination claims failed because the employee had no proof that the employee's supervisor treated similarly situated employees outside of the employee's protected class more favorably regarding the supervisor's vacation pay practice and route assignments. Craig-Wood v. Time Warner NY Cable LLC, 549 Fed. Appx. 505, 2014 FED App. 0106N, 2014 U.S. App. LEXIS 2405 (6th Cir. Ohio 2014).

*Unpublished decision:* As the individual defendants did not participate in the hiring decisions and, even assuming all of the hired candidates were less qualified, a reasonable jury could not infer causation without evidence that the board of education knew about the teacher's job applications or evidence that the hiring decisionmakers knew about the teacher's state civil rights commission complaint. Thus, no reasonable jury could conclude that the teacher established a prima facie case of retaliation. Hopkins v. Canton City Bd. of Educ., 477 Fed. Appx. 349, 2012 FED App. 0437N, 2012 U.S. App. LEXIS 8388 (6th Cir. Ohio 2012).

*Unpublished decision:* Given the lack of similarly situated administrators facing the teacher's disciplinary circumstances, the complete absence of record evidence from which a factfinder could infer pretext for hiring discrimination, and the inconclusive statistical data unaccompanied by any expert analysis, no genuine issue of material fact existed for the jury regarding the state discrimination claim. Hopkins v. Canton City Bd. of Educ., 477 Fed. Appx. 349, 2012 FED App. 0437N, 2012 U.S. App. LEXIS 8388 (6th Cir. Ohio 2012).

*Unpublished decision:* Employee failed to show that his supervisor was liable for his termination; the decision to terminate the employee occurred above, not below, the supervisor, and in a manner that made it unlikely that race discrimination by the supervisor influenced the proceedings. There was ample evidence in the record to support the claim that the employee was terminated for violation of company policy—this was the reason the employer gave in the termination notice, the motion for summary judgment, and on appeal; thus, the employee did not create a question of fact to whether his termination was the product of discriminatory conduct by the supervisor. Butler v. Cooper Std. Auto., Inc., 376 Fed. Appx. 487, 2010 FED App. 0270N, 2010 U.S. App. LEXIS 8968 (6th Cir. Ohio 2010), aff'd, 498 Fed. Appx. 549, 2012 FED App. 0976N, 2012 U.S. App. LEXIS 18720 (6th Cir. Ohio 2012).

*Unpublished decision:* Where an African-American employee's position was eliminated and a white male was hired to fill a new position, summary judgment was inappropriate as to the employee's race discrimination claims because (1) a question of fact existed regarding whether the newly-hired chef replaced the employee, and (2) regarding pretext, defendants' failure to alert the employee to the impending termination or of the chef 1 vacancy created an inference that they were intentionally attempting to get rid of the employee, and the employee offered evidence of a pattern of discrimination. Thompson v. UHHS Richmond Heights Hosp., Inc., 372 Fed. Appx. 620, 2010 FED App. 0225N, 2010 U.S. App. LEXIS 7439 (6th Cir. Ohio 2010).

*Unpublished decision:* Where an African-American employee was terminated for violation of the attendance policy and a union contract, the employee's race discrimination claim failed because the employee was not sufficiently comparable to two white female coworkers since any acts of accommodation of them were done by the employer's predecessor, and not by the employer. Jackson v. Int'l Fiber Corp., 395 Fed. Appx. 275, 2010 FED App. 0594N, 2010 U.S. App. LEXIS 18706 (6th Cir. Ohio 2010), cert. denied, 568 U.S. 814, 133 S. Ct. 111, 184 L. Ed. 2d 25, 2012 U.S. LEXIS 7481 (U.S. 2012).

*Unpublished decision:* District court properly granted an employer's motion for summary judgment in an unsuccessful job applicant's action alleging race discrimination in violation of 42 U.S.C.S. § 2000e-2 of Title VII of the Civil Rights Act of 1964, 42 U.S.C.S. § 2000e et seq., and in violation of R.C. 4112.02(A) because the 24-year-old applicant failed to establish that he was qualified for the sales associate position, which required a high school diploma or a general equivalency degree. Overall v. RadioShack Corp., 202 Fed. Appx. 865, 2006 FED App. 0777N, 2006 U.S. App. LEXIS 26121 (6th Cir. Ohio 2006).

*Unpublished decision:* Employee's testimony that the market consultant told her the company was de-emphasizing the Hispanic market, coupled with the alleged decrease in the employer's presence at Hispanic events and the sales director's admission that she hired the employee because she was Hispanic, was not a sufficient basis on which a jury may infer racial discrimination in the employee's displacement and termination two years after the consultant's statement was made because two years was a long gap over which to infer a causal connection. Lopez v. Am. Family Ins. Co., 618 Fed. Appx. 794, 2015 FED App. 0474N, 2015 U.S. App. LEXIS 11020 (6th Cir. Ohio 2015).

**Burden of proof**

*Unpublished decision:* Grant of summary judgment to the employer was affirmed because the employee offered no evidence that the employer replaced her with white or male employees where to the contrary, the employee's part-time slot was picked up by three African-American females and one African-American male. Wilson v. Chipotle Mexican Grill, Inc., 580 Fed. Appx. 395, 2014 FED App. 0729N, 2014 U.S. App. LEXIS 18008 (6th Cir. Ohio 2014).

**—Promotion**

*Unpublished decision:* Employees failed to show that decisions not to promote the employees were based on racial discrimination since the employees failed to show that they possessed the necessary qualifications for a senior account manager or that others without the necessary qualifications were nonetheless promoted. Woods v. FacilitySource, LLC, 640 Fed. Appx. 478, 2016 FED App. 0074N, 2016 U.S. App. LEXIS 1988 (6th Cir. Ohio 2016).

**—Burden of proof**

*Unpublished decision:* District court erred in dismissing employee's race discrimination claim for failure to state claim upon initial screening because employer's alleged inconsistent application of high-school-diploma requirement may have suggested pretext. Freeman v. Shaker Heights City Sch. Dist., 2012 U.S. App. LEXIS 27048 (6th Cir. Ohio Nov. 26, 2012).

*Unpublished decision:* Fire Prevention Bureau officer failed to prove the city's reason for disciplining him to be pretextual sufficiently to defeat summary judgment and merit a jury trial; the city reasonably considered the severity of the officer's insubordination in making decisions regarding the officer, and insufficient evidence suggested any racial or retaliatory animus. No reasonable jury could have concluded that the officer experienced harassment that was sufficiently severe or pervasive to alter the conditions of his employment and create an abusive working environment. Fullen v. City of Columbus, 514 Fed. Appx. 601, 2013 FED App. 0156N, 2013 U.S. App. LEXIS 3306 (6th Cir. Ohio 2013).

*Unpublished decision:* Because plaintiff former employee did not establish that his termination was merely a pretext for race discrimination or retaliation, and he did not provide sufficient evidence of pervasive discrimination to support his hostile work environment claim, defendant former employer was entitled to summary judgment on his federal and Ohio law claims. Plaintiff failed to show that it was his race, and not his actions interfering with a co-worker's productivity, that led to his termination; defendant's proffered reason for plaintiff's termination was consistent, and plaintiff's arguments to the contrary did not show that the company had a discriminatory motive. Butler v. Cooper-Standard Auto., Inc., 498 Fed. Appx. 549, 2012 FED App. 0976N, 2012 U.S. App. LEXIS 18720 (6th Cir. Ohio 2012).

*Unpublished decision:* Employer who terminated an African-American employee for violating a video rental policy was entitled to summary judgment in the employee's race discrimination action under R.C. 4112.02 and 42 U.S.C.S. § 2000e-2(a)(1) of Title VII of the Civil Rights Act of 1964, 42 U.S.C.S. § 2000e et seq.; the employee did not set forth sufficient evidence, direct or circumstantial, from which a reasonable jury could logically infer that race was a motivating factor in the termination decision because she presented no evidence that white employees were treated differently and no evidence that an immediate supervisor with an alleged racial animus was the decisionmaker. Harris v. Giant Eagle Inc., 133 Fed. Appx. 288, 2005 U.S. App. LEXIS 9997 (6th Cir. Ohio 2005).

**—Discharge**

*Unpublished decision:* Terminated employee's race discrimination and retaliation claims failed because (1) the employer presented evidence that it terminated the employee because the employee's altercation with the employee's partner violated the workplace violence policy, and (2) the employee did not demonstrate pretext since the employee did not present any evidence demonstrating that the violation of the policy did not actually motivate the decision to discharge the employee. Blackshear v. Interstate Brands Corp., 495 Fed. Appx. 613, 2012 FED App. 0917N, 2012 U.S. App. LEXIS 17628 (6th Cir. Ohio 2012).

**—Hostile work environment**

*Unpublished decision:* Terminated Caucasian employee's hostile work environment claim failed because the complained-of conduct was not objectively hostile, and the court could not abandon the subjective/objective hostility requirement. Craig-Wood v. Time Warner NY Cable LLC, 549 Fed. Appx. 505, 2014 FED App. 0106N, 2014 U.S. App. LEXIS 2405 (6th Cir. Ohio 2014).

**—Promotion**

*Unpublished decision:* Defendant employer was entitled to summary judgment on plaintiff employee's race discrimination claim that she brought pursuant to Title VII of the Civil Rights Act of 1964 and R.C. ch. 4112 because she did not show that she was qualified for the promotion because she did not obtain pre-election certification as required under a CBA or that she was similarly situated to the promoted employee who obtained the necessary certification. Wilson v. Ford Motor Co., 513 Fed. Appx. 585, 2013 FED App. 0137N, 2013 U.S. App. LEXIS 2671 (6th Cir. Ohio 2013).

**—Salary**

*Unpublished decision:* Employees failed to show a wage disparity based on racial discrimination since higher wages for newly hired account managers were based on new hiring guidelines requiring higher qualifications, and the employees' seniority was not entitled to greater weight than educational and experiential accomplishments. Woods v. FacilitySource, LLC, 640 Fed. Appx. 478, 2016 FED App. 0074N, 2016 U.S. App. LEXIS 1988 (6th Cir. Ohio 2016).

**Reduction in force**

*Unpublished decision:* Mere fact that defendant employer used subjective criteria in deciding to fire plaintiff employee as part of a reduction in force (RIF) could not by itself establish pretext for age and gender discrimination under Ohio law. Plaintiff presented no evidence that defendant terminated women or older workers at a higher rate during the RIF, that defendant deviated from its normal use of subjective evaluation procedures, or that an evaluator lied about her supervisor's comments; in the absence of any such evidence, the mere fact that defendant used subjective criteria could not by itself establish pretext. Beck v. Buckeye Pipeline Servs. Co., 501 Fed. Appx. 447, 2012 FED App. 1041N, 2012 U.S. App. LEXIS 20621 (6th Cir. Ohio 2012).

*Unpublished decision:* Defendant employer was entitled to summary judgment because plaintiff electrician did not present evidence to rebut the most likely race-neutral reason for his layoff—a reduction in force; the fact that an employer facing a work shortage shifted the available work to some employees and laid off the rest (including plaintiff who was African-American)—without more—failed to establish a prima facie case of discrimination. Both plaintiff's single-motive and mixed-motive claims for race discrimination under Title VII of the Civil Rights Act and Ohio's antidiscrimination law failed because plaintiff failed to link his grievances to race. Copeland v. Regent Elec, Inc., 499 Fed. Appx. 425, 2012 FED App. 0984N, 2012 U.S. App. LEXIS 18893 (6th Cir. Ohio 2012).

**Regarded as having a disability**

**—Not shown**

*Unpublished decision:* Terminated employee's disability discrimination claims failed because the employee did not establish a question of fact over whether supervisors perceived the employee as disabled since the reasons for referral to a fitness-for-duty evaluation were directly related to the employee's ability to do the employee's job, and even if the employee could show that the employer "delayed" the employee's return to work because of the employee's interpretation of a form, it would still not establish that the employee's leave was extended because the employer perceived the employee as disabled. Johnson v. Univ. Hosps. Physician Servs., 617 Fed. Appx. 487, 2015 FED App. 0485N, 2015 U.S. App. LEXIS 11862 (6th Cir. Ohio 2015).

**Retaliation**

*Unpublished decision:* Even if a former employee's discrimination complaint to human resources was protected activity and the employee established a causal connection between the complaint and her termination, the employee's retaliation claims under the Age Discrimination in Employment Act, Title VII of the Civil Rights Act of 1964, and Ohio discrimination statute failed because the employee could not show the employer's proffered reasons for her termination were pretextual and could not show the termination was in retaliation for the complaint made six months prior to her discharge. McKinley v. Skyline Chili, Inc., 534 Fed. Appx. 461, 2013 FED App. 0776N, 2013 U.S. App. LEXIS 17641 (6th Cir. Ohio 2013).

*Unpublished decision:* Employee's retaliation claims failed because the employee failed to establish a causal connection between each action and her complaints to the library. Colston v. Cleveland Pub. Library, 522 Fed. Appx. 332, 2013 FED App. 0371N, 2013 U.S. App. LEXIS 7519 (6th Cir. Ohio), modified, 2013 FED App. 0377N, 2013 U.S. App. LEXIS 7690 (6th Cir. Ohio 2013).



*Unpublished decision:* City employees' retaliation claims failed because they did not present sufficient evidence of a causal connection between their discrimination complaints and the adverse employment actions, which included investigations, loss of remote parking privileges, requirement to complete time sheets, and an employee's suspension and transfer. Arnold v. City of Columbus, 515 Fed. Appx. 524, 2013 FED App. 0189N, 2013 U.S. App. LEXIS 3786 (6th Cir. Ohio), cert. denied, 571 U.S. 991, 134 S. Ct. 532, 187 L. Ed. 2d 370, 2013 U.S. LEXIS 7971 (U.S. 2013).

*Unpublished decision:* Former employee's claims against an employer under 29 U.S.C.S. § 2615(a)(2) of the Family and Medical Leave Act of 1993 (FMLA), 29 U.S.C.S. § 2601 et seq., failed under summary judgment because the employee could not establish a causal connection between the employee's FMLA leave complaints and the non-renewal of the employee's contract; the employee's state retaliation claim under R.C. 4112.02(I) that alleged the contract was not renewed on the basis that the employee complained about gender discrimination in violation of R.C. 4112.02(A) also failed under summary judgment because the employee did not identify evidence from which a reasonable jury could conclude that the employer's legitimate, nondiscriminatory reason concerning job performance was pretextual. Fields v. Fairfield County Bd. of Developmental Disabilities, 507 Fed. Appx. 549, 2012 FED App. 1258N, 2012 U.S. App. LEXIS 25124 (6th Cir. Ohio 2012).

*Unpublished decision:* Although plaintiff, a former assistant fire chief, made out a prima facie case of retaliation under Ohio law, allegedly for making complaints that defendant fire chief engaged in sexual harassment, he failed to show that defendant fire chief and mayor's nondiscriminatory reasons for his discipline and termination, i.e., his violation of rules and policies and his failure to return to work, were pretext for retaliation. Horner v. Klein, 497 Fed. Appx. 484, 2012 FED App. 0955N, 2012 U.S. App. LEXIS 18372 (6th Cir. Ohio 2012).

*Unpublished decision:* As the individual defendants did not participate in the hiring decisions and, even assuming all of the hired candidates were less qualified, a reasonable jury could not infer causation without evidence that the board of education knew about the teacher's job applications or evidence that the hiring decisionmakers knew about the teacher's state civil rights commission complaint. Thus, no reasonable jury could conclude that the teacher established a prima facie case of retaliation. Hopkins v. Canton City Bd. of Educ., 477 Fed. Appx. 349, 2012 FED App. 0437N, 2012 U.S. App. LEXIS 8388 (6th Cir. Ohio 2012).

*Unpublished decision:* Employee failed to show that the supervisor took any adverse action against him based on his Equal Employment Opportunity Commission (EEOC) complaints of racial harassment; two of the alleged actions were taken prior to the employee's initial complaints to the EEOC and thus could not serve as the basis for a retaliation claim regardless of whether they constituted adverse employment actions. The last two notices, which included the employee's termination, could not serve as the basis for a retaliation claim because the supervisor's alleged involvement was not sufficient to form a fact question as to whether the notices were the products of discrimination by the supervisor. Butler v. Cooper Std. Auto., Inc., 376 Fed. Appx. 487, 2010 FED App. 0270N, 2010 U.S. App. LEXIS 8968 (6th Cir. Ohio 2010), aff'd, 498 Fed. Appx. 549, 2012 FED App. 0976N, 2012 U.S. App. LEXIS 18720 (6th Cir. Ohio 2012).

*Unpublished decision:* Summary judgment for an employer was proper in an employee's action under R.C. 4112.02(I) and Title VII of the Civil Rights Act of 1964, 42 U.S.C.S. § 2000e et seq., in which the employee alleged retaliation for reporting a harassing comment between coworkers; the employee failed to offer any admissible evidence of pretext in the employer's explanation that a suspension resulted from dishonesty and that a transfer resulted from more employees than necessary in a department. Garcia v. Daimler Chrysler Corp., 320 Fed. Appx. 356, 2009 FED App. 0266N, 2009 U.S. App. LEXIS 7391 (6th Cir. Ohio 2009).

*Unpublished decision:* Legitimacy of an employer's articulated nonretaliatory reason—an employee's deficient performance— for denying that employee a full pay raise three weeks after she complained of age discrimination was sufficiently called into question by the company's history of granting her full pay raises in previous years, despite its criticisms of her work performance and the close temporal proximity between her attorney's letter complaining of age discrimination and the adverse action..Wharton v. Gorman-Rupp Co., 309 Fed. Appx. 990, 2009 FED App. 0116N, 2009 U.S. App. LEXIS 2667 (6th Cir. Ohio 2009).

*Unpublished decision:* Summary judgment for an employer was proper in an employee's action under R.C. 4112.02(I) and Title VII of the Civil Rights Act of 1964, 42 U.S.C.S. § 2000e et seq., in which the employee alleged retaliation for reporting a harassing comment between coworkers; the employee failed to offer any admissible evidence of pretext in the employer's explanation that a suspension resulted from dishonesty and that a transfer resulted from more employees than necessary in a department. Garcia v. Daimler Chrysler Corp., 320 Fed. Appx. 356, 2009 FED App. 0266N, 2009 U.S. App. LEXIS 7391 (6th Cir. Ohio 2009).

*Unpublished decision:* Legitimacy of an employer's articulated nonretaliatory reason—an employee's deficient performance— for denying that employee a full pay raise three weeks after she complained of age discrimination was sufficiently called into question by the company's history of granting her full pay raises in previous years, despite its criticisms of her work performance and the close temporal proximity between her attorney's letter complaining of age discrimination and the adverse action..Wharton v. Gorman-Rupp Co., 309 Fed. Appx. 990, 2009 FED App. 0116N, 2009 U.S. App. LEXIS 2667 (6th Cir. Ohio 2009).

*Unpublished decision:* District court properly granted summary judgment for an employer in a former employee's action alleging retaliation in violation of 29 U.S.C.S. § 623 of the Age Discrimination in Employment Act, 29 U.S.C.S. § 621 et seq., and in violation of R.C. 4112.02(I); the employee failed to challenge the employer's nondiscriminatory reasons for changes in the employee's working conditions following the employee's internal complaint regarding a failure to promote and, therefore, he could not establish pretext for his retaliation claims. Rufo v. Dave & Busters, Inc., 2007 FED App. 0075N, 2007 U.S. App. LEXIS 2366 (6th Cir. Ohio Jan. 31, 2007).

*Unpublished decision:* Employee, who worked as a coating and finishing mechanic, failed to make a prima facie case of retaliation because there was no evidence that there was a causal connection between the employee's filing of a grievance and an employer's decision not to promote the employee; furthermore, the employee's unsupported assertion that the employer customarily promoted the most senior employee did not show that the employer's stated reason that it promoted the most qualified worker was a pretext for discrimination. Martin v. GE, 187 Fed. Appx. 553, 2006 FED App. 0466N, 2006 U.S. App. LEXIS 16810 (6th Cir. Ohio 2006).

*Unpublished decision:* District court properly granted summary judgment for an employer in a former employee's action alleging retaliation in violation of 42 U.S.C.S. § 2000e-3 of Title VII of the Civil Rights Act of 1964, 42 U.S.C.S. § 2000e et seq., and in violation of R.C. 4112.02; although the employee alleged that she received a second unfavorable evaluation after complaining of discrimination following her first unfavorable evaluation, the employee could not meet the causation requirement for her retaliation claim. The employer put forward substantial evidence demonstrating that the employee's job performance was deficient, and the employee put forward no evidence that the employer gave her a poor performance rating because of her protected activities. Sullivan v. Coca-Cola Bottling Co., 182 Fed. Appx. 473, 2006 FED App. 0360N, 2006 U.S. App. LEXIS 12390 (6th Cir. Ohio 2006).

*Unpublished decision:* Employee's claims did not constituted materially adverse employment actions where (1) the foreman's report was not a materially adverse action where regardless of whether the anglecock was closed or open, the foreman investigated but was unable to determine whether it was done for a legitimate reason or sabotage; and (2) the foreman's refusal to exercise his discretion to modify the job assignment was not an adverse action as the employee offered nothing to show that the assigned position the single position as considerably worse than the job she desired. Goodsite v. Norfolk Southern Ry., 573 Fed. Appx. 572, 2014 FED App. 0661N, 2014 U.S. App. LEXIS 16496 (6th Cir. Ohio 2014).

*Unpublished decision:* Grant of summary judgment to defendants was affirmed because the employee abandoned the job site based on her subjective, not objective, belief that the foreman gave her permission to leave work and nothing established that the manager was influenced by the foreman's alleged retaliatory animus for the employee. Goodsite v. Norfolk Southern Ry., 573 Fed. Appx. 572, 2014 FED App. 0661N, 2014 U.S. App. LEXIS 16496 (6th Cir. Ohio 2014).

*Unpublished decision:* Terminated employee's retaliation claims failed because the employee did not show pretext since the employee did not demonstrate that the employee's refusal to complete a form as instructed did not motivate the employer to terminate the employee. Johnson v. Univ. Hosps. Physician Servs., 617 Fed. Appx. 487, 2015 FED App. 0485N, 2015 U.S. App. LEXIS 11862 (6th Cir. Ohio 2015).

**Retaliatory discharge**

*Unpublished decision:* Where an employee was terminated in a layoff after returning from medical leave, the employee's retaliation claim failed because the employee did not show a causal connection since there was no possible way that the protected activity, the employee's email to the human-resources manager, could have caused the termination because the decision, which had not yet been communicated to the employee, had already been made when the employee sent the email. Blosser v. AK Steel Corp., 520 Fed. Appx. 359, 2013 FED App. 0324N, 2013 U.S. App. LEXIS 6845 (6th Cir. Ohio 2013).

*Unpublished decision:* Defendant employer was entitled to summary judgment on plaintiff former employee's retaliation claims under Title VII of the Civil Rights Act of 1964, 42 U.S.C.S. § 1981, and Ohio law because the employee failed to rebut one of defendant's proffered nonpretextual reasons for her termination, namely, that she recorded conversations with customers in violation of company policy. The recordings were made in derogation of company policy, she admittedly recorded the conversations, some even after she knew it violated company policy, and the recordings were a sufficient basis for termination; plaintiff did not show why she needed to violate the recording policy in order to oppose defendants' alleged discrimination, and nothing suggested that the recording policy was illegitimate or that it would have been futile to oppose the alleged discrimination in ways that did not violate the policy. Jones v. St. Jude Med. S.C., Inc., 504 Fed. Appx. 473, 2012 FED App. 1162N, 2012 U.S. App. LEXIS 23227 (6th Cir. Ohio 2012).

*Unpublished decision:* Former employee pled a plausible claim that the former employer retaliated against him, in violation of the Family and Medical Leave Act and R.C. 4112.02, for opposing the employer's unlawful employment and employee benefits practices because the complaint alleged the employer's various unlawful actions, the employee's opposition to these practices, and his termination mere months after expressing this opposition, despite the "great" work he performed while at the company. Rhodes v. R&L Carriers, Inc., 491 Fed. Appx. 579, 2012 FED App. 0841N, 2012 U.S. App. LEXIS 16534 (6th Cir. Ohio 2012).

*Unpublished decision:* African-American employee's retaliation claim failed because although there was a factual dispute as to whether the employee complained about perceived discrimination to a manager, there was no evidence to suggest that such complaints, whether or not they occurred, led to the employee's termination. Thompson v. UHHS Richmond Heights Hosp., Inc., 372 Fed. Appx. 620, 2010 FED App. 0225N, 2010 U.S. App. LEXIS 7439 (6th Cir. Ohio 2010).

*Unpublished decision:* Where an employee was terminated for violating cash handling rules, the employee's retaliation claim failed because the employee could not establish that the employee engaged in protected activity since the employee never spoke with management about being subjected to sexual or age-based harassment. Balding-Margolis v. Cleveland Arcade, 352 Fed. Appx. 35, 2009 FED App. 0732N, 2009 U.S. App. LEXIS 24604 (6th Cir. Ohio 2009).

*Unpublished decision:* After plaintiff, an African-American store employee, complained to human resources about race discrimination at work, a cash shortage was reported and a security camera showed a man who resembled plaintiff taking money out of a register; plaintiff was terminated after his arrest for theft, and he sued his employer for retaliation in violation of R.C. 4112.02. The district court did not err by dismissing his claim upon summary judgment, because plaintiff did not make a sufficient showing of pretext to overcome the employer's proffered legitimate non-discriminatory reason for reporting him to the police; plaintiff was dismissed for violating the employee-discount policy and provided no evidence that his dismissal was retaliatory. Graham v. Best Buy Stores, L.P., 298 Fed. Appx. 487, 2008 FED App. 0645N, 2008 U.S. App. LEXIS 22224 (6th Cir. Ohio 2008).

*Unpublished decision:* District court properly granted summary judgment in favor of a city, as employer, in a retaliation suit filed under R.C. 4112.02 by a terminated employee who admitted her share of blame in a massive wastewater spill at the city's water pollution control plant; the employee failed to establish the requisite elements for a retaliation claim because she failed to show a causal link between the filing of her complaint with the civil service commission and her termination. Conley v. City of Findlay, 266 Fed. Appx. 400, 2008 FED App. 0083N, 2008 U.S. App. LEXIS 2382 (6th Cir. Ohio 2008).

*Unpublished decision:* District court properly held that a fired 48-year-old employee did not establish a prima facie case of retaliation under R.C. 4112.02 because, even assuming the employee engaged in protected activity, he failed to demonstrate the requisite causal connection between the alleged protected activity and his termination, given the attenuated length of time of six weeks to several months. Counts v. Kraton Polymers, U.S. L.L.C., 260 Fed. Appx. 825, 2008 FED App. 0064N, 2008 U.S. App. LEXIS 2187 (6th Cir. Ohio 2008).

*Unpublished decision:* District court properly granted summary judgment in favor of an employer in a former employee's action alleging discrimination retaliation in violation of R.C. 4112.02; although the employee was discharged shortly after requesting the day shift upon her return from a leave under the Family and Medical Leave Act, the employer presented evidence of a legitimate, non-discriminatory reason for terminating the employee, namely, chronic tardiness, and the employee failed to introduce evidence from which an inference could be drawn that the explanation was pretextual. Gembus v. MetroHealth Sys., 290 Fed. Appx. 842, 2008 FED App. 0528N, 2008 U.S. App. LEXIS 18554 (6th Cir. Ohio 2008).

*Unpublished decision:* District court properly granted summary judgment in favor of a city, as employer, in a retaliation suit filed under R.C. 4112.02 by a terminated employee who admitted her share of blame in a massive wastewater spill at the city's water pollution control plant; the employee failed to establish the requisite elements for a retaliation claim because she failed to show a causal link between the filing of her complaint with the civil service commission and her termination. Conley v. City of Findlay, 266 Fed. Appx. 400, 2008 FED App. 0083N, 2008 U.S. App. LEXIS 2382 (6th Cir. Ohio 2008).

*Unpublished decision:* District court properly held that a fired 48-year-old employee did not establish a prima facie case of retaliation under R.C. 4112.02 because, even assuming the employee engaged in protected activity, he failed to demonstrate the requisite causal connection between the alleged protected activity and his termination, given the attenuated length of time of six weeks to several months. Counts v. Kraton Polymers, U.S. L.L.C., 260 Fed. Appx. 825, 2008 FED App. 0064N, 2008 U.S. App. LEXIS 2187 (6th Cir. Ohio 2008).

*Unpublished decision:* Firefighters could not show their termination was retaliatory, in violation of federal or state law, because high percentage of department's runs required EMTs, so village could reasonably discharge firefighters for failing to obtain EMT certification. Firefighters did not establish pretext. McCowen v. Vill. of Lincoln Heights, 624 Fed. Appx. 380, 2015 FED App. 0598N, 2015 U.S. App. LEXIS 14768 (6th Cir. Ohio 2015).

**Reverse discrimination**

*Unpublished decision:* Where a former employee, a Caucasian male, claimed that his termination amounted to reverse race discrimination, he failed to meet his prima facie burden of establishing such a claim because the court found no evidence of any background circumstances suggesting that the employer was the unusual employer that discriminated against the majority. Nelson v. Ball Corp., 656 Fed. Appx. 131, 2016 FED App. 0442N, 2016 U.S. App. LEXIS 14257 (6th Cir. Ohio 2016).

**—Salary**

*Unpublished decision:* Employees failed to show a wage disparity based on racial discrimination since higher wages for newly hired account managers were based on new hiring guidelines requiring higher qualifications, and the employees' seniority was not entitled to greater weight than educational and experiential accomplishments. Woods v. FacilitySource, LLC, 640 Fed. Appx. 478, 2016 FED App. 0074N, 2016 U.S. App. LEXIS 1988 (6th Cir. Ohio 2016).

**Sexual harassment**

*Unpublished decision:* District court's award of summary judgment to the employer was proper, but the court affirmed on different grounds. While the employee appeared to have suffered from poor working relationships with both supervisors, the record offered insufficient evidentiary support for her claims against the employer. Deters v. Rock-Tenn Co., 245 Fed. Appx. 516, 2007 FED App. 0613N, 2007 U.S. App. LEXIS 20422 (6th Cir. Ohio 2007).

*Unpublished decision:* District court's award of summary judgment to the employer was proper, but the court affirmed on different grounds. While the employee appeared to have suffered from poor working relationships with both supervisors, the record offered insufficient evidentiary support for her claims against the employer. Deters v. Rock-Tenn Co., 245 Fed. Appx. 516, 2007 FED App. 0613N, 2007 U.S. App. LEXIS 20422 (6th Cir. Ohio 2007).

*Unpublished decision:* Employee waived her sexual harassment claim under R.C. 4112.02 because the district court's order granting her supervisor's motion to dismiss stated that the employee was seeking relief only under Title VII of the Civil Rights Act, 42 U.S.C.S. § 2000e et seq., the employee did not object to that characterization of her claim, and she failed to mention R.C. 4112.02 in her brief on appeal. Bangas v. Potter, 145 Fed. Appx. 139, 2005 U.S. App. LEXIS 16780 (6th Cir. Ohio 2005).

**—Employer liability**

*Unpublished decision:* Employee can avoid a policy requirement to initiate an internal company complaint about sexual harassment if the plaintiff can demonstrate that she was under a credible threat of retaliation. Shields v. Fed. Express Customer Info. Servs., 499 Fed. Appx. 473, 2012 FED App. 0989N, 2012 U.S. App. LEXIS 18985 (6th Cir. Ohio 2012).

*Unpublished decision:* Faragher/Ellerth defense should not be applied as a matter of law if circumstances suggest that there are questions of material fact for a jury to decide. Shields v. Fed. Express Customer Info. Servs., 499 Fed. Appx. 473, 2012 FED App. 0989N, 2012 U.S. App. LEXIS 18985 (6th Cir. Ohio 2012).

*Unpublished decision:* Company faced with a pattern of harassment must both respond appropriately and take increasingly effective steps designed to end the harassment. Shields v. Fed. Express Customer Info. Servs., 499 Fed. Appx. 473, 2012 FED App. 0989N, 2012 U.S. App. LEXIS 18985 (6th Cir. Ohio 2012).

*Unpublished decision:* While reasonable sexual harassment policies may take many forms, an effective policy should at least require supervisors to report incidents of sexual harassment, allow employees to make both formal and informal complaints of harassment, provide a method for employees to bypass a harassing supervisor when making a complaint, and provide for training concerning the policy. Shields v. Fed. Express Customer Info. Servs., 499 Fed. Appx. 473, 2012 FED App. 0989N, 2012 U.S. App. LEXIS 18985 (6th Cir. Ohio 2012).

*Unpublished decision:* Employees may not rely on their own subjective fear of confrontation, retaliation, or general unpleasantness in the workplace to avoid a duty under Ellerth to alert the employer to the hostile work environment, nor may employees pass their own judgments—absent supporting facts—about how effectively an employer's sexual harassment policies operate. Shields v. Fed. Express Customer Info. Servs., 499 Fed. Appx. 473, 2012 FED App. 0989N, 2012 U.S. App. LEXIS 18985 (6th Cir. Ohio 2012).

**—Hostile work environment**

*Unpublished decision:* Employees presented sufficient evidence to require a jury to decide whether the employer effectively enforced its Anti-Harassment Policy to prevent or correct the supervisor from sexually harassing women he supervised; based on the evidence, the employer could not benefit from the affirmative defense at the summary judgment stage because it failed to show that there was no genuine issue of material fact regarding whether it exercised reasonable care to prevent and correct promptly any sexually harassing behavior. Shields v. Fed. Express Customer Info. Servs., 499 Fed. Appx. 473, 2012 FED App. 0989N, 2012 U.S. App. LEXIS 18985 (6th Cir. Ohio 2012).



**Summary judgment**

*Unpublished decision:* Employee did not develop any arguments as to why the district court erred in granting summary judgment for his former employer and supervisor on his racially hostile work environment claim; the employee's brief mentioned the phrase "hostile work environment" only three times and cited no cases supporting his hostile work environment claim, and his statement of issues did not address the hostile work environment claim specifically. Because the employee did not challenge the district court's opinion regarding his hostile work environment claim, the issue was waived on appeal. Butler v. Cooper Std. Auto., Inc., 376 Fed. Appx. 487, 2010 FED App. 0270N, 2010 U.S. App. LEXIS 8968 (6th Cir. Ohio 2010), aff'd, 498 Fed. Appx. 549, 2012 FED App. 0976N, 2012 U.S. App. LEXIS 18720 (6th Cir. Ohio 2012).

*Unpublished decision:* After plaintiff, an African-American store employee, complained to human resources about race discrimination at work, a cash shortage was reported and a security camera showed a man who resembled plaintiff taking money out of a register; plaintiff was terminated after his arrest for theft, and he sued his employer for retaliation in violation of R.C. 4112.02. The district court did not err by dismissing his claim upon summary judgment, because plaintiff did not make a sufficient showing of pretext to overcome the employer's proffered legitimate nondiscriminatory reason for reporting him to the police; plaintiff was dismissed for violating the employee-discount policy and provided no evidence that his dismissal was retaliatory. Graham v. Best Buy Stores, L.P., 298 Fed. Appx. 487, 2008 FED App. 0645N, 2008 U.S. App. LEXIS 22224 (6th Cir. Ohio 2008).

*Unpublished decision:* Summary judgment in favor of the employer with regard to employee's race discrimination and retaliation claims brought under Title VII of the Civil Rights Act of 1964, 42 U.S.C.S. § 2000e-2 et seq., 42 U.S.C.S. § 1981 and R.C. 4112.02 et seq., was affirmed because the employee failed to establish that he was similarly situated to other employees who were not terminated due to safety violations and the employee did not establish a causal link between his termination and the prior civil rights complaints he had filed. Gibson v. Shelly Co., 314 Fed. Appx. 760, 2008 FED App. 0507N, 2008 U.S. App. LEXIS 17799 (6th Cir. Ohio 2008).

**Union as employer**

*Unpublished decision:* District court properly granted summary judgment in favor of a labor union chairman in an employee's action alleging retaliation in violation of R.C. 4112.02(I); even assuming that the employee could show that the union chairman met the statutory definition of "employer" under R.C. 4112.01(A)(2), there was no liability to attach jointly or severally to the union chairman because neither the employer nor the union were found liable for the alleged retaliation. Garcia v. Daimler Chrysler Corp., 320 Fed. Appx. 356, 2009 FED App. 0266N, 2009 U.S. App. LEXIS 7391 (6th Cir. Ohio 2009).

**Wage discrimination**

*Unpublished decision:* Where an employee was terminated for violating cash handling rules, the employee's wage discrimination claims failed because the employee presented no evidence that (1) other non-protected employees held "substantially equal" jobs and were paid more, or (2) the employee's salary would have been higher but for the employee's sex; those employees who were paid a higher rate had greater seniority and were being paid pursuant to the provisions of the collective bargaining agreement. Balding-Margolis v. Cleveland Arcade, 352 Fed. Appx. 35, 2009 FED App. 0732N, 2009 U.S. App. LEXIS 24604 (6th Cir. Ohio 2009).

## ATTORNEY GENERAL OPINIONS

The Ohio Civil Rights Commission may file an affidavit to cause the prosecution of a suspected violator of R.C. 4112.02(H), 4112.07 or 4112.11, at such time as the commission has a knowledge of the facts, but only the trial judge of a court of competent jurisdiction may impose the penalties as provided by R.C. 4112.99, after the trial and conviction of an accused violator: 1970 Ohio Op. Att'y Gen. No. 108.

Utilization of arrest records which did not result in a conviction as a factor in determining whether an applicant is hired is an unlawful discriminatory practice as defined in R.C. 4112.02(A) to (F), unless the employer can prove that such practice is a valid predictor of job capability, and the Ohio Civil Rights Commission must prohibit all such discrimination in its conciliation agreements. Where recruitment practices, such as word-of-mouth referrals from present or past employees, nepotism, and reliance upon walk-ins, have an adverse differential effect upon minority group members, their use constitutes an unlawful discriminatory practice as defined in R.C. 4112.02(A) to (F), and the Ohio Civil Rights Commission must prohibit all such discrimination in its conciliation agreements: 1972 Ohio Op. Att'y Gen. No. 006 (1972).

## RESEARCH REFERENCES AND PRACTICE AIDS

**Cross-References to Related Sections**

Age discrimination by employers, RC § 4112.14.
Civil remedies for violations, RC § 4112.99.
Civil rights commission to refer violations of fair housing laws to attorney general, RC § 4112.052.
Contracts by political subdivisions, RC § 125.111.
Contract terms for community schools, RC § 3314.03.
Court injunctions, damage awards for housing discrimination violations, RC § 4112.051.
Development department and housing finance agency; loan programs, RC § 175.22.
Elimination of references to discriminatory restrictive covenants, RC §§ 3953.29, 5309.281.
Employer immunity as to job performance information disclosures, RC § 4113.71.
Health insuring corporation discrimination, RC § 124.93.
Housing advisory board loans, RC §§ 176.04, 176.06.
Housing and remedies available to dissatisfied clients to be published in booklets and furnished to public libraries and to brokers, RC § 4735.03.
Housing authorities; monitoring against discrimination, RC § 176.08.
Housing finance agency bonds, RC § 175.05.
Housing finance agency loans for multifamily residential housing, RC § 175.06.
Interference with fair housing rights, RC § 2927.03.
Liberal construction; bar to civil action, RC § 4112.08.
Municipal housing for elderly, RC § 717.01.
Posting of notice, RC § 4112.07.
Powers and duties of the commission, RC § 4112.04.
Prevention of unlawful discriminatory practices by Ohio civil rights commission, procedure, RC § 4112.05.
Public improvement contracts, RC § 153.59.
Public service facilities in state parks, RC § 1501.012.
Real estate agency agreements, RC § 4735.55.
Restrictive covenants in transfers of registered land, RC §§ 317.20, 5309.09, 5309.24, 5309.33.
Revocation of real estate license for unlawful discriminatory practice, RC § 4735.18.

**Ohio Constitution**

Welfare of employees, Ohio Const. art II, § 34.

**Ohio Administrative Code**

Civil rights commission —
Application for bona fide occupational qualification (BFOQ). OAC 4112-3-15.
Discriminatory practices prohibited —
Against the disabled. OAC 4112-5-06 to OAC 4112-5-09.

Housing discrimination. OAC 4112-6-01; OAC 4112-6-03.
Record keeping of race, sex, religion, etc. OAC 4112-5-04.
Sex discrimination; sexual harassment; sex as BFOQ. OAC 4112-5-05.

**Practice Manuals and Treatises**

Anderson's Ohio Civil Practice with Forms § 35.01 Generally
Anderson's Ohio Residential Real Estate Manual § 11.01 Overview of housing discrimination
Anderson's Ohio Residential Real Estate Manual § 11.02 Coverage
Anderson's Ohio Residential Real Estate Manual § 11.03 Discrimination in financing
Anderson's Ohio Residential Real Estate Manual § 11.04 Burial lots

**Practice Manuals & Treatises**

Ohio Transaction Guide: Business & Commercial Law & Forms § 1.51 Employment Relations — State Laws

**Practice Forms**

Couse's Ohio Form Book § 17.10 Discrimination in Employment

**Jury Instructions**

OJI-CV 533.01 General [Rev. 3-22-03]
OJI-CV 533.03 Disparate treatment claim—indirect evidence [Rev. 3-22-03]
OJI-CV 533.13 Reasonable accommodation [Rev. 3-22-03]

### § 4112.024 Discriminatory practices limiting housing accommodations.

(A) Nothing in division (H) of section 4112.02 of the Revised Code shall bar any religious or denominational institution or organization, or any nonprofit charitable or educational organization that is operated, supervised, or controlled by or in connection with a religious organization, from limiting the sale, rental, or occupancy of housing accommodations that it owns or operates for other than a commercial purpose to persons of the same religion, or from giving preference in the sale, rental, or occupancy of such housing accommodations to persons of the same religion, unless membership in the religion is restricted on account of race, color, or national origin.

(B) Nothing in division (H) of section 4112.02 of the Revised Code shall bar any bona fide private or fraternal organization that, incidental to its primary purpose, owns or operates lodgings for other than a commercial purpose, from limiting the rental or occupancy of the lodgings to its members or from giving preference to its members.

(C) Nothing in division (H) of section 4112.02 of the Revised Code limits the applicability of any reasonable local, state, or federal restrictions regarding the maximum number of occupants permitted to occupy housing accommodations. Nothing in that division prohibits the owners or managers of housing accommodations from implementing reasonable occupancy standards based on the number and size of sleeping areas or bedrooms and the overall size of a dwelling unit, provided that the standards are not implemented to circumvent the purposes of this chapter and are formulated, implemented, and interpreted in a manner consistent with this chapter and any applicable local, state, or federal restrictions regarding the maximum number of occupants permitted to occupy housing accommodations.

(D) Nothing in division (H) of section 4112.02 of the Revised Code requires that housing accommodations be made available to an individual whose tenancy would constitute a direct threat to the health or safety of other individuals or whose tenancy would result in substantial physical damage to the property of others.

(E) Nothing in division (H) of section 4112.02 of the Revised Code pertaining to discrimination on the basis of familial status shall be construed to apply to any of the following:

(1) Housing accommodations provided under any state or federal program that have been determined under the "Fair Housing Amendments Act of 1988," 102 Stat. 1623, 42 U.S.C. 3607, as amended, to be specifically designed and operated to assist elderly persons;

(2) Housing accommodations intended for and solely occupied by persons who are sixty-two years of age or older;

(3) Housing accommodations intended and operated for occupancy by at least one person who is fifty-five years of age or older per unit, as determined under the "Fair Housing Amendments Act of 1988," 102 Stat. 1623, 42 U.S.C. 3607, as amended.

(F) Nothing in divisions (H)(1) to (18) of section 4112.02 of the Revised Code shall be construed to require any person selling or renting property to modify the property in any way or to exercise a higher degree of care for a person with a disability, to relieve any person with a disability of any obligation generally imposed on all persons regardless of disability in a written lease, rental agreement, or contract of purchase or sale, or to forbid distinctions based on the inability to fulfill the terms and conditions, including financial obligations, of the lease, agreement, or contract.

**HISTORY:**

2016 hb463, § 1, effective April 6, 2017.

### § 4112.14 Age discrimination by employers.

(A) No employer shall discriminate in any job opening against any applicant or discharge without just cause any employee aged forty or older who is physically able to perform the duties and otherwise meets the established requirements of the job and laws pertaining to the relationship between employer and employee.

(B) Except as otherwise provided in section 4112.052 of the Revised Code and this section, a person aged forty or older who is discriminated against in any job opening or discharged without just cause by an employer in violation of division (A) of this section may institute a civil action against the employer in a court of competent jurisdiction. If the court finds that an employer has discriminated on the basis of age, the court shall order an appropriate remedy which shall include reimbursement to the applicant or employee for the costs, including reasonable attorney's fees, of the action, or to reinstate the employee in the employee's former position with compensation for lost wages and any lost fringe benefits from the date of the illegal discharge and to reimburse the employee for the costs, including reasonable attorney's fees, of the action. Except as otherwise provided in this section, the remedies available under this section are coexistent with remedies available pursuant to sections 4112.01 to 4112.11 of the Revised Code.

(C) The cause of action described in division (B) of this section shall not be available in the case of discharges where the employee has available to the employee the opportunity to arbitrate the discharge or where a discharge has been arbitrated and has been found to be for just cause.

(D)(1) A person is prohibited from bringing a civil action under division (B) of this section if the person brought a civil action under section 4112.052 of the Revised Code that is based, in whole or in part, on the same allegations and practices.

(2) A person is prohibited from bringing a civil action under section 4112.052 of the Revised Code if the person brought a civil action under division (B) of this section that is based, in whole or in part, on the same allegations and practices.

(E)(1) Except as provided in division (E)(2) of this section, a civil action brought under division (B) of this section shall be filed within two years after the alleged discrimination occurred.

(2) The time period to file a civil action shall be tolled for one of the following periods, as applicable:

(a) If a charge that is based, in whole or in part, on the same allegations was filed under section 4112.051 of the Revised Code less than sixty days before the time period specified under that section expires, the time period to file a civil action is tolled for the period beginning on the date the charge was filed and ending on the date that is sixty days after the charge is no longer pending with the commission.

(b) If a charge that is based, in whole or in part, on the same allegations and practices was filed under section 4112.051 of the Revised Code sixty or more days before the time period specified under that section expires, the time period to file a civil action is tolled for the period beginning on the date the charge was filed and ending on the date the charge is no longer pending with the commission.

**HISTORY:**

RC § 4101.17, 129 v 1803 (Eff 8-28-61); 137 v H 598 (Eff 1-4-79); 138 v H 230 (Eff 11-13-79); 143 v H 314 (Eff 5-31-90); RC § 4112.14, 146 v S 162 (Eff 10-29-95); 146 v H 350 (Eff 1-27-97); 149 v S 108, § 2.01. Eff 7-6-2001;

Titles 39 — 57

2016 hb463, § 1, effective April 6, 2017; 2020 hb352, § 1, effective April 15, 2021.

**Publisher's Note:**

Section 2.02(B) of SB 108 (149 v —) repeals the HB 350 (146 v —) version and section 3(A)(3) revives and amends the former version.

**Amendment Notes**

The 2020 amendment by HB 352, in (B), substituted "Except as otherwise provided in section 4112.052 of the Revised Code and this section, a" for "Any" in the first sentence and rewrote the last sentence, which formerly read: "The remedies available under this section are coexistent with remedies available pursuant to sections 4112.01 to 4112.11 of the Revised Code; except that any person instituting a civil action under this section is, with respect to the practices complained of, thereby barred from instituting a civil action under division (L) of section 4112.02 of the Revised Code or from filing a charge with the Ohio civil rights commission under section 4112.05 of the Revised Code"; deleted "and any remedies available pursuant to sections 4112.01 to 4112.11 of the Revised Code" following "of this section" in (C); and added (D) and (E).

The 2016 amendment by HB 463 substituted "division (L)" for "division (N)" in (B).

## NOTES TO DECISIONS

Analysis





**Constitutionality**

Amended Substitute HB No. 350 violates the one-subject provision of Ohio Const. art II, § 15(D) and is unconstitutional in toto: State ex rel. Ohio Academy of Trial Lawyers v. Sheward, 1999-Ohio-123, 86 Ohio St. 3d 451, 715 N.E.2d 1062, 1999 Ohio LEXIS 2580 (Ohio 1999).

**Generally**

R.C. 4112.14 does present a claim for relief for age discrimination. Nuovo v. Ohio State Univ., 726 F. Supp. 2d 829, 2010 U.S. Dist. LEXIS 71590 (S.D. Ohio 2010).

Consistently with the statutory framework for age-discrimination claims set forth within R.C. ch. 4112, and with precedents interpreting that framework, an age-discrimination claim brought pursuant to R.C. 4112.99 is subject to the substantive provisions of R.C. 4112.02 and 4112.14. Meyer v. UPS, 2009-Ohio-2463, 122 Ohio St. 3d 104, 909 N.E.2d 106, 2009 Ohio LEXIS 1598 (Ohio 2009).

Age discrimination claim brought pursuant to R.C. 4112.99 is subject to the substantive provisions of R.C. 4112.02 and 4112.14. Pursuant to R.C. 4112.14(C), when the discharge of an employee has been arbitrated and the discharge has been found to be for just cause, the discharged employee is barred from pursuing an action for age discrimination: Meyer v. UPS, 2009-Ohio-2463, 122 Ohio St. 3d 104, 909 N.E.2d 106, 2009 Ohio LEXIS 1598 (Ohio 2009).

If an employee who was terminated in a reorganization established a prima facie claim of age discrimination in employment, he could not show that his employer's asserted reason for terminating him was a pretext for discrimination because the employer terminated him for not possessing computer skills, which were required of every employee in his department, after the reorganization. Pierce v. Brown Publ. Co., 2007-Ohio-1657, 2007 Ohio App. LEXIS 1510 (Ohio Ct. App., Fayette County 2007).

In order to establish pretext in an employment discrimination claim, an employee must show by a preponderance of the evidence that the proffered reasons for his termination had no basis in fact, did not actually motivate his termination, or were insufficient to motivate his termination. Pierce v. Brown Publ. Co., 2007-Ohio-1657, 2007 Ohio App. LEXIS 1510 (Ohio Ct. App., Fayette County 2007).

Employer's reasons for discharging the plaintiff were not a pretext for age discrimination where the employer believed that it would eliminate costs in the division and jump start the sales department: Chandler v. Dunn Hardware, Inc., 2006-Ohio-4376, 168 Ohio App. 3d 496, 860 N.E.2d 1042, 2006 Ohio App. LEXIS 4293 (Ohio Ct. App., Cuyahoga County 2006).

Sixty-year-old employee was within the statutorily-protected class defined in 19 U.S.C.S. § 631(A) and R.C. 4112.14(A) for purposes of an age discrimination claim. Hoffman v. CHSHO, Inc., 2005-Ohio-3909, 2005 Ohio App. LEXIS 3597 (Ohio Ct. App., Clermont County 2005).

Because the employee filed an administrative action with the Equal Employment Opportunities Commission (EEOC) and the Ohio Civil Rights Commission he was precluded from later asserting a claim pursuant to any provision of R.C. 4112.14. Kaltenmark v. K-Mart, Inc., 2005 U.S. Dist. LEXIS 21699 (N.D. Ohio Sept. 28, 2005).

Because an employee's statutory age discrimination claims failed, the employee's corresponding claim that the employee was terminated in violation of Ohio's public policy against age discrimination likewise failed. Weller v. Titanium Metals Corp., 361 F. Supp. 2d 712, 2005 U.S. Dist. LEXIS 8373 (S.D. Ohio 2005).

Plaintiff may establish a prima facie case of age discrimination by showing that he or she: (1) was a member of a statutorily protected class, (2) was discharged, (3) was qualified for the position, and (4) was replaced by, or the discharge permitted the retention of, a person of substantially younger age, so a plaintiff may establish a prima facie case even if he or she was replaced by an individual who was 40 or more years of age, as long as that individual is "substantially younger," and a bright-line rule defining the requisite age differential has not been established. Temple v. City of Dayton, 2005-Ohio-57, 2005 Ohio App. LEXIS 40 (Ohio Ct. App., Montgomery County 2005).

Polish doctor's language difficulties constituted a legitimate, nondiscriminatory reason for a decision to place her on academic probation and deny her course credit; the doctor failed to show that a university's motives were motivated by discriminatory reasons. Sarach-Kozlowska v. Univ. of Cincinnati College of Med., 2004-Ohio-1926, 2004 Ohio Misc. LEXIS 142 (Ohio Ct. Cl. 2004).

When considering whether a favored employee is substantially younger than a protected employee, courts must keep in mind that the purpose of R.C. 4112.14(A) is to prevent employment discrimination on the basis of age, and that whether an employee is substantially younger is but a single factor in a broader analysis. Coryell v. Bank One Trust Co. N.A., 2004-Ohio-723, 101 Ohio St. 3d 175, 803 N.E.2d 781, 2004 Ohio LEXIS 337 (Ohio 2004).

Requirement of evidence that an employee's replacement is outside the protected class is logically disconnected from the employment discrimination that R.C. 4112.14(A) seeks to prevent; because § 4112.14(A) prohibits employment discrimination on the basis of age, the ultimate inquiry is whether evidence of age discrimination is present. Coryell v. Bank One Trust Co. N.A., 2004-Ohio-723, 101 Ohio St. 3d 175, 803 N.E.2d 781, 2004 Ohio LEXIS 337 (Ohio 2004).

An employer's multiple reference to negative, age-related stereotypes may be evidence of discriminatory intent. Although an absence of discrimination may be inferred where the same individual hired and fired an employee, such inference is not required: Wexler v. White's Fine Furniture, Inc., 317 F.3d 564, 2003 FED App. 0029P, 2003 U.S. App. LEXIS 1223 (6th Cir. Ohio 2003).

There was no nexus between the defendants' general remarks concerning age and plaintiff's discharge. Where a former employee's duties are assumed by a variety of people, at least one of whom is in the age-protected class, discriminatory intent is not established indirectly: Smith v. E.G. Baldwin & Assocs., 119 Ohio App. 3d 410, 695 N.E.2d 349, 1997 Ohio App. LEXIS 1763 (Ohio Ct. App., Franklin County 1997).

The phrase "absent direct evidence of age discrimination," as used in Kohmescher v. Kroger Co. (1991), 61 Ohio St.3d 501, 575 N.E.2d 439, at the syllabus, refers to a method of proof, not a type of evidence. It means that a plaintiff may establish a prima facie case of age discrimination directly by presenting evidence, of any nature, to show that an employer more likely than not was motivated by discriminatory intent. Irrespective of whether an inference of discriminatory intent is created directly or indirectly, the plaintiff must show that she was "discharged" in order to establish a prima facie case of age discrimination under former R.C. 4101.17: Mauzy v. Kelly Servs., 1996-Ohio-265, 75 Ohio St. 3d 578, 664 N.E.2d 1272, 1996 Ohio LEXIS 366 (Ohio 1996).

An employee alleging age discrimination must prove a causal link or nexus between evidence of a discriminatory statement or conduct and that employee: Byrnes v. LCI Communs. Holdings, 1996-Ohio-307, 77 Ohio St. 3d 125, 672 N.E.2d 145, 1996 Ohio LEXIS 1837 (Ohio 1996), cert. denied, 521 U.S. 1104, 117 S. Ct. 2480, 138 L. Ed. 2d 989, 1997 U.S. LEXIS 3885 (U.S. 1997).

An employer's use of records containing an employee's age is not proof of discrimination. Age-related statements about other employees do not constitute direct proof of discrimination: Miller v. Loral Defense Sys., 109 Ohio App. 3d 379, 672 N.E.2d 227, 1996 Ohio App. LEXIS 479 (Ohio Ct. App., Summit County 1996).

An isolated, ambiguous reference to plaintiff's age was not direct evidence of discrimination. Retained employees were not similarly qualified. The statistical evidence was flawed: Stair v. Phoenix Presentations, 116 Ohio App. 3d 500, 688 N.E.2d 582, 1996 Ohio App. LEXIS 5781 (Ohio Ct. App., Butler County 1996).

The employer did not commit age discrimination when it consolidated an employee's job into a more technical position for which the employee was admittedly not qualified: Norman v. Honeywell, Inc., 105 Ohio App. 3d 658, 664 N.E.2d 1017, 1995 Ohio App. LEXIS 5314 (Ohio Ct. App., Montgomery County 1995).

The factfinder's disbelief of the employer's reasons for the adverse employment action, especially if that disbelief is coupled with a suspicion of duplicity, may, along with the elements of a prima facie case, be sufficient to demonstrate intentional age discrimination: Atkinson v. International Technegroup, 106 Ohio App. 3d 349, 666 N.E.2d 257, 1995 Ohio App. LEXIS 3933 (Ohio Ct. App., Hamilton County 1995).

The employer's alleged statement concerning older employees, made three years prior to the discharge, did not constitute direct evidence of age discrimination: Street v. Gerstenslager Co., 103 Ohio App. 3d 156, 658 N.E.2d 1105, 1995 Ohio App. LEXIS 1855 (Ohio Ct. App., Wayne County 1995).

A "belief," unsubstantiated by direct evidence, that an employee was discharged from employment because of age discrimination, is insufficient to sustain a cause of action pursuant to R.C. 4101.17: Stramowski v. Fairview Medical Center, 1993 Ohio App. LEXIS 1094 (Ohio Ct. App., Cuyahoga County Feb. 18, 1993).

Remark by immediate supervisor to discharged employee that they "needed new blood" was insufficient to create material factual issue as to whether discharge was motivated by age: Gagne v. Northwestern Nat'l Ins. Co., 881 F.2d 309, 1989 U.S. App. LEXIS 11123 (6th Cir. Ohio 1989).

**Adverse employment action**

Former employer was entitled to judgment as a matter of law on age discrimination claims, under the Age Discrimination in Employment Act, 29 U.S.C.S. § 621 et seq., and R.C. ch. 4112, because (1) the former employee had not demonstrated that a material dispute of fact existed as to whether, in fact, she voluntarily resigned her employment from the hospital, and the employee's voluntary resignation from the employer did not qualify as an adverse employment action; (2) the employee had not submitted sufficient evidence upon which a jury could have concluded that she suffered an adverse action as to the transfer positions because the transfers sought would not have constituted promotions; and (3) with the exception of one position, the employee had not demonstrated that a material dispute of fact existed as to whether the employer's stated reasons for its transfer position hiring decisions were pretextual. Sturgeon v. S. Ohio Med. Ctr., 2011 U.S. Dist. LEXIS 135469 (S.D. Ohio Nov. 23, 2011).

Denial of a transfer into a position of increased prestige, at least in the eyes of some employees, could constitute an adverse employment action even though the new position would not have entitled the employee to greater pay, benefits, or rank: Campolieti v. City of Cleveland, 2009-Ohio-5224, 184 Ohio App. 3d 419, 921 N.E.2d 286, 2009 Ohio App. LEXIS 4417 (Ohio Ct. App., Cuyahoga County 2009).

**Age discrimination**

State employer was not entitled to summary judgment in an employee's age discrimination claim because the employer hired a co-worker shortly after the parties and the union entered into a last chance agreement, the co-worker was 15 or 16 years younger than the employee when he was hired, and several of the employee's job duties were reassigned to the co-worker; thus, there was an issue of material fact as to whether the employee was replaced by someone substantially younger than her. Meggitt v. Ohio Dep't of Pub. Safety, 2020-Ohio-4412, 2020 Ohio Misc. LEXIS 128 (Ohio Ct. Cl. 2020).

State employer was not entitled to summary judgment in an employee's age discrimination claim because a genuine issue of material fact existed as to whether the employer's proffered reason for terminating the employee, or its reasons for the prior escalating discipline, was pretextual; a union representative testified that she was not aware of any other employee being recommended for termination based upon a speeding ticket, and the employee performed sufficiently at her job duties. Meggitt v. Ohio Dep't of Pub. Safety, 2020-Ohio-4412, 2020 Ohio Misc. LEXIS 128 (Ohio Ct. Cl. 2020).

Genuine issue of material fact existed as to whether an employee's age discrimination claim was barred by subsection (C) of this statute because the State employer did not submit an arbitration agreement or provision into evidence, and the relevant paragraph of the parties' last chance agreement did not in and of itself set forth an arbitration procedure sufficient to invoke this statute. Meggitt v. Ohio Dep't of Pub. Safety, 2020-Ohio-4412, 2020 Ohio Misc. LEXIS 128 (Ohio Ct. Cl. 2020).

State employer was not entitled to summary judgment on an employee's age discrimination claim because the employee's affidavit was sufficient to raise a genuine issue of material fact as to whether, after an investigation was initiated and human resources recommended removal, a reasonable person would have believed that termination was imminent. Meggitt v. Ohio Dep't of Pub. Safety, 2020-Ohio-4412, 2020 Ohio Misc. LEXIS 128 (Ohio Ct. Cl. 2020).

Because the former employee elected to bring his claim under the statute with a 180-day statute of limitations, he was barred from amending his complaint to assert a claim under the other statute in order to take advantage of the six-year statute of limitations. Juergens v. House of Larose, Inc., 2019-Ohio-94, 2019 Ohio App. LEXIS 118 (Ohio Ct. App., Cuyahoga County 2019).

Employee failed to establish the fourth prong of the prima facie case for age discrimination that she was replaced by a person substantially younger because the 24-year-old man worked in a different department, reported to a different supervisor, and had different duties. At most, his purchasing duties from three vendors, not just the two the employee handled, made up 20-25 percent of his workday and the employee acknowledged that, after she left, many of her duties were redistributed to other employees. Nist v. Nexeo Solutions, LLC, 2015-Ohio-3363, 2015 Ohio App. LEXIS 3244 (Ohio Ct. App., Franklin County 2015).

*Unpublished decision:* In an age discrimination case in which an employee appealed summary judgment in favor of his municipal employer and the mayor, they cited multiple instances in which the employee behaved inappropriately and unprofessionally, the undisputed evidence showed that he was repeatedly insubordinate and unprofessional with the mayor and others, and the employee failed to demonstrate that the stated reasons for his termination were pretextual. Franks v. Village of Bolivar, 583 Fed. Appx. 534, 2014 FED App. 0829N, 2014 U.S. App. LEXIS 21162 (6th Cir. Ohio 2014).

Applicant's age discrimination claims failed because age-plus-sex claims under the Age Discrimination in Employment Act do not exist, and the applicant's charge filed with the Equal Employment Opportunity Commission precluded the applicant's state law age discrimination claims. Thompson v. City of Columbus, 2014 U.S. Dist. LEXIS 63119 (S.D. Ohio May 7, 2014).

Although characterized as a lateral transfer, the vacant lieutenant position constituted a "job opening," and therefore the firefighter was entitled to pursue an age discrimination claim. Campolieti v. Cleveland Dep't of Pub. Safety, 2013-Ohio-5123, 2013 Ohio App. LEXIS 5332 (Ohio Ct. App., Cuyahoga County 2013).

Former employee was entitled to judgment on the issue of liability when the employee alleged discrimination on the basis of age against the employee's former employer, in violation of R.C. 4112.14 and 4112.99, because the employer, a state administrative agency, failed to demonstrate that its actions in not hiring the employee, who had previously retired from the agency, were based upon a reasonable factor other than age. There was an absence of proof that a policy by the agency against double-dipping promoted the public trust, and each of the members of the interview panel testified that the employee was the most qualified applicant for the position and received the highest interview score. Warden v. Ohio Dep't of Natural Res., 2012-Ohio-3854, 2012 Ohio Misc. LEXIS 109 (Ohio Ct. Cl. 2012).

In a former employee's suit for age discrimination, the employer's motion for summary judgment was denied because the former employee set forth a prima facie case based on the evidence that he was discharged from his job and replaced by a younger person. Wind v. Walgreen Co., 2011 U.S. Dist. LEXIS 154972 (S.D. Ohio June 22, 2011).

State trooper was barred from pursuing a claim of age discriminatino pursuant to the plain language of R.C. 4112.14(C) as an arbitrator issued an opinion and award wherein she found that the trooper's employer had just cause to remove him. Lajoye v. Ohio Highway Patrol, 2009-Ohio-7028, 2009 Ohio Misc. LEXIS 368 (Ohio Ct. Cl. 2009).

Mere filing of an age discrimination charge with the Equal Employment Opportunity Commission (EEOC) pursuant to § 626 of the Age Discrimination in Employment Act (ADEA), 29 U.S.C.S. § 621 et seq., is not equivalent to the election of an administrative remedy within the meaning of R.C. 4112.05. Thus, where it is shown that the plaintiffs only filed charges with the EEOC pursuant to the requirements of the ADEA, the fact of such filing does not constitute an election of the remedy set forth in R.C. 4112.05 and such plaintiffs are not precluded from seeking a judicial remedy under R.C. 4112.14 or 4112.99. Reminder v. Roadway Express, Inc., 2006 U.S. Dist. LEXIS 1899 (N.D. Ohio Jan. 10, 2006).

Where no reasonable jury could have found that the employer's state reasons for promotion another instead of the employee were pretextual, and where R.C. 4112.14 did not protect against harassment on the basis of age, but instead was limited to protecting against age discrimination in connection with a job opening or a discharge without cause, the court granted the employee's motion for summary judgment pursuant to Fed. R. Civ. P. 56. Linkinhoker v. CSX Transp., Inc., 2006 U.S. Dist. LEXIS 195 (S.D. Ohio Jan. 5, 2006).

Employer's motion for summary judgment was denied because the employee stated a prima facie case of age discrimination because a reasonable jury could find that she was qualified for the job and that the training provided to the employee was not of the same quality as the training offered to the younger worker. The employee also showed that the employer's explanation for her termination was a pretext for discrimination because the employer had shifted its articulated reasons for her termination. DeLoach v. Island Dental Co., 2005 U.S. Dist. LEXIS 38213 (S.D. Ohio Dec. 22, 2005).

Employer's Fed. R. Civ. P. 12(c) motion was granted because 180-day limitations period applied because the employee's R.C. 4112.99 age discrimination claim could not fairly be read as based on R.C. 4112.14. Because the employee filed an administrative action with the Equal Employment Opportunities Commission (EEOC) and the Ohio Civil Rights Commission he was precluded from later asserting a claim pursuant to any provision of R.C. 4112.14. Kaltenmark v. K-Mart, Inc., 2005 U.S. Dist. LEXIS 21699 (N.D. Ohio Sept. 28, 2005).

Sixty-year-old employee was within the statutorily-protected class defined in 19 U.S.C.S. § 631(A) and R.C. 4112.14(A) for purposes of an age discrimination claim. Hoffman v. CHSHO, Inc., 2005-Ohio-3909, 2005 Ohio App. LEXIS 3597 (Ohio Ct. App., Clermont County 2005).

Because an employee's statutory age discrimination claims failed, the employee's corresponding claim that the employee was terminated in violation of Ohio's public policy against age discrimination likewise failed. Weller v. Titanium Metals Corp., 361 F. Supp. 2d 712, 2005 U.S. Dist. LEXIS 8373 (S.D. Ohio 2005).

**Appeal**

Claimant's contention that the trial court committed reversible error by adding an additional requirement for her establishment of a prima facie case of age discrimination under R.C. 4112.14(A) failed, as the case was fully tried on the merits and the ultimate question of discrimination vel non was the crucial consideration; the appellate court found that since both parties proffered evidence in the case, and because the trial court had all the evidence it needed to determine whether the employer intentionally discriminated against the claimant, it was not required to resolve whether the prima facie case was actually proven, nor was it a necessary consideration on appeal. Ullmann v. Ohio Bureau of Job & Family Servs., 2004-Ohio-1622, 2004 Ohio App. LEXIS 1433 (Ohio Ct. App., Franklin County 2004).

**Applicability**

In an employment discrimination action, an appellate court improperly denied a motion for reconsideration, which claimed that a decision regarding the appropriate statute of limitations, either R.C. 2743.16(A) or 4101.17 (now 4112.14), was invalid because it resolved an intradistrict conflict without an en banc proceeding, as an en banc proceeding did not violate Ohio Const. art. IV, § 3A; the requirement of three judges in art. IV, § 3(A) was a quorum requirement rather than a cap on the number of judges who could sit on a panel, and the need to definitively and efficiently resolve intradistrict conflicts presented a special circumstance warranting a larger appellate panel as every court of appeals in the state was composed of at least four judges. McFadden v. Cleveland State Univ., 2008-Ohio-4914, 120 Ohio St. 3d 54, 896 N.E.2d 672, 2008 Ohio LEXIS 2590 (Ohio 2008).

**Arbitration**

Age discrimination claim by terminated public school teacher was barred because the teacher termination administrative proceeding, in which the referee found that the teacher was fired for just cause, was the functional equivalent of arbitration for purposes of R.C. 4112.14(C). Smith v. Perkins Bd. of Educ., 708 F.3d 821, 2013 FED App. 0055P, 2013 U.S. App. LEXIS 4006 (6th Cir. Ohio 2013).

Because the employee had an opportunity to arbitrate his discharge but failed to do so, and further failed to assert a claim for breach of duty against the union, his age discrimination claim was barred by the arbitration exhaustion requirement set forth in R.C. 4112.14(C). Dobrski v. Ford Motor Co., 698 F. Supp. 2d 966, 2010 U.S. Dist. LEXIS 24470 (N.D. Ohio 2010).

Summary judgment was properly granted to a former employer in an age discrimination case because a former employee's challenge of his discharge in a step four grievance procedure set forth in a collective bargaining agreement between the employer and a local union was the functional equivalent of arbitration under R.C. 4112.14(C). Tatman v. Kaiser Aluminum Corp., 2010-Ohio-6402, 2010 Ohio App. LEXIS 5355 (Ohio Ct. App., Licking County 2010).

Age-discrimination claim brought pursuant to R.C. 4112.99 is subject to the substantive provisions of R.C. 4112.02 and 4112.14, including R.C. 4112.14(C), and, pursuant to § 4112.14(C), when the discharge of an employee has been arbitrated and the discharge has been found to be for just cause, the discharged employee is barred from pursuing an action for age discrimination. Meyer v. UPS, 2009-Ohio-2463, 122 Ohio St. 3d 104, 909 N.E.2d 106, 2009 Ohio LEXIS 1598 (Ohio 2009).

Employee's age discrimination claim brought under R.C. 4112.99 was barred by R.C. 4112.14(C) because, inter alia, (1) § 4112.14(C) barred age discrimination claims when an employee who was allegedly discriminated against had pursued arbitration which resulted in a finding that the employee was terminated for just cause, and (2) the grievance procedure which the employee pursued was equivalent to the arbitration referred to in § 4112.14(C). Meyer v. UPS, 2009-Ohio-2463, 122 Ohio St. 3d 104, 909 N.E.2d 106, 2009 Ohio LEXIS 1598 (Ohio 2009).

Employee's age discrimination claim brought under R.C. 4112.99 was barred by R.C. 4112.14(C) because, inter alia, R.C. 4112.14's substantive provisions applied to age-discrimination claims brought under R.C. 4112.99, as the provisions of R.C. 4112.14, specifically addressing age discrimination claims, prevailed over the provisions of R.C. 4112.99, which generally allowed civil discrimination suits. Meyer v. UPS, 2009-Ohio-2463, 122 Ohio St. 3d 104, 909 N.E.2d 106, 2009 Ohio LEXIS 1598 (Ohio 2009).

Employer was granted summary judgment with regard to the employee's age discrimination claim because the claim was barred under R.C. 4112.14(C), as the employee had an opportunity to arbitrate his discharge but failed to do so. York v. AK Steel Corp., 2005 U.S. Dist. LEXIS 31846 (S.D. Ohio Dec. 8, 2005).

Arbitration provision contained in an employer's employment dispute policy was enforceable, and the court granted the employer's motion to dismiss and compel arbitration of the employee's age discrimination complaint. Raasch v. NCR Corp., 254 F. Supp. 2d 847, 2003 U.S. Dist. LEXIS 11561 (S.D. Ohio 2003).

The plain language of R.C. 4112.14(C) indicates the general assembly's intent to bar civil actions for race discrimination, as well as age discrimination, when the employee has the ability to arbitrate his claims: Hopkins v. UPS, 2000 Ohio App. LEXIS 443 (Ohio Ct. App., Hamilton County Feb. 11, 2000), dismissed, 89 Ohio St. 3d 1426, 729 N.E.2d 1196, 2000 Ohio LEXIS 1484 (Ohio 2000).

**Association**

An association by-law forbidding the election of any delegate over sixty-six years of age violates the prohibition in R.C. 4101.17(A), as amended, against employers denying eligibility for a "job opening" to an applicant solely due to the applicant's age, where the applicant is between the ages of forty and seventy. However, such a by-law does not violate former R.C. 4101.17(A), which provided protection only to those persons between the ages of forty and sixty-five: Mizenko v. First Catholic Slovak Ladies Asso., 49 Ohio App. 3d 6, 550 N.E.2d 541, 1989 Ohio App. LEXIS 3030 (Ohio Ct. App., Cuyahoga County 1989).

**Attorney's fees**

State employee who established age discrimination against the Ohio Department of Natural Resources was entitled to an award of costs and attorney's fees under R.C. 4112.14(B), as he established that the sums sought were reasonable. Warden v. Ohio Dep't of Natural Res., 2013-Ohio-1512, 2013 Ohio Misc. LEXIS 12 (Ohio Ct. Cl. 2013), aff'd in part and rev'd in part, 2014-Ohio-35, 7 N.E.3d 533, 2014 Ohio App. LEXIS 25 (Ohio Ct. App., Franklin County 2014).

**Burden of proof**

Appellant failed to establish a prima facie case of age discrimination because he failed to establish that the allegedly younger managers were treated more favorably than he was for similar paid time off (PTO) issues as appellant had at least 20 violations where he was absent from work but did not submit PTO, but the other managers only had one to four days where they were absent from work and did not submit PTO. Sullivan v. Ikea, 2020-Ohio-6661, 2020 Ohio App. LEXIS 4526 (Ohio Ct. App., Butler County 2020).

Trial court did not err by granting summary judgment for the employer on the former nursing home administrator's age discrimination claim because he failed to produce sufficient evidence from which a reasonable jury could have rejected as pretextual the employer's legitimate nondiscriminatory reasons for termination of poor and substandard work performance. Brehm v. Macintosh Co., 2019-Ohio-5322, 2019 Ohio App. LEXIS 5396 (Ohio Ct. App., Franklin County 2019).

In the terminated university employee's action against her former university employer, the university was entitled to summary judgment on discrimination and retaliation claims because the employee failed to demonstrate discriminatory intent under the McDonnell Douglas framework where there was evidence she had been terminated for insubordination, and she failed to demonstrate retaliation where she failed to show her opposition to any unlawful discriminatory practice. You v. Ne. Ohio Med. Univ., 2018-Ohio-4838, 2018 Ohio App. LEXIS 5161 (Ohio Ct. App., Franklin County 2018).

Trial court did not err in determining that the employee could not prevail on her age discrimination claim because the employer came forward with sufficient evidence of a nondiscriminatory reason for the firing, and the employee did not rebut that evidence to show the reason was only pretextual. Abrigg v. Mercy Med. Ctr., 2011-Ohio-2112, 2011 Ohio App. LEXIS 1806 (Ohio Ct. App., Stark County 2011).

Although an employee was a 57-year-old female at the time of her termination from employment, she failed to show age or gender discrimination under R.C. 4112.02 and 4112.14 where she was fired for poor performance and someone who was already working in the department assumed her duties; she failed to show that the employer's reason for firing her was a mere pretext. Goodyear v. Waco Holdings, Inc., 2009-Ohio-619, 2009 Ohio App. LEXIS 546 (Ohio Ct. App., Cuyahoga County 2009).

State college employee's age discrimination claim lacked merit where there was no convincing evidence presented that the employee's age played a role in the decision to terminate his employment or that the college's reasons for nonrenewal were pretextual; the college had asserted that the nonrenewal was based on poor performance, which claim was supported by multiple student complaints and a showing that the employee lacked initiative. Hannahs v. Edison State Cmty. College, 2008-Ohio-4798, 2008 Ohio Misc. LEXIS 205 (Ohio Ct. Cl. 2008).

Employee could not establish a prima facie case of age discrimination where he failed to do what was required of him by supervisors and thus, could not show that he met his employer's legitimate expectations: Wheelwright v. Clairol, Inc., 770 F. Supp. 396, 1991 U.S. Dist. LEXIS 18215 (S.D. Ohio 1991).

The employer's burden regarding the legitimate nondiscriminating rationale is one of production only. Once an explanation "legally sufficient to justify judgment" for the employer is presented, the plaintiff then bears the burden of persuasion upon the ultimate question of wrongful discrimination: Manofsky v. Goodyear Tire & Rubber Co., 69 Ohio App. 3d 663, 591 N.E.2d 752, 1990 Ohio App. LEXIS 4434 (Ohio Ct. App., Summit County 1990).

**Collateral estoppel**

A finding by the referee of the unemployment compensation board of review that an employee was discharged for just cause in connection with work, within the meaning of R.C. 4141.29(D)(2)(a), based on her refusal to follow orders collaterally estops that employee from raising the issue of the cause of her discharge under R.C. 4101.17, age discrimination: 21 Ohio App. 3d 288, 488 N.E.2d 486.

**Collective bargaining agreements**

Collective bargaining agreement did not require an employee to exhaust administrative remedies before pursuing a statutory age discrimination claim where the agreement contained no reference to discrimination claims: Campolieti v. City of Cleveland, 2009-Ohio-5224, 184 Ohio App. 3d 419, 921 N.E.2d 286, 2009 Ohio App. LEXIS 4417 (Ohio Ct. App., Cuyahoga County 2009).

Collective bargaining agreement, even if it contains an antidiscrimination clause, does not supersede an employee's rights under R.C. Chapter 4112: Haynes v. Ohio Tpk. Comm'n, 2008-Ohio-133, 177 Ohio App. 3d 1, 893 N.E.2d 850, 2008 Ohio App. LEXIS 121 (Ohio Ct. App., Cuyahoga County 2008).

**Constructive discharge**

Intervention specialist failed to establish a prima facie case of age discrimination because, while she certainly suffered a materially adverse effect on her salary and status through the loss of hours, she was not, effectively, required to retire. She had employment at the time she retired, and the prospect of increased hours in the future. Ruez v. Lake Cty. Educ. Serv. Ctr., 2017-Ohio-4125, 82 N.E.3d 21, 2017 Ohio App. LEXIS 2180 (Ohio Ct. App., Lake County 2017).

City employee alleged a prima facie case of constructive discharge based on age discrimination and that his retirement was not voluntary: Gessner v. City of Union, 2004-Ohio-5770, 159 Ohio App. 3d 43, 823 N.E.2d 1, 2004 Ohio App. LEXIS 5206 (Ohio Ct. App., Montgomery County 2004).

Constructive discharge may be found where an employee accepts retirement in the absence of any desirable alternative. An employer decision to redeploy younger employees while not redeploying older ones is a recognized form of adverse employment action: Scott v. Goodyear Tire & Rubber Co., 160 F.3d 1121, 1998 FED App. 0343P, 1998 U.S. App. LEXIS 30479 (6th Cir. Ohio 1998).

Where a plaintiff alleging unlawful age discrimination chooses termination in lieu of transfer, her decision cannot be construed as an actual discharge under former R.C. 4101.17. However, she may establish by sufficient evidence that she was constructively discharged. The test for determining whether an employee was constructively discharged is whether the employer's actions made working conditions so intolerable that a reasonable person under the circumstances would have felt compelled to resign: Mauzy v. Kelly Servs., 1996-Ohio-265, 75 Ohio St. 3d 578, 664 N.E.2d 1272, 1996 Ohio LEXIS 366 (Ohio 1996).

**Damages**

Trial court erred in relying on the general statute in awarding damages because the firefighter was limited to the relief provided under the specific age discrimination statute. Campolieti v. Cleveland Dep't of Pub. Safety, 2013-Ohio-5123, 2013 Ohio App. LEXIS 5332 (Ohio Ct. App., Cuyahoga County 2013).

State employee who established age discrimination against the Ohio Department of Natural Resources under R.C. 4112.14 and 4112.99 was entitled to post-judgment interest on his award of back pay pursuant to R.C. 2743.18(B) at the current statutory rate. Warden v. Ohio Dep't of Natural Res., 2013-Ohio-1512, 2013 Ohio Misc. LEXIS 12 (Ohio Ct. Cl. 2013), aff'd in part and rev'd in part, 2014-Ohio-35, 7 N.E.3d 533, 2014 Ohio App. LEXIS 25 (Ohio Ct. App., Franklin County 2014).

Insurance company, as former employer, was not entitled to remittitur after a jury awarded a terminated insurance executive $6 million in compensatory damages and $10 million in punitive damages in his action alleging age discrimination in violation of R.C. 4112.14(A); the jury adopted the compensatory damages figure from the calculations of the executive's expert, and the past economic compensatory damages award did not exceed the maximum damages that the jury reasonably could find to be compensatory for the executive's loss. Morgan v. New York Life Ins. Co., 507 F. Supp. 2d 808, 2007 U.S. Dist. LEXIS 60217 (N.D. Ohio 2007), aff'd in part, vacated in part, 559 F.3d 425, 2009 FED App. 0096P, 2009 U.S. App. LEXIS 5088 (6th Cir. Ohio 2009).

Insurance company, as former employer, was not entitled to judgment notwithstanding the verdict after a jury awarded a terminated insurance executive $6 million in compensatory damages and $10 million in punitive damages in his action alleging age discrimination in violation of R.C. 4112.14(A); for purposes of the punitive damages award, the executive showed clear and convincing evidence that the employer acted with a conscious disregard for his rights and that this conscious disregard had a greater probability of causing substantial harm. Further, the 1.67:1 ratio between punitive and compensatory damages was reasonable and comported with due process. Morgan v. New York Life Ins. Co., 507 F. Supp. 2d 808, 2007 U.S. Dist. LEXIS 60217 (N.D. Ohio 2007), aff'd in part, vacated in part, 559 F.3d 425, 2009 FED App. 0096P, 2009 U.S. App. LEXIS 5088 (6th Cir. Ohio 2009).

Insurance company, as former employer, was not entitled to remittitur after a jury awarded a terminated insurance executive $6 million in compensatory damages and $10 million in punitive damages in his action alleging age discrimination in violation of R.C. 4112.14(A); the jury adopted the compensatory damages figure from the calculations of the executive's expert, and the past economic compensatory damages award did not exceed the maximum damages that the jury reasonably could find to be compensatory for the executive's loss. Morgan v. New York Life Ins. Co., 507 F. Supp. 2d 808, 2007 U.S. Dist. LEXIS 60217 (N.D. Ohio 2007), aff'd in part, vacated in part, 559 F.3d 425, 2009 FED App. 0096P, 2009 U.S. App. LEXIS 5088 (6th Cir. Ohio 2009).

Insurance company, as former employer, was not entitled to judgment notwithstanding the verdict after a jury awarded a terminated insurance executive $6 million in compensatory damages and $10 million in punitive damages in his action alleging age discrimination in violation of R.C. 4112.14(A); for purposes of the punitive damages award, the executive showed clear and convincing evidence that the employer acted with a conscious disregard for his rights and that this conscious disregard had a greater probability of causing substantial harm. Further, the 1.67:1 ratio between punitive and compensatory damages was reasonable and comported with due process. Morgan v. New York Life Ins. Co., 507 F. Supp. 2d 808, 2007 U.S. Dist. LEXIS 60217 (N.D. Ohio 2007), aff'd in part, vacated in part, 559 F.3d 425, 2009 FED App. 0096P, 2009 U.S. App. LEXIS 5088 (6th Cir. Ohio 2009).

**—Back pay**

State employee who was not offered a full-time position based on the Ohio Department of Natural Resources' policy not to rehire a retiree suffered age discrimination under R.C. 4112.14 and 4112.99, such that he was entitled to recover back pay; there was evidence that he exercised reasonable diligence in looking for other suitable employment, and that he did not decline any job opportunities for substantially equivalent employment. Warden v. Ohio Dep't of Natural Res., 2013-Ohio-1512, 2013 Ohio Misc. LEXIS 12 (Ohio Ct. Cl. 2013), aff'd in part and rev'd in part, 2014-Ohio-35, 7 N.E.3d 533, 2014 Ohio App. LEXIS 25 (Ohio Ct. App., Franklin County 2014).

**Direct evidence**

Pursuant to R.C. 4112.02(A), the employee failed to establish her age discrimination claim by the direct method of proof because her own deposition testimony established that the hiring manager did not inquire about her age or retirement intentions until after she made the decision to hire the other candidate. Dautartas v. Abbott Labs., 2012-Ohio-1709, 2012 Ohio App. LEXIS 1495 (Ohio Ct. App., Franklin County 2012).

With respect to plaintiff's age discrimination claim under R.C. 4112.14 of the Age Discrimination in Employment Act of 1967, R.C. Chapter 4112, evidence that an employee remarked that "they were not going to hire any old guys back" was not sufficient direct evidence of unlawful discrimination. Dunaway v. Univ. of Cincinnati, 2012-Ohio-1248, 2012 Ohio Misc. LEXIS 28 (Ohio Ct. Cl. 2012).

*Unpublished decision:* Where an employee was terminated in an alleged reduction-in-force, the employee failed to provide direct evidence of age discrimination because (1) an email from a human resources manager described the tenures of the employee and a coworker, which was not the same as their age, (2) remarks about "new eyes and tools" and "new ideas" were ambiguous and did not necessarily refer to age, (3) mentioning a coworker's plan for retirement did not show age-based animus, and (4) a statement about a coworker's transfer did not mention the employee or anything about age. Metz v. Titanium Metals Corp., 475 Fed. Appx. 33, 2012 FED App. 0345N, 2012 U.S. App. LEXIS 6497 (6th Cir. Ohio), cert. denied, 568 U.S. 929, 133 S. Ct. 265, 184 L. Ed. 2d 235, 2012 U.S. LEXIS 7649 (U.S. 2012).

*Unpublished decision:* Human Resources Vice-President's explanation about why an employee was not hired for the position she applied for constituted direct evidence of age discrimination when he stated that the company was "looking down the road," "wanted longevity," he characterized her as a "baby boomer" in response to her request for an explanation about what he meant by "longevity," he asked questions about the employee's age and how much longer she had before she retired, and commented that she would be retiring "before too long" and that the company "went with a younger person"Wharton v. Gorman-Rupp Co., 309 Fed. Appx. 990, 2009 FED App. 0116N, 2009 U.S. App. LEXIS 2667 (6th Cir. Ohio 2009).

*Unpublished decision:* Human Resources vice-president's explanation about why an employee was not hired for the position she applied for constituted direct evidence of age discrimination when he stated that the company was "looking down the road," "wanted longevity," he characterized her as a "baby boomer" in response to her request for an explanation about what he meant by "longevity," he asked questions about the employee's age and how much longer she had before she retired, and commented that she would be retiring "before too long" and that the company "went with a younger person"Wharton v. Gorman-Rupp Co., 309 Fed. Appx. 990, 2009 FED App. 0116N, 2009 U.S. App. LEXIS 2667 (6th Cir. Ohio 2009).

Trial court properly granted summary judgment to a judge in an age discrimination action under R.C. 4112.02(A) and 4112.14(A) by deputy clerks who were terminated when the judge took office in a county probate judge capacity, as the clerks did not show direct evidence of the discrimination; statements by a co-worker were not evidence, as she had no decisionmaking authority and accordingly, the statements were not reflective of the judge's discriminatory intent, and as the clerks were unaware of the ages of those who replaced them, there was no statistical evidence to support their claims. Molnar v. Klammer, 2005-Ohio-6905, 2005 Ohio App. LEXIS 6227 (Ohio Ct. App., Lake County 2005).

**Disparate impact**

With respect to plaintiff's disparate impact claim regarding age discrimination under R.C. 4112.14 of the Age Discrimination in Employment Act of 1967, R.C. Chapter 4112, although plaintiff showed a prima facie case of indirect discrimination, defendant's policy not to re-hire retirees in order to promote succession planning and employee development constituted a valid business justification. Dunaway v. Univ. of Cincinnati, 2012-Ohio-1248, 2012 Ohio Misc. LEXIS 28 (Ohio Ct. Cl. 2012).

Trial court properly granted summary judgment to the employer on the disparate-impact age discrimination claim because, even if the employee had identified a specific employment practice to support her claim, she did not present a statistically relevant analysis to prove that the employment practice caused an adverse impact on employees over 40. Leeds v. Weltman, Weinberg & Reis Co., L.P.A., 2021-Ohio-4123, 2021 Ohio App. LEXIS 4038 (Ohio Ct. App., Cuyahoga County 2021).

**Disparate treatment**

Because the employee raised a genuine issue of material fact as to whether a substantially younger, similarly-situated co-worker was treated more favorably despite engaging in substantially similar conduct, the employee demonstrated that the reason for his termination was insufficient. Bowditch v. Mettler Toledo Int'l, Inc., 2013-Ohio-4206, 2013 Ohio App. LEXIS 4380 (Ohio Ct. App., Franklin County 2013).

Trial court erred by granting summary judgment for the employer and the human resources leader. Because reasonable minds could have differed as to whether similarly-situated employees were treated more favorably than the employee, he established the fourth element of his prima facie case for age discrimination. Bowditch v. Mettler Toledo Int'l, Inc., 2013-Ohio-4206, 2013 Ohio App. LEXIS 4380 (Ohio Ct. App., Franklin County 2013).

With respect to plaintiff's disparate treatment claim regarding age discrimination under R.C. 4112.14 of the Age Discrimination in Employment Act of 1967, R.C. Chapter 4112, although plaintiff showed a prima facie case of indirect discrimination, defendant's policy not to re-hire retirees was a legitimate, non-discriminatory reason for not hiring plaintiff. Dunaway v. Univ. of Cincinnati, 2012-Ohio-1248, 2012 Ohio Misc. LEXIS 28 (Ohio Ct. Cl. 2012).

In a disparate impact discrimination case, a city was not entitled to a new trial on the ground that claims under both R.C. 4112.14 and R.C. 4112.02 should not have been presented to the jury because, although the statutes required plaintiffs to select under which statute an age discrimination claim would be pursued, the proofs of disparate impact under both statutes were substantially the same. Howe v. City of Akron, 789 F. Supp. 2d 786, 2010 U.S. Dist. LEXIS 137344 (N.D. Ohio 2010).

Where younger employees who were alleged to have been treated differently by an employer were not "similarly situated" with older discharged employees, evidence of dissimilar treatment was no indication of age discrimination by the company: Merkel v. Scovill, Inc., 787 F.2d 174, 1986 U.S. App. LEXIS 23433 (6th Cir. Ohio), cert. denied, 479 U.S. 990, 107 S. Ct. 585, 93 L. Ed. 2d 587, 1986 U.S. LEXIS 4981 (U.S. 1986).

The fact that an employer had no written company policy defining and prohibiting theft of company merchandise failed to establish any reasonable implication of disparate treatment toward older employees who were discharged after having been found removing company property without authorization: Merkel v. Scovill, Inc., 787 F.2d 174, 1986 U.S. App. LEXIS 23433 (6th Cir. Ohio), cert. denied, 479 U.S. 990, 107 S. Ct. 585, 93 L. Ed. 2d 587, 1986 U.S. LEXIS 4981 (U.S. 1986).

Trial court properly granted the employer's summary judgment motion on the former employee's disparate-treatment age discrimination claim because she offered no evidence that, after being terminated as part of the reduction in force, she was replaced by anyone, let alone replaced by a substantially younger employee. Because her job duties were redistributed among employees all of whom are members of the same protected class, the fourth element of the prima facie case was not satisfied. Leeds v. Weltman, Weinberg & Reis Co., L.P.A., 2021-Ohio-4123, 2021 Ohio App. LEXIS 4038 (Ohio Ct. App., Cuyahoga County 2021).

**Early retirement incentives**

Employer who used age data forms and offered early retirement incentive programs did not violate Ohio's age discrimination statute: Bowman v. Firestone Tire & Rubber Co., 724 F. Supp. 493, 1989 U.S. Dist. LEXIS 12930 (N.D. Ohio 1989).

**Election of remedies**

Summary judgment was properly granted because the nurse's assistant was barred from bringing a private age discrimination claim under R.C. 4112.02 and 4112.99. Because the nurse's assistant filed a charge with the Equal Employment Opportunity Commission (EEOC) and never indicated that she would forego an investigation (and was filing for technical purposes only), her charge to the EEOC was likewise deemed filed with the Ohio Civil Rights Commission. Neal v. Franklin Plaza Nursing Home, 2009-Ohio-2034, 2009 Ohio App. LEXIS 1724 (Ohio Ct. App., Cuyahoga County 2009).

When the judicial secretary filed her suit in federal court, she clearly elected to pursue the remedies available under R.C. 4112.14 and, once she instituted her federal suit, she could not seek administrative remedies because she had locked herself in pursuing remedies under R.C. 4112.14; that did not change merely because the secretary's federal suit was voluntarily dismissed. Thus, the secretary was prevented from receiving any remedy under Ohio law in her administrative claim; R.C. 4112.14 still prevented her from receiving any administrative remedy since she had previously instituted a civil action under R.C. 4112.14 and thus, the secretary's original election to seek a remedy via a civil lawsuit was still effective. Dunn v. Bruzzese, 2007-Ohio-3500, 172 Ohio App. 3d 320, 874 N.E.2d 1221, 2007 Ohio App. LEXIS 3222 (Ohio Ct. App., Jefferson County 2007).

When the employee filed her age discrimination claim in federal court, she clearly elected to pursue the remedies available under R.C. 4112.14. Once the employee instituted her federal suit, she could not seek administrative remedies. That did not change merely because the federal action was voluntarily dismissed. Employee's dismissal was not a pretext for age discrimination where undisputed evidence showed that her behavior had been a consistent distraction in the workplace and the employer had tried resolving the issue in different ways to no avail: Dunn v. Bruzzese, 2007-Ohio-3500, 172 Ohio App. 3d 320, 874 N.E.2d 1221, 2007 Ohio App. LEXIS 3222 (Ohio Ct. App., Jefferson County 2007).

Mere filing of an age discrimination charge with the Equal Employment Opportunity Commission (EEOC) pursuant to § 626 of the Age Discrimination in Employment Act (ADEA), 29 U.S.C.S. § 621 et seq., is not equivalent to the election of an administrative remedy within the meaning of R.C. 4112.05. Thus, where it is shown that the plaintiffs only filed charges with the EEOC pursuant to the requirements of the ADEA, the fact of such filing does not constitute an election of the remedy set forth in R.C. 4112.05 and such plaintiffs are not precluded from seeking a judicial remedy under R.C. 4112.14 or 4112.99. Reminder v. Roadway Express, Inc., 2006 U.S. Dist. LEXIS 1899 (N.D. Ohio Jan. 10, 2006).

Because the employee filed a charge with the Ohio Civil Rights Commission (OCRC) before initiating his current federal action for age discrimination, he elected the remedy made available under R.C. 4112.05. Therefore, he elected the remedy made available by § 4112.05, which precluded later pursuit of the remedy made available by either R.C. 4112.14 or 4112.99 for age discrimination. Gray v. Allstate Ins. Co., 2005 U.S. Dist. LEXIS 40793 (S.D. Ohio Sept. 26, 2005).

The plaintiff was barred from bringing an age discrimination claim pursuant to R.C. 4112.14 where he earlier filed a charge with OCR.C. pursuant to R.C. 4112.05 without stating that the administrative charge was filed for the sole purpose of perfecting an ADEA claim: Fowler v. Hudson Foods, 96 Ohio Misc. 2d 19, 708 N.E.2d 792, 1998 Ohio Misc. LEXIS 57 (Ohio C.P. 1998).

Ohio Administrative Code 4112-3-01(D), which provides that a charge filed with the EEOC is also deemed to be filed with the OCRC, is not inconsistent with R.C. 4112.02(N) and 4412.14 since these sections merely require an election between administrative and judicial remedies: Williams v. Rayle Coal Co., 1997 Ohio App. LEXIS 4302 (Ohio Ct. App., Belmont County Sept. 19, 1997).

The 1987 amendment to R.C. 4112.99 did not alter the election of remedies requirement as to age discrimination claims: Balent v. National Revenue Corp., 93 Ohio App. 3d 419, 638 N.E.2d 1064, 1994 Ohio App. LEXIS 935 (Ohio Ct. App., Franklin County 1994).

Plaintiff who had filed age discrimination charge with the Ohio Civil Rights Commission for the sole purpose of meeting the requirements of a suit under federal law could pursue state remedies in federal court even though Ohio law requires an election of remedies: Baker v. Siemens Energy & Automation, 838 F. Supp. 1227, 1993 U.S. Dist. LEXIS 16769 (S.D. Ohio 1993).

Even though R.C. 4112.02(N) and 4101.17 each preclude filing of age discrimination claims under both provisions, a court should not simply dismiss an action alleging both. The special provision of R.C. 4112.02(N) prevails over the general relief afforded by R.C. 4112.99: Giambrone v. Spalding & Evenflo Co., 79 Ohio App. 3d 308, 607 N.E.2d 106, 1992 Ohio App. LEXIS 2070 (Ohio Ct. App., Miami County 1992).

A party who has potential remedies for alleged age discrimination under R.C. 4101.17, 4112.02 and 4112.99 may not pursue an administrative action under R.C. 4112.05, fail to appeal an adverse determination and then bring an action under R.C. 4112.99: Gallant v. Toledo Pub. Sch., 84 Ohio App. 3d 378, 616 N.E.2d 1156, 1992 Ohio App. LEXIS 6324 (Ohio Ct. App., Lucas County 1992).

R.C. 4101.17, 4112.02 and 4112.05 are exclusive and once an action is brought under one of these sections a plaintiff is barred from bringing an action under either of the other two provisions: Pater v. Health Care & Retirement Corp., 808 F. Supp. 573, 1992 U.S. Dist. LEXIS 20568 (S.D. Ohio 1992).

Protection against age discrimination is provided under Ohio law by three statutory sections: (1) R.C. 4101.17(B), which permits a civil action for violation of subsection (A) of that section; (2) R.C. 4112.02(N), which permits a civil action to be brought against those who violate the other subsections of that section; and (3) R.C. 4112.05, which permits a complaint to be brought with the Ohio Civil Rights Commission for violations of R.C. 4112.02 and 4112.02.1. Each of these statutory remedies is exclusive—the choice of one remedy precludes recourse to other remedies: Pozzobon v. Parts for Plastics, 770 F. Supp. 376, 1991 U.S. Dist. LEXIS 11655 (N.D. Ohio 1991).

Where the Equal Employment Opportunity Commission refers an employee's age discrimination charge to a state agency there is no election of remedies by the employee to seek an administrative rather than a judicial remedy: Carr v. French Oil Mill Machinery Co., 746 F. Supp. 700, 1989 U.S. Dist. LEXIS 17139 (S.D. Ohio 1989).

A claimant who has previously filed a claim with the Ohio Civil Rights Commission for purposes of meeting the requirements of the ADEA, is not precluded from filing an age discrimination action under R.C. 4101.17: Pitts v. Dayton Power & Light Co., 748 F. Supp. 531 (S.D. 1989).

While the argument, that plaintiff filed complaint with Ohio Civil Rights Commission only in order to comply with Age Discrimination in Employment Act, 29 USC § 621 et seq., and did not intend to pursue state administrative remedy, points out inconsistency between state statutory scheme and federal statute, it does not keep plaintiff from being barred from bringing a claim under R.C. 4101.17 by R.C. 4112.08: Keister v. Delco Products, 680 F. Supp. 281, 1987 U.S. Dist. LEXIS 13098 (S.D. Ohio 1987).

Simply because Ohio's age discrimination law has the effect of requiring a litigant to choose between his or her state and federal remedies does not invalidate that law or require the court to construe the terms of that law inconsistently with its plain meaning: Keister v. Delco Products, 680 F. Supp. 281, 1987 U.S. Dist. LEXIS 13098 (S.D. Ohio 1987).

A plaintiff who files a charge of age discrimination with the OCR.C. under R.C. 4112.05 seeking administrative enforcement of the right against age discrimination is barred from bringing a civil action under R.C. 4101.17 or 4112.02(N): Smith v. L.M. Berry & Co., 654 F. Supp. 11, 1986 U.S. Dist. LEXIS 21317 (S.D. Ohio 1986).

A claimant who has previously filed an age discrimination action under R.C. 4101.17 is not barred from filing a claim with the Ohio Civil Rights Commission pursuant to R.C. 4112.05 in order to satisfy the mandatory prerequisite to an action under the federal Age Discrimination in Employment Act: Morris v. Kaiser Engineers, Inc., 14 Ohio St. 3d 45, 471 N.E.2d 471, 1984 Ohio LEXIS 1240 (Ohio 1984).

Allowing a plaintiff to proceed simultaneously under 29 U.S.C. § 621 et seq., the Age Discrimination in Employment Act, and R.C. 4101.17 does not contravene the federal scheme: Mason v. Midwestern Fid. Corp., 589 F. Supp. 751, 1984 U.S. Dist. LEXIS 14867 (S.D. Ohio 1984), aff'd, 1996 U.S. App. LEXIS 17692 (4th Cir. July 19, 1996).

Where an age discrimination plaintiff has elected to proceed administratively by filing a claim with the Ohio Civil Rights Commission, he is precluded from proceeding with a state judicial remedy, but where plaintiff has elected to proceed with his state judicial remedy and federal judicial remedy jointly, prior to commencing state administrative proceedings, he may proceed with his state claim under R.C. 4101.17: Ackman v. Ohio Knife Co., 589 F. Supp. 768, 1984 U.S. Dist. LEXIS 14833 (S.D. Ohio 1984).

Where an age discrimination plaintiff filed an administrative charge with the Ohio Civil Rights Commission two weeks after he filed state and federal claims in federal court, he has commenced state proceedings as required by the Age Discrimination in Employment Act: Venezia v. Scovill, Inc., 592 F. Supp. 3, 1983 U.S. Dist. LEXIS 13898 (S.D. Ohio 1983).

An action involving age discrimination is not foreclosed by the plaintiff's choice to sue under Ohio as well as federal law: Bailey v. Container Corp. of America, 594 F. Supp. 629, 1984 U.S. Dist. LEXIS 23120 (S.D. Ohio 1984), vacated in part, 594 F. Supp. 629, 1985 U.S. Dist. LEXIS 24066 (S.D. Ohio 1985), limited, Adleta v. GE (S.D. Ohio 1996).

Where a plaintiff files suit under R.C. 4101.17, alleging age discrimination, and later files a charge under R.C. 4112.05 with the Ohio Civil Rights Commission, his private right of action under R.C. 4101.17 is not barred: Krenning v. Darling & Co., 572 F. Supp. 923, 1983 U.S. Dist. LEXIS 18990 (S.D. Ohio 1983).



**Emotional distress**

(Former) R.C. 4101.17 does not provide damages for emotional distress. Even though an employee is not reinstated, the court may award damages for lost wages and fringe benefits: Holda v. Skilken Properties Co., 1991 Ohio App. LEXIS 517 (Ohio Ct. App., Richland County Jan. 23, 1991).

**Employee construed**

Trial court properly granted summary judgment to an employer in an action by a terminated independent contractor (IC), alleging claims of age discrimination in violation of R.C. 4112.14, negligence, and violations of Ohio's public policy, as the sales agent agreement executed by the IC clearly indicated that he was not an employee within R.C. 4112.01(A)(3), such that he was not entitled to the statutory age discrimination protections or to other requested relief; there were multiple indicators of the IC status, and the alleged indicia of control by the employer were not sufficient to raise a genuine issue of material fact regarding the IC's status. Perron v. Hood Indus., 2007-Ohio-4478, 2007 Ohio App. LEXIS 4040 (Ohio Ct. App., Lucas County 2007).

Certified public accountant who sued his accounting firm for age discrimination was an "employee" of firm, rather than a partner, and as such, was entitled to the protections of the Ohio age discrimination law where he made no capital contribution to the firm, he received salary rather than sharing profits, he had no right to examine the firm's books and records, he had little management authority, there was no fiduciary relationship, and he lacked any meaningful control or voting rights in the firm: Simpson v. Ernst & Young, 850 F. Supp. 648, 1994 U.S. Dist. LEXIS 5463 (S.D. 1994), affirmed by 100 F.3d 436, 1996 U.S. App. LEXIS 29131, 1996 FED App. 0356P (6th Cir.), 70 Empl. Prac. Dec. (CCH) P44577, 20 Employee Benefits Cas. (BNA) 2088, 72 Fair Empl. Prac. Cas. (BNA) 343 (6th Cir. Ohio 1996)supra.

Whether a claimant under R.C. 4101.17 is an independent contractor or an employee depends on whether the alleged employer reserved the right to control the manner or means of doing the work: Kurtz v. Harcourt Brace Jovanovich, Inc., 69 Ohio App. 3d 267, 590 N.E.2d 772, 1990 Ohio App. LEXIS 3694 (Ohio Ct. App., Cuyahoga County 1990).

R.C. 4101.17, age discrimination by employer, does not apply to independent contractors: Cavanaugh v. Nationwide Mut. Ins. Co., 65 Ohio App. 2d 123, 19 Ohio Op. 3d 74, 416 N.E.2d 1059, 1976 Ohio App. LEXIS 5932 (Ohio Ct. App., Summit County 1976).

**Employment-at-will**

Since the employee was not an at-will employee, he could not assert a claim for wrongful discharge in violation of Ohio law; further and contrary to the employee's argument that, even though his employment was governed by the collective bargaining agreement, his union representatives did not adequately represent him in connection with his discharge, the union's conduct, no matter how inadequate, could not change the fact that the employee was not an at-will employee. Given that fact, he simply could not assert a claim that only existed as an exception to the employment at-will doctrine. Dobrski v. Ford Motor Co., 698 F. Supp. 2d 966, 2010 U.S. Dist. LEXIS 24470 (N.D. Ohio 2010).

Tort claim for wrongful discharge in violation of the public policy against age discrimination did not exist because the jeopardy element of such a tort could not be established as Ohio Rev. Code ch. 4112 protected the policy through the remedies it offered in (1) R.C. 4112.02(N), allowing for any legal or equitable relief that would effectuate an individual's rights, (2) R.C. 4112.05(G), allowing enforcement actions by the Ohio Civil Rights Commission, (3) R.C. 4112.14(B), allowing "an appropriate remedy," which could include damages and injunctive relief, and (4) R.C. 4112.99, which subjected violators to a civil action for damages, injunctive relief, or other appropriate relief. Leininger v. Pioneer Nat'l Latex, 2007-Ohio-4921, 115 Ohio St. 3d 311, 875 N.E.2d 36, 2007 Ohio LEXIS 2229 (Ohio 2007).

There is no need to carve out an exception to the employment-at-will doctrine to recognize a cause of action for wrongful discharge in violation of public policy because, the legislature has already carved out the exception by enacting R.C. 4101.17, 4112.02(N), 4112.05, and 4112.99: Napier v. VGC Corp., 797 F. Supp. 602, 1992 U.S. Dist. LEXIS 12914 (S.D. Ohio 1992).

**Equitable award**

State employee who established age discrimination against the Ohio Department of Natural Resources under R.C. 4112.14 and 4112.99 was entitled to an equitable award to compensate him for his increased tax burden as a result of a lump sum award, as such helped make the employee whole and assured him the most complete relief possible. Warden v. Ohio Dep't of Natural Res., 2013-Ohio-1512, 2013 Ohio Misc. LEXIS 12 (Ohio Ct. Cl. 2013), aff'd in part and rev'd in part, 2014-Ohio-35, 7 N.E.3d 533, 2014 Ohio App. LEXIS 25 (Ohio Ct. App., Franklin County 2014).



**Evidence**

Granting of the employer's motion for summary judgment in the employee's action for age discrimination and retaliation pursuant to the Age Discrimination in Employment Act, 29 U.S.C.S. §§ 623, et seq., and R.C. 4112.02(I) and 4112.14. was proper where a former employee's statement of opinion could not be considered a statement of the party opponent for purposes of Fed. R. Evid. 801(d)(2)(D) because that employee had left the company. Further, the employee failed to identify evidence suggesting that the employer's articulated reason for the alleged adverse actions was mere pretext. Rufo v. Dave & Busters, Inc., 2005 U.S. Dist. LEXIS 33395 (S.D. Ohio Dec. 16, 2005), aff'd, 2007 FED App. 0075N, 2007 U.S. App. LEXIS 2366 (6th Cir. Ohio Jan. 31, 2007).

**—Insufficient**

There were no genuine issues of material fact regarding the former employee's age discrimination claim because he failed to establish that he was replaced by an employee of a substantially younger age who was not a member of the protected class and failed to meet his burden of showing that the employer's reasons for the adverse employment action were a pretext for unlawful age discrimination. The employee was hired at the age of 52 and terminated at the age of 53 and the person who replaced him was only seven years younger. Brown v. O'Reilly Auto. Stores, Inc., 2015-Ohio-5146, 54 N.E.3d 638, 2015 Ohio App. LEXIS 5125 (Ohio Ct. App., Cuyahoga County 2015).

Employee did not prove her age discrimination claim under R.C. 4112.14 as the employee did not demonstrate that the employer's legitimate, nondiscriminatory reason was false, that those reasons did not actually motivate its decision to discharge the employee, or that its reasons were insufficient to motivate discharge. Mittler v. Ohiohealth Corp., 2013-Ohio-1634, 2013 Ohio App. LEXIS 1524 (Ohio Ct. App., Franklin County 2013).

Employee did not prove her age discrimination claim under R.C. 4112.14 as she did not show that she was replaced by, or that her discharge permitted the retention of, a person not belonging in the protected class. The evidence showed that the employee was not replaced but that her duties were redistributed among other nurses, some of whom were older than the employee. Mittler v. Ohiohealth Corp., 2013-Ohio-1634, 2013 Ohio App. LEXIS 1524 (Ohio Ct. App., Franklin County 2013).

Plaintiff's age discrimination claim under R.C. 4112.14(A) failed where the evidence did not support plaintiff's claim that she was replaced by a younger person; rather, the younger person undertook a new, different position that entailed different duties than plaintiff's former job. Spencer v. Cent. State Univ., 2012-Ohio-1245, 2012 Ohio Misc. LEXIS 29 (Ohio Ct. Cl. 2012).

State university employee's age discrimination claim under R.C. 4112.14(A) failed, as the university provided evidence that it had legitimate, non-discriminatory reasons for terminating the employee's position; the evidence showed that the position was abolished as a cost-cutting measure. Kellogg v. Ohio State Univ., 2011-Ohio-4848, 2011 Ohio Misc. LEXIS 411 (Ohio Ct. Cl. 2011).

Employee did not establish a prima facie case of age discrimination because he presented no evidence that the employer's reason for the transfer was pretextual and did not demonstrate a genuine issue of material fact regarding the employer's legitimate, non-discriminatory reasons for promoting younger employees. The employee did not show that his termination was a pretext for impermissible age discrimination. Horsley v. Burton, 2010-Ohio-6315, 2010 Ohio App. LEXIS 5277 (Ohio Ct. App., Scioto County 2010).

Employee who was terminated in a reorganization could not establish a prima facie claim of age discrimination in employment, even though he was 70 years old when he was terminated, because he offered no evidence of the ages of employees who remained employed after the reorganization, so he could not prove that he was replaced by, or that his discharge permitted the retention of, a person of substantially younger age, and his vague assertions that he was replaced by substantially younger employees were insufficient. Pierce v. Brown Publ. Co., 2007-Ohio-1657, 2007 Ohio App. LEXIS 1510 (Ohio Ct. App., Fayette County 2007).

Plaintiff did not establish indirect evidence of age discrimination where he was not replaced. Age-related comments that are isolated, vague, or ambiguous, or that refer to other employees, cannot support a finding of age discrimination: Abrams v. Am. Computer Tech., 2006-Ohio-4032, 168 Ohio App. 3d 362, 860 N.E.2d 123, 2006 Ohio App. LEXIS 3973 (Ohio Ct. App., Hamilton County 2006).

Trial court's grant of summary judgment to an employer in an age discrimination action by an employee pursuant to R.C. 4112.02(A) and 4112.14(A) was proper, as the employer's claim that the employee was terminated for financial reasons was a legitimate, nondiscriminatory reason, and the employee failed to show that it was a mere pretext. Chandler v. Dunn Hardware, Inc., 2006-Ohio-4376, 168 Ohio App. 3d 496, 860 N.E.2d 1042, 2006 Ohio App. LEXIS 4293 (Ohio Ct. App., Cuyahoga County 2006).

Deputy clerks who were discharged when a new county probate judge took office did not show indirect evidence of age discrimination under R.C. 4112.04(A) and 4112.14(A) in order to avoid summary judgment to the judge, although they offered sufficient evidence of the first three factors of the four-part Coryell test, as they were unable to show that the persons who replaced them were "substantially younger" in two out of the three clerks' cases, and as to the third, the judge's claim that the replacement was due to a reorganization of the court and issues of loyalty represented a legitimate, nondiscriminatory reason, which was not shown to be pretextual. Molnar v. Klammer, 2005-Ohio-6905, 2005 Ohio App. LEXIS 6227 (Ohio Ct. App., Lake County 2005).

Plaintiff produced no evidence of age discrimination other than being replaced by an employee under forty: Beauchamp v. CompuServe, Inc., 126 Ohio App. 3d 17, 709 N.E.2d 863, 1998 Ohio App. LEXIS 1482 (Ohio Ct. App., Franklin County 1998).

The direct, circumstantial and statistical evidence did not prove age discrimination: Sobolewski v. Manoir Electroalloys Corp., 120 Ohio App. 3d 225, 697 N.E.2d 688, 1997 Ohio App. LEXIS 2511 (Ohio Ct. App., Lorain County 1997).

A claim of age discrimination was properly held to fail as a matter of law when it was raised in an effort to obfuscate the parties' real dispute over the payment of post-employment commissions, when the mere hiring of a younger employee in the same protected class did not create an inference of discrimination, and when there was nothing to support the plaintiff's assertion that the hiring of a replacement seven years his junior could reasonably be said to reflect discriminatory conduct: Weiper v. W.A. Hill & Assocs., 104 Ohio App. 3d 250, 661 N.E.2d 796, 1995 Ohio App. LEXIS 2202 (Ohio Ct. App., Hamilton County 1995).

**—Sufficient**

Competent, credible evidence supported the finding that the employee did not provide direct evidence of disparate treatment age discrimination, R.C. 4112.14, as the employer offered evidence that the retiree policy was motivated by a desire to prevent double-dipping;the employer's hiring decision was not motivated by inaccurate and stigmatizing stereotypes about age. Warden v. Ohio Dep't of Natural Res., 2014-Ohio-35, 7 N.E.3d 533, 2014 Ohio App. LEXIS 25 (Ohio Ct. App., Franklin County 2014).

Trial court did not err in finding that the department of public safety failed to present a legitimate, nondiscriminatory basis for its decision because the manner in which the fire chief relied on Cleveland, Ohio, Codified Ordinances 135.07 to deny the firefighter a more desirable position was based on his age, in violation of Ohio anti-discrimination statutes. The chief's reasons were mere pretext for age discrimination because all requests for employment extensions for employees age 65 and older had been granted. Campolieti v. Cleveland Dep't of Pub. Safety, 2013-Ohio-5123, 2013 Ohio App. LEXIS 5332 (Ohio Ct. App., Cuyahoga County 2013).

*Unpublished decision:* Terminated employee's age discrimination claims failed because the employer articulated a legitimate, non-discriminatory reason for terminating the employee's employment based on a finding that the employee had falsified a meter reading, and the employee failed to show pretext since all three investigations reached the conclusion that the employee had falsified the reading and the employee failed to put forth evidence that the employer did not have an honest belief, at the time of termination, that the employee falsified the reading. Terry v. United States Enrichment Corp., 482 Fed. Appx. 87, 2012 FED App. 0564N, 2012 U.S. App. LEXIS 11178 (6th Cir. Ohio 2012).

Judgment was not against the manifest weight of the evidence in that competent, credible evidence existed to support a jury's verdict in an age discrimination case because a 67-year-old employee, who had more experience in the hotel and hospitality business, had more management experience, and had more tenure with the employer, was replaced by a worker who was 20 years younger and the employee's supervisor told a coworker that they (the supervisor's superiors) told the supervisor that the supervisor had to let the old one go — the oldest one go. Additionally, when the employee begged to keep the employee's job and offered to take a pay cut, the supervisor informed the employee that it was the employee they wanted gone. Thomas v. Columbia Sussex Corp., 2011-Ohio-17, 2011 Ohio App. LEXIS 9 (Ohio Ct. App., Franklin County 2011).

Insurance company, as former employer, was not entitled to a new trial under Fed. R. Civ. P. 59(a) after a jury awarded a terminated insurance executive $6 million in compensatory damages and $10 million in punitive damages in his action alleging age discrimination in violation of R.C. 4112.14(A); the judgment was not contrary to the weight of the evidence, the evidentiary rulings and jury instructions did not result in an unfair trial, and the closing argument of the executive's counsel did not infect the jury with passion and prejudice. Morgan v. New York Life Ins. Co., 507 F. Supp. 2d 808, 2007 U.S. Dist. LEXIS 60217 (N.D. Ohio 2007), aff'd in part, vacated in part, 559 F.3d 425, 2009 FED App. 0096P, 2009 U.S. App. LEXIS 5088 (6th Cir. Ohio 2009).

**Exhaustion of administrative remedies**

Court erred in granting summary judgment in favor of the school board, because a public employee alleging disability discrimination in violation of R.C. Chapter 4112 need not exhaust the administrative remedy of appeal to a civil service commission before pursuing the civil action allowed in R.C. 4112.99. Worley v. Newton Falls Exempted Vill. Sch. Bd. of Educ., 2014-Ohio-5385, 2014 Ohio App. LEXIS 5211 (Ohio Ct. App., Trumbull County 2014).

**Failure to transfer**

In a suit under R.C. 4112.14, a former employer was entitled to summary judgment on former employees' age discrimination claims arising out of the failure to select the employees for positions at another facility because the positions in question were awarded to older applicants and the employer's general policy of hiring local residents was in effect at the time the employees applied for the positions. Zeman v. Goodrich Corp., 2005 U.S. Dist. LEXIS 37004 (N.D. Ohio July 15, 2005).

**Federal age discrimination in employment ac**

Trial court properly held that a county probate court was an arm of the state and as such, it was immune from liability pursuant to U.S. Const. amend. 11 under the Federal Age Discrimination in Employment Act, 29 U.S.C.S. §§ 621-634, in an action by deputy clerks against a county probate judge, who had replaced them when he took office; dismissal of the action with respect to both money damages and injunctive relief was proper, as there was no merit to the claim for injunctive relief because it had already been determined that there was no merit to a statutory claim under R.C. 4112.14, which was modeled after the federal act. Molnar v. Klammer, 2005-Ohio-6905, 2005 Ohio App. LEXIS 6227 (Ohio Ct. App., Lake County 2005).

**Federal discrimination law**

In reviewing age discrimination claims under R.C. 4101.17, Ohio courts apply the federal evidentiary standards and guidelines applicable to claims brought under the Age Discrimination in Employment Act: Scheid v. Fanny Farmer Candy Shops, Inc., 859 F.2d 434, 1988 U.S. App. LEXIS 14192 (6th Cir. Ohio 1988).

**Federal jurisdiction**

Federal district court would decline to exercise pendent jurisdiction over claims under R.C. 4101.17 in an action brought under the ADEA in the interests of comity, justice to the parties, and fairness to all litigants, in the absence of any clearly articulable reason to make an exception to similar rulings in similar cases: Taber v. Christ Hosp., 723 F. Supp. 1236, 1989 U.S. Dist. LEXIS 12696 (S.D. Ohio 1989).

Federal court would decline pendent jurisdiction over claim under R.C. 4101.17(A) in action under ADEA where Ohio courts had not yet addressed the issue whether a bona fide occupational qualification exception was incorporated into the Ohio statute: Rasberg v. Nationwide Life Ins. Co., 671 F. Supp. 494, 1987 U.S. Dist. LEXIS 11996 (S.D. Ohio 1987).

In an action brought in federal district court under the Age Discrimination in Employment Act (29 USC § 621 et seq), pendent claims under R.C. 4101.17 would be dismissed as a matter of comity and to promote justice to the parties and to insure fairness to all litigants, especially where the state law on which the claims were based was still developing: Foltzer v. Lodge & Shipley Co., 636 F. Supp. 843, 1986 U.S. Dist. LEXIS 24224 (S.D. Ohio 1986).

Pendent claims under R.C. 4101.17 in a federal age discrimination suit brought in federal district court would be dismissed in the interests of judicial economy, comity, and fairness to litigants with federal claims where the state claims overshadowed the federal claim and involved legal theories, issues and remedies separate and distinct from those involved in the federal claim: Goff v. Kroger Co., 647 F. Supp. 87, 1986 U.S. Dist. LEXIS 17959 (S.D. Ohio 1986).

**Federal preemption**

The Federal Home Loan Bank Act specifically empowers the institutions it governs to dismiss an employee "at pleasure" and thus preempts any contrary right created by state law: Kispert v. Federal Home Loan Bank, 778 F. Supp. 950, 1991 U.S. Dist. LEXIS 19868 (S.D. Ohio 1991).

**Former law**

When enacting and then amending R.C. 4101.17, the General Assembly declined to include the remedy of compensatory or punitive damages. It may therefore be presumed that it did not intend to confer the right to such a remedy under the statute: Hoops v. United Tel. Co., 50 Ohio St. 3d 97, 553 N.E.2d 252, 1990 Ohio LEXIS 157 (Ohio 1990), limited, Adleta v. GE (S.D. Ohio 1996).

Where the plaintiff alleged age discrimination in employment, his only available damages were lost wages and benefits, liquidated damages under ADEA, and other damages stemming from breach of implied contract; compensatory and punitive damages are not available under R.C. 4101.17: Hawley v. Dresser Industries, Inc., 737 F. Supp. 445, 1990 U.S. Dist. LEXIS 5956 (S.D. Ohio 1990), aff'd in part and rev'd in part, 958 F.2d 720, 1992 U.S. App. LEXIS 3946 (6th Cir. Ohio 1992), disapproved, Humphreys v. Bellaire Corp., 966 F.2d 1037, 1992 U.S. App. LEXIS 12543 (6th Cir. Ohio 1992).

Where plaintiff claimed age discrimination under R.C. 4101.17 because he was demoted, the court found discriminatory demotion is not actionable under R.C. 4101.17 because its plain language imposes liability only for hiring and termination decisions, if failure to promote constituted discrimination in a job opening against an applicant, the plaintiff would have to assert this as a separate claim, since demotion is an event which is distinct from a failure to promote and it therefore does not fall under the prohibition of R.C. 4101.17: Hawley v. Dresser Industries, Inc., 737 F. Supp. 445, 1990 U.S. Dist. LEXIS 5956 (S.D. Ohio 1990), aff'd in part and rev'd in part, 958 F.2d 720, 1992 U.S. App. LEXIS 3946 (6th Cir. Ohio 1992), disapproved, Humphreys v. Bellaire Corp., 966 F.2d 1037, 1992 U.S. App. LEXIS 12543 (6th Cir. Ohio 1992).

R.C. 4101.17(B) (age discrimination) does not authorize an award of either compensatory or punitive damages: South v. Toledo Edison Co., 32 Ohio App. 3d 24, 513 N.E.2d 800, 1986 Ohio App. LEXIS 10175 (Ohio Ct. App., Lucas County 1986).

Where there is no evidence that age was a determining factor in an employer's discharge of employees after they had been found removing company property without authorization, there is no violation of R.C. 4101.17: Merkel v. Scovill, Inc., 787 F.2d 174, 1986 U.S. App. LEXIS 23433 (6th Cir. Ohio), cert. denied, 479 U.S. 990, 107 S. Ct. 585, 93 L. Ed. 2d 587, 1986 U.S. LEXIS 4981 (U.S. 1986).

Within the context of R.C. 4101.17, "just cause" for discharge is established if plaintiff was terminated for reasons other than those explicitly prohibited by the statute: Barker v. Scovill, Inc., Schrader Bellows Div., 6 Ohio St. 3d 146, 451 N.E.2d 807, 1983 Ohio LEXIS 794 (Ohio 1983).

**Front pay**

State employee who was not offered a full-time position based on the Ohio Department of Natural Resources' policy not to rehire a retiree suffered age discrimination under R.C. 4112.14 and 4112.99, and he was entitled to an award of front pay, as he would have accepted the position for a five-year period if it had been offered to him, and he did not have a reasonable prospect of obtaining comparable employment. Warden v. Ohio Dep't of Natural Res., 2013-Ohio-1512, 2013 Ohio Misc. LEXIS 12 (Ohio Ct. Cl. 2013), aff'd in part and rev'd in part, 2014-Ohio-35, 7 N.E.3d 533, 2014 Ohio App. LEXIS 25 (Ohio Ct. App., Franklin County 2014).

**Governmental immunity, liability**

Trial court properly held that a county probate court was an arm of the state and as such, it was immune from liability pursuant to U.S. Const. amend. 11 under the Federal Age Discrimination in Employment Act, 29 U.S.C.S. §§ 621-634, in an action by deputy clerks against a county probate judge, who had replaced them when he took office. Dismissal of the action with respect to both money damages and injunctive relief was proper, as there was no merit to the claim for injunctive relief because it had already been determined that there was no merit to a statutory claim under R.C. 4112.14, which was modeled after the federal act. Molnar v. Klammer, 2005-Ohio-6905, 2005 Ohio App. LEXIS 6227 (Ohio Ct. App., Lake County 2005).

A state employee may bring an action in the court of claims alleging age discrimination under R.C. 4101.17 (See now R.C. 4112.14) by a state agency: Harris v. Ohio Dept. of Adm. Serv., 63 Ohio App. 3d 115, 577 N.E.2d 1180 (1989).

**Harmless error**

Even if a trial court erred in excluding evidence of a terminated employee's damages in an age discrimination case, no prejudicial harm occurred, because the evidence related to damages, not to liability. Therefore, because no liability on the part of the employer was found by the trial court, any error in the exclusion of evidence of damages was harmless. Davis v. Goodwill Indus., 2009-Ohio-6133, 2009 Ohio App. LEXIS 5147 (Ohio Ct. App., Montgomery County 2009).

**Hiring**

Facts alleged supported a possible claim for age discrimination as to hiring practices in that defendant alleged that he was 56, that he was neither interviewed nor hired for positions for which he was qualified, and that substantially younger candidates were interviewed and/or hired. Richardson v. Clinical Computing PLC, 2016-Ohio-8065, 2016 Ohio App. LEXIS 4926 (Dec. 7, 2016)., Ohio App. LEXIS 4926 (Dec. 7, 2016).

**Insufficient**

An employer and a supervisor were properly granted summary judgment on an employee's age discrimination claims under the Age Discrimination in Employment Act, 29 U.S.C.S. § 621 et seq., and R.C. 4112.14 as the employee did not produce sufficient evidence to show that the employer's justification for the termination of the employee, because of the employee's insubordination towards the employee's supervisor, was pretextual. Hausler v. GE, 134 Fed. Appx. 890, 2005 FED App. 0485N, 2005 U.S. App. LEXIS 10983 (6th Cir. Ohio 2005).

**Judgment N.O.V.**

Insurance company, as former employer, was not entitled to judgment notwithstanding the verdict after a jury awarded a terminated insurance executive $6 million in compensatory damages and $10 million in punitive damages in his action alleging age discrimination in violation of R.C. 4112.14(A); the executive gave the jury sufficient evidence to demonstrate that the discharge was motivated by his age because the evidence showed that the employer treated similarly situated younger employees more favorably and that the employer's proffered job performance reason for the executive's discharge was a pretext for age discrimination animus. The executive also offered direct evidence of numerous allegedly ageist comments made by four of the employer's highest ranking members of management. Morgan v. New York Life Ins. Co., 507 F. Supp. 2d 808, 2007 U.S. Dist. LEXIS 60217 (N.D. Ohio 2007), aff'd in part, vacated in part, 559 F.3d 425, 2009 FED App. 0096P, 2009 U.S. App. LEXIS 5088 (6th Cir. Ohio 2009).

Trial court erred in granting defendants' motion for JNOV on an age discrimination claim: Jelinek v. Abbott Labs., 2005-Ohio-5696, 164 Ohio App. 3d 607, 843 N.E.2d 807, 2005 Ohio App. LEXIS 5122 (Ohio Ct. App., Franklin County 2005).

Since a jury could not within reason find that age was a determining factor in the defendant's discharge of the plaintiffs, the district court erred in refusing to grant the defendant's request for a judgment n.o.v. on the plaintiffs' claims under both the ADEA and R.C. 4101.17: Merkel v. Scovill, Inc., 787 F.2d 174, 1986 U.S. App. LEXIS 23433 (6th Cir. Ohio), cert. denied, 479 U.S. 990, 107 S. Ct. 585, 93 L. Ed. 2d 587, 1986 U.S. LEXIS 4981 (U.S. 1986).

**Judgment on pleadings**

Employee sufficiently alleged a claim of age discrimination, under R.C. 4112.14(A), when he said (1) his employer and supervisor were employers under R.C. 4112.01(A)(2), (2) at the time of the elimination of his position, a substantially younger and far less qualified employee was retained, (3) he was over 50 years of age when his job was terminated, and (4) he was treated less favorably than the younger employee, who performed a similar function, due to his age, so it was error to grant an Civ.R. 12(C) motion for judgment on the pleadings as to this claim. Fearn v. Longaberger Co., 2006-Ohio-6234, 2006 Ohio App. LEXIS 6219 (Ohio Ct. App., Licking County 2006).

**Jury instructions**

Taken as a whole, the instructions accurately stated the law, and adequately instructed the jury in a case where a former employee alleged that the employee was terminated by the former employer because of the employee's age. The instructions made clear that the burden to prove discrimination based on age belonged to the employee and informed the jury that they had to find that the employer discriminated against the employee because of the employee's age and on the basis of age. Thomas v. Columbia Sussex Corp., 2011-Ohio-17, 2011 Ohio App. LEXIS 9 (Ohio Ct. App., Franklin County 2011).

Trial court abused its discretion by providing the jurors with an incomplete instruction on a former employee's claim of age discrimination because the trial court's instruction only informed the jurors of one of the two alternative ways to prove age discrimination, replacement, but not the retention of a younger employee. Fearn v. Longaberger Co., 2010-Ohio-1736, 2010 Ohio App. LEXIS 1445 (Ohio Ct. App., Muskingum County 2010).

**Jury trial**

Actions for employment discrimination, such as that provided by R.C. 4101.17, did not exist at common law and thus there is no right to a jury trial under R.C. 4101.17 guaranteed by Ohio Const. art I, § 5. Further, neither the current language nor the legislative history of R.C. 4101.17 indicate an intent to require jury trials under that section: Hoops v. United Tel. Co., 50 Ohio St. 3d 97, 553 N.E.2d 252, 1990 Ohio LEXIS 157 (Ohio 1990), limited, Adleta v. GE (S.D. Ohio 1996).

R.C. 4101.17(B) (age discrimination) does not entitle a litigant to a jury trial: South v. Toledo Edison Co., 32 Ohio App. 3d 24, 513 N.E.2d 800, 1986 Ohio App. LEXIS 10175 (Ohio Ct. App., Lucas County 1986).

**Just cause for discharge**

*Unpublished decision:* Although the former employee established a prima facie case of age discrimination by showing that he was replaced by a substantially younger individual, the district court properly granted summary judgment to his former employer on his age discrimination claim because the employee's racially derogatory comment on a client's voice mail, which the employee did not dispute, provided a sufficient nondiscriminatory reason for firing the employee, regardless of whether he felt remorse after-the-fact. Additionally, the other employees who allegedly made age-discriminatory comments did not have any influence over the persons who made the decision to fire the employee; furthermore, another employee, who was not fired, was not similarly situated and, thus, the employee did not provide evidence that the stated reason for his termination was not sufficient to support the decision to terminate his employment. Hagedorn v. Veritas Software Corp., 129 Fed. Appx. 1000, 2005 U.S. App. LEXIS 7967 (6th Cir. Ohio 2005).

**Liability of supervisor**

Employee adequately alleged a claim of age discrimination, under R.C. 4112.14(A), against his supervisor because the supervisor could be held liable for his own discriminatory conduct occurring in the workplace environment. Fearn v. Longaberger Co., 2006-Ohio-6234, 2006 Ohio App. LEXIS 6219 (Ohio Ct. App., Licking County 2006).

**Non-pretextual reason for discharge**

Former employee's age discrimination suit was properly dismissed on summary judgment because, although the employee established a prima facie case of discrimination, the employer articulated a legitimate, nondiscriminatory reason for the employee's termination, his violation of a known directive ordering him to cease communicating with other employees regarding a complaint, and the employee failed to establish that the employer's reason was pretextual. Vossman v. AirNet Sys., 2013-Ohio-4675, 2013 Ohio App. LEXIS 4894 (Ohio Ct. App., Franklin County 2013).

Although a prima facie case of age discrimination had been established, there was a legitimate, nondiscriminatory reason for the judicial secretary's discharge and she failed to demonstrate that the judge's reason for discharging her was pretextual. As a member of the unclassified civil service, pursuant to R.C. 124.11, the secretary was an at-will employee and the undisputed evidence showed that her behavior had been a consistent distraction in the workplace and that the judge had tried resolving the issue in different ways to no avail. Dunn v. Bruzzese, 2007-Ohio-3500, 172 Ohio App. 3d 320, 874 N.E.2d 1221, 2007 Ohio App. LEXIS 3222 (Ohio Ct. App., Jefferson County 2007).

If an employee who was terminated in a reorganization established a prima facie claim of age discrimination in employment, he could not show that his employer's asserted reason for terminating him was a pretext for discrimination because the employer terminated him for not possessing computer skills, which were required of every employee in his department, after the reorganization. Pierce v. Brown Publ. Co., 2007-Ohio-1657, 2007 Ohio App. LEXIS 1510 (Ohio Ct. App., Fayette County 2007).

Even if the court assumed that an employee met his burden of demonstrating that his former employer discharged him because of his age, the employer met its summary judgment burden of production by asserting a non-discriminatory reason for discharging the employee: the employer's evidence showed that it discharged the employee because he was an unsafe truck driver. The employee, on the other hand, did not provide evidence to indicate that the employer did not honestly believe a trainer's assessment that the employee was not a safe driver. Wylie v. Arnold Transp. Servs., 494 F. Supp. 2d 717, 2006 U.S. Dist. LEXIS 96474 (S.D. Ohio 2006).

**Nondiscriminatory reason**

Because the elements and burden of proof under this section parallel the federal analysis of an age discrimination claim, an employer that showed it was entitled to summary judgment on a federal age discrimination claim alleging failure to hire a part-time employee for full-time work also defeated a claim under this section; its concerns about the employee's discipline history and failure to disclose a complete work history established a nondiscriminatory reason for hiring a younger applicant. Rosecrans v. Vill. of Wellington, 2018 U.S. App. LEXIS 8366 (6th Cir. Ohio Apr. 2, 2018).

Summary judgment was properly granted for the employer on the claims for age discrimination and sex/gender discrimination because no reasonable person could have rejected the employer's proffered reason for discharging the employee or inferred that it intentionally discriminated against her. The evidence overwhelmingly supported that the employee failed to establish the fourth element of a prima facie case—that she was replaced by a male or treated differently than a similarly situated male—and she failed to present any evidence, outside of her own assumptions and conjecture that age or gender played a factor in her discharge. Manion v. Interbrand Design Forum, LLC, 2015-Ohio-348, 27 N.E.3d 1007, 2015 Ohio App. LEXIS 328 (Ohio Ct. App., Montgomery County 2015).

Former employee failed to show that the employee was unlawfully terminated based on age since the employer had legitimate, nondiscriminatory reasons for the termination based on the employee's history of numerous infractions, warnings, and reprimands concerning misconduct by the employee. Amstutz v. Liberty Ctr. Bd. of Educ., 127 F. Supp. 3d 846, 2015 U.S. Dist. LEXIS 119913 (N.D. Ohio 2015).

Although an applicant, who was not hired after interviewing for either of two entry-level academic advisor positions with a community college district, presented a prima facie case of age discrimination, as two younger people were hired for the positions, the employer was entitled to summary judgment because the employer offered legitimate nondiscriminatory reasons for its hiring decisions, which were not rebutted. The people on the employer's committee which made the hiring decisions were concerned that the applicant was overqualified for the entry level positions and that the younger people who were hired were more suited for the positions. Silberstein v. Montgomery County Cmty. College Dist., 2009-Ohio-6138, 2009 Ohio App. LEXIS 5154 (Ohio Ct. App., Montgomery County 2009).

While a former employee, who was a manger of one of the former employer's retail outlet stores, established a prima facie case of age discrimination by the employer when the employer terminated the employee from the employee's position and replaced the employee with a younger worker, the employer, by its witnesses, provided a nondiscriminatory reason for the employee's termination, the employee's violation of the employer's sales policy. Further, the employee failed to overcome the presumption that the trial court, as the finder of fact, applied the law correctly in rendering its decision. Davis v. Goodwill Indus., 2009-Ohio-6133, 2009 Ohio App. LEXIS 5147 (Ohio Ct. App., Montgomery County 2009).

**Pleadings**

Trial court erred by dismissing a former employee's age discrimination claim under R.C. 4112.02(A) and 4112.14(A) for failure to state a claim under Civ. R. 12(B)(6) because the court improperly required the employee to plead age was the "but-for" cause of the employee's termination. Morrissette v. DFS Servs., LLC, 2011-Ohio-2369, 2011 Ohio App. LEXIS 2023 (Ohio Ct. App., Franklin County 2011).

With respect to whether a prima facie case of age-based employment discrimination in violation of R.C. 4112.14(A) has been pleaded, trial courts are vested with the discretion to determine, based on the circumstances of the case, whether an employee is substantially younger than a protected employee. Coryell v. Bank One Trust Co. N.A., 2004-Ohio-723, 101 Ohio St. 3d 175, 803 N.E.2d 781, 2004 Ohio LEXIS 337 (Ohio 2004).

Plaintiff may plead a prima facie case of age-based employment discrimination in violation of R.C. 4112.14(A) by making a short and plain statement of the claim that includes an allegation that he has been replaced by a person substantially younger than himself. Coryell v. Bank One Trust Co. N.A., 2004-Ohio-723, 101 Ohio St. 3d 175, 803 N.E.2d 781, 2004 Ohio LEXIS 337 (Ohio 2004).

Plaintiff's claim under R.C. 4101.17 was properly dismissed where she failed to allege, directly or inferentially, any facts supporting her conclusory allegation that she was replaced by a younger person or that age was a factor in her termination: Scheid v. Fanny Farmer Candy Shops, Inc., 859 F.2d 434, 1988 U.S. App. LEXIS 14192 (6th Cir. Ohio 1988).

**Pretext**

Even if the clerk had been able to show that she had been replaced by a substantially younger person, she failed to demonstrate pretext because the employer's stated reason for her termination was her poor attitude towards her employer, co-workers, and the general public. Ryncarz v. Belmont Cty. Court of Common Pleas Juvenile Court Div., 2017-Ohio-4423, 93 N.E.3d 190, 2017 Ohio App. LEXIS 2476 (Ohio Ct. App., Belmont County 2017).

Employee raised a fact issue as to whether the reason given for his discharge was pretextual as: (1) he offered evidence that the security provision he was discharged for violating was not enforced; (2) he raised a fact issue as to whether his actions were grossly negligent since he testified that he repeatedly asked to see evidence that the thief was entitled to take the scrap metal, he attempted to contact the person with whom the thief had indicated that he was working, and he did not believe the thief would be able to leave because the thief was blocked in; and (3) the employee offered to reimburse the employer for the loss of the metal. Skidmore v. Nat'l Bronze & Metals (Ohio), Inc., 2014-Ohio-4423, 2014 Ohio App. LEXIS 4339 (Ohio Ct. App., Lorain County 2014).

Although a six-and-a-half year age difference between plaintiff former employee and an employee who replaced her was not the best evidence to create an inference of age discrimination, it was sufficient to create an issue of material fact at the summary judgment stage; however, defendant employer proffered nondiscriminatory reasons for plaintiff's termination, namely, performance failures using new software and a disinclination to learn how to use the software, and although plaintiff created a genuine issue of fact as to the falsity of the reasons, she failed to overcome defendant's honest belief by establishing that the reasons had no basis in fact. Age-related comments to which plaintiff pointed did not relate to the firing decision, and the employee to whom she pointed as receiving favorable treatment was not similarly situated; thus, plaintiff failed to show that defendant's reasons were pretext for discrimination. Blizzard v. Marion Tech. College, 698 F.3d 275, 2012 FED App. 0362P, 2012 U.S. App. LEXIS 21846 (6th Cir. Ohio 2012), cert. denied, 569 U.S. 975, 133 S. Ct. 2359, 185 L. Ed. 2d 1068, 2013 U.S. LEXIS 3626 (U.S. 2013).

In order to establish pretext in an employment discrimination claim, an employee must show by a preponderance of the evidence that the proffered reasons for his termination had no basis in fact, did not actually motivate his termination, or were insufficient to motivate his termination. Pierce v. Brown Publ. Co., 2007-Ohio-1657, 2007 Ohio App. LEXIS 1510 (Ohio Ct. App., Fayette County 2007).

**Pretextual**

In an age discrimination case, plaintiff failed to show that the articulated reasons for terminating her were pretextual because, inter alia, plaintiff violated defendant's rules on at least eight occasions, the violations were independently investigated, resulting in justified discipline and ultimately a recommendation that she be terminated, and plaintiff did not show that younger people received less discipline for similar violations. Meggitt v. Ohio Dep't of Pub. Safety, 2021-Ohio-1140, 2021 Ohio Misc. LEXIS 25 (Ohio Ct. Cl. 2021).

**Prima facie case**

In an appeal against a grant of summary judgment on claimant's claims for race and age discrimination, claimant had established a prima facie case of race and age discrimination because despite having the qualifications for the applied position, a white woman who was substantially younger than claimant was hired since she was African American and was 55 years old; therefore, she was a member of protected race and age classes. Defendant did not dispute that she was qualified for the position. Drummond v. Ohio Dep't of Rehab. & Corr., 2022-Ohio-1096, 2022 Ohio App. LEXIS 985 (Ohio Ct. App., Franklin County 2022).

Plaintiff established a prima facie case of age discrimination because plaintiff was a member of a protected class, clearly qualified for her position, and although plaintiff voluntarily resigned before being officially terminated her, the court concluded that plaintiff was constructively discharged. Meggitt v. Ohio Dep't of Pub. Safety, 2021-Ohio-1140, 2021 Ohio Misc. LEXIS 25 (Ohio Ct. Cl. 2021).

Trial court properly granted summary judgment for the city because the former employee failed to establish a prima facie case of age discrimination. The former employee failed to establish the fourth element of either prima facie case, as he failed to present evidence indicating that he was replaced by a substantially younger person, that a comparable non-protected employee was treated better, or that other reasonable evidence existed to raise an inference that the city refused to rehire him because of his age. Tilley v. City of Dublin, 2013-Ohio-4930, 2013 Ohio App. LEXIS 5130 (Ohio Ct. App., Franklin County 2013).

Appellant failed to offer any evidence tending to show discriminatory intent by appellant's former employer, precluding the showing of a prima facie case of age discrimination, as the former employer faced challenges including the loss of clients, a client's bankruptcy, and the departure of one of its shareholders; in light of these conditions, it took a number of measures to improve efficiency and cut costs, and appellant failed to offer any evidence tending to show discriminatory intent in appellant's dismissal. Karsnak v. Chess Fin. Corp., 2012-Ohio-1359, 2012 Ohio App. LEXIS 1181 (Ohio Ct. App., Cuyahoga County 2012).

Where an employee who was terminated from employment for bringing a knife to work in violation of the employer's weapons policy showed that younger employees brought in knives and were not terminated or disciplined, she met the four prong test of McDonell-Douglas, such that she was entitled to a trial on the age discrimination claim under R.C. 4112.02(A) and 4112.14. Cittadini v. Southwest Gen. Health Sys., 2011-Ohio-6464, 2011 Ohio App. LEXIS 5335 (Ohio Ct. App., Cuyahoga County 2011).

Employee did not establish a prima facie case of age discrimination under R.C. 4112.14(A) and R.C. 4112.02(A) because the evidence presented at a deposition did not show that the employee was replaced by a substantially younger person or whether an employer was able to retain such a person due to the employee's discharge. Gradisher v. Barberton Citizens Hosp., 2011-Ohio-6243, 2011 Ohio App. LEXIS 5119 (Ohio Ct. App., Summit County 2011).

Former employee's age discrimination suit was properly dismissed on summary judgment as the 64-year-old employee was not "replaced" by a 28-year-old employee; instead, the younger employee was hired three years before the employee was discharged, and the employee's discharge did not permit the younger employee's retention as he was transferred to a different position two years earlier. Kowach v. Ohio Presbyterian Ret. Servs., 2010-Ohio-4428, 2010 Ohio App. LEXIS 3771 (Ohio Ct. App., Trumbull County 2010).

Discharged employee failed to establish a prima facie claim of age discrimination because he failed to establish that he was replaced by a substantially younger employee. Because the discharged employee's position was eliminated and some of his duties were eliminated while other duties were assigned to several other employees, he failed to establish that he was replaced; the reassignment of his duties to various employees, who happened to be younger, did not constitute his replacement by a younger employee. Yannarell v. GBS Corp., 2009-Ohio-5254, 2009 Ohio App. LEXIS 4428 (Ohio Ct. App., Stark County 2009).

Assumption of duties does not constitute replacement, and a discharged employee is not "replaced" when another employee is assigned to perform the the discharged employee's duties in addition to other duties. The discharged employee is replaced only when another employee is hired or reassigned to perform his or her duties. Yannarell v. GBS Corp., 2009-Ohio-5254, 2009 Ohio App. LEXIS 4428 (Ohio Ct. App., Stark County 2009).

*Unpublished decision:* District court properly held that a fired 48-year-old employee did not establish a prima facie case of age discrimination under R.C. 4112.14 and 4112.99 because, although the employee was temporarily replaced by a 42-year-old man, the employee was ultimately replaced by a 54-year-old man. Counts v. Kraton Polymers, U.S. L.L.C., 260 Fed. Appx. 825, 2008 FED App. 0064N, 2008 U.S. App. LEXIS 2187 (6th Cir. Ohio 2008).

*Unpublished decision:* District court properly held that a fired 48-year-old employee did not establish a prima facie case of age discrimination under R.C. 4112.14 and 4112.99 because, although the employee was temporarily replaced by a 42-year-old man, the employee was ultimately replaced by a 54-year-old man. Counts v. Kraton Polymers, U.S. L.L.C., 260 Fed. Appx. 825, 2008 FED App. 0064N, 2008 U.S. App. LEXIS 2187 (6th Cir. Ohio 2008).



Employee's age discrimination claim was properly dismissed because the employee failed to demonstrate that he was replaced by, or that the employer retained, a person of substantially younger age as a result of the employee's discharge. While the employee presented evidence that showed that two substantially younger drivers had accidents but, unlike him, were not discharged, there was no evidence indicating that these two younger drivers took over the employee's route or that the employee's discharge allowed the younger men to remain drivers. Murphy v. Penske Logistics, 2007-Ohio-6407, 2007 Ohio App. LEXIS 5612 (Ohio Ct. App., Geauga County 2007).

Absent direct evidence, a party seeking to establish a prima facie case of age discrimination in violation of R.C. 4112.14(A) must show that he or she: (1) was a member of a statutorily-protected class; (2) was discharged; (3) was qualified for the position; and (4) was replaced by, or his or her discharge permitted the retention of, a person of substantially younger age. Pierce v. Brown Publ. Co., 2007-Ohio-1657, 2007 Ohio App. LEXIS 1510 (Ohio Ct. App., Fayette County 2007).

Absent direct evidence, a party seeking to establish a prima facie case of age discrimination in violation of R.C. 4112.14(A) must show that he or she: (1) was a member of a statutorily-protected class; (2) was discharged; (3) was qualified for the position; and (4) was replaced by, or his or her discharge permitted the retention of, a person of substantially younger age. Pierce v. Brown Publ. Co., 2007-Ohio-1657, 2007 Ohio App. LEXIS 1510 (Ohio Ct. App., Fayette County 2007).

Employee adequately alleged a claim of age discrimination, under R.C. 4112.14(A), against his supervisor because the supervisor could be held liable for his own discriminatory conduct occurring in the workplace environment. Fearn v. Longaberger Co., 2006-Ohio-6234, 2006 Ohio App. LEXIS 6219 (Ohio Ct. App., Licking County 2006).

Employee sufficiently alleged a claim of age discrimination, under R.C. 4112.14(A), when he said (1) his employer and supervisor were employers under R.C. 4112.01(A)(2), (2) at the time of the elimination of his position, a substantially younger and far less qualified employee was retained, (3) he was over 50 years of age when his job was terminated, and (4) he was treated less favorably than the younger employee, who performed a similar function, due to his age, so it was error to grant an Civ.R. 12(C) motion for judgment on the pleadings as to this claim. Fearn v. Longaberger Co., 2006-Ohio-6234, 2006 Ohio App. LEXIS 6219 (Ohio Ct. App., Licking County 2006).

Employee terminated after he failed to pass a drug test failed to establish a prima facie case of age discrimination under R.C. 4112.14 and 4112.99 because he was not replaced by a substantially younger employee, his replacement was older notwithstanding that he was his duties were temporary assigned to a younger replacement. Counts v. Kraton Polymers U.S. LLC, 2006 U.S. Dist. LEXIS 65312 (S.D. Ohio Sept. 13, 2006), aff'd, 260 Fed. Appx. 825, 2008 FED App. 0064N, 2008 U.S. App. LEXIS 2187 (6th Cir. Ohio 2008).

District court granted a motion for summary judgment that was filed by an employer and its top executive and thereby dismissed a former salesman's age discrimination claims under the Age Discrimination in Employment Act, 29 U.S.C.S. § 621 et seq., and R.C. 4112.14 because the salesman did not adduce any direct evidence of discrimination, failed to make out a prima facie case of discrimination based on the characteristics of the person who replaced him, failed to identify any similarly situated salesmen who were treated differently, and failed to show that the employer's explanation for its treatment of him was pretextual. Swanson v. McKesson Corp., 2006 U.S. Dist. LEXIS 1512 (S.D. Ohio Jan. 18, 2006).

Employee terminated after he failed to pass a drug test failed to establish a prima facie case of age discrimination under R.C. 4112.14 and 4112.99 because he was not replaced by a substantially younger employee, his replacement was older notwithstanding that he was his duties were temporary assigned to a younger replacement. Counts v. Kraton Polymers U.S. LLC, 2006 U.S. Dist. LEXIS 65312 (S.D. Ohio Sept. 13, 2006), aff'd, 260 Fed. Appx. 825, 2008 FED App. 0064N, 2008 U.S. App. LEXIS 2187 (6th Cir. Ohio 2008).

Because a replacement employee was only four years younger than the former employee who was being replaced, the replacement employee was not "substantially younger" than the former employee for the purposes of the latter's prima facie case of discrimination under § 626 of the Age Discrimination in Employment Act, 29 U.S.C.S. § 621 et seq., and under R.C. 4112.14. By reason thereof, the former employee was precluded as a matter of law from establishing a prima facie case of discriminatory discharge. Swanson v. McKesson Corp., 2006 U.S. Dist. LEXIS 1512 (S.D. Ohio Jan. 18, 2006).

Former employer was entitled to summary judgment on a former employee's age discrimination claim under R.C. 4112.14 because the employee was not meeting the employer's legitimate expectations in his role as a quality inspection supervisor at the time the decision was made to terminate his employment. Thus, the employee failed to establish a prima facie case of age discrimination. Zeman v. Goodrich Corp., 2005 U.S. Dist. LEXIS 37004 (N.D. Ohio July 15, 2005).

In reversing and remanding judgment against dismissed employee under R.C. 4112.02, 4112.14(A), highest court held that a dismissed employee could plead prima facie case of age discrimination by alleging that he was replaced by substantially younger person even if that person was in the over-40 protected class. Coryell v. Bank One Trust Co. N.A., 2004-Ohio-723, 101 Ohio St. 3d 175, 803 N.E.2d 781, 2004 Ohio LEXIS 337 (Ohio 2004).

Former principal failed to establish a prima facie case of age discrimination under R.C. 4112.14(A) where the school district had a legitimate reason for her transfer due to her inability to adequately perform her duties as principal and poor performance reviews Rollins v. Mad River Green Local Sch. Dist., 2003-Ohio-3058, 2003 Ohio App. LEXIS 2735 (Ohio Ct. App., Clark County 2003).

To establish a prima facie case of age discrimination, a plaintiff need not prove that he or she was replaced by a person under forty: Ahern v. Ameritech Corp., 137 Ohio App. 3d 754, 739 N.E.2d 1184, 2000 Ohio App. LEXIS 2015 (Ohio Ct. App., Cuyahoga County), dismissed, 90 Ohio St. 3d 1413, 735 N.E.2d 453, 2000 Ohio LEXIS 2341 (Ohio 2000).

Absent direct evidence of age discrimination, in order to establish a prima facie case of a violation of R.C. 4101.17 in an employment discharge action, a plaintiff-employee must demonstrate (1) that he or she was a member of the statutorily protected class, (2) that he or she was discharged, (3) that he or she was qualified for the position, and (4) that he or she was replaced by, or that the discharge permitted the retention of, a person not belonging to the protected class: Kohmescher v. Kroger Co., 61 Ohio St. 3d 501, 575 N.E.2d 439, 1991 Ohio LEXIS 2078 (Ohio 1991).

One of the criteria for establishing a prima facie case of age discrimination under Title 29, § 621 et seq, is that the employee must have applied for re-employment with the employer for a position for which the employer was taking applications: Strong v. Ohio Gas Co., 64 Ohio App. 3d 635, 582 N.E.2d 638, 1989 Ohio App. LEXIS 3722 (Ohio Ct. App., Lucas County 1989).

In order to establish a prima facie case of age discrimination, violative of R.C. 4101.17, in an employment discharge action, plaintiff-employee must demonstrate (1) that he was a member of the statutorily-protected class, (2) that he was discharged, (3) that he was qualified for the position, and (4) that he was replaced by, or that his discharge permitted the retention of, a person not belonging to the protected class. Defendant-employer may then overcome the presumption inherent in the prima facie case by propounding a legitimate, nondiscriminatory reason for plaintiff's discharge. Finally, plaintiff must be allowed to show that the rationale set forth by defendant was only a pretext for unlawful discrimination: Barker v. Scovill, Inc., Schrader Bellows Div., 6 Ohio St. 3d 146, 451 N.E.2d 807, 1983 Ohio LEXIS 794 (Ohio 1983).

**Public employer**

State employee who was not offered a full-time position based on the Ohio Department of Natural Resources' policy not to rehire a retiree suffered age discrimination under R.C. 4112.14 and 4112.99, and he was entitled to an award based on a lump sum payment from the Money Purchase Plan that he would have received pursuant to the pension through the Ohio Public Employees Retirement System. Warden v. Ohio Dep't of Natural Res., 2013-Ohio-1512, 2013 Ohio Misc. LEXIS 12 (Ohio Ct. Cl. 2013), aff'd in part and rev'd in part, 2014-Ohio-35, 7 N.E.3d 533, 2014 Ohio App. LEXIS 25 (Ohio Ct. App., Franklin County 2014).

**Punitive damages**

Former employee presented sufficient evidence to warrant an award of punitive damages as the employee proved that the employer terminated the employee's employment with a conscious disregard for the employee's rights. Thomas v. Columbia Sussex Corp., 2011-Ohio-17, 2011 Ohio App. LEXIS 9 (Ohio Ct. App., Franklin County 2011).

The employees established a prima facie case of age discrimination. The employer's conduct supported an award of punitive damages: Srail v. RJF Int'l Corp., 126 Ohio App. 3d 689, 711 N.E.2d 264, 1998 Ohio App. LEXIS 862 (Ohio Ct. App., Cuyahoga County), dismissed, 82 Ohio St. 3d 1473, 696 N.E.2d 602, 1998 Ohio LEXIS 1991 (Ohio 1998).

**Qualified employee**

Employee who was terminated in a reorganization could not establish a prima facie claim of age discrimination in employment, even though he was 70 years old when he was terminated, because, as a result of the reorganization, all jobs in his department required computer skills, which he did not have, and he declined his employer's offer to pay for him to learn such skills, so he could not show he was qualified. Pierce v. Brown Publ. Co., 2007-Ohio-1657, 2007 Ohio App. LEXIS 1510 (Ohio Ct. App., Fayette County 2007).

Employee who was terminated in a reorganization could not establish a prima facie claim of age discrimination in employment, even though he was 70 years old when he was terminated, because, as a result of the reorganization, all jobs in his department required computer skills, which he did not have, and he declined his employer's offer to pay for him to learn such skills, so he could not show he was qualified. Pierce v. Brown Publ. Co., 2007-Ohio-1657, 2007 Ohio App. LEXIS 1510 (Ohio Ct. App., Fayette County 2007).

**Reconsideration**

Motion for reconsideration was granted where the court erred in finding age discrimination; discharged worker could not show age discrimination where one of the workers to whom his duties were reassigned was within the protected class of persons 40 and over. Fenton v. Time Warner Entm't Co., 2003-Ohio-6317, 2003 Ohio App. LEXIS 5660 (Ohio Ct. App., Montgomery County 2003).

**Reduction in force**

*Unpublished decision:* Terminated employee's age discrimination claim based on circumstantial evidence failed because, inter alia, (1) there was a reduction-in-force since the reduction decreased the number of supervisors in the scrap and shipping areas from three to two, and one of the remaining supervisors absorbed the employee's responsibilities, and (2) the employee's disagreement with an assessment of the employee's value did not show age discrimination. Metz v. Titanium Metals Corp., 475 Fed. Appx. 33, 2012 FED App. 0345N, 2012 U.S. App. LEXIS 6497 (6th Cir. Ohio), cert. denied, 568 U.S. 929, 133 S. Ct. 265, 184 L. Ed. 2d 235, 2012 U.S. LEXIS 7649 (U.S. 2012).

Employee failed to prove age discrimination under R.C. 4112.14(A) as the evidence showed that she was not singled out for layoff because of her age but instead, primarily because she was the only one who had a salary above the threshold appropriation reduction level of $36,000, which the clerk of courts had been directed to cut from his budget. The totality of the evidence did not suggest that the employee was targeted for discharge because of age or that age was a motivating factor in the termination decision. Kightlinger v. McGee, 2012-Ohio-5295, 2012 Ohio App. LEXIS 4626 (Ohio Ct. App., Belmont County 2012).

Former employee did not present evidence of age-related discrimination, in violation of R.C. 4112.02(A) and 4112.14, because a valid work force reduction occurred as the employee's position was abolished, the employee was not replaced, and the employee's duties were redistributed to other employees in the employee's unit at work, in addition to their existing duties. Wise v. Ohio State Univ., 2011-Ohio-6566, 2011 Ohio App. LEXIS 5403 (Ohio Ct. App., Franklin County 2011).

Employee did not establish a prima facie case of age discrimination where his termination was part of a companywide reduction in force and his position was not refilled: Cassel v. Schuster Elecs., Inc., 2004-Ohio-6276, 159 Ohio App. 3d 224, 823 N.E.2d 519, 2004 Ohio App. LEXIS 5713 (Ohio Ct. App., Summit County 2004).

Due to a reduction-in-force and reorganization of job duties, an age discrimination plaintiff was no longer qualified for the position: Mack v. B.F. Goodrich Co., 121 Ohio App. 3d 99, 699 N.E.2d 97, 1997 Ohio App. LEXIS 2112 (Ohio Ct. App., Cuyahoga County 1997).

Where an unlawful discriminatory purpose is the reason for a reduction in force layoff, that layoff is a discharge for the purposes of R.C. 4101.17. R.C. 4101.17 does not give rise to a claim for compensatory or punitive damages against an offending employer. The remedies available under section (B) are the exclusive remedy available to a victim of age discrimination in employment: Pence v. General Dynamics Land Systems Div., 75 Ohio App. 3d 660, 600 N.E.2d 384, 1991 Ohio App. LEXIS 4479 (Ohio Ct. App., Allen County 1991).

Where an employer implements a plan to reduce the work force due to economic necessity, an employee's burden of establishing a prima facie case of age discrimination is somewhat heavier: Wang v. Goodyear Tire & Rubber Co., 68 Ohio App. 3d 13, 587 N.E.2d 387, 1990 Ohio App. LEXIS 2356 (Ohio Ct. App., Summit County 1990).

When there is a reduction in force, a prima facie case of age discrimination is not established unless the employee shows that she was replaced by a younger person. The mere termination of a competent employee when an employer is making cutbacks due to economic necessity is insufficient to establish a prima facie case of age discrimination. An employee in such reorganization cases must come forward with additional direct, circumstantial, or statistical evidence that age was a factor in her termination in order to establish a prima facie case: Murphy v. East Akron Community House, 56 Ohio App. 3d 54, 564 N.E.2d 742, 1989 Ohio App. LEXIS 4548 (Ohio Ct. App., Summit County 1989).

The elimination by duly adopted ordinance of the position of full-time police officer on a village's police force that was occupied by a forty-five-year-old man does not violate R.C. 4101.17(A), where the officer was neither discharged nor replaced. The municipality's decision to save money by reducing the police force is beyond judicial review in the absence of bad faith, arbitrary action or abuse of power: Baurichter v. Addyston, 31 Ohio App. 3d 121, 509 N.E.2d 80, 1986 Ohio App. LEXIS 10128 (Ohio Ct. App., Hamilton County 1986).

**Reinstatement**

State employee who was not offered a full-time position based on the Ohio Department of Natural Resources' policy not to rehire a retiree suffered age discrimination under R.C. 4112.14 and 4112.99, but he was not entitled to reinstatement in the circumstances, as the person hired to the position had already been there for three years, and the employee had only intended to work in the position for five years. Warden v. Ohio Dep't of Natural Res., 2013-Ohio-1512, 2013 Ohio Misc. LEXIS 12 (Ohio Ct. Cl. 2013), aff'd in part and rev'd in part, 2014-Ohio-35, 7 N.E.3d 533, 2014 Ohio App. LEXIS 25 (Ohio Ct. App., Franklin County 2014).

**Religion**

Parochial school teacher who entered into a marriage that was invalid under church doctrine, in violation of her contract, did not produce proof of age discrimination: Potts v. Catholic Diocese, 2004-Ohio-6816, 159 Ohio App. 3d 315, 823 N.E.2d 917, 2004 Ohio App. LEXIS 6319 (Ohio Ct. App., Mahoning County 2004).

The fact that the employees' conduct violated tenets of the employing church provided a sufficient, nondiscriminatory justification for termination: Basinger v. Pilarczky, 137 Ohio App. 3d 325, 738 N.E.2d 814, 2000 Ohio App. LEXIS 1357 (Ohio Ct. App., Hamilton County), dismissed, 89 Ohio St. 3d 1466, 732 N.E.2d 998, 2000 Ohio LEXIS 1916 (Ohio 2000).

**Remedies**

Jury's award of front pay was supported by sufficient evidence because, although a former employee found a comparable job at the same salary, the award of front pay was consistent with a finding that, had the not been discriminated against on the basis of age, the employee would have been entitled to receive a bonus consistent with past years that was based on performance. Thomas v. Columbia Sussex Corp., 2011-Ohio-17, 2011 Ohio App. LEXIS 9 (Ohio Ct. App., Franklin County 2011).

Insurance company's motion to dismiss an individual's state public policy claim was granted over a magistrate's contrary recommendation because no public policy remedy or common-law action for wrongful discharge was needed when the statutory remedies allowed under R.C. 4112.14 adequately protect the interests of the citizens of Ohio. Williams v. Allstate Ins. Co., 2005 U.S. Dist. LEXIS 40800 (N.D. Ohio May 31, 2005).

**Replacement**

Trial court did not err by granting the employer summary judgment on the employee's age discrimination claim because she failed to show that she was replaced, as she admitted that tasks related to grants was only a portion of her job, the new employee was hired to do data entry for the new accounting system which was not part of the employee's job, there was no evidence that the new employee assumed any or all of the job responsibilities of the business retention and expansion coordinator, which was the employee's job title at the time of her termination, and the employee's responsibilities as manger of finance and administration were absorbed by multiple employees. Ksiazek v. Columbiana Cty. Port Auth., 2021-Ohio-1267, 171 N.E.3d 394, 2021 Ohio App. LEXIS 1251 (Ohio Ct. App., Columbiana County 2021).

Trial court did not err by entering summary judgment against the employees on the age discrimination claims because, although the younger employee, who was let go at the same time, was rehired, he was rehired in a different position. Therefore, he did not "replace" either employee. Robinson v. Vanex Tube Corp., 2016-Ohio-268, 58 N.E.3d 430, 2016 Ohio App. LEXIS 235 (Ohio Ct. App., Trumbull County 2016).

Plaintiff could not establish directly or indirectly a prima facie case of age discrimination, as merely having oversight of plaintiff's former duties for a short while until other co-workers were trained did support the proposition that a co-employee took over a substantial portion of plaintiff's duties and was plaintiff's replacement; the trial court properly found that plaintiff failed to demonstrate that she was replaced by a person of substantially younger age. Alexander v. Columbus State Cmty. Coll.,

2015-Ohio-2170, 35 N.E.3d 949, 2015 Ohio App. LEXIS 2079 (Ohio Ct. App., Franklin County 2015).

Because a replacement employee was only four years younger than the former employee who was being replaced, the replacement employee was not "substantially younger" than the former employee for the purposes of the latter's prima facie case of discrimination under § 626 of the Age Discrimination in Employment Act, 29 U.S.C.S. § 621 et seq., and under R.C. 4112.14. By reason thereof, the former employee was precluded as a matter of law from establishing a prima facie case of discriminatory discharge. Swanson v. McKesson Corp., 2006 U.S. Dist. LEXIS 1512 (S.D. Ohio Jan. 18, 2006).

Where a 60-year-old employee was terminated for poor performance due to a supervisor's evaluations and was replaced by a 47-year-old and a 40-year-old, the employee's age discrimination claims failed to survive summary judgment because the employer articulated a legitimate, nondiscriminatory reason for the employee's discharge and the employee could not show pretext based solely upon replacement by significantly younger persons. Weller v. Titanium Metals Corp., 361 F. Supp. 2d 712, 2005 U.S. Dist. LEXIS 8373 (S.D. Ohio 2005).

**Res judicata**

The federal court judgment rejecting the employee's claims of violation of federal age discrimination provisions was res judicata in the state court action based on R.C. 4112.99. However, the retaliation claim was not barred: Borowski v. State Chem. Mfg. Co., 97 Ohio App. 3d 635, 647 N.E.2d 230, 1994 Ohio App. LEXIS 4207 (Ohio Ct. App., Cuyahoga County 1994).

**Sale of employer**

Employees in division were not discharged when the division was sold and employees retained their same positions: Bowman v. Firestone Tire & Rubber Co., 724 F. Supp. 493, 1989 U.S. Dist. LEXIS 12930 (N.D. Ohio 1989).



**Similarly situation employee**

Summary judgment was properly granted for the employer on the claims for age discrimination and sex/gender discrimination because there was insufficient evidence to find that another employee's situation was similar because there was no evidence that his performance failings were comparable to the employee's, no evidence of his unwillingness and failure to overcome his performance issues, no evidence that he failed to recognize, embrace, and implement the new direction and focus of the company under the new leadership, and no evidence that the other employee had a team of subordinates that he was failing to properly supervise. Manion v. Interbrand Design Forum, LLC, 2015-Ohio-348, 27 N.E.3d 1007, 2015 Ohio App. LEXIS 328 (Ohio Ct. App., Montgomery County 2015).

**Substantially younger employee**

Employee, a deputy court clerk, failed to establish age discrimination because she failed to show that her termination allowed them to hire or retain a person of a substantially younger age. Based on unrebutted testimony, the clerk's replacement was in her sixties at the time she was promoted to fill the position and, of the four the employees hired after the clerk was terminated, two were older than the clerk, one was a truant officer, and another was hired approximately a year after the clerk was terminated to replace another deputy clerk. Ryncarz v. Belmont Cty. Court of Common Pleas Juvenile Court Div., 2017-Ohio-4423, 93 N.E.3d 190, 2017 Ohio App. LEXIS 2476 (Ohio Ct. App., Belmont County 2017).

Trial court did not err in finding that the employee failed to present a prima facie case of age discrimination through the indirect method of proof because the person hired was not substantially younger than the employee, since the employee was 50 and the person hired was 48. Dautartas v. Abbott Labs., 2012-Ohio-1709, 2012 Ohio App. LEXIS 1495 (Ohio Ct. App., Franklin County 2012).

Employee who was terminated in a reorganization could not establish a prima facie claim of age discrimination in employment, even though he was 70 years old when he was terminated, because he offered no evidence of the ages of employees who remained employed after the reorganization, so he could not prove that he was replaced by, or that his discharge permitted the retention of, a person of substantially younger age, and his vague assertions that he was replaced by substantially younger employees were insufficient. Pierce v. Brown Publ. Co., 2007-Ohio-1657, 2007 Ohio App. LEXIS 1510 (Ohio Ct. App., Fayette County 2007).

Although an employee alleged that he was discharged from his position as a trainee truck driver because of his age, he did not meet his prima facie summary judgment burden of demonstrating that he was replaced by a substantially younger person after being discharged from his position, or even present evidence that his former employer treated a substantially younger person more favorably. Wylie v. Arnold Transp. Servs., 494 F. Supp. 2d 717, 2006 U.S. Dist. LEXIS 96474 (S.D. Ohio 2006).

**Summary judgment**

It was error to grant summary judgment for defendants as to plaintiff's age discrimination claim. Plaintiff had established a prima facie case, and there was a question of fact as to whether defendants' stated reason for his termination, violating a spousal opt-out policy, was pretextual in that plaintiff was terminated months after defendants learned of the violation and there was a question of when an employee had to notify the company of his spouse's eligibility for coverage through the spouse's employer. Kudla v. Olympic Steel, Inc., 2014-Ohio-5142, 2014 Ohio App. LEXIS 5003 (Ohio Ct. App., Cuyahoga County 2014).

Medical center's motion for summary judgment was granted in a nurse's suit against it for age discrimination, in violation of the Age Discrimination and Employment Act, 29 U.S.C.S. § 623, and the Age Discrimination in Employment Act, R.C. 4112.02(A) and R.C. 4112.14, because the nurse failed to demonstrate the existence of a genuine dispute over the fact that the medical center had a reasonably-held belief about her work-performance problems based on two work performance plans she had been placed on and an email listing reasons for her termination, thus, the nurse failed to show that the medical center did not reasonably rely on the existence of those sources for terminating her employment. Fischbach v. Cmty. Mercy Health Partners, 2012 U.S. Dist. LEXIS 139019 (S.D. Ohio Sept. 27, 2012).

Summary judgment in favor of the employer in the age discrimination suit was proper, because the employee's performance review did contain negative feedback, and the employee admitted in his deposition that he never submitted any cost-saving ideas, never took a welding class, and never passed the welding tests that the employer scheduled for him. Cozzuli v. Sandridge Food Corp., 2011-Ohio-4878, 2011 Ohio App. LEXIS 4035 (Ohio Ct. App., Medina County 2011).

In an age discrimination claim by a former high school counselor who was passed over for the counselor's own vacant position, the trial court improperly granted summary judgment to the school board and a school superintendent, as there was a genuine issue of material fact regarding whether the reason the superintendent gave for recommending the hired candidate was the true reason; testimony indicated the hiring committee was not unanimous. Welch v. Norton City Sch. Dist. Bd. of Educ., 2010-Ohio-6131, 2010 Ohio App. LEXIS 5157 (Ohio Ct. App., Summit County 2010).

Employer was not entitled to summary judgment on a claim of age discrimination where the employee established a prima facie case and the employer did not establish that the reasons for termination were a pretext: Peters v. Rock-Tenn Co., 2008-Ohio-6444, 180 Ohio App. 3d 10, 903 N.E.2d 1256, 2008 Ohio App. LEXIS 5384 (Ohio Ct. App., Delaware County 2008).

Granting of the employer's motion for summary judgment in the employee's action for age discrimination and retaliation pursuant to the Age Discrimination in Employment Act, 29 U.S.C.S. §§ 623, et seq., and R.C. 4112.02(I) and 4112.14. was proper where a former employee's statement of opinion could not be considered a statement of the party opponent for purposes of Fed. R. Evid. 801(d)(2)(D) because that employee had left the company. Further, the employee failed to identify evidence suggesting that the employer's articulated reason for the alleged adverse actions was mere pretext. Rufo v. Dave & Busters, Inc., 2005 U.S. Dist. LEXIS 33395 (S.D. Ohio Dec. 16, 2005), aff'd, 2007 FED App. 0075N, 2007 U.S. App. LEXIS 2366 (6th Cir. Ohio Jan. 31, 2007).

Where no reasonable jury could have found that the employer's stated reasons for promoting another instead of the employee were pretextual, and where R.C. 4112.14 did not protect against harassment on the basis of age, but instead was limited to protecting against age discrimination in connection with a job opening or a discharge without cause, the court granted the employee's motion for summary judgment pursuant to Fed. R. Civ. P. 56. Linkinhoker v. CSX Transp., Inc., 2006 U.S. Dist. LEXIS 195 (S.D. Ohio Jan. 5, 2006).

*Unpublished decision:* District court properly granted summary judgment for an employer in a former employee's action alleging age discrimination in violation of 29 U.S.C.S. § 623 of the Age Discrimination in Employment Act, 29 U.S.C.S. § 621 et seq., and in violation of R.C. 4112.14, 4112.99 in relation to the failure to promote; the employee failed to challenge the employer's assertion that the employee's violation of company policies amounted to poor performance rendering him unfit for promotion and, therefore, the employee did not meet his burden of establishing pretext. Rufo v. Dave & Busters, Inc., 2007 FED App. 0075N, 2007 U.S. App. LEXIS 2366 (6th Cir. Ohio Jan. 31, 2007).

Trial court's grant of summary judgment to an employer in an age discrimination action by an employee pursuant to R.C. 4112.02(A) and 4112.14(A) was proper, as the employer's claim that the employee was terminated for financial reasons was a legitimate, nondiscriminatory reason, and the employee failed to show that it was a mere pretext. Chandler v. Dunn Hardware, Inc., 2006-Ohio-4376, 168 Ohio App. 3d 496, 860 N.E.2d 1042, 2006 Ohio App. LEXIS 4293 (Ohio Ct. App., Cuyahoga County 2006).

District court granted a motion for summary judgment that was filed by an employer and its top executive and thereby dismissed a former salesman's age discrimination claims under the Age Discrimination in Employment Act, 29 U.S.C.S. § 621 et seq., and R.C. 4112.14 because the salesman did not adduce any direct evidence of discrimination, failed to make out a prima facie case of discrimination based on the characteristics of the person who replaced him, failed to identify any similarly situated salesmen who were treated differently, and failed to show that the employer's explanation for its treatment of him was pretextual. Swanson v. McKesson Corp., 2006 U.S. Dist. LEXIS 1512 (S.D. Ohio Jan. 18, 2006).

Employer was granted summary judgment with regard to the employee's age discrimination claim because the claim was barred under R.C. 4112.14(C), as the employee had an opportunity to arbitrate his discharge but failed to do so. York v. AK Steel Corp., 2005 U.S. Dist. LEXIS 31846 (S.D. Ohio Dec. 8, 2005).

District court properly granted summary judgment for an employer in an employee's action alleging age discrimination in violation of 29 U.S.C.S. § 623 of the Age Discrimination in Employment Act, 29 U.S.C.S. § 621 et seq. and in violation of R.C. 4112.14(A); no reasonable jury could have found that the employee's sales accounts were reassigned as a result of the employee's age because the evidence showed that the customers requested reassignment of the accounts due to the fact that the employee missed deadlines and assignments and failed to follow through on commitments to the customers. Further, the employee presented no evidence that similarly situated younger workers received better treatment from the employer. Stefanski v. W.W. Grainger, Inc., 155 Fed. Appx. 177, 2005 FED App. 0843N, 2005 U.S. App. LEXIS 22216 (6th Cir. Ohio 2005).

Former employer's motion for summary judgment on a terminated employee's age discrimination claim was denied because genuine issues of material fact existed as to whether the employee was otherwise qualified for the position which he held, whether he was replaced by a substantially younger employee, and whether the employer's proffered reason for terminating the employee was pretextual. Hutchens v. Weltman, Weinberg & Reis Co., LPA, 2005 U.S. Dist. LEXIS 21397 (S.D. Ohio Sept. 27, 2005).

Employer's motion for summary judgment was denied because the employee stated a prima facie case of age discrimination because a reasonable jury could find that she was qualified for the job and that the training provided to the employee was not of the same quality as the training offered to the younger worker. The employee also showed that the employer's explanation for her termination was a pretext for discrimination because the employer had shifted its articulated reasons for her termination. DeLoach v. Island Dental Co., 2005 U.S. Dist. LEXIS 38213 (S.D. Ohio Dec. 22, 2005).

Trial court properly granted summary judgment to a judge in an age discrimination action under R.C. 4112.02(A) and 4112.14(A) by deputy clerks who were terminated when the judge took office in a county probate judge capacity, as the clerks did not show direct evidence of the discrimination. Statements by a co-worker were not evidence, as she had no decisionmaking authority and accordingly, the statements were not reflective of the judge's discriminatory intent, and as the clerks were unaware of the ages of those who replaced them, there was no statistical evidence to support their claims. Molnar v. Klammer, 2005-Ohio-6905, 2005 Ohio App. LEXIS 6227 (Ohio Ct. App., Lake County 2005).

Deputy clerks who were discharged when a new county probate judge took office did not show indirect evidence of age discrimination under R.C. 4112.04(A) and 4112.14(A) in order to avoid summary judgment to the judge, although they offered sufficient evidence of the first three factors of the four-part Coryell test, as they were unable to show that the persons who replaced them were "substantially younger" in two out of the three clerks' cases, and as to the third, the judge's claim that the replacement was due to a reorganization of the court and issues of loyalty represented a legitimate, nondiscriminatory reason, which was not shown to be pretextual. Molnar v. Klammer, 2005-Ohio-6905, 2005 Ohio App. LEXIS 6227 (Ohio Ct. App., Lake County 2005).

District court properly granted summary judgment for an employer in an employee's action alleging age discrimination in violation of 29 U.S.C.S. § 623 of the Age Discrimination in Employment Act, 29 U.S.C.S. § 621 et seq. and in violation of R.C. 4112.14(A) because no reasonable jury could have found that the employee's sales accounts were reassigned as a result of the employee's age; evidence showed that the customers requested reassignment of the accounts due to the fact that the employee missed deadlines and assignments and failed to follow through on commitments to the customers. Stefanski v. W.W. Grainger, Inc., 155 Fed. Appx. 177, 2005 FED App. 0843N, 2005 U.S. App. LEXIS 22216 (6th Cir. Ohio 2005).

Former employer was entitled to summary judgment on a former employee's age discrimination claim under R.C. 4112.14 because the employee was not meeting the employer's legitimate expectations in his role as a quality inspection supervisor at the time the decision was made to terminate his employment. Thus, the employee failed to establish a prima facie case of age discrimination. Zeman v. Goodrich Corp., 2005 U.S. Dist. LEXIS 37004 (N.D. Ohio July 15, 2005).

Trial court's grant of summary judgment to an employer in an employee's age discrimination action, based on alleged violations of public policy and of R.C. 4112.02(A) and 4112.14(A), was proper, as the employee failed to meet his burden of either directly or indirectly establishing a prima facie case of discrimination, as he was laid off due to a general work force reduction, and there was no showing that he was singled out for impermissible reasons or that the employer had a discriminatory intent. Ramacciato v. Argo-Tech Corp., 2005-Ohio-506, 2005 Ohio App. LEXIS 541 (Ohio Ct. App., Cuyahoga County 2005).

Where a 60-year-old employee was terminated for poor performance due to a supervisor's evaluations and was replaced by a 47-year-old and a 40-year-old, the employee's age discrimination claims failed to survive summary judgment because the employer articulated a legitimate, nondiscriminatory reason for the employee's discharge and the employee could not show pretext based solely upon replacement by significantly younger persons. Weller v. Titanium Metals Corp., 361 F. Supp. 2d 712, 2005 U.S. Dist. LEXIS 8373 (S.D. Ohio 2005).

Summary judgment against terminated 53-year-old employee was proper where he failed to establish a prima facie case of age discrimination under either direct or indirect evidence standards and the employer showed that the termination was due in part to the seasonal nature of the business and a decline in the employee's job performance after he took a second job. Wilson v. Precision Envtl. Co., 2003-Ohio-2873, 2003 Ohio App. LEXIS 2595 (Ohio Ct. App., Cuyahoga County 2003).

Court erred in granting summary judgment for the employer where there was conflicting evidence: Sheets v. Rockwell Int'l Corp., 68 Ohio App. 3d 345, 588 N.E.2d 271, 1990 Ohio App. LEXIS 4260 (Ohio Ct. App., Franklin County 1990).

**Time limitations**

Former county employee's age discrimination claims were barred by the limitations periods of 29 U.S.C.S. § 626(d)(1)(B) and R.C. 4112.02(N) because the employee never asserted a claim that a six-year limitation period applied under R.C. 4112.14 and there was an insufficient basis for tolling of the limitations period. Wood v. Summit County Fiscal Office, 377 Fed. Appx. 512, 2010 FED App. 0301N, 2010 U.S. App. LEXIS 9999 (6th Cir. Ohio 2010).

Age discrimination claims by city employees against a city as to promotional examinations were not time-barred, even though the statute of limitations for most age discrimination claims brought under R.C. 4112.99 was 180 days, because the statute of limitations for age discrimination claims brought under R.C. 4112.14 was six years, and the employees' first amended complaint was within six years of the posting of the promotion eligibility list by the city. Howe v. City of Akron, 789 F. Supp. 2d 786, 2010 U.S. Dist. LEXIS 137344 (N.D. Ohio 2010).

180-day limitations period applied because the employee's R.C. 4112.99 age discrimination claim could not fairly be read as based on R.C. 4112.14. Kaltenmark v. K-Mart, Inc., 2005 U.S. Dist. LEXIS 21699 (N.D. Ohio Sept. 28, 2005).

The limitations period applicable to R.C. 4112.14 age-discrimination claims is six years. Ohio law recognizes a claim for tortious wrongful termination in violation of public policy based on age discrimination: Ferraro v. B.F. Goodrich Co., 2002-Ohio-4398, 149 Ohio App. 3d 301, 777 N.E.2d 282, 2002 Ohio App. LEXIS 4549 (Ohio Ct. App., Lorain County 2002).

The statute of limitations period applicable to age discrimination claims brought under R.C. Chapter 4112. begins to run on the date of the employee-plaintiff's termination from the defendant-employer: Oker v. Ameritech Corp., 2000-Ohio-139, 89 Ohio St. 3d 223, 729 N.E.2d 1177, 2000 Ohio LEXIS 1587 (Ohio 2000).

Since appellant's R.C. 4112.14 claim was governed by the six-year statute of limitations which applied before the 1997 amendment, the trial court erred in dismissing appellant's cause of action as untimely: Leonardi v. Lawrence Indus., 1997 Ohio App. LEXIS 4014 (Ohio Ct. App., Cuyahoga County Sept. 4, 1997).

Where a person is denied eligibility for reelection to office in violation of R.C. 4101.17, a cause of action under that statute accrues not when the person's last term of office expires, but when such a person is denied the opportunity to run for reelection: Mizenko v. First Catholic Slovak Ladies Asso., 49 Ohio App. 3d 6, 550 N.E.2d 541, 1989 Ohio App. LEXIS 3030 (Ohio Ct. App., Cuyahoga County 1989).

Where plaintiff's Age Discrimination Employment Act case is time barred, he cannot successfully seek to amend his complaint to add an age discrimination claim based solely on former R.C. 4101.17: (see now §4112.14) Baer v. R & F Coal Co., 782 F.2d 600, 1986 U.S. App. LEXIS 21499 (6th Cir. Ohio 1986).

The statute of limitations applicable to an action for age discrimination in employment pursuant to former R.C. 4101.17 (see now §4112.14) is the six-year period contained in R.C. 2305.07: Morris v. Kaiser Engineers, Inc., 14 Ohio St. 3d 45, 471 N.E.2d 471, 1984 Ohio LEXIS 1240 (Ohio 1984).

Where plaintiff has filed an age discrimination action pursuant to former R.C. 4101.17(B), (see now §4112.14) and therefore is barred from filing a charge with the Ohio Civil Rights Commission under R.C. 4112.05, the 300-day limit in 29 U.S.C. § 626(d) for filing an age discrimination charge with the Equal Employment Opportunity Commission is nevertheless applicable: Morris v. Russell, Burdsall & Ward Corp., 577 F. Supp. 147, 1983 U.S. Dist. LEXIS 14441 (N.D. Ohio 1983).

**Transfer of duties**

In response to an employee's allegation that he was transferred from the position of yard jockey to that of trainee truck driver because of his age, his former employer produced evidence that it transferred him because he could not back up trucks or keep up with the fast pace in the truck yard. Although the employee attempted to refute the employer's assertions, his evidence did not suggest that the stated reasons for transferring him were a pretext for age discrimination. Wylie v. Arnold Transp. Servs., 494 F. Supp. 2d 717, 2006 U.S. Dist. LEXIS 96474 (S.D. Ohio 2006).

Age discrimination may be established where a discharged employee's duties are transferred to another person already employed by the defendant: Cruz v. South Dayton Urological Assocs., 121 Ohio App. 3d 655, 700 N.E.2d 675, 1997 Ohio App. LEXIS 3652 (Ohio Ct. App., Montgomery County 1997).

### RESEARCH REFERENCES AND PRACTICE AIDS

**Cross-References to Related Sections**
Civil remedies for violation, RC § 4112.99.
Liberal construction of civil rights commission powers; bar to civil action, RC § 4112.08.
Unlawful discriminatory practices, RC § 4112.02.

**Ohio Administrative Code**
Discrimination. OAC ch. 4112-5.

**Comparative Legislation**
Age Discrimination in Employment Act:
29 USCS § 621 et seq
Age discrimination:
CA—Cal Gov Code § 12941
FL—Fla. Stat. § 112.043 et seq
IL—775 ILCS § 5/2-102 et seq
IN—Burns Ind. Code Ann. § 22-9-2-1 et seq
KY—KRS § 344.040
MI—MCLS § 37.2202
NY—NY CLS Exec § 296
PA—43 P.S. § 953

**Practice Manuals and Treatises**
Anderson's Ohio Civil Practice with Forms § 35.01 Generally



# NEW AFRICAN IMMIGRANTS COMMISSION

## § 4112.99 Civil remedies for violation.

(A) Whoever violates this chapter is subject to a civil action for damages, injunctive relief, or any other appropriate relief. Except as otherwise provided in division (B) of this section, a person may bring such a civil action in a court of competent jurisdiction.

(B) A person is prohibited from bringing a civil action for employment discrimination under this section.

**HISTORY:**
128 v 12 (Eff 7-29-59); 133 v H 432 (Eff 11-12-69); 136 v S 162 (Eff 7-23-76); 142 v H 5 (Eff 9-28-87); 146 v H 350 (Eff 1-27-97); 149 v S 108, § 2.01. Eff 7-6-2001; 2020 hb352, § 1, effective April 15, 2021.

**Publisher's Note:**
Section 2.02(B) of SB 108 (149 v —) repeals the HB 350 (146 v —) version and section 3(A)(4) revives the former version.

**Amendment Notes**
The 2020 amendment by HB 352 rewrote the section, which formerly read: "Whoever violates this chapter is subject to a civil action for damages, injunctive relief, or any other appropriate relief."

### NOTES TO DECISIONS

Analysis



**Generally**
R.C. 4112.99 is a remedial statute and is subject to R.C. 2305.07's six-year statute of limitations. Race and disability discrimination claims were not precluded where a party filed prior administrative proceedings. "Prima facie case" requirement is an evidentiary standard, not a pleading standard: Jackson v. Int'l Fiber, 2006-Ohio-5799, 169 Ohio App. 3d 395, 863 N.E.2d 189, 2006 Ohio App. LEXIS 5750 (Ohio Ct. App., Champaign County 2006).

Ohio does not require a filing with the Ohio Civil Rights Commission as a prerequisite for pursuing a discrimination claim directly in court, as individual claims for employment discrimination are authorized by R.C. 4112.99, which provides for a private right of action, stating that whoever violates R.C. 4112.01 et seq. is subject to a civil action for damages. Dworning v. City of Euclid, 2006-Ohio-6772, 2006 Ohio App. LEXIS 6685 (Ohio Ct. App., Cuyahoga County 2006), aff'd, 2008-Ohio-3318, 119 Ohio St. 3d 83, 892 N.E.2d 420, 2008 Ohio LEXIS 1768 (Ohio 2008).

Employer defendants' motion to dismiss a claim for "adverse employment action in violation of public policy" was granted because the employee had adequate statutory remedies under Title VII of the Civil Rights Act of 1964, 42 U.S.C.S. § 2000e et seq., the Equal Pay Act, 29 U.S.C.S. § 206(d), and R.C. 4112.99, and because Ohio did not recognize a cause of action for violation of public policy outside the context of a wrongful discharge. Stange v. Deloitte & Touche, 2006 U.S. Dist. LEXIS 16444 (S.D. Ohio Apr. 5, 2006).

R.C. 4112.99 is to be liberally construed to promote its object (elimination of discrimination) and protect those to whom it is addressed (victims of discrimination), so § 4112.99 must be interpreted to afford victims of handicap discrimination the right to pursue a civil action. Dworning v. City of Euclid, 2006-Ohio-6772, 2006 Ohio App. LEXIS 6685 (Ohio Ct. App., Cuyahoga County 2006), aff'd, 2008-Ohio-3318, 119 Ohio St. 3d 83, 892 N.E.2d 420, 2008 Ohio LEXIS 1768 (Ohio 2008).

Company's credo and employee handbook provisions were not specific promises of job security or continued employment that would support a breach of implied contract agreement action: Allen v. Ethicon, 919 F. Supp. 1093, 1996 U.S. Dist. LEXIS 8135 (S.D. Ohio 1996).

**Age discrimination**
Applicant's age discrimination claims failed because age-plus-sex claims under the Age Discrimination in Employment Act do not exist, and the applicant's charge filed with the Equal Employment Opportunity Commission precluded the applicant's state law age discrimination claims. Thompson v. City of Columbus, 2014 U.S. Dist. LEXIS 63119 (S.D. Ohio May 7, 2014).

Trial court did not err in finding that the department of public safety failed to present a legitimate, nondiscriminatory basis for its decision because the manner in which the fire chief relied on Cleveland, Ohio, Codified Ordinances 135.07 to deny the firefighter a more desirable position was based on his age, in violation of Ohio anti-discrimination statutes. The chief's reasons were mere pretext for age discrimination because all requests for employment extensions for employees age 65 and older had been granted. Campolieti v. Cleveland Dep't of Pub. Safety,

2013-Ohio-5123, 2013 Ohio App. LEXIS 5332 (Ohio Ct. App., Cuyahoga County 2013).

Appellant did not establish an age discrimination claim, as there was no link or nexus between an offer of retirement and the refusal to reinstate appellant that supported an inference that the refusal to reinstate appellant was the result of discriminatory intent, and appellant had not demonstrated that substantially younger employees were treated more favorably; appellant testified that appellant was "in kind of a unique position." Griffin v. Springfield Reg'l Med. Ctr., 2013 Ohio 1819, 2013 Ohio App. LEXIS 1698 (May 3, 2013).

Former employee was entitled to judgment on the issue of liability when the employee alleged discrimination on the basis of age against the employee's former employer, in violation of R.C. 4112.14 and 4112.99, because the employer, a state administrative agency, failed to demonstrate that its actions in not hiring the employee, who had previously retired from the agency, were based upon a reasonable factor other than age. There was an absence of proof that a policy by the agency against double-dipping promoted the public trust, and each of the members of the interview panel testified that the employee was the most qualified applicant for the position and received the highest interview score. Warden v. Ohio Dep't of Natural Res., 2012-Ohio-3854, 2012 Ohio Misc. LEXIS 109 (Ohio Ct. Cl. 2012).

State university employee's age discrimination claim under R.C. 4112.99 failed, as he failed to show that he was subjected to age-based harassment. Kellogg v. Ohio State Univ., 2011-Ohio-4848, 2011 Ohio Misc. LEXIS 411 (Ohio Ct. Cl. 2011).

Trial court erred by dismissing a former employee's age discrimination claim under R.C. 4112.02(A) and 4112.14(A) for failure to state a claim under Civ. R. 12(B)(6) because the court improperly required the employee to plead age was the "but-for" cause of the employee's termination. Morrissette v. DFS Servs., LLC, 2011-Ohio-2369, 2011 Ohio App. LEXIS 2023 (Ohio Ct. App., Franklin County 2011).

University was entitled to summary judgment in a former employee's wrongful discharge case because the employee could not prove age discrimination under R.C. 4112.02(A) and 4112.99 as there was no evidence that the employee was replaced by, or the discharge permitted the retention of, a person of substantially younger age. Pursuant to a reduction of force as part of a necessary cost cutting by the university, the duties of the employee were divided among three employees who were retained, including a younger employee who only did a part of the employee's work. Woods v. Capital Univ., 2009-Ohio-5672, 2009 Ohio App. LEXIS 4770 (Ohio Ct. App., Franklin County 2009).

Even if a trial court erred in excluding evidence of a terminated employee's damages in an age discrimination case, no prejudicial harm occurred, because the evidence related to damages, not to liability. Therefore, because no liability on the part of the employer was found by the trial court, any error in the exclusion of evidence of damages was harmless. Davis v. Goodwill Indus., 2009-Ohio-6133, 2009 Ohio App. LEXIS 5147 (Ohio Ct. App., Montgomery County 2009).

Age-discrimination claim brought pursuant to R.C. 4112.99 is subject to the substantive provisions of R.C. 4112.02 and 4112.14, including R.C. 4112.14(C), and, pursuant to § 4112.14(C), when the discharge of an employee has been arbitrated and the discharge has been found to be for just cause, the discharged employee is barred from pursuing an action for age discrimination. Meyer v. UPS, 2009-Ohio-2463, 122 Ohio St. 3d 104, 909 N.E.2d 106, 2009 Ohio LEXIS 1598 (Ohio 2009).

Consistently with the statutory framework for age-discrimination claims set forth within R.C. ch. 4112, and with precedents interpreting that framework, an age-discrimination claim brought pursuant to R.C. 4112.99 is subject to the substantive provisions of R.C. 4112.02 and 4112.14. Meyer v. UPS, 2009-Ohio-2463, 122 Ohio St. 3d 104, 909 N.E.2d 106, 2009 Ohio LEXIS 1598 (Ohio 2009).

Employee's age discrimination claim brought under R.C. 4112.99 was barred by R.C. 4112.14(C) because, inter alia, (1) § 4112.14(C) barred age discrimination claims when an employee who was allegedly discriminated against had pursued arbitration which resulted in a finding that the employee was terminated for just cause, and (2) the grievance procedure which the employee pursued was equivalent to the arbitration referred to in § 4112.14(C). Meyer v. UPS, 2009-Ohio-2463, 122 Ohio St. 3d 104, 909 N.E.2d 106, 2009 Ohio LEXIS 1598 (Ohio 2009).

Employee's age discrimination claim brought under R.C. 4112.99 was barred by R.C. 4112.14(C) because, inter alia, R.C. 4112.14's substantive provisions applied to age-discrimination claims brought under R.C. 4112.99, as the provisions of R.C. 4112.14, specifically addressing age discrimination claims, prevailed over the provisions of R.C. 4112.99, which generally allowed civil discrimination suits. Meyer v. UPS, 2009-Ohio-2463, 122 Ohio St. 3d 104, 909 N.E.2d 106, 2009 Ohio LEXIS 1598 (Ohio 2009).

Age discrimination claim brought pursuant to R.C. 4112.99 is subject to the substantive provisions of R.C. 4112.02 and 4112.14. Pursuant to R.C. 4112.14(C), when the discharge of an employee has been arbitrated and the discharge has been found to be for just cause, the discharged employee is barred from pursuing an action for age discrimination: Meyer v. UPS, 2009-Ohio-2463, 122 Ohio St. 3d 104, 909 N.E.2d 106, 2009 Ohio LEXIS 1598 (Ohio 2009).

Employee's age discrimination suit under R.C. 4112.99 was properly dismissed on summary judgment as the 51-year-old employee could not show that the reasons proffered by the employer for hiring a 21-year-old individual, not the employee, were pretextual. he younger individual was hired because she had more recent relevant business experience and because the younger individual viewed the position with long-term interest, while the employee indicated that she was interested in using the job as a stepping stone for a better accounting position. Dabney-Hall v. Cleveland Clinic Found., 2008-Ohio-1080, 2008 Ohio App. LEXIS 945 (Ohio Ct. App., Cuyahoga County 2008).

In a former employee's claim of age discrimination in violation of R.C. 4112.02(A), 4112.99 the trial court erred in granting summary judgment in favor of the former employer and two employees, as there was sufficient evidence from which reasonable minds could disbelieve the proffered reason for removing the former employee from the former employee's position as managing director; all evidence suggested the former employee was successfully performing in that position. Coryell v. Bank One Trust Co., N.A., 2008-Ohio-2698, 2008 Ohio App. LEXIS 2323 (Ohio Ct. App., Franklin County 2008).

Employee's age discrimination claim was not untimely because the age discrimination claims brought under R.C. 4112.99 were subject to a six-year statute of limitations and the employee filed her claim well within the limitation period. Compton v. Swan Super Cleaners, Inc., 2008 U.S. Dist. LEXIS 39526 (S.D. Ohio Apr. 29, 2008).

Employee's age discrimination suit under R.C. 4112.99 was properly dismissed on summary judgment as the 51-year-old employee could not show that the reasons proffered by the employer for hiring a 21-year-old individual, not the employee, were pretextual. he younger individual was hired because she had more recent relevant business experience and because the younger individual viewed the position with long-term interest, while the employee indicated that she was interested in using the job as a stepping stone for a better accounting position. Dabney-Hall v. Cleveland Clinic Found., 2008-Ohio-1080, 2008 Ohio App. LEXIS 945 (Ohio Ct. App., Cuyahoga County 2008).

Although the nurse was a member of a statutorily protected class (she was 50 years old) and she was discharged, she failed to provide evidence that she was qualified for the job as a heart catheter lab registered nurse and, thus, failed to establish a prima facie case of age discrimination. When asked during her deposition whether, at the time of her termination, she was capable of handling the workload of a heart catheter lab R.N., she responded that she was not (she was terminated for making three medical mistakes in three consecutive days) and she also failed to produce evidence that she was replaced by, or that her discharge permitted the retention of, a person outside of the protected class. Guy v. Q.H.G. of Massillon, Inc., 2007 Ohio App. LEXIS 394 (Ohio Ct. App., Stark County Jan. 29, 2007).

Summary judgment was properly granted to an employer in an employee's age discrimination claim, as stray remarks regarding her age by her supervisor did not support a prima facie case of age discrimination, and the employer's non-discriminatory reason for her termination from employment, based on the fact that she had exceeded the allowable leave of absence time under the Family and Medical Leave Act, 9 U.S.C.S. § 2601 et seq., was not shown to have been pretextual. Hershberger v. Altercare, Inc., 2007-Ohio-1452, 2007 Ohio App. LEXIS 1314 (Ohio Ct. App., Stark County 2007).

Summary judgment was properly granted to an employer in an employee's age discrimination claim, as stray remarks regarding her age by her supervisor did not support a prima facie case of age discrimination, and the employer's non-discriminatory reason for her termination from employment, based on the fact that she had exceeded the allowable leave of absence time under the Family and Medical Leave Act, 9 U.S.C.S. § 2601 et seq., was not shown to have been pretextual. Hershberger v. Altercare, Inc., 2007-Ohio-1452, 2007 Ohio App. LEXIS 1314 (Ohio Ct. App., Stark County 2007).

Employee terminated after he failed to pass a drug test failed to establish a prima facie case of age discrimination under R.C. 4112.14 and 4112.99 because he was not replaced by a substantially younger employee, his replacement was older notwithstanding that he was his duties were temporary assigned to a younger replacement. Counts v. Kraton Polymers U.S. LLC, 2006 U.S. Dist. LEXIS 65312 (S.D. Ohio Sept. 13, 2006), aff'd, 260 Fed. Appx. 825, 2008 FED App. 0064N, 2008 U.S. App. LEXIS 2187 (6th Cir. Ohio 2008).

Former employee who was over 40 could not succeed on his action against his former employer under the Age Discrimination in Employment Act, 29 U.S.C.S. §§ 623, 631, R.C. 4112.02, 4112.99, and Ohio public policy because the employer showed a legitimate nondiscriminatory reason for the employee's termination; the employer had hired the employee to increase its sales, and the employee had not increased sales. Shiffman v. Thermal Indus., Inc., 2006 U.S. Dist. LEXIS 64351 (S.D. Ohio Sept. 8, 2006).

Former employee could not maintain an age discrimination case under R.C. 4412.02 and 4112.99, which claims were scrutinized under the same standard as claims under the Age Discrimination in Employment Act, because he did not present circumstantial or direct evidence of discrimination; statements made by co-workers did not constitute direct evidence as co-workers were not decision-makers with regard to the employee's job, and the employee did not establish an adverse employment decision. Because of the failure to establish an adverse employment decision, the employee's retaliation claim under R.C. 4112.02(I) and public policy violation claim also failed. Zivkovic v. Juniper Networks, Inc., 450 F. Supp. 2d 815, 2006 U.S. Dist. LEXIS 63785 (N.D. Ohio 2006).

Mere filing of an age discrimination charge with the Equal Employment Opportunity Commission (EEOC) pursuant to § 626 of the Age Discrimination in Employment Act (ADEA), 29 U.S.C.S. § 621 et seq., is not equivalent to the election of an administrative remedy within the meaning of R.C. 4112.05. Thus, where it is shown that the plaintiffs only filed charges with the EEOC pursuant to the requirements of the ADEA, the fact of such filing does not constitute an election of the remedy set forth in R.C. 4112.05 and such plaintiffs are not precluded from seeking a judicial remedy under R.C. 4112.14 or 4112.99. Reminder v. Roadway Express, Inc., 2006 U.S. Dist. LEXIS 1899 (N.D. Ohio Jan. 10, 2006).

Former employee could not maintain an age discrimination case under R.C. 4412.02 and 4112.99, which claims were scrutinized under the same standard as claims under the Age Discrimination in Employment Act, because he did not present circumstantial or direct evidence of discrimination. Statements made by co-workers did not constitute direct evidence as co-workers were not decision-makers with regard to the employee's job, and the employee did not establish an adverse employment decision. Because of the failure to establish an adverse employment decision, the employee's retaliation claim under R.C. 4112.02(I) and public policy violation claim also failed. Zivkovic v. Juniper Networks, Inc., 450 F. Supp. 2d 815, 2006 U.S. Dist. LEXIS 63785 (N.D. Ohio 2006).

Employee terminated after he failed to pass a drug test failed to establish a prima facie case of age discrimination under R.C. 4112.14 and 4112.99 because he was not replaced by a substantially younger employee, his replacement was older notwithstanding that his duties were temporary assigned to a younger replacement. Counts v. Kraton Polymers U.S. LLC, 2006 U.S. Dist. LEXIS 65312 (S.D. Ohio Sept. 13, 2006), aff'd, 260 Fed. Appx. 825, 2008 FED App. 0064N, 2008 U.S. App. LEXIS 2187 (6th Cir. Ohio 2008).



Former employee who was over 40 could not succeed on his action against his former employer under the Age Discrimination in Employment Act, 29 U.S.C.S. §§ 623, 631, R.C. 4112.02, 4112.99, and Ohio public policy because the employer showed a legitimate nondiscriminatory reason for the employee's termination. The employer had hired the employee to increase its sales, and the employee had not increased sales. Shiffman v. Thermal Indus., Inc., 2006 U.S. Dist. LEXIS 64351 (S.D. Ohio Sept. 8, 2006).

There was sufficient evidence to support a jury's determination that an employee discriminated against a 53-year-old employee on the basis of his age, in violation of R.C. 4112.02(A) and 4112.99, where the employee's manager position was eliminated due to downsizing, and the new position offered to the employee was not in a competitive area and constituted a demotion in the sales hierarchy; further, the position that the employee could have been offered was given to a person who was younger and who did not have the seniority with the employer that the employee had, such that the trial court's grant of a judgment notwithstanding the verdict in favor of the employer and others, pursuant to Civ.R. 50(B), was error. Jelinek v. Abbott Labs., 2005-Ohio-5696, 164 Ohio App. 3d 607, 843 N.E.2d 807, 2005 Ohio App. LEXIS 5122 (Ohio Ct. App., Franklin County 2005).

Trial court properly granted summary judgment to an employer and co-workers of an employee in his age discrimination action pursuant to R.C. 4112.02(A) and 4112.99, as the employee's prima facie case of age discrimination was offset by the showing that his poor job performance and poor behavior were legitimate, nondiscriminatory reasons for the termination; the employee did not meet his burden under any of the Manzer factors of showing that the reasons for the discharge were pretextual. Sweet v. Abbott Foods, 2005-Ohio-6880, 2005 Ohio App. LEXIS 6216 (Ohio Ct. App., Franklin County 2005).

Employer's Fed. R. Civ. P. 12(c) motion was granted because 180-day limitations period applied because the employee's R.C. 4112.99 age discrimination claim could not fairly be read as based on R.C. 4112.14. Because the employee filed an administrative action with the Equal Employment Opportunities Commission (EEOC) and the Ohio Civil Rights Commission he was precluded from later asserting a claim pursuant to any provision of R.C. 4112.14. Kaltenmark v. K-Mart, Inc., 2005 U.S. Dist. LEXIS 21699 (N.D. Ohio Sept. 28, 2005).

Summary judgment was properly granted, dismissing an age discrimination claim, under R.C. 4112.02(N) and 4112.99, brought by a former employee and his wife against the employee's former employer and various managers, because plaintiffs' claim was not filed until more than 180 days after the employee's employment was terminated. Even if plaintiffs could bring suit pursuant to R.C. 4112.02(N) and 4112.99, defendants were entitled to summary judgment because the evidence showed that the work that the employee would have received was distributed among the retained workers, several of which were in the protected class; further, defendants offered a legitimate, non-discriminatory reason for the employee's discharge, a reduction in force, and plaintiffs failed to prove that defendants' work force reduction explanation was a pretext for age discrimination. Vickers v. Wren Indus., 2005-Ohio-3656, 2005 Ohio App. LEXIS 3366 (Ohio Ct. App., Montgomery County 2005).

Employer's motion for summary judgment was denied because the employee stated a prima facie case of age discrimination because a reasonable jury could find that she was qualified for the job and that the training provided to the employee was not of the same quality as the training offered to the younger worker. The employee also showed that the employer's explanation for her termination was a pretext for discrimination because the employer had shifted its articulated reasons for her termination. DeLoach v. Island Dental Co., 2005 U.S. Dist. LEXIS 38213 (S.D. Ohio Dec. 22, 2005).

Trial court properly granted summary judgment to an employer and co-workers of an employee in his age discrimination action pursuant to R.C. 4112.02(A) and 4112.99, as the employee's prima facie case of age discrimination was offset by the showing that his poor job performance and poor behavior were legitimate, nondiscriminatory reasons for the termination. The employee did not meet his burden under any of the Manzer factors of showing that the reasons for the discharge were pretextual. Sweet v. Abbott Foods, 2005-Ohio-6880, 2005 Ohio App. LEXIS 6216 (Ohio Ct. App., Franklin County 2005).

Summary judgment was properly granted, dismissing an age discrimination claim, under R.C. 4112.02(N) and 4112.99, brought by a former employee and his wife against the employee's former employer and various managers, because plaintiffs' claim was not filed until more than 180 days after the employee's employment was terminated. Even if plaintiffs could bring suit pursuant to R.C. 4112.02(N) and 4112.99, defendants were entitled to summary judgment because the evidence showed that the work that the employee would have received was distributed among the retained workers, several of which were in the protected class; further, defendants offered a legitimate, non-discriminatory reason for the employee's discharge, a reduction in force, and plaintiffs failed to prove that defendants' work force reduction explanation was a pretext for age discrimination. Vickers v. Wren Indus., 2005-Ohio-3656, 2005 Ohio App. LEXIS 3366 (Ohio Ct. App., Montgomery County 2005).

180-day limitations period applied because the employee's R.C. 4112.99 age discrimination claim could not fairly be read as based on R.C. 4112.14. Kaltenmark v. K-Mart, Inc., 2005 U.S. Dist. LEXIS 21699 (N.D. Ohio Sept. 28, 2005).

Former employer's failure to hire a former worker, which it had recently terminated, for a subsequent position was an alleged discrete discriminatory act and actionable under Ohio's age discrimination statute. Yovanno v. Ryder Sys., 2003-Ohio-6824, 2003 Ohio App. LEXIS 6159 (Ohio Ct. App., Summit County 2003).

**Appeals**

As a county employee failed to comply with the statutory filing requirements pursuant to R.C. 4112.06(H) with respect to her appeal of a decision from the Ohio Civil Rights Commission regarding her disability discrimination claim against her employer, the appeal had to be dismissed; R.C. 2506.01(A) was not applicable, and the employee could not rely on the independent remedy of R.C. 4112.99 where she did not file a separate civil action under that statutory remedy. Toliver v. Montgomery County Jobs & Family Servs. Div., 2009-Ohio-3521, 2009 Ohio App. LEXIS 3001 (Ohio Ct. App., Montgomery County 2009).

The state employment relations board may participate as a party in appellate review of its decisions. However, it is not necessary or indispensible party to the review proceedings: Hamilton County Bd. of Mental Retardation etc. v. Professionals Guild of Ohio, 46 Ohio St. 3d 147, 545 N.E.2d 1260, 1989 Ohio LEXIS 270 (Ohio 1989).

An order of the State Employment Relations board must comply with R.C. 2505.02 to be appealable: Hamilton County Bd. of Mental Retardation etc. v. Professionals Guild of Ohio, 46 Ohio St. 3d 147, 545 N.E.2d 1260, 1989 Ohio LEXIS 270 (Ohio 1989).

**Arbitration**

Age discrimination claim by terminated public school teacher was barred because the teacher termination administrative proceeding, in which the referee found that the teacher was fired for just cause, was the functional equivalent of arbitration for purposes of R.C. 4112.14(C). Smith v. Perkins Bd. of Educ., 708 F.3d 821, 2013 FED App. 0055P, 2013 U.S. App. LEXIS 4006 (6th Cir. Ohio 2013).

Summary judgment was properly granted to a former employer in an age discrimination case because a former employee's challenge of his discharge in a step four grievance procedure set forth in a collective bargaining agreement between the employer and a local union was the functional equivalent of arbitration under R.C. 4112.14(C). Tatman v. Kaiser Aluminum Corp., 2010-Ohio-6402, 2010 Ohio App. LEXIS 5355 (Ohio Ct. App., Licking County 2010).

**Attorney fees**

Trial court erred by ordering the board of trustees to pay attorney fees; because the trial court could not award punitive damages against a political subdivision, attorney fees could be awarded on that basis. There was no provision under R.C. ch. 2744 that allowed for recovery of attorney fees against a municipality; in the absence of such a provision, attorney fees may not be awarded against a municipality. Henderhan v. Jackson

Twp. Police Dep't, 2009-Ohio-949, 2009 Ohio App. LEXIS 794 (Ohio Ct. App., Stark County 2009).

When an employee alleged that an employer's suit against the employee, after the employee had unsuccessfully sued the employer for sexual harassment, was retaliation, the employee was equitably and judicially estopped from recovering the employee's attorney fees incurred in defending against the employer's lawsuit because (1) the employee's liability for the fees was discharged pursuant to the employee's bankruptcy petition, and (2) the employee took an inconsistent factual position by failing to list the employee's retaliation claim as an asset in the employee's bankruptcy petition. Greer-Burger v. Temesi, 2007-Ohio-6442, 116 Ohio St. 3d 324, 879 N.E.2d 174, 2007 Ohio LEXIS 3049 (Ohio 2007).

In an employee's age discrimination action, as the arbitration provision in the employment agreement was substantively unconscionable because it deprived the employee of his right to seek reimbursement of attorney fees pursuant to R.C. 4112.99 and the rights of the parties were imbalanced, the trial court erred in not holding a hearing on the issue of whether the arbitration provision was procedurally unconscionable pursuant to R.C. 2711.03. As there was a severability provision in the employment agreement, the trial court needed to determine whether it was applicable, whether the offending provisions could be excised, and whether the arbitration provision could then be enforced. Post v. ProCare Auto. Serv. Solutions, 2007-Ohio-2106, 2007 Ohio App. LEXIS 1964 (Ohio Ct. App., Cuyahoga County 2007).

In an employee's age discrimination action, as the arbitration provision in the employment agreement was substantively unconscionable because it deprived the employee of his right to seek reimbursement of attorney fees pursuant to R.C. 4112.99 and the rights of the parties were imbalanced, the trial court erred in not holding a hearing on the issue of whether the arbitration provision was procedurally unconscionable pursuant to R.C. 2711.03; further, as there was a severability provision in the employment agreement, the trial court needed to determine whether it was applicable, whether the offending provisions could be excised, and whether the arbitration provision could then be enforced. Post v. ProCare Auto. Serv. Solutions, 2007-Ohio-2106, 2007 Ohio App. LEXIS 1964 (Ohio Ct. App., Cuyahoga County 2007).

R.C. 4112.99 does not provide for an award of attorney fees in the absence of any of the recognized exceptions to the American rule: Sutherland v. Nationwide Gen. Ins. Co., 102 Ohio App. 3d 297, 657 N.E.2d 281, 1995 Ohio App. LEXIS 1303 (Ohio Ct. App., Franklin County), dismissed, 73 Ohio St. 3d 1426, 652 N.E.2d 799, 1995 Ohio LEXIS 1715 (Ohio 1995).

**Availability**

Dismissal of an assistant principal's request for punitive damages and attorney fees against a board of education, arising from discipline imposed against her, was warranted because they were not expressly authorized by statute. Speller v. Toledo Pub. Sch. Dist. Bd. of Educ., 2015-Ohio-2672, 38 N.E.3d 509, 2015 Ohio App. LEXIS 2562 (Ohio Ct. App., Lucas County 2015).

**Burden of proof**

In an action stemming from termination of employment, a grant of summary judgment in favor of the employer and president (employer) was proper because the employee's arguments for claiming that the employer's proffered reason was insufficient to motivate her termination lacked support in the record. The employee did not provide evidence that a similarly situated comparator was treated more favorably for engaging in similar conduct and failed to demonstrate pretext with regard to gender and age discrimination. Housden v. Wilke Global, Inc., 2018-Ohio-3959, 111 N.E.3d 1264, 2018 Ohio App. LEXIS 4330 (Ohio Ct. App., Franklin County 2018).

In the terminated university employee's action against her former university employer, the university was entitled to summary judgment on discrimination and retaliation claims because the employee failed to demonstrate discriminatory intent under the McDonnell Douglas framework where there was evidence she had been terminated for insubordination, and she failed to demonstrate retaliation where she failed to show her opposition to any unlawful discriminatory practice. You v. Ne. Ohio Med. Univ., 2018-Ohio-4838, 2018 Ohio App. LEXIS 5161 (Ohio Ct. App., Franklin County 2018).

Ohio's requirements for civil rights claims such as those under R.C. 4112.02 and R.C. 4112.99 are the same as those of Title VII of the Civil Rights Act of 1964, 42 U.S.C.S. § 2000e-2000e-17. Carter v. Univ. of Toledo, 349 F.3d 269, 2003 FED App. 0401P, 2003 U.S. App. LEXIS 23054 (6th Cir. Ohio 2003).

**Class actions**

District court properly denied two employees' motion for class certification under Fed. R. Civ. P. 23 in their action claiming race discrimination in promotions in violation of 42 U.S.C.S. § 2000e-2 of Title VII of the Civil Rights Act of 1964, 42 U.S.C.S. § 2000e et seq., and in violation of R.C. 4112.99; the employees' disparate treatment claim failed the prerequisites of Fed. R. Civ. P. 23(a)(2) because the employees did not show that the wide range of class members, which included both hourly and salaried positions with different qualifications and varying levels of seniority in automobile manufacturing plants, were all subject to the same, exclusively-subjective, decision-making process. The employees' disparate impact claim failed the prerequisites of Rule 23(a)(3) because neither employee was a typical member of the class in that their personal choices, independent of any disparate impact practices, rendered them ineligible for promotion. Bacon v. Honda of Am. Mfg., 370 F.3d 565, 2004 FED App. 0155P, 2004 U.S. App. LEXIS 10437 (6th Cir. Ohio 2004), cert. denied, 543 U.S. 1151, 125 S. Ct. 1334, 161 L. Ed. 2d 115, 2005 U.S. LEXIS 1537 (U.S. 2005).

**Collateral estoppel, res judicata**

When an employee sued his former employer in federal court under both 42 U.S.C.S. § 2000-e and R.C. 4112.99, and the federal court dismissed the federal claim and exercised pendent jurisdiction over the state law claim and dismissed it on its merits, res judicata barred the employee from subsequently bringing a suit in state court against the employer in which he raised a whistleblower claim. Watson v. Parma Cmty. Gen. Hosp., 2006-Ohio-712, 2006 Ohio App. LEXIS 628 (Ohio Ct. App., Cuyahoga County 2006).

An OCR.C. finding of no probable cause in a sexual discrimination case does not collaterally estop an employee from claiming sexual discrimination in a civil action pending in the court of common pleas: Delekta v. Snyder Farm, 1995 Ohio App. LEXIS 6090 (Ohio Ct. App., Tuscarawas County Dec. 19, 1995).

The federal court judgment rejecting the employee's claims of violation of federal age discrimination provisions was res judicata in the state court action based on R.C. 4112.99. However, the retaliation claim was not barred. As a general rule, filing with the OCR.C. precludes a subsequent suit under R.C. 4112.99: Borowski v. State Chem. Mfg. Co., 97 Ohio App. 3d 635, 647 N.E.2d 230, 1994 Ohio App. LEXIS 4207 (Ohio Ct. App., Cuyahoga County 1994).

**Collective bargaining agreements**

Collective bargaining agreement, even if it contains an antidiscrimination clause, does not supersede an employee's rights under R.C. Chapter 4112: Haynes v. Ohio Tpk. Comm'n, 2008-Ohio-133, 177 Ohio App. 3d 1, 893 N.E.2d 850, 2008 Ohio App. LEXIS 121 (Ohio Ct. App., Cuyahoga County 2008).

**Common law**

Common law tort claim for wrongful discharge based on Ohio's public policy against age discrimination does not exist, because the remedies in R.C. Chapter 4112 provide complete relief for a statutory claim for age discrimination: Leininger v. Pioneer Nat'l Latex, 2007-Ohio-4921, 115 Ohio St. 3d 311, 875 N.E.2d 36, 2007 Ohio LEXIS 2229 (Ohio 2007).

Availability of remedies under R.C. 4112.99 did not defeat a former employee's common law cause of action for wrongful discharge in violation of public policy based on sexual harassment and discrimination. Burgett v. BFI Waste Sys. of N. Am., Inc., 328 F. Supp. 2d 769, 2004 U.S. Dist. LEXIS 15117 (N.D. Ohio 2004).

R.C. 4112.99 contains its own remedies for employment discrimination. Thus there is no need to recognize a common law claim of wrongful discharge in violation of public policy: Lewis v. Fairview Hosp., 2004-Ohio-1108, 156 Ohio App. 3d 387, 806 N.E.2d 185, 2004 Ohio App. LEXIS 975 (Ohio Ct. App., Cuyahoga County 2004).

It is an unlawful discriminatory practice for an employee to be discharged because of a handicap, and the employee may bring a common law wrongful discharge claim without seeking relief under R.C. Chapter 4112.: Clipson v. Schlessman, 89 Ohio App. 3d 230, 624 N.E.2d 220, 1993 Ohio App. LEXIS 2999 (Ohio Ct. App., Erie County 1993).

**Common law action**

Employer defendants' motion to dismiss a claim for "adverse employment action in violation of public policy" was granted because the employee had adequate statutory remedies under Title VII of the Civil Rights Act of 1964, 42 U.S.C.S. § 2000e et seq., the Equal Pay Act, 29 U.S.C.S. § 206(d), and R.C. 4112.99, and because Ohio did not recognize a cause of action for violation of public policy outside the context of a wrongful discharge. Stange v. Deloitte & Touche, 2006 U.S. Dist. LEXIS 16444 (S.D. Ohio Apr. 5, 2006).

**Complaint sufficient**

Allegations in the employee's complaint indicated that: the employee was terminated after working for the employer for over 30 years; the employee fell within two legally protected classifications based upon his age and a handicap; and the employee said he was abruptly fired after an incident in which he was falsely accused of sleeping on the job and retaliatory conduct, and was replaced by employees outside of his protected classifications. Therefore, the employee's complaint was sufficient to establish plausible age and handicap discrimination claims under R.C. 4112.99. Rodriguez v. PPG Indus., 2011 U.S. Dist. LEXIS 119708 (N.D. Ohio Oct. 17, 2011).

Where an employee sufficiently pleaded the elements of his claims for race and disability discrimination under R.C. 4112.02(A) and 4112.99, he met the pleading requirements of Civ.R. 8(A) and the trial court erred in granting the employer's motion to dismiss the complaint for failure to state a claim; the "prima facie case" requirement was an evidentiary standard for purposes of R.C. 4112.02(A) and not a pleading standard. Jackson v. Int'l Fiber, 2006-Ohio-5799, 169 Ohio App. 3d 395, 863 N.E.2d 189, 2006 Ohio App. LEXIS 5750 (Ohio Ct. App., Champaign County 2006).

**Construction**

R.C. 4112.99 is to be liberally construed to promote its object (elimination of discrimination) and protect those to whom it is addressed (victims of discrimination), so § 4112.99 must be interpreted to afford victims of handicap discrimination the right to pursue a civil action. Dworning v. City of Euclid, 2006-Ohio-6772, 2006 Ohio App. LEXIS 6685 (Ohio Ct. App., Cuyahoga County 2006), aff'd, 2008-Ohio-3318, 119 Ohio St. 3d 83, 892 N.E.2d 420, 2008 Ohio LEXIS 1768 (Ohio 2008).

**Damages**

Trial court erred in relying on the general statute in awarding damages because the firefighter was limited to the relief provided under the specific age discrimination statute. Campolieti v. Cleveland Dep't of Pub. Safety, 2013-Ohio-5123, 2013 Ohio App. LEXIS 5332 (Ohio Ct. App., Cuyahoga County 2013).

State employee who established age discrimination against the Ohio Department of Natural Resources under R.C. 4112.14 and 4112.99 was entitled to post-judgment interest on his award of back pay pursuant to R.C. 2743.18(B) at the current statutory rate. Warden v. Ohio Dep't of Natural Res., 2013-Ohio-1512, 2013 Ohio Misc. LEXIS 12 (Ohio Ct. Cl. 2013), aff'd in part and rev'd in part, 2014-Ohio-35, 7 N.E.3d 533, 2014 Ohio App. LEXIS 25 (Ohio Ct. App., Franklin County 2014).



**—Back pay**

State employee who was not offered a full-time position based on the Ohio Department of Natural Resources' policy not to rehire a retiree suffered age discrimination under R.C. 4112.14 and 4112.99, such that he was entitled to recover back pay; there was evidence that he exercised reasonable diligence in looking for other suitable employment, and that he did not decline any job opportunities for substantially equivalent employment. Warden v. Ohio Dep't of Natural Res., 2013-Ohio-1512, 2013 Ohio Misc. LEXIS 12 (Ohio Ct. Cl. 2013), aff'd in part and rev'd in part, 2014-Ohio-35, 7 N.E.3d 533, 2014 Ohio App. LEXIS 25 (Ohio Ct. App., Franklin County 2014).

**Disability discrimination**

Trial court erred in granting summary judgment to a school district, superintendent, and high school principal in a teacher's suit alleging they engaged in disability discrimination because there was an issue of fact as to whether they took an adverse employment action against the teacher based on her disability in the form of a constructive discharge; one could infer the denial of additional accommodation made the teacher's working conditions intolerable and that she was compelled to resign. Caldwell v. Niles City Schs, 2021-Ohio-1543, 2021 Ohio App. LEXIS 1506 (Ohio Ct. App., Trumbull County 2021).

It was error to grant summary judgment to a school district, superintendent, and principal in a teacher's suit alleging disability discrimination because there was a genuine issue of fact as to whether they made a good faith effort to assist the teacher in seeking an additional accommodation; since there was a genuine issue as to whether the teacher voluntarily resigned or was constructively discharged, there was a genuine issue as to whether she terminated the interactive process by resigning. Caldwell v. Niles City Schs, 2021-Ohio-1543, 2021 Ohio App. LEXIS 1506 (Ohio Ct. App., Trumbull County 2021).

In a case alleging a failure to accommodate a disability under R.C. 4112.02 and R.C. 4112.99, an appellate court was unable to determine if proposed jury instructions on the interactive process an employer and an employee had to engage in to find a reasonable accommodation of a disability contained a correct statement of the law applicable to the facts of the case because they were not in the record; the case was reviewed under a plain error standard because a former employee did not object to the magistrate's handling of the jury trial. Even absent the proposed instructions, there was no plain error committed because the instruction given by the magistrate generally conformed to prevailing Ohio law. Ziadeh v. City of Columbus, 2010-Ohio-1323, 2010 Ohio App. LEXIS 1103 (Ohio Ct. App., Franklin County 2010).

Employee's disability discrimination claim under R.C. 4112.02 and § 4112.99 failed because the employee failed to introduce sufficient evidence to establish a genuine issue of material fact on the question of whether he was disabled for purposes of such where: (1) with respect to the employee's assertion that his sexual impotence constituted a disability to support his claim, the employer correctly pointed out that there was no evidence in the record that the employer was in any way aware of this purported disability at the time of termination, and since the disability had to be known to the employer at the time of an adverse job action, that physical condition could not support his § 4112.02 claim; and (2) the employee was unable to safely and substantially perform the essential functions of the job in question since his medical limitations prevented the employee from safely and substantially performing the work required by his former position. Niles v. Nat'l Vendor Servs., 2010-Ohio-4610, 2010 Ohio App. LEXIS 3885 (Ohio Ct. App., Franklin County 2010).

Trial court properly granted summary judgment to an employer in the former employee's disability discrimination claim under R.C. 4112.99, as she failed to show that her supervisors regarded her as disabled pursuant to R.C. 4112.01(A)(13). She also failed to show that her employer and supervisors took adverse employment action against her due to the disability, as her termination from employment was based on the fact that she exceeded the allowable leave of absence under the Family and Medical Leave Act, 29 U.S.C.S. § 2601 et seq. Hershberger v. Altercare, Inc., 2007-Ohio-1452, 2007 Ohio App. LEXIS 1314 (Ohio Ct. App., Stark County 2007).

Trial court's judgment in favor of a state agency in an employee's disability discrimination claim under R.C. 4112.99 was supported by substantial evidence, as the agency was unaware that the employee had a "disability" within the meaning of R.C. 4112.01(A)(13) when it terminated her for a disciplinary infraction and accordingly, she was not terminated because she was disabled; she had fallen asleep at her desk, which she initially claimed was just a moment with her eyes closed in order to allow eyedrops for "dry eye syndrome" to take effect, but she later claimed that she had sleep apnea, which was a disability, and that she was not reasonably accommodated by the agency. Lee v. Ohio Dep't of Job & Family Servs., 2006-Ohio-6658, 2006 Ohio App. LEXIS 6504 (Ohio Ct. App., Franklin County 2006).

A former employee asserted state law claims for handicap discrimination under R.C. 4112.01 and 4112.99. Summary judgment for the employer on those claims was not proper because those claims involved the same essential elements as the employee's Americans with Disabilities Act claim under 42 U.S.C.S. § 12112(a) and summary judgment was not appropriate on that claim. Downs v. AOL Time Warner, Inc., 2006 U.S. Dist. LEXIS 4848 (S.D. Ohio Jan. 20, 2006).

Employer was not entitled to summary judgment on an employee's disability discrimination claims where there were issues of fact as to whether the employer considered the employee disabled or unable to perform the functions of his job, whether the employee's perceived disability limited his ability to work, and whether the employer discriminated against the employee as a result of the perceived disability. Allen v. Deerfield Mfg., 424 F. Supp. 2d 987, 2006 U.S. Dist. LEXIS 13870 (S.D. Ohio 2006).

Where a maintenance repair worker had permanent work restrictions due to his back injury, which impeded his ability to perform his job, such that he received an involuntary separation notice, his disability discrimination claim under R.C. 4112.02 failed, as he did not show that he was disabled under R.C. 4112.01(A)(13) and he did not show that he had requested an accommodation from his employer. Although he failed to exhaust his administrative remedies, such did not impede his ability to bring the discrimination action, based on the liberal construction given to the remedial law, pursuant to R.C. 4112.99, but the fact that he could not lift more than 50 pounds and could not twist, bend, or stoop was not sufficient to demonstrate a disability that allowed consideration of recovery to him. McClenaghan v. Ohio DOC, 2005-Ohio-1284, 2005 Ohio Misc. LEXIS 101 (Ohio Ct. Cl. 2005).

Employer did not fail to reasonably accommodate back injury where employer allowed employee to go on medical leave several times and, although employee was asked to scrub the floor, there was no evidence that doing so was part of a malicious concerted effort to terminate him: Perdue v. Northern Can Sys., 935 F. Supp. 924, 1996 U.S. Dist. LEXIS 3283 (N.D. Ohio 1996).

"Handicapped person" includes a person who is regarded as handicapped by the employer. Front pay is available for handicap discrimination where reinstatement is inappropriate. Punitive damages are available for a handicap discrimination claim under R.C. 4112.99: Potocnik v. Sifco Indus., 103 Ohio App. 3d 560, 660 N.E.2d 510, 1995 Ohio App. LEXIS 964 (Ohio Ct. App., Cuyahoga County 1995).

**Discovery of defendant's net worth**

There was no compelling reason not to allow the discovery regarding the employer's net worth as the employee had requested punitive damages pursuant to this section, but a protective order preventing the employee from divulging any information regarding the employer's net worth to third parties without prior authorization from the court was required. Smith v. Tech. House, Ltd., 2019-Ohio-2670, 2019 Ohio App. LEXIS 2780 (Ohio Ct. App., Portage County 2019).

**Dismissal**

Former employee's reverse discrimination complaint warranted dismissal because he failed to satisfy the McDonnell Douglas elements, as the complaint lacked operative facts to support an inference of discriminatory intent because he did not allege that the employer unlawfully considered his race when it refused his scheduling requests, disciplined him, or terminated him. Martin v. Block Communs., 2017-Ohio-1474, 2017 Ohio App. LEXIS 1480 (Ohio Ct. App., Lucas County 2017).

Former employee's state law claims for sex and pregnancy discrimination were not dismissed for failure to exhaust administrative remedies as such exhaustion was not required in actions under R.C. 4112.99. Skelton v. Health Alliance, 2006 U.S. Dist. LEXIS 74073 (S.D. Ohio Oct. 11, 2006).

Where an employee sufficiently pleaded the elements of his claims for race and disability discrimination under R.C. 4112.02(A) and 4112.99, he met the pleading requirements of Civ.R. 8(A) and the trial court erred in granting the employer's motion to dismiss the complaint for failure to state a claim. The "prima facie case" requirement was an evidentiary standard for purposes of R.C. 4112.02(A) and not a pleading standard. Jackson v. Int'l Fiber, 2006-Ohio-5799, 169 Ohio App. 3d 395, 863 N.E.2d 189, 2006 Ohio App. LEXIS 5750 (Ohio Ct. App., Champaign County 2006).

In an employment discrimination case alleging violations of 42 U.S.C.S. §§ 1981, 1985, and 2000e-5 and R.C. 4112.02 and 4112.99 in which the former employee had failed to comply with his discovery obligations, had not complied with court orders, and had already been sanctioned, the court determined that any sanction other than dismissal would be ineffective and granted defendants' Fed. R. Civ. P. 36(b)(2)(C) and Fed. R. Civ. P. 41(b) motion to dismiss. Moses v. Sterling Commerce, 2003 U.S. Dist. LEXIS 13390 (S.D. Ohio July 1, 2003), aff'd, 122 Fed. Appx. 177, 2005 U.S. App. LEXIS 19 (6th Cir. Ohio 2005).

Where plaintiff's complaint clearly alleges violations of Ohio's anti-discrimination law after the effective date of the statute, defendant must do more than merely characterize plaintiff's claim as "contrived" to warrant its dismissal: Robinson v. N & C Constr. Co., 767 F. Supp. 843, 1991 U.S. Dist. LEXIS 9838 (N.D. Ohio 1991).

**Election of remedies**

Trial court erred by granting summary judgment on the basis that it lacked subject matter jurisdiction because its analysis prevented the daughter from asserting an independent civil action and limited her remedy to only being permitted to challenge the conciliation agreement and consent order she had signed. She did not have to elect remedies in her disability discrimination claims. Reid v. Plainsboro Partners, III, 2010-Ohio-4373, 2010 Ohio App. LEXIS 3694 (Ohio Ct. App., Franklin County 2010).

Former employee was barred under R.C. 4112.08 from bringing a civil action for age discrimination under R.C. 4112.02 and R.C. 4112.99 because the employee elected to pursue a charge of age discrimination in an administrative action with the Ohio Civil Rights Commission, and there was no evidence to suggest that the limited exception to the election of remedies doctrine applied. Moore v. Dep't of Rehab. & Corr., 2010-Ohio-3739, 2010 Ohio Misc. LEXIS 157 (Ohio Ct. Cl. 2010), aff'd, 2011-Ohio-1607, 2011 Ohio App. LEXIS 1376 (Ohio Ct. App., Franklin County 2011).

Summary judgment was properly granted because the nurse's assistant was barred from bringing a private age discrimination claim under R.C. 4112.02 and 4112.99. Because the nurse's assistant filed a charge with the Equal Employment Opportunity Commission (EEOC) and never indicated that she would forego an investigation (and was filing for technical purposes only), her charge to the EEOC was likewise deemed filed with the Ohio Civil Rights Commission. Neal v. Franklin Plaza Nursing Home, 2009-Ohio-2034, 2009 Ohio App. LEXIS 1724 (Ohio Ct. App., Cuyahoga County 2009).

Employer's motion to dismiss was granted because the employee's claim of age discrimination under R.C. 4112.99 was barred by R.C. 4112.05's age discrimination election of remedies scheme and the employee failed to file her age discrimination claim within the applicable statute of limitations under R.C. 4112.02(N). Hillery v. Fifth Third Bank, 2009 U.S. Dist. LEXIS 39658 (S.D. Ohio May 11, 2009).

State university employee's age discrimination claim under R.C. 4112.99 was not barred by the election of remedies requirement of R.C. 4112.08, as 4112.99 provided an independent civil action to seek redress for discrimination; the employee had asserted that he was not rehired to a new position after his original employment position was abolished due to his age. Knepper v. Ohio State Univ., 2008-Ohio-4796, 2008 Ohio Misc. LEXIS 207 (Ohio Ct. Cl. 2008), aff'd, 2011-Ohio-6054, 2011 Ohio App. LEXIS 4943 (Ohio Ct. App., Franklin County 2011).

Remedial nature of R.C. 4112.99, allowing civil actions for employment discrimination, trumps the availability of an administrative appeal which cannot consider a disability discrimination claim or provide relief in a manner consistent with the purposes of the exhaustion doctrine, and this conclusion is compelled by the nature of the claims involved: one being a statutory right; the other being a judge-made rule of convenience, as the convenience of the courts cannot overcome a right so remedial in purpose as expressed by the general assembly and a long line of court decisions, but this does not apply to employment relationships defined by contract, whether private or by way of a collective bargaining agreement, which set forth agreed upon disciplinary procedures, regardless of whether the right to invoke those procedures is couched in discretionary language, but, unless and until the general assembly expressly incorporates an exhaustion requirement into R.C. 4112.01 et seq., there is no basis for requiring it as a matter of course to those workers who have available civil service remedies. Dworning v. City of Euclid, 2006-Ohio-6772, 2006 Ohio App. LEXIS 6685 (Ohio Ct. App., Cuyahoga County 2006), aff'd, 2008-Ohio-3318, 119 Ohio St. 3d 83, 892 N.E.2d 420, 2008 Ohio LEXIS 1768 (Ohio 2008).

Ohio does not require a filing with the Ohio Civil Rights Commission as a prerequisite for pursuing a discrimination claim directly in court, as individual claims for employment discrimination are authorized by R.C. 4112.99, which provides for a private right of action, stating that whoever violates R.C. 4112.01 et seq. is subject to a civil action for damages. Dworning v. City of Euclid, 2006-Ohio-6772, 2006 Ohio App. LEXIS 6685 (Ohio Ct. App., Cuyahoga County 2006), aff'd, 2008-Ohio-3318, 119 Ohio St. 3d 83, 892 N.E.2d 420, 2008 Ohio LEXIS 1768 (Ohio 2008).

When a fire chief who was separated from his employment sued a city for disability discrimination, under R.C. 4112.99, he did not have to exhaust his administrative remedies in the city's civil service commission as a predicate to filing suit because he was not claiming age discrimination, and the doctrine of exhaustion of administrative remedies was a judge-made "rule of convenience" which could not contradict the general assembly's provision of a clear statutory right which had priority over any other law, including the civil service commission's rules. Dworning v. City of Euclid, 2006-Ohio-6772, 2006 Ohio App. LEXIS 6685 (Ohio Ct. App., Cuyahoga County 2006), aff'd, 2008-Ohio-3318, 119 Ohio St. 3d 83, 892 N.E.2d 420, 2008 Ohio LEXIS 1768 (Ohio 2008).

Summary judgment was properly granted to an employer on a job applicant's age discrimination claim under R.C. 4112.02, .99 because the applicant elected to pursue an administrative remedy that precluded her from filing a civil action; before filing the civil action, she filed charges with the Ohio Civil Rights Commission and the United States Equal Employment Opportunity Commission, no exception to the election of remedies requirement was shown to exist, and the requirement applied to claims under both R.C. 4112.02 and R.C. 4112.99. McNeely v. Ross Corr. Inst., 2006-Ohio-5414, 2006 Ohio App. LEXIS 5408 (Ohio Ct. App., Franklin County 2006).

Mere filing of an age discrimination charge with the Equal Employment Opportunity Commission (EEOC) pursuant to § 626 of the Age Discrimination in Employment Act (ADEA), 29 U.S.C.S. § 621 et seq., is not equivalent to the election of an administrative remedy within the meaning of R.C. 4112.05. Thus, where it is shown that the plaintiffs only filed charges with the EEOC pursuant to the requirements of the ADEA, the fact of such filing does not constitute an election of the remedy set forth in R.C. 4112.05 and such plaintiffs are not precluded from seeking a judicial remedy under R.C. 4112.14 or 4112.99. Reminder v. Roadway Express, Inc., 2006 U.S. Dist. LEXIS 1899 (N.D. Ohio Jan. 10, 2006).

Summary judgment was properly granted to an employer on a job applicant's age discrimination claim under R.C. 4112.02, .99 because the applicant elected to pursue an administrative remedy that precluded her from filing a civil action; before filing the civil action, she filed charges with the Ohio Civil Rights Commission and the United States Equal Employment Opportunity Commission, no exception to the election of remedies requirement was shown to exist, and the requirement applied to claims under both R.C. 4112.02 and R.C. 4112.99. McNeely v. Ross Corr. Inst., 2006-Ohio-5414, 2006 Ohio App. LEXIS 5408 (Ohio Ct. App., Franklin County 2006).

In regard to handicap discrimination claims, the general assembly has not manifested an intent similar to that manifested regarding age discrimination claims, which requires a plaintiff to elect between an administrative or judicial remedy. If the general assembly intended that individuals alleging handicap discrimination be forced to choose between an administrative or civil proceeding, it would have specifically stated so, as it did with respect to age discrimination. The Latin maxim expressio unius est exclusio alterius, which translated means that the expression of one item of a class implicitly excludes other items of the class that are not specifically mentioned, is instructive, as the general assembly has specifically limited an individual's ability to bring both an administrative and civil proceeding in the context of age discrimination only. Its exclusion of other forms of discrimination from this limitation makes clear that it intended that both remedies be available for other forms of discrimination. Dworning v. City of Euclid, 2006-Ohio-6772, 2006 Ohio App. LEXIS 6685 (Ohio Ct. App., Cuyahoga County 2006), aff'd, 2008-Ohio-3318, 119 Ohio St. 3d 83, 892 N.E.2d 420, 2008 Ohio LEXIS 1768 (Ohio 2008).

Claimants with claims before the Ohio Civil Rights Commission could file separate actions in federal and state court pursuant to 28 U.S.C.S. § 1331 and R.C. 4112.99; as the claims were not age discrimination claims, no election of remedies had to be made. Yeager v. Ohio Civ. Rights Comm'n, 2005-Ohio-6151, 2005 Ohio App. LEXIS 5541 (Ohio Ct. App., Trumbull County 2005).

Because the employee filed a charge with the Ohio Civil Rights Commission (OCRC) before initiating his current federal action for age discrimination, he elected the remedy made available under R.C. 4112.05. Therefore, he elected the remedy made available by § 4112.05, which precluded later pursuit of the remedy made available by either R.C. 4112.14 or 4112.99 for age discrimination. Gray v. Allstate Ins. Co., 2005 U.S. Dist. LEXIS 40793 (S.D. Ohio Sept. 26, 2005).

Claimants with claims before the Ohio Civil Rights Commission could file separate actions in federal and state court pursuant to 28 U.S.C.S. § 1331 and R.C. 4112.99; as the claims were not age discrimination claims, no election of remedies had to be made. Yeager v. Ohio Civ. Rights Comm'n, 2005-Ohio-6151, 2005 Ohio App. LEXIS 5541 (Ohio Ct. App., Trumbull County 2005).

Because the employee filed an administrative action with the Equal Employment Opportunities Commission (EEOC) and the Ohio Civil Rights Commission he was precluded from later asserting a claim pursuant to any provision of R.C. 4112.14. Kaltenmark v. K-Mart, Inc., 2005 U.S. Dist. LEXIS 21699 (N.D. Ohio Sept. 28, 2005).

Job applicant claiming to have been denied employment due to her age denied herself the ability to pursue almost all age discrimination claims under R.C. 4112 et seq. by filing a charge with the Ohio Civil Rights Commission and the Equal Employment Opportunity Commission rather than an R.C. 4112.99 claim based on R.C. 4112.02(A). Sterry v. Safe Auto Ins. Co., 2003 U.S. Dist. LEXIS 17363 (S.D. Ohio Aug. 25, 2003).

The election of remedies requirement does not apply to claims of sex discrimination: Noday v. Mahoning County Sheriff, 2002-Ohio-609, 147 Ohio App. 3d 38, 768 N.E.2d 726, 2002 Ohio App. LEXIS 596 (Ohio Ct. App., Mahoning County 2002).

The act of filing an age discrimination charge with the state civil rights commission bars a civil suit in a court: Vinson v. Diamond Triumph Auto Glass, Inc., 2002-Ohio-5596, 149 Ohio App. 3d 605, 778 N.E.2d 149, 2002 Ohio App. LEXIS 5599 (Ohio Ct. App., Montgomery County 2002).

The filing of an unlawful discriminatory practice charge with the Ohio civil rights commission under R.C. 4112.05(B)(1) does not preclude a person alleging handicap discrimination from instituting an independent civil action under R.C. 4112.99: Smith v. Friendship Vill. of Dublin, 2001-Ohio-1272, 92 Ohio St. 3d 503, 751 N.E.2d 1010, 2001 Ohio LEXIS 2127 (Ohio 2001).

Plaintiff was not collaterally estopped from bringing an action for retaliatory discharge where he did not have a full and fair opportunity to litigate the issue at the civil rights commission hearing: Doan v. S. Ohio Admin. Dist. Council, 145 Ohio App. 3d 482, 763 N.E.2d 639, 2001 Ohio App. LEXIS 3659 (Ohio Ct. App., Franklin County 2001).

Claimant was not barred from filing her handicap discrimination complaint with the trial court pursuant to R.C. 4112.99 simply because she had previously filed an administrative claim pursuant to R.C. 4112.05; the trial court erred when it found that she was required to file an appeal with the commission pursuant to R.C. 4112.06 before filing her case with the trial court: Smith v. Friendship Vill. of Dublin, Ohio, Inc., 2000 Ohio App. LEXIS 2867 (Ohio Ct. App., Franklin County June 29, 2000), aff'd, 2001-Ohio-1272, 92 Ohio St. 3d 503, 751 N.E.2d 1010, 2001 Ohio LEXIS 2127 (Ohio 2001).

R.C. 4112.02 does not mandate an election of administrative or court remedies for claimants pursuing discrimination claims other than age discrimination claims: Bourquin v. KeyBank, 138 Ohio App. 3d 435, 741 N.E.2d 584, 2000 Ohio App. LEXIS 2881 (Ohio Ct. App., Lucas County 2000).

Employee did not have to choose between state and federal remedies for sex discrimination: Griswold v. Fresenius USA, 964 F. Supp. 1166, 1997 U.S. Dist. LEXIS 3741 (N.D. Ohio 1997).

The 1987 amendment to R.C. 4112.99 did not alter the election of remedies requirement as to age discrimination claims: Balent v. National Revenue Corp., 93 Ohio App. 3d 419, 638 N.E.2d 1064, 1994 Ohio App. LEXIS 935 (Ohio Ct. App., Franklin County 1994).

Pursuant to OAC 4112-3-01(D), a charge filed with EEOC is deemed filed with Ohio's civil rights commission, precluding a private right of action under R.C. 4112.99: Schwartz v. Comcorp, Inc., 91 Ohio App. 3d 639, 633 N.E.2d 551, 1993 Ohio App. LEXIS 89 (Ohio Ct. App., Cuyahoga County 1993).

Plaintiff who had filed age discrimination charge with the Ohio Civil Rights Commission for the sole purpose of meeting the requirements of a suit under federal law could pursue state remedies in federal court even though Ohio law requires an election of remedies: Baker v. Siemens Energy & Automation, 838 F. Supp. 1227, 1993 U.S. Dist. LEXIS 16769 (S.D. Ohio 1993).

Even though R.C. 4112.02(N) and 4101.17 each preclude filing of age discrimination claims under both provisions, a court should not simply dismiss an action alleging both. The special provision of R.C. 4112.02(N) prevails over the general relief afforded by R.C. 4112.99: Giambrone v. Spalding & Evenflo Co., 79 Ohio App. 3d 308, 607 N.E.2d 106, 1992 Ohio App. LEXIS 2070 (Ohio Ct. App., Miami County 1992).

A party who has potential remedies for alleged age discrimination under R.C. 4101.17, 4112.02 and 4112.99 may not pursue an administrative action under R.C. 4112.05, fail to appeal an adverse determination and then bring an action under R.C. 4112.99: Gallant v. Toledo Pub. Sch., 84 Ohio App. 3d 378, 616 N.E.2d 1156, 1992 Ohio App. LEXIS 6324 (Ohio Ct. App., Lucas County 1992).

The filing of an administrative proceeding under R.C. 4112.05 does not preclude the filing of an age discrimination suit under R.C. 4112.99: Pater v. Health Care & Retirement Corp., 808 F. Supp. 573, 1992 U.S. Dist. LEXIS 20568 (S.D. Ohio 1992).

The Ohio legislature has not manifested an intent to require a plaintiff alleging sex discrimination to elect between various remedies: Larkins v. G.D. Searle & Co., 68 Ohio App. 3d 746, 589 N.E.2d 488, 1991 Ohio App. LEXIS 3669 (Ohio Ct. App., Franklin County 1991).

R.C. 4112.99 does not allow a private right of action for age discrimination where the plaintiff-employee has previously filed a claim with the Civil Rights Commission under R.C. 4112.05: Pozzobon v. Parts for Plastics, 770 F. Supp. 376, 1991 U.S. Dist. LEXIS 11655 (N.D. Ohio 1991).

R.C. 4112.99 creates a private cause of action for alleged victims of discrimination in an original action. R.C. 4112.99, however, does not nullify the effect of R.C. 4112.08 which operates to bar suits by plaintiffs who have previously filed a claim with the Ohio Civil Rights Commission: Emser v. Curtis Industries, Inc., 774 F. Supp. 1076, 1991 U.S. Dist. LEXIS 14190 (N.D. Ohio 1991).

**Eleventh amendment**

The eleventh amendment barred plaintiff's suit against state in federal court for violations of the Ohio statutes prohibiting employment discrimination: Williams v. Ohio Dep't of Mental Health, 960 F. Supp. 1276, 1997 U.S. Dist. LEXIS 5429 (S.D. Ohio 1997).

**Employer liability**

Trial court did not err in denying an employer's motion for judgment notwithstanding the verdict pursuant to Civ.R. 50 in an employee's sexual harassment claim based on her supervisor's allegedly improper conduct towards her, as her settlement with the supervisor did not preclude a finding of liability on the part of the employer; the supervisor was subject to liability because he met the definition of an employer pursuant to R.C. 4112.01(A)(2), and as the supervisor and employer were jointly and severally liable pursuant to R.C. 4112.02(A) and 4112.99, the settlement of the supervisor did not relieve the employer from potential vicarious liability. Edwards v. Ohio Inst. of Cardiac Care, 2007-Ohio-1333, 170 Ohio App. 3d 619, 868 N.E.2d 721, 2007 Ohio App. LEXIS 1214 (Ohio Ct. App., Greene County 2007).

**Employment-at-will**

There is no need to carve out an exception to the employment-at-will doctrine to recognize a cause of action for wrongful discharge in violation of public policy because, the legislature has already carved out the exception by enacting R.C. 4101.17, 4112.02(N), 4112.05, 4112.99: Napier v. VGC Corp., 797 F. Supp. 602, 1992 U.S. Dist. LEXIS 12914 (S.D. Ohio 1992).

**Equitable award**

State employee who established age discrimination against the Ohio Department of Natural Resources under R.C. 4112.14 and 4112.99 was entitled to an equitable award to compensate him for his increased tax burden as a result of a lump sum award, as such helped make the employee whole and assured him the most complete relief possible. Warden v. Ohio Dep't of Natural Res., 2013-Ohio-1512, 2013 Ohio Misc. LEXIS 12 (Ohio Ct. Cl. 2013), aff'd in part and rev'd in part, 2014-Ohio-35, 7 N.E.3d 533, 2014 Ohio App. LEXIS 25 (Ohio Ct. App., Franklin County 2014).

**Exhaustion of administrative remedies**

Court erred in granting summary judgment in favor of the school board, because a public employee alleging disability discrimination in violation of R.C. Chapter 4112 need not exhaust the administrative remedy of appeal to a civil service commission before pursuing the civil action allowed in this provision. Worley v. Newton Falls Exempted Vill. Sch. Bd. of Educ., 2014-Ohio-5385, 2014 Ohio App. LEXIS 5211 (Ohio Ct. App., Trumbull County 2014).

In a gender discrimination suit brought against an organization by a former member of the organization, the member's suit could not be deemed frivolous under R.C. 2323.51(A)(2)(a)(ii) by virtue of the fact that she failed to seek judicial review of a proceeding finding no probable cause to support the member's gender discrimination claim as an individual who opted to pursue a gender discrimination claim under R.C. ch. 4112 was not required to exhaust all of his or her administrative remedies prior to instituting a gender discrimination action at law. Gallagher v. AMVETS Post 17, 2009-Ohio-6348, 2009 Ohio App. LEXIS 5315 (Ohio Ct. App., Erie County 2009).

Terminated city fire chief who alleged employment discrimination in violation of R.C. ch. 4112 properly filed suit against the city and others under R.C. 4112.99 without first exhausting the internal administrative remedy of appeal to the city's civil service commission, as the failure to exhaust administrative remedies did not preclude such civil action. Dworning v. City of Euclid, 2008-Ohio-3318, 119 Ohio St. 3d 83, 892 N.E.2d 420, 2008 Ohio LEXIS 1768 (Ohio 2008).

When a fire chief who was separated from his employment sued a city for disability discrimination, under R.C. 4112.99, he did not have to exhaust his administrative remedies in the city's civil service commission as a predicate to filing suit because he was not claiming age discrimination, and the doctrine of exhaustion of administrative remedies was a judge-made "rule of convenience" which could not contradict the general assembly's provision of a clear statutory right which had priority over any other law, including the civil service commission's rules. Dworning v. City of Euclid, 2006-Ohio-6772, 2006 Ohio App. LEXIS 6685 (Ohio Ct. App., Cuyahoga County 2006), aff'd, 2008-Ohio-3318, 119 Ohio St. 3d 83, 892 N.E.2d 420, 2008 Ohio LEXIS 1768 (Ohio 2008).

**Federal jurisdiction**

In a removal action, former employer met its burden of showing that the amount-in-controversy exceeded the $50,000 jurisdictional minimum for removing the action to a federal court on diversity grounds: Szalay v. Yellow Freight Sys., 999 F. Supp. 972, 1996 U.S. Dist. LEXIS 22128 (N.D. Ohio 1996).

Federal District Court declined to exercise supplemental jurisdiction over plaintiff's state law discrimination claims alleging that employer paid male employees more than females for lack of substantial federal claim: Bielawski v. AMI, Inc., 870 F. Supp. 771, 1994 U.S. Dist. LEXIS 18385 (N.D. Ohio 1994).

**Federal preemption**

The federal reserve act does not preempt state employment discrimination claims against federal reserve banks: White v. Federal Reserve Bank, 103 Ohio App. 3d 534, 660 N.E.2d 493, 1995 Ohio App. LEXIS 1720 (Ohio Ct. App., Cuyahoga County), dismissed, 74 Ohio St. 3d 1416, 655 N.E.2d 737, 1995 Ohio LEXIS 2742 (Ohio 1995).

The Federal Home Loan Bank Act specifically empowers the institutions it governs to dismiss an employee "at pleasure" and thus preempts any contrary right created by state law: Kispert v. Federal Home Loan Bank, 778 F. Supp. 950, 1991 U.S. Dist. LEXIS 19868 (S.D. Ohio 1991).

**Front pay**

State employee who was not offered a full-time position based on the Ohio Department of Natural Resources' policy not to rehire a retiree suffered age discrimination under R.C. 4112.14 and 4112.99, and he was entitled to an award of front pay, as he would have accepted the position for a five-year period if it had been offered to him, and he did not have a reasonable prospect of obtaining comparable employment. Warden v. Ohio Dep't of Natural Res., 2013-Ohio-1512, 2013 Ohio Misc. LEXIS 12 (Ohio Ct. Cl. 2013), aff'd in part and rev'd in part, 2014-Ohio-35, 7 N.E.3d 533, 2014 Ohio App. LEXIS 25 (Ohio Ct. App., Franklin County 2014).

**Gender discrimination generally**

Employer was granted summary judgment on the gender discrimination claim under Ohio state law where the evidence did not show that the employer's decisional process was unworthy of credence, that any of the male comparators were proper, or that the sheer weight of the evidence suggested that the employer's proffered reasons were a cover-up for discrimination. Hale v. Mercy Health Partners, 20 F. Supp. 3d 620, 2014 U.S. Dist. LEXIS 67564 (S.D. Ohio 2014), aff'd, 617 Fed. Appx. 395, 2015 FED App. 270N, 2015 U.S. App. LEXIS 6283 (6th Cir. Ohio 2015).

Summary judgment on employee's claims brought under Equal Pay Act (EPA), 29 U.S.C.S. § 206 (d)(1), and R.C. 4111.17, 4112.02 and 4112.99 was denied because although a comparison of the work performed by the employee to the work performed by the male co-workers, during the relevant time-period, led the court to conclude that the employee's positions did not require equal effort and responsibility, the court was unable to conclude that the evidence presented by the employee was such that a reasonable jury could not return a verdict for the employee. Gonzalez v. Abercrombie & Fitch Co., 2008 U.S. Dist. LEXIS 52171 (S.D. Ohio July 7, 2008).

Police officer's claims of pregnancy discrimination under Title VII, 42 U.S.C.S. §§ 2000e-2(a)(1), 2000e(k), and R.C. 4112.02(A), 4112.99 failed because, even assuming that she made out a prima facie case, the officer failed to rebut a city's legitimate and nondiscriminatory reason for not granting her request for a restricted duty assignment, that it had a policy prohibiting such assignment, by showing it to be a pretext for unlawful discrimination. The officer presented no evidence refuting the police chief's position that the city had a policy of no light duty, and, thus, she failed to demonstrate the falsity of the city's reason for not accommodating her condition. Tysinger v. Police Dep't, 463 F.3d 569, 2006 FED App. 0363P, 2006 U.S. App. LEXIS 24144 (6th Cir. Ohio 2006).

Police officer's claims of pregnancy discrimination under Title VII, 42 U.S.C.S. §§ 2000e-2(a)(1), 2000e(k), and R.C. 4112.02(A), 4112.99 need not have also been evaluated as sex discrimination claims where her complaint, which contained two counts, each alleging "pregnancy discrimination, a form of sex discrimination," did not allege sex discrimination apart from pregnancy discrimination; the officer's allegations regarding the city police department's refusal to grant her a position in a detective bureau or a position processing impound lot vehicles were included as support for her claims that the department wrongfully failed to accommodate her pregnancy, not to substantiate separate sex discrimination claims. Moreover, the claims would not be evaluated under separate standards, and, the merits of such claims were fatally undercut by the officer's acknowledgement that the opening she applied for was really not an opening. Tysinger v. Police Dep't, 463 F.3d 569, 2006 FED App. 0363P, 2006 U.S. App. LEXIS 24144 (6th Cir. Ohio 2006).

Where the Equal Employment Opportunity Commission (EEOC) sued an employer, alleging gender discrimination under Title VII, 42 U.S.C.S. §§ 2000e-5, 2000e-6, a motion to intervene was granted as a matter of right under Fed. R. Civ. P. 24(a)(1) where an individual's federal claims paralleled those of the EEOC and her claim under R.C. 4112.99 did not reach beyond its complaint. Moreover, pendent jurisdiction would not violate federal policy that specifically limited the scope of federal jurisdiction, and, finally, the district court's hearing the individual's state law claim, pursuant to 28 U.S.C.S. § 1367(a), along with the Title VII claim would serve the interests of judicial economy. EEOC v. Pitt-Ohio Express, Inc., 2006 U.S. Dist. LEXIS 54989 (N.D. Ohio Aug. 8, 2006).

After reviewing evidence presented, the court found that a nursing student had presented sufficient evidence to establish a prima facie case of pregnancy discrimination. It was undisputed that she was pregnant when she was subjected to an adverse employment decision, and evidence was submitted that the student was qualified for the job that she was seeking, and therefore the court denied the nursing facility's motion for summary judgment pursuant to Fed. R. Civ. P. 56. Davis v. E. Galbraith Health Care Ctr., 2005 U.S. Dist. LEXIS 33574 (S.D. Ohio July 11, 2005).

The employer was not entitled to a directed verdict in a gender discrimination case where the employee presented sufficient evidence that comparable male employees were "similarly situated" in all relevant respects: Kroh v. Cont'l Gen. Tire, Inc., 2001-Ohio-59, 92 Ohio St. 3d 30, 748 N.E.2d 36, 2001 Ohio LEXIS 1527 (Ohio 2001).

**Handicap discrimination**

In regard to handicap discrimination claims, the general assembly has not manifested an intent similar to that manifested regarding age discrimination claims, which requires a plaintiff to elect between an administrative or judicial remedy, so, had the general assembly intended that individuals alleging handicap discrimination be forced to choose between an administrative or civil proceeding, it would have specifically stated so, as it did with respect to age discrimination, and the Latin maxim expressio unius est exclusio alterius, which translated means that the expression of one item of a class implicitly excludes other items of the class that are not specifically mentioned, is instructive, as the general assembly has specifically limited an individual's ability to bring both an administrative and civil proceeding in the context of age discrimination only, and its exclusion of other forms of discrimination from this limitation makes clear that it intended that both remedies be available for other forms of discrimination. Dworning v. City of Euclid, 2006-Ohio-6772, 2006 Ohio App. LEXIS 6685 (Ohio Ct. App., Cuyahoga County 2006), aff'd, 2008-Ohio-3318, 119 Ohio St. 3d 83, 892 N.E.2d 420, 2008 Ohio LEXIS 1768 (Ohio 2008).

Employer was not entitled to summary judgment on an employee's disability discrimination claims where there were issues of fact as to whether the employer considered the employee disabled or unable to perform the functions of his job, whether the employee's perceived disability limited his ability to work, and whether the employer discriminated against the employee as a result of the perceived disability. Allen v. Deerfield Mfg., 424 F. Supp. 2d 987, 2006 U.S. Dist. LEXIS 13870 (S.D. Ohio 2006).

A former employee asserted state law claims for handicap discrimination under R.C. 4112.01 and 4112.99; summary judgment for the employer on those claims was not proper because those claims involved the same essential elements as the employee's Americans with Disabilities Act claim under 42 U.S.C.S. § 12112(a) and summary judgment was not appropriate on that claim. Downs v. AOL Time Warner, Inc., 2006 U.S. Dist. LEXIS 4848 (S.D. Ohio Jan. 20, 2006).

**Housing discrimination**

Because emotional-distress damages were not inherent in the claim for housing discrimination, the inferred-intent doctrine was inapplicable. It could not be said that the personal injury was intended, nor that emotional distress was inherent in the very nature of housing discrimination. Granger v. Auto-Owners Ins., 2015-Ohio-3279, 144 Ohio St. 3d 57, 40 N.E.3d 1110, 2015 Ohio LEXIS 2080 (Ohio 2015).

The tenant's counterclaim based on alleged racial discrimination was properly raised in an eviction action for nonpayment of rent: Lable & Co. v. Flowers, 104 Ohio App. 3d 227, 661 N.E.2d 782, 1995 Ohio App. LEXIS 2295 (Ohio Ct. App., Lorain County 1995).

**Individual liability**

Individual employees may be liable for violations of the Ohio antidiscrimination law: DeLoach v. American Red Cross, 967 F. Supp. 265, 1997 U.S. Dist. LEXIS 9128 (N.D. Ohio 1997).

R.C. 4112.99 permits individual liability for acts that violate Ohio's employment discrimination law, despite the fact that this construction means that a broader class of individuals may be liable under state law than under federal law: Garraway v. Diversified Material Handling, 975 F. Supp. 1026, 1997 U.S. Dist. LEXIS 12918 (N.D. Ohio 1997).

There is no basis for individual liability under R.C. 4112.02: Dalton v. Jefferson Smurfit Corp. (U.S.), 979 F. Supp. 1187, 1997 U.S. Dist. LEXIS 15506 (S.D. Ohio 1997).

Employee's co-worker and supervisor could be held liable for sexual harassment in their individual capacities: Griswold v. Fresenius USA, 964 F. Supp. 1166, 1997 U.S. Dist. LEXIS 3741 (N.D. Ohio 1997).

**Intentional infliction of emotional distress**

Plaintiff's action for intentional infliction of emotional distress could be maintained against employer even though the actions of her supervisor were not calculated to promote the employer's business: Crihfield v. Monsanto Co., 844 F. Supp. 371, 1994 U.S. Dist. LEXIS 2614 (S.D. Ohio 1994).

**Judgment on pleadings**

In a case in which 16 police officers alleged employment discrimination in violation of 42 U.S.C.S. §§ 1983 and 2000e-2(a) and R.C. 4112.02 and 4112.99, the court denied defendants' motion for judgment on the pleadings because the allegations in the complaint permitted the officers to offer direct evidence of the discrimination complained of, and even if the McDonnell Douglas prima face case standard was applicable, that standard did not apply to the standard the officers had to satisfy to survive the motion for judgment on the pleadings. Grizzell v. City of Columbus, 2003 U.S. Dist. LEXIS 13393 (S.D. Ohio July 8, 2003).

**Jury trial**

A plaintiff may demand a jury trial on claims under R.C. 4112.99 where the gravamen of the claims is discrimination on the basis of sex: Taylor v. National Group of Cos., 1992-Ohio-68, 65 Ohio St. 3d 482, 605 N.E.2d 45, 1992 Ohio LEXIS 3130 (Ohio 1992).

**Just cause**

Employer and supervisors were entitled to summary judgment on a former employee's claim of age discrimination, in violation of R.C. 4112.02(A) and 4112.99, because multiple legitimate, nondiscriminatory reasons were asserted for terminating the employee's employment, and the employee failed to discredit the reasons that were offered as being a mere pretext. The multiple legitimate, nondiscriminatory reasons that were asserted for terminating the 51 year old employee's employment and, apparently, replacing the employee with a 43 year old employee included: (1) the employee hoarded relevant information; (2) the employee resisted change; (3) the employee's negative attitude and behavior towards co-workers; and (4) the employee's difficulty in responding to stressful situations. Wigglesworth v. Mettler Toledo Int'l, Inc., 2010-Ohio-1019, 2010 Ohio App. LEXIS 843 (Ohio Ct. App., Franklin County 2010).

Dishonesty, per se, is insufficient to render an individual unqualified, as a matter of law, to hold a position as a park ranger where there is evidence that it was a pretextual basis for racial discrimination: Smith v. Five Rivers Metroparks, 134 Ohio App. 3d 754, 732 N.E.2d 422, 1999 Ohio App. LEXIS 4286 (Ohio Ct. App., Montgomery County 1999).

Where employee repeatedly received reprimands for inaccurate test results, and revealed that she was not qualified for her position since she did not perform the essential functions of her job, employee's termination did not violate R.C. 4112.99 and did not amount to handicap discrimination: Bennett v. University Hosps., 981 F. Supp. 1065, 1997 U.S. Dist. LEXIS 17348 (N.D. Ohio 1997).



**McDonnell Douglas/Burdine formula**

Trial court erred by not granting a city's motion for a directed verdict in a police officer's employment discrimination action because the officer, who had been discharged upon pleading guilty to a charge of aggravated menacing in connection with a domestic violence incident in which he broke his wife's jaw and rendered her unconscious, did not offer evidence that he was replaced by a person outside of the protected classification and while the other officers who he offered as "comparables" may not have been exemplary officers, their offenses, which ranged from time sheet falsification to domestic violence resulting in lesser physical harm than that inflicted by the officer, did not make them "similarly situated." Williams v. City of Akron, 2003-Ohio-7197, 2003 Ohio App. LEXIS 6648 (Ohio Ct. App., Summit County 2003), aff'd, 2005-Ohio-6268, 107 Ohio St. 3d 203, 837 N.E.2d 1169, 2005 Ohio LEXIS 2836 (Ohio 2005).

The McDonnell Douglas/Burdine formula is the evidentiary framework applicable to claims brought under Title VII, but also to claims of discrimination under Ohio state law: Mitchell v. Toledo Hosp., 964 F.2d 577, 1992 U.S. App. LEXIS 11505 (6th Cir. Ohio 1992).

**Prima facie case**

Ethnic Arab-American employee met his burden of proof in response to the employer's summary judgment motion with respect to his claim of disparate treatment and retaliatory discharge under 42 U.S.C.S. § 2000e-2(a) of Title VII of the Civil Rights Act of 1964, as amended, 42 U.S.C.S. § 2000e et seq., and R.C. 4112.02(A) and 4112.99 of the Ohio Civil Rights Act, R.C. 4112.01 et seq., as he established a genuine issue of material fact regarding an adverse employment action by his constructive discharge, evidence that the employer created conditions with the intention of forcing the employee to resign, and that the employer's explanation was a mere pretext. Mohanna v. Jake Sweeney Auto., 2012 U.S. Dist. LEXIS 97413 (S.D. Ohio July 13, 2012).

Police officer's claims of pregnancy discrimination under Title VII, 42 U.S.C.S. §§ 2000e-2(a)(1), 2000e(k), and R.C. 4112.02(A), 4112.99 failed because she did not show a causal connection between the adverse action and the fact that her infirmity was the result of pregnancy; she could have continued working if able, but her doctor prescribed her light duty, which was unavailable. Further, the employees that she presented as comparable were not similarly situated in that, while they also suffered from temporary infirmities, they presented themselves as willing and able to continue working. Tysinger v. Police Dep't, 463 F.3d 569, 2006 FED App. 0363P, 2006 U.S. App. LEXIS 24144 (6th Cir. Ohio 2006).

Police officer's claims of pregnancy discrimination under Title VII, 42 U.S.C.S. §§ 2000e-2(a)(1), 2000e(k), and R.C. 4112.02(A), 4112.99 failed because, inter alia, even under a mixed motive analysis, she did not demonstrate that pregnancy discrimination was a motivating factor in the decision to deny her an accommodating restricted duty assignment. The police chief's statement that pregnancy was not a disability that the city was required to accommodate did not indicate unlawful discriminatory animus but, rather, was entirely consistent with the law; moreover, even if the chief's testimony was construed as potentially revealing a personal bias, it was undisputed that the decision to deny the officer a restricted duty assignment was consistent with the city's policy prohibiting light duty assignments, a policy that even the chief had no authority to alter or circumvent. Tysinger v. Police Dep't, 463 F.3d 569, 2006 FED App. 0363P, 2006 U.S. App. LEXIS 24144 (6th Cir. Ohio 2006).

After reviewing evidence presented, the court found that a nursing student had presented sufficient evidence to establish a prima facie case of pregnancy discrimination. It was undisputed that she was pregnant when she was subjected to an adverse employment decision, and evidence was submitted that the student was qualified for the job that she was seeking, and therefore the court denied the nursing facility's motion for summary judgment pursuant to Fed. R. Civ. P. 56. Davis v. E. Galbraith Health Care Ctr., 2005 U.S. Dist. LEXIS 33574 (S.D. Ohio July 11, 2005).

African American employee's disparate treatment claim survived summary judgment because, while the employer contended that the employee crossed off her name for a position that was filled by a less senior white person, the employee raised a genuine issue of material fact that she was led to believe by her supervisor that she should cross her name off the intent sheet in order to obtain another position. Then the supervisor prevented her from applying for the other position and from re-signing her name on the intent sheet for the original position. Clay v. UPS, 2005 U.S. Dist. LEXIS 13016 (N.D. Ohio June 30, 2005), aff'd in part and rev'd in part, 501 F.3d 695, 2007 FED App. 0354P, 2007 U.S. App. LEXIS 20945 (6th Cir. Ohio 2007).

African American employee's disparate treatment claim failed on summary judgment because, while the employee alleged that she was denied a position for which she was qualified and the most senior, and the position was filled by a white employee, the position was posted for the required period of time, albeit earlier than normal in relation to the time of the opening, and the employee failed to sign her name to the intent sheet. The employee showed no knowledge on behalf of management that she was interested in the job and no unique disadvantage on her part, given that several others who might have been eligible were subject to the same job posting schedule. Clay v. UPS, 2005 U.S. Dist. LEXIS 13016 (N.D. Ohio June 30, 2005), aff'd in part and rev'd in part, 501 F.3d 695, 2007 FED App. 0354P, 2007 U.S. App. LEXIS 20945 (6th Cir. Ohio 2007).

Employee's hostile work environment claim failed on summary judgment because, while the employee alleged that her supervisor berated her for minor conduct such as eating a donut on work time, there was insufficient evidence that the employee was harassed back on race. Also, the treatment was not so severe or pervasive as to unreasonably interfere with the employee's work performance. Clay v. UPS, 2005 U.S. Dist. LEXIS 13016 (N.D. Ohio June 30, 2005), aff'd in part and rev'd in part, 501 F.3d 695, 2007 FED App. 0354P, 2007 U.S. App. LEXIS 20945 (6th Cir. Ohio 2007).

African American employee failed to make a prima facie case of retaliation where he failed to allege facts to show that the adverse employment action, his termination, was caused by his filing of a discrimination charge some six months prior. Clay v. UPS, 2005 U.S. Dist. LEXIS 13016 (N.D. Ohio June 30, 2005), aff'd in part and rev'd in part, 501 F.3d 695, 2007 FED App. 0354P, 2007 U.S. App. LEXIS 20945 (6th Cir. Ohio 2007).

African American employee's disparate treatment claim failed on summary judgment because, while the employee alleged that he was suspended and eventually terminated due to an unequal application of policies, the employee could not make out a prima facie case because the employer did not make the suspension and termination decisions. Instead, the decisions were made by a joint labor management committee and the employer could not be held responsible. Clay v. UPS, 2005 U.S. Dist. LEXIS 13016 (N.D. Ohio June 30, 2005), aff'd in part and rev'd in part, 501 F.3d 695, 2007 FED App. 0354P, 2007 U.S. App. LEXIS 20945 (6th Cir. Ohio 2007).

**Public employer**

State employee who was not offered a full-time position based on the Ohio Department of Natural Resources' policy not to rehire a retiree suffered age discrimination under R.C. 4112.14 and 4112.99, and he was entitled to an award based on a lump sum payment from the Money Purchase Plan that he would have received pursuant to the pension through the Ohio Public Employees Retirement System. Warden v. Ohio Dep't of Natural Res., 2013-Ohio-1512, 2013 Ohio Misc. LEXIS 12 (Ohio Ct. Cl. 2013), aff'd in part and rev'd in part, 2014-Ohio-35, 7 N.E.3d 533, 2014 Ohio App. LEXIS 25 (Ohio Ct. App., Franklin County 2014).

Public employee alleging employment discrimination in violation of R.C. Chapter 4112 need not exhaust the administrative remedy of appeal to a civil service commission before pursuing the civil action allowed in R.C. 4112.99: Dworning v. City of Euclid, 2008-Ohio-3318, 119 Ohio St. 3d 83, 892 N.E.2d 420, 2008 Ohio LEXIS 1768 (Ohio 2008).

A metropolitan housing authority is a "public employer" as defined in R.C. 4117.01(B): Cincinnati Metro. Housing Authority v. State Employment Relations Bd., 53 Ohio St. 3d 221, 560 N.E.2d 179, 1990 Ohio LEXIS 360 (Ohio 1990).

**Public policy claims**

Tort claim for wrongful discharge in violation of the public policy against age discrimination did not exist because the jeopardy element of such a tort could not be established as Ohio Rev. Code ch. 4112 protected the policy through the remedies it offered in (1) R.C. 4112.02(N), allowing for any legal or equitable relief that would effectuate an individual's rights, (2) R.C. 4112.05(G), allowing enforcement actions by the Ohio Civil Rights Commission, (3) R.C. 4112.14(B), allowing "an appropriate remedy," which could include damages and injunctive relief, and (4) R.C. 4112.99, which subjected violators to a civil action for damages, injunctive relief, or other appropriate relief. Leininger v. Pioneer Nat'l Latex, 2007-Ohio-4921, 115 Ohio St. 3d 311, 875 N.E.2d 36, 2007 Ohio LEXIS 2229 (Ohio 2007).

Where a former employee alleged that the employer's co-owner sexually harassed her, the claim of wrongful discharge in violation of public policy failed to survive summary judgment because the Greeley claim did not satisfy the jeopardy requirement since the Ohio Civil Rights Act contained a sufficient remedy. Hollar v. RJ Coffey Cup, LLC, 505 F. Supp. 2d 439, 2007 U.S. Dist. LEXIS 52630 (N.D. Ohio 2007).

After citing a laundry list of case law in support, the employer argued that virtually every Ohio court had refused to recognize public policy claims premised on Ohio R.C. ch. 4112; the district court acknowledged that the Sixth Circuit Court of Appeals had often address public policy claims related to ch. 4112 by finding them necessarily invalid based on the circumstances in particular cases. Miller v. Burrows Paper Corp., 2007 U.S. Dist. LEXIS 27140 (S.D. Ohio Apr. 12, 2007).

An employee could not assert a wrongful discharge claim based on violation of public policy because the Americans with Disabilities Act (ADA), 42 U.S.C.S. § 12101 et seq., the Family and Medical Leave Act (FMLA), 29 U.S.C.S. § 2601 et seq., and the Ohio Civil Rights Act, R.C. 4112.01 et seq., all provided the employee with complete relief and adequately protected society's interests. Garcia v. Third Fed. S&L Ass'n of Cleveland, 2007 U.S. Dist. LEXIS 30887 (N.D. Ohio Apr. 26, 2007).

Broad scope of remedies available under R.C. 4112.99 is sufficient to vindicate Ohio's public policy against discrimination and thus forecloses a separate cause of action for violation of public policy. Schirmer v. Enerfab, Inc., 2006 U.S. Dist. LEXIS 64344 (S.D. Ohio Sept. 8, 2006).

Assistant nursing director and a nurse could not maintain their action for violation of Ohio's public policy arising out of their termination because they had a statutory cause of action in R.C. 4112.99. Reynolds v. Extendicare Health Servs., 2006 U.S. Dist. LEXIS 53406 (S.D. Ohio Aug. 1, 2006).

Since R.C. 4112.99 contained its own remedies for a violation of discrimination laws, a plaintiff could not assert a public policy claim under that statute in order to bring a wrongful discharge claim. Lewis v. Fairview Hosp., 2004-Ohio-1108, 156 Ohio App. 3d 387, 806 N.E.2d 185, 2004 Ohio App. LEXIS 975 (Ohio Ct. App., Cuyahoga County 2004).

Employee's claim that she was discharged because of her perceived disability satisfied the clarity element required for the tort of wrongful discharge in derogation of public policy: Kramer v. Windsor Park Nursing Home, 943 F. Supp. 844, 1996 U.S. Dist. LEXIS 16093 (S.D. Ohio 1996).

**Punitive damages**

Judgment notwithstanding the verdict was properly denied; because R.C. ch. 2744 did not apply to the officer's causes of action (gender-based discrimination, hostile work environment, and retaliation) because they were causally connected to her employment, R.C. 2744.05 could not be applied to prevent the imposition of punitive damages. However, since there was no language in R.C. 4112.02 or R.C. 4112.99 expressly authorizing an award of punitive damages against a political subdivision, the officer could not recover punitive damages against the board of trustees. Henderhan v. Jackson Twp. Police Dep't, 2009-Ohio-949, 2009 Ohio App. LEXIS 794 (Ohio Ct. App., Stark County 2009).

The $250,000 punitive damage award (permitted by R.C. 4112.99), based on race discrimination, was found not grossly excessive or arbitrary so as to constitute an arbitrary deprivation of property in violation of the Due Process Clause of the Fourteenth Amendment Waddell v. Roxane Labs., 2004-Ohio-2499, 2004 Ohio App. LEXIS 2021 (Ohio Ct. App., Franklin County 2004).

R.C. 4112.99 authorizes an award of punitive damages in civil employment discrimination actions: Rice v. CertainTeed Corp., 1999-Ohio-361, 84 Ohio St. 3d 417, 704 N.E.2d 1217, 1999 Ohio LEXIS 250 (Ohio 1999).

The employees established a prima facie case of age discrimination. The employer's conduct supported an award of punitive damages: Srail v. RJF Int'l Corp., 126 Ohio App. 3d 689, 711 N.E.2d 264, 1998 Ohio App. LEXIS 862 (Ohio Ct. App., Cuyahoga County), dismissed, 82 Ohio St. 3d 1473, 696 N.E.2d 602, 1998 Ohio LEXIS 1991 (Ohio 1998).

**Race discrimination**

African-American employee who was discharged during a reduction in force (RIF) presented evidence of aberrations in his RIF interview, evidence of his superior qualifications, and evidence of a discriminatory employment atmosphere which, when viewed in the aggregate, and in the light most favorable to the employee, established a genuine question of material fact under Fed. R. Civ. P. 56 as to whether the employer singled out the employee for discharge because of his race. Rachells v. Cingular Wireless Emple. Servs., LLC, 732 F.3d 652, 2013 FED App. 0295P, 2013 U.S. App. LEXIS 20979 (6th Cir. Ohio 2013).

Defendant was entitled to summary judgment on the plaintiff's claim that the defendant failed to promote him based on his race because the record established that the defendant repeatedly promoted the plaintiff, and as to the five promotions denied the plaintiff, the defendant awarded two of those positions, one of which would be a lateral move for the plaintiff, to minority males. Moreover, the defendant established that it selected candidates who were more qualified than the plaintiff or who performed better during interviews; accordingly, the record established that the defendant selected other applicants for those positions for legitimate, nondiscriminatory reasons. Rush v. E.I.duPont De Nemours & Co., 911 F. Supp. 2d 545, 2012 U.S. Dist. LEXIS 166356 (S.D. Ohio 2012).

Plaintiff could not establish a prima facie case of race discrimination based on discipline related to his attendance infractions since the written warning given to the plaintiff did not constitute adverse actions sufficient to establish a prima facie case of discrimination. Moreover, the plaintiff had not identified similarly situated comparators who were treated more favorably than he. Rush v. E.I.duPont De Nemours & Co., 911 F. Supp. 2d 545, 2012 U.S. Dist. LEXIS 166356 (S.D. Ohio 2012).

Employee could not assert race discrimination claims under R.C. 4112.02 and R.C. 4112.99 against the U.S. Postal Service because Title VII of the Civil Rights Act of 1964, 42 U.S.C.S. § 2000e et seq., provided the exclusive remedy for discrimination against federal employees. Williams v. United States Postal Serv., 2011 U.S. Dist. LEXIS 69396 (S.D. Ohio June 28, 2011).

Former employee's race discrimination claim under R.C. 4112.02(A) was dismissed for failure to state a claim under Civ. R. 12(B)(6) because the employee failed to state a claim of reverse race discrimination. The employee alleged that (1) an African-American coworker made unsubstantiated and untruthful claims accusing the employee, a Caucasian, of using racially derogatory and improper language; (2) the employer, through the actions of its African-American human resources manager, then involuntarily terminated the employee from the employee's employment; and (3) similar action was not taken regarding other employees. Morrissette v. DFS Servs., LLC, 2011-Ohio-2369, 2011 Ohio App. LEXIS 2023 (Ohio Ct. App., Franklin County 2011).

Court sustained defendants' motion for summary judgment on an African-American employee's hostile work environment claims brought under 42 U.S.C.S. § 1981 and R.C. 4112.02, 4112.99 because the employee allegations of being called a racially offensive name on two occasions between 1989-1991, seeing racially discriminatory graffiti on approximately 13 occasions between 2000-2005, learning that his coworkers had made a racially offensive statement in 2002-2003, and hearing a racially discriminatory word over his computerized system in approximately 2004, while reprehensible, was sufficiently not sufficiently severe and pervasive, as a matter of law, to be said to have altered the conditions of the employee's employment, and further, the employee also failed to satisfy his burden to set forth evidence indicating that the employer knew about the harassment but failed to take appropriate remedial action. Berryman v. SuperValu Holdings, Inc., 2010 U.S. Dist. LEXIS 32968 (S.D. Ohio Mar. 31, 2010), aff'd, 669 F.3d 714, 2012 FED App. 0053P, 2012 U.S. App. LEXIS 3823 (6th Cir. Ohio 2012).

Court sustained defendants' motion for summary judgment with regard to an African-American employee's racial discrimination claims based on disparate treatment under Title VII, 42 U.S.C.S. § 1981 and R.C. 4112.02, 4112.99 because the employee had not set forth sufficient evidence to create a genuine issue of material fact as to whether the individuals with whom he sought to compare his treatment were similarly situated with regard to any of his claims except the claim regarding a supervisor holding open a temporary job assignment for white coworker, rather than offering the assignment to the employee, and the employee had not pointed to sufficient evidence to demonstrate that the giving of a temporarily vacant job to a less senior employee than the employee was an adverse employment action as there was no evidence indicating that the reassignment included a salary or work hour change. Berryman v. SuperValu Holdings, Inc., — F. Supp. 2d —, 2010 U.S. Dist. LEXIS 32960 (S.D. Ohio Mar. 31, 2010), affirmed by 669 F.3d 714, 2012 U.S. App. LEXIS 3823, 2012 FED App. 53P (6th Cir.), 2012 FED App. 053P (6th Cir.), 95 Empl. Prac. Dec. (CCH) P44429, 114 Fair Empl. Prac. Cas. (BNA) 808 (6th Cir. Ohio 2012)supra.

Court sustained defendants' motion for summary judgment on an African-American employee's hostile work environment claims brought under 42 U.S.C.S. § 1981 and R.C. 4112.02, 4112.99 because (1) the facts did not indicate any racial connotation associated with the leave of absence incidents; (2) the seven instances of harassment occurred over a period that spanned greater than 20 years, and while the conduct was reprehensible, it was not sufficiently severe and pervasive to be said to have altered the conditions of the employee's employment; and (3) the employee had not satisfied his burden to set forth evidence indicating that the employer knew about the harassment but failed to take appropriate remedial action. Berryman v. SuperValu Holdings, Inc., — F. Supp. 2d —, 2010 U.S. Dist.

LEXIS 32960 (S.D. Ohio Mar. 31, 2010), affirmed by 669 F.3d 714, 2012 U.S. App. LEXIS 3823, 2012 FED App. 53P (6th Cir.), 2012 FED App. 053P (6th Cir.), 95 Empl. Prac. Dec. (CCH) P44429, 114 Fair Empl. Prac. Cas. (BNA) 808 (6th Cir. Ohio 2012)supra.

Job applicant failed to prove his claim of employment discrimination based on his race because, regardless of whether the applicant misunderstood the senior director and the administrative director when they offered him the position, or if the parties simply failed to reach mutually agreeable terms of compensation, the hospital did not reject the applicant for the position. Rather, the applicant failed to obtain the position because he did not accept any of the hospital's offers. Refaei v. Ohio State Univ. Hosp., 2010-Ohio-5911, 2010 Ohio Misc. LEXIS 346 (Ohio Ct. Cl. 2010), aff'd, 2011-Ohio-6727, 2011 Ohio App. LEXIS 5545 (Ohio Ct. App., Franklin County 2011).

Job applicant failed to prove his claim of employment discrimination based on his race because he did not meet his burden of proving that the hospital's stated reasons for not offering him the position were a pretext for discrimination. The applicant failed to prove that the senior director was untruthful in testifying that the chosen applicant's experience in performing computed tomography (CT) scans made him a more preferable candidate than the applicant and did not prove that discrimination was the reason for his not being hired. Refaei v. Ohio State Univ. Hosp., 2010-Ohio-5911, 2010 Ohio Misc. LEXIS 346 (Ohio Ct. Cl. 2010), aff'd, 2011-Ohio-6727, 2011 Ohio App. LEXIS 5545 (Ohio Ct. App., Franklin County 2011).

Summary judgment was granted in favor of the employer in race discrimination action brought under 42 U.S.C.S. § 2000e-2 of Title VII of the Civil Rights Act of 1964, 42 U.S.C.S. §§ 2000e et seq, 1981, 1983 and R.C. 4112.99 because the employee failed to show that the employer's reason for her demotion and termination were a pretext for discrimination and the employer submitted documents, deposition testimony, and affidavits supporting the factual predicate for her demotion and termination. Brown v. Ohio State Univ., 616 F. Supp. 2d 740, 2009 U.S. Dist. LEXIS 23476 (S.D. Ohio 2009), aff'd, 385 Fed. Appx. 486, 2010 FED App. 0418N, 2010 U.S. App. LEXIS 14298 (6th Cir. Ohio 2010).



Summary judgment was properly granted because the employee's bare assertions were not enough to make a prima facie case of discrimination; the employer proffered a legitimate, nondiscriminatory reason for the discharge—that the employee was terminated for violating company rules. Although the employee offered a different account of the events, he admitted using profanities; the employee did not present any evidence establishing that the employer discharged him for any reason other than having violated company rules. Harris v. Greater Cleveland Reg'l Transit Auth., 2008-Ohio-676, 2008 Ohio App. LEXIS 591 (Ohio Ct. App., Cuyahoga County 2008).

When a former teacher brought a race discrimination action against a public school district and certain of its administrators under federal law and R.C. 4112.02, 4112.99, and 4113.52, the teacher's inability to make a prima facie case of race discrimination under federal law resulted in summary judgment on his state law claims as well because the standard for the state law claims was the same as the standard for the federal claims. Pittman v. Cuyahoga Valley Career Ctr., 451 F. Supp. 2d 905, 2006 U.S. Dist. LEXIS 60411 (N.D. Ohio 2006).

When a former teacher brought a race discrimination action against a public school district and certain of its administrators under federal law and R.C. 4112.02, 4112.99, and 4113.52, the teacher's inability to make a prima facie case of race discrimination under federal law resulted in summary judgment on his state law claims as well because the standard for the state law claims was the same as the standard for the federal claims. Pittman v. Cuyahoga Valley Career Ctr., 451 F. Supp. 2d 905, 2006 U.S. Dist. LEXIS 60411 (N.D. Ohio 2006).

Employer was not entitled to summary judgment on an employee's racial discrimination claim where a reasonable jury could have found that the employer thwarted his attempts to submit an application, thereby committing racial discrimination. Allen v. Deerfield Mfg., 424 F. Supp. 2d 987, 2006 U.S. Dist. LEXIS 13870 (S.D. Ohio 2006).

In an action in which a former employee filed suit against his former employer alleging race discrimination in violation of Title VII, 42 U.S.C.S. § 2000e et seq., and Ohio's civil rights statute, R.C. 4112.02/4112.99; hostile work environment; wrongful discharge; and retaliation in violation of R.C. 4112.02(I), 4112.99, the employer's motion for summary judgment was denied on the race discrimination claim; a reasonable juror could conclude that the reason given for his termination was a pretext for discrimination because it had no basis in fact, did not motivate his discharge, and was insufficient to warrant his discharge. The court reasoned in part that the employee presented evidence that the employer's substance abuse policy did not require termination for a violation. Satterwhite v. Faurecia Exhaust Sys., 2005 U.S. Dist. LEXIS 10282 (S.D. Ohio May 31, 2005).

African American employee's disparate treatment claim survived summary judgment because, while the employer contended that the employee crossed off her name for a position that was filled by a less senior white person, the employee raised a genuine issue of material fact that she was led to believe by her supervisor that she should cross her name off the intent sheet in order to obtain another position. Then the supervisor prevented her from applying for the other position and from re-signing her name on the intent sheet for the original position. Clay v. UPS, 2005 U.S. Dist. LEXIS 13016 (N.D. Ohio June 30, 2005), aff'd in part and rev'd in part, 501 F.3d 695, 2007 FED App. 0354P, 2007 U.S. App. LEXIS 20945 (6th Cir. Ohio 2007).

Employee's hostile work environment claim failed on summary judgment because, while the employee alleged that her supervisor berated her for minor conduct such as eating a donut on work time, there was insufficient evidence that the employee was harassed back on race. Also, the treatment was not so severe or pervasive as to unreasonably interfere with the employee's work performance. Clay v. UPS, 2005 U.S. Dist. LEXIS 13016 (N.D. Ohio June 30, 2005), aff'd in part and rev'd in part, 501 F.3d 695, 2007 FED App. 0354P, 2007 U.S. App. LEXIS 20945 (6th Cir. Ohio 2007).

African American employee's disparate treatment claim that alleged a failure to train did not survive summary judgment because, while the employee alleged that he was denied certain training that had been promised to him, there was no issue of fact that similarly situated employees were treated more favorably. Notably, the employee's initial grievance regarding this matter was brought on behalf of himself and a group of white employees. Clay v. UPS, 2005 U.S. Dist. LEXIS 13016 (N.D. Ohio June 30, 2005), aff'd in part and rev'd in part, 501 F.3d 695, 2007 FED App. 0354P, 2007 U.S. App. LEXIS 20945 (6th Cir. Ohio 2007).

District court erred by granting summary judgment to defendant university in a professor's discrimination suit under Title VII of the Civil Rights Act of 1964, 42 U.S.C.S. §§ 2000e-2000e-17; R.C. 4112.02; and R.C. 4112.99; administrator's comments that a department head was racist and trying to "whitewash" the department, though not direct evidence of discrimination, were evidence of pretext and were not "isolated" because they were a response to the professor's inquiry. Carter v. Univ. of Toledo, 349 F.3d 269, 2003 FED App. 0401P, 2003 U.S. App. LEXIS 23054 (6th Cir. Ohio 2003).

**Reinstatement**

State employee who was not offered a full-time position based on the Ohio Department of Natural Resources' policy not to rehire a retiree suffered age discrimination under R.C. 4112.14 and 4112.99, but he was not entitled to reinstatement in the circumstances, as the person hired to the position had already been there for three years, and the employee had only intended to work in the position for five years. Warden v. Ohio Dep't of Natural Res., 2013-Ohio-1512, 2013 Ohio Misc. LEXIS 12 (Ohio Ct. Cl. 2013), aff'd in part and rev'd in part, 2014-Ohio-35, 7 N.E.3d 533, 2014 Ohio App. LEXIS 25 (Ohio Ct. App., Franklin County 2014).

**Res judicata**

When an employee sued his former employer in federal court under both 42 U.S.C.S. § 2000-e and R.C. 4112.99, and the federal court dismissed the federal claim and exercised pendent jurisdiction over the state law claim and dismissed it on its merits, res judicata barred the employee from subsequently bringing a suit in state court against the employer in which he raised a whistleblower claim. Watson v. Parma Cmty. Gen. Hosp., 2006-Ohio-712, 2006 Ohio App. LEXIS 628 (Ohio Ct. App., Cuyahoga County 2006).

**Reverse discrimination**

While an employer took an adverse action with respect to an employee's employment, by terminating the employee's employment, there was no evidence to support the employee's reverse race discrimination claim that the employer discriminated against non-minority employees and/or treated the employee disparately than other employees similarly situated as no other similarly situated, minority employee had two active suspensions, such as the employee had, nor did any other employee commit a dishonest act, such as the employee did. Hunter v. Bureau of Workers' Comp., 2016-Ohio-8577, 2016 Ohio Misc. LEXIS 131 (Ohio Ct. Cl. 2016).

Where an employee at a residential care facility alleged reverse gender discrimination relating to employment opportunities, the claim survived summary judgment because a genuine issue of material fact existed regarding whether the employee was qualified for a position and whether the employee refused, or was even asked, to take a computer proficiency test. Turner v. Grande Pointe Healthcare Cmty., 631 F. Supp. 2d 896, 2007 U.S. Dist. LEXIS 66711 (N.D. Ohio 2007).

Where an employee at a residential care facility alleged reverse gender discrimination relating to unequal pay, the claim failed because the employer met its burden of proof on an affirmative defense since the employer's interest in controlling attrition was a factor other than sex, and the employee could not show that the employer's affirmative defense was pretext. Turner v. Grande Pointe Healthcare Cmty., 631 F. Supp. 2d 896, 2007 U.S. Dist. LEXIS 66711 (N.D. Ohio 2007).

Where an employee at a residential care facility alleged reverse gender discrimination relating to employment opportunities, the claim survived summary judgment because a genuine issue of material fact existed regarding whether the employee was qualified for a position and whether the employee refused, or was even asked, to take a computer proficiency test. Turner v. Grande Pointe Healthcare Cmty., 631 F. Supp. 2d 896, 2007 U.S. Dist. LEXIS 66711 (N.D. Ohio 2007).

Where an employee at a residential care facility alleged reverse gender discrimination relating to unequal pay, the claim failed because the employer met its burden of proof on an affirmative defense since the employer's interest in controlling attrition was a factor other than sex, and the employee could not show that the employer's affirmative defense was pretext. Turner v. Grande Pointe Healthcare Cmty., 631 F. Supp. 2d 896, 2007 U.S. Dist. LEXIS 66711 (N.D. Ohio 2007).

Summary judgment was properly granted on a former employee's reverse discrimination claim against the company for which the employee had worked and the African American owners of the company because there was no genuine issue of material fact that the employee was replaced by a Caucasian employee after he was terminated; thus, the employee was unable to prove that he was replaced by someone outside the protected class. The African American employee, by whom the employee alleged that he was replaced, was not hired until eight months after the employee was terminated. James v. Bob Ross Buick, Inc., 2006-Ohio-2638, 167 Ohio App. 3d 338, 855 N.E.2d 119, 2006 Ohio App. LEXIS 2490 (Ohio Ct. App., Montgomery County 2006).

The fact that the person in charge of hiring was an African-American was sufficient to satisfy the "background circumstances" requirement, creating an issue of material fact on a claim of reverse discrimination: Zambetti v. Cuyahoga Cmty. College, 314 F.3d 249, 2002 FED App. 0430P, 2002 U.S. App. LEXIS 26196 (6th Cir. Ohio 2002).

**Sexual harassment**

Summary judgment to a moving company owner and employee in an action by a former employee (FE), alleging sexual harassment and other claims as a result of the employer-owner's alleged actions, was error because the owner was within the statutory definition of "employer," he was a supervisor, the FE established his conduct that constituted sexual harassment, and he could be held individually liable. Retuerto v. Berea Moving Storage & Logistics, 2015-Ohio-2404, 38 N.E.3d 392, 2015 Ohio App. LEXIS 2448 (Ohio Ct. App., Cuyahoga County 2015).

Trial court did not err in denying an employer's motion for judgment notwithstanding the verdict pursuant to Civ.R. 50 in an employee's sexual harassment claim based on her supervisor's allegedly improper conduct towards her, as her settlement with the supervisor did not preclude a finding of liability on the part of the employer. The supervisor was subject to liability because he met the definition of an employer pursuant to R.C. 4112.01(A)(2), and as the supervisor and employer were jointly and severally liable pursuant to R.C. 4112.02(A) and 4112.99, the settlement of the supervisor did not relieve the employer from potential vicarious liability. Edwards v. Ohio Inst. of Cardiac Care, 2007-Ohio-1333, 170 Ohio App. 3d 619, 868 N.E.2d 721, 2007 Ohio App. LEXIS 1214 (Ohio Ct. App., Greene County 2007).

Admonishing an employee for frequent tardiness and absenteeism and for wasting supplies and making costly mistakes does not constitute sexual or racial harassment: Bell v. Cuyahoga Community College, 129 Ohio App. 3d 461, 717 N.E.2d 1189, 1998 Ohio App. LEXIS 3741 (Ohio Ct. App., Cuyahoga County 1998).

Sexual harassment on the job is undoubtedly an intentional infliction of emotional distress. Such claims are subject to the statute of limitations for R.C. 4112.99: Johnson v. Cox, 1997 Ohio App. LEXIS 1346 (Ohio Ct. App., Adams County Mar. 28, 1997).

**Sexually hostile work environment**

Although explicitly sexual comments and conversations in an office where common and indiscriminate, the fact that the offensive conduct was explicitly sexual and patently degrading to women showed that it was based on sex for purposes of establishing a prima facie case of a sexually hostile work environment under Ohio Rev. Stat. Ann. § 4112.99. Gallagher v. C.H. Robinson Worldwide, Inc., 567 F.3d 263, 2009 FED App. 0184P, 2009 U.S. App. LEXIS 10933 (6th Cir. Ohio 2009).

**State employees**

Employee's state law claims under R.C. 4112.02 and 4112.99, alleging disability discrimination by the state agency that employed her, were time-barred pursuant to R.C. 2743.16(A), as she failed to commence her state action within the two-year period after she was "unequivocally informed" of the alleged adverse action underlying the complaint. Longstreet v. Indus. Comm'n of Ohio, 2007-Ohio-1883, 2007 Ohio Misc. LEXIS 79 (Ohio Ct. Cl. 2007).

Where a corrections officer's racial and sexual discrimination claim, based on her termination, was brought against a correctional institution and alleged a claim under R.C. 4112.02(A) and 4112.99, the two-year limitations period of R.C. 2743.16(A) was applicable and barred the complaint; as R.C. 4112.99 was not amended to provide that the State had "consented to be sued" for such a claim prior to the enactment of the Court of Claims Act, for purposes of R.C. 2743.02, the two-year period was applicable. McCoy v. Toledo Corr. Inst., 2005-Ohio-1848, 2005 Ohio App. LEXIS 1753 (Ohio Ct. App., Franklin County 2005).

The court of claims has exclusive jurisdiction over a state employee's age discrimination claim under R.C. 4112.99: Honnold v. Wagenknecht, 113 Ohio App. 3d 427, 680 N.E.2d 1312, 1996 Ohio App. LEXIS 3451 (Ohio Ct. App., Franklin County 1996), dismissed, 77 Ohio St. 3d 1514, 674 N.E.2d 370, 1997 Ohio LEXIS 81 (Ohio 1997).

**Statute of limitations**

Retiree's R.C. 4112.02(A) and 4112.99 claim alleging racial discrimination was pre-empted by federal law and was time-barred under 29 U.S.C.S. § 160(b) even though it was originally based upon state law, as the claim was based on the Special Attrition Plan, which was an agreement directly resulting from the collective bargaining process between an employer and the union, and it was necessary to construe the plan in order to decide if a violation of R.C. ch. 4112 had occurred; the six-year limitations period under R.C. 2305.07 did not apply. Gordon v. GMC, 2012-Ohio-863, 2012 Ohio App. LEXIS 759 (Ohio Ct. App., Trumbull County 2012).

Former employee failed to show that the six-year statute of limitation in R.C. 2305.07, which was applicable to claims brought under R.C. 4112.99 for violations of R.C. ch. 4112.02(I), governed the employee's common law claims of wrongful discharge and retaliation against two former supervisors. Therefore, the four-year statute of limitations under R.C. 2305.09(D), which provided the general limitation period for tort actions not specifically covered by other statutory sections, applied to the employee's common law claims. Davenport v. Big Bros. & Big Sisters of the Greater Miami Valley, Inc., 2010-Ohio-2503, 2010 Ohio App. LEXIS 2046 (Ohio Ct. App., Montgomery County 2010).

As an employee failed to file her age discrimination claims pursuant to R.C. 4112.02 and 4112.99 within the 180-day statute of limitations, they were properly dismissed pursuant to Civ.R. 12(B)(6). Goodyear v. Waco Holdings, Inc., 2009-Ohio-619, 2009 Ohio App. LEXIS 546 (Ohio Ct. App., Cuyahoga County 2009).

Employer was entitled to summary judgment in a pro se action filed by a former employee; the employee's discrimination claim under R.C. 4112.99 regarding the denial of a transfer was barred under the six-year statute of limitations, R.C. 2305.07, and the savings statute, R.C. 2305.19. While the employee's refiling of her case the first time was within the statute of limitations and an appropriate use of the savings statute, her third complaint was not. Rogers v. Daimlerchrysler Corp., 588 F. Supp. 2d 804, 2008 U.S. Dist. LEXIS 97487 (N.D. Ohio 2008).

State university employee's claim under R.C. 4112.99, alleging that the university failed to rehire the employee after his original position was abolished due to age discrimination, was not time-barred because the action was filed within the two-year limitations period under R.C. 2743.16. Knepper v. Ohio State Univ., 2008-Ohio-4796, 2008 Ohio Misc. LEXIS 207 (Ohio Ct. Cl. 2008), aff'd, 2011-Ohio-6054, 2011 Ohio App. LEXIS 4943 (Ohio Ct. App., Franklin County 2011).

When an employee sued a state university for money damages for discrimination, R.C. 2743.16 stated the applicable statute of limitations, rather than R.C. 2305.07 or 4112.99, which provided a six-year limitations period, because the state did not consent to be sued for money damages for discrimination until a 1987 amendment to R.C. 4112.99, so it did not so consent prior to the enactment of R.C. 2743.01 et seq. in 1975, as it could not have so consented because it could not consent to waive sovereign immunity for purposes of a remedy that was not available at the time of the waiver. McFadden v. Cleveland State Univ., 2007-Ohio-298, 2007 Ohio App. LEXIS 244 (Ohio Ct. App., Franklin County 2007).

Employee's state law claims under R.C. 4112.02 and 4112.99, alleging disability discrimination by the state agency that employed her, were time-barred pursuant to R.C. 2743.16(A), as she failed to commence her state action within the two-year period after she was "unequivocally informed" of the alleged adverse action underlying the complaint. Longstreet v. Indus. Comm'n of Ohio, 2007-Ohio-1883, 2007 Ohio Misc. LEXIS 79 (Ohio Ct. Cl. 2007).

Trial court committed plain error in dismissing an employee's race and disability discrimination action under R.C. 4112.99 where it relied on the wrong limitations period; as the limitations period was controlled by R.C. 2305.07 and the action was brought within that six-year period, dismissal was error. Jackson v. Int'l Fiber, 2006-Ohio-5799, 169 Ohio App. 3d 395, 863 N.E.2d 189, 2006 Ohio App. LEXIS 5750 (Ohio Ct. App., Champaign County 2006).

Job applicant's age discrimination claim under R.C. 4112.02, .99 against her employer, an Ohio correctional institution, which she originally filed in federal court, voluntarily dismissed for lack of jurisdiction, and refiled in state court four months later, was properly dismissed as untimely because it was not filed within the 180-day limitations period of R.C. 4112.02(N); the doctrine of equitable tolling did not save the claims because the applicant did not show why she did not file the claim originally in state court or why it took her four months to refile it in state court after the voluntary dismissal of the federal claim, nor did she claim that she somehow was misled or tricked into filing the claim originally in the wrong court. McNeely v. Ross Corr. Inst., 2006-Ohio-5414, 2006 Ohio App. LEXIS 5408 (Ohio Ct. App., Franklin County 2006).

Trial court committed plain error in dismissing an employee's race and disability discrimination action under R.C. 4112.99 where it relied on the wrong limitations period; as the limitations period was controlled by R.C. 2305.07 and the action was brought within that six-year period, dismissal was error. Jackson v. Int'l Fiber, 2006-Ohio-5799, 169 Ohio App. 3d 395,

863 N.E.2d 189, 2006 Ohio App. LEXIS 5750 (Ohio Ct. App., Champaign County 2006).

Job applicant's age discrimination claim under R.C. 4112.02, .99 against her employer, an Ohio correctional institution, which she originally filed in federal court, voluntarily dismissed for lack of jurisdiction, and refiled in state court four months later, was properly dismissed as untimely because it was not filed within the 180-day limitations period of R.C. 4112.02(N). The doctrine of equitable tolling did not save the claims because the applicant did not show why she did not file the claim originally in state court or why it took her four months to refile it in state court after the voluntary dismissal of the federal claim, nor did she claim that she somehow was misled or tricked into filing the claim originally in the wrong court. McNeely v. Ross Corr. Inst., 2006-Ohio-5414, 2006 Ohio App. LEXIS 5408 (Ohio Ct. App., Franklin County 2006).

Former worker's age discrimination action met the statute of limitations requirement as the time began to run when the former employer made the decision not to hire the former worker and instead hire a younger worker. Yovanno v. Ryder Sys., 2003-Ohio-6824, 2003 Ohio App. LEXIS 6159 (Ohio Ct. App., Summit County 2003).

Employee filed claim of disability discrimination pursuant to R.C. 4112.99 within the six-year time period; since the trial court ruled on the based solely on statute of limitations grounds, its grant of summary judgment was in error. Barlowe v. AAAA Int'l Driving, 2003-Ohio-5748, 2003 Ohio App. LEXIS 5097 (Ohio Ct. App., Montgomery County 2003).

The limitations period applicable to R.C. 4112.14 age-discrimination claims is six years. Ohio law recognizes a claim for tortious wrongful termination in violation of public policy based on age discrimination: Ferraro v. B.F. Goodrich Co., 2002-Ohio-4398, 149 Ohio App. 3d 301, 777 N.E.2d 282, 2002 Ohio App. LEXIS 4549 (Ohio Ct. App., Lorain County 2002).

Since R.C. Chapter 4112. is the proper foundation for a claim of intentional infliction of emotional distress premised on sexual harassment, the six-year statute of limitations applicable to claims under R.C. 4112.99 applies to such claims: Johnson v. Cox, 1997 Ohio App. LEXIS 1346 (Ohio Ct. App., Adams County Mar. 28, 1997).

Employee's age discrimination claim was time barred where the alleged discriminatory act occurred on August 11, 1995, and employee did not file her complaint until September 26, 1996: Wallace v. Trumbull Mem. Hosp., 970 F. Supp. 618, 1997 U.S. Dist. LEXIS 11544 (N.D. Ohio 1997).

The 180-day limitations period is applicable to age based discrimination claims under R.C. 4112.02 and 4112.99 not the six-year statute of limitations under R.C. 2305.07: Dunn v. Medina Gen. Hosp., 917 F. Supp. 1185, 1996 U.S. Dist. LEXIS 6311 (N.D. Ohio 1996).

The statute of limitations for claims under R.C. 4112.99 is six years. A school bus driver's termination is not a result of sex discrimination where her motor vehicle violations render her uninsurable: Gaus v. Westerville City Sch. Dist. Bd. of Educ., 99 Ohio App. 3d 170, 650 N.E.2d 148, 1994 Ohio App. LEXIS 5505 (Ohio Ct. App., Franklin County 1994).

R.C. 4112.99 is a remedial statute, and is thus subject to R.C. 2305.07's six-year statute of limitations: Cosgrove v. Williamsburg of Cincinnati Management Co., 1994-Ohio-295, 70 Ohio St. 3d 281, 638 N.E.2d 991, 1994 Ohio LEXIS 2064 (Ohio 1994).

Ohio age discrimination claims brought under R.C. 4112.99 are not governed by a six-year statute of limitations, but are governed by either a one year or 180 day period of limitations: Vana v. Mallinckrodt Medical, 849 F. Supp. 576, 1994 U.S. Dist. LEXIS 5245 (N.D. Ohio 1994), aff'd, 70 F.3d 116, 1995 U.S. App. LEXIS 37592 (6th Cir. Ohio 1995).

Statute of limitations for actions brought under R.C. 4112.99 is either four or six years; R.C. 4112.99 is remedial, not penal: Gatlin v. Stark County Bd. of Mental Retardation & Developmental Disabilities, 1993 Ohio App. LEXIS 5462 (Ohio Ct. App., Stark County Nov. 8, 1993), aff'd, 1995-Ohio-90, 74 Ohio St. 3d 2, 655 N.E.2d 406, 1995 Ohio LEXIS 2275 (Ohio 1995).

The statute of limitations for claims brought under R.C. 4112.99 is one year. The six month limitation of R.C. 4112.05 does not apply: Lewis v. Cotton Club Bottling Co., 87 Ohio App. 3d 63, 621 N.E.2d 862, 1993 Ohio App. LEXIS 2053 (Ohio Ct. App., Summit County 1993).

Former employee's claim for sexual harassment, brought within one year, was not time barred because whether R.C. 4112.99 is viewed as a penalty or remedy, the statute of limitations is no shorter than one year, and at most six years: Kester v. Lake Area Recovery Ctr., 834 F. Supp. 226, 1993 U.S. Dist. LEXIS 11825 (N.D. Ohio 1993).

The one year statute of limitations found in R.C. 2305.11, applies to claims brought under R.C. 4112.99: Duvall v. Titan Equip. Corp., 1992 Ohio App. LEXIS 3310 (Ohio Ct. App., Cuyahoga County June 25, 1992), dismissed, 65 Ohio St. 3d 1454, 602 N.E.2d 251, 1992 Ohio LEXIS 2828 (Ohio 1992).

Special provision of R.C. 4112.02(N) imposing a 180-day limit on claims of age discrimination prevails over the general relief afforded by R.C. 4112.99: Napier v. VGC Corp., 797 F. Supp. 602, 1992 U.S. Dist. LEXIS 12914 (S.D. Ohio 1992).

**Summary judgment**

Trial court lacked authority to grant summary judgment to an employer on an employee's entire complaint because the employer sought summary judgment solely on the claim of wrongful termination in violation of public policy but the employee had also raised claims for breach of contract regarding wages, expenses, and monies owed and violations of the Ohio Civil Rights Act. Clucas v. Rt. 80 Express, Inc., 2015-Ohio-2838, 2015 Ohio App. LEXIS 2743 (Ohio Ct. App., Summit County 2015).

Trial court erred by granting summary judgment to an employer in a sex discrimination case, brought under Ohio Code Rev. Ann. §§ 4112.02(A) and 4112.99, because a former employee introduced sufficient direct evidence of discrimination and sufficient evidence for summary judgment purposes that the reasons advanced by the employer for requesting the employee's resignation were pretextual. The employee presented evidence that board members of the employer stated they did not want a woman as head golf professional at the employer's golf course, that the employee knew that the president of the employer would have fired the employee if the employee had not resigned when requested, and that two of the employer's board members who voted to demand the employee's resignation were consistently hostile to the employee's employment on the basis of the employee's sex. Egli v. Congress Lake Club, 2010-Ohio-2444, 2010 Ohio App. LEXIS 2003 (Ohio Ct. App., Stark County 2010).

Defendants were granted summary judgment on an African-American employee's claim for retaliation under Title VII and/or R.C. 4112.02, 4112.99 because the employee conceded that he experienced no retaliation for engaging in activity protected by Title VII, and the employee made no argument and presented no facts in support of his retaliation claim. Berryman v. Supervalu Holdings, Inc., — F. Supp. 2d —, 2010 U.S. Dist. LEXIS 32969 (S.D. Ohio Mar. 31, 2010), affirmed by 669 F.3d 714, 2012 U.S. App. LEXIS 3823, 2012 FED App. 53P (6th Cir.), 2012 FED App. 053P (6th Cir.), 95 Empl. Prac. Dec. (CCH) P44429, 114 Fair Empl. Prac. Cas. (BNA) 808 (6th Cir. Ohio 2012)supra.

Defendants were granted summary judgment on an African-American employee's claim for retaliation under Title VII and/or R.C. 4112.02, 4112.99 because the employee conceded that he experienced no retaliation for engaging in activity protected by Title VII, and the employee made no argument and presented no facts in support of his retaliation claim. Berryman v. SuperValu Holdings, Inc., 2010 U.S. Dist. LEXIS 32968 (S.D. Ohio Mar. 31, 2010), aff'd, 669 F.3d 714, 2012 FED App. 0053P, 2012 U.S. App. LEXIS 3823 (6th Cir. Ohio 2012).

Defendants were granted summary judgment on an African-American employee's claim for retaliation under Title VII and/or R.C. 4112.02, 4112.99 because the employee conceded that he experienced no retaliation for engaging in activity protected by Title VII, and the employee made no argument and presented no facts in support of his retaliation claim. Berryman v. SuperValu Holdings, Inc., — F. Supp. 2d —, 2010 U.S. Dist. LEXIS 32960 (S.D. Ohio Mar. 31, 2010), affirmed by 669 F.3d 714, 2012 U.S. App. LEXIS 3823, 2012 FED App. 53P (6th Cir.), 2012 FED App. 053P (6th Cir.), 95 Empl. Prac. Dec. (CCH) P44429, 114 Fair Empl. Prac. Cas. (BNA) 808 (6th Cir. Ohio 2012)supra.

In a former employee's disability discrimination suit, a trial court erred by granting summary judgment to his former supervisor based on determining that the former employee failed to state a separate claim against him because the definition of "employer" under R.C. 4112.01(A)(2) included supervisors in the definition of an employer and the complaint did state separate allegations against the former supervisor, including allegations of intentional infliction of emotional distress. However, the trial court properly granted summary judgment to the former employer based on claim preclusion because a federal jury's verdict in favor of the former employer disposed of all the claims against it, including the state claims. Price v. Carter Lumber Co., 2010-Ohio-4328, 2010 Ohio App. LEXIS 3658 (Ohio Ct. App., Summit County 2010).

Former employer was granted summary judgment in a former Hispanic employee's action alleging constructive discharge, discrimination on the basis of race, national origin or ancestry, and retaliation in violation of Title VII, 42 U.S.C.S. § 1981, and R.C. 4112.99, because (1) the fact that the employee was repeatedly passed over for promotions that he felt he should have received did not rise to the level of severity needed to show a constructive discharge; (2) the employee's failure to promote claim failed because he was not chosen for positions either because he was not the most qualified or had not applied; and (3) the employee's retaliation claim failed because the fact that he was subject to increased supervision following his internal complaints about discrimination was not tantamount to an adverse employment action. Alcala v. Whirlpool Corp., 675 F. Supp. 2d 765, 2009 U.S. Dist. LEXIS 118629 (N.D. Ohio 2009).

Employer was entitled to summary judgment in a former employee's action alleging retaliation under Title VII of the Civil Rights Act of 1964, 42 U.S.C.S. § 2000e et seq., and under R.C. 4112.99 of the Ohio Civil Rights Act, R.C. 4112.01 et seq.; the employee contended that she was terminated for complaining to the regional store manager of racist comments made by co-workers, but she failed to demonstrate temporal proximity between her complaints and her discharge. Johnson-Romaker v. Kroger Ltd. P'ship One, 609 F. Supp. 2d 719, 2009 U.S. Dist. LEXIS 19071 (N.D. Ohio 2009).

Employer was not entitled to summary judgment on an applicant's claims that the employer committed race discrimination, in violation of R.C. 4112.02(A), and retaliated against him, in violation of R.C. 4112.02(I). Although the employer claimed that it did not hire the applicant because he had felony convictions, evidence showed that the employer hired

Caucasian applicants who had felony convictions, and that evidence raised genuine issues of material fact about whether the employer used the fact that the applicant had felony convictions as a pretext for rejecting his application because he was African-American. Barrow v. Terminix Int'l Co., L.P., 2009 U.S. Dist. LEXIS 6433 (S.D. Ohio Jan. 29, 2009).

Summary judgment was precluded by genuine issues of material fact regarding whether a state university's failure to rehire an employee after his original position was abolished was due to age discrimination, or whether the university had a legitimate, nondiscriminatory reason for not rehiring the employee; questions regarding whether the university's reason was a mere pretext existed. Knepper v. Ohio State Univ., 2008-Ohio-4796, 2008 Ohio Misc. LEXIS 207 (Ohio Ct. Cl. 2008), aff'd, 2011-Ohio-6054, 2011 Ohio App. LEXIS 4943 (Ohio Ct. App., Franklin County 2011).

Trial court properly granted summary judgment to an employer in the former employee's disability discrimination claim under R.C. 4112.99, as she failed to show that her supervisors regarded her as disabled pursuant to R.C. 4112.01(A)(13); further, she also failed to show that her employer and supervisors took adverse employment action against her due to the disability, as her termination from employment was based on the fact that she exceeded the allowable leave of absence under the Family and Medical Leave Act, 29 U.S.C.S. § 2601 et seq. Hershberger v. Altercare, Inc., 2007-Ohio-1452, 2007 Ohio App. LEXIS 1314 (Ohio Ct. App., Stark County 2007).

Where an employee's position was eliminated while on maternity leave and the employee was terminated after returning, the state law discrimination claims survived summary judgment because, inter alia, factual disputes existed as to whether the employee's position, as opposed to that of a subordinate, was eliminated because the employee was on leave when a supervisor quit, and as to the legitimacy of the reasons advanced by defendants for the termination. Nocella v. Basement Experts of Am., 499 F. Supp. 2d 935, 2007 U.S. Dist. LEXIS 47384 (N.D. Ohio 2007).

Trial court's grant of summary judgment to a police chief in an action by a police dispatcher and her husband, alleging a variety of tort claims and work-related statutory claims in violation of R.C. 4112.02(A) and 4112.99, was proper as to the hostile environment sexual harassment claim against the chief, as he was not specifically included within that count of the complaint; rather, that form of discrimination was only alleged against the city and accordingly, the chief was properly granted summary judgment on that claim. Armaly v. City of Wapakoneta, 2006-Ohio-3629, 2006 Ohio App. LEXIS 3562 (Ohio Ct. App., Auglaize County 2006).

Trial court's grant of summary judgment to a police chief in an action by a police dispatcher and her husband, alleging a variety of tort claims and work-related statutory claims in violation of R.C. 4112.02(A) and 4112.99, was proper as to the hostile environment sexual harassment claim against the chief, as he was not specifically included within that count of the complaint; rather, that form of discrimination was only alleged against the city and accordingly, the chief was properly granted summary judgment on that claim. Armaly v. City of Wapakoneta, 2006-Ohio-3629, 2006 Ohio App. LEXIS 3562 (Ohio Ct. App., Auglaize County 2006).

Material fact disputes precluded summary judgment for an employer and a public official in an employee's gender discrimination lawsuit brought under 42 U.S.C.S. § 1983 for an alleged violation of the Equal Protection Clause of the Fourteenth Amendment and under R.C. 4112.02(A) and R.C. 4112.99. The employee offered sufficient evidence of pretext to create a triable issue: The employee proffered evidence that her successor was paid more than the employee for the same work and later was promoted to another managerial position over the employee; that while the successor had more budgeting experience than the employee, he had considerably less managerial experience in the public sector; that in addition to budgeting, managerial and supervisory tasks were primary components of the successor's positions while he worked for defendants; that, before posting the announcement for the position to which the successor was promoted, defendant official changed the job description for that position, apparently eliminating a requirement the successor did not meet; that the official expressed a preference for the successor during the hiring process; and that the official offered a different reason to the employee for not promoting her than was being offered in the instant lawsuit to justify that same decision. Herman v. Montgomery County Combined Health Dist., 2005 U.S. Dist. LEXIS 9333 (S.D. Ohio May 4, 2005).

District court properly granted summary judgment under Fed. R. Civ. P. 56 in an action against an automobile manufacturing employer by two employees who alleged racial discrimination in promotions in violation of 42 U.S.C.S. § 2000e-2 of Title VII of the Civil Rights Act of 1964, 42 U.S.C.S. § 2000e et seq., and in violation of R.C. 4112.99. As to the employees' disparate treatment claim, the employees failed to show that they were denied promotions for which they were eligible and failed to show that their applications for promotions would have been futile; as to the employees' disparate impact claim, the employees failed to show that the employer's requirements for attendance, time in a department, testing, and overtime activities in determining eligibility for promotion injured them personally. Bacon v. Honda of Am. Mfg., 370 F.3d 565, 2004 FED App. 0155P, 2004 U.S. App. LEXIS 10437 (6th Cir. Ohio 2004), cert. denied, 543 U.S. 1151, 125 S. Ct. 1334, 161 L. Ed. 2d 115, 2005 U.S. LEXIS 1537 (U.S. 2005).

Since a lack of a common law tort remedy would not jeopardize the public policy expressed by R.C. 4112.99 and the employee had to pursue her claim under that statute in order to vindicate whatever rights it granted her, summary judgment on the ground that she failed to meet the jeopardy element of her claim was not erroneous. Barlowe v. AAAA Int'l Driving, 2003-Ohio-5748, 2003 Ohio App. LEXIS 5097 (Ohio Ct. App., Montgomery County 2003).

Because the court found that the employee's direct and indirect claims under the Age Discrimination in Employment Act, 29 U.S.C.S. § 621 et seq., survived summary judgment, the court likewise found that her statutory claims under R.C. 4112.99 survived summary judgment. Abrams v. Millikin & Fitton Law Firm, 267 F. Supp. 2d 868, 2003 U.S. Dist. LEXIS 10459 (S.D. Ohio 2003).

Summary judgment was proper where the employee could not establish a prima facie case by showing that a comparable nonprotected employee was treated more favorably. The lapse of time precluded a claim of retaliation for protected activity: Baker v. Buschman Co., 127 Ohio App. 3d 561, 713 N.E.2d 487, 1998 Ohio App. LEXIS 2185 (Ohio Ct. App., Butler County 1998).

Summary judgment for the employer was proper where it articulated legitimate, nondiscriminatory reasons for not renewing the employee and the employee did not produce substantial evidence to support the claims of gender, age and religious discrimination: Doerter v. Bluffton College, 98 Ohio App. 3d 95, 647 N.E.2d 876, 1994 Ohio App. LEXIS 5661 (Ohio Ct. App., Allen County 1994).

**Summary judgment proper**

Dismissal of the employee's retaliation claims was appropriate because the employer provided an overwhelming amount of evidence substantiating its decision to terminate the employee; the employee was disciplined approximately 15 times for attendance violations and she provided inaccurate information about prior traffic citations. Gaither v. Toledo Area Reg'l Transit Auth., 2013-Ohio-3181, 2013 Ohio App. LEXIS 3247 (Ohio Ct. App., Lucas County 2013).

Ethnic Arab-American employee failed to meet his burden of proof in response to the employer's summary judgment motion with respect to his claim of hostile work environment under 42 U.S.C.S. § 2000e-2(a) of Title VII of the Civil Rights Act of 1964, as amended, 42 U.S.C.S. § 2000e et seq., and R.C. 4112.02(A) and 4112.99 of the Ohio Civil Rights Act, R.C. 4112.01 et seq., as to his damage claim for lost commissions and lost wages, as pursuant to Fed. R. Civ. P. 26 and 37, he failed to provide a calculation of those damages, and such failure was not substantially justified or harmless. Mohanna v. Jake Sweeney Auto., 2012 U.S. Dist. LEXIS 97413 (S.D. Ohio July 13, 2012).

Ethnic Arab-American employee failed to meet his burden of proof in response to the employer's summary judgment motion with respect to his claim of religious discrimination under 42 U.S.C.S. § 2000e-2(a) of Title VII of the Civil Rights Act of 1964, as amended, 42 U.S.C.S. § 2000e et seq., and R.C. 4112.02(A) and 4112.99 of the Ohio Civil Rights Act, R.C. 4112.01 et seq., as he failed to demonstrate a genuine issue of material fact on his failure to accommodate claims where he did not show that his constructive discharge related to his failure to comply with an employment requirement. Mohanna v. Jake Sweeney Auto., 2012 U.S. Dist. LEXIS 97413 (S.D. Ohio July 13, 2012).

Summary judgment to a city was properly granted in a hostile environment sexual harassment claim by a police dispatcher and her husband, in violation of R.C. 4112.02(A) and 4112.99, as they failed to satisfy two of the three necessary elements of the claim where there was no showing that the alleged harassment by a police chief to the dispatcher was unwelcome, and that the harassing conduct was sufficiently severe or pervasive to affect the terms, conditions, or privileges of employment, or any matter directly or indirectly related to employment. Armaly v. City of Wapakoneta, 2006-Ohio-3629, 2006 Ohio App. LEXIS 3562 (Ohio Ct. App., Auglaize County 2006).

**Wrongful discharge tort**

employee could not assert a wrongful discharge claim based on violation of public policy because the Americans with Disabilities Act (ADA), 42 U.S.C.S. § 12101 et seq., the Family and Medical Leave Act (FMLA), 29 U.S.C.S. § 2601 et seq., and the Ohio Civil Rights Act, R.C. 4112.01 et seq., all provided the employee with complete relief and adequately protected society's interests. Garcia v. Third Fed. S&L Ass'n of Cleveland, 2007 U.S. Dist. LEXIS 30887 (N.D. Ohio Apr. 26, 2007).

Broad scope of remedies available under R.C. 4112.99 is sufficient to vindicate Ohio's public policy against discrimination and thus forecloses a separate cause of action for violation of public policy. Schirmer v. Enerfab, Inc., 2006 U.S. Dist. LEXIS 64344 (S.D. Ohio Sept. 8, 2006).

Assistant nursing director and a nurse could not maintain their action for violation of Ohio's public policy arising out of their termination because they had a statutory cause of action in R.C. 4112.99. Reynolds v. Extendicare Health Servs., 2006 U.S. Dist. LEXIS 53406 (S.D. Ohio Aug. 1, 2006).

Assistant nursing director and a nurse could not maintain their action for retaliation in violation of R.C. 4112.99 because their employers had legitimate non-discriminatory reasons for terminating them when the director had consistently below-average performance and a lack of interest in improvement and the nurse repeatedly showed attitude problems and made negative comments. Reynolds v. Extendicare Health Servs., 2006 U.S. Dist. LEXIS 53406 (S.D. Ohio Aug. 1, 2006).

Employee's wrongful discharge in violation of public policy claim against his former employer failed as there already existed statutory remedies in 29 U.S.C.S. § 626(c)(1) and R.C. 4112.99 that adequately protected society's interests from age discrimination. Hutchens v. Weltman, Weinberg & Reis Co., LPA, 2005 U.S. Dist. LEXIS 21397 (S.D. Ohio Sept. 27, 2005).

## NOTES TO UNPUBLISHED DECISIONS

Analysis

Age discrimination
Summary judgment proper

**Age discrimination**

*Unpublished decision:* Where an employee was terminated for violating cash handling rules, the employee's age discrimination claims failed because the employee was unable to show that the employee was replaced by a younger worker or that a similarly situated employee was treated more favorably; misappropriation of funds and marrying alcohol were different circumstances involving distinguishable conduct. Balding-Margolis v. Cleveland Arcade, 352 Fed. Appx. 35, 2009 FED App. 0732N, 2009 U.S. App. LEXIS 24604 (6th Cir. Ohio 2009).

*Unpublished decision:* Where an employee was terminated for violating cash handling rules, the employee's age discrimination claims failed because the employee was unable to show that the employee was replaced by a younger worker or that a similarly situated employee was treated more favorably; misappropriation of funds and marrying alcohol were different circumstances involving distinguishable conduct. Balding-Margolis v. Cleveland Arcade, 352 Fed. Appx. 35, 2009 FED App. 0732N, 2009 U.S. App. LEXIS 24604 (6th Cir. Ohio 2009).

*Unpublished decision:* District court properly held that a fired 48-year-old employee did not establish a prima facie case of age discrimination under R.C. 4112.14 and 4112.99 because, although the employee was temporarily replaced by a 42-year-old man, the employee was ultimately replaced by a 54-year-old man. Counts v. Kraton Polymers, U.S. L.L.C., 260 Fed. Appx. 825, 2008 FED App. 0064N, 2008 U.S. App. LEXIS 2187 (6th Cir. Ohio 2008).

*Unpublished decision:* Where a 48-year-old employee was fired for failing a drug test, and claimed that three younger employees who were similarly situated to him were allowed to retake drug tests while he was not, the district court properly found that the employee was not similarly situated because the three alleged comparators' specimens could not be tested for reasons beyond their control, which stood in contrast to the employee's situation where his specimen was found to be not consistent with human urine. Counts v. Kraton Polymers, U.S. L.L.C., 260 Fed. Appx. 825, 2008 FED App. 0064N, 2008 U.S. App. LEXIS 2187 (6th Cir. Ohio 2008).

*Unpublished decision:* District court properly held that a fired 48-year-old employee did not establish a prima facie case of age discrimination under R.C. 4112.14 and § 4112.99 because, although the employee was temporarily replaced by a 42-year-old man, the employee was ultimately replaced by a 54-year-old man. Counts v. Kraton Polymers, U.S. L.L.C., 260 Fed. Appx. 825, 2008 FED App. 0064N, 2008 U.S. App. LEXIS 2187 (6th Cir. Ohio 2008).

*Unpublished decision:* Jury could reasonably have concluded that the employer chose the employee for the reduction in force at least, in part, to satisfy the expressed desire to "go after" older employees and stop losing young ones, and another's expressed belief that the company should look "young and aggressive" and not employ "old, tired programmers;" six of the seven RIF'd employees were over 40 years old, with plaintiff the oldest at 55. Coburn v. Rockwell Automation, Inc., 238 Fed. Appx. 112, 2007 FED App. 0467N, 2007 U.S. App. LEXIS 16632 (6th Cir. Ohio 2007).

**Summary judgment proper**

*Unpublished decision:* District court properly granted summary judgment for an employer in a former employee's action alleging age discrimination in violation of 29 U.S.C.S. § 623 of the Age Discrimination in Employment Act, 29 U.S.C.S. § 621 et seq., and in violation of R.C. 4112.14, 4112.99 in relation to the failure to promote; the employee failed to challenge the employer's assertion that the employee's violation of company policies amounted to poor performance rendering him unfit for promotion and, therefore, the employee did not meet his burden of establishing pretext. Rufo v. Dave & Busters, Inc., 2007 FED App. 0075N, 2007 U.S. App. LEXIS 2366 (6th Cir. Ohio Jan. 31, 2007).

## RESEARCH REFERENCES AND PRACTICE AIDS

**Cross-References to Related Sections**

Interference with fair housing rights, RC § 2927.03.
Liberal construction; bar to civil action, RC § 4112.08.

**Ohio Administrative Code**

Failure to file or filing a willfully false progress report. OAC 4112-7-01.
Punitive damages. OAC 4112-6-02.
Subpeonas. OAC 4112-3-13.

**Practice Manuals and Treatises**

Anderson's Ohio Civil Practice with Forms § 35.01 Generally
Anderson's Ohio Civil Practice with Forms § 35.02 Ohio Civil Rights Commission
Anderson's Ohio Consumer Law Manual § 12.28 Remedies
Anderson's Ohio Consumer Law Manual § 12.30 Civil Action

# TITLE 45

# MOTOR VEHICLES — AERONAUTICS — WATERCRAFT



# CHAPTER 4503

# LICENSING OF MOTOR VEHICLES

Homestead Exemption



Collegiate License Plates



## HOMESTEAD EXEMPTION

### § 4503.064 Definitions.

As used in sections 4503.064 to 4503.069 of the Revised Code:

(A) "Sixty-five years of age or older" means a person who will be age sixty-five or older in the calendar year following the year of application for reduction in the assessable value of the person's manufactured or mobile home.

(B) "Permanently and totally disabled" means that a person other than a disabled veteran has, on the first day of January of the year of application, including late application, for reduction in the assessable value of a manufactured or mobile home, some impairment in body or mind that makes the person unable to work at any substantially remunerative employment which the person is reasonably able to perform and which will, with reasonable probability, continue for an indefinite period of at least twelve months without any present indication of recovery therefrom or has been certified as permanently and totally disabled by a state or federal agency having the function of so classifying persons.

(C) "Homestead exemption" means the reduction in taxes allowed under division (A) of section 323.152 of the Revised Code for the year in which an application is filed under section 4503.066 of the Revised Code.

(D) "Manufactured home" has the meaning given in division (C)(4) of section 3781.06 of the Revised Code, and includes a structure consisting of two manufactured homes that were purchased either together or separately and are combined to form a single dwelling, but does not include a manufactured home that is taxed as real property pursuant to division (B) of section 4503.06 of the Revised Code.

(E) "Mobile home" has the meaning given in division (O) of section 4501.01 of the Revised Code and includes a structure consisting of two mobile homes that were purchased together or separately and combined to form a single dwelling, but does not include a mobile home that is taxed as real property pursuant to division (B) of section 4503.06 of the Revised Code.

(F) "Late application" means an application filed with an original application under division (A)(3) of section 4503.066 of the Revised Code.

(G) "Total income," "disabled veteran," "public service officer," and "killed in the line of duty" have the same meanings as in section 323.151 of the Revised Code.

**HISTORY:**
141 v H 182 (Eff 3-13-87); 142 v H 693 (Eff 3-17-89); 144 v H 66 (Eff 7-11-91); 147 v S 142 (Eff 3-30-99); 148 v S 6. Eff 8-12-99; 150 v H 369, § 1, eff. 11-26-04; 152 v H 119, § 101.01, eff. 6-30-07; 2013 HB 59, § 101.01, eff. Sept. 29, 2013; 2014 HB 85, § 1, eff. Sept. 11, 2014; 2020 hb17, § 1, effective January 15, 2021.

**Editor's Notes**

Acts 2020, HB 17, § 3 provides: "The amendment by this act of sections 323.151, 323.152, and 323.153 of the Revised Code applies to tax year 2020 and every tax year thereafter. The amendment by this act of sections 4503.064, 4503.065, and 4503.066 of the Revised Code applies to tax year 2021 and every tax year thereafter."

The provisions of § 803.06 of 152 v H 119 read as follows:

SECTION 803.06. The amendments by this act to sections 323.151, 323.152, 323.153, and 323.154 of the Revised Code are first effective for tax year 2007, and the amendments to sections 4503.064, 4503.065, 4503.066, and 4503.067 of the Revised Code are first effective for tax year 2008, and the following provisions shall apply:

(A) Notwithstanding the filing deadlines set forth in sections 323.153 and 4503.066 of the Revised Code, original applications requesting reductions pursuant to division (A) of section 323.152 or section 4503.065 of the Revised Code may be filed not later than October 1, 2007. Notwithstanding the deadlines set forth in division (A) of section 323.153 of the Revised Code for homesteads in a housing cooperative, not later than August 1, 2007, the nonprofit corporation that owns and operates the housing cooperative shall obtain original applications from the county auditor and provide one to each occupant in the cooperative. Not later than September 1, 2007, any occupant who may be eligible for the reduction in taxes under division (A) of section 323.152 of the Revised Code shall submit the completed application to the corporation. Not later than October 1, 2007, the corporation shall file all completed applications and the information required by division (B) of section 323.159 of the Revised Code with the county auditor of the county in which the occupants' homesteads are located.

(B) Notwithstanding the deadlines set forth in sections 323.154 and 4503.067 of the Revised Code, if an application requesting the reduction under division (A) of section 323.152 of the Revised Code for tax year 2007 or under section 4503.065 of the Revised Code for tax year 2008 is not approved or the county auditor otherwise determines that the homestead does not qualify for a reduction in taxes, the auditor's deadline to notify the applicant of the reasons for such denial shall be extended to November 1, 2007.

The provisions of § 3(B) of SB 6 (148 v —) read as follows:

SECTION 3. * * *

(B)(1) Except as otherwise provided in division (B)(2) of this section, the amendments made by this act to sections 4503.064 and 4503.065 of the Revised Code first apply to tax year 2000. A person whose manufactured or mobile home first becomes eligible for the reduction in assessable value or is entitled to an increased reduction for tax year 2000 because of the amendments made to either of those sections may apply for the reduction or increase therein for that year not later than 90 days after the effective date of this section, notwithstanding the filing requirements to the contrary under division (A)(2) of section 4503.066 of the Revised Code.

(2) Notwithstanding division (B)(2) of section 4503.065 of the Revised Code, as amended by this act, the adjustment to the dollar amount by which taxable value is reduced under that division shall be made first in calendar year 2002 and thereafter. The reduction resulting from that adjustment first applies to tax years 2003 and thereafter.

**Amendment Notes**

The 2020 amendment by HB 17, in (G), added "public service officer" and "killed in the line of duty"; and made related changes.

The 2014 amendment by HB 85 substituted "that a person other than a disabled veteran" for "a person who" in (B); and rewrote (G), which formerly read: "'Total income' has the same meaning as in section 323.151 of the Revised Code"; and made a stylistic change.

The 2013 amendment added (G).

152 v H 119, effective June 30, 2007, deleted (B) and (C), defining "total income" and "old age and survivors benefits received pursuant to the 'Social Security Act' " and "tier I railroad retirement benefits received pursuant to the 'Railroad Retirement Act' ", and redesignated the remaining subsections accordingly.

**RESEARCH REFERENCES AND PRACTICE AIDS**

**Cross-References to Related Sections**

County employees, RC § 4503.069.

State to reimburse county for tax reduction, RC § 4503.068.

### § 4503.065 Tax reduction for certain owners.

(A)(1) Division (A) of this section applies to any of the following persons:

Titles 39 — 57

(a) An individual who is permanently and totally disabled;

(b) An individual who is sixty-five years of age or older;

(c) An individual who is the surviving spouse of a deceased person who was permanently and totally disabled or sixty-five years of age or older and who applied and qualified for a reduction in assessable value under this section in the year of death, provided the surviving spouse is at least fifty-nine but not sixty-five or more years of age on the date the deceased spouse dies.

(2) The manufactured home tax on a manufactured or mobile home that is paid pursuant to division (C) of section 4503.06 of the Revised Code and that is owned and occupied as a home by an individual whose domicile is in this state and to whom this section applies, shall be reduced for any tax year for which an application for such reduction has been approved, provided the individual did not acquire ownership from a person, other than the individual's spouse, related by consanguinity or affinity for the purpose of qualifying for the reduction. An owner includes a settlor of a revocable or irrevocable inter vivos trust holding the title to a manufactured or mobile home occupied by the settlor as of right under the trust.

(a) For manufactured and mobile homes for which the tax imposed by section 4503.06 of the Revised Code is computed under division (D)(2) of that section, the reduction shall equal one of the following amounts, as applicable to the person:

(i) If the person received a reduction under this section for tax year 2007, the greater of the reduction for that tax year or the amount computed under division (A)(2)(b) of this section;

(ii) If the person received, for any homestead, a reduction under division (A) of this section for tax year 2014 or under division (A)(1) of section 323.152 of the Revised Code for tax year 2013 or the person is the surviving spouse of such a person and the surviving spouse is at least fifty-nine years of age on the date the deceased spouse dies, the amount computed under division (A)(2)(b) of this section. For purposes of divisions (A)(2)(a)(ii) and (iii) of this section, a person receives a reduction under division (A) of this section or division (A)(1) of section 323.152 of the Revised Code for tax year 2014 or 2013, respectively, if the person files a late application for that respective tax year that is approved by the county auditor under section 4503.066 or 323.153 of the Revised Code.

(iii) If the person is not described in division (A)(2)(a)(i) or (ii) of this section and the person's total income does not exceed thirty thousand dollars, as adjusted under division (A)(2)(e) of this section, the amount computed under division (A)(2)(b) of this section.

(b) The amount of the reduction under division (A)(2)(b) of this section equals the product of the following:

(i) Twenty-five thousand dollars of the true value of the property in money;

(ii) The assessment percentage established by the tax commissioner under division (B) of section 5715.01 of the Revised Code, not to exceed thirty-five per cent;

(iii) The effective tax rate used to calculate the taxes charged against the property for the current year, where "effective tax rate" is defined as in section 323.08 of the Revised Code;

(iv) The quantity equal to one minus the sum of the percentage reductions in taxes received by the property for the current tax year under section 319.302 of the Revised Code and division (B) of section 323.152 of the Revised Code.

(c) For manufactured and mobile homes for which the tax imposed by section 4503.06 of the Revised Code is computed under division (D)(1) of that section, the reduction shall equal one of the following amounts, as applicable to the person:

(i) If the person received a reduction under this section for tax year 2007, the greater of the reduction for that tax year or the amount computed under division (A)(2)(d) of this section;

(ii) If the person received, for any homestead, a reduction under division (A) of this section for tax year 2014 or under division (A)(1) of section 323.152 of the Revised Code for tax year 2013 or the person is the surviving spouse of such a person and the surviving spouse is at least fifty-nine years of age on the date the deceased spouse dies, the amount computed under division (A)(2)(d) of this section. For purposes of divisions (A)(2)(c)(ii) and (iii) of this section, a person receives a reduction under division (A) of this section or under division (A)(1) of section 323.152 of the Revised Code for tax year 2014 or 2013, respectively, if the person files a late application for a refund of overpayments for that respective tax year that is approved by the county auditor under section 4503.066 of the Revised Code.

(iii) If the person is not described in division (A)(2)(c)(i) or (ii) of this section and the person's total income does not exceed thirty thousand dollars, as adjusted under division (A)(2)(e) of this section, the amount computed under division (A)(2)(d) of this section.

(d) The amount of the reduction under division (A)(2)(d) of this section equals the product of the following:

(i) Twenty-five thousand dollars of the cost to the owner, or the market value at the time of purchase, whichever is greater, as those terms are used in division (D)(1) of section 4503.06 of the Revised Code;

(ii) The percentage from the appropriate schedule in division (D)(1)(b) of section 4503.06 of the Revised Code;

(iii) The assessment percentage of forty per cent used in division (D)(1)(b) of section 4503.06 of the Revised Code;

(iv) The tax rate of the taxing district in which the home has its situs.

(e) Each calendar year, the tax commissioner shall adjust the income threshold described in divisions (A)(2)(a)(iii) and (A)(2)(c)(iii) of this section by completing the following calculations in September of each year:

(i) Determine the percentage increase in the gross domestic product deflator determined by the bureau of economic analysis of the United States department of commerce from the first day of January of the preceding calendar year to the last day of December of the preceding calendar year;

(ii) Multiply that percentage increase by the total income threshold for the ensuing tax year;

(iii) Add the resulting product to the total income threshold for the ensuing tax year;

(iv) Round the resulting sum to the nearest multiple of one hundred dollars.

The commissioner shall certify the amount resulting from the adjustment to each county auditor not later than the first day of December each year. The certified amount applies to the second ensuing tax year. The commissioner shall not make the adjustment in any calendar year in which the amount resulting from the adjustment would be less than the total income threshold for the ensuing tax year.

(B) The manufactured home tax levied pursuant to division (C) of section 4503.06 of the Revised Code on a manufactured or mobile home that is owned and occupied by a disabled veteran shall be reduced for any tax year for which an application for such reduction has been approved, provided the disabled veteran did not acquire ownership from a person, other than the disabled veteran's spouse, related by consanguinity or affinity for the purpose of qualifying for the reduction. An owner includes an owner within the meaning of division (A)(2) of this section.

(1) For manufactured and mobile homes for which the tax imposed by section 4503.06 of the Revised Code is computed under division (D)(2) of that section, the reduction shall equal the product obtained by multiplying fifty thousand dollars of the true value of the property in money by the amounts described in divisions (A)(2)(b)(ii) to (iv) of this section.

(2) For manufactured and mobile homes for which the tax imposed by section 4503.06 of the Revised Code is computed under division (D)(1) of that section, the reduction shall equal the product obtained by multiplying fifty thousand dollars of the cost to the owner, or the market value at the time of purchase, whichever is greater, as those terms are used in division (D)(1) of section 4503.06 of the Revised Code, by the amounts described in divisions (A)(2)(d)(ii) to (iv) of this section.

The reduction is in lieu of any reduction under section 4503.0610 of the Revised Code or division (A) or (C) of this section. The reduction applies to only one manufactured or mobile home owned and occupied by a disabled veteran.

If a manufactured or mobile home qualifies for a reduction in taxes under this division for the year in which the disabled veteran dies, and the disabled veteran is survived by a spouse who occupied the home when the disabled veteran died and who acquires ownership of the home, the reduction shall continue through the year in which the surviving spouse dies or remarries.

(C) The manufactured home tax levied pursuant to division (C) of section 4503.06 of the Revised Code on a manufactured or mobile home that is owned and occupied by the surviving spouse of a public service officer killed in the line of duty shall be reduced for any tax year for which an application for such reduction has been approved, provided the surviving spouse did not acquire ownership from a person, other than the surviving spouse's deceased public service officer spouse, related by consanguinity or affinity for the purpose of qualifying for the reduction. An owner includes an owner within the meaning of division (A)(2) of this section.

(1) For manufactured and mobile homes for which the tax imposed by section 4503.06 of the Revised Code is computed under division (D)(2) of that section, the reduction shall equal the product obtained by multiplying fifty thousand dollars of the true value of the property in money by the amounts described in divisions (A)(2)(b)(ii) to (iv) of this section.

(2) For manufactured and mobile homes for which the tax imposed by section 4503.06 of the Revised Code is computed under division (D)(1) of that section, the reduction shall equal the product obtained by multiplying fifty thousand dollars of the cost to the owner, or the market value at the time of purchase, whichever is greater, as those terms are used in division (D)(1) of section 4503.06 of the Revised Code, by the amounts described in divisions (A)(2)(d)(ii) to (iv) of this section.

The reduction is in lieu of any reduction under section 4503.0610 of the Revised Code or division (A) or (B) of this section. The reduction applies to only one manufactured or mobile home owned and occupied by such a surviving spouse. A manufactured or mobile home qualifies for a reduction in taxes under this division for the tax year in which the public service officer dies through the tax year in which the surviving spouse dies or remarries.

(D) If the owner or the spouse of the owner of a manufactured or mobile home is eligible for a homestead exemption on the land upon which the home is located, the reduction to which the owner or spouse is entitled under this section shall not exceed the difference between the reduction to which the owner or spouse is entitled under division (A), (B), or (C) of this section and the amount of the reduction under the homestead exemption.

(E) No reduction shall be made with respect to the home of any person convicted of violating division (C) or (D) of section 4503.066 of the Revised Code for a period of three years following the conviction.

**HISTORY:**

141 v H 182 (Eff 3-13-87); 144 v H 66 (Eff 7-11-91); 144 v H 641 (Eff 10-6-92); 146 v H 117 (Eff 6-30-95); 147 v S 142 (Eff 3-30-99); 148 v S 6 (Eff 8-12-99); 149 v S 200. Eff 9-6-2002; 150 v H 127, § 1, eff. 3-11-04; 152 v H 119, § 101.01, eff. 6-30-07; 152 v H 130, § 1, eff. 4-7-09; 2013 HB 59, § 101.01, eff. Sept. 29, 2013; 2013 HB 72, § 1, eff. Jan. 30, 2014; 2013 HB 311, § 1, eff. Jan. 30, 2014; 2020 hb17, § 1, effective January 15, 2021.

**Editor's Notes**

Acts 2020, HB 17, § 3 provides: "The amendment by this act of sections 323.151, 323.152, and 323.153 of the Revised Code applies to tax year 2020 and every tax year thereafter. The amendment by this act of sections 4503.064, 4503.065, and 4503.066 of the Revised Code applies to tax year 2021 and every tax year thereafter."

Acts 2019, HB 166, § 757.150 provides: "(A) The amendment by this act of section 323.151 of the Revised Code applies to section 323.152 of the Revised Code for tax year 2020 and every tax year thereafter and to section 4503.065 of the Revised Code for tax year 2021 and every tax year thereafter."

The provisions of § 10, H.B. 127 (150 v —), read as follows:

SECTION 10. * (B) The amendment by this act of section 4503.065 of the Revised Code applies to taxes levied in 2005 and thereafter.

Acts 2013, HB 311, § 6 provides: "Sections 323.152 and 4503.065 of the Revised Code are amended by this act and also by H.B. 72 of the 130th General Assembly (effective January 30, 2014). The amendments of H.B. 72 are included in this act to confirm the intention to retain them, but are not intended to be effective until January 30, 2014."

**Amendment Notes**

The 2020 amendment by HB 17 added "or (C)" in the first sentence of the second paragraph of (B)(2); added (C); and redesignated former (C) and (D) as (D) and (E).

The 2013 amendment by HB 311, inserted "for any homestead" in the first sentence of (B)(1)(b) and (B)(3)(b).

The 2013 amendment by HB 72, inserted "or the person is the surviving spouse of such a person and the surviving spouse is at least fifty-nine years of age on the date the deceased spouse dies" in the first sentence of (B)(1)(b) and (B)(3)(b); substituted "is not described in division (B)(1)(a) or (b) of this section" for "did not receive a reduction under this section for tax year 2014 or under division (A) of section 323.152 of the Revised Code for tax year 2013" in (B)(1)(c); and substituted "is not described in division (B)(3)(a) or (b) of this section" for "did not receive a reduction under this section for tax year 2014 or under division (A) of section 323.152 of the Revised Code for tax year 2013" in (B)(3)(c).

The 2013 amendment by HB 59, added "persons" to the end of the introductory language of (A); substituted "one of the following amounts, as applicable to the person" for "the greater of the reduction granted for the tax year preceding the first tax year to which this section applies pursuant to Section 803.06 of Am. Sub. H.B. 119 of the 127th general assembly, if the taxpayer received a reduction for that preceding tax year, or" in the introductory language of (B)(1) and (B)(3); added (B)(1)(a) through (B)(1)(c), (B)(3)(a) through (B)(3)(c) and (B)(5); added the (B)(2) and (B)(4) designations; added "The amount of the reduction under division (B)(2) of this section equals" to the beginning of the introductory language of (B)(2); redesignated former (B)(2) as (B)(3); added "The amount of the reduction under division (B)(4) of this section equals" to the beginning of the introductory language of (B)(4); and made a related change.

152 v H 130, effective April 7, 2009, in the introductory paragraph of (B), substituted "an application for such reduction has been approved" for "the owner obtains a certificate of reduction from the county auditor under section 4503.067 of the Revised Code", and inserted "or irrevocable".

152 v H 119, effective June 30, 2007, rewrote the section.



### RESEARCH REFERENCES AND PRACTICE AIDS

**Cross-References to Related Sections**

Application for reduction; notice of change in eligibility, RC § 4503.066.
Approval or denial of reduction; appeal, RC § 4503.067.
Computation of tax on manufactured home, RC § 4503.06.
County employees, RC § 4503.069.
Homestead exemption definitions, RC § 4503.064.
Partial manufactured home tax exemption in counties with major league team, RC § 4503.0610.
State to reimburse county for tax reduction, RC § 4503.068.

## § 4503.066 Application for reduction; notice of change in eligibility.

(A)(1) To obtain a tax reduction under section 4503.065 of the Revised Code, the owner of the home shall file an application with the county auditor of the county in which the home is located. An application for reduction in taxes based upon a physical disability shall be accompanied by a certificate signed by a physician, and an application for reduction in taxes based upon a mental disability shall be accompanied by a certificate signed by a physician or psychologist licensed to practice in this state. The certificate shall attest to the fact that the applicant is permanently and totally disabled, shall be in a form that the department of taxation requires, and shall include the definition of totally and permanently disabled as set forth in section 4503.064 of the Revised Code. An application for reduction in taxes based upon a disability certified as permanent and total by a state or federal agency having the function of so classifying persons shall be accompanied by a certificate from that agency.

An application by a disabled veteran for the reduction under division (B) of section 4503.065 of the Revised Code shall be accompanied by a letter or other written confirmation from the United States department of veterans affairs, or its predecessor or successor agency, showing that the veteran qualifies as a disabled veteran.

An application by the surviving spouse of a public service officer killed in the line of duty for the reduction under division (C) of section 4503.065 of the Revised Code shall be accompanied by a letter or other written confirmation from an officer or employee of the board of trustees of a retirement or pension fund in this state or another state or from the chief or other chief executive of the department, agency, or other employer for which the public service officer served when killed in the line of duty affirming that the public service officer was killed in the line of duty.

(2) Each application shall constitute a continuing application for a reduction in taxes for each year in which the manufactured or mobile home is occupied by the applicant. Failure to receive a new application or notification under division (B) of this section after an application for reduction has been approved is prima-facie evidence that the original applicant is entitled to the reduction calculated on the basis of the information contained in the original application. The original application and any subsequent application shall be in the form of a signed statement and shall be filed on or before the thirty-first day of December of the year preceding the year for which the reduction is sought. The statement shall be on a form, devised and supplied by the tax commissioner, that shall require no more information than is necessary to establish the applicant's eligibility for the reduction in taxes and the amount of the reduction to which the applicant is entitled. The form shall contain a statement that signing such application constitutes a delegation of authority by the applicant to the tax commissioner or the county auditor, individually or in consultation with each other, to examine any tax or financial records that relate to the income of the applicant as stated on the application for the purpose of determining eligibility under, or possible violation of, division (C) or (D) of this section. The form also shall contain a statement that conviction of willfully falsifying information to obtain a reduction in taxes or failing to comply with division (B) of this section shall result in the revocation of the right to the reduction for a period of three years.



(3) A late application for a reduction in taxes for the year preceding the year for which an original application is filed may be filed with an original application. If the auditor determines that the information contained in the late application is correct, the auditor shall determine both the amount of the reduction in taxes to which the applicant would have been entitled for the current tax year had the application been timely filed and approved in the preceding year, and the amount the taxes levied under section 4503.06 of the Revised Code for the current year would have been reduced as a result of the reduction. When an applicant is permanently and totally disabled on the first day of January of the year in which the applicant files a late application, the auditor, in making the determination of the amounts of the reduction in taxes under division (A) (3) of this section, is not required to determine that the applicant was permanently and totally disabled on the first day of January of the preceding year.

The amount of the reduction in taxes pursuant to a late application shall be treated as an overpayment of taxes by the applicant. The auditor shall credit the amount of the overpayment against the amount of the taxes or penalties then due from the applicant, and, at the next succeeding settlement, the amount of the credit shall be deducted from the amount of any taxes or penalties distributable to the county or any taxing unit in the county that has received the benefit of the taxes or penalties previously overpaid, in proportion to the benefits previously received. If, after the credit has been made, there remains a balance of the overpayment, or if there are no taxes or penalties due from the applicant, the auditor shall refund that balance to the applicant by a warrant drawn on the county treasurer in favor of the applicant. The treasurer shall pay the warrant from the general fund of the county. If there is insufficient money in the general fund to make the payment, the treasurer shall pay the warrant out of any undivided manufactured or mobile home taxes subsequently received by the treasurer for distribution to the county or taxing district in the county that received the benefit of the overpaid taxes, in proportion to the benefits previously received, and the amount paid from the undivided funds shall be deducted from the money otherwise distributable to the county or taxing district in the county at the next or any succeeding distribution. At the next or any succeeding distribution after making the refund, the treasurer shall reimburse the general fund for any payment made from that fund by deducting the amount of that payment from the money distributable to the county or other taxing unit in the county that has received the benefit of the taxes, in proportion to the benefits previously received. On the second Monday in September of each year, the county auditor shall certify the total amount of the reductions in taxes made in the current year under division (A) (3) of this section to the tax commissioner who shall treat that amount as a reduction in taxes for the current tax year and shall make reimbursement to the county of that amount in the manner prescribed in section 4503.068 of the Revised Code, from moneys appropriated for that purpose.

(B)(1) If in any year for which an application for reduction in taxes has been approved the owner no longer qualifies for the reduction, the owner shall notify the county auditor that the owner is not qualified for a reduction in taxes.

(2) If the county auditor or county treasurer discovers that an owner not entitled to the reduction in manufactured home taxes under section 4503.065 of the Revised Code failed to notify the county auditor as required by division (B)(1) of this section, a charge shall be imposed against the manufactured or mobile home in the amount by which taxes were reduced under that section for each tax year the county auditor ascertains that the manufactured or mobile home was not entitled to the reduction and was owned by the current owner. Interest shall accrue in the manner prescribed by division (G)(2) of section 4503.06 of the Revised Code on the amount by which taxes were reduced for each such tax year as if the reduction became delinquent taxes at the close of the last day the second installment of taxes for that tax year could be paid without penalty. The county auditor shall notify the owner, by ordinary mail, of the charge, of the owner's right to appeal the charge, and of the manner in which the owner may appeal. The owner may appeal the imposition of the charge and interest by filing an appeal with the county board of revision not later than the last day prescribed for payment of manufactured home taxes under section 4503.06 of the Revised Code following receipt of the notice and occurring at least ninety days after receipt of the notice. The appeal shall be treated in the same manner as a complaint relating to the valuation or assessment of manufactured or mobile homes under section 5715.19 of the Revised Code. The charge and any interest shall be collected as other delinquent taxes.

(3) During January of each year, the county auditor shall furnish each person whose application for reduction has been approved, by ordinary mail, a form on which to report any changes in total income, ownership, occupancy, disability, and other information earlier furnished the auditor relative to the application. The form shall be completed and returned to the auditor not later than the thirty-first day of December if the changes would affect the person's eligibility for the reduction.

(C) No person shall knowingly make a false statement for the purpose of obtaining a reduction in taxes under section 4503.065 of the Revised Code.

(D) No person shall knowingly fail to notify the county auditor of any change required by division (B) of this section that has the effect of maintaining or securing a reduction in taxes under section 4503.065 of the Revised Code.

(E) No person shall knowingly make a false statement or certification attesting to any person's physical or mental condition for purposes of qualifying such person for tax relief pursuant to sections 4503.064 to 4503.069 of the Revised Code.

(F) Whoever violates division (C), (D), or (E) of this section is guilty of a misdemeanor of the fourth degree.

**HISTORY:**

141 v H 182 (Eff 3-13-87); 142 v H 693 (Eff 3-17-89); 144 v H 641 (Eff 10-6-92); 147 v S 142. Eff 3-30-99; 149 v S 123, § 1, eff. 1-1-04; 152 v H 119, § 101.01, eff. 6-30-07; 152 v H 130, § 1, eff. 4-7-09; 2013 HB 59, § 101.01, eff. Sept. 29, 2013; 2014 HB 85, § 1, eff. Sept. 11, 2014; 2017 hb49, § 101.01, effective September 29, 2017; 2018 hb292, § 1, effective September

13, 2018; 2020 hb17, § 1, effective January 15, 2021; 2021 hb110, § 101.01, effective September 30, 2021.

**Editor's Notes**

Acts 2020, HB 17, § 3 provides: "The amendment by this act of sections 323.151, 323.152, and 323.153 of the Revised Code applies to tax year 2020 and every tax year thereafter. The amendment by this act of sections 4503.064, 4503.065, and 4503.066 of the Revised Code applies to tax year 2021 and every tax year thereafter."

Acts 2018, HB 292, § 14 provides: "(A)(1) To obtain a tax reduction under section 4503.065 of the Revised Code, the owner of the home shall file an application with the county auditor of the county in which the home is located. An application for reduction in taxes based upon a physical disability shall be accompanied by a certificate signed by a physician, and an application for reduction in taxes based upon a mental disability shall be accompanied by a certificate signed by a physician or psychologist licensed to practice in this state. The certificate shall attest to the fact that the applicant is permanently and totally disabled, shall be in a form that the department of taxation requires, and shall include the definition of totally and permanently disabled as set forth in section 4503.064 of the Revised Code. An application for reduction in taxes based upon a disability certified as permanent and total by a state or federal agency having the function of so classifying persons shall be accompanied by a certificate from that agency. An application by a disabled veteran for the reduction under division (B) of section 4503.065 of the Revised Code shall be accompanied by a letter or other written confirmation from the United States department of veterans affairs, or its predecessor or successor agency, showing that the veteran qualifies as a disabled veteran.

"(2) Each application shall constitute a continuing application for a reduction in taxes for each year in which the manufactured or mobile home is occupied by the applicant. Failure to receive a new application or notification under division (B) of this section after an application for reduction has been approved is prima-facie evidence that the original applicant is entitled to the reduction calculated on the basis of the information contained in the original application. The original application and any subsequent application shall be in the form of a signed statement and shall be filed on or before the thirty-first day of December of the year preceding the year for which the reduction is sought. The statement shall be on a form, devised and supplied by the tax commissioner, that shall require no more information than is necessary to establish the applicant's eligibility for the reduction in taxes and the amount of the reduction to which the applicant is entitled. The form shall contain a statement that signing such application constitutes a delegation of authority by the applicant to the tax commissioner or the county auditor, individually or in consultation with each other, to examine any tax or financial records that relate to the income of the applicant as stated on the application for the purpose of determining eligibility under, or possible violation of, division (C) or (D) of this section. The form also shall contain a statement that conviction of willfully falsifying information to obtain a reduction in taxes or failing to comply with division (B) of this section shall result in the revocation of the right to the reduction for a period of three years.

"(3) A late application for a reduction in taxes for the year preceding the year for which an original application is filed may be filed with an original application. If the auditor determines that the information contained in the late application is correct, the auditor shall determine both the amount of the reduction in taxes to which the applicant would have been entitled for the current tax year had the application been timely filed and approved in the preceding year, and the amount the taxes levied under section 4503.06 of the Revised Code for the current year would have been reduced as a result of the reduction. When an applicant is permanently and totally disabled on the first day of January of the year in which the applicant files a late application, the auditor, in making the determination of the amounts of the reduction in taxes under division (A)(3) of this section, is not required to determine that the applicant was permanently and totally disabled on the first day of January of the preceding year.

The amount of the reduction in taxes pursuant to a late application shall be treated as an overpayment of taxes by the applicant. The auditor shall credit the amount of the overpayment against the amount of the taxes or penalties then due from the applicant, and, at the next succeeding settlement, the amount of the credit shall be deducted from the amount of any taxes or penalties distributable to the county or any taxing unit in the county that has received the benefit of the taxes or penalties previously overpaid, in proportion to the benefits previously received. If, after the credit has been made, there remains a balance of the overpayment, or if there are no taxes or penalties due from the applicant, the auditor shall refund that balance to the applicant by a warrant drawn on the county treasurer in favor of the applicant. The treasurer shall pay the warrant from the general fund of the county. If there is insufficient money in the general fund to make the payment, the treasurer shall pay the warrant out of any undivided manufactured or mobile home taxes subsequently received by the treasurer for distribution to the county or taxing district in the county that received the benefit of the overpaid taxes, in proportion to the benefits previously received, and the amount paid from the undivided funds shall be deducted from the money otherwise distributable to the county or taxing district in the county at the next or any succeeding distribution. At the next or any succeeding distribution after making the refund, the treasurer shall reimburse the general fund for any payment made from that fund by deducting the amount of that payment from the money distributable to the county or other taxing unit in the county that has received the benefit of the taxes, in proportion to the benefits previously received. On the second Monday in September of each year, the county auditor shall certify the total amount of the reductions in taxes made in the current year under division (A)(3) of this section to the tax commissioner who shall treat that amount as a reduction in taxes for the current tax year and shall make reimbursement to the county of that amount in the manner prescribed in section 4503.068 of the Revised Code, from moneys appropriated for that purpose.

"(B) If in any year for which an application for reduction in taxes has been approved the owner no longer qualifies for the reduction, the owner shall notify the county auditor that the owner is not qualified for a reduction in taxes.

During January of each year, the county auditor shall furnish each person whose application for reduction has been approved, by ordinary mail, a form on which to report any changes in total income, ownership, occupancy, disability, and other information earlier furnished the auditor relative to the application. The form shall be completed and returned to the auditor not later than the thirty-first day of December if the changes would affect the person's eligibility for the reduction.

"(C) No person shall knowingly make a false statement for the purpose of obtaining a reduction in taxes under section 4503.065 of the Revised Code.

"(D) No person shall knowingly fail to notify the county auditor of any change required by division (B) of this section that has the effect of maintaining or securing a reduction in taxes under section 4503.065 of the Revised Code.

"(E)No person shall knowingly make a false statement or certification attesting to any person's physical or mental condition for purposes of qualifying such person for tax relief pursuant to sections 4503.064 to 4503.069 of the Revised Code.

"(F) Whoever violates division (C), (D), or (E) of this section is guilty of a misdemeanor of the fourth degree.

Acts 2017, HB 49, § 803.330 provides: "The amendment by this act of section 4503.066 of the Revised Code shall apply to applications and forms due to the county auditor in tax year 2017 and thereafter."

**Amendment Notes**

The 2021 amendment by HB 110 redesignated former (B) as (B)(1) and (B)(3); and added (B)(2).

The 2020 amendment by HB 17 redesignated the former last sentence of the first paragraph of (A)(1) as the second paragraph of (A)(1); and added the last paragraph of (A)(1).

The 2018 amendment by HB 292 added "preceding the year" in the third sentence of (A)(2); deleted the former second paragraph of (A)(2), which read: "If an application filed for the current tax year is approved after the taxes have been paid for the current year, the amount of the reduction in taxes for the current year shall be treated as an overpayment of taxes in the same manner as a late application under division (A)(3) of this section"; added "On the second Monday in September of each year" in the last sentence of the second paragraph of (A)(3); and substituted "January" for "February" in the first sentence of the second paragraph of (B).

The 2017 amendment by HB 49 substituted "on or before the thirty-first day of December of the year for which the reduction is sought" for "not later than the first Monday in June" in the third sentence of (A)(2); added the second paragraph of (A)(2); deleted "On the second Monday in September of each year" at the beginning of the last sentence of the second paragraph of (A)(3); and in the second paragraph of (B), substituted "February" for "January" in the first sentence and "thirty-first day of December" for "first Monday in June" in the second sentence.

The 2014 amendment by HB 85 added the last sentence to (A)(1).

The 2013 amendment inserted the fifth sentence of (A)(2); and in the second paragraph of (B), inserted "total income" in the first sentence and added the second sentence.

152 v H 130, effective April 7, 2009, in (A)(2), substituted "an application for reduction has been approved" for "a certificate of reduction has been issued under section 4503.067 of the Revised Code"; and rewrote (B).

152 v H 119, effective June 30, 2007, rewrote the section.

### RESEARCH REFERENCES AND PRACTICE AIDS

**Cross-References to Related Sections**

Approval or denial of reduction; appeal, RC § 4503.067.
County employees, RC § 4503.069.
Homestead exemption definitions, RC § 4503.064.
State to reimburse county for tax reduction, RC § 4503.068.
Tax reduction for certain owners, RC § 4503.065.

## § 4503.067 Approval or denial of reduction; appeal.

The county auditor shall approve or deny an application for reduction under section 4503.065 of the Revised Code and shall so notify the applicant not later than the first Monday in October. Notification shall be provided on a form prescribed by the tax commissioner. If a person believes that the person's application for reduction in taxes has been improperly denied or is for less than that to which the person is entitled, the person may file an appeal with the county board of revision no later than the thirty-first day of January of the following calendar year. The appeal shall be treated in the same manner as a complaint relating to the valuation or assessment of real property under Chapter 5715. of the Revised Code.

**HISTORY:**

141 v H 182 (Eff 3-13-87); 142 v H 693 (Eff 3-17-89); 147 v S 142 (Eff 3-30-99); 148 v H 672. Eff 4-9-2001; 152 v H 119, § 101.01, eff. 6-30-07; 152 v H 130, § 1, eff. 4-7-09.

**Amendment Notes**

152 v H 130, effective April 7, 2009, rewrote the section.

152 v H 119, effective June 30, 2007, rewrote (A); and substituted "taxes" for "assessable value of a home" for (B).

**RESEARCH REFERENCES AND PRACTICE AIDS**

**Cross-References to Related Sections**

Application for reduction; notice of change in eligibility, RC § 4503.066.
County employees, RC § 4503.069.
Homestead exemption definitions, RC § 4503.064.
State to reimburse county for tax reduction, RC § 4503.068.
Tax reduction for certain owners, RC § 4503.065.



### § 4503.068 State to reimburse county for tax reduction; distribution.

On or before the second Monday in September of each year, the county treasurer shall total the amount by which the manufactured home taxes levied in that year were reduced pursuant to section 4503.065 of the Revised Code, and certify that amount to the tax commissioner. Within ninety days of the receipt of the certification, the commissioner shall provide for payment to the county treasurer, from the general revenue fund, of the amount certified, which shall be credited upon receipt to the county's undivided income tax fund, and an amount equal to two per cent of the amount by which taxes were reduced, which shall be credited upon receipt to the county general fund as a payment, in addition to the fees and charges authorized by sections 319.54 and 321.26 of the Revised Code, to the county auditor and county treasurer for the costs of administering sections 4503.064 to 4503.069 of the Revised Code.

Immediately upon receipt of funds into the county undivided income tax fund under this section, the county auditor shall distribute the full amount thereof among the taxing districts in the county as though it had been received as taxes under section 4503.06 of the Revised Code from each person for whom taxes were reduced under sections 4503.065 of the Revised Code.

**HISTORY:**

141 v H 182 (Eff 3-13-87); 142 v H 693. Eff 3-17-89; 151 v H 699, § 101.01, eff. 3-29-07; 152 v H 130, § 1, eff. 4-7-09; 153 v H 1, § 101.01, eff. 7-17-09.

**Amendment Notes**

153 v H 1, effective July 17, 2009, rewrote the first paragraph; and substituted "funds into the county undivided income tax fund under this section, the county auditor shall distribute the full amount thereof" for "the payment in the full amount by which taxes were reduced, the full amount of the payment shall be distributed" in the second paragraph.

152 v H 130, effective April 7, 2009, corrected internal references.

151 v H 699, effective March 29, 2007, in the first paragraph, substituted "director of budget and management and the director" for "auditor of state and the auditor".

**RESEARCH REFERENCES AND PRACTICE AIDS**

**Cross-References to Related Sections**

Application for reduction; notice of change in eligibility, RC § 4503.066.
County employees, RC § 4503.069.
Homestead exemption definitions, RC § 4503.064.

### § 4503.069 County employees.

Each county treasurer and county auditor shall employ the assistants, clerks, and other employees necessary to carry out the duties imposed by sections 4503.064 to 4503.069 of the Revised Code.

**HISTORY:**

141 v H 182. Eff 3-13-87.

**RESEARCH REFERENCES AND PRACTICE AIDS**

**Cross-References to Related Sections**

Homestead exemption definitions, RC § 4503.064.

## COLLEGIATE LICENSE PLATES

### § 4503.558 "Stop Elder Abuse" license plates.

(A) The owner or lessee of any passenger car, noncommercial motor vehicle, recreational vehicle, or other vehicle of a class approved by the registrar of motor vehicles may apply to the registrar for the registration of the vehicle and issuance of "Stop Elder Abuse" license plates. The application may be combined with a request for a special reserved license plate under section 4503.40 or 4503.42 of the Revised Code. Upon receipt of the completed application and compliance by the applicant with divisions (B) and (C) of this section, the registrar shall issue to the applicant the appropriate vehicle registration and a set of "Stop Elder Abuse" license plates and a validation sticker, or a validation sticker alone when required by section 4503.191 of the Revised Code.

In addition to the letters and numbers ordinarily inscribed on the license plates, "Stop Elder Abuse" license plates shall display the words "Stop Elder Abuse" and any other logo or words chosen by the registrar. "Stop Elder Abuse" license plates shall display county identification stickers that identify the county of registration as required under section 4503.19 of the Revised Code.

(B) "Stop Elder Abuse" license plates and a validation sticker, or validation sticker alone, shall be issued upon receipt of an application for registration of a motor vehicle under this section; payment of the regular license tax as prescribed under section 4503.04 of the Revised Code, any applicable motor vehicle license tax levied under Chapter 4504. of the Revised Code, any applicable additional fee prescribed by section 4503.40 or 4503.42 of the Revised Code, and an additional administrative fee of ten dollars; and compliance with all other applicable laws relating to the registration of motor vehicles.

(C) For each application for registration and registration renewal notice the registrar receives under this section, the registrar shall collect an administrative fee of ten dollars, the purpose of which is to compensate the bureau of motor vehicles for additional services required in the issuing of "Stop Elder Abuse" license plates. The registrar shall deposit the fee into the state treasury to the credit of the public safety - highway purposes fund created in section 4501.06 of the Revised Code.

**HISTORY:**

2020 sb163, § 1, effective October 23, 2020.

# TITLE 47

# OCCUPATIONS — PROFESSIONS



## CHAPTER 4717

## EMBALMERS, FUNERAL DIRECTORS, CREMATORIES



## PRENEED FUNERAL CONTRACTS

### § 4717.31 Preneed funeral contracts generally.

(A) Only a funeral director licensed pursuant to this chapter may sell a preneed funeral contract that includes funeral services. Sections 4717.31 to 4717.38 of the Revised Code do not prohibit a person who is not a licensed funeral director from selling funeral goods pursuant to a preneed funeral contract; however, when a seller sells funeral goods pursuant to a preneed funeral contract, that seller shall comply with those sections unless the seller is specifically exempt from compliance under section 4717.38 of the Revised Code.

(B) An insurance agent licensed pursuant to Chapter 3905. of the Revised Code may sell, solicit, or negotiate the sale of an insurance policy or annuity that will be used to fund a preneed funeral contract, but in so doing the insurance agent may not offer advice or make recommendations about funeral services and may not discuss the advantages or disadvantages of any funeral service. In selling, soliciting, or negotiating the sale of an insurance policy or annuity that will be used to fund a preneed funeral contract, the insurance agent may do any of the following:

(1) Provide the person purchasing the insurance policy or annuity with price lists from one or more funeral homes and other materials that may assist the person in determining the cost of funeral goods and services;

(2) Discuss the cost of funeral goods and services with the person in order to assist the person in selecting the appropriate amount of life insurance or annuity coverage;

(3) Complete a worksheet or other record to calculate the estimated cost of a funeral.

(C) Activities conducted pursuant to division (B) of this section by an insurance agent licensed pursuant to Chapter 3905. of the Revised Code do not constitute funeral directing, funeral arranging, the business of directing and supervising funerals for profit, or the sale of a preneed funeral contract.

(D) No seller shall fail to comply with the requirements and duties specified in this section and sections 4717.32 to 4717.38 of the Revised Code.

(E) No trustee of a preneed funeral contract trust shall fail to comply with sections 4717.33, 4717.34, 4717.36, and 4717.37 of the Revised Code.

(F) No insurance agent or insurance company that sells or offers life insurance policies or annuities used to fund a preneed funeral contract shall fail to comply with this section and sections 4717.33, 4717.34, 4717.35, and 4717.37 of the Revised Code. To the extent this section and sections 4717.33, 4717.34, 4717.35, and 4717.37 of the Revised Code apply to insurance companies or insurance agents, those sections constitute laws of this state relating to insurance for purposes of sections 3901.03 and 3901.04 of the Revised Code and the superintendent of insurance shall enforce those sections with respect to insurance companies and insurance agents. The superintendent may adopt rules in accordance with Chapter 119. of the Revised Code for purposes of administering and enforcing this section and sections 4717.33, 4717.34, 4717.35, and 4717.37 of the Revised Code as those sections apply to insurance companies or insurance agents.

(G) A preneed funeral contract may be funded by the purchase or assignment of an insurance policy or annuity in accordance with section 3905.45 of the Revised Code. A preneed funeral contract that is funded by the purchase or assignment of an insurance policy or annuity in accordance with section 3905.45 of the Revised Code is not subject to section 4717.36 of the Revised Code.

(H) The board of embalmers and funeral directors shall administer and enforce the provisions of sections 4717.31 to 4717.38 of the Revised Code concerning the requirements for and sale of preneed funeral contracts. The superintendent of insurance shall enforce sections 4717.31, 4717.33, 4717.34, 4717.35, and 4717.37 of the Revised Code to the extent those sections apply to insurance companies and insurance agents. Payments from a trust, insurance policy, or annuity, including any fraudulent activities in which a person engages to obtain payments from a trust, insurance policy, or annuity, shall be regulated in accordance with Chapter 1111. or Title XXXIX of the Revised Code, as applicable.

(I) Except as provided in division (K) of this section, a seller of a preneed funeral contract that is funded by insurance or otherwise annually shall submit to the board the reports the board requires pursuant to division (J) of this section.

(J) Except as provided in division (K) of this section, the board shall adopt rules specifying the procedures and requirements for annual reporting of the sales of all preneed funeral contracts sold by every seller who is subject to sections 4717.31 to 4717.38 of the Revised Code.

(K) A cemetery company or cemetery association that sells merchandise or services pursuant to a preneed cemetery merchandise and services contract and that also sells funeral goods pursuant to a preneed funeral contract shall be deemed to have met the requirements in divisions (I) and (J) of this section by submitting the annual preneed funeral contract report to the division of real estate of the department of commerce along with or as part of the annual cemetery merchandise and services contract affidavit required under division (F)(1) of section 1721.211 of the Revised Code.

**HISTORY:**

152 v S 196, § 1, eff. 7-7-09; 153 v H 1, § 101.01, eff. 10-16-09.

**Amendment Notes**

153 v H 1, effective October 16, 2009, added "Except as provided in division (K) of this section" to the beginning of (I) and (J); added (K); and made stylistic changes.

### § 4717.32 Contract to be in writing; required contents.

(A) Any preneed funeral contract that involves the payment of money or the purchase or assignment of an insurance policy or annuity shall be in writing and shall include all of the following information:

(1) The name, address, and phone number of the seller and the name and address of the purchaser of the contract, and, if the contract beneficiary is someone other than the purchaser of the contract, the name and address of the contract beneficiary, and if the contract involves the payment of money but not the purchase or assignment of an insurance policy or annuity, the social security number of the purchaser of the contract or if the contract beneficiary is someone other than the purchaser, the social security number of the contract beneficiary;

(2) A statement of the funeral goods and funeral services purchased, which disclosure may be made by attaching a copy of the completed statement of funeral goods and services selected to the preneed funeral contract;

(3) A disclosure informing the purchaser whether the contract is either a guaranteed preneed funeral contract or a nonguaranteed preneed funeral contract, and, if the contract is guaranteed only in part, a disclosure specifying the funeral goods or funeral services included in the guarantee;

(4) If the preneed funeral contract is a guaranteed contract, a disclosure that the seller, in exchange for all of the proceeds of the trust, insurance policy, or annuity, shall provide the funeral goods and funeral services set forth in the preneed funeral contract without regard to the actual cost of such funeral goods and funeral services prevailing at the time of performance and that the seller may receive any excess funds remaining after all expenses for the funeral have been paid.

(5) If the preneed funeral contract is a nonguaranteed contract, a disclosure that the proceeds of the trust, insurance policy, or annuity shall be applied to the retail prices in effect at the time of the funeral for the funeral goods and funeral services set forth in the contract, that any excess funds remaining after all expenses for the funeral have been paid shall be paid to the estate of the decedent or the beneficiary named in the life insurance policy if the preneed funeral contract is funded by a life insurance policy, and that, in the event of an insufficiency in funds, the seller shall not be required to perform until payment arrangements satisfactory to the seller have been made.

Titles 39 — 57

(6) A disclosure that the purchaser has the right to make the contract irrevocable and that if the preneed funeral contract is irrevocable, the purchaser does not have a right to revoke the contract;

(7) A disclosure informing the purchaser of the initial right to cancel the preneed funeral contract within seven days as provided in division (A) of section 4717.34 of the Revised Code and the right to revoke a revocable preneed funeral contract in accordance with section 4717.35 or division (G) of section 4717.36 of the Revised Code, as applicable;

(8) A disclosure that the seller may substitute funeral goods or funeral services of equal quality, value, and workmanship if those specified in the preneed funeral contract are unavailable at the time of need;

(9) A disclosure that any purchaser of funeral goods and funeral services is entitled to receive price information prior to making that purchase in accordance with the federal trade commission's funeral industry practices revised rule, 16 C.F.R. part 453;

(10) The following notice in boldface print and in substantially the following form:

**NOTICE: Under Ohio law, the person holding the right of disposition of the remains of the individual contract beneficiary pursuant to section 2108.70 or 2108.81 of the Revised Code will have the right to make funeral arrangements inconsistent with the arrangements set forth in this contract. However, the individual contract beneficiary is encouraged to state his or her preferences as to funeral arrangements in a declaration of the right of disposition pursuant to section 2108.72 of the Revised Code, including that the arrangements set forth in this contract shall be followed.**

(11) The notice described in division (A) of section 4717.34 of the Revised Code;

(12) A disclosure that any purchaser of funeral goods or funeral services funded in whole or in part in advance of death under a preneed funeral contract sold by a licensee under this chapter may be eligible for reimbursement of financial loses suffered as a result of malfeasance, misfeasance, default, failure, or insolvency of the licensee.

(B) If a preneed funeral contract is funded by any means other than an insurance policy or policies, or an annuity or annuities, the preneed funeral contract shall include all of the following information in addition to the information required to be included under division (A) of this section:

(1) Disclosures that identify the name and address of the trustee of the preneed funeral contract trust established pursuant to section 4717.36 of the Revised Code, that direct that any payments made by the purchaser of the preneed funeral contract shall be made directly to the trustee identified in the preneed funeral contract, that indicate whether fees, expenses, and taxes will be deducted from the trust, and that identify whether the trust or the purchaser will be responsible for the taxes owed on the trust earnings;

(2) A disclosure explaining the form in which the purchase price must be paid and, if the price is to be paid in installments, a disclosure to the purchaser regarding what constitutes a default under the preneed funeral contract and the consequences of the default;

(3) The following notice in boldface print and in substantially the following form:

"NOTICE: You, as the purchaser of this contract, will be notified in writing when the trustee of this contract has received a deposit of the funds you paid the seller under this contract. If you do not receive that notice within sixty days after the date you paid the funds to the seller, you should contact the trustee identified in the contract."

(4) A disclosure that if a preneed funeral contract stipulates a fixed or firm or guaranteed price for the funeral goods and services provided under the preneed funeral contract whether the seller will charge any initial service fee as permitted by division (B) of section 4717.36 and a cancellation or transfer fee as permitted by division (G)(2), (H), or (J) of section 4717.36 of the Revised Code.

(C) If a preneed funeral contract is funded by the purchase or assignment of one or more insurance policies or annuities, the preneed funeral contract shall include all of the following information in addition to the information required to be included under division (A) of this section:

(1) The name and address of each applicable insurance company and any right the purchaser has regarding canceling or transferring the applicable insurance policies or annuities;

(2) A directive that any payment made by the purchaser of the preneed funeral contract shall be made directly to the insurance company and, if premiums are being paid in installments, a description of the terms of payment for any remaining payments due;

(3) A list of actions that constitute default under a preneed funeral contract and the consequences of a default;

(4) The following notice in boldface print and in substantially the following form:

"NOTICE: You, as the purchaser of this contract, will be notified in writing by the insurance company identified in this contract when the insurance policy or policies, or annuity or annuities, that will fund this contract have been issued. If you do not receive the notice within sixty days after the date you paid the funds to the seller, you should contact the insurance company identified in the contract."

(D) The seller of a preneed funeral contract that is funded by the purchase or assignment of one or more insurance policies or annuities does not need to include in the contract the information described in divisions (C)(2) and (3) of this section if those disclosures are provided in the application for a life insurance policy or annuity or in the life insurance policy or annuity.

**HISTORY:**

152 v S 196, § 1, eff. 7-7-09; 2017 hb49, § 101.01, effective September 29, 2017.

**Amendment Notes**

The 2017 amendment by HB 49 substituted "division (G)" for "division (E)" in (A)(7); added (A)(12); rewrote (B)(1) and (B)(4); in (C)(2), added "directive that any payment made by the purchaser of the preneed funeral contract shall be made directly to the insurance company and, if premiums are being paid in installments, a" and deleted "if the funding is to be paid in installments" at the end; and made a related change.

### § 4717.33 Trustee or insurance company to notify purchaser of receipt of payment.

(A) If a preneed funeral contract is funded by any means other than an insurance policy or policies, or an annuity or annuities, the trustee of the trust created pursuant to section 4717.36 of the Revised Code shall notify the purchaser of the preneed funeral contract in writing, within fifteen days after the trustee receives any payment to be deposited into the trust, that the trustee has received payment. The notice shall include all of the following information:

(1) The amount the trustee received;

(2) The name and address of the institution described in division (D) of section 4717.36 of the Revised Code where the trust is being held; (3) The name of the beneficiary of that trust.

(B) If a preneed funeral contract is funded by the purchase or assignment of one or more insurance policies or annuities, the insurance company shall notify the purchaser of the preneed funeral contract in writing within sixty days after the insurance company receives an initial premium payment applicable to that preneed funeral contract. The notice shall include all of the following information that is pertinent to that preneed funeral contract:

(1) The amount the insurance company received;

(2) The name and address of the insurance company;

(3) The name of the insured;

(4) The amount of the death benefit;

(5) The policy or contract number of the insurance policy, annuity, or contract.

(C) For purposes of division (B) of this section, delivery of an insurance policy, certificate, annuity, or contract to the purchaser shall satisfy the notice requirement specified in that division.

**HISTORY:**

152 v S 196, § 1, eff. 7-7-09; 2017 hb49, § 101.01, effective September 29, 2017.

**Amendment Notes**

The 2017 amendment by HB 49 substituted "division (D)" for "division (B)" in (A)(2).

### § 4717.34 Right to rescind contract and receive refund; irrevocable contracts.

(A) Any purchaser, on initially entering into a preneed funeral contract may, within seven days after entering into that contract, rescind the contract and request and receive from the seller of the contract one hundred per cent of all payments made under the contract. Each preneed funeral contract shall contain the following notice in boldface print and in substantially the following form:

"NOTICE: Under Ohio law, you, as the purchaser of this contract, may rescind it and receive a refund of all payments you made under the contract. To rescind the contract, you must notify the seller within seven days of signing the contract."

(B) No preneed funeral contract shall contain a provision that restricts the purchaser from making the contract irrevocable. On the purchase by an individual of an irrevocable preneed funeral contract, the funeral director who sold the contract assumes the legal obligation to provide for the funeral of the individual pursuant to the terms of the contract. No money deposited in a trust fund for an irrevocable preneed funeral contract shall be withdrawn to purchase an insurance policy or annuity, except that a trustee may use money in the trust fund to purchase a life insurance policy or annuity as an investment for the trust fund.

**HISTORY:**

152 v S 196, § 1, eff. 7-7-09.

### § 4717.35 Duties of insurance agent; cancellation of contract and change of beneficiary; transfer of irrevocable contract to successor seller.

If a preneed funeral contract contains a provision stating that the preneed funeral contract will be funded by the purchase of an insurance policy, the insurance agent who sold the policy that will fund that preneed funeral contract shall require that any payment made by the purchaser be made in the form of a check, cashier's check, money order, or debit or credit card, payable only to the insurance company. The insurance agent shall remit the application for insurance and the premium paid to the insurance company designated in the preneed funeral contract within the time period specified in division (B)(15) of section 3905.14 of the Revised Code, unless the purchaser rescinds the preneed funeral contract in accordance with division (A) of section 4717.34 of the Revised Code.

If the purchaser of a preneed funeral contract that is revocable and that is funded by an insurance policy or annuity elects to cancel the preneed funeral contract, the purchaser shall provide a written notice to the seller and the insurance company designated in the contract stating that the purchaser intends to cancel that contract. Fifteen days after the purchaser provides the notice to the seller of the contract and the insurance company, the purchaser may cancel the preneed funeral contract and change the beneficiary of the insurance policy or annuity or reassign the benefits under the policy or annuity.

The purchaser of a preneed funeral contract that is irrevocable and that is funded by an insurance policy or annuity may transfer the preneed funeral contract to a successor seller by notifying the original seller of the designation of a successor seller. Within fifteen days after receiving the written notice of the designation of the successor seller from the purchaser, the original seller shall assign the seller's rights to the proceeds of the policy to the successor seller. The insurance company shall confirm the change of assignment by providing written notice to the policyholder.

**HISTORY:**

152 v S 196, § 1, eff. 7-7-09; 2017 hb49, § 101.01, effective September 29, 2017.

**Amendment Notes**

The 2017 amendment by HB 49 redesignated the former first paragraph as the first and second sentences of the first paragraph; added "require that any payment made by the purchaser be made in the form of a check, cashier's check, money order, or debit or credit card, payable only to the insurance company" in the first sentence of the first paragraph; and added "The insurance agent shall" in the second sentence of the first paragraph.

### § 4717.36 Preneed funeral contract trusts generally.

(A) This section applies only to preneed funeral contracts that are funded by any means other than an insurance policy or policies, or an annuity or annuities.

No money in a preneed funeral contract trust shall be distributed from the trust except as provided in this section.

(B) A seller of a preneed funeral contract that stipulates a fixed or firm or guaranteed price for funeral services and funeral goods to be provided under a preneed funeral contract may charge an initial service fee not to exceed ten per cent of the total amount of all payments to be paid under the preneed funeral contract for such guaranteed price funeral services and funeral goods. If the amount to be paid by the purchaser is to be paid in installments, the seller may collect the initial service fee only after all of the installments have been paid.

(C) All payments made by the purchaser of a preneed funeral contract, except for the initial service fee permitted by division (B) of this section and any applicable sales tax, shall be made in the form of a check, cashier's check, money order, or debit or credit card, payable only to the trustee of the preneed funeral contract trust or to the trustee's designated depository. Within thirty days of the seller receiving any form of payment made payable to the trustee or the trustee's designee, the seller shall remit the payment to the trustee or the trustee's designee unless the purchaser rescinds the preneed funeral contract in accordance with division (A) of section 4717.34 of the Revised Code. The funds deposited with the trustee shall remain intact and held in trust for the contract beneficiary.

(D) The seller shall establish a preneed funeral contract trust at one of the following types of institutions and shall designate that institution as the trustee of the preneed funeral contract trust:

(1) A trust company licensed under Chapter 1111. of the Revised Code;

(2) A national bank, federal savings bank, or federal savings association that pledges securities in accordance with section 1111.04 of the Revised Code;

(3) A credit union authorized to conduct business in this state pursuant to Chapter 1733. of the Revised Code.

(E) Moneys deposited in a preneed funeral contract trust fund shall be held and invested in the manner in which trust funds are permitted to be held and invested pursuant to Chapter 1111. of the Revised Code.

(F) The seller shall establish a separate preneed funeral contract trust for the moneys paid under each preneed funeral contract, unless the purchaser or purchasers of a preneed funeral contract or contracts authorize the seller to place the moneys paid for that contract or those contracts in a combined preneed funeral contract trust. The trustee of a combined preneed funeral contract trust shall keep exact records of the corpus, income, expenses, and disbursements with regard to each purchaser and contract beneficiary for whom moneys are held in the trust. The terms of a preneed funeral contract trust are governed by this section and the payments from that trust are governed by Chapter 1111. of the Revised Code, except as otherwise provided in this section.

A trustee of a preneed funeral contract trust may pay taxes and expenses for a preneed funeral contract trust and may charge a fee for managing a preneed funeral contract trust. The fee shall not exceed the amount regularly or usually charged for similar services rendered by the institutions described in division (D) of this section when serving as a trustee.



(G) If the purchaser of a preneed funeral contract that is revocable elects to cancel the contract, the purchaser shall provide a written notice to the seller of the contract and the trustee of the preneed funeral contract trust stating that the purchaser intends to cancel the contract. Fifteen days after the purchaser provides that notice to the seller and trustee, the purchaser may cancel the contract. Upon canceling a preneed funeral contract pursuant to this division, one of the following shall occur, as applicable:

(1) If the preneed funeral contract does not stipulate a firm or fixed or guaranteed price for funeral goods and funeral services to be provided under the preneed funeral contract, the trustee shall give to the purchaser all of the assets of the trust that exist at the time of cancellation, less any fees charged, distributions paid, and expenses incurred by the trustee pursuant to division (F) of this section.

(2) If the preneed funeral contract does stipulate a firm or fixed or guaranteed price for funeral goods and funeral services to be provided under the contract, the purchaser may request and receive from the trustee all of the assets of the trust at the time of cancellation, less a cancellation fee that the original seller may collect from the trustee that is equal to or less than ten per cent of the value of the assets of the trust on the date the trust is cancelled, provided, however, that to the extent the original seller took an initial service fee as permitted by division (B) of this section, the aggregate amount of the cancellation fee and the initial service fee may not exceed ten per cent of the value of those assets. In addition to any cancellation fee, there may also be deducted any fees charged, distributions paid, and expenses incurred by the trustee pursuant to division (F) of this section.

If more than one purchaser enters into the contract, all of those purchasers must request cancellation of the contract for it to be effective under this division, and the trustee shall refund to each purchaser only those funds that purchaser has paid under the contract and any income earned on those funds in an amount that is in direct proportion to the amount of funds that purchaser paid relative to the total amount of payments deposited in that trust, less any fees charged, distributions paid, and expenses incurred by the trustee pursuant to division (F) of this section, the amount of which are in direct proportion to the amount of funds that purchaser paid relative to the total amount of payments deposited in that trust.

(H) The purchaser of a preneed funeral contract that is irrevocable may transfer the preneed funeral contract to a successor seller. A purchaser who elects to make such a transfer shall provide a written notice of the designation of a successor seller to the trustee and the original seller. Within fifteen days after receiving the written notice of the new designation from the purchaser, the trustee shall list the successor seller as the seller of the preneed funeral contract and the original seller shall relinquish and transfer all rights under the preneed funeral contract to the successor seller. The trustee shall confirm the transfer by providing written notice of the transfer to the original seller, the successor seller, and the purchaser. If the preneed funeral contract stipulates a firm or fixed or guaranteed price for the funeral goods and funeral services to be provided under the preneed funeral contract, the original seller may collect from the trustee a transfer fee from the trust that equals up to ten per cent of the value of the assets of the trust on the date the trust is transferred, provided, however, that to the extent the original seller took an initial service fee as permitted by division (B) of this section, the aggregate amount of the transfer fee and the initial service fee may not exceed ten per cent of the value of those assets. If the preneed funeral contract does not stipulate a firm or fixed or guaranteed price for funeral goods and funeral services to be provided under the preneed funeral contract, no transfer fee shall be collected by the original seller.

(I) If a seller of a preneed funeral contract elects to transfer a preneed funeral contract trust from an institution listed in divisions (D)(1) to (3) of this section to a different institution, the trustee of the original trust shall notify the purchaser of the preneed funeral contract of that transfer in writing within thirty days after the transfer occurred and shall provide the purchaser with the name of and the contact information for the institution where the new trust is maintained. Upon receipt of the trust, the trustee of the transferred trust shall notify the purchaser of the receipt of the trusts in accordance with division (A) of section 4717.33 of the Revised Code.

(J) If a seller receives a notice that the contract beneficiary has died and that funeral goods and funeral services have been provided by a provider other than the seller, except as otherwise specified in this section, the seller shall direct the trustee, within thirty days after receiving that notice, to pay to the provider that provided the funeral goods and services, if still unpaid, or the estate of the contract beneficiary all funds held by the trustee, less any fees charged, distributions paid, and expenses incurred by the trustee pursuant to division (F) of this section. In the event the preneed funeral contract stipulates a firm or fixed or guaranteed price for funeral goods and funeral services that were to be provided under the preneed funeral contract, the seller may collect from the trustee a cancellation fee not exceeding ten per cent of the value of the assets of the trust on the date the trust is transferred, provided, however, that to the extent the original seller took an initial service fee as permitted by division (B) of this section, the aggregate amount of the transfer fee and the initial service fee shall not exceed ten per cent of the value of those assets. If the preneed funeral trust does not stipulate a firm or fixed or guaranteed price for funeral goods and funeral services to be provided under the preneed funeral contract, no cancellation fees shall be collected by the original seller.

(K) A certified copy of the certificate of death or other evidence of death satisfactory to the trustee shall be furnished to the trustee as evidence of death, and the trustee shall promptly pay the accumulated payments and income, if any, according to the preneed funeral contract. Such payment of the accumulated payments and income pursuant to this section and, when applicable, the preneed funeral contract, relieves the trustee of any further liability on the accumulated payments and income.

**HISTORY:**

152 v S 196, § 1, eff. 7-7-09; 2017 hb49, § 101.01, effective September 29, 2017; 2018 hb168, § 1, effective October 29, 2018.

**Amendment Notes**

The 2018 amendment by HB 168, in (B), rewrote the second sentence and deleted the third sentence; and, in (C), added "or to the trustee's designated depository" at the end of the first sentence and added "or the trustee's designee" twice in the second sentence.

The 2017 amendment by HB 49 substituted "division (F)" for "division (D)" wherever it appears in (G)(1), (G)(2) and (J); rewrote the second paragraph of (A); added (B) and (C);rewrote the second paragraph of (F); rewrote (G)(2); added "provided, however, that to the extent the original seller took an initial service fee as permitted by division (B) of this section, the aggregate amount of the transfer fee and the initial service fee may not exceed ten per cent of the value of those assets" in the second to the last sentence of (H); substituted "divisions (D)(1) to (3)" for "divisions (B)(1) to (3)" in the first sentence of (I); in (J), added "provider that provided the funeral goods and services, if still unpaid, or the estate of the" in the first sentence and "provided, however, that to the extent the original seller took an initial service fee as permitted by division (B) of this section, the aggregate amount of the transfer fee and the initial service fee shall not exceed ten per cent of the value of those assets" in the second sentence; and made related changes.

### § 4717.37 Delivery of funeral goods.

For purposes of sections 4717.31 to 4717.38 of the Revised Code, a seller is considered to have delivered funeral goods pursuant to a preneed funeral contract when the seller makes actual delivery of the goods to the contract beneficiary.

**HISTORY:**
152 v S 196, § 1, eff. 7-7-09.

### § 4717.38 Construction of provisions; exemption of church or denomination; exemption from attachment.

Sections 4717.31 to 4717.38 of the Revised Code shall be construed as a limitation on the manner in which a person is permitted to accept funds in prepayment for funeral services to be performed in the future, or funeral goods to be used in connection with the funeral or final disposition of human remains, to the end that at all times members of the public may have an opportunity to arrange and pay for a funeral for themselves and their families in advance of need while at the same time providing all possible safeguards to ensure that prepaid funds cannot be dissipated, whether intentionally or not, but remain available for payment for funeral goods and funeral services in connection with the funeral or final disposition of dead human bodies.

Sections 4717.31 to 4717.38 of the Revised Code do not apply to a seller if that seller is an established and legally cognizable church or denomination that is exempt from federal income taxation under section 501(c) (3) of the "Internal Revenue Code of 1986," 100 Stat. 2085, 26 U.S.C. 501, as amended, and the preneed funeral contract pertains to a cemetery owned and operated entirely and exclusively by the church or denomination, on the condition that the church or denomination adopts, on a voluntary basis, rules and other measures to safeguard and secure all funds received under any preneed funeral contract.

Any money, insurance policies, annuities, or other items delivered in payment of a preneed funeral contract, and any funds held in trust pursuant to section 4717.36 of the Revised Code, are exempt from levy, attachment, or sale to satisfy a judgment or order.

**HISTORY:**
152 v S 196, § 1, eff. 7-7-09.

### § 4717.39 Required compliance with R.C. § 4776.20.

The board of embalmers and funeral directors shall comply with section 4776.20 of the Revised Code.

**HISTORY:**
2012 HB 247, § 1, eff. Mar. 22, 2013.

### § 4717.41 Preneed recovery fund.

(A) There is hereby created the preneed recovery fund, which shall be in the custody of the treasurer of state but shall not be part of the state treasury. All fees collected under division (A)(14) of section 4717.07 of the Revised Code shall be deposited into the fund. The fund shall be used to reimburse purchasers of preneed funeral contracts who have suffered financial loss as a result of the malfeasance, misfeasance, default, failure, or insolvency in connection with the sale of a preneed funeral contract by any licensee under this chapter, regardless of whether the sale of such contract occurred before or after the establishment of the fund. The fund, and all investment earnings thereon, shall only be used for the purposes set forth in this section and shall not be used for any other purposes. The fund shall be administered by the board of embalmers and funeral directors.

(B) All fees collected under division (A)(14) of section 4717.07 of the Revised Code shall be deposited into the fund. Deposits to and disbursements from the fund account shall be subject to rules established by the board.

(C) If at the end of any fiscal year for this state, the balance in the fund exceeds two million dollars, the fee required by division (A)(14) of section 4717.07 of the Revised Code for the upcoming fiscal year shall be reduced by fifty per cent. If the balance in the fund at the end of a fiscal year exceeds three million dollars, the payment of the fee required by division (A)(14) of section 4717.07 of the Revised Code shall be suspended for the upcoming fiscal year.

(D) The board shall adopt rules governing management of the fund, the presentation and processing of applications for reimbursement, subrogation, or assignment of the rights of any reimbursed applicant.

(E) The board may expend moneys in the fund for the following purposes:

(1) To make reimbursements on approved applications;

(2) To purchase insurance to cover losses as considered appropriate by the board and not inconsistent with the purposes of the fund;

(3) To invest such portions of the fund as are not currently needed to reimburse losses and maintain adequate reserves, as are permitted to be made by fiduciaries under the laws of this state;

(4) To pay the expenses of the board for administering the fund, including employment of local counsel to prosecute subrogation claims.

(F) Reimbursements from the fund shall be made only to the extent to which those losses are not bonded or otherwise covered, protected, or reimbursed and only after the applicant has complied with all applicable rules of the board.

(G) The board shall investigate all applications made and may reject or allow such claims in whole or in part to the extent that moneys are available in the fund. The board shall have complete discretion to determine the order and manner of payment of approved applications. All payments shall be a matter of privilege and not of right, and no person shall have any right in the fund as a third-party beneficiary or otherwise. No attorney may be compensated by the board for prosecuting an application for reimbursement.

(H) If reimbursement is made to an applicant under this section, the board shall be subrogated in the reimbursement amount and may bring any action it considers advisable against any person. The board may enforce any claims it may have for restitution or otherwise and may employ and compensate consultants, agents, legal counsel, accountants, and other persons it considers appropriate.

**HISTORY:**
2017 hb49, § 101.01, effective September 29, 2017; 2019 hb166, § 101.01, effective October 17, 2019.

**Amendment Notes**
The 2019 amendment by HB 166 substituted "division (A)(14)" for "division (A)(15)" wherever it appears in (A) through (C).

## PENALTIES

### § 4717.99 Penalties.

Whoever violates any provision of sections 4717.01 to 4717.15; division (A) or (B) of section 4717.23; division (B)(1) or (2), (C)(1) or (2), (D), (E), or (F)(1) or (2), or divisions (H) to (K) of section 4717.26; division (D)(1) of section 4717.27; or divisions (A) to (C) of section 4717.28 of the Revised Code shall be fined not less than one hundred nor more than five thousand dollars, or imprisoned for not more than one year, or both, for the first offense. For each subsequent offense such a person shall be fined not less than one hundred nor more than ten thousand dollars, or imprisoned for not more than one year, or both.

Whoever purposely violates division (D) or (E) of section 4717.31 of the Revised Code is guilty of a misdemeanor of the third degree. If the purpose of a violation of that division is to commit or facilitate the commission of a felony, whoever violates that division is guilty of a felony of the fourth degree.

**HISTORY:**

147 v S 117. Eff 8-5-98; 152 v S 196, § 1, eff. 7-7-09.

**Amendment Notes**

152 v S 196, effective July 7, 2009, added the last paragraph.

# CHAPTER 4751

# NURSING HOME ADMINISTRATORS

Section



## § 4751.01 Definitions.

As used in this chapter:

(A) "Health-care licensing agency" means any department, division, board, section of a board, or other government unit that is authorized by a statute of this or another state to issue a license, certificate, permit, card, or other authority to do either of the following in the context of health care:

(1) Engage in a specific profession, occupation, or occupational activity;

(2) Have charge of and operate certain specified equipment, machinery, or premises.

(B) "Licensed health services executive" means an individual who holds a valid health services executive license.

(C) "Licensed nursing home administrator" means an individual who holds a valid nursing home administrator license.

(D) "Licensed temporary nursing home administrator" means an individual who holds a valid temporary nursing home administrator license.

(E) "Long-term services and supports setting" means any institutional or community-based setting in which medical, health, psychosocial, habilitative, rehabilitative, or personal care services are provided to individuals on a post-acute care basis.

(F) "Nursing home" means a nursing home as defined by or under the authority of section 3721.01 of the Revised Code, or a nursing home operated by a governmental agency.

(G) "Nursing home administration" means planning, organizing, directing, and managing the operation of a nursing home.

(H) "Nursing home administrator" means any individual who engages in the practice of nursing home administration, whether or not the individual shares the functions and duties of nursing home administration with one or more other individuals.

(I) "Valid health services executive license" means a health services executive license to which all of the following apply:

(1) It was issued by the board of executives of long-term services and supports under section 4751.21, 4751.23, 4751.25, or 4751.33 of the Revised Code;

(2) It was not sold, fraudulently furnished, or fraudulently obtained in violation of division (F) of section 4751.10 of the Revised Code;

(3) It is current and in good standing.

(J) "Valid nursing home administrator license" means a nursing home administrator license to which all of the following apply:

(1) It was issued by the board under section 4751.20, 4751.201, 4751.23, 4751.24, or 4751.33 of the Revised Code;

(2) It was not sold, fraudulently furnished, or fraudulently obtained in violation of division (F) of section 4751.10 of the Revised Code;

(3) It is current and in good standing.

(K) "Valid temporary nursing home administrator license" means a temporary nursing home administrator license to which all of the following apply:

(1) It was issued by the board under section 4751.202, 4751.23, or 4751.33 of the Revised Code;

(2) It was not sold, fraudulently furnished, or fraudulently obtained in violation of division (F) of section 4751.10 of the Revised Code;

(3) It is current and in good standing.

**HISTORY:**

133 v S 481 (Eff 4-12-70); 135 v S 322 (Eff 8-30-73); 144 v S 132 (Eff 7-22-91); 144 v H 298. Eff 7-26-91; 2013 HB 59, § 101.01, eff. Sept. 29, 2013; 2019 hb166, § 101.01, effective October 17, 2019.

**Amendment Notes**

The 2019 amendment by HB 166 rewrote the introductory language, which formerly read: "As used in sections 4751.01 to 4751.13 of the Revised Code"; added (A) through (D); redesignated and rewrote former (A) as (E); deleted former (B), which read: "'Nursing home administrator' means any individual responsible for planning, organizing, directing, and managing the operation of a nursing home, or who in fact performs such function, whether or not such functions and duties are shared by one or more other persons"; redesignated former (C) as (F); deleted former (D), which read: "'Temporary license' means a license for a period not to exceed one hundred eighty days issued pursuant to division (B) of section 4751.06 of the Revised Code"; redesignated and rewrote former (E) as (J) and (J)(3); and added (G) through (K).

The 2013 amendment substituted "sections 4751.01 to 4751.13" for "sections 4751.01 to 4751.11" in the introductory language; added (A); and redesignated former (A) through (D) as (B) through (E).

### ATTORNEY GENERAL OPINIONS

A "county home" is not necessarily a "nursing home operated by a governmental agency," which would require the licensing of the superintendent as a nursing home administrator, as provided by R.C. Chapter 4751.: 1970 Ohio Op. Att'y Gen. No. 164.

RESEARCH REFERENCES AND PRACTICE AIDS

**Ohio Administrative Code**
Board of examiners of nursing home administrators — Definitions. OAC 4751-1-02.

### § 4751.02 Establishment of board; requirements of members.

(A) There is hereby established in the department of aging a board of executives of long-term services and supports, which board shall be composed of the following eleven members:

(1) Four members who are nursing home administrators, owners of nursing homes, or officers of corporations owning nursing homes, and who shall have an understanding of person-centered care, and experience with a range of long-term services and supports settings;

(2)(a) Three members who work in long-term services and supports settings that are not nursing homes, and who shall have an understanding of person-centered care, and experience with a range of long-term services and supports settings;

(b) At least one of the members described in division (A)(2)(a) of this section shall be a home health administrator, hospice administrator, an owner of a home health agency or hospice care program, or an officer of a home health agency or hospice care program.

(3) One member who is a member of the academic community;

(4) One member who is a consumer of services offered in a long-term services and supports setting;

(5) One nonvoting member who is a representative of the department of health, designated by the director of health, who is involved in the nursing home survey and certification process, who shall serve in an advisory capacity only;

(6) One nonvoting member who is a representative of the office of the state long-term care ombudsman, designated by the state long-term care ombudsman, who shall serve in an advisory capacity only.

All members of the board shall be citizens of the United States and residents of this state. No member of the board who is appointed under divisions (A)(3) to (6) of this section may have or acquire any direct financial interest in a nursing home or long-term services and supports settings.

(B) The term of office for each appointed member of the board shall be for three years, commencing on the twenty-eighth day of May and ending on the twenty-seventh day of May. Each member shall serve from the date of appointment until the end of the term for which appointed. No member shall serve more than two consecutive full terms.

(C) Appointments to the board shall be made by the governor. Any member appointed to fill a vacancy occurring prior to the expiration of the term for which the member's predecessor was appointed shall hold office for the remainder of such term. Any appointed member shall continue in office subsequent to the expiration date of the member's term until the member's successor takes office, or until a period of sixty days has elapsed, whichever occurs first.

(D) The governor may remove any member of the board for misconduct, incapacity, incompetence, or neglect of duty after the member so charged has been served with a written statement of charges and has been given an opportunity to be heard.

(E) Each member of the board, except the member designated by the director of health and the member designated by the ombudsman, shall be paid in accordance with section 124.15 of the Revised Code and each member shall be reimbursed for the member's actual and necessary expenses incurred in the discharge of such duties.

(F) The board shall elect annually from its membership a chairperson and a vice-chairperson.

(G) The board shall hold and conduct meetings quarterly and at such other times as its business requires. A majority of the voting members of the board shall constitute a quorum. The affirmative vote of a majority of the voting members of the board is necessary for the board to act.

(H) The board shall appoint a secretary who has no financial interest in a long-term services and supports setting, and may employ and prescribe the powers and duties of such employees and consultants as are necessary to carry out this chapter and the rules adopted under it.

**HISTORY:**
133 v S 481 (Eff 4-12-70); 135 v S 131 (Eff 8-21-73); 135 v S 322 (Eff 8-30-73); 136 v H 1 (Eff 6-13-75); 136 v H 155 (Eff 6-29-75); 143 v H 623. Eff 7-24-90; 2013 HB 59, § 101.01, eff. Sept. 29, 2013; 2017 hb49, § 101.01, effective September 29, 2017; renumbered from § ORC Ann. 4751.03 by 2019 hb166, § 101.01, effective October 17, 2019.

**Editor's Notes**
Former § 4751.02 [133 v S 481 (Eff 4-12-70); 135 v S 322. Eff8-30-73; 2013 HB 59, § 101.01, eff. Sept. 29,2013], concerning the duties of the board's fiscal agent, was repealed by 2019 HB 166, § 105.01 effective October 17, 2019.

**Amendment Notes**
The 2019 amendment by HB 166, in (A)(2)(b), added "hospice administrator" and "or hospice care program" twice.

The 2017 amendment by HB 49 substituted "One nonvoting member" for "One member" in (A)(5) and (A)(6); added " "who shall serve in an advisory capacity only" in (A)(5) and (A)(6); in (G), added "voting members of the" in the second sentence and substituted "the voting members" for "the members" in the last sentence.

The 2013 amendment rewrote (A); substituted "member designated by the director of health and the member designated by the ombudsman" for "director of health or his designated representative" in (E); substituted "chairperson and a vice-chairperson" for "chairman and a vice-chairman" in (F); in (H), substituted "long-term services and supports setting" for "nursing home" and deleted the second sentence, which read: "Administrative, technical, or other services shall be performed, insofar as practicable, by personnel of the department of health"; and made stylistic changes.

ATTORNEY GENERAL OPINIONS

R.C. 4751.03(H) authorizes the Ohio Board of Examiners of Nursing Home Administrators to employ such employees as are necessary to carry out the work of the Board that is not performed by Department of Health employees who provide administrative, technical, and other services for the Board. The Ohio Board of Examiners of Nursing Home Administrators is, for purposes of R.C. Chapter 124, the appointing authority of the persons it employs under R.C. 4751.03(H). 2009 Ohio Op. Att'y Gen. No. 052 (2009).

RESEARCH REFERENCES AND PRACTICE AIDS

**Cross-References to Related Sections**
Report to legislative service commission, RC § 4743.01.
Restricting entry into occupations by limiting number of accredited institutions by boards prohibited, RC § 4743.03.

**Ohio Administrative Code**
Board of examiners of nursing home administrators — Meetings. OAC 4751-1-04.
Officers and duties. OAC 4751-1-03.

### § 4751.021 Duties of the board's fiscal agent.

(A) The board of executives of long-term services and supports shall enter into a written agreement with the department of aging for the department to serve as the board's fiscal agent. The fiscal agent shall be responsible for all the board's fiscal matters and financial transactions, as specified in the agreement. The written agreement shall specify the fees that the board shall pay to the fiscal agent for services performed under the agreement, and such fees shall be in proportion to the services performed for the board.

(1) The agreement shall require the fiscal agent to provide the following services:

(a) Preparation and processing of payroll and other personnel documents that the board approves;

(b) Maintenance of ledgers of accounts and reports of account balances, and monitoring of budgets and allotment plans in consultation with the board;

(c) Performance of other routine support services, specified in the agreement, that the fiscal agent considers appropriate to achieve efficiency.

Titles 39 — 57

(2) The agreement may require the fiscal agent to provide the following services:

(a) Any shared services between the board and the fiscal agent;

(b) Any other services agreed to by the board and the department, including administrative or technical services.

(B) The board, in conjunction and consultation with the fiscal agent, has the following authority and responsibility relative to fiscal matters:

(1) Sole authority to expend funds from the board's accounts for programs and any other necessary expenses the board may incur;

(2) Responsibility to cooperate with and inform the fiscal agent fully of all financial transactions.

(C) The board shall follow all state procurement, fiscal, human resources, information technology, statutory, and administrative rule requirements.

(D) In its role as fiscal agent for the board, the department shall serve as a contractor of the board, and does not assume responsibility for the debts or fiscal obligations of the board.

**HISTORY:**

2013 HB 59, § 101.01, eff. Sept. 29, 2013; renumbered from § ORC Ann. 4751.042 by 2019 hb166, § 101.01, effective October 17, 2019.



## § 4751.03 Creation of long term services and support fund.

There is hereby created in the state treasury the board of executives of long-term services and supports fund. The fund shall consist of the amounts the board of executives of long-term services and supports collects under this chapter as fees, civil penalties, and fines. The board shall use the money in the fund to administer and enforce this chapter and the rules adopted under section 4751.04 of the Revised Code. Investment earnings of the fund shall be credited to the fund.

**HISTORY:**

2013 HB 59, § 101.01, eff. Sept. 29, 2013; 2017 hb49, § 101.01, effective September 29, 2017; renumbered from § ORC Ann. 4751.14 by 2019 hb166, § 101.01, effective October 17, 2019.

**Amendment Notes**

The 2019 amendment by HB 166, in the first paragraph, in the second sentence, added "of executives of long-term services and supports" and deleted "license and registration fees, other" preceding "fees," and in the third sentence, substituted "The board shall use the money in the fund" for "Money in the fund shall be used by the board of executives of long-term services and supports" and "section 4751.04 of the Revised Code" for "it" at the end.

The 2017 amendment by HB 49, in the second sentence, added "the amounts the board collects under this chapter as" and substituted "other fees, civil penalties, and fines" for "collected under this chapter."

## § 4751.04 Rules adoption.

The board of executives of long-term services and supports shall adopt rules in accordance with Chapter 119. of the Revised Code as necessary to implement and enforce this chapter.

**HISTORY:**

2019 hb166, § 101.01, effective October 17, 2019.

**Editor's Notes**

Former § 4751.04 [133 v S 481 (Eff 4-12-70); 135 v S 322 (Eff8-30-73); 144 v H 298 (Eff 7-26-91); 145 v H 152(Eff 7-1-93); 148 v H 640. Eff 9-14-2000; 2013 HB 59, § 101.01, eff. Sept. 29, 2013; 2017 hb49, § 101.01, effective September 29, 2017], concerning powers and duties, was repealed by 2019 HB 166, § 105.01 effective October 17, 2019.

## § 4751.041 Disclosure of examination materials. [Renumbered]

**HISTORY:**

148 v H 640. Eff 9-14-2000; 2013 HB 59, § 101.01, eff. Sept. 29, 2013; renumbered to § ORC Ann. 4751.151 by 2019 hb166, § 101.01, effective October 17, 2019.

## § 4751.042 Duties of the board's fiscal agent. [Renumbered]

**HISTORY:**

2013 HB 59, § 101.01, eff. Sept. 29, 2013; renumbered to § ORC Ann. 4751.021 by 2019 hb166, § 101.01, effective October 17, 2019.

## § 4751.043 Training and education programs in person or through electronic media [Renumbered]

**HISTORY:**

2017 hb49, § 101.01, effective September 29, 2017; renumbered to § ORC Ann. 4751.381 by 2019 hb166, § 101.01, effective October 17, 2019.

## § 4751.044 Approval of continuing education courses for nursing home administrators [Renumbered]

**HISTORY:**

2017 hb49, § 101.01, effective September 29, 2017; renumbered to § ORC Ann. 4751.26 by 2019 hb166, § 101.01, effective October 17, 2019.

## § 4751.05 Requirements for examination and license. [Renumbered]

**HISTORY:**

133 v S 481 (Eff 4-12-70); 135 v S 1 (Eff 1-1-74); 135 v S 322 (Eff 8-30-73); 136 v H 1 (Eff 6-13-75); 140 v H 291 (Eff 7-1-83); 144 v H 298 (Eff 7-26-91); 147 v H 243 (Eff 5-21-98); 148 v H 640 (Eff 9-14-2000); 148 v H 511. Eff 4-10-2001; 2013 HB 59, § 101.01, eff. Sept. 29, 2013; renumbered to § ORC Ann. 4751.15 by 2019 hb166, § 101.01, effective October 17, 2019.

## § 4751.06 Issuance of license; temporary license; duplicates. [Renumbered]

**HISTORY:**

133 v S 481 (Eff 4-12-70); 135 v S 322 (Eff 8-30-73); 140 v H 291 (Eff 7-1-83); 147 v H 215 (Eff 9-29-97); 148 v H 640. Eff 9-14-2000; 150 v H 95, § 1, eff. 9-26-03; 2013 HB 59, § 101.01, eff. Sept. 29, 2013; renumbered to § ORC Ann. 4751.20 by 2019 hb166, § 101.01, effective October 17, 2019.

## § 4751.07 Registration certificate; duty to display license. [Renumbered]

**HISTORY:**

133 v S 481 (Eff 4-12-70); 135 v S 322 (Eff 8-30-73); 140 v H 291 (Eff 7-1-83); 144 v H 298 (Eff 7-26-91); 147 v H 215. Eff 9-29-97; 150 v H 95, § 1, eff. 9-26-03; 153 v H 1, § 101.01, eff. 10-16-09; 2013 HB 59, § 101.01, eff. Sept. 29, 2013; renumbered to § ORC Ann. 4751.24 by 2019 hb166, § 101.01, effective October 17, 2019.

## § 4751.08 Waiver of examination. [Renumbered]

**HISTORY:**

133 v S 481 (Eff 4-12-70); 140 v H 291 (Eff 7-1-83); 144 v H 298. Eff 7-26-91; 2013 HB 59, § 101.01, eff. Sept. 29, 2013; renumbered to § ORC Ann. 4751.201 by 2019 hb166, § 101.01, effective October 17, 2019.

## § 4751.09 Prohibitions. [Repealed]

**HISTORY:**

133 v S 481 (Eff 4-12-70); 135 v S 322. Eff 8-30-73; repealed by 2019 hb166, § 105.01, effective October 17, 2019.

## § 4751.10 Prohibitions.

No person shall knowingly do any of the following:

(A) Operate a nursing home unless it is under the supervision of an administrator whose principal occupation is nursing home administration or hospital administration and who is a licensed nursing home administrator or licensed temporary nursing home administrator;

(B) Practice or offer to practice nursing home administration unless the person is a licensed nursing home administrator or licensed temporary nursing home administrator;

(C) Use any of the following unless the person is a licensed nursing home administrator:

(1) The title "licensed nursing home administrator," "nursing home administrator," "licensed assistant nursing home administrator," or "assistant nursing home administrator;"

(2) The acronym "LNHA," "L.N.H.A.," "NHA," "N.H.A.," "LANHA," "L.A.N.H.A.," "ANHA," or "A.N.H.A." after the person's name;

(3) Any other words, letters, signs, cards, or devices that tend to indicate or imply that the person is a licensed nursing home administrator.

(D) Use any of the following unless the person is a licensed temporary nursing home administrator:

(1) The title "licensed temporary nursing home administrator," "temporary nursing home administrator," "licensed temporary assistant nursing home administrator," or "temporary assistant nursing home administrator;"

(2) The acronym "LTNHA," "L.T.N.H.A.," "TNHA," "T.N.H.A.," "LTANHA," "L.T.A.N.H.A.," "TANHA," or "T.A.N.H.A." after the person's name;

(3) Any other words, letters, signs, cards, or devices that tend to indicate or imply that the person is a licensed temporary nursing home administrator.

(E) Use any of the following unless the person is a licensed health services executive:

(1) The title "licensed health services executive" or "health services executive;"

(2) The acronym "LHSE," "L.H.S.E.," "HSE," or "H.S.E." after the person's name;

(3) Any other words, letters, signs, cards, or devices that tend to indicate or imply that the person is a licensed health services executive.

(F) Sell, fraudulently furnish, fraudulently obtain, or aid or abet another person in selling, fraudulently furnishing, or fraudulently obtaining any of the following:

(1) A nursing home administrator license;

(2) A temporary nursing home administrator license;

(3) A health services executive license.

(G) Otherwise violate any of the provisions of this chapter or the rules adopted under section 4751.04 of the Revised Code.

**HISTORY:**

2019 hb166, § 101.01, effective October 17, 2019.

**Editor's Notes**

Former § 4751.10 [133 v S 481 (Eff 4-12-70); 135 v S 322. Eff8-30-73; 2013 HB 59, § 101.01, eff. Sept. 29,2013; 2017 hb49, § 101.01, effective September 29, 2017; 2019 hb166, § 101.01, effective October 17, 2019] was renumbered as § 4751.32 by 2019 HB 166, § 101.01, effective October 17, 2019.

### § 4751.101 Limitation on construing chapter.

Nothing in this chapter or the rules adopted under it shall be construed as requiring either of the following:

(A) An individual to be a licensed health services executive in order to do either of the following:

(1) Practice nursing home administration;

(2) Serve in a leadership position at a long-term services and supports setting or direct the practices of others in such a setting.

(B) An applicant for a nursing home administrator license or temporary nursing home administrator license who is employed by an institution for the care and treatment of the sick to demonstrate proficiency in any medical techniques or to meet any medical educational qualifications or medical standards not in accord with the remedial care and treatment provided by the institution if all of the following apply to the institution:

(1) It is operated exclusively for patients who use spiritual means for healing and for whom the acceptance of medical care is inconsistent with their religious beliefs.

(2) It is accredited by a national accrediting organization.

(3) It is exempt from federal income taxation under section 501 of the "Internal Revenue Code of 1986," 26 U.S.C. 501.

(4) It provides twenty-four hour nursing care pursuant to the exemption in division (E) of section 4723.32 of the Revised Code from the licensing requirements of Chapter 4723. of the Revised Code.

**HISTORY:**

2019 hb166, § 101.01, effective October 17, 2019.

### § 4751.102 Names and license numbers to be provided to board of executives.

Every operator of a nursing home shall report to the board of executives of long-term services and supports the name and license number of each licensed nursing home administrator and licensed temporary nursing home administrator who practices nursing home administration at the nursing home not later than ten days after the following dates:

(A) The date the licensed nursing home administrator or licensed temporary nursing home administrator begins to practice nursing home administration at the nursing home;

(B) The date the licensed nursing home administrator or licensed temporary nursing home administrator ceases to practice nursing home administration at the nursing home.

**HISTORY:**

2019 hb166, § 101.01, effective October 17, 2019.

### § 4751.11 Reissuance of license. [Renumbered]

**HISTORY:**

133 v S 481. Eff 4-12-70; 2013 HB 59, § 101.01, eff. Sept. 29, 2013; renumbered to § ORC Ann. 4751.33 by 2019 hb166, § 101.01, effective October 17, 2019.

### § 4751.12 Effect of child support default. [Renumbered]

**HISTORY:**

146 v H 167 (Eff 11-15-96); 148 v S 180. Eff 3-22-2001; 2013 HB 59, § 101.01, eff. Sept. 29, 2013; renumbered to § ORC Ann. 4751.35 by 2019 hb166, § 101.01, effective October 17, 2019.

### § 4751.13 Required compliance with R.C. § 4776.20. [Renumbered]

**HISTORY:**

2012 HB 247, § 1, eff. Mar. 22, 2013; 2013 HB 59, § 101.01, eff. Sept. 29, 2013; renumbered to § ORC Ann. 4751.36 by 2019 hb166, § 101.01, effective October 17, 2019.

### § 4751.14 Creation of long term services and support fund. [Renumbered]

**HISTORY:**

2013 HB 59, § 101.01, eff. Sept. 29, 2013; 2017 hb49, § 101.01, effective September 29, 2017; renumbered to § ORC Ann. 4751.03 by 2019 hb166, § 101.01, effective October 17, 2019.

### § 4751.15 Requirements for examination and license.

The board of executives of long-term services and supports shall administer, or contract with a government or private entity to administer, examinations that an individual must pass to obtain a nursing home administratorlicense under section 4751.20 or 4751.201 of the Revised Code. If the board contracts with a government or private entity to administer the examinations, the contract may authorize the entity to collect and keep, as all or part of the entity's compensation under the contract, any fee an individual pays to take the examination. The entity is not required to deposit the fee into the state treasury.

To be admitted to an examination administered under this section, an individual must pay the examination fee charged by the board or government or privateentity. If an individual fails three times to pass the examination, the individual, before being admitted to the examination a subsequent time, also must satisfy any education requirements, experience requirements, or both, that may be prescribed in rules adopted under section 4751.04 of the Revised Code in addition to any education requirements or experience requirements that must be satisfied to obtain a nursing home administrator license under section 4751.20 or 4751.201 of the Revised Code.

**HISTORY:**
133 v S 481 (Eff 4-12-70); 135 v S 1 (Eff 1-1-74); 135 v S 322 (Eff 8-30-73); 136 v H 1 (Eff 6-13-75); 140 v H 291 (Eff 7-1-83); 144 v H 298 (Eff 7-26-91); 147 v H 243 (Eff 5-21-98); 148 v H 640 (Eff 9-14-2000); 148 v H 511. Eff 4-10-2001; 2013 HB 59, § 101.01, eff. Sept. 29, 2013; renumbered from § ORC Ann. 4751.05 by 2019 hb166, § 101.01, effective October 17, 2019.

**Amendment Notes**
The 2019 amendment by HB 166 rewrote the section.
The 2013 amendment substituted "board of executives of long-term services and supports" for "board of examiners of nursing home administrators" in the introductory language of (A).

**RESEARCH REFERENCES AND PRACTICE AIDS**

**Cross-References to Related Sections**
Issuance of license; temporary license, RC § 4751.06.

**Ohio Administrative Code**
Licensing examinations —
Examination and passing grade. OAC 4751-1-07.
Pre-examination requirements; conditions precedent to application for admission to examination. OAC 4751-1-05.
Subjects for examination. OAC 4751-1-06.
Training and instruction —
Administrator-in-training program; practical training and experience. OAC 4751-1-09.
Continuing education. OAC 4751-1-13.
Registration of institutions and training agencies; approval of courses of study and programs of instruction. OAC 4751-1-08; approval of training agency for continuing education. OAC 4751-1-081.



## § 4751.151 Disclosure of examination materials.

Except when the board of executives of long-term services and supports considers it necessary, the board shall not disclose test materials, examinations, or evaluation tools used in an examination administered under section 4751.15 of the Revised Code.

**HISTORY:**
148 v H 640. Eff 9-14-2000; 2013 HB 59, § 101.01, eff. Sept. 29, 2013; renumbered from § ORC Ann. 4751.041 by 2019 hb166, § 101.01, effective October 17, 2019.

**Amendment Notes**
The 2019 amendment by HB 166 substituted "administered under section 4751.15 of the Revised Code" for "for licensure as a nursing home administrator that the board administers under section 4751.04 of the Revised Code or contracts under that section with a private or government entity to administer."
The 2013 amendment substituted "board of executives of long-term services and supports" for "board of examiners of nursing home administrators".

## § 4751.20 Issuance of license; temporary license; duplicates.

(A) Subject to section 4751.32 of the Revised Code, the board of executives of long-term services and supports shall issue a nursing home administrator license to an individual under this section if all of the following requirements are satisfied:

(1) The individual has submitted to the board a completed application for the license in accordance with rules adopted under section 4751.04 of the Revised Code.

(2) If the individual is required by rules adopted under section 4751.04 of the Revised Code to serve as a nursing home administrator in training, the individual has paid to the board the administrator in training fee of fifty dollars.

(3) The individual is at least twenty-one years of age.

(4) The individual has successfully completed educational requirements and work experience specified in rules adopted under section 4751.04 of the Revised Code, including, if so required by the rules, experience obtained as a nursing home administrator in training.

(5) The individual has complied with section 4776.02 of the Revised Code regarding a criminal records check.

(6) The board, in accordance with section 9.79 of the Revised Code, has determined that the results of the criminal records check do not make the individual ineligible for the license.

(7) The individual has passed the licensing examination administered under section 4751.15 of the Revised Code.

(8) The individual has paid to the board a license fee of two hundred fifty dollars.

(9) The individual has satisfied any additional requirements as may be prescribed in rules adopted under section 4751.04 of the Revised Code.

(B) A nursing home administrator license shall certify that the individual to whom it was issued has met the applicable requirements of this chapter and any applicable rules adopted under section 4751.04 of the Revised Code and is authorized to practice nursing home administration while the license is valid.

**HISTORY:**
133 v S 481 (Eff 4-12-70); 135 v S 322 (Eff 8-30-73); 140 v H 291 (Eff 7-1-83); 147 v H 215 (Eff 9-29-97); 148 v H 640. Eff 9-14-2000; 150 v H 95, § 1, eff. 9-26-03; 2013 HB 59, § 101.01, eff. Sept. 29, 2013; renumbered from § ORC Ann. 4751.06 by 2019 hb166, § 101.01, effective October 17, 2019; 2020 hb263, § 1, effective October 9, 2021.

**Amendment Notes**
The 2020 amendment by HB 263 deleted former (A)(5), which read: "The individual is of good moral character"; redesignated former (A)(6) through (A)(10) as (A)(5) through (A)(9); and substituted "accordance with section 9.79 of the Revised Code" for "its discretion" in (A)(6).
The 2019 amendment by HB 166 rewrote the section.
The 2013 amendment substituted "board of executives of long-term services and supports" for "board of examiners of nursing home administrators" in the first sentence of (A).

**ATTORNEY GENERAL OPINIONS**

When a county operates a separate facility, or a distinct portion of the county home, as a nursing home, the superintendent or person charged with the general administration of the facility shall be licensed as provided in R.C. Chapter 4751.: 1970 Ohio Op. Att'y Gen. No. 164.

**RESEARCH REFERENCES AND PRACTICE AIDS**

**Cross-References to Related Sections**
Registration certificate, RC § 4751.24.
Temporary license defined, RC § 4751.01.

**Ohio Administrative Code**
Fees. OAC 4751-1-16.
Licenses and registrations. OAC 4751-1-10.
Temporary license. OAC 4751-1-11.

## § 4751.201 Waiver of examination.

(A) Subject to section 4751.32 of the Revised Code, the board of executives of long-term services and supports may issue a nursing home administrator license to an individual under this section if all of the following requirements are satisfied:

(1) The individual is legally authorized to practice nursing home administration in another state.

(2) The individual has submitted to the board a completed application for the license in accordance with rules adopted under section 4751.04 of the Revised Code.

(3) The individual is at least twenty-one years of age.

(4) The individual holds at least a bachelor's degree from an accredited educational institution.

(5) The individual is of good moral character.

(6) The individual has complied with section 4776.02 of the Revised Code regarding a criminal records check.

(7) The board, in its discretion, has determined that the results of the criminal records check do not make the individual ineligible for the license.

(8) The individual has passed the licensing examination administered under section 4751.15 of the Revised Code.

(9) The individual has paid to the board a license fee of two hundred fifty dollars.

(10) The individual has satisfied any additional requirements as may be prescribed in rules adopted under section 4751.04 of the Revised Code.

(B) A nursing home administrator license shall certify that the individual to whom it was issued has met the applicable requirements of this chapter and any applicable rules adopted under section 4751.04 of the Revised Code and is authorized to practice nursing home administration while the license is valid.

**HISTORY:**

133 v S 481 (Eff 4-12-70); 140 v H 291 (Eff 7-1-83); 144 v H 298. Eff 7-26-91; 2013 HB 59, § 101.01, eff. Sept. 29, 2013; renumbered from § ORC Ann. 4751.08 by 2019 hb166, § 101.01, effective October 17, 2019.

**Amendment Notes**

The 2019 amendment by HB 166 rewrote the section.

The 2013 amendment substituted "board of executives of long-term services and supports" for "board of examiners of nursing home administrators" in the introductory language; and made a stylistic change.

**RESEARCH REFERENCES AND PRACTICE AIDS**

**Ohio Administrative Code**

Recognition of out-of-state license. OAC 4751-1-14.

### § 4751.202 Temporary nursing home administrator license.

(A) Subject to section 4751.32 of the Revised Code, the board of executives of long-term services and supports may issue a temporary nursing home administrator license to an individual if all of the following requirements are satisfied:

(1) The operator of a nursing home has requested that the board issue a temporary nursing home administrator license to the individual to authorize the individual to temporarily practice nursing home administration at the nursing home because of a vacancy in the position of nursing home administrator at the nursing home resulting from a death, illness, or other unexpected cause.

(2) The individual is at least twenty-one years of age.

(3) The individual has complied with section 4776.02 of the Revised Code regarding a criminal records check.

(4) The board, in accordance with section 9.79 of the Revised Code, has determined that the results of the criminal records check do not make the individual ineligible for the license.

(5) The individual has paid to the board a fee for the temporary license of one hundred dollars.

(6) The individual has satisfied any additional requirements as may be prescribed in rules adopted under section 4751.04 of the Revised Code.

(B) A temporary nursing home administrator license shall certify that the individual to whom it was issued has met the applicable requirements of this chapter and any applicable rules adopted under section 4751.04 of the Revised Code and is authorized to practice nursing home administration while the temporary license is valid.

(C) Except as provided in section 4751.32 of the Revised Code, a temporary nursing home administrator license is valid for a period of time the board shall specify on the temporary license. That period shall not exceed one hundred eighty days. If that period is less than one hundred eighty days, the individual holding the temporary license may apply to the board for renewal of the temporary license in accordance with rules the board shall adopt under section 4751.04 of the Revised Code. Except as provided in section 4751.32 of the Revised Code, a renewed temporary nursing home administrator license is valid for a period of time the board shall specify on the renewed temporary license. That period shall not exceed the difference between one hundred eighty days and the number of days for which the original temporary license was valid. A renewed temporary nursing home administrator license shall not be renewed. A licensed temporary nursing home administrator who intends to continue to practice nursing home administration after the temporary license, including, if applicable, the renewed temporary license, expires must obtain a nursing home administrator license under section 4751.20 of the Revised Code.

**HISTORY:**

2019 hb166, § 101.01, effective October 17, 2019; 2020 hb263, § 1, effective October 9, 2021.

**Amendment Notes**

The 2020 amendment by HB 263 deleted former (A)(3), which read: "The individual is of good moral character"; redesignated former (A)(4) through (A)(7) as (A)(3) through (A)(6); and substituted "accordance with section 9.79 of the Revised Code" for "its discretion" in (A)(4).

### § 4751.21 Health services executive license.

(A) Subject to section 4751.32 of the Revised Code, the board of executives of long-term services and supports shall issue a health services executive license to an individual if all of the following requirements are satisfied:

(1) The individual has submitted to the board a completed application for the license in accordance with rules adopted under section 4751.04 of the Revised Code.

(2) The individual is a licensed nursing home administrator.

(3) The individual has obtained the health services executive qualification through the national association of long-term care administrator boards.

(4) The individual has complied with section 4776.02 of the Revised Code regarding a criminal records check.

(5) The board, in accordance with section 9.79 of the Revised Code, has determined that the results of the criminal records check do not make the individual ineligible for the license.

(6) The individual has paid to the board a license fee of one hundred dollars.

(B) A health services executive license shall certify that the individual to whom it was issued has met the applicable requirements of this chapter and any applicable rules adopted under section 4751.04 of the Revised Code and is a licensed health services executive while the license is valid.

**HISTORY:**

2019 hb166, § 101.01, effective October 17, 2019; 2020 hb263, § 1, effective October 9, 2021.

**Amendment Notes**

The 2020 amendment by HB 263 substituted "accordance with section 9.79 of the Revised Code" for "its discretion" in (A)(5).



### § 4751.22 Signatures required on licenses.

All licenses and temporary licenses that the board of executives of long-term services and supports issues under this chapter shall include the signatures of the board's chairperson and secretary.

**HISTORY:**

2019 hb166, § 101.01, effective October 17, 2019.

### § 4751.23 Duplicate license.

(A) Subject to section 4751.32 of the Revised Code, the board of executives of long-term services and supports may issue to a licensed nursing home administrator, licensed temporary nursing home administrator, or licensed health services executive a duplicate of the individual's nursing home administrator license, temporary nursing home administrator license, or health services executive license if the license or temporary license has been lost, mutilated, or destroyed and the individual does both of the following:

(1) Submits to the board a notarized statement explaining the conditions of the loss, mutilation, or destruction;

(2) Pays to the board a fee of twenty-five dollars.

(B) Subject to section 4751.32 of the Revised Code, the board may issue to a licensed nursing home administrator, licensed temporary nursing home administrator, or licensed health services executive whose name has been legally changed a duplicate of the individual's nursing home administrator license, temporary nursing home administrator license, or health services executive license that has the individual's new name if the individual does all of the following:

(1) Submits to the board a certified copy of the court order or marriage license establishing the change of name;

(2) Returns to the board the license or temporary license that has the individual's previous name;

(3) Pays to the board a fee of twenty-five dollars.

**HISTORY:**

2019 hb166, § 101.01, effective October 17, 2019.

### § 4751.24 Registration certificate; duty to display license.

(A) Subject to section 4751.32 of the Revised Code, a nursing home administrator license is valid for one year and may be renewed and reinstated in accordance with this section.

(B) If a licensed nursing home administrator intends to continue to practice nursing home administration without interruption after the administrator's license expires, the administrator shall apply to the board of executives of long-term services and supports for a renewed nursing home administrator license. Subject to section 4751.32 of the Revised Code, the board shall renew the license if the administrator does all of the following before the license expires:

(1) Submits to the board a completed application for license renewal in accordance with rules adopted under section 4751.04 of the Revised Code;

(2) Pays to the board the license renewal fee of three hundred dollars;

(3) Submits to the board satisfactory evidence of having attended such continuing education programs or courses of study as may be prescribed in rules adopted under section 4751.04 of the Revised Code;

(4) Satisfies any other requirements as may be prescribed in rules adopted under section 4751.04 of the Revised Code.

(C) If a nursing home administrator license issued under section 4751.20 or 4751.201 of the Revised Code is not renewed before it expires, the individual who held the license may apply to the board for the license's reinstatement. Subject to section 4751.32 of the Revised Code, the board shall reinstate the license if the individual does all of the following not later than one year after the date the license expired:

(1) Submits to the board the completed application for license reinstatement in accordance with rules adopted under section 4751.04 of the Revised Code;

(2) Pays to the board the license reinstatement fee equal to the sum of the following:

(a) Three hundred dollars;

(b) Fifty dollars for each calendar quarter that occurs during the period beginning on the date the license expires and ending on the last day of the calendar quarter during which the individual applies for license reinstatement, up to a maximum of two hundred dollars.

(3) Submits to the board satisfactory evidence of having attended such continuing education programs or courses of study as may be prescribed in rules adopted by the board under section 4751.04 of the Revised Code;

(4) Satisfies any other requirements as may be prescribed in rules adopted under section 4751.04 of the Revised Code.

(D) A licensed nursing home administrator who determines to temporarily abandon the practice of nursing home administration shall notify the board in writing immediately. The former administrator may thereafter resume the practice of nursing home administration within the state upon complying with the requirements of this section regarding annual license renewal or license reinstatement, whichever is applicable.

**HISTORY:**

133 v S 481 (Eff 4-12-70); 135 v S 322 (Eff 8-30-73); 140 v H 291 (Eff 7-1-83); 144 v H 298 (Eff 7-26-91); 147 v H 215. Eff 9-29-97; 150 v H 95, § 1, eff. 9-26-03; 153 v H 1, § 101.01, eff. 10-16-09; 2013 HB 59, § 101.01, eff. Sept. 29, 2013; renumbered from § ORC Ann. 4751.07 by 2019 hb166, § 101.01, effective October 17, 2019.

**Amendment Notes**

The 2019 amendment by HB 166 redesignated and rewrote former (A) as (A) and (B); deleted former (B); rewrote (C); deleted former (D); redesignated and rewrote former (E) as (D); and deleted former (F) through (H).

The 2013 amendment substituted "board of executives of long-term services and supports" for "board of examiners of nursing home administrators" in the first sentence of (A).

153 v H 1, effective October 16, 2009, substituted "three hundred dollars" for "two hundred fifty dollars" in (B).

**RESEARCH REFERENCES AND PRACTICE AIDS**

**Cross-References to Related Sections**

Board of examiners of nursing home administrators; powers and duties, RC § 4751.04.

Extension of continuing education reporting period for active duty military service, RC § 5903.12.

**Ohio Administrative Code**

Fees. OAC 4751-1-16.

Licenses and registrations. OAC 4751-1-10.

### § 4751.25 License expiration and renewal.

(A) Subject to section 4751.32 of the Revised Code, a health services executive license is valid for one year and may be renewed and reinstated in accordance with this section.

(B) A licensed health services executive may apply to the board of executives of long-term services and supports for a renewed license. Subject to section 4751.32 of the Revised Code, the board shall renew the license if the licensed health services executive does all of the following before the license expires:

(1) Submits to the board the completed application for license renewal in accordance with rules adopted under section 4751.04 of the Revised Code;

(2) Pays to the board the license renewal fee of fifty dollars;

(3) Submits to the board satisfactory evidence of having attended such continuing education programs or courses of study as may be prescribed in rules adopted under section 4751.04 of the Revised Code.

(C)(1) If a health services executive license is not renewed before it expires, the individual who held the license may apply to the board for the license's reinstatement. Subject to section 4751.32 of the Revised Code, the board shall reinstate the license if the individual does all of the following not later than one year after the date the license expired:

(a) Submits to the board the completed application for license reinstatement in accordance with rules adopted under section 4751.04 of the Revised Code;

(b) Pays to the board the license reinstatement fee specified in division (C)(2) of this section;

(c) Submits to the board satisfactory evidence of having attended such continuing education programs or courses of study as may be prescribed in rules adopted under section 4751.04 of the Revised Code.

(2) The fee to reinstate a health services executive license under division (C)(1) of this section is the following:

(a) If the individual applying for reinstatement has, at the same time, applied for reinstatement of a nursing home administrator license under division (C) of section 4751.24 of the Revised Code and paid the reinstatement fee required by division (C)(2) of that section, one hundred dollars;

(b) If division (C)(2)(a) of this section does not apply to the individual, the sum of the following:

(i) One hundred dollars;

(ii) Twenty-five dollars for each calendar quarter that occurs during the period beginning on the date the license expired and ending on the last day of the calendar quarter during which the individual applies for license reinstatement, up to a maximum of one hundred dollars.

**HISTORY:**

2019 hb166, § 101.01, effective October 17, 2019.

### § 4751.26 Approval of continuing education courses for nursing home administrators.

The board of executives of long-term services and supports shall approve continuing education courses for licensed nursing home administrators and licensed health services executives. The board may establish a fee for approval of such courses that is adequate to cover any expense the board incurs in the approval process.

**HISTORY:**

2017 hb49, § 101.01, effective September 29, 2017; renumbered from § ORC Ann. 4751.044 by 2019 hb166, § 101.01, effective October 17, 2019.

**Amendment Notes**

The 2019 amendment by HB 166, in the first sentence, added "licensed" and "and licensed health services executives."

### § 4751.30 Complaints.

(A) Any person may submit to the board of executives of long-term services and supports a complaint that the person reasonably believes that another person has violated, or failed to comply with a requirement of, this chapter or a rule adopted under section 4751.04 of the Revised Code. All of the following apply to complaints submitted to the board under this section:

(1) They are not subject to discovery in any civil action.

(2) They are not public records for purposes of section 149.43 of the Revised Code.

(3) They are not subject to inspection or copying under section 1347.08 of the Revised Code.

(B) Except as provided in division (D) of section 4751.31 of the Revised Code, the board shall protect the confidentiality of each person who submits a complaint to the board under this section.

**HISTORY:**

2019 hb166, § 101.01, effective October 17, 2019.

### § 4751.31 Investigation of and action on complaints.

(A) The board of executives of long-term services and supports shall receive, investigate, and take appropriate action with respect to any complaint submitted to the board under section 4751.30 of the Revised Code and any other credible information the board possesses that indicates a person may have violated, or failed to comply with a requirement of, this chapter or a rule adopted under section 4751.04 of the Revised Code.

(B) In conducting an investigation under this section, the board may do any of the following:

(1) Question witnesses;

(2) Conduct interviews;

(3) Inspect and copy any books, accounts, papers, records, or other documents;

(4) Issue subpoenas;

(5) Compel the attendance of witnesses and the production of documents and testimony.

(C) No member of the board who supervises an investigation conducted under this section shall participate in any adjudication arising from the investigation.

(D) The board may disclose any information it receives as part of an investigation conducted under this section, including the identity of a person who submits a complaint under section 4751.30 of the Revised Code, to a law enforcement agency, licensing board, or other government agency that investigates, prosecutes, or adjudicates alleged violations of statutes or rules. An agency or board that receives such information shall protect the confidentiality of a person who submits a complaint under section 4751.30 of the Revised Code in the same manner as the board of executives of long-term services and supports, notwithstanding any other information that the agency or other board possesses.

**HISTORY:**

2019 hb166, § 101.01, effective October 17, 2019.

### § 4751.32 Revocation of license.

(A) Except as provided in division (D) of this section, the board of executives of long-term services and supports may take any of the actions authorized by division (B) of this section against an individual who has applied for or holds a nursing home administrator license, temporary nursing home administrator license, or health services executive license if any of the following apply to the individual:

(1) The individual has failed to satisfy any requirement established by this chapter or the rules adopted under section 4751.04 of the Revised Code that must be satisfied to obtain the license or temporary license.

(2) The individual has violated, or failed to comply with a requirement of, this chapter or a rule adopted under section 4751.04 of the Revised Code regarding the practice of nursing home administration, including the requirements of sections 4751.40 and 4751.41 of the Revised Code.

(3) The individual is unfit or incompetent to practice nursing home administration, serve in a leadership position at a long-term services and supports setting, or direct the practices of others in such a setting by reason of negligence, habits, or other causes, including the individual's habitual or excessive use or abuse of drugs, alcohol, or other substances.

(4) The individual has acted in a manner inconsistent with the health and safety of either of the following:

(a) The residents of the nursing home at which the individual practices nursing home administration;

(b) The consumers of services and supports provided by a long-term services and supports setting at which the individual serves in a leadership position or directs the practices of others.

(5) The individual has been convicted of, or pleaded guilty to, either of the following in a court of competent jurisdiction, either within or without this state:

(a) A felony;

(b) An offense of moral turpitude that constitutes a misdemeanor in this state.

(6) The individual made a false, fraudulent, deceptive, or misleading statement in seeking to obtain, or obtaining, a nursing home administrator license, temporary nursing home administrator license, or health services executive license.

(7) The individual made a fraudulent misrepresentation in attempting to obtain, or obtaining, money or anything of value in the practice of nursing home administration or while serving in a leadership position at a long-term services and supports setting or directing the practices of others in such a setting.

(8) The individual has substantially deviated from the board's code of ethics.

(9) Another health care licensing agency has taken any of the following actions against the individual for any reason other than nonpayment of a fee:

(a) Denied, refused to renew or reinstate, limited, revoked, or suspended, or accepted the surrender of, a license or other authorization to practice;

(b) Imposed probation;

(c) Issued a censure or other reprimand.

(10) The individual has failed to do any of the following:

(a) Cooperate with an investigation conducted by the board under section 4751.31 of the Revised Code;

(b) Respond to or comply with a subpoena issued by the board in an investigation of the individual;

(c) Comply with any disciplinary action the board has taken against the individual pursuant to this section.

(B) The following are the actions that the board may take for the purpose of division (A) of this section:

(1) Deny the individual any of the following:

(a) A nursing home administrator license under section 4751.20, 4751.201, 4751.23, or 4751.24 of the Revised Code;

(b) A temporary nursing home administrator license under section 4751.202 or 4751.23 of the Revised Code;

(c) A health services executive license under section 4751.21, 4751.23, or 4751.25 of the Revised Code.

(2) Suspend the individual's nursing home administrator license, temporary nursing home administrator license, or health services executive license;

(3) Revoke the individual's nursing home administrator license, temporary nursing home administrator license, or health services executive license, either permanently or for a period of time the board specifies;

(4) Place a limitation on the individual's nursing home administrator license, temporary nursing home administrator license, or health services executive license;

(5) Place the individual on probation;

(6) Issue a written reprimand of the individual;

(7) Impose on the individual a civil penalty, fine, or other sanction specified in rules adopted under section 4751.04 of the Revised Code.

(C) The board shall take actions authorized by division (B) of this section in accordance with Chapter 119. of the Revised Code, except that the board may enter into a consent agreement with an individual to resolve an alleged violation of this chapter or a rule adopted under section 4751.04 of the Revised Code in lieu of making an adjudication regarding the alleged violation. A consent agreement constitutes the board's findings and order with respect to the matter addressed in the consent agreement if the board ratifies the consent agreement. Any admissions or findings included in a proposed consent agreement have no force or effect if the board refuses to ratify the consent agreement.

(D) The board shall not refuse to issue an initial nursing home administrator license, temporary nursing home administrator license, or health services executive license, unless the refusal is in accordance with section 9.79 of the Revised Code.

**HISTORY:**

133 v S 481 (Eff 4-12-70); 135 v S 322. Eff 8-30-73; 2013 HB 59, § 101.01, eff. Sept. 29, 2013; 2017 hb49, § 101.01, effective September 29, 2017; renumbered from § ORC Ann. 4751.10 by 2019 hb166, § 101.01, effective October 17, 2019; 2020 hb263, § 1, effective October 9, 2021.

**Amendment Notes**

The 2020 amendment by HB 263 added "Except as provided in division (D) of this section" in the introductory language of (A); and added (D).

The 2019 amendment by HB 166 redesignated the former introductory language as the introductory language of (A); redesignated and rewrote former (A) as (A)(3); added (A)(1) and (A)(2); redesignated and rewrote former (B) as (A)(4) and (A)(4)(a); deleted former (C); redesignated and rewrote former (D) as (A)(5); and added (A)(6) through (A)(10), (B), and (C).

The 2017 amendment by HB 49 deleted former concluding language which read: "Proceedings under this section shall be instituted by the board or shall be begun by filing with the board charges in writing and under oath."

The 2013 amendment substituted "board of executives of long-term services and supports" for "board of examiners of nursing home administrators" in the introductory language; and made stylistic changes.



**NOTES TO DECISIONS**

Analysis

Evidence
Power of appellate court to modify sanction

**Evidence**

Administrator's conviction for Medicaid fraud was reliable, probative, and substantial evidence to support revocation of the administrator's license despite the failure of the board of examiners to rule on or consider any objections; while the board might have erred in admitting the certified transcript of the administrator's sentencing hearing, the statements in question were not of a prejudicial nature. Reynolds v. Ohio State Bd. of Examiners of Nursing Home Adm'rs, 2003-Ohio-4958, 2003 Ohio App. LEXIS 4435 (Ohio Ct. App., Franklin County 2003).

**Power of appellate court to modify sanction**

Appellate court was without power to modify the board of examiners' sanction, the revocation of a license, where such penalty was permitted under R.C. 4751.10. Reynolds v. Ohio State Bd. of Examiners of Nursing Home Adm'rs, 2003-Ohio-4958, 2003 Ohio App. LEXIS 4435 (Ohio Ct. App., Franklin County 2003).

**RESEARCH REFERENCES AND PRACTICE AIDS**

**Cross-References to Related Sections**

Drug offense convictions to be reported to professional licensing authorities, RC § 2925.38.

Report of abuse or neglect of resident or misappropriation of property at long-term care facility by health care professional, RC § 3721.22.

**Ohio Administrative Code**

Suspension or revocation of license. OAC 4751-1-12.

**Comparative Legislation**

Grounds for revocation, etc.:
FL—Fla. Stat. § 468.1745
IN—Burns Ind. Code Ann. § 25-19-1-11
KY—KRS § 216A.070
NY—NY CLS Pub Health § 2897
PA—63 P.S. § 1112

## § 4751.33 Reissuance of license.

(A) The board of executives of long-term services and supports may, in its discretion, reissue a nursing home administrator license, temporary nursing home administrator license, or health services executive license to any individual whose license or temporary license has beenrevoked. Application for the reissuance shall not be made prior to one year after revocation and shall be made in such manner as the board may direct.

(B) If an individual who has been convicted of, or pleaded guilty to, a felony is subsequently pardoned by the governor of the state where such conviction or plea was had or by the president of the United States, or receives a final release granted by the adult parole authority of this state or its equivalent agency of another state, the board may, in its discretion, on application of the individual and on the submission of evidence satisfactory to the board, restore the individual's nursing home administrator license, temporary nursing home administrator license, or health services executive license.

**HISTORY:**

133 v S 481. Eff 4-12-70; 2013 HB 59, § 101.01, eff. Sept. 29, 2013; renumbered from § ORC Ann. 4751.11 by 2019 hb166, § 101.01, effective October 17, 2019.

**Amendment Notes**

The 2019 amendment by HB 166 redesignated and rewrote former (A) and (B) as (A); redesignated former (C) as (B); and rewrote (B), which formerly read: "If a person convicted of a felony is subsequently pardoned by the governor of the state where such conviction was had or by the president of the United States, or receives a final release granted by the adult parole authority of this state or its equivalent agency of another state, the board may, in its discretion, on application of such person and on the submission of evidence satisfactory to the board, restore to such person the nursing home administrator's license or registration, or both."

The 2013 amendment substituted "board of executives of long-term services and supports" for "board of examiners of nursing home administrators" in (A).

## § 4751.35 Effect of child support default.

On receipt of a notice pursuant to section 3123.43 of the Revised Code, the board of executives of long-term services and supports shall comply with sections 3123.41 to 3123.50 of the Revised Code and any applicable rules adopted under section 3123.63 of the Revised Code with respect to a license or temporary license issued pursuant to this chapter.

**HISTORY:**

146 v H 167 (Eff 11-15-96); 148 v S 180. Eff 3-22-2001; 2013 HB 59, § 101.01, eff. Sept. 29, 2013; renumbered from § ORC Ann. 4751.12 by 2019 hb166, § 101.01, effective October 17, 2019.

**Amendment Notes**

The 2019 amendment by HB 166 added "or temporary license."

The 2013 amendment substituted "board of executives of long-term services and supports" for "board of examiners of nursing home administrators".

**RESEARCH REFERENCES AND PRACTICE AIDS**

**Ohio Administrative Code**

Department of job and family services, division of public assistance—

Suspension of professional license upon default of child support order; notice and enforcement methods. OAC 5101:12-55-25.

## § 4751.36 Required compliance with R.C. § 4776.20.

The board of executives of long-term services and supports shall comply with section 4776.20 of the Revised Code.

**HISTORY:**

2012 HB 247, § 1, eff. Mar. 22, 2013; 2013 HB 59, § 101.01, eff. Sept. 29, 2013; renumbered from § ORC Ann. 4751.13 by 2019 hb166, § 101.01, effective October 17, 2019.

**Amendment Notes**

The 2013 amendment substituted "board of executives of long-term services and supports" for "board of examiners of nursing home administrators".

## § 4751.37 Board authorized to take action to comply with Social Security Act.

The board of executives of long-term services and supports shall take such actions as may be necessary to enable the state to meet the requirements set forth in section 1908 of the "Social Security Act," 42 U.S.C. 1396g.

**HISTORY:**
2019 hb166, § 101.01, effective October 17, 2019.

### § 4751.38 Opportunities for education, training and credentialing.

The board of executives of long-term services and supports shall create opportunities for the education, training, and credentialing of nursing home administrators, persons in leadership positions who practice in long-term services and supports settings or who direct the practices of others in those settings, and persons interested in serving in those roles. In carrying out this duty, the board shall do both the following:

(A) Identify core competencies and areas of knowledge that are appropriate for nursing home administrators, credentialed individuals, and others working within the long-term services and supports settings system, with an emphasis on all of the following:

(1) Leadership;

(2) Person-centered care;

(3) Principles of management within both the business and regulatory environments;

(4) An understanding of all post-acute settings, including transitions from acute settings and between post-acute settings.

(B) Assist in the development of a strong, competitive market in this state for making training, continuing education, and degree programs available to individuals seeking to practice nursing home administration, serve in a leadership position at a long-term services and support setting, or direct the practice of others in such a setting.

**HISTORY:**
2019 hb166, § 101.01, effective October 17, 2019.

### § 4751.381 Training and education programs in person or through electronic media.

(A) Training and education programs developed by the board of executives of long-term services and supports pursuant to section 4751.38 of the Revised Code may be conducted in person or through electronic media. The board may establish and charge a fee for the education and training programs.

(B) The board may enter into a contract with a government or private entity to perform the board's duties under section 4751.38 of the Revised Code to develop and conduct education and training programs. If the board enters into such a contract, the contract may authorize the entity to pay any or all costs associated with the education or training programs and to collect and keep, as all or part of the entity's compensation under the contract, any fee an applicant for education or training pays to enroll in the education or training program.

**HISTORY:**
2017 hb49, § 101.01, effective September 29, 2017; renumbered from § ORC Ann. 4751.043 by 2019 hb166, § 101.01, effective October 17, 2019.

**Amendment Notes**
The 2019 amendment by HB 166 substituted "section 4751.38" for "division (A)(10) of section 4751.04" in the first sentence of (A); and substituted "section 4751.38" for "division (A)(10) of section 4751.04" in the first sentence of (B).

### § 4751.40 Change of address to be reported to the board.

Each licensed nursing home administrator, licensed temporary nursing home administrator, and licensed health services executive shall report to the board of executives of long-term services and supports any change in any of the following not later than ten days after the change:

(A) The individual's residence mailing address;

(B) The name and address of each place at which the individual practices nursing home administration;

(C) The name and address of each long-term services and supports setting at which the individual serves in a leadership position or directs the practices of others.

**HISTORY:**
2019 hb166, § 101.01, effective October 17, 2019.

### § 4751.41 License to be displayed.

Every licensed nursing home administrator, licensed temporary nursing home administrator, and licensed health services executive shall display the individual's license or temporary license in the place at which the individual practices nursing home administration and the long-term services and supports setting at which the individual serves in a leadership position or directs the practices of others.

**HISTORY:**
2019 hb166, § 101.01, effective October 17, 2019.

### § 4751.45 Request that another state be provided with verification of licensing board.

An individual who is a licensed nursing home administrator, licensed temporary nursing home administrator, or licensed health services executive may request that the board of executives of long-term services and supports provide to a licensing board or agency of another state verification of the individual's licensure status under this chapter and other related information in the board's possession. The board shall provide the licensing board or agency of the other state the verification and other related information so requested if the individual pays to the board the fee for this service. The board shall adopt a rule under section 4751.04 of the Revised Code establishing the fee.

**HISTORY:**
2019 hb166, § 101.01, effective October 17, 2019.

### § 4751.99 Penalties.

Whoever violates section 4751.10 of the Revised Code may be fined not more than five hundred dollars for the first offense; for each subsequent offense such person may be fined not more than five hundred dollars or imprisoned for not more than ninety days, or both.

The imposition of fines pursuant to this section does not preclude the imposition of any civil penalties or fines authorized by section 4751.32 or any other section of the Revised Code.

**HISTORY:**
133 v S 481 (Eff 4-12-70); 135 v S 322. Eff 8-30-73; 2017 hb49, § 101.01, effective September 29, 2017; 2019 hb166, § 101.01, effective October 17, 2019.

**Amendment Notes**
The 2019 amendment by HB 166 substituted "4751.10" for "4751.02 or 4751.09" in the first paragraph; and substituted "by section 4751.32" for "under section 4751.04" in the second paragraph.

The 2017 amendment by HB 49 substituted "may be fined more than five hundred dollars" for "shall be fined not less than fifty nor more than five hundred dollars" twice in the first paragraph; and added the second paragraph.

# TITLE 51

# PUBLIC WELFARE



# CHAPTER 5101

# DEPARTMENT OF JOB AND FAMILY SERVICES — GENERAL PROVISIONS



## DISCLOSURE OF INFORMATION

### § 5101.314 Repealed.

Repealed, 148 v S 180, § 2 [GC § 10503-15; 114 v 320(342); Bureau of Code Revision, RC § 2105.18, 10-1-53; 125 v 347; 136 v S 145; 137 v H 1; 139 v H 245; 143 v H 15; 143 v S 3; 144 v S 10; RC § 5101.31.4, 147 v H 352; 148 v H 471]. Eff 3-22-2001.

**Editor's Notes**
This section concerned acknowledgment of paternity.

## ADULT PROTECTIVE SERVICES

### § 5101.60 Definitions.

As used in sections 5101.60 to 5101.73 of the Revised Code:

(A) "Abandonment" means desertion of an adult by a caretaker without having made provision for transfer of the adult's care.

(B) "Abuse" means the infliction upon an adult by self or others of injury, unreasonable confinement, intimidation, or cruel punishment with resulting physical harm, pain, or mental anguish.

(C) "Adult" means any person sixty years of age or older within this state who is handicapped by the infirmities of aging or who has a physical or mental impairment which prevents the person from providing for the person's own care or protection, and who resides in an independent living arrangement.

(D) "Area agency on aging" means a public or private nonprofit entity designated under section 173.011 of the Revised Code to administer programs on behalf of the department of aging.

(E) "Caretaker" means the person assuming the primary responsibility for the care of an adult by any of the following means:

(1) On a voluntary basis;
(2) By contract;
(3) Through receipt of payment for care;
(4) As a result of a family relationship;
(5) By order of a court of competent jurisdiction.

(F) "Community mental health agency" means any agency, program, or facility with which a board of alcohol, drug addiction, and mental health services contracts to provide the mental health services listed in section 340.99 of the Revised Code.

(G) "Court" means the probate court in the county where an adult resides.

(H) "Emergency" means that the adult is living in conditions which present a substantial risk of immediate and irreparable physical harm or death to self or any other person.

(I) "Emergency services" means protective services furnished to an adult in an emergency.

(J) "Exploitation" means the unlawful or improper act of a person using, in one or more transactions, an adult or an adult's resources for monetary or personal benefit, profit, or gain when the person obtained or exerted control over the adult or the adult's resources in any of the following ways:

(1) Without the adult's consent or the consent of the person authorized to give consent on the adult's behalf;

(2) Beyond the scope of the express or implied consent of the adult or the person authorized to give consent on the adult's behalf;

(3) By deception;

(4) By threat;

(5) By intimidation.

(K) "In need of protective services" means an adult known or suspected to be suffering from abuse, neglect, or exploitation to an extent that either life is endangered or physical harm, mental anguish, or mental illness results or is likely to result.

(L) "Incapacitated person" means a person who is impaired for any reason to the extent that the person lacks sufficient understanding or capacity to make and carry out reasonable decisions concerning the person's self or resources, with or without the assistance of a caretaker. Refusal to consent to the provision of services shall not be the sole determinative that the person is incapacitated.

(M) "Independent living arrangement" means a domicile of a person's own choosing, including, but not limited to, a private home, apartment, trailer, or rooming house. "Independent living arrangement" includes a residential facility licensed under section 5119.22 of the Revised Code that provides accommodations, supervision, and personal care services for three to sixteen unrelated adults, but does not include any other institution or facility licensed by the state or a facility in which a person resides as a result of voluntary, civil, or criminal commitment.

(N) "Mental illness" means a substantial disorder of thought, mood, perception, orientation, or memory that grossly impairs judgment, behavior, capacity to recognize reality, or ability to meet the ordinary demands of life.

(O) "Neglect" means any of the following:

(1) Failure of an adult to provide for self the goods or services necessary to avoid physical harm, mental anguish, or mental illness;

(2) Failure of a caretaker to provide such goods or services;

(3) Abandonment.

(P) "Outpatient health facility" means a facility where medical care and preventive, diagnostic, therapeutic, rehabilitative, or palliative items or services are provided to outpatients by or under the direction of a physician or dentist.

(Q) "Peace officer" means a peace officer as defined in section 2935.01 of the Revised Code.

(R) "Physical harm" means bodily pain, injury, impairment, or disease suffered by an adult.

(S) "Protective services" means services provided by the county department of job and family services or its designated agency to an adult who has been determined by evaluation to require such services for the prevention, correction, or discontinuance of an act of as well as conditions resulting from abuse, neglect, or exploitation. Protective services may include, but are not limited to, case work services, medical care, mental health services, legal services, fiscal management, home health care, homemaker services, housing-related services, guardianship services, and placement services as well as the provision of such commodities as food, clothing, and shelter.

(T) "Reasonable decisions" means decisions made in daily living that facilitate the provision of food, shelter, clothing, and health care necessary for life support.

(U) "Senior service provider" means a person who provides care or specialized services to an adult.

(V) "Working day" means Monday, Tuesday, Wednesday, Thursday, and Friday, except when such day is a holiday as defined in section 1.14 of the Revised Code.

**HISTORY:**

139 v H 694 (Eff 11-15-81); 141 v H 428 (Eff 12-23-86); 143 v S 2 (Eff 11-1-89); 143 v H 253 (Eff 11-15-90); 148 v H 471. Eff 7-1-2000; 153 v H 1, § 101.01, eff. 10-16-09; 2011 HB 153, § 101.01, eff. July 1, 2011; 2012 HB 487, § 101.01, eff. Sept. 10, 2012; 2013 HB 59, § 101.01, eff. Sept. 29, 2013; 2015 hb64, § 101.01, effective September 29, 2015; 2017 hb49, § 130.31, effective September 29, 2018; 2018 sb158, § 1, effective March 20, 2019.

**Amendment Notes**

The 2018 amendment by SB 158 deleted "except that it does not include the state long-term care ombudsman or a regional long-term care ombudsman" at the end of (U).

The 2015 amendment by HB 64 added "when the caretaker obtained or exerted control over the adult or the adult's resources in any of the following ways" to the end of the introductory language of (G); and added (G)(1) through (G)(5).

The 2013 amendment substituted "section 5119.34" for "section 5119.22" in the last sentence of (B).

The 2012 amendment, in the last sentence of (B), substituted "a residential facility licensed under section 5119.22" for "an adult care facility licensed pursuant to Chapter 5119." and inserted "that provides accommodations, supervision, and personal care services for three to sixteen unrelated adults".

The 2011 amendment substituted "Chapter 5119" for "Chapter 3722" in the last sentence of (B).

153 v H 1, effective October 16, 2009, in (B), rewrote the last sentence, and deleted the last sentence, which read: "'Independent living arrangement' does include adult care facilities licensed pursuant to Chapter 3722. of the Revised Code".

## NOTES TO DECISIONS

**Generally**

The policy of the Ohio Adult Protective Services Act, R.C. 5101.60 et seq., is to help maintain the dignity and relative independence of the recipients in their homes in that the economic savings engendered by support and assistance, as opposed to commitment, are beneficial and desirable for both the individual and the state: In re Protective Service of Stitt, 24 Ohio App. 3d 204, 493 N.E.2d 1377, 1985 Ohio App. LEXIS 10174 (Ohio Ct. App., Franklin County 1985).

## RESEARCH REFERENCES AND PRACTICE AIDS

**Cross-References to Related Sections**

Case referrals, RC § 5101.64.

County department of job and family services to implement provisions, RC § 5101.61.

Duty to report abuse, neglect or exploitation of adult, RC § 5101.63.

Reimbursement of county departments; internal management rules, RC § 5101.611.

**Ohio Administrative Code**

Department of job and family services, division of social services— Adult protective services. OAC ch. 5101:2-20.

Definitions. OAC 5101:2-20-01.

## § 5101.61 Duty to report abuse, neglect or exploitation of adult. [Renumbered]

**HISTORY:**

139 v H 694 (Eff 11-15-81); 141 v H 66 (Eff 3-6-86); 142 v S 124 (Eff 10-1-87); 143 v S 2 (Eff 11-1-89); 143 v H 253 (Eff 11-15-90); 143 v H 317 (Eff 10-10-89); 146 v H 117 (Eff 9-29-95); 148 v H 471. Eff 7-1-2000; 153 v H 1, § 101.01, eff. 10-16-09; 2011 HB 153, § 101.01, eff. July 1, 2011; 2012 HB 487, § 101.01, eff. Sept. 10, 2012; 2013 HB 59, § 101.01, eff. Sept. 29, 2013; 2014 HB 232, § 1, eff. July 10, 2014; 2015 hb64, § 101.01, effective September 29, 2015; 2017 hb49, § 101.01, effective September 29, 2017; renumbered to § 5101.63 by 2017 hb49, § 130.31, effective September 29, 2018.

## § 5101.61 County departments of job and family services to implement provisions; training.

(A) The county departments of job and family services shall implement sections 5101.60 to 5101.71 of the Revised Code.

(B) The director of job and family services may adopt rules in accordance with section 111.15 of the Revised Code to carry out the purposes of sections 5101.60 to 5101.71 of the Revised Code. The rules adopted pursuant to this division may include a requirement that the county departments provide on forms prescribed by the rules a plan of proposed expenditures, and a report of actual expenditures, of funds necessary to implement sections 5101.60 to 5101.71 of the Revised Code and other requirements for intake procedures, investigations, case management, and the provision of protective services.

**HISTORY:**

139 v H 694 (Eff 11-15-81); 141 v H 428 (Eff 12-23-86); 143 v H 111 (Eff 7-1-89); 144 v H 298 (Eff 7-26-91); 148 v H 471. Eff 7-1-2000; 2015 hb64, §

101.01, effective September 29, 2015; renumbered from § 5101.71 by 2017 hb49, § 130.31, effective September 29, 2018.

**Amendment Notes**

The 2017 amendment by HB 49 deleted the former second through the last sentences of (A), which read: "The department of job and family services shall provide a program of ongoing, comprehensive, formal training regarding the implementation of sections 5101.60 to 5101.71 of the Revised Code and require all adult protective services caseworkers and their supervisors to undergo the training. Training shall not be limited to the procedures for implementing section 5101.62 of the Revised Code. The department of job and family services shall adopt any rules it deems necessary regarding the training."

The 2015 amendment by HB 64, in (A), in the second sentence, substituted "shall provide" for "may provide," substituted "regarding the implementation of" for "to county departments and other agencies authorized to implement," and added "and require all adult protective services caseworkers and their supervisors to undergo the training" to the end and added the last sentence; and, in (B), substituted "to carry out the purposes" for "governing the county departments' implementation" in the first sentence and added "and other requirements for intake procedures, investigations, case management, and the provision of protective services" to the end of the second sentence.

### RESEARCH REFERENCES AND PRACTICE AIDS

**Cross-References to Related Sections**

Case referrals, RC § 5101.64.
Definitions, RC § 5101.60.
Reimbursement of county departments; internal management rules, RC § 5101.611.

**Ohio Administrative Code**

Department of job and family services, division of social services—Adult protective services. OAC ch. 5101:2-20.

## § 5101.611 Case referrals. [Renumbered]

**HISTORY:**

142 v H 403 (Eff 3-16-89); 148 v H 471. Eff 7-1-2000; 153 v S 79, § 1, eff. 10-6-09; 2015 hb64, § 101.01, effective September 29, 2015; renumbered to § 5101.64 by 2017 hb49, § 130.31, effective September 29, 2018.

## § 5101.611 Reimbursement of county departments; internal management rules.

The department of job and family services may reimburse county departments of job and family services for all or part of the costs they incur in implementing sections 5101.60 to 5101.73 of the Revised Code. The director of job and family services shall adopt internal management rules in accordance with section 111.15 of the Revised Code that provide for reimbursement of county departments of job and family services under this section.

The director shall adopt internal management rules in accordance with section 111.15 of the Revised Code that do both of the following:

(A) Implement sections 5101.60 to 5101.71 of the Revised Code;

(B) Require the county departments to collect and submit to the department, or ensure that a designated agency collects and submits to the department, data concerning the implementation of sections 5101.60 to 5101.73 of the Revised Code.

**HISTORY:**

143 v H 111 (Eff 7-1-89); 148 v H 471 . Eff 7-1-2000; 151 v S 238 , § 1, eff. 9-21-06; 2015 hb64, § 101.01, effective September 29, 2015; renumbered from § 5101.72 by 2017 hb49, § 130.31, effective September 29, 2018.

**Editor's Notes**

Amendments by Act 2017, HB 49 were partially vetoed by the governor. Section is presented without the vetoed provisions.

**Amendment Notes**

The 2017 amendment by HB 49 added "local law enforcement agencies, and county prosecutors" in the first and second sentences of the first paragraph and in (B); and substituted "5101.73" for "5101.71" in the first sentence of the first paragraph and in (B).

## § 5101.612 Uniform statewide automated adult protective services information system. [Renumbered]

**HISTORY:**

2015 hb64, § 101.01, effective September 29, 2015; renumbered to § 5101.631 by 2017 hb49, § 130.31, effective September 29, 2018.

## § 5101.62 Investigation of report; written notice of intent; report of conclusion. [Renumbered]

**HISTORY:**

139 v H 694 (Eff 11-15-81); 141 v H 428 (Eff 12-23-86); 142 v H 403 (Eff 3-16-89); 148 v H 471. Eff 7-1-2000; 2015 hb64, § 101.01, effective September 29, 2015; renumbered to § 5101.65 by 2017 hb49, § 130.31, effective September 29, 2018.

## § 5101.62 Implementing adult protective services program.

The department of job and family services shall do all of the following:

(A) Provide a program of ongoing, comprehensive, formal training on the implementation of sections 5101.60 to 5101.73 of the Revised Code and require all protective services caseworkers and their supervisors to undergo the training;

(B) Develop and make available educational materials for individuals who are required under section 5101.63 of the Revised Code to make reports of abuse, neglect, and exploitation;

(C) Facilitate ongoing cooperation among state agencies on issues pertaining to the abuse, neglect, or exploitation of adults.

**HISTORY:**

2017 hb49, § 130.31, effective September 29, 2018.

## § 5101.621 Memorandum of understanding.

(A) Each county department of job and family services shall prepare a memorandum of understanding that is signed by all of the following:

(1) The director of the county department of job and family services;

(2) If the county department has entered into an agreement or contract with a private or government entity pursuant to section 5101.652 of the Revised Code, the director of the entity;

(3) The county peace officer;

(4) The chief peace officer of the largest municipality within the county;

(5) Other law enforcement officers handling adult abuse, neglect, and exploitation cases in the county;

(6) The prosecuting attorney of the county;

(7) The coroner of the county.

(B) The memorandum of understanding shall set forth the procedures to be followed by the persons listed in division (A) of this section in the execution of their respective responsibilities related to cases of adult abuse, neglect, and exploitation. The memorandum of understanding shall establish all of the following:

(1) An interdisciplinary team to coordinate efforts related to the prevention, reporting, and treatment of abuse, neglect, and exploitation of adults;

(2) The roles and responsibilities for handling cases that have been referred by the county department to another agency pursuant to section 5101.64 of the Revised Code;

(3) The roles and responsibilities for filing criminal charges against persons alleged to have abused, neglected, or exploited adults.

Failure to follow the procedure set forth in the memorandum of understanding is not grounds for, and shall not result in, the dismissal of any charge or complaint arising from a report of abuse, neglect, or exploitation or the suppression of any evidence obtained as a result of a report of abuse, neglect, or exploitation and does not give any rights or grounds for appeal or post-conviction relief to any person.

(C) The memorandum of understanding may, in addition, be signed by any of the following persons who are also members of the interdisciplinary team described in division (B)(1) of this section:

(1) A representative of the area agency on aging, as defined in section 173.14 of the Revised Code;

(2) A representative of the regional long-term care ombudsman program;

(3) A representative of the board of alcohol, drug addiction, and mental health services;

(4) A representative of the board of health of a city or general health district;

(5) A representative of the county board of developmental disabilities;

(6) A representative of a victim assistance program;

(7) A representative of a local housing authority;

(8) Any other person whose participation furthers the goals of the memorandum of understanding.

**HISTORY:**

2015 hb64, § 101.01, effective September 29, 2015; 2018 sb158, § 1, effective March 20, 2019.

**Amendment Notes**

The 2018 amendment by SB 158 rewrote (A)(2), which formerly read: "If the county department has entered into an interagency agreement with a local agency pursuant to section 5101.622 of the Revised Code, the director of the local agency"; rewrote (A)(4), which formerly read: "All chief municipal peace officers within the county"; substituted "section 5101.64" for "section 5101.611" in (B)(2); and in (C)(2), added "A representative of" and "program."



### § 5101.622 Authority to contract with another person or government entity. [Renumbered]

**HISTORY:**

2015 hb64, § 101.01, effective September 29, 2015; renumbered to § 5101.652 by 2017 hb49, § 130.31, effective September 29, 2018.

### § 5101.63 Temporary restraining order to prevent interference or obstruction of investigation. [Renumbered]

**HISTORY:**

139 v H 694 (Eff 11-15-81); 141 v H 428 (Eff 12-23-86); 142 v H 403 (Eff 3-16-89); 148 v H 471. Eff 7-1-2000; renumbered to § 5101.651 by 2017 hb49, § 130.31, effective September 29, 2018.

### § 5101.63 Duty to report abuse, neglect or exploitation of adult.

(A)(1) Any individual listed in division (A)(2) of this section having reasonable cause to believe that an adult is being abused, neglected, or exploited, or is in a condition which is the result of abuse, neglect, or exploitation shall immediately report such belief to the county department of job and family services.

(2) All of the following are subject to division (A)(1) of this section:

(a) An attorney admitted to the practice of law in this state;

(b) An individual authorized under Chapter 4731. of the Revised Code to practice medicine and surgery, osteopathic medicine and surgery, or podiatric medicine and surgery;

(c) An individual licensed under Chapter 4734. of the Revised Code as a chiropractor;

(d) An individual licensed under Chapter 4715. of the Revised Code as a dentist;

(e) An individual licensed under Chapter 4723. of the Revised Code as a registered nurse or licensed practical nurse;

(f) An individual licensed under Chapter 4732. of the Revised Code as a psychologist;

(g) An individual licensed under Chapter 4757. of the Revised Code as a social worker, independent social worker, professional counselor, professional clinical counselor, marriage and family therapist, or independent marriage and family therapist;

(h) An individual licensed under Chapter 4729. of the Revised Code as a pharmacist;

(i) An individual holding a certificate to practice as a dialysis technician issued under Chapter 4723. of the Revised Code;

(j) An employee of a home health agency, as defined in section 3740.01 of the Revised Code;

(k) An employee of an outpatient health facility;

(*l*) An employee of a hospital, as defined in section 3727.01 of the Revised Code;

(m) An employee of a hospital or public hospital, as defined in section 5122.01 of the Revised Code;

(n) An employee of a nursing home or residential care facility, as defined in section 3721.01 of the Revised Code;

(o) An employee of a residential facility licensed under section 5119.22 of the Revised Code that provides accommodations, supervision, and personal care services for three to sixteen unrelated adults;

(p) An employee of a health department operated by the board of health of a city or general health district or the authority having the duties of a board of health under section 3709.05 of the Revised Code;

(q) An employee of a community mental health agency, as defined in section 5122.01 of the Revised Code;

(r) A humane society agent appointed under section 1717.06 of the Revised Code;

(s) An individual who is a firefighter for a lawfully constituted fire department;

(t) An individual who is an ambulance driver for an emergency medical service organization, as defined in section 4765.01 of the Revised Code;

(u) A first responder, emergency medical technician-basic, emergency medical technician-intermediate, or paramedic, as those terms are defined in section 4765.01 of the Revised Code;

(v) An official employed by a local building department to conduct inspections of houses and other residential buildings;

(w) A peace officer;

(x) A coroner;

(y) A member of the clergy;

(z) An individual who holds a certificate issued under Chapter 4701. of the Revised Code as a certified public accountant or is registered under that chapter as a public accountant;

(aa) An individual licensed under Chapter 4735. of the Revised Code as a real estate broker or real estate salesperson;

(bb) An individual appointed and commissioned under section 147.01 of the Revised Code as a notary public;

(cc) An employee of a bank, savings bank, savings and loan association, or credit union organized under the laws of this state, another state, or the United States;

(dd) A dealer, investment adviser, sales person, or investment advisor representative licensed under Chapter 1707. of the Revised Code;

(ee) A financial planner accredited by a national accreditation agency;

(ff) Any other individual who is a senior service provider, other than a representative of the office of the state long-term care ombudsman program as defined in section 173.14 of the Revised Code.

(B) Any person having reasonable cause to believe that an adult has suffered abuse, neglect, or exploitation may report, or cause a report to be made of such belief to the county department of job and family services.

This division applies to a representative of the office of the state long-term care ombudsman program only to the extent permitted by federal law.

(C) The reports made under this section shall be made orally or in writing except that oral reports shall be followed by a written report if a written report is requested by the department. Written reports shall include:

(1) The name, address, and approximate age of the adult who is the subject of the report;

(2) The name and address of the individual responsible for the adult's care, if any individual is, and if the individual is known;

(3) The nature and extent of the alleged abuse, neglect, or exploitation of the adult;

(4) The basis of the reporter's belief that the adult has been abused, neglected, or exploited.

(D) Any person with reasonable cause to believe that an adult is suffering abuse, neglect, or exploitation who makes a report pursuant to this section or who testifies in any administrative or judicial proceeding arising from such a report, or any employee of the state or any of its subdivisions who is discharging responsibilities under section 5101.65 of the Revised Code shall be immune from civil or criminal liability on account of such investigation, report, or testimony, except liability for perjury, unless the person has acted in bad faith or with malicious purpose.

(E) No employer or any other person with the authority to do so shall do any of the following as a result of an employee's having filed a report under this section:

(1) Discharge, demote, transfer, or prepare a negative work performance evaluation;

(2) Reduce benefits, pay, or work privileges;

(3) Take any other action detrimental to an employee or in any way retaliate against the employee.

(F) The written or oral report provided for in this section and the investigatory report provided for in section 5101.65 of the Revised Code are confidential and are not public records, as defined in section 149.43 of the Revised Code. In accordance with rules adopted by the department of job and family services, information contained in the report shall upon request be made available to the adult who is the subject of the report and to legal counsel for the adult. If it determines that there is a risk of harm to a person who makes a report under this section or to the adult who is the subject of the report, the county department of job and family services may redact the name and identifying information related to the person who made the report.

(G) The county department of job and family services shall be available to receive the written or oral report provided for in this section twenty-four hours a day and seven days a week.

**HISTORY:**

139 v H 694 (Eff 11-15-81); 141 v H 66 (Eff 3-6-86); 142 v S 124 (Eff 10-1-87); 143 v S 2 (Eff 11-1-89); 143 v H 253 (Eff 11-15-90); 143 v H 317 (Eff 10-10-89); 146 v H 117 (Eff 9-29-95); 148 v H 471. Eff 7-1-2000; 153 v H 1, § 101.01, eff. 10-16-09; 2011 HB 153, § 101.01, eff. July 1, 2011; 2012 HB 487, § 101.01, eff. Sept. 10, 2012; 2013 HB 59, § 101.01, eff. Sept. 29, 2013; 2014 HB 232, § 1, eff. July 10, 2014; 2015 hb64, § 101.01, effective September 29, 2015; renumbered from § 5101.61 by 2017 hb49, § 130.31, effective September 29, 2018; 2018 sb158, § 1, effective March 20, 2019; 2020 hb24, § 1, effective March 31, 2021; 2021 hb110, § 101.01, effective September 30, 2021.

**Amendment Notes**

The 2021 amendment by HB 110 substituted "3740.01" for "3701.881" in (A)(2)(j).

The 2020 amendment by HB 24 rewrote (A)(2)(r), which formerly read: "An agent of a county humane society organized under section 1717.05 of the Revised Code."

The 2018 amendment by SB 158 added "ombudsman" in (A)(2)(ff) an in the second paragraph of (B); and rewrote (A)(2)(dd), which formerly read: "An investment adviser, as defined in section 1707.01 of the Revised Code."

The 2017 amendment by HB 49 rewrote (A); in (B), substituted "cause a report" for "cause reports" and "county department of job and family services" for "department"; substituted "section 5101.65" for "section 5101.62" in (D); redesignated and revised former (E) as the introductory language of (E) and (E)(1) through (E)(3); and in (F), substituted "section 5101.65" for "section 5101.62" in the first sentence and added the last sentence.

The 2015 amendment by HB 64, in (F), in the first sentence, deleted "Neither" from the beginning, substituted "and the" for "nor the", and substituted "are confidential and are not public records" for "shall be considered a public record" and in the second sentence, added "In accordance with rules adopted by the department of job and family services" to the beginning and deleted "to agencies authorized by the department to receive information contained in the report" following "of the report"; added (G).

The 2014 amendment by HB 232 substituted "professional counseling, social work or marriage and family therapy" for "social work or counseling" in the first sentence of the second paragraph of (A).

The 2013 amendment substituted "department of mental health and addiction services" for "department of alcohol and drug addiction services" in (A)(2)(i); and substituted "section 5119.34" for "section 5119.22" in the first sentence of the second paragraph of (A).

The 2012 amendment, in the first sentence of the second paragraph of (A), substituted "a residential facility licensed under section 5119.22" for "an adult care facility as defined in section 5119.70", inserted "that provides accommodations, supervision, and personal care services for three to sixteen unrelated adults", and substituted "member of the clergy" for "clergyman".

The 2011 amendment substituted "section 5119.70" for "section 3722.01" in the first sentence of the second paragraph of (A).

153 v H 1, effective October 16, 2009, deleted "any employee of a community alternative home as defined in section 3724.01 of the Revised Code" preceding "any employee of a nursing" in the first sentence of the second paragraph of (A)(6); and made a stylistic change.

## NOTES TO DECISIONS

Analysis

Cause for termination
Duty to report
Privilege

**Cause for termination**

Assuming arguendo that an employee established a prima facie case of retaliation in violation of public policy, the employer articulated a legitimate business reason for terminating the employee because the employee's supervisor lost trust and confidence in the employee's ability to serve as police chief of a health care center. Accordingly, the employee's claim for wrongful termination in violation of the public policy embodied in R.C. 5101.61 was without merit. Boyd v. Ohio Dep't of Mental Health, 2010-Ohio-4306, 2010 Ohio Misc. LEXIS 219 (Ohio Ct. Cl. 2010), aff'd, 2011-Ohio-3596, 2011 Ohio App. LEXIS 3037 (Ohio Ct. App., Franklin County 2011).

**Duty to report**

In a complaint filed asserting causes of action for defamation per se, which arose after defendant allegedly overheard that plaintiffs were stealing narcotics in medical center and reported the same to her friend who was working at medical center without verifying the statements, trial court properly found that defendant was not mandatory reporter; at that time, defendant was retired; therefore, not employee of nursing home or residential care facility, thus, she did not have duty to report. Al-Aroud v. McCoy, 2021-Ohio-3832, 2021 Ohio App. LEXIS 3742 (Ohio Ct. App., Stark County 2021).

**Privilege**

As there was sufficient evidence that appellant acted with actual malice in submitting a complaint, appellant was not entitled to summary judgment based on either the common-law qualified privilege or the statutory privilege provided in R.C. 5101.61(D); rather than submitting the complaint at the time he purportedly drafted it, appellant waited and only filed the complaint immediately after he and appellee had a heated argument. Swoope v. Osagie, 2016-Ohio-8046, 76 N.E.3d 686, 2016 Ohio App. LEXIS 4921 (Ohio Ct. App., Cuyahoga County 2016).

## RESEARCH REFERENCES AND PRACTICE AIDS

**Cross-References to Related Sections**

Penalty, RC §§ 5101.99, 5123.99.

Abuse or neglect of patient, RC § 2903.34.

Case referrals, RC § 5101.64.

Case review and investigation, RC § 5126.31.

County department of job and family services to implement provisions, RC § 5101.61.

Department of developmental disabilities shall establish a registry office for the purpose of maintaining reports of abuse and neglect, RC § 5123.61.

Investigation within twenty-four hours of report, RC § 5101.65.

Reimbursement of county departments; internal management rules, RC § 5101.611.

Temporary restraining order to prevent interference or obstruction of investigation, RC § 5101.651.

**Ohio Administrative Code**

Department of health—

Adult care facilities: inspections; access to facilities; standards of conduct. OAC 5122-33-06.

Department of job and family services, division of social services—

Adult protective services. OAC ch. 5101:2-20.

Department of mental health—

Residential facilities: incident reporting. OAC 5122-30-16.

Department of developmental disabilities—

Complaint resolution; major unusual incidents. OAC ch. 5123:2-17.

**Comparative Legislation**

Duty to report abuse:

CA—Cal Wel & Inst Code § 15600 et seq
FL—Fla. Stat. § 415.101 et seq
IN—Burns Ind. Code Ann. § 12-10-3-1 et seq
KY—KRS § 209.010 et seq
MI—MCLS § 400.11 et seq
NY—NY CLS Soc Serv § 473 et seq
PA—35 P.S. § 10225.101 et seq

### § 5101.631 Uniform statewide automated adult protective services information system.

(A) The department of job and family services shall establish and maintain a uniform statewide automated adult protective services information system. The information system shall contain records regarding all of the following:

(1) All reports of abuse, neglect, or exploitation of adults made to county departments of job and family services under section 5101.63 of the Revised Code;

(2) Investigations conducted under section 5101.65 of the Revised Code;

(3) Protective services provided to adults pursuant to sections 5101.60 to 5101.73 of the Revised Code;

(4) Any other information related to adults in need of protective services that state or federal law, regulation, or rule requires the department or a county department to maintain.

(B) The department shall plan implementation of the information system on a county-by-county basis. The department shall promptly notify all county departments of the initiation and completion of statewide implementation of the information system.

(C)(1) The department shall, upon request, release information in the information system to county departments conducting investigations pursuant to section 5101.65 of the Revised Code and to local law enforcement agencies conducting criminal investigations. The department may release information in the information system to law enforcement agencies through the Ohio law enforcement gateway established under section 109.57 of the Revised Code. Information contained in the information system may be accessed or used only in a manner, to the extent, and for the purposes authorized by this section and rules adopted by the department.

(2) Except as provided in division (C) (1) of this section and in rules adopted by the department pursuant to that division, no person shall knowingly do either of the following:

(a) Access or use information contained in the information system;

(b) Disclose information obtained from the information system.

**HISTORY:**

2015 hb64, § 101.01, effective September 29, 2015; renumbered from § 5101.612 by 2017 hb49, § 130.31, effective September 29, 2018.

**Amendment Notes**

The 2017 amendment by HB 49 substituted "section 5101.63" for "section 5101.61" in (A)(1); substituted "5101.65" for "section 5101.62" in (A)(2); substituted "5101.73" for "5101.71" in (A)(3); and rewrote (C).

### § 5101.632 Access to the educational materials.

Each entity that employs or is responsible for licensing or regulating the individuals required under section 5101.63 of the Revised Code to make reports of abuse, neglect, or exploitation of adults shall ensure that the individuals have access to the educational materials developed under division (B) of section 5101.62 of the Revised Code.

**HISTORY:**

2017 hb49, § 130.31, effective September 29, 2018.

### § 5101.64 Request or consent to receiving protective services. [Renumbered]

**HISTORY:**

139 v H 694. Eff 11-15-81; renumbered to § 5101.66 by 2017 hb49, § 130.31, effective September 29, 2018.

### § 5101.64 Case referrals.

(A) If a county department of job and family services knows or has reasonable cause to believe that the subject of a report made under section 5101.63 of the Revised Code or of an investigation conducted under section 5101.65 of the Revised Code is an individual with a developmental disability as defined in section 5126.01 of the Revised Code, the county department shall refer the case to the county board of developmental disabilities of that county for review pursuant to section 5126.31 of the Revised Code.

If a county board of developmental disabilities refers a case to the county department of job and family services in accordance with section 5126.31, the county department of job and family services shall proceed with the case in accordance with sections 5101.60 to 5101.71 of the Revised Code.

(B) If a county department of job and family services knows or has reasonable cause to believe that the subject of a report made under section 5101.63 of the Revised Code or of an investigation conducted under section 5101.65 of the Revised Code is a resident of a long-term care facility, as defined in section 173.14 of the Revised Code, the department shall refer the case to the office of the state long-term care ombudsman program for review pursuant to section 173.19 of the Revised Code.

If the state ombudsman or regional long-term care ombudsman program refers a case to the county department of job and family services in accordance with rules adopted pursuant to section 173.20 of the Revised Code, the county department shall proceed with the case in accordance with sections 5101.60 to 5101.71 of the Revised Code.

(C) If a county department of job and family services knows or has reasonable cause to believe that the subject of a report made under section 5101.63 of the Revised Code or of an investigation conducted under section 5101.65 of the Revised Code is a resident of a nursing home, as defined in section 3721.01 of the Revised Code, and has allegedly been abused, neglected, or exploited by an employee of the nursing home, the department shall refer the case to the department of health for investigation pursuant to section 3721.031 of the Revised Code.

(D) If a county department of job and family services knows or has reasonable cause to believe that the subject of a report made under section 5101.63 of the Revised Code or of an investigation conducted under section 5101.65 of the Revised Code is a child, as defined in section 5153.01 of the Revised Code, the department shall refer the case to the public children services agency of that county.

(E) If a county department of job and family services knows or has reasonable cause to believe that the subject of a report made under section 5101.63 of the Revised Code or of an investigation conducted under section 5101.65 of the Revised Code is being or has been criminally exploited, the department shall notify a local law enforcement agency with jurisdiction over the area where the subject resides.

(F) A referral by the county department of job and family services of a case to another public regulatory agency or investigatory entity pursuant to this section shall be made in accordance with rules adopted by the department of job and family services.

**HISTORY:**

142 v H 403 (Eff 3-16-89); 148 v H 471. Eff 7-1-2000; 153 v S 79, § 1, eff. 10-6-09; 2015 hb64, § 101.01, effective September 29, 2015; renumbered from § 5101.611 by 2017 hb49, § 130.31, effective September 29, 2018.

**Amendment Notes**

The 2017 amendment by HB 49, in the first paragraphs of (A) and (B) and in (C) and (D), substituted "section 5101.63 of the Revised Code" for "section 5101.61" and "section 5101.65" for "sections 5101.62 to 5101.64"; added (E); and redesignated former (E) as (F).

The 2015 amendment by HB 64 added the (A) designation; in (A), in the first paragraph, substituted "of the Revised Code is an individual with a developmental disability" for "or on the initiative of the department is mentally retarded or developmentally disabled" and inserted "county" preceding "department shall" and substituted "county department of job and family services" for "department" in the second paragraph; and added (B) through (E).

153 v S 79, effective October 6, 2009, deleted "mental retardation and" preceding "developmental disabilities" throughout.

RESEARCH REFERENCES AND PRACTICE AIDS

**Cross-References to Related Sections**

County board of developmental disabilities shall review reports of abuse and neglect, RC § 5126.31.

## § 5101.65 Petition for authority to provide protective services; proposed plan. [Renumbered]

**HISTORY:**

139 v H 694 (Eff 11-15-81); 141 v H 428 (Eff 12-23-86); 148 v H 471. Eff 7-1-2000; renumbered to § 5101.68 by 2017 hb49, § 130.31, effective September 29, 2018.

## § 5101.65 Investigation of report; written notice of intent; report of conclusion.

The county department of job and family services or its designee shall be responsible for the investigation of all reports provided for in section 173.20 or 5101.63 and all cases referred to it under section 5126.31 of the Revised Code and for evaluating the need for and, to the extent of available funds, providing or arranging for the provision of protective services.

Investigation of the report provided for in section 5101.63 or a case referred to the department under section 5126.31 of the Revised Code shall be initiated within twenty-four hours after the department receives the report or case if any emergency exists; otherwise investigation shall be initiated within three working days.

Investigation of the need for protective services shall include a face-to-face visit with the adult who is the subject of the report, preferably in the adult's residence, and consultation with the person who made the report, if feasible, and agencies or persons who have information about the adult's alleged abuse, neglect, or exploitation.

The department shall give written notice of the intent of the investigation and an explanation of the notice in language reasonably understandable to the adult who is the subject of the investigation, at the time of the initial interview with that person.

Upon completion of the investigation, the department shall determine from its findings whether or not the adult who is the subject of the report is in need of protective services. No adult shall be determined to be abused, neglected, or in need of protective services for the sole reason that, in lieu of medical treatment, the adult relies on or is being furnished spiritual treatment through prayer alone in accordance with the tenets and practices of a church or religious denomination of which the adult is a member or adherent. The department shall write a report which confirms or denies the need for protective services and states why it reached this conclusion.

**HISTORY:**

139 v H 694 (Eff 11-15-81); 141 v H 428 (Eff 12-23-86); 142 v H 403 (Eff 3-16-89); 148 v H 471. Eff 7-1-2000; 2015 hb64, § 101.01, effective September 29, 2015; renumbered from § 5101.62 by 2017 hb49, § 130.31, effective September 29, 2018.

**Amendment Notes**

The 2017 amendment by HB 49 substituted "5101.63" for "5101.61" in the first and second paragraphs.

The 2015 amendment by HB 64, in the first paragraph, inserted "or its designee", substituted "section 173.20 or 5101.61" for "section 5101.61" and deleted the second sentence, which read: "The department may designate another agency to perform the department's duties under this section."

RESEARCH REFERENCES AND PRACTICE AIDS

**Cross-References to Related Sections**

County department of job and family services to implement provisions, RC § 5101.61.

Definitions, RC § 5101.60.

Reimbursement of county departments; internal management rules, RC § 5101.611.

Protective services only after investigation determines need, RC § 5101.66.

Referrals of abuse cases to board of mental retardation, RC § 5101.64.

Report of adult abuse not to be public record, RC § 5101.63.

Temporary restraining order may be issued to prevent interference, RC § 5101.651.

**Ohio Administrative Code**

Department of job and family services, division of social services—Adult protective services. OAC ch. 5101:2-20.

## § 5101.651 Temporary restraining order to prevent interference or obstruction of investigation.

If, during the course of an investigation conducted under section 5101.65 of the Revised Code, any person, including the adult who is the subject of the investigation, denies or obstructs access to the residence of the adult, the county department of job and family services may file a petition in court for a temporary restraining order to prevent the interference or obstruction. The court shall issue a temporary restraining order to prevent the interference or obstruction if it finds there is reasonable cause to believe that the adult is being or has been abused, neglected, or exploited and access to the person's residence has been denied or obstructed. Such a finding is prima-facie evidence that immediate and irreparable injury, loss, or damage will result, so that notice is not required. After obtaining an order restraining the obstruction of or interference with the access of the protective services representative, the representative may be accompanied to the residence by a peace officer.

**HISTORY:**

139 v H 694 (Eff 11-15-81); 141 v H 428 (Eff 12-23-86); 142 v H 403 (Eff 3-16-89); 148 v H 471. Eff 7-1-2000; renumbered from § 5101.63 by 2017 hb49, § 130.31, effective September 29, 2018.

**Amendment Notes**

The 2017 amendment by HB 49 substituted "section 5101.65" for "5101.62" in the first sentence.

## § 5101.652 Authority to contract with another person or government entity.

The county department of job and family services may enter into an agreement or contract with any private or government entity to perform the following duties:

(A) In accordance with division (G) of section 5101.63 of the Revised Code, receive reports made under that section;

(B) Perform the county department's duties under section 5101.65 of the Revised Code;

(C) Petition the court pursuant to section 5101.68 or 5101.70 of the Revised Code for an order authorizing the provision of protective services.

**HISTORY:**

2015 hb64, § 101.01, effective September 29, 2015; renumbered from § 5101.622 by 2017 hb49, § 130.31, effective September 29, 2018; 2018 sb158, § 1, effective March 20, 2019.

**Amendment Notes**

The 2018 amendment by SB 158 substituted "any private or government entity" for "another person or government entity" in the introductory language.

The 2017 amendment by HB 49 substituted "section 5101.63" for "5101.61" in (A); substituted "section 5101.65" for "section 5101.62" in (B); and substituted "section 5101.68 or 5101.70" for "section 5101.65 or 5101.69" in (C).

## § 5101.66 Notice of petition; adult to be informed of rights. [Renumbered]

**HISTORY:**

139 v H 694. Eff 11-15-81; renumbered to § 5101.681 by 2017 hb49, § 130.31, effective September 29, 2018.

## § 5101.66 Request or consent to receiving protective services.

Any person who requests or consents to receive protective services shall receive such services only after an investigation and determination of a need for protective services. The investigation shall be performed in the same manner as the investigation of a report pursuant to section 5101.65 of the Revised Code. If the person withdraws consent, the protective services shall be terminated.

**HISTORY:**

139 v H 694. Eff 11-15-81; renumbered from § 5101.64 by 2017 hb49, § 130.31, effective September 29, 2018.

**Amendment Notes**

The 2017 amendment by HB 49 redesignated and rewrote the former first sentence as the first and second sentences.

### § 5101.67 Hearing on petition; order; placement; transfer; duration of order. [Renumbered]

**HISTORY:**

139 v H 694 (Eff 11-15-81); 141 v H 428 (Eff 12-23-86); 148 v H 471. Eff 7-1-2000; renumbered to § 5101.682 by 2017 hb49, § 130.31, effective September 29, 2018.

### § 5101.68 Temporary restraining order to prevent interference with provision of services. [Renumbered]

**HISTORY:**

139 v H 694 (Eff 11-15-81); 141 v H 428. Eff 12-23-86; renumbered to § 5101.69 by 2017 hb49, § 130.31, effective September 29, 2018.

### § 5101.68 Petition for authority to provide protective services; proposed plan.

If the county department of job and family services determines that an adult is in need of protective services and is an incapacitated person, the department may petition the court for an order authorizing the provision of protective services. If the adult is in need of protective services as a result of exploitation, the county prosecutor may file the petition. The petition shall state the specific facts alleging the abuse, neglect, or exploitation and shall include a proposed protective service plan. Any plan for protective services shall be specified in the petition.



**HISTORY:**

139 v H 694 (Eff 11-15-81); 141 v H 428 (Eff 12-23-86); 148 v H 471. Eff 7-1-2000; renumbered from § 5101.65 by 2017 hb49, § 130.31, effective September 29, 2018.

**Amendment Notes**

The 2017 amendment by HB 49 added the second sentence.

### § 5101.681 Notice of petition; adult to be informed of rights.

Notice of a petition for the provision of court-ordered protective services as provided for in section 5101.68 of the Revised Code shall be personally served upon the adult who is the subject of the petition at least five working days prior to the date set for the hearing as provided in section 5101.682 of the Revised Code. Notice shall be given either orally or in writing in language reasonably understandable to the adult. The notice shall include the names of all petitioners, the basis of the belief that protective services are needed, the rights of the adult in the court proceedings, and the consequences of a court order for protective services. The adult shall be informed of the right to counsel and the right to appointed counsel if the adult is indigent and if appointed counsel is requested. Written notice by certified mail shall also be given to the adult's guardian, legal counsel, caretaker, and spouse, if any, or if the adult has none of these, to the adult's adult children or next of kin, if any, or to any other person as the court may require. The adult who is the subject of the petition may not waive notice as provided in this section.

**HISTORY:**

139 v H 694. Eff 11-15-81; renumbered from § 5101.66 by 2017 hb49, § 130.31, effective September 29, 2018.

**Amendment Notes**

The 2017 amendment by HB 49, in the first sentence, substituted "section 5101.68" for "section 5101.65" and "section 5101.682" for "section 5101.67"; substituted "either orally or in writing" for "orally and in writing" in the second sentence; in the third to the last sentence, substituted "the right" for "his right" twice and "the adult" for "he"; and in the second to the last sentence, substituted "the adult" for "he" and "the adult's" for "his."

### § 5101.682 Hearing on petition; order; placement; transfer; duration of order.

(A) The court shall hold a hearing on the petition as provided in section 5101.68 of the Revised Code within fourteen days after its filing. The adult who is the subject of the petition shall have the right to be present at the hearing, present evidence, and examine and cross-examine witnesses. The adult shall be represented by counsel unless the right to counsel is knowingly waived. If the adult is indigent, the court shall appoint counsel to represent the adult. If the court determines that the adult lacks the capacity to waive the right to counsel, the court shall appoint counsel to represent the adult's interests.

(B) If the court finds, on the basis of clear and convincing evidence, that the adult has been abused, neglected, or exploited, is in need of protective services, and is incapacitated, and no person authorized by law or by court order is available to give consent, it shall issue an order requiring the provision of protective services only if they are available locally.

(C) If the court orders placement under this section it shall give consideration to the choice of residence of the adult. The court may order placement in settings which have been approved by the department of job and family services as meeting at least minimum community standards for safety, security, and the requirements of daily living. The court shall not order an institutional placement unless it has made a specific finding entered in the record that no less restrictive alternative can be found to meet the needs of the individual. No individual may be committed to a hospital or public hospital as defined in section 5122.01 of the Revised Code pursuant to this section.

(D) The placement of an adult pursuant to court order as provided in this section shall not be changed unless the court authorized the transfer of placement after finding compelling reasons to justify the transfer. Unless the court finds that an emergency exists, the court shall notify the adult of a transfer at least thirty days prior to the actual transfer.

(E) A court order provided for in this section shall remain in effect for no longer than six months. Thereafter, the county department of job and family services shall review the adult's need for continued services and, if the department determines that there is a continued need, it shall apply for a renewal of the order for additional periods of no longer than one year each. The adult who is the subject of the court-ordered services may petition for modification of the order at any time.

**HISTORY:**

139 v H 694 (Eff 11-15-81); 141 v H 428 (Eff 12-23-86); 148 v H 471. Eff 7-1-2000; renumbered from § 5101.67 by 2017 hb49, § 130.31, effective September 29, 2018.

**Amendment Notes**

The 2017 amendment by HB 49 substituted "section 5101.68" for "section 5101.65" in the first sentence of (A).

### § 5101.69 Order authorizing provision of protective services on emergency basis. [Renumbered]

**HISTORY:**

139 v H 694 (Eff 11-15-81); 141 v H 428. Eff 12-23-86; 2015 hb64, § 101.01, effective September 29, 2015; renumbered to § 5101.70 by 2017 hb49, § 130.31, effective September 29, 2018.

### § 5101.69 Temporary restraining order to prevent interference with provision of services.

(A) If an adult has consented to the provision of protective services but any other person refuses to allow such provision, the county department of job and family services or the county prosecutor may petition the court for a temporary restraining order to restrain the person from interfering with the provision of protective services for the adult.

(B) The petition shall state specific facts sufficient to demonstrate the need for protective services, the consent of the adult, and the refusal of some other person to allow the provision of these services.

(C) Notice of the petition shall be given in language reasonably understandable to the person alleged to be interfering with the provision of services;

(D) The court shall hold a hearing on the petition within fourteen days after its filing. If the court finds that the protective services are necessary, that the adult has consented to the provision of such services, and that the person who is the subject of the petition has prevented such provision, the court shall issue a temporary restraining order to restrain the person from interfering with the provision of protective services to the adult.

**HISTORY:**

139 v H 694 (Eff 11-15-81); 141 v H 428. Eff 12-23-86; renumbered from § 5101.68 by 2017 hb49, § 130.31, effective September 29, 2018.

**Amendment Notes**

The 2017 amendment by HB 49 substituted "job and family services or the county prosecutor" for "human services"; and substituted "consented to the provision" for "consented to the provisions" in the second sentence of (D).

### § 5101.691 Authority of judge or magistrate to issue ex parte emergency order by telephone. [Renumbered]

**HISTORY:**

2015 hb64, § 101.01, effective September 29, 2015; renumbered to § 5101.701 by 2017 hb49, § 130.31, effective September 29, 2018.

### § 5101.692 Probable cause hearing. [Renumbered]

**HISTORY:**

2015 hb64, § 101.01, effective September 29, 2015; renumbered to § 5101.702 by 2017 hb49, § 130.31, effective September 29, 2018.

### § 5101.70 Evaluation of adult's ability to pay for services; counsel for indigents. [Renumbered]

**HISTORY:**

139 v H 694 (Eff 11-15-81); 141 v H 428 (Eff 12-23-86); 148 v H 471. Eff 7-1-2000; renumbered to § 5101.71 by 2017 hb49, § 130.31, effective September 29, 2018.

### § 5101.70 Order authorizing provision of protective services on emergency basis.

(A) Upon petition by the county department of job and family services, the department's designee, or the county prosecutor, the court may issue an order authorizing the provision of protective services on an emergency basis to an adult. The petition for any emergency order shall include all of the following:

(1) The name, age, and address of the adult in need of protective services;

(2) The nature of the emergency;

(3) The proposed protective services;

(4) The petitioner's reasonable belief, together with facts supportive thereof, as to the existence of the circumstances described in divisions (D)(1) to (3) of this section;

(5) Facts showing the petitioner's attempts to obtain the adult's consent to the protective services.

(B) Notice of the filing and contents of the petition provided for in division (A) of this section, the rights of the person in the hearing provided for in division (C) of this section, and the possible consequences of a court order, shall be given to the adult. Notice shall also be given to the spouse of the adult or, if the adult has none, to the adult's adult children or next of kin, and the adult's guardian, if any, if the guardian's whereabouts are known. The notice shall be given in language reasonably understandable to its recipients at least twenty-four hours prior to the hearing provided for in this section. The court may waive the twenty-four hours' notice requirement upon a showing that both of the following are the case:

(1) Immediate and irreparable physical harm or immediate and irreparable financial harm to the adult or others will result from the twenty-four hour delay;

(2) Reasonable attempts have been made to notify the adult, the adult's spouse, or, if the adult has none, the adult's adult children or next of kin, if any, and the adult's guardian, if any, if the guardian's whereabouts are known.

Notice of the court's determination shall be given to all persons receiving notice of the filing of the petition provided for in this division.

(C) Upon receipt of a petition for an order for emergency services, the court shall hold a hearing no sooner than twenty-four and no later than seventy-two hours after the notice provided for in division (B) of this section has been given, unless the court has waived the notice. The adult who is the subject of the petition shall have the right to be present at the hearing, present evidence, and examine and cross-examine witnesses.

(D) The court shall issue an order authorizing the provision of protective services on an emergency basis if it finds, on the basis of clear and convincing evidence, all of the following:

(1) The adult is an incapacitated person;

(2) An emergency exists;

(3) No person authorized by law or court order to give consent for the adult is available or willing to consent to emergency services.

(E) In issuing an emergency order, the court shall adhere to the following limitations:

(1) The court shall order only such protective services as are necessary and available locally to remove the conditions creating the emergency, and the court shall specifically designate those protective services the adult shall receive;

(2) The court shall not order any change of residence under this section unless the court specifically finds that a change of residence is necessary;

(3) The court may order emergency services only for fourteen days. The county department, the department's designee, or the county prosecutor may petition the court for a renewal of the order for a fourteen-day period upon a showing that continuation of the order is necessary to remove the emergency.

(4) In its order the court shall authorize the director of the county department, the director's designee, or a representative of the department's designee to give consent for the person for the approved emergency services until the expiration of the order;

(5) The court shall not order a person to a hospital or public hospital as defined in section 5122.01 of the Revised Code.

(F) If the county department or its designee determines that the adult continues to need protective services after the order provided for in division (D) of this section has expired, the county department, the department's designee, or the county prosecutor may petition the court for an order to continue protective services, pursuant to section 5101.68 of the Revised Code. After the filing of the petition, the county department or its designee may continue to provide protective services pending a hearing by the court.

**HISTORY:**

139 v H 694 (Eff 11-15-81); 141 v H 428. Eff 12-23-86; 2015 hb64, § 101.01, effective September 29, 2015; renumbered from § 5101.69 by 2017 hb49, § 130.31, effective September 29, 2018.

**Amendment Notes**

The 2017 amendment by HB 49 substituted "the department's designee, or the county prosecutor" for "or its designee" in the first sentence of the introductory paragraph of (A), in (E)(3), and in the first sentence of (F); and substituted "section 5101.68" for "section 5101.65" in the first sentence of (F).

### § 5101.701 Authority of judge or magistrate to issue ex parte emergency order by telephone.

(A) A court, through a probate judge or a magistrate under the direction of a probate judge, may issue by telephone an ex parte emergency order authorizing the provision of protective services, including the relief available under division (B) of section 5101.702 of the Revised Code, to an adult on an emergency basis if all of the following are the case:

(1) The court receives notice from the county department of job and family services, an authorized employee of the county department, the department's designee, or an authorized employee of the department's designee, that the county depart-

ment, designee, or employee believes an emergency order is needed as described in this section.

(2) There is reasonable cause to believe that the adult is incapacitated.

(3) There is reasonable cause to believe that there is a substantial risk to the adult of immediate and irreparable physical harm, immediate and irreparable financial harm, or death.

(B)(1) The judge or magistrate shall journalize any order issued under this section.

(2) An order issued under this section shall be in effect for not longer than twenty-four hours, except that if the day following the day on which the order is issued is not a working day, the order shall remain in effect until the next working day.

(C)(1) Except as provided in division (C)(2) of this section, not later than twenty-four hours after an order is issued under this section, a petition shall be filed with the court in accordance with division (A) of section 5101.70 of the Revised Code.

(2) If the day following the day on which the order was issued is not a working day, the petition shall be filed with the court on the next working day.

(3) Except as provided in section 5101.702 of the Revised Code, proceedings on the petition shall be conducted in accordance with section 5101.70 of the Revised Code.

**HISTORY:**

2015 hb64, § 101.01, effective September 29, 2015; renumbered from § 5101.691 by 2017 hb49, § 130.31, effective September 29, 2018.

**Amendment Notes**

The 2017 amendment by HB 49 substituted "section 5101.702" for "section 5101.692" in the introductory language of (A); substituted "section 5101.70" for "section 5101.69" in (C)(1); and in (C)(3), substituted "section 5101.702" for "section 5101.692" and "section 5101.70" for "section 5101.69."



### § 5101.702 Probable cause hearing.

(A) If an order is issued pursuant to section 5101.701 of the Revised Code, the court shall hold a hearing not later than twenty-four hours after the issuance to determine whether there is probable cause for the order, except that if the day following the day on which the order is issued is not a working day, the court shall hold the hearing on the next working day.

(B) At the hearing, the court:

(1) Shall determine whether protective services are the least restrictive alternative available for meeting the adult's needs;

(2) May issue temporary orders to protect the adult from immediate and irreparable physical harm or immediate and irreparable financial harm, including, but not limited to, temporary protection orders, evaluations, and orders requiring a party to vacate the adult's place of residence or legal settlement;

(3) May order emergency services;

(4) May freeze the financial assets of the adult.

(C) A temporary order issued pursuant to division (B)(2) of this section is effective for thirty days. The court may renew the order for an additional thirty-day period.

Information contained in the order may be entered into the law enforcement automated data system.

**HISTORY:**

2015 hb64, § 101.01, effective September 29, 2015; renumbered from § 5101.692 by 2017 hb49, § 130.31, effective September 29, 2018.

**Amendment Notes**

The 2017 amendment by HB 49 substituted "section 5101.701" for "section 5101.691" in (A).

### § 5101.71 County departments of job and family services to implement provisions; training. [Renumbered]

**HISTORY:**

139 v H 694 (Eff 11-15-81); 141 v H 428 (Eff 12-23-86); 143 v H 111 (Eff 7-1-89); 144 v H 298 (Eff 7-26-91); 148 v H 471. Eff 7-1-2000; 2015 hb64, § 101.01, effective September 29, 2015; renumbered to § 5101.61 by 2017 hb49, § 130.31, effective September 29, 2018.

### § 5101.71 Evaluation of adult's ability to pay for services; counsel for indigents.

(A) If it appears that an adult in need of protective services has the financial means sufficient to pay for such services, the county department of job and family services shall make an evaluation regarding such means. If the evaluation establishes that the adult has such financial means, the department shall initiate procedures for reimbursement pursuant to rules adopted under section 5101.61 of the Revised Code. If the evaluation establishes that the adult does not have such financial means, the services shall be provided in accordance with the policies and procedures established by the department of job and family services for the provision of welfare assistance. An adult shall not be required to pay for court-ordered protective services unless the court determines that the adult is financially able to pay and the court orders the adult to pay.

(B) Whenever the county department of job and family services or the county prosecutor has petitioned the court to authorize the provision of protective services and the adult who is the subject of the petition is indigent, the court shall appoint legal counsel.

**HISTORY:**

139 v H 694 (Eff 11-15-81); 141 v H 428 (Eff 12-23-86); 148 v H 471. Eff 7-1-2000; renumbered from § 5101.70 by 2017 hb49, § 130.31, effective September 29, 2018.

**Amendment Notes**

The 2017 amendment by HB 49, in (A), substituted "adopted under section 5101.61 of the Revised Code" for "promulgated by the department" in the second sentence and deleted "upon a showing by the department" following "court determines" in the last sentence; and substituted "county department of job and family services or the county prosecutor" for "department" in (B).

### § 5101.72 Reimbursement of county departments; internal management rules. [Renumbered]

**HISTORY:**

143 v H 111 (Eff 7-1-89); 148 v H 471. Eff 7-1-2000; 151 v S 238, § 1, eff. 9-21-06; 2015 hb64, § 101.01, effective September 29, 2015; renumbered to § 5101.611 by 2017 hb49, § 130.31, effective September 29, 2018.

### § 5101.73 Temporary restraining order to prevent interference or obstruction of investigation related to residence of adult victim.

If, during the course of an investigation by a local law enforcement agency of criminal exploitation, any person, including the adult who is the alleged victim, denies or obstructs access to the residence of the adult, the county prosecutor may file a petition in court for a temporary restraining order to prevent the interference or obstruction. The court shall issue a temporary restraining order to prevent the interference or obstruction if it finds there is reasonable cause to believe that the adult is being or has been abused, neglected, or exploited and access to the person's residence has been denied or obstructed. Such a finding is prima facie evidence that immediate and irreparable injury, loss, or damage will result, so that notice is not required. After obtaining an order restraining the obstruction of or interference with the access of the local law enforcement agency representative, the representative may be accompanied to the residence by a peace officer.

**HISTORY:**

2017 hb49, § 101.01, effective September 29, 2018.

### § 5101.74 Elder abuse commission.

(A) There is hereby created the elder abuse commission. The commission shall consist of the following members:

(1) The following members, appointed by the attorney general:

(a) One representative of the AARP;

(b) One representative of the buckeye state sheriffs' association;

(c) One representative of the county commissioners' association of Ohio;

(d) One representative of the Ohio association of area agencies on aging;

(e) One representative of the board of nursing;

(f) One representative of the Ohio coalition for adult protective services;

(g) One person who represents the interests of elder abuse victims;

(h) One person who represents the interests of elderly persons;

(i) One representative of the Ohio domestic violence network;

(j) One representative of the Ohio prosecuting attorneys association;

(k) One representative of the Ohio victim witness association;

(*l*) One representative of the Ohio association of chiefs of police;

(m) One representative of the Ohio association of probate judges;

(n) One representative of the Ohio job and family services directors' association;

(o) One representative of the Ohio bankers league;

(p) One representative of the Ohio credit union league;

(q) Two representatives of national organizations that focus on elder abuse or sexual violence;

(r) One representative of the state medical board;

(s) One representative of the community bankers association of Ohio;

(t) One representative of an organization representing the interests of senior centers;

(u) One representative of an organization representing the policy interests of seniors;

(v) One representative of a research-based academia representing elder abuse research.

(2) The following ex officio members:

(a) The attorney general or the attorney general's designee;

(b) The chief justice of the supreme court of Ohio or the chief justice's designee;

(c) The governor or the governor's designee;

(d) The director of aging or the director's designee;

(e) The director of job and family services or the director's designee;

(f) The director of health or the director's designee;

(g) The director of mental health and addiction services or the director's designee;

(h) The director of developmental disabilities or the director's designee;

(i) The superintendent of insurance or the superintendent's designee;

(j) The director of public safety or the director's designee;

(k) The state long-term care ombudsman or the ombudsman's designee;

(*l*) One member of the house of representatives, appointed by the speaker of the house of representatives;

(m) One member of the senate, appointed by the president of the senate;

(n) One member of the house of representatives, appointed by the minority leader of the house of representatives;

(o) One member of the senate, appointed by the minority leader of the senate;

(p) The director of commerce, or the director's designee.

(B) Members who are appointed shall serve at the pleasure of the appointing authority. Vacancies shall be filled in the same manner as original appointments.

(C) All members of the commission shall serve as voting members. The attorney general shall select from among the appointed members a chairperson. The commission shall meet at the call of the chairperson, but not less than four times per year. Special meetings may be called by the chairperson and shall be called by the chairperson at the request of the attorney general. The commission may establish its own quorum requirements and procedures regarding the conduct of meetings and other affairs.

(D) Members shall serve without compensation, but may be reimbursed for mileage and other actual and necessary expenses incurred in the performance of their official duties.

(E) Sections 101.82 to 101.87 of the Revised Code do not apply to the elder abuse commission.

**HISTORY:**

2017 hb49, § 130.31, effective September 29, 2018; 2018 sb158, § 1, effective March 20, 2019.

**Amendment Notes**

The 2018 amendment by SB 158 added (A)(1)(r) through (A)(1)(v); and added (A)(2)(n) through (A)(2)(p); and made a related change.

### § 5101.741 Duties of elder abuse commission.

(A) The elder abuse commission shall formulate and recommend strategies on all of the following:

(1) Increasing awareness of and improving education on elder abuse;

(2) Increasing research on elder abuse;

(3) Improving policy, funding, and programming related to elder abuse, including estimated funding necessary to implement specific recommendations;

(4) Improving the judicial response to elder abuse victims;

(5) Identifying ways to coordinate statewide efforts to address elder abuse.

(B) The commission shall prepare and issue a biennial report on a plan of action that may be used by local communities to aid in the development of efforts to combat elder abuse. The report shall include the commission's recommendations made under division (A) of this section.

(C) The attorney general may adopt rules as necessary for the commission to carry out its duties. The rules shall be adopted in accordance with section 111.15 of the Revised Code.

**HISTORY:**

2017 hb49, § 130.31, effective September 29, 2018; 2021 hb110, § 101.01, effective September 30, 2021.

**Amendment Notes**

The 2021 amendment by HB 110 added "including estimated funding necessary to implement specific recommendations" in (A)(3); deleted former (B), which read: "The commission shall review current funding of adult protective services and shall report on the cost to the state and county departments of job and family services of implementing its recommendations"; redesignated former (C) and (D) as (B) and (C); and substituted "recommendations made under division (A)" for "findings and recommendations made under divisions (A) and (B)" in the second sentence of (C).



# CHAPTER 5119

# DEPARTMENT OF MENTAL HEALTH



### § 5119.41 Residential state supplement program.

(A) The department of mental health and addiction services shall implement the residential state supplement program under which the state supplements the amounts received by aged, blind, or disabled adults as supplemental security income payments under Title XVI of the "Social Security Act," 42 U.S.C. 1381 et seq., or as social security benefits or social security disability insurance benefits under Title II of the "Social Security Act," 42 U.S.C. 401 et seq. Residential state supplement payments shall be used for the provision of accommodations, supervision, and personal care services to recipients of supplemental security income payments, social security benefits, and social security disability insurance benefits who the department determines are at risk of needing institutional care.

In implementing the program, the department may designate one or more entities to be responsible for providing administrative services regarding the program. The department may designate an entity either by entering into a contract with the entity to provided the services or by otherwise delegating to the entity the responsibility to provide the services.

(B) To be eligible for residential state supplement payments, an individual must satisfy all eligibility requirements established by rules adopted under this section.

(C) The director of mental health and addiction services and the medicaid director shall adopt rules as necessary to implement the residential state supplement program, including the requirements that an individual must satisfy to be eligible for payments under the program. The rules shall be adopted in accordance with Chapter 119. of the Revised Code.

The rules adopted by the director of mental health and addiction services may establish the method to be used to determine the payment an eligible individual will receive under the program. The amount the general assembly appropriates for the program may be a factor included in the method that director establishes.

To the extent permitted by Title XVI of the "Social Security Act and any other provision of federal law, the rules adopted by the medicaid director may establish standards for adjusting the eligibility requirements concerning the level of impairment an individual must have so that the amount appropriated for the program by the general assembly is adequate for the number of eligible individuals. The rules shall not limit the eligibility of individuals who are disabled solely on a basis classifying disabilities as physical or mental.

(D) The county department of job and family services of the county in which an applicant for the residential state supplement program resides or the department of medicaid shall determine whether the applicant meets income and resource requirements for the program.

The county department of job and family services or the department of medicaid shall notify each individual who is denied approval for payments under the program of the individual's right to a hearing. On request, the hearing shall be provided in accordance with section 5101.35 of the Revised Code.

(E) An individual in a licensed or certified living arrangement receiving state supplementation on November 15, 1990, under former section 5101.531 of the Revised Code shall not become ineligible for payments under this program solely by reason of the individual's living arrangement as long as the individual remains in the living arrangement in which the individual resided on November 15, 1990.



**HISTORY:**

145 v H 152 (Eff 7-1-93); 146 v H 117 (Eff 6-30-95); 148 v H 283 (Eff 9-29-99); 148 v H 471 (Eff 7-1-2000); 149 v H 94. Eff 9-5-2001; 152 v H 119, § 101.01, eff. 6-30-07; 153 v H 1, § 101.01, eff. 10-16-09; 2011 HB 153, § 101.01, eff. Sept. 29, 2011; 2012 HB 487, § 101.01, eff. Sept. 10, 2012; 2013 HB 59, § 101.01, eff. Sept. 29, 2013; 2015 hb64, § 101.01, effective September 29, 2015; 2016 sb319, § 1, effective July 1, 2017; 2017 hb49, § 101.01, effective September 29, 2017.

**Editor's Notes**

This section was formerly codified as RC § 5119.69.

**Amendment Notes**

The 2017 amendment by HB 49 rewrote the section.

The 2016 amendment by SB 319 substituted "section 173.51" for "section 5111.89" in (D)(1)(a) and added "class two" in (D)(1)(b).

The 2015 amendment by HB 64 deleted "and section 5119.411 of the Revised Code" from the end of the introductory language of (A); rewrote (D); substituted "Chapter 119." for "section 111.15" in the first paragraph of (E); inserted "or the department of medicaid" in (F) and in the first sentence of present (H); deleted (G), pertaining to procedures and requirements for placing an individual on the waiting list and priorities for the order in which individuals placed on the waiting list are to begin to receive residential state supplement payments; redesignated former (H) and (I) as (G) and (H); and substituted "section 5101.35" for "Chapter 119." in the second sentence of present (H).

The 2013 amendment substituted "section 5119.411" for "section 5119.691" in the introductory language of (A); deleted (A)(1) and (A)(2), pertaining to the meaning of "Long-term care consultation program" and "Long-term care consultation program administrator" or "administrator"; redesignated former (A)(3) through (A)(5) as (A)(1) through (A)(3); substituted "section 5165.01" for "section 5111.20" in present (A)(1); substituted "mental health and addiction services" for "mental health" throughout in present (A)(2) and in (B) and (G); in (B), substituted "42 U.S.C. 1381 et seq." for "49 Stat. 620 (1935), 42 U.S.C.A., as amended" and "social security, supplemental security income, and social security disability insurance" for "supplemental security income"; rewrote (D)(1); in (C)(2), inserted "social security payments" and substituted "services provider" for "agency"; rewrote (E); in the fourth sentence of (G), inserted "social security payments, social security disability insurance, or" and substituted "42 U.S.C. 1381, et seq" for "86 Stat. 1475 (1972), 42 U.S.C. 1381, as amended"; substituted "county department of job and family services from which the person is receiving benefits" for "department of mental health" in (I).

**NOTES TO DECISIONS**

**Authority**

Plain reading of the statute made clear that the Ohio General Assembly granted the Ohio Department of Mental Health and Addiction Services (ODMHAS) broad authority to adopt rules necessary to operate the Residential State Supplement (RSS) program and that authority was not limited to establishing benefit amounts. Hinton Adult Care Facility v. Ohio Dep't of Mental Health & Addiction Servs., 2017-Ohio-4113, 2017 Ohio App. LEXIS 2166 (Ohio Ct. App., Ross County 2017).

### § 5119.411 Home first component. [Repealed]

**HISTORY:**

152 v H 119, § 101.01, eff. 7-1-07; 2011 HB 153, § 101.01, eff. July 1, 2011; 2012 HB 487, § 101.01, eff. June 11, 2012; 2013 HB 59, § 101.01, eff. Sept. 29, 2013; repealed by 2015 hb64, § 105.01, effective September 29, 2015.

## SHELTERS FOR RUNAWAY MINORS

### § 5119.69 Residential state supplement program [Renumbered].

**Editor's Notes**

This section was renumbered as RC § 5119.41 by 2013 HB 59, § 101.01, effective September 29, 2013.

### § 5119.691 Home first component [Renumbered].

**Editor's Notes**

This section was renumbered as RC § 5119.411 by 2013 HB 59, § 101.01, effective September 29, 2013.

### § 5119.692 Standards for certification of adult foster homes [Repealed].

Repealed by 2012 HB 487, § 105.01, September 10, 2012.

**HISTORY:**

145 v H 152. Eff 7-1-93; 2011 HB 153, § 101.01, eff. July 1, 2011.

# CHAPTER 5162

# MEDICAID PROGRAM; MEDICAL ESTATE RECOVERY PROGRAMS; MEDICAID FUNDS

Section

### § 5162.01 Definitions.

(A) As used in the Revised Code:

(1) "Medicaid" and "medicaid program" mean the program of medical assistance established by Title XIX of the "Social Security Act," 42 U.S.C. 1396 et seq., including any medical assistance provided under the medicaid state plan or a federal medicaid waiver granted by the United States secretary of health and human services.

(2) "Medicare" and "medicare program" mean the federal health insurance program established by Title XVIII of the "Social Security Act," 42 U.S.C. 1395 et seq.

(B) As used in this chapter:

(1) "Exchange" has the same meaning as in 45 C.F.R. 155.20.

(2) "Expansion eligibility group" has the same meaning as in section 5163.01 of the Revised Code.

(3) "Federal financial participation" has the same meaning as in section 5160.01 of the Revised Code.

(4) "Federal poverty line" means the official poverty line defined by the United States office of management and budget based on the most recent data available from the United States bureau of the census and revised by the United States secretary of health and human services pursuant to the "Omnibus Budget Reconciliation Act of 1981," section 673(2), 42 U.S.C. 9902(2).

(5) "Healthcheck" has the same meaning as in section 5164.01 of the Revised Code.

(6) "Healthy start component" means the component of the medicaid program that covers pregnant women and children and is identified in rules adopted under section 5162.02 of the Revised Code as the healthy start component.

(7) "Home and community-based services" means services provided under a home and community-based services medicaid waiver component.

(8) "Home and community-based services medicaid waiver component" has the same meaning as in section 5166.01 of the Revised Code.

(9) "ICF/IID" has the same meaning as in section 5124.01 of the Revised Code.

(10) "Individualized education program" has the same meaning as in section 3323.011 of the Revised Code.

(11) "Medicaid managed care organization" has the same meaning as in section 5167.01 of the Revised Code.

(12) "Medicaid MCO plan" has the same meaning as in section 5167.01 of the Revised Code.

(13) "Medicaid provider" has the same meaning as in section 5164.01 of the Revised Code.

(14) "Medicaid services" has the same meaning as in section 5164.01 of the Revised Code.

(15) "Medicaid waiver component" has the same meaning as in section 5166.01 of the Revised Code;

(16) "Nursing facility" and "nursing facility services" have the same meanings as in section 5165.01 of the Revised Code.

(17) "Ordering or referring only provider" means a medicaid provider who orders, prescribes, refers, or certifies a service or item reported on a claim for medicaid payment but does not bill for medicaid services.

(18) "Political subdivision" means a municipal corporation, township, county, school district, or other body corporate and politic responsible for governmental activities only in a geographical area smaller than that of the state.

(19) "Prescribed drug" has the same meaning as in section 5164.01 of the Revised Code.

(20) "Provider agreement" has the same meaning as in section 5164.01 of the Revised Code.

(21) "Qualified medicaid school provider" means the board of education of a city, local, or exempted village school district, the governing board of an educational service center, the governing authority of a community school established under Chapter 3314. of the Revised Code, the state school for the deaf, and the state school for the blind to which both of the following apply:

(a) It holds a valid provider agreement.

(b) It meets all other conditions for participation in the medicaid school component of the medicaid program established in rules authorized by section 5162.364 of the Revised Code.

(22) "State agency" means every organized body, office, or agency, other than the department of medicaid, established by the laws of the state for the exercise of any function of state government.

(23) "Vendor offset" means a reduction of a medicaid payment to a medicaid provider to correct a previous, incorrect medicaid payment to that provider.

**HISTORY:**

2013 HB 59, § 101.01, eff. Sept. 29, 2013; 2013 SB 206, § 1, eff. Mar. 20, 2014; 2015 hb64, § 101.01, effective September 29, 2015; 2016 hb89, § 1, effective March 21, 2017; 2016 sb332, § 1, effective April 6, 2017; 2019 hb166, § 101.01, effective October 17, 2019.

**Amendment Notes**

The 2019 amendment by HB 166 deleted former (B)(1), which read: "'Dual eligible individual' has the same meaning as in section 5160.01 of the Revised Code" redesignated former (B)(2) as (B)(1); added (B)(2); added (B)(12); redesignated former (B)(12) as (B)(13); redesignated former (B)(13) through (B)(22) as (B)(14) through (B)(23); and added "the governing board of an educational service center" in the introductory language of (B)(21).

The 2016 amendment by SB 332 added (B)(5); added (B)(6) designation; and renumbered former (B)(6) through (B)(19) as (B)(7) through (B)(20).

The 2016 amendment by HB 89 inserted (9); redesignated former (9) through (13) as (10) through (14); inserted (15); and redesignated former (14) through (19) as (16) through (21).

The 2015 amendment, by HB 64, inserted (B)(12); and redesignated former (B)(12) through (B)(18) as (B)(13) through (B)(19).

The 2013 amendment inserted (B)(2), (B)(6), and (B)(7); redesignated former (B)(2) through (B)(15) as (B)(3) through (B)(5) and (B)(8) through (B)(18); inserted "and 'nursing facility services'" in present (B)(12); and made stylistic changes.

## § 5162.02 Adoption of rules.

The medicaid director shall adopt rules as necessary to implement this chapter.

**HISTORY:**

2013 HB 59, § 101.01, eff. Sept. 29, 2013.

## § 5162.021 Adoption of rules related to Medicaid by other state agencies.

The medicaid director shall adopt rules under sections 5160.02, 5162.02, 5163.03, 5163.02, 5164.02, 5165.02, 5166.02, and 5167.02 of the Revised Code as necessary to authorize the directors of other state agencies to adopt rules regarding medicaid components, or aspects of medicaid components, the other state agencies administer pursuant to contracts entered into under section 5162.35 of the Revised Code.



**HISTORY:**

2013 HB 59, § 101.01, eff. Sept. 29, 2013; 2017 hb49, § 101.01, effective September 29, 2017.

**Editor's Notes**

Amendments by Act 2017, HB 49 were partially vetoed by the governor. Section is presented without the vetoed provisions.

**Amendment Notes**

The 2017 amendment by HB 49 substituted "sections 5160.02, 5162.02, 5163.02, 5164.02, 5165.02, 5166.02, and 5167.02 of the Revised Code" for "sections 5160.02, 5162.02, 5163.03, 5164.04, 5165.05, 5166.02, and 5167.02 of the Revised Code" in the first paragraph; and added the second paragraph.

## § 5162.022 Effect of director's rules on other agencies.

The medicaid director's rules governing medicaid are binding on other state agencies and political subdivisions that administer one or more components of the medicaid program, or one or more aspects of a component, pursuant to contracts entered into under section 5162.35 of the Revised Code. No state agency or political subdivision may establish, by rule or otherwise, a policy governing medicaid that is inconsistent with a medicaid policy established, in rule or otherwise, by the director.

**HISTORY:**

2013 HB 59, § 101.01, eff. Sept. 29, 2013.

## § 5162.03 Supervision of administration of medicaid program; eligibility; rules establishing standards, procedures, and other requirements.

For the purpose of the "Social Security Act," section 1902(a)(5), 42 U.S.C. 1396a(a)(5), the department of medicaid shall act as the single state agency to supervise the administration of the medicaid program. As the single state agency, the department shall comply with 42 C.F.R. 431.10(e) and all other federal requirements applicable to the single state agency.

**HISTORY:**

143 v H 672 (Eff 11-14-89); 143 v H 822 (Eff 12-13-90); 144 v H 298 (Eff 7-26-91); 144 v H 478 (Eff 1-14-93); 146 v H 167 (Eff 11-15-95); 146 v H 710 (Eff 6-11-96); 147 v H 215 (Eff 6-3-97); 147 v H 408 (Eff 10-1-97); 148 v H 283 (Eff 9-29-99); 148 v H 471 (Eff 7-1-2000); 149 v H 94. Eff 9-5-2001; 152 v H 119, § 101.01, eff. 9-29-07; 153 v H 1, § 101.01, eff. 10-16-09; 2012 HB 487, § 101.01, eff. Sept. 10, 2012; 2013 HB 59, § 101.01, eff. Sept. 29, 2013.

**Editor's Notes**

This section was formerly codified as RC § 5111.01.

**Amendment Notes**

The 2013 amendment rewrote the section.

The 2012 amendment added the (A) and (B) designations; rewrote (A) and (B); redesignated former (A) through (D) as (C) through (F); substituted "office of medical assistance" for "department of job and family services" in the introductory language of present (C); substituted "42 U.S.C. 1396a(f)" for "42 U.S.C.A. 1396a(f)" in present (C)(2)(b)(i); inserted "medical assistance" preceding "director" in the second sentence of present (C)(4) and the first sentence of present (F); substituted "office of medical assistance" for "department" in present (D) and in the first sentence of present (E); substituted "office" for "department" following "unless the" in the first sentence of present (E); substituted "office" for "department" wherever it appears in the second sentence of present (E) and the last sentence of present (F); and made stylistic changes.

153 v H 1, effective October 16, 2009, in (A)(1)(a), substituted "section 5111.0120" for "section 5111.019" in the first sentence and "division (E)" for "division (D)" in the second sentence; and substituted "section 5111.014 or 5111.0120" for "section 5111.014 or 5111.019" in the last sentence of (D).

152 v H 119, effective September 29, 2007, in the first paragraph, substituted "centers for medicare and medicaid services" for "health care financing administration"; substituted "medicaid" for "medical assistance" in (A)(1)(a) and (b), (A)(2)(b)(iii), (A)(3), and three times in (D); in (B), substituted "sufficient funds are appropriated for the medicaid program" for "funds are appropriated for such purpose by the general assembly", and inserted "under the medicaid program"; twice inserted "under the medicaid program" in (D); and corrected internal references.

### NOTES TO DECISIONS

Analysis



**Annuities**

Annuity payments made to a Medicaid recipient were not a countable resource for purposes of calculating patient liability. However, creation of the annuity may have constituted an improper transfer for purposes of a restricted Medicaid coverage period: Rayburn v. Ohio Dep't of Job & Family Servs., 2009-Ohio-1842, 182 Ohio App. 3d 113, 911 N.E.2d 954, 2009 Ohio App. LEXIS 1545 (Ohio Ct. App., Fayette County 2009).

There was insufficient evidence to support the nursing home residents' claims that annuities purchased with a balloon payment provision were not improper transfers of assets for the purpose of meeting eligibility requirements for Medicaid: Fire v. Ohio Dep't of Job & Family Servs., 2005-Ohio-5214, 163 Ohio App. 3d 392, 837 N.E.2d 1257, 2005 Ohio App. LEXIS 4737 (Ohio Ct. App., Stark County 2005).

**Countable resource**

Despite the spendthrift provision, the appellant's interest in the trust was a countable resource for purposes of Medicaid eligibility: Metz v. Ohio Dep't of Human Servs., 145 Ohio App. 3d 304, 762 N.E.2d 1032, 2001 Ohio App. LEXIS 3630 (Ohio Ct. App., Ottawa County 2001).

A non-self-settled trust was not an available resource for purposes of Medicaid eligibility: Carnahan v. Ohio Dep't of Human Servs., 139 Ohio App. 3d 214, 743 N.E.2d 473, 2000 Ohio App. LEXIS 4571 (Ohio Ct. App., Lake County 2000).

The community spouse's retirement account proceeds were properly included as a countable resource under the Medicare catastrophic coverage act: Mannix v. Ohio Dep't of Human Servs., 134 Ohio App. 3d 594, 731 N.E.2d 1154, 1999 Ohio App. LEXIS 3219 (Ohio Ct. App., Montgomery County 1999).

A community spouse's IRA is a countable resource for purposes of an institutionalized spouse's eligibility for Medicaid: Martin v. State Dep't of

Human Servs., 130 Ohio App. 3d 512, 720 N.E.2d 576, 1998 Ohio App. LEXIS 5475 (Ohio Ct. App., Champaign County 1998).

A Medicaid qualifying trust is a countable resource: Martin v. Ohio Dep't of Human Servs., 122 Ohio App. 3d 679, 702 N.E.2d 915, 1997 Ohio App. LEXIS 4145 (Ohio Ct. App., Clark County 1997).

A testamentary trust that expressly prohibited any distribution that would affect the beneficiary's Medicaid benefits was not a "countable resource": Young v. Ohio Dep't of Human Servs., 1996-Ohio-70, 76 Ohio St. 3d 547, 668 N.E.2d 908, 1996 Ohio LEXIS 632 (Ohio 1996).

**Determination of resources**

**—Timing**

Determination of the amount of resources of an institutionalized spouse takes place at the time of the application for benefits, and an undetermined, unbilled prior obligation to a nursing home cannot be deducted from those resources: Lewis v. Ohio Dep't of Human Servs., 137 Ohio App. 3d 458, 738 N.E.2d 1264, 2000 Ohio App. LEXIS 1404 (Ohio Ct. App., Lake County 2000).

**Exhaustion of administrative remedies**

Trial court lacked jurisdiction to hear a son's complaint seeking the transfer of real estate based upon OAC 5101:1-39-31(C)(2)(b), renumbered to OAC 5160:1-3-31 because the son did not exhaust his administrative remedies by first seeking a decision from the Ohio Department of Job and Family Services. The son did not seek a hearing or an administrative appeal prior to filing his lawsuit. Fhiaras v. Boyko, 2010-Ohio-2353, 2010 Ohio App. LEXIS 1938 (Ohio Ct. App., Cuyahoga County 2010).

**Fraudulent transfers**

Merely because a transfer is improper as to a Medicaid application does not necessarily mean the transfer is also improper as a fraudulent conveyance. Anyone, of any age, who transfers their major asset without consideration, leaving little or no assets, is liable to creditors who shortly thereafter extend credit without knowledge of the transfer: Lifesphere v. Sahnd, 2008-Ohio-6507, 179 Ohio App. 3d 685, 903 N.E.2d 379, 2008 Ohio App. LEXIS 5393 (Ohio Ct. App., Hamilton County 2008).

**Incompetent applicant**

The incompetent applicant did not have a legal interest in the joint bank accounts or legal ability to access them where the co-depositor's expenditures for the incompetent exceeded the amount in the accounts: Zolla v. Ohio Dep't of Human Servs., 74 Ohio Misc. 2d 120, 659 N.E.2d 1301, 1994 Ohio Misc. LEXIS 89 (Ohio Ct. App., Lucas County 1994).

**Life estate**

A medicaid applicant's life estate in her condominium had no value in reducing the amount of an improper transfer of the condominium because the life estate was nonassignable and inalienable: Gruber v. Ohio Dep't of Job & Family Servs., 2003-Ohio-2528, 153 Ohio App. 3d 6, 790 N.E.2d 800, 2003 Ohio App. LEXIS 2297 (Ohio Ct. App., Lucas County 2003).

**Medicaid qualifying trust**

The amount which is available from a Medicaid qualifying trust is the maximum the trust could disburse to the applicant if the trustee exercised full discretion to do so: Miller v. Ohio Dep't of Human Servs., 105 Ohio App. 3d 539, 664 N.E.2d 619, 1995 Ohio App. LEXIS 3204 (Ohio Ct. App., Cuyahoga County 1995).

**Medical necessity**

Opinion of the treating physician of a child with autism that ABA therapy was a "medical necessity" was entitled to substantial deference. "Medically necessary service" encompasses "Medical service": Hummel v. Ohio Dep't of Job & Family Servs., 2005-Ohio-6651, 164 Ohio App. 3d 776, 844 N.E.2d 360, 2005 Ohio App. LEXIS 5975 (Ohio Ct. App., Lucas County 2005).

In Ohio, the idea of "medical necessity" is the fundamental concept underlying the Medicaid program: Holman v. State Dep't of Human Servs., 2001-Ohio-3155, 143 Ohio App. 3d 44, 757 N.E.2d 382, 2001 Ohio App. LEXIS 132 (Ohio Ct. App., Monroe County 2001).

**Remedies of provider**

Mandamus was the proper remedy for a nursing home seeking Medicaid reimbursement to which it claimed to be entitled. The court of common pleas lacked jurisdiction to grant an injunction compelling payment or to award a declaratory judgment with money damages: Morning View Care Ctr. - Fulton v. Ohio Dep't of Job & Family Servs., 2004-Ohio-5436, 158 Ohio App. 3d 689, 821 N.E.2d 1046, 2004 Ohio App. LEXIS 4486 (Ohio Ct. App., Franklin County 2004).

**Transfer of resources**

Trial court did not abuse its discretion in finding that substantial evidence supported the Ohio Department of Job and Family Services' decision that annuities with balloon payments after a period of comparatively small monthly payments were improper transfers for Medicaid purposes where a doctor stated that the applicants "could" possibly live for the monthly payment period, but did not state that the applicants were "expected" to live for that long; the annuities' features indicated that the transfers were made with the intent to avoid using the resources for nursing home care. Fire v. Ohio Dep't of Job & Family Servs., 2005-Ohio-5214, 163 Ohio App. 3d 392, 837 N.E.2d 1257, 2005 Ohio App. LEXIS 4737 (Ohio Ct. App., Stark County 2005).

### RESEARCH REFERENCES AND PRACTICE AIDS

**Cross-References to Related Sections**

Administration of program for medically handicapped children; cystic fibrosis program, RC § 3701.023.

Determination of county's share of expenses, RC § 3701.024.

Collection of overpayments of public assistance from refunds; welfare overpayment intercept fund, RC § 5747.122.

County planning committee to review assistance programs, RC § 329.06.

Director of job and family services; acceptance of applications, determination of eligibility and performance of administrative activities for certain programs, RC § 5101.47.

Detection and reporting of violations within governmental health care programs and amount of refund to assistance program, RC § 4731.71.

Disability medical assistance program, RC § 5115.20.

Healthcheck program for recipients of medical assistance, RC § 3313.714.

District school board may request identification numbers of students who are medicaid recipients, RC § 3313.715.

Health insurer not to consider eligibility for medical assistance when determining coverage or making payments, RC § 3924.41.

Assignment of rights to health insurer, RC § 3924.42.

Match of agency records to determine overpayment of assistance; notice to auditor of state; prosecution, RC § 5101.181.

Income tax returns examined to determine overpayment of assistance, RC § 5101.182.

Collection of overpayments from state and federal income tax refunds, RC § 5101.184.

Medicaid investigations, RC § 109.85.

Nursing homes; residential care facilities —

Authorization to handle residents' financial affairs; accounts; return of funds, RC § 3721.15.

Residents' rights when medical assistance program terminated or denied, RC §§ 3721.13, 3721.16.

PASSPORT program or alternative to nursing facility placement, RC § 173.52.

Payments treated as income in determining aid; effect of increased social security benefits, RC § 5101.18.

Recovery rights of state and county job and family services departments for cost of medical services and care, RC § 5160.37.

Reimbursement of counties for children services, RC § 5101.14.

Request for information on assistance recipient from third parties; disclosure and use, RC § 5160.39.

**Ohio Administrative Code**

Department of job and family services, division of medical assistance —

General provisions; providers, programs and services in the medicaid program. OAC ch. 5160-1 et seq.

Medicaid: relationship to medicare (Title XVIII). OAC 5160-1-05.

Department of job and family services, division of public assistance—

Application process and determination of eligibility for public assistance programs. OAC ch. 5101:1-2.

Voter registration requirement. OAC 5101:1-2-15.

Application; verification; pre-termination review; redetermination of medicaid eligibility. OAC ch. 5160-1.

Breast and cervical cancer project (BCCP) medicaid. OAC 5160-1-5-02.4.

Covered groups. OAC 5101:1-40-011.

Income: exempt, non-exempt. OAC 5160-1-2-02.

Medicaid program: eligibility. OAC ch. 5160-1-1.

HCBS waivers financial eligibility, patient liability determinations. OAC ch. 5160-33.

Pregnancy related services. OAC ch. 5101:1-26.

Residential state supplement (RSS) program. OAC ch. 5101:1-17.

Department of job and family services, division of social services—

Medicaid eligibility for special needs children who are receiving state adoption subsidy. OAC 5101:2-44-05.1.

## § 5162.031 Department's duties under medicare prescription drug, improvement, and modernization act of 2003.

(A) The medicaid director may do all of the following as necessary for the department of medicaid to fulfill the duties it has, as the single state agency for the medicaid program, under the "Medicare Prescription Drug, Improvement, and Modernization Act of 2003" Pub. L. No. 108-173:

(1) Adopt rules in accordance with division (B) of this section;

(2) Assign duties to county departments of job and family services;

(3) Make payments to the United States department of health and human services from appropriations made to the department of medicaid for this purpose.

(B) Rules authorized by division (A)(1) of this section shall be adopted as follows:

(1) If the rules concern the department's duties regarding medicaid providers, under sections 5164.02 and 5165.02 of the Revised Code, as appropriate;

(2) If the rules concern the department's duties concerning individuals' eligibility for medicaid services, under section 5163.02 of the Revised Code;

(3) If the rules concern the department's duties concerning financial and operational matters between the department and county departments of job and family services, under section 5162.02 of the Revised Code.

**HISTORY:**

151 v H 66, § 101.01, eff. 6-30-05; 2013 HB 59, § 101.01, eff. Sept. 29, 2013.



**Editor's Notes**

This section was formerly codified as RC § 5111.98.

**Amendment Notes**

The 2013 amendment, in the introductory language of (A), substituted "medicaid director" for "director of job and family services" and deleted "117 Stat. 2066" from the end; substituted "department of medicaid" for "department of job and family services " in the introductory language of (A) and in (A)(3); added "in accordance with division (B) of this section" to the end of (A)(1); substituted "authorized by" for "adopted under" in the introductory language of (B); in (B)(1), substituted "medicaid providers, under sections 5164.02 and 5165.02" for "service providers, in accordance with Chapter 119." and added "as appropriate" to the end; inserted "medicaid" in (B)(2); substituted "under section 5163.02" for "in accordance with section 111.15" in (B)(2) and (B)(3); and deleted "as if the rules were internal management rules" from the end of (B)(3).

## § 5162.04 Private causes of action to enforce state medicaid laws.

As used in this section, "state agency" has the same meaning as in section 9.23 of the Revised Code.

No provision of Title LI of the Revised Code or any other law of this state that incorporates any provision of federal medicaid law, or that may be construed as requiring the state, a state agency, or any state official or employee to comply with that federal provision, shall be construed as creating a cause of action to enforce such state law beyond the causes of action available under federal law for enforcement of the provision of federal law.

**HISTORY:**

152 v H 119, § 101.01, eff. 9-29-07; 2013 HB 59, § 101.01, eff. Sept. 29, 2013.

**Editor's Notes**

This section was formerly codified as RC § 5111.102.

**Amendment Notes**

The 2013 amendment substituted "medicaid law" for "Medicaid law, Title XIX of the Social Security Act, 79 Stat. 286 (1965), 42 U.S.C. 1396" in the second paragraph.

### NOTES TO DECISIONS

**Standing**

Trial court acted properly in granting the medical center's motion to dismiss for failure to state a claim because the letter that the medical center sent to the accident victim was not demand for payment but a letter requesting information for subrogation; thus, there was no violation of the Ohio Medicaid Billing regulations. The accident victim also did not have standing to assert her breach of contract and negligence claims against the medical center based on R.C. 5111.102. Hunt v. Mercy Med. Ctr., 2011-Ohio-3678, 2011 Ohio App. LEXIS 3113 (Ohio Ct. App., Stark County 2011).

Trial court acted properly in granting the medical center's motion to dismiss for failure to state a claim because the letter that the medical center sent to the accident victim was not demand for payment but a letter requesting information for subrogation; thus, there was no violation of the Ohio Medicaid Billing regulations. The accident victim also did not have standing to assert her breach of contract and negligence claims against the medical center based on R.C. 5111.102. Hunt v. Mercy Med. Ctr., 2011-Ohio-3678, 2011 Ohio App. LEXIS 3113 (Ohio Ct. App., Stark County 2011).

## § 5162.05 Implementation in accordance with federal and state rules.

The medicaid program shall be implemented in accordance with all of the following:

(A) The medicaid state plan approved by the United States secretary of health and human services, including amendments to the plan approved by the United States secretary;

(B) Federal medicaid waivers granted by the United States secretary, including amendments to waivers approved by the United States secretary;

(C) Other types of federal approval, including demonstration grants, that establish requirements for components of the medicaid program;

(D) Except as otherwise authorized by a federal medicaid waiver granted by the United States secretary, all applicable federal statutes, regulations, and policy guidances;

(E) All applicable state statutes.

**HISTORY:**

2013 HB 59, § 101.01, eff. Sept. 29, 2013.

## § 5162.06 Preconditions for the implementation of Medicaid components.

(A) Notwithstanding any other state statute except for section 5164.061 of the Revised Code, no component, or aspect of a component, of the medicaid program shall be implemented without all of the following:

(1) Subject to division (B) of this section, if the component, or aspect of the component, requires federal approval, receipt of the federal approval;

(2) Sufficient federal financial participation for the component or aspect of the component;

(3) Sufficient nonfederal funds for the component or aspect of the component that qualify as funds needed to obtain the federal financial participation.

(B) A component, or aspect of a component, of the medicaid program that requires federal approval may begin to be implemented before receipt of the federal approval if federal law authorizes implementation to begin before receipt of the federal approval. Implementation shall cease if the federal approval is ultimately denied.

**HISTORY:**

2013 HB 59, § 101.01, eff. Sept. 29, 2013; 2022 hb136, § 1, effective June 13, 2022.

## § 5162.07 Federal approval for certain components.

The medicaid director shall seek federal approval for all components, and aspects of components, of the medicaid program for which federal approval is needed, except that the director is permitted rather than required to seek federal approval for components, and aspects of components, that state statutes permit rather than require be implemented. Federal approval shall be sought in the following forms as appropriate:

(A) The medicaid state plan;

(B) Amendments to the medicaid state plan;

(C) Federal medicaid waivers;

(D) Amendments to federal medicaid waivers;

(E) Other types of federal approval, including demonstration grants.

**HISTORY:**

2013 HB 59, § 101.01, eff. Sept. 29, 2013.

## § 5162.10 Reviews of medicaid program; corrective action plan; sanctions.

The medicaid director may conduct reviews of the medicaid

program. The reviews may include physical inspections of records and sites where medicaid services are provided and interviews of medicaid providers and medicaid recipients. If the director determines pursuant to a review that a person or government entity has violated a rule governing the medicaid program, the director may establish a corrective action plan for the violator and impose fiscal, administrative, or both types of sanctions on the violator in accordance with rules adopted under section 5162.02 of the Revised Code.

**HISTORY:**

151 v H 66, § 101.01, eff. 10-1-05; 152 v H 119, § 101.01, eff. 9-29-07; 2013 HB 59, § 101.01, eff. Sept. 29, 2013.

**Editor's Notes**

This section was formerly codified as RC § 5111.10.

**Amendment Notes**

The 2013 amendment substituted "medicaid director" for "director of job and family services" in the first sentence; in the second sentence, substituted "where medicaid" for "where medicaid-funded" and "medicaid providers and medicaid recipients" for "providers and recipients of the services"; and susbtituted "adopted under section 5162.02 of the Revised Code" for "governing the medicaid program" in the last sentence.

152 v H 119, effective September 29, 2007, deleted the last sentence, which read: "Such action to be taken against a responsible entity, as defined in section 5101.24 of the Revised Code, shall be taken in accordance with that section".

## § 5162.11 Medicaid data system.

(A) The department of medicaid shall enter into an agreement with the department of administrative services for the department of administrative services to contract through competitive selection pursuant to section 125.07 of the Revised Code with a vendor to perform an assessment of the data collection and data warehouse functions of the medicaid data warehouse system, including the ability to link the data sets of all agencies serving medicaid recipients.

The assessment of the data system shall include functions related to fraud and abuse detection, program management and budgeting, and performance measurement capabilities of all agencies serving medicaid recipients, including the departments of aging, health, job and family services, medicaid, mental health and addiction services, and developmental disabilities.

A qualified vendor with whom the department of administrative services contracts to assess the data system shall also assist the medicaid agencies in the definition of the requirements for an enhanced data system or a new data system and assist the department of administrative services in the preparation of a request for proposals to enhance or develop a data system.

(B) Based on the assessment performed pursuant to division (A) of this section, the department of administrative services shall seek a qualified vendor through competitive selection pursuant to Chapter 125. of the Revised Code to develop or enhance a data collection and data warehouse system for the department of medicaid and all agencies serving medicaid recipients.

The department of medicaid shall seek enhanced federal financial participation for ninety per cent of the funds required to establish or enhance the data system. The department of administrative services shall not award a contract for establishing or enhancing the data system until the department of medicaid receives approval from the United States secretary of health and human services for the ninety per cent federal financial participation.

**HISTORY:**

151 v H 66, § 101.01, eff. 9-29-05; 153 v S 79, § 1, eff. 10-6-09; 2013 HB 59, § 101.01, eff. Sept. 29, 2013; 2015 hb64, § 101.01, effective September 29, 2015.

**Editor's Notes**

This section was formerly codified as RC § 5111.915.

**Amendment Notes**

The 2015 amendment, by HB 64, substituted "Chapter 125." for "section 125.07" in the first paragraph of (B).

The 2013 amendment substituted "department of medicaid" for "department of job and family services" wherever it appears in the first paragraph of (A) and in (B); in the second paragraph of (A), deleted "alcohol and drug addiction services" following "departments of aging" and substituted "medicaid, mental health and addiction services" for "mental health"; deleted the third paragraph of (A), which read: "The department of administrative services shall enter into this contract within thirty days after September 29, 2005. The contract shall require the vendor to complete the assessment within ninety days after September 29, 2005"; in the first sentence of the second paragraph of (B), deleted "Within ninety days after September 29, 2005" from the beginning and substituted "financial participation" for "funding"; in the second sentence of the second paragraph of (B), substituted "United States secretary" for "secretary of the United States department" and "financial participation" for "match"; and made a stylistic change.

153 v S 79, effective October 6, 2009, deleted "mental retardation and" preceding "developmental disabilities" throughout; and substituted "September 29, 2005" for "the effective date of this section" three times throughout.

## § 5162.12 Use of contractor to process data; Limits on use of information.

(A) The medicaid director shall enter into a contract with one or more persons to receive and process, on the director's behalf, requests for medicaid recipient or claims payment data, data from reports of audits conducted under section 5165.109 of the Revised Code, or extracts or analyses of any of the foregoing data made by persons who intend to use the items prepared pursuant to the requests for commercial or academic purposes.

(B) At a minimum, a contract entered into under this section shall do both of the following:

(1) Authorize the contracting person to engage in the activities described in division (A) of this section for compensation, which must be stated as a percentage of the fees paid by persons who are provided the items;

(2) Require the contracting person to charge for an item prepared pursuant to a request a fee in an amount equal to one hundred two per cent of the cost the department of medicaid incurs in making the data used to prepare the item available to the contracting person.

(C) Except as required by federal or state law and subject to division (E) of this section, both of the following conditions apply with respect to a request for data described in division (A) of this section:

(1) The request shall be made through a person who has entered into a contract with the medicaid director under this section.

(2) An item prepared pursuant to the request may be provided to the department of medicaid and is confidential and not subject to disclosure under section 149.43 or 1347.08 of the Revised Code.

(D) The medicaid director shall use fees the director receives pursuant to a contract entered into under this section to pay obligations specified in contracts entered under this section. Any money remaining after the obligations are paid shall be deposited in the health care/medicaid support and recoveries fund created under section 5162.52 of the Revised Code.

(E) This section does not apply to requests for medicaid recipient or claims payment data, data from reports of audits conducted under section 5165.109 of the Revised Code, or extracts or analyses of any of the foregoing data that are for any of the following purposes:

(1) Treatment of medicaid recipients;

(2) Payment of medicaid claims;

(3) Establishment or management of medicaid third party liability pursuant to sections 5160.35 to 5160.43 of the Revised Code;

(4) Compliance with the terms of an agreement the medicaid director enters into for purposes of administering the medicaid program.

**HISTORY:**

2013 HB 59, § 101.01, eff. Jan. 1, 2014; 2015 hb64, § 101.01, effective September 29, 2015; 2017 hb49, § 101.01, effective September 29, 2017; 2019 hb166, § 101.01, effective October 17, 2019.

**Amendment Notes**

The 2019 amendment by HB 166 deleted former (E)(5), which read: "Compliance with an operating protocol the executive director of the office of health transformation or the executive director's designee adopts under division (D) of section 191.06 of the Revised Code."

The 2017 amendment by HB 49 substituted "the health care/medicaid support and recoveries fund created under section 5162.52 of the Revised Code" for "the health care services administration fund created under section 5162.54 of the Revised Code" in the second sentence of (D).

The 2015 amendment, by HB 64, in (A), substituted "shall" for "may" and inserted "prepared pursuant to the requests"; and rewrote (B)(2), which formerly read: "Specify the schedule of fees the contracting person is to charge for the items."

## § 5162.13 Annual report on meeting needs of low-income pregnant women, infants and children.

(A) On or before the first day of January of each year, the department of medicaid shall complete a report on the effectiveness of the medicaid program in meeting the health care needs of low-income pregnant women, infants, and children. The report shall include all of the following, delineated by race and ethnic group:

(1) The estimated number of pregnant women, infants, and children eligible for the program;

(2) The actual number of eligible persons enrolled in the program;

(3) The actual number of enrolled pregnant women categorized by estimated gestational age at time of enrollment;

(4) The average number of days between the following events:

(a) A pregnant woman's application for medicaid and enrollment in the fee-for-service component of medicaid;

(b) A pregnant woman's application for enrollment in a medicaid managed care organization and enrollment in the managed care organization.

The information described in divisions (A)(4)(a) and (b) of this section shall also be delineated by county and the urban and rural communities specified in rules adopted under section 3701.142 of the Revised Code.

(5) The number of prenatal, postpartum, and child health visits;

(6) The estimated number of enrolled women of child-bearing age who use a tobacco product;

(7) The estimated number of enrolled women of child -bearing age who participate in a tobacco cessation program or who use a tobacco cessation product;

(8) The rates at which enrolled pregnant women receive addiction or mental health services, progesterone therapy, and any other service specified by the department;

(9) A report on birth outcomes, including a comparison of low-birthweight births and infant mortality rates of medicaid recipients with the general female child-bearing and infant population in this state;

(10) A comparison of the prenatal, delivery, and child health costs of the program with such costs of similar programs in other states, where available;

(11) A report on performance data generated by the component of the state innovation model (SIM) grant pertaining to episode-based payments for perinatal care that was awarded to this state by the center for medicare and medicaid innovation in the United States centers for medicare and medicaid services;

(12) A report on funds allocated for infant mortality reduction initiatives in the urban and rural communities specified in rules adopted under section 3701.142 of the Revised Code;

(13) A report on the results of client responses to questions related to pregnancy services and healthcheck that are asked by the personnel of county departments of job and family services;

(14) A comparison of the performance of the fee-for-service component of medicaid with the performance of each medicaid managed care organization on perinatal health metrics.

(B) The department shall submit the report to the general assembly in accordance with section 101.68 of the Revised Code and to the joint medicaid oversight committee. The department also shall make the report available to the public.

**HISTORY:**

142 v H 231 (Eff 10-5-87); 142 v S 386 (Eff 3-29-88); 144 v H 298 (Eff 7-26-91); 147 v H 408 (Eff 10-1-97); 148 v H 471. Eff 7-1-2000; 2013 HB 59, § 101.01, eff. Sept. 29, 2013; 2013 SB 206, § 1, eff. Mar. 20, 2014; 2015 hb64, § 101.01, effective September 29, 2015; 2016 sb332, § 1, effective April 6, 2017.

**Editor's Notes**

This section was formerly codified as RC § 5111.09.

**Amendment Notes**

The 2018 amendment by HB 24 substituted "with a medicaid-certified capacity exceeding eight" for "in peer group 1" throughout the section.

The 2015 amendment, by HB 64, added the (A), (A)(1), (A)(2), (A)(4), (A)(6), (A)(7), and (B) designations; added "all of the following" to the end of the second sentence of the introductory language of (A); inserted (A)(3) and (A)(5); and made a related change.

The 2013 amendment substituted "complete" for "submit to the speaker and minority leader of the house of representatives and the president and minority leader of the senate, and shall make available to the public" in the first sentence; and added the last two sentences.

The 2013 amendment, in the first sentence, substituted "department of medicaid" for "department of job and family services" and "medicaid program" for "Ohio works first program established under Chapter 5107. of the Revised Code and the medical assistance medicaid program established under this chapter"; in the second sentence, deleted "persons eligible for health care services to" following "estimated number of," substituted "eligible for the program" for "under the programs," inserted "enrolled in the program," and substituted "medicaid recipients" for "program participants"; and made a stylistic change.

## § 5162.131 Cost containment reports and promotion of better health outcomes.

Semiannually, the medicaid director shall complete a report on the establishment and implementation of programs designed to control the increase of the cost of the medicaid program, increase the efficiency of the medicaid program, and promote better health outcomes. The director shall submit the report to the general assembly in accordance with section 101.68 of the Revised Code and to the joint medicaid oversight committee. In each calendar year, one report shall be submitted not later than the last day of June and the subsequent report shall be submitted not later than the last day of December.

**HISTORY:**

149 v S 261. Eff 6-5-2002; 152 v H 562, § 101.01, eff. 6-24-08; 2012 HB 487, § 101.01, eff. Sept. 10, 2012; 2013 HB 59, § 101.01, eff. Sept. 29, 2013; 2013 SB 206, § 1, eff. Mar. 20, 2014.

**Editor's Notes**

This section was formerly codified as RC § 5111.091.

**Amendment Notes**

The 2013 amendment substituted "complete" for "submit to the president and minority leader of the senate, speaker and minority leader of the house of representatives, and the chairpersons of the standing committees of the senate and house of representatives with primary responsibility for legislation making biennial appropriations" in the first sentence; and inserted the second sentence.

The 2013 amendment substituted "medicaid director" for "director of job and family services" in the first sentence.

The 2012 amendment, in the first sentence, substituted "Semiannually" for "Not later than the first day of each calendar quarter", deleted "a report" following "shall submit", inserted "standing", substituted "with primary responsibility for legislation" for "that hear bills", and inserted "a report" and added the second sentence; and deleted the second paragraph, which read: "The report shall include information regarding all of the following: (A) Provider network management; (B) Electronic claims submission and payment systems; (C) Limited provider contracts and payments based on performance; (D) Efforts to enforce third party liability; (E) Implementation of the medicaid information technology system; (F) Expansion of the medicaid data warehouse and decision support system; (G) Development of infrastructure policies for electronic health records and e-prescribing."

152 v H 562, effective June 24, 2008, rewrote the section.

## § 5162.1310 Periodic evaluation of the success members of expansion eligibility group.

(A) The department of medicaid shall periodically evaluate the success that members of the expansion eligibility group have with the following:

(1) Obtaining employer-sponsored health insurance coverage;

(2) Improving health conditions that would otherwise prevent or inhibit stable employment;

(3) Improving the conditions of their employment, including duration and hours of employment.

(B) For the purpose of aiding the department's evaluations under this section, medicaid managed care organizations shall collect and submit to the department relevant data about members of the expansion eligibility group who are enrolled in the organizations' medicaid MCO plans. The department may request that a medicaid managed care organization collect and submit to the department additional data the department needs for the evaluation.

(C) The department shall complete a report for each evaluation conducted under this section. The director shall provide a copy of the report to the general assembly and joint medicaid oversight committee. The copy to the general assembly shall be provided in accordance with section 101.68 of the Revised Code.

**HISTORY:**

2019 hb166, § 101.01, effective October 17, 2019.

## § 5162.132 Annual report on efforts to minimize fraud, waste, and abuse.

Annually, the department of medicaid shall prepare a report on the department's efforts to minimize fraud, waste, and abuse in the medicaid program.

Each report shall be made available on the department's web site. The department shall submit a copy of each report to the governor, general assembly, and joint medicaid oversight committee. The copy to the general assembly shall be submitted in accordance with section 101.68 of the Revised Code. Copies of the report also shall be made available to the public on request.

**HISTORY:**

153 v H 1, § 101.01, eff. 10-16-09; 2013 HB 59, § 101.01, eff. Sept. 29, 2013; 2013 SB 206, § 1, eff. Mar. 20, 2014.

**Editor's Notes**

This section was formerly codified as RC § 5111.092.

The enactment of RC § 5111.092 by 153 v H 1 was disapproved in part by the Governor.

**Amendment Notes**

The 2013 amendment, in the second paragraph, in the second sentence, inserted "general assembly" and added "joint medicaid oversight committee" to the end and in the third sentence, added "The copy to the general assembly shall be submitted" to the beginning and deleted "the general assembly" from the end; and made a related change.

The 2013 amendment deleted the (A) and (B) designations; and substituted "Annually, the department of medicaid" for "Not later than January 1, 2010, and each year thereafter, the department of job and family services".

## § 5162.133 Reports by director.

Not less than once each year, the medicaid director shall submit a report on the medicaid buy-in for workers with disabilities program to the governor, general assembly, and joint medicaid oversight committee. The copy to the general assembly shall be submitted in accordance with section 101.68 of the Revised Code. The report shall include all of the following information:

(A) The number of individuals who participated in the medicaid buy-in for workers with disabilities program;

(B) The cost of the program;

(C) The amount of revenue generated by premiums that participants pay under section 5163.094 of the Revised Code;

(D) The average amount of earned income of participants' families;

(E) The average amount of time participants have participated in the program;

(F) The types of other health insurance participants have been able to obtain.

**HISTORY:**

152 v H 119, § 101.01, eff. 9-29-07; 2013 HB 59, § 101.01, eff. Sept. 29, 2013; 2013 SB 206, § 1, eff. Mar. 20, 2014.

**Editor's Notes**

This section was formerly codified as RC § 5111.7011.

This section was formerly codified as RC § 5163.0910.

**Amendment Notes**

The 2013 amendment, in the introductory language, substituted "general assembly, and joint medicaid oversight committee" for "speaker and minority leader of the house of representatives, president and minority leader of the senate, and chairpersons of the house and senate committees to which the biennial operating budget bill is referred" in the first sentence and inserted the second sentence.

The 2013 amendment substituted "medicaid director" for "director of job and family services" in the first sentence of the introductory language; and substituted "section 5163.094" for "section 5111.704" in (C).

## § 5162.134 Integrated care delivery system report.

Not later than the first day of each July, the medicaid director shall complete a report of the evaluation conducted under section 5164.911 of the Revised Code regarding the integrated care delivery system. The director shall provide a copy of the report to the general assembly and joint medicaid oversight committee. The copy to the general assembly shall be provided in accordance with section 101.68 of the Revised Code. The director also shall make the report available to the public.

**HISTORY:**

2013 SB 206, § 1, eff. Mar. 20, 2014.

## § 5162.135 Creation of an infant morality scorecard by department of medicaid.

(A) As used in this section, "stillbirth" has the same meaning as in section 3701.97 of the Revised Code.

(B) The department of medicaid shall create an infant mortality scorecard. The scorecard shall report all of the following:

(1) The performance of the fee-for-service component of medicaid and each medicaid managed care organization on population health measures, including the infant mortality rate, preterm birth rate, and low-birthweight rate, stillbirth rate, delineated in accordance with division (C) of this section;

(2) The performance of the fee-for-service component of medicaid and each medicaid managed care organization on service utilization and outcome measures using claims data and data from vital records;

(3) The number and percentage of women who are at least fifteen but less than forty-four years of age who are medicaid recipients;

(4) The number of medicaid recipients who delivered a newborn and the percentage of those who reported tobacco use at the time of delivery;

(5) The number of prenatal, postpartum, and adolescent wellness visits made by medicaid recipients;

(6) The percentage of pregnant medicaid recipients who initiated progesterone therapy during pregnancy;

(7) The percentage of female medicaid recipients of childbearing age who participate in a tobacco cessation program or use a tobacco cessation product;

(8) The percentage of female medicaid recipients of childbearing age who use long-acting reversible contraception;

(9) A comparison of the low-birthweight rate of medicaid recipients with the low-birthweight rate of women who are not medicaid recipients;

(10) Any other information on maternal and child health that the department considers appropriate.

(C) To the extent possible, the performance measures described in division (B)(1) of this section shall be delineated in the scorecard as follows:

(1) For each region of the state and the state as a whole, by race and ethnic group;

(2) For the urban and rural communities specified in rules adopted under section 3701.142 of the Revised Code, as well as for any other communities that are the subject of targeted infant mortality reduction initiatives administered by one or more state agencies, by race, ethnic group, and census tract.

The scorecard shall be updated each calendar quarter and made available on the department's internet web site.

(D) The department shall make available the data sources and methodology used to complete the scorecard to any person or government entity on request.

**HISTORY:**

2016 sb332, § 1, effective April 6, 2017.

### § 5162.136 Department of Medicaid review of access to programs intended to reduce tobacco use, prevent prematurity, and promote optimal birth spacing; Presentation of report; Contents of Report.

(A) The department of medicaid shall conduct periodic reviews to determine the barriers that medicaid recipients face in gaining full access to interventions intended to reduce tobacco use, prevent prematurity, and promote optimal birth spacing. The first review shall occur not later than sixty days after the effective date of this section. Thereafter, reviews shall be conducted every six months. The department shall prepare a report that summarizes the results of each review, which must contain the information specified in division (C)(1) or (2) of this section, as applicable. Each report shall be submitted to the commission on infant mortality, the joint medicaid oversight committee, and the general assembly. Submissions to the general assembly shall be made in accordance with section 101.68 of the Revised Code.

(B) The department shall make a presentation on each report at the first meeting of the commission on infant mortality that follows the report's submission to the commission.



(C)(1) All of the following shall be in the first report submitted in accordance with division (A) of this section:

(a) Identification of the access barriers described in division (A) of this section, the individuals affected by the barriers, and whether the barriers result from policies implemented by the department, medicaid managed care organizations, providers, or others;

(b) Recommendations for the expedient removal of the access barriers;

(c) An analysis of the performance of the fee-for-service component of medicaid and the performance of each medicaid managed care organization on health metrics pertaining to tobacco cessation, prematurity prevention, and birth spacing;

(d) Any other information the department considers pertinent to the report's topic.

(2) All of the following shall be in each subsequent report submitted in accordance with division (A) of this section:

(a) The progress that has been made on removing the access barriers described in division (A) of this section and the impact such progress has had on reducing the infant mortality rate in this state;

(b) A performance analysis of the fee-for-service component of medicaid and each medicaid managed care organization on health metrics pertaining to tobacco cessation, prematurity prevention, and birth spacing;

(c) Any other information the department considers pertinent.

**HISTORY:**

2016 sb332, § 1, effective April 6, 2017.

### § 5162.15 Fraud, waste, and abuse prevention and detection.

(A) As used in this section;

"Agent" and "contractor" include any agent, contractor, subcontractor, or other person who, on behalf of an entity, furnishes or authorizes the furnishing of medicaid services, performs billing or coding functions, or is involved in monitoring of health care that an entity provides.

"Employee" includes any officer or employee (including management employees) of an entity.

"Entity" includes a governmental entity or an organization, unit, corporation, partnership, or other business arrangement, including any medicaid managed care organization, irrespective of the form of business structure or arrangement by which it exists, whether for-profit or not-for-profit. "Entity" does not include a government entity that administers one or more components of the medicaid program, unless the government entity receives medicaid payments for providing medicaid services.

"Federal health care programs" has the same meaning as in the "Social Security Act," section 1128B, 42 U.S.C. 1320a-7b(f).

(B) Each entity that receives or makes in a federal fiscal year payments under the medicaid program, either through the medicaid state plan or a federal medicaid waiver, totaling at least five million dollars shall, as a condition of receiving such payments, do all of the following not later than the first day of the succeeding calendar year:

(1) Establish written policies for all of the entity's employees, contractors, and agents that provide detailed information about the role of all of the following in preventing and detecting fraud, waste, and abuse in federal health care programs:

(a) Federal false claims law under 31 U.S.C. 3729 to 3733;

(b) Federal administrative remedies for false claims and statements available under 31 U.S.C. 3801 to 3812;

(c) Sections 124.341, 2913.40, 2913.401, and 2921.13 of the Revised Code and any other state laws pertaining to civil or criminal penalties for false claims and statements;

(d) Whistleblower protections under the laws specified in divisions (B)(1)(a) to (c) of this section.

(2) Include as part of the written policies required by division (B)(1) of this section detailed provisions regarding the entity's policies and procedures for preventing and detecting fraud, waste, and abuse.

(3) Disseminate the written policies required by division (B)(1) of this section to each of the entity's employees, contractors, and agents in a paper or electronic form and make the written policies readily available to the entity's employees, contractors, and agents.

(4) If the entity has an employee handbook, include in the employee handbook a specific discussion of the laws specified in division (B)(1) of this section, the rights of employees to be protected as whistleblowers, and the entity's policies and procedures for preventing and detecting fraud, waste, and abuse.

(5) Require the entity's contractors and agents to adopt the entity's written policies required by division (B)(1) of this section.

(C) An entity that furnishes medicaid services at multiple locations or under multiple contractual or other payment arrangements is required to comply with division (B) of this section if the entity receives in a federal fiscal year medicaid payments totaling in the aggregate at least five million dollars. This applies regardless of whether the entity submits claims for medicaid payments using multiple provider identification or tax identification numbers.

**HISTORY:**

151 v H 530, § 101.01, eff. 6-30-06; 152 v H 119, § 101.01, eff. 9-29-07; 2013 HB 59, § 101.01, eff. Sept. 29, 2013.

**Editor's Notes**

This section was formerly codified as RC § 5111.101.

**Amendment Notes**

The 2013 amendment, in (A), substituted "medicaid services" for "health care items or services under the medicaid program" in the second paragraph, substituted "providing medicaid" for "providing items or" in the fourth paragraph, and inserted "the 'Social Security Act,' section 1128B" in the last paragraph; substituted "medicaid state" for "state medicaid" in the introductory language of (B); and substituted "medicaid services" for "items or services" in the first sentence of (C).

152 v H 119, effective September 29, 2007, rewrote the section.

### § 5162.16 Report of medicaid fraud, abuse or waste; reasonable cause.

A government entity that administers one or more components of the medicaid program and has reasonable cause to believe that an instance of fraud, waste, or abuse has occurred in the medicaid program shall inform the department of medicaid. The department shall collect the information in the medicaid data warehouse system established under section 5162.11 of the Revised Code.

**HISTORY:**

2017 hb49, § 101.01, effective September 29, 2017.

### § 5162.20 Cost-sharing program.

(A) The department of medicaid shall institute cost-sharing requirements for the medicaid program. The department shall not institute cost-sharing requirements in a manner that does either of the following:

(1) Disproportionately impacts the ability of medicaid recipients with chronic illnesses to obtain medically necessary medicaid services;

(2) Violates section 5164.09 or 5164.10 of the Revised Code.

(B)(1) No provider shall refuse to provide a service to a medicaid recipient who is unable to pay a required copayment for the service.

(2) Division (B)(1) of this section shall not be considered to do either of the following with regard to a medicaid recipient who is unable to pay a required copayment:

(a) Relieve the medicaid recipient from the obligation to pay a copayment;

(b) Prohibit the provider from attempting to collect an unpaid copayment.

(C) Except as provided in division (F) of this section, no provider shall waive a medicaid recipient's obligation to pay the provider a copayment.

(D) No provider or drug manufacturer, including the manufacturer's representative, employee, independent contractor, or agent, shall pay any copayment on behalf of a medicaid recipient.

(E) If it is the routine business practice of a provider to refuse service to any individual who owes an outstanding debt to the provider, the provider may consider an unpaid copayment imposed by the cost-sharing requirements as an outstanding debt and may refuse service to a medicaid recipient who owes the provider an outstanding debt. If the provider intends to refuse service to a medicaid recipient who owes the provider an outstanding debt, the provider shall notify the recipient of the provider's intent to refuse service.

(F) In the case of a provider that is a hospital, the cost-sharing program shall permit the hospital to take action to collect a copayment by providing, at the time services are rendered to a medicaid recipient, notice that a copayment may be owed. If the hospital provides the notice and chooses not to take any further action to pursue collection of the copayment, the prohibition against waiving copayments specified in division (C) of this section does not apply.

(G) The department of medicaid may collaborate with a state agency that is administering, pursuant to a contract entered into under section 5162.35 of the Revised Code, one or more components, or one or more aspects of a component, of the medicaid program as necessary for the state agency to apply the cost-sharing requirements to the components or aspects of a component that the state agency administers.

**HISTORY:**

149 v S 261. Eff 6-5-2002; 150 v H 95, § 1, eff. 9-26-03; 151 v H 66, § 101.01, eff. 9-29-05; 151 v H 530, § 101.01, eff. 6-30-06; 152 v H 119, § 101.01, eff. 9-29-07; 2011 HB 153, § 101.01, eff. Oct. 1, 2011; 2013 HB 59, § 101.01, eff. Sept. 29, 2013; 2013 SB 206, § 1, eff. Mar. 20, 2014; 2014 SB 99, § 1, eff. Sept. 17, 2014; 2020 hb11, § 1, effective September 18, 2020.

**Editor's Notes**

This section was formerly codified as RC § 5111.0112.

**Amendment Notes**

The 2020 amendment by HB 11 added "or 5164.10" in (A)(2).

The 2013 amendment, in (A), added the second sentence and deleted the last two sentences, which read: "The cost-sharing requirements shall include a copayment requirement for at least dental services, vision services, nonemergency emergency department services, and prescribed drugs. The cost-sharing requirements also shall include requirements regarding premiums, enrollment fees, deductions, and similar charges."

The 2013 amendment rewrote (A); deleted the introductory language of (B), which read: "The cost-sharing program shall, to the extent permitted by federal law, provide for all of the following with regard to any providers participating in the medicaid program"; redesignated former (B)(3) through (B)(5), (C), and (D) as (C) through (G); substituted "requirements" for "program" in the first sentence of present (E) and in present (G); substituted "recipient" for "individual" in the second sentence of present (E); in present (G), substituted "medicaid may collaborate" for "job and family services may work," "section 5162.35" for "section 5111.91," and "a component" for "the medicaid program"; and made stylistic changes.

The 2011 amendment deleted the former third sentence of (A), which read: "In the case of an individual participating in the children's buy-in program established under sections 5101.5211 to 5101.5216 of the Revised Code, the cost-sharing program shall be consistent with sections 5101.5213 and 5101.5214 of the Revised Code if the children's buy-in program is a component of the medicaid program."

152 v H 119, effective September 29, 2007, rewrote (A); in the introductory language of (B), (B)(5), and (C), substituted "cost-sharing" for "copayment"; and added (D).

151 v H 530, effective June 30, 2006, in (A), added "program" to the end of the first sentence and "To the extent permitted by federal law" to the beginning, and deleted "to the extent permitted by federal statutes and regulations" from the end of the second sentence; added the exception to the beginning of (B)(3); and added (C).

151 v H 66, effective September 29, 2005, rewrote the section.

The 2014 amendment by SB 99 added "does either of the following" to the end of the introductory language of (A); added (A)(2); and made a related change.

### § 5162.21 Medicaid estate recovery program.

(A) As used in this section and section 5162.211 of the Revised Code:

(1) "Estate" includes both of the following:

(a) All real and personal property and other assets to be administered under Title XXI of the Revised Code and property that would be administered under that title if not for section 2113.03 or 2113.031 of the Revised Code;

(b) Any other real and personal property and other assets in which an individual had any legal title or interest at the time of death (to the extent of the interest), including assets conveyed to a survivor, heir, or assign of the individual through joint tenancy, tenancy in common, survivorship, life estate, living trust, or other arrangement.

(2) "Institution" means a nursing facility, ICF/IID, or a medical institution.

(3) "Permanently institutionalized individual" means an individual to whom all of the following apply:

(a) Is an inpatient in an institution;

(b) Is required, as a condition of the medicaid program paying for the individual's services in the institution, to spend for costs of medical or nursing care all of the individual's income except for an amount for personal needs specified by the department of medicaid;

(c) Cannot reasonably be expected to be discharged from the institution and return home as determined by the department of medicaid.

(4) "Qualified state long-term care insurance partnership program" means the program established under section 5164.86 of the Revised Code.

(5) "Time of death" shall not be construed to mean a time after which a legal title or interest in real or personal property or other asset may pass by survivorship or other operation of law due to the death of the decedent or terminate by reason of the decedent's death.

(B) To the extent permitted by federal law, the department of medicaid shall institute a medicaid estate recovery program under which the department shall, except as provided in divisions (C) and (E) of this section, and subject to division (D) of this section, do all of the following:

(1) For the costs of medicaid services the medicaid program correctly paid or will pay on behalf of a permanently institutionalized individual of any age, seek adjustment or recovery from the individual's estate or on the sale of property of the individual or spouse that is subject to a lien imposed under section 5162.211 of the Revised Code;

(2) For the costs of medicaid services the medicaid program correctly paid or will pay on behalf of an individual fifty-five years of age or older who is not a permanently institutionalized individual, seek adjustment or recovery from the individual's estate;

(3) Seek adjustment or recovery from the estate of other individuals as permitted by federal law.

(C)(1) No adjustment or recovery may be made under division (B)(1) of this section from a permanently institutionalized individual's estate or on the sale of property of a permanently institutionalized individual that is subject to a lien imposed under section 5162.211 of the Revised Code or under division

Titles 39 — 57

(B)(2) or (3) of this section from an individual's estate while either of the following are alive:

(a) The spouse of the permanently institutionalized individual or individual;

(b) The son or daughter of a permanently institutionalized individual or individual if the son or daughter is under age twenty-one or, under the "Social Security Act," section 1614, 42 U.S.C. 1382c, is considered blind or disabled.

(2) No adjustment or recovery may be made under division (B)(1) of this section from a permanently institutionalized individual's home that is subject to a lien imposed under section 5162.211 of the Revised Code while either of the following lawfully reside in the home:

(a) The permanently institutionalized individual's sibling who resided in the home for at least one year immediately before the date of the permanently institutionalized individual's admission to the institution and on a continuous basis since that time;

(b) The permanently institutionalized individual's son or daughter who provided care to the permanently institutionalized individual that delayed the permanently institutionalized individual's institutionalization and resided in the home for at least two years immediately before the date of the permanently institutionalized individual's admission to the institution and on a continuous basis since that time.

(D) In the case of a participant of the qualified state long-term care insurance partnership program, adjustment or recovery required by this section may be reduced in accordance with rules authorized by division (G) of this section.

(E) The department shall, in accordance with procedures and criteria established in rules authorized by division (G) of this section, waive seeking an adjustment or recovery otherwise required by this section if the medicaid director determines that adjustment or recovery would work an undue hardship. The department may limit the duration of the waiver to the period during which the undue hardship exists.

(F) For the purpose of determining whether an individual meets the definition of "permanently institutionalized individual" established for this section, a rebuttable presumption exists that the individual cannot reasonably be expected to be discharged from an institution and return home if either of the following is the case:

(1) The individual declares that he or she does not intend to return home.

(2) The individual has been an inpatient in an institution for at least six months.

(G) Rules adopted under section 5162.02 of the Revised Code shall do both of the following:

(1) For the purpose of division (D) of this section and consistent with the "Social Security Act," section 1917(b)(1)(C), 42 U.S.C. 1396p(b)(1)(C), provide for reducing an adjustment or recovery in the case of a participant of the qualified state long-term care insurance partnership program;

(2) For the purpose of division (E) of this section and consistent with the standards specified by the United States secretary of health and human services under the "Social Security Act," section 1917(b)(3), 42 U.S.C. 1396p(b)(3), establish procedures and criteria for waiving adjustment or recovery due to an undue hardship.



**HISTORY:**

RC § 5111.33, 139 v H 694 (Eff 11-15-81); 140 v H 291 (Eff 7-1-83); 141 v H 428 (Eff 12-23-86); 143 v H 111 (Eff 7-1-89); RC § 5111.11, 143 v H 822 (Eff 12-13-90); 145 v H 152 (Eff 7-1-93); 146 v H 167 (Eff 11-15-95); 147 v H 215 (Eff 9-29-97); 148 v H 471 (Eff 7-1-2000); 148 v H 313. Eff 8-29-2000; 151 v H 66, § 101.01, eff. 6-30-05; 151 v H 530, § 101.01, eff. 6-30-06; 152 v H 119, § 101.01, eff. 9-29-07; 2013 HB 59, § 101.01, eff. Sept. 29, 2013.

**Editor's Notes**

This section was formerly codified as RC § 5111.11.

**Amendment Notes**

The 2013 amendment substituted "section 5162.211" for " section 5111.111" in the introductory language of (A), (C)(1), and (C)(2) and in (B)(1); substituted "ICF/IID" for "intermediate care facility for the mentally retarded" in (A)(2); deleted (A)(3), pertaining to the meaning of the terms "Intermediate care facility for the mentally retarded" and "nursing facility"; redesignated former (A)(4) through (A)(6) as (A)(3) through (A)(5); substituted "department of medicaid" for "department of job and family services" in present (A)(3)(b) and (A)(3)(c), and in the introductory language of (B); inserted "the 'Social Security Act,' section 1614" in (C)(1)(b); substituted "authorized by" for "adopted under" in (D) and the first sentence of (E); substituted "medicaid director" for "director of job and family services" in the first sentence of (E); rewrote the introductory language of (G); inserted "the 'Social Security Act,' section 1917(b)(1)(C)" in (G)(1); and inserted "the 'Social Security Act,' section 1917(b)(3)" in (G)(2).

152 v H 119, effective September 29, 2007, inserted "medicaid" in the introductory languages of (B) and (G); in the introductory language of (B), substituted "divisions (C) and (E) of this section, and subject to division (D) of this section, do all" for "divisions (C), (D), and (E) of this section, do both"; added (B)(3); and corrected internal references.

151 v H 530, effective June 30, 2006, inserted (A)(5) and redesignated former (A)(5) as (6); inserted (D) and redesignated the remaining subsections accordingly; in present (E), inserted "in accordance with procedures and criteria established in rules adopted under division (G) of this section", and deleted the last paragraph, pertaining to the adoption of rules regarding the estate recovery program; added (G); and corrected internal references.

151 v H 66, effective June 30, 2005, rewrote the section.

## NOTES TO DECISIONS

Analysis



**Constitutionality**

Lien by the Ohio Department of Job and Family Services against the decedent's property, seeking repayment of Medicaid benefits, did not amount to a taking in violation of constitutional prohibitions because the Department was not attempting to recover against the remainder interests held by the decedent's children; rather, the Department sought to recover against the decedent's estate in general, and the amount that was subject to recovery was limited to the value of the decedent's life estate. Phillips v. McCarthy, 2016-Ohio-2994, 55 N.E.3d 20, 2016 Ohio App. LEXIS 1854 (Ohio Ct. App., Preble County 2016).

**Assets of estate**

Under the expanded definition of "estate" in R.C. 5162.21(A)(1)(b), which included non-probate assets, the decedent's legal interest in the child support arrearages owed to her represented a quantifiable asset of her estate for the purposes of the Medicaid Estate Recovery Program; thus, the trial court did not err when it approved the administrator's inventory listing the arrearages as an asset of her estate. In re Estate of Anderson, 2020-Ohio-6924, 165 N.E.3d 406, 2020 Ohio App. LEXIS 4754 (Ohio Ct. App., Shelby County 2020).

**Claims against estate**

Under the statute, the Ohio Department of Medicaid was entitled to recover one-half of a refund paid by the retirement community to the father's estate, because the mother's ownership interest in her half of the retirement community endured post-mortem and was subject to recovery for Medicaid medical assistance benefits previously paid on her behalf. Ohio Dep't of Medicaid v. French, 2020-Ohio-2744, 154 N.E.3d 426, 2020 Ohio App. LEXIS 1708 (Ohio Ct. App., Darke County 2020).

Probate court determined correctly that the Ohio Department of Medicaid's (ODM's) claim had priority over the nursing home's claim because ODM recorded a valid, statutory lien against the decedent's real property, and ODM's claim was thus entitled to priority over that of the nursing home. The estate recovery statute did not apply exclusively to living, permanently institutionalized recipients of Medicaid benefits, and thus, ODM was not required to record its lien against the decedent's property before she died. Wiesenmayer v. Vaspory, 2019-Ohio-1805, 135 N.E.3d 1237, 2019 Ohio App. LEXIS 1880 (Ohio Ct. App., Montgomery County 2019).

Court erred in dismissing the claim under the Ohio Medicaid Estate Recovery Program because real property located in foreign lands was subject to the Ohio Medicaid Estate Recovery Program, as this provision indicated that any and all real property, regardless of location, was subject to Medicaid estate recovery. Adm'r, State Medicaid Estate Recovery Program v. Miracle, 2015-Ohio-1516, 31 N.E.3d 658, 2015 Ohio App. LEXIS 1577 (Ohio Ct. App., Washington County 2015).

The time limits in R.C. 2117.06 do not apply to an action by the state pursuant to R.C. 5111.11: Ohio Dep't of Human Servs. v. Eastman, 145 Ohio App. 3d 369, 763 N.E.2d 193, 2001 Ohio App. LEXIS 3373 (Ohio Ct. App., Summit County 2001).

**Life estate**

Ohio Department of Job and Family Services was entitled to file a lien against real property, in which the decedent held a life estate, seeking repayment of Medicaid benefits disbursed on the decedent's behalf, because the recipient's life estate interest transcended physical death and was subject to posthumous encumbrance by the Department. Phillips v. McCarthy, 2016-Ohio-2994, 55 N.E.3d 20, 2016 Ohio App. LEXIS 1854 (Ohio Ct. App., Preble County 2016).

**Medical malpractice**

The department of human services did not have a right of subrogation against the surviving spouse for medical services furnished to the decedent, former R.C. 2305.27 governed subrogation rights in medical malpractice claims: Ohio Dep't of Human Servs. v. Crespo, 99 Ohio App. 3d 709, 651 N.E.2d 1037, 1994 Ohio App. LEXIS 5952 (Ohio Ct. App., Cuyahoga County 1995).

### RESEARCH REFERENCES AND PRACTICE AIDS

**Cross-References to Related Sections**

Letters of administration, RC § 2113.06.

**Ohio Administrative Code**

Department of job and family services, division of public assistance—Medicaid estate recovery. OAC 5160:1-2-07.

Medicaid: recipient-caused overpayment; determination, recovery. OAC 5160:1-2-04 et seq.

**Practice Manuals and Treatises**

Anderson's Ohio Elder Law Practice Manual § 4.14 Estate Recovery and Liens

## § 5162.211 Medicaid estate recovery liens.

(A) Except as provided in division (B) of this section and section 5162.23 of the Revised Code, no lien may be imposed against the property of an individual before the individual's death on account of medicaid services correctly paid or to be paid on the individual's behalf.

(B) Except as provided in division (C) of this section, the department of medicaid may impose a lien against the real property of a medicaid recipient who is a permanently institutionalized individual and against the real property of the recipient's spouse, including any real property that is jointly held by the recipient and spouse. The lien may be imposed on account of medicaid paid or to be paid on the recipient's behalf.

(C) No lien may be imposed under division (B) of this section against the home of a medicaid recipient if any of the following lawfully resides in the home:

(1) The recipient's spouse;

(2) The recipient's son or daughter who is under twenty-one years of age or, under the "Social Security Act," section 1614, 42 U.S.C. 1382c, considered to be blind or disabled;

(3) The recipient's sibling who has an equity interest in the home and resided in the home for at least one year immediately before the date of the recipient's admission to the institution.

(D) The medicaid director or a person designated by the director shall sign a certificate to effectuate a lien required to be imposed under this section. The county department of job and family services shall file for recording and indexing the certificate, or a certified copy, in the real estate mortgage records in the office of the county recorder in every county in which real property of the recipient or spouse is situated. From the time of filing the certificate in the office of the county recorder, the lien attaches to all real property of the recipient or spouse described in the certificate for all amounts for which adjustment or recovery may be made under section 5162.21 of the Revised Code and, except as provided in division (E) of this section, shall remain a lien until satisfied.

Upon filing the certificate in the office of the recorder, all persons are charged with notice of the lien and the rights of the department of medicaid thereunder.

The county recorder shall keep a record of every certificate filed showing its date, the time of filing, the name and residence of the recipient or spouse, and any release, waivers, or satisfaction of the lien.

The priority of the lien shall be established in accordance with state and federal law.

The department may waive the priority of its lien to provide for the costs of the last illness as determined by the department, administration, attorney fees, administrator fees, a sum for the payment of the costs of burial, which shall be computed by deducting from five hundred dollars whatever amount is available for the same purpose from all other sources, and a similar sum for the spouse of the decedent.

(E) A lien imposed with respect to a medicaid recipient under this section shall dissolve on the recipient's discharge from the institution and return home.

**HISTORY:**

146 v H 167 (Eff 11-15-95); 147 v H 215 (Eff 9-29-97); 148 v H 471. Eff 7-1-2000; 150 v H 95, § 1, eff. 9-26-03; 151 v H 66, § 101.01, eff. 6-30-05; 2013 HB 59, § 101.01, eff. Sept. 29, 2013.

**Editor's Notes**

This section was formerly codified as RC § 5111.111.

**Amendment Notes**

The 2013 amendment substituted "section 5162.23" for "section 5111.12" in (A); substituted "medicaid" for "job and family services" in the first sentence of (B); inserted "the 'Social Security Act,' section 1614" in (C)(2); in the first paragraph (D), substituted "medicaid director" for "director of job and family services" in the first sentence and substituted "section 5162.21" for "section 5111.11" in the last sentence; and substituted "medicaid" for "job and family services" in the second paragraph of (D).

151 v H 66, effective June 30, 2005, rewrote the section.

### NOTES TO DECISIONS

**Claims against estate**

Probate court determined correctly that the Ohio Department of Medicaid's (ODM's) claim had priority over the nursing home's claim because ODM recorded a valid, statutory lien against the decedent's real property, and ODM's claim was thus entitled to priority over that of the nursing home. The estate recovery statute did not apply exclusively to living, permanently institutionalized recipients of Medicaid benefits, and thus, ODM was not required to record its lien against the decedent's property before she died. Wiesenmayer v. Vaspory, 2019-Ohio-1805, 135 N.E.3d 1237, 2019 Ohio App. LEXIS 1880 (Ohio Ct. App., Montgomery County 2019).

### RESEARCH REFERENCES AND PRACTICE AIDS

**Cross-References to Related Sections**

Letters of administration, RC § 2113.06.

Long-term care insurance program; exclusion of resources, RC § 5164.86.

**Practice Manuals and Treatises**

Anderson's Ohio Elder Law Practice Manual § 4.14 Estate Recovery and Liens

## § 5162.212 Attorney general may contract for collection of amounts due under estate recovery program.

The department of medicaid shall certify amounts due under the medicaid estate recovery program instituted under section 5162.21 of the Revised Code to the attorney general pursuant to section 131.02 of the Revised Code. The attorney general may enter into a contract with any person or government entity to collect the amounts due on behalf of the attorney general.

The attorney general, in entering into a contract under this section, shall comply with all of the requirements that must be met for the state to receive federal financial participation for the costs incurred in entering into the contract and carrying out actions under the contract. The contract may provide for the person or government entity with which the attorney general contracts to be compensated from the property recovered under the medicaid estate recovery program or may provide for another manner of compensation agreed to by the parties to the contract.

Regardless of whether the attorney general collects the amounts due under the medicaid estate recovery program or contracts with a person or government entity to collect the amounts due on behalf of the attorney general, the amounts due shall be collected in accordance with applicable requirements of federal statutes and regulations and state statutes and rules.

**HISTORY:**

151 v H 66, § 101.01, eff. 6-30-05; 152 v H 119, § 101.01, eff. 9-29-07; 2013 HB 59, § 101.01, eff. Sept. 29, 2013.

**Editor's Notes**

This section was formerly codified as RC § 5111.112.

**Amendment Notes**

The 2013 amendment, in the first sentence of the first paragraph, substituted "medicaid" for "job and family services" and "section 5162.21" for "section 5111.11".

152 v H 119, effective September 29, 2007, inserted "medicaid" preceding "estate recovery" throughout.

## § 5162.22 Duty of adult care facility or home to transfer decedent's personal needs allowance account.

(A) As used in this section:

(1) "Commissioner" means a person appointed by a probate court under division (E) of section 2113.03 of the Revised Code to act as a commissioner.

(2) "Home" has the same meaning as in section 3721.10 of the Revised Code.

(3) "Personal needs allowance account" means an account or petty cash fund that holds the money of a resident of a residential facility or home and that the facility or home manages for the resident.

(4) "Residential facility" means a residential facility licensed under section 5119.34 of the Revised Code that provides accommodations, supervision, and personal care services for three to sixteen unrelated adults.

(B) Except as provided in divisions (C) and (D) of this section, the owner or operator of a home or residential facility shall transfer to the department of medicaid the money in the personal needs allowance account of a resident of the home or facility who was a medicaid recipient no earlier than sixty days but not later than ninety days after the resident dies. The home or facility shall transfer the money even though the owner or operator of the facility or home has not been issued letters testamentary or letters of administration concerning the resident's estate.

(C) If funeral or burial expenses for a resident of a home or residential facility who has died have not been paid and the only resource the resident had that could be used to pay for the expenses is the money in the resident's personal needs allowance account, or all other resources of the resident are inadequate to pay the full cost of the expenses, the money in the resident's personal needs allowance account shall be used to pay for the expenses rather than being transferred to the department of medicaid pursuant to division (B) of this section.

(D) If, not later than sixty days after a resident of a home or residential facility dies, letters testamentary or letters of administration are issued, or an application for release from administration is filed under section 2113.03 of the Revised Code, concerning the resident's estate, the owner or operator of the home or facility shall transfer the money in the resident's personal needs allowance account to the administrator, executor, commissioner, or person who filed the application for release from administration.

(E) The transfer or use of money in a resident's personal needs allowance account in accordance with division (B), (C), or (D) of this section discharges and releases the home or residential facility, and the owner or operator of the home, from any claim for the money from any source.

(F) If, sixty-one or more days after a resident of a home or residential facility dies, letters testamentary or letters of administration are issued, or an application for release from administration under section 2113.03 of the Revised Code is filed, concerning the resident's estate, the department of medicaid shall transfer the funds to the administrator, executor, commissioner, or person who filed the application, unless the department is entitled to recover the money under the medicaid estate recovery program instituted under section 5162.21 of the Revised Code.

**HISTORY:**

146 v H 167 (Eff 11-15-95); 148 v H 471. Eff 7-1-2000; 151 v H 66, § 101.01, eff. 6-30-05; 152 v H 119, § 101.01, eff. 9-29-07; 2011 HB 153, § 101.01, eff. July 1, 2011; 2011 SB 124, § 1, eff. Jan. 13, 2012; 2012 HB 487, § 101.01, eff. Sept. 10, 2012; 2013 HB 59, § 101.01, eff. Sept. 29, 2013.

**Editor's Notes**

This section was formerly codified as RC § 5111.113.

This section was renumbered from RC § 5111.112 by 151 v H 66, effective June 30, 2005.

**Amendment Notes**

The 2013 amendment substituted "a residential" for "an adult care" in (A)(3); substituted "section 5119.34" for "section 5119.22" in (A)(4); substituted "department of medicaid" for "department of job and family services" in the first sentence of (B) and in (C) and (F); substituted "medicaid recipient" for "recipient of the medical assistance program" in the first sentence of (B); and substituted "section 5162.21" for "section 5111.11" in (F).

The 2012 amendment deleted (A)(1), which read: " 'Adult care facility' has the same meaning as in section 5119.70 of the Revised Code"; redesignated former (A)(2) through (A)(4) as (A)(1) through (A)(3); added (A)(4); substituted "a home or residential facility" for "an adult care facility or home" in the first sentence of (B) and in (C), (D), and (F); substituted "home or facility" for "adult care facility or home" in the second sentence of (B); in (E), substituted "home or residential facility" for "adult care facility or home" and deleted "facility or" following "operator of the"; and made stylistic changes.

The 2011 amendment substituted "division (E)" for "division (B)" in (A)(2).

The 2011 amendment by HB 153 substituted "section 5119.70" for "section 3722.01" in (A)(1).

152 v H 119, effective September 29, 2007, inserted "medicaid" in (F).

**RESEARCH REFERENCES AND PRACTICE AIDS**

**Cross-References to Related Sections**

Authorization to handle residents' financial affairs; accounts; return of funds, RC § 3721.15.

Consent of tax commissioner to transfer of decedent's assets, RC § 5731.39.

**Ohio Administrative Code**

Protection of residents' funds and management of personal needs allowance —

Intermediate care facilities for Medicaid coverage of targeted case management services provided to individuals with developmental disabilities, OAC 5160-48-01, 5123:2-7-14.and 5123-7-14.

Nursing facilities (NF) medicaid cost reports, OAC ch. 5160.

## § 5162.23 Action to recover benefits incorrectly paid.

(A) The medicaid director shall adopt rules under section 5162.02 of the Revised Code permitting county departments of job and family services to take action to recover benefits incorrectly paid on behalf of medicaid recipients. The rules shall provide for recovery by the following methods:

(1) Soliciting voluntary payments from recipients or from persons holding property in which a recipient has a legal or equitable interest;

(2) Obtaining a lien on property pursuant to division (B) of this section.

(B) A county department of job and family services may bring a civil action in a court of common pleas against a medicaid recipient for the recovery of any medicaid payments determined by the court to have been paid incorrectly on behalf of the recipient. All persons holding property in which the recipient has a legal or equitable interest may be joined as parties. The court may issue pre-judgment orders, including injunctive relief or attachment under Chapter 2715. of the Revised Code, for the preservation of real or personal property in which the recipient may have a legal or equitable interest. If the court determines that medicaid payments were made incorrectly and issues a judgment to that effect, the county department may obtain a lien upon property of the recipient in accordance with Chapter 2329. of the Revised Code.

(C) The county department of job and family services shall retain fifty per cent of the balance remaining after deduction from the recovery of the amount required to be returned to the federal government and shall pay the other fifty per cent of the balance to the department of medicaid.

(D) Recovery of medicaid payments incorrectly made on behalf of a medicaid recipient may not be accomplished by reducing the amount of benefits the recipient is entitled to receive under another government assistance program.

(E) The remedies provided pursuant to this section do not affect any other remedies county departments of job and family services may have to recover benefits incorrectly paid on behalf of medicaid recipients.

**HISTORY:**

RC § 5111.34, 143 v H 111 (Eff 7-1-89); RC § 5111.12, 143 v H 822 (Eff 12-13-90); 148 v H 471. Eff 7-1-2000; 2013 HB 59, § 101.01, eff. Sept. 29, 2013.

**Editor's Notes**

This section was formerly codified as RC § 5111.12.

**Amendment Notes**

The 2013 amendment substituted "medicaid director shall adopt rules under section 5162.02 of the Revised Code permitting" for "director of job and family services shall establish" in the first sentence of (A); substituted "medicaid recipients" for "recipients of medical assistance" in the first sentence of (A) and (B) and in (E); substituted "medicaid payments" for "medical assistance benefits" in the first sentence of (B); substituted "medicaid payments were made" for "benefits were paid" in the last sentence of (B); substituted "department of medicaid" for "job and family services" in (C); and substituted "medicaid payments incorrectly made on behalf of a medicaid" for "medical assistance benefits incorrectly paid to a" in (D).

**RESEARCH REFERENCES AND PRACTICE AIDS**

**Cross-References to Related Sections**

Offenses by providers; penalties; recovery of excess payments, RC § 5164.35.

**Ohio Administrative Code**

Department of job and family services, division of public assistance—Medicaid: recipient-caused overpayment; determination, recovery. OAC 5160:1-2-04 et seq.

## § 5162.24 Recovery of cost of health care provided to child.

(A) As used in this section, "third party" has the same meaning as in section 5160.35 of the Revised Code.

(B) In addition to the authority granted under section 5160.38 of the Revised Code, the department of medicaid may, to the extent necessary to reimburse its costs, garnish the wages, salary, or other employment income of, and withhold amounts from state tax refunds to, any person to whom both of the following apply:

(1) The person is required by a court or administrative order to provide coverage of the cost of health care services to a child eligible for medicaid.

(2) The person has received payment from a third party for the costs of such services but has not used the payment to reimburse either the other parent or guardian of the child or the provider of the services.

(C) Claims for current and past due child support shall take priority over claims under division (B) of this section.

**HISTORY:**

145 v S 295 (Eff 6-30-94); 148 v H 471. Eff 7-1-2000; 2013 HB 59, § 101.01, eff. Sept. 29, 2013.

**Editor's Notes**

This section was formerly codified as RC § 5111.121.

**Amendment Notes**

The 2013 amendment substituted "section 5160.35" for "section 5101.571" in (A); in the introductory language of (B), substituted "section 5160.38" for "section 5101.59" and "department of medicaid" for "department of job and family services"; and substituted "medicaid" for "medical assistance under this chapter" in (B)(1).

## § 5162.30 Medicaid administrative claiming program.

(A) The medicaid director shall create a medicaid administrative claiming program under which federal financial participation is received for the administrative costs incurred by the department of health and the Arthur G. James cancer hospital and Richard J. Solove research institute of the Ohio state university in analyzing and evaluating both of the following pursuant to sections 3701.261 and 3701.262 of the Revised Code:

(1) Cancer reports under the Ohio cancer incidence surveillance system;

(2) The incidence, prevalence, costs, and medical consequences of cancer on medicaid recipients and other low-income populations.

(B) The medicaid director shall consult with the director of health in creating the medicaid administrative claiming program.

**HISTORY:**

2011 HB 153, § 101.01, eff. June 30, 2011; 2013 HB 59, § 101.01, eff. Sept. 29, 2013.

**Editor's Notes**

This section was formerly codified as RC § 5111.83.

**Amendment Notes**

The 2013 amendment substituted "The medicaid director shall create" for "Not later than January 1, 2012, the director of job and family services shall apply to the United States secretary of health and human services for approval of," substituted "received for the" for "received as reimbursement for," inserted "cancer hospital," and substituted "sections 3701.261 and 3701.262" for "sections 3701.261 to 3701.236"; and, in (B), substituted "medicaid director" for "director of job and family services," substituted "creating" for "seeking approval of," and deleted the second sentence, which read: "The directors shall cooperate in seeking the approval to the extent they find the approval necessary for the effective and efficient administration of the medicaid program."

## § 5162.31 Treatment of local healthy start medicaid expenditures.

Local funds, whether from public or private sources, expended by a county department of job and family services for administration of the healthy start component shall be considered to have been expended by the state for the purpose of determining the extent to which the state has complied with any federal requirement that the state provide funds to match federal financial participation for the medicaid program. This section does not affect the amount of funds a county is entitled to receive under sections 5101.16 and 5101.161 of the Revised Code.

**HISTORY:**

2013 HB 59, § 101.01, eff. Sept. 29, 2013.

## § 5162.32 Contracts with subdivisions to pay nonfederal share.

The department of medicaid may enter into contracts with political subdivisions to use funds of the political subdivision to pay the nonfederal share of expenditures under the medicaid program. The determination and provision of federal financial participation to a subdivision entering into a contract under this section shall be determined by the department, subject to section 5162.40 of the Revised Code.

**HISTORY:**

RC § 5111.10, 144 v H 298 (Eff 7-26-91); 148 v H 471 (Eff 7-1-2000); RC § 5111.90, 149 v S 261. Eff 6-5-2002; 2013 HB 59, § 101.01, eff. Sept. 29, 2013.

**Editor's Notes**

This section was formerly codified as RC § 5111.90.

**Amendment Notes**

The 2013 amendment rewrote the section.

## § 5162.35 Contracts for administration of components; medicaid administrative reimbursement fund.

The department of medicaid may enter into contracts with one or more other state agencies or political subdivisions to have the state agency or political subdivision administer one or more components of the medicaid program, or one or more aspects of a component, under the department's supervision. A state agency or political subdivision that enters into such a contract shall comply with the terms of the contract and any rules the medicaid director has adopted governing the component, or aspect of the component, that the state agency or political subdivision is to administer, including any rules establishing review, audit, and corrective

Titles 39 — 57

action plan requirements. A contract with a state agency shall be in the form of an interagency agreement.

A state agency or political subdivision that enters into a contract with the department under this section shall reimburse the department for the nonfederal share of the cost to the department of performing, or contracting for the performance of, a fiscal audit of the component of the medicaid program, or aspect of the component, that the state agency or political subdivision administers if rules governing the component, or aspect of the component, require that a fiscal audit be conducted.

**HISTORY:**

2013 HB 59, § 101.01, eff. Sept. 29, 2013.

**Editor's Notes**

This section was formerly codified as RC § 5111.91.

**Amendment Notes**

The 2013 amendment, in the first paragraph, substituted "medicaid" for "job and family services" in the first sentence and substituted "medicaid director" for "director of job and family services" in the second sentence; and deleted the last sentence, which read: "There is hereby created in the state treasury the medicaid administrative reimbursement fund. The department shall use money in the fund to pay for the nonfederal share of the cost of a fiscal audit for which a state agency or political subdivision is required by this section to reimburse the department. The department shall deposit the reimbursements into the fund."



### § 5162.36 Creation of medicaid school component.

The medicaid director shall create, in accordance with sections 5162.36 to 5162.366 of the Revised Code, the medicaid school component of the medicaid program.

**HISTORY:**

152 v H 562, § 101.01, eff. 6-24-08; 2013 HB 59, § 101.01, eff. Sept. 29, 2013; 2015 hb64, § 101.01, effective September 29, 2015; 2016 hb89, § 1, effective March 21, 2017.

**Editor's Notes**

This section was formerly codified as RC § 5111.71.

**Amendment Notes**

The 2016 amendment by HB 89 substituted "5162.666" for "5162.365".

The 2015 amendment, by HB 64, substituted "sections 5162.36 to 5162.365" for "sections 5162.36 to 5162.364".

The 2013 amendment rewrote the section.

### § 5162.361 Qualified medicaid school provider may submit claim for federal financial participation; certification of expenditures.

A qualified medicaid school provider participating in the medicaid school component of the medicaid program may submit a claim to the department of medicaid for federal financial participation for providing, in schools, services covered by the medicaid school component to medicaid recipients who are eligible for the services. No qualified medicaid school provider may submit such a claim before the provider incurs the cost of providing the service.

The claim shall include certification of the qualified medicaid school provider's expenditures for the service. The certification shall show that the money the qualified medicaid school provider used for the expenditures was nonfederal money the provider may legally use for providing the service and that the amount of the expenditures was sufficient to pay the full cost of the service.

Except as otherwise provided in sections 5162.36 to 5162.366 of the Revised Code, a qualified medicaid school provider is subject to all conditions of participation in the medicaid program that generally apply to providers of goods and services under the medicaid program, including conditions regarding claims, audits, and recovery of overpayments.

**HISTORY:**

152 v H 562, § 101.01, eff. 6-24-08; 2013 HB 59, § 101.01, eff. Sept. 29, 2013; 2015 hb64, § 101.01, effective September 29, 2015; 2016 hb89, § 1, effective March 21, 2017.

**Editor's Notes**

This section was formerly codified as RC § 5111.711.

**Amendment Notes**

The 2016 amendment by HB 89, substituted "5162.36 to 5162.366" for "5162.36 to 5162.365" in the last paragraph.

The 2015 amendment, by HB 64, in the last paragraph, substituted "sections 5162.36 to 5162.365" for "sections 5162.36 to 5162.364", deleted "and rules authorized by sections 5162.363 and 5162.364 of the Revised Code" following "Revised Code", inserted "claims"; and made a stylistic change.

The 2013 amendment substituted "medicaid" for "job and family services" in the first sentence of the first paragraph; and, in the last paragraph, substituted " sections 5162.36 to 5162.364" for " sections 5111.71 to 5111.715" and "authorized by sections 5162.363 and 5162.364" for "adopted under sections 5111.713 and 5111.715".

### § 5162.362 Department to seek and disburse federal financial participation.

The department of medicaid shall seek federal financial participation for each claim a qualified medicaid school provider properly submits to the department under section 5162.361 of the Revised Code. The department shall disburse the federal financial participation the department receives from the federal government for such a claim to the qualified medicaid school provider that submitted the claim. The department may not pay the qualified medicaid school provider the nonfederal share of the cost of the services for which the claim was submitted.

**HISTORY:**

152 v H 562, § 101.01, eff. 6-24-08; 2013 HB 59, § 101.01, eff. Sept. 29, 2013.

**Editor's Notes**

This section was formerly codified as RC § 5111.712.

**Amendment Notes**

The 2013 amendment, in the first sentence, substituted "medicaid" for "job and family services" and "section 5162.361" for "section 5111.711".

### § 5162.363 Interagency agreement with department of education.

The department of medicaid shall enter into an interagency agreement with the department of education under section 5162.35 of the Revised Code that provides for the department of education to administer the medicaid school component of the medicaid program other than the aspects of the component that sections 5162.36 to 5162.366 of the Revised Code require the department of medicaid to administer. The interagency agreement may include a provision that provides for the department of education to pay to the department of medicaid the nonfederal share of a portion of the administrative expenses the department of medicaid incurs in administering the aspects of the component that the department of medicaid administers.

To the extent authorized by rules authorized by section 5162.021 of the Revised Code, the department of education shall adopt rules establishing a process by which qualified medicaid school providers participating in the medicaid school component pay to the department of education the nonfederal share of the department's expenses incurred in administering the component. The rules shall be adopted in accordance with Chapter 119. of the Revised Code.

**HISTORY:**

152 v H 562, § 101.01, eff. 6-24-08; 2013 HB 59, § 101.01, eff. Sept. 29, 2013; 2015 hb64, § 101.01, effective September 29, 2015; 2016 hb89, § 1, effective March 21, 2017.

**Editor's Notes**

This section was formerly codified as RC § 5111.713.

**Amendment Notes**

The 2016 amendment by HB 89, substituted "5162.36 to 5162.366" for "5162.36 to 5162.365" in the first sentence of the first paragraph.

The 2015 amendment, by HB 64, substituted "sections 5162.36 to 5162.365" for "sections 5162.36 to 5162.364" in the first sentence of the first paragraph; and substituted "adopt rules establishing" for "establish, in rules adopted under section 5162.02 of the Revised Code" in the first sentence of the second paragraph.

The 2013 amendment substituted "department of medicaid" for "department of job and family services" wherever it appears in the first paragraph; in the first sentence of the first paragraph, substituted "section 5162.35" for "section 5111.91" and "sections 5162.36 to 5162.364" for "sections 5111.71 to 5111.715"; in the first sentence of the second paragraph, added "To the extent authorized by rules authorized by section 5162.021 of the Revised Code" to the end and substituted "section 5162.02" for "Chapter 119."; and added the second sentence to the second paragraph.

### § 5162.364 Rules to implement program.

The medicaid director shall adopt rules under section 5162.02 of the Revised Code as necessary to implement the medicaid school component of the medicaid program, including rules that establish or specify all of the following:

(A) Conditions a board of education of a city, local, or exempted school district, a governing board of an educational service center, governing authority of a community school established under Chapter 3314. of the Revised Code, the state school for the deaf, and the state school for the blind must meet to participate in the component;

(B) Services the component covers;

(C) Payment rates for the services the component covers.

The rules shall be adopted in accordance with Chapter 119. of the Revised Code.

**HISTORY:**

152 v H 562, § 101.01, eff. 6-24-08; 2013 HB 59, § 101.01, eff. Sept. 29, 2013; 2019 hb166, § 101.01, effective October 17, 2019.

**Editor's Notes**

This section was formerly codified as RC § 5111.715.

**Amendment Notes**

The 2019 amendment by HB 166 added "a governing board of an educational service center" in (A).

The 2013 amendment, in the introductory language, substituted "medicaid director" for "director of job and family services" and "section 5162.02" for "Chapter 119."; substituted "Payment" for "Reimbursement" in (C); and added the second paragraph.

### § 5162.365 Timely repayment of overpayment by medicaid school provider.

(A) A qualified medicaid school provider is solely responsible for timely repaying any overpayment that the provider receives under the medicaid school component of the medicaid program and that is discovered by a federal or state audit. This is the case regardless of whether the audit's finding identifies the provider, department of medicaid, or department of education as being responsible for the overpayment.

(B) The department of medicaid shall not do any of the following regarding an overpayment for which a qualified medicaid school provider is responsible for repaying:

(1) Make a payment to the federal government to meet or delay the provider's repayment obligation;

(2) Assume the provider's repayment obligation;

(3) Forgive the provider's repayment obligation.

(C) Each qualified medicaid school provider shall indemnify and hold harmless the department of medicaid for any cost or penalty resulting from a federal or state audit finding that a claim submitted by the provider under section 5162.361 of the Revised Code did not comply with a federal or state requirement applicable to the claim, including a requirement of a medicaid waiver component.

**HISTORY:**

2015 hb64, § 101.01, effective September 29, 2015.

### § 5162.366 Medicaid referrals for school services relating to an Individualized Education Program.

(A) Subject to division (B) of this section and for the purpose of a medicaid recipient receiving, in accordance with the recipient's individualized education program, physical therapy services, occupational therapy services, speech-language pathology services, or audiology services under the medicaid school component of the medicaid program:

(1) A physical therapist is a licensed practitioner of the healing arts for the purpose of 42 C.F.R. 440.110(a)(1) and may make a referral for physical therapy services for the recipient.

(2) An occupational therapist is a licensed practitioner of the healing arts for the purpose of 42 C.F.R. 440.110(b)(1) and may make a referral for occupational therapy services for the recipient.

(3) A speech-language pathologist is a licensed practitioner of the healing arts for the purpose of 42 C.F.R. 440.110(c)(1) and may make a referral for speech-language pathology services for the recipient.

(4) An audiologist is a licensed practitioner of the healing arts for the purpose of 42 C.F.R. 440.110(c)(1) and may make a referral for audiology services for the recipient.

(B) To be able to make a referral for a service under this section, a physical therapist, occupational therapist, speech-language pathologist, or audiologist must have a provider agreement. This does not preclude a physical therapist, occupational therapist, speech-language pathologist, or audiologist from being an ordering or referring only provider.

**HISTORY:**

2016 hb89, § 1, effective March 21, 2017.

### § 5162.37 Contracts subject to approval of director of budget and management.

Any contract the department of medicaid enters into with the department of mental health and addiction services under section 5162.35 of the Revised Code is subject to the approval of the director of budget and management and shall require or specify all of the following:

(A) That section 5162.371 of the Revised Code be complied with;

(B) How providers will be paid for providing the services;

(C) The responsibilities of the department of mental health and addiction services with regard to providers, including program oversight and quality assurance.



**HISTORY:**

150 v H 95, § 1, eff. 6-26-03; 2011 HB 153, § 101.01, eff. July 1, 2011; 2013 HB 59, § 101.01, eff. Sept. 29, 2013.

**Editor's Notes**

This section was formerly codified as RC § 5111.911.

**Amendment Notes**

The 2013 amendment rewrote the section.

The 2011 amendment substituted "with regard to" for "for reimbursing" in (D).

### § 5162.371 Payment of nonfederal share under contract with mental health department.

If the department of medicaid enters into a contract with the department of mental health and addiction services under section 5162.35 of the Revised Code, the department of medicaid shall pay the nonfederal share of any medicaid payment to a provider for services under the component, or aspect of the component, the department of mental health and addiction services administers.

**HISTORY:**

150 v H 95, § 1, eff. 6-26-03; 2011 HB 153, § 101.01, eff. July 1, 2011; 2013 HB 59, § 101.01, eff. Sept. 29, 2013.

**Editor's Notes**

This section was formerly codified as RC § 5111.912.

**Amendment Notes**

The 2013 amendment substituted "department of medicaid" for "department of job and family services" twice; substituted "mental health and addiction services" for "mental health" twice; substituted "section 5162.35" for "section 5111.91"; and deleted the second sentence, which read: "If necessary, the director of job and family services shall submit a medicaid state plan amendment to the United States secretary of health and human services regarding the department of job and family services' duty under this section."

The 2011 amendment substituted "job and family" for "mental health and boards of alcohol, drug addiction, and mental health" preceding "services shall pay" in the first sentence; and added the second sentence.

### § 5162.40 Department may retain or collect percentage of federal financial participation.

(A) If a state agency or political subdivision administers one or more components of the medicaid program or administers one or more aspects of such a component, the department of medicaid may retain or collect not more than ten per cent of the federal financial participation the state agency or political subdivision obtains through an approved, administrative claim regarding the component or aspect of the component. If the department retains or collects a percentage of such federal financial participation, the percentage the department retains or collects shall be specified in a contract the department enters into with the state agency or political subdivision under section 5162.35 of the Revised Code.

(B) All amounts the department retains or collects under this section shall be deposited into the health care/medicaid support and recoveries fund created under section 5162.52 of the Revised Code.

**HISTORY:**

149 v S 261. Eff 6-5-2002; 2013 HB 59, § 101.01, eff. Sept. 29, 2013; 2017 hb49, § 101.01, effective September 29, 2017.

**Editor's Notes**

This section was formerly codified as RC § 5111.92.

The amendment of RC § 5111.92 by Am. Sub. H.B. 95 (150 v —) was disapproved by the Governor.

**Amendment Notes**

The 2017 amendment by HB 49 redesignated and rewrote former (A)(1) as (A); deleted former (A)(2); and substituted "the health care/medicaid support and recoveries fund created under section 5162.52 of the Revised Code" for "the health care services administration fund created under section 5162.54 of the Revised Code" in (B).

The 2013 amendment, in (A)(1) and (A)(2), substituted "department of medicaid" for "department of job and family services" in the first sentence and substituted "section 5162.35" for "section 5111.91" in the second sentence; deleted (B), which read: "The department of job and family services may retain or collect a percentage of federal financial participation under divisions (A)(1) and (2) of this section only to the extent permitted by federal statutes and regulations"; redesignated former (C) as (B); and substituted "section 5162.54" for "section 5111.94" in present (B).

### § 5162.41 Retention or collection of percentage of supplemental payment.

The department of medicaid may retain or collect a percentage of the federal financial participation included in a supplemental medicaid payment to one or more medicaid providers owned or operated by a state agency or political subdivision that brings the payment to such provider or providers to the upper payment limit established by 42 C.F.R. 447.272. If the department retains or collects a percentage of that federal financial participation, the medicaid director shall adopt a rule under section 5162.02 of the Revised Code specifying the percentage the department is to retain or collect. All amounts the department retains or collects under this section shall be deposited into the health care/medicaid support and recoveries fund created under section 5162.52 of the Revised Code.

**HISTORY:**

149 v S 261. Eff 6-5-2002; 2013 HB 59, § 101.01, eff. Sept. 29, 2013; 2017 hb49, § 101.01, effective September 29, 2017.

**Editor's Notes**

This section was formerly codified as RC § 5111.93.

**Amendment Notes**

The 2017 amendment by HB 49 substituted "the health care/medicaid support and recoveries fund created under section 5162.52 of the Revised Code" for "the health care services administration fund created under section 5162.54 of the Revised Code" in the last sentence.

The 2013 amendment substituted "department of medicaid" for "department of job and family services" in the first sentence; in the second sentence, substituted "medicaid director" for "department" and "section 5162.02" for "Chapter 119."; and substituted "section 5162.54" for "section 5111.94" in the last sentence.

### § 5162.50 Health care — federal fund.

(A) The health care — federal fund is hereby created in the state treasury. All of the following shall be credited to the fund:

(1) Funds that division (B) of section 5168.11 of the Revised Code requires be credited to the fund;

(2) The federal share of all rebates paid by drug manufacturers to the department of medicaid in accordance with a rebate agreement required by the "Social Security Act," section 1927, 42 U.S.C. 1396r-8;

(3) The federal share of all supplemental rebates paid by drug manufacturers to the department of medicaid in accordance with the supplemental drug rebate program established under section 5164.755 of the Revised Code;

(4) Except as otherwise provided by statute or as authorized by the controlling board, the federal share of all other medicaid-related revenues, collections, and recoveries.

(B) All money credited to the health care — federal fund pursuant to division (B) of section 5168.11 of the Revised Code shall be used solely for distributing funds to hospitals under section 5168.09 of the Revised Code. The department of medicaid shall use all other money credited to the fund to pay for other medicaid services and contracts.

**HISTORY:**

151 v H 530, § 101.01, eff. 7-1-06; 2013 HB 59, § 101.01, eff. Sept. 29, 2013.

**Editor's Notes**

This section was formerly codified as RC § 5111.943.

**Amendment Notes**

The 2013 amendment substituted "section 5168.11" for "section 5112.18" in (A)(1); substituted "department of medicaid" for "department of job and family services" in (A)(2), (A)(3), and the second sentence of (B); inserted "the 'Social Security Act,' section 1927" in (A)(2); substituted "section 5164.755" for "section 5111.081"in (A)(3); and, in the first sentence of (B), substituted "section 5168.11" for "section 5112.18" and "section 5168.09" for "section 5112.08".

### § 5162.52 Medicaid revenue and collections fund.

(A) The health care/medicaid support and recoveries fund is hereby created in the state treasury. All of the following shall be credited to the fund:

(1) Except as otherwise provided by statute or as authorized by the controlling board, the nonfederal share of all medicaid-related revenues, collections, and recoveries;

(2) Federal reimbursement received for payment adjustments made pursuant to section 1923 of the "Social Security Act," 42 U.S.C. 1396r-4, under the medicaid program to state mental health hospitals maintained and operated by the department of mental health and addiction services under division (A) of section 5119.14 of the Revised Code;

(3) Revenues the department of medicaid receives from another state agency for medicaid services pursuant to an interagency agreement;

(4) The money the department of medicaid receives in a fiscal year for performing eligibility verification services necessary for compliance with the independent, certified audit requirement of 42 C.F.R. 455.304;

(5) The nonfederal share of all rebates paid by drug manufacturers to the department of medicaid in accordance with a rebate agreement required by section 1927 of the "Social Security Act," 42 U.S.C. 1396r-8;

(6) The nonfederal share of all supplemental rebates paid by drug manufacturers to the department of medicaid in accordance with the supplemental drug rebate program established under section 5164.755 of the Revised Code;

(7) Amounts deposited into the fund pursuant to sections 5162.12, 5162.40, and 5162.41 of the Revised Code;

(8) The application fees charged to providers under section 5164.31 of the Revised Code;

(9) The fines collected under section 5165.1010 of the Revised Code;

Titles 39 — 57

(10) Amounts from assessments on hospitals under section 5168.06 of the Revised Code and intergovernmental transfers by governmental hospitals under section 5168.07 of the Revised Code that are deposited into the fund in accordance with the law.

(B) The department of medicaid shall use money credited to the health care/medicaid support and recoveries fund to pay for all of the following:

(1) Medicaid services;

(2) Costs associated with the administration of the medicaid program;

(3) Programs that serve youth involved with multiple government agencies;

(4) Innovative programs that the department has statutory authority to implement and that promote access to health care or help achieve long-term cost savings to the state.

**HISTORY:**

151 v H 530, § 101.01, eff. 7-1-06; 152 v H 562, § 101.01, eff. 9-23-08; 2011 HB 153, § 101.01, eff. Oct. 1, 2011; 2012 HB 487, § 101.01, eff. Sept. 10, 2012; 2013 HB 59, § 101.01, eff. Sept. 29, 2013; 2017 hb49, § 101.01, effective September 29, 2017; 2019 hb166, § 101.01, effective October 17, 2019.

**Editor's Notes**

This section was formerly codified as RC §. 5111.941.

**Amendment Notes**

The 2019 amendment by HB 166 substituted "section 1923 of the 'Social Security Act'" for "the 'Social Security Act,' section 1923" in (A)(2); substituted "section 1927 of the 'Social Security Act'" for "the 'Social Security Act,' section 1927" in (A)(5); redesignated and rewrote former (B) as the introductory language of (B), (B)(1) and (B)(2); and added (B)(3) and (B)(4).

The 2017 amendment by HB 49 deleted "other than such revenues required to be deposited into the health care services administration fund created under section 5162.54 of the Revised Code" at the end of (A)(3); substituted "The money the department of medicaid" for "The first seven hundred fifty thousand dollars the department" in (A)(4); added (A)(7) through (A)(10); substituted "medicaid services and costs associated with the administration of the medicaid program" for "medicaid services and contracts" in (B); and made a related change.

The 2013 amendment rewrote (2), which formerly read: "Federal reimbursement received for payment adjustments made pursuant to section 1923 of the 'Social Security Act,' 101 Stat. 1330-148 (1987), 42 U.S.C. 1396r-4, as amended, under the medicaid program to state mental health hospitals maintained and operated by the department of mental health under division (A) of section 5119.02 of the Revised Code"; substituted "medicaid" for "job and family services" in (A)(3) and (B); substituted "section 5162.54" for "section 5111.94" in (A)(3); added (A)(5) and (A)(6); and made related change.

The 2012 amendment rewrote the section, which formerly read: "The medicaid revenue and collections fund is hereby created in the state treasury. Except as otherwise provided by statute or as authorized by the controlling board, the nonfederal share of all medicaid-related revenues, collections, and recoveries shall be credited to the fund. The department of job and family services shall use money credited to the medicaid revenue and collections fund to pay for medicaid services and contracts."

The 2011 amendment deleted the (A), (A)(1), and (B) designations; in the second sentence of the present first paragraph, deleted "both of the following shall be credited to the fund" following "controlling board" and added "shall be credited to the fund" to the end; deleted (A)(2), which read: "The monthly premiums charged under the children's buy-in program pursuant to section 5101.5213 of the Revised Code"; deleted "and the children's buy-in program established under sections 5101.5211 to 5101.5216 of the Revised Code" from the end of the second paragraph; and made related changes.

152 v H 562, effective September 23, 2008, rewrote the section.

## § 5162.54 Health care services administration fund. [Repealed]

**HISTORY:**

149 v S 261. Eff 6-5-2002; 150 v H 95, § 1, eff. 9-26-03; 152 v H 562, § 101.01, eff. 6-24-08; 2011 HB 153, § 101.01, eff. Sept. 29, 2011; 2013 HB 59, § 101.01, eff. Sept. 29, 2013; repealed by 2017 hb49, § 105.01, effective September 29, 2017.

## § 5162.56 Health care special activities fund.

There is created in the state treasury the health care special activities fund. The department of medicaid shall deposit all funds it receives pursuant to the administration of the medicaid program into the fund, other than any such funds that are required by law to be deposited into another fund. The department shall use the money in the fund to pay for expenses related to the services provided under, and the administration of, the medicaid program.

**HISTORY:**

2011 HB 153, § 101.01, eff. June 30, 2011; 2013 HB 59, § 101.01, eff. Sept. 29, 2013.

**Editor's Notes**

This section was formerly codified as RC § 5111.945.

**Amendment Notes**

The 2013 amendment substituted "medicaid" for "job and family services" in the second sentence.

## § 5162.58 Integrated care delivery systems fund. [Repealed]

**HISTORY:**

2011 HB 153, § 101.01, eff. Sept. 29, 2011; 2013 HB 59, § 101.01, eff. Sept. 29, 2013; repealed by 2019 hb166, § 105.01, effective October 17, 2019.

## § 5162.60 Creation of managed care performance payment fund. [Repealed]

**HISTORY:**

2013 HB 59, § 101.01, eff. Sept. 29, 2013; repealed by 2019 hb166, § 105.01, effective October 17, 2019.

## § 5162.62 Creation of Medicaid administration reimbursement fund. [Repealed]

**HISTORY:**

2013 HB 59, § 101.01, eff. Sept. 29, 2013; repealed by 2019 hb166, § 105.01, effective October 17, 2019.

## § 5162.64 Medicaid school program administrative fund. [Repealed]

**HISTORY:**

152 v H 562, § 101.01, eff. 6-24-08; 2013 HB 59, § 101.01, eff. Sept. 29, 2013; repealed by 2019 hb166, § 105.01, effective October 17, 2019.

## § 5162.65 Refunds and reconciliation fund; purpose.

There is hereby created in the state treasury the refunds and reconciliation fund.

Money the department of medicaid receives from a refund or reconciliation shall be deposited into the refunds and reconciliation fund if the department does not know the appropriate fund for the money at the time the department receives the money or if the money is to go to another government entity. Money transferred from the department of job and family services under section 5101.074 of the Revised Code also shall be deposited into the refunds and reconciliation fund.

Money in the refunds and reconciliation fund, including money transferred from the department of job and family services, shall be transferred to the appropriate fund once the appropriate fund is identified or shall be transferred to another government entity, as appropriate.

**HISTORY:**

2017 hb49, § 101.01, effective September 29, 2017.

## § 5162.66 Deposit of fines in residents protection fund.

(A) There is hereby created in the state treasury the residents protection fund. All of the following shall be deposited into the fund:

(1) The proceeds of all fines, including interest, collected under sections 5165.60 to 5165.89 of the Revised Code;

(2) The proceeds of all fines, including interest, collected under section 173.42 of the Revised Code;

(3) The portions of civil money penalties and corresponding interest that are disbursed on or after July 1, 2017, to the department of medicaid pursuant to 42 C.F.R. 488.845.

(B)(1) Money deposited into the fund pursuant to divisions (A)(1) and (2) of this section shall be used for all of the following:

(a) Protection of the health or property of residents of nursing facilities in which the department of health finds deficiencies, including payment for the costs of relocation of residents to other facilities;

(b) Maintenance of operation of a facility pending correction of deficiencies or closure;

(c) Reimbursement of residents for the loss of money managed by the facility under section 3721.15 of the Revised Code;

(d) Provision of funds for costs incurred by a temporary resident safety assurance manager appointed under section 5165.78 of the Revised Code.

(2) Subject to 42 C.F.R. 488.845(g)(2), money deposited into the fund pursuant to division (A)(3) of this section shall be used to improve the quality of medicaid services provided by medicare-certified home health agencies.

(C) The fund shall be maintained and administered by the department of medicaid under rules developed in consultation with the departments of health and aging and adopted under section 5162.02 of the Revised Code. The rules shall be adopted in accordance with Chapter 119. of the Revised Code.



**HISTORY:**

143 v H 822 (Eff 12-13-90); 148 v H 471 (Eff 7-1-2000); 148 v H 403. Eff 7-1-2000; 151 v H 66, § 101.01, eff. 9-29-05; 2011 HB 153, § 101.01, eff. Sept. 29, 2011; 2013 HB 59, § 101.01, eff. Sept. 29, 2013; 2017 hb49, § 101.01, effective September 29, 2017.

**Editor's Notes**

This section was formerly codified as RC § 5111.62.

**Amendment Notes**

The 2017 amendment by HB 49 rewrote the section.

The 2013 amendment added the first paragraph; substituted "sections 5165.60 to 5165.89" for "sections 5111.35 to 5111.62" in the first sentence of the second paragraph; substituted "section 5165.78" for "section 5111.511" in the second sentence of the third paragraph; in the first sentence of the last paragraph, substituted "department of medicaid" for "department of job and family services" and "under section 5162.02" for "by the director of job and family services under Chapter 119."; and added the second sentence of the last paragraph.

The 2011 amendment added the second sentence of the second paragraph.

151 v H 66, effective September 29, 2005, redesignated the former provisions as three paragraphs; and added the last sentence to the present first paragraph.

### RESEARCH REFERENCES AND PRACTICE AIDS

**Cross-References to Related Sections**

Amount and number of fines; means of collection, RC § 5165.83.

Assessment of non-medicaid recipients; disposition of fines collected, RC § 173.42.

Definitions, RC § 5165.60.

**Ohio Administrative Code**

Resident protection fund (RPF) for NFs and collection of fines. OAC 5160-3-03.2.

## § 5162.70 Medicaid reforms.

(A) As used in this section:

(1) "CPI" means the consumer price index for all urban consumers as published by the United States bureau of labor statistics.

(2) "CPI medical inflation rate" means the inflation rate for medical care, or the successor term for medical care, for the midwest region as specified in the CPI.

(3) "JMOC projected medical inflation rate" means the following:

(a) The projected medical inflation rate for a fiscal biennium determined by the actuary with which the joint medicaid oversight committee contracts under section 103.414 of the Revised Code if the committee agrees with the actuary's projected medical inflation rate for that fiscal biennium;

(b) The different projected medical inflation rate for a fiscal biennium determined by the joint medicaid oversight committee under section 103.414 of the Revised Code if the committee disagrees with the projected medical inflation rate determined for that fiscal biennium by the actuary with which the committee contracts under that section.

(4) "Successor term" means a term that the United States bureau of labor statistics uses in place of another term in revisions to the CPI.

(B) The medicaid director shall implement reforms to the medicaid program that do all of the following:

(1) Limit the growth in the per recipient per month cost of the medicaid program, as determined on an aggregate basis for all eligibility groups, for a fiscal biennium to not more than the lesser of the following:

(a) The average annual increase in the CPI medical inflation rate for the most recent three-year period for which the necessary data is available as of the first day of the fiscal biennium, weighted by the most recent year of the three years;

(b) The JMOC projected medical inflation rate for the fiscal biennium.

(2) Achieve the limit in the growth of the per recipient per month cost of the medicaid program under division (B)(1) of this section by doing all of the following:

(a) Improving the physical and mental health of medicaid recipients;

(b) Providing for medicaid recipients to receive medicaid services in the most cost-effective and sustainable manner;

(c) Removing barriers that impede medicaid recipients' ability to transfer to lower cost, and more appropriate, medicaid services, including home and community-based services;

(d) Establishing medicaid payment rates that encourage value over volume and result in medicaid services being provided in the most efficient and effective manner possible;

(e) Implementing fraud and abuse prevention and cost avoidance mechanisms to the fullest extent possible;

(3) Reduce the prevalence of comorbid health conditions among, and the mortality rates of, medicaid recipients;

(4) Reduce infant mortality rates among medicaid recipients.

(C) The medicaid director shall implement the reforms under this section in accordance with evidence-based strategies that include measurable goals.

(D) The reforms implemented under this section shall, without making the medicaid program's eligibility requirements more restrictive, reduce the relative number of individuals enrolled in the medicaid program who have the greatest potential to obtain the income and resources that would enable them to cease enrollment in medicaid and instead obtain health care coverage through employer-sponsored health insurance or an exchange.

**HISTORY:**

2013 SB 206, § 1, eff. Mar. 20, 2014; 2017 hb49, § 101.01, effective September 29, 2017.

**Amendment Notes**

The 2017 amendment by HB 49 deleted former (B)(1)(f), which read: "Integrating in the care management system established under section 5167.03 of the Revised Code the delivery of physical health, behavioral health, nursing facility, and home and community-based services covered by Medicaid."

## § 5162.71 Implementation of medicaid program systems.

The medicaid director shall implement within the medicaid program systems that do both of the following:

(A) Improve the health of medicaid recipients through the use of population health measures;

(B) Reduce health disparities, including, but not limited to, those within racial and ethnic populations.

**HISTORY:**

2013 SB 206, § 1, eff. Mar. 20, 2014.

### § 5162.72 Strategy implementation.

The medicaid director shall implement within the medicaid program strategies that address social determinants of health, including employment, housing, transportation, food, interpersonal safety, and toxic stress.

**HISTORY:**
2019 hb166, § 101.01, effective October 17, 2019.

### § 5162.73 Dental services for pregnant Medicaid recipients; reimbursement rates.

(A) The Department of Medicaid may establish and administer a program to provide dental services to pregnant Medicaid recipients. If the program is established, all of the following shall apply:

(1) Medicaid recipients who are members of the group described in section 5163.06 of the Revised Code shall be eligible to receive two dental cleanings per year.

(2) The Department shall give priority to those Medicaid recipients residing in areas of the state with high preterm birth rates.

(3) The Department shall inform Medicaid recipients about the program and market the program to Medicaid recipients.

(B) The Department of Medicaid shall establish reimbursement rates for entities that educate Medicaid recipients about the importance of prenatal and postnatal dental care as part of the program described in section 3701.615 of the Revised Code, including reimbursement rates for all or part of the costs associated with developing and distributing educational materials related to the importance of prenatal and postnatal dental care.

**HISTORY:**
2020 hb11, § 3, effective September 18, 2020.

### § 5162.80 Reasonable good-faith estimate of provider's non-emergency medical products, services, or procedures.

(A) A provider of medical services licensed, accredited, or certified under Chapter 3721., 3727., 4715., 4725., 4731., 4732., 4734., 4747., 4753., 4755., 4757., or 4779. of the Revised Code shall provide in writing, before products, services, or procedures are provided, a reasonable, good-faith estimate of all of the following for the provider's non-emergency products, services, or procedures:

(1) The amount the provider will charge the patient or the consumer's health plan issuer for the product, service, or procedure;

(2) The amount the health plan issuer intends to pay for the product, service, or procedure;

(3) The difference, if any, that the consumer or other party responsible for the consumer's care would be required to pay to the provider for the product, service, or procedure.

(B) Any health plan issuer contacted by a provider described in division (A) of this section in order for the provider to obtain information so that the provider can comply with division (A) of this section shall provide such information to the provider within a reasonable time of the provider's request.

(C) As used in this section, "health plan issuer" means an entity subject to the insurance laws and rules of this state, or subject to the jurisdiction of the superintendent of insurance, that contracts, or offers to contract, to provide, deliver, arrange for, pay for, or reimburse any of the costs of health care services under a health benefit plan, including a sickness and accident insurance company and a health insuring corporation. "Health plan issuer" also includes a managed care organization under contract with the department of medicaid and, if the services are to be provided on a fee-for-service basis, the Medicaid program.

(D) The medicaid director shall adopt rules, in accordance with Chapter 119. of the Revised Code, to carry out this section.

**HISTORY:**
2015 hb52, § 1, effective January 1, 2017.

#### NOTES TO DECISIONS

Analysis

Constitutionality.
Motion to intervene denied.

**Constitutionality.**
In a dispute between healthcare entities and state defendants over the constitutionality of a statute, even though statutes had a strong presumption of constitutionality, the court found that R.C. 5162.80 was unconstitutional because it violated the one-subject and three-considerations rule of the Ohio Constitution where, inter alia, the statute was unnaturally combined with budget and operations law and the subject matter of the original bill was vitally altered. Cmty. Hosps. & Wellness Ctrs. v. State, 2020-Ohio-401, 151 N.E.3d 1113, 2020 Ohio App. LEXIS 376 (Ohio Ct. App., Williams County 2020).

**Motion to intervene denied.**
In a dispute between healthcare entities and state defendants over the constitutionality of a statute, the trial court did not err in denying the motion to intervene as of right filed by the legislator who authored the statute because the motion was untimely and he lacked a legally protected interest. Further, permissive intervention was not warranted because it would unduly delay the adjudication without addition of any genuine issue of material fact for summary judgment purposes. Cmty. Hosps. & Wellness Ctrs. v. State, 2020-Ohio-401, 151 N.E.3d 1113, 2020 Ohio App. LEXIS 376 (Ohio Ct. App., Williams County 2020).

### § 5162.82 Notification required for increases in payment rate.

Before making any payment rate increases greater than ten per cent under the medicaid program, the medicaid director shall notify the joint medicaid oversight committee of the increase and be available to testify before the joint medicaid oversight committee regarding the increase.

**HISTORY:**
2021 hb110, § 101.01, effective September 30, 2021.



# CHAPTER 5163

# ELIGIBILITY FOR MEDICAID

Section

## § 5163.01 Definitions.

As used in this chapter:

"Caretaker relative" has the same meaning as in 42 C.F.R. 435.4 as that regulation is amended effective January 1, 2014.

"Expansion eligibility group" means the medicaid eligibility group described in section 1902(a)(10)(A)(i)(VIII) of the "Social Security Act," 42 U.S.C. 1396a(a)(10)(A)(i)(VIII).

"Federal financial participation" has the same meaning as in section 5160.01 of the Revised Code.

"Federal poverty line" has the same meaning as in section 5162.01 of the Revised Code.

"Healthy start component" has the same meaning as in section 5162.01 of the Revised Code.

"Home and community-based services medicaid waiver component" has the same meaning as in section 5166.01 of the Revised Code.

"Intermediate care facility for individuals with intellectual disabilities" and "ICF/IID" have the same meanings as in section 5124.01 of the Revised Code.

"Mandatory eligibility groups" means the groups of individuals that must be covered by the medicaid state plan as a condition of the state receiving federal financial participation for the medicaid program.

"Medicaid buy-in for workers with disabilities program" means the component of the medicaid program established under sections 5163.09 to 5163.098 of the Revised Code.

"Medicaid services" has the same meaning as in section 5164.01 of the Revised Code.

"Medicaid waiver component" has the same meaning as in section 5166.01 of the Revised Code.

"Nursing facility" and "nursing facility services" have the same meanings as in section 5165.01 of the Revised Code.

"Optional eligibility groups" means the groups of individuals who may be covered by the medicaid state plan or a federal medicaid waiver and for whom the medicaid program receives federal financial participation.

"Other medicaid-funded long-term care services" has the meaning specified in rules adopted under section 5163.02 of the Revised Code.

"Supplemental security income program" means the program established by Title XVI of the "Social Security Act," 42 U.S.C. 1381 et seq.

**HISTORY:**

2013 HB 59, § 101.01, eff. Sept. 29, 2013; 2013 SB 206, § 1, eff. Mar. 20, 2014; 2016 sb332, § 1, effective April 6, 2017; 2017 hb49, § 101.01, effective September 29, 2017.

**Editor's Notes**

Amendments by Act 2017, HB 49 were partially vetoed by the governor. Section is presented without the vetoed provisions.

**Amendment Notes**

The 2017 amendment by HB 49 added the second and fourth paragraphs.

The 2016 amendment by SB 332 deleted "'Children's hospital' has the same meaning as in section 2151.86 of the Revised Code" preceding "Federal financial participation"" and "'Federally qualified health center' has the same meaning as in the 'Social Security Act,' section 1905(l)(2)(B), 42 U.S.C. 1396d(l)(2)(B). 'Federally qualified health center look-alike' has the same meaning as in section 3701.047 of the Revised Code" preceding "Federal poverty line"".

The 2013 amendment substituted " sections 5163.09 to 5163.098" for " sections 5163.09 to 5163.0910" in the definition of "Medicaid buy-in for workers with disabilities program".

## § 5163.02 Rules establishing eligibility requirements for medicaid program.

The medicaid director shall adopt rules as necessary to implement this chapter. The rules shall establish eligibility requirements for the medicaid program. The rules may establish requirements for applying for medicaid and determining and verifying eligibility for medicaid. The rules shall be adopted in accordance with section 111.15 of the Revised Code.

Notwithstanding any provision of state law, including statutes, administrative rules, common law, and court rules, regarding real or personal property or domestic relations, the standards established under rules adopted under this section shall be used to determine eligibility for medicaid.

**HISTORY:**

143 v H 672 (Eff 11-14-89); 145 v H 152 (Eff 7-1-93); 147 v H 215 (Eff 6-30-97); 148 v H 471. Eff 7-1-2000; 151 v H 66, § 101.01, eff. 9-29-05; 151 v H 530, § 101.01, eff. 3-30-06; 2011 HB 153, § 101.01, eff. Sept. 29, 2011; 2013 HB 59, § 101.01, eff. Sept. 29, 2013.

**Editor's Notes**

This section was formerly codified as RC § 5111.011.

**Amendment Notes**

The 2013 amendment rewrote the section.

The 2011 amendment, in (A)(5), substituted "For the purpose of division (C) of section 5111.0116 of the Revised Code, establish procedures for granting waivers of all or a portion of" for "Establish exceptions to" and "that section and additional reasons for which such waivers may be granted" for "section 5111.0116 of the Revised Code."

151 v H 530, effective March 30, 2006, rewrote the section.

151 v H 66, effective September 29, 2005, rewrote the section.

### NOTES TO DECISIONS

**Shifting of resources**

Under the Medicare catastrophic coverage act, resources, not income, are to be shifted first so that the community spouse retains a sufficient income level: Gruber v. Ohio Dep't of Human Servs., 98 Ohio App. 3d 72, 647 N.E.2d 861, 1994 Ohio App. LEXIS 5310 (Ohio Ct. App., Delaware County 1994).

### RESEARCH REFERENCES AND PRACTICE AIDS

**Cross-References to Related Sections**

Resource exclusions —

Life insurance policies on recipients, RC § 5163.22.

Long-term care insurance policy, RC § 5164.86.

**Ohio Administrative Code**

Department of job and family services, division of medical assistance —

General provisions; medicaid programs, providers and services. OAC ch. 5160-1 et seq.

Department of job and family services, division of public assistance—

Application process and determination of eligibility for public assistance programs. OAC ch. 5101:1-2.

Determination of eligibility for applications and re-applications. OAC 5101:1-2-10.

Verification and reporting requirements. OAC 5101:1-2-20.

Application; verification; pre-termination review; redetermination of medicaid eligibility. OAC ch. 5160-1.

General provisions. OAC ch. 5101:1-1.

Automatic assignment of third-party and medical-support payments, right of recovery of third party resources, and role of state and county departments regarding third party resources. OAC ch. 5101:12-50.

Disclosure of recipient information, nondiscrimination, and treatment of information received from the IRS and social security administration. OAC 5101:1-1-03.

Medicaid program: eligibility. OAC ch. 5160-1-1.

Residential state supplement (RSS) program. OAC ch. 5101:1-17.

## § 5163.03 Medicaid eligibility.

(A) Subject to section 5163.05 of the Revised Code, the medicaid program shall cover all mandatory eligibility groups.

(B) The medicaid program shall cover all of the optional eligibility groups that state statutes require the medicaid program to cover.

(C) The medicaid program may cover any of the optional eligibility groups to which either of the following applies:

(1) State statutes expressly permit the medicaid program to cover the optional eligibility group.

(2) The medicaid program covers the optional eligibility group on the effective date of this amendment.

(D) The medicaid program shall not cover an optional eligibility group to which either of the following applies:

(1) State statutes prohibit the medicaid program from covering the optional eligibility group.

(2) Except as provided in divisions (B) and (C)(1) of this section, the medicaid program does not cover the optional eligibility group on the effective date of this amendment.

**HISTORY:**

2013 HB 59, § 101.01, eff. Sept. 29, 2013; 2017 hb49, § 101.01, effective September 29, 2017.

**Editor's Notes**

Some portions of section as enacted by Acts 2013, HB 59 were partially vetoed by governor.

**Amendment Notes**

The 2017 amendment by HB 49, in (C)(2), deleted "State statutes do not address whether" at the beginning, substituted "program covers" for "program may cover," and added "on the effective date of this amendment"; redesignated and revised former (D) as the introductory language of (D) and (D)(1); and added (D)(2).

### § 5163.05 Eligibility for aged, blind and disabled.

The medicaid program's eligibility requirements for aged, blind, and disabled individuals may be more restrictive than the eligibility requirements for the supplemental security income program. Any such more restrictive eligibility requirements shall be consistent with the 209(b) option described in the "Social Security Act," section 1902(f), 42 U.S.C. 1396a(f).

**HISTORY:**

2013 HB 59, § 101.01, eff. Sept. 29, 2013.

### § 5163.06 Coverage for optional eligibility groups.

The medicaid program shall cover all of the following optional eligibility groups:

(A) The group consisting of children placed with adoptive parents who are specified in the "Social Security Act," section 1902(a)(10)(A)(ii)(VIII), 42 U.S.C. 1396a(a)(10)(A)(ii)(VIII);

(B) Subject to section 5163.061 of the Revised Code, the group consisting of women during pregnancy and the maximum postpartum period permitted under 42 U.S.C. 1396a(e) beginning on the last day of the pregnancy, infants, and children who are specified in the "Social Security Act," section 1902(a)(10)(A)(ii)(IX), 42 U.S.C. 1396a(a)(10)(A)(ii)(IX);

(C) Subject to sections 5163.09 to 5163.098 of the Revised Code, the group consisting of employed individuals with disabilities who are specified in the "Social Security Act," section 1902(a)(10)(A)(ii)(XV), 42 U.S.C. 1396a(a)(10)(A)(ii)(XV);

(D) Subject to sections 5163.09 to 5163.098 of the Revised Code, the group consisting of employed individuals with medically improved disabilities who are specified in the "Social Security Act," section 1902(a)(10)(A)(ii)(XVI), 42 U.S.C. 1396a(a)(10)(A)(ii)(XVI);

(E) The group consisting of independent foster care adolescents who are specified in the "Social Security Act," section 1902(a)(10)(A)(ii)(XVII), 42 U.S.C. 1396a(a)(10)(A)(ii)(XVII);

(F) The group consisting of women in need of treatment for breast or cervical cancer who are specified in the "Social Security Act," section 1902(a)(10)(A)(ii)(XVIII), 42 U.S.C. 1396a(a)(10)(A)(ii)(XVIII);.

**HISTORY:**

2013 HB 59, § 101.01, eff. Sept. 29, 2013; 2013 SB 206, § 1, eff. Mar. 20, 2014; 2015 hb64, § 101.01, effective September 29, 2015; 2021 hb110, § 101.01, effective September 30, 2021.

**Editor's Notes**

Acts 2020, HB 11, File 37, § 3, effective Sept. 18, 2020, provides:

"SECTION 3. (A) The Department of Medicaid may establish and administer a program to provide dental services to pregnant Medicaid recipients. If the program is established, all of the following shall apply:

"(1) Medicaid recipients who are members of the group described in section 5163.06 of the Revised Code shall be eligible to receive two dental cleanings per year.

"(2) The Department shall give priority to those Medicaid recipients residing in areas of the state with high preterm birth rates.

"(3) The Department shall inform Medicaid recipients about the program and market the program to Medicaid recipients.

"(B) The Department of Medicaid shall establish reimbursement rates for entities that educate Medicaid recipients about the importance of prenatal and postnatal dental care as part of the program described in section 3701.615 of the Revised Code, including reimbursement rates for all or part of the costs associated with developing and distributing educational materials related to the importance of prenatal and postnatal dental care."

**Amendment Notes**

The 2021 amendment by HB 110 substituted "maximum postpartum period permitted under 42 U.S.C. 1396a(e)" for "sixty-day period" in (B).

The 2015 amendment, by HB 64, deleted (G), which read: "The group consisting of nonpregnant individuals who may receive family planning services and supplies and are specified in the 'Social Security Act,' section 1902(a)(10)(A)(ii)(XXI), 42 U.S.C. 1396a(a)(10)(A)(ii)(XXI)."

The 2013 amendment substituted "sections 5163.09 to 5163.098" for "sections 5163.09 to 5163.0910" in (C) and (D).

### § 5163.061 Income eligibility threshold during pregnancy and 60 days after.

The income eligibility threshold is two hundred per cent of the federal poverty line for women during pregnancy and the postpartum period beginning on the last day of the pregnancy who are covered by the medicaid program under division (B) of section 5163.06 of the Revised Code.

**HISTORY:**

2013 HB 59, § 101.01, eff. Sept. 29, 2013; 2021 hb110, § 101.01, effective September 30, 2021.

**Amendment Notes**

The 2021 amendment by HB 110 substituted "postpartum period" for "sixty-day period."

### § 5163.07 Income eligibility threshold for parents and caregivers.

The medicaid director shall implement the option authorized by the "Social Security Act," section 1931(b)(2)(C), 42 U.S.C. 1396u-1(b)(2)(C), to set the income eligibility threshold at ninety per cent of the federal poverty line for parents and caretaker relatives who are covered by the medicaid program under that section of the "Social Security Act."

**HISTORY:**

2013 HB 59, § 101.01, eff. Sept. 29, 2013.

### § 5163.08 Eligibility for transitional Medicaid. [Repealed]

**HISTORY:**

2013 HB 59, § 101.01, eff. Sept. 29, 2013; repealed by 2015 hb64, § 105.01, effective September 29, 2015.

### § 5163.09 Definitions; director to seek federal approval to implement buy-in option.

(A) As used in sections 5163.09 to 5163.098 of the Revised Code:

"Applicant" means an individual who applies to participate in the medicaid buy-in for workers with disabilities program.

"Earned income" has the meaning established by rules authorized by section 5163.098 of the Revised Code.

"Employed individual with a medically improved disability" has the same meaning as in the "Social Security Act," section 1905(v), 42 U.S.C. 1396d(v).

"Family" means an applicant or participant and the spouse and dependent children of the applicant or participant. If an applicant or participant is under eighteen years of age, "family" also means the parents of the applicant or participant.

"Health insurance" has the meaning established by rules authorized by section 5163.098 of the Revised Code.

"Income" means earned income and unearned income.

"Participant" means an individual who has been determined eligible for the medicaid buy-in for workers with disabilities program and is participating in the program.

"Resources" has the meaning established by rules authorized by section 5163.098 of the Revised Code.

"Spouse" has the meaning established by rules authorized by section 5163.098 of the Revised Code.

"Unearned income" has the meaning established by rules authorized by section 5163.098 of the Revised Code.

(B) The medicaid program's coverage of the optional eligibility groups specified in the "Social Security Act," section 1902(a)(10)(A)(ii)(XV) and (XVI), 42 U.S.C. 1396a(a)(10)(A)(ii)(XV) and (XVI) shall be known as the medicaid buy-in for workers with disabilities program.

**HISTORY:**

152 v H 119, § 101.01, eff. 9-29-07; 2013 HB 59, § 101.01, eff. Sept. 29, 2013; 2013 SB 206, § 1, eff. Mar. 20, 2014.

**Editor's Notes**

This section was formerly codified as RC § 5111.70.

**Amendment Notes**

The 2013 amendment substituted "sections 5163.09 to 5163.098" for "sections 5163.09 to 5163.0910" in the introductory language of (A); and made a stylistic change.

The 2013 amendment rewrote the section.

Titles 39 — 57

### § 5163.091 Qualification for program.

Under the medicaid buy-in for workers with disabilities program, an individual who does all of the following in accordance with rules authorized by section 5163.098 of the Revised Code qualifies for the medicaid program:

(A) Applies for the medicaid buy-in for workers with disabilities program;

(B) Provides satisfactory evidence of all of the following:

(1) That the individual is at least sixteen years of age and under sixty-five years of age;

(2) Except as provided in section 5163.096 of the Revised Code, that one of the following applies to the individual:

(a) The individual is considered disabled for the purpose of the supplemental security income program, regardless of whether the individual receives supplemental security income benefits, and the individual has earnings from employment.

(b) The individual is an employed individual with a medically improved disability.

(3) That the value of the individual's resources, less amounts disregarded pursuant to rules authorized by section 5163.098 of the Revised Code, does not exceed the amount provided for by section 5163.092 of the Revised Code;

(4) That the individual's income, less amounts disregarded pursuant to section 5163.093 of the Revised Code, does not exceed two hundred fifty per cent of the federal poverty line;

(5) That the individual meets the additional eligibility requirements for the medicaid buy-in for workers with disabilities program established in rules authorized by section 5163.098 of the Revised Code.

(C) To the extent required by section 5163.094 of the Revised Code, pays the premium established under that section.

**HISTORY:**

152 v H 119, § 101.01, eff. 9-29-07; 2013 HB 59, § 101.01, eff. Sept. 29, 2013.

**Editor's Notes**

This section was formerly codified as RC § 5111.701.

**Amendment Notes**

The 2013 amendment substituted "authorized by section 5163.098" for "adopted under section 5111.708" in the introductory language and in (B)(3); deleted "medical assistance under" following "qualifies for" in the introductory language; substituted "section 5163.096" for "section 5111.706" in the introductory language of (B)(2); substituted "section 5163.092" for "section 5111.702" in (B)(3); substituted "section 5163.093" for "section 5111.703" in (B)(4); substituted "established in rules authorized by section 5163.098" for "that the director of job and family services establishes in rules adopted under section 5111.708" in (B)(5); and substituted "section 5163.094" for "section 5111.704" in (C).

### § 5163.0910 Reports by director [Renumbered].

**Editor's Notes**

This section was renumbered as RC § 5162.133 by 2013 SB 206, § 1, effective March 20, 2014.

### § 5163.092 Resource eligibility limit.

(A) Except as provided in division (B) of this section, the maximum value of resources, less amounts disregarded pursuant to rules authorized by section 5163.098 of the Revised Code, that an individual may have without the individual exceeding the resource eligibility limit for the medicaid buy-in for workers with disabilities program shall not exceed ten thousand dollars.

(B) Each calendar year, the medicaid director shall adjust the resource eligibility limit specified in division (A) of this section by the change in the consumer price index for all items for all urban consumers for the previous calendar year, as published by the United States bureau of labor statistics. The annual adjustment shall go into effect on the earliest date possible.

**HISTORY:**

152 v H 119, § 101.01, eff. 9-29-07; 2013 HB 59, § 101.01, eff. Sept. 29, 2013.

**Editor's Notes**

This section was formerly codified as RC § 5111.702.

**Amendment Notes**

The 2013 amendment substituted "authorized by section" for "adopted under section 5111.708" in (A); and substituted "medicaid director" for "director of job and family services" in the first sentence of (B).

### § 5163.093 Determination of income eligibility limit.

For the purpose of determining whether an individual is within the income eligibility limit for the medicaid buy-in for workers with disabilities program, all of the following apply:

(A) Twenty thousand dollars of the individual's earned income shall be disregarded.

(B) No amount that the individual's employer pays to obtain health insurance for one or more members of the individual's family, including any amount of a premium established under section 5163.094 of the Revised Code that the employer pays, shall be treated as the individual's income.

(C) Any other amounts, if any, specified in rules authorized by section 5163.098 of the Revised Code shall be disregarded from the individual's earned income, unearned income, or both.

**HISTORY:**

152 v H 119, § 101.01, eff. 9-29-07; 2013 HB 59, § 101.01, eff. Sept. 29, 2013.

**Editor's Notes**

This section was formerly codified as RC § 5111.703.

**Amendment Notes**

The 2013 amendment substituted "section 5163.094" for "section 5111.704" in (B); and substituted "section 5163.098" for "adopted under section 5111.708" in (C).

### § 5163.094 Premium requirements.

An individual whose income exceeds one hundred fifty per cent of the federal poverty line shall pay an annual premium as a condition of qualifying for the medicaid buy-in for workers with disabilities program. The amount of the premium shall be determined as follows:

(A) Subtract one hundred fifty per cent of the federal poverty line, as applicable for a family size equal to the size of the individual's family, from the amount of the income of the individual's family;

(B) Subtract an amount specified in rules authorized by section 5163.098 of the Revised Code from the difference determined under division (A) of this section;

(C) Multiply the difference determined under division (B) of this section by one tenth.

**HISTORY:**

152 v H 119, § 101.01, eff. 9-29-07; 2013 HB 59, § 101.01, eff. Sept. 29, 2013.

**Editor's Notes**

This section was formerly codified as RC § 5111.704.

**Amendment Notes**

The 2013 amendment substituted "line" for "guidelines" in the first sentence of the introductory language and in (A); and substituted "authorized by section 5163.098" for "adopted under section 5111.708" in (B).

### § 5163.095 Dual eligibility for buy-in and home or community-based services.

No individual shall be denied eligibility for the medicaid buy-in for workers with disabilities program on the basis that the individual receives services under a home and community-based services medicaid waiver component.

**HISTORY:**

152 v H 119, § 101.01, eff. 9-29-07; 153 v H 1, § 101.01, eff. 10-16-09; 2013 HB 59, § 101.01, eff. Sept. 29, 2013.

**Editor's Notes**

This section was formerly codified as RC § 5111.705.

**Amendment Notes**

The 2013 amendment deleted "as defined in section 5111.85 of the Revised Code" from the end.

153 v H 1, effective October 16, 2009, substituted "section 5111.85" for ""section 5111.851".

### § 5163.096 Six months extended eligibility.

An individual participating in the medicaid buy-in for workers with disabilities program may continue to participate in the program for up to six months even though the individual ceases to have earnings from employment or to be an employed individual with a medically improved disability due to ceasing to be employed if the individual continues to meet all other eligibility requirements for the program.

**HISTORY:**

152 v H 119, § 101.01, eff. 9-29-07; 2013 HB 59, § 101.01, eff. Sept. 29, 2013.

**Editor's Notes**

This section was formerly codified as RC § 5111.706.

### § 5163.097 Change or removal required by secretary of health and human services.

If the United States secretary of health and human services requires that a provision of the medicaid buy-in for workers with disabilities program be changed or removed in order for the secretary to approve the program or to avoid an extended delay in the secretary's approval, the medicaid director shall make the change or removal. The change or removal may cause the medicaid buy-in for workers with disabilities program to include a provision that is inconsistent with sections 5163.09 to 5163.096 of the Revised Code. Such a change or removal shall be made only to the extent necessary to obtain the United States secretary's approval or avoid an extended delay in the secretary's approval and shall be reflected in rules authorized by section 5163.098 of the Revised Code.

**HISTORY:**

152 v H 119, § 101.01, eff. 9-29-07; 2013 HB 59, § 101.01, eff. Sept. 29, 2013.

**Editor's Notes**

This section was formerly codified as RC § 5111.707.

**Amendment Notes**

The 2013 amendment, in the first sentence, substituted "of the medicaid buy-in for workers with disabilities program" for "in the amendment to the state medicaid plan or the federal waiver request submitted under section 5111.70 of the Revised Code," "the program" for "the amendment or waiver," "medicaid director" for "director of job and family services"; substituted "sections 5163.09 to 5163.096" for "sections 5111.70 to 5111.706" in the second sentence; and substituted "authorized by section" for "adopted under section 5111.708" in the last sentence.

### § 5163.098 Rules to implement program and specify amounts of income to be disregarded.

(A) The medicaid director shall adopt rules under section 5163.02 of the Revised Code as necessary to implement the medicaid buy-in for workers with disabilities program. The rules shall do all of the following:

(1) Specify assets, asset values, and amounts to be disregarded in determining asset and income eligibility limits for the program;

(2) Establish meanings for the terms "earned income," "health insurance," "resources," "spouse," and "unearned income";

(3) Establish additional eligibility requirements for the program that must be established for the United States secretary of health and human services to approve the program;

(4) For the purpose of division (B) of section 5163.094 of the Revised Code, specify an amount to be subtracted from the difference determined under division (A) of that section.

(B) The director may adopt rules under section 5163.02 of the Revised Code to specify amounts to be disregarded from an individual's earned income, unearned income, or both under division (C) of section 5163.093 of the Revised Code for the purpose of determining whether the individual is within the income eligibility limit for the medicaid buy-in for workers with disabilities program.

**HISTORY:**

152 v H 119, § 101.01, eff. 9-29-07; 2011 SB 171, § 1, eff. June 30, 2011; 2013 HB 59, § 101.01, eff. Sept. 29, 2013.

**Editor's Notes**

This section was formerly codified as RC § 5111.708.

**Amendment Notes**

The 2013 amendment substituted "medicaid director" for "director of job and family services" in the first sentence of the introductory language of (A); substituted "under section 5163.02" for "in accordance with Chapter 119." in the first sentence of the introductory language of (A) and in (B); substituted "section 5163.094" for "section 5111.704" in (A)(4); and substituted "section 5163.093" for "section 5111.703" in (B).

The 2011 amendment deleted "after consulting with the medicaid buy-in advisory council" following "services" in (A) and following "director" in (B).

### § 5163.099 Advisory council created [Repealed].

Repealed by 2013 SB 206, § 3, effective March 20, 2014.

**HISTORY:**

2011 HB 153, § 120.20, eff. Oct. 1, 2012; 2013 HB 59, § 101.01, eff. Sept. 29, 2013.

### § 5163.10 Presumptive eligibility for pregnant women option; creation.

(A) As used in this section:

(1) "Presumptive eligibility for pregnant women option" means the option available under section 1920 of the "Social Security Act," 42 U.S.C. 1396r-1, to make ambulatory prenatal care available to pregnant women under the medicaid program during presumptive eligibility periods.

(2) "Qualified provider" has the same meaning as in section 1920(b)(2) of the "Social Security Act," 42 U.S.C. 1396r-1(b)(2).

(B) The medicaid director shall implement the presumptive eligibility for pregnant women option. Any entity that is eligible to be a qualified provider and requests to serve as a qualified provider may serve as a qualified provider for purposes of the presumptive eligibility for pregnant women option if the department of medicaid determines the entity is capable of making determinations of presumptive eligibility for pregnant women.

**HISTORY:**

2011 HB 153, § 101.01, eff. Sept. 29, 2011; 2013 HB 59, § 101.01, eff. Sept. 29, 2013; 2016 sb332, § 1, effective April 6, 2017.

**Editor's Notes**

This section was formerly codified as RC § 5111.0124.

**Amendment Notes**

The 2016 amendment by SB 332 added (A)(1) and (A)(2) designations; substituted "under section 1920 of the 'Social Security Act,' 42 U.S.C. 1396r-1" for "under the 'Social Security Act,' section 1920, 42 U.S.C. 1396r-1" in (A)(1); substituted "in section 1920(b)(2) of the 'Social Security Act,' 42 U.S.C. 1396r-1(b)(2)" for "in the 'Social Security Act,' section 1920(b)(2), 42 U.S.C. 1396r-1(b)(2)" in (A))(2); and in (B), rewrote the second sentence which formerly read "Children's hospitals, federally qualified health centers, and federally qualified health center look-alikes, if they are eligible to be a qualified providers and request to serve as qualified providers, may serve as a qualified providers for purposes of the presumptive eligibility for pregnant women option", and deleted the last sentence which read "The director may authorize other types of providers that are eligible to be qualified providers and request to serve as qualified providers to serve as qualified providers for purposes of the presumptive eligibility for pregnant women option".

The 2013 amendment rewrote the section.

## § 5163.101 Presumptive eligibility for children option retained.

Titles 39 — 57

(A) As used in this section:

(1) "Children's hospital" has the same meaning as in section 2151.86 of the Revised Code.

(2) "Federally qualified health center" has the same meaning as in section 1905(*l*)(2)(B) of the "Social Security Act," 42 U.S.C. 1396d(*l*)(2)(B).

(3) "Federally qualified health center look-alike" has the same meaning as in section 3701.047 of the Revised Code.

(4) "Presumptive eligibility for children option" means the option available under section 1920A of the "Social Security Act," 42 U.S.C. 1396r-1a, to make medical assistance with respect to health care items and services available to children under the medicaid program during presumptive eligibility periods.

(5) "Qualified entity" has the same meaning as in section 1920A(b)(3) of the "Social Security Act," 42 U.S.C. 1396r-1a(b)(3).

(B) The medicaid director shall implement the presumptive eligibility for children option. Children's hospitals, federally qualified health centers, and federally qualified health center look-alikes, if they are eligible to be qualified entities and request to serve as qualified entities, may serve as qualified entities for purposes of the presumptive eligibility for children option. The director may authorize other types of entities that are eligible to be qualified entities and request to serve as qualified entities to serve as qualified entities for purposes of the presumptive eligibility for children option.

**HISTORY:**

2011 HB 153, § 101.01, eff. Sept. 29, 2011; 2013 HB 59, § 101.01, eff. Sept. 29, 2013; 2016 sb332, § 1, effective April 6, 2017.

**Editor's Notes**

This section was formerly codified as RC § 5111.0125.

**Amendment Notes**

The 2016 amendment by SB 332, in (A), added (1) through (3) and redesignated the former two paragraphs of (A) accordingly; substituted "under section 1920A of the 'Social Security Act,' 42 U.S.C. 1396r-1a" for "under the 'Social Security Act,' section 1920A, 42 U.S.C. 1396r-1a" in (A)(4); and substituted "in section 1920A(b)(3) of the 'Social Security Act,' 42 U.S.C. 1396r-1a(b)(3)" for "in the 'Social Security Act,' section 1920A(b)(3), 42 U.S.C. 1396r-1a(b)(3)" in (A)(5).

The 2013 amendment rewrote the section.

## § 5163.20 Beneficiary of disability trust.

If a medicaid recipient is the beneficiary of a trust created pursuant to section 5815.28 of the Revised Code, then, notwithstanding any contrary provision of this chapter or of a rule adopted under section 5163.02 of the Revised Code, divisions (C) and (D) of that section shall apply in determining the assets or resources of the recipient, the recipient's estate, the settlor, or the settlor's estate and to claims arising under this chapter against the recipient, the recipient's estate, the settlor, or the settlor's estate.

**HISTORY:**

144 v S 124 (Eff 4-16-93); 149 v H 178. Eff 10-26-2001; 151 v H 416, § 1, eff. 1-1-07; 2013 HB 59, § 101.01, eff. Sept. 29, 2013.

**Editor's Notes**

This section was formerly codified as RC § 5111.15.

**Amendment Notes**

The 2013 amendment substituted "medicaid recipient" for "recipient of medical assistance"; and substituted "under section 5163.02 of the Revised Code" for "pursuant to this chapter".

151 v H 416, effective January 1, 2007, corrected internal references.

## § 5163.21 Eligibility determinations where applicant or recipient is trust beneficiary.

(A)(1) This section applies only to either of the following:

(a) Initial eligibility determinations for the medicaid program;

(b) An appeal from an initial eligibility determination pursuant to section 5160.31 of the Revised Code.

(2)(a) Except as provided in division (A)(2)(b) of this section, this section shall not be used by a court to determine the effect of a trust on an individual's initial eligibility for the medicaid program.

(b) The prohibition in division (A)(2)(a) of this section does not apply to an appeal described in division (A)(1)(b) of this section.

(B) As used in this section:

(1) "Trust" means any arrangement in which a grantor transfers real or personal property to a trust with the intention that it be held, managed, or administered by at least one trustee for the benefit of the grantor or beneficiaries. "Trust" includes any legal instrument or device similar to a trust.

(2) "Legal instrument or device similar to a trust" includes, but is not limited to, escrow accounts, investment accounts, partnerships, contracts, and other similar arrangements that are not called trusts under state law but are similar to a trust and to which all of the following apply:

(a) The property in the trust is held, managed, retained, or administered by a trustee.

(b) The trustee has an equitable, legal, or fiduciary duty to hold, manage, retain, or administer the property for the benefit of the beneficiary.

(c) The trustee holds identifiable property for the beneficiary.

(3) "Grantor" is a person who creates a trust, including all of the following:

(a) An individual;

(b) An individual's spouse;

(c) A person, including a court or administrative body, with legal authority to act in place of or on behalf of an individual or an individual's spouse;

(d) A person, including a court or administrative body, that acts at the direction or on request of an individual or the individual's spouse.

(4) "Beneficiary" is a person or persons, including a grantor, who benefits in some way from a trust.

(5) "Trustee" is a person who manages a trust's principal and income for the benefit of the beneficiaries.

(6) "Person" has the same meaning as in section 1.59 of the Revised Code and includes an individual, corporation, business trust, estate, trust, partnership, and association.

(7) "Applicant" is an individual who applies for medicaid or the individual's spouse.

(8) "Recipient" is an individual who receives medicaid or the individual's spouse.

(9) "Revocable trust" is a trust that can be revoked by the grantor or the beneficiary, including all of the following, even if the terms of the trust state that it is irrevocable:

(a) A trust that provides that the trust can be terminated only by a court;

(b) A trust that terminates on the happening of an event, but only if the event occurs at the direction or control of the grantor, beneficiary, or trustee.

(10) "Irrevocable trust" is a trust that cannot be revoked by the grantor or terminated by a court and that terminates only on the occurrence of an event outside of the control or direction of the beneficiary or grantor.

(11) "Payment" is any disbursal from the principal or income of the trust, including actual cash, noncash or property disbursements, or the right to use and occupy real property.

(12) "Payments to or for the benefit of the applicant or recipient" is a payment to any person resulting in a direct or indirect benefit to the applicant or recipient.

(13) "Testamentary trust" is a trust that is established by a will and does not take effect until after the death of the person who created the trust.

(C)(1) If an applicant or recipient is a beneficiary of a trust, the applicant or recipient shall submit a complete copy of the trust instrument to the county department of job and family services and the department of medicaid. A copy shall be considered complete if it contains all pages of the trust instrument and all schedules, attachments, and accounting statements referenced in or associated with the trust. The copy is confidential and is not subject to disclosure under section 149.43 of the Revised Code.

(2) On receipt of a copy of a trust instrument or otherwise determining that an applicant or recipient is a beneficiary of a trust, the county department of job and family services shall determine what type of trust it is and shall treat the trust in accordance with the appropriate provisions of this section and rules adopted under section 5163.02 of the Revised Code governing trusts. The county department of job and family services may determine that any of the following is the case regarding the trust or portion of the trust:

(a) It is a resource available to the applicant or recipient;

(b) It contains income available to the applicant or recipient;

(c) Divisions (C)(2)(a) and (b) of this section are both applicable;

(d) Neither division (C)(2)(a) nor (b) of this section is applicable.

(3) Except as provided in division (F) of this section, a trust or portion of a trust that is a resource available to the applicant or recipient or contains income available to the applicant or recipient shall be counted for purposes of determining medicaid eligibility.

(D)(1) A trust or legal instrument or device similar to a trust shall be considered a medicaid qualifying trust if all of the following apply:

(a) The trust was established on or prior to August 10, 1993.

(b) The trust was not established by a will.

(c) The trust was established by an applicant or recipient.

(d) The applicant or recipient is or may become the beneficiary of all or part of the trust.

(e) Payment from the trust is determined by one or more trustees who are permitted to exercise any discretion with respect to the distribution to the applicant or recipient.

(2) If a trust meets the requirement of division (D)(1) of this section, the amount of the trust that is considered by the county department of job and family services to be a resource available to the applicant or recipient shall be the maximum amount of payments permitted under the terms of the trust to be distributed to the applicant or recipient, assuming the full exercise of discretion by the trustee or trustees. The maximum amount shall include only amounts that are permitted to be distributed but are not distributed from either the income or principal of the trust.

(3) Amounts that are actually distributed from a medicaid qualifying trust to a beneficiary for any purpose shall be treated in accordance with rules adopted under section 5163.02 of the Revised Code governing income.

(4) Availability of a medicaid qualifying trust shall be considered without regard to any of the following:

(a) Whether or not the trust is irrevocable or was established for purposes other than to enable a grantor to qualify for medicaid;

(b) Whether or not the trustee actually exercises discretion.

(5) If any real or personal property is transferred to a medicaid qualifying trust that is not distributable to the applicant or recipient, the transfer shall be considered an improper disposition of assets and shall be subject to section 5163.30 of the Revised Code and rules to implement that section adopted under section 5163.02 of the Revised Code.

(6) The baseline date for the look-back period for disposition of assets involving a medicaid qualifying trust shall be the date on which the applicant or recipient is both institutionalized and first applies for medicaid.

(E)(1) A trust or legal instrument or device similar to a trust shall be considered a self-settled trust if all of the following apply:

(a) The trust was established on or after August 11, 1993.

(b) The trust was not established by a will.

(c) The trust was established by an applicant or recipient, spouse of an applicant or recipient, or a person, including a court or administrative body, with legal authority to act in place of or on behalf of an applicant, recipient, or spouse, or acting at the direction or on request of an applicant, recipient, or spouse.

(2) A trust that meets the requirements of division (E)(1) of this section and is a revocable trust shall be treated by the county department of job and family services as follows:

(a) The corpus of the trust shall be considered a resource available to the applicant or recipient.

(b) Payments from the trust to or for the benefit of the applicant or recipient shall be considered unearned income of the applicant or recipient.

(c) Any other payments from the trust shall be considered an improper disposition of assets and shall be subject to section 5163.30 of the Revised Code and rules to implement that section adopted under section 5163.02 of the Revised Code.

(3) A trust that meets the requirements of division (E)(1) of this section and is an irrevocable trust shall be treated by the county department of job and family services as follows:

(a) If there are any circumstances under which payment from the trust could be made to or for the benefit of the applicant or recipient, including a payment that can be made only in the future, the portion from which payments could be made shall be considered a resource available to the applicant or recipient. The county department of job and family services shall not take into account when payments can be made.

(b) Any payment that is actually made to or for the benefit of the applicant or recipient from either the corpus or income shall be considered unearned income.

(c) If a payment is made to someone other than to the applicant or recipient and the payment is not for the benefit of the applicant or recipient, the payment shall be considered an improper disposition of assets and shall be subject to section 5163.30 of the Revised Code and rules to implement that section adopted under section 5163.02 of the Revised Code.

(d) The date of the disposition shall be the later of the date of establishment of the trust or the date of the occurrence of the event.

(e) When determining the value of the disposed asset under this provision, the value of the trust shall be its value on the date payment to the applicant or recipient was foreclosed.

(f) Any income earned or other resources added subsequent to the foreclosure date shall be added to the total value of the trust.

(g) Any payments to or for the benefit of the applicant or recipient after the foreclosure date but prior to the application date shall be subtracted from the total value. Any other payments shall not be subtracted from the value.

(h) Any addition of assets after the foreclosure date shall be considered a separate disposition.

(4) If a trust is funded with assets of another person or persons in addition to assets of the applicant or recipient, the applicable provisions of this section and rules adopted under

section 5163.02 of the Revised Code governing trusts shall apply only to the portion of the trust attributable to the applicant or recipient.

(5) The availability of a self-settled trust shall be considered without regard to any of the following:

(a) The purpose for which the trust is established;

(b) Whether the trustees have exercised or may exercise discretion under the trust;

(c) Any restrictions on when or whether distributions may be made from the trust;

(d) Any restrictions on the use of distributions from the trust.

(6) The baseline date for the look-back period for dispositions of assets involving a self-settled trust shall be the date on which the applicant or recipient is both institutionalized and first applies for medicaid.

(F) The principal or income from any of the following shall not be a resource available to the applicant or recipient:

(1)(a) A special needs trust that meets all of the following requirements:

(i) The trust contains assets of an applicant or recipient under sixty-five years of age and may contain the assets of other individuals.

(ii) The applicant or recipient is disabled as defined in rules adopted under section 5163.02 of the Revised Code.

(iii) The trust is established for the benefit of the applicant or recipient by any of the following: the applicant or recipient, if established on or after December 13, 2016; a parent, grandparent, or legal guardian of the applicant or recipient; or a court.

(iv) The trust requires that on the death of the applicant or recipient the state will receive all amounts remaining in the trust up to an amount equal to the total amount of medicaid payments made on behalf of the applicant or recipient.

(b) If a special needs trust meets the requirements of division (F)(1)(a) of this section and has been established for a disabled applicant or recipient under sixty-five years of age, the exemption for the trust granted pursuant to division (F) of this section shall continue after the disabled applicant or recipient becomes sixty-five years of age if the applicant or recipient continues to be disabled as defined in rules adopted under section 5163.02 of the Revised Code. Except for income earned by the trust, the grantor shall not add to or otherwise augment the trust after the applicant or recipient attains sixty-five years of age. An addition or augmentation of the trust by the applicant or recipient with the applicant's own assets after the applicant or recipient attains sixty-five years of age shall be treated as an improper disposition of assets.

(c) Cash distributions to the applicant or recipient shall be counted as unearned income. All other distributions from the trust shall be treated as provided in rules adopted under section 5163.02 of the Revised Code governing in-kind income.

(d) Transfers of assets to a special needs trust shall not be treated as an improper transfer of resources. An asset held prior to the transfer to the trust shall be considered as a resource available to the applicant or recipient, income available to the applicant or recipient, or both a resource and income available to the individual.

(2)(a) A qualifying income trust that meets all of the following requirements:

(i) The trust is composed only of pension, social security, and other income to the applicant or recipient, including accumulated interest in the trust.

(ii) The income is received by the individual and the right to receive the income is not assigned or transferred to the trust.

(iii) The trust requires that on the death of the applicant or recipient the state will receive all amounts remaining in the trust up to an amount equal to the total amount of medicaid payments made on behalf of the applicant or recipient.

(b) No resources shall be used to establish or augment the trust.

(c) If an applicant or recipient has irrevocably transferred or assigned the applicant's or recipient's right to receive income to the trust, the trust shall not be considered a qualifying income trust by the county department of job and family services.

(d) Income placed in a qualifying income trust shall not be counted in determining an applicant's or recipient's eligibility for medicaid. The recipient of the funds may place any income directly into a qualifying income trust without those funds adversely affecting the applicant's or recipient's eligibility for medicaid. Income generated by the trust that remains in the trust shall not be considered as income to the applicant or recipient.

(e) All income placed in a qualifying income trust shall be combined with any income available to the individual that is not placed in the trust to arrive at a base income figure to be used for spend down calculations.

(f) The base income figure shall be used for post-eligibility deductions, including personal needs allowance, monthly income allowance, family allowance, and medical expenses not subject to third party payment. Any income remaining shall be used toward payment of patient liability. Payments made from a qualifying income trust shall not be combined with the base income figure for post-eligibility calculations.

(g) The base income figure shall be used when determining the spend down budget for the applicant or recipient. Any income remaining after allowable deductions are permitted as provided under rules adopted under section 5163.02 of the Revised Code shall be considered the applicant's or recipient's spend down liability.

(3)(a) A pooled trust that meets all of the following requirements:

(i) The trust contains the assets of the applicant or recipient of any age who is disabled as defined in rules adopted under section 5163.02 of the Revised Code.

(ii) The trust is established and managed by a nonprofit organization.

(iii) A separate account is maintained for each beneficiary of the trust but, for purposes of investment and management of funds, the trust pools the funds in these accounts.

(iv) Accounts in the trust are established by the applicant or recipient, the applicant's or recipient's parent, grandparent, or legal guardian, or a court solely for the benefit of individuals who are disabled.

(v) The trust requires that, to the extent that any amounts remaining in the beneficiary's account on the death of the beneficiary are not retained by the trust, the trust pay to the state the amounts remaining in the trust up to an amount equal to the total amount of medicaid payments made on behalf of the beneficiary.

(b) Cash distributions to the applicant or recipient shall be counted as unearned income. All other distributions from the trust shall be treated as provided in rules adopted under section 5163.02 of the Revised Code governing in-kind income.

(c) Transfers of assets to a pooled trust shall not be treated as an improper disposition of assets. An asset held prior to the transfer to the trust shall be considered as a resource available to the applicant or recipient, income available to the applicant or recipient, or both a resource and income available to the applicant or recipient.

(4) A supplemental services trust that meets the requirements of section 5815.28 of the Revised Code and to which all of the following apply:

(a) A person may establish a supplemental services trust pursuant to section 5815.28 of the Revised Code only for another person who is eligible to receive services through one of the following agencies:

(i) The department of developmental disabilities;

(ii) A county board of developmental disabilities;

(iii) The department of mental health and addiction services;

(iv) A board of alcohol, drug addiction, and mental health services.

(b) A county department of job and family services shall not determine eligibility for another agency's program. An applicant or recipient shall do one of the following:

(i) Provide documentation from one of the agencies listed in division (F)(4)(a) of this section that establishes that the applicant or recipient was determined to be eligible for services from the agency at the time of the creation of the trust;

(ii) Provide an order from a court of competent jurisdiction that states that the applicant or recipient was eligible for services from one of the agencies listed in division (F)(4)(a) of this section at the time of the creation of the trust.

(c) At the time the trust is created, the trust principal does not exceed the maximum amount permitted. The maximum amount permitted in calendar year 2006 is two hundred twenty-two thousand dollars. Each year thereafter, the maximum amount permitted is the prior year's amount plus two thousand dollars.

(d) A county department of job and family services shall review the trust to determine whether it complies with the provisions of section 5815.28 of the Revised Code.

(e) Payments from supplemental services trusts shall be exempt as long as the payments are for supplemental services as defined in rules adopted under section 5163.02 of the Revised Code. All supplemental services shall be purchased by the trustee and shall not be purchased through direct cash payments to the beneficiary.

(f) If a trust is represented as a supplemental services trust and a county department of job and family services determines that the trust does not meet the requirements provided in division (F)(4) of this section and section 5815.28 of the Revised Code, the county department of job and family services shall not consider it an exempt trust.

(G)(1) A trust or legal instrument or device similar to a trust shall be considered a trust established by an individual for the benefit of the applicant or recipient if all of the following apply:

(a) The trust is created by a person other than the applicant or recipient.

(b) The trust names the applicant or recipient as a beneficiary.

(c) The trust is funded with assets or property in which the applicant or recipient has never held an ownership interest prior to the establishment of the trust.

(2) Any portion of a trust that meets the requirements of division (G)(1) of this section shall be a resource available to the applicant or recipient only if the trust permits the trustee to expend principal, corpus, or assets of the trust for the applicant's or recipient's medical care, care, comfort, maintenance, health, welfare, general well being, or any combination of these purposes.

(3) A trust that meets the requirements of division (G)(1) of this section shall be considered a resource available to the applicant or recipient even if the trust contains any of the following types of provisions:

(a) A provision that prohibits the trustee from making payments that would supplant or replace medicaid or other public assistance;

(b) A provision that prohibits the trustee from making payments that would impact or have an effect on the applicant's or recipient's right, ability, or opportunity to receive medicaid or other public assistance;

(c) A provision that attempts to prevent the trust or its corpus or principal from being a resource available to the applicant or recipient.

(4) A trust that meets the requirements of division (G)(1) of this section shall not be counted as a resource available to the applicant or recipient if at least one of the following circumstances applies:

(a) If a trust contains a clear statement requiring the trustee to preserve a portion of the trust for another beneficiary or remainderman, that portion of the trust shall not be counted as a resource available to the applicant or recipient. Terms of a trust that grant discretion to preserve a portion of the trust shall not qualify as a clear statement requiring the trustee to preserve a portion of the trust.

(b) If a trust contains a clear statement requiring the trustee to use a portion of the trust for a purpose other than medical care, care, comfort, maintenance, welfare, or general well being of the applicant or recipient, that portion of the trust shall not be counted as a resource available to the applicant or recipient. Terms of a trust that grant discretion to limit the use of a portion of the trust shall not qualify as a clear statement requiring the trustee to use a portion of the trust for a particular purpose.

(c) If a trust contains a clear statement limiting the trustee to making fixed periodic payments, the trust shall not be counted as a resource available to the applicant or recipient and payments shall be treated in accordance with rules adopted under section 5163.02 of the Revised Code governing income. Terms of a trust that grant discretion to limit payments shall not qualify as a clear statement requiring the trustee to make fixed periodic payments.

(d) If a trust contains a clear statement that requires the trustee to terminate the trust if it is counted as a resource available to the applicant or recipient, the trust shall not be counted as such. Terms of a trust that grant discretion to terminate the trust do not qualify as a clear statement requiring the trustee to terminate the trust.

(e) If a person obtains a judgment from a court of competent jurisdiction that expressly prevents the trustee from using part or all of the trust for the medical care, care, comfort, maintenance, welfare, or general well being of the applicant or recipient, the trust or that portion of the trust subject to the court order shall not be counted as a resource available to the applicant or recipient.

(f) If a trust is specifically exempt from being counted as a resource available to the applicant or recipient by a provision of the Revised Code, rules, or federal law, the trust shall not be counted as such.

(g) If an applicant or recipient presents a final judgment from a court demonstrating that the applicant or recipient was unsuccessful in a civil action against the trustee to compel payments from the trust, the trust shall not be counted as a resource available to the applicant or recipient.

(h) If an applicant or recipient presents a final judgment from a court demonstrating that in a civil action against the trustee the applicant or recipient was only able to compel limited or periodic payments, the trust shall not be counted as a resource available to the applicant or recipient and payments shall be treated in accordance with rules adopted under section 5163.02 of the Revised Code governing income.

(i) If an applicant or recipient provides written documentation showing that the cost of a civil action brought to compel payments from the trust would be cost prohibitive, the trust shall not be counted as a resource available to the applicant or recipient.

(5) Any actual payments to the applicant or recipient from a trust that meet the requirements of division (G)(1) of this section, including trusts that are not counted as a resource available to the applicant or recipient, shall be treated as provided in rules adopted under section 5163.02 of the Revised Code governing income. Payments to any person other than the applicant or recipient shall not be considered income to the applicant or recipient. Payments from the trust to a person other than the applicant or recipient shall not be considered an improper disposition of assets.

**HISTORY:**

150 v H 85, § 1, eff. 3-9-04; 151 v H 530, § 101.01, eff. 3-30-06; 151 v H 416, § 1, eff. 1-1-07; 153 v S 79, § 1, eff. 10-6-09; 2011 HB 153, § 101.01, eff. Sept. 29, 2011; 2012 HB 267, § 1, eff. May 22, 2012; 2013 HB 59, § 101.01, eff. Sept. 29, 2013; 2018 hb595, § 1, effective March 22, 2019.

**Editor's Notes**

This section was formerly codified as RC § 5111.151.

The enactment of RC § 5111.151 by H.B. 95 (150 v —) was disapproved by the Governor.

**Amendment Notes**

The 2018 amendment by HB 595 in (F)(1)(a)(iii), added "any of the following: the applicant or recipient, if established on or after December 13,

2016" and substituted "or legal guardian of the applicant or recipient" for "legal guardian."

The 2013 amendment deleted "made by the department of job and family services pursuant to section 5101.47 of the Revised Code or by a county department of job and family services pursuant to section 5111.012 of the Revised Code" from the end of (A)(1)(a); substituted "an initial eligibility determination pursuant to section 5160.31" for "a determination described in division (A)(1)(a) of this section pursuant to section 5101.35" in (A)(1)(b); rewrote (C); substituted "under section 5163.02 of the Revised Code" for "by the department of job and family services" in (D)(3), (D)(4), (F)(1)(a)(ii), (F)(3)(a)(i), and (G)(4)(h), in the first sentence of (F)(1)(b), (F)(4)(e), (G)(4)(c), and (G)(5), and in the second sentence of (F)(1)(c), (F)(2)(g), and (F)(3)(b); deleted "medical assistance for covered families and children, or as a qualified medicare beneficiary, specified low-income medicare beneficiary, qualifying individual-1, or qualifying individual-2" form the end of (D)(4)(a); in (D)(5), (E)(2)(c), and (E)(3)(c), substituted "section 5163.30" for "section 5111.0116" and substituted "section 5163.02" for "section 5111.011"; added "and addiction services" to the end of (F)(4)(a)(iii); and made stylistic changes.

The 2012 amendment substituted "organization" for "association" in (F)(3)(a)(ii); and made a stylistic change.

The 2011 amendment rewrote (A); rewrote (C); rewrote the introductory language of (F); rewrote the second sentence of (F)(1)(d); substituted "income available to the individual that is" for "countable income" in (F)(2)(e); rewrote the second sentence of (F)(3)(c); substituted "a resource available to the applicant or recipient" for "an available resource" throughout (G); deleted "counted as" following "being" in (G)(3)(c); substituted "such" for "an available resource" in the first sentence of (G)(4)(d); added "available to the applicant or recipient" in (G)(4)(e); substituted "such" for "a resource" in (G)(4)(f); and made stylistic changes.

153 v S 79, effective October 6, 2009, deleted "mental retardation and" preceding "developmental disabilities" throughout.

151 v H 416, effective January 1, 2007, corrected internal references.

151 v H 530, effective March 30, 2006, in (A), (F)(1)(a)(iv), (F)(2)(a)(iii), twice in (F)(2)(d), in (F)(3)(a)(v), and (G)(3)(a) and (b), substituted "medicaid" for "medical assistance"; substituted "medicaid" for "medical assistance benefits" in (B)(7) and (8); rewrote (D)(5) and (6) and (E); in (F)(1)(b) and (F)(3)(c), substituted "disposition of assets" for "transfer of resources"; in (F)(4)(c), substituted "2006 is two hundred twenty-two" for "2002 is two hundred fourteen"; and, in (G)(5), substituted "disposition" for "transfer".



## NOTES TO DECISIONS

Analysis



**Applicability**

Ohio Supreme Court holds that eligibility for Medicaid benefits by a trust beneficiary is to be determined by the rules in effect when the application is filed pursuant to R.C. 5111.151 and OAC 5101:1-39-27.1, rather than at the time the trust is created; accordingly, a court had to determine what type of trust the beneficiary's interest was in and whether it was a countable resource under the applicable rules for purposes of a Medicaid-eligibility determination. Pack v. Osborn, 2008-Ohio-90, 117 Ohio St. 3d 14, 881 N.E.2d 237, 2008 Ohio LEXIS 26 (Ohio 2008).

**Applicable law**

When a trust beneficiary applies for public assistance, the eligibility rules in effect at the time of the application must be applied to the applicant: Pack v. Osborn, 2008-Ohio-90, 117 Ohio St. 3d 14, 881 N.E.2d 237, 2008 Ohio LEXIS 26 (Ohio 2008).

**Available resource**

Because the trust specifically mentioned health and welfare as two of the specified purposes for which the trustee could distribute trust assets, it had to be considered an available resource for Medicaid eligibility since none of the specified exceptions applied. Because the Medicaid applicant failed to present the trial court with an interpretation from a declaratory judgment action, the trial court correctly determined that she failed to meet the requirements for the exceptions. Cook v. Ohio Dep't of Job & Family Servs., 2015-Ohio-4966, 2015 Ohio App. LEXIS 4806 (Ohio Ct. App., Franklin County 2015).

**Declaratory judgment**

Successor trustee of an inter vivos trust properly commenced a declaratory judgment action pursuant to R.C. 2721.05(C) and 5802.01(C) to determine whether the trust assets could be considered in determining a beneficiary's eligibility for Medicaid benefits, as the court had authority to interpret the terms of the trust in the Medicaid-eligibility context pursuant to R.C. 5111.151(G)(4)(e), (g), and (h), as well as OAC 5101:1-39-27.1(C)(4)(c)(v), (vii), and (viii). Pack v. Osborn, 2008-Ohio-90, 117 Ohio St. 3d 14, 881 N.E.2d 237, 2008 Ohio LEXIS 26 (Ohio 2008).

**Self-settled trust**

Even if the county job and family services used incorrect terminology, it correctly determined that the Medicaid nursing home benefits applicant's trust was a self-settled trust and that the funds in the trust were resources that were available to the applicant under the Ohio Administrative Code. Accordingly, the applicant's estate did not demonstrate that the agency violated R.C. 5111.151(C). Gsellman v. Ohio Dep't of Job & Family Servs., 2012-Ohio-1620, 2012 Ohio App. LEXIS 1421 (Ohio Ct. App., Summit County 2012).

**Special needs trust**

Probate court possessed the jurisdiction to carry out the only relief that the guardian requested—the establishment of a trust account with the pooled special needs trust on the ward's behalf for the purpose of Medicaid eligibility. The probate court was not required to declare that a pooled trust account that it opened on a ward's behalf complied with R.C. 5111.151(F)(3)(a) and OAC 5101:1-39-27.1(C)(3)(c). Kormanik v. Cooper, 2011-Ohio-5617, 195 Ohio App. 3d 790, 961 N.E.2d 1187, 2011 Ohio App. LEXIS 4596 (Ohio Ct. App., Franklin County 2011).

## § 5163.22 Life insurance policies on recipients.

(A) The general assembly hereby finds that the state has an insurable interest in medicaid recipients because of the state's statutory right to recover from the estate of a recipient state funds used to provide the recipient with medicaid services.

(B) As used in this section:

(1) "Beneficiary" means the person or entity designated in a life insurance policy to receive the proceeds of the policy on the death of the insured or maturity of the policy.

(2) "Owner" means the person who has the right to designate the beneficiary of a life insurance policy and to change the designation.

(C) The value of a life insurance policy that would otherwise be considered a resource in determining eligibility for the medicaid program shall be excluded from any determination of a person's eligibility for the medicaid program if the owner designates the department of medicaid as beneficiary of the policy. The department may pay premiums to keep the policy in force. Premiums paid by the department are medicaid payments correctly paid on behalf of a medicaid recipient and subject to recovery under section 5162.21 of the Revised Code.

(D) The medicaid director shall deposit the proceeds of a life insurance policy that do not exceed the amount the department may recover against the property and estate of the owner under section 5162.21 of the Revised Code into the general revenue fund. The director shall pay any remaining proceeds to the person designated by the owner. If the owner failed to designate a person, the director shall pay the remaining proceeds to the surviving spouse, or, if there is no surviving spouse, to the estate of the owner.

(E) If the owner designates the department of medicaid as the policy's beneficiary, the department shall notify the owner that the owner may designate a person to receive proceeds of the policy that exceed the amount the department may recover against the owner's property and estate under section 5162.21 of the Revised Code. The designation shall be made on a form provided by the department.

**HISTORY:**

145 v H 152 (Eff 7-1-93); 148 v H 471. Eff 7-1-2000; 2013 HB 59, § 101.01, eff. Sept. 29, 2013.

**Editor's Notes**

This section was formerly codified as RC § 5111.181.

**Amendment Notes**

The 2013 amendment substituted "medicaid" for "medical care and" wherever it appears in (A) and (C) through (E); deleted "Notwithstanding section 5111.011 of the Revised Code" to the beginning of the first sentence of (C); substituted "section 5162.21" for "section 5111.11" in the second sentence of (C) and the first sentence of (D) and (E); and deleted (F), which read: "The department of job and family services shall not implement this section if implementation would violate any federal requirement unless the department receives a waiver of the requirement from the United States department of health and human services."

## § 5163.30 Ineligibility of institutionalized individual based on disposing of assets for less than fair market value.

(A) As used in this section:

(1) "Assets" include all of an individual's income and resources and those of the individual's spouse, including any income or resources the individual or spouse is entitled to but does not receive because of action by any of the following:

(a) The individual or spouse;

(b) A person or government entity, including a court or administrative agency, with legal authority to act in place of or on behalf of the individual or spouse;

(c) A person or government entity, including a court or administrative agency, acting at the direction or on the request of the individual or spouse.

(2) "Home and community-based services" means home and community-based services furnished under a medicaid waiver granted by the United States secretary of health and human services under the "Social Security Act," section 1915(c) or (d), 42 U.S.C. 1396n(c) or (d).

(3) "Institutionalized individual" means a resident of a nursing facility, an inpatient in a medical institution for whom a payment is made based on a level of care provided in a nursing facility, or an individual described in the "Social Security Act," section 1902(a)(10)(A)(ii)(VI), 42 U.S.C. 1396a(a)(10)(A)(ii)(VI).

(4) "Look-back date" means the date that is a number of months specified in rules adopted under section 5163.02 of the Revised Code immediately before either of the following:

(a) The date an individual becomes an institutionalized individual if the individual is eligible for medicaid on that date;

(b) The date an individual applies for medicaid while an institutionalized individual.

(5) "Nursing facility equivalent services" means services that are covered by the medicaid program, equivalent to nursing facility services, provided by an institution that provides the same level of care as a nursing facility, and provided to an inpatient of the institution who is a medicaid recipient eligible for medicaid-covered nursing facility equivalent services.

(6) "Undue hardship" means being deprived of either of the following:

(a) Medical care such that an individual's health or life is endangered;

(b) Food, clothing, shelter, or other necessities of life.

(B) Except as provided in division (C) of this section and rules adopted under section 5163.02 of the Revised Code, an institutionalized individual is ineligible for nursing facility services, nursing facility equivalent services, and home and community-based services if the individual or individual's spouse disposes of assets for less than fair market value on or after the look-back date. The institutionalized individual's ineligibility shall begin on a date determined in accordance with rules adopted under section 5163.02 of the Revised Code and shall continue for a number of months determined in accordance with such rules.

(C)(1) An institutionalized individual may be granted a waiver of all or a portion of the period of ineligibility to which the individual would otherwise be subjected under division (B) of this section if the ineligibility would cause an undue hardship for the individual.

(2) An institutionalized individual shall be granted a waiver of all or a portion of the period of ineligibility if the administrator of the nursing facility in which the individual resides has notified the individual of a proposed transfer or discharge under section 3721.16 of the Revised Code due to failure to pay for the care the nursing facility has provided to the individual, the individual or the individual's sponsor requests a hearing on the proposed transfer or discharge in accordance with section 3721.161 of the Revised Code, and the transfer or discharge is upheld by a final determination that is not subject to further appeal.

(3) An institutionalized individual may be granted a waiver of all of the period of ineligibility if all of the assets that were disposed of for less than fair market value are returned to the individual or individual's spouse or if the individual or individual's spouse receives cash or other personal or real property that equals the difference between what the individual or individual's spouse received for the assets and the fair market value of the assets. Except as provided in division (C)(1) or (2) of this section, no waiver of any part of the period of ineligibility shall be granted if the amount the individual or individual's spouse receives is less than the difference between what the individual or individual's spouse received for the assets and the fair market value of the assets.

(4) Waivers shall be granted in accordance with rules adopted under section 5163.02 of the Revised Code.

(D) To secure compliance with this section, the medicaid director may require an individual, as a condition of initial or continued eligibility for medicaid, to provide documentation of the individual's assets up to five years before the date the individual becomes an institutionalized individual if the individual is eligible for medicaid on that date or the date the individual applies for medicaid while an institutionalized individual. Documentation may include tax returns, records from financial institutions, and real property records.

**HISTORY:**

151 v H 530, § 101.01, eff. 3-30-06; 2011 HB 153, § 101.01, eff. Sept. 29, 2011; 2013 HB 59, § 101.01, eff. Sept. 29, 2013; 2015 hb64, § 101.01, effective September 29, 2015.

**Editor's Notes**

This section was formerly codified as RC § 5111.0116.

**Amendment Notes**

The 2015 amendment, by HB 64, added the (C)(1), (C)(2), and (C)(4) designation; and inserted (C)(3).

The 2013 amendment inserted "the 'Social Security Act,' section 1915(c) or (d)" in (A)(2); inserted "the 'Social Security Act,' section 1902(a)(10)(A)(ii)(VI)" in (A)(3); substituted "section 5163.02" for "section 5111.011" in the introductory language of (A)(4); deleted (A)(5), which read: " 'Nursing facility' has the same meaning as in section 5111.20 of the Revised Code"; redesignated former (A)(6) and (A)(8) as (A)(5) and (A)(6); deleted (A)(7), which read: " 'Nursing facility services' means nursing facility services covered by the medicaid program that a nursing facility provides to a resident of the nursing facility who is a medicaid recipient eligible for medicaid-covered nursing facility services"; substituted "section 5163.02" for "section 5111.011" in the first and second sentences of (B) and in the last sentence of (D); and substituted "medicaid director" for "director of job and family services" in the first sentence of (D).

The 2011 amendment added (A)(8); inserted "division (C) of this section and" in the first sentence of (B); inserted (C); and redesignated former (C) as (D).

### NOTES TO DECISIONS

Analysis



**Generally**

Six-month period of restrictive coverage began when the deeds to the parent's property were recorded, not when they were executed: Kinasz-Reagan v. Ohio Dep't of Job & Family Servs., 2005-Ohio-5848, 164 Ohio App. 3d 458, 842 N.E.2d 1067, 2005 Ohio App. LEXIS 5273 (Ohio Ct. App., Cuyahoga County 2005).

**Relations with other laws**

R.C. 5163.30, which was amended effective September 29, 2015, to eliminate the half loaf method for persons with substantial personal assets to make themselves eligible for Medicaid benefits without spending down their assets, was not in conflict with Ohio Admin. Code 5160:1-3-07 before the regulation was amended to reflect the change in law as that Reg. 5160:1-3-07 did not reflect the amendment to R.C. 5163.30 for several months did not diminish the effect of the amended statute; the regulation could not supersede the amended statute. Paczko v. Ohio Dep't of Job & Family Servs., 2017-Ohio-9024, 101 N.E.3d 1052, 2017 Ohio App. LEXIS 5527 (Ohio Ct. App., Cuyahoga County 2017).

**Retroactive application**

Application of amended R.C. 5163.30 to appellant's request did not violate Ohio Const. art. II, § 28's prohibition of retroactive laws as the amended statute was only applied to appellant's request for a recalculation of the restricted Medicaid coverage period that was made after the statute had been amended; appellant had no vested right in a continuation of the law as it existed when she made her initial Medicaid application. Paczko v. Ohio Dep't of Job & Family Servs., 2017-Ohio-9024, 101 N.E.3d 1052, 2017 Ohio App. LEXIS 5527 (Ohio Ct. App., Cuyahoga County 2017).

**Undue hardship**

Trial court did not err by granting the Job and Family Services' motion to dismiss the administrative appeal from the nursing facility's efforts to obtain an undue hardship exemption to a restricted Medicaid coverage period (or RMCP) limiting the patient's award of long term care facility benefits because nothing in the Authorized Representative Designation Form could reasonably have been construed as authorizing the facility to prosecute an appeal on the patient's behalf or even to seek the undue hardship exemption. Peck v. Ohio Dep't of Job & Family Servs., 2018-Ohio-2353, 2018 Ohio App. LEXIS 2557 (Ohio Ct. App., Geauga County 2018).

## § 5163.31 When real property ceases to be considered principal place of residence.

(A) Except as provided by division (A) of this section and for the purpose of determining whether an aged, blind, or disabled individual is eligible for nursing facility services, ICF/IID services, or other medicaid-funded long-term care services, the medicaid director may consider an aged, blind, or disabled individual's real property to not be the individual's homestead or principal place of residence once the individual has resided in a nursing facility, ICF/IID, or other medical institution for at least thirteen months.

(B) Division (A) of this section does not apply to an individual if any of the following reside in the individual's real property that, because of this division, continues to be considered the individual's homestead or principal place of residence:

(1) The individual's spouse;

(2) The individual's child if any of the following apply:

(a) The child is under twenty-one years of age.

(b) The child is considered blind or disabled under the "Social Security Act," section 1614, 42 U.S.C. 1382c.

(c) The child is financially dependent on the individual for housing as determined in accordance with rules adopted under section 5163.02 of the Revised Code.

(3) The individual's sibling if the sibling has a verified equity interest in the real property and resided in the real property for at least one year immediately before the date the individual was admitted to the nursing facility, ICF/IID, or other medical institution.

**HISTORY:**

151 v H 530, § 101.01, eff. 3-30-06; 2013 HB 59, § 101.01, eff. Sept. 29, 2013.

**Editor's Notes**

This section was formerly codified as RC § 5111.0117.

**Amendment Notes**

The 2013 amendment deleted (A), pertaining to the meaning of the terms "ICF/MR services", "Intermediate care facility for the mentally retarded", "Nursing facility", "Nursing facility services" and "Other medicaid-funded long-term care services"; redesignated former (B) and (C) as (A) and (B); in present (A), substituted "division (A)" for "division (C)," "ICF/IID services" for "ICF/MR services," and "medicaid director" for "director of job and family services"; and substituted "ICF/IID, or other" for "intermediate care facility for the mentally retarded, or other" in present (A) and (B)(3); inserted "the 'Social Security Act,' section 1614" in (B)(2)(b); substituted "section 5163.02" for "section 5111.011" in (B)(2)(c); and made a stylistic change.

## § 5163.32 Ineligibility due to substantial home equity.

(A) Except as otherwise provided by this section, no individual shall qualify for nursing facility services or other medicaid-funded long-term care services if the individual's equity interest in the individual's home exceeds five hundred thousand dollars. The medicaid director shall increase this amount effective January 1, 2011, and the first day of each year thereafter, by the percentage increase in the consumer price index for all urban consumers (all items; United States city average), rounded to the nearest one thousand dollars.

(B) This section does not apply to an individual if either of the following applies:

(1) Either of the following lawfully reside in the individual's home:

(a) The individual's spouse;

(b) The individual's child if the child is under twenty-one years of age or, under the "Social Security Act," section 1614, 42 U.S.C. 1382c, considered blind or disabled.

(2) The individual qualifies, pursuant to the process established under division (C) of this section, for a waiver of this section due to a demonstrated hardship.

(C) The director shall establish a process by which individuals may obtain a waiver of this section due to a demonstrated hardship. The process shall be consistent with the process for such waivers established by the United States secretary of health and human services under the "Social Security Act," section 1917(f)(4), 42 U.S.C. 1396p(f)(4).

(D) Nothing in this section shall be construed as preventing an individual from using a reverse mortgage or home equity loan to reduce the individual's total equity interest in the home.

**HISTORY:**

151 v H 530, § 101.01, eff. 3-30-06; 2013 HB 59, § 101.01, eff. Sept. 29, 2013.

**Editor's Notes**

This section was formerly codified as RC § 5111.0118.

**Amendment Notes**

The 2013 amendment substituted "medicaid director" for "director of job and family services" in the two sentence of (A); inserted "the 'Social Security Act,' section 1614" in (B)(1)(b); and inserted "the 'Social Security Act,' section 1917(f)(4)" in the second sentence of (C).

## § 5163.33 Deduction of personal needs allowance from recipient's income.

(A) In determining the amount of income that a medicaid recipient must apply monthly toward payment of the cost of care in a nursing facility or ICF/IID, a county department of job and family services shall deduct from the recipient's monthly income a monthly personal needs allowance in accordance with the "Social Security Act," section 1902(q), 42 U.S.C. 1396a(q).

(B) In the case of a resident of a nursing facility, the monthly personal needs allowance shall be

not less than fifty dollars for an individual resident and not less than one hundred dollars for a married couple if both spouses are residents of a nursing facility and their incomes are considered available to each other in determining eligibility.

(C) In the case of a resident of an ICF/IID, the monthly personal needs allowance shall be as follows:

(1) Prior to January 1, 2016, forty dollars unless the resident has earned income, in which case the monthly personal needs allowance shall be determined by the department of medicaid, or the department's designee, but shall not exceed one hundred five dollars;

(2) For calendar year 2016 and each calendar year thereafter, not less than fifty dollars for an individual resident and not less than one hundred dollars for a married couple if both spouses are residents of an ICF/IID and their incomes are considered available to each other in determining eligibility.

**HISTORY:**

147 v H 408 (Eff 10-1-97); 147 v H 283 (Eff 9-29-99); 148 v H 471. Eff 7-1-2000; 151 v H 66, § 101.01, eff. 6-30-05; 2013 HB 59, § 101.01, eff. Sept. 29, 2013; 2015 hb64, § 101.01, effective September 29, 2015.

**Editor's Notes**

This section was formerly codified as RC § 5111.114.

This section was amended and renumbered from RC § 5111.113 by 151 v H 66, effective June 30, 2005.

**Amendment Notes**

The 2015 amendment, by HB 64, deleted (B)(1) and (B)(2), which read: "(1) Prior to January 1, 2014, not less than forty dollars for an individual resident and not less than eighty dollars for a married couple if both spouses are residents of a nursing facility and their incomes are considered available to each other in determining eligibility; (2) For calendar year 2014, not less than forty-five dollars for an individual resident and not less than ninety dollars for a married couple if both spouses are residents of a nursing facility and their incomes are considered available to each other in determining eligibility"; deleted the (B)(3) designation; deleted "For calendar year 2015 and each calendar year thereafter" preceding "not less" in (B); added "as follows" to the end of the introductory language of (C); added "Prior to January 1, 2016" to the beginning of (C)(1); added (C)(2); and made related changes.

The 2013 amendment rewrote the section.

151 v H 66, effective June 30, 2005, substituted "mentally" for "mental" in the first paragraph.

### RESEARCH REFERENCES AND PRACTICE AIDS

**Ohio Administrative Code**

Department of job and family services, division of public assistance—Medicaid: personal needs allowance. OAC 5123:2-7-09, 5160-3-16.5.

## § 5163.40 Healthy start program applications.

(A) The department of medicaid shall do all of the following with regard to the application procedures for the healthy start component of the medicaid program:

(1) Establish a short application form for the component that requires the applicant to provide no more information than is necessary for making determinations of eligibility for the component, except that the form may require applicants to provide their social security numbers. The form shall include a statement, which must be signed by the applicant, indicating that she does not choose at the time of making application for the component to apply for assistance provided under any other program administered by the department or the department of job and family services and that she understands that she is permitted at any other time to apply at the county department of job and family services of the county in which she resides for other assistance administered by the department or the department of job and family services.

(2) Do one or both of the following:

(a) Distribute the application form for the component to each public or private entity that serves as a women, infants, and children clinic or as a child and family health clinic and to each administrative body for such clinics and train employees of each such clinic or administrative body to provide applicants assistance in completing the form;

(b) In cooperation with the department of health, develop arrangements under which employees of county departments of job and family services are stationed at public or private entities selected by the department of medicaid that serve as women, infants, and children clinics; child and family health clinics; or administrative bodies for such clinics for the purpose both of assisting applicants for the component in completing the application form and of making determinations at that location of eligibility for the component.

(3) Establish performance standards by which a county department of job and family services' level of enrollment of persons potentially eligible for the component can be measured, and establish acceptable levels of enrollment for each county department.

(4) Direct any county department of job and family services whose rate of enrollment of potentially eligible enrollees in the component is below acceptable levels established under division (A)(3) of this section to implement corrective action. Corrective action may include but is not limited to any one or more of the following:

(a) Establishing formal referral and outreach methods with local health departments and local entities receiving funding through the bureau of maternal and child health;

(b) Designating a specialized intake unit within the county department for healthy start applicants;

(c) Establishing abbreviated timeliness requirements to shorten the time between receipt of an application and the scheduling of an initial application interview;

(d) Establishing a system for telephone scheduling of intake interviews for applicants;

(e) Establishing procedures to minimize the time an applicant must spend in completing the application and eligibility determination process, including permitting applicants to complete the process at times other than the regular business hours of the county department and at locations other than the offices of the county department.

(B) A county department of job and family services that maintains offices at more than one location shall accept applications for the healthy start component at all of those locations.

**HISTORY:**

143 v H 764 (Eff 4-10-91); 144 v H 298 (Eff 7-26-91); 144 v H 478 (Eff 1-14-93); 147 v H 408 (Eff 10-1-97); 148 v H 471. Eff 7-1-2000; 2011 HB 153, § 101.01, eff. Sept. 29, 2011; 2012 HB 487, § 101.01, eff. Sept. 10, 2012; 2013 HB 59, § 101.01, eff. Sept. 29, 2013.

**Editor's Notes**

This section was formerly codified as RC § 5111.013.

**Amendment Notes**

The 2013 amendment rewrote the section.

The 2012 amendment substituted "division (C)(3)" for "division (A)(3)" in (A).

The 2011 amendment deleted (D), pertaining to the job and family services done by the director; and redesignated former (E) and (F) as (D) and (E).

### RESEARCH REFERENCES AND PRACTICE AIDS

**Ohio Administrative Code**

Department of job and family services, division of public assistance—Covered families and children medicaid. OAC 5101:1-40.

Expedited medicaid eligibility determinations. OAC 5101:1-40-60.

Healthy start. OAC 5101:1-40-08.

Income: nonrecurring lump-sum period of ineligibility for health-start. OAC 5101:1-23-075.

Pregnancy related services. OAC 5101:1-38-06.

## § 5163.45 Suspension of eligibility of certain prisoners.

(A)(1) As used in this section, subject to division (A)(2) of this section, "state or local correctional facility" means any of the following:

(a) A "state correctional institution," as defined in section 2967.01 of the Revised Code;

(b) A "local correctional facility," as defined in section 2903.13 of the Revised Code;

(c) A correctional facility that is privately operated and managed pursuant to section 9.06 of the Revised Code.

(2) "State or local correctional facility" does not include any facility operated directly by or at the direction of the department of youth services.

(B) If a person who is confined in a state or local correctional facility was a medicaid recipient immediately prior to being confined in the facility, all of the following apply:

(1) The person's eligibility for medicaid while so confined shall be suspended due to the confinement.

(2) No medicaid payment shall be made for any care, services, or supplies provided to the person during the suspension described in division (B)(1) of this section.

(3) The suspension described in division (B)(1) of this section shall end upon the release of the person from the confinement.

(4) Except as provided in division (C) of this section, the person shall not be required to reapply or undergo a redetermination of eligibility for medicaid when the suspension described in division (B)(1) of this section ends.

(C) A person may be disenrolled from medicaid any time after the suspension described in division (B)(1) of this section ends if the person is no longer eligible for medicaid. A person may be required to undergo a redetermination of eligibility for medicaid any time after the suspension described in division (B)(1) of this section ends if it is time or past time for the person's eligibility redetermination or the person's circumstances have changed in a manner warranting a redetermination.

**HISTORY:**

152 v H 215, § 1, eff. 4-7-09; 2013 HB 59, § 101.01, eff. Sept. 29, 2013.

**Editor's Notes**

This section was formerly codified as RC § 5111.0119.

**Amendment Notes**

The 2013 amendment deleted (D), which read: "The department of job and family services shall take the steps necessary to begin implementation of this section not later than September 1, 2009."

### § 5163.52 Federal funding that is contingent on limitation of department's ability to disenroll ineligible recipients.

If the department of medicaid receives federal funding for the medicaid program that is contingent on a temporary maintenance of effort restriction or that otherwise limits the department's ability to disenroll ineligible medicaid recipients, such as the requirements under Section 6008 of the "Families First Coronavirus Response Act," Pub. L. No. 116-127, the department shall do both of the following:

(A) Continue to conduct eligibility redeterminations under the medicaid program and act on those redeterminations to the fullest extent permitted under federal law and regulations.

(B) Within sixty days of the expiration of the restriction or limitation, complete an audit in which the department does all of the following:

(1) Completes and acts on eligibility redeterminations for all medicaid recipients for whom a redetermination has not been conducted in the past twelve months;

(2) Requests approval from the United States centers for medicare and medicaid services to conduct and act on eligibility redeterminations on all medicaid recipients who were enrolled for three or more months, or other time period consistent with federal law or federal guidelines, during the period of restriction or limitation; the department shall, within ninety days of any such approval, conduct and act on the redeterminations. Any county department of job and family services assisting the department of medicaid with acting on redeterminations under this section may request from the department of job and family services, in consultation with the department of medicaid, up to thirty additional days to act on redeterminations.

(3) Submits a report summarizing the results of the audit to the speaker of the house of representatives and senate president in accordance with section 101.68 of the Revised Code.

**HISTORY:**

2021 hb110, § 101.01, effective January 1, 2022.



# CHAPTER 5164

# SERVICES UNDER STATE MEDICAID PROGRAM

Section



Section

### § 5164.01 Definitions.

As used in this chapter:

(A) "Adjudication" has the same meaning as in section 119.01 of the Revised Code.

(B) "Behavioral health redesign" means revisions to the medicaid program's coverage of community behavioral health services beginning July 1, 2017, including revisions that update medicaid billing codes and payment rates for community behavioral health services.

(C) "Clean claim" has the same meaning as in 42 C.F.R. 447.45(b).

(D) "Community behavioral health services" means both of the following:

(1) Alcohol and drug addiction services provided by a community addiction services provider, as defined in section 5119.01 of the Revised Code;

(2) Mental health services provided by a community mental health services provider, as defined in section 5119.01 of the Revised Code.

(E) "Early and periodic screening, diagnostic, and treatment services" has the same meaning as in the "Social Security Act," section 1905(r), 42 U.S.C. 1396d(r).

(F) "Federal financial participation" has the same meaning as in section 5160.01 of the Revised Code.

(G) "Federal poverty line" has the same meaning as in section 5162.01 of the Revised Code.

(H) "Healthcheck" means the component of the medicaid program that provides early and periodic screening, diagnostic, and treatment services.

(I) "Home and community-based services medicaid waiver component" has the same meaning as in section 5166.01 of the Revised Code.

(J) "Hospital" has the same meaning as in section 3727.01 of the Revised Code.

(K) "ICDS participant" means a dual eligible individual who participates in the integrated care delivery system.

(L) "ICF/IID" has the same meaning as in section 5124.01 of the Revised Code.

(M) "Integrated care delivery system" and "ICDS" mean the demonstration project authorized by section 5164.91 of the Revised Code.

(N) "Mandatory services" means the health care services and items that must be covered by the medicaid state plan as a condition of the state receiving federal financial participation for the medicaid program.

(O) "Medicaid managed care organization" has the same meaning as in section 5167.01 of the Revised Code.

(P) "Medicaid provider" means a person or government entity with a valid provider agreement to provide medicaid services to medicaid recipients. To the extent appropriate in the context, "medicaid provider" includes a person or government entity applying for a provider agreement, a former medicaid provider, or both.

(Q) "Medicaid services" means either or both of the following:

(1) Mandatory services;

(2) Optional services that the medicaid program covers.

(R) "Nursing facility" has the same meaning as in section 5165.01 of the Revised Code.

(S) "Optional services" means the health care services and items that may be covered by the medicaid state plan or a federal medicaid waiver and for which the medicaid program receives federal financial participation.

(T) "Prescribed drug" has the same meaning as in 42 C.F.R. 440.120.

(U) "Provider agreement" means an agreement to which all of the following apply:

(1) It is between a medicaid provider and the department of medicaid;

(2) It provides for the medicaid provider to provide medicaid services to medicaid recipients;

(3) It complies with 42 C.F.R. 431.107(b).

(V) "State plan home and community-based services" means home and community-based services that, as authorized by section 1915(i) of the "Social Security Act," 42 U.S.C. 1396n(i), may be covered by the medicaid program pursuant to an amendment to the medicaid state plan.

(W) "Terminal distributor of dangerous drugs" has the same meaning as in section 4729.01 of the Revised Code.

**HISTORY:**

2013 HB 59, § 101.01, eff. Sept. 29, 2013; 2015 hb64, § 101.01, effective September 29, 2015; 2017 hb49, § 101.01, effective September 29, 2017; 2019 hb166, § 101.01, effective October 17, 2019.

**Amendment Notes**

The 2019 amendment by HB 166 deleted "proposals developed in a collaborative effort by the office of health transformation, department of medicaid, and department of mental health and addiction services to make" preceding "revisions" in (B).

The 2017 amendment by HB 49 added (B) through (D); redesignated former (B) and (C) as (E) and (F); added (G); redesignated former (D) through (Q) as (H) through (U); added (V); and redesignated former (R) as (W).

The 2015 amendment, by HB 64, added (A); and redesignated former (A) through (Q) as (B) through (R).

### § 5164.02 Rules establishing amount, duration, and scope of medicaid services; procedures for enforcement.

(A) The medicaid director shall adopt rules as necessary to implement this chapter. The rules shall be adopted in accordance with Chapter 119. of the Revised Code.

(B) The rules shall establish all of the following:

(1) The amount, duration, and scope of the medicaid services covered by the medicaid program;

(2) The medicaid payment rate for each medicaid service or, in lieu of the rate, the method by which the rate is to be determined for each medicaid service;

(3) Procedures for enforcing the rules adopted under this section that provide due process protections, including procedures for corrective action plans for, and imposing financial and administrative sanctions on, persons and government entities that violate the rules.

(C) The rules may be different for different medicaid services.

(D) The medicaid director is not required to adopt a rule establishing the medicaid payment rate for a medicaid service if the director adopts a rule establishing the method by which the rate is to be determined for the medicaid service and makes the rate available on the internet web site maintained by the department of medicaid.

**HISTORY:**

151 v H 66, § 101.01, eff. 6-30-05; 2013 HB 59, § 101.01, eff. Sept. 29, 2013; 2017 hb49, § 101.01, effective September 29, 2017.

**Editor's Notes**

Acts 2020, HB 197, § 14, effective March 27, 2020 provides:

"(A) As used in this section, 'Medicaid provider' has the same meaning as in section 5164.01 of the Revised Code.

"(B) During the state of emergency due to COVID-19, declared by Executive Order 2020-01D, issued on March 9, 2020, or until December 1, 2020, whichever is earlier, the Medicaid Director may do any of the following:

"(1) Classify certain Medicaid providers as COVID-19 community providers;

"(2) Direct Medicaid payments to COVID-19 community providers from previously appropriated Medicaid funds;

"(3) Request the Director of Budget and Management to designate additional funds related to the COVID-19 outbreak for Medicaid payments to COVID-19 community providers;

"(4) Make Medicaid payments to COVID-19 community providers from funds designated under division (B)(3) of this section;

"(5) Facilitate payments to COVID-19 community providers by transferring funds designated under division (B)(2) or (3) of this section to the Departments of Developmental Disabilities and Mental Health and Addiction Services via intrastate transfer vouchers.

"(C) The Medicaid Director shall specify all of the following regarding the Medicaid payments authorized by this section:

"(1) Any requirements that a COVID-19 community provider must meet;

"(2) Enhanced rates or additional services reimbursement;

"(3) Methods of payment.

"(D) Section 5162.07 of the Revised Code as it pertains to seeking federal approval for components of the Medicaid program applies to this section.

"(E) All amounts in this section are hereby appropriated."

Amendments by Act 2017, HB 49 were partially vetoed by the governor. Section is presented without the vetoed provisions.

This section was formerly codified as RC § 5111.02.

**Amendment Notes**

The 2017 amendment by HB 49 added "Subject to section 5164.021 of the Revised Code" in the first sentence of (A); in (B)(2), substituted "The medicaid payment rate" for "The payment amount" and substituted "the rate" for "the payment amount" twice; and in (D), substituted "The medicaid payment rate" for "The payment amount" and substituted "the rate" for "the payment amount" twice.

The 2013 amendment rewrote the section.

### NOTES TO DECISIONS

**Mandamus**

When a state agency's decision is discretionary and by statute not subject to appeal, an action in mandamus is the sole avenue of relief available to a party challenging the agency's decision: Ohio Acad. of Nursing Homes v. Ohio Dep't of Job & Family Servs., 2007-Ohio-2620, 114 Ohio St. 3d 14, 867 N.E.2d 400, 2007 Ohio LEXIS 1458 (Ohio 2007).



## § 5164.03 Coverage of services.

(A) The medicaid program shall cover all mandatory services.

(B) The medicaid program shall cover all of the optional services that state statutes require the medicaid program to cover.

(C) The medicaid program may cover any of the optional services to which either of the following applies:

(1) State statutes expressly permit the medicaid program to cover the optional service;

(2) State statutes do not address whether the medicaid program may cover the optional service.

(D) The medicaid program shall not cover any optional services that state statutes prohibit the medicaid program from covering.

**HISTORY:**

2013 HB 59, § 101.01, eff. Sept. 29, 2013.

## § 5164.05 Outpatient health facilities.

(A) As used in this section:

(1) "Outpatient health facility" means a facility that provides comprehensive primary health services by or under the direction of a physician at least five days per week on a forty-hour per week basis to outpatients, is operated by the board of health of a city or general health district or another public agency or by a nonprofit private agency or organization under the direction and control of a governing board that has no health-related responsibilities other than the direction and control of one or more such outpatient health facilities, and receives at least seventy-five per cent of its operating funds from public sources, except that it does not include an outpatient hospital facility or a federally qualified health center as defined in the "Social Security Act," section 1905(*l*)(2)(B), 42 U.S.C. 1396d(*l*)(2)(B).

(2) "Comprehensive primary health services" means preventive, diagnostic, therapeutic, rehabilitative, or palliative items or services that include all of the following:

(a) Services of physicians, physician assistants, and certified nurse practitioners;

(b) Diagnostic laboratory and radiological services;

(c) Preventive health services, such as children's eye and ear examinations, perinatal services, well child services, and family planning services;

(d) Arrangements for emergency medical services;

(e) Transportation services.

(3) "Certified nurse practitioner" has the same meaning as in section 4723.01 of the Revised Code.

(B) Subject to division (C) of this section, the medicaid program shall cover comprehensive primary health services provided by outpatient health facilities with valid provider agreements. The department of medicaid shall prospectively determine the medicaid payment rates for such comprehensive primary health services not less often than once each year. The rates shall not be subject to retroactive adjustment based on actual costs incurred. The rates shall not exceed the maximum fee schedule or rates of payment, limitations based on reasonable costs or customary charges, and limitations based on combined payments received for furnishing comparable services, as are applicable to outpatient hospital facilities under the medicare program. In determining an outpatient health facility's rate prospectively, the department shall take into account the historic expenses of the facility, the operating requirements and services offered by the facility, and the geographical location of the facility, shall provide incentives for the efficient and economical utilization of the facility's resources, and shall ensure that the facility does not discriminate between classes of persons for whom or by whom payment for the services is made.

(C) An outpatient health facility does not qualify for medicaid payments under this section unless it:

(1) Has health and medical care policies developed with the advice of and subject to review by an advisory committee of professional personnel, including one or more physicians, one or more dentists if dental care is provided, and one or more registered nurses;

(2) Has a medical director, a dental director, if dental care is provided, and a nursing director responsible for the execution of such policies, and has physicians, dentists, nursing, and ancillary staff appropriate to the scope of services provided;

(3) Requires that the care of every patient be under the supervision of a physician, provides for medical care in case of emergency, has in effect a written agreement with one or more hospitals and one or more other outpatient facilities, and has an established system for the referral of patients to other resources and a utilization review plan and program;

(4) Maintains clinical records on all patients;

(5) Provides nursing services and other therapeutic services in compliance with applicable laws and rules and under the supervision of a registered nurse, and has a registered nurse on duty at all times when the facility is in operation;

(6) Follows approved methods and procedures for the dispensing and administration of drugs and biologicals;

(7) Maintains the accounting and record-keeping system required under federal laws and regulations for the determination of reasonable and allowable costs.

**HISTORY:**

140 v H 291 (Eff 7-1-83); 141 v H 428 (Eff 12-23-86); 143 v H 672 (Eff 11-14-89); 143 v H 174 (Eff 4-10-91); 146 v S 143 (Eff 3-5-96); 146 v S 154 (Eff 9-10-96); 148 v H 471 (Eff 7-1-2000); 148 v H 511. Eff 4-10-2001; 2013 HB 59, § 101.01, eff. Sept. 29, 2013.

**Editor's Notes**

This section was formerly codified as RC § 5111.04.

**Amendment Notes**

The 2013 amendment substituted "the 'Social Security Act,' section 1905(l)(2)(B), 42 U.S.C." for "Sec. 1905(l) (2)(B) of the 'Social Security Act,' 103 Stat. 2264 (1989), 42 U.S.C.A." in (A)(1); rewrote (B); and, in the introductory language of (C), substituted "An outpatient health" for "A" and "medicaid payments" for "classification as an outpatient health facility".

### ATTORNEY GENERAL OPINIONS

Reimbursement for the delivery of primary health services performed by a nurse practitioner or physician's assistant, as described in R.C. 5101.512, is authorized under the Ohio Medicaid program if the particular services are lawfully provided under R.C. Chapters 4723, 4730, and 4731 and are in accordance with applicable federal law: (decided under former analogous section) 1979 Ohio Op. Att'y Gen. No. 080 (1979).

**RESEARCH REFERENCES AND PRACTICE AIDS**

**Ohio Administrative Code**

Department of job and family services, division of medical assistance —
Ambulatory health care clinic services. OAC ch. 5160.13.
Ambulatory surgery center services. OAC ch. 5160-22.
Federally qualified health center services. OAC ch. 5160:28.
Outpatient health facility services. OAC ch. 5160:29.
Outpatient hospital services: payment policies. OAC 5160-2-21.1.
Rural health clinics. OAC ch. 5160-16.
Transportation —
Ambulance, ambulette / wheelchair vehicle services. OAC ch. 5160-15.
Nonemergency transportation. OAC ch. 5160-24.

### § 5164.06 Occupational therapy services.

The medicaid program shall cover occupational therapy services provided by an occupational therapist licensed under section 4755.08 of the Revised Code. Coverage shall not be limited to services provided in a hospital or nursing facility. Any licensed occupational therapist may enter into a provider agreement with the department of medicaid to provide occupational therapy services under the medicaid program.

**HISTORY:**

152 v H 119, § 101.01, eff. 9-29-07; 2013 HB 59, § 101.01, eff. Sept. 29, 2013.

**Editor's Notes**

This section was formerly codified as RC § 5111.029.

**Amendment Notes**

The 2013 amendment, in the third sentence, deleted "medicaid" preceding "provider agreement with" and substituted "medicaid to" for "job and family services".

### § 5164.061 Medicaid coverage of chiropractic services; payments to chiropractor.

(A) As used in this section:

(1) "Prescriber" has the same meaning as in section 4729.01 of the Revised Code, but does not include a dentist, optometrist, or veterinarian.

(2) "Prior authorization requirement" means any practice in which coverage of a health care service, device, or drug is dependent upon a recipient or health care practitioner obtaining approval from the medicaid program prior to the service, device, or drug being performed, received, or prescribed, as applicable.

(B)(1) The medicaid program shall cover evaluation and management services provided by a chiropractor if the chiropractor is licensed to practice chiropractic under Chapter 4734. of the Revised Code.

(2) The medicaid director may adopt rules under section 5164.02 of the Revised Code to cover other services provided by a chiropractor under the medicaid program.

(3) With respect to the coverage described in this section, all of the following apply:

(a) A chiropractor may provide covered services in any location, including a hospital or nursing facility.

(b) The medicaid program shall not impose a prior authorization requirement on covered services.

(c) The medicaid program shall not make coverage contingent upon the medicaid recipient first receiving a referral, prescription, or treatment from a prescriber.

(C) If a service described in this section could be provided by either a chiropractor licensed under Chapter 4734. of the Revised Code or a licensed health professional other than a chiropractor, the medicaid program shall pay the chiropractor the same amount for the service that it pays the licensed health professional.

**HISTORY:**

2022 hb136, § 1, effective June 13, 2022.

### § 5164.07 Inpatient and follow-up care minimums for mother and newborn; prohibitions.

(A) The medicaid program shall include coverage of inpatient care and follow-up care for a mother and her newborn as follows:

(1) The medicaid program shall cover a minimum of forty-eight hours of inpatient care following a normal vaginal delivery and a minimum of ninety-six hours of inpatient care following a cesarean delivery. Services covered as inpatient care shall include medical, educational, and any other services that are consistent with the inpatient care recommended in the protocols and guidelines developed by national organizations that represent pediatric, obstetric, and nursing professionals.

(2) The medicaid program shall cover a physician-directed source of follow-up care or a source of follow-up care directed by an advanced practice registered nurse. Services covered as follow-up care shall include physical assessment of the mother and newborn, parent education, assistance and training in breast or bottle feeding, assessment of the home support system, performance of any medically necessary and appropriate clinical tests, and any other services that are consistent with the follow-up care recommended in the protocols and guidelines developed by national organizations that represent pediatric, obstetric, and nursing professionals. The coverage shall apply to services provided in a medical setting or through home health care visits. The coverage shall apply to a home health care visit only if the health care professional who conducts the visit is knowledgeable and experienced in maternity and newborn care.

When a decision is made in accordance with division (B) of this section to discharge a mother or newborn prior to the expiration of the applicable number of hours of inpatient care required to be covered, the coverage of follow-up care shall apply to all follow-up care that is provided within forty-eight hours after discharge. When a mother or newborn receives at least the number of hours of inpatient care required to be covered, the coverage of follow-up care shall apply to follow-up care that is determined to be medically necessary by the health care professionals responsible for discharging the mother or newborn.

(B) Any decision to shorten the length of inpatient stay to less than that specified under division (A)(1) of this section shall be made by the physician attending the mother or newborn, except that if a certified nurse-midwife is attending the mother in collaboration with a physician, the decision may be made by the certified nurse-midwife. Decisions regarding early discharge shall be made only after conferring with the mother or a person responsible for the mother or newborn. For purposes of this division, a person responsible for the mother or newborn may include a parent, guardian, or any other person with authority to make medical decisions for the mother or newborn.

(C) The department of medicaid, in administering the medicaid program, may not do either of the following:

(1) Terminate the provider agreement of a health care professional or health care facility solely for making recommendations for inpatient or follow-up care for a particular mother or newborn that are consistent with the care required to be covered by this section;

(2) Establish or offer monetary or other financial incentives for the purpose of encouraging a person to decline the inpatient or follow-up care required to be covered by this section.

(D) This section does not do any of the following:

(1) Require the medicaid program to cover inpatient or follow-up care that is not received in accordance with the program's terms pertaining to the health care professionals and facilities from which a medicaid recipient is authorized to receive health care services.

(2) Require a mother or newborn to stay in a hospital or other inpatient setting for a fixed period of time following delivery;

(3) Require a child to be delivered in a hospital or other inpatient setting;

(4) Authorize a certified nurse-midwife to practice beyond the authority to practice nurse-midwifery in accordance with Chapter 4723. of the Revised Code;

(5) Establish minimum standards of medical diagnosis, care, or treatment for inpatient or follow-up care for a mother or newborn. A deviation from the care required to be covered under this section shall not, on the basis of this section, give rise to a medical claim or derivative medical claim, as those terms are defined in section 2305.113 of the Revised Code.

**HISTORY:**

146 v S 199 (Eff 10-17-96); 148 v H 471 (Eff 7-1-2000); 149 v S 281. Eff 4-11-2003; 2013 HB 59, § 101.01, eff. Sept. 29, 2013; 2016 hb216, § 1, effective April 6, 2017.

**Editor's Notes**

The provisions of § 6 of SB 281 (149 v —) read as follows:

SECTION 6. (A) Sections 1751.67, 2117.06, 2305.11, 2305.15, 2305.234, 2317.02, 2317.54, 2323.56, 2711.21, 2711.22, 2711.23, 2711.24, 2743.02, 2743.43, 2919.16, 3923.63, 3923.64, 3929.71, and 5111.018 of the Revised Code, as amended by this act, and sections 2303.23, 2305.113, 2323.41, 2323.42, 2323.43, and 2323.55 of the Revised Code, as enacted by this act, apply to civil actions upon a medical claim, dental claim, optometric claim, or chiropractic claim in which the act or omission that constitutes the alleged basis of the claim occurs on or after the effective date of this act.

(B) As used in this section, "medical claim," "dental claim," "optometric claim," and "chiropractic claim" have the same meanings as in section 2305.113 of the Revised Code.

This section was formerly codified as RC § 5111.018.

**Amendment Notes**

The 2016 amendment by HB 216 inserted "or a source of follow-up care directed by an advanced practice registered nurse" in the first sentence of (A)(2); and inserted "certified" twice in (B) and in (D)(4).

The 2013 amendment substituted "medicaid program" for "provision of medical assistance under this chapter" in the introductory language of (A); substituted "medicaid" for "medical assistance" in the first sentence of (A)(1) and (A)(2); substituted "medicaid, in administering the medicaid" for "job and family services, in administering the medical assistance" in the introductory language of (C); in (C)(1), substituted "provider agreement" for "participation" and deleted "as a provider under the program" following "health care facility"; and, in (D)(1), substituted "medicaid program" for "medical assistance program" and "a medicaid recipient" for "an individual".



## § 5164.08 Provisions for screening mammography and cytologic screening for cervical cancer.

(A) As used in this section, "screening mammography" means a radiologic examination utilized to detect unsuspected breast cancer at an early stage in asymptomatic women and includes the x-ray examination of the breast using equipment that is dedicated specifically for mammography, including the x-ray tube, filter, compression device, screens, film, and cassettes, and that has an average radiation exposure delivery of less than one rad mid-breast. "Screening mammography" includes two views for each breast. The term also includes the professional interpretation of the film.

"Screening mammography" does not include diagnostic mammography.

(B) The medicaid program shall cover both of the following:

(1) Screening mammography to detect the presence of breast cancer in adult women;

(2) Cytologic screening for the presence of cervical cancer.

(C) The medicaid program's coverage of screening mammography pursuant to division (B)(1) of this section shall be provided in accordance with all of the following:

(1) If a woman is at least thirty-five years of age but under forty years of age, one screening mammography;

(2) If a woman is at least forty years of age but under fifty years of age, either of the following:

(a) One screening mammography every two years;

(b) If a licensed physician has determined that the woman has risk factors to breast cancer, one screening mammography every year.

(3) If a woman is at least fifty years of age but under sixty-five years of age, one screening mammography every year.

(D) The medicaid program's coverage of screening mammographies pursuant to division (B)(1) of this section shall be provided only for screening mammographies that are performed in a facility or mobile mammography screening unit that is accredited under the American college of radiology mammography accreditation program or in a hospital as defined in section 3727.01 of the Revised Code.

(E) The medicaid program's coverage of cytologic screenings pursuant to division (B)(2) of this section shall be provided only for cytologic screenings that are processed and interpreted in a laboratory certified by the college of American pathologists or in a hospital as defined in section 3727.01 of the Revised Code.

**HISTORY:**

144 v H 142 (Eff 7-1-92); 146 v S 150. Eff 11-24-95; 2013 HB 59, § 101.01, eff. Sept. 29, 2013.

**Editor's Notes**

This section was formerly codified as RC § 5111.024.

**Amendment Notes**

The 2013 amendment rewrote the introductory language of (B); deleted "Effective July 1, 1993" from the beginning of (B)(1) and (B)(2); and substituted "medicaid program's coverage of screening mammography pursuant to" for "service provided under" in the introductory language of (C) and in (D) and (E).

**RESEARCH REFERENCES AND PRACTICE AIDS**

**Ohio Administrative Code**

Early and periodic screening, diagnosis, and treatment program. OAC ch. 5101:3-14; OAC 5160-14.

**Comparative Legislation**

Coverage for mammography and cytologic screenings:

42 USCS § 300k et seq
CA—Cal Wel & Inst Code § 14132.16
IL—20 ILCS § 2305/2
KY—KRS § 304.32-1591
MI—MCLS § 333.9501
NY—NY CLS Pub Health § 2409

## § 5164.09 Required coverage for orally administered cancer chemotherapy treatment by Medicaid program.

(A) Except as provided in division (C) of this section, the medicaid program shall cover prescribed, orally administered cancer medications on at least the same basis that it covers intraveneously administered or injected cancer medications. In implementing this section, the department of medicaid shall not institute cost-sharing requirements under section 5162.20 of the Revised Code for prescribed, orally administered cancer medications that are greater than any cost-sharing requirements instituted under that section for intraveneously administered or injected cancer medications.

(B) Division (A) of this section does not preclude the department from requiring a medicaid recipient to obtain prior authorization before a prescribed, orally administered cancer medication is dispensed to the recipient.

(C) This section shall not be implemented during a fiscal year if the medicaid director determines that this section's implementation would cause the costs of the medicaid program's coverage of prescribed drugs to increase by more than one per cent over such costs for the most recent previous fiscal year for which the amount of such costs is known.

**HISTORY:**

2014 SB 99, § 1, eff. Sept. 17, 2014.

## § 5164.091 Prior authorization requirements or other review measures for opioid analgesics for treatment of chronic pain; exceptions.

(A) As used in this section:

(1) "Benzodiazepine" has the same meaning as in section 3719.01 of the Revised Code.

(2) "Chronic pain" has the same meaning as in section 4731.052 of the Revised Code.

(3) "Hospice care program" and "hospice patient" have the same meanings as in section 3712.01 of the Revised Code.

(4) "Opioid analgesic" has the same meaning as in section 3719.01 of the Revised Code.

(5) "Prescriber" has the same meaning as in section 4729.01 of the Revised Code.

(6) "Terminal condition" means an irreversible, incurable, and untreatable condition that caused by disease, illness, or injury and will likely result in death. A terminal condition is one in which there can be no recovery, although there may be periods of remission.

(B)(1) With respect to the medicaid program's coverage of prescribed drugs, the department of medicaid shall apply prior authorization requirements or other utilization review measures as conditions of providing coverage of an opioid analgesic prescribed for the treatment of chronic pain , except when the drug is prescribed under one of the following circumstances:

(a) To an individual who is a hospice patient in a hospice care program;

(b) To an individual who has been diagnosed with a terminal condition but is not a hospice patient in a hospice care program;

(c) To an individual who has cancer or another condition associated with the individual's cancer or history of cancer.

(2) When implementing division (B)(1) of this section, the department shall consider either or both of the following, as applicable to the case in which the opioid analgesic is prescribed:

(a) If the course of treatment with the drug continues for more than ninety days, the requirements of section 4731.052 of the Revised Code;

(b) If the morphine equivalent daily dose for the drug exceeds eighty milligrams or the individual is being treated with a benzodiazepine at the time the opioid analgesic is prescribed, the guidelines established by the governor's cabinet opiate action team and presented in the document titled "Ohio Guidelines for Prescribing Opioids for the Treatment of Chronic, Non-terminal Pain 80 mg of a Morphine Equivalent Daily Dose (MED) "Trigger Point"" or a successor document, unless the guidelines are no longer in effect at the time the opioid analgesic is prescribed.

(C) If the department measures the efficiency, quality of care, or clinical performance of a prescriber, including through the use of patient satisfaction surveys, it shall not penalize the prescriber, financially or otherwise, for deciding not to prescribe an opioid analgesic.

**HISTORY:**

2016 sb319, § 1, effective April 6, 2017.

### § 5164.10 Eligibility for home and community-based services. [Renumbered]

The medicaid program may cover one or more state plan home and community-based services that the department of medicaid selects for coverage. A medicaid recipient of any age may receive a state plan home and community-based service if the recipient has countable income not exceeding two hundred twenty-five per cent of the federal poverty line, has a medical need for the service, and meets all other eligibility requirements for the service specified in rules adopted under section 5164.02 of the Revised Code. The rules may not require a medicaid recipient to undergo a level of care determination to be eligible for a state plan home and community-based service.

**HISTORY:**

2017 hb49, § 101.01, effective September 29, 2017; renumbered to § ORC Ann. 5164.16 by; 2020 hb11, § 1, effective September 18, 2020.

### § 5164.10 Tobacco cessation medication and services.

(A) The medicaid program shall cover both of the following, subject to division (C) of this section:

(1) All tobacco cessation medications approved by the United States food and drug administration;

(2) All forms of tobacco cessation services recommended by the United States preventive services task force, including individual, group, and telephone counseling and any combination thereof.

(B) The department of medicaid shall not impose any of the following conditions with respect to the coverage required by this section:

(1) Counseling requirements for tobacco cessation medications;

(2) Except as provided in division (B)(4) of this section, limits on the duration of services, including annual or lifetime limits on the number of covered attempts to quit using tobacco;

(3) Cost-sharing requirements under section 5162.20 of the Revised Code;

(4) Prior authorization requirements, step therapy protocols as defined in section 5164.7512 of the Revised Code, or any other utilization management requirements, except that prior authorization may be required for either of the following:

(a) Treatment that exceeds the duration recommended in the United States public health service clinical practice guidelines on treating tobacco use and dependence;

(b) Services associated with more than two attempts to quit using tobacco within a twelve-month period.

(C) The director of health shall adopt rules in accordance with Chapter 119. of the Revised Code that establish standards and procedures for approving the forms of tobacco cessation medications and services that must be covered under this section. The rules shall also establish standards and procedures for updating the approved forms of tobacco cessation medications and services that must be covered under this section when the approved forms are modified by the United States food and drug administration, United States public health service, or United States preventive services task force.

(D) With respect to the coverage required by this section, the department of medicaid shall do both of the following:

(1) Inform medicaid recipients about the coverage;

(2) Market the coverage to Medicaid recipients.

**HISTORY:**

2020 hb11, § 1, effective September 18, 2020.

**Editor's Notes**

Former RC § 5164.10 was renumbered as RC § 5164.16 by 2020 hb11, § 1, effective September 18, 2020.

### § 5164.14 Medicaid program may cover pharmacist's service.

The medicaid program may cover a health care service that a pharmacist provides to a medicaid recipient in accordance with Chapter 4729. of the Revised Code, including any of the following services:

(A) Managing drug therapy under a consult agreement pursuant to section 4729.39 of the Revised Code;

(B) Administering immunizations in accordance with section 4729.41 of the Revised Code;

(C) Administering drugs in accordance with section 4729.45 of the Revised Code.

**HISTORY:**

2018 sb265, § 1, effective April 5, 2019; 2020 hb203, § 1, effective December 16, 2020.

**Amendment Notes**

The 2020 amendment by HB 203 deleted "with a physician" following "consult agreement" in (A).

### § 5164.15 Mental health services to be included in state plan.

(A) As used in this section:

(1) "Community mental health services provider or facility" means a community mental health services provider or facility that has its community mental health services certified by the department of mental health and addiction services under section 5119.36 of the Revised Code or by the department of job and family services under section 5103.03 of the Revised Code.

(2) "Mental health professional" means a person qualified to work with mentally ill persons under the standards established by the director of mental health and addiction services pursuant to section 5119.36 of the Revised Code.

(B) The medicaid program may cover the following mental health services when provided by community mental health services providers or facilities:

(1) Outpatient mental health services, including, but not limited to, preventive, diagnostic, therapeutic, rehabilitative, and palliative interventions rendered to individuals in an individual or group setting by a mental health professional in accordance with a plan of treatment appropriately established, monitored, and reviewed;

(2) Partial-hospitalization mental health services rendered by persons directly supervised by a mental health professional;

(3) Unscheduled, emergency mental health services of a kind ordinarily provided to persons in crisis when rendered by persons supervised by a mental health professional;

(4) Assertive community treatment and intensive home-based mental health services.

(C) The department of medicaid shall enter into a separate contract with the department of mental health and addiction services under section 5162.35 of the Revised Code with regard to the mental health services the medicaid program covers pursuant to this section.

**HISTORY:**

139 v H 694 (Eff 11-15-81); 139 v S 530 (Eff 6-25-82); 140 v H 291 (Eff 7-1-83); 141 v H 428 (Eff 12-23-86); 143 v H 317 (Eff 10-10-89); 145 v H 152 (Eff 7-1-93); 148 v H 283 (Eff 9-29-99); 148 v H 471 (Eff 7-1-2000); 149 v H 94. Eff 9-5-2001; 150 v H 95, § 1, eff. 6-26-03; 150 v S 189, § 1, eff. 3-30-04; 151 v H 66, § 101.01, eff. 10-1-05; 152 v H 119, § 101.01, eff. 9-29-07; 2011 HB 153, § 101.01, eff. July 1, 2011; 2013 HB 59, § 101.01, eff. Sept. 29, 2013.

**Editor's Notes**

This section was formerly codified as RC § 5111.023.

This section was amended and renumbered from RC § 5111.022 by 151 v H 66, effective October 1, 2005.

**Amendment Notes**

The 2013 amendment substituted "services provider" for "agency" or variants wherever it appears in (A)(1) and the introductory language of (B); added "under section 5103.03 of the Revised Code" to the end of (A)(1); in (A)(1) and (A)(2), inserted "and addiction services" and substituted "section 5119.36" for "section 5119.611"; substituted "medicaid program may cover" for "state medicaid plan may include provision of" in the introductory language of (B); deleted "Subject to receipt of federal approval" from the beginning of (B)(4); and rewrote (C), which formerly read: "The department of job and family services shall enter into a separate contract with the department of mental health under section 5111.91 of the Revised Code with regard to the component of the medicaid program provided for by this section."

The 2011 amendment, in (A)(1), inserted "agency or" both times it appears, substituted "its community mental health services" for "a quality assurance program accredited by the joint commission on accreditation of healthcare organizations or is," and substituted "under section 5119.611 of the Revised Code or by the" for "or"; in the introductory language of (B), substituted "may" for "shall" and inserted "agencies or"; deleted former (C), which read: "The comprehensive annual plan shall certify the availability of sufficient unencumbered community mental health state subsidy and local funds to match federal medicaid reimbursement funds earned by community mental health facilities"; redesignated former (D) as (C); and deleted (E) and (F), pertaining to the approval for providing assertive community treatment and intensive home-based mental health services.

152 v H 119, effective September 29, 2007, deleted "of three to fourteen hours per service day" following "health services" in (B)(2).

151 v H 66, effective October 1, 2005, in (E), substituted "2006" for "2004".

**ATTORNEY GENERAL OPINIONS**

An alcohol, drug addiction and mental health services board (ADAMH board) established pursuant to R.C. Chapter 340, or a provider with which the ADAMH board contracts, may only access Medicaid funding when authorized by statute and rule, including R.C. 5111.023, R.C. 5111.025, 14 Ohio Admin. Code Chapter 5101:3-27, and 14 Ohio Admin. Code Chapter 5101:3-30. Neither an ADAMH board nor a provider with which the board contracts may access Medicaid funding for services provided to an individual who is not eligible for Medicaid. The determination as to whether a particular individual meets all Medicaid eligibility requirements is made, in the first instance, by the county department of job and family services, except with regard to the Ohio breast and cervical cancer project, where eligibility is determined by the Ohio Department of Health or its designated local agencies or subgrantees. 2006 Ohio Op. Att'y Gen. No. 019 (2006).

**RESEARCH REFERENCES AND PRACTICE AIDS**

**Ohio Administrative Code**

Department of job and family services, division of medical assistance — Alcohol and drug addiction services. OAC ch. 5160-30.

Community mental health agency services. OAC ch. 5160-27.

Hospital services: inpatient psychiatric services, alcohol and drug abuse rehabilitation. OAC ch. 5160-2.

## § 5164.16 Eligibility for home and community-based services.

The medicaid program may cover one or more state plan home and community-based services that the department of medicaid selects for coverage. A medicaid recipient of any age may receive a state plan home and community-based service if the recipient has countable income not exceeding two hundred twenty-five per cent of the federal poverty line, has a medical need for the service, and meets all other eligibility requirements for the service specified in rules adopted under section 5164.02 of the Revised Code. The rules may not require a medicaid recipient to undergo a level of care determination to be eligible for a state plan home and community-based service.

**HISTORY:**

2017 hb49, § 101.01, effective September 29, 2017; renumbered from § ORC Ann. 5164.10 by 2020 hb11, renumbered from § ORC Ann. 5164.10 by 2020 HB 11, § 1, effective Sep 18, 2020, effective September 18, 2020.

## § 5164.17 Coverage of tobacco cessation services.

The medicaid program may cover tobacco cessation services in addition to the services that must be covered under section 5164.10 of the Revised Code or may exclude coverage of additional tobacco cessation services.

**HISTORY:**

2020 hb11, § 1, effective September 18, 2020.

## § 5164.20 Reimbursement for erectile dysfunction drugs prohibited.

The medicaid program shall not cover prescribed drugs for treatment of erectile dysfunction.

**HISTORY:**

151 v H 66, § 101.01, eff. 9-29-05; 2013 HB 59, § 101.01, eff. Sept. 29, 2013.

**Editor's Notes**

This section was formerly codified as RC § 5111.027.

**Amendment Notes**

The 2013 amendment rewrote the section, which formerly read: "If the medicaid program provides prescription drug services to medicaid recipients, the program shall not provide reimbursement for prescription drugs for treatment of erectile dysfunction."

## § 5164.25 Actions affecting services for recipient with developmental disability.

The departments of developmental disabilities and medicaid may approve, reduce, deny, or terminate a medicaid service included in the individual service plan developed for a medicaid recipient with a developmental disability who is eligible for medicaid case management services. If either department approves, reduces, denies, or terminates a service, that department shall timely notify the medicaid recipient that the recipient may appeal pursuant to section 5160.31 of the Revised Code.

**HISTORY:**

149 v H 94. Eff 6-6-2001; 151 v H 66, § 101.01, eff. 7-1-05; 153 v S 79, § 1, eff. 10-6-09; 2013 HB 59, § 101.01, eff. Sept. 29, 2013; 2016 hb158, § 1, effective October 12, 2016.

**Editor's Notes**

This section was formerly codified as RC § 5111.042.

**Amendment Notes**

The 2016 amendment by HB 158, substituted "a developmental disability" for "mental retardation or other developmental disability" in the first sentence; and made a stylistic change.

The 2013 amendment, in the first sentence, substituted "medicaid may" for "job and family services may" and inserted "medicaid" following "terminate a"; and substituted "appeal pursuant to section 5160.31" for "request a hearing under section 5101.35" in the second sentence.

153 v S 79, effective October 6, 2009, deleted "mental retardation and" preceding "developmental disabilities" throughout.

151 v H 66, effective July 1, 2005, deleted the second sentence, which read: "The departments shall consider the recommendations a county board of mental retardation and developmental disabilities makes under division (B)(1) of section 5126.055 of the Revised Code."

## § 5164.26 Dissemination of information concerning healthcheck.

The department of medicaid shall establish a combination of written and oral methods designed to provide information about healthcheck to all persons eligible for the program or their parents or guardians. The department shall ensure that its methods of providing information are effective.

Each entity that distributes or accepts applications for medicaid shall prominently display a notice that complies with the methods of providing information about healthcheck established under this section.

**HISTORY:**

145 v H 152 (Eff 7-1-93); 148 v H 471. Eff 7-1-2000; 150 v H 95, § 1, eff. 9-26-03; 152 v H 119, § 101.01, eff. 9-29-07; 2013 HB 59, § 101.01, eff. Sept. 29, 2013.

**Editor's Notes**

This section was formerly codified as RC § 5111.016.

The addition of (C) to RC § 5111.016 by Am. Sub. H.B. 95 (150 v —) was disapproved by the Governor.

**Amendment Notes**

The 2013 amendment deleted (A), which read: "As used in this section, 'healthcheck' has the same meaning as in section 3313.714 of the Revised Code"; deleted the (B) designation; in the first paragraph, substituted "medicaid shall establish" for "job and family services medicaid shall adopt rules in accordance with Chapter 119. of the Revised Code establishing" in the first sentence and deleted the last sentence, which read: "The methods shall comply with federal law and regulations"; and in the present second paragraph, deleted "county department of job and family services or other" preceding "entity that distributes," substituted "entity that distributes" for "medical assistance shall," and substituted "methods of providing information about healthcheck established under this" for "rules adopted under this division".

152 v H 119, effective September 29, 2007, rewrote (B).

### RESEARCH REFERENCES AND PRACTICE AIDS

**Ohio Administrative Code**

Early and periodic screening, diagnosis, and treatment Program (EPSDT). OAC ch. 5160-14.

## § 5164.29 Plan for single system of records; medicaid providers.

Not later than December 31, 2018, the department of medicaid shall develop and implement revisions to the system by which persons and government entities become and remain medicaid providers so that there is a single system of records for the system and the persons and government entities do not have to submit duplicate data to the state to become or remain medicaid providers for any component or aspect of a component of the medicaid program, including a component or aspect of a component administered by another state agency or political subdivision pursuant to a contract entered into under section 5162.35 of the Revised Code. The departments of aging, developmental disabilities, and mental health and addiction services shall participate in the development of the revisions and shall utilize the revised system.

**HISTORY:**

2017 hb49, § 101.01, effective September 29, 2017.

## § 5164.291 Credentialing program and committee.

The department of medicaid shall establish a credentialing program that includes a credentialing committee to review the competence, professional conduct, and quality of care provided by medicaid providers.

Any activities performed by the credentialing committee shall be considered activities of a peer review committee of a health care entity and shall be subject to sections 2305.25 to 2305.253 of the Revised Code.

The medicaid director may adopt rules under section 5164.02 of the Revised Code as necessary to implement this section. Any rules adopted shall be consistent with the requirements that apply to medicare advantage organizations under 42 C.F.R. 422.204.

**HISTORY:**

2021 hb122, § 1, effective March 23, 2022.

## § 5164.30 Requirements for provider participation.

No person or government entity may participate in the medicaid program as a medicaid provider without a valid provider agreement with the department of medicaid.

**HISTORY:**

2013 HB 59, § 101.01, eff. Sept. 29, 2013.

## § 5164.301 Claim for reimbursement; physician assistant.

(A) As used in this section, "group practice" has the same meaning as in section 4731.65 of the Revised Code.

(B) The department of medicaid shall establish a process by which a physician assistant may enter into a provider agreement.

(C)(1) Subject to division (C)(2) of this section, a claim for medicaid payment for a medicaid service provided by a physician assistant to a medicaid recipient may be submitted by the physician assistant who provided the service or the physician, group practice, clinic, or other health care facility that employs the physician assistant.

(2) A claim for medicaid payment may be submitted by the physician assistant who provided the service only if the physician assistant has a valid provider agreement. When submitting the claim, the physician assistant shall use only the medicaid provider number the department has assigned to the physician assistant.

**HISTORY:**

2011 HB 153, § 101.01, eff. Sept. 29, 2011; 2013 HB 59, § 101.01, eff. Sept. 29, 2013.

**Editor's Notes**

This section was formerly codified as RC § 5111.053.

**Amendment Notes**

The 2013 amendment, in (B), substituted "medicaid shall" for "job and family services shall" and deleted "medicaid" preceding "provider agreement"; substituted "medicaid payment" for "reimbursement" in (C)(1) and in the first sentence of (C)(2); inserted "medicaid" preceding "service provided by" in (C)(1); and deleted (D), which read: "The director of job and family services may adopt rules under section 5111.02 of the Revised Code to implement this section."

## § 5164.31 Application fee for provider seeking to enter or renew medicaid provider agreement.

(A) For the purpose of raising funds necessary to pay the expenses of implementing the provider screening requirements of subpart E of 42 C.F.R. Part 455 and except as provided in division (B) of this section, the department of medicaid shall collect an application fee from a medicaid provider before doing any of the following:

(1) Entering into a provider agreement with a medicaid provider that seeks initial enrollment as a provider;

(2) Entering into a provider agreement with a former medicaid provider that seeks re-enrollment as a provider;

(3) Revalidating a medicaid provider's continued enrollment as a provider.

(B) The department is not to collect an application fee from a medicaid provider that is exempt from paying the fee under 42 C.F.R. 455.460(a).

(C) The application fees shall be deposited into the health care/medicaid support and recoveries fund created under section 5162.52 of the Revised Code. Application fees are nonrefundable when collected in accordance with 42 C.F.R. 455.460(a).

(D) The medicaid director shall adopt rules under section 5164.02 of the Revised Code as necessary to implement this section, including a rule establishing the amount of the application fee to be collected under this section. The amount of the application fee shall not be set at an amount that is more than necessary to pay for the expenses of implementing the provider screening requirements.

**HISTORY:**

2011 HB 153, § 101.01, eff. Sept. 29, 2011; 2013 HB 59, § 101.01, eff. Sept. 29, 2013; 2017 hb49, § 101.01, effective September 29, 2017.

**Editor's Notes**

This section was formerly codified as RC § 5111.063.

**Amendment Notes**

The 2017 amendment by HB 49 substituted "the health care/medicaid support and recoveries fund created under section 5162.52 of the Revised Code" for "the health care services administration fund created under section 5162.54 of the Revised Code" in (C).

The 2013 amendment rewrote the section.



### § 5164.32 Time-limited provider agreements.

(A) Each medicaid provider agreement shall expire not later than five years from its effective date. If a provider agreement entered into before the effective date of this amendment does not have a time limit, the department of medicaid shall convert the agreement to a provider agreement with a time limit.

(B) The medicaid director shall adopt rules under section 5164.02 of the Revised Code as necessary to implement this section. The rules shall be consistent with subpart E of 42 C.F.R. Part 455 and include a process for revalidating medicaid providers' continued enrollments as providers. All of the following apply to the revalidation process:

(1) The department shall refuse to revalidate a provider's provider agreement when the provider fails to file a complete application for revalidation within the time and in the manner required under the revalidation process.

(2) If a provider files a complete application for revalidation within the time and in the manner required under the revalidation process, but the provider agreement expires before the department acts on the application or before the effective date of the department's decision on the application, the provider, subject to division (B)(3) of this section, may continue operating under the terms of the expired provider agreement until the effective date of the department's decision.

(3) If a provider continues operating under the terms of an expired provider agreement pursuant to division (B)(2) of this section and the department denies the provider's application for revalidation, medicaid payments shall not be made for services or items the provider provides during the period beginning on the date the provider agreement expired and ending on the effective date of a subsequent provider agreement, if any, the department enters into with the provider.

**HISTORY:**

152 v H 119, § 101.01, eff. 9-29-07; 153 v H 1, § 101.01, eff. 10-16-09; 2013 HB 59, § 101.01, eff. Sept. 29, 2013.

**Editor's Notes**

This section was formerly codified as RC § 5111.028.

**Amendment Notes**

The 2013 amendment rewrote the section.

153 v H 1, effective October 16, 2009, substituted "January 1, 2015" for "January 1, 2011" in the second paragraph of (A); substituted "seven years" for "three years" in (B)(1); added (E)(4); and made a related change.

### § 5164.33 Director's authority to exclude.

(A) The medicaid director may do the following for any reason permitted or required by federal law and when the director determines that the action is in the best interests of medicaid recipients or the state:

(1) Deny, refuse to revalidate, suspend, or terminate a provider agreement;

(2) Exclude an individual, provider of services or goods, or other entity from participation in the medicaid program.

(B) No individual, provider, or entity excluded from participation in the medicaid program under this section shall do any of the following:

(1) Own, or provide services to, any other medicaid provider or risk contractor;

(2) Arrange for, render, or order services for medicaid recipients during the period of exclusion;

(3) During the period of exclusion, receive direct payments under the medicaid program or indirect payments of medicaid funds in the form of salary, shared fees, contracts, kickbacks, or rebates from or through any other medicaid provider or risk contractor.

(C) An individual, provider, or entity excluded from participation in the medicaid program under this section may request a reconsideration of the exclusion. The director shall adopt rules under section 5164.02 of the Revised Code governing the process for requesting a reconsideration.

(D) Nothing in this section limits the applicability of section 5164.38 of the Revised Code to a medicaid provider.

**HISTORY:**

2013 HB 59, § 101.01, eff. Sept. 29, 2013.

### § 5164.34 Criminal records check as condition of becoming or continuing to be a provider or affiliated person.

(A) As used in this section:

(1) "Criminal records check" has the same meaning as in section 109.572 of the Revised Code.

(2) "Disqualifying offense" means any of the offenses listed or described in divisions (A)(3)(a) to (e) of section 109.572 of the Revised Code.

(3) "Owner" means a person who has an ownership interest in a medicaid provider in an amount designated in rules authorized by this section.

(4) "Person subject to the criminal records check requirement" means the following:

(a) A medicaid provider who is notified under division (E)(1) of this section that the provider is subject to a criminal records check;

(b) An owner or prospective owner, officer or prospective officer, or board member or prospective board member of a medicaid provider if, pursuant to division (E)(1)(a) of this section, the owner or prospective owner, officer or prospective officer, or board member or prospective board member is specified in information given to the provider under division (E)(1) of this section;

(c) An employee or prospective employee of a medicaid provider if both of the following apply:

(i) The employee or prospective employee is specified, pursuant to division (E)(1)(b) of this section, in information given to the provider under division (E)(1) of this section.

(ii) The provider is not prohibited by division (D)(3)(b) of this section from employing the employee or prospective employee.

(5) "Responsible entity" means the following:

(a) With respect to a criminal records check required under this section for a medicaid provider, the department of medicaid or the department's designee;

(b) With respect to a criminal records check required under this section for an owner or prospective owner, officer or prospective officer, board member or prospective board member, or employee or prospective employee of a medicaid provider, the provider.

(B) This section does not apply to any of the following:

(1) An individual who is subject to a criminal records check under section 3712.09, 3721.121, 5123.081, or 5123.169 of the Revised Code;

(2) An individual who is subject to a database review or criminal records check under section 173.38, 173.381, 3740.11, or 5164.342 of the Revised Code;

(3) An individual who is an applicant or independent provider, both as defined in section 5164.341 of the Revised Code.

(C) The department of medicaid may do any of the following:

(1) Require that any medicaid provider submit to a criminal records check as a condition of obtaining or maintaining a provider agreement;

(2) Require that any medicaid provider require an owner or prospective owner, officer or prospective officer, or board member or prospective board member of the provider submit to a criminal records check as a condition of being an owner, officer, or board member of the provider;

(3) Require that any medicaid provider do the following:

(a) If so required by rules authorized by this section, determine pursuant to a database review conducted under division (F)(1)(a) of this section whether any employee or prospective employee of the provider is included in a database;

(b) Unless the provider is prohibited by division (D)(3)(b) of this section from employing the employee or prospective employee, require the employee or prospective employee to submit to a criminal records check as a condition of being an employee of the provider.

(D)(1) The department or the department's designee shall deny or terminate a medicaid provider's provider agreement if the provider is a person subject to the criminal records check requirement and either of the following applies:

(a) The provider fails to obtain the criminal records check after being given the information specified in division (G)(1) of this section.

(b) Except as provided in rules authorized by this section, the provider is found by the criminal records check to have been convicted of or have pleaded guilty to a disqualifying offense, regardless of the date of the conviction or the date of entry of the guilty plea.

(2) No medicaid provider shall permit a person to be an owner, officer, or board member of the provider if the person is a person subject to the criminal records check requirement and either of the following applies:

(a) The person fails to obtain the criminal records check after being given the information specified in division (G)(1) of this section.

(b) Except as provided in rules authorized by this section, the person is found by the criminal records check to have been convicted of or have pleaded guilty to a disqualifying offense, regardless of the date of the conviction or the date of entry of the guilty plea.

(3) Except as provided in division (I) of this section, no medicaid provider shall employ a person if any of the following apply:

(a) The person has been excluded from being a medicaid provider, a medicare provider, or provider for any other federal health care program.

(b) If the person is subject to a database review conducted under division (F)(1)(a) of this section, the person is found by the database review to be included in a database and the rules authorized by this section regarding the database review prohibit the provider from employing a person included in the database.

(c) If the person is a person subject to the criminal records check requirement, either of the following applies:

(i) The person fails to obtain the criminal records check after being given the information specified in division (G)(1) of this section.

(ii) Except as provided in rules authorized by this section, the person is found by the criminal records check to have been convicted of or have pleaded guilty to a disqualifying offense, regardless of the date of the conviction or the date of entry of the guilty plea.

(E)(1) The department or the department's designee shall inform each medicaid provider whether the provider is subject to a criminal records check. For providers with valid provider agreements, the information shall be given at times designated in rules authorized by this section. For providers applying to be medicaid providers, the information shall be given at the time of initial application. When the information is given, the department or the department's designee shall specify the following:

(a) Which of the provider's owners or prospective owners, officers or prospective officers, or board members or prospective board members are subject to a criminal records check;

(b) Which of the provider's employees or prospective employees are subject to division (C)(3) of this section.

(2) At times designated in rules authorized by this section, a medicaid provider that is a person subject to the criminal records check requirement shall do the following:

(a) Inform each person specified under division (E)(1)(a) of this section that the person is required to submit to a criminal records check as a condition of being an owner, officer, or board member of the provider;

(b) Inform each person specified under division (E)(1)(b) of this section that the person is subject to division (C)(3) of this section.

(F)(1) If a medicaid provider is a person subject to the criminal records check requirement, the department or the department's designee shall require the conduct of a criminal records check by the superintendent of the bureau of criminal identification and investigation. A medicaid provider shall require the conduct of a criminal records check by the superintendent with respect to each of the persons specified under division (E)(1)(a) of this section. With respect to each employee and prospective employee specified under division (E)(1)(b) of this section, a medicaid provider shall do the following:

(a) If rules authorized by this section require the provider to conduct a database review to determine whether the employee or prospective employee is included in a database, conduct the database review in accordance with the rules;

(b) Unless the provider is prohibited by division (D)(3)(b) of this section from employing the employee or prospective employee, require the conduct of a criminal records check of the employee or prospective employee by the superintendent.

(2) If a person subject to the criminal records check requirement does not present proof of having been a resident of this state for the five-year period immediately prior to the date the criminal records check is requested or provide evidence that within that five-year period the superintendent has requested information about the person from the federal bureau of investigation in a criminal records check, the responsible entity shall require the person to request that the superintendent obtain information from the federal bureau of investigation as part of the criminal records check of the person. Even if the person presents proof of having been a resident of this state for the five-year period, the responsible entity may require that the person request that the superintendent obtain information from the federal bureau of investigation and include it in the criminal records check of the person.

(G) Criminal records checks required by this section shall be obtained as follows:

(1) The responsible entity shall provide each person subject to the criminal records check requirement information about accessing and completing the form prescribed pursuant to division (C)(1) of section 109.572 of the Revised Code and the standard impression sheet prescribed pursuant to division (C)(2) of that section.

(2) The person subject to the criminal records check requirement shall submit the required form and one complete set of the person's fingerprint impressions directly to the superintendent for purposes of conducting the criminal records check using the applicable methods prescribed by division (C) of section 109.572 of the Revised Code. The person shall pay all fees associated with obtaining the criminal records check.

(3) The superintendent shall conduct the criminal records check in accordance with section 109.572 of the Revised Code. The person subject to the criminal records check requirement shall instruct the superintendent to submit the report of the criminal records check directly to the responsible entity. If the department or the department's designee is not the responsible entity, the department or designee may require the responsible entity to submit the report to the department or designee.

(H)(1) A medicaid provider may employ conditionally a person for whom a criminal records check is required by this section prior to obtaining the results of the criminal records check if both of the following apply:

(a) The provider is not prohibited by division (D)(3)(b) of this section from employing the person.

(b) The person submits a request for the criminal records check not later than five business days after the person begins conditional employment.

(2) Except as provided in division (I) of this section, a medicaid provider that employs a person conditionally under division (H)(1) of this section shall terminate the person's employment if either of the following apply:

(a) The results of the criminal records check request are not obtained within the period ending sixty days after the date the request is made.

(b) Regardless of when the results of the criminal records check are obtained, the results indicate that the person has been convicted of or has pleaded guilty to a disqualifying offense, unless circumstances specified in rules authorized by this section exist that permit the provider to employ the person and the provider chooses to employ the person.

(I) As used in this division, "behavioral health services" means alcohol and drug addiction services, mental health services, or both.

A medicaid provider of behavioral health services may choose to employ a person who the provider would be prohibited by division (D)(3) of this section from employing or would be required by division (H)(2) of this section to terminate the person's employment if both of the following apply:

(1) The person holds a valid health professional license issued under the Revised Code granting the person authority to provide behavioral health services, holds a valid peer recovery supporter certificate issued pursuant to rules adopted by the department of mental health and addiction services, or is in the process of obtaining such a license or certificate.

(2) The provider does not submit any medicaid claims for any services the person provides.

(J) The report of a criminal records check conducted pursuant to this section is not a public record for the purposes of section 149.43 of the Revised Code and shall not be made available to any person other than the following:

(1) The person who is the subject of the criminal records check or the person's representative;

(2) The medicaid director and the staff of the department who are involved in the administration of the medicaid program;

(3) The department's designee;

(4) The medicaid provider who required the person who is the subject of the criminal records check to submit to the criminal records check;

(5) An individual receiving or deciding whether to receive, from the subject of the criminal records check, home and community-based services available under the medicaid state plan;

(6) A court, hearing officer, or other necessary individual involved in a case dealing with any of the following:

(a) The denial or termination of a provider agreement;

(b) A person's denial of employment, termination of employment, or employment or unemployment benefits;

(c) A civil or criminal action regarding the medicaid program.

(K) The medicaid director may adopt rules under section 5164.02 of the Revised Code to implement this section. If the director adopts such rules, the rules shall designate the times at which a criminal records check must be conducted under this section. The rules may do any of the following:

(1) Designate the categories of persons who are subject to a criminal records check under this section;

(2) Specify circumstances under which the department or the department's designee may continue a provider agreement or issue a provider agreement when the medicaid provider is found by a criminal records check to have been convicted of or pleaded guilty to a disqualifying offense;

(3) Specify circumstances under which a medicaid provider may permit a person to be an employee, owner, officer, or board member of the provider when the person is found by a criminal records check conducted pursuant to this section to have been convicted of or have pleaded guilty to a disqualifying offense;

(4) Specify all of the following:

(a) The circumstances under which a database review must be conducted under division (F)(1)(a) of this section to determine whether an employee or prospective employee of a medicaid provider is included in a database;

(b) The procedures for conducting the database review;

(c) The databases that are to be checked;

(d) The circumstances under which, except as provided in division (I) of this section, a medicaid provider is prohibited from employing a person who is found by the database review to be included in a database.

**HISTORY:**

152 v H 119, § 101.01, eff. 9-29-07; 152 v H 562, § 101.01, eff. 9-23-08; 153 v H 1, § 101.01, eff. 10-16-09; 2012 SB 337, § 1, eff. Sept. 28, 2012; 2012 HB 487, § 101.01, eff. Jan. 1, 2013; 2013 HB 59, § 101.01, eff. Sept. 29, 2013; 2014 HB 483, § 101.01, eff. Sept. 15, 2014; 2017 hb49, § 101.01, effective September 29, 2017; 2018 sb229, § 1, effective March 22, 2019; 2018 hb420, § 1, effective April 5, 2019; 2021 hb110, § 101.01, effective September 30, 2021.

**Editor's Notes**

This section was formerly codified as RC § 5111.032.

Acts 2013, HB 59, § 815.10 provides: "The General Assembly, applying the principle stated in division (B) of section 1.52 of the Revised Code that amendments are to be harmonized if reasonably capable of simultaneous operation, finds that the following sections, presented in this act as composites of the sections as amended by the acts indicated, are the resulting versions of the sections in effect prior to the effective date of the sections as presented in this act:

"Section 5111.032 of the Revised Code as amended by both Am. Sub. H.B. 487 and Am. Sub. S.B. 337 of the 129th General Assembly."

**Amendment Notes**

The 2021 amendment by HB 110 substituted "3740.11" for "3701.881" in (B)(2).

The 2018 amendment by SB 229 added "Except as provided in division (I) of this section" at the beginning of the introductory language of (D)(3); redesignated and rewrote former (H)(2) as the introductory language of (H)(2), (H)(2)(a), and (H)(2)(b); added (I); redesignated former (I) and (J) as (J) and (K); deleted "been found eligible for intervention in lieu of conviction for" in (K)(2); added "except as provided in division (I) of this section" in (K)(4)(d); and made a related change.

The 2017 amendment by HB 49 redesignated and revised former (B) as the introductory language of (B), (B)(1) and (B)(2); and added (B)(3).

The 2013 amendment rewrote the section.

The 2012 amendment by HB 487 rewrote the section.

The 2012 amendment by SB 337 substituted " 49 Stat. 620" for "49 State 620" in (A)(4); and inserted "2925.141" to the sections list of (G)(1).

153 v H 1, effective October 16, 2009, added the language beginning "regardless of" to the end of the introductory language of (G); rewrote (G)(1); and substituted "A violation of an existing or former municipal ordinance or law" for "An existing or former law" in (G)(2).

152 v H 562, effective September 23, 2008, corrected internal references.

The 2014 amendment by HB 483 inserted "173.381" in the sections list of (B).

### § 5164.341 Criminal records check of independent provider; ineligibility due to certain convictions.

(A) As used in this section:

"Anniversary date" means the later of the effective date of the provider agreement relating to the independent provider or sixty days after September 26, 2003.

"Applicant" means a person who has applied for a provider agreement to provide home and community-based services as an independent provider under a home and community-based medicaid waiver component administered by the department of medicaid.

"Criminal records check" has the same meaning as in section 109.572 of the Revised Code.

"Disqualifying offense" means any of the offenses listed or described in divisions (A)(3)(a) to (e) of section 109.572 of the Revised Code.

"Independent provider" means a person who has a provider agreement to provide home and community-based services as an independent provider in a home and community-based services medicaid waiver component administered by the department of medicaid.

(B) The department of medicaid or the department's designee shall deny an applicant's application for a provider agreement and shall terminate an independent provider's provider agreement if either of the following applies:

(1) After the applicant or independent provider is given the information and notification required by divisions (D)(2)(a) and (b) of this section, the applicant or independent provider fails to do either of the following:

(a) Access, complete, or forward to the superintendent of the bureau of criminal identification and investigation the form prescribed pursuant to division (C)(1) of section 109.572 of the Revised Code or the standard impression sheet prescribed pursuant to division (C)(2) of that section;

(b) Instruct the superintendent to submit the completed report of the criminal records check required by this section directly to the department or the department's designee.

(2) Except as provided in rules authorized by this section, the applicant or independent provider is found by either of the following to have been convicted of or have pleaded guilty to a disqualifying offense, regardless of the date of the conviction or the date of entry of the guilty plea:

(a) A criminal records check required by this section;

(b) In the case of an independent provider, a notice provided by the bureau of criminal identification and investigation under division (D) of section 109.5721 of the Revised Code.

(C)(1) The department or the department's designee shall inform each applicant, at the time of initial application for a provider agreement, that the applicant is required to provide a set of the applicant's fingerprint impressions and that a criminal records check is required to be conducted as a condition of the department's approving the application.

(2) Unless the department elects to receive notices about independent providers from the bureau of criminal identification and investigation pursuant to division (D) of section 109.5721 of the Revised Code, the department or the department's designee shall inform each independent provider on or before the time of the anniversary date of the provider agreement that the independent provider is required to provide a set of the independent provider's fingerprint impressions and that a criminal records check is required to be conducted.

(D)(1) The department or the department's designee shall require an applicant to complete a criminal records check prior to entering into a provider agreement with the applicant. The department or the department's designee shall require an independent provider to complete a criminal records check at least annually unless the department elects to receive notices about independent providers from the bureau of criminal identification and investigation pursuant to division (D) of section 109.5721 of the Revised Code. If an applicant or independent provider for whom a criminal records check is required by this section does not present proof of having been a resident of this state for the five-year period immediately prior to the date the criminal records check is requested or provide evidence that within that five-year period the superintendent of the bureau of criminal identification and investigation has requested information about the applicant or independent provider from the federal bureau of investigation in a criminal records check, the department or the department's designee shall request that the applicant or independent provider obtain through the superintendent a criminal records request from the federal bureau of investigation as part of the criminal records check of the applicant or independent provider. Even if an applicant or independent provider for whom a criminal records check request is required by this section presents proof of having been a resident of this state for the five-year period, the department or the department's designee may request that the applicant or independent provider obtain information through the superintendent from the federal bureau of investigation in the criminal records check.

(2) The department or the department's designee shall provide the following to each applicant and independent provider for whom a criminal records check is required by this section:

(a) Information about accessing, completing, and forwarding to the superintendent of the bureau of criminal identification and investigation the form prescribed pursuant to division (C)(1) of section 109.572 of the Revised Code and the standard impression sheet prescribed pursuant to division (C)(2) of that section;

(b) Written notification that the applicant or independent provider is to instruct the superintendent to submit the completed report of the criminal records check directly to the department or the department's designee.

(3) Each applicant and independent provider for whom a criminal records check is required by this section shall pay to the bureau of criminal identification and investigation the fee prescribed pursuant to division (C)(3) of section 109.572 of the Revised Code for the criminal records check conducted of the applicant or independent provider.

(E) Neither the report of any criminal records check conducted by the bureau of criminal identification and investigation in accordance with section 109.572 of the Revised Code and pursuant to a request made under this section nor a notice provided by the bureau under division (D) of section 109.5721 of the Revised Code is a public record for the purposes of section 149.43 of the Revised Code. Such a report or notice shall not be made available to any person other than the following:

(1) The person who is the subject of the criminal records check or the person's representative;

(2) The medicaid director and the staff of the department who are involved in the administration of the medicaid program;

(3) The department's designee;

(4) An individual receiving or deciding whether to receive home and community-based services from the person who is the subject of the criminal records check or notice from the bureau;

(5) A court, hearing officer, or other necessary individual involved in a case dealing with either of the following:

(a) A denial or termination of a provider agreement related to the criminal records check or notice from the bureau;

(b) A civil or criminal action regarding the medicaid program.

(F) The medicaid director shall adopt rules under section 5164.02 of the Revised Code to implement this section. The rules shall specify circumstances under which the department or the department's designee may either approve an applicant's application or allow an independent provider to maintain an existing provider agreement even though the applicant or independent provider is found by either of the following to have been convicted of or have pleaded guilty to a disqualifying offense:

(1) A criminal records check required by this section;

(2) In the case of an independent provider, a notice provided by the bureau of criminal identification and investigation under division (D) of section 109.5721 of the Revised Code.

**HISTORY:**

150 v H 95, § 1, eff. 9-26-03; 152 v H 119, § 101.01, eff. 9-29-07; 153 v H 1, § 101.01, eff. 10-16-09; 2012 SB 337, § 1, eff. Sept. 28, 2012; 2012 HB 487, § 101.01, eff. Jan. 1, 2013; 2013 HB 59, § 101.01, eff. Sept. 29, 2013; 2017 hb49, § 101.01, effective September 29, 2017.

**Editor's Notes**

This section was formerly codified as RC § 5111.034.

Acts 2013, HB 59, § 815.10 provides: "The General Assembly, applying the principle stated in division (B) of section 1.52 of the Revised Code that amendments are to be harmonized if reasonably capable of simultaneous operation, finds that the following sections, presented in this act as composites of the sections as amended by the acts indicated, are the resulting versions of the sections in effect prior to the effective date of the sections as presented in this act:

"Section 5111.034 of the Revised Code as amended by both Am. Sub. H.B. 487 and Am. Sub. S.B. 337 of the 129th General Assembly."

This section was amended and renumbered from RC § 5111.96 by 152 v H 119, effective September 29, 2007.

**Amendment Notes**

The 2017 amendment by HB 49 rewrote (B); deleted "Beginning on September 26, 2003" at the beginning of (C)(2); added "unless the department elects to receive notices about independent providers from the bureau of criminal identification and investigation pursuant to division (D) of section 109.5721 of the Revised Code" in (C)(2) and in the second sentence of (D)(1); redesignated and rewrote the former introductory language of (E) as the first and second sentences of the introductory paragraph of (E); added "or notice from the bureau" in (E)(4) and (E)(5)(a); and rewrote (F).

The 2013 amendment deleted "medicaid" preceding "provider agreement" in the third and last paragraphs of (A), in the introductory language of (B), in (C)(1) and (C)(2), in the first sentence of (D)(1), and in the second sentence of (F); substituted "department of medicaid" for "department of job and family services" in the third and last paragraphs of (A) and in the introductory language of (B); deleted the last paragraph of (A), which read: "'Home and community-based services medicaid waiver component' has the same meaning as in section 5111.85 of the Revised Code"; rewrote (B)(2); substituted "medicaid director" for "director of job and family services" in (E)(2) and in the first sentence of (F); substituted "receiving or deciding whether to receive" for "who receives" in (E)(4); substituted "under section 5164.02" for "in accordance with Chapter 119." in the first sentence of (F); deleted "or been found eligible for intervention in lieu of conviction for" preceding "a disqualifying" in the second sentence of (F); and made a related change.

The 2012 amendment by HB 487 rewrote the section.

The 2012 amendment by SB 337 inserted "2925.141" to the sections list of (D)(1).

153 v H 1, effective October 16, 2009, added the language beginning "regardless of" to the end of the introductory language of (D); rewrote (D)(1); substituted "A violation of an existing or former municipal ordinance or law" for "An existing or former law" in (G)(2); and substituted "division (D)(1) or (2)" for "division (C)(1)" in the second sentence of (G).

152 v H 119, effective September 29, 2007, rewrote the section.

### NOTES TO DECISIONS

Analysis





**Equal protection**

When an amendment to R.C. 5111.034, concerning the disqualification of Ohio Medicaid providers due to having disqualifying offenses, caused a provider to have convictions for two such offenses, requiring a termination of the provider's provider agreement with the Ohio Department of Job and Family Services, the provider's equal protection rights were not violated because (1) the statute did not create different classifications, as the provider did not show that the provider was similarly situated to providers of services referred to in R.C. 5104.01, nor (2) did the statute create a suspect classification, classify individuals in a way not rationally related to a legitimate governmental interest, or violate a fundamental right. Dukes v. Dir., 2009-Ohio-6781, 2009 Ohio App. LEXIS 5682 (Ohio Ct. App., Franklin County 2009).

**Expungement**

When an amendment to R.C. 5111.034, concerning the disqualification of Ohio Medicaid providers due to having disqualifying offenses, caused a provider to have convictions for two such offenses, requiring a termination of the provider's provider agreement with the Ohio Department of Job and Family Services, the fact that the offenses, which arose from the same event, were treated as one offense for purposes of the provider's request, under R.C. 2953.31, to seal the provider's criminal record did not require that the offenses be treated as one offense for purposes of the provider's provider agreement because § 2953.31 only applied to sealing a criminal record. Dukes v. Dir., 2009-Ohio-6781, 2009 Ohio App. LEXIS 5682 (Ohio Ct. App., Franklin County 2009).

**Retroactive application of amendment**

When an amendment to R.C. 5111.034, concerning the disqualification of Ohio Medicaid providers due to having disqualifying offenses, caused a provider to have convictions for two such offenses, requiring a termination of the provider's provider agreement with the Ohio Department of Job and Family Services, this amendment could be retroactively applied to the provider's agreement, which was entered into before the amendment became effective, because (1) the language of the statute indicated the intent of the general assembly to apply the amendment retroactively, and (2) a retroactive application did not violate Ohio Const. art. II, § 28 since the provider did not have a vested right in the agreement, so such an application did not affect a substantive right. Dukes v. Dir., 2009-Ohio-6781, 2009 Ohio App. LEXIS 5682 (Ohio Ct. App., Franklin County 2009).

## § 5164.342 Criminal records check of applicant for employment in providing home and community-based waiver services to persons with disabilities; ineligibility due to certain convictions; application to current employees.

(A) As used in this section:

"Applicant" means a person who is under final consideration for employment with a waiver agency in a full-time, part-time, or temporary position that involves providing home and community-based services.

"Community-based long-term care provider" means a provider as defined in section 173.39 of the Revised Code.

"Community-based long-term care subcontractor" means a subcontractor as defined in section 173.38 of the Revised Code.

"Criminal records check" has the same meaning as in section 109.572 of the Revised Code.

"Disqualifying offense" means any of the offenses listed or described in divisions (A)(3)(a) to (e) of section 109.572 of the Revised Code.

"Employee" means a person employed by a waiver agency in a full-time, part-time, or temporary position that involves providing home and community-based services.

"Waiver agency" means a person or government entity that provides home and community-based services under a home and community-based services medicaid waiver component administered by the department of medicaid, other than such a person or government entity that is certified under the medicare program. "Waiver agency" does not mean an independent provider as defined in section 5164.341 of the Revised Code.

(B) This section does not apply to any individual who is subject to a database review or criminal records check under section 3740.11 of the Revised Code. If a waiver agency also is a community-based long-term care provider or community-based long-term care subcontractor, the waiver agency may provide for any of its applicants and employees who are not subject to database reviews and criminal records checks under section 173.38 of the Revised Code to undergo database reviews and criminal records checks in accordance with that section rather than this section.

(C) No waiver agency shall employ an applicant or continue to employ an employee in a position that involves providing home and community-based services if any of the following apply:

(1) A review of the databases listed in division (E) of this section reveals any of the following:

(a) That the applicant or employee is included in one or more of the databases listed in divisions (E)(1) to (5) of this section;

(b) That there is in the state nurse aide registry established under section 3721.32 of the Revised Code a statement detailing findings by the director of health that the applicant or employee abused, neglected, or exploited a long-term care facility or residential care facility resident or misappropriated property of such a resident;

(c) That the applicant or employee is included in one or more of the databases, if any, specified in rules authorized by this section and the rules prohibit the waiver agency from employing an applicant or continuing to employ an employee included in such a database in a position that involves providing home and community-based services.

(2) After the applicant or employee is given the information and notification required by divisions (F)(2)(a) and (b) of this section, the applicant or employee fails to do either of the following:

(a) Access, complete, or forward to the superintendent of the bureau of criminal identification and investigation the form prescribed to division (C)(1) of section 109.572 of the Revised Code or the standard impression sheet prescribed pursuant to division (C)(2) of that section;

(b) Instruct the superintendent to submit the completed report of the criminal records check required by this section directly to the chief administrator of the waiver agency.

(3) Except as provided in rules authorized by this section, the applicant or employee is found by a criminal records check required by this section to have been convicted of or have pleaded guilty to a disqualifying offense, regardless of the date of the conviction or date of entry of the guilty plea.

(D) At the time of each applicant's initial application for employment in a position that involves providing home and community-based services, the chief administrator of a waiver agency shall inform the applicant of both of the following:

(1) That a review of the databases listed in division (E) of this section will be conducted to determine whether the waiver agency is prohibited by division (C)(1) of this section from employing the applicant in the position;

(2) That, unless the database review reveals that the applicant may not be employed in the position, a criminal records check of the applicant will be conducted and the applicant is required to provide a set of the applicant's fingerprint impressions as part of the criminal records check.

(E) As a condition of employing any applicant in a position that involves providing home and community-based services, the chief administrator of a waiver agency shall conduct a database review of the applicant in accordance with rules authorized by this section. If rules authorized by this section so require, the chief administrator of a waiver agency shall conduct a database review of an employee in accordance with the rules as a condition of continuing to employ the employee in a position that involves providing home and community-based services. A database review shall determine whether the applicant or employee is included in any of the following:

(1) The excluded parties list system that is maintained by the United States general services administration pursuant to subpart 9.4 of the federal acquisition regulation and available at the federal web site known as the system for award management;

(2) The list of excluded individuals and entities maintained by the office of inspector general in the United States department of health and human services pursuant to the "Social Security Act," sections 1128 and 1156, 42 U.S.C. 1320a-7 and 1320c-5;

(3) The registry of developmental disabilities employees established under section 5123.52 of the Revised Code;

(4) The internet-based sex offender and child-victim offender database established under division (A)(11) of section 2950.13 of the Revised Code;

(5) The internet-based database of inmates established under section 5120.66 of the Revised Code;

(6) The state nurse aide registry established under section 3721.32 of the Revised Code;

(7) Any other database, if any, specified in rules authorized by this section.

(F)(1) As a condition of employing any applicant in a position that involves providing home and community-based services, the chief administrator of a waiver agency shall require the applicant to request that the superintendent of the bureau of criminal identification and investigation conduct a criminal records check of the applicant. If rules authorized by this section so require, the chief administrator of a waiver agency shall require an employee to request that the superintendent conduct a criminal records check of the employee at times specified in the rules as a condition of continuing to employ the employee in a position that involves providing home and community-based services. However, a criminal records check is not required for an applicant or employee if the waiver agency is prohibited by division (C)(1) of this section from employing the applicant or continuing to employ the employee in a position that involves providing home and community-based services. If an applicant or employee for whom a criminal records check request is required by this section does not present proof of having been a resident of this state for the five-year period immediately prior to the date the criminal records check is requested or provide evidence that within that five-year period the superintendent has requested information about the applicant or employee from the federal bureau of investigation in a criminal records check, the chief administrator shall require the applicant or employee to request that the superintendent obtain information from the federal bureau of investigation as part of the criminal records check. Even if an applicant or employee for whom a criminal records check request is required by this section presents proof of having been a resident of this state for the five-year period, the chief administrator may require the applicant or employee to request that the superintendent include information from the federal bureau of investigation in the criminal records check.

(2) The chief administrator shall provide the following to each applicant and employee for whom a criminal records check is required by this section:

(a) Information about accessing, completing, and forwarding to the superintendent of the bureau of criminal identification and investigation the form prescribed pursuant to division (C)(1) of section 109.572 of the Revised Code and the standard impression sheet prescribed pursuant to division (C)(2) of that section;

(b) Written notification that the applicant or employee is to instruct the superintendent to submit the completed report of the criminal records check directly to the chief administrator.

(3) A waiver agency shall pay to the bureau of criminal identification and investigation the fee prescribed pursuant to division (C)(3) of section 109.572 of the Revised Code for any criminal records check required by this section. However, a waiver agency may require an applicant to pay to the bureau the fee for a criminal records check of the applicant. If the waiver agency pays the fee for an applicant, it may charge the applicant a fee not exceeding the amount the waiver agency pays to the bureau under this section if the waiver agency notifies the applicant at the time of initial application for employment of the amount of the fee and that, unless the fee is paid, the applicant will not be considered for employment.

(G)(1) A waiver agency may employ conditionally an applicant for whom a criminal records check is required by this section prior to obtaining the results of the criminal records check if both of the following apply:

(a) The waiver agency is not prohibited by division (C)(1) of this section from employing the applicant in a position that involves providing home and community-based services.

(b) The chief administrator of the waiver agency requires the applicant to request a criminal records check regarding the applicant in accordance with division (F)(1) of this section not later than five business days after the applicant begins conditional employment.

(2) A waiver agency that employs an applicant conditionally under division (G)(1) of this section shall terminate the applicant's employment if the results of the criminal records check, other than the results of any request for information from the federal bureau of investigation, are not obtained within the period ending sixty days after the date the request for the criminal records check is made. Regardless of when the results of the criminal records check are obtained, if the results indicate that the applicant has been convicted of or has pleaded guilty to a disqualifying offense, the waiver agency shall terminate the applicant's employment unless circumstances specified in rules authorized by this section exist that permit the waiver agency to employ the applicant and the waiver agency chooses to employ the applicant.

(H) The report of any criminal records check conducted pursuant to a request made under this section is not a public record for the purposes of section 149.43 of the Revised Code and shall not be made available to any person other than the following:

(1) The applicant or employee who is the subject of the criminal records check or the representative of the applicant or employee;

(2) The chief administrator of the waiver agency that requires the applicant or employee to request the criminal records check or the administrator's representative;

(3) The medicaid director and the staff of the department who are involved in the administration of the medicaid program;

(4) The director of aging or the director's designee if the waiver agency also is a community-based long-term care provider or community-based long-term care subcontractor;

(5) An individual receiving or deciding whether to receive home and community-based services from the subject of the criminal records check;

(6) A court, hearing officer, or other necessary individual involved in a case dealing with any of the following:

(a) A denial of employment of the applicant or employee;

(b) Employment or unemployment benefits of the applicant or employee;

(c) A civil or criminal action regarding the medicaid program.

(I) The medicaid director shall adopt rules under section 5164.02 of the Revised Code to implement this section.

(1) The rules may do the following:

(a) Require employees to undergo database reviews and criminal records checks under this section;

(b) If the rules require employees to undergo database reviews and criminal records checks under this section, exempt one or more classes of employees from the requirements;

(c) For the purpose of division (E)(7) of this section, specify other databases that are to be checked as part of a database review conducted under this section.

(2) The rules shall specify all of the following:

(a) The procedures for conducting a database review under this section;

(b) If the rules require employees to undergo database reviews and criminal records checks under this section, the times at which the database reviews and criminal records checks are to be conducted;

(c) If the rules specify other databases to be checked as part of a database review, the circumstances under which a waiver agency is prohibited from employing an applicant or continuing to employ an employee who is found by the database review to be included in one or more of those databases;

(d) The circumstances under which a waiver agency may employ an applicant or employee who is found by a criminal records check required by this section to have been convicted of or have pleaded guilty to a disqualifying offense.

(J) The amendments made by H.B. 487 of the 129th general assembly to this section do not preclude the department of medicaid from taking action against a person for failure to comply with former division (H) of this section as that division existed on the day preceding January 1, 2013.



**HISTORY:**

150 v H 95, § 1, eff. 9-26-03; 152 v H 119, § 101.01, eff. 9-29-07; 153 v H 1, § 101.01, eff. 10-16-09; 2012 SB 337, § 1, eff. Sept. 28, 2012; 2012 HB 487, § 101.01, eff. Jan. 1, 2013; 2013 HB 59, § 101.01, eff. Sept. 29, 2013; 2016 hb158, § 1, effective October 12, 2016; 2017 hb49, § 101.01, effective September 29, 2017; 2019 hb166, § 101.01, effective October 17, 2019; 2021 hb110, § 101.01, effective September 30, 2021.

**Editor's Notes**

This section was formerly codified as RC § 5111.033.

Acts 2013, HB 59, § 815.10 provides: "The General Assembly, applying the principle stated in division (B) of section 1.52 of the Revised Code that amendments are to be harmonized if reasonably capable of simultaneous operation, finds that the following sections, presented in this act as composites of the sections as amended by the acts indicated, are the resulting versions of the sections in effect prior to the effective date of the sections as presented in this act:

"Section 5111.033 of the Revised Code as amended by both Am. Sub. H.B. 487 and Am. Sub. S.B. 337 of the 129th General Assembly."

This section was amended and renumbered from RC § 5111.95 by 152 v H 119, effective September 29, 2007.

**Amendment Notes**

The 2021 amendment by HB 110 substituted "section 3740.11" for "section 3701.881" in the first sentence of (B).

The 2019 amendment by HB 166, in the second sentence of (B), substituted "any of its applicants and employees who are not subject to database reviews and criminal records checks under section 173.38 of the Revised Code" for "applicants and employees" and "accordance with that section" for "accordance with section 173.38 of the Revised Code."

The 2017 amendment by HB 49 substituted "employee abused, neglected, or exploited a long-term care" for "employee neglected or abused a long-term care" in (C)(1)(b).

The 2016 amendment by HB 158, substituted "developmental disabilities" for "MR/DD" in (E)(3).

The 2013 amendment rewrote (A); rewrote the second sentence of (B); substituted "authorized by" for "adopted under" in (C)(1)(c), (C)(3), and (E)(7), in the first and second sentences of the introductory language of (E), and in the second sentence of (F)(1) and (G)(2); in (C)(3), deleted "or been found eligible for intervention in lieu of conviction for" preceding "a disqualifying" and deleted "or the date the applicant or employee was found eligible for intervention in lieu of conviction" from the end; added "and available at the federal web site known as the system for award management" to the end of (E)(1); rewrote (E)(2); deleted "or has been found eligible for intervention in lieu of conviction for" preceding "a disqualifying offense" in the second sentence of (G)(2); substituted "medicaid director" for "director of job and family services" in (H)(3); substituted "provider or community-based long-term care subcontractor" for "agency" in (H)(4); added (H)(5); redesigned former (H)(5) as (H)(6); and made related changes.

The 2012 amendment by HB 487 rewrote the section.

The 2012 amendment by SB 337 inserted "2925.141" to the sections list of (C)(1)(a).

153 v H 1, effective October 16, 2009, added the language beginning "regardless of" to the end of the introductory language of (C)(1); rewrote (C)(1)(a); and substituted "A violation of an existing or former municipal ordinance or law" for "An existing or former law" in (C)(1)(b).

152 v H 119, effective September 29, 2007, rewrote the section.

### § 5164.35 Offenses by providers; penalties; termination of agreement; exclusion of individual, provider, or entity.

(A) As used in this section, "owner" means any person having at least five per cent ownership in a medicaid provider.

(B)(1) No medicaid provider shall do any of the following:

(a) By deception, obtain or attempt to obtain payments under the medicaid program to which the provider is not entitled pursuant to the provider's provider agreement, or the rules of the federal government or the medicaid director relating to the program;

(b) Willfully receive payments to which the provider is not entitled;

(c) Willfully receive payments in a greater amount than that to which the provider is entitled;

(d) Falsify any report or document required by state or federal law, rule, or provider agreement relating to medicaid payments.

(2) A medicaid provider engages in "deception" for the purpose of this section when the provider, acting with actual knowledge of the representation or information involved, acting in deliberate ignorance of the truth or falsity of the representation or information involved, or acting in reckless disregard of the truth or falsity of the representation or information involved, deceives another or causes another to be deceived by any false or misleading representation, by withholding information, by preventing another from acquiring information, or by any other conduct, act, or omission that creates, confirms, or perpetuates a false impression in another, including a false impression as to law, value, state of mind, or other objective or subjective fact. No proof of specific intent to defraud is required to show, for purposes of this section, that a medicaid provider has engaged in deception.

(C) Any medicaid provider who violates division (B) of this section shall be liable, in addition to any other penalties provided by law, for all of the following civil penalties:

(1) Payment of interest on the amount of the excess payments at the maximum interest rate allowable for real estate mortgages under section 1343.01 of the Revised Code on the date the payment was made to the provider for the period from the date upon which payment was made, to the date upon which repayment is made to the state;

(2) Payment of an amount equal to three times the amount of any excess payments;

(3) Payment of a sum of not less than five thousand dollars and not more than ten thousand dollars for each deceptive claim or falsification;

(4) All reasonable expenses which the court determines have been necessarily incurred by the state in the enforcement of this section.

(D) In addition to the civil penalties provided in division (C) of this section, the medicaid director, upon the conviction of, or the entry of a judgment in either a criminal or civil action against, a medicaid provider or its owner, officer, authorized agent, associate, manager, or employee in an action brought pursuant to section 109.85 of the Revised Code, shall terminate the provider's provider agreement and stop payment to the provider for medicaid services rendered from the date of conviction or entry of judgment. No such medicaid provider, owner, officer, authorized agent, associate, manager, or employee shall own or provide medicaid services to any other medicaid provider or risk contractor or arrange for, render, or order medicaid services for medicaid recipients, nor shall such provider, owner, officer, authorized agent, associate, manager, or employee receive direct payments under the medicaid program or indirect payments of medicaid funds in the form of salary, shared fees, contracts, kickbacks, or rebates from or through any other medicaid provider or risk contractor. The provider agreement shall not be terminated, and payment shall not be terminated, if the medicaid provider or owner can demonstrate that the provider or owner did not directly or indirectly sanction the action of its authorized agent, associate, manager, or employee that resulted in the conviction or entry of a judgment in a criminal or civil action brought pursuant to section 109.85 of the Revised Code. Nothing in this division prohibits any owner, officer, authorized agent, associate, manager, or employee of a medicaid provider from entering into a provider agreement if the person can demonstrate that the person had no knowledge of an action of the medicaid provider the person was formerly associated with that resulted in the conviction or entry of a judgment in a criminal or civil action brought pursuant to section 109.85 of the Revised Code.

Nursing facility and ICF/IID providers whose provider agreements are terminated pursuant to this section may continue to receive medicaid payments for up to thirty days after the effective date of the termination if the provider makes reasonable efforts to transfer medicaid recipients to another facility or to alternate care and if federal financial participation is provided for the payments.

(E) The attorney general on behalf of the state may commence proceedings to enforce this section in any court of competent jurisdiction; and the attorney general may settle or compromise any case brought under this section with the approval of the department of medicaid. Notwithstanding any other provision of law providing a shorter period of limitations, the attorney general may commence a proceeding to enforce this section at any time within six years after the conduct in violation of this section terminates.

(F) All moneys collected by the state pursuant to this section shall be deposited in the state treasury to the credit of the general revenue fund.

**HISTORY:**

RC § 5101.51.1, 137 v S 159 (Eff 4-24-78); RC § 5111.03, 138 v H 176 (Eff 7-1-80); 140 v H 291 (Eff 7-1-83); 141 v H 428 (Eff 12-23-86); 142 v S 196 (Eff 10-20-87); 143 v H 111 (Eff 7-1-89); 144 v H 904 (Eff 12-22-92); 145 v H 152 (Eff 7-1-93); 148 v H 471. Eff 7-1-2000; 150 v H 95, § 1, eff. 6-26-03; 152 v H 119, § 101.01, eff. 9-29-07; 2013 HB 59, § 101.01, eff. Sept. 29, 2013.

**Editor's Notes**

This section was formerly codified as RC § 5111.03.

**Amendment Notes**

The 2013 amendment rewrote the section.

152 v H 119, effective September 29, 2007, in the second paragraph of (C), deleted "for a period of up to five years" preceding "from the date" and twice deleted "during the period of termination as provided in division (C) of this section" following "medicaid recipients" and preceding "shall such provider", respectively, and substituted "division" for "chapter"; and inserted (D) and redesignated the remaining subsections accordingly.

### NOTES TO DECISIONS

**Multiple charges**

A provider who is charged with Medicaid fraud and theft by deception may properly be convicted of the latter offense where knowingly false billings are submitted and paid: State v. Brown, 99 Ohio App. 3d 604, 651 N.E.2d 470, 1994 Ohio App. LEXIS 6056 (Ohio Ct. App., Franklin County 1994).

### RESEARCH REFERENCES AND PRACTICE AIDS

**Cross-References to Related Sections**

Costs of investigation and prosecution for medicaid fraud to be paid by defendant in addition to other penalties, RC § 2913.40.

Rules for payments to health care providers, RC § 4121.44.

## § 5164.36 Creditable allegations of fraud; suspension; termination.

(A) As used in this section:

(1) "Credible allegation of fraud" has the same meaning as in 42 C.F.R. 455.2, except that for purposes of this section any reference in that regulation to the "state" or the "state medicaid agency" means the department of medicaid.

(2) "Disqualifying indictment" means an indictment of a medicaid provider or its officer, authorized agent, associate, manager, employee, or, if the provider is a noninstitutional provider, its owner, if either of the following applies:

(a) The indictment charges the person with committing an act to which both of the following apply:

(i) The act would be a felony or misdemeanor under the laws of this state or the jurisdiction within which the act occurred.

(ii) The act relates to or results from furnishing or billing for medicaid services under the medicaid program or relates to or results from performing management or administrative services relating to furnishing medicaid services under the medicaid program.

(b) If the medicaid provider is an independent provider, the indictment charges the person with committing an act that would constitute a disqualifying offense.

(3) "Disqualifying offense" means any of the offenses listed or described in divisions (A)(3)(a) to (e) of section 109.572 of the Revised Code.

(4) "Independent provider" has the same meaning as in section 5164.341 of the Revised Code.

(5) "Noninstitutional medicaid provider" means any person or entity with a provider agreement other than a hospital, nursing facility, or ICF/IID.

(6) "Owner" means any person having at least five per cent ownership in a noninstitutional medicaid provider.

(B)(1) Except as provided in division (C) of this section and in rules authorized by this section, the department of medicaid shall suspend the provider agreement held by a medicaid provider on determining either of the following:

(a) There is a credible allegation of fraud against any of the following for which an investigation is pending under the medicaid program:

(i) The medicaid provider;

(ii) The medicaid provider's owner, officer, authorized agent, associate, manager, or employee.

(b) A disqualifying indictment has been issued against any of the following:

(i) The medicaid provider;

(ii) The medicaid provider's officer, authorized agent, associate, manager, or employee;

(iii) If the medicaid provider is a noninstitutional provider, its owner.

(2) Subject to division (C) of this section, the department shall also suspend all medicaid payments to a medicaid provider for services rendered, regardless of the date that the services are rendered, when the department suspends the provider's provider agreement under this section.

(3) The suspension of a provider agreement shall continue in effect until either of the following occurs:

(a) If the suspension is the result of a credible allegation of fraud, the department or a prosecuting authority determines that there is insufficient evidence of fraud by the medicaid provider;

(b) Regardless of whether the suspension is the result of a credible allegation of fraud or a disqualifying indictment, the proceedings in any related criminal case are completed through dismissal of the indictment or through conviction, entry of a guilty plea, or finding of not guiltyor, if the department commences a process to terminate the suspended provider agreement, the termination process is concluded.

(4)(a) When a provider agreement is suspended under this section, none of the following shall take, during the period of the suspension, any of the actions specified in division (B)(4)(b) of this section:

(i) The medicaid provider;

(ii) If the suspension is the result of an action taken by an officer, authorized agent, associate, manager, or employee of the medicaid provider, that person;

(iii) If the medicaid provider is a noninstitutional provider and the suspension is the result of an action taken by the owner of the provider, the owner.

(b) The following are the actions that persons specified in division (B)(4)(a) of this section cannot take during the suspension of a provider agreement:

(i) Own services provided, or provide services, to any other medicaid provider or risk contractor;

Titles 39 — 57

(ii) Arrange for, render to, or order services to any other medicaid provider or risk contractor;

(iii) Arrange for, render to, or order services for medicaid recipients;

(iv) Receive direct payments under the medicaid program or indirect payments of medicaid funds in the form of salary, shared fees, contracts, kickbacks, or rebates from or through any other medicaid provider or risk contractor.

(C) The department shall not suspend a provider agreement or medicaid payments under division (B) of this section if the medicaid provider or, if the provider is a noninstitutional provider, the owner can demonstrate through the submission of written evidence that the provider or owner did not directly or indirectly sanction the action of its authorized agent, associate, manager, or employee that resulted in the credible allegation of fraud or disqualifying indictment.

(D) After suspending a provider agreement under division (B) of this section, the department shall send notice of the suspension to the affected medicaid provider or, if the provider is a noninstitutional provider, the owner in accordance with the following time frames:

(1) Not later than five days after the suspension, unless a law enforcement agency makes a written request to temporarily delay the notice;

(2) If a law enforcement agency makes a written request to temporarily delay the notice, not later than thirty days after the suspension occurs subject to the conditions specified in division (E) of this section.

(E) A written request for a temporary delay described in division (D)(2) of this section may be renewed in writing by a law enforcement agency not more than two times except that under no circumstances shall the notice be issued more than ninety days after the suspension occurs.

(F) The notice required by division (D) of this section shall do all of the following:

(1) State that payments are being suspended in accordance with this section and 42 C.F.R. 455.23;

(2) Set forth the general allegations related to the nature of the conduct leading to the suspension, except that it is not necessary to disclose any specific information concerning an ongoing investigation;

(3) State that the suspension continues to be in effect until either of thecircumstances specified in division (B)(3) of this section occur;

(4) Specify, if applicable, the type or types of medicaid claims or business units of the medicaid provider that are affected by the suspension;

(5) Inform the medicaid provider or owner of the opportunity to submit to the department, not later than thirty days after receiving the notice, a request for reconsideration of the suspension in accordance with division (G) of this section.

(G)(1) Pursuant to the procedure specified in division (G)(2) of this section, a medicaid provider subject to a suspension under this section or, if the provider is a noninstitutional provider, the owner may request a reconsideration of the suspension. The request shall be made not later than thirty days after receipt of a notice required by division (D) of this section. The reconsideration is not subject to an adjudication hearing pursuant to Chapter 119. of the Revised Code.

(2) In requesting a reconsideration, the medicaid provider or owner shall submit written information and documents to the department. The information and documents may pertain to any of the following issues:

(a) Whether the determination to suspend the provider agreement was based on a mistake of fact, other than the validity of an indictment in a related criminal case.

(b) If there has been an indictment in a related criminal case, whether the indictment is a disqualifying indictment.

(c) Whether the provider or owner can demonstrate that the provider or owner did not directly or indirectly sanction the action of its authorized agent, associate, manager, or employee that resulted in the suspension under this section or an indictment in a related criminal case.

(H) The department shall review the information and documents submitted in a request made under division (G) of this section for reconsideration of a suspension. After the review, the suspension may be affirmed, reversed, or modified, in whole or in part. The department shall notify the affected provider or owner of the results of the review. The review and notification of its results shall be completed not later than forty-five days after receiving the information and documents submitted in a request for reconsideration.

(I) Rules adopted under section 5164.02 of the Revised Code may specify circumstances under which the department would not suspend a provider agreement pursuant to this section.

**HISTORY:**

2011 HB 153, § 101.01, eff. Sept. 29, 2011; 2013 HB 59, § 101.01, eff. Sept. 29, 2013; 2019 hb166, § 101.01, effective October 17, 2019.

**Editor's Notes**

This section was formerly codified as RC § 5111.035.

**Amendment Notes**

The 2019 amendment by HB 166 rewrote the section.

The 2013 amendment substituted "credible" for "creditable" in (A)(1) and (C) and in the first sentence of (B)(1); substituted "medicaid" for "job and family services" in (A)(1); deleted (2), which read: " 'Provider' has the same meaning as in section 5111.032 of the Revised Code"; redesignated former (A)(3) and (B)(4) as (A)(2) and (B)(3); substituted "section 5164.37" for "section 5111.031" in present (A)(2) and in (H)(2)(b); in the first sentence of (B)(1), substituted "authorized by" for "adopted by the department of job and family services under division (J) of" and inserted "of medicaid"; inserted "medicaid" preceding "provider" in the first sentence of (B)(1), (H)(1), and (H)(2), in (B)(2)(a)(i), (C), (G)(4), and (G)(5), in the second sentence of (D), and in the introductory language of (E); deleted (B)(3), pertaining to issuing an order; rewrote present (B)(3); substituted "payment" for "reimbursement" or variants wherever it appears in (C) and (D); and rewrote (J).

## NOTES TO DECISIONS

**Appealability**

Provider was not entitled to an appeal of the suspension of his provider agreement due to a credible allegation of fraud as the language of this section did not expressly permit an appeal. Ikemefuna Nkanginieme v. Ohio Dep't of Medicaid, 2015-Ohio-656, 29 N.E.3d 281, 2015 Ohio App. LEXIS 622 (Ohio Ct. App., Franklin County 2015).

### § 5164.37 Suspension of medicaid provider's provider agreement.

(A) The department of medicaid may suspend a medicaid provider's provider agreement without prior notice if the department has evidence that the provider presents a danger of immediate and serious harm to the health, safety, or welfare of medicaid recipients. The department also shall suspend all medicaid payments to the medicaid provider for services rendered, regardless of the date that the services were rendered, when the department suspends the provider agreement under this section.

(B) If the department suspends a medicaid provider's provider agreement under this section, the department shall do both of the following:

(1) Not later than five days after suspending the provider agreement, notify the medicaid provider of the suspension;

(2) Not later than ten business days after suspending the provider agreement, notify the medicaid provider that the department intends to terminate the provider agreement.

(C) The notice that the department provides to a medicaid provider under division (B)(2) of this section shall include the allegation that the provider presents a danger of immediate and serious harm to the health, safety, or welfare of medicaid recipients. It may also include other grounds for terminating the provider agreement. Section 5164.38 of the Revised Code applies to the termination of the provider agreement.

(D) The suspension of a medicaid provider's provider agreement and medicaid payments shall cease at the earliest of the following:

(1) The department's failure to provide a notice required by division (B) of this section by the time specified in that division;

(2) The department rescinds its notice to terminate the provider agreement.

(3) The department issues an order regarding the termination of the provider agreement pursuant to an adjudication conducted in accordance with Chapter 119. of the Revised Code.

(E) This section does not limit the department's authority to suspend or terminate a provider agreement or medicaid payments to a medicaid provider under any other provision of the Revised Code.

**HISTORY:**

2019 hb166, § 101.01, effective October 17, 2019.

**Editor's Notes**

Former section 5164.37 (152 v H 119, § 101.01, eff. 9-29-07; 2011 HB 153, § 101.01, eff. June 30, 2011; 2012 HB 487, § 101.01, eff. Jan. 1, 2013; 2013 HB 59, § 101.01, eff. Sept. 29, 2013) was repealed by 2019 hb166, § 105.01, effective October 17, 2019.

### § 5164.38 Department to act by adjudication order; appeals; exceptions; withholding payment.

(A) As used in this section:

(1) "Party" has the same meaning as in division (G) of section 119.01 of the Revised Code.

(2) "Revalidate" means to approve a medicaid provider's continued enrollment as a medicaid provider in accordance with the revalidation process established in rules authorized by section 5164.32 of the Revised Code.

(B) This section does not apply to either of the following:

(1) Any action taken or decision made by the department of medicaid with respect to entering into or refusing to enter into a contract with a managed care organization pursuant to section 5167.10 of the Revised Code;

(2) Any action taken by the department under division (D)(2) of section 5124.60, division (D)(1) or (2) of section 5124.61, or sections 5165.60 to 5165.89 of the Revised Code.

(C) Except as provided in division (E) of this section and section 5164.58 of the Revised Code, the department shall do any of the following by issuing an order pursuant to an adjudication conducted in accordance with Chapter 119. of the Revised Code:

(1) Refuse to enter into a provider agreement with a medicaid provider;

(2) Refuse to revalidate a medicaid provider's provider agreement;

(3) Suspend or terminate a medicaid provider's provider agreement;

(4) Take any action based upon a final fiscal audit of a medicaid provider.

(D) Any party who is adversely affected by the issuance of an adjudication order under division (C) of this section may appeal to the court of common pleas of Franklin county in accordance with section 119.12 of the Revised Code.

(E) The department is not required to comply with division (C)(1), (2), or (3) of this section whenever any of the following occur:

(1) The terms of a provider agreement require the medicaid provider to hold a license, permit, or certificate or maintain a certification issued by an official, board, commission, department, division, bureau, or other agency of state or federal government other than the department of medicaid, and the license, permit, certificate, or certification has been denied, revoked, not renewed, suspended, or otherwise limited.

(2) The terms of a provider agreement require the medicaid provider to hold a license, permit, or certificate or maintain certification issued by an official, board, commission, department, division, bureau, or other agency of state or federal government other than the department of medicaid, and the provider has not obtained the license, permit, certificate, or certification.

(3) The medicaid provider's application for a provider agreement is denied, or the provider's provider agreement is terminated or not revalidated, because of or pursuant to any of the following:

(a) The termination, refusal to renew, or denial of a license, permit, certificate, or certification by an official, board, commission, department, division, bureau, or other agency of this state other than the department of medicaid, notwithstanding the fact that the provider may hold a license, permit, certificate, or certification from an official, board, commission, department, division, bureau, or other agency of another state;

(b) Division (D) or (E) of section 5164.35 of the Revised Code;

(c) The provider's termination, suspension, or exclusion from the medicare program or from another state's medicaid program and, in either case, the termination, suspension, or exclusion is binding on the provider's participation in the medicaid program in this state;

(d) The provider's pleading guilty to or being convicted of a criminal activity materially related to either the medicare or medicaid program;

(e) The provider or its owner, officer, authorized agent, associate, manager, or employee having been convicted of one of the offenses that caused the provider's provider agreement to be suspended pursuant to section 5164.36 of the Revised Code;

(f) The provider's failure to provide the department the national provider identifier assigned the provider by the national provider system pursuant to 45 C.F.R. 162.408.

(4) The medicaid provider's application for a provider agreement is denied, or the provider's provider agreement is terminated or suspended, as a result of action by the United States department of health and human services and that action is binding on the provider's medicaid participation.

(5) The medicaid provider's provider agreement and medicaid payments to the provider are suspended under section 5164.36 or 5164.37 of the Revised Code.

(6) The medicaid provider's application for a provider agreement is denied because the provider's application was not complete;

(7) The medicaid provider's provider agreement is converted under section 5164.32 of the Revised Code from a provider agreement that is not time-limited to a provider agreement that is time-limited.

(8) Unless the medicaid provider is a nursing facility or ICF/IID, the provider's provider agreement is not revalidated pursuant to division (B)(1) of section 5164.32 of the Revised Code.

(9) The medicaid provider's provider agreement is suspended, terminated, or not revalidated because of either of the following:

(a) Any reason authorized or required by one or more of the following: 42 C.F.R. 455.106, 455.23, 455.416, 455.434, or 455.450;

(b) The provider has not billed or otherwise submitted a medicaid claim for two years or longer.

(F) In the case of a medicaid provider described in division (E)(3)(f), (6), (7), or (9)(b) of this section, the department may take its action by sending a notice explaining the action to the provider. The notice shall be sent to the medicaid provider's address on record with the department. The notice may be sent by regular mail.

(G) The department may withhold payments for medicaid services rendered by a medicaid provider during the pendency of proceedings initiated under division (C)(1), (2), or (3) of this section. If the proceedings are initiated under division (C)(4) of this section, the department may withhold payments only to the extent that they equal amounts determined in a final fiscal audit as being due the state. This division does not apply if the department fails to comply with section 119.07 of the Revised Code, requests a continuance of the hearing, or does not issue a decision within thirty days after the hearing is completed. This division does not apply to nursing facilities and ICFs/IID.

**HISTORY:**

RC § 5101.51.4, 138 v H 204 (Eff 7-30-79); RC § 5111.06, 138 v H 176 (Eff 7-1-80); 141 v H 428 (Eff 12-23-86); 142 v S 196 (Eff 10-20-87); 143 v H 822 (Eff 12-13-90); 148 v H 471. Eff 7-1-2000; 150 v H 95, § 1, eff. 6-26-03; 151 v H 66, § 101.01, eff. 7-1-05, 10-1-05; 152 v H 119, § 101.01, eff. 9-29-07; 153 v H 1, § 101.01, eff. 10-16-09; 2011 HB 153, § 101.01, eff. Sept. 29, 2011; 2012 HB 487, § 101.01, eff. Sept. 10, 2012; 2013 HB 59, § 101.01, eff. Sept. 29, 2013; 2015 hb64, § 101.01, effective September 29, 2015; 2019 hb166, § 101.01, effective October 17, 2019.

**Editor's Notes**

This section was formerly codified as RC § 5111.06.

The amendment of RC § 5111.06 by 153 v H 1 was disapproved in part by the Governor.

**Amendment Notes**

The 2015 amendment, by HB 64, deleted (A)(1), which read: "'Adjudication' has the same meaning as in division (D) of section 119.01 of the Revised Code"; redesignated former (A)(2) and (A)(3) as (A)(1) and (A)(2); and inserted "division (D)(2) of section 5124.60, division (D)(1) or (2) of section 5124.61, or" in (B)(2).

The 2019 amendment by HB 166 rewrote (E)(5), which formerly read: "Pursuant to either section 5164.36 or 5164.37 of the Revised Code, the medicaid provider's provider agreement is suspended and payments to the provider are suspended pending indictment of the provider."

The 2013 amendment rewrote the section.

The 2012 amendment rewrote (A)(2), which formerly read: "This section does not apply to any action taken by the department of job and family services under sections 5111.16 to 5111.177 or sections 5111.35 to 5111.62 of the Revised Code."

The 2011 amendment substituted "sections 5111.061 and 5111.063" for "sections 5111.061 and 5111.062" in the introductory language of (A)(1); inserted "5111.16 to 5111.177 or sections" in (A)(2); in (D)(5), inserted "or from another state's medicaid program," inserted "in either case," and added "in this state"; in (D)(8), added "Pursuant to either section 5111.031 or 5111.035 of the Revised Code" and substituted "and payments to the provider are suspended" for "pursuant to section 5111.031 of the Revised Code"; inserted (D)(12); redesignated former (D)(12) and (D)(13) as (D)(13) and (D)(14); substituted "division (D)(13) or (14)" for "division (D)(12) or (13)" in the first sentence of the second paragraph of (D); and made a stylistic change.

153 v H 1, effective October 16, 2009, inserted "or its owner, officer, authorized agent, associate, manager, or employee" in (D)(9); deleted "and the department has determined that the provider has moved from the address on record with the department without leaving an active forwarding address with the department" from the end of (D)(12); added (D)(13); rewrote the last paragraph of (D); substituted "medicaid program" for "medical assistance program" in the first sentence of (E); and made stylistic changes.

152 v H 119, effective September 29, 2007, rewrote (D)(1); inserted (D)(2), (3), and (8) through (11) and redesignated the remaining subdivisions accordingly; and corrected internal references.

151 v H 66, effective October 1, 2005, except the amendment to (A)(1) that inserts the reference to 5111.061, effective June 30, 2005, added "and in sections 5111.061 and 5111.062 of the Revised Code" to the end of the introductory language of (A)(1); inserted "and section 5111.914 of the Revised Code" in the introductory language of (B); and added (D)(6).



## NOTES TO DECISIONS

Analysis



**Appeal**

Letter informing nursing facilities that the Ohio Department of Job and Family Services would not pay the disputed Medicaid claims did not result from an audit and could not constitute an action taken based upon a final fiscal audit. Consequently, the facilities could not appeal from the letter under R.C. 5111.06 and R.C. 119.12, and the appeal was properly dismissed for lack of jurisdiction. Clifton Care Ctr. v. Ohio Dep't of Job & Family Servs., 2013-Ohio-2742, 994 N.E.2d 879, 2013 Ohio App. LEXIS 2761 (Ohio Ct. App., Franklin County 2013).

**Notice**

Although the corporation's request for an R.C. 119.09 and 5111.06 hearing before the Ohio Department of Job and Family Services was filed well beyond the 30-day deadline that was stated in the notice, the appellate court found that it could review whether the notice satisfied due process; the notice did not satisfy due process under Ohio Const., art. I, § 16, because it did not state that the Department had to receive the request for hearing within 30 days. Bryant Health Ctr., Inc. v. Ohio Dep't of Job & Family Servs., 2004-Ohio-545, 2004 Ohio App. LEXIS 359 (Ohio Ct. App., Franklin County 2004).

**Reopening of reimbursement period**

Unless a prior agreement has been reached with a provider reserving certain claims or rights for future determination, the department cannot reopen a reimbursement period after it has been closed absent evidence of fraud: Ohio Acad. of Nursing Homes, Inc. v. Ohio Dep't of Job & Family Servs., 2002-Ohio-4721, 149 Ohio App. 3d 413, 777 N.E.2d 875, 2002 Ohio App. LEXIS 4797 (Ohio Ct. App., Franklin County 2002).

**Suspension of provider agreement**

Provider could not appeal the suspension of his Medicaid provider agreement due to a credible allegation of fraud as the action was not an adjudication order, and the R.C. 119.12 appeal right granted by R.C. 5164.38 did not attach. Ikemefuna Nkanginieme v. Ohio Dep't of Medicaid, 2015-Ohio-656, 29 N.E.3d 281, 2015 Ohio App. LEXIS 622 (Ohio Ct. App., Franklin County 2015).

Provider was not entitled to an R.C. 119.12 appeal as cases involving credible allegations of fraud were carved out of R.C. 5164.38, and suspensions of provider agreements involving credible allegations of fraud were not specifically made subject to an R.C. 119.12 appeal. Ikemefuna Nkanginieme v. Ohio Dep't of Medicaid, 2015-Ohio-656, 29 N.E.3d 281, 2015 Ohio App. LEXIS 622 (Ohio Ct. App., Franklin County 2015).

**Termination of provider agreement**

Trial court properly denied a Medicaid provider's motion to permit late filing or delayed appeal and dismissed its appeal of the termination of its Medicaid provider agreement by the Ohio Department of Medicaid (ODM) because the original notice of appeal did not invoke the jurisdiction of the trial court where it was not accepted by the clerk of court inasmuch as no appellee was identified, and although the clerk's office advised the provider of the issue three days before the deadline for the provider to timely file a notice of appeal, the provider did not seek to amend the notice of appeal until after the conclusion of the 15-day period following the mailing of ODM's order; consequently, the second/corrected notice of appeal was untimely and did not independently invoke the trial court's jurisdiction over the provider's appeal. Home Health Accessibility, LLC v. Ohio Dep't of Medicaid, 2019-Ohio-487, 2019 Ohio App. LEXIS 505 (Ohio Ct. App., Franklin County 2019).

When ODH terminates a facility's Medicaid certification, ODHS is required to terminate the facility's provider agreement. Where the termination of a provider agreement is mandated in a given situation by the Revised Code, such termination amounts to a mere ministerial act: Bayside Nursing Ctr. v. Ohio Dep't of Health, 96 Ohio App. 3d 754, 645 N.E.2d 1314, 1994 Ohio App. LEXIS 3946 (Ohio Ct. App., Franklin County 1994).

## RESEARCH REFERENCES AND PRACTICE AIDS

**Ohio Administrative Code**

Department of job and family services —
Division of hearings —
RC Chapter 119 hearings. OAC ch. 5101:6-50.
Division of medical assistance —
Availability of payment during the appeals process for denial or termination of a provider agreement. OAC 5160-3-04 et seq.
Process for provider appeals from proposed departmental actions. OAC 5160:1-57.

## § 5164.39 Final medicaid orders when hearing is not requested.

In any action taken by the department of medicaid under section 5164.38 or 5164.57 of the Revised Code or any other state statute governing the medicaid program that requires the department to give notice of an opportunity for a hearing in accordance with Chapter 119. of the Revised Code, if the department gives notice of the opportunity for a hearing but the medicaid provider or other entity subject to the notice does not request a hearing or timely request a hearing in accordance with section 119.07 of the Revised Code, the department is not required to hold a hearing. The medicaid director may proceed by issuing a final adjudication order in accordance with Chapter 119. of the Revised Code.

**HISTORY:**

151 v H 66, § 101.01, eff. 10-1-05; 2013 HB 59, § 101.01, eff. Sept. 29, 2013.

**Editor's Notes**

This section was formerly codified as RC § 5111.062.

**Amendment Notes**

The 2013 amendment, in the first sentence, substituted "medicaid under section 5164.38 or 5164.57" for "job and family services under section 5111.06 or 5111.061," substituted "state statute governing the medicaid program" for "provision of this chapter," inserted "medicaid" preceding "provider or other"; and substituted "medicaid director" for "director of job and family service" in the second sentence.

## § 5164.44 Independent provider is not an employee of the state.

(A) As used in this section:

(1) "Aide services" means all of the following:

(a) Home health aide services covered by the medicaid program as part of the home health services benefit pursuant to 42 C.F.R. 440.70(b)(2);

(b) Home care attendant services covered by a participating medicaid waiver component, as defined in section 5166.30 of the Revised Code;

(c) Any of the following covered by a home and community-based services medicaid waiver component:

(i) Personal care aide services;

(ii) Homemaker/personal care services;

(iii) Community inclusion services.

(2) "Independent provider" means an individual who personally provides aide services or nursing services under the medicaid program and is not employed by, under contract with, or affiliated with another entity that provides the services.

(3) "Nursing services" means all of the following:

(a) Nursing services covered by the medicaid program as part of the home health services benefit pursuant to 42 C.F.R. 440.70(b)(1);

(b) Private duty nursing services, as defined in 42 C.F.R. 440.80, covered by the medicaid program;

(c) Nursing services covered by a home and community-based services medicaid waiver component.

(B) Notwithstanding any provision of the Revised Code to the contrary, an independent provider is not an employee of the state, or any political subdivision of the state, for any purpose under state law due to being an independent provider or any actions taken to become or remain an independent provider.

**HISTORY:**

2015 hb56, § 1, effective March 23, 2016.

### § 5164.45 Contracts for examination, processing, and determination of medical assistance claims.

(A) The department of medicaid may contract with any person or persons as a fiscal agent for the examination, processing, and determination of medicaid claims. The contracting party may provide any of the following services, as required by the contract:

(1) Design and operate medicaid management information systems, including the provision of data processing services;

(2) Determine the amounts of payments to be made upon claims for medicaid;

(3) Prepare and furnish to the department lists and computer tapes of such claims for payment;

(4) In addition to audits which may be conducted by the department and by the auditor of state, make audits of providers and the claims of medicaid providers according to the standards set forth in the contract;

(5) Assist medicaid providers in the development of procedures relating to utilization practices, make studies of the effectiveness of such procedures and methods for their improvement, implement and enforce standards of medical policy, and assist in the application of safeguards against unnecessary utilization;

(6) Assist any institution, facility, or agency to qualify as a medicaid provider;

(7) Establish and maintain fiscal records for the medicaid program;

(8) Perform statistical and research studies;

(9) Develop and implement programs for medicaid cost containment;

(10) Perform such other duties as are necessary to carry out the medicaid program.

(B) The department may contract with any person or persons as an insuring agent for the examination, processing, and determination of medicaid claims, as provided in division (A) of this section, and for the payment of medicaid claims through an underwritten program in which the state pays the insuring agent a monthly premium and the insuring agent pays for medicaid services. The person with whom the department contracts, with respect to the awarding, provisions, and performance of such contract, shall not be subject to the provisions of Title XXXIX of the Revised Code or to regulation by the department of insurance, nor to taxation as an insurance company pursuant to section 5725.18 or 5729.03 of the Revised Code. A contract with an insuring agent shall specify the qualifications, including capital and surplus requirements, and other conditions with which the insuring agent must comply.

(C) In entering into a contract under this section, the department, in cooperation with the director of budget and management, shall determine that the contracting party is qualified to perform the required services and shall follow applicable procedures required of the department of administrative services in sections 125.07 to 125.11 of the Revised Code. A contract shall be awarded to the bidder who, with due consideration to the bidder's experience and financial capability, offers the lowest and best bid to the state for control of the costs of the medicaid program consistent with meeting the obligations under that program for fair and equitable treatment of medicaid recipients and medicaid providers. Any arrangement whereby funds are paid to an insuring or fiscal agent for administrative functions under this section shall, for the purposes of section 125.081 of the Revised Code, be deemed to be a contract or purchase by the department of administrative services; however, money to be used by an insuring agent to pay for medicaid services shall not be deemed a contract or purchase within the meaning of such section.

**HISTORY:**

RC § 5101.51.3, 138 v H 204 (Eff 7-30-79); RC § 5111.05, 138 v H 176 (Eff 7-1-80); 139 v H 694 (Eff 11-15-81); 141 v H 201 (Eff 7-1-85); 142 v S 124 (Eff 10-1-87); 148 v H 471. Eff 7-1-2000; 2013 HB 59, § 101.01, eff. Sept. 29, 2013.

**Editor's Notes**

This section was formerly codified as RC § 5111.05.

**Amendment Notes**

The 2013 amendment, in the first sentence of the introductory language of (A), substituted "department of medicaid" for "department of job and family services" and "medicaid claims" for "medical assistance claims under this chapter"; substituted "medicaid" for "medical assistance" in (A)(2), (A)(7), (A)(9), and (A)(10); substituted "medicaid providers" for "providers of medical assistance" in (A)(4) through (A)(6); in the first sentence of (B), deleted "of job and family services" following "The department," substituted "determination of medicaid" for "determination of medical assistance," and substituted "medicaid claims" for "medical assistance claims"; substituted "medicaid services" for "medical services authorized under the state's medical assistance program" in the first sentence of (B) and the last sentence of (C); and, in the second sentence of (C), substituted "medicaid program" for "medical assistance program" and "medicaid recipients and medicaid providers" for "recipients and providers of medical services".

### § 5164.46 Medicaid reimbursement electronic funds transfer mandatory; exceptions.

(A) As used in this section, "electronic claims submission process" means any of the following:

(1) Electronic interchange of data;

(2) Direct entry of data through an internet-based mechanism implemented by the department of medicaid;

(3) Any other process for the electronic submission of claims that is specified in rules adopted under section 5162.02 of the Revised Code.

(B) Not later than January 1, 2013, and except as provided in division (C) of this section, each medicaid provider shall do both of the following:

(1) Use only an electronic claims submission process to submit to the department of medicaid claims for medicaid payment for medicaid services provided to medicaid recipients;

(2) Arrange to receive medicaid payment from the department by means of electronic funds transfer.

(C) Division (B) of this section does not apply to any of the following:

(1) A nursing facility;

(2) An ICF/IID;

(3) A medicaid managed care organization;

(4) Any other medicaid provider or type of medicaid provider designated in rules adopted under section 5162.02 of the Revised Code.

(D) The department shall not process a medicaid claim submitted on or after January 1, 2013, unless the claim is submitted through an electronic claims submission process in accordance with this section.

**HISTORY:**

2011 HB 153, § 101.01, eff. Sept. 29, 2011; 2013 HB 59, § 101.01, eff. Sept. 29, 2013.

**Editor's Notes**

This section was formerly codified as RC § 5111.052.

**Amendment Notes**

The 2013 amendment rewrote the section.

### § 5164.47 Department of job and family services contract to perform services.

(A) As used in this section, "OCHSPS" means the private, not-for-profit corporation known as the Ohio children's hospital solutions for patient safety, which was formed for the purpose of improving pediatric patient care in this state, which performs functions that are included within the functions of a peer review committee as defined in section 2305.25 of the Revised Code, and which consists of all of the following members: Akron children's hospital, Cincinnati children's hospital medical center, Cleveland clinic children's hospital, Dayton children's medical center, mercy children's hospital, nationwide children's hospital, rainbow babies & children's hospital, and Toledo children's hospital.

(B) If, as authorized by section 5160.10 of the Revised Code, the medicaid director chooses to contract with a person to perform either or both of the following services, the director may contract with any qualified person, including OCHSPS, to perform the service or services on behalf of the department of medicaid:

(1) Review and analyze claims for medicaid services provided to children in accordance with all state and federal laws governing the confidentiality of patient-identifying information;

(2) Perform quality assurance and quality review functions, other than those described in division (B)(1) of this section, related to medicaid services provided to children.

The functions specified in division (B)(2) of this section may include those recommended by the best evidence for advancing child health in Ohio now (BEACON) council.

(C) If the director enters into a contract with OCHSPS for OCHSPS to perform either or both of the services described in division (B) of this section, OCHSPS shall, only for purposes of section 5160.12 of the Revised Code, be considered a public entity and the director shall seek federal financial participation for costs incurred by OCHSPS in performing the service or services.

**HISTORY:**

2011 HB 153, § 101.01, eff. Sept. 29, 2011; 2013 HB 59, § 101.01, eff. Sept. 29, 2013.

**Editor's Notes**

This section was formerly codified as RC § 5111.054.

**Amendment Notes**

The 2013 amendment deleted (A)(1), which read: " 'Federal financial participation' means the federal government's share of expenditures made by an entity in implementing the medicaid program"; deleted the (A)(2) designation; in the introductory language of (B), substituted "section 5160.10" for "section 5101.10," "medicaid director" for "department of job and family services," and "behalf of the department of medicaid" for "the department's behalf"; substituted "medicaid services provided" for "medical assistance made under this chapter" in (B)(1) and (B)(2); in (C), substituted "director" for "department" and "section 5160.12" for "section 5101.11"; and made a stylistic changes.

### § 5164.471 Department of Medicaid to make summary data available.

Not less than once each year and in accordance with all state and federal laws governing the confidentiality of patient-identifying information, the department of medicaid shall make summary data regarding perinatal services available on request to local organizations concerned with infant mortality reduction initiatives and recipients of grants administered by the division of family and community health services in the department of health.

**HISTORY:**

2016 sb332, § 1, effective April 6, 2017.

### § 5164.48 Medicaid state plan amendment or request for a federal waiver.

The medicaid director may implement a system under which medicaid payments for medicaid services are made to an organization on behalf of medicaid providers. The system may not provide for an organization to receive an amount that exceeds, in aggregate, the amount the medicaid program would have paid directly to medicaid providers if not for this section.

**HISTORY:**

2011 HB 153, § 101.01, eff. Sept. 29, 2011; 2013 HB 59, § 101.01, eff. Sept. 29, 2013.

**Editor's Notes**

This section was formerly codified as RC § 5111.051.

**Amendment Notes**

The 2013 amendment rewrote the section, which read: "The director of job and family services may submit a medicaid state plan amendment or request for a federal waiver to the United States secretary of health and human services as necessary to implement, at the director's discretion, a system under which payments for medical assistance provided under the medicaid program are made to an organization on behalf of the providers of the medical assistance. The system may not provide for an organization to receive an amount that exceeds, in aggregate, the amount the department would have paid directly to the providers if not for this section."

### § 5164.55 Final fiscal audits of providers.

The department of medicaid may conduct final fiscal audits of medicaid providers in accordance with the applicable requirements set forth in federal laws and regulations and determine any amounts the provider may owe the state. When conducting final fiscal audits, the department shall consider generally accepted auditing standards, which include the use of statistical sampling.

**HISTORY:**

2013 HB 59, § 101.01, eff. Sept. 29, 2013.

### § 5164.56 State's lien for amount owed by provider; cancellation of claim.

Under the medicaid program, any amount determined to be owed the state by a final fiscal audit conducted pursuant to section 5164.55 of the Revised Code, upon the issuance of an adjudication order pursuant to Chapter 119. of the Revised Code that contains a finding that there is a preponderance of the evidence that a medicaid provider will liquidate assets or file bankruptcy in order to prevent payment of the amount determined to be owed the state, becomes a lien upon the real and personal property of the provider. Upon failure of the provider to pay the amount to the state, the medicaid director shall file notice of the lien, for which there shall be no charge, in the office of the county recorder of the county in which it is ascertained that the provider owns real or personal property. The director shall notify the provider by mail of the lien, but absence of proof that the notice was sent does not affect the validity of the lien. The lien is not valid as against the claim of any mortgagee, pledgee, purchaser, judgment creditor, or other lienholder of record at the time the notice is filed.

If the provider acquires real or personal property after notice of the lien is filed, the lien shall not be valid as against the claim of any mortgagee, pledgee, subsequent bona fide purchaser for value, judgment creditor, or other lienholder of record to such after-acquired property unless the notice of lien is refiled after the property is acquired by the provider and before the competing lien attaches to the after-acquired property or before the conveyance to the subsequent bona fide purchaser for value.

When the amount has been paid, the provider may record with the recorder notice of the payment. For recording such notice of payment, the recorder shall charge and receive from the provider a base fee of one dollar for services and a housing trust fund fee of one dollar pursuant to section 317.36 of the Revised Code.

In the event of a distribution of the provider's assets pursuant to an order of any court under the law of this state including any receivership, assignment for benefit of creditors, adjudicated insolvency, or similar proceedings, amounts then or thereafter due the state under the medicaid program have the same priority as provided by law for the payment of taxes due the state and shall be paid out of the receivership trust fund or other such trust fund in the same manner as provided for claims for unpaid taxes due the state.

If the attorney general finds after investigation that any amount due the state under the medicaid program is uncollectable, in whole or in part, the attorney general shall recommend to the director the cancellation of all or part of the claim. The director may thereupon effect the cancellation.

**HISTORY:**

142 v S 196 (Eff 10-20-87); 143 v H 672 (Eff 11-14-89); 144 v H 904 (Eff 12-22-92); 145 v H 152 (Eff 7-1-93); 148 v H 471. Eff 7-1-2000; 150 v H 95, § 1, eff. 8-1-03; 151 v H 66, § 101.01, eff. 10-1-05; 2013 HB 59, § 101.01, eff. Sept. 29, 2013.

**Editor's Notes**

This section was formerly codified as RC § 5111.022.

This section was amended and renumbered from RC § 5111.021 by 151 v H 66, effective October 1, 2005.

**Amendment Notes**

The 2013 amendment, in the first sentence of the first paragraph, substituted "section 5164.55" for "division (D) of section 5111.021" and "a medicaid" for "the"; substituted "medicaid director" for "director of job and family services" in the second sentence of the first paragraph; substituted "the medicaid program" for "this chapter" in the fourth paragraph; and substituted "the medicaid program" for "this chapter" in the first sentence of the last paragraph.

151 v H 66, effective October 1, 2005, in the first paragraph, substituted "medicaid" for "medical assistance", and corrected internal references.

### RESEARCH REFERENCES AND PRACTICE AIDS

**Cross-References to Related Sections**

Records to be kept by county recorder, RC § 317.08.

## § 5164.57 Recovery of medicaid overpayments.

(A)(1) Except as provided in division (A)(2) of this section, the department of medicaid may recover a medicaid payment or portion of a payment made to a medicaid provider to which the provider is not entitled if the department notifies the provider of the overpayment during the five-year period immediately following the end of the state fiscal year in which the overpayment was made.

(2) In the case of a hospital medicaid provider, if the department determines as a result of a medicare or medicaid cost report settlement that the provider received an amount under the medicaid program to which the provider is not entitled, the department may recover the overpayment if the department notifies the provider of the overpayment during the later of the following:

(a) The five-year period immediately following the end of the state fiscal year in which the overpayment was made;

(b) The one-year period immediately following the date the department receives from the United States centers for medicare and medicaid services a completed, audited, medicare cost report for the provider that applies to the state fiscal year in which the overpayment was made.

(B) Among the overpayments that may be recovered under this section are the following:

(1) Payment for a medicaid service, or a day of service, not rendered;

(2) Payment for a day of service at a full per diem rate that should have been paid at a percentage of the full per diem rate;

(3) Payment for a medicaid service, or day of service, that was paid by, or partially paid by, a third party, as defined in section 5160.35 of the Revised Code, and the third party's payment or partial payment was not offset against the amount paid by the medicaid program to reduce or eliminate the amount that was paid by the medicaid program;

(4) Payment when a medicaid recipient's responsibility for payment was understated and resulted in an overpayment to the provider.

(C) The department may recover an overpayment under this section prior to or after any of the following:

(1) Adjudication of a final fiscal audit that section 5164.38 of the Revised Code requires to be conducted in accordance with Chapter 119. of the Revised Code;

(2) Adjudication of a finding under any other provision of state statutes governing the medicaid program or the rules adopted under those statutes;

(3) Expiration of the time to issue a final fiscal audit that section 5164.38 of the Revised Code requires to be conducted in accordance with Chapter 119. of the Revised Code;

(4) Expiration of the time to issue a finding under any other provision of state statutes governing the medicaid program or the rules adopted under those statutes.

(D)(1) Subject to division (D)(2) of this section, the recovery of an overpayment under this section does not preclude the department from subsequently doing the following:

(a) Issuing a final fiscal audit in accordance with Chapter 119. of the Revised Code, as required under section 5164.38 of the Revised Code;

(b) Issuing a finding under any other provision of state statutes governing the medicaid program or the rules adopted under those statutes.

(2) A final fiscal audit or finding issued subsequent to the recovery of an overpayment under this section shall be reduced by the amount of the prior recovery, as appropriate.

(E) Nothing in this section limits the department's authority to recover overpayments pursuant to any other provision of the Revised Code.

**HISTORY:**

151 v H 66, § 101.01, eff. 6-30-05; 151 v H 530, § 101.01, eff. 3-30-06; 2011 HB 153, § 101.01, eff. Sept. 29, 2011; 2013 HB 59, § 101.01, eff. Sept. 29, 2013; 2015 hb64, § 101.01, effective September 29, 2015.

**Editor's Notes**

This section was formerly codified as RC § 5111.061.

**Amendment Notes**

The 2015 amendment, by HB 64, deleted (A), which read: "As used in this section, 'adjudication' has the same meaning as in section 119.01 of the Revised Code"; redesignated former (B) through (F) as (A) through (E); and made stylistic changes.

The 2013 amendment added (A); redesignated former (A) through (E) as (B) through (F); substituted "department of medicaid" for "department of job and family services" in (B)(1); inserted "medicaid" preceding "provider" in (B)(1) and the introductory language of (B)(2); inserted "medicaid" preceding "service, or" in present (C)(1) and (C)(3); substituted "section 5160.35" for "section 5101.571" in present (C)(3); substituted "section 5164.38" for "section 5111.06" in present (D)(1), (D)(3), and (E)(1)(a); substituted "state statutes governing the medicaid program" for "this chapter" in (D)(2), (D)(4), and (E)(1)(b); and made stylistic changes.

The 2011 amendment added the exception in (A)(1); added (A)(2); and made stylistic changes.

151 v H 530, effective March 30, 2006, in (A), substituted "if the department notifies the provider of the overpayment" for "The recovery may occur at any time"; and, in the introductory language of (C), deleted "During the period specified in division (A) of this section" from the beginning.

### NOTES TO DECISIONS

**Construction**

Affirming an Ohio Department of Medicaid (ODM) order to recover alleged overpayments made to a Medicaid provider was error because ODC failed notify the provider of the alleged overpayment under R.C. 5164.57(A), which expressly conditioned ODM's authority to recover overpayments on timely provision of notice within five years and was mandatory. Clovernook Health Care Pavilion v. Ohio Dep't of Medicaid, 2021-Ohio-337, 167 N.E.3d 1057, 2021 Ohio App. LEXIS 339 (Ohio Ct. App., Franklin County 2021).

## § 5164.58 Recovery of medicaid overpayments by other state agencies.

(A) If a state agency that enters into a contract with the department of medicaid under section 5162.35 of the Revised

Code identifies that a medicaid overpayment has been made to a medicaid provider, the state agency may commence actions to recover the overpayment on behalf of the department.

(B) In recovering an overpayment pursuant to this section, a state agency shall comply with the following procedures:

(1) The state agency shall attempt to recover the overpayment by notifying the medicaid provider of the overpayment and requesting voluntary repayment. Not later than five business days after notifying the medicaid provider, the state agency shall notify the department in writing of the overpayment. The state agency may negotiate a settlement of the overpayment and notify the department of the settlement. A settlement negotiated by the state agency is not valid and shall not be implemented until the department has given its written approval of the settlement.

(2) If the state agency is unable to obtain voluntary repayment of an overpayment, the agency shall give the medicaid provider notice of an opportunity for a hearing in accordance with Chapter 119. of the Revised Code. If the medicaid provider timely requests a hearing in accordance with section 119.07 of the Revised Code, the state agency shall conduct the hearing to determine the legal and factual validity of the overpayment. On completion of the hearing, the state agency shall submit its hearing officer's report and recommendation and the complete record of proceedings, including all transcripts, to the medicaid director for final adjudication. The director may issue a final adjudication order in accordance with Chapter 119. of the Revised Code. The state agency shall pay any attorney's fees imposed under section 119.092 of the Revised Code. The department of medicaid shall pay any attorney's fees imposed under section 2335.39 of the Revised Code.

(C) In any action taken by a state agency under this section that requires the agency to give notice of an opportunity for a hearing in accordance with Chapter 119. of the Revised Code, if the agency gives notice of the opportunity for a hearing but the medicaid provider subject to the notice does not request a hearing or timely request a hearing in accordance with section 119.07 of the Revised Code, the agency is not required to hold a hearing. The agency may request that the medicaid director issue a final adjudication order in accordance with Chapter 119. of the Revised Code.

(D) This section does not preclude the department of medicaid from adjudicating a final fiscal audit under section 5164.38 of the Revised Code, recovering overpayments under section 5164.57 of the Revised Code, or making findings or taking other actions authorized by state statutes governing the medicaid program.



**HISTORY:**

151 v H 66, § 101.01, eff. 10-1-05; 2013 HB 59, § 101.01, eff. Sept. 29, 2013.

**Editor's Notes**

This section was formerly codified as RC § 5111.914.

**Amendment Notes**

The 2013 amendment deleted (A), which read: "As used in this section, 'provider' has the same meaning as in section 5111.06 of the Revised Code"; redesignated former (B) through (E) as (A) through (D); substituted "medicaid under section 5162.35" for "job and family services under section 5111.91" in present (A); added "medicaid" preceding "provider" wherever it appears in present (A) through (C); substituted "medicaid director" for "director of job and family services" in the present third sentence of (B)(2) and the present second sentence of (C); substituted "medicaid" for "job and family services" in the last sentence of present (B)(2) and in present (D); and in present (D), substituted "section 5164.38" for "section 5111.06," "section 5164.57" for "section 5111.061," and "state statutes governing the medicaid program" for "this chapter".

**NOTES TO DECISIONS**

**Overpayment**

Pursuant to the authority granted by statute, the Ohio Department of Developmental Disabilities (ODDD) was performing a government function by identifying a Medicaid overpayment to a provider and commencing an action to recover the overpayment; the provider compliance review dated September 19, 2012 and testimony from the ODDD audit chief about the same provided evidence that the caregiver had been previously informed his documentation was not in compliance with applicable administrative code provisions. Mocznianski v. Ohio Dep't of Medicaid, 2020-Ohio-165, 2020 Ohio App. LEXIS 139 (Ohio Ct. App., Franklin County 2020).

In an action to recover Medicaid overpayments, the trial court did not abuse its discretion in failing to find the hearing examiner relied on inherently unreliable evidence in admitting the e-mail exchange because the e-mail exchange itself was prompted by a request from the agency to gather information as part of an internal review, and the service coordinator dealt directly with the Medicaid provider and the client and had personal knowledge of the information at issue. Katsande v. Ohio Dep't of Medicaid, 2020-Ohio-5488, 2020 Ohio App. LEXIS 4349 (Ohio Ct. App., Franklin County 2020).

### § 5164.59 Deduction from future payments for overpayments.

The department of medicaid may deduct from medicaid payments for medicaid services rendered by a medicaid provider any amounts the provider owes the state as the result of incorrect medicaid payments the department has made to the provider.

**HISTORY:**

2013 HB 59, § 101.01, eff. Sept. 29, 2013.

### § 5164.60 Interest liability on overpayments.

Any medicaid provider who, without intent, obtains payments under the medicaid program in excess of the amount to which the provider is entitled is liable for payment of interest on the amount of the excess payments for the period from the date on which payment was made to the date on which repayment is made to the state. The interest shall be paid at the average bank prime rate in effect on the first day of the calendar quarter during which the provider receives notice of the excess payment. The department of medicaid shall determine the average bank prime rate using statistical release H.15, "selected interest rates," a weekly publication of the federal reserve board, or any successor publication. If statistical release H.15, or its successor, ceases to contain the bank prime rate information or ceases to be published, the department shall request a written statement of the average bank prime rate from the federal reserve bank of Cleveland or the federal reserve board.

**HISTORY:**

2013 HB 59, § 101.01, eff. Sept. 29, 2013.

### § 5164.61 State and federal authority to recover excess Medicaid payments.

The authority, under state and federal law, of the department of medicaid or a county department of job and family services to recover excess medicaid payments made to a medicaid provider is not limited by the availability of remedies under sections 5162.21 and 5162.23 of the Revised Code for recovering benefits paid on behalf of medicaid recipients.

**HISTORY:**

2013 HB 59, § 101.01, eff. Sept. 29, 2013.

### § 5164.70 Medicaid payment limitations.

Except as otherwise required by federal statute or regulation, no medicaid payment for any medicaid service provided by a hospital, nursing facility, or ICF/IID shall exceedthe limits established under Subpart C of 42 C.F.R. Part 447.

**HISTORY:**

RC § 5101.51, 131 v 1210 (Eff 11-5-65); 133 v H 740 (Eff 11-14-69); 135 v S 318 (Eff 1-1-74); 135 v S 174 (Eff 12-4-73); 136 v H 1 (Eff 6-13-75); 136 v H 1546 (Eff 10-7-76); 137 v S 221 (Eff 11-23-77); 138 v H 204 (Eff 7-30-79); RC § 5111.02, 138 v H 176 (Eff 7-1-80); 138 v H 964 (Eff 7-1-80); 138 v H 1237 (Eff 9-30-80); 139 v H 1 (Eff 8-5-81); 139 v H 694 (Eff 11-15-81); 139 v S 550 (Eff 11-26-82); 140 v H 100 (Eff 2-24-83); 140 v H 291 (Eff 7-1-83); 140 v H 794 (Eff 7-6-84); 141 v H 238 (Eff 7-1-85); 142 v H 171 (Eff 7-1-87); 142 v S 196 (Eff 10-20-87); 142 v H 708 (Eff 4-19-88); 143 v H 111 (Eff 7-1-89); 143 v H 672 (Eff 11-14-89); 143 v H 822 (Eff 12-13-90); 144 v H 904 (Eff 12-22-92); 145 v H 152 (Eff 7-1-93); 146 v S 154 (Eff 9-10-96); 147 v S 67 (Eff 6-4-97); 148 v H 471 (Eff 7-1-2000); 149 v S 261. Eff 6-5-2002; 150 v H 95, § 1, eff. 6-26-03; 151 v H 66, § 101.01, eff. 7-1-05, 10-1-05; 2011 HB

153, § 101.01, eff. Sept. 29, 2011; 2013 HB 59, § 101.01, eff. Sept. 29, 2013; 2017 hb49, § 101.01, effective September 29, 2017.

**Editor's Notes**

This section was formerly codified as RC § 5111.021.

This section was amended and renumbered from RC § 5111.02 by 151 v H 66, effective October 1, 2005.

**Amendment Notes**

The 2017 amendment by HB 49 rewrote the section.

The 2013 amendment rewrote the section.

The 2011 amendment, in the introductory language of (A), substituted "required" for "permitted," deleted "and at the department's discretion" following "regulation," deleted "reimbursement by" preceding "the department," substituted "shall not reimburse" for "to," substituted "assistance" for "service," and substituted "an amount that exceeds the following" for "shall not exceed"; added (A)(1); added the (A)(2) designation; and in (A)(2), added "If the provider is other than a provider described in division (A)(1) of this section" and substituted "limits" for "level."

151 v H 66, effective October 1, 2005, except the amendment striking the last sentence of (B), effective July 1, 2005, rewrote the section.

## NOTES TO DECISIONS

Analysis



**Acceptance as Medicaid patient**

Medicaid regulations require the provider of medical services to accept as full payment the amount received from Medicaid if the patient is accepted as a Medicaid patient: Sparks v. George A. Sawaya, M.D., Inc., 9 Ohio App. 3d 275, 459 N.E.2d 901, 1983 Ohio App. LEXIS 11062 (Ohio Ct. App., Franklin County 1983).

**Audits**

Because the common pleas court determined that the audit did not compare rates for the same service, the court properly reversed and remanded the repayment order: HCMC, Inc. v. Ohio Dep't of Job & Family Servs., 2008-Ohio-6223, 179 Ohio App. 3d 707, 903 N.E.2d 660, 2008 Ohio App. LEXIS 5204 (Ohio Ct. App., Franklin County 2008).

**Cost cap**

The cost cap provision in Ohio's medically fragile waiver program does not violate social security law: Ash v. Ohio Dep't of Human Servs., 126 Ohio App. 3d 211, 709 N.E.2d 1257, 1998 Ohio App. LEXIS 562 (Ohio Ct. App., Washington County 1998).

**Cutoff of funds**

There is no due process violation in not affording notice and hearing to the residents of an intermediate care facility for the mentally retarded when federal and state funds are cut off to the facility, due to failure to meet the requirements of Medicaid certification, and the state proposes to relocate or transfer the residents. (O'Bannon v. Town Court Nursing Center, 447 U.S. 773, 100 S. Ct. 2467, 65 L. Ed. 2d 506, 1980 U.S. LEXIS 17 (U.S. 1980).

**Enforcement of provider rights**

Medicaid providers may bring an injunction or declaratory judgment action pursuant to Section 1983, Title 42, U.S. Code, in order to seek enforcement of their rights under Section 1396(a)(13)(A), Title 42, U.S. Code (Wilder v. Virginia Hosp. Assn. [1990], 496 U.S. 498, 110 LEd2d 455, 110 SCt 2510, followed.): Ohio Academy of Nursing Homes v. Barry, 56 Ohio St. 3d 120, 564 N.E.2d 686, 1990 Ohio LEXIS 1735 (Ohio 1990).

Mandamus will not issue to compel the state to make timely Medicaid payments to pharmacists in the future: State ex rel. Home Care Pharmacy, Inc. v. Creasy, 67 Ohio St. 2d 342, 21 Ohio Op. 3d 215, 423 N.E.2d 482, 1981 Ohio LEXIS 588 (Ohio 1981).

**Group homes**

Where the owner of group homes for the mentally retarded, under contract with the state to provide care to such individuals and required under the contract to meet all statutory licensing and certification regulations, brings suit against the state for breach of said contract, it is proper for the trial court to admit evidence presented by the defendant concerning the substandard condition of the homes, as a means of rebutting her claim that all contractual requirements had been met: Humphrey v. State, Dep't of Mental Health & Mental Retardation, 14 Ohio App. 3d 15, 469 N.E.2d 981, 1984 Ohio App. LEXIS 11228 (Ohio Ct. App., Franklin County 1984).

**Guarantors**

A long-term care facility must comply strictly with OAC 5101:3-3-03 and 5101:3-3-08, and OAC 5101:13-1-07 to have a valid claim against a Medicaid patient's guarantor for bedhold days which are reimbursable by Medicaid but are not submitted to Medicaid by the facility: VOA Autumnwood Care Center v. Shiff, 44 Ohio Misc. 2d 39, 542 N.E.2d 1121, 1988 Ohio Misc. LEXIS 25 (Ohio Mun. Ct. 1988).

**Nursing home reimbursement**

The adoption by the General Assembly of fixed ceilings for reimbursement of nursing homes does not create a presumption that costs up to those ceilings are reasonable, but rather, the Department of Public Welfare is given the responsibility of determining what costs are reasonable within those ceilings: Worthington Nursing Home, Inc. v. Creasy, 4 Ohio App. 3d 92, 446 N.E.2d 841, 1982 Ohio App. LEXIS 10963 (Ohio Ct. App., Franklin County 1982).

**Records**

Where a provider agreement with the Ohio Department of Human Services requires the provider to maintain such records as are necessary "to fully disclose the extent of services provided," a record of invoices submitted to the department for payment may be sufficient to satisfy the above requirement, depending on the information contained therein and absent a requirement of validation or support: McBroom Eastside Ambulance Service v. Ohio Dep't of Human Services, 53 Ohio App. 3d 76, 558 N.E.2d 1039, 1988 Ohio App. LEXIS 3882 (Ohio Ct. App., Franklin County 1988), dismissed, 41 Ohio St. 3d 703, 534 N.E.2d 1203, 1989 Ohio LEXIS 514 (Ohio 1989).

**Removal of drug from list**

A decision of the director of the department of human services to remove a drug from its automatic reimbursement list under the Medicaid program is a policy decision which is immune from liability under R.C. 2743.02: Upjohn Co. v. Ohio Dep't of Human Services, 77 Ohio App. 3d 827, 603 N.E.2d 1089, 1991 Ohio App. LEXIS 5170 (Ohio Ct. App., Franklin County 1991).

**Statistical sampling**

Statistical sampling methods used to extrapolate a total disallowance figure have been consistently upheld provided there exists an opportunity to rebut the initial determination of overpayment to a provider: In re Bailey, 64 Ohio App. 3d 291, 581 N.E.2d 577, 1989 Ohio App. LEXIS 3549 (Ohio Ct. App., Franklin County 1989).

## ATTORNEY GENERAL OPINIONS

Neither federal law nor R.C. 149.43 exempts from disclosure records concerning amounts paid to individual providers by the State of Ohio in connection with the Medicaid program: 1981 Ohio Op. Att'y Gen. No. 051 (1981).

## RESEARCH REFERENCES AND PRACTICE AIDS

**Cross-References to Related Sections**

Chiropractor with valid certificate to practice considered physician in re medical aid program, RC § 4734.09.

Medicaid fraud as theft offense; definitions; elements, RC § 2913.40.

Payments to medically handicapped program by counties for expenses incurred but not paid by federal funds or medical assistance program, RC § 3701.023.

Reimbursement of counties for children services, RC § 5101.14

**Ohio Administrative Code**

Department of job and family services, division of medical assistance — General information. OAC ch. 5160-1.

Third-party liability. OAC 5160-1-08.

Reimbursement to providers; covered programs and services—

Abortions. OAC ch. 5160-17.

Alcohol and drug addiction services. OAC ch. 5160-30.

Ambulatory health care clinic services. OAC ch. 5160.13.

Ambulatory surgery center services. OAC ch. 5160-22.

Community mental health agency. OAC ch. 5160-27.

Dental program. OAC ch. 5160-5.

Early and periodic screening, diagnosis, and treatment program (EPSDT aka HEALTHCHEK). OAC ch. 5160-14; OAC 5160-38-05.

Federally qualified health center. OAC ch. 5160-28.

Home and community-based services (HCBS) waiver programs — Generally. OAC 5160-1-06.

Home care services, Ohio. OAC ch. 5160-12.
Residential facility waiver. OAC ch. 5160-43.
Waiver portion of the PASSPORT program. OAC ch. 5160-31.
Waiver VI program. OAC ch. 5160-40.
Waiver VII program. OAC ch. 5160-41.
Hospice program. OAC ch. 5160-56.
Hospital services. OAC ch. 5160-2.
Independent laboratory and X-ray services. OAC ch. 5160-11.
Long-term care facilities; nursing facilities; intermediate car facilities for individuals with developmental disabilities. OAC ch. 5160-3.
Managed care plan. OAC ch. 5160-26.
Medical supplies and equipment. OAC ch. 5160-10.
Outpatient health facility. OAC ch. 5160-29.
Pharmacy services; medicaid drug formulary. OAC ch. 5160-9.
Physician services. OAC ch. 5160-4.
Podiatric services. OAC ch. 5160-7.
Primary alternative care and treatment (PACT) program. OAC ch. 5160-20.
Rural health services. OAC ch. 5160-16.
Sterilization. OAC ch. 5160-21.
Transportation. OAC ch. 5160-15; OAC ch. 5160-24.
Vision care. OAC ch. 5160-1.
Department of job and family services, division of public assistance—
Application; verification; pre-termination review; redetermination of medicaid eligibility. OAC ch. 5160-1.
Medicaid and CFC medicaid: introduction; general provisions. OAC ch. 5160-37.



**Comparative Legislation**
State medicaid program:
CA—Cal Wel & Inst Code § 14131 et seq
IL—305 ILCS § 5/5-1
IN—Burns Ind. Code Ann. § 12-15-1-1
KY—KRS § 205.510 et seq
MI—MCLS § 400.105 et seq
NY—NY CLS Soc Serv § 363 et seq
PA—62 P.S. § 441.1 et seq

## § 5164.71 Freestanding medical laboratory charges.

Medicaid payments for freestanding medical laboratory charges shall not exceed the customary and usual fee for laboratory profiles.

**HISTORY:**
2013 HB 59, § 101.01, eff. Sept. 29, 2013.

## § 5164.72 Limits on inpatient hospital care coverage.

The number of days of inpatient hospital care for which a medicaid payment is made on behalf of a medicaid recipient to a hospital that is not paid under a diagnostic-related-group prospective payment system shall not exceed thirty days during a period beginning on the day of the recipient's admission to the hospital and ending sixty days after the termination of that hospital stay, except that the department of medicaid may make exceptions to this limitation. The limitation does not apply to children participating in the program for medically handicapped children established under section 3701.023 of the Revised Code.

**HISTORY:**
2013 HB 59, § 101.01, eff. Sept. 29, 2013.

## § 5164.721 Hospitals and free-standing birthing centers may submit claims to the department of medicaid.

A hospital or freestanding birthing center that is a medicaid provider may submit to the department of medicaid or the department's fiscal agent a medicaid claim that is both of the following:

(A) For a long-acting reversible contraceptive device that is covered by medicaid and provided to a medicaid recipient during the period after the recipient gives birth in the hospital or center and before the recipient is discharged from that location;

(B) Separate from another medicaid claim for other inpatient care the hospital or center provides to the medicaid recipient.

**HISTORY:**
2016 sb332, § 1, effective April 6, 2017.

## § 5164.73 Limits on payments to nurses.

The division of any medicaid payment between a collaborating physician or podiatrist and a clinical nurse specialist, certified nurse-midwife, or certified nurse practitioner for services performed by the nurse shall be determined and agreed on by the nurse and collaborating physician or podiatrist. In no case shall the medicaid payment exceed the medicaid payment that the physician or podiatrist would have received had the physician or podiatrist provided the entire service.

**HISTORY:**
2013 HB 59, § 101.01, eff. Sept. 29, 2013.

## § 5164.74 Graduate medical education costs.

The medicaid director shall adopt rules under section 5164.02 of the Revised Code governing the calculation and payment of, and the allocation of payments for, graduate medical education costs associated with medicaid services rendered to medicaid recipients. Subject to section 5164.741 of the Revised Code, the rules shall provide for payment of graduate medical education costs associated with medicaid services rendered to medicaid recipients, including recipients enrolled in a medicaid managed care organization, that the department of medicaid determines are allowable and reasonable.

**HISTORY:**
145 v H 152 (Eff 7-1-93); 147 v S 67 (Eff 6-4-97); 148 v H 471. Eff 7-1-2000; 151 v H 66, § 101.01, eff. 6-30-05; 2013 HB 59, § 101.01, eff. Sept. 29, 2013.

**Editor's Notes**
This section was formally codified as RC § 5111.19.
Acts 2013, HB 59, § 812.40 provides:
"The amendments to sections 5101.573 (5160.40), 5101.58 (5160.37), 5111.07 (5164.752), 5111.071 (5164.753), 5111.083 (5164.757), 5111.17 (5167.10), and 5111.19 (5164.74) of the Revised Code are subject to the referendum under Ohio Constitution, Article II, Section 1c and section 1.471 of the Revised Code, and therefore take effect on the ninety-first day after this act is filed with the Secretary of State. However:
"(A) In section 5101.573 (5160.40) of the Revised Code, the new matter inserted into division (C) takes effect January 1, 2014.
"(B) In section 5101.58 (5160.37) of the Revised Code, the insertion of division (K) takes effect January 1, 2014.
"(C)(1) In section 5111.07 (5164.752) of the Revised Code, all of the amendments take effect July 1, 2014, except for the following amendments:
"(a) The renumbering of the section;
"(b) The strike through of "job and family services" and insertion of " medicaid " in the first sentence as the section appears on the day immediately preceding the effective date of this section.
"(2) The reference to "director of job and family services" in the last sentence shall be read as if it reads the "director of medicaid" while the last sentence remains in effect.
"(D) In section 5111.071 (5164.753) of the Revised Code, the insertion in the last sentence of " and the extent to which each terminal distributor participates in the medicaid program as a provider of drugs " takes effect July 1, 2014.
"(E) In section 5111.083 (5164.757) of the Revised Code, all of the amendments take effect January 1, 2014, except for the following amendments:
"(1) The renumbering of the section;
"(2) The insertion of "medicaid" before "director" in the first sentence of division (B);
"(3) The strike through of "of job and family services".
"(F) In section 5111.17 (5167.10) of the Revised Code, the amendments to division (B)(2) take effect January 1, 2014.
"(G) In section 5111.19 (5164.74) of the Revised Code, the following amendments take effect January 1, 2014:
"(1) The insertion of ", and the allocation of payments for, " in the first paragraph;
"(2) The strike through of the second paragraph and divisions (A), (B), and (C)."

**Amendment Notes**
The 2013 amendment rewrote the section.
151 v H 66, effective June 30, 2005, rewrote the section.

### RESEARCH REFERENCES AND PRACTICE AIDS

**Ohio Administrative Code**
Medical education. OAC 5160-2-67.

### § 5164.741 Denial of payment for direct graduate medical education costs.

(A) Except as provided in division (B) of this section, the department of medicaid may deny medicaid payment to a hospital for direct graduate medical education costs associated with the delivery of medicaid services to any medicaid recipient if the hospital refuses without good cause to contract with a medicaid managed care organization that serves the area in which the hospital is located.

(B) A hospital is not subject to division (A) of this section if all of the following are the case:

(1) The hospital is located in a county in which participants in the care management system are required before January 1, 2006, to be enrolled in a medicaid managed care organization that is a health insuring corporation.

(2) The hospital has entered into a contract before January 1, 2006, with at least one health insuring corporation serving the participants specified in division (B)(1) of this section.

(3) The hospital remains under contract with at least one health insuring corporation serving participants in the care management system who are required to be enrolled in a health insuring corporation.

(C) The medicaid director shall specify in the rules adopted under section 5164.02 of the Revised Code what constitutes good cause for a hospital to refuse to contract with a medicaid managed care organization.

**HISTORY:**

151 v H 66, § 101.01, eff. 6-30-05; 2013 HB 59, § 101.01, eff. Sept. 29, 2013.

**Editor's Notes**

This section was formerly codified as RC § 5111.191.

**Amendment Notes**

The 2013 amendment, in (A), substituted "department of medicaid may deny medicaid" for "department of job and family services may deny," inserted "medicaid" preceding "services to any" and "managed care," and deleted "serves participants in the care management system established under section 5111.16 of the Revised Code who are required to be enrolled in a managed care organization and the managed care organization" following "organization that"; and in (C), substituted "medicaid director" for "director of job and family services," substituted "section 5164.02" for "section 5111.19," and inserted "medicaid" preceding "managed care".

### § 5164.75 Drug reimbursement limit.

As used in this section, "federal upper reimbursement limit" means the limit established pursuant to the "Social Security Act," section 1927(e), 42 U.S.C. 1396r-8(e).

The medicaid payment for a drug that is subject to a federal upper reimbursement limit shall not exceed, in the aggregate, the federal upper reimbursement limit for the drug.

**HISTORY:**

2011 HB 153, § 101.01, eff. Sept. 29, 2011; 2013 HB 59, § 101.01, eff. Sept. 29, 2013.

**Editor's Notes**

This section was formerly codified as RC § 5111.086.

**Amendment Notes**

The 2013 amendment, in the first paragraph, deleted "section 1927(e) of" following "established pursuant to" and substituted "section 1927(e), 42 U.S.C. 1396r-8(e)" for "104 Stat. 1388-151 (1990), 42 U.S.C. 1396r-8(e)"; and deleted the second sentence of the second paragraph, which read: "The director of job and family services shall adopt rules under section 5111.02 of the Revised Code as necessary to implement this section."

### § 5164.751 State maximum allowable cost program for medicaid drug reimbursement.

(A) As used in this section, "state maximum allowable cost" means the per unit amount the medicaid program pays a terminal distributor of dangerous drugs for a prescribed drug included in the state maximum allowable cost program established under division (B) of this section. "State maximum allowable cost" excludes dispensing fees and copayments, coinsurance, or other cost-sharing charges, if any.

(B) Subject to section 5167.123 of the Revised Code, the medicaid director shall establish a state maximum allowable cost program for purposes of managing medicaid payments to terminal distributors of dangerous drugs for prescribed drugs identified by the director pursuant to this division. The director shall do all of the following with respect to the program:

(1) Identify and create a list of prescribed drugs to be included in the program.

(2) Update the list of prescribed drugs described in division (B)(1) of this section on a weekly basis.

(3) Review the state maximum allowable cost for each prescribed drug included on the list described in division (B)(1) of this section on a weekly basis.

**HISTORY:**

151 v H 66, § 101.01, eff. 9-29-05; 151 v H 530, § 101.01, eff. 7-1-06; 2013 HB 59, § 101.01, eff. Sept. 29, 2013; 2020 sb263, § 1, effective April 12, 2021.

**Editor's Notes**

This section was formerly codified as RC § 5111.082.

This section was renumbered from RC § 5111.083 by 151 v H 530, effective July 1, 2006.

**Amendment Notes**

The 2020 amendment by SB 263 added "Subject to section 5167.123 of the Revised Code" in the first sentence of the introductory paragraph of (B).

The 2013 amendment deleted the (A)(1) designation; substituted "medicaid program pays" for "department of job and family services reimburses" in the first sentence of (A); substituted "prescribed" for "prescription" in the first sentence of (A) and (B) and in (B)(1) and (B)(2); deleted (A)(2), which read: " 'Terminal distributor of dangerous drugs' has the same meaning as in section 4729.01 of the Revised Code"; in the first sentence of (B), substituted "medicaid director" for "director of job and family services" and "medicaid payments" for "reimbursement"; deleted (C), which read: "The director may adopt rules in accordance with Chapter 119. of the Revised Code to implement this section"; made a related change.



### § 5164.7510 Pharmacy and therapeutics committee.

(A) There is hereby established the pharmacy and therapeutics committee of the department of medicaid. The committee shall assist the department with developing and maintaining a preferred drug list for the medicaid program.

The committee shall review and recommend to the medicaid director the drugs that should be included on the preferred drug list. The recommendations shall be made based on the evaluation of competent evidence regarding the relative safety, efficacy, and effectiveness of prescribed drugs within a class or classes of prescribed drugs.

(B) The committee shall consist of ten members and shall be appointed by the medicaid director. The director shall seek recommendations for membership from relevant professional organizations. A candidate for membership recommended by a professional organization shall have professional experience working with medicaid recipients.

The membership of the committee shall include:

(1) Three pharmacists licensed under Chapter 4729. of the Revised Code;

(2) Two doctors of medicine and two doctors of osteopathy who hold licenses issued under Chapter 4731. of the Revised Code, one of whom is a family practice physician;

(3) A registered nurse licensed under Chapter 4723. of the Revised Code;

(4) A pharmacologist who has a doctoral degree;

(5) A psychiatrist who holds a license to practice medicine and surgery or osteopathic medicine and surgery issued under Chapter 4731. of the Revised Code and specializes in psychiatry.

(C) The committee shall elect from among its members a chairperson. Five committee members constitute a quorum.

The committee shall establish guidelines necessary for the committee's operation.

The committee may establish one or more subcommittees to investigate and analyze issues consistent with the duties of the committee under this section. The subcommittees may submit proposals regarding the issues to the committee and the committee may adopt, reject, or modify the proposals.

A vote by a majority of a quorum is necessary to make recommendations to the director. In the case of a tie, the chairperson shall decide the outcome.

(D) The director shall act on the committee's recommendations not later than thirty days after the recommendation is posted on the department's web site under division (F) of this section. If the director does not accept a recommendation of the committee, the director shall present the basis for this determination not later than fourteen days after making the determination or at the next scheduled meeting of the committee, whichever is sooner.

(E) An interested party may request, and shall be permitted, to make a presentation or submit written materials to the committee during a committee meeting. The presentation or other materials shall be relevant to an issue under consideration by the committee and any written material, including a transcript of testimony to be given on the day of the meeting, may be submitted to the committee in advance of the meeting.

(F) The department shall post the following on the department's web site:

(1) Guidelines established by the committee under division (C) of this section;

(2) A detailed committee agenda not later than fourteen days prior to the date of a regularly scheduled meeting and not later than seventy-two hours prior to the date of a special meeting called by the committee;

(3) Committee recommendations not later than seven days after the meeting at which the recommendation was approved;

(4) The director's final determination as to the recommendations made by the committee under this section.



**HISTORY:**

RC § 5111.47, 143 v H 257 (Eff 8-3-89); RC § 5111.81, 143 v H 822 (Eff 12-13-90); 144 v S 206, § 1 (Eff 6-29-91); 144 v H 298, § 1 (Eff 7-26-91); 144 v H 478 (Eff 1-14-93); 146 v H 350 (Eff 1-27-97); 147 v H 698 (Eff 3-22-99); 148 v H 471 (Eff 7-1-2000); 149 v S 108, § 2.01. Eff 7-6-2001; 151 v H 66, § 101.01, eff. 9-29-05; 151 v H 530, § 101.01, eff. 7-1-06; 152 v H 119, § 101.01, eff. 9-29-07; 152 v H 562, § 101.01, eff. 9-23-08; 153 v H 1, § 101.01, eff. 10-16-09; 2013 HB 59, § 101.01, eff. Sept. 29, 2013; 2019 hb166, § 101.01, effective October 17, 2019.

**Editor's Notes**

The provisions of § 4 of H.B. 516 (150 v —) read in part as follows:

SECTION 4. The following agencies shall be retained pursuant to division (D) of section 101.83 of the Revised Code and shall expire on December 31, 2010:

| AGENCY NAME | REVISED CODE OR UNCODIFIED SECTION |
|---|---|
| ○○○ | ○○○ |
| Pharmacy and Therapeutics Committee of the Dept. of Job and Family Services | 5111.81 |
| ○○○ | ○○○ |

This section was formerly codified as RC § 5111.084.

Section 2.02(A) of SB 108 (149 v —) repeals the existing version and section 3(A)(1) amends this SB 108 version to remove HB 350 matter or to revive matter removed by HB 350.

The amendment of RC § 5111.084 by 153 v H 1 was disapproved in part by the Governor.

**Amendment Notes**

The 2019 amendment by HB 166 substituted "licenses" for "certificates to practice" in (B)(2); and substituted "license to practice medicine and surgery or osteopathic medicine and surgery" for "certificate to practice" in (B)(5).

The 2013 amendment, in the first paragraph of (A), substituted "medicaid" for "job and family services" in the first sentence and added "for the medicaid program" to the end of the second sentence; substituted "medicaid director" for "director of job and family services" in the first sentence of the second paragraph of (A) and the first sentence of the introductory language of (B); and substituted "prescribed" for "prescription" twice in second sentence of the second paragraph of (A).

153 v H 1, effective October 16, 2009, rewrote the section.

152 v H 562, effective September 23, 2008, rewrote the section.

152 v H 119, effective September 29, 2007, inserted the next to last sentence.

151 v H 66, effective September 29, 2005, substituted "nine" for "eight" and "three" for "two".

**NOTES TO DECISIONS**

**Constitutionality**

Amended Substitute HB No. 350 violates the one-subject provision of Ohio Const. art II, § 15(D) and is unconstitutional in toto: State ex rel. Ohio Academy of Trial Lawyers v. Sheward, 1999-Ohio-123, 86 Ohio St. 3d 451, 715 N.E.2d 1062, 1999 Ohio LEXIS 2580 (Ohio 1999).

## § 5164.7511 Medication synchronization for a medicaid recipient.

(A) As used in this section:

(1) "Cost-sharing" means any cost-sharing requirements instituted for the medicaid program under section 5162.20 of the Revised Code.

(2) "Medication synchronization" means a pharmacy service that synchronizes the filling or refilling of prescriptions in a manner that allows the dispensed drugs to be obtained on the same date each month.

(3) "Prescriber" has the same meaning as in section 4729.01 of the Revised Code.

(B) With respect to coverage of prescribed drugs, the medicaid program shall provide for medication synchronization for a medicaid recipient if all of the following conditions are met:

(1) The recipient elects to participate in medication synchronization.

(2) The recipient, the prescriber, and a pharmacist at a pharmacy participating in the medicaid program agree that medication synchronization is in the best interest of the recipient.

(3) The prescribed drug to be included in the medication synchronization meets the requirements of division (C) of this section.

(C) To be eligible for inclusion in medication synchronization for a medicaid recipient, a prescribed drug must meet all of the following requirements:

(1) Be covered by the medicaid program;

(2) Be prescribed for the treatment and management of a chronic disease or condition and be subject to refills;

(3) Satisfy all relevant prior authorization criteria;

(4) Not have quantity limits, dose optimization criteria, or other requirements that would be violated if synchronized;

(5) Not have special handling or sourcing needs, as determined by the medicaid program, that require a single, designated pharmacy to fill or refill the prescription;

(6) Be formulated so that the quantity or amount dispensed can be effectively divided in order to achieve synchronization;

(7) Not be a schedule II controlled substance, opioid analgesic, or benzodiazepine, as those terms are defined in section 3719.01 of the Revised Code.

(D)(1) To provide for medication synchronization under division (B) of this section, the medicaid program shall authorize coverage of a prescribed drug subject to medication synchronization when the drug is dispensed in a quantity or amount that is less than a thirty-day supply.

(2) The requirement of division (D)(1) of this section applies only once for each prescribed drug subject to medication synchronization for the same medicaid recipient, except when either of the following occurs:

(a) The prescriber changes the dosage or frequency of administration of the prescribed drug subject to medication synchronization.

(b) The prescriber prescribes a different drug.

(E)(1) In providing for medication synchronization under division (B) of this section, the medicaid program shall apply a prorated daily cost-sharing rate for a supply of a prescribed drug subject to medication synchronization that is dispensed at a pharmacy participating in the program.

(2) Division (E)(1) of this section does not require the medicaid program to waive any cost-sharing requirement in its entirety.

(F) In providing for medication synchronization under division (B) of this section, the medicaid program shall not use payment structures that incorporate dispensing fees that are determined by calculating the days' supply of drugs dispensed. Dispensing fees shall be based exclusively on the total number of prescriptions that are filled or refilled.

(G) This section does not require the medicaid program to provide to a pharmacy participating in the program or a pharmacist at a participating pharmacy any monetary or other financial incentive for the purpose of encouraging the pharmacy or pharmacist to recommend medication synchronization to a medicaid recipient.

**HISTORY:**

2016 hb116, § 1, effective August 31, 2016; 2018 sb229, § 1, effective March 22, 2020.

**Editor's Notes**

Acts 2016, HB 116, § 3 provides: "Sections 1739.05 and 1751.68 of the Revised Code, as amended or enacted by this act, apply only to arrangements, policies, contracts, and agreements that are created, delivered, issued for delivery, or renewed in this state on or after January 1, 2017. Section 3923.602 of the Revised Code, as enacted by this act, applies only to policies of sickness and accident insurance delivered, issued for delivery, or renewed in this state and public employee benefit plans that are established or modified in this state on or after January 1, 2017. Sections 5164.7511 and 5167.12 of the Revised Code, as amended or enacted by this act, apply to the Medicaid program on or after January 1, 2017."

**Amendment Notes**

The 2018 amendment by SB 229 substituted "opioid analgesic" for "opiate" in (C)(7).

## § 5164.7512 Step therapy protocol.

(A) As used in sections 5164.7512 to 5164.7514 of the Revised Code:

(1) "Clinical practice guidelines" means a systematically developed statement to assist providers and medicaid recipients in making decisions about appropriate health care for specific clinical circumstances and conditions.

(2) "Clinical review criteria" means the written screening procedures, decision abstracts, clinical protocols, and clinical practice guidelines used by the medicaid program to determine whether or not a health care service or drug is appropriate and consistent with medical or scientific evidence.

(3) "Medical or scientific evidence" has the same meaning as in section 3922.01 of the Revised Code.

(4) "Step therapy exemption" means an overriding of a step therapy protocol in favor of immediate coverage of a medicaid provider's selected prescription drug.

(5) "Step therapy protocol" means a protocol under which it is determined through a specific sequence whether the medicaid program, under either a pharmacy or medical benefit, will pay for a prescribed drug that a medicaid provider, consistent with medical or scientific evidence, prescribes for a medicaid recipient's specified medical condition, including both self-administered and physician-administered drugs.

(6) "Urgent care services" has the same meaning as in section 3922.041 of the Revised Code.

(B) If the department of medicaid utilizes a step therapy protocol for the medicaid program under which it is recommended that prescribed drugs be taken in a specific sequence, the department shall do all of the following:

(1) Implement that step therapy protocol using clinical review criteria that are based on clinical practice guidelines or medical or scientific evidence. The department shall take into account the needs of atypical patient populations and diagnoses when establishing clinical review criteria.

(2) In a manner consistent with section 5164.7514 of the Revised Code, establish and implement a step therapy exemption process under which medicaid recipients and medicaid providers who prescribe prescribed drugs for medicaid recipients may request and receive a step therapy exemption;

(3)(a) Make available, to all medicaid providers, a list of all drugs covered by the medicaid program that are subject to a step therapy protocol;

(b) Along with the information required under division (B)(3)(a) of this section, the department of medicaid shall indicate what information or documentation must be provided to the department for a step therapy exemption request to be considered complete. Such information shall be provided for each drug, if the requirements vary according to the drug or protocol in question.

(c) The list required under division (B)(3)(a) of this section, along with all of the required information or documentation described in division (B)(3)(b) of this section, shall be made available on the department of medicaid's web site or provider portal.

(C) This section shall not be construed as requiring the department to set up a new entity to develop clinical review criteria for step therapy protocols.

**HISTORY:**

2018 sb265, § 1, effective April 5, 2019.

## § 5164.7514 Step therapy exemption.

(A) All of the following shall apply to the step therapy exemption process established and implemented by the department of medicaid pursuant to division (B)(2) of section 5164.7512 of the Revised Code:

(1) The process shall be clear and convenient.

(2) The process shall be easily accessible on the department's web site.

(3) The process shall require that a medicaid provider initiate a step therapy exemption request on behalf of a medicaid recipient.

(4) The process shall require supporting documentation and rationale be submitted with each request for a step therapy exemption.

(5) The process shall, pursuant to a step therapy exemption request made under division (B)(2) of section 5164.7512 of the Revised Code or an appeal made under division (B)(2) of this section, require the department to grant a step therapy exemption if either of the following applies:

(a) Either of the following apply to the prescribed drug that would otherwise have to be used under the step therapy protocol:

(i) The required prescription drug is contraindicated for that specific medicaid recipient, pursuant to the drug's United States food and drug administration prescribing information.

(ii) The medicaid recipient tried the required prescription drug while enrolled in medicaid or other health care coverage, or another United States food and drug administration approved AB-rated prescription drug, and such prescription drug was discontinued due to lack of efficacy or effectiveness, diminished effect, or an adverse event.

(b) The medicaid recipient is stable on the prescribed drug selected by the recipient's medicaid provider for the medical condition under consideration, regardless of whether or not the drug was prescribed while the individual in question was a medicaid recipient, or has already gone through a step therapy protocol. However, the department may require a stable medicaid recipient to try a pharmaceutical alternative, per the federal food and drug administration's orange book, purple book, or their successors, prior to providing coverage for the prescribed drug.

(6) On granting a step therapy exemption, the department shall authorize payment for the prescribed drug prescribed by the medicaid recipient's medicaid provider.

(B)(1) From the time a step therapy exemption request is received, the department shall either grant or deny the request within the following time frames:

(a) Forty-eight hours for requests related to urgent care services;

(b) Ten calendar days for all other requests.

(2)(a) If an exemption request is denied, a medicaid provider may appeal the denial on behalf of the medicaid recipient.

(b) From the time a step therapy appeal is received, the department shall either grant or deny the appeal within the following time frames:

(i) Forty-eight hours for appeals related to urgent care services;

(ii) Ten calendar days for all other appeals.

(3) The appeal shall be between the medicaid provider making the appeal and a clinical peer appointed by or contracted by the department or the department's designee.

(4) If the department does not either grant or deny an exemption request or an appeal within the time frames prescribed in division (B)(1) or (2) of this section, then such an exemption request or appeal shall be deemed to be granted.

(C) If an appeal is rejected, the medicaid recipient in question may make a further appeal in accordance with section 5160.31 of the Revised Code.

(D) This section shall not be construed to prevent either of the following:

(1) The department from requiring a medicaid recipient to try any new or existing pharmaceutical alternative, per the federal food and drug administration's orange book, purple book, or their successors, before authorizing a medicaid payment for the prescribed drug;

(2) A medicaid provider from prescribing a prescribed drug that is determined to be consistent with medical or scientific evidence.

**HISTORY:**

2018 sb265, § 1, effective April 5, 2019.

### § 5164.7515 Annual benchmark for prescribed drug spending growth.



(A) Not later than July 1, 2020, the medicaid director shall establish an annual benchmark for prescribed drug spending growth under the medicaid program. If the director determines that prescribed drug spending in a given year is projected to exceed the benchmark for that year, the director shall identify specific prescribed drugs that significantly contribute to exceeding the benchmark.

(B) For a prescribed drug identified by the director under division (A) of this section, the director shall determine if there is a current supplemental rebate for that drug between the drug's manufacturer and the department or its designee. If there is a current supplemental rebate for the drug, the director may renegotiate the supplemental rebate agreement. If there is not a supplemental rebate for the drug, the director shall evaluate whether to pursue a supplemental rebate agreement for the drug with the drug manufacturer. In making that evaluation, the director may consider any of the following:

(1) The prescribed drug's actual cost to the state;

(2) Whether the drug's manufacturer is providing significant discounts or rebates for other prescribed drugs under the medicaid program;

(3) Any other information the director considers relevant.

(C)(1) If the director determines that a prescribed drug rebate agreement renegotiation is warranted under division (B) of this section, the director shall establish a target rebate amount. In determining the target rebate amount, the director may consider any of the following:

(a) Publicly available information relevant to pricing the prescribed drug;

(b) Information the department has that is relevant to the pricing of the drug;

(c) Information relating to value-based pricing of the drug for medicaid recipients;

(d) The seriousness and prevalence of the conditions for which the drug is prescribed;

(e) The drug's volume of use among medicaid recipients;

(f) The effectiveness of the drug in treating conditions for which it is prescribed or improving a patient's health, quality of life, or overall health outcomes;

(g) The likelihood that use of the drug will reduce the need for other medical care, including hospitalization;

(h) The average wholesale price, wholesale acquisition cost, and retail price of the drug, and the cost of the drug under the medicaid program, not including any rebates received for the drug under the program;

(i) In the case of generic drugs, the number of manufacturers that produce the drug;

(j) Whether there are pharmaceutical equivalents to the drug;

(k) Any other information the director considers relevant.

(2) In negotiating a new rebate agreement under division (B) of this section, the director shall seek to negotiate an amount that is equal to the target rebate amount under division (C)(1) of this section. The director shall not enter into a rebate agreement that is less than sixty per cent of the target rebate amount. If no rebate agreement is established or renegotiated under this section, the director may consider removing the drug from the medicaid program's preferred drug list and imposing a prior authorization requirement on the drug in accordance with section 5160.34 of the Revised Code.

(D) The director shall publish a list of the prescribed drugs it identifies as being responsible for increasing spending above the annual benchmark for prescribed drug spending growth.

**HISTORY:**

2019 hb166, § 101.01, effective October 17, 2019.

### § 5164.752 Survey of retail pharmacies to determine maximum dispensing fee.

In July of every even-numbered year, the department of medicaid shall initiate a confidential survey of the cost of dispensing drugs incurred by terminal distributors of dangerous drugs in this state. The survey shall be used as the basis for establishing the medicaid program's dispensing fees for terminal distributors in accordance with section 5164.753 of the Revised Code. The survey shall be completed and its results published not later than the last day of November of the year in which it is conducted.

Each terminal distributor that is a provider of drugs under the medicaid program shall participate in the survey. Except as necessary to publish the survey's results, a terminal distributor's responses to the survey are confidential and not a public record under section 149.43 of the Revised Code.

The survey shall be conducted in conformance with the requirements set forth in 42 C.F.R. 447.500 to 447.518. The survey shall include operational data and direct prescription expenses, professional services and personnel costs, and usual and customary overhead expenses of the terminal distributors surveyed. The survey shall compute and report the cost of dispensing by terminal distributors.

**HISTORY:**

140 v S 240 (Eff 4-11-85); 148 v H 471. Eff 7-1-2000; 2013 HB 59, § 101.01, eff. Sept. 29, 2013; 2017 hb49, § 101.01, effective September 29, 2017.

**Editor's Notes**

This section was formerly codified as RC § 5111.07.

Acts 2013, HB 59, § 812.40 provides:

"The amendments to sections 5101.573 (5160.40), 5101.58 (5160.37), 5111.07 (5164.752), 5111.071 (5164.753), 5111.083 (5164.757), 5111.17 (5167.10), and 5111.19 (5164.74) of the Revised Code are subject to the referendum under Ohio Constitution, Article II, Section 1c and section 1.471 of the Revised Code, and therefore take effect on the ninety-first day after this act is filed with the Secretary of State. However:

"(A) In section 5101.573 (5160.40) of the Revised Code, the new matter inserted into division (C) takes effect January 1, 2014.

"(B) In section 5101.58 (5160.37) of the Revised Code, the insertion of division (K) takes effect January 1, 2014.

"(C)(1) In section 5111.07 (5164.752) of the Revised Code, all of the amendments take effect July 1, 2014, except for the following amendments:

"(a) The renumbering of the section;

"(b) The strike through of "job and family services" and insertion of " medicaid " in the first sentence as the section appears on the day immediately preceding the effective date of this section.

"(2) The reference to "director of job and family services" in the last sentence shall be read as if it reads the "director of medicaid" while the last sentence remains in effect.

"(D) In section 5111.071 (5164.753) of the Revised Code, the insertion in the last sentence of " and the extent to which each terminal distributor participates in the medicaid program as a provider of drugs " takes effect July 1, 2014.

"(E) In section 5111.083 (5164.757) of the Revised Code, all of the amendments take effect January 1, 2014, except for the following amendments:

"(1) The renumbering of the section;

"(2) The insertion of "medicaid" before "director" in the first sentence of division (B);

"(3) The strike through of "of job and family services".

"(F) In section 5111.17 (5167.10) of the Revised Code, the amendments to division (B)(2) take effect January 1, 2014.

"(G) In section 5111.19 (5164.74) of the Revised Code, the following amendments take effect January 1, 2014:

"(1) The insertion of ", and the allocation of payments for, " in the first paragraph;

"(2) The strike through of the second paragraph and divisions (A), (B), and (C)."

**Amendment Notes**

The 2017 amendment by HB 49, in the first paragraph, substituted "dispensing fees for terminal" for "dispensing fee for terminal" in the second sentence, substituted "last day of November" for "last day of October" in the last sentence; and substituted "dispensing by terminal distributors" for "dispensing on a basis of the usual and customary charges by terminal distributors to their customers for dispensing drugs" in the second sentence of the second paragraph.

The 2013 amendment rewrote the section.

### RESEARCH REFERENCES AND PRACTICE AIDS

**Cross-References to Related Sections**

Dispensing fee, RC § 5164.753.

**Ohio Administrative Code**

Pharmacy services. OAC ch. 5160-9.

## § 5164.753 Dispensing fee for pharmacist-providers.

In December of every even-numbered year, the medicaid director shall establish dispensing fees, effective the following July, for terminal distributors of dangerous drugs that are providers of drugs under the medicaid program. In establishing dispensing fees, the director shall take into consideration the results of the survey conducted under section 5164.752 of the Revised Code. The director may establish dispensing fees that vary by terminal distributor, taking into consideration the volume of drugs a terminal distributor dispenses under the medicaid program or any other criteria the director considers relevant.

**HISTORY:**

141 v H 812 (Eff 9-24-86); 148 v H 471. Eff 7-1-2000; 150 v H 95, § 1, eff. 6-26-03; 2013 HB 59, § 101.01, eff. Sept. 29, 2013; 2017 hb49, § 101.01, effective September 29, 2017.

**Editor's Notes**

This section was formerly codified as RC § 5111.071.

Acts 2013, HB 59, § 812.40 provides:

"The amendments to sections 5101.573 (5160.40), 5101.58 (5160.37), 5111.07 (5164.752), 5111.071 (5164.753), 5111.083 (5164.757), 5111.17 (5167.10), and 5111.19 (5164.74) of the Revised Code are subject to the referendum under Ohio Constitution, Article II, Section 1c and section 1.471 of the Revised Code, and therefore take effect on the ninety-first day after this act is filed with the Secretary of State. However:

"(A) In section 5101.573 (5160.40) of the Revised Code, the new matter inserted into division (C) takes effect January 1, 2014.

"(B) In section 5101.58 (5160.37) of the Revised Code, the insertion of division (K) takes effect January 1, 2014.

"(C)(1) In section 5111.07 (5164.752) of the Revised Code, all of the amendments take effect July 1, 2014, except for the following amendments:

"(a) The renumbering of the section;

"(b) The strike through of "job and family services" and insertion of " medicaid " in the first sentence as the section appears on the day immediately preceding the effective date of this section.

"(2) The reference to "director of job and family services" in the last sentence shall be read as if it reads the "director of medicaid" while the last sentence remains in effect.

"(D) In section 5111.071 (5164.753) of the Revised Code, the insertion in the last sentence of " and the extent to which each terminal distributor participates in the medicaid program as a provider of drugs " takes effect July 1, 2014.

"(E) In section 5111.083 (5164.757) of the Revised Code, all of the amendments take effect January 1, 2014, except for the following amendments:

"(1) The renumbering of the section;

"(2) The insertion of "medicaid" before "director" in the first sentence of division (B);

"(3) The strike through of "of job and family services".

"(F) In section 5111.17 (5167.10) of the Revised Code, the amendments to division (B)(2) take effect January 1, 2014.

"(G) In section 5111.19 (5164.74) of the Revised Code, the following amendments take effect January 1, 2014:

"(1) The insertion of ", and the allocation of payments for, " in the first paragraph;

"(2) The strike through of the second paragraph and divisions (A), (B), and (C)."

This section was formerly RC § 5111.08. It was renumbered by H.B. 95 (150 v —), effective June 26, 2003.

**Amendment Notes**

The 2017 amendment by HB 49 substituted "establish dispensing fees" for "establish a dispensing fee" in the first sentence and "establishing dispensing fees" for "establishing the dispensing fee" in the second sentence; and added the last sentence.

The 2013 amendment rewrote the section, which formerly read: "Commencing in December, 1986, and every second December thereafter, the director of job and family services shall establish a dispensing fee, effective the following January, for licensed pharmacists who are providers under this chapter. The dispensing fee shall take into consideration the results of the survey conducted under section 5111.07 of the Revised Code."

## § 5164.754 Multiple-state drug purchasing program.

(A) As used in this section, "dangerous drug" and "manufacturer of dangerous drugs" have the same meaning as in section 4729.01 of the Revised Code.

(B) The medicaid director may enter into or administer an agreement or cooperative arrangement with other states to create or join a multiple-state prescription drug purchasing program for the purpose of negotiating with manufacturers of dangerous drugs to receive discounts or rebates for dangerous drugs covered by the medicaid program.

**HISTORY:**

151 v H 66, § 101.01, eff. 9-29-05; 2013 HB 59, § 101.01, eff. Sept. 29, 2013.

**Editor's Notes**

This section was formerly codified as RC § 5111.0114.

**Amendment Notes**

The 2013 amendment, in (B), substituted "medicaid director" for "director of job and family services" and "covered by" for "dispensed under".



## § 5164.755 Supplemental drug rebate program.

The medicaid director, in rules adopted under section 5164.02 of the Revised Code, may establish and implement a supplemental drug rebate program under which drug manufacturers may be required to provide the department of medicaid a supplemental rebate as a condition of having the drug manufacturers' drug products covered by the medicaid program without prior approval. The department may receive a supplemental rebate negotiated under the program for a drug dispensed to a medicaid recipient pursuant to a prescription or a drug purchased by a medicaid provider for administration to a medicaid recipient in the provider's primary place of business.

If the director establishes a supplemental drug rebate program, the director shall consult with drug manufacturers regarding the establishment and implementation of the program.

**HISTORY:**

149 v S 261. Eff 6-5-2002; 151 v H 66, § 101.01, eff. 6-30-05; 151 v H 530, § 101.01, eff. 7-1-06; 2013 HB 59, § 101.01, eff. Sept. 29, 2013.

**Editor's Notes**

This section was formerly codified as RC § 5111.081.

The amendment of RC § 5111.082 by Am. Sub. H.B. 95 (150 v —) was disapproved by the Governor.

This section was renumbered from RC § 5111.082 by 151 v H 530, effective July 1, 2006.

**Amendment Notes**

The 2013 amendment, in the first sentence of the first paragraph, substituted "medicaid director" for "director of job and family services," "section 5164.02" for "section 5111.02," "department of medicaid" for "department of job and family services"; and deleted the last sentence of the first paragraph, which read: "If necessary, the director may apply to the United States secretary of health and human services for a waiver of federal statutes and regulations to establish the supplemental drug rebate program."

151 v H 66, effective June 30, 2005, inserted the second sentence in the first paragraph; and deleted the third paragraph and (A) and (B), pertaining to exemptions from a supplemental drug rebate program.

### § 5164.756 Confidentiality of information regarding drug rebate agreement.

Any record, data, pricing information, or other information regarding a drug rebate agreement or a supplemental drug rebate agreement for the medicaid program that the department of medicaid receives from a pharmaceutical manufacturer or creates pursuant to negotiation of the agreement is not a public record under section 149.43 of the Revised Code and shall be treated by the department as confidential information.

**HISTORY:**

150 v H 40, § 1, eff. 6-9-03; 153 v H 1, § 101.01, eff. 10-16-09; 2013 HB 59, § 101.01, eff. Sept. 29, 2013.

**Editor's Notes**

The provisions of § 19 of H.B. 40 (150 v —) read as follows:

SECTION 19. Sections 5101.31, 5104.01, 5104.04, 5104.30, 5104.32, 5104.34, 5104.35, 5104.38, 5104.382, and 5104.39 of the Revised Code as amended or enacted by this act, and the items of law of which such sections as amended or enacted by this act are composed, are subject to the referendum. Therefore, under Ohio Constitution, Article II, Section 1c and section 1.471 of the Revised Code, such sections as amended or enacted by this act, and the items of law of which such sections as amended or enacted by this act are composed, take effect on the ninety-first day after this act is filed with the Secretary of State. If, however, a referendum petition is filed against any such section as amended or enacted by this act, or against any item of law of which any such section as amended or enacted by this act is composed, the section as amended or enacted, or item of law, unless rejected at the referendum, takes effect at the earliest time permitted by law.

This section was formerly codified as RC § 5101.31.

**Amendment Notes**

The 2013 amendment deleted "established under Chapter 5111. of the Revised Code" following "the medicaid program"; substituted "medicaid receives" for "job and family services receives".

153 v H 1, effective October 16, 2009, deleted "or the disability medical assistance program established under section 5115.10 of the Revised Code" preceding "that the department".

### § 5164.757 Medicaid e-prescribing system.

(A) As used in this section, "licensed health professional authorized to prescribe drugs" has the same meaning as in section 4729.01 of the Revised Code.

(B) The medicaid director may acquire or specify technologies to provide information regarding medicaid recipient eligibility, claims history, and drug coverage to medicaid providers through electronic health record and e-prescribing applications.

If such technologies are acquired or specified, the e-prescribing applications shall enable a medicaid provider who is a licensed health professional authorized to prescribe drugs to use an electronic system to prescribe a drug for a medicaid recipient. The purpose of the electronic system is to eliminate the need for such medicaid providers to issue prescriptions for medicaid recipients by handwriting or telephone. The technologies acquired or specified by the director also shall provide such medicaid providers with an up-to-date, clinically relevant drug information database and a system of electronically monitoring medicaid recipients' medical history, drug regimen compliance, and fraud and abuse.

**HISTORY:**

151 v H 66, § 101.01, eff. 9-29-05; 151 v H 530, § 101.01, eff. 7-1-06; 2013 HB 59, § 101.01, eff. Sept. 29, 2013.

**Editor's Notes**

This section was formerly codified as RC § 5111.083.

Acts 2013, HB 59, § 812.40 provides:

"The amendments to sections 5101.573 (5160.40), 5101.58 (5160.37), 5111.07 (5164.752), 5111.071 (5164.753), 5111.083 (5164.757), 5111.17 (5167.10), and 5111.19 (5164.74) of the Revised Code are subject to the referendum under Ohio Constitution, Article II, Section 1c and section 1.471 of the Revised Code, and therefore take effect on the ninety-first day after this act is filed with the Secretary of State. However:

"(A) In section 5101.573 (5160.40) of the Revised Code, the new matter inserted into division (C) takes effect January 1, 2014.

"(B) In section 5101.58 (5160.37) of the Revised Code, the insertion of division (K) takes effect January 1, 2014.

"(C)(1) In section 5111.07 (5164.752) of the Revised Code, all of the amendments take effect July 1, 2014, except for the following amendments:

"(a) The renumbering of the section;

"(b) The strike through of "job and family services" and insertion of " medicaid " in the first sentence as the section appears on the day immediately preceding the effective date of this section.

"(2) The reference to "director of job and family services" in the last sentence shall be read as if it reads the "director of medicaid" while the last sentence remains in effect.

"(D) In section 5111.071 (5164.753) of the Revised Code, the insertion in the last sentence of " and the extent to which each terminal distributor participates in the medicaid program as a provider of drugs " takes effect July 1, 2014.

"(E) In section 5111.083 (5164.757) of the Revised Code, all of the amendments take effect January 1, 2014, except for the following amendments:

"(1) The renumbering of the section;

"(2) The insertion of "medicaid" before "director" in the first sentence of division (B);

"(3) The strike through of "of job and family services".

"(F) In section 5111.17 (5167.10) of the Revised Code, the amendments to division (B)(2) take effect January 1, 2014.

"(G) In section 5111.19 (5164.74) of the Revised Code, the following amendments take effect January 1, 2014:

"(1) The insertion of ", and the allocation of payments for, " in the first paragraph;

"(2) The strike through of the second paragraph and divisions (A), (B), and (C)."

This section was renumbered from RC § 5111.084 by 151 v H 530, effective July 1, 2006.

**Amendment Notes**

The 2013 amendment rewrote (B); and deleted (C), which read: "If the director establishes an e-prescribing system under division (B) of this section, the director shall do all of the following: (1) Require that a medicaid provider who is a licensed health professional authorized to prescribe drugs use the e-prescribing system during a fiscal year if the medicaid provider was one of the ten medicaid providers who, during the calendar year that precedes that fiscal year, issued the most prescriptions for medicaid recipients receiving hospital services; (2) Before the beginning of each fiscal year, determine the ten medicaid providers that issued the most prescriptions for medicaid recipients receiving hospital services during the calendar year that precedes the upcoming fiscal year and notify those medicaid providers that they must use the e-prescribing system for the upcoming fiscal year; (3) Seek the most federal financial participation available for the development and implementation of the e-prescribing system."

### § 5164.758 Implementation of a coordinated services for Medicaid receipients.

The medicaid director shall adopt rules under section 5164.02 of the Revised Code to implement a coordinated services program for medicaid recipients who are found to have obtained prescribed drugs under the medicaid program at a frequency or in an amount that is not medically necessary. The program shall be implemented in a manner that is consistent with the "Social Security Act," section 1915(a)(2), 42 U.S.C. 1396n(a)(2), and 42 C.F.R. 431.54(e).

**HISTORY:**

2011 HB 93, § 1, eff. May 20, 2011; 2013 HB 59, § 101.01, eff. Sept. 29, 2013.

**Editor's Notes**

This section was formerly codified as RC § 5111.085.

The enactment of RC § 5111.085 by 152 v H 119 was disapproved by the Governor.

**Amendment Notes**

The 2013 amendment, in the first sentence, substituted "The medicaid director shall adopt rules under section 5164.02" for "Not later than July 1, 2012, the department of job and family services shall adopt rules in accordance with Chapter 119." and "prescribed" for "prescription"; and, in the second sentence, deleted "section 1915(a)(2) of" following "is consistent with" and substituted "section 1915(a)(2), 42 U.S.C. 1396n(a)(2)" for "95 Stat. 810 (1981), 42 U.S.C. 1396n(a)(2), as amended."

### § 5164.759 Outpatient drug use review program.

In accordance with the "Social Security Act," section 1927(g), 42 U.S.C. 1396r-8(g), the department of medicaid shall establish

Titles 39 — 57

an outpatient drug use review program to assure that prescriptions obtained by medicaid recipients are appropriate, medically necessary, and unlikely to cause adverse medical results.

**HISTORY:**
145 v H 152 (Eff 7-1-93); 148 v H 471. Eff 7-1-2000; 150 v H 95, § 1, eff. 6-26-03; 2013 HB 59, § 101.01, eff. Sept. 29, 2013.

**Editor's Notes**
This section was formerly codified as RC § 5111.08.
Former RC § 5111.08 was renumbered to be § 5111.071 by H.B. 95 (150 v —), effective June 26, 2003. This section was renumbered from § 5111.16 by H.B. 95.

**Amendment Notes**
The 2013 amendment substituted "the 'Social Security Act,' section 1927(g), 42 U.S.C. 1396r-8(g), the department of medicaid" for "subsection (g) of section 1927 of the 'Social Security Act,' 49 Stat. 320 (1935), 42 U.S.C.A. 1396r-8(g), as amended, the department of job and family services"; and substituted "medicaid recipients" for "recipients of medical assistance under this chapter."

**RESEARCH REFERENCES AND PRACTICE AIDS**

**Ohio Administrative Code**
Pharmacy services. OAC ch. 5160-9.

## § 5164.76 Manner of paying for community mental health services and alcohol and drug addiction services.

(A) In rules adopted under section 5164.02 of the Revised Code, the medicaid director shall modify the manner or establish a new manner in which the following are paid under medicaid:

(1) Community mental health service providers or facilities for providing community mental health services covered by the medicaid program pursuant to section 5164.15 of the Revised Code;

(2) Providers of alcohol and drug addiction services for providing alcohol and drug addiction services covered by the medicaid program.

(B) The director's authority to modify the manner, or to establish a new manner, for medicaid to pay for the services specified in division (A) of this section is not limited by any rules adopted under section 5119.22 or 5164.02 of the Revised Code that are in effect on June 26, 2003, and govern the way medicaid pays for those services. This is the case regardless of what state agency adopted the rules.

**HISTORY:**
150 v H 95, § 1, eff. 6-26-03; 151 v H 66, § 101.01, eff. 10-1-05; 2011 HB 153, § 101.01, eff. July 1, 2011; 2013 HB 59, § 101.01, eff. Sept. 29, 2013.

**Editor's Notes**
This section was formerly codified as RC § 5111.025.

**Amendment Notes**
The 2013 amendment, in the introductory language of (A), substituted "section 5164.02" for "section 5111.02" and "medicaid director" for "director of job and family services"; in (A)(1), substituted "service providers" for "agencies" and "medicaid program pursuant to section5164.15" for "state medicaid plan pursuant to section 5111.023"; substituted "covered by" for "included in" in (A)(1) and (A)(2); deleted "pursuant to rules adopted under section 5111.02 of the Revised Code" from the end of (A)(2); and substituted "section 5119.22 or 5164.02" for "section 5111.02 or 5119.61" in the first sentence of (B).

The 2011 amendment, in (A)(1), inserted "agencies or" and inserted "community" following "providing."

151 v H 66, effective October 1, 2005, corrected internal references in (A)(1); and substituted "June 26, 2003" for "the effective date of this section" in (B).

**ATTORNEY GENERAL OPINIONS**

An alcohol, drug addiction and mental health services board (ADAMH board) established pursuant to R.C. Chapter 340, or a provider with which the ADAMH board contracts, may only access Medicaid funding when authorized by statute and rule, including R.C. 5111.023, R.C. 5111.025, 14 Ohio Admin. Code Chapter 5101:3-27, and 14 Ohio Admin. Code Chapter 5101:3-30. Neither an ADAMH board nor a provider with which the board contracts may access Medicaid funding for services provided to an individual who is not eligible for Medicaid. The determination as to whether a particular individual meets all Medicaid eligibility requirements is made, in the first instance, by the county department of job and family services, except with regard to the Ohio breast and cervical cancer project, where eligibility is determined by the Ohio Department of Health or its designated local agencies or subgrantees. 2006 Ohio Op. Att'y Gen. No. 019 (2006).

## § 5164.761 Requirement for updating medicaid billing codes or rates.

Before the department of medicaid or department of mental health and addiction services updates medicaid billing codes or medicaid payment rates for community behavioral health services as part of the behavioral health redesign, the departments shall conduct a beta test of the updates. Any medicaid provider of community behavioral health services may volunteer to participate in the beta test. An update may not begin to be implemented outside of the beta test until at least half of the medicaid providers participating in the beta test are able to submit under the beta test a clean claim for community behavioral health services that is properly adjudicated not later than thirty days after the date the clean claim is submitted.

**HISTORY:**
2017 hb49, § 101.01, effective September 29, 2017.

## § 5164.77 Reduction and adjustment of medicaid fees and services. [Repealed]

**HISTORY:**
2011 HB 153, § 101.01, eff. June 30, 2011; 2013 HB 59, § 101.01, eff. Sept. 29, 2013; repealed by 2019 hb166, § 105.01, effective October 17, 2019.



## § 5164.78 Medicaid payment rates for neonatal and newborn services.

(A) The medicaid payment rates for the following neonatal and newborn services shall equal seventy-five per cent of the medicare payment rates for the services in effect on the date the services are provided to medicaid recipients eligible for the services:

(1) Initial care for normal newborns;

(2) Subsequent day, hospital care for normal newborns;

(3) Same day, initial history and physical examination and discharge for normal newborns;

(4) Initial neonatal critical care for children not more than twenty-eight days old;

(5) Subsequent day, neonatal critical care for children not more than twenty-eight days old;

(6) Subsequent day, pediatric critical care for children at least twenty-nine days but less than two years old;

(7) Initial neonatal intensive care;

(8) Subsequent day, neonatal intensive noncritical care for children weighing less than one thousand five hundred grams;

(9) Subsequent day, neonatal intensive noncritical care for children weighing at least one thousand five hundred grams but not more than two thousand five hundred grams;

(10) Subsequent day, neonatal noncritical care for children weighing more than two thousand five hundred grams but not more than five thousand grams.

(B) The medicaid payment rates for other medicaid services selected by the medicaid director shall be less than the amount of the rates in effect on the effective date of this section so that the cost of the rates set pursuant to division (A) of this section do not increase medicaid expenditures. The director may not select any medicaid service for which the medicaid payment rate is determined in accordance with state statutes.

**HISTORY:**
2017 hb49, § 101.01, effective September 29, 2017.

## § 5164.80 Public notification of changes to medicaid reimbursement rates.

As necessary to comply with the "Social Security Act," section 1902(a)(13)(A), 42 U.S.C. 1396a(a)(13)(A), and any other federal law that requires public notice of proposed changes to payment rates for medicaid services, the medicaid director shall give public notice in the register of Ohio of any change to a method or standard used to determine the medicaid payment rate for a medicaid service.

**HISTORY:**

2011 HB 153, § 101.01, eff. Sept. 29, 2011; 2013 HB 59, § 101.01, eff. Sept. 29, 2013.

**Editor's Notes**

This section was formerly codified as RC § 5111.0212.

**Amendment Notes**

The 2013 amendment deleted "section 1902(a)(13)(A) of" following "comply with"; substituted "section 1902(a)(13)(A)" for "111 Stat. 507 (1997)"; deleted "as amended" preceding "and any other"; substituted "payment" for "reimbursement" twice; substituted "medicaid services, the medicaid director" for "medical assistance provided under the medicaid program, the director of job and family services"; and substituted "a medicaid service" for "medical assistance".

### § 5164.82 Medicaid payment for a provider-preventable condition.

The department of medicaid shall not knowingly make a medicaid payment for a provider-preventable condition for which federal financial participation is prohibited by regulations adopted under the "Patient Protection and Affordable Care Act," section 2702, 42 U.S.C. 1396b-1.

**HISTORY:**

2011 HB 153, § 101.01, eff. Sept. 29, 2011; 2013 HB 59, § 101.01, eff. Sept. 29, 2013.

**Editor's Notes**

This section was formerly codified as RC § 5111.0214.

**Amendment Notes**

The 2013 amendment substituted "department of medicaid" for "department of job and family services"; deleted "section 2702 of" following "regulations adopted under"; substituted "section 2702" for "124 Stat. 318 (2010)"; and deleted the second sentence, which read: "The director of job and family services shall adopt rules under section 5111.02 of the Revised Code as necessary to implement this section."



### § 5164.85 Enrollment in group health plan.

(A) As used in this section, "cost-effective" and "group health plan" have the same meanings as in the "Social Security Act," section 1906, 42 U.S.C. 1396e, and any regulations adopted under that section.

(B) The department of medicaid may implement a program pursuant to the "Social Security Act," section 1906, 42 U.S.C. 1396e, for the enrollment of medicaid-eligible individuals in group health plans when the department determines that enrollment is cost-effective.

**HISTORY:**

144 v H 298 (Eff 7-26-91); 145 v H 152 (Eff 7-1-93); 148 v H 471. Eff 7-1-2000; 2011 HB 153, § 101.01, eff. Sept. 29, 2011; 2013 HB 59, § 101.01, eff. Sept. 29, 2013.

**Editor's Notes**

This section was formerly codified as RC § 5111.13.

**Amendment Notes**

The 2013 amendment substituted "the 'Social Security Act,' section 1906, 42 U.S.C. 1396e" for "section 1906 of the 'Social Security Act,' 104 Stat. 1388-161 (1990), 42 U.S.C. 1396e, as amended" in (A) and (B); substituted "medicaid may implement" for "job and family services may submit a medicaid state plan amendment to the United States secretary of health and human services for the purpose of implementing"; and deleted (C), which read: "The director of job and family services may adopt rules in accordance with Chapter 119. of the Revised Code as necessary to implement this section."

The 2011 amendment rewrote the section.

### § 5164.86 Qualified state long-term care insurance partnership program.

The medicaid director shall establish a qualified state long-term care insurance partnership program consistent with the definition of that term in the "Social Security Act," section 1917(b)(1)(C)(iii), 42 U.S.C. 1396p(b)(1)(C)(iii). An individual participating in the program who is subject to the medicaid estate recovery program instituted under section 5162.21 of the Revised Code shall be eligible for the reduced adjustment or recovery under division (D) of that section.

**HISTORY:**

151 v H 530, § 101.01, eff. 6-30-06; 2013 HB 59, § 101.01, eff. Sept. 29, 2013.

**Editor's Notes**

This section was formerly codified as RC § 5111.18.

**Amendment Notes**

The 2013 amendment, in the first sentence, substituted "The medicaid director" for "Not later than September 1, 2007, the director of job and family services" and inserted "the "Social Security Act," section 1917(b)(1)(C)(iii)"; substituted "section 5162.21" for "section 5111.11" in the second sentence; and deleted the second paragraph, which read: "The director of job and family services may adopt rules in accordance with Chapter 119. of the Revised Code as necessary to implement this section."

### § 5164.88 Coordinated care health homes.

The medicaid director may implement within the medicaid program a system under which medicaid recipients with chronic conditions are provided with coordinated care through health homes, as authorized by the "Social Security Act," section 1945, 42 U.S.C. 1396w-4.

**HISTORY:**

2011 HB 153, § 101.01, eff. Sept. 29, 2011; 2013 HB 59, § 101.01, eff. Sept. 29, 2013.

**Editor's Notes**

A former RC § 5111.14 was amended and renumbered as RC § 5111.141 by 2011 HB 153, § 101.01, eff. September 29, 2011.

This section was formerly codified as RC § 5111.14.

**Amendment Notes**

The 2013 amendment substituted "medicaid director may" for "director of job and family services may submit to the United States secretary of health and human services an amendment to the medicaid state plan in order to"; substituted "the 'Social Security Act,' section 1945" for "section 1945 of the 'Social Security Act,' 124 Stat. 319(2010)"; and deleted the second paragraph, which read: "The director may adopt rules under section 5111.02 of the Revised Code to implement this section."

### § 5164.881 Home health care for developmentally disabled chronically ill.

The medicaid director, in consultation with the director of developmental disabilities, may develop and implement within the medicaid program a system under which eligible individuals with chronic conditions, as defined in the "Social Security Act," section 1945 (h)(1), 42 U.S.C. 1396w-4(h)(1), who also have developmental disabilities may receive health home services, as defined in the "Social Security Act," section 1945 (h)(4), 42 U.S.C. 1396w-4(h)(4). Any such system shall focus on the needs of individuals and have as its goal improving services and outcomes under the medicaid program by improving integration of long-term care services and supportive services with primary and acute health care services.

In developing any system under this section, the directors shall consult with representatives of county boards of developmental disabilities, the Ohio provider resource association, and the arc of Ohio. The directors may consult with any other individuals or entities that have an interest in the well being of individuals with developmental disabilities.

**HISTORY:**

2013 HB 59, § 101.01, eff. Sept. 29, 2013; 2016 hb158, § 1, effective October 12, 2016.

**Amendment Notes**

The 2016 amendment by HB 158, deleted "mental retardation or other" following "who also have" in the first sentence.

### § 5164.89 Case management of nonemergency transportation services; federal reimbursement.

The department of medicaid may require county departments of job and family services to provide case management of nonemergency transportation services provided under the medicaid program. County departments shall provide the case management if required by the department in accordance with rules adopted under section 5164.02 of the Revised Code.

The department shall determine, for the purposes of claiming federal financial participation, whether it will claim expenditures for nonemergency transportation services as administrative or program expenditures.

**HISTORY:**

145 v H 152 (Eff 7-1-93); 148 v H 471. Eff 7-1-2000; 2011 HB 153, § 101.01, eff. Sept. 29, 2011; 2013 HB 59, § 101.01, eff. Sept. 29, 2013.

**Editor's Notes**

This section was formerly codified as RC § 5111.14.
This section was formerly codified as RC § 5111.141.

**Amendment Notes**

The 2013 amendment, in the first sentence of the first paragraph, substituted "department of medicaid" for "department of job and family services" and "medicaid program" for "medical assistance program"; substituted "under section 5164.02 of the Revised Code" for "by the director of job and family services" in the second sentence of the first paragraph; and substituted "financial participation" for "reimbursement under the medical assistance program" in the second paragraph.

### § 5164.90 Department permitted to operate helping Ohioans move, expanding (HOME) choice demonstration component of medicaid program to extent funds available under MFP demonstration.

(A) As used in this section, "MFP demonstration project" means a money follows the person demonstration project that the United States secretary of health and human services is authorized to award under section 6071 of the " Deficit Reduction Act of 2005 " (Pub. L. No. 109-171, as amended).

(B) To the extent funds are available under an MFP demonstration project awarded to the department of medicaid, the director of medicaid may operate the helping Ohioans move, expanding (HOME) choice demonstration component of the medicaid program to transition medicaid recipients who qualify for the demonstration component to community settings.

**HISTORY:**

2012 HB 487, § 101.01, eff. Sept. 10, 2012; 2013 HB 59, § 101.01, eff. Sept. 29, 2013.

**Editor's Notes**

This section was formerly codified as RC § 5111.96.

**Amendment Notes**

The 2013 amendment in (B), substituted "medicaid, the director of" for "job and family services, the director of job and family services" and deleted the second sentence, which read: "The director may adopt rules in accordance with Chapter 119. of the Revised Code for the administration and operation of the demonstration component."

### § 5164.91 Demonstration project to test dual eligible individuals.

The medicaid director may implement a demonstration project called the integrated care delivery system to test and evaluate the integration of the care that dual eligible individuals receive under medicare and medicaid. No provision of Title LI of the Revised Code applies to the integrated care delivery system if that provision implements or incorporates a provision of federal law governing medicaid and that provision of federal law does not apply to the system.

**HISTORY:**

2011 HB 153, § 101.01, eff. Sept. 29, 2011; 2012 HB 303, § 1, eff. Mar. 20, 2013; 2013 HB 59, § 101.01, eff. Sept. 29, 2013.

**Editor's Notes**

This section was formerly codified as RC § 5111.981.

**Amendment Notes**

The 2013 amendment deleted (A), which read: "As used in this section and section 5111.982 of the Revised Code: 'Dual eligible individual' has the same meaning as in the 'Social Security Act,' section 1915(h)(2)(B), 42 U.S.C. 1396n(h)(2)(B). 'Medicare' means the program created in the 'Social Security Act,' Title XVIII, 42 U.S.C. 1395 et seq., as amended"; deleted the (B) designation; substituted "The medicaid" for "Subject to division (C) of this section, the medical assistance" in the first sentence; and deleted (C), which read: "Before implementing the integrated care delivery system under division (B) of this section, the director shall obtain the approval of the United States secretary of health and human services in the form of a federal medicaid waiver, medicaid state plan amendment, or demonstration grant. The director is required to seek the federal approval only if the director seeks to implement the integrated care delivery system. The director shall implement the integrated care delivery system in accordance with the terms of the federal approval, including the terms regarding the duration of the system."

The 2012 amendment, in (A), added "and section 5111.982 of the Revised Code" to the end of the introductory language, in the definition of "Dual eligible individual", deleted "section 1915(h)(2)(B) of" following "meaning as in" and substituted "section 1915(h)(2)(B)" for "124 Stat. 315 (2010)", and in the definition of "Medicare", substituted "Medicare" for "Medicare program", substituted "in" for "under Title XVIII of" following "program created", and substituted "Title XVIII, 42 U.S.C. 1395et seq." for "79 Stat. 286 (1965), 42 U.S.C. 1395"; in the first sentence of (B), substituted "medical assistance director" for "director of job and family services", inserted "called the integrated care delivery system", and deleted "programs" from the end; substituted "integrated care delivery system" for "demonstration project" wherever it appears in the second sentence of (B) and in (C); in the second sentence of (B), substituted "medicaid" for "the medicaid program" and substituted "system" for "demonstration project" at the end; substituted "system" for "demonstration project" at the end of the last sentence of (C); and made a stylistic change.

### § 5164.911 Annual evaluations of the integrated care delivery system.

(A) If the medicaid director implements the integrated care delivery system and except as provided in division (C) of this section, the director shall annually evaluate all of the following:

(1) The health outcomes of ICDS participants;

(2) How changes to the administration of the ICDS affect all of the following:

(a) Claims processing;

(b) The appeals process;

(c) The number of reassessments requested;

(d) Prior authorization requests for services.

(3) The provider panel selection process used by medicaid managed care organizations participating in the ICDS.

(B) When conducting an evaluation under division (A) of this section, the director shall do all of the following:

(1) For the purpose of division (A)(1) of this section, do both of the following:

(a) Compare the health outcomes of ICDS participants to the health outcomes of individuals who are not ICDS participants;

(b) Use both of the following:

(i) A control group consisting of ICDS participants who receive health care services from providers not participating in ICDS;

(ii) A control group consisting of ICDS participants who receive health care services from alternative providers that are not part of a participating medicaid managed care organization's provider panel but provide health care services in the geographic service area in which ICDS participants receive health care services.

(2) For the purpose of division (A)(2) of this section, do all of the following:

(a) To the extent the data is available, use data from all of the following:

(i) The fee-for-service component of the medicaid program;

(ii) Medicaid managed care organizations;

(iii) Managed care organizations participating in the medicare advantage program established under Part C of Title XVIII of the "Social Security Act," 42 U.S.C. 1395w-21 et seq.

(b) Identify all of the following:

(i) Changes in the amount of time it takes to process claims and the number of claims denied and the reasons for the changes;

(ii) The impact that changes to the administration of the ICDS had on the appeals process and number of reassessments requested;

(iii) The number of prior authorization denials that were overturned and the reasons for the overturned denials.

(3) Require medicaid managed care organizations participating in the ICDS to submit to the director any data the director needs for the evaluation.

(C) The director is not required to conduct an evaluation under this section for a year if the same evaluation is conducted for that year by an organization under contract with the United States department of health and human services.

**HISTORY:**

2013 HB 59, § 101.01, eff. Sept. 29, 2013; 2013 SB 206, § 1, eff. Mar. 20, 2014.

**Amendment Notes**

The 2013 amendment deleted (C), which read: "Not later than the first day of each July, the director shall complete a report of the evaluation conducted under this section. The director shall provide a copy of the report to the general assembly in accordance with section 101.68 of the Revised Code and make the report available to the public"; redesignated former (D) as (C); and made a stylistic change.

Titles 39 — 57

### § 5164.912 Standardized claim form.

The medicaid director shall select from among universally accepted claim forms used in the United States a standardized claim form for each type of medicaid provider that provides medicaid services under the integrated care delivery system. The director shall create standardized claim codes to be used on the standardized claim forms. Each medicaid provider and medicaid provider's designee that bills for medicaid services provided under the integrated care delivery system shall use the appropriate standardized claim form and standardized claim codes.

**HISTORY:**

2019 hb166, § 101.01, effective October 17, 2019.

**Editor's Notes**

This section, as added by 2019 HB 166, was vetoed in part by the Governor.

### § 5164.92 Advanced diagnostic imaging services.

As used in this section, "advanced diagnostic imaging services" means magnetic resonance imaging services, computed tomography services, positron emission tomography services, cardiac nuclear medicine services, and similar imaging services.

The department of medicaid shall implement evidence-based, best practice guidelines or protocols and decision support tools for advanced diagnostic imaging services covered by the fee-for-service component of the medicaid program.

**HISTORY:**

153 v H 1, § 101.01, eff. 10-16-09; 2013 HB 59, § 101.01, eff. Sept. 29, 2013.

**Editor's Notes**

This section was formerly codified as RC § 5111.0210.

**Amendment Notes**

The 2013 amendment, in the second paragraph, substituted "The department of medicaid" for "Not later than January 1, 2010, the department of job and family services" and "covered by" for "available under".

### § 5164.93 Medicaid provider's electronic health record incentive payment.

(A) The department of medicaid may establish a program under which it provides incentive payments, as authorized by the " Social Security Act," section 1903(a)(3)(F) and (t), 42 U.S.C. 1396b(a)(3)(F) and (t), to encourage the adoption and use of electronic health record technology by medicaid providers who are identified under that federal law as eligible professionals.

(B) After the department has made a determination regarding the amount of a medicaid provider's electronic health record incentive payment or the denial of an incentive payment, the department shall notify the provider. The provider may request that the department reconsider its determination.

A request for reconsideration shall be submitted in writing to the department not later than fifteen days after the provider receives notification of the determination. The request shall be accompanied by written materials setting forth the basis for, and supporting, the reconsideration request.

On receipt of a timely request, the department shall reconsider the determination. On the basis of the written materials accompanying the request, the department may uphold, reverse, or modify its original determination. The department shall mail to the provider by certified mail a written notice of the reconsideration decision.

In accordance with Chapter 2505. of the Revised Code, the medicaid provider may appeal the reconsideration decision by filing a notice of appeal with the court of common pleas of Franklin county. The notice shall identify the decision being appealed and the specific grounds for the appeal. The notice of appeal shall be filed not later than fifteen days after the department mails its notice of the reconsideration decision. A copy of the notice of appeal shall be filed with the department not later than three days after the notice is filed with the court.

(C) The medicaid director may adopt rules under section 5162.02 of the Revised Code as necessary to implement this section. The rules, if any, shall be adopted in accordance with Chapter 119. of the Revised Code.

**HISTORY:**

2011 HB 153, § 101.01, eff. June 30, 2011; 2013 HB 59, § 101.01, eff. Sept. 29, 2013.

**Editor's Notes**

This section was formerly codified as RC § 5111.0215.

**Amendment Notes**

The 2013 amendment, in (A), substituted "department of medicaid" for "department of job and family services" and " 'Social Security Act,' section 1903(a)(3)(F) and (t), 42 U.S.C. 1396b(a)(3)(F) and (t)" for " 'Health Information Technology for Economic and Clinical Health Act,' 123 Stat. 489 (2009), 42 U.S.C. 1396b(a)(3)(F) and 1396b(t), as amended"; and, in (C), substituted "medicaid director may adopt rules under section 5162.02" for "director of job and family services may adopt rules in accordance with Chapter 119." in the first sentence and added the second sentence.

### § 5164.94 Medicaid services to Medicaid recipients in culturally and linguistically appropriate manners.

The medicaid director shall implement within the medicaid program a system that encourages medicaid providers to provide medicaid services to medicaid recipients in culturally and linguistically appropriate manners.

**HISTORY:**

2013 SB 206, § 1, eff. Mar. 20, 2014.

### § 5164.95 Standards for medicaid payments for telehealth care services.

(A) As used in this section, "telehealth service" means a health care service delivered to a patient through the use of interactive audio, video, or other telecommunications or electronic technology from a site other than the site where the patient is located.

(B) The department of medicaid shall establish standards for medicaid payments for health care services the department determines are appropriate to be covered by the medicaid program when provided as telehealth services. The standards shall be established in rules adopted under section 5164.02 of the Revised Code.

In accordance with section 5162.021 of the Revised Code, the medicaid director shall adopt rules authorizing the directors of other state agencies to adopt rules regarding the medicaid coverage of telehealth services under programs administered by the other state agencies. Any such rules adopted by the medicaid director or the directors of other state agencies are not subject to the requirements of division (F) of section 121.95 of the Revised Code.

(C)(1) To the extent permitted under rules adopted under section 5164.02 of the Revised Code and applicable federal law, the following practitioners are eligible to provide telehealth services covered pursuant to this section:

(a) A physician licensed under Chapter 4731. of the Revised Code to practice medicine and surgery, osteopathic medicine and surgery, or podiatric medicine and surgery;

(b) A psychologist or school psychologist licensed under Chapter 4732. of the Revised Code or under rules adopted in accordance with sections 3301.07 and 3319.22 of the Revised Code;

(c) A physician assistant licensed under Chapter 4730. of the Revised Code;

(d) A clinical nurse specialist, certified nurse-midwife, or certified nurse practitioner licensed under Chapter 4723. of the Revised Code;

(e) An independent social worker, independent marriage and family therapist, or professional clinical counselor licensed under Chapter 4757. of the Revised Code;

(f) An independent chemical dependency counselor licensed under Chapter 4758. of the Revised Code;

(g) A supervised practitioner or supervised trainee;

(h) An audiologist or speech-language pathologist licensed under Chapter 4753. of the Revised Code;

(i) An audiology aide or speech-language pathology aide, as defined in section 4753.072 of the Revised Code, or an individual holding a conditional license under section 4753.071 of the Revised Code;

(j) An occupational therapist or physical therapist licensed under Chapter 4755. of the Revised Code;

(k) An occupational therapy assistant or physical therapist assistant licensed under Chapter 4755. of the Revised Code.

(*l*) A dietitian licensed under Chapter 4759. of the Revised Code;

(m) A chiropractor licensed under Chapter 4734. of the Revised Code;

(n) A pharmacist licensed under Chapter 4729. of the Revised Code;

(o) A genetic counselor licensed under Chapter 4778. of the Revised Code;

(p) An optometrist licensed under Chapter 4725. of the Revised Code to practice optometry under a therapeutic pharmaceutical agents certificate;

(q) A respiratory care professional licensed under Chapter 4761. of the Revised Code;

(r) A certified Ohio behavior analyst certified under Chapter 4783. of the Revised Code;

(s) A practitioner who provides services through a medicaid school program;

(t) Subject to section 5119.368 of the Revised Code, a practitioner authorized to provide services and supports certified under section 5119.36 of the Revised Code through a community mental health services provider or community addiction services provider;

(u) Any other practitioner the medicaid director considers eligible to provide telehealth services.

(2) In accordance with division (B) of this section and to the extent permitted under rules adopted under section 5164.02 of the Revised Code and applicable federal law, the following provider types are eligible to submit claims for medicaid payments for providing telehealth services:

(a) Any practitioner described in division (C)(1) of this section, except for those described in divisions (C)(1)(g), (i), and (k) of this section;

(b) A professional medical group;

(c) A federally qualified health center or federally qualified health center look-alike, as defined in section 3701.047 of the Revised Code;

(d) A rural health clinic;

(e) An ambulatory health care clinic;

(f) An outpatient hospital;

(g) A medicaid school program;

(h) Subject to section 5119.368 of the Revised Code, a community mental health services provider or community addiction services provider that offers services and supports certified under section 5119.36 of the Revised Code;

(i) Any other provider type the medicaid director considers eligible to submit the claims for payment.

(D)(1) When providing telehealth services under this section, a practitioner shall comply with all requirements under state and federal law regarding the protection of patient information. A practitioner shall ensure that any username or password information and any electronic communications between the practitioner and a patient are securely transmitted and stored.

(2) When providing telehealth services under this section, every practitioner site shall have access to the medical records of the patient at the time telehealth services are provided.

**HISTORY:**

2014 HB 123, § 1, eff. May 20, 2014; 2021 hb122, § 1, effective March 23, 2022.

**Editor's Notes**

Section originally enacted as R.C. § 5164.94, but was renumbered to avoid conflicting enactment by 2013 SB 206.

**Amendment Notes**

The 2021 amendment by HB 122 added the second paragraph of (B); and added (C) and (D).

### § 5164.951 Standards for medicaid payments for teledentistry services.

As used in this section, "teledentistry" has the same meaning as in section 4715.43 of the Revised Code.

The department of medicaid shall establish standards for medicaid payments for services provided through teledentistry. The standards shall provide coverage for services to the same extent that those services would be covered by the medicaid program if the services were provided without the use of teledentistry.

**HISTORY:**

2018 sb259, § 1, effective March 20, 2019.



# CHAPTER 5165

# NURSING FACILITIES SERVICES—MEDICAID COVERAGE

Section

Titles 39 — 57

### § 5165.01 Definitions.

As used in this chapter:

(A) "Affiliated operator" means an operator affiliated with either of the following:

(1) The exiting operator for whom the affiliated operator is to assume liability for the entire amount of the exiting operator's debt under the medicaid program or the portion of the debt that represents the franchise permit fee the exiting operator owes;

(2) The entering operator involved in the change of operator with the exiting operator specified in division (A)(1) of this section.

(B) "Allowable costs" are a nursing facility's costs that the department of medicaid determines are reasonable. Fines paid under sections 5165.60 to 5165.89 and section 5165.99 of the Revised Code are not allowable costs.

(C) "Ancillary and support costs" means all reasonable costs incurred by a nursing facility other than direct care costs, tax costs, or capital costs. "Ancillary and support costs" includes, but is not limited to, costs of activities, social services, pharmacy consultants, habilitation supervisors, qualified intellectual disability professionals, program directors, medical and habilitation records, program supplies, incontinence supplies, food, enterals, dietary supplies and personnel, laundry, housekeeping, security, administration, medical equipment, utilities, liability insurance, bookkeeping, purchasing department, human resources, communications, travel, dues, license fees, subscriptions, home office costs not otherwise allocated, legal services, accounting services, minor equipment, maintenance and repairs, help-wanted advertising, informational advertising, start-up costs, organizational expenses, other interest, property insurance, employee training and staff development, employee benefits, payroll taxes, and workers' compensation premiums or costs for self-insurance claims and related costs as specified in rules adopted under section 5165.02 of the Revised Code, for personnel listed in this division. "Ancillary and support costs" also means the cost of equipment, including vehicles, acquired by operating lease executed before December 1, 1992, if the costs are reported as administrative and general costs on the nursing facility's cost report for the cost reporting period ending December 31, 1992.

(D) "Applicable calendar year" means the calendar year immediately preceding the calendar year that precedes the first of the state fiscal years for which a rebasing is conducted.

(E) For purposes of calculating a critical access nursing facility's occupancy rate and utilization rate under this chapter, "as of the last day of the calendar year" refers to the occupancy and utilization rates during the calendar year identified in the cost report filed under section 5165.10 of the Revised Code.

(F)(1) "Capital costs" means the actual expense incurred by a nursing facility for all of the following:

(a) Depreciation and interest on any capital assets that cost five hundred dollars or more per item, including the following:

(i) Buildings;

(ii) Building improvements;

(iii) Except as provided in division (D) of this section, equipment;

(iv) Transportation equipment.

(b) Amortization and interest on land improvements and leasehold improvements;

(c) Amortization of financing costs;

(d) Lease and rent of land, buildings, and equipment.

(2) The costs of capital assets of less than five hundred dollars per item may be considered capital costs in accordance with a provider's practice.

(G) "Capital lease" and "operating lease" shall be construed in accordance with generally accepted accounting principles.

(H) "Case-mix score" means a measure determined under section 5165.192 of the Revised Code of the relative direct-care resources needed to provide care and habilitation to a nursing facility resident.

(I) "Change of operator" means an entering operator becoming the operator of a nursing facility in the place of the exiting operator.

(1) Actions that constitute a change of operator include the following:

(a) A change in an exiting operator's form of legal organization, including the formation of a partnership or corporation from a sole proprietorship;

(b) A transfer of all the exiting operator's ownership interest in the operation of the nursing facility to the entering operator, regardless of whether ownership of any or all of the real property or personal property associated with the nursing facility is also transferred;

(c) A lease of the nursing facility to the entering operator or the exiting operator's termination of the exiting operator's lease;

(d) If the exiting operator is a partnership, dissolution of the partnership;

(e) If the exiting operator is a partnership, a change in composition of the partnership unless both of the following apply:

(i) The change in composition does not cause the partnership's dissolution under state law.

(ii) The partners agree that the change in composition does not constitute a change in operator.

(f) If the operator is a corporation, dissolution of the corporation, a merger of the corporation into another corporation that is the survivor of the merger, or a consolidation of one or more other corporations to form a new corporation.

(2) The following, alone, do not constitute a change of operator:

(a) A contract for an entity to manage a nursing facility as the operator's agent, subject to the operator's approval of daily operating and management decisions;

(b) A change of ownership, lease, or termination of a lease of real property or personal property associated with a nursing facility if an entering operator does not become the operator in place of an exiting operator;

(c) If the operator is a corporation, a change of one or more members of the corporation's governing body or transfer of ownership of one or more shares of the corporation's stock, if the same corporation continues to be the operator.

(J) "Cost center" means the following:

(1) Ancillary and support costs;

(2) Capital costs;

(3) Direct care costs;

(4) Tax costs.

(K) "Custom wheelchair" means a wheelchair to which both of the following apply:

(1) It has been measured, fitted, or adapted in consideration of either of the following:

(a) The body size or disability of the individual who is to use the wheelchair;

(b) The individual's period of need for, or intended use of, the wheelchair.

(2) It has customized features, modifications, or components, such as adaptive seating and positioning systems, that the supplier who assembled the wheelchair, or the manufacturer from which the wheelchair was ordered, added or made in accordance with the instructions of the physician of the individual who is to use the wheelchair.

(L)(1) "Date of licensure" means the following:

(a) In the case of a nursing facility that was required by law to be licensed as a nursing home under Chapter 3721. of the Revised Code when it originally began to be operated as a nursing home, the date the nursing facility was originally so licensed;

(b) In the case of a nursing facility that was not required by law to be licensed as a nursing home when it originally began to be operated as a nursing home, the date it first began to be operated as a nursing home, regardless of the date the nursing facility was first licensed as a nursing home.

(2) If, after a nursing facility's original date of licensure, more nursing home beds are added to the nursing facility, the nursing facility has a different date of licensure for the additional beds. This does not apply, however, to additional beds when both of the following apply:

(a) The additional beds are located in a part of the nursing facility that was constructed at the same time as the continuing beds already located in that part of the nursing facility;

(b) The part of the nursing facility in which the additional beds are located was constructed as part of the nursing facility at a time when the nursing facility was not required by law to be licensed as a nursing home.

(3) The definition of "date of licensure" in this section applies in determinations of nursing facilities' medicaid payment rates but does not apply in determinations of nursing facilities' franchise permit fees.

(M) "Desk-reviewed" means that a nursing facility's costs as reported on a cost report submitted under section 5165.10 of the Revised Code have been subjected to a desk review under section 5165.108 of the Revised Code and preliminarily determined to be allowable costs.

(N) "Direct care costs" means all of the following costs incurred by a nursing facility:

(1) Costs for registered nurses, licensed practical nurses, and nurse aides employed by the nursing facility;

(2) Costs for direct care staff, administrative nursing staff, medical directors, respiratory therapists, and except as provided in division (N)(8) of this section, other persons holding degrees qualifying them to provide therapy;

(3) Costs of purchased nursing services;

(4) Costs of quality assurance;

(5) Costs of training and staff development, employee benefits, payroll taxes, and workers' compensation premiums or costs for self-insurance claims and related costs as specified in rules adopted under section 5165.02 of the Revised Code, for personnel listed in divisions (N)(1), (2), (4), and (8) of this section;

(6) Costs of consulting and management fees related to direct care;

(7) Allocated direct care home office costs;

(8) Costs of habilitation staff (other than habilitation supervisors), medical supplies, emergency oxygen, over-the-counter pharmacy products, physical therapists, physical therapy assistants, occupational therapists, occupational therapy assistants, speech therapists, audiologists, habilitation supplies, and universal precautions supplies;

(9) Costs of wheelchairs other than the following:

(a) Custom wheelchairs;

(b) Repairs to and replacements of custom wheelchairs and parts that are made in accordance with the instructions of the physician of the individual who uses the custom wheelchair.

(10) Costs of other direct-care resources that are specified as direct care costs in rules adopted under section 5165.02 of the Revised Code.

(O) "Dual eligible individual" has the same meaning as in section 5160.01 of the Revised Code.

(P) "Effective date of a change of operator" means the day the entering operator becomes the operator of the nursing facility.

(Q) "Effective date of a facility closure" means the last day that the last of the residents of the nursing facility resides in the nursing facility.

(R) "Effective date of an involuntary termination" means the date the department of medicaid terminates the operator's provider agreement for the nursing facility.

(S) "Effective date of a voluntary withdrawal of participation" means the day the nursing facility ceases to accept new medicaid residents other than the individuals who reside in the nursing facility on the day before the effective date of the voluntary withdrawal of participation.

(T) "Entering operator" means the person or government entity that will become the operator of a nursing facility when a change of operator occurs or following an involuntary termination.

(U) "Exiting operator" means any of the following:

(1) An operator that will cease to be the operator of a nursing facility on the effective date of a change of operator;

(2) An operator that will cease to be the operator of a nursing facility on the effective date of a facility closure;

(3) An operator of a nursing facility that is undergoing or has undergone a voluntary withdrawal of participation;

(4) An operator of a nursing facility that is undergoing or has undergone an involuntary termination.

(V)(1) Subject to divisions (V)(2) and (3) of this section, "facility closure" means either of the following:

(a) Discontinuance of the use of the building, or part of the building, that houses the facility as a nursing facility that results in the relocation of all of the nursing facility's residents;

(b) Conversion of the building, or part of the building, that houses a nursing facility to a different use with any necessary license or other approval needed for that use being obtained and one or more of the nursing facility's residents remaining in the building, or part of the building, to receive services under the new use.

(2) A facility closure occurs regardless of any of the following:

(a) The operator completely or partially replacing the nursing facility by constructing a new nursing facility or transferring the nursing facility's license to another nursing facility;

(b) The nursing facility's residents relocating to another of the operator's nursing facilities;

(c) Any action the department of health takes regarding the nursing facility's medicaid certification that may result in the transfer of part of the nursing facility's survey findings to another of the operator's nursing facilities;

(d) Any action the department of health takes regarding the nursing facility's license under Chapter 3721. of the Revised Code.

(3) A facility closure does not occur if all of the nursing facility's residents are relocated due to an emergency evacuation and one or more of the residents return to a medicaid-certified bed in the nursing facility not later than thirty days after the evacuation occurs.

(W) "Franchise permit fee" means the fee imposed by sections 5168.40 to 5168.56 of the Revised Code.

(X) "Inpatient days" means both of the following:

(1) All days during which a resident, regardless of payment source, occupies a licensed bed in a nursing facility;

(2) Fifty per cent of the days for which payment is made under section 5165.34 of the Revised Code.

(Y) "Involuntary termination" means the department of medicaid's termination of the operator's provider agreement for the nursing facility when the termination is not taken at the operator's request.

(Z) "Low resource utilization resident" means a medicaid recipient residing in a nursing facility who, for purposes of calculating the nursing facility's medicaid payment rate for direct care costs, is placed in either of the two lowest resource utilization groups, excluding any resource utilization group that is a default group used for residents with incomplete assessment data.

(AA) "Maintenance and repair expenses" means a nursing facility's expenditures that are necessary and proper to maintain an asset in a normally efficient working condition and that do not extend the useful life of the asset two years or more. "Maintenance and repair expenses" includes but is not limited to the costs of ordinary repairs such as painting and wallpapering.

(BB) "Medicaid-certified capacity" means the number of a nursing facility's beds that are certified for participation in medicaid as nursing facility beds.

(CC) "Medicaid days" means both of the following:

(1) All days during which a resident who is a medicaid recipient eligible for nursing facility services occupies a bed in a nursing facility that is included in the nursing facility's medicaid-certified capacity;

(2) Fifty per cent of the days for which payment is made under section 5165.34 of the Revised Code.

(DD)(1) "New nursing facility" means a nursing facility for which the provider obtains an initial provider agreement following medicaid certification of the nursing facility by the director of health, including such a nursing facility that replaces one or more nursing facilities for which a provider previously held a provider agreement.

(2) "New nursing facility" does not mean a nursing facility for which the entering operator seeks a provider agreement pursuant to section 5165.511 or 5165.512 or (pursuant to section 5165.515) section 5165.07 of the Revised Code.

(EE) "Nursing facility" has the same meaning as in the "Social Security Act," section 1919(a), 42 U.S.C. 1396r(a).

(FF) "Nursing facility services" has the same meaning as in the "Social Security Act," section 1905(f), 42 U.S.C. 1396d(f).

(GG) "Nursing home" has the same meaning as in section 3721.01 of the Revised Code.

(HH) "Occupancy rate" means the percentage of licensed beds that, regardless of payer source, are either of the following:

(1) Reserved for use under section 5165.34 of the Revised Code;

(2) Actually being used.

(II) "Operator" means the person or government entity responsible for the daily operating and management decisions for a nursing facility.

(JJ)(1) "Owner" means any person or government entity that has at least five per cent ownership or interest, either directly, indirectly, or in any combination, in any of the following regarding a nursing facility:

(a) The land on which the nursing facility is located;

(b) The structure in which the nursing facility is located;

(c) Any mortgage, contract for deed, or other obligation secured in whole or in part by the land or structure on or in which the nursing facility is located;

(d) Any lease or sublease of the land or structure on or in which the nursing facility is located.

(2) "Owner" does not mean a holder of a debenture or bond related to the nursing facility and purchased at public issue or a regulated lender that has made a loan related to the nursing facility unless the holder or lender operates the nursing facility directly or through a subsidiary.

(KK) "Per diem" means a nursing facility's actual, allowable costs in a given cost center in a cost reporting period, divided by the nursing facility's inpatient days for that cost reporting period.

(LL) "Provider" means an operator with a provider agreement.

(MM) "Provider agreement" means a provider agreement, as defined in section 5164.01 of the Revised Code, that is between the department of medicaid and the operator of a nursing facility for the provision of nursing facility services under the medicaid program.

(NN) "Purchased nursing services" means services that are provided in a nursing facility by registered nurses, licensed practical nurses, or nurse aides who are not employees of the nursing facility.

(OO) "Reasonable" means that a cost is an actual cost that is appropriate and helpful to develop and maintain the operation of patient care facilities and activities, including normal standby costs, and that does not exceed what a prudent buyer pays for a given item or services. Reasonable costs may vary from provider to provider and from time to time for the same provider.

(PP) "Rebasing" means a redetermination of each of the following using information from cost reports for an applicable calendar year that is later than the applicable calendar year used for the previous rebasing:

(1) Each peer group's rate for ancillary and support costs as determined pursuant to division (C) of section 5165.16 of the Revised Code;

(2) Each peer group's rate for capital costs as determined pursuant to division (C) of section 5165.17 of the Revised Code;

(3) Each peer group's cost per case-mix unit as determined pursuant to division (C) of section 5165.19 of the Revised Code;

(4) Each nursing facility's rate for tax costs as determined pursuant to section 5165.21 of the Revised Code.

(QQ) "Related party" means an individual or organization that, to a significant extent, has common ownership with, is associated or affiliated with, has control of, or is controlled by, the provider.

(1) An individual who is a relative of an owner is a related party.

(2) Common ownership exists when an individual or individuals possess significant ownership or equity in both the provider and the other organization. Significant ownership or equity exists when an individual or individuals possess five per cent ownership or equity in both the provider and a supplier. Significant ownership or equity is presumed to exist when an individual or individuals possess ten per cent ownership or equity in both the provider and another organization from which the provider purchases or leases real property.

(3) Control exists when an individual or organization has the power, directly or indirectly, to significantly influence or direct the actions or policies of an organization.

(4) An individual or organization that supplies goods or services to a provider shall not be considered a related party if all of the following conditions are met:

(a) The supplier is a separate bona fide organization.

(b) A substantial part of the supplier's business activity of the type carried on with the provider is transacted with others than the provider and there is an open, competitive market for the types of goods or services the supplier furnishes.

(c) The types of goods or services are commonly obtained by other nursing facilities from outside organizations and are not a basic element of patient care ordinarily furnished directly to patients by nursing facilities.

(d) The charge to the provider is in line with the charge for the goods or services in the open market and no more than the charge made under comparable circumstances to others by the supplier.

(RR) "Relative of owner" means an individual who is related to an owner of a nursing facility by one of the following relationships:

(1) Spouse;

(2) Natural parent, child, or sibling;

(3) Adopted parent, child, or sibling;

(4) Stepparent, stepchild, stepbrother, or stepsister;

(5) Father-in-law, mother-in-law, son-in-law, daughter-in-law, brother-in-law, or sister-in-law;

(6) Grandparent or grandchild;

(7) Foster caregiver, foster child, foster brother, or foster sister.

(SS) "Residents' rights advocate" has the same meaning as in section 3721.10 of the Revised Code.

(TT) "Skilled nursing facility" has the same meaning as in the "Social Security Act," section 1819(a), 42 U.S.C. 1395i-3(a).

(UU) "State fiscal year" means the fiscal year of this state, as specified in section 9.34 of the Revised Code.

(VV) "Sponsor" has the same meaning as in section 3721.10 of the Revised Code.

(WW) "Tax costs" means the costs of taxes imposed under Chapter 5751. of the Revised Code, real estate taxes, personal property taxes, and corporate franchise taxes.

(XX) "Title XIX" means Title XIX of the "Social Security Act," 42 U.S.C. 1396 et seq.

(YY) "Title XVIII" means Title XVIII of the "Social Security Act," 42 U.S.C. 1395 et seq.

(ZZ) "Voluntary withdrawal of participation" means an operator's voluntary election to terminate the participation of a nursing facility in the medicaid program but to continue to provide service of the type provided by a nursing facility.

**HISTORY:**

138 v H 176 (Eff 7-1-80); 139 v S 550 (Eff 11-26-82); 141 v H 428 (Eff 12-23-86); 143 v H 672 (Eff 11-14-89); 143 v H 822 (Eff 12-13-90); 144 v H 904 (Eff 12-22-92); 145 v H 152 (Eff 7-1-93); 145 v H 715 (Eff 7-22-94); 146 v H 117 (Eff 6-30-95); 148 v H 471 (Eff 7-1-2000); 148 v H 403 (Eff 7-1-2000); 148 v H 448. Eff 10-5-2000; 150 v H 95, § 1, eff. 6-26-03; 151 v H 66, § 101.01, eff. 7-1-05; 151 v H 530, § 101.01, eff. 3-30-06; 152 v H 119, § 101.01, eff. 6-30-07, 9-29-07; 153 v H 1, § 101.01, eff. 7-17-09; 2011 HB 153, § 101.01, eff. Sept. 29, 2011; 2012 HB 487, § 101.01, eff. Sept. 10, 2012; 2013 HB 59, § 101.01, eff. Sept. 29, 2013; 2016 hb483, § 101.01, effective October 12, 2016; 2016 hb158, § 1, effective October 12, 2016; 2017 hb49, § 101.01, effective September 29, 2017; 2020 hb481, § 29, effective September 18, 2020; 2021 hb110, § 101.01, effective September 30, 2021.

**Editor's Notes**

The provisions of § 821.12 of 152 v H 119 read as follows:

SECTION 821.12. (A) Except as otherwise provided in division (B) of this section, the amendments by this act to section 5111.20 of the Revised Code are subject to the referendum. Therefore, under Ohio Constitution, Article II, Section 1c and section 1.471 of the Revised Code, the amendments take effect on the ninety-first day after this act is filed with the Secretary of State. If, however, a referendum petition is filed against the amendments, the amendments, unless rejected at the referendum, take effect at the earliest time permitted by law.

(B) The amendment to division (H)(3)(a) of section 5111.20 of the Revised Code is not subject to the referendum. Therefore, under Ohio Constitution, Article II, Section 1d and section 1.471 of the Revised Code, the amendment goes into immediate effect.

The provisions of § 206.66.24 of 151 v H 66 read as follows:

SECTION 206.66.24. TRANSITION METHODOLOGY FOR MEDICAID REIMBURSEMENT FOR NURSING FACILITIES.

(A) There is hereby created the Nursing Facility Rate Transition Advisory Council. The Council shall consist of all of the following:

(1) The Director of Job and Family Services or the Director's designee;

(2) The Deputy Director of the Office of Ohio Health Plans of the Department of Job and Family Services or the Deputy Director's designee;

(3) The Director of Health or the Director's designee;

(4) One representative of Medicaid recipients residing in nursing facilities appointed by the Governor;

(5) One representative of each of the following organizations appointed by the organization:

(a) The Ohio Academy of Nursing Homes;

(b) The Association of Ohio Philanthropic Homes and Housing for the Aging;

(c) The Ohio Health Care Association.

(B) Members of the Nursing Facility Rate Transition Advisory Council shall receive no compensation for serving on the Council.

(C) The Director of Job and Family Services shall serve as chair of the Nursing Facility Rate Transition Advisory Council.

(D) The Nursing Facility Rate Transition Advisory Council shall develop recommendations on the methodology to be used to phase in the nursing facility reimbursement formula established under sections 5111.20 to 5111.33 of the Revised Code. The Council shall prepare quarterly progress reports and, not later than nine months after the effective date of this section, a final report. The Council shall submit copies of the report to the Governor, the President and Minority Leader of the Senate, and the Speaker and Minority Leader of the House of Representatives. The Council shall cease to exist on the issuance of the final report.

The provisions of § 206.66.23 of 151 v H 66 read as follows:

SECTION 206.66.23. FISCAL YEAR 2007 MEDICAID REIMBURSEMENT SYSTEM FOR NURSING FACILITIES.

(A) As used in this section:

"Franchise permit fee" means the fee imposed by sections 3721.50 to 3721.58 of the Revised Code.

"Nursing facility" and "provider" have the same meanings as in section 5111.20 of the Revised Code.

"Nursing facility services" means nursing facility services covered by the Medicaid program that a nursing facility provides to a resident of the nursing facility who is a Medicaid recipient eligible for Medicaid-covered nursing facility services.

(B) Except as provided in division (C) of this section, the provider of a nursing facility that has a valid Medicaid provider agreement on June 30, 2006, and a valid Medicaid provider agreement for fiscal year 2007 shall be paid, for nursing facility services the nursing facility provides during fiscal year 2007, the rate determined for the nursing facility under sections 5111.20 to 5111.33 of the Revised Code.

(C) If the rate determined for a nursing facility under sections 5111.20 to 5111.33 of the Revised Code for nursing facility services provided during fiscal year 2007 is more than one hundred two per cent of the rate the provider is paid for nursing facility services the nursing facility provides on June 30, 2006, the Department of Job and Family Services shall reduce the nursing facility's fiscal year 2007 rate so that the rate is no more than one hundred two per cent of the nursing facility's rate for June 30, 2006. If the rate determined for a nursing facility under sections 5111.20 to 5111.33 of the Revised Code for nursing facility services provided during fiscal year 2007 is less than ninety-eight per cent of the rate the provider was paid for nursing facility services the nursing facility provides on June 30, 2006, the Department shall increase the nursing facility's fiscal year 2007 rate so that the rate is no less than ninety-eight per cent of the nursing facility's rate for June 30, 2006.

(D) If the United States Centers for Medicare and Medicaid Services requires that the franchise permit fee be reduced or eliminated, the Department of Job and Family Services shall reduce the amount it pays providers of nursing facilities under this section as necessary to reflect the loss to the state of the revenue and federal financial participation generated from the franchise permit fee.

(E) The Department of Job and Family Services shall follow this section in determining the rate to be paid to the provider of a nursing facility that has a valid Medicaid provider agreement on June 30, 2006, and a valid Medicaid provider agreement for fiscal year 2007 notwithstanding anything to the contrary in sections 5111.20 to 5111.33 of the Revised Code.

The provisions of § 232 of H.B. 95 (150 v —) read as follows:

SECTION 232. Section 5111.20 of the Revised Code is presented in this act as a composite of the section as amended by both Sub. H.B. 403 and Sub. H.B. 448 of the 123rd General Assembly. The General Assembly, applying the principle stated in division (B) of section 152 of the Revised Code that amendments are to be harmonized if reasonably capable of simultaneous operation, finds that the composite is the resulting version of the section in effect prior to the effective date of the section as presented in this act.

This section was formerly codified as RC § 5111.20.



**Amendment Notes**

The 2021 amendment by HB 110 added (E); redesignated former (E) through (FF) as (F) through (GG); substituted "division (D)" for "division (C)" in (F)(1)(a)(iii); substituted "division (N)(8)" for "division (M)(8)" in (N)(2); substituted "divisions (N)(1)" for "divisions (M)(1)" in (N)(5); substituted "divisions (V)(2)" for "divisions (U)(2)" in the introductory language of (V)(1); substituted "licensed bed in a nursing facility" for "bed in a nursing facility that is included in the nursing facility's medicaid-certified capacity" in in (X)(1); added (HH); and redesignated former (GG) through (XX) as (II) through (ZZ).

The 2020 amendment by HB 481 deleted former (E), which read: "Budget reduction adjustment factor' means the factor specified pursuant to or in section 5165.361 of the Revised Code for a state fiscal year"; and redesignated former (F) through (CC) as (E) through (BB); substituted "division (M)(8)" for "division (N)(8)" in (M)(2); substituted "divisions (M)(1)" for "divisions (N)(1)" in (M)(5); substituted "divisions (U)(2)" for "divisions (V)(2)" in the introductory language of (U)(1); deleted former (DD), which read: "'Medicare skilled nursing facility market basket index' means the index established by the United States secretary of health and human services under section 1888(e)(5) of the 'Social Security Act,' 42 U.S.C. 1395yy(e)(5)"; and redesignated former (EE) through (ZZ) for (CC) through (XX).

The 2017 amendment by HB 49 rewrote the section.

The 2016 amendment by HB 158 substituted "intellectual disability" for "mental retardation" in the second sentence of (C).

The 2016 amendment by HB 483 deleted "behavioral and mental health services" following "pharmacy products" in (L)(8).

The 2013 amendment rewrote the section.

The 2012 amendment, in (B), inserted "tax costs" in the first sentence and deleted "wheelchairs, resident transportation" following "minor equipment" in the second sentence; inserted "wheelchairs, resident transportation" in (H)(2); rewrote (L), which formerly read: " 'Inpatient days' means all days during which a resident, regardless of payment source, occupies a bed in a nursing facility or intermediate care facility for the mentally retarded that is included in the facility's certified capacity under Title XIX. Therapeutic or hospital leave days for which payment is made under section 5111.33 or 5111.331 of the Revised Code are considered inpatient days proportionate to the percentage of the facility's per resident per day rate paid for those days"; rewrote (O); inserted (CC); and redesignated former (CC) and (DD) as (DD) and (EE).

The 2011 amendment substituted "sections 5111.20 to 5111.331" for "sections 5111.20 to 5111.34" in the introductory language; inserted "behavioral and mental health services" in (H)(2); and substituted "section 5111.33 or 5111.331" for "section 5111.33" in the second sentence of (L) and (O).

153 v H 1, effective July 17, 2009, inserted "wheelchairs, resident transportation" in the second sentence of (B); and substituted "oxygen, over-the-counter pharmacy products, physical therapists, physical therapy assistants, occupational therapists, occupational therapy assistants, speech therapists, audiologists" for "emergency oxygen" in (H)(2).

152 v H 119, effective September 29, 2007, except amendments to division (H)(3)(a), effective June 30, 2007, added (F)(2) and made related changes; inserted "off-site day programming" in (H)(3)(a); and rewrote (J).

151 v H 530, effective March 30, 2006, in (B), inserted "habilitation supervisors, qualified mental retardation professionals, program directors"; in (H)(1)(b), deleted "habilitation staff, qualified mental retardation professionals, program directors" following "medical directors" and "habilitation supervisors" following "respiratory therapists"; in (H)(2), inserted "costs of habilitation staff (other than habilitation supervisors)"; in (H)(3)(a), inserted "habilitation staff (including habilitation supervisors), qualified mental retardation professionals, program directors"; and corrected internal references.

151 v H 66, effective July 1, 2005, rewrote the section.

## RESEARCH REFERENCES AND PRACTICE AIDS

**Cross-References to Related Sections**

Offenses by providers; penalties; termination of agreement, RC § 5164.35.

Payments to reserve bed during temporary absence of resident, RC § 5124.34.

Reimbursement of providers and facilities; rules to be consistent, RC § 5164.02.

**Ohio Administrative Code**

Department of job and family services, division of medical assistance — Medicaid coverage of targeted case management services provided to individuals with developmental disabilities, OAC 5160-48-01.

Nursing facilities (NF) medicaid cost reports, OAC ch. 5160-3.

Definitions. OAC 5160-3-01.

Nursing facilities (NFs): relationship of NF services to other covered medicaid services. OAC 5160-3-19.

**Comparative Legislation**

Licensing of nursing homes:

42 USCS § 3012
CA—Cal Health & Saf Code § 1417 et seq; Cal Wel & Inst Code § 9201
FL—Fla. Stat. § 400.011 et seq
IL—210 Ill. Comp. Stat. § 45/3-101 et seq
KY—KRS § 216B.010 et seq
MI—MCLS § 333.21711
NY—NY CLS Pub Health § 2805 et seq
PA—62 P.S. § 1001 et seq

## § 5165.011 Reference to or designation of particular type of facility.

(A) Except as provided in division (B) of this section, whenever "skilled nursing facility," "intermediate care facility," or "dual skilled nursing and intermediate care facility" is referred to or designated in any statute, rule, contract, provider agreement, or other document pertaining to the medicaid program, the reference or designation is deemed to refer to a nursing facility.

(B) A reference to or designation of an "intermediate care facility for individuals with intellectual disabilities" or "ICF/IID" is not deemed to refer to a nursing facility.

**HISTORY:**

143 v H 822. Eff 12-13-90; 2013 HB 59, § 101.01, eff. Sept. 29, 2013.

**Editor's Notes**

This section was formerly codified as RC § 5111.201.

**Amendment Notes**

The 2013 amendment added the (A) and (B) designation; in (A), added the exception to the beginning, substituted "medicaid program" for "medical assistance program," and deleted "except that" from the end; and substituted "'individuals with intellectual disabilities' or 'ICF/IID'" for "the mentally retarded" in (B).

**RESEARCH REFERENCES AND PRACTICE AIDS**

**Ohio Administrative Code**

Eligible providers and provider types. OAC 5160-3-02.3.

## § 5165.02 Adoption of rules.

The medicaid director shall adopt rules as necessary to implement this chapter. The rules shall be adopted in accordance with Chapter 119. of the Revised Code.

**HISTORY:**

2013 HB 59, § 101.01, eff. Sept. 29, 2013.

## § 5165.03 Conditions for admission of mentally ill person to nursing facility.

(A) As used in this section:

(1) "Dementia" includes Alzheimer's disease or a related disorder.

(2) "Serious mental illness" means "serious mental illness," as defined by the United States department of health and human services in regulations adopted under the "Social Security Act," section 1919(e)(7)(G)(i), 42 U.S.C. 1396r(e)(7)(G)(i).

(3) "Mentally ill individual" means an individual who has a serious mental illness other than either of the following:

(a) A primary diagnosis of dementia;

(b) A primary diagnosis that is not a primary diagnosis of dementia and a primary diagnosis of something other than a serious mental illness.

(4) "Mentally retarded individual" means an individual who is mentally retarded or has a related condition, as described in the "Social Security Act," section 1905(d), 42 U.S.C. 1396d(d).

(5) "Specialized services" means the services specified by the United States department of health and human services in regulations adopted under the "Social Security Act," section 1919(e)(7)(G)(iii), 42 U.S.C. 1396r(e)(7)(G)(iii).

(B)(1) Except as provided in division (D) of this section, no nursing facility shall admit as a resident any mentally ill individual unless the facility has received evidence that the department of mental health and addiction services has determined both of the following under section 5119.40 of the Revised Code:

(a) That the individual requires the level of services provided by a nursing facility because of the individual's physical and mental condition;

(b) Whether the individual requires specialized services for mental illness.

(2) Except as provided in division (D) of this section, no nursing facility shall admit as a resident any mentally retarded individual unless the facility has received evidence that the department of developmental disabilities has determined both of the following under section 5123.021 of the Revised Code:

(a) That the individual requires the level of services provided by a nursing facility because of the individual's physical and mental condition;

(b) Whether the individual requires specialized services for mental retardation.

(C) The department of medicaid shall not make medicaid payments to a nursing facility on behalf of any individual who is admitted to the facility in violation of division (B) of this section for the period beginning on the date of admission and ending on the date the requirements of division (B) of this section are met.

(D) A determination under division (B) of this section is not required for any individual who is exempted from the requirement that a determination be made by division (B)(2) of section 5119.40 of the Revised Code or rules adopted by the department of mental health and addiction services under division (E)(3) of that section, or by division (B)(2) of section 5123.021 of the Revised Code or rules adopted by the department of developmental disabilities under division (E)(3) of that section.

**HISTORY:**

144 v S 124 (Eff 4-16-93); 146 v H 629 (Eff 3-13-97); 148 v H 471. Eff 7-1-2000; 153 v S 79, § 1, eff. 10-6-09; 2013 HB 59, § 101.01, eff. Sept. 29, 2013.

**Editor's Notes**

This section was formerly codified as RC § 5111.202.

**Amendment Notes**

The 2013 amendment substituted "the 'Social Security Act,' section 1919(e)(7)(G)(i), 42 U.S.C. 1396r(e)(7)(G)(i)" for "section 1919(e)(7)(G)(i) of the 'Social Security Act,' 49 Stat. 620 (1935), section 1919(e)(7)(G)(i) of the 'Social Security Act,' 49 Stat. 620 (1935)" in (A)(2); substituted "the 'Social Security Act,' section 1905(d), 42 U.S.C. 1396d(d)" for "section 1905(d) of the 'Social Security Act.'" in (A)(4); substituted "the 'Social Security Act,' section 1919(e)(7)(G)(iii), 42 U.S.C. 1396r(e)(7)(G)(iii)" for "section 1919(e)(7)(G)(iii) of the 'Social Security Act.'" in (A)(5); in the introductory language of (B)(1) and in (D), substituted "mental health and addiction services" for "mental health" and "section 5119.40" for "section 5119.061"; and substituted "medicaid shall not make medicaid payments" for "job and family services shall not make payments under the medical assistance program" in (C).

153 v S 79, effective October 6, 2009, deleted "mental retardation and" preceding "developmental disabilities" throughout.

**RESEARCH REFERENCES AND PRACTICE AIDS**

**Cross-References to Related Sections**

Determination of whether individual requires nursing facility services and, if so, whether specialized services are needed, RC §§ 5119.40, 5123.021.

**Ohio Administrative Code**

Department of job and family services, division of medical assistance — Institutions for mental disease (IMDs). OAC 5160-3-061.

## § 5165.031 Hearing on adverse determination on need for nursing facility services.

An individual who applies for admission to or resides in a nursing facility shall provide notice and an opportunity for a hearing to any applicant for admission to a nursing facility or resident of a nursing facility who ismay appeal if adversely affected by a determination made by the department of mental health and addiction services under section 5119.40 of the Revised Code or by the department of developmental disabilities under section 5123.021 of the Revised Code. If the individual is an applicant for or recipient of medicaid, the individual may appeal pursuant to section 5160.31 of the Revised Code. If the individual is not an applicant for or recipient of medicaid, the individual may appeal pursuant to a process the department of medicaid shall establish, which shall be similar to the appeals process established by section 5101.35 of the Revised Code. The department of medicaid shall provide notice of the right to appeal to individuals adversely affected by determinations made under sections 5119.40 and 5123.021 of the Revised Code. Any decision made on the basis of such an appeal is binding on the department of mental health and addiction services and the department of developmental disabilities.

**HISTORY:**

144 v S 124 (Eff 4-16-93); 148 v H 471. Eff 7-1-2000; 153 v S 79, § 1, eff. 10-6-09; 2013 HB 59, § 101.01, eff. Sept. 29, 2013.

**Editor's Notes**

This section was formerly codified as RC § 5111.203.

**Amendment Notes**

The 2013 amendment rewrote the section, which formerly read: "Regardless of whether or not an applicant for admission to a nursing facility or resident of a nursing facility is an applicant for or recipient of medical assistance, the department of job and family services shall provide notice and an opportunity for a hearing to any applicant for admission to a nursing facility or resident of a nursing facility who is adversely affected by a determination made by the department of mental health under section 5119.061 of the Revised Code or by the department of developmental disabilities under section 5123.021 of the Revised Code. The hearing shall be conducted in the same manner as hearings conducted under section

5101.35 of the Revised Code. Any decision made by the department of job and family services on the basis of the hearing is binding on the department of mental health and the department of developmental disabilities."

153 v S 79, effective October 6, 2009, deleted "mental retardation and" preceding "developmental disabilities" throughout.

### RESEARCH REFERENCES AND PRACTICE AIDS

**Ohio Administrative Code**

Availability of payment during the appeals process for denial or termination of a provider agreement. OAC 5160-3-04 et seq.

## § 5165.04 Assessment of whether recipient needs level of care provided by nursing facility.

(A) As used in this section, "representative" means a person acting on behalf of an applicant for or recipient of medicaid. A representative may be a family member, attorney, hospital social worker, or any other person chosen to act on behalf of an applicant or recipient.

(B) The department of medicaid may require each applicant for or recipient of medicaid who applies or intends to apply for admission to a nursing facility or resides in a nursing facility to undergo an assessment to determine whether the applicant or recipient needs the level of care provided by a nursing facility. The assessment may be performed concurrently with a long-term care consultation provided under section 173.42 of the Revised Code.

To the maximum extent possible, the assessment shall be based on information from the resident assessment instrument specified in rules authorized by section 5165.191 of the Revised Code. The assessment shall also be based on criteria and procedures established in rules authorized by division (F) of this section and information provided by the person being assessed or the person's representative.

The department of medicaid, or if the assessment is performed by an agency under contract with the department pursuant to division (G) of this section, the agency, shall, not later than the time the level of care determination based on the assessment is required to be provided under division (C) of this section, give written notice of its conclusions and the basis for them to the person assessed and, if the department or agency under contract with the department has been informed that the person has a representative, to the representative.

(C) The department or agency under contract with the department, whichever performs the assessment, shall provide a level of care determination based on the assessment as follows:

(1) In the case of a person applying or intending to apply for admission to a nursing facility while hospitalized, not later than one of the following:

(a) One working day after the person or the person's representative submits the application or notifies the department of the person's intention to apply and submits all information required for providing the level of care determination, as specified in rules authorized by division (F)(2) of this section;

(b) A later date requested by the person or the person's representative.

(2) In the case of a person applying or intending to apply for admission to a nursing facility who is not hospitalized, not later than one of the following:

(a) Five calendar days after the person or the person's representative submits the application or notifies the department of the person's intention to apply and submits all information required for providing the level of care determination, as specified in rules authorized by division (F)(2) of this section;

(b) A later date requested by the person or the person's representative.

(3) In the case of a person who resides in a nursing facility, not later than one of the following:

(a) Five calendar days after the person or the person's representative submits an application for medicaid and submits all information required for providing the level of care determination, as specified in rules authorized by division (F)(2) of this section;

(b) A later date requested by the person or the person's representative.

(4) In the case of an emergency, as specified in rules authorized by division (F)(4) of this section, within the number of days specified in the rules.

(D) A person assessed under this section or the person's representative may appeal the conclusions reached by the department or agency under contract with the department on the basis of the assessment. The appeal shall be made pursuant to section 5160.31 of the Revised Code. The department or agency under contract with the department shall provide to the person or the person's representative and the nursing facility written notice of the person's right to request a state hearing. The notice shall include an explanation of the procedure for requesting a state hearing. If a state hearing is requested, the state shall be represented in the hearing by the department or the agency under contract with the department, whichever performed the assessment.

(E) A nursing facility that admits or retains a person determined pursuant to an assessment required under this section not to need the level of care provided by the nursing facility shall not be paid under the medicaid program for the person's care.

(F) The medicaid director shall adopt rules under section 5165.02 of the Revised Code to implement and administer this section. The rules shall include all of the following:

(1) Criteria and procedures to be used in determining whether admission to a nursing facility or continued stay in a nursing facility is appropriate for the person being assessed;

(2) Information the person being assessed or the person's representative must provide to the department or agency under contract with the department for purposes of the assessment and providing a level of care determination based on the assessment;

(3) Circumstances under which a person is not required to be assessed;

(4) Circumstances that constitute an emergency for purposes of division (C)(4) of this section and the number of days within which a level of care determination must be provided in the case of an emergency.

(G) Pursuant to section 5162.35 of the Revised Code, the department of medicaid may enter into contracts in the form of interagency agreements with one or more other state agencies to perform the assessments required under this section. The interagency agreements shall specify the responsibilities of each agency in the performance of the assessments.

**HISTORY:**

145 v H 152 (Eff 7-1-93); 145 v H 715 (Eff 7-22-94); 148 v H 471. Eff 7-1-2000; 151 v H 66, § 101.01, eff. 9-29-05; 2013 HB 59, § 101.01, eff. Sept. 29, 2013.

**Editor's Notes**

The provisions of § 203.21.03 of 151 v H 66 read as follows:

SECTION 203.21.03. PRE-ADMISSION REVIEW FOR NURSING FACILITY ADMISSION.

Pursuant to an interagency agreement, the Department of Job and Family Services shall designate the Department of Aging to perform assessments under sections 173.42 and 5111.204 of the Revised Code. Of the foregoing appropriation item 490-403, PASSPORT, the Department of Aging may use not more than $2,586,648 in fiscal year 2006 and $2,651,315 in fiscal year 2007 to perform the assessments for persons not eligible for Medicaid under the department's interagency agreement with the Department of Job and Family Services and to assist individuals in planning for their long-term health care needs.

This section was formerly codified as RC § 5111.204.

**Amendment Notes**

The 2013 amendment substituted "department of medicaid" for "department of job and family services" in the first sentence of the first paragraph and the last paragraph of (B) and in the first sentence of (G); substituted "authorized by section 5165.191" for "adopted by the director of job and family services under division (E) of section 5111.232" in the first sentence of the second paragraph of (B); substituted "authorized by" for "adopted under" in the second sentence of the second paragraph of (B) and in (C)(1)(a), (C)(2)(a), (C)(3)(a), and (C)(4); deleted "of job and family services" preceding "or agency under" in the last paragraph of (B) and the introductory language of (C); substituted "medicaid" for "medical assistance" in (C)(3)(a); rewrote (D); substituted "paid" for "reimbursed" in (E); substituted "medicaid director shall adopt rules under section 5165.02" for "director of job and family services shall adopt rules in accordance with Chapter 119." in the introductory language of (F); and substituted "section 5162.35" for "section 5111.91" in the first sentence of (G).

151 v H 66, effective September 29, 2005, rewrote the section.

RESEARCH REFERENCES AND PRACTICE AIDS

**Ohio Administrative Code**

Criteria for the protective level of care, OAC 5160-3-06.

Criteria for nursing facility-based level of care. OAC 5160-3-08.

In-person assessments and level of care review process for medicaid covered long term care services. OAC 5160-3-15.

Institutions for mental disease. (IMDs). OAC 5160-3-061.

Skilled level of care (SLOC). OAC 5160-3-05.

## § 5165.06 Operator's duties to be eligible for medicaid payments.

Subject to section 5165.072 of the Revised Code, an operator is eligible to enter into a provider agreement for a nursing facility if all of the following apply:

(A) The nursing facility is certified by the director of health for participation in medicaid;

(B) The nursing facility is licensed by the director of health as a nursing home if so required by law;

(C) The operator and nursing facility comply with all applicable state and federal laws and rules.

**HISTORY:**

138 v H 176 (Eff 7-1-80); 141 v H 428 (Eff 12-23-86); 143 v H 672 (Eff 11-14-89); 143 v H 822 (Eff 12-13-90); 148 v H 471. Eff 7-1-2000; 150 v H 95, § 1, eff. 6-26-03; 151 v H 66, § 101.01, eff. 7-1-05; 153 v H 1, § 101.01, eff. 7-17-09; 153 v H 449, § 1, eff. 6-18-10; 2011 HB 153, § 101.01, eff. Sept. 29, 2011; 2013 HB 59, § 101.01, eff. Sept. 29, 2013.

**Editor's Notes**

This section was formerly codified as RC § 5111.21.

**Amendment Notes**

The 2013 amendment rewrote the section.

The 2011 amendment, in (B), inserted "former," "of the Revised Code as enacted by Am. Sub. H.B. 1 of the 128th general assembly," and "section" preceding "5123.197."

153 v H 449, effective June 18, 2010, in (C)(2), substituted "department of veterans services" for "Ohio veteran's home agency".

153 v H 1, effective July 17, 2009, added "Subject to division (B) of this section" to the beginning of (A)(3); inserted (B); redesignated former (B) as (C); and made a stylistic change.

151 v H 66, effective July 1, 2005, rewrote the section.

NOTES TO DECISIONS

Analysis



**Amount of reimbursement**

Under the current Medicaid reimbursement standard, a state is not required to reimburse every efficient and economic facility for its reasonable, actual costs: Drake Ctr. v. Department of Human Servs., 125 Ohio App. 3d 678, 709 N.E.2d 532, 1998 Ohio App. LEXIS 1118 (Ohio Ct. App., Franklin County 1998).

**Enforcement of operator's rights**

Medicaid providers may bring an injunction or declaratory judgment action pursuant to Section 1983, Title 42, U.S. Code, in order to seek enforcement of their rights under Section 1396(a)(13)(A), Title 42, U.S. Code (Wilder v. Virginia Hosp. Assn. [1990], 496 US 498, 110 LEd2d 455, 110 SCt 2510, followed): Ohio Academy of Nursing Homes v. Barry, 56 Ohio St. 3d 120, 564 N.E.2d 686, 1990 Ohio LEXIS 1735 (Ohio 1990).

**Reimbursement rate**

In a due process determination, Medicaid providers have a legitimate property interest in the reimbursement rate provided under R.C. 5111.21, 5111.22 and Section 1396a(a)(13)(A), Title 42, U.S. Code: Ohio Academy of Nursing Homes v. Barry, 56 Ohio St. 3d 120, 564 N.E.2d 686, 1990 Ohio LEXIS 1735 (Ohio 1990).

**Reopening of reimbursement period**

Unless a prior agreement has been reached with a provider reserving certain claims or rights for future determination, the department cannot reopen a reimbursement period after it has been closed absent evidence of fraud: Ohio Acad. of Nursing Homes, Inc. v. Ohio Dep't of Job & Family Servs., 2002-Ohio-4721, 149 Ohio App. 3d 413, 777 N.E.2d 875, 2002 Ohio App. LEXIS 4797 (Ohio Ct. App., Franklin County 2002).

ATTORNEY GENERAL OPINIONS

R.C. 3517.13(I) and (J) are not applicable to Medicaid provider agreements entered into by the Ohio Department of Human Services pursuant to R.C. 5111.21(A)(1) and 42 C.F.R. 431.107: Ohio Elections Commission Advisory Opinion 86-3 (1986).

RESEARCH REFERENCES AND PRACTICE AIDS

**Cross-References to Related Sections**

Process by which facility may seek reconsideration of rate; appeals from adverse actions, RC § 5165.38.

Required provisions of provider agreements, RC § 5165.07.

**Ohio Administrative Code**

Long-term care facilities; nursing facilities (NFs); intermediate care facilities for individuals with developmental disabilities. OAC ch. 5160-3.

Availability of payment during the administrative appeals process for denial, termination, or failure to renew a provider agreement or certification for a facility. OAC 5160-3-04 et seq.

## § 5165.07 Required provisions of provider agreements; term; renewal; department's discretion to avoid agreement.

(A) Except as provided in section 5165.072 of the Revised Code, the department of medicaid shall enter into a provider agreement with a nursing facility operator who applies, and is eligible, for the provider agreement.

(B) A provider agreement shall require the department to make medicaid payments to the provider in accordance with this chapter for nursing facility services the nursing facility provides to its residents who are medicaid recipients eligible for nursing facility services.

(C) A provider agreement shall require the provider to do all of the following:

(1) Maintain eligibility for the provider agreement as provided in section 5165.06 of the Revised Code;

(2) Keep records relating to a cost reporting period for the greater of seven years after the cost report is filed or, if the department issues an audit report in accordance with section 5165.109 of the Revised Code, six years after all appeal rights relating to the audit report are exhausted;

(3) File reports as required by the department;

(4) Open all records relating to the costs of the nursing facility's services for inspection and audit by the department;

(5) Open its premises for inspection by the department, the department of health, and any other state or local authority having authority to inspect;

(6) Supply to the department such information as it requires concerning the nursing facility's services to residents who are, or are eligible to be, medicaid recipients;

(7) Comply with section 5165.08 of the Revised Code.

(D) A provider agreement may contain other provisions that are consistent with law and considered necessary by the department.

**HISTORY:**

138 v H 176 (Eff 7-1-80); 140 v S 239 (Eff 1-1-85); 143 v H 822 (Eff 12-13-90); 144 v H 904 (Eff 12-22-92); 145 v H 152 (Eff 7-1-93); 148 v H 471 (Eff 7-1-2000); 149 v H 94. Eff 6-6-2001; 150 v H 95, § 1, eff. 6-26-03; 151 v H 66, § 101.01, eff. 7-1-05; 2011 HB 153, § 101.01, eff. Sept. 29, 2011; 2013 HB 59, § 101.01, eff. Sept. 29, 2013.

**Editor's Notes**

This section was formerly codified as RC § 5111.22.

**Amendment Notes**

The 2013 amendment rewrote the section.

The 2011 amendment substituted "sections 5111.20 to 5111.331" for "sections 5111.20 to 5111.33" in the first sentence of (A).

151 v H 66, effective July 1, 2005, rewrote (A); in (B)(6), substituted "residents" for "patients"; in the final paragraph, substituted "under section 5111.02" for "by the director pursuant to Chapter 119"; and made minor stylistic changes.

#### NOTES TO DECISIONS

Analysis

Generally
Provider agreements
Reimbursement rate

**Generally**

Provisions in former R.C. 5126.035(C) and (D) governing direct service contracts (DSCs) between a county board of mental retardation and developmental disabilities and a provider are different from those governing the content of Medicaid provider agreements, which can be found at R.C. 5111.22. Thompson v. Hayes, 2006-Ohio-6000, 2006 Ohio App. LEXIS 5940 (Ohio Ct. App., Franklin County 2006).

**Provider agreements**

Provisions in R.C. 5126.035(C) and (D) governing direct service contracts (DSCs) between a county board of mental retardation and developmental disabilities and a provider are different from those governing the content of Medicaid provider agreements, which can be found at R.C. 5111.22. Thompson v. Hayes, 2006-Ohio-6000, 2006 Ohio App. LEXIS 5940 (Ohio Ct. App., Franklin County 2006).

**Reimbursement rate**

In a due process determination, Medicaid providers have a legitimate property interest in the reimbursement rate provided under R.C. 5111.21, 5111.22 and Section 1396a(a)(13)(A), Title 42, U.S. Code: Ohio Academy of Nursing Homes v. Barry, 56 Ohio St. 3d 120, 564 N.E.2d 686, 1990 Ohio LEXIS 1735 (Ohio 1990).



#### RESEARCH REFERENCES AND PRACTICE AIDS

**Cross-References to Related Sections**

Assessment of non-medicaid recipients as to whether alternative source of long-term care is more appropriate than admission to nursing facility, RC § 173.42.

**Ohio Administrative Code**

Long-term care facilities; nursing facilities (NFs); intermediate care facilities for individuals with developmental disabilities. OAC ch. 5160-3.

Provider agreements; termination, denial. OAC 5160-3-02 et seq.

### § 5165.071 Provider agreements covering multiple facilities.

A nursing facility operator may enter into provider agreements for more than one nursing facility.

**HISTORY:**

151 v H 66, § 101.01, eff. 7-1-05; 2013 HB 59, § 101.01, eff. Sept. 29, 2013.

**Editor's Notes**

This section was formerly codified as RC § 5111.223.

**Amendment Notes**

The 2013 amendment substituted "A nursing facility operator" for "The operator of a nursing facility or intermediate care facility for the mentally retarded"; and deleted "or intermediate care facility for the mentally retarded" from the end.

### § 5165.072 Revalidation of nursing facility provider agreement.

The department of medicaid shall not revalidate a nursing facility provider agreement if the provider fails to maintain eligibility for the provider agreement as provided in section 5165.06 of the Revised Code.

**HISTORY:**

2013 HB 59, § 101.01, eff. Sept. 29, 2013.

### § 5165.073 Termination of agreement for non-compliance with fire protection duties.

The department of medicaid shall terminate the provider agreement with a nursing facility provider that does not comply with the requirements of section 3721.071 of the Revised Code for the installation of fire extinguishing and fire alarm systems.

**HISTORY:**

138 v H 176 (Eff 7-1-80); 141 v H 428 (Eff 12-23-86); 143 v H 822 (Eff 12-13-90); 148 v H 471. Eff 7-1-2000; 151 v H 66, § 101.01, eff. 7-1-05; 2013 HB 59, § 101.01, eff. Sept. 29, 2013.

**Editor's Notes**

This section was formerly codified as RC § 5111.30.

**Amendment Notes**

The 2013 amendment substituted "medicaid" for "job and family services"; and inserted "nursing facility".

151 v H 66, effective July 1, 2005, substituted "a provider" for "a nursing facility or intermediate care facility for the mentally retarded".

#### NOTES TO DECISIONS

**Property interest**

Given the strict limits on the Ohio Department of Medicaid's authority and discretion, Ohio law creates a constitutionally protected property interest in continued participation in the Medicaid program; ODM has no discretion with respect to whether to enter a Medicaid provider agreement with a nursing facility, and participation in Ohio's Medicaid program is not terminable at the will of the state, but only where specified conditions are met. CT Ohio Portsmouth, LLC v. Ohio Dep't of Medicaid, 2020-Ohio-5091, 161 N.E.3d 803, 2020 Ohio App. LEXIS 3937 (Ohio Ct. App., Franklin County 2020).

#### RESEARCH REFERENCES AND PRACTICE AIDS

**Cross-References to Related Sections**

Automatic fire alarm and extinguishing systems, RC § 3721.071.

### § 5165.08 Agreement to prohibit certain discriminatory actions.

(A) As used in this section:

"Bed need" means the number of long-term care beds a county needs as determined by the director of health pursuant to division (B)(3) of section 3702.593 of the Revised Code.

"Bed need excess" means that a county's bed need is such that one or more long-term care beds may be relocated from the county according to the director's determination of the county's bed need.

(B) Every provider agreement with a nursing facility provider shall do both of the following:

(1) Permit the provider to exclude one or more parts of the nursing facility from the provider agreement, even though those parts meet federal and state standards for medicaid certification, if all of the following apply:

(a) The nursing facility initially obtained both its nursing home license under Chapter 3721. of the Revised Code and medicaid certification on or after January 1, 2008.

(b) The nursing facility is located in a county that has a bed need excess at the time the provider excludes the parts from the provider agreement.

(c) Federal law permits the provider to exclude the parts from the provider agreement.

(d) The provider gives the department of medicaid written notice of the exclusion not less than forty-five days before the first day of the calendar quarter in which the exclusion is to occur.

(2) Prohibit the provider from doing either of the following:

(a) Discriminating against a resident on the basis of race, color, sex, creed, or national origin;

(b) Subject to division (D) of this section, failing or refusing to do either of the following:

(i) Except as otherwise prohibited under section 5165.82 of the Revised Code, admit as a resident of the nursing facility an individual because the individual is, or may (as a resident of the nursing facility) become, a medicaid recipient unless at least twenty-five per cent of the nursing facility's medicaid-certified beds are occupied by medicaid recipients at the time the person would otherwise be admitted;

(ii) Retain as a resident of the nursing facility an individual because the individual is, or may (as a resident of the nursing facility) become, a medicaid recipient.

(C) For the purpose of division (B)(2)(b)(ii) of this section, a medicaid recipient who is a resident of a nursing facility shall be considered a resident of the nursing facility during any hospital stays totaling less than twenty-five days during any twelve-month period.

(D) Nothing in this section shall bar a provider from doing any of the following:

(1) If the provider is a religious organization operating a religious or denominational nursing facility from giving preference to persons of the same religion or denomination;

(2) Giving preference to persons with whom the provider has contracted to provide continuing care;

(3) If the nursing facility is a county home organized under Chapter 5155. of the Revised Code, admitting residents exclusively from the county in which the county home is located;

(4) Retaining residents who have resided in the provider's nursing facility for not less than one year as private pay patients and who subsequently become medicaid recipients, but refusing to accept as a resident any person who is, or may (as a resident of the nursing facility) become a medicaid recipient, if all of the following apply:

(a) The provider does not refuse to retain any resident who has resided in the provider's nursing facility for not less than one year as a private pay resident because the resident becomes a medicaid recipient, except as necessary to comply with division (D)(4)(b) of this section;

(b) The number of medicaid recipients retained under division (D)(4) of this section does not at any time exceed ten per cent of all the residents in the nursing facility;

(c) On July 1, 1980, all the residents in the nursing facility were private pay residents.

(E) No provider shall violate the provider agreement obligations imposed by this section.

(F) A nursing facility provider who excludes one or more parts of the nursing facility from a provider agreement pursuant to division (B)(1) of this section does not violate division (C) of section 3702.53 of the Revised Code.

**HISTORY:**

138 v H 176 (Eff 7-1-80); 139 v H 694 (Eff 11-15-81); 140 v H 100 (Eff 2-24-83); 140 v H 291 (Eff 7-1-83); 141 v H 428 (Eff 12-23-86); 143 v H 822 (Eff 12-13-90); 145 v H 152 (Eff 7-1-93); 148 v H 471. Eff 7-1-2000; 151 v H 66, § 101.01, eff. 7-1-05; 151 v H 530, § 101.01, eff. 6-30-06; 152 v H 562, § 101.01, eff. 6-24-08; 2013 HB 59, § 101.01, eff. Sept. 29, 2013; 2014 sb276, § 1, effective January 1, 2015; 2014 hb394, § 1, effective January 1, 2015.

**Editor's Notes**

Acts 2014, HB 394, § 9 and Acts 2014, SB 276, § 8 provides: "The versions of sections 5165.08, 5165.513, 5165.515, and 5165.99 of the Revised Code presented in this act are the versions of the sections that result from Sections 110.25, 110.26, and 110.27 of Am. Sub. H.B. 59 of the 130th General Assembly."

This section was formerly codified as RC § 5111.31.

**Amendment Notes**

The 2014 amendment by SB 276 and HB 394, added (A), (B)(1), and (F); redesignated former (A), (A)(1), (A)(2), (A)(2)(a), (A)(2)(b), and (B) through (C) as (B), (B)(2)(a), (B)(2)(b), (B)(2)(b)(i), (B)(2)(b)(ii), and (C) through (E); added "do both of the following" to the end of the present introductory language of (B); added the (B)(2) designation; substituted "twenty-five per cent" for "eighty per cent" in present (B)(2)(b)(i); and made stylistic changes.

The 2013 amendment rewrote the section.

151 v H 530, effective June 30, 2006, added (B)(1)(c).

### ATTORNEY GENERAL OPINIONS

Pursuant to R.C. 5111.31(A)(4), a nursing home which participates as a provider in Ohio's Medicaid program may not require a prospective nursing home patient who is, becomes, or who may, as a patient in the home, become a recipient of Medicaid benefits, or the patient's family, to enter into an agreement, as a condition of the patient's admission to the home, wherein the patient or his family agrees to relieve the home from accepting Medicaid payments in lieu of payments at private rates until the patient has resided in the home for a period of one year as a private patient, if less than eighty per cent of the patients in the home are Medicaid recipients, unless the home meets the exception set forth in R.C. 5111.31(F): 1985 Ohio Op. Att'y Gen. No. 063 (1985).

Pursuant to 42 U.S.C. § 1396h(d)(2)(A) and applicable state law, a nursing home that participates as a provider in Ohio's Medicaid program may not require a prospective nursing home patient who is, becomes, or who may, as a patient in the home, become a recipient of Medicaid benefits, or the patient's family, to enter into an agreement, as a condition of the patient's admission to the home, wherein the patient or his family agrees to pay to the home the difference between the private rate established by the home and the amount reimbursed to the home through the Medicaid program for the patient's care: 1985 Ohio Op. Att'y Gen. No. 063 (1985).

### RESEARCH REFERENCES AND PRACTICE AIDS

**Cross-References to Related Sections**

Penalty, RC § 5165.99.

Access to records of resident, recipient or provider of long-term care; subpoenas; injunction; referral of complaints, RC § 173.20.

Patient's cause of action for breach of provider agreement, RC § 5165.081.

Required provisions of provider agreements, RC § 5165.07.

**Ohio Constitution**

Equal protection, Ohio Const. art I, § 2.

**Practice Manuals and Treatises**

Anderson's Ohio Elder Law Practice Manual § 4.10 Transfer Rules

## § 5165.081 Patient's cause of action against provider for breach of agreement or other duties.



A nursing facility resident has a cause of action against a nursing facility provider for breach of the provider agreement obligations or other duties imposed by section 5165.08 of the Revised Code. The action may be commenced by the resident, or on the resident's behalf by the resident's sponsor or a residents' rights advocate, by the filing of a civil action in the court of common pleas of the county in which the nursing facility is located, or in the court of common pleas of Franklin county.

If a court of common pleas finds that a provider has breached a provider agreement obligation or other duty imposed by section 5165.08 of the Revised Code, the court may do one or more of the following:

(A) Enjoin the provider from engaging in the practice;

(B) Order such affirmative relief as may be necessary;

(C) Award to a resident and a sponsor or government entity that brings the action on behalf of a resident actual damages, costs, and reasonable attorney's fees.

**HISTORY:**

138 v H 176 (Eff 7-1-80); 143 v H 822. Eff 12-13-90; 151 v H 66, § 101.01, eff. 7-1-05; 2013 HB 59, § 101.01, eff. Sept. 29, 2013.

**Editor's Notes**

This section was formerly codified as RC § 5111.32.

**Amendment Notes**

The 2013 amendment rewrote the section.

151 v H 66, effective July 1, 2005, in the first paragraph, inserted "the provider of"; substituted "provider from" for "facility from" in the second paragraph; and made gender neutral changes.

### RESEARCH REFERENCES AND PRACTICE AIDS

**Comparative Legislation**

Civil Rights of Institutionalized Persons Act:
42 USCS § 1997 et seq

## § 5165.082 Qualification of all Medicaid beds in Medicare program.

(A) Except as provided in division (B) of this section, the operator of a nursing facility that elects to have the nursing facility participate in the medicaid program shall qualify all of the nursing facility's medicaid-certified beds in the medicare program. The medicaid director may adopt rules under section 5165.02 of the Revised Code to establish the time frame in which a nursing facility must comply with this requirement.

(B) The department of veterans services is not required to qualify all of the medicaid-certified beds in a nursing facility the department maintains and operates under section 5907.01 of the Revised Code in the medicare program.

**HISTORY:**
2013 HB 59, § 101.01, eff. Sept. 29, 2013.

### § 5165.10 Annual cost report for each facility; report by new provider.

(A) Except as provided in division (C) of this section, each nursing facility provider shall file with the department of medicaid an annual cost report for each of the provider's nursing facilities that participate in the medicaid program. The cost report for a year shall cover the calendar year or the portion of the calendar year during which the nursing facility participated in the medicaid program. Except as provided in division (D) of this section, the cost report is due not later than ninety days after the end of the calendar year, or portion of the calendar year, that the cost report covers.

(B) If a nursing facility undergoes a change of provider that the department determines, in accordance with rules adopted under section 5165.02 of the Revised Code, is not an arm's length transaction, the new provider shall file the nursing facility's cost report in accordance with division (A) of this section and the cost report shall cover the portion of the calendar year during which the new provider operated the nursing facility and the portion of the calendar year during which the previous provider operated the nursing facility.

(C) The provider of a new nursing facility is not required to file a cost report in accordance with division (A) of this section for the first calendar year that the provider has a provider agreement for the nursing facility if the initial provider agreement goes into effect after the first day of October of that calendar year. The provider shall file a cost report for the nursing facility in accordance with division (A) of this section for the immediately following calendar year.

(D) The department may grant to a provider a fourteen-day extension to file a cost report under this section if the provider provides the department a written request for the extension and the department determines that there is good cause for the extension.

**HISTORY:**
138 v H 176 (Eff 7-1-80); 140 v H 291 (Eff 7-1-83); 141 v H 428 (Eff 12-23-86); 143 v H 822 (Eff 12-13-90); 144 v H 904 (Eff 12-22-92); 145 v H 152 (Eff 7-1-93); 145 v H 715 (Eff 7-22-94); 148 v H 471. Eff 7-1-2000; 151 v H 66, § 101.01, eff. 7-1-05; 2013 HB 59, § 101.01, eff. Sept. 29, 2013; 2014 HB 483, § 101.01, eff. Sept. 15, 2014.

**Editor's Notes**
This section was formerly codified as RC § 5111.26.

**Amendment Notes**
The 2014 amendment by HB 483 deleted (C), which read: "If the medicaid payment rate for a new nursing facility was most recently determined in accordance with section 5165.151 of the Revised Code, the provider shall file with the department a cost report for the new nursing facility not later than, except as provided in division (E) of this section, ninety days after the end of the new nursing facility's first three full calendar months of operation. The cost report shall cover the period that begins with the nursing facility's first day of operation and ends on the first day of the month immediately following the first three full months of operation"; redesignated former (D) and (E) as (C) and (D); rewrote present (C); and made stylistic changes.
The 2013 amendment rewrote the section.
151 v H 66, effective July 1, 2005, rewrote the section.

**NOTES TO DECISIONS**

Analysis

Mandamus
New facilities

**Mandamus**
Where a new nursing facility Medicaid provider's initial Medicaid reimbursement rate was determined pursuant to R.C. 5111.255 and it thereafter failed to comply with the requirement of R.C. 5111.26 to file a timely cost report in order for the state agency to determine the facility's actual rate of Medicaid reimbursement until after the effective date of Am.Sub. H.B. 66, Gen. Assem. (Ohio 2005), the facility could not benefit from its lack of compliance by obtaining the higher, initially-set reimbursement rate; accordingly, a magistrate found that as the facility could not show that it had a clear legal right to a particular reimbursement rate for a certain fiscal year, its request for a writ of mandamus under R.C. 2731.04 to compel the agency to reimburse it at the set rate lacked merit. State ex rel. Autumn Health Care of Coshocton, Inc. v. Ohio Dep't of Job & Family Servs., 2007-Ohio-3223, 2007 Ohio App. LEXIS 2977 (Ohio Ct. App., Franklin County 2007).

**New facilities**
Where a new nursing facility Medicaid provider's initial Medicaid reimbursement rate was determined pursuant to R.C. 5111.255 and it thereafter failed to comply with the requirement of R.C. 5111.26 to file a timely cost report in order for the state agency to determine the facility's actual rate of Medicaid reimbursement until after the effective date of Am.Sub. H.B. 66, Gen. Assem. (Ohio 2005), the facility could not benefit from its lack of compliance by obtaining the higher, initially-set reimbursement rate. A magistrate found that as the facility could not show that it had a clear legal right to a particular reimbursement rate for a certain fiscal year, its request for a writ of mandamus under R.C. 2731.04 to compel the agency to reimburse it at the set rate lacked merit. State ex rel. Autumn Health Care of Coshocton, Inc. v. Ohio Dep't of Job & Family Servs., 2007-Ohio-3223, 2007 Ohio App. LEXIS 2977 (Ohio Ct. App., Franklin County 2007).

**RESEARCH REFERENCES AND PRACTICE AIDS**

**Cross-References to Related Sections**
Penalty, RC § 5165.99.
Annual audit of each home; desk review of cost report, RC § 5165.101.
Desk-reviewed defined, RC § 5165.01.
Initial rates for facilities licensed on or after 1-1-93; adjustment of rates, RC § 5124.151.
Nursing home residents needing skilled nursing care; prohibitions.
Special diets, administration of medication to rest home residents; admission or retention of persons needing skilled nursing care, RC § 3721.011.

**Ohio Administrative Code**
Medicaid coverage of targeted case management services provided to individuals with developmental disabilities, OAC 5160-48-01.
Nursing facilities (NF) medicaid cost reports, OAC ch. 5160.

### § 5165.101 Franchise permit fee reported as nonreimbursable expense.

A nursing facility provider filing the nursing facility's cost report with the department of medicaid under section 5165.10 or 5165.522 of the Revised Code shall report as a nonreimbursable expense the cost of the nursing facility's franchise permit fee.

**HISTORY:**
151 v H 66, § 101.01, eff. 7-1-05; 2013 HB 59, § 101.01, eff. Sept. 29, 2013.

**Editor's Notes**
This section was formerly codified as RC § 5111.266.

**Amendment Notes**
The 2013 amendment substituted "nursing facility provider filing the nursing" for "provider of a nursing facility filing the"; and substituted "medicaid under section 5165.10 or 5165.522" for "job and family services under section 5111.26".

### § 5165.1010 Nursing facility fines.

(A) Subject to division (D) of this section, the department of medicaid shall fine the provider of a nursing facility if the report of an audit conducted under section 5165.109 of the Revised Code regarding a cost report for the nursing facility includes either of the following:

(1) Adverse findings that exceed three per cent of the total amount of medicaid-allowable costs reported in the cost report;

(2) Adverse findings that exceed twenty per cent of medicaid-allowable costs for a particular cost center reported in the cost report.

(B) A fine issued under this section shall equal the greatest of the following:

(1) If the adverse findings exceed three per cent but do not exceed ten per cent of the total amount of medicaid-allowable costs reported in the cost report, the greater of three per cent of those reported costs or ten thousand dollars;

(2) If the adverse findings exceed ten per cent but do not exceed twenty per cent of the total amount of medicaid-allowable costs reported in the cost report, the greater of six per cent of those reported costs or twenty-five thousand dollars;

(3) If the adverse findings exceed twenty per cent of the total amount of medicaid-allowable costs reported in the cost report, the greater of ten percent of those reported costs or fifty thousand dollars;

(4) If the adverse findings exceed twenty per cent but do not exceed twenty-five per cent of medicaid-allowable costs for a particular cost center reported in the cost report, the greater of three per cent of the total amount of medicaid-allowable costs reported in the cost report or ten thousand dollars;

(5) If the adverse findings exceed twenty-five per cent but do not exceed thirty per cent of medicaid-allowable costs for a particular cost center reported in the cost report, the greater of six per cent of the total amount of medicaid-allowable costs reported in the cost report or twenty-five thousand dollars;

(6) If the adverse findings exceed thirty per cent of medicaid-allowable costs for a particular cost center reported in the cost report, the greater of ten per cent of the total amount of medicaid-allowable costs reported in the cost report or fifty thousand dollars.

(C) Fines paid under this section shall be deposited into the health care/medicaid support and recoveries fund created under section 5162.52 of the Revised Code.

(D) The department may not collect a fine under this section until all appeal rights relating to the audit report that is the basis for the fine are exhausted.

**HISTORY:**

2011 HB 153, § 101.01, eff. Sept. 29, 2011; 2013 HB 59, § 101.01, eff. Sept. 29, 2013; 2017 hb49, § 101.01, effective September 29, 2017.

**Editor's Notes**

This section was formerly codified as RC § 5111.271.

**Amendment Notes**

The 2017 amendment by HB 49 substituted "the health care/medicaid support and recoveries fund created under section 5162.52 of the Revised Code" for "the health care services administration fund created under section 5162.54 of the Revised Code" in (C).

The 2013 amendment, in the introductory language of (A), substituted "department of medicaid" for "department of job and family services" and "section 5165.109" for "division (B) of section 5111.27"; substituted "medicaid-allowable" for "medicaid-reimbursable" wherever it appears in (A)(1), (A)(2), and (B)(1) through (B)(6); and substituted "section 5162.54" for "section 5111.94" in (C).

## § 5165.102 Fines not included in cost report.

No nursing facility provider shall report fines paid under sections 5165.60 to 5165.89 or section 5165.99 of the Revised Code in a cost report filed under section 5165.10 or 5165.522 of the Revised Code.

**HISTORY:**

2013 HB 59, § 101.01, eff. Sept. 29, 2013.

## § 5165.103 Cost reporting.

Cost reports shall be completed using the form prescribed under section 5165.104 of the Revised Code and in accordance with the guidelines established under that section.

**HISTORY:**

2013 HB 59, § 101.01, eff. Sept. 29, 2013.

## § 5165.104 Cost reporting forms.

The department of medicaid shall do all of the following:

(A) Prescribe the form to be used for completing a cost report and a uniform chart of accounts for the purpose of reporting costs on the form;

(B) Distribute a paper copy of the form, or computer software for electronic submission of the form, to each provider at least sixty days before the date the cost report is due;

(C) Establish guidelines for completing the form.

**HISTORY:**

2013 HB 59, § 101.01, eff. Sept. 29, 2013.

## § 5165.105 Addendum to cost report for potentially disputed costs.

The department of medicaid shall develop an addendum to the cost report form that a nursing facility provider may use to set forth costs that the provider believes the department may dispute. The department may consider such costs in determining a nursing facility's medicaid payment rate. If the department does not consider such costs in determining a nursing facility's medicaid payment rate, the provider may seek reconsideration of the determination in accordance with section 5165.38 of the Revised Code. If the department subsequently includes such costs in a nursing facility's medicaid payment rate, the department shall pay the provider interest at a reasonable rate established in rules adopted under section 5165.02 of the Revised Code for the period that the rate excluded the costs.

**HISTORY:**

2013 HB 59, § 101.01, eff. Sept. 29, 2013.

Titles 39 — 57

## § 5165.106 Penalties for failure to file cost report.

If a nursing facility provider required by section 5165.10 of the Revised Code to file a cost report for the nursing facility fails to file the cost report by the date it is due or the date, if any, to which the due date is extended pursuant to division (D) of that section, or files an incomplete or inadequate report for the nursing facility under that section, the department of medicaid shall provide immediate written notice to the provider that the provider agreement for the nursing facility will be terminated in thirty days unless the provider submits a complete and adequate cost report for the nursing facility within thirty days. During the thirty-day termination period or any additional time allowed for an appeal of the proposed termination of a provider agreement, the provider shall be paid the nursing facility's then current per medicaid day payment rate, minus the dollar amount by which nursing facility's per medicaid day payment rates are reduced during state fiscal year 2013 in accordance with division (A)(2) of section 5111.26 of the Revised Code (renumbered as section 5165.10 of the Revised Code by H.B. 59 of the 130th general assembly) as that section existed on the day immediately preceding September 29, 2013. On the first day of each July, the department shall adjust the amount of the reduction in effect during the previous twelve months to reflect the rate of inflation during the preceding twelve months, as shown in the consumer price index for all items for all urban consumers for the north central region, published by the United States bureau of labor statistics.

**HISTORY:**

2013 HB 59, § 101.01, eff. Sept. 29, 2013; 2014 HB 483, § 101.01, eff. Sept. 15, 2014; 2017 hb49, § 101.01, effective September 29, 2017.

**Amendment Notes**

The 2017 amendment by HB 49 substituted "reduced during state fiscal year 2013" for "reduced during fiscal year 2013" in the second sentence.

The 2014 amendment by HB 483 substituted "division (D)" for "division (E)" in the first sentence; and substituted "September 29, 2013" for "the effective date of this section" in the second sentence.

### NOTES TO DECISIONS

**Property interest**

Given the strict limits on the Ohio Department of Medicaid's authority and discretion, Ohio law creates a constitutionally protected property interest in continued participation in the Medicaid program; ODM has no discretion with respect to whether to enter a Medicaid provider agreement with a nursing facility, and participation in Ohio's Medicaid program is not terminable at the will of the state, but only where specified conditions are met. CT Ohio Portsmouth, LLC v. Ohio Dep't of Medicaid, 2020-Ohio-5091,

161 N.E.3d 803, 2020 Ohio App. LEXIS 3937 (Ohio Ct. App., Franklin County 2020).

### § 5165.107 Amendment of cost reports.

(A) Except as provided in division (B) of this section and not later than three years after a nursing facility provider files a cost report with the department of medicaid under section 5165.10 of the Revised Code, the provider may amend the cost report if the provider discovers a material error in the cost report or additional information to be included in the cost report. The department shall review the amended cost report for accuracy and notify the provider of its determination.

(B) A provider may not amend a cost report if the department has notified the provider that an audit of the cost report or a cost report of the provider for a subsequent cost reporting period is to be conducted under section 5165.109 of the Revised Code. The provider may, however, provide the department information that affects the costs included in the cost report. Such information may not be provided after the adjudication of the final settlement of the cost report.

**HISTORY:**

2011 HB 153, § 101.01, eff. Sept. 29, 2011; 2013 HB 59, § 101.01, eff. Sept. 29, 2013.

**Editor's Notes**

This section was formerly codified as RC § 5111.261.

**Amendment Notes**

The 2013 amendment, in the first sentence of (A), inserted "nursing facility" and substituted "medicaid under section 5165.10" for "job and family services under section 5111.26"; and substituted "section 5165.109" for "section 5111.27" in the first sentence of (B).



### § 5165.108 Desk review of cost report; preliminary determination; audits; exception reviews of assessment information; withholding of payments; rate adjustments.

(A) The department of medicaid shall conduct a desk review of each cost report it receives under section 5165.10 or 5165.522 of the Revised Code. Based on the desk review, the department shall make a preliminary determination of whether the reported costs are allowable costs. The department shall notify each nursing facility provider of whether any of the reported costs are preliminarily determined not to be allowable, the medicaid payment rate determined under this chapter that results from that determination, and the reasons for the determination and resulting rate. The department shall allow the provider to verify the calculation and submit additional information.

**HISTORY:**

138 v H 176 (Eff 7-1-80); 140 v H 291 (Eff 7-1-83); 141 v H 238 (Eff 7-1-85); 143 v H 822 (Eff 12-13-90); 144 v S 351 (Eff 7-1-92); 144 v H 904 (Eff 12-22-92); 145 v H 152 (Eff 7-1-93); 145 v H 715 (Eff 7-22-94); 148 v H 471. Eff 7-1-2000; 151 v H 66, § 101.01, eff. 7-1-05; 151 v H 530, § 101.01, eff. 3-30-06; 2011 HB 153, § 101.01, eff. Sept. 29, 2011; 2013 HB 59, § 101.01, eff. Sept. 29, 2013.

**Editor's Notes**

This section was formerly codified as RC § 5111.27.

**Amendment Notes**

The 2013 amendment, in the first sentence of (A), substituted "department of medicaid" for "department of job and family services" and "section 5165.10 or 5165.522" for "section 5111.26"; in the second sentence of (A), inserted "nursing facility" and substituted "medicaid payment rate determined under this chapter" for "rate calculation under sections 5111.20 to 5111.331 of the Revised Code"; and deleted (B) through (F), pertaining to conduction of an audit, as defined by rule adopted.

The 2011 amendment substituted "sections 5111.20 to 5111.331" for "sections 5111.20 to 5111.33" in the third sentence of (A) and in (E) and (F); deleted "and shall notify the provider of its findings" from the end of the first paragraph of (B); rewrote the second paragraph of (B); in (B)(3), deleted "fairly" following "presented" and substituted "state and federal laws and regulations" for "generally accepted accounting principles and department rules"; substituted "included in the government auditing standards produced by the United States government accountability office" for "established by the American institute of certified public accountants" in (B)(6); and made a stylistic change.

151 v H 530, effective March 30, 2006, in (F), deleted "nursing facilities and" preceding "intermediate care".

151 v H 66, effective July 1, 2005, rewrote (A) and the first paragraph of (B); deleted "of the 'Social Security Act,' 49 Stat. 620 (1935), 42 U.S.C.A. 301, as amended" from the end of (B)(1); in (B)(8), substituted "provider complete" for "nursing facility or intermediate care facility for the mentally retarded complete" and "permit the provider" for "permit the facility", and inserted "provider's"; deleted "of the 'Social Security Act' " from the end of (C)(1); substituted "provider" for "facility" in (C)(4), three times in (D), and in (E); in (E), substituted "medicaid" for "medical assistance"; and corrected internal references and made stylistic changes.

#### NOTES TO DECISIONS

Analysis



**Audit reports**

R.C. 5111.27(B) did not impose a mandatory duty on the department to issue audit reports corresponding to the first of two six-month cost reports within three years of the filing of each of those cost reports: AmCare, Inc. v. Ohio Dep't of Job & Family Servs., 2005-Ohio-2714, 161 Ohio App. 3d 350, 830 N.E.2d 406, 2005 Ohio App. LEXIS 2540 (Ohio Ct. App., Franklin County 2005).

**Documentation**

When a nursing home sought Medicaid reimbursement for certain medical supplies, reimbursement was properly disallowed, under R.C. 5111.27(B)(3), because the supplies either should have been directly billed to Medicaid, so they were not reimbursable as part of the cost report by which the home sought reimbursement, or the documents submitted to substantiate them were illegible. Meadowwood Nursing Facility v. Ohio Dep't of Job & Family Servs., 2005-Ohio-1263, 2005 Ohio App. LEXIS 5762 (Ohio Ct. App., Franklin County 2005).

When a nursing home sought Medicaid reimbursement for renovation interest expenses for two years, reimbursement was properly disallowed, under R.C. 5111.27(B)(3), because (1) the home provided no original documentation from the lender showing the borrower, the loan's purpose, and whether it was reasonable, necessary, and related to patient care or that the loan proceeds were to be used for the home's operation, (2) the home's owner admitted he did not provide such documentation, and (3) practices of the Ohio Department of Job and Family Services regarding documentation in past years were irrelevant. Meadowwood Nursing Facility v. Ohio Dep't of Job & Family Servs., 2005-Ohio-1263, 2005 Ohio App. LEXIS 5762 (Ohio Ct. App., Franklin County 2005).

When a nursing home sought Medicaid reimbursement for property taxes for a certain year, reimbursement was properly disallowed, under R.C. 5111.27(B)(3), because the home provided no documentation verifying the costs, as the tax bills that were submitted contained no date. Meadowwood Nursing Facility v. Ohio Dep't of Job & Family Servs., 2005-Ohio-1263, 2005 Ohio App. LEXIS 5762 (Ohio Ct. App., Franklin County 2005).

**Mandamus**

When a state agency's decision is discretionary and by statute not subject to appeal, an action in mandamus is the sole avenue of relief available to a party challenging the agency's decision: Ohio Acad. of Nursing Homes v. Ohio Dep't of Job & Family Servs., 2007-Ohio-2620, 114 Ohio St. 3d 14, 867 N.E.2d 400, 2007 Ohio LEXIS 1458 (Ohio 2007).

When nursing facilities and the facilities' trade association sought review of the decision of the Ohio Department of Job and Family Services denying the facilities' request, under R.C. 5111.27(F), for a Medicaid reimbursement rate adjustment, the facilities' and association's sole remedy was pursuant to a petition for a writ of mandamus in which the facilities and association would have to demonstrate the Department's abuse of discretion because (1) R.C. 5111.29(A)(5) explicitly provided that the Department's discretionary decision was not subject to appeal, and (2) a declaratory judgment action, under R.C. 2721.03, to obtain a declaration of the facilities' rights was unavailable because the only rights the facilities had was to have the Department consider their reimbursement request without abusing its discretion. Ohio Acad. of Nursing Homes v. Ohio Dep't of Job & Family Servs., 2007-Ohio-2620, 114 Ohio St. 3d 14, 867 N.E.2d 400, 2007 Ohio LEXIS 1458 (Ohio 2007).

Trial court erred in dismissing an action by nursing home operators against the Ohio Department of Job & Family Services (ODJFS) upon finding that the trial court lacked subject matter jurisdiction because the money damage claims, which were ostensibly against the State, were inextricably intertwined with other claims, as the only available mechanism for review of the denial by the ODJFS of the operators' rate reconsideration requests under R.C. 5111.27(F) and 5111.29 and OAC

5101:3-3-24.1 and 5101:3-3-24(C) was by mandamus; as the Ohio Court of Claims lacked subject matter jurisdiction over such a claim pursuant to R.C. 2731.02, jurisdiction was proper in the trial court and dismissal under Civ. R. 12(B)(1) was error. PNP, Inc. v. Ohio Dep't of Job & Family Servs., 2006-Ohio-1159, 2006 Ohio App. LEXIS 973 (Ohio Ct. App., Franklin County 2006), aff'd, 2007-Ohio-2880, 114 Ohio St. 3d 70, 868 N.E.2d 265, 2007 Ohio LEXIS 1577 (Ohio 2007).

Dismissal of a mandamus action pursuant to Ohio Rev Code Ann. § 2731.01 by nursing homes and an agency, seeking to compel the Ohio Department of Job and Family Services to exercise its discretion and adjust the Medicaid reimbursement rate pursuant to R.C. 5111.27(F) and OAC 5101:3-3-24.1, was error, as the trial court had subject matter jurisdiction over the action pursuant to R.C. 2731.02 because such a discretionary decision was not subject to direct appeal, and a mandamus action was a provider's only pappropriate vehicle to challenge such a decision; however, there was no claim stated where the mandamus sought to compel the exercise of the Department's jurisdiction, which was the second step in a two-step process, and the first step had yet to be undertaken, necessitating a remand for amendment of the complaint. Ohio Acad. of Nursing Homes v. Ohio Dep't of Job & Family Servs., 2005-Ohio-6888, 164 Ohio App. 3d 808, 844 N.E.2d 384, 2005 Ohio App. LEXIS 6211 (Ohio Ct. App., Franklin County 2005), aff'd, 2007-Ohio-2620, 114 Ohio St. 3d 14, 867 N.E.2d 400, 2007 Ohio LEXIS 1458 (Ohio 2007).

**Overpayment determination**

Three-year time restriction for issuance of audit reports by the Ohio Department of Job and Family Services, pursuant to R.C. 5111.27(B) and 5111.28(B), was a directory duty on the Department, rather than a mandatory one, despite use of the word "shall" in the statutory language of R.C. 5111.27(B); accordingly, the Department's issuance of a report and a determination that an overpayment was due from a nursing home was not invalid due to failure to abide by the time limitation, and the overpayment determination was supported by probative, reliable, and substantive evidence, pursuant to R.C. 119.12. AmCare, Inc. v. Ohio Dep't of Job & Family Servs., 2005-Ohio-2714, 161 Ohio App. 3d 350, 830 N.E.2d 406, 2005 Ohio App. LEXIS 2540 (Ohio Ct. App., Franklin County 2005).

**Rate adjustments**

Nursing homes' rate adjustment requests for fiscal year 2002 were untimely since the instructions advised the nursing homes that to be to be eligible for a rate adjustment due to the government mandate effective October 1, 2001, providers had to submit such requests before the end of fiscal year 2002, which the nursing homes did not do. PNP, Inc. v. Ohio Dep't of Job & Family Servs., 2013-Ohio-4344, 2013 Ohio App. LEXIS 4577 (Ohio Ct. App., Franklin County 2013).

Nursing homes' requests for a rate adjustment due to a government mandate to provide extra nursing staff was properly rejected since the rate adjustment requests submitted to the Ohio Department of Job and Family Services on October 30, 2001, did not request a rate adjustment for fiscal years 2002 and 2004; further, the record lacked evidence that the nursing homes' rate adjustment requests sought rate adjustments for fiscal year 2002. PNP, Inc. v. Ohio Dep't of Job & Family Servs., 2013-Ohio-4344, 2013 Ohio App. LEXIS 4577 (Ohio Ct. App., Franklin County 2013).

Nursing homes' rate adjustment requests for fiscal year 2003 were untimely since the instructions advised the nursing homes that a rate adjustment for a government mandate would not be granted if the additional costs to be incurred should have been incurred previously to comply with the existing standards unless the facility could demonstrate a change in the on-going interpretation of the applicable standard; the nursing homes' timing issues were created by their lack of compliance with the government mandate until eight months after it went into effect. PNP, Inc. v. Ohio Dep't of Job & Family Servs., 2013-Ohio-4344, 2013 Ohio App. LEXIS 4577 (Ohio Ct. App., Franklin County 2013).

## RESEARCH REFERENCES AND PRACTICE AIDS

**Cross-References to Related Sections**

Desk-reviewed defined, RC § 5165.01.

Determination of case-mix score for each facility, RC § 5165.19.

Operators required to refund certain payments; interest, penalties; rate adjustments, RC § 5165.40.

Process by which facility may seek reconsideration of rate; appeals from adverse actions, RC § 5165.38.

Required provisions of provider agreements, RC § 5165.07.

**Ohio Administrative Code**

Medicaid coverage of targeted case management services provided to individuals with developmental disabilities, OAC 5160-48-01.

Nursing facilities (NF) medicaid cost reports, OAC ch. 5160.

## § 5165.109 Audit of cost reports; Establishment of audit manual.

(A) The department of medicaid may conduct an audit, as defined in rules adopted under section 5165.02 of the Revised Code, of any cost report filed under section 5165.10 or 5165.522 of the Revised Code. The decision whether to conduct an audit and the scope of the audit, which may be a desk or field audit, may be determined based on prior performance of the provider, a risk analysis, or other evidence that gives the department reason to believe that the provider has reported costs improperly. A desk or field audit may be performed annually, but is required whenever a provider does not pass the risk analysis tolerance factors.

(B) Audits shall be conducted by auditors under contract with the department, auditors working for firms under contract with the department, or auditors employed by the department.

The department may establish a contract for the auditing of nursing facilities by outside firms. Each contract entered into by bidding shall be effective for one to two years.

(C) The department shall notify a provider of the findings of an audit of a cost report by issuing an audit report. The audit report shall include notice of any fine imposed under section 5165.1010 of the Revised Code. The department shall issue the audit report not later than three years after the earlier of the following:

(1) The date the cost report is filed;

(2) The date a desk or field audit of the cost report or a cost report for a subsequent cost reporting period is completed.

(D) The department shall prepare a written summary of any audit disallowance that is made after the effective date of the rate that is based on the cost. Where the provider is pursuing judicial or administrative remedies in good faith regarding the disallowance, the department shall not withhold from the provider's current payments any amounts the department claims to be due from the provider pursuant to section 5165.41 of the Revised Code.

(E)(1) The department shall establish an audit manual and program for field audits conducted under this section. Each auditor conducting a field audit under this section shall follow the audit manual and program, regardless of whether the auditor is under contract with the department, works for a firm under contract with the department, or is employed by the department. The manual and program shall do both of the following:

(a) Require each field audit to be conducted by an auditor to whom all of the following apply:

(i) During the period of the auditor's contract, firm's contract, or auditor's employment with the department, the auditor or firm does not have and is not committed to acquire any direct or indirect financial interest in the ownership, financing, or operation of nursing facilities in this state.

(ii) The auditor does not audit any provider that has been a client of the auditor or the auditor's firm.

(iii) The auditor is otherwise independent as determined by the standards of independence included in the government auditing standards produced by the United States government accountability office.

(b) Require each auditor conducting a field audit to do all of the following:

(i) Comply with applicable rules prescribed pursuant to Title XVIII and Title XIX;

(ii) Consider generally accepted auditing standards prescribed by the American institute of certified public accountants;

(iii) Include a written summary as to whether the costs included in the cost report examined during the audit are allowable and are presented in accordance with state and federal laws and regulations, and whether, in all material respects, allowable costs are documented, reasonable, and related to patient care;

(iv) Complete the audit within the time period specified by the department;

(v) Provide to the provider complete written interpretations that explain in detail the application of all relevant contract provisions, regulations, auditing standards, rate formulae, and departmental policies, with explanations and examples, that are sufficient to permit the provider to calculate with reasonable certainty those costs that are allowable and the rate to which the provider's nursing facility is entitled.

(2) For the purpose of division (E)(1)(a)(i) of this section, employment of a member of an auditor's family by a nursing facility that the auditor does not audit does not constitute a direct or indirect financial interest in the ownership, financing, or operation of the nursing facility.

**HISTORY:**

2013 HB 59, § 101.01, eff. Sept. 29, 2013.

### § 5165.15 Amount of payments to provider; adjustments.

Except as otherwise provided by sections 5165.151 to 5165.157 and 5165.34 of the Revised Code, the total per medicaid day payment rate that the department of medicaid shall pay a nursing facility provider for nursing facility services the provider's nursing facility provides during a state fiscal year shall be determined as follows:

(A) Determine the sum of all of the following:

(1) The per medicaid day payment rate for ancillary and support costs determined for the nursing facility under section 5165.16 of the Revised Code;

(2) The per medicaid day payment rate for capital costs determined for the nursing facility under section 5165.17 of the Revised Code;

(3) The per medicaid day payment rate for direct care costs determined for the nursing facility under section 5165.19 of the Revised Code;

(4) The per medicaid day payment rate for tax costs determined for the nursing facility under section 5165.21 of the Revised Code;

(5) If the nursing facility qualifies as a critical access nursing facility, the nursing facility's critical access incentive payment paid under section 5165.23 of the Revised Code.

(B) To the sum determined under division (A) of this section, add sixteen dollars and forty-four cents.

(C) From the sum determined under division (B) of this section, subtract one dollar and seventy-nine cents.

(D) To the sum determined under division (C) of this section, add, for state fiscal year 2022 and for state fiscal year 2023, the per medicaid day quality incentive payment rate determined for the nursing facility under section 5165.26 of the Revised Code.

**HISTORY:**

151 v H 66, § 101.01, eff. 7-1-05; 151 v H 530, § 101.01, eff. 6-30-06; 2011 HB 153, § 101.01, eff. July 1, 2011; 2011 SB 264, § 1, eff. July 1, 2012; 2012 HB 487, § 101.01, eff. Sept. 10, 2012; 2012 HB 303, § 1, eff. July 1, 2013; 2013 HB 59, § 101.01, eff. Sept. 29, 2013; 2014 HB 483, § 101.01, eff. Sept. 15, 2014; 2015 hb64, § 101.01, effective July 1, 2016; 2017 hb49, § 101.01, effective September 29, 2017; 2019 hb166, § 101.01, effective October 17, 2019; 2020 hb481, § 29, effective September 18, 2020; 2021 hb110, § 101.01, effective June 30, 2021.

**Editor's Notes**

This section was formerly codified as RC § 5111.222.

**Effective Dates**

Acts 2019, HB 166, § 812.12 rovides: "(A) The amendment by this act to division (B) of section 5165.15 of the Revised Code takes effect July 1, 2021.

"(B) The amendment by this act to section 5165.15 of the Revised Code that adds a division (E) to that section takes effect on the ninety-first day after this act is filed with the Secretary of State."

**Amendment Notes**

The 2021 amendment by HB 110 deleted former (D), which read: "To the difference determined under division (C) of this section, add the per medicaid day quality payment rate determined for the nursing facility under section 5165.25 of the Revised Code"; redesignated former (E) as (D); and in (D), substituted "division (C)" for "division (D)" and "2022 and for state fiscal year 2023" for "2021."

The 2020 amendment by HB 481 substituted "state fiscal year 2021" for "for the second half of state fiscal year 2020 and all of each state fiscal year thereafter" in (E).

The 2019 amendment by HB 166 redesignated and rewrote the former introductory language of (B) and (B)(1) as (B); deleted former (B)(2) and (B)(3); and added (E).

The 2017 amendment by HB 49 substituted "during a state fiscal" for "during a fiscal" in the introductory language; redesignated and revised former (A)(6) as (B); redesignated former (B) and (C) as (C) and (D); substituted "under division (B)" for "under division (A)" in (C); substituted "under division (C)" for "under division (B)" in (D); and made a related change.

The 2015 amendment, by HB 64, substituted "be determined as follows" for "equal" in the introductory language; added "Determine" to the beginning of the introductory language of (A); rewrote (A)(6), which formerly read: "The quality incentive payment paid to the nursing facility under section 5165.25 of the Revised Code"; rewrote (B), which formerly read: "In addition to paying a nursing facility provider the nursing facility's total rate determined under division (A) of this section for a fiscal year, the department shall pay the provider a quality bonus under section 5165.26 of the Revised Code for that fiscal year if the provider's nursing facility is a qualifying nursing facility, as defined in that section, for that fiscal year. The quality bonus shall not be part of the total rate"; and added (C).

The 2014 amendment by HB 483 substituted "sections 5165.151 to 5165.157 and 5165.34" for "sections 5165.151 to 5165.156 and 5165.34" in the introductory language of (A).

The 2013 amendment rewrote the section.

The 2012 amendment by HB 303 added (A); redesignated former (A) and (C) as (B) and (D); substituted "division (C)" for "division (B)" in the introductory language of present (B); deleted (B), which read: "The department shall adjust the rates otherwise determined under division (A) of this section as directed by the general assembly through the enactment of law governing medicaid payments to providers of nursing facilities, including any law that establishes factors by which the rates are to be adjusted"; inserted (C); substituted "division (B) or (C)" for "division (A)" in the first sentence of present (D); and made stylistic changes.

The 2012 amendment by HB 487 inserted (A)(5); and redesignated former (A)(5) as (A)(6).

The 2011 amendment by SB 264, in the introductory language of (A), substituted "total rate" for "payments" and "pay for a fiscal year" for "make"; and added (C).

The 2011 amendment by HB 153 substituted "sections 5111.20 to 5111.331" for "sections 5111.20 to 5111.33" in the introductory language of (A); deleted former (A)(4), which read: "The rate for franchise permit fees determined for the nursing facility under section 5111.243 of the Revised Code"; redesignated former (A)(5) and (A)(6) as (A)(4)and (A)(5); in (A)(5), deleted "median" preceding "rate for," inserted "determined," deleted "nursing facilities in the" preceding "nursing," and deleted "as determined" following "group"; in (B), substituted "division (A)" for "divisions (A)(1), (2), (3), and (6)" and deleted "does either of the following" following "any law that"; deleted former (B)(2), which read: "Establishes a methodology for phasing in the rates determined for fiscal year 2006 under uncodified law the general assembly enacts to rates determined for subsequent fiscal years under sections 5111.20 to 5111.33 of the Revised Code"; and made a related change.

151 v H 530, effective June 30, 2006, in (A)(5), substituted "facility" for "facility's quality tier group"; in the introductory language of (B), substituted "rates otherwise determined under divisions (A)(1), (2), (3), and (6)" for "payment otherwise determined under division (A)"; and, in (B)(1), substituted "rates" for "payments".

### § 5165.151 Initial rates for new or replacement facility or newly certified facility.

(A) The total per medicaid day payment rate determined under section 5165.15 of the Revised Code shall not be the initial rate for nursing facility services provided by a new nursing facility. Instead, the initial total per medicaid day payment rate for nursing facility services provided by a new nursing facility shall be determined in the following manner:

(1) The initial rate for ancillary and support costs shall be the rate for the new nursing facility's peer group determined under division (C) of section 5165.16 of the Revised Code.

(2) The initial rate for capital costs shall be the rate for the new nursing facility's peer group determined under division (C) of section 5165.17 of the Revised Code;

(3) The initial rate for direct care costs shall be the product of the cost per case-mix unit determined under division (C) of section 5165.19 of the Revised Code for the new nursing facility's peer group and the new nursing facility's case-mix score determined under division (B) of this section.

(4) The initial rate for tax costs shall be the following:

(a) If the provider of the new nursing facility submits to the department of medicaid the nursing facility's projected tax costs for the calendar year in which the provider obtains an initial provider agreement for the new nursing facility, an amount determined by dividing those projected tax costs by the number of inpatient days the nursing facility would have for that calendar year if its occupancy rate were one hundred per cent;

Titles 39 — 57

(b) If division (A)(4)(a) of this section does not apply, the median rate for tax costs for the new nursing facility's peer group in which the nursing facility is placed under division (B) of section 5165.16 of the Revised Code.

(5) Fourteen dollars and sixty-five cents shall be added to the sum of the rates and payment specified in divisions (A)(1) to (4) of this section.

(B) For the purpose of division (A)(3) of this section, a new nursing facility's case-mix score shall be the following:

(1) Unless the new nursing facility replaces an existing nursing facility that participated in the medicaid program immediately before the new nursing facility begins participating in the medicaid program, the median annual average case-mix score for the new nursing facility's peer group;

(2) If the nursing facility replaces an existing nursing facility that participated in the medicaid program immediately before the new nursing facility begins participating in the medicaid program, the semiannual case-mix score most recently determined under section 5165.192 of the Revised Code for the replaced nursing facility as adjusted, if necessary, to reflect any difference in the number of beds in the replaced and new nursing facilities.

(C) Subject to division (D) of this section, the department of medicaid shall adjust the rates established under division (A) of this section effective the first day of July, to reflect new rate calculations for all nursing facilities under this chapter.

(D) If a rate for direct care costs is determined under this section for a new nursing facility using the median annual average case-mix score for the new nursing facility's peer group, the rate shall be redetermined to reflect the new nursing facility's actual semiannual average case-mix score determined under section 5165.192 of the Revised Code after the new nursing facility submits its first two quarterly assessment data that qualify for use in calculating a case-mix score in accordance with rules authorized by section 5165.192 of the Revised Code. If the new nursing facility's quarterly submissions do not qualify for use in calculating a case-mix score, the department shall continue to use the median annual average case-mix score for the new nursing facility's peer group in lieu of the new nursing facility's semiannual case-mix score until the new nursing facility submits two consecutive quarterly assessment data that qualify for use in calculating a case-mix score.

**HISTORY:**

151 v H 66, § 101.01, eff. 7-1-05; 2011 HB 153, § 101.01, eff. July 1, 2011; 2012 HB 487, § 101.01, eff. Sept. 10, 2012; 2013 HB 59, § 101.01, eff. Sept. 29, 2013; 2015 hb64, § 101.01, effective July 1, 2016; 2017 hb49, § 101.01, effective September 29, 2017; 2021 hb110, § 101.01, effective June 30, 2021.

**Editor's Notes**

This section was formerly codified as RC § 5111.254.

**Amendment Notes**

The 2021 amendment by HB 110 deleted former (A)(5), which read: "The quality payment shall be the mean quality payment rate determined for nursing facilities under section 5165.25 of the Revised Code"; redesignated former (A)(6) as (A)(5); and substituted "divisions (A)(1) to (4)" for "divisions (A)(1) to (5)" in (A)(5).

The 2017 amendment by HB 49 substituted "under division (C)" for "under division (D)" in (A)(1) through (A)(3); redesignated and revised former (A)(4) as the introductory language of (A)(4), (A)(4)(a) and (A)(4)(b); and substituted "the department of medicaid shall adjust" for "the department shall adjust" in (C).

The 2015 amendment, by HB 64, in (A)(5), deleted "incentive" following "The quality" and substituted "quality payment rate determined for" for "payment made to"; and added (A)(6).

The 2013 amendment rewrote the section.

The 2012 amendment deleted "as defined in section 5111.242 of the Revised Code" preceding "shall be the" in (A)(4).

The 2011 amendment deleted "median" following "shall be the" in (A)(3); substituted "made to nursing facilities under" for "specified in division (B) of" in (A)(5); and substituted "sections 5111.20 to 5111.331" for "sections 5111.20 to 5111.33" in (B).

## § 5165.152 Medicaid payment rate for low resource utilization residents.

The total per medicaid day payment rate determined under section 5165.15 of the Revised Code shall not be paid for nursing facility services provided to low resource utilization residents. Instead, the total rate for such nursing facility services shall beone hundred fifteen dollars per medicaid day.

**HISTORY:**

2013 HB 59, § 101.01, eff. Sept. 29, 2013; 2015 hb64, § 101.01, effective July 1, 2016; 2019 hb166, § 101.01, effective October 17, 2019.

**Amendment Notes**

The 2019 amendment by HB 166 redesignated and rewrote the former introductory language and (A) as the introductory paragraph; and deleted former (B), which read: "Ninety-one dollars and seventy cents per medicaid day if division (A) of this section does not apply to the nursing facility."

The 2015 amendment, by HB 64, rewrote the section, which formerly read: "The total per medicaid day payment rate determined under section 5165.15 of the Revised Code shall not be paid for nursing facility services provided to low resource utilization residents. Instead, the total rate for such nursing facility services shall be one hundred thirty dollars per medicaid day."

## § 5165.153 Methodology for calculating prospective rates for facilities with residents whose care costs are not otherwise adequately measured.

(A) The total per medicaid day payment rate determined under section 5165.15 of the Revised Code shall not be paid for nursing facility services provided by a nursing facility, or discrete unit of a nursing facility, designated by the department of medicaid as an outlier nursing facility or unit. Instead, the provider of a designated outlier nursing facility or unit shall be paid each state fiscal year a total per medicaid day payment rate that the department shall prospectively determine in accordance with a methodology established in rules authorized by this section.

(B) The department may designate a nursing facility, or discrete unit of a nursing facility, as an outlier nursing facility or unit if the nursing facility or unit serves residents who have either of the following:

(1) Diagnoses or special care needs that require direct care resources that are not measured adequately by the resident assessment instrument specified in rules authorized by section 5165.191 of the Revised Code;

(2) Diagnoses or special care needs specified in rules authorized by this section as otherwise qualifying for consideration under this section.

(C) Notwithstanding any other provision of this chapter (except section 5165.156 of the Revised Code), the costs incurred by a designated outlier nursing facility or unit shall not be considered in establishing medicaid payment rates for other nursing facilities or units.

(D) The medicaid director shall adopt rules under section 5165.02 of the Revised Code as necessary to implement this section.

(1)(a) The rules shall do both of the following:

(i) Specify the criteria and procedures the department will apply when designating a nursing facility, or discrete unit of a nursing facility, as an outlier nursing facility or unit;

(ii) Establish a methodology for prospectively determining the total per medicaid day payment rate that will be paid each state fiscal year for nursing facility services provided by a designated outlier nursing facility or unit.

(b) The rules authorized by division (D)(1)(a)(i) of this section regarding the criteria for designating outlier nursing facilities and units shall do both of the following:

(i) Provide for consideration of whether all of the allowable costs of a nursing facility, or discrete unit of a nursing facility, would be paid by a rate determined under section 5165.15 of the Revised Code;

(ii) Specify the minimum number of nursing facility beds that a nursing facility, or discrete unit of a nursing facility, must have to be designated an outlier nursing facility or unit, which may vary based on the diagnoses or special care needs of the residents served by the nursing facility or unit.

(c) The rules authorized by division (D)(1)(a)(i) of this section regarding the criteria for designating outlier nursing facilities and units shall not limit the designation to nursing facilities, or discrete units of nursing facilities, located in large cities.

(d) The rules authorized by division (D)(1)(a)(ii) of this section regarding the methodology for prospectively determining the rates of designated outlier nursing facilities and units shall provide for the methodology to consider the historical costs of providing nursing facility services to the residents of designated outlier nursing facilities and units.

(2)(a) The rules may do both of the following:

(i) Include for designation as an outlier nursing facility or unit, a nursing facility, or discrete unit of a nursing facility, that serves medically fragile pediatric residents; residents who are dependent on ventilators; residents who have severe traumatic brain injury, end-stage Alzheimer's disease, or end-stage acquired immunodeficiency syndrome; or residents with other diagnoses or special care needs specified in the rules;

(ii) Require that a designated outlier nursing facility receive authorization from the department before admitting or retaining a resident.

(b) If the director adopts rules authorized by division (D)(2)(a)(ii) of this section regarding the authorization of a designated outlier nursing facility or unit to admit or retain a resident, the rules shall specify the criteria and procedures the department will apply when granting that authorization.



**HISTORY:**

144 v H 904 (Eff 12-22-92); 145 v H 152 (Eff 7-1-93); 148 v H 471. Eff 7-1-2000; 151 v H 66, § 101.01, eff. 7-1-05; 2011 HB 153, § 101.01, eff. Sept. 29, 2011; 2013 HB 59, § 101.01, eff. Sept. 29, 2013; 2017 hb49, § 101.01, effective September 29, 2017.

**Editor's Notes**

This section was formerly codified as RC § 5111.258.

This section was amended and renumbered from RC § 5111.257 by 151 v H 66, effective July 1, 2005.

**Amendment Notes**

The 2017 amendment by HB 49 substituted "each state fiscal year" for "each fiscal year" in the second sentence of (A) and in (D)(1)(a)(ii).

The 2013 amendment rewrote the section.

The 2011 amendment substituted "sections 5111.20 to 5111.331" for "sections 5111.20 to 5111.33" throughout the section; and inserted "(except section 5111.259 of the Revised Code)" in the first sentence of the introductory language of (A), in the last paragraph of (A), and in the first sentence of (B).

151 v H 66, effective July 1, 2005, rewrote the section.

**NOTES TO DECISIONS**

**Reimbursement standard**

Under the current Medicaid reimbursement standard, a state is not required to reimburse every efficient and economic facility for its reasonable, actual costs: Drake Ctr. v. Department of Human Servs., 125 Ohio App. 3d 678, 709 N.E.2d 532, 1998 Ohio App. LEXIS 1118 (Ohio Ct. App., Franklin County 1998).

## § 5165.154 Medicaid payment for residents who meet criteria for designated outlier facility.

(A) To the extent, if any, provided for in rules authorized by this section, the total per medicaid day payment rate determined under section 5165.15 of the Revised Code shall not be paid for nursing facility services that a nursing facility not designated as an outlier nursing facility or unit provides to a resident who meets the criteria for admission to a designated outlier nursing facility or unit, as specified in rules authorized by section 5165.153 of the Revised Code. Instead, the provider of a nursing facility providing nursing facility services to such a resident shall be paid each fiscal year a total per medicaid day payment rate that the department of medicaid shall prospectively determine in accordance with a methodology established in rules authorized by this section.

(B) The medicaid director may adopt rules under section 5165.02 of the Revised Code to implement this section. The rules may require that a nursing facility receive authorization from the department before admitting or retaining a resident who meets the criteria for admission to a designated outlier nursing facility or unit. If the director adopts such rules, the rules shall specify the criteria and procedures the department will apply when granting the authorization.

**HISTORY:**

2013 HB 59, § 101.01, eff. Sept. 29, 2013.

## § 5165.155 Nursing facility payments.

(A) As used in this section, "medicaid maximum allowable amount" means one hundred per cent of a nursing facility's total per medicaid day payment rate.

(B) Instead of paying the total per medicaid day payment rate determined under section 5165.15 of the Revised Code, the department of medicaid shall pay the provider of a nursing facility the lesser of the following for nursing facility services the nursing facility provides on or after January 1, 2012, to a dual eligible individual who is eligible for nursing facility services under the medicaid program and post-hospital extended care services under Part A of Title XVIII:

(1) The coinsurance amount for the services as provided under Part A of Title XVIII;

(2) The medicaid maximum allowable amount for the services, less the amount paid under Part A of Title XVIII for the services.

**HISTORY:**

2011 HB 153, § 101.01, eff. Sept. 29, 2011; 2013 HB 59, § 101.01, eff. Sept. 29, 2013.

**Editor's Notes**

This section was formerly codified as RC § 5111.225.

**Amendment Notes**

The 2013 amendment deleted the first paragraph of (A), which read: "'Dual eligible individual' has the same meaning as in section 1915(h)(2)(B) of the 'Social Security Act,' 124 Stat. 315 (2010), 42 U.S.C. 1396n(h)(2)(B)"; substituted "total per medicaid day payment rate" for "per diem rate for a medicaid day" in (A); in the introductory language of (B), added "Instead of paying the total per medicaid day payment rate determined under section 5165.15 of the Revised Code" to the beginning and substituted "medicaid shall" for "job and family services shall"; and made a related change.

## § 5165.156 Centers of excellence component; purpose; rules.

The medicaid director may establish a centers of excellence component of the medicaid program. The purpose of the centers of excellence component is to increase the efficiency and quality of nursing facility services provided to medicaid recipients with complex nursing facility service needs. The director may adopt rules under section 5165.02 of the Revised Code governing the component, including rules that establish a method of determining the medicaid payment rates for nursing facilities providing nursing facility services to medicaid recipients participating in the component. The rules may specify the extent to which, if any, of the provisions of sections 5165.153 and 5165.154 of the Revised Code are to apply to the centers of excellence component. If such rules are adopted, the nursing facilities that provide nursing facility services to medicaid recipients participating in the centers of excellence component shall be paid for those services in accordance with the method established in the rules instead of the total per medicaid day payment rate determined under section 5165.15 of the Revised Code.

**HISTORY:**

2011 HB 153, § 101.01, eff. Sept. 29, 2011; 2013 HB 59, § 101.01, eff. Sept. 29, 2013.

**Editor's Notes**

This section was formerly codified as RC § 5111.259.

**Amendment Notes**

The 2013 amendment substituted "medicaid director" for "director of job and family services may submit a request to the United States secretary of health and human services for approval to" in the first sentence; in the third sentence, deleted "If federal approval for the centers of excellence component is granted" from the beginning and substituted "payment" for "reimbursement"; substituted "sections 5165.153 and 5165.154" for "section 5111.258" in the fourth sentence; and substituted "instead of the total per medicaid day payment rate determined under section 5165.15" for "notwithstanding anything to the contrary in sections 5111.20 to 5111.331" in the last sentence.

### § 5165.157 Alternative purchasing model for nursing facility services.

(A) The medicaid director shall establish an alternative purchasing model for nursing facility services provided by designated discrete units of nursing facilities to medicaid recipients with specialized health care needs. The director shall do all of the following with regard to the model:

(1) Establish criteria that a discrete unit of a nursing facility must meet to be designated as a unit that, under the alternative purchasing model, may admit and provide nursing facility services to medicaid recipients with specialized health care needs;

(2) Specify the health care conditions that medicaid recipients must have to have specialized health care needs, which may include dependency on a ventilator, severe traumatic brain injury, the need to be admitted to a long-term acute care hospital or rehabilitation hospital if not for nursing facility services, and other serious health care conditions;

(3) For each fiscal year, set the total per medicaid day payment rate for nursing facility services provided by designated discrete units of nursing facilities under the alternative purchasing model at either of the following:

(a) Thirty-four per cent of the statewide average of the total per medicaid day payment rate for long-term acute care hospital services as of the first day of the fiscal year;

(b) Another amount determined in accordance with an alternative methodology that includes improved health outcomes as a factor in determining the payment rate.

(4) Require, to the extent the director considers necessary, a medicaid recipient to obtain prior authorization for admission to a long-term acute care hospital or rehabilitation hospital as a condition of medicaid payment for long-term acute care hospital or rehabilitation hospital services.

(B) The criteria established under division (A)(1) of this section shall provide for a discrete unit of a nursing facility to be excluded from the alternative purchasing model if the unit is paid for nursing facility services in accordance with section 5165.153, 5165.154, or 5165.156 of the Revised Code. The criteria may require the provider of a nursing facility that has a discrete unit designated for participation in the alternative purchasing model to report health outcome measurement data to the department of medicaid.

(C) A discrete unit of a nursing facility that provides nursing facility services to medicaid recipients with specialized health care needs under the alternative purchasing model shall be paid for those services in accordance with division (A)(3) of this section instead of the total per medicaid day payment rate determined under section 5165.15, 5165.153, 5165.154, or 5165.156 of the Revised Code.

**HISTORY:**

2013 HB 59, § 101.01, eff. Sept. 29, 2013; 2014 HB 483, § 101.01, eff. Sept. 15, 2014; 2015 hb64, § 101.01, effective September 29, 2015; 2017 hb49, § 101.01, effective September 29, 2017.

**Amendment Notes**

The 2017 amendment by HB 49 added "by designated discrete units of nursing facilities" in the introductory language of (A)(3); substituted "Thirty-four per cent" for "Sixty per cent" in (A)(3)(a); and made a related change.

The 2015 amendment, by HB 64, in the introductory language of (A), substituted "shall" for "may" in the first sentence and deleted "If the alternative purchasing model is established" from the beginning of the second sentence.

### § 5165.16 Per resident per day rate ancillary and support costs; determination of rate for each peer group.

(A) The department of medicaid shall determine each nursing facility's per medicaid day payment rate for ancillary and support costs. A nursing facility's rate shall be the rate determined under division (C) of this section for the nursing facility's peer group.

(B) For the purpose of determining nursing facilities' rates for ancillary and support costs, the department shall establish six peer groups composed as follows:

(1) Each nursing facility located in any of the following counties shall be placed in peer group one or two: Brown, Butler, Clermont, Clinton, Hamilton, and Warren. Each nursing facility located in any of those counties that has fewer than one hundred beds shall be placed in peer group one. Each nursing facility located in any of those counties that has one hundred or more beds shall be placed in peer group two.

(2) Each nursing facility located in any of the following counties shall be placed in peer group three or four: Allen, Ashtabula, Champaign, Clark, Cuyahoga, Darke, Delaware, Fairfield, Fayette, Franklin, Fulton, Geauga, Greene, Hancock, Knox, Lake, Licking, Lorain, Lucas, Madison, Mahoning, Marion, Medina, Miami, Montgomery, Morrow, Ottawa, Pickaway, Portage, Preble, Ross, Sandusky, Seneca, Stark, Summit, Trumbull, Union, and Wood. Each nursing facility located in any of those counties that has fewer than one hundred beds shall be placed in peer group three. Each nursing facility located in any of those counties that has one hundred or more beds shall be placed in peer group four.

(3) Each nursing facility located in any of the following counties shall be placed in peer group five or six: Adams, Ashland, Athens, Auglaize, Belmont, Carroll, Columbiana, Coshocton, Crawford, Defiance, Erie, Gallia, Guernsey, Hardin, Harrison, Henry, Highland, Hocking, Holmes, Huron, Jackson, Jefferson, Lawrence, Logan, Meigs, Mercer, Monroe, Morgan, Muskingum, Noble, Paulding, Perry, Pike, Putnam, Richland, Scioto, Shelby, Tuscarawas, Van Wert, Vinton, Washington, Wayne, Williams, and Wyandot. Each nursing facility located in any of those counties that has fewer than one hundred beds shall be placed in peer group five. Each nursing facility located in any of those counties that has one hundred or more beds shall be placed in peer group six.

(C)(1) The department shall determine the rate for ancillary and support costs for each peer group established under division (B) of this section. The rate for ancillary and support costs determined under this division for a peer group shall be used for subsequent years until the department conducts a rebasing. To determine a peer group's rate for ancillary and support costs, the department shall do all of the following:

(a) Determine the rate for ancillary and support costs for each nursing facility in the peer group for the applicable calendar year by using the greater of the nursing facility's actual inpatient days for the applicable calendar year or the inpatient days the nursing facility would have had for the applicable calendar year if its occupancy rate had been ninety per cent;

(b) Subject to division (C)(2) of this section, identify which nursing facility in the peer group is at the twenty-fifth percentile of the rate for ancillary and support costs for the applicable calendar year determined under division (C)(1)(a) of this section;

(c) Multiply the rate for ancillary and support costs determined under division (C)(1)(a) of this section for the nursing facility identified under division (C)(1)(b) of this section by the rate of inflation for the eighteen-month period beginning on the first day of July of the applicable calendar year and ending the last day of December of the calendar year immediately following the applicable calendar year using the following:

(i) Except as provided in division (C)(1)(c)(ii) of this section, the consumer price index for all items for all urban consumers for the midwest region, published by the United States bureau of labor statistics;

(ii) If the United States bureau of labor statistics ceases to publish the index specified in division (C)(1)(c)(i) of this section, the index the bureau subsequently publishes that covers urban consumers' prices for items for the region that includes this state.

(2) In making the identification under division (C)(1)(b) of this section, the department shall exclude both of the following:

Titles 39 — 57

(a) Nursing facilities that participated in the medicaid program under the same provider for less than twelve months in the applicable calendar year;

(b) Nursing facilities whose ancillary and support costs are more than one standard deviation from the mean desk-reviewed, actual, allowable, per diem ancillary and support cost for all nursing facilities in the nursing facility's peer group for the applicable calendar year.

(3) The department shall not redetermine a peer group's rate for ancillary and support costs under this division based on additional information that it receives after the rate is determined. The department shall redetermine a peer group's rate for ancillary and support costs only if the department made an error in determining the rate based on information available to the department at the time of the original determination.

**HISTORY:**

151 v H 66, § 101.01, eff. 7-1-05; 153 v H 1, § 101.01, eff. 7-17-09; 2011 HB 153, § 101.01, eff. July 1, 2011; 2012 HB 303, § 1, eff. July 1, 2013; 2013 HB 59, § 101.01, eff. Sept. 29, 2013; 2015 hb64, § 101.01, effective September 29, 2015; 2017 hb49, § 101.01, effective September 29, 2017; 2020 hb481, § 29, effective September 18, 2020; 2021 hb110, § 101.01, effective September 30, 2021.

**Editor's Notes**

This section was formerly codified as RC § 5111.24.

**Amendment Notes**

The 2021 amendment by HB 110 deleted "Subject to division (C)(2) of this section" at the beginning of (C)(1)(a); substituted "division (C)(2)" for "division (C)(3)" in (C)(1)(b); deleted former (C)(2), which read: "For the purpose of determining a nursing facility's occupancy rate under division (C)(1)(a) of this section, the department shall include any beds that the nursing facility removes from its medicaid-certified capacity unless the nursing facility also removes the beds from its licensed bed capacity"; and redesignated former (C)(3) and (C)(4) as (C)(2) and (C)(3).

The 2020 amendment by HB 481 deleted former (C)(1)(d), which read: "For state fiscal year 2020 and each state fiscal year thereafter (other than the first state fiscal year in a group of consecutive state fiscal years for which a rebasing is conducted), adjust the amount calculated under division (C)(1)(c) of this section using the difference between the following: (i) The medicare skilled nursing facility market basket index determined for the federal fiscal year that begins during the state fiscal year immediately preceding the state fiscal year for which the adjustment is being made under division (C)(1)(d) of this section; (ii) The budget reduction adjustment factor for the state fiscal year for which the adjustment is being made under division (C)(1)(d) of this section."

The 2017 amendment by HB 49 rewrote the section.

The 2015 amendment, by HB 64, substituted "Allen, Mahoning, Stark, or Trumbull" for "Mahoning or Stark" in (C)(2)(a) and (C)(2)(b).

The 2013 amendment substituted "medicaid's" for "job and family services'" in (A)(1)(a); substituted "group's" for "groups'" in (A)(2); rewrote (B); substituted "rates" for "rate" in the introductory language of (C); added (C)(1); redesignated the former undesignated paragraphs of (C) as (C)(1)(a) through (c); and added (C)(2).

The 2012 amendment, in the third sentence of the introductory language of (D)(1), deleted "by this act" following "amendments made" and inserted "by Am. Sub. H.B. 153 and Sub. H.B. 303, both of the 129th general assembly"; and added (D)(1)(d).

The 2011 amendment rewrote (A) and (D).

153 v H 1, effective July 17, 2009, rewrote (D)(1)(d).

Titles 39 — 57

## NOTES TO DECISIONS

**Breach of contract**

Where the owner of group homes for the mentally retarded, under contract with the state to provide care to such individuals and required under the contract to meet all statutory licensing and certification regulations, brings suit against the state for breach of said contract, it is proper for the trial court to admit evidence presented by the defendant concerning the substandard condition of the homes, as a means of rebutting her claim that all contractual requirements had been met: Humphrey v. State, Dep't of Mental Health & Mental Retardation, 14 Ohio App. 3d 15, 469 N.E.2d 981, 1984 Ohio App. LEXIS 11228 (Ohio Ct. App., Franklin County 1984).

## RESEARCH REFERENCES AND PRACTICE AIDS

**Ohio Administrative Code**

Method for establishing the indirect care costs component of the prospective rate for nursing facilities (NFs). OAC 5160-3-57 et seq.

## § 5165.17 Contracts with managed care organizations.

(A) The department of medicaid shall determine each nursing facility's per medicaid day payment rate for capital costs. A nursing facility's rate shall be the rate determined under division (C) of this section for the nursing facility's peer group.

(B) For the purpose of determining nursing facilities' rates for capital costs, the department shall establish six peer groups.

(1) Each nursing facility located in any of the following counties shall be placed in peer group one or two: Brown, Butler, Clermont, Clinton, Hamilton, and Warren. Each nursing facility located in any of those counties that has fewer than one hundred beds shall be placed in peer group one. Each nursing facility located in any of those counties that has one hundred or more beds shall be placed in peer group two.

(2) Each nursing facility located in any of the following counties shall be placed in peer group three or four: Allen, Ashtabula, Champaign, Clark, Cuyahoga, Darke, Delaware, Fairfield, Fayette, Franklin, Fulton, Geauga, Greene, Hancock, Knox, Lake, Licking, Lorain, Lucas, Madison, Mahoning, Marion, Medina, Miami, Montgomery, Morrow, Ottawa, Pickaway, Portage, Preble, Ross, Sandusky, Seneca, Stark, Summit, Trumbull, Union, and Wood. Each nursing facility located in any of those counties that has fewer than one hundred beds shall be placed in peer group three. Each nursing facility located in any of those counties that has one hundred or more beds shall be placed in peer group four.

(3) Each nursing facility located in any of the following counties shall be placed in peer group five or six: Adams, Ashland, Athens, Auglaize, Belmont, Carroll, Columbiana, Coshocton, Crawford, Defiance, Erie, Gallia, Guernsey, Hardin, Harrison, Henry, Highland, Hocking, Holmes, Huron, Jackson, Jefferson, Lawrence, Logan, Meigs, Mercer, Monroe, Morgan, Muskingum, Noble, Paulding, Perry, Pike, Putnam, Richland, Scioto, Shelby, Tuscarawas, Van Wert, Vinton, Washington, Wayne, Williams, and Wyandot. Each nursing facility located in any of those counties that has fewer than one hundred beds shall be placed in peer group five. Each nursing facility located in any of those counties that has one hundred or more beds shall be placed in peer group six.

(C)(1) The department shall determine the rate for capital costs for each peer group established under division (B) of this section. The rate for capital costs determined under this division for a peer group shall be used for subsequent years until the department conducts a rebasing. A peer group's rate for capital costs shall be the rate for capital costs for the nursing facility in the peer group that is at the twenty-fifth percentile of the rate for capital costs for the applicable calendar year.

(2) To identify the nursing facility in a peer group that is at the twenty-fifth percentile of the rate for capital costs for the applicable calendar year, the department shall do both of the following:

(a) Use the greater of each nursing facility's actual inpatient days for the applicable calendar year or the inpatient days the nursing facility would have had for the applicable calendar year if its occupancy rate had been one hundred per cent;

(b) Exclude both of the following:

(i) Nursing facilities that participated in the medicaid program under the same provider for less than twelve months in the applicable calendar year;

(ii) Nursing facilities whose capital costs are more than one standard deviation from the mean desk-reviewed, actual, allowable, per diem capital cost for all nursing facilities in the nursing facility's peer group for the applicable calendar year.

(3) The department shall not redetermine a peer group's rate for capital costs under this division based on additional information that it receives after the rate is determined. The department shall redetermine a peer group's rate for capital costs only if the department made an error in determining the rate based on information available to the department at the time of the original determination.

(D) Buildings shall be depreciated using the straight line method over forty years or over a different period approved by the department. Components and equipment shall be depreciated using the straight-line method over a period designated in rules adopted under section 5165.02 of the Revised Code, consistent with the guidelines of the American hospital association, or over a different period approved by the department. Any rules authorized by this division that specify useful lives of buildings, components, or equipment apply only to assets acquired on or after July 1, 1993. Depreciation for costs paid or reimbursed by any government agency shall not be included in capital costs unless that part of the payment under this chapter is used to reimburse the government agency.

(E) The capital cost basis of nursing facility assets shall be determined in the following manner:

(1) Except as provided in division (E)(3) of this section, for purposes of calculating the rates to be paid for facilities with dates of licensure on or before June 30, 1993, the capital cost basis of each asset shall be equal to the desk-reviewed, actual, allowable, capital cost basis that is listed on the facility's cost report for the calendar year preceding the state fiscal year during which the rate will be paid.

(2) For facilities with dates of licensure after June 30, 1993, the capital cost basis shall be determined in accordance with the principles of the medicare program, except as otherwise provided in this chapter.

(3) Except as provided in division (E)(4) of this section, if a provider transfers an interest in a facility to another provider after June 30, 1993, there shall be no increase in the capital cost basis of the asset if the providers are related parties or the provider to which the interest is transferred authorizes the provider that transferred the interest to continue to operate the facility under a lease, management agreement, or other arrangement. If the previous sentence does not prohibit the adjustment of the capital cost basis under this division, the basis of the asset shall be adjusted by one-half of the change in the consumer price index for all items for all urban consumers, as published by the United States bureau of labor statistics, during the time that the transferor held the asset.

(4) If a provider transfers an interest in a facility to another provider who is a related party, the capital cost basis of the asset shall be adjusted as specified in division (E)(3) of this section if all of the following conditions are met:

(a) The related party is a relative of owner;

(b) Except as provided in division (E)(4)(c)(ii) of this section, the provider making the transfer retains no ownership interest in the facility;

(c) The department determines that the transfer is an arm's length transaction pursuant to rules adopted under section 5165.02 of the Revised Code. The rules shall provide that a transfer is an arm's length transaction if all of the following apply:

(i) Once the transfer goes into effect, the provider that made the transfer has no direct or indirect interest in the provider that acquires the facility or the facility itself, including interest as an owner, officer, director, employee, independent contractor, or consultant, but excluding interest as a creditor.

(ii) The provider that made the transfer does not reacquire an interest in the facility except through the exercise of a creditor's rights in the event of a default. If the provider reacquires an interest in the facility in this manner, the department shall treat the facility as if the transfer never occurred when the department calculates its reimbursement rates for capital costs.

(iii) The transfer satisfies any other criteria specified in the rules.

(d) Except in the case of hardship caused by a catastrophic event, as determined by the department, or in the case of a provider making the transfer who is at least sixty-five years of age, not less than twenty years have elapsed since, for the same facility, the capital cost basis was adjusted most recently under division (E)(4) of this section or actual, allowable capital costs was determined most recently under division (F)(9) of this section.

(F) As used in this division:

"Imputed interest" means the lesser of the prime rate plus two per cent or ten per cent.

"Lease expense" means lease payments in the case of an operating lease and depreciation expense and interest expense in the case of a capital lease.

"New lease" means a lease, to a different lessee, of a nursing facility that previously was operated under a lease.

(1) Subject to division (A) of this section, for a lease of a facility that was effective on May 27, 1992, the entire lease expense is an actual, allowable capital cost during the term of the existing lease. The entire lease expense also is an actual, allowable capital cost if a lease in existence on May 27, 1992, is renewed under either of the following circumstances:

(a) The renewal is pursuant to a renewal option that was in existence on May 27, 1992;

(b) The renewal is for the same lease payment amount and between the same parties as the lease in existence on May 27, 1992.

(2) Subject to division (A) of this section, for a lease of a facility that was in existence but not operated under a lease on May 27, 1992, actual, allowable capital costs shall include the lesser of the annual lease expense or the annual depreciation expense and imputed interest expense that would be calculated at the inception of the lease using the lessor's entire historical capital asset cost basis, adjusted by one-half of the change in the consumer price index for all items for all urban consumers, as published by the United States bureau of labor statistics, during the time the lessor held each asset until the beginning of the lease.

(3) Subject to division (A) of this section, for a lease of a facility with a date of licensure on or after May 27, 1992, that is initially operated under a lease, actual, allowable capital costs shall include the annual lease expense if there was a substantial commitment of money for construction of the facility after December 22, 1992, and before July 1, 1993. If there was not a substantial commitment of money after December 22, 1992, and before July 1, 1993, actual, allowable capital costs shall include the lesser of the annual lease expense or the sum of the following:

(a) The annual depreciation expense that would be calculated at the inception of the lease using the lessor's entire historical capital asset cost basis;

(b) The greater of the lessor's actual annual amortization of financing costs and interest expense at the inception of the lease or the imputed interest expense calculated at the inception of the lease using seventy per cent of the lessor's historical capital asset cost basis.

(4) Subject to division (A) of this section, for a lease of a facility with a date of licensure on or after May 27, 1992, that was not initially operated under a lease and has been in existence for ten years, actual, allowable capital costs shall include the lesser of the annual lease expense or the annual depreciation expense and imputed interest expense that would be calculated at the inception of the lease using the entire historical capital asset cost basis of one-half of the change in the consumer price index for all items for all urban consumers, as published by the United States bureau of labor statistics, during the time the lessor held each asset until the beginning of the lease.

(5) Subject to division (A) of this section, for a new lease of a facility that was operated under a lease on May 27, 1992, actual, allowable capital costs shall include the lesser of the annual new lease expense or the annual old lease payment. If the old lease was in effect for ten years or longer, the old lease payment from the beginning of the old lease shall be adjusted by one-half of the change in the consumer price index for all items for all urban consumers, as published by the United States bureau of labor statistics, from the beginning of the old lease to the beginning of the new lease.

(6) Subject to division (A) of this section, for a new lease of a facility that was not in existence or that was in existence but not operated under a lease on May 27, 1992, actual, allowable capital costs shall include the lesser of annual new lease expense or the annual amount calculated for the old lease under division (F)(2), (3), (4), or (6) of this section, as applicable. If the old lease was in effect for ten years or longer, the lessor's historical capital asset cost basis shall be, for purposes of calculating the annual amount under division (F)(2), (3), (4), or

(6) of this section, adjusted by one-half of the change in the consumer price index for all items for all urban consumers, as published by the United States bureau of labor statistics, from the beginning of the old lease to the beginning of the new lease.

In the case of a lease under division (F)(3) of this section of a facility for which a substantial commitment of money was made after December 22, 1992, and before July 1, 1993, the old lease payment shall be adjusted for the purpose of determining the annual amount.

(7) For any revision of a lease described in division (F)(1), (2), (3), (4), (5), or (6) of this section, or for any subsequent lease of a facility operated under such a lease, other than execution of a new lease, the portion of actual, allowable capital costs attributable to the lease shall be the same as before the revision or subsequent lease.

(8) Except as provided in division (F)(9) of this section, if a provider leases an interest in a facility to another provider who is a related party or previously operated the facility, the related party's or previous operator's actual, allowable capital costs shall include the lesser of the annual lease expense or the reasonable cost to the lessor.

(9) If a provider leases an interest in a facility to another provider who is a related party, regardless of the date of the lease, the related party's actual, allowable capital costs shall include the annual lease expense, subject to the limitations specified in divisions (F)(1) to (7) of this section, if all of the following conditions are met:

(a) The related party is a relative of owner;

(b) If the lessor retains an ownership interest, it is, except as provided in division (F)(9)(c)(ii) of this section, in only the real property and any improvements on the real property;

(c) The department determines that the lease is an arm's length transaction pursuant to rules adopted under section 5165.02 of the Revised Code. The rules shall provide that a lease is an arm's length transaction if all of the following apply:

(i) Once the lease goes into effect, the lessor has no direct or indirect interest in the lessee or, except as provided in division (F)(9)(b) of this section, the facility itself, including interest as an owner, officer, director, employee, independent contractor, or consultant, but excluding interest as a lessor.

(ii) The lessor does not reacquire an interest in the facility except through the exercise of a lessor's rights in the event of a default. If the lessor reacquires an interest in the facility in this manner, the department shall treat the facility as if the lease never occurred when the department calculates its reimbursement rates for capital costs.

(iii) The lease satisfies any other criteria specified in the rules.

(d) Except in the case of hardship caused by a catastrophic event, as determined by the department, or in the case of a lessor who is at least sixty-five years of age, not less than twenty years have elapsed since, for the same facility, the capital cost basis was adjusted most recently under division (E)(4) of this section or actual, allowable capital costs were determined most recently under division (F)(9) of this section.

(10) This division does not apply to leases of specific items of equipment.

Titles 39 — 57

**HISTORY:**

144 v H 904 (Eff 12-22-92); 145 v H 152 (Eff 7-1-93); 145 v H 715 (Eff 7-22-94); 146 v H 117 (Eff 6-30-95); 147 v H 698 (Eff 3-22-99); 148 v H 471 (Eff 7-1-2000); 148 v H 403 (Eff 9-27-2000); 149 v H 94. Eff 6-6-2001; 151 v H 66, § 101.01, eff. 7-1-05; 153 v H 1, § 101.01, eff. 7-17-09; 2011 HB 153, § 101.01, eff. July 1, 2011; 2012 HB 303, § 1, eff. July 1, 2013; 2013 HB 59, § 101.01, eff. Sept. 29, 2013; 2015 hb64, § 101.01, effective September 29, 2015; 2017 hb49, § 101.01, effective September 29, 2017; 2020 hb481, § 29, effective September 18, 2020; 2021 hb110, § 101.01, effective September 30, 2021.

**Editor's Notes**

This section was formerly codified as RC § 5111.17.

**Amendment Notes**

The 2021 amendment by HB 110 deleted "Subject to division (C)(3) of this section" at the beginning of (C)(2)(a); deleted former (C)(3), which read: "For the purpose of determining a nursing facility's occupancy rate under division (C)(2)(a) of this section, the department shall include any beds that the nursing facility removes from its medicaid-certified capacity after June 30, 2005, unless the nursing facility also removes the beds from its licensed bed capacity"; and redesignated former (C)(4) as (C)(3).

The 2020 amendment by HB 481 added "for the nursing facility's peer group" in the second sentence of (A); and rewrote (C)(1).

The 2017 amendment by HB 49 rewrote the section.

The 2015 amendment, by HB 64, substituted "Allen, Mahoning, Stark, or Trumbull" for "Mahoning or Stark" in (C)(2)(a) and (C)(2)(b).

The 2013 amendment substituted "department of medicaid's" for "department of job and family services'" in (A)(1)(a); rewrote (B); added the (C)(1) and (C)(1)(a) through (C)(1)(c) designations; added the introductory language to (C)(1); added (C)(2); substituted "section 5165.02" for "section 5111.02" in the second sentence of (E); substituted "this chapter" for "sections 5111.20 to 5111.331 of the Revised Code" in the last sentence of (E) and in (F)(2); deleted "established under Title XVIII" following "the medicare program" in (F)(2); in the first sentence of the introductory language of (F)(4)(c) and (G)(9)(c), deleted "of job and family services" following "department" and substituted "section 5165.02" for "section 5111.02"; substituted "capital costs" for "cost of ownership" in (F)(4)(d); and made stylistic changes.

The 2012 amendment, in the introductory language of (D)(1), in the third sentence, deleted "by this act" following "amendments made" and inserted "by Am. Sub. H.B. 153 and Sub. H.B. 303, both of the 129th general assembly" and in the last sentence, added "To determine" to the beginning and substituted "the department shall do both of the following" for "shall be"; added (D)(1)(b); inserted "in a peer group that is at the twenty-fifth percentile of the rate for capital costs for the applicable calendar year" in the introductory language of present (D)(2); redesignated former (D)(2) and (D)(3) as (D)(3) and (D)(4); and made related and stylistic changes.

The 2011 amendment rewrote (A) and (B); rewrote the introductory language of (D)(1); added (D)(3); substituted "sections 5111.20 to 5111.331" for "sections 5111.20 to 5111.33" in the last sentence of (E) and in (F)(2); deleted "the lesser of the following" following "adjusted by" in the second sentence of (F)(3) and (G)(5); deleted (F)(3)(a); deleted the (F)(3)(b) designation; deleted "the lesser of the following amounts" following "adjusted by" in (G)(2); deleted (G)(2)(a); deleted the (G)(2)(b) designation; deleted "the lessor, adjusted by the lesser of the following" following "cost basis of" in (G)(4); deleted (G)(4)(a); deleted the (G)(4)(b) designation; deleted (G)(5)(a); deleted the (G)(5)(b) designation; in the seconds sentence of the first paragraph of (G)(6), deleted "adjusted by the lesser of the following" following "basis shall be" and inserted "adjusted by"; deleted (G)(6)(a); deleted the (G)(6)(b) designation; and made related changes.

153 v H 1, effective July 17, 2009, deleted former (H), pertaining to the causes of excess depreciation.

151 v H 66, effective July 1, 2005, rewrote the section.

## NOTES TO DECISIONS

Analysis



**Interest expenses**

When a nursing home sought Medicaid reimbursement for certain interest expenses associated with the cost of ownership, and a trial court found reimbursement was improperly disallowed, the trial court abused discretion because many of the documents submitted in support of this expense did not identify that the document was produced by the lender and none of the documents showed the loan proceeds were related to patient care or were to be used for the home's operation. Meadowwood Nursing Facility v. Ohio Dep't of Job & Family Servs., 2005-Ohio-1263, 2005 Ohio App. LEXIS 5762 (Ohio Ct. App., Franklin County 2005).

**Reimbursement rates**

OAC 5101:3-3-51.6(B)(3) (repealed 2/2/06) did not require the Ohio Department of Job and Family Services to enter into a new provider agreement and allow for an increase in reimbursement rates to a nursing facility where only the independent entity that owned of the facility changed, but the actual provider remained constant; OAC 5101:3-3-51.6(B)(3) was deemed facially ambiguous for purposes of the reimbursement rates under R.C. 5111.25, based on the review of other sections of the administrative code as well as on the federal regulation pursuant to R.C. 1.49(D). Meadowwood Manor, Inc. v. Ohio Dep't of Health, 2007-Ohio-2067, 2007 Ohio App. LEXIS 1932 (Ohio Ct. App., Brown County 2007).

OAC 5101:3-3-51.6(B)(3) (repealed 2/2/06) did not require the Ohio Department of Job and Family Services to enter into a new provider agreement and allow for an increase in reimbursement rates to a nursing facility where only the independent entity that owned of the facility changed, but the actual provider remained constant; OAC 5101:3-3-51.6(B)(3) was deemed facially ambiguous for purposes of the reimbursement rates under R.C. 5111.25, based on the review of other sections of the administrative code as well as on the federal regulation pursuant to R.C. 1.49(D). Meadowwood Manor, Inc. v. Ohio Dep't of Health, 2007-Ohio-2067, 2007 Ohio App. LEXIS 1932 (Ohio Ct. App.; Brown County 2007).

### RESEARCH REFERENCES AND PRACTICE AIDS

**Cross-References to Related Sections**

Calculating indirect care costs; per diem defined, RC § 5165.01.

Calculating prospective rates for facilities with residents whose care costs are not otherwise adequately measured, RC § 5165.153.

Department of job and family services to act by adjudication order; appeal from order, RC § 5164.38.

Initial rates for facilities licensed on or after 1-1-93, RC § 5124.151.

Pass-through of related party costs, RC § 5165.30.

Penalty for not providing notice of sale, RC § 5165.40.

Process by which facility may seek reconsideration of rate; appeals from adverse actions, RC § 5165.38.

**Ohio Administrative Code**

Nursing facilities generally. OAC ch. 5160-3.

## § 5165.19 Determination of cost per case-mix unit for each peer group.

(A) Semiannually, the department of medicaid shall determine each nursing facility's per medicaid day payment rate for direct care costs by multiplying the facility's semiannual case-mix score determined under section 5165.192 of the Revised Code by the cost per case-mix unit determined under division (C) of this section for the facility's peer group.

(B) For the purpose of determining nursing facilities' rates for direct care costs, the department shall establish three peer groups.

(1) Each nursing facility located in any of the following counties shall be placed in peer group one: Brown, Butler, Clermont, Clinton, Hamilton, and Warren.

(2) Each nursing facility located in any of the following counties shall be placed in peer group two: Allen, Ashtabula, Champaign, Clark, Cuyahoga, Darke, Delaware, Fairfield, Fayette, Franklin, Fulton, Geauga, Greene, Hancock, Knox, Lake, Licking, Lorain, Lucas, Madison, Mahoning, Marion, Medina, Miami, Montgomery, Morrow, Ottawa, Pickaway, Portage, Preble, Ross, Sandusky, Seneca, Stark, Summit, Trumbull, Union, and Wood.

(3) Each nursing facility located in any of the following counties shall be placed in peer group three: Adams, Ashland, Athens, Auglaize, Belmont, Carroll, Columbiana, Coshocton, Crawford, Defiance, Erie, Gallia, Guernsey, Hardin, Harrison, Henry, Highland, Hocking, Holmes, Huron, Jackson, Jefferson, Lawrence, Logan, Meigs, Mercer, Monroe, Morgan, Muskingum, Noble, Paulding, Perry, Pike, Putnam, Richland, Scioto, Shelby, Tuscarawas, Van Wert, Vinton, Washington, Wayne, Williams, and Wyandot.

(C)(1) The department shall determine a cost per case-mix unit for each peer group established under division (B) of this section. The cost per case-mix unit determined under this division for a peer group shall be used for subsequent years until the department conducts a rebasing. To determine a peer group's cost per case-mix unit, the department shall do all of the following:

(a) Determine the cost per case-mix unit for each nursing facility in the peer group for the applicable calendar year by dividing each facility's desk-reviewed, actual, allowable, per diem direct care costs for the applicable calendar year by the facility's annual average case-mix score determined under section 5165.192 of the Revised Code for the applicable calendar year;

(b) Subject to division (C)(2) of this section, identify which nursing facility in the peer group is at the twenty-fifth percentile of the cost per case-mix units determined under division (C)(1)(a) of this section;

(c) Calculate the amount that is two per cent above the cost per case-mix unit determined under division (C)(1)(a) of this section for the nursing facility identified under division (C)(1)(b) of this section;

(d) Using the index specified in division (C)(3) of this section, multiply the rate of inflation for the eighteen-month period beginning on the first day of July of the applicable calendar year and ending the last day of December of the calendar year immediately following the applicable calendar year by the amount calculated under division (C)(1)(c) of this section.

(2) In making the identification under division (C)(1)(b) of this section, the department shall exclude both of the following:

(a) Nursing facilities that participated in the medicaid program under the same provider for less than twelve months in the applicable calendar year;

(b) Nursing facilities whose cost per case-mix unit is more than one standard deviation from the mean cost per case-mix unit for all nursing facilities in the nursing facility's peer group for the applicable calendar year.

(3) The following index shall be used for the purpose of the calculation made under division (C)(1)(d) of this section:

(a) Except as provided in division (C)(3)(b) of this section, the employment cost index for total compensation, nursing and residential care facilities occupational group, published by the United States bureau of labor statistics;

(b) If the United States bureau of labor statistics ceases to publish the index specified in division (C)(3)(a) of this section, the index the bureau subsequently publishes that covers nursing facilities' staff costs.

(4) The department shall not redetermine a peer group's cost per case-mix unit under this division based on additional information that it receives after the peer group's per case-mix unit is determined. The department shall redetermine a peer group's cost per case-mix unit only if it made an error in determining the peer group's cost per case-mix unit based on information available to the department at the time of the original determination.

**HISTORY:**

151 v H 66, § 101.01, eff. 7-1-05; 151 v H 530, § 101.01, eff. 3-30-06; 153 v H 1, § 101.01, eff. 7-17-09; 2011 HB 153, § 101.01, eff. July 1, 2011; 2012 HB 303, § 1, eff. July 1, 2013; 2013 HB 59, § 101.01, eff. Sept. 29, 2013; 2015 hb64, § 101.01, effective September 29, 2015; 2017 hb49, § 101.01, effective September 29, 2017; 2020 hb481, § 29, effective September 18, 2020.

**Editor's Notes**

This section was formerly codified as RC § 5111.231.

**Amendment Notes**

The 2020 amendment by HB 481 deleted former (C)(1)(e), which read: "For state fiscal year 2020 and each state fiscal year thereafter (other than the first state fiscal year in a group of consecutive state fiscal years for which a rebasing is conducted), adjust the amount calculated under division (C)(1)(d) of this section using the difference between the following: (i) The medicare skilled nursing facility market basket index determined for the federal fiscal year that begins during the state fiscal year immediately preceding the state fiscal year for which the adjustment is being made under division (C)(1)(e) of this section; (ii) The budget reduction adjustment factor for the state fiscal year for which the adjustment is being made under division (C)(1)(e) of this section."

The 2017 amendment by HB 49 rewrote the section.

The 2015 amendment, by HB 64, substituted "Allen, Mahoning, Stark, or Trumbull" for "Mahoning or Stark" in (C)(2).

The 2013 amendment substituted "department of medicaid's" for "department of job and family services" in (A)(1)(a); rewrote (B); added the (C)(1), (C)(1)(a) through (C)(1)(c), and (D)(1)(e)(i) designations; added the introductory language to (C)(1) and (D)(1)(e); added (C)(2) and (D)(1)(e)(ii); inserted "and H.B. 59 of the 130th general assembly" in the second sentence of (D)(1); substituted "section 5165.192" for "section 5111.232" in (D)(1)(a); and made stylistic changes.

The 2012 amendment, in the third sentence of the introductory language of (D)(1), deleted "by this act" following "amendments made" and inserted "by Am. Sub. H.B. 153 and Sub. H.B. 303, both of the 129th general assembly"; added (D)(1)(f); and made a related change.

The 2011 amendment added the (A)(1) designation; redesignated former (A)(1) and (A)(2) as (A)(1)(a) and (A)(1)(b); substituting "rebasings" for "subsequent determinations under division (D) of this section of each peer group's cost per case-mix unit" in (A)(1)(b); added (A)(2); deleted "At least once every ten years" from the beginning of the introductory language of (D)(1); inserted the second sentence of the introductory language of (D)(1); in the third sentence of the introductory language of (D)(1), added the exception and substituted "conducts a rebasing" for "redetermines it"; substituted "two per cent" for "seven per cent" in (D)(1)(c); in (D)(1)(d), substituted "Using the index specified in division (D)(3) of this section, multiply" for "Multiply the amount calculated under division (D)(1)(c) of this section by" and "by the amount calculated under division (D)(1)(c) of this section" for "using the following"; deleted former (D)(1)(d)(i) through (D)(1)(d)(iii), pertaining to the publication of the employment cost index by the United States bureau of labor statistics; added (D)(1)(e); inserted (D)(3); redesignated former (D)(3) as (D)(4); and made related and stylistic changes.

153 v H 1, effective July 17, 2009, rewrote (D)(1)(d).

151 v H 530, effective March 30, 2006, in (D)(2)(b), substituted the first instance of "cost per case-mix unit is" for "direct care costs are" and the second instance for "desk reviewed, actual, allowable, per diem direct care"; and made minor stylistic changes.

## § 5165.191 Submission of quarterly resident assessment data.

Each calendar quarter, each nursing facility provider shall compile complete assessment data for each resident of each of the provider's nursing facilities, regardless of payment source, who is in the nursing facility, or on hospital or therapeutic leave from the nursing facility, on the last day of the quarter. A resident assessment instrument specified in rules authorized by this section shall be used to compile the resident assessment data. Each provider shall submit the resident assessment data to the department of health and, if required by the rules, the department of medicaid. The resident assessment data shall be submitted not later than fifteen days after the end of the calendar quarter for which the data is compiled. If the resident assessment data is to be submitted to the department of medicaid, it shall be submitted to the department through the medium or media specified in the rules.

Rules adopted under section 5165.02 of the Revised Code shall do all of the following:

(A) In a manner consistent with the "Social Security Act," section 1919(e)(5), 42 U.S.C. 1396r(e)(5), specify a resident assessment instrument to be used by nursing facility providers under this section;

(B) Specify whether nursing facility providers must submit the resident assessment data to the department of medicaid;

(C) Specify any resident assessment data that is excluded from the case mix calculation made under section 5165.192 of the Revised Code;

(D) If the rules specify that nursing facility providers must submit the resident assessment data to the department, specify the medium or media through which the data is to be submitted.

Titles 39 — 57

**HISTORY:**

2013 HB 59, § 101.01, eff. Sept. 29, 2013; 2021 hb110, § 101.01, effective September 30, 2021.

**Amendment Notes**

The 2021 amendment by HB 110 added (C); and redesignated former (C) as (D).

## § 5165.192 Determination of case-mix scores for each facility.

(A)(1) Except as provided in division (B) of this section and in accordance with the process specified in rules authorized by this section, the department of medicaid shall do all of the following:

(a) Every quarter, determine the following two case-mix scores for each nursing facility:

(i) A quarterly case-mix score that includes each resident who is a medicaid recipient and is not a low resource utilization resident;

(ii) A quarterly case-mix score that includes each resident regardless of payment source.

(b) Every six months, determine a semiannual average case-mix score for each nursing facility by using the quarterly case-mix scores determined for the nursing facility pursuant to division (A)(1)(a)(i) of this section;

(c) After the end of each calendar year, determine an annual average case-mix score for each nursing facility by using the quarterly case-mix scores determined for the nursing facility pursuant to division (A)(1)(a)(ii) of this section.

(2) When determining case-mix scores under division (A)(1) of this section, the department shall use all of the following:

(a) Data from a resident assessment instrument specified in rules authorized by section 5165.191 of the Revised Code;

(b) Except as provided in rules authorized by this section, the case-mix values established by the United States department of health and human services;

(c) Except as modified in rules authorized by this section, the grouper methodology used on June 30, 1999, by the United States department of health and human services for prospective payment of skilled nursing facilities under the medicare program.

(B)(1) Subject to division (B)(2) of this section, the department, for one or more months of a calendar quarter, may assign to a nursing facility a case-mix score that is five per cent less than the nursing facility's case-mix score for the immediately preceding calendar quarter if any of the following apply:

(a) The provider does not timely submit complete and accurate resident assessment data necessary to determine the nursing facility's case-mix score for the calendar quarter;

(b) The nursing facility was subject to an exception review under section 5165.193 of the Revised Code for the immediately preceding calendar quarter;

(c) The nursing facility was assigned a case-mix score for the immediately preceding calendar quarter.

(2) Before assigning a case-mix score to a nursing facility due to the submission of incorrect resident assessment data, the department shall permit the provider to correct the data. The department may assign the case-mix score if the provider fails to submit the corrected resident assessment data not later than the earlier of the forty-fifth day after the end of the calendar quarter to which the data pertains or the deadline for submission of such corrections established by regulations adopted by the United States department of health and human services under Title XVIII and Title XIX.

(3) If, for more than six months in a calendar year, a provider is paid a rate determined for a nursing facility using a case-mix score assigned to the nursing facility under division (B)(1) of this section, the department may assign the nursing facility a cost per case-mix unit that is five per cent less than the nursing facility's actual or assigned cost per case-mix unit for the immediately preceding calendar year. The department may use the assigned cost per case-mix unit, instead of determining the nursing facility's actual cost per case-mix unit in accordance with section 5165.19 of the Revised Code, to establish the nursing facility's rate for direct care costs for the fiscal year immediately following the calendar year for which the cost per case-mix unit is assigned.

(4) The department shall take action under division (B)(1), (2), or (3) of this section only in accordance with rules authorized by this section. The department shall not take an action that affects rates for prior payment periods except in accordance with sections 5165.41 and 5165.42 of the Revised Code.

(C) The medicaid director shall adopt rules under section 5165.02 of the Revised Code as necessary to implement this section.

(1) The rules shall do all of the following:

(a) Specify the process for determining the semiannual and annual average case-mix scores for nursing facilities;

(b) Adjust the case-mix values specified in division (A)(2)(b) of this section to reflect changes in relative wage differentials that are specific to this state;

(c) Express all of those case-mix values in numeric terms that are different from the terms specified by the United States department of health and human services but that do not alter the relationship of the case-mix values to one another;

(d) Modify the grouper methodology specified in division (A)(2)(c) of this section as follows:

(i) Establish a different hierarchy for assigning residents to case-mix categories under the methodology;

(ii) Allow the use of the index maximizer element of the methodology;

(iii) Incorporate changes to the methodology the United States department of health and human services makes after June 30, 1999;

(iv) Make other changes the department determines are necessary.

(e) Establish procedures under which resident assessment data shall be reviewed for accuracy and providers shall be notified of any data that requires correction;

(f) Establish procedures for providers to correct resident assessment data and specify a reasonable period of time by which providers shall submit the corrections. The procedures may limit the content of corrections in the manner required by regulations adopted by the United States department of health and human services under Title XVIII and Title XIX.

(g) Specify when and how the department will assign case-mix scores or costs per case-mix unit to a nursing facility under division (B) of this section if information necessary to calculate the nursing facility's case-mix score is not provided or corrected in accordance with the procedures established by the rules.

(2) Notwithstanding any other provision of this chapter, the rules may provide for the exclusion of case-mix scores assigned to a nursing facility under division (B) of this section from the determination of the nursing facility's semiannual or annual average case-mix score and the cost per case-mix unit for the nursing facility's peer group.

**HISTORY:**

144 v H 904 (Eff 12-22-92); 145 v H 152 (Eff 7-1-93); 145 v H 715 (Eff 7-22-94); 146 v H 670 (Eff 12-2-96); 148 v H 283 (Eff 6-30-99); 148 v H 471 (Eff 7-1-2000); 149 v H 94. Eff 6-6-2001; 151 v H 66, § 101.01, eff. 7-1-05; 153 v H 1, § 101.01, eff. 10-16-09; 2011 HB 153, § 101.01, eff. Sept. 29, 2011; 2013 HB 59, § 101.01, eff. Sept. 29, 2013; 2017 hb49, § 101.01, effective September 29, 2017.

**Editor's Notes**

This section was formerly codified as RC § 5111.232.

This section was amended and renumbered from RC § 5111.231 by 151 v H 66, effective July 1, 2005.

**Amendment Notes**

The 2017 amendment by HB 49 substituted "Allow the use" for "Prohibit the use" in (C)(1)(d)(ii).

The 2013 amendment rewrote the section.

The 2011 amendment inserted "for fiscal year 2012" in (A)(1)(a)(i); inserted (A)(1)(a)(ii); redesignated former (A)(1)(a)(ii) as (A)(1)(a)(iii); and substituted "sections 5111.20 to 5111.331" for "sections 5111.20 to 5111.33" in the second sentence of the introductory language of (E)(5).

153 v H 1, effective October 16, 2009, substituted "forty-sixth day" for "eighty-first day" in the last sentence of the third paragraph of (D)(1); and made stylistic changes.

151 v H 66, effective July 1, 2005, rewrote the section.

**RESEARCH REFERENCES AND PRACTICE AIDS**

**Cross-References to Related Sections**

Assessment of non-medicaid recipients as to whether alternative source of long-term care is more appropriate than admission to nursing facility, RC § 173.42.

Calculating prospective rates for facilities with residents whose care costs are not otherwise adequately measured, RC § 5165.153.

Case-mix score defined, RC § 5165.01.

Exception reviews of assessment information, RC § 5165.108.

Initial rates for facilities licensed on or after 1-1-93, RC § 5124.151.

**Ohio Administrative Code**

Medicaid coverage of targeted case management services provided to individuals with developmental disabilities, OAC 5160-48-01.

Nursing facilities (NF) medicaid cost reports, OAC ch. 5160-3.

## § 5165.193 Exception review of resident assessment data.

(A) The department of medicaid may, pursuant to rules authorized by this section, conduct an exception review of resident assessment data submitted by a nursing facility provider under section 5165.191 of the Revised Code. The department may conduct an exception review based on the findings of a medicaid certification survey conducted by the department of health, a risk analysis, or prior performance of the provider.

Exception reviews shall be conducted at the nursing facility by appropriate health professionals under contract with or employed by the department. The professionals may review resident assessment forms and supporting documentation, conduct interviews, and observe residents to identify any patterns or trends of inaccurate resident assessments and resulting inaccurate case-mix scores.

(B) If an exception review is conducted before the effective date of a nursing facility's rate for direct care costs that is based on the resident assessment data being reviewed and the review results in findings that exceed tolerance levels specified in the rules authorized by this section, the department, in accordance with those rules, may use the findings to redetermine individual resident case-mix scores, the nursing facility's case-mix score for the quarter, and the nursing facility's annual average case-mix score. The department may use the nursing facility's redetermined quarterly and annual average case-mix scores to determine the nursing facility's rate for direct care costs for the appropriate calendar quarter or quarters.

(C) The department shall prepare a written summary of any exception review finding that is made after the effective date of a nursing facility's rate for direct care costs that is based on the resident assessment data that was reviewed. Where the provider is pursuing judicial or administrative remedies in good faith regarding the finding, the department shall not withhold from the provider's current payments any amounts the department claims to be due from the provider pursuant to section 5165.41 of the Revised Code.

(D)(1) The medicaid director shall adopt rules under section 5165.02 of the Revised Code as necessary to implement this section. The rules shall establish an exception review program that does all of the following:

(a) Requires each exception review to comply with Title XVIII and Title XIX;

(b) Requires a written summary for each exception review that states whether resident assessment forms have been completed accurately;

(c) Prohibits each health professional who conducts an exception review from doing either of the following:

(i) During the period of the professional's contract or employment with the department, having or being committed to acquire any direct or indirect financial interest in the ownership, financing, or operation of nursing facilities in this state;

(ii) Reviewing any provider that has been a client of the professional.

(2) For the purposes of division (D)(1)(c)(i) of this section, employment of a member of a health professional's family by a nursing facility that the professional does not review does not constitute a direct or indirect financial interest in the ownership, financing, or operation of the nursing facility.

**HISTORY:**

2013 HB 59, § 101.01, eff. Sept. 29, 2013.

## § 5165.21 Per resident per day rate for tax costs.

The department of medicaid shall determine each nursing facility's per medicaid day payment rate for tax costs. The rate for tax costs determined under this division for a nursing facility shall be used for subsequent years until the department conducts a rebasing. To determine a nursing facility's rate for tax costs, the department shall divide the nursing facility's desk-reviewed, actual, allowable tax costs paid for the applicable calendar year by the number of inpatient days the nursing facility would have had if its occupancy rate had been one hundred per cent during the applicable calendar year.

**HISTORY:**

151 v H 66, § 101.01, eff. 7-1-05; 153 v H 198, § 1, eff. 6-8-10; 2012 HB 487, § 101.01, eff. Sept. 10, 2012; 2012 HB 303, § 1, eff. July 1, 2013; 2013 HB 59, § 101.01, eff. Sept. 29, 2013; 2017 hb49, § 101.01, effective September 29, 2017; 2019 hb166, § 101.01, effective July 1, 2021.

**Editor's Notes**

This section was formerly codified as RC § 5111.242.

**Amendment Notes**

The 2019 amendment by HB 166 rewrote the section.

The 2017 amendment by HB 49 rewrote the section.

The 2013 amendment substituted "department of medicaid's" for "department of job and family services'" in (A)(1)(a); deleted (B), which read: "The department of job and family services shall pay a provider for each of the provider's eligible nursing facilities a per resident per day rate for tax costs determined under division (C) of this section"; redesignated former (C) and (D) as (B) and (C); in the first sentence of (B), substituted "of medicaid shall determine each nursing facility's per medicaid day payment" for "shall determine the" and deleted "for each nursing facility" from the end; and made stylistic changes.

The 2012 amendment by HB 303, added the (A)(1) designation; redesignated former (A)(1) and (A)(2) as (A)(1)(a) and (A)(1)(b); substituted "rebasings" for "subsequent determinations under division (C) of this section of nursing facilities' rate for tax costs" in present (A)(1)(b); added (A)(2), (C)(2), and (D)(2); in the introductory language of (C), deleted "At least once every ten years" from the beginning of the first sentence, inserted the second sentence, in the present third sentence, added the exception to the beginning and substituted "conducts a rebasing" for "redetermines it", and added "do both of the following" to the end of the last sentence; in the introductory language of (D), inserted "as follows" and substituted "conducts a rebasing" for "redetermines all nursing facilities' rate for tax costs under division (C) of this section by dividing"; added "Divide" to the beginning of present (D)(1); and made related changes.

The 2012 amendment by HB 487, deleted the (A)(1) designation; redesignated former (A)(1)(a) and (A)(1)(b) as (A)(1) and (A)(2); deleted (A)(2), which read: "'Tax costs' means the costs of taxes imposed under Chapter 5751. of the Revised Code, real estate taxes, personal property taxes, and corporate franchise taxes"; and made a related change.

## § 5165.23 Critical access incentive payment; requirements.

Titles 39 — 57

(A) Each state fiscal year, the department of medicaid shall determine the critical access incentive payment for each nursing facility that qualifies as a critical access nursing facility. To qualify as a critical access nursing facility for a state fiscal year, a nursing facility must meet all of the following requirements:

(1) The nursing facility must be located in an area that, on December 31, 2011, was designated an empowerment zone under the "Internal Revenue Code of 1986," section 1391, 26 U.S.C. 1391.

(2) The nursing facility must have an occupancy rate of at least eighty-five per cent as of the last day of the calendar year immediately preceding the state fiscal year.

(3) The nursing facility must have a medicaid utilization rate of at least sixty-five per cent as of the last day of the calendar year immediately preceding the state fiscal year.

(B) A critical access nursing facility's critical access incentive payment for a state fiscal year shall equal five per cent of the portion of the nursing facility's total per medicaid day payment rate for the state fiscal year that is the sum of the rates identified in divisions (A)(1) to (4) of section 5165.15 of the Revised Code.

### HISTORY:

2012 HB 487, § 101.01, eff. Sept. 10, 2012; 2012 HB 303, § 1, eff. July 1, 2013; 2013 HB 59, § 101.01, eff. Sept. 29, 2013; 2014 HB 483, § 101.01, eff. Sept. 15, 2014; 2017 hb49, § 101.01, effective September 29, 2017.

### Editor's Notes

This section was formerly codified as RC § 5111.246.

### Amendment Notes

The 2017 amendment by HB 49 substituted "state fiscal year" for "fiscal year" throughout the section; deleted former (A)(4), which read: "The nursing facility must have been awarded at least five points for meeting accountability measures under section 5165.25 of the Revised Code for the fiscal year and at least one of the five points must have been awarded for meeting the accountability measures identified in divisions (C)(9), (10), (11), (12), and (14) of section 5165.25 of the Revised Code"; in (B), added "per medicaid day payment" and substituted "rates identified in divisions (A)(1) to (4)" for "rates and payment identified in divisions (A)(1) to (4) and (6)."

The 2014 amendment by HB 483 deleted (A)(4)(a), which read: "For fiscal year 2014, the accountability measures identified in divisions (C)(10), (11), (12), and (13) of section 5165.25 of the Revised Code"; in (A)(4), deleted "For fiscal year 2015 and each fiscal year thereafter, the" preceding "accountability measures identified" and substituted "divisions (C)(9), (10), (11), (12), and (14)" for "divisions (D)(9), (10), (11), (12), and (14)"; and made a related change.

The 2013 amendment, in the introductory language of (A), substituted "medicaid shall determine the" for "job and family services shall pay a" and "payment for" for "payment to the provider of"; in (A)(1), deleted "section 1391 of" following "empowerment zone under" and substituted "section 1391, 26 U.S.C. 1391" for " 107 Stat. 543, 26 U.S.C. 1391, as amended"; inserted "immediately" in (A)(2) and (A)(3); added (A)(4); and substituted "divisions (A)(1) to (4) and (6) of section 5165.15" for "divisions (B)(1) to (4) and (6) of section 5111.222" in (B).

The 2012 amendment substituted "divisions (B)(1) to (4) and (6)" for "divisions (A)(1) to (4) and (6)" in (B).

### NOTES TO DECISIONS

**Interpretation.**

Statute did not specify how that rate was to be determined, and it was susceptible to more than one reasonable interpretation by using either licensed beds or certified beds; there was a lack of legislative guidance on the formula or methodology to be applied in calculating occupancy rate for purposes of determining critical access incentive payments, and the Ohio Department of Medicaid's (ODM) interpretation of occupancy rate that resulted in denying critical access incentive payments to the nursing facility for state fiscal year 2017 was not contrary to law. State ex rel. Peregrine Health Servs. of Columbus, LLC v. Sears, 2020-Ohio-3426, 2020 Ohio App. LEXIS 2368 (Ohio Ct. App., Franklin County 2020), dismissed, 2021-Ohio-1825, 163 Ohio St. 3d 1436, 168 N.E.3d 1189, 2021 Ohio LEXIS 1077 (Ohio 2021).

## § 5165.25 Per medicaid day quality payment rate. [Repealed]

### HISTORY:

2015 hb64, § 101.01, effective July 1, 2016; 2017 hb49, § 101.01, effective September 29, 2017; 2019 hb166, § 101.01, effective October 17, 2019; repealed by 2021 hb110, § 105.01, effective September 30, 2021.

## § 5165.26 Nursing facility per medicaid day quality incentive payment rate.

(A) As used in this section:

(1) "Base rate" means the portion of a nursing facility's total per medicaid day payment rate determined under divisions (A), (B), and (C) of section 5165.15 of the Revised Code.

(2) "CMS" means the United States centers for medicare and medicaid services.

(3) "Force majeure event" means an uncontrollable force or natural disaster not within the power of a nursing facility's operator.

(4) "Long-stay resident" means an individual who has resided in a nursing facility for at least one hundred one days.

(5) "Nursing facilities for which a quality score was determined" includes nursing facilities that are determined to have a quality score of zero.

(6) "SFF list" means the list of nursing facilities that the United States department of health and human services creates under the special focus facility program.

(7) "Special focus facility program" means the program conducted by the United States secretary of health and human services pursuant to section 1919(f)(10) of the "Social Security Act," 42 U.S.C. 1396r(f)(10).

(B) For state fiscal year 2022 and state fiscal year 2023, and subject to divisions (D), (E), and (F), and except as provided in division (G) of this section, the department of medicaid shall determine each nursing facility's per medicaid day quality incentive payment rate as follows:

(1) Determine the sum of the quality scores determined under division (C) of this section for all nursing facilities.

(2) Determine the average quality score by dividing the sum determined under division (B)(1) of this section by the number of nursing facilities for which a quality score was determined.

(3) Determine the sum of the total number of medicaid days for all of the calendar year preceding the fiscal year for which the rate is determined for all nursing facilities for which a quality score was determined.

(4) Multiply the average quality score determined under division (B)(2) of this section by the sum determined under division (B)(3) of this section.

(5) Determine the value per quality point by determining the quotient of the following:

(a) The sum determined under division (F)(2) of this section.

(b) The product determined under division (B)(4) of this section.

(6) Multiply the value per quality point determined under division (B)(5) of this section by the nursing facility's quality score determined under division (C) of this section.

(C)(1) Except as provided in division (C)(2) of this section, a nursing facility's quality score for state fiscal year 2022 and state fiscal year 2023 shall be the sum of the total number of points that CMS assigned to the nursing facility under CMS's nursing facility five-star quality rating system for the following quality metrics based on the most recent four-quarter average data available in the database maintained by CMS and known as nursing home compare in the most recent month of the calendar year during which the fiscal year for which the rate is determined begins:

(a) The percentage of the nursing facility's long-stay residents at high risk for pressure ulcers who had pressure ulcers;

(b) The percentage of the nursing facility's long-stay residents who had a urinary tract infection;

(c) The percentage of the nursing facility's long-stay residents whose ability to move independently worsened;

(d) The percentage of the nursing facility's long-stay residents who had a catheter inserted and left in their bladder.

(2) In determining a nursing facility's quality score for state fiscal year 2022 and state fiscal year 2023, the department shall make the following adjustment to the number of points that CMS assigned to the nursing facility for each of the quality metrics specified in division (C)(1) of this section:

(a) Unless division (C)(2)(b) or (c) of this section applies, divide the number of the nursing facility's points for the quality metric by twenty.

(b) If CMS assigned the nursing facility to the lowest percentile for the quality metric, reduce the number of the nursing facility's points for the quality metric to zero.

(c) If the nursing facility's total number of points for state fiscal year 2022 or for state fiscal year 2023 for all of the quality metrics specified in division (C)(1) of this section is less than a number of points that is equal to the twenty-fifth percentile of all nursing facilities, reduce the nursing facility's points to zero for that fiscal year.

(3) A nursing facility's quality score shall be zero for state fiscal year 2021 if it is not to receive a quality incentive payment for that state fiscal year because of division (D) of this section.

(D)(1) Except as provided in division (D)(2) of this section, a nursing facility shall not receive a quality incentive payment for state fiscal year 2021 if the nursing facility's licensed occupancy percentage is less than eighty per cent.

(2) Division (D)(1) of this section does not apply to a nursing facility if any of the following apply:

(a) The nursing facility has a quality score under division (C) of this section for state fiscal year 2021 of at least fifteen points;

(b) The nursing facility was initially certified for participation in the medicaid program on or after January 1, 2019;

(c) Subject to division (D)(4) of this section, one or more of the beds that are part of the nursing facility's licensed capacity could not be used for resident care during calendar year 2019 due to causes beyond the reasonable control of the nursing facility's operator, including a force majeure event;

(d) Subject to division (D)(5) of this section, the nursing facility underwent a renovation during the period beginning January 1, 2018, and ending January 1, 2020, to which both of the following apply:

(i) The renovation involved capital expenditures of at least fifty thousand dollars, excluding expenditures for equipment, staffing, or operational costs.

(ii) The renovation directly impacted the area of the nursing facility in which the beds that are part of the nursing facility's licensed capacity are located.

(3) A nursing facility's licensed occupancy percentage for the purpose of division (D)(1) of this section shall be determined as follows:

(a) Determine the product of the following:

(i) The nursing facility's licensed capacity as of December 31, 2019, as identified on the nursing facility's cost report filed with the department pursuant to section 5165.10 of the Revised Code;

(ii) Three hundred sixty-five.

(b) Determine the quotient of the following:

(i) The total number of the nursing facility's inpatient days for calendar year 2019, as identified on the nursing facility's cost report filed with the department pursuant to section 5165.10 of the Revised Code;

(ii) The product determined under division (D)(3)(a) of this section.

(c) Multiply the quotient determined under division (D)(3)(b) of this section by one hundred.

(4) For a nursing facility to be exempt from division (D)(1) of this section on account of division (D)(2)(c) of this section, the nursing facility's operator must provide to the department written documentation of the number of days during calendar year 2019 that one or more of the beds that are part of the nursing facility's licensed capacity could not be used and the specific reason why they could not be used.

(5) For a nursing facility to be exempt from division (D)(1) of this section on account of division (D)(2)(d) of this section, the nursing facility's operator must provide to the department written documentation that confirms the renovation and capital expenditures.

(E) A nursing facility shall not receive a quality incentive payment for state fiscal year 2022 or state fiscal year 2023 if the Department of Health assigned the nursing facility to the SFF list under the special focus facility program and the nursing facility is listed in table A, table B, or table C on the first day of May of the calendar year for which the rate is being determined.

(F) The total amount to be spent on quality incentive payments under division (B) of this section for each fiscal year during state fiscal years 2022 and 2023 shall be determined as follows:

(1) Determine the following amount for each nursing facility, including those that do not receive a quality incentive payment because of division (D) of this section:

(a) The amount that is five and two-tenths per cent of the nursing facility's base rate for nursing facility services provided on the first day of the state fiscal year plus one dollar and seventy-nine cents;

(b) Multiply the amount determined under division (F)(1)(a) of this section by the number of the nursing facility's medicaid days for the calendar year preceding the fiscal year for which the rate is determined.

(2) Determine the sum of the products determined under division (F)(1)(b) of this section for all nursing facilities for which the product was determined for the state fiscal year.

(3) To the sum determined under division (F)(2) of this section, add twenty-five million dollars for fiscal year 2022 and one hundred twenty-five million dollars for fiscal year 2023.

(G) A new nursing facility or a nursing facility that undergoes a change of operator during fiscal year 2022 or fiscal year 2023 shall not receive a quality incentive payment for the fiscal year in which the new facility obtains an initial provider agreement or the change of operator occurred, whichever is applicable. For the immediately following state fiscal year, the quality incentive payment shall be determined under division (C) of this section.

(H) Divisions (C)(3) and (D) of this section are suspended beginning July 1, 2021, and ending June 30, 2023.

**HISTORY:**

2019 hb166, § 101.01, effective October 17, 2019; 2020 hb481, § 29, effective September 18, 2020; 2021 hb110, § 101.01, effective June 30, 2021.

**Editor's Notes**

A proposed amendment of section 5165.26 by Acts 2021, HB 110 was partially vetoed by the Governor.

This section, as added by 2019 HB 166, was vetoed in part by the Governor.

Former 5165.26 (2011 SB 264, § 1, eff. July 1, 2012; 2013 HB 59, § 101.01, eff. Sept. 29, 2013) was repealed by 2015 hb64, § 105.01, effective July 1, 2016.

**Amendment Notes**

The 2021 amendment by HB 110 substituted "means an individual who has resided in a nursing facility for at least one hundred one days" for "has the same meaning as in section 5165.25 of the Revised Code" in (A)(4); added (A)(6) and (A)(7); in the introductory language of (B), substituted

"2022 and state fiscal year 2023" for "2021" and added "and except as provided in division (G)"; in (B)(3), deleted "For state fiscal year 2021" at the beginning and substituted "the calendar year preceding the fiscal year for which the rate is determined" for "calendar year 2019"; deleted "For state fiscal year 2021" at the beginning of (B)(5)(a); in the introductory language of (C), substituted "division (C)(2)" for "divisions (C)(2) and (3)," "2022 and state fiscal year 2023" for "2021," and "CMS and known as nursing home compare in the most recent month of the calendar year during which the fiscal year for which the rate is determined begins" for "the United States centers for medicare and medicaid services and known as nursing home compare in May of 2020"; substituted "2022 and state fiscal year 2023" for "2021" in the introductory language of (C)(2); added "or (c)" in (C)(2)(a); added (C)(2)(c); rewrote (E); substituted "under division (B) of this section for each fiscal year during state fiscal years 2022 and 2023" for "state fiscal year 2021" in the introductory language of (F); added "plus one dollar and seventy-nine cents" in (F)(1)(a); substituted "preceding the fiscal year for which the rate is determined" for "2019" in (F)(1)(b); added (F)(3); and added (G) and (H).

The 2020 amendment by HB 481 rewrote the section.

### § 5165.261 Nursing facility payment commission.

(A) There is hereby established the nursing facility payment commission. The commission shall consist of the following members:

(1) Four members appointed by the speaker of the house of representatives, three from the majority party and one from the minority party;

(2) Four members appointed by the president of the senate, three from the majority party and one from the minority party.

(B) Appointments to the commission shall be made not later than December 31, 2021. In the event of a vacancy, a replacement member shall be appointed in the same manner as initial appointments. Members shall serve without compensation.

At the initial meeting, commission members shall elect one member from the majority party of the house of representatives and one member from the majority party of the senate to serve as joint co-chairpersons of the commission.

(C) The commission shall analyze the efficacy of all of the following:

(1) The current quality incentive payment formula under section 5165.26 of the Revised Code for efficacy;

(2) The nursing facility base rate calculation, as defined under section 5165.26 of the Revised Code;

(3) The nursing facility cost centers, which are redetermined as part of the rebasing process under section 5165.36 of the Revised Code;

(4) Establishing a bed buyback program under which a nursing facility operator can permanently surrender one or more long-term care beds due to a decrease in bed utilization.

(D) Not later than August 31, 2022, the commission shall submit a report to the general assembly, in accordance with section 101.68 of the Revised Code, with its recommendations and determinations on the items listed under division (C) of this section.



**HISTORY:**

2021 hb110, § 101.01, effective September 30, 2021.

### § 5165.28 Rate for added, replaced, or renovated bed.

If a provider of a nursing facility adds or replaces one or more medicaid certified beds to or at the nursing facility, or renovates one or more of the nursing facility's beds, the medicaid payment rate for the added, replaced, or renovated beds shall be the same as the medicaid payment rate for the nursing facility's existing beds.

**HISTORY:**

151 v H 66, § 101.01, eff. 7-1-05; 2013 HB 59, § 101.01, eff. Sept. 29, 2013.

**Editor's Notes**

This section was formerly codified as RC § 5111.257.

**Amendment Notes**

The 2013 amendment inserted "medicaid payment" twice.

### § 5165.29 Amortization cost concerning relocated beds not allowable cost.

If one or more medicaid-certified beds are relocated from one nursing facility to another nursing facility owned by a different person or government entity and the application for the certificate of need authorizing the relocation is filed with the director of health on or after July 1, 2005, amortization of the cost of acquiring operating rights for the relocated beds is not an allowable cost for the purpose of determining the nursing facility's medicaid payment rate.

**HISTORY:**

151 v H 66, § 101.01, eff. 7-1-05; 2013 HB 59, § 101.01, eff. Sept. 29, 2013.

**Editor's Notes**

This section was formerly codified as RC § 5111.265.

**Amendment Notes**

The 2013 amendment substituted "July 1, 2005" for "the effective date of this section"; and substituted "payment" for "reimbursement".

### § 5165.30 Pass-through of related party costs.

Except as provided in section 5165.17 of the Revised Code, the costs of goods, services, and facilities, furnished to a nursing facility provider by a related party are includable in the allowable costs of the provider at the reasonable cost to the related party.

**HISTORY:**

144 v H 904 (Eff 12-22-92); 145 v H 152 (Eff 7-1-93); 147 v H 698. Eff 3-22-99; 151 v H 66, § 101.01, eff. 7-1-05; 2013 HB 59, § 101.01, eff. Sept. 29, 2013.

**Editor's Notes**

This section was formerly codified as RC § 5111.264.

**Amendment Notes**

The 2013 amendment substituted "section 5165.17" for "section 5111.25 or 5111.251"; and inserted "nursing facility".

151 v H 66, effective July 1, 2005, corrected internal references.

**RESEARCH REFERENCES AND PRACTICE AIDS**

**Cross-References to Related Sections**

Compensation cost limits for owners and relatives of owners, RC § 5165.107.

### § 5165.32 Effect of lower rate charged to non-Medicaid patients.

The department of medicaid shall not reduce a nursing facility's medicaid payment rate determined under this chapter on the basis that the provider charges a lower rate to any resident who is not eligible for medicaid.

**HISTORY:**

2013 HB 59, § 101.01, eff. Sept. 29, 2013.

### § 5165.33 Payments for day of discharge.

No medicaid payment shall be made to a nursing facility provider for the day a medicaid recipient is discharged from the nursing facility.

**HISTORY:**

2013 HB 59, § 101.01, eff. Sept. 29, 2013.

### § 5165.34 Temporary absence; bed reservation rates.

(A) The department of medicaid may make medicaid payments to a nursing facility provider under this chapter to reserve a bed for a recipient during a temporary absence under conditions prescribed by the department, to include hospitalization for an acute condition, visits with relatives and friends, and participation in therapeutic programs outside the facility, when the resident's plan of care provides for such absence and federal financial participation for the payments is available.

(B) The maximum period for which payments may be made to reserve a bed in a nursing facility shall not exceed thirty days in a calendar year.

(C) The department shall establish the per medicaid day payment rates for reserving beds under this section. In establishing the per medicaid day payment rates, the department shall set the per medicaid day payment rate at an amount equal to the following:

(1) In the case of a nursing facility that had an occupancy rate exceeding ninety-five per cent, an amount not exceeding fifty per cent of the per medicaid day payment rate the provider would be paid if the recipient were not absent from the nursing facility that day;

(2) In the case of a nursing facility that had an occupancy rate not exceeding ninety-five per cent, an amount not exceeding eighteen per cent of the per medicaid day payment rate the provider would be paid if the recipient were not absent from the nursing facility that day.

(D) For the purpose of setting a nursing facility's per medicaid day payment rate to reserve a bed for a day during the period beginning on September 29, 2013, and ending December 31, 2013, the department shall determine the nursing facility's occupancy rate by using information reported on the nursing facility's cost report for calendar year 2012. For the purpose of setting a nursing facility's per medicaid day payment rate to reserve a bed for January 1, 2014, or thereafter, the department shall determine the nursing facility's occupancy rate by using information reported on the nursing facility's cost report for the calendar year preceding the state fiscal year in which the reservation falls.

**HISTORY:**

2011 HB 153, § 101.01, eff. Sept. 29, 2011; 2013 HB 59, § 101.01, eff. Sept. 29, 2013; 2017 hb49, § 101.01, effective September 29, 2017.

**Editor's Notes**

This section was formerly codified as RC § 5111.331.

**Amendment Notes**

The 2017 amendment by HB 49, in (D), substituted "September 29, 2013" for "the effective date of this amendment" in the first sentence and "the state fiscal year" for "the fiscal year" in the second sentence.

The 2013 amendment, in (A), substituted "medicaid may make medicaid payments to a nursing facility provider under this chapter" for "job and family services may make payments to a provider of a nursing facility under sections 5111.20 to 5111.331 of the Revised Code" and inserted "financial"; rewrote (C); added (D); and made a stylistic change.

### § 5165.35 Medicaid payments made after termination of facility.

Medicaid payments may be made for nursing facility services provided not later than thirty days after the effective date of an involuntary termination of the nursing facility that provides the services if the services are provided to a medicaid recipient who is eligible for the services and resided in the nursing facility before the effective date of the involuntary termination.

**HISTORY:**

2011 HB 153, § 101.01, eff. Sept. 29, 2011; 2013 HB 59, § 101.01, eff. Sept. 29, 2013.

**Editor's Notes**

This section was formerly codified as RC § 5111.212.

**Amendment Notes**

The 2013 amendment deleted the first paragraph, which read: "As used in this section, 'effective date of an involuntary termination' and 'involuntary termination' have the same meanings as in section 5111.65 of the Revised Code"; deleted "and intermediate care facility for the mentally retarded services" following "facility services" and substituted "the nursing facility" for "the facility".

### § 5165.36 Medicaid rebasing.

(A) The department of medicaid shall conduct a rebasing at least once every five state fiscal years. Except as provided in division (B) of this section, when the department conducts a rebasing for a state fiscal year, it shall conduct the rebasing for only the direct care, ancillary and support, and tax cost centers. A nursing facility provider shall spend money received from the rebasing conducted in state fiscal year 2022 on the direct care, ancillary and support, and tax cost centers only.

(B) A nursing facility provider shall spend seventy per cent of any additional dollars received by the provider as a result of a rebasing on direct care costs, including employee salaries. The department may recover any amounts that are not spent in accordance with this requirement. This requirement applies to the department's rebasing in fiscal year 2022 and all subsequent rebasings. The director shall adopt rules authorized under section 5165.02 of the Revised Code as necessary to implement this division, including to ensure that nursing facility operators spend at least seventy per cent of the additional dollars resulting from a rebasing on direct care costs.

**HISTORY:**

2017 hb49, § 101.01, effective September 29, 2017; 2021 hb110, § 101.01, effective June 30, 2021.

**Amendment Notes**

The 2021 amendment by HB 110 rewrote the section.

### § 5165.37 Time table for calculating rates and making payments; adjustments.

The department of medicaid shall make its best efforts each year to calculate nursing facilities' medicaid payment rates under this chapter in time to pay the rates by the fifteenth day of August of each state fiscal year. If the department is unable to calculate the rates so that they can be paid by that date, the department shall pay each provider the rate calculated for the provider's nursing facilities under this chapter at the end of the previous state fiscal year. If the department also is unable to calculate the rates to pay the rates by the fifteenth day of September and the fifteenth day of October, the department shall pay the previous state fiscal year's rate to make those payments. The department may increase by five per cent the previous state fiscal year's rate paid for any nursing facility pursuant to this section at the request of the provider. The department shall use rates calculated for the current state fiscal year to make the payments due by the fifteenth day of November.

If the rate paid to a provider for a nursing facility pursuant to this section is lower than the rate calculated for the nursing facility for the current state fiscal year, the department shall pay the provider the difference between the two rates for the number of days for which the provider was paid for the nursing facility pursuant to this section. If the rate paid for a nursing facility pursuant to this section is higher than the rate calculated for it for the current state fiscal year, the provider shall refund to the department the difference between the two rates for the number of days for which the provider was paid for the nursing facility pursuant to this section.

**HISTORY:**

146 v H 117 (Eff 6-30-95); 148 v H 471. Eff 7-1-2000; 151 v H 66, § 101.01, eff. 7-1-05; 2011 HB 153, § 101.01, eff. Sept. 29, 2011; 2013 HB 59, § 101.01, eff. Sept. 29, 2013; 2017 hb49, § 101.01, effective September 29, 2017.

**Editor's Notes**

This section was formerly codified as RC § 5111.221.

**Amendment Notes**

The 2017 amendment by HB 49 substituted "state fiscal year" for "fiscal year" throughout the section.

The 2013 amendment, in the first paragraph, rewrote the first sentence, substituted "under this chapter" for "and intermediate care facilities for the mentally retarded under those sections" in the second sentence, substituted "pay the rates" for "make the payments due" in the third sentence; and inserted "nursing" throughout the fourth sentence of the first paragraph and in the second paragraph.

The 2011 amendment substituted "sections 5111.20 to 5111.331" for "sections 5111.20 to 5111.33" in the first sentence of the first paragraph.

151 v H 66, effective July 1, 2005, rewrote the section.

**RESEARCH REFERENCES AND PRACTICE AIDS**

**Ohio Administrative Code**

Nursing facility provider agreements. OAC 5160-3-02.

### § 5165.38 Process by which facility may seek reconsideration of rate; appeals from adverse actions.

The medicaid director shall adopt rules under section 5165.02 of the Revised Code that establish a process under which a nursing facility provider, or a group or association of nursing facility providers, may seek reconsideration of medicaid payment rates established under this chapter, including a rate for direct care costs recalculated before the effective date of the rate as a result of an exception review of resident assessment data conducted under section 5165.193 of the Revised Code. The only issue that a provider, group, or association may raise in the rate reconsideration shall be whether the rate was calculated in accordance with this chapter and the rules adopted under section 5165.02 of the Revised Code. The provider, group, or association may submit written arguments or other materials that support its position. The provider, group, or association and department of medicaid shall take actions regarding the rate reconsideration within time frames specified in rules authorized by this section.

If the department determines, as a result of the rate reconsideration, that the rate determined for one or more nursing facilities is less than the rate to which the nursing facility is entitled, the department shall increase the rate. If the department has paid the incorrect rate for a period of time, the department shall pay the provider the difference between the amount the provider was paid for that period for the nursing facility and the amount the provider should have been paid for the nursing facility.

Titles 39 — 57

**HISTORY:**

144 v H 904 (Eff 12-22-92); 145 v H 152 (Eff 7-1-93); 146 v H 117 (Eff 6-30-95); 148 v H 471 (Eff 7-1-2000); 149 v H 94. Eff 6-6-2001; 151 v H 66, § 101.01, eff. 7-1-05; 2011 HB 153, § 101.01, eff. Sept. 29, 2011; 2013 HB 59, § 101.01, eff. Sept. 29, 2013.

**Editor's Notes**

This section was formerly codified as RC § 5111.29.

**Amendment Notes**

The 2013 amendment rewrote the section.

The 2011 amendment substituted "sections 5111.20 to 5111.331" for "sections 5111.20 to 5111.33" throughout (A).

151 v H 66, effective July 1, 2005, rewrote the section.

**NOTES TO DECISIONS**

Analysis

Hardship
Mandamus

**Hardship**

An intermediate care facility seeking additional reimbursement due to extreme hardship does not have a constitutionally protected property interest in the adjusted reimbursement rate it seeks. There was a genuine issue of fact as to whether the department abused its discretion: Morning View Care Center-Fulton v. Ohio Dep't of Human Servs., 2002-Ohio-2878, 148 Ohio App. 3d 518, 774 N.E.2d 300, 2002 Ohio App. LEXIS 2822 (Ohio Ct. App., Franklin County 2002).

**Mandamus**

Nursing homes' claim that the Ohio Department of Job and Family Services (ODJFS) misapplied the offsets when it awarded rate adjustments for extreme circumstances was rejected since the nursing homes' petition for mandamus relief contained no allegation that their rate adjustments for extreme circumstances were in error due to ODJFS's failure to correctly consider efficiency incentives and equity offsets and did not mention seeking a writ of mandamus to correct the rate adjustments awarded for extreme circumstances. PNP, Inc. v. Ohio Dep't of Job & Family Servs., 2013-Ohio-4344, 2013 Ohio App. LEXIS 4577 (Ohio Ct. App., Franklin County 2013).

When a state agency's decision is discretionary and by statute not subject to appeal, an action in mandamus is the sole avenue of relief available to a party challenging the agency's decision: Ohio Acad. of Nursing Homes v. Ohio Dep't of Job & Family Servs., 2007-Ohio-2620, 114 Ohio St. 3d 14, 867 N.E.2d 400, 2007 Ohio LEXIS 1458 (Ohio 2007).

When nursing facilities and the facilities' trade association sought review of the decision of the Ohio Department of Job and Family Services denying the facilities' request, under R.C. 5111.27(F), for a Medicaid reimbursement rate adjustment, the facilities' and association's sole remedy was pursuant to a petition for a writ of mandamus in which the facilities and association would have to demonstrate the Department's abuse of discretion because (1) R.C. 5111.29(A)(5) explicitly provided that the Department's discretionary decision was not subject to appeal, and (2) a declaratory judgment action, under R.C. 2721.03, to obtain a declaration of the facilities' rights was unavailable because the only rights the facilities had was to have the Department consider their reimbursement request without abusing its discretion. Ohio Acad. of Nursing Homes v. Ohio Dep't of Job & Family Servs., 2007-Ohio-2620, 114 Ohio St. 3d 14, 867 N.E.2d 400, 2007 Ohio LEXIS 1458 (Ohio 2007).

Trial court erred in dismissing an action by nursing home operators against the Ohio Department of Job & Family Services (ODJFS) upon finding that the trial court lacked subject matter jurisdiction because the money damage claims, which were ostensibly against the State, were inextricably intertwined with other claims, as the only available mechanism for review of the denial by the ODJFS of the operators' rate reconsideration requests under former R.C. 5111.27(F) and 5111.29 and former OAC 5101:3-3-24.1 and 5101:3-3-24(C) was by mandamus; as the Ohio Court of Claims lacked subject matter jurisdiction over such a claim pursuant to R.C. 2731.02, jurisdiction was proper in the trial court and dismissal under Civ. R. 12(B)(1) was error. PNP, Inc. v. Ohio Dep't of Job & Family Servs., 2006-Ohio-1159, 2006 Ohio App. LEXIS 973 (Ohio Ct. App., Franklin County 2006), aff'd, 2007-Ohio-2880, 114 Ohio St. 3d 70, 868 N.E.2d 265, 2007 Ohio LEXIS 1577 (Ohio 2007).

Mandamus was the proper remedy for a nursing home seeking Medicaid reimbursement to which it claimed to be entitled. The court of common pleas lacked jurisdiction to grant an injunction compelling payment or to award a declaratory judgment with money damages: Morning View Care Ctr. - Fulton v. Ohio Dep't of Job & Family Servs., 2004-Ohio-5436, 158 Ohio App. 3d 689, 821 N.E.2d 1046, 2004 Ohio App. LEXIS 4486 (Ohio Ct. App., Franklin County 2004).

**RESEARCH REFERENCES AND PRACTICE AIDS**

**Ohio Administrative Code**

Bureau of workers' compensation premium increases. OAC 5101:3-3-242.

Termination, denial, and non-revalidation of provider agreements. OAC 5160-3-02.2.

### § 5165.40 Operators required to refund certain payments; interest, penalties; rate adjustments.

If a nursing facility provider properly amends a cost report for the nursing facility under section 5165.107 of the Revised Code and the amended report shows that the provider received a lower medicaid payment rate under the original cost report than the provider was entitled to receive, the department of medicaid shall adjust the provider's rate for the nursing facility prospectively to reflect the corrected information. The department shall pay the adjusted rate beginning two months after the first day of the month after the provider files the amended cost report.

If the department finds, from an exception review of resident assessment data conducted pursuant to section 5165.193 of the Revised Code after the effective date of a nursing facility's rate for direct care costs that is based on the resident assessment data, that inaccurate resident assessment data resulted in the provider receiving a lower rate for the nursing facility than it was entitled to receive, the department prospectively shall adjust the provider's rate accordingly. The department shall make payments to the provider using the adjusted rate for the remainder of the six-month period for which the resident assessment data is used to determine the rate, beginning one month after the first day of the month after the exception review is completed.

**HISTORY:**

138 v H 176 (Eff 7-1-80); 140 v H 100 (Eff 2-24-83); 140 v H 291 (Eff 7-1-83); 141 v H 238 (Eff 7-1-85); 143 v H 111 (Eff 7-1-89); 143 v H 672 (Eff 11-14-89); 143 v H 822 (Eff 12-13-90); 144 v H 904 (Eff 12-22-92); 145 v H 152 (Eff 7-1-93); 149 v H 94. Eff 6-6-2001; 151 v H 66, § 101.01, eff. 7-1-05; 2011 HB 153, § 101.01, eff. Sept. 29, 2011; 2013 HB 59, § 101.01, eff. Sept. 29, 2013.

**Editor's Notes**

This section was formerly codified as RC § 5111.28.

**Amendment Notes**

The 2013 amendment rewrote the section.

The 2011 amendment substituted "section 5111.261" for "section 5111.27" in the first sentence of (A) and in the first sentence of the first paragraph of (B); inserted "5111.27 of the Revised Code" both times it appears in the first sentence of the first paragraph of (B); and made stylistic changes.

151 v H 66, effective July 1, 2005, in (A), inserted "of job and family services"; rewrote (C)(2); and substituted "medicaid" for "medical assistance" in (D).

NOTES TO DECISIONS

**Time limitations**

Three-year time restriction for issuance of audits report by the Ohio Department of Job and Family Services, pursuant to R.C. 5111.27(B) and 5111.28(B), was a directory duty on the Department, rather than a mandatory one, despite use of the word "shall" in the statutory language of R.C. 5111.27(B); accordingly, the Department's issuance of a report and a determination that an overpayment was due from a nursing home was not invalid due to failure to abide by the time limitation, and the overpayment determination was supported by probative, reliable, and substantive evidence, pursuant to R.C. 119.12. AmCare, Inc. v. Ohio Dep't of Job & Family Servs., 2005-Ohio-2714, 161 Ohio App. 3d 350, 830 N.E.2d 406, 2005 Ohio App. LEXIS 2540 (Ohio Ct. App., Franklin County 2005).

RESEARCH REFERENCES AND PRACTICE AIDS

**Cross-References to Related Sections**

Determination of case-mix score for each facility; assignment of score and rates, RC § 5165.19.

Exception reviews of assessment information; withholding of payments; rate adjustments, RC § 5165.108.

Process by which facility may seek reconsideration of rate; appeals from adverse actions, RC § 5165.38.

**Ohio Administrative Code**

Termination, denial, and non-revalidation of provider agreements. OAC 5160-3-02.2.

## § 5165.41 Redetermining Medicaid payment rate; Interest for overpayment.

(A) The department of medicaid shall redetermine a provider's medicaid payment rate for a nursing facility using revised information if any of the following results in a determination that the provider received a higher medicaid payment rate for the nursing facility than the provider was entitled to receive:

(1) The provider properly amends a cost report for the nursing facility under section 5165.107 of the Revised Code;

(2) The department makes a finding based on an audit under section 5165.109 of the Revised Code;

(3) The department makes a finding based on an exception review of resident assessment data conducted under section 5165.193 of the Revised Code after the effective date of the nursing facility's rate for direct care costs that is based on the resident assessment data;

(4) The department makes a finding based on a post-payment review conducted under section 5165.49 of the Revised Code.

(B) The department shall apply the redetermined rate to the periods when the provider received the incorrect rate to determine the amount of the overpayment. The provider shall refund the amount of the overpayment. The department may charge the provider the following amount of interest from the time the overpayment was made:

(1) If the overpayment resulted from costs reported for calendar year 1993, the interest shall be no greater than one and one-half times the current average bank prime rate.

(2) If the overpayment resulted from costs reported for a subsequent calendar year:

(a) The interest shall be no greater than two times the current average bank prime rate if the overpayment was no more than one per cent of the total medicaid payments to the provider for the state fiscal year for which the overpayment was made.

(b) The interest shall be no greater than two and one-half times the current average bank prime rate if the overpayment was more than one per cent of the total medicaid payments to the provider for the state fiscal year for which the overpayment was made.

**HISTORY:**

2013 HB 59, § 101.01, eff. Sept. 29, 2013; 2017 hb49, § 101.01, effective September 29, 2017.

**Amendment Notes**

The 2017 amendment by HB 49 substituted "state fiscal year" for "fiscal year" in (B)(2)(a) in (B)(2)(b).

## § 5165.42 Fines for failure to produce documentation during audit.

In addition to the other penalties authorized by this chapter, the department of medicaid may impose the following penalties on a nursing facility provider:

(A) If the provider does not furnish invoices or other documentation that the department requests during an audit within sixty days after the request, a fine of no more than the greater of the following:

(1) One thousand dollars per audit;

(2) Twenty-five per cent of the cumulative amount by which the costs for which documentation was not furnished increased the total medicaid payments to the provider during the state fiscal year for which the costs were used to determine a rate.

(B) If an exiting operator or owner fails to provide notice of a facility closure or voluntary withdrawal of participation in the medicaid program as required by section 5165.50 of the Revised Code, or an exiting operator or owner and entering operator fail to provide notice of a change of operator as required by section 5165.51 of the Revised Code, a fine of not more than the current average bank prime rate plus four per cent of the last two monthly payments.

**HISTORY:**

2013 HB 59, § 101.01, eff. Sept. 29, 2013; 2017 hb49, § 101.01, effective September 29, 2017.

**Amendment Notes**

The 2017 amendment by HB 49 substituted "state fiscal year" for "fiscal year" in (A)(2).

## § 5165.43 Determination of interest rate for penalties.

For the purposes of sections 5165.41 and 5165.42 of the Revised Code, the department of medicaid shall determine the current average bank prime rate using statistical release H.15, "selected interest rates," a weekly publication of the federal reserve board, or any successor publication. If statistical release H.15, or its successor, ceases to contain the bank prime rate information or ceases to be published, the department shall request a written statement of the average bank prime rate from the federal reserve bank of Cleveland or the federal reserve board.

**HISTORY:**

2013 HB 59, § 101.01, eff. Sept. 29, 2013.

## § 5165.44 Penalties, refunds and interest charges deducted from payments.

(A) Except as provided in division (B) of this section, the department of medicaid shall deduct the following from the next available medicaid payment the department makes to a nursing facility provider who continues to participate in medicaid:

(1) Any amount the provider is required to refund, and any interest charged, under section 5165.41 of the Revised Code;

(2) The amount of any penalty imposed on the provider under section 5165.42 of the Revised Code.

(B) The department and a nursing facility provider may enter into an agreement under which a deduction required by division (A) of this section is taken in installments from payments the department makes to the provider.

**HISTORY:**

2013 HB 59, § 101.01, eff. Sept. 29, 2013.

## § 5165.45 Deposit of penalties, refunds and interest charges.

The department of medicaid shall transmit to the treasurer of state for deposit in the general revenue fund amounts collected from the following:

(A) Refunds required by, and interest charged under, section 5165.41 of the Revised Code;

(B) Amounts collected from penalties imposed under section 5165.42 of the Revised Code.

**HISTORY:**

2013 HB 59, § 101.01, eff. Sept. 29, 2013.

### § 5165.46 Audits, adverse findings, and penalties subject to adjudication.

All of the following are subject to an adjudication conducted in accordance with Chapter 119. of the Revised Code:

(A) Any audit disallowance that the department of medicaid makes as the result of an audit under section 5165.109 of the Revised Code;

(B) Any adverse finding that results from an exception review of resident assessment data conducted for a nursing facility under section 5165.193 of the Revised Code after the effective date of the nursing facility's medicaid payment rate for direct care costs that is based on the resident assessment data;

(C) Any medicaid payment deemed an overpayment under section 5165.523 of the Revised Code;

(D) Any penalty the department imposes under section 5165.42 of the Revised Code or section 5165.523 of the Revised Code.

**HISTORY:**

2013 HB 59, § 101.01, eff. Sept. 29, 2013.



### § 5165.47 Prohibited reimbursement claims.

No person, other than a nursing facility provider, shall submit a claim for medicaid payment for a service provided to a nursing facility resident if the service is included in a medicaid payment made to the nursing facility provider under this chapter or in the allowable expenses reported on a provider's cost report for a nursing facility. No nursing facility provider shall submit a separate claim for medicaid payment for a service provided to a resident of the nursing facility if the service is included in a medicaid payment made to the provider under this chapter or in the allowable expenses on the provider's cost report for the nursing facility.

**HISTORY:**

153 v H 1, § 101.01, eff. 7-17-09; 2011 HB 153, § 101.01, eff. Sept. 29, 2011; 2013 HB 59, § 101.01, eff. Sept. 29, 2013.

**Editor's Notes**

This section was formerly codified as RC § 5111.262.

**Amendment Notes**

The 2013 amendment rewrote the section.

The 2011 amendment substituted "sections 5111.20 to 5111.331" for "sections 5111.20 to 5111.33" in the second sentence.

### § 5165.48 Medicaid claims for Medicare cost-sharing expenses of nursing facility residents.

The provider of a nursing facility is not required to submit a claim to the department of medicaid regarding the medicare cost-sharing expenses of a resident of the nursing facility who, under federal law, is eligible to have the medicaid program pay for a part of the cost-sharing expenses if the provider determines that, under rules adopted under section 5165.02 of the Revised Code, the nursing facility would not receive a medicaid payment for any part of the medicare cost-sharing expenses. In such a situation, a claim for the medicare cost-sharing expenses shall be considered to have been adjudicated at no payment.

**HISTORY:**

153 v H 215, § 1, eff. 9-13-10; 2013 HB 59, § 101.01, eff. Sept. 29, 2013.

**Editor's Notes**

This section was formerly codified as RC § 5111.0211.

**Amendment Notes**

The 2013 amendment deleted the first paragraph, which read: "As used in this section, 'nursing facility' and 'provider' have the same meanings as in section 5111.20 of the Revised Code"; and in the first sentence, substituted "department of medicaid" for "department of job and family services" and "section 5165.02" for "section 5111.02".

### § 5165.49 Post - payment reviews.

The department of medicaid may conduct a post-payment review of a claim submitted by a nursing facility provider and paid by the medicaid program to determine whether the provider was overpaid. The department shall provide the provider a written summary of the review's results. The review's results are not subject to an adjudication under Chapter 119. of the Revised Code; however, the provider may request that the medicaid director reconsider the review's results. The director shall reconsider the review's results on receipt of a request made in good faith. The department shall not deduct any amounts the department claims to be due from the provider as a result of the review from the provider's medicaid payments pursuant to section 5165.44 of the Revised Code until the conclusion of the director's reconsideration, if any, of the review.

**HISTORY:**

2013 HB 59, § 101.01, eff. Sept. 29, 2013.

### § 5165.50 Prior written notice of certain planned actions.

An exiting operator or owner of a nursing facility participating in the medicaid program shall provide the department of medicaid written notice of a facility closure or voluntary withdrawal of participation not less than ninety days before the effective date of the facility closure or voluntary withdrawal of participation. The written notice shall be provided to the department in accordance with the method specified in rules authorized by section 5165.53 of the Revised Code.

The written notice shall include all of the following:

(A) The name of the exiting operator and, if any, the exiting operator's authorized agent;

(B) The name of the nursing facility that is the subject of the written notice;

(C) The exiting operator's medicaid provider agreement number for the nursing facility that is the subject of the written notice;

(D) The effective date of the facility closure or voluntary withdrawal of participation;

(E) The signature of the exiting operator's or owner's representative.

**HISTORY:**

151 v H 66, § 101.01, eff. 7-1-05; 2011 HB 153, § 101.01, eff. Sept. 29, 2011; 2013 HB 59, § 101.01, eff. Sept. 29, 2013.

**Editor's Notes**

This section was formerly codified as RC § 5111.66.

**Amendment Notes**

The 2013 amendment deleted "or intermediate care facility for the mentally retarded" following "nursing facility" in the first sentence of the first paragraph and in (B); substituted "department of medicaid" for "department of job and family services" in the first sentence of the first paragraph; deleted "voluntary termination" following "facility closure" throughout the first sentence of the first paragraph and in (D); substituted "authorized by section 5165.53" for "adopted under section 5111.689" in the first sentence of the first paragraph; and inserted "nursing" in (C).

The 2011 amendment added the second sentence of the first paragraph.

### § 5165.501 Compliance with federal law on voluntary withdrawal.

An operator shall comply with the "Social Security Act," section 1919(c)(2)(F), 42 U.S.C. 1396r(c)(2)(F) if the operator's nursing facility undergoes a voluntary withdrawal of participation.

**HISTORY:**

151 v H 66, § 101.01, eff. 7-1-05; 2013 HB 59, § 101.01, eff. Sept. 29, 2013.

**Editor's Notes**

This section was formerly codified as RC § 511.661.

**Amendment Notes**

The 2013 amendment substituted "the 'Social Security Act,' section 1919(c)(2)(F)" for "section 1919(c)(2)(F) of the 'Social Security Act,' 79 Stat. 286 (1965)".

## § 5165.51 Notice of change of operator where entering operator seeks to continue facility's participation.

(A) An exiting operator or owner and entering operator shall provide the department of medicaid written notice of a change of operator if the nursing facility participates in the medicaid program and the entering operator seeks to continue the nursing facility's participation. The written notice shall be provided to the department in accordance with the method specified in rules authorized by section 5165.53 of the Revised Code. The written notice shall be provided to the department not later than forty-five days before the effective date of the change of operator if the change of operator does not entail the relocation of residents. The written notice shall be provided to the department not later than ninety days before the effective date of the change of operator if the change of operator entails the relocation of residents.

The written notice shall include all of the following:

(1) The name of the exiting operator and, if any, the exiting operator's authorized agent;

(2) The name of the nursing facility that is the subject of the change of operator;

(3) The exiting operator's seven-digit medicaid legacy number and ten-digit national provider identifier number for the nursing facility that is the subject of the change of operator;

(4) The name of the entering operator;

(5) The effective date of the change of operator;

(6) The manner in which the entering operator becomes the nursing facility's operator, including through sale, lease, merger, or other action;

(7) If the manner in which the entering operator becomes the nursing facility's operator involves more than one step, a description of each step;

(8) Written authorization from the exiting operator or owner and entering operator for the department to process a provider agreement for the entering operator;

(9) The names and addresses of the persons to whom the department should send initial correspondence regarding the change of operator;

(10) If the nursing facility also participates in the medicare program, notification of whether the entering operator intends to accept assignment of the exiting operator's medicare provider agreement;

(11) The signature of the exiting operator's or owner's representative.

(B) An exiting operator or owner and entering operator immediately shall provide the department written notice of any changes to information included in a written notice of a change of operator that occur after that notice is provided to the department. The notice of the changes shall be provided to the department in accordance with the method specified in rules authorized by section 5165.53 of the Revised Code.

**HISTORY:**

151 v H 66, § 101.01, eff. 7-1-05; 2011 HB 153, § 101.01, eff. Sept. 29, 2011; 2013 HB 59, § 101.01, eff. Sept. 29, 2013.

**Editor's Notes**

This section was formerly codified as RC § 5111.67.

**Amendment Notes**

The 2013 amendment substituted "department of medicaid" for "department of job and family services" in the first sentence of the first paragraph of (A); deleted "or intermediate care facility for the mentally retarded" following "nursing facility" in the first sentence of the first paragraph of (A) and in (A)(2); inserted "nursing" following "continue the" in the first sentence of the first paragraph of (A); substituted "authorized by section 5165.53" for "adopted under section 5111.689" in the second sentence of the first paragraph of (A) and the second sentence of (B); and inserted "nursing" in (A)(3), (A)(6), and (A)(7).

The 2011 amendment inserted the second sentence of the first paragraph of (A); substituted "seven-digit medicaid legacy number and ten-digit national provider identifier number" for "medicaid provider agreement number" in (A)(3); inserted (A)(9) and (A)(10); redesignated former (A)(9) as (A)(11); and rewrote (B).

## § 5165.511 Requirements for entering into agreement with entering operator immediately upon change of operator.

The department of medicaid may enter into a provider agreement with an entering operator that goes into effect at 12:01 a.m. on the effective date of the change of operator if all of the following requirements are met:

(A) The department receives a properly completed written notice required by section 5165.51 of the Revised Code on or before the date required by that section.

(B) The department receives both of the following in accordance with the method specified in rules authorized by section 5165.53 of the Revised Code and not later than ten days after the effective date of the change of operator:

(1) From the entering operator, a completed application for a provider agreement and all other forms and documents specified in rules authorized by section 5165.53 of the Revised Code;

(2) From the exiting operator or owner, all forms and documents specified in rules authorized by section 5165.53 of the Revised Code.

(C) The entering operator is eligible for medicaid payments as provided in section 5165.06 of the Revised Code.

**HISTORY:**

151 v H 66, § 101.01, eff. 7-1-05; 2011 HB 153, § 101.01, eff. Sept. 29, 2011; 2013 HB 59, § 101.01, eff. Sept. 29, 2013.

**Editor's Notes**

This section was formerly codified as RC § 5111.671.

**Amendment Notes**

The 2013 amendment substituted "department of medicaid" for "department of job and family services" in the introductory language; substituted "section 5165.51" for "section 5111.67" in (A); substituted "authorized by section 5165.53" for "adopted under section 5111.689" throughout (B); and substituted "section 5165.06" for "section 5111.21" in (C).

The 2011 amendment rewrote (B).

## § 5165.512 Determination of different effective date of agreement with entering operator.

(A) The department of medicaid may enter into a provider agreement with an entering operator that goes into effect at 12:01 a.m. on the date determined under division (B) of this section if all of the following are the case:

(1) The department receives a properly completed written notice required by section 5165.51 of the Revised Code.

(2) The department receives, from the entering operator and in accordance with the method specified in rules authorized by section 5165.53 of the Revised Code, a completed application for a provider agreement and all other forms and documents specified in rules adopted under that section.

(3) The department receives, from the exiting operator or owner and in accordance with the method specified in rules authorized by section 5165.53 of the Revised Code, all forms and documents specified in rules adopted under that section.

(4) One or more of the following apply:

(a) The requirement of division (A)(1) of this section is met after the time required by section 5165.51 of the Revised Code;

(b) The requirement of division (A)(2) of this section is met more than ten days after the effective date of the change of operator;

(c) The requirement of division (A)(3) of this section is met more than ten days after the effective date of the change of operator.

(5) The entering operator is eligible for medicaid payments as provided in section 5165.06 of the Revised Code.

(B) The department shall determine the date a provider agreement entered into under this section is to go into effect as follows:

(1) The effective date shall give the department sufficient time to process the change of operator, assure no duplicate payments are made, and make the withholding required by section 5165.521 of the Revised Code.

(2) The effective date shall be not earlier than the latest of the following:

(a) The effective date of the change of operator;

(b) The date that the entering operator complies with section 5165.51 of the Revised Code and division (A)(2) of this section;

(c) The date that the exiting operator or owner complies with section 5165.51 of the Revised Code and division (A)(3) of this section.

(3) The effective date shall be not later than the following after the later of the dates specified in division (B)(2) of this section:

(a) Forty-five days if the change of operator does not entail the relocation of residents;

(b) Ninety days if the change of operator entails the relocation of residents.

**HISTORY:**

151 v H 66, § 101.01, eff. 7-1-05; 2011 HB 153, § 101.01, eff. Sept. 29, 2011; 2013 HB 59, § 101.01, eff. Sept. 29, 2013.

**Editor's Notes**

This section was formerly codified as RC § 5111.672.

**Amendment Notes**

The 2013 amendment substituted "department of medicaid" for "department of job and family services" in the introductory language of (A); substituted "section 5165.51" for "section 5111.67" in (A)(1), (A)(4)(a), (B)(2)(b), and (B)(2)(c); substituted "authorized by section 5165.53" for "adopted under section 5111.689" in (A)(2) and (A)(3); substituted "section 5165.06" for "section 5111.21" in (A)(5); and substituted "section 5165.521" for "section 5111.681" in (B)(1).

The 2011 amendment rewrote (A)(2); inserted (A)(3); redesignated former (A)(3) and (A)(4) as (A)(4) and (A)(5); added the introductory language of (A)(4); added the (A)(4)(a) and (A)(4)(b) designations; added (A)(4)(c); rewrote (B)(1) and (B)(2); and made related changes.



## § 5165.513 Duties of entering operator.

(A) A provider that enters into a provider agreement with the department of medicaid under section 5165.511 or 5165.512 of the Revised Code shall do all of the following:

(1) Comply with all applicable federal statutes and regulations;

(2) Comply with section 5165.07 of the Revised Code and all other applicable state statutes and rules;

(3) Subject to division (B) of this section, comply with all the terms and conditions of the exiting operator's provider agreement, including, but not limited to, all of the following:

(a) Any plan of correction;

(b) Compliance with health and safety standards;

(c) Compliance with the ownership and financial interest disclosure requirements of 42 C.F.R. 455.104, 455.105, and 1002.3;

(d) Compliance with the civil rights requirements of 45 C.F.R. parts 80, 84, and 90;

(e) Compliance with additional requirements imposed by the department;

(f) Any sanctions relating to remedies for violation of the provider agreement, including deficiencies, compliance periods, accountability periods, monetary penalties, notification for correction of contract violations, and history of deficiencies.

(B) Division (A)(3) of this section does not prohibit a nursing facility provider from excluding one or more parts of the nursing facility from the provider agreement pursuant to division (B)(1) of section 5165.08 of the Revised Code.

**HISTORY:**

151 v H 66, § 101.01, eff. 7-1-05; 2013 HB 59, § 101.01, eff. Sept. 29, 2013; 2014 sb276, § 1, effective January 1, 2015; 2014 hb394, § 1, effective January 1, 2015.

**Editor's Notes**

Acts 2014, HB 394, § 9 and Acts 2014, SB 276, § 8 provides: "The versions of sections 5165.08, 5165.513, 5165.515, and 5165.99 of the Revised Code presented in this act are the versions of the sections that result from Sections 110.25, 110.26, and 110.27 of Am. Sub. H.B. 59 of the 130th General Assembly."

This section was formerly codified as RC § 5111.673.

**Amendment Notes**

The 2014 amendment by SB 276 and HB 394, added the (A) designation; redesignated former (A) through (C) and (C)(1) through (C)(6) as (A)(1) through (A)(3) and (A)(3)(a) through (A)(3)(f); and added (B).

The 2013 amendment substituted "medicaid under section 5165.511 or 5165.512" for "job and family services under section 5111.671 or 5111.672" in the introductory language of (A); redesignated former (A) through (C) and (C)(1) through (C)(3) as (A)(1) through (A)(3) and (A)(3)(a) through (A)(3)(c); substituted "section 5165.07" for "section 5111.22" in (A)(2); added "Subject to division (B) of this section" to the beginning of the introductory language of present (A)(3); and added (B).

## § 5165.514 Exiting operator considered to be operator until effective date of new agreement.

In the case of a change of operator, the exiting operator shall be considered to be the operator of the nursing facility for purposes of the medicaid program, including medicaid payments, until the effective date of the entering operator's provider agreement if the provider agreement is entered into under section 5165.511 or 5165.512 of the Revised Code.

**HISTORY:**

151 v H 66, § 101.01, eff. 7-1-05; 2013 HB 59, § 101.01, eff. Sept. 29, 2013.

**Editor's Notes**

This section was formerly codified as RC § 5111.674.

**Amendment Notes**

The 2013 amendment deleted "or intermediate care facility for the mentally retarded" following "nursing facility"; and substituted "section 5165.511 or 5165.512" for "section 5111.671 or 5111.672".

## § 5165.515 Agreement where entering operator does not agree to all terms and conditions of exiting operator's agreement.

The department of medicaid may enter into a provider agreement as provided in section 5165.07 of the Revised Code, rather than section 5165.511 or 5165.512 of the Revised Code, with an entering operator if the entering operator does not agree to a provider agreement that satisfies the requirements of division (A)(3) of section 5165.513 of the Revised Code. The department may not enter into the provider agreement unless the department of health certifies the nursing facility for participation in medicaid. The effective date of the provider agreement shall not precede any of the following:

(A) The date that the department of health certifies the nursing facility;

(B) The effective date of the change of operator;

(C) The date the requirement of section 5165.51 of the Revised Code is satisfied.

**HISTORY:**

151 v H 66, § 101.01, eff. 7-1-05; 2013 HB 59, § 101.01, eff. Sept. 29, 2013; 2014 hb394, § 1, effective January 1, 2015; 2014 sb276, § 1, effective January 1, 2015.

**Editor's Notes**

Acts 2014, HB 394, § 9 and Acts 2014, SB 276, § 8 provides: "The versions of sections 5165.08, 5165.513, 5165.515, and 5165.99 of the Revised Code presented in this act are the versions of the sections that result from Sections 110.25, 110.26, and 110.27 of Am. Sub. H.B. 59 of the 130th General Assembly."

This section was formerly codified as RC § 5111.675.

**Amendment Notes**

The 2014 amendment by SB 276 and HB 394, substituted "division (A)(3)" for "division (C)" in the first sentence of the introductory language.

The 2013 amendment, in the introductory language, in the first sentence, substituted "medicaid" for "job and family services", "section 5165.07" for "section 5111.22", "section 5165.511 or 5165.512" for "section 5111.671 or 5111.672", and "division (A)(3) of section 5165.513" for "division (C) of section 5111.673" and substituted "for participation in medicaid" for "or intermediate care facility for the mentally retarded under Title XIX of the 'Social Security Act,' 79 Stat. 286 (1965), 42 U.S.C. 1396, as amended"; inserted "nursing" in (A); and substituted "section 5165.51" for "section 5111.67" in (C).

### § 5165.516 Rate adjustment following change of operator.

The medicaid director may adopt rules under section 5165.02 of the Revised Code governing adjustments to the medicaid payment rate for a nursing facility that undergoes a change of operator. No rate adjustment resulting from a change of operator shall be effective before the effective date of the entering operator's provider agreement. This is the case regardless of whether the provider agreement is entered into under section 5165.511, section 5165.512, or, pursuant to section 5165.515, section 5165.07 of the Revised Code.

**HISTORY:**

151 v H 66, § 101.01, eff. 7-1-05; 2013 HB 59, § 101.01, eff. Sept. 29, 2013.

**Editor's Notes**

This section was formerly codified as RC § 5111.676.

**Amendment Notes**

The 2013 amendment, in the first sentence, substituted "medicaid director may adopt rules under section 5165.02" for "director of job and family services may adopt rules in accordance with Chapter 119." and "payment" for "reimbursement", and deleted "or intermediate care facility for the mentally retarded" following "nursing facility"; and, in the last sentence, substituted "section 5165.511, section 5165.512" for "section 5111.671, section 5111.672" and "section 5165.515, section 5165.07" for "section 5111.675, section 5111.22".

### § 5165.517 Determinations unaffected by licensing determinations by other departments.

The department of health's determination that a change of operator has or has not occurred for purposes of licensure under Chapter 3721. of the Revised Code shall not affect the department of medicaid's determination of whether or when a change of operator occurs or the effective date of an entering operator's provider agreement under section 5165.511, section 5165.512, or, pursuant to section 5165.515, section 5165.07 of the Revised Code.

**HISTORY:**

151 v H 66, § 101.01, eff. 7-1-05; 153 v S 79, § 1, eff. 10-6-09; 2013 HB 59, § 101.01, eff. Sept. 29, 2013.

**Editor's Notes**

This section was formerly codified as RC § 5111.677.

**Amendment Notes**

The 2013 amendment rewrote the section.

153 v S 79, effective October 6, 2009, deleted "mental retardation and" preceding "developmental disabilities" throughout.

### § 5165.52 Determination of overpayments and other actual or potential debts exiting operator may owe.

(A) On receipt of a written notice under section 5165.50 of the Revised Code of a facility closure or voluntary withdrawal of participation, on receipt of a written notice under section 5165.51 of the Revised Code of a change of operator, or on the effective date of an involuntary termination, the department of medicaid shall estimate the amount of any overpayments made under the medicaid program to the exiting operator, including overpayments the exiting operator disputes, and other actual and potential debts the exiting operator owes or may owe to the department and United States centers for medicare and medicaid services under the medicaid program, including a franchise permit fee.

(B) In estimating the exiting operator's other actual and potential debts to the department and the United States centers for medicare and medicaid services under the medicaid program, the department shall use a debt estimation methodology the medicaid director shall establish in rules authorized by section 5165.53 of the Revised Code. The methodology shall provide for estimating all of the following that the department determines are applicable:

(1) Refunds due the department under section 5165.41 of the Revised Code;

(2) Interest owed to the department and United States centers for medicare and medicaid services;

(3) Final civil monetary and other penalties for which all right of appeal has been exhausted;

(4) Money owed the department and United States centers for medicare and medicaid services from any outstanding final fiscal audit, including a final fiscal audit for the last state fiscal year or portion thereof in which the exiting operator participated in the medicaid program;

(5) Other amounts the department determines are applicable.

(C) The department shall provide the exiting operator written notice of the department's estimate under division (A) of this section not later than thirty days after the department receives the notice under section 5165.50 of the Revised Code of the facility closure or voluntary withdrawal of participation; the department receives the notice under section 5165.51 of the Revised Code of the change of operator; or the effective date of the involuntary termination. The department's written notice shall include the basis for the estimate.

**HISTORY:**

151 v H 66, § 101.01, eff. 7-1-05; 153 v H 398, § 1, eff. 8-31-10; 2011 HB 153, § 101.01, eff. Sept. 29, 2011; 2013 HB 59, § 101.01, eff. Sept. 29, 2013; 2017 hb49, § 101.01, effective September 29, 2017.

**Editor's Notes**

This section was formerly codified as RC § 5111.68.

The amendment of RC § 5111.68 by 153 v H 1 was disapproved by the Governor.

**Amendment Notes**

The 2017 amendment by HB 49 substituted "state fiscal year" for "fiscal year" in (B)(4).

The 2013 amendment substituted "section 5165.50" for "section 5111.66" in (A) and (C); deleted "voluntary termination" following "facility closure" in (A) and (C); substituted "section 5165.51" for "section 5111.67" in (A) and (C); substituted "department of medicaid" for "department of job and family services" in (A); in the second sentence of the introductory language of (B), substituted "medicaid director" for "director of job and family services" and "authorized by section 5165.53" for "adopted under section 5111.689" in the first sentence of the introductory language of (B); and substituted "section 5165.41" for "section 5111.27" in (B)(1).

The 2011 amendment, in (A), inserted "on receipt of" following "participation" and inserted "or on the effective date of an involuntary termination"; in the first sentence of (C), inserted "the department receives" following "participation" and inserted "or the effective date of the involuntary termination"; and made related changes.

153 v H 398, effective August 31, 2010, rewrote the section.

### § 5165.521 Withholding from payment due to exiting operator; successor liability agreement.

(A) Except as provided in divisions (B), (C), and (D) of this section, the department of medicaid may withhold from payment due an exiting operator under the medicaid program the total amount specified in the notice provided under division (C) of section 5165.52 of the Revised Code that the exiting operator owes or may owe to the department and United States centers for medicare and medicaid services under the medicaid program.

(B) In the case of a change of operator and subject to division (E) of this section, the following shall apply regarding a withholding under division (A) of this section if the exiting operator or entering operator or an affiliated operator executes a successor liability agreement meeting the requirements of division (F) of this section:

(1) If the exiting operator, entering operator, or affiliated operator assumes liability for the total, actual amount of debt the exiting operator owes the department and the United States centers for medicare and medicaid services under the medicaid program as determined under section 5165.525 of the Revised Code, the department shall not make the withholding.

(2) If the exiting operator, entering operator, or affiliated operator assumes liability for only the portion of the amount specified in division (B)(1) of this section that represents the franchise permit fee the exiting operator owes, the department shall withhold not more than the difference between the total amount specified in the notice provided under division (C) of section 5165.52 of the Revised Code and the amount for which the exiting operator, entering operator, or affiliated operator assumes liability.

(C) In the case of a voluntary withdrawal of participation or facility closure and subject to division (E) of this section, the following shall apply regarding a withholding under division (A) of this section if the exiting operator or an affiliated operator executes a successor liability agreement meeting the requirements of division (F) of this section:

(1) If the exiting operator or affiliated operator assumes liability for the total, actual amount of debt the exiting operator owes the department and the United States centers for medicare and medicaid services under the medicaid program as determined under section 5165.525 of the Revised Code, the department shall not make the withholding.

(2) If the exiting operator or affiliated operator assumes liability for only the portion of the amount specified in division (C)(1) of this section that represents the franchise permit fee the exiting operator owes, the department shall withhold not more than the difference between the total amount specified in the notice provided under division (C) of section 5165.52 of the Revised Code and the amount for which the exiting operator or affiliated operator assumes liability.

(D) In the case of an involuntary termination and subject to division (E) of this section, the following shall apply regarding a withholding under division (A) of this section if the exiting operator, the entering operator, or an affiliated operator executes a successor liability agreement meeting the requirements of division (F) of this section and the department approves the successor liability agreement:

(1) If the exiting operator, entering operator, or affiliated operator assumes liability for the total, actual amount of debt the exiting operator owes the department and the United States centers for medicare and medicaid services under the medicaid program as determined under section 5165.525 of the Revised Code, the department shall not make the withholding.

(2) If the exiting operator, entering operator, or affiliated operator assumes liability for only the portion of the amount specified in division (D)(1) of this section that represents the franchise permit fee the exiting operator owes, the department shall withhold not more than the difference between the total amount specified in the notice provided under division (C) of section 5165.52 of the Revised Code and the amount for which the exiting operator, entering operator, or affiliated operator assumes liability.

(E) For an exiting operator or affiliated operator to be eligible to enter into a successor liability agreement under division (B), (C), or (D) of this section, both of the following must apply:

(1) The exiting operator or affiliated operator must have one or more valid provider agreements, other than the provider agreement for the nursing facility that is the subject of the involuntary termination, voluntary withdrawal of participation, facility closure, or change of operator;

(2) During the twelve-month period preceding either the effective date of the involuntary termination or the month in which the department receives the notice of the voluntary withdrawal of participation or facility closure under section 5165.50 of the Revised Code or the notice of the change of operator under section 5165.51 of the Revised Code, the average monthly medicaid payment made to the exiting operator or affiliated operator pursuant to the exiting operator's or affiliated operator's one or more provider agreements, other than the provider agreement for the nursing facility that is the subject of the involuntary termination, voluntary withdrawal of participation, facility closure, or change of operator, must equal at least ninety per cent of the sum of the following:

(a) The average monthly medicaid payment made to the exiting operator pursuant to the exiting operator's provider agreement for the nursing facility that is the subject of the involuntary termination, voluntary withdrawal of participation, facility closure, or change of operator;

(b) Whichever of the following apply:

(i) If the exiting operator or affiliated operator has assumed liability under one or more other successor liability agreements, the total amount for which the exiting operator or affiliated operator has assumed liability under the other successor liability agreements;

(ii) If the exiting operator or affiliated operator has not assumed liability under any other successor liability agreements, zero.

(F) A successor liability agreement executed under this section must comply with all of the following:

(1) It must provide for the operator who executes the successor liability agreement to assume liability for either of the following as specified in the agreement:

(a) The total, actual amount of debt the exiting operator owes the department and the United States centers for medicare and medicaid services under the medicaid program as determined under section 5165.525 of the Revised Code;

(b) The portion of the amount specified in division (F)(1)(a) of this section that represents the franchise permit fee the exiting operator owes.

(2) It may not require the operator who executes the successor liability agreement to furnish a surety bond.

(3) It must provide that the department, after determining under section 5165.525 of the Revised Code the actual amount of debt the exiting operator owes the department and United States centers for medicare and medicaid services under the medicaid program, may deduct the lesser of the following from medicaid payments made to the operator who executes the successor liability agreement:

(a) The total, actual amount of debt the exiting operator owes the department and the United States centers for medicare and medicaid services under the medicaid program as determined under section 5165.525 of the Revised Code;

(b) The amount for which the operator who executes the successor liability agreement assumes liability under the agreement.

(4) It must provide that the deductions authorized by division (F)(3) of this section are to be made for a number of months, not to exceed six, agreed to by the operator who executes the successor liability agreement and the department or, if the operator who executes the successor liability agreement and department cannot agree on a number of months that is less than six, a greater number of months determined by the attorney general pursuant to a claims collection process authorized by statute of this state.

(5) It must provide that, if the attorney general determines the number of months for which the deductions authorized by division (F)(3) of this section are to be made, the operator who executes the successor liability agreement shall pay, in addition to the amount collected pursuant to the attorney general's claims collection process, the part of the amount so collected that, if not for division (H) of this section, would be required by section 109.081 of the Revised Code to be paid into the attorney general claims fund.

(G) Execution of a successor liability agreement does not waive an exiting operator's right to contest the amount specified in the notice the department provides the exiting operator under division (C) of section 5165.52 of the Revised Code.

(H) Notwithstanding section 109.081 of the Revised Code, the entire amount that the attorney general, whether by employees or agents of the attorney general or by special counsel appointed pursuant to section 109.08 of the Revised Code, collects under a successor liability agreement, other than the additional amount the operator who executes the agreement is required by division (F)(5) of this section to pay, shall be paid to the department of medicaid for deposit into the appropriate fund. The additional amount that the operator is required to pay shall be paid into the state treasury to the credit of the attorney general claims fund created under section 109.081 of the Revised Code.

**HISTORY:**

151 v H 66, § 101.01, eff. 7-1-05; 153 v H 398, § 1, eff. 8-31-10; 2011 HB 153, § 101.01, eff. Sept. 29, 2011; 2013 HB 59, § 101.01, eff. Sept. 29, 2013.

**Editor's Notes**

This section was formerly codified as RC § 5111.681.

**Amendment Notes**

The 2013 amendment substituted "medicaid" for "job and family services" in (A) and the first sentence of (H); substituted "section 5165.52" for "section 5111.68" in (A), (B)(2), (C)(2), (D)(2), and (G); substituted "section 5165.525" for "section 5111.685" throughout (B)(1), (C)(1), (D)(1), (F)(1)(a), (F)(3); deleted "voluntary termination" preceding "voluntary withdrawal" throughout the introductory language of (C) and in (E); deleted "or intermediate care facility for the mentally retarded" following "nursing facility" in (E)(1) and (E)(2)(a) and the introductory language of (E)(2); in the introductory language of (E)(2), substituted "section 5165.50" for "section 5111.66" and "section 5165.51" for "section 5111.67"; and made a stylistic change.

The 2011 amendment substituted "divisions (B), (C), and (D)" for "divisions (B) and (C)" in (A); in the introductory language of (B) and (C), substituted "division (E)" for "division (D)" and "division (F)" for "division (E)"; inserted (D); redesignated former (D) through (G) as (E) through (H); substituted "division (B), (C), or (D)" for "division (B) or (C)" in the introductory language of (E); inserted "involuntary termination" in (E)(1) and (E)(2)(a); in the introductory language of (E)(2), inserted "either the effective date of the involuntary termination or" and "involuntary termination" following "subject of the"; substituted "division (F)(1)(a)" for "division (E)(1)(a)" in (F)(1)(b); substituted "division (F)(3)" for "division (E)(3)" in (F)(4) and (F)(5); substituted "division (H)" for "division (G)" in (F)(5); and substituted "division (F)(5)" for "division (E)(5)" in the first sentence of (H).

153 v H 398, effective August 31, 2010, rewrote the section.

### § 5165.522 Exiting operator to file cost report.

(A) Except as provided in division (B) of this section, an exiting operator shall file with the department of medicaid a cost report not later than ninety days after the last day the exiting operator's provider agreement is in effect or, in the case of a voluntary withdrawal of participation, the effective date of the voluntary withdrawal of participation. The cost report shall cover the period that begins with the day after the last day covered by the operator's most recent previous cost report required by section 5165.10 of the Revised Code and ends on the last day the exiting operator's provider agreement is in effect or, in the case of a voluntary withdrawal of participation, the effective date of the voluntary withdrawal of participation. The cost report shall include, as applicable, all of the following:

(1) The sale price of the nursing facility;

(2) A final depreciation schedule that shows which assets are transferred to the buyer and which assets are not transferred to the buyer;

(3) Any other information the department requires.

(B) The department, at its sole discretion, may waive the requirement that an exiting operator file a cost report in accordance with division (A) of this section.

**HISTORY:**

151 v H 66, § 101.01, eff. 7-1-05; 2013 HB 59, § 101.01, eff. Sept. 29, 2013.

**Editor's Notes**

This section was formerly codified as RC § 5111.682.

**Amendment Notes**

The 2013 amendment, in the introductory language of (A), substituted "medicaid" for "job and family services" in the first sentence and substituted "section 5165.10" for "section 5111.26" in the second sentence; and deleted "or intermediate care facility for the mentally retarded" following "nursing facility" in (A)(1).

### § 5165.523 Sanctions for failing to file complying cost report.

If an exiting operator required by section 5165.522 of the Revised Code to file a cost report with the department of medicaid fails to file the cost report in accordance with that section, all payments under the medicaid program for the period the cost report is required to cover are deemed overpayments until the date the department receives the properly completed cost report. The department may impose on the exiting operator a penalty of one hundred dollars for each calendar day the properly completed cost report is late.

**HISTORY:**

151 v H 66, § 101.01, eff. 7-1-05; 2013 HB 59, § 101.01, eff. Sept. 29, 2013.

**Editor's Notes**

This section was formerly codified as RC § 5111.683.

**Amendment Notes**

The 2013 amendment, in the first sentence, substituted "section 5165.522" for "section 5111.682" and "department of medicaid" for "department of job and family services".

### § 5165.524 Final payment prohibited until cost reports received.

The department of medicaid may not provide an exiting operator final payment under the medicaid program until the department receives all properly completed cost reports the exiting operator is required to file under sections 5165.10 and 5165.522 of the Revised Code.

**HISTORY:**

151 v H 66, § 101.01, eff. 7-1-05; 2013 HB 59, § 101.01, eff. Sept. 29, 2013.

**Editor's Notes**

This section was formerly codified as RC § 5111.684.

**Amendment Notes**

The 2013 amendment substituted "department of medicaid" for "department of job and family services"; substituted "sections 5165.10 and 5165.522" for "sections 5111.26 and 5111.682".

### § 5165.525 Determination of actual debt owed by exiting operator; debt summary report.

The department of medicaid shall determine the actual amount of debt an exiting operator owes the department and the United States centers for medicare and medicaid services under the medicaid program by completing all final fiscal audits not already completed and performing all other appropriate actions the department determines to be necessary. The department shall issue an initial debt summary report on this matter not later than sixty days after the date the exiting operator files the properly completed cost report required by section 5165.522 of the Revised Code with the department or, if the department waives the cost report requirement for the exiting operator, sixty days after the date the department waives the cost report requirement. The initial debt summary report becomes the final debt summary report thirty-one days after the department issues the initial debt summary report unless the exiting operator, or an affiliated operator who executes a successor liability agreement under section 5165.521 of the Revised Code, requests a review before that date.

The exiting operator, and an affiliated operator who executes a successor liability agreement under section 5165.521 of the Revised Code, may request a review to contest any of the department's findings included in the initial debt summary report. The request for the review must be submitted to the department not later than thirty days after the date the department issues the initial debt summary report. The department shall conduct the review on receipt of a timely request and issue a revised debt summary report. If the department has withheld money from payment due the exiting operator under division (A) of section 5165.521 of the Revised Code, the department shall issue the revised debt summary report not later than ninety days after the date the department receives the timely request for the review unless the department and exiting operator or affiliated operator agree to a later date. The exiting operator or affiliated operator may submit information to the department explaining what the operator contests before and during the review, including documentation of the amount of any debt the department owes the operator. The exiting operator or affiliated operator may submit additional information to the department not later than thirty days after the department issues the revised debt summary report. The revised debt summary report becomes the final debt summary report thirty-one days after the department issues the revised debt summary report unless the exiting operator or affiliated operator timely submits additional information to the department. If the exiting operator or affiliated operator timely submits additional information to the department, the department shall consider the additional information and issue a final debt summary report not later than sixty days after the department issues the revised debt summary report unless the department and exiting operator or affiliated operator agree to a later date.

Each debt summary report the department issues under this section shall include the department's findings and the amount of debt the department determines the exiting operator owes the department and United States centers for medicare and medicaid services under the medicaid program. The department shall explain its findings and determination in each debt summary report.

The exiting operator, and an affiliated operator who executes a successor liability agreement under section 5165.521 of the Revised Code, may request, in accordance with Chapter 119. of the Revised Code, an adjudication regarding a finding in a final debt summary report that pertains to an audit or alleged overpayment made under the medicaid program to the exiting operator. The adjudication shall be consolidated with any other uncompleted adjudication that concerns a matter addressed in the final debt summary report.

**HISTORY:**

151 v H 66, § 101.01, eff. 7-1-05; 153 v H 398, § 1, eff. 8-31-10; 2013 HB 59, § 101.01, eff. Sept. 29, 2013.

**Editor's Notes**

This section was formerly codified as RC § 5111.685.

The amendment of RC § 5111.685 by 153 v H 1 was disapproved by the Governor.

**Amendment Notes**

The 2013 amendment, in the first paragraph, substituted "department of medicaid" for "department of job and family services" in the first sentence and substituted "section 5165.522" for "section 5111.682" in the second sentence; and substituted "section 5165.521" for "section 5111.681" in the last sentence of the first paragraph, the first and fourth sentences of the second paragraph, and the first sentence of the last paragraph.

153 v H 398, effective August 31, 2010, rewrote the section.



### § 5165.526 Time frames for release of amount withheld.

The department of medicaid shall release the actual amount withheld under division (A) of section 5165.521 of the Revised Code, less any amount the exiting operator owes the department and United States centers for medicare and medicaid services under the medicaid program, as follows:

(A) Unless the department issues the initial debt summary report required by section 5165.525 of the Revised Code not later than sixty days after the date the exiting operator files the properly completed cost report required by section 5165.522 of the Revised Code, sixty-one days after the date the exiting operator files the properly completed cost report;

(B) If the department issues the initial debt summary report required by section 5165.525 of the Revised Code not later than sixty days after the date the exiting operator files a properly completed cost report required by section 5165.522 of the Revised Code, not later than the following:

(1) Thirty days after the deadline for requesting an adjudication under section 5165.525 of the Revised Code regarding the final debt summary report if the exiting operator, and an affiliated operator who executes a successor liability agreement under section 5165.521 of the Revised Code, fail to request the adjudication on or before the deadline;

(2) Thirty days after the completion of an adjudication of the final debt summary report if the exiting operator, or an affiliated operator who executes a successor liability agreement under section 5165.521 of the Revised Code, requests the adjudication on or before the deadline for requesting the adjudication.

(C) Unless the department issues the initial debt summary report required by section 5165.525 of the Revised Code not later than sixty days after the date the department waives the cost report requirement of section 5165.522 of the Revised Code, sixty-one days after the date the department waives the cost report requirement;

(D) If the department issues the initial debt summary report required by section 5165.525 of the Revised Code not later than sixty days after the date the department waives the cost report requirement of section 5165.522 of the Revised Code, not later than the following:

(1) Thirty days after the deadline for requesting an adjudication under section 5165.525 of the Revised Code regarding the final debt summary report if the exiting operator, and an affiliated operator who executes a successor liability agreement under section 5165.521 of the Revised Code, fail to request the adjudication on or before the deadline;

(2) Thirty days after the completion of an adjudication of the final debt summary report if the exiting operator, or an affiliated operator who executes a successor liability agreement under section 5165.521 of the Revised Code, requests the adjudication on or before the deadline for requesting the adjudication.

**HISTORY:**

151 v H 66, § 101.01, eff. 7-1-05; 153 v H 398, § 1, eff. 8-31-10; 2013 HB 59, § 101.01, eff. Sept. 29, 2013.

**Editor's Notes**

The amendment of RC § 5111.686 by 153 v H 1 was disapproved by the Governor.

This section was formerly codified as RC § 5111.686.

**Amendment Notes**

The 2013 amendment substituted "department of medicaid" for "department of job and family services" in the introductory language; substituted "section 5165.521" for "section 5111.681" in the introductory language and in (B)(2) and (D)(2); and, in (A), the introductory language of (B) and (D), in (B)(1), (C), and (D)(1), substituted "section 5165.525" for "section 5111.685" and "section 5165.522" for "section 5111.682".

153 v H 398, effective August 31, 2010, rewrote the section.

### § 5165.527 Release of withholding where action is postponed or canceled.

The department of medicaid, at its sole discretion, may release the amount withheld under division (A) of section 5165.521 of the Revised Code if the exiting operator submits to the department written notice of a postponement of a change of operator, facility closure, or voluntary withdrawal of participation and the transactions leading to the change of operator, facility closure, or voluntary withdrawal of participation are postponed for at least thirty days but less than ninety days after the date originally proposed for the change of operator, facility closure, or voluntary withdrawal of participation as reported in the written notice required by section 5165.50 or 5165.51 of the Revised Code. The department shall release the amount withheld if the exiting operator submits to the department written notice of a cancellation or postponement of a change of operator, facility closure, or voluntary withdrawal of participation and the transactions leading to the change of operator, facility closure, or voluntary withdrawal of participation are canceled or postponed for more than ninety days after the date originally proposed for the change of operator, facility closure, or voluntary withdrawal of participation as reported in the written notice required by section 5165.50 or 5165.51 of the Revised Code. A written notice shall be provided to the department in accordance with the method specified in rules authorized by section 5165.53 of the Revised Code.

After the department receives a written notice regarding a cancellation or postponement of a facility closure or voluntary withdrawal of participation, the exiting operator or owner shall provide new written notice to the department under section 5165.50 of the Revised Code regarding any transactions leading to a facility closure or voluntary withdrawal of participation at a future time. After the department receives a written notice regarding a cancellation or postponement of a change of operator, the exiting operator or owner and entering operator shall provide new written notice to the department under section 5165.51 of the Revised Code regarding any transactions leading to a change of operator at a future time.

**HISTORY:**

151 v H 66, § 101.01, eff. 7-1-05; 2011 HB 153, § 101.01, eff. Sept. 29, 2011; 2013 HB 59, § 101.01, eff. Sept. 29, 2013.

**Editor's Notes**

This section was formerly codified as RC § 5111.687.

**Amendment Notes**

The 2013 amendment deleted "voluntary termination" following "facility closure" throughout the section; in the first paragraph, in the first sentence, substituted "medicaid" for "job and family services" and "section 5165.521" for "section 5111.681", substituted "section 5165.50 or 5165.51" for "section 5111.66 or 5111.67" in the first and second sentences, and substituted "authorized by section 5165.53" for "adopted under section 5111.689" in the last sentence; and, in the second paragraph, substituted "section 5165.50" for "section 5111.66" in the first sentence and substituted "section 5165.51" for "section 5111.67".

The 2011 amendment added the last sentence of the first paragraph.

## § 5165.528 Deposits into medicaid payment withholding fund.

(A) All amounts withheld under section 5165.521 of the Revised Code from payment due an exiting operator under the medicaid program shall be deposited into the medicaid payment withholding fund created by the controlling board pursuant to section 131.35 of the Revised Code. Money in the fund shall be used as follows:

(1) To pay an exiting operator when a withholding is released to the exiting operator under section 5165.526 or 5165.527 of the Revised Code;

(2) To pay the department of medicaid and United States centers for medicare and medicaid services the amount an exiting operator owes the department and United States centers under the medicaid program.

(B) Amounts paid from the medicaid payment withholding fund pursuant to division (A)(2) of this section shall be deposited into the appropriate department fund.

**HISTORY:**

153 v H 398, § 1, eff. 8-31-10; 2013 HB 59, § 101.01, eff. Sept. 29, 2013.

**Editor's Notes**

The enactment of RC § 5111.688 by 153 v H 1 was disapproved by the Governor.

This section was formerly codified as RC § 5111.688.

**Amendment Notes**

The 2013 amendment substituted "section 5165.521" for "section 5111.681" in the introductory language of (A); substituted "section 5165.526 or 5165.527" for "section 5111.686 or 5111.687" in (A)(1); and substituted "department of medicaid" for "department of job and family services" in (A)(2).

## § 5165.53 Rules.

The medicaid director shall adopt rules under section 5165.02 of the Revised Code to implement sections 5165.50 to 5165.53 of the Revised Code, including rules applicable to an exiting operator that provides written notification under section 5165.50 of the Revised Code of a voluntary withdrawal of participation. Rules adopted under this section shall comply with the "Social Security Act," section 1919(c)(2)(F), 42 U.S.C. 1396r(c)(2)(F), regarding restrictions on transfers or discharges of nursing facility residents in the case of a voluntary withdrawal of participation. The rules may prescribe a medicaid payment methodology and other procedures that are applicable after the effective date of a voluntary withdrawal of participation that differ from the payment methodology and other procedures that would otherwise apply. The rules shall specify all of the following:

(A) The method by which written notices to the department required by sections 5165.50 to 5165.53 of the Revised Code are to be provided;

(B) The forms and documents that are to be provided to the department of medicaid under sections 5165.511 and 5165.512 of the Revised Code, which shall include, in the case of such forms and documents provided by entering operators, all the fully executed leases, management agreements, merger agreements and supporting documents, and fully executed sales contracts and any other supporting documents culminating in the change of operator;

(C) The method by which the forms and documents identified in division (B) of this section are to be provided to the department.

**HISTORY:**

151 v H 66, § 101.01, eff. 7-1-05; 153 v H 398, § 1, eff. 8-31-10; 2011 HB 153, § 101.01, eff. Sept. 29, 2011; 2013 HB 59, § 101.01, eff. Sept. 29, 2013.

**Editor's Notes**

This section was formerly codified as RC § 5111.689.

This section was amended and renumbered from RC § 5111.688 by 153 v H 398, effective August 31,2010.

The renumbering of RC § 5111.689 from RC§ 5111.688 by 153 v H 1 was disapproved by the Governor.

**Amendment Notes**

The 2013 amendment, in the introductory language, in the first sentence, substituted "medicaid director" for "director of job and family services", "section 5165.02" for "section 5111.02", "under section 5165.50" for "under section 5111.66", and "the 'Social Security Act,' section 1919(c)(2)(F)" for "section 1919(c)(2)(F) of the 'Social Security Act,' 79 Stat. 286 (1965)" and substituted "payment" for "reimbursement" twice in the second sentence; substituted "sections 5165.50 to 5165.53" for "sections 5111.65 to 5111.689" in the first sentence of the introductory language and in (A); and substituted "of medicaid under sections 5165.511 and 5165.512" for "under sections 5111.671 and 5111.672" in (B).

The 2011 amendment added the last sentence of the introductory language; and added (A) through (C).

153 v H 398, effective August 31, 2010, corrected internal references.

## § 5165.60 Definitions.

As used in this section, "a resident's rights" means the rights of a nursing facility resident under sections 3721.10 to 3721.17 of the Revised Code, the "Social Security Act," sections 1819(c) and 1919(c), 42 U.S.C. 1395i-3(c) and 1396r(c), and federal regulations issued under those sections of the "Social Security Act."

As used in sections 5165.60 to 5165.89 of the Revised Code:

(A) "Certification requirements" means the requirements for nursing facilities established under the "Social Security Act, "sections 1819 and 1919, 42 U.S.C. 1395i-3 and 1396r.

(B) "Compliance" means substantially meeting all applicable certification requirements.

(C) "Contracting agency" means a state agency that has entered into a contract with the department of medicaid under section 5165.63 of the Revised Code.

(D)(1) "Deficiency" means a finding cited by the department of health during a survey, on the basis of one or more actions, practices, situations, or incidents occurring at a nursing facility, that constitutes a severity level three finding, severity level four finding, scope level three finding, or scope level four finding. Whenever the finding is a repeat finding, "deficiency" also includes any finding that is a severity level two and scope level one finding, a severity level two and scope level two finding, or a severity level one and scope level two finding.

(2) "Cluster of deficiencies" means deficiencies that result from noncompliance with two or more certification requirements and are causing or resulting from the same action, practice, situation, or incident.

(E) "Emergency" means either of the following:

(1) A deficiency or cluster of deficiencies that creates a condition of immediate jeopardy;

(2) An unexpected situation or sudden occurrence of a serious or urgent nature that creates a substantial likelihood that one or more residents of a nursing facility may be seriously harmed if allowed to remain in the facility, including the following:

(a) A flood or other natural disaster, civil disaster, or similar event;

(b) A labor strike that suddenly causes the number of staff members in a nursing facility to be below that necessary for resident care.

(F) "Finding" means a finding of noncompliance with certification requirements determined by the department of health under section 5165.66 of the Revised Code.

(G) "Immediate jeopardy" means that one or more residents of a nursing facility are in imminent danger of serious physical or life-threatening harm.

(H) "Medicaid eligible resident" means a person who is a resident of a nursing facility, or is applying for admission to a nursing facility, and is eligible for nursing facility services under the medicaid program.

(I) "Noncompliance" means failure to substantially meet all applicable certification requirements.

(J) "Nursing facility" includes a skilled nursing facility to the extent the context requires.

(K) "Repeat finding" or "repeat deficiency" means a finding or deficiency cited pursuant to a survey, to which both of the following apply:

(1) The finding or deficiency involves noncompliance with the same certification requirement, and the same kind of actions, practices, situations, or incidents caused by or resulting from the noncompliance, as were cited in the immediately preceding standard survey or another survey conducted subsequent to the immediately preceding standard survey of the facility. For purposes of this division, actions, practices, situations, or incidents may be of the same kind even though they involve different residents, staff, or parts of the facility.

(2) The finding or deficiency is cited subsequent to a determination by the department of health that the finding or deficiency cited on the immediately preceding standard survey, or another survey conducted subsequent to the immediately preceding standard survey, had been corrected.

(L)(1) "Scope level one finding" means a finding of noncompliance by a nursing facility in which the actions, situations, practices, or incidents causing or resulting from the noncompliance affect one or a very limited number of facility residents and involve one or a very limited number of facility staff members.

(2) "Scope level two finding" means a finding of noncompliance by a nursing facility in which the actions, situations, practices, or incidents causing or resulting from the noncompliance affect more than a limited number of facility residents or involve more than a limited number of facility staff members, but the number or percentage of facility residents affected or staff members involved and the number or frequency of the actions, situations, practices, or incidents in short succession does not establish any reasonable degree of predictability of similar actions, situations, practices, or incidents occurring in the future.

(3) "Scope level three finding" means a finding of noncompliance by a nursing facility in which the actions, situations, practices, or incidents causing or resulting from the noncompliance affect more than a limited number of facility residents or involve more than a limited number of facility staff members, and the number or percentage of facility residents affected or staff members involved or the number or frequency of the actions, situations, practices, or incidents in short succession establishes a reasonable degree of predictability of similar actions, situations, practices, or incidents occurring in the future.

(4) "Scope level four finding" means a finding of noncompliance by a nursing facility causing or resulting from actions, situations, practices, or incidents that involve a sufficient number or percentage of facility residents or staff members or occur with sufficient regularity over time that the noncompliance can be considered systemic or pervasive in the facility.

(M)(1) "Severity level one finding" means a finding of noncompliance by a nursing facility that has not caused and, if continued, is unlikely to cause physical harm to a facility resident, mental or emotional harm to a resident, or a violation of a resident's rights that results in physical, mental, or emotional harm to the resident.

(2) "Severity level two finding" means a finding of noncompliance by a nursing facility that, if continued over time, will cause, or is likely to cause, physical harm to a facility resident, mental or emotional harm to a resident, or a violation of a resident's rights that results in physical, mental, or emotional harm to the resident.

(3) "Severity level three finding" means a finding of noncompliance by a nursing facility that has caused physical harm to a facility resident, mental or emotional harm to a resident, or a violation of a resident's rights that results in physical, mental, or emotional harm to the resident.

(4) "Severity level four finding" means a finding of noncompliance by a nursing facility that has caused life-threatening harm to a facility resident or caused a resident's death.

(N) "State agency" has the same meaning as in section 1.60 of the Revised Code.

(O) "Substandard care" means care furnished in a facility in which the department of health has cited a deficiency or deficiencies that constitute one of the following:

(1) A severity level four finding, regardless of scope;

(2) A severity level three and scope level four finding, in the quality of care provided to residents;

(3) A severity level three and scope level three finding, in the quality of care provided to residents.

(P)(1) "Survey" means a survey of a nursing facility conducted under section 5165.64 of the Revised Code.

(2) "Standard survey" means a survey conducted by the department of health under division (A) of section 5165.64 of the Revised Code and includes an extended survey.

(3) "Follow-up survey" means a survey conducted by the department of health to determine whether a nursing facility has substantially corrected deficiencies cited in a previous survey.

**HISTORY:**

143 v H 822 (Eff 12-13-90); 148 v H 471. Eff 7-1-2000; 2011 HB 153, § 101.01, eff. Sept. 29, 2011; 2013 HB 59, § 101.01, eff. Sept. 29, 2013.

**Editor's Notes**

This section was formerly codified as RC § 5111.35.

**Amendment Notes**

The 2013 amendment rewrote the first paragraph; substituted "sections 5165.60 to 5111.62" for "sections 5111.35 to 5165.89" in the introductory language; rewrote (A); substituted "medicaid under section 5165.63" for "job and family services under section 5111.38" in (C); substituted "section 5165.66" for "section 5111.41" in (F); substituted "for nursing facility services under the medicaid program" for "to receive financial assistance under the medical assistance program for the care the person receives in such a facility" in (H); rewrote (J); deleted (K) and (L), which read: "(K) 'Provider' means a person, institution, or entity that furnishes nursing facility services under a medical assistance program provider agreement. (L) 'Provider agreement' means a contract between the department of job and family services and a provider for the provision of nursing facility services under the medicaid program"; redesignated former (M) through (R) as (K) through (P); and substituted "section 5165.64" for "section 5111.39" in present (P)(1) and (P)(2).

The 2011 amendment inserted (L); and redesignated former (L) through (Q) as (M) through (R).

## NOTES TO DECISIONS

**Enhancement of penalty**

Enhancement of a civil monetary penalty that the Ohio Department of Health imposed on a nursing facility after finding non-compliance was proper under R.C. 5111.49(A)(1)(g); the record indicated that the violation was a repeat deficiency under R.C. 5111.35(L). Pineview Manor, Inc. v. Ohio Dep't of Health, 2003-Ohio-5762, 2003 Ohio App. LEXIS 5132 (Ohio Ct. App., Franklin County 2003).

## RESEARCH REFERENCES AND PRACTICE AIDS

**Cross-References to Related Sections**

Administration of survey and certification requirements for facilities; review of cited deficiencies, RC § 3721.022.

Resident may file grievance; procedure upon complaint to department of health, RC § 3721.17.

Residents' rights concerning transfer or discharge, RC §§ 3721.13, 3721.16.

## § 5165.61 Rules for administration and enforcement.

The medicaid director may adopt rules under section 5165.02 of the Revised Code that are consistent with regulations, guidelines, and procedures issued by the United States secretary of health and human services under the "Social Security Act," sections 1819 and 1919, 42 U.S.C. 1395i-3 and 1396r, and necessary for administration and enforcement of sections 5165.60 to 5165.89 of the Revised Code. If the secretary does not issue appropriate regulations for enforcement of those sections of the "Social Security Act" on or before December 13, 1990, the medicaid director may adopt, under section 5165.02 of the Revised Code, rules that are consistent with those sections and with sections 5165.60 to 5165.89 of the Revised Code.

Titles 39 — 57

**HISTORY:**
143 v H 822 (Eff 12-13-90); 148 v H 471. Eff 7-1-2000; 2013 HB 59, § 101.01, eff. Sept. 29, 2013.

**Editor's Notes**
This section was formerly codified as RC § 5111.36.

**Amendment Notes**
The 2013 amendment rewrote the section.

**RESEARCH REFERENCES AND PRACTICE AIDS**

**Cross-References to Related Sections**
Definitions, RC § 5165.60.
Department may enforce provisions directly or through contracting agencies, RC § 5165.62.

### § 5165.62 Department may enforce provisions directly or through contracting agencies.

The department of medicaid is hereby authorized to enforce sections 5165.60 to 5165.89 of the Revised Code. The department may enforce the sections directly or through contracting agencies. The department and agencies shall enforce the sections in accordance with the requirements of the "Social Security Act," sections 1819 and 1919, 42 U.S.C. 1395i-3 and 1396r, that apply to nursing facilities; with regulations, guidelines, and procedures adopted by the United States secretary of health and human services for the enforcement of those sections of the "Social Security Act"; and with the rules authorized by section 5165.61 of the Revised Code. The department and agencies shall enforce sections 5165.60 to 5165.89 of the Revised Code for purposes of the medicare program only to the extent prescribed by the regulations, guidelines, and procedures issued by the secretary under the "Social Security Act," section 1819, 42 U.S.C. 1395i-3.

**HISTORY:**
143 v H 822 (Eff 12-13-90); 148 v H 471. Eff 7-1-2000; 2013 HB 59, § 101.01, eff. Sept. 29, 2013.

**Editor's Notes**
This section was formerly codified as RC § 5111.37.

**Amendment Notes**
The 2013 amendment substituted "medicaid" for "job and family services" in the first sentence; substituted "sections 5165.60 to 5165.89" for "sections 5111.35 to 5111.62" in the first and last sentences; in the third sentence, substituted "the 'Social Security Act,' sections 1819 and 1919, 42 U.S.C. 1395i-3 and 1396r" for "sections 1819 and 1919 of the 'Social Security Act,' 49 Stat. 620 (1935), 42 U.S.C.A. 301, as amended", "those sections" for "sections 1819 and 1919", and "authorized by section 5165.61" for "adopted under section 5111.36"; and in the last sentence, deleted "Title XVIII of the 'Social Security Act'" following "medicare program" and substituted "the 'Social Security Act,' section 1819, 42 U.S.C. 1395i-3" for "section 1819 of that act".

**RESEARCH REFERENCES AND PRACTICE AIDS**

**Cross-References to Related Sections**
Definitions, RC § 5165.60.

### § 5165.63 Contracts with other state agencies.

The department of medicaid may enter into contracts with other state agencies pursuant to section 5162.35 of the Revised Code that authorize the agencies to perform all or part of the duties assigned to the department of medicaid under sections 5165.60 to 5165.89 of the Revised Code. Each contract shall specify the duties the agency is authorized to perform and the sections of the Revised Code under which the agency is authorized to perform those duties.

**HISTORY:**
143 v H 822 (Eff 12-13-90); 148 v H 471. Eff 7-1-2000; 2013 HB 59, § 101.01, eff. Sept. 29, 2013.

**Editor's Notes**
This section was formerly codified as RC § 5111.38.

**Amendment Notes**
The 2013 amendment, in the first sentence, substituted "medicaid" for "job and family services" twice, inserted "pursuant to section 5162.35 of the Revised Code", and substituted "sections 5165.60 to 5165.89" for "sections 5111.35 to 5111.62".

**RESEARCH REFERENCES AND PRACTICE AIDS**

**Cross-References to Related Sections**
Contracts for administration of components; medicaid administrative reimbursement fund, RC § 5162.35.

### § 5165.64 Surveys of every nursing facility.

(A) The department of health shall conduct a survey, titled a standard survey, of every nursing facility in this state on a statewide average of not more than once every twelve months. Each nursing facility shall undergo a standard survey at least once every fifteen months as a condition of meeting certification requirements. The department may extend a standard survey; such a survey is titled an extended survey.

(B) The department may conduct surveys in addition to standard surveys when it considers them necessary.

(C) The department shall conduct surveys in accordance with the regulations, guidelines, and procedures issued by the United States secretary of health and human services under Title XVIII and Title XIX, sections 5165.65 to 5165.68 of the Revised Code, and rules adopted under section 3721.022 of the Revised Code.

**HISTORY:**
143 v H 822. Eff 12-13-90; 2013 HB 59, § 101.01, eff. Sept. 29, 2013.

**Editor's Notes**
This section was formerly codified as RC § 5111.39.

**Amendment Notes**
The 2013 amendment, in (C), substituted "Title XVIII and Title XIX" for "Titles XVIII and XIX of the 'Social Security Act,' 49 Stat. 620 (1935), 42 U.S.C.A. 301, as amended" and substituted "sections 5165.65 to 5165.68" for "sections 5111.40 to 5111.42".

**NOTES TO DECISIONS**

Analysis

Discovery
Standard survey

**Discovery**
Nursing home failed to properly invoke the peer review privilege of R.C. 2305.252 with regard to any complaint reports included in survey materials collected by the Ohio Department of Health concerning the nursing home. The affidavit the nursing home cited as the basis of its privilege claim contained no reference to "family/patient complaints" and the material was not generated by or at the request of the peer review committee by rather by the Department of Health pursuant to R.C. 5111.39 and related provisions. Large v. Heartland-Lansing of Bridgeport Ohio, LLC, 2013-Ohio-2877, 995 N.E.2d 872, 2013 Ohio App. LEXIS 2923 (Ohio Ct. App., Belmont County 2013).

**Standard survey**
Evidence supported affirming an Ohio Department of Health order under R.C. 119.12, holding a nursing facility in violation of 42 C.F.R. § 483.25, and imposing a civil monetary penalty; a standard survey pursuant to R.C. 5111.39(A) revealed that a resident had developed a second pressure sore that would have been avoidable with the proper plan in place, a deficiency under R.C. 5111.41(A). Pineview Manor, Inc. v. Ohio Dep't of Health, 2003-Ohio-5762, 2003 Ohio App. LEXIS 5132 (Ohio Ct. App., Franklin County 2003).

**RESEARCH REFERENCES AND PRACTICE AIDS**

**Cross-References to Related Sections**
Resident may file grievance; procedure upon complaint to department of health; retaliation prohibited, RC § 3721.17.
Survey, standard survey defined, RC § 5165.60.

### § 5165.65 Survey team to conduct exit interview.

(A) A department of health survey team shall conclude each survey of a nursing facility not later than one business day after the survey team ceases to need to be on site at the facility for the survey. Not later than the day that the survey team concludes the survey, the survey team shall conduct an exit interview with the administrator or other person in charge of the facility and any other facility staff members designated by the administrator or person in charge of the facility. During the exit interview, at the request of the administrator or other person in charge of the facility, the survey team shall provide one of the following, as selected by the survey team:

(1) Copies of all survey notes and any other written materials created during the survey;

(2) A written summary of the survey team's recommendations regarding findings of noncompliance with certification requirements;

(3) An audio or audiovisual recording of the interview. If the survey team selects this option, at least two copies of the recording shall be made and the survey team shall select one copy to be kept by the survey team for use by the department of health.

(B) All expenses of copying under division (A)(1) of this section or recording under division (A)(3) of this section, including the cost of the copy of the recording kept by the survey team, shall be paid by the facility.

**HISTORY:**

143 v H 822. Eff 12-13-90; 2013 HB 59, § 101.01, eff. Sept. 29, 2013; 2014 HB 483, § 101.01, eff. Sept. 15, 2014.

**Editor's Notes**

This section was formerly codified as RC § 5111.40.

**Amendment Notes**

The 2014 amendment by HB 483, in the introductory language of (A), added the first sentence and in the second sentence, substituted "Not later than the day that the survey team concludes the survey, the" for "At the conclusion of each survey, the department of health" and deleted "nursing" following "charge of the".

The 2013 amendment made no changes.



**RESEARCH REFERENCES AND PRACTICE AIDS**

**Cross-References to Related Sections**

Definitions, RC § 5165.60.

Surveys of every nursing facility, RC § 5165.64.

### § 5165.66 Determination of whether actions, practices, situations or incidents can be justified; declaration and citing of findings.

(A) Except as provided in section 3721.17 of the Revised Code, a finding shall be cited only on the basis of a survey and a determination that one or more actions, practices, situations, or incidents at a nursing facility caused or resulted from the facility's failure to comply with one or more certification requirements. The department of health shall determine whether the actions, practices, situations, or incidents can be justified by either of the following:

(1) The actions, practices, situations, or incidents resulted from a resident exercising the resident's rights guaranteed under the laws of the United States or of this state;

(2) The actions, practices, situations, or incidents resulted from a facility following the orders of a person licensed under Chapter 4731. of the Revised Code to practice medicine or surgery or osteopathic medicine and surgery.

(B) If the department of health determines both that the actions, practices, situations, or incidents cannot be justified by the factors identified in division (A) of this section and that one or more of the following are applicable, the department shall declare that the actions, practices, situations, or incidents constitute a finding:

(1) The actions, practices, situations, or incidents could have been prevented by one or more persons involved in the facility's operation;

(2) No person involved in the facility's operation identified the actions, practices, situations, or incidents prior to the survey;

(3) Prior to the survey, no person involved in the facility's operation initiated action to correct the noncompliance caused by or resulting in the actions, practices, situations, or incidents;

(4) The facility does not have in effect, if needed, a contingency plan that is reasonably calculated to prevent physical, mental, or emotional harm to residents while permanent corrective action is being taken.

(C) The department of health shall determine the severity level and scope level of each finding.

(D) A deficiency that is substantially corrected within the time limits specified in sections 5165.79 to 5165.83 of the Revised Code and for which no remedy is imposed, shall be counted as a deficiency for the purpose of determining whether a deficiency is a repeat deficiency.

(E) Whenever the department of health determines that during the period between two surveys a finding existed at the facility, but the facility substantially corrected it prior to the second survey, the department shall cite it. However, the department of medicaid or a contracting agency shall impose a remedy only as provided in division (C) of section 5165.72 of the Revised Code.

(F) Immediately upon determining the severity and scope of a finding at a nursing facility, the department of health shall notify the department of medicaid and any contracting agency of the finding, the severity and scope of the finding, and whether the finding creates immediate jeopardy. Immediately upon determining that an emergency exists at a facility that does not result from a deficiency that creates immediate jeopardy, the department of health shall notify the department of medicaid and any contracting agency.

**HISTORY:**

143 v H 822 (Eff 12-13-90); 148 v H 471. Eff 7-1-2000; 2013 HB 59, § 101.01, eff. Sept. 29, 2013.

**Editor's Notes**

This section was formerly codified as RC § 5111.41.

**Amendment Notes**

The 2013 amendment substituted "sections 5165.79 to 5165.83" for "sections 5111.52 to 5111.56" in (D); substituted "medicaid" for "job and family services" throughout (E) and (F); and substituted "section 5165.72" for "section 5111.46" in (E).

**NOTES TO DECISIONS**

**Appeal**

Evidence supported affirming an Ohio Department of Health order under R.C. 119.12, holding a nursing facility in violation of 42 C.F.R. § 483.25, and imposing a civil monetary penalty; a standard survey pursuant to R.C. 5111.39(A) revealed that a resident had developed a second pressure sore that would have been avoidable with the proper plan in place, a deficiency under R.C. 5111.41(A). Pineview Manor, Inc. v. Ohio Dep't of Health, 2003-Ohio-5762, 2003 Ohio App. LEXIS 5132 (Ohio Ct. App., Franklin County 2003).

**RESEARCH REFERENCES AND PRACTICE AIDS**

**Cross-References to Related Sections**

Delivery or mailing of notice, statement or order, RC § 5165.86.

Facility to submit plan of correction for each finding cited, RC § 5165.69.

Finding defined, RC § 5165.60.

On-site monitoring of nursing facility; qualifications of monitors, RC § 5165.70.

Remedies for uncorrected deficiencies constituting severity level four findings; fines, RC § 5165.72.

Statement of deficiencies; notice of possible issuance of order denying payment or terminating facility's participation, RC § 5165.68.

Surveys of every nursing facility, RC § 5165.64.

### § 5165.67 Use of results of survey.

The results of a survey of a nursing facility that is conducted under section 5165.64 of the Revised Code, including any statement of deficiencies and all findings and deficiencies cited in the statement on the basis of the survey, shall be used solely to determine the nursing facility's compliance with certification requirements or with this chapter or another chapter of the Revised Code. Those results of a survey, that statement of deficiencies, and the findings and deficiencies cited in that statement shall not be used in either of the following:

(A) Any court or in any action or proceeding that is pending in any court and are not admissible in evidence in any action or proceeding unless that action or proceeding is an appeal of an administrative action by the department of medicaid or contracting agency under this chapter or is an action by any department or agency of the state to enforce this chapter or another chapter of the Revised Code;

(B) An advertisement, unless the advertisement includes all of the following:

(1) The date the survey was conducted;

(2) A statement that the department of health conducts a survey of all nursing facilities at least once every fifteen months;

(3) If a finding or deficiency cited in the statement of deficiencies has been substantially corrected, a statement that the finding or deficiency has been substantially corrected and the date that the finding or deficiency was substantially corrected;

(4) The number of findings and deficiencies cited in the statement of deficiencies on the basis of the survey;

(5) The average number of findings and deficiencies cited in a statement of deficiencies on the basis of a survey conducted under section 5165.64 of the Revised Code during the same calendar year as the survey used in the advertisement;

(6) A statement that the advertisement is neither authorized nor endorsed by the department or any other government agency.

Nothing in this section prohibits the results of a survey, a statement of deficiencies, or the findings and deficiencies cited in that statement on the basis of the survey under this section from being used in a criminal investigation or prosecution.

**HISTORY:**

149 v H 412. Eff 11-7-2002; 2013 HB 59, § 101.01, eff. Sept. 29, 2013; 2014 hb290, § 1, effective March 23, 2015.

**Editor's Notes**

The provisions of § 4 of HB 412 (149 v —) read as follows:

SECTION 4. If any provision of section 2305.11, 2315.21, 3721.02, or 3721.17 of the Revised Code, as amended by this act, any provision of section 5111.411 of the Revised Code, as enacted by this act, or the application of any provision of those sections to any person or circumstance is held invalid, the invalidity does not affect other provisions or applications of the particular section or related sections that can be given effect without the invalid provision or application, and to this end the provisions of the particular section are severable.

This section was formerly codified as RC § 5111.411.

**Amendment Notes**

The 2014 amendment by HB 290, added "either of the following" to the end of the introductory language; added the (A) designation; added (B); and made a related change.

The 2013 amendment, in the first sentence, substituted "section 5165.64" for "section 5111.39" in the first sentence and substituted "medicaid" for "job and family services" in the second sentence.

### NOTES TO DECISIONS

**Inadmissibility**

Trial court did not err in finding the nursing facility survey documents inadmissible at trial because one statute was inapplicable and the documents were inadmissible pursuant to the other statute, since the documents proffered were in compliance with the Revised Code Chapter. The documents proffered were not related to the licensing of the nursing home; instead, they were related to the facility's compliance with Medicare and Medicaid requirements. Sliwinski v. Vill. of St. Edwards, 2014-Ohio-4655, 2014 Ohio App. LEXIS 4539 (Ohio Ct. App., Summit County 2014).

## § 5165.68 Statement of deficiencies; notice of possible issuance of order denying payment or terminating facility's participation.

(A) Not later than ten days after an exit interview, including an exit interview at which a department of health survey team discloses a finding that immediate jeopardy exists, the department of health shall deliver to the nursing facility a detailed statement, titled a statement of deficiencies, setting forth all findings and deficiencies cited on the basis of the survey, including any finding cited pursuant to division (E) of section 5165.66 of the Revised Code. The statement shall indicate the severity and scope level of each finding and fully describe the incidents or other facts that form the basis of the department's determination of the existence of each finding and deficiency. A failure by the survey team to completely disclose in the exit interview every finding that may result from the survey does not affect the validity of any finding or deficiency cited in the statement of deficiencies. On request of the facility, the department shall provide a copy of any written worksheet or other document produced by the survey team in making recommendations regarding scope and severity levels of findings and deficiencies.

(B) At the same time the department of health delivers a statement of deficiencies, it also shall deliver to the facility a separate written notice that states all of the following:

(1) That the department of medicaid or a contracting agency will issue an order under section 5165.84 of the Revised Code denying payment for any medicaid eligible residents admitted on and after the effective date of the order if the facility does not substantially correct, within ninety days after the exit interview, the deficiency or deficiencies cited in the statement of deficiencies in accordance with the plan of correction it submitted under section 5165.69 of the Revised Code;

(2) If a condition of substandard care has been cited on the basis of a standard survey and a condition of substandard care was also cited on the immediately preceding standard survey, that the department of medicaid or a contracting agency will issue an order under section 5165.84 of the Revised Code denying payment for any medicaid eligible residents admitted on and after the effective date of the order if a condition of substandard care is cited on the basis of the next standard survey;

(3) That the department of medicaid or a contracting agency will issue an order under section 5165.88 of the Revised Code terminating the facility's participation in the medicaid program if either of the following applies:

(a) The facility does not substantially correct the deficiency or deficiencies in accordance with the plan of correction it submitted under section 5165.69 of the Revised Code within six months after the exit interview.

(b) The facility substantially corrects the deficiency or deficiencies within the six-month period, but after correcting it, the department of health, based on a follow-up survey conducted during the remainder of the six-month period, determines that the facility has failed to maintain compliance with certification requirements.

**HISTORY:**

143 v H 822 (Eff 12-13-90); 148 v H 471. Eff 7-1-2000; 2013 HB 59, § 101.01, eff. Sept. 29, 2013; 2014 HB 483, § 101.01, eff. Sept. 15, 2014.

**Editor's Notes**

This section was formerly codified as RC § 5111.42.

**Amendment Notes**

The 2014 amendment by HB 483 inserted "including an exit interview at which a department of health survey team discloses a finding that immediate jeopardy exists" in the first sentence of (A).

The 2013 amendment substituted "section 5165.66" for "section 5111.41" in the first sentence of (A); substituted "department of medicaid" for "department of job and family services" in (B)(1), (B)(2), and the introductory language of (B)(3); substituted "section 5165.84" for "section 5111.57" in (B)(1) and (B)(2); substituted "section 5165.69" for "section 5111.43" in (B)(1) and (B)(3)(a); and, in the introductory language of (B)(3), substituted "section 5165.88" for "section 5111.58" and "medicaid program" for "medical assistance program".

### RESEARCH REFERENCES AND PRACTICE AIDS

**Cross-References to Related Sections**

Definitions, RC § 5165.60.

Facility to submit plan of correction for each finding cited, RC § 5165.69.

Most recent statement of deficiencies to be readily accessible to residents, RC § 3721.12.

Review of cited deficiencies, RC § 3721.022.

Surveys of every nursing facility, RC § 5165.64.

**Ohio Administrative Code**
Department of health—
Medicaid certification appeal process. OAC 3701-63-01.

## § 5165.69 Facility to submit plan of correction for each finding cited.

(A) Whenever a nursing facility receives a statement of deficiencies under section 5165.68 of the Revised Code, the facility shall submit to the department of health for its approval a plan of correction for each finding cited in the statement. The plan shall include all of the following:

(1) Detailed descriptions of the actions the facility will take to correct each finding, including actions the facility will take to protect residents situated similarly to the residents affected by the causes of the findings;

(2) The date by which each finding will be corrected;

(3) A detailed description of an ongoing monitoring and improvement process to be used at the facility that is focused on preventing any recurrence of the causes of the findings;

(4) If the plan concerns a finding assigned a severity level indicating that a resident was harmed or immediate jeopardy exists, all of the following:

(a) Detailed analyses of the facts and circumstances of the finding, including identification of its cause;

(b) A detailed explanation of how the corrective actions described pursuant to division (A)(1) of this section relate to the cause of the finding identified pursuant to division (A)(4)(a) of this section;

(c) A detailed explanation of the relationship between the ongoing monitoring and improvement process described pursuant to division (A)(3) of this section and the cause of the finding identified pursuant to division (A)(4)(a) of this section.

(5) If the plan concerns a finding cited pursuant to division (E) of section 5165.66 of the Revised Code, a description of the actions the facility took to correct the finding and the date on which it was corrected.

(B)(1) The department shall approve any plan, and any modification of an existing plan a nursing facility submits to the department, that does both of the following:

(a) Conforms to the requirements for approval of plans of corrections, and modifications, established in the regulations, guidelines, and procedures issued by the United States secretary of health and human services under Title XVIII and Title XIX;

(b) Includes all the information required by division (A) of this section.

(2) The department may consult with the department of medicaid, department of aging, and office of the state long-term care ombudsman program when determining whether a plan, or modification of an existing plan, to which division (A)(4) of this section applies conforms to the requirements for approval. The department of health has sole authority to make the determination regardless of whether it consults with the other departments or office. The department shall not reject a facility's plan of correction or modification on the ground that the facility disputes the finding, if the plan or modification is reasonably calculated to correct the finding.

(C) A facility that complies with this section shall not be considered to have admitted the existence of a finding cited by the department.

**HISTORY:**
143 v H 822. Eff 12-13-90; 2013 HB 59, § 101.01, eff. Sept. 29, 2013.

**Editor's Notes**
This section was formerly codified as RC § 5111.43.

**Amendment Notes**
The 2013 amendment rewrote the section.

### RESEARCH REFERENCES AND PRACTICE AIDS

**Cross-References to Related Sections**
Conditions for continuing participation where certain deficiencies not corrected; order of termination, RC § 5165.71.
Definitions, RC § 5165.60.
Delivery or mailing of notice, statement or order, RC § 5165.86.
Implementation of plan; effect of correction of deficiency, RC § 5165.83.
Notice of correction of deficiency; follow-up survey, RC § 5165.82.
Order denying payment when deficiency is not corrected within ninety days or after three consecutive findings of substandard care, RC § 5165.84.
Remedies for uncorrected deficiencies —
Severity level four finding; termination order, RC § 5165.72.
Severity level one or two or severity level three, scope level two finding, RC § 5165.74.
Severity level three and scope level three or four finding, RC § 5165.68.
Statement of deficiencies; notice of possible issuance of order denying payment or terminating facility's participation, RC § 5165.68.
Termination of participation for failure to correct deficiency within six months, RC § 5165.85.

**Ohio Administrative Code**
Department of health—
Plan of correction; informal review process for deficiency citations. OAC 3701-63-02.

## § 5165.70 On-site monitoring of nursing facility; qualifications of monitors.

The department of health may appoint employees of the department to conduct on-site monitoring of a nursing facility whenever a finding is cited, including any finding cited pursuant to division (E) of section 5165.66 of the Revised Code, or an emergency is found to exist. Appointment of monitors under this section is not subject to appeal under section 5165.87 or any other section of the Revised Code. No employee of a facility for which monitors are appointed, no person employed by the facility within the previous two years, and no person who currently has a consulting or other contract with the department or the facility, shall be appointed as a monitor under this section. Every monitor appointed under this section shall have the professional qualifications necessary to monitor correction of the finding or elimination of the emergency.

**HISTORY:**
143 v H 822. Eff 12-13-90; 2013 HB 59, § 101.01, eff. Sept. 29, 2013.

**Editor's Notes**
This section was formerly codified as RC § 5111.44.

**Amendment Notes**
The 2013 amendment substituted "section 5165.66" for "section 5111.41" in the first sentence; and substituted "section 5165.87" for "section 5111.60" in the second sentence.

### RESEARCH REFERENCES AND PRACTICE AIDS

**Cross-References to Related Sections**
Appointment of on-site monitors, RC § 5165.82.
Definitions, RC § 5165.60.

## § 5165.71 Conditions for continuing participation where certain deficiencies not corrected; order of termination.

(A) If the department of health cites a deficiency or deficiencies that was not substantially corrected before a survey and that does not constitute a severity level four finding or create immediate jeopardy, the department of medicaid or a contracting agency shall permit the nursing facility to continue participating in the medicaid program for up to six months after the exit interview, if all of the following apply:

(1) The facility meets the requirements, established in regulations issued by the United States secretary of health and human services under Title XIX for certification of nursing facilities that have a deficiency.

(2) The department of health has approved a plan of correction submitted by the facility under section 5165.69 of the Revised Code for each deficiency.

(3) The provider agrees to repay the department of medicaid, in accordance with section 5165.85 of the Revised Code, the federal share of all payments made by the department to the facility during the six-month period following the exit interview if the facility does not within the six-month period substantially correct the deficiency or deficiencies in accordance with

the plan of correction submitted under section 5165.69 of the Revised Code.

(B) If any of the conditions in divisions (A)(1) to (3) of this section do not apply, the department of medicaid or contracting agency shall issue an order terminating the facility's participation in the medicaid program. An order issued under this division is subject to appeal under Chapter 119. of the Revised Code. The order shall not take effect prior to the later of the thirtieth day after it is delivered to the facility or, if the order is appealed, the date on which a final adjudication order upholding the termination becomes effective pursuant to Chapter 119. of the Revised Code.

(C) At the time the department of medicaid or contracting agency issues an order under division (B) of this section terminating a nursing facility's participation in the medicaid program, it may also impose, subject to section 5165.76 of the Revised Code, other remedies under sections 5165.72 to 5165.74 of the Revised Code.

**HISTORY:**

143 v H 822 (Eff 12-13-90); 145 v H 152 (Eff 7-1-93); 148 v H 471. Eff 7-1-2000; 2013 HB 59, § 101.01, eff. Sept. 29, 2013.

**Editor's Notes**

This section was formerly codified as RC § 5111.45.

**Amendment Notes**

The 2013 amendment substituted "department of medicaid" for "department of job and family services" throughout the section; substituted "medicaid program" for "medical assistance program" throughout the section; deleted "of the 'Social Security Act,' 49 Stat. 620 (1935), 42 U.S.C.A. 301, as amended" following "Title XIX" in (A)(1); substituted "section 5165.69" for "section 5111.43" in (A)(2) and (A)(3); substituted "section 5165.85" for "section 5111.58" in (A)(3); and, in (C), substituted "section 5165.76" for "section 5111.50" and "sections 5165.72 to 5165.74" for "sections 5111.46 to 5111.48".

**RESEARCH REFERENCES AND PRACTICE AIDS**

**Cross-References to Related Sections**

Definitions, RC § 5165.60.

Fine collected if termination order does not take effect, RC § 5165.76.

Remedies subject to appeal under RC Chapter 119, RC § 5165.87.

Transfer of residents when facility is closed; appointment of temporary manager or special master, RC § 5165.80.

## § 5165.72 Remedies for uncorrected deficiencies constituting severity level four findings; termination order.

(A) If the department of health cites a deficiency, or cluster of deficiencies, that was not substantially corrected before a survey and constitutes a severity level four finding, the department of medicaid or contracting agency shall, subject to sections 5165.79 to 5165.83 of the Revised Code, impose a remedy for the deficiency or cluster of deficiencies. The department or agency may act under either division (A)(1) or (2) of this section:

(1) The department or agency may impose one or more of the following remedies:

(a) Issue an order terminating the nursing facility's participation in the medicaid program.

(b) Do either of the following:

(i) Regardless of whether the provider consents, appoint a temporary manager of the facility.

(ii) Apply to the common pleas court of the county in which the facility is located for such injunctive or other equitable relief as is necessary for the appointment of a special master with such powers and authority over the facility and length of appointment as the court considers necessary.

(c) Do either of the following:

(i) Issue an order denying medicaid payments to the facility for all medicaid eligible residents admitted after the effective date of the order;

(ii) Impose a fine.

(d) Issue an order denying medicaid payments to the facility for medicaid eligible residents admitted after the effective date of the order who have certain diagnoses or special care needs specified by the department or agency.

(2) The department or agency may impose one or more of the following remedies:

(a) Appoint, subject to the continuing consent of the provider, a temporary manager of the facility;

(b) Do either of the following:

(i) Regardless of whether the provider consents, appoint a temporary manager of the facility;

(ii) Apply to the common pleas court of the county in which the facility is located for such injunctive or other equitable relief as is necessary for the appointment of a special master with such powers and authority over the facility and length of appointment as the court considers necessary.

(c) Do either of the following:

(i) Issue an order denying medicaid payments to the facility for all medicaid eligible residents admitted after the effective date of the order;

(ii) Impose a fine.

(d) Issue an order denying medicaid payments to the facility for medicaid eligible residents admitted after the effective date of the order who have certain diagnoses or special care needs specified by the department or agency;

(e) Issue an order requiring the facility to correct the deficiency or cluster of deficiencies under the plan of correction submitted by the facility and approved by the department of health under section 5165.69 of the Revised Code.

(B) The department of medicaid or contracting agency shall deliver a written order issued under division (A)(1) of this section terminating a nursing facility's participation in the medicaid program to the facility within five days after the exit interview. If the facility alleges, at any time prior to the later of the twentieth day after the exit interview or the fifteenth day after it receives the order, that the deficiency or cluster of deficiencies for which the order was issued has been substantially corrected, the department of health shall conduct a follow-up survey to determine whether the deficiency or cluster of deficiencies has been substantially corrected. The order shall take effect and the facility's participation shall terminate on the twentieth day after the exit interview, unless the facility has substantially corrected the deficiency or cluster of deficiencies that constituted a severity level four finding or did not receive notice from the department of medicaid or contracting agency within five days after the exit interview. In the latter case, the order shall take effect and the facility's participation shall terminate on the fifteenth day after the facility received the order.

(C) If the department of health cites a deficiency or cluster of deficiencies pursuant to division (E) of section 5165.66 of the Revised Code that constituted a severity level four finding, the department of medicaid or a contracting agency shall, subject to section 5165.83 of the Revised Code, impose a fine. The fine shall be in effect for a period equal to the number of days the deficiency or cluster of deficiencies existed at the facility.

**HISTORY:**

143 v H 822 (Eff 12-13-90); 148 v H 471. Eff 7-1-2000; 2013 HB 59, § 101.01, eff. Sept. 29, 2013.

**Editor's Notes**

This section was formerly codified as RC § 5111.46.

**Amendment Notes**

The 2013 amendment substituted "department of medicaid" for "department of job and family services" in the first sentence of the introductory language of (A), in the first and third sentences of (B), and in the first sentence of (C); substituted "sections 5165.79 to 5165.83" for "sections 5111.52 to 5111.56" in the first sentence of the introductory language of (A); substituted "medicaid program" for "medical assistance program" in (A)(1)(a) and the first sentence of (B); substituted "medicaid payments to the facility" for "payment to the facility under the medical assistance program" in (A)(1)(c)(i), (A)(1)(d), (A)(2)(c)(i), and (A)(2)(d); substituted "section 5165.69" for "section 5111.43" in (A)(2)(e); and, in (C), substituted "section 5165.66" for "section 5111.41" and "section 5165.83" for "section 5111.56".

**RESEARCH REFERENCES AND PRACTICE AIDS**

**Cross-References to Related Sections**

Amount and number of fines; effect of correction of deficiency; interest; means of collection, RC § 5165.83.

Conditions for continuing participation where certain deficiencies not corrected, RC § 5165.71.
Considerations in imposing remedies and fines; statement provided to facility, RC § 5165.75.
Definitions, RC § 5165.60.
Determination of whether actions, practices, situations or incidents can be justified; declaration and citing of findings, RC § 5165.66.
Fine collected if termination order does not take effect, RC § 5165.76.
Remedies subject to appeal under RC Chapter 119, RC § 5165.87.
Remedies where emergency exists, RC § 5165.77.
Residents to whom denial of medicaid payments applies; publication of orders, RC § 5165.82.
Transfer of residents when facility is closed; appointment of temporary manager or special master, RC § 5165.80.
Qualifications, compensation and powers of temporary manager or special master; warning notice prior to action, RC § 5165.81.

**Ohio Rules**

Injunctions, CivR 65.

### § 5165.73 Remedies for uncorrected deficiencies constituting severity level three and scope level three or four findings.

If the department of health cites a deficiency, or cluster of deficiencies, that was not substantially corrected before a survey and constitutes a severity level three and scope level three or four finding, the department of medicaid or a contracting agency may, subject to sections 5165.82 and 5165.83 of the Revised Code, impose one or more of the following remedies:

(A) Do either of the following:

(1) Issue an order denying medicaid payments to the facility for all medicaid eligible residents admitted after the effective date of the order;

(2) Impose a fine.

(B) Issue an order denying medicaid payments to the facility for medicaid eligible residents admitted after the effective date of the order who have certain diagnoses or special care needs specified by the department or agency;

(C) Issue an order requiring the facility to correct the deficiency or cluster of deficiencies under the plan of correction submitted by the facility and approved by the department of health under section 5165.69 of the Revised Code.

**HISTORY:**

143 v H 822 (Eff 12-13-90); 148 v H 471. Eff 7-1-2000; 2013 HB 59, § 101.01, eff. Sept. 29, 2013.

**Editor's Notes**

This section was formerly codified as RC § 5111.47.

**Amendment Notes**

The 2013 amendment, in the introductory language, substituted "medicaid" for "job and family services" and "sections 5165.82 and 5165.83" for "sections 5111.55 and 5111.56"; substituted "medicaid payments to the facility" for "payment to the facility under the medical assistance program" in (A)(1) and (B); and substituted "section 5165.69" for "section 5111.43" in (C).

#### RESEARCH REFERENCES AND PRACTICE AIDS

**Cross-References to Related Sections**

Amount and number of fines; effect of correction of deficiency; interest; means of collection, RC § 5165.83.
Conditions for continuing participation where certain deficiencies not corrected; order of termination, RC § 5165.71.
Considerations in imposing remedies and fines; statement provided to facility, RC § 5165.75.
Definitions, RC § 5165.60.
Fine collected if termination order does not take effect, RC § 5165.76.
Remedies subject to appeal under RC Chapter 119, RC § 5165.87.
Remedies where emergency exists, RC § 5165.77.
Residents to whom denial of medicaid payments applies; publication of orders, RC § 5165.82.

### § 5165.74 Remedies for uncorrected deficiencies constituting severity level one or two or severity level three, scope level two finding.

(A) If the department of health cites a deficiency, or cluster of deficiencies, that was not substantially corrected before a survey and constitutes a severity level three and scope level two finding, the department of medicaid or a contracting agency may, subject to sections 5165.82 and 5165.83 of the Revised Code, impose one or more of the following remedies:

(1) Do either of the following:

(a) Issue an order denying medicaid payments to the facility for all medicaid eligible residents admitted after the effective date of the order;

(b) Impose a fine.

(2) Issue an order denying medicaid payments to the facility for medicaid eligible residents admitted after the effective date of the order who have certain diagnoses or special care needs specified by the department or agency;

(3) Issue an order requiring the facility to correct the deficiency or cluster of deficiencies under the plan of correction proposed by the facility and approved by the department of health under section 5165.69 of the Revised Code.

(B) If the department of health cites a deficiency, or cluster of deficiencies, that was not substantially corrected before a survey and constitutes a severity level three and scope level one finding, the department of medicaid or a contracting agency may, subject to sections 5165.82 and 5165.83 of the Revised Code, impose one or more of the following remedies:

(1) Impose a fine;

(2) Issue an order denying medicaid payments to the facility for medicaid eligible residents admitted after the effective date of the order who have certain diagnoses or special care needs specified by the department or agency;

(3) Issue an order requiring the facility to correct the deficiency or cluster of deficiencies under the plan of correction proposed by the facility and approved by the department of health under section 5165.69 of the Revised Code.

(C) If the department of health cites a deficiency, or cluster of deficiencies, that was not substantially corrected before a survey and constitutes a severity level two and a scope level three or four finding, the department of medicaid or a contracting agency may, subject to sections 5165.82 and 5165.83 of the Revised Code, impose one or more of the following remedies:

(1) Impose a fine;

(2) Issue an order denying medicaid payments to the facility for medicaid eligible residents admitted after the effective date of the order who have certain diagnoses or special care needs specified by the department or agency;

(3) Issue an order requiring the facility to correct the deficiency or cluster of deficiencies under the plan of correction submitted by the facility and approved by the department of health under section 5165.69 of the Revised Code.

(D) If the department of health cites a deficiency, or cluster of deficiencies, that was not substantially corrected before a survey, constitutes a severity level two and scope level one or two finding, and is a repeat finding, the department of medicaid or a contracting agency may issue an order requiring the facility to correct the deficiency or cluster of deficiencies under the plan of correction submitted by the facility and approved by the department of health under section 5165.69 of the Revised Code.

(E) If the department of health cites a deficiency, or cluster of deficiencies, that was not substantially corrected before a survey and constitutes a severity level one and scope level three or four finding, the department of medicaid or a contracting agency may issue an order requiring the facility to correct the deficiency or cluster of deficiencies under the plan of correction submitted by the facility and approved by the department of health under section 5165.69 of the Revised Code.

(F) If the department of health cites a deficiency, or cluster of deficiencies, that was not substantially corrected before a survey, constitutes a severity level one and scope level two finding, and is a repeat finding, the department of medicaid or a contracting agency may issue an order requiring the facility to correct the deficiency or cluster of deficiencies under the plan of correction submitted by the facility and approved by the department of health under section 5165.69 of the Revised Code.

**HISTORY:**

143 v H 822 (Eff 12-13-90); 148 v H 471. Eff 7-1-2000; 2013 HB 59, § 101.01, eff. Sept. 29, 2013.

**Editor's Notes**

This section was formerly codified as RC § 5111.48.

**Amendment Notes**

The 2013 amendment substituted "medicaid" for "job and family services" in the introductory language of (A) through (C) and in (D) through (F); substituted "sections 5165.82 and 5165.83" for "sections 5111.55 and 5111.56" in the introductory language of (A) through (C); substituted "medicaid payments to the facility" for "payment to the facility under the medical assistance program" in (A)(1)(a), (A)(2), (B)(2), and (C)(2); and substituted "section 5165.69" for "section 5111.43" in (A)(3), (B)(3), (C)(3), and (D) through (F).

**RESEARCH REFERENCES AND PRACTICE AIDS**

**Cross-References to Related Sections**

Amount and number of fines; effect of correction of deficiency; interest; means of collection, RC § 5165.83.

Conditions for continuing participation where certain deficiencies not corrected; order of termination, RC § 5165.71.

Considerations in imposing remedies and fines; statement provided to facility, RC § 5165.75.

Definitions, RC § 5165.60.

Fine collected if termination order does not take effect, RC § 5165.76.

Remedies subject to appeal under RC Chapter 119, RC § 5165.87.

Remedies where emergency exists, RC § 5165.77.

Residents to whom denial of medicaid payments applies; publication of orders, RC § 5165.82.

## § 5165.75 Considerations in imposing remedies and fines; statement provided to facility.

(A) In determining which remedies to impose under section 5165.72, 5165.73, or 5165.74 of the Revised Code, including whether a fine should be imposed, the department of medicaid or a contracting agency shall do both of the following:

(1) Impose the remedies that are most likely to achieve correction of deficiencies, encourage sustained compliance with certification requirements, and protect the health, safety, and rights of facility residents, but that are not directed at punishment of the facility;

(2) Consider all of the following:

(a) The presence or absence of immediate jeopardy;

(b) The relationships of groups of deficiencies to each other;

(c) The facility's history of compliance with certification requirements generally and in the specific area of the deficiency or deficiencies;

(d) Whether the deficiency or deficiencies are directly related to resident care;

(e) The corrective, long-term compliance, resident protective, and nonpunitive outcomes sought by the department or agency;

(f) The nature, scope, and duration of the noncompliance with certification requirements;

(g) The existence of repeat deficiencies;

(h) The category of certification requirements with which the facility is out of compliance;

(i) Any period of noncompliance with certification requirements that occurred between two certifications by the department of health that the facility was in compliance with certification requirements;

(j) The facility's degree of culpability;

(k) The accuracy, extent, and availability of facility records;

(*l*) The facility's financial condition, exclusive of any moneys donated to a facility that is an organization described in subsection 501(c)(3) and is tax exempt under subsection 501(a) of the "Internal Revenue Code of 1986," 100 Stat. 2085, 26 U.S.C.A. 1;

(m) Any adverse effect that the action or fine would have on the health and safety of facility residents;

(n) If the noncompliance that resulted in the citation of a deficiency or cluster of deficiencies existed before a change in ownership of the facility, whether the new owner or owners have had sufficient time to correct the noncompliance.

(B) Whenever the department or agency imposes remedies under section 5165.72, 5165.73, or 5165.74 of the Revised Code, it shall provide a written statement to the nursing facility that specifies all of the following:

(1) The effective date of each remedy;

(2) The deficiency or cluster of deficiencies for which each remedy is imposed;

(3) The severity and scope of the deficiency or cluster of deficiencies;

(4) The rationale, including all applicable factors specified in division (A) of this section, for imposing the remedies.

**HISTORY:**

143 v H 822 (Eff 12-13-90); 148 v H 471. Eff 7-1-2000; 2013 HB 59, § 101.01, eff. Sept. 29, 2013.

**Editor's Notes**

This section was formerly codified as RC § 5111.49.

**Amendment Notes**

The 2013 amendment substituted "section 5165.72, 5165.73, or 5165.74" for "section 5111.46, 5111.47, or 5111.48" in the introductory language of (A) and (B); and substituted "medicaid" for "job and family services" in the introductory language of (A).

**NOTES TO DECISIONS**

**Enhancement of penalty**

Enhancement of a civil monetary penalty that the Ohio Department of Health imposed on a nursing facility after finding non-compliance was proper under R.C. 5111.49(A)(1)(g); the record indicated that the violation was a repeat deficiency under R.C. 5111.35(L). Pineview Manor, Inc. v. Ohio Dep't of Health, 2003-Ohio-5762, 2003 Ohio App. LEXIS 5132 (Ohio Ct. App., Franklin County 2003).

**RESEARCH REFERENCES AND PRACTICE AIDS**

**Cross-References to Related Sections**

Amount and number of fines; effect of correction of deficiency; interest; means of collection, RC § 5165.83.

Definitions, RC § 5165.60.

Warning notice prior to action to appoint temporary manager, RC § 5111.54.

## § 5165.76 Fine collected if termination order does not take effect.

At the time the department of medicaid or a contracting agency, under section 5165.71, 5165.72, or 5165.77 of the Revised Code, issues an order terminating a nursing facility's participation in the medicaid program, the department or agency may also impose a fine, in accordance with sections 5165.72 to 5165.74 and 5165.83 of the Revised Code, to be collected in the event the termination order does not take effect. The department or agency shall not collect this fine if the termination order takes effect.

**HISTORY:**

143 v H 822 (Eff 12-13-90); 148 v H 471. Eff 7-1-2000; 2013 HB 59, § 101.01, eff. Sept. 29, 2013.

**Editor's Notes**

This section was formerly codified as RC § 5111.50.

**Amendment Notes**

The 2013 amendment, in the first sentence, substituted "department of medicaid" for "department of job and family services", "section 5165.71, 5165.72, or 5165.77" for "section 5111.45, 5111.46, or 5111.51", "medicaid program" for "medical assistance program", and "sections 5165.72 to 5165.74 and 5165.83" for "sections 5111.46 to 5111.48 and 5111.56".

**RESEARCH REFERENCES AND PRACTICE AIDS**

**Cross-References to Related Sections**

Conditions for continuing participation where certain deficiencies not corrected; order of termination, RC § 5165.71.

Definitions, RC § 5165.60.

## § 5165.77 Remedies where emergency exists.

(A) If the department of health finds during a survey that an emergency exists at a nursing facility, as the result of a deficiency or cluster of deficiencies that creates immediate jeopardy, the department of medicaid or a contracting agency shall impose one or more of the remedies described in division (A)(1) of this section and, in addition, may take one or both of the actions described in division (A)(2) of this section.

(1) The department or agency shall impose one or more of the following remedies:

(a) Appoint, subject to the continuing consent of the provider, a temporary manager of the facility;

(b) Apply to the common pleas court of the county in which the facility is located for a temporary restraining order, preliminary injunction, or such other injunctive or equitable relief as is necessary to close the facility, transfer one or more residents to other nursing facilities or other appropriate care settings, or otherwise eliminate the condition of immediate jeopardy. If the court grants such an order, injunction, or relief, it may appoint a special master empowered to implement the court's judgment under the court's direct supervision.

(c) Issue an order terminating the facility's participation in the medicaid program;

(d) Regardless of whether the provider consents, appoint a temporary manager of the facility.

(2) The department or agency may do one or both of the following:

(a) Issue an order denying medicaid payments to the facility for all medicaid eligible residents admitted after the effective date of the order;

(b) Impose remedies under sections 5165.72 to 5165.74 of the Revised Code appropriate to the severity and scope of the deficiency or cluster of deficiencies, except that the department or agency shall not impose a fine for the same deficiency for which the department or agency has issued an order under division (A)(2)(a) of this section.

(B) If the department of health, department of medicaid, or a contracting agency finds on the basis of a survey or other visit to the facility by representatives of that department or agency that an emergency exists at a facility that is not the result of a deficiency or cluster of deficiencies that constitutes immediate jeopardy, the department of medicaid or contracting agency may do either of the following:

(1) Appoint, subject to the continuing consent of the provider, a temporary manager of the facility;

(2) Apply to the common pleas court of the county in which the facility is located for a temporary restraining order, preliminary injunction, or such other injunctive or equitable relief as is necessary to close the facility, transfer one or more residents to other nursing facilities or other appropriate care settings, or otherwise eliminate the emergency. If the court grants such an order, injunction, or relief, it may appoint a special master empowered to implement the court's judgment under the court's direct supervision.

(C)(1) Prior to acting under division (A)(1)(b), (c), (d), or (2), or (B)(2) of this section, the department of medicaid or contracting agency shall give written notice to the facility specifying all of the following:

(a) The nature of the emergency, including the nature of any deficiency or deficiencies that caused the emergency;

(b) The nature of the action the department or agency intends to take unless the department of health determines that the facility, in the absence of state intervention, possesses the capacity to eliminate the emergency;

(c) The rationale for taking the action.

(2) If the department of health determines that the facility does not possess the capacity to eliminate the emergency in the absence of state intervention, the department of medicaid or contracting agency may immediately take action under division (A) or (B) of this section. If the department of health determines that the facility possesses the capacity to eliminate the emergency, the department of medicaid or contracting agency shall direct the facility to eliminate the emergency within five days after the facility's receipt of the notice. At the end of the five-day period, the department of health shall conduct a follow-up survey that focuses on the emergency. If the department of health determines that the facility has eliminated the emergency within the time period, the department of medicaid or contracting agency shall not act under division (A)(1)(b), (c), (d), or (2)(a), or (B)(2) of this section. If the department of health determines that the facility has failed to eliminate the emergency within the five-day period, the department of medicaid or contracting agency shall take appropriate action under division (A)(1)(b), (c), (d), or (2), or (B)(2) of this section.

(3) Until the written notice required by division (C)(1) of this section is actually delivered, no action taken by the department of medicaid or contracting agency under division (A)(1)(b), (c), (d), or (2), or (B)(2) of this section shall have any legal effect. In addition to the written notice, the department of health survey team shall give oral notice to the facility, at the time of the survey, concerning any recommendations the survey team intends to make that could form the basis of a determination that an emergency exists.

(D) The department of medicaid or contracting agency shall deliver a written order issued under division (A)(1) of this section terminating a nursing facility's participation in the medicaid program to the facility within five days after the exit interview. If the facility alleges, at any time prior to the later of the twentieth day after the exit interview or the fifteenth day after it receives the order, that the condition of immediate jeopardy for which the order was issued has been eliminated, the department of health shall conduct a follow-up survey to determine whether the immediate jeopardy has been eliminated. The order shall take effect and the facility's participation shall terminate on the twentieth day after the exit interview, unless the facility has eliminated the immediate jeopardy or did not receive notice from the department of medicaid or contracting agency within five days after the exit interview. In the latter case, the order shall take effect and the facility's participation shall terminate on the fifteenth day after the facility received the order.

(E) Any action taken by the department of medicaid or a contracting agency under division (A)(1)(c), (d), or (2)(a) of this section is subject to appeal under Chapter 119. of the Revised Code, except that the department or agency may take such action prior to and during the pendency of any proceeding under that chapter. No action taken by a facility under division (C) of this section to eliminate an emergency cited by the department of health shall be considered an admission by the facility of the existence of an emergency.

**HISTORY:**

143 v H 822 (Eff 12-13-90); 148 v H 471. Eff 7-1-2000; 2013 HB 59, § 101.01, eff. Sept. 29, 2013.

**Editor's Notes**

This section was formerly codified as RC § 5111.51.

**Amendment Notes**

The 2013 amendment substituted "department of medicaid" for "department of job and family services" throughout the section; substituted "medicaid program" for "medical assistance program" in (A)(1)(c) and the first sentence of (D); substituted "medicaid payments" for "payment" in (A)(2)(a); and substituted "sections 5165.72 to 5165.74" for "sections 5111.46 to 5111.48" in (A)(2)(b).

### RESEARCH REFERENCES AND PRACTICE AIDS

**Cross-References to Related Sections**

Definitions, RC § 5165.60.

Fine collected if termination order does not take effect, RC § 5165.76.

Injunction against operation of home without a license; elimination of real and present danger, RC § 3721.08.

Qualifications, compensation and powers of temporary manager or special master; warning notice prior to action, RC § 5165.81.

Remedies subject to appeal under RC Chapter 119, RC § 5165.87.

Residents to whom denial of medicaid payments applies; publication of orders, RC § 5165.82.

Transfer of residents when facility is closed; appointment of temporary manager or special master, RC § 5165.80.

**Ohio Rules**

Temporary restraining order, CivR 65.

## § 5165.771 Special focus facility program; Mandatory improvement schedule.

(A) As used in this section:

"SFF list" means the list of nursing facilities that the United States department of health and human services creates under the special focus facility program.

"Special focus facility program" means the program conducted by the United States secretary of health and human services pursuant to the "Social Security Act," section 1919(f)(10), 42 U.S.C. 1396r(f)(10).

"Table A" means the table included in the SFF list that identifies nursing facilities that are newly added to the SFF list.

"Table B" means the table included in the SFF list that identifies nursing facilities that have not improved.

"Table C" means the table included in the SFF list that identifies nursing facilities that have shown improvement.

"Table D" means the table included in the SFF list that identifies nursing facilities that have recently graduated from the special focus facility program.

(B) The department of medicaid shall issue an order terminating a nursing facility's participation in the medicaid program if any of the following apply:

(1) The nursing facility is listed in table A or table B on the effective date of this section and fails to be placed in table C not later than twelve months after the effective date of this section.

(2) The nursing facility is listed in table A, table B, or table C on the effective date of this section and fails to be placed in table D not later than twenty-four months after the effective date of this section.

(3) The nursing facility is placed in table A after the effective date of this section and fails to be placed in table C not later than twelve months after the nursing facility is placed in table A.

(4) The nursing facility is placed in table A after the effective date of this section and fails to be placed in table D not later than twenty-four months after the nursing facility is placed in table A.

(C) An order issued under this section is not subject to appeal under Chapter 119. of the Revised Code.

(D) To help a nursing facility avoid having its participation in the medicaid program terminated pursuant to division (B) of this section, the department of aging shall provide the nursing facility technical assistance through the nursing home quality initiative established under section 173.60 of the Revised Code at least four months before the department of medicaid would be required to terminate the nursing facility's participation.

**HISTORY:**

2013 HB 59, § 101.01, eff. Sept. 29, 2013.

**Amendment Notes**

The 2021 amendment by HB 110 rewrote the section.

### NOTES TO DECISIONS

Analysis

Due process
Property interest

**Due process**

Given the severity of the remedy imposed on a nursing facility under the statute for failure to be deemed to have shown improvement within 12 months, the inherent delays involved in the informal dispute resolution process, and that the Special Focus Facility program tables may not be based on the latest data, the ability to challenge survey results does not constitute an opportunity to be heard at a meaningful time and in a meaningful manner with respect to termination of a provider agreement. CT Ohio Portsmouth, LLC v. Ohio Dep't of Medicaid, 2020-Ohio-5091, 161 N.E.3d 803, 2020 Ohio App. LEXIS 3937 (Ohio Ct. App., Franklin County 2020).

Because of the inherent delays in challenging individual survey results and the Special Focus Facility list tables may not be based on the most recent survey data, there was a risk of erroneous deprivation due to the 12-month time limit contained in R.C. 5165.771; with respect to the government's interest, there are other provisions under R.C. Chapter 5165 that allow termination of a nursing facility's Medicaid provider agreement due to survey related deficiency findings. CT Ohio Portsmouth, LLC v. Ohio Dep't of Medicaid, 2020-Ohio-5091, 161 N.E.3d 803, 2020 Ohio App. LEXIS 3937 (Ohio Ct. App., Franklin County 2020).

Because Ohio law creates a constitutionally protected property interest in continued participation in the Medicaid program for nursing facilities and R.C. 5165.771 does not contain adequate procedural protections to prevent the deprivation of that interest without due process of law, the common pleas court did not err by finding R.C. 5165.771 to be facially unconstitutional in violation of the Due Process Clauses of the United States Constitution and the Ohio Constitution. CT Ohio Portsmouth, LLC v. Ohio Dep't of Medicaid, 2020-Ohio-5091, 161 N.E.3d 803, 2020 Ohio App. LEXIS 3937 (Ohio Ct. App., Franklin County 2020).

Because R.C. 5165.771 violates the Due Process Clause of the United States Constitution and the Due Course Clause of the Ohio Constitution, the common pleas court did not err by granting a permanent injunction prohibiting enforcement of R.C. 5165.771. CT Ohio Portsmouth, LLC v. Ohio Dep't of Medicaid, 2020-Ohio-5091, 161 N.E.3d 803, 2020 Ohio App. LEXIS 3937 (Ohio Ct. App., Franklin County 2020).

Given the severity of the remedy imposed on a nursing facility under the statute for failure to be deemed to have shown improvement within 12 months, the inherent delays involved in the informal dispute resolution process, and that the Special Focus Facility program tables may not be based on the latest data, the ability to challenge survey results does not constitute an opportunity to be heard at a meaningful time and in a meaningful manner with respect to termination of a provider agreement. CT Ohio Portsmouth, LLC v. Ohio Dep't of Medicaid, 2020-Ohio-5091, 161 N.E.3d 803, 2020 Ohio App. LEXIS 3937 (Ohio Ct. App., Franklin County 2020).

**Property interest**

Given the strict limits on the Ohio Department of Medicaid's authority and discretion, Ohio law creates a constitutionally protected property interest in continued participation in the Medicaid program; ODM has no discretion with respect to whether to enter a Medicaid provider agreement with a nursing facility, and participation in Ohio's Medicaid program is not terminable at the will of the state, but only where specified conditions are met. CT Ohio Portsmouth, LLC v. Ohio Dep't of Medicaid, 2020-Ohio-5091, 161 N.E.3d 803, 2020 Ohio App. LEXIS 3937 (Ohio Ct. App., Franklin County 2020).

Termination of a skilled nursing facility's Medicaid provider agreement, would deprive it of a constitutionally protected property interest because the facility had a constitutionally protected property interest in continued participation in the Medicaid program. CT Ohio Portsmouth, LLC v. Ohio Dep't of Medicaid, 2020-Ohio-5091, 161 N.E.3d 803, 2020 Ohio App. LEXIS 3937 (Ohio Ct. App., Franklin County 2020).



### § 5165.771 Special focus facility program; Mandatory improvement schedule.

(A) As used in this section:

(1) "SFF list" means the list of nursing facilities that the United States department of health and human services creates under the special focus facility program.

(2) "Special focus facility program" means the program conducted by the United States secretary of health and human services pursuant to the "Social Security Act," section 1919(f)(10), 42 U.S.C. 1396r(f)(10).

(3) "Table A" means the table included in the SFF list that identifies nursing facilities that are newly added to the SFF list.

(4) "Table B" means the table included in the SFF list that identifies nursing facilities that have not improved.

(5) "Table C" means the table included in the SFF list that identifies nursing facilities that have shown improvement.

(6) "Table D" means the table included in the SFF list that identifies nursing facilities that have recently graduated from the special focus facility program.

(B) The department of medicaid shall issue an order terminating a nursing facility's participation in the medicaid program if any of the following apply:

(1) The nursing facility is placed in table A or table B and fails to be placed in table C not later than twelve months after the facility is placed in table A or table B.

(2) The nursing facility is placed in table A, table B, or table C and fails to be placed in table D not later than twenty-four months after the facility is placed in table A, table B, or table C.

(3) The nursing facility is placed in table A and fails to be placed in table C not later than twelve months after the nursing facility is placed in table A.

(4) The nursing facility is placed in table A and fails to be placed in table D not later than twenty-four months after the nursing facility is placed in table A.

(C) A nursing facility may appeal, under Chapter 119. of the Revised Code, the length of time the facility is listed in a table as described under division (B) of this section. The medicaid director shall adopt rules under section 5165.02 of the Revised Code as necessary to provide for an appeal under this division. Notwithstanding the timeframes listed in section 119.07 of the Revised Code, the rules may provide for an expedited appeal under this division.

(D) A nursing facility shall take all steps necessary to improve its quality of care to avoid having its participation in the medicaid program terminated pursuant to division (B) of this section. Technical assistance and quality improvement initiatives to help a nursing facility avoid having its participation in the medicaid program terminated pursuant to division (B) of this section are available through the nursing home quality initiative established under section 173.60 of the Revised Code or initiatives offered through a quality improvement organization under contract with the United States secretary of health and human services to carry out in this state the functions described in section 1154 of the "Social Security Act," 42 U.S.C. 1320c-3.

**HISTORY:**

2013 HB 59, § 101.01, eff. Sept. 29, 2013; 2021 hb110, § 101.01, effective September 30, 2021.



### § 5165.78 Temporary resident safety assurance manager.

(A) If the department of medicaid determines that a nursing facility is experiencing or is likely to experience a serious financial loss or failure that jeopardizes or is likely to jeopardize the health, safety, and welfare of its residents, the department, subject to the provider's consent, may appoint a temporary resident safety assurance manager in the nursing facility to take actions the department determines are appropriate to ensure the health, safety, and welfare of the residents.

(B) A temporary resident safety assurance manager appointed under this section is vested with the authority necessary to take actions the department of medicaid determines are appropriate to ensure the health, safety, and welfare of the residents.

(C) A temporary resident safety assurance manager appointed under this section may use any of the following funds to pay for costs the manager incurs on behalf of the nursing facility:

(1) Medicaid payments made in accordance with the provider agreement for the nursing facility;

(2) Funds from the residents protection fund that the department provides the manager under section 5162.66 of the Revised Code;

(3) Other funds the department determines are appropriate if such use of the funds is consistent with the appropriations that authorize the use of the funds and all other state and federal laws governing the use of the funds.

(D) The provider is liable to the department for the amount of any payments the department makes to the temporary resident safety assurance manager, other than payments specified in division (C)(1) of this section. The department may recover the amount the provider owes the department by doing any of the following:

(1) Offsetting medicaid payments made to the provider in accordance with the provider agreement;

(2) Placing a lien on any of the provider's real and personal property;

(3) Initiating other collection actions.

(E) No action the department takes under this section is subject to appeal under Chapter 119. of the Revised Code.

(F) In rules authorized by section 5165.61 of the Revised Code, the medicaid director may establish all of the following:

(1) Qualifications persons must meet to be appointed temporary resident safety assurance managers under this section;

(2) Procedures for maintaining a list of qualified temporary resident safety assurance managers;

(3) Procedures consistent with federal law for paying for the services of temporary resident safety assurance managers;

(4) Accounting and reporting requirements for temporary resident safety assurance managers;

(5) Other procedures and requirements the director determines are necessary to implement this section.

**HISTORY:**

2011 HB 153, § 101.01, eff. Sept. 29, 2011; 2013 HB 59, § 101.01, eff. Sept. 29, 2013.

**Editor's Notes**

This section was formerly codified as RC § 5111.511.

**Amendment Notes**

The 2013 amendment substituted "department of medicaid" for "department of job and family services" in (A) and (B); substituted "section 5162.66" for "section 5111.62" in (C)(2); and, in the introductory language of (F), substituted "authorized by section 5165.61" for "adopted under section 5111.36" and "medicaid director" for "director of job and family services".

### § 5165.79 Procedure for terminating provider agreements; payments after termination.

(A) As used in this section, "terminating" includes not renewing.

(B) A nursing facility's participation in the medicaid program shall be terminated under sections 5165.60 to 5165.89 of the Revised Code as follows:

(1) If the department of medicaid is terminating the facility's participation, it shall issue an order terminating the facility's provider agreement.

(2) If the department of health, acting as a contracting agency, is terminating the facility's participation, it shall issue an order terminating certification of the facility's compliance with certification requirements. When the department of health terminates certification, the department of medicaid shall terminate the facility's provider agreement. The department of medicaid is not required to provide an adjudication hearing when it terminates a provider agreement following termination of certification by the department of health.

(3) If a state agency other than the department of health, acting as a contracting agency, is terminating the facility's participation, it shall notify the department of medicaid, and the department of medicaid shall issue an order terminating the facility's provider agreement. The contracting agency shall conduct any administrative proceedings concerning the order.

(C) If the following conditions are met, the department of medicaid may make medicaid payments to a nursing facility for a period not exceeding thirty days after the effective date of termination under sections 5165.60 to 5165.89 of the Revised Code of the facility's participation in the medicaid program:

(1) The payments are for medicaid eligible residents admitted to the facility prior to the effective date of the termination;

(2) The provider is making reasonable efforts to transfer medicaid eligible residents to other care settings.

The period during which payments may be made under this division begins on the later of the effective date of the termination or, if the facility has appealed a termination order, the date of issuance of the adjudication order upholding termination.

**HISTORY:**

143 v H 822 (Eff 12-13-90); 148 v H 471. Eff 7-1-2000; 2011 HB 153, § 101.01, eff. Sept. 29, 2011; 2013 HB 59, § 101.01, eff. Sept. 29, 2013.

**Editor's Notes**

This section was formerly codified as RC § 5111.52.

**Amendment Notes**

The 2013 amendment substituted "department of medicaid" for "department of job and family services" throughout the section; substituted "medicaid program" for "medical assistance program" in the introductory language of (B) and (C); substituted "sections 5165.60 to 5165.89" for "sections 5111.35 to 5111.62" in the introductory language of (B) and (C); and substituted "medicaid payments" for "medical assistance payments" in the introductory language of (C).

The 2011 amendment deleted former (A)(1), which read: "'Provider agreement' means a contract between the department of job and family services and a nursing facility for the provision of nursing facility services under the medical assistance program"; and made a related change.

#### NOTES TO DECISIONS

**Generally**

When ODH terminates a facility's Medicaid certification, ODHS is required to terminate the facility's provider agreement. Where the termination of a provider agreement is mandated in a given situation by the Revised Code, such termination amounts to a mere ministerial act: Bayside

Nursing Ctr. v. Ohio Dep't of Health, 96 Ohio App. 3d 754, 645 N.E.2d 1314, 1994 Ohio App. LEXIS 3946 (Ohio Ct. App., Franklin County 1994).

### RESEARCH REFERENCES AND PRACTICE AIDS

**Cross-References to Related Sections**

Definitions, RC § 5165.60.

Determination of whether actions, practices, situations or incidents can be justified; declaration and citing of findings, RC § 5165.66.

Remedies for uncorrected deficiencies constituting severity level four finding; termination order, RC § 5165.72.

## § 5165.80 Public notification of changes to medicaid reimbursement rates.

(A) Whenever a nursing facility is closed under sections 5165.60 to 5165.89 of the Revised Code, the department of medicaid or contracting agency shall arrange for the safe and orderly transfer of all residents, including residents who are not medicaid eligible residents, to other appropriate care settings. Whenever a nursing facility's participation in the medicaid program is terminated under sections 5165.60 to 5165.89 of the Revised Code, the department or agency shall arrange for the safe and orderly transfer of all medicaid eligible residents or, if the termination results in the closure of the facility, of all residents. The provider and all persons involved in the facility's operation shall cooperate with and assist in the transfer of residents.

(B) After a nursing facility's participation in the medicaid program is terminated under section 5165.71, 5165.72, 5165.77, 5165.771, or 5165.85 of the Revised Code, the department of medicaid or contracting agency may appoint a temporary manager subject to the continuing consent of the provider, or may apply to the common pleas court of the county in which the facility is located for such injunctive relief as is necessary for the appointment of a special master, to ensure the transfer of medicaid eligible residents to other appropriate care settings and, if applicable, the orderly closure of the facility.

**HISTORY:**

2011 HB 153, § 101.01, eff. Sept. 29, 2011; 2013 HB 59, § 101.01, eff. Sept. 29, 2013.

**Editor's Notes**

This section was formerly codified as RC § 5111.53.

**Amendment Notes**

The 2013 amendment, in (A), substituted "sections 5165.60 to 5165.89" for "sections 5111.35 to 5111.62" in the first and second sentences and inserted "nursing" in the second sentence; substituted "department of medicaid" for "department of job and family services" in the first sentence of (A) and in (B); substituted "medicaid program" for "medical assistance program" in the second sentence of (A) and in (B); and substituted "section 5165.71, 5165.72, 5165.77, 5165.771, or 5165.85" for "section 5111.45, 5111.46, 5111.51, or 5111.58" in (B).

## § 5165.81 Qualifications, compensation and powers of temporary manager or special master; warning notice prior to action; termination of court's jurisdiction.

(A) A temporary manager of a nursing facility appointed by the department of medicaid or a contracting agency under sections 5165.60 to 5165.89 of the Revised Code shall meet all of the following qualifications:

(1) Be licensed as a nursing home administrator under Chapter 4751. of the Revised Code;

(2) Have demonstrated competence as a nursing home administrator;

(3) Have had no disciplinary action taken against the temporary manager by any licensing board or professional society in this state.

(B) The salary of a temporary manager or special master appointed under sections 5165.60 to 5165.89 of the Revised Code shall be paid by the facility and set by the department of medicaid or contracting agency, in the case of a temporary manager, or by the court, in the case of a special master, at a rate not to exceed the maximum allowable compensation for an administrator under the medicaid program. The extent to which this compensation is allowable under the medicaid program is subject to and limited by this chapter and rules adopted under section 5165.02 of the Revised Code.

Subject to division (C) of this section, any costs incurred on behalf of a nursing facility by a temporary manager or special master appointed under sections 5165.60 to 5165.89 of the Revised Code shall be paid by the facility. The allowability of these costs under the medicaid program shall be subject to and governed by this chapter and rules adopted under section 5165.02 of the Revised Code. This division does not prohibit a facility from applying for or receiving any waiver of cost ceilings available under the rules.

(C) No temporary manager or special master appointed under sections 5165.60 to 5165.89 of the Revised Code shall enter into any employment contract on behalf of a facility, or purchase any capital goods using facility funds totaling more than ten thousand dollars, unless the temporary manager or special master has obtained prior approval for the contract or purchase from either the provider or the court.

(D)(1) A temporary manager appointed for a nursing facility under section 5165.72 of the Revised Code is hereby vested, subject to division (C) of this section, with the legal authority necessary to correct any deficiency or cluster of deficiencies at a facility, bring the facility into compliance with certification requirements, and otherwise ensure the health and safety of the residents.

(2) A temporary manager appointed under section 5165.77 of the Revised Code is hereby vested, subject to division (C) of this section, with the authority necessary to eliminate the emergency, bring the facility into compliance with certification requirements, and otherwise ensure the health and safety of the residents.

(3) A temporary manager appointed under section 5165.80 of the Revised Code is hereby vested, subject to division (C) of this section, with the authority necessary to ensure the transfer of medicaid eligible residents to other appropriate care settings and, if applicable, the orderly closure of the facility, and to otherwise ensure the health and safety of the residents.

(E) Prior to acting under division (A)(1)(b) or (2)(b) of section 5165.72 of the Revised Code to appoint a temporary manager or apply for a special master, the department of medicaid or contracting agency shall order the facility to substantially correct the deficiency or deficiencies within five days after receiving the statement and inform the facility, in the statement it provides pursuant to division (B) of section 5165.75 of the Revised Code, of the order and that it will not take that action unless the facility fails to substantially correct the deficiency or deficiencies within that five-day period. At the end of the five-day period, the department of health shall conduct a follow-up survey that focuses on the deficiency or deficiencies. If the department of health determines that the facility has substantially corrected the deficiency or deficiencies within that time, the department of medicaid or contracting agency shall not appoint a temporary manager or apply for a special master. If the department of health determines that the facility has failed to substantially correct the deficiency or deficiencies within that time, the department of medicaid or contracting agency may proceed with appointment of the temporary manager or application for a special master. Until the statement required under division (B) of section 5165.75 of the Revised Code is actually delivered, no action taken by the department or agency to appoint a temporary manager or apply for a temporary manager under division (A)(1)(b) or (2)(b) of section 5165.72 of the Revised Code shall have any legal effect. No action taken by a facility under this division to substantially correct a deficiency or deficiencies shall be considered an admission by the facility of the existence of a deficiency or deficiencies.

(F) Appointment of a temporary manager under division (A)(1)(b) or (2)(b) of section 5165.72 or division (A)(1)(d) of section 5165.77 of the Revised Code shall expire at the end of the seventh day following the appointment. If the department of medicaid or contracting agency finds that the deficiency or deficiencies that prompted the appointment under division (A)(1)(b) or (2)(b) of section 5165.72 of the Revised Code cannot be substantially corrected, or the condition of immediate jeopardy that prompted the appointment under division (A)(1)(d) of section 5165.77 of the Revised Code cannot be eliminated, prior to the expiration of the appointment, it may take one of the following actions:

Titles 39 — 57

(1) Appoint, subject to the continuing consent of the provider, a temporary manager for the facility;

(2) Apply to the common pleas court of the county in which the facility is located for an order appointing a special master who, under the authority and direct supervision of the court and subject to divisions (B) and (C) of this section, may take such additional actions as are necessary to correct the deficiency or deficiencies or eliminate the condition of immediate jeopardy and bring the facility into compliance with certification requirements.

(G) The court, on finding that the deficiency or deficiencies for which a special master was appointed under division (F)(2) of this section or division (A)(1)(b) or (2)(b) of section 5165.72 of the Revised Code has been substantially corrected, or the emergency for which a special master was appointed under division (F)(2) of this section or division (A)(1)(b) or (B)(2) of section 5165.77 of the Revised Code has been eliminated, that the facility has been brought into compliance with certification requirements, and that the provider has established the management capability to ensure continued compliance with the certification requirements, shall immediately terminate its jurisdiction over the facility and return control and management of the facility to the provider. If the deficiency or deficiencies cannot be substantially corrected, or the emergency cannot be eliminated practicably within a reasonable time following appointment of the special master, the court may order the special master to close the facility and transfer all residents to other nursing facilities or other appropriate care settings.

(H) This section does not apply to temporary resident safety assurance managers appointed under section 5165.78 of the Revised Code.



**HISTORY:**

143 v H 822 (Eff 12-13-90); 148 v H 471. Eff 7-1-2000; 2011 HB 153, § 101.01, eff. Sept. 29, 2011; 2013 HB 59, § 101.01, eff. Sept. 29, 2013.

**Editor's Notes**

This section was formerly codified as RC § 5111.54.

**Amendment Notes**

The 2013 amendment substituted "department of medicaid" for "department of job and family services" throughout the section; substituted "sections 5165.60 to 5165.89" for "sections 5111.35 to 5111.62" throughout (A) and (B); substituted "medicaid program" for "medical assistance program" throughout (B); in (B), substituted "adopted under section 5165.02 of the Revised Code" for "of the department" in the second sentence of the first and second paragraphs and deleted "of the department" from the end of the second paragraph; substituted "section 5165.72" for "section 5111.46" in (D)(1), in the first and fifth sentences of (E), in the first and second sentences of the introductory language of (F), and in the first sentence of (G); substituted "section 5165.77" for "section 5111.51" in (D)(2), in the first and second sentences of the introductory language of (F), and in the first sentence of (G); substituted "section 5165.75" for "section 5111.49" in the first and fifth sentences of (E); substituted "section 5165.78" for "section 5111.511" in (H); and made a stylistic change.

The 2011 amendment added (H).

## RESEARCH REFERENCES AND PRACTICE AIDS

**Cross-References to Related Sections**

Definitions, RC § 5165.60.

Determination of whether actions, practices, situations or incidents can be justified; declaration and citing of findings, RC § 5165.66.

Remedies for uncorrected deficiencies constituting severity level four finding; termination order, RC § 5165.72.

## § 5165.82 Residents to whom denial of medicaid payments applies; effective date; restrictions on new admissions; notice of correction of deficiency; follow-up survey; publication of orders.

(A) An order issued under section 5165.72, 5165.73, 5165.74, 5165.77, or 5165.84 of the Revised Code denying medicaid payments to a nursing facility for all medicaid eligible residents admitted after its effective date, or an order issued under section 5165.72, 5165.73, or 5165.74 of the Revised Code denying medicaid payments to a nursing facility for medicaid eligible residents admitted after the effective date of the order who have specified diagnoses or special care needs, shall also apply to individuals admitted to the facility on and after the effective date of the order who are not medicaid eligible residents but become medicaid eligible residents after admission. Such an order shall not apply to any of the following:

(1) An individual who was a medicaid eligible resident of the facility on the day immediately preceding the effective date of the order and continues to be a medicaid eligible resident on and after that date;

(2) An individual who was a resident of the facility on the day immediately preceding the effective date of the order, continues to be a resident on and after that date, and becomes medicaid eligible on or after that date;

(3) An individual who was a medicaid eligible resident of the facility prior to the effective date of the order, is temporarily absent from the facility on that or a subsequent date due to hospitalization or participation in therapeutic programs outside the facility, and chooses to return to the facility;

(4) An individual who was a resident of the facility prior to the effective date of the order, is temporarily absent from the facility on that or a subsequent date due to hospitalization or participation in therapeutic programs outside the facility, becomes medicaid eligible on or after that date, and chooses to return to the facility.

(B) An order issued under section 5165.72 of the Revised Code denying medicaid payments to a nursing facility for all medicaid eligible residents admitted after its effective date, or denying medicaid payments to a facility for medicaid eligible residents admitted after the effective date of the order who have specified diagnoses or special care needs shall not take effect prior to the fifth day after the order is delivered to the facility. Such an order issued under section 5165.73 or 5165.74 of the Revised Code shall not take effect prior to the twentieth day after it is delivered to the facility.

(C) No nursing facility that has received an order under section 5165.72, 5165.73, 5165.74, 5165.77, or 5165.84 of the Revised Code denying medicaid payments for all new admissions of medicaid eligible residents shall admit a medicaid eligible resident on or after the effective date of the order, unless the resident is described in division (A)(3) or (4) of this section, until the order is terminated pursuant to this section. No nursing facility that has received an order under section 5165.72, 5165.73, or 5165.74 of the Revised Code denying medicaid payments to a nursing facility for new admissions of medicaid eligible residents with specified diagnoses or special care needs shall admit such a resident on or after the effective date of the order, unless the resident is described in division (A)(3) or (4) of this section, until the order is terminated pursuant to this section.

(D) In the case of an order imposed under division (B) of section 5165.84 of the Revised Code, the department or agency shall appoint monitors in accordance with section 5165.70 of the Revised Code to conduct on-site monitoring.

(E)(1) A facility may give written notice to the department of health whenever any of the following apply:

(a) With respect to an order denying payment issued under section 5165.72, 5165.73, or 5165.74 of the Revised Code, either of the following is the case:

(i) The facility has completed implementation of the plan of correction it submitted under section 5165.69 of the Revised Code and substantially corrected all deficiencies for which the order was issued.

(ii) The facility has reduced the severity or scope of all of the deficiencies to a level at which sections 5165.72 to 5165.74 of the Revised Code do not authorize the order.

(b) With respect to an order denying payment issued under section 5165.77 of the Revised Code, the facility has eliminated the immediate jeopardy.

(c) With respect to an order denying medicaid payments issued under division (A) of section 5165.84 of the Revised Code, the facility has completed implementation of the plan of correction it submitted under section 5165.69 of the Revised Code and substantially corrected all deficiencies for which the order was issued.

(d) With respect to an order denying medicaid payments issued under division (B) of section 5165.84 of the Revised Code, both of the following are the case:

(i) The facility has completed implementation of the plan of correction it submitted under section 5165.69 of the Revised Code and substantially corrected all deficiencies for which the order was issued.

(ii) The facility is in compliance with certification requirements and has provided adequate assurance that it will remain in compliance with them.

(2) Within ten working days after it receives the notice under division (E)(1) of this section, the department of health shall conduct a follow-up survey that focuses on the cited deficiency or deficiencies, unless the department is able to determine, on the basis of documentation provided by the facility, that the facility has completed the applicable action described in divisions (E)(1)(a) to (d) of this section. If the department of health makes that determination on the basis of the documentation, the department of medicaid or contracting agency shall terminate the order denying medicaid payments as of the date the facility completed the applicable action, as subsequently verified by the department of health. If the department of health conducts a follow-up survey, the department of medicaid or contracting agency shall terminate the order denying medicaid payments as of the date the department of health makes the determination that the facility completed the applicable action.

(F) The department of medicaid or contracting agency shall provide public notice implementing an order under section 5165.72, 5165.73, 5165.74, 5165.77, or 5165.84 of the Revised Code denying medicaid payments to a nursing facility for all medicaid eligible residents by publishing in a newspaper of general circulation in the county in which the facility is located an announcement stating: "By order of the (Ohio Department of Medicaid or name of contracting agency), effective on and after (effective date of order), (name of facility) is no longer authorized to admit Medicaid eligible residents." Immediately following termination of any such order, the department or agency shall publish in a newspaper of general circulation in the county in which the facility is located an announcement stating: "By order of the (Ohio Department of Medicaid or name of contracting agency), effective on and after (effective date of termination), (name of facility) is hereby authorized to admit Medicaid eligible residents." Neither the department nor the contracting agency shall issue public notice of an order under section 5165.72, 5165.73, or 5165.74 of the Revised Code denying payment to a nursing facility for medicaid eligible residents with specified diagnoses or special care needs; public notice is not required for such an order to take effect.

(G) A facility that complies with division (E) of this section shall not be considered to have admitted to the existence of the deficiency that constitutes the basis of the department's or agency's order.

**HISTORY:**

143 v H 822 (Eff 12-13-90); 148 v H 471. Eff 7-1-2000; 2013 HB 59, § 101.01, eff. Sept. 29, 2013.

**Editor's Notes**

This section was formerly codified as RC § 5111.55.

**Amendment Notes**

The 2013 amendment rewrote the section.

**RESEARCH REFERENCES AND PRACTICE AIDS**

**Cross-References to Related Sections**

Agreement to prohibit certain discriminatory actions, RC § 5165.08.

Determination of whether actions, practices, situations or incidents can be justified; declaration and citing of findings, RC § 5165.66.

Order denying payment when deficiency is not corrected within 90 days or after three consecutive findings of substandard care, RC § 5165.84.

Remedies for uncorrected deficiencies —

Severity level four finding; termination order, RC § 5165.72.

Severity level one or two or severity level three, scope level two finding, RC § 5165.74.

Severity level three and scope level three or four finding, RC § 5165.68.

## § 5165.83 Amount and number of fines; effect of correction of deficiency; interest; means of collection.

(A) As used in this section, "certified beds" means beds certified under Title XVIII or Title XIX.

(B) If the department of medicaid or a contracting agency imposes a fine on a nursing facility under section 5165.72, 5165.73, or 5165.74 of the Revised Code, it may impose one or more of the following:

(1) One hundred sixty per cent of the amount calculated under division (C) of this section for any deficiency or cluster of deficiencies that constitutes a severity level four and scope level four finding;

(2) One hundred forty per cent of the amount calculated under division (C) of this section for any deficiency or cluster of deficiencies that constitutes a severity level four and scope level three finding;

(3) One hundred twenty per cent of the amount calculated under division (C) of this section for any deficiency or cluster of deficiencies that constitutes a severity level four and scope level two finding;

(4) The amount calculated under division (C) of this section for any deficiency or cluster of deficiencies that constitutes a severity level four and scope level one finding or any deficiency or cluster of deficiencies that constitutes a severity level three and scope level four finding;

(5) Ninety per cent of the amount calculated under division (C) of this section for any deficiency or cluster of deficiencies that constitutes a severity level three and scope level three finding;

(6) Eighty per cent of the amount calculated under division (C) of this section for any deficiency or cluster of deficiencies that constitutes a severity level three and scope level two finding;

(7) Seventy per cent of the amount calculated under division (C) of this section for any deficiency or cluster of deficiencies that constitutes a severity level three and scope level one finding;

(8) Fifty per cent of the amount calculated under division (C) of this section for any deficiency or cluster of deficiencies that constitutes a severity level two and scope level four finding;

(9) Forty per cent of the amount calculated under division (C) of this section for any deficiency or cluster of deficiencies that constitutes a severity level two and scope level three finding.



(C) The amount subject to division (B) of this section shall be the product of multiplying two dollars and fifty cents for each day the fine is in effect by the total number of licensed nursing home beds or certified beds, whichever is greater, in the facility as of the date the deficiency or cluster of deficiencies that is the reason for the fine was cited.

(D)(1) The department of medicaid or contracting agency shall not impose on a facility, at any one time, more than four fines as a result of any one survey.

(2) The department of medicaid or contracting agency shall not impose more than one fine based on a deficiency or cluster of deficiencies. However, if the department of health, in a follow-up or other subsequent survey, finds a change in the scope or severity of the deficiency or cluster of deficiencies, the department of medicaid or contracting agency may increase or decrease the fine in accordance with division (B) of this section to reflect the change in scope or severity. The department or agency shall give the facility written notice of the change in the amount of the fine. The change shall take effect on the date the follow-up or other subsequent survey is completed.

If the department of health finds that a deficiency is a repeat deficiency, the department of medicaid or contracting agency may impose a fine that is one hundred per cent greater than the fine specified in division (B) of this section for the deficiency.

(E) The total amount of fines the department of medicaid or contracting agency may impose on a facility in a single calendar year shall not exceed five hundred dollars for each licensed nursing home bed or certified bed, whichever is greater in number, in the facility.

(F)(1) Except as provided in division (F)(2) of this section, the department of medicaid or contracting agency shall not impose a fine under section 5165.72, 5165.73, or 5165.74 of the Revised Code if the deficiency or cluster of deficiencies is substantially corrected within twenty days after the nursing facility receives the statement provided under division (B) of section 5165.75 of the Revised Code. The department or agency shall inform the nursing facility in that statement that the fine will not be imposed if the deficiency or cluster of deficiencies is substantially corrected within the twenty-day period.

(2) If a nursing facility has substantially corrected a deficiency or cluster of deficiencies within six months after the exit interview of a survey that was the basis for citing a deficiency or cluster of deficiencies, but after correcting it has been cited for the same deficiency or cluster of deficiencies by the department of health on the basis of a subsequent survey conducted during the remainder of the six-month period, the department of medicaid or contracting agency may impose a fine beginning on the date of the exit interview of the subsequent survey.

(G) Whenever a facility believes that it has completed implementation of the plan of correction it submitted under section 5165.69 of the Revised Code and substantially corrected the cited deficiency or cluster of deficiencies that is the basis for a fine, it may give written notice to that effect to the department of health. After receiving the notice, the department shall conduct a follow-up survey of the facility that focuses on the deficiency or cluster, unless the department is able to determine, on the basis of documentation provided by the facility, that the facility has substantially corrected the deficiency or cluster. If, based on the follow-up survey, the department establishes that the facility had not completed implementation of the plan of correction at the time the department received the notice, any fine based on the deficiency or cluster shall be doubled effective from the date the department received the notice. A facility that complies with this division shall not be considered to have admitted the existence of the deficiency or cluster that is the basis for the fine.



(H) Except for a fine imposed under division (C) of section 5165.72 of the Revised Code and as provided in division (F)(2) of this section, the department of medicaid or contracting agency shall impose a fine only if the facility fails to give notice under division (G) of this section within twenty days after it receives the statement required by division (B) of section 5165.75 of the Revised Code or if the department of health determines, based on a follow-up survey, that the deficiency or cluster of deficiencies for which the fine is proposed has not been substantially corrected within the twenty-day period. The fine shall be imposed effective on the twenty-first day after the facility receives the statement under division (B) of section 5165.75 of the Revised Code. The fine shall remain in effect until the earliest of the following:

(1) The date the department of health receives notice under division (G) of this section, unless the department determines, on the basis of a follow-up survey, that the deficiency or cluster of deficiencies that is the basis for the fine has not been substantially corrected as of that date;

(2) The date on which the department of health makes a determination, on the basis of a follow-up survey, that the deficiency or cluster of deficiencies has been substantially corrected;

(3) The date the facility substantially corrected the deficiency or cluster, as subsequently determined by the department of health on the basis of documentation provided by the facility.

(I) Any fine imposed by the department of medicaid or contracting agency under this section is subject to appeal under Chapter 119. of the Revised Code. If the facility does not request a hearing under Chapter 119. of the Revised Code and either pays or agrees in writing to pay the fine when payment becomes due under division (J) of this section, the department or agency shall reduce the fine by fifty per cent. The department or agency may compromise any claim for payment of a fine under sections 5165.60 to 5165.89 of the Revised Code.

(J) The department of medicaid or contracting agency shall collect interest on fines, at the rate per calendar month that equals one-twelfth of the rate per year prescribed by section 5703.47 of the Revised Code for the calendar year that includes the month for which the interest charge accrues. Payment of a fine is due, and interest begins to accrue on the unpaid fine or balance, on the thirty-first day after the department or agency issues a final adjudication order imposing the fine. If the deficiency or deficiencies on which the fine is based have not been corrected when the final adjudication order is issued, the payment is due, and interest begins to accrue on the unpaid fine or balance, on the thirty-first day after the deficiency or deficiencies are corrected and the department or agency mails a notice specifying the amount of the fine to the facility.

(K) The department of medicaid or contracting agency shall collect fines and interest imposed under this section through one of the following means:

(1) A lump sum payment from the provider;

(2) Periodic payments for a period not to exceed twelve months, in accordance with a schedule approved by the department or agency;

(3) Appropriately reducing the amounts of medicaid payments made to the facility for nursing facility services provided to medicaid eligible residents for a period not to exceed twelve months following the date on which payment of the fine becomes due under division (J) of this section. An amount equal to the amount by which each payment is reduced shall be deposited to the credit of the residents protection fund in accordance with section 5162.66 of the Revised Code.

**HISTORY:**

143 v H 822 (Eff 12-13-90); 145 v H 152 (Eff 7-1-93); 148 v H 471. Eff 7-1-2000; 2013 HB 59, § 101.01, eff. Sept. 29, 2013.

**Editor's Notes**

This section was formerly codified as RC § 5111.56.

**Amendment Notes**

The 2013 amendment rewrote (A); substituted "department of medicaid" for "department of job and family services" throughout the introductory language of (B) and (K) and in (D), (E), (F), (H), (I), and (J); substituted "section 5165.72, 5165.73, or 5165.74" for "section 5111.46, 5111.47, or 5111.48" in the introductory language of (B) and in the first sentence of (F)(1); substituted "section 5165.75" for "section 5111.49" in the first sentence of (F)(1) and in the first and second sentences of the introductory language of (H); substituted "section 5165.69" for "section 5111.43" in the first sentence of (G); substituted "section 5165.72" for "section 5111.46" in the first sentence of the introductory language of (G); substituted "sections 5165.60 to 5165.89" for "sections 5111.35 to 5111.62" in the second sentence of (I); and in (K)(3), in the first sentence, inserted "medicaid" following "amounts of" and substituted "nursing facility services" for "care" and substituted "section 5162.66" for "section 5111.62" in the second sentence.

**RESEARCH REFERENCES AND PRACTICE AIDS**

**Cross-References to Related Sections**

Definitions, RC § 5165.60.

Determination of whether actions, practices, situations or incidents can be justified; declaration and citing of findings, RC § 5165.66.

Fine collected if termination order does not take effect, RC § 5165.76.

Remedies for uncorrected deficiencies —

Severity level four finding; termination order, RC § 5165.72.

Severity level one or two or severity level three, scope level two finding, RC § 5165.74.

Severity level three and scope level three or four finding, RC § 5165.68.

## § 5165.84 Order denying payment when deficiency is not corrected within 90 days or after three consecutive findings of substandard care.

(A) The department of medicaid or a contracting agency shall issue an order denying medicaid payments to a nursing facility for all medicaid eligible residents admitted to the facility on or after the effective date of the order, if the facility has failed to substantially correct within ninety days after the exit interview a deficiency or cluster of deficiencies in accordance with the plan of correction it submitted under section 5165.69 of the Revised Code, as determined by the department of health on the basis of a follow-up survey.

(B) The department of medicaid or contracting agency shall issue an order denying medicaid payments to a nursing facility for all medicaid eligible residents admitted to the facility on or after the effective date of the order, if during three consecutive standard surveys conducted after December 13, 1990, the department of health has found a condition of substandard care in a facility.

(C) An order issued under division (A) or (B) of this section shall take effect on the later of the date the facility receives the order or the date the public notice required under division (F) of section 5165.82 of the Revised Code is published. The order is subject to appeal under Chapter 119. of the Revised Code;

however the order may take effect prior to or during the pendency of any hearing under that chapter. In that case, the department or agency shall provide the facility an opportunity for a hearing in accordance with section 5165.87 of the Revised Code.

**HISTORY:**

143 v H 822 (Eff 12-13-90); 148 v H 471. Eff 7-1-2000; 2013 HB 59, § 101.01, eff. Sept. 29, 2013.

**Editor's Notes**

This section was formerly codified as RC § 5111.57.

**Amendment Notes**

The 2013 amendment substituted "department of medicaid" for "department of job and family services" in (A) and (B); substituted "medicaid payments" for "payment" in (A) and (B); substituted "section 5165.69" for "section 5111.43" in (A); and, in (C), substituted "section 5165.82" for "section 5111.55" in the first sentence and substituted "section 5165.87" for "section 5111.60" in the last sentence.

### RESEARCH REFERENCES AND PRACTICE AIDS

**Cross-References to Related Sections**

Definitions, RC § 5165.60.

Remedies subject to appeal under RC Chapter 119, RC § 5165.87.

Residents to whom denial of medicaid payments applies; publication of orders, RC § 5165.82.

Statement of deficiencies; notice of possible issuance of order denying payment or terminating facility's participation, RC § 5165.68.

## § 5165.85 Termination of participation for failure to correct deficiency within six months; repayment of interim payments.

(A) If a nursing facility notifies the department of medicaid or a contracting agency, at any time during the six-month period following the exit interview of a survey that was the basis for citing a deficiency or deficiencies, that the deficiency or deficiencies have been substantially corrected in accordance with the plan of correction submitted and approved under section 5165.69 of the Revised Code, the department of health shall conduct a follow-up survey to determine whether the deficiency or deficiencies have been substantially corrected in accordance with the plan.

(B) The department of medicaid or a contracting agency shall terminate a nursing facility's participation in the medicaid program whenever the facility has not substantially corrected, within six months after the exit interview of the survey on the basis of which it was cited, a deficiency or deficiencies in accordance with the plan of correction submitted under section 5165.69 of the Revised Code, as determined by the department of health on the basis of a follow-up survey.

(C) Unless the facility has substantially corrected the deficiency or deficiencies in accordance with the plan of correction, as determined by the department of health on the basis of a follow-up survey, the department of medicaid or contracting agency shall deliver to the facility, at least thirty days prior to the day that is six months after the exit interview, a written order terminating the facility's participation in the medicaid program. The order shall take effect and the facility's participation shall terminate on the day that is six months after the exit interview. The order shall not take effect if, after it is delivered to the facility and prior to the effective date of the order, the department of health determines on the basis of a follow-up survey that the facility has corrected the deficiency or deficiencies.

An order issued under this section is subject to appeal under Chapter 119. of the Revised Code; however, the order may take effect prior to or during the pendency of any hearing under that chapter. In that case, the department of medicaid or contracting agency shall provide the facility an opportunity for a hearing in accordance with section 5165.87 of the Revised Code.

(D) Except as provided in division (E) of this section, whenever the department of medicaid or a contracting agency terminates a facility's participation in the medicaid program pursuant to this section, the provider shall repay the department the federal share of all medicaid payments made by the department to the facility during the six-month period following the exit interview of the survey that was the basis for citing the deficiency or cluster of deficiencies. The provider shall repay the department within thirty days after the department repays to the federal government the federal share of medicaid payments made to the facility during that six-month period.

(E) A provider is not required to repay the department of medicaid if either of the following is the case:

(1) The facility has brought an appeal under Chapter 119. of the Revised Code of termination of its participation in the medicaid program, except that the provider shall repay the department of medicaid within thirty days after the facility exhausts its right to appeal under that chapter.

(2) The facility complied with the plan of correction approved by the department of health and the obligation to repay resulted from the department's failure to provide timely verification to the United States department of health and human services of the facility's compliance with the plan of correction.

(F) If a provider's obligation to repay the department of medicaid under division (D) of this section results from disallowance of federal financial participation by the United States department of health and human services, the provider shall not be required to repay the department of medicaid until the federal disallowance becomes final.

(G) Any fines paid under sections 5165.60 to 5165.89 of the Revised Code during any period for which the facility is required to repay the department of medicaid under division (D) of this section shall be offset against the amount the provider is required to repay the department for that period.

(H) Prior to a change of ownership of a facility for which a provider has an obligation to repay the department of medicaid under division (D) of this section that has not become final, or has become final but not been paid, the department may do one or more of the following:

(1) Require the provider to place money in escrow, or obtain a bond, in sufficient amount to indemnify the state against the provider's failure to repay the department after the change of ownership occurs;

(2) Place a lien on the facility's real property;

(3) Use any method to recover the medicaid payments that is available to the attorney general to recover payments on behalf of the department of medicaid.

**HISTORY:**

143 v H 822 (Eff 12-13-90); 145 v H 152 (Eff 7-1-93); 148 v H 471. Eff 7-1-2000; 2013 HB 59, § 101.01, eff. Sept. 29, 2013.

**Editor's Notes**

This section was formerly codified as RC § 5111.58.

**Amendment Notes**

The 2013 amendment substituted "department of medicaid" for "department of job and family services" throughout the section; substituted "section 5165.69" for "section 5111.43" in (A) and (B); substituted "medicaid program" for "medical assistance program" in (B), the first sentence of the first paragraph of (C), in the first sentence of (D), and in (E)(1); substituted "section 5165.87" for "section 5111.60" in the second paragraph of (C); inserted "medicaid" preceding "payments" in the first and second sentences of (D); substituted "sections 5165.60 to 5165.89" for "sections 5111.35 to 5111.62" in (G); and inserted "medicaid" following "to recover the" in (H)(3).

### RESEARCH REFERENCES AND PRACTICE AIDS

**Cross-References to Related Sections**

Conditions for continuing participation where certain deficiencies not corrected; order of termination, RC § 5165.71.

Definitions, RC § 5165.60.

Remedies subject to appeal under RC Chapter 119, RC § 5165.87.

Statement of deficiencies; notice of possible issuance of order denying payment or terminating facility's participation, RC § 5165.68.

Transfer of residents when facility is closed; appointment of temporary manager or special master, RC § 5165.80.

## § 5165.86 Delivery or mailing of notice, statement or order.

The department of medicaid, the department of health, and any contracting agency shall deliver a written notice, statement, or order to a nursing facility under sections 5165.60 to 5165.66 and 5165.69 to 5165.89 of the Revised Code by certified mail or hand delivery. If the notice, statement, or order is mailed, it shall be addressed to the administrator of the facility as indicated in the department's or agency's records. If it is hand delivered, it shall be delivered to a person at the facility who would appear to the average prudent person to have authority to accept it.

Delivery of written notice by a nursing facility to the department of health, the department of medicaid, or a contracting agency under sections 5165.60 to 5165.89 of the Revised Code shall be by certified mail or hand delivery to the appropriate department or the agency.

**HISTORY:**

143 v H 822 (Eff 12-13-90); 148 v H 471. Eff 7-1-2000; 2013 HB 59, § 101.01, eff. Sept. 29, 2013.

**Editor's Notes**

This section was formerly codified as RC § 5111.59.

**Amendment Notes**

The 2013 amendment substituted "medicaid" for "job and family services" in the first sentence of the first paragraph and in the second paragraph; substituted "sections 5165.60 to 5165.66 and 5165.69 to 5165.89" for "sections 5111.35 to 5111.41 and 5111.43 to 5111.62" in the first sentence of the first paragraph; and substituted "sections 5165.60 to 5165.89" for "sections 5111.35 to 5111.62" in the second paragraph.

**RESEARCH REFERENCES AND PRACTICE AIDS**

**Cross-References to Related Sections**

Definitions, RC § 5165.60.



## § 5165.87 Remedies subject to appeal under RC Chapter 119.

(A) Except as provided in division (B) of this section, the following remedies are subject to appeal under Chapter 119. of the Revised Code:

(1) An order issued under section 5165.71, 5165.72, 5165.77, or 5165.85 of the Revised Code terminating a nursing facility's participation in the medicaid program;

(2) Appointment of a temporary manager of a facility under division (A)(1)(b) or (2)(b) of section 5165.72, or division (A)(1)(d) of section 5165.77 of the Revised Code;

(3) An order issued under section 5165.72, 5165.73, 5165.74, 5165.77, or 5165.84 of the Revised Code denying medicaid payments to a facility for all medicaid eligible residents admitted after the effective date of the order;

(4) An order issued under section 5165.72, 5165.73, or 5165.74 of the Revised Code denying medicaid payments to a facility for medicaid eligible residents admitted after the effective date of the order who have certain diagnoses or special care needs specified by the department or agency;

(5) A fine imposed under section 5165.72, 5165.73, or 5165.74 of the Revised Code.

(B) The department of medicaid or contracting agency may do any of the following prior to or during the pendency of any proceeding under Chapter 119. of the Revised Code:

(1) Issue and execute an order under section 5165.72, 5165.77, or 5165.85 of the Revised Code terminating a nursing facility's participation in the medicaid program;

(2) Appoint a temporary manager under division (A)(1)(b) or (2)(b) of section 5165.72 or division (A)(1)(d) of section 5165.77 of the Revised Code;

(3) Issue and execute an order under section 5165.72, 5165.73, 5165.77, or 5165.84 of the Revised Code denying medicaid payments to a facility for all medicaid eligible residents admitted after the effective date of the order;

(4) Issue and execute an order under section 5165.72 or 5165.73 or division (A), (B), or (C) of section 5165.74 of the Revised Code denying medicaid payments to a facility for medicaid eligible residents admitted after the effective date of the order who have specified diagnoses or special care needs.

(C) Whenever the department or agency imposes a remedy listed in division (B) of this section prior to or during the pendency of a proceeding, all of the following apply:

(1) The provider against whom the action is taken shall have ten days after the date the facility actually receives the notice specified in section 119.07 of the Revised Code to request a hearing.

(2) The hearing shall commence within thirty days after the date the department or agency receives the provider's request for a hearing.

(3) The hearing shall continue uninterrupted from day to day, except for Saturdays, Sundays, and legal holidays, unless other interruptions are agreed to by the provider and the department or agency.

(4) If the hearing is conducted by a hearing examiner, the hearing examiner shall file a report and recommendations within ten days after the close of the hearing.

(5) The provider shall have five days after the date the hearing officer files the report and recommendations within which to file objections to the report and recommendations.

(6) Not later than fifteen days after the date the hearing officer files the report and recommendations, the medicaid director or the director of the contracting agency shall issue an order approving, modifying, or disapproving the report and recommendations of the hearing examiner.

(D) If the department or agency imposes more than one remedy as the result of deficiencies cited in a single survey, the proceedings for all of the remedies shall be consolidated. If any of the remedies are imposed during the pendency of a hearing, as permitted by division (B) of this section, the consolidated hearing shall be conducted in accordance with division (C) of this section. The consolidation of the remedies for purposes of a hearing does not affect the effective dates prescribed in sections 5165.60 to 2165.85 of the Revised Code.

(E) If a contracting agency conducts administrative proceedings pertaining to remedies imposed under sections 5165.60 to 5165.89 of the Revised Code, the department of medicaid shall not be considered a party to the proceedings.

**HISTORY:**

143 v H 822 (Eff 12-13-90); 148 v H 471. Eff 7-1-2000; 2013 HB 59, § 101.01, eff. Sept. 29, 2013.

**Editor's Notes**

This section was formerly codified as RC § 5111.60.

**Amendment Notes**

The 2013 amendment rewrote (A) and (B); substituted "medicaid director" for "director of job and family services" in (C)(6); substituted "sections 5165.60 to 2165.85" for "sections 5111.35 to 5111.58" in the last sentence of (D); and, in (E), substituted "sections 5165.60 to 5165.89" for "sections 5111.35 to 5111.62" and "medicaid" for "job and family services".

**NOTES TO DECISIONS**

**Generally**

Given the strict limits on the Ohio Department of Medicaid's authority and discretion, Ohio law creates a constitutionally protected property interest in continued participation in the Medicaid program; ODM has no discretion with respect to whether to enter a Medicaid provider agreement with a nursing facility, and participation in Ohio's Medicaid program is not terminable at the will of the state, but only where specified conditions are met. CT Ohio Portsmouth, LLC v. Ohio Dep't of Medicaid, 2020-Ohio-5091, 161 N.E.3d 803, 2020 Ohio App. LEXIS 3937 (Ohio Ct. App., Franklin County 2020).

Certification of a health care provider by ODH for compliance with federal Medicaid requirements constitutes a "license" for purposes of R.C. 119.12; it is not an arrangement whereby a person, institution, or entity furnishes Medicaid services under a provider agreement with ODHS. R.C. 119.12 does not require orders consolidated into a single action under R.C. 5111.60(D) to be separately appealed in two distinct counties, especially when they arise out of the same set of facts: Bayside Nursing Ctr. v. Ohio Dep't of Health, 96 Ohio App. 3d 754, 645 N.E.2d 1314, 1994 Ohio App. LEXIS 3946 (Ohio Ct. App., Franklin County 1994).

**RESEARCH REFERENCES AND PRACTICE AIDS**

**Cross-References to Related Sections**

Definitions, RC § 5165.60.

Order denying payment when deficiency is not corrected within 90 days or after three consecutive findings of substandard care, RC § 5165.84.

Termination of participation for failure to correct deficiency within six months, RC § 5165.85.

### § 5165.88 Confidentiality of information; false complaints.

(A)(1) Except as required by court order, as necessary for the administration or enforcement of any statute relating to nursing facilities, or as provided in division (C) of this section, the department of medicaid and any contracting agency shall not release any of the following information without the permission of the individual or the individual's legal representative:

(a) The identity of any resident of a nursing facility;

(b) The identity of any individual who submits a complaint about a nursing facility;

(c) The identity of any individual who provides the department or agency with information about a nursing facility and has requested confidentiality;

(d) Any information that reasonably would tend to disclose the identity of any individual described in division (A)(1)(a) to (c) of this section.

(2) An agency or individual to whom the department or contracting agency is required, by court order or for the administration or enforcement of a statute relating to nursing facilities, to release information described in division (A)(1) of this section shall not release the information without the permission of the individual who would be or would reasonably tend to be identified, or of the individual's legal representative, unless the agency or individual is required to release it by division (C) of this section, by court order, or for the administration or enforcement of a statute relating to nursing facilities.

(B) Except as provided in division (C) of this section, any record that identifies an individual described in division (A)(1) of this section or that reasonably would tend to identify such an individual is not a public record for the purposes of section 149.43 of the Revised Code, and is not subject to inspection and copying under section 1347.08 of the Revised Code.

(C) If the department or a contracting agency, or an agency or individual to whom the department or contracting agency was required by court order or for administration or enforcement of a statute relating to nursing facilities to release information described in division (A)(1) of this section, uses information in any administrative or judicial proceeding against a facility that reasonably would tend to identify an individual described in division (A)(1) of this section, the department, agency, or individual shall disclose that information to the facility. However, the department, agency, or individual shall not disclose information that directly identifies an individual described in divisions (A)(1)(a) to (c) of this section, unless the individual is to testify in the proceedings.

(D) No person shall knowingly register a false complaint about a nursing facility with the department or a contracting agency, or knowingly swear or affirm the truth of a false complaint, when the allegation is made for the purpose of incriminating another.

**HISTORY:**

143 v H 822 (Eff 12-13-90); 148 v H 471. Eff 7-1-2000; 2013 HB 59, § 101.01, eff. Sept. 29, 2013.

**Editor's Notes**

This section was formerly codified as RC § 5111.61.

**Amendment Notes**

The 2013 amendment substituted "medicaid" for "job and family services" in the introductory language of (A)(1).

**RESEARCH REFERENCES AND PRACTICE AIDS**

**Cross-References to Related Sections**

Penalty, RC § 5165.99.
Definitions, RC § 5165.60.

### § 5165.89 Hearing on transfer or discharge of resident.

The department of health shall be the designee of the department of medicaid for the purpose of conducting a hearing pursuant to section 3721.162 of the Revised Code concerning a nursing facility's decision to transfer or discharge a resident if the resident is a medicaid recipient or medicare beneficiary.

**HISTORY:**

149 v H 94. Eff 9-5-2001; 2013 HB 59, § 101.01, eff. Sept. 29, 2013.

**Editor's Notes**

This section was formerly codified as RC § 5111.63.

**Amendment Notes**

The 2013 amendment deleted the first paragraph, which read: "For the purposes of this section, 'facility,' 'medicare,' and 'medicaid' have the same meanings as in section 3721.10 of the Revised Code"; substituted "department of medicaid" for "department of job and family services"; and inserted "nursing".

### § 5165.99 Penalties.

(A) Whoever violates section 5165.102 or division (E) of section 5165.08 of the Revised Code shall be fined not less than five hundred dollars nor more than one thousand dollars for the first offense and not less than one thousand dollars nor more than five thousand dollars for each subsequent offense. Fines paid under this section shall be deposited in the state treasury to the credit of the general revenue fund.

(B) Whoever violates division (D) of section 5165.88 of the Revised Code is guilty of registering a false complaint, a misdemeanor of the first degree.

**HISTORY:**

138 v H 176 (Eff 7-1-80); 138 v S 403 (Eff 10-2-80); 143 v H 822. Eff 12-13-90; 151 v H 66, § 101.01, eff. 9-29-05; 2013 HB 59, § 101.01, eff. Sept. 29, 2013; 2014 hb394, § 1, effective January 1, 2015; 2014 sb276, § 1, effective January 1, 2015.

**Editor's Notes**

Acts 2014, SB 276, § 8 and Acts 2014, HB 394, § 9 provides: "The versions of sections 5165.08, 5165.513, 5165.515, and 5165.99 of the Revised Code presented in this act are the versions of the sections that result from Sections 110.25, 110.26, and 110.27 of Am. Sub. H.B. 59 of the 130th General Assembly."

This section was formerly codified as RC § 5111.99.

**Amendment Notes**

The 2014 amendment by SB 276 and HB 394, substituted "division (E)" for "division (D)" in the first sentence of (A).

The 2013 amendment, in the first sentence of (A), substituted "section 5165.102" for "division (B) of section 5111.26" and "section 5165.08" for "section 5111.31"; and substituted "section 5165.88" for "section 5111.61" in (B).

151 v H 66, effective September 29, 2005, corrected internal references in (A).

**RESEARCH REFERENCES AND PRACTICE AIDS**

**Cross-References to Related Sections**

Penalty for misdemeanor, RC § 2929.21 et. seq.

Titles 39 — 57

# CHAPTER 5166

# FEDERAL MEDICAID WAIVER COMPONENTS

Section



### § 5166.01 Definitions.

As used in this chapter:

"209(b) option" means the option described in section 1902(f) of the "Social Security Act," 42 U.S.C. 1396a(f), under which the medicaid program's eligibility requirements for aged, blind, and disabled individuals are more restrictive than the eligibility requirements for the supplemental security income program.

"Administrative agency" means, with respect to a home and community-based services medicaid waiver component, the department of medicaid or, if a state agency or political subdivision contracts with the department under section 5162.35 of the Revised Code to administer the component, that state agency or political subdivision.

"Care management system" has the same meaning as in section 5167.01 of the Revised Code.

"Dual eligible individual" has the same meaning as in section 5160.01 of the Revised Code.

"Enrollee" has the same meaning as in section 5167.01 of the Revised Code.

"Expansion eligibility group" has the same meaning as in section 5163.01 of the Revised Code.

"Federal poverty line" has the same meaning as in section 5162.01 of the Revised Code.

"Home and community-based services medicaid waiver component" means a medicaid waiver component under which home and community-based services are provided as an alternative to hospital services, nursing facility services, or ICF/IID services.

"Hospital" has the same meaning as in section 3727.01 of the Revised Code.

"Hospital long-term care unit" has the same meaning as in section 5168.40 of the Revised Code.

"ICDS participant" has the same meaning as in section 5164.01 of the Revised Code.

"ICF/IID" and "ICF/IID services" have the same meanings as in section 5124.01 of the Revised Code.

"Integrated care delivery system" and "ICDS" have the same meanings as in section 5164.01 of the Revised Code.

"Level of care determination" means a determination of whether an individual needs the level of care provided by a hospital, nursing facility, or ICF/IID and whether the individual, if determined to need that level of care, would receive hospital services, nursing facility services, or ICF/IID services if not for a home and community-based services medicaid waiver component.

"Medicaid buy-in for workers with disabilities program" has the same meaning as in section 5163.01 of the Revised Code.

"Medicaid MCO plan" has the same meaning as in section 5167.01 of the Revised Code.

"Medicaid provider" has the same meaning as in section 5164.01 of the Revised Code.

"Medicaid services" has the same meaning as in section 5164.01 of the Revised Code.

"Medicaid waiver component" means a component of the medicaid program authorized by a waiver granted by the United States department of health and human services under section 1115 or 1915 of the "Social Security Act," 42 U.S.C. 1315 or 1396n. "Medicaid waiver component" does not include the care management system or services delivered under a prepaid inpatient health plan, as defined in 42 C.F.R. 438.2.

"Medically fragile child" means an individual who is under eighteen years of age, has intensive health care needs, and is considered blind or disabled under section 1614(a)(2) or (3) of the "Social Security Act," 42 U.S.C. 1382c(a)(2) or (3).

"Nursing facility" and "nursing facility services" have the same meanings as in section 5165.01 of the Revised Code.

"Ohio home care waiver program" means the home and community-based services medicaid waiver component that is known as Ohio home care and was created pursuant to section 5166.11 of the Revised Code.

"Provider agreement" has the same meaning as in section 5164.01 of the Revised Code.

"Residential treatment facility" means a residential facility licensed by the department of mental health and addiction services under section 5119.34 of the Revised Code, or an institution certified by the department of job and family services under section 5103.03 of the Revised Code, that serves children and either has more than sixteen beds or is part of a campus of multiple facilities or institutions that, combined, have a total of more than sixteen beds.

"Skilled nursing facility" has the same meaning as in section 5165.01 of the Revised Code.

"Unified long-term services and support medicaid waiver component" means the medicaid waiver component authorized by section 5166.14 of the Revised Code.

**HISTORY:**

2013 HB 59, § 101.01, eff. Sept. 29, 2013; 2015 hb64, § 101.01, effective September 29, 2015; 2016 hb483, § 101.01, effective October 12, 2016; 2017 hb49, § 101.01, effective September 29, 2017; 2019 hb166, § 101.01, effective October 17, 2019; 2020 hb481, § 29, effective September 18, 2020; 2021 hb110, § 101.01, effective September 30, 2021.

**Amendment Notes**

The 2021 amendment by HB 110, in the definition of the "Medicaid waiver component," in the first sentence, added "section 1115 or 1915 of" and deleted "section 1115 or 1915" preceding "42 U.S.C. 1315," and added "or services delivered under a prepaid inpatient health plan, as defined in 42 C.F.R. 438.2" in the second sentence.

The 2020 amendment by HB 481 deleted the former seventh to the last paragraph, which read: "'Medicare skilled nursing facility market basket index' has the same meaning as in section 5165.01 of the Revised Code."

The 2019 amendment by HB 166 substituted "has the same meaning as in section 5167.01" for "means the system established under 5167.03" in the definition of "'Care management system'"; added the definition of "'Enrollee'"; added the definition of "'Medicaid MCO plan'"; in the second sentence in the definition of "'Medicaid waiver component'," substituted "the care management system" for "a care management system" and deleted "established under section 5167.03 of the Revised Code" at the end; and added the definition of "'Medicare skilled nursing facility market basket index.'"

The 2017 amendment by HB 49 added the definition of "Expansion eligibility group" and deleted former definition of "Ohio transitions II aging carve-out program" which read: "means the home and community-based services medicaid waiver component that is known as Ohio transitions II aging carve-out and was created pursuant to section 5166.11 of the Revised Code."

The 2016 amendment by HB 483, inserted the definitions of "Medicaid provider" and "Medically fragile child".

The 2015 amendment, by HB 64, added the definition of "209(b) option"; and inserted the definitions of "Care management system" and "Federal poverty line".

## § 5166.02 Rules governing medicaid waiver components.

(A) The medicaid director shall adopt rules in accordance with Chapter 119. of the Revised Code governing medicaid waiver components. The rules may establish all of the following:

(1) Eligibility requirements for the medicaid waiver components;

(2) The type, amount, duration, and scope of medicaid services the medicaid waiver components cover;

(3) The conditions under which the medicaid waiver components cover medicaid services;

(4) The amounts the medicaid waiver components pay for medicaid services or the methods by which the amounts are determined;

(5) The manners in which the medicaid waiver components pay for medicaid services;

(6) Safeguards for the health and welfare of medicaid recipients receiving medicaid services under a medicaid waiver component;

(7) Procedures for prioritizing and approving for enrollment individuals who are eligible for a home and community-based services medicaid waiver component and choose to be enrolled in the component;

(8) Procedures for enforcing the rules, including establishing corrective action plans for, and imposing financial and administrative sanctions on, persons and government entities that violate the rules. Sanctions shall include terminating provider agreements. The procedures shall include due process protections.

(9) Other policies necessary for the efficient administration of the medicaid waiver components.

(B) The director may adopt different rules for the different medicaid waiver components. The rules shall be consistent with the terms of the waiver authorizing the medicaid waiver component.

(C) The following apply to procedures established under division (A)(7) of this section:

(1) Any such procedures established for the medicaid-funded component of the PASSPORT program shall be consistent with section 173.521 of the Revised Code.

(2) Any such procedures established for the medicaid-funded component of the assisted living program shall be consistent with section 173.542 of the Revised Code.

(3) Any such procedures established for the Ohio home care waiver program shall be consistent with section 5166.121 of the Revised Code.

(4) Any such procedures established for the unified long-term services and support medicaid waiver program shall be consistent with section 5166.141 of the Revised Code.

**HISTORY:**

149 v H 94. Eff 9-5-2001; 150 v H 95, § 1, eff. 6-26-03; 151 v H 66, § 101.01, eff. 10-1-05; 153 v H 1, § 101.01, eff. 10-16-09; 2011 HB 153, § 101.01, eff. Sept. 29, 2011; 2013 HB 59, § 101.01, eff. Sept. 29, 2013.

**Editor's Notes**

The provisions of § 63.26 of HB 94 (149 v —) read as follows:

SECTION 63.26. As used in this section, "Medicaid waiver component" has the same meaning as in section 5111.85 of the Revised Code.

A rule adopted by the Director of Job and Family Services governing a Medicaid waiver component that is in effect on the effective date of this section shall remain in effect until amended or rescinded as part of the adoption of rules under section 5111.85 of the Revised Code.

The rule of this act that items in uncodified sections do not have effect after June 30, 2003, does not apply to this section.

This section was formerly codified as RC § 5111.85.

**Amendment Notes**

The 2013 amendment rewrote the section.

The 2011 amendment rewrote (B)(7) and (D).

153 v H 1, effective October 16, 2009, rewrote (A); inserted (B)(7) and redesignated remaining subsections accordingly; and added (D).

151 v H 66, effective October 1, 2005, in (A), inserted "and sections 5111.851 to 5111.856 of the Revised Code"; and deleted (D), pertaining to reviews of the medicaid waiver components.

**RESEARCH REFERENCES AND PRACTICE AIDS**

**Ohio Administrative Code**

Department of job and family services, division of medical services—Home and community-based waiver programs. OAC ch. 5160-40 et seq.

### § 5166.03 Request for waiver concerning demonstration projects.

The medicaid director may not submit a request to the United States secretary of health and human services for a medicaid waiver under the "Social Security Act," section 1115, 42 U.S.C. 1315, unless the director provides the speaker of the house of representatives and president of the senate written notice of the director's intent to submit the request at least ten days before the date the director submits the request to the United States secretary. The notice shall include a detailed explanation of the medicaid waiver the director proposes to seek.

**HISTORY:**

152 v H 119, § 101.01, eff. 9-29-07; 2013 HB 59, § 101.01, eff. Sept. 29, 2013.

**Editor's Notes**

This section was formerly codified as RC § 5111.84.

**Amendment Notes**

The 2013 amendment, in the first sentence, substituted "medicaid director" for "director of job and family services" and "the 'Social Security Act,' section 1115" for "section 1115 of the 'Social Security Act of 1935'"

### § 5166.04 Requirements applicable to home and community-based services medicaid waiver components.

The following requirements apply to each home and community-based services medicaid waiver component:

(A) Only an individual who qualifies for a component shall receive that component's medicaid services.

(B) A level of care determination shall be made as part of the process of determining whether an individual qualifies for a component and shall be made each year after the initial determination if, during such a subsequent year, the administrative agency determines there is a reasonable indication that the individual's needs have changed.

(C) A written plan of care or individual service plan based on an individual assessment of the medicaid services that an individual needs to avoid needing admission to a hospital, nursing facility, or ICF/IID shall be created for each individual determined eligible for a component.

(D) Each individual determined eligible for a component shall receive that component's medicaid services in accordance with the individual's level of care determination and written plan of care or individual service plan.

(E) No individual may receive medicaid services under a component while the individual is a hospital inpatient or resident of a skilled nursing facility, nursing facility, or ICF/IID.

(F) No individual may receive prevocational, educational, or supported employment services under a component if the individual is eligible for such services that are funded with federal funds provided under 29 U.S.C. 730 or the "Individuals with Disabilities Education Act," 111 Stat. 37 (1997), 20 U.S.C. 1400, as amended.

(G) Safeguards shall be taken to protect the health and welfare of individuals receiving medicaid services under a component, including safeguards established in rules adopted under section 5166.02 of the Revised Code and safeguards established by licensing and certification requirements that are applicable to the providers of that component's medicaid services.

(H) No medicaid services may be provided under a component by a provider that is subject to standards that the "Social Security Act," section 1616(e)(1), 42 U.S.C. 1382e(e)(1), requires be established if the provider fails to comply with the standards applicable to the provider.

(I) Individuals determined to be eligible for a component, or such individuals' representatives, shall be informed of that component's medicaid services, including any choices that the individual or representative may make regarding the component's medicaid services, and given the choice of either receiving medicaid services under that component or, as appropriate, hospital services, nursing facility services, or ICF/IID services.

(J) No individual shall lose eligibility for services under a component, or have the services reduced or otherwise disrupted, on the basis that the individual also receives services under the medicaid buy-in for workers with disabilities program.

(K) No individual shall lose eligibility for services under a component, or have the services reduced or otherwise disrupted, on the basis that the individual's income or resources increase to an amount above the eligibility limit for the component if the individual is participating in the medicaid buy-in for workers with disabilities program and the amount of the individual's income or resources does not exceed the eligibility limit for the medicaid buy-in for workers with disabilities program.

(L) No individual receiving services under a component shall be required to pay any cost sharing expenses for the services for any period during which the individual also participates in the medicaid buy-in for workers with disabilities program.

**HISTORY:**

151 v H 66, § 101.01, eff. 10-1-05; 152 v H 119, § 101.01, eff. 9-29-07; 153 v H 1, § 101.01, eff. 10-16-09; 2013 HB 59, § 101.01, eff. Sept. 29, 2013.

**Editor's Notes**

This section was formerly codified as RC § 5111.851.

**Amendment Notes**

The 2013 amendment deleted (A); deleted the (B) designation; redesignated former (B)(1) through (B)(12) as (A) through (L); inserted "medicaid" in present (A), (C) through (E), and (G) through (I); substituted "ICF/IID" for "intermediate care facility for the mentally retarded" in present (C), (E), and (I); substituted "section 5166.02" for "section 5111.85" in present (G); inserted "the 'Social Security Act,' section 1616(e)(1)" in present (H); and substituted "hospital services, nursing facility services" for "hospital, nursing facility" in present (I).

153 v H 1, effective October 16, 2009, in (A), deleted the definitions of "Home and community-based services medicaid waiver component", "Hospital", "Intermediate care facility for the mentally retarded", and "Nursing facility".

152 v H 119, effective September 29, 2007, inserted the seventh paragraph in (A); and added (B)(10) through (12).

### § 5166.041 Providing nursing services in a group visit under a home and community-based services medicaid waiver component.

A medicaid provider of nursing services may provide nursing services in a group visit under a home and community-based services medicaid waiver component if the component covers the nursing services, the number of medicaid recipients who receive the nursing services during the group visit does not exceed four, and all of the following apply to all of those medicaid recipients:

(A) They are enrolled in the component;

(B) They are medically fragile children;

(C) They are siblings;

(D) They reside together in the home of their caretaker relative.

**HISTORY:**

2016 hb483, § 101.01, effective October 12, 2016.

### § 5166.05 Review, approval, modification, or denial of written plans of care and individual service plans.

The department of medicaid may review and approve, modify, or deny written plans of care and individual service plans that section 5166.04 of the Revised Code requires be created for individuals determined eligible for a home and community-based services medicaid waiver component. If a state agency or political subdivision contracts with the department under section 5162.35 of the Revised Code to administer a home and community-based services medicaid waiver component and approves, modifies, or denies a written plan of care or individual service plan pursuant to the agency's or subdivision's administration of the component, the department may review the agency's or subdivision's approval, modification, or denial and order the agency or subdivision to reverse or modify the approval, modification, or denial. The state agency or political subdivision shall comply with the department's order.

The department of medicaid shall be granted full and immediate access to any records the department needs to implement its duties under this section.

**HISTORY:**

151 v H 66, § 101.01, eff. 10-1-05; 2013 HB 59, § 101.01, eff. Sept. 29, 2013.

**Editor's Notes**

This section was formerly codified as RC § 5111.852.

**Amendment Notes**

The 2013 amendment substituted "department of medicaid" for "department of job and family services" in the first sentence of the first paragraph and the second paragraph; and, in the first paragraph, substituted "section 5166.04" for "section 5111.851" in the first sentence and substituted "section 5162.35" for "section 5111.91" in the second sentence.

### § 5166.12 Ohio Home Care Program.

If the unified long-term services and support medicaid waiver component is created, the departments of aging and medicaid shall collaborate to determine whether the Ohio home care waiver program should continue to operate as a separate medicaid waiver component or be terminated. If the departments determine that the Ohio home care waiver program should be terminated, the program shall cease to exist on a date the departments shall specify.

**HISTORY:**

2011 HB 153, § 101.01, eff. Sept. 29, 2011; 2013 HB 59, § 101.01, eff. Sept. 29, 2013.

**Editor's Notes**

Former 5111.861, as enacted by 153 v H 1, § 101.01 was repealed by 2011 HB 153, § 105.01, effective Sept. 29, 2011.

This section was formerly codified as RC § 5111.861.

**Amendment Notes**

The 2013 amendment deleted (A) and (B), which read: "(A) As used in this section: 'Medicaid waiver component' has the same meaning as in section 5111.85 of the Revised Code. 'Unified long-term services and support medicaid waiver component' means the medicaid waiver component authorized by section 5111.864 of the Revised Code. (B) Subject to division (C) of this section, there is hereby created the Ohio home care program. The program shall provide home and community-based services. The department of job and family services medicaid shall administer the program"; deleted the (C) designation; substituted "medicaid shall collaborate" for "job and family services shall work together" in the first sentence; and inserted "waiver" preceding "program" in the first and second sentences.

### § 5166.121 Ohio Home Care Program; home first component.

(A) Unless the Ohio home care waiver program is terminated pursuant to section 5165.12 of the Revised Code, the department of medicaid shall establish a home first component for the Ohio home care waiver program. An individual is eligible for the Ohio home care waiver program's home first component if the individual has been determined to be eligible for the Ohio home care waiver program and at least one of the following applies:

(1) If the individual is under twenty-one years of age, the individual received inpatient hospital services for at least fourteen consecutive days, or had at least three inpatient hospital stays during the twelve months, immediately preceding the date the individual applies for the Ohio home care waiver program.

(2) If the individual is at least twenty-one but less than sixty years of age, the individual received inpatient hospital services for at least fourteen consecutive days immediately preceding the date the individual applies for the Ohio home care waiver program.

(3) The individual received private duty nursing services under the medicaid program for at least twelve consecutive months immediately preceding the date the individual applies for the Ohio home care waiver program.

(4) The individual does not reside in a nursing facility or hospital long-term care unit at the time the individual applies for the Ohio home care waiver program but is at risk of imminent admission to a nursing facility or hospital long-term care unit due to a documented loss of a primary caregiver.

(5) The individual resides in a nursing facility at the time the individual applies for the Ohio home care waiver program.

(6) At the time the individual applies for the Ohio home care waiver program, the individual participates in the money follows the person demonstration project authorized by section 6071 of the "Deficit Reduction Act of 2005," Pub. L. No. 109-171, as amended, and either resides in a residential treatment facility or inpatient hospital setting.

(B) An individual determined to be eligible for the home first component of the Ohio home care waiver program shall be enrolled in the program in accordance with rules adopted under section 5166.02 of the Revised Code.

**HISTORY:**

2011 HB 153, § 101.01, eff. Sept. 29, 2011; 2012 HB 487, § 101.01, eff. Sept. 10, 2012; 2013 HB 59, § 101.01, eff. Sept. 29, 2013.

**Editor's Notes**

This section was formerly codified as RC § 5111.862.

**Amendment Notes**

The 2013 amendment deleted (A), pertaining to the meaning of "Hospital long-term care unit", "Nursing facility", "Ohio home care program" and "Residential treatment facility"; redesignated former (B) and (C) as (A) and (B); in the first sentence of the introductory language present (A), substituted "Unless the Ohio home care waiver program is terminated pursuant to section 5165.12" for "Subject to division (C) of section 5111.861", substituted "medicaid" for "job and family services", and inserted "waiver" preceding "program" at the end; inserted "waiver" in the second sentence of the introductory language of present (A)and in present (A)(1) through (A)(6) and (B); and, in present (B), deleted "Ohio home care" preceding "program in accordance" and substituted "section 5166.02" for "section 5111.85".

### § 5166.13 Ohio transitions II aging carve-out program. [Repealed]

**HISTORY:**

2011 HB 153, § 101.01, eff. Sept. 29, 2011; 2013 HB 59, § 101.01, eff. Sept. 29, 2013; repealed by 2017 hb49, § 105.01, effective September 29, 2017.

### § 5166.301 Agreement authorizing home care attendant services to consumers.

The medicaid director shall enter into a provider agreement with an individual to authorize the individual to provide home care attendant services to consumers if the individual does both of the following:

(A) Agrees to comply with the requirements of sections 5166.30 to 5166.3010 and rules adopted under section 5166.02 of the Revised Code;

(B) Provides the director evidence satisfactory to the director of all of the following:

(1) That the individual either meets the personnel qualifications specified in 42 C.F.R. 484.4 for home health aides or has successfully completed at least one of the following:

(a) A competency evaluation program or training and competency evaluation program approved or conducted by the director of health under section 3721.31 of the Revised Code;

(b) A training program approved by the appropriate director that includes training in at least all of the following and provides training equivalent to a training and competency evaluation program specified in division (B)(1)(a) of this section or meets the requirements of 42 C.F.R. 484.36(a):

(i) Basic home safety;

(ii) Universal precautions for the prevention of disease transmission, including hand-washing and proper disposal of bodily waste and medical instruments that are sharp or may produce sharp pieces if broken;

(iii) Personal care aide services;

(iv) The labeling, counting, and storage requirements for schedule II, III, IV, and V medications.

(2) That the individual has obtained a certificate of completion of a course in first aid from a first aid course to which all of the following apply:

(a) It is not provided solely through the internet.

(b) It includes hands-on training provided by a first aid instructor who is qualified to provide such training according to standards set in rules adopted under section 5166.02 of the Revised Code.

(c) It requires the individual to demonstrate successfully that the individual has learned the first aid taught in the course.

(3) That the individual meets any other requirements for the medicaid provider agreement specified in rules adopted under section 5166.02 of the Revised Code.

**HISTORY:**

153 v H 1, § 101.01, eff. 10-16-09; 2013 HB 59, § 101.01, eff. Sept. 29, 2013.

**Editor's Notes**

This section was formerly codified as RC § 5111.881.

**Amendment Notes**

The 2013 amendment, in the introductory language, substituted "medicaid director" for "director of job and family services" and deleted "medicaid" preceding "provider"; substituted "sections 5166.30 to 5166.3010" for "sections 5111.88 to 5111.8810" in (A); substituted "section 5166.02" for "section 5111.8811" in (A), (B)(2)(b), and (B)(3); and substituted "appropriate director" for "department of job and family services" in the introductory language of (B)(1)(b).

# CHAPTER 5168

# HOSPITAL CARE ASSURANCE PROGRAM

Section



### § 5168.40 Definitions.

As used in sections 5168.40 to 5168.56 of the Revised Code:

(A) "Bed surrender" means the following:

(1) In the case of a nursing home, the removal of a bed from a nursing home's licensed capacity in a manner that reduces the total licensed capacity of all nursing homes and makes it impossible for the bed to ever be a part of any nursing home's licensed capacity;

(2) In the case of a hospital, the removal of a hospital bed from registration under section 3701.07 of the Revised Code as a skilled nursing facility bed or long-term care bed in a manner that reduces the total number of hospital beds registered under that section as skilled nursing facility beds or long-term care beds and makes it impossible for the bed to ever be registered as a skilled nursing facility bed or long-term care bed.

(B) "Change of operator" means an entering operator becoming the operator of a nursing home or hospital in the place of the exiting operator.

(1) Actions that constitute a change of operator include the following:

(a) A change in an exiting operator's form of legal organization, including the formation of a partnership or corporation from a sole proprietorship;

(b) A transfer of all the exiting operator's ownership interest in the operation of the nursing home or hospital to the entering operator, regardless of whether ownership of any or all of the real property or personal property associated with the nursing home or hospital is also transferred;

(c) A lease of the nursing home or hospital to the entering operator or the exiting operator's termination of the exiting operator's lease;

(d) If the exiting operator is a partnership, dissolution of the partnership;

(e) If the exiting operator is a partnership, a change in composition of the partnership unless both of the following apply:

(i) The change in composition does not cause the partnership's dissolution under state law.

(ii) The partners agree that the change in composition does not constitute a change in operator.

(f) If the operator is a corporation, dissolution of the corporation, a merger of the corporation into another corporation that is the survivor of the merger, or a consolidation of one or more other corporations to form a new corporation.

(2) The following, alone, do not constitute a change of operator:

(a) A contract for an entity to manage a nursing home or hospital as the operator's agent, subject to the operator's approval of daily operating and management decisions;

(b) A change of ownership, lease, or termination of a lease of real property or personal property associated with a nursing home or hospital if an entering operator does not become the operator in place of an exiting operator;

(c) If the operator is a corporation, a change of one or more members of the corporation's governing body or transfer of ownership of one or more shares of the corporation's stock, if the same corporation continues to be the operator.

(C) "Effective date of a change of operator" means the day an entering operator becomes the operator of a nursing home or hospital.

(D) "Entering operator" means the person or government entity that will become the operator of a nursing home or hospital on the effective date of a change of operator.

(E) "Exiting operator" means an operator that will cease to be the operator of a nursing home or hospital on the effective date of a change of operator.

(F) "Franchise permit fee rate" means the rate determined in accordance with section 5168.41 of the Revised Code.

(G) "Hospital" has the same meaning as in section 3727.01 of the Revised Code.

(H) "Hospital long-term care unit" means any distinct part of a hospital in which any of the following beds are located:

(1) Beds registered pursuant to section 3701.07 of the Revised Code as skilled nursing facility beds or long-term care beds;

(2) Beds licensed as nursing home beds under section 3721.02 or 3721.09 of the Revised Code.

(I) "Indirect guarantee percentage" means the percentage specified in the "Social Security Act," section 1903(w)(4)(C)(ii), 42 U.S.C. 1396b(w)(4)(C)(ii), that is to be used in determining whether a class of providers is indirectly held harmless for any portion of the costs of a broad-based health-care-related tax. If the indirect guarantee percentage changes during a fiscal year, the indirect guarantee percentage is the following:

(1) For the part of the fiscal year before the change takes effect, the percentage in effect before the change;

(2) For the part of the fiscal year beginning with the date the indirect guarantee percentage changes, the new percentage.

(J) "Medicaid days" and "nursing facility" have the same meanings as in section 5165.01 of the Revised Code.

(K)(1) "Nursing home" means all of the following:

(a) A nursing home licensed under section 3721.02 or 3721.09 of the Revised Code, including any part of a home for the aging licensed as a nursing home;

(b) A facility or part of a facility, other than a hospital, that is certified as a skilled nursing facility under Title XVIII;

(c) A nursing facility, other than a portion of a hospital certified as a nursing facility.

(2) "Nursing home" does not include either of the following:

(a) A county home, county nursing home, or district home operated pursuant to Chapter 5155. of the Revised Code;

(b) A nursing home maintained and operated by the department of veterans services under section 5907.01 of the Revised Code.

(L) "Operator" means the person or government entity responsible for the daily operating and management decisions for a nursing home or hospital.

(M) "Title XIX" means Title XIX of the "Social Security Act," 42 U.S.C. 1396 et seq.

(N) "Title XVIII" means Title XVIII of the "Social Security Act," 42 U.S.C. 1395 et seq.



**HISTORY:**

145 v H 152. Eff 7-1-93; 151 v H 66, § 101.01, eff. 7-1-05; 153 v H 1, § 101.01, eff. 7-17-09; 153 v H 449, § 1, eff. 6-18-10; 2011 HB 153, § 101.01, eff. July 1, 2011; 2012 HB 487, § 101.01, eff. Sept. 10, 2012; 2013 HB 59, § 101.01, eff. Sept. 29, 2013; 2015 hb64, § 101.01, effective September 29, 2015.

**Editor's Notes**

This section was formerly codified as RC § 3721.50.

Acts 2013, HB 59, § 812.30 provides: "The sections that are listed in the left-hand column of the following table combine amendments by this act that are and that are not exempt from the referendum under Ohio Constitution, Article II, sections 1c and 1d and section 1.471 of the Revised Code.

"The middle column identifies the amendments to the listed sections that are subject to the referendum under Ohio Constitution, Article II, Section 1c and therefore take effect on the ninety-first day after this act is filed with the Secretary of State or, if a later effective date is specified, on that date.

"The right-hand column identifies the amendments to the listed sections that are exempt from the referendum under Ohio Constitution, Article II, Section 1d and section 1.471 of the Revised Code and therefore take effect immediately when this act becomes law or, if a later effective date is specified, on that date.

Acts 2013, HB 59, § 812.30 provides: "The sections that are listed in the left-hand column of the following table combine amendments by this act that are and that are not exempt from the referendum under Ohio Constitution, Article II, sections 1c and 1d and section 1.471 of the Revised Code.

"The middle column identifies the amendments to the listed sections that are subject to the referendum under Ohio Constitution, Article II, Section 1c and therefore take effect on the ninety-first day after this act is filed with the Secretary of State or, if a later effective date is specified, on that date.

"The right-hand column identifies the amendments to the listed sections that are exempt from the referendum under Ohio Constitution, Article II, Section 1d and section 1.471 of the Revised Code and therefore take effect immediately when this act becomes law or, if a later effective date is specified, on that date.

| "Section of "law | Amendments subject to referendum | Amendments exempt from referendum |
|---|---|---|
| "3745.11 | Amendments to division (M)(5) | All amendments except as described in the middle column |
| "3721.50 "(5168.40) | All Amendments except as described in the right-hand column | Amendments to division (F) |
| "5112.30 "(5168.60) | All Amendments except as described in the right-hand column | Amendments to division (A) take effect July 1, 2013 |
| "5739.02 "except as | All Amendments described in the right-hand column | Amendments to division (A) |
| "6109.21 | The stricken sentence in division (E) | All amendments except as described in the middle column" |

**Amendment Notes**

The 2015 amendment, by HB 64, added "and makes it impossible for the bed to ever be a part of any nursing home's licensed capacity" to the end of (A)(1); and added "and makes it impossible for the bed to ever be registered as a skilled nursing facility bed or long-term care bed" to the end of (A)(2).

The 2013 amendment substituted "sections 5168.40 to 5168.56" for "sections 3721.50 to 3721.58" in the introductory language; rewrote (F), which formerly read: " 'Franchise permit fee rate' means the following: (1) For fiscal year 2012, eleven dollars and forty-seven cents; (2) For fiscal year 2013 and each fiscal year thereafter, eleven dollars and sixty-seven cents"; in the first sentence of (I), deleted "section 1903(w)(4)(C)(ii) of" following "specified in" and substituted "section 1903(w)(4)(C)(ii)" for "120 Stat. 2994 (2006)"; rewrote former (J) and (L) as present (J); deleted (K), which read: " 'Medicare' means the program established by Title XVIII"; redesignated former (M) through (P) as (K) through (N); substituted "42 U.S.C. 1396, et seq" for "79 Stat. 286 (1965), 42 U.S.C. 1396, as amended" in present (M) and (N); and made a stylistic change.

The 2012 amendment deleted (J), which read: " 'Inpatient days' means all days during which a resident of a nursing facility, regardless of payment source, occupies a bed in the nursing facility that is included in the facility's certified capacity under Title XIX. Therapeutic or hospital leave days for which payment is made under section 5111.26 of the Revised Code are considered inpatient days proportionate to the percentage of the facility's per resident per day rate paid for those days"; redesignated former (K) and (M) through (R) as (J) through (P); deleted (L), pertaining to the definition of "Medicaid day"; deleted present (M)(2)(c), pertaining to the certification of the nursing home or part of a nursing home; and made related and stylistic changes.

The 2011 amendment rewrote the section.

153 v H 449, effective June 18, 2010, in (I)(2)(b), substituted "department of veterans services" for "Ohio veterans' home agency".

153 v H 1, effective July 17, 2009, rewrote the section.

151 v H 66, effective July 1, 2005, rewrote the section.

**RESEARCH REFERENCES AND PRACTICE AIDS**

**Cross-References to Related Sections**

Exemptions from fees, RC § 3721.511.

Franchise permit fees for funding of home and community-based services for elderly and disabled persons, RC § 5168.42.

Investigations; enforcement actions, RC § 5168.55.

Recategorization of hospital beds to skilled nursing beds; nursing home placement clearinghouses, RC § 3702.521.

Rules for implementation or ceasing implementation of provisions and for distributing moneys, RC § 5168.56.

**Ohio Administrative Code**

Ohio department of job and family services, division of medical assistance—

Definition of nursing home beds subject to the franchise permit fee. OAC 5160-3-30.4.

## § 5168.41 Franchise permit fee rate; Determination of net patient revenue.

(A) The franchise permit fee rate shall be determined for each fiscal year as follows:

(1) Determine the estimated total net patient revenues for all nursing homes and hospital long-term care units for the fiscal year;

(2) Multiply the estimated total net patient revenues determined under division (A)(1) of this section by the lesser of the following:

(a) The indirect guarantee percentage;

(b) Six per cent.

(3) Divide the product determined under division (A)(2) of this section by the number of days in the fiscal year;

(4) Determine the sum of the following:

(a) The total number of beds in all nursing homes and hospital long-term care units that are subject to the franchise permit fee for the fiscal year;

(b) The total number of nursing home beds that are exempt from the franchise permit fee for the fiscal year because of the waiver obtained pursuant to section 5168.43 of the Revised Code.

(5) Divide the quotient determined under division (A)(3) of this section by the sum determined under division (A)(4) of this section.

(B) In determining the estimated total net patient revenues for all nursing homes and hospital long-term care units for a fiscal year, the department of medicaid shall use at least all of the following:

(1) Information from medicaid cost reports filed under section 5165.10 of the Revised Code that are the most recent at the time the determination is made;

(2) The projected total medicaid payment rates for nursing facility services for the fiscal year;

(3) The projected total number of medicaid days for the fiscal year.

**HISTORY:**

2013 HB 59, § 101.01, eff. Sept. 29, 2013.

## § 5168.42 Annual franchise permit fee.

The department of medicaid shall do all of the following:

(A) Subject to sections 5168.44, 5168.45, and 5168.48 of the Revised Code and divisions (C) and (D) of this section and for the purposes specified in section 5168.54 of the Revised Code, determine an annual franchise permit fee on each nursing home in an amount equal to the franchise permit fee rate multiplied by the product of the following:

(1) The number of beds licensed as nursing home beds, plus any other beds certified as skilled nursing facility beds under Title XVIII or nursing facility beds under Title XIX on the first day of May of the calendar year in which the fee is determined pursuant to division (A) of section 5168.47 of the Revised Code;

(2) The number of days in the fiscal year beginning on the first day of July of the calendar year in which the fee is determined pursuant to division (A) of section 5168.47 of the Revised Code.

(B) Subject to sections 5168.44, 5168.45, and 5168.48 of the Revised Code and divisions (C) and (D) of this section and for the purposes specified in section 5168.54 of the Revised Code, determine an annual franchise permit fee on each hospital in an amount equal to the franchise permit fee rate multiplied by the product of the following:

(1) The number of beds registered pursuant to section 3701.07 of the Revised Code as skilled nursing facility beds or long-term care beds, plus any other beds licensed as nursing home beds under section 3721.02 or 3721.09 of the Revised Code, on the first day of May of the calendar year in which the fee is determined pursuant to division (A) of section 5168.47 of the Revised Code;

(2) The number of days in the fiscal year beginning on the first day of July of the calendar year in which the fee is determined pursuant to division (A) of section 5168.47 of the Revised Code.

(C) If the total amount of the franchise permit fee assessed under divisions (A) and (B) of this section for a fiscal year exceeds the indirect guarantee percentage of the actual net patient revenue for all nursing homes and hospital long-term care units for that fiscal year and seventy-five per cent or more of the combined total number of nursing homes and hospital long-term care units receive enhanced medicaid payments or other state payments equal to seventy-five per cent or more of their total franchise permit fee assessments, do both of the following:

(1) Recalculate the assessments under divisions (A) and (B) of this section using a per bed per day rate equal to the indirect guarantee percentage of actual net patient revenue for all nursing homes and hospital long-term care units for that fiscal year;

(2) Refund the difference between the amount of the franchise permit fee assessed for that fiscal year under divisions (A) and (B) of this section and the amount recalculated under division (C)(1) of this section as a credit against the assessments imposed under divisions (A) and (B) of this section for the subsequent fiscal year.

(D) If the United States centers for medicare and medicaid services determines that the franchise permit fee established by sections 5168.40 to 5168.56 of the Revised Code is an impermissible health care-related tax under the "Social Security Act," section 1903(w), 42 U.S.C. 1396b(w), take all necessary actions to cease implementation of sections 5168.40 to 5168.56 of the Revised Code in accordance with rules adopted under section 5168.56 of the Revised Code.

**HISTORY:**

145 v H 152 (Eff 7-1-93); 148 v H 471 (Eff 7-1-2000); 149 v H 94 (Eff 6-6-2001); 149 v S 261. Eff 6-5-2002; 151 v H 66, § 101.01, eff. 7-1-05; 152 v H 119, § 101.01, eff. 6-30-07; 153 v H 1, § 101.01, eff. 7-17-09; 2011 HB 153, § 101.01, eff. July 1, 2011; 2012 HB 487, § 101.01, eff. Sept. 10, 2012; 2013 HB 59, § 101.01, eff. Sept. 29, 2013.

**Editor's Notes**

151 v H 66, effective July 1, 2005, rewrote the section.

This section was formerly codified as RC § 3721.51.

**Amendment Notes**

The 2013 amendment substituted "medicaid" for "job and family services" in the introductory language; in the introductory language of (A) and (B), substituted "sections 5168.44, 5168.45, and 5168.48" for "sections 3721.512, 3721.513, and 3721.531" and "section 5168.54" for "section 3721.56"; substituted "section 5168.47" for "section 3721.53" in (A)(1), (A)(2), (B)(1), and (B)(2); and in (D), substituted "sections 5168.40 to 5168.56" for "sections 3721.50 to 3721.58" twice, substituted "the 'Social Security Act,' section 1903(w), 42 U.S.C. 1396b(w)" for "section 1903(w) of the 'Social Security Act,' 49 Stat. 620 (1935) section 1903(w), 42 U.S.C. 1396b(w), as amended", and substituted "section 5168.56" for "section 3721.58".

The 2012 amendment inserted "and seventy-five per cent or more of the combined total number of nursing homes and hospital long-term care units receive enhanced medicaid payments or other state payments equal to seventy-five per cent or more of their total franchise permit fee assessments" in the introductory language of (C).

The 2011 amendment, in the introductory language of (A) and (B), inserted "and 3721.531" and substituted "section 3721.56" for "sections 3721.56 and 3721.561"; substituted "the indirect guarantee percentage" for "five and one-half per cent" in the introductory language of (C) and in (C)(1); and made related changes.

153 v H 1, effective July 17, 2009, in the introductory language of (A) and (B), substituted "sections 3721.512 and 3721.513 of the Revised Code and divisions (C) and (D)" for "division (C)" and "the franchise permit fee rate" for "six dollars and twenty-five cents"; inserted (C); and redesignated former (C) as (D).

152 v H 119, effective June 30, 2007, in the introductory languages of (A) and (B), deleted "for fiscal years 2006 and 2007 and one dollar for each fiscal year thereafter" preceding "multiplied by the product".

### NOTES TO DECISIONS

**Certificate of need application**

Decision to grant a certificate of need (CON) to a nursing facility was supported by reliable, probative, and substantial evidence because deference was given to the director of the Ohio Department of Health's decision that the omission of a franchise fee from the CON application did not result in understating the costs involved; the director concluded that the applicant would not have included franchise fee costs unless the application indicated that the beds that were the subject of the CON would have remained licensed after the CON was approved and while a project was under construction. Even if funds should have been allocated for franchise permit fees as part of the reviewable project costs, the contingency amounts allowed for the project appeared adequate to cover those fees. In re Heritage [at Heather Hill], 2009-Ohio-6480, 2009 Ohio App. LEXIS 5425 (Ohio Ct. App., Franklin County 2009).

### RESEARCH REFERENCES AND PRACTICE AIDS

**Cross-References to Related Sections**

Annual report of number of licensed beds in each facility, RC § 5168.46.
Appeal of amount of fee, RC § 5168.53.
Determination and payment of annual fee, RC § 5168.47.

**Ohio Administrative Code**

Ohio department of job and family services, division of medical assistance—
Franchise permit fee. OAC 5101:3-3-49.1 to OAC 5160-3-30.4.

## § 5168.43 Redetermining nursing homes' and hospitals' franchise permit fees.

(A) Not later than four months after July 17, 2009, the department of medicaid shall apply to the United States secretary of health and human services for a waiver under the "Social Security Act," section 1903(w)(3)(E), 42 U.S.C. 1396b(w)(3)(E), as necessary to do both of the following regarding the franchise permit fee assessed under section 5168.42 of the Revised Code:

(1) Reduce the franchise permit fee rate to zero dollars for each nursing home licensed under section 3721.02 or 3721.09 of the Revised Code to which either of the following applies:

(a) The nursing home:

(i) Is exempt from state taxation under section 140.08 of the Revised Code or is exempt from state taxation as a home for the aged as defined in section 5701.13 of the Revised Code;

(ii) Is exempt from federal income taxation under section 501 of the Internal Revenue Code of 1986;

(iii) Does not participate in medicaid or medicare; and

(iv) Provides services for the life of each resident without regard to the resident's ability to secure payment for the services.

(b) The nursing home:

(i) Has had a written affiliation agreement with a university in this state for education and research related to Alzheimer's disease for each of the twenty years preceding July 17, 2009, and has such an agreement on July 17, 2009;

(ii) Was constructed pursuant to a certificate of need granted under Section 3 of Am. Sub. S.B. 256 of the 116th general assembly; and

(iii) Does not participate in medicaid or medicare.

(2) For each nursing facility with more than two hundred beds certified as nursing facility beds under Title XIX, reduce the franchise permit fee rate for a number of the nursing facility's beds specified by the department to the amount necessary to obtain approval of the waiver sought under this section.

(B) The effective date of the waiver sought under this section shall be the first day of the quarter beginning after the United States secretary approves the waiver.

**HISTORY:**

153 v H 1, § 101.01, eff. 7-17-09; 2011 HB 153, § 101.01, eff. July 1, 2011; 2013 HB 59, § 101.01, eff. Sept. 29, 2013.

**Editor's Notes**

This section was formerly codified as RC § 3721.511.

**Amendment Notes**

The 2013 amendment, in the introductory language of (A), substituted "medicaid" for "job and family services", inserted "the 'Social Security Act,' section 1903(w)(3)(E)", ad substituted "section 5168.42" for "section 3721.51"; and made a stylistic change.

The 2011 amendment substituted "July 17, 2009" for "the effective date of this section" wherever it appears in the introductory language of (A) and in (A)(1)(b)(i); substituted "assessed under" for "imposed by" in the introductory language of (A); inserted "rate" in the introductory language of (A)(1) and in (A)(2); and deleted "calendar" preceding "quarter" in (B).

## § 5168.44 Proceedings after approval of waiver.

If the United States secretary of health and human services approves the waiver sought under section 5168.43 of the Revised Code, the department of medicaid shall, for each nursing home and hospital that qualifies for a reduction of its franchise permit fee rate under the waiver, reduce the franchise permit fee rate in accordance with the terms of the waiver. For purposes of the first fiscal year during which the waiver takes effect, the department shall determine the amount of the reduction not later than the effective date of the waiver and shall mail to each nursing home and hospital qualifying for the reduction notice of the reduction not later than the last day of the first month of the quarter that begins after the United States secretary approves the waiver. For purposes of subsequent fiscal years, the department shall make such determinations and notify the nursing homes and hospitals in accordance with section 5168.47 of the Revised Code.

**HISTORY:**

153 v H 1, § 101.01, eff. 7-17-09; 2011 HB 153, § 101.01, eff. July 1, 2011; 2013 HB 59, § 101.01, eff. Sept. 29, 2013; 2015 hb64, § 101.01, effective September 29, 2015.

**Editor's Notes**

This section was formerly codified as RC § 3721.512.

**Amendment Notes**

The 2015 amendment, by HB 64, substituted "notify the nursing homes and hospitals" for "mail such notices" in the last sentence.

The 2013 amendment in the first sentence, substituted "section 5168.43" for "section 3721.511" and "medicaid" for "job and family services"; and substituted "section 5168.47" for "section 3721.53" in the last sentence.

The 2011 amendment inserted "rate" twice in the first sentence and deleted "calendar" preceding "quarter" in the second sentence.

## § 5168.45 Increase in fee after waiver.

(A) If the United States secretary of health and human services approves the waiver sought under section 5168.43 of the Revised Code, the department of medicaid may do both of the following regarding the franchise permit fee assessed under section 5168.42 of the Revised Code:

(1) Determine how much money the franchise permit fee would have raised in a fiscal year if not for the waiver;

(2) For each nursing home and hospital subject to the franchise permit fee, other than a nursing home or hospital that has its franchise permit fee rate reduced under section 5168.44 of the Revised Code, uniformly increase the amount of the franchise permit fee rate for a fiscal year to an amount that will have the franchise permit fee raise an amount of money that does not exceed the amount determined under division (A)(1) of this section for that fiscal year.

(B) If the department increases the franchise permit fee rate in accordance with division (A) of this section for the first fiscal year during which the waiver takes effect, the department shall determine the amount of the increase not later than the effective date of the waiver and shall mail to each nursing home and hospital subject to the increase notice of the increase not later than the last day of the first month of the quarter that begins after the United States secretary approves the waiver. If the department increases the franchise permit fee rate in accordance with division (A) of this section for a subsequent fiscal year, the department shall make such determinations and notify the nursing homes and hospitals in accordance with section 5168.47 of the Revised Code.

**HISTORY:**

153 v H 1, § 101.01, eff. 7-17-09; 2011 HB 153, § 101.01, eff. July 1, 2011; 2013 HB 59, § 101.01, eff. Sept. 29, 2013; 2015 hb64, § 101.01, effective September 29, 2015.

**Editor's Notes**

This section was formerly codified as RC § 3721.513.

**Amendment Notes**

The 2015 amendment, by HB 64, substituted "notify the nursing homes and hospitals" for "mail such notices" in the last sentence of (B).

The 2013 amendment, in the introductory language, substituted "section 5168.43" for "section 3721.511", "medicaid" for "job and family services", "section 5168.42" for "section 3721.51"; substituted "section 5168.44" for "section 3721.512" in (A)(2); and substituted "section 5168.47" for "section 3721.53" in (B).

The 2011 amendment substituted "assessed under" for "imposed by" in the introductory language of (A); inserted "rate" throughout (A)(2) and (B); and deleted "calendar" preceding "quarter that" in the first sentence of (B).

## § 5168.46 Annual report of number of licensed beds in each facility.

The department of health shall do all of the following:

(A) For the purpose of the determinations made under divisions (A) and (B) of section 5168.42 of the Revised Code and not later than the first day of each June, report to the department of medicaid the following:

(1) For each nursing home, the number of beds in the nursing home licensed on the preceding first day of May under section 3721.02 or 3721.09 of the Revised Code or certified on that date under Title XVIII or Title XIX;

(2) For each hospital, the number of beds in the hospital registered on the preceding first day of May pursuant to section 3701.07 of the Revised Code as skilled nursing facility or long-term care beds or licensed on that date under section 3721.02 or 3721.09 of the Revised Code as nursing home beds.

(B) For the purpose of the redetermination under section 5168.48 of the Revised Code and not later than the fifteenth day of each January, report to the department of medicaid, for each nursing home and hospital, the number of beds for which a bed surrender occurred during the period beginning on the first day of May of the preceding calendar year and ending on the first day of January of the calendar year in which the redetermination is made.

**HISTORY:**

145 v H 152 (Eff 7-1-93); 145 v H 715 (Eff 7-22-94); 148 v H 471. Eff 7-1-2000; 151 v H 66, § 101.01, eff. 7-1-05; 2011 HB 153, § 101.01, eff. July 1, 2011; 2013 HB 59, § 101.01, eff. Sept. 29, 2013.

**Editor's Notes**

This section was formerly codified as RC § 3721.52.

**Amendment Notes**

The 2013 amendment substituted "section 5168.42" for "section 3721.51" in the introductory language of (A); substituted "medicaid" for "job and family services" in the introductory language of (A) and in (B); substituted "Title XVIII or Title XIX" for "Title XVIII or XIX" in (A)(1); and substituted "section 5168.48" for "section 3721.531" in (B).

The 2011 amendment rewrote the section.

151 v H 66, effective July 1, 2005, rewrote the section.

### RESEARCH REFERENCES AND PRACTICE AIDS

**Ohio Administrative Code**

Identification of nursing facility (NF) and hospital beds subject to the franchise permit fee (FPF). OAC 5101:3-3-49.2.

## § 5168.47 Determination and payment of annual fee.

(A) Not later than the fifteenth day of September of each year, the department of medicaid shall determine the annual franchise permit fee for each nursing home and hospital in accordance with section 5168.42 of the Revised Code and any adjustments made in accordance with sections 5168.44 and 5168.45 of the Revised Code.

(B) Not later than the first day of October of each year, the department shall notify, electronically or by United States postal service, each nursing home and hospital of the amount of the franchise permit fee that has been determined for the nursing home or hospital.

(C) Subject to section 5168.48 of the Revised Code, each nursing home and hospital shall pay its fee under section 5168.42 of the Revised Code, as adjusted in accordance with sections 5168.44 and 5168.45 of the Revised Code, to the department in four installment payments not later than forty-five days after the last day of each October, December, March, and June.

**HISTORY:**

145 v H 152 (Eff 7-1-93); 148 v H 471. Eff 7-1-2000; 153 v H 1, § 101.01, eff. 7-17-09; 2011 HB 153, § 101.01, eff. July 1, 2011; 2013 HB 59, § 101.01, eff. Sept. 29, 2013; 2015 hb64, § 101.01, effective September 29, 2015.

**Editor's Notes**

This section was formerly codified as RC § 3721.53.

**Amendment Notes**

The 2015 amendment, by HB 64, in (B), substituted "notify, electronically or by United States postal service" for "mail to" and deleted "notice" following "and hospital".

The 2013 amendment substituted "medicaid" for "job and family services" in (A); substituted "section 5168.42" for "section 3721.51" in (A) and (C); substituted "sections 5168.44 and 5168.45" for "sections 3721.512 and 3721.513" in (A) and (C); and substituted "section 5168.48" for "section 3721.531" in (C).

The 2011 amendment added "Subject to section 3721.531 of the Revised Code" to the beginning of (C); and deleted (D), which read: "No nursing home or hospital shall directly bill its residents for the fee paid under this section, or otherwise directly pass the fee through to its residents."

153 v H 1, effective July 17, 2009, rewrote (A); substituted "October" for "September" in (B) and (C); and in (C), inserted "as adjusted in accordance with sections 3721.512 and 3721.513 of the Revised Code", and substituted "four installment" for "quarterly installment".

### RESEARCH REFERENCES AND PRACTICE AIDS

**Cross-References to Related Sections**

Franchise permit fees for funding of home and community-based services for elderly and disabled persons, RC § 5168.42.

Nursing home franchise permit fee fund, RC § 5168.54.

Per resident per day rate for other protected costs, RC § 5124.23.

**Ohio Administrative Code**

Calculation, billing, collection and appeal process for the franchise permit fee. OAC 5160-3-30.4.

## § 5168.48 Redetermining nursing homes' and hospitals' franchise permit fees.

(A) Not later than the last day of February of each year, the department of medicaid shall redetermine each nursing home's and hospital's franchise permit fee if one or more bed surrenders occur during the period beginning on the first day of May of the preceding calendar year and ending on the first day of January of the calendar year in which the redetermination is made.

(B) In redetermining nursing homes' and hospitals' franchise permit fees under this section, the department shall do both of the following:

(1) Provide for the redetermination to be conducted in a manner consistent with the terms of the waiver sought under section 5168.43 of the Revised Code;

(2) Recalculate each nursing home's and hospital's franchise permit fee in accordance with division (A) or (B) of section 5168.42 of the Revised Code with the following changes:

(a) In the case of a nursing home or hospital for which one or more bed surrenders occurred during the period beginning on the first day of May of the preceding calendar year and ending on the first day of January of the calendar year in which the redetermination is made, the number of beds included in the calculation for the purpose of division (A)(1) or (B)(1) of section 5168.42 of the Revised Code shall exclude the beds for which bed surrenders occurred during that period.

(b) The number of days used in the calculation under division (A)(2) or (B)(2) of section 5168.42 of the Revised Code shall be the number of days in the first half of the calendar year in which the redetermination is made.

(c) The franchise permit fee rate shall reflect adjustments made under sections 5168.44 and 5168.45 of the Revised Code.

(C) Not later than the first day of March of each year, the department shall notify, electronically or by United States postal service, each nursing home and hospital of the amount of its redetermined franchise permit fee.

(D) Each nursing home and hospital shall pay its redetermined fee to the department in two installment payments not later than forty-five days after the last day of March and June of the calendar year in which the redetermination is made.

**HISTORY:**

2011 HB 153, § 101.01, eff. July 1, 2011; 2013 HB 59, § 101.01, eff. Sept. 29, 2013; 2015 hb64, § 101.01, effective September 29, 2015.



**Editor's Notes**

This section was formerly codified as RC § 3721.531.

**Amendment Notes**

The 2015 amendment, by HB 64, in (C), substituted "notify, electronically or by United States postal service" for "mail to" and deleted "notice" following "and hospital".

The 2013 amendment substituted "medicaid" for "job and family services" in (A); substituted "section 5168.43" for "section 3721.511" in (B)(1); substituted "section 5168.42" for "section 3721.51" in the introductory language of (B)(2) and in (B)(2)(a) and (B)(2)(b); and substituted "sections 5168.44 and 5168.45" for "sections 3721.512 and 3721.513" in (B)(2)(c).

### § 5168.49 Franchise permit fee when nursing home or hospital undergoes change of operator.

If a nursing home or hospital undergoes a change of operator during a fiscal year, the responsibility for paying the franchise permit fee that was determined for the nursing home or hospital under section 5168.47 of the Revised Code, or redetermined for the nursing home or hospital under section 5168.48 of the Revised Code, for that fiscal year shall be divided proportionally. The exiting operator shall be responsible for paying the amount of the fee that is for the part of the fiscal year that ends on the day before the effective date of the change of operator. The entering operator shall be responsible for paying the amount of the fee that is for the part of the fiscal year that begins on the effective date of the change of operator. The department of medicaid is not required to notify the entering operator regarding the amount of that fiscal year's fee for which the entering operator is responsible.

**HISTORY:**

2011 HB 153, § 101.01, eff. July 1, 2011; 2013 HB 59, § 101.01, eff. Sept. 29, 2013; 2015 hb64, § 101.01, effective September 29, 2015.

**Editor's Notes**

This section was formerly codified as RC § 3721.532.

**Amendment Notes**

The 2015 amendment, by HB 64, substituted "notify" for "mail a notice to" in the last sentence.

The 2013 amendment, in the first sentence, substituted "section 5168.47" for "section 3721.53" and "section 5168.48" for "section 3721.531"; and substituted "medicaid" for "job and family services" in the last sentence.

### § 5168.50 Franchise permit fee not to be passed through to residents.

No nursing home or hospital shall directly bill its residents for the franchise permit fee paid under section 5168.47 or 5168.48 of the Revised Code or otherwise directly pass the fee through to its residents.

**HISTORY:**

2011 HB 153, § 101.01, eff. July 1, 2011; 2013 HB 59, § 101.01, eff. Sept. 29, 2013.

**Editor's Notes**

This section was formerly codified as RC § 3721.533.

**Amendment Notes**

The 2013 amendment substituted "section 5168.47 or 5168.48" for "section 3721.53 or 3721.531".

### § 5168.51 Penalty for overdue installments.

If a nursing home or hospital fails to pay the full amount of a franchise permit fee installment when due, the department of medicaid may assess a five per cent penalty on the amount due for each month or fraction thereof the installment is overdue.

**HISTORY:**

145 v H 152 (Eff 7-1-93); 148 v H 471. Eff 7-1-2000; 2013 HB 59, § 101.01, eff. Sept. 29, 2013.

**Editor's Notes**

This section was formerly codified as RC § 3721.54.

**Amendment Notes**

The 2013 amendment substituted "medicaid" for "job and family services".

**RESEARCH REFERENCES AND PRACTICE AIDS**

**Cross-References to Related Sections**

Nursing home franchise permit fee fund, RC § 5168.54.

**Ohio Administrative Code**

Calculation, billing, collection and appeal process for the franchise permit fee. OAC 5160-3-30.4.

### § 5168.52 Additional sanctions for failing to pay required installment.

(A) In addition to assessing a penalty pursuant to section 5168.51 of the Revised Code, the department of medicaid may do any of the following if a nursing facility or hospital fails to pay the full amount of a franchise permit fee installment when due:

(1) Withhold an amount less than or equal to the installment and penalty assessed under section 5168.51 of the Revised Code from a medicaid payment due the nursing facility or hospital until the nursing facility or hospital pays the installment and penalty;

(2) Offset an amount less than or equal to the installment and penalty assessed under section 5168.51 of the Revised Code from a medicaid payment due the nursing facility or hospital;

(3) Terminate the nursing facility or hospital's medicaid provider agreement.

(B) The department may offset a medicaid payment under division (A) of this section without providing notice to the nursing facility or hospital and without conducting an adjudication under Chapter 119. of the Revised Code.

**HISTORY:**

151 v H 66, § 101.01, eff. 6-30-05; 152 v H 119, § 101.01, eff. 6-30-07; 2013 HB 59, § 101.01, eff. Sept. 29, 2013.

**Editor's Notes**

This section was formerly codified as RC § 3721.541.

**Amendment Notes**

The 2013 amendment substituted "section 5168.51" for "section 3721.54" in the introductory language of (A) and in (A)(1) and (A)(2); substituted "medicaid" for "job and family services" in the introductory language of (A); and made a stylistic change.

152 v H 119, effective June 30, 2007, in (A)(1), inserted "less than or"; inserted (A)(2) and redesignated former (A)(2) as (3) and made related changes; in (B), substituted "offset" for "withhold"; and corrected internal references.

### § 5168.53 Appeal of amount of fee.

(A) A nursing home or hospital may appeal the fee assessed under section 5168.42 of the Revised Code, as adjusted under section 5168.44 or 5168.45 of the Revised Code, and redetermined under section 5168.48 of the Revised Code solely on the grounds that the department of medicaid committed a material error in determining or redetermining the amount of the fee. A request for an appeal must be received by the department not later than fifteen days after the date the department notifies the nursing home or hospital of the fee and must include written materials setting forth the basis for the appeal.

(B) If a nursing home or hospital submits a request for an appeal within the time required under division (A) of this section, the department shall hold a public hearing in Columbus not later than thirty days after the date the department receives the request for an appeal. The department shall, not later than ten days before the date of the hearing, notify, electronically or by United States postal service, the nursing home or hospital of the date, time, and place of the hearing. The department may hear all the requested appeals in one public hearing.

(C) On the basis of the evidence presented at the hearing or any other evidence submitted by the nursing home or hospital, the department may adjust a fee. The department's decision is final.

**HISTORY:**
145 v H 152 (Eff 7-1-93); 148 v H 471. Eff 7-1-2000; 153 v H 1, § 101.01, eff. 7-17-09; 2011 HB 153, § 101.01, eff. July 1, 2011; 2013 HB 59, § 101.01, eff. Sept. 29, 2013; 2015 hb64, § 101.01, effective September 29, 2015.

**Editor's Notes**
This section was formerly codified as RC § 3721.55.

**Amendment Notes**
The 2015 amendment, by HB 64, substituted "notifies the nursing home or hospital" for "mails the notice" in the second sentence of (A); and, in the second sentence of (B), substituted "notify, electronically or by United States postal service, the nursing home or hospital" for "mail a notice" and deleted "to the nursing home or hospital" from the end.

The 2013 amendment, in the first sentence of (A), substituted "section 5168.42" for "section 3721.51", "section 5168.44 or 5168.45" for "section 3721.512 or 3721.513", "section 5168.48" for "section 3721.531", and "medicaid" for "and family services"; and deleted "of job and family services" preceding "shall hold a" in the first sentence of (B).

The 2011 amendment, in the first sentence of (A), substituted "assessed" for "imposed", inserted "and redetermined under section 3721.531 of the Revised Code", and inserted "or redetermining".

153 v H 1, effective July 17, 2009, inserted "as adjusted under section 3721.512 or 3721.513 of the Revised Code" in the first sentence of (A).

**RESEARCH REFERENCES AND PRACTICE AIDS**

**Ohio Administrative Code**
Calculation, billing, collection and appeal process for the franchise permit fee (FPF). OAC 5160-3-30.4.

### § 5168.54 Nursing home franchise permit fee fund.

(A) There is hereby created in the state treasury the nursing home franchise permit fee fund. All payments and penalties paid by nursing homes and hospitals under sections 5168.47, 5168.48, and 5168.51 of the Revised Code shall be deposited into the fund. The fund shall also consist of money deposited into it pursuant to sections 3769.08 and 3769.26 of the Revised Code. Subject to division (B) of section 3769.08 of the Revised Code, the department of medicaid shall use the money in the fund to make medicaid payments to providers of nursing facility services and providers of home and community-based services. Money in the fund may also be used for the residential state supplement program established under section 5119.41 of the Revised Code.

(B) Any money remaining in the nursing home franchise permit fee fund after payments specified in division (A) of this section are made shall be retained in the fund. Any interest or other investment proceeds earned on money in the fund shall be credited to the fund and used to make medicaid payments in accordance with division (A) of this section.

**HISTORY:**
151 v H 66, § 101.01, eff. 7-1-05; 2011 HB 153, § 101.01, eff. July 1, 2011; 2013 HB 59, § 101.01, eff. Sept. 29, 2013.

**Editor's Notes**
This section was formerly codified as RC § 3721.561.

Former § 3721.56 [145 v H 152 (Eff 7-1-93); 146 v H 117 (Eff 6-30-95); 148 v H 471 (Eff 7-1-2000); 149 v H 94 (Eff 6-6-2001); 149 v S 261. Eff 6-5-2002; 151 v H 66, § 101.01, eff. 7-1-05; 152 v H 119, § 101.01, eff. 6-30-07; 153 v H 1, § 101.01, eff. 7-17-09; 2011 HB 153, § 101.01, eff. July 1, 2011], concerning the home and community-based services for the aged fund, was repealed by 2011 HB 153, § 105.01, effective July 1, 2011.

This section was formerly codified as RC § 3721.56.

**Amendment Notes**
The 2013 amendment, in (A), substituted "sections 5168.47, 5168.48, and 5168.51" for "sections 3721.53, 3721.531, and 3721.54" in the second sentence, substituted "medicaid" for "and family services" in the fourth sentence, and substituted "section 5119.41" for "section 5119.69" in the last sentence.

The 2011 amendment rewrote (A), which formerly read: "There is hereby created in the state treasury the nursing facility stabilization fund. All payments and penalties paid by nursing homes and hospitals under sections 3721.53 and 3721.54 of the Revised Code that are not deposited into the home and community-based services for the aged fund shall be deposited into the fund. The department of job and family services shall use the money in the fund to make medicaid payments to nursing facilities"; and substituted "home franchise permit fee" for "facility stabilization" in the first sentence of (B).

### § 5168.55 Investigations; enforcement actions.

The department of medicaid may make any investigation it considers appropriate to obtain information necessary to fulfill its duties under sections 5168.40 to 5168.56 of the Revised Code. At the request of the department, the attorney general shall aid in any such investigations. The attorney general shall institute and prosecute all necessary actions for the enforcement of sections 5168.40 to 5168.56 of the Revised Code, except that at the request of the attorney general, the county prosecutor of the county in which a nursing home or hospital that has failed to comply with sections 5168.40 to 5168.56 of the Revised Code is located shall institute and prosecute any necessary action against the nursing home or hospital.

**HISTORY:**
145 v H 152 (Eff 7-1-93); 148 v H 471. Eff 7-1-2000; 2013 HB 59, § 101.01, eff. Sept. 29, 2013.

**Editor's Notes**
This section was formerly codified as RC § 3721.57.

**Amendment Notes**
The 2013 amendment substituted "medicaid" for "and family services" in the first sentence; and substituted "sections 5168.40 to 5168.56" for "sections 3721.50 to 3721.58" throughout the section.

**RESEARCH REFERENCES AND PRACTICE AIDS**

**Ohio Administrative Code**
Enforcement of franchise permit fee program. OAC 5160-3-30.4.

### § 5168.56 Rules for implementation or ceasing implementation of provisions and for distributing moneys.

The medicaid director shall adopt rules in accordance with Chapter 119. of the Revised Code to do both of the following:

(A) Prescribe the actions the department of medicaid will take to cease implementation of sections 5168.40 to 5168.56 of the Revised Code if the United States centers for medicare and medicaid services determines that the franchise permit fee established by those sections is an impermissible health-care related tax under the "Social Security Act," section 1903(w), 42 U.S.C. 1396b(w);

(B) Establish any requirements or procedures the director considers necessary to implement sections 5168.40 to 5168.56 of the Revised Code.

**HISTORY:**
145 v H 152 (Eff 7-1-93); 148 v H 471. Eff 7-1-2000; 151 v H 66, § 101.01,

eff. 7-1-05; 2011 HB 153, § 101.01, eff. July 1, 2011; 2013 HB 59, § 101.01, eff. Sept. 29, 2013.

**Editor's Notes**

This section was formerly codified as RC § 3721.58.

**Amendment Notes**

The 2013 amendment substituted "medicaid director" for "director of job and family services" in the introductory language; in (A), substituted "department of medicaid" for "department of job and family services", "sections 5168.40 to 5168.56" for "sections 3721.50 through 3721.57", and "the 'Social Security Act,' section 1903(w), 42 U.S.C. 1396b(w)" for "section 1903(w) of the 'Social Security Act,' 105 Stat. 1793 (1991), 42 U.S.C. 1396b(w), as amended"; and substituted "sections 5168.40 to 5168.56" for "sections 3721.50 to 3721.58" in (B).

The 2011 amendment substituted "105 Stat. 1793 (1991)" for "49 Stat. 620 (1935)" in (A); deleted (B), which read: "Establish the method of distributing moneys in the home and community-based services for the aged fund created under section 3721.56 of the Revised Code"; redesignated former (C) as (B); and made a related change.

151 v H 66, effective July 1, 2005, in (A), substituted "centers for medicare and Medicaid services" for "health care financing administration"; and corrected internal references and made minor stylistic changes.

## RESEARCH REFERENCES AND PRACTICE AIDS

**Cross-References to Related Sections**

Exemptions from fees, RC § 3721.511.

Franchise permit fees for funding of home and community-based services for elderly and disabled persons, RC § 5168.42.

Investigations; enforcement actions, RC § 5168.55.

Recategorization of hospital beds to skilled nursing beds; nursing home placement clearinghouses, RC § 3702.521.

**Ohio Administrative Code**

Method of distribution of franchise permit fee proceeds: use for programs. OAC 5101:3-3-49.7.

Procedure for terminating the franchise permit fee program for nursing facilities (NFs) and hospitals. OAC 5160-3-30.4.

# TITLE 53

# REAL PROPERTY



## CHAPTER 5302

## STATUTORY FORMS OF LAND CONVEYANCE



### § 5302.02 Rules and definitions to apply to all instruments relating to real estate.

The rules and definitions contained in sections 5302.03, 5302.04, 5302.06, 5302.08, 5302.10, 5302.13, 5302.17, 5302.18, 5302.19, 5302.20, and 5302.21 of the Revised Code apply to all deeds or other instruments relating to real estate, whether the statutory forms or other forms are used, where the instruments are executed on or after October 1, 1965. The rules and definitions contained in section 5302.22 of the Revised Code, as it existed prior to the effective date of this amendment, apply to instruments executed on or after August 29, 2000, and prior to the effective date of this amendment. The rules and definitions contained in section 5302.22 of the Revised Code apply to instruments executed on or after the effective date of this amendment.

**HISTORY:**

131 v 1251 (Eff 10-30-65); 142 v H 502 (Eff 5-31-88); 148 v H 313. Eff 8-29-2000; 153 v S 124, § 1, eff. 12-28-09.

**Amendment Notes**

153 v S 124, effective December 28, 2009, rewrote the section.

**NOTES TO DECISIONS**

Analysis

Construction
Seller's knowledge
—Liability

**Construction**

Summary judgment to deed contestants was proper in their declaratory judgment action, seeking to invalidate a purported transfer of real property from a decedent to a deed grantee, as a transfer on death deed was invalid pursuant to R.C. 5302.02 where it was not executed after the effective date of R.C. 5302.22; as no transfer of real property occurred pursuant thereto, the real property belonged to the decedent's estate. Rickels v. Goyings, 2008-Ohio-2119, 2008 Ohio App. LEXIS 1833 (Ohio Ct. App., Paulding County 2008).

**Seller's knowledge**

**—Liability**

Trial court erred in finding that the property seller was liable for the cost of replacing an air conditioner that the property purchaser found did not work, as the trial court was required to find that the property seller had "actual knowledge" of the inoperative air conditioner and competent, credible evidence in the record did not support such a finding; accordingly, the trial court's ruling in favor of the property purchaser was against the manifest weight of the evidence. Reiter v. Davidson, 2004-Ohio-2800, 2004 Ohio App. LEXIS 2476 (Ohio Ct. App., Seneca County 2004).

**RESEARCH REFERENCES AND PRACTICE AIDS**

**Cross-References to Related Sections**

Designation of transfer on death beneficiary, RC § 5302.23.

## CO-OWNERSHIP

### § 5302.22 Transfer on death designation affidavit.

(A) As used in sections 5302.22, 5302.222, 5302.23, and 5302.24 of the Revised Code:

(1) "Affidavit of confirmation" means an affidavit executed under division (A) of section 5302.222 of the Revised Code.

(2) "Survivorship tenancy" means an ownership of real property or any interest in real property by two or more persons that is created by executing a deed pursuant to section 5302.17 of the Revised Code.

(3) "Survivorship tenant" means one of the owners of real property or any interest in real property in a survivorship tenancy.

(4) "Tenants by the entireties" mean only those persons who are vested as tenants in an estate by the entireties with survivorship pursuant to any deed recorded between February 9, 1972, and April 3, 1985, under section 5302.17 of the Revised Code as it existed during that period of time. Nothing in sections 5302.22, 5302.222, 5302.23, and 5302.24 of the Revised Code authorizes the creation of a tenancy by the entireties or recognizes a tenancy by the entireties created outside that period of time.

(5) "Transfer on death designation affidavit" means an affidavit executed under this section.

(6) "Transfer on death beneficiary or beneficiaries" means the beneficiary or beneficiaries designated in a transfer on death designation affidavit.

(B) Any individual who, under the Revised Code or the common law of this state, owns real property or any interest in real property as a sole owner, as a tenant in common, or as a survivorship tenant, or together with the individual's spouse owns an indivisible interest in real property as tenants by the entireties, may designate the entire interest, or any specified part that is less than the entire interest, in that real property as transferable on death to a designated beneficiary or beneficiaries by executing, together with the individual's spouse, if any, a transfer on death designation affidavit as provided in this section. If the affidavit is executed by an individual together with the individual's spouse, if any, the dower rights of the spouse are subordinate to the vesting of title to the interest in the real property in the transfer on death beneficiary or beneficiaries designated under this section. The affidavit shall be recorded in the office of the county recorder in the county in which the real property is located, and, when so recorded, the affidavit or a certified copy of the affidavit shall be evidence of the transfer on death beneficiary or beneficiaries so designated in the affidavit insofar as the affidavit affects title to the real property.

(C)(1) If an individual who owns real property or an interest in real property as a sole owner or as a tenant in common executes a transfer on death designation affidavit, upon the death of that individual, title to the real property or interest in the real property specified in the affidavit vests in the transfer on death beneficiary or beneficiaries designated in the affidavit.

(2) If an individual who owns real property or an interest in real property as a survivorship tenant executes a transfer on death designation affidavit, upon the death of that individual or of one but not all of the surviving survivorship tenants, title to the real property or interest in the real property specified in the affidavit vests in the surviving survivorship tenant or tenants. Upon the death of the last surviving survivorship tenant, title to the real property or interest in the real property vests in the

Titles 39 — 57

transfer on death beneficiary or beneficiaries designated in the affidavit, subject to division (B)(7) of section 5302.23 of the Revised Code.

(3) If an individual who together with the individual's spouse owns an indivisible interest in real property as tenants by the entireties executes a transfer on death designation affidavit, upon the death of that individual, title to the real property or interest in the real property vests in the remaining tenant by the entireties. Upon the death of the remaining tenant by the entireties, title to the real property or interest in the real property vests in the transfer on death beneficiary or beneficiaries designated in the affidavit, subject to division (B)(7) of section 5302.23 of the Revised Code.

(D) A transfer on death designation affidavit shall be verified before any person authorized to administer oaths and shall include all of the following:

(1) A description of the real property the title to which is affected by the affidavit and a reference to an instrument of record containing that description;

(2) If less than the entire interest in the real property is to be transferred on death under the affidavit, a statement of the specific interest or part of the interest in the real property that is to be so transferred;

(3) A statement by the individual executing the affidavit that the individual is the person appearing on the record of the real property as the owner of the real property or interest in the real property at the time of the recording of the affidavit and the marital status of that owner. If the owner is married, the affidavit shall include a statement by the owner's spouse stating that the spouse's dower rights are subordinate to the vesting of title to the real property or interest in the real property in the transfer on death beneficiary or beneficiaries designated in the affidavit.

(4) A statement designating one or more persons, identified by name, as transfer on death beneficiary or beneficiaries.

(E) The county recorder of the county in which a transfer on death designation affidavit is offered for recording shall receive the affidavit and cause it to be recorded in the same manner as deeds are recorded. The county recorder shall collect a fee for recording the affidavit in the same amount as the fee for recording deeds. The county recorder shall index the affidavit in the name of the owner of record of the real property or interest in the real property who executed the affidavit.

(F) A transfer on death designation affidavit need not be supported by consideration and need not be delivered to the transfer on death beneficiary or beneficiaries designated in the affidavit to be effective. However, in order to be effective, that affidavit shall be recorded with the county recorder as described in this section prior to the death of the individual who executed the affidavit.

(G) Subject to division (C) of this section, upon the death of any individual who owns real property or an interest in real property that is subject to a transfer on death beneficiary designation made under a transfer on death designation affidavit as provided in this section, that real property or interest in real property of the deceased owner shall be transferred only to the transfer on death beneficiary or beneficiaries who are identified in the affidavit by name and who survive the deceased owner or that are in existence on the date of death of the deceased owner.

For purposes of this division, if a natural or legal person designated by name in the affidavit as a transfer on death beneficiary or as a contingent transfer on death beneficiary as provided in division (B)(2) of section 5302.23 of the Revised Code solely in that person's capacity as a trustee of a trust has died, has resigned, or otherwise has been replaced by a successor trustee of the trust on the date of death of the deceased owner, the successor trustee of the trust shall be considered the transfer on death beneficiary or contingent transfer on death beneficiary in existence on the date of death of the deceased owner in full compliance with this division, notwithstanding that the successor trustee is not named as a transfer on death beneficiary or contingent transfer on death beneficiary in the affidavit.

(H) Any person who knowingly makes any false statement in a transfer on death designation affidavit is guilty of falsification under division (A)(6) of section 2921.13 of the Revised Code.



**HISTORY:**

148 v H 313 (Eff 8-29-2000); 149 v H 279 (Eff 2-1-2002); 149 v H 470. Eff 2-1-2002; 153 v S 124, § 1, eff. 12-28-09.

**Editor's Notes**

See provisions, § 4 of HB 470 (149 v —), following RC § 5302.05.

**Amendment Notes**

153 v S 124, effective December 28, 2009, rewrote the section.

**NOTES TO DECISIONS**

Analysis



**Fee simple**

Appellants' complaint was properly dismissed under Civ.R. 12(B)(6) for failure to state a claim because a fee simple interest in the subject real estate was transferred to the transferees; the deed conveyed "a remainder over in fee simple" which indicated that a fee simple title was conveyed. Because appellants did not follow the statutory form in conveying the land under former R.C. 5302.22(A), they could not claim its benefits; the language that the deed transferred on death to appellants was ineffectual in view of the fee simple interest already transferred to the transferees. Brannan v. Easter, 2012-Ohio-2045, 2012 Ohio App. LEXIS 1796 (Ohio Ct. App., Scioto County 2012).

**Oil and gas rights**

When the decedent died, the oil company which leased the decedent's farm property held a fee simple determinable interest in the oil and gas subject to a reverter and the decedent owned the surface rights and the right to reversion in the oil and gas upon expiration of the lease. The lease remained with the farm property even though title to the property transferred from the decedent to the decedent's grandchild, as the transfer-on-death beneficiary, so that the grandchild owned the decedent's interest in the property subject to the lease. In re Estate of Ball, 2016-Ohio-4917, 67 N.E.3d 28, 2016 Ohio App. LEXIS 2718 (Ohio Ct. App., Belmont County 2016).

**Recording**

Public policy supports the requirement that a transfer on death deed be recorded before the death of the grantor because the designation of a transfer on death beneficiary can be revoked or changed at any time, without the consent of the beneficiary, by the owner's executing and recording a deed to one or more persons, including the owner, with or without the designation of another transfer on death beneficiary, so the requirement that the deed be recorded before the grantor's death helps alleviate concerns about fraud and undue influence, and the formality of the recording process helps ensure that the owner intended to make the transfer. Mattia v. Hall, 2008-Ohio-180, 2008 Ohio App. LEXIS 152 (Ohio Ct. App., Summit County 2008).

R.C. 5302.22 clearly requires both execution and recordation of a transfer on death deed, as the language of the statute makes explicit that execution and recordation together create a present interest as sole owner or as a tenant in common in the grantee and creates a transfer on death interest in the beneficiary or beneficiaries, under R.C. 5302.22(A), so the interests in the property are not created until the grantor executes and records the deed. Mattia v. Hall, 2008-Ohio-180, 2008 Ohio App. LEXIS 152 (Ohio Ct. App., Summit County 2008).

Recordation of a transfer on death deed must occur before the grantor's death because R.C. 5302.22 allows any person who owns real property, by executing and recording a transfer on death deed, to create in a transfer on death beneficiary an interest in the property that is transferable on the death of the property owner. Mattia v. Hall, 2008-Ohio-180, 2008 Ohio App. LEXIS 152 (Ohio Ct. App., Summit County 2008).

Deed purporting to transfer real estate from the grantor to the grantor and to grant the grantor's ex-wife a transfer on death interest in the property was invalid because the deed was not recorded before the grantor died, and, under R.C. 5302.22, both execution and recordation of the deed were required to make any transfer effective, so, when the deed was recorded, a present interest in the property could not have been transferred to the grantor as grantee, since property could not be transferred to a deceased person, nor could any interest have been created in the ex-wife. Mattia v. Hall, 2008-Ohio-180, 2008 Ohio App. LEXIS 152 (Ohio Ct. App., Summit County 2008).

When a transfer on death deed was not recorded before the death of the grantor, it did not effectuate a transfer of the subject property, so it had to be included in an inventory of the decedent's estate. In re Estate of Scott,

2005-Ohio-5917, 164 Ohio App. 3d 464, 842 N.E.2d 1071, 2005 Ohio App. LEXIS 5339 (Ohio Ct. App., Miami County 2005).

Since the transfer on death deed was not recorded prior to the grantor's death, the grantor did not effectuate a transfer upon her death to the grantee: In re Estate of Scott, 2005-Ohio-5917, 164 Ohio App. 3d 464, 842 N.E.2d 1071, 2005 Ohio App. LEXIS 5339 (Ohio Ct. App., Miami County 2005).

**Sale**

No sale of condominium property took place for purposes of a declaration and bylaws, or for purposes of the Ohio Condominium Act, R.C. ch. 5311, when a dentist conveyed the dentist's office unit in a professional office building by way of a quit-claim deed, with a transfer-on-death provision, to the dentist's wife because the dentist conveyed the dentist's fee simple interest to the dentist's wife after signing the condominium documents. The dentist, under R.C. 2103.02, retained a dower interest in the property, which was an estate for life in one-third of the property, and was not a legal interest, as the dentist's wife held full legal title to the property. DiPasquale v. Costas, 2010-Ohio-832, 186 Ohio App. 3d 121, 926 N.E.2d 682, 2010 Ohio App. LEXIS 676 (Ohio Ct. App., Montgomery County 2010).

**Standing**

Executor lacked standing to bring a quiet-title action against the beneficiaries under the decedent's transfer-on-death (TOD) affidavit because there was no allegation in the complaint, nor was it anywhere claimed, that the executor was in possession of the decedent's house or that the executor, individually as the decedent's son, or the estate had an interest in remainder or reversion in the house. Lomelino v. Lomelino, 2020-Ohio-1645, 2020 Ohio App. LEXIS 1591 (Ohio Ct. App., Montgomery County 2020).

**Validity**

Transfer-on-death designation affidavit was effective to transfer title of the property because the beneficiaries presented unchallenged evidence of the decedent's testamentary capacity sufficient to overcome the presumption of lack of capacity. Lomelino v. Lomelino, 2020-Ohio-1645, 2020 Ohio App. LEXIS 1591 (Ohio Ct. App., Montgomery County 2020).

Imposition of a constructive trust on an 80-acre parcel transferred to the beneficiaries upon the owner's death was not warranted because the transfer on death (TOD) deed followed the form prescribed by the former version of this statute and was duly recorded, there was no finding of unjust enrichment, and, while the owner executed a new last will and testament and power of attorney in favor of the objectors, there was no direct evidence to show that the owner intended to execute a new TOD deed. Blausey v. VanNess, 2016-Ohio-5068, 2016 Ohio App. LEXIS 2885 (Ohio Ct. App., Ottawa County 2016).

Transfer on death deed was not in substantial compliance with the statute because the deed lacked any indication of its date of execution, and the acknowledgment clause was "blank" since it listed neither a mother as the grantor nor the date of its acknowledgment. Fragola v. Graham, 2016-Ohio-8281, 78 N.E.3d 277, 2016 Ohio App. LEXIS 5129 (Ohio Ct. App., Summit County 2016), vacated in part, 2017 Ohio Misc. LEXIS 13378 (Ohio C.P. Dec. 12, 2017).

Summary judgment to deed contestants was proper in their declaratory judgment action, seeking to invalidate a purported transfer of real property from a decedent to a deed grantee, as a transfer on death deed was invalid pursuant to R.C. 5302.02 where it was not executed after the effective date of R.C. 5302.22; as no transfer of real property occurred pursuant thereto, the real property belonged to the decedent's estate. Rickels v. Goyings, 2008-Ohio-2119, 2008 Ohio App. LEXIS 1833 (Ohio Ct. App., Paulding County 2008).

### RESEARCH REFERENCES AND PRACTICE AIDS

**Practice Manuals and Treatises**

Anderson's Ohio Elder Law Practice Manual § 4.5 Resource Limits and Statutory Exemptions

Anderson's Ohio Residential Real Estate Manual § 9.09 "Void" or "Voidable"

Anderson's Ohio Probate Practice and Procedure Form 16.18 Transfer on death deed

**Practice Guides**

Anderson's Ohio Probate Practice and Procedure § 13.03 Preparation and content of the inventory

Anderson's Ohio Probate Practice and Procedure § 16.03 Evidence of title

Anderson's Ohio Probate Practice and Procedure § 16.10 Transfer on death deeds

Anderson's Ohio Probate Practice and Procedure § 21.15 Distributing real estate

Anderson's Ohio Probate Practice and Procedure § 21.18 Disclaimers

**Practice Forms**

Affidavit for Transfer of Interest Created by Transfer on Death Deed 1, 11 OH Forms of Pleading & Practice — Probate Form 6:6

Disclaimer of Interest Created by Transfer on Death Deed 1, 12 OH Forms of Pleading & Practice — Probate Form 24:1A

## § 5302.221 Medicaid estate recovery program form.

(A) As used in this section, "medicaid estate recovery program" means the program instituted under section 5162.21 of the Revised Code.

(B) The administrator of the medicaid estate recovery program shall prescribe a form on which a beneficiary of a transfer on death designation affidavit as provided in section 5302.22 of the Revised Code, who survives the deceased owner of the real property or an interest in the real property or that is in existence on the date of death of the deceased owner, or that beneficiary's representative is to indicate both of the following:

(1) Which of the following applies to the deceased owner:

(a) The deceased owner had been a medicaid recipient.

(b) The deceased owner had never been a medicaid recipient.

(c) The beneficiary or representative does not know whether the deceased owner had ever been a medicaid recipient.

(2) If the spouse of the deceased owner died before the owner died, which of the following applies to the predeceased spouse:

(a) The predeceased spouse had been a medicaid recipient.

(b) The predeceased spouse had never been a medicaid recipient.

(c) The beneficiary or representative does not know whether the predeceased spouse had ever been a medicaid recipient.

(C) The administrator of the medicaid estate recovery program shall make the form prescribed under division (B) of this section available to county recorders. A county recorder shall provide a copy of the form to a beneficiary of a transfer on death designation affidavit or the beneficiary's representative before recording the transfer of the real property or interest in the real property under section 5302.222 of the Revised Code. A beneficiary or beneficiary's representative shall submit a copy of the properly completed form to the administrator of the medicaid estate recovery program if the beneficiary or representative indicates any of the following on the form:

(1) That the deceased owner had been a medicaid recipient or that the beneficiary or representative does not know whether the deceased owner had ever been a medicaid recipient;

(2) That the predeceased spouse of the deceased owner had been a medicaid recipient or that the beneficiary or representative does not know whether the predeceased spouse had ever been a medicaid recipient.

**HISTORY:**

152 v H 119, § 101.01, eff. 9-29-07; 153 v S 124, § 1, eff. 12-28-09; 2013 HB 59, § 101.01, eff. Sept. 29, 2013; 2016 sb227, § 1, effective April 6, 2017.

**Amendment Notes**

The 2016 amendment by SB 227 rewrote (A) and (B); in (C), added the first sentence, in the second sentence, substituted "provide a copy of the form to a beneficiary" for "obtain a properly completed form prescribed under division (B) of this section from the beneficiary" and deleted "and send a copy of the form to the administrator of the medicaid estate recovery program" following "beneficiary's representative", and added the last sentence; and added (C)(1) and (C)(2).

The 2013 amendment substituted "section 5162.21" for "section 5111.11" twice in (A).

153 v S 124, effective December 28, 2009, in (B) and (C), substituted "designation affidavit" for "deed"; and corrected internal references and made stylistic changes.

## § 5302.222 Recording of transfer on death designation affidavit; affidavit of confirmation.

(A) The transfer of a deceased owner's real property or interest in real property as designated in a transfer on death designation affidavit provided in section 5302.22 of the Revised Code shall be recorded by presenting to the county auditor of the county in which the real property is located and filing with the county recorder of that county an affidavit of confirmation executed by any transfer on death beneficiary to whom the transfer is made. The affidavit of confirmation shall be verified before a person authorized to administer oaths and shall be accompanied by a certified copy of the death certificate for the deceased owner. The affidavit of confirmation shall contain all of the following information:

(1) The name and address of each transfer on death beneficiary who survived the deceased owner or that is in existence on the date of death of the deceased owner. If a named beneficiary was designated as a transfer on death beneficiary solely in that person's capacity as a trustee of a trust and that trustee subsequently has been replaced by a successor trustee, the affidavit of confirmation shall include the name and address of the successor trustee and shall be accompanied by a copy of the recorded successor trustee affidavit described in section 5302.171 of the Revised Code.

(2) The date of death of the deceased owner;

(3) A description of the subject real property or interest in real property;

(4) The name of each transfer on death beneficiary who has not survived the deceased owner or that is not in existence on the date of death of the deceased owner.

(B) The affidavit of confirmation shall be accompanied by a certified copy of the death certificate for each transfer on death beneficiary who has not survived the deceased owner.

(C) The county recorder shall record in the official records any affidavit of confirmation filed under this section.

(D) Upon the death of any individual holding real property or an interest in real property that is the subject of a transfer on death designation affidavit as provided in section 5302.22 of the Revised Code, if the title to the real property is registered pursuant to Chapter 5309. of the Revised Code, the procedure for the transfer of the interest of the deceased owner to the transfer on death beneficiary or beneficiaries designated in the affidavit shall be pursuant to section 5309.081 of the Revised Code.

(E) Any person who knowingly makes any false statement in an affidavit of confirmation is guilty of falsification under division (A)(6) of section 2921.13 of the Revised Code.



**HISTORY:**

153 v S 124, § 1, eff. 12-28-09; 2013 HB 72, § 1, eff. Jan. 30, 2014.

**Amendment Notes**

The 2013 amendment, in (C), substituted "record in the official records" for "make an index reference in the record of deeds to" and deleted "with the county recorder" following "confirmation filed".

### § 5302.23 Designation of transfer on death beneficiary.

(A) Any affidavit containing language that shows a clear intent to designate a transfer on death beneficiary shall be liberally construed to do so.

(B) Real property or an interest in real property that is the subject of a transfer on death designation affidavit as provided in section 5302.22 of the Revised Code or as described in division (A) of this section has all of the following characteristics and ramifications:

(1) An interest of a deceased owner shall be transferred to the transfer on death beneficiaries who are identified in the affidavit by name and who survive the deceased owner or that are in existence on the date of the deceased owner's death. If there is a designation of more than one transfer on death beneficiary, the beneficiaries shall take title to the interest in equal shares as tenants in common, unless the deceased owner has specifically designated other than equal shares or has designated that the beneficiaries take title as survivorship tenants, subject to division (B)(3) of this section. If a transfer on death beneficiary does not survive the deceased owner or is not in existence on the date of the deceased owner's death, and the deceased owner has designated one or more persons as contingent transfer on death beneficiaries as provided in division (B)(2) of this section, the designated contingent transfer on death beneficiaries shall take the same interest that would have passed to the transfer on death beneficiary had that transfer on death beneficiary survived the deceased owner or been in existence on the date of the deceased owner's death. If none of the designated transfer on death beneficiaries survives the deceased owner or is in existence on the date of the deceased owner's death and no contingent transfer on death beneficiaries have been designated, have survived the deceased owner, or are in existence on the date of death of the deceased owner, the interest of the deceased owner shall be distributed as part of the probate estate of the deceased owner of the interest. If there are two or more transfer on death beneficiaries and the deceased owner has designated that title to the interest in the real property be taken by those beneficiaries as survivorship tenants, no designated contingent transfer on death beneficiaries shall take title to the interest unless none of the transfer on death beneficiaries survives the deceased owner on the date of death of the deceased owner.

(2) A transfer on death designation affidavit may contain a designation of one or more persons as contingent transfer on death beneficiaries, who shall take the interest of the deceased owner that would otherwise have passed to the transfer on death beneficiary if that named transfer on death beneficiary does not survive the deceased owner or is not in existence on the date of death of the deceased owner. Persons designated as contingent transfer on death beneficiaries shall be identified in the affidavit by name.

(3) Any transfer on death beneficiary or contingent transfer on death beneficiary may be a natural or legal person, including, but not limited to, a bank as trustee of a trust, except that if two or more transfer on death beneficiaries are designated as survivorship tenants, all of those beneficiaries shall be natural persons and if two or more contingent transfer on death beneficiaries are designated as survivorship tenants, all of those contingent beneficiaries shall be natural persons. A natural person who is designated a transfer on death beneficiary or contingent transfer on death beneficiary solely in that natural person's capacity as a trustee of a trust is not considered a natural person for purposes of designating the transfer on death beneficiaries or contingent transfer on death beneficiaries as survivorship tenants under division (B)(3) of this section.

(4) The designation of a transfer on death beneficiary has no effect on the present ownership of real property, and a person designated as a transfer on death beneficiary has no interest in the real property until the death of the owner of the interest.

(5) The designation in a transfer on death designation affidavit of any transfer on death beneficiary may be revoked or changed at any time, without the consent of that transfer on death beneficiary, by the owner of the interest, by the surviving survivorship tenants of the interest, or by the remaining tenant by the entireties of the interest, by executing and recording, prior to the death of the owner of the interest, of the surviving survivorship tenants of the interest, or of the remaining tenant by the entireties of the interest, as the case may be, a new transfer on death designation affidavit pursuant to section 5302.22 of the Revised Code stating the revocation or change in that designation. The new transfer on death designation affidavit shall automatically supersede and revoke all prior recorded transfer on death designation affidavits with respect to the real property or the interest in real property identified in the new affidavit, provided that the prior recorded affidavit was executed before the later recorded affidavit.

(6) A fee simple title or any fractional interest in a fee simple title may be subjected to a transfer on death beneficiary designation.

(7)(a) A transfer on death beneficiary takes only the interest that the deceased owner or owners of the interest held on the date of death, subject to all encumbrances, reservations, and exceptions.

(b) If the owners hold title to the interest in a survivorship tenancy, the death of all except the last survivorship tenant automatically terminates and nullifies any transfer on death beneficiary designations made solely by the deceased survivorship tenant or tenants without joinder by the last surviving survivorship tenant. The termination or nullification of any transfer on death beneficiary designations under division (B)(7)(b) of this section is effective as of the date of death of a deceased survivorship tenant. No affirmative act of revocation is required of the last surviving survivorship tenant for the termination or nullification of the transfer on death beneficiary designations to occur as described in division (B)(7)(b) of this section. If the last surviving survivorship tenant dies with no transfer on death beneficiary designation, the entire interest of that last surviving survivorship tenant shall be distributed as part of the tenant's probate estate.

(c) If the owners hold title to the interest in a tenancy by the entireties, the death of the first tenant by the entireties automatically terminates and nullifies any transfer on death beneficiary designations made solely by that deceased first tenant without joinder by the remaining tenant by the entireties. The termination or nullification of any transfer on death beneficiary designations under division (B)(7)(c) of this section is effective as of the date of death of the first tenant by the entireties. No affirmative act of revocation is required of the remaining tenant by the entireties for the termination or nullification of the transfer on death beneficiary designations to occur as described in division (B)(7)(c) of this section. If the remaining tenant by the entireties dies with no transfer on death beneficiary designation, the entire interest of that remaining tenant shall be distributed as part of the tenant's probate estate.

(8) No rights of any lienholder, including, but not limited to, any mortgagee, judgment creditor, or mechanic's lien holder, shall be affected by the designation of a transfer on death beneficiary pursuant to this section and section 5302.22 of the Revised Code. If any lienholder takes action to enforce the lien, by foreclosure or otherwise through a court proceeding, it is not necessary to join any transfer on death beneficiary as a party defendant in the action unless the transfer on death beneficiary has another interest in the real property.

(9) Any transfer on death of real property or of an interest in real property that results from a transfer on death designation affidavit designating a transfer on death beneficiary is not testamentary. That transfer on death shall supersede any attempted testate or intestate transfer of that real property or interest in real property.

(10) The execution and recording of a transfer on death designation affidavit shall be effective to terminate the designation of a transfer on death beneficiary in a transfer on death deed involving the same real property or interest in real property and recorded prior to the effective date of this section.

(11) The execution and recording of a transfer on death designation affidavit shall be effective to bar the vesting of any rights of dower in a subsequent spouse of the owner of the real property who executed that affidavit unless the affidavit is revoked or changed.

(12) If, after the execution and recording of a transfer on death designation affidavit under which the owner of the real property's spouse is designated the transfer on death beneficiary, the owner of the real property and such owner's spouse are divorced, obtain a dissolution of the marriage, or have the marriage annulled, then the designation of the owner's spouse as a transfer on death beneficiary on such instrument shall be terminated and the spouse shall be deemed to have predeceased the owner of the real property.

(C) If, after the execution and recording of a transfer on death deed under which the owner of the real property's spouse is designated the transfer on death beneficiary, the owner of the real property and such owner's spouse are divorced, obtain a dissolution of the marriage, or have the marriage annulled, then the designation of the owner's spouse as a transfer on death beneficiary on such instrument shall be terminated and the spouse shall be deemed to have predeceased the owner of the real property.

**HISTORY:**

148 v H 313. Eff 8-29-2000; 153 v S 124, § 1, eff. 12-28-09; 2016 sb232, § 1, effective March 14, 2017.

**Amendment Notes**

153 v S 124, effective December 28, 2009, rewrote the section.
The 2016 amendment by SB 232 added (B)(12) and (C).

**NOTES TO DECISIONS**

Analysis

Applicability
Condominium
Oil and gas interests
Validity

**Applicability**

Trial court did not err in failing to apply the former version of the statute to preclude the daughter's claim for intentional interference with an expectancy of inheritance and specific performance because it was clear from the name of the claim itself that the inheritance was not a present interest in the property but only an expectancy of an inheritance. Thus, the claim did not require a present interest in the property. Brown v. Ralston, 2016-Ohio-4916, 67 N.E.3d 15, 2016 Ohio App. LEXIS 2720 (Ohio Ct. App., Belmont County 2016).

**Condominium**

No sale of condominium property took place for purposes of a declaration and bylaws, or for purposes of the Ohio Condominium Act, R.C. ch. 5311, when a dentist conveyed the dentist's office unit in a professional office building by way of a quit-claim deed, with a transfer-on-death provision, to the dentist's wife because the dentist conveyed the dentist's fee simple interest to the dentist's wife after signing the condominium documents. The dentist, under R.C. 2103.02, retained a dower interest in the property, which was an estate for life in one-third of the property, and was not a legal interest, as the dentist's wife held full legal title to the property. DiPasquale v. Costas, 2010-Ohio-832, 186 Ohio App. 3d 121, 926 N.E.2d 682, 2010 Ohio App. LEXIS 676 (Ohio Ct. App., Montgomery County 2010).

**Oil and gas interests**

When the decedent died, the oil company which leased the decedent's farm property held a fee simple determinable interest in the oil and gas subject to a reverter and the decedent owned the surface rights and the right to reversion in the oil and gas upon expiration of the lease. The lease remained with the farm property even though title to the property transferred from the decedent to the decedent's grandchild, as the transfer-on-death beneficiary, so that the grandchild owned the decedent's interest in the property subject to the lease. In re Estate of Ball, 2016-Ohio-4917, 67 N.E.3d 28, 2016 Ohio App. LEXIS 2718 (Ohio Ct. App., Belmont County 2016).

**Validity**

Imposition of a constructive trust on an 80-acre parcel transferred to the beneficiaries upon the owner's death was not warranted because the transfer on death (TOD) deed followed the form required by the former version of this statute and was duly recorded, there was no finding of unjust enrichment, and, while the owner executed a new last will and testament and power of attorney in favor of the objectors, there was no direct evidence to show that the owner intended to execute a new TOD deed. Blausey v. VanNess, 2016-Ohio-5068, 2016 Ohio App. LEXIS 2885 (Ohio Ct. App., Ottawa County 2016).

**RESEARCH REFERENCES AND PRACTICE AIDS**

**Practice Guides**

Anderson's Ohio Probate Practice and Procedure § 16.10 Transfer on death deeds

Anderson's Ohio Probate Practice and Procedure § 12.03 Non-probate assets

Anderson's Ohio Probate Practice and Procedure § 21.15 Distributing real estate

**Practice Forms**

Affidavit for Transfer of Interest Created by Transfer on Death Deed 1, 11 OH Forms of Pleading & Practice — Probate Form 6:6

## § 5302.24 Validity of transfer on death deed or beneficiary designation prior to SB 124.

Except as otherwise provided in divisions (B)(12) and (C) of section 5302.23 of the Revised Code, sections 5302.22, 5302.222, and 5302.23 of the Revised Code do not affect any deed that was executed and recorded prior to December 28, 2009, or any transfer on death beneficiary designation made, pursuant to section 5302.22 of the Revised Code as it existed prior to that date. If that deed or designation is valid on the day prior to that date, the deed or designation continues to be valid on and after that date. A grantee of that deed need not execute a transfer on death designation affidavit that designates the same transfer on death beneficiary or beneficiaries as in the deed unless the grantee chooses to do so.

**HISTORY:**

153 v S 124, § 1, eff. 12-28-09; 2016 sb232, § 1, effective March 14, 2017.

**Amendment Notes**

The 2016 amendment by SB 232 § 1 substituted "that date" for "the effective date of this section" at the end of the first sentence and twice in the second sentence; in the first sentence, added "Except as otherwise provided in divisions (B)(12) and (C) of section 5302.23 of the Revised Code" at the beginning and substituted "prior to December 28, 2009" for "prior to the effective date of this section"; and made a stylistic change.

# CHAPTER 5305

# DOWER

Section





## § 5305.01 Assignment of dower.

When the lands of a deceased person are not encumbered by mortgage, or by judgment obtained against such decedent during life, the heir, guardian of an heir, or other person having the next immediate estate of inheritance, may assign in writing to the surviving spouse, dower therein, particularly describing such estate, which, if approved in writing on the deed of assignment by the probate judge of the county, and also by the probate judge of the county appointing such guardian, and accepted by such spouse, in writing thereon, shall be a valid assignment.

**HISTORY:**

RS § 5707; S&C 520; 29 v 249, § 8; 81 v 198; 85 v 17; 86 v 184; GC § 12004; Bureau of Code Revision. Eff 10-1-53.

### NOTES TO DECISIONS

Analysis

Antenuptial contract
Inchoate dower
Mortgage
—Release of dower by
Property not subject to dower
Property subject to dower
Purchase money mortgage
Release of dower
Relinquishment of dower
Spouse's share

**Antenuptial contract**

If an antenuptial contract is not performed by one of the parties thereto, the other party may treat such breach as a discharge, and may set up a claim to dower and a distributive share of the property of the other party: Stotler v. Stotler, 27 Ohio Dec. 303, 19 Ohio N.P. (n.s.) 369, 1916 Ohio Misc. LEXIS 47 (Ohio C.P. 1916).

Dower may be barred by an antenuptial contract when it is shown that the husband acted with the utmost good faith and made a full and fair disclosure of his financial condition: Duttenhofer v. Duttenhofer, 12 Ohio Dec. 736 (Ohio Cincinnati Super. Ct. 1902).

**Inchoate dower**

The wife of an heir is entitled in a sale in partition to the present value of her inchoate right of dower in her husband's interest in such estate, even as against his creditors: In re Hays, 104 C.C.A. 656, 181 F. 674 (1910), sub nomine, Hays v. Hays, 16 Ohio Fed. 436, 8 Ohio L. Rep. 155.

The inchoate dower of the wife is an incident of the seizin of the husband and can only be conveyed by her in connection with the husband's transfer of title: Thoms v. Thoms, 1 Hosea 185 (1905), affirmed, without report, 73 Ohio St. 333.].

Judgment creditor of husband cannot subject dower interest of wife to the payment of the husband's debts; the inchoate dower of the wife is not a lien upon the land of the husband, but is an interest in it: Jewett v. Feldheiser, 68 Ohio St. 523, 67 N.E. 1072, 1 Ohio L. Rep. 509, 1903 Ohio LEXIS 243 (Ohio 1903).

**Mortgage**

**—Release of dower by**

A husband and wife joined in a mortgage, which was afterward avoided as a fraud of creditors of the husband. It was held that the avoidance of the mortgage avoided the wife's release of her inchoate right of dower, and the mortgagee cannot on distribution require that the value of her dower interest be paid to him: In re Lingafelter, 8 Ohio L. 231 (1909), affirmed, 181 F. 24.].

In a case of amicable partition by mutual conveyances of unequal purparts, a mortgage given by one tenant in common (his wife not joining) to another to equalize the allotments, is subordinate to the wife's inchoate right of dower in the undivided interest acquired by descent of such mortgagor in the purpart so allotted to him, but is superior to dower in the share acquired by purchase from the mortgagee: Fleming v. Morningstar, 17 Ohio Dec. 430, 4 Ohio N.P. (n.s.) 405, 1904 Ohio Misc. LEXIS 153 (Ohio C.P. 1904).

**Property not subject to dower**

In lands acquired by her husband subsequent to the termination of the marriage relation by divorce granted to the husband: Spaulding v. Spaulding, 11 Ohio App. 143, 30 Ohio C.A. 475, 30 Ohio C.C. (n.s.) 475, 1919 Ohio App. LEXIS 215 (Ohio Ct. App., Clermont County 1919).

In entire proceedings of the sale on foreclosure of property mortgaged before marriage, but only to surplus remaining after satisfaction of mortgage: Pelton v. Smith, 35 Ohio Cir. Dec. 137, 26 Ohio C.C. 271 (1912).

**Property subject to dower**

Widow taking life estate in one third of one-sixth interest in land, subsequently leased, with her consent, by owners of remaining interest to parties taking and selling oil therefrom, held entitled only to income from one third of such interest, though dower had not been set apart for her: Fourth & Central Trust Co. v. Woolley, 31 Ohio App. 259, 165 N.E. 742, 28 Ohio L. Rep. 497, 1928 Ohio App. LEXIS 320 (Ohio Ct. App., Hamilton County 1928).

A bankrupt's wife is entitled to her inchoate right of dower in his real estate, and if she consents to the sale of the same, free from her dower, she is entitled to the value of such dower as fixed by the laws of the state of the bankrupt's residence. Taxes and costs and expenses of administering the bankrupt's estate have priority over dower: In re Forbes (1901).

**Purchase money mortgage**

The widow of a purchase-money mortgagor, mortgage given before marriage, and property sold by executors to pay the mortgage debt, is not dowable of the whole proceeds, but only of the surplus remaining after satisfying the mortgage: Nichols v. French, 83 Ohio St. 162, 93 N.E. 897 (1910), [following Culver v. Harper, 27 Ohio St. 464; distinguishing Kling v. Ballentine, 40 Ohio St. 391, 1883 Ohio LEXIS 325 (Ohio 1883); Mandel v. McClave, 46 Ohio St. 407, 22 N.E. 290, 1889 Ohio LEXIS 100 (Ohio 1889); Sprague v. Law, 17 Ohio C.C. 735, 8 Ohio Cir. Dec. 428 affirming 7 Ohio N.P. 554, 5 Ohio Dec. 384.].

**Release of dower**

A contract to convey by "good warranty deed" does not include a release of dower by the wife: Peoples Sav. Bank Co. v. Parisette, 68 Ohio St. 450, 67 N.E. 896, 96 AmSt 672 (1903).

**Relinquishment of dower**

Where a widow relinquished her dower when executor sold farm of her late husband, and she died before payment, it was held that, even though dower had not been assigned, it was an estate in land which could be relinquished, and the dower money goes to her administrators: In re Mowry, 26 Ohio N.P. 573 (1927).

**Spouse's share**

Where land is directed by a will to be sold and the proceeds distributed to certain persons, such persons acquire no title under the will by electing to take the land, nor can any such election be made to defeat the widow's right to her distributive share out of the proceeds of such land: Bullock v. Bullock, 15 Ohio Dec. 783, 3 Ohio N.P. (n.s.) 190, 1905 Ohio Misc. LEXIS 77 (Ohio C.P. 1905), aff'd, 75 Ohio St. 574, 80 N.E. 1124, 4 Ohio L. Rep. 462 (Ohio 1906).

### RESEARCH REFERENCES AND PRACTICE AIDS

**Cross-References to Related Sections**

Commissioners to assign dower, RC § 5307.18.
Dower—
General provisions in re, RC Chapter 2103.
Not abated by death, RC § 2311.22.
Not affected by execution against property, RC § 2329.83.

**Comparative Legislation**

Dower:
11 USCS § 363
CA—Cal Prob Code § 6412
FL— Fla. Stat. §§ 708.10, 732.111
IN—Burns Ind. Code Ann. §§ 29-1-2-3.1, 29-1-2-11
KY—KRS §§ 381.135, 392.010 et seq
MI— MCLS § 558.1 et seq
NY—NY CLS Real P § 189 et seq

## § 5305.02 Petition for dower.

A surviving spouse may file a petition for dower in the court of common pleas, against the heir, or other person having the next immediate estate of inheritance or other estate or interest therein, setting forth the right thereto, and describing the tracts of land in which dower is claimed. On the hearing the court shall render such judgment as appears just and consistent with the rights of the parties interested.

**HISTORY:**

RS § 5708; S&C 520; S&S 310; 63 v 33, § 9; 86 v 184; GC § 12005; Bureau of Code Revision. Eff 10-1-53.

### NOTES TO DECISIONS

Analysis

Assignment of dower
Effect of divorce
Parties
Remedy of surviving spouse

**Assignment of dower**

Revised Code § 5305.02 does not divest court of appeals of power to assign dower as incident to equitable relief: McCormick v. McCormick, 124 Ohio St. 440, 179 N.E. 286, 11 Ohio Law Abs. 64, 1931 Ohio LEXIS 216 (Ohio 1931).

**Effect of divorce**

A wife may maintain an action against persons who conspire with her husband to defraud her of her dower in an equitable estate, although she had not recovered a judgment for alimony at the time of such fraudulent conveyance: Iddings v. Whitacre, 1 Ohio App. 223, 24 Ohio Cir. Dec. 427, 19 Ohio C.A. 336, 19 Ohio C.C. (n.s.) 336, 1913 Ohio App. LEXIS 138 (Ohio Ct. App. 1913).

**Parties**

In an action to set off dower, one who has conveyed such land with covenants of general warranty may be made a party and may defend: Rohn v. Leach, 24 Ohio N.P. (n.s.) 459, 1922 Ohio Misc. LEXIS 289 (Ohio C.P. 1922), aff'd, 1 Ohio Law Abs. 700, 1923 Ohio Misc. LEXIS 2008 (Ohio Ct. App., Defiance County Feb. 8, 1923), [affirmed by Court of Appeals.].

**Remedy of surviving spouse**

Revised Code § 5305.02 gives the only remedy to a surviving spouse who holds a dower interest in the realty of the decedent. If such surviving spouse does not employ the remedy given by R.C. 5305.02, he cannot interfere with the management of the property, collect the rents therefor, or take possession thereof: Bates v. Creed, 2 Ohio App. 59, 26 Ohio Cir. Dec. 338, 15 Ohio C.C. (n.s.) 433, 1913 Ohio App. LEXIS 191 (Ohio Ct. App., Hamilton County 1913), aff'd, 90 Ohio St. 288, 107 N.E. 770, 12 Ohio L. Rep. 78, 1914 Ohio LEXIS 191 (Ohio 1914), [for opinion below, see Creed v. Bates, 14 Ohio N.P. (n.s.) 81; affirmed, Industrial School v. Bates, 90 Ohio St. 288.].

### RESEARCH REFERENCES AND PRACTICE AIDS

**Cross-References to Related Sections**

Commissioners to assign dower, RC § 5307.18.

**Law Review**

Equivalence of right of entry and right of reverter. Comment. 18 Ohio St. L.J. 120 (1957).

## § 5305.03 Encumbrances presented.

When the rights of a lessee or lienor are shown by cross-petition filed before judgment, such rights and liens shall be regarded by the court of common pleas, and no inequality shall be allowed or injustice done to such lessee or lienor.

**HISTORY:**

RS § 5709; S&C 520; 29 v 249, § 10; GC § 12006; Bureau of Code Revision. Eff 10-1-53.

### NOTES TO DECISIONS

**Liens**

Summons must be issued and served upon the wife in order to bar her dower in a foreclosure under a cross-petition in a suit to marshal liens: Kaufman v. Heckman, 13 Ohio C.C. (n.s.) 309, 22 Ohio Cir. Dec. 277 (1908), affirmed, without report, Heckman v. Kaufman, 82 Ohio St. 453.].

Where real estate is sold to pay the debts of decedent, which real estate is encumbered by a purchase-money mortgage of decedent and also by one assumed by the decedent, and such land is sold for a sum more than the amount of both of said mortgages, the widow is entitled to have her dower in said land computed from and based on the entire proceeds of the sale, after satisfying said mortgages: Hickey v. Conine, 6 Ohio C.C. (n.s.) 321, 17 Ohio Cir. Dec. 369 (1904), affirmed, without report, 71 Ohio St. 548.].

### RESEARCH REFERENCES AND PRACTICE AIDS

**Cross-References to Related Sections**

Commissioners to assign dower, RC § 5307.18.

## § 5305.04 Land situated in different counties.

When the lands in which dower is claimed lie in several counties, the petition for dower may be filed by the surviving spouse in any county in which a part of the estate is situated. The court of common pleas of such county has complete jurisdiction, and may order the whole dower of such spouse to be assigned in one or more of such counties, and out of one or more of such tracts of land, if it may be done without prejudice to the rights of any person claiming title to or holding a lien on the land.

**HISTORY:**

RS § 5710; S&C 520; 29 v 249, § 11; 82 v 142; 86 v 184; GC § 12007; Bureau of Code Revision. Eff 10-1-53.

### RESEARCH REFERENCES AND PRACTICE AIDS

**Cross-References to Related Sections**

Commissioners to assign dower, RC § 5307.18.

**Ohio Rules**

Commencement of action; venue. CivR 3.
There is a partial or possible conflict between CivR 3(B), venue, and RC § 5305.04. See also CivR 1(C) concerning exceptions to applicability of Civil Rules.

## § 5305.05 Death of plaintiff before assignment.

When a plaintiff in an action to assign dower dies before the assignment, or before entry of the final judgment, the action may be revived in the name of the executor or administrator. The court of common pleas shall determine, if not before decided, whether the plaintiff was entitled to dower in such action. If the plaintiff was so entitled, the court shall adjudge in favor of such executor or administrator a sum equal to one third of the rental value of the real estate in which the plaintiff was entitled to dower, from the filing of the petition until death, after deducting one third of the necessary expenses. The sum so adjudged in favor of such executor or administrator is a lien upon such real estate, and its payment may be enforced by sale as upon execution.

**HISTORY:**
RS § 5711; S&S 311; 60 v 10; 86 v 184; GC § 12008; Bureau of Code Revision. Eff 10-1-53.

### NOTES TO DECISIONS

**Construction**
The expenses referred to in R.C. 5305.05 are those attending the assignment of dower by commissioners. Revised Code § 5303.05 does not authorize the recovery of counsel fees in ordinary actions for the assignment of dower: Watson v. Watson, 11 Ohio Cir. Dec. 463, 21 Ohio C.C. 249, 1901 Ohio Misc. LEXIS 305 (Ohio Ct. App., Fairfield County 1901).

### RESEARCH REFERENCES AND PRACTICE AIDS

**Cross-References to Related Sections**
Action not to abate by death of either or both parties to action, RC § 2311.21.
Commissioners to assign dower, RC § 5307.18.



## § 5305.06 Appointment of commissioners to assign dower.

When dower is adjudged, the court of common pleas shall appoint three judicious, disinterested men of the county in which the action to assign dower is pending, who are not of kin to either of the parties interested, to be commissioners. The court shall issue its order to the sheriff of that county, commanding him that by the oaths of the commissioners which may be administered by him, he cause such dower to be set off and assigned to the plaintiff in the manner set forth in the judgment.

**HISTORY:**
RS § 5712; S&C 521, 522; 38 v 37; 54 v 27, § 12; GC § 12009; Bureau of Code Revision. Eff 10-1-53.

### NOTES TO DECISIONS

Analysis

Interest on proceeds
Power of court

**Interest on proceeds**
The dower of the widow of a decedent includes interest earned by the proceeds of real estate while in the hands of the executor: Estate of Arnold, 1 Ohio N.P. (n.s.) 167, 1902 Ohio Misc. LEXIS 252 (Ohio P. Ct. June 21, 1902).

**Power of court**
The court of common pleas has power to assess the value of the dower interest at a gross sum and charge the same upon land under certain circumstances, and where this is done, it will be presumed that the requisite circumstances existed and that the judgment is valid: Weyer v. Sager, 12 Ohio Cir. Dec. 193, 21 Ohio C.C. 710, 1901 Ohio Misc. LEXIS 345 (Ohio Ct. App., Allen County Apr. 1, 1901).

### RESEARCH REFERENCES AND PRACTICE AIDS

**Cross-References to Related Sections**
Assignment of dower when estate indivisible, RC § 5305.08.
Commissioners to assign dower, RC § 5307.18.
Dower during pendency of petition, RC § 5305.11.
Fees of commissioners, RC § 2335.01.
Proceedings upon return of assignment of dower, RC § 5305.07.
Timberlands or other unimproved lands or lots, RC § 5305.09.

## § 5305.07 Proceedings upon return of assignment of dower.

The commissioners provided for in section 5305.06 of the Revised Code and the sheriff shall obey the order to assign dower, and return their proceedings thereon to the court of common pleas at such time as it appoints. If the court approves the assignment, it shall be entered on its records, and thenceforth the assignment is valid. Thereupon execution shall be issued, directing the sheriff to put the surviving spouse in full possession of the dower assigned.

**HISTORY:**
RS § 5713; S&C 521; 54 v 27, § 12; 86 v 184; GC § 12010; Bureau of Code Revision. Eff 10-1-53.

### RESEARCH REFERENCES AND PRACTICE AIDS

**Cross-References to Related Sections**
Commissioners to assign dower, RC § 5307.18.

## § 5305.08 Assignment of dower when estate indivisible.

When an estate of which a surviving spouse is dowable is entire, and no division of it can be made by metes and bounds, dower shall be assigned as of a third part of the rents, issues, and profits thereof, to be computed and ascertained by the commissioners provided for in section 5305.06 of the Revised Code.

**HISTORY:**
RS § 5714; S&C 521; 29 v 249, § 14; 86 v 184; GC § 12011; Bureau of Code Revision. Eff 10-1-53.

### RESEARCH REFERENCES AND PRACTICE AIDS

**Cross-References to Related Sections**
Commissioners to assign dower, RC § 5307.18.

## § 5305.09 Timberlands or other unimproved lands or lots.

When an estate of which a surviving spouse is dowable, or in which such spouse owns a dower interest assigned to or vested in such spouse, consists in whole or in part of timberlands or other unimproved lands or lots, the commissioners, appointed as provided in section 5305.06 of the Revised Code, shall return to the court of common pleas a true appraisement of such lands in money, and also a true appraisement of their annual rental value. Upon the hearing of such report, if it appears to the court that the assignment of dower in such lands, either by metes and bounds, or as of the rents, issues, and profits, cannot be or has not been made so as to provide such surviving spouse with an income from the lands or lots so charged commensurate with their value, as fixed by such commissioners, the court shall determine the value of such dower in money, and make an order directing the sheriff to advertise and sell such lands, or so much thereof as is necessary, as upon execution. The sheriff shall not cause the lands to be appraised, but their value as returned by the commissioners shall be the appraised value, and they shall not be sold for less than two thirds of that value. Upon the confirmation of such sale, the court shall order the payment to the surviving spouse out of the money arising therefrom the value of the dower so determined by it.

**HISTORY:**
RS § 5714a; 89 v 131; 92 v 314; GC § 12012; Bureau of Code Revision. Eff 10-1-53.

### NOTES TO DECISIONS

**Timber land**
An unproductive orchard is not timber land or unimproved land within the meaning of R.C. 5305.09: Schenk v. Swank, 15 Ohio Law Abs. 725, 1933 Ohio Misc. LEXIS 1497 (Ohio Ct. App., Miami County Apr. 28, 1933).

### RESEARCH REFERENCES AND PRACTICE AIDS

**Cross-References to Related Sections**
Commissioners to assign dower, RC § 5307.18.
Election by owner of lands to pay value of dower, RC § 5305.10.

## § 5305.10 Election by owner of lands to pay value of dower.

The person owning lands or lots mentioned in section 5305.09 of the Revised Code, at the time the order for the sale of such lands is made, may elect to pay to the surviving spouse the value of the dower. If such payment is made within ten days or such further reasonable time as the court of common pleas grants not exceeding ninety days from such election, the court shall make a decree divesting such spouse of any interest by way of dower in such lands. A surviving spouse owning a dower interest in timber lands or other unimproved lots or lands assigned to or vested in such spouse may maintain an action for relief in accordance with section 5305.09 of the Revised Code.

**HISTORY:**
RS § 5714a; 89 v 131; 92 v 314; GC § 12013; Bureau of Code Revision. Eff 10-1-53.

**RESEARCH REFERENCES AND PRACTICE AIDS**

**Cross-References to Related Sections**
Commissioners to assign dower, RC § 5307.18.

## § 5305.11 Dower during pendency of petition.

When the commissioners provided for in section 5305.06 of the Revised Code have set off and assigned dower, they shall make a true appraisement of the yearly value, after deducting necessary expenses, of the real estate in which the surviving spouse is entitled to dower, estimating such value from the day of filing the petition for dower to the day of assigning dower, and return such appraisement and assignment. The court of common pleas shall adjudge the payment of one third of the whole sum so returned to the surviving spouse out of the real estate not covered by the dower, upon which judgment execution may issue. This section does not require execution to be issued against such of the defendants in dower as are minors. In such cases the dower shall operate as a lien upon the real estate, for their proportion of the judgment, until it is paid.

**HISTORY:**
RS § 5715; S&C 522; 41 v 6; 86 v 184; GC § 12014; Bureau of Code Revision. Eff 10-1-53.

**NOTES TO DECISIONS**

**Necessary expenses**
The term "necessary expenses" does not include counsel fees; they are expenses attending the assignment of dower by commissioners under R.C. 5305.11: Watson v. Watson, 11 Ohio Cir. Dec. 463, 21 Ohio C.C. 249, 1901 Ohio Misc. LEXIS 305 (Ohio Ct. App., Fairfield County 1901).

**RESEARCH REFERENCES AND PRACTICE AIDS**

**Cross-References to Related Sections**
Commissioners to assign dower, RC § 5307.18.
Exemptions in estimating yearly value of dower, RC § 5305.12.

## § 5305.12 Exemptions in estimating yearly value of dower.

In making the appraisement of the yearly value of the real estate provided for in section 5305.11 of the Revised Code, the commissioners must exclude all permanent or valuable improvements made thereon after the deceased consort of the surviving spouse ceased to be its owner.

**HISTORY:**
RS § 5716; S&C 522; 41 v 6, § 2; 86 v 184; GC § 12015; Bureau of Code Revision. Eff 10-1-53.

**RESEARCH REFERENCES AND PRACTICE AIDS**

**Cross-References to Related Sections**
Commissioners to assign dower, RC § 5307.18.

## § 5305.13 Minor heir not to be prejudiced by collusive assignment of dower.

During the minority of an heir, if dower is assigned to a surviving spouse not entitled thereto, or, if such dower was recovered by the default, fraud, or collusion of the guardian, such heir, on coming of age, may have an action against such spouse to recover the lands wrongfully awarded.

**HISTORY:**
RS § 5717; S&C 521; 86 v 184; GC § 12016; Bureau of Code Revision. Eff 10-1-53.

**RESEARCH REFERENCES AND PRACTICE AIDS**

**Cross-References to Related Sections**
Commissioners to assign dower, RC § 5307.18.

## § 5305.14 Costs.

If the petition of a person claiming dower is contested, and the court of common pleas finds that such person is entitled to dower as claimed therein, the defendant so contesting shall pay all costs of the suit. If the petition is not contested, the plaintiff shall pay one third, and the legal owner of the real estate two thirds of the costs.

**HISTORY:**
RS § 5718; S&C 522; 41 v 6, § 22; 73 v 127, § 38; 86 v 184; GC § 12017; Bureau of Code Revision. Eff 10-1-53.

**NOTES TO DECISIONS**

Analysis

Costs
Suit for assignment of dower

**Costs**
The word "costs," as used in R.C. 5305.14, does not include attorney fees: Watson v. Watson, 11 Ohio Cir. Dec. 463, 21 Ohio C.C. 249, 1901 Ohio Misc. LEXIS 305 (Ohio Ct. App., Fairfield County 1901).

**Suit for assignment of dower**
In a suit for the assignment of dower, the defendant set up an agreement claimed to have been made by the plaintiff with the defendants, whereby the defendants should hold the premises without an assignment of dower for a certain length of time, unexpired at the time suit was brought. It was held that this constituted a resistance to the plaintiff's rights of assignment of dower, within the meaning of R.C. 5305.14: Watson v. Watson, 11 Ohio Cir. Dec. 463, 21 Ohio C.C. 249, 1901 Ohio Misc. LEXIS 305 (Ohio Ct. App., Fairfield County 1901).

**RESEARCH REFERENCES AND PRACTICE AIDS**

**Cross-References to Related Sections**
Commissioners to assign dower, RC § 5307.18.

## § 5305.15 Surviving spouse may elect to be endowed out of proceeds of sale.

In actions for partition, when an estate cannot be divided, and is ordered to be sold, and in actions for the sale of real estate by executors, administrators, guardians, and assignees, acting under a general assignment for the benefit of creditors, and in all other actions and proceedings in which the court orders the sale of real estate to satisfy a judgment or decree, the surviving spouse who has a dower interest in such real estate, and is a party, may file an answer, waive the assignment of dower by metes and bounds, and ask to have the estate sold free of dower and to be allowed, in lieu thereof, such money out of the proceeds of sale as the court deems the just value of the dower interest therein.

**HISTORY:**
RS § 5719; S&C 622; 74 v 201; 79 v 37; 85 v 180; 86 v 184; 91 v 35; GC § 12018; Bureau of Code Revision. Eff 10-1-53.

**NOTES TO DECISIONS**

Analysis

Contingent right to dower
Value of dower

**Contingent right to dower**

The contingent right of dower of a wife in the proceeds from the sale of real estate located in Ohio and sold to pay a purchase-money mortgage of her husband, extends as against other creditors of the husband only to the surplus remaining after payment of such mortgage, and does not extend to the whole proceeds: Hays v. Hays, 16 Ohio Fed. 436, 181 F. 674, 8 Ohio L. Rep. 155 (1910).

**Value of dower**

Where dower has been assigned by metes and bounds at the widow's request, she cannot thereafter have the assigned land sold and the value of dower paid from the proceeds: Schenk v. Swank, 15 Ohio Law Abs. 725, 1933 Ohio Misc. LEXIS 1497 (Ohio Ct. App., Miami County Apr. 28, 1933).

Where an interest in real estate is sold to pay debts of the decedent, the value of a widow's dower is payable to her in money out of the proceeds; and the reasonable value is the present value of one third of the proceeds computed in accordance with her expectancy of life under the mortality tables: Ralston Steel Car Co. v. Ralston, 112 Ohio St. 306, 147 N.E. 513, 3 Ohio Law Abs. 200, 1925 Ohio LEXIS 331 (Ohio 1925).

#### RESEARCH REFERENCES AND PRACTICE AIDS

**Cross-References to Related Sections**

Commissioners to assign dower, RC § 5307.18.
Election by answer is a release of dower, RC § 5305.16.
Guardian may elect for surviving spouse, RC § 5305.17.
Sale of real estate by fiduciary to be free of dower rights; allowance in money to person having dower interest, RC § 2127.16.

**Practice Guides**

Anderson's Ohio Probate Practice and Procedure § 58.01 General



### § 5305.16 Election by answer is a release of dower.

The answer of a surviving spouse under section 5305.15 of the Revised Code has the same effect, in all respects, as a deed of release to the purchaser of such estate of the dower interest therein of such spouse.

**HISTORY:**

RS § 5720; 74 v 201, § 2; 86 v 184; GC § 12019; Bureau of Code Revision. Eff 10-1-53.

#### NOTES TO DECISIONS

**Action to sell realty on execution**

In an action to sell realty on execution, an answer, consenting to sale and waiving assignment of inchoate right of dower, does not transfer the lien of judgment creditor to purchase money (R.C. 5305.16), as inchoate right of dower is not an interest in realty: Good v. Crist, 23 Ohio App. 484, 156 N.E. 146, 5 Ohio Law Abs. 178, 1926 Ohio App. LEXIS 327 (Ohio Ct. App., Butler County 1926).

#### RESEARCH REFERENCES AND PRACTICE AIDS

**Cross-References to Related Sections**

Commissioners to assign dower, RC § 5307.18.

### § 5305.17 Guardian may elect for surviving spouse.

As used in this section and sections 5305.18 to 5305.22 of the Revised Code, "incompetent person" means a person who is so mentally impaired, as a result of a mental or physical illness or disability, as a result of an intellectual disability, or as a result of chronic substance abuse, that the person is incapable of taking proper care of the person's self or property or fails to provide for the person's family or other persons for whom the person is charged by law to provide.

The guardian of a surviving spouse who has been adjudged to be an incompetent person may appear and answer for such incompetent person in an action under section 5305.15 of the Revised Code, subject to the approval of the court in which it is pending. Such answer has the same effect as if such spouse answered personally. The guardian shall be liable to such spouse, or the heirs, for all damage or loss sustained by the guardian's fraud or collusion, notwithstanding the approval of the court.

**HISTORY:**

RS § 5721; 74 v 201, § 3; 86 v 184; GC § 12020; Bureau of Code Revision. Eff 10-1-53; 152 v H 53, § 1, eff. 8-7-07; 2016 hb158, § 1, effective October 12, 2016.

**Editor's Notes**

See provisions of § 3 of 152 v H 53 following RC § 5301.22.

**Amendment Notes**

The 2016 amendment by HB 158 substituted "as a result of an intellectual disability" for "or mental retardation" in the first paragraph; and made a related change.

152 v H 53, effective August 7, 2007, added the first paragraph; twice substituted "incompetent person" for "insane"; and made minor stylistic and gender neutral changes.

#### RESEARCH REFERENCES AND PRACTICE AIDS

**Cross-References to Related Sections**

Commissioners to assign dower, RC § 5307.18.
Guardian may sell, compromise or release dower right of ward upon approval of probate court, RC § 2111.21.

### § 5305.18 Petition to discharge land of dower of incompetent person.

A person owning real property in this state, encumbered by the contingent of vested right of dower of an incompetent person, may apply, by petition to the court of common pleas of the county in which the real estate, or any part thereof, is situated, making defendants thereto such incompetent person, and the spouse and guardian, if such incompetent person has either or both, for leave to sell any part of such real property, discharged and unencumbered of such contingent or vested right of dower. The petition must set forth the grounds for the incompetency of the person, together with a description of the land proposed to be sold. Thereupon the court shall appoint a committee of six competent individuals, of whom at least three are physicians, who, under oath, shall inquire into the competence of such person, and hear testimony to be produced by the spouse or guardian, or, if there is no such guardian, by a guardian ad litem to be appointed in the action. The committee shall make a report, in writing, of the result of its investigation, signed by its members.

**HISTORY:**

RS § 5722; S&C 852; S&S 439; 35 v 105; 60 v 24; 86 v 184; GC § 12021; Bureau of Code Revision, 10-1-53; 136 v H 390. Eff 8-6-76; 152 v H 53, § 1, eff. 8-7-07.

**Editor's Notes**

See provisions of § 3 of 152 v H 53 following RC § 5301.22.

**Amendment Notes**

152 v H 53, effective August 7, 2007, substituted "incompetent" for "insane" and made similar and related changes throughout, and made gender neutral changes.

#### RESEARCH REFERENCES AND PRACTICE AIDS

**Cross-References to Related Sections**

Commissioners to assign dower, RC § 5307.18.
Dower of incompetent person may be barred, RC § 5305.21.
Appraisal by freeholders, RC § 5305.19.

### § 5305.19 Appraisal by freeholders.

If the committee provided for in section 5305.18 of the Revised Code unanimously reports that the person having a contingent or vested right of dower, in its opinion, is a permanently incompetent person, the court of common pleas shall appoint three judicious freeholders to appraise the real estate described in the petition mentioned in said section, whether or not such real estate is in one or several counties. Such freeholders shall report in writing the value of each tract.

**HISTORY:**

RS § 5723; S&C 852; S&S 439; 35 v 105, § 2; 60 v 24, § 2; 86 v 184; GC § 12022; Bureau of Code Revision. Eff 10-1-53; 152 v H 53, § 1, eff. 8-7-07.

**Editor's Notes**

See provisions of § 3 of 152 v H 53 following RC § 5301.22.

**Amendment Notes**

152 v H 53, effective August 7, 2007, substituted "incompetent person" for "insane".

**RESEARCH REFERENCES AND PRACTICE AIDS**

**Cross-References to Related Sections**

Commissioners to assign dower, RC § 5307.18.
Dower of incompetent person may be barred, RC § 5305.21.
Conveyance or assignment to incompetent person or investment on person's behalf, RC § 5305.20.

### § 5305.20 Conveyance or assignment to incompetent person or investment on person's behalf.

When the report provided for in section 5305.19 of the Revised Code is filed, the court of common pleas may direct the petitioner, by a sufficient deed of conveyance, to convey to the incompetent person, to be held by such person in fee, such proportion of the real estate described in the petition as seems just, or the court may assign to such incompetent person, to be held by the incompetent person during life, after the death of the spouse of such person, such proportion of the real estate described in the petition as seems just, for the incompetent person's support, or the court may order the petitioner to invest an amount by it fixed, in the stock of a company, or stocks created by the laws of this state, as the court designates, the profits, and dividends or distributions arising from such investment to be applied to the support and maintenance of the incompetent person after the death of the spouse of such person. The petitioner, upon compliance with the order of the court, may sell all the real property the petitioner is possessed of, described in the petition, free and unencumbered of the contingent or vested right of dower of such incompetent person.

**HISTORY:**

RS § 5724; S&C 852; S&S 439; 35 v 105, § 3; 60 v 24, § 3; 86 v 184; GC § 12023; Bureau of Code Revision, 10-1-53; 140 v H 250. Eff 7-30-84; 152 v H 53, § 1, eff. 8-7-07.

**Editor's Notes**

See provisions of § 3 of 152 v H 53 following RC § 5301.22.

**Amendment Notes**

152 v H 53, effective August 7, 2007, substituted "incompetent" for "insane" and made similar and related changes throughout, and made gender neutral changes.

**RESEARCH REFERENCES AND PRACTICE AIDS**

**Cross-References to Related Sections**

Commissioners to assign dower, RC § 5307.18.
Dower of incompetent person may be barred, RC § 5305.21.

### § 5305.21 Dower of incompetent person may be barred.

When the spouse of an incompetent person conveys real estate in this state, in which such person has a contingent or vested right of dower, and the incompetent person does not join the spouse in the conveyance, the spouse may apply by petition to the court of common pleas of the county in which the incompetent person resides, or, if such incompetent person resides out of the state, then in the county in which the real estate is situated, for leave to have part or all of such real estate so conveyed, released of the dower right therein. Such petition shall set forth the grounds for incompetency of the incompetent person, and a description of the land proposed to be affected. The incompetent person, guardian, if there is one, and all persons in interest, shall be made defendants, and the action shall be proceeded with as prescribed in sections 5305.18 to 5305.20 of the Revised Code, except that instead of ordering the petitioner to sell the real estate or to convey or assign to such incompetent person any part of it, the court shall direct the petitioner to make such investment as is provided in section 5305.20 of the Revised Code, or require the petitioner to secure the amount to the use of the incompetent person by mortgage of unencumbered real estate of at least double the value thereof. Upon compliance by the petitioner with the order made, the court shall enter a judgment releasing and discharging the real estate from the encumbrance of such right of dower, and adjudge the holder of the legal title, or other party liable, to pay to the petitioner any sum withheld or retained as indemnity against such dower right.

**HISTORY:**

RS § 5725; S&S 440; 61 v 99; 86 v 184; GC § 12024; Bureau of Code Revision. Eff 10-1-53; 152 v H 53, § 1, eff. 8-7-07.

**Editor's Notes**

See provisions of § 3 of 152 v H 53 following RC § 5301.22.

**Amendment Notes**

152 v H 53, effective August 7, 2007, substituted "incompetent" for "insane" and made similar and related changes throughout, and made gender neutral changes.

**NOTES TO DECISIONS**

**Dower**

Dower in Ohio is regulated entirely by statute and does not depend upon common law, and it is therefore subject to legislative control and may be modified at will by the legislature: In re Russell, 14 Ohio Fed. 364, 13 AmBankRep 24 (1904).

**RESEARCH REFERENCES AND PRACTICE AIDS**

**Cross-References to Related Sections**

Commissioners to assign dower, RC § 5307.18.



### § 5305.22 Conveyance free from dower if spouse adjudged mentally ill person subject to hospitalization by court order.

(A) Any real estate or interest in real estate coming to a person by purchase, inheritance, or otherwise, after the spouse of the person is adjudged a mentally ill person subject to court order and admitted to either a hospital for persons with mental illness in this or any other state of the United States or the psychiatric department of any hospital of the United States, may be conveyed by the person while the person's spouse who is a mentally ill person subject to court order remains a patient of that hospital, free and clear from any dower right or expectancy of the person's spouse who is a mentally ill person subject to court order. Dower shall not attach to any real estate so acquired and conveyed during the time described in this section in favor of such spouse who is a mentally ill person subject to court order. The indorsement upon the instrument of conveyance, by the superintendent of the hospital to which the spouse was admitted, that the spouse of the person conveying the real estate is a mentally ill person subject to court order who has been admitted to that hospital, stating when received in that hospital and signed officially by the superintendent, shall be sufficient evidence of the fact that the spouse of the person conveying the real estate is a mentally ill person subject to court order. This indorsement shall be a part of the instrument of conveyance.

(B) As used in this section, "mentally ill person subject to court order" has the same meaning as in section 5122.01 of the Revised Code.

**HISTORY:**

RS § 5725a; 87 v 281; 95 v 65; GC § 12025; 119 v 26; Bureau of Code Revision. Eff 10-1-53; 152 v H 53, § 1, eff. 8-7-07; 152 v S 157, § 1, eff. 5-14-08; 2014 SB 43, § 1, eff. Sept. 17, 2014.

**Editor's Notes**

See provisions of § 3 of 152 v H 53 following RC § 5301.22.

**Amendment Notes**

The 2014 amendment by SB 43 deleted "hospitalization by" following "person subject to" throughout the section.
152 v S 157, effective May 14, 2008, rewrote the section.
152 v H 53, effective August 7, 2007, rewrote the section.

**ATTORNEY GENERAL OPINIONS**

The words "in this state" in the line "is an inmate of an asylum [hospital] for the insane in this state" mean an asylum provided by the state; a state institution: 1920 OAG vol. 1, p. 746 (1920).

# TITLE 57
# TAXATION



## CHAPTER 5748
## SCHOOL DISTRICT INCOME TAX



**§ 5748.06 Tax credit for senior citizens.**

For a taxpayer sixty-five years of age or older during the taxable year, a credit shall be permitted against the tax otherwise due under this chapter for such year equal to fifty dollars for each return required to be filed under section 5747.08 of the Revised Code for taxes levied under this chapter. The credit allowed under this section shall not exceed the tax otherwise due.

**HISTORY:**
143 v S 28. Eff 6-13-89.

Titles 39 — 57

# OHIO ADMINISTRATIVE CODE

## 4501:1

## BUREAU OF MOTOR VEHICLES.



## CHAPTER 4501:1-1

## DRIVER LICENSES.



### 4501:1-1-01. Examination of license holders competency.

The registrar of motor vehicles, upon determination that any person has twelve or more points charged against him or her under section 4510.037 of the Revised Code, and is not subject to the provisions of section 4510.038 of the Revised Code, or, having good cause to believe that the holder of a driver's or commercial driver's license is incompetent or otherwise not qualified to be licensed, shall upon written notice of at least five days, sent by mail in accordance with rule 4501:1-10-01 of the Administrative Code to the licensee's last known address, require him or her to submit to a physical exam or to a driver's license examination or a commercial driver's license examination, if appropriate, or both. Good cause shall be established by a report of a peace officer; by a report of a court; by information from a physician, a nurse, a relative of the licensee, or a friend of the licensee; or by a court order. The report of the peace officer shall be approved by the chief of police, sheriff, or the designee of either unless the peace officer is a member of the Ohio state highway patrol. The report or information shall be based on the personal observation of the licensee by the reporter and shall include the details of the incident giving rise to it. The report shall include a request that the licensee be reexamined in the interest of public safety based on the professional judgment of the reporter. A report or an order from a court shall be signed by the judge or his designee. In no case shall a report be accepted if it appears that the sole basis is the age of the licensee. Information received from a nurse, a relative of the licensee, or a friend of the licensee shall not be accepted unless it is corroborated in essential details by an investigation performed by the bureau of motor vehicles. No information shall be received anonymously. A court order ordering a reexamination shall be accepted without further information.

Effective: 04/10/2016.
Five Year Review (FYR) Dates: 01/19/2016 and 01/15/2021.
Promulgated Under: 119.03.
Statutory Authority: 4501.02, 4507.01.
Rule Amplifies: 4507.20
Prior Effective Dates: 2/8/68, 12/27/89 (Emer.), 6/4/90, 4/20/96, 4/23/06, 8/13/07.

Admin Code

# 5101:4

# DIVISION OF FOOD STAMPS

Chapter
5101:4-6. Determining Eligibility for Specific Groups

## CHAPTER 5101:4-6

## DETERMINING ELIGIBILITY FOR SPECIFIC GROUPS

Rule
5101:4-6-29. Food assistance: elderly and disabled individuals living with others.

### 5101:4-6-29. Food assistance: elderly and disabled individuals living with others.

(A) Can individuals who are elderly and disabled be certified for supplemental nutrition assistance program (SNAP) benefits separately from individuals they purchase food and prepare meals with?

(1) Elderly individuals, age sixty and older, who are disabled as described in paragraph (B) of this rule may be permitted separate assistance group status when they meet the following criteria:

(a) The income of the individuals with whom the elderly and disabled individual resides does not exceed one hundred sixty-five per cent of the poverty level; and

(b) The disabled individual is unable to purchase food and prepare his or her own meals.

(2) If an individual meets these criteria, both the individual and their spouse may be granted separate assistance group status, even if the spouse does not meet the criteria.

(B) What is the disability criteria to be certified for SNAP separately?

The disability shall be considered permanent under the Social Security Act of 1935 or be a nondisease-related, severe, permanent disability. "Disability" as defined in this rule is not the same as "disabled member" as found in rule 5101:4-1-03 of the Administrative Code. The key factor in determining whether or not disability would qualify an individual for separate assistance group status under this provision is an inability to purchase food and prepare meals.

(C) How is a disability verified for separate assistance group status? Disability shall be verified by one of the following procedures:

(1) A county agency shall use the social security administration's most current list of disabilities as the initial step for verifying if a person has a disability considered permanent under the Social Security Act. A person who suffers from one of the disabilities listed under the Social Security Act must also be unable to purchase and prepare meals because of the disability in order to meet the designation of a separate assistance group status.

(2) When it is obvious to the county agency that the person is unable to purchase and prepare meals because he or she suffers from a severe physical or mental disability, even if the disability is not specifically mentioned on the Social Security Act list, additional verification is not needed and the nature of the disability shall be documented in the case file.

(3) When the disability is not obvious to the county agency, the person shall be required to provide a statement from a physician or licensed or certified psychologist certifying that the person is unable to purchase and prepare meals because he or she suffers from one of the non obvious disabilities mentioned in the Social Security Act list or is unable to purchase and prepare meals because he or she suffers from some other severe, permanent physical or mental disease or nondisease-related disability.

(D) How is the income of the other individuals in the home determined?

(1) After an elderly individual has been determined disabled in accordance with this rule the following must occur:

(a) The gross income of the others with whom the individual resides must be considered, as if the others were applying for participation; and

(b) The income of the individual who is elderly and disabled and their spouse shall not be included in the calculation, nor are the elderly and disabled individual and their spouse to be considered assistance group members for this purpose.

(2) The gross monthly income of the others shall be compared to the one hundred sixty-five per cent of the federal poverty level for that assistance group size. If the gross income of the others with whom the elderly and disabled individual resides is no more than one hundred sixty-five per cent of the federal poverty level the elderly and disabled individual (and their spouse) shall be granted separate assistance group status.

(3) The elderly and disabled individuals who wish to be a separate assistance group shall be responsible for obtaining the cooperation of the individuals with whom they reside in providing necessary income information to the county agency.

(4) Income of the others with whom the elderly and disabled individuals live shall be verified as if the others were also applying for program participation, as discussed in rule 5101:4-2-09 of the Administrative Code.

(E) How are shared expenses handled?

Once separate assistance group status has been established, county agencies shall prorate any expenses shared by the elderly and disabled individual's assistance group and the others with whom the elderly and disabled assistance group resides. If the assistance group is eligible for one of the utility allowances, the utility allowance shall not be prorated.

Effective: 9/1/2018.
Five Year Review (FYR) Dates: 5/23/2018 and 09/01/2023.
Promulgated Under: 111.15.
Statutory Authority: 5101.54.
Rule Amplifies: 329.042, 5101.54
Prior Effective Dates: 06/01/1983, 09/24/1983, 12/31/1984 (Emer.), 04/01/1985, 10/01/1995 (Emer.), 12/15/1995, 02/01/1999, 02/01/2004, 01/01/2009, 06/01/2013.

# 5160

# MEDICAID SERVICES



## CHAPTER 5160-31

## PASSPORT HCBS WAIVER PROGRAM



### 5160-31-02. Pre-admission screening system providing options and resources today (PASSPORT) HCBS waiver program definitions.

(A) The purpose of this rule is to define the terms used in Chapter 5160-31 of the Administrative Code governing the pre-admission screening system providing options and resources today (PASSPORT) home and community-based services (HCBS) waiver program.

As used in this chapter:

(B) "Activities of Daily Living (ADL)" means activities of daily living as defined in rule 5160-3-05 of the Adminstrative Code.

(C) "Assessment" means a face-to-face evaluation used to obtain information about an individual including his or her condition, personal goals and preferences, functional limitations, health status and other factors that are relevant to the authorization and provision of services. Assessment information supports the determination that an individual requires waiver services as well as the development of the person-centered services plan.

(D) "Authorized representative" has the same meaning as defined in rule 5160-1-33 of the Administrative Code.

(E) "C.F.R." means the code of federal regulations.

(F) "Caregiver" means relatives, friend, and/or significant others who voluntarily provide assistance to the individual enrolled in PASSPORT and are responsible for the individual's care on a continuing basis.

(G) "Case manager" means the registered nurse, licensed social worker or licensed independent social worker that ODA's designee employs to plan, coordinate, monitor, evaluate, and authorize services received by individuals enrolled in PASSPORT.

(H) "Case management" means the administrative activities to assess, plan, coordinate, monitor, evaluate, and authorize services, supports and resources provided to an individual enrolled in PASSPORT.

(I) "Centers for medicare and medicaid services (CMS)" means the federal agency that is part of the U.S. department of health and human services, and that administers the medicaid program and approves home and community-based services waivers.

(J) "Certification" means providers are approved by the Ohio department of aging (ODA) to provide services for PASSPORT as established in Chapter 173-39 of the Administrative Code.

(K) "Financial management service (FMS)" is a support provided to waiver participants who direct some or all of their waiver services. In the PASSPORT waiver, this support is conducted as an administrative activity through an entity under contract with the state of Ohio. When used in conjunction with the participant-directed authorities available to individuals enrolled in PASSPORT, this support includes operating a payroll service for participant-employed workers and making required payroll withholdings.

(L) "HCBS" or " Home and community-based services (HCBS)" means services provided under the provisions set forth in 42 C.F.R. 441 Subpart G ( October 1, 2018) that permit individuals to live in a home setting rather than a nursing facility (NF) or hospital. HCBS waiver services are approved by CMS for specific populations and are not otherwise available under the medicaid state plan.

(M) "Home First" means the component of the PASSPORT HCBS waiver program that offers priority enrollment for certain individuals in accordance with section 173.521 of the Revised Code.

(N) "Individual" means a medicaid recipient, a medicaid recipient enrolled in a HCBS program, or person with pending medicaid eligibility who is applying for HCBS waiver enrollment, or other long-term care services

(O) "Individual provider" means a person with a signed medicaid provider agreement with ODM to provide PASSPORT services in rule 5160-31-05 of the Administrative Code, and who meets the PASSPORT waiver program's conditions of participation set forth in rule 5160-31-06 of the Administrative Code and who is not the spouse, parent, stepparent, and/or legal guardian of the individual.

(P) "Instrumental activities of daily living (IADL)" has the same meaning as defined in rule 5160-3-05 of the Administrative Code.

(Q) "Level of care" or "LOC" means the designation describing a person's functional levels and nursing needs pursuant to the criteria defined in rule 5160-3-05 of the Administrative Code.

(R) "Nursing Facility (NF)" has the same meaning as defined in section 5165.01 of the Revised Code.

(S) "ODA's designee" means an entity to which ODA delegates one or more of daily waiver operations. ODA's current designees include the area agencies on aging that ODA lists in rule 173-2-04 of the Administrative Code and catholic social services of the Miami Valley.

(T) "ODM's administrative agency" has the same meaning as "administrative agency" in rule 5160:1-1-01 of the Administrative Code.

(U) "Participant-directed individual provider" means a person with a signed medicaid provider agreement with ODM to provide PASSPORT services in rule 5160-31-05 of the Administrative Code, and who meets the PASSPORT waiver program's conditions of participation set forth in rule 5160-31-06 of the Administrative Code and who is not the spouse, parent, stepparent, and/or legal guardian of the consumer individual.

(V) "PASSPORT" or "PASSPORT HCBS waiver program" means the medicaid-funded component of the PASSPORT program created under section 173.52 of the Revised Code.

(W) "Person-centered services plan" has the same meaning as in rule 5160-44-02 of the Administrative Code.

(X) "Region" means the geographic area in which ODA's designee operates the PASSPORT program.

(Y) "Subregion" means a geographic area located within ODA's designee's region for the purpose of establishing PASSPORT unit rates in rule 5160-31-07 of the Administrative Code.

(Z) "Waiver service provider" means an agency or person with a signed medicaid provider agreement with ODM to provide HCBS waiver services, and who meets the conditions of participation set forth in rule 5160-31-06 of the Administrative Code.

Replaces: 5160-31-02.
Effective: 1/1/2019.
Five Year Review (FYR) Dates: 01/01/2024.
Promulgated Under: 119.03.
Statutory Authority: 5166.02.
Rule Amplifies: 173.52

Admin Code

Prior Effective Dates: 07/16/1984, 12/22/1986 (Emer.), 03/23/1987, 07/01/1990, 01/14/1996, 09/01/1998, 03/01/2000, 03/03/2001, 07/01/2006, 03/17/2011, 09/29/2011, 03/06/2014.

**5160-31-03. Eligibility for enrollment in the PASSPORT HCBS waiver program.**

(A) To be eligible for the medicaid-funded component of the pre-admission screening system providing options and resources today (PASSPORT) program, an individual must meet all of the following requirements:

(1) The individual must have been determined eligible for medicaid in accordance with Chapters 5160:1-1 to 5160:1-6 of the Administrative Code.

(2) The cost of waiver services in the person-centered services plan does not exceed the individual cost limit at the time of initial enrollment. The individual cost limit is equal to fourteen thousand and seven hundred dollars per month for waiver services.

(a) If ODA's designee determines that the applicant's waiver service needs cannot be met within the individual cost limit, the individual shall not be enrolled.

(b) Once enrolled in PASSPORT, additional waiver services may be authorized in excess of the individual cost limit with prior approval from ODA.

(c) When additional waiver services that exceed the individual cost limit are not approved, the individual shall be disenrolled from the waiver.

(3) The needed services are not readily available through another source at the level required to allow the individual to live in the community.

(4) The individual agrees to participate in PASSPORT and while enrolled in PASSPORT, shall not be simultaneously enrolled in the state-funded component of the PASSPORT program, the state-funded component of the assisted living program, another medicaid home and community-based program, the residential state supplement (RSS) program, or the program of all inclusive care for the elderly (PACE).

(5) The individual's health related needs can be safely met in a home and community-based setting as determined by ODA's designee.

(6) The individual will participate in the development of a person-centered services plan in accordance with the process and requirements set forth in rule 5160-44-02 of the Administrative Code.

(7) The individual must require the provision of at least one waiver service on a monthly basis as documented in the individual's approved person-centered services plan.

(8) Services in the person-centered services plan are to be approved by one of the medical practitioners in paragraphs (A)(8)(a) to (A)(8)(c) of this rule, within the scope of his/her or their practice. Approval may be verbal or written and is to be obtained prior to initial enrollment. Written approval may be satisfied via electronic signature.

(a) A licensed physician;

(b) A licensed certified nurse practitioner;

(c) A licensed physician assistant.

(9) While enrolled in PASSPORT, the individual must reside in a setting that possesses the home and community-based setting characteristics set forth in rule 5160-44-01 of the Administrative Code and not reside in a hospital, nursing facility (NF), intermediate care facility for individuals with an intellectual disability (ICF-IID) or another licensed/certified facility, any facility covered by section 1616(e) of the Social Security Act (42 U.S.C. 1382e(e) (January 1, 2021) residential care facility, adult foster home or another group living arrangement subject to state licensure or certification.

(10) The individual is age sixty or older at the time of enrollment.

(11) The individual must be determined to meet the criteria for an intermediate or skilled level of care in accordance with rule 5160-3-08 of the Administrative Code and, in the absence of PASSPORT, would require NF services as defined in 42 C.F.R. 440.40 (as in effect on October 1, 2020).

(12) PASSPORT has not reached the CMS-authorized limit on the number of individuals who may enroll on the waiver during the current year.



(B) If the individual does not meet any of the eligibility requirements identified in this rule, the individual shall be denied enrollment in PASSPORT. In such instances, the individual shall be notified of his or her hearing rights in accordance with division 5101:6 of the Administrative Code.

(C) An individual will not be disenrolled from the PASSPORT waiver if disenrollment will result in losing eligibility for Ohio medicaid, unless the individual requests disenrollment, moves out of state, or dies.

Effective: 7/16/2021.
Five Year Review (FYR) Dates: 06/30/2026.
Promulgated Under: 119.03.
Statutory Authority: 5166.02.
Rule Amplifies: 173.52.
Prior Effective Dates: 12/22/1986 (Emer.), 3/23/1987, 1/14/1996, 2/22/2001, 1/31/2005, 7/1/2008, 3/17/2011, 3/1/2014, 4/1/2015, 11/25/2016, 1/1/2019, 6/12/2020 (Emer.), 10/17/2020.

**5160-31-04. Enrollment process for PASSPORT HCBS waiver program.**

(A) The Ohio department of aging (ODA) is responsible for the daily operation of the pre-admission screening system providing options and resources today (PASSPORT) home and community-based services (HCBS) waiver. ODA will operate this waiver pursuant to an interagency agreement with the Ohio department of medicaid (ODM) in accordance with sections 5162.35 and 5166.21 of the Revised Code. ODA will establish processes and procedures to enroll individuals on this waiver.

(B) Individuals who wish to enroll in PASSPORT must have his/her medicaid eligibility determination made by ODM's administrative agency and an assessment of his/her PASSPORT eligibility made by ODA's designee.

(C) If the individual has been determined eligible and a waiver slot is available, the individual shall be enrolled in accordance with the PASSPORT HCBS waiver program's home first component, if applicable, and rule 173-42-03 of the Administrative Code.

(D) ODA's designee shall make the determination of PASSPORT eligibility using the requirements set forth in rule 5160-31-03 of the Administrative Code.

(E) Any applicant for PASSPORT HCBS waiver program services is entitled to notice and hearing rights as set forth in section 5101.35 of the Revised Code and division 5101:6 of the Administrative Code.

Replaces: 5160-31-04.
Effective: 1/1/2019.
Five Year Review (FYR) Dates: 01/01/2024.
Promulgated Under: 119.03.
Statutory Authority: 5166.02.
Rule Amplifies: 173.52
Prior Effective Dates: 07/16/1984, 12/22/1986 (Emer.), 03/23/1987, 07/01/1990, 01/14/1996, 02/22/2001, 10/03/2005 (Emer.), 01/01/2006, 03/17/2011, 09/29/2011, 03/06/2014.

**5160-31-05. PASSPORT HCBS waiver program covered services.**

(A) The purpose of this rule is to establish the services covered by the pre-admission screening system providing options and resources today (PASSPORT) home and community based services (HCBS) program.

(B) The PASSPORT program benefit package is limited to the following services:

(1) Adult day as set forth in rule 173-39-02.1 of the Administrative Code;

(2) Alternative meal as set forth in rule 173-39-02.2 of the Administrative Code;

(3) Choices home care attendant as set forth in rule 173-39-02.4 of the Administrative Code;

(4) Community integration as set forth in rule 173-39-02.15 of the Administrative Code;

(5) Community transition as set forth in rule 173-39-02.17 of the Administrative Code;

(6) Enhanced community living as set forth in rule 173-39-02.20 of the Administrative Code;

(7) Homemaker as set forth in rule 173-39-02.8 of the Administrative Code;

(8) Home care attendant as set forth in rule 173-39-02.24 of the Administrative Code;

(9) Home delivered meal as set forth in rule 173-39-02.14 of the Administrative Code;

(10) Home maintenance and chore as set forth in rule 173-39-02.5 of the Administrative Code;

(11) Home medical equipment and supplies as set forth in rule 173-39-02.7 of the Administrative Code;

(12) Home modification as set forth in rule 173-39-02.9 of the Administrative Code;

(13) Non-emergency medical transportation as set forth in rule 173-39-02.13 of the Administrative Code;

(14) Non-medical transportation as set forth in rule 173-39-02.18 of the Administrative Code;

(15) Nutrition consultation as set forth in rule 173-39-02.10 of the Administrative Code;

(16) Out-of-home respite as set forth in rule 173-39-02.23 of the Administrative Code;

(17) Personal care as set forth in rule 173-39-02.11 of the Administrative Code;

(18) Personal emergency response system as set forth in rule 173-39-02.6 of the Administrative Code;

(19) Social work counseling as set forth in rule 173-39-02.12 of the Administrative Code; and

(20) Waiver nursing as set forth in rule 173-39-02.22 of the Administrative Code.

(C) Services shall be delivered by providers in a manner that is consistent with the individual's person-centered services plan as documented in the PASSPORT information management system (PIMS).

(D) In accordance with the federally approved PASSPORT waiver, the services identified in this paragraph are subject to employer and/or budget authority if elected by the individual. Services shall be provided in accordance with the requirements in paragraph (B) of this rule:

(1) The following services are subject to employer authority, including the ability to hire, fire, and train employees:

(a) Choices home care attendant; and

(b) Personal care.

(2) The following services are subject to budget authority, including the ability to negotiate reimbursement rates paid to providers furnishing services:

(a) Alternative meals;

(b) Choices home care attendant;

(c) Home medical equipment and supplies;

(d) Home maintenance and chore; and

(e) Home modification

(E) An individual who elects to direct any of the services provided in paragraph (D) of this rule shall be assessed by their case manager to determine the individual's ability to direct their services as set forth in rule 173-42-06 of the Administrative Code.

(1) If an individual demonstrates the ability to direct their services, the case manager may initiate the orientation process to familiarize the individual with the participant direction of services including the role of the financial management service (FMS).

(2) If an individual is unable to demonstrate the ability to direct his or her care and to assume the responsibilities associated with the participant direction authorities in paragraph (D) of this rule, the individual may choose an authorized representative to act on his or her behalf.

(3) If no authorized representative is available, the case manager shall assist the individual with obtaining services through ODA-certified long-term care agency providers.

(F) If an individual who is seeking to direct his or her services chooses an authorized representative to act on his or her behalf in accordance with paragraph (E)(2) of this rule, the authorized representative shall not simultaneously serve as the individual's authorized representative and the individual's provider.

Effective: 7/1/2019.
Five Year Review (FYR) Dates: 4/9/2019 and 07/01/2024.
Promulgated Under: 119.03.
Statutory Authority: 5166.02.
Rule Amplifies: 173.52
Prior Effective Dates: 07/16/1984, 12/22/1986 (Emer.), 03/23/1987, 07/01/1990, 01/14/1996, 09/01/1998, 07/01/2006, 07/01/2008, 06/28/2009, 03/17/2011, 03/01/2014, 07/01/2014, 01/01/2019.

### 5160-31-06. Provider conditions of participation for the PASSPORT HCBS waiver program.

(A) The purpose of this rule is to establish the conditions under which providers are able to participate in the preadmission screening system providing options and resources today (PASSPORT) home and community based services (HCBS) waiver program.

(B) In order to obtain a medicaid provider agreement to be a PASSPORT provider furnishing services in rule 5160-31-05 of the Administrative Code the provider shall be certified by the Ohio department of aging (ODA) in accordance with the provisions of Chapter 173-39 of the Administrative Code.

(C) Individuals enrolled in the PASSPORT HCBS waiver shall be given a free choice of qualified providers in accordance with rule 173-42-06 of the Administrative Code.

(D) ODA is authorized to deem any provider approved by the Ohio department of medicaid (ODM) or certified by the Ohio department of developmental disabilities (DODD) to provide waiver services as having satisfied the requirements for certification by ODA for the same or similar services.

Effective: 10/07/2020
Promulgated Under: 119.03.
Statutory Authority: 5166.02
Rule Amplifies: 173.52
Prior Effective Dates: 07/16/1984, 12/22/1986 (Emer.), 03/23/1987, 07/01/1990, 01/14/1996, 09/01/1998, 07/01/2006, 03/17/2011, 07/01/2014, 01/01/2019, 06/11/2020 (Emer.), 10/05/2020.

### 5160-31-07. PASSPORT HCBS waiver program rate setting.

The purpose of this rule is to describe the methods used to determine provider rates for the PASSPORT program.

(A) Rates determined under this rule shall not exceed the maximum allowable rate for PASSPORT services in appendix A to rule 5160-1-06.1 of the Administrative Code. Payment for PASSPORT waiver services constitutes payment in full and shall not be construed as a partial payment when the payment amount is less than the provider's usual and customary rate. The provider shall not bill the individual for any difference between the medicaid payment and the provider's rate or request the individual to share in the cost through a co-payment or other similar charge.

(B) PASSPORT rates are established for the services in rule 5160-31-05 of the Administrative Code under the following categories:

(1) Per-job bid rate;

(2) Per-item rate; and

(3) Unit rate.

(C) Rates set within the categories in paragraph (B) of this rule may be:

(1) Participant-directed, in which the individual or his/her designated authorized representative, who is acting on the individual's behalf, may negotiate the rate for services furnished by providers as specified in paragraphs (D)(3), (E)(3), and (H)(1) of this rule.

(2) Statewide, in which the state establishes a rate used on a statewide basis to pay for services specified in paragraph (F)(1) of this rule.

(3) Regional, in which the state establishes a regional rate for services specified in paragraph (G)(1) of this rule. The regions in which applicable rates are calculated shall be designated by ODA.

(a) The regional rate for each service shall be the weighted average rate paid in the region using cost and unit data either from the most recently completed state fiscal year or the most recent twelve calendar months for which complete data is available, whichever is later.

(b) ODA or its designee shall enter into a provider agreement with providers in each region. The provider agreement shall do all of the following:

(i) Specify the time period for which the rates shall be in effect;

Admin Code

(ii) Specify the timelines for contracting;

(iii) Define the region/subregions for which the rates are established;

(iv) Base rates on the units of service as set forth in appendix A to rule 5160-1-06.1 of the Administrative Code;

(v) Reflect the agreed upon rate and

(vi) Adjust the regional rate up to the nearest number that is divisible by four, out to two decimal places.

(c) Regional provider rates shall be established as follows:

(i) No provider shall have a rate exceeding the maximum allowable rate for the service as established in appendix A to rule 5160-1-06.1 of the Administrative Code.

(ii) If the state recalculates regional rates for the services in paragraph (G) of this rule, certified providers may either accept the new regional rate or continue to be paid at the rate paid for services prior to the calculation of the regional rate.

(iii) Providers certified after the regional rate is established shall have a provider rate less than or equal to the regional rate.

(4) Group rates are seventy-five per cent of the rate the provider would be paid for providing PASSPORT services as specified in paragraphs (D)(2), (F)(2), (G) (2), and (G)(3) of this rule.

(D) For the services listed in this paragraph, a per-job bid rate shall be negotiated between the provider and the individual's case manager.

(1) A per-job bid rate shall be used for the following services:

(a) Community transition;

(b) Home maintenance and repair;

(c) Home modification,

(d) Non-emergency medical transportation;

(e) Non-medical transportation;

(2) Non-emergency medical transportation and non-medical transportation rendered simultaneously by the same provider to more than one individual enrolled in PASSPORT residing in the same household and traveling in the same vehicle to the same destination shall be paid using the group rate that is equal to seventy-five per cent of the provider's per-job bid rate. This shall apply to any combination of nonemergency medical transportation and/or non-medical transportation services.

(3) Home modification and Home maintenance and chore services may be participant-directed services in which the individual enrolled on PASSPORT or his/her authorized representative, acting on the individual's behalf, may negotiate rates.

(a) The negotiated rate shall be reviewed by ODA's designee and reflected on the individual's person-centered service plan prior to service delivery.

(b) Should the individual choose not to negotiate a rate the service shall be paid at a rate proposed by the provider and accepted by the individual and ODA's designee. The accepted rate shall be reflected on the individual's person-centered services plan.

(E) A per-item rate shall be determined for home medical equipment and supplies service.

(1) The cost of the item shall not exceed the medicaid state plan rate.

(2) The cost of an item that does not have an established medicaid rate shall be paid at a per-item bid rate submitted and agreed to in writing by ODA's designee prior to delivery of the item.

(3) Home medical equipment and supplies services may be participant directed in which the individual enrolled on PASSPORT or the authorized representative, acting on the individual's behalf, may negotiate rates.

(a) The negotiated rate shall be reviewed by ODA's designee and reflected on the individual's person-centered service plan prior to service delivery.

(b) Should the individual choose not to negotiate a rate the service shall b paid at a rate agreed upon between the provider, the individual and ODA's designee. The agreed upon rate shall be reflected on the individual's person-centered service plan.

(F) ODA shall establish unit rates for the services listed in this paragraph. No service shall have both a regional and statewide rate set pursuant to this rule.

(1) Statewide unit rates shall be established and used for the following services:

(a) Adult day;

(b) Community integration;

(c) Enhanced community living;

(d) Home care attendant;

(e) Home delivered meals

(f) Out-of-home respite;

(g) Personal care;

(h) Personal emergency response system; and

(i) Waiver nursing.

(2) The services in paragraphs (F)(1)(d), (F)(1)(g), and (F)(1)(i) of this rule, when rendered consecutively during the same visit to more than one but fewer than four PASSPORT individuals in the same household, as identified in the individuals' person-centered service plans, shall be paid to one hundred per cent of the provider's per unit rate set in accordance with paragraph (C) of this rule for one PASSPORT individual and paid a group rate for each. subsequent PASSPORT individual in the household receiving services during the visit.

(G) ODA shall establish regional unit rates for the services listed in this paragraph pursuant to the methodology in paragraph (C)(3) of this rule. No service shall have both a regional and statewide rate set pursuant to this rule.

(1) Regional unit rates shall be set for the following services:

(a) Adult day transportation;

(b) Homemaker;

(c) Social work counseling; and

(d) Nutritional consultation

(2) Adult day transportation services rendered simultaneously by the same provider to more than one individual residing in the same household and traveling in the same vehicle to the same destination shall be paid using a group rate equal to seventy-five per cent of the provider's regional unit rate.

(3) Personal care rendered during the same visit by the same provider to more than one but less than four PASSPORT individuals in the same household, as identified in the individuals' person-centered services plans, shall be paid one hundred per cent of the provider's per unit rate set in accordance with paragraph (C) of this rule for one PASSPORT individual and paid the group rate for each subsequent PASSPORT individual in the household receiving services during the visit.

(H) The services in this paragraph are participant directed and the individual may negotiate unit rates with providers.

(1) The participant directed services include:

(a) Alternative meals; and

(b) Choices home care attendant.

(2) The individual shall have in effect, before choices home care attendant services are delivered, a signed provider agreement with each ODA-certified participant-directed individual provider delivering services to the individual. The provider agreement shall:

(a) Include the rate negotiated with the provider;

(b) Specify the time period the rates shall be in effect;

(c) Base rates on the units of service as set forth in Chapter 173-39 of the Administrative Code; and

(d) Be signed by the individual receiving the choices home care attendant service and the HCBS provider.

(3) The rates negotiated by the individual with providers of services in paragraph (H)(1) of this rule shall not exceed the maximum allowed per unit of service as specified in appendix A to rule 5160-1-06.1 of the Administrative Code. The negotiated rate shall be reviewed by the ODA's designee and reflected on the individual's person-centered service plan prior to service delivery.

(4) Should the individual choose not to negotiate a rate for any of the services in paragraph (H)(1) of this rule, the service shall be paid at a rate agreed upon by the provider and the individual and the individual's case manager. The agreed upon rate shall be reflected on the individual's person-centered service plan.

(I) The Ohio department of medicaid, or its designee, shall evaluate unit rates within two years of the effective date of this rule and every two years thereafter.

Effective: 7/1/2019.
Five Year Review (FYR) Dates: 4/9/2019 and 07/01/2024.
Promulgated Under: 119.03.
Statutory Authority: 5166.02.
Rule Amplifies: 173.52
Prior Effective Dates: 09/01/1998, 03/01/2000, 07/01/2006, 07/01/2008, 03/17/2011, 07/01/2011 (Emer.), 09/29/2011, 03/01/2014, 07/01/2014, 01/01/

2017, 01/01/2019.

# CHAPTER 5160-33

# ASSISTED LIVING HCBS WAIVER PROGRAM



## 5160-33-02. Definitions for the assisted living home and community based services waiver (HCBS) program.

(A) The purpose of this rule is to define the terms used in Chapter 5160-33 of the Administrative Code governing the medicaid assisted living HCBS waiver program.

As used in this chapter:

(B) "ADL" means activities of daily living including bathing; grooming; toileting; dressing; eating; and mobility, which refers to bed mobility, transfer, and locomotion as these are defined in 5160-3-05 of the Administrative Code.

(C) "Assessment" means a face-to-face evaluation used to obtain information about an individual including his or her condition, personal goals and preferences, functional limitations, health status and other factors that are relevant to the authorization and provision of services. Assessment information supports the determination that an individual requires waiver services as well as the development of a service plan.

(D) "Assisted living waiver" (ALW) means the home and community based services waiver, approved by the centers for medicare and medicaid services, that is administered by the Ohio department of aging.

(E) "Authorized representative" has the same meaning as in rule 5160-1-33 of the Administrative Code.

(F) "CDJFS" means a county department of job and family services.

(G) "C.F.R." means the code of federal regulations.

(H) "CMS" means the centers for medicare and medicaid services, a federal agency that is part of the United States department of health and human services, and that administers the medicaid program and approves HCBS waivers.

(I) "Case management" means a set of person centered activities provided by ODA's designee that are undertaken to ensure that the individual receives appropriate and necessary services. Under a HCBS waiver, these activities may include, but are not necessarily limited to, assessment, service plan development, service plan implementation and service monitoring as well as assistance in accessing waiver, state plan, and other non-medicaid services and resources.

(J) "Certified" or "certification" means providers certified by the Ohio department of aging (ODA) to provide services for assisted living HCBS waiver individual pursuant to Chapter 173-39 of the Administrative Code.

(K) "HCBS" or "home and community-based services" means services furnished under the provisions set forth in 42 C.F.R 441 Subpart G (October 1, 2016) that permit individuals to live in a home setting rather than a nursing facility (NF) or hospital. HCBS waiver services are approved by CMS for specific populations and are not otherwise available under the medicaid state plan.

(L) "Home first" means the component of the assisted living HCBS waiver program that offers priority enrollment in the waiver for certain individuals in accordance with section 173.542 of the Revised Code.

(M) "Individual" is a person enrolled on the assisted living HCBS waiver.

(N) "Level of care" (LOC) means the designation describing an individual's functional levels and nursing needs pursuant to the criteria set forth in rules 5160-3-05, 5160-3-06, 5160-3-07, and 5160-3-08 of the Administrative Code.

(O) "NF" means a nursing facility as defined in section 5165.01 of the Revised Code.

(P) "ODA" means the Ohio department of aging.

(Q) "ODJFS" means the Ohio department of job and family services.

(R) "PASSPORT" means preadmission screening system providing options and resources today.

(S) "ODA's designee" has the same meaning as in rule 173-39-01 of the Administrative Code.

(T) "Residential care facility" means a residential care facility as defined in section 3721.01 of the Revised Code that is issued a license pursuant to section 3721.02 of the Revised Code.

(U) "Room and board" means a payment made by an individual enrolled in the assisted living waiver directly to the ODA certified assisted living waiver provider. When paying "room" the individual shall not be charged for the same furnishings and other shelter expenses the residential care facility provides at no cost to private pay non-waiver residents pursuant to the facility's resident agreement. The term "board" means three meals a day or any other full nutritional regimen.

Room and board does not include charges for ancillary items, services, and/or social activities purchased or paid for by the individual including hygiene and supplies not provided through medicaid and reflected on the individual care plan, recreation and activities, and/or other items or services purchased by the individual; however ODA certified assisted living providers may, at their own discretion, provide ancillary items, services and/or social activities as part of the room and board payment.

(V) "Service Plan" has the same meaning as the person-centered service plan in paragraph (B) in rule 5160-44-02 of the Administrative Code.

Effective: 04/01/2017.
Five Year Review (FYR) Dates: 12/27/2016 and 04/01/2022.
Promulgated Under: 119.03.
Statutory Authority: 5166.02.
Rule Amplifies: 173.54
Prior Effective Dates: 7/1/06, 12/31/09, 9/29/2011.



## 5160-33-03. Eligibility for the medicaid funded component of the assisted living program.

(A) The purpose of this rule is to outline the requirements that must be met for an individual to be eligible to enroll in the medicaid funded component of the assisted living program.

(B) To be eligible for the medicaid funded component of the assisted living program, an individual must meet all of the following:

(1) Be eligible for medicaid in accordance with Chapters 5160:1-3 to 5160:1-6 of the Administrative Code.

(2) Have an intermediate or skilled level of care in accordance with rule 5160-3-08 of the Administrative Code. If the individual requires skilled nursing care beyond supervision of special diets, application of dressings, or administration of medication, it must be provided in accordance with rule 3701-16-09.1 of the Administrative Code.

(3) Be age twenty-one years old or older at the time of enrollment.

(4) Participate in the development of a person-centered services plan in accordance with the process and requirements set forth in rule 5160-44-02 of the Administrative Code.

(5) Have the ability to make room and board payments calculated at the current supplemental security income (SSI) federal benefit level minus fifty dollars. Providers shall not charge or collect room and board payments from individuals in excess of the room and board payment calculated in accordance with this paragraph. In the event an individual does not have sufficient personal income:

(a) An individual may arrange for informal supports to provide a supplemental payment to the provider in order to meet room and board requirements;

(i) The supplemental payment shall represent no more than the difference between the individual's personal income and the maximum room and board payment established in paragraph (B)(5) of this rule.

(ii) The amount of the supplemental payment shall not be considered when calculating the individual's patient liability as described in rule 5160:1-6-07.1 of the Administrative Code.

(b) A provider may elect to accept a reduced room and board rate.

(6) Have health and safety related needs met, as determined by the Ohio department of aging's (ODA) designee.

(C) The individual must reside in a residential care facility (RCF) licensed by the Ohio department of health. At the time of initial and continued enrollment, the individual must reside in a certified living unit, in an RCF certified by ODA that possesses the home and community-based setting characteristics set forth in rule 5160-44-01 of the Administrative Code.

(D) If the individual fails to meet any of the eligibility requirements identified in this rule, the individual shall be denied enrollment in the assisted living HCBS waiver. In such instances, the individual shall be notified of his or her hearing rights in accordance with division 5101:6 of the Administrative Code.

(E) An individual will not be disenrolled from the assisted living HCBS waiver if disenrollment will result in losing eligibility for Ohio medicaid, unless the individual requests disenrollment, moves out of state, or dies.

Effective: 7/1/2021.
Promulgated Under: 119.03.
Statutory Authority: 5166.02.
Rule Amplifies: 173.54.
Prior Effective Dates: 7/1/2006, 3/22/2008, 9/19/2009, 9/29/2011, 10/4/2015, 11/25/2016, 10/1/2019, 6/12/2020 (Emer.), 10/17/2020.

**5160-33-04. Enrollment process for medicaid-funded component of the assisted living waiver program.**

(A) The purpose of this rule is to outline the requirement that must be met for an individual to enroll in the medicaid-funded component of the assisted living waiver program.

(B) To be eligible for enrollment, an individual must:

(1) Have been determined to meet the eligibility requirements set forth in rule 5160-33-03 of the Administrative Code; and

(2) Upon initial and continued enrollment, reside in an approved living unit in accordance with paragraph (C) of rule 173-38-03 of the administrative code, located in a licensed residential care facility (RCF) certified by the Ohio department of aging (ODA) that possesses the home and community-based setting characteristics set forth in rule 5160-44-01 of the Administrative Code.

(C) If the individual has been determined eligible and the medicaid component of the assisted living waiver program has not reached the centers for medicare and medicaid services (CMS) authorized limit of participants for the current year, the individual shall be enrolled in accordance with the assisted living waiver program's home first component, if applicable, and rule 173-38-03 of the Administrative Code.

(D) Pursuant to chapters 5160:1-3 to 5160:1-6 of the Administrative Code, if an individual is determined eligible for medicaid by the county department of job and family services, the individual shall not enroll in the assisted living waiver program until ODA's designee establishes a waiver program enrollment date and authorizes the provision of waiver services by an ODA certified assisted living provider. The waiver program enrollment date shall in no way restrict retroactive eligibility for non-assisted living waiver services available to individuals through the medicaid state plan.

(E) Any applicant for the assisted living waiver program is entitled to notice and hearing rights as set forth in section 5101.35 of the Revised Code and division 5101:6 of the Administrative Code.

Effective: 10/17/2020
Promulgated Under: 119.03.
Statutory Authority: 5166.02.
Rule Amplifies: 173.54
Prior Effective Dates: 07/01/2006, 03/22/2008, 09/19/2009, 09/29/2011, 04/01/2017, 10/01/2019, 06/11/2020 (Emer.), 10/05/2020.

Admin Code

**5160-33-05. Provider conditions of participation for the assisted living home and community based services (HCBS) waiver program.**

(A) The purpose of this rule is to establish the conditions under which providers are able to participate in the assisted living HCBS waiver program.

(B) In order to obtain a medicaid provider agreement to be an assisted living services provider, the provider must be certified by the Ohio department of aging (ODA) or its designee in accordance with the provisions of rule 173-39-03 of the Administrative Code.

(C) Individuals enrolled in the assisted living HCBS waiver shall be given a free choice of qualified providers in accordance with rule 173-42-06 of the Administrative Code and 42 C.F.R. 431.51 (as in effect on October 1, 2016).

Effective: 04/01/2017.
Five Year Review (FYR) Dates: 12/27/2016 and 04/01/2022.
Promulgated Under: 119.03.
Statutory Authority: 5166.02.
Rule Amplifies: 173.54
Prior Effective Dates: 7/1/206, 9/29/2011.

**5160-33-06. Covered services for the assisted living services home and community based services (HCBS) waiver program.**

(A) The purpose of this rule is to establish the services covered by the assisted living HCBS waiver program.

(B) The assisted living HCBS waiver benefit package is limited to the following services:

(1) Assisted living services as set forth in rule 173-39-02.16 of the Administrative Code, and

(2) Community transition services as set forth in rule 173-39-02.17 of the Administrative Code.

(C) Services will be delivered consistent with the individual's person-centered service plan.

Effective: 04/01/2017.
Five Year Review (FYR) Dates: 12/27/2016 and 04/01/2022.
Promulgated Under: 119.03.
Statutory Authority: 5166.02.
Rule Amplifies: 173.54
Prior Effective Dates: 7/1/2016, 9/29/2011.

**5160-33-07. Assisted living home and community based services (HCBS) waiver rate setting.**

(A) The purpose of this rule is to describe the methods used to determine provider rates for the assisted living HCBS waiver as set forth in appendix A to rule 5160-1-06.5 of the Administrative Code.

(B) Provider rates are determined for the following categories:

(1) Per-job bid rate or deposit made.

(2) Unit rate.

(C) A per-job bid rate or deposit made shall be determined on a per-job basis for the community transition service as set forth in rule 173-39-02.17 of the Administrative Code. The cost per job shall be paid at a per-job bid rate that is negotiated and approved by Ohio department of aging's (ODA) designee and accepted by the individual. The per-job bid rate includes the items and supports set forth in rule 173-39-02.17 of the Administrative Code and authorized on the person-centered services plan.

(D) A unit rate shall be based on a three-tiered model, and shall not exceed the amounts in appendix A to rule 5160-1-06.5 of the Administrative Code. These rates are used for assisted living services as set forth in rule 173-39-02.16 of the Administrative Code.

(1) The rate for assisted living services for each individual shall be determined by the ODA's designee through an assessment of the individual service needs in four areas:

(a) Cognitive impairments,

(b) Medication administration,

(c) Nursing services, and

(d) Functional impairments.

(2) The ODA-certified assisted living provider must agree to provide the services in the individual's person-centered service plan at the rate determined by the assessment.

(E) ODA certified assisted living providers shall only be paid for assisted living services authorized by ODA's designee and reflected on the individual's person-centered service plan.

(F) Assisted living service payment constitutes payment in full and may not be construed as a partial payment when the payment amount is less than the provider's charge. The provider may not bill an individual enrolled in the assisted living program for any difference between the medicaid payment and the provider's charge or request that the individual share in the cost through a co-payment or other similar charge.

(G) The assisted living service payment is for assisted living services as defined in rule 173-39-02.16 of the Administrative Code and does not include payment for room and board as calculated pursuant to rule 5160-33-03 of the Administrative Code, which is the responsibility of the individual.

Effective: 7/1/2019.
Five Year Review (FYR) Dates: 4/9/2019 and 07/01/2024.
Promulgated Under: 119.03.
Statutory Authority: 5166.02.
Rule Amplifies: 173.54
Prior Effective Dates: 07/01/2006, 03/22/2008, 09/19/2009, 09/29/2011, 04/01/2017.

# CHAPTER 5160-36

# PROGRAM OF ALL-INCLUSIVE CARE FOR THE ELDERLY (PACE)

Rule



## 5160-36-01. Program of all-inclusive care for the elderly (PACE) definitions.

(A) "Authorized representative" has the same meaning as in rule 5160:1-1-01 of the Administrative Code.

(B) "Capitated payment" means the monthly payment paid to the program of all inclusive care for the elderly PACE organization by the Ohio department of medicaid ( ODM) for medical care and services provided to medicaid recipients enrolled in PACE.

(C) "Individual" is the applicant for or recipient of a medical assistance program such as medicaid.

(D) "Involuntary disenrollment" means the disenrollment of a participant from PACE at the request of the PACE organization or a county department of job and family services.

(E) "PACE" means the 'program of all-inclusive care for the elderly' as set forth in 42 C.F.R. Part 460 as in effect on October 1, 2019.

(F) "PACE center" means a facility operated by a PACE organization where primary care or other related services offered by PACE are provided to participants.

(G) "PACE organization" means an entity that has a medicaid provider agreement and also has in effect a PACE agreement with the centers for medicare and medicaid services (CMS) and the Ohio department of aging ( ODA).

(H) "PACE agreement" means an agreement between a PACE organization, CMS, and ODA.

(I) "Participant" means a person enrolled in and receiving services through PACE.

(J) "Private pay participant" means an individual who does not meet the medicaid eligibility criteria but chooses to participate in PACE and is responsible for payment of the PACE organization's private pay premium.

(K) "Service area" means the geographic area in which a PACE organization is approved by CMS and ODA to provide services to PACE participants.

(L) "State administering agency" means the state agency responsible for administering the PACE agreement. Pursuant to section 173.50 of the Revised Code ODA shall serve as the state administering agency for PACE in Ohio.

(M) "Voluntary disenrollment" means the disenrollment of a participant from PACE at the request of the participant or the participant's authorized representative.

Effective: 1/1/2020.
Five Year Review (FYR) Dates: 10/15/2019 and 01/01/2025.
Promulgated Under: 119.03.
Statutory Authority: 5164.02.
Rule Amplifies: 5162.35, 173.50.
Prior Effective Dates: 03/28/2009, 07/01/2011 (Emer.), 09/29/2011, 01/01/2015.

## 5160-36-02. Program of all-inclusive care for the elderly (PACE) administration.

(A) In accordance with section 173.50 of the Revised Code, the Ohio department of aging (ODA) shall serve as the designated state administering agency for PACE and shall adhere to and monitor the implementation of all applicable requirements for the program's administration as set forth in 42 C.F.R Part 460 as in effect on October 1, 2019.

(B) ODA shall:

(1) Facilitate the process in which prospective PACE organizations apply to the centers for medicare and medicaid services (CMS) for approval to provide PACE services;

(2) Enter into a PACE agreement with (CMS) and each PACE organization approved by CMS to provide PACE services to participants in Ohio who reside in the PACE organization's designated service area. The content and duration of that agreement shall conform to standards set forth in 42 C.F.R. Part 460 as in effect on October 1, 2019.

(3) Verify that PACE organizations providing PACE services have signed medicaid provider agreements as required by rule 5160-1-17 of the Administrative Code.

(4) Work with PACE organizations to assist individuals seeking enrollment in PACE.

(5) Manage PACE enrollment.

(6) Adopt rules including, but not limited to, participant eligibility, participant enrollment, participant voluntary disenrollment and participant involuntary disenrollment.

(7) Confer as necessary and appropriate with the Ohio department of medicaid (ODM) on matters including but not limited to:

(a) Participant eligibility;

(b) Participant enrollment and disenrollment, and program waiting list;

(c) Establishing the payment for PACE organizations operating in Ohio;

(d) Designating each PACE organization's service area;

(e) The enrollment and disenrollment of PACE organizations; and

(f) The termination of PACE agreements.

(C) ODM shall be responsible for the capitated payments made to PACE organizations for medicaid services rendered to PACE participants.

Effective: 1/1/2020.
Five Year Review (FYR) Dates: 10/15/2019 and 01/01/2025.
Promulgated Under: 119.03.
Statutory Authority: 5164.02.
Rule Amplifies: 5162.35; 173.50.
Prior Effective Dates: 03/28/2009, 07/01/2011 (Emer.), 09/29/2011, 01/01/2015.

## 5160-36-03. Program of all-inclusive care for the elderly (PACE) eligibility.

(A) To be eligible and maintain eligibility for PACE an individual shall meet the requirements for PACE participant eligibility set forth in rule 173-50-02 of the Administrative Code.

(B) Individuals seeking enrollment in PACE through medicaid shall be determined by their county department of job and family services (CDJFS) to be eligible for Ohio medicaid in accordance with Chapters 5160:1-3 to 5160:1-6 of the Administrative Code.

(C) If a PACE participant who is also enrolled in medicaid has a period of continuous institutionalization as defined in rule 5160:1-6-01.1 of the Administrative Code that individual's patient liability amount is to be recalculated by the appropriate CDJFS as directed in rule 5160:1-6-07.1 of the Administrative Code.

(D) Participants who fail to meet the eligibility requirements in paragraph (A) of this rule shall be denied enrollment in PACE.

(E) PACE participants who no longer meet the medicaid eligibility requirements in paragraph (B) of this rule shall be given the opportunity to remain enrolled in PACE as a medicare only or as a private pay participant.

(F) Participants who no longer meet the medicaid financial eligibility criteria but choose to remain enrolled in PACE through private resources shall be charged no less than the medicaid rate for services by the PACE organization.

Effective: 10/17/2020
Promulgated Under: 119.03.
Statutory Authority: 5164.02.
Rule Amplifies: 5162.35, 173.50.
Prior Effective Dates: 03/28/2009, 01/01/2015, 01/01/2020, 06/11/2020 (Emer.), 10/05/2020.

### 5160-36-04. Program of all-inclusive care for the elderly (PACE): enrollment and disenrollment.

(A) Individuals eligible and seeking to enroll in PACE shall enroll in the manner established in rule 173-50-03 of the Administrative Code unless paragraph (B) of this rule applies.

(B) A participant may choose to voluntarily disenroll from PACE at any time without cause if the participant or the participant's authorized representative informs the PACE organization orally or in writing.

(1) Should a participant choose to voluntarily disenroll from PACE, ODA shall, prior to the participant's disenrollment, verify that the voluntary disenrollment was initiated by the individual or the individual's authorized representative.

(2) The voluntary disenrollment of a participant shall occur in the manner prescribed in rule 173-50-04 of the Administrative Code.

(C) Subject to paragraph (D) of this rule, a PACE organization may initiate the involuntary disenrollment of a participant if either of the conditions set forth in paragraph (C)(1) or (C)(2) of this rule are met.

(1) The participant no longer meets the PACE requirements set forth in rule 173-50-02 of the Administrative Code.

(2) The participant meets the criteria for involuntary disenrollment set forth in rule 173-50-05 of the Administrative Code.

(3) The involuntary disenrollment of a PACE participant shall occur in the manner prescribed in rule 173-50-05 of the Administrative Code.

(D) Once enrolled in PACE, a participant will not be disenrolled if disenrollment results in the loss of medicaid eligibility, unless the participant requests disenrollment pursuant to paragraph (B) of this rule, moves out of state, or dies.

Effective: 10/1/2021.
Promulgated Under: 119.03.
Statutory Authority: 5164.02.
Rule Amplifies: 5162.35, 173.50, 5162.35.
Prior Effective Dates: 3/28/2009, 1/1/2015, 1/1/2020, 6/12/2020 (Emer.), 10/17/2020.

Admin Code

### 5160-36-05. Program of all-inclusive care for the elderly (PACE): care coordination.

(A) Each PACE organization shall establish and maintain at each PACE center an interdisciplinary team to assess the care and service needs of participants. The composition, qualifications, and activities of the interdisciplinary team shall be consistent with 42 C.F.R. Part 460 as in effect on October 1, 2019.

(B) PACE organizations shall ensure that all participants have access to all medically necessary services including, but not limited to, services covered by Ohio's medicaid program, in addition to those prescribed in 42 C.F.R. Part 460.92 as in effect on October 1, 2019 to 42 C.F.R. Part 460.96 as in effect on October 1, 2019.

(1) Services provided shall be sufficient in their amount, duration and scope to meet the participant's medical, physical, emotional, and social needs as identified in the comprehensive assessment to achieve the measurable outcomes identified in the participant's plan of care.

(2) Services provided shall be reflected in the participant's plan of care unless the services are an emergency service.

Effective: 1/1/2020.
Five Year Review (FYR) Dates: 10/15/2019 and 01/01/2025.
Promulgated Under: 119.03.
Statutory Authority: 5164.02.
Rule Amplifies: 5162.35, 173.50.
Prior Effective Dates: 03/28/2009, 01/01/2015.

### 5160-36-06. Program of all-inclusive care for the elderly (PACE) organization reimbursement.

(A) PACE is a full-risk program in which the PACE organization assumes all financial risk for the cost of the medical care and services provided to participants.

(B) PACE organizations shall receive a monthly capitated payment from the Ohio department of medicaid (ODM) for each PACE participant enrolled in the medicaid program including individuals enrolled in both medicaid and medicare.

(C) The amount of the capitated payment shall be established in the PACE agreement.

(D) The amount paid in accordance with paragraph (B) of this rule represents the total maximum payment obligation of the state administering agency to the PACE organization for the cost of medical care and services provided to participants enrolled in medicaid including those participants enrolled in both medicaid and medicare.

(E) The PACE organization shall accept the capitation payment amount as payment in full for medicaid participants and shall not bill, charge, collect, or receive any other form of payment from ODM or from, or on behalf of, the participant, except as permitted under 42 C.F.R. Part 460.182(c) as in effect on October 1, 2019.

Effective: 1/1/2020.
Five Year Review (FYR) Dates: 10/15/2019 and 01/01/2025.
Promulgated Under: 119.03.
Statutory Authority: 119.03.
Rule Amplifies: 5164.02, 173.50, 5162.35.
Prior Effective Dates: 03/28/2009, 07/01/2011 (Emer.), 09/29/2011, 01/01/2015.

# CHAPTER 5160-56

# MEDICAID HOSPICE PROGRAM

Rule


### 5160-56-01. Hospice services: definitions.

This rule set forth terms used throughout Chapter 5160-56 of the Administrative Code.

(A) "Advance directive" refers to written instructions recognized under state law that are related to the provisions of health care when the individual is incapacitated. Samples of advance directive documents include a living will, a declaration as defined in Chapter 2133. of the Revised Code, and a durable power of attorney for health care as defined in Chapter 1337. of the Revised Code.

(B) "Advanced practice registered nurse (APRN)" refers to a registered nurse (RN) authorized to practice as a clinical nurse specialist, certified registered nurse anesthetist, certified nurse midwife or certified nurse practitioner in accordance with section 4723.43 of the Revised Code.

(C) "Attending physician" refers to a health professional identified by the individual at the time of the election of hospice, as having primary responsibility in the determination and delivery of the individual's medical care while under hospice, and one who is:

(1) A doctor of medicine or osteopathy licensed and legally authorized under Chapter 4731. of the Revised Code to practice medicine and surgery or osteopathic medicine and surgery; or

(2) A "nurse practitioner" who meets the training, education, and experience requirements of a certified, advanced practice nurse in accordance with section 4723.43 of the Revised Code. APRNs are prohibited from certifying or recertifying a terminal diagnosis.

(3) A "physician assistant" (PA) who meets the training, education, and other specifications of a licensed physician assistant in accordance with section 4730 of the Revised Code. PAs are prohibited from certifying or recertifying a terminal diagnosis.

(D) "Authorized representative" has the same meaning as a person, in accordance with rule 5160:1-1-01 of the Administrative Code, who is at least eighteen years old, or a legal entity who stands in place of the individual as defined in this rule. If an individual has designated an authorized representative, all references to "individual" in regards to an individual's responsibilities shall include the individual's authorized representative. Actions or failures of an authorized representative will be accepted as the action or failure of the individual. An authorized representative may make health care decisions on behalf of the individual who is mentally or physically incapacitated, or at the request of the terminally ill individual. These decisions may include the termination of medical care, the election of the hospice benefit, or the revocation of election of the hospice benefit on behalf of a terminally ill individual. Documentation of the authorization must be maintained in the individual's hospice record.

(E) "Beginning date of service" means the first billable date on which a designated hospice provider delivers hospice services to an individual.

(F) "Benefit period" or "election benefit period" refers to a span for which the individual is enrolled in the hospice benefit. Benefit periods consist of two ninety day benefit periods, followed by an unlimited number of sixty day benefit periods. The benefit periods may be used consecutively or at intervals. The election benefit period is subject to the conditions set forth in this chapter to include revocation, and must be utilized in sequential order:

(1) An initial ninety-day period (limited to one during the individual's lifetime);

(2) A second subsequent ninety-day period (limited to one during the individual's lifetime);

(3) An unlimited number of subsequent sixty-day periods.

(G) "Bereavement counseling" refers to counseling services furnished to the individual's immediate family or caregiver before and after the individual's death, to assist the family with issues related to grief, loss, and adjustment. Bereavement counseling must be made available by the designated hospice for a period up to one year following the individual's death.

(H) "Certification of the terminal illness" refers to the clinical judgment made by a medical director or physician member of the interdisciplinary group (IDG) and the individual's attending physician about the life expectancy of an individual should a terminal illness run its normal course. As a requirement pursuant to 42 C.F.R. 418.22 (October 1, 2017), in order to receive hospice care, the individual must be certified by a hospice medical director or physician member of the IDG and the individual's attending physician as being terminally ill with a medical prognosis that the individual's life expectancy is six months or less.

(I) "Concurrent care for children" refers to a federal provision which allows for curative treatment and hospice care to be covered simultaneously for individuals under age twenty-one.

(J) "Continuous home care" is a level of hospice care covered by medicaid in accordance with 42 C.F.R. 418.302 (October 1, 2017). A continuous home care day is one on which an individual who has elected to receive hospice care is at home and not in an inpatient facility, and when the care provided in the home consists predominantly of nursing care. Continuous home care may involve a home health aide (also known as a hospice aide) or homemaker services, or both. Continuous home care is only furnished during brief periods of crisis and only as necessary to maintain the terminally ill individual at home.

(K) "Core hospice services" are nursing care, medical social services, counseling services, and physician services that must routinely be afforded and/or provided directly to the individual by employees of the hospice.

(L) "Corresponding federal fiscal year" refers to the annual period from October first to September thirtieth, as set by the federal government for accounting and budgeting purposes.

(M) "Counseling services" are services provided to the terminally ill individual and the family members or other persons caring for the individual at home, including dietary counseling, training the individual's family or other caregiver to provide care, and for the purpose of helping the individual and the family members and/or caregiver with adjustment to the approaching death.

(N) "Designated hospice provider" refers to the hospice responsible for the professional management of care provided to the individual while enrolled in hospice.

(O) "Dietary counseling" means intervention and education regarding appropriate nutritional intake that is provided to the individual and/or the individual's family by a qualified professional including, but not limited to, a registered nurse, a dietitian and/or a physician.

(P) "Dietitian" means a person licensed to practice dietetics who meets the criteria set forth in Chapter 4759. of the Revised Code.

(Q) "Election statement," "election of hospice statement" and the "hospice election statement" refer to the required, written acknowledgment of the individual's decision to receive hospice care in lieu of curative care or treatment of the terminal illness.

(R) "Ending date of service" means the date on which a designated hospice stops delivering hospice services to the individual because of revocation of the medicaid hospice benefit, discharge from the hospice benefit, change by the individual of the designated hospice, or death of the individual in accordance with Chapter 5160-56 of the Administrative Code.

(S) "Episode of Care" or "Hospice Episode of Care" is a hospice election period or series of election periods separated by no more than a sixty day gap. Each episode is initiated by a start of care and is ended by a discharge to death or a gap in hospice services of more than sixty days. An episode of care may include multiple election benefit periods; however, a benefit period cannot span more than one episode of care.

(T) "General inpatient care" is a level of hospice care covered in accordance with 42 C.F.R. 418.302 (October 1, 2017). A general inpatient care day is a day on which an individual who has elected hospice care receives care in an inpatient facility for pain control or acute or chronic symptom management which cannot be managed in other settings.

(U) "Home and community based services (HCBS) waivers" refers to medicaid programs operated in accordance with Section 1915 (c) of the Social Security Act (the Act), 42 U.S.C. 1396n(c) (as in effect January 1, 2017) that allow individuals to receive covered services in their own home or community rather than institutions or other isolated settings. The HCBS waiver programs include those waivers administered by the Ohio department of medicaid (ODM), the Ohio department of aging (ODA), and the Ohio department of developmental disabilities (DODD).

(V) "Hospice" refers to a public agency, a private organization, or a subdivision of either, subject to the conditions of participation pursuant to 42 C.F.R. Part 418 (October 1, 2017), that is licensed in the state of Ohio and approved by the ODM to engaged in providing care to terminally ill individuals.

(W) "Hospice aide" refers to one who has successfully completed a training and competency evaluation program for hospice aide services, who meets the conditions of participation prescribed in 42 C.F.R. 418.76 (October 1, 2017), and who provides home care services pursuant to rule 3701-19-16 of the Administrative Code. For purposes of this chapter, hospice aide is interchangeable with the term, "home health aide".

(X) "Hospice care" refers to a comprehensive set of home based, inpatient and/or outpatient services coordinated by an interdisciplinary group of health professionals and volunteers as part of a written plan of care, to provide for the physical, psychosocial, spiritual, and emotional needs of a terminally ill individual and/or the individual's family members. Hospice stresses palliative care as opposed to curative care.

(Y) "Hospice enrollment" refers to the process of entering hospice data, such as benefit periods pursuant to rule 5160-56-03.3 of the Administrative Code, into the Ohio medicaid information technology system (MITS) for an individual in receipt of hospice care.

(Z) "Hospice quality reporting program" refers to a federal mandate pursuant to the Section 3004 of Affordable Care Act of 2010 (as in effect January 1, 2017). HQRP requires all Medicare-certified hospice providers to comply with data reporting requirements prescribed by the centers for medicare and medicaid services (CMS). Annually, by October 1, CMS publishes the quality measures a hospice must report. The act of submitting data is what determines compliance with HQRP requirements. If the required quality data is not reported by each designated submission deadline, the hospice will be subject to a two percentage point reduction in their annual payment update.

(AA) "Hospice provider span" refers to the date range (begin date to end date) that a valid provider is considered the designated hospice provider. It is an assignment in MITS that refers to the period of time during which an individual receives hospice services from the designated hospice.

(BB) "Individual" refers to the beneficiary eligible for medicaid, who is in need of, or under the care of the designated hospice, and who is considering and/or who has elected the hospice benefit. For decision making purposes, an individual may designate an authorized representative to act on his or her behalf, in place of the individual.

(CC) "Inpatient facility" refers to a facility that is either operated by or under contract with a hospice for the purpose of providing general inpatient and/or respite care to the individual.

(DD) "Inpatient respite care" is a level of hospice care covered in accordance with 42 C.F.R. 418.302 (October 1, 2017). An inpatient respite care day is a day on which the individual who has elected hospice care receives care in an approved facility on a short-term basis for the purpose of providing relief and respite for caregivers.

(EE) "Interdisciplinary group (IDG)" refers to a group of professionals and volunteer staff who provide or supervise the care and the services offered by the hospice in accordance with 42 C.F.R. 418.56 (October 1, 2017).

(FF) "Intermediate care facility for individuals with intellectual disabilities" has the same meaning as in rule 5123:2-7-01 of the Administrative Code.

(GG) "Licensed occupational therapist" means a person holding a valid license under Chapter 4755. of the Revised Code as an occupational therapist.

(HH) "Licensed occupational therapy assistant" means a person holding a valid license under Chapter 4755. of the Revised Code as an occupational therapy assistant (OTA).

(II) "Licensed physical therapist" means a person holding a valid license under Chapter 4755. of the Revised Code as a physical therapist.

(JJ) "Licensed physical therapy assistant" means a person holding a valid license under Chapter 4755. of the Revised Code as a physical therapist assistant (PTA).

(KK) "Licensed speech-language pathologist" means a person holding a valid license under Chapter 4753. of the Revised Code as a speech-language pathologist and who is eligible for or meets the educational requirements for a certificate of clinical competence in speech language pathology granted by the "American Speech- Language-Hearing Association."

(LL) "Licensed speech-language pathology aide" means a person holding a valid license under Chapter 4753. of the Revised Code as a speech-language pathology aide.

(MM) "Long Term Care Facility (LTCF)" as defined in section 3721.21 of the Revised Code is a term used interchangeably in the Ohio medicaid information technology system to refer to a nursing home, a facility or part of a facility that is certified as a skilled nursing facility or a nursing facility under Title XVIII or XIX of the "Social Security Act.

(NN) "Medicaid Information Technology System (MITS)" refers to the information management system utilized by ODM, hospice and other providers, and state agencies for medicaid billing and data management purposes. The "MITS Hospice Portal" refers to the functionality in MITS maintained by ODM that gives authorized entities access to data such as medicaid eligibility, hospice enrollment status, claim and payment status, election and hospice service spans, benefit periods, and payer and provider information.

(OO) "Medicaid Managed Care Plan" or a "Managed Care Plan" has the same meaning as in rule 5160-26-01 of the Administrative Code.

(PP) "Medical director" refers to the doctor of medicine or osteopathy employed by the designated hospice to assume overall responsibility for the medical component of the individual's plan of care, including consulting with other members of the interdisciplinary team and collaborating with the individual's attending physician if any.

(QQ) "Medicare" is the federally financed medical assistance program operated under Title XVIII of the Social Security Act (as in effect January 1, 2017).

(RR) "Non-core hospice services" are hospice services that are the responsibility of the hospice to ensure are provided directly to the individual by hospice employees or under a contractual arrangement made by the hospice.

(SS) "Nursing facility" (NF) has the same meaning as in section 5165.01 of the Revised Code.

(TT) "Nursing services" are services that require the skills of a RN, or a LPN under the supervision of an RN. Services provided by an advanced practice registered nurse (APRN) who is not the individual's attending physician or are not provided by a physician in the absence of an APRN are included under nursing services.

(UU) "Oral Physician Certification Date" refers to the date the verbal certification of the individual's terminally ill is obtained by the hospice medical director (or physician member of the IDG), and the patient's attending physician, if he/she has one.

(VV) "Palliative care" refers to patient and family-centered care that optimizes quality of life by anticipating, preventing, and treating suffering. Palliative care is at the core of hospice philosophy and care practices, and is a critical component of the medicaid hospice benefit.

(WW) "Physician" means an individual who is currently licensed and authorized under Chapter 4731. of the Revised Code to practice as a doctor of medicine and surgery or osteopathic medicine and surgery. An unlicensed individual who is authorized to practice under the laws of the state in which the services are performed is not a physician, even if the individual holds a staff or faculty appointment.

(XX) "Physician assistant" means an individual practicing in accordance with Chapter 4730 of the Revised Code.

(YY) "Physician services" refers to services as defined in Chapter 5160-4 of the Administrative Code. Physician services may be provided by a physician, or an advanced practice registered nurse acting within his or her scope of practice as defined in section 4723.01 of the Revised Code, or a physician assistant acting within his or her scope of practice under the supervision, control, and direction of one or more physicians as defined in section 4730.01 of the Revised Code.

(ZZ) "Plan of Care" refers to an individualized written plan established at the start of hospice care by the hospice interdisciplinary group in collaboration with the attending physician (if any), the individual and the primary caregiver (when feasible). The plan of care must specify the hospice care and services necessary to meet the individual and family-specific needs identified in the comprehensive assessment as such needs relate to the terminal illness and related conditions.

(AAA) "Registered nurse" (RN) refers to a person licensed to practice as a RN in accordance with the criteria set forth in Chapter 4723. of the Revised Code.

(BBB) "Routine Home Care" is a level of hospice care covered in accordance with 42 C.F.R. 418.302 (as in effect January 1, 2016). Routine home care shall be afforded to an individual in the individual's residence when the individual is not receiving continuous home care.

(CCC) "Social worker" means a person registered under Chapter 4757. of the Revised Code to practice as a social worker or independent social worker.

(DDD) "Telehealth" has the same meaning as in rule 5160-1-18 of the Administrative Code.

(EEE) "Terminally ill" means that a physician has certified that the individual has a medical prognosis that his or her life expectancy is six months or less if the illness runs its normal course.

(FFF) "Written Physician Certification Date" refers to the date the completed certification of the individual's terminally ill is signed by the hospice medical director (or physician member of the IDG, and the patient's attending physician, if he or she has one.

Effective: 1/30/2021.
Five Year Review (FYR) Dates: 10/1/2022.
Promulgated Under: 119.03.
Statutory Authority: 5164.02.
Rule Amplifies: 5162.03.
Prior Effective Dates: 04/16/1990, 12/01/1991, 04/01/1994, 09/26/2002, 02/16/2004, 03/02/2008, 04/01/2015, 10/01/2017, 06/12/2020.

**5160-56-02. Hospice services: eligibility and election requirements.**

This rule sets forth the criteria that must be met for an individual eligible for medicaid to receive the Ohio medicaid hospice benefit.

(A) To be covered under Ohio medicaid, the designated hospice must ensure the following criteria are met prior to furnishing hospice care:

(1) The designated hospice has a certification of the terminal illness on behalf of the individual, obtained in accordance with 42 C.F.R. 418.22 (October 1, 2017). ODM will allow this requirement to be met via telehealth where face-to-face interactions are required;

(2) A hospice election statement, completed by the individual, has been obtained by the designated hospice pursuant to paragraphs (B) and (C) of this rule;

(3) The individual has a hospice plan of care initiated, pursuant to paragraph (F) of this rule;

(4) Other applicable criteria are met which pertain to the individual and the election of hospice:

(a) The designated hospice shall ensure an individual eligible for both medicare and medicaid hospice elects the hospice benefit under both programs. Hospice services furnished to individuals who are dual eligible shall be billed to medicare first.

(b) If the individual has or later obtains third-party coverage of hospice, the individual must elect the third-party coverage of hospice to cover the same days the medicaid hospice benefit covers in order to ensure medicaid is the secondary payor. If the individual revokes his or her thirdparty coverage of hospice, the medicaid hospice benefit must be revoked at the same time.

(c) If the individual is a participant in the program of all-inclusive care for the elderly (PACE), the individual must access hospice services through the PACE site's network of providers.

(d) If the individual is enrolled in a medicaid managed care plan (MCP), the individual must access hospice services through the MCP's network of providers.

(e) If the individual is enrolled in a home and community based services (HCBS) waiver, the designated hospice shall assist the individual in coordinating concurrent care and waiver services in accordance with rule 5160-56-04 of the Administrative Code.

(B) At the time hospice is elected, the designated hospice must:

(1) Assist the individual with the election process; and

(2) Provide the individual with the following materials and written information:

(a) A copy of the agency's grievance procedures;

(b) Information regarding advance directives in accordance with Chapter 2133. of the Revised Code; and

(c) Any policies the hospice has regarding the implementation of advance directives, including ensuring the individual's right to formulate an advance directive, and the right to request a "do not resuscitate" order. The hospice must maintain the individual's advance directive in an accessible part of the individual's current hospice record and include a notation in the individual's plan of care.

(C) The designated hospice shall maintain a record of the election statement completed by the individual.

(1) The election statement shall be in writing and a notice of the election filed by the designated hospice in accordance with 42 C.F.R. 418.24 (October 1, 2017). The medicaid election statement may be combined with the medicare election statement or on a separate form, provided it is clear the form denotes medicaid hospice has been elected.

(2) The election statement shall contain the following:

(a) Documentation that the individual elected the medicaid hospice benefit;

(b) The identity of the designated hospice responsible for providing hospice care to the individual;

(c) The individual's acknowledgment that he or she has been given a full explanation of the palliative rather than curative nature of hospice care as it relates to the individual's terminal illness and the provisions and limitations of services as specified in this chapter;

(d) Acknowledgment that the individual understands that certain medicaid services are waived by the election, except when the individual is under age twenty-one;

(e) The identification of the individual's attending physician (if any) with an acknowledgment that the identified attending physician was the individual's own choice;

(f) The individual's acknowledgment that the attending physician was the individual's choice;

(g) The effective date of the election which may be the first day of hospice care or a later date, but shall be no earlier than the date of the election statement;

(h) The individual's signature; and

(i) The date the election statement was signed.

(3) A copy of the completed election statement shall be scanned and uploaded to the medicaid information technology system (MITS) pursuant to rule 5160-56-03.3 of the Administrative Code. The original form as completed, shall remain on file with the designated hospice.

(4) The election statement shall remain in effect as long as the individual continues to meet all eligibility requirements of this rule.

(D) While a hospice election is in effect, the designated hospice shall commence hospice care to the individual, beginning with enrolling the individual in the appropriate benefit period as defined in rule 5160-56-01 of the Administrative Code and pursuant to the remainder of this rule.

(1) The initial benefit period shall commence with hospice care on or after the date of election and end on the ninetieth day, unless a discharge pursuant to rule 5160-56-03 of the Administrative Code disrupts hospice care.

(2) If at the end of the initial ninety day period, the individual is recertified as terminally ill, the designated hospice shall ensure the individual is enrolled in the second subsequent ninety-day benefit period, continuing hospice services uninterrupted until the end the second ninety-period, to the onehundred eightieth day, unless a discharge pursuant to rule 5160-56-03 of the Administrative Code disrupts hospice care.

(3) If at the end of the subsequent ninety day period, the individual is recertified as terminally ill, the designated hospice shall ensure the individual is enrolled in a subsequent sixty day benefit period, and shall continue hospice services uninterrupted for increments of sixty additional days as recertifications occur, unless a discharge pursuant to rule 5160-56-03 of the Administrative Code disrupts hospice care.

(E) For the duration of the election of hospice care, the individual must waive medicaid services if the services:

(1) Are provided by a hospice other than the hospice designated by the individual, unless provided under arrangement made by the designated hospice;

(2) Are related to the curative treatment of the terminal condition for which hospice care was elected or a related condition, except for the individual under age twenty-one; or

(3) Are equivalent to hospice care such as non-waiver services provided through home health and private duty nursing services.

(F) The designated hospice shall follow the requirements as prescribed in this rule for an individual previously discharged from hospice, who has subsequently re-elected hospice care in accordance with paragraph (A)(3) of rule 5160-56-03 of the Administrative Code.

Effective: 6/12/2020.
Promulgated Under: 119.03.
Statutory Authority: 5164.02.
Rule Amplifies: 5162.03
Prior Effective Dates: 05/15/1990, 05/16/1990, 12/01/1991, 04/01/1994, 09/26/2002, 01/01/2004, 04/01/2005, 03/02/2008, 02/01/2011, 04/01/2015, 10/01/2017.

**5160-56-03. Hospice services: discharge requirements.**

This rule sets forth the requirements for discharging an individual from the designated hospice's care and/or the hospice benefit.

(A) Discharge refers to the end the hospice benefit and/or the designated hospice's care:

(1) Discharge from the designated hospice's care shall occur when the individual:

(a) Dies/expires;

(b) No longer meets the hospice enrollment or eligibility criteria;

(c) No longer is terminally ill, e.g., physician discharges or does not recertify the individual;

(d) Moves out of the service area;

(e) Enters a facility where the designated hospice has no access and/or cannot enter to provide care;

(f) Revokes the hospice benefit in accordance with paragraph (B) of this rule;

(g) Transfers to another hospice in accordance with paragraph (D) of this rule; or

(h) Is discharged for cause, such as compromising the safety of self or the safety of the hospice staff.

(2) The hospice provider must notify the Ohio department of medicaid (ODM) through the medicaid information technology system (MITS) or its designee of the individual's discharge from the designated hospice's care so that the designated hospice's services and billings coincide with the date of the individual's discharge and/or so that hospice services may continue with the new hospice when applicable, e.g., following a transfer.

(3) Except for the reason cited in paragraph (A)(1)(a) of this rule, the designated hospice shall complete a written summary statement which clearly states the reason(s) for the individual's discharge from the designated hospice's care. The original statement of discharge shall be retained by the hospice for its records, with a copy provided to the individual. As a reason for discharge, a hospice provider may not automatically or routinely discharge an individual at its "discretion" or request or demand that the individual revoke his or her election.

(4) With the exception of paragraph (A)(1)(g) of this rule, when an individual is discharged from a designated hospice's care, the current election period (as defined in rule 5160-56-01 of the Administrative Code) shall end and the individual shall be discharged from the hospice benefit entirely, making him or her no longer eligible to receive medicaid hospice services.

(B) The designated provider shall respect the right of the individual to revoke the election of the hospice benefit at any time during any given election period.

(1) Upon notice of the individual's intent to revoke, the designated hospice shall:

(a) Obtain a written statement, signed and dated by the individual, which states that the election of hospice care has been revoked by the individual for the remainder of the applicable benefit period. The designated hospice shall not accept a verbal revocation of the hospice benefit;

(b) Discharge the individual from hospice care, such that hospice coverage for the remaining days in that election period is forfeited and medicaid coverage of the benefits waived when hospice care was elected may resume; and

(c) Provide the individual with a copy of the written revocation statement and maintain the original for its record.

(2) An individual shall be permitted to re-elect the medicaid hospice benefit at any time after revocation pursuant to paragraph (C) of this rule, provided the individual meets all hospice eligibility requirements.

(C) If the individual remains eligible for hospice, a designated hospice may enroll an individual at any time after the re-election.

(1) The individual discharged from hospice care during the initial ninety-day period, who re-elects the hospice benefit, shall be enrolled in the second ninety-day benefit period; or

(2) The individual who revoked the hospice benefit or who was discharged from hospice care during the second ninety-day benefit period, or any subsequent sixty-day benefit period, who re-elects the hospice benefit, shall be enrolled in a subsequent sixty-day benefit period.

(D) The following requirements apply when an individual is discharged from the designated hospice's care due to individual's transfer to another hospice:

(1) The individual may change the designation of the hospice from which care is received once during each benefit period. The change of the designated hospice is not considered a revocation of the election from the period in which it is made.

(2) To change the designated hospice, the individual must file, with the hospice from which the individual has received care and the newly designated hospice, a signed statement which includes the following information:

(a) The name of the hospice from which the individual has received care;

(b) The name of the hospice from which the individual plans to receive care; and

(c) The date the change is to be effective.

(3) When an individual transfers from one hospice to another, his or her medicaid hospice benefit shall continue without interruption of care.

(E) The individual who has elected the hospice benefit and decided to revoke, terminate, or transfer his or her hospice benefit must do so on the same effective date for both the third-party covered or medicare hospice benefit and the medicaid hospice benefit. When the dual eligible individual revokes his or her medicare hospice benefit, the provider shall ensure the medicaid hospice benefit is revoked by the individual at the same time.

(F) Any denial or termination of hospice care which is the result of an Ohio department of medicaid (ODM) decision shall be subject to the notice and hearing rights contained in Chapters 5101:6-1 to 5101:6-9 of the Administrative Code.

Replaces: 5160-56-03.
Effective: 10/1/2017.
Five Year Review (FYR) Dates: 10/01/2022.
Promulgated Under: 119.03.
Statutory Authority: 5164.02.
Rule Amplifies: 5162.03
Prior Effective Dates: 5/16/90, 12/1/91, 4/1/94, 9/26/02, 1/1/04, 3/2/08, 4/1/15.

**5160-56-03.3 Hospice services: reporting requirements.**

This rule sets forth the requirement for recording the hospice provider span for individuals receiving medicaid hospice care in accordance with Chapter 5160-56 of the Administrative Code, including individuals who may be covered by third-party insurance, such as medicare, for which the hospice seeks reimbursement.

(A) The designated hospice shall report the required enrollment information to the Ohio department of medicaid using the medicaid information technology system (MITS) for the following:

(1) Individuals in fee-for-service (FFS) medicaid hospice under the designated hospice's care on the effective date of this rule; and

(2) Individuals in which the hospice seeks to file an original or adjusted claim to ODM for medicaid hospice services rendered under codes T2042 and T2046, including:

(a) All individuals with FFS claims for routine home care, code T2042, for the dates of service on or after January 1, 2016 ,whether or not the claim has previously been submitted and paid.

(b) Individuals in the care of hospice prior to the effective date of this rule, if the provider is submitting an original FFS claim for hospice services other than the services specified in paragraph (A)(2)(a) of this rule.

(c) Individuals in the care of hospice prior to the effective date of this rule, if the provider is submitting an adjusted FFS claim or if ODM must adjust a FFS claim for hospice services other than the services specified in paragraph (A)(2)(a) of this rule.

(B) The designated hospice shall ensure the following information is entered into MITS prior to submitting a claim for reimbursement:

(1) The individual's recipient identification number (also referred to as the medicaid billing number) as shown on the individual's medicaid card;

(2) The date the individual elected hospice;

(3) The begin date and end date of every benefit period recognized under paragraph (D) of rule 5160-56-02 of the Administrative Code. For each benefit period, the designated hospice shall identify the benefit period as either the initial one time ninety-day period, the subsequent one time ninety-day period, or one of the subsequent unlimited sixty-day periods as applicable;

(4) The national provider identifier for the medical doctor who serves on the hospice interdisciplinary group (IDG) for each benefit period;

(5) The national provider identifier for the attending physician or the advanced practice registered nurse for each benefit period;

(6) The oral certification date(s), if applicable;

(7) The written physician certification date(s);

(8) The hospice terminal illness diagnosis code(s);

(a) At least one but not more than three terminal diagnosis codes for the individual;

(b) The effective dates (begin and ending date) that apply to the terminal diagnosis code(s) shall be entered in MITS by the designated hospice;

(9) The county (or counties if more than one) where hospice services were or will be provided during the benefit period;

(10) The national provider identifier of the long term care facility (LTFC) and the corresponding effective date and end date, if the individual resides in a LTCF and provider will be billing for hospice room and board services;

(11) Supporting documentation, as required to be attached to the claim, including:

(a) Copy of the current certification of the terminal illness;

(b) Copy of the individual's election statement;

(12) The date of death, when applicable; and

(13) Any updates or changes to be made to the benefit period as a result of a discharge pursuant to rule 5160-56-03 of the Administrative Code.

(C) The information specified in paragraph (B) of this rule shall be submitted to ODM only through the system in accordance with the requirements of the MITS system.

Replaces: 5160-56-03.3.
Effective: 10/1/2017.
Five Year Review (FYR) Dates: 10/01/2022.
Promulgated Under: 119.03.
Statutory Authority: 5164.02.
Rule Amplifies: 5162.03
Prior Effective Dates: 9/1/07, 4/1/15.

## 5160-56-04. Hospice services: provider requirements.

This rule sets forth the responsibilities, including the conditions of participation for a hospice engaged in the provision of medicaid hospice services. To be eligible to provide and to request reimbursement for hospice services, a designated hospice must:

(A) Be eligible to participate in the Ohio medicaid program upon execution of a provider agreement in accordance with rule 5160-1-17.2 of the Administrative Code.

(B) Meet the medicare guidelines in accordance with 42 C.F.R. part 418 (October 1, 2017).

(C) Be licensed under Ohio law in accordance with Chapter 3712. of the Revised Code by the Ohio department of health.

(D) Comply with all requirements for medicaid providers in Chapter 5160-1 of the Administrative Code.

(E) Ensure that all hospice employees, volunteers, and contracted staff who provide direct services to hospice individuals are trained, licensed, certified, and/or registered in accordance with applicable federal and state law. ODM will allow hospices to utilize pseudo-patients, such as a person trained to participate in a role-play situation or a computer-based mannequin device instead of real patients, in competency testing of hospice aides and allow individuals who are competency tested only in the tasks for which they will be assigned to function as hospice aides.

(F) Not discontinue or diminish the hospice care provided to the individual because of the inability of the individual to pay or receipt of medicaid reimbursement for such care pursuant to the medicare requirements outlined in Section 1861 (dd)(2)(D) of the Social Security Act, 42 U.S.C. 1395x(dd)(2)(D) (as in effect January 1, 2017).

(G) Arrange for another individual or entity to furnish services to the individual in accordance with 42 C.F.R. 418.56 (October 1, 2017) when the designated hospice cannot provide services to the individual. This arrangement must include a signed agreement which shall remain on file at the hospice agency.

(H) Assume responsibility for the professional management of the individual's hospice care. Professional management involves the assessment, planning, monitoring, directing and evaluation of the individual's hospice care across all settings. The designated hospice must provide for and ensure the ongoing sharing of information between all disciplines providing care and services in all settings, whether the care and services are provided directly or under arrangement.

(I) Facilitate concurrent care and services with other medicaid providers for which the individual under age twenty-one is eligible. As a responsibility for the professional management of the individual's hospice care, the designated hospice shall:

(1) Ensure hospice services are maintained and coordinated with concurrent care services;

(2) Document the delineation in which services and the assessment process are coordinated between medicaid hospice and non-hospice providers to avoid the duplication of equivalent or similar scope of services; and

(3) Maintain up-to-date contact information for providers of concurrent care and services.

(J) Have a signed agreement with the nursing facility, the intermediate care facility for individuals with intellectual disabilities (ICF-IID), the general inpatient facility, and/or the inpatient respite care facility in which the individual resides and/or receives services. The terms of the agreement must not violate the medicaid provider agreement as set forth in rule 5160-1-17.2 of the Administrative Code and must not violate the individual's freedom of choice of providers. This agreement must remain on file at the hospice agency and contain, at a minimum, the following:

(1) A stipulation that the designated hospice maintains responsibility for the professional management of the individual's hospice care;

(2) A delineation of the manner in which contracted services are coordinated and supervised by the hospice;

(3) A delineation of the role of the hospice and the facility in the admissions process, patient/family assessments, and the interdisciplinary group conferences; and

(4) A stipulation that the facility must have a valid medicaid provider agreement in accordance with rule 5160-1-17.2 of the Administrative Code and accept the payment from the hospice as payment in full as negotiated.

(K) Ensure all necessary care and services set forth in this chapter are furnished to the individual and that such care and services are specified in the individual's plan of care in accordance with the standards set forth in 42 C.F.R. 418.56 (October 1, 2017) for:

(1) Approaching service delivery;

(2) Care planning;

(3) Contents of the plan of care;

(4) Reviewing and revising the plan; and

(5) Coordinating hospice and non-hospice services.

(L) Designate a registered nurse who is a member of the interdisciplinary group to provide coordination of care and to ensure continuous assessment of each individual's and family's needs and implementation of the plan of care.

(M) Ensure hospice care is coordinated for an individual enrolled in a home and community based waiver program. A collaborative effort must occur between the designated hospice and the waiver case manager or the service and support administrator (SSA) as applicable to maintain a continuum of the overall care provided to the individual.

(1) Case management of hospice services shall be provided by the designated hospice in accordance with this chapter;

(2) Case management of waiver services shall be provided by the waiver case manager; and

(3) The hospice must provide services to a waiver individual in accordance with a comprehensive plan for the concurrent provision of waiver services by waiver and hospice providers. The administrating agency of the waiver or its designee shall assist in the coordination of care by:

(a) Reviewing and approving the comprehensive plan for the concurrent provision of waiver services by waiver and hospice providers;

(b) Resolving any issues resulting from the comprehensive plan for the concurrent provision of waiver services by waiver and hospice providers;

(c) Resolving any issues of interpretation when implementing the requirements in this chapter; and

(d) Applying any exceptions to the requirements of this chapter on a case-bycase basis.

Effective: 1/30/2021.
Five Year Review (FYR) Dates: 10/1/2022.
Promulgated Under: 119.03.
Statutory Authority: 5164.02.
Rule Amplifies: 5162.02.
Prior Effective Dates: 05/01/1990, 05/15/1990, 05/16/1990, 12/01/1991, 04/01/1994, 09/26/2002, 02/03/2005, 04/01/2005, 03/02/2008, 02/01/2011, 04/01/2015, 10/01/2017, 06/12/2020.

**5160-56-05. Hospice services: covered services.**

This rule sets forth medicaid covered services that hospice providers may or must furnish to individuals to the extent specified by the individual's plan of care.

(A) The designated hospice shall ensure the hospice services furnished to an individual in accordance with this rule are reasonable and necessary for the palliation and management of the terminal illness and related conditions.

(B) Unless otherwise specified, covered services shall be furnished to the individual in his or her residence, including the individual's home, a relative's home or any other type of living arrangement, a skilled nursing facility (SNF), a nursing facility (NF), an intermediate care facility for individuals with intellectual disabilities (ICF-IID), or a hospice inpatient unit.

(C) The designated hospice shall ensure covered services provided to the individual are furnished by qualified personnel pursuant to 42 C.F.R. 418.114 (October 1, 2017), who are employed by the hospice, under an individual contract, or under arrangement with another provider.

(D) The following services are covered by medicaid when furnished or arranged by the designated hospice based on the individual's needs, appropriate level of care, and plan of care:

(1) Core hospice services may be provided through a combination of contracting services and telehealth services as necessary:

(a) Nursing care;

(b) Medical social services, provided by a social worker under the direction of a physician or attending provider;

(c) Physicians' services, including attending physician services, and services rendered by advance nurse practitioners or physician assistants acting as attending physicians; and

(d) Counseling services, including but not limited to dietary counseling, bereavement counseling and spiritual counseling.

(2) Non-core hospice services may be provided through a combination of contracting services and telehealth services as necessary and appropriate:

(a) Physical therapy, occupational therapy, and speech-language pathology provided for symptom control or to enable the individual to maintain activities of daily living and basic functional skills;

(b) Hospice aide, home health aide and homemaker services that enable the individual to carry out the plan of care;

(c) Volunteers;

(d) Medical appliances and supplies, including drugs and biologicals;

(e) Short-term inpatient care provided in hospital, hospice inpatient unit, or a participating SNF or NF on an intermittent, non routine basis for relief of the individual's caregivers, and/or general inpatient care for the purpose of respite, pain control and acute or chronic symptom management that cannot feasibly be provided in other settings; and

(f) Any other item or service provided in relation to the terminal condition, when medically indicated, included in the plan of care and for which payment may otherwise be made under medicaid.

(3) Ambulance transports or an individual that are related to the terminal illness and that occur after the effective date of election, are covered to the extent specified by the individual's plan of care, when deemed the responsibility of the hospice as specified in section 40.1.9 of the "medicare benefit policy manual, chapter nine: coverage of hospice services under hospital insurance" under hospital insurance, www.cms.gov (revised May 08, 2015).

(a) Transports to an individual's home which occur on the effective date of the hospice election, the date of admission, prior to the initial assessment or prior to establishing the plan of care are not covered under the hospice benefit.

(b) If the hospice determines that the individual's need for transportation is for any reason other than receiving care related to the terminal illness, the hospice may make arrangements pursuant to paragraph (G) of this rule for the appropriate level or type of transportation and the service to be covered under the ambulance benefit for medicaid in accordance with Chapter 5160-15 of the Administrative Code.

(E) Coverage for individuals who reside in a NF or ICF-IID:

(1) Pursuant to rule 5160-56-06 of the Administrative Code, the room and board shall be covered for the individual when all of the following applies:

(a) The individual has elected hospice and is receiving hospice care;

(b) The individual resides in a NF, SNF or ICF-IID; and

(c) All other payments for room and board have been exhausted, making medicaid the payer of last resort.

(2) The designated hospice shall pay the facility per diem reimbursed to the designated hospice by the Ohio department of medicaid in accordance with rule 5160-56-06 of the Administrative Code. The following room and board services are covered pursuant to section 20.3 of the "medicare benefit policy manual, chapter nine: coverage of hospice services under hospital insurance" under hospital insurance, www.cms.gov (revised May 08, 2015):

(a) Performing personal care services;

(b) Assisting with ADLs;

(c) Administering medication;

(d) Socializing activities;

(e) Maintaining the cleanliness of the individual's room; and

(f) Supervising and assisting in the use of durable medical equipment and prescribed therapies.

(F) Hospice care for individuals enrolled in a home and community based services (HCBS) waiver program:

(1) Waiver services are provided by approved waiver providers in the amount and scope approved on the individual's plan of care.

(2) The designated hospice has the responsibility to cover hospice services pursuant to paragraph (M) of rule 5160-56-04 of the Administrative Code.

(G) For any medicaid services that are unrelated to the treatment of the terminal condition for which hospice care was elected, non-designated hospices and/or non-hospice providers must:

(1) Follow all applicable medicaid authorization policies and procedures; and

(2) Contact the designated hospice to coordinate the individual's care and to clarify provider payment responsibility.

Effective: 1/30/2021.
Five Year Review (FYR) Dates: 10/1/2022.
Promulgated Under: 119.03.
Statutory Authority: 5162.02.
Rule Amplifies: 5162.03
Prior Effective Dates: 05/15/1990, 05/16/1990, 12/01/1991, 04/01/1994, 09/26/2002, 01/01/2004, 04/01/2005, 03/02/2008, 04/01/2015, 10/01/2017, 06/12/2020.

**5160-56-06. Hospice services: reimbursement.**

This rule sets forth the Ohio department of medicaid (ODM) payment for hospice services and care.

(A) ODM will directly pay the designated hospice to care for an individual enrolled in medicaid hospice. Payment to the designated hospice shall cover the array of services listed in rule 5160-56-05 of the Administrative Code, except for:

(1) Services pursuant to paragraph (E) of this rule which are paid directly to the physician; and

(2) Services furnished by a non-hospice provider pursuant to paragraph (I) of this rule for the concurrent care of an individual under the age of twenty-one.

(B) Reimbursement rates paid by ODM to the designated hospice shall be based on the level of care that is appropriate for the individual for each day while receiving hospice care. Based on the methodology set forth in 42 C.F.R. 418.302 (as in effect January 1, 2016), the medicaid payment for hospice care is made at predetermined rates in accordance with paragraph (C) of this rule for levels of care as defined in rule 5160-56-01 of the Administrative Code.

(1) The medicaid payment for hospice covers the cost of services rendered by the hospice either directly or under contractual arrangement.

(2) For designated hospices that are compliant with the hospice quality reporting program in accordance with 42 C.F.R. 418.312 (as in effect January 1, 2016), ODM will reimburse the full medicaid payment rate for hospice services, up to the maximum payment rate prescribed for the county where services were provided.

(3) For designated hospices that fail to comply with the hospice quality reporting program as federally mandated, ODM will reimburse the payment amount minus a two percentage point reduction, as prescribed by CMS for the corresponding federal fiscal year.

(C) The designated hospice shall bill ODM the appropriate code and unit(s) for the appropriate level of care. ODM will allow telehealth services to be provided where in-person visits are mandated:

(1) Hospice providers must use code T2042 for one unit per day to bill for routine home care afforded to an individual in his or her home, who is not receiving continuous home care.

(a) Routine home care days shall be paid using a two-tiered system in accordance with 42 C.F.R 418.302 (as in effect January 1, 2016), where the per diem for the first sixty days of hospice care is paid at a higher rate and days sixty-one and thereafter are paid at a lower rate for the duration of the individual's hospice episode of care. A minimum of a sixty day gap in hospice services is required to reset the counter that determines which per diem to apply.

(b) In accordance with 42 C.F.R 418.302 (as in effect January 1, 2016), routine home care may be eligible for an add-on payment for services provided by a registered nurse (RN) authorized to practice under Chapter 4723. of the Revised Code, and/or a social worker licensed to practice under Chapter 4757. of the Revised Code during the last seven days of an individual's life, when the discharge from hospice care is due to death.

The service intensity add-on (SIA) payment shall be billed using code G0299 for the direct care provided in an in-person visit completed by an RN. The SIA payment shall be billed using code G0155 for the direct care provided during an in-person visit completed by a social worker.

The reimbursement rate for the SIA payment shall be equal to the continuous home care hourly rate converted into fifteen minute increments, up to a maximum of four hours (sixteen units) combined total per day for RN and social worker visits. Visits solely for the pronouncement of death shall not be counted for the service intensity add-on payment.

(2) Hospice providers must use code T2043 for one unit per hour, with a minimum of eight hours per day, to bill for continuous home care.

(3) Hospice providers must use code T2044 for one unit per day to bill for inpatient respite care.

(4) Hospice providers must use code T2045 for one unit per day to bill for general inpatient care.

(5) Hospice providers that deliver any component of services via telehealth will add the GT modifier on those claims, in addition to the appropriate procedure code above.

(6) Services billed with T2044 and T2045 are not eligible to be provided via telehealth.

(D) When the individual is a resident of a nursing facility (NF) or an intermediate care facility for individuals with intellectual disabilities (ICF-IID), the hospice may be reimbursed for room and board. This additional per diem amount is reimbursable at ninety-five per cent of the rate established for the long-term care facility, as reported to ODM for the individual pursuant to rule 5160-56-06 of the Administrative Code, and only on days where the individual receives routine home care or continuous home care. To receive reimbursement, the hospice:

(1) Must bill for room and bill using code T2046.

(2) Must bill patient liability until consumed to zero dollars.

(3) Must bill only for days that the individual is in the NF or ICF-IID overnight and is medicaid eligible.

(4) Must bill for individuals who are medicare and medicaid eligible, medicare for services provided under the medicare hospice benefit and medicaid for the individual's room and board.

(5) Hospice providers that deliver any component of services via telehealth will add the GT modifier on those claims, in addition to the procedure code above.

(E) Separate payment may be made to a physician for services involving direct patient care. The physician may be an employee of the hospice, a practitioner under contractual arrangement with the hospice, or an attending practitioner who is not an employee of the hospice but is an eligible medicaid provider. Separate payment cannot be made, however, for the following services:

(1) A physician service furnished on a volunteer basis or on an administrative basis;

(2) A procedure classified as a technical service; or

(3) Laboratory or radiography services performed in connection with the physician service.

(F) After receipt of all third-party resources, including private insurance, and taking into account patient liability for room and board, ODM may be billed for the balance owed to the designated hospice, except for services covered by individuals receiving hospice through managed care. For each day the medicaid eligible individual is enrolled in hospice, the total reimbursement for hospice services cannot exceed the medicaid per diem reimbursement rate.

(G) Medicaid eligible residents of NFs or ICF-IIDs who are enrolled in a medicare or medicaid hospice program are not entitled to medicaid-covered bed-hold days. It is the hospice's responsibility to contract with and pay the NF in accordance with rule 5160-3-16.4 of the Administrative Code. It is the hospice's responsibility to contract with and pay the ICF-IID in accordance with rule 5123:2-7-08 of the Administrative Code.

(H) Pursuant to Section 1861(dd)(2)(A)(iii) of the Social Security Act, 42 U.S.C. 1395x(dd) (2)(A)(iii) (as in effect January 1, 2017) there shall be a limitation on reimbursement for inpatient care during the hospice cap period.

(I) For any services related to the terminal illness, non-hospice providers must bill the designated hospice provider directly unless the services were for concurrent care of the terminal illness for individuals under age twenty-one. Providers billing for concurrent care must comply with, and will only be reimbursed according to, all the requirements for medicaid providers in Chapter 5160-1 of the Administrative Code.

Effective: 1/30/2021.
Five Year Review (FYR) Dates: 10/1/2022.
Promulgated Under: 119.03.
Statutory Authority: 5164.02.
Rule Amplifies: 5162.03
Prior Effective Dates: 05/01/1990, 05/15/1990, 05/16/1990, 12/01/1991, 04/01/1994, 09/26/2002, 01/01/2004, 04/01/2005, 03/02/2008, 02/01/2011, 04/01/2015, 10/01/2017, 06/12/2020.

# CHAPTER 5160-58

# MYCARE OHIO PLANS

Rule



Admin Code

### 5160-58-01. MyCare Ohio plans: definitions.

(A) The definitions set forth in rule 5160-26-01 of the Administrative Code apply to the MyCare Ohio rules set forth in Chapter 5160-58 of the Administrative Code.

(B) In addition to the definitions set forth in rule 5160-26-01 of the Administrative Code, the following definitions apply to Chapter 5160-58 of the Administrative Code:

(1) "Assessment" means a comprehensive evaluation of an individual's medical, behavioral health, long-term services and supports, and social needs. Results of the assessment process are used to develop the integrated, individualized care plan, inclusive of the waiver services plan.

(2) "Creditable insurance" or "creditable coverage" means health insurance coverage as defined in 42 U.S.C. 300gg-3(c) ( October 1, 2020).

(3) "Dual benefits member" or "opt-in member" means a member for whom a MyCare Ohio plan is responsible for the coordination and payment of both medicare and medicaid benefits.

(4) "Financial management service (FMS)" means a support that is provided to waiver participants who direct some or all of their waiver services. When used in conjunction with the employer authority, this support includes, but is not limited to, operating a payroll service for participant employed workers and making required payroll withholdings. When used in conjunction with the budget authority, this support includes, but is not limited to, paying invoices for waiver goods and services and tracking expenditures against the participant-directed budget.

(5) "Health and welfare" means a requirement that necessary safeguards are taken to protect the health and welfare of individuals enrolled in a home and community-based services (HCBS) waiver. It includes the following:

(a) Risk and safety planning and evaluations;

(b) Critical incident management;

(c) Housing and environmental safety evaluations;

(d) Behavioral interventions;

(e) Medication management; and

(f) Natural disaster and public emergency response planning.

(6) "Home and community-based services (HCBS)" means services available to individuals to help maintain their health and safety in a community setting in lieu of institutional care as described in 42 C.F.R. 440 subpart A (October 1, 2020).

(7) "Individual care plan" means an integrated, individualized, person-centered care plan developed by the member and his or her MyCare Ohio plan's trans-disciplinary care management team that addresses clinical and non-clinical needs identified in the assessment and includes goals, interventions, and expected outcomes.

(8) "Medicaid only member" or "opt-out member" means a member for whom a MyCare Ohio plan is responsible for coordination and payment of medicaid benefits.

(9) "MyCare Ohio plan (MCOP)" means a health insuring corporation (HIC) contracted to comprehensively manage medicaid benefits for medicare and medicaid eligible members, including HCBS. MCOPs are also managed care plans in accordance with rule 5160-26-01 of the Administrative Code. For the purpose of this chapter, an MCOP does not include entities approved to operate as a program for the all-inclusive care of the elderly (PACE) site as defined in rule 5160-36-01 of the Administrative Code.

(10) "Nursing facility-based level of care" means the intermediate and skilled levels of care, as described in rule 5160-3-08 of the Administrative Code.

(11) "Participant direction" means the opportunity for a MyCare Ohio waiver member to exercise choice and control in identifying, accessing, and managing waiver services and other supports in accordance with their needs and personal preferences.

(12) "Significant change event" is a change experienced by a member that warrants further evaluation. Significant changes include, but are not limited to, a change in health status, caregiver status, or location/residence; referral to or active involvement on the part of a protective service agency; institutionalization; and when the waiver-enrolled individual has not received MyCare Ohio waiver services for ninety calendar days.

(13) "Trans-disciplinary care management team" means a team of appropriately qualified individuals comprised of the member, the member's family/caregiver, the MyCare Ohio plan manager, the waiver service coordinator, if appropriate, the primary care provider, specialists, and other providers, as applicable, that is designed to effectively meet the enrollee's needs.

(14) "Waiver services plan" is a component of the care plan that identifies specific goals, objectives and measurable outcomes for a waiver-enrolled member's health and functioning expected as a result of HCBS provided by both formal and informal caregivers, and that addresses the physical and medical conditions of the individual. At a minimum, the waiver services plan shall include:

(a) Essential information needed to provide care to the member that assures the member's health and welfare;

(b) Signatures indicating the member's acceptance or rejection of the waiver services plan. If the member is unable to provide the signature when the services plan is initially developed, the individual will submit an electronic signature or standard signature via regular mail, or otherwise provide a signature in no instance any later than at the next face-to-face visit with the case manager; and

(c) Information that the waiver services plan is not the same as the physician's plan of care.

Effective: 10/12/2020.
Five Year Review (FYR) Dates: 7/1/2022.
Promulgated Under: 119.03.
Statutory Authority: 5164.02, 5166.02, 5167.02.
Rule Amplifies: 5164.02, 5166.02, 5167.02
Prior Effective Dates: 03/01/2014, 07/01/2017.

### 5160-58-01.1 MyCare Ohio plans: application of general managed care rules.

(A) MyCare Ohio plans must comply with all of the requirements applicable to managed care plans (MCPs) in the following rules:

(1) Rule 5160-26-05 of the Administrative Code;

(2) Rule 5160-26-05.1 of the Administrative Code;

(3) Rule 5160-26-06 of the Administrative Code;

(4) Rule 5160-26-08.3 of the Administrative Code;

(5) Rule 5160-26-09 of the Administrative Code;

(6) Rule 5160-26-09.1 of the Administrative Code;

(7) Rule 5160-26-10 of the Administrative Code; and

(8) Rule 5160-26-11 of the Administrative Code.

(B) MyCare Ohio plans must comply with all of the requirements applicable to MCPs in rule 5160-26-03.1 of the Administrative Code, however, the following language replaces all of paragraph (B)(3)(h) for MyCare Ohio plans: "Prior authorization decisions for covered outpatient drugs as defined in 42 U.S.C. 1396r-8(k)(2) (as in effect January 1, 2017) must be made within the timeframes specified in 42 C.F.R. 423.568(b) (October 1, 2017) for standard decisions and 42 C.F.R. 423.572(a) (October 1, 2017) for expedited decisions. When an emergency situation exists, a seventy-two hour supply of the covered outpatient drug that was prescribed must be authorized. If the plan is unable to obtain the information needed to make the prior authorization decision within seventy-two hours, the decision timeframe has expired and the MCP must give notice to the member as specified in rule 5160-58-08.4 of the Administrative Code."

(C) For all rules listed in paragraphs (A) and (B) of this rule, the following provisions apply to the MyCare Ohio program described in Chapter 5160-58 of the Administrative Code:

(1) All cross-references to rule 5160-26-01 of the Administrative Code are replaced by cross-references to rule 5160-58-01 of the Administrative Code.

(2) All cross-references to rule 5160-26-02 of the Administrative Code are replaced by cross-references to rule 5160-58-02 of the Administrative Code.

(3) All cross-references to rule 5160-26-02.1 of the Administrative Code are replaced by cross-references to rule 5160-58-02.1 of the Administrative Code.

(4) All cross-references to rule 5160-26-03 of the Administrative Code are replaced by cross-references to rule 5160-58-03 of the Administrative Code.

(5) All cross-references to rule 5160-26-08.4 of the Administrative Code are replaced by cross-references to rule 5160-58-08.4 of the Administrative Code.

(D) The following rules in Chapter 5160-26 of the Administrative Code do not apply to MyCare Ohio, as they are replaced by corresponding rules in Chapter 5160-58 of the Administrative Code:

(1) Rule 5160-26-02 of the Administrative Code

(2) Rule 5160-26-02.1 of the Administrative Code

(3) Rule 5160-26-03 of the Administrative Code, and

(4) Rule 5160-26-08.4 of the Administrative Code.

(E) When an MCP holds provider agreements with the Ohio department of medicaid (ODM) for the MyCare Ohio and medicaid managed care programs, ODM may apply all of the applicable provisions in Chapter 5160-26 of the Administrative Code separately to each of the contracts.

Effective: 1/1/2018.
Five Year Review (FYR) Dates: 7/1/2022.
Promulgated Under: 119.03.
Statutory Authority: 5164.02, 5166.02, 5167.02.
Rule Amplifies: 5160.34, 5164.02, 5166.02, 5167.02
Prior Effective Dates: 03/01/14, 07/01/17.

## 5160-58-02. MyCare Ohio plans: eligibility and enrollment.

(A) Eligibility.

(1) Except as specified in paragraph (A)(2) of this rule, in mandatory service areas as permitted by 42 C.F.R. 438.52 (October 1, 2016), an individual must be enrolled in a MyCare Ohio plan (also known as "plan") if he or she meets all of the following criteria:

(a) Age eighteen or older at the time of enrollment in the plan;

(b) Eligible for medicare parts A, B and D, and full benefits under the medicaid program; and

(c) Reside in a plan demonstration county in Ohio. A list of demonstration counties, and the plans available in those counties, is available at http://medicaid. ohio.gov.

(2) Indians who are members of federally recognized tribes may voluntarily choose to enroll in a plan.

(3) The following individuals are not eligible for enrollment in a plan:

(a) Individuals enrolled in the program of all inclusive care for the elderly (PACE);

(b) Individuals who have other third party creditable health care coverage, except medicare coverage as authorized by 42 U.S.C. 1395 (January 1, 2017);

(c) Individuals who are inmates of public institutions as defined in 42 C.F.R. 435.1010 (October 1, 2016);

(d) Individuals with intellectual disabilities who have a level of care that meets the criteria specified in rule 5123:2-8-01 of the Administrative Code and receive services through a home and community-based services (HCBS) waiver administered by the Ohio department of developmental disabilities (DODD); and

(e) Individuals with intellectual disabilities who receive services through an intermediate care facility for individuals with intellectual disabilities (ICF-IID).

(4) Individuals are eligible for plan enrollment in the manner prescribed in this rule if the Ohio department of medicaid (ODM) has a provider agreement with the plan applicable to the eligible individual's county of residence.

(5) Nothing in this rule shall be construed to limit or in any way jeopardize an eligible individual's basic medicaid eligibility or eligibility for medicare or other non-medicaid benefits to which he or she may be entitled.

(B) MyCare Ohio plan enrollment.

(1) The following applies to plan enrollment:

(a) The plan must accept eligible individuals without regard to race, color, religion, gender, sexual orientation, age, disability, national origin, veteran's status, military status, genetic information, ancestry, ethnicity, mental ability, behavior, mental or physical disability, use of services, claims experience, appeals, medical history, evidence of insurability, geographic location within the service area, health status or need for health services. The plan will not use any discriminatory policy or practice in accordance with 42 C.F.R. 438.3(d) (October 1, 2016).

(b) The plan must accept eligible individuals who request plan membership without restriction.

(c) If a plan member loses managed care eligibility and is disenrolled from the plan, and subsequently regains eligibility, his or her membership in the same plan shall be re-instated back to the date eligibility was regained in accordance with procedures established by ODM.

(d) The plan must cover all members designated by ODM in an ODM-produced Health Insurance Portability and Accountability Act of 1996 (HIPAA) compliant 834 daily or monthly enrollment file of new members, continuing members, and terminating members.

(e) The plan shall not be required to provide medicaid coverage to an individual until the individual's membership in the plan is confirmed via an ODM-produced HIPAA compliant 834 daily or monthly enrollment file or upon mutual agreement between ODM and the plan.

(2) Should a service area change from voluntary to mandatory, the notice rights in this rule must be followed.

(a) When a service area is initially designated by ODM as mandatory for eligible individuals specified in paragraph (A)(1) of this rule, ODM shall confirm the eligibility of each individual as prescribed in paragraph (A)(1) of this rule. Upon the confirmation of eligibility:

(i) Eligible individuals residing in the service area who are currently plan members are deemed participants in the mandatory program; and

(ii) All other eligible individuals residing in the mandatory service area may request plan membership at any time but must select a plan following receipt of a notification of mandatory enrollment (NME) issued by ODM.

(b) MyCare Ohio plan membership selection procedures for the mandatory program:

(i) A newly eligible individual who does not make a choice following issuance of a NME by ODM and one additional notice, will be assigned to a plan by ODM, the medicaid consumer hotline, or other ODM-approved entity.

(ii) ODM or the medicaid consumer hotline shall assign the individual to a plan based on prior medicaid fee-for-service or plan membership history, whenever available, or at the discretion of ODM.

(C) Commencement of coverage.

Coverage of plan members will be effective on the first day of the calendar month specified on the ODM-produced HIPAA compliant 834 daily or monthly enrollment file to the plan.

Effective: 01/01/2017.
Five Year Review (FYR) Dates: 10/14/2016 and 01/01/2022.
Promulgated Under: 119.03.
Statutory Authority: 5164.02, 5166.02, 5167.02.
Rule Amplifies: 5164.02, 5166.02, 5167.02
Prior Effective Dates: 3/1/2014, 8/1/2016.

## 5160-58-02.1 MyCare Ohio plans: termination of enrollment.

(A) A member will be terminated from enrollment in a MyCare Ohio plan ("plan") for any of the following reasons:

(1) The member becomes ineligible for full medicaid or medicare parts A or B or D. Termination of plan enrollment is effective the end of the last day of the month in which the member became ineligible.

(2) The member's permanent place of residence is moved outside the plan's service area. Termination of plan enrollment is effective the end of the last day of the month in which the member moved from the service area.

(3) The member dies, in which case plan enrollment ends on the date of death.

(4) The member is found by the Ohio department of medicaid (ODM), or their designee, to meet the criteria for the developmental disabilities (DD) level of care and has a stay in an intermediate care facility for individuals with intellectual disabilities (ICF-IID) or is enrolled in a DD waiver. After the plan notifies ODM this has occurred, termination of plan enrollment takes effect on the last day of the month preceding the ICF-IID facility stay or enrollment on the DD waiver.

(5) The member has third party coverage, excepting medicare coverage, and ODM determines it is not in the best interest of the member to continue in the plan. The effective date of termination shall be determined by ODM but in no event shall the termination date be later than the last day of the month in which ODM approves the termination.

(6) The provider agreement between ODM and the plan is terminated or not renewed. The effective date of termination shall be the last day of the month of the provider agreement termination or nonrenewal.

(7) The member is not eligible for enrollment in a plan for one of the reasons set forth in rule 5160-58-02 of the Administrative Code.

(B) All of the following apply when enrollment in a MyCare Ohio plan is terminated for any of the reasons set forth in paragraph (A) of this rule:

(1) Such terminations may occur either in a mandatory or voluntary service area;

(2) All such terminations occur at the individual level;

(3) Such terminations do not require completion of a consumer contact record (CCR);

(4) If ODM fails to notify the plan of a member's termination from the plan, ODM shall continue to pay the plan the applicable monthly premium rate for the member. The plan shall remain liable for the provision of covered services as set forth in rule 5160-58-03 of the Administrative Code, until ODM provides the plan with documentation of the member's termination; and

(5) ODM shall recover from the plan any premium paid for retroactive enrollment termination occurring as a result of paragraph (A) of this rule.

(C) Member-initiated terminations.

(1) A dual-benefits member may request disenrollment from the plan and transfer between plans on a month-to-month basis any time during the year. Plan coverage continues until the end of the month of disenrollment.

(2) A medicaid-only member may request a different plan in a mandatory service area as follows:

(a) From the date of initial enrollment through the first three months of plan enrollment, whether the first three months of enrollment are dual-benefits or medicaid-only enrollment periods;

(b) During an open enrollment month for the member's service area as described in paragraph (E) of this rule; or

(c) At any time, if the just cause request meets one of the reasons for just cause as specified in paragraph (C)(4)(e) of this rule.

(3) A medicaid-only member may request a different plan if available or be returned to medicaid fee-for-service in a voluntary service area as follows:

(a) From the date of enrollment through the initial three months of plan enrollment;

(b) During an open enrollment month for the member's service area as described in paragraph (E) of this rule; or

(c) At any time, if the just cause request meets one of the reasons for just cause as specified in paragraph (C)(4)(e) of this rule.

(4) The following provisions apply when a member either requests a different plan in a mandatory service area, requests disenrollment in a voluntary service area:

(a) The request may be made by the member, or by the member's authorized representative.

(b) All member-initiated changes or terminations must be voluntary. Plans are not permitted to encourage members to change or terminate enrollment due to a member's race, color, religion, gender, gender identity, sexual orientation, age, disability, national origin, veteran's status, military status, genetic information, ancestry, ethnicity, mental ability, behavior, mental or physical disability, use of services, claims experience, appeals, medical history, evidence of insurability, geographic location within the service area, health status or need for health services. Plans may not use a policy or practice that has the effect of discrimination on the basis of the above criteria.

(c) If a member requests disenrollment because he or she meets any of the requirements in rule 5160-58-02 of the Administrative Code, the member will be disenrolled after the member notifies the consumer hotline.

(d) Disenrollment will take effect on the last day of the calendar month as specified by an ODM-produced HIPAA compliant 834 daily or monthly file sent to the plan.

(e) In accordance with 42 C.F.R. 438.56 (October 1, 2019), a change or termination of plan enrollment may be permitted for any of the following just cause reasons:

(i) The member moves out of the plan's service area and a non-emergency service must be provided out of the service area before the effective date of a termination that occurs for one of the reasons set forth in paragraph (A) of this rule;

(ii) The plan does not, for moral or religious objections, cover the service the member seeks;

(iii) The member needs related services to be performed at the same time in a coordinated manner; however, not all related services are available within the plan network, and the member's primary care provider (PCP) or another provider determines that receiving services separately would subject the member to unnecessary risk;

(iv) The member has experienced poor quality of care and the services are not available from another provider within the plan's network;

(v) The member receiving long-term services and supports would have to change their residential, institutional, or employment supports provider based on that provider's change in status from an in-network to and out-of-network provider with the plan and, as a result, would experience a disruption in their residence or employment;

(vi) The member cannot access medically necessary medicaid-covered services or cannot access the type of providers experienced in dealing with the member's health care needs;

(vii) ODM determines that continued enrollment in the plan would be harmful to the interests of the member.

(f) The following provisions apply when a member seeks a change or termination in plan enrollment for just cause:

(i) The member or an authorized representative must contact the plan to identify providers of services before seeking a determination of just cause from ODM.

(ii) The member may make the request for just cause directly to ODM or an ODM-approved entity, either orally or in writing.

(iii) ODM shall review all requests for just cause within seven working days of receipt. ODM may request documentation as necessary from both the member and the plan. ODM shall make a decision within ten working days of receipt of all necessary documentation, or forty-five days from the date ODM receives the just cause request. If ODM fails to make the determination within this timeframe, the just cause request is considered approved.

(iv) ODM may establish retroactive termination dates and/or recover premium payments as determined necessary and appropriate.

(v) Regardless of the procedures followed, the effective date of an approved just cause request must be no later than the first day of the second month following the month in which the member requests change or termination.

(vi) If the just cause request is not approved, ODM shall notify the member or the authorized representative of the member's right to a state hearing.

(vii) Requests for just cause may be processed at the individual level or case level as ODM determines necessary and appropriate.

(viii) If a member submits a request to change or terminate enrollment for just cause, and the member loses medicaid eligibility prior to action by ODM on the request, ODM shall assure that the member's plan enrollment is not automatically renewed if eligibility for medicaid is reauthorized.

(g) A member who is in a medicare Part D drug management program and is in a potentially at-risk or at-risk status as defined in 42 C.F.R. 423.100 (October 1, 2019) is precluded from changing plans.

Admin Code

(D) The following provisions apply when a termination in plan enrollment is initiated by a plan for a medicaid-only member:

(1) A plan may submit a request to ODM for the termination of a member for the following reasons:

(a) Fraudulent behavior by the member; or

(b) Uncooperative or disruptive behavior by the member or someone acting on the member's behalf to the extent that such behavior seriously impairs the plan's ability to provide services to either the member or other plan members.

(2) The plan may not request termination due to a member's race, color, religion, gender, gender identity, sexual orientation, age, disability, national origin, veteran's status, military status, genetic information, ancestry, ethnicity, mental ability, behavior, mental or physical disability, use of services, claims experience, appeals, medical history, evidence of insurability, geographic location within the service area, health status or need for health services.

(3) The plan must provide covered services to a terminated member through the last day of the month in which the plan enrollment is terminated.

(4) If ODM approves the plan's request for termination, ODM shall notify in writing the member, the authorized representative, the medicaid consumer hotline and the plan.

(E) Open enrollment.

Open enrollment months will occur at least annually. At least sixty days prior to the designated open enrollment month, ODM will notify eligible individuals by mail of the opportunity to change or terminate enrollment in a plan and will explain how the individual can obtain further information.

Effective: 02/15/2020.
Five Year Review (FYR) Dates: 1/1/2025.
Promulgated Under: 119.03.
Statutory Authority: 5164.02.
Rule Amplifies: 5164.02, 5166.02, 5167.02
Prior Effective Dates: 03/01/2014, 08/01/2016, 01/01/2018.

### 5160-58-02.2. MyCare Ohio waiver: eligibility and enrollment.

(A) To be eligible for enrollment in the MyCare Ohio waiver, a member must meet all of the following requirements:

(1) Be enrolled in the MyCare Ohio demonstration at the time of application for the MyCare Ohio waiver;

(2) Be determined to have a nursing facility based level of care (i.e., intermediate or skilled) in accordance with rule 5160-3-08 or 5160-3-09 of the Administrative Code;

(3) In the absence of the MyCare Ohio waiver, require hospitalization or institutionalization in a nursing facility to meet his or her needs;

(4) Be determined to require at least one waiver service monthly that is otherwise unavailable through another source (including the medicaid state plan) and in an amount sufficient to meet the member's assessed needs;

(5) Reside in a setting that possesses the home and community-based setting characteristics set forth in rule 5160-44-01 of the Administrative Code, and is not a hospital, nursing facility, intermediate care facility for individuals with intellectual disabilities (ICF-IID) or another licensed/certified facility, any facility covered by section 1616(e) of the Social Security Act ( October 1, 2020), residential care facility (except an assisted living facility as described in rule 173-39-02.16 of the Administrative Code), adult foster home or another group living arrangement subject to state licensure or certification.

(6) Sign an agreement prior to waiver enrollment confirming that the member has been informed of service alternatives, choice of qualified providers available in the MyCare Ohio plan's provider panel and the options of institutional and community-based care, and he or she elects to receive MyCare Ohio waiver services. If the individual is unable to sign the agreement prior to waiver enrollment, the individual will submit an electronic signature or standard signature via regular mail, or otherwise provide a signature in no instance any later than at the next face-to-face visit with the case manager; and

(7) Be able to have waiver services that can be identified in person-centered services plan as described in rule 5160-44-02 of the Administrative Code that will safely meet his or her assessed needs.

(B) To be enrolled, and maintain enrollment in the MyCare Ohio waiver, a member must be determined by the MyCare Ohio plan to meet all of the following requirements:

(1) Be determined eligible for the MyCare Ohio waiver in accordance with paragraph (A) of this rule;

(2) Be able to have his or her health and welfare ensured through the waiver;

(3) Participate in the development and implementation of an integrated, individualized care plan that includes a person-centered services plan in accordance with the process and requirements set forth in rule 5160-44-02 of the Administrative Code, and sign and date the plan as a condition of its acceptance. If the individual is unable to sign the plan when initially developed, the individual will submit an electronic signature or standard signature via regular mail, or otherwise provide a signature in no instance any later than at the next face-to-face visit with the case manager;

(4) Agree to receive waiver service coordination from the MyCare Ohio plan or its designee; and

(5) Agree to participate in quality management and evaluation activities during his or her enrollment on the MyCare Ohio waiver.

(C) If a member fails to meet any of the requirements set forth in paragraph (A) and/or paragraph (B) of this rule, the member shall be denied enrollment on the MyCare Ohio waiver.

(D) Once enrolled in the MyCare Ohio waiver, a member's level of care shall be reassessed at least annually, and more frequently if there is a significant change in the member's situation that may impact his or her health and welfare. If the reassessment determines the member no longer meets the requirements set forth in paragraph (A) or paragraph (B) of this rule, he or she shall be disenrolled from the MyCare Ohio waiver.

(E) If a member enrolled in the MyCare Ohio waiver does not receive at least one waiver service for ninety consecutive days, the MyCare Ohio plan shall, within ten days of the ninetieth day, reassess the member's need for waiver services. If it is determined the member no longer meets the requirements set forth in paragraph (A) or paragraph (B) of this rule, he or she shall be disenrolled from the MyCare Ohio waiver.

(F) If, at any other time, it is determined that a member enrolled in the MyCare Ohio waiver no longer meets the requirements set forth in paragraph (A) or paragraph (B) of this rule, he or she shall be disenrolled from the MyCare Ohio waiver.

(G) If a member is denied enrollment in the MyCare Ohio waiver pursuant to paragraph (C) of this rule, or is disenrolled from the waiver pursuant to paragraph (D), (E) or (F) of this rule, the member will be afforded notice and hearing rights in accordance with division 5101:6 of the Administrative Code.

Effective: 10/12/2020.
Five Year Review (FYR) Dates: 1/1/2024.
Promulgated Under: 119.03.
Statutory Authority: 5164.02, 5166.02.
Rule Amplifies: 5164.02, 5164.91, 5166.02, 5166.16
Prior Effective Dates: 03/01/2014, 08/01/2016, 01/01/2019.

### 5160-58-03. MyCare Ohio plans: covered services.

(A) A MyCare Ohio plan (MCOP) must ensure members have access to all medically-necessary medical, drug, behavioral health, nursing facility and home and community-based services (HCBS) covered by Ohio medicaid. After consideration of verified third party liability including medicare coverage pursuant to rule 5160-26-09.1 of the Administrative Code, the MCOP must ensure:

(1) Services are sufficient in amount, duration or scope to reasonably be expected to achieve the purpose for which the services are furnished;

(2) The amount, duration, or scope of a required service is not arbitrarily denied or reduced solely because of the diagnosis, type of illness, or condition;

(3) Prior authorization is available for services on which an MCOP has placed a preidentified limitation to ensure the limitation may be exceeded when medically necessary, unless the MCOP's limitation is also a limitation for fee-for-service medicaid coverage;

(4) Medicaid coverage decisions are based on the coverage and medical necessity criteria published in agency 5160 of the Administrative Code; and practice guidelines specified in rule 5160-26-05.1 of the Administrative Code; and

(5) If a member is unable to obtain medically-necessary medicaid services from an MCOP panel provider, the plan must adequately and timely cover the services out of panel until the plan is able to provide the services from a panel provider.

(B) The MCOP may place appropriate limits on a service;

(1) On the basis of medical necessity for the member's condition or diagnosis; or;

(2) Except as otherwise specified in this rule, to available panel providers; or

(3) For the purposes of utilization control, provided the services furnished can be reasonably expected to achieve their purpose as specified in paragraph (A)(1) of this rule.

(C) The MCOP must cover annual physical examinations for adults.

(D) At the request of a member, an MCOP must provide for a second opinion from a qualified health care professional within the panel. If a qualified health care professional is not available within the plan's panel, the plan must arrange for the member to obtain a second opinion outside the panel, at no cost to the member.

(E) The MCOP must ensure emergency services as defined in rule 5160-26-01 of the Administrative Code are provided and covered twenty-four hours a day, seven days a week. At a minimum, such services must be provided and reimbursed in accordance with the following:

(1) The MCOP may not deny payment for treatment obtained when a member had an emergency medical condition as defined in rule 5160-26-01 of the Administrative Code.

(2) The MCOP cannot limit what constitutes an emergency medical condition on the basis of diagnoses or symptoms.

(3) The MCOP must cover all emergency services without requiring prior authorization.

(4) The MCOP must cover medicaid-covered services related to the member's emergency medical condition when the member is instructed to go to an emergency facility by a representative of the plan including but not limited to the member's primary care provider (PCP) or the plan's twenty-four-hour toll-free call-in-system.

(5) The MCOP cannot deny payment of emergency services based on the treating provider, hospital, or fiscal representative not notifying the member's PCP of the visit.

(6) For the purposes of this rule, "non-contracting provider of emergency services" means any person, institution, or entity who does not contract with the MCOP but provides emergency services to a plan member, regardless of whether that provider has a medicaid provider agreement with ODM. The plan must cover emergency services as defined in rule 5160-26-01 of the Administrative Code when the services are delivered by a non-contracting provider of emergency services. Claims for these services cannot be denied regardless of whether the services meet an emergency medical condition as defined in rule 5160-26-01 of the Administrative Code. Such services must be reimbursed by the plan at the lesser of billed charges or one hundred per cent of the Ohio medicaid program fee-for-service reimbursement rate (less any payments for indirect costs of medical education and direct costs of graduate medical education that is included in the Ohio medicaid program fee-for-service reimbursement rate) in effect for the date of service. If an inpatient admission results, the plan is required to reimburse at this rate only until the member can be transferred to a provider designated by the plan.

(7) The MCOP must cover emergency services until the member is stabilized and can be safely discharged or transferred.

(8) The MCOP must adhere to the judgment of the attending provider when the attending provider requests a member's transfer to another facility or discharge. The plan may establish arrangements with hospitals whereby the plan may designate one of its contracting providers to assume the attending provider's responsibilities to stabilize, treat and transfer the member.

(9) A member who has had an emergency medical condition may not be held liable for payment of any subsequent screening and treatment needed to diagnose the specific condition or stabilize the member.

(F) The MCOP must establish, in writing, the process and procedures for the submission of claims for services delivered by non-contracting providers, including non-contracting providers of emergency services as described in paragraph (E)(6) of this rule. These written policies and procedures must be made available to non-contracting providers, including non-contracting providers of emergency services, on request. The plan may not establish claims filing and processing procedures for non-contracting providers, including non-contracting providers of emergency services, that are more stringent than those established for their contracting providers.

(G) The MCOP must ensure post-stabilization care services as defined in rule 5160-26-01 of the Administrative Code are provided and covered twenty-four hours a day, seven days a week.

(1) The MCOP must designate a telephone line to receive provider requests for coverage of post-stabilization care services. The line must be available twenty-four hours a day, seven days a week. The plan must document the telephone number and process for obtaining authorization has been provided to each emergency facility in the service area. The plan must maintain a record of any request for coverage of post-stabilization care services that is denied including, at a minimum, the time of the provider's request and the time the plan communicated the decision in writing to the provider.

(2) At a minimum, post-stabilization care services must be provided and reimbursed in accordance with the following:

(a) The MCOP must cover services obtained within or outside the plan's panel that have not been pre-approved in writing by a plan provider or other plan representative.

(b) If the MCOP does not respond within one hour of a provider's request for preapproval of further services administered to maintain the member's stabilized condition, the plan must cover the services, whether or not they were provided within the plan's panel.

(c) The MCOP must cover services obtained within or outside the plan's panel that are not pre-approved by a plan provider or other plan representative but are administered to maintain, improve or resolve the member's stabilized condition if:

(i) The MCOP fails to respond within one hour to a provider request for authorization to provide such services.

(ii) The MCOP cannot be contacted.

(iii) The MCOP's representative and treating provider cannot reach an agreement concerning the member's care and a plan provider is not available for consultation. In this situation, the plan must give the treating provider the opportunity to consult with a plan provider and the treating provider may continue with care until a plan provider is reached or one of the criteria specified in paragraph (G)(3) of this rule is met.

(3) The MCOP's financial responsibility for post stabilization care services not pre-approved ends when:

(a) A plan provider with privileges at the treating hospital assumes responsibility for the member's care;

(b) A plan provider assumes responsibility for the member's care after the member is transferred to another facility;

(c) A plan representative and the treating provider reach an agreement concerning the member's care; or

(d) The member is discharged.

(H) MCOP responsibilities for payment of other services.

(1) The MCOP must permit members to self-refer to Title X services provided by any qualified family planning provider (QFPP). The plan is responsible for payment of claims for Title X services delivered by QFPPs not contracting with the plan at the lesser of one hundred per cent of the Ohio medicaid program fee-for-service reimbursement rate or billed charges, in effect for the date of service.

(2) The MCOP must permit members to self-refer to any women's health specialist within the plan's panel for covered care necessary to provide women's routine and preventative health care services. This is in addition to the member's designated primary care provider (PCP) if that PCP is not a women's health specialist.

(3) The MCOP must ensure access to covered services provided by all federally qualified health centers (FQHCs) and rural health clinics (RHCs).

(4) Where available, the MCOP must ensure access to covered services provided by a certified nurse practitioner.

(5) The MCOP is not responsible for payment of services provided through the medicaid schools program pursuant to Chapter 5160-35 of the Administrative Code.

(6) The MCOP must provide all early and periodic screening, diagnosis and treatment (EPSDT) services, also known as healthchek services, in accordance with rule 5160-1-14 of the Administrative Code, to healthchek eligible members and ensure healthchek exams:

(a) Include the components specified in rule 5160-1-14 of the Administrative Code. All components of exams must be documented and included in the medical record of each healthchek eligible member and made available for the ODM annual external quality review.

(b) Are completed within ninety days of the initial effective date of membership for those children found to have a possible ongoing condition likely to require care management services.

(7) An MCOP is not required to cover services provided to members outside the United States.

(8) When a member is determined to be no longer eligible for enrollment in an MCOP during a stay in an institution for mental disease (IMD), the MCOP is not responsible for payment of that IMD stay after the date of disenrollment from the plan.

Effective: 1/1/2018.
Five Year Review (FYR) Dates: 10/17/2017 and 01/01/2023.
Promulgated Under: 119.03.
Statutory Authority: 5164.02, 5166.02, 5167.02.
Rule Amplifies: 5166.02, 5167.02, 5164.02
Prior Effective Dates: 3/1/14.

**5160-58-03.2. MyCare Ohio waiver: member choice, control, responsibilities and participant direction.**

A member and/or an authorized representative who is acting on behalf of a member (hereinafter "member") who is enrolled in the MyCare Ohio waiver in accordance with rule 5160-58-02.2 of the Administrative Code has choice and control over the arrangement and provision of home and community-based services (HCBS). Members also have choice over the selection and control over the direction of approved waiver service providers.

(A) A member may choose to receive MyCare Ohio waiver services from any combination of providers on the provider panel of the MyCare Ohio plan selected by the member pursuant to paragraph (B) of rule 5160-58-04 of the Administrative Code.

(B) A member receiving waiver services from any MyCare Ohio waiver provider shall:

(1) Participate with the waiver service coordinator in the development of the person-centered services plan as defined in rule 5160-44-02 of the Administrative Code.

(2) Decide who from their trans-disciplinary care management team will participate in the face-to-face development of the person-centered services plan.

(3) Communicate to the service provider and, as appropriate, the provider's management staff, personal preferences about the manner in which duties, tasks and procedures are to be performed.

(4) Work with the waiver service coordinator and the provider to identify and secure additional service provider orientation, training and/or continuing education within the provider's scope of practice in order to meet the member's specific needs.

(5) Not direct the provider to act in a manner that is contrary to any relevant MyCare Ohio waiver requirements, medicaid rules and regulations, or the provider's policies and procedures.

(6) Understand the incident management and reporting responsibilities of the member as set forth in rule 5160-58-05.3 or 5160-44-05 of the Administrative Code.

(7) Communicate to the waiver service coordinator and/or MyCare Ohio plan care manager any significant changes, as defined in rule 5160-58-01 of the Administrative Code, that may affect the provision of services or result in a need for more or fewer hours of service.

(8) Sign a complete and accurate timesheet or other documentation, as appropriate, to verify services have been furnished. The member shall never approve blank timesheets, or timesheets that have been completed before services have been furnished. Verification may be written or electronic at the discretion of the MyCare Ohio plan, unless otherwise required by rule 5160-1-40 of the Administrative Code. If the individual is unable to provide the signature required to verify a service at the time of the service, the individual will submit an electronic signature or standard signature via regular mail, or otherwise provide a signature in no instance any later than at the next face-to-face visit with the provider.

(9) Participate in the recruitment, selection and dismissal of providers in collaboration with the trans-disciplinary care management team.

(10) In the manner specified by the waiver service coordinator, notify the provider if the member is going to miss a scheduled visit.

(11) Notify the waiver service coordinator if the assigned provider misses a scheduled visit.

(12) Notify the waiver service coordinator when any change in provider is necessary. Notification shall include the desired end date of the current provider.

(13) Participate in the monitoring of the performance of the provider.

(C) If a member chooses to receive waiver services from any non-agency provider, or is exercising participant-direction over the services in paragraph (F) of rule 5160-58-04 of the Administrative Code using one or more participant-directed individual providers or participant-directed personal care providers, the following additional requirements shall apply as appropriate to the service being furnished:

(1) In accordance with paragraph (B)(9) of this rule, members shall take a proactive role in the delivery of their MyCare Ohio waiver services. This includes identifying prospective providers, recruiting and training MyCare Ohio providers to furnish tasks in accordance with the member's needs and preferences, and working with the MyCare Ohio care manager or waiver service coordinator to schedule and manage the delivery of authorized MyCare Ohio waiver services.

(2) The member shall designate a location in their home in which the member and, as appropriate, the provider can safely store a copy of the member's records in a manner that protects the confidentiality of the records, and for the purpose of contributing to the continuity of the member's care.

(3) The member or, as appropriate, the provider shall make the member's records available upon request by the MyCare Ohio plan, the Ohio department of medicaid (ODM) and/or ODM's designee.

(4) The member shall not aid the provider in furnishing a service in a manner that does not comply with any rule or law that regulates the provider.

(5) Members who exercise participant-direction of providers under the MyCare Ohio waiver shall work with ODM's designated financial management service.

(D) If the member elects to receive services from a participant-directed provider, the waiver service coordinator shall assess the member's strengths and weaknesses (and if the member has an authorized representative, the authorized representative's strengths and weaknesses) and ability to direct a provider. The waiver service coordinator shall allow the member to direct a provider if the waiver service coordinator determines that the member demonstrates the following:

(1) An understanding of the elements of the service the provider shall furnish;

(2) An understanding of how to direct the provider; and

(3) An ability to perform the responsibilities of an employer, including:

(a) Completion of any training required by ODM or the MyCare Ohio plan;

(b) Understanding which service activities are covered according to rule 5160-58-04 of the Administrative Code;

(c) Understanding the methods for selecting and dismissing participant-directed service providers including the requirements for providers to furnish services in the MyCare Ohio waiver;

(d) Understanding the methods for entering into written agreements with participant-directed service providers for specific activities;

(e) Understanding the methods for training participant-directed service providers to meet the member's specific needs;

(f) Understanding the methods for supervising and monitoring the participant-directed service provider's performance of specific activities, including written approval of the provider's time sheets;

(g) Development of a back-up plan if a provider is unable to furnish the agreed-upon service;

(h) Understanding the methods for filing grievances, including use of the regional and state long term care ombudsman;

(i) Familiarity with the MyCare Ohio plan grievance process and the state appeal and fair hearing request procedures;

(j) Understanding and compliance with the state's record-retention requirements; and,

(k) An ability to manage the participant-directed service provider when he or she furnishes a service.

(E) If the waiver service coordinator determines that the member cannot meet the requirements set forth in paragraph (C) or (D) of this rule, as appropriate, the waiver service coordinator may require the member to appoint an authorized representative to assist the member with directing services.

(F) If the waiver service coordinator, in consultation with the trans-disciplinary care management team, determines that the member and/or the member's authorized representative cannot meet the requirements set forth in paragraph (C) or (D) of this rule, or the health and welfare of the member receiving services from a non-agency or participant-directed provider cannot be ensured, the waiver service coordinator may require the member to receive services from only agency providers. The member will be afforded notice and hearing rights in accordance with division 5101:6 of the Administrative Code.

Effective: 10/12/2020.
Five Year Review (FYR) Dates: 1/1/2024.
Promulgated Under: 119.03.
Statutory Authority: 5164.02, 5166.02.
Rule Amplifies: 5164.02, 5164.91, 5166.02 , 5166.16
Prior Effective Dates: 03/01/2014, 01/01/2019.

### 5160-58-04. MyCare Ohio waiver: covered services and providers.

(A) The purpose of this rule is to establish both the services covered by the MyCare Ohio home and community based services (HCBS) waiver program and the providers eligible to furnish those services to members enrolled in the MyCare Ohio waiver.

(B) Providers seeking to furnish services in the MyCare Ohio waiver program shall meet the requirements in Chapter 173-39, 5160-45 or 5160-44 of the Administrative Code, as appropriate. Prior to furnishing services to MyCare Ohio waiver recipients, the services must be documented on the member's person-centered services plan as described in rule 5160-44-02 of the Administrative Code.

(C) MyCare Ohio waiver covered services are limited to the following and exclude any reimbursement provisions in the Ohio Administrative Code rules cited therein:

(1) Adult day health services as set forth in rule 173-39-02.1 or 5160-46-04 of the Administrative Code;

(2) Alternative meal services as set forth in rule 173-39-02.2 of the Administrative Code;

(3) Assisted living services as set forth in rule 173-39-02.16 of the Administrative Code;

(4) Choices home care attendant services as set forth in rule 173-39-02.4 of the Administrative Code;

(5) Community integration services as set forth in rule 173-39-02.15 or 5160-44-14 of the Administrative Code;

(6) Community transition services as set forth in rule 173-39-02.17 or 5160-44-26 of the Administrative Code;

(7) Enhanced community living services as set forth in rule 173-39-02.20 of the Administrative Code.

(8) Homemaker services as set forth in rule 173-39-02.8 of the Administrative Code;

(9) Home care attendant services as set forth in rule 173-39-02.24 or 5160-44-27 of the Administrative Code;

(10) Home delivered meal services as set forth in rule 173-39-02.14 or 5160-44-11 of the Administrative Code;

(11) Home maintenance and chore services as set forth in rule 173-39-02.5 or 5160-44-12 of the Administrative Code.

(12) Home medical equipment and supplemental adaptive and assistive devices services as set forth in rule 173-39-02.7 or 5160-46-04 of the Administrative Code;

(13) Home modification services as set forth in rule 173-39-02.9 or 5160-44-13 of the Administrative Code;

(14) Nutrition consultation services as set forth in rule 173-39-02.10 of the Administrative Code;

(15) Out-of- home respite services as set forth in rule 173-39-02.23 or 5160-44-17 of the Administrative Code;

(16) Personal care aide services as set forth in rule 173-39-02.11 or 5160-46-04 of the Administrative Code;

(17) Personal emergency response services as set forth in rule 173-39-02.6 or 5160-44-16 of the Administrative Code;

(18) Pest control services as set forth in rule 173-39-02.3 of the Administrative Code;

(19) Social work counseling services as set forth in rule 173-39-02.12 of the Administrative Code;

(20) Waiver nursing services as set forth in rule 173-39-02.22 or 5160-44-22 of the Administrative Code; and

(21) Waiver transportation services as set forth in rules 173-39-02.13 and 173-39-02.18 or 5160-46-04 of the Administrative Code.

(D) If a member enrolled in the MyCare Ohio waiver is also a participant in the helping ohioans move, expanding (HOME) choice demonstration program pursuant to Chapter 5160-51 of the Administrative Code, the member may use the HOME choice community transitions service in lieu of, but not in addition to, the community transition service available through the MyCare Ohio waiver.

(E) If a member receives enhanced community living services, the member shall not also receive personal care or homemaker services available through the MyCare Ohio waiver.

(F) The following services may be participant directed using budget and/or employer authority. To exercise these authorities, members must demonstrate the ability to direct providers in accordance with paragraph (D) of rule 5160-58-03.2 of the Administrative Code:

(1) Employer authority which includes, but is not limited to, the ability of the member to hire, fire, and train employees is available for the following services:

(a) Choices home care attendant services provided by a participant- directed individual provider; and

(b) Personal care services provided by a participant-directed personal care provider.

(2) Budget authority which includes the ability of the member to negotiate rates of reimbursement is available in the following services:

(a) Alternative meals;

(b) Choices home care attendant services;

(c) Home maintenance and chore services;

(d) Home modification services; and

(e) Home medical equipment and supplemental adaptive and assistive devices.

Effective: 7/1/2019.
Five Year Review (FYR) Dates: 1/1/2024.
Promulgated Under: 119.03.
Statutory Authority: 5164.02, 5166.02.
Rule Amplifies: 5164.02, 5164.91, 5166.02, 5166.16
Prior Effective Dates: 03/01/2014, 01/01/2019.

### 5160-58-05.3. MyCare Ohio waiver and 1915(i) specialized recovery services program (SRSP): incident management system. [RESCINDED]

Rescinded Effective: 7/1/2019.
Five Year Review (FYR) Dates: 4/15/2019.
Promulgated Under: 119.03.
Statutory Authority: 5164.02, 5164.91.
Rule Amplifies: 5164.02, 5167.02, 5166.02, 5164.91
Prior Effective Dates: 03/01/2014, 08/01/2016.

### 5160-58-08.4 Appeals and grievances for "MyCare Ohio."

(A) Definitions. —

(1) "Adverse benefit determination" is a MyCare Ohio plan (MCOP)'s:

(a) Denial or limited authorization of a requested service, including determinations based on the type or level of service, requirements for medical necessity, appropriateness, setting, or effectiveness of a covered benefit;

(b) Reduction, suspension, or termination of services prior to the member receiving the services previously authorized by the MCOP;

(c) Denial, in whole or part, of payment for a service not covered by medicaid, including a service denied through the MCOP's prior authorization process as not medically necessary;

(d) Denial of a request for a specific MCOP-contracted non-agency or participant-directed waiver services provider pursuant to paragraph (G) of rule 5160-58-03.2 of the Administrative Code;

(e) Failure to provide services in a timely manner as specified in rules 5160-26-03.1 and 5160-58-01.1 of the Administrative Code;

(f) Failure to act within the resolution time frames specified in this rule; or

(g) Denial of a member's request to dispute a financial liability, including cost sharing, copayments, premiums, deductibles, coinsurance and other member financial liabilities, if applicable.

(2) "Appeal" is the member's request for an MCOP's review of an adverse benefit determination.

(3) "Grievance" is the member's expression of dissatisfaction about any matter other than an adverse benefit determination. Grievances may include, but are not limited to, the quality of care or services provided, and aspects of interpersonal relationships such as rudeness of a provider or employee, or failure to respect the member's rights regardless of whether remedial action is requested. Grievance includes a member's right to dispute an extension of time proposed by the MCOP to make an authorization decision.

(4) "Notice of action (NOA)" is the written notice an MCOP must provide to members when an MCOP adverse benefit determination has occurred or will occur.

(B) NOA by an MCOP.

(1) When an MCOP adverse benefit determination has or will occur, the MCOP shall provide the affected member with a NOA.

(2) The NOA shall explain:

(a) The adverse benefit determination the MCOP has taken or intends to take;

(b) The reasons for the adverse benefit determination, including the right of the member to be provided, upon request and free of charge, reasonable access to copies of all documents, records, and other relevant determination information;

(c) The member's right to file an appeal to the MCOP;

(d) Information related to exhausting the MCOP appeal;

(e) The member's right to request a state hearing through the state's hearing system upon exhausting the MCOP appeal;

(f) Procedures for exercising the member's rights to appeal the adverse benefit determination;

(g) Circumstances under which expedited resolution is available and how to request it;

(h) If applicable, the member's right to have benefits continue pending the resolution of the appeal, how to request that benefits be continued, and the circumstances under which the member may be required to pay for the cost of those services;

(i) The date the notice is issued;

(3) The following language and format requirements apply to a NOA issued by an MCOP:

(a) It shall be provided in a manner and format that may be easily understood;

(b) It shall explain that oral interpretation is available for any language, written translation is available in prevalent non-English languages as applicable, and written alternative formats may be available as needed;

(c) It shall explain how to access the MCOP's interpretation and translation services as well as alternative formats that can be provided by the MCOP;

(d) When directed by ODM, it shall be printed in the prevalent non-English languages of members in the MCOP's service area; and

(e) It shall be available in alternative formats, and in an appropriate manner, taking into consideration the special needs of members, including but not limited to members who are visually limited and members who have limited reading proficiency.

(4) An MCOP shall issue a NOA within the following time frames:

(a) For a decision to deny or limit authorization of a requested service, the MCOP shall issue a NOA simultaneously with the MCOP's decision.

(b) For reduction, suspension, or termination of services prior to the member receiving the services previously authorized by the MCOP, the MCOP shall give notice at least fifteen calendar days before the effective date of the adverse benefit determination except:

(i) If probable recipient fraud has been verified, the MCOP shall give notice five calendar days before the effective date of the adverse benefit determination.

(ii) Under the circumstances set forth in 42 CFR 431.213 (October 1, 2017), the MCOP shall give notice on or before the effective date of the adverse benefit determination.

(c) For denial of payment for a non-covered service, the MCOP shall give notice simultaneously with the MCOP's action to deny the claim, in whole or part, for a service that is not covered by medicaid, including a service that was determined through the MCOP's prior authorization process as not medically necessary.

(d) For denial of a request for a provider pursuant to paragraph (A)(1)(d) of this rule, the MCOP shall give notice simultaneously with the MCOP's decision.

(e) For untimely prior authorization, appeal, or grievance resolution, the MCOP shall give notice simultaneously with the MCOP becoming aware of the untimely resolution. Service authorization decisions not reached within the time frames specified in rules 5160-26-03.1 and 5160-58-01.1 of the Administrative Code constitutes a denial and is thus considered to be an adverse benefit determination. Notice shall be given on the date the authorization decision time frame expires.

(C) Grievances to an MCOP. —

(1) A member may file a grievance with an MCOP orally or in writing at any time. An authorized representative must have the member's written consent to file a grievance on the member's behalf.

(2) An MCOP shall acknowledge the receipt of each grievance to the member filing the grievance. Oral acknowledgment by an MCOP is acceptable. If the grievance is filed in writing, written acknowledgment shall be made within three business days of receipt of the grievance.

(3) An MCOP shall review and resolve all grievances as expeditiously as the member's health condition requires. Grievance resolutions, including member notification, shall meet the following time frames:

(a) Within two business days of receipt if the grievance is regarding access to services.

(b) Within thirty calendar days of receipt for all other grievances that are not regarding access to services.

(4) At a minimum, an MCOP shall provide oral notification to the member of a grievance resolution. If an MCOP is unable to speak directly with the member, or the resolution includes information that must be confirmed in writing, the resolution shall be provided in writing simultaneously with the MCOP's resolution.

(5) If an MCOP's resolution to a grievance is to affirm the denial, reduction, suspension, or termination of a service, denial of a provider pursuant to paragraph (A)(1)(d) of this rule, or billing of a member due to the MCOP's denial of payment for that service, the MCOP shall notify the member of his or her right to request a state hearing as specified in paragraph (G) of this rule, if the member has not previously been notified.

(D) Standard appeal to an MCOP. —

(1) A member, a member's authorized representative, or a provider may file an appeal orally or in writing within sixty calendar days from the date that the NOA was issued. An oral appeal filing must be followed by a written appeal. An MCOP shall:

(a) Immediately convert an oral appeal filing to a written appeal on behalf of the member; and

(b) Consider the date of the oral appeal filing as the filing date.

(2) Any provider acting on the member's behalf shall have the member's written consent to file an appeal. An MCOP must begin processing the appeal upon receipt of the written consent.

(3) An MCOP shall acknowledge receipt of each appeal to the member filing the appeal. At a minimum, acknowledgment shall be made in the same manner the appeal was filed. If an appeal is filed in writing, written acknowledgment shall be made by an MCOP within three business days of receipt of the appeal.

(4) An MCOP shall provide members a reasonable opportunity to present evidence and allegations of fact or law, in person as well as in writing, and inform the member of this opportunity sufficiently in advance of the resolution time frame. Upon request, the member and/or member's authorized representative shall be provided, free of charge and sufficiently in advance of the resolution time frame, the case file, including medical records, and any other documents and records, and any new or additional evidence considered, relied upon or generated by an MCOP, or at the direction of an MCOP, in connection with the appeal of the adverse benefit determination.

(5) An MCOP shall consider the member, the member's authorized representative, or an estate representative of a deceased member as parties to the appeal.

(6) An MCOP shall review and resolve each appeal as expeditiously as the member's health condition requires, but the resolution time frame shall not exceed fifteen calendar days from the receipt of the appeal unless the resolution time frame is extended as outlined in paragraph (F) of this rule.

(7) An MCOP shall provide written notice of the appeal's resolution to the member, and to the member's authorized representative if applicable. At a minimum, the written notice shall include the resolution decision and date of the resolution.

(8) For appeal resolutions not resolved wholly in the member's favor, the written notice to the member shall also include the following information:

(a) The right to request a state hearing through the state's hearing system;

(b) How to request a state hearing; and if applicable:

(i) The right to continue to receive benefits pending a state hearing; and

(ii) How to request the continuation of benefits.

(c) Oral interpretation is available for any language;

(d) Written translation is available in prevalent non-English languages as applicable;

(e) Written alternative formats may be available as needed; and

(f) How to access the MCOP's interpretation and translation services as well as alternative formats that can be provided by the MCOP.

(9) For appeal resolutions decided in favor of the member, an MCOP shall:

(a) Authorize or provide the disputed services promptly and as expeditiously as the member's health condition requires, but no later than seventy-two hours from the appeal resolution date, if the services were not furnished while the appeal was pending.

(b) Pay for the disputed services if the member received the services while the appeal was pending.

(E) Expedited appeals to an MCOP. —

(1) An MCOP shall establish and maintain an expedited review process to resolve appeals when the member requests and the MCOP determines, or the provider indicates in making the request on the member's behalf or supporting the member's request, that taking the time for a standard resolution could seriously jeopardize the member's life, physical or mental or health or ability to attain, maintain, or regain maximum function.

(2) In utilizing an expedited appeal process, an MCOP shall comply with the standard appeal process specified in paragraph (D) of this rule, except the MCOP shall:

(a) Determine within one business day of the appeal request whether to expedite the appeal resolution;

(b) Make reasonable efforts to provide prompt oral notification to the member of the decision to expedite or not expedite the appeal resolution;

(c) Inform the member of the limited time available for the member to present evidence and allegations of fact or law in person or in writing;

(d) Resolve the appeal as expeditiously as the member's health condition requires, but the resolution time frame shall not exceed seventy-two hours from the date the MCOP received the appeal unless the resolution time frame is extended as outlined in paragraph (F) of this rule;

(e) Make reasonable efforts to provide oral notice of the appeal resolution in addition to the required written notification;

(f) Ensure punitive action is not taken against a provider who requests an expedited resolution or supports a member's appeal; and

(g) Notify ODM within one business day of any appeal that meets the criteria for expedited resolution as specified by ODM.

(3) If an MCOP denies the request for expedited resolution of an appeal, the MCOP shall:

(a) Transfer the appeal to the standard resolution time frame of fifteen calendar days from the date the appeal was received unless the resolution time frame is extended as outlined in paragraph (F) of this rule; and

(b) Make reasonable efforts to provide the member prompt oral notification of the decision not to expedite, and within two calendar days of the receipt of the appeal, provide the member written notice of the reason for the denial, including information that the member can grieve the decision.

(F) Grievance and appeal resolution extensions. —

(1) A member may request the time frame for an MCOP to resolve a grievance or standard or expedited appeal be extended up to fourteen calendar days.

(2) An MCOP may request that the time frame to resolve a grievance or standard or expedited appeal be extended up to fourteen calendar days. The following requirements apply:

(a) The MCOP shall seek such an extension from ODM prior to the expiration of the standard or expedited appeal or grievance resolution time frame;

(b) The MCOP request shall be supported by documentation of the need for additional information and that the extension is in the member's best interest; and

(c) If ODM approves the extension, the MCOP shall immediately give the member written notice of the reason for the extension and the date a decision shall be made.

(3) The MCOP shall maintain documentation of any extension request.

(G) Access to state's hearing system. —

(1) In accordance with 42 CFR 438.402 (October 1, 2017), members may request a state hearing only after exhausting the MCOP's appeal process. If an MCOP fails to adhere to the notice and timing requirements for appeals set forth in this rule, the member is deemed to have exhausted the MCOP appeal process and may request a state hearing.

(2) When required by paragraph (D)(8) of this rule, and in accordance with division 5101:6 of the Administrative Code, an MCOP shall notify members, and any authorized representatives on file with the MCOP, of the right to a state hearing subject to the following requirements:

(a) If an MCOP appeal resolution upholds the denial of a request for the authorization of a service, in whole or in part, the MCOP shall simultaneously issue the "Notice of Denial of Medical Services By Your Managed Care Plan" (ODM 04043, 1/2018).

(b) If an MCOP appeal resolution upholds the decision to reduce, suspend, or terminate services prior to the member receiving the services as authorized by the MCOP, the MCOP shall issue the "Notice of Reduction, Suspension or Termination of Medical Services By Your Managed Care Plan" (ODM 04066, 1/2018).

(c) If an MCOP appeal resolution upholds the denial of a request for the authorization to receive waiver services from a provider pursuant to paragraph (A)(1)(d) of this rule, the MCOP shall simultaneously issue the required notice of state hearing rights.

(d) If an MCOP learns a member has been billed for services received by the member due to the MCOP's denial of payment, and the MCOP upholds the denial of payment, the MCOP shall immediately issue the "Notice of Denial of Payment for Medical Services By Your Managed Care Plan" (ODM 04046, 1/2018).

(3) The member or the member's authorized representative may request a state hearing within one hundred twenty days from the date of an adverse appeal resolution by contacting the ODJFS bureau of state hearings or local county department of job and family services (CDJFS).

(4) There are no state hearing rights for a member terminated from an MCOP pursuant to an MCOP-initiated membership termination as permitted in rule 5160-58-02.1 of the Administrative Code.

(5) Following the bureau of state hearing's notification to an MCOP that a member has requested a state hearing, the MCOP shall:

(a) Complete the "Appeal Summary for Managed Care Plans" (ODM 01959, 7/2014) with appropriate supporting attachments, and file it with the bureau of state hearings, at least three business days prior to the scheduled hearing date. The appeal summary shall include all facts and documents relevant to the issue, in accordance with rule 5160-26-03.1 of the Administrative Code, and be sufficient to demonstrate the basis for the MCOP's adverse benefit determination;

(b) Send a copy of the completed ODM 01959 to the member and the member's authorized representative, if applicable, the CDJFS, and the designated ODM contact; and

(c) If benefits were continued through the appeal process in accordance with paragraph (H)(1) of this rule, continue or reinstate the benefit(s) if the MCOP is notified the member's state hearing request was received within fifteen days from the date of the appeal resolution.

(6) An MCOP shall participate in the state hearing, in person or by telephone, on the date indicated on the "Notice to Appear for a Scheduled Hearing" (JFS 04002, 1/2015) sent to the MCOP by the bureau of state hearings.

(7) An MCOP shall comply with the state hearing decision provided to the MCOP via the "State Hearing Decision" (JFS 04005, 1/2015). If the state hearing decision sustains the member's appeal, the MCOP shall submit the information required by the "Order of Compliance" (JFS 04068, 1/2015) to the bureau of state hearings. The information, including applicable supporting documentation, is due to the bureau of state hearings and the designated ODM contact by no later than the compliance date specified in the hearing decision. If applicable, the MCOP shall:

(a). Authorize or provide the disputed services promptly and as expeditiously as the member's health condition requires, but no later than seventytwo hours from the date it receives notice reversing the adverse benefit determination if services were not furnished while the appeal was pending.

(b) Pay for the disputed services if the member received the services while the appeal was pending.

(H) Continuation of benefits while the appeal to an MCOP or state hearing are pending. —

(1) Unless a member requests that previously authorized benefits not be continued, an MCOP shall continue a member's benefits when all the following conditions are met:

(a) The member requests an appeal within fifteen days of the MCOP issuing the NOA;

(b) The appeal involves the termination, suspension, or reduction of services prior to the member receiving the previously authorized services;

(c) The services were ordered by an authorized provider; and

(d) The authorization period has not expired.

(2) If an MCOP continues or reinstates the member's benefits while the appeal or state hearing are pending, the benefits shall be continued until one of the following occurs:

(a) The member withdraws the appeal or the state hearing request;

(b) The member fails to request a state hearing within fifteen days after the MCOP issues an adverse appeal resolution; or

(c) The bureau of state hearings issues a state hearing decision upholding the reduction, suspension or termination of services.

(3) If the final resolution of the appeal or state hearing upholds an MCOP's original adverse benefit determination, at the discretion of ODM, the MCOP may recover the cost of the services furnished to the member while the appeal and/ or state hearing was pending.

(I) Other duties of an MCOP regarding appeals and grievances. —

(1) An MCOP shall give members all reasonable assistance filing a grievance, an appeal, or a state hearing request including but not limited to:

(a) Explaining the MCOP's process to be followed in resolving the member's appeal or grievance;

(b) Completing forms and taking other procedural steps as outlined in this rule; and

(c) Providing oral interpretation and oral translation services, sign language assistance, and access to the grievance system through a toll-free number with text telephone yoke (TTY) and interpreter capability.

(2) An MCOP shall ensure the individuals who make decisions on appeals and grievances are individuals who:

(a) Were neither involved in any previous level of review or decision-making nor a subordinate of any such individual; and

(b) Are health care professionals who have the appropriate clinical expertise in treating the member's condition or disease, if deciding any of the following:

(i) An appeal of a denial based on lack of medical necessity;

(ii) A grievance regarding the denial of an expedited resolution of an appeal; or

(iii) An appeal or grievance involving clinical issues.

(3) In reaching an appeal resolution, the MCOP shall take into account all comments, documents, records, and other information submitted by the member or their representative without regard to whether such information was submitted or considered in the initial adverse benefit determination.

Replaces: 5160-58-08.4.
Effective: 1/1/2018.
Five Year Review (FYR) Dates: 01/01/2023.
Promulgated Under: 119.03.
Statutory Authority: 5164.02, 5166.02, 5167.02.
Rule Amplifies: 5164.02, 5166.02, 5167.02
Prior Effective Dates: 03/01/2014, 12/01/2014, 08/01/2016.

# 5160:1

# MEDICAID GENERAL PRINCIPLES

Chapter
5160:1-3. Medicaid for the Aged, Blind, or Disabled (ABD)

# CHAPTER 5160:1-3

# MEDICAID FOR THE AGED, BLIND, OR DISABLED (ABD)

Rule
5160:1-3-01. Medicaid: coverage for the aged, blind, or disabled.
5160:1-3-01.1. Medicare premium assistance programs (MPAP). [RESCINDED]
5160:1-3-01.2. Medicare: qualified disabled and working individuals (QDWI). [RESCINDED]
5160:1-3-02. Medicaid: criteria for age, blindness, or disability.
5160:1-3-02.1. Medicare premium assistance programs (MPAP).
5160:1-3-02.2. Medicare buy-in.
5160:1-3-02.3. Medicaid: coverage for individuals receiving supplemental security income (SSI) benefits.
5160:1-3-02.4. Medicaid: coverage for the categorically needy.
5160:1-3-02.5. Medicaid: supplemental security income (SSI) recipients qualifying under section 1619 of the Social Security Act for continued medical assistance coverage.
5160:1-3-02.6. Medicaid: grandfathering provisions and deemed eligibility.
5160:1-3-02.7. Medicaid: continuing care communities, life care communities and philanthropic long-term care facilities. [RESCINDED]
5160:1-3-02.8. Medicaid: treatment of qualified long-term care insurance policies. [RESCINDED]
5160:1-3-02.9. Medicaid: disability determination process.
5160:1-3-03. Medicaid: limiting physical factor. [RESCINDED]
5160:1-3-03.1. Medicaid: income.
5160:1-3-03.2. Medicaid: income exclusions.
5160:1-3-03.3. Medicaid: deeming of income.
5160:1-3-03.4. Medicaid: continued medicaid coverage for children who lost their eligibility for supplemental security income (SSI) due to a change in the disability determination. [RESCINDED]
5160:1-3-03.5. Medicaid: application of income standards.
5160:1-3-03.6. Medicaid: treatment of rental income.
5160:1-3-03.7. Medicaid: treatment of sick pay and sick leave.
5160:1-3-03.8. Medicaid: in-kind support and maintenance.
5160:1-3-03.9. Medicaid: deeming of income. [RESCINDED]
5160:1-3-03.10. Medicaid: retirement funds.
5160:1-3-03.11. Medicaid: income exclusions. [RESCINDED]
5160:1-3-04. Medicaid: living arrangement requirement. [RESCINDED]
5160:1-3-04.1. Medicaid: eligibility through the spenddown process. [RESCINDED]
5160:1-3-04.2. Medicaid: income computations for determining eligibility using the special income level. [RESCINDED]
5160:1-3-04.3. Medicaid: determining patient liability. [RESCINDED]
5160:1-3-04.4. Medicaid: income and patient liability determinations for individuals under the assisted living home and community based waiver. [RESCINDED]
5160:1-3-05. Medicaid: resource requirement. [RESCINDED]
5160:1-3-05.1. Medicaid: resource requirement.
5160:1-3-05.2. Medicaid: trusts.
5160:1-3-05.3. Medicaid: annuities.
5160:1-3-05.4. Medicaid: cash and checking and savings accounts and time deposits.
5160:1-3-05.5. Medicaid: promissory notes, property agreements, and loans.
5160:1-3-05.6. Medicaid: burial funds and contracts.
5160:1-3-05.7. Medicaid: burial spaces.
5160:1-3-05.8. Medicaid: lump-sum payments.
5160:1-3-05.9. Medicaid: dividends and interest.
5160:1-3-05.10. Medicaid: household goods and personal effects as resources.
5160:1-3-05.11. Medicaid: automobiles and other modes of transportation as resources.
5160:1-3-05.12. Medicaid: life insurance.
5160:1-3-05.13. Medicaid: treatment of the home.
5160:1-3-05.14. Medicaid: resource exclusions.

Rule
5160:1-3-05.15. Medicaid: exclusion of property no longer the principal place of residence. [RESCINDED]
5160:1-3-05.16. Medicaid: home replacement exclusion.
5160:1-3-05.17. Medicaid: life estates.
5160:1-3-05.18. Medicaid: stocks, mutual funds, and bonds.
5160:1-3-05.19. Medicaid: real or personal property essential to self-support.
5160:1-3-05.20. Medicaid: deeming of resources.
5160:1-3-06. Medicaid: social security administration reporting alleged transfer of resources by supplemental security income (SSI) applicants to the Ohio department of job and family services (ODJFS). [RESCINDED]
5160:1-3-06.1. Medicaid: treatment of income and resources of institutionalized individuals. [RESCINDED]
5160:1-3-06.2. Medicaid: resource assessment. [RESCINDED]
5160:1-3-06.3. Medicaid: treatment of resources for institutionalized individuals with a spouse in the community. [RESCINDED]
5160:1-3-06.4. Medicaid: resource budgeting methodology for institutionalized individuals with a spouse in the community. [RESCINDED]
5160:1-3-06.5. Medicaid: transfer of resources for institutionalized spouses with a spouse in the community. [RESCINDED]
5160:1-3-07. Medicaid: transfer of resources. [RESCINDED]
5160:1-3-07.1. Medicaid: social security administration reporting alleged transfer of resources by supplemental security income (SSI) applicants to the Ohio department of medicaid (ODM). [RESCINDED]
5160:1-3-07.2. Medicaid: transfer of resources. [RESCINDED]
5160:1-3-07.3. Medicaid: disposal of resources for Ohio department of developmental disabilities and/or Ohio department of mental health and addiction services individuals. [RESCINDED]
5160:1-3-08. Medicaid: income. [RESCINDED]
5160:1-3-10. Medicaid: eligibility through the spenddown process. [RESCINDED]
5160:1-3-11. Medicaid eligibility for persons living in state institutions for the mentally ill and mentally retarded. [RESCINDED]
5160:1-3-12.2. Medicaid: information sharing with long term care facility (LTCF) providers. [Rescinded.]
5160:1-3-14.4. Medicaid: sheltered workshop earnings. [RESCINDED]
5160:1-3-15.1. Medicaid: treatment of rental income. [RESCINDED]
5160:1-3-15.2. Medicaid: treatment of sick pay. [RESCINDED]
5160:1-3-17. Medicaid: in-kind support and maintenance. [RESCINDED]
5160:1-3-18. Medicaid: income exemptions and disregards. [RESCINDED]
5160:1-3-19. Medicaid: deeming of income. [RESCINDED]
5160:1-3-21. Medicaid: standards and allocations. [RESCINDED]
5160:1-3-22. Medicaid: treatment of income and resources of institutionalized individuals. [RESCINDED]
5160:1-3-22.7. Medicaid: retirement and income supplementing accounts (RISAs). [RESCINDED]
5160:1-3-22.8. Medicaid: the disclosure and treatment of annuities for recipients or applicants for medical assistance programs. [RESCINDED]
5160:1-3-23. Medicaid: income computations for determining eligibility using the special income level. [RESCINDED]
5160:1-3-24. Medicaid: determining patient liability. [RESCINDED]
5160:1-3-24.1. Medicaid: income and patient liability determinations for individuals under the assisted living home and community based waiver. [RESCINDED]
5160:1-3-26. Medicaid: resource exemption. [RESCINDED]
5160:1-3-27. Medicaid: liquid assets as resources. [RESCINDED]
5160:1-3-27.1. Medicaid: trusts. [RESCINDED]
5160:1-3-27.2. Medicaid: cash and checking and savings accounts and time deposits. [RESCINDED]
5160:1-3-27.3. Medicaid: promissory notes, mortgages, stocks, bonds and loans. [RESCINDED]
5160:1-3-27.4. Medicaid: preneed funeral contracts. [RESCINDED]
5160:1-3-27.5. Medicaid: lump-sum payments. [RESCINDED]
5160:1-3-27.6. Medicaid: dividends and interest. [RESCINDED]
5160:1-3-28. Household goods and personal effects as resources. [RESCINDED]
5160:1-3-29. Automobiles and other modes of transportation as resources. [RESCINDED]
5160:1-3-30. Medicaid: life insurance. [RESCINDED]
5160:1-3-31. Medicaid: treatment of the home. [RESCINDED]
5160:1-3-31.3. Medicaid: exemption of property no longer the principal place of residence. [RESCINDED]
5160:1-3-31.4. Medicaid: home replacement exclusion. [RESCINDED]
5160:1-3-32. Medicaid: life estates and life leases. [RESCINDED]
5160:1-3-32.1. Medicaid: property agreements. [RESCINDED]
5160:1-3-32.2. Medicaid: burial spaces. [RESCINDED]

### 5160:1-3-01. Medicaid: coverage for the aged, blind, or disabled.

(A) The medicaid program provides coverage for individuals who meet the aged, blind, or disability status as set forth in section 1902 of the Social Security Act (as in effect on February 1, 2016). The provisions of Chapter 5160:1-3 of the Administrative Code establish eligibility criteria, standards, and procedures that apply to individuals enrolling in an aged, blind or disability categorical coverage group.

(B) The rules of this chapter are organized as follows:

(1) Rules under principal rule 5160:1-3-02 of the Administrative Code set forth base eligibility requirements of the aged, blind, or disabled eligibility covered groups.

(2) Rules under principal rule 5160:1-3-03 of the Administrative Code set forth income eligibility requirements.

(3) Rules under principal rule 5160:1-3-05 of the Administrative Code set forth resource eligibility requirements.

Replaces: 5160:1-3-01.
Effective: 08/01/2016.
Five Year Review (FYR) Dates: 08/01/2021.
Promulgated Under: 111.15.
Statutory Authority: 5160.02, 5163.02.
Rule Amplifies: 5160.02, 5163.02
Prior Effective Dates: 1/22/15.

### 5160:1-3-01.1 Medicare premium assistance programs (MPAP). [RESCINDED]

Rescinded effective: 01/22/2015.
Five Year Review (FYR) Dates: 10/14/2014.
Promulgated Under: 111.15.
Statutory Authority: 5111.01.
Rule Amplifies: 5111.01, 5111.011
Prior Effective Dates: 1/1/89 (Emer.), 4/1/89, 1/1/90 (Emer.), 1/5/90 (Emer.), 4/1/90, 7/1/90 (Emer.), 9/8/90, 9/28/90 (Emer.), 12/24/90, 1/1/92 (Emer.), 3/20/92, 7/1/92, 1/1/93 (Emer.), 3/18/93, 6/11/93, 8/15/93, 3/1/94 (Emer.), 4/18/94 (Emer.), 6/1/98, 8/12/98 (Emer.), 11/1/98, 10/1/02, 7/1/05, 1/1/10.



### 5160:1-3-01.2 Medicare: qualified disabled and working individuals (QDWI). [RESCINDED]

Rescinded effective: 01/22/2015.
Five Year Review (FYR) Dates: 10/14/2014.
Promulgated Under: 111.15.
Statutory Authority: 5111.01.
Rule Amplifies: 5111.01, 5111.011
Prior Effective Dates: 7/1/90 (Emer.), 9/8/90, 1/1/91, 10/1/02, 1/1/10.

### 5160:1-3-02. Medicaid: criteria for age, blindness, or disability.

(A) The medicaid program provides coverage for individuals who have been determined to meet the criteria for the limiting physical factors of age, blindness, or disability as set forth in section 1902 of the Social Security Act (as in effect on October 1, 2016). Age is determined by county departments of job and family services (CDJFS). Blindness and disability are determined by either the social security administration (SSA) or the Ohio department of medicaid (ODM) in accordance with rule 5160:1-3-02.9 of the Administrative Code. The criteria are as follows:

(1) Age: A person who is age sixty-five years or older meets the age requirement for medicaid. Verification of age is required.

(2) Blindness: A person is considered to be blind if he or she has central visual acuity of 20/200 or less in the better eye with correcting glasses, or a limited visual field of twenty degrees or less in the better eye.

(3) Disability. Disability is defined differently for adults and children. An individual is disabled if the individual is:

(a) An adult who is unable to do any substantial gainful activity by reason of any medically determinable physical or mental impairment or combination of impairments which can be expected to result in death or which has lasted or can be expected to last for a continuous period of not less than twelve months.

(b) A child under the age of eighteen who has a medically determinable physical or mental impairment or combination of impairments that causes marked and severe functional limitations, and that can be expected to cause death or that has lasted or can be expected to last for a continuous period of not less than twelve months. No individual under the age of eighteen who engages in substantial gainful activity may be considered disabled.

(B) If SSA makes a finding of presumptive disability based upon the available evidence which reflects a high degree of probability that the individual will meet the disability requirements, the applicant for medical assistance meets the disability requirements necessary to qualify for medical assistance. If it is later determined that the SSA decision was erroneously made and the individual was without fault in the determination, no attempt shall be made to recover payments for medical assistance made on behalf of the individual.

Replaces: 5160:1-3-02.
Effective: 9/1/2017.
Five Year Review (FYR) Dates: 09/01/2022.
Promulgated Under: 111.15.
Statutory Authority: 5160.02, 5163.02.
Rule Amplifies: 5160.02, 5163.02
Prior Effective Dates: 9/3/77, 1/1/81, 9/6/84, 8/1/85, 8/1/86 (Emer.), 10/3/86, 7/1/87 (Emer.), 8/3/87, 1/1/88 (Emer.), 3/28/88, 10/1/88 (Emer.), 12/20/88, 4/1/90, 10/1/91 (Emer.), 12/1/91, 12/2/91, 12/20/91, 1/1/92 (Emer.), 3/20/92, 12/22/92 (Emer.), 1/1/93 (Emer.), 2/11/93, 3/20/93, 9/1/93, 8/1/95 (Emer.), 10/30/95, 4/1/99, 10/1/02, 11/25/02, 1/1/05, 1/22/15, 8/1/16.

### 5160:1-3-02.1 Medicare premium assistance programs (MPAP).

(A) This rule sets forth the eligibility criteria and benefits for the medicare premium assistance programs (MPAP). The programs are: qualified medicare beneficiary (QMB), specified low-income medicare beneficiary (SLMB), qualified individuals (QI-1), and qualified disabled and working individuals (QDWI).

(B) Definitions.

(1) "Eligible," for the purpose of this rule, means an individual meets all the requirements to enroll in MPAP.

(2) "Enrolled," for the purpose of this rule, means an individual is in receipt of benefits under a medicare health plan.

(3) "Entitled" for the purpose of this rule, means an individual has coverage under medicare through the social security administration (SSA).

(4) "Family," for the purposes of MPAP, means the following persons living in the same household as the individual for whom medicare premium assistance is sought or received:

(a) The individual; and

(b) If the individual is a minor, the biological parents, adoptive parents, step-parents, legal guardians, or legal custodians of the individual; and

(c) The spouse of the individual and of any persons described in paragraph (B)(4)(b) of this rule; and

(d) The minor biological, adopted, or stepchild(ren) of the individual and of any persons described in paragraphs (B)(4)(b) and (B)(4)(c) of this rule.

(5) "Family of the size involved" means "family" as defined in paragraph (B)(4) of this rule.

(6) "MPAP" means any or all of the medicare premium assistance programs: QMB, SLMB, QI-1, and QDWI.

(7) "MPAP resource limit" means the maximum amount of countable resources allowed under section 1905(p)(1) of the Social Security Act (as in effect October 1, 2019), as adjusted annually according to the change in the consumer price index for urban areas (CPI-U).

(8) "Qualified," for the purpose of this rule, means an individual is eligible to receive benefits under a medicare health plan, whether or not the individual has applied for those benefits.

(9) "QDWI" means the qualified disabled and working individuals program established by section 1905(s) of the Social Security Act (as in effect October 1, 2019). This program is sometimes referred to as the qualified working disabled individuals (QWDI) program.

(10) "QI-1" means the qualified individual group, described in section 1902(a)(10)(E)(iv) of the Social Security Act (as in effect October 1, 2019).

(11) "QMB" means the qualified medicare beneficiary group described in section 1905(p)(1) of the Social Security Act (as in effect October 1, 2019).

(12) "SLMB" means the specified low-income medicare beneficiary group described in section 1902(a)(10)(E)(iii) of the Social Security Act (as in effect October 1, 2019).

(C) The income standards for the medicare premium assistance programs (MPAP) are as follows:

(1) The QMB income standard is one hundred per cent of the federal poverty level for the family of the size involved.

(2) The SLMB income standard is greater than one hundred per cent of the federal poverty level and up to a maximum one hundred twenty per cent of the federal poverty level for the family of the size involved.

(3) The QI-1 income standard is greater than one hundred twenty per cent of the federal poverty level and up to a maximum one hundred thirty-five per cent of the federal poverty level for the family of the size involved.

(4) The QDWI income standard is two hundred per cent of the federal poverty level for the family of the size involved.

(D) To be eligible for a medicare premium assistance program, an individual must meet all of the following conditions:

(1) Be qualified for coverage under medicare part A (part A).

(a) An individual otherwise qualified for QMB must be enrolled in either part A or medicare part B (part B) for the administrative agency to provide benefits under this rule.

(b) An individual otherwise qualified for SLMB must be enrolled in part A for the administrative agency to provide benefits under this rule.

(c) An individual otherwise qualified for QI-1 must be enrolled in part A for the administrative agency to provide benefits under this rule.

(d) An individual otherwise qualified for QDWI must be enrolled in part A under section 1818A of the Social Security Act (as in effect October 1, 2019). Coverage can be identified as being provided under section 1818A of the Social Security Act when the individual meets the following criteria:

(i) Has not reached sixty-five years of age; and

(ii) Has lost disability benefits under Title II of the Social Security Act (as in effect October 1, 2019) solely due to earnings in excess of the substantial gainful activity (SGA) level established by the SSA; and

(iii) Is paying a premium for part A coverage; and

(iv) Has provided no document or communication from the SSA indicating another basis for part A coverage.

(2) For QMB, SLMB, and QI-1, have countable resources that do not exceed the MPAP resource limit as defined in paragraph (B)(7) of this rule, for an individual or the MPAP resource limit for a couple (the individual and the individual's spouse). Countable resources shall be determined in accordance with Chapter 5160:1-3 of the Administrative Code.

(3) For QDWI, have countable resources that do not exceed twice the maximum amount of resources that an individual or couple (the individual and the individual's spouse) may have under the supplemental security income (SSI) program. Countable resources shall be determined in accordance with Chapter 5160:1-3 of the Administrative Code.

(4) Have countable income, as determined in accordance with paragraph (E) of this rule, within the MPAP income standards as set forth in paragraph (C) of this rule.

(5) For QI-1 and QDWI, be otherwise ineligible for medical assistance in accordance with Chapters 5160:1-3, 5160:1-4, 5160:1-5, and 5160:1-6 of the Administrative Code.

(6) Meet the application, conditions of eligibility, and verification requirements set forth in Chapter 5160:1-2 of the Administrative Code.

(E) Countable income shall be determined in accordance with Chapter 5160:1-3 of the Administrative Code.

(1) The annual cost of living adjustment (COLA) shall be deducted from the individual's income beginning in January of each year and continuing through the end of the month after the month in which the updated federal poverty guidelines are published in the Federal Register.

(2) The income of both the individual and the individual's spouse shall be determined in accordance with rule 5160:1-3-03.1 of the Administrative Code and applying all exclusions listed in rule 5160:1-3-03.2 of the Administrative Code, except that the twenty-dollar general income exclusion and the exclusion of the first sixty-five dollars of earned income shall be applied only once to a married couple in the MPAP eligibility determination.

(3) The deeming provisions set forth in rule 5160:1-3-03.3 of the Administrative Code do not apply to MPAP eligibility determinations.

(F) Application of income standards.

(1) When the individual is a minor, the countable income of the following individuals is combined and compared to the income standards set forth in paragraph (C) of this rule for the family of the size involved:

(a) The individual; and

(b) The individual's biological parents, adoptive parents, stepparents, legal guardians, or legal custodians; and

(c) If married, the individual's spouse.

(2) The income of the individual combined with the income of the individual's spouse is compared to the income standards set forth in paragraph (C) of this rule for the family of the size involved.

(G) Application of resource standards.

(1) The countable resources of the individual combined with the countable resources of the individual's spouse are compared to the resource standards set forth in paragraphs (D)(2) and (D)(3) of this rule.

(2) The deeming provisions set forth in rule 5160:1-3-05.20 of the Administrative Code do not apply to MPAP eligibility determinations.

(H) Coordination of enrollment. When the individual is eligible for benefits under this rule, the county department of job and family services (CDJFS) shall coordinate the individual's receipt of benefits.

(1) When the individual is or has ever been in receipt of part A or part B benefits, the CDJFS shall approve MPAP benefits for the individual in the electronic eligibility system.

(2) When the individual has never received part A or part B benefits, the CDJFS shall:

(a) Inform the individual that the Ohio department of medicaid (ODM) can not pay medicare premiums until the individual has enrolled in part A or part B through the SSA; and

(b) Advise the individual to apply for part A or part B benefits through the SSA, and advise the individual that the CDJFS will assist upon request; and

(c) Advise the individual to report the approval of part A or part B benefits to the CDJFS immediately, so payment of premiums can be approved; and

(d) Approve MPAP benefits for the individual in the electronic eligibility system upon being informed that the individual has been enrolled in part A or part B by the SSA.

(I) Coverage periods.

(1) The effective date of QMB coverage is the first day of the month after the month in which the administrative agency approves QMB benefits. No retroactive coverage is available for QMB.

(2) Eligibility for SLMB benefits begins no earlier than the third month prior to the month of application, provided the individual met all eligibility criteria including enrollment in part A during the three-month period.

(3) Eligibility for QI-1 benefits begins no earlier than the third month prior to the month of application, provided the individual met all eligibility criteria including enrollment in part A during the three-month period.

(4) Eligibility for QDWI benefits begins no earlier than the third month prior to the month of application, provided the individual met all eligibility criteria including enrollment in part A during the three-month period.

(5) Eligibility for payment of medicare premiums under this rule ends on the earliest of the following dates:
(a) The last day of the month in which the individual dies; or
(b) The last day of the last month in which the individual is entitled to part B benefits; or
(c) The last day of the last month in which the individual meets the eligibility criteria for MPAP, if notice was provided to the centers for medicare and medicaid (CMS) no later than the twenty-fifth day of the second month of ineligibility; or
(d) The last day of the second month before CMS receives notice the individual was no longer eligible for MPAP, if notice was not provided within the time limit identified in paragraph (I)(5)(c) of this rule.
(J) Benefits.
(1) When the individual is eligible for QMB, the administrative agency shall pay the individual's:
(a) Premiums for part B and, when a premium is charged, for part A; and
(b) Medicare deductibles; and
(c) Medicare co-pays; and
(d) Medicare coinsurance costs.
(2) When the individual is eligible for SLMB or QI-1, the administrative agency shall pay the individual's part B premiums.
(3) When the individual is eligible for QDWI, the administrative agency shall pay the individual's part A premiums.
(4) The medicare prescription drug benefit program (part D) is not covered by MPAP.
(K) Administrative agency responsibilities. The administrative agency shall:
(1) Explore eligibility for medical assistance and for all MPAP categories when a medical assistance applicant is qualified for part A. The agency shall advise the individual:
(a) Of the categories of medical assistance or MPAP for which the individual is eligible, the individual's right to decline payment of premiums, co-pays, or coinsurance costs, and the effect of declining MPAP payments; and
(b) That when the individual is qualified for benefits under part A or part B, ODM is prohibited from paying for prescriptions on behalf of that individual, whether or not a premium would be charged for those benefits.
(2) Determine the individual's eligibility for QMB and when eligible:
(a) Approve QMB benefits effective the month after the administrative agency approves QMB coverage; and
(b) For individuals who are not receiving free part A, but who could receive part A benefits by paying a premium, coordinate enrollment in parts A and B with SSA.
(3) Determine the individual's eligibility for SLMB and, when eligible, approve SLMB benefits in accordance with paragraph (I)(2) of this rule.
(4) Determine the individual's eligibility for QI-1 and, when eligible, approve QI-1 benefits in accordance with paragraph (I)(3) of this rule.
(5) Determine the individual's eligiblity for QDWI and, when eligible, approve QDWI benefits in accordance with paragraph (I)(4) of this rule.
(6) Deny benefits under this rule when:
(a) Any criterion under this rule is not met; or
(b) Any of the conditions for denial set forth in rule 5160:1-2-01 of the Administrative Code are met.
(7) Discontinue benefits under this rule when the individual was eligible for benefits under QI-1 or QDWI but becomes eligible for another category of medical assistance.
(8) Coordinate enrollment with the individual, the SSA, and ODM's buy-in unit.
(L) Individual responsibilities.
(1) Inform the CDJFS of any actions by the SSA on the individual's application for part A or part B, or any changes in the individual's part A or part B coverage.
(2) Adhere to the individual responsibilities set forth in rule 5160:1-2-08 of the Administrative Code.

Effective: 12/14/2020.
Five Year Review (FYR) Dates: 9/29/2020 and 12/14/2025.
Promulgated Under: 111.15.
Statutory Authority: 5162.03, 5163.02.
Rule Amplifies: 5162.03, 5163.02 , 5163.45
Prior Effective Dates: 01/01/1989 (Emer.), 04/01/1989, 01/01/1990 (Emer.), 01/05/1990 (Emer.), 04/01/1990, 07/01/1990 (Emer.), 09/08/1990, 09/28/1990 (Emer.), 12/24/1990, 01/01/1991, 01/01/1992 (Emer.), 03/20/1992, 07/01/1992, 01/01/1993 (Emer.), 03/18/1993, 06/11/1993, 08/15/1993, 03/01/1994 (Emer.), 04/18/1994 (Emer.), 06/01/1998, 08/12/1998 (Emer.), 11/01/1998, 10/01/2002, 07/01/2005, 01/01/2010, 01/22/2015, 07/01/2016, 07/08/2020 (Emer.).

**5160:1-3-02.2 Medicare buy-in.**

(A) This rule sets forth:
(1) The eligibility criteria for benefits under the medicare part B buy-in agreement between the social security administration (SSA) and the Ohio department of medicaid (ODM), which allows ODM to pay medicare part B (supplemental medical insurance) premiums for certain medicaid-eligible individuals even if those individuals are not eligible for a medicare premium assistance program (MPAP) set out in rule 5160:1-3-02.1 of the Administrative Code; and
(2) The beginning date of payment of medicare part B (part B) benefits under this rule; and
(3) The date and effect of termination of benefits under medicare part B buy-in.
(4) The process of coordinating enrollment with ODM and the SSA.
(B) Definitions.
(1) "Medicare buy-in" means the program and process of paying part A or part B benefits on behalf of an eligible individual.
(2) "Part B buy-in" means the agreement under which ODM pays part B premiums on behalf of an eligible individual.
(C) Eligibility criteria. To be eligible for payment of the part B premium under the medicare buy-in agreement, an individual must meet all three of the following requirements:
(1) Be eligible for part B.
(2) Be eligible for a category of medicaid other than:
(a) Breast and cervical cancer project medicaid as set forth in rules 5160:1-5-02 to 5160:1-5-02.4 of the Adminstrative Code; or
(b) Presumptive medicaid as set forth in rule 5160:1-2-13 of the Administrative Code.
(3) Be receiving at least one of the following:
(a) Medicare premium assistance under rule 5160:1-3-02.1 of the Administrative Code.
(b) One of the following kinds of cash assistance:
(i) Ohio works first (OWF); or
(ii) Supplemental security income (SSI); or
(iii) Residential state supplement.
(c) Four-month extended coverage as set forth in rule 5160:1-4-05 of the Administrative Code.
(d) Grandfathered medicaid as set forth in rule 5160:1-3-02.6 of the Administrative Code.
(e) Foster care maintenance payments or adoption assistance payments as set forth in rule 5160:1-2-14 of the Administrative Code.
(f) Medicaid as a result of section 1619(b) of the Social Security Act (as in effect October 1, 2019) as set forth in rule 5160:1-3-02.8 of the Administrative Code.
(g) Deemed OWF as described in 42 C.F.R 435.115 (as in effect October 1, 2019).
(h) Long-term care services in a Title XIX certified nursing facility (NF) or intermediate care facility for individuals with intellectual disabilities (ICF-IID).
(i) Home and community-based (HCB) services, including the program of all inclusive care for the elderly (PACE), under a waiver described in agency 5160 of the Administrative Code.
(D) Coordination of enrollment. If an individual is eligible for benefits under this rule or would be eligible if the individual were enrolled in part A or part B, the county department of job and family services (CDJFS) shall coordinate the individual's receipt of benefits. If the individual:
(1) Is or has ever been in receipt of part A or part B benefits, the CDJFS shall approve part B buy-in benefits for the individual in the electronic eligibility system.
(2) Has never received part A or part B benefits, the CDJFS shall:

Admin Code

(a) Inform the individual that the Ohio department of medicaid (ODM) cannot pay medicare premiums until the individual has enrolled in part A or part B through the SSA; and

(b) Advise the individual to apply for part A or part B benefits, and advise the individual that the CDJFS will assist upon request; and

(c) Advise the individual to report the approval of part A or part B benefits to the CDJFS immediately, so payment of premiums can be approved; and

(d) Approve part B buy-in benefits for the individual in the electronic eligibility system upon being informed that the individual has been enrolled by the SSA in part A or part B.

(E) Coverage period.

(1) Start date.

(a) For MPAP benefits under rule 5160:1-3-02.1 of the Administrative Code, the beginning date for payment of premiums is addressed in those rules. If an individual is eligible for MPAP benefits under rule 5160:1-3-02.1 of the Administrative Code and also eligible for part B buy-in under this rule, payment of part B premiums begins on the earlier of the coverage date under rule 5160:1-3-02.1 of the Administrative Code or the coverage date under this rule.

(b) For individuals eligible for payment of premiums under the part B buy-in agreement, eligibility begins:

(i) The first month an individual is eligible for both medicare and cash assistance as defined in paragraph (C)(3)(b) of this rule; or

(ii) The first day of the second month after the administrative agency made the determination the individual was eligible for medicaid, if the individual is not in receipt of cash assistance as defined in paragraph (C)(3)(b) of this rule.

(2) Termination date. Eligibility for payment of medicare premiums under this rule ends on the last day of the month in which the individual dies.

Effective: 12/14/2020.
Five Year Review (FYR) Dates: 9/29/2020 and 12/14/2025.
Promulgated Under: 111.15.
Statutory Authority: 5160.02, 5163.02.
Rule Amplifies: 5160.02, 5163.02
Prior Effective Dates: 08/15/1982, 10/01/2002, 01/01/2010, 01/22/2015, 07/01/2016, 07/08/2020 (Emer.).

### 5160:1-3-02.3 Medicaid: coverage for individuals receiving supplemental security income (SSI) benefits.

(A) This rule describes eligibility for medical assistance for aged, blind or disabled individuals who receive SSI benefits authorized by the social security administration under Title XVI of the Social Security Act (as in effect on October 1, 2017). Eligibility for this category shall be determined for applications for medical assistance filed on or after August 1, 2016.

(B) Eligibility criteria. To be eligible for coverage under this group an individual must be receiving SSI benefits based on the social security administration's determination of eligibility for SSI payments. In addition, certain requirements specific to medical assistance must be met in order for an individual to be eligible under this group. Failure to comply with the following requirements will prevent an individual from being determined eligible under this provision:

(1) Consistent with rule 5160:1-2-10 of the Administrative Code:

(a) An individual must assign to the state of Ohio any rights to medical support and payments for medical care from any third party; and

(b) An individual must cooperate with the child support enforcement agency (CSEA) in establishing the paternity of any child eligible for medical assistance and in obtaining medical support and payments for medical care from any third party, in accordance with 42 C.F.R. 433.147 (as in effect on October 1, 2017); and

(c) An individual must cooperate with the administrative agency in identifying and providing information to assist the state with pursuing any third party who may be liable to pay for care and services; and

(2) An individual who is the beneficiary of a trust must provide documentation of the trust as required by rule 5160:1-3-05.2 of the Administrative Code.

(C) Retroactive coverage is available for this program in accordance with rule 5160:1-2-01 of the Administrative Code, but coverage under this rule shall not begin prior to August 1, 2016, and shall not provide reimbursement of services rendered prior to August 1, 2016.

Replaces: 5160:1-3-02.3.
Effective: 4/1/2018.
Five Year Review (FYR) Dates: 04/01/2023.
Promulgated Under: 111.15.
Statutory Authority: 5160.02, 5163.02.
Rule Amplifies: 5160.02, 5163.02
Prior Effective Dates: 08/01/2016.

### 5160:1-3-02.4 Medicaid: coverage for the categorically needy.

(A) This rule describes eligibility for aged, blind or disabled individuals who meet the income and resource requirements of the supplemental security income (SSI) program authorized by the social security administration (SSA) under Title XVI of the Social Security Act (as in effect on February 1, 2016) but do not receive cash benefits under the program. Eligibility for this program shall be determined for applications for medical assistance filed on or after the effective date of this rule.

(B) Eligibility criteria. To be eligible under this group, an individual must meet all of the following critiera:

(1) Be aged, blind or disabled;

(2) Determinations of blindness and disability must be in accordance with SSA policy;

(3) Have countable income, as determined under Chapter 5160:1-3 of the Administrative Code, which does not exceed the income standard described in rule 5160:1-3-03.5 of the Administrative Code;

(4) Have countable resources, as determined under Chapter 5160:1-3 of the Administrative Code, which do not exceed the resource limit described in rule 5160:1-3-05.1 of the Administrative Code;

(5) Not be receiving cash benefits from the SSI program; and

(6) Meet the conditions of eligibility outlined in rule 5160:1-2-10 of the Administrative Code.

(C) Retroactive coverage is available for this program in accordance with rule 5160:1-2-01 of the Administrative Code, but coverage shall not begin prior to the effective date of this rule and shall not provide reimbursement of services rendered prior to the effective date of this rule.

Effective: 08/01/2016.
Five Year Review (FYR) Dates: 08/01/2021.
Promulgated Under: 111.15.
Statutory Authority: 5160.02, 5163.02
Rule Amplifies: 5160.02, 5163.02.

### 5160:1-3-02.5 Medicaid: supplemental security income (SSI) recipients qualifying under section 1619 of the Social Security Act for continued medical assistance coverage.

(A) This rule describes the eligibility criteria for an individual receving SSI benefits under section 1619 of the Social Security Act for continued medical assistance coverage.

(B) Section 1619 of the Social Security Act (as in effect January 10, 2016) comprises two basic provisions:

(1) Section 1619(a) extends special SSI cash to individuals whose earnings preclude eligibility for regular SSI cash benefits. Individuals in 1619(a) status may still receive an SSI cash benefit in addition to the individual's earned income.

(2) Section 1619(b) extends medicaid coverage to individuals whose earnings, although high enough to preclude eligibility for regular SSI cash benefits or special SSI cash benefits under section 1619(a), may not be enough for medical care.

(C) To determine initial medicaid eligibility for sections 1619(a) and 1619(b), the administrative agency shall verify that the individual is currently in 1619(a) or 1619(b) status, as determined by the social security administration.

(D) Protection of benefits under 1619 status.

(1) An individual who has been determined eligible for medicaid because of 1619 status is protected from losing medicaid

benefits under this provision as long as the individual remains in 1619(a) or (b) status.

(2) The individual may have income or resources in excess of the medicaid requirements and remain eligible for regular medicaid under the 1619 provisions.

(3) If the individual's 1619 status ends, the individual's medicaid protection is lost.

Replaces: 5160:1-3-02.4.
Effective: 08/01/2016.
Five Year Review (FYR) Dates: 08/01/2021.
Promulgated Under: 111.15.
Statutory Authority: 5160.02, 5163.02.
Rule Amplifies: 5160.02, 5163.02
Prior Effective Dates: 7/1/87 (Emer.), 8/3/87, 1/1/88, 4/1/89 (Emer.), 6/18/89, 9/1/93, 10/1/02, 1/22/15.

**5160:1-3-02.6 Medicaid: grandfathering provisions and deemed eligibility.**

(A) Various grandfathering provisions and deemed eligibility requirements were enacted to assure that aged, blind, or disabled individuals previously eligible for cash assistance and medicaid under former programs of aid would not be disadvantaged by eligibility conditions when the supplemental security income (SSI) program was implemented.

(B) Definitions.

(1) "Cash assistance," for the purpose of this rule, means the receipt of at least one of the following: Ohio works first (OWF), SSI or residential state supplement (RSS), or the former programs of aid known as aid for dependent children (ADC), aid for the aged (AFA), aid for the blind (AFB), and aid for the disabled (AFD).

(2) "Essential spouse" for the purpose of this rule means one who is living with the individual whose needs were included in determining the amount of cash assistance and who is determined essential to the individual's well-being.

(C) Under the grandfathering provisions, certain individuals who were eligible for medicaid in December 1973 are entitled to continued medicaid eligibility coverage even though they may not meet the medicaid eligibility requirements imposed beginning in January 1974 for the coverage of the aged, blind, and disabled.

(1) The grandfathered groups are the following:

(a) Individuals receiving mandatory state supplements as described in 42 C.F.R. 435.130 (as in effect October 1, 2019): an individual who is the recipient of mandatory state supplement payments (SSP) administered by the social security administration is automatically eligible for medicaid.

(b) Individuals who are essential spouses as described in 42 C.F.R. 435.131 as in effect October 1, 2019): any individual who was eligible in December 1973 as an essential spouse remains eligible under the following criteria:

(i) The aged, blind or disabled spouse continues to meet the December 1973 eligibility requirements of the applicable cash assistance programs; and

(ii) The essential spouse continues to be the spouse of and lives with the spouse described in paragraph (C)(1)(b)(i) of this rule; and

(iii) The essential spouse continues to meet the conditions that were in effect in December 1973 under the applicable cash assistance program for having his or her needs included in computing the payment to the individual described in paragraph (C)(1)(b)(i) of this rule.

(c) Blind or disabled individuals eligible in 1973 as described in 42 C.F.R. 435.133 (as in effect October 1, 2019): an individual who was eligible for medicaid in December 1973 because the individual met the definition of blindness or disability in effect under the former programs of AFB or AFD and meets the following criteria:

(i) The individual meets all current requirements for medicaid eligibility except for blindness or disability; and

(ii) The individual was eligible for medicaid in December 1973 as blind or disabled, whether or not the individual received cash assistance in December 1973; and

(iii) For each consecutive month after December 1973, the individual has continued to meet the December 1973 criteria for blindness or disability; and

(iv) For each consecutive month after December 1973, the individual has continued to meet all other eligibility requirements which were in effect December 1973.

(d) Individuals who lost eligibility for SSI due to an increase in retirement, survivors and disability insurance (RSDI) as described in 42 C.F.R. 435.134 (as in effect October 1, 2019): individuals eligible despite the October 1972 twenty per cent general increase:

(i) An individual who would currently be eligible for SSI or cash assistance except for the amount of increased income resulting from the October 1972 twenty per cent general increase in RSDI is eligible for medicaid if, for the month of August 1972, the individual met the following criteria:

(*a*) The individual was eligible for and receiving cash assistance under the ADC, AFA, AFB, or AFD programs, and

(*b*) The individual received and was entitled to monthly RSDI benefits.

(ii) Only the October 1972 RSDI increase is disregarded. Any subsequent increases in RSDI are not disregarded.

(iii) Although the amount of the October 1972 RSDI increase is disregarded in determining financial eligibility, the individual must meet all of the current eligibility requirements for medicaid.

(e) Institutionalized individuals continuously eligible since 1973 as described in 42 C.F.R. 435.132 (as in effect October 1, 2019): an individual who was eligible for medicaid in December 1973 as an inpatient or resident of a Title XIX institution and for each consecutive month after December 1973 meets the following criteria:

(i) Continues to meet the requirements for medicaid eligibility that were in effect in December 1973 for institutionalized individuals; and

(ii) Remains institutionalized; and

(iii) Is determined to continue to need institutional care.

(f) Individuals who would be eligible for SSI but not for RSDI COLA increases since April 1977 (Pickle Amendment Group) as described in 42 C.F.R. 435.135 (as in effect October 1, 2019): an individual receiving RSDI and meets the following criteria:

(i) Became ineligible for SSI after April 1977; and

(ii) Would continue to be eligible for SSI if all of the RSDI cost-of-living increases received by the individual, the individual's spouse or other family member after April 1977 were deducted from current RSDI benefits.

(g) Ineligible for SSI due to requirements prohibited by Medicaid as described in 42 C.F.R. 435.122 (as in effect October 1, 2019): individuals who would be eligible for SSI or residential state supplements except for an eligibility requirement used in those programs that is specifically prohibited under medicaid.

(2) Failure to meet any one of the conditions listed in paragraph (C)(1) of this rule renders the individual ineligible for grandfathered status under the blind or disabled grandfathering provisions.

(3) An individual described in paragraph (C)(1)(c) of this rule permanently loses grandfathered status when the individual fails to meet any December 1973 eligibility requirement for any one month.

(4) Any change in circumstances requires a redetermination of eligibility based upon all the conditions set forth in paragraph (C)(1) of this rule.

(5) Eligibility under a grandfathered group does not apply to individuals in a long-term care facility or enrolled in a home and community-based services waiver.

(D) Under deemed eligibility, certain individuals who were ineligible for SSI, due to receipt of social security benefits, are entitled to continued medicaid coverage for the aged, blind and disabled if certain criteria are met.

(1) The deemed eligibility groups are the following:

(a) Disabled widows(ers) ineligible for SSI or RSS due to increase in RSDI as described in 42 C.F.R. 435.137 (as in effect October 1, 2019): disabled widows(ers) who became ineligible for SSI or RSS benefits as a result of the elimination of the additional reduction factor for disabled widows(ers) under age sixty and meet all of the following criteria:

(i) Entitled to a monthly RSDI benefit for December 1983, and

(ii) Entitled to and received a social security widow(er)'s disability benefit in January 1984, and

(iii) Became ineligible for SSI benefits in the first month in which the increase in social security disabled widows(ers) benefits, as a result of the elimination of the additional reduction factor, was received, and

(iv) Continuously entitled to widow(er)'s disability benefits from the first month that the increase was received, and

(v) Would be eligible for SSI or RSS if the increase in RSDI benefits due to the elimination of the reduction factor and subsequent cost-of-living adjustments in RSDI benefits were excluded, and

(vi) Filed a medicaid application or renewal on or before June 30, 1988 for deemed eligibility.

(b) Disabled adult children as described in section 1634 of the Social Security Act (as in effect October 1, 2019): disabled individuals who have attained the age of eighteen and received SSI benefits on the basis of blindness or disability which began before he or she attained the age of twenty-two and meet all of the following criteria:

(i) Entitled to social security child's insurance benefits on the basis of disability or an increase in the amount of the child's insurance benefits which are payable, and

(ii) Became ineligible for SSI benefits solely because of their receipt of social security child's insurance benefits or increase in social security child's insurance benefits, and

(iii) Would be eligible for SSI if the social security child's insurance benefits were excluded.

(c) Disabled widows(ers) ineligible for SSI due to early receipt of social security as described in 42 C.F.R. 435.138 (as in effect October 1, 2019): disabled widows(ers) at least age sixty who became ineligible for SSI as a result of the receipt of widows(ers) social security disability benefits and meet all of the following criteria:

(i) Receives widows(ers) social security disability benefits, and

(ii) Became ineligible for SSI benefits solely because of the receipt of widows(ers) social security disability benefits, and

(iii) Received a SSI benefit in the month before the month of receipt of widows(ers) social security disability benefits, and

(iv) Not entitled to medicare part A.

(v) Although the amount of the widows(ers) social security disability benefits is excluded in determining financial eligibility, the individual must meet all of the current eligibility requirements for medical assistance.

(2) Any changes in circumstances requires a redetermination of eligibility based upon all conditions set forth in paragraph (D)(1) of this rule.

(3) Eligibility under a deemed group does not apply to individuals in a long-term care facility or enrolled in a home and community-based services waiver.

Effective: 12/14/2020.
Five Year Review (FYR) Dates: 9/29/2020 and 12/14/2025.
Promulgated Under: 111.15.
Statutory Authority: 5160.02, 5163.02.
Rule Amplifies: 5160.02, 5163.02
Prior Effective Dates: 09/03/1977, 10/26/1978, 05/01/1979, 09/21/1979, 02/21/1980, 04/17/1989 (Emer.), 06/30/1989, 08/01/1990 (Emer.), 10/25/1990, 10/24/1991 (Emer.), 01/20/1992, 07/01/1994, 10/15/1998, 10/01/2002, 01/22/2015, 08/01/2016, 07/08/2020 (Emer.).

### 5160:1-3-02.7 Medicaid: continuing care communities, life care communities and philanthropic long-term care facilities. [RESCINDED]

Effective: 12/12/2016.
Five Year Review (FYR) Dates: 09/15/2016.
Promulgated Under: 111.15.
Statutory Authority: 5160.02, 5163.02.
Rule Amplifies: 5160.02, 5163.02
Prior Effective Dates: 9/3/77, 10/26/78, 5/1/79, 9/21/79, 2/21/80, 6/18/89, 10/1/02, 10/1/06, 1/1/16.

### 5160:1-3-02.8 Medicaid: treatment of qualified long-term care insurance policies. [RESCINDED]

Replaces: 5160:1-2-11.
Rescinded effective: 11/1/2017.
Five Year Review (FYR) Dates: 8/15/2017.
Promulgated Under: 119.03.
Statutory Authority: 5162.21, 5163.02, 5164.86.
Rule Amplifies: 5162.21, 5164.86
Prior Effective Dates: 9/1/2007, 12/1/2014.

### 5160:1-3-02.9 Medicaid: disability determination process.

(A) This rule addresses the process of determining blindness or disability for medical assistance eligibility purposes.

(B) Definitions.

(1) "Administrative agency," for the purpose of this rule, means the county department of job and family services (CDJFS).

(2) "Current medical information" means medical records that originated within eighteen months of the date of initial application.

(3) "Deferred" means the delay in the determination for a disability packet due to incomplete or a insufficient amount of current medical information for the disability determination area (DDA) to approve, deny or continue the blindness or disability claim.

(4) "Disability begin date" means the date the individual is otherwise eligible for medical assistance and meets the limiting physical factor.

(5) "Disability determination" is the process by which the DDA determines whether the individual meets the social security administration's definition of "blind" or "disabled" for medical assistance eligibility. The DDA determines blindness and disability in accordance with SSA policy.

(6) "Disability packet" consists of all required forms specified in paragraph (C) of this rule and all available current medical information to support the individual's blindness or disability claim. The disability packet is submitted by the administrative agency to the DDA for a disability determination.

(7) "Disability review date" means the date, determined by the DDA, that the individual's current blindness or disability approval will expire.

(8) "Limiting physical factor" is a non-financial eligibility criterion consisting of a physical or mental characteristic or impairment, or a combination of physical or mental characteristics or impairments, that may limit the individual's ability to work. An individual meets the limiting physical factor by meeting the criteria of age, blindness or disability as set forth in rule 5160:1-3-02 of the Administrative Code.

(9) "SSA disability" means a determination of blindness or disability, as set forth in section 1902 of the Social Security Act (as in effect on October 1, 2017), by the social security administration (SSA).

(C) Administrative agency responsibilities. The administrative agency shall:

(1) Determine eligibility for medical assistance in accordance with the eligibility rules contained in Chapters 5160:1-1 to 5160:1-6 of the Administrative Code.

(2) Determine the limiting physical factor is met and shall not submit a disability packet to the DDA when the individual:

(a) Is sixty-five years of age or older; or

(b) Has been approved for SSA disability for the individual's own blindness or disability.

(3) Determine the limiting physical factor is not met and shall submit a disability packet to the DDA for a disability determination when the individual is potentially eligible for one of the following:

(a) Alien emergency medical assistance (AEMA) in accordance with rule 5160:1-5-06 of the Administrative Code; or

(b) Medicaid buy-in for workers with disabilities (MBIWD) in accordance with rule 5160:1-5-03 of the Administrative Code when an individual has not yet been determined disabled by the SSA; or

(c) Medical assistance for an individual who has died and retroactive eligibility is requested in accordance with rule 5160:1-2-01 of the Administrative Code; or

(d) An individual has an initial application for SSA disability pending with the SSA for ninety days or more.

(4) Presume the limiting physical factor is met and shall not submit a disability packet to the DDA for a disability determination when the individual is determined to have a presumptive disability by the SSA and has an application for SSA disability pending.

(5) Upon request, assist the individual with obtaining medical documentation to support the blindness or disability claim, including, if necessary, using administrative funds to assist the individual with receiving a medical, psychological or eye examination to determine whether the individual is blind or disabled.

(6) Obtain and/or assist the individual in obtaining all available current medical information that pertains to the individual's alleged impairment(s) or combination of impairments, as well as any other information requested by the DDA, and submit it in the disability packet. This includes existing medical information, tests, services or records from other entities such as the SSA, opportunities for Ohioans with disabilities, workers' compensation, etc.

(7) Provide the forms listed in this paragraph to the individual, the individual's legal representative, another person applying on behalf of the individual, or the treating physician(s).

(a) ODM 07302 "Basic Medical" (rev. 5/2018); and

(b) ODM 07308 "Mental Functional Capacity Assessment" (rev. 5/2018) when the individual has or appears to have a mental impairment; and

(c) JFS 03606 "Medication Dependencies" (rev. 5/2006) when applicable.

(8) Complete the ODM 07004 "Social Summary Report for Disability Determination" (rev. 5/2018).

(9) Obtain signed copies of form ODM 03397 "Authorization for the Release or Use of Protected Health Information (PHI)" (rev. 2/2016) from the individual for all providers who have or may have current medical information.

(10) Complete the JFS 03605 "CDJFS Referral to DDU" (rev. 6/2006) using current medical information.

(11) Submit the disability packet to the DDA for a blindness or disability determination.

(12) When the DDA has deferred a disability determination, and the administrative agency is unable to obtain all of the requested additional medical information, resubmit the initial disability packet and any additional information to the DDA for a final decision.

(D) Individual responsibilities.

(1) When the individual alleges a blindness or disability, the individual shall assist the administrative agency with obtaining all available current medical information that supports the blindness or disability claim.

(2) As a condition of eligibility for medical assistance, the individual is required to apply for any disability benefits to which the individual may be entitled in accordance with rule 5160:1-2-10 of the Administrative Code.

(E) Disability determination area (DDA) responsibilities.

(1) The DDA shall approve, deny or defer disability determinations, and shall notify the administrative agency via the electronic eligibility system.

(2) The DDA shall determine the disability begin date and end date, as appropriate, for approved blindness or disability claims, and shall inform the administrative agency via the electronic eligibility system.

(3) In accordance with paragraph (C)(12) of this rule, when the initial disability packet is resubmitted to the DDA because the administrative agency was unable to obtain the requested additional medical information, the DDA shall make a final decision on the case based upon the information available in the initial disability packet, and shall notify the administrative agency of the decision via the electronic eligibility system.

(F) Eligibility for medical assistance during initial disability determination.

(1) If the individual meets all other medical assistance eligibility criteria and also meets the limiting physical factor in accordance with paragraph (C)(2) of this rule, the administrative agency shall approve eligibility for medical assistance, and shall not submit a disability packet to the DDA.

(2) If the individual meets all other medical assistance eligibility criteria, but has not yet been determined to meet the limiting physical factor, the administrative agency shall not approve eligibility for medical assistance and shall submit a disability packet to the DDA for a disability determination in accordance with paragraph (C)(3) of this rule.

(3) When the individual's SSA disability application is pending for ninety days or more, the administrative agency shall submit a disability packet to the DDA for a disability determination.

(a) If the DDA approves the blindness or disability, the limiting physical factor is met, and the individual meets all other medical assistance eligibility criteria, the administrative agency shall approve eligibility for medical assistance until the date the SSA makes a decision on the SSA application.

(b) If the DDA denies the blindness or disability, the limiting physical factor is not met and the administrative agency shall deny eligibility for medical assistance until the SSA makes a decision on the SSA application.

(i) If the SSA approves SSA disability, the limiting physical factor is met and the administrative agency shall determine eligibility for medical assistance based upon the initial application for medical assistance and continue eligibility for medical assistance until a renewal is required.

(ii) If the SSA denies SSA disability, the limiting physical factor is not met and the administrative agency shall deny eligibility for medical assistance programs where blindness or disability is an eligibility requirement.

(G) Renewal for medical assistance. When an individual is terminated from medical assistance and reapplies:

(1) Within twelve months after the disability begin date, the individual meets the limiting physical factor for the remainder of the twelve months. The administrative agency shall not submit a new disability packet to the DDA. The administrative agency shall apply the existing disability review date.

(2) Beyond twelve months of the disability begin date, the limiting physical factor is not met. The administrative agency shall submit a new disability packet to the DDA for a new disability determination, in accordance with paragraphs (C) to (F) of this rule.

(H) Eligibility for medical assistance when SSA denials are appealed.

(1) When the SSA makes a decision denying SSA disability, the individual has a right to appeal the SSA decision.

(2) An individual shall not be eligible for medical assistance programs, where blindness or disability is an eligibility requirement, during the SSA appeals process.

Effective: 7/1/2018.
Five Year Review (FYR) Dates: 8/1/2021.
Promulgated Under: 111.15.
Statutory Authority: 5163.02, 5160.02.
Rule Amplifies: 5160.02, 5163.02
Prior Effective Dates: 9/3/77, 1/1/81, 9/6/84, 8/1/85, 7/1/87 (Emer.), 8/3/87, 1/1/88 (Emer.), 3/28/88, 10/1/88 (Emer.), 12/20/88, 4/1/90, 10/1/91 (Emer.), 12/1/91, 12/2/91, 12/20/91, 1/1/92 (Emer.), 3/20/92, 12/22/92 (Emer.), 1/1/93 (Emer.), 2/11/93, 3/20/93, 9/1/93, 8/1/95 (Emer.), 10/30/95, 4/1/99, 10/1/02, 11/25/02, 1/1/05, 2/23/15, 8/1/16.

### 5160:1-3-03. Medicaid: limiting physical factor. [RESCINDED]

Rescinded effective: 01/22/2015.
Five Year Review (FYR) Dates: 10/14/2014.
Promulgated Under: 111.15.
Statutory Authority: 5111.01, 5111.011.
Rule Amplifies: 5111.01, 5111.011, 5111.012
Prior Effective Dates: 9/3/77, 1/1/81, 9/6/84, 8/1/85, 7/1/87 (Emer.), 8/3/87, 1/1/88 (Emer.), 3/28/88, 10/1/88 (Emer.), 12/20/88, 4/1/90, 10/1/91 (Emer.), 12/1/91, 12/2/91, 12/20/91, 1/1/92 (Emer.), 3/20/92, 12/22/92 (Emer.), 1/1/93(Emer.), 2/11/93, 3/20/93, 9/1/93, 8/1/95 (Emer.), 10/30/95, 4/1/99, 10/1/02, 11/25/02, 1/1/05.

### 5160:1-3-03.1 Medicaid: income.

(A) This rule describes how income, as defined in rule 5160:1-1-01 of the Administrative Code, is treated for the purpose of determining eligibility for medical assistance for aged, blind, or disabled individuals.

(B) Treatment of income.

(1) Eligibility for medical assistance is dependent in part upon the amount of monthly income available to or received by the individual.

(a) Gross income, prior to any deductions or exclusions, that can be reliably anticipated is considered available in calculating countable income for a month. Thus, when an individual is receiving a pension or is regularly employed or self-employed, the expected amount of income is counted.

(i) Wages are counted as earned income in the calendar month in which they are paid even if all of the work which produced the wages is performed in a prior month.

(ii) When the time of receipt of the income is at the employee's discretion, the employee shall avail himself/herself of such wages.

(iii) When the payment of wages is deferred at the employee's request, the administrative agency shall determine when the wages would normally have been paid and allocate them as income for the month in which the wages would have normally been paid. The administrative agency shall assume the wages were payable in equal segments throughout the applicable period and determine eligibility accordingly. When the payment of wages is deferred due to circumstances beyond the control of the employee, the administrative agency shall consider the wages as income when the income is actually received.

(b) Receipt of cash, income in-kind, or something of value in a particular month is considered income to the individual for that month. Any portion of the income which is retained by an individual into the next month becomes a resource.

(2) All income, except income excluded in rule 5160:1-3-03.2 of the Administrative Code, shall be considered in determining the amount of income that is available to an individual.

(3) When an eligible individual resides with an ineligible spouse or parent(s), a portion of the ineligible spouse's or parent's income shall be deemed as available income to the eligible individual. This deeming of income is subject to conditions and limitations as described in rule 5160:1-3-03.3 of the Administrative Code.

(4) Net-earnings from self-employment are the gross income from any trade or business minus allowable deductions for that trade or business.

(a) When the individual has filed taxes for the previous year, use all tax forms that were filed with the internal revenue service (IRS).

(b) When the individual has not filed taxes for the previous year, the following may be used:

(i) Business records including receipts for the costs of doing business, or

(ii) Estimated net income.

(5) The monthly income allowance (MIA) from an institutionalized individual to a community spouse as described in rules 5160:1-6-07 and 5160:1-6-07.1 of the Administrative Code, shall be treated as unearned income to the community spouse in the determination of the community spouse's eligibility for medical assistance.

(C) Under certain circumstances, the amount of income determined available to an individual may be greater than the amount of income that the individual actually receives for his or her own use. The following types of income deductions are not subtracted from the individual's countable income for purposes of determining eligibility for medical assistance. This list is not all-inclusive.

(1) Court-ordered income deductions.

(a) This includes child and/or spousal support, even if such support is paid directly to the former spouse or child's guardian by the employer or benefit payer.

(b) A division of marital property in a divorce settlement, which may include a retirement pension, is not considered a court ordered income deduction.

(2) Deductions due to a repayment of an overpayment, loan, or other debt, unless the amount being withheld to reduce a previous overpayment was included when determining the amount of unearned income for a previous month in the determination of medical assistance eligibility.

(3) Garnishments and liens placed against earned or unearned income of the individual, regardless of the purpose for the garnishment or lien.

(D) Potential income must be explored prior to approving medical assistance. An individual who does not avail himself/herself of potential income is presumed to fail to do so in order to make himself/herself eligible for medical assistance. Such non-utilization of income constitutes ineligibility unless good cause can be shown. Such income includes but is not limited to:

(1) Retirement, survivors, disability insurance (RSDI);

(2) Prouty benefits;

(3) Railroad retirement;

(4) Veterans benefits;

(5) Other public/private retirement benefits;

(E) The following items are not considered income, in accordance with 20 C.F.R. 416.1103 (as in effect October 1, 2019). This list is not all inclusive:

(1) A personal service performed for an individual is not income to the individual where the service is not convertible to cash.

(2) Payments made on behalf of an individual under credit life or credit disability policies directly to loan companies, mortgage companies, etc.

(3) Money an individual borrows or money received as the repayment of the principal of a bona fide loan. Any interest received on the money loaned is unearned income. If the proceeds of the loan are retained in the month following the month of receipt, they are counted as a resource.

(4) A bill paid directly to a creditor or vendor by a third party on behalf of the individual, unless payment is for food or shelter to include:

(a) A premium payment for supplementary medical insurance.

(b) Medical insurance premiums.

(5) An arrearage of child support which is payable to an individual on behalf of an adult child unless the individual retains the income and does not give it to the adult child.

(6) Receipts from the sale, exchange or replacement of a resource are not income but remain resources.

(7) A rebate, refund, or other return of money an individual has already paid. The money returned is not income.

(8) Any amount refunded on income taxes already paid.

(9) The replacement of an individual's income that was lost, stolen, or destroyed and was previously used in determining eligibility.

(10) A return of erroneously received payments.

(11) Cash or in-kind assistance from a governmental or non-governmental program for medical or social services that are not food or shelter.

(F) Verification of income.

(1) The individual's statements of source and amount of income are subject to verification. At the time of application/renewal, the individual and household member(s) whose income affects the individual, shall be verified electronically or documents shall be required to be submitted which verifies all sources of income. When necessary, the administrative agency shall obtain a signed release of information and contact other sources to verify income.

(a) When the administrative agency is unable to verify the income through electronic sources, the administrative agency will contact the individual to collect the information needed. If the individual declares the verifications cannot be accessed or submitted, the individual's statement is to be accepted.

(b) If the administrative agency is unable to make contact with the individual, a written (electronic or paper) request for the necessary information or verification documents is to be sent as set forth in rule 5160:1-2-01 of the Administrative Code.

(2) An individual's report of income is subject to verification when a review is conducted by the ODM quality assurance review section.

(3) The individual has the burden of verifying the sources and amounts of income, and has the responsibility of reporting income changes to the administrative agency in accordance with rule 5160:1-2-08 of the Administrative Code.

(4) When an individual claims to have no income at the time of application/ renewal, the administrative agency shall review the application/renewal for inconsistencies requiring resolution. It is the individual's responsibility to support the claim of no income. However, when verification is not available and the individual has cooperated in trying to obtain it, the administrative agency may process the case based on the individual's statement as long as there is no evidence to cast doubt on the income allegations. Reference rule 5160:1-2-10 of the Administrative Code for additional information on acceptable verification.

(5) When income in-kind is received, the administrative agency shall determine whether in-kind support and maintenance is being received in accordance with rule 5160:1-3-03.8 of the Administrative Code.

Effective: 12/14/2020.
Five Year Review (FYR) Dates: 1/1/2023.
Promulgated Under: 111.15.

Statutory Authority: 5160.02, 5163.02.
Rule Amplifies: 5160.02, 5163.02
Prior Effective Dates: 09/03/1977, 12/31/1977, 03/01/1979, 10/01/1979, 12/07/1979, 01/03/1980, 12/01/1984 (Emer.), 02/10/1985, 08/01/1985, 10/01/1988 (Emer.), 12/20/1988, 09/01/1992, 10/01/2002, 07/01/2005, 10/01/2006, 01/25/2015, 08/01/2016, 01/01/2018, 07/08/2020 (Emer.).

**5160:1-3-03.2. Medicaid: income exclusions.**

(A) When determining eligibility for medical assistance for the aged, blind, or disabled, certain types of income, including income from certain sources, are not counted. This rule sets forth the types of income that are to be excluded, and the order in which they are excluded from the individual's income.

(B) Definitions.

(1) "Blind work expense" (BWE) means the portion of the individual's earned income used to meet any expenses reasonably attributable to the earning of the income if the individual is blind; and

(a) Is under age sixty-five; or

(b) Is age sixty-five or older and received SSI payments due to blindness for the month before attaining age sixty-five.

(2) "Countable income" means the total earned and unearned income minus the income exclusions set forth in this rule. Countable income is compared to the appropriate income standard when determining eligibility for medical assistance.

(3) "Exclusion" means an amount of income which does not count when determining eligibility for medical assistance.

(C) Order of exclusions. Unearned income exclusions are applied before earned income exclusions. The specific order of exclusions are described in paragraphs (D) to (F) of this rule.

(D) Unearned income exclusions.

(1) Unearned income excluded by federal laws other than the Social Security Act, in accordance with 20 C.F.R 416 subpart K appendix (as in effect October 1, 2020) unless otherwise noted. The exclusions listed in this paragraph are applied before the exclusions listed in paragraph (D)(2) of this rule:

(a) Agent orange settlement fund payments received on or after January 1, 1989, as a result of the Agent Orange Compensation Exclusion Act (Pub. L. No. 101-201).

(b) Child care assistance under the Child Care and Development Block Grant Act (Pub. L. No. 113-186).

(c) The first two thousand dollars per calendar year received as compensation for participation in clinical trials that meet the criteria detailed in section 1612(b) of the Social Security Act (as in effect October 1, 2020).

(d) Payments made for supporting services or reimbursement of out-of-pocket expenses to volunteers participating in corporation for national and community service (CNCS, formerly ACTION) programs in accordance with 42 U.S.C. 1382a (as in effect October 1, 2020):

(i) AmeriCorps VISTA program; and

(ii) Special and demonstration volunteer program; and

(iii) Retired senior volunteer program (RSVP); and

(iv) Foster grandparents program; and

(v) Senior companion program.

(e) Payments made to individuals under the Energy Employees Occupational Illness Compensation Program Act of 2000 (Pub. L. No. 106-398).

(f) Federal food and nutrition programs:

(i) Supplemental nutrition assistance program (SNAP), formerly known as food stamps or food assistance; and

(ii) The value of foods donated by the U.S. department of agriculture commodity supplemental food program; and

(iii) The value of supplemental food assistance received under the Child Nutrition Act of 1966 (Pub. L. No. 89-642) and the special food service program for children under the National School Lunch Act (Pub. L. No. 90-302); and

(iv) The special supplemental nutrition program for women, infants, and children (WIC); and

(v) Nutrition program benefits provided for the elderly under Title VII of the Older Americans Act of 1965 (Pub. L. No. 89-73).

(g) Student financial assistance received under the Higher Education Act of 1965 (as in effect October 1, 2020) or bureau of Indian affairs is excluded from income and resources, regardless of use:

(i) Pell grants; and

(ii) Student services incentives; and

(iii) Academic achievement incentive scholarships; and

(iv) Federal supplemental education opportunity grants; and

(v) Federal educational loans (Stafford loans, William D. Ford federal direct and direct PLUS loans, etc.); and

(vi) Upward bound; and

(vii) Gear up (gaining early awareness and readiness for undergraduate programs); and

(viii) State educational assistance programs funded by the leveraging educational assistance program; and

(ix) Work-study programs.

(h) Home energy assistance provided on the basis of need, in accordance with 20 C.F.R. 416.1157 (as in effect October 1, 2020).

(i) Matching funds that are deposited into individual development accounts (IDAs), either demonstration project or TANF-funded, in accordance with 42 U.S.C. 604 (as in effect October 1, 2020).

(j) Restitution payments under the Civil Liberties Act of 1988, to U.S. citizens of Japanese ancestry and permanent resident Japanese non-citizens who were interned during World War II, or their survivors, in accordance with 50 U.S.C. 4215 (as in effect October 1, 2020).

(k) Restitution payments under the Aleutian and Pribilof Island Restitution Act in accordance with 50 U.S.C. 4236 (as in effect October 1, 2020).

(*l*) Payments to victims of Nazi persecution.

(m) Payments from the Dutch government under the Netherlands' Benefit Act for victims of persecution from 1940-1945 (Dutch acronym, WUV) (Pub. L. No. 103-286).

(n) Department of defense payments to certain persons captured and interned in North Vietnam, in accordance with the Departments of Labor, Health and Human Services, and Education, and Related Agencies Appropriations Act of 1998 (Pub. L. No. 105-78).

(o) Radiation exposure compensation trust fund payments, in accordance with the Radiation Exposure Compensation Act of 1990 (Pub. L. No. 101-426).

(p) Veterans affairs payments made to or on behalf of:

(i) Certain Vietnam veterans' natural children, regardless of age or marital status, for any disability resulting from spina bifida suffered by such children; and

(ii) Certain Korea service veterans' natural children, regardless of age or marital status, for any disability resulting from spina bifida suffered by such children; and

(iii) The natural children, regardless of age or marital status, with certain birth defects born to a woman who served in Vietnam.

(q) Austrian social insurance payments based, in whole or in part, on wage credits received under the provisions of the Austrian General Social Insurance Act, paragraphs 500 to 506 (as in effect October 1, 2020). These payments are to be documented and identifiable from countable insurance.

(r) Payments made to Native Americans as listed in section IV of 20 C.F.R. 416 subpart K appendix (as in effect October 1, 2020).

(s) Payments from the Ricky Ray Hemophilia Relief Fund Act of 1998 (Pub. L. No. 105-369) or payments made from any fund established pursuant to a class settlement in the case of Susan Walker v. Bayer corporation, 96-C-5024 (N.D. Ill).

(t) Accounts under the Stephen Beck, Jr., Achieving a Better Life Experience (ABLE) Act of 2014 (Pub. L. No. 113-295). The following are not considered income to the account holder:

(i) Contributions to an ABLE account by another individual or third party.

(ii) Interest earned on an ABLE account.

(iii) Distributions from an ABLE account.

(2) Unearned income excluded by the Social Security Act, in accordance with 20 C.F.R. 416.1124 (as in effect October 1, 2020) unless otherwise noted. The exclusions listed in this paragraph are applied after the exclusions listed in paragraph (D)(1) of this rule, and in the following order:

(a) Any public agency's refund of taxes on real property or food.

(b) Assistance based on need which is provided under a program which uses income as a factor of eligibility and is wholly funded by a state or political subdivision. Residential state supplement (RSS) payments are included in this category.

(c) Grants, scholarships, fellowships, or gifts used for paying educational expenses are either excluded or countable, depending upon their use:

(i) Any portion of a grant, scholarship, fellowship, or gift used for paying tuition, fees, or other necessary educational expenses at any educational institution, including vocational or technical education, is excluded from income.

(ii) Any portion of such educational assistance that is not used to pay current tuition, fees, or other necessary educational expenses but is set aside to be used for paying this type of educational expense at a future date is excluded from income in the month of receipt. If these funds are not spent after nine months, they become a countable resource as of the tenth month following receipt.

(iii) Any portion of a grant, scholarship, fellowship, or gift that is not used or set aside for paying tuition, fees, or other necessary educational expenses is income in the month received and a resource the month after the month of receipt, if retained.

(d) Food which an individual or his/her spouse grows or raises if it is consumed by the household.

(e) Assistance received under the Robert T. Stafford Disaster Relief and Emergency Assistance Act (Pub. L. No. 100-707) and assistance provided under any federal statute because of a presidentially-declared disaster.

(f) The first sixty dollars of infrequent or irregular unearned income received in a calendar quarter.

(g) Alaska senior benefits program payments.

(h) Foster care payments.

(i) Any interest earned on an excluded burial fund and any appreciation in the value of an excluded burial arrangement which are left to accumulate and become a part of that burial fund.

(j) Support and maintenance assistance based on need:

(i) Provided in-kind by a private non-profit agency; or

(ii) Provided in cash or in-kind by a supplier of home heating oil or gas, or by a private or municipal utility company.

(k) One-third of child support payments made by an absent parent.

(*l*) Twenty dollar general income exclusion. This exclusion does not apply to income/assistance based on need that uses income as a factor of eligibility and is wholly or partially funded by the federal government or by a non-governmental agency, in accordance with 20 C.F.R. 416.1124(c)(12)(as in effect October, 1, 2020). Catholic charities and the salvation army are non-governmental agencies.

(m) Unearned income used to fulfill an approved plan to achieve self-support (PASS).

(n) Federal housing assistance, in accordance with 1612(b)(14) of the Social Security Act (as in effect October 1, 2020), provided by:

(i) The office of housing and urban development (HUD); or

(ii) The U.S. department of agriculture's rural housing service (RHS), formally known as the farmers home administration (FHA).

(o) Any interest earned on an excluded burial space purchase agreement if left to accumulate as part of the value of the agreement.

(p) The value of any commercial transportation ticket which is received as a gift and is not converted to cash.

(q) Payments from a state compensation fund for victims of crime.

(r) Relocation assistance provided under title II of the Uniform Relocation Assistance and Real Property Acquisitions Policies Act of 1970 (Pub. L. No. 91-646) provided to individuals displaced by or through any federal, federally-assisted, state, state-assisted, local, or locally-assisted government project in the acquisition of real property.

(s) Combat fire pay received from the uniformed services.

(t) Interest on a dedicated account in a financial institution for an individual under the age of eighteen, that is maintained by a representative payee, the sole purpose of which is to receive and maintain past-due supplemental security income (SSI) benefits which are allowed to be paid into such an account, and the use of which is restricted by section 1631(a)(2)(F) of the Social Security Act (as in effect October 1, 2020).

(u) Gifts to children with life-threatening conditions, in accordance with section 1612(b)(22) of the Social Security Act (as in effect October 1, 2020), from an organization described in section 501(c)(3) of the Internal Revenue Code of 1986, within the following limitations:

(i) In-kind gifts not converted to cash; and

(ii) The first two thousand dollars of any cash gifts within a calendar year.

(v) Interest and dividend income from a countable resource or from a resource excluded under a federal statute other than section 1613(a) of the Social Security Act (as in effect October 1, 2020).

(w) A state annuity paid by a state, to an individual and/or the individual's spouse, on the basis of the state's determination that the individual is a veteran and is blind, disabled, or aged.

(E) Earned income excluded by the Social Security Act, in accordance with 20 C.F.R. 416.1112 (as in effect October 1, 2020) unless otherwise noted. The exclusions listed in this paragraph are applied after the unearned income exclusions, and in the following order:

(1) Earned income tax credit payments and child tax credit payments.

(2) The first thirty dollars of infrequent or irregular earned income received in a calendar quarter.

(3) Student earned income exclusion (SEIE):

(a) Earned income of blind or disabled student children under the age of twenty-two, up to the SEIE monthly limit, and not more than the SEIE yearly limit. The SEIE monthly and yearly limits are updated and published annually in a medicaid eligibility procedure letter that includes standards and limits that have been updated due to the social security administration's cost of living adjustment (COLA).

(b) Available to a student attending school to include college, university, or a course of vocational or technical training designed to prepare students for gainful employment.

(4) Any portion of the twenty-dollar monthly general income exclusion which has not been excluded from unearned income in that same month.

(5) The first sixty-five dollars of earned income in a month.

(6) Earned income of disabled individuals used to pay impairment-related work expenses (IRWEs), as described in 20 C.F.R. 404.1576 (as in effect October 1, 2020).

(7) One-half of remaining earned income in a month.

(8) BWEs, as defined in paragraph (B) of this rule.

(9) Earned income used to fulfill an approved plan to achieve self-support (PASS).

(F) As a state-selected option under section 1902(r)(2) of the Social Security Act (as in effect October 1, 2020), exclude all income received from temporary employment with the decennial census.

(G) Unused exclusions.

(1) Exclusions never reduce earned or unearned income below zero.

(2) Unused portions of a monthly exclusion cannot be carried over for use in subsequent months.

(3) Unused earned income exclusions are never applied to unearned income.

(4) Other than the twenty-dollar general income exclusion, no unused unearned income exclusion may be applied to earned income.

(H) The twenty-dollar general and sixty-five-dollar earned income exclusions are applied only once to an eligible couple, even when both members have income, since the couple's earned income is combined in determining eligibility for medical assistance.

Replaces: 5160:1-3-03.2.
Effective: 7/1/2021.
Five Year Review (FYR) Dates: 7/1/2026.
Promulgated Under: 111.15.
Statutory Authority: 5160.02, 5163.02.
Rule Amplifies: 5160.02, 5163.02
Prior Effective Dates: 9/3/1977, 12/31/1977, 3/1/1979, 10/1/1979, 12/1/1979, 1/3/1980, 3/1/1984, 10/1/1988 (Emer.), 12/20/1988, 7/1/1989 (Emer.), 9/23/1989, 10/1/1989 (Emer.), 12/16/1989, 2/7/1991 (Emer.), 5/1/1991, 7/18/1991, 10/1/1991, 1/1/1992, 4/1/1992, 6/1/1992 (Emer.), 8/13/1992, 10/1/1992 (Emer.), 12/21/1992, 8/18/1993 (Emer.), 11/1/1993, 3/1/1994 (Emer.), 4/18/1994, 7/1/1994, 10/7/1994, 1/1/1995, 4/1/1995, 7/1/1996 (Emer.), 9/1/1996,

5/1/1997, 10/31/1997 (Emer.), 1/26/1998, 3/1/1998 (Emer.), 5/1/1998, 9/10/1999, 1/25/2015, 8/1/2016.

**5160:1-3-03.3 Medicaid: deeming of income.**

(A) This rule describes the process for calculating the amount of income to deem from an ineligible spouse, ineligible parent, or sponsor when determining eligibility for medical assistance for an eligible spouse, eligible child, or sponsored alien.

(1) When an eligible spouse resides in the same household with his or her ineligible spouse, or an eligible child under age eighteen resides in the same household with his or her ineligible parent(s), a portion of the income and resources of such spouse or parent are included in determining the eligible spouse's or eligible child's financial eligibility for medical assistance for the aged, blind, or disabled. For spouse-to-spouse deeming to apply, the eligible spouse must be eligible based on his or her own income.

(2) If a sponsored alien is sponsored by his or her ineligible spouse or ineligible parent(s), apply spouse-to-spouse or parent-to-child deeming calculations.

(3) If a sponsored alien has a sponsor and also has an ineligible spouse or ineligible parent(s) who is not his or her sponsor, apply both sponsor-to-alien and spouseto- spouse (or parent-to-child) deeming calculations.

(B) Definitions:

(1) "Allocation," for the purpose of this rule, means an amount deducted from income subject to deeming, which is considered to be set aside for the support of certain individuals other than the eligible individual.

(2) "Child," for deeming purposes, means an individual under age eighteen who lives in a household with one or both parents and who is neither married nor head of household. The deeming of parental income applies through the month in which the child becomes eighteen years old. An eligible or ineligible child's income and/or resources are never deemed to parent(s) or sibling(s).

(3) "Deemed income" means income attributed to another person whether or not the income is actually available to the person to whom it is deemed.

(4) "Eligible child" means a child in the household who has applied for medical assistance for the blind or disabled, and who meets all the applicable nonfinancial eligibility criteria for medical assistance.

(5) "Eligible parent" means a parent in the household who has applied for medical assistance for the aged, blind, or disabled, and who meets all the applicable non-financial eligibility criteria for medical assistance.

(6) "Eligible spouse" means the member of the married couple who has applied for medical assistance for the aged, blind, or disabled, and who meets all the applicable non-financial eligibility criteria for medical assistance.

(7) "Household" means the eligible spouse, the ineligible spouse, and any of the couple's children or the children of either member of the couple; or the eligible child, the eligible child's parent(s), and other children of the parent(s).

(a) A household does not exist if an individual or a group of individuals does not have a residence. In such a case, only the eligible individual's income is used to determine eligibility for medical assistance.

(b) If a child is born in an institution (e.g., a hospital), the child is a member of the household at the time of birth unless the parents have completed the required paperwork to give the child up for adoption or the child has been placed in the temporary custody of a public children's services agency.

(c) An eligible individual or an ineligible spouse or ineligible parent who is temporarily absent, as defined in rule 5160:1-1-01 of the Administrative Code, is still considered to be a member of the household for deeming purposes.

(8) "Ineligible child" means a child in the household who has not applied for medical assistance for the blind or disabled.

(9) "Ineligible parent" means an eligible child's parent who has not applied for medical assistance for the aged, blind, or disabled.

(10) "Ineligible spouse" means an eligible spouse's husband or wife who has not applied for medical assistance for the aged, blind, or disabled.

(11) "Parent" means a natural or adoptive father or mother living in the same household as the eligible child. The income of a step-parent who lives with the eligible child is deemed to the child only when the natural or adoptive parent also lives in the household with the step-parent and the child. If the natural or adoptive parent divorces a step-parent and the child is living with the stepparent, the step-parent is not a parent or spouse for deeming purposes.

(12) "Sponsor" means an individual who signs an affidavit of support agreeing to support an alien as a condition of the alien's admission for permanent residence in the U.S. A sponsored alien may have more than one sponsor. For deeming purposes, a sponsor does not include an organization such as the congregation of a church or a service club, or an employer who only guarantees employment for an alien upon entry but does not sign an affidavit of support.

(13) "Sponsored alien," for purposes of this rule, means an individual lawfully admitted for permanent residence in the U.S. who is supported by a sponsor(s). Such an individual has applied for medical assistance for the aged, blind, or disabled, and meets all the applicable non-financial eligibility criteria for medical assistance.

(14) "Spouse" means a person who is legally married to another under Ohio law.

(C) In accordance with 20 C.F.R. 416.1161 (as in effect on October 1, 2018), when determining the income of an ineligible spouse, ineligible parent, or sponsor of an alien, or of an ineligible child in the household, the following items shall not be considered income:

(1) Income excluded by federal laws other than the Social Security Act as described in paragraph (D)(1) of rule 5160:1-3-03.2 of the Administrative Code;

(2) Items not considered income as described in paragraph (E) of rule 5160:1-3-03.1 of the Administrative Code;

(3) Any public income-maintenance (PIM) payments, as defined in 20 C.F.R. 416.1142(a) (as in effect on October 1, 2018), received by the ineligible spouse, ineligible parent(s), or ineligible child in the household, and any income which was counted or excluded in figuring the amount of that payment;

(4) Any of the income of the ineligible spouse or ineligible parent that is used to determine the amount of a PIM payment to someone else;

(5) Any portion of a grant, scholarship, fellowship, or gift used or set aside to pay tuition, fees, or other necessary educational expenses;

(6) Money received for providing foster care to an ineligible child;

(7) The value of food assistance and the value of foods donated by the department of agriculture;

(8) Food raised and consumed by members of the household;

(9) Tax refunds on income, real property, or food purchased by the family;

(10) Income used to fulfill an approved plan to achieve self-support (PASS), as defined in 20 C.F.R. 416.1181 (as in effect on October 1, 2018);

(11) The amount of court-ordered child support payments paid by a household member for a child outside the home;

(12) The value of in-kind support and maintenance;

(13) Alaska longevity bonus payments made to an individual who is a resident of Alaska and who, prior to October 1, 1985, met the twenty-five-year residency requirement for receipt of such payments in effect prior to January 1, 1983, and was eligible for supplemental security income (SSI);

(14) Disaster assistance as described in 20 C.F.R. 416.1150 and 416.1151 (as in effect on October 1, 2018);

(15) Income received infrequently or irregularly, as defined in 20 C.F.R. 416.1112(c) (2) and 416.1124(c)(6) (as in effect on October 1, 2018);

(16) Blind work expenses, as defined in rule 5160:1-3-03.2 of the Administrative Code, of the ineligible spouse or parent;

(17) Income of the ineligible spouse or ineligible parent which was paid under a federal, state, or local government program to provide the eligible individual with chore, attendant, or homemaker services;

(18) Certain support and maintenance assistance as described in 20 C.F.R. 416.1157(c) (as in effect on October 1, 2018);

(19) The value of a commercial transportation ticket as described in 20 C.F.R. 416.1124(c)(16) (as in effect on October 1,

2018); however, if such a ticket is converted to cash, the cash is income in the month the ineligible spouse or ineligible parent receives the cash;

(20) Refunds of federal income taxes and advances made by an employer relating to an earned income tax credit, as described in 20 C.F.R. 416.1112(c) (as in effect on October 1, 2018);

(21) Payments from a fund established by a state to aid victims of crime, as described in 20 C.F.R. 416.1124(c)(17) (as in effect on October 1, 2018);

(22) Combat pay received from one of the uniformed services pursuant to 37 U.S.C. 310 (as in effect on October 1, 2018);

(23) Impairment-related work expenses, as described in 20 C.F.R. 404.1576 (as in effect on October 1, 2018), incurred and paid by an ineligible spouse or ineligible parent, if the ineligible spouse or ineligible parent receives disability benefits under title II of the act;

(24) Interest earned on excluded burial funds and appreciation in the value of excluded burial arrangements which are left to accumulate and become part of separate burial funds, and interest accrued on and left to accumulate as part of the value of agreements representing the purchase of excluded burial spaces, as described in 20 C.F.R. 416.1124(c)(9) and (15) (as in effect on October 1, 2018);

(25) Interest and dividend income from a countable resource or from a resource excluded under a federal statute other than section 1613(a) of the Social Security Act, in accordance with 20 C.F.R. 416.1124(c)(22) (as in effect on October 1, 2018);

(26) Earned income of a student as described in 20 C.F.R. 416.1112(c)(3) (as in effect on October 1, 2018);

(27) Any additional increment in pay, other than any increase in basic pay, received while serving as a member of the uniformed services if:

(a) The ineligible spouse or ineligible parent received the pay as a result of deployment to or service in a combat zone; and

(b) The ineligible spouse or ineligible parent was not receiving additional pay immediately prior to deployment to or service in a combat zone.

(D) If the eligible spouse or eligible parent(s) is/are receiving Ohio works first (OWF) or SSI payments, then the payments themselves and any of the OWF- or SSI-eligible individual's own income that was used to compute eligibility for such payments are not considered available for deeming.

(E) When an eligible spouse is living in the same household with an ineligible spouse who has income, perform the following steps to calculate the amount of income to deem to the eligible spouse:

(1) Determine the ineligible spouse's income, applying any appropriate exclusions listed in paragraph (C) of this rule;

(2) Deduct the appropriate allocation for each ineligible child in the household:

(a) There is no allocation for an ineligible child receiving PIM payments as described in paragraph (C)(3) of this rule.

(b) The allocation amount is the current SSI federal benefit rate (FBR), as published annually in the Federal Register, for a couple minus the current SSI FBR for an individual.

(c) The allocation for each ineligible child in the household is reduced by the amount of that ineligible child's income, minus any appropriate exclusions listed in paragraph (C) of this rule.

(d) The ineligible child allocation(s) must first be taken from the ineligible spouse's unearned income; any remaining allocation amount will be subtracted from the ineligible spouse's earned income.

(3) If the ineligible spouse's remaining income after subtracting the ineligible child allocation(s) is less than or equal to the current SSI FBR for a couple minus the current SSI FBR for an individual:

(a) Do not deem any income to the eligible spouse.

(b) Combine the eligible spouse's unearned and earned income, applying the appropriate exclusions listed in rule 5160:1-3-03.2 of the Administrative Code.

(c) If the eligible spouse's countable income is less than or equal to the current income standard for an individual, the eligible spouse is financially eligible for medical assistance.

(4) If the ineligible spouse's remaining income after subtracting the ineligible child allocation(s) is greater than the current SSI FBR for a couple minus the current SSI FBR for an individual, treat the spouses as if they were an eligible couple:

(a) Combine both the ineligible spouse's post-allocation unearned and earned income and the eligible spouse's unearned and earned income, applying any appropriate exclusions listed in rule 5160:1-3-03.2 of the Administrative Code;

(b) Subtract the twenty-dollar general exclusion from the couple's combined unearned income; if there is less than twenty dollars of unearned income, subtract the remainder of the exclusion from the couple's combined earned income;

(c) Subtract sixty-five dollars from the couple's combined earned income, then subtract one-half of the remaining earned income.

(d) If the couple's countable income is less than or equal to the current income standard for a couple, the eligible spouse is financially eligible for medical assistance.

(F) When an eligible child(ren) reside(s) with an ineligible parent(s), perform the following steps to calculate the amount of income to deem to the eligible child(ren):

(1) Determine the income of each ineligible parent, applying any appropriate exclusions listed in paragraph (C) of this rule;

(2) Deduct the appropriate allocation for each ineligible child in the household:

(a) There is no allocation for an ineligible child receiving PIM payments as described in paragraph (C)(3) of this rule.

(b) The allocation amount is the current SSI federal benefit rate (FBR), as published annually in the Federal Register, for a couple minus the current SSI FBR for an individual.

(c) The allocation for each ineligible child in the household is reduced by the amount of that ineligible child's income, minus any appropriate exclusions listed in paragraph (C) of this rule.

(d) The ineligible child allocation(s) must first be taken from the ineligible parent(s) combined unearned income; any remaining allocation amount will be subtracted from the ineligible parent(s)'s combined earned income.

(3) Subtract the twenty-dollar general exclusion from the combined unearned income of the ineligible parent(s); if there is less than twenty dollars of unearned income, subtract the remainder of the exclusion from the combined earned income of the ineligible parent(s);

(4) Subtract sixty-five dollars from the combined earned income of the ineligible parent(s), then subtract one-half of the remaining earned income;

(5) Combine the ineligible parent(s)' remaining earned and unearned income;

(6) Subtract the appropriate parental living allowance for each ineligible parent;

(a) There is no parental living allowance deducted for an ineligible parent who receives PIM payments as described in paragraph (C)(3) of this rule.

(b) If one ineligible parent resides in the household with the child(ren), subtract the current SSI FBR for an individual.

(c) If two ineligible parents (or one ineligible parent and an ineligible stepparent) reside in the household with the child(ren), subtract the current SSI FBR for a couple.

(d) If both ineligible natural or adoptive parents and an ineligible step-parent reside in the household with the child(ren), subtract both the current SSI FBR for a couple and the current SSI FBR for an individual.

(7) Divide the remaining income by the number of eligible children in the household, and the resulting amount (rounded to the second decimal place) is deemed to each eligible child.

(8) Any income deemed to an eligible child from an ineligible parent is added to the eligible child's own unearned income.

(9) Combine the eligible child's unearned and earned income, applying any appropriate exclusions listed in rule 5160:1-3-03.2 of the Administrative Code.

(10) If the eligible child's resulting countable income is less than or equal to the current income standard for an individual, the eligible child is financially eligible for medical assistance.

(G) When a household is comprised of an ineligible spouse, an eligible spouse, and one or more eligible children, the ineligible spouse's income is deemed first to the eligible spouse and the remainder deemed to the eligible child(ren).

(1) Determine the income of the ineligible spouse, applying any appropriate exclusions listed in paragraph (C) of this rule;

(2) Deduct the appropriate allocation for each ineligible child in the household, as described in paragraph (E)(2) of this rule.

(3) If the ineligible spouse's remaining income after subtracting the ineligible child allocation(s) is less than or equal to the current SSI FBR for a couple minus the current SSI FBR for an individual:

(a) Do not deem any income to the eligible spouse or eligible child(ren); and

(b) Compare the eligible spouse's and each eligible child(ren)'s own countable income, applying any appropriate exclusions listed in rule 5160:1-3-03.2 of the Administrative Code, to the current income standard for an individual.

(c) If the eligible spouse's and/or each eligible child(ren)'s own income is less than or equal to the current income standard for an individual, the eligible spouse and/or each eligible child(ren) is financially eligible for medical assistance.

(4) If the ineligible spouse's remaining income after subtracting the ineligible child allocation(s) is greater than the current SSI FBR for a couple minus the current SSI FBR for an individual:

(a) Combine both the ineligible spouse's post-allocation unearned and earned income and the eligible spouse's unearned and earned income, applying any appropriate exclusions listed in rule 5160:1-3-03.2 of the Administrative Code;

(b) Subtract the twenty-dollar general exclusion from the couple's combined unearned income; if there is less than twenty dollars of unearned income, then subtract the remainder of the exclusion from the couple's combined earned income;

(c) Subtract sixty-five dollars from the couple's combined earned income, then subtract one-half of the remaining earned income.

(d) If the couple's countable income is less than or equal to the current income standard for a couple, the eligible spouse is financially eligible for medical assistance and no income is deemed to the eligible child(ren).

(e) If the couple's countable income is greater than the current income standard for a couple, the eligible spouse is not financially eligible for medical assistance.

(f) The amount of the couple's income in excess of the need standard for a couple is divided by the number of eligible children in the household and the resulting amount (rounded to the second decimal place) is deemed to each eligible child.

(5) Any income deemed to an eligible child under paragraph (G)(4)(f) of this rule is added to the eligible child's own unearned income.

(6) Combine each eligible child's unearned and earned income, applying any appropriate exclusions listed in rule 5160:1-3-03.2 of the Administrative Code.

(7) If each eligible child's resulting countable income is less than or equal to the current income standard for an individual, the eligible child is financially eligible for medical assistance.

(H) Sponsor-to-alien deeming shall apply regardless of whether the sponsor and the sponsored alien live in the same household or whether the sponsor actually provides the sponsored alien any support.

(1) Determine the income of the sponsor and the sponsor's spouse (if applicable), applying unearned income excluded by federal laws other than the Social Security Act, in accordance with 20 C.F.R. 416 Subpart K appendix (as in effect on October 1, 2018), unless otherwise noted;

(2) Deduct the appropriate allocation for each sponsor, each sponsor's spouse, and child of each sponsor.

(a) The allocation amount for each sponsor is the current SSI FBR for an individual.

(b) The allocation amount for each sponsor's spouse and child of each sponsor is one-half of the current SSI FBR for an individual.

(3) The remaining amount is deemed to the sponsored alien as unearned income.

(4) If there are multiple sponsored aliens who are sponsored by the same sponsor, the deemed amount is applied in full to each sponsored alien.

(5) Combine the sponsored alien's unearned and earned income, applying any appropriate exclusions listed in rule 5160:1-3-03.2 of the Administrative Code.

(6) If the sponsored alien's resulting countable income is less than or equal to the current income standard for an individual, the sponsored alien is financially eligible for medical assistance.

Replaces: 5160:1-3-03.3.
Effective: 4/1/2019.
Five Year Review (FYR) Dates: 04/01/2024.
Promulgated Under: 111.15.
Statutory Authority: 5160.02, 5163.02.
Rule Amplifies: 5160.02, 5163.02
Prior Effective Dates: 09/03/1977, 12/31/1977, 03/01/1979, 10/01/1979, 12/07/1979, 01/03/1980, 02/15/1985 (Emer.), 05/14/1985 (Emer.), 06/10/1985, 10/01/1988 (Emer.), 12/20/1988, 01/01/1991, 01/01/1992, 07/01/1992, 08/18/1993 (Emer.), 11/01/1993, 03/01/1994 (Emer.), 04/18/1994, 04/01/1995 (Emer.), 06/11/1995, 10/01/1995, 10/01/1996 (Emer.), 12/15/1996, 10/01/2002, 03/01/2013, 01/25/2015, 08/01/2016, 01/01/2019 (Emer).

### 5160:1-3-03.4 Medicaid: continued medicaid coverage for children who lost their eligibility for supplemental security income (SSI) due to a change in the disability determination. [RESCINDED]

Rescinded effective: 01/22/2015.
Five Year Review (FYR) Dates: 10/14/2014.
Promulgated Under: 111.15.
Statutory Authority: 5111.01, 5111.011.
Rule Amplifies: 5111.01, 5111.011
Prior Effective Dates: 10/1/02.

### 5160:1-3-03.5 Medicaid: application of income standards.

(A) The purpose of this rule is to set forth the application of income standards used in medicaid eligibility determinations for aged, blind, or disabled individuals.

(B) Definitions.

(1) "Income standard" means the income limit above which an individual is ineligible for a given category of medicaid for the aged, blind or disabled.

(2) "Couple income standard" is equal to the current supplemental security income (SSI) benefit rate for a couple. The updated figure is published annually by the social security administration.

(3) "Individual income standard" is equal to the current supplemental security income (SSI) benefit rate for an individual. The updated figure is published annually by the social security administration.

(C) Application of income standards.

(1) For an individual, countable income is compared to the appropriate individual income standard.

(2) For a married couple:

(a) If both members of the married couple are categorically eligible, countable income is compared to the appropriate couple income standard.

(b) If only one member of the married couple is categorically eligible, countable income may be compared to either the individual income standard or the couple income standard, in accordance with the deeming provisions set forth in rule 5160:1-3-03.3 of the Administrative Code.

Effective: 03/01/2017.
Five Year Review (FYR) Dates: 07/01/2021.
Promulgated Under: 111.15.
Statutory Authority: 5160.02, 5163.02.
Rule Amplifies: 5160.02, 5163.02
Prior Effective Dates: 9/3/77, 12/31/77, 3/1/79, 10/1/79, 12/7/79, 1/3/80, 7/1/80, 8/1/81, 7/1/82, 12/1/82, 7/1/83 (Temp.), 9/24/83, 1/1/85 (Emer.), 4/1/85, 5/1/85 (Emer.), 7/31/85, 1/1/86 (Emer.), 4/1/86, 1/1/87 (Emer.), 3/20/87, 1/1/88 (Emer.), 2/1/88 (Emer.), 3/21/88, 1/1/89 (Emer.), 4/1/89, 5/1/89 (Emer.), 7/8/89, 1/1/90 (Emer.), 4/1/90, 4/2/90 (Emer.), 6/22/90, 1/1/91 (Emer.), 4/1/91, 4/2/91 (Emer.), 6/17/91, 1/1/92 (Emer.), 3/20/92, 4/1/92 (Emer.), 6/30/92, 1/1/93 (Emer.), 3/18/93, 3/25/93, 6/11/93, 9/1/93, 3/18/94, 2/1/95, 4/01/95 (Emer.), 6/11/95, 4/1/96, 1/1/97 (Emer.), 2/9/97, 12/3/97 (Emer.), 2/1/98, 1/8/99 (Emer.), 4/1/99, 1/1/00 (Emer), 4/1/01, 6/2/01, 5/12/02, 1/25/15, 7/1/16.

### 5160:1-3-03.6 Medicaid: treatment of rental income.

(A) The purpose of this rule is to describe the calculation and treatment of rental income and expenses for medical assistance eligibility determinations.

(B) Definitions.

(1) "Net rental income" means gross rent less the ordinary and necessary expenses paid in the same taxable year. Net rental income is treated as unearned income unless the individual is in the business of renting properties, in which case the income is treated as earned income from self-employment.

(2) "Ordinary and necessary expenses" are those expenses necessary for the production or collection of rental income. In general, these expenses include interest on debts, state and local taxes on real and personal property, state and local taxes on motor fuel, general sales taxes, and expenses for managing or maintaining property.

(3) "Rent" means a payment which an individual receives for the use of real or personal property, such as land, housing, or machinery.

(C) To determine net rental income:

(1) Identify countable rental income.

(a) Rental deposits.

(i) Rental deposits are not income to the landlord while subject to return to the tenant.

(ii) Rental deposits used to pay rental expenses become income to the landlord at the point of use.

(b) Do not consider rents received in months prior to the individual's eligibility for medical assistance.

(2) Calculate allowable expenses.

(a) Deductible expenses include:

(i) Interest and escrow portions of a mortgage payment (at the point the payment is made to the mortgage holder).

(ii) Real estate insurance.

(iii) Repairs (i.e., minor correction to an existing structure).

(iv) Property taxes.

(v) Lawn care.

(vi) Snow removal.

(vii) Advertising for tenants.

(viii) Utilities.

(b) Nondeductible expenses include:

(i) Depreciation or depletion of property.

(ii) Principal portion of a mortgage payment.

(iii) Capital expenditures (i.e., an expense for an addition or increase in the value of property which is subject to depreciation for income tax purposes).

(c) Proration to determine allowable amount of expenses.

(i) In multiple family residences, if the units in the building are of approximately equal size, prorate allowable expenses based on the number of units designated for rent compared to the total number of units. If the units are not of approximately equal size, prorate allowable expenses based on the number of rooms in the rental units compared to the total number of rooms in the building. The rooms do not have to be occupied.

(ii) For rooms in a single residence, prorate allowable expenses based on the number of rooms designated for rent compared to the number of rooms in the house. Do not count bathrooms as rooms in the house. Basements and attics are counted only if they have been converted to living spaces (e.g., recreation rooms).

(iii) For rented land, prorate expenses based on the percentage of total acres that are for rent.

(d) Do not consider expenses paid in months prior to the individual's eligibility for medical assistance.

(e) Expenses are deducted when paid, not when incurred.

(3) Subtract the deductible expenses paid in a month from gross rent received in the same month.

(a) If deductible expenses exceed gross rent in a month, subtract the excess expenses from the next month's gross rent and continue doing this as necessary until the end of the tax year in which the expenses are paid.

(b) If there are still excess expenses, subtract them from the gross rent received in the month prior to the month the expenses were paid and continue doing this as necessary to the beginning of the tax year involved.

(c) Do not carry excess expenses over to other tax years or use them to offset other income.

(4) Use evidence from the previous months to estimate net rental income for the next twelve months; however, deduct only predictable expenses (e.g., utilities, interest payments, taxes, etc.).

(5) If an unpredictable expense is reported at a later date (e.g., a repair), deduct the expense in the month paid. If the expense exceeds the rent for that month, recalculate the rest of the estimated period in accordance with paragraph (C)(3) of this rule.

(6) Absent evidence to the contrary, apportion net rental income in proportion to the percentage of ownership. If the gross rent is split between the individual and another joint owner before expenses are paid, deduct expenses paid by the individual from the individual's portion of the gross rent.

(D) Verification of income and expenses. Use documents in the individual's possession (e.g., bills, receipts, etc.) to verify the gross rent and the dates received, and expenses and the dates paid. The individual's most recent federal income tax return including "Schedule E" may assist with identifying past expenses and estimating future rental income.

(1) The administrative agency will contact the individual to collect the information needed. If the individual declares the verifications cannot be accessed or submitted, the individual's statement is to be accepted.

(2) If the administrative agency is unable to make contact with the individual, a written (electronic or paper) request for the necessary information or verification documents is to be sent as set forth in rule 5160:1-2-01 of the Administrative Code.

(3) If a determination cannot be made regarding whether an expense is allowable (e.g., whether the expense is an incidental repair or a capital expenditure), the administrative agency may contact the internal revenue service (IRS) for assistance.

Effective: 12/14/2020.
Five Year Review (FYR) Dates: 9/29/2020 and 12/14/2025.
Promulgated Under: 111.15.
Statutory Authority: 5160.02, 5163.02.
Rule Amplifies: 5160.02, 5163.02
Prior Effective Dates: 09/03/1977, 12/31/1977, 03/01/1979, 10/01/1979, 12/07/1979, 01/03/1980, 10/01/1988 (Emer.), 12/20/1988, 10/01/1989 (Emer.), 12/16/1989, 05/01/1991 (Emer.), 06/17/1991, 07/17/1991, 09/01/1994, 10/01/2002, 01/25/2015, 08/01/2016, 07/08/2020 (Emer.).

### 5160:1-3-03.7 Medicaid: treatment of sick pay and sick leave.

(A) The purpose of this rule is to set forth the treatment of sick pay and sick leave for eligibility for medical assistance.

(B) Definitions.

(1) "Sick pay" means a payment made to or on behalf of an employee by an employer or a private third party for sickness or accident disability.

(2) "Sick leave" means a paid absence from duty for personal or family medical reasons and considered a continuation of salary.

(C) Treatment of sick pay.

(1) Sick pay is treated as earned income (wages) if the individual receives sick pay within six months after stopping work and the income is not attributable to the employee's own contributions toward a sick pay plan.

(2) Sick pay is treated as unearned income if:

(a) The individual receives sick pay within six months after stopping work and the income is attributable to the employee's own contributions toward a sick pay plan; or

(b) The individual receives sick pay more than six months after stopping work.

(3) To determine the six months' period after stopping work, begin with the first day of non-work, include the remainder of that calendar month, and include the next six full calendar months.

(D) Treatment of sick leave.

(1) Sick leave payments are treated as earned income.

(2) Sick leave that is donated to the individual is treated the same as if it were the individual's own leave.

Effective: 08/01/2016.
Five Year Review (FYR) Dates: 01/25/2020.
Promulgated Under: 111.15.
Statutory Authority: 5160.02, 5163.02.
Rule Amplifies: 5160.02, 5163.02
Prior Effective Dates: 9/1/94, 1/25/15.

### 5160:1-3-03.8 Medicaid: in-kind support and maintenance.

(A) This rule sets forth how in-kind support and maintenance is valued for purposes of determining eligibility for medical assistance.

(B) Definitions.

(1) "Actual value" is the dollar amount that an individual paid for an item or service, or for his/her share of an item or service.

(2) "Current market value" is the dollar amount for which an item would sell on the local open market.

(3) "Household" is a personal place of residence in which individuals share common living quarters and function as a single economic unit.

(4) "Household of another income standard" is equal to two-thirds of the income standard for an individual or couple as applicable.

(5) "In-kind support and maintenance" is unearned income in the form of food or shelter, or something that can be used to get food or shelter, that a person is given or receives because someone else pays for it.

(6) "Living in household of another" means that the individual does not live in his/her own household as defined in paragraph (B)(7) of this rule.

(7) "Living in own household" means that:

(a) The individual has ownership interest or life estate in the home; or,

(b) The individual is liable for payment of any part of a rental charge; or,

(c) The individual pays a pro-rated share of living expenses; or,

(d) The individual lives in a non-institutional care situation.

(8) "Non-institutional care situation" means that:

(a) The individual has been placed by a public or private agency under a specific program of protective placement; and,

(b) The placement is in a private household that is licensed or otherwise approved by the state to provide protective care; and,

(c) The placing agency retains responsibility for continuing supervision of the need for placement and of the services provided; and,

(d) The individual, the placing agency, or some other party pays for the services provided, or has a written agreement to pay for the services provided.

(9) "Presumed maximum value" is one-third the value of the individual income standard, as set forth in rule 5160:1-3-03.5 of the Administrative Code, plus twenty dollars.

(10) "Public assistance household" is a household in which all individuals receive some type of public income-maintenance payments, including but not limited to Ohio works first (OWF), supplemental security income (SSI), disaster relief and emergency assistance, or state or local government assistance programs based on need.

(11) "Shelter" means living quarters for an individual in the individual's permanent living arrangement.

(12) "Shelter costs" means rent, mortgage payments, real property taxes, heating fuel, gas, electricity, water, sewerage, and garbage collection services.

(C) In-kind support and maintenance received by an individual is excluded if:

(1) It is identified as excluded in accordance with rule 5160:1-3-03.2 of the Administrative Code; or,

(2) It is received from another member of a public assistance household; or,

(3) The individual receives SSI and the social security administration does not reduce the individual's SSI benefit because of in-kind support and maintenance.

(D) In-kind support and maintenance received by an individual is valued by applying the household of another income standard when:

(1) The individual is a recipient of SSI benefits and receives the one-third reduction in the SSI benefit; or,

(2) The individual lives for an entire month in another person's household, and receives both food and shelter for the entire month from someone living in that household.

(E) In-kind support and maintenance received by an individual is valued by treating the in-kind support and maintenance as countable unearned income, using the presumed maximum value if the individual:

(1) Receives in-kind support and maintenance but lives in his own household, or

(2) Does not live for the entire month in another person's household, or

(3) Does not receive all his food and shelter from another person in that household for the entire month, or

(4) Receives in-kind support and maintenance from someone outside the household.

(F) In-kind support and maintenance received by an individual is valued by treating the in-kind support and maintenance as countable unearned income, using the current market value or actual value, whichever is less, when the individual demonstrates that:

(1) The current market value of any in-kind support and maintenance received, minus any payment the individual makes for them, is less than the presumed maximum value; or,

(2) The actual amount someone else pays for the individual's in-kind support and maintenance is less than the presumed maximum value.

(G) The administrative agency shall, for purposes of determining eligibility for medical assistance, determine the value of in-kind support and maintenance received by an individual in accordance with this rule.

Effective: 08/01/2016.
Five Year Review (FYR) Dates: 01/25/2020.
Promulgated Under: 111.15.
Statutory Authority: 5160.02, 5163.02.
Rule Amplifies: 5160.02, 5163.02
Prior Effective Dates: 9/3/77, 12/31/77, 3/1/79, 10/1/79, 12/7/79, 1/3/80, 12/1/84 (Emer.), 2/10/85, 7/1/87 (Emer.), 8/3/87, 1/1/99, 7/1/05, 1/25/15.

### 5160:1-3-03.9 Medicaid: deeming of income. [RESCINDED]

Rescinded effective: 08/01/2016.
Five Year Review (FYR) Dates: 04/14/2016.
Promulgated Under: 111.15.
Statutory Authority: 5160.02, 5163.02.
Rule Amplifies: 5160.02, 5163.02
Prior Effective Dates: 9/3/77, 12/31/77, 3/1/79, 10/1/79, 12/7/79, 1/3/80, 2/15/85 (Emer.), 5/14/85 (Emer.), 6/10/85, 10/1/88 (Emer.), 12/20/88, 1/1/91, 1/1/92, 7/1/92, 8/18/93 (Emer.), 11/1/93, 3/1/94 (Emer.), 4/18/94, 4/1/95 (Emer.), 6/11/95, 10/1/95, 10/1/96 (Emer.), 12/15/96, 10/1/02, 3/1/13.

### 5160:1-3-03.10 Medicaid: retirement funds.

(A) This rule describes how retirement funds are treated for purposes of determining medical assistance eligibility.

(B) Definition. "Retirement funds" are plans designed to provide unearned income to supplant or supplement earned income. Retirement funds may include, but are not limited to such plans as: public and private pension, disability, or retirement plans; defined benefit employer pension plans, profit sharing pension plans, 403(b) pension plans, money purchase pension plans, employee stock ownership plans, individual retirement accounts (IRA); KEOGH pension plans, Roth IRAs, simplified employee pension plans (SEP-IRA), and 401k pension plans; or any other pension or retirement plans authorized under 401, 403, 408 of the Internal Revenue Code (IRC) as outlined in 26 U.S.C. (as in effect on February 1, 2016), or any other enacted IRC provisions providing for a pension or retirement plan or any other similar financial vehicles administered by an individual, employer, or union. A retirement fund converted into an annuity shall be considered in accordance with rule 5160:1-3-05.3 of the Administrative Code.

(C) Retirement funds treated as income.

(1) A retirement fund in which an individual has the legal ability to receive regular guaranteed lifetime payments will be treated as a source of unearned income rather than as a resource. A defined benefit employer pension plan is an example of this type of retirement.

(2) The individual is required to obtain the maximum available amount of payment from the plan. If the maximum available amount of payment requires the individual's spouse to consent to a waiver of the spouse's survivor benefits, the individual must document a good faith attempt to obtain that consent, and whether consent was obtained or refused. If consent is not obtained, the individual must elect the minimum spousal survivor benefit required by the plan.

Admin Code

(3) If allowed in the plan, the individual may elect a lesser payment in favor of retaining a minimum survivor benefit for a child who can be documented to be blind or disabled, as defined in rule 5160:1-3-02 of the Administrative Code.

(4) If the retirement fund is determined to not be income, then the retirement fund shall be evaluated as a potential resource.

(D) Retirement funds treated as a resource.

(1) The retirement fund shall be evaluated as a potential resource only after it is determined to not be income.

(2) A retirement fund is a countable resource if the individual or the individual's spouse has an ownership interest in the retirement fund and the legal ability to convert it to cash.

(a) The value of a retirement fund is the amount an individual can currently withdraw from the fund.

(b) This determination shall be made by reference to documentation describing the retirement fund and/or a letter from the plan administrator.

(c) Self-defined retirement plans such as an IRA or KEOGH plan are examples of this type of retirement fund.

(3) If there is a financial penalty imposed by the plan administrator in order to convert the account to cash, the amount of the countable resource is the net amount payable to the individual after deducting the penalty. The amount payable may not be further reduced by the amount of any tax incurred by the individual as a result of the conversion of the account to cash.

(4) A retirement fund is not a resource if an individual must terminate employment in order to obtain any lump sum or payment.

(5) A retirement fund determined to be a resource in accordance with paragraph (D) of this rule, which is owned by an ineligible spouse or parent or spouse of an ineligible parent, shall not be considered for deeming purposes described in rule 5160:1-3-03.20 of the Administrative Code.

(E) Administrative agency responsibilities.

(1) The administrative agency must evaluate any retirement fund of which the individual is a beneficiary.

(2) The administrative agency shall obtain the summary plan description or other document describing the rights and benefits under the retirement fund. A letter from the plan administrator may also be obtained to make the determinations required under this rule.

(F) Individual responsibilities. An individual is required to provide all available documentation to aid the administrative agency in evaluating any retirement fund of which the individual is a beneficiary.

Replaces: 5160:1-3-03.10.
Effective: 08/01/2016.
Five Year Review (FYR) Dates: 08/01/2021.
Promulgated Under: 111.15.
Statutory Authority: 5160.02, 5163.02.
Rule Amplifies: 5160.02, 5163.02
Prior Effective Dates: 1/1/93, 7/1/94, 12/1/04, 10/1/06, 1/25/15.

### 5160:1-3-03.11 Medicaid: income exclusions. [RESCINDED]

Rescinded effective: 08/01/2016.
Five Year Review (FYR) Dates: 04/14/2016.
Promulgated Under: 111.15.
Statutory Authority: 5160.02, 5163.02.
Rule Amplifies: 5160.02, 5163.02
Prior Effective Dates: 9/3/77, 12/31/77, 3/1/79, 10/1/79, 12/1/79, 1/3/80, 3/1/84, 10/1/88 (Emer.), 12/20/88, 7/1/89 (Emer.), 9/23/89, 10/1/89 (Emer.), 12/16/89, 2/ 7/91 (Emer.), 5/1/91, 7/18/91, 10/1/91, 1/1/92, 4/1/92, 6/1/92 (Emer.), 8/13/92, 10/1/92 (Emer.), 12/21/92, 8/ 18/93 (Emer.), 11/1/93, 3/1/94 (Emer.), 4/18/94, 7/1/94, 10/7/94, 1/1/95, 4/1/95, 7/1/96 (Emer.), 9/1/96, 5/1/97, 10/31/97 (Emer.), 1/26/98, 3/1/98 (Emer.), 5/1/98, 9/10/99.

### 5160:1-3-04. Medicaid: living arrangement requirement. [RESCINDED]

Rescinded effective: 01/22/2015.
Five Year Review (FYR) Dates: 10/14/2014.
Promulgated Under: 111.15.
Statutory Authority: 5111.011, 5111.01.
Rule Amplifies: 5111.011, 5111.01
Prior Effective Dates: 9/3/97, 12/31/77, 1/1/81, 12/1/82, 12/1/84 (Emer.), 2/10/85, 4/1/88 (Emer.), 6/30/88, 8/1/88 (Emer.), 10/30/88, 10/1/90, 4/1/91, 1/1/03, 3/1/09 (Emer.), 5/29/09.

#### NOTES TO DECISIONS

(1995) In determining whether Ohio Medicaid eligibility continues to exist in changed circumstances, the county department of human services should examine and apply relevant provisions of law, including 12 OAC 5101:1-39-04(D), 5101:1-39-22(B), and 5101:1-39-54(B)(1), which indicate that the transfer of temporary custody of a child who resides in a long term care facility in Ohio from a county department of human services to the child's grandparent who resides in another state will not, in itself, render the child ineligible for Medicaid benefits under the Ohio medical assistance program: OAG No. 95-002.

### 5160:1-3-04.1. Medicaid: eligibility through the spend-down process. [RESCINDED]

Rescinded Effective: 7/1/2021.
Five Year Review (FYR) Dates: 3/24/2021.
Promulgated Under: 111.15.
Statutory Authority: 5162.02, 5163.02.
Rule Amplifies: 5162.02, 5163.02
Prior Effective Dates: 09/03/1977, 12/31/1977, 03/01/1979, 10/01/1979, 12/07/1979, 02/21/1980, 10/10/1984 (Emer.), 12/29/1984, 04/01/1986, 08/01/1986 (Emer.), 10/03/1986, 11/01/1986 (Emer.), 12/22/1986, 10/01/1988, 12/20/1988, 01/01/1989 (Emer.), 04/01/1989, 10/01/1989 (Emer.), 12/16/1989, 01/01/1990 (Emer.), 04/01/1990, 09/28/1990 (Emer.), 12/24/1990, 10/01/1991, 01/01/1993 (Emer.), 03/18/1993, 09/10/1993 (Emer.), 12/10/1993, 12/01/1997 (Emer.), 02/01/1998, 10/01/2002, 04/01/2015, 08/01/2016.

### 5160:1-3-04.2 Medicaid: income computations for determining eligibility using the special income level. [RESCINDED]

Rescinded effective: 9/1/2017.
Five Year Review (FYR) Dates: 6/16/2017.
Promulgated Under: 119.03.
Statutory Authority: 5163.02.
Rule Amplifies: 5163.02
Prior Effective Dates: 6/1/88 (Emer.), 8/1/88 (Emer.), 10/30/88, 1/1/90 (Emer.), 3/1/90 (Emer.), 3/30/90 (Emer.), 4/1/90, 6/29/90, 7/1/90, 10/1/90, 1/1/91 (Emer.), 4/1/91, 1/1/92 (Emer.), 3/20/92, 5/1/92 (Emer.), 7/1/92, 8/14/92 (Emer.), 11/1/92, 5/1/93, 9/1/93, 7/1/94, 1/1/95 (Emer.), 3/20/95, 10/1/95, 4/1/96, 1/1/97 (Emer.), 2/9/97, 12/31/97 (Emer.), 2/1/98, 4/1/99, 1/1/00, 1/1/01, 5/12/02, 7/1/05.

#### NOTES TO DECISIONS

(1995) In determining whether Ohio Medicaid eligibility continues to exist in changed circumstances, the county department of human services should examine and apply relevant provisions of law, including 12 OAC 5101:1-39-04(D), 5101:1-39-22(B), and 5101:1-39-54(B)(1), which indicate that the transfer of temporary custody of a child who resides in a long term care facility in Ohio from a county department of human services to the child's grandparent who resides in another state will not, in itself, render the child ineligible for Medicaid benefits under the Ohio medical assistance program: OAG No. 95-002.

### 5160:1-3-04.3 Medicaid: determining patient liability. [RESCINDED]

Rescinded effective: 9/1/2017.
Five Year Review (FYR) Dates: 6/16/2017.
Promulgated Under: 111.15.
Statutory Authority: 5160.02, 5163.02.
Rule Amplifies: 5163.33
Prior Effective Dates: 6/1/88 (Emer.), 8/1/88 (Emer.), 10/30/88, 1/1/90 (Emer.), 3/1/90 (Emer.), 3/30/90 (Emer.), 4/1/90, 6/29/90, 7/1/90, 10/1/90, 1/1/91 (Emer.), 4/1/91, 1/1/92 (Emer.), 3/20/92, 5/1/92 (Emer.), 7/1/92, 8/14/92 (Emer.), 11/1/92, 5/1/93, 9/1/93, 7/1/94, 1/1/95 (Emer.), 3/20/95, 10/1/95, 4/1/96, 1/1/97 (Emer.), 2/9/97, 12/31/97 (Emer.), 2/1/98, 4/1/99, 1/1/00, 1/1/01, 5/12/02, 7/01/05, 12/01/06, 11/1/13.

### 5160:1-3-04.4 Medicaid: income and patient liability determinations for individuals under the assisted living home and community based waiver. [RESCINDED]

Rescinded effective: 9/1/2017.
Five Year Review (FYR) Dates: 6/16/2017.
Promulgated Under: 111.15.
Statutory Authority: 5160.02, 5163.02.

Rule Amplifies: 5160.02, 5163.02
Prior Effective Dates: 7/1/06 (Emer.), 9/15/06.

**5160:1-3-05. Medicaid: resource requirement. [RESCINDED]**

Rescinded effective: 01/15/2015.
Five Year Review (FYR) Dates: 10/30/2014.
Promulgated Under: 111.15.
Statutory Authority: 5111.01, 5111.011.
Rule Amplifies: 5111.01, 5111.011
Prior Effective Dates: 9/3/77, 2/1/79, 10/1/79 1/3/80, 1/1/81, 2/15/85 (Emer.), 5/14/85 (Emer.), 6/10/85, 10/1/90, 1/1/91, 9/1/92, 1/1/93 (Emer.), 3/18/93, 9/1/94, 1/1/95, 10/1/95, 11/7/02, 7/1/05.

**5160:1-3-05.1 Medicaid: resource requirement.**

(A) This rule describes how resources are treated for purposes of determining eligibility for medical assistance.

(B) Definitions.

(1) "Countable resources" mean those resources remaining after all exclusions have been applied.

(2) An "encumbrance" means a claim, lien, charge, or liability attached to and binding on an identified piece of real or personal property.

(3) "Equity value" means the fair market value of a resource minus any encumbrance on it.

(4) "Fair market value" of a resource means the going price, for which real or personal property can reasonably be expected to sell on the open market, in the particular geographic area involved.

(5) "Personal property" means any property that is not real property. The term includes, but is not limited to, such things as cash, jewelry, household goods, tools, life insurance policies, automobiles, promissory notes, etc.

(6) "Real property" means land, including buildings or immovable objects, attached permanently to the land.

(7) "Resources" is defined in rule 5160:1-1-01 of the Administrative Code.

(8) "Resource limit" means the maximum combined value of all resources an individual can have an ownership interest in and still qualify for medical assistance.

(a) For an individual, the resource limit is two thousand dollars.

(b) For a married couple, whether both are eligible or one is ineligible, the resource limit is three thousand dollars.

(c) A child living with a parent is considered to be an individual and has a resource limit of two thousand dollars.

(9) "Trust" is defined in rule 5160:1-3-05.2 of the Administrative Code.

(C) Treatment of non-excluded resources and determination of resource availability.

(1) The administrative agency shall evaluate and calculate the value of all resources held by an individual and the individual's spouse. An individual is ineligible for medical assistance if he or she has an ownership interest in resources with an aggregate or total countable value greater than the resource limit. The following provisions govern that process.

(a) Receipt and retention of cash or in-kind items.

(i) An individual or the individual's spouse may receive cash or in-kind items during a calendar month (the "month of receipt"). The administrative agency must treat the cash or in-kind items as a possible source of countable income for the month of receipt under the rules governing income.

(ii) If the individual or the individual's spouse retains the cash or in-kind items beyond the month of receipt, the administrative agency shall determine the availability of the cash or in-kind items as a possible countable resource under the rules governing resources.

(iii) Receipt of cash or in-kind items from the sale or exchange of timber, minerals, or other like items that are part of the land must be governed by this provision.

(b) If the individual or the individual's spouse receives cash or in-kind items as the result of an exchange, sale, replacement, or conversion of a resource, the administrative agency must consider the availability of the cash or in-kind items under the rules governing the treatment of resources, even in the first calendar month.

(2) Changes in the value of resources.

(a) The administrative agency shall review any change (increase or decrease), in the total value of an individual's resources, if the change may affect the individual's eligibility for medical assistance.

(b) The review may be initiated by the administrative agency based upon information derived from any reliable source indicating the value of an individual's available resources has increased or decreased.

(c) The administrative agency shall conduct the review of any changes as soon as possible.

(3) Discovery of previously unknown ownership interests.

(a) Any individual alleging lack of knowledge of an ownership interest in a resource must provide a signed statement attesting to the lack of knowledge and explaining the circumstances resulting in its discovery.

(b) The individual shall obtain supporting documentation, which may include signed statements from other individuals who are familiar with the individual's situation, that confirms the individual's claim.

(c) If the administrative agency obtains both the signed statement and adequate supporting documentation from the individual, the administrative agency will not count an individual's ownership interest as an available resource during any period in which the individual was unaware of the ownership interest.

(d) The administrative agency shall evaluate the value of previously unknown ownership interests, including any monies (interest, dividends, or other earnings) that have accumulated on it, under income-counting rules for that item.

(e) If either the signed statement or the supporting documentation is not provided, the administrative agency shall count an individual's ownership interest as an available resource during any period in which the individual claimed to be unaware of the ownership interest. When appropriate, the administrative agency may refer the case to the administrative agency's benefit recovery unit.

(4) Shared ownership.

(a) If the individual shares ownership with another person (co-owner) and the individual is unable to make the resource available because one of the owners cannot be located, the cost of a legal action is prohibitive, or the individual was unsuccessful in a legal action, the resource is not counted. Availability of the resource is reexamined at each eligibility review.

(b) If the co-owner is the individual's spouse, parent (if the individual is under age eighteen), or child under age eighteen, the ability to use or dispose of the resource is assumed to exist unless the individual can provide documentation of the contrary.

(5) Continuing verification.

(a) The administrative agency shall verify the value of real and personal property with each application or renewal and any time information is provided that indicates that a change in the individual's resources may have occurred.

(b) The administrative agency shall record the verification and place all supporting documents in the case record.

(D) Resources of family members, households, and aliens.

(1) The resources of spouses residing together are addressed in accordance with the deeming of resources in rule 5160:1-3-05.20 of the Administrative Code.

(2) The administrative agency shall apply the resource limitation for an individual effective with the month following the month a married couple separates or divorces or one member dies.

(3) The resources of a child under the age of eighteen are addressed in accordance with the deeming of resources in rule 5160:1-3-05.20 of the Administrative Code.

(4) The resources of an alien and sponsor(s) are addressed in accordance with the sponsor-to-alien deeming requirements in Chapter 5101:1-2 of the Administrative Code.

(E) Resources determined excluded from the applicable resource limit for medical assistance remain excluded at the time of the individual's death. Excluded resources are part of the deceased individual's estate and are subject to the estate recovery provisions in accordance with section 5162.21 of the Revised Code.

(F) For purposes of determining or renewing eligibility for medical assistance on or after February 8, 2006, the entrance fee

Admin Code

for individuals residing in a continuing care retirement community or a life care community must be considered an available resource in accordance with rule 5160:1-6-01.8 of the Administrative Code.

Effective: 9/1/2017.
Five Year Review (FYR) Dates: 8/1/2021.
Promulgated Under: 111.15.
Statutory Authority: 5160.02, 5163.02.
Rule Amplifies: 5160.02, 5163.02
Prior Effective Dates: 9/3/77, 2/1/79, 10/1/79, 1/3/80, 1/1/81, 2/15/85 (Emer.), 5/14/85 (Emer.), 6/10/85, 10/1/90, 1/1/91, 9/1/92, 1/1/93 (Emer.), 3/18/93, 9/1/94, 1/1/95, 10/1/95, 11/7/02, 7/1/05, 10/1/06, 1/15/15, 8/1/16

**5160:1-3-05.2 Medicaid: trusts.**

(A) This rule defines the treatment of a trust for the purposes of determining eligibility for medical assistance programs. This rule is only enforceable to the same extent as section 5163.21 of the Revised Code.

(B) Definitions.

(1) "Beneficiary" means any person benefiting in some way from the trust. The beneficiary can be the grantor or another person. There may be more than one beneficiary of a trust.

(2) "Grantor" means any person who creates a trust. For purposes of this rule, the term grantor includes:

(a) An individual;

(b) An individual's spouse;

(c) A person, including a court or administrative body, with legal authority to act in place of, or on behalf of, an individual or the individual's spouse; and

(d) A person, including a court or administrative body, acting at the direction or upon the request of an individual or the individual's spouse.

(3) "Irrevocable trust" means a trust that cannot be revoked by the grantor or terminated by a court. A trust terminating only upon the occurrence of an event outside the control or direction of the beneficiary or the grantor is irrevocable.

(4) "Legal instrument or device similar to a trust" means any legal instrument, device, or arrangement that is not called a trust under state law, but is similar to a trust. This includes, but is not limited to, escrow accounts, investment accounts, partnerships, contracts and other similar arrangements. To constitute a legal instrument or device similar to a trust, all of the following must be present.

(a) There must be a person holding, managing, retaining, or administering the property. For the purposes of this rule, the person holding, managing, retaining or administering the property is referred to as the trustee.

(b) The trustee must have an equitable, legal, or fiduciary duty to hold, manage, retain, or administer the property for the benefit of another person. For the purposes of this rule, this other person is referred to as the beneficiary.

(c) The trustee must hold identifiable property for the beneficiary.

(5) "Payment" means any disbursal from the principal or income of the trust. A payment may include actual cash, non-cash or property disbursements, or the right to use and occupy real property.

(6) "Payments to or for the benefit of the individual" means any payment to any person resulting in any direct or indirect benefit to the individual.

(7) "Person" has the same meaning as set forth in section 1.59 of the Revised Code and includes an individual, corporation, business trust, estate, trust, partnership and association.

(8) "Revocable trust" means a trust that can be revoked by the grantor or the beneficiary. For the purposes of the medicaid program, the following trusts are "revocable trusts" even if the terms of the trust state it is irrevocable:

(a) A trust providing the trust can be terminated only by a court; or

(b) A trust terminating upon the happening of an event, if the event can occur at the direction or control of the grantor, the beneficiary, or the trustee.

(9) "Testamentary trust" means a trust that is established by a will. This type of trust does not take effect until after the death of the person (testator) who created the trust.

(10) "Trust", for the purpose of this rule, means any arrangement in which a grantor transfers property (real or personal) to a trust with the intention that it be held, managed, or administered by a trustee(s) for the benefit of the grantor or certain designated individuals (beneficiaries). In this rule, the term trust includes any legal instrument or device that is similar to a trust.

(11) "Trustee" means any person who manages a trust. A trustee manages a trust's principal and income for the benefit of the beneficiaries.

(C) The five categories of trusts.

(1) Category one: self-settled trusts established before August 11, 1993, also referred to as medicaid qualifying trusts.

(a) A trust, or legal instrument or device similar to a trust, falls under this category if it meets all the following criteria:

(i) The trust was established before August 11, 1993;

(ii) The trust was not established by a will;

(iii) The trust was established by the individual;

(iv) The individual is or may become the beneficiary of all or part of the trust; and

(v) Payment from the trust is determined by one or more trustees who are permitted to exercise any discretion with respect to the distribution to the individual.

(b) The amount of the trust deemed to be an available resource to the individual is the maximum amount of payments that may be permitted under the terms of the trust to be distributed to the individual, assuming the full exercise of discretion by the trustee or trustees. The maximum amount includes only amounts that may be, but are not, distributed from either the income (interest) or principal of the trust.

(c) Amounts actually distributed to the beneficiary for any purpose are treated under the rules governing income.

(d) The availability of a trust in this category shall be considered whether or not:

(i) The medicaid qualifying trust is irrevocable or is established for purposes other than to enable a grantor to qualify for medicaid, or medicare premium assistance programs described in rule 5160:1-3-02.1 of the Administrative Code; and

(ii) The trustee actually exercises discretion.

(2) Category two: self-settled trusts established on or after August 11, 1993.

(a) A trust, or legal instrument or device similar to a trust, falls under this category if it meets all of the following criteria:

(i) The trust was established on or after August 11, 1993;

(ii) The assets of the individual were used to form all or part of the corpus of the trust;

(iii) The trust was not established by a will; and

(iv) The trust was established by the individual, the spouse of the individual, a person, including a court or administrative body, with legal authority to act in place of or on behalf of the individual or on behalf of the spouse of the individual, or a person, including a court or administrative body, acting at the direction or upon the request of the individual or the spouse of the individual.

(b) Revocable trusts in this category are treated as follows.

(i) The corpus of the trust is considered a resource available to the individual.

(ii) Payments from the trust to, or for the benefit of, the individual are considered unearned income.

(c) Irrevocable trusts in this category are treated as follows.

(i) If there are any circumstances under which payment from the trust could be made to, or for the benefit of, the individual, the portion from which payments could be made is considered a resource available to the individual. The administrative agency shall not take into account when payments can be made. A payment that can be made only in the future satisfies this provision.

(ii) Any payments actually made to, or for the benefit of, the individual from either the corpus or income are considered unearned income.

(d) Where a trust is funded with assets of another person or persons, as well as assets of the individual, the rule provisions governing this category of trust applies only to the portion of the trust attributable to the individual.

(e) The availability of a trust in this category is considered without regard to:

(i) The purpose for which a trust is established;

Admin Code

(ii) Whether the trustees have or exercise any discretion under the trust;

(iii) Any restrictions on when or whether distributions may be made from the trust; and

(iv) Any restrictions on the use of distributions from the trust.

(3) Category three: exempt trusts. The principal or income from any one of these trusts is exempt from being counted as a resource.

(a) Special needs trusts are not countable resources. A trust qualifies as a special needs trust if the following conditions are met.

(i) The trust contains the assets of an individual under age sixty-five. The trust may also contain the assets of other individuals.

*(a)* When such a trust was established for a disabled individual under age sixty-five, the exception for the trust continues even after the individual becomes age sixty-five, provided the individual continues to be disabled as defined in rule 5160:1-3-02 of the Administrative Code.

*(b)* The trust cannot be added to or otherwise augmented after the individual reaches age sixty-five, with the exception of income earned by the trust.

(ii) The individual is disabled as defined in rule 5160:1-3-02 of the Administrative Code.

(iii) The trust is established for the benefit of the individual.

(iv) The trust is established by one of the following:

*(a)* The individual, if established on or after December 13, 2016;

*(b)* A parent;

*(c)* A grandparent;

*(d)* A legal guardian; or

*(e)* A court.

(v) The trust requires, upon the death of the individual, the state will receive all amounts remaining in the trust, up to an amount equal to the total amount of medical assistance paid on behalf of the individual.

(vi) Cash distributions to the individual are counted as unearned income. All other distributions from the trust are treated under the rules governing in-kind income.

(vii) Distributions from an individual's special needs trust to the same individual's own achieving a better life experience (ABLE) account shall be treated in accordance with rule 5160:1-3-05.14 of the Administrative Code.

(b) Qualified income trusts (QIT) are not countable resources. A trust qualifies as a QIT if the trust meets the requirements in rule 5160:1-6-03.2 of the Administrative Code.

(c) Pooled trusts are not countable resources. A trust qualifies as a pooled trust only under all of the following conditions.

(i) The trust contains the assets of an individual of any age who is disabled as defined in rule 5160:1-3-02 of the Administrative Code.

(ii) A separate account is maintained for each beneficiary of the trust but, for purposes of investment and management of funds, the trust pools the funds in these accounts.

(iii) Accounts in the trust are established by the individual, the individual's parent, grandparent, or legal guardian, or a court solely for the benefit of individuals who are disabled.

(iv) To the extent that any amounts remaining in the beneficiary's account upon the death of the beneficiary are not retained by the trust, the trust pays to the state the amount remaining in the account equal to the total amount of medical assistance paid on behalf of the beneficiary. To meet this requirement, the trust must include a provision specifically providing for such payment.

(v) Cash distributions to the individual are counted as unearned income. All other distributions from the trust are treated under the rules governing in-kind income.

(vi) Distributions from an individual's pooled trust to the same individual's own achieving a better life experience (ABLE) account shall be treated in accordance with rule 5160:1-3-05.14 of the Administrative Code.

(d) Supplemental services trusts are not countable resources. A trust qualifies as a supplemental services trust only if it meets the requirements of section 5815.28 of the Revised Code.

(i) Any person may establish a trust under section 5815.28 of the Revised Code only for another person who is eligible to receive services through one of the following agencies: the department of developmental disabilities; a county board of developmental disabilities; the department of mental health and addiction services.

*(a)* The administrative agency shall not determine eligibility for another agency's program.

*(b)* An individual must provide documentation from one of these agencies establishing that the individual was determined to be eligible for services from that agency at the time of the creation of the trust.

*(c)* An individual may provide an order from a court of competent jurisdiction that states the individual was eligible for services from one of the agencies at the time of the creation of the trust.

(ii) At the time the trust is created, the trust principal does not exceed the maximum amount permitted. In 2006, the maximum amount permitted was two hundred twenty-two thousand dollars. The maximum amount each year thereafter is the prior year's amount plus two thousand dollars.

(iii) The administrative agency shall review the trust to determine whether it complies with the remaining provisions of section 5815.28 of the Revised Code.

(iv) Payments from supplemental services trusts are exempt as long as the payments are for supplemental services as defined in section 5815.28 of the Revised Code. All supplemental services shall be purchased by the trustee, not through direct cash payments to the beneficiary.

(e) If a trust is represented to be an exempt trust, but the administrative agency determines that it does not meet the requirements for one of the exempt trusts, then it is not an exempt trust and will fall under one of the four other categories of trusts.

(4) Category four: trusts established by someone else for the benefit of the individual.

(a) A trust, or legal instrument or device similar to a trust, falls under this category if it meets the following criteria:

(i) The trust is created by someone other than the individual;

(ii) The trust names the individual as a beneficiary; and

(iii) The trust is funded with assets or property that the individual never held an ownership interest in prior to the establishment of the trust.

(b) Any portion of a trust in this category is an available resource only if the trust permits the trustee to expend principal, corpus or assets of the trust for the individual's medical care, care, comfort, maintenance, health, welfare, general well-being, or a combination of these purposes. The trust is still considered an available resource even if the trust contains any of the following types of provisions:

(i) Any provision prohibiting the trustee from making payments that would supplant or replace medicaid or public assistance, or other government assistance;

(ii) Any provision prohibiting the trustee from making payments that would impact or affect the individual's right or ability or opportunity to receive medicaid, or public assistance, or other government assistance; or

(iii) Any provision attempting to prevent the trust or its corpus or principal from counting as an available resource under this rule.

(c) A trust in this category normally considered as an available resource is not counted as an available resource under the following circumstances.

(i) If the trust contains a clear statement requiring the trustee to preserve a portion of the trust for another beneficiary or remainderman, then that portion of the trust is not counted as an available resource. Terms of a trust granting discretion to preserve a portion of the trust do not qualify as a clear statement requiring the trustee to preserve a portion of the trust.

(ii) If the trust contains a clear statement requiring the trustee to use a portion of the trust for a purpose other than the medical care, care, comfort, maintenance, welfare, or general well-being of the individual, then that portion of the trust is not counted as an available resource. Terms of a trust that grant discretion to limit the use of a portion of the trust do not qualify as a clear statement requiring the trustee to use a portion of the trust for a particular purpose.

(iii) If the trust contains a clear statement limiting the trustee to making fixed periodic payments, then the trust is not counted as an available resource; however, the payments are treated under the rules governing income. Terms of a trust that grant discretion to limit payments do not qualify as a clear statement requiring the trustee to make fixed periodic payments.

(iv) If the trust contains a clear statement requiring the trustee to terminate the trust if it is counted as an available resource, then it is not counted as an available resource. Terms of a trust granting discretion to terminate the trust do not qualify as a clear statement requiring the trustee to terminate the trust.

(v) If any person obtains a judgment from a court of competent jurisdiction expressly preventing the trustee from using part or all of the trust for the medical care, care, comfort, maintenance, welfare, or general well-being of the individual, then the trust or that portion subject to the court order is not counted as a resource.

(vi) If the trust is specifically exempt from counting as an available resource by this rule, another rule, the Revised Code, or the U.S. Code, it is not counted as a resource.

(vii) If the individual presents a final judgment from a court demonstrating that he or she was unsuccessful in a civil action against the trustee to compel payments from the trust, then it is not counted as an available resource.

(viii) If the individual presents a final judgment from a court demonstrating that in a civil action against the trustee the individual was only able to compel limited or periodic payments, then it is not counted as an available resource; however, the payments are treated under rules governing income.

(ix) If the individual provides written documentation showing the cost of a civil action brought to compel payments from the trust are cost prohibitive, then it is not counted as an available resource.

(d) For trusts under this category, even if the trust is not counted as an available resource, any actual payments from the trust to the individual are treated under the rules governing income.

(5) Category five: trusts established by will for the benefit of a surviving spouse.

(a) A trust, or legal instrument or device similar to a trust, can be established by the will of a deceased spouse.

(i) If there are any circumstances under which payment from the trust could be made to, or for the benefit of, the surviving spouse, the portion from which payments could be made is considered an available resource. The administrative agency shall not take into account when payments can be made. A payment that can be made only in the future satisfies this provision.

(ii) Any payments actually made to, or for the benefit of, the surviving spouse from either the corpus or income are considered unearned income.

(D) This rule supersedes all previous rules governing trusts and the administrative agency shall apply it prospectively to all determinations and renewals of eligibility for all individuals. Any determination or renewal made in accordance with this rule shall not be affected by or governed by any prior eligibility determinations made under former rules governing trusts nor shall this rule be applied retroactively to determine an individual's eligibility or liability for any prior period.

Effective: 3/1/2018.
Five Year Review (FYR) Dates: 9/1/2022.
Promulgated Under: 111.15.
Statutory Authority: 5160.02, 5163.02.
Rule Amplifies: 5160.02, 5163.02
Prior Effective Dates: 09/03/1977, 02/01/1979, 10/01/1979, 01/03/1980, 12/01/1984 (Emer.), 02/10/1985, 05/03/1985 (Emer.), 08/01/1985, 09/01/1985 (Emer.), 11/25/1985, 10/01/1989 (Emer.), 12/16/1989, 10/01/1991, 09/01/1992, 02/01/1995 (Emer.), 04/27/1995, 07/01/1996, 11/07/2002, 10/01/2006, 01/15/2015, 08/01/2016, 09/01/2017.

**5160:1-3-05.3 Medicaid: annuities.**

(A) This rule describes the treatment of annuities for the purposes of determining eligibility for medical assistance

(B) Definition. An "annuity" provides fixed, periodic payments, either for life or a term of years. When an individual purchases an annuity, he or she generally pays the entity issuing the annuity a lump sum of money, in return for which the issuing entity promises regular payments in a specified amount to the individual or designated beneficiary. These payments may continue for a fixed period of time or for the lifetime of the individual or designated beneficiary. The annuity typically contains a remainder clause under which, if the annuitant dies, the contracting entity converts whatever is remaining in the annuity into a lump sum and pays it to a designated beneficiary.

(C) Treatment of annuities in the determination of eligibility for medical assistance.

(1) Any resource meeting the definition of an annuity in paragraph (B) of this rule shall be considered an excluded resource.

(2) Any payments from an annuity shall be considered as unearned income to the individual or designated beneficiary.

Replaces: 5160:1-3-05.3.
Effective: 9/1/2017.
Five Year Review (FYR) Dates: 09/01/2022.
Promulgated Under: 111.15.
Statutory Authority: 5163.02, 5160.02.
Rule Amplifies: 5160.02, 5163.02
Prior Effective Dates: 5/1/97, 10/28/02, 10/1/06, 1/15/15, 1/1/16, 8/1/16.

**5160:1-3-05.4 Medicaid: cash and checking and savings accounts and time deposits.**

(A) This rule describes the treatment of cash, checking and savings accounts, and time deposits for purposes of determining eligibility for medical assistance.

(B) Definitions.

(1) "Cash" means money on hand or available in the form of currency or coins. Foreign currency or coins are cash to the extent that they can be exchanged for U.S. currency.

(a) Monthly income is not counted when evaluating cash on hand.

(b) The individual's statement of actual cash on hand is accepted without verification.

(2) "Checking account" or "savings account" is the same as having cash on hand because deposits are payable on demand. An individual should be able to withdraw money from a checking account or savings account on the same day the individual requests it.

(3) "Dedicated account" means an account in a financial institution, the sole purpose of which is to receive and maintain supplemental security income (SSI) past-due benefits which are required or allowed to be paid into such an account and the use of which is restricted by section 1631(a)(2)(F) of the Social Security Act (as in effect October 1, 2019).

(4) "Depository account", for the purpose of this rule, means a checking account, savings account, or time deposit at a financial institution that allows money to be deposited and withdrawn by the account owner.

(5) "Depository account signature card" means a contract with the financial institution that shows who has access to the depository account and whether or not the signatures of more than one owner of the depository account are needed to withdraw funds.

(6) "Passbook" means a financial institution record which shows deposits, withdrawals, and interest.

(7) "Past-due benefits" mean any of the following:

(a) SSI benefits due but unpaid which accrue prior to the month payment was effectuated; or

(b) SSI benefits due but unpaid which accrue during a period of suspension from SSI payments for which the individual was subsequently determined to have been eligible; or

(c) Any adjustment to SSI benefits that results in an accrual of unpaid benefits.

(8) "Time deposit" means a contract between an individual and a financial institution whereby the individual agrees to leave funds on deposit for a specified period and the financial institution agrees to pay interest at a specified rate for that period.

(a) Certificates of deposit (CDs) and saving certificates are common forms of time deposits.

(b) Withdrawal of a time deposit before the specified period expires incurs a penalty, which usually is imposed against the principal. This penalty does not prevent the time deposit from being a resource, but does reduce its value as a resource. On rare occasions, the terms of a time deposit will prohibit early withdrawal.

Admin Code

(C) Access to depository accounts.

(1) When the individual is:

(a) The account owner and has the legal right to withdraw funds from the account, all of the funds in the account are a resource to the individual.

(b) A co-owner of the account with another individual who is applying for or in receipt of medical assistance, the funds in the account are equally divided and a resource to each of the co-owners.

(c) A co-owner of the account with someone who is not applying for or in receipt of medical assistance, all of the funds in the account are a resource to the individual.

(2) The depository account signature card identifies who has access to the funds. In the absence of the depository account signature card, a statement from the financial institution is acceptable documentation.

(3) In situations where a depository account is shared with others and the amount of funds has an effect on the individual's eligibility for medical assistance, the administrative agency shall inform the individual that if he or she has restricted access to the depository account according to the contract with the financial institution or if a portion of the depository account was contributed by another person, the individual must provide documentation to support his or her statements regarding the account situation.

(4) When the individual provides documentation showing that access to the depository account is restricted through the need for the signature of other owners, all of the funds are still considered a resource of the individual unless documentation is provided of the percentage the other owners have contributed.

(a) When the other owners refuse to allow the individual to withdraw funds from the depository account, the individual must provide documentation that the resource is unavailable and take any action necessary to obtain the resource.

(b) When the individual is institutionalized, a determination of whether an improper transfer has occurred must be completed in accordance with rule 5160:1-6-06.5 of the Administrative Code. If the individual's signature is all that is needed to access the depository account, then the depository account is his or hers in its entirety unless documentation is provided that indicates which percentage of the funds the other person(s) deposited.

(5) When the individual provides documentation showing that another person, who is not applying for or in receipt of medical assistance, has an ownership interest in and contributed to the depository account, then only the portion contributed by the individual shall be considered as a resource.

(a) Interest accrued on the depository account shall be allocated according to the portions of ownership.

(b) Documentation necessary to show the individual does not own the funds in the depository account includes:

(i) A statement from the individual giving his or her allegation regarding ownership of the funds, the reason for establishing the co-owned depository account, who made deposits to and withdrawals from the depository account, how withdrawals were spent, etc.; and

(ii) Corroborating statements from the other depository account holder(s); and

(iii) Where ownership for prior periods needs to be established, the evidence must include a financial institution record or income statement. This may result in determinations that the individual owned varying dollar amounts for the prior period.

(6) When the co-owner of the depository account is incompetent or a minor, it is unnecessary to obtain a corroborating statement from that person. That person's incompetency or age may be the reason why the claimant is listed as a depository account co-owner. In the event this occurs, the administrative agency shall:

(a) Obtain a corroborating statement from a third party who has knowledge of the circumstances surrounding the establishment of the co-owned depository account.

(b) Make the decision without a corroborating statement if there is no third party and document the basis for the decision and why no corroborating statement was obtained.

(7) When, following the evaluation of ownership, it is determined that the individual's share of the resource is within the allowable limit, medical assistance is to be approved or continued. The individual shall:

(a) Remove his or her assets from the co-owned depository account within sixty days from the date his or her eligibility is approved; and

(b) Provide documentation that the change has been made.

(8) The name and address of the financial institution, the depository account number, the name(s) on the depository account, and the amount of money in the depository account must be documented in the individual's case record. If the authority to withdraw money from the depository account does not belong to those whose names are shown on the depository account, that fact must also be documented.

(D) The checking or savings account is not a resource when:

(1) The account restricts the right to withdraw funds from the account to a specific account owner; or

(2) Withdrawals from the account require authorization from a third party; or

(3) Use is restricted by a court order; or

(4) The account is restricted to a special purpose.

(E) Time deposits.

(1) When the owner of a time deposit cannot under any circumstances withdraw funds before the time deposit matures, it is not a resource. The time deposit becomes a resource (not income) on the date of maturity, and may affect countable resources in the month in which the time deposit matures. If the owner has no access to the interest before the time deposit matures, accrued interest is not a resource and is income in the month the deposit matures.

(2) When an individual has transferred his or her resources into a time deposit in which early withdrawal is prohibited, a determination of whether an improper transfer has occurred must be completed in accordance with rule 5160:1-6-06.5 of the Administrative Code. The determination shall include consideration of the length of the period of inaccessibility, the individual's life expectancy, and the amount of the time deposit.

(3) A time deposit for which early withdrawal is prohibited is still considered a countable resource for the purposes of determining a community spouse resource allowance for an institutionalized individual as described in rule 5160:1-6-04 of the Administrative Code.

(4) A time deposit's resource value at any given time, if early withdrawal is permitted, is the amount the owner would receive upon withdrawing it at that time, excluding interest paid that month. Generally, this is the amount originally deposited; plus accrued interest for past months; minus any penalty specified on the time deposit certificate for early withdrawal.

(F) Verifying depository accounts.

(1) A checking account is verified by examining the printout from online banking or the last monthly bank statement and the checkbook record to arrive at the current bank balance. A copy of the monthly bank statement and checkbook record shall be retained in the case record.

(a) When the printout or statement shows deposit and withdrawal activity or cash flow inconsistent with the individual's stated financial situation, the administrative agency shall investigate fully to establish the source of income.

(b) When the printout, bank statement, or checkbook record is not available or there is some reason to doubt the accuracy of the checkbook record, verification shall be obtained by contact with the financial institution after obtaining the individual's written authorization.

(2) A savings account is verified by examining the printout from online banking, last monthly bank statement, or current balance of the passbook.

(a) The administrative agency shall retain a copy of the page(s) that show activity in the last sixty days. When the printout, bank statement, or passbook shows deposit and withdrawal activity inconsistent with the individual's stated financial situation, the administrative agency shall investigate fully to establish the source of income.

(b) When the printout, bank statement, or passbook is not available or appears to have been materially altered, the administrative agency shall obtain verification by contact with the financial institution after securing the individual's written authorization.

(c) All the information obtained shall be retained in the individual's case record.

(3) A time deposit is verified by viewing the time deposit certificate or document and the account records of interest accrual. The administrative agency may also obtain verification of the time deposit or early withdrawal provisions by contacting the financial institution after securing the individual's authorization. All the information obtained shall be retained in the individual's case record.

(4) The administrative agency will contact the individual to collect the information needed. If the individual declares the verifications cannot be accessed or submitted, the individual's statement is to be accepted.

(5) If the administrative agency is unable to make contact with the individual, a written (electronic or paper) request for the necessary information or verification documents is to be sent as set forth in rule 5160:1-2-01 of the Administrative Code.

(G) Dedicated account.

(1) Past-due benefits deposited into a dedicated financial institution account and any accrued interest or other earnings on such an account are excluded from income and resources.

(2) For any month that funds other than accrued interest or other earnings on the account are commingled in this account, the exclusion does not apply to any funds in the account.

(a) An exception is when the financial institution requires the individual to deposit money to open an account, such as a minimum deposit, a small amount of other funds can be used to open the dedicated account.

(i) The funds that were used to open the account are not excluded as a resource and must be removed from the account once the account has been established and the past-due benefits paid into it.

(ii) The funds that were used to open the account must be withdrawn before the end of the month following the month that the past-due benefits are paid.

(b) Funds other than those described in paragraph (G)(2)(a) of this rule shall not be deposited into a dedicated account.

(3) The individual must provide verification that a dedicated account has been established. The verification must include the name and address of the financial institution, account number, account title, type of account, and the amount of money in the account.

(4) The individual's representative payee shall use funds in the account to pay for the following allowable expenses: education or job skills training, personal needs assistance, special equipment, housing modification, medical treatment, therapy or rehabilitation, or any other item or service that the social security administration determines to be appropriate provided that such expense benefits the individual and, in the case of personal needs assistance, special equipment, housing modification, therapy or rehabilitation, or other approved item, is related to the impairment (or combination of impairments) of the individual. These expenditures do not affect an individual's income or resources.

(5) Restrictions on the use of funds in a dedicated account continue to apply during a period of suspension from SSI payments, non-pay status, and SSI eligibility but no payment.

(a) The exclusion of the funds in the account from the individual's countable resources continues to apply until SSI eligibility is terminated.

(b) Once an individual's SSI eligibility has been terminated, the exclusion of the funds in a dedicated account cannot be carried over if the individual establishes a new period of SSI eligibility by filing a new application for SSI. Any remaining funds are a countable resource.

(c) Reopening of a prior period of SSI eligibility following termination is not a new period of eligibility and, therefore, the exclusion may be reapplied.

(6) When an individual receives past-due benefits that may be, but have not yet been, deposited into a dedicated account, the payment is excluded from resources for nine months until the payee deposits the payment into a dedicated account. Such payments are not required to be deposited into a dedicated account at the option of the representative payee.

Effective: 12/14/2020.
Five Year Review (FYR) Dates: 9/29/2020 and 12/14/2025.
Promulgated Under: 111.15.
Statutory Authority: 5160.02, 5163.02.
Rule Amplifies: 5160.02, 5163.02
Prior Effective Dates: 09/03/1977, 02/01/1979, 01/03/1980, 12/01/1984 (Emer.), 02/10/1985, 05/03/1985 (Emer.), 08/01/1985, 09/01/1985 (Emer.), 11/25/1985, 04/01/1991, 09/01/1994, 05/01/1998, 10/01/2002, 10/02/2014, 08/01/2016, 07/08/2020 (Emer.).

**5160:1-3-05.5 Medicaid: promissory notes, property agreements, and loans.**

(A) This rule describes the treatment of promissory notes, property agreements, and loans for purposes of determining eligibility for medical assistance.

(B) Definitions.

(1) "Promissory note" means a written, unconditional promise signed by a person to pay a specified sum of money at a specified time, or on demand, to the person, corporation, or institution named on the note. It may be given in return for goods, money loaned, or services rendered. A promissory note making periodic payments is not considered an annuity.

(2) "Property agreement" means a pledge or security of particular property for the payment of a debt or the performance of some other obligation within a specified period.

(a) Property agreements on real estate generally are referred to as mortgages but also may be called real estate or land contracts, contracts for deed, deeds of trust, etc.

(b) Personal property agreements (e.g., pledges of crops, fixtures, inventory, etc.) are commonly known as chattel mortgages.

(C) Promissory notes or property agreements held by an individual.

(1) A promissory note or property agreement is an available resource.

(a) The resource value is its outstanding principal balance unless the individual furnishes evidence that it has a lower cash value.

(b) The property itself is not a resource.

(2) Payments received by an individual toward the principal balance of a promissory note or property agreement are not income. The interest portion of payments received is unearned income to the individual.

(3) A copy of the property agreement must be recorded with the county auditor, county recorder, or other appropriate government agency charged with the responsibility of recording property agreements.

(a) For the purposes of this rule, a property agreement is not considered effective until the date it is recorded with the county auditor, county recorder, or other appropriate government agency charged with the responsibility of recording property agreements. The administrative agency shall disregard any property agreement that is not properly recorded and shall consider the entire property as an available resource to the individual.

(b) For the purposes of this rule, the property agreement recording date held by the appropriate government agency is considered the date of transfer.

(4) Documentation must be provided by the individual verifying his or her proportionate share of the note or agreement if ownership of the note or agreement is shared.

(5) A promissory note or property agreement has no value if the individual adequately documents the obligations under the promissory note or property agreement were discharged by order of a bankruptcy court.

(D) Loans held by an individual.

(1) Money an individual borrows or money received as the principal repayment of a bona fide loan is not considered income.

(a) Any interest received on money loaned is unearned income.

(b) Retained proceeds of a loan in the month following the month of receipt are counted as a resource.

(2) The value of the loan is the outstanding balance due as of the individual's application date for medical assistance.

Replaces: 5160:1-3-05.5.
Effective: 9/1/2017.
Five Year Review (FYR) Dates: 09/01/2022.
Promulgated Under: 111.15.
Statutory Authority: 5163.02, 5160.02.
Rule Amplifies: 5160.02, 5163.02
Prior Effective Dates: 9/3/77, 2/1/79, 10/1/79, 1/3/80, 12/1/84 (Emer.), 2/10/85, 5/3/85 (Emer.), 8/1/85, 9/1/85 (Emer.), 11/25/85, 8/1/86 (Emer.),

10/3/86, 11/1/86 (Emer.), 12/22/86, 10/1/91, 7/1/94, 9/1/94, 5/1/97, 11/7/02, 10/1/06, 10/2/14, 1/1/16, 8/1/16.

**5160:1-3-05.6 Medicaid: burial funds and contracts.**

(A) This rule describes the treatment of burial funds and burial contracts for purposes of determining eligibility for medical assistance.

(B) Definitions.

(1) "Burial funds" are revocable burial contracts, revocable burial trusts, other revocable burial arrangements (including the value of certain installment contract for burial spaces), cash, financial accounts (checking or savings accounts), or other financial instruments with a definite cash value (e.g. stocks, bonds, etc.).

(2) "Prepaid burial contract" means an agreement whereby the buyer pays in advance for a burial that the seller agrees to furnish upon the death of the buyer or other designated individual.

(C) Burial funds exclusion.

(1) Up to one thousand five hundred dollars for each person can be excluded in burial funds set aside for:

(a) The burial expenses of the individual; and

(b) The burial expenses of the individual's spouse.

(2) Burial funds must be clearly designated for the individual's or the individual's spouse's burial and must be kept separate from nonburial-related assets in order to be excluded.

(3) The burial funds exclusion is separate from and in addition to the burial space exclusion described in rule 5160:1-3-05.7 of the Administrative Code.

(4) Any accural of interest or appreciation in the value of excluded burial funds is excluded from resources and income, even if the total value of the burial funds exceeds one thousand five hundred dollars.

(5) Expenses included for burial funds purposes are generally those related to preparing a body for burial and any services prior to burial to include transportation of the body, embalming, cremation, flowers, clothing, services of the funeral director and staff, etc.

(6) Any burial funds that exceed the burial funds exclusion are combined with all other countable resources and compared to the resource limit described in rule 5160:1-3-05.1 of the Administrative Code.

(D) Irrevocable prepaid burial contracts.

(1) Irrevocable prepaid burial contracts are not a resource.

(2) Any portion of the contract that represents burial funds reduces the amount available under the burial funds exclusion described in paragraph (C) of this rule.

(3) Any portion of the contract that represents the purchase of burial spaces has no effect on the burial funds exclusion.

(E) Revocable or salable prepaid burial contracts.

(1) If a prepaid burial contract is revocable or salable it is a countable resource and treated as a burial fund.

(2) Any portion of the contract that clearly represents the purchase of a burial space is excludable as a countable resource if it meets the requirements of rule 5160:1-3-05.7 of the Administrative Code.

(3) The value of a revocable or salable burial contract is:

(a) The amount payable to the buyer upon revocation; or

(b) If the contract is not revocable but is salable, its current market value.

(F) Burial space contract.

(1) The burial space exclusion described in rule 5160:1-3-05.7 of the Administrative Code is applied to any single-purpose burial space contract if:

(a) The contract lists all of the burial spaces and either includes a value for each space or the total value of all the spaces combined; and

(b) The seller's obligations to provide those items is not contingent on further payment, as in certain installment contracts (ie. the items are actually being held for the individual's future use).

(2) Treat the burial space contract as burial funds when:

(a) The unidentified portion of a contract that implies it covers only burial spaces but does not identify some or all of the spaces or does not include either a value for each burial space or the total of all the spaces combined; or

(b) The amount paid on an installment contract for burial spaces if the contract does not entitle the individual to the spaces until the full purchase price has been paid.

(G) Life insurance funded burial contracts.

(1) A life insurance funded burial contract involves an individual owning/purchasing a life insurance policy on his or her own life and then assigning, revocably or irrevocably, either the ownership or proceeds of the policy to a third party, generally a funeral provider. The purpose of the assignment is to fund a burial contract.

(a) Assignment of ownership.

(i) Revocable assignment of ownership.

(*a*) The burial space exclusion described in rule 5160:1-3-05.7 of the Administrative Code does not apply because the funeral provider has not received payment and no purchase of burial spaces has been made. The provider has no obligation to provide any spaces until the individual dies and, therefore, no spaces are being held for the individual.

(*b*) The resource value of the burial contract is equal to the cash surrender value (CSV) of the life insurance policy, subject to the burial funds exclusion described in paragraph (C) of this rule.

(ii) Irrevocable assignment of ownership.

(*a*) The burial space exclusion described in rule 5160:1-3-05.7 of the Administrative Code may apply if the burial space contract with a funeral service company for specified burial spaces represents current right to the use of the items at the amount shown. Any portion of the burial contract that represents the purchase of a burial space has no effect on the burial funds exclusion described in paragraph (C) of this rule.

(*b*) The life insurance policy and burial contract are not resources. The face value (FV) of the burial funds portion of the contract is subject to the burial funds exclusion described in paragraph (C) of this rule.

(b) Assignment of proceeds.

(i) Revocable assignment of proceeds.

(*a*) The burial space exclusion described in rule 5160:1-3-05.7 of the Administrative Code does not apply to the CSV of the life insurance policy because the funeral provider has not received payment and no purchase of burial spaces has been made. The provider has no obligation to provide any spaces until the individual dies and, therefore, no spaces are being held for the individual.

(*b*) The resource value of the burial contract is equal to the CSV of the life insurance policy.

(*i*) If the FV of all life insurance policies on the individual's life is one thousand five hundred dollars or less, the CSV is excluded under the life insurance exclusion described in rule 5160:1-3-05.12 of the Administrative Code.

(*ii*) If the FV of all life insurance polices exceeds one thousand five hundred dollars, treat the CSV of the policy according to the burial funds exclusion described in paragraph (C) of this rule.

(ii) Irrevocable assignment of proceeds. The irrevocable assignment of proceeds is not premitted without requiring the irrevocable assignment of ownership.

(2) When an individual irrevocably transfers ownership of a revocable life insurance policy that funds a burial contract to a trust, the CSV of the policy is evaluated under the trust rule 5160:1-3-05.2 of the Administrative Code.

(3) Life insurance funded burial contracts are not burial insurance.

(4) Dividend accumulations of a life insurance policy as part of the value of the policy or the prepaid burial contract are not excluded. Dividend accumulations are separate resources and must be designated separately in order to qualify for the burial funds exclusion.

(H) Burial insurance.

(1) Burial insurance is a contract whose terms prevents the use of its proceeds for anything other than payment of the insured's burial expenses.

(2) Treat burial insurance as burial funds described in paragraph (C) of this rule.

(3) The value of the burial insurance policy is the FV of the policy.

(I) Contracts for both burial spaces and burial funds. If a contract does not indicate which amounts represent the purchase of burial spaces and which amount represents burial funds, and which parts, if any, are irrevocable, the entire contract shall be considered a resource in the form of burial funds.

Effective: 9/1/2017.
Five Year Review (FYR) Dates: 8/1/2021.
Promulgated Under: 111.15.
Statutory Authority: 5160.02, 5163.02.
Rule Amplifies: 5160.02, 5163.02
Prior Effective Dates: 9/3/77, 2/1/79, 10/1/79, 1/3/80, 12/1/84 (Emer.), 2/1/85, 5/3/85 (Emer.), 8/1/85, 9/1/85 (Emer.), 11/25/85, 10/1/88 (Emer.), 12/20/88, 10/1/02, 10/2/14.

**5160:1-3-05.7 Medicaid: burial spaces.**

(A) This rule describes the treatment of burial spaces for the purposes of determining eligibility for medical assistance.

(B) Definitions.

(1) "Agreement," for the purpose of this rule, means a contract with a burial provider for a burial space held for the individual or a member of the individual's immediate family.

(2) "Burial space," means a burial plot, gravesite, crypt, mausoleum, casket, urn, niche, or other repository customarily and traditionally used for the deceased's bodily remains. The term also includes a contract for care and maintenance of the gravesite, sometimes referred to as an endowment or perpetual care and necessary and reasonable improvements or additions to such spaces, including but not limited to vaults, headstones, markers, or plaques, burial containers (e.g., for caskets) and arrangements for the opening and closing of the gravesite.

(3) "Immediate family" includes the individual's:

(a) Parents, including adoptive parents;

(b) Minor or adult children, including adoptive and stepchildren;

(c) Siblings, including adoptive and stepsiblings; or

(d) Spouses of immediate family if the marriage is in effect at the time of determination or renewal of eligibility for medical assistance.

(C) A burial space or burial space contract, described in rule 5160:1-3-05.6 of the Administrative Code which represents the purchase of a burial space held for the burial of the individual, the individual's spouse, or any other member of the individual's immediate family is an excluded resource, regardless of value.

(D) A burial space is held for an individual when someone currently has:

(1) Title to and/or possesses a burial space intended for the individual's use (e.g., has title to a burial plot or owns a burial urn stored for his own use); or

(2) A contract with a funeral service company for specified burial spaces for the individual's burial (i.e., an agreement which represents the individual's current right to the use of the items at the amount shown).

(E) Until the purchase price is paid in full, a burial space is not held for an individual under an installment sales contract or similar device and the installment payments shall be considered burial funds in accordance with rule 5160:1-3-05.6 of the Administrative Code.

(F) Administrative agency responsibilities. The administrative agency shall:

(1) Determine whether the burial space is held for the individual or member of the individual's immediate family if the agreement shows the purchase of a specified burial space at a specified price.

(2) Of items that serve the same purpose, exclude only one per person. For example, exclude a cemetery lot and a casket for the same person, but not a casket and an urn.

(3) If the agreement calls for installment payments, determine whether the value of the burial space must be treated as burial funds in accordance with rule 5160:1-3-05.6 of the Administrative Code.

Replaces: 5160:1-3-05.7.
Effective: 08/01/2016.
Five Year Review (FYR) Dates: 08/01/2021.
Promulgated Under: 111.15.
Statutory Authority: 5160.02, 5163.02.
Rule Amplifies: 5160.02, 5163.02
Prior Effective Dates: 9/3/77, 2/1/79, 10/1/79, 1/3/80, 12/1/84 (Emer.), 2/10/85, 9/1/94, 10/2/14.

**5160:1-3-05.8 Medicaid: lump-sum payments.**

(A) This rule describes the treatment of lump-sum payments for purposes of determining eligibility for medical assistance.

(B) Definition. "Lump-sum payment" means income which is accrued over two or more months or a money payment which is not related to any time period, such as a death benefit or inheritance.

(C) An anticipated nonrecurring lump-sum payment is considered unearned income unless otherwise excluded. It is unearned income in the month received and a countable resource in the month following the month of receipt. The following are some types of anticipated lump-sum payments that are considered unearned income:

(1) Gifts, prizes, or awards.

(2) Retirement or pension funds.

(3) Judgments and out-of-court settlements.

(4) Proceeds received as the beneficiary of a life insurance policy, including social security lump-sum death benefits.

(5) Workers compensation payments when received as a lump-sum.

(D) An unanticipated nonrecurring lump-sum payment is not considered unearned income in the month of receipt and is a resource in the month following the month of receipt. The following are some types of unanticipated lump-sum payments that are considered resources, that are not unearned income:

(1) Proceeds received from the surrender or maturing of insurance policies.

(2) Proceeds received for the sale of real property.

(3) Replacement of income that was lost, destroyed or stolen if the original income was used to determine eligibility.

(E) Retroactive payments from supplemental security income (SSI) or retirement, survivors, disability insurance (RSDI) are unearned income in the month received and excluded as countable resources for nine months following the month of receipt. The source, amount, and the date of receipt of the retroactive payment must be verified and the information recorded in the case record.

(1) As long as the funds from the retroactive payment are not spent, they are excluded for the full nine month period. Unspent money must be identifiable from other resources for this exclusion to apply. The money may be commingled with other funds, but if this is done in such a fashion that the retroactive amount can no longer be separately identified, that amount will count toward the resource limit.

(2) Once the money is spent, this exclusion does not apply to items purchased with the money even if the nine month period has not expired. However, other exclusions may apply.

(F) Federal income tax refunds, and advance payments with respect to refundable income tax credits, are not considered income and are excluded as a countable resource for a period of twelve months beginning the month after the month of receipt, in accordance with 26 U.S.C. 6409 (as in effect October 1, 2020).

(G) When an individual eligible for medical assistance receives a lump-sum payment, he or she may increase his or her personal property holdings up to the maximums allowed. Then the CDJFS compares the amount received to the amount of medicaid payments made on behalf of the individual. The individual has the choice of:

(1) Purchasing household goods or personal effects, as described in rule 5160:1-3-05.10 of the Administrative Code, to ensure that resources remain within allowable limits; or

(2) Using some or all of the lump-sum payment to pay personal debts; or

(3) Using some or all of the lump-sum payment for his or her own personal care, including but not limited to hygiene products, toiletries, and assistance with daily living activities; or

(4) Repaying the medicaid program for medicaid payments made on his or her behalf in order to preserve continuing eligibility for medical assistance. The amount paid by medicaid for past care can be recovered only if the individual agrees and if the repayment amount will continue to ensure the individual's resources remain within the allowable limits; or

(5) Requesting that his or her medicaid be discontinued.

Effective: 12/14/2020.
Five Year Review (FYR) Dates: 9/1/2022.

Admin Code

Promulgated Under: 111.15.
Statutory Authority: 5160.02, 5163.02.
Rule Amplifies: 5160.02, 5163.02
Prior Effective Dates: 09/03/1977, 02/01/1979, 10/01/1979, 01/03/1980, 12/01/1984 (Emer.), 02/10/1985, 05/03/1985 (Emer.), 08/01/1985, 09/01/1985 (Emer.), 11/25/1985, 09/01/1986, 05/01/1991 (Emer.), 07/01/1991, 06/11/1993, 09/01/1994, 10/01/2002, 10/02/2014, 08/01/2016, 09/01/2017, 07/08/2020 (Emer.).

**5160:1-3-05.9 Medicaid: dividends and interest.**

(A) This rule describes the treatment of dividends and interest for the purposes of determining eligibility for medical assistance.

(B) Definitions. "Dividends" and "interest", for the purpose of this rule, are returns on financial institution accounts. A cash gift or incentive payment to open an account is considered interest.

(C) If the resource that produced the dividends or interest is:

(1) A countable resource, the dividends and interest are excluded.

(2) Excluded under a federal statute other than the Social Security Act, the dividends and interest are excluded.

(3) Excluded under section 1613(a) of the Social Security Act as described in rule 5160:1-3-05.14 of the Administrative Code, the dividends and interest may or may not be excluded, depending on the specific resource.

Replaces: 5160:1-3-05.9.
Effective: 08/01/2016.
Five Year Review (FYR) Dates: 08/01/2021.
Promulgated Under: 111.15.
Statutory Authority: 5160.02, 5163.02.
Rule Amplifies: 5160.02, 5163.02
Prior Effective Dates: 9/3/77, 2/1/79, 10/1/79, 1/3/80, 12/1/84 (Emer.), 2/10/85, 5/3/85 (Emer.), 8/1/85, 9/1/85 (Emer.), 11/25/85, 4/1/91, 10/1/02, 10/2/14.

**5160:1-3-05.10 Medicaid: household goods and personal effects as resources.**

(A) This rule describes the treatment of household goods and personal effects for the purposes of determining eligibility for medical assistance.

(B) Definitions.

(1) "Encumbrance" means a claim, lien, charge, or liability attached to and binding on an identified piece of real or personal property.

(2) "Household goods", for the purpose of this rule, are all personal property customarily found in or near the home and used on a regular basis in connection with the maintenance, use and occupancy of the premises. This encompasses items necessary for an adequate standard of sustenance, accommodation, comfort, information and entertainment of occupants and guests. Such items include furniture, household appliances, carpets, dishes, cooking and eating utensils, televisions and personal computers.

(3) "Personal effects", for the purpose of this rule, are other personal property normally held and recognized as incidental items intended for personal use by one or more household members. Such items include clothing, personal jewelry, pets, personal care items musical instruments, books, or items of cultural or religious significance.

(C) Household goods and personal effects are excluded as resources.

(D) Items acquired or are held for their value or as an investment are not considered personal effects and are countable resources. Such items can include but are not limited to gems, jewelery that is not worn or held for family significance, collectibles, or animals for investment purposes.

(1) The current market value is the countable resource amount.

(2) If there is an encumbrance on the items, the equity value is the countable resource amount.

Replaces: 5160:1-3-05.10.
Effective: 08/01/2016.
Five Year Review (FYR) Dates: 08/01/2021.
Promulgated Under: 111.15.
Statutory Authority: 5160.02, 5163.02.
Rule Amplifies: 5160.02, 5163.02

Admin Code

Prior Effective Dates: 9/3/77, 2/1/79, 10/1/79, 1/3/80, 10/1/02, 10/2/14.

**5160:1-3-05.11. Medicaid: automobiles and other modes of transportation as resources.**

(A) This rule describes the treatment of automobiles and other modes of transportation for purposes of determining eligibility for medical assistance.

(B) Definition. "Automobile", for the purpose of this rule, means any vehicle used for transportation. It can include, in addition to cars and trucks: motorcycles, boats, snowmobiles, animal-drawn vehicles, and animals.

(C) One automobile is excluded for the individual, regardless of value, if a member of the individual's household uses the automobile for transportation.

(1) For the purpose of determining the community spouse resource allowance for couples when one spouse is institutionalized, one automobile is considered totally excluded, regardless of its use and value in accordance with rule 5160:1-6-04 of the Administrative Code.

(2) If an automobile is not excluded, count the equity value of the automobile as a resource.

(3) Any automobile an individual owns in addition to the one wholly excluded and which cannot be excluded under another rule (e.g., property essential for self-support) is a resource in the amount of its equity value.

(4) If one of two automobiles can be excluded because of one of the reasons listed above, and the other is a countable resource, the exclusion applies to the automobile with the greater equity value regardless of which automobile is actually used.

(5) The equity value for all additional automobiles, regardless of the type of vehicle, is counted as a resource.

(6) The equity value for all vehicles that are not used for transportation (e.g., pleasure boats, snowmobiles, etc.) or excluded under another rule (e.g., necessary for self-employment) is counted as a resource. These vehicles are considered countable personal effects.

(D) For the purpose of determining whether a vehicle is used for transportation, accept the individual's account of its use. If a vehicle is not being used for transportation, determine the reason why.

(1) A temporarily broken-down vehicle normally used for transportation still qualifies as an automobile. One that has been junked or that is used only as a recreational vehicle (e.g., a boat used weekends on the lake) does not qualify as an automobile.

(2) Vehicles that do not meet the definition of an automobile are personal effects. The value they have as a resource is their equity value, and the personal effects exclusion, described in rule 5160:1-3-05.10 of the Administrative Code, does not apply to them.

(E) The fair market value of an automobile is determined by the average trade-in value shown for the vehicle in the most recently published "National Automobile Dealers Association (NADA) Guide". The description of the car must be complete enough to enable the administrative agency to locate it in the appropriate NADA guide. The description is to include the year, make, model, number of doors, equipment, etc. Absent evidence to the contrary, assume the vehicle to be in average condition.

(1) If the NADA guide cannot be used (e.g., animal-drawn vehicle), obtain a fair market value estimate from a disinterested knowledgeable source.

(2) An individual who disagrees with the value of the vehicle can rebut the value by obtaining a written appraisal of the vehicle's fair market value from a disinterested knowledgeable source, such as a used car or truck dealer or an automobile insurance company. The administrative agency is not bound by this appraisal but the appraisal is to be considered in the evaluation of the vehicle.

(3) Always verify the collector value of an antique or other collectible vehicle.

Effective: 6/1/2021.
Five Year Review (FYR) Dates: 6/1/2026.
Promulgated Under: 111.15.
Statutory Authority: 5160.02, 5163.02.
Rule Amplifies: 5160.02, 5163.02

Prior Effective Dates: 9/3/1977, 2/1/1979, 10/1/1979, 1/3/1980, 4/1/1986, 7/1/1988 (Emer.), 9/1/1988, 1/1/1990 (Emer.), 4/1/1990, 7/1/1993, 10/1/2002, 10/2/2014, 8/1/2016.

**5160:1-3-05.12 Medicaid: life insurance.**

(A) This rule describes how life insurance policies are treated for purposes of determining medical assistance eligibility.

(B) Definitions of terms contained within life insurance policies.

(1) "Accelerated life insurance payments" means some or all of the proceeds from the life insurance policy are paid out to the policy owner prior to the death of the insured.

(2) "Beneficiary" means an individual or entity named in the contract to receive the policy proceeds upon the death of the insured.

(3) "Cash surrender value (CSV)" means a form of equity value that the policy acquires over time. The owner of a policy can obtain its CSV only by turning the policy in for cancellation before it matures or the insured dies. A loan against a policy reduces its CSV. The value usually increases with the age of the policy.

(4) "Dividend accumulations" are dividends which accrue in an account that the insurance company controls for the policy owner. The policy owner can access the funds without penalty at any time without affecting the policy's face value (FV) or CSV. Dividend accumulations cannot be excluded from resources under the life insurance exclusion, even if the policy that pays the accumulations is excluded from resources. Unless they can be excluded under another provision, they are a countable resource.

(5) "Dividend additions" are amounts of insurance purchased with dividends and added to the policy, increasing its death benefit and CSV. The table of CSV's that comes with a policy does not reflect the added CSV of any dividend additions.

(6) "Dividends", for the purpose of this rule, means periodically (annually, as a rule), the insurer may pay a share of any surplus company earnings to the policy owner as a dividend. Depending on the life insurance company and type of policy involved, dividends can be applied to premiums due, paid by check to the owner, or by an addition or accumulation to an existing policy.

(7) "Face value" (FV) means the amount of basic death benefit contracted for at the time the policy is purchased. It is the amount to be paid out when the insured dies.

(8) "Insured" means the individual whose life is covered by the life insurance policy.

(9) "Insurer" means the company or association which contracts with the owner.

(10) "A life insurance policy" means a contract under which the insurer agrees to pay a specified amount to a designated beneficiary upon the death of the insured.

(11) "Owner" means the individual with the right to change such policy. It is normally the person who pays the premiums.

(12) "Term life insurance" means an insurance policy that provides coverage for a specified period at a guaranteed rate. Usually does not have a CSV. Policy owners have the option of converting some term life policies into universal life or whole life insurance policies.

(13) "Universal life insurance" means an insurance policy that provides insurance over a specified period with greater flexibility on premium payment and potential for higher internal rates of return and builds CSV for policy owners over time.

(14) "Whole life insurance" means an insurance policy that applies part of the premium payments to build CSV for the policy owner.

(C) A life insurance policy is a countable resource to the policy owner for medical assistance purposes if it generates a CSV. Its value as a resource is the amount of the CSV.

(1) The total CSV of all life insurance policies for an individual is excluded if the total face value of the policies is equal to or less than one thousand five hundred dollars for any one individual. If the total face value of all life insurance policies for any one individual is more than one thousand five hundred dollars, then the total CSV of all the policies for that individual is counted toward the applicable resource limit. Policies in which a CSV has not yet accrued are still considered available when determining the total face value of the individual's life insurance policies.

(2) Life insurance policies in which no CSV will ever accrue (e.g., term life insurance), are not considered in determining the face value of the insurance policies, and are excluded from all computations. In addition, burial insurance policies are not considered in computing face value. Burial insurance is insurance which by its terms can only be used to pay the burial expense of the insured and will not accrue any CSV.

(3) When the face value of all countable life insurance policies on an ineligible individual exceeds one thousand five hundred dollars and deeming is required, the cash value of the policies is combined with the ineligible individual's other countable resources and appropriately deemed to the eligible individual.

(D) The individual must submit all policies that the individual and spouse own. The following information must be recorded in the case record:

(1) Name of insured;

(2) Name of owner;

(3) Type of insurance (whole life, universal life, or term life);

(4) Date the policy was purchased;

(5) Maturity date of policy, if specified;

(6) Face value;

(7) Cash surrender value, if applicable;

(8) Amount of loans outstanding against the policy, if applicable;

(9) For term insurance, amount of premium and frequency;

(10) Contact information for the insurance company to include address and phone number; and

(11) Policy number;

(E) Factors to consider when determining whether a life insurance policy is a resource:

(1) If the policy does not have a CSV due to the type of policy, further examination is not necessary. If the policy does have a CSV, the administrative agency must distinguish between the owner of the policy and the insured.

(2) The owner of the policy is the only individual who can receive the proceeds under the cash surrender provisions of the policy. Therefore, it is not material that the individual (or spouse) is the insured individual if the individual is not also the owner of the policy. If this is the case, there is no resource available.

(3) A life insurance policy is an available resource only when the policy is owned by the individual or person whose resources are deemed to the individual. If the consent of another person is needed to surrender a policy for its full CSV, the policy is available as a resource after the individual has obtained the consent. The individual must make a reasonable effort to obtain consent. If the consent cannot be obtained, the policy is not available. Any doubt about possible availability is resolved by contacting the insurance company. A determination would need to be made as to whether an improper transfer had occurred.

(4) The exclusion of a total of one thousand five hundred dollars face value of countable insurance policies applies to each individual separately and does not mean an average of one thousand five hundred dollars per person. An individual and spouse are each allowed one thousand five hundred dollars but not any combination of values for a three thousand dollar total for both.

(5) CSV of a policy is determined by contacting the insurance company whenever there is any question regarding the current value.

(6) The insurance exclusion does not apply to a matured endowment policy since the owner may elect to receive the total face value at any time. If the individual leaves the matured policy on deposit with the insurance company, it is no longer classified as insurance but is considered an investment at interest (the same as money in a savings account).

(F) Evaluating the insurance policy.

(1) Face value. The face value on the insurance policy may be labeled the "face amount," "sum insured," "amount of insurance" or "amount of this policy."

(a) The face value does not include additional benefits payable because of special conditions such as double indemnity riders, which apply in the event of accidental death.

(b) If the face value cannot be determined, the insurance company or local agent must be contacted for clarification. For example, the insurance company must be contacted to clarify the value when there has been a lapse in the policy because of nonpayment of premiums which results in some other insurance option becoming effective. If the information is obtained by telephone, the name, title and telephone number of the person contacted, and the name and address of the insurance company and the details of the conversation are documented in the case record.

(2) Cash surrender value. To compute the cash surrender value of a life insurance policy, it is necessary to know whether the premiums are up-to-date or in default (have not been paid) and to read the conditions in the policy affecting cash surrender. The anniversary date of a policy is the same day and month as the date of issuance. Verification of the cash surrender value must be obtained from the insurance company if the CSV, on its own, or in conjunction with other resources is close to the applicable resource limit.

(3) Dividends.

(a) Dividend additions.

(i) The FV of dividend additions are not included when determining whether a life insurance policy is countable or excluded as a resource.

(ii) If the life insurance policy is a countable resource, include the CSV of dividend additions when determining the resource value of the policy.

(iii) If the life insurance policy is an excluded resource, the CSV of the dividend additions is not included when determining the individual's countable resources.

(b) Dividend accumulations.

(i) Dividend accumulations are not excluded under the life insurance provision, even if the life insurance policy that pays the dividend accumulation is excluded.

(ii) Unless the dividend accumulations are excluded under another provision, dividend accumulations are countable as a resource, even if the life insurance policy is excluded because the policy's FV is one thousand five hundred dollars or less.

(c) Dividends count as income if the total FV of all the life insurance policies on any one person does not exceed one thousand five hundred dollars. Dividends are excluded as income if the life insurance policy is countable as a resource.

(4) An owner's failure to pay the premiums on the life insurance policy or failure to elect an option within a certain period of time after defaulting on the premiums generally causes an option to apply automatically. The CSV is usually applied by the company along with any dividends to buy extended life insurance. Under these circumstances, the face amount of the life insurance is uncertain and there is a possibility that a certain option or options have come into play. It is necessary for the insurance company to compute the actual CSV before a determination of eligibility can be made. The current face value and CSV must be obtained from the insurance company.

(5) When an individual has borrowed on a life insurance policy, the amount of the CSV depends upon the outstanding loan. Under these circumstances, the administrative agency must contact the insurance company to determine the amount of the CSV.

(G) Treatment of accelerated life insurance payments.

(1) Most accelerated payment plans fall into three basic types, depending on the circumstances which cause or trigger the payments to be accelerated. These types are the following:

(a) Long term care model, which allows the policyholders to access their death benefits should they require extended confinement in a care facility or, in some instances, health care services at home;

(b) Dread disease or catastrophic illness model, which allows policyholders to access their death benefits if they contract or acquire one of a number of specified covered conditions; and

(c) Terminal illness model, which allows policyholders to access their death benefits following a diagnosis of terminal illness where death is likely to occur within a specified number of months.

(2) Some companies refer to these types of payments as "living needs" or "accelerated death" payments.

(3) Depending on the type of accelerated payment plan, receipt of accelerated payments may reduce the policy's face value by the amount of the payments and may reduce the CSV in a manner proportionate to the reduction in face value. In some cases, a lien may be attached to the policy in the amount of the accelerated payments and a proportionate reduction in CSV results.

(4) Accelerated payments are not "benefits" for purposes of exploring potential income. It is not required that a policyholder apply for accelerated payments as a condition of obtaining or retaining medical assistance eligibility.

(5) Since accelerated payments can be used to meet food or shelter needs, the payments are income in the month received and a resource if retained into the following month and not otherwise excludable.

(6) The receipt of an accelerated payment is not treated as a conversion of a resource for medicaid purposes. This is because, under an accelerated arrangement, an individual receives proceeds from the policy, not the policy's resource value, which is its CSV.

Effective: 9/1/2017.
Five Year Review (FYR) Dates: 8/1/2021.
Promulgated Under: 111.15.
Statutory Authority: 5160.02, 5163.02.
Rule Amplifies: 5160.02, 5163.02
Prior Effective Dates: 9/3/77, 2/1/79, 10/1/79, 1/3/80, 11/1/87, 7/1/88 (Emer.), 9/1/88, 9/1/92, 8/13/02, 10/1/06, 10/2/14.

**5160:1-3-05.13 Medicaid: treatment of the home.**

(A) This rule describes the treatment of an individual's home for purposes of determining eligibility for medical assistance.

(B) Definitions.

(1) "Home", for the purpose of this rule, means any property in which an individual has an ownership interest in and which serves as the individual's principal place of residence. Home includes the structures and land appertaining to the home property. Appertaining land must adjoin the land on which the home property is located and must not be separated by intervening land property owned by others.

(2) "Principal place of residence" means the dwelling the individual considers his or her established or principal home and to which, if absent, he or she intends to return. Principal place of residence can be real or personal property, fixed or mobile, and located on land or water.

(a) Only one living place may be established as the principal place of residence.

(b) The administrative agency must obtain a signed statement, declaring the principal place of residence, when there is an indication the individual resides in or has ownership of more than one place.

(C) The home lived in, owned by, and considered the principal place of residence by the individual, the couple, or the parents with whom the eligible child is living is an excluded resource, regardless of value.

(1) For the value of the home to be excluded:

(a) The home must be the individual's, the individual's spouse's, or the parents' with whom the eligible child is living principal place of residence; and

(b) The deed to the home must be in the individual's, individual's spouse's, or the eligible child's parents' name; or

(c) The home must be deeded to a revocable trust so long as the principal of the trust remains a resource of the individual or the individual's spouse.

(2) The home is no longer considered to be the principal place of residence and shall be treated as a countable resource if the individual does not intend to return to the home.

(3) A temporary absence from the home does not affect the principal place of residence exclusion so long as the individual provides a signed statement of his or her intentions to return to the home and has not established permanent residence elsewhere.

(4) If the individual leaves the home with no intentions of returning, the home remains an excluded resource for as long as:

(a) A spouse or dependent relative of the individual continues to live there while the individual is receiving long-term care services, in accordance with Chapter 5160:1-6 of the Administrative Code.

(i) Dependency may be of any kind (e.g. financial, medical, etc.).

(ii) Relative means:

(*a*) Child, stepchild, or grandchild;
(*b*) Parent, stepparent, or grandparent;
(*c*) Aunt, uncle, niece, or nephew;
(*d*) Brother, sister, stepbrother or stepsister, half brother or half sister;
(*e*) Cousin; or
(*f*) In-law.

(b) Its sale would cause undue hardship, due to loss of housing for co-owner of the property and the co-owner provides a signed statement that he or she:
(i) Uses the property as his or her principal place of residence; and
(ii) Would have to move if the property were sold; and
(iii) Has no other living quarter readily available.

(c) The individual leaves his or her home due to domestic abuse and has not established a new principal place of residence, or has not taken action to render the home no longer excludable.

(d) The property satifies the provisions governing the treatment of property essential for self-support described in rule 5160:1-3-05.19 of the Administrative Code.

Replaces: 5160:1-3-05.13.
Effective: 9/1/2017.
Five Year Review (FYR) Dates: 09/01/2022.
Promulgated Under: 111.15.
Statutory Authority: 5160.02, 5163.02.
Rule Amplifies: 5160.02, 5163.02
Prior Effective Dates: 9/3/77, 2/1/79, 10/1/79, 1/3/80, 12/1/84 (Emer.), 2/10/85, 11/1/86 (Emer.), 12/22/86, 7/1/96 (Emer.), 9/1/96, 11/7/02, 10/1/06, 9/1/07, 10/2/14.

### 5160:1-3-05.14. Medicaid: resource exclusions.

(A) This rule describes excluded resources for the purpose of determining medical assistance eligibility for the aged, blind, or disabled.

(B) Resource exclusions.

(1) Resources excluded by federal laws other than the Social Security Act, in accordance with 20 C.F.R. 416.1236 (as in effect October 1, 2020), unless otherwise noted. This list contains unspent income from exempt sources:

(a) Agent orange settlement payments received on or after January 1, 1989, under the Agent Orange Compensation Exclusion Act (Pub. L. No. 101-201).

(b) Restitution payments under the Civil Liberties Act of 1988, to U.S. citizens of Japanese ancestry and permanent resident Japanese non-citizens who were interned during World War II, or their survivors, in accordance with 50 U.S.C. 4215 (as in effect October 1, 2020).

(c) Restitution payments under the Aleutian and Pribilof Island Restitution Act in accordance with 50 U.S.C. 4236 (as in effect October 1, 2020).

(d) Payments to victims of Nazi persecution.

(e) Payments received under the Radiation Exposure Compensation Act of 1990 (Pub. L. No. 101-426).

(f) Austrian social insurance payments, based in whole or in part, on wage credits paid under paragraphs 500 to 506 of the Austrian General Social Insurance Act (as in effect October 1, 2020).

(g) Payments received from the Dutch government as a result of the Netherlands' Benefit Act for victims of persecution from 1940-1945 (Dutch acronym, WUV) (Pub. L. No. 103-286).

(h) Payments made to Native Americans as listed in section IV of 20 C.F.R 416 subpart K appendix (as in effect October 1, 2020).

(i) Payments from the Ricky Ray Hemophilia Relief Fund Act of 1998 (Pub. L. No. 105-369) or payments made from any fund established pursuant to a class settlement in the case of Susan Walker v. Bayer corporation, 96-C-5024 (N.D. Ill).

(j) The first two thousand dollars per calendar year received as compensation for participation in clinical trials that meet the criteria detailed in section 1612(b)(26) of the Social Security Act (as in effect October 1, 2020).

(k) Payments made for supporting services or reimbursement of out-of-pocket expenses to volunteers participating in corporation for national and community service (CNCS, formerly ACTION) programs in accordance with 42 U.S.C. 1382a (as in effect October 1, 2020):
(i) AmeriCorps VISTA program; and
(ii) Special and demonstration volunteer program; and
(iii) Retired senior volunteer program (RSVP); and
(iv) Foster grandparents program; and
(v) Senior companion program.

(*l*) Payments received under the Energy Employees Occupational Illness Compensation Program Act of 2000 (Pub. L. No. 106-398). Interest received on any unspent payment is a countable resource.

(m) Student financial assistance received under the Higher Education Act of 1965 (as in effect October 1, 2020) or bureau of Indian affairs is excluded from income and resources, regardless of use:
(i) Pell grants; and
(ii) Student services incentives; and
(iii) Academic achievement incentive scholarships; and
(iv) Federal supplemental education opportunity grants; and
(v) Federal educational loans (Stafford loans, William D. Ford federal direct and direct PLUS loans, etc.); and
(vi) Upward bound; and
(vii) Gear up (gaining early awareness and readiness for undergraduate programs); and
(viii) State educational assistance programs funded by the leveraging educational assistance program; and
(ix) Work-study programs.

(n) Home energy assistance payments or allowances in accordance with 20 C.F.R. 416.1157 (as in effect October 1, 2020).

(o) Contributions, matching funds, or interest in individual development accounts (IDAs), either demonstration project or TANF-funded, in accordance with 42 U.S.C. 604 (as in effect October 1, 2020).

(p) Veterans affairs payments made to or on behalf of:
(i) Certain Vietnam veterans' natural children, regardless of age or marital status, for any disability resulting from spina bifida suffered by such children; and
(ii) Certain Korea service veterans' natural children, regardless of age or marital status, for any disability resulting from spina bifida suffered by such children; and
(iii) The natural children, regardless of age or marital status, with certain birth defects born to a woman who served in Vietnam.

(q) Funds and interest held in an account under the Stephen Beck, Jr., Achieving a Better Life Experience (ABLE) Act of 2014 (Pub. L. No. 113-295):
(i) A contribution to an ABLE account by another individual or by a third party is neither income nor a resource to the ABLE account holder. If the individual who made the contribution later requests medical assistance for long-term care services, the contribution will be evaluated in accordance with rule 5160:1-6-06 of the Administrative Code.
(ii) A distribution from an ABLE account may be used to pay for a qualified disability expense (QDE). A QDE is any expense related to the blindness or disability of the individual and made for the benefit of the individual. QDEs include but are not limited to:
(*a*) Education; and
(*b*) Housing; and
(*c*) Transportation; and
(*d*) Employment training and support; and
(*e*) Assistive technology; and
(*f*) Health; and
(*g*) Prevention and wellness; and
(*h*) Financial management and administrative services; and
(*i*) Legal fees; and
(*j*) Expenses for ABLE account oversight and monitoring; and
(*k*) Funeral and burial; and
(*l*) Basic living expenses.
(iii) A distribution from an ABLE account with the intent of paying for a QDE, except for housing, is excluded as income and will be excluded as a resource while:
(*a*) The individual continues to maintain the ABLE account; and
(*b*) The distribution is unspent; and
(*c*) The distribution is identifiable even if commingled with non-excluded funds; and

*(d)* The individual's intent to use the distribution for a QDE, other than housing, has not changed.

*(i)* If the intent has changed and the individual spent the distribution for a non-QDE or for housing, the distribution is counted as a resource for the month in which the distribution was spent.

*(ii)* If the intent has changed and the individual has decided to use the distribution for a non-QDE or for housing, but has not yet spent the distribution, the retained portion of the distribution is a countable resource the first day of the month following the month in which the intent changed.

(iv) A distribution from an ABLE account with the intent of paying for a non-QDE or for a housing expense is:

*(a)* Not countable income.

*(b)* A countable resource if retained into the following month.

(2) Resources excluded by the Social Security Act, in accordance with 20 C.F.R. 416.1210 (as in effect October 1, 2020), unless otherwise noted:

(a) Household goods and personal effects of a reasonable value as described in rule 5160:1-3-05.10 of the Administrative Code.

(b) One automobile or other mode of transportation as described in rule 5160:1-3-05.11 of the Administrative Code.

(c) Life insurance policies as described in rule 5160:1-3-05.12 of the Administrative Code.

(d) The home considered the principal place of residence as described in rule 5160:1-3-05.13 of the Administrative Code.

(e) Real or personal property considered essential to the means of self-support as described in rule 5160:1-3-05.19 of the Administrative Code.

(f) Certain burial funds and contracts as described in rule 5160:1-3-05.6 of the Administrative Code.

(g) Value of a burial space as described in rule 5160:1-3-05.7 of the Administrative Code.

(h) Cash or in-kind replacement received from any source for purposes of replacing or repairing an excluded resource which is lost, damaged, or stolen. Any interest earned on such cash payments is not income. The total amount of cash (including interest earned) or the value of the in-kind replacement is excluded as a resource for a period of nine months from the date of receipt.

(i) If the exclusion time expires and the individual has not used all of the cash, any remaining cash (as well as interest earned on such cash) is a countable resource effective the first day of the month following the month in which the time period expires.

(ii) The exclusion time may be extended for good cause for a reasonable period not to exceed an additional nine months (a total of eighteen months from the date the cash is received).

(iii) Good cause may be found if circumstances beyond the individual's control:

*(a)* Prevent repair or replacement of the lost, damaged, or stolen property; or

*(b)* Keep the individual from contracting for such repair or replacement.

(iv) Any cash and interest retained become a resource the first day of the month following the month in which the eighteen-month period ends.

(v) Temporary housing received by an individual whose home was destroyed or damaged is also excluded for a period of nine months beginning with the month the temporary housing is first provided. For purposes of this rule, temporary housing includes the value of support and maintenance. When a home is damaged or destroyed and temporary housing is furnished to an individual who owned the home, any form of in-kind support and maintenance is not counted as income.

(i) Funds held in a plan to achieve self-support (PASS) account in accordance with section 1613(a)(4) of the Social Security Act (as in effect October 1, 2020).

(j) Federal tax refunds and advance tax payments with respect to refundable credits received on or after January 1, 2010, are excluded for twelve months beginning the month following the month of receipt under the American Taxpayer Relief Act of 2012 (Pub. L. No. 112-240).

(k) Funds or interest held in a dedicated account in a financial institution for an individual under the age of eighteen, that is maintained by a representative payee, from past-due supplemental security income (SSI) benefits that exceed six times the monthly SSI payment which are allowed to be deposited into such an account, and the use of which is restricted by section 1631(a)(2)(F) of the Social Security Act (as in effect October 1, 2020), are excluded as income and resources as defined in rule 5160:1-3-05.4 of the Administrative Code.

(*l*) Payments received from a fund established by a state to aid victims of crime are excluded for nine months beginning the month following the month of receipt in accordance with section 1613(a)(9) of the Social Security Act (as in effect October 1, 2020). Interest earned on any unspent payment is a countable resource.

(m) Relocation assistance in accordance with section 1613(a)(10) of the Social Security Act (as in effect October 1, 2020).

(i) Payments under Title II of the Uniform Relocation Assistance and Real Property Acquisitions Policies Act of 1970 (Pub. L. No. 91-646) provided to individuals displaced by projects in the acquisition of real property are excluded with no time limits.

(ii) Relocation assistance payments from a state or local government are excluded for nine months.

(iii) Interest earned on unspent relocation assistance is a countable resource.

(n) Grants, scholarships, fellowships, and gifts used or intended to be used to pay the cost of tuition, fees, or other necessary educational expenses, in accordance with section 1613(A)(15) of the Social Security Act (as in effect October 1, 2020) are excluded for nine months.

(o) Filipino veteran equity compensation fund payments in accordance with section 1002 of the American Recovery and Reinvestment Act of 2009 (Pub. L. No. 111-5). Interest earned on the payment is a countable resource.

(p) Value of food or assistance provided under federal food and nutrition programs.

(q) Unspent portion of retroactive SSI and retirement, survivors, and disability insurance (RSDI) payments are excluded for nine months following the month of receipt in accordance with section 1613(a)(7) of the Social Security Act (as in effect October 1, 2020).

(r) Payments provided for flood mitigation activities under section 1324 of the National Flood Insurance Act of 1968 (Pub. L. No. 109-64).

(s) Payments received under the Robert T. Stafford Disaster Relief and Emergency Assistance Act (Pub. L. No. 100-707) and assistance provided under any federal statute because of a presidentially-declared disaster in accordance with section 1613(a)(6) of the Social Security Act (as in effect October 1, 2020).

(t) The value of federal housing assistance in accordance with section 1613(a)(8) of the Social Security Act (as in effect October 1, 2020) provided by:

(i) The office of housing and urban development (HUD); or

(ii) The U.S. department of agriculture's rural housing service (RHS), formally known as the farmers home administration (FHA).

(u) Gifts to children with life-threatening conditions in accordance with section 1613(a)(13) of the Social Security Act (as in effect October 1, 2020) from an organization described in section 501(c)(3) of the Internal Revenue Code of 1986, within the following limitations:

(i) In-kind gifts not converted to cash.

(ii) The first two thousand dollars of any cash gifts within a calendar year.

(iii) Interest or dividends earned on any gift is a countable resource.

(v) Restitution payments for misused benefits for beneficiaries of RSDI, special benefits for certain world war II veterans, and SSI are excluded for nine months following the month of receipt in accordance with section 1613(a)(14) of the Social Security Act (as in effect October 1, 2020). Payments are made to the beneficiary or the beneficiary's representative payee in the amount equal to the benefits misused in the following situations:

(i) The misuse resulted from the negligent failure of the social security administration (SSA) to investigate or monitor a representative payee; or

(ii) An organization or individual payee misused the benefits, without regard to whether SSA was negligent.

(w) A state annuity paid by a state, to an individual and/or the individual's spouse, on the basis of the state's determination that the individual is a veteran and is blind, disabled, or aged in accordance with section 1613(a)(16) of the Social Security Act (as in effect October 1, 2020).

(C) Payments or benefits listed in this rule that have been commingled with countable resources need to be identifiable in order to be excluded as a resource.

(D) Administrative agency responsibilities.

(1) Evaluate interest received on excluded resources in accordance with rule 5160:1-3-05.9 of the Administrative Code.

(2) Consider any resource purchased with funds listed in this rule as not automatically excluded and subject to medicaid resource requirements.

Replaces: 5160:1-3-05.14.
Effective: 7/1/2021.
Five Year Review (FYR) Dates: 7/1/2026.
Promulgated Under: 111.15.
Statutory Authority: 5160.02, 5163.02.
Rule Amplifies: 5160.02, 5163.02
Prior Effective Dates: 9/3/1977, 2/1/1979, 10/1/1979, 1/3/1980, 5/29/1980, 2/15/1985 (Emer.), 5/14/1985 (Emer.), 6/10/1985, 4/1/1986, 11/1/1986 (Emer.), 12/22/1986, 10/1/1987 (Emer.), 11/1/1987, 7/1/1988 (Emer.), 9/1/1988, 6/1/1990 (Emer.), 6/1/1990, 8/31/1990, 2/7/1991 (Emer.), 5/1/1991, 10/1/1991, 4/1/1992, 6/1/1992 (Emer.), 8/13/1992, 10/1/1992 (Emer.), 12/21/1992, 10/7/1994, 10/31/1997 (Emer.), 1/26/1998, 3/1/1998 (Emer.), 5/1/1998, 10/1/2006, 10/2/2014, 8/1/2016, 1/1/2018.

### 5160:1-3-05.15 Medicaid: exclusion of property no longer the principal place of residence. [RESCINDED]

Rescinded effective: 08/01/2016.
Five Year Review (FYR) Dates: 04/15/2016.
Promulgated Under: 111.15.
Statutory Authority: 5160.02, 5163.02.
Rule Amplifies: 5160.02, 5163.02
Prior Effective Dates: 9/3/77, 2/1/79, 10/1/79, 1/3/80, 12/1/84 (Emer.), 2/10/85, 11/1/86 (Emer.), 12/22/86, 5/1/94, 11/7/02.

### 5160:1-3-05.16 Medicaid: home replacement exclusion.

(A) This rule describes the application of the home replacement exclusion for purposes of determining eligibility for medical assistance. When the home is being replaced due to loss or damage resulting from a disaster, refer to rule 5160:1-3-05.14 of the Administrative Code.

(B) Definitions.

(1) "Proceeds" mean the net payments received by the seller after satisfaction of all encumbrances and sale expenses.

(2) "Sale expenses" mean all expenses that must be paid by the seller in connection with the sale of the home, including but not limited to broker fees, commissions, legal fees, mortgage-related fees such as points paid by the seller, inspection and settlement fees, and transfer and other accrued taxes paid by the seller.

(C) The home replacement exclusion allows an individual to sell an excluded home that was the individual's principal place of residence without having the proceeds of the sale count as a resource if used for the purchase of, and costs incidental to occupying, another excluded home.

(1) This exclusion from resources applies to the proceeds of the sale of the excluded home when they are used or obligated to purchase and occupy another excluded home by the last day of the third full month following the month of receipt.

(2) When the home is not replaced within this period, the proceeds are to be counted as a resource beginning with the month following the month they were received by the individual.

(3) The exclusion does not apply to interest earned on the proceeds of the sale.

(4) The administrative agency shall not implement the exclusion until the statement described in paragraph (E) of this rule is obtained.

(D) The home replacement period begins on the date the proceeds of the sale are received by the individual. The home replacement period ends on the last day of the third full month following the month the proceeds are received.

(E) When the individual states that the home is being replaced, the administrative agency shall obtain a signed statement from the individual containing the following required information:

(1) Date and amount of proceeds received from the sale of the home; and

(2) The individual's intent to replace the home with another home by a specific date that is on or before the last day of the third full month following the month of receipt of the proceeds; and

(3) An acknowledgement that any proceeds of the sale not used for another excluded home by the date identified in paragraph (E)(2) of this rule are to count in determining eligibility for medical assistance beginning on a specific date that is the first day of the first month following receipt of the proceeds.

(4) The administrative agency will contact the individual to collect the information needed. If the individual declares the verifications cannot be accessed or submitted, the individual's statement is to be accepted.

(5) If the administrative agency is unable to make contact with the individual, a written (electronic or paper) request for the necessary information or verification documents is to be sent as set forth in rule 5160:1-2-01 of the Administrative Code.

(F) The administrative agency shall verify the amount of the proceeds and the date they were received by obtaining a copy of the settlement sheet or other documents prepared at settlement and received by the individual from the sale.

(G) By the last day of the month in which the home replacement period expires, the administrative agency shall contact the individual to verify the date and amount of any allowable costs or deductions for the replacement home by obtaining written evidence (e.g., contracts, bills, receipts, settlement sheets) regarding the substitute home.

(1) The administrative agency shall charge any retained proceeds not used or contracted to be used toward the replacement home before expiration of the replacement period as a resource beginning with the month following the month of receipt.

(2) When the individual has not replaced the home as intended, all of the proceeds will count as a resource beginning with the month following the month of receipt.

Effective: 12/14/2020.
Five Year Review (FYR) Dates: 9/29/2020 and 12/14/2025.
Promulgated Under: 111.15.
Statutory Authority: 5160.02, 5163.02.
Rule Amplifies: 5160.02, 5163.02
Prior Effective Dates: 11/01/1986 (Emer.), 12/22/1986, 11/07/2002, 11/02/2014, 07/08/2020 (Emer.).

### 5160:1-3-05.17 Medicaid: life estates.

(A) This rule describes the treatment of life estates for the purposes of determining eligibility for medical assistance.

(B) Definitions.

(1) "Date of signature" is the date on which an individual with authority to transfer the property actually signed.

(2) "Life estate" means an ownership interest in property wherein one person holds the right to possess, use, and obtain profits from the property as long as he or she lives, while another person holds the actual ownership interest in the property.

(a) A life estate is a form of legal ownership.

(b) It is usually created through an instrument such as deed or will or by operation of law.

(c) A life estate instrument often identifies remaindermen who will take possession of the property upon the expiration of the life estate.

(d) A life estate owner owns the property only for the duration of the life estate. The owner can sell only his or her interest in the life estate. The owner cannot take any action concerning the interest of the remainderman.

(3) "Recording date" means the date that the deed is recorded with the county auditor, county recorder, or other appropriate government agency charged with the responsibility for recording real estate transfers and titles.

(4) A "remainderman" has an ownership interest in the physical property but normally does not have the right to possess and use the property until termination of the life estate.

(C) Unless specifically prohibited by the instrument establishing the life estate or remainder interest:

(1) The life estate owner has the right to possess, use, and obtain profits from the property and to sell his or her life estate interest.

(2) The remainderman has the right to sell his or her interest in the physical property even before the life estate interest expires.

(D) Categories of life estates.

(1) Life estates established with the individual's property.

(a) A life estate held by an individual falls within this category if the life estate is established with property that the individual held an ownership interest.

(b) If the individual has the right to transfer or sell the life estate, the life estate's fair market value is considered a countable resource unless it qualifies as an excluded resource as described in rule 5160:1-3-05.14 of the Administrative Code.

(2) Life estates not established by the individual.

(a) A life estate held by an individual falls within this category if the life estate is established with property that the individual did not hold an ownership interest in at the time of the establishment of the life estate.

(b) If the individual has the right to transfer or sell the life estate, the life estate's fair market value is considered a countable resource unless it qualifies as an excluded resource as described in rule 5160:1-3-05.14 of the Administrative Code.

(E) If the life estate is the individual's principal place of residence, as described in rule 5160:1-3-05.13 of the Administrative Code, the fair market value of the life estate is excluded as a resource.

(F) Effective date of the creation of a life estate.

(1) For life estates that are recorded within six months after the date of signature, the date of signature is the date of transfer.

(2) If a life estate is recorded more than six months after the date of signature, the individual must produce documentation from other sources verifying that the transfer occurred on the date of signature rather than the date of recording.

(a) Such documentation may consist of financial records from lending institutions, tax records from governmental agencies, or records from other agencies or private or public instititutions.

(b) The individual may provide statements of persons holding a remainder interest, or other persons who participated in the creation of the life estate.

(G) Calculating the fair market value of a life estate.

(1) The administrative agency must first determine the fair market value of the property as established by the county auditor. If a valuation by a county auditor is unavailable, the value shall be based upon a valuation by the appropriate governmental agency charged with the responsibility for valuation of real property.

(2) The administrative agency must deduct from the fair market value of the property all liens and encumbrances that have been placed against the property.

(3) The administrative agency must deduct from the fair market value of the property all liens and encumbrances that have been placed against the life estate.

(4) After the deductions, the balance is the equity value of the property.

(5) The administrative agency must multiply the equity value of the property by the product that corresponds to the life estate owner's age at the time of determination for medical assistance on the following life estate table:

| AGE | LIFE ESTATE | REMAINDER |
|---|---|---|
| 0 | .97188 | .02812 |
| 1 | .98988 | .01012 |
| 2 | .99017 | .00983 |
| 3 | .99008 | .00992 |
| 4 | .98981 | .01019 |
| 5 | .98938 | .01062 |
| 6 | .98884 | .01116 |
| 7 | .98822 | .01178 |
| 8 | .98748 | .01252 |
| 9 | .98663 | .01337 |
| 10 | .98565 | .01435 |
| 11 | .98453 | .01547 |
| 12 | .98329 | .01671 |
| 13 | .98198 | .01802 |
| 14 | .98066 | .01934 |
| 15 | .97937 | .02063 |
| 16 | .97815 | .02185 |
| 17 | .97700 | .02300 |
| 18 | .97590 | .02410 |
| 19 | .97480 | .02520 |
| 20 | .97365 | .02635 |
| 21 | .97245 | .02755 |
| 22 | .97120 | .02880 |
| 23 | .96986 | .03014 |
| 24 | .96841 | .03159 |
| 25 | .96678 | .03322 |
| 26 | .96495 | .03505 |
| 27 | .96290 | .03710 |
| 28 | .96062 | .03938 |
| 29 | .95813 | .04187 |
| 30 | .95543 | .04457 |
| 31 | .95254 | .04746 |
| 32 | .94942 | .05058 |
| 33 | .94608 | .05392 |
| 34 | .94250 | .05750 |
| 35 | .93868 | .06132 |
| 36 | .93460 | .06540 |
| 37 | .93026 | .06974 |
| 38 | .92567 | .07433 |
| 39 | .92083 | .07917 |
| 40 | .91571 | .08429 |
| 41 | .91030 | .08970 |
| 42 | .90457 | .09543 |
| 43 | .89855 | .10145 |
| 44 | .89221 | .10779 |
| 45 | .88558 | .11442 |
| 46 | .87863 | .12137 |
| 47 | .87137 | .12863 |
| 48 | .86374 | .13626 |
| 49 | .85578 | .14422 |
| 50 | .84743 | .15257 |
| 51 | .83674 | .16126 |
| 52 | .82969 | .17031 |
| 53 | .82028 | .17972 |
| 54 | .81054 | .18946 |
| 55 | .80046 | .19954 |
| 56 | .79006 | .20994 |
| 57 | .77931 | .22069 |
| 58 | .76822 | .23178 |
| 59 | .75675 | .24325 |
| 60 | .74491 | .25509 |
| 61 | .73267 | .26733 |
| 62 | .72002 | .27998 |
| 63 | .70696 | .29304 |
| 64 | .69352 | .30648 |
| 65 | .67970 | .32030 |
| 66 | .66551 | .33449 |
| 67 | .65098 | .34902 |
| 68 | .63610 | .36390 |
| 69 | .62086 | .37914 |
| 70 | .60522 | .39478 |
| 71 | .58914 | .41086 |
| 72 | .57261 | .42739 |
| 73 | .55571 | .44429 |
| 74 | .53862 | .46138 |
| 75 | .52149 | .47851 |
| 76 | .50441 | .49559 |
| 77 | .48742 | .51258 |
| 78 | .47049 | .52951 |
| 79 | .45357 | .54643 |
| 80 | .43659 | .56341 |
| 81 | .41967 | .58033 |
| 82 | .40295 | .59705 |
| 83 | .38642 | .61358 |
| 84 | .36998 | .63002 |
| 85 | .35359 | .64641 |
| 86 | .33764 | .66236 |
| 87 | .32262 | .67738 |
| 88 | .30859 | .69141 |
| 89 | .29526 | .70474 |
| 90 | .28221 | .71779 |
| 91 | .26955 | .73045 |

| AGE | LIFE ESTATE | REMAINDER |
|---|---|---|
| 92 | .25771 | .74229 |
| 93 | .24692 | .75308 |
| 94 | .23728 | .76272 |
| 95 | .22887 | .77113 |
| 96 | .22181 | .77819 |
| 97 | .21550 | .78450 |
| 98 | .21000 | .79000 |
| 99 | .20486 | .79514 |
| 100 | .19975 | .80025 |
| 101 | .19532 | .80468 |
| 102 | .19054 | .80946 |
| 103 | .18437 | .81563 |
| 104 | .17856 | .82144 |
| 105 | .16962 | .83038 |
| 106 | .15488 | .84512 |
| 107 | .13409 | .86591 |
| 108 | .10068 | .89932 |
| 109 | .04545 | .95455 |

(H) If the individual disagrees with the county auditor's determination of the fair market value of the property as described in paragraph (G)(1) of this rule, the individual may have a licensed real estate broker perform an appraisal of the property's value, which may be substituted as the fair market value of the property in paragraph (G)(1) of this rule. Such appraisal services may be provided through the use of administrative funds if the individual is unable to obtain an appraisal due to insufficient funds of his or her own.

(I) Administrative agency responsibilities. The administrative agency shall:

(1) Determine the effective date of the creation of a life estate.

(2) Accept the statements of persons holding a remainder interest, or other persons who participated in the creation of the life estate, only upon a finding that their statements are corroborated and credible.

(3) Use the date of recording as the effective date of the creation of the life estate if the individual fails to produce documentation verifying that the transfer occurred on the date of signature.

(4) If the life estate has not been recorded, the administrative agency shall request that the individual verify transfer by recording the life estate and, unless the life estate was created within the prior six months, provide documentation as required in paragraph (E)(2) of this rule. If the individual does not provide documentation that the life estate has been recorded, disregard the life estate and consider the entire property as an available resource to the individual.

Replaces: 5160:1-3-05.17.
Effective: 9/1/2017.
Five Year Review (FYR) Dates: 09/01/2022.
Promulgated Under: 111.15.
Statutory Authority: 5163.02, 5160.02.
Rule Amplifies: 5160.02, 5163.02
Prior Effective Dates: 9/3/77,/1/79, 10/1/79, 1/3/80, 7/1/88 (Emer.), 9/1/88, 1/1/90 (Emer.), 4/1/90, 4/1/91 (Emer.), 6/17/91, 9/1/94, 11/7/02, 10/1/06, 11/1/13, 8/1/16.

### NOTES TO DECISIONS

Analysis

Improper transfer
Life estate value

**Improper transfer**

Medicaid recipient did not establish that the administrative code was unreasonable, and her reliance on the general definition of "fair market value" to value her life estate was improper. She also failed to rebut the presumption of an improper transfer by clear and convincing evidence by selling her life estate to her sons for $1,800. Stutz v. Ohio Dep't of Job & Family Servs., 2017-Ohio-7287, 96 N.E.3d 963, 2017 Ohio App. LEXIS 3580 (Ohio Ct. App., Van Wert County 2017).

**Life estate value**

Trial court correctly determined the value of the Medicaid recipient's life estate because she failed to demonstrate that the general statute defining "fair market value" should be used by the Agency instead of the specific administrative code to value life estates. As such, by its plain and unambiguous meaning, the specific administrative code had be used to value the life estate. Stutz v. Ohio Dep't of Job & Family Servs., 2017-Ohio-7287, 96 N.E.3d 963, 2017 Ohio App. LEXIS 3580 (Ohio Ct. App., Van Wert County 2017).

### 5160:1-3-05.18 Medicaid: stocks, mutual funds, and bonds.

(A) This rule describes the treatment of stocks, mutual funds, and bonds for purposes of determining eligibility for medical assistance.

(B) Stocks held by an individual, including preferred stocks, warrants and rights, and stock option purchases.

(1) Stock shares represent ownership in a business corporation. Their value shifts with demand and may fluctuate widely.

(2) The current market value of publicly traded stock as of the first moment of a given month is its closing price on the last business day of the preceding month. The stock closing price, on a given day, can usually be found in the next day's regulator or financial newspaper. The value of over-the-counter stocks are shown on a "bid" and "asked" basis. The bid price is used to determine the stock's value.

(a) If the closing or bid price of a stock is not shown, a local securities firm must determine its value.

(b) The stock of some corporations not publicly traded is held within close groups and traded very infrequently. The sale of such stock is often handled privately and subject to restrictions. The burden of proof for establishing the value of this kind of stock is on the individual. The preferred evidence is a letter or other written statement from the firm's accountants giving their best estimate of the stock's value and the basis for the estimate, and can include the most recent sale, the most recent offer from outsiders, the current market value of assets less debts on them, cessation of activity and sale of assets, and bankruptcy.

(3) The county prosecutor or the administrative agency's legal staff shall be consulted for assistance in determining the value of the stock when the verification of the current value of the stock of a closely held corporation is questionable, including when there are indications that the extent of an individual's ownership is being manipulated to reduce the value of the stock as a countable resource.

(4) If the ownership of the stock is shared (i.e., more than one name is on the face of the stock certificate), each owner owns an equal share of the value of the stock.

(5) Shares of stock in an Alaskan native regional or village corporation, as defined in 43 U.S.C. 1601 - 1624 (as in effect on February 1, 2016), are excluded from resources.

(C) A mutual fund is determined in the same manner as the value of a stock.

(D) The current market value of a municipal, corporate, or government bond is counted as a resource. If the ownership of a bond is shared, each owner owns an equal share of the current market value of the bond.

(E) The current redemption value of a U.S. savings bond is a countable resource. If the ownership of the U.S. savings bond is shared, each owner owns equal shares of the redemption value of the bond.

Replaces: 5160:1-3-05.5.
Effective: 09/12/2016.
Five Year Review (FYR) Dates: 09/12/2021.
Promulgated Under: 111.15.
Statutory Authority: 5160.02, 5163.02.
Rule Amplifies: 5160.02, 5163.02
Prior Effective Dates: 9/3/77, 2/1/79, 10/1/79, 1/3/80, 12/1/84 (Emer.), 2/10/85, 5/3/85 (Emer.), 8/1/85, 9/1/85 (Emer.), 11/25/85, 10/1/91, 9/1/94, 11/7/02, 10/1/06, 10/2/14, 1/1/16.

### 5160:1-3-05.19. Medicaid: real or personal property essential to self-support.

(A) This rule describes exclusions when real or personal property is essential to an individual's means of self-support.

(B) Definition.

(1) "Basic daily living needs", for the purpose of this rule, means any food, basic clothing, basic shelter, and any medical

care that are not provided by medicaid. Items for entertainment or leisure are not basic daily living needs.

(2) "Maximum allowable equity" means an individual's equity in income-producing property, up to a maximum of six thousand dollars.

(C) Categories of property essential to self-support.

(1) Property used in a trade or business, government permits that represent authority granted by a government agency to engage in an income-producing activity, or property used by an individual as an employee for work.

(a) Is excluded as a resource regardless of value or rate of return.

(b) Government permits includes any permit, license, or similiar instrument issued by a federal, state, or local government agency.

(c) Personal property used by an employee for work includes farm machinery, tools, safety equipment, uniforms, etc.

(2) Nonbusiness real or personal property used to produce goods or services essential to basic daily living needs.

(a) Up to six thousand dollars of the equity value is excluded, regardless of rate of return.

(b) Any portion of the property's equity value in excess of six thousand dollars is a countable resource.

(c) Nonbusiness property used to produce goods or services includes growing produce or livestock solely for personal consumption in the individual's household or performing activities essential to the production of food solely for home consumption.

(3) Nonbusiness income-producing property.

(a) Up to six thousand dollars of the equity value is excluded as a resource if the property produces a net annual return equal to at least six per cent of the excluded equity.

(b) Any portion of the property's equity value in excess of six thousand dollars is a countable resource.

(c) If the property produces less than a six per cent return, the exclusion can only apply if the lower return is for reasons beyond the individual's control and there is a reasonable expectation that the property will again produce a six per cent return. Otherwise, none of the equity value is excluded under this section.

(d) If the earnings decline was for reasons beyond the individual's control, up to twenty-four months are to be allowed for the property to resume producing a six per cent return. The twenty-four month period begins with the first day of the tax year following the tax year in which the return dropped to below six per cent.

(e) If the tax return shows that the property has operated at a loss for the two most recent years or longer, the property cannot be excluded unless the individual submits current receipts and records to show that the property currently is producing a six per cent return.

(f) If an individual owns more than one piece of income-producing property, the six per cent return requirement applies individually to each property and the six thousand dollar equity value limit applies to the total equity value of all the properties meeting the six per cent return requirement.

(g) If all properties meet the six per cent return requirement but the total equity value exceeds six thousand dollars, that portion of the total equity value in excess of six thousand dollars is a countable resource.

(D) For any of the exclusions to apply, the property is to be in current use in the type of activity that qualifies it as essential.

(E) Property not in current use. If the property is not in current use, it must be for reasons beyond the individual's control and there must be a reasonable expectation that the use will resume within twelve months of last use.

(1) Property not in current use is to be excluded for twelve months as essential for self-support if the property has been in use and there is reasonable expectation that the use will resume. The individual is to provide a signed statement of last date of use, reason the property is not in use, and when the individual expects to resume the self-support activity.

(2) If an individual alleges that self-support property is not in current use because of a disabling condition of the individual, the individual is to provide a signed statement of the nature of the condition, the date the individual ceased the self-support activity, and when the individual intends to resume activity to receive up to an additional twelve months.

(3) If the individual does not intend to resume the self-support activity, the property is a countable resource in the month after the month of last use.

(4) If, after property has been excluded because an individual intends to resume self-support activity, the individual decides not to resume such activity, the exclusion ceases to apply as of the date of the change of intent. The property is a resource in the following month.

(F) Individual responsibilities. The individual is to:

(1) Provide a copy of the tax return for the tax year prior to application or renewal if the property is used in a trade or business in order for the administrative agency to determine the net income earned by the individual.

(2) Provide pertinent documents and a signed statement if the individual alleges owning a government license, permit, or other property that represents government authority to engage in an income-producing activity, and has value as a resource. The statement is to include:

(a) The type of license, permit, or other property; and

(b) The name of the issuing agency, if appropriate; and

(c) Whether the law requires such license, permit, or property for engaging in the income-producing activity at issue; and

(d) How the license, permit, or other property is being used; or

(e) Why the license, permit, or other property is not being used.

(3) Provide a signed statement if the individual alleges owning items used in his or her work as an employee. The statement is to include:

(a) The name, address, and telephone number of the employer; and

(b) A general description of the items; and

(c) A general description of the individual's duties; and

(d) Whether the items are currently being used.

(4) Provide a signed statement if the individual alleges owning property used to produce goods or services essential to basic daily living needs. The statement is to include:

(a) A description of the property; and

(b) How the property is used; and

(c) An estimate of the property's fair market value and any encumbrances on the property.

(G) Administrative agency responsibilities. The administrative agency is to:

(1) Determine whether the property qualifies under one of the three categories identified in paragraph (C) of this rule if the individual asserts his or her property is essential for self-support.

(2) Determine whether to exclude equity in property that provides either a product or a service that supplies basic daily living needs for the individual as described in paragraph (C)(2) of this rule.

(a) If the property does provide basic daily living needs for the individual, then the individual's equity up to a maximum of six thousand dollars is not to be counted as a resource. Any equity in excess of six thousand dollars is to be counted as a resource.

(b) If the property does not provide basic daily living needs for the individual, then the entire equity is a countable resource.

(3) Determine whether to exclude equity in nonbusiness income-producing property described in paragraph (C)(3) of this rule as follows:

(a) Determine the individual's maximum allowable equity in the property.

(b) Multiply the individual's maximum allowable equity by six per cent.

(c) Establish the net annual income the property produces for the individual.

(i) If the income to the individual is equal to or greater than the six per cent calculated in paragraph (G)(3)(b) of this rule, then the maximum allowable equity is not counted as a resource.

(ii) If the income to the individual is less than the six per cent calculated in paragraph (G)(3)(b) of this rule, then the individual's entire equity is counted as an available resource.

(d) If there is more than one potentially excluded property, the six per cent return requirement applies individually to each property and the six thousand dollars equity value limit applies to the total equity value of all the properties meeting the six per cent return requirement.

(4) Apply only the provision that is most beneficial to the individual if the individual's property falls under more than one of the categories in paragraph (C) of this rule.

(5) Request any other documentation necessary to fully and adequately distinguish between the income from the income-producing property, and income from other sources.

(6) Consider the individual's entire equity as a countable resource if the individual fails to cooperate with providing the appropriate documentation.

Effective: 6/1/2021.
Five Year Review (FYR) Dates: 6/1/2026.
Promulgated Under: 111.15.
Statutory Authority: 5160.02, 5163.02.
Rule Amplifies: 5160.02, 5163.02
Prior Effective Dates: 9/3/1977, 2/1/1979, 10/1/1979, 1/3/1980, 10/1/1995, 11/7/2002, 11/2/2014, 8/1/2016.

**5160:1-3-05.20. Medicaid: deeming of resources.**

(A) This rule describes the deeming of resources from an ineligible spouse to an eligible spouse or from parent(s) to an eligible child who are living in the same household when determining eligibility for medical assistance.

(B) Definitions.

(1) "Child," for deeming purposes, means an individual under age eighteen who lives in the household with one or both parents and is neither married nor head of household. The deeming of parental resources applies through the month in which the eligible child becomes eighteen years old. An eligible or ineligible child's resources are never deemed to parent(s) or sibling(s).

(2) "Deemed resources" means resources attributed to another person whether or not the resource is actually available to the person to whom they are deemed.

(3) "Eligible child" means a child in the household who has applied for medical assistance for the blind or disabled, and who meets all the applicable non-financial and income eligibility criteria for medical assistance.

(4) "Eligible spouse" means the member of a married couple who has applied for medical assistance for the aged, blind, or disabled, and who meets all the applicable non-financial and income eligibility criteria for medical assistance.

(5) "Household" means the eligible spouse, ineligible spouse, and any of the couple's children or the children of either member of the couple; or the eligible child, and the eligible child's parent(s), and other children of the parent(s).

(a) A household does not exist if an individual or a group of individuals does not have a residence. In such a case, only the eligible individual's resources are used to determine eligibility for medical assistance.

(b) If a child is born in an institution (e.g., hospital), the child is a member of the household at the time of birth unless the parents have completed the required paperwork to surrender the child for adoption or the child has been placed in the temporary custody of a public children's services agency (PCSA) or private child placing agency (PCPA).

(c) An eligible individual or an ineligible spouse or ineligible parent who is temporarily absent, as defined in rule 5160:1-1-01 of the Administrative Code, is still considered to be a member of the household for deeming purposes.

(6) "Ineligible child" means a child in the household who has not applied for medical assistance for the blind or disabled.

(7) "Ineligible parent" means an eligible child's parent who has not applied for medical assistance for the aged, blind, or disabled.

(8) "Ineligible spouse" means an eligible spouse's husband or wife who has not applied for medical assistance for the aged, blind, or disabled.

(9) "Parent" means a natural or adoptive father or mother living in the same household as the eligible child. The resources of a step-parent who lives with the eligible child are deemed to the eligible child only when the natural or adoptive parent also lives in the household with the step-parent and eligible child. If the natural or adoptive parent divorces a step-parent and the eligible child is living with the step-parent, the step-parent is not a parent for deeming purposes.

(10) "Sponsor" means an individual who signs an affidavit of support agreeing to support a non-citizen as a condition of the non-citizen's admission for permanent residence in the U.S. A sponsored non-citizen may have more than one sponsor. For deeming purposes, a sponsor does not include an organization such as the congregation of a church or a service club, or an employer that only guarantees employment for a non-citizen upon entry but does not sign an affidavit of support.

(11) "Sponsored non-citizen", for the purpose of this rule, means an individual lawfully admitted for permanent residence in the U.S. who is supported by a sponsor(s). Such an individual has applied for medical assistance for the aged, blind, or disabled, and meets all the applicable non-financial eligibility criteria for medical assistance.

(12) "Spouse" means a person who is legally married to another under Ohio law.

(C) In deeming resources from an ineligible spouse to an eligible spouse, only the resources of those two individuals are considered. In deeming resources from a parent(s) to an eligible child, only the resources of the parent(s) are considered.

(D) Retirement funds, described in rule 5160:1-3-03.10 of the Administrative Code, owned by an ineligble spouse, parent(s), or sponsor are excluded from resources for deeming purposes.

(E) Spouse to spouse deeming.

(1) When an eligible spouse and his or her ineligible spouse live together, all resources are combined and the couple is permitted resources in the amount described in rule 5160:1-3-05.1 of the Administrative Code in addition to what is excluded as described in rule 5160:1-3-05.14 of the Administrative Code.

(2) The couple's resource limitation is not affected by whether the spouse of the eligible individual is eligible or ineligible for medical assistance.

(3) If the couple's countable resources are less than or equal to the resource limit for a couple described in rule 5160:1-3-05.1 of the Administrative Code, the eligible spouse is resource eligible for medical assistance.

(4) When spouses are no longer living together, each person is considered as an individual living alone beginning the month after separation. The individual resource limit, as described in rule 5160:1-3-05.1 of the Administrative Code, is then applicable.

(a) For the month of separation, the spouses are treated as an eligible couple or as an eligible spouse and ineligible spouse living together in the same household with a resource limit for a couple described in rule 5160:1-3-05.1 of the Administrative Code.

(b) In the month after the month of separation, resources are computed separately because each person is considered to be an individual without a spouse.

(F) Parent to child deeming.

(1) The resource limit for a child is described in rule 5160:1-3-05.1 of the Administrative Code in addition to what is excluded as described in rule 5160:1-3-05.14 of the Administrative Code.

(2) The resources of an eligible child consist of whatever resources the eligible child has in his or her own right plus whatever resources are deemed to the eligible child from his or her parent(s).

(3) In determining the amount of resources to be deemed to an eligible child, the resources of the eligible child and of the parent(s) are computed separately and both the eligible child and the parent(s) are each allowed all of the resource exclusions they would normally be eligible for in their own right. Only one home and one automobile are excluded.

(a) After the exclusions are applied, only the countable resources over the resource limit of the parent(s) living in the household are deemed to the eligible child when there is only one eligible child.

(i) If there is one parent in the household the parental resource limit is two thousand dollars.

(ii) If both parents are in the household the parental resource limit is three thousand dollars.

(iii) If both natural or adoptive parents and a step-parent are in the household the parental resource limit is two thousand dollars for one natural or adoptive parent plus three thousand dollars for the other natural or adoptive parent with the step-parent.

(b) When there is more than one eligible child, the resources available for deeming are shared equally among the eligible child(ren).

(c) None of the parents' resources are deemed to any ineligible children.

(4) An eligible child is not eligible for medical assistance if his or her own countable resources plus the value of the parent(s)'s

resources deemed to the eligible child exceed the resource limit for a child described in rule 5160:1-3-05.1 of the Administrative Code.

(G) Sponsor to non-citizen deeming.

(1) Sponsor to non-citizen deeming is to apply:

(a) Regardless of whether the sponsor and the sponsored non-citizen live in the same household or whether the sponsor actually provides the sponsored non-citizen any support; and

(b) For a period of three years following a sponsored non-citizen's lawful admission to the U.S. as a permanent resident or the sponsored non-citizen's status is adjusted to permanent resident.

(2) If a sponsored non-citizen is sponsored by his or her ineligible spouse or ineligible parent(s), apply spouse to spouse and parent to child deeming calculations.

(3) If a sponsored non-citizen has a sponsor and also has an ineligible spouse or ineligible parent(s) who is not his or her sponsor, apply both sponsor to non-citizen and spouse to spouse or parent to child deeming calculations.

(4) In determining the amount of resources to be deemed to a sponsored non-citizen, combine the resources of the sponsor (and sponsor's spouse, if applicable) and apply any appropriate exclusions described in rule 5160:1-3-05.14 of the Administrative Code.

(a) After the exclusions are applied, only the countable resources over the resource limit of the sponsor are deemed to the sponsored non-citizen.

(i) If the sponsor does not live with a spouse, the resource limit is two thousand dollars.

(ii) If the sponser lives with a spouse and the spouse is not the non-citizen's sponsor, the resource limit is three thousand dollars.

(iii) If the sponser lives with a spouse and the spouse is also a sponsor of the non-citizen, the resource limit is four thousand dollars.

(b) A sponsored non-citizen is not eligible for medical assistance if his or her countable resources plus the value of the sponsor's resources deemed to the sponsored non-citizen exceed the resource limit for an individual described in rule 5160:1-3-05.1 of the Administrative Code.

Effective: 6/1/2021.
Five Year Review (FYR) Dates: 6/1/2026.
Promulgated Under: 111.15.
Statutory Authority: 5160.02, 5163.02.
Rule Amplifies: 5160.02, 5163.02
Prior Effective Dates: 9/3/1977, 2/1/1979, 10/1/1979, 1/3/1980, 2/15/1985 (Emer.), 5/14/1985 (Emer.), 6/10/1985, 1/1/1991, 7/1/1994, 10/1/1995, 10/1/1996 (Emer.), 12/15/1996, 11/2/2014, 8/1/2016, 9/1/2017.



### 5160:1-3-06. Medicaid: social security administration reporting alleged transfer of resources by supplemental security income (SSI) applicants to the Ohio department of job and family services (ODJFS). [RESCINDED]

Rescinded effective: 01/15/2015.
Five Year Review (FYR) Dates: 10/30/2014.
Promulgated Under: 111.15.
Statutory Authority: 5111.01, 5111.011.
Rule Amplifies: 5111.01, 5111.011
Prior Effective Dates: 8/9/90.

### 5160:1-3-06.1 Medicaid: treatment of income and resources of institutionalized individuals. [RESCINDED]

Rescinded effective: 9/1/2017.
Five Year Review (FYR) Dates: 6/16/2017.
Promulgated Under: 111.15.
Statutory Authority: 5163.02, 5160.02.
Rule Amplifies: 5160.02, 5163.02
Prior Effective Dates: 9/3/77, 12/31/77, 3/1/79, 10/1/79, 12/179/79, 1/21/80, 9/1/82, 12/7/83, 7/25/84 (Temp.), 10/1/84, 10/1/88 (Emer.), 12/20/88, 1/1/90 (Emer.), 4/1/90, 4/1/91, 10/1/02, 11/2/14.

### 5160:1-3-06.2 Medicaid: resource assessment. [RESCINDED]

Rescinded effective: 9/1/2017
Five Year Review (FYR) Dates: 6/16/2017.
Promulgated Under: 111.15.
Statutory Authority: 5160.02.
Rule Amplifies: 5160.02
Prior Effective Dates: 1/1/90 (Emer.), 4/1/90, 10/1/90, 2/7/91 (Emer.), 5/1/91, 7/1/92, 9/1/94, 10/1/02, 7/1/05, 10/1/06, 11/2/14.

### 5160:1-3-06.3 Medicaid: treatment of resources for institutionalized individuals with a spouse in the community. [RESCINDED]

Rescinded effective: 9/1/2017.
Five Year Review (FYR) Dates: 6/16/2017.
Promulgated Under: 111.15.
Statutory Authority: 5163.02, 5160.02.
Rule Amplifies: 5160.02, 5163.02
Prior Effective Dates: 1/1/90 (Emer.), 4/1/90, 1/1/91 (Emer.), 4/1/91, 1/1/92 (Emer.), 3/30/92, 2/12/93 (Emer.), 5/13/93, 3/18/94, 9/1/94, 4/1/96, 5/1/97, 4/1/98 (Emer.), 6/1/98, 4/1/99, 1/1/00 (Emer.), 4/1/00, 1/1/01, 5/12/02, 11/2/14.

### 5160:1-3-06.4 Medicaid: resource budgeting methodology for institutionalized individuals with a spouse in the community. [RESCINDED]

Rescinded effective: 9/1/2017.
Five Year Review (FYR) Dates: 6/16/2017.
Promulgated Under: 111.15.
Statutory Authority: 5163.02, 5160.02.
Rule Amplifies: 5160.02, 5163.02
Prior Effective Dates: 1/1/90 (Emer.), 4/1/90, 6/1/90 (Emer.), 8/1/90, 10/1/90 (Emer.), 12/24/90, 1/1/91 (Emer.), 4/1/91, 1/1/92 (Emer.), 3/30/92, 2/12/93 (Emer.), 5/13/93, 9/1/94, 11/7/02, 7/1/03, 9/20/03, 10/1/06, 11/2/14.

### 5160:1-3-06.5 Medicaid: transfer of resources for institutionalized spouses with a spouse in the community. [RESCINDED]

Rescinded effective: 9/1/2017.
Five Year Review (FYR) Dates: 6/16/2017.
Promulgated Under: 111.15.
Statutory Authority: 5163.02, 5160.02.
Rule Amplifies: 5160.02, 5163.02
Prior Effective Dates: 1/1/90 (Emer.), 4/1/90, 6/1/90 (Emer.), 8/1/90, 1/1/92, 7/1/95, 10/1/02, 11/2/14.

### 5160:1-3-07. Medicaid: transfer of resources. [RESCINDED]

Rescinded effective: 01/01/2016.
Five Year Review (FYR) Dates: 10/16/2015.
Promulgated Under: 111.15.
Statutory Authority: 5111.01, 5111.011.
Rule Amplifies: 5111.01, 5111.011
Prior Effective Dates: 9/3/77, 7/1/82, 7/15/84, 1/1/85 (Emer.), 4/1/85, 11/1/86 (Emer.), 12/22/86, 7/1/87 (Emer.), 8/3/87, 1/1/90 (Emer.), 4/1/90, 10/1/90, 4/1/95 (Emer.), 6/11/95, 3/15/96 (Emer.), 6/1/96, 11/7/02.

### 5160:1-3-07.1 Medicaid: social security administration reporting alleged transfer of resources by supplemental security income (SSI) applicants to the Ohio department of medicaid (ODM). [RESCINDED]

Rescinded effective: 9/1/2017.
Five Year Review (FYR) Dates: 6/16/2017.
Promulgated Under: 111.15.
Statutory Authority: 5160.02, 5163.02.
Rule Amplifies: 5160.02, 5163.02
Prior Effective Dates: 8/9/90, 10/1/02.

### 5160:1-3-07.2 Medicaid: transfer of resources. [RESCINDED]

Rescinded effective: 9/1/2017.
Five Year Review (FYR) Dates: 6/16/2017.
Promulgated Under: 111.15.
Statutory Authority: 5160.02, 5163.02.
Rule Amplifies: 5160.02, 5163.02
Prior Effective Dates: 9/3/77, 7/1/82, 7/15/84, 1/1/85 (Emer.), 4/1/85, 11/1/86 (Emer.), 12/22/86, 7/1/87 (Emer.), 8/3/87, 1/1/90 (Emer.), 4/1/90, 10/1/90, 4/1/95 (Emer.), 6/11/95, 3/15/96 (Emer.), 6/1/96, 11/7/02, 10/20/06.

**5160:1-3-07.3 Medicaid: disposal of resources for Ohio department of developmental disabilities and/or Ohio department of mental health and addiction services individuals. [RESCINDED]**

Rescinded effective: 9/1/2017.
Five Year Review (FYR) Dates: 6/16/2017.
Promulgated Under: 111.15.
Statutory Authority: 5160.02, 5163.02.
Rule Amplifies: 5160.02, 5163.02
Prior Effective Dates: 4/1/89 (Emer.), 11/7/02.

**5160:1-3-08. Medicaid: income. [RESCINDED]**

Rescinded effective: 01/25/2015.
Five Year Review (FYR) Dates: 10/20/2014.
Promulgated Under: 111.15.
Statutory Authority: 5111.01, 5111.012.
Rule Amplifies: 5111.01, 5111.012
Prior Effective Dates: 9/3/77, 12/31/77, 3/1/79, 10/1/79, 12/7/79, 1/3/80, 12/1/84 (Emer.), 2/10/85, 8/1/85, 10/1/88 (Emer.), 12/20/88, 9/1/92, 10/1/02, 7/1/05, 10/1/06.

**5160:1-3-10. Medicaid: eligibility through the spenddown process. [RESCINDED]**

Rescinded effective: 04/01/2015.
Five Year Review (FYR) Dates: 12/23/2014.
Promulgated Under: 111.15.
Statutory Authority: 5111.01, 5111.011.
Rule Amplifies: 5111.01, 5111.011
Prior Effective Dates: 9/3/77, 12/31/77, 3/1/79, 10/1/79, 12/7/79, 2/21/80, 10/10/84 (Emer.), 12/29/84, 4/1/86, 8/1/86 (Emer.), 10/3/86, 11/1/86 (Emer.), 12/22/86, 10/1/88, 12/20/88, 1/1/89 (Emer.), 4/1/89, 10/1/89 (Emer.), 12/16/89, 1/1/90 (Emer.), 4/1/90, 9/28/90 (Emer.), 12/24/90, 10/1/91, 1/1/93 (Emer.), 3/18/93, 9/10/93 (Emer.), 12/10/93, 12/1/97 (Emer.), 2/1/98.

**5160:1-3-11. Medicaid eligibility for persons living in state institutions for the mentally ill and mentally retarded. [RESCINDED]**

Rescinded effective: 01/22/2015.
Five Year Review (FYR) Dates: 10/14/2014.
Promulgated Under: 111.15.
Statutory Authority: 5111.01, 5111.011.
Rule Amplifies: 5111.01, 5111.011
Prior Effective Dates: 9/3/77, 8/1/86 (Emer.), 10/3/86, 10/1/02.

**5160:1-3-12.2 Medicaid: information sharing with long term care facility (LTCF) providers. [Rescinded.]Eff 8-1-9010-1-029-1-03Rescinded eff. 1-6-05.**

Rule promulgated under: RC 111.15.
Rule authorized by: RC 5111.01, 5111.011.
Rule amplifies: RC 5111.01, 5111.012
Prior Effective Dates: 8-1-90, 10-1-2002, 9-1-2003.

**5160:1-3-14.4 Medicaid: sheltered workshop earnings. [RESCINDED]**

Rescinded effective: 01/25/2015.
Five Year Review (FYR) Dates: 10/20/2014.
Promulgated Under: 111.15.
Statutory Authority: 5111.01, 5111.011.
Rule Amplifies: 5111.01, 5111.011
Prior Effective Dates: 9/3/77, 12/31/77, 3/1/79, 10/1/79, 1/3/80, 10//1/88 (Emer.), 12/20/88, 10/1/89 (Emer.), 12/16/89, 5/1/91 (Emer.), 6/17/91, 9/1/94, 10/1/02.

**5160:1-3-15.1 Medicaid: treatment of rental income. [RESCINDED]**

Rescinded effective: 01/25/2015.
Five Year Review (FYR) Dates: 10/20/2014.
Promulgated Under: 111.15.
Statutory Authority: 5111.01, 5111.011.
Rule Amplifies: 5111.01, 5111.011
Prior Effective Dates: 9/3/77, 12/31/77, 3/1/79, 10/1/79, 12/7/79, 1/3/80, 10/1/88 (Emer.), 12/20/88, 10/1/89 (Emer.), 12/16/89, 5/1/91 (Emer.), 6/17/91, 7/17/91, 9/1/94, 10/1/02.

**5160:1-3-15.2 Medicaid: treatment of sick pay. [RESCINDED]**

Rescinded effective: 01/25/2015.
Five Year Review (FYR) Dates: 10/20/2014.
Promulgated Under: 111.15.
Statutory Authority: 5111.01, 5111.011.
Rule Amplifies: 5111.01, 5111.011
Prior Effective Dates: 9/1/94.

**5160:1-3-17. Medicaid: in-kind support and maintenance. [RESCINDED]**

Rescinded effective: 01/25/2015.
Five Year Review (FYR) Dates: 10/20/2014.
Promulgated Under: 111.15.
Statutory Authority: 5111.01.
Rule Amplifies: 5111.01, 5111.012
Prior Effective Dates: 9/3/77, 12/31/77, 3/1/79, 10/1/79, 12/7/79, 1/3/80, 12/1/84 (Emer.), 2/10/85, 7/1/87 (Emer.), 8/3/87, 1/1/99, 7/1/05.

**5160:1-3-18. Medicaid: income exemptions and disregards. [RESCINDED]**

Rescinded effective: 01/25/2015.
Five Year Review (FYR) Dates: 10/20/2014.
Promulgated Under: 111.15.
Statutory Authority: 5101.01, 5101.011.
Rule Amplifies: 5101.01, 5101.011
Prior Effective Dates: 9/3/77, 12/31/77, 3/1/79, 10/1/79, 12/1/79, 1/3/80, 3/1/84, 10/1/88 (Emer.), 12/20/88, 7/1/89 (Emer.), 9/23/89, 10/1/89 (Emer.), 12/16/89, 2/ 7/91 (Emer.), 5/1/91, 7/18/91, 10/1/91, 1/1/92, 4/1/92, 6/1/92 (Emer.), 8/13/92, 10/1/92 (Emer.), 12/21/92, 8/ 18/93 (Emer.), 11/1/93, 3/1/94 (Emer.), 4/18/94, 7/1/94, 10/7/94, 1/1/95, 4/1/95, 7/1/96 (Emer.), 9/1/96, 5/1/97, 10/31/97 (Emer.), 1/26/98, 3/1/98 (Emer.), 5/1/98, 9/10/99.

**5160:1-3-19. Medicaid: deeming of income. [RESCINDED]**

Rescinded effective: 01/25/2015.
Five Year Review (FYR) Dates: 10/20/2014.
Promulgated Under: 111.15.
Statutory Authority: 5111.01.
Rule Amplifies: 5111.01, 5111.011
Prior Effective Dates: 9/3/77, 12/31/77, 3/1/79, 10/1/79, 12/7/79, 1/3/80, 2/15/85 (Emer.), 5/14/85 (Emer.), 6/10/85, 10/1/88 (Emer.), 12/20/88, 1/1/91, 1/1/92, 7/1/92, 8/18/93 (Emer.), 11/1/93, 3/1/94 (Emer.), 4/18/94, 4/1/95 (Emer.), 6/11/95, 10/1/95, 10/1/96 (Emer.), 12/15/96, 10/1/02, 3/1/13.

**5160:1-3-21. Medicaid: standards and allocations. [RESCINDED]**

Rescinded effective: 01/25/2015.
Five Year Review (FYR) Dates: 10/20/2014.
Promulgated Under: 111.15.
Statutory Authority: 5111.01, 5111.011, 5101.531.
Rule Amplifies: 5111.01, 5111.011, 5101.531
Prior Effective Dates: 9/3/77, 12/31/77, 3/1/79, 10/1/79, 12/7/79, 1/3/80, 7/1/80, 8/1/81, 7/1/82, 12/1/82, 7/1/83 (Temp.), 9/24/83, 1/1/85 (Emer.), 4/1/85, 5/1/85 (Emer.), 7/31/85, 1/1/86 (Emer.), 4/1/86, 1/1/87 (Emer.), 3/20/87, 1/1/88 (Emer.), 2/1/88 (Emer.), 3/21/88, 1/1/89 (Emer.), 4/1/89, 5/1/89 (Emer.), 7/8/89, 1/1/90 (Emer.), 4/1/90, 4/2/90 (Emer.), 6/22/90, 1/1/91 (Emer.), 4/1/91, 4/2/91 (Emer.), 6/17/91, 1/1/92 (Emer.), 3/20/92, 4/1/92 (Emer.), 6/30/92, 1/1/93 (Emer.), 3/18/93, 3/25/93, 6/11/93, 9/1/93, 3/18/94, 2/1/95, 4/01/95 (Emer.), 6/11/95, 4/1/96, 1/1/97 (Emer.), 2/9/97, 12/3/97 (Emer.), 2/1/98, 1/8/99 (Emer.), 4/1/99, 1/1/00, 6/2/01, 5/12/02.

**5160:1-3-22. Medicaid: treatment of income and resources of institutionalized individuals. [RESCINDED]**

Rescinded effective: 11/02/2014.
Five Year Review (FYR) Dates: 08/07/2014.
Promulgated Under: 111.15.
Statutory Authority: 5111.01, 5111.011.
Rule Amplifies: 5111.01, 5111.011
Prior Effective Dates: 9/3/77, 12/31/77, 3/1/79, 10/1/79, 12/17/79, 1/21/80, 9/1/82, 12/7/83, 7/25/84 (Temp.), 10/1/84, 10/1/88 (Emer.), 12/20/88, 1/1/90 (Emer.), 4/1/90, 4/1/91.

NOTES TO DECISIONS

(1995) In determining whether Ohio Medicaid eligibility continues to exist in changed circumstances, the county department of human services

Admin Code

should examine and apply relevant provisions of law, including 12 OAC 5101:1-39-04(D), 5101:1-39-22(B), and 5101:1-39-54(B)(1), which indicate that the transfer of temporary custody of a child who resides in a long term care facility in Ohio from a county department of human services to the child's grandparent who resides in another state will not, in itself, render the child ineligible for Medicaid benefits under the Ohio medical assistance program: OAG No. 95-002.

### 5160:1-3-22.7 Medicaid: retirement and income supplementing accounts (RISAs). [RESCINDED]

Rescinded effective: 01/25/2015.
Five Year Review (FYR) Dates: 10/20/2014.
Promulgated Under: 111.15.
Statutory Authority: 5111.01, 5111.11.
Rule Amplifies: 5111.01, 5111.11
Prior Effective Dates: 1/1/93, 7/1/94, 12/1/04, 10/1/06.

### 5160:1-3-22.8 Medicaid: the disclosure and treatment of annuities for recipients or applicants for medical assistance programs. [RESCINDED]

Rescinded effective: 01/15/2015.
Five Year Review (FYR) Dates: 10/30/2014.
Promulgated Under: 111.15.
Statutory Authority: 5111.01, 5111.011.
Rule Amplifies: 5111.01, 5111.011
Prior Effective Dates: 5/1/97, 10/28/02.

### 5160:1-3-23. Medicaid: income computations for determining eligibility using the special income level. [RESCINDED]

Rescinded effective: 01/25/2015.
Five Year Review (FYR) Dates: 10/14/2014.
Promulgated Under: 119.03.
Statutory Authority: 173.40, 5111.01, 5111.871.
Rule Amplifies: 173.40, 5111.01, 5111.012, 5111.205, 5111.87, 5111.871, 5111.91
Prior Effective Dates: 6/1/88 (Emer.), 8/1/88 (Emer.), 10/30/88, 1/1/90 (Emer.), 3/1/90 (Emer.), 3/30/90 (Emer.), 4/1/90, 6/29/90, 7/1/90, 10/1/90, 1/1/91 (Emer.), 4/1/91, 1/1/92 (Emer.), 3/20/92, 5/1/92 (Emer.), 7/1/92, 8/14/92 (Emer.), 11/1/92, 5/1/93, 9/1/93, 7/1/94, 1/1/95 (Emer.), 3/20/95, 10/1/95, 4/1/96, 1/1/97 (Emer.), 2/9/97, 12/31/97 (Emer.), 2/1/98, 4/1/99, 1/1/00, 1/1/01, 5/12/02.

Admin Code

### 5160:1-3-24. Medicaid: determining patient liability. [RESCINDED]

Rescinded effective: 01/01/2016.
Five Year Review (FYR) Dates: 09/21/2015.
Promulgated Under: 111.15.
Statutory Authority: 5111.01, 5111.011.
Rule Amplifies: 5111.01, 5111.011
Prior Effective Dates: 6/1/88 (Emer.), 8/1/88 (Emer.), 10/30/88, 1/1/90 (Emer.), 3/1/90 (Emer.), 3/30/90 (Emer.), 4/1/90, 6/29/90, 7/1/90, 10/1/90, 1/1/91 (Emer.), 4/1/91, 1/1/92 (Emer.), 3/20/92, 5/1/92 (Emer.), 7/1/92, 8/14/92 (Emer.), 11/1/92, 5/1/93, 9/1/93, 7/1/94, 1/1/95 (Emer.), 3/20/95, 10/1/95, 4/1/96, 1/1/97 (Emer.), 2/9/97, 12/31/97 (Emer.), 2/1/98, 4/1/99, 1/1/00, 1/1/01, 5/12/02, 7/01/05, 12/01/06, 1/1/13.

### 5160:1-3-24.1 Medicaid: income and patient liability determinations for individuals under the assisted living home and community based waiver. [RESCINDED]

Rescinded effective: 01/01/2016.
Five Year Review (FYR) Dates: 09/21/2015.
Promulgated Under: 111.15.
Statutory Authority: 5111.01.
Rule Amplifies: 173.40, 5111.01, 5111.89
Prior Effective Dates: 7/1/06 (Emer.), 9/15/06.

### 5160:1-3-26. Medicaid: resource exemption. [RESCINDED]

Rescinded effective: 10/02/2014.
Five Year Review (FYR) Dates: 07/01/2014.
Promulgated Under: 111.15.
Statutory Authority: 5111.01, 5111.011.
Rule Amplifies: 5111.01, 5111.011
Prior Effective Dates: 10/1/06.

### 5160:1-3-27. Medicaid: liquid assets as resources. [RESCINDED]

Rescinded effective: 08/01/2016.
Promulgated Under: 111.15.
Statutory Authority: 5111.02.
Rule Amplifies: 5111.02
Prior Effective Dates: 9/3/77, 2/1/79, 10/1/79, 1/3/80, 12/1/84 (Emer.), 2/10/85, 5/3/85 (Emer.), 8/1/85, 9/1/85 (Emer.), 11/25/85.

### 5160:1-3-27.1 Medicaid: trusts. [RESCINDED]

Rescinded effective: 01/15/2015.
Five Year Review (FYR) Dates: 10/30/2014.
Promulgated Under: 111.15.
Statutory Authority: 5111.01, 5111.011.
Rule Amplifies: 5111.01, 5111.011
Prior Effective Dates: 9/3/77, 2/1/79, 10/1/79, 1/3/80, 12/1/84 (Emer.), 2/10/85, 5/3/85 (Emer.), 8/1/85, 9/1/85 (Emer.), 11/25/85, 10/1/89 (Emer.), 12/16/89, 10/1/91, 9/1/92, 2/1/95 (Emer.), 4/27/95, 7/1/96, 11/7/02.

### 5160:1-3-27.2 Medicaid: cash and checking and savings accounts and time deposits. [RESCINDED]

Rescinded effective: 10/02/2014.
Five Year Review (FYR) Dates: 07/01/2014.
Promulgated Under: 111.15.
Statutory Authority: 5111.01, 5111.011.
Rule Amplifies: 5111.01, 5111.011
Prior Effective Dates: 9/3/77, 2/1/79, 1/3/80, 12/1/84 (Emer.), 2/10/85, 5/3/85 (Emer.), 8/1/85, 9/1/85 (Emer.), 11/25/85, 4/1/91, 9/1/94, 5/1/98.

### 5160:1-3-27.3 Medicaid: promissory notes, mortgages, stocks, bonds and loans. [RESCINDED]

Rescinded effective: 10/02/2014.
Five Year Review (FYR) Dates: 07/01/2014.
Promulgated Under: 111.15.
Statutory Authority: 5111.01, 5111.011.
Rule Amplifies: 5111.01, 5111.011
Prior Effective Dates: 9/3/77, 2/1/79, 10/1/79, 1/3/80, 12/1/84 (Emer.), 2/10/85, 5/3/85 (Emer.), 8/1/85, 9/1/85 (Emer.), 11/25/85, 10/1/91, 9/1/94, 11/7/02.

### 5160:1-3-27.4 Medicaid: preneed funeral contracts. [RESCINDED]

Rescinded effective: 10/02/2014.
Five Year Review (FYR) Dates: 07/01/2014.
Promulgated Under: 111.15.
Statutory Authority: 5111.01, 5111.011.
Rule Amplifies: 5111.01, 5111.011
Prior Effective Dates: 9/3/77, 2/1/79, 10/1/79, 1/3/80, 12/1/84 (Emer.), 2/1/85, 5/3/85 (Emer.), 8/1/85, 9/1/85 (Emer.), 11/25/85, 10/1/88 (Emer.), 12/20/88.

### 5160:1-3-27.5 Medicaid: lump-sum payments. [RESCINDED]

Rescinded effective: 10/02/2014.
Five Year Review (FYR) Dates: 07/01/2014.
Promulgated Under: 111.15.
Statutory Authority: 5111.01, 5111.011.
Rule Amplifies: 5111.01, 5111.011
Prior Effective Dates: 9/3/77, 2/1/79, 10/1/79, 1/3/80, 12/1/84 (Emer.), 2/10/85, 5/3/85 (Emer.), 8/1/85, 9/1/85 (Emer.), 11/25/85, 9/1/86, 5/1/91 (Emer.), 7/1/91, 6/11/93, 9/1/94.

### 5160:1-3-27.6 Medicaid: dividends and interest. [RESCINDED]

Rescinded effective: 10/02/2014.
Five Year Review (FYR) Dates: 07/01/2014.
Promulgated Under: 111.15.
Statutory Authority: 5111.01, 5111.011.
Rule Amplifies: 5111.01, 5111.011
Prior Effective Dates: 9/3/77, 2/1/79, 10/1/79, 1/3/80, 12/1/84 (Emer.), 2/10/85, 5/3/85 (Emer.), 8/1/85, 9/1/85 (Emer.), 11/25/85, 4/1/91.

### 5160:1-3-28. Household goods and personal effects as resources. [RESCINDED]

Rescinded effective: 10/02/2014.
Five Year Review (FYR) Dates: 07/01/2014.

Promulgated Under: 111.15.
Statutory Authority: 5111.01, 5111.011.
Rule Amplifies: 5111.01, 5111.011
Prior Effective Dates: 9/3/77, 2/1/79, 10/1/79, 1/3/80.

**5160:1-3-29. Automobiles and other modes of transportation as resources. [RESCINDED]**

Rescinded effective: 10/02/2014.
Five Year Review (FYR) Dates: 07/01/2014.
Promulgated Under: 111.15.
Statutory Authority: 5111.01, 5111.011.
Rule Amplifies: 5111.01, 5111.011
Prior Effective Dates: 9/3/77, 2/1/79, 10/1/79, 1/3/80, 4/1/89, 7/1/88 (Emer.), 9/1/88, 1/1/90 (Emer.), 4/1/90, 7/1/93.

**5160:1-3-30. Medicaid: life insurance. [RESCINDED]**

Rescinded effective: 10/02/2014.
Five Year Review (FYR) Dates: 07/01/2014.
Promulgated Under: 111.15.
Statutory Authority: 5111.01, 5111.011.
Rule Amplifies: 5111.01, 5111.011
Prior Effective Dates: 9/3/77, 2/1/79, 10/1/79, 1/3/80, 11/1/87, 7/1/88 (Emer.), 9/1/88, 9/1/92, 8/13/02.

**5160:1-3-31. Medicaid: treatment of the home. [RESCINDED]**

Rescinded effective: 10/02/2014.
Five Year Review (FYR) Dates: 07/01/2014.
Promulgated Under: 111.15.
Statutory Authority: 5111.01, 5111.011.
Rule Amplifies: 5111.11, 5111.18
Prior Effective Dates: 09/3/77, 2/1/79, 10/1/79, 1/3/80, 12/1/84 (Emer.), 2/10/85, 11/1/86 (Emer.), 12/22/86, 7/1/96 (Emer.), 9/1/96, 11/7/02, 10/1/06.

**5160:1-3-31.3 Medicaid: exemption of property no longer the principal place of residence. [RESCINDED]**

Rescinded effective: 10/02/2014.
Five Year Review (FYR) Dates: 07/01/2014.
Promulgated Under: 111.15.
Statutory Authority: 5111.01, 5111.011.
Rule Amplifies: 5111.01, 5111.011
Prior Effective Dates: 9/3/77, 2/1/79, 10/1/79, 1/3/80, 12/1/84 (Emer.), 2/10/85, 11/1/86 (Emer.), 12/22/86, 5/1/94.

**5160:1-3-31.4 Medicaid: home replacement exclusion. [RESCINDED]**

Rescinded effective: 11/02/2014.
Five Year Review (FYR) Dates: 08/07/2014.
Promulgated Under: 111.15.
Statutory Authority: 5111.01, 5111.011.
Rule Amplifies: 5111.01, 5111.011
Prior Effective Dates: 11/1/86 (Emer.), 12/22/86.

**5160:1-3-32. Medicaid: life estates and life leases. [RESCINDED]**

Rescinded effective: 11/02/2014.
Five Year Review (FYR) Dates: 08/07/2014.
Promulgated Under: 111.15.
Statutory Authority: 5111.01, 5111.011.
Rule Amplifies: 5111.01, 5111.011
Prior Effective Dates: 9/3/77, 2/1/79, 10/1/79, 1/3/80, 7/1/88 (Emer.), 9/1/88, 1/1/90 (Emer.), 4/1/90, 4/1/91 (Emer.), 6/17/91, 9/1/94, 11/7/02, 10/1/06, 11/1/13.

**5160:1-3-32.1 Medicaid: property agreements. [RESCINDED]**

Rescinded effective: 01/01/2016.
Five Year Review (FYR) Dates: 10/16/2015.
Promulgated Under: 111.15.
Statutory Authority: 5111.01, 5111.011.
Rule Amplifies: 5111.01, 5111.011
Prior Effective Dates: 8/1/86 (Emer.), 10/3/86, 11/1/86 (Emer.), 12/22/86, 7/1/94, 5/1/97, 11/7/02.

**5160:1-3-32.2 Medicaid: burial spaces. [RESCINDED]**

Rescinded effective: 10/02/2014.
Five Year Review (FYR) Dates: 07/01/2014.
Promulgated Under: 111.15.
Statutory Authority: 5111.01, 5111.011.
Rule Amplifies: 5111.01, 5111.011
Prior Effective Dates: 9/3/77, 2/1/79, 10/1/79, 1/3/80, 12/1/84 (Emer.), 2/10/85.

**5160:1-3-33. Real or personal property essential to self-support. [RESCINDED]**

Rescinded effective: 11/02/2014.
Five Year Review (FYR) Dates: 08/07/2014.
Promulgated Under: 111.15.
Statutory Authority: 5111.01, 5111.011.
Rule Amplifies: 5111.01, 5111.011
Prior Effective Dates: 9/3/77, 2/1/79, 10/1/79, 1/3/80, 10/1/95.

**5160:1-3-34. Deeming of resources. [RESCINDED]**

Rescinded effective: 11/02/2014.
Five Year Review (FYR) Dates: 08/07/2014.
Promulgated Under: 111.15.
Statutory Authority: 5111.01.
Rule Amplifies: 5111.01, 5111.011
Prior Effective Dates: 9/37//, 2/1/79, 10/1/79, 1/3/80, 2/15/85 (Emer.), 5/14/85 (Emer.), 6/10/85, 1/1/91, 7/1/94, 10/1/95, 10/1/96 (Emer.).

**5160:1-3-35. Medicaid: resource assessment. [RESCINDED]**

Rescinded effective: 11/02/2014.
Five Year Review (FYR) Dates: 08/07/2014.
Promulgated Under: 111.15.
Statutory Authority: 5111.01.
Rule Amplifies: 5111.01
Prior Effective Dates: 1/1/90 (Emer.), 4/1/90, 10/1/90, 2/7/91 (Emer.), 5/1/91, 7/1/92, 9/1/94, 10/1/02, 7/1/05.

**5160:1-3-36. Medicaid: treatment of resources for institutionalized individuals with a spouse in the community. [RESCINDED]**

Rescinded effective: 11/02/2014.
Five Year Review (FYR) Dates: 08/07/2014.
Promulgated Under: 111.15.
Statutory Authority: 5111.01, 5111.011.
Rule Amplifies: 5111.01, 5111.011
Prior Effective Dates: 1/1/90 (Emer.), 4/1/90, 1/1/91 (Emer.), 4/1/91, 1/1/92 (Emer.), 3/30/92, 2/12/93 (Emer.), 5/13/93, 3/18/94, 9/1/94, 4/1/96, 5/1/97, 4/1/98 (Emer.), 6/1/98, 4/1/99, 1/1/00 (Emer.), 4/1/00, 1/1/01.

NOTES TO DECISIONS

(1994) In determining the medicaid eligibility of an institutionalized spouse where the other spouse is not institutionalized, the federal statutes and Ohio administrative rules allow the transfer of resources first to the latter spouse in order to meet that spouse's income needs: Kimnach v. Ohio Dep't of Human Servs., 96 Ohio App. 3d 640, 645 N.E.2d 825, 1994 Ohio App. LEXIS 3957.

**5160:1-3-36.1 Medicaid: resource budgeting methodology for institutionalized individuals with a spouse in the community. [RESCINDED]**

Rescinded effective: 11/02/2014.
Five Year Review (FYR) Dates: 08/07/2014.
Promulgated Under: 111.15.
Statutory Authority: 5111.01, 5111.011.
Rule Amplifies: 5111.01, 5111.011
Prior Effective Dates: 1/1/90 (Emer.), 4/1/90, 6/1/90 (Emer.), 8/1/90, 10/1/90 (Emer.), 12/24/90, 1/1/91 (Emer.), 4/1/91, 1/1/92 (Emer.), 3/30/92, 2/12/93 (Emer.), 5/13/93, 9/1/94, 10/28/02, 9/20/03.

**5160:1-3-36.2 Medicaid: transfer of resources for institutionalized spouses with a spouse in the community. [RESCINDED]**

Rescinded effective: 11/02/2014.
Five Year Review (FYR) Dates: 08/07/2014.

Promulgated Under: 111.15.
Statutory Authority: 5111.01, 5111.011.
Rule Amplifies: 5111.01, 5111.011

Prior Effective Dates: 1/1/90 (Emer.), 4/1/90, 6/1/90 (Emer.), 81/190, 1/1/92, 7/1/95.

# INDEX



Index

Index

Index

Index

Index